Index to Poetry in Music

A Guide to the Poetry Set as Solo Songs by 125 Major
Song Composers

Carol June Bradley

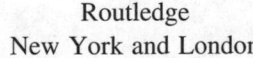

Routledge
New York and London

Published in 2003 by
Routledge
29 West 35th Street
New York, NY 10001
www.routledge-ny.com

Published in Great Britain by
Routledge
11 New Fetter Lane
London EC4P 4EE
www.routledge.com.uk

Copyright © 2003 by Taylor and Francis Books, Inc.
Routledge is an imprint of the Taylor & Francis Group.

Printed in the United States of America on acid-free paper.

10 9 8 7 6 5 4 3 2 1

Cataloging-in-Publication Data is available from the Library of Congress

ISBN 0-415-94302-7

For my dear sister,

Janice Bradley Newman

and

my colleague,

James B. Coover

TABLE OF CONTENTS

ACKNOWLEDGMENTS

This has truly been a career-long project. Begun as the result of a reference question I couldn't answer in 1960, it has evolved during the last forty years into an expandable, emendable data base and a comprehensive collection of art songs at the State University of New York at Buffalo. Members of the University's Computing Center; Dr. Richard H. Lesniak, Director of Academic Services, Computing and Information Technology; Geraldine Sonnesso, Associate Director for User Services, Academic Services; and Dr. Hinrich Martens, Associate Vice President for Computing and Information Technology, supported the automation of my data. Roger Campbell, the programmer with whom I worked, was unendingly patient, kind, thoughtful, and competent; he made the mechanical stages of the project interesting, even fun. Two graduate students, David Gates and William C. Borucki, patiently taught me the necessary machine skills to convert the data into pages. The University granted me two sabbatical leaves for which this study was the major project.

The interlibrary loan facilities at Vassar College and SUNY at Buffalo borrowed literally hundreds of volumes, both scores and books, for my use in this project. Anne Clifford, formerly interlibrary loan librarian here, was especially effective in securing sources from behind the then Iron Curtain.

Over the years I visited some of the major art song collections in the United States; for their courtesies and considerations my thanks go to the staffs of the Music Division, Library of Congress; the Music Department, Boston Public Library; Forbes Library; New England Conservatory; School of Music Library, Yale University; and the Sibley Music Library, Eastman School of Music. The late Ruth S. Bleecker of the Boston Public Library was particularly helpful by collecting dozens of volumes for my use during the very limited amount of time I could spend in Boston.

Diane Parr Walker searched the holdings of the Deutsche Staatsbibliothek for Lassen songs; Robert Orledge responded to several requests for information about d'Indy; Jean-Michel Nectoux sent information about d'Indy manuscripts in the Bibliothèque nationale; Jean Geil provided information about Kilpinen songs. Three librarians searched their collections for songs I needed to see: Frederick Kent, Free Library of Philadelphia; Morris Martin, University of North Texas; and Joan Falconer, University of Iowa. Walter Foster of Sam Houston State University suggested libraries which might hold fugitive materials. Others responded to individual queries: Garrett H. Bowles, Nicholas Chadwick, Lenore Coral, David Diamond, Miriam Gideon, Eric A. Gordon, Susan Halpert, Don A. Hennessee, Ernst Krenek, Hans Lenneberg, François Lesure, Kenneth A. Lohf, Margery M. Lowens, Otto Luening, Jerry McBride, Carolyn Mankell, O. W. Neighbour, P. Nelson-Safinor, Vittorio Rieti, Jean Rivier, Joaquín Rodrigo, Ned Rorem, Harold Samuel, Henri Sauguet, Lieselotte Sievers, Susan T. Sommer, Dan Stehman, Thomas Stoner, Igor Stravinsky, Karen Sturges, Virgil Thomson, David Francis Urrows, Geoffrey Wexler, Marlene Wong, and James B. Wright.

David Nuzzo, Acquisitions Librarian, SUNY at Buffalo, conducted a lengthy correspondence with publishers searching for out-of-print songs. Frequently he was granted permission to photocopy an out-of-print song in exchange for providing the publisher with a copy; other times publishers sent a photocopy of their archival copy.

Several graduate assistants searched general reference sources for poet information; among them were Alan Green and Edward Komara.

My colleague, James B. Coover, supported this project in every conceivable way. If something could be bought, be it source material or mechanical aid, he engineered its purchase. If University officials needed to be convinced about some aspect or need of the project, he helped convince them. Over the years, it has become second nature for him to think of 'the song index' and SUNY at Buffalo's song holdings.

A sad point is that so few songs are available in American libraries—many are known from bibliographies only. In my travels to major song collections, desiderata in hand, too often I found only one or two of a cycle of four or six songs. Thanks to interlibrary loan and microfilm, I've seen more than I thought possible.

Errors and omissions are mine. Corrections and additions will be welcomed; if readers have access to songs and/or sources omitted here, please send the information to me at the postal address: Music Library, Baird Hall, SUNY at Buffalo, Buffalo, New York 14260; the electronic mailing address is: muscarol@acsu.buffalo.edu.

INTRODUCTION

This guide—intended for researchers, performers, teachers, students, and music librarians—includes

*comprehensive lists of the art songs of 125 composers of the Western world
*identities of the poets who wrote the lyrics
*song titles used by the respective composers together with cross references from variant titles used by other composers who set the same text
*cross references from first lines
*publishers of the individual songs
*location of individual songs within the collected works of individual composers
*date of composition when it could be ascertained

It answers the questions: "What songs did X compose?" "Who published this song?" "Which composers set this poem?" [For the purposes of this book, a song is defined as a short composition for solo voice, usually accompanied by piano, which is based on a poetic text.] Occasionally a composition generally regarded as a song has an obbligato or second accompanying instrument; such are included here.

HOW TO USE THIS BOOK

The data are arranged in a single alphabetical sequence with major subdivisions by composer and poet. The information provided for each song is:

COMPOSER
Poet
Song title, op. no./composition date [publication information] "first line" OR same

("First line" is omitted if it is the **same** as the song title; it will be lacking if no copy of the song could be located.)

Complete information for each song is included only within the composer subdivision, which is arranged alphabetically by poet, then song title. That is,

COMPOSER
Poet A
Song a
Song b
etc.

Poet B
Song a
Song b
etc.
(Publisher and first line are included here only.)

In the poet subdivision, composers arc listcd alphabetically, then song titles, also alphabetically.

Poet
COMPOSER A
Song a
Song b

COMPOSER B
Song a
Song b

If the poetic text is an excerpt from a larger work, the title of the whole is listed under poet, followed by another composer and title sequence.

Poet
TITLE OF THE WHOLE.
COMPOSER A
Song a
Song b

COMPOSER B
Song a
Song b

Entered alphabetically among these major subdivisions are *see* references from titles, first lines, translations and transliterations of titles. Consistent type fonts are used so that one may readily distinguish among **COMPOSER**, Poet, *TITLE OF THE WHOLE*, *Title*, and "First line" references.

Technical Considerations

Sets of folk songs are excluded. Individual settings of folk texts are included; for them, as for 'Traditional' and liturgical texts, **Anonymous** is used as author of text. For vocalises, **No author** is used and for unidentified authors of texts, **Unknown**.

Poets' names follow the form used in the *National Union Catalog* and its *Supplement*, the New York Public Library catalogue, Library of Congress usage, or other standard library sources of information. There are poets for whom no information could be located; they are included here as found or as printed on the music itself. Several times there is confusion in author attribution; in those cases, supposed author is added to the author's name and dates.

Cities are included for obscure publishers; e.g., Amsterdam: Broekmans & Van Poppel (Pijper) and Trieste: Schmidl (Pizzetti). For Rossini, only city and date of publication are known for some songs.

Borodin song titles are German, Russian or English according to the exemplar seen; **all** known variant titles and English titles are used as cross references.

Composers with small song output are included because they set major poets; e.g., Bruckner.

Transliterations of Russian (Cyrillic) titles are by the chart in the *A.L.A. Cataloging Rules for Author and Title Entries*, 2nd ed., edited by Clara Beetle (Chicago: ALA, 1949), p. 246 or from *The New Grove*.

Most of the data was compiled before AACR2[1] usage; if the AACR2 form of name affects alphabetization, appropriate cross references are provided for composers, not poets.

Transliterated titles appear in { } before publication information if the title and text of the song are in a language other than Russian; this occurs in songs by Borodin, Chaĭkovskiĭ, Medtner, Rachmaninoff and Stravinskiĭ. For instance, the Medtner song

The prayer, op. 61 no. 5 {*Molitva*} [GA, v. 6, p. 246] "When life becomes unbearable"

Cycle titles are capitalized. Few cycle titles which begin with a number are indexed. If the number precedes a distinctive title, they are indexed; e.g., TROIS MELODIES SANS PAROLES, ACHT LIEDER NACH VERSCHIEDENEN DICHTEN. DEUX IDYLLES appears in the index as IDYLLES.

The composers Lassen and Seiber set major poets, yet their works are not generally available in the United States. Because of the poets, known information is included here.

Only solo songs from an opus or cycle are included; piano interludes or songs for other media are usually omitted.

German spellings vary according to the date of available information. Nineteenth century sources use *Thränen*, twentieth century *Tränen*.

Titles and first lines are reproduced as printed in the songs or other sources, hence spellings vary.

In general, fragments are excluded. Fragments of Schubert songs are included because they are printed in his collected works.

Publisher information is cited as found on songs; to trace sale of plates/stock, consult Krummel and Sadie, eds. *Music Printing and Publishing* (New York: W. W. Norton, 1990).

---

[1]*Anglo-American Cataloguing Rules.* Second edition. (Chicago: American Library Association, 1978).

BACKGROUND INFORMATION ABOUT THE DATA COLLECTION

The composers whose songs are included were selected by collating the major song composers identified in *Grove's Dictionary of Music and Musicians*, 5th ed. (London: Macmillan, 1954), James Hall's *The Art Song* (Norman: University of Oklahoma Press, 1953), and Philip L. Miller's *The Ring of Words* (Garden City: Doubleday, 1963). From the data in those and other peripheral sources I compiled a list of composers to be included. Then I examined the song holdings of several American libraries recognized for the quality of their collections. After that revision of the list, I consulted with musicologists and librarians knowledgeable in the subject. In these consultations there were the added considerations of availability and performance issues. Finally, over the years, a few composers had to be eliminated because it was impossible to locate their songs in libraries or to purchase them. The composers included are recognized for their song production and the quality of the texts they set. Settings of Biblical texts and folk song arrangements are included, as are unpublished songs. Sketches and most incomplete songs are not.

Complete lists of individual composers' songs are very rare; usually they must be laboriously compiled from various reference sources, biographies, and publishers' catalogues. Most of the lists in *Die Musik in Geschichte und Gegenwart*[2] and *The New Grove Dictionary of Music and Musicians*[3] are selective; many of these use cycle name only—e.g., *Myrthen*, a cycle of 26 individual songs—opus number or publication title—e.g., *Drei Lieder* or *Lieder und Gesange*—rather than individual song titles. Only 24 of the song lists in *The New Grove* were sufficiently detailed to be of value in this study. That small percentage reflects the general dearth of thorough coverage of songs in biographies, periodical literature, and other encyclopedias. The *Song Catalogue* of the BBC Music Library[4] was of limited value because it omits authors of texts unless there are "different poems with identical titles." Many sources carry complete lists of the larger works, e.g., operas and symphonies, but trickle down to "92 songs," "many songs," "1 vol. songs, 1922-37" for this smaller form of composition. The lists in this book provide information about all the songs of the composers included.

Beyond knowledge of a song's existence is the need to acquire it by purchase or locating it in a library. Of the composers represented in this study, *The New Grove* includes publisher information for Stravinskiĭ only. Those wishing to purchase a particular song or cycle need to search elsewhere for publisher information. Although modern biographies of composers usually include lists of works, they seldom include all the elements of information provided here: e.g., publication information and titles of individual songs within opus numbers; virtually none quote first lines of songs if variant from the song title.

There are collected editions for 33 of the composers included here but songs had not yet been published in nine of them when data collection ended in 1988. There is also a collected edition of Richard Strauss songs and Weber's *Reliquienschrein* which include previously unpublished compositions. Even in those instances where the songs have been published in collected editions, the publication may not include all of the composer's songs. For instance, some 19 Schumann songs are not included in the Breitkopf & Härtel complete edition.[5] Several heavily-edited 19th century collected editions are being replaced by new editions prepared according to contemporary

---

[2]Kassel: Bärenreiter-Verlag, 1949-1968.
[3]London: Macmillan, 1980.
[4]London: British Broadcasting Company, 1966.
[5]*Robert Schumanns Werke*. Hrsg. von Clara Schumann (Leipzig: Breitkopf & Härtel, 1888-1893).

standards of musical scholarship. This guide provides quick location of individual songs within those otherwise un-indexed modern editions, e. g., Mozart and Wagner.[6]

Thematic catalogues of some composers' works are excellent, but others are practically worthless for those seeking information about individual songs and authors of texts. For instance, the Chaĭkovskiĭ thematic catalogue, published in 1987, cites only the original Russian publication of Chaĭkovskiĭ's works; again, it does not provide the location of individual songs within the collected edition. Even recent thematic catalogues are incomplete; the 1982 *Robert Schumann Thematisches Verzeichnis* compiled by Kurt Hofmann omits 8 unpublished songs which are included in Eric Sams' *New Grove* list. To compile the list of Schumann songs indexed here, the songs in the 1881-93 Breitkopf & Härtel collected edition, the 1982 thematic catalogue, Eric Sams' *Songs of Robert Schumann* (1969) and his more recent list in *The New Grove* (1980) were collated.

Songs are poorly represented in the *National Union Catalog* and its *Supplement*.[7] For instance, only 48 individual songs and 15 collections of Gounod's more than 200 songs are included, 2 individual songs and 5 collections of Franz Ries. Collating the holdings represented in the *National Union Catalog*, the catalogues of the New York Public Library and the Boston Public Library, and the shelf list of the Library of Congress, it was possible to locate only a little more than half of Gounod's songs in American libraries. Many libraries own collections published by Choudens in the 19th century but few individual songs published separately have made their way into American libraries. For this study, desiderata lists were circulated to European antiquarians; microfilm and photocopies of many Gounod songs were acquired, but not all. 49 Gounod songs—one quarter of his output—have not been located. A Ries list was compiled from opus numbers listed in *Die Musik in Geschichte und Gegenwart*; title, first line, and publisher information was gathered from the Hofmeister catalogues.[8] Ultimately that incomplete data was deleted from this volume.

Similarly, the Lassen information was developed from caption title-pages, songs found in American libraries and the Deutsche Staatsbibliothek, antiquarian offerings, and Pazdírek.[9] The indexed list includes the 180 titles included in the Hainauer caption title series plus nos. 1-6 of the 8 identified as op. 4; opp. 5, 12, 88, 89, 92, 93; and 25 without any numerical identification. Certainly there can be no representation that this is a complete list of Lassen's songs and some poet information is lacking. Zelter presents a parallel situation. The indexed list was compiled from various sources, including the valuable Barr dissertation.[10] Although secondary sources cite a Schlesinger edition, the Künst und Industrie Comptoir edition seen at Yale is cited as publisher in this list. Again, there is information lacking; unfortunately, Zelter is poorly represented in the Challier *Grosser Lieder-Katalog*.[11]

Contemporary composers fare no better in the *National Union Catalog*. Of the songs of Samuel Barber, 7 opus numbers can be located; two of Ned Rorem. Of Yrjö Kilpinen, one of the foremost song writers of the 20th century, only 18 of the 53 opus numbers devoted to solo songs are present. Contemporary composers present other problems as well. To identify the songs indexed here, information was collated from biographical sources, catalogues of publishers, periodical literature, published library catalogues, and the national bibliographic utilities; the resultant lists were sent to the individual composers for additions and emendations. Composers responded graciously, usually expanding their lists to include unpublished songs.

Heretofore it was difficult to answer the question "Who set this text?" Questions about texts cut across all the humanities bringing literature, language, history, and art scholars into the music library. Traditionally, music librarians have been hampered by the lack of readily accessible information about texts. Both the New York Public Library and the Boston Public Library catalogues provide analytical entries for authors of texts. When those great catalogues were published—1964-

---

[6]W. A. Mozart, *Neue Ausgabe sämtlicher Werke*, in Verbindung mit den Mozartstädten, Augsburg, Salzburg und Wien . . . (Kassel: Bärenreiter, 1955-) and Richard Wagner, *Sämtliche Werke in Zusammenarbeit mit der Bayerischen Akademie der Schönen Künste, München*. Hrsg. von Carl Dahlhaus. (Mainz: Schott, 1970-)

[7]*The National Union Catalog, pre-1956 imprints* and *Supplement* (London: Mansell, 1968-1981).

[8]*Handbuch der musikalischen Literatur* (Leipzig: Friedrich Hofmeister, 1844-1933).

[9]Franz Pazdírek, *Universal-Handbuch der Musikliteratur aller Zeiten und Völker...* (Wien: Pazdírek & Co., 1904-1910).

[10]Raymond Arthur Barr, "Carl Friedrich Zelter, a study of the Lied in Berlin during the late eighteenth and early nineteenth centuries" (Ph.D. diss., University of Wisconsin, 1968).

[11](Berlin: Ernst Challier's Selbstverlag, 1885- ; reprint ed., Wiesbaden: Dr. Martin Sändig, 1979).

76 and 1972-77 respectively—they were of immeasurable aid to other music librarians. Their impact, however, is limited by their holdings. The aggregate of their song holdings is small compared to the scope of this study.

There are several indexes to the settings of a single poet, e.g., Burton Pollin's *Music for Shelley's poetry; an annotated bibliography of musical settings of Shelley's poetry* (New York: Da Capo Press, 1974), three titles by Gooch and Thatcher which index settings of 19th century English language texts,[12] and guides to musical settings of American and German poetry[13] but no other source indexes the major song literature by poet and poem title. This aspect reveals multiple settings of the same text. For instance, performers and scholars will now be able to compare the four different composers' settings of Apollinaire's *Automne*. (An inquiry by song title, *Automne*, will lead to the poet Apollinaire and the composers Lennox Berkeley, Arthur Honegger, Jean Rivier, and Ned Rorem, all of whom set it. Authors of the six settings of Goethe's *Der Fischer* are identified: Loewe, Schubert, Schumann, Strauss, Wolf, and Zelter. Four settings of a Geibel text, using three different titles, are identified: There are two entitled *Für Musik* by Franz and Strauss, one entitled *Nun die Schatten dunkeln* by Jensen, and one entitled *Lied* by Rubinstein.) Errors in text authorship are corrected; e.g., Reger's *Helle Nacht*, op. 37 no. 1, is attributed to Verlaine in the Reger complete works. In fact, the text is by Richard Dehmel, an excerpt from his *Weib und Welt*.

It was originally intended to provide, as a separate element of information, the title of the poem or larger work from which a text was excerpted. As the project developed, it became apparent the overwhelming percentage of texts bear the poem title as song title; frequently the first lines of the poem and song are identical. Locating the variants in an author's *oeuvre* often proved impossible. Many not found were by authors unidentifiable except as song text authors. Some texts appear to be from unpublished works or excerpts from prose works. The infinite pursuit of these fugitive texts would have delayed completion and publication of the rest of the data indefinitely. Usually an individual querying the data has the title or first line of the text sought; that type of query is easily answered by the present data. If the title of the work from which a text is taken is readily available, as are the titles of Shakespeare plays, it is included.

Performers frequently compare performance editions with the more scholarly collected works. This guide facilitates that some sometimes difficult step. For instance, the popular Chaĭkovskiĭ song, *None but the lonely heart*, can be readily located in Chaĭkovskiĭ's collected works, v. 44, p. 39, where it is entitled *Niet″, tol'ko tot″, kto znal″*, with Russian (Cyrillic) text only.

Although song data collection was completed by 1988, new sources were checked against existing data until about 1992. The most recent sources of information were used to compile complete lists of songs. Discrepancies among sources are noted if they affect numbering; e.g., Schumann op. 125 which is numbered variantly in Eric Sams' *Songs of Schumann*[14] and the thematic catalogue than in the collected works. The songs are numbered here according to the recent research, not the collected works. The collected edition is, however, used as the source of publication.

In several instances German translations of English language texts are cited in English with the German translations—as set by the composers—used as cross references only; e.g., Schumann *Gedichte der Königin Maria Stuart*, op. 135. This brings English language texts together under poet.

Composition dates are cited when known; all numbers of an opus may not be assumed to have been composed within a given year or span of years.

---

[12]*Musical settings of British romantic literature* (New York: Garland Publications, 1982); *Musical settings of early and mid-Victorian literature* (New York: Garland, 1979); and *Musical settings of late Victorian and modern British literature* (New York: Garland, 1976).

[13]Michael A. Hovland, *Musical settings of American poetry: A bibliography* (Westport, Conn.: Greenwood Press, 1986) and Lawrence D. Snyder, *German poetry in song: An index of Lieder* (Berkeley, Calif.: Fallen Leaf Press, 1995).

[14]London: Methuen, 1969. There is also a "revised and enlarged" 1993 edition.

LIST OF COMPOSERS

Aubert, Louis François Marie, 1877-1968.
Auric, Georges, 1899-1983.
Balakirev, Miliĭ Alekseevich, 1837-1910.
Barber, Samuel, 1910-1981.
Bartók, Béla, 1881-1945.
Beethoven, Ludwig van, 1770-1827.
Bennett, William Sterndale, 1816-1875.
Berg, Alban, 1885-1935.
Berkeley, Lennox, 1903-1989.
Berlioz, Hector, 1803-1869.
Bernstein, Leonard, 1918-1990.
Bizet, Georges, 1838-1875.
Blacher, Boris, 1903-1975.
Blitzstein, Marc, 1905-1964.
Bloch, Ernest, 1880-1959.
Borodin, Alcksandr Porfir'evich, 1833-1887.
Boulanger, Lili, 1893-1918.
Brahms, Johannes, 1833-1897.
Britten, Benjamin, 1913-1976.
Bruckner, Anton, 1824-1896.
Carpenter, John Alden, 1876-1951.
Carter, Elliott, 1908-
Casella, Alfredo, 1883-1947.
Chabrier, Emmanuel, 1841-1894.
Chaĭkovskiĭ, Petr Il'ich, 1840-1893.
Chanler, Theodore, 1902-1961.
Chausson, Ernest, 1855-1899.
Chopin, Fryderyk Franciszek, 1810-1849.
Copland, Aaron, 1900-1991.
Cornelius, Peter, 1824-1874.
Debussy, Claude, 1862-1918.
Delibes, Léo, 1836-1891.
Delius, Frederick, 1862-1934.
Diamond, David, 1915-
Duparc, Henri, 1848-1933.
Dvořák, Antonín, 1841-1904.
Falla, Manuel de, 1876-1946.
Fauré, Gabriel Urbain, 1845-1924.
Franck, César Auguste, 1822-1890.
Franz, Robert, 1815-1892.
Gideon, Miriam, 1906-1996.
Gluck, Christoph Willibald, 1714-1787.
Gounod, Charles François, 1818-1893.
Grieg, Edvard, 1843-1907.
Griffes, Charles Tomlinson, 1884-1920.
Hahn, Reynaldo, 1875-1947.
Harris, Roy, 1898-1979.
Heseltine, Philip Arnold, 1894-1930.

Hindemith, Paul, 1895-1963.
Honegger, Arthur, 1892-1955.
Ibert, Jacques, 1890-1962.
Indy, Vincent d', 1851-1931.
Ireland, John, 1879-1962.
Ives, Charles Edward, 1874-1954.
Janáček, Leoš, 1854-1928.
Jensen, Adolf, 1837-1879.
Jolivet, André, 1905-1974.
Kilpinen, Yrjö, 1892-1959.
Koechlin, Charles, 1867-1950.
Krenek, Ernst, 1900-1991.
Lalo, Edouard, 1823-1892.
Lassen, Eduard, 1830-1904.
Liszt, Franz, 1811-1886.
Loeffler, Charles Martin, 1861-1935.
Loewe, Karl, 1796-1869.
Luening, Otto, 1900-1996.
MacDowell, Edward Alexander, 1861-1908.
Mahler, Gustav, 1860-1911.
Malipiero, Gian Francesco, 1882-1973.
Martinů, Bohuslav, 1890-1959.
Massenet, Jules, 1842-1912.
Medtner, Nikolaĭ Karlovich, 1880-1951.
Mendelssohn-Bartholdy, Felix, 1809-1847.
Messiaen, Olivier, 1908-1992.
Milhaud, Darius, 1892-1974.
Mompou, Federico, 1893-1987.
Mozart, Wolfgang Amadeus, 1756-1791.
Musorgskiĭ, Modest Petrovich, 1839-1881.
Nielson, Carl, 1865-1931.
Pfitzner, Hans, 1869-1949.
Pijper, Willem, 1894-1947.
Pizzetti, Ildebrano, 1880-1968.
Poulenc, Francis, 1899-1963.
Prokofiev, Sergeĭ Sergeevich, 1891-1953.
Quilter, Roger, 1877-1953.
Rachmaninoff, Sergei, 1873-1943.
Ravel, Maurice, 1875-1937.
Reger, Max, 1873-1916.
Respighi, Ottorino, 1879-1936.
Riegger, Wallingford, 1885-1961.
Rieti, Vittorio, 1898-1994.
Rimskiĭ-Korsakov, Nikola Andreevich, 1844-1908.
Rivier, Jean, 1896-1987.
Rodrigo, Joaquín, 1901-1999.
Rorem, Ned, 1923-
Rossini, Gioacchino, 1792-1868.

Roussel, Albert, 1869-1937.
Rubinstein, Anton, 1829-1894.
Saint-Saëns, Camille, 1835-1921.
Satie, Erik, 1866-1925.
Sauguet, Henri, 1901-1989.
Schmitt, Florent, 1870-1958.
Schoeck, Othmar, 1886-1957.
Schönberg, Arnold, 1874-1951.
Schubert, Franz, 1797-1828.
Schumann, Robert, 1810-1856.
Seiber, Mátyás, 1905-1960.
Séverac, Déodat, de, 1873-1921.
Sibelius, Jean, 1865-1957.
Spohr, Louis, 1784-1859.
Strauss, Richard, 1864-1949.

Stravinskiĭ, Igor' Fedorovich, 1882-1971.
Szymanowski, Karol, 1882-1937.
Thompson, Randall, 1899-1984.
Thomson, Virgil, 1896-1989.
Turina, Joaquín, 1882-1949.
Varèse, Edgar, 1883-1965.
Vaughan Williams, Ralph, 1872-1958.
Verdi, Giuseppe, 1813-1901.
Wagner, Richard, 1813-1883.
Weber, Karl Maria von, 1786-1826.
Webern, Anton von, 1883-1945.
Weisgall, Hugo, 1912-1997.
Wolf, Hugo, 1860-1903.
Zelter, Karl Friedrich, 1758-1832.

COLLECTED WORKS USED AS PUBLISHER[15]

Beethoven, Ludwig van
Werke. Leipzig: Breifkopf & Härtel, 1864-1890; reprint ed., New York: Kalmus, 1967-
Siglum: GA
Supplemente, 1959-

Berlioz, Hector
Werke. Leipzig: Breifkopf & Härtel, 1900-1907; reprint ed., New York: Kalmus, 1971.
Siglum: Werke

Brahms, Johannes
Sämtliche Werke; Ausgabe der Gesellschaft der Musikfreunde in Wien. Wiesbaden:
Breifkopf & Härtel, 1965. **Siglum: GA**

Bruckner, Anton
[Göllerich, August. *Anton Bruckner, ein Lebens- und Schaffens-Bild.* Regensburg: G.
Bosse, 1922, 1937.] **Siglum: Göllerich *Anton Bruckner***

Chaĭkovskiĭ, Petr Il'ich
[Complete works. Moscow: State Music Publishers, 1940-197__] **Siglum: GA**

Chopin, Fryderyk Franciszek
Complete works . . . Editor, Ignacy J. Paderewski . . . Warsaw: Fryderyk Chopin Institute,
1949-1962. **Siglum: GA**

Cornelius, Peter
Musikalische Werke. Erste Gesamtausgabe, im Auftrage seiner Familie hrsg. von Max
Hasse. Leipzig: Breifkopf & Härtel, 1905-1906; reprint ed., Farnborough, Hants.,
England: Gregg International Publishers, 1971. **Siglum: Werke**

Dvořák, Antonín
Souborné vydání del Antonína Dvořáka. Prague: Artia, 1955- **Siglum: GA**

Grieg, Edvard
Samlede verker. Frankfurt: C. F. Peters, 1977- **Siglum: GA**

Ives, Charles Edward
114 songs. [Redding, Conn.: C. E. Ives, 1922]
Thirty four songs. [San Francisco: New Music, 1933]
18 [i.e., 19]songs. New York: New Music Society, 1935.

Liszt, Franz
Musikalische Werke. Hrsg. von der Franz Liszt-Stiftung. Leipzig: Breifkopf & Härtel,
1907-1936; reprint ed., Farnborough, Hants., England: Gregg, 1970. **Siglum: GA**

Loewe, Karl
Gesamtausgabe der Balladen, Legenden, Lieder und Gesänge für eine Singstimme, in
Auftrage der Loeweschen Familie hrsg. von Dr. Max Runze. Leipzig: Breifkopf &
Härtel, 1899-1904; reprint ed., Farnborough, Hants., England: Gregg, 1970. **Siglum: GA**

Medtner, Nikolaĭ Karlovich
[Collected works. Moscow: State Music Publishers, 1959-] **Siglum: GA**

Mendelssohn-Bartholdy, Felix
Werke. Kritisch durchgesehene Ausgabe von Julius Rietz. Leipzig: Breifkopf & Härtel,
1874-1877; reprint ed.: Farnborough, Hants., England: Gregg Press, 1967-
Siglum: GA

---

[15]To achieve as much uniformity as possible in the sigla representing the various collected works, the initials **GA** (Gesamtausgaben) were selected in most cases. GA is the common term used in many music libraries to describe the collected editions.

Mozart, Wolfgang Amadeus
Werke. Leipzig: Breifkopf & Härtel, 1877-1905. **Siglum: GA**
Neue Ausgabe sämtlicher Werke . . . Kassel: Bärenreiter, 1955- **Siglum: NMA**

Musorgskiĭ, Modest Petrovich
Sämtliche Werke. Hrsg. von Paul Lamm. Moskau: Staatsmusikverlag, 1928-1934; reprint ed., New York: Kalmus, 1969. **Siglum: GA**

Prokofiev, Sergeĭ Sergeevich
Sobranie sochinenii. Moskva: Gos. muzyk. Izd-vo, 1955- **Siglum: GA**

Rachmaninoff, Sergei
[Collected works. Moscow: State Music Publishers, 1947- ; reprint ed.: *Romansy*. Moscow: State Music Publishers, 1963. **Siglum: State Music Publ.**

Reger, Max
Sämtliche Werke. Wiesbaden: Breifkopf & Härtel, 1954- **Siglum: GA**

Rimskiĭ-Korsakov, Nikolaĭ Andreevich
[Collected works. Moscow: State Music Publishers, 1948-] **Siglum: GA**

Rossini, Gioacchino
Quaderni Rossiniani, a cura della Fondazione Rossini. Pesaro: Fondazione Rossini, 1954-

Schönberg, Arnold
Sämtliche Werke. Hrsg. von Josef Rufer . . . Mainz: Schott, 1966- **Siglum: GA**

Schubert, Franz
Werke. Kritisch durchgesehene Gesammtausgabe. Leipzig: Breifkopf & Härtel, 1884- 1897; reprint ed., New York: Dover, 1971. **Siglum: GA**
Neue Ausgabe sämtlicher Werke. Kassel, New York: Bärenreiter, 1964- **Siglum: NGA**

Schumann, Robert
Werke. Leipzig: Breifkopf & Härtel, 1881-1893; reprint ed., Farnborough, Hants., England: Gregg Press, 1967. **Siglum: GA**

Strauss, Richard
Lieder. Gesamtausgabe. Hrsg. von Dr. Franz Trenner. [n.p.] Fürstner, Boosey & Hawkes, 1964-1965. **Siglum: Lieder GA**

Szymanowski, Karol
Gesamtausgabe. Kraków: PWM-Edition, 1973- **Siglum: GA**

Wagner, Richard
Musikalische Werke. Leipzig: Breitkopf & Härtel, 1912-ca.1929; reprint ed., New York: Da Capo Press, 1971. **Siglum: GA**
Sämtliche Werke in Zusammenarbeit mit der Bayerischen Akademic der Schönen Künste, München. Hrsg. von Carl Dahlhaus. Mainz: Schott, 1970- **Siglum: SW**

Weber, Karl Maria von
Reliquienschrein des Meisters Carl Maria von Weber, in seinem hundertsten Todesjahr aufgestellt von Leopold Hirschberg. Berlin: Morawe & Scheffelt Verlag, 1927. **Siglum: *Reliquienschrein***

Wolf, Hugo
Sämtliche Werke. Wien: Musikwissenschaftlicher Verlag [1960- **Siglum: GA**

Zelter, Karl Friedrich
Sämtlicher Lieder, Balladen, und Romanzen für das Pianoforte. Berlin: Im Kunst- und Industrie- Comptoir [1810-1813] **Siglum: Kunst und Industrie Comptoir**
Fünfzig Lieder: 32 Lieder nach Gedichten von Goethe und 18 Lieder nach Worten verschiedener Dichter, für eine Singstimme und Klavier. Ausgewählt . . . von Ludwig Landshoff. Mainz: Schott [1932] **Siglum: Schott (Landshoff), 1932**

A

A b c d e f und g see No author **BLACHER**

"A ce malheur qui jour et jour me point" see
L'amant malheureux Ronsard
SAINT-SAËNS

À *Cécile see* Dubufe **GOUNOD**

À *celle qui part see* Silvestre **LALO**

A *cette heure du dèpart see* Tagore
GITANJALI. **CASELLA**

"A cette place, chez nous" see *L'azalée*
Patmore **MILHAUD**

"A che più debb' io mai l'intensa voglia" see
Sonetto XXXI Buonarroti
BRITTEN

A *Chloris see* Théophile **HAHN**

À *Clymène see* Verlaine **FAURÉ**

À *Colombine see* Gallet **MASSENET**

"Å, der var en Jente som vi så ombord" see
Ragnhild Drachmann **GRIEG**

A *des roses sous la neige see* Lamartine
SAUGUET

"A deux pas de la mer qu'on entend
bourdonner" see *Paysage* Theuriet **HAHN**

À *deux pleurer! see* Croze, J. L.
MASSENET

"A dónde te escondiste, Amado" see *Cantico
de la esposa* San Juan de la Cruz
RODRIGO

"A douvres un original tombe" see *Adèle*
Giraudoux **HONEGGER**

"A fasci s'effonde per l'aria tranquilla" see
Luce Negri **RESPIGHI**

"A gdzie pod lasem podlasina" see *Zielone
slowa* Tuwim **SZYMANOWSKI**

A *goccia a goccia see* Sappho **RIETI**

À *Grenade see* Pacini **ROSSINI**

"Å hipp og hoppe og tipp og toppe" see
Killingdans Garborg **GRIEG**

"A já mám doma bratra rybáře" see *Touha*
Anon. **MARTINŮ**

A *jótevök see* Havas **BARTÓK**
The benefactors

A *kdybys písní stvořená see* Heyduk
DVOŘÁK

"Å Kyri mi vene" see *Ku-Lok* Garborg
GRIEG

À *la brise see* Unknown **GOUNOD**

"A la chapelle Notre Dâme" see *Cinq mars, à
la mémoire de Max Jacob* Salmon
SAUGUET

"A la fenêtre recélant" see *Sainte* Mallarmé
RAVEL

À *la lune see* Anon. **SAINT-SAËNS**

À *la lune see* Châteaubriand **MILHAUD**

À *la Madone see* Barbier, J. **GOUNOD**

À *la nuit see* Gounod **GOUNOD**

A *la Santé see* Apollinaire *ALCOOLS.*
HONEGGER

À *la trépassée see* Silvestre **MASSENET**
Lève-toi, lève-toi

"A la très chère" see *Hymne* Baudelaire
FAURÉ

"A la tua culla vennero le fate" see *Tanto
bella* Unknown **RESPIGHI**

A *l'aube dans la Montagne see* Séverac
SÉVERAC

A *les je tichý kolem kol see* Heyduk
DVOŘÁK

A *ma belle mère see* Unknown **ROSSINI**

À *ma mignonne see* Renaut, J. **DELIBES**

A *magyarok Istene see* Petöfi **LISZT**

"A mes pas le plus doux chemin" see *Le plus
doux chemin* Silvestre **FAURÉ**

A *mesure qu'on avance see* Guérin, E.
MILHAUD

À *Mignonne see* Chouquet **MASSENET**

A *nos morts ignorés see* Hennevé, Louis
HAHN

"A pas lents, et suivis du chien de la maison"
see *Automne* Samain **KOECHLIN**

A *Phidylé see* Leconte de Lisle *ÉTUDES
LATINES.* **HAHN**

A *pod borem siwe kunie see* Anon.
SZYMANOWSKI

"A quoi bon à quoi bon entendre" see *Ruy
Blas* Hugo **CHABRIER**

À *quoi bon entendre les oiseaux des bois see*
Hugo **SAINT-SAËNS**

"A quoi bon entendre les oiseaux des bois?"
see *Liebeswunder* Hugo **RUBINSTEIN**

"A quoi bon vouloir m'exprimer" see *Silence*
Docquois **SAINT-SAËNS**

"A quoi, dans ce matin d'Avril" see *Dans la
pénombre* Lerberghe **FAURÉ**

A *QUOI RÊVENT LES JEUNES FILLES. see*
Musset *Sérénade à Ninon* **DELIBES**

À *sa guitare see* Ronsard **POULENC**

À *Saint-Blaise see* Ronsard **SAINT-SAËNS**

À *Saint-Blaize à la Zuecca see* Musset
RUBINSTEIN

"A Saint Blaise à la Zuecca vous étiez" see
Souvenir de Venise Musset **MASSENET**
La Zuecca Musset **LALO**

"A Scheveningue sur la plage òu l'ensable le
vent du nord" see
La sirène de Scheveningue Gilson
RIVIER

"A Séville, belles Señoras" *see Sévillana*
  Anon. **MASSENET**
A son Altesse la Princesse Antoinette Murat
  see Rohan **THOMSON**
A son page see Ronsard **POULENC**
"A Strasbourg en dix-neuf-cent-quatre" *see*
  1904 Apollinaire **POULENC**
"A te, che benedetta fra tutte sei, Maria" *see*
  Ave Maria (su due note)
  Unknown **ROSSINI**
À toi mon coeur see Barbier, J. **GOUNOD**
"A toi qui sais combien je l'aime" *see Prière*
  du soir Ligny, Charles **GOUNOD**
A toutes brides see Éluard **POULENC**
"A traduire en esthonien . . . " *see* Chalupt
  RIVIER
"A travers la lande pierreuse" *see Noël*
  pastoral Hettich **AUBERT**
À une bourse see Augier **GOUNOD**
A une élégante sans fortune see Fernandez,
  Jeanne **SAUGUET**
A une femme see Verlaine **LOEFFLER**
À une fleur see Musset **BIZET, LALO**
À une jeune fille see Augier **GOUNOD**
À une jeune grecque see Sappho **GOUNOD**
A une rose pâlissant au soleil see Richter
  SAUGUET
A une sainte le jour de sa fête see Jacob, M.
  SAUGUET
À une soeur see Pradère-Niquet **GOUNOD**
A unos ojos see Rodríguez Marin,
  Francisco **TURINA**
A vágyak éjjele see Gleiman, W. **BARTÓK**
  Night of desire
"A Vardari, a Vardari, nel campo di Vardari"
  see Bebro e il suo cavallo Anon.
  PIZZETTI
"Å veit du den Draum og veit du den Song"
  see Det synge Garborg **GRIEG**
 A Vénus see Labé **SAUGUET**
"A' Versle, a' g'spassig's" *see Mei Bua*
  Sommerstorff **REGER**
"A Vesta, portez vos offrandes" *see*
  Invocation à Vesta Barbier, J. **GOUNOD**
"A vous ces vers de par la grâce consolante"
  see A une femme Verlaine
  LOEFFLER
A vous, oiseau des plaines see Anon.
  RAVEL
Aakjaer, Jeppe, 1866-1930.
  NIELSEN
    Det danske Brød paa Sletten gror
    Den føreste laerke
    Høgen
    Jens Vejmand
    HISTORIENS SANG.
      NIELSEN *Som dybest Brønd*

JYLLAND.
  NIELSEN *Der dukker af Disen min*
    Faedrenejord
MORS ROK.
  NIELSEN *Spurven sidder stum bag*
    Kvist
PIGER PAA ENGEN.
  NIELSEN *Nu er Dagen fuld af Sang*
SE DIGUD.
  NIELSEN *Se dig ud en Sommerdag*
SUNDT BLOD.
  NIELSEN *Jeg baerer med Smil min*
    Byrde
SVALEN.
  NIELSEN *Hør, hvor let dens Vinger*
    smaekker
"Aallot solisevat" *see Kevättä* Lamberg
  KILPINEN
Aamu see Jalkanen **KILPINEN**
Aamulaulu see Jalkanen **KILPINEN**
Aamulla see Lönnbohm **KILPINEN**
"Der Aar den Kukuk" *see Der Adler und der*
  Kukuk Krylov **RUBINSTEIN**
Aarestrup, Emil, 1800-1856.
  NIELSEN *Angst*
L'abandon see Latil **MILHAUD**
L'abandonée see Escudier, M. **VERDI**
Abandonée, je suis abandonée see Hugnet
  ROREM
L'abandonnée see Mendès **BIZET**
Abandonnée see Supervielle **MILHAUD**
Abbandono see Vivanti **RESPIGHI**
"L'abbé divague" *see Sur l'Herbe* Verlaine
  RAVEL
Abbitte see Hölderlin **PFITZNER**
Abel see Capetanakis **ROREM**
Der Abend see Eichendorff **LASSEN**
Der Abend see Kosegarten *DER ABEND*
  BLÜHT, TEMORA GLÜHT. **SCHUBERT**
Der Abend see Lenau **SCHOECK**
Der Abend see Matthisson **SCHUBERT**
Abend see Schäfer, T. **REGER**
DER ABEND AM WALDBRUNNEN. see
  Kind, F.
  Bach, Echo, Kuss **WEBER**
"Der Abend blüht, Temora glüht" *see*
  Der Abend Kosegarten **SCHUBERT**
DER ABEND BLÜHT, TEMORA GLÜHT. see
  Kosegarten
  Der Abend **SCHUBERT**
"Der Abend graut" *see Stiller Gang* Dehmel
  STRAUSS
"Abend ist's" *see Abendempfindung an Laura*
  Campe **MOZART**
"Der Abend röthet nun das Thal" *see*
  Abendlied der Fürstin Mayrhofer
  SCHUBERT

"Der Abend schleiert Flur und Hain" *see Geist der Liebe* Matthisson SCHUBERT

Abend- und Morgenrot see Hoffmann von Fallersleben STRAUSS

Abendbild see Ernst LASSEN

Abendbilder see Lenau WOLF

Abendbilder see Silbert SCHUBERT

Abenddämmerung see Schack BRAHMS, LASSEN

Abendempfindung an Laura see Campe MOZART

Abendfantasie see Brun, S. ZELTER
  Abendphantasie

Abendfrieden see Braungart REGER

Abendgebet, nach einer erlittenen Kränkung see Gerstenberg LOEWE

Abendgefühl see Hebbel CORNELIUS
  Two settings: 1862 and 1863.

Abendgesang see Stieglitz LOEWE

ABENDGEWÖLKE SCHWEBEN HELL. see Matthisson
  Stimme der Liebe SCHUBERT
  Two settings: D. 187 and D. 418.

"Abendgewölke schweben hell" *see Stimme der Liebe* Matthisson SCHUBERT
  Two settings: D. 187 and D. 418.

"Abendglockenhalle zittern" *see Der Herbstabend* Salis-Seewis SCHUBERT

Abendglockenläuten see Rückert *SCHWANENGESANG.* LASSEN

Abendglöcklein see Zusner WOLF

"Abendglokkenläuten" *see Abendglockenläuten* Rückert *SCHWANENGESANG.* LASSEN

Abendlandschaft see Eichendorff SCHOECK

Abendlandschaft see Unknown LASSEN

"Abendlich schon rauscht der Wald" *see Abends* Eichendorff FRANZ
  Abschied Eichendorff PFITZNER, SCHOECK

Abendlied see Becker, J. SPOHR

Abendlied see Claudius, M. GIDEON, SCHOECK, SCHUBERT

Abendlied see Giesebrecht LOEWE

Abendlied see Keller, G. SCHOECK

Abendlied see Kinkel SCHUMANN

Abendlied see Mayrhofer SCHUBERT
  Schlaflied

Abendlied see Müchler ZELTER

Abendlied see Rückert LOEWE

Abendlied see Stolberg SCHUBERT

Abendlied see Sturm, J. PFITZNER

Abendlied see Unknown REGER, SCHUBERT

Abendlied see Voss MENDELSSOHN-BARTHOLDY, ZELTER

Abendlied see Wildenbruch LASSEN

Abendlied an die Natur see Keller, G. SCHOECK

Abendlied der Fürstin see Mayrhofer SCHUBERT

Abendlied für den Falben see Rolfsen GRIEG *Kveldssang for Blakken*

Abendlied für die Entfernte see Schlegel SCHUBERT

Abendlied im Freien see Kind, F. ZELTER

Abendlied unterm gestirnten Himmel see Goeble BEETHOVEN

Abendliedchen see Pleshcheyev MUSORGSKIĬ *Vecherniaia pesenka*

Abendmahlslied see Neus LOEWE

Abendphantasie see Brun, S. ZELTER

Abendphantasie see Hölderlin HINDEMITH

Abendregen see Keller, G. BRAHMS

Abendröte see Schlegel, F. *ABENDRÖTE.* SCHUBERT

ABENDRÖTE. see Schlegel, F.
  Abendröte SCHUBERT
  Die Berge SCHUBERT
  Der Fluss SCHUBERT
  Die Gebüsche SCHUBERT
  Der Knabe SCHUBERT
  Das Mädchen SCHUBERT
  Die Rose SCHUBERT
  Der Schmetterling SCHUBERT
  Die Sterne SCHUBERT
  Die Vögel SCHUBERT
  Der Wanderer SCHUBERT

Abendrot see Leinhard, Friedrich PFITZNER

Das Abendrot see Schreiber SCHUBERT

Abends see Eichendorff FRANZ

Abends see Hesse SCHOECK

Abends see Osterwald FRANZ

Abends see Unknown FRANZ

Abends am Strand see Heine SCHUMANN

"Abends gehn die Liebespaare" *see Abends* Hesse SCHOECK

Abends unter der Linde see Kosegarten SCHUBERT
  Two settings: D. 235 and D. 237.

"Abendschwärmer zogen um die Linden" *see Michaelskirchplatz* Busse PFITZNER

Abendsegen see Anon. *FLIEGENDES BLATT.* WEBER

Der Abendsegen see Unknown MENDELSSOHN-BARTHOLDY

Die Abendsonne see Urner LOEWE

Abendständchen: An Lina see Batsányi SCHUBERT

Der Abendstern see Enslin **LOEWE**
Der Abendstern see Hoffmann von
   Fallersleben **SCHUMANN**
Abendstern see Mayrhofer **SCHUBERT**
Abendstimmung see Bjørnson **DELIUS**
Abendstunde see Rose, Karl **LOEWE**
Abendwolke see Meyer **SCHOECK**
Abendwolken see Uhland **SCHOECK**
"Aber auch den Föhrenwald" *see Aus den*
   Waldliedern II Keller, G. **SCHOECK**
ABER DIE LIEBE. see Dehmel
   Nächtliche Scheu **WEBERN**
Aber die Nächte see Sauter, Lilly von
   KRENEK
Aber die Winter! see Rilke **KRENEK**
"Aber Efeu nenn' ich jene Mädchen" *see Efeu*
   Dahn **STRAUSS**
"Aber ein kleiner goldener Stern" *see Aus:*
   Ein Tagewerk II Keller, G. **SCHOECK**
Die abgeblühte Linde see Széchényi
   SCHUBERT
Abgeguckt see Mayr **REGER**
Die Abgeschiedenen see Uhland **LOEWE**
"Abi Abirounère, qui que tu n'etais don?" *see*
   Air du Rat Fargue **SATIE**
Abide with me see Lyle **IVES**
Abkehr see Leuthold **SCHOECK**
Ablösung im Sommer see Anon. *DES*
   KNABENWUNDERHORN: Ablösung.
   MAHLER
About my garden see Carpenter, Rue
   CARPENTER
"About the field they piped full right" *see*
   Tyrley Tyrlow Anon. **HESELTINE**
"Above the gulf that has no name" *see Day*
   and night Tiutchev **MEDTNER**
Abraham's request see Barbier, J.
   GOUNOD *Prière d'Abraham*
Ábrányi, Cornel *see* Ábrányi, Kornél,
   1822-1903.
Ábrányi, Kornél, 1822-1903.
   LISZT *Magyar király-dal*
L'abri see Rodès **BLOCH**
Abril galan see Machado y Ruiz
   RODRIGO
Absalom see Goodman **ROREM**
Abschatz, Johann Erasmus Assmann,
   freiherr von, 1646-1699.
   ZELTER *Mut*
Abschied see Anon. **VAUGHAN**
   WILLIAMS *Entlaubet ist der Walde*
Abschied see Eichendorff **PFITZNER,**
   SCHOECK
Abschied see Gerstenberg **LOEWE**
ABSCHIED. see Haringer
   Mädchenlied **SCHÖNBERG**
   Tot **SCHÖNBERG**

Abschied see Heine **FRANZ, GRIEG**
Abschied see Heyse **JENSEN**
Abschied see Kapper **FRANZ**
Abschied see Levetzow *HÖHENLIEDER.*
   SCHÖNBERG
Abschied see Löwenstein **RUBINSTEIN**
Abschied see Mayrhofer *LUNZ.*
   SCHUBERT
Abschied see Mörike **WOLF**
Abschied see Monsterberg-Münckeman
   BERG
Abschied see Paulsen **GRIEG** *Farvel*
Abschied see Rellstab **SCHUBERT**
Abschied see Roquette **JENSEN**
Abschied see Schubert **SCHUBERT**
Abschied see Uhland **LOEWE,**
   SCHOECK
Abschied see Unknown **MENDELSSOHN-**
   BARTHOLDY, ZELTER
Abschied see Wiener, Oskar **REGER**
Abschied, Böhmisch see Wenzig
   WESTSLAWISCHEM MÄRCHENSCHATZ.
   BRAHMS
Abschied vom Leben see Körner **WEBER**
Abschied vom Walde see Schöpff
   SCHUMANN
Abschied von der Erde see Pratobevera
   SCHUBERT
Abschied von der Harfe see Salis-Seewis
   SCHUBERT
Abschied von der Welt see Mary
   SCHUMANN
Abschied von Frankreich see Mary
   SCHUMANN
Abschiedsgesang an Wiens Bürger see
   Friedelberg **BEETHOVEN**
Absence see Gautier **BERLIOZ, BIZET;**
   DUPARC *Au pays où se fait la guerre*
Absence see Ségur **GOUNOD**
L'absent see Gounod **GOUNOD**
L'absent see Hugo **FAURÉ**
Absorbed and alone see Tiutchev
   MEDTNER *Dejection*
L'Académie Française nous a nommés tous
   trois see Indy **INDY**
Accept just once see Shenshin
   CHAÏKOVSKIĬ *Poymi khotraz*
Accompagnement see Samain **FAURÉ,**
   KOECHLIN
"Accoudés sur la table et déjà noyés d'ombre"
   see Le sommeil de canope Samain
   KOECHLIN
"Ach!" *see Taniec* Szymanowska, Zafia
   SZYMANOWSKI

"Ach! ach!" *see*
Pieśń o fali Szymanowska, Zafia
SZYMANOWSKI
Samotny ksiezyc Szymanowska, Zafia
SZYMANOWSKI
"Ach! ach! ach!" *see Slowik* Szymanowska,
Zafia **SZYMANOWSKI**
ACH! AUS DIESES TALES GRÜNDEN. see
Schiller
Sehnsucht **SCHUBERT**
Two settings: D. 52 and D. 636.
"Ach, aus dieses Tales Gründen" *see*
Sehnsucht Schiller **SCHUBERT**
Two settings: D. 52 and D. 636.
"Ach! aus Träumen fahr ich in die graue Luft"
see Enführung Dehmel
SZYMANOWSKI
"Ach, dass die innre Schöpfungskraft" *see*
Künstlers Abendlied Goethe **ZELTER**
Ach, dass du kamst see Osterwald **FRANZ**
"Ach, der Gebirgssohn hängt mit kindlicher
Lieb' " *see Das Heimweh* Pyrker
SCHUBERT
Ach, des Knaben Augen sind see López dc
Ubeda **WOLF**
"Ach du klar blauer Himmel" *see Wohin mit
der Freud?* Reinick **WOLF**
Ach du, um die Blumen sich verliebt see Lenz
GIDEON
"Ach, es ist so dunkel in des Todes Kammer"
see Der Tod Claudius, M.
SCHOECK, WEBERN
"Ach, Herr, wie lange willst du mein so ganz
vergessen?" *see Der 13. Psalm* Bible
SCHUBERT
Ach, ich denke see Köstlin **FRANZ**
Ach ihr lieben Aeuglein see Anon.
SPANISCHES LIEDERBUCH: Ay ojuelos
verdes. **JENSEN**
"Ach, ihr Wälder, dunkle Wälder" *see*
Der Verlassene Anon. **FRANZ**
Ach, im Maien wär's, im Maieh see Anon.
WOLF
"Ach, könnt ich, könnt vergessen sie!" *see*
Sonett aus dem 13. Jahrhundert Thibaut
IV **ZELTER**
Ein Sonnett Thibaut IV **BRAHMS**
Ach könnt' ich nimmer vergessen' see
Unknown **ZELTER**
"Ach, Lejbo, Lejbo, jakze ci nie wstyd?" *see*
Zly Lebja Iłłakowiczówna
SZYMANOWSKI
Ach Lieb', nun muss ich scheiden see Dahn
SCHLICHTE WEISEN, no. 12 (?).
STRAUSS

Ach, Liebster, in Gedanken see Scholz
REGER
"Ach! mein kühler Wasserquell!" *see*
Mädchen und Rose Jacob, T. **LOEWE**
"Ach, mich hält der Gram gefangen" *see*
Abschied, Böhmisch Wenzig **BRAHMS**
"Ach mir fehlt, nicht ist da" *see Klage I*, Aus
dem Böhmischen *see* Wenzig **BRAHMS**
"Ach, mir ist das Herz so schwer" *see Lied in
der Abwesenheit* Stolberg **SCHUBERT**
Ach! Mir ist das Herz so schwer see
Stolberg **ZELTER**
"Ach mir schallt's dorten so lieblich hervor"
see Der Wachtelschlag Sauter
BEETHOVEN, SCHUBERT
"Ach! musstest du denn scheiden" *see Kurzes
Wiedersehen* Osterwald **FRANZ**
"Ach neige, du Schmerzenreiche" *see*
*Gretchen vor dem Andachtsbild der Mater
dolorosa* Goethe **WOLF**
Gretchen vor der Mater dolorosa Goethe
SCHUBERT
Melodram Gretchens Goethe **WAGNER**
Szene aus "Faust" Goethe **LOEWE**
Ach není, není tu see Anon. **DVOŘÁK**
"Ach, nun taucht die Klosterzelle einsam aus
des Wassers Welle" *see Nonnenwerth*
Lichnowsky **LISZT**
"Ach! Od wrót mojego palacu" *see Zlote
trzewiczki* Szymanowska, Zafia
SZYMANOWSKI
"Ach Schwester, liebe Schwester" *see*
Der Spuk Löns **KILPINEN**
"Ach ty róże, krásná róže" *see Róže*
Unknown **DVOŘÁK**
"Ach, um deine feuchten Schwingen" *see*
Suleika Goethe **MENDELSSOHN-
BARTHOLDY, ZELTER**
Suleika II Willemer **SCHUBERT**
"Ach, und du mein kühles Wasser!" *see*
Mädchenlied Kapper **BRAHMS**
"Ach unsre leuchtenden Tage" *see Leuchtende
Tage* Jacobowski **PFITZNER**
"Ach vy lesí, tmaví losi" *see Opuščená*
Unknown **DVOŘÁK**
"Ach, vychodí, vychodí" *see Opuštěný milý*
Anon. **MARTINŮ**
Ach, wär' es nie geschehen see Anon.
FRANZ
"Ach, wär' ich doch zu dieser Stund" *see*
Mein Verlangen Förster, F. **WEBER**
"Ach, wär' ich nur ein Vögelein!" *see Lied
aus Aslauga's Ritter* La Motte-Fouque
SPOHR

Ach, warum blict dein Auge zuweilen see
Pleshcheyev MUSORGSKIĬ
Akh, zachem tvoi glazki poroĭu
"Ach, was bin ich aufgewacht?" *see Schlaf
nur ein* Heyse JENSEN
"Ach! was ist Leben doch so schwer" *see Sei
stille* Schorn LASSEN, LISZT
Ach was Kummer, Qual und Schmerzen see
Mündel *ELSÄSSISCHE VOLKSLIEDER.*
STRAUSS
"Ach! was soll der Mensch verlangen?" *see
Benerzigung* Goethe WOLF
"Ach was soll ich beginnen" *see Delphine*
Schütz SCHUBERT
Ach, was wird uns hier bereitet? see Kafka
KRENEK
Ach, weh mir verglückhaftem Mann see Dahn
SCHLICHTE WEISEN, no. 10. STRAUSS
Ach, wende diesen Blick see Daumer
FRAUENBILDER UND HULDIGUNGEN.
BRAHMS
"Ach, wenn es nun die Mutter wüsst' " *see
Mädchenlied* Remer SCHÖNBERG
Ach, wenn ich doch ein Immchen wär see
Osterwald FRANZ
"Ach wenn ich nur ein Liebchen hätt" *see
Die kleine Fritz an seine jungen Freunde*
Anon. WEBER
"Ach, wenn's nur der König auch wüsst' " *see
Die Soldatenbraut* Mörike
SCHUMANN
"Ach wenn's nur der König wüsst" *see
Die Soldatenbraut* Mörike BERG
"Ach wer bringt die schönen Tage" *see Erster
Verlust* Goethe BERG, MEDTNER,
MENDELSSOHN-BARTHOLDY,
SCHOECK, SCHUBERT, WOLF,
ZELTER
ACH, WER DOCH DAS KÖNNTE! see
Blüthgen
Kinderliedchen SCHOECK
"Ach, wer nimmt von meiner Seele" *see
Todessehnen* Schenkendorf BRAHMS
"Ach, wie brenn' ich vor Verlangen" *see
Galathea* Wedekind SCHÖNBERG
"Ach, wie ich mich doch schinde" *see
Rosalinde* Krenek KRENEK
Ach, wie komm' ich da hinüber? see Heine
FRANZ
Ach, wie lang die Seele schlummert! see
Anon. WOLF
Ach, wie richtete, so klagt ich see Hafiz
SCHOECK
"Ach wie schnell die Tage fliehen" *see Im
Herbst* Klingemann
MENDELSSOHN-BARTHOLDY

*Ach, wie schön ist Nacht und Dämmerschein
see* Hafiz SCHOECK
Ach, you drunken woodcock see Musorgskiĭ
MUSORGSKIĬ
Akh, ty, p'ianaia teteri͡a!
"Achille aux pieds légers" *see Mouton Blanc*
Bibesco SAUGUET
ACHT LIEDER NACH VERSCHIEDENEN
DICHTEN, no. 1
HINDEMITH Bock, K. *Die trunkene
Tänzerin*
ACHT LIEDER NACH VERSCHIEDENEN
DICHTEN, no. 2
HINDEMITH Morgenstern *Wie Sankt
Franciscus schweb' in der Luft*
ACHT LIEDER NACH VERSCHIEDENEN
DICHTEN, no. 3
HINDEMITH Lasker-Schüler *Traum*
ACHT LIEDER NACH VERSCHIEDENEN
DICHTEN, no. 4
HINDEMITH Morgenstern *Auf der
Treppe sitzen meine Öhrchen*
ACHT LIEDER NACH VERSCHIEDENEN
DICHTEN, no. 5
HINDEMITH Morgenstern *Vor dir
schein' ich aufgewacht*
ACHT LIEDER NACH VERSCHIEDENEN
DICHTEN, no. 6
HINDEMITH Lasker-Schüler *Du machst
mich traurig-hör'*
ACHT LIEDER NACH VERSCHIEDENEN
DICHTEN, no. 7
HINDEMITH Schilling *Durch die
abendlichen Gärten*
ACHT LIEDER NACH VERSCHIEDENEN
DICHTEN, no. 8
HINDEMITH Trakl *Trompeten*
Achtzehn Lieder see Unknown
HINDEMITH
"Ack, vänskap, ljufva blomma" *see
Vänskapens blomma* Josephson, E.
SIBELIUS
Ackermann, Louise Victorine (Choquet),
1813-1890.
CHAUSSON *Hébé*
Acqua see Rubino RESPIGHI
"Acqua, e tu ancora sul tuo flauto lene" *see
Acqua* Rubino RESPIGHI
"Across the hill of late" *see Spring song* Ives,
Harmony IVES
Across the midnight sky see Lermontov
RIMSKIĬ-KORSAKOV *Po nebu
polunochi*
"Across the summer meadows fair" *see
The camp meeting* Elliot IVES
Action de grâces see Messiaen MESSIAEN

COMPOSER Poet *Title* ''First Line''

Ad Jesum Christum, Dominum et Salvatorem meum see Böhmer **LOEWE**

Ad una stella see Maffei **VERDI**

Adagio see Bergman **KILPINEN**

Adam lay ybounden see Anon. **HESELTINE**

Addio ai viennesi see Unknown **ROSSINI**

Addio di Rossini see Unknown **ROSSINI** *Addio ai viennesi*

Ade denn, du stolze see Osterwald **FRANZ**

"*Ade! du muntre, do fröhliche Stadt*" see *Abschied* Rellstab **SCHUBERT**

"*Ade, mein Schatz, du mochtst mich nicht*" see *Seemanns Abschied* Eichendorff **WOLF**

Ade! (Nach dem Böhmischen) see Kapper **BRAHMS**

Adela see Anon. **RODRIGO**

Adelaide see Matthisson **BEETHOVEN, SCHUBERT, ZELTER**

Adèle see Giraudoux *SUZANNE ET LA PACIFIQUE.* **HONEGGER**

Adelina à la promenade see Garcia Lorca **POULENC**

Adelwold und Emma see Bertrand **SCHUBERT**

Adenis, Eugène, pseud. see Colombeau, Eugène Adenis de, 1854-

L'adieu see Apollinaire *ALÇOOLS.* **IIONEGGER, MARTINŮ, RIVIER**

Adieu see Desbordes-Valmore **SAUGUET**

Adieu see Gilbert **MASSENET** *Stances*

Adieu see Grandmougin **FAURÉ**

L'adieu see Lunel **MILHAUD**

Adieu see Messiaen **MESSIAEN**

Adieu see Musset **INDY**

Adieu see Radiguet **SATIE**

Un adieu see Silvestre **MASSENET**

Adieu see Silvestre **MASSENET** *Complainte*

L'adieu see Toussaint *JARDIN DES CARESSES.* **AUBERT**

L'adieu see Unknown **POULENC**

L'ADIEU À LA VIE, no. 1 **CASELLA** Tagore *O toi, suprême accomplissement de ma vie*

L'ADIEU À LA VIE, no. 2 **CASELLA** Tagore *Mort, ta servante est à ma porte*

L'ADIEU À LA VIE, no. 3 **CASELLA** Tagore *A cette heure du départ*

L'ADIEU À LA VIE, no. 4 **CASELLA** Tagore *Dans une salutation suprême*

"*Adieu! Adieu! bergère chérie*" see *Adieux à la prairie* Silvestre **MASSENET**

"*Adieu, adieu! my native shore fades*" see *A farewell to land* Byron **IVES**

"*Adieu, amour nuage qui fuis*" see *Voyage* Apollinaire **POULENC**

Adieu, Bessy! see Moore, T. **BERLIOZ**

"*Adieu, charmant pays de France*" see *Les adieux de Marie Stuart* Béranger **WAGNER**

"*Adieu! je crois qu'en cette vie*" see *Adieu* Musset **INDY**

"*Adieu, patrie, l'onde est en furie!*" see *Le chant de ceux qui s'en vont sur mer* Hugo **SAINT-SAËNS**

Adieu pour jamais see Kahn *LES PALAIS NOMADES*: Intermède XIV. **LOEFFLER**

"*Adieu, Suzon, adieu, ma rose blonde*" see *Adieux à Suzon* Musset **BIZET**

"*Adieu toi, colombe verte*" see *Adieu* Messiaen **MESSIAEN**

"*Adieu, va, mon homme, adieu*" see *Chanson espagnole* Anon. **RAVEL**

Adieux see Régnier **ROUSSEL**

Les adieux à la maison see Dennery **GOUNOD**

Adieux à la prairie see Silvestre **MASSENET**

Adieux à la vie! (Élégie sur une seule note) see Unknown **ROSSINI**

Les adieux à Rome see Delavigne **ROSSINI**

Adieux à Suzon see Musset **BIZET, CHABRIER**

Adieux au désert see Flobert, A. **LALO**

Adieux de l'hôtesse arabe see Hugo **BIZET**

Les adieux de Marie Stuart see Béranger **WAGNER**

Les Adieux du berger see Silvestre **MASSENET** *Adieux à la prairie*

Adil **SPOHR** *Ghasel*

Adjuro vos, filiae Jerusalem see Canticum Canticorum **PIZZETTI** Two settings: 1908 and 1932-33.

ADJUTANTENRITTE UND ANDERE GEDICHTE. see Liliencron *Meiner Mutter* **WEBERN**

"*Der Adler lauscht auf seinem Horst*" see *Der Feind* Scherenberg **LOEWE**

Der Adler und der Kukuk see Krylov **RUBINSTEIN**

Admiral Trash see Maĭakovskii **PROKOFIEV** *Pesnya*

L'adolescent see Carême **SAUGUET**

The adoration see Symons **IRELAND**

ADRIANO: Act II, scene 6. see Metastasio *L'amante impatiente* **BEETHOVEN** Two settings: Op. 82 nos. 3 and 4.

The advent see Meynell **IRELAND**

COMPOSER Poet *Title* . "First Line"

Ady, Endre, 1877-1918.
  BARTÓK
    Alone with the sea
    Autumn echoes
    Autumn tears
    I cannot come to you
    Lost content
  SEIBER
    Jó Csönd herceg elött
    Tüzes seb vagyok
AE Lastrae see Berntsen **NIELSEN**
AEbleblomst see Holstein **NIELSEN**
"Die Ähren nur noch niken" *see Wiegenlied*
  Hoffmann von Fallersleben **STRAUSS**
Älvan och kardinalen see Josephson, E.
  KILPINEN
Älvan och snigeln see Josephson, E.
  SIBELIUS
AENEID. see Vergilius
  Lutheri Vespera **ZELTER**
Aeolsharfe see Lingg **REGER**
Äppelträd och päronträd see Blomberg
  KILPINEN
Den aergjerrige see Paulsen **GRIEG**
Aeschylus Ca. 525-456 B.C.
  SCHUBERT *Fragment aus dem Aeschylus*
"Der Affe, Herr von Putzig" *see Das Quartett*
  Krylov **RUBINSTEIN**
"Afin que ton renom coule parmi la plaine"
  see La fontaine d'Hélène Ronsard
  AUBERT
Afinogenov, Aleksandr Nikolaevich,
  1904-1941.
  PROKOFIEV
    Chetyre pesni
    Skvoz' shega i tumany
Afraid see De La Mare **BERKELEY**
Afsked see Heine **GRIEG** *Abschied*
"Aftenen kommer, Solen står rød" *see Fra*
  Monte Pincio Bjørnson **GRIEG**
"Aftensolens Hygge ikke kan mit Vindu naa"
  see Suk Bjørnson **GRIEG**
after all white horses are in bed see
  Cummings **BLITZSTEIN**
After Antwerp see Cammaerts **COPLAND**
After Atlantis see Ayer, Ethan **ROREM**
After sunset see Symons **RIEGGER**
After the birth of her son see Mary
  SCHUMANN *Nach der Geburt ihres*
  Sohnes
After the dazzle of day see Whitman
  BLITZSTEIN
After two years see Aldington *IMAGES*
  (1910-1915). **HESELTINE**
Afterglow see Cooper, James **IVES**
Afterthought see Bernstein **BERNSTEIN**

Afton water see Burns **BRITTEN**
Again, as before, alone see Rathaus
  CHAĬKOVSKIĬ *Weil' ich wie einstmals*
  allein
Again I am alone see Shevchenko
  RACHMANINOFF
Again you leapt, my heart see Grekov
  RACHMANINOFF
"Against these turbid turquoise skies" *see*
  Les ballons Wilde **GRIFFES**
Aganoor-Pompilj, Vittoria Antonia
  Maria, 1855-1910.
  RESPIGHI
    E se un Giorno Tornasse
    Pioggia
Agathas see Pound **DIAMOND**
L'ÂGE D'OR, no. 9
  GOUNOD Barbier, J. *À la Madone*
L'ÂGE D'OR, no. 13
  GOUNOD Pradère-Niquet *À une soeur*
L'ÂGE D'OR, no. 20
  GOUNOD Barbier, J. *Parlez pour moi*
Agee, James, 1909-1955.
  PERMIT ME VOYAGE: Description of
    Elysium.
    BARBER *Sure on this shining night*
  SONNET 1.
    DIAMOND *So it begins*
  SONNET 2.
    DIAMOND *Our doom is in our being*
  SONNET 4.
    DIAMOND *I have been fashioned*
  SONNET 8.
    DIAMOND *What curious thing is love*
  SONNET 9.
    DIAMOND *Why am I here*
  SONNET 10.
    DIAMOND *Wring me no more*
  SONNET 17.
    DIAMOND *I nothing saw in you*
  SONNET XX.
    CARPENTER *Morning fair*
  SONNET 20.
    DIAMOND *Now stands our love*
  SONNET 23.
    DIAMOND *This little time*
Ages and ages see Whitman **BLITZSTEIN**
"Ages and ages returning at intervals
  unde[s]troyed" *see Ages and ages*
  Whitman **BLITZSTEIN**
"Agite, bon cheval, ta crinière fuyante" *see*
  Le galop Sully-Prudhomme **DUPARC**
Aglaé see Cocteau **AURIC**
AGNES. see Kosegarten
  Von Ida **SCHUBERT**
Agnes see Mörike **BRAHMS, WOLF**

COMPOSER   Poet   *Title*   "First Line"

Agnete see Plönnies **LOEWE**
Agnivt͡sev, Nikolaĭ I͡Akovlevich, d. 1932.
PROKOFIEV *Kudesnik*
AGNUS DEI. see Boito
Pietà, Signor **VERDI**
Agnus Dei see No author **CHANLER**
L'agriculteur see Lunel **MILHAUD**
Agrippa d'Aubigné, Théodore *see*
Aubigné, Théodore Agrippa d', 1552-
1630.
"Agua quisiera ser" *see Anhelos* Rodríguez
Marin, Francisco **TURINA**
Aguet, William
HONEGGER *Chanson de marin*
IBERT
Je penais épouser un fier à bras
Mon bien aimé siffle bien
SAUGUET *Chanson de la fille de bar*
SAINT-SAËNS *Angélus*
Aguétant, Pierre
SAINT-SAËNS *Où nous avons aimé*
"Ah, ah, ah, nacht liegt auf den fremden
Wegen" *see Süsser Mond* Heine
WEISGALL
"Ah! Ah! Dans les prés fleuris" *see Dans les*
pré fleuris Anon. **SZYMANOWSKI**
"Ah! ce soir là vraiment tout était si paisible"
see Cloche du soir Fort **HONEGGER**
"Ah, comme vous souriez" *see Le bal*
d'enfants Richter **SAUGUET**
"Ah dit la fille frivole que le vent y vire" *see*
Chanson de la fille frivole
Fombeure **POULENC**
Ah dove siete? see Unknown **WEBER**
"Ah! du moins, pour toi je veux être" *see Mon*
amour l'a bien mérité Silvestre
MASSENET
"Ah! fuyez à présent" *see Air grave* Moréas
POULENC
"Ah grief to think" *see La tiranna* Unknown
BEETHOVEN
Ah! if you knew see Pleshcheyev
CHAĬKOVSKIĬ *O, eslib" znali vy*
"Ah, Ikharus sa oot, et enempää" *see Ikarus*
Koskenniemi **KILPINEN**
Ah, is it an honor for a young man to weave
flax? see Tolstoĭ **MUSORGSKIĬ**
Oĭ, chest' li to molodt͡su len priasti?
"Ah! je ne savais pas qu'il pouvait m'être
doux" *see La délaissée* Blanchecotte
HAHN
"Ah! la charmante chose" *see Voyage à Paris*
Apollinaire **POULENC**
"Ah! les cornes: c'est un colimaçon" *see*
Déjeuner de soleil Radiguet **AURIC**
"Ah! Luceros radiantes" *see A unos ojos*
Rodríguez Marin, Francisco **TURINA**

Ah, missä lienet nyt see Jalkanen
KILPINEN
"Ah, miten kimmeltää keväinen hanki" *see*
Kevätlaulu Lehtinen **KILPINEN**
"Ah! mon cher docteur" *see Le petit garçon*
trop bien portant Nohain, Jean
POULENC
"Ah! ne repousse pas" *see Repentir* Anon.
GOUNOD
Ah! Petit démons! see Musset **CHABRIER**
"Ah! que ces gens continuent à dormir!" *see*
La descente Claudel **MILHAUD**
"Ah! que je plains ta flamme" *see Boléro*
Barbier, J. **GOUNOD**
"Ah! reste, reste dans mon coeur" *see La*
chanson du printemps Bard, Chevalier
MILHAUD
"Ah! sad are they who know not love" *see*
Spurned love Aldrich **COPLAND**
"Ah! si vous saviez comme on pleure" *see*
Prière Sully-Prudhomme **GOUNOD**
"Ah! si vraiment l'indifférence" *see Le doute!*
Ferrier **BIZET**
"Ah! s'il est dans votre village" *see Chanson*
de Florian Florian **IVES**
Ah! sun-flower see Blake, William *AH!*
SUN-FLOWER.
BRITTEN, VAUGHAN WILLIAMS
AH! SUN-FLOWER. see Blake, William
Ah! sun-flower **BRITTEN, VAUGHAN**
WILLIAMS
"Ah, sunflower weary of love" *see*
The sunflower Blake, William
THOMSON
"Ah, Sun-flower! weary of time" *see Ah! Sun-*
flower Blake, William
BRITTEN, VAUGHAN WILLIAMS
"Ah, there were many of us there" *see Arion*
Pushkin **MEDTNER**
"Ah! To be all alone in a little cell" *see*
The desire for hermitage
O'Faolain, Sean, translator. **BARBER**
"Ah! vous l'aurez, plus tard" *see Quand*
l'enfant prie Boyer, Charles **GOUNOD**
Ah! When thine eyes of azure see Heine
LASSEN *Mit deinen blauen Augen*
"Ahi! Ahi! Ahi! Ahi!" *see Répétition*
planétaire Messiaen **MESSIAEN**
"Ahidi, ich liebe, Ahidi, ich liebe!" *see*
Hänflings Liebeswerbung Kind, F.
SCHUBERT
Ahlefeldt, Ottilie von
LASSEN
Die Erde steht in süssem Beben
Ich gehe durch die stille Nacht
Jüngst, als ich über'n Friedhof ging
Könnt ich mit den Vöglein fliegen

Ahlefeldt, Ottilie von *(continued)*
   LASSEN *(continued)*
    Still ist's auf dem Erdenkreise
    Wenn ich ein kleines Mücklein wär
Ahnung see Becker, K. **ZELTER**
AHNUNG UND GEGENWART. see
   Eichendorff
   Wehmuth **SCHUMANN**
   Zwielicht **SCHUMANN**
"Aĭ, aĭ, aĭ, aĭ, mama!" *see Kot matros*
   Musorgskiĭ **MUSORGSKIĬ**
Aicard, Jean François Victor, 1848-1921.
   MARTINŮ *La poule a couvé*
   MASSENET
    Chant de nourrice
    Loin de moi ta lèvre qui ment
    Le Noël des humbles
   SAINT-SAËNS *Vogue, vogue la galère*
Aigues-Marines see Vivien **AUBERT**
Aiken, Conrad Potter, 1889-1973.
   DISCORDANTS.
    COPLAND *Music I heard*
    ROREM *Discordants*
"Aimable bijou de famille" *see L'éventail*
   Morel-Retz **MASSENET**
"Aimè, io tremo!" *see Il traditor deluso*
   Metastasio **SCHUBERT**
Aimer see Méry **FRANCK**
Aimons, rêvons! see Ferrier **BIZET**
Aimons-nous see Banville *ODELETTES.*
   SAINT-SAËNS
Aimons-nous see Barbier, J. **GOUNOD**
Aimons-nous et dormons see Banville
   ODELETTES. **DEBUSSY**
Aina laulan see Kanteletar **KILPINEN**
"Ainsi qu'un fier guerrier" *see L'heure douce*
   Chabroux, Ernest **MASSENET**
"Ainsi qu'une jeune beauté" *see* Anon.
   SAINT-SAËNS
L'air see Banville **HAHN, KOECHLIN**
Air champêtre see Moréas **POULENC**
Air du Poète see Fargue *LUDIONS.* **SATIE**
Air du Rat see Fargue *LUDIONS.* **SATIE**
L'air du soir emportait see Silvestre
   MASSENET
"L'air est embaumé" *see Nuit d'Espagne*
   Gallet **MASSENET**
Air grave see Moréas **POULENC**
The air is the only see Moss **ROREM**
Air romantique see Moréas **POULENC**
"L'air s'embrume" *see Le nénuphar*
   Haraucourt **KOECHLIN**
Air vif see Moréas **POULENC**
"L'aire est chauve" *see L'hiver* Hölderlin
   SAUGUET
Aire y Donaire see Anon. **RODRIGO**

"Airey donaire!" *see Aire y Donaire* Anon.
   RODRIGO
AIRS CHANTÉS, no. 1
   POULENC Moréas *Air romantique*
AIRS CHANTÉS, no. 2
   POULENC Moréas *Air champêtre*
AIRS CHANTÉS, no. 3
   POULENC Moréas *Air grave*
AIRS CHANTÉS, no. 4
   POULENC Moréas *Air vif*
"Aiusi quand la fleur printa-nière dans le
   bois" *see Marie* Musset **LOEFFLER**
Aj! Kterak trojhranec muj přerozkošně see
   Heyduk **DVOŘÁK**
"Aj! Stupaj, stupaj, stupaj" *see Cesta k milé*
   Unknown **MARTINŮ**
"Aj, veža, veža" *see Vysoká veža* Anon.
   MARTINŮ
Akahito see Akahito, 8th cent.
   STRAVINSKIĬ
Akahito, 8th cent.
   STRAVINSKIĬ *Akahito*
"Akh, a to nigde" *see IA nigde druzhka ne*
   vizhu Anon. **PROKOFIEV**
Akh igry i tantsy see Goethe **MEDTNER** *So*
   tanzet
"Akh, kari glazki" *see Kari glazki* Anon.
   PROKOFIEV
Akh, ty, p'ianaia teteria! see Musorgskiĭ
   MUSORGSKIĬ
"Akh, ty, prokaznik!" *see V uglu* Musorgskiĭ
   MUSORGSKIĬ
"Akh! uĭmis' ty, buria!" *see Kolybel'naia*
   pesn' v Pleshcheyev **CHAĬKOVSKIĬ**
Akh, zachem tvoi glazki poroiu see
   Pleshcheyev **MUSORGSKIĬ**
Akhmatova, Anna Andreevna, 1888-
   1966.
   PROKOFIEV
    Nastoiashchuiu
    Pamiat' o solntse
    Seroglazyĭ korol'
    Solntse komnatu napolnilo
    Zdravstvuĭ!
Akhtamar, Grégoire d'
   MASSENET *Ivre d'amour*
Aksakov, Konstantin Sergeevich, 1817-
   1860.
   BALAKIREV *Sredi tsvetov pori osenney*
   CHAĬKOVSKIĬ *Detskaya pesnya*
"Al comenzar la noche de aquel dia" *see*
   Los dos miedos
   Campoamor y Campoosorio **TURINA**
Al Marchesén, povrén, ch'l'era un bulot see
   Zerbini, Alfredo **PIZZETTI**
"Al paño fino" *see El pano moruno* Anon.
   FALLA

COMPOSER Poet *Title* ''First Line''

Al val de Fuente Ovejuna *see* Vega Carpio
   FUENTE OVEJUNA. **TURINA**
"Alack and woe that love is so akin to pain!"
   see Melancholy: a song "à la Debussy"
   Farnol **COPLAND**
"Alahan' on allin mieli" *see Armottoman osa*
   Kanteletar **KILPINEN**
Alas, for I outlive my yearnings see Pushkin
   MEDTNER
"Alas! for them their day is o'er" *see*
   The Indians Sprague **IVES**
Alas, how easily things go wrong see
   McDonald, George **CARPENTER**
"Alas, I am a heavy child" *see Stout*
   Carpenter, Rue **CARPENTER**
"Alas! my heart is not my own" *see Old love*
   song Anon. **LOEFFLER**
Albada a l'Estela see Rey, Paul **SÉVERAC**
Albado see Marguerite d'Angoulême
   SÉVERAC
L'Albatros see Baudelaire **CHAUSSON**
"L'albero a cui tendevi" *see Pianto antico*
   Carducci **CASELLA**
"Albertine blanc pur" *see Les jacinthes*
   Daudet, L. **MILHAUD**
 Alberus, Erasmus, d. 1553.
   MORGENLIED.
     REGER
     Morgengesang
     O Jesu Christ, wir warten dein
Album see Radiguet **AURIC**
L'ALBUM DE LILIAN, no. 1
   KOECHLIN Koechlin *Gardez ce teint de*
   jeune fille
L'ALBUM DE LILIAN, no. 2
   KOECHLIN Koechlin *Tout va bien*
Albumblatt see Krenek **KRENEK**
EL ALCALDE DE ZALAMEA. see Calderon
   Liebesliedchen **STRAUSS**
   Lied der Chispa **STRAUSS**
L'alchimiste a la voix d'ambre see Raphaël,
   Cluzel **SAUGUET**
L'alchimiste au cher visage see Raphaël,
   Cluzel **SAUGUET**
L'alchimiste au regard d'ambre see Raphaël,
   Cluzel **SAUGUET**
L'alchimiste est dans le grenier see Raphaël,
   Cluzel **SAUGUET**
ALCIDE AL BIVIO. see Metastasio
   Pensa, che questo istante **SCHUBERT**
ALCOOLS. see Apollinaire
   A la Santé **HONEGGER**
   L'adieu **HONEGGER, MARTINŮ,**
     RIVIER
   Aubade **RIVIER**
   Automne **BERKELEY, HONEGGER,**
     RIVIER, ROREM

   Les cloches **HONEGGER, RIVIER**
   Clotilde **HONEGGER, RIVIER**
   Les colchiques **RIVIER**
   Le pont Mirabeau **RIVIER**
   Rosemonde **POULENC**
   Saltimbanques **HONEGGER, RIVIER**
ALCYONE. see Annunzio
   Ditirambo terzo (dalle laudi di Gabriele
     d'Annunzio, 1923) **MALIPIERO**
   La sera fiesolana **CASELLA**
Les Alcyons see Autran **MASSENET**
Aldington, Richard, 1892-1962.
   IMAGES (1910-1915).
     HESELTINE *After two years*
"Áldott légyen Magyarok királya!" *see*
   Magyar király-dal Ábrányi **LISZT**
Aldrich, Thomas Bailey, 1836-1907.
   IVES *Maple leaves*
   THE BETROTHAL.
     LASSEN *Verlobung*
   TWO SONGS FROM THE PERSIAN, II.
     COPLAND *Spurned love*
Aldrig hans Ord kan jeg glemme see
   Unknown **NIELSEN**
Alexander, Cecil Francis (Humphreys),
   1818-1895.
   GOUNOD *There is a green hill far away*
Alexander, Griffith
   CARPENTER *My sweetheart*
Alexandre, André
   MASSENET
     Amours bénis
     Extase printanière
     La mélodie des baisers
     Mousmé
ALEXANDRIE. see Vincendon, Mireille
   Antennes **SCHMITT**
Alexis, Wilibald, pseud. *see* Häring,
   Wilhelm, 1798-1871.
Alford, Henry, 1810-1871.
   IVES
     Forward into light
     Naught that country needeth
Alguna vez see Castillejo *SPANISCHES*
   LIEDERBUCH: Alguna vez.
   GRIEG *Dereinst, Gedanke mein*
   JENSEN *Alguna vez*
   WOLF *Dereinst, dereinst, Gedanke mein*
Ali im Garten see Stieglitz **LOEWE**
Ali mat' menia rozhala see Mickiewicz
   CHAÏKOVSKIĬ
Ali Pascha *see* Ali, pasha, of Janima,
   1741-1822.
Ali, pasha, of Janima, 1741-1822.
   LASSEN *Die Rosen von Jericho*
Alice Rodd see De La Mare *DING DONG*
   BELL: Benighted. **CHANLER**

Alinde see Rochlitz **SCHUBERT**
ALISSA, no. 1
   MILHAUD Gide *Jérôme*
ALISSA, no. 2
   MILHAUD Gide *Jérôme et Alissa*
ALISSA, no. 3
   MILHAUD Gide *Jérôme et Alissa*
ALISSA, no. 4
   MILHAUD Gide *Lettre d'Alissa*
ALISSA, no. 5
   MILHAUD Gide *Jérôme et Alissa*
ALISSA, no. 6
   MILHAUD Gide *Lettres d'Alissa*
   NB: No. 7 is a prelude for piano only.
ALISSA, no. 8
   MILHAUD Gide *Journal d'Alissa*
Alix, Marie
   SAUGUET *Pour Nicolas*
Alkanzor und Zaide see Kind, F. *DAS*
NACHTLAGER VON GRANADA.
   WEBER
All in a garden green see Howell, Thomas
   IRELAND
All in green my love went riding see
   Cummings **ROREM**
"All is darkness, naught I see" *see Sleepless*
   Pushkin **MEDTNER**
All is vanity see Byron **DIAMOND**
All mein Gedanken see Dahn *SCHLICHTE*
   WEISEN, no. 11. **STRAUSS**
All' mein Gedanken, mein Herz und mein Sinn
   see Dahn **REGER**
"All' mein Wirken" *see Als ich sie erröten*
   sah Ehrlich **SCHUBERT**
All men are mad some way see Goodman
   ROREM
"All nature sings to God Almighty" *see Glory*
   to God Teternikov **RACHMANINOFF**
All night a wind of music see Beddoes
   BERKELEY
All once I gladly owned see Tiutchev
   RACHMANINOFF *He took all from me*
All poison the song that I sing thee see Heine
   BORODIN *Vergiftet sind meine Lieder*
All round about the woods are still see
   Heyduk **DVOŘÁK** *A les je tichý kolem*
   kol
All sudden by the wind see Brooke
   BLITZSTEIN
"All suddenly the wind comes soft" *see*
   Spring sorrow Brooke **IRELAND**
"All summer long we boys dreamed" *see*
   Circus band Ives **IVES**
All that's past see De La Mare **BERKELEY**
"All the little birds I see that flutter" *see*
   Serenade Shenshin **MEDTNER**

"All the way from Illinois to a little old town
   in France" *see Khaki Sammy*
   Carpenter, John **CARPENTER**
All things depart see Rathaus
   RACHMANINOFF *All things pass by*
All things pass by see Rathaus
   RACHMANINOFF
All this is what only remains see Sládek
   MARTINŮ
All through the long day see Rivas, Reyna
   THOMSON *Todas las horas*
All through the night a bird will sing see
   Hálek **DVOŘÁK**
   Ten ptáček, ten se nazpívá
All ye that labour come unto Me see Hálek
   DVOŘÁK *Vy všichni kdo jste stísněni*
Alla dem som vilse fara see Ullman
   KILPINEN
Alla riva del tebro see Anon.
   SAINT-SAËNS
Allah, Allah, Akbar see Iwaszkiewicz
   SZYMANOWSKI
Alle see Meyer **SCHOECK**
Alle gingen, Herz, zu Ruh see Anon. **WOLF**
"Alle Mädchen erwarten" *see Die Näherin*
   Rilke **BERG**
Alle meine Wünsche schweigen see Schoeck,
   P. **SCHOECK**
"Alle Menschen gross und klein" *see*
   Sinnspruch Goethe **STRAUSS**
Alle sind gekommen see Anon.
   SZYMANOWSKI *Wsyscy przyjechali*
"Alle Sternelein, die am Himmel steh'n" *see*
   Bitte Holst **REGER**
Une allée du Luxembourg see Gérard de
   Nerval **AURIC**
L'allée est sans fin see Verlaine **HAHN**
Allegro see Ives, Harmony **IVES**
Allein see Hesse **KILPINEN**
Allein see Michell **LASSEN**
Allein see Ritter **REGER**
"Allein: du mit den Worten" *see Worte* Benn
   BLACHER
"Allein in sonniger Herbstlaube sitz' ich beim
   Wein" *see Trinklied* Krenek **KRENEK**
"Allein, nachdenklich, wie gelähmt vom
   Krampfe" *see Sonett II* Petrarca
   SCHUBERT
"Allein zu sein!" *see Einsamkeit* Stotterfoth,
   Adelheid von **LASSEN**
"Alleluia . . . " *see Alleluia* No author
   ROREM
Alleluia see No author **ROREM**
"Alleluia, alleluia" *see Résurrection*
   Messiaen **MESSIAEN**
Allen Welten abgewandt see Scholz **REGER**

COMPOSER Poet *Title* "First Line"

The all-enduring see Brewster, Lyman
 IVES
Allerseelen see Gilm zu Rosenegg *LETZTE
 BLÄTTER.* LASSEN, PIJPER,
 STRAUSS
Alles see Dehmel *IM ZWIELICHT.*
 SCHÖNBERG
"Alles dunkel, alles still" *see Nacht* Huber,
 B. KILPINEN
Alles endet, was entstehet see Buonarroti
 WOLF
Alles in dir see Branco LOEWE
"Alles in mir glühet, zu lieben!" *see Gebet um
 die Geliebte* Gubitz WEBER
Alles ist eitel, spricht der Prediger see Byron
 LOEWE
"Alles kündet dich an" *see Gegenwart*
 Goethe FRANZ
"Alles kündigt dich an!" *see Gegenwart*
 Goethe WEBERN
Alles scheidet liebes Herz see Hoffmann
 von Fallersleben LASSEN
Alles um Liebe see Kosegarten
 SCHUBERT
"Alles, was Odem hat, lobe den Herrn!" *see
 Lobgesang* Buerde LOEWE
"Alles wiegt die stille Nacht" *see Ständchen*
 Körner WOLF
"Allgütiger, ich bringe dir" *see Lied* Recke,
 Ewald von der ZELTER
Allievo, Biago
 MASSENET *L'hymne des fleurs*
Die Allmacht see Pyrker SCHUBERT
Allmacht Gottes see Branco LOEWE
Die Allmächtige see Hafiz STRAUSS
Allmers, Hermann, 1821-1902.
 BRAHMS *Feldeinsamkeit*
 IVES *In summer fields*
Allnächtlich im Traume see Heine FRANZ,
 MENDELSSOHN-BARTHOLDY,
 SCHUMANN
Allons plus vite see Apollinaire *IL Y A.*
 POULENC
Allons-y Chochotte see Durante, D. SATIE
Allorge, Henri
 MASSENET *Effusion*
ALL'S WELL THAT ENDS WELL. see
 Shakespeare
 Was this fair face THOMSON
Almaïde d'Étremont see Jammes
 MILHAUD
Almers, Hermann *see* Allmers,
 Hermann, 1821-1902.
Almquist, C. J. L. 1793-1866.
 NIELSEN *Balladen om Bjørnen*
"Alone and lost in dreams" *see Twilight*
 Guyot RACHMANINOFF

"Alone by the bars at the window I lay" *see
 The prisoner* Pushkin MEDTNER
Alone with the sea see Ady BARTÓK
"Along the faint shores of the foamless gulf"
 see Venilia Sharp, W. LUENING
Along the field see Housman *A
 SHROPSHIRE LAD*: XXVI.
 VAUGHAN WILLIAMS
ALONG THE FIELD, no. 1
 VAUGHAN WILLIAMS Housman
 We'll go to the woods no more
ALONG THE FIELD, no. 2
 VAUGHAN WILLIAMS Housman
 Along the field
ALONG THE FIELD, no. 3
 VAUGHAN WILLIAMS Housman
 The half-moon westers low
ALONG THE FIELD, no. 4
 VAUGHAN WILLIAMS Housman
 In the morning
ALONG THE FIELD, no. 5
 VAUGHAN WILLIAMS Housman
 The sigh that heaves the grasses
ALONG THE FIELD, no. 6
 VAUGHAN WILLIAMS Housman
 Goodbye
ALONG THE FIELD, no. 7
 VAUGHAN WILLIAMS Housman
 Fancy's knell
ALONG THE FIELD, no. 8
 VAUGHAN WILLIAMS Housman
 With rue my heart is laden
"Along the field as we came by" *see Along
 the field* Housman
 VAUGHAN WILLIAMS
Along the stream see Li Po HESELTINE
"Alors qu'en tes mains de lumière" *see
 Exaucement* Lerberghe FAURÉ
"Alors vers sa douzième année" *see Présage
 de la croix* Bordése SAINT-SAËNS
"Die Alpen werden von wilden Nomaden
 bewohnt" *see Alpenbewohner* Krenek
 KRENEK
Alpenbewohner see Krenek KRENEK
Der Alpenjäger see Mayrhofer SCHUBERT
Der Alpenjäger see Schiller SCHUBERT
Der Alpenjäger see Schiller *WILHELM
 TELL.* LISZT
ALPHABET, no. 1
 AURIC Radiguet *Album*
ALPHABET, no. 2
 AURIC Radiguet *Bateau*
ALPHABET, no. 3
 AURIC Radiguet *Domino*
ALPHABET, no. 4
 AURIC Radiguet *Filet à papillons*

COMPOSER Poet *Title* "First Line"

ALPHABET, no. 5
  AURIC Radiguet *Mallarmé*
ALPHABET, no. 6
  AURIC Radiguet *Hirondelle*
ALPHABET, no. 7
  AURIC Radiguet *Escarpin*
Alphonso Maria [de' Liguori] Saint,
  Bishop of Sant'Agata dei Goti *see*
  Liguori, Alfonso Maria de', Saint,
  1696-1787.
Alphorn see Kerner **STRAUSS**
"Ein Alphorn hör' ich schallen" *see Alphorn*
  Kerner **STRAUSS**
Alpin's Klage um Morar see Goethe
  LOEWE
Alplied see Krummacher **LOEWE**
"Already autumn has come, bringing death"
  see In the valley Gombossy **BARTÓK**
"Als bei dem Kreuz Maria stand" *see Vom*
  Mitleiden Mariae Schlegel, F.
  SCHUBERT
"Als das Christkind ward zur Welt gebracht"
  see Weihnachtlied Andersen
  SCHUMANN
"Als der Frühling sich vom" *see*
  Vergissmeinnicht Schober **SCHUBERT**
Als die Geliebte sich trennen wollte see
  Breuning **BEETHOVEN**
"Als die Linden trieben" *see Bei der Linde*
  Osterwald **FRANZ**
"Als ein unergründlich Wonnemeer strahlte"
  see Scheideblick Lenau
  SCHOECK, WOLF
Als einst von deiner Schöne see Hafiz
  JENSEN
Als er sein Weib und 's Kind schlafend fand
  see Claudius, M. **SCHOECK**
Als ich auf dem Euphrat schiffte see Goethe
  WESTÖSTLICHER DIVAN:
  Buch Suleika. **WOLF**
"Als ich das erste Veilchen erblickt" *see*
  Das erste Veilchen Ebert
  MENDELSSOHN-BARTHOLDY
Als ich dich kaum gesehn see Storm
  LASSEN
"Als ich ein junger Geselle war" *see Der alte*
  Goethe Förster, F. **LOEWE**
"Als ich gieng zum Eichenwalde" *see*
  Rozmarýna Erben **DVOŘÁK**
"Als ich ging die Flur entlang" *see*
  Dichtersegen Uhland **SCHOECK**
"Als ich noch ein Knabe war" *see Der neue*
  Amadis Goethe **WOLF**
"Als ich noch Knabe war" *see Der neue*
  Amadis Goethe **KRENEK**
Als ich sie erröten sah see Ehrlich
  SCHUBERT

"Als ich still und ruhig spann" *see*
  Die Spinnerin Goethe **SCHUBERT**
"Als ich zuerst dich hab' geseh'n" *see Nichts*
  Schöneres Reinick
  SCHUMANN, SPOHR
"Als kaum wir geöffnet des Feldherren" *see*
  Sem' noyabrya Khomyakov
  BALAKIREV
"Als Kinder glaubten wir an Zauberwesen"
  see Die Hexe Wolf, F. **BLACHER**
"Als Lenz die Erde wieder mit erstem Kuss
  umschloss" *see Die Reigerbaize*
  Auersperg **LOEWE**
Als Luise die Briefe ihres ungetreuen
  Liebhabers verbrannte see Batsányi
  MOZART
"Als Maria heut' entwich" *see Der Weichdorn*
  Rückert **LOEWE**
"Als mein Auge sie fand" *see Sehnsucht*
  Zedlitz **SCHÖNBERG**
"Als mein Leben vol Blumen hing" *see*
  Schwermut Mahlmann **SPOHR**
Als mich dein Blick beim Scheiden traf see
  Träger **JENSEN**
Als mir dein Lied erklang see Brentano
  STRAUSS
"Als mir noch die Thräne" *see Lied aus der*
  Ferne Reissig **BEETHOVEN**
"Als nachts ich überm Gebirge ritt" *see Jung*
  Hexenlied Bierbaum **STRAUSS**
Als Neuling trat ich ein in dein Gehege see
  George *DAS BUCH DER HÄNGENDEN*
  GÄRTEN. **SCHÖNBERG**
"Als noch dem blinden Heidenwahn" *see*
  Otto-Lied Kugler, Johann, Consul in
  Stettin **LOEWE**
Als trüg' man die Liebe zu Grab see Röser,
  Otto **FRANZ**
"Als über den Flieder das Mondlicht rann" *see*
  Brautring Ritter **REGER**
Als Weibesarm in jungen Jahren see
  Giesebrecht **LOEWE**
"Als wir Beiden mussten scheiden" *see*
  Abschied Heyse **JENSEN**
Als wir hinter dem beblümten Tore see
  George *DAS BUCH DER HÄNGENDEN*
  GÄRTEN. **SCHÖNBERG**
"Also auch wir vergeben unsern Schuldigern"
  see Vater unser VII Cornelius
  CORNELIUS
"Also ihr lebt noch" *see Siehe, auch ich—lebe*
  Morgenstern **KILPINEN**
"Also lieb' ich euch, Geliebte" *see Geständnis*
  Vimioso **SCHUMANN**
Alt Heidelberg, du feine see Scheffel
  JENSEN

COMPOSER Poet *Title* ''First Line''

Alt Mütterlein see Nietzsche **MEDTNER**
Altassyrisch see Scheffel *GAUDEAMUS.*
    JENSEN
Altdeutsches Frühlingslied see Spee
    MENDELSSOHN-BARTHOLDY
Altdeutsches Lied see Schreiber, H.
    MENDELSSOHN-BARTHOLDY
Der Alte see Falke **REGER**
Die Alte see Hagedorn **MOZART**
Der alte Dessauer see Fitzau *DER SELTENE*
    BETER. **LOEWE**
Der alte Goethe see Förster, F. **LOEWE**
"Alte Gruben schaufle um" *see Sehnsucht*
    Jacobowski **REGER**
Die alte Jungfer see Vinje **GRIEG**
    Attegløyma
Der alte König see Vogl **LOEWE**
Alte Laute see Kerner **SCHUMANN**
Alte Liebe see Candidus **BRAHMS**
Alte Liebe rostet nie see Mayrhofer
    SCHUBERT
Das alte Lied see Heine **GRIEG, LASSEN**
"Der alte Müller Jakob" *see Der Raubschütz*
    Lenau **WOLF**
Die alte Mutter see Vinje **GRIEG** *Gamle*
    Mor
Der alte Schiffsherr see Vogl **LOEWE**
Der alte Vagabund see Béranger **LISZT**
    Le vieux vagabond
Alte Weiber see Nicolai *DER KLEINE,*
    FEINE ALMANACH. **WEBER**
ALTE WEISEN. see Keller, G.
    Mir glänzen die Augen **PFITZNER,**
    SCHOECK
ALTE WEISEN, no. 1
    PFITZNER Keller, G. *Mir glänzen die*
    Augen
    WOLF Keller, G. *Tretet ein, hoher*
    Krieger
ALTE WEISEN, no. 2
    PFITZNER Keller, G. *Ich fürcht' nit*
    Gespenster
    WOLF Keller, G. *Singt mein Schatz wie*
    ein Fink
ALTE WEISEN, no. 3
    PFITZNER, WOLF Keller, G. *Du*
    milchjunger Knabe
ALTE WEISEN, no. 4
    PFITZNER, WOLF Keller, G. *Wandl' ich*
    in dem Morgentau
ALTE WEISEN, no. 5
    PFITZNER Keller, G. *Singt mein Schatz*
    wie ein Fink
    WOLF Keller, G. *Das Köhlerweib ist*
    trunken

ALTE WEISEN, no. 6
    PFITZNER Keller, G. *Rös'chen biss den*
    Apfel an
    WOLF Keller, G. *Wie glänzt der helle*
    Mond
ALTE WEISEN, no. 7
    PFITZNER Keller, G. *Tretet ein, hoher*
    Krieger
ALTE WEISEN, no. 8
    PFITZNER Keller, G. *Wie glänzt der*
    helle Mond
Die alten, bösen Lieder see Heine
    SCHUMANN
Altenberg, Peter, 1859-1919.
    WAS DER TAG MIR ZUTRÄGT':
    Flötenspielerin.
    BERG *Flötenspielerin*
    WAS DER TAG MIR ZUTRÄGT':
    Hoffnung.
    BERG *Hoffnung*
    WAS DER TAG MIR ZUTRÄGT':
    Traurigkeit.
    BERG *Traurigkeit*
Das Alter see Eichendorff **PFITZNER**
"Alter Mann, grimmer Mann" *see Scene . . .*
    Pushkin **RUBINSTEIN**
Altes Lied see Heine **FRANZ**
"Altho' my bed were yonder muir" *see*
    Montgomery-Gretchen Burns **FRANZ**
"Although at times the load is heavy" *see*
    The coach of life Pushkin **MEDTNER**
ALTRE CINQUE LIRICHE, no. 1
    PIZZETTI Canticum Canticorum
    Adjuro vos, filiae Jerusalem
ALTRE CINQUE LIRICHE, no. 2
    PIZZETTI Sappho *Oscuro è il ciel*
ALTRE CINQUE LIRICHE, no. 3
    PIZZETTI Anon. *Augurio*
ALTRE CINQUE LIRICHE, no. 4
    PIZZETTI Anon. *Mirologio per un*
    bambino
ALTRE CINQUE LIRICHE, no. 5
    PIZZETTI Anon. *Canzone per ballo*
Ein altschottische Ballade see Herder
    SCHUBERT
Alvarez Quintero, Serafín, 1871-1938.
    TURINA *Saeta en forma de Salve a la*
    Virgen de la Esperanza
Alvaro Fernandez de Almeida
    SPANISCHES LIEDERBUCH: Tango vos,
    el mi Pandero.
    JENSEN, RUBINSTEIN, WOLF
    Klinge, klinge, mein Pandero
Always for Thee see Apukhtin
    CHAĬKOVSKIĬ *Den' li t͡sarit*
Am Abend see Geibel **BERG**

COMPOSER Poet *Title* "First Line"

Am Abend see Unknown **REGER**
"Am Abgrund leitet der schwindliche Steg"
  see Berglied Schiller **ZELTER**
"Am Bach, am Bach, im flüsternden Gras" *see*
  Verlust Zimmermann, B. **SPOHR**
Am Bach im Frühling see Schober
  SCHUBERT
"Am Bach viel kleine Blumen steh'n" *see*
  Des Müllers Blumen Müller, Wilhelm
  SCHUBERT
Am Bach see Kleinschrod **DVOŘÁK**
  U potoka
Am Bergbach see Garborg *HAUGTUSSA.*
  GRIEG *Ved Gjaetle-Bekken*
Am Brünnele see Gersdorff **REGER**
"Am Brunnen vor dem Thore" *see*
  Der Lindenbaum Müller, Wilhelm
  SCHUBERT
Am Dnjepr see Shevchenko **MUSORGSKÏ**
  Na Dnepre
Am Dorfsee see Wiener, Oskar **REGER**
"Am Dorfsee neigt die Weide ihr kahles
  Haupt" *see Am Dorfsee* Wiener, Oskar
  REGER
Am Erlafsee see Mayrhofer **SCHUBERT**
  Erlafsee
Am ersten Maimorgen see Claudius, M.
  SCHUBERT
Am Feierabend see Müller, Wilhelm
  SCHUBERT
"Am Felsenvorgebirge schroff" *see Vision*
  Platen-Hallermünde **CORNELIUS**
Am Fenster see Huber, B. **KILPINEN**
Am Fenster see Seidl **SCHUBERT**
Am fernen Horizonte see Heine **FRANZ**
"Am fernen Horizonte" *see Die Stadt* Heine
  SCHUBERT
Am Feste der Vorsterbenen see
  Krummacher **LOEWE** *Gebet*
Am Flusse see Goethe **SCHUBERT**
  Two settings: D. 160 and D. 766.
Am Flusse see Golenishchev-Kutuzov
  MUSORGSKÏ *Nad rekoǐ*
"Am frisch geschnittnen Wanderstab" *see*
  Fussreise Mörike **WOLF**
Am Grabe Anselmo's see Claudius, M.
  SCHUBERT
Am Grabe der Mutter see Benzon **GRIEG**
  Ved Moders Grav
Am Haidenhügel geht ein Singen see Löns
  KILPINEN
"Am Himmel wächst der Sonne Glut" *see*
  Lenzfahrt Meyer **SCHOECK**
"Am Himmelsantlitz wandelt ein Gedanke"
  see Himmelstrauer Lenau **SCHOECK**
"Am Himmelsgrund da schiessen so lustig die
  Stern' " *see Der Bote* Eichendorff
  JENSEN

"Am Himmelsgrund schiessen lustig die
  Stern" *see Der Bote* Eichendorff
  PFITZNER
"Am Himmelsgrund schiessen so lustig die
  Stern" *see Der Bote* Eichendorff
  FRANZ
Am Himmelstor see Meyer **SCHOECK**
"Am hohen, hohen Thurm" *see Ammenlied*
  Lubi **SCHUBERT**
"Am jüngsten Tag ich aufersteh" *see*
  Mädchenlied Heyse **BRAHMS**
"Am Kirchhof ging ich jüngst vorbei" *see*
  Gruss Michaeli **REGER**
Am Klosterbrunne see Vogl **LOEWE**
"Am Kreuzweg, da lausche ich" *see*
  Die Zigeunerin Eichendorff **WOLF**
Am Kreuzweg wird begraben see Heine
  LYRISCHES INTERMEZZO, no. 67.
  GRIFFES
Am leuchtenden Sommermorgen see Heine
  FRANZ, SCHUMANN
Am Meer! see Glücklich **REGER**
Am Meer see Heine **SCHUBERT**
Am Meeresstrand see Tolstoï **RUBINSTEIN**
Am Morgen see Cornelius **CORNELIUS**
Am Rhein see Cornelius **CORNELIUS**
Am Rhein see Heine **LISZT** *Im Rhein, im*
  schönen Strome
Am Rheinfall see Hahn-Hahn **FRANZ**
Am schönsten Sommerabend war's see
  Paulsen **GRIEG**
  Jeg reiste en deilig Sommerkvaeld
Am schönsten Sommerabend war's see
  Paulsen
  JEG REISTE ENDEILIG
  SOMMERKVAELD. **DELIUS**
Am See see Bruchmann **SCHUBERT**
Am See see Cornelius **CORNELIUS**
Am See see Mayrhofer *SITZ' ICH IM GRAS.*
  SCHUBERT
AM SEEGESTAD'. see Matthisson
  Erinnerungen **SCHUBERT**
"Am Seegestad', in lauden
  Vollmondsnächten" *see Erinnerungen*
  Matthisson **SCHUBERT**
Am Sonntag Morgen see Heyse
  ITALIENISCHES LIEDERBUCH.
  BRAHMS
Am Strand see Unknown **RIEGGER**
Am Strande see Rilke **SCHÖNBERG**
Am Strande see Scherer **BERG,**
  RUBINSTEIN
Am Strande see Stieler **LASSEN**
Am Strom see Eichendorff **FRANZ**
Am Strome see Mayrhofer **SCHUBERT**

Am Strome *see* Vinje **GRIEG** *Langs ei Å*
"Am Tag nich meiner Heimkehr geh' ich" *see*
    Epilog Krenek **KRENEK**
Am Tage aller Seelen *see* Jacobi
    SCHUBERT
Am Tage der sieben Brüder *see* Anon.
    ZELTER
Am Ufer *see* Dehmel *WEIB UND WELT.*
    STRAUSS, WEBERN
Am Ufer des Flusses, des Manzanares *see*
    Anon.
        SPANISCHES LIEDERBUCH: Ribericas del
        Rio. **JENSEN**
Am Walde *see* Mörike **SCHOECK**
"Am Waldsaum kann ich lange Nachmittage"
    see Am Walde Mörike **SCHOECK**
Am Wegrand *see* Mackay **SCHÖNBERG**
"Am Wiesenhügel schlummert' ich" *see*
    Der Traum Zhukovski **RUBINSTEIN**
"Amada, el aura dice" *see Mi corazon te
    aguarda* Machado y Ruiz **RODRIGO**
Amalia *see* Anna Amalia von Sachsen-
    Weimar, 1739-1807.
Amalia *see* Schiller *DIE RÄUBER.*
    SCHUBERT
Amanda *see* Unknown **LOEWE**
L'amant malheureux *see* Ronsard **SAINT-
    SAËNS**
L'amante discreto *see* Metastasio **ROSSINI**
    Mi lagnerò tacendo
L'amante impaziente *see* Metastasio
    ADRIANO: Act II, scene 6. **BEETHOVEN**
    Two settings: Op. 82 no. 3 and op. 82 no.
    4.
Amante sono, vaghiccia, di voi *see* Anon.
    CASELLA
"Amants, heureux amants, voulez-vous
    voyager?" *see Les deux pigeons*
    La Fontaine **GOUNOD**
AMARANTH. see Redwitz
    Nur das thut mir so bitterweh'
        SCHÖNBERG
    Reiterlied **LOEWE**
    Sängers Gebet **LOEWE**
Amaranths' Waldeslieder *see* Redwitz
    BRUCKNER
Amaryllis at the fountain *see* Anon.
    QUILTER
"Amaryllis rit au pâtre Daphnis" *see*
    Les bergers Banville **AURIC**
"Amaste á Pedro" *see Vade retro!* Rodríguez
    Marin, Francisco **TURINA**
L'âme de Claude Debussy *see* Unknown
    DIAMOND
L'âme de la morte *see* Banville **GOUNOD**
L'âme délaissée *see* Delavigne **ROSSINI**

L'âme des fleurs *see* Delair **MASSENET**
L'âme d'un ange *see* Banville **GOUNOD**
"L'âme d'une flûte soupire" *see Arpège*
    Samain **FAURÉ**
L'âme errante *see* Samain **AUBERT**
L'âme évaporée *see* Bourget *LES AVEUX.*
    DEBUSSY
"L'âme évaporée et souffrante" *see L'âme
    évaporée* Bourget **DEBUSSY**
L'âme humaine est pareille au doux ciel *see*
    Lamartine **BIZET**
L'âme oiseaux *see* Văcărescu **MASSENET**
Âme triste *see* Docquois **SAINT-SAËNS**
Die Ameise und die Libelle *see* Krylov
    RUBINSTEIN
"Amelette Ronsardelette, Mignonnelette" *see*
    Ronsard à son âme Ronsard **RAVEL**
L'Américain de ma soeur *see* Unknown
    SÉVERAC *Marche Américaine*
Les âmes *see* Demouth, Paul **MASSENET**
Âmes obscures *see* France **MASSENET**
Améthyste *see* Samain **KOECHLIN**
AMÉTHYSTES. see Banville
    Caprice **DEBUSSY**
    Le rossignol **SAINT-SAËNS**
"Amiamo, cantiamo" *see L'orgia* Pepoli
    ROSSINI
Amid the din of the ball *see* Tolstoĭ
    CHAĬKOVSKIĬ *Sred' shumnago bala*
"Amiral, ne crois pas déchoir" *see Adieu*
    Radiguet **SATIE**
"Amis, c'est Dieu qui nous envoie" *see Chant
    des sauveteurs Bretons* Ségalas
    GOUNOD
"Amis, vive l'orgie" *see Chanson à boire*
    Hugo **LALO**
Amis, vive, vive l'orgie *see* Hugo **LALO**
    Chanson à boire
Amitié *see* Gaillard, Roger **SAUGUET**
L'amitié *see* Paté **HAHN**
Ammann, Heinrich
    SCHÖNBERG *Jane Grey*
Ammenlied *see* Lubi **SCHUBERT**
Die Ammenuhr *see* Des Knaben
    Wunderhorn **SCHUMANN**
Ammosov, A
    MUSORGSKIĬ *Chto vam slova liubvi*
"Amo l'ora del giorno che muore" *see*
    Il tramonto Maffei **VERDI**
L'amoire de campagne *see* Laporte
    SAUGUET
"Among the leaves the small birds sing" *see*
    Lauds Auden **BERKELEY**
Amor *see* Brentano **STRAUSS**
"Amor mi fa sovente" *see Canzone* Donini
    RESPIGHI

"Amor, nicht das Kind" *see Der neue Amor*
Goethe **ZELTER**
AMOR TIMIDO (Cantata XVI). *see*
Metastasio
Liebes-Klage **BEETHOVEN**
AMORETTI. see Spenser
Sweet is the rose **BLITZSTEIN**
"Amori scendete" *see Beltà crudele* Santo-
Magno, N. di **ROSSINI**
Amoroso see Docquois **SAINT-SAËNS**
Amour see Alexandre, André **MASSENET**
Amours bénis
Amour see Émié **JOLIVET**
Amour see Labé **SAUGUET**
L'amour à Pekin see Pacini **ROSSINI**
"Amour, amour cruel et tendre" *see Reviens*
(Epilogue) Docquois **SAINT-SAËNS**
"L'amour auquel tout invite" *see Duo* Bédat
de Monlaur, Pierre **HONEGGER**
L'amour blessé see Ronsard **SAINT-SAËNS**
L'AMOUR CHANTE, no. 1
MILHAUD Du Bellay *Le vrai amour*
L'AMOUR CHANTE, no. 2
MILHAUD Musset *J'aime*
L'AMOUR CHANTE, no. 3
MILHAUD Labé *Sonnet*
L'AMOUR CHANTE, no. 4
MILHAUD Du Bellay *De sa peine, et des
beautés de sa Dame*
L'AMOUR CHANTE, no. 5
MILHAUD Scève *Moins je la vois*
L'AMOUR CHANTE, no. 6
MILHAUD Verlaine *Nevermore*
L'AMOUR CHANTE, no. 7
MILHAUD Rimbaud *Veillées*
L'AMOUR CHANTE, no. 8
MILHAUD Ronsard *Plusieurs de leurs
corps dénués*
L'AMOUR CHANTE, no. 9
MILHAUD France, Marie de *Le Lai du
Chevrefeuille*
Amour d'antan see Bouchor, M.
CHAUSSON
"L'amour de la femme est l'ombre" *see
Le destin* Toussaint **AUBERT**
L'amour de moy see Anon.
VAUGHAN WILLIAMS
L'amour de Piroutcha see Messiaen
MESSIAEN
L'amour d'un mort see Lermontov
CHAĬKOVSKIĬ *Liubov' mertvetsa*
"L'amour est assis sur le crâne de
l'Humanité" *see L'amour et le crane*
Baudelaire **INDY**
L'amour et le crane see Baudelaire
LES FLEURS DU MAL. **INDY**

Amour et sommeil see Swinburne
SAUGUET
"Amour, mon coeur languit tout le jour" *see
Love, my heart longs day and night*
Tagore **MILHAUD**
Amour oiseau d'étoile see Messiaen
MESSIAEN
L'amour oyseau see Ronsard **SAINT-
SAËNS**
L'amour pleure see Postel, Madeleine
MASSENET
Amour sans espoir ("Tirana all'espagnole
rossinize") *see* Pacini **ROSSINI**
Amour viril see Boyer, Georges
SAINT-SAËNS
Amoureuse see Morel-Retz **MASSENET**
Amoureuses see Éluard **POULENC**
"Les amoureuses aux matelots" *see
Complainte* Mauclair **BLOCH**
Les amoureuses sont des folles see
Macdonald, Jacques **MASSENET**
L'amoureux see Carême **MILHAUD**
Amoureux appel see Dubor **MASSENET**
Amoureux séparés see Roché **ROUSSEL**
Les amoureux sont seuls au monde see
Marcy, Claude **SAUGUET**
Les amours see Ronsard **SÉVERAC**
Amours bénis see Alexandre, André
MASSENET
Amphiaraos see Körner **SCHUBERT**
Amphion see Tennyson **IVES** *from*
"*Amphion*"
Amphise et Melitta see Samain *AUX
FLANCS DU VASE.* **KOECHLIN**
"Die Amsel flötet" *see Abendstunde* Rose,
Karl **LOEWE**
"Amselchen mein" *see Amselliedchen*
Asenijeff **REGER**
Amselliedchen see Asenijeff **REGER**
An see Koch, E. **SPOHR**
An** see Lenau **WOLF**
An Anna I see Kerner **SCHUMANN**
An Anna II see Kerner **SCHUMANN**
"An Babylons Wassern gefangen" *see An den
Wassern zu Babel* Byron **LOEWE**
An Bachesranft die einzigen Frühen see
George *DER SIEBENTE RING.*
WEBERN
AN BERTHA, I
CORNELIUS Cornelius *Sei mein!*
AN BERTHA, II
CORNELIUS Cornelius *Wie lieb ich dich
hab'*
AN BERTHA, III
CORNELIUS Cornelius *In der Ferne*
AN BERTHA, IV
CORNELIUS Cornelius *Dein Bildnis*

"An Birkenzweigen blättert" *see Frühlingslied*
  Unknown **LOEWE**
"An Celia's Baum in stiller Nacht hängt" *see*
  Der Blumenkranz Moore, T.
  MENDELSSOHN-BARTHOLDY
An Chloe see Jacobi **MOZART**
An Chloen see Jacobi **SCHUBERT**
AN CIDLI. see Klopstock
  Furcht der Geliebten **SCHUBERT**
An das Herz see Keller, G. **SCHOECK**
An das Vaterland see Paulsen **GRIEG** *Til*
  Norge
An deinem Finger, dem weissen, schlanken see
  Träger **JENSEN**
"An dem Brünnle" *see Am Brünnele*
  Gersdorff **REGER**
"An dem Feuer sass das Kind Amor" *see*
  Amor Brentano **STRAUSS**
An dem jungen Morgenhimmel see Fouqué
  DER ZAUBERRING. **SCHUBERT**
"An dem reinsten Frühlingsmorgen" *see*
  Die Spröde Goethe
  MEDTNER, WOLF, ZELTER
An dem schlummernden Strom see Rathaus
  CHAÏKOVSKIÏ
"An dem Seegestade düster" *see Am See*
  Cornelius **CORNELIUS**
An dem Traume see Cornelius **LUENING**
An den fernen Geliebten see Reissig
  BEETHOVEN
An den Frühling see Lenau **RUBINSTEIN**
An den Frühling see Schiller **SCHUBERT**
  Three settings: D. 245, D. 283, and D. 587
An den Frühlingsregen see Kiesekamo
  REGER
An den Mond see Byron *HEBREW*
  MELODIES. **SCHUMANN**
An den Mond see Goethe **PFITZNER,**
  SCHUBERT, ZELTER
  Two Schubert settings: D. 259 and D. 296
An den Mond see Hölty **SCHUBERT**
  Two settings: D. 193 and D. 468
An den Mond see Schink **ZELTER**
An den Mond see Simrock **BRAHMS**
An den Mond see Unknown **LASSEN**
An den Mond in einer Herbstnacht see
  Schreiber **SCHUBERT**
"An den Mondes strahlen gleiten meine
  Küsse" *see Allen Welten abgewandt*
  Scholz **REGER**
"An den Rhein, an den Rhein" *see Warnung*
  vor dem Rhein Simrock
  MENDELSSOHN-BARTHOLDY
An den Schlaf see Mörike **WOLF**
An den Schlaf see Unknown **SCHUBERT**
An den See see Anon. **ZELTER**

An den Sonnenschein see Reinick
  LIEDERBUCH EINES MALERS.
  SCHUMANN
An den Sturmwind see Rückert **LOEWE**
  Dem Allmächtigen
An den Tod see Klopstock **GLUCK**
  Der Tod
An den Tod see Schubart **SCHUBERT**
An den Traum see Cornelius **CORNELIUS**
An den Wassern zu Babel see Byron
  LOEWE
An den Wind see Lenau *LIEBESKLÄNGE.*
  FRANZ, GRIFFES
An der Bahre einer jungen Frau see Monrad
  GRIEG *Ved en ung Hustrus Båre*
An der Linden see Roquette **JENSEN**
"An der Quelle sass der Knabe" *see Der*
  Jüngling am Bache Schiller **SCHUBERT**
  Three settings: D. 30, D. 192, and D. 638.
"An der Rose Busen schmiegt" *see Lied*
  Hoffmann von Fallersleben
  RUBINSTEIN
"An des lust'gen Brunnens Rand" *see Suleika*
  und Hatem Goethe **SCHOECK**
An dich see Itzerott **REGER**
An die Apfelbäume, wo ich Julien erblickte
  see Hölty **SCHUBERT**
An die Bienen see Bürger **PFITZNER**
"An die blaue Himmelsdecke" *see Auf dem*
  Meere Heine **FRANZ**
"An die bretterne Schiffswand" *see Auf dem*
  Meere Heine **FRANZ**
An die Einsamkeit see Hermes **MOZART**
  Sei du mein Trost
An die Entfernte see Goethe **SCHUBERT,**
  ZELTER
An die Entfernte see Lenau
  MENDELSSOHN-BARTHOLDY,
  SCHOECK
  Two Schoeck settings: Op. 5 no. 2 and op.
  24a no. 3.
AN DIE FERNE GELIEBTE, no. 1
  BEETHOVEN Jeitteles *Auf dem Hügel*
  sitz ich spähend
AN DIE FERNE GELIEBTE, no. 2
  BEETHOVEN Jeitteles *Wo die Berge so*
  blau
AN DIE FERNE GELIEBTE, no. 3
  BEETHOVEN Jeitteles *Leichte Segler in*
  den Höhen
AN DIE FERNE GELIEBTE, no. 4
  BEETHOVEN Jeitteles *Diese Wolken in*
  den Höhen
AN DIE FERNE GELIEBTE, no. 5
  BEETHOVEN Jeitteles *Es kehret der*
  Maien

COMPOSER Poet *Title* "First Line"

AN DIE FERNE GELIEBTE, no. 6
  BEETHOVEN Jeitteles *Nimm sie hin denn diese Lieder*
AN DIE FLEISIGE CHLOE. see Krauseneck
  An die fleissige Spinnerin **LOEWE**
An die fleissige Spinnerin see Krauseneck
AN DIE FLEISIGE CHLOE. **LOEWE**
An die Freude see Schiller **SCHUBERT, ZELTER**
An die Freude see Uz **MOZART**
An die Freunde see Mayrhofer **SCHUBERT**
An die Geliebte see Falke **REGER**
An die Geliebte see Gotter **LOEWE**
An die Geliebte see Hugo *RUY BLAS.* **SPOHR**
An die Geliebte see Mörike **WOLF**
An die Geliebte see Stoll **BEETHOVEN, SCHUBERT**
An die Grille see Anacreon **LOEWE**
An die Grille see Unknown **LOEWE**
An die Harmonie see Salis-Seewis **SCHUBERT** *Gesang an die Harmonie*
An die Harmonien see Salis-Seewis **SCHUBERT** *Gesang an die Harmonie*
An die Hoffnung see Hermes **MOZART** *Ich würd' auf meinem Pfad*
An die Hoffnung see Hölderlin **REGER**
An die Hoffnung see Tiedge *URANIA.* **BEETHOVEN**
An die Hoffnung see Tiedge *URANIA:* Klagen des Zweiflers. **BEETHOVEN** The above two songs, op. 32 and 94, use different texts.
An die Königin Elisabeth see Mary **SCHUMANN**
An die Laute see Rochlitz **SCHUBERT**
An die Leier see Anacreon **LOEWE**
An die Leyer see Anacreon **SCHUBERT**
An die Lützowschen Jäger see Eichendorff **SCHOECK**
An die Mark see Wackernagel, I. **PFITZNER**
An die Morgenröte see Bürger **PFITZNER**
An die Muse see Dionysius **LOEWE**
An die Musik see Schober **SCHUBERT**
An die Nacht see Bernays **LASSEN**
An die Nacht see Brentano **STRAUSS**
An die Nacht see Shelley **JENSEN**
An die Nachtigall see Claudius, M. **SCHUBERT**
An die Nachtigall see Hölty *GEUSS NICHT SO LAUT.* **BRAHMS, SCHUBERT**
An die Nachtigall see Schmidt, F. **LOEWE**
An die Natur see Stolberg **LOEWE, SCHUBERT**
An die Natur see Unknown **LOEWE**
An die Parzen see Hölderlin **HINDEMITH**
An die Preisverteilerin bei einem Ritterspiele see Anon. **ZELTER**
An die Sonne see Batsányi **SCHUBERT**
An die Sonne see Tiedge **SCHUBERT**
An die Stolze see Fleming **BRAHMS**
An die Thüren will ich schleichen see Goethe *WILHELM MEISTER.* Harfenspieler. **SCHUMANN**
"*An die Thüren will ich schleichen*" *see Harfenspieler II* Goethe **SCHUBERT**
An die Trauben see Schenkendorf **BRAHMS**
An die Türen will ich schleichen see Goethe *WILHELM MEISTER.* Harfenspieler. **MEDTNER, ZELTER**
"*An die Türen will ich schleichen*" *seeHarfenspieler II* Goethe **WOLF**
"*An die Türen will ich schleichen*" *see Lied des Harfenspielers* Goethe **MUSGORSKIĭ**
An die untergehende Sonne see Kosegarten **SCHUBERT**
An die Vögel see Hamerling **JENSEN, LASSEN, RUBINSTEIN**
An die welke Rose see Rudolphi **ZELTER**
An die Wolke see Lenau **FRANZ**
"*An dies Schifflein schmiege*" *see Auf dem See* Köstlin **BRAHMS**
"*An dir allein, an dir hab' ich gesündigt*" *see Busslied* Gellert **BEETHOVEN**
"*An Edens Thor ein Engel*" *see Der Engel* Pushkin **RUBINSTEIN**
An Edlitam, zur silbernen Hochzeit see Bodenstedt **LISZT**
An ein Bild see Schenkendorf **BRAHMS**
An ein Veilchen see Hölty **BRAHMS**
An eine Äolsharfe see Mörike **BRAHMS, WOLF**
An eine Freudin see Voigt **WEBER**
An eine Mutter see Asenijeff **REGER**
An eine Mutter, deren Tochter als Kind starb see Sonnleithner **ZELTER**
An eine Quelle see Claudius, M. **SCHUBERT**
An eine Teufelin see Benzon **GRIEG** *To a devil*
"*An einem Abend*" *see Die geheimnisvolle Flöte* Li Po **WEBERN**
An einem Bache see Vinje **GRIEG** *Langs ei Å*
"*An einem Baum, am Weidenbaum*" *see Lied der Desdemona* Herder **JENSEN**
An einem heitern Morgen see Uhland **SCHOECK**

An einem Wintermorgan, vor Sonnenaufgang see Mörike **SCHOECK**

An einen Säugling see Döhring **BEETHOVEN**

An Emma see Schiller **SCHUBERT**

AN FANNY. see Klopstock
Wenn einst ich tot bin **LOEWE**

"L'An fuit vers son déclin" see Pensée *d'automne* Silvestre **MASSENET**

An Gott see Hohlfeld **SCHUBERT**

"An ihrem Grabe kniet ich fest" see *Rückleben* Uhland **STRAUSS**

"An ihren bunten Liedern klettert die Lerche" see Liebesfeier Lenau **FRANZ**

"An jedem Abend geh'ich aus" see Lauf der Welt Uhland **GRIEG**

An junge spröde Schöne see Müchler **ZELTER**

An kleine Mädchen see Faktor **SZYMANOWSKI**

An Laura see Matthisson **BEETHOVEN, SCHUBERT**

An Leukon see Gleim **BERG**

An Lina see Kleist **ZELTER**

An Marie see Unknown **MENDELSSOHN-BARTHOLDY**

An mein Herz see Schulze **SCHUBERT**

An mein Klavier see Schubart **SCHUBERT**
Seraphine an ihr Klavier

An meine Grossmutter see Leuthold **SCHOECK**

An meine Mutter see Mörike **SCHOECK**

An meinem Herzen, an meiner Brust see Chamisso **LOEWE, SCHUMANN**

An meinen Sohn see Benzon **GRIEG** *Til min Dreng*

An Mignon see Goethe *WILHELM MEISTER.* **SCHUBERT, SPOHR, ZELTER**

An Minna see Unknown **BEETHOVEN**

"An mir vorüber ging ein Geist" see Eliphas' *Gesicht* Byron **LOEWE**

An Philomele see Mörike **SCHOECK**

An Rosa I see Kosegarten **SCHUBERT**

An Rosa II see Kosegarten **SCHUBERT**

An Rosa Maria see Anna Amalia **SPOHR**

An Schwager Kronos see Goethe **SCHUBERT**

An Sich see Fleming **KRENEK**

An sie am Klavier see Braun von Braunthal **SPOHR**
Sonatine, B flat minor, op. 138 "An sie am Klavier"

An Sie see Klopstock *ODE.* **SCHUBERT, STRAUSS**

An Sie see Wargentin **WEBER**

An Sie. I see Paulsen **GRIEG** *Til Én.* I

An Sie. II see Paulsen **GRIEG** *Til Én.* II

"An soleil couchant, toi qui vas cherchant fortune" see La chanson du fou Hugo **BIZET**

An Sylvia see Shakespeare *TWO GENTLEMEN OF VERONA.* **SCHUBERT**

"An wolken reinem Himmel geht" see Vor der *Ernte* Meyer **SCHOECK**

An Zeppelin see Glücklich **REGER**

Anacreon, b.ca.570 B.C.
LOEWE
An die Grille
An die Leier
Auf sich selbst
Two settings.
ROUSSEL
Qu'il faut boire
Sur lui-même
Two settings: Op. 31 no. 1 and op. 32 no. 1.
Sur une jeune fille
Two settings: Op. 31 no. 3 and op. 32 no. 2.
Sur une songe
SCHOECK
Ruheplatz
SCHUBERT
An die Leyer

Anacreontica see Unknown **ROSSINI**
La passeggiata

ANACREONTICHE, no. 1
ROREM Vittorelli *Zitto, La Bella Irene*

ANACREONTICHE, no. 2
ROREM Vittorelli *O platano felice*

ANACREONTICHE, no. 3
ROREM Vittorelli *Guarda che bianca luna!*

ANACREONTICHE, no. 4
ROREM Vittorelli *Non t'accostare all'urna*

Anakreon's Grab see Goethe **WOLF**

Anbetung see Rückert *LIEBESFRÜHLING.* **STRAUSS**

Anchar–Tree of death see Pushkin **RIMSKIÏ-KORSAKOV** *Anchar-drevo smerti*

Anchar-drevo smerti see Pushkin **RIMSKIÏ-KORSAKOV**

"And can the physician make sick men well?" see Robin Good-fellow Anon. **HESELTINE**

And did those feet see Blake, William **THOMSON**

"And did you not hear of a mirth that befell" see Away to Twiver Anon. **HESELTINE**

"And have you heard the singer in the night"
see *The singer* Pushkin **MEDTNER**
"And he cast it down, down, on the green
grass" *see The new ghost* Shove
VAUGHAN WILLIAMS
And I questioned them no further see
Runeberg **SIBELIUS**
Se'n har jag ej frågat mera
"And in September" *see September* San
Geminiano **IVES**
And is there a thought? see Tavaststjerna
SIBELIUS *Och finns det en tanke?*
"And like a dying lady, lean and pale" *see*
The moon Shelley **HINDEMITH**
"And, lo, the Angel of the Lord" *see An angel*
speaks to the shepherds Bible **ROREM**
"And so goodbye to the war" *see The real*
war will never get in the books
Whitman **ROREM**
"And so he came from the prairie cabin" *see*
from "Lincoln, the great commoner"
Markham **IVES**
"And so unless I'm going to see your face"
see Poem Koch **ROREM**
"And why your moaning, winds of night?" *see*
Night winds Tiutchev **MEDTNER**
And wilt thou leave me thus? see Wyatt
HESELTINE
Andando a uccellare see Burchiello
MALIPIERO
Andělíčku muj see Des Knaben
Wunderhorn **MARTINŮ** *My little angel*
Andenken see Matthisson **BEETHOVEN,**
SCHUBERT, WOLF
Ein Anderes see Weckherlin **KRENEK**
"Die andern Mädchen wissen's nicht" *see*
Geheimnis Evers **REGER**
"Anders wird die Welt mit jedem Schritt" *see*
Heimweh Mörike **WOLF**
Andersen, Hans Christian, 1805-1875.
DELIUS *Zwei braune Augen*
GRIEG
En Digters sidste Sang
Du fatter ei Bølgernes evige Gang
Hun er saa hvid
Hytten
Jeg elsker Dig!
Kjaerlighed
Langelandsk Folkemelodi
Min lille Fugl
Min Tanke er et maegtigt Fjeld
Poesien
Rosenknoppen
Soldaten
Taaren

To brune Øjne
Vandring i Skoven
NIELSEN
Højt ligger paa Marken den hvide Sne
Hun har mig glemt!
Min lille Fugl, hvor flyver du
Studie efter Naturen
PROKOFIEV *Gadkiĭ utenok"*
SCHUMANN
Märzveilchen
Muttertraum
Der Soldat
Der Spielmann
Weihnachtlied
André, Johann, 1741-1799.
LOEWE
Mädchen sind wie der Wind
Romanze
"André ne connaît pas la dame" *see La dame*
d'André Vilmorin **POULENC**
Andres Maienlied see Hölty
MENDELSSOHN-BARTHOLDY
"Ane ou vache coq ou cheval" *see Marc*
Chagall Éluard **POULENC**
The anemone see Franzén **SIBELIUS**
Blåsippan
"L'anèmone et l'ancolie" *see Clothilde*
Apollinaire **HONEGGER, RIVIER**
Anfangs wollt' ich fast verzagen see Heine
LISZT, SCHUMANN
L'ange a perdu son auréole see Gabory
AURIC
"L'ange Amabed a cueilli des roses" *see*
La ange et l'enfant Barbier, M.
MASSENET
L'ange et l'enfant see Barbier, M.
MASSENET
L'ange et l'enfant see Reboul **FRANCK**
L'ange gardien see Quételart, A. **GOUNOD**
"Ange silencieux" *see Antienne du silence*
Messiaen **MESSIAEN**
Angedenken see Cornelius **CORNELIUS**
Angel see Capetanakis **ROREM**
The angel see Lermontov **MEDTNER**
Angel see Pushkin **BRITTEN, MEDTNER**
An angel one midnight see Lermontov
RIMSKIĬ-KORSAKOV *Po nebu*
polunochi
An angel speaks to the shepherds see Bible:
LUKE 2: 9-15. **ROREM**
"Die Angel zuckt, die Rute bebt" *see Wie*
Ulfru fischt Mayrhofer **SCHUBERT**
Angeleca see Giacomo **PIZZETTI**
"Angelehnt an die Efeuwand" *see An eine*
Äolsharfe Mörike **BRAHMS, WOLF**

Angélus see Aguétant, Pierre
SAINT-SAËNS
Les Angélus see LeRoy *LA CHANSON DU
PAUVRE* ... **DEBUSSY**
Angelus Domini apparuit see Bible
HINDEMITH
"Das Angenehme dieser Welt hab ich
genossen" *see Fragment* Hölderlin
HINDEMITH
Les anges see Contamine **SATIE**
Les anges musiciens see Carême **POULENC**
Angiolin dal biondo crin see Bocella **LISZT**
Angiolini, Carlo
VERDI *Nell' orror di notte oscura*
Angoisse see Bazenery, F. **INDY**
Angst see Aarestrup **NIELSEN**
*Angst und Hoffen wechselnd mich beklemmen
see* George
DAS BUCH DER HÄNGENDEN GÄRTEN.
SCHÖNBERG
L'anguille see Apollinaire **POULENC**
Anhelos see Rodríguez Marin, Francisco
TURINA
LES ANIMAUX ET LEURS HOMMES, no.
1
SAUGUET Éluard *Cheval*
LES ANIMAUX ET LEURS HOMMES, no.
2
SAUGUET Éluard *Vache*
LES ANIMAUX ET LEURS HOMMES, no.
3
SAUGUET Éluard *Oiseau*
LES ANIMAUX ET LEURS HOMMES, no.
4
SAUGUET Éluard *Chien*
LES ANIMAUX ET LEURS HOMMES, no.
5
SAUGUET Éluard *Chat*
LES ANIMAUX ET LEURS HOMMES, no.
6
SAUGUET Éluard *Poule*
LES ANIMAUX ET LEURS HOMMES, no.
7
SAUGUET Éluard *Porc*
Aniutka see Anon. **PROKOFIEV**
Anklänge see Eichendorff **BRAHMS**
Anmutiger Vertrag see Morgenstern
KILPINEN, REGER
Ann Poverty see De La Mare *DING DONG
BELL*: Benighted. **CHANLER**
Ann street see Pool, Morris W. **IVES**
Anna Amalia von Sachsen-Weimar,
1739-1807.
SPOHR *An Rosa Maria*
"Anna Banna, nash otriad" *see Porosiata*
Kvitko, L. **PROKOFIEV**

ANNA BRYDE. see Benzon
Lys Nat **GRIEG**
Se dig for, når du vaelger din Vej **GRIEG**
Anna Kiesus antajalle see Kanteletar
KILPINEN
Anna Maata Maariainen see Kanteletar
KILPINEN
Anne Boleyn, queen consort of Henry
VIII, 1507-1536.
ROREM *Defiled is my name*
"Anne por jeu me jecta de la neige" *see*
D'Anne qui me jecta de la neige Marot
RAVEL
Anniversaire see Silvestre **MASSENET**
L'anniversaire des martyrs see Dallet
GOUNOD
Anniversary see Kubly **ROREM**
Anniversary in a country cemetery see Porter
DIAMOND
Annunciata see Vogl *SCHNEEGLÖCKCHEN.*
LOEWE *Blumenballade*
L'annuncio see Teresa of Avila **PIZZETTI**
Annunzio, Gabriele d', 1863-1938.
PIZZETTI *Erotica*
REGER *Wenn lichter Mondenschein*
RESPIGHI
La donna sul sarcofago
La statua
ALCYONE.
CASELLA *La sera fiesolana*
MALIPIERO *Ditirambo terzo* (dalle
laudi di Gabriele d'Annunzio, 1923)
CANTO NOVO: Canto dell'Ospite, no. VI.
RESPIGHI *Van li effluvi de le rose*
CANTO NOVO: Canto dell'Ospite, no. VII.
RESPIGHI *O falce di luna*
LA CHIMERA.
MALIPIERO
Eliana
Grasinda
Melusina
Mirinda
Morgana
Oriana–Oriana infedele
RESPIGHI *Mattinata*
LAUDI.
PIZZETTI *I Pastori*
POEMA PARADISIACO.
RESPIGHI
La najade
La sera
Un sogno
Sopra un'aria antica
ANOMALIE. see Rey, Paul
Le chevrier **SÉVERAC**

Anonymous
BLITZSTEIN *Court song*
BORODIN
Arabian melody
Merciful God
BRAHMS
Dort in den Weiden
Der Gang zum Liebchen
Gang zur Liebsten
Gold überwiegt die Liebe
Ich schell mein Horn ins Jammertal
Klage
Murrays Ermordung
Sehnsucht
　Two settings: Op. 14 no. 8 and op. 49
　　no. 3.
Spannung
Ständchen
Die Trauernde
Trennung
　Two settings: Op. 14 no. 5 and op. 97
　　no. 6.
Vergangen ist mir Glück und Heil
Vergebliches Standchen
Volkslied
Vom verwundeten Knaben
Vor dem Fenster
BRITTEN
Begone, dull care
Ee-Oh!
May
A new year carol
Old Abram Brown
There was a man of Newington
There was a monkey
The useful plough
BRUCKNER *Ave Maria*
CASELLA
Amante sono, vaghiccia, di voi
Flaiolet
Fuor de la bella gaiba
Ninna nanna corbellina
Rêves d'or pour ton sommeil
CHAUSSON
Nous nous aimerons
Pour un arbre de Noël
CHOPIN *Piosnka litewska*
COPLAND
Ching-a-ring chaw
The dodger
The golden willow tree
I bought me a cat
The little horses
Long time ago
Simple gifts
Zion's walls
CORNELIUS *Ave Maria*

DEBUSSY *Rondel chinois*
DELIBES *Le rossignol*
DIAMOND
As life what is so sweet
This world is not my home
DVOŘÁK
Ach není, není tu
Dobrú noc, má milá
Ej, mám já koňa faku
Když tě vidím
Koljas
Lásce neujdeš
Nereidy
Panenka a tráva
Připamatování
Spi, mé dítě, spi
Výklad znamení
Žalo dievča, žalo trávu
Žalozpěv Pargy
FALLA
Asturiana
Cancion
Jota
Nana (berceuse)
El pano moruno
Polo
Seguidilla Murciana
FAURÉ
Après un rêve
Ave Maria
O Salutaris
Salve Regina
Sérénade toscane
FRANCK
Messe solennelle: O salutaris
Tantum Ergo, motet no. 3
FRANZ
Ach, wär' es nie geschehen
Dies und Das
Frühlings Ankunft
Frühlingswonne
Hatte Liebchen zwei
Herziges Schätzle du
Rote Äuglein
Die Trauernde
Der Verlassene
Volkslied
Wird er wohl noch meiner gedenken?
Wozu?
GIDEON *Song from without the world*
GOUNOD
L'Ave Marie de l'enfant
Bethléem
Chant d'automne
Chidiock Tichborne
Crépuscule

La distribution des prix
My daddy is a cankered carl
Prière à la Vierge
Repentir
Roy's wife of Aldivalloch
Le temps qui fuit
Welcome to Skye

GRIFFES
Djakoan
Hampelas
Kinanti
Song of the dagger
Two birds flew into the sunset glow

HAHN
L'avertimento
La barcheta
La Biondina in gondoleta
Che pecà!
O Salutaris
La primavera
Sopra l'acqua indormenzada . . .

HARRIS La primavera

HESELTINE
Adam lay ybounden
As ever I saw
The bachelor
The bayly berith the bell away
The distracted maid
The droll lover
Elore lo
Good ale
Hey, troly loly lo
Jenny Gray
Jillian of Berry
Johnnie wi' the tye
The jolly shepherd
Love for love
My little sweet darling
Passing by
Peter Warlock's fancy
Piggesnie
Play acting
Rest, sweet nymphs
Robin Good-fellow
The shoemaker
There is a lady sweet and kind
Tom Tyler
Twelve oxen
Tyrley Tyrlow
Walking the woods

HINDEMITH
In principio erat Verbum
Lieder in Aargauer Mundart

HONEGGER O salutaris

IRELAND
Friendship in misfortune

I have twelve oxen
The three ravens
Variations sur "Cadet rousselle"

IVES
Charlie Rutlage
A Christmas carol
My native land
A son of a gambolier

JENSEN Wenn ich ein Vöglein wär'

LALO Veni Creator

LOEFFLER
By-an'-by
Credo
Old love song

LOEWE
Elvershöh
Friede und Ruhe in Gott
Gesang der Königin Maria Stuart auf den
    Tod Franz II
Jesus mit seinen Jüngern auf dem Meere
Kyrie
Der Treuergebene

LUENING
The dawn
For like a chariot's wheel

MAHLER Es fiel ein Reif in der
    Frühlingsnacht

MALIPIERO Canto della neve

MARTINŮ
Bohatá milá
Boží muka
Děvče z Moravy
The gnat's wedding
Hlásný
In the garden at the castle
Let there be light, O God
A love carol
Mother mine, I have a laddie
Naděje
Opuštěný milý
Le petit oiseau
Prosba
Le sapin de Noel
Smutný milý
Le soir
Súsedova stajňa
Tajná láska
Touha
    Two settings: 1932 and 1942.
Ukolébavka
Veselá dievča
Vysoká veža
Zvědavá dievča
Zvolenovcí chlapci

MASSENET
Mélancolie

Anonymous *(continued)*
    MASSENET *(continued)*
      Poésie de Mytis
      Le poète et le fantôme
      Sévillana
    MENDELSSOHN-BARTHOLDY
      Erntelied
      Minnelied
      O Jugend, O schöne Rosenzeit!
      Winterlied
    MILHAUD
      Beata viscera Mariae
      Berceuse
      Bonjour, messieurs les libérateurs
      Le chant du veilleur
      Chant Hassidique
      Chante de délivrance
      Confidence
      Le Funeste Retour: chanson de marin
      Gam hayom
      Gloire à Dieu
      Hodie nobis de coelo
      Holem tsaudi
      Jeunesse
      Long distance
      Maintenant que les portes de
        bienveillance
      Marronniers
      Le mistral
      O magnum mysterium
      Prenez courage, Ô enfants d'Israël!
      Prière de l'après-dîner
      Prière du matin
      Prière du soir
      Salve Regina mater
      Le seigneur est roi
      Seigneur par le son du schophar vous
        ferez entendre
      La séparation
      Toi
      Toute l'année
      Trois ans de souffrance
      Verbum caro factum
    MOMPOU
      Aserrin, aserran
      D'alt d'un cotxe n'hi ha una nina qu'en
      Hevist dins la lluna tres petits conills
      Margot la pie a fait son nid
      Petite fille de Paris
      Pito, pito, colorito
    NIELSEN *Der boede en Mand i Ribe By*
    PFITZNER *Untreu und Trost*
    PIJPER
      Het wasser te nacht
      Het windetje die uyt den oosten waeyt
    PIZZETTI
      Augurio

      Bebro e il suo cavallo
      Bella lucente luna
      Canzone per ballo
      Il Clefta prigione
      Mirologio per un bambino
      San Basilio
    POULENC
      La belle jeuness
      Chanson à boire
      Couplets bachiques
      Invocations aux Parques
      Madrigal
      La maîtresse volage
      L'Offrande
      Sérénade
    PROKOFIEV
      Aniutka
      Chernets
      Duniushka
      Geĭ, po doroge
      IA nigde druzhka ne vizhu
      Kari glazki
      Katerina
      Na gore-to kalina
      Provody
      Sashen'ka
      Snezhki belye
      Son
      V lete kalina
      Za goroĭu
      Za lesochkom
      Zelenaĭa roshchitsa
    QUILTER
      Amaryllis at the fountain
      Brown is my love
      Damask roses
      Fair house of joy
      The faithless shepherdess
      The fuchsia tree
      Love is a bable
      An old carol
      Weep you no more
    RAVEL
      A vous, oiseau des plaines
      Chanson de pâtre épirote
      Chanson des cueilleuses de lentisques
      Chanson espagnole
      Chanson française
      Chanson hébraïque
      Chanson italienne
      L'Enigme éternelle
      Kaddisch
      Là-bas vers l'èglise
      Mon mouchoir, hélas, est perdu
      Quel galant
      Le réveil de la mariée

COMPOSER Poet *Title* "First Line"

Tout gai!
Tripatos
REGER
  Böses Weib
  Elternstolz
  Hoffnungstrost
  Der Knabe an die Mutter
  Lied eines Mädchens
  Das Mägdlein und der Spatz
  Minnelied
  Schlimm für die Männer
  Wären wir zwei kleine Vögel
  Waldeinsamkeit
  Wenn alle Welt so einig wär'
  Wiegenlied
RIEGGER
  Charmant bocage
  Toi, dont les yeux
RIETI
  Balow
  E lo mio cor s'inchina
  E per un bel cantar
  Fain would I have a pretty thing
  Love me little, love me long
  Madrigal
      Two settings: 1949 and 1967.
RIMSKIĬ-KORSAKOV
  Gde ty, tam mysl' moĭa letaet
  Vikhodi ko mne, signora
RODRIGO
  Adela
  Aire y Donaire
  Canción de baile con pandero
  Canción de cuna
  Cancion del grumete
  Con qué la lavaré?
  Corderito blanco
  De dónde venis, amore?
  De los álamos vengo, madre!
  De ronda
  En Jerez de la Frontera
  En las montañas de Asturias
  Estando yo en mi majada
  Folias Canarias
  "Morena" me llaman
  Nani, nani (Cancion de cuna)
  Una Palomita blanca
  Una pastora yo ami
  Porque toco el pandero
  Quedito
  Respóndemos
  Romance de la infantina de francia
  Romancillo
  San José y Maria
  Tararán
  Viva la novia y el novio!
  Vos me matásteis

ROREM
  Ave Maria
  The call
  A Christmas carol
  Epitaph
  Knight of the Grail
  The mild mother
  The nightingale
  Roundel
ROUSSEL *O bon vin, où as-tu crû?*
RUBINSTEIN *Räthsel*
SAINT-SAËNS
  À la lune
  Alla riva del tebro
  Ariel
  Canzonetta toscana
  La chasse du Burgrave
  Dans ce beau mois
  L'echo de la harpe
  Heureux qui du coeur de Marie
  Le lever de la lune
  Nous qu'en ces lieux
  Pourquoi t'exiler
  Reçois mes hommages
  Reine des cieux
  Tandis que sur vos ans
SATIE *Chanson*
SAUGUET *Cette attirance de la brume*
SCHOECK *Die Verlassene*
SCHÖNBERG
  Es gingen zwei Gespielen gut
  Der Mai tritt ein mit Freuden
  Mein Herz in steten Treuen
  Mein Herz ist mir gemenget
SCHUMANN
  Requiem
  Schneeglöckchen
  Verrathene Liebe
  Vom Reitersmann
  Zigeunerliedchen
SEIBER
  Farewell
  Lament
  Quarrel
  Soldier's song
  Tears
SÉVERAC *Philis*
STRAUSS *Liebesgeschenk*
STRAVINSKIĬ
  Canard
  Les canards, les cygnes, les oies . . .
  Chanson de l'ours
  Chanson pour compter
  Chant dissident
  Le moineau est assis
  Tilim-bom

COMPOSER Poet *Title* ''First Line''

Anonymous *(continued)*

SZYMANOWSKI
A pod borem siwe kunie
Bzicem kunia
Ciamna nocka, ciamna
Dans les pré fleuris
Four folk songs
Idom se siuhaje, dołu, śpiewajecy
Leć, glosie, po rosie
Lecioly zurazie
Ściani dumbek
U jeziorecka
Uwoz, mamo
Wsyscy przyjechali
Wysla burzycka
Wysly rybki, sysly
Zarzyjze, kuniu

THOMPSON, R. *My master hath a garden*

THOMSON
Before sleeping
The feast of love
The holly and the ivy, a carol of Nativity
and Lent
Jerusalem, my happy home
Mass for solo voice
My Master hath a garden
Remember Adam's fall

VAUGHAN WILLIAMS
L'amour de moy
La ballade de Jésus Christ
Chanson de quête
Entlaubet ist der Walde
Jean Renaud
Le paradis
Quand le rossignol
Que Dieu se montre seulement
Réveillez-vous, Piccarz
The Spanish ladies
Wanderlied
The willow song

VERDI *Stornello*

WEBER
Bettlerlied
Canzonetta: Italienisches Ständchen
Heimlicher Liebe Pein
Herzchen, mein Schätzchen
Die kleine Fritz an seine jungen Freunde
Lebensansicht
Der Sänger und der Maler
Umsonst
Unbefangenheit
Volkslied
Two settings: Op. 54 no. 6 and op. 54
no. 7.

WEBERN
Du bist mein, ich bin dein

Der Tag ist vergangen

WEISGALL
Baleboste Zisinke
Di goldene pave
Lomir zikh bafrayen
Mayn harts veynt in mir
No more I will thy love importune
Nuptial song
Der Rebe Elimeylekh
Schlof mayn kind, schlof keseyder zingen
Undzer Rebenyu

WOLF
Ach, im Maien wär's, im Maieh
Ach, wie lang die Seele schlummert!
Alle gingen, Herz, zu Ruh
Auf den grünen Balkon mein Mädchen
Bitt' ihn, O Mutter, bitte den Knaben
Da nur Leid und Leidenschaft
Eide, so die Liebe schwur
Führ' mich, Kind, nach Bethlehem!
Geh, Geliebter
Herr, was trägt der Boden hier
Herz, verzage nicht geschwind
Ich fuhr über Meer
Liebe mir im Busen zündet
Mögen alle bösen Zungen
Morgentau
Sagt ihm, dass er zu mir komme
Sagt, seid Ihr es, feiner Herr
Schmerzliche Wonnen
Seltsam ist Juanas Weise
Sie blasen zum Abmarsch, lieb Mütterlein
Trau' nicht der Liebe
Treibe nur mit Lieben Spott
Wanderlied
Wer sein holdes Lieb verloren
Wer tat deinem Füsslein weh?

ZELTER
Am Tage der sieben Brüder
An den See
An die Preisverteilerin bei einem
Ritterspiele
Auf den Tod eines Kindes
Beglückt, wer in des Herbstes
Beim lieben hellen Mondenschein
Chloe, kennst du noch die Stunde?
Mein Wunsch
Ständchen
Tiefe grauenvolle Stille
Das Veilchen

DES KNABEN WUNDERHORN: Ablösung.
MAHLER *Ablösung im Sommer*
DES KNABEN WUNDERHORN: Abschied
für immer.
MAHLER *Aus! Aus!*

DES KNABEN WUNDERHORN: Drei Reiter am Tor.
MAHLER *Scheiden und Meiden*
DES KNABEN WUNDERHORN: Nicht Wiedersehen.
MAHLER *Nicht Wiedersehen!*
DES KNABEN WUNDERHORN: Der Schweizer.
FRANZ, MAHLER *Zu Strassburg auf der Schanz*
DES KNABEN WUNDERHORN: Selbstgefühl.
MAHLER *Selbstgefühl*
DES KNABEN WUNDERHORN: Starke Einbildungskraft.
MAHLER *Starke Einbildungskraft*
DES KNABEN WUNDERHORN: Um die Kinder still und artig zu machen.
MAHLER *Um schlimme Kinder artig zu machen*
DES KNABEN WUNDERHORN: Waldvöglein.
MAHLER *Ich ging mit Lust durch einen grünen Wald*
EBRO CAUDOLOSE.
SCHUMANN *Flutenreicher Ebro*
THE FAMOUS HISTORY OF FRIAR BACON (printed before 1600).
HESELTINE *Away to Twiver*
FLIEGENDES BLATT.
WEBER
  Abendsegen
  Liebesgruss aus der Ferne
  Liebeslied
  Volkslied
JENSEIT DES TWEED.
LOEWE *Thomas der Reimer*
MAIDMENT'S NORTH COUNTRIE GARLAND (1824).
HESELTINE *Burd Ellen and young Tamlane*
NURSE LOVECHILD'S LEGACY (London: The Poetry Bookshop, 1916).
HESELTINE
  Arthur o' Bower
  How many miles to Babylon?
  I had a little pony
  I won't be my father's Jack
  Little Jack Jingle
  Little Tommy Tucker
  O my kitten
  Robin and Richard
  Suky, you shall be my wife
  There was a man of Thessaly
  There was an old man
  There was an old woman

THE NUT-BROWNE MAYD.
LOEWE *Das braune Mädchen*
SPANISCHES LIEDERBUCH.
RUBINSTEIN, WOLF *Bedeckt mich mit Blumen*
SPANISCHES LIEDERBUCH: Aunque con semblante airado.
JENSEN, WOLF *Ob auch finstre Blicke glitten*
SPANISCHES LIEDERBUCH: Ay ojuelos verdes.
JENSEN *Ach ihr lieben Aeuglein*
SPANISCHES LIEDERBUCH: En campaña madre.
JENSEN *En campaña, madre*
SPANISCHES LIEDERBUCH: Niña, si la huerta vas.
JENSEN, WOLF *Wenn du zu den Blumen gehst*
SPANISCHES LIEDERBUCH: Pensamientos me quitan.
JENSEN *Pensamientos me quitan*
SPANISCHES LIEDERBUCH: Ribericas del rio.
JENSEN *Am Ufer des Flusses, des Manzanares*
SPANISCHES LIEDERBUCH: Ventecico murmurador.
JENSEN *Murmelndes Lüftchen*
Another epitaph see Herrick **ROREM**
"Another good cow-puncher has gone" *see* Charlie Rutlage Anon. **IVES**
Another spring see De La Mare
BERKELEY
ANOTHER SPRING, no. 1
BERKELEY De La Mare *Poetry*
ANOTHER SPRING, no. 2
BERKELEY De La Mare *Another spring*
ANOTHER SPRING, no. 3
BERKELEY De La Mare *Afraid*
Anouilh, Jean, 1910-1987.
LÉOCADIA.
POULENC *Les chemins de l'amour*
Anschütz, Ernst, 1797-1855.
LOEWE *Johann von Nepomuk*
The answer see Binyon **QUILTER**
The answer see Hugo **RACHMANINOFF**
  They answered
Answer not a fool according to his folly see Bible **LUENING**
Antennes see Vincendon, Mireille
ALEXANDRIE. **SCHMITT**
"Antennes du silence" *see Antennes* Vincendon, Mireille **SCHMITT**
Antienne see Van Ormelingen *GLOSES ORPHIQUES.* **MASSENET**

COMPOSER Poet *Title* "First Line"

Antienne du silence see Messiaen
  MESSIAEN
Antigone und Oedip see Mayrhofer
  SCHUBERT
Antike Poesie see Mörike **SCHOECK**
Antipater, of Sidon, fl.120 B.C.
  BERKELEY *Spring song*
Antonio de Villegas
  SPANISCHES LIEDERBUCH: En la peña,
  suso la peña.
    JENSEN *En la peña, suso la peña*
ANTONY AND CLEOPATRA. *see*
  Shakespeare
  Trinklied **SCHUBERT**
Antwort see Uhland **SAINT-SAËNS**
Anzkiis kwanzkiis kurschpiis kluus see No
  author **BLACHER**
Anzoleta avanti la regata see Unknown
  ROSSINI
Anzoleta co passa la regata see Unknown
  ROSSINI
Anzoleta dopo la regata see Unknown
  ROSSINI
A-ou see Bal'mont **RACHMANINOFF**
  The quest
Aoua! see Parny, Evariste **RAVEL**
"Aoua! Aoua!" *see Aoua!* Parny, Evariste
  RAVEL
Apaisement see Verlaine *LA BONNE*
  CHANSON. **CHAUSSON**
Apel, Theodor
  DER ENTFERNTEN.
    WAGNER *Glockentöne*
An Aphrodite see Sappho **LOEWE**
Ein Aphroditen see Sappho **LOEWE** *An*
  Aphrodite
Apollinaire, Guillaume, 1880-1918.
  MARTINŮ
    La blanche neige
    Saltimbanques
  POULENC
    L'anguille
    Avant le cinéma
    Bleuet
    Carte postale
    Chanson d'Orkenise
    Voyage à Paris
  RIVIER *Crépuscule*
  ALCOOLS.
    BERKELEY *Automne*
    HONEGGER
      A la Santé
      L'adieu
      Automne
      Les cloches
      Clotilde
      Saltimbanques

  MARTINŮ *L'adieu*
  POULENC *Rosemonde*
  RIVIER
    L'adieu
    Aubade
    Automne
    Les cloches
    Clothilde
    Les colchiques
    Le pont Mirabeau
    Saltimbanques
  ROREM *Automne*
  LE BESTIAIRE.
    POULENC
      Le carpe
      La chèvre du Thibet
      Le dauphin
      Le dromadaire
      L'écrevisse
      La sauterelle
      La souris
  CALLIGRAMMES.
    POULENC
      Aussi bien que les cigales
      L'espionne
      La grâce exilée
      Il pleut
      Mutation
      Vers le sud
      Voyage
  LE GUETTEUR MÉLANCOLIQUE.
    POULENC *Hôtel*
  IL Y A.
    POULENC
      Allons plus vite
      Chanson
      Dans le jardin d'Anna
      Fagnes de Wallonie
      La grenouillère
      Hyde Park
      Montparnasse
      1904
      Un poème
      Le pont
      Sanglots
  IL Y A: Les dicts d'amour à Linda.
    RIVIER *Linda*
  OBUS COULEUR DE LUNE.
    RIVIER *Carte postale*
  LA TÊTE ÉTOILÉE.
    RIVIER *Le départ*
"Apollo, lebet noch dein hold Verlangen" *see*
  Sonett I Petrarca **SCHUBERT**
Der Apotheker als Nebenbuhler see Gruppe
  LOEWE
Apparition see Mallarmé **DEBUSSY**

The apparition see Roethke **ROREM**
L'apparition see Schiller **SAUGUET**
The appeal see Wyatt **ROREM**
Apple tree, O apple tree see Unknown
    RACHMANINOFF
"Apprendre n'est pas un pensum" *see Album*
    Radiguet **AURIC**
Aprel'! veshniĭ prazdnichnyĭ den' see
    Pailleron *AVRIL*: Chanson.
    RACHMANINOFF
Après l'hiver see Hugo **BIZET**
"Après ma mort, je te feray la guerre" *see*
    Epître imprécatoire Germain-Colin
    JOLIVET
Après minuit see Vildrac *LIVRE D'AMOUR.*
    IBERT
Après un rêve see Anon. **FAURÉ**
"Après un temps d'averse pas trop épaisse"
    see Crépuscule de mi juillet, huit heures
    Laforgue **SAUGUET**
APRÈSLUDE, no. 1
    BLACHER Benn *Gedichte*
APRÈSLUDE, no. 2
    BLACHER Benn *Worte*
APRÈSLUDE, no. 3
    BLACHER Benn *Eure Etüden*
APRÈSLUDE, no. 4
    BLACHER Benn *Letzter Frühling*
April see Storm **SCHOECK**
April see Watson **QUILTER**
"April, April, Laugh thy girlish laughter" *see*
    April Watson **QUILTER**
April love see Quilter **QUILTER**
Aprillaunen see Osterwald **FRANZ**
"Aprilwind; alle Knospen" *see*
    Mädchenfrühling Dehmel **SCHÖNBERG**
Apukhtin, Aleksyeĭ Nikolayevich, 1841-
    1893.
    CHAĬKOVSKIĬ
      Den' li t͡sarit
      Kto idyot?
      Nochi bezumnye
      On tak menia li͡ubil
      Zabyt' tak skoro!
    PROKOFIEV *Otchalila lodka*
    RACHMANINOFF
      Fate
      Oh, do not grieve!
AQUARELLES. see Verlaine
    Green **DEBUSSY, FAURÉ**
    Spleen **DEBUSSY, IRELAND**
"Aquella eterna fuerte esta escondida" *see*
    Cantar del alma John, Saint, apostle
    MOMPOU
"Aquest cami tan fi tan fi qui sap ou mena"
    see Cançoneta incerta Carner **MOMPOU**

Aquesta nit un mateix vent see Janés i Olivé
    MOMPOU
"År, som stundar, aldrig kände jag nyår" *see*
    Hälsning till ett nytt år
    Österling **KILPINEN**
Arab love song see Shelley **QUILTER**
L'Arabe jaloux see Florian **BERLIOZ**
    Le maure jaloux
Arabian melody see Anon. **BORODIN**
Arabskaya melodiya see Anon. **BORODIN**
    Arabian melody
Aragon, Louis, 1897-1982.
    AURIC
      Richard II Quarante
      La rose et la Réséda
    POULENC
      C
      Fêtes galantes
Aragonese see Metastasio **ROSSINI**
Aram, Kurt, pseud. *see* Fischer, Hans,
    1869-1934.
"Arbeitsam und wacker" *see Pflügerlied*
    Salis-Seewis **SCHUBERT**
Der Arbeitsmann see Dehmel **PFITZNER,**
    STRAUSS
ARBOURS AND ENDURANCES. see Nichols
    The water lily **HESELTINE**
L'arbre see Moréas **SAINT-SAËNS**
"Arbre charmant qui me rappelle" *see*
    Paysage Silvestre **MASSENET**
"Arbe de marbre où je sais" *see Ritournelle*
    Richaud **SAUGUET**
L'arbre exotique see Gosse, Chevalier
    MILHAUD
Arc-en-ciel d'innocence see Messiaen
    MESSIAEN
L'archet see Cros *LE COFFRET DE*
    SANTAL, CHANSONS PERPÉTUELLES.
    DEBUSSY, MALIPIERO
Archibald Douglas see Fontane, T. **LOEWE**
Ardeur see Claudel **MILHAUD**
"Are not the joys of morning sweeter" *see*
    Young love Blake, William **LUENING**
"Are ye the ghosts of fallen leaves" *see*
    Phantoms Tabb **GRIFFES**
"Are you divine?" *see The way you are*
    Blitzstein **BLITZSTEIN**
Arens, Egmont
    RIEGGER *The somber pine*
Argizagi ederra see Unknown
    SZYMANOWSKI
Argwohn Josephs see Rilke **HINDEMITH**
Aria see James, E. **SAUGUET**
Aria see No author **IBERT** *Vocalise-étude*
    (Aria, 1930)
Arie see Metastasio *DIDONE*
    ABBANDONATA. **SCHUBERT**

Arie aus dem Spiegel von Arcadien see
  Schikaneder *SPIEGEL VON ARCADUA.*
  SCHÖNBERG
Ariel see Anon. **SAINT-SAËNS**
Arietta all'antica, dedotta dal "O salutaris
  Hostia" *see* Metastasio **ROSSINI**
Ariette see Ferrand, A. **MOZART**
Ariette see Goldoni **SCHUBERT**
  La pastorella
Ariette see Lamotte **MOZART**
Ariette see Moréas **MALIPIERO**
Ariette à l'ancienne see Rousseau **ROSSINI**
Ariette pour Tina see Indy **INDY**
Ariette villageoise see Rousseau **ROSSINI**
ARIETTES DOULOUREUSES. see Marès
  Ballade de la reine morte d'aimer **RAVEL**
ARIETTES OUBLIÉES, no. 1
  DEBUSSY Verlaine *C'est l'extase*
    langoureuse
ARIETTES OUBLIÉES, no. 2
  DEBUSSY Verlaine *Il pleure dans mon*
    coeur
ARIETTES OUBLIÉES, no. 3
  DEBUSSY Verlaine *L'ombre des arbres*
ARIETTES OUBLIÉES, no. 4
  DEBUSSY Verlaine *Chevaux de bois*
ARIETTES OUBLIÉES, no. 5
  DEBUSSY Verlaine *Green*
ARIETTES OUBLIÉES, no. 6
  DEBUSSY Verlaine *Spleen*
Arion see Pushkin **MEDTNER,**
  RACHMANINOFF
Arioso see Runeberg **SIBELIUS**
Arioso see Silvestre **DELIBES**
Ariosto, Lodovico, 1474-1533.
  IVES *La fède*
Arise, come down! see Mei **RIMSKĬĬ-**
  KORSAKOV
  Vstan', soĭdi! davno dennitsa
L'arithmétique see Turpin, Charles
  GOUNOD
"Arm am Beutel, krank am Herzen" *see*
  Der Schatzgräber Goethe
  LOEWE, SCHUBERT
"Arm in Arm und Kron' an Krone" *see Aus*
  den Waldliedern I Keller, G.
  SCHOECK
Armas arkussa ajavi see Kanteletar
  KILPINEN
DER ARME MINNESINGER. see Kotzebue
  Lass mich schlummern **WEBER**
  Rase, Sturmwind, blase **WEBER**
  Über die Berge mit Ungestüm **WEBER**
  Umringt vom muterfüllten Heere **WEBER**
Der arme Peter see Heine **SCHUMANN**

Der arme Thoms see Falk **ZELTER**
Das arme Vögelein see Gilm zu Rosenegg
  REGER
"Der Arme, wie seufzend am Ahorn sass sie!"
  see Lied der Desdemona
  Shakespeare **LOEWE**
Armes Blünchen see Hoffmann von
  Fallersleben **LASSEN**
Armottoman osa see Kanteletar **KILPINEN**
Armstrong, Martin Donisthorpe, 1882-
  1974.
  ROREM *On a little bird*
Arndt, Ernst Moritz, 1769-1860.
  LASSEN *Ballade*
  LOEWE *Liebesnähe*
  REGER *Grablied*
Arndt, Johann, 1555-1621.
  FRANZ *Im Frühling*
ARNE. see Bjørnson
  Kleine Venevil **DELIUS**
  Over the mountains high **DELIUS**
Arnim, Ludwig Achim, Freiherr von,
  1781-1831.
  STRAUSS
    Einerlei
    Der Pokal
    Der Stern
Arnold, Matthew, 1822-1888.
  IVES *West London*
Arnoux, Alexandre, 1884-1973.
  IBERT
    Berceuse de Galiane
    Complainte de Florinde
Arosa, Paul, b. 1874.
  SCHMITT
    Belle Meunière
    Chanson bretonne
Around a twisted snake of flame see
  MacDowell **MACDOWELL**
"Around the globe the mighty seas extend"
  see Song of night Tiutchev
  MEDTNER
"Around were all the roses red" *see Spleen*
  Verlaine **IRELAND**
Arpège see Samain **FAURÉ**
"Arrête! écoute-moi voyageur!" *see La prière*
  du mort Hérédia **KOECHLIN**
The arrow and the song see Longfellow
  GOUNOD
Arsen'ev, Aleksandr Vasil'evich, 1854-
  1896.
  BALAKIREV
    Barkarola
    Kolibel'naya pesnya
Arsenieff, A *see* Arsen'ev, Aleksandr
  Vasil'evich, 1854-1896.

Art see Maĭkov **RIMSKIĬ-KORSAKOV**
 Iskusstvo
"L'art de compter avec exactitude" *see*
 L'arithmétique Turpin, Charles
 GOUNOD
Die Art, ein Weib zu nehmen see Unknown
 SCHUBERT *Il modo di prender mogli*
"Art thou poor, yet hast thou golden
 slumbers?" *see Sweet content* Dekker
 HESELTINE
ARTASERSE. see Metastasio
 Leiden der Trennung **SCHUBERT**
Arteaga, Cristina de
 TURINA
  Corazón de mujer
  Cunas
  Lo mejor del amor
Arthur o' Bower see Anon. *NURSE*
 LOVECHILD'S LEGACY. **HESELTINE**
"Arthur o' Bower has broken his band" *see*
 Arthur o' Bower Anon. **HESELTINE**
Arvers, Félix, 1806-1850.
 BIZET *Ma vie a son secret*
"As a perfume doth remain" *see Memory*
 London Atheneum **CARPENTER**
As Adam see Whitman **BLITZSTEIN**
"As Adam early in the morning" *see As Adam*
 Whitman **BLITZSTEIN**
As Adam early in the morning see Whitman
 ROREM
"As areas de ouro aureana do Sil" *see*
 Aureana do sil Cabanillas **MOMPOU**
"As down the road she wambled slow" *see*
 Bessie Bobtail Stephens, James
 BARBER
As ever I saw see Anon. **HESELTINE**
As fair as day in blaze of noon see Vilenkin
 RACHMANINOFF
 She is as lovely as the moon
"As I rode down to Yarmouth Fair" *see*
 Yarmouth Fair Collins, Hal **HESELTINE**
"As I sat musing" *see The song of the soldiers*
 De La Mare **BERKELEY**
"As I walked with my love, one evening" *see*
 The right number Mužik **MARTINŮ**
"As I wander'd the forest" *see The wild*
 flower's song Blake, William
 HINDEMITH
"As I wandered in the forest" *see The wild*
 flower's song Blake, William **QUILTER**
As if a phantom caress'd me see Whitman
 BLITZSTEIN
As it fell upon a day see Barnefield
 COPLAND
"As it fell upon a day" *see Philomel*
 Barnefield **ROREM**

As it is, plenty see Auden *HIS*
 EXCELLENCY. **BRITTEN**
As life what is so sweet see Anon.
 DIAMOND
As lonesome through the woods I stray see
 Klingemann *WALDEINSAMKEIT.*
 BENNETT
As o'er the burning ashes see Tiutchev
 CHAĬKOVSKIĬ
 Kak" nad" goriacheiu zoloĭ
As the gloaming shadows creep see
 MacDowell **MACDOWELL**
As they reiterated: "Fool" see Mei *PESNYA.*
 CHAĬKOVSKIĬ
 Kak naladili: Durak
As though on hot ashes see Tiutchev
 CHAĬKOVSKIĬ
 Kak" nad" goriacheiu zoloĭ
AS YOU LIKE IT. see Shakespeare
 In spring **CARPENTER**
 It was a lover and his lass **DELIUS,**
 QUILTER, RIETI
 Komm herbei, komm herbei, Tod! **LOEWE**
 Pretty ring time **HESELTINE**
 Under the greenwood tree **QUILTER**
Ascendente Jesu in naviculam see Bible
 HINDEMITH
Asenijeff, Elsa von
 REGER
  Amselliedchen
  An eine Mutter
  Klage
Aserrin, aserran see Anon. **MOMPOU**
Ashbery, John, 1927-
 SELF PORTRAITS IN A CONVEX
 MIRROR.
 ROREM *Fear of death*
 TENNIS COURT OATH.
 ROREM *Thoughts of a young girl*
An aside see Henry VIII **IRELAND**
Ask me no more see Tennyson **ROREM**
"Ask me not, dear, what thing it is" *see*
 The answer Binyon **QUILTER**
ASMUS. see Claudius, M.
 Der Zahn **LOEWE**
Aspergi il corpo tuo see Sappho **RIETI**
Aspiration see Carpenter, Rue
 CARPENTER
Asquith, Herbert, 1881-1947.
 THE VOLUNTEER.
 BRITTEN *Epitaph: The clerk*
Der Asra see Heine **LOEWE,**
 RUBINSTEIN
Assad mit dem Selam see Stieglitz **LOEWE**
Assad und Gulhinde see Stieglitz **LOEWE**
 Assad mit dem Selam

COMPOSER Poet *Title* "First Line"

"Assez dormir ma belle" *see Le lever*
　Musset **GOUNOD**
"Assis au bord du lac où baignent leurs pieds
　nus" *see Amphise et Melitta* Samain
　KOECHLIN
"Assis sur cette blanche tombe" *see Au
　cimetière* Renaud **SAINT-SAËNS**
"Assise sur la plaine" *see Le châle* Vilmorin
　AURIC
Assunta see Giacomo **PIZZETTI**
Astray see Tavaststjerna **SIBELIUS** *Vilse*
L'astre rouge see Leconte de Lisle
　KOECHLIN
ASTRONOMICA: Book 4, livre 16. *see*
　Manilius *Vita* **IVES**
ASTROPHEL AND STELLA (1591): First
　song. *see* Sidney, Sir Philip
　Dedication **HESELTINE**
Asturiana see Anon. **FALLA**
Asturias, Miguel Angel, 1899-1974.
　LOS INDIOS BAJAN DE MIXCO.
　　GIDEON *Mixco*
At bedtime see Ogarev **CHAĭKOVSKIĭ**
　Na son" griadushchiĭ
At Christmas time see Hesse **LUENING**
"At Christmas time I travel far" *see At
　Christmas time* Hesse **LUENING**
At close of day see Binyon **QUILTER**
At day-close in November see Hardy
　BRITTEN
"At Eden's gate a gentle angel" *see Angel*
　Pushkin **BRITTEN**
"At Heaven's gate there stood an angel" *see
　The angel* Pushkin **MEDTNER**
At home see Unknown **MARTINŮ**
　U maměnky
At home among real people see Nekrasov
　BORODIN *U lyudey-to v domu*
"At Martinmas, when I was born" *see Mr.
　Belloc's fancy* Squire, Sir John
　HESELTINE
"At midnight an angel flew over the sky"
　see The angel Lermontov
　MEDTNER
At night see Mayer, R. **MARTINŮ**
At parting see Peterson **IVES**
At sea see Johnson **IVES**
At St. Patrick's Purgatory see O'Faolain,
　Sean, translator. *THE SILVER BRANCH.*
　BARBER
At the aquarium see Eastman **GIDEON**
At the brook see Kleinschrod **DVOŘÁK**
　U potoka
At the cloister gate see Lermontov
　MEDTNER

"At the cry of the first bird" *see The
　crucifixion* Jones, Howard Mumford,
　translator. **BARBER**
"At the dance and supper room I could not
　help thinking" *see Inauguration ball*
　Whitman **ROREM**
"At the feäst, I do mind very well, all the
　vo'ks" *see Don't Ceäre* Barnes
　CARPENTER
"At 'The Fox Inn' the tattered ears" *see
　The fox* Blunt **HESELTINE**
At the gate of the Holy Abode see
　Lermontov *NISCHCHIY.*
　RACHMANINOFF
At the last see Whitman **LUENING**
"At the quiet close of day" *see Afterglow*
　Cooper, James **IVES**
At the railway station, Upway see Hardy
　BRITTEN
"At the red of the dawn" *see The lilacs*
　Beketova **RACHMANINOFF**
At the river see Lowry **COPLAND, IVES**
At the round Earth's imagined corners see
　Donne **BRITTEN**
At the spring see Fisher, J. **THOMSON**
"At the spring birds do sing" *see At the spring*
　Fisher, J. **THOMSON**
"At the time when the near return of Christ"
　see The millennium Blixen
　DIAMOND
ATALANTA. see Wied
　Gudhjaelp **NIELSEN**
"Atherische ferne Stimmen" *see
　Lerchengesang* Candidus **BRAHMS**
Der Atlas see Heine **SCHUBERT**
"Atme nur leise zieh ich die Kreise hier" *see
　Ständchen* Simrock **SPOHR**
　Two settings: Op. 139 no. 1 and WoO 94.
Attard, Josefina de
　TURINA *Melpómene*
Attegløyma see Vinje **GRIEG**
Attendez le prochain bateau see Vilmorin
　AURIC
L'attente see Hasselt **MASSENET** *Sur une
　poésie de Van Hasselt*
Attente see Hugo *LES ORIENTALES.* **INDY**
L'attente see Hugo *LES ORIENTALES.*
　SAINT-SAËNS, WAGNER
Attente see Maeterlinck **BOULANGER**
Attributs see Ronsard **POULENC**
Atys see Mayrhofer **SCHUBERT**
Au! see Bal'mont **RACHMANINOFF**
　The quest
"Au banquet de la vie" *see Stances* Gilbert
　MASSENET

"Au beau milieu de l'ile verte" *see Poupette et Patata* Vildrac **MILHAUD**

Au beau soleil see Jammes **MILHAUD**

Au bord de la cheminée see D'Harcourt, Antoniette **SAUGUET**

Au bord de l'eau see Sully-Prudhomme **FAURÉ**

Au bord de l'eau verte see Jammes **MILHAUD**

"Au bord de l'île on voit" *see La grenouillère* Apollinaire **POULENC**

"Au bord d'un torrent, Ophélie" *see La mort d'Ophélie* Legouvé **SAINT-SAËNS**

"Au bord d'une fontaine" *see Félicité passée* Rousseau **ZELTER**

"Au bosquet de ta lèvre" *see Soir de rêve* Lugnier, Antonin **MASSENET**

Au chevet d'un mourant (élégie) *see* Pacini **ROSSINI**

"Au ciel, en d'immenses vergers" *see Les feuilles* Carême **MILHAUD**

"Au ciel sept chérubins silencieux comme les rêves" *see Lamentation* Unknown **MILHAUD**

Au cimetière see Gautier **BERLIOZ**

Au cimetière see Renaud **SAINT-SAËNS**

Au cimetière see Richepin **FAURÉ**

"Au coin d'une rue" *see Deux soeurs qui sont pas soeurs* Stein **THOMSON**

AU COURANT DE LA VIE. Stances, sonnets, poèmes (1885). *see* Guinand *Barcarolle* **DEBUSSY**

"Au cyprès que j'ai fait planter là-bas" *see Pour un cyprés* Desnoux, Lucienne **SAUGUET**

Au delà du rêve see Hirsch **MASSENET**

"Au détour du chemin" *see Néére* Carré **MASSENET**

"Au Dieu d'Amour" *see L'Offrande* Anon. **POULENC**

"Au fleuve le ruisseau se mêle" *see Aimons-nous* Barbier, J. **GOUNOD**

Au galop see Bonnières **INDY**

"Au gibet noir, manchot aimable" *see Bal des pendus* Rimbaud **HINDEMITH**

"Au jardin de ma fantaisie" *see Mousmé* Alexandre, André **MASSENET**

"Au levant làbas" *see Chansonette* Wailly **BERLIOZ**

"Au loin, dans la mer" *see Lied maritime* Indy **INDY**

"Au long de ces montagnes douces" *see La Romance d'Ariel* Bourget **DEBUSSY**

Au matin see Ferrière, S. **GOUNOD**

Au milieu du jardin see Moréas **RESPIGHI**

Au pays see Fargue **AUBERT**

Au pays see Follain **SAUGUET**

"Au pays de Papouasie, J'ai caressé la Pouasie . . . " *see Air du Poète* Fargue **SATIE**

Au pays des rêves see Silvestre **FAURÉ** *Le pays des rêves*

Au pays où se fait la guerre see Gautier *LA COMÉDIE DE LA MORT*: Romance. **DUPARC**

Au pied de mon lit see Jammes *TRISTESSES.* **BOULANGER**

"Au pied de sontrône d'amour" *see Prière à la Vierge* Anon. **GOUNOD**

Au printemps see Barbier, J. **GOUNOD**

Au rossignol see Guillot de Saix **HAHN**

Au rossignol see Lamartine **GOUNOD**

Au très aimé see Duer **MASSENET**

Aubade see Apollinaire *ALCOOLS.* **RIVIER**

Aubade see Béranger **BERLIOZ** *Les champs*

Aubade see Ferrier **BIZET**

Aubade see Hugo **GOUNOD**

Aubade see Marguerite d'Angoulême **SÉVERAC** *Albado*

Aubade see Pommey, Louis **FAURÉ**

Aubade see Prévost, Gabriel **MASSENET**

Aubade see Wilder **LALO**

Aubanel, T **SCHMITT** *Si mon coeur avait des ailes . . .*

Aube see Lefilleul, G. **JOLIVET**

Aube see Rimbaud **MILHAUD**

L'aube blanche see Lerberghe **FAURÉ**

"Une aube fraîche . . . et printanière" *see Amours bénis* Alexandre, André **MASSENET**

"L'aube nait et ta porte est close" *see Aubade* Hugo **GOUNOD**

L'aube nait et ta porte est close see Hugo **LALO**

Aube païenne see Rocha, Lucien **MASSENET**

AUBERT, LOUIS FRANÇOIS MARIE, 1877-1968.
  Barbusse, Henri, 1874-1935.
    La lettre (1900) [Durand, 1909]
      "Je t'écris et la lampe écoute"
  Bengy-Puyvallée, Antoine de, 1854-
    Hélène (1901) [Durand, 1908-09]
      "Je suis la blonde fleur d'amour qui resplendis"
    Première (1904) [Durand, 1907-09]
      "J'habite avec toi seule un sommet de lumière"
  Catteau, Robert
    Grisaille (1908) [Durand, 1909]
      "La pluie, hésitante et sans bruit"

AUBERT, LOUIS FRANÇOIS MARIE, 1877-1968 (continued)
Chalupt, René, 1885-1957.
De Ceylan (1920) [Durand, 1920]
"Une odeur délicate de thé"
La mauvaise prière (1932) [Durand, 1932] "Sur un trois-mâts de la Marine"
Champlay, R
Berceuse du marin (1933) [Durand, 1933] "Tu seras loin, loin de moi"
Tendresse (1934) [Durand, 1934] "Pour toi j'ai toute donné"
Dommange, René Auguste Louis Henri, b. 1888.
L'heure captive (1928) [Durand, 1928] "Ne parlons plus"
Voice, violin & piano.
Fargue, Léon-Paul, 1878-1947.
Au pays (1920) [Durand, 1920] "Un nom: Cromac, nous fait parler"
Giraud, Henri, 1869-
Déclaration (1901) [Durand, 1909] "Tes yeux sont de claires fontaines"
Haraucourt, Edmond, 1857-1941.
Secret aveu (1901) [Durand, 1912] "Les vierges fleurs ouvrant leur minces corsets verts"
Hérold, André-Ferdinand, b. 1865.
Prélude (1908) [Durand, 1909] "La flûte amère de l'automne"
Hettich, Amédée Louis Landely, 1856-1937.
D'un berceau (1900) [Durand, 1912] "Dors, ma petit mère, ah!"
Melancholia (1897) [Durand, 1909] "Il est au fond des bois des fleurs"
Noël pastoral (1899) [Salabert; R. Deiss, 1927] "A travers la lande pierreuse"
Houssaye, Arsène, 1815-1896.
Vieille chanson espagnole (1894) [Salabert, 1909; Durand, 1909] "En mes belles années j'étais un arbe en fleurs"
Jean-Aubry, Georges, 1882-1950.
Sérénade mélancolique (1923) [Durand, 1924] "Le soir s'afaisse sur lui même"
Ludana
Péché véniel (1899) [Salabert; R. Deiss, 1927] "En priant chaque soir la Madone"
Marès, Roland de, 1874-1955.
Légende (1899) [Salabert; R. Deiss, 1927] "Sais-tu bien le destin"

Mauclair, Camille, 1872-1945.
Brodeuses (1908) [Durand, 1909] "Les mains lentes sous la lampe"
Oeris, Arsène
Fatum (1897) [Salabert, 1912]
Sur le bord (1899) [Salabert; R. Deiss, 1927] "J'ai pleuré j'ai lutté"
Régnier, Henri François Joseph de, 1864-1936.
Odelette (1910) [Durand, 1911] "Si j'ai parlé de mon amour"
Ronsard, Pierre de, 1524-1585.
La fontaine d'Hélène (1924) [Durand; Suppl. to **La Revue Musicale,** May 1924] "Afin que ton renom coule parmi la plaine"
Samain, Albert Victor, 1858-1900.
L'âme errante (1908) [Durand, 1909] "Le Séraphin des soirs passe le long des fleurs"
Silence (1908) [Durand, 1909] "Le silence descend en nous"
Schneider, Édouard
Pays sans nom (1926) [Durand, 1926] "Les pays, tu sais bien"
Silvestre, Paul Armond, 1837-1901.
Quand, à tes genoux! op. 4, no. 1 (1898) [Durand, 1909] same
Also voice & orchestra; orchestral version published 1900.
Si de mon premier rêve, op. 4, no. 2 (1898) [Durand, 1909] same
Also voice & orchestra; orchestral version published 1900.
Souvent de nos biens le meilleur, op. 4, no. 3 (1898) [Durand, 1909] same
Also voice & orchestra; orchestral version published 1900.
Sully-Prudhomme, René François Armand, 1839-1907.
Chanson de mer (1900) [Durand, 1908-09] "Ton sourire infini m'est cher"
Les yeux (1900) [Durand, 1909] "Bleus ou noirs, tous aimés"
Tonquédec, Marthe de
L'inconnu (1899) [Salabert; R. Deiss, 1927] "Il s'est envolé comme un rêve"
Toussaint, Franz, 1879-1955.
JARDIN DES CARESSES.
L'adieu (1915-17) [Durand, 1917] "Quand, pour me faire ce geste"
Also voice & orchestra; orchestral version published 1921.
Le destin (1915-17) [Durand, 1917] "L'amour de la femme est l'ombre"

Also voice & orchestra; orchestral version published 1921.

Le mirage (1915-17) [Durand, 1917]
"Je m'étais endormi, et je faisais un rêve"
Also voice & orchestra; orchestral version published 1921.

Le sommeil des colombes (1915-17) [Durand, 1917]
"Dans le cèndre, des colombes se sont posées"
Also voice & orchestra; orchestral version published 1921.

Le vaincu (1915-17) [Durand, 1917]
"Je ne veux que te meurtrir de caresses"
Also voice & orchestra; orchestral version published 1921.

Le visage penché (1915-17) [Durand, 1917]
"Reste ainsi, penchée sur ton coeur"
Also voice & orchestra; orchestral version published 1921.

Unknown
Sous-bois (1892) [Durand, 1892]

Văcărescu, Elena, 1868-1947.
Sérénade (1906) [Durand, 1907-09]
"La lune s'est bâti dans les flots cette nuit"

Vivien, Renée, 1877-1907.
Aigues-Marines (1918) [Durand, 1919]
"Des gouttes d'eau"
Feuilles sur l'eau (1908) [Durand, 1909]
"L'onde porte le poids des feuilles en détresse"
Nuit mauresque (1911) [Durand, 1911]
"La nuit est façonée avec un art subtil"
Roses du soir (1919) [Durand, 1919]
"Des roses sur la mer"

Aubigné, Théodore Agrippa d', 1552-1630.
MILHAUD *Préparatif a la mort en allégorie maritime*
"Auch das schönste Blumenleben" *see*
Himmelsblüthen Gerstenberg **LOEWE**
Auch kleine Dinge see Heyse **WOLF**
Auch mein Sinn see Goethe **ZELTER**
"Aucun plaisir sur terre" *see Nessun maggior,*
page d'album Dante **BERLIOZ**

Auden, Wystan Hugh, 1907-1973.
BERKELEY
Carry her over the water
Eyes look into the well
Lauds
O lurcher-loving collier, black as night
What's in your mind, my dove

BRITTEN
Calypso
Fish in the unruffled lakes
Funeral blues
Johnny
Tell me the truth about love
ROREM *Stop all the clocks*
THE DOG BENEATH THE SKIN.
BRITTEN *Nocturne*
HIS EXCELLENCY.
BRITTEN *As it is, plenty*
LOOK, STRANGER!
BRITTEN
Let the florid music praise!
Now the leaves are falling fast
ON THIS ISLAND.
BRITTEN *Seascape*
ROREM *Look stranger, on this island*

Auden, Wystan Hugh, 1907-1973, translator.
BARBER
The monk and his cat
The praises of God

Audigier, Georges
SAINT-SAËNS *Le fleuve*
SÉVERAC *Prends mon âme*

Auersperg, Anton Alexander, Graf von, 1806-1876.
LOEWE
Die Leiche zu St. Just
Die Reigerbaize
Das Wiegenfest zu Gent
REGER *Das Blatt im Buche*
EIN FRIEDHOFKRANZ.
LOEWE *Die Grabrose*
DER LETZTE RITTER.
LOEWE
Max' Abschied von Augsburg
Max in Augsburg
Max und Dürer

"Auf, Brüder, auf! Der Tag bricht an" *see*
Morgenlied Rudolphi **LOEWE**
"Auf das Feuer mit dem goldnen Strahle" *see*
Das Heilige Feuer Meyer **SCHOECK**
Auf dein Wohl trink'ich see Pushkin
RUBINSTEIN
"Auf deinem Bild in schwarzem Rahmen" *see*
Dein Bild Jacobowski **REGER**
"Auf deinem Grunde" *see Auf dem Rhein*
Immermann **SCHUMANN**
Auf dem Berge dort, am Fluss see Kol'tsov
MUSORGSKIĬ
Po nad Donom sad tsvetet
"Auf dem Dache sitzt der Spatz" *see Spatz und Spätzin* Meyer, K. **REGER**

COMPOSER Poet *Title* "First Line"

"Auf dem Dorf' in den Spinnstuben" *see*
  Die Spinnerin Heyse **SCHUMANN**
Auf dem Flusse see Müller, Wilhelm
  SCHUBERT
Auf dem Hügel sitz ich spähend see Jeitteles
  BEETHOVEN
Auf dem Kirchhofe see Liliencron **BRAHMS**
Auf dem Krankenbette see Mörike
  SCHOECK
Auf dem Landgut see Musorgskiĭ
  MUSORGSKIĬ *Poekhal na polochke*
Auf dem Meere see Heine **FRANZ**
  Six settings: Op. 5 no. 3, op. 6 no. 3, op. 9
  no. 6, op. 11 no. 5, op. 25 no. 6, and op.
  36 no. 1.
Auf dem Rhein see Eichendorff **SCHOECK**
Auf dem Rhein see Immermann
  SCHUMANN
Auf dem Schiffe see Köstlin **BRAHMS**
Auf dem See see Goethe **LOEWE,**
  MEDTNER, SCHUBERT, WOLF
Auf dem See see Köstlin **BRAHMS**
Auf dem See see Simrock **BRAHMS**
"Auf dem stillen, schwülen Pfuhle tanzt" *see*
  Schwalbenmärchen Freiligrath **LOEWE**
Auf dem Strome see Rellstab **SCHUBERT**
Auf dem Teich, dem regungslosen see Lenau
  SCHILFLIEDER. **FRANZ, GRIFFES**
"Auf dem Teich, dem regungslosen" *see*
  Schilflied Lenau
  MENDELSSOHN-BARTHOLDY
Auf dem Wasser zu singen see Stolberg
  SCHUBERT
"Auf dem Wege vom Tanzsaal nach Haus"
  see Müde Liliencron **PFITZNER**
Auf den Bergen see Lemcke **JENSEN**
"Auf den Blumen" *see Nach einem Gewitter*
  Mayrhofer **SCHUBERT**
Auf den grünen Balkon mein Mädchen see
  Anon. **WOLF**
Auf den Tod einer Kaiserin see Claudius, M.
  SCHOECK
Auf den Tod einer Nachtigall see Hölty
  SCHUBERT
Auf den Tod eines Kindes see Anon.
  ZELTER
Auf den Tod eines Kindes see Uhland
  SCHOECK
"Auf den Wassern wohnt mein stilles Leben"
  see Lebensmelodien Schlegel
  SCHUBERT
Auf der Bahre einer jungen Frau see Monrad
  GRIEG *Ved en ung Hustrus Båre*
"Auf der Bank im Walde" *see Anmutiger*
  Vertrag Morgenstern **KILPINEN,**
  REGER

"Auf der Bank, wo sie sonst" *see In der*
  Kirche Rückert **LOEWE**
"Auf der Berge freien Höhen" *see Punschlied.*
  Im Norden zu singen Schiller
  SCHUBERT
Auf der Bruck see Schulze **SCHUBERT**
Auf der Donau see Mayrhofer **SCHUBERT**
"Auf der fernen See" *see Lied des*
  Schiffermädels Bierbaum **BERG**
"Auf der Heide weht der Wind (herzig Kind)"
  see Willst du, dass ich geh'?
  Lemcke **BRAHMS**
"Auf der Messe, da zieht es" *see*
  Der Mohrenfürst auf der Messe
  Freiligrath **LOEWE**
Auf der Reise zur Heimat see Vinje
  FERDAMINNI. **DELIUS**
Auf der Riesenkoppe see Körner
  SCHUBERT
"Auf der schönen, schönen Wiese" *see*
  Ein Tänzchen Boelitz **REGER**
Auf der Sieg der Deutschen see Unknown
  SCHUBERT
Auf der Teck see Mörike **SCHOECK**
Auf der Treppe sitzen meine Öhrchen see
  Morgenstern **HINDEMITH**
AUF DER ÜBERFAHRT. see Uhland
  Die Überfahrt **LOEWE**
Auf der Wanderschaft see Chamisso **WOLF**
Auf der Wanderschaft see Lenau
  LIEBESKLÄNGE.
  MENDELSSOHN-BARTHOLDY
Auf der Wanderung see Hoffmann von
  Fallersleben
  DES FAHRENDEN SCHÜLERS LIEBEN
  UND LEIDEN. **WOLF**
"Auf der Wellen Spiegel schwimmt der Kahn"
  see Auf der Donau Mayrhofer
  SCHUBERT
"Auf des Berges höchstem Scheitel" *see*
  Fernsicht Hertz **JENSEN**
"Auf des Lagers weichem Kissen ruht die
  Jungfrau" *see Der Blumen Rache*
  Freiligrath **LOEWE**
"Auf die Dächer zwischen blassen Wolken"
  see Das Ständchen Eichendorff
  LASSEN, WOLF
"Auf die Nacht in den Spinnstuben" *see*
  Die Einsame Heyse **JENSEN**
"Auf die Nacht in den Spinnstub'n" *see*
  Mädchenlied Heyse **BRAHMS**
"Auf die stürm'sche See hinaus" *see Des*
  Künstlers Abschied Dusch **WEBER**
Auf ein altes Bild see Mörike **WOLF**
Auf ein Ei geschrieben see Mörike
  SCHOECK

Auf ein Kind see Mörike SCHOECK
Auf ein Kind see Uhland SCHOECK,
STRAUSS
Auf ein schlummerndes Kind see Hebbel
CORNELIUS
Auf eine Christblume see Mörike WOLF
Two settings: M 20 and M 21.
Auf eine Lampe see Mörike SCHOECK
Auf eine Unbekannte see Hebbel
CORNELIUS
"Auf einem Grab in Stükken liegt ein
zerrissner Kranz" see Der zerrissne
Grabkranz Unknown REGER
Auf einem verfallenen Kirchhof see
Morgenstern KILPINEN
Auf einen Kirchhof see Schlechta IM
KIRCHHOF. SCHUBERT
Auf einen Klavierspieler see Mörike
SCHOECK
"Auf einen Totenacker" see Das Wirtshaus
Müller, Wilhelm SCHUBERT
Auf einer Burg see Eichendorff SCHOECK,
SCHUMANN
Auf einer Wanderung see Mörike WOLF
"Auf! es dunkelt; silbern funkelt" see Lied
beim Rundetanz Salis-Seewis SPOHR
Auf Flügeln des Gesanges see Heine
MENDELSSOHN-BARTHOLDY
"Auf frisch gemähtem Weideplatz" see Die
Zeitlose Gilm zu Rosenegg STRAUSS
Auf geheimem Waldespfade see Lenau
SCHILFLIEDER.
FRANZ, GRIFFES, SCHOECK
Auf geheimen Waldespfade see Lenau
SCHILFLIEDER. PIJPER
"Auf geheimen Waldespfade" see Schilflied
Lenau BERG
Auf Hamars Ruinen see Vinje GRIEG Paa
Hamars Ruiner
"Auf hebe die funkelnde Schalc" see
Heimliche Aufforderung Mackay
STRAUSS
"Auf hohem Bergesrücken" see
Der Alpenjäger Mayrhofer
SCHUBERT
"Auf hoher Alp wohnt auch der liebe Gott"
see Alplied Krummacher LOEWE
Auf ihrem Grab see Heine TRAGÖDIE.
GRIFFES
"Auf ihrem Grabe" see Vier trübe Monden
sind entfloh'n Unknown
MENDELSSOHN-BARTHOLDY
"Auf ihrem Leibrösslein" see Der Gärtner
Mörike SCHUMANN, WOLF
"Auf jener Flucht, von welcher nun das
Morgenland" see Das Wunder auf der
Flucht Rückert LOEWE

"Auf Jordan's grünen Borden" see Nebo
Freiligrath LOEWE
"Auf Jordans Ufer streifen wilde Horden" see
Jordans Ufer Byron LOEWE
"Auf Kieseln im Bache" see Wechsel Goethe
LOEWE
"Auf meinem Tische stehn" see Der
Kornblumenstrauss Wildenbruch REGER
Auf meines Kindes Tod see Eichendorff
SCHOECK
Auf mondbeschienenen Wegen see
Huggenberger REGER
Auf Morgen ist Sanct Valentinstag see
Shakespeare HAMLET. LASSEN
"Auf, Preussenherz! mit deinen Jubeltönen"
see Dem Könige Hildebrandt
LOEWE
"Auf schicke dich recht feierlich" see
Weihnachtslied Baur, Albert
MENDELSSOHN-BARTHOLDY
Auf See see Dehmel SZYMANOWSKI
"Auf seinem gold'nen Throne" see Liedesend
Mayrhofer SCHUBERT
"Auf seinen Nasen schreitet" see
Das Nasobem Morgenstern SEIBER
Auf sich selbst see Anacreon LOEWE
Two setttings.
"Auf steilem Felsen steht" see Der Sturm
Pushkin RUBINSTEIN
Auf und Ab see Krenek KRENEK
"Auf und ab wie die Narren rennen die
Menschen" see Auf und Ab Krenek
KRENEK
"Auf Wogen gezogen, von Klängen,
Gesängen" see Schifferlied der Wasserfee
Tieck SPOHR
Aufblick see Dehmel SZYMANOWSKI,
WEBERN
Aufblick see Rodès BLOCH Invocation
Aufbruch see Lenau SCHOECK
Aufbruch see Osterwald FRANZ
Aufenthalt see Rellstab SCHUBERT
Die Auferstehung see Krummacher
LOEWE
Die Aufgeregten see Keller, G.
SCHÖNBERG
"Aufgeschmückt ist der Freudensaal" see
Peregrina Mörike SCHOECK
Auflösung see Mayrhofer SCHUBERT
"Aufs Wohlsein meiner Dame" see
Der Schreckenberger Eichendorff WOLF
"Aufsteigt der Strahl und fallend giesst" see
Der römische Brunnen Meyer
SCHOECK
Aufstieg see Hesse KILPINEN
"Aufhaute die Erde vom Strahle" see
Maiblümelein Unknown LOEWE

COMPOSER Poet *Title* "First Line"

Aufträge see L'Egru **SCHUMANN**
Auftrag see Hölty **CORNELIUS**
Auftrag see Mörike **WOLF**
"Augen, meine lieben Fensterlein" *see*
    Abendlied Keller, G. **SCHOECK**
Augenblicke see Hamerling **BERG**
"Augenblicke gibt es zage" *see Augenblicke*
    Hamerling **BERG**
Augenlied see Mayrhofer **SCHUBERT**
Augier, Emile, 1820-1889.
    GOUNOD
        À une bourse
        À une jeune fille
        Boire à l'ombre
        La chanson du pâtre
        Envoi de fleurs
    LE DÉPART.
        DELIBES, GOUNOD *Départ*
Auguries of innocence see Blake, William
    LUENING
AUGURIES OF INNOCENCE. see Blake,
    William
        Every night and every morn **BRITTEN**
        Proverb VII **BRITTEN**
Augurio see Anon. **PIZZETTI**
August see San Geminiano **IVES**
August, Emil Leopold, Herzog von
    Sachsen-Gotha und Altenburg, 1772-
    1822.
        WEBER *Um Rettung biete ein güld'nes
        Geschmeide*
Augustinus, Aurelius, Saint, Bp. of
    Hippo, 354-430.
        LOEWE *Wie du deine Sonne hast lassen
        aufgehn*
The auld aik see Soutar **BRITTEN**
"Aunque todoen el mundo fuese mentira" *see*
    Canzon Andaluza: El pan de ronda
    Martinez Sierra **FALLA**
"Auprès de cette grotte sombre" *see La grotte*
    Tristan L'Hermite **DEBUSSY**
"Auprès d'un torrent Ophélie cueillait" *see*
    La mort d'Ophélie Shakespeare
    BERLIOZ
"Aura gentil che mormori" *see À la brise*
    Unknown **GOUNOD**
Aura gentil che mormori see Unknown
    GOUNOD *À la brise*
Aureana do sil see Cabanillas **MOMPOU**
AURIC, GEORGES, 1899-1983.
    Aragon, Louis, 1897-1982.
        Richard II Quarante (1943) [Salabert,
        1947]
            "Ma patrie est comme une barque"
        La rose et la Réséda (1943) [Salabert,
        1947] "Ce lui qui croyait au ciel"

Banville, Théodore Faullain de, 1823-
    1891.
    LES CARIATIDES, livre 3, no. III.
        Fête galante (1927) [Heugel, 1928]
            "Voilà Silvandre et Lycas et Myrtil"
    LES CARIATIDES, livre 3, no. V.
        Les bergers (1927) [Heugel, 1928]
            "Amaryllis rit au pâtre Daphnis"
    LES CARIATIDES, livre 3, no. X.
        Parade (1927) [Heugel, 1928]
            "La Saltimbanque aux yeux pleins
            de douceur"
Chalupt, René, 1885-1957.
    Le gloxinia (1914) [Eschig, 1965]
        "Je voudrais qu'à ma fenêtre"
    Le pouf (1914) [Eschig, 1965]
        "Entre les poufs de satin capitonné"
    Le tilbury (1914) [Eschig, 1965]
        "Si j'avais le talent de Constantin
        Guys"
Cocteau, Jean, 1889-1963.
    Aglaé (1919) [Eschig, 1963]
        "Je bois l'eau froide par saccades"
    Biplan le matin (1919) [Eschig, 1963]
        "Le bruit de l'aéro se fane à la
        descente"
    École de guerre (1919) [Eschig, 1963]
        "Que la vie est ennuyeuse"
    Hommage à Erik Satie (1919) [Eschig,
        1963]
        "Madame Henri Rousseau monte en
        ballon captif"
    Marie Laurencin (1919) [Eschig, 1963]
        "Entre les fauves et les cubistes"
    Place des Invalides (1919) [Eschig, 1963]
        "Ecoute Dieu ronronne dans son beau
        ciel vide"
    Portrait d'Henri Rousseau (1919)
        [Eschig, 1963]
        "Des aloès et des mésanges"
    Réveil (1919) [Eschig, 1963]
        "Bouches graves des lions"
Desbordes-Valmore, Marceline
    Félicité Josèphe, 1786-1859.
    Le premier amour (1926) [Heugel, 1927]
        "Vous souvient-il de cette jeune amie"
    Le réveil... (1926) [Heugel, 1927]
        "On sonne, on sonne!"
Eluard, Paul, 1895-1952.
    Elle se penche sur moi... (1941)
        [Heugel, 1948] same
    Le front aux vitres... (1941) [Heugel,
        1948] same
    Je te l'ai dit (1941) [Heugel, 1948] same
    Mon amour... (1941) [Heugel, 1948]
        "Mon amour pour avoir figuré mes
        désirs"

COMPOSER   Poet   *Title*   "First Line"

Nous ne vous chantons pas (1943)
[Salabert, 1947] same
On ne peut me connaitre . . . (1941)
[Heugel, 1948] same
Also in *La Table Ronde* (Paris, 1945).
Cahier 2, after p. 235.
Tout disparut . . . (1941) [Heugel, 1948]
"Tout disparut même les toits"
Fargue, Léon-Paul, 1878-1947.
Enfance (1940) [Eschig, 1951]
"Voici mes plus beaux"
Nuit blanche (1940) [Eschig, 1951]
"Loin de la ville sitôt crépite"
Regrets (1940) [Eschig, 1951]
"O misère de trop aimer"
Gabory, Georges, 1899-
L'ange a perdu son auréole (1927) [La
Sirène Musicale, 1928] same
Ma vie est la feuille (1927) [La Sirène
Musicale, 1928] same
Miroir (1927) [La Sirène Musicale, 1928]
"Miroir puisque le temps emporte"
La voix (1927) [La Sirène Musicale,
1928] "La voix d'un démon familier"
**Gérard de Nerval, Gérard Labrunie,
1808-1855.**
Une allée du Luxembourg (1925)
[Heugel, 1925] "Elle a passé"
Avril . . . (1925) [Heugel, 1925]
"Déjà les beaux jours"
Chanson gothique (1925) [Heugel, 1925]
"Belle épousée, j'aime tes pleurs"
Les cydalises (1925) [Heugel, 1925]
"Où sont nos amoureuses?"
Fantaisie (1925) [Heugel, 1925]
"Il est un air pour qui je donnerais"
Hirtz, Lise
Il était une petite pie (1929) [Heugel,
1930] same
Les pâquerettes (1929) [Heugel, 1930]
"Les pâquerettes trop simplettes"
Une petite pomme (1929) [Heugel, 1930]
same
Les petits ânes (1929) [Heugel, 1930]
same
La poule noire (1929) [Heugel, 1930]
same
Jacob, Max, 1876-1944.
Il se peut qu'un rêve étrange . . . (1946)
[Heugel, 1948] same
Lord Bolingbroke (1946) [Heugel, 1948]
"Lord Bolingbroke est en voyage"
Pour demain soir . . . (1946) [Heugel,
1948] "Où allez-vous?"
No author
Vocalise (1926) [Leduc, 1927]
Wordless.

Radiguet, Raymond, 1903-1923.
Album (1922) [Eschig, 1924]
"Apprendre n'est pas un pensum"
Bateau (1922) [Eschig, 1924]
"Bateau debout bateau hagard"
Déjeuner de soleil (1920) [Ed. de la
Sirène, 1921]
"Ah! les cornes: c'est un colimaçon"
Domino (1922) [Eschig, 1924]
"Le domino jeu des ménages"
Escarpin (1922) [Eschig, 1924]
"Grand bal dans la forêt ce soir"
Filet à papillons (1922) [Eschig, 1924]
"Papillon, tu es inhumain!"
Hirondelle (1922) [Eschig, 1924]
"Comme chacun sait l'hirondelle"
Les joues en feu (1920) [Ed. de la Sirène,
1921]
"Insolemment à la beauté je me voue"
Mallarmé (1922) [Eschig, 1924]
"Un éventail qui fut l'oiselle"
Pelouse (1920) [Ed. de la Sirène, 1921]
"Bulle de savon Egayant ta pipe
Gambier"
Ronsard, Pierre de, 1524-1585.
Printemps [Durand, 1935]
"Quand ce beau printemps je voy"
Supervielle, Jules, 1884-1960.
Le petit bois (1943) [Salabert, 1947]
"J'étais un petit bois de France"
Vilmorin, Louise de, 1902-1969.
Attendez le prochain bateau (1940)
[Eschig, 1951]
"Belle, sous la mauvaise étoile"
Le châle (1940) [Eschig, 1951]
"Assise sur la plaine"
La jeune sanguine (1940) [Eschig, 1951]
"Une jeune sanguine"
Auringon nousu see Koskenniemi
KILPINEN
Auriol, J.-G.
SAUGUET *Chanson de Calypso*
Aurore see Turquety AURORE.
CHAïKOVSKIï *Serenada*
L'aurore see Châteaubriand **MILHAUD**
L'aurore see Hugo CHANTS DU
CRÉPUSCULE. **FAURÉ**
Aurore see Silvestre **FAURÉ, MASSENET**
AURORE. see Turquety
Serenada **CHAïKOVSKIï**
"L'aurore s'allume" *see L'aurore* Hugo
FAURÉ
"L'aurore s'allume" *see Le matin* Hugo
SAINT-SAËNS
Aus alten Märchen winkt es see Heine
SCHUMANN

Aus! Aus! see Anon. *DES KNABEN WUNDERHORN*: Abschied für immer. **MAHLER**

"Aus bangen Träumen der Winternacht die Ros' " see *Zu spät* Osterwald **FRANZ**

Aus banger Brust see Dehmel **SIBELIUS**

"Aus Bois de Boulogne, l'hiver" see *L'hiver* Banville **KOECHLIN**

Aus "Claudine von Villa-Bella" see Goethe *CLAUDINE VON VILLA-BELLA.* **MEDTNER**

Aus das Trinkglas eines verstorbenen Freundes see Kerner **SCHUMANN**

Aus deinen Augen fliessen meine Lieder see Heine **DELIUS**

"Aus dem dunkeln Thor wallt" see *Husarenabzug* Candidus **SCHUMANN**

Aus dem "Glühenden" see Mombert **BERG**

Aus dem hohen Liede see Cornelius **CORNELIUS**

"Aus dem meergrünen Teiche" see *Erwartung* Dehmel **SCHÖNBERG**

"Aus dem Notizbüchlein der Liebe" see *Trinklied* Henckell **BERG**

"Aus dem Rosenstokke vom Grabe des Christ" see *Die schwarze Laute* Bierbaum **SZYMANOWSKI**

Aus dem See zur Weichsel see Anon. **SZYMANOWSKI** *Wysly rybki, sysly*

Aus dem Süden see Leuthold **SCHOECK**

"Aus dem Walde tritt die Nacht" see *Die Nacht* Gilm zu Rosenegg **STRAUSS**

Aus den "Hebräischen Gesängen" see Byron **SCHUMANN**

Aus den Himmelsaugen see Heine **REGER**

"Aus den Himmelsaugen droben fallen" see *Auf dem Meere* Heine **FRANZ**

Aus den Liedern der Trauer see Schack **STRAUSS** *Dem Herzen ähnlich*

Aus den Liedern der Trauer see Schack **STRAUSS** *Von dunklem Schleier umsponnen*

Aus den "Östlichen Rosen" see Rückert **SCHUMANN**

"Aus den Trümmern einer hohen Schönheit" see *Abschied* Levetzow **SCHÖNBERG**

Aus den Waldliedern I see Keller, G. **SCHOECK**

Aus den Waldliedern II see Keller, G. **SCHOECK**

"Aus der Bedrängnis" see *Auf ein Kind* Uhland **SCHOECK, STRAUSS**

"Aus der Eltern Macht und Haus" see *Hochzeitslied* Meyer **SCHOECK**

Aus der Ferne see Goethe **ZELTER**

Aus der Ferne see Mörike **SCHOECK**

Aus der Ferne in der Nacht see Bierbaum **REGER**

"Aus der Ferne schallen Gesänge" see *Frühe Klage* Osterwald **FRANZ**

AUS DER FRÜHLINGSZEIT, no. 1 **LASSEN** Ahlefeldt, Ottilie von *Die Erde steht in süssem Beben*

AUS DER FRÜHLINGSZEIT, no. 2 **LASSEN** Ahlefeldt, Ottilie von *Still ist's auf dem Erdenkreise*

AUS DER FRÜHLINGSZEIT, no. 3 **LASSEN** Ahlefeldt, Ottilie von *Jüngst, als ich über'n Friedhof ging*

AUS DER FRÜHLINGSZEIT, no. 4 **LASSEN** Ahlefeldt, Ottilie von *Könnt ich mit den Vöglein fliegen*

AUS DER FRÜHLINGSZEIT, no. 5 **LASSEN** Ahlefeldt, Ottilie von *Ich gehe durch die stille Nacht*

"Aus der Heimat hinter den Blitzen" see *In der Fremde* Eichendorff **BRAHMS**

"Aus der Heimath hinter den Blitzen" see *In der Fremde* Eichendorff **SCHUMANN**

"Aus der Schiffsbank mach' ich neinen Pfühl" see *Im Spätboot* Meyer **STRAUSS**

"Aus der Tiefe tauchte sie nach oben" see *Die Nixe* Falke **REGER**

"Aus des Abends weissen Wogen taucht ein Stern" see *Tief von fern* Dehmel **WEBERN**

Aus Diego Manazares see Schlechta **SCHUBERT**

"Aus dunkler Nacht ein Brunnenlied klang hell" see *Brunnensang* Flemes **REGER**

Aus: Ein Tagewerk I see Keller, G. **SCHOECK**

Aus: Ein Tagewerk II see Keller, G. **SCHOECK**

Aus Goethes Faust see Goethe *FAUST.* **BEETHOVEN**

Aus "Heliopolis" see Mayrhofer **SCHUBERT** Two settings: D. 753 and D. 754.

Aus meinen grossen Schmerzen see Heine *LIEDERSTRAUSS.* **FRANZ, WOLF**

Aus meinen Thränen spriessen see Heine **SCHUMANN**

Aus meinen Tränen see Heine *LYRICAL INTERMEZZO.* **BORODIN**

Aus meinen Tränen spriessen see Heine **MUSORGSKIĬ** *Iz slez moikh vyroslo mnogo*

Aus meiner Erinnerung see Heine **FRANZ**

AUS OSTEN, no. 1 **FRANZ** Anon. *Wozu?*

AUS OSTEN, no. 2
  FRANZ Bodenstedt *Die helle Sonne leuchtet*
AUS OSTEN, no. 3
  FRANZ Petöfi *Selige Nacht!*
AUS OSTEN, no. 4
  FRANZ Hafiz *Weisst du noch?*
AUS OSTEN, no. 5
  FRANZ Bodenstedt *Es hat die Rose sich beklagt*
AUS OSTEN, no. 6
  FRANZ Bodenstedt *Wenn der Frühling auf die Berge steigt*
Aus *"Pfingsten ein Gedichtsreigen" see*
  Evers **BERG**
"Aus Rosen, Phlox, Zinienflor" see Malven
  Knobel **STRAUSS**
"Aus Sanct Justi Klosterhallen" see Die Leiche zu St. Just Auersperg **LOEWE**
"Aus schweren Träumen" see Motto
  Eichendorff **SCHOECK**
Aus zwei Tälern see Hesse **KILPINEN, SCHOECK**
Ausblick nach Süden see Krenek **KRENEK**
Aus-delà see Vilmorin **POULENC**
Ausfahrt see Munch **GRIEG** *Udfarten*
Ausfahrt see Scheffel *GAUDEAMUS.* **JENSEN**
Ausklang see Huber, B. **KILPINEN**
Auskunft see Hesse **SCHOECK**
Aussi bien que les cigales see Apollinaire *CALLIGRAMMES.* **POULENC**
AUSSICHT. see Eichendorff *Serenade* **MEDTNER**
Austin, Mary (Hunter), 1868-1934.
  CARPENTER *Young man, chieftan!*
Der Auswanderer see Paulsen **GRIEG** *Udvandreren*
Automne see Apollinaire *ALCOOLS.* **BERKELEY, HONEGGER, RIVIER, ROREM**
L'automne see Banville **HAHN, KOECHLIN**
Automne see Collin **MASSENET**
L'automne see Lamartine **SAINT-SAËNS**
Automne see Samain **KOECHLIN**
Automne see Silvestre **FAURÉ**
"Automne au ciel brumeux" see Automne Silvestre **FAURÉ**
"Les automobilistes qui pasent sur la route" see Le château Paliard **MILHAUD**
"Autour de la Sainte Vierge il fait chaud ce sont les cierges" see Ex-voto Cocteau **HONEGGER**
"Autour du vieux chêne qui penche" see Le nid Quételart, A. **GOUNOD**

Autran, Joseph Antoine, 1813-1877.
  MASSENET *Les Alcyons*
"L'autre jour, sous l'ombrage" see Musette Florian **MASSENET**
L'autre matin see Zaffira **GOUNOD** *Siam' iti l'altro giorno*
Autrefois, à présent see Guilliaume **LASSEN**
"Autrefois, autrefois souviens t'en farouche" see Autrefois, à présent Guilliaume **LASSEN**
"Autrefois un roi de Thulé" see Le roi de Thulé Gérard de Nerval **BERLIOZ**
Autumn see De La Mare **BRITTEN**
Autumn see Eristavi, D. **RUBINSTEIN**
Autumn see Ives, Harmony **IVES**
Autumn see Holstein **DELIUS** *Herbst*
Autumn see Pleshcheyev **CHAĬKOVSKIĬ** *Osen'*
Autumn breeze see Pósa **BARTÓK** *Őszi szellő*
Autumn echoes see Ady **BARTÓK**
Autumn evening see Maquarie, Arthur **QUILTER**
Autumn evening see Rydberg **SIBELIUS** *Höstkväll*
Autumn song see Dixon **SIBELIUS**
Autumn tears see Ady **BARTÓK**
Autumn twilight see Symons *LONDON NIGHTS*: "12 Sep 1891" (1895-97). **HESELTINE**
The autumn wind see Wu-Ti, Han dynasty **BERKELEY, BRITTEN**
"Autumn wind rises; white clouds fly" see The autumn wind Wu-Ti, Han dynasty **BERKELEY, BRITTEN**
AUTUMN'S LEGACY, no. 1
  BERKELEY Beddoes *The mighty thoughts of an old world*
AUTUMN'S LEGACY, no. 2
  BERKELEY Beddoes *All night a wind of music*
AUTUMN'S LEGACY, no. 3
  BERKELEY Durrell, L. *Lesbos*
AUTUMN'S LEGACY, no. 4
  BERKELEY Tennyson *Tonight the winds begin to rise*
AUTUMN'S LEGACY, no. 5
  BERKELEY Hopkins *Hurrahing in harvest*
AUTUMN'S LEGACY, no. 6
  BERKELEY Davies, W. H. *Rich days*
AUTUMN'S LEGACY, no. 7
  BERKELEY Coleridge, H. *When we were idlers with the loitering rills*
AUX FLANCS DU VASE. see Samain *Amphise et Melitta* **KOECHLIN** *Le cortège d'amphitrite* **KOECHLIN**

AUX FLANCS DU VASE. see Samain
  (continued)
  L'ile ancienne KOECHLIN
  La maison du matin KOECHLIN
  Le repas préparé KOECHLIN
  Le sommeil de canope KOECHLIN
Aux officiers de la Garde Blanche see
  Vilmorin POULENC
Aux rayons du couchant see Moréas HAHN
Aux temps des fées see Haraucourt
  KOECHLIN
"Aux temps jadis, aux temps rêveurs" *see Aux*
  temps des fées Haraucourt
  KOECHLIN
"Avant de m'exiler pour jamais de ce lieu"
  see Les adieux à la maison Dennery
  GOUNOD
"Avant de quitter ces lieux" *see Invocation*
  Pradère-Niquet GOUNOD
Avant le cinéma see Apollinaire POULENC
Avant que tu ne t'en ailles see Verlaine *LA*
  BONNE CHANSON. DELIUS, FAURÉ
"Ave, ave Maria!" *seeAve Maria* Anon.
  CORNELIUS
Ave Margarita (prière d'amour, 1902) *see*
  Noël, Édouard MASSENET
Ave Maria see Anon. BRUCKNER,
  CORNELIUS, FAURÉ, ROREM
"Ave Maria" *see Ave Maria* Anon. FAURÉ
"Ave Maria!" *see Ave Maria* Geibel FRANZ
Ave Maria see Geibel FRANZ
Ave Maria see Lamartine GOUNOD
  Premier prélude de Bach
Ave Maria see No author DVOŘÁK
Ave Maria see Scott MENDELSSOHN-
  BARTHOLDY
Ave Maria see Unknown LASSEN
Ave Maria (su due note) *see* Unknown
  ROSSINI
Ave Maria see Unknown TURINA
"Ave Maria, ave Maria" *see Tantum Ergo,*
  motet no. 3 Anon. FRANCK
"Ave Maria gratia plena gratia" *see Un rien*
  Unknown ROSSINI
"Ave Maria, Jungfrau mild" *see Ave Maria*
  Scott MENDELSSOHN-BARTHOLDY
"Ave Maria! Jungfrau mild!" *see Ellens*
  Gesang III Scott SCHUBERT
"Ave Maria, Toi qui fus mère sur cette terre"
  see Premier prélude de Bach
  Lamartine GOUNOD
L'Ave Marie de l'enfant see Anon.
  GOUNOD
Ave maris stella see No author DVOŘÁK,
  GRIEG

"Avec mon face à main" *see La tragique*
  histoire du petit René Nohain, Jean
  POULENC
"Avec sa belle prestance" *see Le départ*
  Bédat de Monlaur, Pierre HONEGGER
"Avec ses caprices la lune" *see La lune*
  Banville KOECHLIN
"Avec ses quatre dromadaires" *see*
  Le dromadaire Apollinaire POULENC
"Avec son chant doux et plaintif" *see*
  Le ramier Silvestre FAURÉ
Avec tes yeux, Mignonne see Heine LASSEN
  Mit deinen blauen Augen
Avec toi see Gruaz, Julien MASSENET
"Avec toi courir dans les plaines" *see Avec toi*
  Gruaz, Julien MASSENET
Avec ton parapluie see Jammes MILHAUD
"Avec une si belle main" *see Sérénade* Anon.
  POULENC
Avenarius, Ferdinand, 1856-1923.
  BERG *Wandert ihr Wolken*
  STIMMEN UND BILDER.
    WEBERN *Wolkennacht*
  STIMMEN UND BILDER: Ehe.
    WEBERN
      Freunde
      Gefunden
  STIMMEN UND BILDER: Jahrbuch.
    WEBERN
      Vorfrühling
      Vorfrühling II
      Wehmut
  STIMMEN UND BILDER: Stimmungen.
    WEBERN *Gebet*
L'Aventure see Tardieu SAUGUET
L'avertimento see Anon. HAHN
L'aveu see Rameau GOUNOD
L'aveu see Villiers CHAUSSON
LES AVEUX. see Bourget *L'âme évaporée*
  DEBUSSY
  Les cloches DEBUSSY
LES AVEUX: Amour. *see* Bourget
  Musique DEBUSSY
  Paysage sentimental DEBUSSY
  Regret: Devant le ciel DEBUSSY
LES AVEUX: Romance. *see* Bourget
  Romance, musique pour éventail
    DEBUSSY
LES AVEUX: Souvenirs du Nord, no. 5. *see*
  Bourget *La Romance d'Ariel*
  DEBUSSY
LES AVEUX: Souvenirs du Nord, no. 7. *see*
  Bourget *Beau soir* DEBUSSY
Avril see Belleau DELIBES,
  SAINT-SAËNS
Avril . . . see Gérard de Nerval AURIC

COMPOSER Poet *Title* "First Line"

AVRIL: Chanson. *see* **Pailleron**
   Aprel'! veshniǐ prazdnichnyǐ den'
   RACHMANINOFF
"Avril dort sous la lune blanche" *see Avril est*
   amoureux Halmont, Jacques d'
   MASSENET
Avril est amoureux see Halmont, Jacques
   d' **MASSENET**
"Avril est de retour" *see Tristesse* Gautier
   FAURÉ
Avril est là! see Ferrand, François
   MASSENET
"Avril, et c'est le point du jour" *see*
   La messagère Lerberghe **FAURÉ**
"Avril, la gràce et le ris De Cypris" *see Avril*
   Belleau **DELIBES**
"Avril, l'honneur et des bois" *see Avril*
   Belleau **SAINT-SAËNS**
"Avril parait" *see Mazatsumi* Mazatsumi
   STRAVINSKIǏ
"Awake, awake, my little boy!" *see The land*
   of dreams Blake, William **THOMSON**
Awakening see Pushkin **RIMSKIǏ-**
   KORSAKOV *Probuzhden'e*
Aware see Lawrence **RIETI**
Away to Twiver see Anon.
   THE FAMOUS HISTORY OF FRIAR
   BACON (printed before1600).
   HESELTINE
AXEL UND WALBURG: Romanze. *see*
   Oehlenschläger
   Romanze **ZELTER**

"Ay! Ay! Más cerca de mí te siento" *see*
   Cantares Campoamor y Campoosorio
   TURINA
Ayelet hashakhar see Goldberg **GIDEON**
   Morning star
Ayer, Ethan
   ROREM
   After Atlantis
   Blood is not blood
Ayez pitié de votre serviteur see Tagore
   GARDENER. **MILHAUD**
Az ágyam hívogat see Ady **BARTÓK** *Lost*
   content
Až budeme staří see Klášterský **MARTINŮ**
   When we are old
"Az der Rebe Elimeylekh iz gevorn zeyer
   freylekh" *see Der Rebe Elimeylekh*
   Anon. **WEISGALL**
Az én szerelmem see Gombossy **BARTÓK**
   My love
Az őszi lárma see Ady **BARTÓK** *Autumn*
   echoes
Až přijde den see Sládek **MARTINŮ** *When*
   the day comes
L'azalée see Patmore *THE UNKNOWN*
   EROS: The azalea. **MILHAUD**
"L'azur si pur des cieux joyeux ruisselle" *see*
   Sur une poésie de Van Hasselt
   Hasselt **MASSENET**
"L'azur sourit; le vent tiédit" *see C'est le*
   printemps Gillouin **MASSENET**

B

Ba, be, bi, bo, bu *see* Carême **POULENC**
Babochka see Bal'mont **PROKOFIEV**
Babochka see Shenshin **MEDTNER**
   Butterfly
Babushka i vnuchek see Pleshcheyev
   CHAǏKOVSKIǏ
Baby see Rossetti, Christina **IRELAND**
"A baby watch'd a ford, whereto a wagtail
   came for drinking" *see Wagtail and baby*
   Hardy **BRITTEN**
Bacchisches Lied see Pushkin
   RUBINSTEIN
"Bacchus, feister Furst des Wiens" *see*
   Trinklied Shakespeare **SCHUBERT**

Bach, Echo, Kuss see Kind, F. *DER ABEND*
   AM WALDBRUNNEN. **WEBER**
Le bachelier de Salamanque see Chalupt
   ROUSSEL
The bachelor see Anon. **HESELTINE**
Backody
   RUBINSTEIN *Wir drei*
Das Bächlein see Goethe **STRAUSS**
"Bächlein, lass dein Rauschen sein" *see Mein!*
   Müller, Wilhelm **SCHUBERT**
Baëlen, Mme.
   GOUNOD
   Hommage à Madame La Comtesse
   Herminie de Léautaud

COMPOSER Poet *Title* "First Line"

Baëlen, Mme. *(continued)*
  GOUNOD *(continued)*
    *Prière pour l'Empereur et la famille
      impériale*
De bägge rosorna see Franzén **SIBELIUS**
"Die Bäume blüh'n, die Vöglein singen" *see
  Lenz* Lenau **FRANZ, SCHOECK**
"Die Bäume tropfen vom Gewittergruss" *see
  Sommernacht* Hesse **SCHOECK**
Die Bäume wurden gelb see Cossmann
  PFITZNER
Baggesen, Jens, 1764-1826.
  WEBER
    Die Lethe des Lebens
    Serenade
Baïf, Jean Antoine de, 1532-1589.
  GOUNOD *O ma belle rebelle*
  ROREM *L'Hymne de la paix*
Bail avec Mi see Messiaen **MESSIAEN**
The bailey beareth the bell away see Anon.
  HESELTINE *The bayly berith the bell
    away*
"Baĩu bai, baĩ" *see Kolybel'naĩa Eremushki*
  Nekrasov **MUSORGSKIĩ**
"Baĩu, baĩu, milvnu chenochek" *see
  Kolybel'naĩa pesnia* Ostrovski
  MUSORGSKIĩ
"Baĩu, baĩushki, baĩu" *see Kolybel'naĩa pesnia*
  Mei **RIMSKIĩ-KORSAKOV**
Baker, Mary Ely
  THOMPSON, R. *The echo child*
**Baker, Sir Henry Williams, bart., 1821-
  1877.**
  GOUNOD *The King of love my shepherd*
Le bal d'enfants see Richter **SAUGUET**
Bal des pendus see Rimbaud **HINDEMITH**
"Le bal, sur le parc incendié" *see Jazz dans la
  nuit* Dommange **ROUSSEL**
Balada letní see Herold, Jĩří **MARTINŮ**
  Summer ballad
**BALAKIREV, MILĩĩ ALEKSEEVICH,
  1837-1910.**
  **Aksakov, Konstantin Sergeevich,
    1817-1860.**
    Sredi tsvetov pori osenney (1895-96)
      [Muzgiz, 1937] same
  **Arsen'ev, Aleksandr Vasil'evich, 1854-
    1896.**
    Barkarola (1858) [Muzgiz, 1937]
      "Prelestna ĩa rybachka"
      Text "after Heine"
    Kolibel'naya pesnya (1858) [Muzgiz,
      1937] "Spi, malĩutka moĩ prekrasnyĩ"
  **Golenishchev-Kutuzov, Arseniĩ
    Arkad'yevich, graf, 1848-1913.**
    Nad ozerom (1895-96) [Muzgiz, 1937]
      "Me sĩats zadumchivyĩ"

Golovinsky, A
  Ti plenitel'noy negi polna (1855)
    [Muzgiz, 1937] same
ĨAtsevicha, M
  Vzoshol na nebo mesyats yasnĩy (1858)
    [Muzgiz, 1937] same
**Khomyakov, Aleksyeĩ Stepanovich,
  1804-1860.**
  Bezzvezdnaya polnoch' (1903-04)
    [Zimmermann, 1904]
    "Bezzvĩezdnaĩa polnoch' dyshala
      prokhaladoĩ"
    Also orchestrated by Liapunow.
  Nachstück (1895-96) [Muzgiz, 1937]
    "Vcherashniaĩa noch' byla tak svetna"
  Sem' noyabrya (1903-04) [Zimmermann,
    1904?] "Als kaum wir geöffnet des
    Feldherren"
  Spi! (1903-04) [Muzgiz, 1937]
    "Dnem naigravshis"
  Zarya (1909) [Muzgiz, 1937]
    "Vvozdushnykh vysotakh"
**Kol'tsov, Alekseĩ Vasil'yevich, 1809-
  1842.**
  ĨA lĩubila ego (1895-96) [Muzgiz, 1937]
    same
  Isstupleniye (1859) [Muzgiz, 1937]
    "Dukhi neba, daĩte mne"
  Mne li, molodtsu razudalomu (1858)
    [Muzgiz, 1937] same
  Oboymi, potsaluy (1858) [Muzgiz, 1937]
    same
  Pesnya razboynika (1858) [Muzgiz,
    1937] "Ne strashna mne"
  Pesnya starika (1863) [Muzgiz, 1937]
    "Osedlaĩu konĩa, Konĩa bystrova"
  Pridi ko mne (1858) [Muzgiz, 1937]
    same
  Tak i rvetsya dusha (1858) [Muzgiz,
    1937] same
Krasov, V
  Vzglyani, moy drug (1903-04) [Muzgiz,
    1937] same
Kulchinsky, V
  Dogorayet rumyanĩy zakat (1895-96)
    [Muzgiz, 1937] same
**Lermontov, Mikhail Yuryevich, 1814-
  1841.**
  Evreyskaya melodiya (1859) [Muzgiz,
    1937] "Dusha moĩa mrachna"
    Text "after Byron"
  Iz-pod tainstvennoy kholodnoy polumaski
    (1903-04) [Muzgiz, 1937] same
  Kogda volnuyetsya zhelteyushchaya niva
    (1895-96) [Muzgiz, 1937] same

Otchevo (1860) [Muzgiz, 1937] "Mne grustno, lotomu"

Pesnya Selima (1858) [Muzgiz, 1937] "Mesiats plyvet I tikh i spokoen"

Pesnya: Zholtïy list (1903-04) [Muzgiz, 1937] "Zheltyï list o stebel' b'etsia"

Pesnya zolotoy rïbki (1860) [Muzgiz, 1937] "Ditia moë, Ostan' sia zdes' so mnoï"

Slïshu li golos tvoy (1863) [Muzgiz, 1937] same

Son (1903-04) [Muzgiz, 1937] "V poldnevnyï zhar"
Also orchestrated by S. Liapunow.

Sosna (1895-96) [Muzgiz, 1937] "Na severe dikom stoit"
Text after Heine.

Utes (1909) [Muzgiz, 1937] "Nochevala tuchka zolotaïa"

Maïkov, Apollon Nikolayevich, 1821-1897.

Vvedi menya, O noch, taykom (1859) [Muzgiz, 1937] same

Mei, Lev Aleksandrovich, 1822-1862.

Zapevka (1903-04) [Muzgiz, 1937] "Okh, pora tebe na voliu"

PESNYA.

Kak naladidi: Durak (1895-96) [Muzgiz, 1937] same

Mikhailov, Mikhail Larionovich, 1826-1865.

Ispanskaya pensyna (1855) [Muzgiz, 1937] "Spish'li ty, moiadevitsa?"

Son (1863) [Muzgiz, 1937] "Snilas' mne devushka"

Pushkin, Aleksandr Sergeevich, 1799-1837.

Gruzinskaya pesnya (1863) [Muzgiz, 1937] "Ne poï, krasavitsa"

Shenshin, Afanasiï Afanas'evich, 1820-1892.

Shopot, robkoye dïkhan'ye (1903-04) [Muzgiz, 1937] same

Ya prishol k tebe s privetom (1903-04) [Muzgiz, 1937] same

Tolstoï, Alekseï Konstantinovich, Graf, 1817-1875.

Ne penitsya more (1895-96) [Muzgiz, 1937] same

Tumanskiï, Vasiliï Ivanovich, 1800-1860.

Zveno (1855) [Muzgiz, 1937] "Bylykh strasteï"

Wilde, Ch

Kogda bezzabotno, ditya, tïrezvish'sya (1858) [Muzgiz, 1937] same

Rïysar (1858) [Muzgiz, 1937] "Vlaty zakovan, Vshleme zlatom"

Zhemchuzhnikov, Alekseï Mikhaïlovich, 1821-1908.

Pustïnya (1895-96] [Muzgiz, 1937] "U zhe davno idu ia utomlennyï"

La balançoire see **Stevenson, Robert Louis** *A CHILD'S GARDEN OF VERSES.* **HAHN** *The swing*

"Balayant la contrée et ce vallon feuillu" *see Décembre* **Claudel MILHAUD**

Le Balcon see **Baudelaire** *FLEURS DU MAL.* **DEBUSSY**

"Bald ist der Nacht ein End gemacht" *see Morgenstimmung* **Reinick WOLF**

Baleboste Zisinke see **Anon. WEISGALL**

"Balesboste zisinke, zisinke zise Baleboste" *see Baleboste Zisinke* **Anon. WEISGALL**

Balestra, Luigi
VERDI *La seduzione*

A ballad see **Moses, Elizabeth Ann THOMPSON, R.**

Ballad of the foxhunter see **Yeats LOEFFLER**

The ballad of the railroads see **Krenek KRENEK**

Ballada see **Turgenev RUBINSTEIN**

Ballade see **Arndt LASSEN**

Ballade see **Bechstein CORNELIUS**
Der König und der Sänger

Ballade see **Goethe ZELTER**

BALLADE. see **Hölty**
Der Traum **SCHUBERT**

Ballade see **Kenner SCHUBERT**

Ballade see **Mauclair CHAUSSON**

Ballade see **Reinbeck**
GORDON UND MONTROSE ODER DER KAMPFDER GEFÜHLE. **WEBER**

Ballade see **Uhland SCHUMANN**

Ballade à la lune see **Musset** *CONTES D'ESPAGNE ET D'ITALIE.* **DEBUSSY, LALO**

Ballade de David Rizzio see **Chouquet MASSENET**

La ballade de Jésus Christ see **Anon. VAUGHAN WILLIAMS**

Ballade de la reine morte d'aimer see **Marès** *ARIETTES DOULOUREUSES.* **RAVEL**

Ballade de Villon à s'amye see **Villon** *LE TESTAMENT.* **DEBUSSY**

Ballade des äusseren Lebens see **Hofmannsthal BERG**

Ballade des femmes de Paris see **Villon** *LE TESTAMENT.* **DEBUSSY**

Ballade des gros dindons see **Rostand CHABRIER**

COMPOSER Poet *Title* "First Line"

Ballade des Harfners see Goethe *WILHELM MEISTER.* **SCHUMANN**

Ballade des pendus see Villon **MESSIAEN**

Ballade que Villon feit à requeste de sa mère . . . see Villon *LE TESTAMENT.* **DEBUSSY**

Ballade vom Fest see Krenek **KRENEK**

Ballade vom Haideknaben see Hebbel **SCHUMANN**

Die Ballade vom König Lobesam see Goering **KRENEK**

Ballade vom vertriebenen und zurückkehrenden Grafen see Goethe **LOEWE**

Die Ballade von den Eisenbahnen see Krenek **KRENEK** *The ballad of the railroads*

Ballade von den Schiffen see Krenek **KRENEK**

Balladen om Bjørnen see Almquist, C. J. L. **NIELSEN**

Ballade-nocturne see Vilmorin **MILHAUD**

BALLADS AND POEMS. see Masefield
   Captain Stratton's fancy **HESELTINE**

Ballata see Boccaccio **RESPIGHI**

Ballata see Poliziano **MALIPIERO**

Ballet see Ronsard **POULENC**

Les ballons see Wilde *FANTAISIES DÉCORATIVES,* no. 2. **GRIFFES**

Bal'mont, Konstantin Dmitriyevich, 1867-1943.
  PROKOFIEV
    Babochka
    Est' drugie planety
    Golos" ptīṡ"
    Pomni menia!
    Stolby
    V moem sadu
    Zaklinanie vody i orniā
  RACHMANINOFF
    The migrant wind
    The quest
  STRAVINSKIĬ
    The dove
    Forget-me-nots

Balow see Anon. **RIETI**

"Balow, my babe, lie still and sleep!" *see Balow* Anon. **RIETI**

Balslev, Harald
  NIELSEN *Der gaar et stille Tog*

Balulalow see Luther **HESELTINE**

Balzac, Honoré de, 1799-1850.
  SAUGUET *Sur une page d'Album*

BANALITÉS, no. 1
  POULENC Apollinaire *Chanson d'Orkenise*

BANALITÉS, no. 2
  POULENC Apollinaire *Hôtel*

BANALITÉS, no. 3
  POULENC Apollinaire *Fagnes de Wallonie*

BANALITÉS, no. 4
  POULENC Apollinaire *Voyage à Paris*

BANALITÉS, no. 5
  POULENC Apollinaire *Sanglots*

Le banc de pierre see Choudens **GOUNOD**

"Bangt dir mein Lieb?" *see Im Sturme* Siebel **LOEWE**

Banville, Théodore Faullain de, 1823-1891.
  CHABRIER *Lied*
  GOUNOD
    L'âme de la morte
    L'âme d'un ange
  HAHN
    L'air
    L'automne
    Dernier voeu
    Les étoiles
    La nuit
    La paix
    La pêche
    Le printemps
  KOECHLIN
    L'air
    L'automne
    La chasse
    L'eau
    L'été
    Les étoiles
    La guerre
    L'hiver
    Le jour
    La lune
    Le matin
    Les métaux
    Le midi
    La nuit
    La paix
    La pêche
    Les Pierreries
    Le printemps
    Le terre
    Le Thé
    Le vin
  SAINT-SAËNS *Les fées*

AMÉTHYSTES.
  DEBUSSY *Caprice*
  SAINT-SAËNS *Le rossignol*

LES CARIATIDES, livre 2, Amours d'Élise . . . no. V.
  DEBUSSY *Rêverie*

LES CARIATIDES, livre 3, no. II.
   DEBUSSY *Zéphyr*
LES CARIATIDES, livre 3, no. III.
   AURIC, DEBUSSY *Fête galante*
LES CARIATIDES, livre 3, no. V.
   AURIC *Les bergers*
LES CARIATIDES, livre 3, no. VI.
   DEBUSSY *Pierrot*
LES CARIATIDES, livre 3, no. VII.
   DEBUSSY *Sérénade*
LES CARIATIDES, livre 3, no. X.
   AURIC *Parade*
LES CARIATIDES, livre 3, no. XV.
   DEBUSSY *Les roses*
LES CARIATIDES, livre 3, no. XVII.
   DEBUSSY *Les lilas*
LES EXILÉS.
   HAHN *L'énamourée*
HYMNIS.
   DEBUSSY *Il dort encore*
ODELETTES.
   DEBUSSY *Aimons-nous et dormons*
   SAINT-SAËNS *Aimons-nous*
RIMES DORÉES.
   KOECHLIN *Promenade galante*
LES STALACTITES.
   DEBUSSY *Souhait*
LES STALACTITES. La Dernière Pensée de
   Weber.
   DEBUSSY *Nuit d'étoiles*
Bar see Dreman, J. **MARTINŮ**
"Bara du går över markerna" *see Melodi*
   Bergman **KILPINEN**
BARBER, SAMUEL, 1910-1981.
   Agee, James, 1909-1955.
     PERMIT ME VOYAGE. Description of
     Elysium.
       Sure on this shining night, op. 13 no. 3
       (1938) [G. Schirmer, 1941] same
       Also voice & orchestra.
   Auden, Wystan Hugh, 1907-1973,
     translator.
     The monk and his cat, op. 29 no. 8
     (1952-53) [G. Schirmer, 1954]
     "Pangur, white Pangur, how happy we
     are"
     The praises of God, op. 29 no. 9 (1952-
     53) [G. Schirmer, 1954]
     "How foolish the man"
   Graves, Robert, 1895-1985.
     Despite and still, op. 41 no. 5 [G.
     Schirmer, 1969]
     "Have you not read the words in my
     head"

In the wilderness, op. 41 no. 3 [G.
   Schirmer, 1969]
   "He, of his gentleness, Thirsting and
   hungering"
A LAST POEM.
   A last song, op. 41 no. 1 [G. Schirmer,
   1969]
   "A last song, and a very last"
Harasymowicz, Jerzy, 1933-
   A green lowland of pianos, op. 45 no. 2
   [G. Schirmer, 1974] "In the evening as
   far as the eye can see"
Heym, Georg, 1887-1912.
   O boundless, boundless evening, op. 45
   no. 3 [G. Schirmer, 1974] same
Hopkins, Gerard Manley, 1844-1889.
   A nun takes the veil, op. 13 no. 1 (1937)
   [G. Schirmer, 1941] "I have desired to
   go where springs not fail"
Horan, Robert, 1922-1981.
   The queen's face on the summery coin,
   op. 18 no. 1 (1942) [G. Schirmer,
   1944] same
Housman, Alfred Edward, 1859-1936.
   A SHROPSHIRE LAD: LIV.
     With rue my heart is laden, op. 2 no. 2
     (1928) [G. Schirmer, 1936] same
Jackson, Kenneth, translator.
   A CELTIC MISCELLANY.
     Promiscuity, op. 29 no. 7 (1952-53)
     [G. Schirmer, 1954] "I do not know
     with whom Edan will sleep"
Jones, Howard Mumford, 1892-1980.
   translator.
   ROMANESQUE LYRIC.
     Church bell at night, op. 29 no. 2
     (1952-53) [G. Schirmer, 1954]
     "Sweet little bell"
     The crucifixion, op. 29 no. 5 (1952-53)
     [G. Schirmer, 1954]
     "At the cry of the first bird"
Joyce, James, 1882-1941.
   CHAMBER MUSIC.
     I hear an army, op. 10 no. 3 [G.
     Schirmer, 1939] same
     Also voice & orchestra.
     Rain has fallen, op. 10 no. 1 [G.
     Schirmer, 1939]
     "Rain has fallen all the day"
     Sleep now, op. 10 no. 2 [G. Schirmer,
     1939] "Sleep now, O sleep now"
   FINNEGANS WAKE.
     Nuvoletta, op. 25 (1947) [G. Schirmer,
     1952] "Nuvoletta in her light dress"

BARBER, SAMUEL, 1910-1981 *(continued)*
Joyce, James, 1882-1941 *(continued)*
ULYSSES.
　Solitary hotel, op. 41 no. 4 [G.
　　Schirmer, 1969]
　"Solitary hotel in mountain pass"
Kallman, Chester Simon, 1921-1975,
translator.
　St. Ita's vision, op. 29 no. 3 (1952-53)
　　[G. Schirmer, 1954] "I will take
　　nothing from my Lord, said she"
Keller, Gottfried, 1819-1890.
　Now have I fed and eaten up the rose,
　　op. 45 no. 1 [G. Schirmer, 1974] same
O'Faolain, Sean, 1900- translator.
　Sea-snatch, op. 29 no. 6 (1952-53) [G.
　　Schirmer, 1954] "It has broken us"
THE SILVER BRANCH.
　At St. Patrick's Purgatory, op. 29 no. 1
　　(1952-53) [G. Schirmer, 1954]
　　"Pity me on my pilgrimage to Loch
　　Derg!"
　The desire for hermitage, op. 29 no. 10
　　(1952-53) [G. Schirmer, 1954]
　　"Ah! To be all alone in a little
　　cell"3142
　The heavenly banquet, op. 29 no. 4
　　(1952-53) [G. Schirmer, 1954]
　　"I would like to have the men of
　　Heaven in my own house"
Prokosch, Frederic, 1908-
THE CARNIVAL.
　Nocturne, op. 13 no. 4 (1940) [G.
　　Schirmer, 1941]
　　"Close my darling both your eyes"
　　Also voice & orchestra.
Rilke, Rainer Maria, 1875-1926.
POÈMES FRANCAIS.
　Le clocher chante, op. 27 no. 4 [G.
　　Schirmer, 1952]
　　"Mieux qu'une tour profane"
　Un cygne, op. 27 no. 2 [G. Schirmer,
　　1952] "Un cygne avance sur l'eau"
　Départ, op. 27 no. 5 [G. Schirmer,
　　1952]
　　"Mon amie, il faut que je parte"
　Puisque tout passe, op. 27 no. 1[G.
　　Schirmer, 1952] same
　Tombeau dans un parc, op. 27 no. 3
　　[G. Schirmer, 1952]
　　"Dors au fond de l'allée"
Roethke, Theodore, 1908-1963.
WISH FOR A YOUNG WIFE.
　My lizard, op. 41 no. 2 [G. Schirmer,
　　1969] "My lizard, my lively writher"

Stephens, James, 1882-1950.
　Bessie Bobtail, op. 2 no. 3 (1934) [G.
　　Schirmer, 1936]
　　"As down the road she wambled slow"
　The daisies, op. 2 no. 1 (1927) [G.
　　Schirmer, 1936]
　　"In the scented bud of the morning o"
Villa, José Garcia, 1914-1997.
HAVE COME, AM HERE.
　Monks and raisins, op. 18 no. 2 (1943)
　　[G. Schirmer, 1944] "I have
　　observed pink monks eating blue
　　raisins"
Yeats, William Butler, 1865-1939.
　The secrets of the old, op. 13 no. 2
　　(1938) [G. Schirmer, 1941]
　　"I have old women's secrets now"
BARBERINE. *see* Musset
Beau chevalier qui partez pour la guerre
　DELIBES
Chanson de Barberine **LALO,**
　RUBINSTEIN
Barberinen's Lied **see** Musset *BARBERINE.*
　RUBINSTEIN *Chanson de Barberine*
Barbier, Jules, 1825-1901.
　BIZET
　　La chanson de la rose
　　N'oublions pas!
　GOUNOD
　　À la Madone
　　À toi mon coeur
　　Aimons-nous
　　Au printemps
　　Bienheureux le coeur sincère
　　Boléro
　　Chanson printanière
　　Chantez noël
　　Clos ta paupière
　　Hymne à la nuit
　　Invocation à Vesta
　　Medjé
　　Mon amour a mon coeur
　　Parlez pour moi
　　Prends garde
　　Prière d'Abraham
　　Rêverie
　　Sur la montagne
　　Viens, les gazons sont verts
Barbier, Marie Anne, d.1742.
　GOUNOD *Réponse de Medjé*
　MASSENET *L'ange et l'enfant*
　CONTES BLANCS.
　SAINT-SAËNS *La sérénité*
Barbier, Pierre
　GOUNOD
　　Le départ du mousse
　　Vincenette

Barbusse, Henri, 1874-1935.
AUBERT *La lettre*
Barcarola see Kamhi, Victoria **RODRIGO**
Barcarola see Piave **VERDI**
Barcarole see Heiberg **JENSEN**
Barcarolle see Arsen'ev **BALAKIREV**
Barkarola
Barcarolle see Guinand
*AU COURANT DE LA VIE. STANCES,
   SONNETS, POÈMES* (1885). **DEBUSSY**
Barcarolle see Monnier, M. **FAURÉ**
Barcarolle see Prölss **LASSEN**
Barcarolle, Le tribut de Zamora see
   Unknown **GOUNOD** *Voguons sur les
   flots*
La barcheta see Anon. **HAHN**
Bard, Chevalier
MILHAUD *La chanson du printemps*
Der Bardengeist see Hermann
BEETHOVEN
"Bardzo raniuchno wschodzilo sloneczko" *see*
   Piosnka litewska Anon. **CHOPIN**
"Barin moǐ milen'kiǐa" *see Sirotka*
   Musorgskiǐ **MUSORGSKIǐ**
Barkarola see Arsen'ev **BALAKIREV**
Barkarole see Schack **STRAUSS**
"Barn af våren" *see Blommans öde*
   Runeberg **SIBELIUS**
Barn, som jag smekt see Lagerkvist
KILPINEN
Barnefield, Richard, 1574-1627.
COPLAND *As it fell upon a day*
ROREM *Philomel*
Barnes, William, 1801-1886.
CARPENTER *Don't Ceäre*
VAUGHAN WILLIAMS
   In the spring
   The winter's willow, a country song
BLACKMWORE MAIDENS.
   VAUGHAN WILLIAMS *Blackmwore
   by the Stour*
COME.
   CARPENTER *Wull ye come in the eärly
   spring*
MY ORCHA'D IN LINDEN LEA.
   VAUGHAN WILLIAMS *Linden Lea*
Barnets Sang see Dam **NIELSEN**
BARNLIGE SANGE, no. 1
GRIEG Rolfsen *Havet*
BARNLIGE SANGE, no. 2
GRIEG Krohn *Sang til juletraeet*
BARNLIGE SANGE, no. 3
GRIEG Bjørnson *Lok*
BARNLIGE SANGE, no. 4
GRIEG Dass *Fiskervise*
BARNLIGE SANGE, no. 5
GRIEG Rolfsen *Kveldssang for Blakken*

BARNLIGE SANGE, no. 6
GRIEG Rolfsen *De norske fjelde*
BARNLIGE SANGE, no. 7
GRIEG Rolfsen *Faedrelandssalme*
Baron, Jacques, b. 1905.
SAUGUET
   En attendant
   Lied
   La tour prends garde
Les barques see Montesquiou- **SCHMITT**
"Les barques sont les cygnes blancs" *see*
   Les barques Montesquiou- **SCHMITT**
Bartels, Adolf, 1862-1945.
PFITZNER *Wenn sich Liebes von dir
   lösen will*
Barth, Emil, 1900-1958.
KRENEK
   Heller als Glassteine
   Ihr Schwüre
   Der Schatten
   Schwarze Muse
   Spruchband
   Wechselrahmen
Bartholdy, Dr.
LOEWE
   Dem Herrscher
   Polterabendlied
Barto, A
PROKOFIEV *Boltun'ia*
BARTÓK, BÉLA, 1881-1945.
Ady, Endre, 1877-1918.
   Alone with the sea, op. 16 no. 4
      [Universal-Edition, 1923; Boosey &
      Hawkes, 1939] "Empty the room we
      once knew together"
   Autumn echoes [Universal-Edition, 1923;
      Boosey & Hawkes, 1939]
      "Have you heard it yet?"
   Autumn tears, op. 16 no. 1 [Universal-
      Edition, 1923; Boosey & Hawkes,
      1939] "Sad am I on autumn mornings"
   I cannot come to you, op. 16 no. 5
      [Universal-Edition, 1923; Boosey &
      Hawkes, 1939] "Is it summer?"
   Lost content, op. 16 no. 3 [Universal-
      Edition, 1923; Boosey & Hawkes,
      1939]
      "Now I come, lonely bed, lonely bed"
Bodenstedt, Friedrich Martin von,
   1819-1892.
   Die Gletscher leuchten im Mondenlicht,
      DD.54,3 [unpubl.] same
   Ich fühle deinen Odem, DD.62,4 [Editio
      Musica; Schott, 1963] same
   Text variously attributed to Rückert
      and Lenau.

COMPOSER Poet *Title* "First Line"

BARTÓK, BÉLA, 1881-1945 *(continued)*
Gleiman, W
  Night of desire, op. 15 no. 3 [Universal, 1961]
    "Kisses! my lips now cry for kisses!"
Goethe, Johann Wolfgang von, 1749-1832.
  Du meine Liebe, du mein Herz, DD.62,1 [unpubl.] same
  Wie herrlich leuchtet, DD.62,5 [unpubl.] same
Gombossy, K
  In the valley, op. 15 no. 5 [Universal, 1961] "Already autumn has come, bringing death"
  In vivid dreams, op. 15 no. 4 [Universal, 1961]
    "In vivid dreams I've seen you before"
  My love, op. 15 no. 1 [Universal, 1961] "My love bears no resemblance to the moon"
  Summer, op. 15 no. 2 [Universal, 1961] "Lying and longing, thirsting for breezes"
Harsányi, Kálmán, 1876-1929.
  Est, DD.73 [Editio Musica; Schott, 1963] "Csőndes minden, csőndes, Hallgatnak a lombok"
Havas, István
  The benefactors (1904?) [Ödön Geszler, *Enekiskala* I: 74]
Heine, Heinrich, 1797-1856.
  Im wunderschönen Monat Mai, DD.54,1 [*Lev.* I, pp. 203-05 (facsimile of holograph)] same
    NB: **Levelei**. Szerkeszti: Demény János. (Budapest: Zenemükiadó Vallalat, 1948, 1951, 1955).
Lenau, Nicolaus, 1802-1850.
  Diese Rose pflück ich hier, DD.62,2 [Editio Musica; Schott, 1963] same
Peros, Sándor
  Evening song (1904?) [Ödön Geszler, *Enekiskala* I: 56]
Pósa, Lajos, 1850-1914.
  Ejnye! Ejnye! DD.67,4 [Bárd, 1904] same
  Még azt vetik szememre, DD.67,2 [Bárd, 1904] "Még azt vetik a szememre"
  Nincs olyan bú, DD.67,3 [Bárd, 1904] same
  Őszi szellő, DD.67,1 [Bárd, 1904] same
Rückert, Friedrich, 1788-1866.
  Herr! der du alles wohl gemacht, DD.62,6 [unpubl.] same
Siebel, Carl, 1836-1868.
  Nacht am Rheine, DD.54,2 [unpubl.] "Es waren drei lust'ge Gesellen"

Sztankó, Béla
  Bell sound (1904?) [Ödön Geszler, *Enekiskala* II: 36]
Unknown
  Du geleitest mich zum Grave, DD.62,3 [unpubl.] same
Bartrumsen
  FRA ROLD TIL REBILD.
    NIELSEN *Vi Jyder*
Bassewitz, Karl, 1809-1907.
  SPOHR *Erwartung*
Bassus *see* Johanus Bassus, Frater, 16th cent.
Bateau see Radiguet **AURIC**
"Bateau debout bateau hagard" *see Bateau* Radiguet **AURIC**
Batsányi, Gabriele (von Baumberg), 1775-1839.
  MOZART *Als Luise die Briefe ihres ungetreuen Liebhabers verbrannte*
  SCHUBERT
    Abendständchen: An Lina
    An die Sonne
    Cora an die Sonne
    Lob des Tokayers
  DER MORGENKUSS NACH EINEM BALL.
    SCHUBERT *Der Morgenkuss*
Battements d'ailes see Dortzal **MASSENET**
Batter my heart see Donne **BRITTEN**
BATTLE OF LORA. see Macpherson
  Lorma **SCHUBERT**
    Two settings: D. 327 and D. 376.
Baudelaire, Charles Pierre, 1821-1867.
  CASELLA *La cloche fêlée*
  CHAUSSON *L'Albatros*
  DUPARC *La vie antérieure*
  FAURÉ
    Chant d'automne
    Hymne
    La rançon
  HINDEMITH *Le revenant*
  LOEFFLER
    La cloche fêlée
    Le flambeau vivant
  SAUGUET *Le chat*
    Two settings, 1938.
  SÉVERAC *Les hiboux*
  LES FLEURS DU MAL.
    CHABRIER *L'invitation au voyage*
    DEBUSSY
      Le Balcon
      Harmonie du soir
      Le Jet d'eau
      La Mort des amants
      Recueillement
    DUPARC *L'Invitation au voyage*
    INDY *L'amour et le crane*

COMPOSER   Poet   *Title*   "First Line"

Bauditz, O
  NIELSEN *Christianshavn*
Bauern unter der Linde see Goethe *FAUST.*
  WAGNER
Bauernfeld, Eduard von, 1802-1890.
  SCHUBERT *Der Vater mit dem Kind*
Bauernfest see Kol'tsov **MUSORGSKII**
  Pirushka
DAS BAUERNLIED. see Claudius, M.
  Im Anfang und jetzt **LOEWE**
Bauernregel see Uhland **LOEWE, REGER**
Baumbach, Rudolf, 1840-1905.
  BERG *Scheidelied*
  REGER *Der Schwur*
  RUBINSTEIN
    Das begraben Lied
    Seefahrt
Baumberg, Gabriele von *see* Batsányi,
  Gabriele (von Baumberg), 1775-1839.
Baur, Albert, 1803-1886.
  MENDELSSOHN-BARTHOLDY
    Weihnachtslied
Bawling blues see Goodman **ROREM**
The bayly berith the bell away see Anon.
  HESELTINE
Bazan, Noël
  MASSENET *Les mains*
Bazenery, F
  INDY *Angoisse*
"Be composed–be at case with me" *see To a*
  common prostitute Whitman **ROREM**
Be music, night see Patchen **DIAMOND**
"Be nimble, quick, away" *see Nuptial song*
  Anon. **WEISGALL**
"Be still, my sweet sweeting" *see Cradle song*
  Phillip, John **HESELTINE**
Be still, the hanging gardens were a dream
  see Stickney **GIDEON**
Be very quiet now see De La Mare *DING*
  DONG BELL: Benighted. **CHANLER**
The beacon barn see O'Malley, Patrick
  BERKELEY
The beast see Roethke **ROREM**
Beata viscera Mariae see Anon. **MILHAUD**
"Beau chevalier qui partez pour la guerre" *see*
  Chanson de Barberine Musset
  LALO, RUBINSTEIN
Beau chevalier qui partez pour la guerre see
  Musset *BARBERINE.* **DELIBES**
Le beau navire see Carême **MILHAUD**
Beau soir see Bourget *LES AVEUX:*
  Souvenirs du Nord, no. 7. **DEBUSSY**
Beaucoup d'amour see Béranger **LALO**
Beaumont, Germaine, 1891-1983.
  SAUGUET *Eaux douces*

Beauquier, Charles, 1833-1916.
  LALO *Humoresque*
"A beautiful angel came and stood" *see*
  The flight Feeney **CHANLER**
The beautiful fishermaiden see Heine
  BORODIN *Das schöne Fischermädchen*
The beauty see Pushkin **RIMSKII-**
  KORSAKOV *Krasavítsa*
Beauty see Shenshin **MEDTNER**
"Beauty and youth, with manners sweet" *see*
  Epitaph Melville **DIAMOND**
"Beauty fired by the coals of art" *see Beauty*
  touch me Cox, Oscar **HINDEMITH**
Beauty touch me see Cox, Oscar
  HINDEMITH
Beauvoir, Roger de, 1806-1866.
  BERLIOZ *Zäide* (Boléro, 1845, 1850)
Les beaux gars s'assemblent see Anon.
  SZYMANOWSKI *Wsyscy przyjechali*
"Beaux jours que le coeur envie" *see*
  L'abandonée Escudier, M. **VERDI**
Beaux yeux que j'aime see Maquet,
  Thérèse **MASSENET**
Bebro e il suo cavallo see Anon. **PIZZETTI**
Because I liked you better see Housman
  BERKELEY
"Because I would not stop for Death" *see*
  The chariot Dickinson **COPLAND**
"Because it is the day of palms" *see Santa*
  Chiara (Palm Sunday; Naples, 1925)
  Symons **IRELAND**
Bechstein, Ludwig, 1801-1860.
  CORNELIUS *Der König und der Sänger*
Bechtolsheim, Julie, Freifrau von (geb.
  Freiin von Keller), 1747-1847.
  ZELTER *Die beiden Schalen*
Bechtoldsheim, Julie von *see*
  Bechtolsheim, Julie, Freifrau von
    (geb. Freiin von Keller), 1747-1847.
Beck, Karl Isidor, 1817-1879.
  JENSEN
    Über Nacht
    Wo Tauben sind
  EINE THRÄNE.
    JENSEN *Eine Thräne*
Becker, Julius, 1811-1859.
  SPOHR *Abendlied*
Becker, Karl Friedrich, 1777-1806,
  supposed author.
  ZELTER
    Ahnung
    Romanze
    Der Sommerabend
Becker, Konstantin Julius *see* Becker,
  Julius, 1811-1859.

Beckon to me to come see Hardy **IRELAND**
Bécquer, Gustavo Adolfo, 1836-1870.
   FALLA
    Dios mio, que solos se quedan los
     muertos!
    Olas gigantes
   TURINA
    Besa el aura que gimé blandamente
    Olas gigantes
    Rima
      Two settings: Op. 6 and op. 26 no. 3.
    Tu pupila es azul y cuando ríes
Bed in summer see Stevenson, Robert
   Louis **IRELAND**
"Bedächtig stieg die Nacht ans Land" *see*
   Um Mitternacht Mörike **FRANZ**
Bédat de Monlaur, Pierre
   HONEGGER
    Le château du Bartas
    Le départ
    Duo
    Nérac en fête
    La promenade
    Tout le long de la Baïse
Bedat de Monlaur, Pierre *see* Bédat de
   Monlaur, Pierre
Beddoes, Thomas Lovell, 1803-1849.
   BERKELEY
    All night a wind of music
    The mighty thoughts of an old world
   IRELAND *If there were dreams to sell*
   QUILTER *If thou would'st ease thine*
    heart
"Bedecke deinen Himmel, Zeus" *see*
   Prometheus Goethe **SCHUBERT, WOLF**
Bedeckt mich mit Blumen see Anon.
   SPANISCHES LIEDERBUCH.
   RUBINSTEIN, WOLF
Bedlam see Bishop **ROREM** *Visits to St.*
   Elizabeths
Bed-time see Soutar **BRITTEN**
Die Beere see Vinje **GRIEG** *Tyteberet*
"Das Beet, schon lockert sich's in die Höh'!"
   see Frühling übers Jahr Goethe **LOEWE,**
   WOLF
BEETHOVEN, LUDWIG VAN, 1770-1827.
   Breuning, Stephan von, 1774-1827.
    Als die Geliebte sich trennen wollte,
     WoO 132 [GA Serie 23, Nr. 21]
     "Der Hoffnung letzter Schimmer"
   Bürger, Gottfried August, 1747-1794.
    Das Blümchen Wunderhold, op. 52 no. 8
     [GA Serie 23, Nr. 4]
     "Es blüht ein Blümchen irgendwo"
    Gegenliebe, WoO 118 no. 2 [GA Serie
     23, Nr. 40]
     "Wüsst ich, dass du mich lieb"

    Mollys Abschied, op. 52 no. 5 [GA Serie
     23, Nr. 4] "Lebe wohl, du Mann der
     Lust und Schmerzen"
    Seufzer eines Ungeliebten, WoO 118 no.
     1 [GA Serie 23, Nr. 40]
     "Hast du nicht Liebe zugemessen"
   Carpani, Giuseppe, 1752-1825.
    In questa tomba oscura, WoO 133 [GA
     Serie 23, Nr. 39] same
   Claudius, Matthias, 1740-1815.
    Urians Reise um die Welt, op. 52 no. 1
     [GA Serie 23, Nr. 4]
     "Wenn jemand eine Reise tut"
   Döhring, J von?
    An einen Säugling, WoO 108 [GA Serie
     23, Nr. 15] "Noch weisst du nicht wess
     Kind du bist"
   Friedelberg, d. 1800.
    Abschiedsgesang an Wiens Bürger, WoO
     121 [GA Serie 23, Nr. 16]
     "Keine Klage soll erschallen"
    Kriegslied der Österreicher, WoO 122
     [GA Serie 23, Nr. 17]
     "Ein grosses deutsches Volk sind wir"
   Gellert, Christian Fürchtegott, 1715-
   1769.
    Bitten, op. 48 no. 1 [GA Serie 23, Nr. 3]
     "Gott, deine Güte reicht so weit"
    Busslied, op. 48 no. 6 [GA Serie 23, Nr.
     3; Supplemente, v. 5, p. 28]
     "An dir allein, an dir hab' ich
     gesündigt"
    Die Ehre Gottes aus der Natur, op. 48
     no. 4 [GA Serie 23, Nr. 3]
     "Die Himmel rühmen"
    Gottes Macht und Vorschung, op. 48 no.
     5 [GA Serie 23, Nr. 3]
     "Gott ist mein Lied"
    Die Liebe des Nächsten, op. 48 no. 2
     [GA Serie 23, Nr. 3]
     "So jemand spricht: ich liebe Gott"
    Vom Tode, op. 48 no. 3 [GA Serie 23,
     Nr. 3 "Meine Lebenszeit verstreicht"
   Gleim, Johann Wilhelm Ludwig,
   1719-1803.
    Selbstgespräch, WoO 114 [GA Serie 25,
     Nr. 275]
     "Ich, der mit flatterndem Sinn"
   Goeble, H
    Abendlied unterm gestirnten Himmel,
     WoO 150 [GA Serie 23, Nr. 34]
     "Wenn die Sonne nieder sinket"
   Goethe, Johann Wolfgang von, 1749-
   1832.
    Erlkönig, WoO 131 [Leipzig, J.
     Schuberth, 1897; NY: Luckhardt &
     Belder, 1898] "Wer reitet so spät durch
     Nacht und Wind?"

Ich denke dein, WoO 74 [GA Serie 15, Nr. 4] same
Accompaniment for piano, 4 hands.
Maigesang, op. 52 no. 4 [GA Serie 23, Nr. 4]
"Wie herrlich leuchtet mir die Natur"
Marmotte, op. 52 no. 7 [GA Serie 23, Nr. 4] "Ich komme schon durch manche Land"
Mit einem gemalten Band, op. 83 no. 3 [GA Serie 23, Nr. 7]
"Kleine Blumen, kleine Blätter"
Neue Liebe, neues Leben, op. 75 no. 2 [GA Serie 23, Nr. 5]
"Herz, mein Herz, was soll das geben?"
Neue Liebe, neues Leben, WoO 127 [Supplemente, v. 5, p. 20]
"Herz, mein Herz, was soll das geben?"
Wonne der Wehmut, op. 83 no. 1 [GA Serie 23, Nr. 7]
"Trocknet nicht, trocknet nicht"
FAUST.
Aus Goethes Faust, op. 75 no. 3 [GA Serie 23, Nr. 5]
"Es war einmal ein König"
DAS GÖTTLICHE (last verse).
Der edle Mensch sei hülfreich und gut, WoO 151 [Supplemente, v. 5, p. 38] same
SEHNSUCHT.
Sehnsucht, op. 83 no. 2 [GA Serie 23, Nr. 7] "Was zieht mir das Herz so?"
WILHELM MEISTER. Mignon's song: Kennst du das Land?
Mignon, op. 75 no. 1 [GA Serie 23, Nr. 5] "Kennst du das Land"
WILHELM MEISTER. Mignon's song: Nur wer die Sehnsucht kennt
Sehnsucht, WoO 134 [GA Serie 23, Nr. 37]
"Nur wer die Sehnsucht kennt"
Halem, Gerhard Anton von, 1752-1819.
Gretels Warnung, op. 75 no. 4 [GA Serie 23, Nr. 5]
"Mit Liebesblick und Spiel und Sang"
Haugwitz, Paul von, Bp. of Naumberg
Resignation, WoO 149 [GA Serie 23, Nr. 33] "Lisch aus, lisch aus, mein Licht!"
Herder, Johann Gottfried von, 1744-1803.
Der Gesang der Nachtigal, WoO 141 [GA Serie 25, Nr. 277]
"Höre, die Nachtigall singt"

Die laute Klage, WoO 135 [GA Serie 23, Nr. 41] "Turteltaube, du klagest so laut"
Hermann, Franz Rudolf, 1787-1823.
Der Bardengeist, WoO 142 [GA Serie 23, Nr. 27]
"Dort auf dem hohen Felsen sang"
Herrosee, Karl Friedrich, 1754-1821.
Zärtliche Liebe, WoO 123 [GA Serie 23, Nr. 36] "Ich liebe dich"
Hölty, Ludwig Heinrich Christoph, 1748-1776.
Klage, WoO 113 [GA Serie 25, Nr. 283] "Dein Silber schien durch Eichengrün"
Jeitteles, Alois, 1794-1858.
Auf dem Hügel sitz ich spähend, op. 98 no. 1 [GA Serie 23, Nr. 10] same
Diese Wolken in den Höhen, op. 98 no. 4 [GA Serie 23, Nr. 10] same
Es kehret der Maien, op. 98 no. 5 [GA Serie 23, Nr. 10] same
Leichte Segler in den Höhen, op. 98 no. 3 [GA Serie 23, Nr. 10] same
Nimm sie hin denn diese Lieder, op. 98 no. 6 [GA Scric 23, Nr. 10] same
Wo die Berge so blau, op. 98 no. 2 [GA Serie 23, Nr. 10] same
Kleinschmid, Friedrich August, b. 1749.
Der Mann von Wort, op. 99 [GA Scric 23, Nr. 11]
"Du sagtest, Freund, an diesen Ort"
Lappe, Karl, 1773-1843.
So oder so, WoO 148 [GA Serie 23, Nr. 31] "Nord oder Süd!"
Lessing, Gotthold Ephraim, 1729-1781.
Die Liebe, op. 52 no. 6 [GA Serie 23, Nr. 4] "Ohne Liebe lebe wer da kann"
Matthisson, Friedrich von, 1761-1831.
Adelaide, op. 46 [GA Serie 23, Nr. 2]
"Einsam wandelt dein Freund im Frühlings Garten"
An Laura, WoO 112 [Supplemente, v. 5, p. 7] "Freund' umblühe dich auf allen Wegen"
Andenken, WoO 136 [GA Serie 23, Nr. 35] "Ich denke dein, wenn durch den Hain"
Opferlied, WoO 126 [GA Serie 23, Nr. 19; another version, Supplemente v. 5, p. 15] "Die Flamme lodert"
Mereau, Sophie (Schubert), 1773?-1806.
Feuerfarb', Hess 144 [Supplemente, v. 5, p. 10] "Ich weiss eine Farbe"
Erste Fassung.

BEETHOVEN, LUDWIG VAN, 1770-1827
(continued)
Mereau, Sophie (Schubert), 1773?-1806 *(continued)*
Feuerfarb', op. 52 no. 2 [GA Serie 23, Nr. 4; Supplemente v. 5, p. 10]
"Ich weiss eine Farbe"
Metastasio, Pietro Antonio Domenico Buonaventura, 1698-1782.
O care selve, WoO 119 [GA Serie 25, Nr. 279] same
La partenza, WoO 124 [GA Serie 23, Nr. 38] "Ecco quel fiero istante!"
ADRIANO: Act II, scene 6.
L'amante impaziente, op. 82 no. 3 [GA Serie 23, Nr. 6] "Che fa il mio bene?"
Arietta buffa.
L'amante impaziente, op. 82 no. 4 [GA Serie 23, Nr. 6] "Che fa il mio bene?"
Ariette assai seriosa.
AMOR TIMIDO (Cantata XVI).
Liebes-Klage, op. 82 no. 2 [GA Serie 23, Nr. 6] "T'intendo, si, mio cor"
LA PACE FRA LA VIRTÙ E LA BELLEZZA.
Lebens-Genuss, op. 82 no. 5 [GA Serie 23, Nr. 6]
"Odi l'aura che dolce sospira"
Duet for soprano and tenor.
Pfeffel, Gottlieb Conrad, 1736-1809.
Der freie Mann, WoO 117 [GA Serie 23, Nr. 18; Supplemente v. 5, p. 41]
"Wer, wer ist ein freier Mann?"
Reissig, Christian Ludwig, 1783-1822.
An den fernen Geliebten, op. 75 no. 5 [GA Serie 23, Nr. 5]
"Einst wohnten süsse Ruh"
Des Kriegers Abschied, WoO 143 [GA Serie 23, Nr. 26] "Ich zieh' ins Feld"
Der Jüngling in der Fremde, WoO 138 [GA Serie 23, Nr. 23]
"Der Frühling entblühet"
Der Liebende, WoO 139 [GA Serie 23, Nr. 24]
"Welch ein wunderbares Leben"
Lied aus der Ferne, WoO 137 [GA Serie 23, Nr. 22]
"Als mir noch die Thräne"
Sehnsucht, WoO 146 [GA Serie 23, Nr. 25] "Die stille Nacht umdunkelt"
Der Zufriedene, op. 75 no. 6 [GA Serie 23, Nr. 5]
"Zwar schuf das Glück hienieden"
Rousseau, Jean Jacques, 1712-1778.
Que le temps me dure, WoO 116 [Supplemente, v. 5, pp. 11, 13] same

Rupprecht, Johann Baptist, 1776-1846.
Merkenstein, WoO 144 [GA Serie 25, Nr. 276]
"Merkenstein, Merkenstein! Wo ich wandle denk' ich dein"
Also for 2 voices & piano as op. 100.
Sauter, Samuel Friedrich, 1766-1846.
IL CANTO DELLA QUAGLIA.
Der Wachtelschlag, WoO 129 [GA Serie 23, Nr. 20] "Ach mir schallt's dorten so lieblich hervor"
Stoll, Johann Ludwig, 1778-1815.
An die Geliebte, WoO 140 (2 versions) [GA Serie 23, Nr. 30, 29]
"O dass ich dir vom stillen Auge"
Tiedge, Christoph August, 1752-1841.
URANIA.
An die Hoffnung, op. 32 [GA Serie 23, Nr. 1] "Die du so gern in heilgen Nächten feierst"
URANIA: Klagen des Zweiflers.
An die Hoffnung, op. 94 [GA Serie 23, Nr. 9] "Ob ein Gott sei"
Treitschke, Georg Friedrich, 1776-1842.
Ruf vom Berge, WoO 147 [GA Serie 23, Nr. 28] "Wenn ich ein Vöglein wär"
Ueltzen, Hermann Wilhelm Franz, 1759-1808.
Das Liebchen von der Ruhe, op. 52 no. 3 [GA Serie 23, Nr. 4]
"Im Arm der Liebe"
Unknown
An Minna, WoO 115 [GA Serie 25, Nr. 280] "Nur bei dir, an deinem Herzen"
Elegie auf den Tod eines Pudels, WoO 110 [GA Serie 25, Nr. 284]
"Stirb immerhin, es welken ja so viele der Freuden"
Gedenke mein, WoO 130 [GA Serie 25, Nr. 281] same
Das Glück der Freundschaft, op. 88 [GA Serie 23, Nr. 8]
"Der lebt ein Leben wonniglich"
Hoffnung, op. 82 no. 1 [GA Serie 23, Nr. 6] "Dimmi, ben mio che m'ami"
Man strebt die Flamme zu verhehlen, WoO 120 [GA Serie 25, Nr. 278] same
Plaisir d'aimer, WoO 128 [Supplemente zur GA, v. 5, p. 27] same
Punschlied, WoO 111 [Supplemente, v. 5, p. 39] "Wer nicht, wenn warm von Hand zu Hand"
Schilderung eines Mädchens, WoO 107 [GA Serie 23, Nr. 14]

"Schildern, willst du Freund, soll ich
dir Elisen?"
La tiranna, WoO 125 [Supplemente, v. 5,
p. 16] "Ah grief to think"
English translation by W. Wennington.
Traute Henriette, Hess 151
[Supplemente, v. 5, p. 14] same
Trinklied, WoO 109 [GA Serie 25, Nr.
282] "Erhebt das Glas"
Weisse, Christian Felix, 1726-1804.
Der Kuss, op. 128 [GA Serie 23, Nr. 13]
"Ich war bei Chloen ganz allein"
**Wessenberg, Ignaz Heinrich Karl,
Freiherr von, 1774-1860.**
Das Geheimnis, WoO 145 [GA Serie 23,
Nr. 32] "Wo blüht das Blümchen"
The beetle see Musorgskiĭ **MUSORGSKIĬ**
Zhuk
Before life and after see Hardy **BRITTEN**
Before my window see Einerling
RACHMANINOFF
Before sleeping see Anon. **THOMSON**
Before the court see Goethe **MEDTNER**
Vor Gericht
"Before the holy cloister gate" *see At the
cloister gate* Lermontov **MEDTNER**
Before the icon see Golenishchev-Kutuzov
RACHMANINOFF
Before the image see Golenishchev-
Kutuzov **RACHMANINOFF** *Before the
icon*
"Before we leave this deadly Land of Fear"
see The land of fear Capetanakis
ROREM
Before you know see Červenka, Jan
MARTINŮ
Die Befreier Europas in Paris see Mikan
SCHUBERT
Befreit see Dehmel **STRAUSS**
Befriad är dagen see Lagerkvist **KILPINEN**
Begegnung see Gruppe **STRAUSS**
Begegnung see Mörike **REGER, WOLF**
Die Begegnung am Meeresstrand see Fick,
Heinrich
THE MEETING ON THE SEASHORE.
LOEWE
The beggar see Goethe *WILHELM
MEISTER.* Harfenspieler. **MEDTNER**
An die Türen will ich schleichen
"Beginne deine heilige Feier" *see An die
Nacht* Bernays **LASSEN**
"Beglückt, beglückt, wer dich erblickt" *see
Der Liebende* Hölty **SCHUBERT**
Beglückt, wer in des Herbstes see Anon.
ZELTER
Begone, dull care see Anon. **BRITTEN**

Le bégonia see Daudet, L. **MILHAUD**
"Bégonia Aurora" *see Le bégonia* Daudet, L.
MILHAUD
Das begraben Lied see Baumbach
RUBINSTEIN
"Begrüsset mit Tönen und Liedern den Tag"
*see Gesang zum Jahresfeste der
Luisenstiftung* Ianke **ZELTER**
Beherzigung see Goethe **WOLF**
Behind the window in the shadow see
Polonsky *VIZOV.* **CHAĬ KOVSKIĬ**
Za oknom v teni mel'kaet
"Behold, bless ye the Lord" *see Psalm 134*
Bible **ROREM**
"Behold, my friend, the daisies sweet and
tender" *see Daisies* Lotarev
RACHMANINOFF
Behold my visionary soul see Tiutchev
MEDTNER
"Behold the brand of beauty tossed!" *see
The dancer* Waller **ROREM**
"Behold the dust of Timas dead" *see Epitaph
of Timas* Sappho **BERKELEY**
"Bei dem angenehmsten Wetter" *see
Der Scholar* Eichendorff **WOLF**
Bei dem Glanz der Abendröte see Goethe
MACDOWELL *In the woods*
"Bei dem Glanz der Abendröthe" *see
Die Bekehrte* Goethe **WOLF**
"Bei dem Glanze der Abendröte" *see
Die Bekehrte* Goethe **MEDTNER**
Bei dem Grabe meines Vaters see Claudius,
M. **SCHUBERT**
"Bei den Bienenkörben im Garten" *see
Unruhe* Roquette **JENSEN**
"Bei der Abendsonne Wandern" *see Requiem*
Meyer **SCHOECK**
Bei der Kirche see Rüeger, Armin
SCHOECK
"Bei der Liebe reinsten Flammen" *see An
Chloen* Jacobi **SCHUBERT**
Bei der Linde see Osterwald **FRANZ**
Bei der Wiege see Klingemann
MENDELSSOHN-BARTHOLDY
"Bei diesen kalten Wehen" *see Winterreise*
Uhland **STRAUSS**
Bei dir see Grosse **JENSEN**
Bei dir allein see Seidl **SCHUBERT**
"Bei dir allein empfind' ich" *see Bei dir allein*
Seidl **SCHUBERT**
Bei dir sind meine Gedanken see Münch-
Bellinghausen **BRAHMS**
"Bei einem Wirte wundermild" *see Einkehr*
Uhland **STRAUSS**
Two settings: AV 3 and op. 47 no. 4.

Bei einer Trauung see Mörike **WOLF**
"Bei euren Taten, euren Siegen" *see Nach
    dem Kriege* Mörike **SCHOECK**
"Bei jeder Wendung deiner Lebensbahn" *see
    Zu einer Konfirmation* Mörike **SCHOECK**
"Bei Nacht im Dorf der Wächter rief" *see
    Elfenlied* Mörike **WOLF**
Bei Rondane see Vinje **FERDAMINNI.**
    GRIEG *Ved Rondane*
Bei Sonnenuntergang see Munch
    SOLNEDGANG. GRIEG *Solnedgang*
Die Beiden see Hofmannsthal
    SCHÖNBERG
Die beiden Grenadiere see Heine
    SCHUMANN
Die beiden Schalen see Bechtolsheim
    ZELTER
Die beiden Wolken see Hamerling **LASSEN**
Beim Abschied see Münch-Bellinghausen
    BRAHMS
Beim Auszug in das Feld see Unknown
    MOZART
Beim Fenstergehn see Löwenstein
    RUBINSTEIN
Beim Kirchgang von allen see Groth **GRIEG**
Beim lieben hellen Mondenschein see Anon.
    ZELTER
Beim Mähen see Garborg **HAUGTUSSA.**
    GRIEG *I Slåtten*
Beim Maitrank see Unknown **LOEWE**
Beim Scheiden see Kugler, Johann, Consul
    in Stettin **LOEWE**
"Beim Scheiden der Sonne erschimmert der
    Metilstein" *see Walther von der Vogelweide*
    Scheffel **LISZT**
Beim Schneewetter see Unknown **REGER**
Beim Sonnenuntergang see Munch
    SOLNEDGANG. DELIUS
Beim Tanze see Jacob, T. **LOEWE**
Beim Winde see Mayrhofer **SCHUBERT**
Beissier, Fernand, 1858-1936.
    MASSENET *Petite mireille*
Die Bekehrte see Goethe **MEDTNER,
    WOLF, ZELTER**
Beketova, Ekaterina Andreevna, 1855-
    1892.
    SIREN'
        RACHMANINOFF *The lilacs*
Bekmann, Mathilde
    SPOHR *Lied aus dem "Märlein von der
        Wasserfee"*
Bel aubépin see Ronsard **RIVIER**
"Bel aubépin verdissant fleurissant" *see Bel
    aubépin* Ronsard **RIVIER**
Believe it not see Tolstoï
    RACHMANINOFF *Believe me not, friend*

Believe me see Vérine, Boris **PROKOFIEV**
    Dover'sia mne
Believe me not, friend see Tolstoï
    RACHMANINOFF
Believe not, friend of mine see Tolstoï
    CHAÏKOVSKIÏ *Ne ver', moĭ drug*
The bell doth toll see Heywood **THOMSON**
Bell sound see Sztankó **BARTÓK**
Bella lucente luna see Anon. **PIZZETTI**
Bella porta di rubini see Unknown
    RESPIGHI
"Bell'astro della terra" *see Ad una stella*
    Maffei **VERDI**
Bellay, Joachim du *see* Du Bellay,
    Joachim, ca.1525-1560.
"Belle âme qui fus mon flambeau" *see
    Épitaphe* Malherbe **POULENC**
La Belle au bois dormant see Hyspa
    DEBUSSY
Belle dame de mon émoi see Valmy-Baysse
    MILHAUD
La belle dame sans merci see Keats
    HINDEMITH
LA BELLE EN DORMANT, no. 1
    THOMSON Hugnet *Pour chercher sur la
        carte des mers*
LA BELLE EN DORMANT, no. 2
    THOMSON Hugnet *La première de
        toutes*
LA BELLE EN DORMANT, no. 3
    THOMSON Hugnet *Mon amour est bon à
        dire*
LA BELLE EN DORMANT, no. 4
    THOMSON Hugnet *Partis les vaisseaux*
"Belle épousée, j'aime tes pleurs" *see
    Chanson gothique* Gérard de Nerval
    AURIC
La belle Isabeau see Dumas the elder
    BERLIOZ
La belle jeunesse see Anon. **POULENC**
Belle lune d'argent see Moréas **HAHN**
"Belle, méchante, menteuse, injuste" *see
    Le portrait* Colette **POULENC**
Belle Meunière see Arosa **SCHMITT**
La belle morte see Brimont **SAUGUET**
"Belle nymphes blondes des forêts profondes"
    see Le sylvain Pacini **ROSSINI**
"Belle source, belle source" *see Air champêtre*
    Moréas **POULENC**
"Belle, sous la mauvaise étoile" *see Attendez
    le prochain bateau* Vilmorin **AURIC**
La belle voyageuse see Moore, T. **BERLIOZ**
Belleau, Rémy, 1527?-1577.
    DELIBES, SAINT-SAËNS *Avril*
Les belles de nuit see Maquet, Thérèse
    MASSENET

COMPOSER Poet *Title* "First Line"

"Belles frileuses qui sont nées" *see Roses d'Octobre* Collin **MASSENET**

"Belles journées" *see La souris* Apollinaire **POULENC**

Belloc, Hilaire, 1870-1953.
BRITTEN *The birds*
HESELTINE
The birds
Ha'nacker mill
The night
THE FOUR MEN. His own country: I shall go without companions.
HESELTINE *My own country*

BELLOC SONGS, no. 1
HESELTINE Belloc, Hilaire *Ha'nacker mill*

BELLOC SONGS, no. 2
HESELTINE Belloc, Hilaire *The night*

BELLOC SONGS, no. 3
HESELTINE Belloc, Hilaire *My own country*

Bells see Hayes **GIDEON**
The Bells of San Marie see Masefield **IRELAND**
Beloved, let us fly see Golenishchev-Kutuzov **RACHMANINOFF**
Below here in the valley see Gombossy **BARTÓK** *In the valley*
BELSATZAR. see Heine
Belsatzar **SCHUMANN**
Belsatzar see Heine *BELSATZAR.*
SCHUMANN
Belsazar's Gesicht see Byron *HEBREW MELODIES.* **LOEWE**
Beltà crudele see Santo-Magno, N di **ROSSINI**
Bely, Andrey, pseud. *see* Bugayev, Boris Nikolaevich, 1880-1934.
"Bemesst den Schritt" *see Säerspruch* Meyer **PFITZNER**
Benedeit die sel'ge Mutter see Heyse **WOLF**
Benedetto sia'l giorno see Petrarca **LISZT**
Benediktov, Vladimir Grigor'evich, 1807-1873.
RUBINSTEIN *Lied*
The benefactors see Havas **BARTÓK**
Benerzigung see Goethe **WOLF**
Bengoechea, Hernando de, 1889-1915.
CRÉPUSCULES DU MATIN.
SCHMITT *Prise aux réseaux d'or*
Bengy-Puyvallée, Antoine de, 1854-
AUBERT
Hélène
Première
"Béni soit le Seigneur, notre Dieu" *see Prière du soir* Anon. **MILHAUD**

Benn, Gottfried, 1886-1956.
BLACHER
Eure Etüden
Gedichte
Letzter Frühling
Worte
Bennett, Rodney, 1890-1948.
QUILTER
The cradle in Bethlehem
Freedom
BENNETT, WILLIAM STERNDALE, 1816-1875.
Bryan, Waller Procter, 1787-1874.
Dawn, gentle flower, op. 35 no. 3 [Kistner, 1856] same
Indian love, op. 35 no. 1 [Kistner, 1856] "Tell me not that thou dost love me"
Sing, maiden, sing, op. 35 no. 6 [Kistner, 1856] same
Burns, Robert, 1759-1796.
Castle Gordon, or The young Highland rover, op. 35 no. 4 [Kistner, 1856] "Loud blaw the frosty breezes"
Musing on the roaring ocean, op. 23 no. 1 [Kistner, 1842] same
Stay, my charmer, op. 47 no. 4 (ca.1839) [Chappell, 1875] same
To Chloe in sickness, op. 23 no. 4 [Kistner, 1842] "Long, long is the night"
Case, Thomas, 1844-1925.
Dancing lightly, op. 47 no. 3 (ca.1871) [Chappell, 1875] "Dancing lightly comes the summer"
Maiden mine, op. 47 no. 1 [Chappell, 1875] "Maiden mine with lips so rosy" 1861, rev. 1866.
Sunset, op. 47 no. 2 [Chappell, 1875] "Star of day"
Tell me where, ye summer breezes (1861) [unpubl.]
Clare, John, 1793-1864.
Winter's gone, op. 35 no. 2 [Kistner, 1856] same
Hemans, Felicia Dorothea (Browne), 1793-1835.
The better land [advertised under "New Music," Nov. 1839] "I hear thee speak"
Klingemann, Carl, 1798-1862.
WALDEINSAMKEIT.
As lonesome through the woods I stray, op. 35 no. 5 [Kistner, 1856] same
Landon, Letitia, 1802-1838.
Forget-me-not, op. 23 no. 3 [Kistner, 1842] "Wave that wand'rest"

**BENNETT, WILLIAM STERNDALE,
1816-1875** *(continued)*
Montgomery, James, 1771-1854.
  Resignation (1835?) [*The Sacred
    Melodist,* Jan. 1, 1836]
    "Oh thou whose mercy"
Shelley, Percy Bysshe, 1792-1822.
  The past, op. 23 no. 5 [Kistner, 1842]
    "Wilt thou forget?"
Uhland, Ludwig, 1787-1862.
  O'er the woodlands, op. 23 no. 2
    [Kistner, 1842]
Unknown
  Gentle Zephyr, op. 23 no. 6 [Kistner,
    1842]
Benz, Friedrich, 1878-1904.
  REGER *Schlummerlied*
Benzon, Carl Otto Valdemar, 1856-
  1927.
  GRIEG
    Der gynger en Båd på Bølge
    Digtervise
    Drømme
    Eros
    Jeg lever et Liv i Laengsel
    Snegl, Snegl!
    Til min Dreng
    To a devil
    Ved Moders Grav
  ANNA BRYDE.
  GRIEG
    Lys Nat
    Se dig for, når du vaelger din Vej
Benzon, Otto *see* Benzon, Carl Otto
  Valdemar, 1856-1927.
Beppa la napolitaine see Metastasio
  ROSSINI *Mi lagnerò tacendo*
Béranger, Pierre Jean de, 1780-1857.
  BERLIOZ, GOUNOD *Les champs*
  GOUNOD *Mon habit*
  LALO
    Beaucoup d'amour
    La pauvre femme
    Les petits coups
    Si j'étais petit oiseau
    Le suicide
    Le vieux vagabond
  LISZT *Le vieux vagabond*
  WAGNER *Les adieux de Marie Stuart*
  LES CARTES, OU L'HOROSCOPE.
  SCHUMANN *Die Kartenlegerin*
  *JEANNE LA ROUSSE, OU, LA FEMME
    DU BRACONNIER.*
  SCHUMANN *Die rothe Hanne*
  LE JUIF ERRANT: Chrétien, au voyageur
    souffrant.
  GOUNOD, LISZT *Le juif errant*

Le Berceau de Gertrude Stein see Hugnet
  THOMSON
Les berceaux see Sully-Prudhomme
  FAURÉ
Berceuse see Anon. **MILHAUD**
Berceuse see Chouquet **MASSENET**
Berceuse see Desbordes-Valmore **BIZET**
Berceuse see Gibout, Henri **MASSENET**
Berceuse see Ives **IVES**
Berceuse see Jacob, M. **POULENC**
Berceuse see Olivier, Pierre **SAUGUET**
  L'enfant qui dort
Berceuse see Peter, René **DEBUSSY**
Berceuse see Stravinskiĭ **STRAVINSKIĭ**
Berceuse de Galiane see Arnoux **IBERT**
Berceuse de la guerre see Cammaerts
  MESSINES . . . **CARPENTER**
Berceuse du marin see Champlay, R.
  AUBERT
Berceuse populaire see Unknown **INDY**
"Bereifte Kiefern, atemlose Seen" *see An die
  Mark* Wackernagel, I. **PFITZNER**
Berent, Waclav, 1873-1941.
  SZYMANOWSKI *Lebedź*
BERG, ALBAN, 1885-1935.
Altenberg, Peter, 1859-1919.
  WAS DER TAG MIR ZUTRÄGT':
    Flötenspielerin.
  Flötenspielerin (ca.1902) [unpubl.]
    "Von der Last"
    Jugendlieder, no. 56
  WAS DER TAG MIR ZUTRÄGT':
    Hoffnung.
  Hoffnung (ca.1902) [unpubl.] "Was
    erhofftest Du Dir"
    Jugendlieder, no. 55
  WAS DER TAG MIR ZUTRÄGT':
    Traurigkeit.
  Traurigkeit (ca.1902) [unpubl.]
    "Weinet, sanfte Mädchen"
    Jugendlieder, no. 54
Avenarius, Ferdinand, 1856-1923.
  Wandert ihr Wolken (1904-05) [unpubl.]
    Jugendlieder, no. 29
Baumbach, Rudolf, 1840-1905.
  Scheidelied (1904-05) [unpubl.]
    "Die Schwalben zieh'n"
    Jugendlieder, no. 24
Bierbaum, Otto Julius, 1865-1910.
  Lied des Schiffermädels (ca.1902)
    [Universal-Edition, 1985]
    "Auf der fernen See"
    Jugendlieder, no. 6.
  Nachtgesang (1904-05) [unpubl.] "Wir
    gingen durch die dunkle milde Nacht"
    Jugendlieder, no. 26

COMPOSER Poet *Title* "First Line"

Bjørnson, Bjornstjerne, 1832-1910.
Im Walde (ca.1902) [unpubl.] "Langsam
erzählet der rauschende Wald"
Jugendlieder, no. 64. Duet.

Burns, Robert, 1759-1796.
O wär' mein Lieb' jen' Röslein rot
(ca.1902) [unpubl.]
Jugendlieder, no. 51

Busse, Carl, 1872-1918.
Ich und du (ca.1902) [unpubl.]
"Rebhahnruf und Glockenlaut"
Jugendlieder, no. 39
Das stille Königreich (1908) [unpubl.]
"Es gibt ein stilles Königreich"
Jugendlieder, no. 78
Über den Bergen (1904 or 1905)
[unpubl.]
Jugendlieder, no. 43

Busse-Palma, Georg, 1876-1915.
Furcht (1904-05) [unpubl.] "Mein Hoffen
du und Seligkeit"
Jugendlieder, no. 33

Dörmann, Felix, 1876-1928.
Wenn Gespenster auferstehen (1904-05)
[unpubl.]
"Sieh, Du musst es mir vergeben"
Jugendlieder, no. 21

Eichendorff, Joseph Karl Benedikt,
Freiherr von, 1788-1857.
Es wandelt, was wir schauen (1904-05)
[Universal-Edition, 1985]
Jugendlieder, no. 27

Eichhorn, Maria, 1879-
Über meinen Nächten (ca.1902) [unpubl.]
Jugendlieder, no. 9

Evers, Franz, 1871-1947.
Aus "Pfingsten ein Gedichtsreigen"
(ca.1902) [unpubl.]
"Die Nachigallen schlafen"
Jugendlieder, no. 48
Heilige Himmel, op. 1 (1900) [unpubl.]
"Sommerträume ihr purpurne Abende"
Jugendlieder, no. 1
Leben (1904-05) [unpubl.] "Was will die
Nacht"
Jugendlieder without number.

Falke, Gustav, 1853-1916.
Die Sorglichen (1904-05) [unpubl.]
"Im Frühling"
Jugendlieder, no. 72
MIT DEM LEBEN.
Fromm (1904-05) [unpubl.] "Der
Mond scheint auf mein Lager"
Jugendlieder, no. 40

Finckh, Ludwig, 1876-1964.
Fraue, Du Süsse (?) [unpubl.] "Ich hab'
es nicht gewusst"
Jugendlieder, no. 50

Fischer, Johann Georg, 1816-1897.
Eure Weisheit (1904-05) [unpubl.]
"Ich sah am liebsten"
Jugendlieder, no. 61

Flaischlen, Cäsar, 1864-1920.
So regnet es sich langsam ein (ca.1902)
[unpubl.]
Jugendlieder, no. 60

Fleischer, Siegfried, 1856-1924.
Herbstgefühl (1900-01) [Universal-
Edition, 1985]
"Verwelkte Blätter, entseelte Götter"
Jugendlieder, no. 2

Frey, Friedrich Hermann, 1830-1911.
Schattenleben (1904-05) [Universal-
Edition, 1985]
"Still ist's wo die Gräber sind"
Jugendlieder, no. 19
Schlummerlose Nächte (1904-05)
[Universal-Edition, 1985]
"Legt mir unter's Haupt"
Jugendlieder, no. 25

Geibel, Emanuel, i.e., Franz Emanuel
August, 1815-1884.
Am Abend (1904-05) [Universal-Edition,
1985] "Du feuchter Frühlingsabend"
Jugendlieder, no. 20

Gleim, Johann Wilhelm Ludwig,
1719-1803.
An Leukon (1908) [Reich **Alban Berg** . . .
(Vienna: Herbert Reichner, 1937)]
"Rosen pflücken, Rosen blüh'n"
Jugendlieder, no. 79. In **Beilage,** p.14.

Goethe, Johann Wolfgang von, 1749-
1832.
Erster Verlust (1904-05) [unpubl.]
"Ach wer bringt die schönen Tage"
Jugendlieder, no. 36
Grenzen der Menschheit (ca.1902)
[Universal-Edition, 1985]
"Wenn der uralte, heilige Vater"
Jugendlieder, no. 62
WILHELM MEISTER. Mignon's song:
Kennst du das Land?
Mignon (1904-05) [unpubl.]
"Kennst du das Land"
Jugendlieder, no. 69

Grabbe, Christian Dietrich, 1801-1836.
Ich liebe dich! (1904-05) [Universal-
Edition, 1985]
"Wie ein Goldadler reisst der Blitz"
Jugendlieder, no. 15

Grazie, Marie Eugenie delle, 1864-
1931.
Was zucken die braunen Geigen (1904-
05) [unpubl.]
Jugendlieder, no. 67

BERG, ALBAN, 1885-1935 *(continued)*
Hamerling, Robert, 1830-1889.
Augenblicke (1904-05) [unpubl.]
"Augenblicke gibt es zage"
Jugendlieder, no. 34
Viel Träume (1903) [unpubl.]
"Viele Vögel sind geflogen"
Jugendlieder, no. 65. Duet.
Hartleben, Otto Erich, 1864-1905.
Liebesode (1906) [Universal-Edition, 1928]
"Im Arm der Liebe schliefen wir selig ein"
Also voice & orchestra, 1928; publ. 1955, 1969.
Hauptmann, Carl Ferdinand Maximilian, 1858-1921.
Nacht (1908) [Universal-Edition, 1928]
"Dämmern Wolken über Nacht und Tal"
Also voice & orchestra, 1928; publ. 1955, 1969.
Hebbel, Christian Friedrich, 1813-1863.
Spuk (ca.1902) [unpubl.]
"Ich blicke hinab"
Jugendlieder, no. 47
DEM SCHMERZ SEIN RECHT.
Schlafen, schlafen, op. 2 no. 1 [Schlesinger/Robert Lienau, 1910, 1928]
"Schlafen, schlafen, nichts als schlafen!"
Heine, Heinrich, 1797-1856.
Geliebte Schöne (1904-05) [Universal-Edition, 1985] "Ernst ist der Frühling"
Jugendlieder, no. 18
Sehnsucht II (ca.1902) [Universal-Edition, 1985] "Mir träumte"
Jugendlieder, no. 12
LIEDERSTRAUSS.
Vielgeliebte schöne Frau [Universal-Edition, 1985]
"Spätherbstnebel, kalte Träume"
Jugendlieder, no. 11
Henckell, Karl Friedrich, 1864-1929.
Trinklied (1904-05) [unpubl.]
"Aus dem Notizbüchlein der Liebe"
Jugendlieder, no. 74
Hofmannsthal, Hugo Hofmann, Edler von, 1874-1929.
Ballade des äusseren Lebens (ca.1902) [unpubl.] "Und Kinder wachsen auf"
Jugendlieder, no. 63
Reiselied (ca.1902) [unpubl.]
"Wasser stürzt uns"
Jugendlieder, no. 46

Hohenberg, Paul
Läuterung (1904-05) [unpubl.]
"Heut' aber geh' ich"
Jugendlieder, no. 81
Sehnsucht I (ca.1902) [Universal-Edition, 1985] "Hier in der öden Fremde"
Jugendlieder, no. 10
Sehnsucht III (ca.1902) [Universal-Edition, 1985]
"Wenn die Nacht sich über die Welt senkt"
Jugendlieder, no. 14
Sommertag (1908) [Universal-Edition, 1928]
"Nun ziehen Tage über die Welt"
Also voice & orchestra, 1928; publ. 1955, 1969.
Holz, Arno, 1863-1929.
DAFNIS.
Er klagt, dass der Frühling so kurtz blüht (ca.1904) [unpubl.]
"Kleine Blumen"
Jugendlieder, no. 38
Ibsen, Henrik, 1828-1906.
SPILLEMAEND.
Spielleute (ca.1902) [Universal-Edition, 1985]
"Zu ihr stand all' mein Sehnen"
Jugendlieder, no. 4
Jacobowski, Ludwig, 1868-1900.
Grabschrift (1904-05) [Universal-Edition, 1985]
"Dem Auge fern, dem Herzen han!"
Jugendlieder, no. 31
Knodt, Karl Ernst, 1856-1917.
Süss sind mir die Schollen des Tales (1904-05) [unpubl.]
Jugendlieder, no. 37
Lenau, Nicolaus, 1802-1850.
SCHILFLIEDER.
Schilflied (1908) [Universal-Edition, 1928]
"Auf geheimen Waldespfade"
Also voice & orchestra, 1928; publ. 1955, 1969.
Liliencron, Detlov, Freiherr von, 1844-1909.
Tiefe Sehnsucht (1905) [unpubl.]
"Maienkätzchen, erster Gruss"
Jugendlieder, no. 42
Lorenz, F
Wo der Goldregen steht (ca.1902) [Universal-Edition, 1985]
"Eh' wir weiter gehen"
Jugendlieder, no. 5

Mell, Max, 1882-1971.
Der milde Herbst von Anno 45 (1904-05)
[unpubl.]
"Ich Uralter kann's erzählen"
Jugendlieder, no. 66
Mörike, Eduard Friedrich, 1804-1875.
Die Soldatenbraut (ca.1902) [unpubl.]
"Ach wenn's nur der König wüsst"
Jugendlieder, no. 58
Mombert, Alfred, 1872-1942.
Aus dem "Glühenden" [unpubl.]
"Warm die Lüfte"
Spaziergang (ca.1902) [unpubl.]
"Sie wandeln durch des Waldes
Grün"
Jugendlieder, no. 57
DER GLÜHENDE.
Nun ich der Riesen Stärksten, op. 2 no.
3
[Schlesinger/Robert Lienau, 1910,
1928]
Schlafend trägt man mich, op. 2 no. 2
[Schlesinger/Robert Lienau, 1910,
1928]
Warm die Lüfte, op. 2 no. 4
[Schlesinger/Robert Lienau, 1910,
1928]
**Monsterberg-Münckeman, Elimar
von, b.1877.**
Abschied (ca.1902) [Universal-Edition,
1985]
"Ein Spielmann, der muss reisen"
Jugendlieder, no. 7
No author
Verlassen (ca.1902) [unpubl.]
"Knabe dir gefiel"
Jugendlieder, no. 52
**Puttkamer, Marie Madeleine
(Günther), Freifrau, 1881-**
Vom Ende (1904-05) [unpubl.]
"Das ist aber das Ende"
Jugendlieder, no. 22
Rilke, Rainer Maria, 1875-1926.
Liebe (1904-05) [Universal-Edition,
1985] "Und wie mag die Liebe"
Jugendlieder, no. 28
Die Näherin (1904-05) [unpubl.]
"Alle Mädchen erwarten"
Jugendlieder, no. 35
Traumgekrönt (1907) [Universal-Edition,
1928]
"Das war der Tag der weissen
Chrysanthemen"
Also voice & orchestra, 1928; publ.
1955, 1969.

Roquette, Otto, 1824-1896.
*REBENKRANZ ZU WALDMEISTERS
SILBERNER HOCHZEIT:* In
der Früh.
Über Nacht und Tag (ca.1902)
[unpubl.] "In der Früh"
Jugendlieder, no. 41
**Rosenbaum, Kory Elizabeth, 1868-
1930.**
Liebeslied (ca.1902) [unpubl.]
"Knieend im Staube"
Jugendlieder, no. 8
Rückert, Friedrich, 1788-1866.
Ferne Lieder (1904-05) [Universal-
Edition, 1985] "Rosen!"
Jugendlieder, no. 16
Ich will die Fluren meiden (1904-05)
[Universal-Edition, 1985]
Jugendlieder, no. 17
Scherer, Georg, 1828-1909.
Am Strande (ca.1902) [unpubl.]
"Ich sass am Strand"
Jugendlieder, no. 44
Schlaf, Johannes, 1862-1941.
HELLDUNKEL (1899).
Im Zimmer (1905) [Universal-Edition,
1928]
"Herbstsonnenschein. Der liebe
Abend blickt"
Also voice & orchestra, 1928; publ.
1955, 1969.
Regen (?) [unpubl.]
"Geht ein grauer Mann"
Jugendlieder, no. 53
Winter (ca.1902) [unpubl.]
"Der schönste Cherub kommt"
Jugendlieder, no. 49
**Semler, Frida (Mrs. Mortimer
Seabury)**
Traum (1904-05) [unpubl.]
"Der Mondschein lag auf dem
Wasser"
Jugendlieder, no. 32
Stieler, Karl, 1842-1885.
Im Morgengrauen (1904-05) [Universal-
Edition, 1985]
"So harre ich schweigend"
Jugendlieder, no. 30
Storm, Theodor, 1817-1888.
Die Nachtigall (1905-06) [Universal-
Edition, 1928]
"Das macht, es hat die Nachtigall die
ganze Nacht gesungen"
Also voice & orchestra, 1928; publ.
1955, 1969.

COMPOSER Poet *Title* "First Line"

BERG, ALBAN, 1885-1935 *(continued)*
  Storm, Theodor, 1817-1888 *(continued)*
    Schliesse mir die Augen beide (1907, 2nd
      version 1925) [*Die Musik* 22 Jhrg.,
      Feb. heft, 1930, after p.352]
      Jugendlieder, no. 75. Also published:
      Universal-Edition, 1955.
  Wallpach zu Schwanenfeld, Arthur,
    ritter von, 1866-1946.
    Holophan (1904-05) [unpubl.]
      "Das Schratlein hockt"
      Jugendlieder, no. 68
  Walther von der Vogelweide, 12th
    cent.
    Unter der Linden (1900) [unpubl.]
      "Später der Linden bei der Haide"
      Jugendlieder, no. 3
  Wilhelm, Carl
    Sternenfall (ca.1902) [Universal-Edition,
      1985]
      "Meine Sehnsucht ist zum Licht"
      Jugendlieder, no. 13
  Wisbacher, Franz, 1849-1912.
    Vorüber (1904-05) [Universal-Edition,
      1985] "Die Luft ist kühl"
      Jugendlieder, no. 23
Berg' und Burgen schau'n herunter see
  Heine **SCHUMANN**
Die Berge see Schlegel, F. *ABENDRÖTE.*
  SCHUBERT
Bergerat, Émile, 1845-1923.
  SAINT-SAËNS *Romance pour* ***
Bergère see Clancier **SAUGUET**
"Bergère, bergère dans l'herbe . . . " *see*
  Bergère Clancier **SAUGUET**
Bergerie see Chabrillac, Léon **SAUGUET**
Bergeronnette see Lombard, F.
  SAINT-SAËNS
Les bergers see Banville *LES CARIATIDES*:
  livre 3, no. V. **AURIC**
Berggeist see Hesse **KILPINEN**
"Berggipfel erglühen" *see Ausfahrt* Scheffel
  JENSEN
"Bergkönig ritt durch die Lande" *see Gesang*
  Margit's Ibsen **WOLF**
Berglied see Schiller **ZELTER**
Bergman, Bo Hjalmar, 1869-1967.
  KILPINEN
    Adagio
    Du och jag
    Hjärtat
    Klockan
    Lillebarn
    Lyss till det djupa och stora
    Melodi

    Den sista stjärnan
    Skogen spelar. Älven rinner
    En sommarafton
    Stjärnöga
    Stormen kör i fjällen
    Under vintergatan
Der Bergmann see Unknown **LOEWE**
DER BERGMANN, no. 1
  LOEWE Giesebrecht *Im Schacht der*
    Adern und der Stufen
DER BERGMANN, no. 2
  LOEWE Giesebrecht *Von meines Hauses*
    engen Wänden
DER BERGMANN, no. 3
  LOEWE Giesebrecht *Unser Herzog hat*
    herrliche Taten vollbracht
DER BERGMANN, no. 4
  LOEWE Giesebrecht *Es steht ein Kelch*
    in der Kapelle
DER BERGMANN, no. 5
  LOEWE Giesebrecht *Als Weibesarm in*
    jungen Jahren
"Der Bergmann lebt beim Grubenlicht" *see*
  Der Bergmann Unknown **LOEWE**
Bergstedt, Harald Alfred, 1877-1965.
  NIELSEN
    Jeg ved en Laerkerede
    Solen er saa rød, Mor
Bergstimme see Heine **MEDTNER**
BERKELEY, LENNOX, 1903-1989.
  Antipater, of Sidon, fl.120 B.C.
    Spring song, op. 38 no. 2 (1951) [J. &
      W. Chester, 1953]
      "Now swallows build"
  Apollinaire, Guillaume, 1880-1918.
    ALCOOLS.
    Automne, op. 60/3 (1963) [unpubl.?]
  Auden, Wystan Hugh, 1907-1973.
    Carry her over the water, op. 53 no. 5
      (1958) [J. & W. Chester, 1960] same
    Eyes look into the well, op. 53 no. 4
      (1958) [J. & W. Chester, 1960] same
    Lauds, op. 53 no. 1 (1958) [J. & W.
      Chester, 1960]
      "Among the leaves the small birds
      sing"
    O lurcher-loving collier, black as night,
      op. 53 no. 2 (1958)
      [J. & W. Chester, 1960] same
    What's in your mind, my dove, op. 53 no.
      3 (1958) [J. & W. Chester, 1960]
      same
  Beddoes, Thomas Lovell, 1803-1849.
    All night a wind of music, op. 58 no. 2
      (1962) [J. & W. Chester, 1963] same

The mighty thoughts of an old world, op. 58 no. 1 (1962) [J. & W. Chester, 1963] same

Bridges, Robert Seymour, 1844-1930.
So sweet love seemed (ca.1959) [unpubl.]

Coleridge, Hartley, 1796-1849.
When we were idlers with the loitering rills, op. 58 no. 7 (1962) [J. & W. Chester, 1963] same

Davies, William Henry, 1871-1940.
Rich days, op. 58 no. 6 (1962) [J. & W. Chester, 1963]
"Welcome to you rich autumn days"

De La Mare, Walter, 1873-1956.
Afraid, op. 93 no. 3 (1977) [J. & W. Chester, 1978]
"Here lies, but seven years old"
All that's past, op. 65 no. 3 (1964) [J. & W. Chester, 1966]
"Very old are the woods"
High voice & guitar.
Another spring, op. 93 no. 2 (1977) [J. & W. Chester, 1978]
"What though the first pure snowdrop wilt and die"
The fleeting, op. 65 no. 5 (1964) [J. & W. Chester, 1966]
"The late wind failed"
High voice & guitar.
Full moon, op. 65 no. 2 (1964) [J. & W. Chester, 1966]
"One night, as Dick lay fast asleep"
High voice & guitar.
The horseman, op. 26 no. 1 (1946) [J. & W. Chester, 1948]
"I heard a horseman"
Mistletoe, op. 26 no. 2 (1946) [J. & W. Chester, 1948]
"Sitting under the mistletoe"
The moth, op. 65 no. 4 (1964) [J. & W. Chester, 1966]
"Isled in the midnight air"
High voice & guitar.
Poetry, op. 93 no. 1 (1977) [J. & W. Chester, 1978]
"In stagnant gloom I toil through day"
Poor Henry, op. 26 no. 3 (1946) [J. & W. Chester, 1948] "Think in it's glass"
Rachel, op. 65 no. 1 (1964) [J. & W. Chester, 1966]
"Rachel sings sweet, Oh, yes, at night"
High voice & guitar.
Silver, op. 26 no. 5 (1946) [J. & W. Chester, 1948]
"Slowly, silently, now the moon"

The song of the soldiers, op. 26 no. 4 (1946) [J. & W. Chester, 1948]
"As I sat musing"

Du Bellay, Joachim, ca.1525-1560.
D'UN VANNEUR DE BLÉ AUX VENTS:
A vous troppe légère.
The thresher (1925) [Oxford Univ. Press, 1927]
"You kindly winds who gaily go blowing"

Durrell, Lawrence, 1912-1990.
Lesbos, op. 58 no. 3 (1962) [J. & W. Chester, 1963]
"The Pleiades are sinking cool as paint"

Graves, Robert, 1895-1985.
Counting the beats, op. 60/4 (1963) [unpubl.?]

Herrick, Robert, 1591-1674.
Herrick songs, op. 89 (1974) [unpubl.?]
High voice & harp.
How love came in (1935) [Boosey & Hawkes, 1936] same

Hopkins, Gerard Manley, 1844-1889.
Hurrahing in harvest, op. 58 no. 5 (1962) [J. & W. Chester, 1963]
"Summer ends now"

Housman, Alfred Edward, 1859-1936.
Because I liked you better, op. 14/3 no. 5 (1940) [J. & W. Chester, 1983] same
He would not stay for me, op. 14/3 no. 3 (1940) [J. & W. Chester, 1983] same
Look not in my eyes, op. 14/3 no. 4 (1940) [J. & W. Chester, 1983] same
The street sounds to the soldiers' tread, op. 14/3 no. 2 (1940) [J. & W.Chester, 1983] same
LAST POEMS: XXVI.
The half-moon westers low, op. 14/3 no. 1 (1940) [J. & W. Chester, 1983] same

Labé, Louise Charly, called, 1526-1566.
Tant que mes yeux (A memory) [Oxford Univ. Press, 1941]
"Tant que mes yeux"

O'Malley, Patrick
The beacon barn [J. & W. Chester, 1940]
"Now on another land I turn two quiet eyes"
One of 5 songs, op. 14/2 (ca. 1939-40)

Passerat, Jean, 1534-1602.
Ode du premier jour de Mai [J. & W. Chester, 1945]
"Laisons le litet le sommiel"

BERKELEY, LENNOX, 1903-1989
(*continued*)
Plato, ca.429-347 B.C.
   To Aster, op. 38 no. 3 (1951) [J. & W.
      Chester, 1953]
      "Thou gazest on the stars"
Sappho, 625? B.C.-570 B.C.
   Epitaph of Timas, op. 38 no. 1 (1951)
      [J. & W. Chester, 1953]
      "Behold the dust of Timas dead"
Shên-Yo, 441-513.
   Dreaming of a dead lady, op. 78 no. 3
      (1971) [J. & W. Chester, 1975]
      "I heard at night your long sighs"
Ssu-k'ung Shu, 8th century A. D.
   The riverside village, op. 78 no. 5 (1971)
      [J. & W. Chester, 1975]
      "My fishing done, I have returned"
Tennyson, Alfred Tennyson, 1st
baron, 1809-1892.
   Tonight the winds begin to rise, op. 58
      no. 4 (1962) [J. & W. Chester, 1963]
      same
Unknown
   The Lowlands of Holland (1947)
      [unpubl.]
Wu-Ti, Han dynasty, 157-87 B. C.
   The autumn wind, op. 78 no. 2 (1971)
      [J. & W. Chester, 1975]
      "Autumn wind rises; white clouds fly"
Wu-Ti, Liang dynasty, 464-549.
   People hide their love, op. 78 no. 1
      (1971) [J. & W. Chester, 1975]
      "Who says that it's by my desire"
Yang Knang
   Late spring, op. 78 no. 4 (1971) [J. & W.
      Chester, 1975]
      "Here in Loyang spring tarries"
Berlepsch, Emilie von, 1757-1830.
   DAS GRAB.
      LOEWE *Lied am Grabe*
BERLIOZ, HECTOR, 1803-1869.
Beauvoir, Roger de, 1806-1866.
   Zäide (Boléro, 1845, 1850) [Werke, v.
      17, pp. 191, 197]
      "Ma ville, ma belle ville"
      Later in *Feuillets d'album*, op. 19 no. 1.
Béranger, Pierre Jean de, 1780-1857.
   Les champs (1834, 1850) [Werke, v. 17,
      pp. 107, 115]
      "Rose, partons! voici l'aurore"
      Revised version in *Feuillets d'album*,
         op. 19 no. 2.
Berlioz, Hector, 1803-1869.
   Chant de bonheur (1831-32) [Werke, v.
      17, p. 66] "O mon bonheur, ma vie"

   From *La mort d'Orpheé*; also in *Lélio*,
      op. 14 bis no. 4.
Bouclon, Adolphe de, 1813-1882.
   Le matin (1849 or earlier) [Werke, v. 17,
      p. 227] "Pour chanter le retour du
      jour"
   Petit oiseau (1850) [Werke, v. 17, p.
      235] "Pour chanter le retour du jour"
Brizeux, Julien Auguste Pélage, 1806-
1858.
   Le chant des Bretons (1834; rev. 1850)
      [Werke, v. 17, pp. 220, 223]
      "Oui, nous sommes encor les hommes
         d'Armorique"
      1850 revision in cycle.
   Le jeune pâtre breton (1833) [Werke, v.
      17, p. 101]
      "Dès que la grive est éveille"
      Horn obbligato.
Dante Aligheri, 1265-1321.
   Nessun maggior, page d'album (1847)
      [Werke, v. 17, p. 211]
      "Aucun plaisir sur terre"
Deschamps, Émile, 1791-1871.
   Premiers transports (1839) [Werke, v.
      17, p. 70]
      "Premiers transports que nul n'oublie"
      With cello obbligato, chorus *ad lib.*
Du Boys, Albert, 1804-1889.
   Le pêcheur (ca.1828) [Werke, v. 17, p.
      56] "L'onde frémit, lónde s'agite"
      Later in *Lélio* as op. 14 bis no. 1.
   Toi qui l'amais, verse des pleurs (?1822-
      23) [Werke, v. 17, p. 6]
      "Sous le saule de la prairie"
Dumas, Alexandre, the elder, 1803-
1870.
   La belle Isabeau (1843 or earlier)
      [Werke, v. 17, p. 181]
      "Dans la montagne noire"
      Later *Feuillets d'album*, op. 19 no. 5.
Florian, Jean Pierre Claris de, 1755-
1794.
   Le maure jaloux (?1818-22) [Werke, v.
      17, p. 12]
      "Je vais revoir la beauté que j'adore"
Gautier, Théophile, 1811-1872.
   Absence, op. 7 no. 4 (1840-41) [Werke,
      v. 17, p. 157]
      "Reviens, reviens, ma bien aimée"
   Au cimetière, op. 7 no. 5 (1840-41)
      [Werke, v. 17, p. 161]
      "Connaissez-vous la blanche tombe"
   L'Île inconnue, op. 7 no. 6 (1840-41)
      [Werke, v. 17, p. 173]
      "Dites, la jeune belle"

La spectre de la rose, op. 7 no. 2 (1840-41) [Werke, v. 17, pp. 137, 143] "Souléve ta paupière close"

Sur les lagunes, op. 7 no. 3 (1840-41) [Werke, v. 17, p. 149] "Ma belle amie est morte"

Villanelle, op. 7 no. 1 (1840-41) [Werke, v. 17, p. 131] "Quand viendra la saison nouvelle"

Gérard de Nerval, Gérard Labrunie, 1808-1855.

Le roi de Thulé, op. 1 no. 6 (1828) [To be in New collected works, v. 15] "Autrefois un roi de Thulé"

Guérin, Léon, 1807-ca.1885.

Je crois en vous (1834) [Werke, v. 17, p. 123] "Quand mon âme ravie"

Hugo, Victor Marie, comte, 1802-1885.

La captive, op. 12 (1832) [Werke, v. 17, pp. 79, 85, 93] "Si je n'étais captive" Third version also voice & orchestra.

Leuven, Adolphe de, grefve Ribbing, called, 1800-1884.

Le chasseur danois (1845) [Werke, v. 17, p. 205] "Entendez-vous dans la bruyère?" Later *Feuillets d'album,* op. 19 no. 6.

Moore, Thomas, 1779-1852.

Adieu, Bessy! op. 2 no. 8 (1829) [Werke, v. 17, p. 35] "Loin de toi, loin de toi"

La belle voyageuse, op. 2 no. 4 (1829) [Werke, v. 17, p. 18] "Elle s'en va sculcttc"

Le coucher du soleil! op. 2 no. 1 (1829) [Werke, v. 17, p. 24] "Que j'aime cette heure rêveuse"

Élégie, op. 2 no. 9 (1827-29) [Werke, v. 17, p. 48] "Quand celui qui t'adore"

L'origine de la harpe, op. 2 no. 7 (1829) [Werke, v. 17, p. 28] "Cette harpe, chérie, à te chanter fidèle"

Shakespeare, William, 1564-1616.

La mort d'Ophélie (1847 or earlier) [Werke, v. 17, p. 212] "Auprès d'un torrent Ophélie cueillait" Text "after Shakespeare" by Ernest Legrouvé.

Unknown

Le dépit de la bergère (1819 or earlier) [Werke, v. 17, p. 2] "De mon berger volage"

Wailly, Léon de, 1804-1863.

Chansonette (1835) [To be in New collected works, v. 15] "Au levant làbas"

Berlioz, Hector, 1803-1869.
BERLIOZ *Chant de bonheur*

Bern, Maximilian, 1849-1923.
REGER *Mit Rosen bestreut*

Bernadette see Jammes **MILHAUD**

Bernard, Josef Karl, 1780-1850.
SCHUBERT *Vergebliche Liebe*

Bernays, Michael, 1834-1897.
LASSEN *An die Nacht*

Bernhard, Lily, fl.1840.
SCHUMANN *Mädchen-Schwermuth*

Berni, Francesco, 1497 or 8-1535.
MALIPIERO
Cancheri e beccafichi magri arosto
Chiome d'argento fine, irte e attorte

BERNSTEIN, LEONARD, 1918-1990.

Bernstein, Leonard, 1918-1990.

Afterthought (1945) [G. Schirmer, 1951; withdrawn] "The lost one"

A big Indian and a little Indian (1943) [M. Witmark, 1943] same

Get hep! (1955) [G. Schirmer, 1955] same
Marching song commissioned by Michigan State College.

I hate music! (1943) [M. Witmark, 1943] same

I just found out today (1943) [M. Witmark, 1943] same

Jupiter has seven moons (1943) [M. Witmark, 1943] same

My mother says that babies come in bottles (1943) [M. Witmark, 1943] same

Piccola serenata (1979) [Jalni Publ., 1988] "Da ga da ga dum da lai la lo"

Silhouette (1951) [G. Schirmer, 1951] "A last little bird on a palm feather riding"

Comden, Betty, 1919- and Adolph Green, 1915-2002.

So pretty (1968) [G. Schirmer, 1968] "We were learning in our school today" Text by Comden and Adolph Green.

Dumont, Émile
LA BONNE CUISINE FRANÇAISE.
Civet à toute vitesse (1947) [G. Schirmer, 1949] "Lorsqu'on sera très pressé"

Plum pudding (1947) [G. Schirmer, 1949] "Deux cents cinquante grammes de raisins de Malaga"

Queues de boeuf (1947) [G. Schirmer, 1949] "La queue de boeuf n'est pas"

Tavouk gueunksis (1947) [G. Schirmer, 1949] same

COMPOSER Poet *Title* "First Line"

BERNSTEIN, LEONARD, 1918-1990
(continued)
Rilke, Rainer Maria, 1875-1926.
Extinguish my eyes (1949) [G. Schirmer, 1960] same
When my soul touches yours (1949) [G. Schirmer, 1960] same
Bernstein, Leonard, 1918-1990.
BERNSTEIN
Afterthought
A big Indian and a little Indian
Get hep!
I hate music!
I just found out today
Jupiter has seven moons
My mother says that babies come in bottles
Piccola serenata
Silhouette
Berntsen, Anton
NIELSEN
AE Lastrae
Den jenn a den anden
Jens Madsen a An-Sofi
Wo Daetter
Bertha's Lied in der Nacht see Grillparzer **SCHUBERT**
Bertheroy, Jean, pseud. *see* Le Barillier, Mme. Berthe, 1868-1927.
Berthrams Grablied see Scott *MINSTRELSY OF THE SCOTISH BORDER.* **JENSEN**
Bertin, Louise, 1805-1877.
GOUNOD *Si la mort est le but*
Bertrand, Friedrich Anton Franz, 1787-1830.
SCHUBERT
Adelwold und Emma
Minona
Beruhigung see Löwenstein **RUBINSTEIN**
Beruhigung see Matthisson **ZELTER**
Beruhigung see Unknown **SPOHR**
Besa el aura que gimé blandamente see Bécquer **TURINA**
Bescheidene Liebe see Unknown **WOLF**
Der bescheidene Schäfer see Weisse **REGER**
Das bescheidene Wünschlein see Spitteler **SCHOECK**
Bescheidung see Rückert **LOEWE**
Beschwörung see Sauter, Lilly von, d. ca. 1970. **KRENEK**
Bessie Bobtail see Stephens, James **BARBER**
Bessonnitsa see Tiutchev **MEDTNER**
Sleepless
Beständighet see Josephson, E. **KILPINEN**

"Das beste Bier im ganzen Nest" see Margreth am Thore Roquette **JENSEN**
LE BESTIAIRE. see **APOLLINAIRE**
Le carpe **POULENC**
La chèvre du Thibet **POULENC**
Le dauphin **POULENC**
Le dromadaire **POULENC**
L'écrevisse **POULENC**
La sauterelle **POULENC**
La souris **POULENC**
LE BESTIAIRE, no. 1
POULENC Apollinaire *Le dromadaire*
LE BESTIAIRE, no. 2
POULENC Apollinaire *La chèvre du Thibet*
LE BESTIAIRE, no. 3
POULENC Apollinaire *La sauterelle*
LE BESTIAIRE, no. 4
POULENC Apollinaire *Le dauphin*
LE BESTIAIRE, no. 5
POULENC Apollinaire *L'écrevisse*
LE BESTIAIRE, no. 6
POULENC Apollinaire *Le carpe*
Bestimmung see Huch **PFITZNER, SZYMANOWSKI**
DER BESUCH. see Schiller
Dithyrambe **SCHUBERT**
Besuch im Kuhstall see Iłłakowiczówna **SZYMANOWSKI** *Wizyta u krowy*
Besuch in Urach see Mörike **SCHOECK**
Beta, Ottomar, 1845-1913.
SCHÖNBERG *Wanderlied*
Bête me veut, bête me prend see Birot, P. A. **SAUGUET**
Die Betende see Matthisson **SCHUBERT, ZELTER**
Bêtes et méchants see Éluard **SAUGUET**
BETHANE THE SMITH: Chapter XVI. *see* Farnol *Melancholy:* a song "à la Debussy" **COPLAND**
Bethléem see Anon. **GOUNOD**
Bethlehem see Unknown **LOEWE**
Bethlehem down see Blunt **HESELTINE**
Betragt mit svage spind see Oehlenschläger **NIELSEN**
Die Betrogene spricht see Ritter **REGER**
Die betrogene Welt see Weisse **MOZART**
THE BETROTHAL. see Aldrich
Verlobung **LASSEN**
The betrothed see Witwicki **CHOPIN**
Narzeczony
The better land see Gounod **GOUNOD**
Le pays bienheureux
The better land see Hemans **BENNETT**
Der Bettler see Goethe **LOEWE** *Ballade vom vertriebenen und zurückkehrenden Grafen*

Der Bettler *see* Unknown
  MENDELSSOHN-BARTHOLDY
Bettlerlied see Anon. **WEBER**
"Between the dark and the daylight" *see*
  The children's hour Longfellow **IVES**
"Beugt euch aus euren Wolken nieder" *see*
  Ossians Lied nach dem Falle Nathos'
  Macpherson **SCHUBERT**
Beware see Longfellow **BRITTEN,**
  GOUNOD
Die Bewegung see Voss **ZELTER**
"Beweint die, so geweint in Babels Land!" *see*
  Weint um Israel! Byron **LOEWE**
Bewitched see Mickiewicz **CHAÏKOVSKIÏ**
  Ali mat' menia rozhala
"Bey dem Glanze der Abendröthe" *see*
  Die Bekehrte Goethe **ZELTER**
Beylié, Laurence de
  POULENC *Nuage*
Beyond the hills see Anon. **PROKOFIEV** *Za*
  goroiu
Beyond the window see Polonsky *VIZOV.*
  CHAÏKOVSKIÏ *Za oknom v teni mel'kaet*
Beyond the woods see Anon. **PROKOFIEV**
  Za lesochkom
BEZ SOLNTSA, no. 1
  MUSORGSKIÏ Golenishchev-Kutuzov
    V chetyrekh stenakh
BEZ SOLNTSA, no. 2
  MUSORGSKIÏ Golenishchev-Kutuzov
    Menia ty v tolpe ne uznala
BEZ SOLNTSA, no. 3
  MUSORGSKIÏ Golenishchev-Kutuzov
    Okon'en prazdnyï, shumnyï den'
BEZ SOLNTSA, no. 4
  MUSORGSKIÏ Golenishchev-Kutuzov
    Skuchaï
BEZ SOLNTSA, no. 5
  MUSORGSKIÏ Golenishchev-Kutuzov
    Elegiia
BEZ SOLNTSA, no. 6
  MUSORGSKIÏ Golenishchev-Kutuzov
    Nad rekoï
Bezzvezdnaya polnoch' see Khomyakov
  BALAKIREV
"Bezzviezdnaia polnoch' dyshala prokhaladoï"
  see Bezzvezdnaya polnoch'
  Khomyakov **BALAKIREV**
Bialik, Chaim Nachman *see* Bialik,
  Hayyim Nahman, 1873-1934.
Bialik, Hayyim Nahman, 1873-1934.
  GIDEON
    The nest
    The swing
Bialy krag ksiezyca olbrzymi see
  Iwaszkiewicz **SZYMANOWSKI**

Bianchi, Tommaso
  VERDI *More, Elisa, lo stanco poeta*
Bibesco, Marthe Lucie (Lahovary),
  Princesse, 1887-1945.
  SAUGUET *Mouton Blanc*
Bible
  BLACHER
    Psalm 121
    Psalm 141
    Psalm 142
  DIAMOND *David mourns for Absalmon*
  DVOŘÁK
    Bože! Bože! Píseň novou
    Hospodin jest muj pastýř
    Oblak a mrákota
    Popatřiž na mne a smiluj se nade mnou
    Pozdvihuji očí svých k horám
    Při řekách babylonských
    Skrýše má paveza má Ty jsi
    Slyš, Ó Bože! slyš modlitbu mou
    Slyš, Ó Bože, volání mé
    Zpívejte Hospodinu píseň novou
  GOUNOD
    Entreat me not to leave thee
    My beloved spake
  HINDEMITH
    Angelus Domini apparuit
    Ascendente Jesu in naviculam
    Cum descendisset Jesus de monte
    Cum factus esset Jesus annorum
      duodecim
    Cum natus esset
    Defuncto Herode
    Dicebat Jesus scribis et pharisaeis
    Dixit Jesus Petro
    Erat Joseph et Maria
    Exiit edictum
    Nuptiae factae sunt
    Pastores loquebantur
    Vidit Joannes Jesum venientem
  HONEGGER
    Mimaamaquim
    Psalm XXXIV
    Psalm CXI
    Psalm CXXXVIII
  KRENEK
    The light is sweet
    The 104th Psalm
  LUENING
    Answer not a fool according to his folly
    The mouth of the righteous man
    A righteous man falling down before the
      wicked
    The slothful man saith
    There is a generation that curseth their
      father
    These six things doth the Lord hate

Bible *(continued)*
MENDELSSOHN-BARTHOLDY
Der du die Menschen lässest sterben
Doch der Herr, er leitet die Irrenden
recht
RACHMANINOFF *From the Gospel of St.*
John, XV: 13
SCHOECK
Psalm 23
Psalm 100
SCHUBERT *Der 13. Psalm*
THOMSON
By night
I am my beloved's
Two settings: 1924 and 1926.
O, my dove
Return, O Shulamite
Two settings: 1924 and 1926.
Thou that dwellest in the gardens
Two settings: 1924 and 1926.
VAUGHAN WILLIAMS
The bird's song
The pilgrim's psalm
The song of the leaves of life and the
water of life
Watchful's song
LUKE 2: 9-15.
ROREM *An angel speaks to the*
shepherds
MATTHEW 6: 9-13.
ROREM *The Lord's prayer*
MATTHEW 27: 62-66; 28.
ROREM *The resurrection*
PROVERBS 31.
GIDEON *Eishet chayil*
PSALM 62.
REGER *Meine Seele ist still zu Gott*
PSALM 86.
ROREM *Psalm 86: A prayer of David*
PSALM 100.
ROREM *A psalm of praise*
PSALM 119.
REGER *Geistliches Lied "Wohl denen"*
PSALM 120.
ROREM *A song of David*
PSALM 127.
GIDEON *Hinei nachalat adonai baním*
PSALM 128.
GIDEON *Y' gia kapecha ki Tocheil*
PSALM 134.
ROREM *Psalm 134*
PSALM 142.
ROREM *Psalm 142*
PSALM 148.
ROREM *Psalm 148*
PSALM 150.
ROREM *Psalm 150*

BIBLICAL SONGS, no. 1
DVOŘÁK Bible *Oblak a mrákota*
BIBLICAL SONGS, no. 2
DVOŘÁK Bible *Skrýše má paveza má Ty*
jsi
BIBLICAL SONGS, no. 3
DVOŘÁK Bible *Slyš, Ó Bože! slyš*
modlitbu mou
BIBLICAL SONGS, no. 4
DVOŘÁK Bible *Hospodin jest muj pastýř*
BIBLICAL SONGS, no. 5
DVOŘÁK Bible *Bože! Bože! Píseň novou*
BIBLICAL SONGS, no. 6
DVOŘÁK Bible *Slyš, Ó Bože, volání mé*
BIBLICAL SONGS, no. 7
DVOŘÁK Bible *Při řekách babylonských*
BIBLICAL SONGS, no. 8
DVOŘÁK Bible *Popatřiž na mne a smiluj*
se nade mnou
BIBLICAL SONGS, no. 9
DVOŘÁK Bible *Pozdvihuji očí svých k*
horám
BIBLICAL SONGS, no. 10
DVOŘÁK Bible *Zpívejte Hospodinu píseň*
novou
Bickle, Judith Brundrett
QUILTER *Daisies after rain*
Bid me to live see Herrick **CARPENTER**
"Bid me to live" *see To Anthea, who may*
command him anything Herrick **ROREM**
Biegeleben, Rüdiger, Freiherr von
LISZT *Und sprich*
"Bien courte, hélas! est l'espérance" *see*
Chanson Contamine **SATIE**
"Bienchen, Bienchen, Bienchen wiegt sich im
Sonnenschein" *see Wiegenlied* Dehmel
REGER
"Bienchen, Bienchen wiegt sich im
Sonnenschein" *see Wiegenliedchen*
Dehmel **STRAUSS**
Die Bienen see Kiesekamo **REGER**
"Bienen summen, wie schwer zu tragen" *see*
Bienenweben Giesebrecht **LOEWE**
Bienenweben see Giesebrecht **LOEWE**
Bienheureux le coeur sincère see Barbier, J.
GOUNOD
"Bien-tôt nous plongerous dans les froides
ténèbres" *see Chant d'automne* Baudelaire
FAURÉ
Bierbaum, Otto Julius, 1865-1910.
BERG
Lied des Schiffermädels
Nachtgesang
REGER
Aus der Ferne in der Nacht

Flieder
Frauenhaar
Freundliche Vision
Gegen Abend
Letzte Bitte
Nachtgang
Ritter rät dem Knappen dies
Schmied Schmerz
Traum durch die Dämmerung
SCHÖNBERG *Gigerlette*
STRAUSS
Freundliche Vision,
Nachtgang
Schlagende Herzen
Traum durch die Dämmerung
Wir beide wollen springen
SZYMANOWSKI *Die schwarze Laute*
DER JUNGEN HEXE LIED.
STRAUSS *Jung Hexenlied*
The big chariot see Unknown *THE BOOK*
OF SONGS. **BRITTEN**
A big Indian and a little Indian see
Bernstein **BERNSTEIN**
"*A big October morning*" *see Walking* Ives
IVES
Bigorie, L
GOUNOD *Les vacances*
"*Les bijoux aux poitrines*" *see Mazurka*
Vilmorin **POULENC**
Das Bild see Unknown **SCHUBERT**
Bild der Liebe see Frey, F. **WEBERN**
BILDER DER HEIMAT AUS PERSIEN, Heft
II no. 2
LOEWE Stieglitz *Ali im Garten*
BILDER DER HEIMAT AUS PERSIEN, Heft
II no. 3
LOEWE Stieglitz *Assad mit dem Selam*
BILDER DER HEIMAT AUS PERSIEN, Heft
II no. 4
LOEWE Stieglitz *Taubenpost*
BILDER DER HEIMAT AUS PERSIEN, Heft
II no. 5
LOEWE Stieglitz *Gulhinde am Putztische*
BILDER DER HEIMAT AUS PERSIEN, Heft
II no. 6
LOEWE Stieglitz *Abendgesang*
BILDER DES ORIENTS, Heft I no. 1
LOEWE Stieglitz *Die Geister der Wüste*
BILDER DES ORIENTS, Heft I no. 2
LOEWE Stieglitz *Der verschmachtende*
Pilger
BILDER DES ORIENTS, Heft I no. 3
LOEWE Stieglitz *Melek in der Wüste*
BILDER DES ORIENTS, Heft I no. 4
LOEWE Stieglitz *Die Oasis*

BILDER DES ORIENTS, Heft I no. 5
LOEWE Stieglitz *Lied eines Vögleins in*
der Oasis
BILDER DES ORIENTS, Heft I no. 6
LOEWE Stieglitz *Melek am Quell*
BILDER DES ORIENTS, Heft II no. 1
LOEWE Stieglitz *Maisuna am Brunnen*
Bilder schon entflohner Stunden see Recke,
Ewald von der **ZELTER**
BILLY BUD, FORETOPMAN. see Melville
Billy in the Darbies **DIAMOND**
Billy in the Darbies see Melville *BILLY*
BUD, FORETOPMAN. **DIAMOND**
Bílý sníh see Apollinaire **MARTINŮ**
La blanche neige
"*Bin ein Feuer hell, das lodert*" *see*
Waldmädchen Eichendorff **WOLF**
"*Bin jung gewesen, kann auch mit reden*" *see*
Rat einer Alter Mörike **WOLF**
"*Bin mit dir im Wald gegangen*" *see Traurige*
Wege Lenau **WOLF**
"*Bin nur ein armer Hirtenknab*" *see*
Hirtenknabe Schumann **SCHUMANN**
"*Bin so müde*" *see Du machst mich traurig-*
hör' Lasker-Schüler **HINDEMITH**
Binder, Franz Rudolf Immanuel, 1810-
1846.
LOEWE *Das Grab zu Ephesus*
Binyon, Laurence, 1869-1943.
QUILTER
The answer
At close of day
BIONDINA, no. 1
GOUNOD Zaffira *Da qualche tempo*
BIONDINA, no. 2
GOUNOD Zaffira *Biondina bella*
BIONDINA, no. 3
GOUNOD Zaffira *Ier l'ho scontrata*
BIONDINA, no. 4
GOUNOD Zaffira *Le labbra ella*
compose
BIONDINA, no. 5
GOUNOD Zaffira *E stati al quanto*
BIONDINA, no. 6
GOUNOD Zaffira *Ho messo nuove*
BIONDINA, no. 7
GOUNOD Zaffira *Se come io son poeta*
BIONDINA, no. 8
GOUNOD Zaffira *Siam' iti l'altro giorno*
BIONDINA, no. 9
GOUNOD Zaffira *E le campane hanno*
suonato
BIONDINA, no. 10
GOUNOD Zaffira *Ell' è malata!*
BIONDINA, no. 11
GOUNOD Zaffira *Ier fù mandata*

COMPOSER Poet *Title* "First Line"

BIONDINA, no. 12
  GOUNOD Zaffira *L' ho compagnata*
Biondina bella see Zaffira **GOUNOD**
La Biondina in gondoleta see Anon. **HAHN**
Biplan le matin see Cocteau **AURIC**
"A bird a nest" *see Proverb III* Blake,
  William **BRITTEN**
The bird-catcher see Runeberg **SIBELIUS**
  Fågelfängaren
"A birdless heaven, sea-dusk" *see Tutto è
  sciolto* Joyce **IRELAND**
The birds see Belloc, Hilaire **BRITTEN,
  HESELTINE**
The bird's song see Bible **VAUGHAN
  WILLIAMS**
The bird's story see Ibsen *EN FUGLEVISE.*
  DELIUS *Eine Vogelweise*
"The birds take cover on the ground" *see
  Jägargossen* Runeberg **SIBELIUS**
"Birg, O Veilchen, in deinem blauen Kelche"
  see An ein Veilchen Hölty **BRAHMS**
Birga, Arturo
  RISPETTI TOSCANI.
    RESPIGHI
      Quando nasceste voi
      Razzolan, sopra a l'aja, le galline . . .
      Venitelo a vedere 'l mi'piccino . . .
      Viene di là, lontan lontano . . .
"Birke, Birke, des Waldes Zier" *see
  Der Bräutigam und die Birke* Pfarrius
  SCHUMANN
Biron, Armand de Gontaut, baron de
  MASSENET *La dernière lettre de Werther
    à Charlotte*
Birot, Pierre-Albert
  SAUGUET
    Bête me veut, bête me prend
    Démon des mains, parfait visage
    Pourtant il y a encore autre chose
The birth of pleasure see Unknown
  LUENING
A birthday see Rossetti, Christina
  MILHAUD, ROREM
A BIRTHDAY HANSEL, no. 1
  BRITTEN Burns *Birthday song*
A BIRTHDAY HANSEL, no. 2
  BRITTEN Burns *My early walk*
A BIRTHDAY HANSEL, no. 3
  BRITTEN Burns *Wee Willie*
A BIRTHDAY HANSEL, no. 4
  BRITTEN Burns *My Hoggie*
A BIRTHDAY HANSEL, no. 5
  BRITTEN Burns *Afton water*
A BIRTHDAY HANSEL, no. 6
  BRITTEN Burns *The winter*
A BIRTHDAY HANSEL, no. 7
  BRITTEN Burns *Leezie Lindsay*

Birthday song see Burns **BRITTEN**
La bise see Carême **MILHAUD**
"Une bise aigre et monotone fait grincer les
  girouettes des maisons" *see L'heure du
  retour* Chalupt **ROUSSEL**
Bishop, Elizabeth, 1911-1979.
  ROREM
    Casabianca
    Conversation
    Detective story
    Insomnia
    Letter to New York
    Visits to St. Elizabeths
  SONGS FOR A COLORED SINGER, VI.
    ROREM *What's that shining in the
      leaves*
"Bist auf ewig du gegangen" *see Erwartung*
  Unknown **MENDELSSOHN-
  BARTHOLDY**
Bist du! see Metschersky **LISZT**
"Bist ja noch ganz allein" *see Der Abendstern*
  Enslin **LOEWE**
Biterolf (Im Lager von Akkon 1190) *see*
  Scheffel **WOLF**
Biterolf und der Schmied von Ruhla see
  Scheffel
  *DER BRAUTWILLKOMM AUF
    WARTBURG.* **LISZT**
Bitt' ihn, O Mutter, bitte den Knaben see
  Anon. **WOLF**
Bitte see Glücklich **MACDOWELL**
Bitte see Holst **REGER**
BITTE. see Lenau
  Das dunkle Auge **LOEWE**
Bitte see Lenau **FRANZ, RUBINSTEIN**
Bitte see Unknown **REGER**
Bitte, bitte! see Unknown **SPOHR**
Bitte um einen seligen Tod see Herman
  REGER
Bitte zu Gott um Frieden see Telschow
  LOEWE
Bitten see Gellert **BEETHOVEN**
Bitteres Gedenken see Wildenbruch
  LASSEN
Bitteres zu sagen denkst du see Daumer
  HAFIS. **BRAHMS**
Das bittersüsse Lied see Löns **KILPINEN**
BIZET, GEORGES, 1838-1875.
  Arvers, Félix, 1806-1850.
    Ma vie a son secret (1868) [G.
      Hartmann/Heugel, 1868] same
  Barbier, Jules, 1825-1901.
    La chanson de la rose [Choudens, 1886]
      "Viens à moi! viens à moi!"
    N'oublions pas! (1868) [Choudens, 1886]
      "Elle étais jeune et jolie"

Bouilhet, Louis Hyacinthe, 1822-1869.
Chanson d'avril (1866) [Choudens, 1867]
"Lève-toi! lève-toi! le printemps vient
de maître!"

Courmont, Louis de, 1828-1900.
Rêve de la bien-aimée (1868) [G.
Hartmann/Heugel, 1868] "J'ai rêvé que
mon coeur était comme jadis"

Delavigne, Jean François Casimir,
1793-1843.
Vous ne priez pas [Choudens, 1873]
"Mon bien aimé, dans mes doulcurs"

Desbordes-Valmore, Marceline
Félicité Josèphe, 1786-1859.
Berceuse (1868) [G. Hartmann/Heugel,
1868] "Si l'enfant som meille"

Ferrier, Paul, 1843-1920.
Aimons, rêvons! (1868) [Choudens, 1886]
same
Aubade [Choudens, 1886]
"Ma belle, le jour va paraitre"
Conte [Choudens, 1886]
"Le roi vieilli s'accoude au balcon du
palais"
Le doute! (1868) [Choudens, 1886]
"Ah! si vraiment l'indifférence"
La nuit (1868) [Choudens, 1886]
"Mi nuit! le flat murmure el le ciel
étincè le"

Gautier, Théophile, 1811-1872.
Absence [Choudens, 1872]
"Reviens, reviens, ma bien aimée"

Gille, Philippe Emile François, 1831-
1901.
Pastel [Choudens, 1886]
"C'est un portrait de jeune fille"
Si vous aimez! [Choudens, 1886] same
Voyage [Choudens, 1886] "Tous deux
vers la rive lointaine"

Glan, Alexandre
Le colibri (ca.1870) [unpubl.]

Hugo, Victor Marie, comte, 1802-1885.
Adieux de l'hôtesse arabe (1866)
[Choudens, 1867] "Puisque rien ne
t'arrête en cet heureux pays"
Après l'hiver (1866) [Choudens, 1867]
"Tout revit, ma bien aimée!"
La chanson du fou (1868) [G. Hartmann/
Heugel, 1868] "An soleil couchant, toi
qui vas cherchant fortune"
La coccinelle (1868) [G. Hartmann/
Heugel, 1868] "Elle me dit: quelque
chose, me tourmente"
Guitare (1866) [Heugel, 1866]
"Tra, la, la, la, la, la, comment,
disaient-ils"

Sérénade: Oh, quand je dors [unpubl.]
Voeu [unpubl.]

Lamartine, Alphonse Marie Louis de
Prat de, 1790-1869.
L'âme humaine est pareille au doux ciel
[unpubl.]
Chant d'amour (1872) [Choudens, 1872]
"Viens, cherchons une ombre propice"
Douce mer (1866) [Choudens, 1867]
"Murmure autour de ma nacelle"
Le grillon (1866) [Heugel, 1866]
"Grillon solitaire ici comme moi"

Mendès, Catulle Abraham, 1841-1909.
L'abandonnée (1868?) [Choudens, 1886]
"D'autre femmes m'ont pris son regard
sa pensée!"
Le gascon (1868) [Choudens, 1886]
"Ca dé dis! lorsque je me fâche"
La sirène (1868) [Choudens, 1886]
"Sous le flot qui déferle"
Fragment of *La coupe du Roi de
Thulé.*

Millevoye, Charles Hubert, 1782-1816.
Rose d'amour (1866) [Heugel, 1866]
same
Vieille chanson (1865) [Choudens, 1865]
"Dans les bois l'amoureux Myrtil"

Musset, Alfred de, 1810-1857.
À une fleur (1866) [Heugel, 1866]
"Que me veux-tu, chère fleurette"
Adieux à Suzon (1866) [Heugel, 1866]
"Adieu, Suzon, adieu, ma rose blonde"

No author
Vocalise pour ténor (1849) [unpubl.]
Wordless.

Pailleron, Édouard Jules Henri, 1834-
1899.
Tarantelle [Choudens, 1872]
"Tra la la . . . "

Regnard, Jean François, 1655-1709.
Pastorale (1868) [G. Hartmann/Heugel,
1868] "Un jour de printemps"

Rolland, Olivier
Petite Marguerite (1854) [Cendrier,
1854]
Reissued as *En Avril* with new words
by Silvestre [Choudens, 1888]
La rose et l'abeille (1854) [Cendrier,
1854]
Reissued as *Rive d'amour* with new
words by Silvestre [Choudens, 1888]

Ronsard, Pierre de, 1524-1585.
Sonnet (1866) [Heugel, 1866]
"Vous méprisez nature!"

Silvestre, Paul Armond, 1837-1901.
En Avril [Choudens, 1888]
Originally *Petite Marguerite* with
words by Rolland [Cendrier, 1854]

COMPOSER Poet *Title* "First Line"

BIZET, GEORGES, 1838-1875 *(continued)*
  Silvestre, Paul Armond, 1837-1901
  (continued)
    Rive d'amour [Choudens, 1888]
      Originally *La rose et l'abeille* with
        words by Rolland [Cendrier, 1854]
  Unknown
    L'esprit saint [Choudens, 1869]
      "Quel feu s'allu me dans mon coeur!"
    Sur la Grève [Choudens, n.d.] same
      Text from *L'Age d'Or.*
Bjørnson, Bjornstjerne, 1832-1910.
  BERG *Im Walde*
  DELIUS
    Abendstimmung
    Der Schlaf
    Skogen gir susende, langsom besked
    Verborg'ne Liebe
  GRIEG
    Den blonde Pige
    Den blonde Pige II
    Dulgt Kjaerlighed
    Fra Monte Pincio
    Den hvide, røde Rose
    Jeg elsket
    Lok
    Serenade til Welhaven
    Suk
    Valgsang
  NIELSEN
    Fremtidens Land
    Sangen har lysning
  ARNE.
    DELIUS
      Kleine Venevil
      Over the mountains high
  FISKERJENTEN.
    GRIEG
      Det første møde
      God morgen!
      Jeg giver mit digt til våren
      Takk for dit råd
  PRINSESSEN.
    GRIEG
      Prinsessen
Blåbaeret see Grønvold **GRIEG**
Blåbaer-Li see Garborg *HAUGTUSSA.*
  GRIEG
BLACHER, BORIS, 1903-1975.
  Benn, Gottfried, 1886-1956.
    Eure Etüden, op. 57 no. 3 (1958)
      [Bote & Bock, 1958]
      "Eure Etüden, Arpeggios, Dankchoral"
    Gedichte, op. 57 no. 1 (1958) [Bote &
      Bock, 1958]
      "Und was bedeuten diese Zwänge"

Letzter Frühling, op. 57 no. 4 (1958)
  [Bote & Bock, 1958]
  "Nimm die Forsythien tief in dich
    hinein"
Worte, op. 57 no. 2 (1957) [Bote &
  Bock, 1958]
  "Allein: du mit den Worten"
Bible
  Psalm 121 [Bote & Bock, n.d.]
  Psalm 141 [Bote & Bock, n.d.]
  Psalm 142 [Bote & Bock, n.d.]
Brecht, Bertolt, 1898-1956.
  Zwei chansons (1947) [unpubl.]
Dante Aligheri, 1265-1321.
  DIVINE COMEDY.
    Francesca da Rimini, op. 47 (1954)
      [Bote & Bock, 1955] "Du, der du
      uns besuchst voll Güt' und Huld"
      Soprano & violin.
No author
  A b c d e f und g (1967) [Bote & Bock,
    1970] same
  Anzkiis kwanzkiis kurschpiis kluus (1967)
    [Bote & Bock, 1970] same
  Guete Tag, mon cher Papa! (1967)
    [Bote & Bock, 1970] same
  Ich und du und dem Müller sein Kuh
    (1967) [Bote & Bock, 1970] same
  Madmaselle Pimpernelle (1967) [Bote &
    Bock, 1970] same
  Quunk, quai quenni monni denni monni
    (1967) [Bote & Bock, 1970] same
  Unser Schaulmester es en gelärden Mann
    (1967) [Bote & Bock, 1970] same
Omar Khayyam, 11th c.
  *Fünf Sinnsprüche Omars des
    Zeltmachers,* op. 3 no. 1 (1931)
    [Bote & Bock, 1940]
      "Des Lebens Karawane zieht mit
        Macht dahin"
  *Fünf Sinnsprüche Omars des
    Zeltmachers,* op. 3 no. 2 (1931)
    [Bote & Bock, 1940]
      "Von diesem Kreis"
  *Fünf Sinnsprüche Omars des
    Zeltmachers,* op. 3 no. 3 (1931)
    [Bote & Bock, 1940] "Heut, wo noch
      Rosendüfte mich umschweben"
  *Fünf Sinnsprüche Omars des
    Zeltmachers,* op. 3 no. 4 (1931)
    [Bote & Bock, 1940] "In jener Nacht"
  *Fünf Sinnsprüche Omars des
    Zeltmachers,* op. 3 no. 5 (1931)
    [Bote & Bock, 1940] "Omar, der
      Zeltmacher hat von früh bis spät"
Sandburg, Carl, 1878-1967.
  Nebel (1952) [Bote & Bock, n.d.]

COMPOSER Poet *Title* "First Line"

Shakespeare, William, 1564-1616.
ROMEO AND JULIET.
Die einst'ge Sehnsucht (1943)
[Universal-Edition, 1963] same
*So wilde Freude nimmt ein wildes
Ende* (1943)
[Universal-Edition, 1963] same
*Zwei hohe Häuser, gleich an
Würdigkeit* (1943)
[Universal-Edition, 1963] same
Weisenborn, Günther, 1902-
Das Lied von den Türen (1946) [unpubl.]
Wolf, Friedrich, 1888-1953.
Herzensverstand, op. 25 no. 3 (1947)
[Bote & Bock, 1947]
"Man soll seinem Herzen gehorchen"
Die Hexe, op. 25 no. 4 (1947) [Bote &
Bock, 1947] "Als Kinder glaubten wir
an Zauberwesen"
Kirschkerne, op. 25 no. 1 (1947) [Bote &
Bock, 1947]
"Erste Kirschen hast du mir gebracht"
Das Zirkuspferdchen, op. 25 no. 2 (1947)
[Bote & Bock, 1947]
"Es trabt im Kreis durch die Manege"
Black day see Soutar **BRITTEN**
Black roses see Josephson, E. *SVARTA
ROSOR OCH GULA.*
DELIUS *Schwarze Rosen*
SIBELIUS *Svarta rosor*
Blackenmore by the Stour see Barnes
VAUGHAN WILLIAMS *Blackmwore by
the Stour*
Blackmore by the Stour see Barnes
VAUGHAN WILLIAMS *Blackmwore by
the Stour*
Blackmwore by the Stour see Barnes
BLACKMWORE MAIDENS.
VAUGHAN WILLIAMS
BLACKMWORE MAIDENS. see Barnes
Blackmwore by the Stour **VAUGHAN
WILLIAMS**
Das Blättchen see Zhukovski **RUBINSTEIN**
Blätter lässt die Blume fallen see Petöfi
FRANZ
"Blättlein so fein und rund" *see Allmacht
Gottes* Branco **LOEWE**
Blagoslavlyayu vas, lesa see Tolstoï *JOHN
OF DAMASCUS.* **CHAÏ KOVSKIÏ**
Blagov, A
PROKOFIEV *Stakhanovka*
Blake, Ernest
IRELAND *The journey*
Blake, James Vila, 1842-1925.
IRELAND
Hymn to light

*I will walk on the earth
When lights go rolling round the sky*
Blake, William, 1757-1827.
BRITTEN
*Ah! Sun-flower
The chimney-sweeper
A cradle song
The fly
London
A poison tree
Proverb V*
CARPENTER
*A cradle-song
Little fly*
CHANLER
*The lamb
Memory*
HINDEMITH *The wild flower's song*
IRELAND *Memory*
LUENING
*Auguries of innocence
The Divine image
Earth's answer
Hear the voice of the Bard
Infant joy
The little vagabond
Silent, silent night
To morning
Young love*
QUILTER
*Dream valley
The jocund dance
The wild flower's song*
ROREM *The sick rose*
THOMPSON, R. *Spring*
THOMSON
*And did those feet
The divine image
The land of dreams
The little black boy
The sunflower*
VAUGHAN WILLIAMS
*The divine image
Eternity
Infant joy
The lamb
London
A poison tree
The shepherd*
AH! SUN-FLOWER.
VAUGHAN WILLIAMS *Ah! sun-flower*
AUGURIES OF INNOCENCE.
BRITTEN
*Every night and every morn
Proverb VII*
A DIVINE IMAGE.
VAUGHAN WILLIAMS *Cruelty has a
human heart*

Blake, William, 1757-1827 (continued)
IN A MIRTLE SHADE.
  GRIFFES *In a myrtle shade*
MORNING.
  QUILTER *Daybreak*
NEVER PAIN TO TELL THY LOVE.
  LUENING *Love's secret*
POEMS FROM THE ROSSETTI MS 1793:
  A poem with a moral.
    HESELTINE *I asked a thief to steal me*
    a peach
PROVERBS OF HELL.
  BRITTEN
    Proverb I
    Proverb II
    Proverb III
    Proverb IV
    Proverb VI
SONGS OF INNOCENCE: Introduction.
  VAUGHAN WILLIAMS *The piper*
THE TYGER.
  BRITTEN *The tyger*
  THOMSON
    The tiger
    Tiger! Tiger!
"Le blanc Messie chevauche devant nous" *see*
  Israël est vivant Cohen, A. **MILHAUD**
Blancafort, Manuel, 1897-
  MOMPOU *L' hora grisa*
"Blanche clochette au bal" *see Le muguet*
  Richter **SAUGUET**
Blanche et Rose see Silvestre **DELIBES**
"Blanche madone, notre patronne" *see À la*
  Madone Barbier, J. **GOUNOD**
La blanche neige see Apollinaire
  MARTINŮ
"Blanche sous sa robe blanche" *see Blanche et*
  Rose Silvestre **DELIBES**
Blanchecotte, Augustine Malvine
  (Souville), 1830-1878. *see*
  Blanchecotte, Augustine-Malvina,
  1830-before 1895.
Blanchecotte, Augustine-Malvina, 1830-
  before 1895.
  CHAÏKOVSKIÏ *Les larmes*
  HAHN
    La chère blessure
    La délaissée
  MASSENET *Non, tu n'as pas fini d'aimer*
Les blancs cygnes see Anon.
  SZYMANOWSKI *Lecioly zurazie*
Blancs sont les jours d'été see Lenormand
  FOLLE DU CIEL. **MILHAUD**
"Blank and dull the dingy, heavy stone" *see*
  In the church-yard Bryusov **MEDTNER**
Blanka see Schlegel, F. **SCHUBERT**

Blankenfeldt, Otto
  LOEWE *Frühlingsweihe*
Blankensee, Georg Friedrich Alexander
  von, count, 1792-1867.
  LOEWE *Blumen-Evangelium*
  WEBER *Schmerz*
Blåsippan see Franzén **SIBELIUS**
Eine blasse Wäscherin see Giraud, Albert
  WEISGALL
Das Blatt im Buche see Auersperg **REGER**
"Blau der See, vom hohen Schilfe" *see*
  Zweifelnde Liebe Unknown **PFITZNER**
Die Blaubeere see Grønvold **GRIEG**
  Blåbaeret
Blaue Augen see Leo **LASSEN**
"Die blauen Frühlingsaugen" *see*
  Frühlingslied Heine **RUBINSTEIN**
Die blauen Frühlingsaugen see Heine
  FRANZ
DIE BLAUEN FRÜHLINGSAUGEN. see
  Heine
  Glazki vecny golubye **CHAÏKOVSKIÏ**
"Blauer Himmel, blaue Wogen" *see Auf dem*
  See Simrock **BRAHMS**
Blauer Schmetterling see Hesse **SCHOECK**
Blauer Sommer see Busse **STRAUSS**
"Ein blauer Sommerglanz" *see Blauer*
  Sommer Busse **STRAUSS**
"Le blé jaunissant craint les rêves" *see*
  Le lièvre et le blé Carême **MILHAUD**
Blée, Catulle
  SCHMITT
    Chanson
    Fleurs décloses
"Blegnet, blegnet, hun, midt i Livets Glød"
  see Ved en ung Hustrus Båre Monrad
  GRIEG
"Bleib bi uns!" *see Elfe* Eichendorff
  GRIFFES
"Bleib, mein Bruder!" *see Scholastica*
  Giesebrecht **LOEWE**
"Bleibe, bleibe bei mir" *see Liebesglück*
  Goethe **MARTINŮ**
"Bleiche Blüte, Blüte der Liebe" *see Weisser*
  Jasmin Busse **STRAUSS**
"Der bleiche, kalte Mond erhob sich in Osten"
  see Loda's Gespenst Macpherson
  SCHUBERT
Der Bleicherin Nachtlied see Reinick
  SPOHR
Bleiches Antlitz, sei gegrüsset see Rist
  LOEWE
"Ein blenden des Spitzchen blickt über den
  Wald" *see Das weisse Spitzchen* Meyer
  SCHOECK

COMPOSER Poet *Title* "First Line"

Blès, Numa
  SATIE *La diva de l'Empire*
"Bless the Lord, O my soul" *see The 104th*
  Psalm Bible **KRENEK**
Blessed is the man see Barbier, J.
  GOUNOD *Bienheureux le coeur sincère*
Blessures see Turpin, Henri **GOUNOD**
Bleuet see Apollinaire **POULENC**
"Bleus ou noirs, tous aimés" *see Les yeux*
  Sully-Prudhomme **AUBERT**
Blicher, Steen Steensen, 1782-1848.
  NIELSEN
      De Refsnaesdrenge, de Samsøpiger
      Ud gaar du nu paa Livets Vej
Blick auf, mein Lieb see Krasov, V.
  BALAKIREV *Vzglyani, moy drug*
Blick vom oberen Belvedere see Weinheber
  STRAUSS
"Ein Blick von deinen Augen in die meinen"
  see Die Liebende schreibt Goethe
  BRAHMS, MENDELSSOHN-
      BARTHOLDY, SCHUBERT
"Ein Blick zurück noch von der Schwelle" *see*
  Epilog Drachman **GRIEG**
Blind see Cooper, Eric Thirkell **IRELAND**
The blind boy see Rossetti, Christina
  IRELAND
"Blind from my birth" *see The blind boy*
  Rossetti, Christina **IRELAND**
Der blinde Knabe see Cibber **SCHUBERT**
Blinde Kuh see Kopisch **BRAHMS**
Blindenklage see Henckell **STRAUSS**
Blindes Schauen see Cota **WOLF**
"Blindes Schauen, dunkle Leuchte" *see*
  Blindes Schauen Cota **WOLF**
BLITZSTEIN, MARC, 1905-1964.
  Anon.
      Court song (1958) [Chappell (NY), 1959]
        "Farewell! my joy, my joy"
  Blitzstein, Marc, 1905-1964.
      Displaced (1946) [unpubl.] "I remember
        running and running to my house"
        Holograph at State Historical Society
        of Wisconsin, Madison.
        Later used as "Such a fear" in *Idiots*
        First (1963).
      Quiet girl (1942) [unpubl.]
        "I used to be a QUIET GIRL"
        Holograph at State Historical Society
        of Wisconsin, Madison.
      Three Offenbach songs (1955) [Chappell
        (NY), 1955]
        Neither located nor examined.
      The way you are (1935) [unpubl.]
        "Are you divine?"
        Holograph at State Historical Society
        of Wisconsin, Madison.

Brooke, Rupert, 1887-1915.
  All sudden by the wind (1925) [unpubl.]
      Incomplete.
Cummings, Edward Estlin, 1894-1962.
  after all white horses are in bed (1929)
      [unpubl.]
      Holograph at State Historical Society
      of Wisconsin, Madison.
  Jimmie's got a goil (1929) [Cos Cob
      Press, 1935]
      "Jimmie's got a goil goil goil"
      Holograph at State Historical Society
      of Wisconsin, Madison.
  mister, youse needn't be so spry (1929)
      [unpubl.]
      Holograph at State Historical Society
      of Wisconsin, Madison.
  o by the by (1960) [Chappell (NY), 1962]
      same
  open your heart (1960) [Chappell (NY),
      1962] same
  silent unday by silently not night (1960)
      [Chappell (NY), 1962] same
  until and i heard (1960) [Chappell (NY),
      1962] same
  what if a much of a which of a wind
      (1960) [Chappell (NY), 1962] same
  when life is quite through with (1929)
      [unpubl.]
      Holograph at State Historical Society
      of Wisconsin, Madison.
  when life is quite through with (1960)
      [Chappell (NY), 1962] same
  yes is a pleasant country (1960)
      [Chappell (NY), 1962] same
  you are like the snow (1929) [unpubl.]
      Holograph at State Historical Society
      of Wisconsin, Madison.
Housman, Alfred Edward, 1859-1936.
  Into my heart an air (1925) [unpubl.]
      "Into my heart an air that kills"
      Holograph at State Historical Society
      of Wisconsin, Madison.
Jonson, Ben, 1573?-1637.
  Song of the glove (1958) [Chappell (NY),
      1959]
      "Thou more than most sweet glove"
Shakespeare, William, 1564-1616.
  Lullaby (1958) [Chappell (NY), 1959]
      "Lulla, lulla, lullaby"
  Vendor's song (1958) [Chappell (NY),
      1959] "Lawn as white as driven snow"
  A WINTER'S TALE.
      Shepherd's song (1958) [Chappell
        (NY), 1959]
        "When daffodils begin to peer"

BLITZSTEIN, MARC, 1905-1964
(continued)
Spenser, Edmund, 1552?-1599.
AMORETTI.
Sweet is the rose (1958) [Chappell
(NY), 1959] same
Unknown
Chez Eitingon (1946) [unpubl.]
"Now that there's no more fighting on"
Holograph at State Historical Society
of Wisconsin, Madison.
Text by Blitzstein?
A child writes a letter (1936) [unpubl.]
Whitman, Walt, 1819-1892.
After the dazzle of day (1925) [unpubl.]
same
Holograph at State Historical Society
of Wisconsin, Madison.
Ages and ages (1928) [unpubl.]
"Ages and ages returning at intervals
unde[s]troyed"
Holograph at State Historical Society
of Wisconsin, Madison.
As Adam (1928) [unpubl.]
"As Adam early in the morning"
Holograph at State Historical Society
of Wisconsin, Madison.
As if a phantom caress'd me (1925)
[unpubl.] same
Holograph at State Historical Society
of Wisconsin, Madison.
I am He (1928) [unpubl.]
"I am he with amorous love"
Holograph at State Historical Society
of Wisconsin, Madison.
O Hymen! O Hymenee! (1928) [unpubl.]
"O Hymen! O Hymenee! why do you
tantalize me thus?"
Holograph at State Historical Society
of Wisconsin, Madison.
Blitzstein, Marc, 1905-1964.
BLITZSTEIN
Displaced
Quiet girl
Three Offenbach songs
The way you are
Blixen, Karen, 1885-1962.
OUT OF AFRICA.
DIAMOND *The millennium*
Blizost' milogo see Goethe **MEDTNER**
Nähe des Geliebten
BLOCH, ERNEST, 1880-1959.
Mauclair, Camille, 1872-1945.
Complainte (1903) [Demets/Eschig,
1903] "Les amoureuses aux matelots"
Les fleurs (1903) [Demets/Eschig, 1903]
"Mon amant m'a baisée au cou"

Légende (1903) [Demets/Eschig, 1903]
"Ils l'ont clouée par les mains"
Rondo (1903) [Demets/Eschig, 1903]
"Les trois filles allèrent danser au clair
de lune"
Rodès, Béatrix
L'abri (1906) [G. Schirmer, 1918]
"J'écoute la voix de mon rêve"
Also voice & orchestra.
Le déclin (1906) [G. Schirmer, 1918]
"Dans le verger paisible, bordé là-bas
de peupiliers"
Also voice & orchestra.
Invocation (1906) [G. Schirmer, 1918]
"Les colonnes du temple s'animent"
Also voice & orchestra.
La vagabonde (1906) [G. Schirmer,
1918] "Elle a passé dans le vent
d'automne"
Also voice & orchestra.
Bloch, Jean Richard, 1884-1947.
HONEGGER
Chanson des quatre
Chant de l'émigrant
MILHAUD
Chanson du capitaine
Java de la femme
Blogoslawiona niech bedzie ta chwila see
Kasprowicz, Jan *MOJA PIEŚŃ
WIECZORNA.* **SZYMANOWSKI**
Blomberg, Erik Axel, 1894-1965.
KILPINEN
Äppelträd och päronträd
Desdemonas sång
Den djupa källen
Dyningen
Förledde vän
Förr ägde jag intet
Gravskrift över ett litet barn
Gullvivan
I dina händers mjuka fågelbo
Jag har haft en stor, tyst sorg
Jag väntar ingen lycka
Jag ville vara tårar
Körsbär
Lärksång
Den ljusa nattens ljusa fågeldrillar
Människans hem
Modern
Och stod du i den kalla blåst
Snöblommor
Stjärnorna äro så stilla
Till Elektra
Till en diktare
Till några påskliljor
En ung mor

Var stilla hjärta
Vem är du?
Visa
En blomma stod vid vägen see Josephson,
  E. **SIBELIUS**
Blomman see Josephson, E. **KILPINEN**
"Blomman i solen stod" *see Blomman*
  Josephson, E. **KILPINEN**
Blommans öde see Runeberg **SIBELIUS**
Blomsterne tale see Winther **GRIEG**
Blomstervise see Holstein **NIELSEN**
Das blonde Mädchen see Bjørnson **GRIEG**
  Den blonde Pige
Das blonde Mädchen II see Bjørnson
  GRIEG *Den blonde Pige II*
Den blonde Pige see Bjørnson **GRIEG**
Den blonde Pige II see Bjørnson **GRIEG**
Blondel zu Marien see Unknown
  SCHUBERT
Blondel's Lied see Seidl **SCHUMANN**
Blood is not blood see Ayer, Ethan **ROREM**
"Blossom on the plum" *see Blossom time*
  Chesson **QUILTER**
Blossom time see Chesson **QUILTER**
Blow, blow, thou winter wind see
  Shakespeare **QUILTER**
"Blow, blow, winds of May" *see Cuckoo song*
  Williams **QUILTER**
"Blow high, blow low, O wind from the
  West" *see The wind from the West* Young,
  Ella **HESELTINE**
Blow out, you bugles see Brooke **IRELAND**
Blow winds, wild winds see Kol'tsov
  MUSORGSKIĭ *Duĭut vetry, vetry buĭ nye*
Blue eyes of spring see Heine *DIE BLAUEN*
  FRÜHLINGSAUGEN. **CHAĭ KOVSKIĭ**
  Glazki vecny golubye
"Blue forget-me-not, sweet blossom" *see*
  Forget-me-nots Bal'mont **STRAVINSKIĭ**
Blue gal see Carpenter, John
  CARPENTER
The blue-bell see Deland **MACDOWELL**
"Blüht denn hier an Tauris Strande" *see*
  Iphigenia Mayrhofer **SCHUBERT**
"Blümchen der Demuth, unter dichten Blättern
  birgst" *see Das Veilchen* Anon. **ZELTER**
Das Blümchen Wunderhold see Bürger
  BEETHOVEN
Das Blümlein see Loewe, Helene **LOEWE**
"Die Blümlein auf der Heide" *see In der*
  Ferne Cornelius **CORNELIUS**
"Blümlein im Garten" *see Liebchen ist da!*
  Schröer **FRANZ**
Blüthgen, Viktor, 1844-1920.
  REGER

Die fünf Hühnerchen
Stampelchen
ACH, WER DOCH DAS KÖNNTE!
  SCHOECK *Kinderliedchen*
DAS ERSTE LIED.
  LASSEN *Wer hat das erste Lied erdacht*
Blumauer, Aloys, 1755-1798.
  MOZART *Lied der Freiheit*
Blumauer, Johannes Aloys *see*
  Blumauer, Aloys, 1755-1798.
Die Blume see Haug **WEBER**
Die Blume see Zhukovski **RUBINSTEIN**
Die Blume der Ergebenheit see Rückert
  RUBINSTEIN
Die Blume der Ergebung see Rückert
  LOEWE, SCHUMANN
Blume und Duft see Hebbel **LISZT**
Der Blumen Rache see Freiligrath **LOEWE**
Der Blumen Schmerz see Mayláth
  SCHUBERT
Blumenballade see Vogl
  SCHNEEGLÖCKCHEN. **LOEWE**
Der Blumenbrief see Schreiber **SCHUBERT**
Blumendeutung see Anon. **DVOŘÁK** *Výklad*
  znamení
Blumen-Evangelium see Blankensee
  LOEWE
"Ein Blumenglöckchen vom Boden hervor"
  see Gleich und Gleich Goethe
  FRANZ, MEDTNER, SCHOECK,
  WEBERN, WOLF, ZELTER
BLUMENGRUSS. see Goethe
  Blumengruss **WEBERN, WOLF**
Blumengruss see Goethe *BLUMENGRUSS.*
  WEBERN, WOLF
BLUMENGRUSS. see Goethe
  Willkommen dem 28. August 1749
  ZELTER
Der Blumenkranz see Moore, T.
  MENDELSSOHN-BARTHOLDY
Blumenlied see Hölty **SCHUBERT**
Das Blumenopfer see Zitzmann **LOEWE**
Die Blumensprache see Platner **SCHUBERT**
Blumensprache see Winther **GRIEG**
  Blomsterne tale
Der Blumenstrauss see Klingemann
  MENDELSSOHN-BARTHOLDY
Blunt, Bruce *see* Blunt, George Henry
  Bruce, 1899-1957.
Blunt, George Henry Bruce, 1899-1957.
  HESELTINE
  Bethlehem down
  The cricketers of Hambledon
  The first mercy
  The fox
  The frostbound wood

"Blyszcza krople rosy" *see Wiosna* Witwicki
  CHOPIN
The boatmen's dance see Emmett
  COPLAND
Bobrik, Johann Friedrich Ludwig, 1781-
  1844.
  SCHUBERT *Die drei Sänger*
Boccaccio, Giovanni, 1313-1375.
  RESPIGHI
    Ballata
    L'udir talvolta . . .
  IL NINFALE FIESOLANO, 287.
    RESPIGHI *Ma come potrei . . .*
Bocchialini, Jacopo
  PIZZETTI
    E il mio dolore io canto
    Sei tornato da me
Bocella, Marchese Cesare
  LISZT *Angiolin dal biondo crin*
Bock, Kurt, 1890-1949.
  HINDEMITH *Die trunkene Tänzerin*
Bodden, G von *see* Boddien, G von
Boddien, G von
  RUBINSTEIN
    Es blinkt der Thau
    Die Heimath meiner Lieder
    Die Waldhexe
    Wie eine Lerch' in blauer Luft
Boddien, Helene von *see* Krause, Helene
  von (née Boddien), 1841-1915.
Bodenstedt, Friedrich Martin von, 1819-
  1892.
  BARTÓK
    Die Gletscher leuchten im Mondenlicht
    Ich fühle deinen Odem
  FRANZ
    Es hat die Rose sich beklagt
    Es ragt der alte Elborus
    Die helle Sonne leuchtet
    Wenn der Frühling auf die Berge steigt
  GRIEG *Ein Traum*
  LASSEN
    Die Gletscher leuchten im Mondenlicht
    Die helle Sonne leuchtet
    Hoch auf fliegt mein Herz
    Ich fühle deinen Odem
    Nun liegt die Welt im Traume
    Wenn der Frühling auf die Berge steigt
    Wenn ich dich seh'
  LISZT
    An Edlitam, zur silbernen Hochzeit
    Einst
  LUENING *Wir wandeln alle den Weg*
  QUILTER
    Die helle Sonne leuchtet
    Ich fühle deinen Odem

    My heart adorned with thee
    Neig' schöne Knospe Dich zu mir
    Und was die Sonne glüht
  RUBINSTEIN
    Gelb rollt mir zu Füssen
    Gott hiess die Sonne glühen
    Die helle Sonne leuchtet
    Ich fühle deinen Odem
    Mein Herz schmückt sich mit dir
    Neigl, schöne Knospe, dich zu mir
    Nicht mit Engeln im blauen Himmelszelt
    Die Rose
    Schlag' die Tschadra zurück
    Seh' ich deine zarte Füsschen an
    Thu nicht so spröde, schönes Kind
    Verschliedene Wege
    Die Weise guter Zecher ist
  SPOHR
    Fatima beim Saitenspiel
    Trinklied
    Zuleikha
  SZYMANOWSKI *Zuleikha*
  IVAN.
    BRAHMS *Lied*
Det bødes der for see Jacobsen **NIELSEN**
DET BØDES DER FOR. see Jacobsen
  Through long, long years **DELIUS**
Bodmann, Emanuel von, 1874-1946.
  STRAUSS *Herr Lenz*
A body without love see Moss **ROREM**
Böhm, Hans, 1876-1946.
  WEBERN *Liebeslied*
Böhmer, Wilhelm, 1791-1842.
  LOEWE *Ad Jesum Christum, Dominum et*
    Salvatorem meum
Der böhmische Musikant see Pletzsch,
  Oskar **STRAUSS**
Boelitz, Martin, 1874-1921.
  REGER
    Dämmer
    Das Dorf
    Du bist mir gut!
    Erlöst
    Es blüht ein Blümlein rosenrot
    Knecht Ruprecht
    Lutschemäulchen
    Mädchenlied
    Mariä Wiegenlied
    Notturno
    Ostern
    Präludium
    Reinheit
    Reiterlied
    Schlaf ein
    Soldatenlied
    Ein Tänzchen

Tragt, blaue Träume
Unterwegs
Der verliebte Jäger
Vor dem Sterben
Vorbeimarsch
Wehe
Das Wölklein
Zwei Mäuschen
Zwiesprach
"Böljan och stormen förenade skrida" *see*
    Sången Österling **KILPINEN**
Die böse Farbe see Müller, Wilhelm
    SCHUBERT
Ein böser Tag see Garborg *HAUGTUSSA.*
    GRIEG *Vond Dag*
Böses Weib see Anon. **REGER**
Böttger, Adolf, 1816-1870.
    GRIEG *Osterlied*
    MENDELSSOHN-BARTHOLDY *Ich hör'*
        ein Vöglein
    PFITZNER *Ich hör ein Vöglein locken*
Bogan, Louise, 1897-1970.
    ROREM *Solitary observation brought back*
        from a soujourn in hell
Bøgh, Johan
    GRIEG *Til Generalkonsul Chr. Tønsberg*
Bohatá milá see Anon. **MARTINŮ**
THE BOHEMIAN GIRL. see Bunn
    When other lips shall speak **DELIUS**
La bohémienne la main n'a pris see Pitoëff
    TU NE M'ÉCHAPPERAS JAMAIS.
    MILHAUD
Boileau-Despréaux, Nicolas, 1636-1711.
    SAINT-SAËNS *Chanson à boire du vieux*
        temps
Boire à l'ombre see Augier **GOUNOD**
"Bois chère aux ramiers" *see Nanny* Leconte
    de Lisle **CHAUSSON**
Les bois de pins see Distel, Camille
    MASSENET
Boito, Arrigo, 1842-1918.
    AGNUS DEI.
    VERDI *Pietà, Signor*
Boléro see Barbier, J. **GOUNOD**
Bolero see Hugo **LISZT** *Gastibelza*
Boléro triste see Kahn **LOEFFLER**
Bollspelet vid Trianon see Fröding
    SIBELIUS
"Bol'shi seia liubve nikto zhe imat" *see From*
    the Gospel of St. John, XV: 13 Bible
    RACHMANINOFF
Boltun'ia see Barto, A. **PROKOFIEV**
"Bon chevalier masqué qui chevauche en
    silence" *see Le chevalier Malheur* Verlaine
    CHAUSSON
Bon jour, bon soir see Spenner, M.
    GOUNOD

Un bon petit garçon see Stevenson, Robert
    Louis *A CHILD'S GARDEN OF VERSES.*
    HAHN *A good boy*
"Le bon Pierrot, que la foule contemple" *see*
    Pierrot Banville **DEBUSSY**
"Bon Saint Michel qui me donnez loisir" *see*
    Chanson épique Morand **RAVEL**
Bonaparte im Pestspital zu Kairo see Gruppe
    LOEWE *Der Feldherr*
Le bonheur see Heine *INTERMEZZO.*
    SAUGUET
The bonie lad that's far away see Burns
    SCHUMANN *Weit, weit*
Bonjour, messieurs les libérateurs see Anon.
    MILHAUD
Bonjour, Suzon! see Musset **DELIBES**
"Bonjour, Suzon, ma fleur des bois!" *see*
    Bonjour, Suzon! Musset **DELIBES**
Bonjour toi, colombe vert see Messiaen
    MESSIAEN
Bonnard, A
    KOECHLIN *Choeur des voleurs*
Bonnaud, Dominique, b.1864.
    SATIE *La diva de l'Empire*
La bonne chanson see Verlaine **HAHN**
LA BONNE CHANSON. see Verlaine
    Apaisement **CHAUSSON**
    Avant que tu ne t'en ailles **DELIUS,**
        FAURÉ
    La bonne chanson **STRAVINSKII**
La bonne chanson see Verlaine *LA BONNE*
    CHANSON. **STRAVINSKII**
LA BONNE CHANSON. see Verlaine
    L' heure exquise **HAHN**
    Un jour de juin, que j'étais soucieux
        KOECHLIN
    La lune blanche **DELIUS**
    La lune blanche luit dans les bois **FAURÉ**
    N'est-ce pas? **FAURÉ, KOECHLIN**
    Le soleil du matin **KOECHLIN**
    Va, chanson **KOECHLIN**
LA BONNE CHANSON, no. 1
    FAURÉ Verlaine *Une sainte en son*
        auréole
LA BONNE CHANSON, no. 2
    FAURÉ Verlaine *Puisque l'aube grandit*
LA BONNE CHANSON, no. 3
    FAURÉ Verlaine *La lune blanche luit*
        dans les bois
LA BONNE CHANSON, no. 4
    FAURÉ Verlaine *J'allais par des chemins*
        perfides
LA BONNE CHANSON, no. 5
    FAURÉ Verlaine *J'ai presque peur, en*
        vérité
LA BONNE CHANSON, no. 6
    FAURÉ Verlaine *Avant que tu ne t'en*
        ailles

LA BONNE CHANSON, no. 7
  FAURÉ Verlaine *Donc, ce sera par un clair jour d'été*
LA BONNE CHANSON, no. 8
  FAURÉ Verlaine *N'est-ce pas?*
LA BONNE CHANSON, no. 9
  FAURÉ Verlaine *L' hiver a cessé*
LA BONNE CUISINE, no. 1
  BERNSTEIN Dumont *Plum pudding*
LA BONNE CUISINE, no. 2
  BERNSTEIN Dumont *Queues de boeuf*
LA BONNE CUISINE, no. 3
  BERNSTEIN Dumont *Tavouk gueunksis*
LA BONNE CUISINE, no. 4
  BERNSTEIN Dumont *Civet à toute vitesse*
LA BONNE CUISINE FRANÇAISE. see
  Dumont
  Civet à toute vitesse **BERNSTEIN**
  Plum pudding **BERNSTEIN**
  Queues de boeuf **BERNSTEIN**
  Tavouk gueunksis **BERNSTEIN**
Bonne journée see Éluard **POULENC**
Bonne nuit see Distel, Camille **MASSENET**
La bonne terre see Legrand, Marc **INDY**
Bønnelycke, Emil, 1893-1953.
  NIELSEN *Hjemlige Jul*
Bonnières, Robert de, 1850-1905.
  INDY
    Au galop
    Madrigal
  CONTES DE FÉES.
    DUPARC *Le manoir de Rosemonde*
"Bonté, sagesse et le savoir" see Imploration
  Boulanger, D. **SAUGUET**
THE BOOK OF SONGS. see Unknown
  The big chariot **BRITTEN**
  Dance song **BRITTEN**
"Booth led boldly with his big bass drum" see
  General William Booth enters into Heaven
  Lindsay **IVES**
Det borde vara skatter see Cnattingius,
  Thor **KILPINEN**
Bordèse, Stéphan, b. 1847.
  FAURÉ *En prière*
  MASSENET
    Jour de noces
    La neige
    Le sais-tu?
  SAINT-SAËNS *Présage de la croix*
Borecký, Jaromír, 1869-1951.
  MARTINŮ *I love old parks*
Borgström
  SIBELIUS *Hymn to Thais*
Bornehjaelpsdagens Sang see Jørgensen
  NIELSEN

Bornowski, Theodor, 1829-1892.
  LASSEN *Seufzer*
BORODIN, ALEKSANDR PORFIR'EVICH, 1833-1887.
Anon.
  Arabian melody (1881) {*Arabskaya melodiya*} [W. Bessel; Belaïeff, 1888]
    "Do not flee from my sight"
    Borodin translated traditional text.
  Merciful God (1852-5?) {*Bozhe milostivïy*} [unpubl.]
Borodin, Aleksandr Porfir'evich, 1833-1887.
  Fal'shivaya nota (1868) [Jurgenson, 1870; Muzgiz, 1967]
    "Ona vse vliubviuveriala"
  Morskaya tsarevna (1868) [W. Bessel, 1873; Muzgiz, 1967]
    "Pridi ko mne nochnoǐ poroǐ"
  Die schlafende Prinzessin (1867) {*Spyashchaya knyazhna*} [Jurgenson, 1870; W. Bessel, 1873]
    "Tief in des Waldes Nacht liegt"
  The sea (1870) {*More*} [Jurgenson, 1885; J. & W. Chester, 1920]
    "Ocean thunders and raves"
    Also voice & orchestra, 1884.
  Song of the dark forest (1868) {*Pesnya tyomnovo lesa*} [W. Bessel, 1873]
    "Thro' the forest dark"
Collen, Georges
  SEPTAIN.
    Chudnyǐ sad″ (1885) [Liège: Veuve Muraille, 1885; W. Bessel, 1887; Muzgiz, 1967] same
Heine, Heinrich, 1797-1856.
  Das schöne Fischermädchen (1854-5) {*Krasavitsa rybachka*} [Muzgiz, 1947, 1967] same
    With violoncello obbligato.
  Vergiftet sind meine Lieder (1868) {*Otravoǐ polny moi piesni*} [Jurgenson, 1870; W. Bessel, 1873] same
  LYRICAL INTERMEZZO.
    Aus meinen Tränen (1870-71) {*Iz slyoz moikh*} [W. Bessel, 1873] same
Kruse, E von
  Listen to my song, little friend (ca.1854) {*Slushayte, podruzhen'ki, pesenku moyu*} [Muzgiz, 1947, 1967] same
    With violoncello obbligato.
Nekrasov, Nikolaiǐ Aleksyeyevich, 1821-1877.
  U lyudey-to v domu (1881) [Belaïeff, 1890] same

Originally for voice & orchestra;
arranged for voice & piano, 1890.
Pushkin, Aleksandr Sergeevich, 1799-
1837.
For the shores of thy far native land
(1881) {*Dlya beregov otchiznï dal'noy*}
[Belaïeff, 1888; Muzgiz, 1967] same
Solov'yov, S
Why art thou so early, Dawn? (1852-5?)
{*Chto tï rano, zoren'ka*}
[Muzgiz, 1947, 1967] same
Tolstoĭ, Alekseĭ Konstantinovich, Graf,
1817-1875.
Spes' (1884) [Belaïeff, 1890; Muzgiz,
1967] "Khbdit spes' naduvaĭuchis' "
Vinogradov
Razlyubila krasna devitsa (ca.1854)
[Muzgiz, 1947, 1967] same
With violoncello obbligato.
Borodin, Aleksandr Porfir'evich, 1833-
1887.
BORODIN
Fal'shivaya nota
Morskaya tsarevna
Die schlafende Prinzessin
The sea
Song of the dark forest
Borrelli, Raymond, vicomte de, b. 1837.
DELIBES *Faut-il chanter?*
Borte! see Ibsen **GRIEG**
Bossuet, Jacques Bénigne, bishop of
Meaux, 1627-1704.
THOMSON *Oraison funèbre*
Der Bote see Eichendorff **FRANZ,
JENSEN, PFITZNER**
Der Bote see Fick, K. **REGER**
Both painfully and sweetly see Rostopchina
CHAĬKOVSKIĬ *I bol'no, i sladko*
Botschaft see Cornelius **CORNELIUS**
Botschaft see Daumer **HAFIS. BRAHMS**
"Bouches graves des lions" *see Réveil*
Cocteau **AURIC**
Bouchor, Maurice, 1855-1929.
CHAUSSON
Amour d'antan
Nocturne
Nos souvenirs
Le petit sentier
Printemps triste
DEBUSSY
Chanson triste
DANS LA FORÊT.
CHAUSSON *Lilas, vos frissons sous le
ciel*
*LES POÈMES DE L'AMOUR ET DE LA
MER* (1876).
DEBUSSY *Fleur des eaux*

Bouclon, Adolphe de, 1813-1882.
BERLIOZ
Le matin
Petit oiseau
Boudry, R
JOLIVET *La vie est plate*
Bouilhet, Louis Hyacinthe, 1822-1869.
BIZET *Chanson d'avril*
KOECHLIN
Chanson d'amour
Moisson prochaine
Le boulanger see Paliard **MILHAUD**
Boulanger, Daniel, 1922-
SAUGUET *Imploration*
BOULANGER, LILI, 1893-1918.
Delaquys, Georges, b. 1880
Le retour (1912) [Ricordi, 1919; G.
Schirmer, 1979]
"Ulysses part la voile au vent"
Galéron de Calone, Bertha, b.1859.
DANS LA SOMBRE TRISTESSE.
Dans l'immense Tristesse (1916)
[Ricordi, 1919; G. Schirmer, 1979]
same
Jammes, Francis, 1868-1938.
TRISTESSES.
Au pied de mon lit [Ricordi, 1919;
Durand, 1970] same
Demain fera un an qu'à Audaux
[Ricordi, 1919; Durand, 1970]
same
Deux ancolies se balançaient [Ricordi,
1919; Durand, 1970] same
Elle est gravement gaie [Ricordi, 1919;
Durand, 1970] same
*Elle était descendue au bas de la
prairie* [Ricordi, 1919; Durand,
1970] same
Je garde une médaille d'elle [Ricordi,
1919; Durand, 1970] same
Les lilas qui avaient fleuri [Ricordi,
1919; Durand, 1970] same
*Nous nous aimerons tant que nous
tairons* [Ricordi, 1919; Durand,
1970] same
Par ce que j'ai souffert [Ricordi, 1919;
Durand, 1970] same
Parfois, je suis triste [Ricordi, 1919;
Durand, 1970] same
Un poète disait que [Ricordi, 1919;
Durand, 1970] same
Si tout ceci n'est qu'un pauvre rêve
[Ricordi, 1919; Durand, 1970] same
*Vous m'avez regardé avec tout votre
âme* [Ricordi, 1919; Durand, 1970]
same

COMPOSER Poet *Title* "First Line"

BOULANGER, LILI, 1893-1918 *(continued)*
Maeterlinck, Maurice, 1862-1949.
  Attente (1910) [Ricordi, 1918; G.
    Schirmer, 1979]
    "Mon âme a joint ses mains étranges"
    Also voice & orchestra.
  Reflets (1911) [Ricordi, 1919; G.
    Schirmer, 1979]
    "Sous l'eau du songe qui s'éllève"
Boultenhouse, Charles
  ROREM
    Boy into animal
    Cloudless blue claw
    Now I make a circle
    Squirrel song
    Sun song
Un bouquet à la main see Capri, Agnès
  SAUGUET
LE BOURGEOIS GENTILHOMME. see
Molière
  Sérénade du Bourgeois gentilhomme
    FAURÉ
Bourget, Paul Charles Joseph, 1852-
1935.
  CHAUSSON *Sérénade italienne*
  DEBUSSY *Romance: Voici que le*
    printemps
  KOECHLIN *Novembre*
  LOEFFLER *Madrigal*
LES AVEUX.
  DEBUSSY
    L'âme évaporée
    Les cloches
    Musique
LES AVEUX: Amour.
  DEBUSSY
    Paysage sentimental
    Regret: Devant le ciel
LES AVEUX: Romance.
  DEBUSSY *Romance, musique pour*
    éventail
LES AVEUX: Souvenirs du Nord, no. 5.
  DEBUSSY *La Romance d'Ariel*
LES AVEUX: Souvenirs du Nord, no. 7.
  DEBUSSY *Beau soir*
Bourguignat, Paul
  GOUNOD *Les lilas blancs*
  MASSENET
    Où que s'envole
    Pour Antoinette
    Vous qui passez
Il bove see Carducci **CASELLA**
Die Bowle fort! see Moore, T. **JENSEN**
Bowring, Sir John, 1792-1872.
  IVES *Watchman*
Boy into animal see Boultenhouse, Charles
  ROREM

Boy Johnny see Rossetti, Christina
  VAUGHAN WILLIAMS
Boy with a baseball glove see Goodman
  ROREM
The boy with the ax see Goodman **ROREM**
Boyer, Charles
  GOUNOD *Quand l'enfant prie*
Boyer, Georges, 1850-1931.
  GOUNOD
    Elle sait!
    Notre Dame de France
  MASSENET
    En chantant
    Les enfants
    Les mères
      Two versions: 1891 and 1901.
    Le pauv' petit
    Le petit Jésus
    Royauté
    Si tu veux, Mignonne
    Souvenez-vous, Vierge Marie!
  SAINT-SAËNS *Amour viril*
"The boys are up the woods with day" *see*
  The heart's desire Housman **IRELAND**
Bože! Bože! Píseň novou see Bible
  DVOŘÁK
Bozhe milostivïy see Anon. **BORODIN**
  Merciful God
Boží muka see Anon. **MARTINŮ**
Bozzani, Suzanne
  MASSENET *Je t'aime*
The bracelet see Herrick **QUILTER**
Le brachycome see Daudet, L. **MILHAUD**
"Brachycome Ibéridifolia étoile bleue
  nouveauté" *see Le brachycome* Daudet, L.
  MILHAUD
Bradstreet, Anne, 1612-1672.
  ROREM *To my dear and loving husband*
Der Bräutigam see Gruppe **LOEWE**
Der Bräutigam und die Birke see Pfarrius
  WALDLIEDERN. **SCHUMANN**
BRAHMS, JOHANNES, 1833-1897.
Allmers, Hermann, 1821-1902.
  Feldeinsamkeit, op. 86 no. 2 [GA, v. 25,
    p. 118]
    "Ich ruhe still im hohen grünen Grass"
Anon.
  Dort in den Weiden, op. 97 no. 4 [GA, v.
    25, p. 200] same
    Poem in Zuccalmaglio's **Deutsche**
      Volkslieder... v.2,p.461.
  Der Gang zum Liebchen, op. 48 no. 1
    [GA, v. 24, p. 48]
    "Es glänzt der Mond nieder"
  Gang zur Liebsten, op. 14 no. 6 [GA, v.
    23, p. 63] "Des Abends kann ich nicht
    schlafen gehn"

COMPOSER Poet *Title* "First Line"

From Zuccalmaglio *Deutsche Volkslieder* 1840.

Gold überwiegt die Liebe, op. 48 no. 4 [GA, v. 24, p. 54] "Sternchen mit dem trüben Schein"

Ich schell mein Horn ins Jammertal, op. 43 no. 3 [GA, v. 24, p. 11] same

Klage, op. 105 no. 3 [GA, v. 26, p. 7] "Feins Liebchen, trau' du nicht" Poem in Zuccalmaglio *Deutsche Volkslieder* 1840.

Murrays Ermordung, op. 14 no. 3 [GA, v. 23, p. 55] "O Hochland und O Südland!" From Herder's *Volkslieder* 1779.

Sehnsucht, op. 14 no. 8 [GA, v. 23, p. 66] "Mein Schatz ist nicht da" From Zuccalmaglio *Deutsche Volkslieder* 1840.

Sehnsucht, op. 49 no. 3 [GA, v. 24, p. 70] "Hinter jenen dichten Wäldern"

Spannung, op. 84 no. 5 [GA, v. 25, p. 96] "Gut'n Abend, gut'n Abend"

Ständchen, op. 14 no. 7 [GA, v. 23, p. 64] "Gut Nacht, gut Nacht, mein liebster Schatz" From Zuccalmaglio *Deutsche Volkslieder* 1840.

Die Trauernde, op. 7 no. 5 [GA, v. 23, p. 47] "Mei Mueter mag mi net" From Georg Scherer (collector) *Deutsche Volkslieder* 1851.

Trennung, op. 14 no. 5 [GA, v. 23, p. 60] "Wach auf, wach auf, du junger Gesell" From Zuccalmaglio *Deutsche Volkslieder* 1840.

Trennung, op. 97 no. 6 [GA, v. 25, p. 204] "Da unten im Talle, läuft's Wasser so trub" Poem in Zuccalmaglio's *Deutsche Volkslieder* . . . v.2, p.383

Vergangen ist mir Glück und Heil, op. 48 no. 6 [GA, v. 24, p. 58] same

Vergebliches Standchen, op. 84 no. 4 [GA, v. 25, p. 92] "Guten Abend, mein Schatz, guten Abend"

Volkslied, op. 7 no. 4 [GA, v. 23, p. 46] "Die Schwälble ziehet fort, ziehet fort" From Georg Scherer (collector) *Deutsche Volkslieder* 1851.

Vom verwundeten Knaben, op. 14 no. 2 [GA, v. 23, p. 53] "Es wollt ein Mädchen früh aufstehn" From Herder's *Volkslieder* 1773.

Vor dem Fenster, op. 14 no. 1 [GA, v. 23, p. 50] "Soll sich der Mond nicht heller scheinen" From Karl Simrock, collector *Die deutschen Volkslieder* 1851.

Bodenstedt, Friedrich Martin von, 1819-1892.

IVAN.

Lied, op. 3 no. 4 [GA, v. 23, p. 11] "Weit über das Feld"

Brentano, Clemens Maria, 1778-1842.

O kühler Wald, op. 72 no. 3 [GA, v. 25, p. 70] same

Candidus, Karl August, 1817-1872.

Alte Liebe, op. 72 no. 1 [GA, v. 25, p. 63] "Es kehrt die dunkle Schwalbe"

Geheimnis, op. 71 no. 3 [GA, v. 25, p. 53] "O Frühlingsabenddämmerung!"

Lerchengesang, op. 70 no. 2 [GA, v. 25, p. 37] "Atherische ferne Stimmen"

Schwermut, op. 58 no. 5 [GA, v. 24, p. 122] "Mir ist so weh ums Herz"

Sommerfäden, op. 72 no. 2 [GA, v. 25, p. 68] "Sommerfäden hin und wieder"

Tambourliedchen, op. 69 no. 5 [GA, v. 25, p. 13] "Den Wirbel schlag' ich gar so stark"

Daumer, Georg Friedrich, 1800-1875.

FRAUENBILDER UND HULDIGUNGEN.

Ach, wende diesen Blick, op. 57 no. 4 [GA, v. 24, p. 91] same

In meiner Nächte Sehnen, op. 57 no. 5 [GA, v. 24, p. 94] same

Strahlt zuweilen auch ein mildes Licht, op. 57 no. 6 [GA, v. 24, p. 98] same

Unbewegte laue Luft, op. 57 no. 8 [GA, v. 24, p. 104] same

Von waldbekränzter Hohe, op. 57 no. 1 [GA, v. 24, p. 80] same

HAFIS.

Bitteres zu sagen denkst du, op. 32 no. 7 [GA, v. 23, p. 98] same

Botschaft, op. 47 no. 1 [GA, v. 24, p. 32] "Wehe Luftchen, lind und lieblich"

Liebesglut, op. 47 no. 2 [GA, v. 24, p. 36] "Die Flamme hier, die wilde, zu verhehlen"

Nicht mehr zu dir zu gehen Beschloss ich, op. 32 no. 2 [GA, v. 23, p. 85] same

So stehn wir, ich und meine Weide, op. 32 no. 8 [GA, v. 23, p. 100] same

Wenn du nur zuweilen lächelst, op. 57 no. 2 [GA, v. 24, p. 86] same

BRAHMS, JOHANNES, 1833-1897
(continued)
Daumer, Georg Friedrich, 1800-1875
(continued)
HAFIS (continued)
   Wie bist du, meine Königin, op. 32 no.
     9 [GA, v. 23, p. 103] same
POLYDORA.
   Es träumte mir, op. 57 no. 3 [GA, v.
     24, p. 88] same
   Eine gute, gute Nacht, op. 59 no. 6
     [GA, v. 24, p. 157] same
   Die Kränze, op. 46 no. 1 [GA, v. 24,
     p. 18] "Hier ob dem Eingang seid"
   Magyarisch, op. 46 no. 2 [GA, v. 24,
     p. 22] "Sah' dem edlen Bildnis in
     des Auges"
   Die Schnur, die Perl an Perle, op. 57
     no. 7 [GA, v. 24, p. 100] same
   Schön war, das ich dir weihte, op. 95
     no. 7 [GA, v. 25, p. 178] same
   Wir wandelten, op. 96 no. 2 [GA, v.
     25, p. 182] same
DES KNABEN WUNDERHORN
   Liebesklage des Mädchens, op. 48 no. 3
     [GA, v. 24, p. 52] "Wer sehen will
     zweien lebendige Brunnen"
   Der Überläufer, op. 48 no. 2 [GA, v. 24,
     p. 51]
     "In den Garten wollen wir gehen"
   Wiegenlied, op. 49 no. 4 [GA, v. 24, p.
     73] "Guten Abend, gut' Nacht"
Eichendorff, Joseph Karl Benedikt,
  Freiherr von, 1788-1857.
   Anklänge, op. 7 no. 3 [GA, v. 23, p. 44]
     "Hoch über stillen Höhen"
   In der Fremde, op. 3 no. 5 [GA, v. 23, p.
     14]
     "Aus der Heimat hinter den Blitzen"
   Lied, op. 3 no. 6 [GA, v. 23, p. 16]
     "Lindes Rauschen in den Wipfeln"
   Mondnacht [GA, v. 26, p. 62] "Es war,
     als hätt' der Himmel"
   Vom Strande, Nach dem Spanischen, op.
     69 no. 6 [GA, v. 25, p. 16]
     "Ich rufe vom Ufer verlorenes Glück"
   DICHTER UND IHRE GESELLEN
     (1834).
     Parole, op. 7 no. 2 [GA, v. 23, p. 41]
       "Sie stand wohl am Fensterbogen"
Fleming, Paul, 1606-1640.
   An die Stolze, op. 107 no. 1 [GA, v. 26,
     p. 31] "Und gleichwohl kann ich
     anders nicht"
   O liebliche Wangen, op. 47 no. 4 [GA, v.
     24, p. 42] same

Frey, Adolf, 1855-1920.
   Meine Lieder, op. 106 no. 4 [GA, v. 26,
     p. 26]
     "Wenn mein Herz beginnt zu klingen"
Geibel, Emanuel, i.e., Franz Emanuel
  August, 1815-1884.
   Frühlingslied, op. 85 no. 5 [GA, v. 25, p.
     110] "Mit geheimnisvollen Düften"
SPÄTHERBSTBLÄTTER.
   Mein Herz ist schwer, op. 94 no. 3
     [GA, v. 25, p. 154] same
SPANISCHES LIEDERBUCH.
   Geistliches Wiegenlied, op. 91 no. 2
     [GA, v. 25, p. 140]
     "Die ihr schwebet um diese Palmen"
     Accompaniment for viola & piano.
     Text after Vega Carpio.
Goethe, Johann Wolfgang von, 1749-
  1832.
   Die Liebende schreibt, op. 47 no. 5 [GA,
     v. 24, p. 45] "Ein Blick von deinen
     Augen in die meinen"
   Trost in Tränen, op. 48 no. 5 [GA, v. 24,
     p. 56]
     "Wie kommt's, dass du so traurig bist"
   Unüberwindlich, op. 72 no. 5 [GA, v. 25,
     p. 77]
     "Hab' ich tausendmal geschworen"
   *CHINESISCH- DEUTSCHE JAHRES-
     UND TAGESZEITEN.*
     Dämmrung senkte sich von oben, op.
       59 no. 1 [GA, v. 24, p. 134] same
   CLAUDINE VON VILLA BELLA.
     Serenate, op. 70 no. 3 [GA, v. 25, p.
       40] "Liebliches Kind"
Grohe, Melchior, 1829-1906.
   O Komme, holde Sommernacht, op. 58
     no. 4 [GA, v. 24, p. 119] same
Groth, Klaus, 1819-1899.
   Komm bald, op. 97 no. 5 [GA, v. 25, p.
     202] "Warum denn warten von Tag zu
     Tag?"
   Nachklang, op. 59 no. 4 [GA, v. 24, p.
     150]
     "Regentropfen aus den Bäumen fallen"
   Regenlied, WoO 23 [GA, v. 26, p. 64]
     "Regentropfen aus den Bäumen fallen"
   HUNDERT BLÄTTER . . .
     Dein blaues Auge, op. 59 no. 8 [GA, v.
       24, p. 162] same
     Es hing der Reif, op. 106 no. 3 [GA, v.
       26, p. 23] same
     Heimweh I, op. 63 no. 7 [GA, v. 24, p.
       196]
       "Wie traulich war das Fleckchen"
     Heimweh II, op. 63 no. 8 [GA, v. 24,
       p. 199]
       "O wüsst ich doch den Weg zurück"

Heimweh III, op. 63 no. 9 [GA, v. 24,
   p. 203]
   "Ich sah als Knabe Blumen blühn"
Mein wundes Herz verlangt, op. 59 no.
   7 [GA, v. 24, p. 159] same
Regenlied, op. 59 no. 3 [GA, v. 24, p.
   142] "Walle, Regen, walle nieder"
Wie Melodien zieht es mir, op. 105 no.
   1 [GA, v. 26, p. 1] same

Gruppe, Otto Friedrich, 1804-1876.
Das Mädchen spricht, op. 107 no. 3 [GA,
   v. 26, p. 37] "Schwalbe, sag' mir an"

Häring, Wilhelm, 1798-1871.
Entführung, op. 97 no. 3 [GA, v. 25, p.
   198] "O Lady Judith, spröder Schatz"

Hebbel, Christian Friedrich, 1813-1863.
In der Gasse, op. 58 no. 6 [GA, v. 24, p.
   124] "Ich blicke hinab in die Gasse"
Vorüber, op. 58 no. 7 [GA, v. 24, p. 126]
   "Ich legte mich unter den
   Lindenbaum"

Heine, Heinrich, 1797-1856.
Es schauen die Blumen, op. 96 no. 3
   [GA, v. 25, p. 185] same
FRÜHLING.
   Es liebt sich so lieblich im Lenze, op.
   71 no. 1 [GA, v. 25, p. 46]
   "Die Wellen blinken und fliessen"
HEIMKEHR.
   Mondenschein, op. 85 no. 2 [GA, v.
   25, p. 102] "Nacht liegt auf den
   fremden Wegen"
   Sommerabend, op. 85 no. 1 [GA, v.
   25, p. 100]
   "Dämmernd liegt der Sommerabend"
DIE HEIMKEHR.
   Der Tod, das ist die kühle Nacht, op.
   96 no. 1 [GA, v. 25, p. 180] same
*TRAGÖDIEN NEBST EINEM
   LYRISCHEN INTERMEZZO.*
   Meerfahrt, op. 96 no. 4 [GA, v. 25, p.
   188] "Mein Liebchen, wir sassen
   beisammen"

**Heyse, Paul Johann Ludwig von,
1830-1914.**
Mädchenlied, op. 95 no. 6 [GA, v. 25, p.
   176] "Am jüngsten Tag ich aufersteh"
Mädchenlied, op. 107 no. 5 [GA, v. 26,
   p. 42]
   "Auf die Nacht in den Spinnstub'n"
ITALIENISCHES LIEDERBUCH.
   Am Sonntag Morgen, op. 49 no. 1
   [GA, v. 24, p. 64] same
SPANISCHES LIEDERBUCH (1852).
   Spanisches Lied, op. 6 no. 1 [GA, v.
   23, p. 20]
   "In dem Schatten meiner Locken"

**Hölty, Ludwig Heinrich Christoph,
1748-1776.**
An ein Veilchen, op. 49 no. 2 [GA, v. 24,
   p. 66] "Birg, O Veilchen, in deinem
   blauen Kelche"
Der Küss, op. 19 no. 1 [GA, v. 23, p. 67]
   "Unter Blüten des Mai's"
Die Mainacht, op. 43 no. 2 [GA, v. 24, p.
   7] "Wann der silberne Mond"
Minnelied, op. 71 no. 5 [GA, v. 25, p.
   60] "Holder klingt der Vogelsang"
Die Schale der Vergessenheit, op. 46 no.
   3 [GA, v. 24, p. 24]
   "Eine Schale des Stroms"
GEUSS NICHT SO LAUT.
   An die Nachtigall, op. 46 no. 4 [GA, v.
   24, p. 28]
   "Geuss nicht so laut"

**Hoffmann von Fallersleben, August
Heinrich, 1798-1874.**
Liebe und Frühling, op. 3 no. 2 [GA, v.
   23, no. 4]
   "Wie sich Rebenranken schwingen"
Liebe und Frühling, op. 3 no. 3 [GA, v.
   23, p. 8]
   "Ich muss hinaus, ich muss zu dir"
Nachtigallen schwingen, op. 6 no. 6 [GA,
   v. 23, p. 34] same
Wie die Wolke nach der Sonne, op. 6 no.
   5 [GA, v. 23, p. 32] same

Kalbeck, Max, 1850-1921.
NÄCHTE.
   Nachtwandler, op. 86 no. 3 [GA, v. 25,
   p. 120]
   "Störe nicht den leisen Schlummer"

Kapper, Siegfried, 1821-1879.
Ade! (Nach dem Böhmischen) op. 85 no.
   4 [GA, v. 25, p. 106]
   "Wie scheinen die Sternlein so hell, so
   hell"
Das Mädchen, op. 95 no. 1 [GA, v. 25,
   p. 161] "Stand das Mädchen, stand am
   Bergesabhang"
Mädchenlied, op. 85 no. 3 [GA, v. 25, p.
   104]
   "Ach, und du mein kühles Wasser!"
Vorschneller Schwur, op. 95 no. 5 [GA,
   v. 25, p. 174]
   "Schwor ein junges Mädchen"
DIE GESÄNGE DER SERBEN.
   Mädchenfluch, Nach dem Serbischen,
   op. 69 no. 9 [GA, v. 25, p. 28]
   "Ruft die Mutter, ruft der
   Tochter"

Keller, Gottfried, 1819-1890.
Abendregen, op. 70 no. 4 [GA, v. 25, p.
   42] "Langsam und schimmernd fiel ein
   Regen"

BRAHMS, JOHANNES, 1833-1897
(continued)
Keller, Gottfried, 1819-1890 *(continued)*
  Salome, op. 69 no. 8 [GA, v. 25, p. 25]
    "Singt mein Schatz wie ein Fink"
  Therese, op. 86 no. 1 [GA, v. 25, p. 116]
    "Du milchjunger Knabe"
Köstlin, Christian Reinhold, 1813-
1856.
  Auf dem Schiffe, op. 97 no. 2 [GA, v. 25,
    p. 194]
    "Ein Vögelein fliegt über den Rhein"
  Auf dem See, op. 106 no. 2 [GA, v. 26, p.
    18] "An dies Schifflein schmiege"
  Nachtigall, op. 97 no. 1 [GA, v. 25, p.
    192] "O Nachtigall, dein süsser Schall"
  Ein Wanderer, op. 106 no. 5 [GA, v. 26,
    p. 28]
    "Hier, wo sich die Strassen scheiden"
Kopisch, August, 1799-1853.
  Blinde Kuh, op. 58 no. 1 [GA, v. 24, p.
    109] "Im Finstern geh' ich suchen"
  Die Spröde, op. 58 no. 3 [GA, v. 24, p.
    116] "Ich sahe eine Tig'rin"
  Während des Regens, op. 58 no. 2 [GA,
    v. 24, p. 112]
    "Voller, dichter tropft ums Dach da"
Kugler, Franz Theodor, 1808-1858.
  SKIZZENBUCH.
  Ständchen, op. 106 no. 1 [GA, v. 26,
    p. 15]
    "Der Mond steht über dem Berge"
Lemcke, Karl von, 1831-1913.
  Im Garten am Seegestade, op. 70 no. 1
    [GA, v. 25, p. 35] same
  Im Waldeseinsamkeit, op. 85 no. 6 [GA,
    v. 25, p. 113]
    "Ich sass zu deinen Füssen"
  Salamander, op. 107 no. 2 [GA, v. 26, p.
    35] "Es sass ein Salamander"
  Über die See, op. 69 no. 7 [GA, v. 25,
    no. 23] same
  Verrat, op. 105 no. 5 [GA, v. 26, p. 10]
    "Ich stand in einer lauen Nacht"
  Verzagen, op. 72 no. 4 [GA, v. 25, p. 72]
    "Ich sitz' am Strande der rauschenden
    See"
  Willst du, dass ich geh'? op. 71 no. 4
    [GA, v. 25, p. 56] "Auf der Heide
    weht der Wind (herzig Kind)"
Liliencron, Detlov, Freiherr von, 1844-
1909.
  Auf dem Kirchhofe, op. 105 no. 4 [GA, v.
    26, p. 8] "Der Tag ging regenschwer
    und sturmbewegt"
  Maienkätzchen, op. 107 no. 4 [GA, v. 26,
    p. 40] "Maienkätzchen, erster Gruss"

Lingg, Hermann, 1820-1905.
  Immer leiser wird mein Schlummer, op.
    105 no. 2 [GA, v. 26, p. 4] same
Meissner, Alfred, 1822-1885.
  Nachwirkung, op. 6 no. 3 [GA, v. 23, p.
    26] "Sie ist gegangen"
Mörike, Eduard Friedrich, 1804-1875.
  Agnes, op. 59 no. 5 [GA, v. 24, p. 153]
    "Rosenzeit, wie schnell vorbei"
  An eine Äolsharfe, op. 19 no. 5 [GA, v.
    23, p. 74] "Angelehnt an die
    Efeuwand"
Münch-Bellinghausen, Eligius Franz
Joseph, freiherr von, 1806-1871.
  Bei dir sind meine Gedanken, op. 95 no.
    2 [GA, v. 25, p. 165] same
  Beim Abschied, op. 95 no. 3 [GA, v. 25,
    p. 168] "Ich müh' mich ab, und kann's
    nicht verschmerzen"
  Der Jäger, op. 95 no. 4 [GA, v. 25, p.
    172] "Mein Lieb ist ein Jäger, und
    grün ist sein Kleid"
  Kein Haus, keine Heimat, op. 94 no. 5
    [GA, v. 25, p. 160] same
  Steig' auf, geliebter Schatten, op. 94 no.
    2 [GA, v. 25, p. 152] same
Platen-Hallermünde, August, Graf
von, 1796-1835.
  Du sprichst, dass ich mich täuschte, op.
    32 no. 6 [GA, v. 23, p. 95] same
  Ich schleich umher betrübt, op. 32 no. 3
    [GA, v. 23, p. 88] same
  Der Strom, der neben mir verrauschte,
    op. 32 no. 4 [GA, v. 23, p. 89] same
  Wehe, so willst du mich wieder, op. 32
    no. 5 [GA, v. 23, p. 92] same
  Wie rafft' ich mich auf in der Nacht, op.
    32 no. 1 [GA, v. 23, p. 79] same
Reinick, Robert, 1805-1852.
  Juchhe! op. 6 no. 4 [GA, v. 23, p. 28]
    "Wie ist doch die Erde so schön, so
    schön!"
  Liebestreu, op. 3 no. 1 [GA, v. 23, p. 1]
    "O versenk', O versenk' dein Leid"
Rousseau, Johann Baptist, 1802-1867.
  Der Frühling, op. 6 no. 2 [GA, v. 23, p.
    24]
    "Es lockt und säuselt um den Baum"
Rückert, Friedrich, 1788-1866.
  Gestillte Sehnsucht, op. 91 no. 1 [GA, v.
    25, p. 132]
    "In goldnen Abendschein getauchet"
    Accompaniment for viola & piano.
  Mit vierzig Jahren, op. 94 no. 1 [GA, v.
    25, p. 149] same
Schack, Adolf Friedrich, Graf von,
1815-1894.

Abenddämmerung, op. 49 no. 5 [GA, v. 24, p. 74]
"Sei willkommen, Zwielichtstunde"

Herbstgefühl, op. 48 no. 7 [GA, v. 24, p. 60] "Wie wenn im frost'gen Windhauch tödtlich"

Serenade, op. 58 no. 8 [GA, v. 24, p. 129] "Leise, um dich nicht zu wecken"

Schenkendorf, Max von, 1783-1817.

An die Trauben, op. 63 no. 4 [GA, v. 24, p. 182]
"Fleigt nur aus, geliebte Tauben!"

An ein Bild, op. 63 no. 3 [GA, v. 24, p. 178] "Was schaust du mich so freundlich an"

Erinnerung, op. 63 no. 2 [GA, v. 24, p. 174] "Ihr wunderschönen Augenblicke"

Frühlingstrost, op. 63 no. 1 [GA, v. 24, p. 164]
"Es weht um mich Narzissenduft"

Todessehnen, op. 86 no. 6 [GA, v. 25, p. 128]
"Ach, wer nimmt von meiner Seele"

Schmidt, Hans, 1854-1923.

In den Beeren, op. 84 no. 3 [GA, v. 25, p. 89] "Singe, Mädchen, hell und klar"

Der Kranz, op. 84 no. 2 [GA, v. 25, p. 85] "Mutter, hilf mir armen Tochter"

Sappische Ode, op. 94 no. 4 [GA, v. 25, p. 158] "Rosen brach ich Nachts mir am dunklen Hage"

Sommerabend, op. 84 no. 1 [GA, v. 25, p. 81]
"Geh' schlafen, Tochter, schlafen!"

Schulz, Eduard, 1813-1842.

Treue Liebe, op. 7 no. 1 [GA, v. 23, p. 38]
"Ein Mägdlein sass am Meeresstrand"

Schumann, Felix, 1854-1879.

Junge Lieder I, op. 63 no. 5 [GA, v. 24, p. 188] "Meine Liebe ist grün wie der Fliederbusch"

Junge Lieder II, op. 63 no. 6 [GA, v. 24, p. 193] "Wenn um den Hollunder der Abendwind kost"

Versunken, op. 86 no. 5 [GA, v. 25, p. 124] "Es brausen der Liebe Wogen"

Simrock, Karl Joseph, 1802-1876.

An den Mond, op. 71 no. 2 [GA, v. 25, p. 50]
"Silbermond, mit bleichen Strahlen"

Auf dem See, op. 59 no. 2 [GA, v. 24, p. 138] "Blauer Himmel, blaue Wogen"

Storm, Theodor, 1817-1888.

Über die Heide, op. 86 no. 4 [GA, v. 25, p. 122] same

Thibaut IV, King of Navarre, 1201-1253.

Ein Sonnett, op. 14 no. 4 [GA, v. 23, p. 58]
"Ach könnt' ich, könnte vergessen sie"

Tieck, Johann Ludwig, 1773-1853.

Liebe kam aus fernen Landen, op. 33 no. 4 [GA, v. 23, p. 126] same

Muss es eine Trennung geben, op. 33 no. 12 [GA, v. 23, p. 175] same

Ruhe, Süssliebchen, op. 33 no. 9 [GA, v. 23, p. 158] same

Sind es Schmerzen, op. 33 no. 3 [GA, v. 23, p. 119] same

So willst du des Armen, op. 33 no. 5 [GA, v. 23, p. 132] same

Sulima, op. 33 no. 13 [GA, v. 23, p. 178]
"Geliebter, wo zaudert dein irrender Fuss?"

Traun, Bogen und Pfeil sind gut für den Feind, op. 33 no. 2 [GA, v. 23, p. 116] same

Treue Liebe dauert lange, op. 33 no. 15 [GA, v. 23, p. 189] same

Verzweiflung, op. 33 no. 10 [GA, v. 23, p. 165]
"So tönet denn, schäumende Wellen"

War es dir, dem dies Lippen bebten? op. 33 no. 7 [GA, v. 23, p. 147] same

Wie froh und frisch, op. 33 no. 14 [GA, v. 23, p. 183] same

Wie schnell verschwindet so Licht als Glanz, op. 33 no. 11 [GA, v. 23, p. 171] same

Wie soll ich die Freude, op. 33 no. 6 [GA, v. 23, p. 136] same

Wir müssen uns trennen, op. 33 no. 8 [GA, v. 23, p. 152] same

WUNDERSCHÖNE LIEBESGESCHICHTE . . .

Keinen hat es noch gereut, op. 33 no. 1 [GA, v. 23, p. 107] same

Uhland, Ludwig, 1787-1862.

Heimkehr, op. 7 no. 6 [GA, v. 23, p. 48]
"O brich nicht Steg, du zitterst sehr"

Das Lied von Herrn von Falkenstein, op. 43 no. 4 [GA, v. 24, p. 12]
"Es reit der Herr von Falkenstein"

Der Schmied, op. 19 no. 4 [GA, v. 23, p. 73] "Ich hör' meinen Schatz"

Sonntag, op. 47 no. 3 [GA, v. 24, p. 40]
"So hab' ich doch die ganze Woche"

WANDERLIEDER.

In der Ferne, op. 19 no. 3 [GA, v. 23, p. 70]
"Will ruhen unter den Bäumen hier"

BRAHMS, JOHANNES, 1833-1897
(continued)
Uhland, Ludwig, 1787-1862 (continued)
WANDERLIEDER (continued)
Scheiden und Meiden, op. 19 no. 2
[GA, v. 23, p. 69]
"So soll ich dich nun meiden"
Wenzig, Josef, 1807-1876.
Von ewiger Liebe, op. 43 no. 1 [GA,
v. 24, p. 1] "Dunkel, wie dunkel im
Wald und in Feld!"
WESTSLAWISCHEM
MÄRCHENSCHATZ.
Abschied, Böhmisch, op. 69 no. 3 [GA,
v. 25, p. 7]
"Ach, mich hält der Gram gefangen"
Des Liebsten Schwur, Aus dem
Böhmischen, op. 69 no. 4 [GA,
v. 25, p. 9] "Ei, schmollte mein
Vater nicht wach und im Schlaf"
Klage I, Aus dem Böhmischen, op. 69
no. 1 [GA, v. 25, p. 1]
"Ach mir fehlt, nicht ist da"
Klage II, Slowakisch, op. 69 no. 2
[GA, v. 25, p. 4]
"O Felsen, lieber Felsen"
Branco, Frau Helene [von Rödlich] 1818-
1894.
LOEWE
Alles in dir
Allmacht Gottes
Dein Auge
Des Mädchens Wunsch und Geständnis
Du Geist der reinsten Güte
Frühling
Das Glockenspiel der Phantasie
Mit jedem Pulsschlag leb' ich dir
Mondlicht
Brandenburg, Otto von, 1266-1308.
JENSEN *Räumt den Weg!*
Branders Lied see Goethe *FAUST.*
WAGNER
Braun, Ferdinand, fl.1841.
SCHUMANN *Frühlingslied*
Braun von Braunthal, Johann Karl,
1802-1866.
SPOHR
Gruss
Sonatine, B flat minor, op. 138 "An sie
am Klavier"
Das braune Mädchen see Anon. *THE NUT-*
BROWNE MAYD. **LOEWE**
Braungart, Richard, 1872-1963.
REGER
Abendfrieden
Du brachtest mir deiner Seele Trank

Gebet
Mensch und Natur
Ein Paar
Schlecht' Wetter
Tränen
Warte nur!
Wiegenlied
"Braust des Unglücks Sturm empor" *see Trost*
im Liede Schober **SCHUBERT**
Die Braut see Hamerling **JENSEN**
Die Braut am Gestade see Voss **ZELTER**
Die Braut von Corinth see Goethe **LOEWE,**
ZELTER
Brautkranzlied see Goldtammer, Frau
LOEWE
Brautlied see Brumm, Pauline **LOEWE**
Brautlied see Redwitz *LIEDER DER*
AMARANTH. **LOEWE**
BRAUTLIEDER I
CORNELIUS Cornelius *Ein Myrtenreis*
BRAUTLIEDER II
CORNELIUS Cornelius *Der Liebe Lohn*
BRAUTLIEDER III
CORNELIUS Cornelius *Vorabend*
BRAUTLIEDER IV
CORNELIUS Cornelius *Am Morgen*
BRAUTLIEDER V
CORNELIUS Cornelius *Aus dem hohen*
Liede
BRAUTLIEDER VI
CORNELIUS Cornelius *Märchenwunder*
Brautring see Ritter **REGER**
DER BRAUTWILLKOMM AUF WARTBURG.
see Scheffel
Biterolf und der Schmied von Ruhla **LISZT**
Heinrich von Ofterdingen **LISZT**
Reimar der Alte **LISZT**
Der tugendhafte Schreiber **LISZT**
Walther von der Vogelweide **LISZT**
The breakers are pounding, and surging so
high see Tolstoĭ **RIMSKIĬ-KORSAKOV**
Drobitsĭa, i pleshchet
"Breathe from the gentle south" *see*
The waiting soul Cowper **IVES**
Brecht, Bertolt, 1898-1956.
BLACHER *Zwei chansons*
"Den breda elf genom skogens barm" *see*
Älvan och snigeln Josephson, E.
SIBELIUS
Breden, Christiane (Friderik), 1844-1901.
SCHÖNBERG *Dass schon die Maienzeit*
vorüber
Breit' über mein Haupt see Schack
LOTOSBLÄTTER. **STRAUSS**
Die brennenden Tulpen see Hafiz
SZYMANOWSKI

Brentano, Clemens Maria, 1778-1842.
BRAHMS *O kühler Wald*
HINDEMITH *Zwei Lieder*
STRAUSS
  Als mir dein Lied erklang
  Amor
  An die Nacht
  Ich wollt' ein Sträusslein binden
  Lied der Frauen
  Säusle, liebe Myrthe
Brentano, Fritz, 1840-1914.
REGER *Leise, leise weht ihr Lüfte*
Breton, Nicholas, 1542-1626.
IRELAND *A report song*
MELANCHOLIC HUMOURS (1600).
HESELTINE *Fair and true*
"Die bretterne Kammer der Toten erbebt" *see*
  Der Geistertanz Matthisson **SCHUBERT**
Two settings: D. 15 and D. 116.
Breuning, Stephan von, 1774-1827.
BEETHOVEN *Als die Geliebte sich*
  trennen wollte
Brevier see Prölss **LASSEN**
Brewster, Lyman Dennison, 1832-1904,
  supposed author.
IVES *The all-enduring*
"Bricht das matte Herz" *see Lied*
  Hardenberg **ZELTER**
Bricourt, Louis
MASSENET *Fleurs cueillies*
Bridges, Robert Seymour, 1844-1930.
BERKELEY *So sweet love seemed*
Brief an Danzi see Weber, Karl **WEBER**
  Komisches musikalisches Sendschreiben
Einen Brief soll ich schreiben see Storm
  REGER
Briesen, Otto von
LOEWE *Letzter Seufzer*
Brigand's song see Kol'tsov **BALAKIREV**
  Pesnya razboynika
Bright is the ring of words see Stevenson,
  Robert Louis *SONGS OF TRAVEL*, XIV.
  VAUGHAN WILLIAMS
"Bright is the ring of words" *see To the*
  memory of a great singer
  Stevenson, Robert Louis **HESELTINE**
The bright moon see IAtsevicha
  BALAKIREV *Vzoshol na nebo mesyats*
  yasnïy
"The bright moon, oh so white it shines" *see*
  Old poem Waley, Arthur **COPLAND**
Il Brigidino see Ongaro **VERDI**
Brigid's song see Joyce *A PORTRAIT OF*
  THE ARTIST AS A YOUNG MAN.
  DIAMOND

Brimont, Renée de, Baronne, 1880-1943.
FAURÉ
  Cygne sur l'éau
  Danseuse
  Jardin nocturne
  Reflets dans l'éau
SAUGUET *La belle morte*
Brindisi see Maffei **VERDI**
Two settings: 1835? And 1845.
"Bring us in no beef, sir" *see Peter Warlock's*
  fancy Anon. **HESELTINE**
"Bring us in no brown bread" *see Good ale*
  Anon. **HESELTINE**
"Bringet des treusten Herzens Grüsse" *see*
  Reiselied Ebert
  MENDELSSOHN-BARTHOLDY
La brise see Renaud **SAINT-SAËNS**
Brisieux, Charles *see* Brizeux, Charles
BRITTEN, BENJAMIN, 1913-1976.
Anon.
  Begone, dull care, op. 7 no. 1 [Boosey &
    Hawkes, 1936] same
  Ee-Oh! op. 7 no. 4 [Boosey & Hawkes,
    1936] "The fox and his wife"
  May (1934) [Ascherberg, Hopwood &
    Crew, 1935]
    "Now is the month of maying"
    For unison chorus & piano.
  A new year carol, op. 7 no. 5 [Boosey &
    Hawkes, 1936]
    "Here we bring new water"
  Old Abram Brown, op. 7 no. 12
    [Boosey & Hawkes, 1936] same
  There was a man of Newington, op. 7 no.
    7 [Boosey & Hawkes, 1936] same
  There was a monkey, op. 7 no. 11
    [Boosey & Hawkes, 1936] same
  The useful plough, op. 7 no. 9 [Boosey &
    Hawkes, 1936]
    "A country life is sweet"
Asquith, Herbert, 1881-1947.
THE VOLUNTEER.
  Epitaph: The clerk (1926) [Faber,
    1985]
    "Here lies the clerk who half his life
      had spent"
Auden, Wystan Hugh, 1907-1973.
  Calypso (1939) [Faber, 1980] "Driver,
    drive faster and make a good run"
  Fish in the unruffled lakes (1937)
    [Boosey & Hawkes, 1947] same
  Funeral blues (1937) [Faber, 1980]
    "Stop all the clocks"
  Johnny (1937) [Faber, 1980]
    "O the valley in the summer when I
      and my John"

BRITTEN, BENJAMIN, 1913-1976
(continued)
Auden, Wystan Hugh, 1907-1973
(continued)
Tell me the truth about love (1938)
[Faber, 1980]
"Liebe l'amour amor amoris, Some say
that Love's a little boy"
THE DOG BENEATH THE SKIN.
Nocturne, op. 11 no. 4 [Boosey &
Hawkes, 1938]
"Now thro' night's caressing grip"
HIS EXCELLENCY.
As it is, plenty, op. 11 no. 5 [Boosey &
Hawkes, 1938] same
LOOK, STRANGER!
Let the florid music praise! op. 11 no.
1 [Boosey & Hawkes, 1938]
same
Now the leaves are falling fast, op. 11
no. 2 [Boosey & Hawkes, 1938]
same
ON THIS ISLAND.
Seascape, op. 11 no. 3 [Boosey &
Hawkes, 1938]
"Look, stranger, at this island now"
Belloc, Hilaire, 1870-1953.
The birds (1929, rev. 1934) [Boosey &
Hawkes, 1935] "When Jesus Christ
was four years old"
Blake, William, 1757-1827.
The chimney-sweeper, op. 74 [Faber,
1965]
"A little black thing among the
snow"
A cradle song, op. 41 no. 1 [Boosey &
Hawkes, 1949]
"Sleep! sleep! beauty bright"
Mezzo-soprano & piano.
The fly, op. 74 [Faber, 1965]
"Little fly, little fly"
London, op. 74 [Faber, 1965]
"I wander thro' each charter'd street"
A poison tree, op. 74 [Faber, 1965]
"I was angry with my friend"
Proverb V, op. 74 [Faber, 1965]
"The tygers of wrath are wiser than the
horses of instruction"
AH! SUN-FLOWER.
Ah! Sun-flower, op. 74 [Faber, 1965]
"Ah, Sun-flower! weary of time"
AUGURIES OF INNOCENCE.
Every night and every morn, op. 74
[Faber, 1965] same
Proverb VII, op. 74 [Faber, 1965]
"To see a world in a grain of sand"
PROVERBS OF HELL.
Proverb I, op. 74 [Faber, 1965]

"The pride of the peacock is the
glory of God"
Proverb II, op. 74 [Faber, 1965]
"Prisons are built with stones of
Law"
Proverb III, op. 74 [Faber, 1965]
"The bird a nest"
Proverb IV, op. 74 [Faber, 1965]
"Think in the morning"
Proverb VI, op. 74 [Faber, 1965]
"The hours of folly are measur'd by
the clock"
THE TYGER.
The tyger, op. 74 [Faber, 1965]
"Tyger! Tyger! burning bright"
Buonarroti, Michel Angelo, 1475-1564.
Sonetto XVI, op. 22 no. 1 (1940)
[Boosey & Hawkes, 1943]
"Sì come nella penna e nell'inchiostro"
Tenor & piano.
Sonetto XXIV, op. 22 no. 7 (1940)
[Boosey & Hawkes, 1943] "Spirto ben
nato, in cui si specchia e vede"
Tenor & piano.
Sonetto XXX, op. 22 no. 3 (1940)
[Boosey & Hawkes, 1943] "Veggio co'
bei vostri occhi un dolce lume"
Tenor & piano.
Sonetto XXXI, op. 22 no. 2 [Boosey &
Hawkes, 1943] "A che più debb' io
mai l'intensa voglia"
Tenor & piano.
Sonetto XXXII, op. 22 no. 6 (1940)
[Boosey & Hawkes, 1943]
"S'un casto amor, s'una pietà superna"
Tenor & piano.
Sonetto XXXVIII, op. 22 no. 5 (1940)
[Boosey & Hawkes, 1943]
"Rendete a gli occhi miei, O fonte O
fiume"
Tenor & piano.
Sonetto LV, op. 22 no. 4 (1940)
[Boosey & Hawkes, 1943] "Tu sa'
ch'io so, signior mie, che tu sai"
Tenor & piano.
Burns, Robert, 1759-1796.
Afton water, op. 92 no. 5 [Faber, 1978]
"Flow gently, sweet Afton"
Birthday song, op. 92 no. 1 [Faber, 1978]
"Health to our well-lo'ed Hielan
Chief!"
The highland balou, op. 41 no. 2
[Boosey & Hawkes, 1949]
"Hee balou, my sweet wee Donald"
Mezzo-soprano & piano.
Leezie Lindsay, op. 92 no. 7 [Faber,
1978] "Will ye go to the Hielands,
Leezie Lindsay?"

My early walk, op. 92 no. 2 [Faber,
   1978] "A rose bud by my early walk"
My Hoggie, op. 92 no. 4 [Faber, 1978]
   "What will I do gin my Hoggie die"
O that I'd ne'er been married (1922)
   [Faber, 1985] same
Wee Willie, op. 92 no. 3 [Faber, 1978]
   "Wee Willie Gray, and his leather
   wallet"
The winter, op. 92 no. 6 [Faber, 1978]
   "The winter is past, and the summer
   comes at last"

De La Mare, Walter, 1873-1956.

Autumn (1928-31, rewritten 1968) [Faber,
   1969]
   "There is a wind where the rose was"
Silver (1928-31, rewritten 1968) [Faber,
   1969] "Slowly, silently, now the
   moon"
A song of enchantment (1928-31,
   rewritten 1968) [Faber, 1969]
   "A song of enchantment I sang me
   there"
Tit for tat (1928-31, rewritten 1968)
   [Faber, 1969] "Have you been catching
   of fish, Tom Noddy?"
Vigil (1928-31, rewritten 1968) [Faber,
   1969] "Dark is the night"
PEACOCK PIE.
   The ship of Rio (1963) [Oxford Univ.
   Press, 1964] "There was a ship of
   Rio sail'd out into the blue"
   Arranged by Britten from 1932 two-
   part song.

Donne, John, 1573-1631.

At the round Earth's imagined corners,
   op. 35 no. 7 (1945)
   [Boosey & Hawkes, 1946] same
   High voice & piano.
Batter my heart, op. 35 no. 2 (1945)
   [Boosey & Hawkes, 1946] same
   High voice & piano.
Death, be not proud, op. 35 no. 9 (1945)
   [Boosey & Hawkes, 1946] same
   High voice & piano.
O might those sighes and teares, op. 35
   no. 3 (1945) [Boosey & Hawkes,
   1946] same
   High voice & piano.
Oh my blacke Soule! op. 35 no. 1 (1945)
   [Boosey & Hawkes, 1946] same
   High voice & piano.
Oh, to vex me, op. 35 no. 4 (1945)
   [Boosey & Hawkes, 1946] same
   High voice & piano.

Since she whom I loved, op. 35 no. 6
   (1945) [Boosey & Hawkes, 1946]
   same
   High voice & piano.
Thou hast made me, op. 35 no. 8 (1945)
   [Boosey & Hawkes, 1946] same
   High voice & piano.
What if this present, op. 35 no. 5 (1945)
   [Boosey & Hawkes, 1946] same
   High voice & piano.

Eliot, Thomas Stearns, 1888-1965.

THE DEATH OF SAINT NARCISSUS.
   Canticle V, op. 89 [Faber, 1976]
   "Come under the shadow of this
   gray rock–"
   Tenor & harp.

Farjeon, Eleanor, 1881-1965.

Jazz-man, op. 7 no. 10 [Boosey &
   Hawkes, 1936] "Crash and clang!"

Greene, Robert, ca.1558-1592.

Sephestia's lullaby, op. 41 no. 3
   [Boosey & Hawkes, 1949] "Weep not,
   my wanton, smile upon my knee"
   Mezzo-soprano & piano.

Hardy, Thomas, 1840-1928.

At day-close in November, op. 52 no. 1
   (1953) [Boosey & Hawkes, 1954]
   "The ten hours' light is abating"
   Tenor & piano.
At the railway station, Upway, op. 52
   no. 7 (1953) [Boosey & Hawkes,
   1954]
   "There is not much that I can do"
   Tenor & piano.
Before life and after, op. 52 no. 8 (1953)
   [Boosey & Hawkes, 1954]
   "A time there was as one may guess"
   Tenor & piano.
The choirmaster's burial, op. 52 no. 5
   (1953) [Boosey & Hawkes, 1954]
   "He often would ask us that, when he
   died"
   Tenor & piano.
The little old table, op. 52 no. 4 (1953)
   [Boosey & Hawkes, 1954]
   "Creak, creak, little wood thing"
   Tenor & piano.
Midnight on the Great Western, op. 52
   no. 2 (1953) [Boosey & Hawkes,
   1954] "In the third class seat sat the
   journeying boy"
   Tenor & piano.
Proud songsters, op. 52 no. 6 (1953)
   [Boosey & Hawkes, 1954]
   "The thrushes sing as the sun is going"
   Tenor & piano.

BRITTEN, BENJAMIN, 1913-1976
(continued)
Hardy, Thomas, 1840-1928 *(continued)*
Wagtail and baby, op. 52 no. 3 (1953)
[Boosey & Hawkes, 1954]
"A baby watch'd a ford, whereto a
wagtail came for drinking"
Tenor and piano.
Hölderlin, Friedrich, 1770-1843.
Hälfte des Lebens, op. 61 no. 5 (1958)
[Boosey & Hawkes, 1963]
"Mit gelben Birnen hänget"
Die Heimat, op. 61 no. 2 (1958)
[Boosey & Hawkes, 1963]
"Froh kehrt der Schiffer heim an den
Stillen Strom"
Die Jugend, op. 61 no. 4 (1958)
[Boosey & Hawkes, 1963]
"Da ich ein Knabe war"
Die Linien des Lebens, op. 61 no. 6
(1958) [Boosey & Hawkes, 1963]
same
Menschenbeifall, op. 61 no. 1 (1958)
[Boosey & Hawkes, 1963]
"Ist nicht heilig mein Herz"
Sokrates und Alcibiades, op. 61 no. 3
(1958) [Boosey & Hawkes, 1963]
"Warum huldigest du, heiliger
Sokrates"
Longfellow, Henry Wadsworth, 1807-
1882.
Beware (1923) [Faber, 1985]
"I know a maiden fair to see"
Lu Yu, 1125-1210.
The herd-boy, op. 58 no. 4 (1957)
[Boosey & Hawkes, 1959]
"In the southern village the boy who
minds the ox"
High voice & guitar.
Phillip, John
The nurse's song, op. 41 no. 5
[Boosey & Hawkes, 1949]
"Lullaby baby, lullabylaby bady"
Mezzo-soprano & piano.
Po Chü-i, 772-846.
Depression, op. 58 no. 5 (1957)
[Boosey & Hawkes, 1959]
"Turned to jade are the boy's rosy
cheeks"
High voice & guitar.
The old lute, op. 58 no. 2 (1957)
[Boosey & Hawkes, 1959]
"Of cord and cassiawood is the lute
compounded"
High voice & guitar.

Pushkin, Aleksandr Sergeevich, 1799-
1837.
Angel, op. 76 no. 3 (1965) [Faber, 1967]
"At Eden's gate a gentle angel"
Echo, op. 76 no. 1 (1965) {*Zkho*} [Faber,
1967]
"From leafy woods the savage howl"
Epigram, op. 76 no. 5 (1965)
{*Epigramma*} [Faber, 1967]
"Half a milord, half of a boss"
Lines written during a sleepless night, op.
76 no. 6 (1965) {*Stikhi, sochinennye
noch'iu vo vremia vessonnitsy*} [*Faber,
1967*]
"Sleep forsakes me with the light"
My heart . . . op. 76 no. 2 {*IA dumal,
serdtse pozabylo*} [Faber, 1967]
"My heart, I fancied it was over"
The nightingale and the rose, op. 76 no.
4 (1965) {*Solovei i roza*} [Faber, 1967]
"The garden's dark and still; 'tis
spring"
Quarles, Francis, 1592-1644.
Canticle I, op. 40 (1947) [Boosey &
Hawkes, 1949] "Ev'n like two little
bank divided brooks"
Randolph, Thomas, 1605-1635.
A charm, op. 41 no. 4 [Boosey &
Hawkes, 1949]
"Quiet sleep! or I will make Erinnys
whip thee"
Mezzo-soprano & piano.
Shakespeare, William, 1564-1616.
MERCHANT OF VENICE.
Fancie (1961) [Boosey & Hawkes]
"Tell me, tell me, where is fancie
bred"
First published in Harewood *Classical
songs for children* (London: A.
Blond, 1964), p. 251.
Sitwell, Edith, Dame, 1887-1964.
THE CANTICLE OF THE ROSE.
Canticle III, op. 55 (1954) [Boosey &
Hawkes, 1956]
"Still falls the rain"
Accompaniment for horn & piano.
Soutar, William, 1898-1943.
The auld aik, op. 84 no. 12 (1969)
[Faber, 1972] "The auld aik's doun"
Bed-time, op. 84 no. 5 (1969) [Faber,
1972] "Cuddle-doun, my bairnie"
Black day, op. 84 no. 4 (1969) [Faber,
1972] "A skelp frae his teacher"
The children, op. 84 no. 11 (1969)
[Faber, 1972]
"Upon the street they lie"

A laddie's sang, op. 84 no. 2 (1969)
[Faber, 1972] "O! it's owre the braes
abüne our toun"

The larky lad, op. 84 no. 8 (1969) [Faber,
1972] "The larky lad frae the pantry"

Nightmare, op. 84 no. 3 (1969) [Faber,
1972]
"The tree stood flowering in a dream"

A riddle, op. 84 no. 1 (1969) [Faber,
1972] "There's pairt o' it young"

A riddle, op. 84 no. 7 (1969) [Faber,
1972] "It was your faither and mither"

Slaughter, op. 84 no. 6 (1969) [Faber,
1972]
"Within the violence of the storm"

Supper, op. 84 no. 10 (1969) [Faber,
1972] "Steepies for the bairnie"

Who are these children? op. 84 no. 9
(1969) [Faber, 1972]
"With easy hands upon the rein"

Taylor, Jane, 1783-1824.
Cuckoo! op. 7 no. 3 [Boosey & Hawkes,
1936]
"Cuckoo, Cuckoo, What do you do?"

**Thackeray, William Makepeace, 1811-
1863.**
A tragic story, op. 7 no. 2 [Boosey &
Hawkes, 1936] "There liv'd a sage"

Udall, Nicholas, 1505-1556.
I must be married on Sunday, op. 7 no. 6
[Boosey & Hawkes, 1936] same

Unknown
THE BOOK OF SONGS.
The big chariot, op. 58 no. 1 (1957)
[Boosey & Hawkes, 1959]
"Don't help on the big chariot"
High voice & guitar.

Dance song, op. 58 no. 6 (1957)
[Boosey & Hawkes, 1959]
"The unicorn's hoofs! The unicorn's
hoofs!"
High voice & guitar.

Walton, Izaak, 1593-1683.
Fishing song, op. 7 no. 8 [Boosey &
Hawkes, 1936]
"Oh, the gallant fisher's life"

Wu-Ti, Han dynasty, 157-87 B.C.
The autumn wind, op. 58 no. 3 (1957)
[Boosey & Hawkes, 1959]
"Autumn wind rises; white clouds fly"
High voice & guitar.

Briussov, Valeri *see* **Bryusov, Valery
Yakovlevich, 1873-1924.**

Brizeux, Charles
FRANCK *La procession*

**Brizeux, Julien Auguste Pélage, 1806-
1858.**
BERLIOZ
Le chant des Bretons
Le jeune pâtre breton

Brodeuses see **Mauclair AUBERT**

"Brodí se panenka, brodí se, brodí" *see Lásce
neujdeš* Anon. **DVOŘÁK**

Brontë, Emily Jane, 1818-1848.
IRELAND *Love and friendship*

Brooding see **Shevchenko**
RACHMANINOFF *Meditation*

Brooke, Rupert, 1887-1915.
BLITZSTEIN *All sudden by the wind*
GRIFFES *WaiKiKi*
IRELAND
Blow out, you bugles
The soldier
Spring sorrow
IVES *Grantchester*

Brother see **Carpenter, Rue CARPENTER**

Broughten, James Richard, 1913-1999.
ROREM *The orphan girl in the pleasure
garden*

"Broutez le thym, broutez mes chèvres" *see
La chanson du pâtre* Augier **GOUNOD**

Brown eyes see Anon. **PROKOFIEV** *Kari
glazki*

Brown, Herbert S
IRELAND *The holy boy*

Brown is my love see Anon. **QUILTER**

Brown penny see Yeats **RIETI**

Brown, S
GIDEON *Southern road*

Browning, Robert, 1812-1889.
ROREM *Love in a life*
PARACELSUS.
IVES *from "Paracelsus"*

**Bruchmann, Franz, Ritter von, 1798-
1867.**
SCHUBERT
Am See
Im Haine
Schwestergruss
Der zürnende Barde

BRUCKNER, ANTON, 1824-1896.
Anon.
Ave Maria (1882) [A.Böhm, 1932; Annie
Bank] same
Contralto & organ; Latin words.

Ernst, Heinrich Wilhelm, 1814-1865.
Herbstkummer (ca.1868) [Göllerich
Anton Bruckner . . . iii/2,151]
"Die Blumen vergehen, der Sommer ist
hin"

BRUCKNER, ANTON, 1824-1896
(continued)
Geibel, Emanuel, i.e., Franz Emanuel
  August, 1815-1884.
  Im April (ca.1868) [Doblinger, 1898]
    "Du feuchter Frühlingsabend"
Heine, Heinrich, 1797-1856.
  Frühlingslied (1851) [Göllerich *Anton*
    Bruckner . . . ii/2,44]
    "Leise zieht durch mein Gemüt"
Martinelli?
  Wild wie Bäche (ca.1846-50) [Göllerich
    Anton Bruckner . . . ii/2,59]
    First line in Göllerich illegible.
Platen-Hallermünde, August, Graf
  von, 1796-1835.
  Mein Herz und deine Stimme (ca.1868)
    [Göllerich *Anton Bruckner* . . . iii/
    2,144] "Lass tief in dir mich lesen"
Redwitz, Oskar, Freiherr von, 1823-
  1891.
  Amaranths' Waldeslieder (ca.1858)
    [*Die Musik* i/3 (1902), Suppl.
    (following p.1619)]
    "Wie bist du Frühling gut und treu"
Unknown
  O du liebes Jesukind (ca.1845) [Göllerich
    Anton Bruckner . . . ii/2,13] same
    Tenor & organ.
Einen Bruder hatt' ich, einen Geliebten see
  Unknown **RUBINSTEIN**
Bruder Liederlich see Liliencron **STRAUSS**
Das Brüderchen see Kiesekamo **REGER**
"Le bruit de l'aéro se fane à la descente" *see*
  Biplan le matin Cocteau **AURIC**
"Bruit profond de la mer" *see Sur la grève*
  Humières **KOECHLIN**
Brumm, Pauline
  LOEWE *Brautlied*
Brun, Carl, 1851-1923.
  GRIEG *Odalisken synger*
Brun, Friedericke *see* Brun, Sophie
  Christiane Frederikke (Münter), 1765-
  1835.
Brun, Sophie Christiane Frederikke
  (Münter), 1765-1835.
  ZELTER
    Abendphantasie
    Ich denke dein
Brunnensang see Flemes **REGER**
Bruno, Camille
  MASSENET
    La rivière
    Tes cheveux
    Tout passé
Bruyn, Bertha de

PIJPER
  Meiliedje
  Nachtliedje
  Sneeuwklokjes
  Vlinderliedje
Bruyr, José
  HONEGGER
    L'hymne de la délivrance
    Hymne du sport
Bryan, Waller Procter, 1787-1874.
  BENNETT
    Dawn, gentle flower
    Indian love
    Sing, maiden, sing
Bryusov, Valery Yakovlevich, 1873-1924.
  MEDTNER *In the church-yard*
  RACHMANINOFF The rat-catcher
DAS BUCH DER HÄNGENDEN GÄRTEN.
  see George
  Als Neuling trat ich ein in dein Gehege
    SCHÖNBERG
  Als wir hinter dem beblümten Tore
    SCHÖNBERG
  Angst und Hoffen wechselnd mich
    beklemmen **SCHÖNBERG**
  Da meine Lippen reglos sind und brennen
    SCHÖNBERG
  Du lehnest wider eine Silberweide
    SCHÖNBERG
  Hain in diesen Paradiesen **SCHÖNBERG**
  Jedem Werke bin ich fürder tot
    SCHÖNBERG
  Saget mir auf welchem Pfade
    SCHÖNBERG
  Das schöne Beet betracht ich mir im
    Harren **SCHÖNBERG**
  Sprich nicht immer **SCHÖNBERG**
  Streng ist uns das Glück und spröde
    SCHÖNBERG
  Unterm schutz von dichten Blättergründen
    SCHÖNBERG
  Wenn ich heut nicht deinen Leib berühre
    SCHÖNBERG
  Wenn sich bei heiliger Ruh in tiefen Matten
    SCHÖNBERG
  Wir bevölkerten die abend-düstern
    SCHÖNBERG
DAS BUCH DER HÄNGENDEN GÄRTEN,
  no. 1
  SCHÖNBERG George *Unterm schutz von*
    dichten Blättergründen
DAS BUCH DER HÄNGENDEN GÄRTEN,
  no. 2
  SCHÖNBERG George *Hain in diesen*
    Paradiesen
DAS BUCH DER HÄNGENDEN GÄRTEN,
  no. 3

SCHÖNBERG George *Als Neuling trat ich ein in dein Gehege*
DAS BUCH DER HÄNGENDEN GÄRTEN, no. 4

SCHÖNBERG George *Da meine Lippen reglos sind und brennen*
DAS BUCH DER HÄNGENDEN GÄRTEN, no. 5

SCHÖNBERG George *Saget mir auf welchem Pfade*
DAS BUCH DER HÄNGENDEN GÄRTEN, no. 6

SCHÖNBERG George *Jedem Werke bin ich fürder tot*
DAS BUCH DER HÄNGENDEN GÄRTEN, no. 7

SCHÖNBERG George *Angst und Hoffen wechselnd mich beklemmen*
DAS BUCH DER HÄNGENDEN GÄRTEN, no. 8

SCHÖNBERG George *Wenn ich heut nicht deinen Leib berühre*
DAS BUCH DER HÄNGENDEN GÄRTEN, no. 9

SCHÖNBERG George *Streng ist uns das Glück und spröde*
DAS BUCH DER HÄNGENDEN GÄRTEN, no. 10

SCHÖNBERG George *Das schöne Beet betracht ich mir im Harren*
DAS BUCH DER HÄNGENDEN GÄRTEN, no. 11

SCHÖNBERG George *Als wir hinter dem beblümten Tore*
DAS BUCH DER HÄNGENDEN GÄRTEN, no. 12

SCHÖNBERG George *Wenn sich bei heiliger Ruh in tiefen Matten*
DAS BUCH DER HÄNGENDEN GÄRTEN, no. 13

SCHÖNBERG George *Du lehnest wider eine Silberweide*
DAS BUCH DER HÄNGENDEN GÄRTEN, no. 14

SCHÖNBERG George *Sprich nicht immer*
DAS BUCH DER HÄNGENDEN GÄRTEN, no. 15

SCHÖNBERG George *Wir bevölkerten die abend-düstern*
BUCH DER LIEDER. see Heine
Der Fichtenbaum DELIUS
DAS BUCH DER SAGEN UND SÄNGE:
Sänge eines fahrenden Spielmanns. *see*
George *So ich traurig bin weiss ich nur ein Ding* WEBERN

"Bûcheron Abats mon ombre" *see Chanson de l'oranger sec* Garcia Lorca POULENC
Buchillot, G.
  MASSENET
    Oh! si les fleurs avaient des yeux
    Les yeux clos
Buddeus, Julius, fl.1850.
  SCHUMANN
    Die Meerfee
    Resignation
"The buds are bursting in the brake" *see April love* Quilter QUILTER
Budy, Friedrich, 1809-1856.
  LOEWE *Deutsche Flotte*
BÜHNE UND HAUS. see Harnier
  Immer dasselbe SPOHR
Buerde, Samuel Gottlieb, 1753-1831.
  LOEWE *Lobgesang*
Bürde, Samuel Gottlob *see* Buerde, Samuel Gottlieb, 1753-1831.
Bürger, Gottfried August, 1747-1794.
  BEETHOVEN
    Das Blümchen Wunderhold
    Gegenliebe
    Mollys Abschied
    Seufzer eines Ungeliebten
  CORNELIUS
    Der Entfernten
    Liebe ohne Heimat
    Verlust (Auf Mollys Tod, 1859)
  PFITZNER
    An die Bienen
    An die Morgenröte
    Gegenliebe
    Schön Suschen
    Trauerstille
  STRAUSS *Muttertändelei*
  ZELTER *Lust am Liebchen*
Bürger, J. H.
  WEBER *Liebeszauber*
Die Bürgschaft see Schiller SCHUBERT
Bugayev, Boris Nikolaevich, 1880-1934.
  RACHMANINOFF *To her*
  DRUZBIAM.
    MEDTNER *Epitaph*
The bugle song see Tennyson
  THE PRINCESS. THOMSON
Bulcke, Carl, 1875-1936.
  SZYMANOWSKI *Einsiedel*
"Bulle de savon Egayant ta pipe Gambier" *see Pelouse* Radiguet AURIC
Bulwer-Lytton *see*
  Lytton, Edward George Earle Lytton Bulwer-Lytton, 1st baron, 1803-1873.
Bundeslied see Goethe SCHUBERT

Bunin, Ivan Alekseevich, 1870-1953.
   RACHMANINOFF *Night is mournful*
Bunn, Alfred, 1796?-1860.
   THE BOHEMIAN GIRL.
      DELIUS *When other lips shall speak*
"Bunt sind schon die Wälder" *see Herbstlied*
   Salis-Seewis **SCHUBERT**
BUNTE BEUTE. see Liliencron
   Heimgang in der Frühe **WEBERN**
BUNTE LIEDER, no. 1
   SZYMANOWSKI Bulcke *Einsiedel*
BUNTE LIEDER, no. 2
   SZYMANOWSKI Paquet *Lied des*
   Mädchens am Fenster
BUNTE LIEDER, no. 3
   SZYMANOWSKI Faktor *An kleine*
   Mädchen
BUNTE LIEDER, no. 4
   SZYMANOWSKI Ritter *Das hat die*
   Sommernacht getan
BUNTE LIEDER, no. 5
   SZYMANOWSKI Huch *Bestimmung*
Die bunten Kühe see Falke **REGER**
Bunyan, John, 1628-1688.
   DIAMOND *The shepherd boy sings in the*
   valley of humiliation
   VAUGHAN WILLIAMS
   The song of the pilgrims
   The woodcutter's song
Buonaparty see Hardy THE DYNASTS.
   VAUGHAN WILLIAMS
Buonarroti, Michel Angelo, 1475-1564.
   BRITTEN
   Sonetto XVI
   Sonetto XXIV
   Sonetto XXX
   Sonetto XXXI
   Sonetto XXXII
   Sonetto XXXVIII
   Sonetto LV
   PIZZETTI *Vorrei voler, Signor, quel ch'io*
   non voglio
   SCHOECK *Die Verklärende*
   WOLF
   Alles endet, was entstehet
   Fühlt meine Seele
   Wohl denk' ich oft
   MADRIALE.
      SCHOECK, STRAUSS *Madrigal*
Burchiello, Domenico di Giovanni,
   known as, 1404-1448.
   MALIPIERO
   Andando a uccellare
   Cacio stillato
   Rose spinose
   Va in mercato, Giorgin

Burd Ellen and young Tamlane see Anon.
   MAIDMENT'S NORTH COUNTRIE
   GARLAND (1824). **HESELTINE**
"Burd Ellen sits in her bower windowe" *see*
   Burd Ellen and young Tamlane Anon.
   HESELTINE
"Burgen mit hohen Mauern und Zinnen" *see*
   Lied der Soldaten Goethe **WAGNER**
Buri
   SPOHR *Klagelied von den drei Rosen*
Buria see Pushkin **RACHMANINOFF**
   The storm
EL BURLADOR DE SEVILLA. see Tellez
   Phantasie **MAHLER**
   Serenade **MAHLER**
Burns, Robert, 1759-1796.
   BENNETT
   Castle Gordon, or The young Highland
   rover
   Musing on the roaring ocean
   Stay, my charmer
   To Chloe in sickness
   BERG *O wär' mein Lieb' jen' Röslein rot*
   BRITTEN
   Afton water
   Birthday song
   The highland balou
   Leezie Lindsay
   My early walk
   My Hoggie
   O that I'd ne'er been married
   Wee Willie
   The winter
   FRANZ
   Für Einen
   Ihr Auge
   Ihr Hügel dort am schönen Doon
   Lovely maid!
   Mein Hochland-Kind
   Montgomery-Gretchen
   My heart is in the Highland
   My love is like a red rose
   Nun holt mir eine Kanne Wein
   O wert thou in the cauld blast
   The pleasant summer's come
   So far away
   The sorrowful maiden
   Die süsse Dirn' von Inverness
   Thou hast left me ever, Jame
   Was pocht mein Herz so sehr
   GIDEON
   Epitaph for a wag in Mauchline
   Epitaph on the author
   Epitaph on wee Johnie
   Monody on a lady famed for her caprice
   JENSEN
   Du süsse Dirn' von Inverness

Einen schlimmen Weg ging gestern ich
Für Einen
John Anderson, mein Lieb
Leb' wohl mein Ayr!
Mein Herz ist im Hochland
O säh' ich auf der Heide dort
LASSEN It's nae thy bonnieface
LOEWE Findlay
MACDOWELL
  Deserted
  Menie
  My Jean
NIELSEN Tag Jer i Agt for Anna
RAVEL Chanson écossaise
RIEGGER Ye banks and braes o' Bonnie
  Doon
SCHUMANN
  Dem rothen Röslein gleicht mein Lieb
  Hauptmann's Weib
  Hochländers Abschied
  Die Hochländer-Wittwe
  Hochländisches Wiegenlied
  Im Westen
  Jemand
  Niemand
  Weit, weit
STRAUSS John Anderson
A burnt ship see Donne **ROREM**
Der Bursch see Vinje **GRIEG** Guten
Busch, Wilhelm, 1832-1908.
  HINDEMITH Drei Lieder
  SCHOECK Dilemma
Busse, Carl, 1872-1918.
  BERG
    Ich und du
    Das stille Königreich
    Über den Bergen
  PFITZNER
    Gretel
    Leierkastenmann
    Michaelskirchplatz
    Stimme der Sehnsucht
  REGER
    Der Sausewind
    Schlafliedchen
    Wenn die Linde blüht
  SCHOECK Über den Bergen
  STRAUSS
    Blauer Sommer
    Weisser Jasmin
  HEDWIG.
    STRAUSS Wenn
Busse-Palma, Georg, 1876-1915.
  BERG Furcht
  SIBELIUS Erloschen
Busslied see Gellert **BEETHOVEN,**
  LOEWE

Busslied see Sturm, C. **LOEWE**
Busslied see Unknown **LOEFFLER**
"Busy, curious, thirsty fly!" see On a fly
  drinking out of his cup Oldys
  HINDEMITH
But my bird is long in homing see Fröding
  SIBELIUS Men min fågel märks dock icke
"But perhaps he is a friend of yours?" see
  The epitaph Smith, Logan **DIAMOND**
The butterfly see Bal'mont **PROKOFIEV**
  Babochka
Butterfly see Shenshin **MEDTNER**
By a fountainside see Jonson **QUILTER**
By a lonely forest pathway see Lenau
  SCHILFLIEDER. **GRIFFES**
  Auf geheimem Waldespfade
"By morning's brightest beams" see Allegro
  Ives, Harmony **IVES**
By night see Bible **THOMSON**
"By night on my bed I sought him" see By
  night Bible **THOMSON**
By the fountains of Rome see Unknown
  SEIBER
By the fresh grave see Nadson
  RACHMANINOFF
By the grave see Nadson
  RACHMANINOFF By the fresh
  grave
By the river see Golenishchev-Kutuzov
  MUSORGSKIĬ Nad rekoĭ
By the sea see Quilter **QUILTER**
BY THE SEA, no. 1
  RIMSKIĬ-KORSAKOV Tolstoĭ Drobitsia,
  i pleshchet
BY THE SEA, no. 2
  RIMSKIĬ-KORSAKOV Tolstoĭ Ne
  penitsia more
BY THE SEA, no. 3
  RIMSKIĬ-KORSAKOV Tolstoĭ
  Kolyshetsia more
BY THE SEA, no. 4
  RIMSKIĬ-KORSAKOV Tolstoĭ Ne ver'
  mne, drug
BY THE SEA, no. 5
  RIMSKIĬ-KORSAKOV Tolstoĭ
  Vzdymaiutsia volny
By the shore of the river Babylon see Bible
  DVOŘÁK Při řekách babylonských
"By ways remote and distant waters sped" see
  Catullus: On the burial of his brother
  Catullus **ROREM**
By-an'-by see Anon. **LOEFFLER**
"Byl raz sobie zolnierz, co mial dwie
  kochanki" see O zawiedzionym zolnierzu
  Unknown **SZYMANOWSKI**
"Byl u Khrista mladentsa sad" see Legenda
  Pleshcheyev **CHAĬKOVSKIĬ**

COMPOSER Poet *Title* "First Line"

"Bylo to, ach!" *see Lípy* Pech **DVOŘÁK**
"Bylykh strasteĭ" *see Zveno* Tumanskiĭ
BALAKIREV
Byron, George Gordon Byron, 6th
baron, 1778-1824.
  DIAMOND
    All is vanity
    If that high world
    My soul is dark
    Saul
  GOUNOD *Maid of Athens*
  IVES *from the "Incantation"*
  LASSEN
    Mein Leben, ich liebe dich
    There was a time
  LOEWE
    Alles ist eitel, spricht der Prediger
    An den Wassern zu Babel
    Davids Harfe
    Herodes' Klage um Mariamne
    Die höh're Welt
    Jephthas Tochter
    Jerusalems Zerstörung durch
      Titus
    Jordans Ufer
    Lebewohl
    Mein Geist ist trüb'
    Sanherib's Niederlage
    Saul
    Saul vor seiner letzten Schlacht
    Sie geht in Schönheit
    Die Sonne der Schlaflosen
    Thränen und Lächeln
    Todtenklage
    Wär' ich wirklich so falsch?
    Weint um Israel!
    Die wilde Gazelle

    Wohin, O Seele, wirst du eilen?
LUENING
    The harp the monarch minstrel swept
    She walks in beauty
MENDELSSOHN-BARTHOLDY
    Sun of the sleepless
    There be none of beauty's
      daughters
NIELSEN *Min Sjael er mørk*
QUILTER *There be none of beauty's*
    daughters
RIMSKIĬ-KORSAKOV *Pesnia Ziuleĭki*
SCHUMANN
    Aus den "Hebräischen Gesängen"
    Die Weinende
WOLF *Keine gleicht von allen Schönen*
CHILDE HAROLD'S PILGRIMAGE.
  IVES *A farewell to land*
HEBREW MELODIES.
  LOEWE
    Belsazar's Gesicht
    Eliphas' Gesicht
    Saul und Samuel
  MUSORGSKIĬ *TSar' Saul*
  SCHUMANN
    An den Mond
    Dem Helden
    Die Tochter Jephtha's
MY SOUL IS DARK.
  RUBINSTEIN *Hebräische Melodie*
PORTUGUESE IMITATION.
  RIMSKIĬ-KORSAKOV *V poryve*
    nezhnosti serdechnoĭ
SUN OF THE SLEEPLESS!
  WOLF *Sonne der Schlummerlosen*
Bzicem kunia see Anon. **SZYMANOWSKI**

C

C see Aragon **POULENC**
"Ca dé dis! lorsque je me fâche" *see*
  Le gascon Mendès **BIZET**
"Ĉa n'a pas mordu, ce soir" *see Le Martin-*
  Pêcheur Renard **RAVEL**
Cabanillas, Ramón, 1876-1959.
  MOMPOU *Aureana do sil*
CABARET SONGS, no. 1
  BRITTEN Auden *Tell me the truth about*
    love
CABARET SONGS, no. 2
  BRITTEN Auden *Funeral blues*

CABARET SONGS, no. 3
  BRITTEN Auden *Johnny*
CABARET SONGS, no. 4
  BRITTEN Auden *Calypso*
"Cabré devant la noire escallade du mur" *see*
  Pégase Margueritte **MALIPIERO**
Cache la fée see Hugnet **SAUGUET**
Cacio stillato see Burchiello **MALIPIERO**
"Cadet-Rousselle a trois chapeaux" *see*
  Variations sur "Cadet rousselle" Anon.
  IRELAND
Cäcilie see Hart, J. **STRAUSS**

The cage see Ives **IVES**
Cake and Sack see De La Mare *PEACOCK*
PIE. **CHANLER**
Calamnius, Ilmari *see* Kianto, Ilmari,
1874-1970.
Calderon de la Barca, Pedro, 1600-1681.
EL ALCALDE DE ZALAMEA.
    STRAUSS
      Liebesliedchen
      Lied der Chispa
The call see Anon. **ROREM**
The call see Pushkin **MEDTNER**
    The summons
"Call for the robin red-breast and the wren"
    see Dirge Webster **THOMSON**
Callanau, I
    NIELSEN *Serenade*
CALLIGRAMMES. see Apollinaire
    Aussi bien que les cigales **POULENC**
    L'espionne **POULENC**
    La grâce exilée **POULENC**
    Il pleut **POULENC**
    Mutation **POULENC**
    Vers le sud **POULENC**
    Voyage **POULENC**
CALLIGRAMMES, no. 1
    POULENC Apollinaire *L'espionne*
CALLIGRAMMES, no. 2
    POULENC Apollinaire *Mutation*
CALLIGRAMMES, no. 3
    POULENC Apollinaire *Vers le sud*
CALLIGRAMMES, no. 4
    POULENC Apollinaire *Il pleut*
CALLIGRAMMES, no. 5
    POULENC Apollinaire *La grâce exilée*
CALLIGRAMMES, no. 6
    POULENC Apollinaire *Aussi bien que les*
    cigales
CALLIGRAMMES, no. 7
    POULENC Apollinaire *Voyage*
Callimachus, ca.305-ca.240 B.C.
    HESELTINE *Heracleitus*
"Calmes dans le demi-jour" *see En sourdine*
    Verlaine **DEBUSSY**
    Two settings: 1882 and 1892.
"Calmes dans le demijour" *see En sourdine*
    Verlaine **FAURÉ, HAHN**
Calypso see Auden **BRITTEN**
"Los caminos de la tarde" *see Pastoral*
    Jimenez **MOMPOU**
Cammaerts, Emile Leon, 1878-1953.
    COPLAND *After Antwerp*
    MESSINES . . .
      CARPENTER *Berceuse de la guerre*
    DE DENTRO TENGO MI MAL.
    SCHUMANN *Tief im Herzen*
    WOLF *Tief im Herzen trag' ich Pein*

The camp meeting see Elliot **IVES**
Campbell
    GOUNOD *Woe's me! woe's me!*
Campbell, Joan
    CARPENTER *The pools of peace*
Campe, Joachim Heinrich, 1746-1818.
    MOZART *Abendempfindung an Laura*
Campion, Thomas, 1567-1619.
    QUILTER *My life's delight*
    THOMSON
      Follow thy fair sun
      Follow your saint
      Rose cheek'd Laura, come
      There is a garden in her face
      What is it?
    GILES EARLE, HIS BOOKE (1616-1625).
    HESELTINE *The lover's maze*
Campoamor, Ramón *see* Campoamor y
    Campoosorio, Ramón María . . . ,
    1817-1901.
Campoamor y Campoosorio, Ramón
    María . . . , 1817-1901.
    TURINA
      Cantares
      Los dos miedos
      Farruca
      Las locas por amor
      Nunca olvida
Canard see Anon. **STRAVINSKIĬ**
Les canards, les cygnes, les oies . . . see
    Anon. **STRAVINSKIĬ**
Canary see Mei **CHAĬKOVSKIĬ** *Kanareyka*
Cancheri e beccafichi magri arosto see Berni
    MALIPIERO
Cancion see Anon. **FALLA**
Canción de baile con pandero see Anon.
    RODRIGO
Canción de cuna see Anon. **RODRIGO**; *see*
    also his *Nani, nani* (Cancion de cuna, 1968)
Cancion del cucu see Kamhi, Victoria
    RODRIGO
Canción del duero see Machado y Ruiz
    RODRIGO
Cancion del grumete see Anon. **RODRIGO**
Cançó de la Fira see Garcés **MOMPOU**
Cançó del teuladí see Llorente **RODRIGO**
La canço dels invadits see Mestres
    SÉVERAC
Cançoneta incerta see Carner **MOMPOU**
Candidus, Karl August, 1817-1872.
    BRAHMS
      Alte Liebe
      Geheimnis
      Lerchengesang
      Schwermut
      Sommerfäden
      Tambourliedchen
    SCHUMANN *Husarenabzug*

COMPOSER Poet *Title* "First Line"

CANDLELIGHT: A CYCLE OF NURSERY
JINGLES, no. 1
  HESELTINE Anon. *How many miles to
  Babylon?*
CANDLELIGHT: A CYCLE OF NURSERY
JINGLES, no. 2
  HESELTINE Anon. *I won't be my
  father's Jack*
CANDLELIGHT: A CYCLE OF NURSERY
JINGLES, no. 3
  HESELTINE Anon. *Robin and Richard*
CANDLELIGHT: A CYCLE OF NURSERY
JINGLES, no. 4
  HESELTINE Anon. *O my kitten*
CANDLELIGHT: A CYCLE OF NURSERY
JINGLES, no. 5
  HESELTINE Anon. *Little Tommy Tucker*
CANDLELIGHT: A CYCLE OF NURSERY
JINGLES, no. 6
  HESELTINE Anon. *There was an old
  man*
CANDLELIGHT: A CYCLE OF NURSERY
JINGLES, no. 7
  HESELTINE Anon. *I had a little pony*
CANDLELIGHT: A CYCLE OF NURSERY
JINGLES, no. 8
  HESELTINE Anon. *Little Jack Jingle*
CANDLELIGHT: A CYCLE OF NURSERY
JINGLES, no. 9
  HESELTINE Anon. *There was a man of
  Thessaly*
CANDLELIGHT: A CYCLE OF NURSERY
JINGLES, no. 10
  HESELTINE Anon. *Suky, you shall be my
  wife*
CANDLELIGHT: A CYCLE OF NURSERY
JINGLES, no. 11
  HESELTINE Anon. *There was an old
  woman*
CANDLELIGHT: A CYCLE OF NURSERY
JINGLES, no. 12
  HESELTINE Anon. *Arthur o' Bower*
Canon see Moore, T. **IVES**
Cansón pel cabalet see Estieu **SÉVERAC**
Cant per Nadal see Goudouli **SÉVERAC**
Cantaban los niños see Machado y Ruiz
  RODRIGO
Cantar del alma see John, Saint, apostle
  MOMPOU
Cantares see Campoamor y Campoosorio
  TURINA
Cantate sylvestre see Desnoux, Lucienne
  SAUGUET *Pour un cyprés*
Canti oghun see Poliziano **RIETI**
Canticel see Carner **RODRIGO**
Canticle I see Quarles **BRITTEN**

Canticle III see Sitwell *THE CANTICLE OF
  THE ROSE.* **BRITTEN**
Canticle V see Eliot *THE DEATH OF SAINT
  NARCISSUS.* **BRITTEN**
Canticle in memory of Dick Sheppard see
  Quarles **BRITTEN** *Canticle I*
THE CANTICLE OF THE ROSE. see Sitwell
  Canticle III **BRITTEN**
Cantico de la esposa see San Juan de la
  Cruz **RODRIGO**
Canticum Canticorum
  PIZZETTI
  Adjuro vos, filiae Jerusalem
    Two settings: 1908 and 1932-33.
  In lectulo meo
  Surge, propera, amica mia
Cantiga see Vicente, Gil **RODRIGO**
Cantilena see Rivas **TURINA**
CANTILENE ALL'ARIA APERTA. see
  Pàntini, Romualdo
  La Madre al figlio lontano **PIZZETTI**
Un cantique see Montesquiou- **SCHMITT**
Cantique see Ségur **GOUNOD**
Cantique à l'Épouse see Jounet
  CHAUSSON
Cantique pour la première communion see
  Dulong de Rosnay, R. P. **GOUNOD**
Cantique sur le bonheur des justes . . . see
  Racine **HAHN**
Canto della neve see Anon. **MALIPIERO**
IL CANTO DELLA QUAGLIA. see Sauter
  Der Wachtelschlag **BEETHOVEN,
  SCHUBERT**
Canto funebre see Shelley **RESPIGHI**
CANTO NOVO: Canto Dell'ospite, no. VI. *see*
  Annunzio *Van li effluvi de le rose*
  RESPIGHI
CANTO NOVO: Canto Dell'ospite, no. VII.
  see Annunzio *O falce di luna* **RESPIGHI**
Le cantonnier see Mallarmé **MILHAUD**
Canzon Andaluza: El pan de ronda see
  Martinez Sierra **FALLA**
Canzone see Donini **RESPIGHI**
Canzone dans le mode hypolidien see No
  author **SÉVERAC**
*Canzone di ringraziamento per un prussiano
  avendo . . . see* Gounod **GOUNOD**
Canzone per ballo see Anon. **PIZZETTI**
Canzone sacra see Unknown **RESPIGHI**
Canzonetta see Metastasio **WEBER** *Ch' io
  mai vi possa*
Canzonetta see Unknown **WEBER**
  Ah dove siete?
  Ninfe se liete
Canzonetta: Italienisches Ständchen see
  Anon. **WEBER**

Canzonetta spagnuola "En medio a mis
   colores" *see* Unknown **ROSSINI**
Canzonetta toscana *see* Anon.
   SAINT-SAËNS
Canzonette *see* Goethe **LOEWE** *Kanzonette*
Canzonette *see* Rückert **JENSEN**
Capetanakis, Demetrios, 1912-1944.
   ROREM
      Abel
      Angel
      Experienced by two stones
      Guilt
      The land of fear
"Capitaine tu as su des malheurs" *see Chant
   de l'émigrant* Bloch **HONEGGER**
Capitulation *see* Jacob, T. **LOEWE**
   Kapitulation
Capri, Agnès
   SAUGUET *Un bouquet à la main*
Capriccio *see* Lemene **MALIPIERO**
Caprice *see* Banville *AMÉTHYSTES.*
   DEBUSSY
Captain Stratton's fancy *see* Masefield
   BALLADS AND POEMS (1903).
   HESELTINE
The Captain's wife *see* Burns **SCHUMANN**
   Hauptmann's Weib
La captive *see* Hugo **BERLIOZ**
"Captive, et peut-être oubliée" *see L'Esclave*
   Gautier **LALO, MASSENET**
Le carafon *see* Carême **POULENC**
Caralis, pseud. *see* Preetzman, Caspara,
   1792-1876.
La caravane *see* Gautier **CHAUSSON**
"La caravane humaine" *see La caravane*
   Gautier **CHAUSSON**
"Caravelle de mes rêves" *see La crise* Jacob,
   M. **RIETI**
Carducci, Giosuè, 1835-1907.
   CASELLA
      Il bove
      Pianto antico
Carême, Maurice, 1899-1978.
   MILHAUD
      L'amoureux
      Le beau navire
      La bise
      La chance
      Le charme
      Destinée
      La dormeuse
      Les feuilles
      Le lièvre et le blé
      La peine
      La prière
      Sortilège

POULENC
   Les anges musiciens
   Ba, be, bi, bo, bu
   Le carafon
   Lune d'Avril
   Quelle aventure!
   La reine de coeur
   Le sommeil
SAUGUET
   L'adolescent
   Celui que j'aime
   Il vieillissait
   Image
   Ingénuité
   Je marcherai pour toi
   Je sais qu'il existe
   Je serai toujours là
   Je suis un oiseau
   Nul ne se lasse d'être soi
   Le semeur
   Seul sur la terre
   Simplicité
LE LANTERNE MAGIQUE.
   SCHMITT *Le cerlster*
LES CARIATIDES, livre 2, Amours
   d'Élise . . . no. V. *see* Banville
   Rêverie **DEBUSSY**
LES CARIATIDES, livre 3, no. II. *see*
   Banville *Zéphyr* **DEBUSSY**
LES CARIATIDES, livre 3, no. III. *see*
   Banville *Fête galante* **AURIC, DEBUSSY**
LES CARIATIDES, livre 3, no. V. *see*
   Banville *Les bergers* **AURIC**
LES CARIATIDES, livre 3, no. VI. *see*
   Banville *Pierrot* **DEBUSSY**
LES CARIATIDES, livre 3, no. VII. *see*
   Banville *Sérénade* **DEBUSSY**
LES CARIATIDES, livre 3, no. X. *see*
   Banville *Parade* **AURIC**
LES CARIATIDES, livre 3, no. XV. *see*
   Banville *Les roses* **DEBUSSY**
LES CARIATIDES, livre 3, no. XVII. *see*
   Banville *Les lilas* **DEBUSSY**
"Carillon funèbre" *see La sirène au
   coquillage* Gengenbach, Eric de
   SAUGUET
La carità *see* Salustri *LE FAVOLE
   ROMANESCHE.* **CASELLA**
Carlisle Tor *see* Cunningham **JENSEN**
Carner, José, 1884-1971.
   MOMPOU *Cançoneta incerta*
   RODRIGO *Canticel*
Carner, Josep *see* Carner, José, 1884-
   1971.
THE CARNIVAL. see Prokosch
   Nocturne **BARBER**

COMPOSER   Poet   *Title*   "First Line"

Carpani, Giuseppe, 1752-1825.
BEETHOVEN ZELTER *In questa tomba oscura*
Le carpe see Apollinaire *LE BESTIAIRE.*
POULENC
The carpenter see Heine **MEDTNER** *Lieb Liebchen*
CARPENTER, JOHN ALDEN, 1876-1951.
Agee, James, 1909-1955.
SONNET XX.
Morning fair (1935) [G. Schirmer, 1936] "Now stands our love on that still verge of day"
Alexander, Griffith
My sweetheart [Miles & Thompson, 1894] "She's neither scholarly nor wise"
Austin, Mary (Hunter), 1868-1934.
Young man, chieftan! (1929) [G. Schirmer, 1930] "Lord of the Mountain, reared within the Mountain"
Barnes, William, 1801-1886.
Don't Ceäre (1911) [G. Schirmer, 1912] "At the feäst, I do mind very well, all the vo'ks"
COME.
Wull ye come in the eärly spring (1914) [G. Schirmer, 1918] same
Blake, William, 1757-1827.
A cradle-song (1911) [G. Schirmer, 1912] "Sleep, sleep, beauty bright"
Little fly (1909) [G. Schirmer, 1912] "Little fly, thy summer's play"
Cammaerts, Emile Leon, 1878-1953.
MESSINES . . .
Berceuse de la guerre (1918) [G. Schirmer, 1918] "Dodo, l'enfant do, l'enfant dormira tantôt"
Campbell, Joan
The pools of peace (1934) [G. Schirmer, 1938]
"The quiet pools of peace lie far"
Carpenter, John Alden, 1876-1951.
Blue gal (1941) [unpubl.] "When a gal is breathin' sorrow cause her man is far away"
Holograph at the Library of Congress. Also voice & orchestra.
The home-road (1917) [G. Schirmer, 1945] "Sing a Hymn of Freedom, fling the banner high!"
Khaki Sammy (1917) [G. Schirmer, 1917] "All the way from Illinois to a little old town in France"
Carpenter, Rue (Winterbotham), d.1931.
About my garden [A.C.McClurg, 1904] "Out in the sun my garden stands"

Aspiration [A.C.McClurg, 1904] "O what would I give"
Brother [A.C.McClurg, 1904] "My brother he's a funny one"
Also *Improving songs for anxious children* no. 14
Contemplation [A.C.McClurg, 1904] "For days and days I've climbed"
Also *Improving songs for anxious children* no. 16
For careless children [G. Schirmer, 1913] "Oh! children only think of it"
Good Ellen [G. Schirmer, 1913] "Oh, little Ellen never did"
Happy heathen [A.C.McClurg, 1904] "Just think of little heathen boys!"
Humility [G. Schirmer, 1913] "My nature it is very wild"
The liar [G. Schirmer, 1913] "I've done a very frightful thing"
Making calls [A.C.McClurg, 1904] "The most unpleasant thing to do"
Also *Improving songs for anxious children* no. 15
Maria, glutton [G. Schirmer, 1913] "Maria sits in her high chair"
A plan [A.C.McClurg, 1904] "When I'm a big man"
Also *Improving songs for anxious children* no. 13
Practising [A.C.McClurg, 1904] "What's the use of practising"
Also *Improving songs for anxious children* no. 2
Red hair [A.C.McClurg, 1904] "I wish I knew a sea of ink"
Also *Improving songs for anxious children* no. 4
Spring [G. Schirmer, 1913] "I wander far and unrestrained"
Stout [G. Schirmer, 1913] "Alas, I am a heavy child"
The thunderstorm [A.C.McClurg, 1904] "I wonder if God thinks of me"
To cross the street [A.C.McClurg, 1904] "Tell me why do wagons frown"
Vanity [G. Schirmer, 1913] "In evenings of the summer days"
War [G. Schirmer, 1913] "When I hear the blare of trumpet"
When the night comes [A.C.McClurg, 1904] same
Also *Improving songs for anxious children* no. 17
A wicked child [G. Schirmer, 1913] "My parents say that dancing"

COMPOSER Poet *Title* "First Line"

Chesson, Mrs. Nora (Hopper), 1871-1906.
Little John's song [H.B.Stevens, 1897] "Its oh, and oh 'tis merry to go"

Confucius, 551-479 B. C.
NATIONAL ODES OF CHINA.
To a young gentleman (1916) [G. Schirmer, 1916] "Don't come in, sir, please!"

Douglas, Lord Alfred Bruce, 1870-1945.
The green river (1909) [G. Schirmer, 1912] "I know a green grass path that leaves the field"

Dudley, Helen
To one unknown (1912) [G. Schirmer, 1913] "I have seen the proudest stars"

Dunbar, Paul Laurence, 1872-1906.
Treat me nice (1905) [G. Schirmer, 1918, 1932] "Treat me nice, Miss Mandy Jane"

Evans, Mrs. Florence (Wilkinson)
The heart's country (1909) [Oliver Ditson, 1912] "Hill-people long for their hills"

Field, Eugene, 1850-1895.
Norse lullaby [H.B.Stevens, 1896; T.Presser, 1903] "The sky is dark and the hills are white"
Sicilian lullaby [H.B.Stevens, 1897] "Hush my little one, fold your hands"

Fisher, Aileen Lucia, 1906-
THE COFFEE-POT FACE.
Worlds (1934) [G. Schirmer, 1938] "The world is high as a bird can fly"

Florenz, Karl Adolf, 1865-1939.
Endlose Liebe (189_) [unpubl.] "Wo ich ferne des Mikaue Ho her Gipfel ragen seh"
Holograph at the Library of Congress.

Havet, Mireille
Les cheminées rouge (1934) [unpubl.] "Vingt-huit cheminées rouges dansent sur le toit"
Holograph at the Library of Congress.
Le petit cimetière (1934) [unpubl.] "Derrière le mur du petit cimetière"
Holograph at the Library of Congress.

Herrick, Robert, 1591-1674.
Bid me to live (1911) [G. Schirmer, 1912] same

Howells, Mildred, 1872-
Fog-wraiths (1912) [G. Schirmer, 1913] "In from the ocean the white fog creeps"

Hughes, Langston, 1902-1967.
FINE CLOTHES TO THE JEW.
That soothin' song (1926) [G. Schirmer, 1927] "Play de blues for me"
THE WEARY BLUES.
The cryin' blues (1926) [G. Schirmer, 1927] "Hey! hey! that's what the blues singers say"
Jazz-boys (1926) [G. Schirmer, 1927] "Sleek black boys in a cabaret"
Shake your brown feet, Honey (1926) [G. Schirmer, 1927] same

Lanier, Sidney, 1842-1881.
May, the maiden (1908) [Oliver Ditson, 1912] "May, the maiden, violet laden"

Li Po, 701-762.
On a screen (1916) [G. Schirmer, 1916] "A tortoise I see on a lotus-flower resting"

Li-Shê, 9th cent.
Highwaymen (1916) [G. Schirmer, 1916] "The rainy mist sweeps gently o'er the village by the stream"

Livingstone, Mabel
If (1934) [G. Schirmer, 1938] "Oh, would not it be funny, and would not people stare"

London Atheneum, pseud.
Memory [H.B.Stevens, 1896] "As a perfume doth remain"

McDonald, George
Alas, how easily things go wrong [H.B.Stevens, 1896] same

Sassoon, Siegfried Lorraine, 1886-1967.
Serenade (1920) [G. Schirmer, 1921] "You were glad tonight"
Slumber-song (1920) [G. Schirmer, 1921] "Sleep; and my song shall build about your bed"

Shakespeare, William, 1564-1616.
AS YOU LIKE IT.
In spring [H.B.Stevens, 1896] "It was a lover and his lass"
TWELFTH NIGHT.
Mistress mine [H.B.Stevens, 1897] "Mistress mine, where are you roaming"

Simpson, Archibald
The little prayer of I [G. Schirmer, 1915]

Simpson, Mabel
THE DIAL.
Rest (1934) [G. Schirmer, 1936] "No song, no song from far or near"

Stevenson, Robert Louis, 1850-1894.
The cock shall crow (1908) [G. Schirmer, 1912] same

COMPOSER Poet *Title* "First Line"

CARPENTER, JOHN ALDEN, 1876-1951
(continued)
Stevenson, Robert Louis, 1850-1894
(continued)
Looking-glass river (1909) [G. Schirmer,
1912]
"Smooth it slides upon its travel"
Tagore, Rabindranath, 1861-1941.
GITANJALI.
The day is no more (1914) [G.
Schirmer, 1915] same
*I am like a remnant of a cloud of
autumn* (1913) [G. Schirmer, 1914]
same
Light, my light (1913) [G. Schirmer,
1914] same
*On the day when death will knock at
thy door* (1913) [G. Schirmer, 1914]
same
On the seashore of endless worlds
(1913) [G. Schirmer, 1914] same
The sleep that flits on baby's eyes
(1913) [G. Schirmer, 1914] same
When I bring to you colour'd toys
(1913) [G. Schirmer, 1914] same
Unknown
The Lawd is smilin' through the do'
(1917) [G. Schirmer, 1918]
"Sleep, my honey, sleep"
Love whom I have never seen [Miles &
Thompson, 1894]
"Oh, love, whom I have never seen"
Verlaine, Paul, 1844-1896.
Dansons la gigue (1910) [G. Schirmer,
1912] "Dansons la gigue! J'aimais
surtout ses jolis yeux"
Il pleure dans mon coeur (1910) [G.
Schirmer, 1912] same
EN SOURDINE.
When the misty shadows glide (1910)
[Oliver Ditson, 1912] same
POÈMES SATURNIENS.
Chanson d'automne (1910) [G.
Schirmer, 1912] "Les sanglots longs
des violons de l'automne"
SAGESSE.
Le ciel (1910) [G. Schirmer, 1912]
"Le ciel est par-dessus le toit"
Waller, Edmund, 1606-1687.
Go, lovely rose (1908) [G. Schirmer,
1912] same
Wilde, Oscar, 1854-1900.
Her voice (1912) [G. Schirmer, 1913]
"The wild bee reels from bough to
bough"

Les silhouettes (1912) [G. Schirmer,
1913]
"The sea is flecked with bars of gray"
Yeats, William Butler, 1865-1939.
The player queen (1914) [G. Schirmer,
1915]
"My mother dandled me and sang"
Yü-hsi, 772-842.
The Odalisque (1916) [G. Schirmer,
1916] "A gaily dressed damsel steps
forth from her bow'r"
Carpenter, John Alden, 1876-1951.
CARPENTER
Blue gal
The home-road
Khaki Sammy
Carpenter, Rue (Winterbotham), d.1931.
CARPENTER
About my garden
Aspiration
Brother
Contemplation
For careless children
Good Ellen
Happy heathen
Humility
The liar
Making calls
Maria, glutton
A plan
Practising
Red hair
Spring
Stout
The thunderstorm
To cross the street
Vanity
War
When the night comes
A wicked child
Carré, Michel, 1819-1872.
MASSENET
Chant provençal
Nêére
CARRIC-THURA. see Macpherson
Cronnan **SCHUBERT**
Shilrik und Vinvela **SCHUBERT**
CARRIC-THURA: Spirit of Loda. *see*
Macpherson
Loda's Gespenst **SCHUBERT**
Carrier, P.
MASSENET *Tristesse*
Carry her over the water see Auden
BERKELEY
Carte postale see Apollinaire **POULENC**
Carte postale see Apollinaire *OBUS*
COULEUR DE LUNE. **RIVIER**

NB: Poulenc and Rivier set different
Apollinaire texts.
Une carte postale see Radiguet SAUGUET
Carte postale à Délos see Richaud
SAUGUET
CARTER, ELLIOTT, 1908-
Crane, Hart, 1899-1932.
VOYAGES III.
Voyage (1943) [Valley Music Press;
Associated, 1973]
"Infinite consanguinity it bears"
Also voice & small orchestra, 1974.
Frost, Robert, 1874-1963.
The dust of snow (1942 or 43)
[Associated, 1947]
"The way a crow shook down on me"
Low voice & piano; also high voice &
orchestra, 1975.
The line gang (1942 or 43) [Associated,
1975] "Here come the line-gang
pioneering by"
Low voice & piano; also high voice &
orchestra, 1975.
The rose family (1942 or 43) [Associated,
1947] "The rose is a rose, and was
always a rose"
Low voice & piano; also high voice &
orchestra, 1975.
Joyce, James, 1882-1941.
My love is in a light attire (1928)
[unpubl.]
Shakespeare, William, 1564-1616.
MERCHANT OF VENICE.
Tell me where is fancy bred? (1938)
[Associated, 1972] same
Alto voice & guitar.
Van Doren, Mark, 1894-1972.
The difference (1944) [withdrawn]
Soprano, baritone & piano.
Whitman, Walt, 1819-1892.
Warble for lilac time (1943) [Peer
International, 1956]
"Warble me now for joy of lilac-time"
High voice & piano or orchestra.
LES CARTES, OU L'HOROSCOPE. see
Béranger
Die Kartenlegerin SCHUMANN
Cartomancie see Chalupt RIVIER
Casabianca see Bishop ROREM
Case, Thomas, 1844-1925.
BENNETT
Dancing lightly
Maiden mine
Sunset
Tell me where, ye summer breezes

CASELLA, ALFREDO, 1883-1947.
Annunzio, Gabriele d', 1863-1938.
ALCYONE.
La sera fiesolana, op. 37 (1923)
[Ricordi, 1924]
"Fresche le mie parole ne la sera"
Anon.
Amante sono, vaghiccia, di voi, op. 36
no. 3 (1923) [Ricordi, 1924] same
Flaiolet, op. 22 no. 2 (1913) [Mathot,
1922] "En mai quand le rossignolet"
Fuor de la bella gaiba, op. 36 no. 2
(1923) [Ricordi, 1924] same
Ninna nanna corbellina (1934) [De
Santis, 1939] same
Rêves d'or pour ton sommeil, op. 22 no.
1 (1913) [Mathot, 1922] same
Text a 17th century lullaby; perhaps
from Thomas Dekker's
The pleasant comoedy of Patient
Grissill (1603).
Baudelaire, Charles Pierre, 1821-1867.
La cloche fêlée, op. 7 (1903 or 4)
[Suppl.: ***Monde Musical,*** 15 Jan. 1904]
"Il est amer et doux"
Carducci, Giosuè, 1835-1907.
Il bove, op. 21 no. 2 (1913) [Société
Anonyme des Editions Ricordi, 1915]
"T'amo, o pio bove"
Pianto antico, op. 21 no. 1 (1913)
[Société Anonyme des Editions
Ricordi, 1915]
"L'albero a cui tendevi"
Cino da Pistoia, 1270-1336.
Giovane bella luce del mio core, op. 36
no. 1 (1923) [Ricordi, 1924] same
Croisset, Francis de, 1877-1937.
Rêverie, op. 2 no. 4 (1902-3) [Mathot]
Duval, Paul Alexander Martin, 1856-
1906.
C'était un songe, op. 2 no. 2 (1902-3)
[Mathot]
Hettich, Amédée Louis Landely, 1856-
1937.
Temps de neige, op. 2 no. 3 (1902-3)
[Mathot]
No author
Ecce Deus salvator meus (1943) [Suvini
Zerboni, 1946] same
Arr. for baritone & organ, 1943.
Variantly identified as op. 66 or 67.
Ecce odor filii mei (1943) [Suvini
Zerboni, 1946] same
Arr. for baritone & organ, 1943.
Variantly identified as op. 66 or 67.

CASELLA, ALFREDO, 1883-1947
(continued)
No author *(continued)*
  Respice, Domine, familiam tuam (1943)
    [Suvini Zerboni, 1946] same
    Arr. for baritone & organ, 1943.
    Variantly identified as op. 66 or 67.
  Tre vocalizzi (1929) [Ricordi, 1929]
    Wordless.
Olkienizkaia-Naldi, Raissa
  LO SPECCHIO.
    La danza, op. 39 no. 2 (1923) [Ricordi,
      1924] "Nella sala gialla una tazza
      d'ambra"
    Volutta, op. 39 no. 1 (1923) [Ricordi,
      1924] "Fra i casti e freddi lini del
      letto"
Richepin, Jean, 1849-1926.
  En ramant, op. 9 no. 3 [Mathot, 1913]
    "Sur la mer qui brame"
  Larmes, op. 2 no. 1 (1902-3) [Mathot]
  Nuageries, op. 2 no. 5 (1902-3) [Mathot]
    "Les nuages là-haut vont rêvant"
Ronsard, Pierre de, 1524-1585.
  Sonnet, op. 16 (1910) [Mathot, 1913]
    "Comme on voit sur la branche au
      mois de mai"
Salustri, Carlo Alberto, 1871-1950.
  LE FAVOLE ROMANESCHE.
    La carità, op. 38 no. 2 (1923) [Ricordi,
      1924] "Er presidente d'una società"
    L'elezzione der presidente, op. 38 no.
      4 (1923) [Ricordi, 1924]
      "Un giorno tutti quanti l'animali"
    Er coccodrillo, op. 38 no. 1 (1923)
      [Ricordi, 1924]
      "Ner mejo che un signore"
    Er gatto e er cane, op. 38 no. 3 (1923)
      [Ricordi, 1924] "Un gatto soriano"
Samain, Albert Victor, 1858-1900.
  Soir païen, op. 9 no. 2 (1905) [Mathot,
    1922]
    "C'est un beau soir couleur de rose"
Tagore, Rabindranath, 1861-1941.
  GITANJALI.
    A cette heure du départ, op. 26 no. 3
      (1915) [J. & W. Chester, 1921]
      same
      Arr. for voice & 16 instruments as
        op. 26 bis (1926).
    Dans une salutation suprême, op. 26
      no. 4 (1915) [J. & W. Chester,
      1921] same
      Arr. for voice & 16 instruments as
        op. 26 bis (1926).
    Mort, ta servante est à ma porte, op.
      26 no. 2 (1915)

      [J. & W. Chester, 1921] same
      Arr. for voice & 16 instruments as
        op. 26 bis (1926).
    *O toi, suprême accomplissement de ma
      vie,* op. 26 no. 1 (1915)
      [J. & W. Chester, 1921] same
      Arr. for voice & 16 instruments as
        op. 26 bis (1926).
Verlaine, Paul, 1844-1896.
  PAYSAGES TRISTES.
    Soleils couchants, op. 9 no. 1 (1905)
      [Mathot]
Castellani, A
  ROSSINI *Il fanciullo smarrito*
Castelli, Ignaz Franz, 1781-1862.
  SCHUBERT
    Das Echo
    Frohsinn
  WEBER *Wunsch und Entsagung*
  DIANA VON POITIERS.
    WEBER *Ein König einst gefangen sass*
Castelli, Ignaz Friedrich *see* Castelli,
  Ignaz Franz, 1781-1862.
Castillejo, Christoval De, 1490-1556.
  SPANISCHES LIEDERBUCH: Alguna vez.
    GRIEG *Dereinst, Gedanke mein*
    JENSEN *Alguna vez*
    WOLF *Dereinst, dereinst, Gedanke mein*
Castle Gordon, or The young Highland rover
  see Burns **BENNETT**
Castleman, Marion
  ROREM *From "The return"*
Castro, Cristóbal de, 1880-
  FALLA *Tus ojillos negros* (Canzon
    Andaluza, 1902)
Castro, Rosalía de, 1837-1885.
  RODRIGO *Un home, San Antonio!*
The cat is angry see Yalan-Stekelis
  GIDEON
CATALOGUE DE FLEURS, no. 1
  MILHAUD Daudet, L. *La violette*
CATALOGUE DE FLEURS, no. 2
  MILHAUD Daudet, L. *Le bégonia*
CATALOGUE DE FLEURS, no. 3
  MILHAUD Daudet, L. *Les fritillaires*
CATALOGUE DE FLEURS, no. 4
  MILHAUD Daudet, L. *Les jacinthes*
CATALOGUE DE FLEURS, no. 5
  MILHAUD Daudet, L. *Les crocus*
CATALOGUE DE FLEURS, no. 6
  MILHAUD Daudet, L. *Le brachycome*
CATALOGUE DE FLEURS, no. 7
  MILHAUD Daudet, L. *L'eremurus*
Catteau, Robert
  AUBERT *Grisaille*
Catullus, Caius Valerius, 87-57 B.C.
  MILHAUD
    La femme que j'aime

Ma chérie, aimons-nous
Ma chérie, en présence de son mari
Voilà où mon âme en est venue
ROREM *Catullus: On the burial of his*
brother
Catullus: On the burial of his brother see
Catullus **ROREM**
Cavalca, Domenico, d.1342.
MALIPIERO *In memoria d'un amico*
La cavalcata della morte see Pàntini,
Romualdo **MALIPIERO**
Le cavalier see Lunel **MILHAUD**
A cavalry catch see Sharp, W. **SIBELIUS**
Cazalis, Henri, 1840-1909.
CHAUSSON *Sérénade*
DUPARC
Chanson triste
Extase
Sérénade Florentine
HAHN *Nocturne*
MASSENET *La chanson des lèvres*
SAINT-SAËNS *Danse macabre*
CHANSON TRISTE.
SAINT-SAËNS *Dans ton coeur*
Ce bruit de la mer see Supervielle
MILHAUD
Ce doux petit visage see Éluard **POULENC**
"Ce lui qui croyait au ciel" *see La rose et la*
Réséda Aragon **AURIC**
"Ce n'est la rosée ni la pluie" *see Chant de*
Sion Unknown **MILHAUD**
"Ce n'est pas même la souffrance" *see Je ne*
puis espérer Delpit **GOUNOD**
"Ce n'est pas ta beauté qui m'attire . . . " *see*
Rose de Mai Poirson, S. Cuthbert
MASSENET
"Ce n'est pas vous" *see Chinoiserie* Gautier
FALLA, LASSEN
"Ce n'étaient pas là vos grandes et gracieuses
manières" *see Le départ* Patmore
MILHAUD
"Ce paqu'bot ci s'appell' 'La Julie' " *see*
Chanson du capitaine Bloch **MILHAUD**
Ce peu see Supervielle **MILHAUD**
"Ce peu d'océan" *see Ce peu* Supervielle
MILHAUD
Ce que disent les cloches see Vingtrie, Jean
de **MASSENET**
Ce que je suis sans toi see Peyre, L. de
GOUNOD
"Ce qu'est le lierre sans l'ormeau" *see Ce que*
je suis sans toi Peyre, L. de **GOUNOD**
Ce qu'il faut à mon âme see Sédillot, Abbé
Félix **GOUNOD**
"Ce soir, à travers le bonheur" *see Crépuscule*
Lerberghe **FAURÉ**

"Ce soir, mon bien aimé" *see Rêverie*
sentimentale Peyre, Mathylde
MASSENET
"Ce soleil sur la sable" *see Tristesse d'été*
Mallarmé **SAUGUET**
"Ce sont des feuilles mortes" *see La bise*
Carême **MILHAUD**
Ce sont les petits que je veux chanter see
Grieumard, Édouard **MASSENET**
"Ce tendre sentiment, dans mon âme il habite"
see Sonnet Saint-Saëns **SAINT-SAËNS**
Čech, Svatopluk, 1846-1908.
LEŠETÍNSKÝ KOVÁR.
DVOŘÁK *Zpěv z Lešetínského kováře*
Cécile see Giraudoux *SUZANNE ET LA*
PACIFIQUE. **HONEGGER**
La ceinture see Valéry **SAUGUET**
"Celle qui devient mère" *see Les mères*
Boyer, Georges **MASSENET**
Two settings: 1891 and 1901.
A CELTIC MISCELLANY. see Jackson,
Kenneth, translator.
Promiscuity **BARBER**
Celui que j'aime see Carême **SAUGUET**
"Celui qui distingue le sacré du profane" *see*
La séparation Anon. **MILHAUD**
Celui qui dort, à la mémoire de Francis
Poulenc see Éluard **SAUGUET**
LA CENDRE ROUGE, no. 1
SAINT-SAËNS Docquois *Prélude*
LA CENDRE ROUGE, no. 2
SAINT-SAËNS Docquois *Âme triste*
LA CENDRE ROUGE, no. 3
SAINT-SAËNS Docquois *Douceur*
LA CENDRE ROUGE, no. 4
SAINT-SAËNS Docquois *Silence*
LA CENDRE ROUGE, no. 5
SAINT-SAËNS Docquois *Pâques*
LA CENDRE ROUGE, no. 6
SAINT-SAËNS Docquois *Jour de pluie*
LA CENDRE ROUGE, no. 7
SAINT-SAËNS Docquois *Amoroso*
LA CENDRE ROUGE, no. 8
SAINT-SAËNS Docquois *Mai*
LA CENDRE ROUGE, no. 9
SAINT-SAËNS Docquois *Petite main*
LA CENDRE ROUGE, no. 10
SAINT-SAËNS Docquois *Reviens*
(Epilogue)
Le cerisier see Carême *LE LANTERNE*
MAGIQUE. **SCHMITT**
"'Le cerisier,' fable" *see Le cerisier* Carême
SCHMITT
"Cerraron sus ojos que aún teniaabiertos" *see*
Dios mio, que solos se quedan los muertos!
Bécquer **FALLA**

COMPOSER Poet *Title* "First Line"

"Certain mot murmuré Par vous est un baiser"
see *Le sourire* Sauvage MESSIAEN
"Certains Sauvages croient que l'âme des
enfantes mortnés" see *La nuit à la vérandah*
Claudel MILHAUD
"Certes si nous avions vécu" see *Dans le
jardin d'Anna* Apollinaire POULENC
Cerutti, L F
ROSSINI *L'ultimo pensiero* ("Patria,
consorti, figli")
Cervantes Saavedra, Miguel de, 1547-
1616.
CORNELIUS *Preziosas Sprüchlein gegen
Kopfweh*
WOLF *Köpfchen, Köpfchen, nicht
gewimmert*
Červené botičky see *Des Knaben
Wunderhorn* MARTINŮ *Little red
bootees*
Červenka, Jan, 1861-1908.
MARTINŮ *Before you know*
Ces mots qui n'ont plus de sens see Hugnet
SAUGUET
C'est ainsi que tu es see Vilmorin
POULENC
"C'est au petit jour qu'ils trépassent" see
Après minuit Vildrac IBERT
C'est au temps de la Chrysantheme see
Silvestre MASSENET
"C'est aujourd'hui que l'on couronne" see
La distribution des prix Anon. GOUNOD
"C'est la bossue de ma cour" see *La Pintade*
Renard RAVEL
"C'est la douce fiancée" see *La fiancée
perdue* Messiaen MESSIAEN
"C'est la fillette aux yeux cernés" see
Les couronnes Mauclair CHAUSSON
C'est la paix see Debladis, Georgette
FAURÉ
"C'est la paix, c'est la douce pais" see
La douce paix Guillot de Saix HAHN
C'est l'amour see Hugo MASSENET
C'est le joli printemps see Fombeure
CHANSONS DE LA GRANDE HUNE.
POULENC
"C'est le premier matin du monde" see
Paradis Lerberghe FAURÉ
C'est le printemps see Gillouin MASSENET
"C'est le printemps viens t'en Pâquette" see
Aubade Apollinaire RIVIER
"C'est le repos éclairé" see *Veillées* Rimbaud
MILHAUD
"C'est l'espoir des beaux jours qui luit dans le
ciel bleu" see *Pensée de printemps*
Silvestre MASSENET
C'est l'extase . . . see Verlaine *ROMANCES
SANS PAROLES.* FAURÉ

"C'est l'extase langoureuse" see *C'est
l'extase . . .* Verlaine FAURÉ
"C'est l'extase langoureuse" see *Le vent dans
la plaine* Verlaine SAINT-SAËNS
C'est l'extase langoureuse see Verlaine
ROMANCES SANS PAROLES. DEBUSSY
C'est l'heure see Ganzo *LANGAGE.*
SCHMITT
"C'est l'heure où" see *Le Grillon* Renard
RAVEL
"C'est l'heure sainte où la voix des
archanges" see *Chantez, voix bénies* Gallet
GOUNOD
"C'est mon feu, c'est ma cordelle" see *De sa
peine, et des beautés de sa Dame* Du
Bellay MILHAUD
"C'est mon trésor, c'est mon bijou le joli trou
par où" see *Chanson* Anon. SATIE
"C'est permis de fumer gare" see *Fumée*
Cocteau MILHAUD
"C'est ta lettre qui m'a fait revenir" see
Jérôme et Alissa Gide MILHAUD
"C'est toi qui me diras les saisons infinies"
see *Dormons parmi les lis* Picard, Hélène
MASSENET
"C'est un amant" see *Sérénade de Molière*
Molière MASSENET
"C'est un beau soir couleur de rose" see *Soir
païen* Samain CASELLA, KOECHLIN
"C'est un portrait de jeune fille" see *Pastel*
Gille BIZET
"C'est une fille belle à voir!" see *Prends
garde* Barbier, J. GOUNOD
"C'est vous qu'au Palais de Tauride" see
Les journées d'Août Chalupt MILHAUD
Cesta k milé see Unknown MARTINŮ
Cet hiver see Paliard MILHAUD
C'était affreux see Jammes MILHAUD
"C'était dans la nuit brune" see *Ballade à la
lune* Musset DEBUSSY, LALO
C'était en avril see Pailleron *AVRIL:
Chanson.* RACHMANINOFF
Aprel'! veshniï prazdnichnyï den'
"C'était pendant l'horreur du Quatorze Juillet"
see *L'omnibus automobile* Hyspa SATIE
C'était un songe see Duval CASELLA
Cette attirance de la brume see Anon.
SAUGUET
Cette cigarette d'ombre see Jacqueton,
Henry SAUGUET
Cette douleur see Paliard MILHAUD
"Cette fleur, autrefois donnée" see *Fleur fanée*
Dierx HAHN
Cette grande chambre see Derème IBERT
"Cette harpe, chérie, à te chanter fidèle" see
L'origine de la harpe Moore, T.
BERLIOZ

"Cette main abattue sur mon visage" *see*
  Sommeil D'Harcourt, Antoniette
  SAUGUET
"Cette maison nous allons la quitter" *see*
  La maison Messiaen **MESSIAEN**
Cette promenade avec toi see Guérin, E.
  MILHAUD
Chabaleyret, Paul de *see* Bourguignat,
  Paul
Chabaneix, Philippe, 1898-
  IBERT
    Familière
    Fête nationale
    Mélancolie
CHABRIER, EMMANUEL, 1841-1894.
  Banville, Théodore Faullain de, 1823-
  1891.
    Lied (1862) [unpubl.]
      Manuscript in the Bibliothèque
      nationale.
  Baudelaire, Charles Pierre, 1821-1867.
    LES FLEURS DU MAL.
    L'invitation au voyage (1870)
      [Costallat, 1913] "Mon enfant, ma
      soeur"
        Accompaniment includes bassoon
        ad lib.
  Châtillon, M.-A. de
    Sérénade (1862) [unpubl.]
      Manuscript in the Bibliothèque
      nationale.
  Dierx, Marais Victor Léon, 1838-1912.
    Les lèvres closes (1867) [unknown
      Parisian publisher]
  Hugo, Victor Marie, comte, 1802-1885.
    Ruy Blas (1863) [Enoch & Costallat,
      1913] "A quoi bon à quoi bon
      entendre"
    CHANSONS DES RUES ET DES BOIS.
    Sommation irrespectueuse (1880)
      [Enoch & Costallat, 1913, 1929]
      "Rire étant si jolie, c'est mal"
  Leprade, Pierre Marin Victor Richard
  de, 1812-1883.
    Chants d'oiseaux (1862) [unpubl.]
      Manuscript in the Bibliothèque
      nationale.
    Couplets de Mariette (1862) [unpubl.]
      Manuscript in the Bibliothèque
      nationale.
    L'enfant (1862) [unpubl.]
      Manuscript in the Bibliothèque
      nationale.
  Mendès, Catulle Abraham, 1841-1909.
    Chanson pour Jeanne (1886) [Enoch &
      Costallat]
      "Puisque les roses sont jolies"

    Lied (before 1888) [Enoch & Costallat,
      1897]
      "Nez au vent, coeur plein d'ai se"
  Mikhaël, Ephraïm, 1866-1890.
    L'île heureuse (1890) [Enoch &
      Costallat, 1897]
      "Dans le golfe aux jardins ombreux"
  Musset, Alfred de, 1810-1857.
    Adieux à Suzon (1862) [unpubl.]
      Manuscript in the Bibliothèque
      nationale.
    Ah! Petit démons! (1862) [unpubl.]
      Manuscript in the Bibliothèque
      nationale.
  Renaudière, M de La
    Le sentier sombre (1862) [unpubl.]
      Manuscript in the Bibliothèque
      nationale.
  Rollinat, Maurice, 1853-1903.
    Tes yeux bleus (1883) [Enoch &
      Costallat, 1913] same
      First published: *Album du Gaulois,*
      1885.
  Rostand, Edmond, 1868-1918.
    Ballade des gros dindons (1890)
      [Enoch & Costallat, 1897]
      "Les gros dindons, à travers champs"
    Pastorale des cochons roses (1890)
      [Enoch & Costallat, 1897]
      "Le jour s'annonce à l'Orient"
    Toutes les fleurs (1890) [Enoch &
      Costallat, 1897]
      "Toutes les fleurs, certes"
    Les cigales (1890) [Enoch & Costallat,
      1897] "Le soleil est droit sur la sente"
  Rostand, Rosemonde Gérard, b. 1871.
    Villanelle des petits canards (1890)
      [Enoch & Costallat, 1897]
      "Ils vont, les petits canards"
  Silvestre, Paul Armond, 1837-1901.
    Credo d'amour (1883) [Enoch &
      Costallat] "Je crois aux choses
      éternelles"
  Unknown
    Ronde gauloise (1862) [unpubl.]
      Manuscript in the Bibliothèque
      nationale.
Chabrillac, Léon
  SAUGUET *Bergerie*
Chabroux, Ernest
  MASSENET *L'heure douce*
Chacun son tour, les animaux see
  Supervielle *LA PREMIÈRE FAMILLE.*
  MILHAUD
Chaffotte, Jeanne
  MASSENET *Le printemps visite la terre*

COMPOSER Poet *Title* "First Line"

CHAĬKOVSKIĬ, PETR IL'ICH, 1840-1893.

Aksakov, Konstantin Sergeevich, 1817-1860.

Detskaya pesnya, op. 54 no. 16 (1881) [GA, v. 45, p. 64] "Moĭ lizochek tak uzh mal"

Apukhtin, Aleksyeĭ Nikolayevich, 1841-1893.

Den' li t͡sarit, op. 47 no. 6 (1880) [GA, v. 44, p. 280] same

Kto idyot? (1857-60) [lost]

Nochi bezumnye, op. 60 no. 6 (1886) [GA, v. 45, p. 128] same

On tak menia liubil, op. 28 no. 4 (1875) [GA, v. 44, p. 198] "Net, ne liubila ia"

Zabyt' tak skoro! (1870) [GA, v. 44, p. 45] same

Blanchecotte, Augustine-Malvina, 1830-before 1895.

Les larmes, op. 65 no. 5 (1888) {*Slezy*} [GA, v. 45, p. 205] "Si vous donnez le calme aprés tant de secousses"

Chaĭkovskiĭ, Petr Il'ich, 1840-1893.

Pimpinella, op. 38 no. 6 (1878) [GA, v. 44, p. 239] "Esli ty khochesh', zhelannaia"

Prostye solva, op. 60 no. 5 (1886) [GA, v. 45, p. 122] "Ty zvezda na polnochnom nebe"

Strashnaia minuta, op. 28 no. 6 (1875) [GA, v. 44, p. 206] "Tyvnimaesh', vniz skloniv golovku"

Tak chto zhe? op. 16 no. 5 (1872) [GA, v. 44, p. 74] "Tvoĭ obraz svetlyĭ"

Collin, Paul Adrien François, 1845-1915.

Déception, op. 65 no. 2 (1888) {*Razocharovanie*} [GA, v. 45, p. 193] "Le soleil rayonnait encore"

Qu'importe que l'hiver, op. 65 no. 4 (1888) {*Pushaĭ zima*} [GA, v. 45, p. 201] same

Rondel, op. 65 no. 6 (1888) {*Charovnitsa*} [GA, v. 45, p. 209] "Il se cache dans ta grâce"

Sérénade, op. 65 no. 3 (1888) {*Serenada*} [GA, v. 45, p. 196] "J'aime dous le rayon de la limpide aurore"

Gellert, Christian Fürchtegott, 1715-1769.

Kukushka, op. 54 no. 8 (1883) [GA, v. 45, p. 31] "Ty priletel iz goroda" Text adapted by Pleshcheyev.

Goethe, Johann Wolfgang von, 1749-1832.

WILHELM MEISTER. Mignon's song: Heiss mich nicht reden.

Ne sprashivaĭ, op. 57 no. 3 (1884) [GA, v. 45, p. 81] same

WILHELM MEISTER. Mignon's song: Kennst du das Land?

Pesnya Min'ony, op. 25 no. 3 (1874) [GA, v. 44, p. 113] "Ty znaesh' kraĭ"

WILHELM MEISTER. Mignon's song: Nur wer die Sehnsucht kennt.

Niet'', tol'ko tot'', kto znal'', op. 6 no. 6 (1869) [GA, v. 44, p. 39] same

Grekov, Nikolay, 1810-1866.

Ne dolgo nam gulyat (1873?) [GA, v. 44, p. 139] same

Pogodi! op. 16 no. 2 (1872) [GA, v. 44, p. 59] same

STANSĬ.

Smotri, von oblako, op. 27 no. 2 (1875) [GA, v. 44, p. 149] same

Heine, Heinrich, 1797-1856.

DIE BLAUEN FRÜHLINGSAUGEN.

Glazki vecny golubye (1873) [GA, v. 44, p. 95] same

DIE HEIMKEHR.

Khotel by v edinoe slovo (1875) [GA, v. 44, p. 135] same Text adapted by Mei.

WARUM SIND DANN DIE ROSEN SO BLASS?

Otchevo? op. 6 no. 5 (1869) [GA, v. 44, p. 35] "Otchevo poblednela vesnoy"

Karadžić, Vuk Stefanović, 1787-1864.

Soloveĭ, op. 60 no. 4 (1886) [GA, v. 45, p. 117] "Solovei msĭ, soloveiko!" Text adapted by Pushkin.

Khomyakov, Aleksyeĭ Stepanovich, 1804-1860.

Podvig, op. 60 no. 11 (1886) [GA, v. 45, p. 149] "Podvig est' iv srazhen' i"

Vcherashniaia noch', op. 60 no. 1 (1886) [GA, v. 45, p. 101] same

Kondratowicz, Ludwik, 1823-1862.

Korol'ki, op. 28 no. 2 (1875) [GA, v. 44, p. 186] "Kak loshel" ĭas" kazakami" Text adapted by Mei.

Konstantin Konstantinovich, Grand Duke of Russia, 1858-1915.

IA snachala tebia ne liubila, op. 63 no. 1 (1887) [GA, v. 45, p. 161] same

IA vam ne nravlius', op. 63 no. 3 (1887) [GA, v. 45, p. 168] same

Pervoe svidanie, op. 63 no. 4 (1887) [GA, v. 45, p. 171] "Vot" minovala razluka unylaia"

Rastvoril ia okno, op. 63 no. 2 (1887) [GA, v. 45, p. 165] same

Serenada, op. 63 no. 6 (1887) [GA, v. 45, p. 181]
"O ditya, pod okoshkom tvoim"
Uzh gasli v'' komnatakh ogni, op. 63 no. 5 (1887) [GA, v. 45, p. 176] same

Lenartowicz, Teofil, 1822-1893.
Lastochka, op. 54 no. 15 (1883) [GA, v. 45, p. 60] "Idet devochkasirotka"
Text adapted by Surikov.

Lermontov, Mikhail Yuryevich, 1814-1841.
Liubov' mertvetsa, op. 38 no. 5 (1878) [GA, v. 44, p. 233]
"Puskaĭ kholodnoiu zemleiu"

Maĭkov, Apollon Nikolayevich, 1821-1897.
NOVOGRECHESKIYE PESNI.
Kolibel'naya pesnya, op. 16 no. 1 (1873?) [GA, v. 44, p. 53]
"Spi, ditia moe"
Novogrecheskiye pesni, op. 16 no. 6 (1872) [GA, v. 44, p. 81]
"V temnom ade, pod zemleĭ"

Mei, Lev Aleksandrovich, 1822-1862.
Kanareyka, op. 25 no. 4 (1874) [GA, v. 44, p. 120] "Govorit sultansha kanareĭke"
Zachem? op. 28 no. 3 (1875) [GA, v. 44, p. 194] "Zachem zhe ty prisnilasia"
OKTAVI.
Ya s neyu nikogda ne govoril, op. 25 no. 5 (1874) [GA, v. 44, p. 125] same
PESNYA.
Kak naladili: Durak, op. 25 no. 6 (1874) [GA, v. 44, p. 130] same

Merezhkovski, Dmitriĭ Sergyeyevich, 1865-1941.
Smert', op. 57 no. 5 (1884) [GA, v. 45, p. 92] "Esli rozy tikho osypaiutsia"
Usni! op. 57 no. 4 (1884) [GA, v. 45, p. 87] "Usnut' by mne navek v trave"

Mickiewicz, Adam, 1798-1855.
Ali mat' menia rozhala, op. 27 no. 5 (1875) [GA, v. 44, p. 161] same
Text adapted by Mei.
Moia balovnitsa, op. 27 no. 6 (1875) [GA, v. 44, p. 166, 173] same
Text adapted by Mei.
Na zemliu sumrak pal, op. 47 no. 3 (1880) [GA, v. 44, p. 263] same
Text adapted by N.V.Berg.

Musset, Alfred de, 1810-1857.
CHANSON DE FORTUNIO.
Net, nikogda ne nazovu, op. 28 no. 1 (1875) [GA, v. 44, p. 181] same
Text adapted by Grekov.

Nekrasov, Nikolaĭ Aleksyeyevich, 1821-1877.
Prosti, op. 60 no. 8 (1886) [GA, v. 45, p. 137] same

Ogarev, Nikolai Platonovich, 1813-1877.
Na son'' griadushchiĭ, op. 27 no. 1 (1875) [GA, v. 44, p. 145]
"Nochniia t'ma bezmolvie"

Pleshcheyev, Alekseĭ Nikolayevich, 1825-1893.
Babushka i vnuchek, op. 54 no. 1 (1883) [GA, v. 45, p. 3]
"Pod oknom, chulok starushka"
Kolybel'naia pesn' v, op. 54 no. 10 (1883) [GA, v. 45, p. 41]
"Akh! uĭmis' ty, buria!"
Legenda, op. 54 no. 5 (1883) [GA, v. 45, p. 19] "Byl u Khrista mladentsa sad"
Lish' ty odin'', op. 57 no. 6 (1884) [GA, v. 45, p. 95] same
Moĭ sadik, op. 54 no. 4 (1883) [GA, v. 45, p. 15]
"Kak moĭ sadik svezh i zelen!"
Na beregu, op. 54 no. 6 (1883) [GA, v. 45, p. 22] "Domik nad rekoiu"
Ni slova, O drug'' moĭ, op. 6 no. 2 (1869) [GA, v. 44, p. 20] same
O, eslib'' znali vy, op. 60 no. 3 (1886) [GA, v. 45, p. 112] same
O, spoĭ zhe tu pesniu, op. 16 no. 4 (1872) [GA, v. 44, p. 68] same
Osen', op. 54 no. 14 (1883) [GA, v. 45, p. 57] "Skuchnaia kartina!"
Vesennyaya pesnya, op. 54 no. 13 (1883) [GA, v. 45, p. 53]
"V staryĭ sad vykhozhu ia"
Vesna, op. 54 no. 3 (1883) [GA, v. 45, p. 11] "Travka zeleneet"
Vesna, op.54 no. 9 (1883) [GA, v. 45, p. 37] "Uzh taet sneg"
Zima, op. 54 no. 12 (1883) [GA, v. 45, p. 49] "Ded, podniavshis' spozaranku"
Zimniĭ vecher, op. 54 no. 7 (1883) [GA, v. 45, p. 25] "Khorosho vam, detki"
PODSNEZHNIK.
Ptichka, op. 54 no. 2 (1883) [GA, v. 45, p. 7] same
SLOVA DLYA MUZĬKI.
Nam zvezdy krotkie siiali, op. 60 no. 12 (1886) [GA, v. 45, p. 154] same

Polonsky, Yakov Petrovich, 1819-1898.
Noch', op. 60 no. 9 (1886) [GA, v. 45, p. 141] "Otchego ia liubliu tebia"
Pesu', op. 60 no. 7 (1886) [GA, v. 45, p. 132] "Moĭ koster v tumane svetit"

CHAĭKOVSKĭ, PETR IL'ICH, 1840-1893
(*continued*)
Polonsky, Yakov Petrovich, 1819-1898
(*continued*)
VIZOV.
    Za oknom v teni meĺkaet, op. 60 no.
        10 (1886) [GA, v. 45, p. 146] same
Pushkin, Aleksandr Sergeevich, 1799-
    1837.
    Pesnya Zemfiri (ca.1855-60) [GA, v. 44,
        p. 5] "Staryĭ muzh, groznyĭ muzh"
Rathaus, Daniil, 1869-1937.
    An dem schlummernden Strom, op. 73 no.
        1 (1893) {*My sideli s toboĭ*}
        [GA, v. 45, p. 215] same
    In trüber Stund', op. 73 no. 5 (1893)
        {*Sreď mrachnykh dneĭ*}
        [GA, v. 45, p. 229] same
    Nacht, op. 73 no. 2 (1893) {*Noch'*} [GA,
        v. 45, p. 219]
        "Schon erlischt der Kerze Schein"
    O, du mondhelle Nacht, op. 73 no. 3
        (1893) {*V etu lunnuiu noch'*}
        [GA, v. 45, p. 222] same
    Sonne ging zur Ruhe, op. 73 no. 4 (1893)
        {*Zakatilos' solntse*}
        [GA, v. 45, p. 226] same
    Weil' ich wie einstmals allein, op. 73 no.
        6 (1893) {*Snova, kak prezhde*}
        [GA, v. 45, p. 234] same
Ratisbonne, Louis Gustave Fortuné,
    1827-1900.
    Tsvetok, op. 54 no. 11 (1883) [GA, v. 45,
        p. 44]
        "Veselo tsvetiki v pole pestreiut"
        Text adapted by Pleshcheyev.
Rostopchina, Evdokiïa, grafinïa, 1811-
    1858.
    I boĺno, i sladko, op. 6 no. 3 (1869)
        [GA, v. 44, p. 24] same
Shcherbina, Nikelaĭ Fedorovich, 1821-
    1869.
    Primiren'e, op. 25 no. 1 (1875?) [GA, v.
        44, p. 103]
        "O zasni moe serdtse gluboko!"
Shenshin, Afanasiĭ Afanas'evich,
    1820-1892.
    IA tebe nichego ne skazhu', op. 60 no. 2
        (1886) [GA, v. 45, p. 108] same
    Mezza notte (ca.1855-60) [GA, v. 44, p.
        8] "Poco è l'ora omai lontana"
    Moy geniy, moy angel, moy drug
        (ca.1855-60) [GA, v. 44, p. 3]
        "Ne zdes' li ty legkoiu ten'iu"
    Poymi khotraz, op. 16 no. 3 (1872) [GA,
        v. 44, p. 63]
        "Poĭmi khoťraz" tosklivoe priznan'e"

MELODII.
    Ne otkhodi ot menia, op. 27 no. 3
        (1875) [GA, v. 44, p. 154] same
PEVITSE: Unosi moe serdtse.
    Unosi moe serdtse (1873) [GA, v. 44,
        p. 89] same
Shevchenko, Taras, 1814-1861.
    Vecher, op. 27 no. 4 (1875) [GA, v. 44,
        p. 158] "Vishnevyĭ sadik vozle khaty"
        Text adapted by Mei.
Sollogub, Vladimir Aleksandrovich,
    graf, 1814-1882.
    Skazhi, O chem v teni vetveĭ, op. 57 no. 1
        (1884) [GA, v. 45, p. 71] same
Surikov, Ivan Zakharovich, 1841-1880.
    MALOROSSYSKAYA PESNYA.
    IA li v poke da ne travushka byla, op.
        47 no. 7 (1880) [GA, v. 44, p. 288]
        same
Tiutchev, Fĕdor Ivanovich, 1803-1873.
    Kak" nad" goriacheiu zoloĭ, op. 25 no. 2
        (1874) [GA, v. 44, p. 109] same
Tolstoĭ, Alekseĭ Konstantinovich, Graf,
    1817-1875.
    Gornimi tikho letela dusha nebesami, op.
        47 no. 2 (1880) [GA, v. 44, p. 257]
        same
    Kaby znala ia, op. 47 no. 1 (1880) [GA,
        v. 44, p. 249] same
    Na nivy zhelty, op. 57 no. 2 (1884) [GA,
        v. 45, p. 77] same
    Ne ver', moĭ drug, op. 6 no. 1 (1869)
        [GA, v. 44, p. 15] same
    Ni otzyva, ni slova, op. 28 no. 5 (1875)
        [GA, v. 44, p. 203] same
    O, esli b ty mogla, op. 38 no. 4 (1878)
        [GA, v. 44, p. 228] same
    Serenada Don-Zhuana, op. 38 no. 1
        (1878) [GA, v. 44, p. 213]
        "Gasnut daĺneĭ Aĺpukhary"
    Sleza drozhiť, op. 6 no. 4 (1869) [GA, v.
        44 p. 30] same
    Sreď shumnago bala, op. 38 no. 3 (1878)
        [GA, v. 44, p. 224] same
    To bylo ranneiu vesnoĭ, op. 38 no. 2
        (1878) [GA, v. 44, p. 219] same
    Usni pechaĺnyĭ drug", op. 47 no. 4
        (1880) [GA, v. 44, p. 267] same
    JOHN OF DAMASCUS.
    Blagoslavlyayu vas, lesa, op. 47 no. 5
        (1880) [GA, v. 44, p. 274] same
Turquety, Edouard, 1807-1867.
    AURORE.
    Serenada, op. 65 no. 1 (1888) [GA, v.
        45, p. 189] "Ty kuda letish', kak"
        ptitsa"

Chaĭkovskiĭ, Petr Il'ich, 1840-1893.
CHAĭKOVSKIĭ
Pimpinella
Prostye solva
Strashnaĭa minuta
Tak chto zhe?
The chain of roses see Klopstock *ODE.*
MACDOWELL *Das Rosenband*
Le châle see Vilmorin **AURIC**
Le chalet tyrolien see Chalupt **SAUGUET**
Chalkhill, John, 17th cent.
THE COMPLEAT ANGLER (1653):
Corydon's song.
HESELTINE *The countryman*
Chalupt, René, 1885-1957.
AUBERT
De Ceylan
La mauvaise prière
AURIC
Le gloxinia
Le pouf
Le tilbury
MILHAUD
Le Colonel Romanoff
Le convive
La Grand'Mère de la Révolution
L'infidèle
L'irrésolue
Les journées d'Août
La limousine
La martiale
Monsieur Protopopoff
L'orgueilleuse
La perverse
La révoltée
RIVIER
"A traduire en esthonien . . . "
Cartomancie
Hommage à Valery-Larbaud
Le vivier
ROUSSEL
Le bachelier de Salamanque
Coeur en péril
L'heure du retour
Sarabande
SATIE *Le Chapelier*
SAUGUET *Le chalet tyrolien*
SCHMITT *Vendredi XIII*
Chamber music see Kreymborg **THOMSON**
CHAMBER MUSIC. see Joyce
Dear heart **ROREM**
I hear an army **BARBER**
Rain has fallen **BARBER,
SZYMANOWSKI**
Sleep now **BARBER, SZYMANOWSKI**
La chambre de juin see Laporte **SAUGUET**

Chambrun, Marie Jeanne (Godard-Desmarest), comtesse de, 1827-1891.
GOUNOD *Passiflora*
Chamisso, Adelbert von, 1781-1838.
FRANZ
Mitten ins Herz
Tränen
Four settings: Op. 6 no. 6, op. 50 no. 5, op. 51 no. 2, and op. 52 no. 4.
GRIEG
Morgentau
Die Müllerin
Die Waise
Was soll ich sagen?
JENSEN
Denke, denke, mein Geliebter
Ich hab' ihn im Schlafe
Ich habe, bevor der Morgen
Nicht der Tau und nicht der Regen
Was ist's, O Vater
Wie so bleich
LOEWE
An meine Herzen, an meiner Brust
Du Ring an meinem Finger
Er, der Herrlichste von allen
Helft mir, ihr Schwestern!
Ich kann's nicht fassen, nicht glauben
Nun hast du mir den ersten Schmerz gethan
Süsser Freund, du blickest mich verwundert an
Traum der eignen Tage
MEDTNER
Frisch gesungen
Die Quelle
PFITZNER *Tragische Geschichte*
REGER *Scherz*
RIMSKIĭ-KORSAKOV *Taina*
SCHUMANN
An meinem Herzen, an meiner Brust
Du Ring an meinem Finger
Er, der Herrlichste von allen
Helft mir, ihr Schwestern
Ich kann's nicht fassen
Die Löwenbraut
Nun hast du mir den ersten Schmerz gethan
Süsser Freund, du blickest mich verwundert an
Was soll ich sagen!
SPOHR *Tränen*
STRAUSS *Lass ruh'n die Toten*
WOLF
Auf der Wanderschaft
Was soll ich sagen?
FRAUENLIEBE UND LEBEN.
LOEWE *Seit ich ihn gesehn*

Chamisso, Adelbert von, 1781-1838
(continued)
FRAUENLIEBE UND LEBEN (continued)
SCHUMANN *Seit ich ihn gesehen*
KATZENNATUR.
LOEWE *Die Katzenkönigin*
Les champignons see Paliard **MILHAUD**
Champlay, R
AUBERT
Berceuse du marin
Tendresse
Les champs see Béranger **BERLIOZ,**
GOUNOD
Champsaur, Félicien, 1859-1934.
MASSENET *Chanson juanesque*
La chance see Carême **MILHAUD**
LE CHANDELIER. see Musset
Chanson de Fortunio **DELIUS**
"Chandelier du mystère" *see Marronniers*
Anon. **MILHAUD**
Chang-Chi, 8-9th cent.
ROUSSEL *Réponse d'une épouse sage*
Chang Wen-chang, fl. T'ang Dynasty,
905-618 B.C.
GRIFFES *The old temple among the*
mountains
CHANLER, THEODORE, 1902-1961.
Blake, William, 1757-1827.
The lamb (1941) [Associated, 1946,
1974] "Little lamb, who made thee?"
Memory (1934) [Associated, 1946, 1974]
"Memory, hither come, & tune your
merry notes"
De La Mare, Walter, 1873-1956.
A one-eyed tailor (1940) [unpubl.]
"Here's an old Taylor, rest his eye"
A shepherd (1940) [unpubl.]
"A shepherd, Ned Vaughan"
DING DONG BELL: Benighted.
Alice Rodd (1936) [Arrow, 1939;
Boosey & Hawkes, 1966]
"Here lyeth our infant, Alice Rodd"
Ann Poverty (1936) [Arrow, 1939;
Boosey & Hawkes, 1966]
"Stranger, here lies Ann Poverty"
Be very quiet now (1936) [Arrow,
1939; Boosey & Hawkes, 1966]
same
A midget (1936) [Arrow, 1939;
Boosey & Hawkes, 1966]
"Just a span and half a span from
head to heel"
No voice to scold (1936) [Arrow,
1939; Boosey & Hawkes, 1966]
same
Susannah Fry (1936) [Arrow, 1939;
Boosey & Hawkes, 1966]
"Here sleep I, Susannah Fry"

Thomas Logge (1936) [Arrow, 1939;
Boosey & Hawkes, 1966]
"Here lies Thomas Logge"
Three sisters (1936) [Arrow, 1939;
Boosey & Hawkes, 1966]
"Three sisters rest beneath this
cypress shade"
HERE LIES MY THREE HUSBANDS.
Three husbands (1940) [Boosey &
Hawkes, 1962]
"Here lies my husbands; one, two
three"
Sometimes appended to *Eight*
epitaphs as no. 9.
PEACOCK PIE.
Cake and Sack (1940) [Associated,
1948]
"Old King Caraway supped on
cake"
Old Shellover (1940) [Associated,
1948]
"'Come!' said Old Shellover"
The ship of Rio (1940) [Associated,
1948]
"There was a ship of Rio sailed"
Tillie (1940) [Associated, 1948] "Old
Tillie Turveycombe sat to sew"
Feeney, Leonard, 1897-1978.
The children (1945) [G. Schirmer, 1946]
"We are the children who play in the
park"
The doves (1935) [Hargail Music Press,
1946] "The doves, they fly to the
moonlit elms"
The flight (1944) [Associated, 1948]
"A beautiful angel came and stood"
Grandma (1945) [G. Schirmer, 1946]
"Grandma is old"
I rise when you enter (1942) [G.
Schirmer, 1945] "You are so
wonderful, what shall I do?"
Moo is a cow (1945) [G. Schirmer, 1946]
same
Once upon a time (1945) [G. Schirmer,
1946] same
One of us (1945) [G. Schirmer, 1946]
"Husbands and wives!"
The policeman in the park (1948) [G.
Schirmer, 1948]
"When the stars in crowds"
The rose (1945) [G. Schirmer, 1946]
"Superimpose on the petals of a rose"
Sleep (1945) [G. Schirmer, 1946] "Sleep
is not something you worry about"
Spick and span (1945) [G. Schirmer,
1946] same
Wind (1945) [G. Schirmer, 1946] "Wind
is to show how a thing can blow"

Henley, William Ernest, 1849-1903.
  The patient sleeps (1948) [G. Schirmer, 1949]
    "Then they bid you close your eyelids"
MacLeish, Archibald, 1892-1982.
  These, my Ophelia (1925) [*Cos Cob song volume*, 1935; Boosey & Hawkes, 1964] same
  These, my Ophelia (revised version, 1937) [unpubl.; in Kolb diss.: Appendix III, p. 115] same
    Bruce Lanier Kolb, "The published songs of Theodore Chanler." D.M.A. diss., Louisiana State University, 1976.
No author
  Agnus Dei (1930) [G. Schirmer, 1949] same
Shakespeare, William, 1564-1616.
  TWELFTH NIGHT.
    O mistress mine! (1936) [Boosey & Hawkes, 1962]
      "O mistress mine, where are you roaming?"

Chanson see Anon. **SATIE**
Chanson see Apollinaire *IL Y A.* **POULENC**
Chanson see Blée, Catulle **SCHMITT**
Chanson see Contamine **SATIE**
Chanson see Hugo **LASSEN** *Si vous n'avez rien à me dire*
Chanson see Hugo **SAINT-SAËNS** *S'il est un charmant gazon*
Chanson see Louÿs *CHANSONS DE BILITIS.* **GIDEON**
Chanson see Maeterlinck **IBERT**
Chanson see Mendès **HAHN**
Chanson see Régnier **FAURÉ**
Chanson see Shakespeare **SAUGUET**
Chanson à boire see Anon. **POULENC**
Chanson à boire see Hugo **LALO**
Chanson à boire see Morand **RAVEL**
Chanson à boire du vieux temps see Boileau-Despréaux **SAINT-SAËNS**
Chanson andalouse see Unknown **MASSENET**
Chanson au bord de la fontaine, extraite de *Méduse see* Magre **HAHN**
La chanson bien douce see Verlaine **CHAUSSON**
Chanson bretonne see Arosa **SCHMITT**
Chanson bretonne see Jacob, M. **POULENC**
Chanson d'amour see Bouilhet **KOECHLIN**
Chanson d'amour see Hugo **RUBINSTEIN**
Chanson d'amour see Shakespeare *MEASURE FOR MEASURE*: Take, O take those lips away. **CHAUSSON**

Chanson d'amour see Silvestre **FAURÉ**
Chanson d'automne see Claudel **MILHAUD**
Chanson d'automne see Verlaine *POÈMES SATURNIENS.* **CARPENTER, DELIUS, HAHN**
Chanson d'avril see Bouilhet **BIZET**
Chanson d'Avril see Coppée **GOUNOD**
Chanson de Barberine see Musset *BARBERINE.* **LALO, RUBINSTEIN**
Chanson de Barberine see Musset **DELIBES** *Beau chevalier qui partez pour la guerre*
La chanson de blaisine see Magre *L'OUVRIER QUI PLEURE.* **SÉVERAC**
Chanson de Calypso see Auriol, J.-G. **SAUGUET**
Chanson de Capri see Gallet **MASSENET**
Chanson de clown see Shakespeare *TWELFTH NIGHT*: Come away, come away, death. **CHAUSSON**
Chanson de Florian see Florian **IVES**
Chanson de flûte see Leclère, translator. *SHÉHÉRAZADE.* **KOECHLIN**
Chanson de fol see Fort *COMPLAINTES ET DITS.* **HONEGGER**
Chanson de Fortunio see Musset *LE CHANDELIER.* **DELIUS**
Chanson de Fortunio see Musset **SAINT-SAËNS**
CHANSON DE FORTUNIO. see Musset *Net, nikogda ne nazovu* **CHAĬKOVSKIĬ**
Chanson de la fille de bar see Aguet, William **SAUGUET**
Chanson de la fille frivole see Fombeure *CHANSONS DE LA GRANDE HUNE.* **POULENC**
La chanson de la glu see Richepin **GOUNOD**
Chanson de la mariée see Anon. **RAVEL** *Le réveil de la mariée*
Chanson de la nuit durable see Espinasse-Mongenet **SÉVERAC**
La chanson de la rose see Barbier, J. **BIZET**
Chanson de la route see Kerdyk, René **HONEGGER**
Chanson de la route see Richepin **HONEGGER**
La chanson de l'alouette see Leprade **LALO**
Chanson de l'aveugle see Flaubert **MILHAUD**
Chanson de l'eau see Richepin **HONEGGER**
La chanson de l'Escadrille see Kessel **HONEGGER**

COMPOSER Poet *Title* "First Line"

Chanson de l'oiseleur see Lanoux
   SAUGUET
Chanson de l'oiseleur see Lockroy
   DELIBES
Chanson de l'oranger sec see Garcia Lorca
   POULENC
Chanson de l'ours see Anon. **STRAVINSKĬ**
Chanson de marin see Aguet, William
   HONEGGER
Chanson de Mélisande see Maeterlinck
   FAURÉ *Mélisande's song*
Chanson de mer see Sully-Prudhomme
   AUBERT
Chanson de pâtre épirote see Anon. **RAVEL**
Une chanson de porcelaine see Éluard
   POULENC
Chanson de printemps see Tourneux,
   Eugène **GOUNOD**
Chanson de quête see Anon. **VAUGHAN
   WILLIAMS**
Chanson de Zora (La petite Bohémienne) *see*
   Deschamps **ROSSINI**
Chanson d'Engaddi see Leclère, translator.
   SHÉHÉRAZADE. **KOECHLIN**
Chanson des amoureux see Luka,
   Madeleine **SAUGUET**
La chanson des beux amants see Leclère,
   translator. *SHÉHÉRAZADE.* **KOECHLIN**
Chanson des cueilleuses de lentisques see
   Anon. **RAVEL**
CHANSON DES HEURES. see Silvestre
   Le charme **CHAUSSON**
La chanson des ingénues see Verlaine
   KOECHLIN
La chanson des lèvres see Cazalis
   MASSENET
Chanson des quatre see Bloch **HONEGGER**
Chanson désespérée see Teulet, Edmond
   MASSENET
LA CHANSON D'ÈVE, no. 1
   FAURÉ Lerberghe *Paradis*
LA CHANSON D'ÈVE, no. 2
   FAURÉ Lerberghe *Prima verba*
LA CHANSON D'ÈVE, no. 3
   FAURÉ Lerberghe *Roses ardentes*
LA CHANSON D'ÈVE, no. 4
   FAURÉ Lerberghe *Comme Dieu
   rayonne . . .*
LA CHANSON D'ÈVE, no. 5
   FAURÉ Lerberghe *L'aube blanche*
LA CHANSON D'ÈVE, no. 6
   FAURÉ Lerberghe *Eau vivante*
LA CHANSON D'ÈVE, no. 7
   FAURÉ Lerberghe *Veilles-tu, ma senteur
   de soleil*
LA CHANSON D'ÈVE, no. 8
   FAURÉ Lerberghe *Dans un parfum de
   roses blanches*

LA CHANSON D'ÈVE, no. 9
   FAURÉ Lerberghe *Crépuscule*
LA CHANSON D'ÈVE , no. 10
   FAURÉ Lerberghe *O mort, poussière
   d'étoiles*
Chanson d'Ishak de Mossoul see Leclère,
   translator. *SHÉHÉRAZADE.* **KOECHLIN**
Chanson d'Ophélie see Shakespeare
   HAMLET: He is dead & gone, lady.
   CHAUSSON
Chanson d'Orkenise see Apollinaire
   POULENC
La chanson du Bébé see Pacini **ROSSINI**
Chanson du capitaine see Bloch **MILHAUD**
Chanson du chat see Fargue *LUDIONS.*
   SATIE
Chanson du clair tamis see Fombeure
   CHANSONS DE LA GRANDE HUNE.
   POULENC
La chanson du fou see Hugo **BIZET**
Chanson du Jour de Noël see Marot *TRENTE
   ET HUYT CHANSONS MUSICALES . . . :*
   Chanson vingtcinquiesme . . . **HESELTINE**
La chanson du pâtre see Augier **GOUNOD**
LA CHANSON DU PAUVRE . . . see LeRoy
   Les Angélus **DEBUSSY**
Chanson du pêcheur see Gautier **FAURÉ,
   GOUNOD**
La chanson du printemps see Bard,
   Chevalier **MILHAUD**
Chanson du rien see Constantin-Weyer
   IBERT
Chanson du rouet see Leconte de Lisle
   CHANSONS ÉCOSSAISES. **RAVEL**
Chanson écossaise see Burns **RAVEL**
Chanson épique see Morand **RAVEL**
Chanson espagnole see Anon. **RAVEL**
Chanson espagnole see Musset **DELIBES**
   Les filles de Cadix
Chanson flamande see Unknown **RAVEL**
Chanson florentine see Chaïkovskiï
   CHAÏKOVSKIĬ *Pimpinella*
Chanson française see Anon. **RAVEL**
Chanson gothique see Gérard de Nerval
   AURIC
Chanson grecque dans le mode phrygien see
   Ackermann **CHAUSSON** *Hébé*
Chanson hébraïque see Anon. **RAVEL**
Chanson hongroise see Petöfi **DELIBES**
Chanson italienne see Anon. **RAVEL**
Chanson juanesque see Champsaur
   MASSENET
Chanson médiévale see Mendès **SATIE**
Chanson morave see Margueritte
   MALIPIERO
Chanson pour compter see Anon.
   STRAVINSKIĬ

Chanson pour elle see Maigret, Henri
  MASSENET
Chanson pour Jeanne see Mendès
  CHABRIER
Chanson pour le petit cheval see Estieu
  SÉVERAC *Cansón pel cabalet*
Chanson printanière see Barbier, J.
  GOUNOD
Chanson romantique see Morand **RAVEL**
Chanson russe see Unknown **RAVEL**
Chanson triste see Bouchor, M. **DEBUSSY**
Chanson triste see Cazalis **DUPARC**
CHANSON TRISTE. see Cazalis
  Dans ton coeur **SAINT-SAËNS**
Chansonette see Wailly **BERLIOZ**
Chansonette de cabaret ('Le lazzarone') *see*
  Unknown **ROSSINI**
CHANSONS, no. 1
  MILHAUD Vildrac *Les quatre petits lions*
CHANSONS, no. 2
  MILHAUD Vildrac *Poupette et Patata*
CHANSONS, no. 3
  MILHAUD Vildrac *La pomme et*
  l'escargot
CHANSONS, no. 4
  MILHAUD Vildrac *Le malpropre*
CHANSONS, no. 5
  MILHAUD Vildrac *Le jardinier impatient*
CHANSONS BAS, no. 1
  MILHAUD Mallarmé *Le savetier*
CHANSONS BAS, no. 2
  MILHAUD Mallarmé *La Marchande*
  d'herbes aromatiques
CHANSONS BAS, no. 3
  MILHAUD Mallarmé *Le cantonnier*
CHANSONS BAS, no. 4
  MILHAUD Mallarmé *Le Marchand d'ail*
  et d'oignons
CHANSONS BAS, no. 5
  MILHAUD Mallarmé *La femme de*
  l'ouvrier
CHANSONS BAS, no. 7
  MILHAUD Mallarmé *Le crieur*
  d'imprimés
CHANSONS BAS, no. 8
  MILHAUD Mallarmé *La Marchande*
  d'habits
CHANSONS DE BILITIS
  DEBUSSY
    Louÿs
      Le chevelure
      La flûte de Pan
      Le tombeau des Naïdes
CHANSONS DE BILITIS. see Louÿs
  Chanson **GIDEON**
  Chant funèbre **KOECHLIN**

  Le chevelure **DEBUSSY**
  Épitaphe de Bilitis **KOECHLIN**
  La flûte de Pan **DEBUSSY**
  Hymne à Astarté **KOECHLIN**
  Hymne à la nuit **KOECHLIN**
  La pluie au matin **GIDEON, KOECHLIN**
  Le tombeau des Naïdes **DEBUSSY**
CHANSONS DE LA GRANDE HUNE. see
  Fombeure
  C'est le joli printemps **POULENC**
  Chanson de la fille frivole **POULENC**
  Chanson du clair tamis **POULENC**
  Les gars qui vont à la fête **POULENC**
  Le mendiant **POULENC**
  Le retour du sergent **POULENC**
Chansons de marins see Cocteau
  SAUGUET
CHANSONS DE MIARKA, no. 1
  CHAUSSON Richepin *Les morts*
CHANSONS DE MIARKA, no. 2
  CHAUSSON Richepin *La pluie*
CHANSONS DE SHAKESPEARE, no. 1
  CHAUSSON Shakespeare *Chanson de*
  clown
CHANSONS DE SHAKESPEARE, no. 2
  CHAUSSON Shakespeare *Chanson*
  d'amour
CHANSONS DE SHAKESPEARE, no. 3
  CHAUSSON Shakespeare *Chanson*
  d'Ophélie
CHANSONS DES RUES ET DES BOIS. see
  Hugo
  Sommation irrespectueuse **CHABRIER**
CHANSONS ÉCOSSAISES. see Leconte de
  Lisle *Chanson du rouet* **RAVEL**
Chansons espagnoles see Unknown **HAHN**
CHANSONS GAILLARDES, no. 1
  POULENC Anon. *La maîtresse volage*
CHANSONS GAILLARDES, no. 2
  POULENC Anon. *Chanson à boire*
CHANSONS GAILLARDES, no. 3
  POULENC Anon. *Madrigal*
CHANSONS GAILLARDES, no. 4
  POULENC Anon. *Invocations aux*
  Parques
CHANSONS GAILLARDES, no. 5
  POULENC Anon. *Couplets bachiques*
CHANSONS GAILLARDES, no. 6
  POULENC Anon. *L'Offrande*
CHANSONS GAILLARDES, no. 7
  POULENC Anon. *La belle jeunesse*
CHANSONS GAILLARDES, no. 8
  POULENC Anon. *Sérénade*
CHANSONS GRISES, no. 1
  HAHN Verlaine *Chanson d'automne*
CHANSONS GRISES, no. 2
  HAHN Verlaine *Tous deux*

COMPOSER   Poet   *Title*   "First Line"

CHANSONS GRISES, no. 3
 HAHN Verlaine *L'allée est sans fin*
CHANSONS GRISES, no. 4
 HAHN Verlaine *En sourdine*
CHANSONS GRISES, no. 5
 HAHN Verlaine *L'heure exquise*
CHANSONS GRISES, no. 6
 HAHN Verlaine *Paysage triste*
CHANSONS GRISES, no. 7
 HAHN Verlaine *La bonne chanson*
CHANSONS MADÉCASSES, no. 1
 RAVEL Parny, Evariste *Nahandove*
CHANSONS MADÉCASSES, no. 2
 RAVEL Parny, Evariste *Aoua!*
CHANSONS MADÉCASSES, no. 3
 RAVEL Parny, Evariste *Il est doux . . .*
CHANSONS POUR ELLE, no. 20. *see*
 Verlaine *L'incrédule* **HAHN**
CHANSONS POUR GLADYS, no. 1
 KOECHLIN Koechlin *M'a dit amour . . .*
CHANSONS POUR GLADYS, no. 2
 KOECHLIN Koechlin *Tu croyais le tenir,
 et il t'a prise*
CHANSONS POUR GLADYS, no. 3
 KOECHLIN Koechlin *Prise au piège*
CHANSONS POUR GLADYS, no. 4
 KOECHLIN Koechlin *Quand tu nageois
 emmy Sirènes et Tritons*
CHANSONS POUR GLADYS, no. 5
 KOECHLIN Koechlin *Le cyclone*
CHANSONS POUR GLADYS, no. 6
 KOECHLIN Koechlin *La Colombe*
CHANSONS POUR GLADYS, no. 7
 KOECHLIN Koechlin *Fatum*
CHANSONS VILLAGEOISES, no. 1
 POULENC Fombeure *Chanson du clair
 tamis*
CHANSONS VILLAGEOISES, no. 2
 POULENC Fombeure *Les gars qui vont
 à la fête*
CHANSONS VILLAGEOISES, no. 3
 POULENC Fombeure *C'est le joli
 printemps*
CHANSONS VILLAGEOISES, no. 4
 POULENC Fombeure *Le mendiant*
CHANSONS VILLAGEOISES, no. 5
 POULENC Fombeure *Chanson de la fille
 frivole*
CHANSONS VILLAGEOISES, no. 6
 POULENC Fombeure *Le retour du
 sergent*
Chant Breton see Delpit **LALO**
Chant d'amour see Lamartine **BIZET**
Chant d'amour see Unknown **MILHAUD**
Chant d'automne see Anon. **GOUNOD**
Chant d'automne see Baudelaire **FAURÉ**

Chant de bonheur see Berlioz **BERLIOZ**
Le chant de ceux qui s'en vont sur mer see
 Hugo **SAINT-SAËNS**
Chant de feu see Senghor **SAUGUET**
Chant de folie see Vallery-Radot, Pasteur
 IBERT
Chant de forgeron see Unknown
 MILHAUD
Chant de guerre cosaque see Văcărescu
 MASSENET
Chant de la pitié see Unknown **MILHAUD**
Chant de l'almée see Gille **DELIBES**
Chant de l'émigrant see Bloch **HONEGGER**
Chant de Noël see Goudouli **SÉVERAC**
 Cant per Nadal
Chant de nourrice see Aicard **MASSENET**
Chant de nourrice see Unknown
 MILHAUD
Chant de résignation see Unknown
 MILHAUD
Chant de Sion see Unknown **MILHAUD**
Le chant des Bretons see Brizeux **BERLIOZ**
Chant des sauveteurs Bretons see Ségalas
 GOUNOD
Chant dissident see Anon. **STRAVINSKIĭ**
Chant du Destin see Hölderlin **SAUGUET**
Chant du laboureur see Unknown
 MILHAUD
Le chant du veilleur see Anon. **MILHAUD**
Chant funèbre see Louÿs *CHANSONS DE
 BILITIS.* **KOECHLIN**
Chant funèbre pour de nouveaux héros see
 Seghers **SAUGUET**
Chant Hassidique see Anon. **MILHAUD**
Chant provençal see Carré **MASSENET**
"Un chant s'élance, fleur du silence" see Song
 Jean-Aubry **MALIPIERO**
Chante de délivrance see Anon. **MILHAUD**
"Chante! me dit l'oiseau jaseur" see Chanter
 et souffrir Delpit **GOUNOD**
Chantepie, J
 MASSENET *Dors, ami*
Chanter et souffrir see Delpit **GOUNOD**
Chantez noël see Barbier, J. **GOUNOD**
"Chantez un chant funèbre" see Chant funèbre
 Louÿs **KOECHLIN**
Chantez, voix bénies see Gallet **GOUNOD**
"Chantons, voici le temps des roses!" see
 Le temps des roses Roy, Camille
 GOUNOD
CHANTS BAS, no. 6
 MILHAUD Mallarmé *Le vitrier*
CHANTS DE MISÈRE, no. 1
 MILHAUD Paliard *Cet hiver*
CHANTS DE MISÈRE, no. 2
 MILHAUD Paliard *Cette douleur*

COMPOSER Poet *Title* "First Line"

CHANTS DE MISÈRE, no. 3
  MILHAUD Paliard *Silence au fond de l'allée*
CHANTS DE MISÈRE, no. 4
  MILHAUD Paliard *Tant de vagabonds*
CHANTS DE TERRE ET DE CIEL, no. 1
  MESSIAEN Messiaen *Bail avec Mi*
CHANTS DE TERRE ET DE CIEL, no. 2
  MESSIAEN Messiaen *Antienne du silence*
CHANTS DE TERRE ET DE CIEL, no. 3
  MESSIAEN Messiaen *Danse du bébé-Phile*
CHANTS DE TERRE ET DE CIEL, no. 4
  MESSIAEN Messiaen *Arc-en-ciel d'innocence*
CHANTS DE TERRE ET DE CIEL, no. 5
  MESSIAEN Messiaen *Minuit pile et face*
CHANTS DE TERRE ET DE CIEL, no. 6
  MESSIAEN Messiaen *Résurrection*
Chants d'oiseaux see Leprade **CHABRIER**
CHANTS DU CRÉPUSCULE. see Hugo
  L'aurore **FAURÉ**
  S'il est un charmant gazon **FRANCK, LISZT, SAINT-SAËNS**
CHANTS INTIMES, no. 1
MASSENET Chouquet *Déclaration*
CHANTS INTIMES, no. 2
  MASSENET Chouquet *À Mignonne*
CHANTS INTIMES, no. 3
  MASSENET Chouquet *Berceuse*
CHANTS POPULAIRES, no. 1
  RAVEL Anon. *Chanson espagnole*
CHANTS POPULAIRES, no. 2
  RAVEL Anon. *Chanson française*
CHANTS POPULAIRES, no. 3
  RAVEL Anon. *Chanson italienne*
CHANTS POPULAIRES, no. 4
  RAVEL Anon. *Chanson hébraïque*
CHANTS POPULAIRES, no. 5
  RAVEL Burns *Chanson écossaise*
CHANTS POPULAIRES, no. 6
  RAVEL Unknown *Chanson flamande*
CHANTS POPULAIRES, no. 7
  RAVEL Unknown *Chanson russe*
Le Chapelier see Chalupt **SATIE**
"Le chapelier s'étonne de constater que sa montre" *see Le Chapelier* Chalupt **SATIE**
The chariot see Dickinson **COPLAND**
Charles, Duke of Orleans, 1391-1465.
  DEBUSSY
    Pour ce que plaisance est morte
    Le temps a laissié son manteau
  HAHN
    Je me metz en vostre mercy
    Quand je fus pris au pavillon

HESELTINE *My gostly fader*
POULENC *Priez pour paix*
SAINT-SAËNS
  Primavera
  Temps nouveau
Charlie Rutlage see Anon. **IVES**
A charm see Randolph, T. **BRITTEN**
"Charm me asleep, and melt me so" *see To music* Herrick **GIDEON**
"Charm me asleep, and melt me so" *see To music, to becalm his fever* Herrick **HINDEMITH, ROREM**
A CHARM OF LULLABIES, no. 1
  BRITTEN Blake, William *A cradle song*
A CHARM OF LULLABIES, no. 2
  BRITTEN Burns *The highland balou*
A CHARM OF LULLABIES, no. 3
  BRITTEN Greene, R. *Sephestia's lullaby*
A CHARM OF LULLABIES, no. 4
  BRITTEN Randolph, T. *A charm*
A CHARM OF LULLABIES, no. 5
  BRITTEN Phillip, John *The nurse's song*
Charmant bocage see Anon. **RIEGGER**
Le charme see Carême **MILHAUD**
Le charme see Silvestre *CHANSON DES HEURES.* **CHAUSSON**
"Charmé . . . Oh! pauvre fille!" *see Oiseau* Éluard **SAUGUET**
Charovnítsa see Collin **CHAÏKOVSKIĬ**
  Rondel
Chassang, Maurice
  MASSENET *Et puis*
La chasse see Banville **KOECHLIN**
Chasse see Labé **SAUGUET**
La chasse du Burgrave see Anon.
  SAINT-SAËNS
Le chasseur danois see Leuven **BERLIOZ**
Le chasseur perdu en forêt see Fort *COMPLAINTES ET DITS.* **HONEGGER**
"Chaste déese! déesse si pure" *see À la lune* Châteaubriand **MILHAUD**
Le chat see Baudelaire **SAUGUET**
  Two settings, both 1938.
Chat see Cocteau **MILHAUD**
Chat see Éluard **SAUGUET**
Le château see Paliard **MILHAUD**
LE CHÂTEAU, no. 1
  MILHAUD Lunel *Les enfants*
LE CHÂTEAU, no. 2
  MILHAUD Lunel *Le sifflet*
LE CHÂTEAU, no. 3
  MILHAUD Lunel *Les châtelaines*
LE CHÂTEAU, no. 4
  MILHAUD Lunel *Le cavalier*
LE CHÂTEAU, no. 5
  MILHAUD Lunel *Les Libellules*

COMPOSER Poet *Title* "First Line"

LE CHÂTEAU, no. 6
MILHAUD Lunel *L'agriculteur*
LE CHÂTEAU, no. 7
MILHAUD Lunel *L'Octobre*
LE CHÂTEAU, no. 8
MILHAUD Lunel *L'adieu*
Le château du Bartas see Bédat de
Monlaur, Pierre **HONEGGER**
Châteaubriand, François Auguste René,
vicomte de,1768-1848.
FRANCK *Souvenance*
MILHAUD
À la lune
L'aurore
L'Innocence
Les châtelaines see Lunel **MILHAUD**
Châtillon, M.-A. de
CHABRIER *Sérénade*
The chatterbox see Barto, A. **PROKOFIEV**
Boltun'i͡a
Chatterton see Keats **DIAMOND**
Chaucer, Geoffrey, d. 1400.
ROREM *Song*
CHAUSSON, ERNEST, 1855-1899.
Ackermann, Louise Victorine
(Choquet), 1813-1890.
Hébé, op. 2 no. 6 [Hamelle]
"Les yeux boissés"
Anon.
Nous nous aimerons (1882) [unpubl.]
Pour un arbre de Noël, op. 33 (1898)
[unpubl.]
Baudelaire, Charles Pierre, 1821-1867.
L'Albatros (1879) [unpubl.]
Bouchor, Maurice, 1855-1929.
Amour d'antan, op. 8 no. 2 [Rouart
Lerolle, 1910] "Mon amour d'antan"
Nocturne, op. 8 no. 1[Rouart Lerolle,
1910]
"La nuit était pensive et ténébreuse"
Nos souvenirs, op. 8 no. 4 [Rouart
Lerolle, 1910]
"Nos souvenirs, toutes ces choses"
Le petit sentier (1878) [unpubl.]
Printemps triste, op. 8 no. 3 [Rouart
Lerolle, 1910]
"Nos sentiers aimés s'en vont refleurir"
DANS LA FORÊT.
Lilas, vos frissons sous le ciel (1878)
[unpubl.]
Bourget, Paul Charles Joseph, 1852-
1935.
Sérénade italienne, op. 2 no. 5 [Hamelle]
"Partons en barque sur la mer"
Cazalis, Henri, 1840-1909.
Sérénade, op. 13 no. 2 [Hamelle] "Tes
grands yeux doux semblent des îles"

Gautier, Théophile, 1811-1872.
La caravane, op. 14 [Hamelle]
"La caravane humaine"
Also voice & orchestra.
La dernière feuille, op. 2 no. 4 [Hamelle]
"Dans la forêt chauve et rouillée"
Les papillons, op. 2 no. 3 [Hamelle]
"Les papillons couleur de neige"
Jounet, Albert, 1863-1923.
Cantique à l'Épouse, op. 36 no. 1
[Rouart Lerolle, 1910]
"Epouse au front lumineux"
Leconte de Lisle, Charles Marie René,
1818-1894.
La cigale, op. 13 no. 4 [Hamelle]
"O Cigale, née avec les beaux jours"
Le colibri, op. 2 no. 7 [Hamelle]
"Le vert colibri, le roi des collines"
POÈMES ANTIQUES.
Nanny, op. 2 no. 1 [Hamelle]
"Bois chère aux ramiers"
Maeterlinck, Maurice, 1862-1949.
Fauves las, op. 24 no. 4 [Rouart Lerolle,
1910] "O les passions en allées"
Lassitude, op. 24 no. 3 [Rouart Lerolle,
1910] "Ils ne savent plus où se poser
ces baisers"
Oraison, op. 24 no. 5 [Rouart Lerolle,
1910]
"Vous savez, seigneur, ma misère!"
Serre chaude, op. 24 no. 1 [Rouart
Lerolle, 1910]
"O serre au milieu des forêts!"
Serre d'ennui, op. 24 no. 2 [Rouart
Lerolle, 1910]
"O cet ennui bleu dans le coeur!"
Mauclair, Camille, 1872-1945.
Ballade, op. 27 no. 2 [Rouart Lerolle,
1910]
"Quand les anges se sont perdus"
Les couronnes, op. 27 no. 3 [Rouart
Lerolle, 1910]
"C'est la fillette aux yeux cernés"
Les heures, op. 27 no. 1 [Rouart Lerolle,
1910] "Les pâles heures, sous la lune"
Moréas, Jean, 1856-1910.
*Dans la forêt du Charme et de
l'Enchantement*, op. 36 no. 2
[Rouart Lerolle, 1910] "Sous vos
sombres chevelures petites fées"
Musset, Alfred de, 1810-1857.
Le rideau de ma voisine (1879) [unpubl.]
Richepin, Jean, 1849-1926.
Le mort maudit (1884) [unpubl.]
Les morts, op. 17 no. 1 [Bornemann]
"Ne crois pas que les morts soient
morts!"

La pluie, op. 17 no. 2 [Bornemann]
"La pluie, la pluie aux doigts verts"
Shakespeare, William, 1564-1616.
IIAMLET: He is dead & gone, lady.
Chanson d'Ophélie, op. 28 no. 3
[Rouart Lerolle, 1910] "Il est mort
ayant bien souffert, Madame"
MEASURE FOR MEASURE: Take, O
take those lips away.
Chanson d'amour, op. 28 no. 2
[Rouart Lerolle, 1910]
"Loin de mai, loin de mai"
TWELFTH NIGHT: Come away, come
away, death.
Chanson de clown, op. 28 no. 1
[Rouart Lerolle, 1910]
"Fuis, mon âme, fuis!"
Silvestre, Paul Armond, 1837-1901.
CHANSON DES HEURES.
Le charme, op. 2 no. 2 [Hamelle]
"Quand ton sourire me surprit"
Verlaine, Paul, 1844-1896.
La chanson bien douce, op. 34 no. 1
[Rouart Lerolle, 1910]
"Ecoutez la chanson bien douce"
Le chevalier Malheur, op. 34 no. 2
[***Revue Musicale, Supplément,*** 1er
Déc. 1925] "Bon chevalier masqué
qui chevauche en silence"
LA BONNE CHANSON.
Apaisement, op. 13 no. 1 [Hamelle]
"La lune blanche luit dans les bois"
Villiers de l'Isle-Adam, Jean Marie
Mathias . . . , comte de, 1838-1889.
L'aveu, op. 13 no. 3 [Hamelle]
"J'ai perdu la forêt, la plaine"
Chauvinière, Edmond de
GOUNOD
La jeune fille et la fauvette
Sérénade
"Chceme my se, chceme" *see Tajná láska*
Anon. **MARTINŮ**
Che cälma in gir! Che päza sepolcräla! see
Zerbini, Alfredo **PIZZETTI**
"Che fa il mio bene?" *see L'amante*
impatiente Metastasio **BEETHOVEN**
Two settings: Op. 82 no. 3 and op. 84 no.
4.
"Che fai tu, Eco, mentre io ti chiamo?" *see*
L'Eco Poliziano **MALIPIERO**
"Che mi giova cantar: 'Fior di betulla'" *see*
Stornellatrice Zangarini **RESPIGHI**
Che pecà! see Anon. **HAHN**
Le Cheichi see Mahaut **RIVIER**
Chekhov, Anton Pavlovich, 1860-1909.
UNCLE VANYA, Act IV.
RACHMANINOFF *Let us rest*

"Chemin de nuit" *see Voyage* Jacob, M.
SAUGUET
Le chemin des forains see Dréjac, Jean
SAUGUET
"Le chemin près du bois" *see Le secret*
Obaldia **SAUGUET**
Les cheminées rouge see Havet
CARPENTER
Les chemins de l'amour see Anouilh
LÉOCADIA. **POULENC**
"Les chemins qui vont à la mer" *see*
Les chemins de l'amour Anouilh
POULENC
Chénier, André Marie, 1762-1794.
KOECHLIN
La jeune tarentine
Néère
"Chère apparence viens aux couchants
illuminés" *see Adieu pour jamais* Kahn
LOEFFLER
La chère blessure see Blanchecotte **HAHN**
Chernets see Anon. **PROKOFIEV**
Cherry-ripe see Herrick **QUILTER,**
ROREM
" 'Cherry-ripe, ripe, ripe,' I cry" *see Cherry-*
ripe Herrick **QUILTER, ROREM**
Chesson, Mrs. Nora (Hopper), 1871-
1906.
CARPENTER *Little John's song*
QUILTER
Blossom time
June
Spring is at the door
Chetyre pesni see Afinogenov
PROKOFIEV
Cheval see Éluard **SAUGUET**
"Cheval seul, cheval perdu" *see Cheval*
Éluard **SAUGUET**
Le chevalier à l'armure étincelante see
Tardieu **SAUGUET**
Le chevalier Malheur see Verlaine
CHAUSSON
La chevauchée du Cid see Bonnières **INDY**
Au galop
Chevaux de bois see Verlaine *PAYSAGES*
BELGES. **DEBUSSY**
Le chevelure see Louÿs *CHANSONS DE*
BILITIS. **DEBUSSY**
La chèvre du Thibet see Apollinaire
LE BESTIAIRE. **POULENC**
LE CHÈVRE-FEUILLE, no. 1
SAUGUET Hugnet *Je t'adore*
LE CHÈVRE-FEUILLE, no. 2
SAUGUET Hugnet *Laisse ta hanche*
blonde
LE CHÈVRE-FEUILLE, no. 3
SAUGUET Hugnet *Cache la fée*

COMPOSER Poet *Title* "First Line"

LE CHÈVRE-FEUILLE, no. 4
  SAUGUET Hugnet *La reine m'a livré*
LE CHÈVRE-FEUILLE, no. 5
  SAUGUET Hugnet *Je suis hereux*
LE CHÈVRE-FEUILLE, no. 6
  SAUGUET Hugnet *Sois mon amie*
LE CHÈVRE-FEUILLE, no. 7
  SAUGUET Hugnet *Et voici des ans*
LE CHÈVRE-FEUILLE, no. 8
  SAUGUET Hugnet *Ici seront nées mes saisons*
LE CHÈVRE-FEUILLE, no. 9
  SAUGUET Hugnet *Nous avions si chaud*
LE CHÈVRE-FEUILLE, no. 10
  SAUGUET Hugnet *Ces mots qui n'ont plus de sens*
Le chevrier see Rey, Paul *ANOMALIE.*
  SÉVERAC
Chez Eitingon see Unknown **BLITZSTEIN**
Chez le docteur see Hyspa **SATIE**
Chézy, Helmina von *see* Chezy, Wilhelmine Christiane von, 1783-1856.
Chezy, Wilhelmine Christiane von, 1783-1856.
  IVES *Rosamunde*
  LOEWE
    Moosröslein
    St. Johannes und das Würmlein
"Chi colla neve solazzarsi verole" *see Canto della neve* Anon. **MALIPIERO**
Chi i bei di m'adduce ancora see Goethe
  VERDI
"Chi m'ascolta il canto usato" *see Il trovatore*
  Unknown **ROSSINI**
"Chi padre mi fosse" *see La zingara*
  Maggioni, S. Manfredo **VERDI**
"Chi scenderà dal'alta scala" *see La statua*
  Annunzio **RESPIGHI**
CHICAGO POEMS. see Sandburg
  Fog **HARRIS**
Chicher" Iacher" Sobiralsia na vecher" see
  Unknown **STRAVINSKIï**
    Tchitcher-Iatcher
Chidiock Tichborne see Anon. **GOUNOD**
Chien see Éluard **SAUGUET**
"Chien chaud, tout entier dans la voix" *see*
  Chien Éluard **SAUGUET**
CHILD POEMS, no. 1
  MILHAUD Tagore *When and why*
CHILD POEMS, no. 2
  MILHAUD Tagore *Defamation*
CHILD POEMS, no. 3
  MILHAUD Tagore *Paper boats*
CHILD POEMS, no. 4
  MILHAUD Tagore *Sympathy*

CHILD POEMS, no. 5
  MILHAUD Tagore *The gift*
Child song see Trustman, Deborah
  WEISGALL
Child, thou art as beautiful as a flower see
  Heine *DU BIST WIE EINE BLUME.*
  RACHMANINOFF
A child writes a letter see Unknown
  BLITZSTEIN
Childe Harold see Heine **FRANZ, LASSEN**
CHILDE HAROLD'S PILGRIMAGE. see
  Byron *A farewell to land* **IVES**
The children see Feeney **CHANLER**
The children see Soutar **BRITTEN**
THE CHILDREN, no. 1
  CHANLER Feeney *The children*
THE CHILDREN, no. 2
  CHANLER Feeney *Once upon a time*
THE CHILDREN, no. 3
  CHANLER Feeney *Wind*
THE CHILDREN, no. 4
  CHANLER Feeney *Sleep*
THE CHILDREN, no. 5
  CHANLER Feeney *The rose*
THE CHILDREN, no. 6
  CHANLER Feeney *Grandma*
THE CHILDREN, no. 7
  CHANLER Feeney *Spick and span*
THE CHILDREN, no. 8
  CHANLER Feeney *Moo is a cow*
THE CHILDREN, no. 9
  CHANLER Feeney *One of us*
The children of the poor see Hugo
  DIAMOND
The children's hour see Longfellow **IVES**
CHILDREN'S RHYMES, no. 1
  SZYMANOWSKI Iłłakowiczówna *Przed zaśnieciem*
CHILDREN'S RHYMES, no. 2
  SZYMANOWSKI Iłłakowiczówna *Jak sie najlepiej opedzać od szerszenia*
CHILDREN'S RHYMES, no. 3
  SZYMANOWSKI Iłłakowiczówna *Mieszkanie*
CHILDREN'S RHYMES, no. 4
  SZYMANOWSKI Iłłakowiczówna *Prosie*
CHILDREN'S RHYMES, no. 5
  SZYMANOWSKI Iłłakowiczówna *Gwiazdka*
CHILDREN'S RHYMES, no. 6
  SZYMANOWSKI Iłłakowiczówna *Ślub królewny*
CHILDREN'S RHYMES, no. 7
  SZYMANOWSKI Iłłakowiczówna *Trzmiel i zuk*

COMPOSER Poet *Title* "First Line"

CHILDREN'S RHYMES, no. 8
SZYMANOWSKI Iłłakowiczówna
Świetz Krystyna
CHILDREN'S RHYMES, no. 9
SZYMANOWSKI Iłłakowiczówna
Wiosna
CHILDREN'S RHYMES, no. 10
SZYMANOWSKI Iłłakowiczówna
Kolysanka lalek
CHILDREN'S RHYMES, no. 11
SZYMANOWSKI Iłłakowiczówna *Gil i*
sroka
CHILDREN'S RHYMES, no. 12
SZYMANOWSKI Iłłakowiczówna
Smutek
CHILDREN'S RHYMES, no. 13
SZYMANOWSKI Iłłakowiczówna
Wizyta u krowy
CHILDREN'S RHYMES, no. 14
SZYMANOWSKI Iłłakowiczówna
Kolysanka Krzysi
CHILDREN'S RHYMES, no. 15
SZYMANOWSKI Iłłakowiczówna *Kot*
CHILDREN'S RHYMES, no. 16
SZYMANOWSKI Iłłakowiczówna
Kolysanka lalki
CHILDREN'S RHYMES, no. 17
SZYMANOWSKI Iłłakowiczówna *Myszy*
CHILDREN'S RHYMES, no. 18
SZYMANOWSKI Iłłakowiczówna *Zly*
Lejba
CHILDREN'S RHYMES, no. 19
SZYMANOWSKI Iłłakowiczówna
Kolysanka gniadego konia
CHILDREN'S RHYMES, no. 20
SZYMANOWSKI Iłłakowiczówna
Nikczemny szpak
Children's song see Aksakov
CHAÏKOVSKIï *Detskaya pesnya*
A CHILD'S GARDEN OF VERSES. see
Stevenson, Robert Louis
Foreign children **QUILTER**
A good boy **HAHN**
A good child **QUILTER**
The lamplighter **QUILTER**
My ship and I **HAHN**
The stars **HAHN**
The swing **HAHN**
Where go the boats? **QUILTER**
Windy nights **HAHN**
Child's song see Aksakov **CHAÏKOVSKIï**
Detskaya pesnya
Child's song see Mei *RUTHENISCHE*
LIEDER: No. 2. Nane. **MUSORGSKIï**
Detskaia pesenka
Chilman, Eric, 1893-
IRELAND *The east riding*

LA CHIMERA. see Annunzio
Eliana **MALIPIERO**
Grasinda **MALIPIERO**
Mattinata **RESPIGHI**
Melusina **MALIPIERO**
Mirinda **MALIPIERO**
Morgana **MALIPIERO**
Oriana–Oriana infedele **MALIPIERO**
"Chimes of gladness, chimes of sadness" *see*
Spring Gorodetski **STRAVINSKIï**
The chimney-sweeper see Blake, William
BRITTEN
CHINESE SONGS, no. 1
BERKELEY Wu-Ti, Liang dynasty *People*
hide their love
CHINESE SONGS, no. 2
BERKELEY Wu-Ti, Han dynasty
The autumn wind
CHINESE SONGS, no. 3
BERKELEY Shên-Yo *Dreaming of a*
dead lady
CHINESE SONGS, no. 4
BERKELEY Yang Knang *Late spring*
CHINESE SONGS, no. 5
BERKELEY Ssu-k'ung Shu
The riverside village
CHINESISCH- DEUTSCHE JAHRES- UND
TAGESZEITEN. see Goethe
Dämmrung senkte sich von oben
BRAHMS, SCHOECK
Nun weiss man erst, was Rosenknospe sei
WEBERN
Chinesisches see Gautier **LASSEN**
Chinoiserie
Ching-a-ring chaw see Anon. **COPLAND**
"Ching-a-ring-a ring ching ching" *see Ching-*
a-ring chaw Anon. **COPLAND**
Chinoiserie see Gautier *LA COMÉDIE DE*
LA MORT. **FALLA, LASSEN**
Ch'io mai vi possa see Metastasio **WEBER**
"Ch'io mai vi possa lasciar d'amare" *see*
La dichiarazione Metastasio **ROSSINI**
"Ch'io mai vi possa lasciar d'amare" *see*
La promessa Metastasio **ROSSINI**
Chiome d'argento fine, irte e attorte see
Berni **MALIPIERO**
Chloe, kennst du noch die Stunde? see Anon.
ZELTER
Chobanian, Arshag, 1872-1954.
HONEGGER
La douceur de tes yeux
La mort passe
"Chodí hlásný po dědině" *see Hlásný* Anon.
MARTINŮ
Chodníček see Unknown **MARTINŮ**
Choeur des voleurs see Bonnard, A.
KOECHLIN

The choirmaster's burial see Hardy
BRITTEN
Chopcherry see Peele *THE OLD WIVES'*
TALE (1595). **HESELTINE**
CHOPIN, FRYDERYK FRANCISZEK,
1810-1849.
Anon.
  Piosnka litewska, op. 74 no. 16 [GA, v.
    17, p. 57] "Bardzo raniuchno
    wschodzilo sloneczko"
    Text incorrectly attributed to Witwicki.
Krasiński, Zygmunt, 1812-1859.
  Melodia, op. 74 no. 9 [GA, v. 17, p. 38]
    "Z gór, gdzie dźwigali strasznych
    krzyzów brzemie"
Mickiewicz, Adam, 1798-1855.
  Moja pieszczotka, op. 74 no. 12 [GA, v.
    17, p. 45] same
Pol, Wincenty, 1807-1872.
  Leci liście z drzewa, op. 74 no. 17 [GA,
    v. 17, p. 61] same
    Pol's dates are variantly: 1809-1876.
Witwicki, Stefan, 1802-1847.
  Czary [GA, v. 17, p. 67] "To sa czary,
    pewno czary!"
  Gdzie lubi . . . op. 74 no. 5 [GA, v. 17, p.
    27] "Strumyk lubi wdolinie"
  Hulanka, op. 74 no. 4 [GA, v. 17, p. 25]
    "Szynkareczko, szafareczko, bój sie
    Boga, stój!"
  Narzeczony, op. 74 no. 15 [GA, v. 17, p.
    54] "Wiatr zaszumial miedzy krzewy"
  Pierścien, op. 74 no. 14 [GA, v. 17, p.
    52] "Smutno niańki ci śpiewaly"
  Posel, op. 74 no. 7 [GA, v. 17, p. 32]
    "Rośnie trawka, ziólko, zimne dni sie
    mienia"
  Precz z moich oczu . . . op. 74 no. 6 [GA,
    v. 17, p. 29] same
  Smutna rzeka, op. 74 no. 3 [GA, v. 17 p.
    21] "Rzeko z cudzoziemców strony"
  Wiosna, op. 74 no. 2 [GA, v. 17, p. 18]
    "Blyszcza krople rosy"
  Wojak, op. 74 no. 10 [GA, v. 17 p. 40]
    "Rźy mój gniady, ziemie grzebie"
  Zyczenie, op. 74 no. 1 [GA, v. 17, p. 15]
    "Gdybym ja byla sloneczkiem na
    niebie"
Zaleski, Josef Bohdan, 1802-1886.
  Dwojaki koniec, op. 74 no. 11 [GA, v.
    17, p. 43] "Rok sie kochali, a wiek sie
    nie widzieli"
  Nie ma czego trzeba, op. 74 no. 13 [GA,
    v. 17, p. 49]
    "Mgla mi do oczu zawiewa zlona"
  Śliczny chlopiec, op. 74 no. 8 [GA, v. 17,
    p. 36] "Wzniosly, smukly i mlody"

NIE MA CZEGO TRZEBA.
  Dumka [GA, v. 17, p. 69] "Mgla mi do
    oczu zawiewa zlona"
Choudens, Paul de, 1850-1925.
  FAURÉ *Sylvie*
  GOUNOD *Le banc de pierre*
Chouquet, Gustave, 1819-1886.
  MASSENET
    À Mignonne
    Ballade de David Rizzio
    Berceuse
    Déclaration
    Le sentier perdu
Chrétien, au voyageur souffrant see
  Béranger **LISZT** *Le juif errant*
"*Chrétien au voyageur souffrant*" *see Le juif*
  errant Béranger **GOUNOD**
Christ, deines Geistes Süssigkeit see
  Unknown **REGER**
Christ is risen see Merezhkovski
  RACHMANINOFF
Christbaum see Cornelius **CORNELIUS**
Christel see Goethe **ZELTER**
Christels Wiegenlied see Iłłakowiczówna
  SZYMANOWSKI *Kolysanka Krzysi*
Christen, Ada, pseud. *see* Breden,
  Christiane (Friderik), 1844-1901.
Christern, Carl, fl.1840.
  SCHUMANN *Ich wand're nicht*
Christi Huld gegen Petrus see Recke
  LOEWE
Christian & pagan see Manilius **IVES** *Vita*
Christianshavn see Bauditz, O. **NIELSEN**
Christkind see Cornelius **CORNELIUS**
Christkindlein trägt die Sünden der Welt see
  Unknown **WEBERN**
Christkindleins Wiegenlied see Des Knaben
  Wunderhorn **SZYMANOWSKI**
Christkindleins Wiegenlied see Unknown
  REGER
A Christmas carol see Anon. **IVES,**
  ROREM
Christmas tree see Cummings **DIAMOND**
Christnacht see Iłłakowiczówna
  SZYMANOWSKI *Gwiazdka*
Christus der Kinderfreund see Cornelius
  CORNELIUS
Chrysanthème see Fuchs, Paul **DELIBES**
Chto ti rano, zoren'ka see Solov'yov, S.
  BORODIN *Why art thou so early, Dawn?*
Chto ty klonish' nad vodami see Tiutchev
  MEDTNER *Willow*
Chto v imeni tebe moem? see Pushkin
  MEDTNER *What means to thee my*
  humble name?
Chto v imeni tebe moem? see Pushkin
  RIMSKIÏ-KORSAKOV

Chto vam slova li͡ubvi *see* Ammosov, A.
   MUSORGSKIĭ
"Chto zhe ty, Sashen'kara dost' " *see*
   Sashen'ka Anon. **PROKOFIEV**
Chu Ch'ing-yu, 8th cent.?
   GRIFFES *In the harem*
Chudleigh, Mary (Lee), lady, 1656-1710.
   ROREM *To the ladies*
Chudnyĭ sađ" *see* Collen, G. *SEPTAIN.*
   BORODIN
Church bell at night *see* Jones, Howard
   Mumford, translator. *ROMANESQUE*
   LYRIC. **BARBER**
Chybili jsme ráno *see* Manin, J. **MARTINŮ**
   We erred in the morning
"Čí je to dítko" *see* Sirotek Erben **DVOŘÁK**
Ciamna nocka, ciamna *see* Anon.
   SZYMANOWSKI
Ciampoli, Domenico, 1855-1929.
   RUBINSTEIN *Fanciula mia*
Cibber, Colley, 1671-1757.
   SCHUBERT *Der blinde Knabe*
Cidli *see* Klopstock **SCHUBERT**
   Das Rosenband
"Cidli, du weinest, und ich schlumm're
   sicher" *see* Furcht der Geliebten
   Klopstock **SCHUBERT**
Le ciel *see* Verlaine *SAGESSE.*
   CARPENTER
La ciel a visité la terre *see* Ségur **GOUNOD**
Ciel, aer et vens *see* Ronsard **ROUSSEL**
"Le ciel d'hiver, si doux, si triste, si dormant"
   see Paysage sentimental Bourget
   DEBUSSY
"Le ciel est par dessus le toit" *see D'une
   prison* Verlaine **HAHN**
"Le ciel est, par dessus le toit" *see Prison*
   Verlaine **FAURÉ**
"Le ciel est par-dessus le toit" *see Le ciel*
   Verlaine **CARPENTER**
Le ciel est, par-dessus la toit *see* Verlaine
   SAGESSE. **DELIUS, SÉVERAC**
LE CIEL EST PARDESSUS LE TOIT. see
   Verlaine *The sky above the roof*
   VAUGHAN WILLIAMS
"Le ciel et la mer couleur de tableau" *see
   Marine à Roscoff* Jacob, M. **SAUGUET**
"Le ciel, et l'eau qui suit les variations des
   nuage" *see Action de gràces* Messiaen
   MESSIAEN
"Ciel et mer, homme et femme" *see Plain-ciel*
   Jacqueton, Henry **SAUGUET**
"Ciel! les colonies" *see Paul et Virginie*
   Radiguet **POULENC**
"Les cieux resplendissants d'étoiles" *see
   Les étoiles* Banville **HAHN**

La cigale *see* Leconte de Lisle
   CHAUSSON
"La cigale ayant chanté 'Tout l'été' " *see
   La cigale et la fourmi* La Fontaine
   SAINT-SAËNS
La cigale et la fourmi *see* La Fontaine
   SAINT-SAËNS
Les cigales *see* Rostand, R. **CHABRIER**
La Cigogne *see* Unknown **RESPIGHI**
   Kroung (La Cigogne, 1930?)
Cimetière *see* Jacob, M. **POULENC**
Cimetière de campagne *see* Vicaire **HAHN**
Cino da Pistoia, 1270-1336.
   CASELLA *Giovane bella luce del mio core*
CINQ CHANSONS DE LISE HIRTZ, no. 1
   AURIC Hirtz *Il était une petite pie*
CINQ CHANSONS DE LISE HIRTZ, no. 2
   AURIC Hirtz *Une petite pomme*
CINQ CHANSONS DE LISE HIRTZ, no. 3
   AURIC Hirtz *Les pâquerettes*
CINQ CHANSONS DE LISE HIRTZ, no. 4
   AURIC Hirtz *La poule noire*
CINQ CHANSONS DE LISE HIRTZ, no. 5
   AURIC Hirtz *Les petits ânes*
Cinq mars, à la mémoire de Max Jacob *see*
   Salmon **SAUGUET**
CINQ MÉLODIES DITES "DE VENISE,"
   no. 1
   FAURÉ Verlaine *Mandoline*
CINQ MÉLODIES DITES "DE VENISE,"
   no. 2
   FAURÉ Verlaine *En sourdine*
CINQ MÉLODIES DITES "DE VENISE,"
   no. 3
   FAURÉ Verlaine *Green*
CINQ MÉLODIES DITES "DE VENISE,"
   no. 4
   FAURÉ Verlaine *A Clymène*
CINQ MÉLODIES DITES "DE VENISE,"
   no. 5
   FAURÉ Verlaine *C'est l'extase . . .*
CINQ POÈMES DE BAUDELAIRE, no. 1
   DEBUSSY Baudelaire *Le Balcon*
CINQ POÈMES DE BAUDELAIRE, no. 2
   DEBUSSY Baudelaire *Harmonie du soir*
CINQ POÈMES DE BAUDELAIRE, no. 3
   DEBUSSY Baudelaire *Le Jet d'eau*
CINQ POÈMES DE BAUDELAIRE, no. 4
   DEBUSSY Baudelaire *Recueillement*
CINQ POÈMES DE BAUDELAIRE, no. 5
   DEBUSSY Baudelaire *La Mort des
   amants*
CINQ POÈMES DE GERARD DE NERVAL,
   no. 1
   AURIC Gérard de Nerval *Fantaisie*

COMPOSER   Poet   *Title*   "First Line"

CINQ POÈMES DE GERARD DE NERVAL, no. 2
  AURIC Gérard de Nerval *Chanson gothique*
CINQ POÈMES DE GERARD DE NERVAL, no. 3
  AURIC Gérard de Nerval *Les cydalises*
CINQ POÈMES DE GERARD DE NERVAL, no. 4
  AURIC Gérard de Nerval *Avril...*
CINQ POÈMES DE GERARD DE NERVAL, no. 5
  AURIC Gérard de Nerval *Une allée du Luxembourg*
CINQ PRIÈRES, no. 1
  MILHAUD Anon. *Salve Regina mater*
CINQ PRIÈRES, no. 2
  MILHAUD Anon. *Hodie nobis de coelo*
CINQ PRIÈRES, no. 3
  MILHAUD Anon. *O magnum mysterium*
CINQ PRIÈRES, no. 4
  MILHAUD Anon. *Beata viscera Mariae*
CINQ PRIÈRES, no. 5
  MILHAUD Anon. *Verbum caro factum*
CINQUE LIRICHE, no. 1
  CASELLA Richepin *Larmes*
CINQUE LIRICHE, no. 2
  CASELLA Duval *C'était un songe*
CINQUE LIRICHE, no. 3
  CASELLA Hettich *Temps de neige*
CINQUE LIRICHE, no. 4
  CASELLA Croisset *Rêverie*
CINQUE LIRICHE, no. 5
  CASELLA Richepin *Nuageries*
Circus band see Ives **IVES**
CIRQUE, no. 1
  SAUGUET Copperie, Adrien *Haute ecole*
CIRQUE, no. 2
  SAUGUET Copperie, Adrien *Petite écuyère*
CIRQUE, no. 3
  SAUGUET Copperie, Adrien *Ecuyère voltige*
CIRQUE, no. 4
  SAUGUET Copperie, Adrien *Gymnaste aérien*
CIRQUE, no. 5
  SAUGUET Copperie, Adrien *Cloune étoilé*
Cirrus see Goethe *GOTT UND WELT*: Howards Ehrengedächtnis. **WEBERN**
La citerne des mille colonnes see Dampierre **SCHMITT**
A city by the sea see Margolin **WEISGALL**
Civet à toute vitesse see Dumont *LA BONNE CUISINE FRANÇAISE.* **BERNSTEIN**

Clärchen see Goethe *EGMONT.* **ZELTER**
Clärchens Lied see Feddersen *FRIERIET PAA HELGOLAND.* **GRIEG** *Claras Sang*
Clärchens Lied see Goethe *EGMONT.* **RUBINSTEIN**
Clair de lune see Haraucourt **KOECHLIN**
Clair de lune see Hugo *LES ORIENTALES.* **INDY**
Clair de lune see Latil **MILHAUD**
Clair de lune see Mendès **SAINT-SAËNS**
Clair de lune see Verlaine *FÊTES GALANTES.* **DEBUSSY, FAURÉ**
  Two Debussy settings: 1882 and 1892.
Clair de lune de Novembre see Laforgue **SAUGUET**
"Claire Vénus, qui erres par les Cieux" *see* *A Vénus* Labé **SAUGUET**
CLAIRIÈRES DANS LE CIEL (1914)
  BOULANGER
    Jammes
      Au pied de mon lit
      Demain fera un an
      Deux ancolies
      Elle est gravement gaie
      Elle était descendue au bas de la prairie
      Je garde une médaille d'elle
      Les lilas qui avaient fleuri
      Nous nous aimerons tant
      Par ce que j'ai souffert
      Parfois, je suis triste
      Un poète disait...
      Si tout ceci n'est qu'un pauvre rêve
      Vous m'avez regardé avec tout votre âme
Clancier, Georges Emmanuel, 1914-
  SAUGUET
    Bergère
    Comme autrefois
    Le temps et les pays
Clara d'Ellebeuse see Jammes **MILHAUD**
Claras Sang see Feddersen *FRIERIET PAA HELGOLAND.* **GRIEG**
Clare, John, 1793-1864.
  BENNETT *Winter's gone*
  DIAMOND *On death*
Claribel see Tennyson **JENSEN, VAUGHAN WILLIAMS**
Claris de Florian, Jean Pierre *see* Florian, Jean Pierre Claris de, 1755-1794.
The classicist see Musorgskiï **MUSORGSKIï** *Klassik*
Claudel, Paul, 1868-1955.
  HONEGGER
    La delphinium

COMPOSER Poet *Title* "First Line"

Closset, Marie, 1875-1952.
    FAURÉ *Le don silencieux*
Clothilde see Apollinaire *ALCOOLS.*
    RIVIER
The cloths of heaven see Yeats *THE WIND*
    AMONG THE REEDS (1899):
    Aedh wishes for the cloths . . .
        HESELTINE
Clotilde see Apollinaire *ALCOOLS.*
    HONEGGER
The cloud see Grekov *STANSĬ.*
    CHAĬKOVSKIĬ *Smotri, von oblako*
Cloudless blue claw see Boultenhouse,
    Charles **ROREM**
Clouds see Goodman **ROREM**
The clouds begin to scatter see Pushkin
    RIMSKĬĬ-KORSAKOV
    Redeet oblakov letuchaĭa grĭada
Cloune étoilé see Copperie, Adrien
    SAUGUET
"*Cloune, étoile de mer*" *see Cloune étoilé*
    Copperie, Adrien **SAUGUET**
The clover see Deland **MACDOWELL**
Clown's song see Shakespeare *TWELFTH*
    NIGHT: When that I was and a little tiny
    boy. **SCHUMANN** *Schlusslied des Narren*
Cnattingius, Thor, 1880-1929.
    KILPINEN
    Det borde vara skatter
    Danslek
    Dödens vila
    Jag ville bygga ett litet bo
    Lilla Olles visa
    Liten jungfru
    En liten visa om våren
    Min längtans ö
    Minnen
    Mitt gagoland
    Önskekransen
    Ring, ring
    Rosa lill'
    Rosor
    Så dansa!
    Sjung mitt hjärta
    Slumra, slumra sakta
    Solstrålen
    Stämmingsvisa
    Svanevit
    Det var i vårens ljusa tid
    En vårmelodie
The coach of life see Pushkin **MEDTNER**
COCARDES, no. 1
    POULENC Cocteau *Miel de Narbonne*
COCARDES, no. 2
    POULENC Cocteau *Donne d'enfant*
COCARDES, no. 3
    POULENC Cocteau *Enfant de troupe*

La coccinelle see Hugo **BIZET, LASSEN,**
    SAINT-SAËNS
Cocconi, Ildebrando
    PIZZETTI
    Incontro di Marzo
    Remember
    Vigilia Nuziale
The cock shall crow see Stevenson, Robert
    Louis **CARPENTER**
"*Cocorico, le coq chante*" *see* Aurore
    Silvestre **MASSENET**
Cocteau, Jean, 1889-1963.
    AURIC
    Aglaé
    Biplan le matin
    École de guerre
    Hommage à Erik Satie
    Marie Laurencin
    Place des Invalides
    Portrait d'Henri Rousseau
    Réveil
    HONEGGER
    Une danseuse
    Ex-voto
    Locutions
    Madame
    Souvenirs d'enfance
    MILHAUD
    Chat
    Fête de Bordeaux
    Fête de Montmartre
    Fumée
    Pièce de circonstance
    POULENC
    Donne d'enfant
    Enfant de troupe
    Miel de Narbonne
    Toréador
    ROREM *De Don Juan*
    SATIE *Danseuse*
    SAUGUET *Chansons de marins*
    TEMPÉRATURES.
        HONEGGER *Le Nègre*
Coeur en péril see Chalupt **ROUSSEL**
Coeur noir du vent qui passe see Richaud
    SAUGUET
"*Coeur, va vite, pauvre coeur*" *see L'heureuse*
    souffrance Henri IV **MASSENET**
THE COFFEE-POT FACE. see Fisher, A.
    Worlds **CARPENTER**
LE COFFRET DE SANTAL, CHANSONS
    PERPÉTUELLES (1873). *see* Cros
    L'archet **DEBUSSY, MALIPIERO**
    Le coffret d'ébène see Jannet, Victor
        MASSENET

Cohen, Albert, 1895-1981.
MILHAUD
Hymne de Sion
Israël est vivant
"Coi pensieri malinconici" *see Sopra l'acqua*
indormenzada . . . Anon. **HAHN**
Cojo jazmin y clavel see Manuel del Rio,
Don *SPANISCHES LIEDERBUCH*:
Cojo jazmin y clavel. **JENSEN**
Les colchiques see Apollinaire *ALCOOLS.*
RIVIER
Coleridge, Hartley, 1796-1849.
BERKELEY *When we were idlers with the*
loitering rills
Coleridge, Mary Elizabeth, 1861-1907.
IRELAND
Remember
The sacred flame
QUILTER
Through the sunny garden
The valley and the hill
ROREM *We never said farewell*
VAUGHAN WILLIAMS *Cradle song*
Colette, Sidonie Gabrielle, 1873-1954.
POULENC *Le portrait*
Le colibri see Glan **BIZET**
Le colibri see Leconte de Lisle
CHAUSSON, KOECHLIN
Collected poems see Koch **THOMSON**
The collection see Unknown **IVES**
Collen, Georges
SEPTAIN.
BORODIN *Chudnyĭ sad"*
Collerville, Vicomte de
SAINT-SAËNS *Les fleurs*
Collet, Louise, 1810-1876.
MILHAUD *Lassitude*
Le collier see Messiaen **MESSIAEN**
Collin, Heinrich Joseph von, 1772-1811.
GOUNOD *Le souvenir*
Collin, Matthäus, 1779-1824.
SCHUBERT
Herrn Josef Spaun
Licht und Liebe
Nacht und Träume
Wehmut
Der Zwerg
Collin, Paul Adrien François, 1845-1915.
CHAĬKOVSKIĬ
Déception
Qu'importe que l'hiver
Rondel
Sérénade
GOUNOD *Je te rends grâce, Ô Dieu*
MASSENET
Automne

Les marronniers
Narcisse à la fontaine
Pareils à des oiseaux
Prelude
Qu'importe que l'hiver
Roses d'Octobre
Collins, Anne
IVES *The greatest man*
Collins, Hal, d.1929.
HESELTINE *Yarmouth Fair*
Colloque sentimental see Verlaine *FÊTES*
GALANTES. **DEBUSSY**
Colly
SCHÖNBERG *Jedem das Seine*
Colma, ein altschottisches Fragment . . . see
Macpherson **ZELTER** *Colma von Ossian*
Colma von Ossian see Macpherson
ZELTER
La Colombe see Koechlin **KOECHLIN**
"Colombe, colombe verte" *see Syllabes*
Messiaen **MESSIAEN**
Colombeau, Eugène Adenis de, 1854-
SCHMITT *Sémiramis*
Les Colombes see Gautier *LA COMÉDIE DE*
LA MORT. **FALLA**
"Colombine charmante" *see À Colombine*
Gallet **MASSENET**
Le Colonel Romanoff see Chalupt
MILHAUD
"Les colonnes du temple s'animent" *see*
Invocation Rodès **BLOCH**
"Colonnes sans soleil, pâles prisonnières" *see*
La citerne des mille colonnes Dampierre
SCHMITT
Coma's Klage see Macpherson
SCHUBERT *Kolma's Klage*
COMBAT DEL SOMNI, no. 1
MOMPOU Janés i Olivé *Damunt de tu*
només les flors
COMBAT DEL SOMNI, no. 2
MOMPOU Janés i Olivé *Aquesta nit un*
mateix vent
COMBAT DEL SOMNI, no. 3
MOMPOU Janés i Olivé *Jo et pressentia*
com la mar
Combien de bras se sont ouverts see
Lefilleul, G. **JOLIVET**
"Combien j'ai douce souvenance" *see*
Souvenance Châteaubriand **FRANCK**
Comden, Betty, 1919- and Adolph
Green, 1915-2002.
BERNSTEIN *So pretty*
COME. see Barnes
Wull ye come in the eärly spring
CARPENTER
"Come all ye jolly shepherds that whistle thro'
the glen" *see When the kye come hame*

COMPOSER Poet *Title* "First Line"

"Come all ye jolly shepherds that whistle thro' the glen" *(continued)* Unknown **RESPIGHI**

"Come and buy from our booths" *see The song of Vanity Fair* Vaughan Williams, U. **VAUGHAN WILLIAMS**

Come and join the dancing see Heyduk **DVOŘÁK** *Struna naladěna*

Come, arise, for dawn is breaking see Mei **RIMSKIĬ-KORSAKOV** *Vstan', soǐdi! davno dennítsa*

"Come away, come away, death" *see Come away, Death* Shakespeare **QUILTER**

Come away, come away, death see Shakespeare **CHAUSSON** *Chanson de clown*

Come away, Death see Shakespeare *TWELFTH NIGHT.* **QUILTER**

Come away, death see Shakespeare *TWELFTH NIGHT.* **SIBELIUS** *Kom nu hit, död*

Come back see Unknown **QUILTER**

"Come fathers and mothers come" *see Zion's walls* Anon. **COPLAND**

Come hither, you that love see Fletcher **ROREM**

Come into the garden, Maud see Tennyson **MASSENET**

"Come join my humble ditty" *see A son of a gambolier* Anon. **IVES**

Come, lady-day see Pemberton, May **QUILTER**

Come let us rest see Chekhov *UNCLE VANYA*, Act IV. **RACHMANINOFF** *Let us rest*

"Come list and hark" *see The bell doth toll* Heywood **THOMSON**

"Come live with me, and be my love" *see The passionate shepherd* Marlowe **HESELTINE**

"Come l'ombra di cara estinta vita" *see I tempi assai lontani* Shelley **RESPIGHI**

Come love, across the sunlit land see Scollard **GRIFFES**

"Come, O come, my life's delight!" *see My life's delight* Campion **QUILTER**

Come out to me, Signora see Anon. **RIMSKIĬ-KORSAKOV** *Vikhodi ko mne, signora*

Come potrei ma vivere see Unknown **ZELTER**

" 'Come!' said Old Shellover" *see Old Shellover* De La Mare **CHANLER**

Come, shepherds, come see Fletcher **ROREM**

"Come, sleep, and with thy sweet deceiving" *see Sleep* Fletcher **HESELTINE**

Come spring! sweet spring! see Quilter **QUILTER**

Come to me see Kol'tsov **BALAKIREV** *Pridi ko mne*

"Come under the shadow of this gray rock–" *see Canticle V* Eliot **BRITTEN**

Come unto these yellow sands see Shakespeare *THE TEMPEST.* **DIAMOND, QUILTER**

LA COMÉDIE DE LA MORT. see Gautier *Chinoiserie* **FALLA, LASSEN** *Les Colombes* **FALLA** *Lamento* **DUPARC** *Séguidille* **FALLA**

LA COMÉDIE DE LA MORT: Romance. *see* Gautier *Au pays où se fait la guerre* **DUPARC**

Comendador Escriva *see* Escriva Comendador, Joan, d.ca.1520.

Comfort to a youth that had lost his love see Herrick **ROREM**

The coming of Spring see Tavaststjerna **SIBELIUS** *Vår förnimmelser*

Comitat see Uhland **LOEWE** *Abschied*

Comme à la lumière de la lune see Proust **SAUGUET**

Comme à l'aurore see Zaffira **GOUNOD** *Da qualche tempo*

Comme autrefois see Clancier **SAUGUET**

Comme autrefois see Dortzal **MASSENET**

"Comme autrefois la douceur . . . " *see Comme autrefois* Clancier **SAUGUET**

"Comme chacun sait l'hirondelle" *see Hirondelle* Radiguet **AURIC**

"Comme de longs cheveux peignés au vent du soir" *see Accompagnement* Samain **KOECHLIN**

"Comme des chevreaux piqués par un taon" *see La brise* Renaud **SAINT-SAËNS**

Comme Dieu rayonne . . . see Lerberghe **FAURÉ**

"Comme d'un sein ouvert la main arrache une arme" *see La chère blessure* Blanchecotte **HAHN**

Comme elle a les yeux bandés see Vildrac *LIVRE D'AMOUR.* **IBERT**

"Comme elle chante dans ma voix" *see Prima verba* Lerberghe **FAURÉ**

Comme j'allais see Derème **IBERT**

"Comme je m'en retournais de la fontaine" *see Chanson médiévale* Mendès **SATIE**

"Comme la voix d'un mort qui chanterait" *see Sérénade* Verlaine **LOEFFLER**

"Comme les fils étincelants" *see Fils de la Vierge* Ganivet **SCHMITT**

COMPOSER Poet *Title* "First Line"

"Comme l'hirondelle effleurant la rive" *see*
Chrysanthème Fuchs, Paul **DELIBES**
"Comme on voit sur la branche au mois de
mai" *see Sonnet* Ronsard **CASELLA**
"Comme tout meurt vite" *see Adieu*
Grandmougin **FAURÉ**
"Comme un ange qui se dévoile" *see Souvenir*
Hugo **LALO**
"Comme un lierre grimpant" *see Hymne
d'amour* Desachy **MASSENET**
"Comme un rayon qui luit" *see Enchantement!*
Ruelle **MASSENET**
"Comme un rideau sous la blancheur" *see
Crépuscule* Silvestre **MASSENET**
"Comme vous dormiez, je n'ai pas osé" *see À
deux pleurer!* Croze, J. L. **MASSENET**
"Comment, disaient-ils?" *see Guitare* Hugo
LALO, MASSENET
Comment, disaient-ils see Hugo **LISZT**
"Comment, disaient-ils, avec nos nacelles" *see
Guitare* Hugo **SAINT-SAËNS**
Comment disait-il see Hugo **RUBINSTEIN**
Romance, "Comment disait-il"
Commentaire sur Saint Jérome see Sade
THOMSON
*THE COMMODYE OF PACIENT AND
MEEKE GRISSILL* (1566). *see* Phillip,
John *Cradle song* **HESELTINE**
Compagne de l'éther see Moréas **HAHN**
"Compagne de l'éther, indolente fumée" *see
Fumée* Moréas **HAHN**
Compagnons du silence see Supervielle
MILHAUD
Complainte see Mauclair **BLOCH**
Complainte see Silvestre *MIGNONNE.*
MASSENET
Complainte de Florinde see Arnoux **IBERT**
COMPLAINTES ET DITS. see Fort
Chanson de fol **HONEGGER**
Le chasseur perdu en forêt **HONEGGER**
Cloche du soir **HONEGGER**
THE COMPLEAT ANGLER (1653):
Corydon's song. *see* Chalkhill
The countryman **HESELTINE**
Compliment see Dumas the younger
GOUNOD
COMPTINES I, no. 1
MOMPOU Anon. *D'alt d'un cotxe n'hi ha
una nina qu'en*
COMPTINES I, no. 2
MOMPOU Anon. *Margot la pie a fait son
nid*
COMPTINES I, no. 3
MOMPOU Anon. *Hevist dins la lluna tres
petits conills*
COMPTINES II, no. 1
MOMPOU Anon. *Aserrin, aserran*

COMPTINES II, no. 2
MOMPOU Anon. *Petite fille de Paris*
COMPTINES II, no. 3
MOMPOU Anon. *Pito, pito, colorito*
CON ANTONIO MACHADO, no. 1
RODRIGO Machado y Ruiz *Preludio*
CON ANTONIO MACHADO, no. 2
RODRIGO Machado y Ruiz *Mi corazon
te aguarda*
CON ANTONIO MACHADO, no. 3
RODRIGO Machado y Ruiz *Tu voz y tu
mano*
CON ANTONIO MACHADO, no. 4
RODRIGO Machado y Ruiz *Mañana de
Abril*
CON ANTONIO MACHADO, no. 5
RODRIGO Machado y Ruiz *Los sueños*
CON ANTONIO MACHADO, no. 6
RODRIGO Machado y Ruiz *Cantaban
los niños*
CON ANTONIO MACHADO, no. 7
RODRIGO Machado y Ruiz *Recuerdas?*
CON ANTONIO MACHADO, no. 8
RODRIGO Machado y Ruiz *Fiesta en el
Prado*
CON ANTONIO MACHADO, no. 9
RODRIGO Machado y Ruiz *Abril galan*
CON ANTONIO MACHADO, no. 10
RODRIGO Machado y Ruiz *Canción del
duero*
Con qué la lavaré? see Anon. **RODRIGO**
Confidence see Anon. **MILHAUD**
Confidence see MacDowell **MACDOWELL**
Confucius, 551-479 B. C.
NATIONAL ODES OF CHINA.
CARPENTER *To a young gentleman*
"Connaissant, seigneur, mon état d'épouse"
see Réponse d'une épouse sage Chang-Chi
ROUSSEL
"Connaissez-vous la blanche tombc" *see Au
cimetière* Gautier **BERLIOZ**
"Connaissez-vous la blanche tombe" *see
Lamento* Gautier **DUPARC**
"Connaissez-vous qui m'a charmé?" *see
Chanson de Capri* Gallet **MASSENET**
"Le connais-tu, ce radieux pays" *see Romance
de Mignon* Goethe **DUPARC**
"Connais-tu le pays" *see Mignon* Goethe
GOUNOD
Conquered see Goethe **MEDTNER**
Die Bekehrte
Conradi, Hermann, 1862-1890.
LIEDER EINES SÜNDERS. 1. Teil,
"Inferno."
SCHÖNBERG *Verlassen*
Conscience see Goethe *ERWIN UND
ELMIRE.* **MEDTNER**
Inneres Wühlen ewig zu fühlen

Les conscrits see Paliard **MILHAUD**
Consider see Ford **HESELTINE**
Consider, Lord see Donne **THOMSON**
LES CONSOLATIONS DES MISÈRES DE MA
   VIE. *see* Rousseau
   Félicité passée **ZELTER**
Constancy see MacDowell **MACDOWELL**
The constant lover see Suckling **QUILTER**
Constantin-Weyer, Maurice, 1881-1964.
   IBERT *Chanson du rien*
Contamine de Latour, J.P., pseud. *see*
   Contamine, José-Maria Patricio
   Manuel, 1867-1926.
Contamine, José-Maria Patricio Manuel,
   1867-1926.
   SATIE
      Les anges
      Chanson
      Elégie
      Les fleurs
      Imperial-Oxford
      Légende californienne
      Sylvie
Conte see Ferrier **BIZET**
Contemplation see Carpenter, Rue
   CARPENTER
The contented lover see Mabbe
   THE SPANISH BAWD (1631):
   Now sleepe, and take thy rest.
   HESELTINE
"Contented river! in thy dreamy realm" *see*
   The Housatonic at Stockbridge Johnson
   IVES
CONTES BLANCS. *see* Barbier, M.
   La sérénité **SAINT-SAËNS**
CONTES DE FÉES. *see* Bonnières
   Le manoir de Rosemonde **DUPARC**
CONTES D'ESPAGNE ET D'ITALIE. *see*
   Musset
   Ballade à la lune **DEBUSSY, LALO**
   Madrid, Princesse des Espagnes **DEBUSSY**
Der Contrabandiste see Unknown
   SCHUMANN
Contrasto see Zangarini **RESPIGHI**
Conversation see Bishop **ROREM**
The convict and boy with the violin see
   Hardy **BRITTEN** *At the railway station,*
      Upway
Le convive see Chalupt **MILHAUD**
Cool and fragrant is thy garland see
   Shenshin **RIMSKIĬ-KORSAKOV**
   Svezh i dushist tvoĭ
Cooper, Eric Thirkell
   IRELAND
      Blind
      The cost

Cooper, James Fenimore, 1789-1851.
   IVES *Afterglow*
Cophtisches Lied I see Goethe **WOLF**
Cophtisches Lied II see Goethe **WOLF**
Copillas de Belen see Kamhi, Victoria
   RODRIGO
COPLAND, AARON, 1900-1991.
   Aiken, Conrad Potter, 1889-1973.
      DISCORDANTS.
         Music I heard (1920) [unpubl.]
            "Music I heard with you was more
               than music"
   Aldrich, Thomas Bailey, 1836-1907.
      TWO SONGS FROM THE PERSIAN, II.
         Spurned love (1917) [unpubl.] "Ah!
            sad are they who know not love"
         Holograph at Library of Congress.
   Anon.
      Ching-a-ring chaw (1952) [Boosey &
         Hawkes, 1954]
            "Ching-a-ring-a ring ching ching"
      The dodger (1950) [Boosey & Hawkes,
         1950] "Yes, the candidate's a dodger"
         From John and Alan Lomax collection
         Our singing country.
      The golden willow tree (1952) [Boosey &
         Hawkes, 1954] "There was a little ship
         in South Amerikee"
      I bought me a cat (1950) [Boosey &
         Hawkes, 1950] same
      The little horses (1952) [Boosey &
         Hawkes, 1954]
            "Hush you bye, don't you cry"
         Text from Lomax collection, ***Folk
         song U. S. A.***
      Long time ago (1950) [Boosey &
         Hawkes, 1950] "On the lake where
         droop'd the willow"
      Simple gifts (1950) [Boosey & Hawkes,
         1950] "Tis the gift to be simple"
         Text from Shaker rituals, ***The Gift to
         be Simple.***
      Zion's walls (1952) [Boosey & Hawkes,
         1954]
            "Come fathers and mothers come"
         Original melody and words credited to
            John G. McCurry, compiler of the
            Social Harp.
   Barnefield, Richard, 1574-1627.
      As it fell upon a day (1923) [New Music,
         1929; Boosey & Hawkes, 1956]
         same
         Voice, flute & clarinet.
   Cammaerts, Emile Leon, 1878-1953.
      After Antwerp (1917) [unpubl.] "Sing,
         Belgian's [sic] sing"
         Holograph at Library of Congress.

Cummings, Edward Estlin, 1894-1962.
> *Song* (1927) [*Cos Cob Song Volume,*
> 1935; Boosey & Hawkes, 1964]
> "In spite of every thing which breathes
> and moves"

Dickinson, Emily, 1830-1866.
> *The chariot* (1949-50) [Boosey &
> Hawkes, 1951]
> "Because I would not stop for Death"
> *Dear March, come in!* (1949-50)
> [Boosey & Hawkes, 1951] same
> *Going to Heaven!* (1949-50) [Booscy &
> Hawkes, 1951] same
> *Heart, we will forget him* (1949-50)
> [Boosey & Hawkes, 1951] same
> *I felt a funeral in my brain* (1949-50)
> [Boosey & Hawkes, 1951] same
> *I've heard an organ talk sometimes*
> (1949-50) [Boosey & Hawkes, 1951]
> same
> *Nature, the gentlest mother* (1949-50)
> [Boosey & Hawkes, 1951] same
> *Sleep is supposed to be* (1949-50)
> [Boosey & Hawkes, 1951] same
> *There came a wind like a bugle* (1949-
> 50) [Boosey & Hawkes, 1951] same
> *When they come back* (1949-50)
> [Boosey & Hawkes, 1951] same
> *Why do they shut me out of Heaven?*
> (1949-50) [Boosey & Hawkes, 1951]
> same
> *The world feels dusty* (1949-50)
> [Boosey & Hawkes, 1951] same

Emmett, Daniel Decatur, 1815-1904.
> *The boatmen's dance* (1950) [Boosey &
> Hawkes, 1950]
> "High row the boatman row"

Farnol, Jeffrey, 1878-1952.
> *BETHANE THE SMITH*: Chapter XVI.
> *Melancholy: a song "à la Debussy"*
> (1917) [unpubl.] "Alack and woe
> that love is so akin to pain!"
> Holograph at Library of Congress.

Gourmont, Rémy de, 1858-1915.
> *Simone* (1919) [unpubl.] "Simone, white
> as thy throat the snow I see"
> Holograph at Library of Congress.

Kafiristan
> *Pastorale* (1921) [Boosey & Hawkes,
> 1979] "Since you love me and I love
> you the rest matters not"
> Text translated by Edward Powys
> Mathers.

Lowry, Robert, 1826-1899.
> *At the river* (1952) [Boosey & Hawkes,
> 1954] "Shall we gather by the river"

Meredith, George, 1828-1909.
> *Dirge in woods* (1954) [Boosey &
> Hawkes, 1957]
> "A wind sways the pines"

No author
> *Vocalise* (1928) [Alphonse Leduc, 1929;
> Boosey & Hawkes, 1956]
> Wordless.

Schaffer, Aaron, 1894-1957.
> *My heart is in the east* (1918) [unpubl.]
> "While I in western lands do pine"
> Holograph at Library of Congress.
> *Night* (1918) [unpubl.]
> "My heart is placid as the lake"
> Holograph at Library of Congress.
> *A summer vacation* (1918) [unpubl.]
> "Days of joy, how have ye fled?"
> Holograph at Library of Congress.

Waley, Arthur, 1889-1966, translator.
> *Old poem* (1920) [Senart, 1923; Salabert]
> "The bright moon, oh so white it
> shines"
> Translated from the Chinese.

Coplas del pastor enamorado see
Vega Carpio **RODRIGO**

Coppée, François Édouard Joachim,
1842-1908.
GOUNOD
> *Chanson d'Avril*
> *Mélancolie*

HAHN *Mai*
MASSENET *Sérénade de Zanetto*
RIMSKIĭ-KORSAKOV *Ekho*
SAINT-SAËNS
> *Marquise vous souvenez-vous?*
> *Ronde*

SÉVERAC *Ritournelle*
LE RELIQUAIRE.
> **DUPARC** *La vague et la cloche*

Copperie, Adrien
SAUGUET
> *Cloune étoilé*
> *Ecuyère voltige*
> *Fausse alerte*
> *Gymnaste aérien*
> *Haute ecole*
> *Petite écuyère*

Coquetterie posthume see Gautier *EMAUX
ET CAMÉES.* **DEBUSSY**
"*Coquilles d'ailes!*" *see Jardin mystérieux*
Jacob, M. **SAUGUET**
"Le cor appelle comme une cloche" *see Ports
de l'enfer* Jacob, M. **SAUGUET**
Cora an die Sonne see Batsányi
SCHUBERT
Les corails see Kondratowicz
CHAĭKOVSKIĭ *Korol'ki*

COMPOSER   Poet   *Title*   ''First Line''

The corals **see** Kondratowicz
CHAïKOVSKIï *Korol'ki*
Corazón de mujer **see** Arteaga, Cristina de
TURINA
Le corbeau **see** Unknown **STRAVINSKIï**
Corderito blanco **see** Anon. **RODRIGO**
Corneille, Pierre, 1606-1684.
    MILHAUD *Poème de Corneille*
    PSYCHÉ.
    KOECHLIN *Je suis jaloux*
CORNELIUS, PETER, 1824-1874.
    Anon.
        Ave Maria (1862) [Schott, 1930]
          "Ave, ave Maria!"
          Subsequently arranged for voice, string
            quintet & harp.
    Bechstein, Ludwig, 1801-1860.
        Der König und der Sänger (ca.1844)
          [unpubl.] "Ein König sass im Norden"
          Holograph in Österreichische
            Nationalbibliothek, Wien.
    Bürger, Gottfried August, 1747-1794.
        Der Entfernten (1859) [Werke, v. 1, p.
          158] "Du, mein Heil, mein Leben"
        Liebe ohne Heimat [Werke, v. 1, p. 161]
          "Meine Liebe, lange wie die Taube"
        Verlust (Auf Mollys Tod, 1859) [Werke,
          v. 1, p. 166]
          "Wonnelohn getreuer Huldigungen"
          Another setting, same year: Werke, v.
            1, p. 169.
    Cervantes Saavedra, Miguel de, 1547-
    1616.
        Preziosas Sprüchlein gegen Kopfweh
          (1854-55) [Werke, v. 1, p. 83]
          "Köpfchen, Köpfchen"
    Cornelius, Peter, 1824-1874.
        Am Morgen (1856-59) [Werke, v. 1, p.
          112]
          "Die Nacht bergeht nach süsser Ruh"
        Am Rhein (1856) [Werke, v. 1, p. 95]
          "O, Lust am Rheine, am heimischen
            Strande"
        Am See (1848) [Werke, v. 1, p. 18] "An
          dem Seegestade düster"
        An den Traum, op. 3 no. 4 (1854)
          [Werke, v. 1, p. 78]
          "Offne mir die goldne Pforte"
        Angedenken, op. 3 no. 2 (1854) [Werke,
          v. 1, p. 75] "Von stillem Ort"
        Aus dem hohen Liede (1856-59) [Werke,
          v. 1, p. 114] "Mein Freund ist mein,
          und ich bin sein!"
        Botschaft, op. 5 no. 1 (1856) [Werke, v.
          1, p. 92]
          "Liebendes Wort, dich send ich fort"

Christbaum, op. 8 no. 1 [Werke, v. 1, p.
   125] "Wie schön geschmückt der
   festliche Raum"
Christkind, op. 8 no. 6 [Werke, v. 1, p.
   143] "Das einst ein Kind auf Erden
   war"
Christus der Kinderfreund, op. 8 no. 5
   [Werke, v. 1, p. 141]
   "Das zarte Knäblein ward ein Mann"
Dein Bildnis, op. 15 no. 4 (1865) [Werke,
   v. 1, p. 221] "Halb Dämmerschein,
   halb Kerzenlicht"
Denkst du an mich? op. 1 no. 6 (1853)
   [Werke, v. 1, p. 32]
   "Ein grünes Spinnchen gaukelte"
Gedenken (1856) [Werke, v. 1, p. 99]
   "Kehr' ich zum heimischen Rhein"
Die Hirten (1856) [Werke, v. 1, p. 128]
   "Die Hirten wachen nachts im Feld"
Die Hirten, op. 8 no. 2 (1870) [Werke, v.
   1, p. 131] "Hirten wachen im Feld"
Ich bin so froh geworden, op. 4 no. 5
   (1854) [Breitkopf & Härtel, 1922]
   same
   Hofmeister identifies it as op. 4 no. 4.
Im Frühling! Im Frühling (ca.1844)
   [unpubl.] same
   Holograph in Österreichische
     Nationalbibliothek, Wien.
Im Tiefsten Herzen glüht mir eine Wunde
   (1862) [Werke, v. 1, p. 211] same
In der Ferne (1856) [Werke, v. 1, p. 86]
   "Mit hellem Sang und Harfenspiel"
In der Ferne, op. 15 no. 3 (1865)
   [Werke, v. 1, p. 218]
   "Die Blümlein auf der Heide"
In Lust und Schmerzen, op. 4 no. 1
   (1854) [Werke, v. 1, p. 61] same
Komm, wir wandeln zusammen in
   Mondschein, op. 4 no. 2 (1854)
   [Werke, v. 1, p. 66] same
Die Könige (1856) [Werke, v. 1, p. 134]
   "Drei Kön'ge wandern aus
     Morgenland"
Die Könige, op. 8 no. 3 (1870) [Werke,
   v. 1, p. 136] "Drei Kön'ge wandern
   aus Morgenland"
Lieb' ist die Perle, op. 4 no. 6 (1854)
   [Breitkopf & Härtel, 1922] same
   Hofmeister identifies it as op. 4 no. 5.
Der Liebe Lohn (1856-59) [Werke, v. 1,
   p. 104] "Süss tönt Gesanges Hauch"
Märchenwunder (1856-59) [Werke, v. 1,
   p. 118] "Nun lass mich träumen"
Möcht' im Walde mit dir geh'n, op. 4 no.
   3 (1854)

[Werke, v. 1, p. 69; Breitkopf &
Härtel, 1922] same
No. 4 in Breitkopf & Härtel edition.
Ein Myrtenreis (1856-59) [Werke, v. 1, p.
102] "In meinem Herzen regte"
Nachts, op. 1 no. 5 (1853) [Werke, v. 1,
p. 30] "Nachts bin vom Traum
schlaftrunken ich erwacht"
Schmetterling, op. 1 no. 4 (1853) [Werke,
v. 1, p. 28]
"Wer hats doch durchschauet?"
Sei mein! op. 15 no. 1 (1865) [Werke, v.
1, p. 213]
"Tief im Gemüt mir Liebe glüht"
Simeon, op. 8 no. 4 [Werke, v. 1, p. 138]
"Das Knäblein nach acht Tagen"
Ein Ton, op. 3 no. 3 (1854) [Werke, v. 1,
p. 76]
"Mir klingt ein Ton so wunderbar"
Trauer, op. 3 no. 1 (1854) [Werke, v. 1,
p. 73] "Ich wandle einsam"
Treue, op. 3 no. 5 (1854) [Werke, v. 1, p.
79]
"Dein Gedenken lebt in Liedern fort"
Trost, op. 3 no. 6 (1854) [Werke, v. 1, p.
81] "Der Glückes Fülle mir verlieh'n"
Untreu, op. 1 no. 1 (1853) [Werke, v. 1,
p. 24] "Mein Lied ist klein"
Vater unser I, op. 2 no. 1 (1854-55)
[Werke, v. 1, p. 34]
"Vater unser, der du bist im Himmel"
Vater unser II, op. 2 no. 2 (1854-55)
[Werke, v. 1, p. 37]
"Geheiliget werde Dein Name"
Vater unser III, op. 2 no. 3 (1854-55)
[Werke, v. 1, p. 40]
"Zu uns komme Dein Reich"
Vater unser IV, op. 2 no. 4 (1854-55)
[Werke, v. 1, p. 43]
"Dein Wille geschehe"
Vater unser V, op. 2 no. 5 (1854-55)
[Werke, v. 1, p. 46]
"Unser täglich Brot gib uns heute"
Vater unser VI, op. 2 no. 6 (1854-55)
[Werke, v. 1, p. 48]
"Vergib uns unsre Schuld"
Vater unser VII, op. 2 no. 7 (1854-55)
[Werke, v. 1, p. 52] "Also auch wir
vergeben unsern Schuldigern"
Vater unser VIII, op. 2 no. 8 (1854-55)
[Werke, v. 1, p. 55]
"Führe uns nicht in Versuchung"
Vater unser IX, op. 2 no. 9 (1854-55)
[Werke, v. 1, p. 58]
"Erlöse uns vom Übel"
Veilchen, op. 1 no. 2 (1853) [Werke, v.
1, p. 25] "Zu dem Duft, der da würzt
die Lenzesluft"

Vorabend (1856-59) [Werke, v. 1, p. 109]
"Nun, Liebster, geh', nun scheide!"
Wie lieb ich dich hab', op. 15 no. 2
(1865) [Werke, v. 1, p. 215] "Und
sängen die Vögel dir laut meine Lieb"
Wiegenlied, op. 1 no. 3 (1853) [Werke, v.
1, p. 26]
"Vöglein fliegt dem Nestchen zu"

Droste-Hülshoff, Annette Elisabeth,
Freiin von, 1797-1848.
Gesegnet (1862) [Werke, v. 1, p. 207]
"Wer bist du doch, O Mädchen?"
Das Kind (1862) [Werke, v. 1, p. 205]
"Wär' ich ein Kind"
Unerhört, op. 5 no. 5 (1862) [Werke, v.
1, p. 203] "Zum Ossa sprach der
Pelion"

Eichendorff, Joseph Karl Benedikt,
Freiherr von, 1788-1857.
Die Räuberbrüder (1868-69) [Werke, v.
1, p. 231]
"Vorüber ist der blut'ge Strauss"

Hebbel, Christian Friedrich, 1813-
1863.
Abendgefühl (1862) [Werke, v. 1, p. 185]
"Friedlich bekämpfen Nacht sich und
Tag"
Abendgefühl (1863) [Werke, v. 1, p. 187]
"Friedlich bekämpfen Nacht sich und
Tag"
Auf ein schlummerndes Kind, op. 5 no. 2
(1861) [Werke, v. 1, p. 177]
"Wenn ich, O Kindlein"
Auf eine Unbekannte, op. 5 no. 3 (1861)
[Werke, v. 1, p. 180] "Die Dämmerung
war längst hereingebrochen"
Dämmerempfindung (1861) [Werke, v. 1,
p. 172]
"Was treibt mich hier von hinnen?"
Reminiszenz (1862) [Werke, v. 1, p. 189]
"Millionen öder Jahre"

Heine, Heinrich, 1797-1856.
Die Heimkehr (1848) [Werke, v. 1, p. 21]
"Was will die einsame Träne"
Warum sind denn die Rosen so blass?
(1862) [Werke, v. 1, p. 209] same

Heyse, Paul Johann Ludwig von,
1830-1914.
Im Lenz (1848) [Werke, v. 1, p. 2]
"Im Lenz, im Lenz"
Im Walde (1848) [*Die Musik* 14 (1 Dec.
1914)] "Wundervolle Waldeskühle, die
ich tausendmale grüss"
In der Mondnacht (1848) [Werke, v. 1, p.
13] same
Morgenwind (1848) [Werke, v. 1, p. 6]
"Wenn die Hahnen frühe krähen"

COMPOSER   Poet   *Title*   "First Line"

CORNELIUS, PETER, 1824-1874
(continued)
Heyse, Paul Johann Ludwig von,
1830-1914 *(continued)*
Musje Morgenrots Lied (1848) [Werke,
v. 1, p. 4] "Wie trag ich doch im
Sinne"
Schäfers Nachtlied (1848) [Werke, v. 1,
p. 10] "Und bist du jung an Jahren"
Hölderlin, Friedrich, 1770-1843.
Sonnenuntergang (1862) [Werke, v. 1, p.
196] "Wo bist du? Trunken dämmert
die Seele mir"
Hölty, Ludwig Heinrich Christoph,
1748-1776.
Auftrag, op. 5 no. 6 (1862) [Werke, v. 1,
p. 200] "Ihr Freunde, hänget, wenn ich
gestorben bin"
Hood, Thomas, 1799-1845.
Dich lieb ich, op. 4 no. 3 [lost]
Kuh, Emil, 1828-1876.
Du kleine Biene, verfolg mich nicht
(1859) [Werke, v. 1, p. 148] same
Frühling im Sommer (1859) [Werke, v. 1,
p. 151] "Das ist die schönste Stunde"
Hirschlein ging im Wald spazieren
(1859) [Werke, v. 1, p. 146] same
*Mir ist, als zögen Arme mich schaurig
himmelwärts* (1859)
[Werke, v. 1, p. 155] same
Platen-Hallermünde, August, Graf
von, 1796-1835.
Ode, op. 5 no. 4 (1861) [Werke, v. 1, p.
193] "Lange begehrten wir ruhig allein
zu sein"
Vision (1865) [Werke, v. 1, p. 223] "Am
Felsenvorgebirge schroff"
Tieck, Johann Ludwig, 1773-1853.
Herbstlied (1843) [unpubl.] "Feldeinwärts
flog ein Vögelein"
Voice, clarinet & piano. Holograph in
Österreichische Nationalbibliothek,
Wien.
Cornelius, Peter, 1824-1874.
   CORNELIUS
Am Morgen
Am Rhein
Am See
An den Traum
Angedenken
Aus dem hohen Liede
Botschaft
Christbaum
Christkind
Christus der Kinderfreund
Dein Bildnis

Denkst du an mich?
Gedenken
Die Hirten
   Two settings: 1856 and op. 8 no. 2
   (1870).
Ich bin so froh geworden
Im Frühling! Im Frühling
Im Tiefsten Herzen glüht mir eine Wunde
In der Ferne
   Two settings: 1856 and op. 15 no. 3
   (1865).
In Lust und Schmerzen
Die Könige
   Two settings: 1856 and op. 8 no. 3
   (1870).
*Komm, wir wandeln zusammen in
   Mondschein*
Lieb' ist die Perle
Der Liebe Lohn
Märchenwunder
Möcht' im Walde mit dir geh'n
Ein Myrtenreis
Nachts
Schmetterling
Sei mein!
Simeon
Ein Ton
Trauer
Treue
Trost
Untreu
Vater unser I
Vater unser II
Vater unser III
Vater unser IV
Vater unser V
Vater unser VI
Vater unser VII
Vater unser VIII
Vater unser IX
Veilchen
Vorabend
Wie lieb ich dich hab'
Wiegenlied
LASSEN
Du meiner Seele schönster Traum
Ich ging hinaus, um dich zu sehen
Ich weil' in tiefer Einsamkeit
In deiner Nähe weil' ich noch
Der Lenz
Lilienblüthe
Löse, Himmel, meine Seele
Mein Lied verklingt
Nur eine Viertelstund!
Der Sänger
Schönste Rast

COMPOSER   Poet   *Title*   "First Line"

Schon grüsst auf dämmerndem Pfade
Seit du gesagt dein strenges Wort
Vergissmeinnicht
Wieder möcht' ich dir begegnen
Wiegenlied
LISZT
   Weimars Volkslied
   Wieder möcht' ich dir begegnen
LUENING *An dem Traume*
RUBINSTEIN *Lass mich deine Augen*
Cornwall, Barry, pseud. *see* Bryan, Waller Procter, 1787-1874.
A coronal see Dowson **QUILTER**
Coronini, Carl, graf von Cronberg, b.1818.
   LISZT *Die Fischerstochter*
"*Corre, corre, mi barquito*" *see Barcarola* Kamhi, Victoria **RODRIGO**
Les cors see Rey, Paul **SÉVERAC**
Le cortège d'amphitrite see Samain *AUX FLANCS DU VASE.* **KOECHLIN**
"Le cortège léger glisse aux plaines liquides" *see Le cortège d'amphitrite* Samain **KOECHLIN**
A cossack came through the village see Panch **PROKOFIEV** *Shel stanitseĭu kazak*
Cossmann, Paul Nikolaus, 1869-1942.
   PFITZNER
     Die Bäume wurden gelb
     Widmung
The cost see Cooper, Eric Thirkell **IRELAND**
Cota, Rodrigo de, fl.15th cent.
   WOLF *Blindes Schauen*
"Le couchant est si beau" *see Nuit d'automne* Régnier **ROUSSEL**
Le coucher du soleil! see Moore, T. **BERLIOZ**
The coughing of the trees has ceased see Hálek **DVOŘÁK** *Umlklo stromu šumění*
Counting song see Anon. **STRAVINSKIĬ** *Chanson pour compter*
Counting the beats see Graves, Robert **BERKELEY**
"A country life is sweet" *see The useful plough* Anon. **BRITTEN**
The countryman see Chalkhill *THE COMPLEAT ANGLER* (1653): Corydon's song. **HESELTINE**
Coupe d'ivresse see Simoni, H. Ernest **MASSENET**
"Couple amoureux aux accents méconnus" *see Violon* Vilmorin **POULENC**
Couplets bachiques see Anon. **POULENC**
Couplets de Mariette see Leprade **CHABRIER**

Courmont, Louis de, 1828-1900.
   BIZET *Rêve de la bien-aimée*
La couronne see Unknown **POULENC**
Les couronnes see Mauclair **CHAUSSON**
Cours de solfège: Papillon, Papillonnette see Fluchère **MILHAUD**
Court song see Anon. **BLITZSTEIN**
LA COURTE PAILLE, no. 1
   POULENC Carême *Le sommeil*
LA COURTE PAILLE, no. 2
   POULENC Carême *Quelle aventure!*
LA COURTE PAILLE, no. 3
   POULENC Carême *La reine de coeur*
LA COURTE PAILLE, no. 4
   POULENC Carême *Ba, be, bi, bo, bu*
LA COURTE PAILLE, no. 5
   POULENC Carême *Les anges musiciens*
LA COURTE PAILLE, no. 6
   POULENC Carême *Le carafon*
LA COURTE PAILLE, no. 7
   POULENC Carême *Lune d'Avril*
The courtship of the Yongly Bongly Bo see Lear **THOMSON**
"Cousin to Clare washing" *see Preciosilla* Stein **THOMSON**
Cowley, Abraham, 1618-1667.
   SCHUBERT *Der Weiberfreund*
Cowper, William, 1731-1800.
   IVES *The waiting soul*
Cox, Oscar
   HINDEMITH
     Beauty touch me
     Image
"Le crabe sort sur des pointes" *see Une danseuse* Cocteau **HONEGGER**
"Le crabe sort sur ses points" *see Danseuse* Cocteau **SATIE**
Cradle hymn see Unknown **MACDOWELL** *Geistliches Wiegenlied*
The cradle in Bethlehem see Bennett **QUILTER**
Cradle song see Arsen'ev **BALAKIREV** *Kolibel'naya pesnya*
A cradle song see Blake, William **BRITTEN**
Cradle song see Coleridge **VAUGHAN WILLIAMS**
Cradle song see Ibsen *KONGS-EMNERNE.* **DELIUS** *Wiegenlied*
Cradle song see Ives, A. L., Miss **IVES**
Cradle song see Maĭkov *NOVOGRECHESKIYE PESNI.* **CHAĬKOVSKIĬ** *Kolibel'naya pesnya*
Cradle song see Ostrovski **MUSORGSKIĬ** *Kolybel'naĭa pesnia*
Cradle song see Phillip, John *THE COMMODYE OF PACIENT AND MEEKE GRISSILL* (1566). **HESELTINE**

Cradle song see Tennyson **HARRIS**
   Evening song
Cradle song see Yeats **ROREM**
A cradle-song see Blake, William
   CARPENTER
Cradle-song see Golenishchev-Kutuzov
   MUSORGSKĬ *Kolybel'naĭa*
Cradle song from The Maid of Pskov see
   Mei **RIMSKĬ-KORSAKOV**
   Kolybel'naĭa pesnia
The crag see Lermontov **BALAKIREV**
   Utes
Craigher, Jacob Nicolaus de Jachelutta,
   1797-1855.
   SCHUBERT
     Die junge Nonne
     Totengräbers Heimwehe
Crainte frivole see Zaffira **GOUNOD** *E stati*
   al quanto
Cramer, Johann Andreas, 1723-1788.
   LOEWE
     Der Herr ist Gott
     Die Himmel rufen
Crane, Hart, 1899-1932.
   VOYAGES III.
   CARTER *Voyage*
Crane, Walter, 1845-1915.
   THIS BOOK OF HOURS.
   GRIFFES *This book of hours*
Crapsey, Adelaide, 1878-1914.
   WEISGALL
     Dirge
     Oh, lady, let the sad tears fall
     Old love
     Song
"Crash and clang!" *see Jazz-man* Farjeon
   BRITTEN
Crashaw, Richard, 1613?-1649.
   A HYMN TO THE NATIVITY.
   THOMSON *Sung by the shepherds*
"Creak, creak, little wood thing" *see The little*
   old table Hardy **BRITTEN**
Credo see Anon. **LOEFFLER**
Credo d'amour see Silvestre **CHABRIER**
"Credo in unum Deum" *see Credo* Anon.
   LOEFFLER
Crepuscolo see Rubino **RESPIGHI**
Crépuscule see Anon. **GOUNOD**
Crépuscule see Apollinaire **RIVIER**
Crépuscule see Lerberghe **FAURÉ**
Crépuscule see Silvestre **MASSENET**
Crépuscule de mi juillet, huit heures see
   Laforgue **SAUGUET**
CRÉPUSCULES D'AUTOMNE, no. 1
   AUBERT Hérold *Prélude*
CRÉPUSCULES D'AUTOMNE, no. 2
   AUBERT Catteau *Grisaille*

CRÉPUSCULES D'AUTOMNE, no. 3
   AUBERT Samain *Silence*
CRÉPUSCULES D'AUTOMNE, no. 4
   AUBERT Samain *L'âme errante*
CRÉPUSCULES D'AUTOMNE, no. 5
   AUBERT Mauclair *Brodeuses*
CRÉPUSCULES D'AUTOMNE, no. 6
   AUBERT Vivien *Feuilles sur l'eau*
CRÉPUSCULES DU MATIN. see
   Bengoechea
   Prise aux réseaux d'or **SCHMITT**
The cricketers of Hambledon see Blunt
   HESELTINE
Le crieur d'imprimés see Mallarmé
   MILHAUD
"Les cris des chiens" *see La chasse* Banville
   KOECHLIN
La crise see Jacob, M. **RIETI**
Les crocus see Daudet, L. **MILHAUD**
"Les crocus se forcent en potées ou dans des
   soucoupes" *see Les crocus* Daudet, L.
   MILHAUD
Crois mon conseil see Tristan L'Hermite
   DEBUSSY
"La croisée est ouverte" *see Le jardin mouillé*
   Régnier **ROUSSEL**
Croisset, Francis de, 1877-1937.
   CASELLA *Rêverie*
Cronnan see Macpherson *CARRIC-THURA.*
   SCHUBERT
Cronyn, George William, 1888-1969.
   RIEGGER
     Fairy song
     Hi Hi Hi
     Night flowers
     Song of the woman of the wood
Cros, Charles, 1842-1888.
   LE COFFRET DE SANTAL, CHANSONS
     PERPÉTUELLES (1873).
   DEBUSSY, MALIPIERO *L'archet*
"Crouch'd on the pavement" *see West London*
   Arnold **IVES**
"Crowned with flowers I saw fair amaryllis"
   see Amaryllis at the fountain Anon.
   QUILTER
Croze, J. L.
   MASSENET *À deux pleurer!*
   SAINT-SAËNS
     Là-bas
     Peut-être
     Pourquoi rester seulette?
Le crucifix see Hugo **LISZT**
The crucifixion see Jones, Howard
   Mumford, translator. *ROMANESQUE*
   LYRIC. **BARBER**
"Une cruelle abeille piqua une fois" *see*
   Le Kérioklépte Theocritus **ROUSSEL**

COMPOSER Poet *Title* "First Line"

Cruelty has a human heart see Blake,
William A DIVINE IMAGE.
VAUGHAN WILLIAMS
The cryin' blues see Hughes, L.
THE WEARY BLUES. CARPENTER
"Crying my little one, footsore and weary?"
see The only child Rossetti, Christina
IRELAND
"Csőndes minden, csőndes, Hallgatnak a
lombok" see Est Harsányi BARTÓK
Čtrnáct andělíčku see Des Knaben
Wunderhorn MARTINŮ Fourteen little
angels
"Cualquiera que el tejado" see Seguidilla
Murciana Anon. FALLA
"Cuando llegue, ay, yo no sé" see La espera
Kamhi, Victoria RODRIGO
Cuando tan hermosa os miro see Vega
Carpio LA DISCRETA ENAMORADA.
TURINA
The cuckoo see Gellert CHAĬKOVSKIĬ
Kukushka
Cuckoo! see Taylor, J. BRITTEN
The cuckoo see Unknown DVOŘÁK
Zezhulice
"Cuckoo, Cuckoo, What do you do?" see
Cuckoo! Taylor, J. BRITTEN
Cuckoo song see Williams QUILTER
"Cuclillo, cuclillo canta" see Cancion del cucu
Kamhi, Victoria RODRIGO
"Cuddle-doun, my bairnie" see Bed-time
Soutar BRITTEN
Cum descendisset Jesus de monte see Bible
HINDEMITH
Cum factus esset Jesus annorum duodecim see
Bible HINDEMITH
Cum natus esset see Bible HINDEMITH
Cummings, Edward Estlin, 1894-1962.
BLITZSTEIN
after all white horses are in bed
Jimmie's got a goil
mister, youse needn't be so spry
o by the by
open your heart
silent unday by silently not night
until and i heard
what if a much of a which of a wind
when life is quite through with
Two settings: 1929 and 1960.
yes is a pleasant country
you are like the snow
COPLAND Song
DIAMOND
Christmas tree
I shall imagine life
If you can't
Love is more

GIDEON Sonnet
ROREM
All in green my love went riding
Doll's boy
in the rain
Listen beloved
Spring song
IS 5.
DIAMOND Four uncles
Cunas see Arteaga, Cristina de TURINA
"Cunas de los niños misteriosas arcas" see
Cunas Arteaga, Cristina de TURINA
Cunningham, Allan, 1784-1842.
JENSEN
Carlisle Tor
Der Geächtete
Gordon von Brakley
Das Mädchen von Inverness
Cupido, loser see Goethe FRANZ
"Cupido, loser eigensinniger Knabe" see
Cupido, loser Goethe FRANZ
Cupo e il sepolcro mutolo see Unknown
VERDI
Cussy, Ferdinand de Cornot, baron de,
1795-1866.
WEBER Elle était simple et gentillette
CYCLE OF HOLY SONGS, no. 1
ROREM Bible Psalm 134
CYCLE OF HOLY SONGS, no. 2
ROREM Bible Psalm 142
CYCLE OF HOLY SONGS, no. 3
ROREM Bible Psalm 148
CYCLE OF HOLY SONGS, no. 4
ROREM Bible Psalm 150
"Cycliste en jupe culotte" see Halte
Radiguet SAUGUET
Le cyclone see Koechlin KOECHLIN
Les cydalises see Gérard de Nerval AURIC
Le cygne see Claudel MILHAUD
Le Cygne see Renard HISTOIRES
NATURELLES. RAVEL
Un cygne see Rilke POÈMES FRANCAIS.
BARBER
"Un cygne avance sur l'eau" see Un cygne
Rilke BARBER
Cygne sur l'éau see Brimont FAURÉ
Les cygnes see Renaud HAHN
CYMBELINE. see Shakespeare
Fear no more the heat o' the sun
QUILTER
Ständchen SCHUBERT
"Cypris, meiner Phyllis gleich" see
Die Liebesgötter Uz SCHUBERT
CYPŘIŠE, no. 1
DVOŘÁK Pfleger-Moravský Vy vroucí
pìsně spějte

CYPŘIŠE, no. 2
   DVOŘÁK Pfleger-Moravský *Vté sladké moci*
CYPŘIŠE, no. 3
   DVOŘÁK Pfleger-Moravský *Vtak mnohém srdci mrtvojest*
CYPŘIŠE, no. 4
   DVOŘÁK Pfleger-Moravský *Ó duše drahá jedinkájež*
CYPŘIŠE, no. 5
   DVOŘÁK Pfleger-Moravský *Ó byl to krásný zlatý sen*
CYPŘIŠE, no. 6
   DVOŘÁK Pfleger-Moravský *Já vím, že v sladké naději*
CYPŘIŠE, no. 7
   DVOŘÁK Pfleger-Moravský *Ó zlatá ruže, spatnilá*
CYPŘIŠE, no. 8
   DVOŘÁK Pfleger-Moravský *Ó, naší lásce*
CYPŘIŠE, no. 9
   DVOŘÁK Pfleger-Moravský *Kol domuse*
CYPŘIŠE, no. 10
   DVOŘÁK Pfleger-Moravský *Mne často týrá pochyba*
CYPŘIŠE, no. 11
   DVOŘÁK Pfleger-Moravský *Mé srdce často vbolesti*
CYPŘIŠE, no. 12
   DVOŘÁK Pfleger-Moravský *Zde hledím na tendrahý list*

CYPŘIŠE, no. 13
   DVOŘÁK Pfleger-Moravský *Na horách ticho a vúdolí ticho*
CYPŘIŠE, no. 14
   DVOŘÁK Pfleger-Moravský *Zde v lese u potoka*
CYPŘIŠE, no. 15
   DVOŘÁK Pfleger-Moravský *Mou celou duší zádumně bolestné*
CYPŘIŠE, no. 16
   DVOŘÁK Pfleger-Moravský *Tam stojí stará skála*
CYPŘIŠE, no. 17
   DVOŘÁK Pfleger-Moravský *Nad krajem vévodí lehký spánek*
CYPŘIŠE, no. 18
   DVOŘÁK Pfleger-Moravský *Ty se ptáš pročmoje zpěvy bouří*
Czary see Witwicki **CHOPIN**
Czasem gdy dlugo na pól sennie marze see Tetmajer **SZYMANOWSKI**
Czaty see Mickiewicz **LOEWE** *Der Woywode*
"Czemu tak lzy ronisz, dziewczyno droga" *see Do dziewczyny* Unknown **SZYMANOWSKI**
"Czupirzy sie, czupurzy kosmaty trzmiel na rózy" *see Trzmiel i zuk* Iłłakowiczówna **SZYMANOWSKI**
"Czy zdrowa pani krowa" *see Wizyta u krowy* Iłłakowiczówna **SZYMANOWSKI**
Czyzowskiego, Kazimierza Andrzeja **SZYMANOWSKI** *Wyszywala raz Hanka*

D

"Da der Sommer kommen ist" *see Im Sommer* Osterwald **FRANZ**
"Da die Heimath, O Vater" *see Die Tochter Jephtha's* Byron **SCHUMANN**
Da die Stunde kam see Osterwald **FRANZ**
"Da dob'n auf jener Linden" *see Untreu und Trost* Anon. **PFITZNER**
"Da droben am Berge" *see Einsiedel* Bulcke **SZYMANOWSKI**
"Da droben auf jenem Berge" *see Schäfers Klagelied* Goethe **SCHUBERT, ZELTER**
"Da fahr' ich still im Wagen" *see In der Fremde* Eichendorff **SCHOECK, WOLF**

"Da ga da ga dum da lai la lo" *see Piccola serenata* Bernstein **BERNSTEIN**
"Da ging ich hin" *see Die Nachtigall* Unknown **MENDELSSOHN-BARTHOLDY**
Da ich dich einmal gefunden see Rückert *LIEBESFRÜHLING.* **JENSEN**
"Da ich ein Knabe war" *see Die Jugend* Hölderlin **BRITTEN**
"Da ich nun entsagen müssen" *see Der Page* Geibel **JENSEN, SCHUMANN**
"Da kommt ja der liebliche Mai" *see Naturgenuss* Gleim **LOEWE**

Da lieg' ich unter den Bäumen see Unknown
MENDELSSOHN-BARTHOLDY
"Da liegen sie alle, die grauen Höhn" *see Der*
König auf dem Thurme Uhland **LOEWE**
Da liegt der Feinde gestreckte Schaar see
Lenau **SCHUMANN**
Da meine Lippen reglos sind und brennen see
George
DAS BUCH DER HÄNGENDEN GÄRTEN.
SCHÖNBERG
"Da mit Sokrates die Freunde tranken" *see*
Das Ende des Festes Meyer **SCHOECK**
"Da Nachts wir uns küssten O Mädchen" *see*
Verrathene Liebe Anon. **SCHUMANN**
Da nur Leid und Leidenschaft see Anon.
WOLF
Da qualche tempo see Zaffira **GOUNOD**
Da quel sembiante appresi see Metastasio
SCHUBERT
"Da schwimm ich allein auf dem stillen Meer"
see Meerfahrt Freiligrath **LOEWE**
Da sind die bleichen Geister wieder see
Hauenschild **FRANZ**
"Da sitz' ich ohne Bogen" *see Piloktet*
Mayrhofer **SCHUBERT**
"Da unten im Talle, läuft's Wasser so trub"
see Trennung Anon. **BRAHMS**
"Da voi cari lumi" *see L'incanto degli occhi*
Metastasio **SCHUBERT**
"Da voi parto, amate sponde" *see Addio ai*
viennesi Unknown **ROSSINI**
"Da welkt am Fenster" *see Die letzte Rose*
Gottschall **FRANZ**
"Da, wo des Tajo gründlich blauer Strom" *see*
Die Gruft der Liebenden
Puttkamer-Plauth **LOEWE**
Dabelsteen, Chr
NIELSEN *Naar Smaabørn klynker ved*
Aftentide
Dämmer see Boelitz **REGER**
Dämmerempfindung see Hebbel
CORNELIUS
"Dämmern Wolken über Nacht und Tal" *see*
Nacht Hauptmann **BERG**
"Dämmernd liegt der Sommerabend" *see*
Sommerabend Heine **BRAHMS,**
SCHOECK
Dämmerstunde see Storm **WEBERN**
"Die Dämmerung war längst hereingebrochen"
see Auf eine Unbekannte Hebbel
CORNELIUS
"Dämmesung löscht die letzten Lichter" *see*
Seele Falke **SZYMANOWSKI**
"Der Dämm'rung Schein durchblinkt den
Hain" *see Geisternähe* Matthisson
SCHUBERT

Dämmrung senkte sich von oben see Goethe
CHINESISCH- DEUTSCHE JAHRES- UND
TAGESZEITEN. **BRAHMS, SCHOECK**
"Dämm'rung will die Flügel spreiten" *see*
Zwielicht Eichendorff **SCHUMANN**
DAFNIS. see Holz
Er klagt, dass der Frühling so kurtz blüht
BERG
"Dagen er oppe, glaeden er taendt" *see God*
morgen! Bjørnson **GRIEG**
"Daggen har duggat" *see Fågellek*
Tavaststjerna **SIBELIUS**
"The dagger at my belt it dances whene'er I
dance" *see Song of the dagger* Anon.
GRIFFES
Dahn, Felix Ludwig Sophus, 1834-1912.
LASSEN *Germanensang*
REGER
All' mein Gedanken, mein Herz und mein
Sinn
Dein Auge
RUBINSTEIN *Fatme*
STRAUSS
Efeu
Kornblumen
Mohnblumen
Wasserrose
SCHLICHTE WEISEN, no. 7.
REGER, STRAUSS *Du meines Herzens*
Krönelein
SCHLICHTE WEISEN, no. 10.
STRAUSS *Ach, weh mir verglückhaftem*
Mann
SCHLICHTE WEISEN, no. 11.
STRAUSS *All mein Gedanken*
SCHLICHTE WEISEN, no. 12 (?).
STRAUSS *Ach Lieb', nun muss ich*
scheiden
SCHLICHTE WEISEN, no. 13.
STRAUSS *Die Frauen sind oft fromm*
und still
SIND GÖTTER.
LASSEN *Weisse Rose*
Daisies see Lotarev **RACHMANINOFF**
The daisies see Stephens, James **BARBER**
Daisies after rain see Bickle **QUILTER**
The daisy see Dumas the younger
GOUNOD *La Pâquerette*
"The daisy stars are swaying lakes" *see*
Daisies after rain Bickle **QUILTER**
"Daïte bokaly!" *see Zastol'naia pesn'*
Kol'tsov **MUSORGSKIĬ**
Daleko zostal caly świat see Tetmajer
SZYMANOWSKI
Dallet, Claude-Charles, 1829-1878.
GOUNOD *L'anniversaire des martyrs*

COMPOSER Poet *Title* "First Line"

Dalliba, Gerda, 1885-1913.
PIZZETTI *My cry*
D'alt d'un cotxe n'hi ha una nina qu'en see
Anon. **MOMPOU**
Dam, Johannes, 1866-1926.
NIELSEN *Barnets Sang*
"Damals, ganz zuerst am Anfang" *see*
Das bescheidene Wünschlein Spitteler
SCHOECK
Damask roses see Anon. **QUILTER**
La dame d'André see Vilmorin **POULENC**
Dame du ciel see Haraucourt **KOECHLIN**
"Dame du ciel, regente terrienne" *see*
Ballade que Villon feit à requeste de sa
mère . . . Villon **DEBUSSY**
"Dame du soir les anémones" *see Ballade-*
nocturne Vilmorin **MILHAUD**
"A dame of high degree, is she" *see*
The mignonette Deland
MACDOWELL
Damm, M
NIELSEN *Den Spillemand spiller paa*
Strenge
"Der Damm zerreisst, das Feld erbraust" *see*
Johanna Sebus Goethe **SCHUBERT**
Damon und Chloe see Hiemer **WEBER**
Dampierre, Leila de, comtesse, 1891-
1955.
SCHMITT *La citerne des mille colonnes*
Damunt de tu només les flors see Janés i
Olivé **MOMPOU**
The dance see Williams, W. **ROREM**
Dance song see Unknown *THE BOOK OF*
SONGS. **BRITTEN**
The dancer see Waller **ROREM**
Dancing lightly see Case **BENNETT**
"Dancing lightly comes the summer" *see*
Dancing lightly Case **BENNETT**
Daniel, Samuel, 1562-1619.
IRELAND *Love is a sickness full of woes*
Dank see Levetzow *HÖHENLIEDER,*
pp. 41-42. **SCHÖNBERG**
Dank see Winther **GRIEG** *Taksigelse*
Dank des Paria see Goethe **LOEWE,**
WOLF
Danksagung an den Bach see Müller,
Wilhelm **SCHUBERT**
Danmark, nu blunder den lyse Nat see
Larsen **NIELSEN**
"Danmarks Sommer gik sin Gang" *see*
Blomstervise Holstein **NIELSEN**
D'Anne jouant de l'espinette see Marot
RAVEL
D'Anne qui me jecta de la neige see Marot
RAVEL
Dans ce beau mois see Anon.
SAINT-SAËNS

"Dans ce fossé cessons de vivre" *see Le vieux*
vagabond Béranger **LALO, LISZT**
Dans cette étable see Anon. **GOUNOD**
Bethléem
"Dans cette grotte où le silence ignore encor"
see Homenaje a Debussy: "La grotte"
Émié **RODRIGO**
"Dans la brume où se perd la lointaine
colline" *see Le novice* Stupuy, Hippolyte
LALO
"Dans la brume rêveuse où dort" *see*
Fourvières Léna **MASSENET**
"Dans la brûme tiède d'une haleine" *see*
La jeune fille de Budapest Michaux
SAUGUET
"Dans la clarté du matin" *see La vie est belle*
Guillot de Saix **HAHN**
"Dans la familiale demeure" *see En chantant*
Boyer, Georges **MASSENET**
"Dans la feuillée écrin vert tàché d'or" *see*
Tête de faune Rimbaud **RIVIER**
DANS LA FORÊT. see Bouchor, M.
Lilas, vos frissons sous le ciel **CHAUSSON**
"Dans la forêt chauve et rouillée" *see*
La dernière feuille Gautier **CHAUSSON**
Dans la forêt de Septembre see Mendès
FAURÉ
Dans la forêt du Charme et de
l'Enchantement see Moréas **CHAUSSON**
Dans la forêt noire see Anon.
SZYMANOWSKI *Ściani dumbek*
"Dans la forêt que orée un rêve" *see Clair de*
lune Mendès **SAINT-SAËNS**
"Dans la lumière éclatante d'automne" *see*
Chanson d'automne Claudel **MILHAUD**
"Dans la maison refermée" *see Eglogue*
Follain **SAUGUET**
"Dans la montagne noire" *see La belle*
Isabeau Dumas the elder **BERLIOZ**
Dans la nuit see Michaux **SAUGUET**
Dans la nuit see Moréas **HAHN**
Dans la Nymphée see Lerberghe **FAURÉ**
Dans la pénombre see Lerberghe **FAURÉ**
"Dans la plaine les baladins" *see*
Saltimbanques Apollinaire **HONEGGER,**
RIVIER
"Dans la plus haute Eughillydie" *see Aria*
James, E. **SAUGUET**
DANS LA SOMBRE TRISTESSE. see
Galéron de Calone
Dans l'immense Tristesse **BOULANGER**
Dans l'air fraîchi see Rodenbach, G.
SCHMITT
"Dans l'air léger, dans l'azur rose" *see*
Villanelle Leconte de Lisle **KOECHLIN**

Dans l'air plein de fils de soie see Silvestre
  MASSENET
"Dans l'air s'en vont les ailes" *see L'air*
  Banville HAHN, KOECHLIN
"Dans l'après midi chaud où dorment les
  oiseaux" *see Rhodante* Samain
  KOECHLIN
"Dans le brouillard s'en vont un paysan
  cagneux" *see Automne* Apollinaire
  HONEGGER, RIVIER
"Dans le cèndre, des colombes se sont posées"
  see Le sommeil des colombes
  Toussaint AUBERT
Dans le chemin toujours trempé see Jammes
  TRISTESSES. MILHAUD
Dans le ciel est dressé le chéne séculaire see
  Moréas HAHN
"Dans le golfe aux jardins ombreux" *see L'île*
  heureuse Mikhaël CHABRIER
Dans le jardin see Gravollet, Paul
  DEBUSSY
Dans le jardin d'Anna see Apollinaire
  IL Y A. POULENC
"Dans le jardin de grand'mère" *see Le rosier*
  blanc Spenner, M. GOUNOD
Dans le jardin de l'alchimiste see Raphaël,
  Cluzel SAUGUET
"Dans le jardin du Luxembourg" *see Vendredi*
  XIII Chalupt SCHMITT
"Dans le mortel soupir de l'automne" *see*
  Déclin d'amour Sully-Prudhomme
  KOECHLIN
Dans le murmure see Anon.
  SZYMANOWSKI *U jeziorecka*
Dans le noir see Messiaen MESSIAEN
"Dans le parc au noble dessin" *see Promenade*
  galante Banville KOECHLIN
"Dans le parc de cette demoiselle" *see*
  Le chalet tyrolien Chalupt SAUGUET
"Dans le royaume de Yen" *see Amoureux*
  séparés Roché ROUSSEL
Dans le sentier, parmi les roses see
  Le Barillier MASSENET
"Dans le ventre de Maman" *see Les jumeaux*
  de la nuit Obaldia SAUGUET
"Dans le verger paisible, bordé là-bas de
  peupiliers" *see Le déclin* Rodès BLOCH
"Dans le vieux parc solitaire et glacé" *see*
  Colloque sentimental Verlaine DEBUSSY
"Dans le village, il v a deux hôtels" *see*
  Les deux hôtels Paliard MILHAUD
"Dans le village il y a un petit homme tout
  sec" *see Le boulanger* Paliard MILHAUD
"Dans l'ennui si désolément vert de la serre
  de douleur" *see De fleurs* Debussy
  DEBUSSY

"Dans les bois l'amoureux Myrtil" *see*
  La fauvette Millevoye GOUNOD
"Dans les bois l'amoureux Myrtil" *see Vieille*
  chanson Millevoye BIZET
"Dans les campagnes de Pologne" *see*
  Postlude: Polonaise Vilmorin SAUGUET
"Dans les champs de Bethléem" *see Chant de*
  la pitié Unknown MILHAUD
Dans les coins bleus see Sainte-Beuve
  SAINT-SAËNS
Dans les nuages see Anon.
  SZYMANOWSKI *Wysla burzycka*
Dans les pré fleuris see Anon.
  SZYMANOWSKI
Dans les ruines d'une abbaye see Hugo
  FAURÉ
"Dans les sentiers de mai remplis de parfums"
  see Les lilas blancs Bourguignat, Paul
  GOUNOD
Dans les ténèbres du jardin see Éluard
  POULENC
Dans l'herbe see Vilmorin POULENC
Dans l'immense Tristesse see Galéron de
  Calone *DANS LA SOMBRE TRISTESSE.*
  BOULANGER
"Dans Londres, la grande ville" *see Jeanne*
  Giraudoux HONEGGER
"Dans ma cervelle se promène" *see Le chat*
  Baudelaire SAUGUET
"Dans mes coupes d'un prix modique" *see*
  Vile potabis Leconte de Lisle HAHN
"Dans mon indigne main lorsque je
  t'emprisonne" *see Petite main* Docquois
  SAINT-SAËNS
"Dans son potager ma grand mère" *see Le*
  jardinier impatient Vildrac MILHAUD
Dans ton coeur see Cazalis *CHANSON*
  TRISTE. SAINT-SAËNS
"Dans ton coeur dort un clair de lune" *see*
  Chanson triste Cazalis DUPARC
"Dans un baiser l'onde au rivage" *see Seule*
  Gautier FAURÉ, HAHN
"Dans un bois solitaire" *see Ariette* Lamotte
  MOZART
Dans un parfum de roses blanches see
  Lerberghe FAURÉ
"Dans un pré en pente" *see La maison*
  inachevée Paliard MILHAUD
"Dans un sommeil que charmait ton image"
  see Après un rêve Anon. FAURÉ
"Dans un vieux square où l'océan" *see Spleen*
  Fargue SATIE
Dans une salutation suprême see Tagore
  GITANJALI. CASELLA
"Dans Venise la rouge" *see Venise* Musset
  GOUNOD

COMPOSER Poet *Title* "First Line"

"Dans vos viviers dans vos étangs" *see*
  Le carpe Apollinaire **POULENC**
Danse du bébé-Phile see Messiaen
  MESSIAEN
Danse macabre see Cazalis **SAINT-SAËNS**
Danseuse see Brimont **FAURÉ**
Une danseuse see Cocteau **HONEGGER,**
  SATIE
Dansk Arbejde see Rørdam, Valdemar
  NIELSEN
Dansk Vejr see Rode, Ove **NIELSEN**
Det danske Brød paa Sletten gror see
  Aakjaer **NIELSEN**
Den danske Sang er en ung, blond Pige see
  Hoffmann **NIELSEN**
Danslek see Cnattingius, Thor **KILPINEN**
Dansons la gigue see Verlaine
  CARPENTER, LOEFFLER
"Dansons la gigue! J'aimais surtout ses jolis
  yeux" *see Dansons la gigue* Verlaine
  CARPENTER
Dante Aligheri, 1265-1321.
  BERLIOZ *Nessun maggior*, page d'album
  ROSSINI *Recitativo ritmato*
  RUBINSTEIN *Tanto gentile e tanto onesta*
  SAINT-SAËNS *La porta dell'inferno*
  DIVINE COMEDY.
    BLACHER *Francesca da Rimini*
  VITA NUOVA.
    SCHOECK *Du, des Erbarmens Feind,*
      grausamer Tod
La danza see Olkienizkaia-Naldi *LO*
  SPECCHIO. **CASELLA**
La danza see Pepoli **ROSSINI**
Daphénéo see Godebska, Mimie **SATIE**
Daphne am Bach see Stolberg **SCHUBERT**
Darest thou now, O soul see Whitman
  WHISPERS OF HEAVENLY DEATH.
  VAUGHAN WILLIAMS
"Darf ich einer Blume still" *see Wehmut*
  Avenarius **WEBERN**
Daring exploit see Khomyakov
  CHAÏKOVSKIĬ *Podvig*
"Dark brown is the river" *see Where go the*
  boats? Stevenson, Robert Louis
  QUILTER
"Dark, grey twilight comes descending" *see*
  Twilight Tiutchev **MEDTNER**
"Dark is the night" *see Vigil* De La Mare
  BRITTEN
"Dark red roses in a honeyed wind swinging"
  see June Chesson **QUILTER**
"The dark rose of thy mouth" *see The rose of*
  the night Sharp, W. **GRIFFES**
Darkness and thunderclouds are round about
  Him see Bible **DVOŘÁK**
  Oblak a mrákota

Die Darstellung Mariäim Tempel see Rilke
  HINDEMITH
DARTHULA. see Macpherson
  Ossians Lied nach dem Falle Nathos'
  SCHUBERT
Darthula's Grabesgesang see Herder
  STIMMEN DER VÖLKER. **JENSEN**
Darum see Seyboth, Sofie **REGER**
"Das also, das ist der enge Schrein" *see Vor*
  meiner Wiege Leitner **SCHUBERT**
"Das dank' ich deiner Güte" *see Erlöst*
  Boelitz **REGER**
"Das einst ein Kind auf Erden war" *see*
  Christkind Cornelius **CORNELIUS**
"Das glaube mir, so sagte er" *see Dilemma*
  Busch, W. **SCHOECK**
Das hat die Sommernacht getan see Ritter
  SZYMANOWSKI
"Das heiss' ich rechte Augenweide" *see Als er*
  sein Weib und 's Kind schlafend fand
  Claudius, M. **SCHOECK**
"Das ist aber das Ende" *see Vom Ende*
  Puttkamer **BERG**
"Das ist der Liebe schönes Licht" *see*
  Die Memnonsäule Fitger **LASSEN**
"Das ist des Frühlings traurige Lust!" *see*
  Frühlingsfeier Heine **FRANZ, STRAUSS**
"Das ist die Drossel, die da schlägt" *see April*
  Storm **SCHOECK**
"Das ist die schönste Stunde" *see Frühling im*
  Sommer Kuh **CORNELIUS**
"Das ist die Zeit der Rosenpracht" *see*
  Sommerabend Scholz, B. **LASSEN**
Das ist ein Brausen und Heulen see Heine
  LYRISCHES INTERMEZZO, no. 63.
  FRANZ, GRIFFES, WOLF
Das ist ein Flöten und Geigen see Heine
  SCHUMANN
"Das ist ein hohes helles Wort" *see Dem*
  Vaterland Reinick **WOLF**
"Das ist ein schlechtes Wetter" *see Schlechtes*
  Wetter Heine **STRAUSS**
Das macht das dunkelgrüne Laub see
  Roquette **FRANZ**
"Das macht, es hat die Nachtigall die ganze
  Nacht gesungen" *see Die Nachtigall* Storm
  BERG
"Das machte dein stiller, keuscher Blick" *see*
  Glück Schellenberg **REGER**
Das sind so traumheft schöne Stunden see
  Zitelmann **LASSEN**
"Das war der Junker" *see Gute Nacht* Falke
  REGER
"Das war der Junker Emerich" *see*
  Die schwarzen Augen Vogl **LOEWE**
"Das war der Tag der weissen
  Chrysanthemen" *see Traumgekrönt* Rilke
  BERG

COMPOSER Poet *Title* "First Line"

"Das war der Zwerg Perkêo im Heidelberger
Schloss" *see Perkêo* Scheffel **JENSEN**
"Das war des Frühlings warmer Hauch" *see*
Mein Herz, der wilde Rosenstrauch Sergel
KILPINEN
"Das war die Schlacht von Waterloo" *see*
Der Papagei Rückert **LOEWE**
"Das war ein recht abscheuliches Gesicht" *see*
An Sie Wargentin **WEBER**
"Das war ein Tag der Schmerzen" *see*
Heimkehr Nietzsche **MEDTNER**
Das war ich see Körner **SCHUBERT**
Das wirtshaus zu see Marées **SPOHR**
"Dass der Ostwind Düfte" *see Dass sie hier*
gewesen Rückert **SCHUBERT**
Dass doch gemalt all'deine Reize wären see
Heyse **WOLF**
"Dass du bei mir magst weilen" *see Für*
Ninon Hesse **SCHOECK**
"Dass du so krank geworden" *see Wer machte*
dich so krank? Kerner **SCHUMANN**
Dass gestern eine Wespe Dich see Unknown
SCHÖNBERG
"Dass ich an dich denke immerdar" *see Denk*
ich dein! Förster, M. **FRANZ**
"Dass ich dich verloren habe" *see Am Grabe*
Anselmo's Claudius, M. **SCHUBERT**
"Dass Liebe Raum noch hat in solcher Zeit"
see Liebeslied Krenek **KRENEK**
Dass, Petter, 1647-1708.
   GRIEG *Fiskervise*
Dass schon die Maienzeit vorüber see
Breden **SCHÖNBERG**
Dass sie hier gewesen see Rückert
SCHUBERT
Daudet, Alphonse, 1840-1897.
   HAHN *Trois jours de vendange*
   MILHAUD
      Le bégonia
      Le brachycome
      Les crocus
      L'eremurus
      Les fritillaires
      Les jacinthes
      La violette
Dauerhafte Farben see Schmidt, Georg
   ZELTER
Daumer, Georg Friedrich, 1800-1875.
   FRAUENBILDER UND HULDIGUNGEN.
   BRAHMS
      Ach, wende diesen Blick
      In meiner Nächte Sehnen
      Strahlt zuweilen auch ein mildes Licht
      Unbewegte laue Luft
      Von waldbekränzter Hohe
   HAFIS.
   BRAHMS
      Bitteres zu sagen denkst du

Botschaft
Liebesglut
Nicht mehr zu dir zu gehen Beschloss
   ich
So stehn wir, ich und meine Weide
Wenn du nur zuweilen lächelst
Wie bist du, meine Königin
POLYDORA.
   BRAHMS
      Es träumte mir
      Eine gute, gute Nacht
      Die Kränze
      Magyarisch
      Die Schnur, die Perl an Perle
      Schön war, das ich dir weihte
      Wir wandelten
Le dauphin see Apollinaire *LE BESTIAIRE.*
   POULENC
Dauphin, Léopold, b.1847.
   HAHN *Le rossignol des lilas*
"Dauphins, vous jouez dans la mer" *see*
   Le dauphin Apollinaire **POULENC**
Daurat, Jean, 1507-1588.
   ROREM *Sonnet*
"D'autre femmes m'ont pris son regard sa
   pensée!" *see L'abandonnée* Mendès
   BIZET
David, Eugène, 1813-1889.
   FRANCK *Le mariage des roses*
David mourns for Absalmon see Bible
   DIAMOND
David Rizzio see Chouquet **MASSENET**
      Ballade de David Rizzio
"David the King was grievèd and much
   moved" *see David mourns for Absalmon*
   Bible **DIAMOND**
Davidov
   RUBINSTEIN *Der Schiffer*
Davidov, Dmitri
   SZYMANOWSKI
      Kak tolko wostok
      Niebo biez zwiozd
      Osiennieje solnce
Davidova, Mariya A
   RACHMANINOFF *I wait for thee!*
Davids Harfe see Byron **LOEWE**
Davies, William Henry, 1871-1940.
   BERKELEY *Rich days*
Davis, F.
   SAINT-SAËNS *My land*
Davis, Rev. O. S.
   RIEGGER *Prayer on Great Island*
Davis, T. see Davis, F.
Davno l', moĭ drut see Golenishchev-
   Kutuzov **RACHMANINOFF**
   How long, my friend

COMPOSER Poet *Title* ''First Line''

Davno v liubni see Shenshin
 RACHMANINOFF
  For long there has been little consolation
The dawn see Anon. **LUENING**
Dawn see Khomyakov **BALAKIREV** *Zarya*
Dawn see Wilde *THE FOURTH
  MOVEMENT*. Impression: Le Réveillon.
 GRIFFES
Dawn angel see Tyler **ROREM**
Dawn, gentle flower see Bryan **BENNETT**
Dawn in the garden see Shenshin
 MEDTNER
The dawn of spring see Tolstoĭ
 CHAĬKOVSKIĬ *To bylo ranneiu vesnoĭ*
Dawydoff *see* Davidov
Dawydow, Dmitri *see* Davidov, Dmitri
Day and night see Tiutchev **MEDTNER**
"Day by day I float my paper boats" *see*
  Paper boats Tagore **MILHAUD**
THE DAY DREAM. see Tennyson
  The sleeping palace **ROREM**
The day is no more see Tagore *GITANJALI.*
 CARPENTER
*Day to night comparing went the wind her
  way see* Bal'mont **RACHMANINOFF**
  The migrant wind
Daybreak see Blake, William *MORNING.*
 QUILTER
"The days in turn pass all too soon" *see*
  Meditation Shevchenko
 RACHMANINOFF
"Days of joy, how have ye fled?" *see*
  A summer vacation Schaffer **COPLAND**
Daz iuwer min engel walte! see Hertz
 REGER
Dazzi, Manlio
 PIZZETTI *In questa notte carica di stelle*
"De ce soir, je serai joyeux" *see Mienne!*
  Laroche, Ernest **MASSENET**
De Ceylan see Chalupt **AUBERT**
DE DENTRO TENGO MI MAL. see
  Camoens
  Tief im Herzen **SCHUMANN**
  Tief im Herzen trag' ich Pein **WOLF**
"De deux nous voici un" *see Les deux
  guerriers* Messiaen **MESSIAEN**
"De doigts mignons oeuvre mignonne" *see*
  À une bourse Augier **GOUNOD**
De Don Juan see Cocteau **ROREM**
De dónde venis, amore? see Anon.
 RODRIGO
De fleurs see Debussy **DEBUSSY**
De grève see Debussy **DEBUSSY**
"De jour merci" *see Juan Gris* Éluard
 POULENC
"De la belle Timar c'est ici le tombeau" *see*
  À une jeune grecque Sappho **GOUNOD**

"De la douleur n'aît l'espérance" *see Au
  chevet d'un mourant* (élégie) Pacini
 ROSSINI
De La Mare, Walter, 1873-1956.
 BERKELEY
  Afraid
  All that's past
  Another spring
  The fleeting
  Full moon
  The horseman
  Mistletoe
  The moth
  Poetry
  Poor Henry
  Rachel
  Silver
  The song of the soldiers
 BRITTEN
  Autumn
  Silver
  A song of enchantment
  Tit for tat
  Vigil
 CHANLER
  A one-eyed tailor
  A shepherd
 ROREM *Myself*
 THOMPSON, R. *Some one*
DING DONG BELL: Benighted.
 CHANLER
  Alice Rodd
  Ann Poverty
  Be very quiet now
  A midget
  No voice to scold
  Susannah Fry
  Thomas Logge
  Three sisters
HERE LIES MY THREE HUSBANDS.
 CHANLER *Three husbands*
PEACOCK PIE.
 BRITTEN *The ship of Rio*
 CHANLER
  Cake and Sack
  Old Shellover
  The ship of Rio
  Tillie
De la Motte Fouqué, Friedrich Heinrich
  Karl von *see*
  La Motte-Fouque, Friedrich Heinrich
  Karl, freiherr, 1777-1843.
De l'Atlantique ou Pacifique see Féline, J.
 HONEGGER
"De loin, tu parais-sais très grande" *see*
  Mirage Gravollet, Paul **INDY**

De los àlamos vengo, madre! see Anon.
RODRIGO
"De mon berger volage" *see Le dépit de la bergère* Unknown **BERLIOZ**
"De mon coeur une partie" *see Absence* Ségur **GOUNOD**
... *de pleurs d'égrène see* Ganzo **SCHMITT**
De rêve see Debussy **DEBUSSY**
De ronda see Anon. **RODRIGO**
"De sa dent soudaine et vorace" *see Le manoir de Rosemonde* Bonnières **DUPARC**
"De sa fourrure blonde et brune" *see Le chat* Baudelaire **SAUGUET**
De sa peine, et des beautés de sa Dame see Du Bellay **MILHAUD**
De soir see Debussy **DEBUSSY**
"De tristesse amère et profonde" *see Tristesse* Lemaire, Ferdinand **SAINT-SAËNS**
Dead eyes see Martínek **MARTINŮ**
Dead love see Mužik **MARTINŮ**
Dear heart see Joyce **CHAMBER MUSIC.**
ROREM
Dear March, come in! see Dickinson **COPLAND**
"Dear mother, dear mother, the church is cold" *see The little vagabond* Blake, William **LUENING**
Dear one, why are thine eyes sometimes so cold? see Pleshcheyev **MUSORGSKIĭ** *Akh, zachem tvoi glazki poroiu*
Dear, think not that they will forget you see Hardy **IRELAND**
"Dearest, sleep sound" *see Slumber song* MacDowell **MACDOWELL**
Death see Merezhkovski **CHAĬKOVSKIĭ** *Smert'*
Death, be not proud see Donne **BRITTEN**
Death in love see Rossetti, Dante *THE HOUSE OF LIFE,* no. XLVIII. **VAUGHAN WILLIAMS**
THE DEATH OF SAINT NARCISSUS. see Eliot *Canticle V* **BRITTEN**
Death reigns in many a human breast see Pfleger-Moravský **DVOŘÁK** *Vtak mnohém srdci mrtvojest* Two settings: B. 11 no. 3 and B. 160 no. 2.
Death-parting see Rossetti, Christina **IRELAND**
Death's divisions see Zaleski **CHOPIN** *Dwojaki koniec*
LES DÉBÂCLES. see Verhaeren *Si morne!* **RAVEL**

Debladis, Georgette
FAURÉ *C'est la paix*
DEBUSSY, CLAUDE, 1862-1918.
Anon.
Rondel chinois (ca.1881) [unpubl.] "Sur le lac bordé d'azalée"
Banville, Théodore Faullain de, 1823-1891.
AMÉTHYSTES.
Caprice (1880) [Ruschenburg ***Stilkritische Untersuchungen...*** (1966)] "Quand je baise, pâle dc fièvre"
LES CARIATIDES, livre 2, Amours d'Élise ... no. V.
Rêverie (ca.1880) [Jobert, 1984] "Le Zéphir à la douce haleine"
LES CARIATIDES, livre 3, no. II.
Zéphyr (1881) [***Revue illustrée,*** 1.9.1890; Eschig, 1932] "Si j'étais le Zéphyr ailé"
LES CARIATIDES, livre 3, no. III.
Fête galante (1882) [Jobert, 1984] "Voilà Sylvandre et Lucas et Myrtil"
LES CARIATIDES, livre 3, no. VI.
Pierrot (ca.1881) [***Revue Musicale,*** May 1926; Jobert, 1969] "Le bon Pierrot, que la foule contemple"
LES CARIATIDES, livre 3, no. VII.
Sérénade (ca.1882) [Jobert, 1984] "Las, Colombine a fermé le volet"
LES CARIATIDES, livre 3, no. XV.
Les roses (ca.1881) [Jobert, 1984] "Lorsque le ciel de saphir"
LES CARIATIDES, livre 3, no. XVII.
Les lilas (1882) [Jobert, 1984] "O floraison divine des lilas"
HYMNIS.
Il dort encore (188_) [Jobert, 1984] same
ODELETTES.
Aimons-nous et dormons (ca.1881) [unpubl.] same
LES STALACTITES.
Souhait (1881) [Jobert, 1984] "Oh! quand la mort que rien ne saurait apaiser"
LES STALACTITES. La Dernière Pensée de Weber.
Nuit d'étoiles (1880) [E. Bulla, 1882; E. Coutarel, 1907, 1910] same
Baudelaire, Charles Pierre, 1821-1867.
FLEURS DU MAL.
Le Balcon (1888) [Librairie de l'Art Indépendant (Bailly), 1890; Durand, 1902] "Mère des souvenirs"

COMPOSER Poet *Title* "First Line"

DEBUSSY, CLAUDE, 1862-1918
(continued)
Baudelaire, Charles Pierre, 1821-1867
(continued)
Harmonie du soir (1889)
[Librairie de l'Art Indépendant
(Bailly), 1890; Durand, 1902]
"Voici venir les temps où vibrant
sur sa tige"
Le Jet d'eau (1889)
[Librairie de l'Art Indépendant
(Bailly), 1890; Durand, 1902]
"Tes beaux yeux sont las"
La Mort des amants (1887)
[Librairie de l'Art Indépendant
(Bailly), 1890; Durand, 1902]
"Nous aurons des lits pleins
d'odeurs légères"
Recueillement (ca.1888)
[Librairie de l'Art Indépendant
(Bailly), 1890; Durand, 1902]
"Sois sage, Ô ma Douleur"
Bouchor, Maurice, 1855-1929.
Chanson triste (ca.1883) [unpubl.]
"On entend un chant sur l'eau dans la
brume"
*LES POÈMES DE L'AMOUR ET DE LA
MER* (1876).
Fleur des eaux (ca.1883) [unpubl.]
Bourget, Paul Charles Joseph, 1852-
1935.
Romance: Voici que le printemps (1884)
[Société Nouvelle d'Editions
musicales, 1907] "Voici que le
printemps, ce fils léger d'Avril"
Also published by Paul Dupont
(later Eschig), 1907, 1947.
LES AVEUX.
L'âme évaporée (1891) [Durand, 1906]
"L'âme évaporée et souffrante"
Les cloches (1891) [Durand, 1891;
Eschig, 1907] "Les feuilles
s'ouvraient sur le bord des branches"
LES AVEUX: Amour.
Musique (1883) [Salabert, 1980, 1983]
"La lune se levait, pure, mais plus
glacée"
Paysage sentimental (1883)
[**Revue illustrée,** 15 avril 1891; Soc.
Nouvelle, 1907] "Le ciel d'hiver,
si doux, si triste, si dormant"
Also published by Paul Dupont
(later Eschig), 1907, 1947.
Regret: Devant le ciel (1884) [Salabert,
1983]
"Devant le ciel d'été, tiède et calme"

LES AVEUX: Romance.
Romance, musique pour éventail
(1883) [Salabert, 1980, 1983]
"Silence ineffable de l'heure"
LES AVEUX: Souvenirs du Nord, no. 5.
La Romance d'Ariel (1884) [Salabert,
1983]
"Au long de ces montagnes douces"
LES AVEUX: Souvenirs du Nord, no. 7.
Beau soir (ca.1880) [Girod, 1891;
Fromont; Ditson, 1913]
"Lorsque au soleil couchant les
riviéres sont roses"
Charles, Duke of Orleans, 1391-
1465.
Pour ce que plaisance est morte (1904)
[Durand, 1904] same
Le temps a laissié son manteau (1904)
[Durand, 1904] same
Cros, Charles, 1842-1888.
LE COFFRET DE SANTAL, chansons
perpétuelles (1873).
L'archet (ca.1883) [unpubl.]
"Elle avait de beaux cheveux"
Debussy, Claude, 1862-1918.
De fleurs (1893) [Fromont, 1895]
"Dans l'ennui si désolément vert de la
serre de douleur"
De grève (1892) [Fromont, 1895]
"Sur la mer les crépuscules tombent"
De rêve (1892) [Fromont, 1895]
"La nuit a des douceurs de femme"
De soir (1893) [Fromont, 1895]
"Dimanche sur le villes, dimanche
dans les coeurs"
*Noël des enfants qui n'ont plus de
maisons* (1915) [Durand, 1915]
"Nous n'avons plus de maisons!"
Arranged for children's chorus, 2 parts
with piano (1916).
Nuits blanches (1899-1902) [lost]
"Tout à l'heure ses mains plus
délicates"
Gautier, Théophile, 1811-1872.
EMAUX ET CAMÉES.
Coquetterie posthume (1883) [Salabert,
1980] "Quand je mourrai, que l'on
me mette"
ESPAÑA.
Séguidille (ca.1881)
[holograph in Piatigorsky collection;
cf. RISM C/I rev.]
"Un jupon serré sur les hanches"
Girod, André
Fleur des blés (ca.1880) [Girod, 1891;
Leduc, 1919]
"Le long des blés que la brise"

Gravollet, Paul
  Dans le jardin (1891) [Hamelle, 1905]
    "Je regardais dans le jardin"
Guinand, Édouard, b. 1838.
  *AU COURANT DE LA VIE. STANCES,
    SONNETS, POÈMES* (1885).
    Barcarolle (ca.1885) [unpubl.]
    "Viens! l'heure est procice"
Hyspa, Vincent, 1865-1938.
  La Belle au bois dormant (1890)
    [Société Nouvelle d'Editions
    musicales; Dupont (Eschig), 1902]
    "Des trous à son pourpoint
      vermeil"
Leconte de Lisle, Charles Marie René,
  1818-1894.
  POÈMES ANTIQUES.
    La fille aux cheveux de lin (ca.1882)
      [unpubl.] "Sur la luzerne en fleur"
    Jane (ca.1881) [T.Presser, 1982]
      "Je pâlis et tombe en langeur"
LeRoy, Grégoire, 1862-1941.
  LA CHANSON DU PAUVRE . . .
    Les Angélus (1891) [Hamelle, 1891]
      "Cloches chrétiennes pour les
        matines"
Louÿs, Pierre, 1870-1925.
  CHANSONS DE BILITIS.
    Le chevelure (1897) [Fromont,
      1899]
      "Il m'a dit: Cette nuit, j'ai rêve"
    La flûte de Pan (1897) [Fromont,
      1899]
      "Pour le jour des Hyacinthies"
    Le tombeau des Naïdes (1897)
      [Fromont, 1899]"Le long du bois
      couvert de givre je marchais"
Mallarmé, Stéphane, 1842-1898.
  Apparition (1884) [**Revue Musicale**, Mai
    1926; Jobert, 1969]
    "La lune s'attristait"
    Mallarmé's text published in "la revue
    Lutèce (24-30 Nov 1883)."
  Éventail (1913) [Durand, 1913]
    "O rêveuse, pour que je plonte"
  Placet futile (1913) [Durand, 1913]
    "Princesse! à jalouser le destin d'une
      Hébé"
  Soupir (1913) [Durand, 1913]
    "Mon âme vers ton front où rêve"
Musset, Alfred de, 1810-1857.
  CONTES D'ESPAGNE ET D'ITALIE.
    Ballade à la lune (1878) [lost]
      "C'était dans la nuit brune"
    Madrid, Princesse des Espagnes
      (1878) [lost] same

POÉSIES NOUVELLES (1842).
  Rondeau (1882) [Schott, 1932; Eschig,
    1932] "Fut-il jamais douceur de
    coeur pareille"
Peter, René
  Berceuse (1899) [unpubl.]
    "Il était une fois une fée qui avait un
      beau sceptre"
Renaud, Armand, 1836-1895.
  NUITS PERSANES (1870).
    Flots, palmes, sables (1882) [unpubl.]
      "Loin des yeux du monde"
Tristan L'Hermite François, 1601-1655.
  Crois mon conseil (1910) [Durand, 1910]
    same
  La grotte (1904) [Durand, 1904]
    "Auprès de cette grotte sombre"
  Je tremble en voyant ton visage (1910)
    [Durand, 1910] same
Valade, Léon, 1841-1884.
  *NOCTURNES, POÈMES IMITÉS DE H.
    HEINE.*
    Tragédie (ca.1881) [unpubl.]
      "Les petites fleurs n'ont pu vivre"
Verlaine, Paul, 1844-1896.
  L'échelonnement des haies (1891)
    [Hamelle, 1901; Fromont, 1907] same
  Il pleure dans mon coeur (1887) [Girod,
    1888; Fromont, 1903, 1913] same
  La mer est plus belle (1891) [Hamelle,
    1901] same
  AQUARELLES.
    Green (1886) [Girod, 1888; Fromont,
      1903, 1913] "Voici des fruits, des
      fleurs, des feuilles et des branches"
    Spleen (1888) [Girod, 1888; Fromont,
      1903, 1913]
      "Les roses étaient toules rouges"
  FÊTES GALANTES.
    Clair de lune (1882) [**Revue Musicale**,
      Mai 1926; Jobert, 1969]
      "Votre âme est un paysage choisi"
    Clair de lune (1892) [Fromont, 1903]
      "Votre âme est un paysage choisi"
      2nd version.
    Colloque sentimental (1904) [Durand,
      1904] "Dans le vieux parc solitaire
      et glacé"
    En sourdine (1882) [Elkan-Vogel,
      1944] "Calmes dans le demi-jour"
    En sourdine (1892) [Fromont, 1903]
      "Calmes dans le demi-jour"
      2nd version.
    Fantoches (1882)
      [Fromont; **Revue Musicale**, Mai
      1926; Zen-on Music, 197_]
      "Scaramouche et Pulcinella"

DEBUSSY, CLAUDE, 1862-1918
(continued)
 Verlaine, Paul, 1844-1896 *(continued)*
  FÊTES GALANTES. (continued)
   Fantoches (1892?) [Fromont, 1903]
    "Scaramouche et Pulcinella"
    2nd version.
   Le faune (1904) [Durand, 1904]
    "Un vieux faune de terre cuite"
   Les Ingénus (1904) [Durand, 1904]
    "Les hauts talons luttaient avec les
     longues jupes"
   Mandoline (1882) [Durand, 1905]
    "Les donneurs de sérénades"
    2nd version, 1883, published in
     Revue illustrée and by Durand,
     1890.
   Pantomime (1882)
    [***Revue Musicale,*** Mai 1926; Jobert,
     1969; Peters, 1974]
    "Pierrot qui n'a rien d'un Clitandre"
  PAYSAGES BELGES.
   Chevaux de bois (1885) [Girod, 1888;
    Fromont, 1903, 1913] "Tournez,
    tournez, bons chevaux de bois"
  ROMANCES SANS PAROLES.
   C'est l'extase langoureuse (1887)
    [Girod, 1888; Fromont, 1903, 1913]
    same
   L'ombre des arbres (1888) [Girod,
    1888; Fromont, 1903, 1913] same
  SAGESSE.
   Le son du cor s'afflige (1891)
    [Hamelle, 1901; Fromont, 1907]
    "Le son du cor s'afflige vers les
     bois"
 Villon, François, b.1431.
  LE TESTAMENT.
   Ballade de Villon à s'amye (1910)
    [Durand, 1910] "Faulse beauté, qui
    tant me couste cher"
   Ballade des femmes de Paris (1910)
    [Durand, 1910] "Quoy qu'on tient
    belles langagières"
   *Ballade que Villon feit à requeste de
    sa mère . . .* (1910) [Durand, 1910]
    "Dame du ciel, regente terrienne"
Debussy, Claude, 1862-1918.
 DEBUSSY
  De fleurs
  De grève
  De rêve
  De soir
  *Noël des enfants qui n'ont plus de
   maisons*
  Nuits blanches

December see San Geminiano **IVES**
December night see Lawrence **RIETI**
Décembre see Claudel **MILHAUD**
Déception see Collin **CHAÏKOVSKIǐ**
Déclaration see Chouquet **MASSENET**
Déclaration see Giraud, Henri **AUBERT**
Le déclin see Rodès **BLOCH**
Déclin d'amour see Sully-Prudhomme
 KOECHLIN
"Ded, podniavshis' spozaranku" *see Zima*
 Pleshcheyev **CHAÏKOVSKIǐ**
Dedans Paris, ville jolie . . . see Marot
 RIVIER
Dédicace see Leclère, translator
 SHÉHÉRAZADE. **KOECHLIN**
Dedication see Sidney, Sir Philip
 ASTROPHEL AND STELLA (1591): First
 song. **HESELTINE**
"Dee abwärts kam Inveraye" *see Gordon von*
 Brakley Cunningham **JENSEN**
Defamation see Tagore **MILHAUD**
Defiled is my name see Anne Boleyn
 ROREM
Defuncta nascuntur see Van Ormelingen
 GLOSES ORPHIQUES. **MASSENET**
Defuncto Herode see Bible **HINDEMITH**
Deh, pietoso, oh addolorata see Goethe
 FAUST. **VERDI**
Deharme, Lise, d. 1990.
 SAUGUET *Je suis heureuse*
Dehmel, Richard, 1863-1920.
 PFITZNER
  Der Arbeitsmann
  Die stille Stadt
  Venus mater
 REGER
  Jetzt und immer
  Die Liebe
  Waldseligkeit
  Wiegenlied
 SCHOECK *Manche Nacht*
 SCHÖNBERG
  Erhebung
  Erwartung
  Schenk mir deinen goldenen Kamm
  Warnung
 SIBELIUS
  Aus banger Brust
  Die stille Stadt
 STRAUSS
  Der Arbeitsmann
  Befreit
  Leises Lied
  Lied an meinen Sohn
  Mein Auge
  Stiller Gang

Waldseligkeit
Wiegenliedchen
SZYMANOWSKI
 Auf See
 Aufblick
 Enführung
 Geheimnis
 Hoch in der Frühe
 Manche Nacht
 Nach einem Regen
 Stimme im Dunkeln
 Verkündigung
 Werbung
WEBERN
 Aufblick
 Nachtgebet der Braut
ABER DIE LIEBE.
 WEBERN *Nächtliche Scheu*
ERLÖSUNGEN.
 SCHÖNBERG
  Mädchenfrühling
  Nicht doch!
 WEBERN *Tief von fern*
IM ZWIELICHT.
 SCHÖNBERG *Alles*
DIE VERWANDLUNGEN DER VENUS:
 Venus Mater.
 REGER, STRAUSS *Wiegenlied*
WEIB UND WELT.
 REGER *Helle Nacht*
 SCHÖNBERG *Mannesbangen*
 STRAUSS *Am Ufer*
 WEBERN
  Am Ufer
  Helle Nacht
  Himmelfahrt
  Ideale Landschaft
Dein Angesicht see Heine **SCHUMANN**
Dein Auge see Branco **LOEWE**
Dein Auge see Dahn **REGER**
Dein Auge ist mein Himmel see Scholz, B.
 LASSEN
Dein Bild see Jacobowski **REGER**
Dein Bildnis see Cornelius **CORNELIUS**
"Dein Bildniss wunderselig hab' ich im
 Herzens grund" *see Intermezzo*
 Eichendorff **SCHUMANN**
Dein blaues Auge see Groth *HUNDERT*
 BLÄTTER . . . **BRAHMS**
"Dein Gedenken lebt in Liedern fort" *see*
 Treue Cornelius **CORNELIUS**
"Dein Herzlein mild" *see Ueber Nacht* Heyse
 JENSEN
"Dein Leben schliesst, dein Ruhm begann"
 see Saul Byron **LOEWE**

"Dein Liebesfeuer, ach Herr!" *see Seufzer*
 Mörike **WOLF**
"Dein Lied erklang! Ich hab' es gehört!" *see*
 Als mir dein Lied erklang Brentano
 STRAUSS
Dein Rat ist wohl gut see Bjørnson
 FISKERJENTEN. **GRIEG** *Takk for dit råd*
"Dein Schwert, wie ist's von Blut so rot" *see*
 Ein altschottische Ballade Herder
 SCHUBERT
"Dein Schwert, wie ist's von Blut so rot" *see*
 Edward Herder **JENSEN**
"Dein Schwert, wie ist's von Blut so roth" *see*
 Edward Herder **LOEWE**
"Dein Silber schien durch Eichengrün" *see*
 Klage Hölty **BEETHOVEN**
"Dein Silber schien durch Eichengrün" *see*
 Klage an den Mond Hölty **SCHUBERT**
"Dein süsses Bild, Edone" *see Edone*
 Klopstock **SCHUBERT**
"Dein Tag ist aus, dein Ruhm fing an" *see*
 Dem Helden Byron **SCHUMANN**
"Dein Wille geschehe" *see Vater unser IV*
 Cornelius **CORNELIUS**
Dein Wille, Herr, geschehe! see Eichendorff
 REGER
"Deine Finger rühren die Saiten, und die
 Saiten mein Herz" *see Fatima beim*
 Saitenspiel Bodenstedt **SPOHR**
"Dcinc Freuden, deine Leiden zähle nicht von
 Tag" *see Das Ganze, nicht das Einzelne*
 Rückert **HINDEMITH**
"Deine gewälbten Brauen" *see Ihre Augen*
 Hafiz **STRAUSS**
Deine Mutter, süsses Kind see Luis el Chico,
 Don **WOLF**
Deine Rosen an der Brust see Morgenstern
 KILPINEN
"Deine Seele hat die meine einst so wunderbar
 berührt" *see An dich* Itzerott **REGER**
"Deine Stimme lass ertönen" *see Ali im*
 Garten Stieglitz **LOEWE**
Deine weissen Lilienfinger see Heine
 FRANZ
Deinem Blick mich zu bequemen see Goethe
 WESTÖSTLICHER DIVAN.
 SCHÖNBERG
"Deinem Blick mich zu bequemen" *see*
 Suleika Goethe **SCHOECK**
"Deinem sanft flötenden Ton" *see An die*
 Nachtigall Schmidt, F. **LOEWE**
"Deiner bunten Blasen Kinderfreude" *see Tod*
 und Dichter Keller, G. **SCHOECK**
"Deiner gedenk ich im Reden und Schweigen"
 see Mein Alles du Ernst **LASSEN**
"Deiner Liebe goldene Güte trägst du
 lächelnd" *see Reinheit* Boelitz **REGER**

COMPOSER Poet *Title* ''First Line''

Deinhardstein, Johann Ludwig
Ferdinand von, 1794-1859.
SCHUBERT *Skolie*
SPOHR *Lied des verlassenen Mädchens*
"Dej mně, Bože, ten dar" *see Prosba* Anon.
MARTINŮ
"Déjà les beaux jours" *see Avril* . . . Gérard
de Nerval **AURIC**
Dejection see Tiutchev **MEDTNER**
Déjeuner de soleil see Radiguet **AURIC**
Dejte klec jestřábu see Heyduk **DVOŘÁK**
Dekker, Thomas, 1570-1641.
IRELAND *The merry month of May*
QUILTER *O, the month of May*
*THE PLEASANT COMOEDY OF PATIENT
GRISSILL* (1603).
HESELTINE
Lullaby
Sweet content
"Del sonno tra i fantasimi di te sognavo" *see
Serenata indiana* Shelley **RESPIGHI**
"Del tuo celeste foco eterno Iddio un core
accendi" *see Il preghiera del poeta* Sole
VERDI
Delair, Paul, 1842-1894.
MASSENET *L'âme des fleurs*
La délaissée see Blanchecotte **HAHN**
Deland, Margaret Wade (Campbell),
1857-1945.
MACDOWELL
The blue-bell
The clover
The mignonette
The myrtle
The pansy
The yellow daisy
Delaporte, R. P.
INDY *Les noces d'Or du Sacerdoce*
Delaquys, Georges, b. 1880
BOULANGER *Le retour*
Delavigne, Jean François Casimir, 1793-
1843.
BIZET *Vous ne priez pas*
ROSSINI
Les adieux à Rome
L'âme délaissée
Delfosse, Bernard
FRANCK *Les trois exiles*
DELIBES, LÉO, 1836-1891.
Anon.
Le rossignol [G. Hartmann, later Heugel]
"Ecoutez la chanson"
Mezzo-soprano & piano.
Augier, Emile, 1820-1889.
LE DÉPART.
Départ [G. Hartmann, later Heugel]
"Je veux oublier"
Tenor & piano.

Belleau, Rémy, 1527?-1577.
Avril [G. Hartmann, later Heugel]
"Avril, la gràce et le ris De Cypris"
Originally a cappella chorus; included
in his *15 Melodies.*
Borrelli, Raymond, vicomte de, b.
1837.
Faut-il chanter? [Heugel]
"L'oiseau m'a dit"
Fuchs, Paul
Chrysanthème [Heugel]
"Comme l'hirondelle effleurant la rive"
Gille, Philippe Emile François, 1831-
1901.
Chant de l'almée [G. Hartmann, later
Heugel] "Dismoi, jeune captive"
Soprano & piano.
Grenier, Édouard, 1819-1901.
Épithalame [Heugel] "Quand les bruns
matelots des mers orientales"
Hugo, Victor Marie, comte, 1802-
1885.
L'Églogue (1863) [G. Hartmann, later
Heugel] "Viens! une flûte invisible"
Mezzo-soprano or baritone & piano.
LE ROI S'AMUSE.
Vieille chanson (1882) [Heugel]
"Oui, Messieurs, c'est alors"
Voice & mandolin.
Lockroy, Joseph Philippe Simon,
1803-1891.
Chanson de l'oiseleur [G. Hartmann,
later Heugel]
"Un jour, menant ma chevrette"
Tenor & piano.
Musset, Alfred de, 1810-1857.
Bonjour, Suzon! (1863) [G. Hartmann,
later Heugel]
"Bonjour, Suzon, ma fleur des bois!"
Tenor or soprano & piano.
Les filles de Cadix (1874) [G. Hartmann,
later Heugel]
"Nous venions de voir le taureau"
Soprano & piano.
A QUOI RÊVENT LES JEUNES FILLES.
Sérénade à Ninon [Heugel] "Ninon,
Ninon, que fais-tu de la vie?"
Voice & mandolin or harp.
BARBERINE.
*Beau chevalier qui partez pour la
guerre* (1882) [Heugel] same
Voice & harp.
Petöfi, Sándor, 1823-1849.
Chanson hongroise [Heugel]
"J'ai bu deux flacons"
Text adapted by Coppée.

COMPOSER Poet *Title* ''First Line''

Renaut, J
À ma mignonne [Heugel]
"Mignonne, viens voir, ce soir"
Silvestre, Paul Armond, 1837-1901.
Arioso [G. Hartmann, later Heugel] "
Ô mer, ouvre-toi"
Mezzo-soprano & piano.
Blanche et Rose [G. Hartmann, later
Heugel]
"Blanche sous sa robe blanche"
Tenor & piano.
Heure du soir [G. Hartmann, later
Heugel]
"Sur les grands bois noyés de brume"
Tenor & piano.
Myrto [G. Hartmann, later Heugel]
"Myrto ne sait pas de chansons"
Mezzo-soprano & piano.
Peine d'amour [G. Hartmann, later
Heugel] "Je lui rends la rose fletrie"
Regrets! [G. Hartmann, later Heugel]
"Jours passés, Ô jeunesse envolée"
Tenor or mezzo-soprano & piano.
MIGNONNE.
Que l'heure est donc brève! [G.
Hartmann, later Heugel] same
Tenor & piano.
Sully-Prudhomme, René François
Armand, 1839-1907.
Le meilleur moment des amours (1872)
[G. Hartmann, later Heugel] same
DELIUS, FREDERICK, 1862-1934.
Andersen, Hans Christian, 1805-1875.
Zwei braune Augen (1885) [unpubl.]
Bjørnson, Bjornstjerne, 1832-1910.
Abendstimmung (1889-90) [Augener,
1892; Tischer & Jagenberg, 1910;
Oxford Univ. Press, 1930]
"Es sass die Prinzessin im
Frauengemach"
7 Lieder aus dem Norwegischen,
no. 3
Der Schlaf (1888) [Augener, 1890;
Stainer & Bell, 1973]
"Das Kindlein schlief ein"
5 Lieder aus dem Norwegischen, no. 1
Skogen gir susende, langsom besked
(1890-91) [Universal-Edition, 1981]
same
Verborg'ne Liebe (1889-90) [Augener,
1892; Tischer & Jagenberg, 1910;
Oxford Univ. Press, 1930]
"Er schlich sich die Wände entlang"
ARNE.
Kleine Venevil (1889-90) [Augener,
1892; Tischer & Jagenberg,
1910; Oxford Univ. Press, 1930]

"Kleine Venevil hüpfte mit leichtem
Sinn"
Over the mountains high (1885)
[Fac. ed. in Rachel Lowe *Cat. of ...*
Delius Trust, 116-17]
Bunn, Alfred, 1796?-1860.
THE BOHEMIAN GIRL.
When other lips shall speak (ca.1880)
[unpubl.]
Drachmann, Holger Henrik Herholdt,
1846-1908.
Dreamy nights (1891) [Stainer & Bell,
1973] "On shore how still, all nature
seems asleep"
In bliss we walked with laughter (1898)
[Universal-Edition, 1981] same
Jeg hører i natten (1901) [Universal-
Edition, 1981] same
Summer landscape (1902) [Oxford Univ.
Press, 1952, 1970]
"The sun is at rest: its rays are gone"
LYSE NAETTER.
Summer nights (1897) [Stainer & Bell,
1973] "No leaflet stirs upon the
silent shore"
Also voice & orchestra.
Geibel, Emanuel, i.e., Franz Emanuel
August, 1815-1884.
O schneller mein Ross (1888)
[L. Grus fils, 1896; withdrawn from
circulation]
Heine, Heinrich, 1797-1856.
Aus deinen Augen fliessen meine Lieder
(1890-91) [unpubl.] same
Hör' ich das Liedchen klingen (1890-91)
[unpubl.]
Mit deinen blauen Augen (1890-91)
[Fac. ed. in Threlfall *Catalogue ...,*
102]
*Ein schöner Stern geht auf in meiner
Nacht* (1890-91)
[Fac. ed. in Threlfall *Catalogue ...,*
102-3]
BUCH DER LIEDER.
Der Fichtenbaum (1886) [unpubl.]
Heinitz, Marie
Traum rosen (ca.1898) [*Delius Society
Journal,* April 1976]
"Dunkle, schwüle Sommernacht"
Henley, William Ernest, 1849-1903.
LIFE & DEATH (Echoes).
The nightingale has a lyre of gold
(1908 or 1910)
[Tischer & Jagenberg, 1915;
Oxford Univ. Press, 1930, 1970]
same

DELIUS, FREDERICK, 1862-1934
(continued)
Herrick, Robert, 1591-1674.
  HESPERIDES.
    To daffodils (1915)
      [Winthrop Rogers, 1919; Boosey &
      Hawkes, 1952] "Fair daffodils, we
      weep to see you haste away so
      soon"
Holstein, Ludvig Ditlef, greve, 1864-
1943.
  Herbst (1900) [Harmonie-Verlag, 1906;
    Universal-Ed., 1921;
    Boosey & Hawkes, 1952]
    "Vater, wo fliegen die Schwänehin?"
  Das Veilchen (1900) [Harmonie-Verlag,
    1906; Universal-Ed., 1921;
    Boosey & Hawkes, 1952]
    "Mein Blümchenklein"
Ibsen, Henrik, 1828-1906.
  Hochgebirgsleben (1888)
    [Fac. ed. in Rachel Lowe *Cat. of . . .*
      Delius Trust, 118-19]
    "Nun ruht der Sommerabend lind"
  EN FUGLEVISE.
    Eine Vogelweise (1889-90) [Augener,
      1892; Tischer & Jagenberg, 1910;
      Oxford Univ. Press, 1930]
      "Wir gingen an einem Maientag in
      schattiger Allee"
  KONGS-EMNERNE.
    Wiegenlied (1889-90) [Augener, 1892;
      Tischer & Jagenberg, 1910; Oxford
      Univ. Press, 1930]
      "Nun hebt sich Dach und Dekke
      zum Sternenhimmel auf"
  SPILLEMAEND.
    Spielleute (1889-90) [Augener, 1892;
      Tischer & Jagenberg, 1910;
      Oxford Univ. Press, 1930]
      "Zu ihr stand all mein Sehnen"
Jacobsen, Jens Peter, 1847-1885.
  The page sat in the lofty tower (1895?)
    [Stainer & Bell, 1973] same
  Through long, long years (1897)
    [Stainer & Bell, 1973] same
    Also voice & orchestra.
  I SERAILLETS HAVE.
    In the seraglio garden (1897)
      [Harmonie-Verlag, 1906;
      Universal-Ed., 1921; Boosey &
      Hawkes, 1952]
      "With perfume heavily laden the
      roses droop their heads"
      Also voice & orchestra.

IRMELIN ROSE.
  Irmelin (1897) [Harmonie-Verlag,
    1906; Universal-Ed., 1921;
    Boosey & Hawkes, 1952]
    "There was a King in days of
    old"
    Also voice & orchestra.
LAD VAAREN KOMME.
  Let springtime come then (1897)
    [Tischer & Jagenberg, 1915;
    Oxford Univ. Press, 1930] same
    Also voice & orchestra.
LØFT DE KLINGRE GLASPOKALER.
  Wine roses (1897) [Stainer & Bell, 1973]
    "Lift on high & clink the glasses"
    Also voice & orchestra.
SILKESKO OVER GYLDEN LAEST.
  Silken shoes (1897) [Harmonie-Verlag,
    1906; Universal-Ed., 1921;
    Boosey & Hawkes, 1952]
    "Silken shoes upon golden lasts!"
    Also voice & orchestra.
Jonson, Ben, 1573?-1637.
  UNDERWOODS.
    So white, so soft, so sweet is she
      (1915) [Winthrop Rogers, 1919;
      Boosey & Hawkes, 1952]
      "Have you seen but a white lily
      grow"
Josephson, Ernst Abraham, 1851-
1906.
  SVARTA ROSOR OCH GULA.
    Schwarze Rosen (1901) [Tischer &
      Jagenberg, 1915; Oxford Univ.
      Press, 1930, 1970]
      "Sag, warum bist du so traurig
      heut?"
Kjerulf, Theodor, 1825-1888.
  LAENGSEL.
    Sehnsucht (1888) [Augener, 1890;
      Stainer & Bell, 1973]
      "Schnell fliegt der Aar am Himmel
      hell"
      5 Lieder aus dem Norwegischen,
      no. 4
Krag, Vilhelm Andreas Wexels, 1871-
1933.
  Jeg havde en nyskaaren seljefløjte (1892-
    93) [Universal-Edition, 1981] same
Munch, Andreas, 1811-1884.
  SOLNEDGANG.
    Beim Sonnenuntergang (1888)
      [Augener, 1890; Stainer & Bell,
      1973] "Nun sinkt hinab die Sonne"
      5 Lieder aus dem Norwegischen, no. 5

COMPOSER Poet *Title* "First Line"

Musset, Alfred de, 1810-1857.
LE CHANDELIER.
  Chanson de Fortunio (1889)
    [Fac. ed. in Lionel Carley
    Delius . . . , 87-89]
Nashe, Thomas, 1567-1601.
*SUMMER'S LAST WILL AND
  TESTAMENT* (1600).
  Spring, the sweet Spring (1915)
    [Winthrop Rogers, 1919;
    Boosey & Hawkes, 1952] same
Nietzsche, Friedrich Wilhelm, 1844-
1900.
DIE FRÖHLICHE WISSENSCHAFT.
  Der Einsame (1898)
    [Universal-Edition, 1924; Boosey &
    Hawkes, 1952] "Verhasst ist mir
    das Folgen und das Führen"
  Nach neuen Meeren (1898)
    [Universal-Edition, 1924; Boosey &
    Hawkes, 1952] "Dorthin will ich;
    und ich traue mir fortan und
    meinem Griff"
  Der Wanderer (1898)
    [Universal-Edition, 1924; Boosey &
    Hawkes, 1952] "Kein Pfad mehr"
*MENSCHLICHES,
  ALLZUMENSCHLICHES.*
  Der Wanderer und sein Schatten
    (1898) [Universal-Edition, 1924;
    Boosey & Hawkes, 1952]
    "Nicht mehr zurück?"
Paulsen, John Olaf, 1851-1924.
*JEG REISTE ENDEILIG
  SOMMERKVAELD.*
  Am schönsten Sommerabend war's
    (1888) [Augener, 1890; Stainer &
    Bell, 1973] same
    5 Lieder aus dem Norwegischen, no.
    3
Richepin, Jean, 1849-1926.
  Nuages (1893) [Fac. ed. in Lionel Carley
    Delius . . . , 90-92]
    "Nuages, nuages que . . . "
Shakespeare, William, 1564-1616.
AS YOU LIKE IT.
  It was a lover and his lass (1916)
    [Winthrop Rogers, 1919; Boosey &
    Hawkes, 1952] same
Sharp, William, 1885-1905.
THE HOUR OF BEAUTY.
  I-Brasil (1913)
    [Tischer & Jagenberg, 1915; Oxford
    Univ. Press, 1930, 1970] "There's
    sorrow on the wind, my grief"

Shelley, Percy Bysshe, 1792-1822.
  Love's philosophy (1891) [Augener,
    1892; Tischer & Jagenberg;
    Oxford Univ. Press, 1930]
    "The fountains mingle with the
    river"
  To the queen of my heart (1891)
    [Augener, 1892; Tischer & Jagenberg;
    Oxford Univ. Press, 1930]
    "Shall we roam, my love, to the
    twilight grove"
    Authenticity of text doubtful.
THE INDIAN SERENADE.
  Indian love song (1891) [Augener,
    1892; Tischer & Jagenberg;
    Oxford Univ. Press, 1930]
    "I arise from dreams of Thee"
Verlaine, Paul, 1844-1896.
  Il pleure dans mon coeur (1895) [L.
    Grus, 1896; Tischer & Jagenberg,
    1910; Oxford Univ. Press, 1930] same
LA BONNE CHANSON.
  Avant que tu ne t'en ailles (1919)
    [Boosey & Hawkes, 1932, 1952]
    same
  La lune blanche (1910) [Tischer &
    Jagenberg, 1910; Oxford Univ.
    Press, 1930, 1970]
    "La lune blanche luit dans les
    bois"
POÈMES SATURNIENS.
  Chanson d'automne (1911) [Tischer &
    Jagenberg, 1915; Oxford Univ.
    Press, 1930, 1970] "Les sangelots
    longs des violons de l'automne"
SAGESSE.
  Le ciel est, par-dessus la toit (1895)
    [*L'Aube,* 1896; Tischer &
    Jagenberg, 1910; Oxford, 1930]
    same
Vinje, Aasmund Olavsson, 1818-1870.
FERDAMINNI.
  Auf der Reise zur Heimat (1889-90)
    [Augener, 1892; Tischer &
    Jagenberg, 1910; Oxford Univ.
    Press, 1930] "Nun seh' ich meine
    Berg' und Täler wieder"
Welhaven, Johann Sebastian
  Cammermeyer, 1807-1873.
  Sing, sing (1888) [Augener, 1890;
    Stainer & Bell, 1973]
    "Sing, sing Nachtigall Du"
    5 Lieder aus dem Norwegischen, no. 2
delle Grazie, Maria Eugenia *see*
  Grazie, Marie Eugenie delle, 1864-
  1931.
Delphine see Schütz *LACRIMAS.*
SCHUBERT

COMPOSER Poet *Title* "First Line"

La delphinium see Claudel HONEGGER
Delpit, Albert, 1849-1893.
  GOUNOD
    Chanter et souffrir
    Je ne puis espérer
  LALO *Chant Breton*
Dem Allmächtigen see Rückert LOEWE
"Dem Armen, dem niemals die Freude
  gelacht" *see Engelgesang* Hertz, H.
  JENSEN
"Dem Auge fern, dem Herzen han!" *see*
  Grabschrift Jacobowski BERG
"Dem bist du Kind" *see Kunfttag I* George
  WEBERN
Dem Dreieinigen see Klopstock LOEWE
Dem Ew'gen see Fink *HÄUSLICHEN*
  ANDACHTEN. LOEWE
"Dem Ew'gen unsre Lieder!" *see Dem Ew'gen*
  Fink LOEWE
Dem Helden see Byron *HEBREW*
  MELODIES. SCHUMANN
Dem Herrscher see Bartholdy, Dr. LOEWE
Dem Herzen ähnlich see Schack STRAUSS
"Dem hohen Kaiser-Worte treu" *see Beim*
  Auszug in das Feld Unknown MOZART
Dem Könige see Hildebrandt LOEWE
Dem Lenz soll mein Lied erklingen see
  Bjørnson *FISKERJENTEN.* GRIEG
    Jeg giver mit digt til våren
Dem rothen Röslein gleicht mein Lieb see
  Burns SCHUMANN
DEM SCHMERZ SEIN RECHT. see Hebbel
    Schlafen, schlafen BERG
    Schlafen, schlafen, nichts als schlafen
    SCHOECK
"Dem Schnee, dem Regen" *see Rastlose Liebe*
  Goethe FRANZ, SCHOECK,
  SCHUBERT, ZELTER
Dem Unendlichen see Klopstock
  SCHUBERT
"Dem Vater liegt das Kind im Arm" *see*
  Der Vater mit dem Kind Bauernfeld
  SCHUBERT
Dem Vaterland see Reinick WOLF
Demain fera un an qu'à Audaux see
  Jammes *TRISTESSES.*
  BOULANGER, MILHAUD
Demande see Forestier, J. SCHMITT
Demanten på marssnön see Wecksell
  SIBELIUS
*DEMOFOONTE. see*Metastasio
    Misero pargoletto SCHUBERT
"Démon au sourire angélique" *see Fête*
  nationale Chabaneix IBERT
Démon des mains, parfait visage see Birot,
  P. A. SAUGUET

Demouth, Paul
  MASSENET
    Les âmes
    Le nid
"Den Fischer fechten Sorgen" *see*
  Fischerweise Schlechta SCHUBERT
"Den Geborenen schreckt das Licht der Welt"
  see Spruchband Barth KRENEK
Den grünen Zeigern see Lenau
  SCHUMANN
Den Lenz lass kommen see Jacobsen *LAD*
  VAAREN KOMME. DELIUS
    Let springtime come then
Den' li tsarit see Apukhtin CHAÏKOVSKIÏ
"Den Linden ist zu Füssen tief" *see*
  Fahrewohl Keller, G. SCHOECK
"Den Sängling an der Brust" *see Die rothe*
  Hanne Béranger SCHUMANN
"Den Sol, som dukker op i Øst" *see*
  Gudhjaelp Wied NIELSEN
"Den Strauss, den sie gewunden" *see Vergiss*
  mein nicht Osterwald FRANZ
"Den Tag hindurch nur einmal mag ich
  sprechen" *see Memnon* Mayrhofer
  SCHUBERT
"Den Wirbel schlag' ich gar so stark" *see*
  Tambourliedchen Candidus BRAHMS
Den Zweifellosen I see Keller, G.
  SCHOECK
Den Zweifellosen II see Keller, G.
  SCHOECK
Denby, Edward 1903-1983.
  ROREM *First warm days*
Denis, Johann Nepomuk Cosmas
  Michael, 1729-1800.
  MOZART *Gibraltar*
Denk es, O Seele see Mörike PFITZNER,
  WOLF
Denk ich dein! see Förster, M. FRANZ
Denke, denke, mein Geliebter see Chamisso
  JENSEN
"Denke, denke mein Geliebter" *see Tränen*
  Chamisso FRANZ
"Der Denker rechnet wohl einmal" *see Eine*
  Unbekanntschaft Spitteler SCHOECK
DIE DENKMÄLER: Der Reisende oder Die
  Träne. *see* Haringer
    Summermüd SCHÖNBERG
Denkst du an mich? see Cornelius
  CORNELIUS
Denn traut lieb Robin ist all' mein Lust! see
  Shakespeare *HAMLET.* LASSEN
Denn unsere Liebe hat zu heiss geflammt see
  Huch PFITZNER
Dennery, Adolphe Philippe, 1811-1899.
  GOUNOD *Les adieux à la maison*

Denson, Olive M.
  QUILTER *Wild cherry*
Le départ see Apollinaire *LA TÊTE
  ÉTOILÉE.* RIVIER
Départ see Augier *LE DÉPART.* DELIBES,
  GOUNOD
LE DÉPART. see Augier
  Départ DELIBES, GOUNOD
Le départ see Bédat de Monlaur, Pierre
  HONEGGER
Départ see Guérin-Catelin MASSENET
Le départ see Patmore *THE UNKNOWN
  EROS:* Departure. MILHAUD
Le Départ see Régnier ROUSSEL
Départ see Rilke *POÈMES FRANCAIS.*
  BARBER
Le départ see Unknown POULENC
Le départ du mousse see Barbier, Pierre
  GOUNOD
Le dépit de la bergère see Unknown
  BERLIOZ
Depression see Po Chü-i BRITTEN
"Depuis neuf ans et plus dans l'amphore
  scelée" *see Phyllis* Leconte de Lisle
  HAHN
"Depuis un mois, chère exilée" *see Mai*
  Coppée HAHN
Der boede en Mand i Ribe By see Anon.
  NIELSEN
Der du die Menschen lässest sterben see
  Bible MENDELSSOHN-BARTHOLDY
"Der du so lustig rauschtest" *see Auf dem
  Flusse* Müller, Wilhelm SCHUBERT
Der du von dem Himmel bist see Goethe
  WANDRERS NACHTLIED I. LISZT
"Der du von dem Himmel bist" *see
  Wanderers Nachtlied* Goethe PFITZNER,
  WOLF
"Der du von dem Himmel bist" *see Wandrers
  Nachtlied* Goethe LOEWE, MEDTNER,
  SCHUBERT, ZELTER
Der dukker af Disen min Faedrenejord see
  Aakjaer *JYLLAND.* NIELSEN
"Der einst er seine junge sonnige Lieb'
  gebracht" *see Loose* Storm JENSEN
"Der er et herligt Land" *see Poesien*
  Andersen GRIEG
"Der er jo de, som er Ho'de kun" *see
  Digtervise* Benzon GRIEG
Der gaar et stille Tog see Balslev, Harald
  NIELSEN
Der gynger en Båd på Bølge see Benzon
  GRIEG
"D'er Haust. Det ruskar ute med Regn" *see
  Veslemøy ved rokken* Garborg GRIEG
Dér, hvor vi stred og sang see Hostrup
  NIELSEN

Der ich, in Zwischenräumen see Whitman
  HINDEMITH
"Der ich von den Frauen allen bis" *see
  Der Treuergebene* Anon. LOEWE
"Der jag satt i drömmar vid en källa" *see
  Kyssens hopp* Runeberg SIBELIUS
"Der lebt ein Leben wonniglich" *see
  Das Glück der Freundschaft* Unknown
  BEETHOVEN
Der sad en fisker sa tankefuld see Grundtvig
  NIELSEN
"Der sad en Fugl paa Bøgekvist" *see Skovsang*
  Winther GRIEG
Der skreg en Fugl see Krag GRIEG
Der snaekker mødtes see Grundtvig
  NIELSEN
"Der strømmer en Flod" *see Guldfloden*
  Ingemann NIELSEN
"Dereinst, dereinst, Gedanke mein" *see
  Alguna vez* Castillejo JENSEN
Dereinst, dereinst, Gedanke mein see
  Castillejo WOLF
Dereinst, Gedanke mein see Castillejo
  GRIEG; JENSEN *Alguna vez*
Derème, Tristan, 1899-1941.
  IBERT
    Cette grande chambre
    Comme j'allais
    Personne ne saura jamais
    Tiède azur
Derfor kan vort øje Glaedes see Richardt
  NIELSEN
Le dernier mazour see Unknown
  POULENC
Dernier poeme see Desnos POULENC
Dernier voeu see Banville HAHN
La dernière chanson see Lefèbvre
  MASSENET
La dernière feuille see Gautier CHAUSSON
La dernière fleur see Desbordes-Valmore
  SAUGUET
La dernière lettre de Werther à Charlotte see
  Biron MASSENET
Dernières volontés see Veuillot GOUNOD
Déroulède, Paul, 1846-1914.
  GOUNOD *Vive la France*
"Derrière le mur du petit cimetière" *see
  Le petit cimetière* Havet CARPENTER
"Derrière les vallons a peine creusés" *see
  L'horizon* Paliard MILHAUD
"Derrière Murcie en fleurs je connais" *see
  Chanson de marin* Aguet, William
  HONEGGER
"Derweil ich schlafend lag" *see Ein Stündlein
  wohl vor Tag* Mörike FRANZ, WOLF
"Des Abends kann ich nicht schlafen gehn"
  see Gang zur Liebsten Anon. BRAHMS

COMPOSER Poet *Title* "First Line"

"Des Abends Rosen sind abgeblüht" *see*
   Grüssen Jung, Walter **LASSEN**

"Des aloès et des mésanges" *see Portrait*
   d'Henri Rousseau Cocteau **AURIC**

Des Alpenhirten Abschied see Schiller
   STRAUSS

Des Baches Geplauder see Tolstoï
   RUBINSTEIN

Des Baches Wiegenlied see Müller, Wilhelm
   SCHUBERT

"Des Berges Gipfel war erschwungen" *see*
   Der Ferne Lenau **SCHOECK**

Des Bettlers Tochter von Bednall Green see
   Percy *RELIQUES.* **LOEWE**

"Des bons vieux airs très connus" *see*
   Première danse Normand **MASSENET**

Des Buben Schützenlied see Schiller
   WILHELM TELL. **SCHUMANN**

"Des chants, des fleurs et du soleil" *see*
   Les extases Dessirier, Annie
   MASSENET

Des Dichters Abendgang see Uhland
   STRAUSS

Des Dichters Herz see Andersen **GRIEG**
   Du fatter ei Bølgernes evige Gang

Des Dichters letztes Lied see Andersen
   GRIEG *En Digters sidste Sang*

"Des Dorfes heimische Stille that meinem
   trotzigen Sinne weh" *see*
   Die Heimatglokken Urban, Robert
   JENSEN

Des Durstes Erklärung see Fick, K. **REGER**

DES FAHRENDEN SCHÜLERS LIEBEN
UND LEIDEN. see
   Hoffmann von Fallersleben
   Auf der Wanderung **WOLF**
   Ja, die Schönst! **WOLF**

Des Fischers Liebesglück see Leitner
   SCHUBERT

Des fleurs font un broderie see Li-Ho
   ROUSSEL

Des Fräuleins Liebeslauschen see Schlechta
   SCHUBERT *Liebeslauschen*

Des fremden Kindes heiliger Christ see
   Rückert **LOEWE**

Des Fremdlings Abendlied see Schmidt,
   Georg **SCHUBERT** *Der Unglückliche;*
   Der Wanderer

Des Frühlings blaue Augen see Heine
   DIE BLAUEN FRÜHLINGSAUGEN.
   CHAïKOVSKIï *Glazki vecny golubye*

Des Glockenthürmers Töchterlein see
   Rückert **LOEWE**

"Des Glöckleins Schall durchtönt das Tal" *see*
   Abendglöcklein Zusner **WOLF**

"Des gouttes d'eau" *see Aigues-Marines*
   Vivien **AUBERT**

Des Herzens Purpurvogel see Jone
   DIE FREUNDE. **WEBERN**

"Des Himmels frohes Antlitz brannte" *see*
   Aufbruch Lenau **SCHOECK**

"Des jardins de la nuit s'envolent les étoiles"
   see Aurore Silvestre **FAURÉ**

"Des Jünglings Blick erkennt der Liebe
   Zeichen" *see Die Begegnung am*
   Meeresstrand Fick, Heinrich **LOEWE**

Des Jünglings Segen see Jacob, T. **LOEWE**

Des kleinen Friedrichs Geburtstag see
   Schall **MOZART**

Des Knaben Berglied see Uhland
   SCHUMANN

DES KNABEN WUNDERHORN
   BRAHMS
     Liebesklage des Mädchens
     Der Überläufer
     Wiegenlied
   MARTINŮ
     Fourteen little angels
     Little red bootees
     My little angel
     Sleep, infant, sleep
     Thanks to God the Creator
   MENDELSSOHN-BARTHOLDY
     Jagdlied
     Lieblingsplätzchen
   REGER *Hat gesagt- bleibt's nicht dabei*
   SCHÖNBERG *Wie Georg von Frundsberg*
     von sich selber sang
   SCHUMANN
     Die Ammenuhr
     Das Käuzlein
       Two settings: Op. 79 no. 10 and
       another, unpublished setting without
       opus or date.
     Marienwürmchen
   STRAUSS
     Für fünfzehn Pfennige
     Hat gesagt–bleibt's nicht dabei
     Himmelsboten zu Liebchens Himmelbett
     Junggesellenschwur
   SZYMANOWSKI *Christkindleins*
     Wiegenlied

DES KNABEN WUNDERHORN see
   Zuccalmaglio
   Die verlorene Tochter **LOEWE**

DES KNABEN WUNDERHORN: Ablösung.
   see Anon. *Ablösung im Sommer*
   MAHLER

DES KNABEN WUNDERHORN: Abschied für
   immer. *see* Anon. *Aus! Aus!* **MAHLER**

DES KNABEN WUNDERHORN: Der
   Schweizer. *see* Anon.
   Zu Strassburg auf der Schanz **FRANZ,**
   MAHLER

DES KNABEN WUNDERHORN: Drei Reiter am Tor. *see* Anon.
  Scheiden und Meiden **MAHLER**
DES KNABEN WUNDERHORN: Nicht Wiedersehen. *see* Anon.
  Nicht Wiedersehen! **MAHLER**
DES KNABEN WUNDERHORN: Selbstgefühl. *see* Anon. *Selbstgefühl* **MAHLER**
DES KNABEN WUNDERHORN: Starke Einbildungskraft. *see* Anon.
  Starke Einbildungskraft **MAHLER**
DES KNABEN WUNDERHORN: Um die Kinder still und artig zu machen. *see* Anon.
  Um schlimme Kinder artig zu machen **MAHLER**
DES KNABEN WUNDERHORN: Waldvöglein. *see* Anon.
  Ich ging mit Lust durch einen grünen Wald **MAHLER**
Des Königs Zuversicht see Telschow **LOEWE**
Des Kriegers Abschied see Reissig **BEETHOVEN**
Des Künstlers Abschied see Dusch **WEBER**
"Des larmes ont coulé" *see Light* Jean-Aubry **MALIPIERO, ROUSSEL**
"Des Lebens Karawane zieht mit Macht dahin" *see Fünf Sinnsprüche Omars des Zeltmachers* Omar Khayyam **BLACHER**
"Des Lebens Tag ist schwer und schwül" *see Lied* Stolberg **SCHUBERT**
Des Liebsten Schwur, Aus dem Bohmischen see Wenzig *WESTSLAWISCHEM MÄRCHENSCHATZ.* **BRAHMS**
Des Mädchens Klage see Schiller *DIE PICCOLOMINI.*
  MENDELSSOHN-BARTHOLDY, SCHUBERT, ZELTER
    Three Schubert settings: D. 6, D. 191, and D. 389.
Des Mädchens Klage see Schweizer **SPOHR**
Des Mädchens Wunsch und Geständnis see Branco **LOEWE**
"Des Menschen Seele gleicht dem Wasser" *see Gesang der Geister über den Wassern* Goethe **LOEWE, SCHUBERT**
Des Morgens see Hölderlin **HINDEMITH**
Des müden Abendlied see Geibel **FRANZ, GRIFFES**
Des Müllers Blumen see Müller, Wilhelm **SCHUBERT**
"Des noms sont exaltés un à un" *see Quatrain* Jammes **MILHAUD**

"Des Phöbus Strahlen sind dem Aug'entschwunden" *see Zur Namensfeier des Herrn Andreas Siller* Unknown **SCHUBERT**
Des profondeurs de l'abîme see Bible **HONEGGER** *Mimaamaquim*
"Dès que Bakkhos me tient" *see Sur lui-même* Anacreon **ROUSSEL**
"Dès que la grive est éveille" *see Le jeune pâtre breton* Brizeux **BERLIOZ**
"Des roses sur la mer" *see Roses du soir* Vivien **AUBERT**
Des roses sur la mer see Vivien **KOECHLIN**
Des Sängers Habe see Schlechta **SCHUBERT**
"Des Schäfers sein Haus und das steht auf zwei Rad" *see Storchenbotschaft* Mörike **WOLF**
Des Sennen Abschied see Schiller **SCHUMANN**
"Des Sonntags in der Morgenstund' " *see Sonntags am Rhein* Reinick **SCHUMANN**
Des Tages laute Stimmen schweigen see Saar **LISZT**
"Des trous à son pourpoint vermeil" *see La Belle au bois dormant* Hyspa **DEBUSSY**
"Des Waldes Sänger singen" *see Umsonst* Osterwald **FRANZ**
"Des Waldes Wipfel rauschen" *see Die Liebe hat gelogen* Osterwald **FRANZ**
"Des Wassermanns sein Töchterlein" *see Nixe Binsefuss* Mörike **WOLF**
Des Woiewoden Tochter see Geibel **LASSEN**
Desachy, Paul, 1872-1906.
  MASSENET *Hymne d'amour*
Desbordes-Valmore, Marceline Félicité Josèphe, 1786-1859.
  AURIC
    Le premier amour
    Le réveil . . .
  BIZET *Berceuse*
  FRANCK *Les cloches du soir*
  SAINT-SAËNS *Le soir*
  SAUGUET
    Adieu
    La dernière fleur
    Souvenir
"Descendons au jardin" *see Akahito* Akahito, 8th cent. **STRAVINSKIÏ**
La descente see Claudel **MILHAUD**
Deschamps, Émile, 1791-1871.
  BERLIOZ *Premiers transports*
  ROSSINI
    Chanson de Zora (La petite Bohémienne)
    Nizza

COMPOSER Poet *Title* ''First Line''

Deschoulières, Mme.
  SAINT-SAËNS *Idylle*
Desdemonas sång see Blomberg **KILPINEN**
DESEO DE AMOR. see Perpina, D.
  Francisco *Désir d'amour* **SAINT-SAËNS**
Deserted see Burns **MACDOWELL**
Deshoulières, Mme. *see* Deschoulières,
  Mme.
Désir d'amour see Perpina, D. Francisco
  DESEO DE AMOR. **SAINT-SAËNS**
Désir de l'Orient see Saint-Saëns
  SAINT-SAËNS
Desire see Heine **MUSORGSKIĬ** *Zhelanie*
The desire for hermitage see O'Faolain,
  Sean, translator *THE SILVER BRANCH.*
  BARBER
Desnos, Robert, 1900-1945.
  HONEGGER *Les Gars du bâtiment*
  POULENC
    Dernier poeme
    Le disparu
Desnoux, Lucienne
  SAUGUET *Pour un cyprés*
Despair see Nietzsche **MEDTNER**
  Verzweiflung
Despite and still see Graves, Robert
  BARBER
DESPITE AND STILL, no. 1
  BARBER Graves, Robert *A last song*
DESPITE AND STILL, no. 2
  BARBER Roethke *My lizard*
DESPITE AND STILL, no. 3
  BARBER Graves, Robert *In the
  wilderness*
DESPITE AND STILL, no. 4
  BARBER Joyce *Solitary hotel*
DESPITE AND STILL, no. 5
  BARBER Graves, Robert *Despite and
  still*
Dessirier, Annie
  MASSENET *Les extases*
Le destin see Toussaint *JARDIN DES
  CARESSES.* **AUBERT**
Destinée see Carême **MILHAUD**
Det är du som skall bliva den yppersta see
  Lagerkvist **KILPINEN**
Det är höst see Rogberg, Alma **NIELSEN**
Det, som lysner over Vangen see Poulsen,
  Frederik **NIELSEN**
"Det var en daemrende Sommernat" *see*
  Udfarten Munch **GRIEG**
Detective story see Bishop **ROREM**
DETSKAĬA, no. 1
  MUSORGSKIĬ Musorgskiĭ *S nianeĭ*
DETSKAĬA, no. 2
  MUSORGSKIĬ Musorgskiĭ *V uglu*

DETSKAĬA, no. 3
  MUSORGSKIĬ Musorgskiĭ *Zhuk*
DETSKAĬA, no. 4
  MUSORGSKIĬ Musorgskiĭ *S kukloĭ*
DETSKAĬA, no. 5
  MUSORGSKIĬ Musorgskiĭ *Na son
  griadushiĭ'*
DETSKAĬA, no. 6
  MUSORGSKIĬ Musorgskiĭ *Kot matros*
DETSKAĬA, no. 7
  MUSORGSKIĬ Musorgskiĭ *Poekhal na
  polochke*
Detskaĭa pesenka see Mei *RUTHENISCHE
  LIEDER*: No. 2. Nane. **MUSORGSKIĬ**
Detskaya pesnya see Aksakov
  CHAĬKOVSKIĬ
Dětství see Liliencron **MARTINŮ** *From
  childhood*
Deu'i noch' see Tiutchev **MEDTNER** *Day
  and night*
Deutsch, Babette, 1895-1982.
  DIAMOND *Homage to Paul Klee*
Deutsche Barkarole see Prechtler **LOEWE**
Deutsche Flotte see Budy **LOEWE**
"Deutschlands Adler liegt gebunden" *see*
  Deutsche Flotte Budy **LOEWE**
Deux ancolies se balançaient see Jammes
  TRISTESSES. **BOULANGER, MILHAUD**
"Deux cents cinquante grammes de raisins de
  Malaga" *see Plum pudding* Dumont
  BERNSTEIN
DEUX CHANSONS ANCIENNES, no. 1
  CASELLA Anon. *Rêves d'or pour ton
  sommeil*
DEUX CHANSONS ANCIENNES, no. 2
  CASELLA Anon. *Flaiolet*
DEUX CHANSONS DE MELPOMÈNE, no.
  1
  IBERT Aguet, William *Mon bien aimé
  siffle bien*
DEUX CHANSONS DE MELPOMÈNE, no.
  2
  IBERT Aguet, William *Je penais épouser
  un fier à bras*
DEUX CHANSONS ENFANTINES, no. 1
  INDY Legrand, Marc *La bonne terre*
DEUX CHANSONS ENFANTINES, no. 2
  INDY Legrand, Marc *Mon père travaille*
DEUX CHANTS D'ARIEL, no. 1
  HONEGGER Shakespeare *Modéré-Plus
  lent*
DEUX CHANTS D'ARIEL, no. 2
  HONEGGER Shakespeare *Un peu
  animé*
"Deux dames, le long le long du fleuve" *see*
  Le pont Apollinaire **POULENC**

"D'eux deux il était ainsi comme du chèvre
feuille était" *see Le Lai du Chevrefeuille*
France, Marie de **MILHAUD**
Les deux Etoiles see Unknown **LASSEN**
Mein Herz ist wie die dunkle Nacht
Les deux grenadiers see Heine **WAGNER**
Les deux guerriers see Messiaen
MESSIAEN
"Deux heures après diner" *see La sieste*
Claudel **HONEGGER**
Les deux hôtels see Paliard **MILHAUD**
DEUX MÉLODIES, no. 1
CHAUSSON Jounet *Cantique à l'Épouse*
DEUX MÉLODIES, no. 2
CHAUSSON Moréas *Dans la forêt du
Charme et de l'Enchantement*
Deux mélodies en Langue d'Oc see Vabre
SÉVERAC
DEUX MÉLODIES HÉBRAÏQUES, no. 1
RAVEL Anon. *Kaddisch*
DEUX MÉLODIES HÉBRAÏQUES, no. 2
RAVEL Anon. *L'Enigme éternelle*
DEUX PETIT AIRS, no. 1
MILHAUD Mallarmé *Indomptablement a
dû*
DEUX PETITS AIRS, no. 2
MILHAUD Mallarmé *Quelconque une
solitude*
Les deux pigeons see La Fontaine
GOUNOD
DEUX POÈMES, no. 1
CHAUSSON Verlaine *La chanson bien
douce*
DEUX POÈMES, no. 2
CHAUSSON Verlaine *Le chevalier
Malheur*
DEUX POÈMES D'AMOUR, no. 1
MILHAUD Tagore *Love, my heart longs
day and night*
DEUX POÈMES D'AMOUR, no. 2
MILHAUD Tagore *Peace, my heart*
DEUX ROMANCES, no. 1
AURIC Desbordes-Valmore *Le premier
amour*
DEBUSSY Bourget *L'âme évaporée*
DEUX ROMANCES, no. 2
AURIC Desbordes-Valmore
Le réveil . . .
DEBUSSY Bourget *Les cloches*
DEUX ROMANCES SENTIMENTALES, no.
1
HONEGGER Zimmer, Bernard *Quand
tu verras les hirondelles*
DEUX ROMANCES SENTIMENTALES, no.
2
HONEGGER Zimmer, Bernard *Si le
mal d'amour*

Deux soeurs qui sont pas soeurs see Stein
THOMSON
DEUX STÈLES ORIENTÉES, no. 1
IBERT Ségalen *Mon amante a les vertus
de l'eau*
DEUX STÈLES ORIENTÉES, no. 2
IBERT Ségalen *On me dit: . . .*
Deva i solntse see Maĭkov **RIMSKIĬ-
KORSAKOV**
"Devant le ciel d'été, tiède et calme" *see
Regret: Devant le ciel* Bourget **DEBUSSY**
Devant l'infini see Troillet, Émile
MASSENET
Děvče z Moravy see Anon. **MARTINŮ**
Devereux, Penelope, 1562?-1607,
supposed author.
LALO *La Fénaison*
Dévigne, Roger, 1885-1965.
LOEFFLER *Prayer*
"Devochka vseren' kom plat'itse" *see Seroe
plat'itse* Gippius **PROKOFIEV**
"Devotero tisíc ovcí" *see Nereidy* Anon.
DVOŘÁK
Devrient, Eduard, 1801-1877.
MENDELSSOHN-BARTHOLDY
Geständniss
Dew see Unknown **MARTINŮ** *Rosička*
"Dew sat on Julia's hair" *see Julia's hair*
Herrick **QUILTER**
D'Harcourt, Antoniette
SAUGUET
Au bord de la cheminée
Dormeur suspendu
Fenêtre ouverte le soir
Les gens distraits
Invasion
Sommeil
d'Hotelier, A.
LOEFFLER *Les Hirondelles*
Di goldene pave see Anon. **WEISGALL**
THE DIAL. see Simpson, M.
Rest **CARPENTER**
Dialogo no. 3 'con Jacopone da Todi' see
Unknown **MALIPIERO**
Dialogue see Varenne, Marc **MASSENET**
DIAMOND, DAVID, 1915-
Agee, James, 1909-1955.
SONNET 1.
So it begins (1970-71) [Columbia
Univ. Press, 1983) same
SONNET 2.
Our doom is in our being (1970-71)
[Columbia Univ. Press, 1983)
same
SONNET 4.
I have been fashioned (1970-71)
[Columbia Univ. Press, 1983) same

COMPOSER Poet *Title* "First Line"

DIAMOND, DAVID, 1915- *(continued)*
Agee, James, 1909-1955 *(continued)*
SONNET 8.
What curious thing is love (1970-71)
[Columbia Univ. Press, 1983)
same
SONNET 9.
Why am I here (1970-71) [Columbia
Univ. Press, 1983) same
SONNET 10.
Wring me no more (1970-71)
[Columbia Univ. Press, 1983) same
SONNET 17.
I nothing saw in you (1970-71)
[Columbia Univ. Press, 1983) same
SONNET 20.
Now stands our love (1970-71)
[Columbia Univ. Press, 1983) same
SONNET 23.
This little time (1970-71) [Columbia
Univ. Press, 1983) same
Anon.
As life what is so sweet (1940) [Arrow;
Boosey & Hawkes, 1941] same
This world is not my home (1946)
[Elkan-Vogel, 1947] same
Bible
David mourns for Absalmon (1946)
[Mercury Music Corp., 1947]
"David the King was grievèd and
much moved"
Text from Samuel II, 18:33.
Blixen, Karen, 1885-1962.
OUT OF AFRICA.
The millennium (1960) [Southern,
1969] "At the time when the near
return of Christ"
Bunyan, John, 1628-1688.
*The shepherd boy sings in the valley of
humiliation* (1946) [Southern, 1949]
"He that is down needs fear no fall"
Byron, George Gordon Byron, 6th
baron, 1778-1824.
All is vanity (1968) [Southern, 1969]
"Fame, wisdom, love, and power were
mine"
If that high world (1968) [Southern,
1969] same
My soul is dark (1968) [Southern, 1969]
same
Saul (1968) [Southern, 1969] "Thou
whose spell can raise the dead"
Clare, John, 1793-1864.
On death (1943) [Associated, 1944]
"O Life, thy name to me's a galling
sound"

Cummings, Edward Estlin, 1894-1962.
Christmas tree (1970) [Southern, 1972]
"little tree little silent Christmas tree"
I shall imagine life (1962) [Southern,
1968] same
If you can't (1950) [Leeds, 1950] "If you
can't eat you got to smoke"
Love is more (1950) [Southern, 1954]
"Love is more thicker than forget"
IS 5.
Four uncles (1940) [Elkan-Vogel,
1946] "My Uncle Daniel fought in
the Civil War band"
Deutsch, Babette, 1895-1982.
Homage to Paul Klee (1970) [Elkan-
Vogel, 1973] "I-tis-kit, i-tas-ket, a
green and yellow basket"
Eliot, Thomas Stearns, 1888-1965.
For an old man (1943) [Southern, 1951]
"The tiger in the tiger pit"
Hardy, Thomas, 1840-1928.
My spirit will not haunt the mound
(1946) [Southern, 1952] same
Hugo, Victor Marie, comte, 1802-1885.
The children of the poor (1950) [Leeds,
1950] "Take heed of this small child of
earth"
Joyce, James, 1882-1941.
POMES PENYEACH.
A flower given to my daughter (1940)
[Arrow; Boosey & Hawkes, 1942]
"Frail the white rose and frail are
her hands"
*A PORTRAIT OF THE ARTIST AS A
YOUNG MAN.*
Brigid's song (1946) [Mercury Music
Corp., 1947]
"Ding-dong! the castle bell!"
Keats, John, 1795-1821.
Chatterton (1946) [Southern, 1950]
"O Chatterton! How very sad thy
fate!"
La Fontaine, Jean de, 1621-1695.
Sister Jane (1943) [Elkan-Vogel, 1946]
"When Sister Jane, who had produced
a child"
Larson, Jack, b. 1933.
Do I love you? (1968) [Southern, 1971]
"Do I love you more than a look?"
Louchheim, Katie, 1903-1991.
WITH OR WITHOUT ROSES.
The incredible hour (1967-68)
[Southern, 1971] "This is the
summer's incredible hour"
Love's worth (1967-68) [Southern,
1971] "LOVE is of nothing made"

Spring talk (1967-68) [Southern, 1971]
"The lilacs are out"
Whither thou goest (1967-68)
[Southern, 1971]
"Hell has doors and walls and keys"
Lovelace, Richard, 1618-1658.
To Lucasta, on going to the wars (1944)
[Associated, 1946]
"Tell me not, Sweet"
Mansfield, Katherine, 1890-1923.
*THE JOURNAL OF KATHERINE
MANSFIELD.*
My little Mother (1943) [Elkan-Vogel,
1946] "My little Mother, my star"
Souvent j'ai dit a mon mari (1943)
[Elkan-Vogel, 1946] same
McCullers, Carson, 1917-1967.
The twisted Trinity (1943) [Elkan-Vogel,
1946] "There was a time when stone
was stone"
Melville, Herman, 1819-1891.
Monody (1945) [Elkan-Vogel, 1947]
"To have known him"
*A portrait; the Marchioness of
Brinvilliers* (1946) [Elkan-Vogel,
1947] "He toned the sprightly beam of
morning"
BILLY BUD, FORETOPMAN.
Billy in the Darbies (1944) [Elkan-
Vogel, 1946] "Good of the Chaplain
to enter Lone Bay"
*ON THE GRAVE OF A YOUNG
CAVALRY OFFICER.*
Epitaph (1945) [Associated, 1946]
"Beauty and youth, with manners
sweet"
Monroe, Marilyn, 1926-1962.
Don't cry (1981) [G. Schirmer, 1983)
"Don't cry, my doll, don't cry"
No author
Vocalises (1935; rev. 1956) [Southern,
1966]
Voice & viola.
Olson, Elder, 1909-1992.
*I thought once I should have at a man's
age* (1951) [Southern, 1954] same
*Immensity, like the darkness cast from
the cloud above* (1951)
[Southern, 1954] same
*Let children ride the year's sweet
carrousel* (1951) [Southern, 1954]
same
Midnight: I pluck the curtains back
(1951) [Southern, 1954] same
**O'Shaughnessy, Arthur William
Edgar, 1844-1881.**
Ode (1969) [Southern, 1971]
"We are the music-makers"

Patchen, Kenneth, 1911-1972.
Be music, night (1944) [Carl Fischer,
1948] same
Porter, Katherine Anne, 1894-1980.
Anniversary in a country cemetery (1940)
[Arrow; Boosey & Hawkes, 1942]
"This time of year"
Pound, Ezra, 1885-1972.
Agathas (1935; rev. 1962) [Southern,
1966] "Four and forty lovers had
Agathas"
Lesbia Illa (1935) [Southern, 1966]
"Memnon, Memnon, That Lady who
used to walk about"
Passing (1935; rev. 1962) [Southern,
1966] "Flawless as Aphrodite"
Young lady (1935; rev. 1962) [Southern,
1966] "I have fed your lar with
poppies"
Rilke, Rainer Maria, 1875-1926.
SONETTE AN ORPHEUS.
Even though the world keeps changing
(1946) [Carl Fischer, 1948] same
Roethke, Theodore, 1908-1963.
My papa's waltz (1964) [Southern, 1968]
"The whiskey on your breath could
make a small boy dizzy"
Prayer (1964) [Southern, 1968] "If I
must of my senses lose"
Shakespeare, William, 1564-1616.
*For shame deny that thou bear'st love to
any* (1964) [Southern, 1967] same
Let me confess that we two must be twain
(1964) [Southern, 1967] same
My love is as a fever longing still (1964)
[Southern, 1967] same
No longer mourn for me when I am dead
(1964) [Southern, 1967] same
*O from what power hast thou this
powerful might* (1964) [Southern,
1967] same
Shall I compare thee to a summer's day?
(1964) [Southern, 1967] same
Those pretty wrongs that liberty commits
(1964) [Southern, 1967] same
*When in disgrace with fortune and men's
eyes* (1964) [Southern, 1967] same
*When to the sessions of sweet silent
thought* (1964) [Southern, 1967] same
THE TEMPEST.
Come unto these yellow sands (1944)
[Chappell, 1945] same
Full fathom five (1944) [Chappell,
1945] same
No more dams I'll make for fish (1944)
[Chappell, 1945] same

DIAMOND, DAVID, 1915- *(continued)*
Shakespeare, William, 1564-1616
(continued)
THE TEMPEST (continued)
Where the bee sucks (1944) [Chappell, 1945] same
While you here do snoring lie (1944) [Chappell, 1945] same
Shelley, Percy Bysshe, 1792-1822.
Lift not the painted veil (1946) [Southern, 1949] same
POSTHUMOUS POEMS (1824).
Music, when soft voices die (1943) [Associated, 1944] same
Smith, Logan Pearsall, 1865-1946.
MORE TRIVIA.
The epitaph (1946) [Elkan-Vogel, 1947] "But perhaps he is a friend of yours?"
Somewhere (1946) [Elkan-Vogel, 1947] "Somewhere, far below the horizon"
Stein, Gertrude, 1874-1946.
I am rose (1971) [Elkan-Vogel, 1973] "I am rose, my eyes are blue"
Stringham, Edward, 1918-
The lover as mirror (1944) [Elkan-Vogel, 1946] "Down the perspective leading to your horizon"
Teresa of Avila, Saint, 1515-1582.
Let nothing disturb thee (1945) [Associated, 1946] same
Thomas, Dylan, 1914-1953.
I have longed to move away (1944) [Southern, 1968] same
Tichborne, Chidiock, 1558?-1586.
Life and death (1969) [Southern, 1971] "My prime of youth is but a frost of cares"
Unknown
L'âme de Claude Debussy (1949) [unpubl.?]
Reportedly published by Southern, but not located.
Whitman, Walt, 1819-1892.
How it was with them (1950) [Leeds, 1950] "When I peruse the conquer'd fame of heroes"
The diamond on the March snow see
Wecksell **SIBELIUS** *Demanten på marssnön*
DIANA VON POITIERS. see Castelli
Ein König einst gefangen sass **WEBER**
"Diane étant en l'épaisseur d'un bois" *see*
Chasse Labé **SAUGUET**
Diane, Séléné see La Ville de Mirmont
FAURÉ

Dicebat Jesus scribis et pharisaeis see Bible
HINDEMITH
"Dicen que no nos queremos" *see Jota* Anon.
FALLA
Dich bet' ich an, erstand'ner Held see
Unknown **LOEWE**
"Dich blendet Kerzenlicht!" *see Herzen und Augen* Gerstenberg **LOEWE**
Dich lieb ich see Hood **CORNELIUS**
Dich liebe ich! see Preetzman **GRIEG** *Dig elsker jeg!*
Dich soll mein Lied erheben see Rüling
LOEWE
"Dich vor allem, heilige Muttersprache" *see Muttersprache* Leuthold **SCHOECK**
La dichiarazione see Metastasio **ROSSINI**
Der Dichter see Sturm, J. **RUBINSTEIN**
"Der Dichter singt dem Frühling" *see Der Sänger* Cornelius **LASSEN**
DICHTER UND IHRE GESELLEN (1834).
see Eichendorff
Parole **BRAHMS**
Schöne Fremde **SCHUMANN**
"Dichter! was Liebe sei, mir nicht verhehle!" *see Was Liebe sei?* Hagn **LISZT**
DICHTERLIEBE, no. 1
SCHUMANN Heine *Im wunderschönen Monat Mai*
DICHTERLIEBE, no. 2
SCHUMANN Heine *Aus meinen Thränen spriessen*
DICHTERLIEBE, no. 3
SCHUMANN Heine *Die Rose, die Lilie*
DICHTERLIEBE, no. 4
SCHUMANN Heine *Wenn ich in deine Augen seh'*
DICHTERLIEBE, no. 5
SCHUMANN Heine *Ich will meine Seele tauchen*
DICHTERLIEBE, no. 6
SCHUMANN Heine *Im Rhein, im heiligen Strome*
DICHTERLIEBE, no. 7
SCHUMANN Heine *Ich grolle nicht*
DICHTERLIEBE, no. 8
SCHUMANN Heine *Und wüssten's die Blumen*
DICHTERLIEBE, no. 9
SCHUMANN Heine *Das ist ein Flöten und Geigen*
DICHTERLIEBE, no. 10
SCHUMANN Heine *Hör' ich das Liedchen klingen*
DICHTERLIEBE, no. 11
SCHUMANN Heine *Ein Jüngling liebt ein Mädchen*

DICHTERLIEBE, no. 12
   SCHUMANN Heine *Am leuchtenden Sommermorgen*
DICHTERLIEBE, no. 13
   SCHUMANN Heine *Ich hab' im Traum geweinet*
DICHTERLIEBE, no. 14
   SCHUMANN Heine *Allnächtlich im Traume*
DICHTERLIEBE, no. 15
   SCHUMANN Heine *Aus alten Märchen winkt es*
DICHTERLIEBE, no. 16
   SCHUMANN Heine *Die alten, bösen Lieder*
Dichterlos see Vinje **GRIEG** *Guten*
Dichters Genesung see Reinick
   LIEDERBUCH EINES MALERS.
   SCHUMANN
Dichtersegen see Uhland **SCHOECK**
Dichterweise see Benzon **GRIEG** *Digtervise*
"D'ici voyez sur ce sommet" *see Marche du panacheà la grande Maréchale* Indy
   INDY
Dickens, Charles, 1812-1870.
   ODE TO AN EXPIRING FROG.
      HINDEMITH *Recitativo e aria romantica*
Dickinson, Emily, 1830-1866.
   COPLAND
      The chariot
      Dear March, come in!
      Going to Heaven!
      Heart, we will forget him
      I felt a funeral in my brain
      I've heard an organ talk sometimes
      Nature, the gentlest mother
      Sleep is supposed to be
      There came a wind like a bugle
      When they come back
      Why do they shut me out of Heaven?
      The world feels dusty
   LUENING
      Experiment to me Is every one I meet
      Few get enough
      Hope is the thing with feathers
      I felt a cleavage in my mind
      If I can stop one heart from breaking
      Our share of night to bear
      The show is not the show
      Soul, wilt thou toss again?
      When I hoped I feared
   ROREM
      Love's stricken "Why"
      What inn is this
DICKINSON SONG CYCLE, no. 1
   LUENING Dickinson *Our share of night to bear*

DICKINSON SONG CYCLE, no. 2
   LUENING Dickinson *The show is not the show*
DICKINSON SONG CYCLE, no. 3
   LUENING Dickinson *Hope is the thing with feathers*
DICKINSON SONG CYCLE, no. 4
   LUENING Dickinson *If I can stop one heart from breaking*
DICKINSON SONG CYCLE, no. 5
   LUENING Dickinson *Experiment to me Is every one I meet*
DICKINSON SONG CYCLE, no. 6
   LUENING Dickinson *I felt a cleavage in my mind*
DICKINSON SONG CYCLE, no. 7
   LUENING Dickinson *Few get enough*
DICKINSON SONG CYCLE, no. 8
   LUENING Dickinson *Soul, wilt thou toss again?*
DICKINSON SONG CYCLE, no. 9
   LUENING Dickinson *When I hoped I feared*
DIDONE ABBANDONATA. see Metastasio
   Arie **SCHUBERT**
"Die angetrauet am Altare" *see Der König bei der Krönung* Mörike **WOLF**
"Die, du bist so schön und rein" *see Du bist so schön und rein* Heine **FRANZ**
Die du Gott gebarst, du Reine see Nuñez
   WOLF
"Die du so gern in heilgen Nächten feierst"
   see An die Hoffnung Tiedge
   BEETHOVEN
"Die du, über den Sterne weg" *see Gebet*
   Hebbel **PFITZNER, REGER**
"Die ihr den Aether mit seligen Schwingen durch schneidet" *see Sterne* Ritter **REGER**
Die ihr des unermesslichen Weltalls Schöpfer ehrt see Ziegenhagen **MOZART**
"Die ihr dort wallet unter den Palmen" *see Wiegenlied der Jungfrau Maria* Vega Carpio **LASSEN**
"Die ihr einem neuen Grade" *see Lied zur Gesellenreise* Ratschky **MOZART**
"Die ihr Felsen und Bäume bewohnt" *see Einsamkeit* Goethe **MEDTNER, REGER**
"Die ihr schwebet um diese Palmen" *see Geistliches Wiegenlied* Geibel **BRAHMS**
Die ihr schwebet um diese Palmen see Vega Carpio **WOLF**
"Die mich hält am Fädchen" *see Kind und Mädchen* Rückert **LOEWE**
"Die mich recht erkennen" *see Abendgebet, nach einer erlittenen Kränkung* Gerstenberg **LOEWE**

Der Dieb see Schellenberg **REGER**
Diederich, Franz, 1865-1921.
  REGER *Der Mond glüht*
Dierx, Marais Victor Léon, 1838-1912.
  CHABRIER *Les lèvres closes*
  HAHN *Fleur fanée*
"Dies ist ein Herbsttag, wie ich keinen sah"
  see Herbstbild Hebbel **PFITZNER**
Dies ist ein Lied für dich allein see George
  DER SIEBENTE RING. **WEBERN**
Dies und Das see Anon. **FRANZ**
Dies zu deuten bin erbötig! see Goethe
  WESTÖSTLICHER DIVAN: Buch Suleika.
  WOLF
"Diese, die noch eben atemlos flohen" *see*
  Rast auf der Flucht in Ägypten Rilke
  HINDEMITH
Diese Gondel vergleich ich see Goethe
  WESTÖSTLICHER DIVAN. **SCHOECK**
"Diese Rose pflück' ich hier" *see An die*
  Entfernte Lenau
  MENDELSSOHN-BARTHOLDY,
  SCHOECK
Diese Rose pflück ich hier see Lenau
  BARTÓK
"Diese Rose von heimlichen Küssen schwer"
  see Unsere Liebe Morgenstern
  KILPINEN
Diese Wolken in den Höhen see Jeitteles
  BEETHOVEN
DIETÀ SILVANE, no. 1
  RESPIGHI Rubino *I fauni*
DIETÀ SILVANE, no. 2
  RESPIGHI Rubino *Musica in horto*
DIETÀ SILVANE, no. 3
  RESPIGHI Rubino *Egle*
DIETÀ SILVANE, no. 4
  RESPIGHI Rubino *Acqua*
DIETÀ SILVANE, no. 5
  RESPIGHI Rubino *Crepuscolo*
Dieu créa le désert see Grain, Madeleine
  MASSENET
Dieu qui sourit et qui donne see Hugo
  LALO
"Dieu, qu'il la faict bon regarder" *see*
  Madrigal à deux voix Orléans, Charles d'
  INDY
"Dieu s'avance à travers les champs!" *see*
  La procession Brizeux, Ch. **FRANCK**
"Dievča umíralo, ešte zavolalo" *see Zvědavá*
  dievča Anon. **MARTINŮ**
Diez, Heinrich Friedrich von, 1751-1817.
  ZELTER *Die Gegenwart*
The difference see Van Doren **CARTER**
Dig elsker jeg! see Preetzman **GRIEG**
En Digters sidste Sang see Andersen
  GRIEG

Digtervise see Benzon **GRIEG**
Dík Bohu Stvořiteli see Des Knaben
  Wunderhorn **MARTINŮ**
  Thanks to God the Creator
Dilemma see Busch, W. **SCHOECK**
Dilia Helena, pseud. *see* Branco, Frau
  Helene [von Rödlich] 1818-1894.
"Dimanche sur le villes, dimanche dans les
  coeurs" *see De soir* Debussy **DEBUSSY**
"Dimmi, ben mio che m'ami" *see Hoffnung*
  Unknown **BEETHOVEN**
"Din Hånd er barket, Ingebjørg" *see Ingebjørg*
  Drachmann **GRIEG**
Din mun är ljusare än min see Lagerkvist
  KILPINEN
"Dina gropia fingrar" *see En ung mor*
  Blomberg **KILPINEN**
Un dîner à l'Élysée see Hyspa **SATIE**
Les dîners se font en courant see Ganzo
  SCHMITT
Dinesen, Isak *see* Blixen, Karen, 1885-
  1962.
DING DONG BELL: Benighted. *see* De La
  Mare
  Alice Rodd **CHANLER**
  Ann Poverty **CHANLER**
  Be very quiet now **CHANLER**
  A midget **CHANLER**
  No voice to scold **CHANLER**
  Susannah Fry **CHANLER**
  Thomas Logge **CHANLER**
  Three sisters **CHANLER**
"Ding-dong! the castle bell!" *see Brigid's*
  song Joyce **DIAMOND**
Dingelstedt, Franz, Freiherr von, 1814-
  1881.
  LISZT *Schwebe, schwebe, blaues Auge*
    Two settings: 1845 and ca. 1860.
  SPOHR
    Mitternacht
    Unterwegs
Dionysius, 2nd c. after Christ
  LOEWE *An die Muse*
Dios mio, que solos se quedan los muertos!
  see Bécquer **FALLA**
"Dios te salve, Macarena" *see Saeta en forma*
  de Salve a la Virgen de la Esperanza
  Alvarez Quintero, S. **TURINA**
"Dioskuren, Zwillingssterne" *see Lied eines*
  Schiffers an die Dioskuren Mayrhofer
  SCHUBERT
"Dir angetrauet am Altare, O Vaterland" *see*
  Der König bei der Krönung Mörike
  REGER
"Dir zu eröffnen mein Herz verlangt mich"
  see Aus der Ferne Goethe **ZELTER**

"Dir zu eröffnen mein Herz verlangt mich"
  see Liebeslied Goethe **SCHUMANN**
"Dir, kleines Bethlehem, erklang" *see*
  Bethlehem Unknown **LOEWE**
"Dir, Mädchen, schlägt mit leisem Behen" *see*
  Liebesrausch Körner **SCHUBERT**
Dirge see Crapsey **WEISGALL**
Dirge see Webster *THE WHITE DEVIL.*
  THOMSON
Dirge in woods see Meredith **COPLAND**
Discipleship see Wright, Merle St. Croix
  THOMPSON, R.
Disclosure see Ives **IVES**
Discord see Polonsky **RACHMANINOFF**
DISCORDANTS. see Aiken
  Discordants **ROREM**
Discordants see Aiken *DISCORDANTS.*
  ROREM
DISCORDANTS. see Aiken
  Music I heard **COPLAND**
LA DISCRETA ENAMORADA. see
  Vega Carpio
  Cuando tan hermosa os miro **TURINA**
"Dis-moi, Daphénéo, quel est donc cet arbre"
  see Daphénéo Godebska, Mimie
  SATIE
"Dismoi, jeune captive" *see Chant de l'almée*
  Gille **DELIBES**
Le disparu see Desnos **POULENC**
Displaced see Blitzstein **BLITZSTEIN**
Dissident song see Anon. **STRAVINSKIï**
  Chant dissident
Dissolution see Claudel **KOECHLIN,**
  MILHAUD
Dissonance see Borodin **BORODIN**
  Fal'shivaya nota
Dissonance see Polonsky
  RACHMANINOFF *Discord*
Dissonans see Polonsky **RACHMANINOFF**
  Discord
Distel, Camille
  MASSENET
    Les bois de pins
    Bonne nuit
    Le verger
  SAINT-SAËNS *Etoile du matin*
Distichen see Leuthold **SCHOECK**
Distichon see Goethe **STRAUSS** *Xenion*
The distracted maid see Anon. **HESELTINE**
La distribution des prix see Anon. **GOUNOD**
"Dites, la jeune belle" *see L'Île inconnue*
  Gautier **BERLIOZ**
"Dites, la jeune belle" *see Où voulez-vous*
  aller? Gautier **GOUNOD**
Dites-lui que je l'aime see Fleury-
  Daunizeau, Georges **MASSENET**

"Dites-lui que les fleurs ont ouvert leur calice"
  see Dites-lui que je l'aime
  Fleury-Daunizeau, Georges
  MASSENET
"Dites-moi ce que sont les âmes" *see*
  Les âmes Demouth, Paul **MASSENET**
Dithyrambe see Schiller *DER BESUCH.*
  SCHUBERT
Dithyrambe see Schober **LISZT** *Weimars*
  Toten
Ditia! kak tsbetok . . . see Heine
  RACHMANINOFF
  Child, thou art as beautiful as a flower
"Ditia moë, Ostan' sia zdes' so mnoï" *see*
  Pesnya zolotoy rïbki
  Lermontov **BALAKIREV**
Ditirambo terzo (dalle laudi di Gabriele
  d'Annunzio) *see* Annunzio *ALCYONE.*
  MALIPIERO
La diva de l'Empire see Bonnaud **SATIE**
Dívčí píseň see Sládek **MARTINŮ**
  A maiden's song
Dívčí píseň see Sládek **MARTINŮ**
  NB: 1910; variant from the previous, 1911,
  sctting.
Dívčí sny see Huch **Martinů** *Maiden's*
  dreams
DIVINE COMEDY. see Dante
  Francesca da Rimini **BLACHER**
"Divine créature" *see Pardon* Hölderlin
  SAUGUET
A DIVINE IMAGE. see Blake, William
  Cruelty has a human heart
  VAUGHAN WILLIAMS
The Divine image see Blake, William
  LUENING, THOMSON,
  VAUGHAN WILLIAMS
DIVING INTO THE WRECK. see Rich
  The stranger **ROREM**
Dixit Jesus Petro see Bible **HINDEMITH**
Dix-neuf-cent-quatre see Apollinaire
  POULENC *1904*
Dixon, Richard Watson, 1833-1900.
  SIBELIUS *Autumn song*
Djakoan see Anon. **GRIFFES**
"Djup stod färgen på fura och på sten" *see*
  Näcken Josephson, E. **KILPINEN**
"Djup stod färgen pa fura och pa sten" *see*
  Necken Josephson, E. **SIBELIUS**
Den djupa källen see Blomberg **KILPINEN**
Dlïa beregov otchizuy dal'noi see Pushkin
  RIMSKIï-KORSAKOV
Dlouhé putování see Hafiz **MARTINŮ**
  A long pilgrimage
Dlya beregov otchiznï dal'noy see Pushkin
  BORODIN
  For the shores of thy far native land

"Dnem naigravshis" *see Spi!* Khomyakov
BALAKIREV
Do dziewczyny see Unknown
SZYMANOWSKI
Do I love you? see Larson, Jack
DIAMOND, ROREM
"Do I love you more than a day?" *see Do I love you?* Larson, Jack **ROREM**
"Do I love you more than a look?" *see Do I love you?* Larson, Jack **DIAMOND**
Do not ask see Goethe **CHAĬKOVSKIĬ**
Ne sprashivaĭ
Do not believe me, my friend see Tolstoĭ
RIMSKIĬ-KORSAKOV *Ne ver' mne, drug*
Do not believe, my friend see Tolstoĭ
CHAĬKOVSKIĬ *Ne ver', moĭ drug*
"Do not flee from my sight" *see Arabian melody* Anon. **BORODIN**
DO NOT GO GENTLE. see Thomas
The dying of the light **RIEGGER**
"Do not go gentle into that good night"
see The dying of the light Thomas
RIEGGER
Do not leave me see Shenshin *MELODII.*
CHAĬKOVSKIĬ *Ne otkhodi ot menia*
Do not question me see Goethe *WILHELM MEISTER.*
Mignon's song: Heiss mich nicht reden.
CHAĬKOVSKIĬ *Ne sprashivaĭ*
Do not sing to me, O lovely one see Pushkin
RIMSKIĬ-KORSAKOV
Ne poĭ, krasavitsa, pri mne
Do you remember the evening? see Tolstoĭ
RACHMANINOFF
"Do you see the road awinding through the dear green fields below?" *see The journey* Blake, Ernest **IRELAND**
Dobrú noc, má milá see Anon. **DVOŘÁK**
Doch der Herr, er leitet die Irrenden recht see Bible **MENDELSSOHN-BARTHOLDY**
Doch du liessest ihn im Grabe nicht see Händel *MESSIAH.* **REGER**
"Doch hatte niemals tiefere Macht dein Blick" *see Auf See* Dehmel **SZYMANOWSKI**
"Doch immer höher steigt der edle Drang" *see Cirrus* Goethe **WEBERN**
Doch könnt' ich dich im Leben noch einmal wiedersehn see Kurochkin **MUSORGSKIĬ**
No esli by s toboĭu ia vstretit'sia mogla
"Doch schwer hinschnaubend" *see Vorfrühling II* Avenarius **WEBERN**
"Doch vor dem Apostel Thomas" *see Vom Tode Mariä* Rilke **HINDEMITH**

Docquois, Georges, 1863-1927.
SAINT-SAËNS
Âme triste
Amoroso
Douceur
Jour de pluie
Mai
Pâques
Petite main
Prélude
Reviens (Epilogue)
Silence
The dodger see Anon. **COPLAND**
Le dodo des enfants see Unknown **ROSSINI**
"Dodo, l'enfant do, l'enfant dormira tantôt" *see Berceuse de la guerre* Cammaerts **CARPENTER**
Dödens vila see Cnattingius, Thor
KILPINEN
Döhring, J von?
BEETHOVEN *An einen Säugling*
Dörmann, Felix, 1876-1928.
BERG *Wenn Gespenster auferstehen*
Does the day reign? see Apukhtin
CHAĬKOVSKIĬ *Den' li tsarit*
"Does the road wind uphill all the way?" *see Up-hill* Rossetti, Christina **ROREM**
THE DOG BENEATH THE SKIN. see Auden
Nocturne **BRITTEN**
Dogorayet rumyaniy zakat see Kulchinsky, V. **BALAKIREV**
Das *"Dolce far niente" see* Grassmann
LOEWE
Dolce far niente see Tavaststjerna
SIBELIUS
Der Dolch see Lermontov **RUBINSTEIN**
Dold förening see Snoilsky **SIBELIUS**
"Dolgo noch'iu vchera" *see Son v letniuiu noch* Maĭkov **RIMSKIĬ-KORSAKOV**
Doll's boy see Cummings **ROREM**
Dolorosa see Eichhorn, Maria, 1879-
DOLOROSA, no. 1
JENSEN Chamisso *Was ist's, O Vater*
DOLOROSA, no. 2
JENSEN Chamisso *Ich habe, bevor der Morgen*
DOLOROSA, no. 3
JENSEN Chamisso *Nicht der Tau und nicht der Regen*
DOLOROSA, no. 4
JENSEN Chamisso *Denke, denke, mein Geliebter*
DOLOROSA, no. 5
JENSEN Chamisso *Ich hab' ihn im Schlafe*
DOLOROSA, no. 6
JENSEN Chamisso *Wie so bleich*

Doloroso e giocoso see Unknown **RIVIER**
Domaine d'homme see Follain **SAUGUET**
Dømd see Garborg *HAUGTUSSA.* **GRIEG**
"Domik nad rekoĭu" *see Na beregu*
Pleshcheyev **CHAĬKOVSKIĬ**
Dominique, Jean, pseud. *see* Closset, Marie, 1875-1952.
Domino see Radiguet **AURIC**
"Le domino jeu des ménages" *see Domino* Radiguet **AURIC**
Dommange, René Auguste Louis Henri, b. 1888.
AUBERT *L'heure captive*
ROUSSEL *Jazz dans la nuit*
Don Gayseros, Don Gayseros see Fouqué *DER ZAUBERRING.* **SCHUBERT**
DON GAYSEROS, no. 1
SCHUBERT Fouqué *Don Gayseros, Don Gayseros*
DON GAYSEROS, no. 2
SCHUBERT Fouqué *Nächtens klang die süsse Laute*
DON GAYSEROS, no. 3
SCHUBERT Fouqué *An dem jungen Morgenhimmel*
Don Juan see Morand **MILHAUD**
Don Juan's serenade see Tolstoĭ
CHAĬKOVSKIĬ *Serenada Don-Zhuana*
DON QUICHOTTE À DULCINÉE, no. 1
RAVEL Morand *Chanson romantique*
DON QUICHOTTE À DULCINÉE, no. 2
RAVEL Morand *Chanson épique*
DON QUICHOTTE À DULCINÉE, no. 3
RAVEL Morand *Chanson à boire*
Le don silencieux see Closset **FAURÉ**
"Donc Abraham, debout près du tombeau" *see Prière d'Abraham* Barbier, J. **GOUNOD**
"Donc, ce sera par un clair jour d'été" *see Tous deux* Verlaine **HAHN**
Donc, ce sera par un clair jour d'été see Verlaine **FAURÉ**
"Donc il se tourna vers le mur" *see Seul sur la terre* Carême **SAUGUET**
Donc, vous allez fleurir encor see Moréas **HAHN**
Donini, Alberto, 1887-
RESPIGHI
Canzone
Stornello
"La donna in attitudine regale" *see La donna sul sarcofago* Annunzio **RESPIGHI**
La donna sul sarcofago see Annunzio **RESPIGHI**
Donne d'enfant see Cocteau **POULENC**

Donne, John, 1573-1631.
BRITTEN
At the round Earth's imagined corners
Batter my heart
Death, be not proud
O might those sighes and teares
Oh my blacke Soule!
Oh, to vex me
Since she whom I loved
Thou hast made me
What if this present
KRENEK *The flea*
ROREM *A burnt ship*
THOMSON *Consider, Lord*
"Donne mie voi non sapete" *see Ballata* Poliziano **MALIPIERO**
Donne-moi cette fleur see Gozlan **GOUNOD**
"Les donneurs de sérénades" *see Fêtes galantes* Verlaine **HAHN**
"Les donneurs de sérénades" *see Mandoline* Verlaine **DEBUSSY, FAURÉ**
Don't Ceäre see Barnes **CARPENTER**
"Don't come in, sir, please!" *see To a young gentleman* Confucius **CARPENTER**
Don't cry see Monroe **DIAMOND**
"Don't cry, my doll, don't cry" *see Don't cry* Monroe **DIAMOND**
"Don't help on the big chariot" *see The big chariot* Unknown **BRITTEN**
Der Doppelgänger see Heine **SCHUBERT**
Doppelwandlung see Hoffmann von Fallersleben **FRANZ**
Dorat, Jean *see* Daurat, Jean, 1507-1588.
Das Dorf see Boelitz **REGER**
Die Dorfkirche see Zedlitz **LOEWE**
Dorismund, pseud. *see* Dehmel, Richard, 1863-1920.
"Dorme a notte il palagio d'Eliana" *see Eliana* Annunzio **MALIPIERO**
"Dorme Grasinda in mezzo a'suoi tesori" *see Grasinda* Annunzio **MALIPIERO**
Dormeur suspendu see D'Harcourt, Antoniette **SAUGUET**
La dormeuse see Carême **MILHAUD**
"Dormi Jesu!" *see Geistliches Wiegenlied* Unknown **MACDOWELL**
"Dormía en un prado mi pastora hermosa" *see Soneto* Mesa, Juan Bautista de **RODRIGO**
Dormons parmi les lis see Picard, Hélène **MASSENET**
Dornröschen see Osterwald **FRANZ**
Dornröschen (Das Mädchen spricht) *see* Heyse **LASSEN**
"Dornröschen schlägt zum ersten Mal die Augen" *see Dornröschen* Osterwald **FRANZ**

"Dorogoĭ Konstantin Sergeevich" *see Letter to K. S. Stanislavsky from S. R.* Rachmaninoff **RACHMANINOFF**

Dors, ami see Chantepie, J. **MASSENET**

"Dors, ami, dors et que les songes" *see Dors, ami* Chantepie, J. **MASSENET**

"Dors au fond de l'allée" *see Tombeau dans un parc* Rilke **BARBER**

"Dors, dors, dors, ton papa ira au village" *see Berceuse* Anon. **MILHAUD**

"Dors entre mes bras, enfant plein de charmés" *see Dors, mon enfant* Unknown **WAGNER**

"Dors, ma fleur, mon fils chéri" *see Chant de nourrice* Unknown **MILHAUD**

"Dors, ma petit mère, ah!" *see D'un berceau* Hettich **AUBERT**

Dors, Magda see Silvestre **MASSENET**

"Dors, Magda, si blanche et si rose" *see Dors, Magda* Silvestre **MASSENET**

Dors, mon enfant see Unknown **WAGNER**

"Dors, mon petit enfant, dors" *see Chant de nourrice* Aicard **MASSENET**

"Dors pendant que je veille" *see Romance* Musset **RUBINSTEIN**

"Dort am grünen Hügel glänzen schmucke Blümchen" *see Das Schlüsselblumen* Müller, J. **LISZT**

"Dort auf dem hohen Felsen sang" *see Der Bardengeist* Hermann **BEETHOVEN**

"Dort blinket durch Weiden" *see Des Fischers Liebesglück* Leitner **SCHUBERT**

"Dort im Tal hör ich verhallen" *see Die Stimme der Nacht* W., Cäcilie von **SPOHR**

Dort im Wald die Schimmelfohlen see Anon. **SZYMANOWSKI** *A pod borem siwe kunie*

Dort in den Weiden see Anon. **BRAHMS**

"Dort ist ihr Grab, did einst im Schmelz" *see Ihr Grab* Engelhardt **SCHUBERT**

"Dort raget ein Berg aus den Wolken hehr" *see Genügsamkeit* Schober **SCHUBERT**

Dort unterm Lindenbaum see Osterwald **FRANZ**

"Dort, wo der Morgenstern" *see Morgenrot* Rückert **STRAUSS**

"Dort, wo ich bei ihr sass" *see Canzonette* Rückert **JENSEN**

Dort, wo in leichter Kurve see Krenek **KRENEK**

"Dorthin will ich; und ich traue mir fortan und meinem Griff" *see Nach neuen Meeren* Nietzsche **DELIUS**

Dortzal, Jeanne, 1878- **MASSENET** *Battements d'ailes* *Comme autrefois* *Nocturne* *Parfums*

Los dos miedos see Campoamor y Campoosorio **TURINA**

Dos rimas see Bécquer **FALLA** *Dios mio, que solos se quedan los muertos!*

Dos rimas see Bécquer **FALLA** *Olas gigantes*

"Do'st remember child!" *see Kären* Unknown **IVES**

La double rougeur see Richter **SAUGUET**

Doubt see Maĭkov **RIMSKIĬ-KORSAKOV** *Somnenie*

"Doubt you to whom my muse these notes intendeth" *see Dedication* Sidney, Sir Philip **HESELTINE**

Doubts see Dougherty, Eleanor **THOMPSON, R.**

"Douce! Faut-il t'aimer, te chanter tour à tour?" *see Soir de printemps* Martin, Gabriel **MASSENET**

"Douce maîtresse, touche" *see Heureux sera le jour* Ronsard **GOUNOD**

Douce mer see Lamartine **BIZET**

La douce paix see Guillot de Saix **HAHN**

Douceur see Docquois **SAINT-SAËNS**

La douceur de tes yeux see Chobanian **HONEGGER**

Dougherty, Eleanor **THOMPSON, R.** *Doubts*

Douglas, Lord Alfred Bruce, 1870-1945. **CARPENTER** *The green river*

Douglas, William **THOMPSON, R.** *Tapestry*

Doundou tchil see Messiaen **MESSIAEN**

Le doute! see Ferrier **BIZET**

Douwdeuntje see Clercq, René de **PIJPER**

"Le doux printemps à bu dans le creux" *see Vous aimerez demain* Silvestre **MASSENET**

"Doux printemps, remplis mon âme" *see Chanson printanière* Barbier, J. **GOUNOD**

"Le doux printemps vient d'éclater!" *see Maria Lucrezia* Legouvé **SAINT-SAËNS**

"Le doux rêve que tu nias" *see Tristesse au jardin* Tailhade **SCHMITT**

The dove see Bal'mont **STRAVINSKIĬ**

Dove sei mia bella see Unknown **ZELTER**

Dover'sia mne see Vérine, Boris **PROKOFIEV**

The doves see Feeney **CHANLER**
"The doves, they fly to the moonlit elms" *see*
  The doves Feeney **CHANLER**
"Den dovne Fjord som gynger og straekker"
  see Hilsen Holstein **NIELSEN**
Down at the docks see Koch **ROREM,**
  THOMSON
"Down by the salley gardens my love and I
  did meet" *see The salley gardens* Yeats
  IRELAND
Down east see Ives **IVES**
Down in Temesvar's fair glade see Anon.
  DVOŘÁK *Žalo dievča, žalo trávu*
"Down the perspective leading to your
  horizon" *see The lover as mirror*
  Stringham **DIAMOND**
"Down the river comes a noise!" *see The new
  river* Ives **IVES**
Downcast am I, so often with despair see
  Pfleger-Moravský **DVOŘÁK**
    Mé srdce často vbolesti
      Three settings: B. 11 no. 11, B. 123
        no. 6, and B. 124 no. 3.
Dowson, Ernest Christopher, 1867-1900.
  IRELAND
    I was not sorrowful
    If we must part
  QUILTER
    A coronal
    In spring
    A land of silence
    Passing dreams
Der Drachenfels see Lutze **LOEWE**
Drachmann, Holger Henrik Herholdt,
  1846-1908.
  DELIUS
    Dreamy nights
    In bliss we walked with laughter
    Jeg hører i natten
    Summer landscape
  GRIEG
    Du retter tidt dit Øjepar
    Epilog
    Foraarsregn
    Ingebjørg
    Johanne
    Jule-Sne
    Nur er Aftnen lys og lang
    Prolog
    Ragna
    Ragnhild
    Saa du Knøsen, som strøg forbi
    Simpel Sang
    Vaer hilset, I Damer
    Vug, O Vove

NIELSEN *Faedrelandssang*
LYSE NAETTER.
  DELIUS *Summer nights*
"De draebte Bjørnens Unger" *see Balladen om
  Bjørnen* Almquist, C. J. L. **NIELSEN**
Ein Drängen see Zweig **REGER**
"Dränkt i tjära qvarn hjulet gar" *see
  Kvarnhjulet* Josephson, E. **SIBELIUS**
The dragonfly see Levertin **SIBELIUS**
  En slända
The drake see Anon. **STRAVINSKIĬ** *Canard*
Drang in die Ferne see Leitner **SCHUBERT**
Le drapeau blanc see Unknown **POULENC**
"Draussen im weiten Krieg" *see Mädchenlied*
  Morgenstern **REGER**
"Draussen im Winde" *see Am Fenster* Huber,
  B. **KILPINEN**
"Draussen in der weiten Nacht" *see Im Freien*
  Seidl **SCHUBERT**
"Draussen weht es bitterkalt" *see Knecht
  Ruprecht* Boelitz **REGER**
The dream see Anon. **PROKOFIEV** *Son*
A dream see Heine *ICH HATTE EINST EIN
  SCHÖNES VATERLAND.*
  RACHMANINOFF
Dream see Lermontov **BALAKIREV** *Son*
Dream see Mikhailov **BALAKIREV** *Son*
A dream see Moore, T. **RUBINSTEIN**
A DREAM. see Poe
  Un rêve **SÉVERAC**
The dream see Pushkin **RIMSKIĬ-
  KORSAKOV** *Snovidenie*
The dream see Runeberg **SIBELIUS**
  Drömmen
A dream see Teternikov **RACHMANINOFF**
A dream in the summer night see Maĭkov
  RIMSKIĬ-KORSAKOV
  Son v letniuiu noch'
The dream of the Virgin Mary see Unknown
  MARTINŮ *Sen Panny Marie*
Dream valley see Blake, William **QUILTER**
A dream within a dream see Poe
  LOEFFLER
"Dreamily the night comes" *see Drooping
  wings* Sterling-Levis, Edith **QUILTER**
Dreaming of a dead lady see Shên-Yo
  BERKELEY
Dreamland see Rossetti, Christina
  VAUGHAN WILLIAMS
Dreams see Teternikov **RACHMANINOFF**
  A dream
Dreams see Unknown **IVES**
The dreamy lake see Mosen **GRIFFES**
  Der träumende See
Dreamy nights see Drachmann **DELIUS**
Drei Bitten see Geibel **LASSEN**

COMPOSER Poet *Title* "First Line"

"Drei Bitten hab ich" *see Drei Bitten* Geibel
LASSEN
Die drei Budrisse see Mickiewicz **LOEWE**
"Drei bunte Kühe in guter Ruh" *see*
Die bunten Kühe Falke **REGER**
DREI CHANSONS AUS SHAKESPEARES
ROMEO UND JULIA, no. 1
BLACHER Shakespeare *Zwei hohe*
Häuser, gleich an Würdigkeit
DREI CHANSONS AUS SHAKESPEARES
ROMEO UND JULIA, no. 2
BLACHER Shakespeare *Die einst'ge*
Sehnsucht
DREI CHANSONS AUS SHAKESPEARES
ROMEO UND JULIA, no. 3
BLACHER Shakespeare *So wilde*
Freude nimmt ein wildes Ende
Die drei Dörfer see Scheffel *GAUDEAMUS.*
JENSEN
DREI HYMNEN, no. 1
HINDEMITH Whitman *Der ich, in*
Zwischenräumen
DREI HYMNEN, no. 2
HINDEMITH Whitman *O, nun heb du*
an, dort in deinem Moor
DREI HYMNEN, no. 3
HINDEMITH Whitman *Schlagt! Schlagt!*
Trommeln!
"Drei Kön'ge wandern aus Morgenland" *see*
Die Könige Cornelius **CORNELIUS**
Two settings: 1856 and op. 8 no. 3.
Drei Lieder see Busch, W. **HINDEMITH**
Die drei Lieder see Uhland **LOEWE,**
STRAUSS
Drei Lieder see Unknown **HINDEMITH**
Drei Masken sah ich see Kerr **STRAUSS**
DREI PSALMEN, no. 1
BLACHER Bible *Psalm 142*
DREI PSALMEN, no. 2
BLACHER Bible *Psalm 141*
DREI PSALMEN, no. 3
BLACHER Bible *Psalm 121*
Die drei Reiche der Natur see Lessing
ZELTER
"Drei Rosen hielt ich in Händen, um eine der
Liebsten zu spenden" *see*
Klagelied von den drei Rosen Buri **SPOHR**
Die drei Sänger see Bobrik **SCHUBERT**
"Drei Sonne sah ich am Himmel steh'n" *see*
Die Nebensonne Müller, Wilhelm
SCHUBERT
"Drei Tage Regen fort und fort" *see*
Der Jäger Mörike **WOLF**
Die drei Zigeuner see Lenau **LISZT,**
RUBINSTEIN, SCHOECK

"Drei Zigeuner fand ich einmal" *see Die drei*
Zigeuner Lenau **LISZT, RUBINSTEIN,**
SCHOECK
DREIZEHN MOTETTEN.
HINDEMITH
Bible
Angelus Domini apparuit
Ascendente Jesu in naviculam
Cum descendisset Jesus de monte
Cum factus esset Jesus annorum
duodecim
Cum natus esset
Defuncto Herode
Dicebat Jesus scribis et pharisaeis
Dixit Jesus Petro
Erat Joseph et Maria
Exiit edictum
Nuptiae factae sunt
Pastores loquebantur
Vidit Joannes Jesum venientem
Der 13. Psalm see Bible **SCHUBERT**
Dréjac, Jean
SAUGUET *Le chemin des forains*
Dreman, J
MARTINŮ *Bar*
The drifting boat see Apukhtin
PROKOFIEV *Otchalila lodka*
Driftwood see Kianto **SIBELIUS** *Lastu*
lainehilla
A drinking song see Witwicki **CHOPIN**
Hulanka
"Driver, drive faster and make a good run"
see Calypso Auden **BRITTEN**
"Driver, what stream is it?" *see The lordly*
Hudson Goodman **ROREM**
"Droben stehet die Kapelle" *see Die Kapelle*
Uhland **SCHOECK**
Drobitsia, i pleshchet see Tolstoï **RIMSKĬ-**
KORSAKOV
"Dröhnende Hämmer in russiger Hand" *see*
Wehe Boelitz **REGER**
Drömmen see Runeberg **SIBELIUS**
The droll lover see Anon. **HESELTINE**
En Drøm see Bodenstedt **GRIEG**
Ein Traum
Le dromadaire see Apollinaire
LE BESTIAIRE. **POULENC**
Drømme see Benzon **GRIEG**
Drooping wings see Sterling-Levis, Edith
QUILTER
Dropkin, Celia (Levin), 1888-1956.
WEISGALL
Poem
Two settings: 1972 and 197_.
Die Drossel see Uhland **STRAUSS**
"Die Drossel pfeift ihr letztes Stück" *see*
Die Waldbrüder Storm **LASSEN**

Droste-Hülshoff, Annette Elisabeth,
Freiin von, 1797-1848.
CORNELIUS
   Gesegnet
   Das Kind
   Unerhört
Drought see Wright, Merle St. Croix
   THOMPSON, R.
The drowned maiden see Sládek **MARTINŮ**
Droysen, Johann Gustav, 1808-1884.
   MENDELSSOHN-BARTHOLDY
   Entsagung
   Ferne
   Sehnsucht
Drüben see Hesse **KILPINEN**
Drüben beim See dort see Anon.
   SZYMANOWSKI *U jeziorecka*
Drüben geht die Sonne scheiden see Lenau
   FRANZ, SCHOECK
"Drüben geht die Sonne scheiden" *see*
   Schilflied Lenau **SCHÖNBERG**
"Drüben hinterm Dorfe steht ein Leiermann"
   see Der Leiermann Müller, Wilhelm
   SCHUBERT
"Drüben überm Bcrgc" *see Drüben* Hesse
   KILPINEN
Drug dlia druga see Goethe **MEDTNER**
   Gleich und Gleich
"Drunten auf der Gassen stand ich" *see*
   Mädchenlied Heyse **JENSEN**
DRUZBIAM. see Bugayev
   Epitaph **MEDTNER**
THE DRY SALVAGES. see Eliot
   Prayer from "The dry salvages" **ROREM**
Dryaden I see Österling **KILPINEN**
Dryaden II see Österling **KILPINEN**
Dryaden III see Österling **KILPINEN**
Dryden, John, 1631-1700.
   ROREM
   From "Cleomenes"
   Hidden flames
Du alte Mutter see Vinje **IVES** *The old
mother*
"Du arme, kleine Nachtigall" *see Die tote
Nachtigall* Kaufmann, J. **LISZT**
"Du armes Herz, was wünschest du?" *see
Beruhigung* Unknown **SPOHR**
"Du Bächlein silberhell und klar" *see
Das Bächlein* Goethe **STRAUSS**
Du Bellay, Joachim, ca.1525-1560.
   MILHAUD
   De sa peine, et des beautés de sa Dame
   Le vrai amour
   D'UN VANNEUR DE BLÉ AUX VENTS: A
   vous troppe légère.
   BERKELEY *The thresher*

Du bist der junge Lenz see Paulsen **GRIEG**
   Til Én. I
Du bist die Ruh see Rückert *KEHR EIN BEI
MIR.* **SCHUBERT**
"Du bist gestorben" *see Altes Lied* Heine
   FRANZ
"Du bist glücklich, O Cicade" *see An die
Grille* Anacreon **LOEWE**
"Du bist mein Auge" *see Mein Auge* Dehmel
   STRAUSS
"Du bist mein fernes Tal" *see Die Kindheit*
   Hesse **KILPINEN, SCHOECK**
Du bist mein, ich bin dein see Anon.
   WEBERN
Du bist mir gut! see Boelitz **REGER**
"Du bist Orplid, mein Land!" *see Gesang
Weylas* Mörike **WOLF**
Du bist so schön und rein see Heine **FRANZ**
"Du bist vom Schlaf erstanden" *see Stille
Thränen* Kerner **SCHUMANN**
DU BIST WIE EINE BLUME. see Heine
   Child, thou art as beautiful as a flower
   RACHMANINOFF
Du bist wie eine Blume see Heine **LISZT,
SCHUMANN, WOLF**
"Du bist wie eine Blume" *see Lied* Heine
   RUBINSTEIN
"Du blühst schön, schöner als sonst" *see
Stella's Monologue* Goethe **KRENEK**
Du Boys, Albert, 1804-1889.
   BERLIOZ
   Le pêcheur
   Toi qui l'amais, verse des pleurs
"Du brachst sie nun, die kalte Rinde" *see Am
Bach im Frühling* Schober
   SCHUBERT
Du brachtest mir deiner Seele Trank see
   Braungart **REGER**
"Du danske Mand" *see Faedrelandssang*
   Drachmann **NIELSEN**
Du denkst mit einem Fädchen see Heyse
   WOLF
"Du, der die Menschheit stolz" *see
An Zeppelin* Glücklich **REGER**
"Du, der Du bist der Geister Hort" *see
Sängers Gebet* Redwitz **LOEWE**
"Du, der du uns besuchst voll Güt' und Huld"
   see Francesca da Rimini Dante
   BLACHER
"Du, der cwig um mich trauert" *see Pflicht
und Liebe* Gotter **SCHUBERT**
"Du, deren Kunst die Todten ruft" *see Saul
und Samuel* Byron **LOEWE**
Du, des Erbarmens Feind, grausamer Tod see
   Dante *VITA NUOVA.* **SCHOECK**

"Du er den unge vår" *see Til Én. I* Paulsen
GRIEG

"Du er min mor" *see Til Norge* Paulsen
GRIEG

"Du ewig Wandelbare, sieh, du bist die
Brükke" *see Rätelspiel* Goering **KRENEK**

"Du ewigkalter Himmel" *see Gebet*
Braungart **REGER**

Du fatter ei Bølgernes evige Gang see
Andersen **GRIEG**

"Du ferer vidt, og du verdt trøytt" *see Guten*
Vinje **GRIEG**

"Du feuchter Frühlingsabend" *see Am Abend*
Geibel **BERG**

Du feuchter Frühlingsabend see Geibel
JENSEN

"Du feuchter Frühlingsabend" *see Im April*
Geibel **BRUCKNER, LASSEN, REGER**

"Du fine, hvide" *see AEbleblomst* Holstein
NIELSEN

"Du fragst mich, du mein blondes Lieb" *see*
Schweigsamkeit Geibel **LASSEN**

"Du fragst mich, Mädchen" *see*
Das Geheimnis Schack **STRAUSS**

"Du gabst mir längst dein schönes Herz" *see*
An Rosa Maria Anna Amalia **SPOHR**

"Du gamle Mor!" *see Gamle Mor* Vinje
GRIEG

Du Geist der reinsten Güte see Branco
LOEWE

Du geleitest mich zum Grave see Unknown
BARTÓK

"Du giebst die Freude" *see Alles in dir*
Branco **LOEWE**

"Du Grabesrose wurzelst wohl" *see*
Die Grabrose Auersperg **LOEWE**

"Du grønne, glitrende trae" *see Sang til*
juletraeet Krohn **GRIEG**

Du grüne Rast im Haine see Osterwald
FRANZ

"Du gute, gute Mäzze" *see Vatergruss*
Unknown **WEBER**

"Du har saa blød en Vuggeseng" *see Julens*
Vuggesang Langsted **GRIEG**

"Du hast mich belogen, du warst nicht treu"
see Ich habe den Glauben verloren
Lüdt **LASSEN**

Du hast mich verlassen, Jamie see Burns
FRANZ *Thou hast left me ever, Jame*

"Du hattest einen Glanz auf deiner Stirn" *see*
Ideale Landschaft Dehmel **WEBERN**

"Du heilig, glühend Abendrot!" *see*
Das Abendrot Schreiber **SCHUBERT**

"Du Herre, som er sterk og stor" *see*
Faedrelandssalme Rolfsen **GRIEG**

"Du herrlich Glas" *see Aus das Trinkglas*
eines verstorbenen Freundes Kerner
SCHUMANN

"Du holde Kunst, in wie viel grauen Stunden"
see An die Musik Schober
SCHUBERT

"Du in der Schönheit strahlendem Scheim
Entschwundne" *see Todtenklage* Byron
LOEWE

"Du junges Grün" *see Erstes Grün* Kerner
SCHUMANN

"Du kamst, du ginst mit leiser Spur" *see Auf*
den Tod eines Kindes Uhland
SCHOECK

Du kannst dich zurückhalten . . . see Kafka
KRENEK

Du kehrst mir den Rücken see Pfau
SCHÖNBERG

Du kleine Biene, verfolg mich nicht see Kuh
CORNELIUS

"Du kleine bist so lieb und hold" *see Zweifler*
Pfau **SCHÖNBERG**

"Du kleine grünumwachs'ne Quelle" *see An*
eine Quelle Claudius, M. **SCHUBERT**

Du lehnest wider eine Silberweide see
George
DAS BUCH DER HÄNGENDEN GÄRTEN.
SCHÖNBERG

"Du liebe, treue Laute" *see Nachruf*
Eichendorff **SCHOECK, WOLF**

Du liebes Auge see Roquette **FRANZ,**
REGER

"Du liebes Auge willst dich tauchen" *see*
Du liebes Auge Roquette **FRANZ**

"Du liebes Auge willst dich tauchen" *see*
Perlenfischer Roquette **JENSEN, WOLF**

"Du liebes, holdes, himmelsüsses Wesen" *see*
Sonett Streckfuss **WEBER**

"Du lieblicher Stern" *see Der Abendstern*
Hoffmann von Fallersleben
SCHUMANN

Du liebst mich nicht see Heine
MACDOWELL

Du liebst mich nicht see Platen-
Hallermünde **SCHUBERT**

Du machst mich traurig-hör' see Lasker-
Schüler **HINDEMITH**

"Du, mein Heil, mein Leben" *see*
Der Entfernten Bürger **CORNELIUS**

Du meine Liebe, du mein Herz see Goethe
BARTÓK

"Du meine Seele, du mein Herz" *see*
Widmung Rückert **SCHUMANN**

Du meiner Seele schönster Traum see
Cornelius **LASSEN**

Du meines Herzens Krönelein see Dahn
SCHLICHTE WEISEN, no. 7.
REGER, STRAUSS

"Du merkst nicht, wie so flüchtig" *see*
Der Dichter Sturm, J. **RUBINSTEIN**

Du milchjunger Knabe see Keller, G.
   PFITZNER, WOLF
"Du milchjunger Knabe" *see Therese* Keller,
   G. **BRAHMS**
"Du musst nicht meinen" *see Mannesbangen*
   Dehmel **SCHÖNBERG**
Du nennst mich armes Mädchen see
   Kulmann **SCHUMANN**
Du och jag see Bergman **KILPINEN**
Du retter tidt dit Øjepar see Drachmann
   GRIEG
Du Ring an meinem Finger see Chamisso
   LOEWE, SCHUMANN
"Du sagst, mein liebes Mütterlein" *see*
   Herzenstausch Enslin **REGER**
Du sagst mir, dass ich keine Fürstin sei see
   Heyse **WOLF**
"Du sagtest, Freund, an diesen Ort" *see*
   Der Mann von Wort Kleinschmid
   BEETHOVEN
"Du sagtest mir es, Mutter" *see Die Männer*
   sind méchant Seidl **SCHUBERT**
"Du sahst durch meine Seele in die Welt" *see*
   Die Liebe Dehmel **REGER**
"Du sahst mich schwelgen oft im Tonregister"
   see Unmut Leuthold **SCHOECK**
"Du samlar, och du samlar" *see Till en diktare*
   Blomberg **KILPINEN**
"Du schläfst und sachte neig' ich" *see Meinem*
   Kinde Falke **REGER, STRAUSS**
"Du schönes Fischermädchen" *see*
   Das Fischermädchen Heine **SCHUBERT**
Du schönes Fischermädchen see Heine
   LOEWE
"Du Schwert an meiner Linken" *see*
   Schwertlied Körner **SCHUBERT**
"Du sider i Mindets Lund" *see Til*
   Generalkonsul Chr. Tønsberg Bøgh,
   Johan **GRIEG**
"Du siehst mich, Königin, zurück" *see*
   *Lynceus, der Helen*e Goethe **LOEWE**
"Du siehst mich nun schon drei Tage heut"
   see Bitte Unknown **REGER**
"Du Skog! som bøyer deg imot" *see Langs ei*
   Å Vinje **GRIEG**
"Du soleil sur le dos" *see Porc* Éluard
   SAUGUET
"Du, som bland jasminer medan natten går"
   see Dryaden I Österling **KILPINEN**
"Du Sommerabend! Heilig, goldnes Licht!"
   see Sommerabend Weigand **WEBERN**
Du sprichst, dass ich mich täuschte see
   Platen-Hallermünde **BRAHMS**
"Du staunest, O Mensch" *see Die Sterne*
   Schlegel, F. **SCHUBERT**
Du süsse Dirn' von Inverness see Burns
   JENSEN

"Du surlande Bekk" *see Ved Gjaetle-Bekken*
   Garborg **GRIEG**
"Du tatest mir die Tür auf, ernstes Kind" *see*
   Verkündigung Dehmel
   SZYMANOWSKI
"Du Thurm! zu meinem Leide" *see Der Hirt*
   Mayrhofer **SCHUBERT**
Du träumst so heiss im Sommerwind see
   Unknown **WEBERN**
"Du Trotz des Glaubens" *see Marienkirche zu*
   Danzig im Gerüst
   Zwehl, Hans Fritz von **KILPINEN**
"Du trüber Nebel, hüllest mir das Tal" *see*
   Nebel Lenau **FRANZ, STRAUSS**
"Du Unruh' meiner Seelen" *see Friede und*
   Ruhe in Gott Anon. **LOEWE**
"Du vackra slända, som till mig flög in" *see*
   En slända Levertin **SIBELIUS**
"Du Vårens milde, skjønne Barn" *see Med en*
   Primula veris Paulsen **GRIEG**
"Du verstörst uns nicht, O Nacht!" *see*
   Die Nacht Uz **SCHUBERT**
"Du warest mir ein täglich Wanderziel" *see*
   Jetzt rede du! Meyer **SCHOECK**
"Du warst mir ein gar trauter" *see Erinnerung*
   Lenau **SCHOECK**
Du whisky pour Jo see Frank, J. H.
   HONEGGER
"Du wirst nicht weinen" *see Befreit* Dehmel
   STRAUSS
"Du wunderbare Frühlingszeit" *see Frühling*
   Huber, B. **KILPINEN**
Dubor, Georges de, 1848-
   MASSENET *Amoureux appel*
Dubufe, Guillaume
   GOUNOD *À Cécile*
Dubuffe, Guillaume *see* Dubufe,
   Guillaume
Dudley, Helen
   CARPENTER *To one unknown*
DUE CANTI, no. 1
   CASELLA Carducci *Pianto antico*
DUE CANTI, no. 2
   CASELLA Carducci *Il bove*
"Due in confidenzo, dritti come re" *see*
   Passeggiata Papini, Giovanni **PIZZETTI**
DUE LIRICHE, no. 1
   CASELLA Olkienizkaia-Naldi *Volutta*
DUE LIRICHE, no. 2
   CASELLA Olkienizkaia-Naldi *La danza*
DUE SONETTI DEL BERNI, no. 1
   MALIPIERO Berni *Chiome d'argento*
   fine, irte e attorte
DUE SONETTI DEL BERNI, no. 2
   MALIPIERO Berni *Cancheri e beccafichi*
   magri arosto

COMPOSER   Poet   *Title*   "First Line"

Duer, Caroline King, 1865-
MASSENET *Au très aimé*
"Dürft' ich einmal dies Dach durchbrechen!"
see Feuersgedanken Trinius LOEWE
"Duérmete, niño, duerme" *see Nana* Anon.
FALLA
Düster und feucht war der Abend see
Pleshcheyev MUSORGSKiĭ
List'ia shumeli unylo
"Düst're Harmonieen hör' ich klingen" *see*
Leyer und Schwert Körner WEBER
Dufrénoy, Mme. Adélaide Gillette
(Billet), 1765-1825.
MILHAUD *Élégie*
"Det duftet af gran" *see Turisten* Paulsen
GRIEG
"Die duftenden Kräuter auf der Au'" *see Ich*
scheide Hoffmann von Fallersleben
LISZT
Duftet die Lindenblüt' see Groth LASSEN
"Duftreich ist die Erde" *see Ekloge* Vrchlický
SCHÖNBERG
Duiut vetry, vetry buĭnye see Kol'tsov
MUSORGSKiĭ
Duke Magnus see Josephson, E. SIBELIUS
Hertig Magnus
"Dukhi neba, daĭte mne" *see Isstupleniye*
Kol'tsov BALAKIREV
"Dukhovnoĭ zhazhdoiu tomim" *see Prorok*
Pushkin RIMSKIĭ-KORSAKOV
"Dulce Jesús, que estás dormido" *see Oración*
de las madres que tienen . . .
Martinez Sierra FALLA
Dulces árboles sombrosos see Unknown
SPANISCHES LIEDERBUCH: Celestina.
JENSEN
"Dulces exuviae, dum fata deusque sinebat"
see Lutheri Vespera Vergilius ZELTER
"Duld' es still" *see Maienblüten* Jacobowski
REGER
"Dulde, gedulde dich fein!" *see Über ein*
Stündlein Heyse JENSEN, PFITZNER
Dulgt Kjaerlighed see Bjørnson GRIEG
Dulong de Rosnay, R P
GOUNOD *Cantique pour la première*
communion
Duma see Shevchenko RACHMANINOFF
Meditation
Duma za dumoĭ, volna za volnoĭ see
Tiutchev MEDTNER *Waves and thoughts*
Dumas, Alexandre, the elder, 1803-
1870.
BERLIOZ *La belle Isabeau*
FRANCK *Le sylphe*
LISZT *Jeanne d'Arc au bûcher*

Dumas, Alexandre, the younger, 1824-
1895.
GOUNOD
Compliment
La Pâquerette
Si vous n'ouvrez vôtre fenêtre
Dumerki see Tiutchev MEDTNER *Twilight*
Dumka see Zaleski *NIE MA CZEGO*
TRZEBA. CHOPIN
Dumont, Émile
LA BONNE CUISINE FRANÇAISE.
BERNSTEIN
Civet à toute vitesse
Plum pudding
Queues de boeuf
Tavouk gueunksis
"Dumpf rauschts vom hohen Wogenstrand ans
steile Felsengestade" *see*
Die Geister des Sees Helvig ZELTER
"D'un amour tendre et pur" *see Tendrement*
Hyspa SATIE
D'un berceau see Hettich AUBERT
D'UN CAHIER INÉDIT DU JOURNAL
D'EUGÉNIE DE GUÉRIN, no. 1
MILHAUD Guérin, E. *Cette promenade*
avec toi
D'UN CAHIER INÉDIT DU JOURNAL
D'EUGÉNIE DE GUÉRIN, no. 2
MILHAUD Guérin, E. *Nous voilà donc*
exilés
D'UN CAHIER INÉDIT DU JOURNAL
D'EUGÉNIE DE GUÉRIN, no. 3
MILHAUD Guérin, E. *A mesure qu'on*
avance
"D'un même moule, les jours s'écoulent" *see*
Pour Nicolas Alix, Marie SAUGUET
D'UN VANNEUR DE BLÉ AUX VENTS: A
vous troppe légère. *see* Du Bellay
The thresher BERKELEY
Dunbar, Paul Laurence, 1872-1906.
CARPENTER *Treat me nice*
Dunbar, William, 1460?-1520?
SEIBER *Timor mortis*
D'une prison see Verlaine *MES PRISONS*:
Sagesse III, no. 6. HAHN
Duniushka see Anon. PROKOFIEV
"Dunkel sind nun alle Gassen" *see Nach dem*
Abschiede Hoffmann von Fallersleben
WOLF
"Dunkel, wie dunkel im Wald und in Feld!"
see Von ewiger Liebe Wenzig BRAHMS
"Dunkelnd über den See" *see Gruss in die*
Ferne Lingg SCHÖNBERG
Das dunkle Auge see Lenau *BITTE.* LOEWE
Dunkle Augen see Hesse KILPINEN
"Dunkle Giebel, hohe Fenster" *see In Danzig*
Eichendorff PFITZNER

Das dunkle Herz see Jone *VIAE INVIAE.*
WEBERN
"Dunkle, schwüle Sommernacht" *see Traum*
rosen Heinitz, Marie **DELIUS**
"Die dunklen Wolken hingen" *see*
Der schwere Abend Lenau **FRANZ,**
SCHUMANN
"Dunno a heap about the what an' why" *see*
Vagabond Masefield **IRELAND**
Dunyushka see Anon. **PROKOFIEV**
Duniushka
Duo see Bédat de Monlaur, Pierre
HONEGGER
DUPARC, HENRI, 1848-1933.
Baudelaire, Charles Pierre, 1821-1867.
La vie antérieure (1884) [Rouart Lerolle,
1911]
"J'ai longtemps habité sous de vastes
portiques"
Originally voice & orchestra.
LES FLEURS DU MAL.
L'Invitation au voyage (1870)
[Badoux, 1894; Rouart Lerolle,
1911] "Mon enfant, ma soeur"
Bonnières, Robert de, 1850-1905.
CONTES DE FÉES.
Le manoir de Rosemonde (1879)
[Badoux, 1894; Rouart Lerolle,
1911] "De sa dent soudaine et
vorace"
Cazalis, Henri, 1840-1909.
Chanson triste, op. 2 no. 4 (1868)
[G. Flaxland, 1869; Rouart Lerolle,
1911] "Dans ton coeur dort un clair
de lune"
Extase (1878) [Badoux, 1894; Rouart
Lerolle, 1911]
"Sur un lys pàle mon coeur dort"
Sérénade Florentine (1880) [Badoux,
1894; Rouart Lerolle, 1911]
"Etoile dont la beauté luit"
Coppée, François Édouard Joachim,
1842-1908.
LE RELIQUAIRE.
La vague et la cloche (1871) [Badoux,
1894; Rouart Lerolle, 1911]
"Une fois, terrassé par un puissant
breuvage"
Bass & orchestra; voice-piano
reduction by Vincent d'Indy.
Gautier, Théophile, 1811-1872.
LA COMÉDIE DE LA MORT.
Lamento (1883) [Badoux, 1895; Rouart
Lerolle, 1911]
"Connaissez-vous la blanche tombe"

LA COMÉDIE DE LA MORT: Romance.
Au pays où se fait la guerre (1869)
[***Journal de musique d'Armand***
Gouzien, May 19, 1877] same
Also published by Rouart Lerolle,
1911.
Goethe, Johann Wolfgang von, 1749-
1832.
WILHELM MEISTER. Mignon's song:
Kennst du das Land?
Romance de Mignon, op. 2 no. 3
(1868) [G. Flaxland, 1869]
"Le connais-tu, ce radieux pays"
Text adapted by Victor Wilder.
Leconte de Lisle, Charles Marie René,
1818-1894.
Phidylé (1882) [Badoux, 1894; Rouart
Lerolle, 1911]
"L'herbe est molle au sommeil"
Marc, Gabriel
Sérénade, op. 2 no. 2 (1868) [G.
Flaxland, 1869]
"Si j'étais, O mon amoureuse"
Moore, Thomas, 1779-1852.
Élégie (1874) [***Journal de Musique***
d'Armand Gouzien, Jan. 12, 1878]
"Oh! ne murmurez pas son nom!"
Also published by Rouart Lerolle,
1911.
Silvestre, Paul Armond, 1837-1901.
Testament (1883) [Badoux, 1896; Rouart
Lerolle, 1911]
"Pour que le vent te les apporte"
Sully-Prudhomme, René François
Armand, 1839-1907.
Le galop, op. 2 no. 5 (1868) [G.
Flaxland, 1869; Durand, 1948]
"Agite, bon cheval, ta crinière fuyante"
LES SOLITUDES.
Soupir, op. 2 no. 1 (1868) [G.
Flaxland, 1869; Rouart Lerolle,
1911]
"Ne jamais la voir ni l'entendre"
Durante, D
SATIE *Allons-y Chochotte*
Durch allen Schall und Klang see Goethe
WESTÖSTLICHER DIVAN. **STRAUSS**
"Durch alte Marmorhallen" *see*
Venezianisches Intermezzo Zwehl, Hans
Fritz von **KILPINEN**
"Durch Bäume dringt ein leiser Ton" *see*
Stilleben Keller, G. **SCHOECK**
"Durch den Wald, den dunkeln" *see*
Frühlingsblick Lenau
FRANZ, RUBINSTEIN, SCHOECK
"Durch den Wald, den dunkeln" *see*
Frühlingslied Lenau
MENDELSSOHN-BARTHOLDY

COMPOSER Poet *Title* "First Line"

Durch den Wald im Mondenscheine see
Heine **FRANZ**
Durch die abendlichen Gärten see Schilling
HINDEMITH
Durch die Ferne, durch die Nacht see Heyse
JENSEN
"Durch die Freundschaft fest verbunden" *see
Letztes Lied* Kugler, Johann, Consul in
Stettin **LOEWE**
"Durch die Lande auf und ab" *see
Der Säemann* Morgenstern **KILPINEN**
"Durch die laue Nacht" *see Ständchen*
Unknown **RUBINSTEIN**
Durch die Nacht see Kraus *WORTE IN
VERSEN.* **KRENEK**
Durch die Nacht, die dunkle see Anon.
SZYMANOWSKI *Ciamna nocka, ciamna*
"Durch die Strassen von Granada" *see
Der Sturm von Alhama* Huber, V.
LOEWE
"Durch die Tannen und die Linden" *see
Herbstlied* Schöpff **SCHUMANN**
"Durch die Wälder streif ich munter" *see
Herbstlied* Sallet **PFITZNER**
Durch die wolkige Maiennacht see Geibel
JENSEN
"Durch eine ganze Nacht sich nah zu sein"
see Der Morgenkuss Batsányi
SCHUBERT
"Durch Feld u. Buchenhallen" *see Reiselied*
Eichendorff **SCHOECK**
"Durch Feld und Wald zu schweifen" *see
Der Musensohn* Goethe **SCHUBERT,
ZELTER**
"Durch Fichten am Hügel, durch Erlen am
Bach" *see Lied der Liebe* Matthisson
SCHUBERT
"Durch hohe Tannen" *see Vorfrühling* Zwehl,
Hans Fritz von **KILPINEN**
"Durch irr' ich Länder" *see Mein Hochland-
Kind* Burns **FRANZ**
Durch säuselnde Bäume see Osterwald
FRANZ
"Durch Schneegestöber und eisigen Wind" *see
Der Lappländer* Marggraff **LOEWE**
"Durch schöne Augen hab' ich" *see Vom
Auge zum Herzen* Rückert **FRANZ**
"Durch schwankende Wipfel schiesst güldener
Strahl" *see Jagdlied* Eichendorff
FRANZ
"La dure épreuve va finir" *see La bonne
chanson* Verlaine **HAHN**
During music see Rossetti, Dante
IRELAND
During the ball see Tolstoĭ **CHAĬKOVSKIĬ**
Sred' shumnago bala

Durrell, Lawrence, 1912-1990.
BERKELEY *Lesbos*
Dusch, Alexander von, 1789-1876.
WEBER *Des Künstlers Abschied*
"Dusha moĭa mrachna" *see Evreyskaya
melodiya* Lermontov **BALAKIREV**
Dusk fell on the earth see Mickiewicz
CHAĬKOVSKIĬ *Na zemlĭu sumrak pal*
Dusk has fallen see Tolstoĭ
RACHMANINOFF *Twilight has fallen*
The dust of snow see Frost **CARTER**
Duty see Emerson **IVES**
Duval, Paul Alexander Martin, 1856-
1906.
CASELLA *C'était un songe*
Duverne, Anne Girard
MASSENET *Si tu m'aimes*
Dva proshchaniĭa see Kol'tsov
RACHMANINOFF *Two partings,* a
dialogue
DVOŘÁK, ANTONÍN, 1841-1904.
Anon.
Ach není, není tu, B. 146 no. 3 (1886)
[GA, v. VI/2] same
Op. 73 no. 3.
Dobrú noc, má milá, B. 146 no. 1 (1886)
[GA, v. VI/2] same
Op. 73 no. 1.
Ej, mám já koňa faku, B. 146 no. 4
(1886) GA, v. VI/2] same
Op. 73 no. 4.
Když tě vidim, B. 142 no. 2 (1885) [GA,
v. VI/2] same
Koljas, B. 84 no. 1 (1878) [GA, v. VI/1]
"Na vysoké skále sama sedí matka
Koljova"
Op. 50 no. 1; text translated by
Nebesky.
Lásce neujdeš, B. 29 no. 4 (1872?) [GA,
v. VI/1] "Brodí se panenka, brodí se,
brodí"
Op. 6 no. 4.
Nereidy, B. 84 no. 2 (1878) [GA, v. VI/
1] "Devotero tisíc ovcí"
Op. 50 no. 2; text translated by
Nebesky.
Panenka a tráva, B. 29 no. 1 (1872?)
[GA, v. VI/1]
"Usnula panenka usnula vtravičce"
Op. 6 no. 1.
Připamatování, B. 29 no. 2 (1872?) [GA,
v. VI/1] "Nezapomeň, družičko má,
nikdy"
Op. 6 no. 2.
Spi, mé ditě, spi, B. 142 no. 1 (1885)
[GA, v. VI/2] same

Výklad znamení, B. 29 no. 3 (1872?)
[GA, v. VI/1]
"Přání svá, duše, zasázej"
Op. 6 no. 3.

Žalo dievča, žalo trávu, B. 146 no. 2
(1886) [GA, v. VI/2] same
Op. 73 no. 2.

Žalozpěv Pargy, B. 84 no. 3 (1878) [GA,
v. VI/1] "Tré ptáku letí Prevezy"
Op. 50 no. 3; text translated by
Nebesky.

Bible

Bože! Bože! Píseň novou, B. 185 no. 5
(1894) [GA, v. VI/2] same
Op. 99 no. 5.

Hospodin jest muj pastýř, B. 185 no. 4
(1894) [GA, v. VI/2] same
Op. 99 no. 4.

Oblak a mrákota, B. 185 no. 1 (1894)
[GA, v. VI/2] same
Op. 99 no. 1.

Popatřiž na mne a smiluj se nade mnou,
B. 185 no. 8 (1894) [GA, v. VI/2]
same
Op. 99 no. 8.

Pozdvihuji očí svých k horám, B. 185 no.
9 (1894) [GA, v. VI/2] same
Op. 99 no. 9.

Při řekách babylonských, B. 185 no. 7
(1894) [GA, v. VI/2] same
Op. 99 no. 7.

Skrýše má paveza má Ty jsi, B. 185 no. 2
(1894) [GA, v. VI/2] same
Op. 99 no. 2.

Slyš, Ó Bože! slyš modlitbu mou, B. 185
no. 3 (1894) [GA, v. VI/2] same
Op. 99 no. 3.

Slyš, Ó Bože, volání mé, B. 185 no. 6
(1894) [GA, v. VI/2] same
Op. 99 no. 6.

Zpívejte Hospodinu píseň novou, B. 185
no. 10 (1894) [GA, v. VI/2] same
Op. 99 no. 10.

Čech, Svatopluk, 1846-1908.
LEŠETINSKÝ KOVÁR.
Zpěv z Lešetínského kováře, B. 204
(1901) [GA, v. VI/2]
"Sirší jiskry, srší, skovadliny prší"
Op. posth.

Erben, Karel Jaromír, 1811-1870.
Rozmarýna, B. 24a (1871?) [GA, v.
VI/1] "Als ich gieng zum
Eichenwalde"
Sirotek, B. 24 (1871) [GA, v. VI/1]
"Čí je to dítko"

Hálek, Vitezslav, 1835-1874.
Já jstem ten rytîr zpohádky, B. 61 no. 3
(1876?) [GA, v. VI/1] same
Op. 3 no. 3.

Jsem jako lípa košatá, B. 61 no. 9
(1876?) [GA, v. VI/1] same
Op. 31 no. 3.

Když bůh byl nejvíc rozkochán, B. 61 no.
4 (1876?) [GA, v. VI/1] same
Op. 3 no. 4.

Když jsem se díval do nebe, B. 61 no. 7
(1876?) [GA, v. VI/1] same
Op. 31 no. 1.

Mně zdálo se žes umřela, B. 61 no. 2
(1876?) [GA, v. VI/1] same
Op. 3 no. 2.

Přílítlo jaro zdaleka, B. 61 no. 6 (1876?)
[GA, v. VI/1] same
Op. 9 no. 4.

Tak jak ten měsíc vnebes báň, B. 61 no.
12 (1876?) [GA, v. VI/1] same

Ten ptáček, ten se nazpívá, B. 61 no. 11
(1876?) [GA, v. VI/1] same
Op. 31 no. 5.

Ty hvězdičky tam na nebi to veliké, B. 61
no. 1 (1876?) [GA, v. VI/1] same
Op. 3 no. 1.

Umlklo stromu šumění, B. 61 no. 5
(1876?) [GA, v. VI/1] same
Op. 9 no. 3.

Vy malí, drobní ptáčkové, B. 61 no. 8
(1876?) [GA, v. VI/1] same
Op. 31 no. 2.

Vy všichni kdo jste stísněni, B. 61 no. 10
(1876?) [GA, v. VI/1] same
Op. 31 no. 4.

Heyduk, Adolf, 1835-1923.
A kdybys písní stvořená, B. 13 no. 2
(1865) [GA, v. VII] same

A les je tichý kolem kol, B. 104 no. 3
(1880) [GA, v. VI/1] same
Op. 55 no. 3.

Aj! Kterak trojhranec muj přerozkošně,
B. 104 no. 2 (1880) [GA, v. VI/1]
same
Op. 55 no. 2.

Dejte klec jestřábu, B. 104 no. 7 (1880)
[GA, v. VI/1] same
Op. 55 no. 7.

Kdybys, milé děvče, sedalo na truno, B.
13 no. 1 (1865) [GA, v. VII] same

Když mne stará matka, B. 104 no. 4
(1880) [GA, v. VI/1] same
Op. 55 no. 4.

Má píseň zas mi láskouzní, B. 104 no. 1
(1880) [GA, v. VI/1] same
Op. 55 no. 1.

DVOŘÁK, ANTONÍN, 1841-1904
(continued)
Heyduk, Adolf, 1835-1923 *(continued)*
  Široké rukávy, B. 104 no. 6 (1880) [GA,
    v. VI/1] same
    Op. 55 no. 6.
  Struna naladěna, B. 104 no. 5 (1880)
    [GA, v. VI/1] same
    Op. 55 no. 5.
Jelínek, F. L.
  Ukolébavka, B. 194 (1895) [GA, v. VI/4]
    "Spi, mé zaté boubelaté malé dětátko"
Kleinschrod, Ottilie (Stieler), 1836-
1914.
  Jaro, B. 157 no. 3 (1887-88) [GA,
    v. VI/2] "Slunka svit jak líbá zemi"
    Op. 82 no. 3.
  Kéž duch muj sám . . . , B. 157 no. 1
    (1887-88) [GA, v. VI/2]
    "Kéž sám a sám duch muj"
    Op. 82 no. 1.
  Při vyšívání, B. 157 no. 2 (1887-88)
    [GA, v. VI/2] "Jak velké požehnání"
    Op. 82 no. 2.
  U potoka, B. 157 no. 4 (1887-88) [GA, v.
    VI/2] "Šumí potok v tichém lkání"
    Op. 82 no. 4.
No author
  Ave Maria, B. 68 (1877) [GA, v. VI/1]
    same
    Low voice & organ. Op. 19B.
  Ave maris stella, B. 95 (1879) [GA,
    v. VI/1] same
    Op. 19B.
  Hymnus k Nejsvětější Trojici, B. 82 [GA,
    v. VI/1] "Tu Trinitatis unitas"
Pech, Jindřiška, 1847-1926.
  Lípy, B. 23 no. 1 (1871) [GA, v. VI/1]
    "Bylo to, ach!"
  Překážky, B. 23, no. 3 (1871) [GA,
    v. VI/1] "Řekla bych vám, ruže, něco"
  Přemítání, B. 23 no. 4 (1871) [GA,
    v. VI/1] "Koho jen bych se zeptala"
  Proto, B. 23 no. 2 (1871) [GA, v. VI/1]
    "Mezi květy dlela zlatá včela"
  Vzpomínání, B. 23 no. 5 (1871) [GA,
    v. VI/1] "Ó zda vmysli mám jen
    tebe?"
Pfleger-Moravský, Gustav, 1833-1875.
  Já vím, že v sladké naději, B. 11 no. 6
    (1865) [GA, v. VII] same
  Já vím, že v sladké naději, B. 160 no. 4
    (1888) [GA, v. VI/2] same
    Op. 83 no. 4.
  Kol domu se ted potácím, B. 123 no. 3
    (1881-82?) [GA, v. sub VI/2] same

  Kol domu se ted potácím, B. 160 no. 3
    (1888) [GA, v. VI/2] same
    Op. 83 no. 3.
  Kol domuse, B. 11 no. 9 (1865) [GA,
    v. VII] same
  Mé srdce často vbolesti, B. 11 no. 11
    [GA, v. VII] same
    Other settings:
      B. 123 no. 6 (1881-82?) [GA, v. sub
        VI/2] same
      B. 124 no. 3 (1881-82?) [GA, v.
        VI/2] same
    Op. 2 no. 3
  Mne často týrá pochyba, B. 11 no. 10
    (1865) [GA, v. VII] same
  Mou celou duší zádumně bolestné, B.11
    no. 15 [GA, v. VII] same
  Na horách ticho a vúdolí ticho, B. 11 no.
    13 (1865) [GA, v. VII] same
  Na horách ticho a vúdolích ticho, B. 123
    no. 5 (1881-82?)
    [GA, v. sub VI/2] same
  Na horách ticho, vúdolí ticho, B. 124 no.
    4 (1881-82) [GA, v. VI/2] same
    Op. 2 no. 4.
  Nad krajem vévodí lehký spánek, B. 11
    no. 17 (1865) [GA, v. VII] same
    Another setting: B. 160 no. 5 (1888)
      [GA, v. VI/2] same
    Op. 83 no. 5.
  Ó byl to krásný zlatý sen, B. 11 no. 5
    (1865) [GA, v. VII] same
    Other settings:
      B. 123 no. 2 (1881-82?) [GA, v. sub
        VI/2] same
      B. 124 no. 2 (1881-82?) [GA, v.
        VI/2] same
    Op. 2 no. 2.
  Ó, duše drahá, jedinká, B. 160 no. 8
    (1888) [GA, v. VI/2] same
    Op. 83 no. 8.
  Ó duše drahá jedinkájež, B. 11 no. 4
    (1865) [GA, v. VII] same
  Ó, naší lásce, B. 11 no. 8 (1865) [GA, v.
    VII] same
  Ó, naší lásce nekvete, B. 123 no. 4
    (1881-82?) [GA, v. sub VI/2] same
    Another setting: B. 160 no. 1 (1888)
      [GA, v. VI/2] same
  Ó zlatá ruže, spatnilá, B. 11 no. 7 (1865)
    [GA, v. VII] same
  Tam stojí stará skála, B. 11 no. 16 [GA,
    v. VII] same
  Ty se ptáš pročmoje zpěvy bouří, B. 11
    no. 18 [GA, v. VII] same

Vtak mnohém srdci mrtvojest, B. 11 no. 3
(1865) [GA, v. VII] same
Another setting: B. 160 no. 2 (1888)
[GA, v. VI/2] same
Op. 83 no. 2.
Vté sladké moci, B. 11 no. 2 (1865) [GA,
v. VII] same
Vté sladké moci očí tvých, B. 160 no. 7
[GA, v. VI/2] same
Op. 83 no. 7.
Vy vroucí pìsně pějte, B. 11 no. 1 (1865)
[GA, v. VII] same
Vy vroucí pìsně pějte! B. 123 no. 1
(1881-82?) [GA, v. sub VI/2] same)
Vy vroucí písně spějte, B. 124 no. 1
(1881-82?) [GA, v. VI/2] same
Op. 2 no. 1.
Zde hledím na tendrahý list, B. 11 no. 12
(1865) [GA, v. VII] same
Zde v lese u potoka, B. 11 no. 14 (1865)
[GA, v. VII] same
Another setting: B. 160 no. 6 (1888)
[GA, v. VI/2] same
Op. 83 no. 6.
Unknown
Jahody, B. 30 no. 6 (1872) [GA, v. VI/1]
"Jde má milá na jahody na zelená
borka"
Text from the Dvur Králové ms.
Op. 7 no. 6.
Kytice, B. 30 no. 5 (1872) [GA, v. VI/1]
"Věje větříček zkniežeckých lesév"
Text from the Dvur Králové ms.
Op. 7 no. 5.
Opuščená, B. 30 no. 2 (1872) [GA, v.
VI/1] "Ach vy lesí, tmaví losi"

Text from the Dvur Králové ms.
Op. 7 no. 2.
Róže, B. 30 no. 4 (1872) [GA, v. VI/1]
"Ach ty róvž, krásná róže"
Text from the Dvur Králové ms.
Op. 7 no. 4.
Skřivánek, B. 30 no. 3 (1872) [GA, v.
VI/1]
"Pleje děva konopí u panskéhe sada"
Text from the Dvur Králové ms.
Op. 7 no. 3.
Zezhulice, B. 30 no. 1 (1872) [GA, v.
VI/1] "Všírém poli dubec stojí"
Text from the Dvur Králové ms.
Op. 7 no. 1.
Dwojaki koniec see Zaleski **CHOPIN**
"Dybych já měla sukňu červenú" *see Veselá
dievča* Anon. **MARTINŮ**
"Dybych věděl já" *see Bohatá milá* Anon.
MARTINŮ
"D'ye ken John Peel with his coat so gay" *see
John Peel* Graves, John **THOMSON**
The dying child see Geibel **GRIFFES**
Das sterbende Kind
THE DYING CHRISTIAN TO HIS SOUL. see
Pope
Verklärung **SCHUBERT**
The dying of the light see Thomas *DO NOT
GO GENTLE.* **RIEGGER**
THE DYNASTS. see Hardy
Buonaparty **VAUGHAN WILLIAMS**
Dyningen see Blomberg **KILPINEN**
"Dyningen susar med langa slag" *see*
Dyningen Blomberg **KILPINEN**
"Dyž sem u maměnky byla" *see U maměnky*
Unknown **MARTINŮ**

E

"È 'a notte 'e Pasca. A ll'unnece" *see*
Angeleca Giacomo **PIZZETTI**
E il mio dolore io canto see Bocchialini,
Jacopo **PIZZETTI**
È la vita see Unknown **VERDI**
E le campane hanno suonato see Zaffira
GOUNOD
E lo mio cor s'inchina see Anon. **RIETI**
"E lo mio damo se n'è ito a Siena" *see*
Il Brigidino Ongaro **VERDI**
E per un bel cantar see Anon. **RIETI**

"È sdruscito il navil" *see In alto mare*
Panzacchi **RESPIGHI**
E se un Giorno Tornasse see Aganoor-
Pompilj **RESPIGHI**
E stati al quanto see Zaffira **GOUNOD**
"È tempo per me d'andare, mamma, me ne
vado" *see La fine* Tagore **RESPIGHI**
"È vanito l'odor di questo fiore, che" *see Su
una violetta morta* Shelley **RESPIGHI**
Eagel, Paul
ROREM *The freedom song*

Early in the morning see Hillyer **ROREM**
Early in the morning I weed the grain see
Unknown **MARTINŮ**
Early morning in London see Wilde *WIND FLOWERS*: Impression du matin.
GRIFFES
Early spring see Tolstoĭ **RIMSKIĬ-KORSAKOV** *To bylo ranneĭu vesnoĭ*
"Earth rais'd up her head" *see Earth's answer*
Blake, William **LUENING**
"Earth rests!" *see Autumn* Ives, Harmony
IVES
Earth's answer see Blake, William
LUENING
Earth's call see Monro **IRELAND**
The east riding see Chilman **IRELAND**
Easter see Erben **MARTINŮ**
Eastman, Max, 1883-1969.
GIDEON *At the aquarium*
L'eau see Banville **KOECHLIN**
Eau printanière see Moréas **HAHN**
Eau vivante see Lerberghe **FAURÉ**
"Eau-de-vie!" *see Aus-delà* Vilmorin
POULENC
Eaux douces see Beaumont **SAUGUET**
Eben, Bedřich
MARTINŮ *Píseň na starošpanělský text*
*Eben brach der Mond durch Wolkenschatten
see* Unknown **RUBINSTEIN**
"Ebenes Paradefeld" *see Jedem das Seine*
Colly **SCHÖNBERG**
Ebert, Karl Leopold Felix Egon (Ritter
von), 1801-1882.
MENDELSSOHN-BARTHOLDY
Das erste Veilchen
Reiselied
Eberwein, Julius, 1801-1870.
SPOHR *Sangeslust*
Two settings: Op. 101 no. 2 and WoO
95.
"Ebranlez la solitaire" *see Prière exaucée*
Messiaen **MESSIAEN**
EBRO CAUDOLOSE. see Anon.
Flutenreicher Ebro **SCHUMANN**
Ecce Deus salvator meus see No author
CASELLA
Ecce odor filii mei see No author
CASELLA
"Ecco quel fiero istante!" *see La partenza*
Metastasio **BEETHOVEN, ROSSINI**
L'échelonnement des haies see Verlaine
DEBUSSY
Das Echo see Castelli **SCHUBERT**
Echo see Coppée **RIMSKIĬ-KORSAKOV**
Ekho
Echo see Moore, T. **HINDEMITH**

Echo see Pushkin **BRITTEN, MEDTNER; RIMSKIĬ-KORSAKOV** *Ekho*
The echo child see Baker, Mary Ely
THOMPSON, R.
L'echo de la harpe see Anon.
SAINT-SAËNS
"Ein Echo kenn' ich" *see Er an Sie* Lehr,
Hofrath **WEBER**
The echo nymph see Larin-Kyösti
SIBELIUS *Kaiutar*
Echo's song see Jonson **ROREM**
Eckschlager, Joseph August, b. 1784.
WEBER *Maienblümlein*
Ecloge see Vrchlický **SCHÖNBERG** *Ekloge*
ECLOGUES, a Suite in B Minor, no. 1
ROREM Fletcher *Now the lusty spring is
seen*
ECLOGUES, a Suite in B Minor, no. 2
ROREM Fletcher *Hold back thy hours,
dark night*
ECLOGUES, a Suite in B Minor, no. 3
ROREM Fletcher *Come hither, you that
love*
ECLOGUES, a Suite in B Minor, no. 4
ROREM Fletcher *Come, shepherds, come*
ECLOGUES, a Suite in B Minor, no. 5
ROREM Fletcher *Sing his praises*
Une écluse sans brouillard see Éluard
SAUGUET
L'Eco see Poliziano **MALIPIERO**
École de guerre see Cocteau **AURIC**
"Ecoute Dieu ronronne dans son beau ciel
vide" *see Place des Invalides* Cocteau
AURIC
"Ecoute, écoute . . . On dirait un glas qui dans
l'air frissonne" *see Chanson morave*
Margueritte **MALIPIERO**
"Ecoutez la chanson" *see Le rossignol* Anon.
DELIBES
"Ecoutez la chanson bien douce" *see
La chanson bien douce* Verlaine
CHAUSSON
Ecoutez mes enfants see Unknown
MILHAUD
L'écrevisse see Apollinaire *LE BESTIAIRE.*
POULENC
Les Ecrevisses see Hugnet **THOMSON**
Ecuyère voltige see Copperie, Adrien
SAUGUET
Eddy, Mary Baker, 1821-1910.
ROREM *Feed my sheep*
Der Edelfalk see Freiligrath **LOEWE**
Der edle Mensch sei hülfreich und gut see
Goethe *DAS GÖTTLICHE* (last verse).
BEETHOVEN
Edone see Klopstock **SCHUBERT**

Edward see Herder *STIMMEN DER VÖLKER.* **JENSEN, LOEWE**

Edward, Edward see Herder **SCHUBERT**
Ein altschottische Ballade

Edwardes, Richard, 1523-1566.
   IRELAND *The sweet season*
Eelbo, Bruno H., 1853-1917.
   LASSEN *Siehe, noch blühen die Tage der Rose*

Ee-Oh! see Anon. **BRITTEN**
Efeu see Dahn **STRAUSS**
Effacement see Follain **SAUGUET**
"Efforcez vous d'entrer par la porte étroite" *see Jérôme* Gide **MILHAUD**
Effusion see Allorge, Henri **MASSENET**
Efter lång sorg see Österling **KILPINEN**
Efteraarsstoren see Richardt **GRIEG**
EFTERLADTE SANGE
   GRIEG
      Bjørnson *Den blonde Pige*
      Preetzman *Dig elsker jeg!*
      Schultz *Der Jäger*
      Bjørnson *Jeg elsket*
      Langsted *Julens Vuggesang*
      Andersen *Min lille Fugl*
      Vinje *Paa Humars Ruiner*
      Drachmann *Simpel Sang*
      Andersen *Soldaten*
      Bjørnson *Suk*
      Andersen *Taaren*
"Eg hev som vigde Mammons Trael" *see Dømd* Garborg **GRIEG**
Egle see Rubino **RESPIGHI**
Eglogue see Follain **SAUGUET**
L'Églogue see Hugo **DELIBES**
EGMONT. *see* Goethe
   Clärchen **ZELTER**
   Clärchens Lied **RUBINSTEIN**
   Freudvoll und leidvoll **LISZT**
   Die Liebe **SCHUBERT**
Egyedűl a tengerrel see Ady **BARTÓK** *Alone with the sea*
"Eh' die Sonne früh aufersteht" *see Morgenlied* Werner **SCHUBERT**
"Eh' wir weiter gehen" *see Wo der Goldregen steht* Lorenz, F. **BERG**
Eheu fugaces! see Jalkanen **KILPINEN**
Ehlen, Hanns, pseud. *see* Kolbe, Hanna, fl. 1892.
Ehmals und jetzt see Hölderlin
   HINDEMITH
Die Ehre Gottes aus der Natur see Gellert
   BEETHOVEN
"Ehre sei dem Hocherhab'nen" *see Das grosse Halleluja* Klopstock **SCHUBERT**
Ehre sei Gott in der Höhe! see Hamann
   REGER

"Ehre sei Gott in der Höhe" *see Weihnachts-Kantate* Unknown **LOEWE**
Ehrgeiz see Paulsen **GRIEG**
   Den aergjerrige
Ehrlich, Bernhard Ambros, ca.1765-1827.
   SCHUBERT *Als ich sie erröten sah*
"Ei, das tanzt, das lärmt und trinket!" *see Frau Twardowska* Mickiewicz **LOEWE**
"Ei Gjente eg såg" *see Eit Syn* Vinje **GRIEG**
"Ei! Kennt ihr noch das alte Lied" *see Das alte Lied* Heine **LASSEN**
"Ei maailman rikkaan riemuista" *see Nuori Apollo* Lehtinen **KILPINEN**
Ei minusta lienekänä see Kanteletar
   KILPINEN
"Eĭ, pochtenny gospoda" *see Raëk* Musorgskiĭ **MUSORGSKIĭ**
Ei runo rahatta laula see Kanteletar
   KILPINEN
"Ei, schmollte mein Vater nicht wach und im Schlaf" *see Des Liebsten Schwur,* Aus dem Bohmischen Wenzig **BRAHMS**
Ei sula syan surunen see Kanteletar
   KILPINEN
"Ei, wenn ich doch ein Maler wär" *see Der Sänger und der Maler* Anon. **WEBER**
DIE EICHBÄUME. see Hölderlin
   Ihr, ihr Herrlichen! **REGER**
Eiche zu Fall gekommen see Anon.
   SZYMANOWSKI *Ściani dumbek*
Eichendorff, Joseph Karl Benedikt, Freiherr von, 1788-1857.
   BERG *Es wandelt, was wir schauen*
   BRAHMS
      Anklänge
      In der Fremde
      Lied
      Mondnacht
      Vom Strande, Nach dem Spanischen
   CORNELIUS *Die Räuberbrüder*
   FRANZ
      Abends
      Am Strom
      Der Bote
      Gute Nacht!
      Ich wandre durch die stille Nacht
      Jagdlied
      Meeresstille
      Möcht' wissen, was sie schlagen
      Romanze
         Two settings: Op. 35 no. 4 and op. 51 no. 9.
      Der Schalk
      Sonntag
      Der vielschönen Fraue

COMPOSER Poet *Title* "First Line"

Eichendorff, Joseph Karl Benedikt, Freiherr von, 1788-1857 *(continued)*

GIDEON *Lockung*

GRIFFES *Elfe*

JENSEN

Der Bote

Frühlingsnacht

Nacht

Waldesgespräch

LASSEN

Der Abend

Im Herbst

Mittagsruh

Der Morgen

Morgengebet

Die Nacht

Das Ständchen

Verschwiegene Liebe

Vom Strande

MEDTNER

Im Walde

Nachtgruss

Reiselied

Winternacht

MENDELSSOHN-BARTHOLDY

Es weiss und räth es doch Keiner

Nachtlied

Pagenlied

Das Waldschloss

Wanderlied

PFITZNER

Abschied

Das Alter

Der Bote

Die Einsame

Der Gärtner

Im Herbst

In Danzig

Der Kühne

Lockung

Die Nachtigallen

Nachts

Nachtwanderer

Neue Liebe

Sonst

Studentenfahrt

Der verspätete Wanderer

Der Weckruf

Zorn

Zum Abschied meiner Tochter

REGER

Dein Wille, Herr, geschehe!

Gottes Segen

Traum

RUBINSTEIN

Nacht

Waldeinsamkeit

SCHOECK

Abendlandschaft

Abschied

An die Lützowschen Jäger

Auf dem Rhein

Auf einer Burg

Auf meines Kindes Tod

Die Einsame

Ergebung

Erinnerung

   Two settings: Op. 10 no. 1 and op. 17
   no. 7.

Der frohe Wandersmann

Der Gärtner

Gottes Segen

Guter Rat

Im Wandern

In der Fremde

Der Kranke

Kurze Fahrt

Lockung

Motto

Nachklang

Nachruf

Nacht

Nachtgruss

Nachtlied

Reiselied

Sterbeglocken

Trost

Umkehr

Der verspätete Wanderer

Waldeinsamkeit

Wanderlied der Prager Studenten

Winternacht

SCHUMANN

Auf einer Burg

Der Einsiedler

Der frohe Wandersmann

Frühlingsfahrt

Frühlingsnacht

Im Walde

In der Fremde

   Two settings: Op. 39 no. 1 and op. 39
   no. 8.

Intermezzo

Mondnacht

Der Schatzgräber

Die Stille

Waldesgespräch

WOLF

Erwartung

Der Freund

Der Glücksritter

Heimweh

In der Fremde

   Three settings: One in 1881 and two in
   1883.

COMPOSER   Poet   *Title*   ''First Line''

Die Kleine
Lieber alles
Liebesglück
Der Musikant
Nachruf
Die Nacht
Nachtgruss
Nachtzauber
Rückkehr
Der Scholar
Der Schreckenberger
Seemanns Abschied
Der Soldat I
Der Soldat II
Das Ständchen
Unfall
Verschwiegene Liebe
Der verzweifelte Liebhaber
Waldmädchen
Die Zigeunerin
AHNUNG UND GEGENWART.
   SCHUMANN
     Wehmuth
     Zwielicht
AUSSICHT.
   MEDTNER *Serenade*
DICHTER UND IHRE GESELLEN (1834).
   BRAHMS *Parole*
   SCHUMANN *Schöne Fremde*
Eichhorn, Maria, 1879-
   BERG *Über meinen Nächten*
Der Eichwald see Lenau **FRANZ,**
   LUENING, SCHOECK
"Der Eichwald brauset" *see Des Mädchens*
   Klage Schiller
   MENDELSSOHN-BARTHOLDY,
     SCHUBERT, ZELTER
"Der Eichwald brauscht" *see Thekla's Gesang*
   Schiller **JENSEN**
"Der Eichwald braust" *see Des Mädchens*
   Klage Schiller **SCHUBERT**
   Two settings: D. 191 and D. 389.
Eide, so die Liebe schwur see Anon. **WOLF**
Eifersucht und Stolz see Müller, Wilhelm
   SCHUBERT
EIGHT EPITAPHS, no. 1
   CHANLER De La Mare *Alice Rodd*
EIGHT EPITAPHS, no. 2
   CHANLER De La Mare *Susannah Fry*
EIGHT EPITAPHS, no. 3
   CHANLER De La Mare *Three sisters*
EIGHT EPITAPHS, no. 4
   CHANLER De La Mare *Thomas Logge*
EIGHT EPITAPHS, no. 5
   CHANLER De La Mare *A midget*
EIGHT EPITAPHS, no. 6
   CHANLER De La Mare *No voice to*
   scold

EIGHT EPITAPHS, no. 7
   CHANLER De La Mare *Ann Poverty*
EIGHT EPITAPHS, no. 8
   CHANLER De La Mare *Be very quiet*
   now
Eikö totta see Lamberg **KILPINEN**
"Eil' in des Waldes Ruh' " *see Der letzte*
   Wunsch Hemans **JENSEN**
"Eilen kuulsi pilvet, talot, ihmissydämet" *see*
   Muisto Lamberg **KILPINEN**
Einen schlimmen Weg ging gestern ich see
   Burns **JENSEN**
"Einen schlimmen Weg ging gestern ich" *see*
   Ihr Auge Burns **FRANZ**
Einerlei see Arnim **STRAUSS**
Einerling, Countess Adolfovna, 1873-
   1942.
   RACHMANINOFF
     Before my window
     How fair this spot
     How painful for me
"Eines gibt's, darauf ich mich freuen darf" *see*
   Unverlierbare Gewähr Morgenstern
   KILPINEN
"Ein einfaches lichtes Kleid, ein leichter
   Gang" *see Wunsch* Krzyzanowski
   KRENEK
Einfältiges Lied see Salus **SCHÖNBERG**
"Einflüstrerin, Stimme" *see Schwarze Muse*
   Barth **KRENEK**
Eingang see George *DER SIEBENTE RING:*
   Traumdunkel. **WEBERN**
Eingehüllt in graue Wolken see Heine
   GRIEG
Eingelegte Ruder see Meyer **PFITZNER**
"Eingeschlafen auf der Lauer" *see Auf einer*
   Burg Eichendorff **SCHOECK,**
   SCHUMANN
"Eingeschmiegt in Klippenwände" *see*
   Einsamkeit Prölss **LASSEN**
Eingeschneite stille Felder see Sergel
   KILPINEN
"Eingewiegt von Meereswellen" *see Auf dem*
   Meere Heine **FRANZ**
Einglein hold im Lockengold see Bocella
   LISZT *Angiolin dal biondo crin*
Einkehr see Uhland **STRAUSS**
   Two settings: AV 3 and op. 47 no. 4.
Die Einladung see Knapp, A. **LOEWE**
"Einmal aus seinen Blicken" *see Romanze*
   Unknown **MENDELSSOHN-**
   BARTHOLDY
"Einmal, einmal, in viellen hunderttausend
   Tagen oder Jahren" *see Der Genuss des*
   Unendlichen Krenek **KRENEK**
"Einmal in einem tiefen Thal" *see Der Kukuk*
   Herder **LOEWE**

COMPOSER Poet *Title* "First Line"

"Einmal Mekka noch zu sehen" *see Der verschmactende Pilger* Stieglitz **LOEWE**
"Einmal, nach einer lustigen Nacht" *see Zur Warnung* Mörike **WOLF**
Einrichtung see Gruppe **LOEWE**
"Eins, zwei, drei" *see Mausefangen* Schellenberg **REGER**
"Einsam auf blauer Wasserwüste" *see Das Schiff* Lermontov **RUBINSTEIN**
Einsam bin ich und allein see Pfau **SCHÖNBERG**
"Einsam? einsam? nein" *see Lied in der Fremde* Winkler **WEBER**
Einsam ging ich jüngst see Lamotte **MOZART** *Ariette*
"Einsam steh ich und alleine" *see Das Lied der Waise* Steinebach **WOLF**
"Einsam wandelt dein Freund im Frühlings Garten" *see Adelaide* Matthisson **BEETHOVEN, SCHUBERT**
Die Einsame see Eichendorff **PFITZNER, SCHOECK**
Die Einsame see Heyse **JENSEN**
Der Einsame see Lappe **SCHUBERT**
Der Einsame see Mayrhofer **SCHUBERT** *Einsamkeit*
Der Einsame see Nietzsche *DIE FRÖHLICHE WISSENSCHAFT.* **DELIUS**
Der einsame Mond see Szymanowska, Zafia **SZYMANOWSKI** *Samotny ksiezyc*
Der einsame See see Kalbeck **RUBINSTEIN**
Einsamkeit see Goethe **MEDTNER, REGER**
Einsamkeit see Goethe *WILHELM MEISTER.* **ZELTER**
Einsamkeit see Lenau **GIDEON, SCHOECK, SCHUMANN**
Einsamkeit see Mayrhofer **SCHUBERT**
Einsamkeit see Müller, Wilhelm **SCHUBERT**
Einsamkeit see Prölss **LASSEN**
Einsamkeit see Stotterfoth, Adelheid von **LASSEN**
Einsegnungslied see Giesebrecht **LOEWE**
Einsiedel see Bulcke **SZYMANOWSKI**
Die Einsiedelei see Salis-Seewis **SCHUBERT**
   Two settings: D. 393 and D. 563.
Der Einsiedler see Eichendorff **SCHUMANN**
Einst see Bodenstedt **LISZT**
Einst see Leuthold **SCHOECK**
Einst see Unknown **LASSEN**
"Einst am schönen Frühlingsmorgen" *see Der Räuber* Uhland **LOEWE**
"Einst aus meinem Grabe werden ungezählte rote Tulpen" *see Die brennenden Tulpen* Hafiz **SZYMANOWSKI**

Einst hat vor deines Vaters haus see Pfau **SCHÖNBERG**
Einst kam der Bock see Kerr **STRAUSS**
Einst und jetzt see Guilliaume **LASSEN** *Autrefois, à présent*
"Einst warst du meiner Seele Hoffnungsstern" *see Vergangnes Glück* Heyse **JENSEN**
"Einst wohnten süsse Ruh" *see An den fernen Geliebten* Reissig **BEETHOVEN**
"Einst wollt ich einen Kranz dir winden" *see Einst* Bodenstedt **LISZT**
Die einst'ge Sehnsuch see Shakespeare *ROMEO AND JULIET.* **BLACHER**
Die einzige Arzenei see Hafiz **SZYMANOWSKI**
Eine einzige Nacht an deinem Herzen! see Goethe *WESTÖSTLICHER DIVAN.* **SCHOECK**
"Einziger Augenblick, unbemerkt" *see Der Schatten* Barth **KRENEK**
Eis tettiga see Anacreon **LOEWE** *An die Grille*
Eisenmayer, W
   LASSEN *Meine Devise*
Eishet chayil see Bible *PROVERBS 31.* **GIDEON**
"Eishet chayil mi yimtsa" *see Eishet chayil* Bible **GIDEON**
Eit Syn see Vinje **GRIEG**
Ej, mám já koňa faku see Anon. **DVOŘÁK**
"Ej, smutno je mně, smutno" *see Smutný milý* Anon. **MARTINŮ**
Ejnye! Ejnye! see Pósa **BARTÓK**
Ekert, Carl, pseud. *see* Schumann, Robert, 1810-1856.
Ekho see Coppée **RIMSKĬÍ-KORSAKOV**
Ekho see Pushkin **MEDTNER** *Echo*
Ekho see Pushkin **RIMSKĬÍ-KORSAKOV**
Ekloge see Vrchlický **SCHÖNBERG**
El' i pal'ma see Heine *LYRICAL INTERMEZZO.* **RIMSKĬÍ-KORSAKOV**
An election see Ives **IVES**
Electrocution see Ridge *RED FLAG.* **ROREM**
Elegia kaunneudelle see Koskenniemi **KILPINEN**
Elegia satakielelle see Koskenniemi **KILPINEN**
Elegia yksinäisyydelle see Koskenniemi **KILPINEN**
Elegia yölle see Koskenniemi **KILPINEN**
Élégie see Contamine **SATIE**
Élégie see Dufrénoy **MILHAUD**
Elégie see Gallet **IVES, MASSENET**
Elegie see Golenishchev-Kutuzov **MUSORGSKĬÍ** *Elegiia*

COMPOSER Poet *Title* ''First Line''

Elégie see Lamartine **SATIE**
Elegie see Maïkov **RUBINSTEIN**
Élégie see Monnier **LISZT**
Élégie see Moore, T. **BERLIOZ, DUPARC**
Elegie an Emma see Schiller **ZELTER**
Elegie auf den Tod eines Pudels see
   Unknown **BEETHOVEN**
ELÉGIE, no. 1
   SAUGUET Desbordes-Valmore
     Souvenir
ELÉGIE, no. 2
   SAUGUET Desbordes-Valmore *Adieu*
ELÉGIE, no. 3
   SAUGUET Desbordes-Valmore
     La dernière fleur
Elegiia see Golenishchev-Kutuzov
   MUSORGSKIĭ
Elegiia see Pushkin **MEDTNER** *Elegy*
   Two settings: Op. 45 no. 1 and op. 52 no.
   3.
Elegiia: IA perezhil svoi zhelan'ia see
   Pushkin **MEDTNER** *Lost hopes*
ELEGISKE DIGTE, no. 1
   GRIEG Paulsen *Nå jeg vil dø*
ELEGISKE DIGTE, no. 2
   GRIEG Paulsen *På Norges nøgn fjelde*
ELEGISKE DIGTE, no. 3
   GRIEG Paulsen *Til Én. I*
ELEGISKE DIGTE, no. 4
   GRIEG Paulsen *Til Én. II*
ELEGISKE DIGTE, no. 5
   GRIEG Paulsen *Farvel*
ELEGISKE DIGTE, no. 6
   GRIEG Paulsen *Nu hviler du i jorden*
Elegy see Golenishchev-Kutuzov
   MUSORGSKIĭ *Elegiia*
Elegy see Krasiński **CHOPIN** *Melodia*
Elegy see Pushkin **MEDTNER**
   Two settings: Op. 45 no. 1 and op. 52 no.
   3.
Elegy see Tiutchev **MEDTNER**
"The element of air was out of hand" *see*
   Interlude Roethke **ROREM**
Elevation see Werfel **KRENEK**
L'elezzione der presidente see Salustri
   LE FAVOLE ROMANESCHE. **CASELLA**
Elfe see Eichendorff **GRIFFES**
Die Elfenkönigin see Matthisson **LOEWE,**
   ZELTER
ELFENLIED. see Goethe
   Elfenliedchen **MARTINŮ, MEDTNER**
Elfenlied see Kannegiesser **WEBER**
Elfenlied see Mörike **WOLF**
Elfenliedchen see Goethe *ELFENLIED.*
   MARTINŮ, MEDTNER
Les elfes see Leconte de Lisle **GIDEON**

Elfven och snigeln see Josephson, E.
   SIBELIUS *Älvan och snigeln*
"Elia popeia, so leise, so lind" *see Wiegenlied*
   Göchhausen **SPOHR**
Eliana see Annunzio *LA CHIMERA.*
   MALIPIERO
Eliot, Thomas Stearns, 1888-1965.
   DIAMOND *For an old man*
   THE DEATH OF SAINT NARCISSUS.
     BRITTEN *Canticle V*
   THE DRY SALVAGES.
     ROREM *Prayer* from *"The dry*
      salvages"
Eliphas' Gesicht see Byron *HEBREW*
   MELODIES. **LOEWE**
Elisabeth see Hesse **SCHOECK**
Ell' è malata! see Zaffira **GOUNOD**
"Ella pareva un so gno di poeta" *see Storia*
   breve Negri **RESPIGHI**
Elle see Lecocq **SAINT-SAËNS**
"Elle a passé" *see Une allée du Luxembourg*
   Gérard de Nerval **AURIC**
"Elle a passé dans le vent d'automne" *see*
   La vagabonde Rodès **BLOCH**
"Elle avait de beaux cheveux" *see L'archet*
   Cros **DEBUSSY, MALIPIERO**
Elle avait emporté des brasées de lilas see
   Jammes *TRISTESSES.* **MILHAUD**
"Elle avait trois couronnes d'or" *see Chanson*
   Maeterlinck **IBERT**
"Elle devint tout-à-coup très grave" *see*
   Jérôme et Alissa Gide **MILHAUD**
"Elle dormait depuis cent ans" *see*
   La dormeuse Carême **MILHAUD**
"Elle est gentille, Madeleine" *see Madeleine*
   Tranchant, Alfred **SAINT-SAËNS**
Elle est gravement gaie see Jammes
   TRISTESSES. **BOULANGER, MILHAUD**
Elle est malade! see Zaffira **GOUNOD** *Ell' è*
   malata!
"Elle est menue comme une puce" *see*
   La petite bergère Paliard **MILHAUD**
"Elle est si belle, Ma Sylvie" *see Sylvie*
   Contamine **SATIE**
"Elle étais jeune et jolie" *see N'oublions pas!*
   Barbier, J. **BIZET**
Elle était descendue au bas de la prairie see
   Jammes *TRISTESSES.* **BOULANGER**
Elle était descendue au bord de la prairie see
   Jammes *TRISTESSES.* **MILHAUD**
"Elle était jeune, pure et douce" *see L'aveu*
   Rameau **GOUNOD**
Elle était simple et gentillette see Cussy
   WEBER
Elle était venue sur les marches tièdes see
   Vildrac *LIVRE D'AMOUR.* **IBERT,**
   SCHMITT

COMPOSER Poet *Title* "First Line"

"Elle me demandait: 'Que de viennent les roses' " *see Amoroso* Docquois
SAINT-SAËNS
"Elle me dit: quelque chose, me tourmente"
see La coccinelle Hugo
BIZET, LASSEN, SAINT-SAËNS
"Elle partit, le grande errante" *see A son Altesse la Princesse Antoinette Murat* Rohan **THOMSON**
"Elle passe, tranquille, en un rêve divin" *see Épiphanie* Leconte de Lisle **KOECHLIN**
Elle sait! see Boyer, Georges **GOUNOD**
Elle se penche sur moi . . . see Eluard
AURIC
Elle s'en est allée see Solvay, Lucien
MASSENET
"Elle s'en va seulette" *see La belle voyageuse* Moore, T. **BERLIOZ**
Ellens Gesang I see Scott *THE LADY OF THE LAKE.* **SCHUBERT**
Ellens Gesang II see Scott *THE LADY OF THE LAKE.* **SCHUBERT**
Ellens Gesang III see Scott *THE LADY OF THE LAKE.* **SCHUBERT**
"Elles marchent deux par deux" *see Orphelines* Ludana **MASSENET**
"Elles ont les épaules hautes" *see Amoureuses* Éluard **POULENC**
"Elles t'aiment plus que la vie" *see Le convive* Chalupt **MILHAUD**
Elliot, Lady Charlotte, d.1880.
IVES *The camp meeting*
"Eloigne, oh! éloigne ces lèvres" *see Chanson* Shakespeare **SAUGUET**
Elore lo see Anon. **HESELTINE**
"Els seus tresors mostra la fira" *see Cançó de la Fira* Garcés **MOMPOU**
ELSÄSSISCHE VOLKSLIEDER. see Mündel
Ach was Kummer, Qual und Schmerzen **STRAUSS**
Wer lieben will, muss leiden **STRAUSS**
Elsk see Garborg *HAUGTUSSA.* **GRIEG**
Elskov see Garborg *HAUGTUSSA.* **GRIEG**
Elsk
Die Elster see Pushkin **MUSORGSKIĭ**
Strekotun'ia beloboka
Das Elternhaus see Claus, Nicolo **LASSEN**
Elternstolz see Anon. **REGER**
Éluard, Paul, 1895-1952.
AURIC
Elle se penche sur moi . . .
Le front aux vitres . . .
Je te l'ai dit
Mon amour . . .
Nous ne vous chantons pas
On ne peut me connaitre . . .
Tout disparut . . .

POULENC
A toutes brides
Amoureuses
Bonne journée
Ce doux petit visage
Une chanson de porcelaine
Dans les ténèbres du jardin
Figure de force brûlante et farouche
Le front comme un drapeau perdu
Georges Braque
La grande rivière qui va
Une herbe pauvre
Homme au sourire tendre
Il la prend dans ses bras
Jacques Villon
Je n'ai envie que de t'aimer
Je nommerai ton front
Juan Gris
Juan Miró
Main dominée par le coeur
. . . Mais mourir
Marc Chagall
Le matin les branches attisent
Nous avons fait la nuit
Pablo Picasso
Paul Klee
Peut-il se reposer?
Plume d'eau clair
Rayon des yeux
Rôdeuse au front de verre
Une roulotte couverte en tuiles
Une ruine coquille vide
Tout disparut
Tu vois le feu du soir
Unis la fraîcheur et le feu
SAUGUET
Bêtes et méchants
Celui qui dort, à la mémoire de Francis Poulenc
Chat
Cheval
Chien
Une écluse sans brouillard
Fenêtre illusoire à ma taille
Il est midi, il est minuit
Je n'avais d'yeux et de courage
Nuage, premier pas de mon élévation
Oiseau
Plus rien ne me tient aux pieds
Porc
Poule
Tout est un grand secret
Vache
Elvershöh see Anon. **LOEWE**
Elves see Eichendorff **GRIFFES** Elfe
Elysium see Schiller **SCHUBERT**

"Elysium, du Land, wo Friede wird" *see*
   Heimweh Unknown **LOEWE**
EMAUX ET CAMÉES. see Gautier
   Coquetterie posthume **DEBUSSY**
EMBLEMS OF CONDUCT: Chapter "The
   Rain." *see* Windham
   Prologue and Epilogue: from "The Rain"
      ROREM
Embrace, kiss see Kol'tsov **BALAKIREV**
   Oboymi, potsaluy
Emerson, Ralph Waldo, 1803-1882.
   IVES *Duty*
Émié, Louis, 1900-1967.
   JOLIVET
      Amour
      Je veux te voir
      Nous baignons dans une eau tranquille
      Pour te parler
      Tu dors
   RODRIGO *Homenaje a Debussy: "La
      grotte"*
L'Émir de Bengador see Méry **FRANCK**
Emmett, Daniel Decatur, 1815-1904.
   COPLAND *The boatmen's dance*
"Empfangen und genähret" *see Der Mensch*
   Claudius, M. **SCHOECK**
"Emporte ma folie" *see Fleur jetée* Silvestre
   FAURÉ
"Empty the room we once knew together" *see*
   Alone with the sea Ady **BARTÓK**
Emsmann, August Hugo, 1810-1889.
   LOEWE *König Wilhelm*
"En allant se coucher le soleil" *see Il vole*
   Vilmorin **POULENC**
En attendant see Baron **SAUGUET**
"En attendant je serai" *see Abandonnée*
   Supervielle **MILHAUD**
En Avignon, pays d'amour see Silvestre
   KOECHLIN
En Avril see Silvestre **BIZET**
"En Avril sous les branches" *see Sous les
   branches* Silvestre **MASSENET**
"En Bohème était une Reine" *see Ballade de
   la reine morte d'aimer* Marès **RAVEL**
En campaña, madre see Anon. *SPANISCHES
   LIEDERBUCH*: En campaña madre.
   JENSEN
En ces lieux see Monnier **LISZT**
"En ces lieux tout me parle delle" *see Élégie*
   Monnier **LISZT**
En chantant see Boyer, Georges
   MASSENET
"En des visions de la sombre nuit" *see*
   Un rêve Poe **SÉVERAC**
En Digters Bryst see Andersen **GRIEG**
   Du fatter ei Bølgernes evige Gang

"En dolç desmai durant la nit" *see Rosa del
   cami* Mompou **MOMPOU**
"En el mar, hay un pescado" *see Canción de
   baile con pandero* Anon. **RODRIGO**
En flicka sjunger där see Susman,
   Margarete **SIBELIUS** *Im Feld ein
   Mädchen singt*
En Jerez de la Frontera see Anon.
   RODRIGO
"En joukoin kulkevalle näy" *see Lehdokki*
   Koskenniemi **KILPINEN**
"En kulu minä kutsuissa" *see Sanoissa kuluva*
   Kanteletar **KILPINEN**
"En la mar hay una torre" *see Cancion del
   grumete* Anon. **RODRIGO**
En la peña, suso la peña see Antonio de
   Villegas *SPANISCHES LIEDERBUCH*:
   En la peña, suso la peña **JENSEN**
En las montañas de Asturias see Anon.
   RODRIGO
"En le frais silence nageant" *see Le vivier*
   Chalupt **RIVIER**
"En ma tiennyt, kun sun luota läksin" *see
   Vanha laulu* Koskenniemi **KILPINEN**
"En mai quand le rossignolet" *see Flaiolet*
   Anon. **CASELLA**
En même temps que ton amour see Lebey
   MASSENET
"En même temps que tous les bourgeons la
   rose" *see Chant d'amour* Unknown
   MILHAUD
"En mes belles années j'étais un arbe en
   fleurs" *see Vieille chanson espagnole*
   Houssaye **AUBERT**
"En mil neuf cent quarante on nous a dit" *see
   Trois ans de souffrance* Anon. **MILHAUD**
"En priant chaque soir la Madone" *see Péché
   véniel* Ludana **AUBERT**
En prière see Bordèse **FAURÉ**
En ramant see Richepin **CASELLA**
En rêve see Mahaut **RIVIER**
"En robe grise et verte" *see Un jour de juin,
   que j'étais soucieux* Verlaine **KOECHLIN**
En slända see Levertin **SIBELIUS**
En sourdine see Verlaine *FÊTES
   GALANTES.* **DEBUSSY, FAURÉ, HAHN**
   Two Debussy settings: 1882 and 1892.
EN SOURDINE. see Verlaine
   When the misty shadows glide
   CARPENTER
"En tu puerta, Teresa" *see Canción de cuna*
   Anon. **RODRIGO**
"En un rêve, en un rêve étrange" *see
   Le vaisseau* Haraucourt **KOECHLIN**
"En una yegua tordilla" *see Romance* Rivas
   TURINA

"En unta saa" *see Per aspera* Jalkanen **KILPINEN**

En voyage see Maurer **MASSENET**

L'énamourée see Banville *LES EXILÉS.* **HAHN**

"Encare veig al lluny" *see Fortina de fullatge* Mompou **MOMPOU**

Enchantement! see Ruelle **MASSENET**

Encor sur le pavé sonne mon pas nocturne see Moréas **HAHN**

"Encore un mazour avant" *see Le dernier mazour* Unknown **POULENC**

The encounter see Housman *THE SHROPSHIRE LAD.* **IRELAND**

The end of all see Mužik **MARTINŮ**

Das Ende see Huber, B. **KILPINEN**

Das Ende des Festes see Meyer **SCHOECK**

"Endlich hatte Damon sie gefunden" *see Damon und Chloe* Hiemer **WEBER**

"Endlich scheinest der wieder" *see An den Mond* Schink **ZELTER**

"Endlich steh'n die Pforten offen" *see Schwangesang* Kosegarten **SCHUBERT**

Endlose Liebe see Florenz **CARPENTER**

Endymion see Koskenniemi **KILPINEN**

Enfance see Fargue **AURIC**

L'enfant see Leprade **CHABRIER**

"L'enfant cherche sa voix" *see L'enfant muet* Garcia Lorca **POULENC**

"Un enfant court Autour des marhres" *see Rêves* Fargue **RAVEL**

"Un enfant de dans un bocage" *see L'amour oyseau* Ronsard **SAINT-SAËNS**

Enfant de troupe see Cocteau **POULENC**

"L'enfant est nu, Tout en peuple est venu" *see Le Noël des humbles* Aicard **MASSENET**

L'enfant muet see Garcia Lorca **POULENC**

L'enfant qui dort see Olivier, Pierre **SAUGUET**

"Une enfant qui soulève un peu" *see Les images* Follain **SAUGUET**

"Enfant rose, Fleur éclose" *see Berceuse* Chouquet **MASSENET**

Enfant, si j'étais roi see Hugo **LISZT**

Les enfants see Boyer, Georges **MASSENET**

Les enfants see Lunel **MILHAUD**

"Enfants au doux visage Venez charmernos yeux" *see Sérénade* Chauvinière, Edmond de **GOUNOD**

Les enfants du Ruisseau see Vaucaire **SAUGUET**

"Enfin, elles s'en vont" *see Narcisse à la fontaine* Collin **MASSENET**

Enführung see Dehmel **SZYMANOWSKI**

Der Engel see Pushkin **RUBINSTEIN**

Der Engel see Wesendonck **WAGNER**

Engel, Franz, 1834-1920. **REGER** *Verlassen hab ich mein Lieb*

"Die Engel Gottes weinen" *see Das Lied der Trennung* Schmidt, Klamer **MOZART**

"Ein Engel zog durch Flur und Haus" *see Gottesbote* Lutze **LOEWE**

Engelgesang see Hertz, H. **JENSEN**

Engelhardt, Karl August, 1768-1834. **SCHUBERT** *Ihr Grab*

Engelsstimmen am Krankenbette see Geppert family **LOEWE**

Engelwacht see Muth **REGER**

"Die Englein haben's Bett gemacht" *see Beim Schneewetter* Unknown **REGER**

English May see Rossetti, Dante **IRELAND**

ENGLISH SONGS, no. 1 **HIDEMITH** Moore, T. *Echo*

ENGLISH SONGS, no. 2 **HINDEMITH** Thompson, F. *Envoy*

ENGLISH SONGS, no. 3 **HINDEMITH** Shelley *The moon*

ENGLISH SONGS, no. 4 **HINDEMITH** Oldys *On a fly drinking out of his cup*

ENGLISH SONGS, no. 5 **HINDEMITH** Wolfe, C. *On hearing "The last rose of summer"*

ENGLISH SONGS, no. 6 **HINDEMITH** Blake, William *The wild flower's song*

ENGLISH SONGS, no. 7 **HINDEMITH** Lover *The whistlin' thief*

ENGLISH SONGS, no. 8 **HINDEMITH** Whitman *Sing on there in the swamp*

ENGLISH SONGS, no. 9 **HINDEMITH** Herrick *To music, to becalm his fever*

English usage see Moore, M. **THOMSON**

Die engste Nähe see Unknown **LOEWE**

Enigma see Fanshawe **SCHUMANN** *Räthsel*

L'Enigme éternelle see Anon. **RAVEL**

L'enlèvement see Hugo **SAINT-SAËNS**

Ennery, Adolphe Philippe d' *see* Dennery, Adolphe Philippe, 1811-1899.

"Enno ein Gong fekk eg Vetren" *see Våren* Vinje **GRIEG**

"L'ennui d'aller en visite" *see Le Marchand d'ail et d'oignons* Mallarmé **MILHAUD**

Enough of happiness see Liliencron **MARTINŮ**

Enslaved by the rose, the nightingale see Kol'tsov **RIMSKIĬ-KORSAKOV** *Plenivshis' pozoǐ, soloveǐ*

Enslin, Karl, 1819-1875.
   LOEWE
      Der Abendstern
      Schlittschuhlauf
      Der Schwimmer
   REGER *Herzenstausch*
"Entendez-vous dans la bruyère?" *see*
   Le chasseur danois Leuven **BERLIOZ**
AN ENTERLUDE CALLED LUSTY
   JUVENTUS (1565). *see* Wever
   In an arbour green **HESELTINE**
   Lusty juventus **HESELTINE**
Der Entfernten see Bürger **CORNELIUS**
Der Entfernten see Salis-Seewis
   SCHUBERT
DER ENTFERNTEN. see Apel, Theodor
   Glockentöne **WAGNER**
Entflieh mit mir see Heine **GRIFFES**
   Tragödie I
"Entflieh mit mir und sei mein Weib" *see*
   Tragödie Heine **RUBINSTEIN,**
   SCHUMANN
"Entfliehet schnell von mir" *see Lied* Seida
   und Landenberg **WEBER**
Entführung see Häring **BRAHMS**
Die Enthusiasten see Mörike **SCHOECK**
Enticement see Tavaststjerna **SIBELIUS**
   Fågellek
Entlaubet ist der Walde see Anon.
   VAUGHAN WILLIAMS
"Entoure ce citron de blanc d'oeuf informe"
   see Pablo Picasso Éluard **POULENC**
"Entre le lièvre et la tortue" *see La tortue et le
   lièvre* Sanglier, Charles **SCHMITT**
"Entre les fauves et les cubistes" *see Marie
   Laurencin* Cocteau **AURIC**
"Entre les poufs de satin capitonné" *see
   Le pouf* Chalupt **AURIC**
Entreat me not to leave thee see Bible
   GOUNOD
Entsagung see Droysen **MENDELSSOHN-
   BARTHOLDY**
Entscheidung see Krenek **KRENEK**
Entschluss see Osterwald **FRANZ**
Die Entschwundene see Keller, G.
   SCHOECK
Der entsühnte Orest see Mayrhofer
   SCHUBERT
Entzückung see Matthisson **SCHUBERT**
Die Entzückung an Laura see Schiller
   SCHUBERT
   Two settings: D. 390 and D. 577.
Envoi de fleurs see Augier **GOUNOD**
Envoy see Thompson, F. **HINDEMITH**
Epheu see Dahn **STRAUSS** *Efeu*
Das Epheublatt see Krause **LASSEN**

Epigram see O'Donnell, G. M. **ROREM**
Epigram see Pushkin **BRITTEN**
Epigramm see Goethe **SCHOECK**
Epigramma see Pushkin **BRITTEN** *Epigram*
EPIGRAMMES, no. 1
   RAVEL Marot *D'Anne qui me jecta de la
   neige*
EPIGRAMMES, no. 2
   RAVEL Marot *D'Anne jouant de
   l'espinette*
Epilog see Drachmann **GRIEG**
Epilog see Krenek **KRENEK**
Epilogue see Goethe *FAUST.* **SEIBER**
Epilogue see Housman *THE SHROPSHIRE
   LAD.* **IRELAND**
EPIMENIDES ERWACHEN. see Goethe
   In tiefe Sklaverei lag ich gebunden
   ZELTER
Epiphanias see Goethe **WOLF**
Épiphanie see Leconte de Lisle
   KOECHLIN
"Les épis sont à Cérès" *see Attributs*
   Ronsard **POULENC**
"Les épis sont à Cérès" *see Privilèges*
   Ronsard **SCHMITT**
Epistel see Collin, M. **SCHUBERT** *Herrn
   Josef Spaun*
Epitaph see Anon. **ROREM**
Epitaph see Bugayev *DRUZBIAM.*
   MEDTNER
Epitaph see Melville *ON THE GRAVE OF A
   YOUNG CAVALRY OFFICER.* **DIAMOND**
The epitaph see Smith, Logan *MORE
   TRIVIA.* **DIAMOND**
Epitaph for a wag in Mauchline see Burns
   GIDEON
Epitaph for Janet see Goodman **ROREM**
Epitaph of Timas see Sappho **BERKELEY**
Epitaph on the author see Burns **GIDEON**
Epitaph on wee Johnie see Burns **GIDEON**
Epitaph: The clerk see Asquith
   THE VOLUNTEER. **BRITTEN**
Epitaph upon a child that died see Herrick
   ROREM
Epitaphe see Hugo **PIZZETTI**
Épitaphe see Malherbe **POULENC**
Épitaphe see Silvestre **MASSENET**
Épitaphe de Bilitis see Louÿs *CHANSONS
   DE BILITIS.* **KOECHLIN**
EPITAPHS FROM ROBERT BURNS, no. 1
   GIDEON Burns *Epitaph for a wag in
   Mauchline*
EPITAPHS FROM ROBERT BURNS, no. 2
   GIDEON Burns *Epitaph on wee Johnie*
EPITAPHS FROM ROBERT BURNS, no. 3
   GIDEON Burns *Epitaph on the author*

COMPOSER Poet *Title* "First Line"

EPITAPHS FROM ROBERT BURNS, no. 4
  GIDEON Burns *Monody on a lady famed*
    for her caprice
Epitazhiia see Bugayev **MEDTNER** *Epitaph*
Épithalame see Grenier **DELIBES**
Epître à ses amis see Villon **MESSIAEN**
Epître imprécatoire see Germain-Colin
  JOLIVET
L'épouse see Messiaen **MESSIAEN**
"Epouse au front lumineux" *see Cantique à*
  l'Épouse Jounet **CHAUSSON**
Épouvante see Messiaen **MESSIAEN**
Er an Sie see Lehr, Hofrath **WEBER**
Er coccodrillo see Salustri *LE FAVOLE*
  ROMANESCHE. **CASELLA**
Er, der Herrlichste von allen see Chamisso
  LOEWE, SCHUMANN
"Er fiel den Tod fürs Vaterland" *see Grablied*
  Kenner **SCHUBERT**
Er gatto e er cane see Salustri *LE FAVOLE*
  ROMANESCHE. **CASELLA**
"Er hat mich im Traum geküsst" *see Wenn*
  ich's nur wüsst Kolbe **REGER**
"Det er herligt at leve i Drømmenes Land" *see*
  I Drømmes Land Jacobsen **NIELSEN**
"Er ist erstanden, Jesus Christ" *see Unsere*
  Auferstehung durch Christum Münter
  LOEWE
Er ist gekommen see Rückert **FRANZ**
Er ist's! see Mörike **FRANZ, SCHOECK,**
  SCHUMANN, WOLF
"Er kam in der Frühe wie der Morgenwind"
  see Morgens am Brunnen Roquette
  JENSEN
Er klagt, dass der Frühling so kurtz blüht see
  Holz *DAFNIS.* **BERG**
Er liebte mich so sehr! see Girardin **LISZT**
  Il m'aimait tant!
"Er liegt und schläft" *see An die Nachtigall*
  Claudius, M. **SCHUBERT**
"Er presidente d'una società" *see La carità*
  Salustri **CASELLA**
"Er reitet nachts auf einem braunen Ross" *see*
  Nachtwanderer Eichendorff **PFITZNER**
"Er schläft so süss" *see Der Knabe in der*
  Wiege Ottenwalt **SCHUBERT**
"Er schlich sich die Wände entlang" *see*
  Verborg'ne Liebe Bjørnson **DELIUS**
"Er schoss herab" *see Der fallende Stern*
  Rostopchina **RUBINSTEIN**
"Er war ein fauler Schäfer" *see Der Schäfer*
  Goethe **WOLF**
"Era bella com'angiol del cielo" *see*
  La seduzione Balestra, Luigi **VERDI**
"Era una mañana y abril sonreía" *see Mañana*
  de Abril Machado y Ruiz **RODRIGO**

Eräs see Lamberg **KILPINEN**
"Eräs on, on eräs, eräs on" *see Eräs*
  Lamberg **KILPINEN**
Erat Joseph et Maria see Bible
  HINDEMITH
Erben, Karel Jaromír, 1811-1870.
  DVOŘÁK
    Rozmarýna
    Sirotek
  MARTINŮ *Easter*
Erdbeerliedchen see Unknown **LOEWE**
Die Erde ruht see Turgenev **RUBINSTEIN**
"Die Erde ruht, das Herz erwacht" *see*
  Die Nacht Mahlmann **LOEWE**
"Die Erde schläft, des Mondes Schein
  verklärend sie bedeckt" *see Der Bote*
  Fick, K. **REGER**
Die Erde steht in süssem Beben see
  Ahlefeldt, Ottilie von **LASSEN**
L'eremurus see Daudet, L. **MILHAUD**
"Eremurus Isabellinus" *see L'eremurus*
  Daudet, L. **MILHAUD**
Erfüllung see Cornelius **CORNELIUS**
  Märchenwunder
Ergebung see Eichendorff **SCHOECK**
"Ergehst du dich im Abendlicht" *see Des*
  Dichters Abendgang Uhland **STRAUSS**
"Erhalt uns den König" *see Lied für*
  preussischen Patrioten Gleim **ZELTER**
"Erhebt das Glas" *see Trinklied* Unknown
  BEETHOVEN
Erhebung see Dehmel **SCHÖNBERG**
"Erhöhet die prächtigen Pforten der Siege" *see*
  Der Siegesfürst Schmid **LOEWE**
Erindringens Sø see Holstein **NIELSEN**
Erinna an Sappho see Mörike **SCHOECK**
Erinnerung see Eichendorff **SCHOECK**
  Two settings: Op. 10 no. 1 and op. 17 no.
    7.
Erinnerung see Jacobi **SCHUMANN**
Erinnerung see Kosegarten **SCHUBERT**
  Die Erscheinung
Erinnerung see Krzyzanowski **KRENEK**
Erinnerung see Lenau **SCHOECK**
Erinnerung see Matthisson **SCHUBERT**
  Todtenopfer
Erinnerung see Osterwald **FRANZ**
  Two settings: Op. 5 no. 10 and op. 51 no.
    10.
Erinnerung see Schäfer, T. **REGER**
Erinnerung see Schenkendorf **BRAHMS**
Erinnerung see Volkmann **MAHLER**
Erinnerung an einen Freund see Mereau
  ZELTER
Erinnerungen see Goering **KRENEK**
Erinnerungen see Matthisson *AM*
  SEEGESTAD'. **SCHUBERT**

Eristavi, D.
 RUBINSTEIN
  Autumn
  The looking-glass
Das Erkennen see Vogl **LOEWE**
Erkennung see Schink **ZELTER**
Erlafsee see Mayrhofer **SCHUBERT**
Erlkönig see Goethe **BEETHOVEN,**
 LOEWE, SCHUBERT
Der Erlkönig see Goethe **ZELTER**
Erlkönigs Tochter see Herder *STIMMEN*
 DER VÖLKER. **JENSEN; LOEWE** *Herr*
 Oluf
"Erlöse uns vom Übel" *see Vater unser IX*
 Cornelius **CORNELIUS**
Erlöse uns von dem Übel see Cornelius
 CORNELIUS *Vater unser IX*
Erlöst see Boelitz **REGER**
ERLÖSUNGEN. see Dehmel
 Mädchenfrühling **SCHÖNBERG**
 Nicht doch! **SCHÖNBERG**
 Tief von fern **WEBERN**
Erloschen see Busse-Palma **SIBELIUS**
Ermln, pseud. *see* Kumpf, Johann
 Gottfried, 1781-1862.
Ermutigung see Schweizer **SPOHR**
Ernst, Heinrich Wilhelm, 1814-1865.
 BRUCKNER *Herbstkummer*
 LASSEN
  Abendbild
  Ewig jung
  Holger's Brautritt
  Immer bei dir
  Mein Alles du
  Sonntagsruhe
  Trüber Morgen
"Ernst ist der Frühling" *see Geliebte Schöne*
 Heine **BERG**
Ernst ist der Frühling see Heine **WOLF**
"Ernst ritt der Kaiser" *see Kaiser Karl V. in*
 Wittenberg Hohlfeld **LOEWE**
Erntelied see Anon. **MENDELSSOHN-**
 BARTHOLDY
Erntelied see Hölty **SCHUBERT**
Eron hetki see Jalkanen **KILPINEN**
Eros see Benzon **GRIEG**
Erotessa see Jalkanen **KILPINEN**
Erotica see Annunzio **PIZZETTI**
Erotus mielillä see Kanteletar **KILPINEN**
"Erschaffen schon die Erde lag" *see*
 Der Gesang Vogl **LOEWE**
Erschaffen und Beleben see Goethe
 WESTÖSTLICHER DIVAN: Schenkenbuch.
 STRAUSS, WOLF
Die Erscheinung see Kosegarten *ICH LAG*
 AUF GRÜNEN MATTEN. **SCHUBERT**

"Erst sitzt er eine Weile" *see Der Misanthrop*
 Goethe **ZELTER**
Erstarrung see Müller, Wilhelm
 SCHUBERT
Das Erste see Vinje **GRIEG** *Det Første*
"Erste Kirschen hast du mir gebracht" *see*
 Kirschkerne Wolf, F. **BLACHER**
Der erste Kuss see Kartscher **SPOHR**
Die erste Liebe see Fellinger **SCHUBERT**
Erste Liebe see Heine **LOEWE**
DAS ERSTE LIED. see Blüthgen
 Wer hat das erste Lied erdacht **LASSEN**
Das erste Sommergras; Vor der Ernte see
 Frey, F. **RUBINSTEIN**
"Der erste Strahl vom Osten her" *see*
 Der Morgen Sallet **STRAUSS**
Das erste Veilchen see Ebert
 MENDELSSOHN-BARTHOLDY *Das*
 erste Veilchen see Maffei **RUBINSTEIN**
 La prima viola
Die erste Walpurgisnacht see Goethe
 LOEWE
"Die ersten Tropfel fallen aus trübem
 Morgenroth" *see Trüber Morgen* Ernst
 LASSEN
Erster Verlust see Goethe **BERG,**
 MEDTNER, MENDELSSOHN-
 BARTHOLDY, SCHOECK,
 SCHUBERT, WOLF, ZELTER
Erster Verlust see Osterwald **FRANZ**
Erstes Begegnen see Bjørnson
 FISKERJENTEN. **GRIEG** *Det første møde*
Erstes Grün see Kerner **SCHUMANN**
Erstes Liebeslied eines Mädchens see Mörike
 WOLF
"Ertrage du's, lass schneiden dir den
 Schmerz" *see Gebet* Avenarius **WEBERN**
Erwachen see Cornelius **CORNELIUS**
 Am Morgen
Erwachen aus dem tiefsten Traumesschosse
 see George *DAS JAHR DER SEELE:*
 Nachtwachen. **WEBERN**
"Erwacht in neuer Stärke begrüss' ich, Gott"
 see Morgenlied Voss
 MENDELSSOHN-BARTHOLDY,
 ZELTER
"Erwacht zum neuen Leben" *see Der Frühling*
 Sturm, C. **MOZART**
Die erwachte Rose see Sallet **STRAUSS**
Erwartung see Bassewitz **SPOHR**
Erwartung see Dehmel **SCHÖNBERG**
Erwartung see Eichendorff **WOLF**
DIE ERWARTUNG. see Schiller
 Im Garten **ZELTER**
Die Erwartung see Schiller **SCHUBERT**

COMPOSER Poet *Title* "First Line"

Erwartung see Unknown
MENDELSSOHN-BARTHOLDY
ERWIN UND ELMIRE. see Goethe
   Inneres Wühlen ewig zu fühlen **MEDTNER**
   Sie liebt mich! **MEDTNER**
   Sieh mich, Heil'ger, wie ich bin
      MEDTNER
"Erzeugt von heisser Phantasie" *see Als Luise*
   die Briefe ihres ungetreuen Liebhabers
   verbrannte Batsányi **MOZART**
"Es bellen die Hunde, es rasseln die Ketten"
   see Im Dorfe Müller, Wilhelm
   SCHUBERT
Es blasen die blauen Husaren see Heine
   LIEDERSTRAUSS. **WOLF**
Es blinkt der Thau see Boddien, G. von
   RUBINSTEIN
"Es blitzt und kracht" *see Der Spielmann und*
   sein Kind Hoffmann von Fallersleben
   STRAUSS
"Es blühen die Rosen von Jericho" *see*
   Die Rosen von Jericho Ali **LASSEN**
"Es blüht ein Blümchen irgendwo" *see*
   Das Blümchen Wunderhold Bürger
   BEETHOVEN
Es blüht ein Blümlein rosenrot see Boelitz
   REGER
"Es blüht um mich des Abends Stille" *see*
   Abend Schäfer, T. **REGER**
"Es brandet die Welle" *see Am Meeresstrand*
   Tolstoï **RUBINSTEIN**
"Es brausen der Liebe Wogen" *see Versunken*
   Schumann, F. **BRAHMS**
"Es brechen im schallenden Reigen" *see*
   Frühlingslied Klingemann
   MENDELSSOHN-BARTHOLDY
"Es brennt mir unter beiden Sohlen" *see*
   Rückblick Müller, Wilhelm **SCHUBERT**
"Es deuten die Blumen des Herzens Gefühle"
   see Die Blumensprache Platner
   SCHUBERT
"Es donnern die Höhn" *see Der Alpenjäger*
   Schiller **LISZT**
"Es donnert über der Pfaffengass" *see*
   Frühgesicht Keller, G. **SCHOECK**
"Es fährt der Wind gewaltig durch die Nacht"
   see In einer Sturmnacht Meyer
   SCHOECK
Es fällt ein Stern herunter see Heine
   FRANZ, PFITZNER
"Es fahren die Schiffer" *see Der Stern ist die*
   Liebe Unknown **FRANZ**
Es fasst mich wieder der alte Mut see Heine
   PFITZNER
Es fiel ein Reif see Heine **GRIFFES**
   Tragödie II

Es fiel ein Reif in der Frühlingsnacht see
   Anon. **MAHLER**
"Es flimmert der Kranz der Sterne" *see Meine*
   Lilie Hamerling **LASSEN**
"Es flogen drei Schwälbelein über den Rhein"
   see Die verlorene Tochter Zuccalmaglio
   LOEWE
"Es floh die Zeit im Wirbelfluge" *see*
   Der Flug der Zeit Széchényi
   SCHUBERT
"Es flüstern und rauschen die Wogen" *see*
   Loreley Lorenz **SCHUMANN**
"Es flüstert's der Himmel" *see Räthsel*
   Fanshawe **SCHUMANN**
"Es freut sich Alles weit und breit" *see*
   Seemanns Scheidelied Hoffmann von
   Fallersleben
   MENDELSSOHN-BARTHOLDY
"Es führen über die Erde" *see Allein* Hesse
   KILPINEN
"Es gehen zur Kirche die Leute" *see Bei der*
   Kirche Rüeger, Armin **SCHOECK**
"Es geht bei gedämpfter Trommel Klang" *see*
   Mitten ins Herz Chamisso **FRANZ**
"Es geht bei gedämpfter Trommeln Klang"
   see Der Soldat Andersen **SCHUMANN**
"Es geht der Tag zur Neige" *see Warnung*
   Pfarrius **SCHUMANN**
"Es geht ein alter König" *see Der alte König*
   Vogl **LOEWE**
"Es geht mit mir zu Ende" *see Hussens*
   Kerker Meyer **PFITZNER**
"Es gibt ein stilles Königreich" *see Das stille*
   Königreich Busse **BERG**
"Es gibt Regentage die sehr schön sind" *see*
   Regentag Krenek **KRENEK**
"Es ging die Riesentochter" *see Die Riesen*
   und die Zwerge Rückert **LOEWE**
"Es ging ein Mann zur Frühlingszeit" *see*
   Die Perle Jacobi **SCHUBERT**
"Es ging ein Wind durch's weite Land" *see*
   Wir beide wollen springen Bierbaum
   STRAUSS
"Es ging einmal ein Wind" *see Männertreu*
   Löns **KILPINEN**
"Es gingen drei Jäger" *see Der weisse Hirsch*
   Uhland **SCHUMANN, STRAUSS**
Es gingen zwei Gespielen gut see Anon.
   SCHÖNBERG
"Es glänzt der Mond nieder" *see Der Gang*
   zum Liebchen Anon. **BRAHMS**
"Es glänzt der Tulpenflor" *see Sonst*
   Eichendorff **PFITZNER**
"Es glänzt im Abendsonnen golde der stille
   Waldesteich" *see Ein Gruss von Ihr!* Viol
   FRANZ

COMPOSER Poet *Title* "First Line"

Es glänzt so schön die sinkende Sonne *see*
Heine **PFITZNER**
"Es glitten nach rauschendem Regen" *see*
In stiller Nacht Tolstoï **RUBINSTEIN**
"Es grünet ein Nussbaum vor dem Haus" *see*
Der Nussbaum Mosen **SCHUMANN**
"Es haben die liebjungen Mädchen" *see*
Vorbeimarsch Boelitz **REGER**
"Es haben viel Dichter gesungen" *see Trost*
Eichendorff **SCHOECK**
"Es hält der blaue Tag" *see Mittag im*
September Hesse **SCHOECK**
"Es hat das Herz des Menschen" *see Max in*
Augsburg Auersperg **LOEWE**
"Es hat der schimmernde Sonnenstrahl" *see*
Frühlings Seele Giesebrecht **LOEWE**
Es hat die Rose sich beklagt see Bodenstedt
FRANZ
"Es hat die Rose sich beklagt" *see Die Rose*
Bodenstedt **RUBINSTEIN**
Es hat so grün gesäuselt see Müller,
Wilhelm **JENSEN**
ES HEBT DER WALLENDE BUSEN. see
Luhden *Sehnsucht* **ZELTER**
"Es heilt die Nacht des Tages Wunden" *see*
Tröst der Nacht Kinkel **LASSEN**
Es hing der Reif see Groth *HUNDERT*
BLÄTTER . . . **BRAHMS**
"Es ist bestimmt in Gottes Rath" *see Volkslied*
Feuchtersleben
MENDELSSOHN-BARTHOLDY
"Es ist doch im April fürwahr" *see Das*
Mädchen an den Mai Mörike **SCHOECK**
"Es ist doch meine Nachbarin" *see Der*
Goldschmiedsgesell Goethe **SCHUBERT**
"Es ist ein halbes Himmelreich" *see*
Blumenlied Hölty **SCHUBERT**
"Es ist ein Ring gebogen" *see Das Ringlein*
Jacobowski **REGER**
"Es ist ein Schnitter" *see Erntelied* Anon.
MENDELSSOHN-BARTHOLDY
"Es ist ein seliges Prangen" *see Mondnacht*
Evers **REGER**
"Es ist ein stiller Regentag" *see Trübes Wetter*
Keller, G. **SCHOECK**
"Es ist ein süsses Wähnen im Trauern und in
Tränen" *see Mein Verlangen*
Müller von der Werra **SPOHR**
"Es ist immer derselbe Traum" *see Traum*
Hesse **KILPINEN**
"Es ist in den Wald gesungen" *see*
Altdeutsches Lied Schreiber, H.
MENDELSSOHN-BARTHOLDY
"Es ist in Schuss gefallen" *see Der junge*
Jäger Goethe **ZELTER**
"Es ist mein Herz ein kleines Haus" *see*
Die Waldkapelle Siebel **LOEWE**

"Es ist mein Herz verengt, verdorrt" *see*
Frühlingsankunft Ziegler, K. **LOEWE**
"Es ist mir wie den kleinen Waldvögelein zu
Mut" *see Frühlingswonne* Anon. **FRANZ**
Es ist Nacht see Morgenstern **KILPINEN**
"Es ist nicht Selbstsucht und nicht Eitelkeit"
see Den Zweifellosen II Keller, G.
SCHOECK
"Es ist schon spät" *see Waldesgespräch*
Eichendorff **JENSEN, SCHUMANN**
"Es ist so angenehm" *see Lied* Schiller
SCHUBERT
"Es ist so still geworden" *see Abendlied*
Kinkel **SCHUMANN**
"Es ist so still geworden" *see Ein geistlich*
Abendlied Kinkel **LASSEN**
"Es ist so still, so heimlich um mich" *see*
Der Winterabend Leitner **SCHUBERT**
"Es ist so süss zu scherzen" *see Der Hidalgo*
Geibel **LASSEN, SCHUMANN**
"Es kam des Assyers gewaltige Macht" *see*
Sanherib's Niederlage Byron **LOEWE**
"Es kam ein Herr zum Schlösseli" *see*
Um schlimme Kinder artig zu machen
Anon. **MAHLER**
"Es kam zu ihr, leis an die Thür" *see*
Das braune Mädchen Anon. **LOEWE**
Es kehret der Maien see Jeitteles
BEETHOVEN
"Es kehrt die dunkle Schwalbe" *see Alte Liebe*
Candidus **BRAHMS**
"Es klagt im Dunkeln irgendwo" *see Stimme*
im Dunkeln Dehmel **SZYMANOWSKI**
Es klingt in der Luft see Hauenschild
FRANZ
"Es klingt so prächtig" *see Nachklang*
Goethe **SCHOECK**
"Es klopft an das Fenster der Lindenbaum"
see Frühlingsmorgen Volkmann
MAHLER
"Es kommt aus fernem Böhmerland" *see*
Der böhmische Musikant Pletzsch, Oskar
STRAUSS
Es kommt eine Zeit, eine trübe Zeit! see
Moore, T. **JENSEN**
"Es kumt tsu flien di goldene pave" *see*
Di goldene pave Anon. **WEISGALL**
"Es lacht der Mai!" *see Die erste*
Walpurgisnacht Goethe **LOEWE**
"Es lächelt der See" *see Die Fischerknabe*
Schiller **LISZT**
"Es läuft ein fremdes Kind" *see Des fremden*
Kindes heiliger Christ Rückert **LOEWE**
"Es läuten zur Kirche die Glokken" *see*
Kindergottesdienst Gerok **SCHOECK**
"Es lag auf meiner Stirn einst eine Wolke so
schwer und trüb" *see Wolkenbild* Löper,
Lina **LOEWE**

COMPOSER Poet *Title* "First Line"

Es lauschte das Laub so dunkelgrün see
Klingemann MENDELSSOHN-
BARTHOLDY
Es lebt kein König! see Prölss LASSEN
Es leuchtet meine Liebe see Heine
SCHUMANN
"Es leuchtet so schön die Sonne" *see*
Mädchenlied Haringer SCHÖNBERG
Es liebt einst ein Hase see Kerr STRAUSS
"Es liebt' in Welschland irgendwo" *see*
Die Nonne Hölty SCHUBERT
Es liebt sich so lieblich im Lenze see Heine
FRÜHLING. BRAHMS
"Es liegt ein alter Mühlenstein" *see Abgeguckt*
Mayr REGER
"Es lockt und säuselt um den Baum" *see*
Der Frühling Rousseau, J. B. BRAHMS
"Es lockte schöne Wärme" *see Die Rose*
Schlegel, F. SCHUBERT
"Es löst ein Blatt sich" *see Das Ende* Huber,
B. KILPINEN
"Es lokket und zwitschert von Haus zu Haus"
see Das arme Vögelein Gilm zu
Rosenegg REGER
"Es mahnt der Wald" *see Schlaflied*
Mayrhofer SCHUBERT
Es muss ein Wunderbares sein see Redwitz
LISZT
Es ragt der alte Elborus see Bodenstedt
FRANZ
Es ragt ins Meer der Runenstein see Heine
FRANZ
"Es ragt in's Meer der Runenstein" *see*
Wo sind Sie hin? Heine GRIEG
Es rauben Gedanken den Schlaf see Anon.
JENSEN *Pensamientos me quitan*
"Es rauben Gedanken den Schlaf" *see*
Pensamientos me quitan Anon. JENSEN
"Es rauschen die Tannen und Föhren" *see*
Rübezahl Hamerling JENSEN
Es rauschen die Winde see Rellstab LISZT
"Es rauschen die Winde so herbstlich und
kalt" *see Herbst* Rellstab SCHUBERT
"Es rauschen die Wipfel und schauern" *see*
Schöne Fremde Eichendorff
SCHUMANN
"Es rauscht das rote Laub zu meinen Füssen"
see Im Herbst Geibel FRANZ
"Es rauscht der Strom, es weht der Wind" *see*
Erinnerung an einen Freund Mereau
ZELTER
Es rauscht der Wald see Unknown
MENDELSSOHN-BARTHOLDY
Es rauscht des Laub zu meinem Füssen see
Geibel STRAUSS

ES REDEN UND TRÄUMEN DIE
MENSCHEN. see Schiller
Hoffnung SCHUBERT
Two settings: D. 251 and D. 637.
"Es reden und träumen die Menschen viel"
see Hoffnung Schiller SCHUBERT
Two settings: D. 251 and D. 637.
"Es reit der Herr von Falkenstein" *see*
Das Lied von Herrn von Falkenstein
Uhland BRAHMS
"Es reitet schweigend und allein der alte Graf"
see Die verfallene Mühle Vogl LOEWE
"Es rieselt, klar und wehend" *see*
Die Einsiedelei Salis-Seewis
SCHUBERT
Two settings: D. 393 and D. 563.
"Es ritten drei Reiter zum Thore hinaus!" *see*
Scheiden und Meiden Anon. MAHLER
Es rollte kein Donner see Tolstoï
MUSORGSKĬ *Ne bozhiim gromom gore*
udarilo
"Es ruht mit ernstem Sinnen auf mir dein
Blick" *see Glück* Rohrscheidt REGER
"Es sagen mir die Weiber" *see Auf sich selbst*
Anacreon LOEWE
"Es sass die Prinzessin im Frauengemach" *see*
Abendstimmung Bjørnson DELIUS
"Es sass ein Salamander" *see Salamander*
Lemcke BRAHMS
Es schauen die Blumen see Heine BRAHMS
"Es schauet der Morgen mit funkelndem
Schein" *see Frühlingserwachen* Gramberg
LOEWE
Es schaukelt ein Kahn im Fjorde see Benzon
GRIEG *Der gynger en Båd på Bølge*
"Es schaute in die Wogen" *see Agnete*
Plönnies LOEWE
Es schläft ein stiller Garten see Hauptmann
REGER
"Es schlug mein Herz, geschwind zu Pferde!"
see Willkommen und Abschied Goethe
PFITZNER, SCHUBERT
"Es schmachtet eine Blume" *see Räthsel*
Anon. RUBINSTEIN
"Es schritt wohl über die Heide" *see*
Die Vätergruft Uhland LISZT
"Es segeln die Wolken" *see Wanderlied*
Anon. WOLF
"Es senkt sich der Abend über das Meer" *see*
Allein Michell LASSEN
"Es singt der Ros' in Liebesdrang" *see*
Die Nachtigall und die Rose Kol'tsov
RUBINSTEIN
"Es sitzt die Zeit im weissen Kleid" *see*
Die Zeit Stoll WEBER
Es soll mein Gebet dich tragen see Wegerer,
Asta von REGER

"Es sprach der Geist: Sieh auf!" *see Alle Meyer* SCHOECK

"Es stand eine Rose im tieftiefen Grund" *see Unbegehrt Ritter* REGER

"Es stehn in unserm Garten" *see Scherz* Chamisso REGER

"Es steht der Sachsenführer, Herr Wittekind" *see Karl der Grosse und Wittekind* Vogl LOEWE

"Es steht ein altes Gemäuer" *see Lass ruh'n die Toten* Chamisso STRAUSS

"Es steht ein Berg im Feuer" *see Frühlingsgruss* Unknown LASSEN

"Es steht ein Blümchen dort im Thal" *see Wir drei* Backody RUBINSTEIN

Es steht ein Kelch in der Kapelle see Giesebrecht LOEWE

"Es steht eine gold'ne Wiege" *see Das Wiegenfest zu Gent* Auersperg LOEWE

"Es steht im Wald, im tiefen Wald" *see Des Woiewoden Tochter* Geibel LASSEN

"Es steht in der Bibel geschrieben" *see Ich bin bis zum Tode betrübet* Hahn-Hahn FRANZ

"Es steht mein Lied in Nacht und Frost" *see Wer hat's gethan?* Gilm zu Rosenegg STRAUSS

"Es steht sein Bild noch immer da" *see Gedenken* Unknown SCHÖNBERG

"Es streckt der Wald die Zweige so grün" *see Im Walde* Müller von Königswinter FRANZ

Es stürmet am Abendhimmel see Schöpff SCHUMANN

Es stürmt auf der Flur see Rochlitz WEBER

"Es stürzen der Jugend Altäre zusammen" *see Thalatta* Morgenstern KILPINEN

Es stürzt aus Höhen Frische see Jone VIAE INVIAE. WEBERN

"Es tanzen Mond und Sterne" *see Gondelfahrer* Mayrhofer SCHUBERT

"Es tat den Beiden so weh das Scheiden" *see Stummer Abschied* Unknown SCHOECK

"Es tönet sein Lob Feld und Wald" *see Die Gestirne* Klopstock SCHUBERT

"Es tönt des Nöcken Harfenschall" *see Der Nöck* Kopisch LOEWE

"Es trabt im Kreis durch die Manege" *see Das Zirkuspferdchen* Wolf, F. BLACHER

"Es träumen die Wolken" *see Beim Winde* Mayrhofer SCHUBERT

Es träumte mir see Daumer POLYDORA. BRAHMS

"Es träumte mir von einer weiten Haide" *see Auf dem Meere* Heine FRANZ

"Es treibt dich fort" *see In der Fremde* Heine FRANZ

Es treibt mich hin, es treibt mich her see Heine FRANZ, SCHUMANN

"Es tropft auf die Dächer" *see Regen I* Huber, B. KILPINEN

Es vergessen sich . . . see Tolstoï MUSORGSKIĬ *Rassevaetsia, rasstupaetsia*

"Es wälzt der Strom" *see Strom bei Nacht* Huber, B. KILPINEN

"Es wallt und woget schwer" *see Nebel und Gram* Tolstoï RUBINSTEIN

Es wandelt, was wir schauen see Eichendorff BERG

"Es wandelt, was wir schauen" *see Ergebung* Eichendorff SCHOECK

"Es wandert eine schöne Sage" *see Frühlingsglaube* Keller, G. SCHOECK

"Es war, als hätt' der Himmel" *see Mondnacht* Eichendorff BRAHMS, SCHUMANN

"Es war die Zeit, du kennst das Jahr" *see There was a time* Byron LASSEN

Es war doch schön see Fitger LASSEN

"Es war ein alter König" *see Das alte Lied* Heine GRIEG

Es war ein alter König see Heine WOLF

"Es war ein alter König" *see Lied* Heine RUBINSTEIN

"Es war ein Bruder Liederlich" *see Lied der Chispa* Calderon STRAUSS

"Es war ein heit'res, gold'nes Jahr" *see Die Entschwundene* Keller, G. SCHOECK

"Es war ein Jäger wohl keck und kühn" *see Treuröschen* Körner LOEWE

"Es war ein Kind, das wollte nie" *see Die wandelnde Glocke* Goethe LOEWE, SCHUMANN

"Es war ein Knabe frech gerug" *see Der untreue Knabe* Goethe MEDTNER

Es war ein König in Thule see Goethe FAUST. LISZT, SEIBER

"Es war ein König in Thule" *see Der König in Thule* Goethe JENSEN, SCHUBERT

"Es war ein König in Tule" *see Der König von Tule* Goethe ZELTER

"Es war ein König Lobesam" *see Die Ballade vom König Lobesam* Goering KRENEK

Es war ein Traum see Wilder LASSEN *Ich hatte einst ein schönes Vaterland*

"Es war ein wunderschönes Tal" *see Romanze* Becker, K. ZELTER

"Es war eine Ratt' im Kellernest" *see Branders Lied* Goethe WAGNER

Es war einmal ein Bock see Kerr STRAUSS

"Es war einmal ein König" *see Aus Goethes Faust* Goethe BEETHOVEN

"Es war einmal ein König" *see Lied des Mephistopheles* Goethe **WAGNER**

"Es war einmal ein Schneidergesell" *see Schneiderlied* Häring **LOEWE**

"Es war einmal, ihr Leute" *see Des kleinen Friedrichs Geburtstag* Schall **MOZART**

Es war mal eine Wanze see Kerr **STRAUSS**

"Es waren drei lust'ge Gesellen" *see Nacht am Rheine* Siebel **BARTÓK**

"Es waren mal zwei Mäuschen" *see Zwei Mäuschen* Boelitz **REGER**

"Es waren Ruhm und Weisheit mein" *see Alles ist eitel, spricht der Prediger* Byron **LOEWE**

"Es wecket meine Liebe die Lieder immer wieder!" *see Erinnerung* Volkmann **MAHLER**

"Es wehet kühl und leise" *see Die Gebüsche* Schlegel, F. **SCHUBERT**

"Es weht um mich Narzissenduft" *see Frühlingstrost* Schenkendorf **BRAHMS**

Es weiss und räth es doch Keiner see Eichendorff **MENDELSSOHN-BARTHOLDY**

"Es weiss und räth es doch Keiner" *see Die Stille* Eichendorff **SCHUMANN**

"Es will kein Baum so wie die Linde blühen!" *see Erinnerung* Krzyzanowski **KRENEK**

"Es wird wohl Winter" *see Trost* Unknown **LOEWE**

"Es wogt wie steigende Wellen im Herzen hin" *see Immer dasselbe* Harnier **SPOHR**

"Es wohnt ein kleines Vögelein" *see Sie wissen's nicht* Panizza **STRAUSS**

"Es wollt ein Mädchen früh aufstehn" *see Vom verwundeten Knaben* Anon. **BRAHMS**

"Es ziehen die Wolken" *see Die Lerchen* Hamerling **LASSEN**

"Es ziehet den Pilgrim rastlos fort" *see Das Grab zu Ephesus* Binder **LOEWE**

Es ziehn die brausenden Wellen see Heine **FRANZ**

"Es zog ein Jäger in den Wald" *see Der verliebte Jäger* Boelitz **REGER**

"Es zog eine Hochzeit den Berg entlang" *see Im Walde* Eichendorff **MEDTNER, SCHUMANN**

"Es zogen drei Bursche wohl über den Rhein" *see Der Wirthin Töchterlein* Uhland **LOEWE**

"Es zogen zwei rüst'ge Gesellen" *see Frühlingsfahrt* Eichendorff **SCHUMANN**

L'escalier redit, gestes du soleil see Messiaen **MESSIAEN**

Escarpin see Radiguet **AURIC**

L'Esclave see Gautier **LALO, MASSENET**

Escriva Comendador, Joan, d.ca.1520. **WOLF** *Komm, O Tod*

Escudier, Marie Pierre Yves, 1819-1880. **VERDI** *L'abandonée*

"Ein Esel sah die Nachtigall" *see Der Esel und die Nachtigall* Krylov **RUBINSTEIN**

Der Esel und die Nachtigall see Krylov **RUBINSTEIN**

Eshche ĭa poln, O drug moĭ milyĭ see Maĭkov **RIMSKIĬ-KORSAKOV**

"Esli rozy tikho osypaiutsia" *see Smert'* Merezhkovski **CHAĬKOVSKIĬ**

"Esli ty khochesh', zhelannaia" *see Pimpinella* Chaĭkovskiĭ **CHAĬKOVSKIĬ**

Esli zhizn' tebia obmanet see Pushkin **MEDTNER** *If one day you're disillusioned*

L'ESPACE DU DEDANS, no. 1 **SAUGUET** Michaux *Repos dan le malheur*

L'ESPACE DU DEDANS, no. 2 **SAUGUET** Michaux *La jeune fille de Budapest*

L'ESPACE DU DEDANS, no. 3 **SAUGUET** Michaux *Dans la nuit*

ESPAÑA. *see* Gautier *Séguidille* **DEBUSSY**

La espera see Kamhi, Victoria **RODRIGO**

Espinasse-Mongenet, Mme. Louise **SÉVERAC** *Chanson de la nuit durable*

L'espionne see Apollinaire *CALLIGRAMMES.* **POULENC**

L'esprit saint see Unknown **BIZET**

"Esprits d'amour et d'harmonie" *see Le nom de Marie* Ségur **GOUNOD**

Espronceda, José de, 1808-1842. **TURINA** *El pescador*

Est see Harsányi **BARTÓK**

Est' drugie planety see Bal'mont **PROKOFIEV**

Est' mnogo zvukov see Tolstoĭ **RACHMANINOFF** *There are many sounds*

Esta niña se lleva la flor see Figueroa **RODRIGO**

"Está tuimagen, que admiro" *see Farruca* Campoamor y Campoosorio **TURINA**

Estando yo en mi majada see Anon. **RODRIGO**

ESTHER, no. 1 **LOEWE** Giesebrecht *Wie früh das enge Pförtchen knarre*

ESTHER, no. 2 **LOEWE** Giesebrecht *Der König auf dem goldnen Stuhle*

ESTHER, no. 3 **LOEWE** Giesebrecht *Nun auf dem fremden Boden*

ESTHER, no. 4
   LOEWE Giesebrecht *Spielt, Mägdlein, unter eurer Weide!*
ESTHER, no. 5
   LOEWE Giesebrecht *Wie wohnst du in des Reiches Städten*
Esti dal see Peros **BARTÓK** *Evening song*
Estieu, Prosper, 1860-1939.
   SÉVERAC *Cansón pel cabalet*
"Est-il rien de plus beau" *see La Seine* Rohan **THOMSON**
LA ESTRELLA DE SEVILLA. see Vega Carpio *Si con mis deseos* **TURINA**
Estribillo see Polo de Medina **RODRIGO**
Es-tu sorti par cette nuit d'orage? see Tagore **SAUGUET**
L'esule see Solèra **VERDI**
L'esule see Torre, G. **ROSSINI**
Et Håb see Paulsen **GRIEG**
"Et je suis de nouvea reporté sur la mer" *see Dissolution* Claudel **MILHAUD**
"Et le soir vient et les lys meurent" *see Allons plus vite* Apollinaire **POULENC**
"Et leurs visages étaient pâles" *see Le départ* Apollinaire **RIVIER**
Et puis see Chassang, Maurice **MASSENET**
"Et puis ce soir" *see Avant le cinéma* Apollinaire **POULENC**
"Et Sagn nu mig drages til Minde" *see Harpen* Munch **GRIEG**
Et Syn see Vinje **GRIEG** *Eit Syn*
Et Vennestykke see Vinje **GRIEG**
Et voici des ans see Hugnet **SAUGUET**
"Était-ce hier ou dans un temps lointain" *see L'Aventure* Tardieu **SAUGUET**
L'été see Banville **KOECHLIN**
"Eté, j'ai cherché trop longtemps" *see Soir romantique* Noailles **SAINT-SAËNS**
"Étendu au seuil du bassin" *see Reflets dans l'éau* Brimont **FAURÉ**
"Etendue dans le vallon étroit" *see Paresse* Paliard **MILHAUD**
Eternité see Girard, Marguerite **MASSENET**
"L'éternité! je l'ai comprise" *see Eternité* Girard, Marguerite **MASSENET**
Eternity see Blake, William **VAUGHAN WILLIAMS**
Eti letnie nochi see Rathaus **RACHMANINOFF** *These summer nights*
"Eto vovka vydumal" *see Boltun'ia* Barto, A. **PROKOFIEV**
L'etoile see Haïdar-Pacha, Prince **SAINT-SAËNS**

"Etoile dont la beauté luit" *see Sérénade Florentine* Cazalis **DUPARC**
Etoile du matin see Distel, Camille **SAINT-SAËNS**
"Etoile, Ô feu du soir qui te lèves la première" *see L'etoile* Haïdar-Pacha, Prince **SAINT-SAËNS**
Les étoiles see Banville **HAHN, KOECHLIN**
Les étoiles see Stevenson, Robert Louis *A CHILD'S GARDEN OF VERSES.* **HAHN** *The stars*
"Les etoiles effarouchées" *see Sonnet matinal* Silvestre **MASSENET**
Être aimé see Hugo **MASSENET**
Étrennes see Morand **MILHAUD**
En etsi valtaa, loistoa see Topelius **SIBELIUS** *Giv mig ej glans*
Ett enda ord är mitt see Lagerkvist **KILPINEN**
"Ett ensamt stilla segel lyser" *see Kvällning* Ullman **KILPINEN**
ÉTUDES LATINES. see Leconte de Lisle *À Phidylé* **HAHN**
ÉTUDES LATINES, no. 2
   HAHN Leconte de Lisle *Néère*
ÉTUDES LATINES, no. 3
   HAHN Leconte de Lisle *Salinum*
ÉTUDES LATINES, no. 5
   HAHN Leconte de Lisle *Lydé*
ÉTUDES LATINES, no. 6
   HAHN Leconte de Lisle *Vile potabis*
ÉTUDES LATINES, no. 7
   HAHN Leconte de Lisle *Tyndaris*
ÉTUDES LATINES, no. 8
   HAHN Leconte de Lisle *Pholoé*
ÉTUDES LATINES, no. 10
   HAHN Leconte de Lisle *Phyllis*
      NB: Nos. 1, 4, and 9 include chorus; omitted here.
"Euch Blümlein will ich senden zur schönen Jungfrau dort" *see Der Blumenbrief* Schreiber **SCHUBERT**
L'eucharistie see Frère Eucher **GOUNOD**
"Euer Herz erschrecke nicht" *see Der Friedhof* Giesebrecht **LOEWE**
Eure Etüden see Benn **BLACHER**
"Eure Etüden, Arpeggios, Dankchoral" *see Eure Etüden* Benn **BLACHER**
Eure Weisheit see Fischer **BERG**
Evans, Mari E., 1923-
   I AM A BLACK WOMAN.
      WEISGALL *The rebel*
Evans, Mrs. Florence (Wilkinson)
   CARPENTER *The heart's country*
   GIDEON *Farewell tablet to Agathocles*

COMPOSER   Poet   *Title*   "First Line"

Éveil see Gassier **MASSENET**
L'éveil de Pâques see Verhaeren *LES VIGNES DANS MURAILLE.* **SÉVERAC**
Even though the world keeps changing see Rilke *SONETTE AN ORPHEUS.* **DIAMOND**
Evening see Harsányi **BARTÓK** *Est*
Evening see Milton *PARADISE LOST.* **IVES**
Evening see Moore, G. **MARTINŮ**
Evening see Prokosch **ROREM**
Evening see Sappho **ROREM**
Evening see Shevchenko **CHAÏKOVSKÏ** *Vecher*
Evening and morning see Mickiewicz **CHAÏKOVSKÏ** *Na zemliu sumrak pal*
AN EVENING SONG. see Lanier
Evening song **GRIFFES**
Evening song see Lanier *AN EVENING SONG.* **GRIFFES**
Evening song see No author **LUENING**
Evening song see Peros **BARTÓK**
Evening song see Pleshcheyev **MUSORGSKÏ** *Vecherniaia pesenka*
Evening song see Tennyson **HARRIS**
EVENING SONGS, no. 1
   DVOŘÁK Hálek *Ty hvězdičky tam na nebi to veliké*
EVENING SONGS, no. 2
   DVOŘÁK Hálek *Mně zdálo se žes umřela*
EVENING SONGS, no. 3
   DVOŘÁK Hálek *Já jstem ten rytîr zpohádky*
EVENING SONGS, no. 4
   DVOŘÁK Hálek *Když bůh byl nejvíc rozkochán*
EVENING SONGS, no. 5
   DVOŘÁK Hálek *Umlklo stromu šumění*
EVENING SONGS, no. 6
   DVOŘÁK Hálek *Přílítlo jaro zdaleka*
EVENING SONGS, no. 7
   DVOŘÁK Hálek *Když jsem se díval do nebe*
EVENING SONGS, no. 8
   DVOŘÁK Hálek *Vy malí, drobní ptáčkové*
EVENING SONGS, no. 9
   DVOŘÁK Hálek *Jsem jako lípa košatá*
EVENING SONGS, no. 10
   DVOŘÁK Hálek *Vy všichni kdo jste stísněni*
EVENING SONGS, no. 11
   DVOŘÁK Hálek *Ten ptáček, ten se nazpívá*
EVENING SONGS, no. 12
   DVOŘÁK Hálek *Tak jak ten měsíc vnebes báň*
Evening voices see Bjørnson **DELIUS** *Abendstimmung*

Éventail see Mallarmé **DEBUSSY**
L'éventail see Morel-Retz **MASSENET**
"Un éventail qui fut l'oiselle" *see Mallarmé* Radiguet **AURIC**
The everlasting voices see Yeats *THE WIND AMONG THE REEDS* (1899): Aodh to Dectora. **HESELTINE**
Evers, Franz, 1871-1947.
   BERG
      Aus "Pfingsten ein Gedichtsreigen"
      Heilige Himmel
      Leben
   REGER
      Das Fenster klang im Winde
      Flötenspielerin
      Geheimnis
      Märchenland
      Meine Seele
      Mondnacht
      Nachtgeflüster
      Nachtseele
      Nachtsegen
      Ruhe
      Sommernacht
      Traum
Every night and every morn see Blake, William *AUGURIES OF INNOCENCE.* **BRITTEN**
"Everywhere, the impossible is happening" *see Prologue and Epilogue: from "The Rain"* Windham **ROREM**
Evidence see Ives **IVES**
"Ev'n like two little bank divided brooks" *see Canticle I* Quarles **BRITTEN**
Evocation see Pushkin **RIMSKÏ-KORSAKOV** *Zaklinanie*
Evocation see Richepin **SCHMITT**
Evreǐ skaia pesnia see Mei **RIMSKÏ-KORSAKOV**
Evreǐ skaia pesnia see Solomon **MUSORGSKÏ**
Evreyskaya melodiya see Lermontov **BALAKIREV**
"Ev'ry where, far and near, whether resting, whether walking" *see Sehnsucht* Meier, Daniel Eduard **SPOHR**
Ev'rything's still in valley and mountain see Pfleger-Moravský **DVOŘÁK** *Na horách ticho, vúdolí ticho*
Ewig jung see Ernst **LASSEN**
Der ewige Jude see Schreiber **LOEWE**
Ewige Liebe see Wildenbruch **LASSEN**
Exaucement see Lerberghe **FAURÉ**
Exhortation see Jacob, M. **SAUGUET**
Exiit edictum see Bible **HINDEMITH**
LES EXILÉS. see Banville *L'énamourée* **HAHN**

COMPOSER   Poet   *Title*   "First Line"

Experienced by two stones see Capetanakis
ROREM
Experiment to me Is every one I meet see
Dickinson **LUENING**
Exploit see Khomyakov **CHAÏKOVSKIÏ**
Podvig
EXPRESSIONS LYRIQUES, no. 1
MASSENET Varenne, Marc *Dialogue*
EXPRESSIONS LYRIQUES, no. 2
MASSENET Louvencourt *Les nuages*
EXPRESSIONS LYRIQUES, no. 3
MASSENET Maurer *En voyage*
EXPRESSIONS LYRIQUES, no. 4
MASSENET Dortzal *Battements d'ailes*
EXPRESSIONS LYRIQUES, no. 5
MASSENET Biron *La dernière lettre de*
Werther à Charlotte
EXPRESSIONS LYRIQUES, no. 6
MASSENET Dortzal *Comme autrefois*
EXPRESSIONS LYRIQUES, no. 7
MASSENET Dortzal *Nocturne*
EXPRESSIONS LYRIQUES, no. 8
MASSENET Anon. *Mélancolie*

EXPRESSIONS LYRIQUES, no. 9
MASSENET Poirson, S. Cuthbert *Rose*
de Mai
EXPRESSIONS LYRIQUES, no. 10
MASSENET Grain, Madeleine *Feux*
follets d'amour
Extase see Cazalis **DUPARC**
Extase see Hugo **SAINT-SAËNS**
Extase see Hugo *LES ORIENTALES.*
WAGNER
NB: Variant texts set by Saint-Saëns and
Wagner.
Extase printanière see Alexandre, André
MASSENET
Les extases see Dessirier, Annie
MASSENET
Extinct see Busse-Palma **SIBELIUS**
Erloschen
Extinguish my eyes see Rilke **BERNSTEIN**
Ex-voto see Cocteau **HONEGGER**
Eyes look into the well see Auden
BERKELEY

F

FABELBALLADEN, no. 1
LOEWE Reinick *Der verliebte Maikäfer*
FABELBALLADEN, no. 2
LOEWE Herder *Der Kukuk*
FABELBALLADEN, no. 3
LOEWE Chamisso *Die Katzenkönigin*
FABELBALLADEN, no. 4
LOEWE Häring *Wer ist Bär?*
La fable du village see Gilson **RIVIER**
Facklor see Österling **KILPINEN**
"*Facklor i stormen, hell er*" *see Facklor*
Österling **KILPINEN**
Faded and vanished see Zaleski **CHOPIN**
Nie ma czego trzeba
The faded flower see Pushkin **MEDTNER**
"*A faded flower, dried and scentless*" *see The*
faded flower Pushkin **MEDTNER**
Faedrelandssalme see Rolfsen **GRIEG**
Faedrelandssang see Drachmann **NIELSEN**
Faedrelandssang see Paulsen **GRIEG**
Fåfäng önskan see Runeberg **SIBELIUS**
"*En fågel genom natten far*" *see Japansk*
akvarell Josephson, E. **KILPINEN**
Fågelfångaren see Runeberg **SIBELIUS**

Fågellek see Tavaststjerna **SIBELIUS**
Fågelungarna see Josephson, E.
KILPINEN
"*Fågelungarna flögo ur bo*" *see Fågelungarna*
Josephson, E. **KILPINEN**
Fagnes de Wallonie see Apollinaire *IL Y A.*
POULENC
"*Fahr hin! fahr hin für alle Zeiten*" *see Das*
Vaterland Vogl **LOEWE**
Fahrewohl see Keller, G. **SCHOECK**
Die Fahrt ins Heu see Langbein **ZELTER**
Fahrt zum Hades see Mayrhofer
SCHUBERT
"*Fain would I change that note*" *see Fair*
house of joy Anon. **QUILTER**
Fain would I have a pretty thing see Anon.
RIETI
Fair and true see Breton *MELANCHOLIC*
HUMOURS (1600). **HESELTINE**
"*Fair daffodils, we weep to see you haste*
away so soon" *see To daffodils* Herrick
DELIUS
Fair house of joy see Anon. **QUILTER**
Fair lullaby see Quilter **QUILTER**

Fair springtide see MacDowell
   MACDOWELL
"Fair springtide cometh once again" *see Fair*
   springtide MacDowell **MACDOWELL**
The fair young maid no longer loves me see
   Vinogradov **BORODIN**
   Razlyubila krasna devitsa
The fairy and the snail see Josephson, E.
   SIBELIUS *Älvan och snigeln*
Fairy song see Cronyn **RIEGGER**
"Fais rafraîchir mon vin" *see A son page*
   Ronsard **POULENC**
Faisait-il beau quand elle est morte see
   Jammes *TRISTESSES.* **MILHAUD**
"Les Faiseurs de religions" *see Hyde Park*
   Apollinaire **POULENC**
The faithless lad see Goethe *CLAUDINE*
   VON VILLA BELLA. **MEDTNER**
   Der untreue Knabe
The faithless shepherdess see Anon.
   QUILTER
Faktor, Emil, 1876-1942.
   SZYMANOWSKI *An kleine Mädchen*
Falck, Mogens
   NIELSEN *Julesang*
Falk, Johannes, 1768-1826.
   LOEWE *Nordisches Seelied*
   ZELTER *Der arme Thoms*
Falke, Gustav, 1853-1916.
   BERG *Die Sorglichen*
   MARTINŮ *To my child*
   REGER
      Der Alte
      An die Geliebte
      Die bunten Kühe
      Gute Nacht
      Heimat
      Meinem Kinde
      Müde
      Die Nixe
      Der tapfere Schneider
      Trost
      Die Verschmähte
      Viola d'amour
      Wäsche im Wind
      Wir zwei
      Zwischen zwei
   STRAUSS *Meinem Kinde*
   SZYMANOWSKI *Seele*
   MIT DEM LEBEN.
      BERG, REGER, WEBERN *Fromm*
THE FALL, no. 1
   DIAMOND Agee *So it begins*
THE FALL, no. 2
   DIAMOND Agee *Our doom is in our*
      being

THE FALL, no. 3
   DIAMOND Agee *I have been fashioned*
THE FALL, no. 4
   DIAMOND Agee *What curious thing is*
      love
THE FALL, no. 5
   DIAMOND Agee *Wring me no more*
THE FALL, no. 6
   DIAMOND Agee *Why am I here*
THE FALL, no. 7
   DIAMOND Agee *Now stands our love*
THE FALL, no. 8
   DIAMOND Agee *I nothing saw in you*
THE FALL, no. 9
   DIAMOND Agee *This little time*
FALLA, MANUEL DE, 1876-1946.
   Anon.
      Asturiana (1914) [Eschig, 1922]
         "Por ver si me consolaba"
      Cancion (1914) [Eschig, 1922]
         "Por traidores, tus ojos"
      Jota (1914) [Eschig, 1922]
         "Dicen que no nos queremos"
      Nana (berceuse, 1914) [Eschig, 1922]
         "Duérmete, niño, duerme"
      El pano moruno (1914) [Eschig, 1922]
         "Al paño fino"
      Polo (1914) [Eschig, 1922]
         "Guardo una 'Ay!' "
      Seguidilla Murciana (1914) [Eschig,
         1922] "Cualquiera que el tejado"
   Bécquer, Gustavo Adolfo, 1836-1870.
      Dios mio, que solos se quedan los
         muertos! (before 1900)
         [Union Musical Española, 1980]
         "Cerraron sus ojos que aún
            teniaabiertos"
      Olas gigantes (before 1900) [Union
         Musical Española, 1980]
         "Olas gigantes que os rompeis
            bramando"
   Castro, Cristóbal de, 1880-
      Tus ojillos negros (Canzon Andaluza,
         1902) [Union Musical Española, 1940]
         "Yo no se que tienen tus ojillos
            negros"
   Gautier, Théophile, 1811-1872.
      LA COMÉDIE DE LA MORT.
         Chinoiserie (1909) [Rouart Lerolle,
            1910] "Ce n'est pas vous"
         Les Colombes (1909) [Rouart Lerolle,
            1910] "Sur le coteau"
         Séguidille (1909) [Rouart Lerolle,
            1910]
            "Un jupon serré sur les hanches"

COMPOSER Poet *Title* "First Line"

Góngora y Argote, Luis de, 1561-
1627.
SONETO A CÓRDOBA.
Soneto a Córdoba (1927) [Oxford
Univ. Press, 1932]
"Oh excelso muro, oh torres
coronadas"
Voice & harp or piano.
Martinez Sierra, Gregorio, 1881-1947.
Canzon Andaluza: El pan de ronda
(1915) [Union Musical Española,
1980]
"Aunque todoen el mundo fuese
mentira"
Oración de las madres que tienen . . .
(1915) [Union Musical Española,
1980]
"Dulce Jesús, que estás dormido"
Trueba, Antonio de, 1821-1899.
Preludios (before 1900) [Union Musical
Española, 1980]
"Madre, todas las noches junto a mis
rejas"
Der fallende Stern see Rostopchina
RUBINSTEIN
Fallersleben *see* Hoffmann von
Fallersleben, August Heinrich, 1798-
1874.
THE FALLS OF LOVE, no. 1
ROREM Moss *I know so many stories*
THE FALLS OF LOVE, no. 3
ROREM Moss *Only lover's rest*
THE FALLS OF LOVE, no. 5
ROREM Moss *A body without love*
THE FALLS OF LOVE, no. 6
ROREM Moss *They rise up shining*
The false note see Borodin **BORODIN**
Fal'shivaya nota
Fal'shivaya nota see Borodin **BORODIN**
"Fame, wisdom, love, and power were mine"
see All is vanity Byron **DIAMOND**
Familière see Chabaneix **IBERT**
THE FAMOUS HISTORY OF FRIAR BACON
(printed before 1600). *see* Anon.
Away to Twiver **HESELTINE**
Fancie see Shakespeare *MERCHANT OF
VENICE.* **BRITTEN**
Fanciula mia see Ciampoli **RUBINSTEIN**
Il fanciullo smarrito see Castellani, A.
ROSSINI
Fancy see Shakespeare *MERCHANT OF
VENICE.* **POULENC**
Fancy's knell see Housman *LAST POEMS:
XLI.* **VAUGHAN WILLIAMS**
Fanshawe, Catharine, 1765-1834.
SCHUMANN *Räthsel*

Fantaisie see Gérard de Nerval **AURIC**
FANTAISIES DÉCORATIVES, no. 2. *see*
Wilde *Les ballons* **GRIFFES**
Fantoches see Verlaine *FÊTES GALANTES.*
DEBUSSY
Two settings: 1882 and 1892?
*Far, ah how far is flown all happiness I've
known see* Anon. **DVOŘÁK** *Ach není,
není tu*
Far, far away see Tennyson **ROREM**
THE FAR FIELD. see Roethke
From whence cometh song? **ROREM**
"Far from home are you, my brother" *see
Message* Pushkin **MEDTNER**
Die Farben Helgolands see Hoffmann von
Fallersleben **FRANZ**
Farbenkantus see Unknown **SCHOECK**
"Fare you well and adieu to you, Spanish
ladies" *see The Spanish ladies* Anon.
VAUGHAN WILLIAMS
Farewell see Anon. **SEIBER**
Farewell see Nekrasov **CHAĬKOVSKĬ**
Prosti
A farewell see Oliphant **ROUSSEL**
Farewell see Rydberg **SIBELIUS** *Vi ses
igen*
"Farewell! my joy, my joy" *see Court song*
Anon. **BLITZSTEIN**
Farewell tablet to Agathocles see Evans
GIDEON
Farewell to France see Mary **SCHUMANN**
Abschied von Frankreich
A farewell to land see Byron *CHILDE
HAROLD'S PILGRIMAGE.* **IVES**
Farewell to the world see Mary
SCHUMANN *Abschied von der Welt*
Fargue, Léon-Paul, 1878-1947.
AUBERT *Au pays*
AURIC
Enfance
Nuit blanche
Regrets
RAVEL *Rêves*
SATIE *La statue de bronze*
LUDIONS.
SATIE
Air du Poète
Air du Rat
Chanson du chat
La Grenouille américaine
Spleen
TANCRÈDE.
SCHMITT *La petite princesse*
Farjeon, Eleanor, 1881-1965.
BRITTEN *Jazz-man*
A farm picture see Whitman **LUENING**

COMPOSER Poet *Title* "First Line"

Farnie, Henry Brougham, d.1889.
  GOUNOD *Gliding down the river*
"Farò come colui che piange e dice" *see*
  Recitativo ritmato Dante **ROSSINI**
Farnol, Jeffrey, 1878-1952.
  BETHANE THE SMITH: Chapter XVI.
    COPLAND *Melancholy: a song "à la Debussy"*
Farruca see Campoamor y Campoosorio
  TURINA
Farvel see Paulsen **GRIEG**
Farvel, min velsignede Fødeby! see Møller
  NIELSEN
FATAL INTERVIEW. see Millay
  Gone in good sooth you are **GIDEON**
  Moon, that against the lintel of the West
    GIDEON
  Night is my sister **GIDEON**
FATALITÀ. see Negri
  Nevicata **RESPIGHI**
Fate see Apukhtin **RACHMANINOFF**
Fatima beim Saitenspiel see Bodenstedt
  SPOHR
Fatme see Dahn **RUBINSTEIN**
Fatum see Koechlin **KOECHLIN**
Fatum see Oeris **AUBERT**
"Faulse beauté, qui tant me couste cher" *see*
  Ballade de Villon à s'amye Villon
  DEBUSSY
Le faune see Verlaine *FÊTES GALANTES.*
  DEBUSSY
I fauni see Rubino **RESPIGHI**
FAURÉ, GABRIEL URBAIN, 1845-1924.
  Anon.
    Après un rêve, op. 7 no. 1 (ca.1878?)
      [Choudens, 1878; Hamelle]
      "Dans un sommeil que charmait ton image"
    Ave Maria, op. 67 no. 2 (1894-95)
      [Hamelle, 1895] "Ave Maria"
      Voice & organ.
    O Salutaris, op. 47 no. 1 (1878 & 1887)
      [Hamelle, 1888] "O Salutaris hostia"
      Voice & organ; 2nd version with 2
      horns, harp & string quintet.
    Salve Regina, op. 67 no. 1 (1895)
      [Hamelle, 1895] "Salve Regina Mater"
      Voice & organ.
    Sérénade toscane, op. 3 no. 2 (ca.1878?)
      [Choudens, 1879; Hamelle, 1887]
      "Ô toi que berce un rêve enchanteur"
  Baudelaire, Charles Pierre, 1821-1867.
    Chant d'automne, op. 5 no. 1 (1871?)
      [Choudens, 1879; Hamelle, 1887]
      "Bien-tôt nous plongerous dans les froides ténèbres"

  Hymne, op. 7 no. 2 (ca.1870) [G.
    Hartmann, 1871; Choudens, 1879;
    Hamelle, 1887] "A la très chère"
  La rançon, op. 8 no. 2 (1871?)
    [Choudens, 1879; Hamelle, 1887]
    "L'homme a, pour payer sa rançon"
Bordèse, Stéphan, b. 1847.
  En prière (1890) [Durand, 1890;
    Hamelle, 1897] "Si la voix d'un enfant
    peut monter jusqu'à vous"
    Voice & organ; also voice &
    orchestra, orchestration probably
    by Fauré.
Brimont, Renée de, Baronne, 1880-1943.
  Cygne sur l'éau, op. 113 no. 1 (1919)
    [Durand, 1919] "Ma pensée est un
    cygne harmonieux et sage"
  Danseuse, op. 113 no. 4 (1919) [Durand,
    1919] "Soeur des Soeurs tisseuses de violettes"
  Jardin nocturne, op. 113 no. 3 (1919)
    [Durand, 1919] "Nocturne jardin"
  Reflets dans l'éau, op. 113 no. 2 (1919)
    [Durand, 1919]
    "Étendu au seuil du bassin"
Choudens, Paul de, 1850-1925.
  Sylvie, op. 6 no. 3 (1878) [Choudens,
    1879; Hamelle, 1887]
    "Si tu veux savoir ma belle"
Closset, Marie, 1875-1952.
  Le don silencieux, op. 92 (1906) [Heugel,
    1906] "Je mettrai mes deux mains sur ma bouche"
Debladis, Georgette
  C'est la paix, op. 114 (1919) [Durand,
    1920] "Pendant qu'ils étaient partis pour la guerre"
Gautier, Théophile, 1811-1872.
  Chanson du pêcheur, op. 4 no. 1 (1872?)
    [Choudens, 1877, 1879; Hamelle,
    1887] "Ma belle amie est morte"
    Also voice & orchestra, 1876.
  Les matelots, op. 2 no. 2 (ca.1865)
    [Choudens, 1876; Hamelle, 1887]
    "Sur l'eau bleue et profonde"
  Seule, op. 3 no. 1 (1871) [G. Hartmann,
    1871; Choudens, 1877; Hamelle, 1887]
    "Dans un baiser l'onde au rivage"
  Tristesse, op. 6 no. 2 (ca.1873)
    [Choudens, 1876; Hamelle, 1887]
    "Avril est de retour"
Grandmougin, Charles-Jean, 1850-1930.
  Adieu, op. 21 no. 3 (1878) [Durand,
    1880; Hamelle, 1897]
    "Comme tout meurt vite"

Rencontre, op. 21 no. 1 (1878) [Durand, 1880; Hamelle, 1897]
"J'étais triste et pensif"

Toujours, op. 21 no. 2 (1878) [Durand, 1880; Hamelle, 1897]
"Vous me demandez de me taire"

Hugo, Victor Marie, comte, 1802-1885.

L'absent, op. 5 no. 3 (1871) [Choudens, 1879; Hamelle, 1887]
"Sentiers où l'herbe se balance"

Dans les ruines d'une abbaye, op. 2 no. 1 (ca.1865) [Choudens, 1869; Hamelle, 1887]
"Seuls, tous deux, ravis, chantants"

Mai, op. 1 no. 2 (1861?) [G. Hartmann, 1871; Choudens, 1877; Hamelle]
"Puisque Mai tout en fleurs"

Le papillon et la fleur, op. 1 no. 1 (1861) [Choudens, 1869; Hamelle]
"La pauvre fleur disait au papillon céleste"

Rêve d'amour, op. 5 no. 2 (1862?) [Choudens, 1875; Hamelle, 1887]
"S'il est un charmant gazon"

CHANTS DU CRÉPUSCULE.

L'aurore (ca.1870) [Arno Volk Verlag, 1958] "L'aurore s'allume"
Song in album entitled **The solo song outside German speaking countries,** pp. 79-80.

La Ville de Mirmont, Jean de, 1886-1914.

Diane, Séléné, op. 118 no. 3 (1921) [Durand, 1922] same

Je me suis embarqué, op. 118 no. 2 (1921) [Durand, 1922] same

La mer est infinie, op. 118 no. 1 (1921) [Durand, 1922] same

Vaisseaux, nous vous aurons aimés, op. 118 no. 4 (1921) [Durand, 1922] same

Leconte de Lisle, Charles Marie René, 1818-1894.

Lydia, op. 4 no. 2 (ca.1870) [G. Hartmann, 1871; Choudens, 1877; Hamelle, 1887]
"Lydia sur tes roses joues"

Nell, op. 18 no. 1 (1878) [Hamelle, 1880]
"Ta rose de pourpre à ton clair soleil"

Le parfum impérissable, op. 76 no. 1 (1897) [Hamelle, 1897]
"Quand la fleur du soleil"

La rose, op. 51 no. 4 (1889-90?) [Hamelle, 1890] "Je dirai la rose aux plis gracieux"

Les roses d'Ispahan, op. 39 no. 4 (1884) [Hamelle, 1885] "Les roses d'Ispahan dans leur gaîne de mousse"
Also voice & orchestra, 1896; unpublished.

Lerberghe, Charlesvan, 1861-1907.

L'aube blanche, op. 95 no. 5 (1908) [Heugel, 1908] same

Comme Dieu rayonne . . . , op. 95 no. 4 (1909) [Heugel, 1909] same

Crépuscule, op. 95 no. 9 (1906) [Heugel, 1906] "Ce soir, à travers le bonheur"

Dans la Nymphée, op. 106 no. 5 (1914) [Durand, 1915]
"Quoique tes yeux ne la voient pas"

Dans la pénombre, op. 106 no. 6 (1914) [Durand, 1915]
"A quoi, dans ce matin d'Avril"

Dans un parfum de roses blanches, op. 95 no. 8 (1909) [Heugel, 1909] same

Eau vivante, op. 95 no. 6 (1909) [Heugel, 1909] "Que tu es simple et claire"

Exaucement, op. 106 no. 1 (1914) [Durand, 1915]
"Alors qu'en tes mains de lumière"

Il m'est cher, Amour, le bandeau, op. 106 no. 7 (1914) [Durand, 1915] same

Inscription sur le sable, op. 106 no. 8 (1914) [Durand, 1915]
"Toute, avec sa robe et ses fleurs"

Je me poserai sur ton coeur, op. 106 no. 4 (1914) [Durand, 1915] same

La messagère, op. 106 no. 3 (1914) [Durand, 1915]
"Avril, et c'est le point du jour"

O mort, poussière d'étoiles, op. 95 no. 10 (1910) [Heugel, 1910] same

Paradis, op. 95 no. 1 (1906) [Heugel, 1907] "C'est le premier matin du monde"

Prima verba, op. 95 no. 2 (1906) [Heugel, 1907] "Comme elle chante dans ma voix"

Quand tu plonges tes yeux dans mes yeux, op. 106 no. 2 (1914) [Durand, 1915] same

Roses ardentes, op. 95 no. 3 (1908) [Heugel, 1909] same

Veilles-tu, ma senteur de soleil, op. 95 no. 7 (1910) [Heugel, 1910] same

Maeterlinck, Maurice, 1862-1949.

PELLÉAS ET MÉLISANDE.

Mélisande's song, op. posth. (1898) [Hamelle, 1937] "The King's three blind daughters" NB: from Act 3, scene 1, of *Pelléas . . .*

COMPOSER Poet *Title* "First Line"

FAURÉ, GABRIEL URBAIN, 1845-1924
(continued)

Mendès, Catulle Abraham, 1841-1909.
Dans la forêt de Septembre, op. 85 no. 1
(1902) [Hamelle, 1902]
"Ramure aux rumeurs amollies"
La fleur qui va sur l'eau, op. 85 no. 2
(1902) [Hamelle, 1902]
"Sur la mer voilée"

Molière, Jean Baptiste Poquelin,
1622-1673.
LE BOURGEOIS GENTILHOMME.
Sérénade du Bourgeois gentilhomme,
op. posth. (1893) [Heugel, 1957]
"Je languis nuit et jour et ma peine
est extrême"

Monnier, Marc, 1829-1885.
Barcarolle, op. 7 no. 3 (ca.1873)
[Choudens, 1877; Hamelle, 1887]
"Gondolier du Rialto"

No author
Vocalise (1906?) [Leduc, 1907]
In Hettich, ed. **Répertoire moderne de
vocalises-études,** v. 1.
Originally *Pièce* for oboe.

Pommey, Louis
Aubade, op. 6 no. 1 (ca.1873) [Choudens,
1879; Hamelle, 1887]
"L'oiseau dans le buisson"

Régnier, Henri François Joseph de,
1864-1936.
Chanson, op. 94 (1906) [Heugel, 1907]
"Que me fait toute la terre"

Richepin, Jean, 1849-1926.
Au cimetière, op. 51 no. 2 (1888)
[Hamelle, 1888]
"Heureux qui meurt ici"
LA MER.
Larmes, op. 51 no. 1 (1888) [Hamelle,
1888] "Pleurons nos chagrins,
chacun le nôtre"

Samain, Albert Victor, 1858-1900.
Accompagnement, op. 85 no. 3 (1902)
[Hamelle, 1902]
"Tremble argenté, til-leul, bouleau . . ."
Arpège, op. 76 no. 2 (1897) [Hamelle,
1897] "L'âme d'une flûte soupire"
Soir, op. 83 no. 2 (1894) [E. Fromont,
1896; Hamelle, 1897]
"Voici que les jardins de la nuit vont
fleurir"
Froment ed. as op. 68 no. 2;
Hamelle ed. as op. 73 no. 2.

Silvestre, Paul Armond, 1837-1901.
Aurore, op. 39 no. 1 (1884) [Hamelle,
1885] "Des jardins de la nuit
s'envolent les étoiles"

Automne, op. 18 no. 3 (1878) [Hamelle,
1880] "Automne au ciel brumeux"
Chanson d'amour, op. 27 no. 1 (1882)
[Hamelle, 1882] "J'aime tes yeux"
Le Fée aux chansons, op. 27 no. 2 (1882)
[Hamelle, 1883] "Il était une Fée"
Fleur jetée, op. 39 no. 2 (1884)
[Hamelle, 1885] "Emporte ma folie"
Notre amour, op. 23 no. 2 (ca.1879)
[Hamelle, 1881]
"Notre amour est chose légere"
Le pays des rêves, op. 39 no. 3 (1884)
[Hamelle, 1885]
"Veux-tu qu'au beau pays des rêves"
Le plus doux chemin, op. 87 no. 1 (1904)
[Hamelle, 1907]
"A mes pas le plus doux chemin"
Le ramier, op. 87 no. 2 (1904) [Milan:
Gramophone Co., 1904; Hamelle,
1907]
"Avec son chant doux et plaintif"
Le secret, op. 23 no. 3 (1880-81)
[Hamelle, 1881]
"Je veux que le matin l'ignore"
Le voyageur, op. 18 no. 2 (1878?)
[Hamelle, 1880]
"Voyageur, où vas-tu?"

Sully-Prudhomme, René François
Armand, 1839-1907.
Au bord de l'eau, op. 8 no. 1 (1875)
[Choudens, 1877; Hamelle, 1887]
"S'asseoir tous deux au bord du flot
qui passe"
Les berceaux, op. 23 no. 1 (1879)
[Hamelle, 1881] "Le long du Qaui"
Ici-bas, op. 8 no. 3 (ca.1873) [Choudens,
1877; Hamelle, 1887]
"Ici-bas tous les lilas meurent"

Verlaine, Paul, 1844-1896.
A Clymène, op. 58 no. 4 (1891)
[Hamelle, 1891]
"Mystiques barcarolles"
Donc, ce sera par un clair jour d'été, op.
61 no. 7 (1892-94) [Hamelle, 1894]
same
L'hiver a cessé, op. 61 no. 9 (1892-94)
[Hamelle, 1894] same
J'ai presque peur, en vérité, op. 61 no. 5
(1892-94) [Hamelle, 1894] same
J'allais par des chemins perfides, op. 61
no. 4 (1892-94) [Hamelle, 1894] same
Puisque l'aube grandit, op. 61 no. 2
(1892-94) [Hamelle, 1894] same
Une sainte en son auréole, op. 61 no. 1
((1892-94) [Hamelle, 1894] same
Spleen, op. 51 no. 3 (1888) [Hamelle,
1888] "Il pleure dans mon coeur"

COMPOSER Poet *Title* "First Line"

AQUARELLES.
  Green, op. 58 no. 3 (1891) [Hamelle, 1891]
    "Voici des fruits, des fleurs, des feuilles et des branches"
LA BONNE CHANSON.
  Avant que tu ne t'en ailles, op. 61 no. 6 (1892-94) [Hamelle, 1894] same
  La lune blanche luit dans les bois, op. 61 no. 3 (1892-94) [Hamelle, 1894] same
  N'est-ce pas? op. 61 no. 8 (1892-94) [Hamelle, 1894] same
FÊTES GALANTES.
  Clair de lune, op. 46 no. 2 (1887) [Hamelle, 1888]
    "Votre âme est un paysage choisi"
    Also voice & orchestra, 1888; unpublished.
  En sourdine, op. 58 no. 2 (1891) [Hamelle, 1891]
    "Calmes dans le demijour"
  Mandoline, op. 58 no. 1 (1891) |Hamelle, 1891]
    "Les donneurs de sérénades"
ROMANCES SANS PAROLES.
  C'est l'extase . . . , op. 58 no. 5 (1891) [Hamelle, 1891]
    "C'est l'extase langoureuse"
SAGESSE.
  Prison, op. 83 no. 1 (1894) [E. Fromont, 1896; Hamelle, 1897]
    "Le ciel est, par dessus le toit"
    Fromont ed. as op. 51 no. 1; Hamelle ed. as op. 73 no. 1.
Villiers de l'Isle-Adam, Jean Marie Mathias . . . , comte de, 1838-1889.
  Nocturne, op. 43 no. 2 (1886) [Hamelle, 1886] "La nuit, sur le grand mystère"
    Contralto & piano.
  Les présents, op. 46 no. 1 (1887) [Hamelle, 1888]
    "Si tu demandes quelque soir"
Wilder, Victor van, 1835-1892.
  Noël, op. 43 no. 1 (1885) [Hamelle, 1886] "La nuit descend du haut des cieux"
Faure, Maurice Louis Émile, 1850-1919.
  MASSENET *La mort de la cigale*
Fausse alerte see Copperie, Adrien **SAUGUET**
La fausse morte see Valéry **MOMPOU**
Faust, Camille Laurent Célestin, 1872-1945. *see* Mauclair, Camille, 1872-1945.

FAUST. see Goethe
  Aus Goethes Faust **BEETHOVEN**
  Bauern unter der Linde **WAGNER**
  Branders Lied **WAGNER**
  Deh, pietoso, oh addolorata **VERDI**
  Epilogue **SEIBER**
  Es war ein König in Thule **LISZT, SEIBER**
  Gretchen **MENDELSSOHN-BARTHOLDY, SPOHR**
  Gretchen am Spinnrade **SCHUBERT, WAGNER**
  Gretchen vor dem Andachtsbild der Mater dolorosa **WOLF**
  Gretchen vor der Mater dolorosa **SCHUBERT**
  Gretchens Lied aus Faust **ZELTER**
  Invocation **SEIBER**
  Der König in Thule **JENSEN, SCHUBERT**
  Der König von Tulen **ZELTER**
  Lied der Soldaten **WAGNER**
  Lied des Mephistopheles **WAGNER**
    Two settings: Op. 5 no. 4 and op. 5 no. 5.
  Lied Lynceus des Thürmers **SCHUMANN**
  Lynceus, der Helene **LOEWE**
  Lynceus, der Thürmer **LOEWE**
  Mädchen, als du kamst ans Licht **LOEWE**
  Margarethe **ZELTER**
  Meine Ruh' ist hin **LOEWE, SEIBER**
  Melodram Gretchens **WAGNER**
  Nur Platz, nur Blösse! **LOEWE**
  Perduta ho la pace **VERDI**
  Sei mir heute nichts zuwider! **LOEWE**
  Szene aus "Faust" **LOEWE**
  Szene aus Goethe's "Faust" **SCHUBERT**
  Thurmwächter Lynceus **LOEWE**
  Wenn der Blüten Frühlingsregen **LOEWE**
Faut-il chanter? see Borrelli **DELIBES**
Fauves las see Maeterlinck **CHAUSSON**
La fauvette see Millevoye **GOUNOD**
LE FAVOLE ROMANESCHE. see Salustri
  La carità **CASELLA**
  L'elezzione der presidente **CASELLA**
  Er coccodrillo **CASELLA**
  Er gatto e er cane **CASELLA**
Favorite abandonnée see Li-I **ROUSSEL**
Fear no more the heat o' the sun see Shakespeare *CYMBELINE.* **QUILTER**
Fear of death see Ashbery *SELF PORTRAITS IN A CONVEX MIRROR.* **ROREM**
The fearful minute see Chaĭkovskiĭ **CHAĬKOVSKIĬ** *Strashnaia minuta*
The feast see Kol'tsov **MUSORGSKIĬ** *Pirushka*

A feast of lanterns see Yuan Mei **GRIFFES**
The feast of love see Anon. **THOMSON**
"The feathers of the willow" *see Autumn song*
  Dixon **SIBELIUS**
Feddersen, Berend Wilhelm, 1832-1918.
  FRIERIET PAA HELGOLAND.
    GRIEG *Claras Sang*
La fède see Ariosto **IVES**
"La fède mai non debbe esser corrotta" *see*
  La fède Ariosto **IVES**
"Die Feder am Sturmhut" *see Bruder*
  Liederlich Liliencron **STRAUSS**
Le Fée aux chansons see Silvestre **FAURÉ**
Feed my sheep see Eddy **ROREM**
Feeney, Leonard, 1897-1978.
    CHANLER
    The children
    The doves
    The flight
    Grandma
    I rise when you enter
    Moo is a cow
    Once upon a time
    One of us
    The policeman in the park
    The rose
    Sleep
    Spick and span
    Wind
Feenreigen see Matthisson **ZELTER**
Les fées see Banville **SAINT-SAËNS**
"Feiger Gedanken, bängliches Schwanken" *see*
  Beherzigung Goethe **WOLF**
Feillet, Émilie
    MASSENET *Ton souvenir*
"Fein Rösslein, ich beschlage dich" *see Lied*
  eines Schmiedes Lenau **SCHUMANN**
Der Feind see Scherenberg **LOEWE**
"Der Feinde Scharen rüsten sich" *see*
  Des Königs Zuversicht Telschow **LOEWE**
Die feindlichen Brüder see Heine
    SCHUMANN
"Feins Liebchen, trau' du nicht" *see Klage*
  Anon. **BRAHMS**
"Feld einwärts flog ein Vögelein" *see*
  Herbstlied Tieck **ZELTER**
Feldblumen see Huber, B. **KILPINEN**
"Feldblumen, zarte, kleine" *see Feldblumen*
  Huber, B. **KILPINEN**
"Feldein nach einem dürren Baum" *see*
  Die Krähen Lingg **LASSEN**
Feldeinsamkeit see Allmers **BRAHMS;**
  IVES *In summer fields*
"Feldeinwärts flog ein Vögelein" *see*
  Herbstlied Tieck **CORNELIUS, LASSEN**
Der Feldherr see Gruppe **LOEWE**

Feldherr Tod see Golenishchev-Kutuzov
  MUSORGSKIÏ *Polkovodet͡s*
Félicité passée see Rousseau *LES*
  CONSOLATIONS DES MISÈRES DE MA
  VIE. **ZELTER**
Féline, J
    HONEGGER *De l'Atlantique ou Pacifique*
Felix Randal see Hopkins **ROREM**
Fellinger, Johann Georg, 1781-1886.
    SCHUBERT
    Die erste Liebe
    Die Sternenwelten
  WAS FUNKELT IHR SO MILD.
    SCHUBERT *Die Sterne*
"Félre Kislelküek, félre kislelküek" *see*
  A magyarok Istene Petöfi **LISZT**
"Fels auf Felsen hingewälzet" *see Aus*
  "Heliopolis" Mayrhofer **SCHUBERT**
Der Felsen see Lermontov **RUBINSTEIN**
La femme de l'ouvrier see Mallarmé
    MILHAUD
Femme et chatte see Verlaine **SCHMITT**
"La femme l'enfant la soupe" *see La femme*
  de l'ouvrier Mallarmé **MILHAUD**
La femme que j'aime see Catullus
    MILHAUD
"Une femme qui pleurait" *see Mutation*
  Apollinaire **POULENC**
Les femmes de Magdala see Gallet
    MASSENET
La Fénaison see Devereux **LALO**
Fenêtre illusoire à ma taille see Éluard
    SAUGUET
Fenêtre ouverte le soir see D'Harcourt,
  Antoniette **SAUGUET**
"Fenêtre pleine d'après-midi" *see Ta voix*
  Messiaen **MESSIAEN**
"Die Fenster klär'ich zum Feiertag" *see*
  Die Fensterscheibe Ulrich **SCHUMANN**
Das Fenster klang im Winde see Evers
    REGER
Die Fensterscheibe see Ulrich **SCHUMANN**
FERDAMINNI. see Vinje
  Auf der Reise zur Heimat **DELIUS**
  Ved Rondane **GRIEG**
Feridas teneis see Valdivielso *SPANISCHES*
  LIEDERBUCH. **JENSEN**
Das Ferkel see Iłłakowiczówna
    SZYMANOWSKI *Prosie*
"Un fermier du voisinage" *see Le malpropre*
  Vildrac **MILHAUD**
"Fern im Süd' das schöne Spanien" *see*
  Zigeunerbub' im Norden Geibel **LASSEN**
"Fern tobt der Kampf im Palmenthal" *see*
  Die Mohrenfürstin Freiligrath **LOEWE**
"Fern und ferner schallt der Reigen" *see*
  Sehnsucht Droysen **MENDELSSOHN-
  BARTHOLDY**

Fernandez, Jeanne
 SAUGUET *A une élégante sans fortune*
Ferne see Droysen MENDELSSOHN-BARTHOLDY
Der Ferne see Lenau SCHOECK
Ferne Lieder see Rückert BERG
"Ferne von der grossen Stadt" *see Lied* Pichler SCHUBERT
Der Fernen see Gerstenberg LOEWE
"Die fernen, fernen Berge mit ihren Nebelschleiern" *see Mädchenlied* Puttkamer REGER
Fernsicht see Hertz JENSEN
Ferrand, Antoine, 1678-1719.
 MOZART *Ariette*
Ferrand, Eduard, pseud. *see* Schulz, Eduard, 1813-1842.
Ferrand, François
 MASSENET *Avril est là!*
Ferrier, Paul, 1843-1920.
 BIZET
  Aimons, rêvons!
  Aubade
  Conte
  Le doute!
  La nuit
Ferrière, S
 GOUNOD *Au matin*
Ferry me across the water see Rossetti, Christina ROREM
Fersen, I. de
 RESPIGHI
  Par les soirs . . .
  Par l'étreinte . . .
  L'HYMNAIRE D'ADONIS.
 RESPIGHI *Il pleut, bergère*
Fes me la vida transparent see Janés i Olivé
 MOMPOU
Das Fest see Szymanowska, Zafia
 SZYMANOWSKI *Uczta*
DAS FEST AUF SOLHAUG. see Ibsen
  Gesang Margit's WOLF
  Gudmund's erster Gesang WOLF
  Gudmund's zweiter Gesang WOLF
FESTBÜCHLEIN. see Krummacher
  Die Lerche LOEWE
The festive, noisy day has ended see Golenishchev-Kutuzov MUSORGSKIĬ
  Okon'en prazdnyĭ, shumnyĭ den'
Fet, Afanasy, pseud. *see* Shenshin, Afanasiĭ Afanas'evich, 1820-1892.
Fête de Bordeaux see Cocteau MILHAUD
Fête de Montmartre see Cocteau MILHAUD
Fête galante see Banville *LES CARIATIDES:* livre 3, no. III. AURIC, DEBUSSY

Fête nationale see Chabaneix IBERT
Fêtes galantes see Aragon POULENC
FÊTES GALANTES. see Verlaine
  Clair de lune DEBUSSY, FAURÉ
   Two Debussy settings: 1882 and 1892.
  Colloque sentimental DEBUSSY
  En sourdine DEBUSSY, FAURÉ, HAHN
   Two Debussy settings: 1882 and 1892.
  Fantoches DEBUSSY
   Two settings: 1882 and 1892?
  Le faune DEBUSSY
Fêtes galantes see VERLAINE *FÊTES GALANTES.* HAHN
FÊTES GALANTES. see Verlaine
  Fêtes galantes HAHN
  Les Ingénus DEBUSSY
  Mandoline DEBUSSY, FAURÉ
  Pantomime DEBUSSY
FÊTES GALANTES I [no. 1]
 DEBUSSY Verlaine *En sourdine*
FÊTES GALANTES I [no. 2]
 DEBUSSY Verlaine *Clair de lune*
FÊTES GALANTES I [no. 3]
 DEBUSSY Verlaine *Fantoches*
FÊTES GALANTES II [no. 1]
 DEBUSSY Verlaine *Les Ingénus*
FÊTES GALANTES II [no. 2]
 DEBUSSY Verlaine *Le faune*
FÊTES GALANTES II [no. 3]
 DEBUSSY Verlaine *Colloque sentimental*
"Fetter grüne, du Laub" *see Herbstgefühl* Goethe SCHOECK
"Feu que les hommes regardent dans la nuit" *see Chant de feu* Senghor SAUGUET
Feuchtersleben, Ernst, Freiherr von, 1806-1849.
 MENDELSSOHN-BARTHOLDY
  Volkslied
Feuerfarb' see Mereau BEETHOVEN
 Two settings: Hess 144 and op. 52 no. 2.
Der Feuerreiter see Mörike WOLF
"Die Feuerschlünde am Seinstrand" *see Der fünfte Mai* Unknown LOEWE
Feuersgedanken see Trinius LOEWE
La feuille du peuplier see Tastu SAINT-SAËNS
"Feuille mobile et tremblante" *see La feuille du peuplier* Tastu SAINT-SAËNS
Les feuilles see Carême MILHAUD
LES FEUILLES BLESSÉES, no. 1
 HAHN Moréas *Dans le ciel est dressé le chéne séculaire*
LES FEUILLES BLESSÉES, no. 2
 HAHN Moréas *Encor sur le pavé sonne mon pas nocturne*
LES FEUILLES BLESSÉES, no. 3
 HAHN Moréas *Quand reviendra l'automne*

LES FEUILLES BLESSÉES, no. 4
  HAHN Moréas *Belle lune d'argent*
LES FEUILLES BLESSÉES, no. 5
  HAHN Moréas *Quand je viendrai
    m'asseoir*
LES FEUILLES BLESSÉES, no. 6
  HAHN Moréas *Eau printanière*
LES FEUILLES BLESSÉES, no. 7
  HAHN Moréas *Donc, vous allez fleurir
    encor*
LES FEUILLES BLESSÉES, no. 8
  HAHN Moréas *Compagne de l'éther*
LES FEUILLES BLESSÉES, no. 9
  HAHN Moréas *Pendant que je médite*
LES FEUILLES BLESSÉES, no. 10
  HAHN Moréas *Roses en bracelet*
LES FEUILLES BLESSÉES, no. 11
  HAHN Moréas *Aux rayons du couchant*
"Les feuilles dans les airs" *see Devant l'infini*
  Troillet, Émile **MASSENET**
FEUILLES DE TEMPÉRATURE, no. 1
  MILHAUD Morand *Don Juan*
FEUILLES DE TEMPÉRATURE, no. 2
  MILHAUD Morand *Révérence*
FEUILLES DE TEMPÉRATURE, no. 3
  MILHAUD Morand *Étrennes*
"Les feuilles s'ouvraient sur le bord des
  branches" *see Les cloches* Bourget
  DEBUSSY
Feuilles sur l'eau see Vivien **AUBERT**
Feux follets d'amour see Grain, Madeleine
  MASSENET
Few get enough see Dickinson **LUENING**
Fialka see Goethe **MEDTNER** *Das Veilchen*
FIANÇAILLES POUR RIRE, no. 1
  POULENC Vilmorin *La dame d'André*
FIANÇAILLES POUR RIRE, no. 2
  POULENC Vilmorin *Dans l'herbe*
FIANÇAILLES POUR RIRE, no. 3
  POULENC Vilmorin *Il vole*
FIANÇAILLES POUR RIRE, no. 4
  POULENC Vilmorin *Mon cadavre est
    doux comme un gant*
FIANÇAILLES POUR RIRE, no. 5
  POULENC Vilmorin *Violon*
FIANÇAILLES POUR RIRE, no. 6
  POULENC Vilmorin *Fleurs*
La fiancée perdue see Messiaen
  MESSIAEN
Fiat nox see Koskenniemi **KILPINEN**
Der Fichtenbaum see Heine **FRANZ,
  LASSEN, MACDOWELL**
Der Fichtenbaum see Heine *BUCH DER
  LIEDER.* **DELIUS**
  NB: Unpublished; may be same text set by
    Franz, Lassen, and MacDowell.

Der Fichtenbaum see Paulsen **GRIEG**
  På Norges nøgne fjelde
"Ein Fichtenbaum steht einsam" *see
  Der Fichtenbaum* Heine
  FRANZ, LASSEN, MACDOWELL
Ein Fichtenbaum steht einsam see Heine
  LISZT
"Ein Fichtenbaum steht einsem" *see Lyrisches
  Intermezzo* Heine **MEDTNER**
Fick, Heinrich
  THE MEETING ON THE SEASHORE.
    LOEWE *Die Begegnung am
      Meeresstrand*
Fick, K.
  REGER
    Der Bote
    Des Durstes Erklärung
The fiddler of Dooney see Yeats
  LOEFFLER, RIETI
"Fidèle à ma maîtresse et toujours sur ses pas"
  see Ariette pour Tina Indy **INDY**
FIEDELLIEDER AUS DEM "LIEDERBUCH
  DREIER FREUNDE," no. 1
  KRENEK Mommsen *Meine Laute
    nehm'ich wieder*
FIEDELLIEDER AUS DEM "LIEDERBUCH
  DREIER FREUNDE," no. 2
  KRENEK Storm *Musikanten wollen
    wandern durch die Saiten*
FIEDELLIEDER AUS DEM "LIEDERBUCH
  DREIER FREUNDE," no. 3
  KRENEK Mommsen *Im Walde*
FIEDELLIEDER AUS DEM "LIEDERBUCH
  DREIER FREUNDE," no. 4
  KRENEK Mommsen *Und so lasst mich
    weider wandern*
FIEDELLIEDER AUS DEM "LIEDERBUCH
  DREIER FREUNDE," no. 5
  KRENEK Storm *Nun ein Scherflein in
    der Runde*
FIEDELLIEDER AUS DEM "LIEDERBUCH
  DREIER FREUNDE," no. 6
  KRENEK Mommsen *Die Saiten weiss
    ich zu rühren*
FIEDELLIEDER AUS DEM "LIEDERBUCH
  DREIER FREUNDE," no. 7
  KRENEK Mommsen *Wiederum lebt
    wohl*
Fiéffé, Eugène, 1821-1862.
  SAINT-SAËNS *Le rendez-vous*
Field marshal see Golenishchev-Kutuzov
  MUSORGSKIĭ *Polkovodets*
Field, Eugene, 1850-1895.
  CARPENTER
    Norse lullaby
    Sicilian lullaby

COMPOSER Poet *Title* "First Line"

"The fields are full of summer still" *see Late summer* Shanks **HESELTINE**

Fière beauté see Mahot, A. **SAINT-SAËNS**

The fiery man see Hlavsa, Vrat. **MARTINŮ**

Fiesta en el Prado see Machado y Ruiz **RODRIGO**

Fièvre jaune see Frank, J. H. **HONEGGER**

"Fifteen years ago today" *see He is there!* Ives **IVES**

Figueroa, Francisco de, 1536?-1620. **RODRIGO** *Esta niña se lleva la flor*

Figure de force brûlante et farouche see Éluard **POULENC**

Filet à papillons see Radiguet **AURIC**

Fill a glass with golden wine see Henley **QUILTER**

La fille aux cheveux de lin see Leconte de Lisle *POÈMES ANTIQUES.* **DEBUSSY**

"La fille de Tantalos fut" *see Sur une jeune fille* Anacreon **ROUSSEL**

"Fille du ciel, aimable innocence" *see L'Innocence* Châteaubriand **MILHAUD**

"Fille du sourire pur" *see La première dent* La Laurencie **INDY**

"En Fillehytte var dit Bo" *see Johanne* Drachmann **GRIEG**

Les filles de Cadix see Musset **DELIBES**

Film: Two sisters not sisters see Stein **THOMSON**

IL FILOSOFO DI CAMPAGNA. see Goldoni *La pastorella* **SCHUBERT**

Fils de la Vierge see Ganivet **SCHMITT**

Finckh, Ludwig, 1876-1964. **BERG** *Fraue, Du Süsse (?)*

Das Finden see Kosegarten **SCHUBERT**

Findlay see Burns **LOEWE**

La fine see Tagore **RESPIGHI**

FINE CLOTHES TO THE JEW. see Hughes, L. *That soothin' song* **CARPENTER**

FINGAL. see Macpherson *Das Mädchen von Inistore* **SCHUBERT**

Fink, Gottfried Wilhelm, 1783-1847. *HÄUSLICHEN ANDACHTEN.* **LOEWE** *Dem Ew'gen*

Fink und Elster see Iłłakowiczówna **SZYMANOWSKI** *Gil i sroka*

FINNEGANS WAKE. see Joyce *Nuvoletta* **BARBER**

Fino cristal see Rodriguez-Pintos **RODRIGO**

"Fino cristal, mi niño" *see Fino cristal* Rodriguez-Pintos **RODRIGO**

"Die finstere Nacht bricht schnell herein" *see Leb' wohl mein Ayr!* Burns **JENSEN**

La fioraja fiorentina see Unknown **ROSSINI**

"Fiorellin che sorgi appena cosi fresco" *see Barcarola* Piave **VERDI**

The fir and the palm see Heine *LYRICAL INTERMEZZO.* **RIMSKIĬ-KORSAKOV** *El' i pal'ma*

"The fir tree felt it with a thrill" *see The first snowfall* Tabb **GRIFFES**

"The fire of youth is gone, its madness jaded" *see Elegy* Pushkin **MEDTNER**

The fires in the rooms were already extinguished see Konstantin **CHAĬKOVSKIĬ** *Uzh gasli v'' komnatakh ogni*

Firnelicht see Meyer **SCHOECK**

The first kiss see Runeberg **SIBELIUS** *Den första kyssen*

First love see Goethe **MEDTNER** *Erster Verlust*

First love see Mužik **MARTINŮ**

The first meeting see Konstantin **CHAĬKOVSKIĬ** *Pervoe svidanie*

The first mercy see Blunt **HESELTINE**

The first rendezvous see Konstantin **CHAĬKOVSKIĬ** *Pervoe svidanie*

The first snowfall see Tabb **GRIFFES**

The first tryst see Konstantin **CHAĬKOVSKIĬ** *Pervoe svidanie*

First warm days see Denby, Edward **ROREM**

"Fischchen schwimmt wohl hin und her" *see Fischerin und Jägerbursch* Unknown **LOEWE**

Der Fischer see Goethe **LOEWE, SCHUBERT, SCHUMANN, STRAUSS, WOLF, ZELTER**

Fischer, Hans, 1869-1934. **SCHÖNBERG** *Lockung*

Fischer harrt am Brückenbogen see Schlechta **SCHUBERT** *Widerschein*

"Fischer harrt am Brückenbogen" *see Widerschein* Schlechta **SCHUBERT**

Fischer, Johann Georg, 1816-1897. **BERG** *Eure Weisheit* **REGER** *Mein und Dein*

Das Fischergewerbe see Salis-Seewis **LOEWE**

"Das Fischergewerbe gibt rüstigen Mut" *see Das Fischergewerbe* Salis-Seewis **LOEWE**

"Das Fischergewerbe gibt rüstigen Muth!" *see Fischerlied* Salis-Seewis **SCHUBERT** Two settings: D. 351 and D. 562.

Fischerin und Jägerbursch see Unknown **LOEWE**

Die Fischerknabe see Schiller *WILHELM TELL.* **LISZT**

Fischerlied see Salis-Seewis **SCHUBERT**
Two settings: D. 351 and D. 562.
Das Fischermädchen see Heine **SCHUBERT**
Die Fischerstochter see Coronini **LISZT**
"Die Fischerstochter sitzt am Strand" *see*
   Die Fischerstochter Coronini **LISZT**
Fischerweise see Dass **GRIEG** *Fiskervise*
Fischerweise see Schlechta **SCHUBERT**
Fish in the unruffled lakes see Auden
   BRITTEN
Fisher, Aileen Lucia, 1906-
   THE COFFEE-POT FACE.
   CARPENTER *Worlds*
Fisher, Jasper, fl. 1639.
   THOMSON *At the spring*
Fishing song see Walton, I. **BRITTEN**
FISKERJENTEN. see Bjørnson
   Det første møde **GRIEG**
   God morgen! **GRIEG**
   Jeg giver mit digt til våren **GRIEG**
   Takk for dit råd **GRIEG**
Fiskervise see Dass **GRIEG**
Fitger, Arthur, 1840-1909.
   LASSEN
      Es war doch schön
      Ich liege dir zu Füssen
      Die Memnonsäule
   PIJPER
      Ich liege Dir zu Füssen
      Die Spinnerin
         Two settings: 1913 and an undated
            fragment, apparently unpublished.
   SIBELIUS *Lenzgesang*
   LIEDER VOM MAURERGESELLEN.
      PIJPER *Wanderschaft*
Fitzau, Heinrich, 1810-1859.
   LASSEN *Der seltne Beter*
   DER SELTENE BETER.
      LOEWE *Der alte Dessauer*
FIVE GERMAN POEMS, no. 1
   GRIFFES Lenau *Auf dem Teich, dem*
      regungslosen
FIVE GERMAN POEMS, no. 2
   GRIFFES Lenau *Auf geheimem*
      Waldespfade
FIVE GERMAN POEMS, no. 3
   GRIFFES Heine *Nacht liegt auf den*
      fremden Wegen
FIVE GERMAN POEMS, no. 4
   GRIFFES Mosen *Der träumende See*
FIVE GERMAN POEMS, no. 5
   GRIFFES Geibel *Wohl lag ich einst in*
      Gram und Schmerz
FIVE IRISH FANTASIES, no. 1
   LOEFFLER Yeats *The hosting of the*
      Sidhe

FIVE IRISH FANTASIES, no. 2
   LOEFFLER Yeats *The host of the air*
FIVE IRISH FANTASIES, no. 3
   LOEFFLER Yeats *The fiddler of Dooney*
FIVE IRISH FANTASIES, no. 4
   LOEFFLER Yeats *Ballad of the foxhunter*
FIVE IRISH FANTASIES, no. 5
   LOEFFLER Hefferman *The song of*
      Catilin Ni Uallachain
FIVE JACOBEAN LYRICS, no. 1
   QUILTER Rochester *The jealous lover*
FIVE JACOBEAN LYRICS, no. 2
   QUILTER Suckling *Why so pale and*
      wan?
FIVE JACOBEAN LYRICS, no. 3
   QUILTER Herrick *I dare not ask a kiss*
FIVE JACOBEAN LYRICS, no. 4
   QUILTER Lovelace *To Althea from*
      prison
FIVE JACOBEAN LYRICS, no. 5
   QUILTER Suckling *The constant lover*
FIVE LITTLE SONGS, no. 1
   HAHN Stevenson, Robert Louis
      The swing
FIVE LITTLE SONGS, no. 2
   HAHN Stevenson, Robert Louis *Windy*
      nights
FIVE LITTLE SONGS, no. 3
   HAHN Stevenson, Robert Louis *My*
      ship and I
FIVE LITTLE SONGS, no. 4
   HAHN Stevenson, Robert Louis
      The stars
FIVE LITTLE SONGS, no. 5
   HAHN Stevenson, Robert Louis
      A good boy
FIVE PHRASES FROM *The Song of*
   Solomon, no. 1
   THOMSON Bible *Thou that dwellest in*
      the gardens
FIVE PHRASES FROM *The Song of*
   Solomon, no. 2
   THOMSON Bible *Return, O Shulamite!*
FIVE PHRASES FROM *The Song of*
   Solomon, no. 3
   THOMSON Bible *O, my dove*
FIVE PHRASES FROM *The Song of*
   Solomon, no. 4
   THOMSON Bible *I am my beloved's*
FIVE PHRASES FROM *The Song of*
   Solomon, no. 5
   THOMSON Bible *By night*
FIVE POEMS OF ANCIENT CHINA AND
   JAPAN, no. 1
   GRIFFES Wang *So-fei gathering flowers*
FIVE POEMS OF ANCIENT CHINA AND
   JAPAN, no. 2
   GRIFFES Sada-Ihe *Landscape*

COMPOSER Poet *Title* "First Line"

FIVE POEMS OF ANCIENT CHINA AND
JAPAN, no. 3
GRIFFES Chang Wen-chang *The old
temple among the mountains*
FIVE POEMS OF ANCIENT CHINA AND
JAPAN, no. 4
GRIFFES Wang Seng-ju *Tears*
FIVE POEMS OF ANCIENT CHINA AND
JAPAN, no. 5
GRIFFES Yuan Mei *A feast of lanterns*
FIVE XVITH CENTURY POEMS, no. 1
IRELAND Johanus Bassus *A
thanksgiving*
FIVE XVITH CENTURY POEMS, no. 2
IRELAND Howell, Thomas *All in a
garden green*
FIVE XVITH CENTURY POEMS, no. 3
IRELAND Henry VIII *An aside*
FIVE XVITH CENTURY POEMS, no. 4
IRELAND Breton *A report song*
FIVE XVITH CENTURY POEMS, no. 5
IRELAND Edwardes *The sweet season*
FIVE SONGS FROM *The Tempest*, no. 1
DIAMOND Shakespeare *Come unto
these yellow sands*
FIVE SONGS FROM *The Tempest*, no. 2
DIAMOND Shakespeare *Full fathom
five*
FIVE SONGS FROM *The Tempest*, no. 3
DIAMOND Shakespeare *While you here
do snoring lie*
FIVE SONGS FROM *The Tempest*, no. 4
DIAMOND Shakespeare *No more dams
I'll make for fish*
FIVE SONGS FROM *The Tempest*, no. 5
DIAMOND Shakespeare *Where the bee
sucks*
Five songs without words see No author
PROKOFIEV *Piat' pesen bez slov*
Flack're ew'ges Licht im Tal see Keller, G.
SCHOECK
Flaiolet see Anon. **CASELLA**
Flaischlen, Cäsar, 1864-1920.
BERG *So regnet es sich langsam ein*
Le flambeau vivant see Baudelaire
LOEFFLER
"Les flamboyantes Pierreries" *see
Les Pierreries* Banville **KOECHLIN**
Flament, Albert, 1877-1956.
MILHAUD *Quatrain*
"Die Flamme hier, die wilde, zu verhehlen"
see Liebeslut Daumer **BRAHMS**
"Die Flamme lodert" *see Opferlied*
Matthisson **BEETHOVEN, ZELTER**
Flammes see Jean-Aubry **ROUSSEL**
Flaubert, Gustave, 1821-1880.
MILHAUD *Chanson de l'aveugle*

"Flawless as Aphrodite" *see Passing* Pound
DIAMOND
The flea see Donne **KRENEK**
The flea's lament see Norse **ROREM**
The fleeting see De La Mare **BERKELEY**
"Fleigt nur aus, geliebte Tauben!" *see An die
Trauben* Schenkendorf **BRAHMS**
Fleischer, Siegfried, 1856-1924.
BERG *Herbstgefühl*
Flemes, Bernhard, 1875-1940.
REGER *Brunnensang*
Fleming, Paul, 1606-1640.
BRAHMS
An die Stolze
O liebliche Wangen
KRENEK
An Sich
Während der Trennung
MENDELSSOHN-BARTHOLDY
Pilgerspruch
REGER *Lass dich nur nichts nicht dauern*
Flemming, Paul *see* Fleming, Paul, 1606-
1640.
Fletcher, John, 1579-1625.
HESELTINE *Mourn no moe*
ROREM
Come hither, you that love
Come, shepherds, come
Hold back thy hours, dark night
Now the lusty spring is seen
Sing his praises
THE MAID'S TRAGEDY (1619): Aspatia's
song.
HESELTINE *A sad song*
THE WOMAN HATER (1607).
HESELTINE *Sleep*
"Fleur d'Athènes je te quitte" *see Maid of
Athens* Byron **GOUNOD**
"Fleur de nos champs sur la montagne aride
souffrait!" *see La fleur du foyer* Ligny,
Charles **GOUNOD**
Fleur des blés see Girod **DEBUSSY**
Fleur des eaux see Bouchor, M. *LES
POÈMES DE L'AMOUR ET DE LA MER*
(1876). **DEBUSSY**
La fleur du foyer see Ligny, Charles
GOUNOD
La fleur du foyer see Maitland **GOUNOD**
Oh, happy home
Fleur fanée see Dierx **HAHN**
Fleur jetée see Silvestre **FAURÉ**
La fleur qui va sur l'eau see Mendès
FAURÉ
Fleuramye see Van Ormelingen *GLOSES
ORPHIQUES.* **MASSENET**
Les fleurs see Collerville, Vicomte de
SAINT-SAËNS

Les fleurs see Contamine **SATIE**
Les fleurs see Mauclair **BLOCH**
Fleurs see Vilmorin **POULENC**
Fleurs cueillies see Bricourt, Louis
   MASSENET
Fleurs décloses see Blée, Catulle
   SCHMITT
FLEURS DES LANDES, no. 1
   BERLIOZ Bouclon *Le matin*
FLEURS DES LANDES, no. 2
   BERLIOZ Bouclon *Petit oiseau*
     NB: No. 3 is a duet; omitted here.
FLEURS DES LANDES, no. 4
   BERLIOZ Brizeux *Le jeune pâtre breton*
FLEURS DES LANDES, no. 5
   BERLIOZ Brizeux *Le chant des Bretons*
LES FLEURS DU MAL. see Baudelaire
   L'amour et le crane **INDY**
   Le Balcon **DEBUSSY**
   Harmonie du soir **DEBUSSY**
   L'invitation au voyage **CHABRIER,**
    DUPARC
   Le Jet d'eau **DEBUSSY**
   La Mort des amants **DEBUSSY**
   Recueillement **DEBUSSY**
"Les fleurs passent au gré du temps" *see*
   Toujours Nax, Paul **MASSENET**
"Fleurs promises" *see Fleurs* Vilmorin
   POULENC
Fleury-Daunizeau, Georges
   MASSENET *Dites-lui que je l'aime*
Le fleuve see Audigier, Georges
   SAINT-SAËNS
"Flew once where he saw a tow'r" *see*
   The dove Bal'mont **STRAVINSKIÏ**
Flickan kom ifrån sin älsklings möte see
   Runeberg **SIBELIUS**
Flickans årstider see Runeberg **SIBELIUS**
   Arioso
Flieder see Bierbaum **REGER**
"Flieg doch fort, du kleines Tier!" *see*
   Das Vöglein Unknown **LOEWE**
"Fliege auf Windes Schwingen, Blättlein, zu
   ihr!" *see Grüsse* Harnier **SPOHR**
FLIEGENDES BLATT. see Anon.
   Abendsegen **WEBER**
   Liebesgruss aus der Ferne **WEBER**
   Liebeslied **WEBER**
   Volkslied **WEBER**
"Fliegt der erste Morgenstrahl" *see*
   Der Morgen Eichendorff **LASSEN**
"Fliegt der Schnee mir in's Gesicht" *see Mut*
   Müller, Wilhelm **SCHUBERT**
"Flieh, flieh, flieh Täubchen, flieh" *see*
   Mädchens Held Goethe **ZELTER**
Fliehe hin, Nachtigall see Kol'tsov
   RUBINSTEIN

The flight see Feeney **CHANLER**
FLIGHT FOR HEAVEN, no. 1
   ROREM Herrick *To music, to becalm his*
    fever
FLIGHT FOR HEAVEN, no. 2
   ROREM Herrick *Cherry-ripe*
FLIGHT FOR HEAVEN, no. 3
   ROREM Herrick *Upon Julia's clothes*
FLIGHT FOR HEAVEN, no. 4
   ROREM Herrick *To daisies, not to shut so*
    soon
FLIGHT FOR HEAVEN, no. 5
   ROREM Herrick *Epitaph upon a child*
    that died
FLIGHT FOR HEAVEN, no. 6
   ROREM Herrick *Another epitaph*
FLIGHT FOR HEAVEN, no. 7
   ROREM Herrick *To the willow-tree*
FLIGHT FOR HEAVEN, no. 8
   ROREM Herrick *Comfort to a youth that*
    had lost his love
    NB: No. 9 is a piano interlude.
FLIGHT FOR HEAVEN, no. 10
   ROREM Herrick *To Anthea, who may*
    command him anything
The flirt see Goethe **MEDTNER** *Die Spröde*
Flobert, A.
   LALO *Adieux au désert*
"Flockendichte Winternacht" *see Winternacht*
   Morgenstern **KILPINEN**
"Flocking to the Temple" *see Hymn for a*
   child Warner **IRELAND**
Flötenspielerin see Altenberg *WAS DER*
TAG MIR ZUTRÄGT': Flötenspielerin.
   BERG
Flötenspielerin see Evers **REGER**
Floods of spring see Tiutchev
   RACHMANINOFF *Spring waters*
Florenz, Karl Adolf, 1865-1939.
   CARPENTER *Endlose Liebe*
Florian, Jean Pierre Claris de, 1755-
   1794.
   BERLIOZ *Le maure jaloux*
   FRANCK *Robin Gray*
   IVES *Chanson de Florian*
   MASSENET *Musette*
   ZELTER *Helas!*
Florio see Schütz *LACRIMAS.* **SCHUBERT**
FLORS D'OCCITANIA, no. 1
   SÉVERAC Estieu *Cansón pel cabalet*
FLORS D'OCCITANIA, no. 2
   SÉVERAC Marguerite d'Angoulême
    Albado
FLORS D'OCCITANIA, no. 3
   SÉVERAC Goudouli *Cant per Nadal*
"Les flots battent la plage solitaire" *see*
   Les ondines Heine **SAUGUET**

COMPOSER Poet *Title* "First Line"

Flots, palmes, sables see Renaud *NUITS PERSANES* (1870). **DEBUSSY**

"Flow gently, sweet Afton" *see Afton water* Burns **BRITTEN**

"Flow on! happy stream" *see Song of the stream* Williams **QUILTER**

The flower see Bal'mont **STRAVINSKIĭ** *Forget-me-nots*

The flower see Pushkin **MEDTNER** *The faded flower*

The flower see Ratisbonne **CHAĭKOVSKIĭ** *Tsvetok*

A flower given to my daughter see Joyce *POMES PENYEACH.* **DIAMOND, ROUSSEL**

The flower has faded see Rathaus **RACHMANINOFF**

The flower of friendship see Josephson, E. **SIBELIUS** *Vänskapens blomma*

A flower stood by the path see Josephson, E. **SIBELIUS** *En blomma stod vid vägen*

The flower's destiny see Runeberg **SIBELIUS** *Blommans öde*

FLOWERS OF GOLD: Impressions, no. 2. *see* Wilde *La fuite de la lune* **GRIFFES**

"Flowers through the window lavender and yellow" *see Nantucket* Williams, W. **ROREM**

Flowery message see Unknown **DVOŘÁK** *Kytice*

Flowery omens see Anon. **DVOŘÁK** *Výklad znamení*

Fluchère, Henri, 1914-
   MILHAUD *Cours de solfège: Papillon, Papillonnette*

Der Flüchtling see Schiller **SCHUBERT**

Die Flüchtlinge see Shelley **SCHUMANN**

Flügel! Flügel! see Rückert *LIEBESFRÜHLING.* **SCHUMANN**

"Flügelt ein kleiner blauer" *see Blauer Schmetterling* Hesse **SCHOECK**

Flüstern, banges Atmen see Shenshin **BALAKIREV** *Shopot, robkoye dīkhan'ye*

Der Flug der Zeit see Széchényi **SCHUBERT**

Der Fluss see Schlegel, F. *ABENDRÖTE.* **SCHUBERT**

"La flûte amère de l'automne" *see Prélude* Hérold **AUBERT**

La flûte de Pan see Louÿs *CHANSONS DE BILITIS.* **DEBUSSY**

Une flûte invisible see Hugo **SAINT-SAËNS**

Flutenreicher Ebro see Anon. *EBRO CAUDOLOSE.* **SCHUMANN**

The fly see Blake, William **BRITTEN**

A flying bank of clouds disperses see Pushkin **RIMSKIĭ-KORSAKOV** *Redeet oblakov letuchaia griada*

FOAM OF THE PAST. see Sharp, W. *The lament of Ian the proud* **GRIFFES**

"Føden og Klaeden, Baaden og Teltet" *see Dansk Arbejde* Rørdam, Valdemar **NIELSEN**

Förgätmigejer see Österling **KILPINEN**

Förledde vän see Blomberg **KILPINEN**

Förr ägde jag intet see Blomberg **KILPINEN**

Den första kyssen see Runeberg **SIBELIUS**

Förster, Friedrich, 1791-1868.
   LOEWE *Der alte Goethe*
   WEBER
      Die freien Sänger
      Mein Verlangen

Förster, Karl Albert Eleon, 1794-1833.
   WEBER *Triolett*

Förster, Marie Laura, 1817-1856.
   FRANZ
      Denk ich dein!
      O Mond, O lösch' dein gold'nes Licht
      Vorüber der Mai

Förstner, Clara (Müller), 1850-1907.
   REGER *Frühlingsmorgen*

Fog see Sandburg *CHICAGO POEMS.* **HARRIS**

"The fog comes on little cat feet" *see Fog* Sandberg **HARRIS**

Fogazzaro, Antonio
   RESPIGHI *Miranda*

Fogelfängarn see Runeberg **SIBELIUS** *Fågelfängaren*

Fog-wraiths see Howells, M. **CARPENTER**

"Foin du bâtard, illustre Dame" *see Chanson à boire* Morand **RAVEL**

"Une fois, terrassé par un puissant breuvage" *see La vague et la cloche* Coppé **DUPARC**

"Fola, fola, Blakken!" *see Kveldssang for Blakken* Rolfsen **GRIEG**

Folgore da San Geminiano, 13-14 c. *see* San Geminiano, Folgore da, 13th cent.

Folias Canarias see Anon. **RODRIGO**

Folksong see Howells, W. D. **MACDOWELL**

Follain, Jean, 1903-1971.
   ROREM *L'ile*
   SAUGUET
      Au pays
      Domaine d'homme
      Effacement
      Eglogue
      Les images
      Pensées d'octobre
      Promeneur
      Vie des campagnes

COMPOSER Poet *Title* "First Line"

FOLLE DU CIEL. see Lenormand
 Blancs sont les jours d'été **MILHAUD**
 Mes amis les cygnes **MILHAUD**
Follow thy fair sun see Campion
 THOMSON
Follow your saint see Campion **THOMSON**
Fombeure, Maurice, 1906-1981.
 CHANSONS DE LA GRANDE HUNE.
  POULENC
   C'est le joli printemps
   Chanson de la fille frivole
   Chanson du clair tamis
   Les gars qui vont à la fête
   Le mendiant
   Le retour du sergent
Fomicacicadéide see Unknown
 SAINT-SAËNS
La fontaine d'Hélène see Ronsard **AUBERT**
Les fontaines see Régnier **HAHN**
Fontaines, A
 HONEGGER *Sur le basalte*
Fontan see Tiutchev **RACHMANINOFF**
 The fountains
Fontane, Theodor, 1819-1898.
 LOEWE *Archibald Douglas*
 SCHOECK *Der Gast*
The foot path see Unknown **MARTINŮ**
 Chodníček
"*For a life of pain I have giv'n my love*" *see*
 I have grown fond of sorrow Shevchenko
 RACHMANINOFF
For an old man see Eliot **DIAMOND**
"*For August, for August*" *see August* San
 Geminiano **IVES**
For careless children see Carpenter, Rue
 CARPENTER
"*For days and days I've climbed*" *see*
 Contemplation Carpenter, Rue
 CARPENTER
"*Før drømte jeg fast hver eneste Nat*" *see*
 Til Asali Jacobsen **NIELSEN**
For ever with the Lord see Montgomery, J.
 GOUNOD
"*For God is glorified in man*" *see from*
 "*Paracelsus*" Browning, R. **IVES**
For Janet see Goodman **ROREM**
For like a chariot's wheel see Anon.
 LUENING
"*For long I wander'd happily*" *see*
 The world's highway Ives, Harmony
 IVES
For long there has been little consolation see
 Shenshin **RACHMANINOFF**
For Poulenc see O'Hara **ROREM**
For shame deny that thou bear'st love to any
 see Shakespeare **DIAMOND**

For Susan see Goodman **ROREM**
For sweet love's sake see Gardner, W.
 MACDOWELL
"*For the grandeur of Thy nature*" *see*
 His exaltation Robinson **IVES**
For the shores of thy far native land see
 Pushkin **BORODIN**;
 RIMSKIÏ-KORSAKOV
 Dlia beregov otchizuy dal'noi
"*For you my voice is filled tonight with love*
 and longing" *see Night* Pushkin
 MEDTNER
Foraarsregn see Drachmann **GRIEG**
Den Foraeldreløse see Chamisso **GRIEG**
 Die Waise
FORCE ET FAIBLESSE, no. 1
 SAUGUET Éluard *Je n'avais d'yeux et de*
  courage
FORCE ET FAIBLESSE, no. 2
 SAUGUET Éluard *Tout est un grand*
  secret
FORCE ET FAIBLESSE, no. 3
 SAUGUET Éluard *Plus rien ne me tient*
  aux pieds
FORCE ET FAIBLESSE, no. 4
 SAUGUET Éluard *Nuage, premier pas de*
  mon élévation
FORCE ET FAIBLESSE, no. 5
 SAUGUET Éluard *Une écluse sans*
  brouillard
FORCE ET FAIBLESSE, no. 6
 SAUGUET Éluard *Il est midi, il est minuit*
FORCE ET FAIBLESSE, no. 7
 SAUGUET Éluard *Fenêtre illusoire à ma*
  taille
Ford, Ford Madox, 1873-1939.
 HESELTINE *Consider*
Foreign children see Stevenson, Robert
 Louis *A CHILD'S GARDEN OF VERSES.*
 QUILTER
Die Forelle see Schubart **SCHUBERT**
Den føreste laerke see Aakjaer **NIELSEN**
Forestier, J.
 SCHMITT *Demande*
"*La forêt gémit, le nuage roule*" *see Plainte de*
 Thécla Schiller **INDY**
"*Forêt profonde*" *see La rendez-vous* Claudel
 HONEGGER
"*La forêt semble tout en fête*" *see Retour*
 d'oiseau Stuart, Paul **MASSENET**
"*Une forêt surgit des flots*" *see Prelude*
 Vilmorin **SAUGET**
Forever lost see Unknown **LUENING**
Forget not yet see Wyatt **ROREM**
Forget-me-not see Landon **BENNETT**

COMPOSER Poet *Title* "First Line"

Forget-me-nots see Bal'mont
STRAVINSKĬ
Forgive! see Nekrasov **CHAĬKOVSKĬ**
  Prosti
Forgive! Forget our days so hateful see
  Nekrasov **RIMSKĬ-KORSAKOV**
  Prosti! Ne pomni dneĭ paden'ia
Forgive these tearful days see Nekrasov
  RIMSKĬ-KORSAKOV
  Prosti! Ne pomni dneĭ paden'ia
Forgotten see Golenishchev-Kutuzov
  MUSORGSKĬ *Menia ty v tolpe ne uznala*
Forgotten see Golenishchev-Kutuzov
  MUSORGSKĬ *Zebytyĭ*
The forgotten one see Apukhtin
  CHAĬKOVSKĬ *Zabyt' tak skoro!*
Formål see Vinje **GRIEG** *Fyremål*
The forsaken see Unknown **DVOŘÁK**
  Opuščená
Forsman, August Valdemar, pseud. *see*
  Koskimies, Aukusti Valdemar, 1856-
  1929.
Det Første see Vinje **GRIEG**
Det første møde see Bjørnson
  FISKERJENTEN. **GRIEG**
"Fort, fort, mich duldet's nicht" *see*
  Wanderlied Geibel **JENSEN**
"Fort möcht ich reisen weit" *see Wunsch*
  Lenau **WOLF**
Fort, Paul, 1872-1960.
  COMPLAINTES ET DITS.
    HONEGGER
      Chanson de fol
      Le chasseur perdu en forêt
      Cloche du soir
Fortina de fullatge see Mompou **MOMPOU**
Forward! see Mendel'son **PROKOFIEV**
  Smelo vpered!
"Forward flock of Jesus" *see Forward into*
  light Alford, Henry **IVES**
Forward into light see Alford, Henry **IVES**
The fountain mingles with the river see
  Shelley **GOUNOD**
"The fountain murmuring of sleep" *see Tryst*
  Symons **IRELAND**
The fountains see Tiutchev
  RACHMANINOFF
"The fountains mingle with the river" *see*
  Love's philosophy Shelley **DELIUS,**
  QUILTER
Fouqué, Friedrich Heinrich, Baron de la
  Motte, 1777-1843.
  SCHÄFER UND REITER.
    SCHUBERT *Der Schäfer und der Reiter*
  UNDINE.
    SCHUBERT *Lied*

DER ZAUBERRING.
  SCHUBERT
    An dem jungen Morgenhimmel
    Don Gayseros, Don Gayseros
    Nächtens klang die süsse Laute
"Four and forty lovers had Agathas" *see*
  Agathas Pound **DIAMOND**
FOUR CHILD SONGS, no. 1
  QUILTER Stevenson, Robert Louis
    A good child
FOUR CHILD SONGS, no. 2
  QUILTER Stevenson, Robert Louis
    The lamplighter
FOUR CHILD SONGS, no. 3
  QUILTER Stevenson, Robert Louis
    Where go the boats?
FOUR CHILD SONGS, no. 4
  QUILTER Stevenson, Robert Louis
    Foreign children
Four folk songs see Anon.
  SZYMANOWSKI
FOUR IMPRESSIONS, no. 1
  GRIFFES Wilde *Le jardin*
FOUR IMPRESSIONS, no. 2
  GRIFFES Wilde *Early morning in London*
FOUR IMPRESSIONS, no. 3
  GRIFFES Wilde *The sea*
FOUR IMPRESSIONS, no. 4
  GRIFFES Wilde *Dawn*
FOUR LADIES, no. 1
  DIAMOND Pound *Agathas*
FOUR LADIES, no. 2
  DIAMOND Pound *Young lady*
FOUR LADIES, no. 3
  DIAMOND Pound *Lesbia Illa*
FOUR LADIES, no. 4
  DIAMOND Pound *Passing*
THE FOUR MEN. HIS OWN COUNTRY: I
  shall go without companions. *see* Belloc,
  Hilaire *My own country* **HESELTINE**
FOUR NEGRO SONGS, no. 1
  CARPENTER Hughes, L. *Shake your*
    brown feet, Honey
FOUR NEGRO SONGS, no. 2
  CARPENTER Hughes, L. *The cryin'*
    blues
FOUR NEGRO SONGS, no. 3
  CARPENTER Hughes, L. *Jazz-boys*
FOUR NEGRO SONGS, no. 4
  CARPENTER Hughes, L. *That soothin'*
    song
Four nights see Shove
  VAUGHAN WILLIAMS
FOUR OLD ENGLISH LYRICS, no. 1
  DELIUS Shakespeare *It was a lover and*
    his lass

COMPOSER   Poet   *Title*   "First Line"

FOUR OLD ENGLISH LYRICS, no. 2
  DELIUS Jonson *So white, so oft, so sweet is she*
FOUR OLD ENGLISH LYRICS, no. 3
  DELIUS Nashe *Spring, the sweet Spring*
FOUR OLD ENGLISH LYRICS, no. 4
  DELIUS Herrick *To daffodils*
FOUR RHYMES FROM "*Peacock Pie*," no. 1
  CHANLER De La Mare *The ship of Rio*
FOUR RHYMES FROM "*Peacock Pie*," no. 2
  CHANLER De La Mare *Old Shellover*
FOUR RHYMES FROM "*Peacock Pie*," no. 3
  CHANLER De La Mare *Cake and Sack*
FOUR RHYMES FROM "*Peacock Pie*," no. 4
  CHANLER De La Mare *Tillie*
FOUR SAINTS IN 3 ACTS. see Stein
  Pigeons on the grass **THOMSON**
FOUR SHAKESPEARE SONGS, no. 1
  QUILTER Shakespeare *Who is Silvia?*
FOUR SHAKESPEARE SONGS, no. 2
  QUILTER Shakespeare *When daffodils begin to peer*
FOUR SHAKESPEARE SONGS, no. 3
  QUILTER Shakespeare *How should I your true love know?*
FOUR SHAKESPEARE SONGS, no. 4
  QUILTER Shakespeare *Sigh no more, ladies*
FOUR SONGS FOR BARITONE, no. 1
  BLITZSTEIN Whitman *O Hymen! O Hymenee!*
FOUR SONGS FOR BARITONE, no. 2
  BLITZSTEIN Whitman *I am He*
FOUR SONGS FOR BARITONE, no. 3
  BLITZSTEIN Whitman *Ages and ages*
FOUR SONGS FOR BARITONE, no. 4
  BLITZSTEIN Whitman *As Adam*
FOUR SONGS OF MIRZA-SCHAFFY, no. 1
  QUILTER Bodenstedt *Neig' schöne Knospe Dich zu mir*
FOUR SONGS OF MIRZA-SCHAFFY, no. 2
  QUILTER Bodenstedt *Und was die Sonne glüht*
FOUR SONGS OF MIRZA-SCHAFFY, no. 3
  QUILTER Bodenstedt *Ich fühle deinen Odem*
FOUR SONGS OF MIRZA-SCHAFFY, no. 4
  QUILTER Bodenstedt *Die helle Sonne leuchtet*
FOUR SONGS OF SORROW, no. 1
  QUILTER Dowson *A coronal*
FOUR SONGS OF SORROW, no. 2
  QUILTER Dowson *Passing dreams*

FOUR SONGS OF SORROW, no. 3
  QUILTER Dowson *A land of silence*
FOUR SONGS OF SORROW, no. 4
  QUILTER Dowson *In spring*
FOUR SONGS OF THE SEA, no. 1
  QUILTER Quilter *I have a friend*
FOUR SONGS OF THE SEA, no. 2
  QUILTER Quilter *The sea-bird*
FOUR SONGS OF THE SEA, no. 3
  QUILTER Quilter *Moonlight*
FOUR SONGS OF THE SEA, no. 4
  QUILTER Quilter *By the sea*
Four uncles see Cummings *IS 5.*
  DIAMOND
Fourcaud, Louis de Boussés de, 1851-1914.
  FRANCK *Nocturne*
Fournier, Paul, 1853-1935.
  SAINT-SAËNS
    Honneur à l'Amérique
    Victoire
    Vive la France
Fourteen little angels see Des Knaben Wunderhorn **MARTINŮ**
THE FOURTH MOVEMENT. IMPRESSION: Le Réveillon. *see* Wilde
  Dawn **GRIFFES**
Fourvières see Léna **MASSENET**
The fox see Blunt **HESELTINE**
"The fox and his wife" *see* Ee-Oh! Anon.
  BRITTEN
"Fra i casti e freddi lini del letto" *see Volutta* Olkienizkaia-Naldi **CASELLA**
Fra Monte Pincio see Bjørnson **GRIEG**
FRA ROLD TIL REBILD. see Bartrumsen
  Vi Jyder **NIELSEN**
"Fra Vinterens Kulde vi komme" *see Blomsterne tale* Winther **GRIEG**
Das Fräulein am Meere see Heine
  SCHOECK
"Fräulein Gigerlette lud mich ein zum Thee" *see Gigerlette* Bierbaum **SCHÖNBERG**
DAS FRÄULEIN IM THURME. see Matthisson *Romanze* **SCHUBERT**
"Ein Fräulein klagt' " *see Romanze* Matthisson **SCHUBERT**
"Ein Fräulein schaut vom hohen Thurm" *see Ballade* Kenner **SCHUBERT**
"Ein Fräulein stand am Meere" *see Das Fräulein am Meere* Heine **SCHOECK**
"Fråga mig, varför jag ger den första primulan åt er" *see Gullvivan* Blomberg **KILPINEN**
Frage see Kerner **SCHUMANN**
Frage see Lenau **FRANZ**

Frage see Voss MENDELSSOHN-BARTHOLDY

"Frage mich immer, fragest umsonst!" *see Unbefangenheit* Anon. WEBER

Frage nicht see Lenau WOLF

Frage nicht! see Unknown LOEWE

"Frage nicht, wie es gekommen" *see Frage nicht!* Unknown LOEWE

Frage und Antwort see Mörike WOLF

Fragment see Goethe KRENEK

Fragment see Hölderlin HINDEMITH

Fragment aus dem Aeschylus see Aeschylus SCHUBERT

Fragment aus Schillers Gedicht "Die Götter Griechenlands" see Schiller SCHUBERT *Die Götter Griechenlands*

Fragment: Der Glühende see Mombert SZYMANOWSKI

Fragrant and fresh is your garland see Shenshin RIMSKIĭ-KORSAKOV *Svezh i dushist tvoĭ*

"Fragst du mich woher die bange" *see Frage und Antwort* Mörike WOLF

"Fragst du mit den Äugelein" *see Wiegenlied* Cornelius LASSEN

"Fraîche comme une rose" *see Locutions* Cocteau HONEGGER

LA FRAÎCHEUR ET LE FEU, no. 1 POULENC Éluard *Rayon des yeux*

LA FRAÎCHEUR ET LE FEU, no. 2 POULENC Éluard *Le matin les branches attisent*

LA FRAÎCHEUR ET LE FEU, no. 3 POULENC Éluard *Tout disparut*

LA FRAÎCHEUR ET LE FEU, no. 4 POULENC Éluard *Dans les ténèbres du jardin*

LA FRAÎCHEUR ET LE FEU, no. 5 POULENC Éluard *Unis la fraîcheur et le feu*

LA FRAÎCHEUR ET LE FEU, no. 6 POULENC Éluard *Homme au sourire tendre*

LA FRAÎCHEUR ET LE FEU, no. 7 POULENC Éluard *La grande rivière qui va*

"Frail the white rose and frail are her hands" *see A flower given to my daughter* Joyce DIAMOND, ROUSSEL

"Framför en Mariabild vid vägkanten" *see Modern* Blomberg KILPINEN

La française see Zamacoïs SAINT-SAËNS

France, Anatole, 1844-1924.
  MASSENET *Âmes obscures*

France, Marie de
  MILHAUD *Le Lai du Chevrefeuille*

Francesca da Rimini see Dante *DIVINE COMEDY.* BLACHER

Francis of Assisi, Saint, 1182-1226.
  THOMSON *From the canticle of the sun*

FRANCK, CÉSAR, 1822-1890.
  Anon.
    Messe solennelle: O salutaris (1858) [Régnier-Canoux, 1858] Bass & organ. Neither located nor examined.
    Tantum Ergo, motet no. 3 (1858) [Hamelle] "Ave Maria, ave Maria" Bass & organ; chorus ad lib.
  Brizeux, Charles
    La procession (1888) [Leduc, 1893] "Dieu s'avance à travers les champs!" Also voice & orchestra.
  Châteaubriand, François Auguste René, vicomte de,1768-1848.
    Souvenance (1842-43) [Costallat, 1844?] "Combien j'ai douce souvenance"
  David, Eugène, 1813-1889.
    Le mariage des roses (1871) [Enoch, 1873?] "Mignonne, sais-tu comment"
  Delfosse, Bernard
    Les trois exiles (1849) [Mayaud] "Quand l'étranger envahissant la France"
  Desbordes-Valmore, Marceline Félicité Josèphe, 1786-1859.
    Les cloches du soir (1888) [Leduc, 1889] "Quand les cloches du soir"
  Dumas, Alexandre, the elder, 1803-1870.
    Le sylphe (1842-43) [Costallat, 1844?] "Je suis un sylphe, une ombre, un rien" Cello obbligato.
  Florian, Jean Pierre Claris de, 1755-1794.
    Robin Gray (1842-43) [Costallat, 1844?] "Quand les moutons sont dans la bergerie"
  Fourcaud, Louis de Boussés de, 1851-1914.
    Nocturne (1884) [Enoch, 1900] "O fraîche nuit, nuit transparente"
  Hugo, Victor Marie, comte, 1802-1885.
    Passez, passez toujours (1872) [Costallat, 1873?] "Puisque j'ai mis ma lèvre à ta coupe"
    Roses et papillons (1872) [Enoch, 1873; Litolff] same
    CHANTS DU CRÉPUSCULE.
      S'il est un charmant gazon (1857 & 1875) [**Revue Musicale** (1922) iv/2, Suppl.; Enoch, 1927] same 2 versions.

FRANCK, CÉSAR, 1822-1890 *(continued)*
Méry, Joseph, 1798-1865.
  Aimer (1849) [Costallat]
    "J'entendais sa voix si touchante"
  L'Émir de Bengador (1842-43) [Costallat,
    1844?] "Si tu savais que je t'adore"
Musset, Alfred de, 1810-1857.
  Ninon (1842-43) [Costallat, 1844?]
    "Ninon! Ninon! que fais-tu de la vie?"
Paté, Lucien, 1845-1939.
  Lied (1873) [Enoch, 1880?] "Pour moi sa
    main cueillait des roses"
Reboul, Jean, 1795-1864.
  L'ange et l'enfant (1846) [Hamelle,
    1878] "Un ange au radieux visage"
Sully-Prudhomme, René François
  Armand, 1839-1907.
  Le vase brisé (1879) [Enoch, 1900]
    "Le vase, où meurt cette verveine"
Unknown
  Pour les victims (1887) [Hamelle, 1912]
    "Sous les décombres entassés"
  Sinite parvulos [unpubl.]
    Solo voice.
Frank, Jacques Henri, 1904-
HONEGGER
  Du whisky pour Jo
  Fièvre jaune
Frankl, Ludwig August, 1810-1894.
LOEWE *Menschenlose*
FRANZ, ROBERT, 1815-1892.
Anon.
  Ach, wär' es nie geschehen, op. 23 no. 3
    [Siegel] "Meine Mutter hat gewollt"
  Dies und Das, op. 30 no. 5 [Kistner;
    Peters] "Wie traurig sind wir Mädchen
    dran"
  Frühlings Ankunft, op. 23 no. 5 [Siegel]
    "Der Lenz ist angekommen"
  Frühlingswonne, op. 23 no. 2 [Siegel;
    Peters] "Es ist mir wie den kleinen
    Waldvögelein zu Mut"
  Hatte Liebchen zwei, op. 14 no. 4
    [Kistner] same
  Herziges Schätzle du, op. 50 no. 1
    [Leuckart; Peters] same
  Rote Äuglein, op. 23 no. 6 [Siegel]
    "Könnt'st du meine Äuglein seh'n"
  Die Trauernde, op. 17 no. 4 [Siegel;
    Peters] "Mei Mutter mag mi net"
  Der Verlassene, op. 40 no. 5 [Kistner]
    "Ach, ihr Wälder, dunkle Wälder"
  Volkslied, op. 36 no. 3 [Leuckart]
    "Habt ihr sie schon geseh'n?"
  Wird er wohl noch meiner gedenken? op.
    23 no. 1 [Siegel]

    "Mei Schätzel das hat mi verlassen"
  Wozu? op. 42 no. 1 [Siegel] "Wozu wozu
    mir sein sollte das Aug' "
DES KNABEN WUNDERHORN: Der
  Schweizer.
  Zu Strassburg auf der Schanz, op. 12
    no. 2 [J. André] same
Arndt, Johann, 1555-1621.
  Im Frühling, op. 22 no. 3 [Senff]
    "Wenn die Erde leise aufgewacht"
Bodenstedt, Friedrich Martin von,
  1819-1892.
  Es hat die Rose sich beklagt, op. 42 no. 5
    [Siegel; Peters] same
  Es ragt der alte Elborus, op. 43 no. 5
    [Kistner] same
  Die helle Sonne leuchtet, op. 42 no. 2
    [Siegel; Peters] same
  Wenn der Frühling auf die Berge steigt,
    op. 42 no. 6 [Siegel] same
Burns, Robert, 1759-1796.
  Für Einen, op. 1 no. 8 [Peters]
    "Mein Herz ist schwer"
  Ihr Auge, op. 1 no. 1 [Peters] "Einen
    schlimmen Weg ging gestern ich"
  Ihr Hügel dort am schönen Doon, op. 4
    no. 4 [Kistner] same
  Lovely maid! op. 4 no. 3 [Kistner]
    "While larks with little wind fann'd the
    pure air"
  Mein Hochland-Kind, op. 4 no. 1
    [Kistner] "Durch irr' ich Länder"
  Montgomery-Gretchen, op. 4 no. 5
    [Kistner] "Altho' my bed were yonder
    muir"
  My heart is in the Highland, op. 31 no. 5
    [Senff] same
  My love is like a red rose, op. 31 no. 3
    [Senff] same
  Nun holt mir eine Kanne Wein, op. 1 no.
    4 [Peters] same
  O wert thou in the cauld blast, op. 1 no.
    5 [Peters] same
  The pleasant summer's come, op. 3 no. 5
    [Breitkopf & Härtel] same
  So far away, op. 22 no. 6 [Senff]
    "So trieb sie mich"
  The sorrowful maiden, op. 23 no. 4
    [Siegel] "I know, ah! too well why I
    am so sad"
  Die süsse Dirn' von Inverness, op. 4 no.
    2 [Kistner] same
  Thou hast left me ever, Jame, op. 4 no. 6
    [Kistner] same
  Was pocht mein Herz so sehr, op. 9 no. 1
    [Leuckart] same

Chamisso, Adelbert von, 1781-1838.
Mitten ins Herz, op. 52 no. 2 [Kistner] "Es geht bei gedämpfter Trommel Klang"
Text after H.C. Andersen.
Tränen, op. 6 no. 6 [Peters] "Nicht der Thau und nicht der Regen"
Tränen, op. 50 no. 5 [Leuckart] "Denke, denke mein Geliebter"
Tränen, op. 51 no. 2 [Leuckart] "Was ist's, O Vater"
Tränen, op. 52 no. 4 [Kistner] "Ich habe, bevor der Morgen"

Eichendorff, Joseph Karl Benedikt, Freiherr von, 1788-1857.
Abends, op. 16 no. 4 [Siegel; Peters] "Abendlich schon rauscht der Wald"
Am Strom, op. 30 no. 3 [Kistner] "Der Strom glitt einsam hin"
Der Bote, op. 8 no. 1 [Breitkopf & Härtel] "Am Himmelsgrund schiessen so lustig die Stern"
Gute Nacht! op. 5 no. 7 [Siegel; Peters] "Die Höh'n und Wälder schon steigen"
Ich wandre durch die stille Nacht, op. 35 no. 2 [Leuckhart] same
Jagdlied, op. 1 no. 9 [Peters] "Durch schwankende Wipfel schiesst güldener Strahl"
Meeresstille, op. 8 no. 2 [Breitkopf & Härtel] "Ich seh' von des Schiffes Rande"
Möcht' wissen, was sie schlagen, op. 18 no. 5 [Siegel] same
Romanze, op. 35 no. 4 [Leuckhart] "Und wo noch kein Wand'rer 'gangen"
Romanze, op. 51 no. 9 [Leuckhart] "Zur ew'gen Ruh' sie sangen die schöne Müllerin"
Der Schalk, op. 3 no. 1 [Breitkopf & Härtel] "Läuten kaum die Maienglocken leise"
Sonntag, op. 1 no. 7 [Peters] "Die Nacht war kaum verblühet"
Der vielschönen Fraue, op. 10 no. 4 [Peters] "Wohin ich geh' und schaue"

Förster, Marie Laura, 1817-1856.
Denk ich dein! op. 21 no. 2 [Senff; Peters] "Dass ich an dich denke immerdar"
O Mond, O lösch' dein gold'nes Licht, op. 21 no. 3 [Senff] same
Vorüber der Mai, op. 22 no. 2 [Senff] same

Geibel, Emanuel, i.e., Franz Emanuel August, 1815-1884.
Ave Maria, op. 17 no. 1 [Siegel; Peters] "Ave Maria!"

Des müden Abendlied, op. 26 no. 4 [Siegel] "Verglommen ist das Abendrot"
Für Musik, op. 10 no. 1 [Peters] "Nun die Schatten dunkeln"
Gute Nacht, mein Herz, op. 12 no. 5 [J. André] same
Im Herbst, op. 20 no. 6 [Siegel] "Es rauscht das rote Laub zu meinen Füssen"
In meinem Garten die Nelken, op. 1 no. 12 [Peters] same
Die Lotosblume, op. 1 no. 3 [Peters] "Die stille Lotosblume steigt aus dem blauen See"
Nachtlied, op. 28 no. 3 [Siegel] "Der Mond kommt still gegangen"
Vöglein, wohin so schnell, op. 1 no. 11 [Peters] same
Wasserfahrt, op. 9 no. 2 [Leuckart] "Nun wollen Berg' und Tale wieder blüh'n"
Wenn sich zwei Herzen scheiden, op. 35 no. 5 [Leuckhart] same
Wohl waren es, Tage der Sonne, op. 41 no. 3 [Breitkopf & Härtel] same
Wolle keiner mich fragen, op. 52 no. 3 [Kistner] same

Glück, Barbara Elisabeth, 1814-1894.
Gute Nacht, op. 36 no. 5 [Leuckart] "Im tiefsten Innern"

Goethe, Johann Wolfgang von, 1749-1832.
Cupido, loser, op. 33 no. 4 [Peters] "Cupido, loser eigensinniger Knabe"
Gegenwart, op. 33 no. 2 [Peters] "Alles kündet dich an"
Gleich und Gleich, op. 22 no. 1 [Senff; Peters] "Ein Blumenglöckchen vom Boden hervor"
Im Sommer, op. 16 no. 2 [Siegel] "Wie Feld und Au' so blinkend im Tau"
Mailied, op. 33 no. 3 [Peters] "Zwischen Weizen und Korn"
Rastlose Liebe, op. 33 no. 6 [Peters] "Dem Schnee, dem Regen"
Schweizerlied, op. 33 no. 5 [Peters] "Uf'm Bergli bin i gsässe"
Wonne der Wehmuth, op. 33 no. 1 [Peters] "Trocknet nicht, trocknet nicht"

Gottschall, Rudolf von, 1823-1909.
Die letzte Rose, op. 20 no. 2 [Siegel] "Da welkt am Fenster"
Marie, op. 18 no. 1 [Siegel; Peters] "Marie, am Fenster sitzest du"

COMPOSER Poet *Title* "First Line"

FRANZ, ROBERT, 1815-1892 *(continued)*
Hafiz, Muhammad Shums al-Din, d.1388.
Weisst du noch? op. 42 no. 4 [Siegel] same
Hahn-Hahn, Ida Marie Luise Sophie. . . , Gräfin von, 1805-1880.
Am Rheinfall, op. 44 no. 6 [Kistner] "In den Abgrund lass mich schauen"
Ich bin bis zum Tode betrübt, op. 48 no. 5 [Leuckart] "Es steht in der Bibel geschrieben"
Nachtlied, op. 1 no. 2 [Peters] "In der Nacht, in der Nacht da rauschen die Bäume so traurig"
Hauenschild, Georg von, 1825-1855.
Da sind die bleichen Geister wieder, op. 13 no. 6 [Peters] same
Es klingt in der Luft, op. 13 no. 2 [Peters] same
Ein Friedhof, op. 13 no. 3 [Peters] "Schemen erloschener Flammen"
Ich wollte, ich könnte nicht träumen, op. 52 no. 5 [Kistner] same
Rosmarin, op. 13 no. 4 [Peters] "Ich habe mir Rosmarin gepflanzt"
Wenn drüben die Glocken klingen, op. 13 no. 5 [Peters] same
Zwei welke Rosen, op. 13 no. 1 [Peters] "Zwei welke Rosen träumen"
Heine, Heinrich, 1797-1856.
Abschied, op. 31 no. 5 [Senff] "Das gelbe Laub erzittert"
Ach, wie komm' ich da hinüber? op. 41 no. 2 [Breitkopf & Härtel] "In dem Traum"
Allnächtlich im Traume, op. 9 no. 4 [Leuckart] same
Altes Lied, op. 39 no. 6 [Breitkopf & Härtel] "Du bist gestorben"
Am fernen Horizonte, op. 37 no. 3 [Kistner] same
Am leuchtenden Sommermorgen, op. 11 no. 2 [Siegel] same
Auf dem Meere, op. 5 no. 3 [Siegel] "Aus den Himmelsaugen droben fallen"
Auf dem Meere, op. 6 no. 3 [Peters] "An die blaue Himmelsdecke"
Auf dem Meere, op. 9 no. 6 [Leuckart] "Eingewiegt von Meereswellen"
Auf dem Meere, op. 11 no. 5 [Siegel] "Es träumte mir von einer weiten Haide"
Auf dem Meere, op. 25 no. 6 [Siegel; Peters] "An die bretterne Schiffswand"

Auf dem Meere, op. 36 no. 1 [Leuckart; Peters] "Das Meer hat seine Perlen"
Aus meiner Erinnerung, op. 12 no. 4 [J. André] same
Die blauen Frühlingsaugen, op. 20 no. 1 [Siegel; Peters] same
Childe Harold, op. 38 no. 3 [Breitkopf & Härtel] "Eine starke schwarze Barke"
Deine weissen Lilienfinger, op. 34 no. 2 [Leuckhart] same
Du bist so schön und rein, op. 37 no. 1 [Kistner] "Die, du bist so schön und rein"
Durch den Wald im Mondenscheine, op. 8 no. 3 [Breitkopf & Härtel] same
Es fällt ein Stern herunter, op. 44 no. 4 [Kistner] same
Es ragt ins Meer der Runenstein, op. 39 no. 2 [Breitkopf & Härtel] same
Es treibt mich hin, es treibt mich her, op. 34 no. 4 [Leuckhart] same
Es ziehn die brausenden Wellen, op. 40 no. 2 [Kistner] same
Der Fichtenbaum, op. 16 no. 3 [Siegel] "Ein Fichtenbaum steht einsam"
Frühling, op. 38 no. 1 [Breitkopf & Härtel] "Die Wellen blinken"
Frühlingsfeier, op. 39 no. 1 [Breitkopf & Härtel] "Das ist des Frühlings traurige Lust!"
Gekommen ist der Maie, op. 34 no. 6 [Leuckhart] same
Güldne Sternlein schauen nieder, op. 38 no. 5 [Breitkopf & Härtel] same
Hör' ich das Liedchen klingen, op. 5 no. 11 [Siegel] same
Ich hab' im Traum geweinet, op. 25 no. 3 [Siegel] same
Ich lieb' eine Blume, op. 28 no. 1 [Siegel] same
Ich will meine Seele tauchen, op. 43 no. 4 [Kistner] same
Im Rhein, im heiligen Strome, op. 18 no. 2 [Siegel; Peters] same
Im wunderschönen Monat Mai, op. 25 no. 5 [Siegel] same
In der Fremde, op. 38 no. 6 [Breitkopf & Härtel] "Es treibt dich fort"
Ja, du bist elend, op. 7 no. 6 [Peters] same
Kommt feins Liebchen heut'? op. 25 no. 4 [Siegel] "Morgens steh' ich auf und frage"
Lehre, op. 41 no. 5 [Breitkopf & Härtel] "Mutter zum Bienelein"
Leise zieht, durch mein Gemüt, op. 41 no. 1 [Breitkopf & Härtel] same

Lieb' Liebchen, op. 17 no. 3 [Siegel]
same
Die Lotosblume, op. 25 no. 1 [Siegel]
"Die Lotosblume ängstigt sich"
Mädchen mit dem roten Mündchen, op. 5
no. 5 [Siegel; Peters] same
Das Meer erstrahlt im Sonnenschein, op.
39 no. 3 [Breitkopf & Härtel] same
Mir fehlt das Beste, op. 39 no. 5
[Breitkopf & Härtel] "Ein jeder hat zu
diesem Feste"
O lüge nicht! op. 25 no. 2 [Siegel]
"Ein schöner Stern geht auf in meiner
Nacht"
Die Rose, die Lilie, op. 34 no. 5
[Leuckhart] same
*Sag mir! Sag mir, wer einst die Uhren
erfand,* op. 38 no. 4 [Breitkopf &
Härtel] same
Die schlanke Wasserlilie, op. 51 no. 7
[Leuckart] same
*Der Schmetterling ist in die Rose
verliebt,* op. 38 no. 2 [Breitkopf &
Härtel; Peters] same
Die schönen Augen der Frühlingsnacht,
op. 51 no. 5 [Leuckart] same
Sie floh vor mir, op. 40 no. 6 [Kistner]
same
Sie liebten sich beide, op. 31 no. 4
[Senff] same
Traumbild, op. 34 no. 3 [Leuckhart]
"Mir träumte einst von wildem
Liebesglüh'n"
Und wüssten's die Blumen, op. 12 no. 6
[J. André] same
Unter'm weissen Baume sitzend, op. 40
no. 3 [Kistner] same
Verfehlte Liebe, op. 20 no. 3 [Siegel]
"Zuweilen dünkt es mich als trübe"
Wandl' ich in dem Wald des Abends, op.
39 no. 4 [Breitkopf & Härtel] same
Was will die einsame Träne, op. 34 no. 1
[Leuckhart] same
Wasserfahrt, op. 48 no. 3 [Leuckart] "Ich
stand gelehnet an den Mast"
Wenn ich auf dem Lager liege, op. 37 no.
6 [Kistner] same
Wenn ich in deine Augen seh, op. 44 no.
5 [Kistner] same
Wenn Zwei von einander scheiden, op. 48
no. 1 [Leuckart] same
LIEDERSTRAUSS.
Aus meinen grossen Schmerzen, op. 5
no. 1 [Siegel; Peters] same
Sterne mit den goldnen Füsschen, op.
30 no. 1 [Kistner; Peters] same

Wie des Mondes Abbild zittert, op. 6
no. 2 [Peters] same
LYRISCHES INTERMEZZO, no. 63.
Das ist ein Brausen und Heulen, op. 8
no. 4 [Breitkopf & Härtel] same
*TRAGÖDIEN NEBST EINEM
LYRISCHEN INTERMEZZO.*
Meerfahrt, op. 18 no. 4 [Siegel] "Mein
Liebchen, wir sassen beisammen"
VERSCHIEDENE-SERAPHINE, no. 12.
Mit schwarzen Segeln, op. 18 no. 6
[Siegel] same

**Hemans, Felicia Dorothea (Browne),
1793-1835.**
Mutter, O sing mich zur Ruh! op. 10 no.
3 [Peters] same

**Hoffmann von Fallersleben, August
Heinrich, 1798-1874.**
Doppelwandlung, op. 44 no. 3 [Kistner]
"Zum Frühling sprach ich: Weile!"
Die Farben Helgolands, op. 3 no. 2
[Breitkopf & Härtel] "Grün ist das
Eiland"
Frühling und Liebe, op. 3 no. 3
[Breitkopf & Härtel; Peters]
"Im Rosenbusch die Liebe schlief"
Frühlingsliebe, op. 3 no. 4 [Breitkopf &
Härtel] "Komm' zum Garten"
Tanzlied im Mai, op. 1 no. 6 [Peters]
"Zum Reigen herbei im fröhlichen
Mai!"
Wasserfahrt, op. 6 no. 1 [Peters]
"Über die hellen funkelnden Wellen"

Kapper, Siegfried, 1821-1879.
Abschied, op. 11 no. 1 [Siegel; Peters]
"Wie schienen die Sternlein so hell,
so hell"
"Nach dem Böhemischen"; cf. Brahms
setting, *Ade!*

**Körner, Theodor, i.e., Karl Theodor,
1791-1813.**
Waldfahrt, op. 14 no. 3 [Kistner; Peters]
"Im Wald', im Wald' ist's frisch und
grün"

**Köstlin, Christian Reinhold, 1813-
1856.**
Ach, ich denke, op. 51 no. 6 [Leuckart]
same

Lebret, Karl August, 1809-1855.
Frühlingsklage, op. 50 no. 2 [Leuckart]
"Nun wird es wieder grün auf allen
Wiesen"

Lenau, Nicolaus, 1802-1850.
An die Wolke, op. 30 no. 6 [Kistner]
"Zieh' nicht so schnell vorüber"

FRANZ, ROBERT, 1815-1892 *(continued)*
Lenau, Nicolaus, 1802-1850 *(continued)*

Bitte, op. 9 no. 3 [Leuckart; Peters]
"Weil' auf mir, du dunkles Auge"

Drüben geht die Sonne scheiden, op. 2
no. 2 [Breitkopf & Härtel] same

Der Eichwald, op. 51 no. 1 [Leuckart]
"Ich trat in einen heilig düstern
Eichwald"

Frage, op. 14 no. 6 [Kistner] "Wie sehr
ich dein, soll ich dir sagen"

Frühlingsblick, op. 52 no. 6 [Kistner]
"Durch den Wald, den dunkeln"

Frühlingsgedränge, op. 7 no. 5 [Peters]
"Frühlingskinder im bunten Gedränge"

Lenz, op. 14 no. 2 [Kistner] "Die Bäume
blüh'n, die Vöglein singen"

Liebesfeier, op. 21 no. 4 [Senff] "An
ihren bunten Liedern klettert die
Lerche"

Liebesfrühling, op. 14 no. 5 [Kistner]
"Ich sah den Lenz einmal"

Nebel, op. 28 no. 4 [Siegel] "Du trüber
Nebel, hüllest mir das Tal"

Der schwere Abend, op. 37 no. 4
[Kistner] "Die dunklen Wolken
hingen"

*Sonnenuntergang; schwarze Wolken
zieh'n,* op. 2 no. 4 [Breitkopf &
Härtel] same

Stille sicherheit, op. 10 no. 2 [Peters]
"Horch, wie still es wird im dunkeln
Hain"

Trübe wird's, die Wolken jagen, op. 2 no.
3 [Breitkopf & Härtel] same

Winternacht, op. 21 no. 5 [Senff]
"Vor Kälte ist die Luft erstarrt"

LIEBESKLÄNGE.
An den Wind, op. 26 no. 6 [Siegel]
"Ich wand're fort, ins ferne Land"

SCHILFLIEDER.
Auf dem Teich, dem regungslosen, op.
2 no. 5 [Breitkopf & Härtel] same

Auf geheimem Waldespfade, op. 2 no.
1 [Breitkopf & Härtel] same

Mayer, K.
O Herz in meiner Brust! op. 51 no. 4
[Leuckart] "Das Vöglein auf dem
Baum"

Mörike, Eduard Friedrich, 1804-1875.
Er ist's! op. 27 no. 2 [Senff] "Frühling
lässt sein blaues Band"

Herz, ich habe schwer an dir zu tragen,
op. 27 no. 3 [Senff]
"Herz und weisst du selber denn"

In Leid versunken, op. 27 no. 4 [Senff]
"Früh, wenn die Hähne krähn"

Rosenzeit, op. 27 no. 5 [Senff]
"Rosenzeit, wie schnell vorbei"

Ein Stündlein wohl vor Tag, op. 28 no. 2
[Siegel; Peters] "Derweil ich
schlafend lag"

Ein Tännlein grünet wo, op. 27 no. 6
[Senff] same

Um Mitternacht, op. 28 no. 6 [Siegel]
"Bedächtig stieg die Nacht ans Land"

Verborgenheit, op. 28 no. 5 [Siegel]
"Lass', O Welt, O lass mich sein!"

Volker spielt auf! op. 27 no. 1 [Senff]
"Jung Volker ist der
Räuberhauptmann"

Müller von Königswinter, Wolfgang,
1816-1873.
Im Herbst, op. 17 no. 6 [Siegel; Peters]
"Die Heide ist braun, einst blühte sie
rot"

Im Walde, op. 12 no. 3 [J. André] "Es
streckt der Wald die Zweige so grün"

Widmung, op. 14 no. 1 [Kistner; Peters]
"O danke nicht, für diese Lieder"

Natorp, Bernard Christoph Ludwig,
1774-1846.
In meinen Armen wieg ich dich, op. 7 no.
4 [Peters] same

Osterwald, Karl Wilhelm, 1820-1887.
Abends, op. 20 no. 4 [Siegel]
"Der Tag beginnt zu dunkeln"

Ach, dass du kamst, op. 4 no. 12
[Kistner] same

Ach, wenn ich doch ein Immchen wär,
op. 3 no. 6 [Breitkopf & Härtel;
Peters] same

Ade denn, du stolze, op. 31 no. 2 [Senff]
same

Aprillaunen, op. 44 no. 2 [Kistner]
"Liebchen, was willst du?"

Aufbruch, op. 35 no. 6 [Leuckhart]
"Die Lüfte werden heller"

Bei der Linde, op. 36 no. 4 [Leuckart]
"Als die Linden trieben"

Da die Stunde kam, op. 7 no. 3 [Peters]
same

Dornröschen, op. 51 no. 3 [Leuckart]
"Dornröschen schlägt zum ersten Mal
die Augen"

Dort unterm Lindenbaum, op. 31 no. 1
[Senff] same

Du grüne Rast im Haine, op. 41 no. 6
[Breitkopf & Härtel] same

Durch säuselnde Bäume, op. 4 no. 9
[Kistner] same

Entschluss, op. 43 no. 3 [Kistner]
"Scheust dich noch immer"

Erinnerung, op. 5 no. 10 [Siegel]
   "O banger Traum"
Erinnerung, op. 51 no. 10 [Leuckart]
   "Die Sterne flimmern und prangen"
Erster Verlust, op. 36 no. 2 [Leuckart]
   "Gestern hielt er mich im Arme"
Frühe Klage, op. 22 no. 4 [Senff]
   "Aus der Ferne schallen Gesänge"
Gewitternacht, op. 8 no. 6 [Breitkopf &
   Härtel; Peters]
   "Grolle lauter, zürnend Gewitter"
Gleich wie der Mond, op. 43 no. 2
   [Kistner] same
Die Harrende, op. 35 no. 1 [Leuckhart]
   "Hör' ich ein Vöglein singen"
Herbstsorge, op. 4 no. 10 [Kistner]
   "Gleich eines Herzens bangen
      Fieberträumen"
Ich lobe mir die Vögelein, op. 5 no. 8
   [Siegel] same
Im Frühling, op. 17 no. 5 [Siegel] "Im
   Grase lieg' ich manche Stunde"
Im Mai, op. 11 no. 3 [Siegel]
   "Nun grünt der Berg"
Im Mai, op. 22 no. 5 [Senff]
   "Musst nicht allein im Freien"
Im Sommer, op. 11 no. 4 [Siegel]
   "Da der Sommer kommen ist"
In Blüten, op. 43 no. 6 [Kistner]
   "Nun da die Bäum' in Blüten steh'n"
Der junge Tag erwacht, op. 7 no. 1
   [Peters] same
Kurzes Wiedersehen, op. 4 no. 8
   [Kistner] "Ach! musstest du denn
   scheiden"
Die Liebe hat gelogen, op. 6 no. 4
   [Peters] "Des Waldes Wipfel rauschen"
Lieber Schatz, wie wieder gut mir, op. 26
   no. 2 [Siegel; Peters]
   "In dem Dornbusch blüht ein Röslein"
Mein Schatz ist auf der Wanderschaft, op.
   40 no. 1 [Kistner; Peters] same
Nun hat das Lied ein Ende, op. 18 no. 3
   [Siegel] same
Nun hat mein Stecken gute Rast, op. 36
   no. 6 [Leuckart] same
Der Schnee ist zergangen, op. 6 no. 5
   [Peters] same
Schöner Mai, bist über Nacht, op. 30 no.
   4 [Kistner] same
Sonnenwende, op. 37 no. 5 [Kistner]
   "Der Sommer ist zu Ende"
Ständchen, op. 17 no. 2 [Siegel; Peters]
   "Der Mond ist schlafen 'gangen"
Träume, op. 43 no. 1 [Kistner] "Lieblich
   blüh'n die Bäume voller Schmelz und
   Duft"

Treibt der Sommer seinen Rosen, op. 8
   no. 5 [Breitkopf & Härtel] same
Um Mitternacht, op. 16 no. 6 [Siegel]
   "Um Mitternacht ruht die ganze Erde
   nun"
Umsonst, op. 10 no. 6 [Peters]
   "Des Waldes Sänger singen"
Und die Rosen, sie prangen, op. 10 no. 5
   [Peters] same
Und welche Rose blüten treibt, op. 12 no.
   1 [J. André] same
Vergiss mein nicht, op. 26 no. 3 [Siegel]
   "Den Strauss, den sie gewunden"
Verlass' mich nicht! op. 21 no. 6 [Senff]
   "Die Schwalbe zieht, der Sommer
   flieht"
Vom Berge, op. 9 no. 5 [Leuckart] "Jetzt
   steh' ich auf der höchsten Höh' "
Wanderlied, op. 4 no. 11 [Kistner] "Und
   kommt der Frühling wieder her"
Wenn ich's nur wüsste, op. 26 no. 1
   [Siegel; Peters] "Vor meinem Fenster
   regt"
Will über Nacht wohl übers Tal, op. 5 no.
   4 [Siegel] same
Zu spät, op. 37 no. 2 [Kistner] "Aus
   bangen Träumen der Winternacht die
   Ros' "

Petöfi, Sándor, 1823-1849.
   Blätter lässt die Blume fallen, op. 30 no.
   2 [Kistner] same
   Selige Nacht! op. 42 no. 3 [Siegel]
   "Selige Nacht! Ich bin nun bei der
   Liebsten hier"

Prutz, Robert Eduard, 1816-1872.
   Wohl viele tausend Vögelein, op. 52 no. 1
   [Kistner] same

Roquette, Otto, 1824-1896.
   Das macht das dunkelgrüne Laub, op. 20
   no. 5 [Siegel; Peters] same
   Du liebes Auge, op. 16 no. 1 [Siegel;
   Peters] "Du liebes Auge willst dich
   tauchen"
   Die Sonn' ist hin, op. 35 no. 3
   [Leuckhart] same
   Weisst du noch? op. 16 no. 5 [Siegel;
   Peters] same
   Willkommen, mein Wald, op. 21 no. 1
   [Senff; Peters] same

Röser, Otto
   Als trüg' man die Liebe zu Grab, op. 40
   no. 4 [Kistner]
   "Ich sass am einsamen Weiher"
   Liebe, op. 41 no. 4 [Breitkopf & Härtel]
   "In dem frischen, grünen Wald"

Rückert, Friedrich, 1788-1866.
   Er ist gekommen, op. 4 no. 7 [Kistner;
   Peters] same

COMPOSER   Poet   *Title*   "First Line"

FRANZ, ROBERT, 1815-1892 *(continued)*
Rückert, Friedrich, 1788-1866
(continued)
Ich hab' in deinem Auge, op. 5 no. 6
[Siegel] same
Liebesfrühling, op. 50 no. 6 [Leuckart]
"Ich hab' in mein gesogen"
Ständchen, op. 7 no. 2 [Peters]
"Hüttelein still und klein"
Vom Auge zum Herzen, op. 26 no. 5
[Siegel] "Durch schöne Augen hab'
ich"
Wiedersehen, op. 51 no. 8 [Leuckart]
"Leb' wohl, und sehen wir uns wieder"
LIEBESFRÜHLING.
Die Perle, op. 48 no. 4 [Leuckart]
"Der Himmel hat eine Thräne
geweint"
Scheffler, Johann, 1624-1677.
O nimm dich in Acht, op. 44 no. 1
[Kistner] "In meiner Brust eine Glocke
klingt"
Schröer, Karl Julius, 1825-1900.
Genesung, op. 5 no. 12 [Siegel; Peters]
"Und nun ein End' dem Trauern"
Liebchen ist da! op. 5 no. 2 [Siegel;
Peters] "Blümlein im Garten"
Stiller Abend, op. 5 no. 9 [Siegel] "Sel'ge
Abende nieder steigen in mein Herz"
Tieck, Johann Ludwig, 1773-1853.
Schlummerlied, op. 1 no. 10 [Peters;
Oliver Ditson, 1903]
"Ruhe Süssliebchen"
Unknown
Abends, op. 11 no. 6 [Siegel] "O lächle,
Freund der Liebe"
Das Grab der Liebe, op. 48 no. 2
[Leuckart] "Wo süss in Frieden ein
Herze ruht"
Der Stern ist die Liebe, op. 50 no. 3
[Leuckart] "Es fahren die Schiffer"
Viol, Wilhelm, i.e., Friedrich Wilhelm,
1817-1874.
Ein Gruss von Ihr! op. 50 no. 4
[Leuckart]"Es glänzt im Abendsonnen
golde der stille Waldesteich"
Welhaven, Johann Sebastian
Cammermeyer, 1807-1873.
Norwegische Frühlingsnacht, op. 48 no.
6 [Leuckart; Peters]
"Lenz nacht, so still und so kühl"
Franzén, Franz Mikael, bishop, 1772-
1847.
SIBELIUS
De bägge rosorna

Blåsippan
Hvitsippan
"Franziskus einst, der Heil'ge" *see Der heilige
Franziskus* Wessenberg **LOEWE**
"Französ'sche Musika" *see Strafpredigt über
die französische Musik* Unknown
WEBER
"Det frasar af silke" *see Teodora*
Gripenberg **SIBELIUS**
"Frau Amme, Frau Amme, das Kind ist
erwacht!" *see Das Kind am Brunnen*
Hebbel **WOLF**
Frau Twardowska see Mickiewicz **LOEWE**
Fraue, Du Süsse (?) see Finckh **BERG**
Die Frauen sind oft fromm und still see Dahn
SCHLICHTE WEISEN, no. 13. **STRAUSS**
FRAUENBILDER UND HULDIGUNGEN. see
Daumer
Ach, wende diesen Blick **BRAHMS**
In meiner Nächte Sehnen **BRAHMS**
Strahlt zuweilen auch ein mildes Licht
BRAHMS
Unbewegte laue Luft **BRAHMS**
Von waldbekränzter Hohe **BRAHMS**
Frauengebet see Lamartine **RUBINSTEIN**
La prière de femme
Frauenhaar see Bierbaum **REGER**
"Frauenhaar trag' ich am Hute" *see
Frauenhaar* Bierbaum **REGER**
FRAUENLIEBE UND LEBEN. see Chamisso
Seit ich ihn gesehen **SCHUMANN**
Seit ich ihn gesehn **LOEWE**
FRAUENLIEBE UND LEBEN, no. 1
SCHUMANN Chamisso *Seit ich ihn
gesehen*
FRAUENLIEBE UND LEBEN, no. 2
SCHUMANN Chamisso *Er, der
Herrlichste von allen*
FRAUENLIEBE UND LEBEN, no. 3
SCHUMANN Chamisso *Ich kann's nicht
fassen*
FRAUENLIEBE UND LEBEN, no. 4
SCHUMANN Chamisso *Du Ring an
meinem Finger*
FRAUENLIEBE UND LEBEN, no. 5
SCHUMANN Chamisso *Helft mir, ihr
Schwestern*
FRAUENLIEBE UND LEBEN, no. 6
SCHUMANN Chamisso *Süsser Freund,
du blickest mich verwundert an*
FRAUENLIEBE UND LEBEN, no. 7
SCHUMANN Chamisso *An meinem
Herzen, an meiner Brust*
FRAUENLIEBE UND LEBEN, no. 8
SCHUMANN Chamisso *Nun hast du mir
den ersten Schmerz gethan*

Freak show see Norse **ROREM**
Frech und Froh I see Goethe **WOLF**
Frech und Froh II see Goethe **WOLF**
Der freche Star see Iłłakowiczówna
  SZYMANOWSKI *Nikczemny szpak*
Fred see Tegengren **KILPINEN**
Freedom see Bennett **QUILTER**
The freedom song see Eagel, Paul **ROREM**
Freedom's land see MacLeish **HARRIS**
"Frei und froh mit muntern Sinnen" *see*
  Lebensansicht Anon. **WEBER**
Freibeuter see Goethe **LOEWE**
Der freie Mann see Pfeffel **BEETHOVEN**
Die freien Sänger see Förster, F. **WEBER**
Freigeisterei der Leidenschaft see Schiller
  SCHUBERT *Der Kampf*
Freihold see Lingg **SCHÖNBERG**
Freiligrath, Ferdinand, 1810-1876.
  LISZT *O lieb*
  LOEWE
    Der Blumen Rache
    Der Edelfalk
    Meerfahrt
    Der Mohrenfürst
    Der Mohrenfürst auf der Messe
    Die Mohrenfürstin
    Nebo
    Prinz Eugen, der edle Ritter
    Schwalbenmärchen
  TROMPETE VON VIONVILLE.
    LISZT *Und wir dachten der Toten*
Freimauerlied see Claudius, M. **ZELTER**
Freisinn see Goethe *WESTÖSTLICHER*
  DIVAN. **RUBINSTEIN, SCHUMANN**
"Freiwillige vor! Auch du, lieb Mädchen" *see*
  Die Heldenbraut Kurowski-Eichen
  LOEWE
Freiwilliges Versinken see Mayrhofer
  SCHUBERT
"Fremd bin ich eingezogen" *see Gute Nacht*
  Müller, Wilhelm **SCHUBERT**
Das Fremdlings Abendlied see Schmidt,
  Georg **ZELTER**
Fremtidens Land see Bjørnson **NIELSEN**
"Fremtidens Land! Derhen de styrer, de
  tusinde Savn" *see Fremtidens Land*
  Bjørnson **NIELSEN**
Frenzied nights see Apukhtin
  CHAĬKOVSKIĬ *Nochi bezumnye*
Frère Eucher
  GOUNOD *L'eucharistie*
"Fresche le mie parole ne la sera" *see La sera
  fiesolana* Annunzio **CASELLA**
"The fresh air moves like water round a boat"
  see Earth's call Monro **IRELAND**
Freude der Kinderjahre see Köpken
  SCHUBERT

"Freude, die im frühen Lenze" *see Freude der
  Kinderjahre* Köpken **SCHUBERT**
"Freude, Königin der Weisen" *see An die
  Freude* Uz **MOZART**
"Freude, schöner Götterfunken" *see An die
  Freude* Schiller **SCHUBERT**
"Freuden sonder Zahl" *see Seligkeit* Hölty
  SCHUBERT
"Freudig war vor viellen Jahren" *see Parabase*
  Goethe **SCHOECK**
"Freudvoll, freudvoll und leidvoll, Gedanken
  voll seyn" *see Clärchen* Goethe **ZELTER**
"Freudvoll und leidvoll" *see Clärchens Lied*
  Goethe **RUBINSTEIN**
Freudvoll und leidvoll see Goethe *EGMONT.*
  LISZT
"Freudvoll und leidvoll" *see Die Liebe*
  Goethe **SCHUBERT**
Der Freund see Eichendorff **WOLF**
"Freund' umblühe dich auf allen Wegen" *see
  An Laura* Matthisson **BEETHOVEN**
Freunde see Avenarius *STIMMEN UND
  BILDER*: Ehe. **WEBERN**
DIE FREUNDE. see Jone
  Des Herzens Purpurvogel **WEBERN**
  Sterne **WEBERN**
  Wie bin ich Froh! **WEBERN**
"Freunde, deren Grüfte sich schon bemoosten"
  see Die Schatten Matthisson
  SCHUBERT
"Freunde, weihet den Pokal" *see Der Pokal*
  Arnim **STRAUSS**
"Freundig zum Himmel auf blikke mein
  Herz!" *see Ermutigung* Schweizer
  SPOHR
"Freundlich ist dein Antlitz" *see An den Mond
  in einer Herbstnacht* Schreiber
  SCHUBERT
Freundliche Vision see Bierbaum **REGER,
  STRAUSS**
Freundschaft und Wein see Zettler
  SCHUBERT *Trinklied*
Ein Freundschaftsstück see Vinje **GRIEG** *Et
  Vennestykke*
Frey, Adolf, 1855-1920.
  BRAHMS *Meine Lieder*
  LUENING *Mysterium*
  REGER *Unvergessen*
  SCHOECK
    Das Schlummerlied
    Schöner Ort
Frey, Friedrich Hermann, 1830-1911.
  BERG
    Schattenleben
    Schlummerlose Nächte
  PFITZNER *Herbstgefühl*

Frey, Friedrich Hermann, 1830-1911
 (*continued*)
 RUBINSTEIN *Das erste Sommergras; Vor
  der Ernte*
 SCHÖNBERG *Das zerbrochene Krüglein*
 SIBELIUS *Der Wanderer und der Bach*
 STRAUSS *Weihnachtsgefühl*
 SZYMANOWSKI *Liebesnacht*
 WEBERN *Bild der Liebe*
FRIDAY AFTERNOONS, no. 1
 BRITTEN Anon. *Begone, dull care*
FRIDAY AFTERNOONS, no. 2
 BRITTEN Thackeray *A tragic story*
FRIDAY AFTERNOONS, no. 3
 BRITTEN Taylor, J. *Cuckoo!*
FRIDAY AFTERNOONS, no. 4
 BRITTEN Anon. *Ee-Oh!*
FRIDAY AFTERNOONS, no. 5
 BRITTEN Anon. *A new year carol*
FRIDAY AFTERNOONS, no. 6
 BRITTEN Udall *I must be married on
  Sunday*
FRIDAY AFTERNOONS, no. 7
 BRITTEN Anon. *There was a man of
  Newington*
FRIDAY AFTERNOONS, no. 8
 BRITTEN Walton, I. *Fishing song*
FRIDAY AFTERNOONS, no. 9
 BRITTEN Anon. *The useful plough*
FRIDAY AFTERNOONS, no. 10
 BRITTEN Farjeon *Jazz-man*
FRIDAY AFTERNOONS, no. 11
 BRITTEN Anon. *There was a monkey*
FRIDAY AFTERNOONS, no. 12
 BRITTEN Anon. *Old Abram Brown*
Friderici, Daniel, 1584-1638.
 REGER *In einem Rosengärtelein*
Fridericus Rex see Häring **LOEWE**
"Fridericus Rex, unser König und Herr" *see
  Fridericus Rex* Häring **LOEWE**
Friede see Huggenberger **REGER**
 Two settings: op. 76 no. 25 and op. 79c no.
  4.
Der Friede see Unknown **ZELTER**
Friede den Schlummerern! see Moore, T.
 JENSEN
"Der Friede sei mit euch!" *see Pax vobiscum*
 Schober **SCHUBERT**
"Friede sei um diesen Grabstein her" *see Bei
 dem Grabe meines Vaters* Claudius, M.
 SCHUBERT
Friede und Ruhe in Gott see Anon. **LOEWE**
Friedelberg, d. 1800.
 BEETHOVEN
  *Abschiedsgesang an Wiens Bürger
  Kriegslied der Österreicher*

Frieden see Grun, James **PFITZNER**
Frieden see Molbech **JENSEN**
Friedensreigen see Voss **ZELTER**
Friederike, pseud. *see* Robert, Friederike
 (Braun), 1795-1832.
Der Friedhof see Giesebrecht *SANFT
 RUHENDE FLUR.* **LOEWE**
Ein Friedhof see Hauenschild **FRANZ**
Friedhof im Gebirgsdorf see Krenek
 KRENEK
EIN FRIEDHOFKRANZ. see Auersperg
 Die Grabrose **LOEWE**
Friedhofsgang see Kleinschmidt **REGER**
"Friedlich bekämpfen Nacht sich und Tag" *see
 Abendgefühl* Hebbel **CORNELIUS**
 Two settings: 1862 and 1863.
"Friedlich lieg' ich hingegossen" *see
 Der Schiffer* Schlegel, F. **SCHUBERT**
"Friedlicher Abend" *see Abendbilder* Lenau
 WOLF
Friedrich Wilhelm IV, King of Prussia,
 1795-1861?, supposed author.
 LOEWE *Preussisches Hurrahlied*
Friends, hear my song see Kruse **BORODIN**
 Listen to my song, little friend
Friendship in misfortune see Anon.
 IRELAND
FRIERIET PAA HELGOLAND. see
 Feddersen *Claras Sang* **GRIEG**
Frihed er det bedste guld see Thomas af
 Strengnaes **NIELSEN**
"Frisch atmet des Morgens lebendiger Hauch"
 see Der Flüchtling Schiller **SCHUBERT**
Frisch gesungen see Chamisso **MEDTNER**
"Frisch trabe sonder Ruh' und Rast" *see Auf
 der Bruck* Schulze **SCHUBERT**
LES FRISSONS. see Gravollet, Paul
 Manteau de fleurs **RAVEL**
LES FRISSONS, no. 9. see Gravollet, Paul
 Mirage **INDY**
Frithjofs Glück see Unknown **LASSEN**
Les fritillaires see Daudet, L. **MILHAUD**
"Les fritillaires aiment les endroits exposés"
 see Les fritillaires Daudet, L. **MILHAUD**
Frits see Mendel'son **PROKOFIEV**
Fritz see Mendel'son **PROKOFIEV** *Frits*
Fröding, Gustaf, 1860-1911.
 SIBELIUS
  *Bollspelet vid Trianon
  Jag ville jag vore i Indialand
  Men min fågel märks dock icke
  INGALILL.*
  SIBELIUS *Säf, säf, susa*
Fröhlich, Abraham, 1796-1865.
 SCHUMANN *Die Nonne*
Fröhliche Gesellen see Roquette **JENSEN**

DIE FRÖHLICHE WISSENSCHAFT. see
Nietzsche
Der Einsame **DELIUS**
Nach neuen Meeren **DELIUS**
Der Wanderer **DELIUS**
"Frölicher Lebensmut" *see Lebensmut*
Rellstab **SCHUBERT**
Die Fröhlichkeit see Prandstetter
SCHUBERT
"Frog, frog, frog, a name in zoology" *see*
Recitativo e aria romantica Dickens
HINDEMITH
"Froh kehrt der Schiffer heim an den Stillen
Strom" *see Die Heimat* Hölderlin
BRITTEN
"Froh summte nach der Süssen Beute" *see*
Die Lerche Lenau **SCHOECK**
Frohe Botschaft see Reinick **WOLF**
"Die frohe neubelebte Flur" *see Morgenlied*
Unknown **SCHUBERT**
Der frohe Wandersmann see Eichendorff
SCHOECK, SCHUMANN
Frohsinn see Castelli **SCHUBERT**
from "Amphion" see Tennyson **IVES**
FROM AN OLD GARDEN, no. 1
MACDOWELL Deland *The pansy*
FROM AN OLD GARDEN, no. 2
MACDOWELL Deland *The myrtle*
FROM AN OLD GARDEN, no. 3
MACDOWELL Deland *The clover*
FROM AN OLD GARDEN, no. 4
MACDOWELL Deland *The yellow daisy*
FROM AN OLD GARDEN, no. 5
MACDOWELL Deland *The blue-bell*
FROM AN OLD GARDEN, no. 6
MACDOWELL Deland *The mignonette*
From childhood see Liliencron **MARTINŮ**
"From childhood's early days" *see The muse*
Pushkin **RACHMANINOFF**
From Chindara's warbling fount see Moore,
T. **WEBER**
From "Cleomenes" see Dryden **ROREM**
"From leafy woods the savage howl" *see Echo*
Pushkin **BRITTEN**
from "Lincoln, the great commoner" see
Markham **IVES**
FROM MARION'S BOOK, no. 1
BLITZSTEIN Cummings *o by the by*
FROM MARION'S BOOK, no. 2
BLITZSTEIN Cummings *when life is*
quite through with
FROM MARION'S BOOK, no. 3
BLITZSTEIN Cummings *what if a much*
of a which of a wind
FROM MARION'S BOOK, no. 4
BLITZSTEIN Cummings *silent unday by*
silently not night

FROM MARION'S BOOK, no. 5
BLITZSTEIN Cummings *until and i*
heard
FROM MARION'S BOOK, no. 6
BLITZSTEIN Cummings *yes is a*
pleasant country
FROM MARION'S BOOK, no. 7
BLITZSTEIN Cummings *open your*
heart
From my tears see Heine *LYRICAL*
INTERMEZZO.
BORODIN *Aus meinen Tränen*
RIMSKĬ-KORSAKOV *Iz sléz moikh*
mnogo, maliutka
from "Night of frost in May" see Meredith
IVES
FROM NOON TO STARRY NIGHT. see
Whitman *A clear midnight*
VAUGHAN WILLIAMS
from "Paracelsus" see Browning, R.
PARACELSUS. **IVES**
"From reeds on the river" *see The water lily*
Heine **RACHMANINOFF**
From "Sneden's Landing Variations" see
O'Hara *SNEDEN'S LANDING*
VARIATIONS. **THOMSON**
"From the brake the nightingale" *see A last*
year's rose Henley **QUILTER**
From the canticle of the sun see Francis of
Assisi **THOMSON**
From the day that I was born see Mickiewicz
CHAĬKOVSKĬ *Ali mat' menia rozhala*
From the Gospel of St. John, XV: 13 see
Bible **RACHMANINOFF**
FROM THE HILLS OF DREAMS. see Sharp,
W. *Thy dark eyes to mine* **GRIFFES**
from the "Incantation" see Byron **IVES**
From "The return" see Castleman, Marion
ROREM
from "The swimmers" see Untermeyer
IVES
From whence cometh song? see Roethke
THE FAR FIELD. **ROREM**
Fromm see Falke *MIT DEM LEBEN.* **BERG,**
REGER, WEBERN
Die fromme Magd see Ringwaldt **WEBER**
"Ein' fromme Magd von gutem Stand" *see*
Die fromme Magd Ringwaldt **WEBER**
"Ein frommer Knecht war Fridolin" *see*
Der Gang nach dem Eisenhammer Schiller
LOEWE
"Ein frommer Landmann in der Kirche sass"
see Die Einladung Knapp, A. **LOEWE**
"Frondeggia il bosco d'uberi verzure" *see*
Egle Rubino **RESPIGHI**
Le front aux vitres . . . see Eluard **AURIC**

Le front comme un drapeau perdu see Éluard
   POULENC
"Der Frost hat mir bereifet des Hauses Dach"
   see Greisengesang Rückert SCHUBERT
"Der Frost hat mir bereifet des Hauses Dach"
   see Vom künftigen Alter Rückert
   STRAUSS
"Der Frost in letzter Nacht" *see Vor Tau und*
   Tag Sergel KILPINEN
Frost, Robert, 1874-1963.
   CARTER
      The dust of snow
      The line gang
      The rose family
   ROREM *Stopping by woods on a snowy*
      evening
The frostbound wood see Blunt HESELTINE
"Früh am Morgen ging die Maid aus der Tür
   hinaus" *see Das Mägdlein und der Spatz*
   Anon. REGER
"Der Früh hauch hat gefächelt" *see Morgentau*
   Anon. WOLF
"Früh, wann die Hähne krähen" *see*
   Das verlassene Mägdelein Mörike
   PFITZNER
      Two settings: Op. 30 no. 2 and one without
      opus number, published 1933.
"Früh, wann die Hähne krähn" *see*
   Das verlassene Mägdlein Mörike WOLF
"Früh wann die Hähne kräh'n" *see*
   Das verlassne Mägdelein Mörike
   SCHUMANN
"Früh, wenn die Hähne krähn" *see In Leid*
   versunken Mörike FRANZ
"Früh, wenn die Hähne kräh'n" *see*
   Das verlassene Mägdlein Mörike LASSEN
"Frühe geht die Schäferinn, führt die
   Lämmchen" *see Die Schäferinn* Poliziano
   ZELTER
Frühe Klage see Osterwald FRANZ
Die frühe Liebe see Hölty SCHUBERT
Die frühen Gräber see Klopstock GLUCK,
   KRENEK, SCHUBERT
Frühgesicht see Keller, G. SCHOECK
Früh-Lied am Meere see Unknown LOEWE
Frühling see Branco LOEWE
Der Frühling see Claudius, M. SCHOECK
FRÜHLING. see Heine
   Es liebt sich so lieblich im Lenze BRAHMS
Frühling see Heine FRANZ
Frühling see Hesse LUENING, SCHOECK
Der Frühling see Hölty ZELTER
Frühling see Huber, B. KILPINEN
Frühling see Iłakowiczówna
   SZYMANOWSKI *Wiosna*
Frühling see Kleinschrod DVOŘÁK *Jaro*

Frühling see Mörike LASSEN
Der Frühling see Rousseau, J. B.
   BRAHMS
Der Frühling see Sturm, C. MOZART
Frühling see Tolstoï RUBINSTEIN
"Der Frühling begrüsset" *see Frühling*
   Branco LOEWE
"Frühling, der die Welt umblaut" *see Frühling*
   Triumphator Meyer SCHOECK
"Der Frühling entblühet" *see Der Jüngling in*
   der Fremde Reissig BEETHOVEN
Frühling im Sommer see Kuh CORNELIUS
"Der Frühling ist erschienen" *see Trauriger*
   Frühling Hafiz SZYMANOWSKI
"Der Frühling ist herangekommen" *see*
   Rätselhaft Unknown SPOHR
"Der Frühling kehret wieder" *see Die Waise*
   Hoffmann von Fallersleben
   SCHUMANN
"Frühling lässt ein blaues Band" *see Frühling*
   Mörike LASSEN
"Frühling lässt sein blaues Band" *see Er ist's!*
   Mörike FRANZ, SCHOECK,
   SCHUMANN, WOLF
Frühling, Liebster see Rückert WOLF
"Der Frühling naht mit Brausen" *see*
   Frühlingslied Klingemann
   MENDELSSOHN-BARTHOLDY
Frühling Triumphator see Meyer
   SCHOECK
Frühling übers Jahr see Goethe LOEWE,
   WOLF
Der Frühling und die Liebe see Hoffmann
   von Fallersleben LASSEN
Frühling und Liebe see Hoffmann von
   Fallersleben FRANZ
Frühlings Ankunft see Anon. FRANZ
Frühlings Ankunft see Hoffmann von
   Fallersleben SCHUMANN
Frühlings Seele see Giesebrecht LOEWE
Frühlingsanfang see Geibel STRAUSS
Frühlingsankunft see Ziegler, K. *HIMMEL*
   UND ERDE. LOEWE
Frühlingsblick see Lenau FRANZ,
   RUBINSTEIN, SCHOECK
Frühlingsbotschaft see Hoffmann von
   Fallersleben SCHUMANN
Frühlingserwachen see Gramberg LOEWE
Frühlingsfahrt see Eichendorff
   SCHUMANN
Frühlingsfeier see Heine FRANZ,
   STRAUSS
Frühlingsfeier see Uhland SCHOECK
FRÜHLINGSGEDICHTE. see Schlegel, F.
   Der Schiffer SCHUBERT
Frühlingsgedränge see Lenau FRANZ,
   LASSEN, STRAUSS

Frühlingsgefühl see Zhukovski
RUBINSTEIN
Frühlingsglaube see Keller, G. **SCHOECK**
Frühlingsglaube see Uhland
**MENDELSSOHN-BARTHOLDY,
SCHUBERT, SPOHR**
Frühlingsglocken see Reinick **SPOHR,
WOLF**
Frühlingsgruss see Hoffmann von
Fallersleben **SCHUMANN**
Frühlingsgruss see Unknown **LASSEN**
Frühlingsgrüsse see Lenau **SCHUMANN,
WOLF**
"Frühlingskinder im bunten Gedränge" *see
Frühlingsgedränge* Lenau **FRANZ,
LASSEN, STRAUSS**
Frühlingsklage see Lebret **FRANZ**
Frühlingsliebe see Hoffmann von
Fallersleben **FRANZ**
Frühlingslied see Braun **SCHUMANN**
Frühlingslied see Geibel **BRAHMS,
LASSEN**
Frühlingslied see Heine **BRUCKNER,
RUBINSTEIN**
Three Rubinstein settings: Op. 32 nos. 1-3.
Frühlingslied see Klingemann
MENDELSSOHN-BARTHOLDY
Two settings: Op. 34 no. 3 and op. 71 no.
2.
Frühlingslied see Lenau **MENDELSSOHN-
BARTHOLDY**
Frühlingslied see Lichtenstein
MENDELSSOHN-BARTHOLDY
Frühlingslied see Pollak, Aaron
SCHUBERT
Frühlingslied see Robert, F.
MENDELSSOHN-BARTHOLDY
Frühlingslied see Unknown **LOEWE,
SCHUBERT**
Frühlingslied see Voss **LOEWE**
Frühlingslust see Heyse **SCHUMANN**
Frühlingslust see Naumann, L. G. **LOEWE**
Frühlingsmorgen see Förstner **REGER**
Frühlingsmorgen see Volkmann **MAHLER**
Frühlingsnacht see Eichendorff **JENSEN,
SCHUMANN**
Ein Frühlingsnacht see Unknown **LASSEN**
Frühlingsregen see Drachmann **GRIEG**
Foraarsregn
Frühlingsregen see Morgenstern **REGER**
Der Frühlingsregen see Thu-Fu **WEBERN**
Frühlingsruhe see Uhland **SCHOECK**
Frühlingssehnsucht see Rellstab
SCHUBERT
"Der Frühlingssonne holdes Lächeln" *see
Wiedersehn* Schlegel **SCHUBERT**

Frühlingstraum see Müller, Wilhelm
SCHUBERT
Ein Frühlingstraum see Träger **JENSEN**
Frühlingstrost see Schenkendorf **BRAHMS**
Frühlingsweihe see Blankenfeldt, Otto
LOEWE
Frühlingswonne see Anon. **FRANZ**
Frühmorgens see Geibel **RUBINSTEIN**
Frühzeitiger Frühling see Goethe **LOEWE,
ZELTER**
Fuchs, Paul
DELIBES *Chrysanthème*
The fuchsia tree see Anon. **QUILTER**
Fühlt meine Seele see Buonarroti **WOLF**
Führ' mich, Kind, nach Bethlehem! see
Anon. **WOLF**
"Führe mich zum Rosenhaine" *see Jünger des
Weins I* Gamper **SCHOECK**
"Führe uns nicht in Versuchung" *see Vater
unser VIII* Cornelius **CORNELIUS**
Fülle der Liebe see Schlegel, F.
SCHUBERT
"Fülle du!" *see Blick vom oberen Belvedere*
Weinheber **STRAUSS**
"Füllest wieder Busch und Tal" *see An den
Mond* Goethe **PFITZNER, SCHUBERT,
ZELTER**
Two Schubert settings: D. 259 and D. 296.
"Füllt mir das Trinkhorn! reicht es herum!"
see Trinklied Bodenstedt **SPOHR**
"Füllt noch einmal die Gläser" *see
Freimauerlied* Claudius, M. **ZELTER**
Die fünf Hühnerchen see Blüthgen **REGER**
Fünf Sinnsprüche Omars des Zeltmachers see
Omar Khayyam **BLACHER**
Five different settings: Op. 3 nos. 1-5.
Der fünfte Mai see Unknown **LOEWE**
Der Fünfundsechziger see Scheffel
GAUDEAMUS. **JENSEN**
FUENTE OVEJUNA. see Vega Carpio
Al val de Fuente Ovejuna **TURINA**
Für Chr. Tönsberg see Bøgh, Johan **GRIEG**
Til Generalkonsul Chr. Tønsberg
Für Einen see Burns **FRANZ, JENSEN**
Für fünfzehn Pfennige see Des Knaben
Wunderhorn **STRAUSS**
Für Musik see Geibel **FRANZ, STRAUSS**
Für Ninon see Hesse **SCHOECK**
Fürst Rostislav see Tolstoï **RUBINSTEIN**
"Fürst, Trossbub, Ritter, Gauner" *see Max und
Dürer* Auersperg **LOEWE**
"Die Fürstin zog zu Walde" *see Der Edelfalk*
Freiligrath **LOEWE**
En fuglevise see Ibsen **GRIEG**
EN FUGLEVISE. see Ibsen
Eine Vogelweise **DELIUS**

COMPOSER Poet *Title* "First Line"

"Fuis, mon âme, fuis!" *see Chanson de clown* Shakespeare **CHAUSSON**

"Fuit tempus, cum plorarem" *see Ad Jesum Christum, Dominum et Salvatorem meum* Böhmer **LOEWE**

La fuite de la lune see Wilde *FLOWERS OF GOLD.* Impressions, no. 2. **GRIFFES**

Full fathom five see Shakespeare *THE TEMPEST.* **DIAMOND, QUILTER**

"Full many souls the vessels held" *see Arion* Pushkin **RACHMANINOFF**

Full moon see De La Mare **BERKELEY**

Fumée see Cocteau **MILHAUD**

Fumée see Moréas **HAHN**

Fumée légère see Thoreau **SAUGUET**

"Fumée légère, ailée" *see Fumée légère* Thoreau **SAUGUET**

Funeral blues see Auden **BRITTEN**

Funeral song see Pushkin **MEDTNER** *Message*

Le Funeste Retour: chanson de marin *see* Anon. **MILHAUD**

Le funtanelle, canzone dell'Abruzzo *see* Unknown **RESPIGHI**

Fuor de la bella gaiba see Anon. **CASELLA**

Furcht see Busse-Palma **BERG**

Furcht der Geliebten see Klopstock *AN CIDLI.* **SCHUBERT**

Furchthäschen see Schellenberg **REGER**

Fussreise see Mörike **WOLF**

Die Fusswaschung see Morgenstern **KILPINEN**

Fuster, Charles, 1866-1929. **MASSENET** *Passionnément*

"Fut-il jamais douceur de coeur pareille" *see Rondeau* Musset **DEBUSSY**

"Fyldt med Blomster blusser AEbletraeets Gren" *see Sommersang* Holstein **NIELSEN**

Fyremål see Vinje **GRIEG**

Der fyrste see Vinje **GRIEG** *Det Første*

G

Gabory, Georges, 1899-
  AURIC
    L'ange a perdu son auréole
    Ma vie est la feuille
    Miroir
    La voix
  SAUGUET
    O jeunes filles
    Puisque Vénus
    Tombé du ciel dans la mansarde
GABRIELE. see Schopenhauer
  Hippolit's Lied **SCHUBERT**
Gadkiĭ utenok" see Andersen **PROKOFIEV**
Der Gärtner see Eichendorff **PFITZNER,
  SCHOECK**
Der Gärtner see Mörike **SCHUMANN,
  WOLF**
GAFIZ. see Shenshin
  V tsarstvo rozy i vina-pridi **RIMSKIĬ-
    KORSAKOV**
GAĭDAMAKI. see Shevchenko
  Gopak **MUSORGSKIĭ**
Gaillard, Roger
  SAUGUET
    Amitié
    Solitude
"A gaily dressed damsel steps forth from her
  bow'r" *see The Odalisque* Yü-hsi
  CARPENTER
Gaily singing see Chamisso **MEDTNER**
  Frisch gesungen
"Der Gaishirt steht am Felsenrand" *see*
  Das Licht im Tale Kind, F. **WEBER**
Galathea see Wedekind **SCHÖNBERG**
"Galères! les proues et les poupes s'avancent"
  see Régates mystérieuses Jacob, M.
  SAUGUET
Galéron de Calone, Bertha, b.1859.
  DANS LA SOMBRE TRISTESSE.
    BOULANGER *Dans l'immense Tristesse*
Galina, Glafina, pseud. *see* Einerling,
  Countess Adolfovna, 1873-1942.
Gallet, Louis, 1835-1898.
  GOUNOD *Chantez, voix bénies*
  IVES *Elégie*
  MASSENET
    À Colombine
    Chanson de Capri
    Elégie
    Les femmes de Magdala
    Nuit d'Espagne
Galli, Eugenie Tugendreich (nee von
  Loos), 1849-1917.
  REGER *Verlorne Liebe*

"Den galne Guten min Hug hev dåra" *see Elsk*
  Garborg **GRIEG**
Le galop see Sully-Prudhomme **DUPARC**
Gam hayom see Anon. **MILHAUD**
Gamle Mor see Vinje **GRIEG**
Den gamle Vise see Heine **GRIEG** *Das alte
  Lied*
Gammal sorg see Österling **KILPINEN**
"Gammal sorg kan länge sjunga" *see Gammal
  sorg* Österling **KILPINEN**
GAMMER GURTON'S NEEDLE (1575). *see*
  Stevenson, W.
  Maltworms **HESELTINE**
Gamper, Gustav, 1873-1948.
  SCHOECK
    Jünger des Weins I
    Jünger des Weins II
Der Gang nach dem Eisenhammer see
  Schiller **LOEWE**
*En gång skall det brinna ett ljus på min grav
  see* Lagerkvist **KILPINEN**
Der Gang zum Liebchen see Anon.
  BRAHMS
Gang zur Liebsten see Anon. **BRAHMS**
Ganivet, Maurice, 1849-1884.
  SCHMITT
    Fils de la Vierge
    Nature morte
    Neige, coeur et lys
Ganymed see Goethe **LOEWE,
  SCHUBERT, WOLF**
"Ganz verloren, ganz versunken" *see
  Huldigung* Kosegarten **SCHUBERT**
"Die ganz' Welt ist in dich verliebt" *see
  Impromptu* Mörike **SCHOECK**
Das Ganze, nicht das Einzelne see Rückert
  HINDEMITH
Ganzo, Robert, 1898-1995.
  SCHMITT
    C'est l'heure
    . . . de pleurs d'égrène
    Les dîners se font en courant
  LANGAGE.
    SCHMITT
"Gar fröhlich tret ich in die Welt" *see
  Sängers Wanderlied* Körner **LOEWE**
Garbed in flowing linen see Heyduk
  DVOŘÁK *Široké rukávy*
Garborg, Arne, 1851-1925.
  HAUGTUSSA.
    GRIEG
      Blåbaer-Li
      Dømd
      Elsk

Garborg, Arne, 1851-1925 *(continued)*
  HAUGTUSSA (continued)
    GRIEG *(continued)*
      I Slåtten
      Killingdans
      Ku-Lok
      Møte
      Sporven
      Det synge
      Til Deg du hei
      Ved Gjaetle-Bekken
      Veslemøy
      Veslemøy lengtar
      Veslemøy undrast
      Veslemøy ved rokken
      Vond Dag
Garcés, Tomás, 1901-
  MOMPOU *Cançó de la Fira*
Garcia Lorca, Federico, 1899-1936.
  POULENC
    Adelina à la promenade
    Chanson de l'oranger sec
    L'enfant muet
"Un garçon de conte de fée" *see Le garçon de Liège* Vilmorin **POULENC**
Le garçon de Liège see Vilmorin **POULENC**
The garden see Wilde *IMPRESSIONS I*: Le jardin. **GRIFFES** *Le jardin*
GARDENER. see Tagore
  Ayez pitié de votre serviteur **MILHAUD**
  Ne gardez pas **MILHAUD**
"The garden's dark and still; 'tis spring" *see The nightingale and the rose* Pushkin **BRITTEN**
Gardez ce teint de jeune fille see Koechlin **KOECHLIN**
"Gardez les fleurs que je vous ai données" *see L'âme des fleurs* Delair **MASSENET**
Gardner, William Henry, 1865-1932.
  MACDOWELL
    For sweet love's sake
    I ask but this
    O lovely rose
    Sweet blue-eyed maid
    Sweetheart tell me
    Thy beaming eyes
The garland see Moore, T.
  MENDELSSOHN-BARTHOLDY
    Der Blumenkranz
The garland see Rossetti, Christina **IRELAND**
"Garmonii stikha bozhestvennye" *see Oktava* Maĭkov **RIMSKIĬ-KORSAKOV**
Garrigue, Jean, 1914-1972.
  ROREM *Where we came*
Les Gars du bâtiment see Desnos **HONEGGER**

Les gars polonais see Unknown **POULENC**
Les gars qui vont à la fête see Fombeure *CHANSONS DE LA GRANDE HUNE.* **POULENC**
Der Garten des Lebens see Kloentrup **ZELTER**
Der Garten des Lebens see Rosemann **LOEWE**
  Rosemann may be a pseudonym of Johann Aegidius Kloentrup, 1755-1830.
"Der Garten des Lebens ist lieblich und schön" *see Der Garten des Lebens* Rosemann **LOEWE**
Le gascon see Mendès **BIZET**
"Un Gascon à mine fière" *see Le château du Bartas* Bédat de Monlaur, Pierre **HONEGGER**
"Gasnut dal'neĭ Al'pukhary" *see Serenada Don-Zhuana* Tolstoĭ **CHAĬKOVSKIĬ**
Gassier, Alfred, 1849-1907.
  MASSENET *Éveil*
Der Gast see Fontane, T. **SCHOECK**
Gastibelza see Hugo **LISZT**
"Gastibelza, der greise, kühne Jäger" *see Gastibelza* Hugo **LISZT**
Gastibelza, l'homme à la carabine see Hugo **LISZT** *Gastibelza*
Das Gastmahl see Goethe **ZELTER**
Gather ye rosebuds see Herrick **GIDEON**
"Gather ye rosebuds while ye may" *see To the virgins, to make much of time* Herrick **RIETI**
Gathering mushrooms see Mei **MUSORGSKIĬ** *Po griby*
"Un gatto soriano" *see Er gatto e er cane* Salustri **CASELLA**
GAUDEAMUS. see Scheffel
  Altassyrisch **JENSEN**
  Ausfahrt **JENSEN**
  Die drei Dörfer **JENSEN**
  Der Fünfundsechziger **JENSEN**
  Die Heimkehr **JENSEN**
  Hildebrandlied **JENSEN**
  Lied fahrender Schüler **JENSEN**
  Die Malbronner Fuge **JENSEN**
  Perkêo **JENSEN**
  Wer reit't mit sieben Knappen **JENSEN**
  Wer wankt zu Fusse **JENSEN**
  Der Willekumm **JENSEN**
Gauthier-Villars, Henry, 1859-1931.
  SCHMITT *Soir sur le lac*
  SÉVERAC *Temps de neige*
Gautier, Théophile, 1811-1872.
  BERLIOZ
    Absence

Au cimetière
L'Île inconnue
La spectre de la rose
Sur les lagunes
Villanelle
BIZET Absence
CHAUSSON
La caravane
La dernière feuille
Les papillons
FAURÉ
Chanson du pêcheur
Les matelots
Seule
Tristesse
GOUNOD
La chanson du pêcheur
Ma belle amie est morte
Où voulez-vous aller?
Primavera
HAHN
Infidélité
Seule
LALO, MASSENET L'Esclave
SAINT-SAËNS Lamento
SAUGUET Le spectre de la rose
LA COMÉDIE DE LA MORT.
DUPARC Lamento
FALLA
Chinoiserie
Les Colombes
Séguidille
LASSEN Chinoiserie
LA COMÉDIE DE LA MORT: Romance.
DUPARC Au pays où se fait la guerre
EMAUX ET CAMÉES.
DEBUSSY Coquetterie posthume
ESPAÑA.
DEBUSSY Séguidille
La gavotte de Puyjoli see Noël, Édouard
MASSENET
Gay, Delphine see
Girardin, Delphine (Gay) de, "Mme.
Émile de Girardin," 1804-1855.
"Gazelle, die so wild und schnell" see
Die wilde Gazelle Byron **LOEWE**
Gde ty, tam mysl' moia letaet see Anon.
RIMSKIĭ-KORSAKOV
Gde ty, zvezdochka? see Grekov
MUSORGSKIĭ
"Gdy zorza zablysnie na niebie" see Kak tolko
wostok Davidov, Dmitri
SZYMANOWSKI
"Gdyby sie tak zmieścić w kwiatku" see
Mieszkanie Iłłakowiczówna
SZYMANOWSKI

"Gdybym ja byla sloneczkiem na niebie" see
Zyczenie Witwicki **CHOPIN**
Gdzie lubi . . . see Witwicki **CHOPIN**
"Gdziekolwiek zwróce krok" see Pielgrzym
Tetmajer **SZYMANOWSKI**
Der Geächtete see Cunningham **JENSEN**
Gebet see Avenarius STIMMEN UND
BILDER. Stimmungen. **WEBERN**
Gebet see Braungart **REGER**
Gebet see Hebbel **PFITZNER, REGER**
Gebet see Krummacher **LOEWE**
Gebet see Kunze, W. **RUBINSTEIN**
Gebet see Lermontov **LISZT,**
MUSORGSKIĭ Molitva; **RUBINSTEIN**
Gebet see Mary **SCHUMANN**
Gebet see Mörike **SCHOECK, WOLF**
Gebet see Voss **ZELTER**
Gebet auf den Wassern see Strachwitz
LASSEN
Gebet der Fischer see Hesse **KILPINEN**
Das Gebet des Herrn und die
Einsetzungsworte see Unknown **LOEWE**
Gebet des Paria see Goethe **LOEWE**
Gebet um die Geliebte see Gubitz **WEBER**
Gebet während der Schlacht see Körner
SCHUBERT, WEBER
Das gebrochene Herz see Löwenstein
RUBINSTEIN
"Gebt mir meinen Becher" see Schwung Hafiz
STRAUSS
Die Gebüsche see Schlegel, F.
ABENDRÖTE. **SCHUBERT**
Geburt Christi see Rilke **HINDEMITH**
Geburt Mariä see Rilke **HINDEMITH**
Ein Gedanke see Schulz **SCHUMANN**
Gedenke mein see Musset **RUBINSTEIN**
Rappelle-toi quand l'aurore craintive
Gedenke mein see Unknown **BEETHOVEN**
Gedenken see Cornelius **CORNELIUS**
Gedenken see Unknown **SCHÖNBERG**
Gedichte see Benn **BLACHER**
GEDICHTE DER KÖNIGIN MARIA
STUART, no. 1
SCHUMANN Mary Abschied von
Frankreich
GEDICHTE DER KÖNIGIN MARIA
STUART, no. 2
SCHUMANN Mary Nach der Geburt
ihres Sohnes
GEDICHTE DER KÖNIGIN MARIA
STUART, no. 3
SCHUMANN Mary An die Königin
Elisabeth
GEDICHTE DER KÖNIGIN MARIA
STUART, no. 4
SCHUMANN Mary Abschied von der
Welt

COMPOSER   Poet   Title   "First Line"

GEDICHTE DER KÖNIGIN MARIA
STUART, no. 5
SCHUMANN Mary *Gebet*
Gedichte von Heine see Heine **GRIFFES** *Mit
schwarzen Segeln*
Geduld see Gilm zu Rosenegg *LETZTE
BLÄTTER.* **STRAUSS**
Der Gefangene see Pushkin **RUBINSTEIN**
Der gefangene Admiral see Strachwitz
LASSEN, LOEWE
Die gefangenen Sänger see Schenkendorf
WEBER
Die gefangenen Sänger see Schlegel
SCHUBERT
Gefilde des Todes see Reichardt, Heinrich
ZELTER
Gefror'ne Thränen see Müller, Wilhelm
SCHUBERT
"Gefror'ne Tropfen fallen" *see Gefror'ne
Thränen* Müller, Wilhelm **SCHUBERT**
Gefunden see Avenarius *STIMMEN UND
BILDER.* Ehe. **WEBERN**
Gefunden see Goethe **MEDTNER,
STRAUSS**
Gegen Abend see Bierbaum **REGER**
Die Gegend am Meer see Voss **ZELTER**
Gegenliebe see Bürger **BEETHOVEN,
PFITZNER**
Die Gegenwart see Diez **ZELTER**
Gegenwart see Goethe **FRANZ, WEBERN**
Gegrüsst seid, Ihr Damen see Drachmann
GRIEG *Vaer hilset, I Damer*
Geh' bei Tagesanbruch auf die Strasse see
Unknown **RUBINSTEIN**
"Geh! gehorche meinen Winken" *see
Cophtisches Lied II* Goethe **WOLF**
Geh, Geliebter see Anon. **WOLF**
"Geh nicht, die Gott für mich erschuf" *see
Lass scharren deiner Rosse* Hug Meyer
PFITZNER
"Geh' schlafen, Tochter, schlafen!" *see
Sommerabend* Schmidt, Hans **BRAHMS**
"Geheiliget werde Dein Name" *see Vater
unser II* Cornelius **CORNELIUS**
Geheimes see Goethe *WESTÖSTLICHER
DIVAN.* **SCHUBERT**
Geheimnis see Candidus **BRAHMS**
Geheimnis see Dehmel **SZYMANOWSKI**
Geheimnis see Evers **REGER**
Geheimnis see Goethe *WILHELM MEISTER.*
Mignon's song: Heiss mich nicht reden.
ZELTER
Geheimnis see Goethe **ZELTER**
NB: Unpublished 1810 setting of text
different than that of the previous song.
Geheimnis see Heyse **JENSEN**

Geheimnis see Ritter **REGER**
Das Geheimnis see Schack **STRAUSS**
Das Geheimnis see Wessenberg
BEETHOVEN
Geheimnis. An Franz Schubert see
Mayrhofer **SCHUBERT**
Geheimnis voll verbarg die Maske see
Lermontov **BALAKIREV**
Iz-pod tainstvennoy kholodnoy polumaski
Das Geheimniss see Schiller *SIE KONNTE
MIR KEIN WÖRTCHEN SAGEN.*
SCHUBERT
Two settings: D. 250 and D. 793.
Die Geheimnisse see Goethe **ZELTER**
Die geheimnisvolle Flöte see Li Po
WEBERN
"Geheimnisvoller Klang" *see Aeolsharfe*
Lingg **REGER**
"Geht ein grauer Mann" *see Regen (?)* Schlaf
BERG
"Geht nun hin und grabt mein Grab" *see
Grablied* Arndt **REGER**
"Geht nun, ihr Blüthen" *see Assad mit dem
Selam* Stieglitz **LOEWE**
"Geht, suchet in der Waldschlucht" *see Der
Geächtete* Cunningham **JENSEN**
"Geĭ! Gop, gop, gop!" *see Poekhal na
polochke* Musorgskiĭ **MUSORGSKIĬ**
Geĭ, po doroge see Anon. **PROKOFIEV**
Geibel, Emanuel, i.e., Franz Emanuel
August, 1815-1884.
BERG *Am Abend*
BRAHMS *Frühlingslied*
BRUCKNER *Im April*
DELIUS *O schneller mein Ross*
FRANZ
  Ave Maria
  Des müden Abendlied
  Für Musik
  Gute Nacht, mein Herz
  Im Herbst
  In meinem Garten die Nelken
  Die Lotosblume
  Nachtlied
  Vöglein, wohin so schnell
  Wasserfahrt
  Wenn sich zwei Herzen scheiden
  Wohl waren es, Tage der Sonne
  Wolle keiner mich fragen
GRIEG *Siehst du das Meer?*
GRIFFES
  Des müden Abendlied
  Mein Herz ist wie die dunkle Nacht
  Nachtlied
  Das sterbende Kind
  Zwei Könige sassen auf Orkadal

COMPOSER Poet *Title* "First Line"

Gélin, Daniel, 1921-
  ROREM
    Marrant
    Prends bien soin de mourir
    Toute une ville
Gellert, Christian Fürchtegott, 1715-
  1769.
  BEETHOVEN
    Bitten
    Busslied
    Die Ehre Gottes aus der Natur
    Gottes Macht und Vorschung
    Die Liebe des Nächsten
    Vom Tode
  CHAĬKOVSKIĬ *Kukushka*
  LOEWE
    Busslied
    Gott ist mein Lied
    Wie gross ist des Allmächt'gen Güte!
  PREIS DES SCHÖPFERS.
    LOEWE *Wenn ich, O Schöpfer, deine*
      Macht
Gellner, František, 1881-1914.
  MARTINŮ *Miners' song*
Gelobt sei Gott! see Unknown **LOEWE**
"Gemäht sind die Felder" *see Kinderliedchen*
  Blüthgen **SCHOECK**
Gemmingen, Eberhard Friedrich,
  Freiherr von, 1726-1791.
  KRENEK *Das Schweigen*
General Schwerin see Häring
  SCHWERIN, MEIN GENERAL, IST TODT,
    SCHWERIN IST TODT! **LOEWE**
General William Booth enters into Heaven see
  Lindsay **IVES**
Der Genesene an die Hoffung see Mörike
  WOLF
Genesung see Schröer **FRANZ**
Gengenbach, Eric de
  SAUGUET *La sirène au coquillage*
Genialisch Treiben see Goethe **WOLF**
Genrebillede see Jacobsen **NIELSEN**
"Gens de la plaine ou de l'âpre montagne" *see*
  Chanson de Zora (La petite Bohémienne)
  Deschamps **ROSSINI**
Les gens distraits see D'Harcourt,
  Antoniette **SAUGUET**
"Gens du midi, gens du midi" *see Aussi bien*
  que les cigales Apollinaire **POULENC**
Gensichen, Otto Franz, 1847-1933.
  REGER *Gruss*
Gensyn see Paludan-Müller **NIELSEN**
Gentle lady . . . see Joyce **SZYMANOWSKI**
Gentle Zephyr see Unknown **BENNETT**
Gentlemen-Menige see Kipling **GRIEG**

Gentlemen-Rankers see Kipling **GRIEG**
  Gentlemen-Menige
Gentlemen-Soldaten see Kipling **GRIEG**
  Gentlemen-Menige
Gently my soul to the towering heavens
  ascended see Tolstoĭ
  RIMSKIĬ-KORSAKOV *Gornimi tikho*
    letela dusha nebesami
Der genügsame Liebhaber see Salus
  SCHÖNBERG
Genügsamkeit see Schober **SCHUBERT**
Der Genuss des Unendlichen see Krenek
  KRENEK
"Geöffnet sind des Winters Riegel" *see*
  Frühlingslied Pollak, Aaron **SCHUBERT**
George, Stefan, 1868-1933.
  DAS BUCH DER HÄNGENDEN GÄRTEN.
  SCHÖNBERG
    Als Neuling trat ich ein in dein Gehege
    Als wir hinter dem beblümten Tore
    Angst und Hoffen wechselnd mich
      beklemmen
    Da meine Lippen reglos sind und
      brennen
    Du lehnest wider eine Silberweide
    Hain in diesen Paradiesen
    Jedem Werke bin ich fürder tot
    Saget mir auf welchem Pfade
    Das schöne Beet betracht ich mir im
      Harren
    Sprich nicht immer
    Streng ist uns das Glück und spröde
    Unterm schutz von dichten
      Blättergründen
    Wenn ich heut nicht deinen Leib
      berühre
    Wenn sich bei heiliger Ruh in tiefen
      Matten
    Wir bevölkerten die abend-düstern
  DAS BUCH DER SAGEN UND SÄNGE:
    Sänge eines fahrenden Spielmanns.
    WEBERN *So ich traurig bin weiss ich*
      nur ein Ding
  DAS JAHR DER SEELE, p. 27.
    SCHÖNBERG *Ich darf nicht dankend*
  DAS JAHR DER SEELE: Nach der Lese.
    WEBERN *Ja Heil und Dank dir die den*
      Segen brachte!
  DAS JAHR DER SEELE: Nachtwachen.
    WEBERN *Erwachen aus dem tiefsten*
      Traumesschosse
  DAS JAHR DER SEELE: Traurige Tänze.
    WEBERN *Ihr tratet zu dem Herde*
  DAS JAHR DER SEELE: Waller im Schnee.
    WEBERN *Noch zwingt mich Treue über*
      dir zu wachen

COMPOSER Poet *Title* "First Line"

DER SIEBENTE RING.
  WEBERN
    An Bachesranft die einzigen Frühen
    Dies ist ein Lied für dich allein
    Im Morgentaun trittst du hervor
    Im Windesweben war meine Frage
    Kahl reckt der Baum
DER SIEBENTE RING: Gezeiten.
  WEBERN *Das lockere Saatgefilde*
DER SIEBENTE RING: Maximin.
  WEBERN
    Kunfttag I
    Trauer I
DER SIEBENTE RING: Traumdunkel.
  WEBERN *Eingang*
Georges Braque see Éluard **POULENC**
Georgian song see Pushkin **BALAKIREV**
  Gruzinskaya pesnya
Die Georgine see Gilm zu Rosenegg
  LETZTE BLÄTTER. **STRAUSS**
Geppert family: father or one of the
  daughters, Therese or Luise
  LOEWE *Engelsstimmen am Krankenbette*
Der Geprüste see Mörike **SCHOECK**
Gérard de Nerval, Gérard Labrunie,
  1808-1855.
  AURIC
    Une allée du Luxembourg
    Avril . . .
    Chanson gothique
    Les cydalises
    Fantaisie
  BERLIOZ *Le roi de Thulé*
Gérard, Rosemonde *see* Rostand,
  Rosemonde Gérard, 1871-
Gerhardt, Paul, 1607-1676.
  ZELTER *Sonett*
Gerheusser, Rosa
  REGER *Der Maien ist gestorben*
Germain-Colin Bucher, 1475-1545.
  JOLIVET *Epître imprécatoire*
Germanensang see Dahn **LASSEN**
"Gern in stillen Melancholien" *see*
  Der verliebte Schäferin Scapine Goethe
  LOEWE
Gerok, Karl, 1815-1890.
  SCHOECK *Kindergottesdienst*
Gersdorff, Julius, 1849-1907.
  REGER *Am Brünnele*
Gerstenberg
  LOEWE
    Abendgebet, nach einer erlittenen
      Kränkung
    Abschied
    Der Fernen
    Gruss an Züllchow

Gute Nacht!
Herzen und Augen
Himmelsblüthen
Der Komet
Die Sterne
Gerstenberg, Friedrich von
  WEBER *Das Mädchen an das erste*
    Schneeglöckchen
Geruhig seines Weges gehn see Unknown
  LOEWE
"Geruld, sagst du" *see Geduld* Gilm zu
  Rosenegg **STRAUSS**
DIE GESÄNGE DER SERBEN. see Kapper
  Mädchenfluch, Nach dem Serbischen
  BRAHMS
Gesänge des Harfners see Goethe
  SCHUBERT *Harfenspieler I*
GESÄNGE DES ORIENTS, no. 1
  STRAUSS Hafiz *Ihre Augen*
GESÄNGE DES ORIENTS, no. 2
  STRAUSS Hafiz *Schwung*
GESÄNGE DES ORIENTS, no. 3
  STRAUSS Anon. *Liebesgeschenk*
GESÄNGE DES ORIENTS, no. 4
  STRAUSS Hafiz *Die Allmächtige*
GESÄNGE DES ORIENTS, no. 5
  STRAUSS Hafiz *Huldigung*
GESÄNGE DES SPÄTEN JAHRES, no. 1
  KRENEK Krenek *Wanderlied im Herbst*
GESÄNGE DES SPÄTEN JAHRES, no. 2
  KRENEK Krenek *Mauern wachsen*
GESÄNGE DES SPÄTEN JAHRES, no. 3
  KRENEK Krenek *Ballade von den*
    Schiffen
GESÄNGE DES SPÄTEN JAHRES, no. 4
  KRENEK Krenek *Ballade vom Fest*
GESÄNGE DES SPÄTEN JAHRES, no. 5
  KRENEK Krenek *Heimatgefühl*
GESÄNGE DES SPÄTEN JAHRES, no. 6
  KRENEK Krenek *Trinklied*
GESÄNGE DES SPÄTEN JAHRES, no. 7
  KRENEK Krenek *Liebeslied*
GESÄNGE DES SPÄTEN JAHRES, no. 8
  KRENEK Krenek *Und Herbstlaub und*
    Regenschauer
GESÄNGE DES SPÄTEN JAHRES, no. 9
  KRENEK Krenek *Vor dem Tod*
    NB: No. 10 is a piano interlude.
GESÄNGE DES SPÄTEN JAHRES, no. 11
  KRENEK Krenek *Der Genuss des*
    Unendlichen
Gesang see Shakespeare **SCHUBERT**
  An Sylvia
Der Gesang see Vogl **LOEWE**
Gesang an die Harmonie see Salis-Seewis
  SCHUBERT

COMPOSER Poet *Title* "First Line"

Gesang der Geister über den Wassern see
Goethe **LOEWE, SCHUBERT**

Gesang der Königin Maria Stuart auf den Tod Franz II see Anon. **LOEWE**

Der Gesang der Nachtigal see Herder **BEETHOVEN**

Gesang der Norna see Scott *THE PIRATE.* **SCHUBERT**

Gesang des Einsiedlers see Grimmelshausen *SIMPLICIUS SIMPLICISSIMUS.* **JENSEN**

Der Gesang des Meeres see Meyer **SCHOECK**

Gesang Margit's see Ibsen *DAS FEST AUF SOLHAUG.* **WOLF**

Gesang und Kuss see Schlegel **ZELTER**

Gesang Weylas see Mörike **WOLF**

Gesang zu zweien in der Nacht see Mörike **SCHOECK**

Gesang zum Jahresfeste der Luisenstiftung see lanke **ZELTER**

Gesanges Erwachen see Kerner **SCHUMANN**

Das Gescheh'ne, nicht bereut's Hafis see Hafiz **SCHOECK**

Geschieden! see Ibsen **GRIEG** *Borte!*

Gesegnet see Droste-Hülshoff **CORNELIUS**

Gesegnet sei das Grün see Heyse **WOLF**

Gesegnet sei, durch den die Welt entstund see Heyse **WOLF**

Geselle, woll'n wir uns in Kutten hüllen see Heyse **WOLF**

Gesellenlied see Reinick **WOLF**

Gesellenreise see Ratschky **MOZART** *Lied zur Gesellenreise*

GESPENSTER SONATE. see Strindberg *Schien mir's, als ich sah die Sonne* **WEBERN**

Geständnis see Vimioso **SCHUMANN**

Geständniss see Devrient, Eduard **MENDELSSOHN-BARTHOLDY**

"Gestern Abend in der stillen Ruh' " *see Waldeinsamkeit* Anon. **REGER**

"Gestern, als ich vom nächtlichen Lager" *see Johann Kepler* Mörike **SCHOECK**

"Gestern fand ich" *see Der Reisebecher* Meyer **SCHOECK**

"Gestern hielt er mich im Arme" *see Erster Verlust* Osterwald **FRANZ**

"Gestern sasz ich wie ich sasz" *see Die Spinnerin* Fitger **PIJPER**

Gestern war ich Atlas see Rückert **STRAUSS**

Gestillte Sehnsucht see Rückert **BRAHMS**

Die Gestirne see Klopstock **SCHUBERT**

Das gestörte Glück see Körner **SCHUBERT**

Gestorben war ich see Uhland **LISZT**

"Gestorben war ich vor Liebeswonne" *see Gestorben war ich* Uhland **LISZT**

Gesungen see Schöpff **SCHUMANN**

Get hep! see Bernstein **BERNSTEIN**

Der getäuschte Verräter see Metastasio **SCHUBERT** *Il traditor deluso*

Getrennte Liebe see Schmidt, Heinrich **SPOHR**

Der getreue Eckart see Goethe **LOEWE, ZELTER**

Geübtes Herz see Keller, G. **SCHÖNBERG**

"Geuss, lieber Mond" *see An den Mond* Hölty **SCHUBERT**

"Geuss nicht so laut" *see An die Nachtigall* Hölty **BRAHMS, SCHUBERT**

GEUSS NICHT SO LAUT. see Hölty *An die Nachtigall* **BRAHMS, SCHUBERT**

Gewalt der Minne see Walther von der Vogelweide **PFITZNER**

GEWEIHTER PLATZ. see Goethe *Geweihter Platz* **MEDTNER**

Geweihter Platz see Goethe *GEWEIHTER PLATZ.* **MEDTNER**

Geweihter Platz see Goethe *ZAHME XENIEN.* **MEDTNER**

Gewitter see Krenek **KRENEK**

Das Gewitter see Lenau **SCHOECK**

Gewitternacht see Osterwald **FRANZ**

Gewohnt, getan see Goethe **ZELTER**

Geyer, Agnes Emerita, b. 1787. **SPOHR** *Das Schiffermädchen*

Ghasel see Adil **SPOHR**

Ghasel see Keller, G. **SCHÖNBERG**

Ghazél see Platen-Hallermünde **WOLF**

"Gi Husly til to Personwer" *see Husvild* Jensen, J. **NIELSEN**

"Già la luna è in mezzo al mare" *see La danza* Pepoli **ROSSINI**

"Giacinti e violete" *see La primavera* Anon. **HAHN**

Giacomo, Salvatore di, 1862-1934. **PIZZETTI**
  Angeleca
  Assunta

"Gib mir deine Hand" *see Erhebung* Dehmel **SCHÖNBERG**

"Gib mir die Fülle der Einsamkeit!" *see Einsamkeit* Mayrhofer **SCHUBERT**

Gibbons, Orlando, 1583-1625. **ROREM** *The silver swan*

Gibout, Henri **MASSENET** *Berceuse*

Gibraltar see Denis **MOZART**

Gibt es wo einen Rasen grün see Hugo *CHANTS DU CRÉPUSCULE.* **LISZT** *S'il est un charmant gazon*

COMPOSER   Poet   *Title*   "First Line"

"Gick du en morgon i vårsols sken" *see*
   Sångarlön Snoilsky **SIBELIUS**
Gide, André Paul Guillaume, 1869-1951.
   LA PORTE ETROITE.
      MILHAUD
         Jérôme
         Jérôme et Alissa
            Three settings: Op. 9 nos. 2, 3, and
            5.
         Journal d'Alissa
         Lettre d'Alissa
         Lettres d'Alissa
GIDEON, MIRIAM, 1906-1996.
   Anon.
      Song from without the world (1929)
         [unpubl.] "Listen when late at night"
   Asturias, Miguel Angel, 1899-1974.
      LOS INDIOS BAJAN DE MIXCO.
         Mixco (1957) [ACA, 1957]
            "The Indians descend from Mixco"
            Text setting in English only; Spanish
            phrases interspersed.
   Bialik, Hayyim Nahman, 1873-1934.
      The nest (1980) [ACA, 1980]
         "Kan latsipor"
      The swing (1980) [ACA, 1980]
         "Nad, nad"
   Bible
      PROVERBS 31.
         Eishet chayil (1982) [ACA, 1982]
            "Eishet chayil mi yimtsa"
      PSALM 127.
         Hinei nachalat adonai baním (1982)
            [ACA, 1982] same
      PSALM 128.
         Y' gia kapecha ki Tocheil (1982)
            [ACA, 1982] same
   Brown, S.
      Southern road (1938) [unpubl.]
   Burns, Robert, 1759-1796.
      Epitaph for a wag in Mauchline (1952)
         [ACA, 1957]
         "Lament him, Mauchline husbands a' "
      Epitaph on the author (1952) [ACA,
         1957] "He who of Rankine sang"
      Epitaph on wee Johnie (1952) [ACA,
         1957] "Whoe'er thou art, O reader"
      Monody on a lady famed for her caprice
         (1952) [ACA, 1957] "How cold is that
         bosom which folly once fired"
   Claudius, Matthias, 1740-1815.
      Abendlied (1937) [ACA, 1962]
   Cummings, Edward Estlin, 1894-1962.
      Sonnet (1938) [unpubl.]
   Eastman, Max, 1883-1969.
      At the aquarium (1938) [unpubl.]

Eichendorff, Joseph Karl Benedikt,
   Freiherr von, 1788-1857.
   Lockung (1937) [ACA, 1962]
Evans, Mrs. Florence (Wilkinson)
   Farewell tablet to Agathocles (1961)
      [ACA, 1962] "Naked & brave thou
      goest"
Goldberg, Leah, 1911-1970.
   Morning star (1980) [ACA, 1980]
      "Ma Osot Haayalot Balalot?"
Hayes, Marvin, ca.1924-
   Bells (1966) [ACA, 1966] "When
      Abraham Lincoln was born"
Hebbel, Christian Friedrich, 1813-
   1863.
   Das Mädchen im Kampf mit sich selbst
      (1929) [unpubl.]
Heine, Heinrich, 1797-1856.
   Im Traum (1938) [unpubl.]
   Leise zieht durch mein Gemüt (1929)
      [ACA, 1962] same
   Vergiftet sind meine Lieder (1937) [ACA,
      1962]
Herrick, Robert, 1591-1674.
   Gather ye rosebuds (1940) [unpubl.]
   To music (1957) [ACA, 1957, 1964]
      "Charm me asleep, and melt me so"
Joyce, James, 1882-1941.
   She weeps over Rahoon (1939) [unpubl.?]
Leconte de Lisle, Charles Marie René,
   1818-1894.
   Les elfes (1930) [unpubl.]
Lenau, Nicolaus, 1802-1850.
   Einsamkeit (1929) [ACA, 1962]
Lenz, Jakob Michael Reinhold, 1751-
   1792.
   Ach du, um die Blumen sich verliebt
      (1937) [ACA, 1962]
Louÿs, Pierre, 1870-1925.
   CHANSONS DE BILITIS.
      Chanson (1929) [unpubl.]
      La pluie au matin (1930) [unpubl.]
Lowell, Amy, 1814-1925.
   Little ivory figures pulled with string
      (1950) [ACA, 1959] "Is it the tinkling
      of mandolins that disturbs you?"
      Voice & guitar.
MacLeish, Archibald, 1892-1982.
   The too-late born (1939) [unpubl.?]
Millay, Edna St. Vincent, 1892-1950.
   FATAL INTERVIEW.
      Gone in good sooth you are (1952)
         [ACA, 1961] same
         Also voice & string trio.
      Moon, that against the lintel of the
         West (1952) [ACA, 1961] same

COMPOSER   Poet   *Title*   "First Line"

GIDEON, MIRIAM, 1906-1996 *(continued)*
Millay, Edna St. Vincent, 1892-1950.
(continued)
Also voice & string trio.
Night is my sister (1952) [ACA, 1961]
same
Also voice & string trio.
Peabody, Josephine Preston, 1874-1922.
The nightingale unheard (1961) [ACA, 1962] "Yes, nightingale thru all the summertime"
Sassoon, Siegfried Lorraine, 1886-1967.
Slumber song (1931) [unpubl.]
Stickney
Be still, the hanging gardens were a dream (1934) [unpubl.]
Unknown
Orion (1934) [unpubl.]
Yalan-Stekelis, Miriam (Wilensky), 1900-
The cat is angry (1980) [ACA, 1980] "Rogez, Rogez"
Gieb' O heil'ge Geisternacht see Kol'tsov
RUBINSTEIN
"Gieb, Schwester, mir die Harf' herab" *see*
Der Liedler Kenner **SCHUBERT**
Giesebrecht, Heinrich Ludwig Theodor
see Giesebrecht, Ludwig, 1792-1873.
Giesebrecht, Ludwig, 1792-1873.
LOEWE
Abendlied
Als Weibesarm in jungen Jahren
Bienenweben
Einsegnungslied
Es steht ein Kelch in der Kapelle
Frühlings Seele
Das heilige Haus in Loretto
Im Schacht der Adern und der Stufen
Der König auf dem goldnen Stuhle
Nun auf dem fremden Boden
Sang des Moses
Sankt Mariens Ritter
Scholastica
Spielt, Mägdlein, unter eurer Weide!
Taubenlied
Unser Herzog hat herrliche Taten vollbracht
Von meines Hauses engen Wänden
Wie früh das enge Pförtchen knarre
Wie wohnst du in des Reiches Städten
SANFT RUHENDE FLUR.
LOEWE *Der Friedhof*
The gift see Tagore **MILHAUD**

Gigerlette see Bierbaum **SCHÖNBERG**
Gil i sroka see Iłłakowiczówna
SZYMANOWSKI
Gilbert, Laurent, 1751-1780.
MASSENET *Stances*
GILES EARLE, HIS BOOKE (1616-1625). *see*
Campion *The lover's maze* **HESELTINE**
Gille, Philippe Emile François, 1831-1901.
BIZET
Pastel
Si vous aimez!
Voyage
DELIBES *Chant de l'almée*
MASSENET *Printemps dernier*
Gillouin, Adrien, 1861-
MASSENET *C'est le printemps*
Gilm zu Rosenegg, Hermann von, 1812-1864.
REGER *Das arme Vögelein*
STRAUSS *Wer hat's gethan?*
IM FRÜHLING.
STRAUSS *Zueignung*
LETZTE BLÄTTER.
LASSEN, PIJPER, STRAUSS
Allerseelen
STRAUSS
Geduld
Die Georgine
Die Nacht
Nichts
Die Verschwiegenen
Die Zeitlose
Gilson, Paul, 1865-1942.
RIVIER
La fable du village
Passage d'une nurse
La sirène de Scheveningue
"Ging Herr Walther hin im Freien" *see*
Die Schwanenjungfrau Vogl **LOEWE**
Ging heut' Morgens übers Feld see Mahler
MAHLER
Ginner, Isaac
SAINT-SAËNS *Night song to preciosa*
Ginzkey, Franz Karl, 1871-1963.
REGER *Von der Liebe*
"Un giorno tutti quanti l'animali" *see*
L'elezzione der presidente Salustri
CASELLA
Giovane bella luce del mio core see Cino da
Pistoia **CASELLA**
Giovanni, Nikki, 1943-
WEISGALL *Knoxville, Tennessee*
Giovannitti, Arturo, 1884-1959.
GRIFFES *Phantoms*

Gippius, Zinaida Nikolaevna, 1869-1945.
   PROKOFIEV *Seroe plat'itse*
Girard, Marguerite
   MASSENET *Eternité*
Girardin, Delphine (Gay) de, "Mme.
   Émile de Girardin," 1804-1855.
   LISZT *Il m'aimait tant!*
Giraud, Albert, 1860-1929.
   WEISGALL *Eine blasse Wäscherin*
Giraud, Henri, 1869-
   AUBERT *Déclaration*
Giraudoux, Jean, 1882-1944.
   SUZANNE ET LA PACIFIQUE.
      HONEGGER
         Adèle
         Cécile
         Irène
         Jeanne
         Rosemonde
A girl's desire see Witwicki **CHOPIN** *Gdzie
   lubi . . .*
The girls of Szeged scorn me see Pósa
   BARTÓK *Még azt vetik szememre*
Girod, André
   DEBUSSY *Fleur des blés*
"Gisant endormi entre les battements de la
   nuit" *see Amour et sommeil* Swinburne
   SAUGUET
La gita in gondola see Pepoli **ROSSINI**
GITANJALI. see Tagore
   A cette heure du départ **CASELLA**
   Dans une salutation suprême **CASELLA**
   The day is no more **CARPENTER**
   I am like a remnant of a cloud of autumn
      CARPENTER
   Light, my light **CARPENTER**
   Mort, ta servante est à ma porte
      CASELLA
   O toi, suprême accomplissement de ma vie
      CASELLA
   *On the day when death will knock at thy
      door* **CARPENTER**
   On the seashore of endless worlds
      CARPENTER
   Poème du "Gitanjali" **MILHAUD**
   The sleep that flits on baby's eyes
      CARPENTER
   When and why **MILHAUD**
   When I bring to you colour'd toys
      CARPENTER
GITANJALI, no. 1
   CARPENTER Tagore *When I bring to
      you colour'd toys*
GITANJALI, no. 2
   CARPENTER Tagore *On the day when
      death will knock at thy door*

GITANJALI, no. 3
   CARPENTER Tagore *The sleep that flits
      on baby's eyes*
GITANJALI, no. 4
   CARPENTER Tagore *I am like a
      remnant of a cloud of autumn*
GITANJALI, no. 5
   CARPENTER Tagore *On the seashore of
      endless worlds*
GITANJALI, no. 6
   CARPENTER Tagore *Light, my light*
Giv mig ej glans see Topelius **SIBELIUS**
Give a hawk a fine cage see Heyduk
   DVOŘÁK *Dejte klec jestřábu*
Give me no splendor see Topelius
   SIBELIUS *Giv mig ej glans*
"Give me the depth of love that springs" *see
   Friendship in misfortune* Anon. **IRELAND**
"Give to me the life I love" *see The vagabond*
   Stevenson, Robert Louis
   VAUGHAN WILLIAMS
Gjenta see Vinje **GRIEG** *Jenta*
Gjertsen, Fredrik
   GRIEG *Morgenbøn paa Skolen*
Glan, Alexandre
   BIZET *Le colibri*
"Glanz des Guten und des Schönen strahlt mir
   dein hohes Bild" *see Liebesrausch* Körner
   SCHUBERT
Glaube see Vinje **GRIEG** *Trudom*
"Glaube, hoffe, liebe!" *see Glaube, Hoffnung
   und Liebe* Kuffner **SCHUBERT**
Glaube, Hoffnung und Liebe see Kuffner
   SCHUBERT
Glaze, Andrew, 1920-
   ROREM *A journey*
Glazki vecny golubye see Heine
   DIE BLAUEN FRÜHLINGSAUGEN.
   CHAïKOVSKIï
Gleich einer versunkenen Melodie see
   Morgenstern **REGER**
"Gleich eines Herzens bangen Fieberträumen"
   see Herbstsorge Osterwald **FRANZ**
Gleich und Gleich see Goethe
   **FRANZ, MEDTNER, SCHOECK,
      WEBERN, WOLF, ZELTER**
Gleich wie der Mond see Osterwald **FRANZ**
"Gleich wie ein Vogel am Fenster vorbei" *see
   Auf dem Krankenbette* Mörike **SCHOECK**
Gleim, Johann Wilhelm Ludwig, 1719-
   1803.
   BEETHOVEN *Selbstgespräch*
   BERG *An Leukon*
   LOEWE *Naturgenuss*

COMPOSER   Poet   *Title*   "First Line"

Gleim, Johann Wilhelm Ludwig, 1719-
1803 *(continued)*
ZELTER
　Das Hüttchen
　Ich alter Pilger
　Lasst mich sterben
　Lied für preussischen Patrioten
　Weg mit allen euren Klagen
　TRIOLETT: Gebt mir Blumen.
　　ZELTER *Triolett*
Gleiman, W
　BARTÓK *Night of desire*
"Gleite hinan die glänzende Bahn!" *see*
　Kahnlied Unknown **LOEWE**
Die Gletscher leuchten im Mondenlicht see
　Bodenstedt **BARTÓK, LASSEN**
Gliding down the river see Farnie **GOUNOD**
Gliding o'er all see Whitman **LUENING,**
　ROREM
Die Glocke des Glücks see Ritter **REGER**
"Ein Glocke läutet" *see Aus zwei Tälern*
　Hesse **KILPINEN**
"Die Glocken läutens das Ostern" *see*
　Osterlied Böttger **GRIEG**
Die Glocken zu Speier see Oër **LOEWE**
Glockenklänge see Unknown **SPOHR**
Das Glockenspiel der Phantasie see Branco
　LOEWE
Glockentöne see Apel, Theodor
　DER ENTFERNTEN. **WAGNER**
Glockentürmers Töchterlein see Rückert
　SCHUMANN
Glöckleins Klage see Spitteler **SCHOECK**
Gloire à Dieu see Anon. **MILHAUD**
"Eine Glokke läutet" *see Aus zwei Tälern*
　Hesse **SCHOECK**
　Glory to God see Teternikov
　RACHMANINOFF
Glory to Thee my God see Ken **GOUNOD**
GLOSES ORPHIQUES. see Van
　Ormelingen
　Antienne **MASSENET**
　Defuncta nascuntur **MASSENET**
　Fleuramye **MASSENET**
Le gloxinia see Chalupt **AURIC**
GLUCK, CHRISTOPH WILLIBALD,
　1714-1787.
　Klopstock, Friedrich Gottlieb, 1724-
　　1803.
　　Die frühen Gräber [Artaria, 1787]
　　　"Willkommen, O silbener Mond"
　　Der Jüngling [Artaria, 1787]
　　　"Schweigend sahe der May die
　　　　bekränzte"
　　Schlachtgesang [Artaria, 1787]
　　　"Wie erscholl der Gang"

Die Sommernacht [Artaria, 1787]
　"Wenn der Schimmer von dem Monde
　　nun herab"
Die Sommernacht (1785) [Voss *Musen-
　Almanach auf das Jahr 1785*, p. 78]
　"Wenn der Schimmer von dem Monde
　　nun herab"
　　Second setting of text.
Der Tod (1783) [**Der musikalische
　Blumenstrauss**, 1792] "O, Anblick der
　Glanznacht, Sternheere"
Vaterlandslied [Artaria, 1787]
　"Ich bin ein deutsches Mädchen"
Wir und Sie [Artaria, 1787]
　"Was that dir, Thor"
Matthisson, Friedrich von, 1761-1831.
　Siegsgesang für Freie [Voss
　　Musenalmanach, 1795]
Unknown
　Die Neigung [Artaria, 1787] "Nein, ich
　　wiederstrebe nicht mehr"
　　　According to A. Einstein, text not
　　　by Klopstock.
Glück see Hesse **KILPINEN**
Glück see Rohrscheidt **REGER**
Glück see Schellenberg **REGER**
Glück, Barbara Elisabeth, 1814-1894.
　FRANZ *Gute Nacht*
"Glück der Engel! wo geblieben?" *see*
　Erinnerung Jacobi **SCHUMANN**
Das Glück der Freundschaft see Unknown
　BEETHOVEN
"Der Glückes Fülle mir verlieh'n" *see Trost*
　Cornelius **CORNELIUS**
Glückes genug see Liliencron **REGER,**
　STRAUSS
Glücklich, Johann Christian, 1839-1920.
　MACDOWELL *Bitte*
　REGER
　　Am Meer!
　　An Zeppelin
Der Glückliche see Wilbrandt **LISZT**
Glückliche Fahrt see Goethe **MARTINŮ,**
　MEDTNER
Der Glücksritter see Eichendorff **WOLF**
DER GLÜHENDE. see Mombert
　Nun ich der Riesen Stärksten **BERG**
　Schlafend trägt man mich **BERG**
Der Glühende see Mombert
　SZYMANOWSKI *Fragment: Der
　　Glühende*
DER GLÜHENDE. see Mombert
　Warm die Lüfte **BERG**
"Glühwürmchen, steck's Laternchen an" *see*
　Der verliebte Maikäfer Reinick **LOEWE**
The gnat's wedding see Anon. **MARTINŮ**

Go forth my song, delay not see Pfleger-
Moravský **DVOŘÁK**
> *Vy vroucí písně pějte!*
>> Two settings: B. 11 no. 1 and B. 123
>> no. 1.
> *Vy vroucí písně spějte*
Go, lovely rose see Waller **CARPENTER,
QUILTER, ROREM**
"Go my songs!" *see Old home day* Ives **IVES**
Go not, happy day see Tennyson **LISZT**
"Go, songs, for ended is our brief, sweet play"
see Envoy Thompson, F. **HINDEMITH**
Go to sleep, Alexander Smallers, Jr. see
Thomson **THOMSON**
Go to sleep, Pare McTaggett Lorentz see
Thomson **THOMSON**
Goal and wicket see Housman
THE SHROPSHIRE LAD. **IRELAND**
"God groet u coninghinne" *see Mariazang*
Unknown **PIJPER**
God morgen! see Bjørnson *FISKERJENTEN.*
GRIEG
"God of the tender young" *see Prayer*
Dévigne **LOEFFLER**
"God, who gave the world its fairness" *see*
Blind Cooper, Eric Thirkell **IRELAND**
Godebska, Mimie
SATIE *Daphénéo*
"Godete, giovani, godete" *see Canzone per*
ballo Anon. **PIZZETTI**
Godnat see Jensen, J. **NIELSEN**
Gods see Whitman **ROREM**
"God's blessing on this house, to God we
sing" *see Easter* Erben **MARTINŮ**
Goeble, H.
BEETHOVEN *Abendlied unterm gestirnten*
> *Himmel*
Göchhausen, Karl Emil Konstantin von,
1778-1855.
SPOHR
> *Immerdar Liebe*
> *Wiegenlied*
"Gönnt mir goldne Tageshelle" *see Sehnsucht*
Lermontov **RUBINSTEIN**
Goering, Gerd Hans, 1900-ca.1932.
KRENEK
> *Die Ballade vom König Lobesam*
> *Erinnerungen*
> *Im Spiegel*
> *Rätelspiel*
> *Räume*
Goethe, Johann Wolfgang von, 1749-
1832.
BARTÓK
> *Du meine Liebe, du mein Herz*
> *Wie herrlich leuchtet*

BEETHOVEN
> *Erlkönig*
> *Ich denke dein*
> *Maigesang*
> *Marmotte*
> *Mit einem gemalten Band*
> *Neue Liebe, neues Leben*
>> Two settings: Op. 75 no. 2 and WoO
>> 127.
> *Wonne der Wehmut*
BERG
> *Erster Verlust*
> *Grenzen der Menschheit*
BRAHMS
> *Die Liebende schreibt*
> *Trost in Tränen*
> *Unüberwindlich*
FRANZ
> *Cupido, loser*
> *Gegenwart*
> *Gleich und Gleich*
> *Im Sommer*
> *Mailied*
> *Rastlose Liebe*
> *Schweizerlied*
> *Wonne der Wehmuth*
GRIEG
> *Ich denke dein*
> *Zur Rosenzeit*
IVES *Ilmenau: over all the treetops*
JENSEN *Schweizerlied*
KRENEK
> *Fragment*
> *Der neue Amadis*
> *Die Zerstörung Magdeburgs*
LASSEN
> *Maienlied*
> *Nähe des Geliebten*
LISZT *Über allen Gipfeln ist Ruh'*
LOEWE
> *Alpin's Klage um Morar*
> *Auf dem See*
> *Ballade vom vertriebenen und*
>> *zurückkehrenden Grafen*
> *Die Braut von Corinth*
> *Dank des Paria*
> *Erlkönig*
> *Die erste Walpurgisnacht*
> *Der Fischer*
> *Freibeuter*
> *Frühling übers Jahr*
> *Frühzeitiger Frühling*
> *Ganymed*
> *Gebet des Paria*
> *Gesang der Geister über den Wassern*
> *Der getreue Eckart*

COMPOSER   Poet   *Title*   "First Line"

Goethe, Johann Wolfgang von, 1749-
1832 *(continued)*
  LOEWE *(continued)*
    Gottes ist der Orient!
    Gutmann und Gutweib
    Hochzeitlied
    Ich denke dein
    Im Vorübergehen
    Kanzonette
    Legende
    Mädchenwünsche
    Mahomet's Gesang
    Mailied
    Der Schatzgräber
    Der Todtentanz
    Trost in Tränen
    Der verliebte Schäferin Scapine
    Die wandelnde Glocke
    Wechsel
    Wirkung in die Ferne
    Der Zauberlehrling
  MACDOWELL
    Idylle
    Midsummer lullaby
  MARTINŮ
    Glückliche Fahrt
    Liebesglück
  MEDTNER
    Auf dem See
    Die Bekehrte
    Einsamkeit
    Erster Verlust
    Gefunden
    Geistergruss
    Gleich und Gleich
    Glückliche Fahrt
    Im Vorübergehen
    Jägers Abendlied
    Mailied
    Nähe des Geliebten
    Selbstbetrug
    Die Spröde
    Das Veilchen
    Vor Gericht
  MENDELSSOHN-BARTHOLDY
    Erster Verlust
    Die Liebende schreibt
    Lied der Freundin
    Suleika
  MOZART *Das Veilchen*
  MUSORGSKĬ *Pesnia Mefistofelia v*
    pogrebke Auerbakha
  PFITZNER
    An den Mond
    Mailied
    Willkommen und Abschied

  RACHMANINOFF *A prayer*
  REGER *Einsamkeit*
  SCHOECK
    Epigramm
    Erster Verlust
    Geistesgruss
    Gleich und Gleich
    Herbstgefühl
    Im Sommer
    Mailied
    Mit einem gemalten Band
    Nachtgesang
    Parabase
    Rastlose Liebe
    Selbstbetrug
    Sorge
    Ungeduld
  SCHÖNBERG *Mailied*
  SCHUBERT
    Am Flusse
      Two settings: D. 160 and D. 766.
    An den Mond
      Two settings: D. 259 and D. 296.
    An die Entfernte
    An Schwager Kronos
    Auf dem See
    Bundeslied
    Erlkönig
    Erster Verlust
    Der Fischer
    Ganymed
    Geistesgruss
    Gesang der Geister über den Wassern
    Der Goldschmiedsgesell
    Grenzen der Menschheit
    Heidenröslein
    Hoffnung
    Jägers Abendlied
      Two settings: D. 215 and D. 368.
    Johanna Sebus
    Die Liebende schreibt
    Liebhaber in allen Gestalten
    Mahomets Gesang
      Two settings: D. 549 and D. 721.
    Meeres Stille
      Two settings: D. 215A and D. 216.
    Der Musensohn
    Nachtgesang
    Nähe des Geliebten
    Prometheus
    Rastlose Liebe
    Der Rattenfänger
    Schäfers Klagelied
    Der Schatzgräber
    Schweizerlied
    Die Spinnerin

Trost in Thränen
Wer kauft Liebesgötter?
Willkommen und Abschied
Wonne der Wehmut
SCHUMANN
Der Fischer
Nachtlied
Die wandelnde Glocke
SPOHR
Nachgefühl
Neue Liebe, neues Leben
Vanitas! Vanitatum vanitas
Zigeunerlied
STRAUSS
Das Bächlein
Der Fischer
Gefunden
Lust und Qual
Sinnspruch
Xenion
VERDI Chi i bei di m'adduce ancora
WEBERN
Gegenwart
Gleich und Gleich
WOLF
Anakreon's Grab
Auf dem See
Beherzigung
Die Bekehrte
Benerzigung
Cophtisches Lied I
Cophtisches Lied II
Dank des Paria
Epiphanias
Erster Verlust
Der Fischer
Frech und Froh I
Frech und Froh II
Frühling übers Jahr
Ganymed
Genialisch Treiben
Gleich und Gleich
Grenzen der Menschheit
Gutmann und Gutweib
Königlich Gebet
Mai
Der neue Amadis
Prometheus
Der Rattenfänger
Ritter Kurt's Brautfahrt
Der Schäfer
Die Spröde
St. Nepomuk's Vorabend
Wanderlied
ZELTER
An den Mond

An die Entfernte
Auch mein Sinn
Aus der Ferne
Ballade
Die Bekehrte
Die Braut von Corinth
Christel
Der Erlkönig
Erster Verlust
Der Fischer
Frühzeitiger Frühling
Das Gastmahl
Geheimnis
Die Geheimnisse
Geistesgruss
Der getreue Eckart
Gewohnt, getan
Gleich und Gleich
Der Goldschmied
Hochzeitlied
Ich wollt' ich wär ein Fisch
Im Fernen
Jägers Abendlied
Der junge Jäger
Der Junggesell und der Muhlbach
Klagegesang: Jrisch
Künstlers Abendlied
Mädchens Held
Mailied
Mignon als Engel verkleidet
Der Misanthrop
Musen und Grazien in der Mark
Der Musensohn
Nachgefühl
Nachtgesang
Nähe des Geliebten
Der neue Amadis
Der neue Amor
Neue Liebe, neues Leben
Rastlose Liebe
Ruhe
Schäfers Klagelied
Sct. Nepomuks Vorabend
Die Spinnerin
Die Spröde
Stirbt der Fuchs, so gilt der Balg
Das Sträusschen
Suleika
Der Totentanz
Trost in Tränen
Um Mitternacht
Vanitas! Vanitatum vanitas!
Versuch in achtzeiligen Strophen
Wer kauft Liebesgötter?
Wiederfinden
Wirkung in die Ferne

COMPOSER Poet *Title* ''First Line''

Goethe, Johann Wolfgang von, 1749-1832 (*continued*)
ZELTER (*continued*)
Wonne der Wehmut
Der Zauberlehrling
BLUMENGRUSS.
   WEBERN, WOLF *Blumengruss*
   ZELTER *Willkommen dem 28. August 1749*
CHINESISCH- DEUTSCHE JAHRES- UND TAGESZEITEN.
   BRAHMS, SCHOECK *Dämmrung senkte sich von oben*
   WEBERN *Nun weiss man erst, was · Rosenknospe sei*
CLAUDINE VON VILLA BELLA.
   BRAHMS *Serenate*
   MEDTNER
   Aus "Claudine von Villa-Bella"
   Der untreue Knabe
EGMONT.
   LISZT *Freudvoll und leidvoll*
   RUBINSTEIN *Clärchens Lied*
   SCHUBERT *Die Liebe*
   ZELTER *Clärchen*
ELFENLIED.
   MARTINŮ, MEDTNER *Elfenliedchen*
EPIMENIDES ERWACHEN.
   ZELTER *In tiefe Sklaverei lag ich gebunden*
ERWIN UND ELMIRE.
   MEDTNER
   Inneres Wühlen ewig zu fühlen
   Sie liebt mich!
   Sieh mich, Heil'ger, wie ich bin
FAUST.
   BEETHOVEN *Aus Goethes Faust*
   JENSEN *Der König in Thule*
   LISZT *Es war ein König in Thule*
   LOEWE
   Lynceus, der Helene
   Lynceus, der Thürmer
   Mädchen, als du kamst ans Licht
   Meine Ruh' ist hin
   Nur Platz, nur Blösse!
   Sei mir heute nichts zuwider!
   Szene aus "Faust"
   Thurmwächter Lynceus
   Wenn der Blüten Frühlingsregen
   MENDELSSOHN-BARTHOLDY
   Gretchen
   SCHUBERT
   Gretchen am Spinnrade
   Gretchen vor der Mater dolorosa
   Der König in Thule
   Szene aus Goethe's "Faust"

   SCHUMANN *Lied Lynceus des Thürmers*
SEIBER
   Epilogue
   Es war ein König in Thule
   Invocation
   Meine Ruh' ist hin
SPOHR *Gretchen*
VERDI
   Deh, pietoso, oh addolorata
   Perduta ho la pace
WAGNER
   Bauern unter der Linde
   Branders Lied
   Gretchen am Spinnrade
   Lied der Soldaten
   Lied des Mephistopheles
     Two settings: Op. 5 no. 4 and op. 5 no. 5.
   Melodram Gretchens
WOLF *Gretchen vor dem Andachtsbild der Mater dolorosa*
ZELTER
   Gretchens Lied aus Faust
   Der König von Tule
   Margarethe
GEWEIHTER PLATZ.
   MEDTNER *Geweihter Platz*
DAS GÖTTLICHE (last verse).
   BEETHOVEN *Der edle Mensch sei hülfreich und gut*
GOTT UND WELT: Howards Ehrengedächtnis.
   WEBERN *Cirrus*
IM WALDE.
   MACDOWELL *In the woods*
INDISCHE LEGENDE.
   LOEWE, SCHOECK, SCHUBERT, ZELTER *Der Gott und die Bajadere*
LILA.
   MEDTNER *So tanzet*
MAILIED.
   ZELTER *Wo geht's Liebchen?*
MEERESSTILLE.
   GRIFFES, MEDTNER *Meeresstille*
MICH ERGREIFT, ICH WEISS NICHT WIE.
   SCHUBERT, ZELTER *Tischlied*
SCHENKENBUCH.
   WOLF *Ob der Koran von Ewigkeit sei?*
SEHNSUCHT.
   BEETHOVEN, SCHUBERT, WOLF, ZELTER *Sehnsucht*
STELLA: Act 4 scene 1.
   KRENEK *Stella's Monologue*
UF'M BERGLI.
   ZELTER *Schweizer Lied*

COMPOSER Poet *Title* "First Line"

WANDERERS NACHTLIED.
  ZELTER *Die wackelnde Glocke*
WANDRERS NACHTLIED I.
  LISZT *Der du von dem Himmel bist*
  LOEWE, MEDTNER, SCHUBERT,
    ZELTER *Wandrers Nachtlied*
  PFITZNER, WOLF
    Wanderers Nachtlied
WANDRERS NACHTLIED II.
  LOEWE, MEDTNER, SCHUBERT
    Wandrers Nachtlied
WESTÖSTLICHER DIVAN.
  MENDELSSOHN-BARTHOLDY
    Suleika
  RUBINSTEIN *Freisinn*
  SCHOECK
    Diese Gondel vergleich ich
    Eine einzige Nacht an deinem Herzen!
    Haben sie von deinen Fehlen
    Höre den Rat
    Nachklang
    Seh' ich den Pilgrim
    Selige Sehnsucht
    Suleika
    Suleika und Hatem
    Unmut
    Warum leckst du dein Mäulchen
    Wie ich so ehrlich war
    Wie sie klingeln, die Pfaffen!
  SCHÖNBERG *Deinem Blick mich zu*
    bequemen
  SCHUBERT
    Geheimes
    Suleika
    Versunken
  SCHUMANN
    Freisinn
    Liebeslied
    Lied der Suleika
    Lieder aus dem Schenkenbuch . . .
      Two settings: Op. 25 no. 5 and op.
        25 no. 6.
    Talismane
  STRAUSS
    Durch allen Schall und Klang
    Hab' ich euch denn je geraten
    Spruch
    Wanderers Gemütsruhe
    Wer wird von der Welt verlangen
    Zugemessne Rhythmen
  ZELTER
    In tausend Formen
    Selige Sehnsucht
WESTÖSTLICHER DIVAN: Buch des
Sängers.
  WOLF *Phanomen*

WESTÖSTLICHER DIVAN: Buch Suleika.
  WOLF
    Als ich auf dem Euphrat schiffte
    Dies zu deuten bin erbötig!
    Hätt' ich irgend wohl Bedenken
    Hoch beglückt in deiner Liebe
    Komm, Liebchen, komm!
    Locken, haltet mich gefangen
    Nicht Gelegenheit macht Diebe
    Nimmer will ich dich verlieren!
    Wenn ich dein gedenke
    Wie sollt' ich heiter bleiben
WESTÖSTLICHER DIVAN: Schenkenbuch.
  STRAUSS, WOLF *Erschaffen und*
    Beleben
  WOLF
    Sie haben wegen der Trunkenheit
    So land man nüchtern ist
    Trunken müssen wir alle sein!
    Was in der Schenke waren heute
WILHELM MEISTER.
  LISZT *Wer nie sein Brot mit Tränen ass*
  LOEWE *Der Sänger*
  SCHUBERT
    An Mignon
    Harfenspieler
    Harfenspieler I
    Harfenspieler III
    Lied der Mignon
    Mignon
      Two settings: D. 469 and D. 727.
    Der Sänger
  SCHUMANN
    Ballade des Harfners
    Singet nicht in Trauertönen
    So lasst mich scheinen, bis ich werde
    Wer nie sein Brod mit Thränen ass
    Wer sich der Einsamkeit ergiebt
  SPOHR *An Mignon*
  WOLF
    Harfenspieler I
    Harfenspieler III
    Mignon III
    Philine
    Der Sänger
    Spottlied
  ZELTER
    An Mignon
    Einsamkeit
    Klage
    Der Sänger
    Wer nie sein Brot mit Tränen ass
WILHELM MEISTER. Harfenspieler.
  MEDTNER *An die Türen will ich*
    schleichen
  MUSORGSKII *Lied des Harfenspielers*

COMPOSER Poet *Title* ''First Line''

Goethe, Johann Wolfgang von, 1749-1832 *(continued)*

WILHELM MEISTER. Harfenspieler.
   (continued)
   SCHUBERT *Harfenspieler II*
   SCHUMANN *An die Thüren will ich
      schleichen*
   WOLF *Harfenspieler II*
   ZELTER *An die Türen will ich
      schleichen*
WILHELM MEISTER. Mignon's song:
   Heiss mich nicht reden.
   CHAĭKOVSKIĭ *Ne sprashivaĭ*
   SCHUBERT
      Lied der Mignon
      Mignon
   SCHUMANN *Heiss' mich nicht reden*
   WOLF *Mignon I*
   ZELTER *Geheimnis*
WILHELM MEISTER. Mignon's song:
   Kennst du das Land?
   BEETHOVEN, BERG *Mignon*
   CHAĭKOVSKIĭ *Pesnya Min'ony*
   DUPARC *Romance de Mignon*
   GOUNOD, JENSEN *Mignon*
   LISZT *Mignons Lied*
   SCHUBERT *Mignon*
   SCHUMANN *Kennst du das Land?*
   SCHUMANN *Mignon*
   SPOHR *Mignon's Lied*
   WOLF *Mignon IV*
   ZELTER *Kennst du das Land?*
WILHELM MEISTER. Mignon's song: Nur
   wer die Sehnsucht kennt.
   BEETHOVEN *Sehnsucht*
   CHAĭKOVSKIĭ *Niet", tol'ko tot", kto
      znal"*
   LOEWE *Sehnsucht*
   MEDTNER *Mignon*
   SCHUBERT *Lied der Mignon*
      Three settings: D. 359, D. 481, and D.
      877 no. 4.
   SCHUBERT *Mignon und der Harfner*
   SCHUBERT *Sehnsucht*
   SCHUMANN *Nur wer die Sehnsucht
      kennt*
   WOLF *Mignon II*
   ZELTER *Nur wer die Sehnsucht kennt*
   ZELTER *Sehnsucht*
ZAHME XENIEN.
   MEDTNER
      Geweihter Platz
      Praeludium
Die Götter Griechenlands see Schiller *DIE
   GÖTTER GRIECHENLANDS*: 12th stanza.
   SCHUBERT

DIE GÖTTER GRIECHENLANDS: 12th
   stanza. *see* Schiller
   Die Götter Griechenlands **SCHUBERT**
Göttermahl see Meyer **SCHOECK**
"Göttin der Nacht" *see An die Nacht* Shelley
   JENSEN
Die Göttin im Putzzimmer see Rückert
   LOEWE
DAS GÖTTLICHE (last verse). *see* Goethe
   Der edle Mensch sei hülfreich und gut
      BEETHOVEN
"Goï! gol, gol, go laka!" *see Gopak*
   Shevchenko **MUSORGSKIĭ**
Going to Heaven! see Dickinson **COPLAND**
Going to sleep see Musorgskiĭ
   MUSORGSKIĭ *Na son griadushiĭ*
Gold, Alfred, b. 1874.
   SCHÖNBERG *In hellen Träumen hab ich
      Dich oft geschaut*
Gold überwiegt die Liebe see Anon.
   BRAHMS
"The gold-armoured ghost from the Roman
   road" *see The youth with the red-gold hair*
   Sitwell **ROREM**
Goldberg, Leah, 1911-1970.
   GIDEON *Morning star*
The golden cloud had slept see Lermontov
   RIMSKIĭ-KORSAKOV
   Nochevala tuchka zolotaĭa
A golden cloud was gently drowsing see
   Lermontov **RIMSKIĭ-KORSAKOV**
   Nochevala tuchka zolotaĭa
"Golden lacht und glüht der Morgen" *see*
   Der goldene Morgen Unknown **WOLF**
THE GOLDEN PEACOCK, no. 1
   WEISGALL Anon. *Undzer Rebenyu*
THE GOLDEN PEACOCK, no. 2
   WEISGALL Anon. *Der Rebe Elimeylekh*
THE GOLDEN PEACOCK, no. 3
   WEISGALL Anon. *Baleboste Zisinke*
THE GOLDEN PEACOCK, no. 4
   WEISGALL Anon. *Mayn harts veynt in
      mir*
THE GOLDEN PEACOCK, no. 5
   WEISGALL Anon. *Lomir zikh bafrayen*
THE GOLDEN PEACOCK, no. 6
   WEISGALL Anon. *Schlof mayn kind,
      schlof keseyder zingen*
THE GOLDEN PEACOCK, no. 7
   WEISGALL Anon. *Di goldene pave*
Golden shadows have descended see
   Shenshin **RIMSKIĭ-KORSAKOV**
   Tikho vecher dogoraet
Golden slumbers kiss your eyes see Anon.
   CASELLA *Rêves d'or pour ton sommeil*

"Golden slumbers kiss your eyes" *see Lullaby*
  Dekker **HESELTINE**
"Golden thronend, ewige Aphrodite" *see*
  An Aphrodite Sappho **LOEWE**
The golden willow tree see Anon.
  COPLAND
"Die goldene Mittagssonne durch zitternde
  Wipfel dringt" *see Goldenes Lied* Löns
  KILPINEN
Der goldene Morgen see Unknown **WOLF**
"Die goldene Wage des Lebens" *see Lied der*
  Renate Zwehl, Hans Fritz von
  KILPINEN
Die goldenen Pantoffeln see Szymanowska,
  Zafia **SZYMANOWSKI** *Zlote trzewiczki*
Goldenes Lied see Löns **KILPINEN**
"Goldne Abendsonne" *see Die Abendsonne*
  Urner **LOEWE**
"Der goldne Morgen kommt herauf mit Glut"
  see Süsse Ruh' Laubsch, Frieda
  REGER
Goldoni, Carlo, 1707-1793.
  IL FILOSOFO DI CAMPAGNA.
    SCHUBERT *La pastorella*
Der Goldschmied see Goethe **ZELTER**
"Ein Goldschmied in der Bude stand" *see*
  Goldschmieds Töchterlein Uhland
  LOEWE
Goldschmieds Töchterlein see Uhland
  LOEWE
Der Goldschmiedsgesell see Goethe
  SCHUBERT
Goldtammer, Frau
  LOEWE *Brautkranzlied*
Golenishchev-Kutuzov, Arseniĭ
  Arkad'yevich, graf, 1848-1913.
  BALAKIREV *Nad ozerom*
  MUSORGSKIĭ
    Elegiia
    Kolybel'naia
    Menia ty v tolpe ne uznala
    Nad rekoĭ
    Okon'en prazdnyĭ, shumnyĭ den'
    Polkovodets
    Serenada
    Skuchaĭ
    Trepak
    V chetyrekh stenakh
    Zebytyĭ
  RACHMANINOFF
    Before the icon
    Beloved, let us fly
    How long, my friend
  SOMMERNACHT.
    MUSORGSKIĭ *Videnie*

Golenistchev-Koutousov, Count Arseni
  see
  Golenishchev-Kutuzov, Arseniĭ
    Arkad'yevich, graf, 1848-1913.
Le golfe de Baya see Lamartine
  SAINT-SAËNS
Golodnogo, M *see* Golodny, Mikhail
Golodny, Mikhail
  PROKOFIEV *Partizan Zhelezniak*
Golos" ptits" see Bal'mont **PROKOFIEV**
Golovinsky, A
  BALAKIREV *Ti plenitel'noy negi polna*
Gol'ts-Miller, Ivan Ivanovich, 1842-1871.
  MUSORGSKIĭ *Otverzhennaia*
Goltz, Emily von der, d. 1893.
  LOEWE *Spirito santo*
Golub' see Bal'mont **STRAVINSKIĭ**
  The dove
Gombossy, K
  BARTÓK
    In the valley
    In vivid dreams
    My love
    Summer
La gomme coule see Jammes **MILHAUD**
  Two settings: Op. 50 no. 1 and op. 50 no.
  2.
Gondelfahrer see Mayrhofer **SCHUBERT**
Gondelfahrt see Geibel **SPOHR**
"Gondolier du Rialto" *see Barcarolle*
  Monnier, M. **FAURÉ**
Gone are my desires see Pushkin
  MEDTNER *Lost hopes*
Gone in good sooth you are see Millay
  FATAL INTERVIEW. **GIDEON**
Gonets see Heine **RIMSKIĭ-KORSAKOV**
Góngora y Argote, Luis de, 1561-1627.
  SONETO A CÓRDOBA.
    FALLA *Soneto a Córdoba*
Gontant Biron *see* Biron, Armand de
  Gontaut, baron de
Good ale see Anon. **HESELTINE**
A good boy see Stevenson, Robert Louis *A*
  CHILD'S GARDEN OF VERSES. **HAHN**
A good child see Stevenson, Robert Louis
  A CHILD'S GARDEN OF VERSES.
  QUILTER
Good Ellen see Carpenter, Rue
  CARPENTER
Good morning see Akhmatova
  PROKOFIEV *Zdravstvuĭ!*
Good Night! see Moore, T. **RUBINSTEIN**
Good night see Shelley **GOUNOD**
Good night, good night see Anon. **DVOŘÁK**
  Dobrú noc, má milá
"Good night! good night! and is it so?" *see*
  Good Night! Moore, T. **RUBINSTEIN**

COMPOSER Poet *Title* ''First Line''

"Good of the Chaplain to enter Lone Bay" *see*
  Billy in the Darbies Melville **DIAMOND**
Goodbye see Housman *A SHROPSHIRE*
  LAD: V. **VAUGHAN WILLIAMS**
"Goodbye in fear, goodbye in sorrow" *see*
  Death-parting Rossetti, Christina
  IRELAND
Goodbye to penny fate see Norse **ROREM**
Goodbye to the Highlands see Burns
  SCHUMANN *Hochländers Abschied*
Goodman, Paul, 1911-1972.
  ROREM
    Absalom
    All men are mad some way
    Bawling blues
    Boy with a baseball glove
    The boy with the ax
    Clouds
    Epitaph for Janet
    For Janet
    For Susan
    Hallowed be the ordainer
    Jail-bait blues
    Lord, have not by custom
    The lordly Hudson
    Man-like, my God
    The midnight sun
    Near closing time
    Noblesse obligé, my Lord
    Of God, angels . . .
    Rain in spring
    Rest well . . .
    Sally's smile
    Such beauty as hurts to behold
    The tulip tree
    What sparks and wiry cries
Goodnight see Shelley **LUENING**
"Goodnight! ah no; the hour is ill" *see*
  Goodnight Shelley **LUENING**
Gopak see Shevchenko *GAïDAMAKI.*
  MUSORGSKIï
"Gordes, que ferons-nous?" *see Sonnet*
  Magny **ROREM**
GORDON UND MONTROSE ODER DER
  KAMPFDER GEFÜHLE. see Reinbeck
  Ballade **WEBER**
Gordon von Brakley see Cunningham
  JENSEN
Gorgheggi e solfeggi see No author
  ROSSINI
Gorianskogo, V
  PROKOFIEV *Pod krysheï*
Gornimi tikho letela dusha nebesami see
  Tolstoï
  CHAïKOVSKIï, MUSORGSKIï,
  RIMSKIï-KORSAKOV

Gornyĭ golos see Heine **MEDTNER**
  Bergstimme
Gorodetski, Sergey Mitrofanovich, 1884-
  1967.
  STRAVINSKIï
    A song of the dew
    Spring
Goryansky, Valentine *see* Gorianskogo,
  V
"Gospodi pomiluĭ papu i mamu" *see Na son*
  griadushiĭ' Musorgskiĭ
  MUSORGSKIï
Gosse, Chevalier
  MILHAUD *L'arbre exotique*
Les Gosses dans les ruines see Unknown
  SÉVERAC
"Gossip and tennis and clash and clatter" *see*
  Bollspelet vid Trianon Fröding **SIBELIUS**
"Gott, deine Güte reicht so weit" *see Bitten*
  Gellert **BEETHOVEN**
Gott grüss dich, Marie! see Pfau
  SCHÖNBERG
Gott hiess die Sonne glühen see Bodenstedt
  RUBINSTEIN
Gott im Frühlinge see Uz **SCHUBERT**
Gott ist mein Lied see Gellert **LOEWE**
"Gott ist mein Lied" *see Gottes Macht und*
  Vorschung Gellert **BEETHOVEN**
Gott, O Gott, wo ist, wo ist mein
  Auserwählter? see Unknown
  RUBINSTEIN
Der Gott und die Bajadere see Goethe
  INDISCHE LEGENDE.
  LOEWE, SCHOECK, SCHUBERT,
  ZELTER
GOTT UND WELT: Howards
  Ehrengedächtnis. *see* Goethe
  Cirrus **WEBERN**
"Gott, wie sind meine Sünden so schwer" *see*
  Busslied Unknown **LOEFFLER**
Gotter, Friedrich Wilhelm, 1746-1797.
  LOEWE *An die Geliebte*
  SCHUBERT *Pflicht und Liebe*
  ZELTER *Unser süsster Beruf*
"Gottes Atem hin und wieder" *see Magie der*
  Farben Hesse **SCHOECK**
Gottes ist der Orient! see Goethe **LOEWE**
"Gottes ist der Orient!" *see Talismane*
  Goethe **SCHUMANN**
Gottes Macht und Vorschung see Gellert
  BEETHOVEN
Gottes Segen see Eichendorff **REGER,**
  SCHOECK
Gottesbote see Lutze **LOEWE**
Die Gottesmauer see Rückert **LOEWE**

Gottschall, Rudolf von, 1823-1909.
FRANZ
Die letzte Rose
Marie
IVES, JENSEN *Marie*
Goudelin, Pierre *see* Goudouli, Pierre,
1580-1649.
Goudouli, Pierre, 1580-1649.
SÉVERAC *Cant per Nadal*
"La gouénouille améouicaine Me regarde par
dessus" *see La Grenouille américaine*
Fargue **SATIE**
**GOUNOD, CHARLES FRANÇOIS, 1818-
1893.**
Alexander, Cecil Francis (Humphreys),
1818-1895.
There is a green hill far away (1871)
[Novello; G. Schirmer] same
Anon.
L'Ave Marie de l'enfant (1872-73?)
[Lemoine]
Bethléem [Lebeau]
First version, chorus & orchestra; 2nd,
voice & keyboard.
Chant d'automne (1855) [Brandus, 1855;
Choudens, 1867]
"Oh! viens, la fleur déjà fanée"
Chidiock Tichborne (1872-73) [Lemoine]
Crépuscule (1865) [Choudens, 1866]
"Quand sur la colline"
James Harding's **Gounod** cites Bertin
as author of text.
La distribution des prix (1852-58)
[Lebeau; Choudens, 1878]
"C'est aujourd'hui que l'on couronne"
First version for 3-part chorus.
My daddy is a cankered carl [London:
1877]
Old Scots song.
Prière à la Vierge (1868) [Lebeau;
Choudens, 1878]
"Au pied de sontrône d'amour"
Repentir [**Revue de Paris,** 15 Dec. 1894;
Choudens, 1895]
"Ah! ne repousse pas"
Roy's wife of Aldivalloch (1873)
[Lemoine]
Le temps qui fuit [Lebeau; Choudens,
1878] same
Welcome to Skye [London: 1873]
Old Jacobite song.
Augier, Emile, 1820-1889.
À une bourse (1865) [Choudens] "De
doigts mignons oeuvre mignonne"
À une jeune fille (1865) [Choudens]
"Pauvre enfant qui voulez combattre la
nature"

Boire à l'ombre (1868) [Choudens]
"Je n'ai pas soif, vieillard, merci!"
La chanson du pâtre (ca.1850)
[Choudens] "Broutez le thym, broutez
mes chèvres"
Envoi de fleurs (1865-68) [Choudens]
"Si l'on veut savoir qui m'envoie"
LE DÉPART.
Départ (1868) [Choudens] "Je veux
oublier, oublier"
Baëlen, Mme.
*Hommage à Madame La Comtesse
Herminie de Léautaud* (1865-68)
[Lebeau aîné, 1869]
*Prière pour l'Empereur et la famille
impériale* (1869) [Lebeau]
Baïf, Jean Antoine de, 1532-1589.
O ma belle rebelle (1855) [Brandus;
Choudens, 1867] same
Baker, Sir Henry Williams, bart., 1821-
1877.
The King of love my shepherd (1872)
[Philips and Page]
Banville, Théodore Faullain de, 1823-
1891.
L'âme de la morte (1860) [Imp. de
Magnier, 1860]
L'âme d'un ange (1860) [Choudens,
1867] "Ils se dissent, ma colombe"
Barbier, Jules, 1825-1901.
À la Madone [Choudens] "Blanche
madone, notre patronne"
À toi mon coeur (1876) [Choudens]
"La perle est aux ondes"
Aimons-nous (1874) [Choudens]
"Au fleuve le ruisseau se mêle"
Au printemps [Choudens] "Le printemps
chasse les hivers"
Bienheureux le coeur sincère (1872)
[Lemoine] same
For soprano & contralto.
Boléro (1871) [Chappell, 1871;
Choudens]
"Ah! que je plains ta flamme"
Chanson printanière [Choudens, 1895]
"Doux printemps, remplis mon âme"
Barbier noted as "adapter" on music.
Chantez noël [Choudens] "Montez à
Dieu, chants d'allé gresse!"
Also a vocal duo.
Clos ta paupière (1873) [Lemoine] same
Hymne à la nuit [Choudens]
"Viens, lorsque dans l'azur"
Invocation à Vesta [Lemoine]
"A Vesta, portez vos offrandes"
Medjé (1865) [Choudens, 1867]
"O Medjé, qui d'un sourire"

GOUNOD, CHARLES FRANÇOIS, 1818-1893 *(continued)*

Barbier, Jules, 1825-1901 *(continued)*

Mon amour a mon coeur (1875) [Lemoine] same

Parlez pour moi [Choudens]

Prends garde (1871?) [Choudens] "C'est une fille belle à voir!"

Prière d'Abraham (1872-73) [Lemoine] "Donc Abraham, debout près du tombeau"

Rêverie (1878) [Choudens] "Sur le flot des rêves"

Sur la montagne (1874) [Choudens] "Sur cette croix jadis immonde"

Viens, les gazons sont verts (1875) [Lemoine] "Si tu dors, jeune fille"

Barbier, Marie Anne, d.1742.

Réponse de Medjé (1882) [Choudens] "Tu m'aimes!"

Barbier, Pierre

Le départ du mousse (1878) [Choudens] "Tu vas, cruel navire, m'emporter là-bas!"

Vincenette [Lemoine] "Le soleil vient de paraître"

Béranger, Pierre Jean de, 1780-1857.

Les champs [Choudens, 1867] "Rose, partons voici l'aurore"

Mon habit (1855) [Heugel; Choudens, 1867] "Sois-moi fidèle, Ô pauvre habit que j'aime!"

LE JUIF ERRANT: Chrétien, au voyageur souffrant.

Le juif errant (1860) [Choudens, 1861] "Chrétien au voyageur souffrant"

Bertin, Louise, 1805-1877.

Si la mort est le but (1865-66) [Choudens, 1866] same

Bible

Entreat me not to leave thee (1872-73) [Lemoine]

Text from the song of Ruth.

My beloved spake (1873) [Goddard; Lemoine]

Accompaniment for 'cello & piano.

Bigorie, L.

Les vacances [Lebeau; Choudens, 1878] "Vivent les vacances!"

Also for 2 equal voices.

Bourguignat, Paul

Les lilas blancs (1876) [Lemoine] "Dans les sentiers de mai remplis de parfums" Noske identifies poet as Bourguignat; music cites Chabaleyret.

Boyer, Charles

Quand l'enfant prie (1885) [Lemoine] "Ah! vous l'aurez, plus tard"

Boyer, Georges, 1850-1931.

Elle sait! (1882) [Lemoine] "Lorsque Ninon courait dans la forêt prochaine"

Notre Dame de France (1888) [**Le Figaro,** 15 Aug. 1888; Hartmann; Heugel] "Ô vous que Dieu bénit entre toutes les femmes"

Byron, George Gordon Byron, 6th baron, 1778-1824.

Maid of Athens (1872) [Goddard, 1872] "Fleur d'Athènes je te quitte"

Campbell

Woe's me! woe's me! [Chappell, 1871] No additional information about poet located.

Chambrun, Marie Jeanne (Godard-Desmarest), comtesse de, 1827-1891.

Passiflora (1888) [Lemoine] "Voici, sur mon déclin"

Chauvinière, Edmond de

La jeune fille et la fauvette (1860) [Lebeau aîné; Choudens, 1878] "Ma gentille fauvette"

Sérénade [Lebeau; Choudens, 1878] "Enfants au doux visage Venez charmernos yeux"

Choudens, Paul de, 1850-1925.

Le banc de pierre [Choudens] "Sous les grands peupliers"

Collin, Heinrich Joseph von, 1772-1811.

Le souvenir (1871) [Choudens] "Qu'es-tu donc"

Je te rends grâce, Ô Dieu (1892) [Lebeau] same

Coppée, François Édouard Joachim, 1842-1908.

Chanson d'Avril (1872) [Lemoine] "Mignonne, voici l'Avril!"

Mélancolie (1879-80) [**Gil-Blas** (journal); Choudens, 1881] "Odsédé par ces mots le veuvage et l'automne"

Dallet, Claude-Charles, 1829-1878.

L'anniversaire des martyrs (1870) [Choudens] "O Dieu, de tes soldats la cauronne et la gloire!"

Delpit, Albert, 1849-1893.

Chanter et souffrir [Choudens] "Chante! me dit l'oiseau jaseur"

Je ne puis espérer (1870) [Choudens] "Ce n'est pas même la souffrance"

Dennery, Adolphe Philippe, 1811-1899.
   Les adieux à la maison [Lemoine, 1885]
      "Avant de m'exiler pour jamais de ce lieu"
      Text by Dennery and Jules Brésil, ca.1818-1899.
Déroulède, Paul, 1846-1914.
   Vive la France (1877) [Lemoine]
      "Vive la France! O mon pays"'
Dubufe, Guillaume
   À Cécile [Lemoine]
      "Je vous aime, Ô ma fiancée!"
Dulong de Rosnay, R. P.
   Cantique pour la première communion (1872) [Lemoine] "Mon bien aimé"
Dumas, Alexandre, the younger, 1824-1895.
   Compliment (1876) [Lemoine]
      "Quand un regard que rien ne voile"
   La Pâquerette (1871) [Choudens]
      "Pâquerette gentille, sur qui brille"
   Si vous n'ouvrez vôtre fenêtre (1871-72) [Lemoine] "J'ai vu des fleurs qui dans les plaines"
Farnie, Henry Brougham, d.1889.
   Gliding down the river [Pitt and Hatzfeld]
Ferrière, S.
   Au matin [unpubl.]
Frère Eucher
   L'eucharistie [Lemoine]
Gallet, Louis, 1835-1898.
   Chantez, voix bénies (1870) [Choudens]
      "C'est l'heure sainte où la voix des archanges"
Gautier, Théophile, 1811-1872.
   La chanson du pêcheur (1841) [Choudens, 1895]
      "Ma belle amie est morte"
         Lemoine published same text to another melody as "Ma belle amie est morte"; see below.
   Ma belle amie est morte (1872) [Lemoine] same
      New melody to the text of "Chanson du pêcheur."
   Où voulez-vous aller? [J. Meissonnier]
      "Dites, la jeune belle"
   Primavera (1852-59) [Choudens, 1867]
      "Tandis qu'à leurs oeuvres perverses"
Goethe, Johann Wolfgang von, 1749-1832.
   WILHELM MEISTER. Mignon's song: Kennst du das Land?

   Mignon (1871) [Choudens]
      "Connais-tu le pays"
      Text adapted by Louis Gallet.
Gounod, Charles François, 1818-1893.
   À la nuit (1891) [Lemoine]
   L'absent (1876) [Lemoine] "O silence des nuits dont la voix seule est douce"
   Canzone di ringraziamento per un prussiano avendo . . . [unpubl.]
      Holograph at Bibliothèque du Conservatoire, Paris.
   Les cloches [Lemoine]
      "Tintez, tintez, cloches de deuil"
      First version for chorus & piano.
   Loin du pays (1873) [Goddard, 1873]
      "Vallons de ma montagne"
   Le pays bienheureux (1871-72) [Lemoine] "Tu me parles toujours d'un pays radieux"
   Que ta volonté soit faite [Lemoine]
      "Mon Dieu, Seigneur et Père"
   Soir d'automne [Henri Tellier, 1896]
      "Petit ruisseau qui cours à travers la prairie"
Gozlan, Léon, 1806-1866.
   Donne-moi cette fleur (1865-68) [Choudens] same
Henry, Maurice
   La paix de Dieu [Alphonse Leduc]
Hood, Thomas, 1799-1845.
   There is dew my tone love (1871) [Chappell, 1871]
Houghton, Richard Monckton Milnes, 1st baron, 1809-1885.
   Ilala (1873) [Marston and Goddard, 1873]
      Also voice & orchestra.
Hugo, Victor Marie, comte, 1802-1885.
   Aubade (1855) [Brandus, 1855; Choudens, 1867]
      "L'aube nait et ta porte est close"
   Sérénade (1855-57) [Lebeau aîné, 1857; Choudens, 1867]
      "Quand tu chantes bercée"
Ken, Thomas, Bishop of Bath and Wells, 1637-1711.
   Glory to Thee my God (1872) [Philips and Page]
Kingsley, Charles, 1819-1875.
   Oh! that we two are maying (1871) [Duff & Stewart] same
      Harmonium and viola ad lib.
La Fontaine, Jean de, 1621-1695.
   Les deux pigeons (1883) [Lemoine]
      "Amants, heureux amants, voulez-vous voyager?"

GOUNOD, CHARLES FRANÇOIS, 1818-1893 *(continued)*

La Fontaine, Jean de, 1621-1695
(continued)
> *Tout l'univers obéit à l'amour* (1893)
> [Lemoine] same
> *PHILÉMON ET BAUCIS.*
> > *Ni l'or ni la grandeur* [Choudens, 1867] same

Lamartine, Alphonse Marie Louis de Prat de, 1790-1869.
> *Au rossignol* [Choudens, 1867]
> > "Quand ta voix céleste prélude"
> *Premier prélude de Bach* (1852) [Mayaud, 1852; Choudens, 1867]
> > "Ave Maria, Toi qui fus mère sur cette terre"
> *Le soir* (1840-42) [Choudens, 1867]
> > "Le soir ramène le silence"
> *Solitude* (1865) [Choudens, 1867]
> > "Je sais sur la colline"
> *Le vallon* (1840-42) [Choudens, 1861, 1867] "Mon coeur lassé de tout"
> *LA PENSÉE DES MORTS.*
> > *Seul* [Choudens, 1867]
> > > "Voilà les feuilles sans sève qui tombent sur le gazon"

Legouvé, Ernest, 1807-1903.
> *Tombez mes ailes* (1865) [Choudens]
> > "Petite fourmi sérieuse"

Ligny, Charles
> *La fleur du foyer* (1871-72) [Lemoine]
> > "Fleur de nos champs sur la montagne aride souffrait!"
> > Text after Ed. Maitland.
> *Prière du soir* (1871-72) [Lemoine]
> > "A toi qui sais combien je l'aime"

Longfellow, Henry Wadsworth, 1807-1882.
> *The arrow and the song* [London, 1885]
> *Beware* (1871) [Novello]
> *If thou art sleeping maiden, awake* (1872-73) [Lemoine; Chappell]
> *It is not always May* (1871) [Chappell]
> *The sea hath its pearls* (1871) [Duff & Stewart] same
> > Accompaniment for harmonium and violin, ad lib.

Maitland, Edward, 1824-1897.
> *Oh, happy home* (1871-72) [Rudall & Carte, 1872]
> > Also voice & orchestra.

Manuel, Eugène, 1823-1901.
> *Prière du soir* (1873) [Choudens]
> > "Je veux prier: l'heure est propice"

Metastasio, Pietro Antonio Domenico Buonaventura, 1698-1782.
> *Quanti Mai* (1871-72) [Novello]
> > "Se a ciascun l'interno affanno"

Millevoye, Charles Hubert, 1782-1816.
> *La fauvette* (1871-72) [Lemoine, 1872]
> > "Dans les bois l'amoureux Myrtil"

Montgomery, James
> *For ever with the Lord* (1872) [Philips and Page]
> > Author of text may be James Montgomery, 1771-1854.

Musset, Alfred de, 1810-1857.
> *Le lever* (1855) [Brandus; Choudens, 1867] "Assez dormir ma belle"
> *Venise* (1842) [Brandus, 1855; Choudens, 1867] "Dans Venise la rouge"

Nadaud, Gustave, 1820-1893.
> *Pauvre Braga* (1882) [Delanchy]

Palgrave, Francis Turner, 1824-1897.
> *Queen of love* (1871) [Novello, 1871]

Passerat, Jean, 1534-1602.
> *Le premier jour de Mai* (1855) [Brandus; Choudens, 1867]
> > "Laissons le lit et le sommeil"

Pavesi, Corrado Marchese
> *Perchè piangi?* (1871-72) [Novello, 1872] "Mi parve, un giorno"

Peyre, L. de
> *Ce que je suis sans toi* [Choudens]
> > "Ce qu'est le lierre sans l'ormeau"

Porte, A.
> *Jésus de Nazareth* (1856) [Lebeau aîné; Choudens, 1867] "Né dans une crèche"

Pradère-Niquet, Onésime
> *À une soeur* [Choudens]
> > "Si le bonheur à sourire t'invite"
> *Invocation* (1872-73) [Choudens]
> > "Avant de quitter ces lieux"
> *Marguerite* [Choudens]
> > "Si le bonheur à sourire t'invite"

Quételart, A.
> *L'ange gardien* (1854-55) [Lebeau aîné; Choudens]
> > "Près de l'enfant Dieu fait descendre"
> > First version for 4-part chorus.
> *Le nid* [Lebeau; Choudens, 1878]
> > "Autour du vieux chêne qui penche"

Rameau, Jean Philippe, 1683-1764.
> *L'aveu* [Heugel, 1894]
> > "Elle était jeune, pure et douce"

Richepin, Jean, 1849-1926.
> *La chanson de la glu* (1883) [Lemoine]
> > "Y avait un' foix un pauv' gas"

Ronsard, Pierre de, 1524-1585.
> *Heureux sera le jour* (1871-72) [Lemoine] "Douce maîtresse, touche"

Rousseil, R.
Voix d'Alsace-Lorraine (1885) [Lemoine]
Roy, Camille
Le temps des roses (1885) [Lemoine]
"Chantons, voici le temps des roses!"
Sappho, 625? B.C.-570 B.C.
À une jeune grecque (1860) [Choudens, 1862]
"De la belle Timar c'est ici le tombeau"
Saunders, E.
Passed away [London: 1872]
Scribe, Augustin Eugène, 1791-1861.
Le jour des prix [Lebeau]
Sédillot, Abbé Félix
Ce qu'il faut à mon âme (1872) [Lemoine]
Ségalas, Anaïs (Ménard), 1814-1895.
Chant des sauveteurs Bretons (1882) [Lemoine]
"Amis, c'est Dieu qui nous envoie"
Ségur, Anatole Henri Philippe, Marquis de, 1823-1902.
Absence (1870) [Choudens]
"De mon coeur une partie"
Cantique (1868) [Lemoine]
La ciel a visité la terre (1868-69) [Choudens] same
Voice & unison chorus with keyboard.
Le nom de Marie [Choudens]
"Esprits d'amour et d'harmonie"
Notre Dame des petits enfants [Choudens]
"Ô Vierge Sante Virge mère"
Shelley, Percy Bysshe, 1792-1822.
The fountain mingles with the river (1871) [Chappel, 1871]
Good night (1871) [Chappell, 1871]
Skelton, Philipp, 1707-1787.
To God, ye choir above (1872-73) [Goddard]
Spenner, M.
Bon jour, bon soir [Lebeau, 1861; Choudens, 1878]
"Voici le soleil qui se lève"
First version for 3-part chorus.
Patte de velours [Lebeau; Choudens, 1878] "Près de son nid jeune fauvette"
First version for 3-part chorus.
Un rêve [Lebeau; Choudens, 1878]
"Un soir que j'etais endormie"
First version for chorus.
Le rosier blanc [Lebeau; Choudens, 1878] "Dans le jardin de grand'mère"
First version for 3-part chorus.

Sully-Prudhomme, René François Armand, 1839-1907.
Prière (1876) [Lemoine] "Ah! si vous saviez comme on pleure"
Tennyson, Alfred Tennyson, 1st baron, 1809-1892.
Ring out, wild bells [*Songs from the published writings of . . . Tennyson,* edited by W.G.Cusius (London: C. Kegan Paul, 1880), 333] same
Tourneux, Eugène
Chanson de printemps (1860) [J. Meissonnier fils; Choudens, 1867]
"Viens enfant, la terre s'éveille"
Turpin, Charles
L'arithmétique [Lebeau, 1855; Choudens, 1878]
"L'art de compter avec exactitude"
2nd version for 2 voices.
Turpin, Henri
Blessures (1885) [Lemoine]
"Je cheminais, seul et rèveur . . . "
Unknown
À la brise (1875) [Lemoine]
"Aura gentil che mormori"
Text translated by Jules Barbier.
Jésus à la crêche (1878) [Lebeau; Choudens, 1878] same
Ma fille, souviens-toi (1876) [Lemoine]
"L'hiver enveloppait la terre de son ombre"
Venez, douces compagnes [unpubl.]
Ms. in the Bibliothèque du Conservatoire, Paris.
Voguons sur les flots [Lemoine, 1884; Choudens]
"Le soir sous l'abri de ses voiles"
When in the early morning [London: 1876]
Veuillot, Louis François, 1813-1883.
Dernières volontés (1883) [Lemoine]
"Placez à mon côté ma plume"
Weatherly, Frederick Edward, 1848-1929.
The holy vision (1886) [Novello]
The worker (1873) [Goddard] "L'orage mugis sait dans une nuit profonde"
Also voice & orchestra.
Wither, George, 1588-1667.
Sweet baby, sleep! [Novello, 1871]
Text from Sir Roundell Palmers *Book of Praise.*
Zaffira, Giuseppe
Biondina bella [Duff & Stewart, 1872; Lemoine, 1873] same
French text by Jules Barbier.

GOUNOD, CHARLES FRANÇOIS, 1818-1893 *(continued)*
Zaffira, Giuseppe *(continued)*
  Da qualche tempo [Duff & Stewart, 1872; Lemoine, 1873] same
    French text by Jules Barbier.
  E le campane hanno suonato [Duff & Stewart, 1872; Lemoine, 1873] same
    French text by Jules Barbier.
  E stati al quanto [Duff & Stewart, 1872; Lemoine, 1873] same
    French text by Jules Barbier.
  Ell' è malata! [Duff & Stewart, 1872; Lemoine, 1873] same
    French text by Jules Barbier.
  L'ho compagnata [Duff & Stewart, 1872; Lemoine, 1873] same
    French text by Jules Barbier.
  Ho messo nuove [Duff & Stewart, 1872; Lemoine, 1873] same
    French text by Jules Barbier.
  Ier fù mandata [Duff & Stewart, 1872; Lemoine, 1873] same
    French text by Jules Barbier.
  Ier l'ho scontrata [Duff & Stewart, 1872; Lemoine, 1873] same
    French text by Jules Barbier.
  Le labbra ella compone [Duff & Stewart, 1872; Lemoine, 1873] same
    French text by Jules Barbier.
  Oh! dille tu! (1871-72) [Goddard]
  Se come io son poeta [Duff & Stewart, 1872; Lemoine, 1873] same
    French text by Jules Barbier.
  Siam' iti l'altro giorno [Duff & Stewart, 1872; Lemoine, 1873] same
    French text by Jules Barbier.
Gounod, Charles François, 1818-1893.
  GOUNOD
    À la nuit
    L'absent
    Canzone di ringraziamento per un prussiano avendo . . .
    Les cloches
    Loin du pays
    Le pays bienheureux
    Que ta volonté soit faite
    Soir d'automne
Gourmont, Rémy de, 1858-1915.
  COPLAND *Simone*
"Govorit sultansha kanareĭke" *see Kanareyka*
  Mei **CHAĬKOVSKIĬ**
Gozlan, Léon, 1806-1866.
  GOUNOD *Donne-moi cette fleur*
DAS GRAB. see Berlepsch
  Lied am Grabe **LOEWE**

Ein Grab see Peitl **WOLF**
Das Grab see Salis-Seewis **SCHOECK, SCHUBERT**
  Three Schubert settings: D. 330, D. 377, and D. 569.
Das Grab der Liebe see Unknown **FRANZ**
Das Grab des Hafis see Hafiz **SZYMANOWSKI** *Grób Hafiza*
"Das Grab ist tief und stille" *see Das Grab* Salis-Seewis **SCHOECK, SCHUBERT**
  Three Schubert settings: D. 330, D. 377, and D. 569.
Das Grab und die Rose see Hugo **LISZT**
  La tombe et la rose
Das Grab zu Ephesus see Binder **LOEWE**
Grabbe, Christian Dietrich, 1801-1836.
  BERG *Ich liebe dich!*
"Grabe, Spaten, grabe!" *see Todtengräberlied* Hölty **SCHUBERT**
Grablied see Arndt **REGER**
Grablied see Kenner **SCHUBERT**
Grablied auf einen Soldaten see Schubart **SCHUBERT**
Grablied für die Mutter see Unknown **SCHUBERT**
Die Grabrose see Auersperg *EIN FRIEDHOFKRANZ.* **LOEWE**
Grabschrift see Jacobowski **BERG**
Grabstein see Zwehl, Hans Fritz von **KILPINEN**
La grâce exilée see Apollinaire *CALLIGRAMMES.* **POULENC**
Graf, Arturo, 1848-1913.
  RESPIGHI *Povero core*
"Graf Eberhard im Bart" *see Graf Eberhards Weissdorn* Uhland **LOEWE**
Graf Eberhards Weissdorn see Uhland **LOEWE**
Graf Eberstein see Uhland **LOEWE**
Der Graf von Habsburg see Schiller **LOEWE, ZELTER**
Der Graf von Rom see No author **STRAUSS**
Graf-Bartholomew, M
  PFITZNER *Mir bist du tot*
Grain, Madeleine
  MASSENET
    Dieu créa le désert
    Feux follets d'amour
Gramberg, Gerhard Anton Hermann, 1772-1816.
  LOEWE *Frühlingserwachen*
Gramont, T. de
  MARTINŮ *Le poulet*
"Gran Canaria, Gran Canaria se ha dormido" *see Folias Canarias* Anon. **RODRIGO**

"Grand bal dans la forêt ce soir" *see Escarpin*
    Radiguet **AURIC**
Grand bruit de cloches see Zaffira
    GOUNOD *E le campane hanno suonato*
"Le grand chinois de Lancastre" *see Cécile*
    Giraudoux **HONEGGER**
Le grand étang see Tranchant, Jean
    HONEGGER
"Un grand sommeil noir" *see Sagesse*
    Verlaine **STRAVINSKIĬ**
Un grand sommeil noir see Verlaine
    HONEGGER, RAVEL, VARÈSE
"Le grand Turc apprend ce qu'il cuit" *see*
    La martiale Chalupt **MILHAUD**
La grande rivière qui va see Éluard
    POULENC
Grandma see Feeney **CHANLER**
"Grandma is old" *see Grandma* Feeney
    CHANLER
La Grand'Mère de la Révolution see Chalupt
    MILHAUD
Grandmother and grandson see Pleshcheyev
    CHAĬKOVSKIĬ *Babushka i vnuchek*
Grandmougin, Charles-Jean, 1850-1930.
    FAURÉ
        Adieu
        Rencontre
        Toujours
"Les grands bois s'éveillaient" *see Sonnet*
    Pradel, Georges **MASSENET**
Les Grands Vents venus d'outre-mer see
    Régnier **RAVEL**
Granny & grandson see Pleshcheyev
    CHAĬKOVSKIĬ *Babushka i vnuchek*
Grantchester see Brooke **IVES**
Grasinda see Annunzio *LA CHIMERA.*
    MALIPIERO
Grasselette et maigrelette see Ronsard
    SAINT-SAËNS
"Grasses dewpearl'd so tearfully" *see To her*
    Bugayev **RACHMANINOFF**
Grassmann, Newton von, 1809-1877.
    LOEWE *Das "Dolce far niente"*
"Grausame Frühlingssonne" *see Zitronenfalter*
    im April Mörike **WOLF**
Graves, John Woodcock, 1795-1886.
    THOMSON *John Peel*
Graves, Robert, 1895-1985.
    BARBER
        Despite and still
        In the wilderness
    BERKELEY *Counting the beats*
    A LAST POEM.
        BARBER *A last song*

Gravollet, Paul
    DEBUSSY *Dans le jardin*
    MASSENET *Ma petite mère a pleuré*
    LES FRISSONS.
        RAVEL *Manteau de fleurs*
    LES FRISSONS, no. 9.
        INDY *Mirage*
Gravskrift över ett litet barn see Blomberg
    KILPINEN
Gray-eyed king see Akhmatova
    PROKOFIEV *Sieroglazyĭ korol'*
Grazie, Marie Eugenie delle, 1864-
    1931.
    BERG *Was zucken die braunen Geigen*
Great things see Hardy **IRELAND**
The greatest man see Collins, Anne **IVES**
Grechanke see Pushkin **RIMSKIĬ-
    KORSAKOV**
Greek song see Maĭkov
    NOVOGRECHESKIYE PESNI.
    CHAĬKOVSKIĬ
        Novogrecheskiye pesni
Green see Verlaine *AQUARELLES.*
    DEBUSSY, FAURÉ
GREEN. see Verlaine
    Offrande **HAHN**
Green, Adolph, 1915-2002. *see* Comden,
    Betty, 1919-
Green, Julien, 1900-1998.
    ROREM
        He thinks upon his death
        He walks beneath the stars
        Hearing music at his mother's funeral
A green lowland of pianos see
    Harasymowicz **BARBER**
The green river see Douglas **CARPENTER**
Greene, Robert, ca.1558-1592.
    BRITTEN *Sephestia's lullaby*
Greeting see Akhmatova **PROKOFIEV**
    Zdravstvuĭ!
Greeting see Nietzsche **MEDTNER** *Gruss*
Greeting see Shenshin **MEDTNER**
Gregh, Fernand, 1873-1960.
    KOECHLIN *Menuet*
GREGOR AUF DEM STEIN, no. 1
    LOEWE Kugler *Herolde ritten von Ort zu*
    Ort
GREGOR AUF DEM STEIN, no. 2
    LOEWE Kugler *Im Schloss, da brennen*
    der Kerzen viel
GREGOR AUF DEM STEIN, no. 3
    LOEWE Kugler *Der junge König und sein*
    Gemahl
GREGOR AUF DEM STEIN, no. 4
    LOEWE Kugler *Ein Klippeneiland liegt*
    im Meer

COMPOSER   Poet   *Title*   "First Line"

GREGOR AUF DEM STEIN, no. 5
  LOEWE Kugler *Wie bräutlich glänzt das
    heilige Rom*
Greif, Martin, pseud. *see* Frey, Friedrich
  Hermann, 1830-1911.
"Greift zum Becher und lasst das Schelten!"
  see Trinklied Leuthold **SCHOECK**
Der greise Kopf see Müller, Wilhelm
  SCHUBERT
Greisengesang see Rückert *VOM
  KÜNFTIGEN ALTER.* **SCHUBERT**
Grekov, Nikolay, 1810-1866.
  CHAÏKOVSKIÏ
    *Ne dolgo nam gulyat
    Pogodi!*
  MUSORGSKIÏ *Gde ty, zvezdochka?*
  RACHMANINOFF *Again you leapt, my
    heart
    STANSÏ.*
    CHAÏKOVSKIÏ *Smotri, von oblako*
La grenade entr'ouverte see Unknown
  SCHMITT
"Grenade grenadine" *see Grenadine* Hugnet
  THOMSON
Grenadine see Hugnet **THOMSON**
Grendel, Frédéric, supposed author.
  SAUGUET *La marchande d'anémondes*
Grenier, Édouard, 1819-1901.
  DELIBES *Épithalame*
La Grenouille américaine see Fargue
  LUDIONS. **SATIE**
"La grenouille du jeu de tonneau" *see
  La statue de bronze* Fargue **SATIE**
La grenouillère see Apollinaire *IL Y A.*
  POULENC
Grenzen der Menschheit see Goethe **BERG,
  SCHUBERT, WOLF**
Gretchen see Goethe *FAUST.*
  **MENDELSSOHN-BARTHOLDY,
  SPOHR**
Gretchen am Spinnrade see Goethe *FAUST.*
  SCHUBERT, WAGNER
Gretchen im Zwinger see Goethe
  SCHUBERT *Gretchen vor der Mater
    dolorosa*
"Gretchen ligger i Kiste" *see Moderen synger*
  Krag **GRIEG**
*Gretchen vor dem Andachtsbild der Mater
  dolorosa see* Goethe *FAUST.* **WOLF**
Gretchen vor der Mater dolorosa see Goethe
  FAUST. **SCHUBERT**
Gretchens Bitte see Goethe **SCHUBERT**
  Gretchen vor der Mater dolorosa
Gretchens Lied aus Faust see Goethe
  FAUST. **ZELTER**
Gretel see Busse **PFITZNER**

Gretels Warnung see Halem **BEETHOVEN**
Grief disperses and gives way see Tolstoĭ
  MUSORGSKIÏ
    Rassevaetsia, rasstupaetsia
Grief does not crash like God's thunder see
  Tolstoĭ **MUSORGSKIÏ**
    Ne bozhiim gromom gore udarilo
GRIEG, EDVARD, 1843-1907.
  Andersen, Hans Christian, 1805-1875.
    En Digters sidste Sang, op. 18 no. 3
      [GA, v. 14, p. 76]
      "Løft mig kun bort, du staerke Død"
    Du fatter ei Bølgernes evige Gang, op. 5
      no. 2 [GA, v. 14, p. 31] same
    Hun er saa hvid, op. 18 no. 2 [GA, v. 14,
      p. 75] same
    Hytten, op. 18 no. 7 [GA, v. 14, p. 91]
      "Hvor Bølgen høit mod Kysten slaar"
    Jeg elsker Dig! op. 5 no. 3 [GA, v. 14,
      p. 34]
      "Min Tankes Tanke ene du er vorden"
    Kjaerlighed, op. 15 no. 2 [GA, v. 14,
      p. 66]
      "Se, Solen blusser saa elskovsrød"
    Langelandsk Folkemelodi, op. 15 no. 3
      [GA, v. 14, p. 68] "Hun har mig
      glemt"
    Min lille Fugl (1865) [GA, v. 15, p. 175]
      same
    Min Tanke er et maegtigt Fjeld, op. 5
      no. 4 [GA, v. 14, p. 36] same
    Poesien [GA, v. 14, p. 84] "Der er et
      herligt Land"
    Rosenknoppen, op. 18 no. 8 [GA, v. 14,
      p. 93] "Rosenknop saa fast og rund"
    Soldaten (1865) [GA, v. 15, p. 171]
      "Med daempede Hvirvler Trommerne
      gaa"
    Taaren (1865) [GA, v. 15, p. 182]
      "Mit Hjerte er en Himmel graa"
    To brune Øjne, op. 5 no. 1 [GA, v. 14,
      p. 29] "To brune Øjne jeg nylig saa"
    Vandring i Skoven, op. 18 no. 1 [GA,
      v. 14, p. 73]
      "Min søde Brud, min unge Viv"
  Benzon, Carl Otto Valdemar, 1856-
  1927.
    Der gynger en Båd på Bølge, op. 69
      no. 1 (1900) [GA, v. 15, p. 109] same
    Digtervise, op. 70 no. 5 [GA, v. 15,
      p. 151] "Der er jo de, som er Ho'de
      kun"
    Drømme, op. 69 no. 5 [GA, v. 15, p.
      131] "Mit Alt var du blevet"
    Eros, op. 70 no. 1 [GA, v. 15, p. 136]
      "Hør mig, I kølige Hjaerter i Nord"

Jeg lever et Liv i Laengsel, op. 70 no. 2
[GA, v. 15, p. 140]
"Jeg havde betalt, hvad jeg skyldte"
Snegl, Snegl! op. 69 no. 4 [GA, v. 15,
p. 124] same
Til min Dreng, op. 69 no. 2 [GA, v. 15,
p. 115] "Min kaere lille Gentleman"
To a devil [GA, v. 15, p. 266] "I tell you,
if an angel"
GA has English and German texts
only.
Ved Moders Grav, op. 69 no. 3 [GA,
v. 15, p. 121] "Sov nu sødt, du lille
Mor"
ANNA BRYDE.
Lys Nat, op. 70 no. 3 [GA, v. 15,
p. 147] "Var det ej nylig, Solen
sank"
Se dig for, når du vaelger din Vej, op.
70 no. 4 GA, v. 15, p. 149] same
Bjørnson, Bjornstjerne, 1832-1910.
Den blonde Pige (1867) [GA, v. 15,
p. 188] "Jeg elsker dig, du blonde
Pige"
Den blonde Pige II [GA, v. 15, p. 212]
"Jeg elsker dig, du blonde Pige"
Dulgt Kjaerlighed, op. 39 no. 2 [GA,
v. 14, p. 200]
"Han tvaer over Baenkene hang"
Fra Monte Pincio, op. 39 no. 1 [GA,
v. 14, p. 193]
"Aftenen kommer, Solen står rød"
Also voice & orchestra.
Den hvide, røde Rose (1873) [GA, v. 15,
p. 210] same
Jeg elsket (1896) [GA, v. 15, p. 263]
same
Only item from projected oratorio
Fred (Peace), never completed.
Lok, op. 61 no. 3 [GA, v. 15, p. 54]
"Kom, bukken til gutten"
Serenade til Welhaven, op. 18 no. 9 [GA,
v. 14, p. 95]
"Lyt nu, du ludende Sanger"
Suk (1873) [GA, v. 15, p. 203]
"Aftensolens Hygge ikke kan mit
Vindu naa"
Valgsang [GA, v. 15, p. 237] "Hvad siger
de dog om dig"
FISKERJENTEN.
Det første møde, op. 21 no. 1 [GA,
v. 14, p. 98]
"Det første mødes sødme"
God morgen! op. 21 no. 2 [GA, v. 14,
p. 100]
"Dagen er oppe, glaeden er taendt"

Jeg giver mit digt til våren, op. 21 no.
3 [GA, v. 14, p. 102] same
Takk for dit råd, op. 21 no. 4 [GA,
v. 14, p. 104] same
PRINSESSEN.
Prinsessen (1871) [GA, v. 15, p. 200]
"Prinsessen sad højt i sit Jomfrubur"
**Bodenstedt, Friedrich Martin von,
1819-1892.**
Ein Traum, op. 48 no. 6 [GA, v. 14,
p. 256]
"Mir träumte einst ein schöner Traum"
Böttger, Adolf, 1816-1870.
Osterlied (1889) [GA, v. 15, p. 228]
"Die Glokken läuten das Ostern"
Bøgh, Johan
Til Generalkonsul Chr. Tønsberg (1873)
[GA, v. 15, p. 207]
"Du sider i Mindets Lund"
Brun, Carl, 1851-1923.
Odalisken synger (1870) [GA, v. 15,
p. 195] "Nu synker Solen i Asiens
Dale"
Castillejo, Christoval De, 1490-1556.
SPANISCHES LIEDERBUCH: Alguna
vez.
Dereinst, Gedanke mein, op. 48 no. 2
[GA, v. 14, p. 244] same
Geibel, translator.
Chamisso, Adelbert von, 1781-1838.
Morgentau, op. 4 no. 2 [GA, v. 14, p. 16]
"Wir wollten mit Kosen und Lieben"
Die Müllerin, op. 2 no. 1 [GA, v. 14,
p. 1] "Die Mühle, die dreht ihre
Flügel"
Die Waise, op. 4 no. 1 [GA, v. 14, p. 12]
"Sie haben mich geheissen"
Was soll ich sagen? op. 2 no. 4 [GA,
v. 14, p. 10] "Mein Aug' ist trüb"
Dass, Petter, 1647-1708.
Fiskervise, op. 61 no. 4 [GA, v. 15,
p. 56] "Det haender vel ofte"
**Drachmann, Holger Henrik Herholdt,
1846-1908.**
Du retter tidt dit Øjepar (1889) [GA,
v. 15, p. 339] same
Epilog, op. 44 no. 6 [GA, v. 14, p. 236]
"Vi ser på Taersklen os tilbage"
Foraarsregn, op. 49 no. 6 [GA, v. 14,
p. 290] "Det klinger som fra fine
Instrumenter"
Ingebjørg, op. 44 no. 4 [GA, v. 14,
p. 227] "Din Hånd er barket,
Ingebjørg"
Johanne, op. 44 no. 2 [GA, v. 14, p. 218]
"En Fillehytte var dit Bo"

GRIEG, EDVARD, 1843-1907 *(continued)*
Drachmann, Holger Henrik Herholdt,
1846-1908. *(continued)*
   Jule-Sne, op. 49 no. 5 [GA, v. 14, p. 284]
     "Jeg vandrer gennem Skoven ved Jule-
     tid"
   Nur er Aftnen lys og lang, op. 49 no. 4
     [GA, v. 14, p. 281] same
   Prolog, op. 44 no. 1 [GA, v. 14, p. 214]
     "Jeg ved ej hvad der rører sig"
   Ragna, op. 44 no. 5 [GA, v. 14, p. 232]
     "O Ragna, hvor dog Tiden går"
   Ragnhild, op. 44 no. 3 [GA, v. 14,
     p. 223] "Å, der var en Jente som vi så
     ombord"
   Saa du Knøsen, som strøg forbi, op. 49
     no. 1 [GA, v. 14, p. 260] same
   Simpel Sang (1889) [GA, v. 15, p. 231]
     "Naar trofast, varm og redelig jeg bejle
     vil til dig"
   Vaer hilset, I Damer, op. 49 no. 3 [GA,
     v. 14, p. 277] same
   Vug, O Vove, op. 49 no. 2 [GA, v. 14,
     p. 267] same
Feddersen, Berend Wilhelm, 1832-
1918.
   FRIERIET PAA HELGOLAND.
     Claras Sang (1864) [GA, v. 15,
     p. 168] "Jeg priser vort ringe"
Garborg, Arne, 1851-1925.
   HAUGTUSSA.
     Blåbaer-Li, op. 67 no. 3 [GA, v. 15,
     p. 80] "Nei sjå, kor det blåner her!"
     Dømd (1895) [GA, v. 15, p. 253]
       "Eg hev som vigde Mammons
       Trael"
     Elsk, op. 67 no. 5 [GA, v. 15, p. 91]
       "Den galne Guten min Hug hev
       dåra"
     I Slåtten (1895) [GA, v. 15, p. 248]
       "No Ljåen han syng på den saftige
       Voll"
     Killingdans, op. 67 no. 6 [GA, v. 15,
     p. 95]
       "Å hipp og hoppe og tipp og toppe"
     Ku-Lok [GA, v. 15, p. 260]
       "Å Kyri mi vene"
     Møte, op. 67 no. 4 [GA, v. 15, p. 87]
       "Ho sit ein Sundag lengtande i Li"
     Sporven [GA, v. 15, p. 245]
       "Småsporven gjeng i"
     Det synge, op. 67 no. 1 [GA, v. 15,
     p. 72] "Å veit du den Draum og veit
     du den Song"
     Til Deg du hei (1895) [GA, v. 15,
     p. 344] same

     Ved Gjaetle-Bekken, op. 67 no. 8 [GA,
     v. 15, p. 101] "Du surlande Bekk"
     Veslemøy, op. 67 no. 2 [GA, v. 15, p.
     77] "Ho er mager og myrk og mjå"
     Veslemøy lengtar (1895) [GA, v. 15,
     p. 257]
       "No stend ho steller i Kjøkenkrå"
     Veslemøy undrast (1895) [GA, v. 15,
     p. 251]
       "Jenton' breier der Gutan' slaer"
     Veslemøy ved rokken (1895) [GA,
     v. 15, p. 345] "D'er Haust. Det
     ruskar ute med Regn"
     Vond Dag, op. 67 no. 7 [GA, v. 15,
     p. 99] "Ho reknar Dag og Stund og
     seine Kveld"
Geibel, Emanuel, i.e., Franz Emanuel
August, 1815-1884.
   Siehst du das Meer? [GA, v. 15, p. 159]
   same
Gjertsen, Fredrik
   Morgenbøn paa Skolen [GA, v. 115,
     p. 216] "I dit dyrebare Navn"
Goethe, Johann Wolfgang von, 1749-
1832.
   Ich denke dein (1862?) [lost]
   Zur Rosenzeit, op. 48 no. 5 [GA, v. 14,
     p. 253] "Ihr verblühet, süsse Rosen"
Grønvold, Didrik Hegermann, 1855-
1928.
   Blåbaeret (1896) [GA, v. 15, p. 226]
     "På Tunet gik Smågutten med Hugen
     tung af Nag"
Groth, Klaus, 1819-1899.
   Beim Kirchgang von allen [GA, v. 15,
     p. 165] same
Grundtvig, Nicolai Frederik Severin,
1783-1872.
   Den syngende Menighed (1860) [GA,
     v. 15, p. 161] "Guds Menighed, syng
     for vor Skaber i Løn"
Heine, Heinrich, 1797-1856.
   Abschied, op. 4 no. 3 [GA, v. 14, p. 18]
     "Das gelbe Laub erzittert"
   Das alte Lied, op. 4 no. 5 [GA, v. 14,
     p. 23] "Es war ein alter König"
   Eingehüllt in graue Wolken, op. 2 no. 2
     [GA, v. 14, p. 4] same
   Gruss, op. 48 no. 1 [GA, v. 14, p. 242]
     "Leise zieht durch mein Gemüt"
   Hör' ich das Liedchen klingen, op. 39
     no. 6 [GA, v. 14, p. 211] same
     Text adapted by Nordahl Rolfsen.
   Wo sind Sie hin? op. 4 no. 6 [GA, v. 14,
     p. 25]
     "Es ragt in's Meer der Runenstein"

LIEDERSTRAUSS.
 Ich stand in dunkeln Träumen, op. 2
  no. 3 [GA, v. 14, p. 8] same
Ibsen, Henrik, 1828-1906.
 Borte! op. 25 no. 5 [GA, v. 14, p. 130]
  "De sidste gaester vi fulgte til grinden"
 En fuglevise, op. 25 no. 6 [GA, v. 14,
  p. 131] "Vi gik en dejlig vårdag"
 Med en vandlilje, op. 25 no. 4 [GA,
  v. 14, p. 125] "Se, Marie, hvad jeg
  bringer"
 Spillemaend, op. 25 no. 1 [GA, v. 14,
  p. 119] "Til hende stod mine tanker"
 Stambogsrim, op. 25 no. 3 [GA, v. 14,
  p. 124] "Jeg kaldte dig mit lykkebud"
 En svane, op. 25 no. 2 [GA, v. 14,
  p. 122] "Min hvide svane"
KONGS-EMNERNE.
 Margretes Vuggesang, op. 15 no. 1
  [GA, v. 14, p. 65]
  "Nu løftes Laft og Lofte"
Janson, Kristofer Nagel, 1841-1917.
 Millom Roser, op. 39 no. 4 [GA, v. 14,
  p. 206] "I Hagen sat Mod'ri med
  Barnet"
 Vesle Gut (1866) [GA, v. 15, p. 185]
  same
Kipling, Rudyard, 1865-1936.
 Gentlemen-Menige (1900) [GA, v. 15,
  p. 270] "Til de tabtes Legioner"
Krag, Vilhelm Andreas Wexels, 1871-
 1933.
 Der skreg en Fugl, op. 60 no. 4 [GA,
  v. 15, p. 41] same
 Liden Kirsten, op. 60 no. 1 [GA, v. 15,
  p. 31] "Liden Kirsten hun sad så
  silde"
 Mens jeg venter, op. 60 no. 3 [GA, v. 15,
  p. 37]
  "Vildgjaes, Vildgjaes i hvide Flokker"
 Moderen synger, op. 60 no. 2 [GA, v. 15,
  p. 35] "Gretchen ligger i Kiste"
 Og jeg vil ha mig en Hjertenskjaer,
  op. 60 no. 5 [GA, v. 15, p. 43]
  "Og jeg vil ha mig en Silkevest"
Krohn, Johan Jacob, 1841-1925.
 Sang til juletraeet, op. 61 no. 2 [GA,
  v. 15, p. 50] "Du grønne, glitrende
  trae"
Langsted, Adolf, 1864-1919.
 Julens Vuggesang (1900) [GA, v. 15,
  p. 269] "Du har saa blød en
  Vuggeseng"
Lie, Jonas Lauritz Idemil., 1833-1909.
 I Liden højt deroppe, op. 39 no. 3 [GA,
  v. 14, p. 203] same

Moe, Jørgen Engebretsen, 1813-1882.
 Ungbirken, op. 18 no. 6 [GA, v. 14,
  p. 89] "En Ungbirk standder ved
  Fjorden"
Monrad, Olaf Peder, 1849-1920.
 Ved en ung Hustrus Båre, op. 39 no. 5
  [GA, v. 14, p. 208] "Blegnet, blegnet,
  hun, midt i Livets Glød"
Munch, Andreas, 1811-1884.
 Harpen, op. 9 no. 1 [GA, v. 14, p. 39]
  "Et Sagn nu mig drages til Minde"
 Udfarten, op. 9 no. 4 [GA, v. 14, p. 50]
  "Det var en daemrende Sommernat"
 Vuggesang, op. 9 no. 2 [GA, v. 14, p. 42]
  "Sov, min Søn, o slumre sødt"
SOLNEDGANG.
 Solnedgang, op. 9 no. 3 [GA, v. 14,
  p. 48] "Nu daler Solen sagte ned"
Nikolajesen, V.
 Til L.M. Lindemans Sølvbryllup (1873)
  [GA, v. 15, p. 205]
  "Paa Fjeldet Huldren sidder"
No author
 Ave Maris Stella (1898) [GA, v. 15,
  p. 240] same
  Arranged for SATB chorus, a cappella,
  1899.
  Text after the Latin by Thor Lange.
Paulsen, John Olaf, 1851-1924.
 Den aergjerrige, op. 26 no. 3 [GA, v. 14,
  p. 140]
  "I Haven her du hvisked engang"
 Et Håb, op. 26 no. 1 [GA, v. 14, p. 135]
  "Jeg kunde juble for alle Vinde min
  Glaede ud!"
 Faedrelandssang [GA, v. 15, p. 243] "En
  hytte simpelt tjeldet vi har til odel fåt"
 Farvel, op. 59 no. 5 [GA, v. 15, p. 26]
  "En svane strøg mod syd"
 Henrik Wergeland, op. 58 no. 3 [GA,
  v. 15, p. 5]
  "Vandrer jeg i granskogen stille"
 Hjemkomst, op. 58 no. 1 [GA, v. 15,
  p. 1] "Jeg stod på daekket og jeg så"
 Jeg reiste en deilig Sommerkvaeld, op. 26
  no. 2 [GA, v. 14, p. 138] same
 Med en Primula veris, op. 26 no. 4 [GA,
  v. 14, p. 143]
  "Du Vårens milde, skjønne Barn"
 Når jeg vil dø, op. 59 no. 1 [GA, v. 15,
  p. 17] "Når løvet falder traet fra
  skogens kroner"
 Nu hviler du i jorden, op. 59 no. 6 [GA,
  v. 15, p. 27] same
 På Norges nøgne fjelde, op. 59 no. 2
  [GA, v. 15, p. 20] same
  After Heine's *Ein Fichtenbaum.*

GRIEG, EDVARD, 1843-1907 *(continued)*
Paulsen, John Olaf, 1851-1924
(continued)
På Skogstien, op. 26 no. 5 [GA, v. 14,
p. 145] "Sig, husker du i Sommer"
Til Én. I, op. 59 no. 3 [GA, v. 15, p. 22]
"Du er den unge vår"
Til Én. II, op. 59 no. 4 [GA, v. 15, p. 24]
"Hvorfor svømmer dit øje"
Til Norge, op. 58 no. 2 [GA, v. 15,
p. 4] "Du er min mor"
Turisten, op. 58 no. 4 [GA, v. 15, p. 9]
"Det dufted af gran"
Udvandreren, op. 58 no. 5 [GA, v. 15,
p. 13] "Nu vist det våres i Norges
dale"
Preetzman, Caspara, 1792-1876.
Dig elsker jeg! (1865) [GA, v. 15,
p. 179] same
Richardt, Christian Ernst, 1831-1892.
Efteraarsstormen, op. 18 no. 4 [GA,
v. 14, p. 78]
"I Sommer var Skoven saa grøn"
Modersorg, op. 15 no. 4 [GA, v. 14,
p. 71] "Saa du ham min lille Dreng"
Rolfsen, Nordahl, 1848-1928.
Faedrelandssalme, op. 61 no. 7 [GA,
v. 15, p. 68]
"Du Herre, som er sterk og stor"
Havet, op. 61 no. 1 [GA, v. 15, p. 47]
"Skjaer og ø!"
Kveldssang for Blakken, op. 61 no. 5
[GA, v. 15, p. 59]
"Fola, fola, Blakken!"
De norske fjelde, op. 61 no. 6 [GA,
v. 15, p. 64]
"Ifald du følger mig over heien"
Under Juletraeet (1885?) [GA, v. 15,
p. 224] "Vi løfted din Rod!"
Schultz, Wilhelm, 1854-1921.
Der Jäger (1905 or earlier) [GA, v. 15,
p. 276]
"Die Morgensonn die Vöglein weckt"
Uhland, Ludwig, 1787-1862.
Jägerlied, op. 4 no. 4 [GA, v. 14, p. 21]
"Kein' bess're Lust in dieser Zeit"
Lauf der Welt, op. 48 no. 3 [GA, v. 14,
p. 246] "An jedem Abend geh'ich aus"
Vinje, Aasmund Olavsson, 1818-1870.
Attegløyma (1880) [GA, v. 15, p. 222]
"Hardt å halda ut"
Eit Syn, op. 33 no. 6 [GA, v. 14, p. 172]
"Ei Gjente eg såg"
Et Vennestykke, op. 33 no. 10 [GA, v. 14,
p. 182] "Tro ei Venner"
Det Første, op. 33 no. 8 [GA, v. 14,
p. 177] "Det Første du har å gjera,
Mann"

Fyremål, op. 33 no. 12 [GA, v. 14,
p. 186] "Vegen vita, på Villstig venda"
Gamle Mor, op. 33 no. 7 [GA, v. 14,
p. 175] "Du gamle Mor!"
Guten, op. 33 no. 1 [GA, v. 14, p. 156]
"Du ferer vidt, og du verdt trøytt"
Jenta (1880) [GA, v. 15, p. 220]
"Ver ikkje so modlaus"
Langs ei Å, op. 33 no. 5 [GA, v. 14,
p. 170] "Du Skog! som bøyer deg
imot"
Paa Hamars Ruiner (1800) [GA, v. 15,
p. 217]
"Vi står og synge på Hamars Grav"
Den Saerde, op. 33 no. 3 [GA, v. 14,
p. 164]
"Mitt Hjarta har vori i Livets Strid"
Trudom, op. 33 no. 11 [GA, v. 14,
p. 184] "Guds Rike er eit Fredens
Rike"
Tyteberet, op. 33 no. 4 [GA, v. 14,
p. 167] "Tytebaeret opp på Tuva"
Våren, op. 33 no. 2 [GA, v. 14, p. 159]
"Enno ein Gong fekk eg Vetren"
Also voice & orchestra.
FERDAMINNI.
Ved Rondane, op. 33 no. 9 [GA, v. 14,
p. 179]
"No ser eg atter slike Fjell og Dalar"
Walther von der Vogelweide, 12th
cent.
Die verschwiegene Nachtigall, op. 48 no.
4 [GA, v. 14, p. 249]
"Unter den Linden, an der Haide"
Winther, Christian, 1796-1876.
Blomsterne tale, op. 10 no. 3 [GA, v. 14,
p. 60]
"Fra Vinterens Kulde vi komme"
Sang paa Fjeldet, op. 10 no. 4 [GA,
v. 14, p. 62]
"I Aftenens Glans mon gløde"
Skovsang, op. 10 no. 2 [GA, v. 14, p. 58]
"Der sad en Fugl paa Bøgekvist"
Taksigelse, op. 10 no. 1 [GA, v. 14, p.
56] "Jeg takker dig for hver en Stund"
Grieumard, Édouard
MASSENET *Ce sont les petits que je veux
chanter*
**GRIFFES, CHARLES TOMLINSON, 1884-
1920.**
Anon.
Djakoan (1917) [unpubl.]
Hampelas (1917) [unpubl.]
Kinanti (1917) [unpubl.]
Song of the dagger (1912, 1916)
[Henmar Press, 1983]

"The dagger at my belt it dances
whene'er I dance"
Roumanian song taken from *The Bard
of Dimbovitza,* 1902.
Two birds flew into the sunset glow
(1914) [Henmar Press, 1986] same
Blake, William, 1757-1827.
IN A MIRTLE SHADE.
In a myrtle shade, op. 9 no. 1 (1916)
[G. Schirmer, 1918]
"To a lovely myrtle bound"
Brooke, Rupert, 1887-1915.
WaiKiKi, op. 9 no. 2 (1916) [G.
Schirmer, 1918] "Warm perfumes like
a breath from vine and tree"
Chang Wen-chang, fl. T'ang Dynasty,
905-618 B.C.
The old temple among the mountains, op.
10 no. 3 (1916) [G. Schirmer, 1917]
"The temple courts with grasses rank
abound"
Chu Ch'ing-yu, 8th cent.?
In the harem (1917?) [Henmar Press,
1986] "It was the time of flowers"
Crane, Walter, 1845-1915.
THIS BOOK OF HOURS.
This book of hours, op. 4 no. 1 (1914?)
[G. Schirmer, 1915] same
Eichendorff, Joseph Karl Benedikt,
Freiherr von, 1788-1857.
Elfe (1906?) [G. Schirmer, 1941]
"Bleib bi uns!"
Geibel, Emanuel, i.e., Franz Emanuel
August, 1815-1884.
Des müden Abendlied (1906?) [Henmar
Press, 1986]
"Verglommen ist das Abendrot"
Mein Herz ist wie die dunkle Nacht
[Henmar Press, 1986] same
Nachtlied (1912) [Henmar Press, 1983]
"Der Mond kommt still gegangen"
Das sterbende Kind [Henmar Press,
1986]
"Wie doch so still dir am Kerzen"
Zwei Könige sassen auf Orkadal (1906?)
[G. Schirmer, 1910] same
LIEDER ALS INTERMEZZO, no. 2.
*Wohl lag ich einst in Gram und
Schmerz* (1906?) [G. Schirmer,
1909] same
LIEDER ALS INTERMEZZO, no. 19.
So halt' ich endlich dich umfangen
(1906?) [Peters, 1970] same
Giovannitti, Arturo, 1884-1959.
Phantoms, op. 9 no. 3 (1916) [G.
Schirmer, 1918] "When in my night"

Goethe, Johann Wolfgang von, 1749-
1832.
MEERESSTILLE.
Meeresstille (1906?) [Peters, 1970]
"Tiefe Stille herrscht im Wasser"
Song untitled.
Heine, Heinrich, 1797-1856.
DIE HEIMKEHR, no. 98.
Nacht liegt auf den fremden Wegen
(1906?) [G. Schirmer, 1909] same
LYRISCHES INTERMEZZO, no. 63.
Das ist ein Brausen und Heulen
(1906?) [Henmar Press, 1986]
same
LYRISCHES INTERMEZZO, no. 67.
Am Kreuzweg wird begraben (1906?)
[Peters, 1970] same
LYRISCHES INTERMEZZO, no. 68.
Wo ich bin, mich rings umdunkelt
(1906?) [Henmar Press, 1986] same
TRAGÖDIE.
Auf ihrem Grab (1906?) [G. Schirmer,
1941] same
Tragödie I (1906?) [unpubl.]
Tragödie II (1906?) [unpubl.]
VERSCHIEDENE-SERAPHINE, no. 12.
Mit schwarzen Segeln (1906?)
[Henmar Press, 1986] same
Henley, William Ernest, 1849-1903.
We'll to the woods and gather May, op. 3
no. 3 (1914) [G. Schirmer, 1915]
same
Unclear whether a translation of
Charles d'Orléans text or an
original rondel inspired by Charles'
text.
Hugo, Victor Marie, comte, 1802-
1885.
Si mes vers avaient des ailes (1901)
[unpubl.]
Kao, Shih, 707?-765.
Impressions of a traveler (1917)
[unpubl.] "In a silent desolate spot"
Unfinished.
Lanier, Sidney, 1842-1881.
AN EVENING SONG.
Evening song (ca.1912) [G. Schirmer,
1941] "Look off, dear Love, across
the sallow sands"
Lenau, Nicolaus, 1802-1850.
LIEBESKLÄNGE.
An den Wind (1906?) [Peters, 1970]
"Ich wandre fort in's ferne Land"
SCHILFLIEDER.
Auf dem Teich, dem regungslosen
(1906?) [G. Schirmer, 1909] same
Auf geheimem Waldespfade (1906?)
[G. Schirmer, 1909] same

COMPOSER Poet *Title* ''First Line''

GRIFFES, CHARLES TOMLINSON, 1884-1920 *(continued)*
Masefield, John, 1878-1967.
An old song re-sung (1918) [G. Schirmer, 1920] "I saw a ship a-sailing"
SALT WATER BALLADS.
Sorrow of Mydath (1917) [G. Schirmer, 1920]
"Weary the cry of the wind is"
Mosen, Julius, 1803-1867.
Der träumende See (1906?) [G. Schirmer, 1909]
"Der See ruht tief im blauen Traum"
NACHTLIED.
Könnt ich mit dir dort oben gehen (1912) [G. Schirmer, 1941] same
Sada-Ihe, 13th cent.
Landscape, op. 10 no. 2 (1916) [G. Schirmer, 1917]
"Out across the wave all is bare"
Sainte-Beuve, Charles Augustin, 1804-1869.
Sur ma lyre l'autre foix (?1901) [unpubl.]
Scollard, Clinton, 1860-1932.
Come love, across the sunlit land, op. 4 no. 2 (1914?) [G. Schirmer, 1915] same
Sharp, William, 1885-1905.
FOAM OF THE PAST.
The lament of Ian the proud, op. 11 no. 1 (1918) [G. Schirmer, 1918]
"What is this crying that I hear in the wind?"
FROM THE HILLS OF DREAMS.
Thy dark eyes to mine, op. 11 no. 2 (1918) [G. Schirmer, 1918] same
THE HOUR OF BEAUTY.
The rose of the night, op. 11 no. 3 (1918) [G. Schirmer, 1918]
"The dark rose of thy mouth"
Tabb, John Banister, 1845-1909.
Cleopatra to the asp (ca.1912) [Henmar Press, 1986]
"Lie thou where Life hath lain"
The first snowfall (ca.1912) [G. Schirmer, 1941] "The fir tree felt it with a thrill"
The half-ring moon (ca.1912) [G. Schirmer, 1941]
"Over the sea, over the sea"
Phantoms (ca.1912) [Henmar Press, 1986]
"Are ye the ghosts of fallen leaves"
The water lily (1911) [Henmar Press, 1986]
"Whence, O fragrant form of life"

Teasdale, Sara, 1884-1933.
Pierrot (1912) [Henmar Press, 1986]
"Pierrot stands in the garden"
Unknown
Mir war als müsste ich graven (1906?) [unpubl.]
Text may be by Geibel.
Wang, Chang-ling, fl.ca.750.
So-fei gathering flowers, op. 10 no. 1 (1917) [G. Schirmer, 1917]
"In a dress of gauzy fabric"
Wang Seng-ju, fl. 6th cent.
Tears, op. 10 no. 4 (1916) [G. Schirmer, 1917] "High o'er the hill"
Wilde, Oscar, 1854-1900.
Symphony in yellow, op. 3 no. 2 (1912?) [G. Schirmer, 1915]
"An omnibus across the bridge"
FANTAISIES DÉCORATIVES, no. 2.
Les ballons (1915) [Henmar Press, 1986] "Against these turbid turquoise skies"
FLOWERS OF GOLD. Impressions, no. 2.
La fuite de la lune, op. 3 no. 1 (1912) [G. Schirmer, 1915]
"To outer senses there is peace"
THE FOURTH MOVEMENT.
Impression: Le Réveillon.
Dawn (1914) [Peters, 1970]
"The sky is laced with fitful red"
IMPRESSIONS I: Le jardin.
Le jardin (1915) [Peters, 1970]
"The lily's withered chalice falls"
IMPRESSIONS II: La mer.
La mer (1916) [unpubl.] "A white mist drifts across the shrouds"
The sea (1912) [Peters, 1970] "A white mist drifts across the shrouds"
WIND FLOWERS: Impression du matin.
Early morning in London (1915) [Peters, 1970] "The Thames nocturne of blue and gold"
Yuan Mei, 1715-1797.
A feast of lanterns, op. 10 no. 5 (1917) [G. Schirmer, 1917]
"In spring for sheer delight"
Grille und Käfer see Iłłakowiczówna
SZYMANOWSKI *Trzmiel i żuk*
Le grillon see Lamartine **BIZET**
Le Grillon see Renard *HISTOIRES NATURELLES.* **RAVEL**
"Grillon solitaire ici comme moi" *see*
Le grillon Lamartine **BIZET**
Grillparzer, Franz, 1791-1872.
MENDELSSOHN-BARTHOLDY *Italien*
SCHUBERT *Bertha's Lied in der Nacht*

Grimmelshausen, Hans Jacob
  Christoffel von, 1625-1676.
  ZELTER *Der Waldbruder*
  SIMPLICIUS SIMPLICISSIMUS.
    JENSEN *Gesang des Einsiedlers*
"Grince, grince, grince patte en bouleau" *see*
  Chanson de l'ours Anon. **STRAVINSKIÏ**
Grindel, Eugène *see* Éluard, Paul, 1895-
  1952.
Grindelwald see Hesse **KILPINEN**
Gripenberg, Bertil, 1878-1947.
  SIBELIUS
    Narsissi
    Teodora
    Vårtagen
Grisaille see Catteau **AUBERT**
Gròb Hafiza see Hafiz **SZYMANOWSKI**
Grøn er Vaarens Haek see Møller **NIELSEN**
Grønvold, Didrik Hegermann, 1855-1928.
  GRIEG *Blåbaeret*
Grohe, Melchior, 1829-1906.
  BRAHMS *O Komme, holde Sommernacht*
"Grokhochet bitva" *see Polkovodets*
  Golenishchev-Kutuzov **MUSORGSKIÏ**
"Grolle lauter, zürnend Gewitter" *see*
  Gewitternacht Osterwald **Franz**
"Les gros dindons, à travers champs" *see*
  Ballade des gros dindons Rostand
  CHABRIER
Gross, E.
  SPOHR *Lied der Freude*
Gross ist der Herr see Kleist **LOEWE**
"Gross ist Jehovah, der Herr" *see*
  Die Allmacht Pyrker **SCHUBERT**
"Gross und rotentflammet schwebet" *see*
  Abendlied Stolberg **SCHUBERT**
"Gross wuchsen alle Räume" *see Räume*
  Goering **KRENEK**
Der grosse Christoph see Kind, F. **LOEWE**
Das grosse Halleluja see Klopstock
  SCHUBERT
Grosse, Julius Waldemar, 1828-1902.
  JENSEN *Bei dir*
  LASSEN *Sehnsucht*
Der grosse Kurfürst und die Spreejungfrau see
  Kurowski-Eichen **LOEWE**
Die grossen stillen Augen see Scholz, B.
  LASSEN
"Grosser Brama, Herr der Mächte!" *see Gebet*
  des Paria Goethe **LOEWE**
"Grosser Brama! nun erkenn' ich" *see Dank*
  des Paria Goethe **LOEWE, WOLF**
"Grosser Taten tat der Ritter" *see Romanze*
  des Richard Löwenherz Scott **SCHUBERT**
"Ein grosses deutsches Volk sind wir" *see*
  Kriegslied der Österreicher Friedelberg
  BEETHOVEN

"Grosses hast du mir gegeben in jenen
  Hochstunden" *see Dank* Levetzow
  SCHÖNBERG
Grossi, Tommaso, 1791-1853.
  RUBINSTEIN *Die Wanderschwalbe*
Grossmanová-Brodská, Ludmila, 1859-
  MARTINŮ
    The jilted maiden
    Once upon a time
Grot, Yakov Karlovich, 1812-1893.
  RUBINSTEIN *The Siskin*
Groth, Klaus, 1819-1899.
  BRAHMS
    Komm bald
    Nachklang
    Regenlied
  GRIEG *Beim Kirchgang von allen*
  LASSEN
    Duftet die Lindenblüt'
    Mir war das Leben blass und schal
    Mit Ahnungsschauern, O Natur!
  HUNDERT BLÄTTER . . .
    BRAHMS
      Dein blaues Auge
      Es hing der Reif
      Heimweh I
      Heimweh II
      Heimweh III
      Mein wundes Herz verlangt
      Regenlied
      Wie Melodien zieht es mir
La grotte see Tristan L'Hermite **DEBUSSY**
"Grove, rove, night, delight" *see Romanzo di*
  Central Park Hunt **IVES**
Gruaz, Julien
  MASSENET
    Avec toi
    Rondel de la belle au bois
Grün, Anastasius, pseud. *see* Auersperg,
  Anton Alexander, Graf von, 1806-
  1876.
"Grün ist das Eiland" *see Die Farben*
  Helgolands Hoffmann von Fallersleben
  FRANZ
"Grün ist der Jasminenstrauch" *see*
  Jasminenstrauch Rückert **SCHUMANN**
Grüne Lust see Tuwim **SZYMANOWSKI**
  Zielone slowa
"Grüner wird die Au und der Himmel blau"
  see Mailied Hölty **SCHUBERT**
"Ein grünes Spinnchen gaukelte" *see Denkst*
  du an mich? Cornelius **CORNELIUS**
"Grüss euch aus Herzensgrund" *see*
  Erwartung Eichendorff **WOLF**
Grüsse see Harnier **SPOHR**
Grüssen see Jung, Walter **LASSEN**

COMPOSER Poet *Title* "First Line"

Die Gruft der Liebenden see Puttkamer-
Plauth **LOEWE**
Grun, James
PFITZNER
  Frieden
  Wie Frühlingsahnung weht es durch die
    Lande
  Wiegenlied
  Zugvogel
"*Grunda bäckar, där de fara*" *see Den djupa*
  källen Blomberg **KILPINEN**
Grundtvig, Nicolai Frederik Severin,
  1783-1872.
  GRIEG *Den syngende Menighed*
  NIELSEN
    Der sad en fisker sa tankefuld
    Der snaekker mødtes
    Nu skal det abenbares
    Syndfloden
    Udrundne er de gamle Dage
Gruppe aus dem Tartarus see Schiller
  SCHUBERT
Gruppe, Otto Friedrich, 1804-1876.
  BRAHMS *Das Mädchen spricht*
  LOEWE
    Der Apotheker als Nebenbuhler
    Der Bräutigam
    Einrichtung
    Der Feldherr
    Landgraf Ludwig
    Niemand hat's gesehn
  STRAUSS *Begegnung*
Gruss see Braun von Braunthal **SPOHR**
Gruss see Gensichen **REGER**
Gruss see Heine **GRIEG,**
  MENDELSSOHN-BARTHOLDY
Gruss see Michaeli **REGER**
Gruss see Nietzsche **MEDTNER**
Gruss an Züllchow see Gerstenberg
  LOEWE
Gruss in die Ferne see Lingg **SCHÖNBERG**
Gruss seiner Treuen an Friedrich August den
  Geliebten see Wagner **WAGNER**
Gruss vom Meere see Schwarzenberg
  LOEWE
Ein Gruss von Ihr! see Viol **FRANZ**
Gruzinskaya pesnya see Pushkin
  BALAKIREV
Gry see Lorenzen, H. **NIELSEN**
"*Guarda, assisa, la vaga Melusina*" *see*
  Melusina Annunzio **MALIPIERO**
Guarda che bianca luna! see Vittorelli
  ROREM, SCHUBERT
"*Guardami dunque! Io sono sempre quella*"
  see Incontro di Marzo Cocconi,
  Ildebrando **PIZZETTI**

"*Guardo una 'Ay!' " see Polo* Anon. **FALLA**
Gubitz, Friedrich Wilhelm, 1786-1870.
  WEBER
    Gebet um die Geliebte
    Der Geleichmütige
    Der Jüngling und die Spröde
    Der Leichtmütige
    Liebe-Glühen
    Der Liebewütige
    Der Schwermütige
"*Guckst du mir denn immer nach*" *see Hans*
  und Grete Uhland **LOEWE, REGER**
Gudhjaelp see Wied *ATALANTA.* **NIELSEN**
Gudmund's erster Gesan see Ibsen
  DAS FEST AUF SOLHAUG. **WOLF**
Gudmund's zweiter Gesang see Ibsen
  DAS FEST AUF SOLHAUG. **WOLF**
"*Guds Menighed, syng for vor Skaber i Løn*"
  see Den syngende Menighed Grundtvig
  GRIEG
"*Guds Rike er eit Fredens Rike*" *see Trudom*
  Vinje **GRIEG**
Guelder-rose in summer see Anon.
  PROKOFIEV *V lete kalina*
Guelder-rose on the hill see Anon.
  PROKOFIEV *Na gore-to kalina*
Güldne Sternlein schauen nieder see Heine
  FRANZ
Günther, Johann Christian, 1695-1723.
  KRENEK *Das unerkannte Gedicht*
Günther, Paul, pseud. *see* Peitl, Paul,
  1853-
Guérin, Eugénie de, 1805-1848.
  MILHAUD
    A mesure qu'on avance
    Cette promenade avec toi
    Nous voilà donc exilés
Guérin, Léon, 1807-ca.1885.
  BERLIOZ *Je crois en vous*
Guérin, Maurice de, 1810-1839.
  MILHAUD *Les siècles ont creusé*
Guérin-Catelin, Émile-Jean, 1856-after
  1905.
  MASSENET *Départ*
La guerre see Banville **KOECHLIN**
"*La guerre a fait une victime!*" *see Larmes*
  maternelles Nekrasov **MASSENET**
Guete Tag, mon cher Papa! see No author
  BLACHER
LE GUETTEUR MÉLANCOLIQUE. see
  Apollinaire *Hôtel* **POULENC**
Guichard, Abeille
  SAUGUET
    Minuit
    La nef
    Toi

Les guides de la vie see Schiller SAUGUET

Guilliaume, Jules Louis, 1825-1900.
LASSEN
Autrefois, à présent
Mon fils est couché là
Pourquoi?
Question grave

Guillot de Saix, b. 1885.
HAHN
Au rossignol
La douce paix
Je me souviens
Sous l'oranger
Ta main
La vie est belle

Guilt see Capetanakis ROREM

Guinand, Édouard, b. 1838.
AU COURANT DE LA VIE. STANCES,
SONNETS, POÈMES (1885).
DEBUSSY Barcarolle

Guitare see Hugo BIZET, LALO,
MASSENET, SAINT-SAËNS

Guitares et mandolines see Saint-Saëns
SAINT-SAËNS

Guldfloden see Ingemann NIELSEN

Gulhinde am Putztische see Stieglitz
LOEWE

"Gullmor, Gullmor, min hjärtans kär" see
Önskekransen Cnattingius, Thor
KILPINEN

Gullvivan see Blomberg KILPINEN

Gusi, lebedi . . . see Anon. STRAVINSKIĬ
Les canards, les cygnes, les oies...

Gut' Nacht see Moore, T. RUBINSTEIN
Good Night!

"Gut Nacht, gut Nacht, mein liebster Schatz"
see Ständchen Anon. BRAHMS

Eine gute, gute Nacht see Daumer
POLYDORA. BRAHMS

Der gute Hirte see Uz SCHUBERT

Gute Nacht! see Eichendorff FRANZ

Gute Nacht see Falke REGER

Gute Nacht! see Gerstenberg LOEWE

Gute Nacht see Glück FRANZ

Gute Nacht see Müller, Wilhelm
SCHUBERT

Gute Nacht see Schubart LOEWE

"Gute Nacht! Im Mondenschein" see
Ständchen Unknown LOEWE

Gute Nacht, mein Herz see Geibel FRANZ

Der gute Rat see Schatz REGER

"Gute Ruh', gute Ruh', tu' die Augen zu" see
Des Baches Wiegenlied Müller, Wilhelm
SCHUBERT

Guten see Vinje GRIEG

"Guten abend, Freund" see Der Tod und der
einsame Trinker Morgenstern
KILPINEN

"Guten Abend, gut' Nacht" see Wiegenlied
Des Knaben Wunderhorn BRAHMS

"Guten Abend, mein Schatz, guten Abend"
see Vergebliches Standchen Anon.
BRAHMS

Guten Morgen! see Bjørnson
FISKERJENTEN. GRIEG God morgen!

"Guten Morgen, du Sonntagsglockenschall!"
see Jungfrau Lorenz Kugler LOEWE

Guten Morgen, 's ist Sankt Valentinstag see
Shakespeare HAMLET. STRAUSS

"Guten Morgen, schöne Müllerin!" see
Morgengruss Müller, Wilhelm
SCHUBERT

Guter Rat see Eichendorff SCHOECK

"Ein guter Ruf ist wie ein wohnlich Haus" see
Spruch Leuthold SCHOECK

Gutmann und Gutweib see Goethe LOEWE,
WOLF

"Gut'n Abend, gut'n Abend" see Spannung
Anon. BRAHMS

Gutten see Vinje GRIEG Guten

Guyot, Jean-Marie, 1854-1888.
RACHMANINOFF Twilight

Gwiazdka see Iłłakowiczówna
SZYMANOWSKI

"Det gyldenhvide Himmellys" see I Aften
Holstein NIELSEN

Gymnaste aérien see Copperie, Adrien
SAUGUET

The gypsy see Norse ROREM

GYPSY SONGS, no. 1
DVOŘÁK Heyduk Má píseň zas mi
láskouzní

GYPSY SONGS, no. 2
DVOŘÁK Heyduk Aj! Kterak trojhranec
muj přerozkošně

GYPSY SONGS, no. 3
DVOŘÁK Heyduk A les je tichý kolem
kol

GYPSY SONGS, no. 4
DVOŘÁK Heyduk Když mne stará matka

GYPSY SONGS, no. 5
DVOŘÁK Heyduk Struna naladěna

GYPSY SONGS, no. 6
DVOŘÁK Heyduk Široké rukávy

GYPSY SONGS, no. 7
DVOŘÁK Heyduk Dejte klec jestřábu

Gypsy's song see Polonsky CHAĬKOVSKIĬ
Pesu'

Gyr, Agnes see Geyer, Agnes Emerita, b.
1787.

H

"Ha, dort kömmt er, mit Schweiss, mit Römerblut" *see Hermann und Thusnelda* Klopstock **SCHUBERT**

"ha, ha, ha, ha, ha, ha, ha, ho!" *see Épouvante* Messiaen **MESSIAEN**

"Ha, ich bin der Herr der Welt'!" *see Königlich Gebet* Goethe **WOLF**

"Ha, Priester, zitt're!" *see Johann von Nepomuk* Anschütz **LOEWE**

Hab Dank, du güt'ger Weisheitspender see Strauss, R. **STRAUSS**

"Hab Erbarmen, hab Erbarmen!" *see Durch die Ferne, durch die Nacht* Heyse **JENSEN**

Hab' ich euch denn je geraten see Goethe *WESTÖSTLICHER DIVAN.* **STRAUSS**

"Hab ich geträumt?" *see Heinrich von Ofterdingen* Scheffel **LISZT**

"Hab' ich tausendmal geschworen" *see Unüberwindlich* Goethe **BRAHMS**

"Hab oft einen dummen düstern Sinn" *see Christel* Goethe **ZELTER**

"Hab' oft im Kreise der Lieben" *see Frisch gesungen* Chamisso **MEDTNER**

"Hab' Singen für mein Leben gern" *see Darum* Seyboth, Sofie **REGER**

Hab viel Schlösser und Gärten see Kol'tsov **MUSORGSKIĬ**
Mnogo est' u menia teremov i sadov

Haben sie von deinen Fehlen see Goethe *WESTÖSTLICHER DIVAN.* **SCHOECK**

"Habt ihr sie schon geseh'n?" *see Volkslied* Anon. **FRANZ**

"Had I the heaven's embroidered cloths" *see The cloths of heaven* Yeats **HESELTINE**

"El hada más hermosa ha soureido" *see Los sueños* Machado y Ruiz **RODRIGO**

Hadley, Arthur Twining, 1856-1930.
SOME INFLUENCES IN MODERN PHILOSOPHIC THOUGHT.
IVES *Tolerance*

Hälfte des Lebens see Hölderlin **BRITTEN**

Hälsning till ett nytt år see Österling **KILPINEN**

"Hältst mich nun ganz in den Armen" *see Ruhe* Evers **REGER**

Händel, Georg Friedrich, 1685-1759.
MESSIAH.
REGER *Doch du liessest ihn im Grabe nicht*

"Det haender vel ofte" *see Fiskervise* Dass **GRIEG**

Der Händler und die Macher see Kerr **STRAUSS**

Hänflings Liebeswerbung see Kind, F. **SCHUBERT**

"Här hon göms, en vacker knopp" *see Gravskrift över ett litet barn* Blomberg **KILPINEN**

Häring, Wilhelm, 1798-1871.
BRAHMS *Entführung*
LOEWE
Fridericus Rex
Rüberettig
Schneiderlied
Der späte Gast
Walpurgisnacht
Wer ist Bär?

SCHWERIN, MEIN GENERAL, IST TODT, SCHWERIN IST TODT!
LOEWE *General Schwerin*

Hätt' ich das gewusst, hätt' ich das gehant see Tolstoĭ **RUBINSTEIN**

Hätt' ich irgend wohl Bedenken see Goethe *WESTÖSTLICHER DIVAN:* Buch Suleika. **WOLF**

"Hätt' ich tausend Arme zu rühen" *see Am Feierabend* Müller, Wilhelm **SCHUBERT**

"Hättest du der Einfalt nicht" *see Geburt Christi* Rilke **HINDEMITH**

HÄUSLICHEN ANDACHTEN. see Fink
Dem Ew'gen **LOEWE**

HAFIS. see Daumer
Bitteres zu sagen denkst du **BRAHMS**
Botschaft **BRAHMS**
Liebesglut **BRAHMS**
Nicht mehr zu dir zu gehen Beschloss ich **BRAHMS**
So stehn wir, ich und meine Weide **BRAHMS**
Wenn du nur zuweilen lächelst **BRAHMS**
Wie bist du, meine Königin **BRAHMS**

Hafiz, Muhammad Shums al-Din, d.1388.
FRANZ *Weisst du noch?*
JENSEN
Als einst von deiner Schöne
Ich bin ein armes Lämpchen nur
Ich will bis in die Sterne
Lockenstricke sollst du wissen
Wehe mir mein Rosenkränzlein
Wehre nicht, O Lieb
Zu der Rose, zu dem Weine

MARTINŮ
A long pilgrimage
Restored to health
Sweet death
SCHOECK
Ach, wie richtete, so klagt ich
Ach, wie schön ist Nacht und
Dämmerschein
Das Gescheh'ne, nicht bereut's Hafis
Höre mir den Prediger
Horch, hörst du nicht vom Himmel her
Ich habe mich dem Heil entschworen
Ich roch der Liebe himmlischers Arom
Lieblich in der Rosenzeit
Meine Lebenszeit verstreicht
Nicht düstre, Theosoph, so tief!
Sing, O lieblicher Sängermund
Wie stimmst du mich zur Andacht
STRAUSS
Die Allmächtige
Huldigung
Ihre Augen
Schwung
SZYMANOWSKI
Die brennenden Tulpen
Die einzige Arzenei
Grób Hafiza
Tanz
Trauriger Frühling
Der verliebte Ostwind
Wünsche
WEBER *Rosen in Haare*
Hagar's Klage see Schücking **SCHUBERT**
Hagedorn, Friedrich von, 1708-1754.
   MOZART *Die Alte*
"Der Hagel klirrt nieder" *see Die Flüchtlinge*
   Shelley **SCHUMANN**
Hagn, Charlotte von, 1809-1891.
   LISZT *Was Liebe sei?*
"Der Hahn hat gekräht" *see Wach auf!*
   Kurowski-Eichen **LOEWE**
HAHN, REYNALDO, 1875-1947.
   Anon.
      L'avertimento [Heugel] "No corè, puti"
         Name Pietro Buratti above music; ?
      La barcheta [Heugel] "La note è bela"
         Name Pietro Buratti above music; ?
      La Biondina in gondoleta [Heugel] same
         Name Antonio Lamberti above music;
         ?
      Che pecà! [Heugel] "Te recordistu, Nina"
         Name Francesco Dall'Ongaro above
         music; ?
      O Salutaris [Heugel, 1900?] "O Salutaris
         hostia"

La primavera [Heugel] "Giacinti e
   violete"
   Name Alvise Cigogna above music; ?
Sopra l'acqua indormenzada . . . [Heugel]
   "Coi pensieri malinconici"
   Name Pietro Pagello above music; ?
Banville, Théodore Faullain de, 1823-
1891.
L'air [Au Ménestrel, 1898; Heugel,
   1899] "Dans l'air s'en vont les ailes"
L'automne [Au Ménestrel, 1898; Heugel,
   1899] "Sois le bienvenu, rouge
   automne"
Dernier voeu [Heugel, 1894] "Oh! quand
   la mort, que rien ne saurait apaiser"
Les étoiles [Au Ménestrel, 1898; Heugel,
   1899] "Les cieux resplendissants
   d'étoiles"
La nuit [Heugel]
   "Nous bénissons la douce nuit"
La paix [Au Ménestrel, 1898; Heugel,
   1899] "La paix, au milieu des
   moissons"
La pêche [Au Ménestrel, 1898; Heugel,
   1899] "Le pêcheur vidant scs filcts"
Le printemps [Au Ménestrel, 1898;
   Heugel, 1899] "Te voilà, rire du
   printemps"
LES EXILÉS.
   L'énamourée [Heugel, 1892]
      "Ils sc discnt, ma colombe"
Blanchecotte, Augustine-Malvina,
1830-before 1895.
La chère blessure [Heugel, 1900]
   "Comme d'un sein ouvert la main
   arrache une arme"
La délaissée [Heugel, 1896] "Ah! je ne
   savais pas qu'il pouvait m'être doux"
Cazalis, Henri, 1840-1909.
Nocturne [Heugel, 1896]
   "Sur ton sein pâle, mon coeur"
Charles, Duke of Orleans, 1391-1465.
Je me metz en vostre mercy [Au
   Ménestrel, 1898; Heugel, 1899] same
Quand je fus pris au pavillon [Au
   Ménestrel, 1898; Heugel, 1899] same
Coppée, François Édouard Joachim,
1842-1908.
Mai [Heugel]
   "Depuis un mois, chère exilée"
Daudet, Alphonse, 1840-1897.
Trois jours de vendange [Heugel, 1893]
   "Je l'ai rencontrée un jour de
   vendange"

COMPOSER   Poet   *Title*   "First Line"

HAHN, REYNALDO, 1875-1947 *(continued)*
Dauphin, Léopold, b.1847.
Le rossignol des lilas [Heugel, 1913]
  "Ô premier rossignol qui viens dans les
  lilas"
Dierx, Marais Victor Léon, 1838-1912.
Fleur fanée [Heugel, 1894]
  "Cette fleur, autrefois donnée"
Gautier, Théophile, 1811-1872.
Infidélité [Heugel, 1893]
  "Voici l'orme qui balance"
Seule [Heugel, 1892]
  "Dans un basier, l'onde au rivage"
Guillot de Saix, b. 1885.
Au rossignol [Salabert, 1955]
  "Viens tout près et chante"
La douce paix [Heugel, 1921]
  "C'est la paix, c'est la douce pais"
Je me souviens [Salabert, 1955] same
Sous l'oranger [Salabert, 1955]
  "Ton image que mon coeur garde"
Ta main [Salabert, 1955]
  "Jeune fille aux lèvres roses"
La vie est belle [Salabert, 1955]
  "Dans la clarté du matin"
Heine, Heinrich, 1797-1856.
Séraphine [Heugel, 1896]
  "Quand je chemine, le soir"
Hennevé, Louis
A nos morts ignorés (Argonne, 1915)
  [Heugel, 1918]
  "Il n'est pas besoin d'une pierre"
Hugo, Victor Marie, comte, 1802-1885.
Puisque j'ai mis ma lèvre [Heugel, 1917]
  "Puisque j'ai mis ma lèvre à ta coupe"
Quand la nuit n'est pas étoilé [Heugel,
  1900] same
Rêverie [Heugel]
  "Puisqu'ici-bas toute âme"
Si mes vers avaient des ailes! [Heugel]
  "Mes vers fuiraient, doux et frêles"
Leconte de Lisle, Charles Marie René,
  1818-1894.
Lydé [Heugel, 1900]
  "Viens! c'est le jour d'un Dieu"
Néére [Heugel, 1900] "Il me faut
  retourner aux anciennes amours"
Pholoé [Heugel, 1900]
  "Oublie, Ô Pholoé"
Phyllis [Heugel, 1900] "Depuis neuf ans
  et plus dans l'amphore scelée"
Salinum [Heugel, 1900] "Le souci plus
  léger que les vents de l'Epire"
Tyndaris [Heugel, 1900]
  "O blanche Tyndaris"

Vile potabis [Heugel, 1900]
  "Dans mes coupes d'un prix modique"
ÉTUDES LATINES.
A Phidylé [Heugel, 1896] "Offre un
  encens modeste aux Lares familiers"
  Solo voice, chorus & 2 pianos.
Magre, Maurice, 1877-1941.
Chanson au bord de la fontaine, extraite
  de **Méduse** [Heugel, 1912]
  "O blanches colombes du soir"
Le plus beau présent [Heugel, 1917]
  "Tu m'as donné un coussin de soie"
Mendès, Catulle Abraham, 1841-1909.
Chanson [Salabert, 1955]
  "Si ton front est comme un roseau"
Naguère, au temps des églantines
  [Musical suppl. to **L'illustration,** 22
  février 1896] same
Le souvenir davoir chanté [Au Ménestrel,
  1898; Heugel, 1899] same
Moréas, Jean, 1856-1910.
Aux rayons du couchant [Heugel] same
Belle lune d'argent [Heugel] same
Compagne de l'éther [Heugel] same
Dans la nuit [Heugel] "Quand je viendrai
  m'asseoir dans le vent"
Dans le ciel est dressé le chéne séculaire
  [Heugel] same
Donc, vous allez fleurir encor [Heugel]
  same
Eau printanière [Heugel] same
*Encor sur le pavé sonne mon pas
  nocturne* [Heugel] same
Fumée [Heugel] "Compagne de l'éther,
  indolente fumée"
Pendant que je médite [Heugel] same
Quand je viendrai m'asseoir [Heugel]
  same
Quand reviendra l'automne [Heugel]
  same
Roses en bracelet [Heugel] same
Théone [Heugel, 1897]
  "Sauvons-nous du souci d'un jour!"
Paté, Lucien, 1845-1939.
L'amitié [Salabert, 1955]
  "Tu peux m'oublier dans la joie"
Racine, Jean Baptiste, 1639-1699.
Cantique sur le bonheur des justes . . .
  [Heugel, 1896]
  "Heureux qui de la sagesse"
Régnier, Henri François Joseph de,
  1864-1936.
Les fontaines [Heugel, 1910]
  "Pour que ton rire clair, jeune"
Renaud, Armand, 1836-1895.
Les cygnes [Heugel, 1894]
  "Ton âme est un lac d'amour"

COMPOSER Poet *Title* "First Line"

Stevenson, Robert Louis, 1850-1894.
A CHILD'S GARDEN OF VERSES.
A good boy (1915) [Heugel, 1917]
"I woke before the morning"
My ship and I (1915) [Heugel, 1917]
"O it's I that am the captain of a
tidy little ship"
The stars (1915) [Heugel, 1917]
"The lights from the parlour and
kitchen shone out"
The swing (1915) [Heugel, 1917]
"How do you like to go up in a
swing?"
Windy nights (1915) [Heugel, 1917]
"Whenever the moon and the stars
are set"
Sully-Prudhomme, René François
Armand, 1839-1907.
Sur l'eau [Heugel] "Je n'entends que le
bruit de la rive et de l'eau"
Théophile de Viau, 1590-1626.
A Chloris [Heugel, 1916] "S'il est vrai,
Chloris, que tu m'aimes"
Theuriet, André, 1833-1907.
Paysage [Heugel] "A deux pas de la mer
qu'on entend bourdonner"
Unknown
Chansons espagnoles (1957) [unpubl.?]
Naïs [Salabert, 1955] "Naïs vierge blonde
à l'oeil noir"
La nymphe de la source [Salabert, 1955]
"Si tes pas t'ont conduit vers
l'heureuse vallée"
Văcărescu, Elena, 1868-1947.
Ma jeunesse [Heugel, 1918] "Ma
jeunesse, toujours brisée"
Verlaine, Paul, 1844-1896.
L'allée est sans fin [Heugel, 1892] same
La bonne chanson [Heugel, 1892]
"La dure épreuve va finir"
Paysage triste [Heugel, 1892] "L'ombre
des arbres dans la rivière embrumée"
Tous deux [Heugel, 1892]
"Donc, ce sera par un clair jour d'été"
LA BONNE CHANSON.
L'heure exquise [Heugel, 1892]
"La lune blanche luit dans les bois"
CHANSONS POUR ELLE, no. 20.
L'incrédule [Heugel, 1894]
"Tu crois au mare de café"
FÊTES GALANTES.
En sourdine [Heugel, 1892]
"Calmes, dans le demi jour"
Fêtes galantes [Heugel, 1893]
"Les donneurs de sérénades"

GREEN.
Offrande [Heugel] "Voici des fruits,
des fleurs, des feuilles et des
branches"
MES PRISONS: Sagesse III, no. 6.
D'une prison [Heugel, 1894]
"Le ciel est par dessus le toit"
POÈMES SATURNIENS.
Chanson d'automne [Heugel, 1892]
"Les sanglots longs des violons de
l'automne"
Vicaire, Gabriel, 1848-1900.
Cimetière de campagne [Heugel, 1894]
"J'ai revu le cimetière"
Hahn-Hahn, Ida Marie Luise Sophie. . . ,
Gräfin von, 1805-1880.
FRANZ
Am Rheinfall
Ich bin bis zum Tode betrübet
Nachtlied
Haïdar-Pacha, Prince
SAINT-SAËNS *L'etoile*
Hain in diesen Paradiesen **see** George *DAS
BUCH DER HÄNGENDEN GÄRTEN.*
SCHÖNBERG
Hajej, můj malý **see** Raabe **MARTINŮ**
Sleep, my little one
"Halb Dämmerschein, halb Kerzenlicht" **see**
Dein Bildnis Cornelius **CORNELIUS**
Hálek, Vitezslav, 1835-1874.
DVOŘÁK
Já jstem ten rytîr zpohádky
Jsem jako lípa košatá
Když bůh byl nejvíc rozkochán
Když jsem se díval do nebe
Mně zdálo se žes umřela
Přílítlo jaro zdaleka
Tak jak ten měsíc vnebes báň
Ten ptáček, ten se nazpívá
Ty hvězdičky tam na nebi to veliké
Umlklo stromu šumění
Vy malí, drobní ptáčkové
Vy všichni kdo jste stísněni
MARTINŮ *In nature*
Halem, Gerhard Anton von, 1752-1819.
BEETHOVEN *Gretels Warnung*
"Half a milord, half of a boss" **see** *Epigram*
Pushkin **BRITTEN**
The half-moon westers low **see** Housman
LAST POEMS: XXVI.
BERKELEY, VAUGHAN WILLIAMS
The half-ring moon **see** Tabb **GRIFFES**
Hallowed be the ordainer **see** Goodman
ROREM
The hallowed place **see** Goethe *ZAHME
XENIEN.* **MEDTNER** *Geweihter Platz*

COMPOSER Poet *Title* "First Line"

Halm, Friedrich, pseud. *see*
  Münch-Bellinghausen, Eligius Franz
    Joseph, freiherr von, 1806-1871.
Halmont, Jacques d'
  MASSENET *Avril est amoureux*
Halt! see Müller, Wilhelm **SCHUBERT**
Halte see Radiguet **SAUGUET**
Hamann, Ludwig, 1867-died between
  1930 and 1936.
  REGER *Ehre sei Gott in der Höhe!*
Hamerling, Robert, 1830-1889.
  BERG
    Augenblicke
    Viel Träume
  JENSEN
    An die Vögel
    Die Brut
    Geister der Nacht
    Im Schlosshof
    Lebe wohl
    Liebe im Schnee
    Rübezahl
  LASSEN
    An die Vögel
    Die beiden Wolken
    Ich seh' dich heut zum ersten Mal
    Lass' die Rose schlummern
    Lebenslied
    Die Lerchen
    Meine Lilie
    Mit den Sternen
    Mund und Auge
    O selig
    O trockne diese Tränen nicht
    Reisebild
    Sei nur ruhig, lieber Robin
    Trost
    Um Mitternacht
    Viel Träume
  REGER
    Das kleinste Lied
    Die Primeln
  RUBINSTEIN *An die Vögel*
HAMLET. *see* Shakespeare
  Auf Morgen ist Sanct Valentinstag
    LASSEN
  Denn traut lieb Robin ist all' mein Lust!
    LASSEN
  Guten Morgen, 's ist Sankt Valentinstag
    STRAUSS
  How should I your true love know?
    QUILTER, THOMSON
  Ophelia's lament **ROREM**
  Sein Bahrtuch weiss wie Bergesschnee
    LASSEN
  Sein Bart war weiss wie Bergesschnee
    LASSEN

Sie trugen ihn auf der Bahre bloss
  STRAUSS
Sie trugen ihn barhaupt auf der Bahr
  LASSEN
Song for the Gravedigger from **Hamlet**
  THOMSON
They bore him barefac'd on the bier
  THOMSON
Tomorrow is Saint Valentine's day
  THOMSON
Totengräberlied **LOEWE**
Und kommt er denn nimmer zurück?
  LASSEN
Wie erkenn' ich dein Treulieb? **LASSEN**
Wie erkenn' ich mein Treulieb? **STRAUSS**
HAMLET: He is dead & gone, lady. *see*
  Shakespeare
  Chanson d'Ophélie **CHAUSSON**
Hampelas see Anon. **GRIFFES**
"Han tvaer over Baenkene hang" *see Dulgt*
  Kjaerlighed Bjørnson **GRIEG**
Ha'nacker mill see Belloc, Hilaire
  HESELTINE
Hands, eyes and heart see Vaughan
  Williams, U. **VAUGHAN WILLIAMS**
"Hands, give him all the measure of my love"
  see Hands, eyes and heart
  Vaughan Williams, U.
    VAUGHAN WILLIAMS
Der Handschuh see Schiller **SCHUMANN**
Der Handschuh; eine Erzälung see Schiller
  ZELTER
The handsome lad see Zaleski **CHOPIN**
  Śliczny chlopiec
"Hans Adam war ein Erdenkloss" *see*
  Erschaffen und Beleben Goethe
  STRAUSS, WOLF
Hans u. Grethe see Mahler **MAHLER**
  Maitanz im Grünen
"Der Hans und die Grete tanzen herum" *see*
  Der arme Peter Heine **SCHUMANN**
Hans und Grete see Uhland **LOEWE,**
  REGER
Hans und Grethe see Mahler **MAHLER**
Hanson, Pauline
  ROREM *So beautiful is the tree of night*
Happy heathen see Carpenter, Rue
  CARPENTER
Happy hour see Kol'tsov **MUSORGSKIĬ**
  Zastol'naĭa pesn'
Happy voyage see Goethe **MEDTNER**
  Glückliche Fahrt
Har Dagen sanket al sin Sorg see Jacobsen
  NIELSEN
Harald see Uhland **LOEWE**
Harangszó see Sztankó **BARTÓK** *Bell*
  sound

COMPOSER Poet *Title* "First Line"

Harasymowicz, Jerzy, 1933-
BARBER *A green lowland of pianos*
Haraucourt, Edmond, 1857-1941.
AUBERT *Secret aveu*
KOECHLIN
Aux temps des fées
Clair de lune
Dame du ciel
Le nénuphar
Plein eau
Le vaisseau
HARAWI, CHANT D'AMOUR ET DE
MORT, no. 1
MESSIAEN Messiaen *La ville qui
dormait, toi*
HARAWI, CHANT D'AMOUR ET DE
MORT, no. 2
MESSIAEN Messiaen *Bonjour toi,
colombe vert*
HARAWI, CHANT D'AMOUR ET DE
MORT, no. 3
MESSIAEN Messiaen *Montagnes*
HARAWI, CHANT D'AMOUR ET DE
MORT, no. 4
MESSIAEN Messiaen *Doundou tchil*
HARAWI, CHANT D'AMOUR ET DE
MORT, no. 5
MESSIAEN Messiaen *L'amour de
Piroutcha*
HARAWI, CHANT D'AMOUR ET DE
MORT, no. 6
MESSIAEN Messiaen *Répétition
planétaire*
HARAWI, CHANT D'AMOUR ET DE
MORT, no. 7
MESSIAEN Messiaen *Adieu*
HARAWI, CHANT D'AMOUR ET DE
MORT, no. 8
MESSIAEN Messiaen *Syllabes*
HARAWI, CHANT D'AMOUR ET DE
MORT, no. 9
MESSIAEN Messiaen *L'escalier redit,
gestes du soleil*
HARAWI, CHANT D'AMOUR ET DE
MORT, no. 10
MESSIAEN Messiaen *Amour oiseau
d'étoile*
HARAWI, CHANT D'AMOUR ET DE
MORT, no. 11
MESSIAEN Messiaen *Katchikatchi les
étoiles*
HARAWI, CHANT D'AMOUR ET DE
MORT, no. 12
MESSIAEN Messiaen *Dans le noir*
Harcourt Antoniette d' *see* D'Harcourt,
Antoniette

Hardenberg, Friedrich Leopold, Freiherr
von, 1772-1801.
HINDEMITH *Vier Lieder*
LOEWE
Wenn alle untreu werden
Wenn ich ihn nur habe
REGER
Ich sehe dich in tausend Bildern
Wenn in bangen, trüben Stunden
SCHOECK *Marienlied*
SCHUBERT
Hymne I
Hymne II
Hymne III
Hymne IV
Marie
Nachthymne
ZELTER *Lied*
"Hardt å halda ut" *see Attegløyma* Vinje
GRIEG
Hardy, Thomas, 1840-1928.
BRITTEN
At day-close in November
At the railway station, Upway
Before life and after
The choirmaster's burial
The little old table
Midnight on the Great Western
Proud songsters
Wagtail and baby
DIAMOND *My spirit will not haunt the
mound*
IRELAND
Beckon to me to come
Dear, think not that they will forget you
Great things
Her song
In my sage moments
It was what you bore with you, woman
Summer schemes
The tragedy of that moment
Weathers
ROREM *The oxen*, a Christmas carol
THE DYNASTS.
VAUGHAN WILLIAMS *Buonaparty*
Hardÿ de Périni, Édouard, 1843-1908.
MASSENET *La légende du baiser*
Die Harfe see Munch **GRIEG** *Harpen*
"Eine Harfe ist mein Herz" *see Harfenklänge*
Unknown **LASSEN**
Harfenklänge see Unknown **LASSEN**
HARFENKLÄNGEN: Kaiser Karl V. an
Luthers Grabe. *see* Hohlfeld
Kaiser Karl V. in Wittenberg **LOEWE**
Harfenspieler see Goethe **WILHELM
MEISTER. SCHUBERT**

Harfenspieler 1 see Goethe **ZELTER**
Einsamkeit
Harfenspieler 2 see Goethe **ZELTER**
An die Türen will ich schleichen
Harfenspieler 3 see Goethe **ZELTER**
Wer nie sein Brot mit Tränen ass
Harfenspieler I see Goethe *WILHELM*
MEISTER. **SCHUBERT, WOLF**
Harfenspieler II see Goethe *WILHELM*
MEISTER: Harfenspieler. **SCHUBERT,
WOLF**
Harfenspieler III see Goethe *WILHELM*
MEISTER. **SCHUBERT, WOLF**
Der Harfner see Goethe **ZELTER** *Wer nie
sein Brot mit Tränen ass*
Haringer, Jakob, 1883-1948.
  ABSCHIED.
    SCHÖNBERG
      Mädchenlied
      Tot
  DIE DENKMÄLER: Der Reisende oder Die
    Träne.
    SCHÖNBERG *Summermüd*
Hark, hark the lark see Shakespeare
  QUILTER
Hark! how my triangle see Heyduk
  DVOŘÁK *Aj! Kterak trojhranec muj
    přerozkošně*
"Hark ye, hark to the winding horn" *see Hope
the hornblower* Newbolt **IRELAND**
Harmonie du soir see Baudelaire *FLEURS
DU MAL*. **DEBUSSY**
Harnier, Auguste, 1826-1855.
  SPOHR *Grüsse*
  BÜHNE UND HAUS.
    SPOHR *Immer dasselbe*
Három őszi kőnnycsepp see Ady **BARTÓK**
  Autumn tears
The harp the monarch minstrel swept see
  Byron **LUENING**
Harpalus see Percy *RELIQUES*. **IVES**
Harpen see Munch **GRIEG**
The harper and his son see Rydberg
  SIBELIUS *Harpolekaren och hans son*
Harpolekaren och hans son see Rydberg
  SIBELIUS
Die Harrende see Osterwald **FRANZ**
HARRIS, ROY, 1898-1979.
  Anon.
    La primavera (1940) [Belwin-Mills,
      1981] "Ya viene la primavera"
  Harris, Roy, 1898-1979.
    Sons of Uncle Sam (1944?) [Mills Music,
      1944] "We man the ships, we fire the
      guns"

Take the sun and keep the stars (1944)
  [Mills Music, 1944] "We guide the
  ships, we scan the skies"
    Arranged from 1942 band/chorus
    composition.
Waitin' (1939) [Mills Music, 1942;
  Belwin-Mills, 1981] "Oh, Lord, I'm
  lonesome"
    Adapted by the composer from
    Challenge (1940), for solo,
    chorus & orchestra.
MacLeish, Archibald, 1892-1982.
  Freedom's land (1941) [Mills Music,
    1941; Belwin-Mills, 1981]
    "Stand, stand against the rising night"
    Later arranged for chorus (SATB) &
    women's chorus (SSA).
Sandburg, Carl, 1878-1967.
  CHICAGO POEMS.
    Fog (1945) [Carl Fischer, 1948]
    "The fog comes on little cat feet"
Tennyson, Alfred Tennyson, 1st
  baron, 1809-1892.
  Evening song (1940) [Mills Music, 1942;
    Belwin-Mills, 1981]
    "Sweet and low, sweet and low"
Harris, Roy, 1898-1979.
  HARRIS
    Sons of Uncle Sam
    Take the sun and keep the stars
    Waitin'
Harsányi, Kálmán, 1876-1929.
  BARTÓK *Est*
Hart, Julius, 1859-1930.
  SCHÖNBERG *Traumleben*
  STRAUSS *Cäcilie*
Hartleben, Otto Erich, 1864-1905.
  BERG *Liebesode*
  REGER *Im Arm der Liebe*
Hartmann, Yvette von *see* Svetlova,
  Marina, 1922-
Hartwig, Dora, b. 1913.
  REGER *Mutter, tote Mutter*
The harvest of sorrow see Tolstoĭ
  RACHMANINOFF *O thou, my field*
Hasselt, André Henri Constant van,
  1806-1874.
  MASSENET *Sur une poésie de Van
    Hasselt*
Hast du ein Tongedicht see Kerr **STRAUSS**
"Hast du Lianen nicht gesehen?" *see Liane*
  Mayrhofer **SCHUBERT**
"Hast du nicht Liebe zugemessen" *see Seufzer
eines Ungeliebten* Bürger **BEETHOVEN**
Hast du von den Fischerkindern see Müller
  von Königswinter **PFITZNER**

"Hast gesagt, du willst mich nehmen" *see*
  Starke Einbildungskraft Anon. **MAHLER**
Hast never come to thee see Whitman
  LUENING
"Hat der alte Hexenmeister sich doch einmal
  wegbegeben!" *see Der Zauberlehrling*
  Goethe **LOEWE, ZELTER**
"Hat einmal ein Mädel die Muhme gefragt"
  see Pythia Ritter **REGER**
Hat gesagt–bleibt's nicht dabei see
  Des Knaben Wunderhorn **REGER,
  STRAUSS**
"Hat mit frischem Birkenlaube" *see*
  Taubenlied Giesebrecht **LOEWE**
Hatte Liebchen zwei see Anon. **FRANZ**
Hauch, Johannes Carsten, 1790-1872.
  NIELSEN
    Morgendug, der sagte baever
    Naturens aedle dyrker
    Vender sig Lykken fra dig
"Hauche milder, Abendluft" *see Grablied für
  die Mutter* Unknown **SCHUBERT**
Hauenschild, Georg von, 1825-1855.
  FRANZ
    Da sind die bleichen Geister wieder
    Es klingt in der Luft
    Ein Friedhof
    Ich wollte, ich könnte nicht träumen
    Rosmarin
    Wenn drüben die Glocken klingen
    Zwei welke Rosen
Haug, Friedrich, 1761-1829.
  WEBER *Die Blume*
HAUGTUSSA. see Garborg
  Blåbaer-Li **GRIEG**
  Dømd **GRIEG**
  Elsk **GRIEG**
  I Slåtten **GRIEG**
  Killingdans **GRIEG**
  Ku-Lok **GRIEG**
  Møte **GRIEG**
  Sporven **GRIEG**
  Det synge **GRIEG**
  Til Deg du hei **GRIEG**
  Ved Gjaetle-Bekken **GRIEG**
  Veslemøy **GRIEG**
  Veslemøy lengtar **GRIEG**
  Veslemøy undrast **GRIEG**
  Veslemøy ved rokken **GRIEG**
  Vond Dag **GRIEG**
HAUGTUSSA SANG-CYKLUS, no. 1
  GRIEG Garborg *Det synge*
HAUGTUSSA SANG-CYKLUS, no. 2
  GRIEG Garborg *Veslemøy*
HAUGTUSSA SANG-CYKLUS, no. 3
  GRIEG Garborg *Blåbaer-Li*

HAUGTUSSA SANG-CYKLUS, no. 4
  GRIEG Garborg *Møte*
HAUGTUSSA SANG-CYKLUS, no. 5
  GRIEG Garborg *Elsk*
HAUGTUSSA SANG-CYKLUS, no. 6
  GRIEG Garborg *Killingdans*
HAUGTUSSA SANG-CYKLUS, no. 7
  GRIEG Garborg *Vond Dag*
HAUGTUSSA SANG-CYKLUS, no. 8
  GRIEG Garborg *Ved Gjaetle-Bekken*
Haugwitz, Paul von, Bp. of Naumberg
  BEETHOVEN *Resignation*
Hauptmann, Carl Ferdinand Maximilian,
  1858-1921.
  BERG *Nacht*
  REGER *Es schläft ein stiller Garten*
Hauptmann's Weib see Burns **SCHUMANN**
"Einen Haushalt klein und fein hab' ich
  angestellt" *see Kleiner Haushalt* Rückert
  LOEWE
Haut comme trois pommes see Kriéger,
  Jacqueline **MILHAUD**
Haute ecole see Copperie, Adrien
  SAUGUET
"Les hauts talons luttaient avec les longues
  jupes" *see Les Ingénus* Verlaine
  DEBUSSY
Havas, István
  BARTÓK *The benefactors*
"Havde Jeg, O havde jeg en Dattersøn"
  see Vise af "Mogens" Jacobsen
  NIELSEN
HAVE COME, AM HERE. see Villa, J. G.
  Monks and raisins **BARBER**
"Have you been catching of fish, Tom
  Noddy?" *see Tit for tat* De La Mare
  BRITTEN
"Have you heard it yet?" *see Autumn echoes*
  Ady **BARTÓK**
"Have you not read the words in my head"
  see Despite and still Graves, Robert
  BARBER
"Have you seen but a white lily grow" *see*
  So white, so soft, so sweet is she Jonson
  DELIUS
Havet see Rolfsen **GRIEG**
Havet, Mireille
  CARPENTER
    Les cheminées rouge
    Le petit cimetière
Havířská see Gellner **MARTINŮ** *Miners'
  song*
Hawthorn time see Housman *THE
  SHROPSHIRE LAD.* **IRELAND**
"Hay fiesta en el prado verde" *see Fiesta en el
  Prado* Machado y Ruiz **RODRIGO**

COMPOSER Poet *Title* "First Line"

Hayes, Marvin, ca.1924-
GIDEON *Bells*

"He grew in those seasons like corn in the night" *see Thoreau* Ives **IVES**

He is there! see Ives **IVES**

He loved me so much see Apukhtin
CHAĬKOVSKIĬ *On tak menía liubil*

"He, of his gentleness, Thirsting and hungering" *see In the wilderness* Graves, Robert **BARBER**

"He often would ask us that, when he died" *see The choirmaster's burial* Hardy **BRITTEN**

"He! schenket mir im Helme ein!" *see Der Wallensteiner Lanzknecht beim Trunk* Leitner **SCHUBERT**

"He shudders . . . feeling on the shaven spot" *see Electrocution* Ridge **ROREM**

"He that is down need fear no fall" *see The woodcutter's song* Bunyan **VAUGHAN WILLIAMS**

"He that is down needs fear no fall" *see The shepherd boy sings in the valley of humiliation* Bunyan **DIAMOND**

He thinks upon his death see Green **ROREM**

"He toned the sprightly beam of morning" *see A portrait; the Marchioness of Brinvilliers* Melville **DIAMOND**

He took all from me see Tiutchev **RACHMANINOFF**

Hé, va donc see Anon. **SZYMANOWSKI** *Bzicem kunia*

He walks beneath the stars see Green **ROREM**

"He who binds to himself a joy" *see Eternity* Blake, William **VAUGHAN WILLIAMS**

"He who of Rankine sang" *see Epitaph on the author* Burns **GIDEON**

"He would have me go mad who invented this rose" *see Impromptu* Shenshin **MEDTNER**

He would not stay for me see Housman **BERKELEY**

Heald, Arthur
QUILTER *The walled-in garden*

"Health to our well-lo'ed Hielan Chief!" *see Birthday song* Burns **BRITTEN**

Hear me, Lord see Goethe *ERWIN UND ELMIRE.* **MEDTNER** *Sieh mich, Heil'ger, wie ich bin*

Hear, oh hear my prayer, Lord see Bible **DVOŘÁK** *Slyš, Ó Bože! slyš modlitbu mou*

Hear, Oh Lord, my bitter cry see Bible **DVOŘÁK** *Slyš, Ó Bože, volání mé*

"Hear the beautiful tinny voices of the trumpets" *see Hearing* Koch **ROREM**

Hear the skylark sweetly singing see Tolstoĭ **RIMSKIĬ-KORSAKOV** *Zvonche zhavoronka pen'e*

Hear the voice of the Bard see Blake, William **LUENING**

Hearing see Koch **ROREM**

HEARING, no. 1
ROREM Koch *In love with you*

HEARING, no. 2
ROREM Koch *Down at the docks*

HEARING, no. 3
ROREM Koch *Poem*

HEARING, no. 4
ROREM Koch *Spring*

HEARING, no. 5
ROREM Koch *Invitation*

HEARING, no. 6
ROREM Koch *Hearing*

Hearing music at his mother's funeral see Green **ROREM**

Heart, we will forget him see Dickinson **COPLAND**

The heart's country see Evans **CARPENTER**

The heart's desire see Housman *THE SHROPSHIRE LAD.* **IRELAND**

Heart's haven see Rossetti, Dante *THE HOUSE OF LIFE,* no. XXII. **VAUGHAN WILLIAMS**

The heart's morning see Runeberg **SIBELIUS** *Hjärtats morgon*

The heart's secret see Tolstoĭ **RACHMANINOFF** *There are many sounds*

The heavenly banquet see O'Faolain, Sean, translator *THE SILVER BRANCH.* **BARBER**

The Heavens declare see Wright, Merle St. Croix **THOMPSON, R.**

Heavy is the gravestone see Bryusov **MEDTNER** *In the church-yard*

A heavy tear see Tolstoĭ **CHAĬKOVSKIĬ** *Sleza drozhit'*

Heb' auf dein blondes Haupt see Heyse **WOLF**

Hebbel, Christian Friedrich, 1813-1863.
BERG *Spuk*
BRAHMS
  In der Gasse
  Vorüber
CORNELIUS
  Abendgefühl
    Two settings: 1862 and 1863.
  Auf ein schlummerndes Kind

Auf eine Unbekannte
Dämmerempfindung
Reminiszenz
GIDEON *Das Mädchen im Kampf mit sich*
selbst
LISZT *Blume und Duft*
PFITZNER
Gebet
Herbstbild
Ich und Du
REGER *Gebet*
SCHOECK *Das Heiligste*
SCHUMANN
Ballade vom Haideknaben
Sag'an, O lieber Vogel mein
Schön Hedwig
WOLF
Das Kind am Brunnen
Knabentod
Das Vöglein
DEM SCHMERZ SEIN RECHT.
BERG *Schlafen, schlafen*
SCHOECK *Schlafen, schlafen, nichts als*
schlafen
Hébé see Ackermann **CHAUSSON**
Hebräische Melodie see Byron *MY SOUL IS*
DARK. **RUBINSTEIN**
Hebräisches Lied see Solomon
MUSORGSKIĬ *Evreĭskaia pesnia*
Hebraic song see Solomon **MUSORGSKIĬ**
Evreĭskaia pesnia
HEBREW MELODIES. see Byron
An den Mond **SCHUMANN**
Belsazar's Gesicht **LOEWE**
Dem Helden **SCHUMANN**
Eliphas' Gesicht **LOEWE**
Saul und Samuel **LOEWE**
Die Tochter Jephtha's **SCHUMANN**
TSar' Saul **MUSORGSKIĬ**
HEBREW MELODIES, no. 1
DIAMOND Byron *My soul is dark*
HEBREW MELODIES, no. 2
DIAMOND Byron *If that high world*
HEBREW MELODIES, no. 3
DIAMOND Byron *Saul*
HEBREW MELODIES, no. 4
DIAMOND Byron *All is vanity*
Hebrew melody see Lermontov
BALAKIREV *Evreyskaya melodiya*
Hebrew song see Mei **RIMSKIĬ-**
KORSAKOV *Evreĭskaia pesnia*
The Hebrides see Norse **ROREM**
Hedberg, Tor Harald, 1862-1931.
SIBELIUS *Soluppgång*
"Hederlaerken, den liden fugl" *see St. St.*
Blicher Ploug **NIELSEN**

HEDWIG. see Busse
Wenn **STRAUSS**
"Hee balou, my sweet wee Donald"
see
The highland balou Burns **BRITTEN**
Hefferman, William, ca.1720-1803.
LOEFFLER *The song of Catilin Ni*
Uallachain
The he-goat see Musorgskiĭ **MUSORGSKIĬ**
Kozel
Heiberg, Johann Ludvig, 1791-1860.
JENSEN *Barcarole*
"Die Heide ist braun, einst blühte sie rot" *see*
Im Herbst Müller von Königswinter
FRANZ
Die Heideberre see Vinje **GRIEG** *Tyteberet*
Heidenröslein see Goethe **SCHUBERT**
The heights of Tatra see Heyduk **DVOŘÁK**
Dejte klec jestřábu
"Heil! dies ist die letzte Zähre" *see*
Die Sterbende Matthisson **SCHUBERT**
"Heil dir, der du hassen kannst" *see Hymnus*
des Hasses Morgenstern **REGER**
"Heil jenem Tag" *see Liebeshymnus* Henckell
STRAUSS
"Der heilig Geist vom Himmel kam" *see*
Pfingslied Helmbold **LOEWE**
"Ein heilig Säuseln, und ein Gesangeston" *see*
An die Apfelbäume, wo ich Julien erblickte
Hölty **SCHUBERT**
"Heilig Wesen" *see Abbitte* Hölderlin
PFITZNER
Heilige Christine see Iłłakowiczówna
SZYMANOWSKI *Świetz Krystyna*
Das Heilige Feuer see Meyer **SCHOECK**
Der heilige Franziskus see Tuwim
SZYMANOWSKI *Świety Franciszek*
Der heilige Franziskus see Wessenberg
LOEWE
Das heilige Haus in Loretto see Giesebrecht
LOEWE
Heilige Himmel see Evers **BERG**
Der Heilige Lukas see Schlegel **ZELTER**
"Heilige Nacht, du sinkest nieder" *see Nacht*
und Träume Collin, M. **SCHUBERT**
"Heilige Nacht! Heil'ge Nacht!
Sternengeschlossner Himmelsfriede!" *see*
An die Nacht Brentano **STRAUSS**
"Die heiligen drei König' mit ihren Stern" *see*
Ephiphanias Goethe **WOLF**
Die heiligen drei Könige see Heine
STRAUSS
"Die heiligen drei Könige aus Morgenland"
see Die heiligen drei Könige Heine
STRAUSS
Heiligendamm see Sergel **KILPINEN**

COMPOSER Poet *Title* "First Line"

Das Heiligste see Hebbel SCHOECK
Heimat see Falke REGER
Die Heimat see Hölderlin BRITTEN
Heimat see Morgenstern KILPINEN
Heimatgefühl see Krenek KRENEK
Die Heimatglokken see Urban, Robert
   JENSEN
Die Heimath meiner Lieder see Boddien, G.
   von RUBINSTEIN
Heimath und Liebe see Claus, Nicolo
   LASSEN *Heimatliebe*
Heimatliebe see Claus, Nicolo LASSEN
Der Heimatlose see Zwehl, Hans Fritz von
   KILPINEN
Heimgang in der Frühe see Liliencron
   BUNTE BEUTE. WEBERN
Die Heimkehr see Heine CORNELIUS
DIE HEIMKEHR. see Heine
   Khotel by v edinoe slovo CHAĭKOVSKIĭ
   Mondenschein BRAHMS
   Nacht liegt auf den fremden Wegen
      GRIFFES
   Sommerabend BRAHMS, SCHOECK
   Der Tod, das ist die kühle Nacht
      BRAHMS, REGER
Heimkehr see Krenek KRENEK
Heimkehr see Nietzsche MEDTNER
Heimkehr see Paulsen GRIEG *Hjemkomst*
Heimkehr see Schack STRAUSS
Die Heimkehr see Scheffel *GAUDEAMUS.*
   JENSEN
Heimkehr see Strachwitz LASSEN
Heimkehr see Uhland BRAHMS
Heimkehr see Vinje DELIUS *Auf der Reise
   zur Heimat*
Heimliche Aufforderung see Mackay
   STRAUSS
Heimlicher Liebe Pein see Anon. WEBER
Heimliches Lieben see Klenke SCHUBERT
Heimliches Verschwinden see Schöpff
   SCHUMANN
Heimlichkeit see Siebel LOEWE
Heimweh see Eichendorff WOLF
Heimweh see Krenek KRENEK
Heimweh see Leuthold SCHOECK
Heimweh see Mörike WOLF
Heimweh see Nietzsche MEDTNER
Das Heimweh see Pyrker SCHUBERT
Das Heimweh see Robert, F.
   MENDELSSOHN-BARTHOLDY
Heimweh see Sturm, J. REGER
Heimweh see Unknown LOEWE
Das Heimweh see Winkler SCHUBERT
Heimweh I see Groth *HUNDERT
   BLÄTTER...* BRAHMS
Heimweh II see Groth *HUNDERT
   BLÄTTER...* BRAHMS

Heimweh III see Groth *HUNDERT
   BLÄTTER...* BRAHMS
Heine, Heinrich, 1797-1856.
   BARTÓK *Im wunderschönen Monat Mai*
   BERG
      Geliebte Schöne
      Sehnsucht II
   BORODIN
      Das schöne Fischermädchen
      Vergiftet sind meine Lieder
   BRAHMS *Es schauen die Blumen*
   BRUCKNER *Frühlingslied*
   CORNELIUS
      Die Heimkehr
      Warum sind denn die Rosen so blass?
   DELIUS
      Aus deinen Augen fliessen meine Lieder
      Hör' ich das Liedchen klingen
      Mit deinen blauen Augen
      *Ein schöner Stern geht auf in meiner
         Nacht*
   FRANZ
      Abschied
      Ach, wie komm' ich da hinüber?
      Allnächtlich im Traume
      Altes Lied
      Am fernen Horizonte
      Am leuchtenden Sommermorgen
      Auf dem Meere
         Six settings: Op. 5 no. 3, op. 6 no. 3,
            op. 9 no. 6, op. 11 no. 5, op. 25 no.
            6, and op. 36 no. 1.
      Aus meiner Erinnerung
      Die blauen Frühlingsaugen
      Childe Harold
      Deine weissen Lilienfinger
      Du bist so schön und rein
      Durch den Wald im Mondenscheine
      Es fällt ein Stern herunter
      Es ragt ins Meer der Runenstein
      Es treibt mich hin, es treibt mich her
      Es ziehn die brausenden Wellen
      Der Fichtenbaum
      Frühling
      Frühlingsfeier
      Gekommen ist der Maie
      Güldne Sternlein schauen nieder
      Hör' ich das Liedchen klingen
      Ich hab' im Traum geweinet
      Ich lieb' eine Blume
      Ich will meine Seele tauchen
      Im Rhein, im heiligen Strome
      Im wunderschönen Monat Mai
      In der Fremde
      Ja, du bist elend

Kommt feins Liebchen heut'?
Lehre
Leise zieht, durch mein Gemüt
Lieb' Liebchen
Die Lotosblume
Mädchen mit dem roten Mündchen
Das Meer erstrahlt im Sonnenschein
Mir fehlt das Beste
O lüge nicht!
Die Rose, die Lilie
Sag mir! Sag mir, wer einst die Uhren
    erfand
Die schlanke Wasserlilie
Der Schmetterling ist in die Rose verliebt
Die schönen Augen der Frühlingsnacht
Sie floh vor mir
Sie liebten sich beide
Traumbild
Und wüssten's die Blumen
Unter'm weissen Baume sitzend
Verfehlte Liebe
Wandl' ich in dem Wald des Abends
Was will die einsame Träne
Wasserfahrt
Wenn ich auf dem Lager liege
Wenn ich in deine Augen seh
Wenn Zwei von einander scheiden

GIDEON
Im Traum
Leise zieht durch mein Gemüt
Vergiftet sind meine Lieder

GRIEG
Abschied
Das alte Lied
Eingehüllt in graue Wolken
Gruss
Hör' ich das Liedchen klingen
Wo sind Sie hin?

HAHN *Séraphine*

IVES *Ich grolle nicht*

JENSEN
Lehn' deine Wang' an meine Wang'
Nacht liegt auf den fremden Wegen

LASSEN
Das alte Lied
Childe Harold
Der Fichtenbaum
Ich hab' im Traum geweinet
Im Wald
Mein Liebchen
Mit deinen blauen Augen

LISZT
Anfangs wollt' ich fast verzagen
Du bist wie eine Blume
Ein Fichtenbaum steht einsam
Im Rhein, im schönen Strome
Die Loreley

Morgens steh' ich auf und frage
Vergiftet sind meine Lieder

LOEWE
Der Asra
Du schönes Fischermädchen
Erste Liebe
Ich hab' im Traume geweinet
Im Traum sah ich die Geliebte
Leise zieht durch mein Gemüth
Die Lotosblume
Neuer Frühling
Die schlanke Wasserlilie

MACDOWELL
Du liebst mich nicht
Der Fichtenbaum
Mein Liebchen
Oben, wo die Sterne glühen

MAHLER *Im wunderschönen Monat Mai*

MARTINŮ
Hoar-frost fallen in the field
I see you every night, my dear

MEDTNER
Bergstimme
Lieb Liebchen
Lyrisches Intermezzo

MENDELSSOHN-BARTHOLDY
Allnächtlich im Traume
Auf Flügeln des Gesanges
Gruss
Im Kahn
Morgengruss
Neue Liebe
Reiselied
Verlust

MUSORGSKIĬ
Iz slez moikh vyroslo mnogo
Zhelanie

PFITZNER
Es fällt ein Stern herunter
Es fasst mich wieder der alte Mut
Es glänzt so schön die sinkende Sonne
Ich will mich im grünen Wald ergehn
Die schlanke Wasserlilie
Wasserfahrt

REGER *Aus den Himmelsaugen*

RIMSKIĬ-KORSAKOV
Gonets
K moeĭ pesne

RUBINSTEIN
Der Asra
Frühlingslied
    Three settings: Op. 32 no. 1, op. 32 no.
    2, and op. 32 no. 3.
Lied
    Two settings: Op. 32 no. 4 and op. 32
    no. 5.

COMPOSER   Poet   *Title*   ''First Line''

Heine, Heinrich, 1797-1856 *(continued)*

RUBINSTEIN *(continued)*
Tragödie
Wo?
SAUGUET *Les ondines*
SCHOECK
Das Fräulein am Meere
Gekommen ist der Maie
Ja, du bist elend
Vergiftet sind meine Lieder
Warum sind denn die Rosen so blass?
Wo?
SCHUBERT
Am Meer
Der Atlas
Der Doppelgänger
Das Fischermädchen
Die Stadt
SCHUMANN
Abends am Strand
Allnächtlich im Traume
Die alten, bösen Lieder
Am leuchtenden Sommermorgen
Anfangs wollt' ich fast verzagen
Der arme Peter
Aus alten Märchen winkt es
Aus meinen Thränen spriessen
Die beiden Grenadiere
Berg' und Burgen schau'n herunter
Das ist ein Flöten und Geigen
Dein Angesicht
Du bist wie eine Blume
Es leuchtet meine Liebe
Es treibt mich hin, es treibt mich her
Die feindlichen Brüder
Hör' ich das Liedchen klingen
Ich grolle nicht
Ich hab' im Traum geweinet
Ich wandelte unter den Bäumen
Ich will meine Seele tauchen
Im Rhein, im heiligen Strome
Im wunderschönen Monat Mai
Ein Jüngling liebt ein Mädchen
Lehn' deine Wang' an meine Wang'
Lieb' Liebchen
Die Lotosblume
Mein Wagen rollet langsam
Morgens steh' ich auf und frage
Die Rose, die Lilie
Schöne Wiege meiner Leiden
Tragödie
Und wüssten's die Blumen
Warte, warte, wilder Schiffsmann
Was will die einsame Thräne
Wenn ich in deine Augen seh'

STRAUSS
Frühlingsfeier
Die heiligen drei Könige
In Vaters Garten heimlich steht
Mit deinen blauen Augen
Schlechtes Wetter
Waldesfahrt
WAGNER *Les deux grenadiers*
WEISGALL *Süsser Mond*
WOLF
Du bist wie eine Blume
Ernst ist der Frühling
Es war ein alter König
Mädchen mit dem roten Mündchen
Manch Bild vergessener Zeiten
Wenn ich in deinen Augen seh
Wo wird einst?
BELSATZAR.
SCHUMANN *Belsatzar*
DIE BLAUEN FRÜHLINGSAUEN.
CHAÏKOVSKIĬ *Glazki vecny golubye*
BUCH DER LIEDER.
DELIUS *Der Fichtenbaum*
DU BIST WIE EINE BLUME.
RACHMANINOFF *Child, thou art as beautiful as a flower*
FRÜHLING.
BRAHMS *Es liebt sich so lieblich im Lenze*
HEIMKEHR.
BRAHMS
Mondenschein
Sommerabend
Der Tod, das ist die kühle Nacht
CHAÏKOVSKIĬ *Khotel by v edinoe slovo*
GRIFFES *Nacht liegt auf den fremden Wegen*
REGER *Der Tod, das ist die kühle Nacht*
SCHOECK *Sommerabend*
ICH HATTE EINST EIN SCHÖNES VATERLAND.
RACHMANINOFF *A dream*
INTERMEZZO.
SAUGUET
Le bonheur
Le malheur
LIEDERSTRAUSS.
BERG *Vielgeliebte schöne Frau*
FRANZ
Aus meinen grossen Schmerzen
Sterne mit den goldnen Füsschen
Wie des Mondes Abbild zittert
GRIEG *Ich stand in dunkeln Träumen*
PFITZNER *Sie haben heut' Abend Gesellschaft*

COMPOSER Poet *Title* ''First Line''

SCHUBERT *Ihr Bild*
WOLF
   Aus meinen grossen Schmerzen
   Es blasen die blauen Husaren
   Ich stand in dunkeln Träumen
   Mein Liebchen wir sassen beisammen
   Mir träumte von einem Königskind
   Sie haben heut Abend Gesellschaft
   Spätherbstnebel, kalte Träume
   Sterne mit den goldnen Füsschen
   Wie des Mondes Abbild zittert
LYRICAL INTERMEZZO.
   BORODIN *Aus meinen Tränen*
   RIMSKIĬ-KORSAKOV
      El' i pal'ma
      Iz sléz moikh mnogo, maliutka
      Kogda gliazhu tebe v glaza
      Shchekotiu k shcheke ty moeĭ prilozhis'
LYRISCHES INTERMEZZO, no. 63.
   FRANZ, GRIFFES, WOLF *Das ist ein*
      Brausen und Heulen
LYRISCHES INTERMEZZO, no. 67.
   GRIFFES *Am Kreuzweg wird begraben*
LYRISCHES INTERMEZZO, no. 68.
   GRIFFES, WOLF *Wo ich bin, mich*
      rings umdunkelt
DIE SCHLANKE WASSERLILIE.
   RACHMANINOFF *The water lily*
TRAGÖDIE.
   GRIFFES
      Auf ihrem Grab
      Tragödie I
      Tragödie II
TRAGÖDIEN NEBST EINEM LYRISCHEN
INTERMEZZO.
   BRAHMS, FRANZ *Meerfahrt*
VERSCHIEDENE-SERAPHINE, no. 12.
   FRANZ, GRIFFES, WOLF *Mit*
      schwarzen Segeln
WARUM SIND DANN DIE ROSEN SO
BLASS?
   CHAĬKOVSKIĬ *Otchevo?*
Heinitz, Marie
   DELIUS *Traum rosen*
Heinrich der Vogler see Vogl **LOEWE**
Heinrich von Ofterdingen see Scheffel *DER*
   BRAUTWILLKOMM AUF WARTBURG.
   LISZT
Die Heinzelmännchen see Kopisch **LOEWE**
"*Heiss glüht der Pfad*" *see Melek in der Wüste*
   Stieglitz **LOEWE**
"*Heiss mich nicht reden*" *see Geheimnis*
   Goethe **ZELTER**
Heiss mich nicht reden see Goethe
   WILHELM MEISTER. Mignon's song:
   Heiss mich nicht reden.

CHAĬKOVSKIĬ *Ne sprashivaĭ*;
SCHUMANN
"Heiss mich nicht reden" *see Lied der Mignon*
   Goethe **SCHUBERT**
"Heiss mich nicht reden" *see Mignon* Goethe
SCHUBERT
"Heiss mich nicht reden, heiss mich
   schweigen" *see Mignon I* Goethe **WOLF**
Heisser Tag am See see Krenek **KRENEK**
Heiter see Nietzsche **WEBERN**
Hektors Abschied see Schiller **SCHUBERT**
Hela världen är mig så kär see Lagerkvist
   KILPINEN
Helas! see Florian **ZELTER**
"Hélas! les marronniers qui bordent les allées"
   see Les marronniers Collin **MASSENET**
"Hélas! ma soeur, bête bête" *see Poule*
   Éluard **SAUGUET**
Die Heldenbraut see Kurowski-Eichen
   LOEWE
"Helen, thy beauty is to me like those Nicéan
   barks of yore" *see To Helen* Poe
   LOEFFLER
Hélène see Bengy-Puyvallée **AUBERT**
Helene, Herzogin von Orleans, 1814-
   1858 *see*
      Orléans, Hélène Louise Élisabeth,
      Duchesse d', 1814-1858.
Helft mir, ihr Schwestern! see Chamisso
   LOEWE, SCHUMANN
"Helisten soi tiu'ut, kellot" *see Joulukirkkoon*
   Jalkanen **KILPINEN**
"Hell has doors and walls and keys" *see*
   Whither thou goest Louchheim
   DIAMOND
"Hell schimmert das alte Königsschloss" *see*
   Das begraben Lied Baumbach
   RUBINSTEIN
Hell, Theodor, pseud. *see* Winkler, Karl
   Gottfried Theodor, 1775-1856.
HELLDUNKEL (1899). *see* Schlaf
   Im Zimmer **BERG**
   Regen **BERG**
   Winter **BERG**
Helle Nacht see Dehmel *WEIB UND WELT.*
   REGER, WEBERN
"Helle Silberglöcklein klingen" *see*
   Die Meerfee Buddeus **SCHUMANN**
Die helle Sonne leuchtet see Bodenstedt
   FRANZ, LASSEN, QUILTER,
   RUBINSTEIN
Heller als Glassteine see Barth **KRENEK**
Helmbold, Ludwig, 1532-1598.
   LOEWE *Pfingslied*
Helmer, Eduard, pseud. *see* Koch, Ernst,
   1808-1858.

Helvig, Amalie (von Imhof) von, 1766-
1831.
   ZELTER *Die Geister des Sees*
Hemans, Felicia Dorothea (Browne),
1793-1835.
   BENNETT *The better land*
   FRANZ *Mutter, O sing mich zur Ruh!*
   JENSEN
      Der letzte Wunsch
      Mutter, O sing' mich zur Ruh
      Weit entfernt
Henckel, Georg
   SCHÖNBERG *In diesen Wintertagen*
Henckell, Karl Friedrich, 1864-1929.
   BERG *Trinklied*
   REGER *Ich schwebe*
   STRAUSS
      Blindenklage
      Ich schwebe
      Ich trage meine Minne
      Kling
      Das Lied des Steinklopfers
      O süsser Mai!
      Ruhe, meine Seele
      Winterliebe
      Winterweihe
   STEH' ICH IN SEL'GEM TRAUME.
      STRAUSS *Liebeshymnus*
Henley, William Ernest, 1849-1903.
   CHANLER *The patient sleeps*
   GRIFFES *We'll to the woods and gather
      May*
   QUILTER
      Fill a glass with golden wine
      A last year's rose
      Song of the blackbird
   LIFE & DEATH (ECHOES).
      DELIUS *The nightingale has a lyre of
      gold*
Hennes budskap see Runeberg **SIBELIUS**
Hennevé, Louis
   HAHN *A nos morts ignorés*
Henri IV, king of France, 1553-1610.
   MASSENET *L'heureuse souffrance*
Henrik Wergeland see Paulsen **GRIEG**
Henry VIII, king of England, 1491-1547.
   IRELAND *An aside*
Henry, Maurice
   GOUNOD *La paix de Dieu*
"Heponenki hengähtävi matkan pitkän
   mentyämsä" *see Miksi en väsyisi*
   Kanteletar **KILPINEN**
"Her eyes the glow-worm lend thee" *see
   The night-piece* Herrick **QUILTER**
Her message see Runeberg **SIBELIUS**
   Hennes budskap

Her song see Hardy **IRELAND**
Her voice see Wilde **CARPENTER**
"Herab kamst du auf Erden" *see Jesus als
   Kind* Unknown **LOEWE**
Heracleitus see Callimachus **HESELTINE**
"L'herbe a grandi au fossé" *see Effacement*
   Follain **SAUGUET**
"L'herbe est molle au sommeil" *see Phidylé*
   Leconte de Lisle **DUPARC**
Une herbe pauvre see Éluard **POULENC**
"Herbei, heran, auf die glänzende Bahn!" *see
   Schlittschuhlauf* Enslin **LOEWE**
Herbert, Mary Sidney, Countess of
   Pembroke, 1561-1621.
   ROREM *If ever hapless woman had a
      cause*
Herbst see Ady **BARTÓK** *Autumn echoes*
Herbst see Hesse **KILPINEN**
Herbst see Holstein **DELIUS**
Herbst see Lenau **WOLF**
Der Herbst see Lua **SPOHR**
Herbst see Rellstab **SCHUBERT**
Herbst see Rilke **SAUGUET**
Der Herbst see Schulz, J. **LOEWE**
HERBST, no. 1
   KILPINEN Hesse *Jugendflucht*
HERBST, no. 2
   KILPINEN Hesse *Herbst*
HERBST, no. 3
   KILPINEN Hesse *Gebet der Fischer*
HERBST, no. 4
   KILPINEN Hesse *Aus zwei Tälern*
HERBST, no. 5
   KILPINEN Hesse *Drüben*
HERBST, no. 6
   KILPINEN Hesse *Nach dem Fest*
HERBST, no. 7
   KILPINEN Hesse *Die Kindheit*
HERBST, no. 8
   KILPINEN Hesse *Vergänglichkeit*
Der Herbstabend see Salis-Seewis
   SCHUBERT
Herbstbild see Hebbel **PFITZNER**
Herbstenschluss see Lenau **WOLF**
Herbstgedanken see Unknown
   RUBINSTEIN
Herbstgefühl see Fleischer **BERG**
Herbstgefühl see Frey, F. **PFITZNER**
Herbstgefühl see Goethe **SCHOECK**
Herbstgefühl see Schack **BRAHMS**
Herbstgefühl see Schulenburg **LASSEN**
Herbsthauch see Rückert **PFITZNER**
Herbstklage see Lenau **WOLF**
Herbstkummer see Ernst **BRUCKNER**
Herbstlied see Klingemann
   MENDELSSOHN-BARTHOLDY

Herbstlied see Salis-Seewis SCHUBERT
Herbstlied see Sallet PFITZNER
Herbstlied see Schöpff SCHUMANN
Herbstlied see Tieck CORNELIUS,
    LASSEN, ZELTER
Herbstlied see Verlaine *POÈMES*
    SATURNIENS. DELIUS *Chanson*
    d'automne
Herbstnacht see Geibel LASSEN
Die Herbstnacht see Salis-Seewis
    SCHUBERT *Wehmut*
"Herbstsonnenschein. Der liebe Abend blickt"
    see Im Zimmer Schlaf BERG
Herbstsorge see Osterwald FRANZ
Herbststimmung see Paulsen GRIEG *Nå jeg*
    vil dø
Herbststimmung see Paulsen GRIEG *På*
    Skogstien
Herbststurm see Richardt GRIEG
    Efteraarsstormen
Herbsttränen see Ady BARTÓK *Autumn*
    tears
"Der Herbstwind rüttelt die Bäume" *see*
    Reiselied Heine MENDELSSOHN-
    BARTHOLDY
"Der Herbstwind schüttelt die Linde" *see Zum*
    Abschied meiner Tochter Eichendorff
    PFITZNER
The herd-boy see Lu Yu BRITTEN
Herder, Johann Gottfried von, 1744-
    1803.
    BEETHOVEN
        Der Gesang der Nachtigal
        Die laute Klage
    LOEWE
        Der Kukuk
        Das Paradies in der Wüste
        Die Sylphide
    SCHUBERT *Ein altschottische Ballade*
    WEBER *Das neue Lied*
    ZELTER *Macht der Liebe*
    STIMMEN DER VÖLKER.
        JENSEN
            Darthula's Grabesgesang
            Edward
            Erlkönigs Tochter
            Lied der Desdemona
        LOEWE
            Edward
            Herr Oluf
"Here a pretty baby lies" *see Another epitaph*
    Herrick ROREM
"Here come the line-gang pioneering by" *see*
    The line gang Frost CARTER
"Here in Loyang spring tarries" *see Late*
    spring Yang Knang BERKELEY

"Here lies, but seven years old" *see Afraid*
    De La Mare BERKELEY
"Here lies my husbands; one, two three" *see*
    Three husbands De La Mare CHANLER
HERE LIES MY THREE HUSBANDS. see
    De La Mare
    Three husbands CHANLER
"Here lies the clerk who half his life had
    spent" *see Epitaph: The clerk* Asquith
    BRITTEN
"Here lies Thomas Logge" *see Thomas Logge*
    De La Mare CHANLER
"Here lyeth our infant, Alice Rodd" *see Alice*
    Rodd De La Mare CHANLER
"Here she lies, a pretty bud" *see Epitaph upon*
    a child that died Herrick ROREM
"Here sleep I, Susannah Fry" *see Susannah*
    Fry De La Mare CHANLER
Here the frailest leaves of me see Whitman
    LUENING
"Here the tapers I hold" *see The ring*
    Kol'tsov RACHMANINOFF
"Here we bring new water" *see A new year*
    carol Anon. BRITTEN
Hérédia, José María, 1842-1905.
    KOECHLIN *La prière du mort*
"Herein, O du Guter" *see Ballade* Goethe
    ZELTER
"Herein, O du Guter!" *see Ballade vom*
    vertriebenen und zurückkehrenden Grafen
    Goethe LOEWE
"Here's an old Taylor, rest his eye" *see A*
    one-eyed tailor De La Mare CHANLER
Herlossohn, Karl, 1804-1849.
    WOLF *Der Schwalben Heimkehr*
Herman, Nikolaus, d. 1561.
    REGER *Bitte um einen seligen Tod*
Hermann, Franz Rudolf, 1787-1823.
    BEETHOVEN *Der Bardengeist*
Hermann und Thusnelda see Klopstock
    SCHUBERT
Hermes, Johann Timotheus, 1738-1821.
SOPHIENS REISE.
    MOZART
        Ich würd' auf meinem Pfad
        Sei du mein Trost
        Verdankt sei es dem Glanz der
            Grossen
HERMIT SONGS, no. 1
    BARBER O'Faolain, Sean, translator *At*
    St. Patrick's Purgatory
HERMIT SONGS, no. 2
    BARBER Jones, Howard Mumford,
        translator *Church bell at night*
HERMIT SONGS, no. 3
    BARBER Kallman *St. Ita's vision*

COMPOSER   Poet   *Title*   "First Line"

HERMIT SONGS, no. 4
   BARBER O'Faolain, Sean, translator
   The heavenly banquet
HERMIT SONGS, no. 5
   BARBER Jones, Howard Mumford,
   translator *The crucifixion*
HERMIT SONGS, no. 6
   BARBER O'Faolain, Sean, translator
   Sea-snatch
HERMIT SONGS, no. 7
   BARBER Jackson, Kenneth, translator
   Promiscuity
HERMIT SONGS, no. 8
   BARBER Auden, W. H., translator
   The monk and his cat
HERMIT SONGS, no. 9
   BARBER Auden, W. H., translator
   The praises of God
HERMIT SONGS, no. 10
   BARBER O'Faolain, Sean, translator
   The desire for hermitage
Hernández Aquino, Luis, 1907-
   RODRIGO *Sobre el cupey*
The hero see Byron *HEBREW MELODIES.*
   SCHUMANN *Dem Helden*
Herodes' Klage um Mariamne see Byron
   LOEWE
Hérold, André-Ferdinand, b. 1865.
   AUBERT *Prélude*
Herold, Jíří, 1875-1934.
   MARTINŮ *Summer ballad*
Herolde ritten von Ort zu Ort see Kugler
   LOEWE
"Herr, der du alles wohl gemacht" *see*
   Jünglings Gebet Rückert **LOEWE**
Herr! der du alles wohl gemacht see Rückert
   BARTÓK
"Herr Dyring ritt wohl durch das Land" *see*
   Der Mutter Geist Jacob, T. **LOEWE**
"Herr Frühling gibt jetzt ein Konzert" *see*
   Waldkonzert Vogl **STRAUSS**
"Herr Heinrich sitzt am Vogelherd" *see*
   Heinrich der Vogler Vogl **LOEWE**
Der Herr ist Gott see Cramer **LOEWE**
"Der Herr ist Gott und keiner mehr" *see*
   Der Herr ist Gott Cramer **LOEWE**
"Der Herr ist mein Hirte" *see Psalm 23* Bible
   SCHOECK
"Herr Jesu Christ" *see Nach der Geburt ihres*
   Sohnes Mary **SCHUMANN**
Herr Jesus mein see Jone *VIAE INVIAE.*
   WEBERN
Herr Lenz see Bodmann **STRAUSS**
"Herr Lenz springt heute durch die Stadt" *see*
   Herr Lenz Bodmann **STRAUSS**
Herr Oluf see Herder *STIMMEN DER*
   VÖLKER. **LOEWE**

"Herr Oluf reitet spät und weit" *see Erlkönigs*
   Tochter Herder **JENSEN**
"Herr Oluf reitet spät und weit" *see Herr Oluf*
   Herder **LOEWE**
"Herr Pfarrer hat zwei Fräulchen" *see*
   Das Pfarrjüngferchen Rückert **LOEWE**
"Herr! schicke was du Willt" *see Gebet*
   Mörike **WOLF**
"Herr! schikke, was du willt" *see Gebet*
   Mörike **SCHOECK**
Herr, was trägt der Boden hier see Anon.
   WOLF
"Herr, zu dir will ich mich retten" *see*
   Entsagung Droysen **MENDELSSOHN-**
   BARTHOLDY
Herrick, Robert, 1591-1674.
   BERKELEY
   Herrick songs
   How love came in
   CARPENTER *Bid me to live*
   GIDEON
   Gather ye rosebuds
   To music
   HINDEMITH *To music, to becalm his*
   fever
   QUILTER
   The bracelet
   Cherry-ripe
   I dare not ask a kiss
   Julia's hair
   The maiden blush
   The night-piece
   To daisies
   Tulips
   RIETI *To the virgins, to make much of*
   time
   ROREM
   Another epitaph
   Cherry-ripe
   Comfort to a youth that had lost his love
   Epitaph upon a child that died
   To Anthea, who may command him
   anything
   To daisies, not to shut so soon
   To music, to becalm his fever
   To the willow-tree
   Upon Julia's clothes
HESPERIDES.
   DELIUS *To daffodils*
HESPERIDES (1648): Chop-cherry.
   HESELTINE *Thou gav'st me leave to*
   kiss
HESPERIDES (1648): Upon love.
   HESELTINE *I held Love's head*
Herrick songs see Herrick **BERKELEY**
Herrn Josef Spaun see Collin, M.
   SCHUBERT

Herrosee, Karl Friedrich, 1754-1821.
BEETHOVEN *Zärtliche Liebe*
Hertig Magnus see Josephson, E.
SIBELIUS
"Hertig Magnus fran sitt fönster" *see Hertig Magnus* Josephson, E. **SIBELIUS**
Hertz, Henrik, 1798-1870.
JENSEN
   Engelgesang
   Mich treibt's hinaus in's lichte Frühlingsrauschen
Hertz, Wilhelm, 1855-1902.
JENSEN
   Fernsicht
   Letzter Wunsch
   Lied der verlassenen Liebe
   Mein Engel hüte dein
   Mein Herz
   Sternbotschaft
REGER *Daz iuwer min engel walte!*
Herwegh, George, 1817-1875.
JENSEN *Ob die Locken eine Glorie quellen*
LISZT *Ich möchte hingehn*
Herz, ich habe schwer an dir zu tragen see Mörike **FRANZ**
"Das Herz ist gewachsen, Es pocht in der Brust" *see Das Mädchens Sehnsucht* Kind, F. **SPOHR**
Herz, mein Herz see Geibel **STRAUSS**
"Herz, mein Herz, ermanne dich!" *see Schmerz* Blankensee **WEBER**
"Herz, mein Herz, sei nicht beklommen" *see Herz, mein Herz* Geibel **STRAUSS**
"Herz, mein Herz, sei nicht beklommen" *see Neuer Frühling* Heine **LOEWE**
"Herz, mein Herz, warum so fröhlich" *see Neue Liebe* Eichendorff **PFITZNER**
"Herz, mein Herz, was soll das geben?" *see Neue Liebe, neues Leben* Goethe **BEETHOVEN, SPOHR, ZELTER**
   Two Beethoven settings: Op. 75 no. 2 and WoO 127.
"Herz, nun so alt" *see Herbsthauch* Rückert **PFITZNER**
"Herz und weisst du selber denn" *see Herz, ich habe schwer an dir zu tragen* Mörike **FRANZ**
Herz, verzage nicht geschwind see Anon. **WOLF**
Herzchen, mein Schätzchen see Anon. **WEBER**
"Herzchen, mein Schätzchen" *see Minnelied* Anon. **REGER**
Herzeleid see Ulrich **SCHUMANN**
"Herzen, die gen Himmel sich erheben" *see An Laura* Matthisson **SCHUBERT**

Herzen und Augen see Gerstenberg **LOEWE**
Die Herzensrose see Rückert **LOEWE**
Herzenstausch see Enslin **REGER**
Herzensverstand see Wolf, F. **BLACHER**
Herziges Schätzle du see Anon. **FRANZ**
"Herzliebe, gute Mütter" *see Das Echo* Castelli **SCHUBERT**
HESELTINE, PHILIP, 1894-1930.
Aldington, Richard, 1892-1962.
   IMAGES (1910-1915).
     After two years (1930) [Oxford Univ. Press, 1931] "She is all so slight"
Anon.
   Adam lay ybounden (1922) [Oxford Univ. Press, 1923; Oxford Book of Carols, 1928] same
   Text in British Museum MS Sloane 2593.
   As ever I saw (1918) [Winthrop Rogers, 1919] "She is gentle and also wise"
   Text in British Museum MS Harleian 7578.
   The bachelor (1922) [Augener, 1922] "In all this warld nis a meriar life"
   Text in Chambers & Sidgwick *Early English lyrics* (A.H.Bullen, 1907).
   The bayly berith the bell away (1918) [Winthrop Rogers, 1919] "The maidens came when I was in my mother's bow'r"
   Text in Chambers & Sidgwick *Early English lyrics* (A.H.Bullen, 1907).
   The distracted maid (1922) [J. & W. Chester, 1923] "One morning very early, one morning in the spring"
   Poem from *Lillygay* (Steyning, Sussex: Vine Press, 1920).
   The droll lover (1928) [Augener, 1929] "I love thee for thy fickleness"
   Text in British Museum MS Add. 53723 [325 songs by Henry Lawes]
   Elore lo (1928) [Augener, 1929] "In a garden so green in a May morning"
   Text in John Forbes *Cantus, songs and fancies* (Aberdeen, 1662).
   Good ale (1922) [Augener, 1922] "Bring us in no brown bread"
   Hey, troly loly lo (1922) [Augener, 1922] "Hey, troly loly lo, maid, whither go you?"
   Text in British Museum MS Add. 31922 [Music by Henry VIII and others]
   Jenny Gray (1923?) [Thames Publ., 1972] "I had a little nobby mare"

HESELTINE, PHILIP, 1894-1930
(continued)
Anon. *(continued)*

Jillian of Berry (1926) [Oxford Univ. Press, 1927]
"Jillian of Berry she dwells on a hill"
Text in Beaumont & Fletcher *The Knight of the Burning Pestle.*

Johnnie wi' the tye (1922) [J. & W. Chester, 1923] "Johnnie cam' to our toun"
Poem from *Lillygay* (Steyning, Sussex: Vine Press, 1920).

The jolly shepherd (1927) [Winthrop Rogers; Hawkes & Son, 1930]
"The life of a shepherd is void of all care-a"
Poem in *Wit and Drollery* (1661).

Love for love (1919) [Winthrop Rogers, 1920] "My joy it is from her to here"
Text in British Museum MS Harleian 3362.

My little sweet darling (1919) [Winthrop Rogers, 1920] same
Text in MS at Christ Church, Oxford; also in British Museum MS Add. 17786-91.

Passing by (1928) [Oxford Univ. Press, 1929] "There is a lady sweet and kind"
Text in Thomas Ford *Musicke of Sundrie Kindes* (1607).

Peter Warlock's fancy (1924) [Paterson, 1925; Chappell] "Bring us in no beef, sir"
Text in British Museum MS Harleian 541; also in Ritson *Ancient Songs & Ballads* (Payne & Foss, 1829).

Piggesnie (1922) [Augener, 1922] "She is so proper and so pure"
Text in Sidgwick & Chambers *Early English lyrics* (A.H.Bullen, 1907).

Play acting (1920) [Thames Publ., 1972] "There's a jolly lot o' laughter"

Rest, sweet nymphs (1922) [Oxford Univ. Press, 1924]
"Rest, sweet nymphs, let golden sleep"
Text in *Oxford book of English verse* (1900).

Robin Good-fellow (1926) [Oxford Univ. Press, 1927] "And can the physician make sick men well?"

The shoemaker (1922) [J. & W. Chester, 1923]
"Shoemaker, shoemaker, are ye within?"
Poem from *Lillygay* (Steyning, Sussex: Vine Press, 1920).

There is a lady sweet and kind (1919) [Winthrop Rogers, 1920] same
Poem in *Oxford book of English verse* (1900).

Tom Tyler (1928) [Augener, 1929] "I am a poor tiler in simple array"

Twelve oxen (1924) [Oxford Univ. Press, 1924] "I have twelve oxen"
Solo voice with chorus.
Poem in Chambers & Sidgwick *Early English lyrics* (A.H.Bullen, 1907).

Tyrley Tyrlow (1922) [Oxford Univ. Press, 1923; Oxford Book of Carols, 1928]
"About the field they piped full right"
Poem in Chambers & Sidgwick *Early English lyrics* (A.H.Bullen, 1907).

Walking the woods (1927) [Hawkes & Son, 1927] "I would I were Actaeon whom Diana did disguise"
Poem in *A gorgeous gallery of gallant inventions* (1578).

THE FAMOUS HISTORY OF FRIAR BACON (printed before 1600).

Away to Twiver (1926) [Oxford Univ. Press, 1927] "And did you not hear of a mirth that befell"

MAIDMENT'S NORTH COUNTRIE GARLAND (1824).

Burd Ellen and young Tamlane (1922) [J. & W. Chester, 1923] "Burd Ellen sits in her bower windowe"

NURSE LOVECHILD'S LEGACY (London: The Poetry Bookshop, 1916).

Arthur o' Bower (1923) [Augener, 1924] "Arthur o' Bower has broken his band"

How many miles to Babylon? (1923) [Augener, 1924] same

I had a little pony (1923) [Augener, 1924] same

I won't be my father's Jack (1923) [Augener, 1924] same

Little Jack Jingle (1923) [Augener, 1924] "Now what do you think of little Jack Jingle?"

Little Tommy Tucker (1923) [Augener, 1924] same

O my kitten (1923) [Augener, 1924] "O my kitten, a kitten"

Robin and Richard (1923) [Augener, 1924] "Robin and Richard were two pretty men"

Suky, you shall be my wife (1923) [Augener, 1924] same

There was a man of Thessaly (1923) [Augener, 1924] same

There was an old man (1923)[Augener, 1924] same

There was an old woman (1923) [Augener, 1924] same

Belloc, Hilaire, 1870-1953.

The birds (1926) [Joseph Williams Ltd., 1927; Stainer & Bell] "When Jesus Christ was four years old"

Ha'nacker mill (1927) [Oxford Univ. Press, 1927]

"Sally is gone that was so kindly"

The night (1927) [Oxford Univ. Press, 1927] "Most holy night, that still dost keep"

THE FOUR MEN. HIS OWN COUNTRY: I shall go without companions.

My own country (1927) [Oxford Univ. Press, 1927]

"I shall go without companions"

Blake, William, 1757-1827.

POEMS FROM THE ROSSETTI MS 1793: A poem with a moral.

I asked a thief to steal me a peach (1917) [Thames Publ., 1972] same

Blunt, George Henry Bruce, 1899-1957.

Bethlehem down (rewritten, 1930) [Winthrop Rogers, 1931]

"When He is King we will give Him the Kings' gifts"

Voice & organ. Text in *The London Mercury,* Dec. 1927.

The cricketers of Hambledon (1928) [Augener, 1929]

"I'll make a song of Hambledon"

Text in *The London Mercury,* Dec. 1927.

The first mercy (1927) [Hawkes & Son, 1927] "Ox and ass at Bethlehem"

Text in *The London Mercury,* Dec. 1927.

The fox (1930) [Oxford Univ. Press, 1931] "At 'The Fox Inn' the tattered ears"

Text in *The London Mercury,* Dec. 1927.

The frostbound wood (1929) [Oxford Univ. Press, 1931]

"Mary that was the Child's mother"

Text in *The London Mercury,* Dec. 1927.

Breton, Nicholas, 1542-1626.

MELANCHOLIC HUMOURS (1600).

Fair and true (1926) [Oxford Univ. Press, 1927]

"Lovely kind, and kindly loving"

Callimachus, ca.305-ca.240 B.C.

Heracleitus (1917) [J. &. W. Chester, 1923] "They told me, Heracleitus, you were dead"

Poem in *Oxford book of English verse* (1900).

Campion, Thomas, 1567-1619.

GILES EARLE, HIS BOOKE (1616-1625).

The lover's maze (1927) [Oxford Univ. Press, 1928] "O be still, be still, unquiet thoughts"

Chalkhill, John, 17th cent.

THE COMPLEAT ANGLER (1653): Corydon's song.

The countryman (1926) [Hawkes & Son, 1926]

"Oh, the sweet contentment"

Charles, Duke of Orleans, 1391-1465.

My gostly fader (1918-19) [Winthrop Rogers, 1919] same

Text in British Museum MS Harleian 682.

Collins, Hal, d.1929.

Yarmouth Fair (1924) [Oxford Univ. Press, 1925]

"As I rode down to Yarmouth Fair"

Dekker, Thomas, 1570-1641.

THE PLEASANT COMOEDY OF PATIENT GRISSILL (1603).

Lullaby (1918) [Winthrop Rogers, 1919]

"Golden slumbers kiss your eyes"

Sweet content (1919) [Winthrop Rogers, 1920] "Art thou poor, yet hast thou golden slumbers?"

Poem in *Oxford book of English verse* (1900).

Fletcher, John, 1579-1625.

Mourn no moe (1919) [Winthrop Rogers, 1920]

"Weep no more, nor sigh, nor groan"

THE MAID'S TRAGEDY (1619): Aspatia's song.

A sad song (1922) [J. & W. Chester, 1923] "Lay a garland on my hearse"

THE WOMAN HATER (1607).

Sleep (1922) [Oxford Univ. Press, 1924] "Come, sleep, and with thy sweet deceiving"

Poem in *Oxford book of English verse* (1900).

Ford, Ford Madox, 1873-1939.

Consider (1923) [Oxford Univ. Press, 1924] "Now green comes springing o'er the heath"

COMPOSER Poet *Title* "First Line"

HESELTINE, PHILIP, 1894-1930
(continued)
Herrick, Robert, 1591-1674.
  HESPERIDES (1648): Chop-cherry.
    Thou gav'st me leave to kiss (1923)
    [Boosey, 1924] same
  HESPERIDES (1648): Upon love.
    I held Love's head (1923) [Boosey,
    1924] "I held Love's head while it
    did ache"
Hood, Thomas, 1799-1845.
  MINOR POEMS (1846): For music.
    A lake and a fairy boat (1911?)
    [Thames Publ., 1927] same
Li Po, 701-762.
  Along the stream (1917) [J. & W.
    Chester, 1923] "The rustling nightfall
    strews my gown with roses"
Luther, Martin, 1483-1546.
  Balulalow (1919) [Oxford Univ. Press,
    1923; Oxford Book of Carols, 1928]
    "O my deir hert, young Jesus sweit"
Mabbe, James, 1572-1642? translator.
  THE SPANISH BAWD (1631): Now
    sleepe, and take thy rest.
    The contented lover (1928) [Augener,
    1929] "Now sleep and take thy rest"
Marlowe, Christopher, 1564-1593.
  *THE PASSIONATE SHEEPHERD TO
  HIS LOVE.*
    The passionate shepherd (1928) [Elkin,
    1929; Novello] "Come live with me,
    and be my love"
    Text in **England's Helicon** (1600).
Marot, Clément, 1495?-1544.
  *TRENTE ET HUYT CHANSONS
  MUSICALES . . . :* Chanson
  vingtcinquiesme . . .
    Chanson du Jour de Noël (1925?)
    [Winthrop Rogers, 1926]
    "Une pastourelle gentille"
Masefield, John, 1878-1967.
  BALLADS AND POEMS (1903).
    Captain Stratton's fancy (1920)
    [Augener, 1922] "Oh, some are fond
    of red wine and some are fond of
    white"
Nashe, Thomas, 1567-1601.
  *SUMMER'S LAST WILL AND
  TESTAMENT* (1600).
    Spring (1922) [Oxford Univ. Press,
    1924] "Spring, the sweet spring is
    the year's pleasant king"
    Poem in **Oxford Book of English
    Verse** (1900).

Neuburg, Victor B., 1873-1940.
  Rantum Tantum (1922) [J. & W. Chester,
    1923] "Who'll play at Rantum Tantum
    over the fields in May?"
    Poem from **Lillygay** (Steyning, Sussex:
    Vine Press, 1920).
Nichols, Robert Malise Bowyer, 1893-
1944.
  ARBOURS AND ENDURANCES (1917).
    The water lily (1916-17) [Thames
    Publ., 1972]
    "The lily floated white and red"
Peele, George, 1558?-1597?
  THE OLD WIVES' TALE (1595).
    Chopcherry (1922) [J. & W. Chester,
    1923]
    "Whenas the rye reach to the chin"
    Whenas the rye reach to the chin
    (1918) [Winthrop Rogers, 1920]
    same
Phillip, John
  *THE COMMODYE OF PACIENT AND
  MEEKE GRISSILL* (1566).
    Cradle song (1927) [Oxford Univ.
    Press, 1928]
    "Be still, my sweet sweeting"
    Poet may be John Phillips, fl. 1570-
    1591.
Shakespeare, William, 1564-1616.
  AS YOU LIKE IT.
    Pretty ring time (1925) [Oxford Univ.
    Press, 1926]
    "It was a lover and his lass"
  LOVE'S LABOUR'S LOST.
    Mockery (1927) [Oxford Univ. Press,
    1928]
    "When daises pied, and violets blue"
  MEASURE FOR MEASURE.
    Take, O take those lips away (1916-17)
    [J. & W. Chester, 1923] same
    Take, O take those lips away (1918-19)
    [Winthrop Rogers, 1919] same
  MUCH ADO ABOUT NOTHING.
    Sigh no more, ladies (1927) [Oxford
    Univ. Press, 1928] same
  TWELFTH NIGHT.
    Sweet-and-twenty (1924) [Oxford
    Univ. Press, 1924] "O mistress
    mine, where are you roaming?"
  A WINTER'S TALE.
    The sweet o' the year (1928) [Elkin,
    1929; Novello]
    "When daffodils begin to peer"
Shanks, Edward Buxton, 1892-1953.
  *THE QUEEN OF CHINA AND OTHER
  POEMS* (1919).

Late summer (1922) [Augener, 1925]
"The fields are full of summer still"
The singer (1922) [Augener, 1925]
"In the dim light of the golden
lamp"
Shelley, Percy Bysshe, 1792-1822.
POSTHUMOUS POEMS (1824).
Music, when soft voices die (1911?)
[Thames Publ., 1972] same
Sidney, Sir Philip, 1554-1586.
ASTROPHEL AND STELLA (1591): First
song.
Dedication (1919) [Winthrop Rogers,
1919] "Doubt you to whom my
muse these notes intendeth"
Skelton, John, 1460?-1529.
Rutterkin (1922) [J. & W. Chester, 1923]
"Rutterkin is come unto our town"
Poem in British Museum MS Add.
5465 and Chambers & Sidgwick
Early English lyrics (A.H.Bullen,
1907).
Smith, Dr. James, 1605-1667.
LARKSPUR; ed. by Victor Neuburg
(Steyning, Sussex: Vine Press, 1922).
Milkmaids (1923) [Enoch, 1924]
"Walkeing betimes close by a green
wood side"
Text perhaps first published in ***Wit
Restored*** (1658).
Squire, Sir John Collings, 1884-1958.
TRICKS OF THE TRADE (1917).
Mr. Belloc's fancy (1921; rev. 1930)
[Augener, 1922, 1930]
"At Martinmas, when I was born"
Stevenson, Robert Louis, 1850-1894.
SONGS OF TRAVEL (1895).
Romance (1919) [Curwen, 1921]
"I will make you brooches"
To the memory of a great singer
(1918-22) [Augener, 1923]
"Bright is the ring of words"
Stevenson, William, 1521-1575.
GAMMER GURTON'S NEEDLE (1575).
Maltworms (1926) [Oxford Univ.
Press, 1926]
"I cannot eat but little meat"
Text previously attributed to Bishop
Still (1575).
Composed with E. J. Moeran.
Symons, Arthur, 1865-1945.
LONDON NIGHTS.
A prayer to Saint Anthony of Padua
(1925) [Oxford Univ. Press, 1928]

"Saint Anthony of Padua whom I
bear in effigy"
LONDON NIGHTS: "12 Sep 1891"
(1895-97).
Autumn twilight (1922) [Oxford Univ.
Press, 1923]
"The long September evening dies"
THE LOOM OF DREAMS.
The sick heart (1925) [Oxford Univ.
Press, 1928]
"O sick heart, be at rest!"
Udall, Nicholas, 1505-1556.
RALPH ROISTER DOISTER (1550).
Roister doister (1922) [Oxford Univ.
Press, 1924]
"I mun be married a Sunday"
Wever, Robert, fl.ca.1550.
*AN ENTERLUDE CALLED LUSTY
JUVENTUS* (1565).
In an arbour green (1922) [Paterson,
1925] same
Lusty juventus (1922) [Oxford Univ.
Press, 1924] "In a harbour grene
aslepe whereas I lay"
Wyatt, Sir Thomas, 1503?-1542.
And wilt thou leve me thus? (1928)
[Oxford Univ. Press, 1929] same
Text in British Museum MS Add.
17492.
Yeats, William Butler, 1865-1939.
THE WIND AMONG THE REEDS
(1899): Aedh wishes for the cloths . . .
The cloths of heaven (1919) [unpubl.]
"Had I the heaven's embroidered
cloths"
THE WIND AMONG THE REEDS
(1899): Aodh to Dectora.
The everlasting voices (1915) [Thames
Publ., 1975]
"O sweet everlasting voices, be still"
Young, Ella, 1867-1956.
POEMS (1906).
The wind from the West (1911?)
[Thames Publ., 1972] "Blow high,
blow low, O wind from the West"
HESPERIDES. see Herrick
To daffodils **DELIUS**
HESPERIDES (1648): Chop-cherry. *see*
Herrick
Thou gav'st me leave to kiss **HESELTINE**
HESPERIDES (1648): Upon love. *see* Herrick
I held Love's head **HESELTINE**
"Hesperus, der bleiche Funken" *see*
Vergangenheit Lenau **SCHOECK**

Hesse, Hermann, 1877-1962.
KILPINEN
Allein
Aufstieg
Aus zwei Tälern
Berggeist
Drüben
Dunkle Augen
Gebet der Fischer
Glück
Grindelwald
Herbst
Ich fragte dich
Jugendflucht
Die Kindheit
Liebeslied
Nach dem Fest
Schlittenfahrt
Traum
Vergänglichkeit
Wo mag meine Heimat sein?
LUENING
At Christmas time
Frühling
In Weihnachtzeiten
Wie sind die Tage
SCHOECK
Abends
Aus zwei Tälern
Auskunst
Blauer Schmetterling
Elisabeth
Frühling
Für Ninon
Im Krauzgang von St. Stefano
Im Nebel
Jahrestag
Keine Rast
Kennst du das auch?
Die Kindheit
Magie der Farben
Mittag im September
Nachtgefühl
Pfeifen
Ravenna
Sommernacht
Vergänglichkeit
Verwelkende Rosen
Vorwurf
Was lachst du so?
Das Ziel
Het wasser te nacht see Anon. **PIJPER**
Het windetje die uyt den oosten waeyt see
   Anon. **PIJPER**

Hettich, Amédée Louis Landely, 1856-1937.
AUBERT
D'un berceau
Melancholia
Noël pastoral
CASELLA *Temps de neige*
Heuffer, Ford Madox *see* Ford, Ford
   Madox, 1873-1939.
L'heure avance see Anon.
   SZYMANOWSKI *A pod borem siwe kunie*
L'heure captive see Dommange **AUBERT**
L'heure d'amour see Gallet **MASSENET**
   Nuit d'Espagne
L'heure douce see Chabroux, Ernest
   MASSENET
"*Heure du ciel, jour de Dieu*" *see Les noces*
   d'Or du Sacerdoce Delaporte, R. P.
   INDY
L'heure du retour see Chalupt **ROUSSEL**
Heure du soir see Silvestre **DELIBES**
L'heure exquise see Verlaine *LA BONNE*
   CHANSON. **HAHN**
Heure vécue see Jacquet, Mme. M.
   MASSENET
L'heure volée see Mendès **MASSENET**
Les heures see Mauclair **CHAUSSON**
Heures passées see Lenfaut, A.
   SAINT-SAËNS
L'heureuse souffrance see Henri IV
   MASSENET
Heureux qui comme Ulysse see Ronsard
   RIVIER
"*Heureux qui de la sagesse*" *see Cantique sur*
   le bonheur des justes . . . *Racine* **HAHN**
Heureux qui du coeur de Marie see Anon.
   SAINT-SAËNS
"*Heureux qui meurt ici*" *see Au cimetière*
   Richepin **FAURÉ**
Heureux sera le jour see Ronsard **GOUNOD**
Heuska see Vogl **LOEWE**
"*Heut' aber geh' ich*" *see Läuterung*
   Hohenberg **BERG**
Heut' Nacht erhob ich mich im Mitternacht
   see Heyse **WOLF**
"*Heut ward mir bis zum jungen Tag*" *see*
   Unruhige Nacht Meyer **SCHOECK**
"*Heut, wo noch Rosendüfte mich*
   umschweben" *see Fünf Sinnsprüche Omars*
   des Zeltmachers Omar Khayyam
   BLACHER
"*Heute ist Sonntag*" *see Sonntag und Montag*
   Unknown **SPOHR**
"*Heute marschieren wir!*" *see Aus! Aus!*
   Anon. **MAHLER**
"*Heute, nur heute bin ich so schön*" *see*
   Die Zigeunerin Unknown **LASSEN**

"Heute tanzt alles" *see Tanz* Hafiz
  SZYMANOWSKI
"Heute will ich fröhlich, fröhlich sein" *see*
  Am ersten Maimorgen Claudius, M.
  SCHUBERT
"Heute will ich fröhlich, fröhlich sein" *see*
  Der Frühling Claudius, M. **SCHOECK**
Hevist dins la lluna tres petits conills see
  Anon. **MOMPOU**
Die Hexe see Häring **LOEWE**
  Walpurgisnacht
Die Hexe see Wolf, F. **BLACHER**
Hexenlied see Hölty **MENDELSSOHN-**
  BARTHOLDY *Andres Maienlied*
"Hey! hey! that's what the blues singers say"
  see The cryin' blues Hughes, L.
  CARPENTER
Hey, ho, the wind and the rain see
  Shakespeare *TWELFTH NIGHT.*
  QUILTER
Hey! Ring out, my triangle see Heyduk
  DVOŘÁK *Aj! Kterak trojhranec muj*
    přerozkošně
Hey, troly loly lo see Anon. **HESELTINE**
"Hey, troly loly lo, maid, whither go you?"
  see Hey, troly loly lo Anon. **HESELTINE**
Heyduk, Adolf, 1835-1923.
  DVOŘÁK
    A kdybys písní stvořená
    A les je tichý kolem kol
    Aj! Kterak trojhranec muj přerozkošně
    Dejte klec jestřábu
    Kdybys, milé děvče, sedalo na truno
    Když mne stará matka
    Má píseň zas mi láskouzní
    Široké rukávy
    Struna naladěna
  MARTINŮ
    A winter's night
    You write to me
Heyduk, Adolf, 1835-1923, translator.
  IVES *Songs my mother taught me*
Heym, Georg, 1887-1912.
  BARBER *O boundless, boundless evening*
Heyse, Paul Johann Ludwig von, 1830-
  1914.
  BRAHMS *Mädchenlied*
    Two settings: Op. 95 no. 6 and op. 107
      no. 5.
  CORNELIUS
    Im Lenz
    Im Walde
    In der Mondnacht
    Morgenwind
    Musje Morgenrots Lied
    Schäfers Nachtlied

JENSEN
  Abschied
  Durch die Ferne, durch die Nacht
  Die Einsame
  Geheimnis
  Im Walde
  Mädchenlied
  Rosenzeit
  Schlaf nur ein
  Sonnenschein
  Über ein Stündlein
  Ueber Nacht
  Unter den Zweigen in tiefer Nacht
  Vergangnes Glück
LASSEN
  Dornröschen (Das Mädchen spricht)
  Komm, O Verina
PFITZNER *Über ein Stündlein*
SCHÖNBERG
  Mädchenlied
  Waldesnacht
SCHUMANN
  Frühlingslust
  Die Spinnerin
WOLF
  Auch kleine Dinge
  Benedeit die sel'ge Mutter
  Dass doch gemalt all'deine Reize wären
  Du denkst mit einem Fädchen
  Du sagst mir, dass ich keine Fürstin sei
  Gesegnet sei das Grün
  Gesegnet sei, durch den die Welt
    entstund
  Geselle, woll'n wir uns in Kutten hüllen
  Heb' auf dein blondes Haupt
  Heut' Nacht erhob ich mich im
    Mitternacht
  Hoffärtig seid Ihr
  Ich esse nun mein Brot nicht trocken
    mehr
  Ich hab' in Penna
  Ich liess mir sagen und mir ward erzählt
  Ihr jungen Leute
  Ihr seid die Allerschönste weit und breit
  In dem Schatten meiner Locken
  Lass sie nur gehn
  Man sagt mir
  Mein Liebster hat es Tische mich geladen
  Mein Liebster ist so klein
  Mein Liebster singt am Haus
  Mir ward gesagt
  Der Mond hat eine schwere Klag'
  Nein, junger Herr, so triebt
  Nicht länger kann ich singen
  Nun lass uns Frieden schliessen
  O wär' dein Haus durchsichtig

COMPOSER Poet *Title* "First Line"

Heyse, Paul Johann Ludwig von, 1830-
1914 *(continued)*
   WOLF *(continued)*
      O wüsstest du, wie viel ich deinetwegen
      Schon streckt' ich aus
      Schweig' einmal still
      Selig ihr Blinden
      Ein Ständchen Euch zu bringen
      Sterb' ich, so hüllt in Blumen
      Und steht Ihr früh am Morgen auf
      Und willst du deinen Liebsten
      Verschling' der Abgrund meines Liebste
         Hütte
      Was für ein Lied soll dir gesungen
         werden
      Was soll der Zorn
      Wenn du, mein Liebster
      Wenn du mich mit den Augen streifst und
         lachst
      Wer rief dich denn?
      Wie lange schon
      Wie soll ich fröhlich sein und lachen gar
      Wie viele Zeit verlor ich
      Wir haben beide lange Zeit
      Wohl kenn' ich Euren Stand
   ITALIENISCHES LIEDERBUCH.
      BRAHMS *Am Sonntag Morgen*
   MELEAGER.
      JENSEN *Über die Welt*
   SPANISCHES LIEDERBUCH (1852).
      BRAHMS, JENSEN *Spanisches Lied*
   TOSCANISCHER RISPETTO.
      JENSEN *Toscanischer Rispetto*
Heywood, Thomas, d. 1641.
   QUILTER *Morning song*
   THOMSON *The bell doth toll*
   VAUGHAN WILLIAMS *Ye little birds*
Hi Hi Hi see Cronyn **RIEGGER**
Les hiboux see Baudelaire **SÉVERAC**
Der Hidalgo see Geibel **LASSEN,**
   SCHUMANN
Hidden flames see Dryden **ROREM**
Hidden love see Bjørnson **DELIUS**
   Verborg'ne Liebe
Hidden union see Snoilsky **SIBELIUS** *Dold*
   förening
"*Hie und da ist an den Bäumen*" *see Letzte*
   Hoffnung Müller, Wilhelm **SCHUBERT**
"*Hielt die allerschönste Herrin*" *see Frohe*
   Botschaft Reinick **WOLF**
Hiemer, Franz Karl, 1768-1822.
   WEBER
      Damon und Chloe
      Wiegenlied
Hier see Laurencin **POULENC**
"*Hier am Hügel heissen Sandes sitz' ich*" *see*
   Hagar's Klage Schücking **SCHUBERT**

Hier au soir see Hugo **LASSEN**
"*Hier bin ich*" *see Umkehr* Eichendorff
   SCHOECK
"*Hier, c'est ce chapeau fané*" *see Hier*
   Laurencin **POULENC**
"*Hier doch keinem darfst du's zeigen*" *see*
   Mit einem Jugendbildnis Meyer
   SCHOECK
"*Hier ein Weilchen! dort ein Weilchen!*" *see*
   Der gute Rat Schatz **REGER**
"*Hier grub man ein*" *see Grabstein* Zwehl,
   Hans Fritz von **KILPINEN**
"*Hier im Kruge*" *see Fröhliche Gesellen*
   Roquette **JENSEN**
"*Hier im Schatten, O Batyllos*" *see Ruheplatz*
   Anacreon **SCHOECK**
"*Hier in der öden Fremde*" *see Sehnsucht I*
   Hohenberg **BERG**
"*Hier in diesen erdbeklommen Lüften*" *see*
   Zum Schluss Rückert **SCHUMANN**
"*Hier ist alles weich und südlich*" *see Heisser*
   Tag am See Krenek **KRENEK**
"*Hier ist Freude, hier ist Lust*" *see Auf der*
   Teck Mörike **SCHOECK**
Hier je l'ai vue see Zaffira **GOUNOD**
   Ier l'ho scontrata
"*Hier le vent du soir*" *see Hier au soir* Hugo
   LASSEN
"*Hier lieg ich auf dem Frühlingshügel*" *see*
   Im Frühling Mörike **WOLF**
"*Hier ob dem Eingang seid*" *see Die Kränze*
   Daumer **BRAHMS**
"*Hier pflegt Natur mit ihren goldnen Auen*"
   see Heimweh Leuthold **SCHOECK**
"*Hier scheidet die Klosterpforte*" *see Im*
   Klosterkeller Leuthold **SCHOECK**
"*Hier steh' ich einsam auf dem Fels im Meer*"
   see Sankt Helena Kahlert **LOEWE**
"*Hier unten steht ein Ritter im hellen*
   Mondenstrahl*" *see Liebeslauschen*
   Schlechta **SCHUBERT**
"*Hier, wo sich die Strassen scheiden*" *see*
   Ein Wanderer Köstlin **BRAHMS**
"*Hierusalem, my happie home*" *see Jerusalem,*
   my happy home Anon. **THOMSON**
High are the snowdrifts see Joukahainen,
   Wilkku **SIBELIUS** *On hanget korkeat*
High in the Georgian hills see Pushkin
   RIMSKĬĬ-KORSAKOV *Na kholmakh*
   Gruzii
"*High o'er the hill*" *see Tears* Wang Seng-
   ju **GRIFFES**
"*High row the boatman row*" *see*
   The boatmen's dance Emmett **COPLAND**
The highland balou see Burns **BRITTEN**
Highland cradle song see Burns
   SCHUMANN *Hochländisches Wiegenlied*

COMPOSER Poet *Title* "First Line"

The Highland widow see Burns
   SCHUMANN Die Hochländer-Wittwe
Highwaymen see Li-Shê CARPENTER
"Hildebrand und sein Sohn Hadubrand" see
   Hildebrandlied Scheffel JENSEN
Hildebrandlied see Scheffel GAUDEAMUS.
   JENSEN
Hildebrandt
   LOEWE Dem Könige
Hiljaisuus see Jalkanen KILPINEN
"Hiljaisuus, mi henkii" see Hiljaisuus
   Jalkanen KILPINEN
Hill, Susan Benedict
   IVES William Will, a Republican campaign
   song
Hillankukka see Törmänen KILPINEN
"Hill-people long for their hills" see
   The heart's country Evans CARPENTER
Hillyer, Robert Silliman, 1895-1961.
   ROREM Early in the morning
Hilsen see Heine GRIEG Gruss
Hilsen see Holstein NIELSEN
"Himlen mørkner stor og stum" see Julesang
   Falck, Mogens NIELSEN
"Der Himmel glänzt vom reinsten
   Frühlingslichte" see Zu viel Mörike
   SCHOECK
"Der Himmel hat eine Thräne geweint" see
   Die Perle Rückert FRANZ
Der Himmel hat eine Thräne geweint see
   Rückert LIEBESFRÜHLING.
   SCHUMANN
Der Himmel hat eine Träne geweint see
   Rückert LIEBESFRÜHLING. REGER
"Der Himmel ist so weit und hehr" see
   An eine Mutter Asenijeff REGER
"Die Himmel rühmen" see Die Ehre Gottes
   aus der Natur Gellert BEETHOVEN
Die Himmel rufen see Cramer LOEWE
Himmel und Erde see Schöpff SCHUMANN
HIMMEL UND ERDE. see Ziegler, K.
   Frühlingsankunft LOEWE
"Der Himmel wölbt sich rein und blau" see
   Märzveilchen Andersen SCHUMANN
Himmelfahrt see Dehmel WEIB UND WELT.
   WEBERN
"Ein Himmelreich dein Auge ist" see Dein
   Auge Branco LOEWE
Himmelsblüthen see Gerstenberg LOEWE
Himmelsboten zu Liebchens Himmelbett
   see Des Knaben Wunderhorn
   STRAUSS
Die Himmelsbraut see Kerner SPOHR
Himmelsfunken see Silbert SCHUBERT
Himmelstrauer see Lenau SCHOECK
Hinaus! Hinauf! Hinab! see Lasker LOEWE

"Hinaus, hinaus! in freie Luft" see Hinaus!
   Hinauf! Hinab! Lasker LOEWE
Hinaus ins Freie see Hoffmann von
   Fallersleben SCHUMANN
"Hinaus in's Weite" see Neue Liebe Geibel
   RUBINSTEIN
"Hinaus, mein Blick! hinaus in's Tal!" see
   Abendlied für die Entfernte Schlegel
   SCHUBERT
HINDEMITH, PAUL, 1895-1963.
   Anon.
      In principio erat Verbum (1941)
         [unpubl.]
         Motet for soprano & piano.
      Lieder in Aargauer Mundart, op. 5
         (1916) [unpubl.]
         Text in the dialect of the Swiss Canton
            of Aargau.
   Baudelaire, Charles Pierre, 1821-1867.
      Le revenant (1946) [unpubl.]
   Bible
      Angelus Domini apparuit (1958) [Schott,
         1959] same
      Ascendente Jesu in naviculam (1943)
         [Schott, 1959] same
      Cum descendisset Jesus de monte (1960)
         [Schott, 1960] same
      Cum factus esset Jesus annorum
         duodecim (1959) [Schott, 1960] same
      Cum natus esset (1941) [Schott, 1952]
         same
      Defuncto Herode (1958) [Schott, 1959]
         same
      Dicebat Jesus scribis et pharisaeis (1959)
         [Schott, 1959] same
      Dixit Jesus Petro (1959) [Schott, 1959]
         same
      Erat Joseph et Maria (1959) [Schott,
         1959] same
      Exiit edictum (1960) [Schott, 1960] same
      Nuptiae factae sunt (1944) [Schott, 1952]
         same
      Pastores loquebantur (1944) [Schott,
         1952] same
      Vidit Joannes Jesum venientem (1959)
         [Schott, 1960] same
   Blake, William, 1757-1827.
      The wild flower's song (1942)
         [Associated, 1945; Schott] "As I
         wander'd the forest"
   Bock, Kurt, 1890-1949.
      Die trunkene Tänzerin, op. 18 no. 1
         (1920) [Schott, 1922]
         "Sieh, an letzten Himmels Saum
         schwebt die Blume"
   Brentano, Clemens Maria, 1778-1842.
      Zwei Lieder (1936) [unpubl.]

HINDEMITH, PAUL, 1895-1963 *(continued)*
Busch, Wilhelm, 1832-1908.
  Drei Lieder (1933) [unpubl.]
Claudius, Matthias, 1740-1815.
  Vier Lieder (1933) [unpubl.]
Cox, Oscar
  Beauty touch me (1955) [Schott, 1955]
    "Beauty fired by the coals of art"
  Image (1955) [Schott, 1955]
    "Snow in winter's wind"
Dickens, Charles, 1812-1870.
  ODE TO AN EXPIRING FROG.
    Recitativo e aria romantica (1944)
      [unpubl., holograph at Library of
      Congress] "Frog, frog, frog, a name
      in zoology"
    Text from Dickens and
      Encyclopedia Britannica: "Frog."
    Bass & piano.
Hardenberg, Friedrich Leopold,
  Freiherr von, 1772-1801.
  Vier Lieder (1933) [unpubl.]
Herrick, Robert, 1591-1674.
  To music, to becalm his fever (1944)
    [Associated, 1945; Schott]
    "Charm me asleep, and melt me so"
Hölderlin, Friedrich, 1770-1843.
  Abendphantasie (1933) [Schott, 1965]
    "Vor seiner Hütte ruhig im Schatten
    sitzt"
  An die Parzen (1935) [Schott, 1965]
    "Nur einen Sommer gönnt, ihr
    Gewaltigen!"
  Des Morgens (1935) [Schott, 1965]
    "Vom Taue glänzt der Rasen"
  Ehmals und jetzt (1935) [Schott, 1965]
    "In jüng'ren Tagen war ich des
    Morgens froh"
  Fragment (1933) [Schott, 1965]
    "Das Angenehme dieser Welt hab ich
    genossen"
  Sonnenuntergang (1935) [Schott, 1965]
    "Wo bist du? Trunken dämmert die
    Seele mir"
Keats, John, 1795-1821.
  La belle dame sans merci (1942)
    [Associated, 1945; Schott, 1980]
    "O what can ail thee, knight-at-arms"
Keller, Gottfried, 1819-1890.
  Das Köhlerweib (1936) [unpubl.]
Lasker-Schüler, Else, 1869-1945.
  Du machst mich traurig-hör', op. 18 no.
    6 (1920) [Schott, 1922] "Bin so müde"
  Traum, op. 18 no. 3 (1920) [Schott,
    1922] "Der Schlaf entführte mich in
    deine Gärten"

Lover, Samuel, 1797-1868.
  The whistlin' thief (1942) [Associated,
    1945; Schott]
    "When Pat came over the hill"
Moore, Thomas, 1779-1852.
  Echo [Associated, 1944; Schott]
    "How sweet the answer echo makes"
Morgenstern, Christian Otto Joseph
  Wolfgang, 1871-1914.
  Auf der Treppe sitzen meine Öhrchen, op.
    18 no. 4 [Schott, 1922] same
  Vor dir schein' ich aufgewacht, op. 18
    no. 5 (1920) [Schott, 1922] same
  *Wie Sankt Franciscus schweb' in der
    Luft*, op. 18 no. 2 (1920) [Schott,
    1922] same
Nietzsche, Friedrich Wilhelm, 1844-
  1900.
  Three songs (1939) [unpubl.]
Oldys, William, 1696-1761.
  On a fly drinking out of his cup (1942)
    [Associated, 1944; Schott]
    "Busy, curious, thirsty fly!"
Rilke, Rainer Maria, 1875-1926.
  Argwohn Josephs, op. 27, IIa [Schott,
    1924] "Und der Engel sprach"
    Revised version published by Schott,
    1948.
  Die Darstellung Mariä im Tempel, op.
    27, Ib [Schott, 1924]
    "Um zu begreifen, wie sie damals war"
    Revised version published by Schott,
    1948.
  Geburt Christi, op. 27, IIc [Schott, 1924]
    "Hättest du der Einfalt nicht"
    Revised version published by Schott,
    1948.
  Geburt Mariä, op. 27, Ia [Schott, 1924]
    "O was muss es die Engel gekostet
    haben"
    Revised version published by Schott,
    1948.
  Mariä Heimsuchung, op. 27, Id [Schott,
    1924] "Noch erging sie's leicht im
    Anbeginne"
    Revised version published by Schott,
    1948.
  Mariä Verkündigung, op. 27, Ic [Schott,
    1924] "Nicht dass ein Engel eintrat"
    Revised version published by Schott,
    1948.
  Pietà, op. 27, IIIc [Schott, 1924]
    "Jetzt wird mein Elend voll"
    Revised version published by Schott,
    1948.
  Rast auf der Flucht in Ägypten, op. 27,
    IId [Schott, 1924]

"Diese, die noch eben atemlos flohen"
Revised version published by Schott,
1948.
Stillung Mariä mit dem Auferstandenen,
op. 27, IIId [Schott, 1924]
"Was sie damals empfanden"
Revised version published by Schott,
1948.
Verkündigung über den Hirten, op. 27,
IIb [Schott, 1924]
"Seht auf ihr Männer"
Revised version published by Schott,
1948.
Vom Tode Mariä, op. 27, IVa [Schott,
1924] "Der selbe grosse Engel"
Revised version published by Schott,
1948.
Vom Tode Mariä, op. 27, IVb [Schott,
1924] "Wer hat bedacht, dass bis zu
ihrem Kommen"
Revised version published by Schott,
1948.
Vom Tode Mariä, op. 27, IVc [Schott,
1924]
"Doch vor dem Apostel Thomas"
Revised version published by Schott,
1948.
Vor der Hochzeit zu Kana, op. 27, IIIa
[Schott, 1924]
"Konnte sie denn anders"
Revised version published by Schott,
1948.
Vor der Passion, op. 27, IIIb [Schott,
1924] "O hast du dies gewollt"
Revised version published by Schott,
1948.
Rimbaud, Jean Nicolas Arthur, 1854-
1891.
Bal des pendus (1944) [Associated, 1945;
Schott, 1980]
"Au gibet noir, manchot aimable"
Rückert, Friedrich, 1788-1866.
Das Ganze, nicht das Einzelne (1933)
[Bosse, 1933] "Deine Freuden, deine
Leiden zähle nicht von Tag"
In *Zeitschrift für Musik,* 100./1933,
Notenbeil. Nr. 6.
Vier Lieder (1933) [unpubl.]
Scheffler, Johann, 1624-1677.
Vier Lieder (1935) [unpubl.]
Schilling, Heinar, 1894-1955.
Durch die abendlichen Gärten, op. 18 no.
7 [Schott, 1922] same
Shelley, Percy Bysshe, 1792-1822.
The moon (1942) [Associated, 1944;
Schott] "And like a dying lady, lean
and pale"

Thompson, Francis, 1859-1907.
Envoy (1942) [Associated, 1945; Schott]
"Go, songs, for ended is our brief,
sweet play"
Trakl, Georg, 1887-1914.
Trompeten, op. 18 no. 8 (1920) [Schott,
1922] "Unter verschnittenen Weiden"
Unknown
Achtzehn Lieder (1942) [unpubl.]
German, French and Latin texts.
Drei Lieder (1944) [unpubl.]
Whitman, Walt, 1819-1892.
Der ich, in Zwischenräumen, op. 14 no. 1
(1919) [Schott, 1983] same
Baritone & piano.
O, nun heb du an, dort in deinem Moor,
op. 14 no. 2 (1919) [Schott, 1983]
same
Baritone & piano.
Schlgt! Schlagt! Trommeln! op. 14 no. 3
(1919) [Schott, 1983] same
Baritone & piano.
Sing on there in the swamp (1942)
[Associated, 1945; Schott] same
Wolfe, Charles, 1791-1823.
On hearing "The last rose of summer"
(1942) [Associated, 1945; Schott]
"That strain again?"
Hinei nachalat adonai baním see Bible
PSALM 127. **GIDEON**
Hinkende Jamben see Rückert **LOEWE**
"Hinter jenen dichten Wäldern" *see Sehnsucht*
Anon. **BRAHMS**
"Hinterm Berge dort" *see Kapitulation*
Jacob, T. **LOEWE**
Hippolit's Lied see Schopenhauer
GABRIELE. **SCHUBERT**
Hirondelle see Radiguet **AURIC**
Les Hirondelles see d'Hotelier, A.
LOEFFLER
Hirsch, Gaston, b. 1830.
MASSENET *Au delà du rêve*
Hirschlein ging im Wald spazieren see Kuh
CORNELIUS
Der Hirt see Mayrhofer **SCHUBERT**
Der Hirt see Schiller *WILHELM TELL.*
LISZT
Der Hirt auf dem Felsen see Müller,
Wilhelm **SCHUBERT**
Der Hirt auf der Brücke see Ziegler, K.
LOEWE
"Der Hirt bläst seine Weise" *see*
Abendlandschaft Eichendorff **SCHOECK**
"Der Hirt bläst seine Weise" *see*
Abendlandschaft Unknown **LASSEN**
NB: Text may be by Eichendorff; song not
seen.

Der Hirte see Lenau SCHOECK
Die Hirten see Cornelius CORNELIUS
   Two settings: 1856 and op. 8 no. 2 (1870).
Der Hirten Lied am Krippelein see Schubart
   LOEWE
"Hirten wachen im Feld" *see Die Hirten*
   Cornelius CORNELIUS
   Op. 8 no. 2 (1870) setting.
"Die Hirten wachen nachts im Feld" *see*
   Die Hirten Cornelius CORNELIUS
   1856 setting.
Der Hirtenknabe see Mörike SCHOECK
Hirtenknabe see Schumann SCHUMANN
Hirtenlied see Uhland MENDELSSOHN-
   BARTHOLDY
Hirtz, Lise
   AURIC
      Il était une petite pie
      Les pâquerettes
      Une petite pomme
      Les petits ânes
      La poule noire
"Hirüber wall' ich" *see Nachthymne*
   Hardenberg SCHUBERT
His exaltation see Robinson IVES
HIS EXCELLENCY. see Auden
   As it is, plenty BRITTEN
HISTOIRES NATURELLES. see Renard
   Le Cygne RAVEL
   Le Grillon RAVEL
   Le Martin-Pêcheur RAVEL
   Le Paon RAVEL
   La Pintade RAVEL
HISTOIRES NATURELLES, no. 1
   RAVEL Renard *Le Paon*
HISTOIRES NATURELLES, no. 2
   RAVEL Renard *Le Grillon*
HISTOIRES NATURELLES, no. 3
   RAVEL Renard *Le Cygne*
HISTOIRES NATURELLES, no. 4
   RAVEL Renard *Le Martin-Pêcheur*
HISTOIRES NATURELLES, no. 5
   RAVEL Renard *La Pintade*
HISTORIENS SANG. see Aakjaer
   Som dybest Brønd NIELSEN
HISTORIETTES AU CRÉPUSCULE, no. 1
   BLOCH Mauclair *Légende*
HISTORIETTES AU CRÉPUSCULE, no. 2
   BLOCH Mauclair *Les fleurs*
HISTORIETTES AU CRÉPUSCULE, no. 3
   BLOCH Mauclair *Rondo*
HISTORIETTES AU CRÉPUSCULE, no. 4
   BLOCH Mauclair *Complainte*
L'hiver see Banville KOECHLIN
L'hiver see Hölderlin SAUGUET
L'hiver a cessé see Verlaine FAURÉ

"L'hiver enveloppait la terre de son ombre"
   see Ma fille, souviens-toi Unknown
   GOUNOD
Hjärtat see Bergman KILPINEN
"Hjärtat skall gro av drömmar" *see Hjärtat*
   Bergman KILPINEN
Hjärtats morgon see Runeberg SIBELIUS
Hjemkomst see Paulsen GRIEG
Hjemlige Jul see Bønnelycke NIELSEN
Hjemstavn see Poulsen, Frederik NIELSEN
Hlásný see Anon. MARTINŮ
"Hlavěnka mě bolí" *see Naděje* Anon.
   MARTINŮ
Hlavsa, Vrat.
   MARTINŮ
      The fiery man
      Song of the First of November
      Three maidens on a bright night
L'ho compagnata see Zaffira GOUNOD
"Ho er mager og myrk og mjå" *see Veslemøy*
   Garborg GRIEG
Ho messo nuove see Zaffira GOUNOD
"Ho reknar Dag og Stund og seine Kveld" *see*
   Vond Dag Garborg GRIEG
"Ho sit ein Sundag lengtande i Li" *see Møte*
   Garborg GRIEG
Hoar-frost fallen in the field see Heine
   MARTINŮ
"Hoch am dunklen Himmelsbogen glänzt ein
   Stern" *see Ehre sei Gott in der Höhe!*
   Hamann REGER
"Hoch auf dem alten Thurme" *see*
   Geistesgruss Goethe SCHUBERT,
   ZELTER
"Hoch auf dem alten Turme" *see Geistergruss*
   Goethe MEDTNER
"Hoch auf dem alten Turme" *see Geistesgruss*
   Goethe SCHOECK
"Hoch auf dem Gipfel deiner Gebirge" *see*
   Auf der Riesenkoppe Körner SCHUBERT
Hoch auf fliegt mein Herz see Bodenstedt
   LASSEN
"Hoch bäumen sich auf in die Lüfte" *see*
   Vergängliches Tolstoĭ RUBINSTEIN
Hoch beglückt in deiner Liebe see Goethe
   WESTÖSTLICHER DIVAN: Buch Suleika.
   WOLF
"Hoch fand von Evens Töchter scharen ich
   keine" *see Der Weiberfreund* Cowley
   SCHUBERT
"Hoch gewölbte Blätterkronen" *see*
   Im Treibhaus Wesendonck WAGNER
Hoch, hoch sind die Berge see Padrilla
   LA SIERRA ES ALTA. SCHUMANN
Hoch in der Frühe see Dehmel
   SZYMANOWSKI

"Hoch mit den Wolken geht der Vögel Reise"
   see Das Alter Eichendorff **PFITZNER**
"Hoch über stillen Höhen" *see Anklänge*
   Eichendorff **BRAHMS**
"Hoch, und ehern schier von Dauer" *see*
   Adelwold und Emma Bertrand
   SCHUBERT
"Hoch zu Pferd!" *see Hauptmann's Weib*
   Burns **SCHUMANN**
Hochgebirgsleben see Ibsen **DELIUS**
HOCHGEBIRGSWINTER, no. 1
   KILPINEN Hesse *Aufstieg*
HOCHGEBIRGSWINTER, no. 2
   KILPINEN Hesse *Grindelwald*
HOCHGEBIRGSWINTER, no. 3
   KILPINEN Hesse *Berggeist*
HOCHGEBIRGSWINTER, no. 4
   KILPINEN Hesse *Schlittenfahrt*
Hochländers Abschied see Burns
   SCHUMANN
Die Hochländer-Wittwe see Burns
   SCHUMANN
Hochländisches Wiegenlied see Burns
   SCHUMANN
Hochmut see Tolstoï **MUSORGSKIĬ** *Spes'*
Hochstetter, Gustav, 1873-1944.
   SCHÖNBERG *Mahnung*
Hochwald, A von
   SPOHR *Trostlos*
Hochzeitlich Lied see Lindner, Anton
   STRAUSS
Hochzeitlied see Goethe **LOEWE, ZELTER**
Hochzeitlied see Jacobi **SCHUBERT**
Hochzeitslied see Jacobsen **SCHÖNBERG**
Hochzeitslied see Meyer **SCHOECK**
Hodie nobis de coelo see Anon. **MILHAUD**
"Die höchste Macht der Erde" *see*
   Die Allmächtige Hafiz **STRAUSS**
"Högt i det höga slår" *see Under vintergatan*
   Bergman **KILPINEN**
HÖHENLIEDER, pp. 39-40. *see* Levetzow
   Abschied **SCHÖNBERG**
HÖHENLIEDER, pp.41-42. *see* Levetzow
   Dank **SCHÖNBERG**
"Die Höh'n und Wälder schon steigen" *see*
   Gute Nacht! Eichendorff **FRANZ**
Die höh're Welt see Byron **LOEWE**
Hölderlin, Friedrich, 1770-1843.
   BRITTEN
      Hälfte des Lebens
      Die Heimat
      Die Jugend
      Die Linien des Lebens
      Menschenbeifall
      Sokrates und Alcibiades
   CORNELIUS *Sonnenuntergang*

HINDEMITH
   Abendphantasie
   An die Parzen
   Des Morgens
   Ehmals und jetzt
   Fragment
   Sonnenuntergang
PFITZNER *Abbitte*
REGER *An die Hoffnung*
SAUGUET
   Chant du Destin
   L'hiver
   Pardon
   Le printemps
   La vie gaie
DIE EICHBÄUME.
   REGER *Ihr, ihr Herrlichen!*
Hölty, Ludwig Heinrich Christoph, 1748-
1776.
BEETHOVEN *Klage*
BRAHMS
   An ein Veilchen
   Der Küss
   Die Mainacht
   Minnelied
   Die Schale der Vergessenheit
CORNELIUS *Auftrag*
LOEWE *O wunderschön ist Gottes Erde*
MENDELSSOHN-BARTHOLDY
   Andres Maienlied
   Minnelied
MOZART *Das Traumbild*
SCHUBERT
   An den Mond
      Two settings: D. 193 and D. 468.
   An die Apfelbäume, wo ich Julien
      erblickte
   Auf den Tod einer Nachtigall
   Blumenlied
   Erntelied
   Die frühe Liebe
   Klage an den Mond
   Die Knabenzeit
   Die Laube
   Mailied
   Die Mainacht
   Minnelied
   Die Nonne
   Seligkeit
   Todtengräberlied
   Winterlied
WOLF *Mailied*
ZELTER *Der Frühling*
BALLADE.
   SCHUBERT *Der Traum*
GEUSS NICHT SO LAUT.
   BRAHMS, SCHUBERT
      An die Nachtigall

COMPOSER   Poet   *Title*   ''First Line''

Hölty, Ludwig Heinrich Christoph, 1748-1776 (continued)
LIED EINES LIEBENDEN.
   SCHUBERT *Der Liebende*
DIE NACHTIGALL.
   SCHUBERT *Seufzer*
"Hör auf deinen Fahrgesellen" *see Seefahrt*
   Baumbach **RUBINSTEIN**
"Hör, hör, hör en kör av lärkor" *see Lärksång*
   Blomberg **KILPINEN**
Hör' ich das Liedchen klingen see Heine
   DELIUS, FRANZ, GRIEG, SCHUMANN
"Hör' ich das Pförtchen nicht gehen?" *see*
   Die Erwartung Schiller **SCHUBERT**
"Hör ich das Pförtchen nicht gehen?" *see*
   Im Garten Schiller **ZELTER**
"Hör' ich ein Vöglein singen" *see*
   Die Harrende Osterwald **FRANZ**
"Hör mein Liebesliedchen ziehn Isabel" *see*
   Liebesliedchen Calderon **STRAUSS**
Höre den Rat see Goethe *WESTÖSTLICHER*
   DIVAN. **SCHOECK**
"Höre, die Nachtigall singt" *see Der Gesang*
   der Nachtigal Herder **BEETHOVEN**
"Höre mich, Ewiger" *see Hymnus der Liebe*
   Jacobowski **REGER**
Höre mir den Prediger see Hafiz **SCHOECK**
Hörmann, Ludwig von, 1837-1924.
   REGER *Stelldichein*
"Hörnerklänge rufen klagend" *see Trost*
   Mayrhofer **SCHUBERT**
"Hörst du den Vogel singen?" *see Alte Laute*
   Kerner **SCHUMANN**
"Hörst du die Gründe rufen" *see Nacht*
   Eichendorff **RUBINSTEIN, SCHOECK**
"Hörst du nicht die Bäume rauschen" *see*
   Lockung Eichendorff **PFITZNER**
"Hörst du nicht die Quellen gehen" *see*
   Nachtzauber Eichendorff **WOLF**
"Hörst du von den Nachtigallen" *see Die*
   gefangenen Sänger Schlegel **SCHUBERT**
"Hört die Lerche, sie singt" *see Die Lerche*
   Krummacher **LOEWE**
"Hört ihn und seht sein dürftig Instrument!"
   see Auf einen Klavierspieler Mörike
   SCHOECK
"Hört ihr die Hörner erschallen" *see Der Jagd*
   Unknown **LOEWE**
"Hört Ihr dort drüben" *see Die Verlassene*
   Unknown **WOLF**
"Hört ihr im Laube des Regens" *see Gesungen*
   Schöpff **SCHUMANN**
Höstkväll see Rydberg **SIBELIUS**
Hoffärtig seid Ihr see Heyse **WOLF**
"Hoffe, liebe, glaube" *see Blumen-Evangelium*
   Blankensee **LOEWE**

Hoffen und wieder verzagen see Schack
   LOTOSBLÄTTER. **STRAUSS**
Hoffmann, Kai, 1874-1949.
   NIELSEN *Den danske Sang er en ung,*
   blond Pige
Hoffmann von Fallersleben, August
   Heinrich, 1798-1874.
BRAHMS
   Liebe und Frühling
      Two settings: Op. 3 no. 2 and op. 3
      no. 3.
   Nachtigallen schwingen
   Wie die Wolke nach der Sonne
FRANZ
   Doppelwandlung
   Die Farben Helgolands
   Frühling und Liebe
   Frühlingsliebe
   Tanzlied im Mai
   Wasserfahrt
JENSEN *Lasst mich ruhen*
LASSEN
   Alles scheidet liebes Herz
   Armes Blünchen
   Der Frühling und die Liebe
   Im Liebeslust
   Lasst mich ruhen
   Mein Liebchen
   Mein Lied
   Und die Lerchen singen wieder
   Wiegenlied
LISZT
   Ich scheide
   In Liebeslust
   Lasst mich ruhen
   Wie singt die Lerche schön
LOEWE *Jugend und Alter*
MENDELSSOHN-BARTHOLDY
   Seemanns Scheidelied
   Tröstung
RUBINSTEIN
   Lied
      Two settings: Op. 33 no. 2 and op. 33
      no. 5.
SCHOECK *Wiegenlied*
SCHUMANN
   Der Abendstern
   Frühlings Ankunft
   Frühlingsbotschaft
   Frühlingsgruss
   Hinaus ins Freie
   Mein Garten
   Schmetterling
   Soldatenlied
   Sonntag
   Vom Schlaraffenland
   Die Waise

COMPOSER Poet *Title* "First Line"

SPOHR
Mein Vaterland
Was mir wohl übrig bliebe
Two settings: Op. 139 no. 5 and WoO
96.
STRAUSS
Abend- und Morgenrot
Husarenlied
Die müde Wanderer
Ein Röslein zog ich mir im Garten
Soldatenlied
Der Spielmann und sein Kind
Wiegenlied
WOLF
Liebesfrühling
Nach dem Abschiede
DES FAHRENDEN SCHÜLERS LIEBEN
UND LEIDEN.
WOLF
Auf der Wanderung
Ja, die Schönst!
Hoffnung see Altenberg *WAS DER TAG MIR*
ZUTRÄGT': Hoffnung. **BERG**
Hoffnung see Goethe **SCHUBERT**
Hoffnung see Paulsen **GRIEG** *Et Håb*
Hoffnung see Schiller *ES REDEN UND*
TRÄUMEN DIE MENSCHEN.
SCHUBERT
Two settings: D. 251 and D. 637.
Hoffnung see Unknown **BEETHOVEN**
"Der Hoffnung letzter Schimmer" *see Als die*
Geliebte sich trennen wollte Breuning
BEETHOVEN
Hoffnungslos see Obst, Willibald **REGER**
Hoffnungstrost see Anon. **REGER**
Hofmannsthal, Hugo Hofmann, Edler
von, 1874-1929.
BERG
Ballade des äusseren Lebens
Reiselied
SCHÖNBERG *Die Beiden*
Høgen see Aakjaer **NIELSEN**
Hohe Liebe see Uhland **LISZT**
Hohenberg, Paul
BERG
Läuterung
Sehnsucht I
Sehnsucht III
Sommertag
Hohenlohe, Prinzessin Therese von
LISZT *La perla*
Hohlfeld, Christoph Christian, 1776-
1849.
SCHUBERT *An Gott*
HARFENKLÄNGEN: Kaiser Karl V. an
Luthers Grabe.

LOEWE *Kaiser Karl V. in Wittenberg*
Højt ligger paa Marken den hvide Sne see
Andersen **NIELSEN**
"Holà! Qui va là?" *see Le chant du veilleur*
Anon. **MILHAUD**
Hold back thy hours, dark night see Fletcher
ROREM
"Hold fastere omkring mig" *see Angst*
Aarestrup **NIELSEN**
DAS HOLDE BESCHEIDEN, no. 1
SCHOECK Mörike *Widmung*
DAS HOLDE BESCHEIDEN, no. 2
SCHOECK Mörike *An einem*
Wintermorgan, vor Sonnenaufgang
DAS HOLDE BESCHEIDEN, no. 3
SCHOECK Mörike *Gesang zu zweien in*
der Nacht
DAS HOLDE BESCHEIDEN, no. 4
SCHOECK Mörike *Am Walde*
DAS HOLDE BESCHEIDEN, no. 5
SCHOECK Mörike *An Philomele*
DAS HOLDE BESCHEIDEN, no. 6
SCHOECK Mörike *Auf der Teck*
DAS HOLDE BESCHEIDEN, no. 7
SCHOECK Mörike *Das Mädchen an den*
Mai
DAS HOLDE BESCHEIDEN, no. 8
SCHOECK Mörike *Im Park*
DAS HOLDE BESCHEIDEN, no. 9
SCHOECK Mörike *Mein Fluss*
DAS HOLDE BESCHEIDEN, no. 10
SCHOECK Mörike *Lose Ware*
DAS HOLDE BESCHEIDEN, no. 11
SCHOECK Mörike *Ritterliche Werbung*
DAS HOLDE BESCHEIDEN, no. 12
SCHOECK Mörike *Die Schwestern*
DAS HOLDE BESCHEIDEN, no. 13
SCHOECK Mörike *Schön-Rohtraut*
DAS HOLDE BESCHEIDEN, no. 14
SCHOECK Mörike *Peregrina*
DAS HOLDE BESCHEIDEN, no. 15
SCHOECK Mörike *Zu viel*
DAS HOLDE BESCHEIDEN, no. 16
SCHOECK Mörike *Nachts am*
Schreibepult
DAS HOLDE BESCHEIDEN, no. 17
SCHOECK Mörike *Aus der Ferne*
DAS HOLDE BESCHEIDEN, no. 18
SCHOECK Mörike *Nur zu!*
DAS HOLDE BESCHEIDEN, no. 19
SCHOECK Mörike *Auf eine Lampe*
DAS HOLDE BESCHEIDEN, no. 20
SCHOECK Mörike *Nachts*
DAS HOLDE BESCHEIDEN, no. 21
SCHOECK Mörike *Antike Poesie*
DAS HOLDE BESCHEIDEN, no. 22
SCHOECK Mörike *Erinna an Sappho*

COMPOSER   Poet   *Title*   ''First Line''

DAS HOLDE BESCHEIDEN, no. 23
   SCHOECK Mörike *Johann Kepler*
DAS HOLDE BESCHEIDEN, no. 24
   SCHOECK Mörike *Keine Rettung*
DAS HOLDE BESCHEIDEN, no. 25
   SCHOECK Mörike *Nach dem Kriege*
DAS HOLDE BESCHEIDEN, no. 26
   SCHOECK Mörike *In ein Autographen-*
   Album
DAS HOLDE BESCHEIDEN, no. 27
   SCHOECK Mörike *Impromptu*
DAS HOLDE BESCHEIDEN, no. 28
   SCHOECK Mörike *Die Enthusiasten*
DAS HOLDE BESCHEIDEN, no. 29
   SCHOECK Mörike *Trost*
DAS HOLDE BESCHEIDEN, no. 30
   SCHOECK Mörike *Auf ein Ei*
   geschrieben
DAS HOLDE BESCHEIDEN, no. 31
   SCHOECK Mörike *Auf einen*
   Klavierspieler
DAS HOLDE BESCHEIDEN, no. 32
   SCHOECK Mörike *Restauration*
DAS HOLDE BESCHEIDEN, no. 33
   SCHOECK Mörike *Gebet*
DAS HOLDE BESCHEIDEN, no. 34
   SCHOECK Mörike *Der Hirtenknabe*
DAS HOLDE BESCHEIDEN, no. 35
   SCHOECK Mörike *Auf ein Kind*
DAS HOLDE BESCHEIDEN, no. 36
   SCHOECK Mörike *Zu einer Konfirmation*
DAS HOLDE BESCHEIDEN, no. 37
   SCHOECK Mörike *Muse und Dichter*
DAS HOLDE BESCHEIDEN, no. 38
   SCHOECK Mörike *Auf dem Krankenbette*
DAS HOLDE BESCHEIDEN, no. 39
   SCHOECK Mörike *Der Geprüste*
DAS HOLDE BESCHEIDEN, no. 40
   SCHOECK Mörike *Besuch in Urach*
"Holde Königin der Geigen" *see Viola*
   d'amour Falke **REGER**
"Der holde liebe Frühlingsregen" *see*
   Der Frühlingsregen Thu-Fu **WEBERN**
"Holde, schattenreiche Baüme" *see Dulces*
   árboles sombrosos Unknown **JENSEN**
"Der holden Lenzgeschmeide" *see Meine Rose*
   Lenau **SCHUMANN**
"Holder klingt der Vogelsang" *see Minnelied*
   Hölty **BRAHMS, MENDELSSOHN-**
   BARTHOLDY, SCHUBERT
"Holder Lenz, du bist dahin" *see Herbstklage*
   Lenau **WOLF**
"Holder Lenz, mit reichen Gaben" *see*
   Frühlingsweihe Blankenfeldt, Otto
   LOEWE
"Der Holdseligen sonder Wank" *see Minnelied*
   Voss **LOEWE, WEBER**

Holem tsaudi see Anon. **MILHAUD**
Holger's Brautritt see Ernst **LASSEN**
The holly and the ivy, a carol of Nativity and
   Lent *see* Anon. **THOMSON**
"The holly and the ivy, now both are full well
   grown" *see The holly and the ivy*,
   a carol of Nativity and Lent Anon.
   THOMSON
Holm, Mia, 1845-1912.
   LASSEN *März*
Holmes, Oliver Wendell, 1809-1894.
   IVES *The last reader*
Holophan see Wallpach zu Schwanenfeld
   BERG
Holst, Adolf, 1867-1945.
   REGER *Bitte*
Holstein, Ludvig Ditlef, greve, 1864-
   1943.
   DELIUS
     Herbst
     Das Veilchen
   NIELSEN
     AEbleblomst
     Blomstervise
     Erindringens Sø
     Hilsen
     I Aften
     Sang bag Ploven
     Sommersang
The holy boy see Brown, Herbert S.
   IRELAND
THE HOLY SONNETS OF JOHN DONNE,
   no. 1
   BRITTEN Donne *Oh my blacke Soule!*
THE HOLY SONNETS OF JOHN DONNE,
   no. 2
   BRITTEN Donne *Batter my heart*
THE HOLY SONNETS OF JOHN DONNE,
   no. 3
   BRITTEN Donne *O might those sighes*
   and teares
THE HOLY SONNETS OF JOHN DONNE,
   no. 4
   BRITTEN Donne *Oh, to vex me*
THE HOLY SONNETS OF JOHN DONNE,
   no. 5
   BRITTEN Donne *What if this present*
THE HOLY SONNETS OF JOHN DONNE,
   no. 6
   BRITTEN Donne *Since she whom*
   I loved
THE HOLY SONNETS OF JOHN DONNE,
   no. 7
   BRITTEN Donne *At the round Earth's*
   imagined corners

COMPOSER   Poet   *Title*   "First Line"

THE HOLY SONNETS OF JOHN DONNE,
no. 8
BRITTEN Donne *Thou hast made me*
THE HOLY SONNETS OF JOHN DONNE,
no. 9
BRITTEN Donne *Death, be not proud*
The holy vision see **Weatherly GOUNOD**
Holz, Arno, 1863-1929.
DAFNIS.
> **BERG** *Er klagt, dass der Frühling so kurtz blüht*
Holz-Miller, I *see* Gol'ts-Miller, Ivan Ivanovich, 1842-1871.
Homage to Paul Klee see **Deutsch**
> **DIAMOND**
"Home no more home to me" *see Whither must I wander?* **Stevenson, Robert Louis VAUGHAN WILLIAMS**
Home to thy native land see **Pushkin**
> **BORODIN** *For the shores of thy far native land*
Homenaje a Debussy: "La grotte" see **Émié**
> **RODRIGO**
HOMENAJE A LOPE DE VEGA, no. 1
> **TURINA** Vega Carpio *Cuando tan hermosa os miro*
HOMENAJE A LOPE DE VEGA, no. 2
> **TURINA** Vega Carpio *Si con mis deseos*
HOMENAJE A LOPE DE VEGA, no. 3
> **TURINA** Vega Carpio *Al val de Fuente Ovejuna*
The home-road see **Carpenter, John**
> **CARPENTER**
The homeward journey see **Vinje**
> *FERDAMINNI.* **DELIUS** *Auf der Reise zur Heimat*
Hommage à Erik Satie see **Cocteau AURIC**
Hommage à Madame La Comtesse Herminie de Léautaud see **Baëlen, Mme.**
> **GOUNOD**
Hommage à Valery-Larbaud see **Chalupt**
> **RIVIER**
Hommage au travail see **Senart**
> **HONEGGER**
"L'homme a, pour payer sa rançon" *see La rançon* **Baudelaire FAURÉ**
Homme au sourire tendre see **Éluard**
> **POULENC**
"L'homme éternel cultive" *see Domaine d'homme* **Follain SAUGUET**
"L'homme oublie les soucis de l'esprit" *see Le printemps* **Hölderlin SAUGUET**
HONEGGER, ARTHUR, 1892-1955.
> Aguet, William
>> *Chanson de marin* [Salabert, 1947]
>> "Derrière Murcie en fleurs je connais"

Anon.
> *O salutaris* (1940) [Heugel, 1943] "O salutaris hostia"
> Excerpt from film score ***Cavalcade d'amour.***
Apollinaire, Guillaume, 1880-1918.
> *ALCOOLS.*
>> *A la Santé* (1916) [Mathot, 1921; Salabert] "Que lentement passent les heures"
>> *L'adieu* (1917) [Mathot, 1921] "J'ai cueilli ce brin de bruyère"
>> *Automne* (1915) [Mathot, 1921; Salabert] "Dans le brouillard s'en vont un paysan cagneux"
>> *Les cloches* (1917) [Mathot, 1921] "Mon beau tzigane mon amant"
>> *Clotilde* (1916) [Mathot, 1921; Salabert] "L'anèmone et l'ancolie"
>> *Saltimbanques* (1917) [Mathot, 1921; Salabert] "Dans la plaine les baladins"
Bédat de Monlaur, Pierre
> *Le château du Bartas* (1941) [Lemoine, 1942] "Un Gascon à minc fièrc"
> *Le départ* (1941) [Lemoine, 1942] "Avec sa belle prestance"
> *Duo* (1941) [Lemoine, 1942] "L'amour auquel tout invite"
> *Nérac en fête* (1941) [Lemoine, 1942] "Qu'est ce donc sur la garenne?"
> *La promenade* (1941) [Lemoine, 1942] "Marguerite de Navarre"
> *Tout le long de la Baïse* (1941) [Lemoine, 1942] same
Bible
> *Mimaamaquim* (1946) [Salabert, 1947] "Mimaamaquim queratikha Adornaï" Transliteration of Hebrew verses of Psalm 130.
> *Psalm XXXIV* (1940-41) [Salabert, 1943] "Jamais ne cesserai"
> *Psalm CXI* (1940-41) [Salabert, 1943] "O Dieu donne-moi déliverance"
> *Psalm CXXXVIII* (1940-41) [Salabert, 1943] "Il faut que de tous mes esprits"
Bloch, Jean Richard, 1884-1947.
> *Chanson des quatre* (1937) [R. Deiss, 1937; Salabert] "Un, deux, trois et quat'" Excerpt from film score ***La construction d'une cité.***
> *Chant de l'émigrant* (1937) [R. Deiss, 1937; Salabert] "Capitaine tu as su des malheurs" Excerpt from film score ***La construction d'une cité.***

HONEGGER, ARTHUR, 1892-1955
(continued)
Bruyr, José
L'hymne de la délivrance (1945-46)
[Choudens, 1946]
Excerpt from film score *Un ami
viendra ce soir* (1945-46).
Hymne du sport (1943) [Choudens, 1943]
Excerpt from film score *La Boxe en
France* (1943).
Chobanian, Arshag, 1872-1954.
La douceur de tes yeux (1945) [Salabert,
1947] same
La mort passe (1916) [J. & W. Chester,
1921]
"Toute senle silencieuse les yeux"
Claudel, Paul, 1868-1955.
La delphinium (1940) [Salabert, 1942]
"Toute pure comme le ciel"
La rendez-vous (1940) [Salabert, 1942]
"Forêt profonde"
La sieste (1939) [Salabert, 1942]
"Deux heures après diner"
Cocteau, Jean, 1889-1963.
Une danseuse (1923) [Senart, 1924;
Salabert]
"Le crabe sort sur des pointes"
Ex-voto (1923) [Senart, 1924; Salabert]
"Autour de la Sainte Vierge il fait
chaud ce sont les cierges"
Locutions (1920) [Senart, 1924; Salabert]
"Fraîche comme une rose"
Madame (1923) [Senart, 1924; Salabert]
"O Madame voilà ce qu'il faudrait
comprendre vous me"
Souvenirs d'enfance (1920) [Senart,
1924; Salabert] "Pendant la nuit une
rose avance sous feux éteints"
TEMPÉRATURES.
Le Nègre (1920) [Senart, 1924;
Salabert]
"Le nègre mineur de l'azure"
Desnos, Robert, 1900-1945.
Les Gars du bâtiment (1937) [unpubl.]
Excerpt from film score *Les
Batisseurs.*
Féline, J.
De l'Atlantique ou Pacifique (1937) [R.
Ventura, 1937]
Excerpt from film score *Nitchevo.*
Fontaines, A.
Sur le basalte (1914) [J. & W. Chester,
1921] same
Fort, Paul, 1872-1960.
COMPLAINTES ET DITS.
Chanson de fol (1916) [Senart, 1922;
Salabert] "Les sorciers et les fées
dansent sur le côteau"

Le chasseur perdu en forêt (1916)
[Senart, 1922; Salabert]
"Quand le son du cor sendort"
First published *La Revue Musicale*
Jan. 1922.
Cloche du soir (1916) [Senart, 1922;
Salabert] "Ah! ce soir là vraiment
tout était si paisible"
Frank, Jacques Henri, 1904-
Du whisky pour Jo (1936) [La Sirène
Musicale, 1936; Eschig]
Fièvre jaune (1935) [La Sirène Musicale,
1935; Eschig] "Je n'ai jamais connu la
couleur de ses yeux"
Giraudoux, Jean, 1882-1944.
SUZANNE ET LA PACIFIQUE.
Adèle (1941) [Salabert, 1947]
"A douvres un original tombe"
1st published as musical supplement
in *Arthur Honegger* (Paris: Les
Publications Techniques/Galerie
Charpentier, 1942).
Cécile (1941) [Salabert, 1947]
"Le grand chinois de Lancastre"
1st published as musical supplement
in *Arthur Honegger* (Paris: Les
Publications Techniques/Galerie
Charpentier, 1942).
Irène (1941) [Salabert, 1947]
"Le Lord prévôt d'Edinbourg"
1st published as musical supplement
in *Arthur Honegger* (Paris: Les
Publications Techniques/Galerie
Charpentier, 1942).
Jeanne (1941) [Salabert, 1947]
"Dans Londres, la grande ville"
1st published as musical supplement
in *Arthur Honegger* (Paris: Les
Publications Techniques/Galerie
Charpentier, 1942).
Rosemonde (1941) [Salabert, 1947]
"Qu' as-tu vu dans ton exil?"
1st published as musical supplement
in *Arthur Honegger* (Paris: Les
Publications Techniques/Galerie
Charpentier, 1942).
Jammes, Francis, 1868-1938.
Prière (1915) [J. & W. Chester, 1921]
"Mon Dieu vous m'avez appelé parmi
les hommes"
Kerdyk, René
Chanson de la route [Editions Oeuvres
Francaises]
Le naturaliste
On est heureux [Editions Oeuvres
Francaises]

Kessel, Joseph, 1898-1979.
La chanson de l'Escadrille (1934)
[Editions Coda, 1934]
Excerpt from film music *Cessez le feu*
(1934).
Laforgue, Jules, 1860-1887.
Petite Chapelle (1916) [J. & W. Chester,
1921] "Peuple du Christ j'expose"
No author
Vocalise-etude (1929) [Leduc, 1929]
No. 73, v. 8, of A.L.Hettich *Répertoire
moderne de vocalise.* Wordless.
Richepin, Jean, 1849-1926.
Chanson de la route (1938) [Salabert,
1938]
Excerpt from film score *Miarka*
(1938).
Chanson de l'eau (1938) [Salabert, 1938]
Excerpt from film score *Miarka*
(1938).
Ronsard, Pierre de, 1524-1585.
La terre, l'eau, l'air et le vent [Salabert,
1947] "La terre les eaux va bruvant"
Senart, Maurice, 1878-1962.
Hommage au travail (1938) [Senart,
1939; Eschig, 1955] "Quand le matin
l'homme est bien reposé"
Shakespeare, William, 1564-1616.
THE TEMPEST.
Modéré-Plus lent (1923) [Senart, 1925;
Salabert]
"Venez jusqu'à ces sables d'or"
Un peu animé (1923) [Senart, 1925;
Salabert]
"Où butine l'abeille je butine aussi"
Tranchant, Jean
Le grand étang (1932) [unpubl.]
Vaillant-Couturier, Paul, 1892-1937.
Jeunesse (1937) [Le Chant du Monde,
1937] "Nous sommes la jeunesse
ardente"
Verlaine, Paul, 1844-1896.
Un grand sommeil noir (1944) [Salabert,
1947] same
Zimmer, Bernard
Quand tu verras les hirondelles (1943)
[Salabert, 1946]
Excerpt from film score *Un seul
amour* (1943).
Si le mal d'amour (1943) [Salabert,
1946]
Excerpt from film score *Un seul
amour* (1943).
"Honka se humisi ikkunan alla" *see Pieni
ballaadi* Lönnbohm **KILPINEN**
Honneur à l'Amérique see Fournier
SAINT-SAËNS

Hood, Thomas, 1799-1845.
CORNELIUS *Dich lieb ich*
GOUNOD *There is dew my tone love*
QUILTER *The time of roses*
MINOR POEMS (1846): For music.
HESELTINE *A lake and a fairy boat*
Hopak see Shevchenko *GAïDAMAKI.*
MUSORGSKIï *Gopak*
Hope see Anon. **MARTINŮ** *Naděje*
Hope see Rossetti, Christina **IRELAND**
"The hope I dreamed of was a dream" *see
Mirage* Rossetti, Christina **IVES**
Hope is the thing with feathers see Dickinson
LUENING
Hope the hornblower see Newbolt
IRELAND
Hopfen, Hans
SCHOECK *Lieb Seelchen, lass das Fragen
sein*
Hopkins, Gerard Manley, 1844-1889.
BARBER *A nun takes the veil*
BERKELEY *Hurrahing in harvest*
KRENEK
Moonrise
On a piece of music
Patience
Peace
ROREM
Felix Randal
Spring
Spring and fall (to a young child, 1946)
Hopper, Nora *see* Chesson, Mrs. Nora
(Hopper), 1871-1906.
Hør, hvor let dens Vinger smaekker see
Aakjaer *SVALEN.* **NIELSEN**
"Hør mig, I kølige Hjaerter i Nord" *see Eros*
Benzon **GRIEG**
L'hora grisa see Blancafort **MOMPOU**
Horan, Robert, 1922-1981.
BARBER *The queen's face on the summery
coin*
"Horch! auf der Erde feuchtem Grund
gelegen" *see Nachts* Mörike **SCHOECK**
"Horch, Hörnerklang" *see Die Kaiserjagd im
Wienerwald* Vogl **LOEWE**
Horch, hörst du nicht vom Himmel her see
Hafiz **SCHOECK**
"Horch, horch! die Lerch' im Ätherblau" *see
Ständchen* Shakespeare **SCHUBERT**
"Horch, leise horch!" *see Serenade*
Baggesen **WEBER**
"Horch, wie Murmeln des empörten Meeres"
see Gruppe aus dem Tartarus Schiller
SCHUBERT
"Horch, wie still es wird im dunkeln Hain"
see Stille sicherheit Lenau **FRANZ,
WOLF**

COMPOSER Poet *Title* "First Line"

Hører jeg Sangen klinge see Heine GRIEG
  Hör' ich das Liedchen klingen
L'horizon see Paliard MILHAUD
L'HORIZON CHIMÉRIQUE, no. 1
  FAURÉ La Ville de Mirmont *La mer est infinie*
L'HORIZON CHIMÉRIQUE, no. 2
  FAURÉ La Ville de Mirmont *Je me suis embarqué*
L'HORIZON CHIMÉRIQUE, no. 3
  FAURÉ La Ville de Mirmont *Diane, Séléné*
L'HORIZON CHIMÉRIQUE, no. 4
  FAURÉ La Ville de Mirmont *Vaisseaux, nous vous aurons aimés*
Hornez, André
  SAUGUET *L'ombre des rues*
"Hors de la poix rien à faire" *see Le savetier*
  Mallarmé MILHAUD
The horse see Pushkin MEDTNER
  The war horse
The horseman see De La Mare BERKELEY
Horváth, P
  LISZT *Isten veled!*
Hospodin jest muj pastýř see Bible
  DVOŘÁK
"The host is riding from Knocknarea" *see*
  The hosting of the Sidhe Yeats
  LOEFFLER
The host of the air see Yeats *THE WIND AMONG THE REEDS.* LOEFFLER
The hosting of the Sidhe see Yeats *THE WIND AMONG THE REEDS.* LOEFFLER
Hostrup, Jens Christian, 1818-1892.
  NIELSEN
    Dér, hvor vi stred og sang
    Hvad synger du om
    Nar somrens sang er sungen
    Den traenger ud til hvert et sted
    De unges Sang
    Det vi ved at siden Slangens Gift
Hôtel see Apollinaire *LE GUETTEUR MÉLANCOLIQUE.* POULENC
Houdart de Lamotte, Antoine *see*
  Lamotte, Antoine Houdart de, 1672-1731.
Houdek, V.
  MARTINŮ *Why have you laughed at me?*
Houghton, Richard Monckton Milnes, 1st baron, 1809-1885.
  GOUNOD *Ilala*
"The hour I mind me" *see I remember that day* Tiutchev RACHMANINOFF
THE HOUR OF BEAUTY. see Sharp, W.
  I-Brasil DELIUS
  The rose of the night GRIFFES

"The hours of folly are measur'd by the clock" *see Proverb VI* Blake, William
BRITTEN
The Housatonic at Stockbridge see Johnson
IVES
THE HOUSE OF LIFE, no. IV. see Rossetti, Dante
  Lovesight VAUGHAN WILLIAMS
THE HOUSE OF LIFE, no. IX. see Rossetti, Dante
  Love's minstrels VAUGHAN WILLIAMS
THE HOUSE OF LIFE, no. XIX. see
  Rossetti, Dante
  Silent noon VAUGHAN WILLIAMS
THE HOUSE OF LIFE, no. XXII. see
  Rossetti, Dante
  Heart's haven VAUGHAN WILLIAMS
THE HOUSE OF LIFE, no. XLVIII. see
  Rossetti, Dante
  Death in love VAUGHAN WILLIAMS
THE HOUSE OF LIFE, no. LIX. see
  Rossetti, Dante
  Love's last gift VAUGHAN WILLIAMS
THE HOUSE OF LIFE, no. 1
  VAUGHAN WILLIAMS Rossetti, Dante *Lovesight*
THE HOUSE OF LIFE, no. 2
  VAUGHAN WILLIAMS Rossetti, Dante *Silent noon*
THE HOUSE OF LIFE, no. 3
  VAUGHAN WILLIAMS Rossetti, Dante *Love's minstrels*
THE HOUSE OF LIFE, no. 4
  VAUGHAN WILLIAMS Rossetti, Dante *Heart's haven*
THE HOUSE OF LIFE, no. 5
  VAUGHAN WILLIAMS Rossetti, Dante *Death in love*
THE HOUSE OF LIFE, no. 6
  VAUGHAN WILLIAMS Rossetti, Dante *Love's last gift*
Housman, Alfred Edward, 1859-1936.
  BERKELEY
    Because I liked you better
    He would not stay for me
    Look not in my eyes
    The street sounds to the soldiers' tread
  BLITZSTEIN *Into my heart an air*
  IRELAND
    In boyhood
    Spring will not wait
  RIEGGER *We'll to the woods so move*
LAST POEMS: Prologue.
    IRELAND *We'll to the woods no more*
    VAUGHAN WILLIAMS *We'll go to the woods no more*

LAST POEMS: XXIII.
   VAUGHAN WILLIAMS
      In the morning
LAST POEMS: XXVI.
   BERKELEY, VAUGHAN WILLIAMS
      The half-moon westers low
LAST POEMS: XXVII.
   RIEGGER, VAUGHAN WILLIAMS
      The sigh that heaves the grasses
LAST POEMS: XLI.
   VAUGHAN WILLIAMS *Fancy's knell*
THE SHROPSHIRE LAD.
   IRELAND
      The encounter
      Epilogue
      Goal and wicket
      Hawthorn time
      The heart's desire
      Ladslove
      The Lent lily
      The vain desire
A SHROPSHIRE LAD: V.
   VAUGHAN WILLIAMS *Goodbye*
A SHROPSHIRE LAD. XXVI.
   VAUGHAN WILLIAMS *Along the field*
A SHROPSHIRE LAD: XXVII.
   VAUGHAN WILLIAMS *Is my team ploughing?*
A SHROPSHIRE LAD: LIV.
   BARBER, RIEGGER, VAUGHAN WILLIAMS *With rue my heart is laden*
Houssaye, Arsène, 1815-1896.
   AUBERT *Vieille chanson espagnole*
Housset, Arsène *see* Houssaye, Arsène, 1815-1896.
"How all's to one thing wrought!" *see On a piece of music* Hopkins **KRENEK**
"How can I turn from any fire" *see Tolerance* Hadley **IVES**
"How can I wash the lightning away" *see Song for lying in bed during a night rain* Pitchford **ROREM**
"How can the tree but waste and wither away" *see How can the tree but wither?* Vaux **VAUGHAN WILLIAMS**
How can the tree but wither? see Vaux **VAUGHAN WILLIAMS**
"How cold is that bosom which folly once fired" *see Monody on a lady famed for her caprice* Burns **GIDEON**
"How do you like to go up in a swing?" *see The swing* Stevenson, Robert Louis **HAHN**
How everyone loves thee see Tolstoĭ **RACHMANINOFF**

How fair this spot see Einerling **RACHMANINOFF**
How few the joys see Shenshin **RACHMANINOFF** *For long there has been little consolation*
"How foolish the man" *see The praises of God* Auden, W. H., translator **BARBER**
"How it flows, how it grows!" *see Music* Polonsky **RACHMANINOFF**
How it was with them see Whitman **DIAMOND**
"How like a wildflower untended" *see For Susan* Goodman **ROREM**
How long, my friend see Golenishchev-Kutuzov **RACHMANINOFF**
How love came in see Herrick **BERKELEY**
How many miles to Babylon? see Anon. *NURSE LOVECHILD'S LEGACY* (London: The Poetry Bookshop, 1916). **HESELTINE**
"How? my heart aches!" *see How painful for me* Einerling **RACHMANINOFF**
How nice it is here see Einerling **RACHMANINOFF** *How fair this spot*
"How oft a cloud, with envious veil" *see A night thought* Moore, T. **IVES**
"How often at midnight" *see To the children* Khomyakov **RACHMANINOFF**
How painful for me see Einerling **RACHMANINOFF**
How should I your true love know? see Shakespeare *HAMLET.* **QUILTER, THOMSON**
"How sweet is the shepherd's sweet lot!" *see The shepherd* Blake, William **VAUGHAN WILLIAMS**
"How sweet the answer echo makes" *see Echo* Moore, T. **HINDEMITH**
How the mushrooms went to war see Unknown **STRAVINSKIĬ**
"How tossed how lost with all hopes crossed we have been!" *see The song of Catilin Ni Uallachain* Hefferman **LOEFFLER**
"How will I know" *see Child song* Trustman, Deborah **WEISGALL**
Howe, Mark Antony De Wolfe, 1864-1960.
   THOMPSON, R.
      The passenger
      Veritas
Howell, Thomas, fl.1568.
   IRELAND *All in a garden green*
   RIETI *To his lady, of her doubtful answer*
Howells, Mildred, b. 1872
   CARPENTER *Fog-wraiths*

Howells, William Dean, 1837-1920.
MACDOWELL
Folksong
The sea
Through the meadow
Huang-Fu-Ian
ROUSSEL *Vois, de belles filles*
Huber, Berta (Bindschedler), 1893-1958.
KILPINEN
Am Fenster
Ausklang
Das Ende
Feldblumen
Frühling
Der Kirchturm
Kleinstadt im Frühling
Das Licht
Mein Stübchen
Nacht
Regen I
Regen II
Der Ruhelose
Strom bei Nacht
Verbundenheit
Huber, Victor Aimé, 1800-1869.
SKIZZEN AUS SPANIEN.
LOEWE *Der Sturm von Alhama*
Huber-Bindschedler, Berta *see* Huber,
Berta (Bindschedler), 1893-1958.
Huch, Ricarda Octavia, 1864-1947.
MARTINŮ *Maiden's dream*
PFITZNER
Bestimmung
Denn unsere Liebe hat zu heiss geflammt
Ich werde nicht an deinem Herzen satt
Eine Melodie singt mein Herz
Schwill an, mein Strom
Sehnsucht
Wo hast du all die Schönheit
hergenommen
SZYMANOWSKI *Bestimmung*
"Hüll' ein mich in die grünen Dekken" *see*
Abendlied an die Natur Keller, G.
SCHOECK
Hüte dich see Lingg **RUBINSTEIN**
Hütet euch see Geibel **REGER**
Das Hüttchen see Gleim **ZELTER**
Die Hütte see Andersen **GRIEG** *Hytten*
Die Hütte see Pfarrius *WALDLIEDERN.*
SCHUMANN
"Hüttelein still und klein" *see Ständchen*
Rückert **FRANZ**
Hüttenbrenner, Heinrich
SCHUBERT *Der Jüngling auf dem Hügel*
Der Hufschmied see Spitteler **SCHOECK**

Huggenberger, Josef, c. 1865-1938.
REGER
Auf mondbeschienenen Wegen
Friede
Two settings: Op. 76 no. 25 and op.
79c no. 4.
Mein Schätzelein
Schmeichelkätzchen
Züge
Hughes, Langston, 1902-1967.
FINE CLOTHES TO THE JEW.
CARPENTER *That soothin' song*
THE WEARY BLUES.
CARPENTER
The cryin' blues
Jazz-boys
Shake your brown feet, Honey
Hugnet, Georges, 1906-1974.
ROREM
Abandonée, je suis abandonée
Tout beau mon coeur
SAUGUET
Cache la fée
Ces mots qui n'ont plus de sens
Et voici des ans
Ici seront nées mes saisons
Je suis hereux
Je t'adore
Laisse ta hanche blonde
Nous avions si chaud
La reine m'a livré
Sois mon amie
THOMSON
Le Berceau de Gertrude Stein
Les Ecrevisses
Grenadine
Mon amour est bon à dire
Partis les vaisseaux
Pour chercher sur la carte des mers
La première de toutes
La Rosée
Les soirées bagnolaises
La wagon immobile
Hugo, Victor Marie, comte, 1802-1885.
BERLIOZ *La captive*
BIZET
Adieux de l'hôtesse arabe
Après l'hiver
La chanson du fou
La coccinelle
Guitare
Sérénade: Oh, quand je dors
Voeu
CHABRIER *Ruy Blas*
DELIBES *L'Églogue*

DIAMOND *The children of the poor*
FAURÉ
  L'absent
  Dans les ruines d'une abbaye
  Mai
  Le papillon et la fleur
  Rêve d'amour
FRANCK
  Passez, passez toujours
  Roses et papillons
GOUNOD
  Aubade
  Sérénade
GRIFFES *Si mes vers avaient des ailes*
HAHN
  Puisque j'ai mis ma lèvre
  Quand la nuit n'est pas étoilé
  Rêverie
  Si mes vers avaient des ailes!
LALO
  L'aube nait et ta porte est close
  Chanson à boire
  Dieu qui sourit et qui donne
  Guitare
  Oh! quand je dors
  Puisqu'ici-bas toute âme
  Souvenir
LASSEN
  La Coccinelle
  Hier au soir
  Si mes vers avaient des ailes
  Si vous n'avez rien à me dire
LISZT
  Comment, disaient-ils
  Le crucifix
  Enfant, si j'étais roi
  Gastibelza
  Oh! quand je dors
  Quand tu chantes bercée
  La tombe et la rose
MASSENET
  C'est l'amour
  Être aimé
  Guitare
  Nouvelle chanson sur un vieil air
  La nuit
  Soleil couchant
PIZZETTI *Epitaphe*
RACHMANINOFF *They answered*
RESPIGHI *Si tu beux*
RUBINSTEIN
  Chanson d'amour
  Liebeswunder
  Romance, "Comment disait-il"
SAINT-SAËNS
  À quoi bon entendre les oiseaux des bois

Le chant de ceux qui s'en vont sur mer
La cloche
La coccinelle
L'enlèvement
Extase
Une flûte invisible
Guitare
Le matin
La pas d'armes du roi Jean
Rêverie
Si vous n'avez rien à me dire
Soirée en mer
Suzette et Suzon
CHANSONS DES RUES ET DES BOIS.
  CHABRIER *Sommation irrespectueuse*
CHANTS DU CRÉPUSCULE.
  FAURÉ *L'aurore*
  FRANCK, LISZT, SAINT-SAËNS *S'il*
    est un charmant gazon
LES ORIENTALES.
  INDY
    Attente
    Clair de lune
  SAINT-SAËNS, WAGNER *L'attente*
  WAGNER *Extase*
LE ROI S'AMUSE.
  DELIBES *Vieille chanson*
RUY BLAS.
  SPOHR *An die Geliebte*
LES VOIX INTÉRIEURES.
  WAGNER *La tombe dit à la rose*
"Hui! wie die Wolke von Staub und Brand"
  see Die Geister der Wüste Stieglitz
  LOEWE
Huidobro, Vicente, 1893-1948.
  JOLIVET *Voyage imaginaire*
HUIT CHANSONS POLONAISES, no. 1
  POULENC Unknown *La couronne*
HUIT CHANSONS POLONAISES, no. 2
  POULENC Unknown *Le départ*
HUIT CHANSONS POLONAISES, no. 3
  POULENC Unknown *Les gars polonais*
HUIT CHANSONS POLONAISES, no. 4
  POULENC Unknown *Le dernier mazour*
HUIT CHANSONS POLONAISES, no. 5
  POULENC Unknown *L'adieu*
HUIT CHANSONS POLONAISES, no. 6
  POULENC Unknown *Le drapeau blanc*
HUIT CHANSONS POLONAISES, no. 7
  POULENC Unknown *La Vistule*
HUIT CHANSONS POLONAISES, no. 8
  POULENC Unknown *Le lac*
HUIT POÈMES, no. 1
  AURIC Cocteau *Hommage à Erik Satie*
HUIT POÈMES, no. 2
  AURIC Cocteau *Réveil*

COMPOSER Poet *Title* "First Line"

HUIT POÈMES, no. 3
  AURIC Cocteau *École de guerre*
HUIT POÈMES, no. 4
  AURIC Cocteau *Aglaé*
HUIT POÈMES, no. 5
  AURIC Cocteau *Place des Invalides*
HUIT POÈMES, no. 6
  AURIC Cocteau *Marie Laurencin*
HUIT POÈMES, no. 7
  AURIC Cocteau *Biplan le matin*
HUIT POÈMES, no. 8
  AURIC Cocteau *Portrait d'Henri*
    Rousseau
HUIT SCÈNES DE FAUST, op. 1 no. 6
  BERLIOZ Gérard de Nerval *Le roi de*
    Thulé
Hulanka see Witwicki **CHOPIN**
Huldigung see Hafiz **STRAUSS**
Huldigung see Kosegarten *MINNESANG.*
  SCHUBERT
"Humble am I when thunder roars" *see*
  Humble yet valiant Shenshin **MEDTNER**
Humble yet valiant see Shenshin
  MEDTNER
"Humblement, tendrement, sur le tombeau
  charmant" *see La fausse morte* Valéry
  MOMPOU
"L'humide été de pleurs dégrène" *see* . . . *de*
  pleurs d'égrène Ganzo **SCHMITT**
Humières, Robert, Vicomte d', 1868-
  1915.
  KOECHLIN *Sur la grève*
Humility see Carpenter, Rue **CARPENTER**
Humoresque see Beauquier **LALO**
"Hun ae sa møjen hwalle Piig" *see Wo*
  Daetter Berntsen **NIELSEN**
Hun er saa hvid see Andersen **GRIEG**
Hun har mig glemt! see Andersen
  NIELSEN
"Hun har mg glemt" *see Langelandsk*
  Folkemelodi Andersen **GRIEG**
HUNDERT BLÄTTER . . . *see* Groth
  Dein blaues Auge **BRAHMS**
  Es hing der Reif **BRAHMS**
  Heimweh I **BRAHMS**
  Heimweh II **BRAHMS**
  Heimweh III **BRAHMS**
  Mein wundes Herz verlangt **BRAHMS**
  Regenlied **BRAHMS**
  Wie Melodien zieht es mir **BRAHMS**
Hundra vägar see Runeberg **SIBELIUS**
A hundred ways see Runeberg **SIBELIUS**
  Hundra vägar
HUNGARIAN FOLKSONGS, no. 1
  SEIBER Anon. *Lament*

HUNGARIAN FOLKSONGS, no. 2
  SEIBER Anon. *Quarrel*
HUNGARIAN FOLKSONGS, no. 3
  SEIBER Anon. *Farewell*
HUNGARIAN FOLKSONGS, no. 4
  SEIBER Anon. *Soldier's song*
Hunt, Leigh, 1784-1859.
  IVES *Romanzo di Central Park*
Hunter's even-song see Goethe **MEDTNER**
  Jägers Abendlied
Hurrahing in harvest see Hopkins
  BERKELEY
Hus, Jan, 1369-1415.
  LOEWE *Jesus ist mein Hirt*
Der Husar, trara! see Lenau **SCHUMANN**
"Husaren müssen reiten" *see Husarenlied*
  Hoffmann von Fallersleben **STRAUSS**
Husarenabzug see Candidus **SCHUMANN**
Husarenlied see Hoffmann von
  Fallersleben **STRAUSS**
HUSARENLIEDER, no. 1
  SCHUMANN Lenau *Der Husar, trara!*
HUSARENLIEDER, no. 2
  SCHUMANN Lenau *Der leidige Frieden*
    hat lange gewährt
HUSARENLIEDER, no. 3
  SCHUMANN Lenau *Den grünen Zeigern*
HUSARENLIEDER, no. 4
  SCHUMANN Lenau *Da liegt der Feinde*
    gestreckte Schaar
"Husbands and wives!" *see One of us* Feeney
  CHANLER
"Husch, husch, husch, husch" *see Stelldichein*
  Hörmann **REGER**
"Hush my little one, fold your hands" *see*
  Sicilian lullaby Field, Eugene
  CARPENTER
"Hush thee, dear child to slumbers" *see*
  Cradle song Ives, A. L., Miss **IVES**
"Hush you bye, don't you cry" *see The little*
  horses Anon. **COPLAND**
Hussens Kerker see Meyer **PFITZNER**
Husvild see Jensen, J. **NIELSEN**
Huxley, Aldous Leonard, 1894-1963.
  IRELAND *The trellis*
Hva skal jeg si? see Chamisso **GRIEG**
  Was soll ich sagen?
"Hvad lärkan bådat har från skyn" *see*
  Blåsippan Franzén **SIBELIUS**
"Hvad siger de dog om dig" *see Valgsang*
  Bjørnson **GRIEG**
Hvad synger du om see Hostrup **NIELSEN**
"Hvarför är sa flyktig varen" *see Se'n har jag*
  ej frågat mera Runeberg **SIBELIUS**
"Hvem sidder der bag Skjaermen med Klude
  om sin Haand" *see Jens Vejmand* Aakjaer
  NIELSEN

Hvem styrde hit din väg? see Runeberg
   SIBELIUS
Den hvide, røde Rose see Bjørnson **GRIEG**
Hvitsippan see Franzén **SIBELIUS**
"Hvor blev den Blomst" *see Gensyn*
   Paludan-Müller **NIELSEN**
"Hvor Bølgen høit mod Kysten slaar" *see*
   Hytten Andersen **GRIEG**
Hvor er' de nu? see Heine **GRIEG** *Wo sind*
   Sie hin?
Hvor sødt i Sommer-Aftenstunden see
   Oehlenschläger **NIELSEN**
"Hvorfor svømmer dit øje" *see Til Én. II*
   Paulsen **GRIEG**
Hy-Brazil see Sharp, W. *THE HOUR OF*
   BEAUTY. **DELIUS** *I-Brasil*
Hyde Park see Apollinaire *IL Y A.*
   POULENC
Hymn see Tersteegen **IVES**
Hymn for a child see Warner **IRELAND**
Hymn to light see Blake, James **IRELAND**
Hymn to Thais see Borgström **SIBELIUS**
A HYMN TO THE NATIVITY. see Crashaw
   Sung by the shepherds **THOMSON**
L'HYMNAIRE D'ADONIS. see Fersen, I. de
   Il pleut, bergère **RESPIGHI**
Hymne see Baudelaire **FAURÉ**
Hymne see Racine **POULENC**
Hymne à Astarté see Louÿs *CHANSONS DE*
   BILITIS. **KOECHLIN**
Hymne à la nuit see Barbier, J. **GOUNOD**
Hymne à la nuit see Louÿs *CHANSONS DE*
   BILITIS. **KOECHLIN**
Hymne à Venus see Villiers **KOECHLIN**
Hymne an die Kalliope see Dionysius
   LOEWE *An die Muse*

Hymne d'amour see Desachy **MASSENET**
L'hymne de la délivrance see Bruyr, José
   HONEGGER
L'Hymne de la paix see Baïf **ROREM**
Hymne de la patrie see Boyer, Georges
   GOUNOD *Notre Dame de France*
Hymne de Sion see Cohen, A. **MILHAUD**
L'hymne des fleurs see Allievo, Biago
   MASSENET
Hymne du sport see Bruyr, José
   HONEGGER
Hymne I see Hardenberg **SCHUBERT**
Hymne II see Hardenberg **SCHUBERT**
Hymne III see Hardenberg **SCHUBERT**
Hymne IV see Hardenberg **SCHUBERT**
Hymne pour le "Salut Drapeau" du "Prince
   de Byzance"... see Péladin
   LE PRINCE DE BYZANCE. **SATIE**
HYMNIS. see Banville
   Il dort encore **DEBUSSY**
Hymnus der Liebe see Jacobowski *VOM*
   GESCHLECHT DER PROMETHIDEN.
   REGER
Hymnus des Hasses see Morgenstern
   REGER
Hymnus k Nejsvětější Trojici see No author
   DVOŘÁK
Hyökyaalto see Koskenniemi **KILPINEN**
Hyspa, Vincent, 1865-1938.
   DEBUSSY *La Belle au bois dormant*
   SATIE
      Chez le docteur
      Un dîner à l'Élysée
      L'omnibus automobile
      Tendrement
      Le veuf
Hytten see Andersen **GRIEG**

I

I Aften see Holstein **NIELSEN**

"I Aftenens Glans mon gløde" *see Sang paa Fjeldet* Winther **GRIEG**

"I always like summer best" *see Knoxville, Tennessee* Giovanni **WEISGALL**

I AM A BLACK WOMAN. see Evans, M. *The rebel* **WEISGALL**

"I am a poor tiler in simple array" *see Tom Tyler* Anon. **HESELTINE**

I am a tree see Josephson, E. **SIBELIUS** *Jag är ett träd*

I am He see Whitman **BLITZSTEIN**

"I am he with amorous love" *see I am He* Whitman **BLITZSTEIN**

I am like a remnant of a cloud of autumn see Tagore *GITANJALI.* **CARPENTER**

I am my beloved's see Bible **THOMSON** Two settings: 1924 and 1926.

I am rose see Stein **DIAMOND, ROREM**

"I am rose, my eyes are blue" *see I am rose* Stein **DIAMOND**

I am still filled, dear friend see Maïkov **RIMSKIĬ-KORSAKOV** *Eshche ia poln, o drug moĭ milyĭ*

I am that knight of fairy tale see Hálek **DVOŘÁK** *Já jstem ten rytîr zpohádky*

I am the knight of fairy-tale see Hálek **DVOŘÁK** *Já jstem ten rytîr zpohádky*

I am unhappy see Lermontov **RIMSKIĬ-KORSAKOV** *Mne grustno*

"I arise from dreams of Thee" *see Indian love song* Shelley **DELIUS**

I arrived to give you greeting see Shenshin **RIMSKIĬ-KORSAKOV** *ĨA prishel k tebe s privetom*

I ask but this see Gardner, W. **MACDOWELL**

I asked a thief to steal me a peach see Blake, William *POEMS FROM THE ROSSETTI MS 1793:* A poem with a moral. **HESELTINE**

"I aspired to soar in sun-light" *see Epitaph* Bugayev **MEDTNER**

"I awoke in the midsummer not to call night" *see Moonrise* Hopkins **KRENEK**

I beg for mercy see Merezhkovski **RACHMANINOFF**

I believe I love see Pushkin **RIMSKIĬ-KORSAKOV** *ĨA veriu ia liubim*

I Blåbaer-Tuerne see Garborg *HAUGTUSSA.* **GRIEG** *Blåbaer-Li*

I bless you, forests see Tolstoĭ *JOHN OF DAMASCUS.* **CHAĬKOVSKIĬ** *Blagoslavlyayu vas, lesa*

I bol'no, i sladko see Rostopchina **CHAĬKOVSKIĬ**

I bought me a cat see Anon. **COPLAND**

I came to her see Kol'tsov **RACHMANINOFF** *I was with her*

I came to thee with greeting see Shenshin **BALAKIREV** *Ya prishol k tebe s privetom*

I cannot come to you see Ady **BARTÓK**

"I cannot eat but little meat" *see Maltworms* Stevenson, W. **HESELTINE**

"I closed and drew" *see Tarrant moss* Kipling **IVES**

"I come, Inesilla, my sweetest and best" *see Serenade* Pushkin **MEDTNER**

"I cried unto the Lord with my voice" *see Psalm 142* Bible **ROREM**

"I dag är luften blå" *see Snöblommor* Blomberg **KILPINEN**

I dare not ask a kiss see Herrick **QUILTER**

"I did not look upon her eyes" *see Penumbra* Rossetti, Dante **IRELAND**

I did not love you at first see Konstantin **CHAĬKOVSKIĬ** *ĨA snachala tebia ne liubila*

I died from happiness see Uhland **RIMSKIĬ-KORSAKOV** *ĨA umer ot schast'ia*

I died from the rapture see Uhland **RIMSKIĬ-KORSAKOV** *ĨA umer ot schast'ia*

I dina händers mjuka fågelbo see Blomberg **KILPINEN**

"I dina ögons klara morgonljus" *see I dina händers mjuka fågelbo* Blomberg **KILPINEN**

"I dit dyrebare Navn" *see Morgenbøn paa Skolen* Gjertsen **GRIEG**

"I do not know with whom Edan will sleep" *see Promiscuity* Jackson, Kenneth, translator. **BARBER**

I do not please you see Konstantin **CHAĬKOVSKIĬ** *ĨA vam ne nravlius'*

"I dreamed I heard your voice in the night" *see Come back* Unknown **QUILTER**

I dreamed last night that you were dead see Hálek **DVOŘÁK** *Mně zdálo se žes umřela*

I Drømmes Land see Jacobsen **NIELSEN**

"I dug and dug amongst the snow" *see Hope* Rossetti, Christina **IRELAND**

I faint, I perish see Shelley **LUENING**

"I faint, I perish with my love!" *see I faint, I perish* Shelley **LUENING**

I felt a cleavage in my mind see Dickinson **LUENING**

COMPOSER Poet *Title* "First Line"

I felt a funeral in my brain see Dickinson
COPLAND
I FJÄLLGRÄNSEN, no. 1
KILPINEN Bergman *Lyss till det djupa
och stora*
I FJÄLLGRÄNSEN, no. 2
KILPINEN Bergman *Skogen spelar.
Älven rinner*
I FJÄLLGRÄNSEN, no. 3
KILPINEN Bergman *Stormen kör i
fjällen*
"I hab gedacht, dass i allei" *see Abschied*
Löwenstein **RUBINSTEIN**
"I had a little nobby mare" *see Jenny Gray*
Anon. **HESELTINE**
I had a little pony see Anon.
NURSE LOVECHILD'S LEGACY (London:
The Poetry Bookshop, 1916).
HESELTINE
"I Hagen sat Mod'ri med Barnet" *see Millom
Roser* Janson **GRIEG**
"I hat e schön's Schatzerl" *see Beruhigung*
Löwenstein **RUBINSTEIN**
I hate music! see Bernstein **BERNSTEIN**
I HATE MUSIC! no. 1
BERNSTEIN Bernstein *My mother says
that babies come in bottles*
I HATE MUSIC! no. 2
BERNSTEIN Bernstein *Jupiter has seven
moons*
I HATE MUSIC! no. 3
BERNSTEIN Bernstein *I hate music!*
I HATE MUSIC! no. 4
BERNSTEIN Bernstein *A big Indian and
a little Indian*
I HATE MUSIC! no. 5
BERNSTEIN Bernstein *I just found out
today*
I have a friend see Quilter **QUILTER**
I have been fashioned see Agee *SONNET 4.*
DIAMOND
"I have been here before" *see Sudden light*
Rossetti, Dante **LOEFFLER**
I have come to greet thee see Shenshin
RIMSKIĬ-KORSAKOV
IA prishel k tebe s privetom
"I have desired to go where springs not fail"
see A nun takes the veil Hopkins
BARBER
"I have fed your lar with poppies" *see Young
lady* Pound **DIAMOND**
I have grown fond of sorrow see
Shevchenko **RACHMANINOFF**
I have longed to move away see Thomas
DIAMOND
I have many palaces and gardens see
Kol'tsov **MUSORGSKIĬ**
Mnogo est' u menia teremov i sadov

I have never spoken to her see Mei *OKTAVI.*
CHAĬKOVSKIĬ *Ya s neyu nikogda ne
govoril*
"I have no name" *see Infant joy* Blake,
William **LUENING,**
VAUGHAN WILLIAMS
"I have observed pink monks eating blue
raisins" *see Monks and raisins* Villa, J. G.
BARBER
"I have old women's secrets now" *see
The secrets of the old* Yeats **BARBER**
"I have seen the proudest stars" *see To one
unknown* Dudley, Helen **CARPENTER**
*I have trod the upward and the downward
slope see* Stevenson, Robert Louis
SONGS OF TRAVEL, XXII.
VAUGHAN WILLIAMS
I have twelve oxen see Anon. **IRELAND**
"I have twelve oxen" *see Twelve oxen* Anon.
HESELTINE
"I Haven her du hvisked engang" *see
Den aergjerrige* Paulsen **GRIEG**
"I haven't yet seen you asleep" *see Poem*
Dropkin **WEISGALL**
I hear an army see Joyce *CHAMBER
MUSIC.* **BARBER**
I hear in the night see Drachmann **DELIUS**
Jeg hører i natten
"I hear thee speak" *see The better land*
Hemans **BENNETT**
"I heard a horseman" *see The horseman*
De La Mare **BERKELEY**
"I heard a little chicken chirp" *see Thomas
Earp* Lawrence **RIETI**
"I heard a throstle singing at the dawn of day"
see Spring voices Quilter **QUILTER**
"I heard at night your long sighs" *see
Dreaming of a dead lady* Shên-Yo
BERKELEY
I held Love's head see Herrick *HESPERIDES*
(1648): Upon love. **HESELTINE**
"I held Love's head while it did ache" *see
I held Love's head* Herrick **HESELTINE**
I just found out today see Bernstein
BERNSTEIN
"I Knøse, tag, det raader jeg" *see Tag Jer i
Agt for Anna* Burns **NIELSEN**
"I know a green grass path that leaves the
field" *see The green river* Douglas
CARPENTER
"I know a maiden fair to see" *see Beware*
Longfellow **BRITTEN**
"I know, ah! too well why I am so sad" *see
The sorrowful maiden* Burns **FRANZ**
I know so many stories see Moss **ROREM**
I know that I shall meet my fate see Yeats
ROREM

I know that on my . . . see Pfleger-Moravský
  DVOŘÁK *Já vím, že v sladké naději*
    Two settings: B. 11 no. 6 and B. 160 no.
    4.
I Liden højt deroppe see Lie **GRIEG**
I looked back suddenly see Wolfe, H.
  WEISGALL
"I love little pussy, her coat is so warm" *see*
  The wild home pussy Rounds, Emma
  THOMPSON, R.
I love old parks see Borecký, Jaromír
  MARTINŮ
"I love the jocund dance" *see The jocund*
  dance Blake, William **QUILTER**
"I love thee for thy fickleness" *see The droll*
  lover Anon. **HESELTINE**
I love thee, moon see Maĭkov **RIMSKIĬ-**
  KORSAKOV
    Liubliu tebia, mesiats
"I love thee well" *see Morning* Yanova
  RACHMANINOFF
"I love you as a sheriff searches for a walnut"
  see Love song Koch **THOMSON**
"I love your secret hidden flowers" *see Elegy*
  Pushkin **MEDTNER**
I loved him see Kol′tsov **BALAKIREV** *IA*
  liubila ego
I loved thee well see Pushkin **MEDTNER**
  I loved you well
I loved you well see Pushkin **MEDTNER**
"I make my shroud but no one know" *see*
  Song Crapsey **WEISGALL**
"I mun be married a Sunday" *see Roister*
  doister Udall **HESELTINE**
I must be married on Sunday see Udall
  BRITTEN
"I must go down to the seas again" *see Sea*
  fever Masefield **IRELAND**
I natten see Rydberg **SIBELIUS**
I never spoke to her see Mei **OKTAVI.**
  CHAĬKOVSKIĬ *Ya s neyu nikogda ne*
  govoril
I nothing saw in you see Agee **SONNET 17.**
  DIAMOND
I nowhere see my love see Anon.
  PROKOFIEV *IA nigde druzhka ne vizhu*
I once had a newly cut willow pipe see Krag
  DELIUS *Jeg havde en nyskaaren seljefløjte*
I opened the window see Konstantin
  CHAĬKOVSKIĬ *Rastvoril ia okno*
"I pant for the music which is divine" *see*
  Music Shelley **QUILTER**
"I remember running and running to my
  house" *see Displaced* Blitzstein
  BLITZSTEIN

I remember that day see Tiutchev
  RACHMANINOFF
"I ride to you, and happy dreams" *see Visions*
  Pushkin **MEDTNER**
I rise when you enter see Feeney
  CHANLER
I roamed the meadows see Goethe
  MEDTNER *Im Vorübergehen*
I Rosentiden see Goethe **GRIEG** *Zur*
  Rosenzeit
"I sah mal a Blimle" *see Das gebrochene*
  Herz Löwenstein **RUBINSTEIN**
"I sang that song on Sunday" *see Her song*
  Hardy **IRELAND**
"I saw a ship a-sailing" *see An old song re-*
  sung Masefield **GRIFFES**
"I saw a young snake glide" *see Snake*
  Roethke **ROREM**
I saw in Louisiana a live-oak growing see
  Whitman **ROREM**
"I saw the maid on rocky strand" *see*
  The storm Pushkin **RACHMANINOFF**
I see you every night, my dear see Heine
  MARTINŮ
I SERAILLETS HAVE. see Jacobsen
  I Seraillets Have **NIELSEN**
I Seraillets Have see Jacobsen *I*
  SERAILLETS HAVE. **NIELSEN**
I SERAILLETS HAVE. see Jacobsen
  In the seraglio garden **DELIUS**
"I shall go without companions" *see My own*
  country Belloc, Hilaire **HESELTINE**
I shall imagine life see Cummings
  DIAMOND
I shall tell you nothing see Shenshin
  CHAĬKOVSKIĬ *IA tebe nichego ne*
  skazhu′; **RACHMANINOFF**
I should like in a single word see Heine
  DIE HEIMKEHR. **CHAĬKOVSKIĬ**
  Khotel by v edinoe slovo
I should like to sleep for ever see
  Merezhkovski **CHAĬKOVSKIĬ** *Usni!*
"I sing of a maiden that is matchless" *see*
  An old carol Anon. **QUILTER**
"I sit alone in a way station" *see*
  The passenger Howe **THOMPSON, R.**
"I sit dejected and apart" *see Dejection*
  Tiutchev **MEDTNER**
I Skyggen vi vanke see Oehlenschläger
  NIELSEN
I Slåtten see Garborg **HAUGTUSSA. GRIEG**
"I Solen gaar jeg bag min Plov" *see Sang bag*
  Ploven Holstein **NIELSEN**
"I sometimes sit beneath a tree" *see The last*
  reader Holmes, O. **IVES**
"I Sommer var Skoven saa grøn" *see*
  Efteraarsstormen Richardt **GRIEG**

"I stood today by the shimm'ring sea" *see By the sea* Quilter **QUILTER**

I strolled across an open field see Roethke *THE WAKING.* **ROREM**

I systrar, I bröder see Lybeck **SIBELIUS**

"I tell you, if an angel" *see To a devil* Benzon **GRIEG**

"I that in heill was and gladness am" *see Timor mortis* Dunbar, William **SEIBER**

"I think there must be a place in the soul" *see The things our fathers loved* Ives **IVES**

"I thought I woke: the midnight sun flooded" *see The midnight sun* Goodman **ROREM**

I thought once I should have at a man's age see Olson **DIAMOND**

"I thought this heart enkindled lay" *see A dream* Moore, T. **RUBINSTEIN**

I travelled among unknown men see Wordsworth **IVES**

"I und mein junges Weib" *see Bettlerlied* Anon. **WEBER**

"I used to be a QUIET GIRL" *see Quiet girl* Blitzstein **BLITZSTEIN**

"I used to be jail-bait" *see Jail-bait blues* Goodman **ROREM**

I wait for thee! see Davidova, Mariya **RACHMANINOFF**

I waited for thee at the appointed hour see Maĭkov **RIMSKIĬ-KORSAKOV** *IA v grote zhdal tebia v urochnyĭ chas*

I waited there for you within the cove see Maĭkov **RIMSKIĬ-KORSAKOV** *IA v grote zhdal tebia v urochnyĭ chas*

"I wake to sleep" *see The waking* Roethke **ROREM**

I wan' my friends see Wright, Merle St. Croix **THOMPSON, R.** *Spiritual: I wan' my friends*

"I wander far and unrestrained" *see Spring* Carpenter, Rue **CARPENTER**

I wander oft past yondre house see Pfleger-Moravský **DVOŘÁK** *Kol domuse*

"I wander thro' each charter'd street" *see London* Blake, William **BRITTEN, VAUGHAN WILLIAMS**

"I want to give you something, my child" *see The gift* Tagore **MILHAUD**

"I was angry with my friend" *see A poison tree* Blake, William **BRITTEN, VAUGHAN WILLIAMS**

"I was asleep when they worked up the buffalo" *see Collected poems* Koch **THOMSON**

"I was five years old and I stepped up into the street car" *see A journey* Glaze **ROREM**

I was not sorrowful see Dowson **IRELAND**

I was with her see Kol'tsov **RACHMANINOFF**

"I watched a sea-bird flying" *see The sea-bird* Quilter **QUILTER**

"I whispered, 'I am too young' " *see Brown penny* Yeats **RIETI**

I will alwas love you see O'Hara **ROREM** *Poem: I will always love you*

"I will make you brooches" *see The roadside fire* Stevenson, Robert Louis **VAUGHAN WILLIAMS**

"I will make you brooches" *see Romance* Stevenson, Robert Louis **HESELTINE**

"I will put on the whole armour of light" *see The pilgrim's psalm* Bible **VAUGHAN WILLIAMS**

"I will take nothing from my Lord, said she" *see St. Ita's vision* Kallman **BARBER**

I will walk on the earth see Blake, James **IRELAND**

I wish I dwelt in India land see Fröding **SIBELIUS** *Jag ville jag vore i Indialand*

"I wish I knew a sea of ink" *see Red hair* Carpenter, Rue **CARPENTER**

"I woke before the morning" *see A good boy* Stevenson, Robert Louis **HAHN**

"I woke before the morning" *see A good child* Stevenson, Robert Louis **QUILTER**

"I wonder if God thinks of me" *see The thunderstorm* Carpenter, Rue **CARPENTER**

I wonder oft past yondre house see Pfleger-Moravský **DVOŘÁK** *Kol domu se ted potácím* Two settings: B. 123 no. 3 and B. 160 no. 3.

I won't be my father's Jack see Anon. *NURSE LOVECHILD'S LEGACY* (London: The Poetry Bookshop, 1916). **HESELTINE**

"I would I were Actaeon whom Diana did disguise" *see Walking the woods* Anon. **HESELTINE**

"I would like to have the men of Heaven in my own house" *see The heavenly banquet* O'Faolain, Sean, translator. **BARBER**

IA byl u neĭ see Kol'tsov **RACHMANINOFF** *I was with her*

IA dumal, serdtse pozabylo see Pushkin **BRITTEN** *My heart . . .*

"IA gor'ko setoval v pustyne" *see Ekho* Coppée **RIMSKIĬ-KORSAKOV**

IA li v poke da ne travushka byla see Surikov *MALOROSSYSKAYA PESNYA.* **CHAĬKOVSKIĬ**

IA liubila ego see Kol'tsov **BALAKIREV**

"IA, matey' bozhiia" *see Molitva* Lermontov
MUSORGSKIĬ

"Ia Mutter, weine nur! das Schicksal griff und
brach" *see An eine Mutter, deren Tochter
als Kind starb* Sonnleithner **ZELTER**

IA ne prorok see Kruglov
RACHMANINOFF *No prophet I*

"IA ne znaiu chto takoe" *see Pod krysheĭ*
Gorianskogo, V. **PROKOFIEV**

IA nigde druzhka ne vizhu see Anon.
PROKOFIEV

IA opiat' odinok see Shevchenko
RACHMANINOFF *Again I am alone*

IA perezhil svoi zhelan'ia see Pushkin
MEDTNER *Alas, for I outlive my
yearnings*

IA potriasen, kogda krugom see Shenshin
MEDTNER *Humble yet valiant*

"IA prines tebe vkradchibyĭ list" *see Pomni
menia!* Bal'mont **PROKOFIEV**

IA prishel k tebe s privetom see Shenshin
MEDTNER *Greeting;* **RIMSKIĬ-
KORSAKOV**

"IA prost, ia iasen, ia skromen" *see Klassik*
Musorgskiĭ **MUSORGSKIĬ**

"IA sidela do sumerek" *see Katerina* Anon.
PROKOFIEV

IA snachala tebia ne liubila see Konstantin
CHAĬKOVSKIĬ

"IA svet zazhgu, ia svet zazhgu na etom
beregu" *see Zaklinanie vody i ornia*
Bal'mont **PROKOFIEV**

IA tebe nichego ne skazhu' see Shenshin
CHAĬKOVSKIĬ; RACHMANINOFF
I shall tell you nothing

"IA, tsvetok polevoĭ" *see Evreĭskaia pesnia*
Solomon **MUSORGSKIĬ**

IA umer ot schast'ia see Uhland **RIMSKIĬ-
KORSAKOV**

IA v grote zhdal tebia v urochnyĭ chas see
Maĭkov **RIMSKIĬ-KORSAKOV**

IA v subbotu zatepliu svechu see Unknown
MUSORGSKIĬ

IA vac liubil see Pushkin **MEDTNER**
I loved you well

IA vam ne nravlius' see Konstantin
CHAĬKOVSKIĬ

IA veriu ia liubim see Pushkin **RIMSKIĬ-
KORSAKOV**

"IA videl noch'" *see Videnie* Golenishchev-
Kutuzov **MUSORGSKIĬ**

IA zhdu tebia see Davidova, Mariya
RACHMANINOFF *I wait for thee!*

"IA znaiu, otchego" *see Nimfa* Maĭkov
RIMSKIĬ-KORSAKOV

Ianke
ZELTER *Gesang zum Jahresfeste der
Luisenstiftung*

IAtsevicha, M
BALAKIREV *Vzoshol na nebo mesyats
yasnȳĭ*

IBERT, JACQUES, 1890-1962.
Aguet, William
Je penais épouser un fier à bras [Heugel,
1947] same
Mon bien aimé siffle bien [Heugel, 1947]
same
Arnoux, Alexandre, 1884-1973.
Berceuse de Galiane [Leduc, 1957] "Par
les chemins de l'aurore chevauche"
Complainte de Florinde [Leduc, 1957]
"Je suis née un mauvais mardi"
Chabaneix, Philippe, 1898-
Familière [Heugel, 1927] "Tu aimais les
raisins"
Fête nationale [Heugel, 1927] "Démon
au sourire angélique"
Mélancolie [Heugel, 1927] "Tu te
penches et tu souris"
Constantin-Weyer, Maurice, 1881-
1964.
Chanson du rien [Leduc, 1930] "Je vais
vous parler d'un Rien"
Derème, Tristan, 1899-1941.
Cette grande chambre (1923) [Leduc,
1924] same
Comme j'allais (1923) [Leduc, 1924]
same
Personne ne saura jamais (1923) [Leduc,
1924] same
Tiède azur (1923) [Leduc, 1924] same
Also published in **La Revue musicale**
Suppl., 1er fév., 5.année no. 4.
Jean-Aubry, Georges, 1882-1950.
Romance [Heugel, 1927] "Se peut-il
qu'autrefois"
Louÿs, Pierre, 1870-1925.
Le petit âne blanc [Leduc, 1940]
"Va! trotte sans fin, trotte sans trêve"
After *Histoires* no. 2 for piano; also
orchestrated.
Maeterlinck, Maurice, 1862-1949.
Chanson (1910) [Leduc, 1922]
"Elle avait trois couronnes d'or"
Mendès, Catulle Abraham, 1841-1909.
Le jardin du ciel (1910) [Leduc, 1922]
"Un souffle d'ombre éteint"
No author
Vocalise-étude (Aria, 1930) [Leduc,
1931]
Wordless. Also for 2 voices or voice-
flute-piano, etc.

Ségalen, Victor Joseph Ambroise
Désiré, 1878-1919.
  Mon amante a les vertus de l'eau (1925)
    [Heugel, 1926] same
    Voice & flute.
  On me dit: . . . (1925) [Heugel, 1926]
    same
    Voice & flute.
Vallery-Radot, Pasteur
  Chant de folie (1924) [Leduc, 1925]
    "La la la la la"
    Also for 6 solo voices, chorus and
    orchestra.
Vildrac, Charles, 1882-1971.
  LIVRE D'AMOUR.
    Après minuit [Leduc, 1923] "C'est au
      petit jour qu'ils trépassent"
    Comme elle a les yeux bandés [Leduc,
      1923] same
    Elle était venue sur les marches tièdes
      [Leduc, 1923] same
I-Brasil see Sharp, W. *THE HOUR OF*
BEAUTY. DELIUS
Ibsen, Henrik, 1828-1906.
  DELIUS *Hochgebirgsleben*
  GRIEG
    Borte!
    En fuglevise
    Med en vandlilje
    Spillemaend
    Stambogsrim
    En svane
  DAS FEST AUF SOLHAUG.
    WOLF
      Gesang Margit's
      Gudmund's erster Gesang
      Gudmund's zweiter Gesang
  EN FUGLEVISE.
    DELIUS *Eine Vogelweise*
  KONGS-EMNERNE.
    DELIUS *Wiegenlied*
    GRIEG *Margretes Vuggesang*
  SPILLEMAEND.
    BERG, DELIUS *Spielleute*
Ich aber weiss, ich seh' dich manche Nacht
  see Jacobowski PFITZNER
Ich alter Pilger see Gleim ZELTER
"Ich armer Teufel, Herr Baron" *see Spottlied*
  Goethe WOLF
"Ich armes Käuzlein kleine" *see Das Käuzlein*
  Des Knaben Wunderhorn
  SCHUMANN
  Two settings: Op. 79 no. 10 and another
    without opus number.
"Ich auf der Erd', am Himmel du" *see*
  Der Wanderer an den Mond Seidl
  SCHUBERT

"Ich bin auch in Ravenna gewesen" *see*
  Ravenna Hesse SCHOECK
Ich bin bis zum Tode betrübet see Hahn-
  Hahn FRANZ
"Ich bin der Contrabandiste" *see Der*
  Contrabandiste Unknown SCHUMANN
"Ich bin der König vom Morgenland" *see Der*
  König aus dem Morgenland Schellenberg
  REGER
"Ich bin der Trommelschläger laut" *see*
  Trommel-Städchen Moehrcke LOEWE
"Ich bin der wohlbekannte Sänger" *see*
  Der Rattenfänger Goethe SCHUBERT,
  WOLF
"Ich bin die Blum' im Garten" *see Die Blume*
  der Ergebung Rückert LOEWE,
  SCHUMANN
"Ich bin die Blume im Garten" *see Die Blume*
  der Ergebenheit Rückert RUBINSTEIN
Ich bin ein armes Lämpchen nur see Hafiz
  JENSEN
"Ich bin ein deutsches Mädchen" *see*
  Vaterlandslied Klopstock GLUCK,
  SCHUBERT
"Ich bin ein Dieb geworden" *see Der Dieb*
  Schellenberg REGER
"Ich bin ein jung jung Malergesell" *see*
  Wanderschaft Fitger PIJPER
"Ich bin ein leichter Junggesell" *see*
  Der Junggesell Pfizer LOEWE
"Ich bin ein lust'ger Gesell" *see Der Knabe*
  mit dem Wunderhorn Geibel
  JENSEN, SCHUMANN
Ich bin ein Spielmann von Beruf see
  Leuthold SCHOECK
"Ich bin ein Waller auf der Erde" *see*
  Pilgerweise Schober SCHUBERT
"Ich bin eine Blume an Baches Band" *see*
  Vergissmeinnicht Cornelius LASSEN
"Ich bin einmal etwas hinausspaziert" *see*
  Kuriose Geschichte Reinick PFITZNER
"Ich bin gekommen ins Niederland" *see Die*
  Hochländer-Wittwe Burns SCHUMANN
"Ich bin im Mai gegangen und hab' es nicht
  gewusst" *see Kurzes Erwachen* Kerner
  SCHUMANN
"Ich bin kein Minister" *see Das Lied des*
  Steinklopfers Henckell STRAUSS
"Ich bin meiner Mutter einzig Kind" *see*
  Selbstgeständnis Mörike WOLF
"Ich bin so bleich, du bist so rot" *see Des*
  Mädchens Klage Schweizer SPOHR
Ich bin so froh geworden see Cornelius
  CORNELIUS
"Ich bin vergnügt, im Siegeston" *see Lied*
  Claudius, M. SCHUBERT

"Ich bin vergnügt, im Siegeston" *(continued)*
Two settings: D. 362 and D. 501.

"Ich bin vom Berg der Hirtenknab' " *see*
Der Knabe vom Berge Uhland LOEWE

"Ich bin vom Berg der Hirtenknab' " *see Des*
Knaben Berglied Uhland SCHUMANN

"Ich bin von aller Ruh' geschieden" *see Tiefes*
Leid Schulze SCHUBERT

"Ich bin von lockerem Schlage" *see Frohsinn*
Castelli SCHUBERT

"Ich bin wie and're Mädchen nicht" *see*
Bescheidene Liebe Unknown WOLF

"Ich blick' in mein Herz" *see Sehnsucht*
Geibel SCHUMANN

"Ich blicke hinab" *see Spuk* Hebbel BERG

"Ich blicke hinab in die Gasse" *see In der*
Gasse Hebbel BRAHMS

"Ich dachte dein in tiefer Nacht" *see Mirza*
Schaffy Unknown LASSEN

"Ich danke dir, du stummer Stein" *see Die*
Fusswaschung Morgenstern KILPINEN

"Ich danke Gott dir" *see Der Bettler*
Unknown MENDELSSOHN-
BARTHOLDY

"Ich danke Gott und freue mich" *see Täglich*
zu singen Claudius, M. SCHUBERT

Ich darf nicht dankend see George *DAS*
JAHR DER SEELE, p. 27. SCHÖNBERG

Ich denke dein see Brun, S. ZELTER

Ich denke dein see Goethe BEETHOVEN,
GRIEG, LOEWE

Ich denke dein see Matthisson WEBER

"Ich denke dein" *see Nähe des Geliebten*
Goethe LASSEN, MEDTNER,
SCHUBERT, ZELTER

"Ich denke dein, wenn durch den Hain" *see*
Andenken Matthisson BEETHOVEN,
SCHUBERT, WOLF

"Ich denke dein, wenn durch den Hain" *see*
Ich denke dein Matthisson WEBER

"Ich, der mit flatterndem Sinn" *see*
Selbstgespräch Gleim BEETHOVEN

"Ich empfinde fast ein Grauen" *see*
Gelahrtheit Opitz WEBER

Ich esse nun mein Brot nicht trocken mehr see
Heyse WOLF

"Ich faud im Buch ein Epheublatt" *see*
Das Epheublatt Krause LASSEN

"Ich flocht ein Kränzlein schöner Lieder" *see*
Lieben und Schweigen Tischendorf
MENDELSSOHN-BARTHOLDY

"Ich frage keine Blume" *see Der Neugierige*
Müller, Wilhelm SCHUBERT

Ich fragte dich see Hesse KILPINEN

Ich fühle deinen Odem see Bodenstedt
BARTÓK, LASSEN, QUILTER,
RUBINSTEIN

Ich fürcht' nit Gespenster see Keller, G.
PFITZNER

Ich fuhr über Meer see Anon. WOLF

"Ich fuhr wohl über Wasser und in die Ferne
weit" *see Gudmund's zweiter Gesang*
Ibsen WOLF

"Ich geh' auf stillen Auen" *see Das Wölklein*
Boelitz REGER

"Ich geh durch die dunklen Gassen" *see*
In der Fremde Eichendorff WOLF

Ich gehe durch die stille Nacht see Ahlefeldt,
Ottilie von LASSEN

"Ich gehe durch die stille Nacht" *see An den*
Mond Unknown LASSEN

"Ich gehe fremd durch die Menge" *see*
Sonnenregen Ritter REGER

"Ich gieng im Walde so vor mich hin" *see*
Auch mein Sinn Goethe ZELTER

"Ich ging bei Nacht einst über Land" *see*
Unfall Eichendorff WOLF

"Ich ging den Weg entlang" *see Sehnsucht*
Liliencron PFITZNER, STRAUSS

Ich ging hinaus, um dich zu sehen see
Cornelius LASSEN

"Ich ging im Felde so für mich hin" *see*
Im Vorübergehen Goethe LOEWE,
MEDTNER

"Ich ging im grünen Walde" *see*
Der Verehrug Löns KILPINEN

"Ich ging im Walde so für mich hin" *see*
Gefunden Goethe MEDTNER, STRAUSS

Ich ging mit Lust durch einen grünen Wald
see Anon. *DES KNABEN*
WUNDERHORN: Waldvöglein. MAHLER

Ich glaub', lieber Schatz see Ritter REGER

"Ich glaubte, die Schwalbe träumte schon" *see*
Über Nacht Beck JENSEN

Ich grolle nicht see Heine IVES,
SCHUMANN

Ich grüne wie die Weide grünt see
Wackernagel SCHÖNBERG

"Ich grüsse die Sonne" *see In der Campagna*
Mackay STRAUSS

"Ich hab' ein Bächlein funden" *see Daphne*
am Bach Stolberg SCHUBERT

"Ich hab' ein heisses junges Blut" *see*
Das gestörte Glück Körner SCHUBERT

"Ich hab' ein kleines Hüttchen nur" *see*
Das Hüttchen Gleim ZELTER

"Ich hab ein Liebchen lieb recht von Herzen"
see Liebesglück Eichendorff WOLF

"Ich hab' ein Mädchen funden" *see*
Das Finden Kosegarten SCHUBERT

"Ich hab eine alte Muhme" *see Das Blatt im*
Buche Auersperg REGER

"Ich hab' eine Brieftaub' in meinem Sold" *see*
Die Taubenpost Seidl SCHUBERT

"Ich hab eine Wiege so schmuck und nett" *see*
Todes Wiegenlied Schmidt, Georg
ZELTER

"Ich hab' es getragen sieben Jahr" *see*
Archibald Douglas Fontane, T. **LOEWE**

"Ich hab' es nicht gewusst" *see Fraue, Du*
Süsse (?) Finckh **BERG**

Ich hab' ihn im Schlafe see Chamisso
JENSEN

Ich hab' im Traum geweinet see Heine
FRANZ, LASSEN, SCHUMANN

Ich hab' im Traume geweinet see Heine
LOEWE

Ich hab' in deinem Auge see Rückert
FRANZ

"Ich hab' in mein gesogen" *see Liebesfrühling*
Rückert **FRANZ**

Ich hab' in mich gesogen den Frühling treu
see Rückert *LIEBESFRÜHLING.*
SCHUMANN

Ich hab' in Penna see Heyse **WOLF**

"Ich hab' kein' Mutter" *see Und hab' so*
grosse Sehnsucht doch Ritter **REGER**

"Ich hab' mein Sach auf Nichts gestellt" *see*
Vanitas! Vanitatum vanitas! Goethe
ZELTER

"Ich hab' mein Weib allein" *see Niemand*
Burns **SCHUMANN**

"Ich hab' meine Sach' auf nichts gestellt,
juchhe!" *see Vanitas! Vanitatum vanitas*
Goethe **SPOHR**

"Ich hab mir einen Kranz gepflückt" *see*
Liebessuche Löns **KILPINEN**

"Ich hab' mir eins erwählet" *see Liebeslied*
Anon. **WEBER**

"Ich hab' zum Brunnen ein Krüglein
gebracht" *see Das zerbrochene Krüglein*
Frey, F. **SCHÖNBERG**

"Ich habe alle meine Schiffe ausgesendet" *see*
Ballade von den Schiffen Krenek
KRENEK

Ich habe, bevor der Morgen see Chamisso
JENSEN

"Ich habe, bevor der Morgen" *see Tränen*
Chamisso **FRANZ**

Ich habe den Glauben verloren see Lüdt
LASSEN

"Ich habe geliebet" *see Gewohnt, getan*
Goethe **ZELTER**

"Ich habe keine Schulden" *see Der Sorglose*
Unknown **LOEWE**

"Ich habe lieb die helle Sonne" *see Heimat*
Falke **REGER**

"Ich habe mein Kindlein in Schlaf gewiegt"
see Mit Rosen bestreut Bern **REGER**

Ich habe mich dem Heil entschworen see
Hafiz **SCHOECK**

"Ich habe mir Rosmarin gepflanzt" *see*
Rosmarin Hauenschild **FRANZ**

"Ich habe wohl" *see Die Verschwiegenen*
Gilm zu Rosenegg **STRAUSS**

"Ich halte dich in meinem Arm" *see Ghasel*
Keller, G. **SCHÖNBERG**

Ich hat' ein glühend Messer see Mahler
MAHLER

"Ich hatt ein Vöglein, ach wie fein!" *see*
Suschens Vogel Mörike **WOLF**

"Ich hatte eine Nachtigall" *see Verlust*
Lemcke **RUBINSTEIN**

ICH HATTE EINST EIN SCHÖNES
VATERLAND. see Heine
A dream **RACHMANINOFF**

Ich hatte einst ein schönes Vaterland see
Wilder **LASSEN**

"Ich hör' die Bächlein rauschen" *see*
Erinnerung Eichendorff **SCHOECK**

"Ich hör' die Bächlein rauschen" *see In der*
Fremde Eichendorff **SCHUMANN**

Ich hör' ein Vöglein see Böttger
MENDELSSOHN-BARTHOLDY

Ich hör ein Vöglein locken see Böttger
PFITZNER

Ich hör' in der Nacht see Drachmann
DELIUS *Jeg hører i natten*

"Ich hör' meinen Schatz" *see Der Schmied*
Uhland **BRAHMS, JENSEN**

"Ich hört' ein Bächlein rauschen" *see Wohin?*
Müller, Wilhelm **SCHUBERT**

Ich kann nicht zu dir see Ady **BARTÓK**
I cannot come to you

"Ich kann wohl manchmal singen" *see*
Wehmuth Eichendorff **SCHUMANN**

Ich kann's nicht fassen see Chamisso
LOEWE, SCHUMANN

"Ich kenne die Geister, die düstern" *see*
Geister der Nacht Hamerling **JENSEN**

"Ich kenne sieben lustige Brüder" *see Von den*
sieben Zechbrüdern Uhland **STRAUSS**

Ich komm' von Tschindaras tönendem Quell
see Moore, T. **WEBER**
From Chindara's warbling fount

"Ich komme schon durch manche Land" *see*
Marmotte Goethe **BEETHOVEN**

"Ich komme vom Gebirge her" *see*
Der Unglückliche Schmidt, Georg
SCHUBERT

"Ich komme vom Gebirge her" *see Der*
Wanderer Schmidt, Georg **SCHUBERT**

"Ich komme vor dein Angesicht" *see Busslied*
Gellert **LOEWE**

"Ich lag auf grünen Matten" *see Die*
Erscheinung Kosegarten **SCHUBERT**

ICH LAG AUF GRÜNEN MATTEN. see
Kosegarten
Die Erscheinung **SCHUBERT**

Ich lebe ein Leben in Sehnsucht see Benzon
   GRIEG *Jeg lever et Liv i Laengsel*
"Ich legte mein Haupt auf Elvershöh" *see*
   Elvershöh Anon. LOEWE
"Ich legte mich unter den Lindenbaum" *see*
   Vorüber Hebbel BRAHMS
Ich lieb' eine Blume see Heine FRANZ
Ich liebe dich see Andersen GRIEG *Jeg
   elsker Dig!*
Ich liebe dich! see Grabbe BERG
Ich liebe dich see Liliencron STRAUSS
Ich liebe dich see Rückert LISZT
"Ich liebe dich" *see Zärtliche Liebe* Herrosee
   BEETHOVEN
Ich liebte . . . see Bjørnson GRIEG *Jeg
   elsket*
Ich liege dir zu Füssen see Fitger LASSEN,
   PIJPER
Ich liess mir sagen und mir ward erzählt see
   Heyse WOLF
Ich lobe mir die Vögelein see Osterwald
   FRANZ
"Ich mochte zu Fussen liegen dir" *see Nur
   eine Viertelstund!* Cornelius LASSEN
Ich möchte hingehn see Herwegh LISZT
"Ich möchte zieh'n in die Welt hinaus" *see
   Die böse Farbe* Müller, Wilhelm
   SCHUBERT
"Ich müh' mich ab, und kann's nicht
   verschmerzen" *see Beim Abschied* Münch-
   Bellinghausen BRAHMS
"Ich muss hinaus, ich muss zu dir" *see Liebe
   und Frühling* Hoffmann von
   Fallersleben BRAHMS
"Ich pflückte eine kleine Pfirsichblüte" *see
   Liebesgeschenk* Anon. STRAUSS
"Ich raun' dir am Bette" *see Stimme der
   Sehnsucht* Busse PFITZNER
"Ich reise aus, meine Heimat zu entdekken"
   see Motiv Krenek KRENEK
Ich roch der Liebe himmlischers Arom see
   Hafiz SCHOECK
"Ich rufe vom Ufer verlorenes Glück" *see
   Vom Strande* Eichendorff BRAHMS,
   LASSEN
"Ich ruhe still im hohen grünen Grass" *see
   Feldeinsamkeit* Allmers BRAHMS
"Ich sag' es jedem" *see Hymne IV*
   Hardenberg SCHUBERT
"Ich sah als Knabe Blumen blühn" *see
   Heimweh III* Groth BRAHMS
"Ich sah am liebsten" *see Eure Weisheit*
   Fischer BERG
"Ich sah den Helikon in Wolkendunst" *see
   Antike Poesie* Mörike SCHOECK
"Ich sah den Lenz einmal" *see Liebesfrühling*
   Lenau FRANZ, WOLF

"Ich sah' dich einmal" *see Nachhall*
   Mosenthal RUBINSTEIN
Ich sah dich in wogender Menge see
   Golenishchev-Kutuzov MUSORGSKIĬ
   Menia ty v tolpe ne uznala
"Ich sah dich weinen! ach!" *see Die Weinende*
   Byron SCHUMANN
"Ich sah die volle Thräne glüh'n in deines
   Auges Blau" *see Thränen und Lächeln*
   Byron LOEWE
"Ich sah ein Röschen" *see Das Röschen*
   Müchler WEBER
"Ich sah heut früh im Brunnen tief" *see
   Mondmythus* Lingg LASSEN
"Ich sah sie hingesunken" *see Lied* Swoboda
   WEBER
"Ich sah sie nur ein einzigmal" *see Und dann
   nicht mehr* Rückert STRAUSS
"Ich sahe eine Tig'rin" *see Die Spröde*
   Kopisch BRAHMS
Ich sang mich durch das deutsche Land see
   Sergel KILPINEN
"Ich sass am einsamen Weiher" *see Als trüg'
   man die Liebe zu Grab* Röser, Otto
   FRANZ
"Ich sass am Strand" *see Am Strande*
   Scherer BERG, RUBINSTEIN
"Ich sass an einem Rädchen" *see Frühling,
   Liebster* Rückert WOLF
"Ich sass bei jener Lide" *see Die Zufriedenen*
   Uhland LOEWE
"Ich sass in finstrer Trauer, mir war das Herz
   so schwer" *see Sternbotschaft* Hertz
   JENSEN
"Ich sass zu deinen Füssen" *see Im
   Waldeseinsamkeit* Lemcke BRAHMS
"Ich schau' über Forth" *see Im Westen* Burns
   SCHUMANN
"Ich schaukle leicht mich im grünen Laub"
   see Lied eines Vögleins in der Oasis
   Stieglitz LOEWE
Ich scheide see Hoffmann von
   Fallersleben LISZT
Ich schell mein Horn ins Jammertal see
   Anon. BRAHMS
"Ich schiess' den Hirsch im grünen Forst" *see
   Jägers Liebeslied* Schober SCHUBERT
Ich schleich umher betrübt see Platen-
   Hallermünde BRAHMS
"Ich schnitt' es gern in alle Rinden ein" *see
   Ungeduld* Müller, Wilhelm
   SCHUBERT, SPOHR
"Ich schreit' hin an die Waldesbahn" *see
   Herbstnacht* Geibel LASSEN
"Ich schrieb allzeit nur wenig" *see Der
   tugendhafte Schreiber* Scheffel LISZT

Ich schwebe see Henckell **REGER, STRAUSS**

"Ich schwebe wie auf Engelsschwingen" *see Ich schwebe* Henckell **REGER, STRAUSS**

Ich seh' dich heut zum ersten Mal see Hamerling **LASSEN**

"Ich seh' von des Schiffes Rande" *see Meeresstille* Eichendorff **FRANZ**

Ich sehe dich in tausend Bildern see Hardenberg **REGER**

"Ich sehe dich in tausend Bildern" *see Marie* Hardenberg **SCHUBERT**

"Ich sehe dich in tausend Bildern" *see Marienlied* Hardenberg **SCHOECK**

"Ich sehe oft um Mitternacht" *see Die Sternseherin* Claudius, M. **SCHOECK**

Ich sehe wie in einem Spiegel see Rückert **STRAUSS**

"Ich sende einen Gruss" *see Aus den "Östlichen Rosen"* Rückert **SCHUMANN**

"Ich sinke dir ans volle Herz" *see Du Geist der reinsten Güte* Branco **LOEWE**

"Ich sitz' am Strande der rauschenden See" *see Verzagen* Lemcke **BRAHMS**

"Ich sitz' bei der moosigten Quelle" *see Cronnan* Macpherson **SCHUBERT**

Ich sprach zur Taube see Geibel **LASSEN**

"Ich stand auf Berges Halde" *see Abendlied* Rückert **LOEWE**

"Ich stand gelehnet an den Mast" *see Wasserfahrt* Heine **FRANZ, PFITZNER**

"Ich stand in deiner Strasse" *see Das Licht* Huber, B. **KILPINEN**

Ich stand in dunkeln Träumen see Heine *LIEDERSTRAUSS.* **GRIEG, WOLF**

"Ich stand in dunkeln Träumen" *see Ihr Bild* Heine **SCHUBERT**

"Ich stand in einer lauen Nacht" *see Verrat* Lemcke **BRAHMS**

"Ich stehe hier am Jammerstein" *see Jeduch* Löns **SCHÖNBERG**

Ich stehe hoch über'm See see Lieben, Frau von **REGER**

"Ich stehe ihn wieder, den lieblichen Stern" *see Der Stern* Arnim **STRAUSS**

"Ich stehe im Waldesschatten" *see Nachts* Eichendorff **PFITZNER**

"Ich such' im Schnee vergebens" *see Erstarrung* Müller, Wilhelm **SCHUBERT**

"Ich träumte von bunten Blumen" *see Frühlingstraum* Müller, Wilhelm **SCHUBERT**

"Ich trag' ein glückselig Geheimnis" *see Geheimnis* Ritter **REGER**

"Ich trag' eine Liebe im Herzen" *see Stille Liebe* Unknown **LOEWE**

Ich trage meine Minne see Henckell **STRAUSS**

"Ich trage, wo ich gehe" *see Die Uhr* Seidl **LOEWE**

"Ich trat in einen heilig düstern Eichwald" *see Der Eichwald* Lenau **FRANZ, SCHOECK**

"Ich treibe auf des Lebens Meer" *see Selige Welt* Senn **SCHUBERT**

"Ich tummle mich auf der Haide" *see Elfenlied* Kannegiesser **WEBER**

Ich und du see Busse **BERG**

Ich und Du see Hebbel **PFITZNER**

Ich und du und dem Müller sein Kuh see No author **BLACHER**

Ich und mein Gevatter see Rückert **LOEWE**

"Ich unglücksel'ger Atlas" *see Der Atlas* Heine **SCHUBERT**

"Ich, Unglückseliger!" *see Der verliebte Ostwind* Hafiz **SZYMANOWSKI**

"Ich Uralter kann's erzählen" *see Der milde Herbst von Anno 45* Mell **BERG**

Ich verlor die Kraft und das Leben see Musset *TRISTESSE.* **LISZT** *J'ai perdu ma force et ma vie*

"Ich wand ein Sträusschen morgens früh" *see Nelken* Storm **REGER**

"Ich wandelte sinnend allein auf der Halde" *see Gudmund's erster Gesang* Ibsen **WOLF**

Ich wandelte unter den Bäumen see Heine **SCHUMANN**

"Ich wandle einsam" *see Trauer* Cornelius **CORNELIUS**

Ich wandle unter Blumen see Unknown **LASSEN**

Ich wandre durch die stille Nacht see Eichendorff **FRANZ**

"Ich wand're fort, ins ferne Land" *see An den Wind* Lenau **FRANZ, GRIFFES**

"Ich wandre fort in's ferne Land" *see Auf der Wanderschaft* Lenau **MENDELSSOHN-BARTHOLDY**

Ich wand're nicht see Christern **SCHUMANN**

"Ich wandre über Berg und Tal" *see Im Walde* Schulze **SCHUBERT**

"Ich war bei Chloen ganz allein" *see Der Kuss* Weisse **BEETHOVEN**

"Ich war erst sechzehn Sommer alt" *see Phidile* Claudius, M. **SCHOECK, SCHUBERT**

"Ich war mal in dem Dorfe" *see Die fünf Hühnerchen* Blüthgen **REGER**

Ich weil' in tiefer Einsamkeit see Cornelius **LASSEN**

COMPOSER Poet *Title* "First Line"

"Ich weiss eine Farbe" *see Feuerfarb'*
Mereau **BEETHOVEN**
Two settings: Hess 144 and op. 52 no. 2.
"Ich weiss es nicht" *see Das erste*
Sommergras; Vor der Ernte Frey, F.
RUBINSTEIN
"Ich weiss es nicht, was es wohl war" *see*
Heiligendamm Sergel **KILPINEN**
"Ich weiss, ich träume im Grabe schon vielle
tausend Jahre" *see Totensprache*
Jacobowski **REGER**
"Ich weiss ihr liebt das Dunkel nicht" *see An*
kleine Mädchen Faktor **SZYMANOWSKI**
"Ich weiss mir'n Mädchen" *see Mailied*
Unknown **MENDELSSOHN-
BARTHOLDY**
"Ich weiss nicht" *see Frühmorgens* Geibel
RUBINSTEIN
"Ich weiss nicht, was soll's bedeuten" *see*
Die Loreley Heine **LISZT**
"Ich weiss nicht, wie mir ist!" *see Selbstgefühl*
Anon. **MAHLER**
"Ich werde Mama" *see Das Schwesterchen*
Kiesekamo **REGER**
Ich werde nicht an deinem Herzen satt see
Huch **PFITZNER**
"Ich werde Soldat" *see Das Brüderchen*
Kiesekamo **REGER**
"Ich will spiegeln mich in jenen Tagen" *see*
Jugendgedenken Keller, G. **SCHOECK**
Ich will bis in die Sterne see Hafiz **JENSEN**
Ich will die Fluren meiden see Rückert
BERG
"Ich will die lauten Freuden nicht" *see*
Brautlied Redwitz **LOEWE**
"Ich will dir's nimmer sagen" *see Vorsatz*
Prutz **LASSEN**
"Ich will ja nicht in Gerten geh'n" *see*
Die Drossel Uhland **STRAUSS**
Ich will meine Seele tauchen see Heine
FRANZ, SCHUMANN
Ich will mich im grünen Wald ergehn see
Heine **PFITZNER**
"Ich will mit Leides Tönen" *see Trost*
Hamerling **LASSEN**
"Ich will von Atreus Söhnen" *see An die*
Leyer Anacreon **SCHUBERT**
"Ich will von den Atriden" *see An die Leier*
Anacreon **LOEWE**
Ich wollt' ein Sträusslein binden see
Brentano **STRAUSS**
Ich wollt' ich wär ein Fisch see Goethe
ZELTER
"Ich wollt', ich wär' ein Fisch" *see Liebhaber*
in allen Gestalten Goethe **SCHUBERT**
"Ich wollt', ich wär' ein Held" *see*
Der tapfere Schneider Falke **REGER**

"Ich wollt, ich wär ein morgenklarer See und
du" *see Wünsche* Hafiz **SZYMANOWSKI**
"Ich wollt' ich wär' eine Blume" *see*
Liebeslied Hesse **KILPINEN**
Ich wollt' meine Schmerzen ergössen see
Heine **MUSORGSKIï** *Zhelanie*
Ich wollte, ich könnte nicht träumen see
Hauenchild **FRANZ**
Ich würd' auf meinem Pfad see Hermes
SOPHIENS REISE. **MOZART**
Ich würd' es hören see Meyer **SCHOECK**
"Ich zieh' dahin" *see Abschied von Frankreich*
Mary **SCHUMANN**
"Ich zieh' ins Feld" *see Des Kriegers*
Abschied Reissig **BEETHOVEN**
"Ich zieh' so allein in den Wald hinein!" *see*
Im Wald Müller von Königswinter
SCHUMANN
"Ici, d'un repentir célèbre et glorieux" *see*
Sonnet à Madeleine Repentie Le Père
JOLIVET
"Ici et là, partout et même" *see Amour* Émié
JOLIVET
"Ici rien n'est changé dans le jardin" *see*
Lettres d'Alissa Gide **MILHAUD**
Ici seront nées mes saisons see Hugnet
SAUGUET
Ici-bas see Sully-Prudhomme **FAURÉ**
"Ici-bas tous les lilas meurent" *see Ici-bas*
Sully-Prudhomme **FAURÉ**
I'd like in a single word see Heine
DIE HEIMKEHR. **CHAïKOVSKIï** *Khotel*
by v edinoe slovo
Ida's Nachtgesang see Kosegarten
SCHUBERT *Idens Nachtgesang*
Ida's Wunsch see Loewe, Helene **LOEWE**
Die Ideale see Schiller **ZELTER**
Ideale Landschaft see Dehmel *WEIB UND*
WELT. **WEBERN**
Idens Nachtgesang see Kosegarten
SCHUBERT
Idens Schwanenlied see Kosegarten
SCHUBERT
"Idet devochkasirotka" *see Lastochka*
Lenartowicz **CHAïKOVSKIï**
Idle wish see Runeberg **SIBELIUS** *Fåfäng*
önskan
Idom se siuhaje, dolu, śpiewajecy see Anon.
SZYMANOWSKI
Idyll see Goethe **MACDOWELL** *Idylle*
Idylle see Deschoulières, Mme.
SAINT-SAËNS
Idylle see Goethe **MACDOWELL**
IDYLLES, no. 1
ROUSSEL Theocritus *Le Kérioklépte*
IDYLLES, no. 2
ROUSSEL Moskhos *Pan ainmait Ekho*

Ier fù mandata see Zaffira **GOUNOD**
Ier l'ho scontrata see Zaffira **GOUNOD**
If see Livingstone, Mabel **CARPENTER**
If ever hapless woman had a cause see
   Herbert **ROREM**
"If ever two were one, then surely we" *see To*
   my dear and loving husband Bradstreet
   ROREM
"If I am to be preserved from heartache and
   shyness" *see A prayer to Saint Catherine*
   Koch **THOMSON**
If I can stop one heart from breaking see
   Dickinson **LUENING**
If I could but meet you see Kurochkin
   MUSORGSKIĬ *No esli by s toboĭu ĭa*
   vstretit'sĭa mogla
If I could go with you see Mosen
   NACHTLIED. **GRIFFES** *Könnt ich mit dir*
   dort oben gehen
If I knew him see Tolstoĭ **CHAĬKOVSKIĬ**
   Kaby znala ĭa
"If I must of my senses lose" *see Prayer*
   Roethke **DIAMOND**
"If I should die, think only this of me" *see*
   The soldier Brooke **IRELAND**
If I were a queen see Rossetti, Christina
   VAUGHAN WILLIAMS
"If I were only a little puppy" *see Sympathy*
   Tagore **MILHAUD**
If I'd only known see Tolstoĭ
   CHAĬKOVSKIĬ *Kaby znala ĭa*
If one day you're disillusioned see Pushkin
   MEDTNER
If only I had known see Tolstoĭ
   CHAĬKOVSKIĬ *Kaby znala ĭa*
If that high world see Byron **DIAMOND**
If there were dreams to sell see Beddoes
   IRELAND
If thou a reason dost desire to know see
   Kynaston **THOMSON**
If thou art sleeping maiden, awake see
   Longfellow **GOUNOD**
"If thou insist then we will say farewell" *see*
   A farewell Oliphant **ROUSSEL**
If thou wilt hold my heart secure see
   Chaĭkovskiĭ **CHAĬKOVSKIĬ** *Pimpinella*
If thou would'st ease thine heart see
   Beddoes **QUILTER**
"If truth in heart that perish" *see The vain*
   desire Housman **IRELAND**
If we must part see Dowson **IRELAND**
If you can't see Cummings **DIAMOND**
"If you can't eat you got to smoke" *see If you*
   can't Cummings **DIAMOND**
"If you'll busk you as a bride" *see Boy*
   Johnny Rossetti, Christina
   VAUGHAN WILLIAMS

"Ifald du følger mig over heien" *see*
   De norske fjelde Rolfsen **GRIEG**
Der Igel see Schellenberg **REGER**
"Der Igel, der Igel" *see Der Igel*
   Schellenberg **REGER**
Ignoto, pseud. *see* Barnefield, Richard,
   1574-1627.
Ihme see Koskenniemi **KILPINEN**
Ihmisen osa see Jalkanen **KILPINEN**
Ihr Auge see Burns **FRANZ**
Ihr Auge see Rellstab **LISZT**
Ihr Bild see Heine *LIEDERSTRAUSS.*
   SCHUBERT
"Ihr Bilder, die die Zeit begrub" *see Einst*
   Leuthold **SCHOECK**
"Ihr Blümlein alle, die sie mir gab" *see*
   Trockne Blumen Müller, Wilhelm
   SCHUBERT
"Ihr Brüder, hört ein ernstes Wort" *see Politik*
   Krenek **KRENEK**
"Ihr deutschen Länder alle" *see Preussisches*
   Marinelied Randow, Carl **LOEWE**
Ihr ewigen Sterne see Sergel **KILPINEN**
"Ihr Freunde, hänget, wenn ich gestorben bin"
   see Auftrag Hölty **CORNELIUS**
"Ihr Freunde und du gold'ner Wein" *see*
   Trinklied Zettler **SCHUBERT**
IHR FREUNDE UND DU, GOLD'NER
   WEIN. see Zettler
   Trinklied **SCHUBERT**
"Ihr frühlings trunknen Blumen" *see Im*
   Frühling Unknown **MENDELSSOHN-**
   BARTHOLDY
Ihr Glocken von Marling see Kuh **LISZT**
Ihr Grab see Engelhardt **SCHUBERT**
"Ihr habt doch Wein genug im Hause?" *see*
   Rundgesang beim Rheinwein Voss
   ZELTER
"Ihr habt genug getrunken" *see Maisuna am*
   Brunnen Stieglitz **LOEWE**
"Ihr hohen Himmlischen, erhöret der Tochter"
   see Antigone und Oedip Mayrhofer
   SCHUBERT
Ihr Hügel dort am schönen Doon see Burns
   FRANZ
Ihr, ihr Herrlichen! see Hölderlin
   DIE EICHBÄUME. **REGER**
Ihr jungen Leute see Heyse **WOLF**
Ihr Kuss, ihr Wort see Guilliaume **LASSEN**
   Question grave
"Ihr lieben Mauern hold und traut" *see Am*
   Fenster Seidl **SCHUBERT**
"Ihr Mädchen, flieht Damöten ja" *see*
   Der Zauberer Weisse **MOZART**
"Ihr Matten, lebt wohl" *see Des Sennen*
   Abschied Schiller **SCHUMANN**

"Ihr Matten, lebt wohl" *see Der Hirt* Schiller
LISZT

"Ihr Menschenkinder, seid ihr nicht Laub" *see*
Die Nachtigall Kraus KRENEK

"Ihr müsst den Becher trinken" *see Brevier*
Prölss LASSEN

"Ihr Mund ist stets derselbe" *see Einerlei*
Arnim STRAUSS

Ihr nennet Fieberwahn see Ammosov, A.
MUSORGSKIï *Chto vam slova liubvi*

Ihr Schwüre see Barth KRENEK

"Ihr Schwüre gegen das Vergessen" *see Ihr
Schwüre* Barth KRENEK

Ihr seid die Allerschönste weit und breit see
Heyse WOLF

Ihr Spaziergang see Jacob,T. LOEWE

Ihr Sternlein see Träger JENSEN

"Ihr Sternlein, still in der Hohe" *see Der
liebliche Stern* Schulze SCHUBERT

"Ihr Töne schwingt euch" *see Lied zum
Geburtstage meines guten Vaters*
Mendelssohn-Bartholdy
MENDELSSOHN-BARTHOLDY

Ihr tratet zu dem Herde see George *DAS
JAHR DER SEELE*: Traurige Tänze.
WEBERN

"Ihr verblühet, süsse Rosen" *see Zur Rosenzeit*
Goethe GRIEG

"Ihr Vögel im Gesträuch" *see Herbst* Hesse
KILPINEN

"Ihr Vöglein in den Lüften" *see Gruss*
Nietzsche MEDTNER

"Ihr wisset, was für schwere Klagen" *see
Ein Anderes* Weckherlin KRENEK

"Ihr wunderschönen Augenblicke" *see
Erinnerung* Schenkendorf BRAHMS

Ihre Augen see Hafiz STRAUSS

Ihre Stimme see Platen-Hallermünde
SCHUMANN

"Ik hoor hem nog" *see Douwdeuntje* Clercq,
René de PIJPER

Ikävä omia maita see Kanteletar KILPINEN

"Ikävässä kenttäin huojuvaisten" *see Lakeus
IV* Koskenniemi KILPINEN

"Ikävät on illat pitkät" *see Maassa marjani
makaavi* Kanteletar KILPINEN

Ikalos' li tebe, Natasha? see Vyazemsky
RACHMANINOFF *Were you hiccuping?*

Ikarus see Koskenniemi KILPINEN

Ikuinen kevät see Lönnbohm KILPINEN

Ikuinen suru see Kanteletar KILPINEN

"Il aimait se déshabiller" *see Ingénuité*
Carême SAUGUET

"Il brille le sauvage Eté" *see L'été* Banville
KOECHLIN

Il dort encore see Banville *HYMNIS.*
DEBUSSY

"Il éclipsait tous les jeunes gens" *see*
Le souvenir Schiller SAUGUET

"Il est amer et doux" *see La cloche fêlée*
Baudelaire CASELLA, LOEFFLER

"Il est au fond des bois des fleurs" *see*
Melancholia Hettich AUBERT

"Il est comme la tige au milieu des herbes"
see Que penser de mon salut Jacob, M.
SAUGUET

"Il est de doux adieux au seuil des portes" *see*
Adieux Régnier ROUSSEL

"Il est des étoiles aux cieux" *see Beaux yeux
que j'aime* Maquet, Thérèse
MASSENET

"Il est deux génies qui te guident" *see*
Les guides de la vie Schiller SAUGUET

Il est doux . . . see Pary, Evariste RAVEL

"Il est entré" *see Un poème* Apollinaire
POULENC

Il est midi, il est minuit see Éluard
SAUGUET

"Il est minuit" *see Nocturne* Dortzal
MASSENET

"Il est minuit l'étable est sombre" *see*
La veillée du petit Jésus Theuriet
MASSENET

"Il est mort ayant bien souffert, Madame" *see*
Chanson d'Ophélie Shakespeare
CHAUSSON

"Il est un air pour qui je donnerais" *see*
Fantaisie Gérard de Nerval AURIC

"Il est une bébête Tili petit n'enfant" *see*
Chanson du chat Fargue SATIE

"Il est une conception dans la joie" *see*
Tristesse de l'eau Claudel MILHAUD

"Il étaient deux amoureux" *see Chanson des
amoureux* Luka, Madeleine SAUGUET

"Il etait un pauv' petit gas" *see Chanson
bretonne* Arosa SCHMITT

"Il était un petit enfant" *see Le pauv' petit*
Boyer, Georges MASSENET

"Il était une Fée" *see Le Fée aux chansons*
Silvestre FAURÉ

"Il était une fois une fée qui avait un beau
sceptre" *see Berceuse* Peter, René
DEBUSSY

Il était une petite pie see Hirtz AURIC

"Il fait beau, le ciel nous protège" *see Jour de
noces* Bordèse MASSENET

"Il faut nous séparer . . . " *see La dernière
lettre de Werther à Charlotte* Biron
MASSENET

Il faut obéir see Kriéger, Jacqueline
MILHAUD

"Il faut que de tous mes esprits" *see Psalm
CXXXVIII* Bible HONEGGER

"Il faut s'aimer toujours" *see La belle
jeunesse* Anon. **POULENC**

"Il glisse sur le bassin" *see Le Cygne* Renard
RAVEL

Il la prend dans ses bras see Éluard
POULENC

"Il l'aimait tellement" *see L'amoureux*
Carême **MILHAUD**

"Il m'a dit: Cette nuit, j'ai rêve" *see
Le chevelure* Louÿs **DEBUSSY**

Il m'aimait tant see Apukhtin
CHAĬKOVSKIĬ *On tak menia liubil*

Il m'aimait tant! see Girardin **LISZT**

"Il me faut retourner aux anciennes amours"
see Néère Leconte de Lisle **HAHN**

"Il me semblait" *see Sur une songe*
Anacreon **ROUSSEL**

Il m'est cher, Amour, le bandeau see
Lerberghe **FAURÉ**

"Il ne faut pas prier pour les morts" *see
Amitié* Gaillard, Roger **SAUGUET**

"Il ne parle plus" *see L'escalier redit, gestes
du soleil* Messiaen **MESSIAEN**

"Il ne tient plus qu'a un fil" *see Le charme*
Carême **MILHAUD**

"Il neige, il neige et là devant l'église" *see
La pauvre femme* Béranger **LALO**

"Il n'est pas besoin d'une pierre" *see A nos
morts ignorés* Hennevé, Louis **HAHN**

"Il n'est point tant de barques à Venise" *see
Sonnet à une lunatique* Mellin **JOLIVET**

"Il n'y avait qu'un lit" *see Lied* Baron
SAUGUET

"Il pleure dans mon coeur" *see Spleen*
Verlaine **FAURÉ**

Il pleure dans mon coeur see Verlaine
**CARPENTER, DEBUSSY, DELIUS,
KOECHLIN, SCHMITT**

Il pleut see Apollinaire *CALLIGRAMMES.*
POULENC

Il pleut, bergère see Fersen, I. de
L'HYMNAIRE D'ADONIS. **RESPIGHI**

"Il pleut des iris, des jasmins, des roses" *see
Noël des fleurs* Schneider **MASSENET**

"Il pleut des voix de femmes" *see Il pleut*
Apollinaire **POULENC**

Il pleut doucement see Latil **MILHAUD**

Il pleuvait see Silvestre **MASSENET**

"Il plongea ses deux mains" *see Le semeur*
Carême **SAUGUET**

"Il prit un reste de brouillard" *see Sortilège*
Carême **MILHAUD**

"Il se cache dans ta grâce" *see Rondel* Collin
CHAĬKOVSKIĬ

"Il se disait si je pouvais" *see Il vieillissait*
Carême **SAUGUET**

Il se peut qu'un rêve étrange . . . see Jacob,
M. **AURIC**

"Il s'est envolé comme un rêve" *see
L'inconnu* Tonquédec, Marthe de
AUBERT

"Il s'éveille en chantant" *see Le mistral*
Anon. **MILHAUD**

"Il va sûrement se marier aujourd'hui" *see
Le Paon* Renard **RAVEL**

Il vieillissait see Carême **SAUGUET**

Il vole see Vilmorin **POULENC**

"Il voulait que cc soit mon picd" *see
L'adolescent* Carême **SAUGUET**

"Il voulait sortir de lui" *see Nul ne se lasse
d'être soi* Carême **SAUGUET**

IL Y A. see Apollinaire
   Allons plus vite **POULENC**
   Chanson **POULENC**
   Dans le jardin d'Anna **POULENC**
   Fagnes de Wallonie **POULENC**
   La grenouillère **POULENC**
   Hyde Park **POULENC**
   Montparnasse **POULENC**
   1904 **POULENC**
   Un poème **POULENC**
   Le pont **POULENC**
   Sanglots **POULENC**

IL Y A: Les dicts d'amour à Linda. see
Apollinaire *Linda* **RIVIER**

"Il y avait une pomme" *see La pomme et
l'escargot* Vildrac **MILHAUD**

Iłłakowiczówna, Kazimiera, 1892-1983.
SZYMANOWSKI
   Gil i sroka
   Gwiazdka
   Jak sie najlepiej opedzać od szerszenia
   Kolysanka gniadego konia
   Kolysanka Krzysi
   Kolysanka lalek
   Kolysanka lalki
   Kot
   Mieszkanie
   Myszy
   Nikczemny szpak
   Prosie
   Przed zaśnieciem
   Ślub królewny
   Smutek
   Świetz Krystyna
   Trzmiel i zuk
   Wiosna
   Wizyta u krowy
   Zly Lejba

Ilala see Houghton **GOUNOD**

L'ile see Follain **ROREM**

L'ile ancienne see Samain *AUX FLANCS
DU VASE.* **KOECHLIN**

COMPOSER Poet *Title* ''First Line''

L'île heureuse see Mikhaël **CHABRIER**

L'Île inconnue see Gautier **BERLIOZ**

"I'll make a song of Hambledon" *see*
  The cricketers of Hambledon Blunt
  HESELTINE

I'll tell you nothing see Shenshin
  CHAïKOVSKIï *IA tebe nichego ne skazhu'*

I'll tell you nothing see Shenshin
  RACHMANINOFF *I shall tell you nothing*

Illalla see Lönnbohm **KILPINEN**

"Illalla kävelin ma kangasta pitkin" *see Illalla*
  Lönnbohm **KILPINEN**

Illalle see Koskimies **SIBELIUS**

Illanrusko see Jalkanen **KILPINEN**

Ilmenau: over all the treetops see Goethe
  IVES

"Ils avaient décidé de s'en aller" *see Au pays*
  Follain **SAUGUET**

"Ils cheminent depuis longtemps" *see Vers*
  Béthléem Le Moyne **MASSENET**

"Ils l'ont clouée par les mains" *see Légende*
  Mauclair **BLOCH**

Ils marchant devant moi see Baudelaire
  LOEFFLER *Le flambeau vivant*

"Ils n'avait qu'une table" *see Simplicité*
  Carême **SAUGUET**

"Ils ne savent plus où se poser ces baisers"
  see Lassitude Maeterlinck **CHAUSSON**

"Ils ont troué la nuit de paillettes d'argent"
  see Le chemin des forains Dréjac, Jean
  SAUGUET

Ils ont tué trois petites filles see Maeterlinck
  SCHMITT

"Ils se disent, ma colombe" *see L'énamourée*
  Banville **HAHN**

"Ils se dissent, ma colombe" *see L'âme d'un*
  ange Banville **GOUNOD**

"Ils se sont recontrés dans le flot du métro"
  see Les amoureux sont seuls au monde
  Marcy, Claude **SAUGUET**

"Ils sont tous jeunes et beaux sur la 'belle
  cubaine' " *see Chansons de marins*
  Cocteau **SAUGUET**

"Ils vont arriver, la nuit est tombée" *see En*
  attendant Baron **SAUGUET**

"Ils vont, les petits canards" *see Villanelle des*
  petits canards Rostand, R. **CHABRIER**

Ilta see Jalkanen **KILPINEN**

Ilta see Lehtinen **KILPINEN**

"Iltarusko jo sammunut on" *see Kehtolaulu*
  Koskenniemi **KILPINEN**

"Iltaruskon leimu läikehtii" *see Rannalta II*
  Koskenniemi **KILPINEN**

I'm a fine fellow see Kol'tsov **BALAKIREV**
  Mne li, molodtsu razudalomu

I'm a person too see Bernsten **BERNSTEIN**
  I just found out today

"Im Abendgolde glänzet zu Bärenburg das
  Schloss" *see Der alte Dessauer* Fitzau
  LOEWE

"Im Abendgolde glänzet zu Bärenburg das
  Schloss" *see Der seltne Beter* Fitzau
  LASSEN

Im Abendrot see Lappe **SCHUBERT**

"Im Abendschimmer wallt der Quell" *see*
  Naturgenuss Matthisson **SCHUBERT**

"Im alten loderlohen Glanze" *see Jahrestag*
  Hesse **SCHOECK**

Im Anfang und jetzt see Claudius, M. *DAS*
  BAUERNLIED. **LOEWE**

"Im Anfang war's auf Erden" *see Im Anfang*
  und jetzt Claudius, M. **LOEWE**

Im April see Geibel **BRUCKNER, LASSEN,**
  REGER

Im Arm der Liebe see Hartleben **REGER**

"Im Arm der Liebe" *see Das Liebchen von*
  der Ruhe Ueltzen **BEETHOVEN**

"Im Arm der Liebe schliefen wir selig ein"
  see Liebesode Hartleben **BERG**

I'm certain: I am loved see Pushkin
  RIMSKIï-KORSAKOV
  IA veriu ia liubim

IM DORF. see Trakl
  In der Heimat **WEBERN**

Im Dorfe see Müller, Wilhelm **SCHUBERT**

"Im düstern Klostergarten ein einsam
  Brünnlein steht" *see Am Klosterbrunne*
  Vogl **LOEWE**

Im Einschlafen see Iłłakowiczówna
  SZYMANOWSKI *Przed zaśnieciem*

IM ERLENBUSCH, IM TANNENHAIN. see
  Kosegarten
  Die Täuschung **SCHUBERT**

"Im Erlenbusch, im Tannenhain" *see*
  Die Täuschung Kosegarten **SCHUBERT**

Im Feld ein Mädchen singt see Susman,
  Margarete **SIBELIUS**

"Im Felde schleich' ich still und wild" *see*
  Jägers Abendlied Goethe
  MEDTNER, SCHUBERT, ZELTER
    Two Schubert settings: D. 215 and D.
    368.

Im Fernen see Goethe **ZELTER**

"Im Finstern geh' ich suchen" *see Blinde Kuh*
  Kopisch **BRAHMS**

Im Fjeld see Rolfsen **GRIEG** *De norske*
  fjelde

Im Fliederbusch ein Vöglein sass see Reinick
  SCHÖNBERG

Im Freien see Seidl **SCHUBERT**

"Im fremden Land, im Bett des Stroms" *see*
  Fürst Rostislav Tolstoï **RUBINSTEIN**

Im Frühling see Arndt, J. **FRANZ**

IM FRÜHLING. see Gilm zu Rosenegg
  Zueignung **STRAUSS**
Im Frühling see Hugo **LASSEN** *Hier au soir*
Im Frühling see Mörike **WOLF**
Im Frühling see Osterwald **FRANZ**
Im Frühling see Schulze **SCHUBERT**
"Im Frühling" *see Die Sorglichen* Falke
  BERG
Im Frühling see Unknown
  MENDELSSOHN-BARTHOLDY
Im Frühling! Im Frühling see Cornelius
  CORNELIUS
"Im Frühlings Schatten fand ich sie" *see*
  Das Rosenband Klopstock
  MACDOWELL
Im Frühlingsanfang see Sturm, C.
  MOZART *Der Frühling*
"Im Frühlingsgarten fand ich sie" *see*
  Das Rosenband Klopstock **SCHUBERT**
"Im Frühlingsschatten fand ich sie" *see*
  Das Rosenband Klopstock **STRAUSS,**
  ZELTER
"Im ganzen Ort gibts keine Kohlen" *see*
  Notschrei aus den Gefilden Lapplands
  Strauss, R. **STRAUSS**
Im Garten see Schiller *DIE ERWARTUNG.*
  ZELTER
Im Garten am Seegestade see Lemcke
  BRAHMS
"Im Garten rauscht die Sommernacht" *see*
  Sommernacht Triepel, Gertrud **REGER**
"Im Garten steht die Nonne" *see Die Nonne*
  Fröhlich **SCHUMANN**
Im Gebirg see Geibel **JENSEN**
Im Gefälle der Zeit see Krenek **KRENEK**
"Im Gefild zum Strausse wand wilde Blüt' ich
  sonder Acht" *see Unvergessen* Frey
  REGER
Im Glück wir lachend gingen see
  Drachmann **DELIUS** *In bliss we walked
  with laughter*
"Im Grase lieg' ich manche Stunde" *see Im
  Frühling* Osterwald **FRANZ**
Im Grünen see Voss **MENDELSSOHN-
  BARTHOLDY**
Im Haine see Bruchmann **SCHUBERT**
Im Harmesnächten see Meyer **SCHOECK**
Im Herbst see Eichendorff **LASSEN,
  PFITZNER**
Im Herbst see Geibel **FRANZ**
Im Herbst see Klingemann
  MENDELSSOHN-BARTHOLDY
Im Herbst see Müller von Königswinter
  FRANZ
Im Herbst see Träger **JENSEN**
Im Herbste see Kerner **SCHUMANN**

Im Herbste see Uhland **SCHOECK**
Im Hochgebirge see Mayrhofer
  SCHUBERT *Aus "Heliopolis"*
Im Kahn see Heine **MENDELSSOHN-
  BARTHOLDY**
Im Kahne see Krag **GRIEG** *Mens jeg venter*
"Im kalten rauhen Norden" *see Aus
  "Heliopolis"* Mayrhofer **SCHUBERT**
"Im Kerker gefangen" *see Der Gefangene*
  Pushkin **RUBINSTEIN**
IM KIRCHHOF. see Schlechta
  Auf einen Kirchhof **SCHUBERT**
Im Klosterkeller see Leuthold **SCHOECK**
Im Krauzgang von St. Stefano see Hesse
  SCHOECK
"Im Kreise der Vasallen sitzt der Ritter" *see
  Schön Hedwig* Hebbel **SCHUMANN**
Im Lenz see Heyse **CORNELIUS**
Im Lenz see Mahler **MAHLER**
"Im Lenz, im Lenz" *see Im Lenz* Heyse
  CORNELIUS
Im Liebeslust see Hoffmann von
  Fallersleben **LASSEN**
Im Mai see Osterwald **FRANZ**
  Two settings: Op. 11 no. 3 and op. 22 no.
  5.
"Im Mondenschein wall' ich auf und ab" *see
  Schwestergruss* Bruchmann **SCHUBERT**
"Im Morgen grauen schritt ich fort" *see
  Verlassen* Conradi **SCHÖNBERG**
Im Morgengrauen see Stieler **BERG**
Im Morgentaun trittst du hervor see George
  DER SIEBENTE RING. **WEBERN**
"Im Mummelsee, im dunkeln See" *see
  Der Mummelsee* Schnezler **LOEWE**
Im Nebel see Hesse **SCHOECK**
"Im Nebel ruhet noch die Welt" *see
  Septembermorgen* Mörike **SCHOECK**
  Two settings: Op. 7 no. 2 and op. 51 no. 5.
"Im Nebelgeriesel, im tiefen Schnee" *see
  Zigeunerlied* Goethe **SPOHR**
Im Park see Mörike **SCHOECK**
Im Rhein, im heiligen Strome see Heine
  FRANZ, SCHUMANN
Im Rhein, im schönen Strome see Heine
  LISZT
"Im Rosenbusch die Liebe schlief" *see
  Der Frühling und die Liebe*
  Hoffmann von Fallersleben **LASSEN**
"Im Rosenbusch die Liebe schlief" *see
  Frühling und Liebe*
  Hoffmann von Fallersleben **FRANZ**
I'm saddened see Lermontov **RIMSKĪĭ-
  KORSAKOV** *Mne grustno*
Im Schacht der Adern und der Stufen see
  Giesebrecht **LOEWE**

COMPOSER Poet *Title* "First Line"

Im Schloss, da brennen der Kerzen viel see
Kugler LOEWE
Im Schlosshof see Hamerling JENSEN
"Im schönen Land Tirol" *see*
Das Muttergottesbild im Teiche Wetzel
LOEWE
"Im schwarzen Wallfisch zu Ascalon" *see*
Altassyrisch Scheffel JENSEN
"Im Sessel du, und ich zu deinen Füssen" *see*
Dämmerstunde Storm WEBERN
Im Sommer see Goethe FRANZ,
SCHOECK
Im Sommer see Osterwald FRANZ
"Im Sommer such ein Liebchen dir" *see*
Bauernregel Uhland LOEWE, REGER
Im Sonnenschein see Rückert STRAUSS
Im Spätboot see Meyer STRAUSS
Im Spiegel see Goering KRENEK
"Im Städtchen giebt es des Jubels viel" *see*
Der Spielmann Andersen SCHUMANN
"Im stillen Klostergarten eine bleiche Jungfrau
ging" *see Die Nonne* Uhland
MENDELSSOHN-BARTHOLDY
Im Sturme see Siebel LOEWE
Im tiefen Wald verborgen see Unknown
PFITZNER
Im Tiefsten Herzen glüht mir eine Wunde see
Cornelius CORNELIUS
"Im tiefsten Innern" *see Gute Nacht* Glück
FRANZ
Im Traum see Heine GIDEON
Im Traum sah ich die Geliebte see Heine
LOEWE
Im Treibhaus see Wesendonck WAGNER
"Im treuen Sachsenland ertönt die frohe
Kunde" *see Gruss seiner Treuen an
Friedrich August den Geliebten* Wagner
WAGNER
"Im trüben Licht verschwinden schon die
Berge" *see Der Zwerg* Collin, M.
SCHUBERT
Im Verborgnen see Träger LASSEN
Im Vorübergehen see Goethe LOEWE,
MEDTNER
Im Wald see Heine LASSEN
Im Wald see Müller von Königswinter
SCHUMANN
"Im Wald der erste Vogel singt" *see März*
Holm LASSEN
"Im Wald, im Wald, da grabt mich ein" *see
An die Freunde* Mayrhofer SCHUBERT
"Im Wald', im Wald' ist's frisch und grün"
see Waldfahrt Körner FRANZ
"Im Wald, in grüner Runde" *see Die Hütte*
Pfarrius SCHUMANN
Im Walde see Bjørnson BERG

Im Walde see Eichendorff MEDTNER,
SCHUMANN
Im Walde see Geibel STRAUSS
IM WALDE. see Goethe
In the woods MACDOWELL
Im Walde see Heyse CORNELIUS,
JENSEN
Im Walde see Mommsen KRENEK
Im Walde see Müller von Königswinter
FRANZ
Im Walde see Schlegel, F. SCHUBERT
Im Walde see Schulze *POETISCHES
TAGEBUCH.* SCHUBERT
"Im Walde geh' ich wohlgemut" *see Waldlied*
Uhland REGER
Im Walde liegt ein stiller See see Sergel
KILPINEN
"Im Walde rauschen dürre Blätter" *see
Herbstlied* Klingemann
MENDELSSOHN-BARTHOLDY
Im Waldeseinsamkeit see Lemcke BRAHMS
Im Wandern see Eichendorff SCHOECK
"Im Wasser wogt die Lilie, die blanke, hin
und her" *see Ghazél* Platen-Hallermünde
WOLF
"Im Welschland, wo die braunen" *see
Auskunft* Hesse SCHOECK
Im Westen see Burns SCHUMANN
IM WINDE. see Mayrhofer
Der Schiffer SCHUBERT
"Im Winde, im Sturme befahr' ich den Fluss"
see Der Schiffer Mayrhofer SCHUBERT
Im Windesweben war meine Frage see
George *DER SIEBENTE RING.*
WEBERN
Im Winkel see Musorgskiĭ MUSORGSKIĬ
V uglu
"Im Winterboden schläft ein Blumenkeim" *see
Auf eine Christblume* Mörike WOLF
"Im Winterrefektorium zu Maulbronn in dem
Kloster" *see Die Malbronner Fuge*
Scheffel JENSEN
"Im Wirthshaus geht es aus und ein" *see
Das wirtshaus zu* Marées SPOHR
Im wunderschönen Monat Mai see Heine
BARTÓK, FRANZ, MAHLER,
SCHUMANN
Im Zimmer see Schlaf *HELLDUNKEL*
(1899). BERG
IM ZWIELICHT. see Dehmel
Alles SCHÖNBERG
Image see Carême SAUGUET
Image see Cox, Oscar HINDEMITH
IMAGES (1910-1915). *see* Aldington
After two years HESELTINE
Les images see Follain SAUGUET

Imhoff, Amalie von *see* Helvig, Amalie (von Imhof) von, 1766-1831.
Immensity, like the darkness cast from the cloud above see Olson **DIAMOND**
Immer bei dir see Ernst **LASSEN**
"Immer bin ich ohne Ziel gegangen" *see Das Ziel* Hesse **SCHOECK**
"Immer bleibst du lieblich mir" *see An die Geliebte* Falke **REGER**
Immer dasselbe see Harnier *BÜHNE UND HAUS.* **SPOHR**
"Immer fort" *see Reiterlied* Unknown **MENDELSSOHN-BARTHOLDY**
"Immer leiser verrinnst du" *see Vor dem Tod* Krenek **KRENEK**
Immer leiser wird mein Schlummer see Lingg **BRAHMS, PFITZNER**
"Immer mag verklingen muntrer Bögel Sang" *see An die Geliebte* Hugo **SPOHR**
"Immer schwitzend, immer sitzend" *see Des Durstes Erklärung* Fick, K. **REGER**
"Immer wieder in die Weite" *see Ungeduld* Goethe **SCHOECK**
Immerdar Liebe see Göchhausen **SPOHR**
Immermann, Karl Leberecht, 1796-1840.
   MENDELSSOHN-BARTHOLDY
      Todeslied der Bojaren
   SCHUMANN *Auf dem Rhein*
Immortality see Ives **IVES**
"Immortelle! bring' mein 'gute Nacht' ih hin" *see Gruss* Braun von Braunthal **SPOHR**
Imperial-Oxford see Contamine **SATIE**
Imploration see Boulanger, D. **SAUGUET**
IMPRESSIONS I: Le jardin. *see* Wilde *Le jardin* **GRIFFES**
IMPRESSIONS II: La mer. *see* Wilde *La mer* **GRIFFES**
   The sea **GRIFFES**
Impressions du matin see Wilde *WIND FLOWERS*: Impression du matin.
   GRIFFES *Early morning in London*
Impressions of a traveler see Kao, Shih **GRIFFES**
Impromptu see Mörike **SCHOECK**
Impromptu see Shenshin **MEDTNER**
IMPROVING SONGS FOR ANXIOUS CHILDREN, no. 1
   CARPENTER Carpenter, Rue *Stout*
IMPROVING SONGS FOR ANXIOUS CHILDREN, no. 2
   CARPENTER Carpenter, Rue *Practising*
IMPROVING SONGS FOR ANXIOUS CHILDREN, no. 3
   CARPENTER Carpenter, Rue *For careless children*
IMPROVING SONGS FOR ANXIOUS CHILDREN, no. 4
   CARPENTER Carpenter, Rue *Red hair*

IMPROVING SONGS FOR ANXIOUS CHILDREN, no. 5
   CARPENTER Carpenter, Rue *The liar*
IMPROVING SONGS FOR ANXIOUS CHILDREN, no. 6
   CARPENTER Carpenter, Rue *A wicked child*
IMPROVING SONGS FOR ANXIOUS CHILDREN, no. 7
   CARPENTER Carpenter, Rue *Spring*
IMPROVING SONGS FOR ANXIOUS CHILDREN, no. 8
   CARPENTER Carpenter, Rue *Maria, glutton*
IMPROVING SONGS FOR ANXIOUS CHILDREN, no. 9
   CARPENTER Carpenter, Rue *Good Ellen*
IMPROVING SONGS FOR ANXIOUS CHILDREN, no. 10
   CARPENTER Carpenter, Rue *War*
IMPROVING SONGS FOR ANXIOUS CHILDREN, no. 11
   CARPENTER Carpenter, Rue *Vanity*
IMPROVING SONGS FOR ANXIOUS CHILDREN, no. 12
   CARPENTER Carpenter, Rue *Humility*
IMPROVING SONGS FOR ANXIOUS CHILDREN, no. 13
   CARPENTER Carpenter, Rue *A plan*
IMPROVING SONGS FOR ANXIOUS CHILDREN, no. 14
   CARPENTER Carpenter, Rue *Brother*
IMPROVING SONGS FOR ANXIOUS CHILDREN, no. 15
   CARPENTER Carpenter, Rue *Making calls*
IMPROVING SONGS FOR ANXIOUS CHILDREN, no. 16
   CARPENTER Carpenter, Rue *Contemplation*
IMPROVING SONGS FOR ANXIOUS CHILDREN, no. 17
   CARPENTER Carpenter, Rue *When the night comes*
L'improvisatore see Zaffira **MASSENET**
"In a dress of gauzy fabric" *see So-fei gathering flowers* Wang **GRIFFES**
"In a garden so green in a May morning" *see Elore lo* Anon. **HESELTINE**
"In a harbour grene aslepe whereas I lay" *see Lusty juventus* Wever **HESELTINE**
IN A MIRTLE SHADE. see Blake, William *In a myrtle shade* **GRIFFES**
In a myrtle shade see Blake, William *IN A MIRTLE SHADE.* **GRIFFES**

"In a silent desolate spot" *see Impressions of a traveler* Kao, Shih **GRIFFES**

"In all this warld nis a meriar life" *see The bachelor* Anon. **HESELTINE**

"In allen guten Stunden" *see Bundeslied* Goethe **SCHUBERT**

"In aller Früh, ach lang vor Tag" *see Lied eines Verliebten* Mörike **WOLF**

In alto mare see Panzacchi **RESPIGHI**

In an arbour green see Wever *AN ENTERLUDE CALLED LUSTY JUVENTUS (1565).* **HESELTINE**

"In Basra eine Wittwe war" *see Der Traum der Wittwe* Rückert **LOEWE**

"In begrünter Sommerlaube" *see Das Schlummerlied* Frey **SCHOECK**

In bliss we walked with laughter see Drachmann **DELIUS**

In Blüten see Osterwald **FRANZ**

In boyhood see Housman **IRELAND**

"In Breughel's great picture, The Kermess" *see The dance* Williams, W. **ROREM**

In Danzig see Eichendorff **PFITZNER**

In dark Hell see Maĭkov *NOVOGRECHESKIYE PESNI.* **CHAĬKOVSKIĬ** *Novogrecheskiye pesni*

In deepest forest glade I stand see Pfleger-Moravský **DVOŘÁK** *Zde v lese u potoka* Two settings: B. 11 no. 14 and B. 160 no. 6.

"In deine Augen will ich schauen" *see Immer bei dir* Ernst **LASSEN**

"In deinen Liedern lebt mein Leben" *see Eine Seele* Jacobowski **REGER**

In deiner Nähe weil' ich noch see Cornelius **LASSEN**

"In dem Bäumen regt sich's leise" *see Nächtliche Pfade* Stieler **REGER**

"In dem Dornbusch blüht ein Röslein" *see Lieber Schatz* Osterwald **MACDOWELL**

"In dem Dornbusch blüht ein Röslein" *see Lieber Schatz, wie wieder gut mir* Osterwald **FRANZ**

"In dem frischen, grünen Wald" *see Liebe* Röser, Otto **FRANZ**

"In dem Grünebusch" *see Das bittersüsse Lied* Löns **KILPINEN**

"In dem Himmel ruht die Erde" *see Nachtgruss* Reinick **WOLF**

"In dem Mondenschein im Walde sah ich" *see Neue Liebe* Heine **MENDELSSOHN-BARTHOLDY**

In dem Schatten meiner Locken see Heyse **WOLF**

"In dem Schatten meiner Locken" *see Spanisches Lied* Heyse **BRAHMS, JENSEN**

"In dem Traum" *see Ach, wie komm' ich da hinüber?* Heine **FRANZ**

"In dem Walde spriesst's und grünt es" *see Frühlingslied* Heine **RUBINSTEIN**

"In dem Walde, süsse Töne singen kleine Vöglein" *see Frühlingslied* Lichtenstein **MENDELSSOHN-BARTHOLDY**

"In den Abgrund lass mich schauen" *see Am Rheinfall* Hahn-Hahn **FRANZ**

In den Beeren see Schmidt, Hans **BRAHMS**

"In den Garten wollen wir gehen" *see Der Überläufer* Des Knaben Wunderhorn **BRAHMS**

"In den Grünenwald bin ich gegangen" *see Küssekraut* Löns **KILPINEN**

In den Heidelbeeren see Garborg *HAUGTUSSA.* **GRIEG** *Blåbaer-Li*

"In den Lüften schwellen des Gedröhne" *see Neujahrsglocken* Meyer **SCHOECK**

In den Nachtmittag geflüstert see Trakl *TRAUM DES BÖSEN.* **WEBERN**

"In den Schlosshof hernieder rief Held Budris die Brüder" *see Die drei Budrisse* Mickiewicz **LOEWE**

"In den Thalen der Provence" *see Provençalisches Lied* Uhland **SCHUMANN**

"In den Wassern der Laguna" *see Gondelfahrt* Geibel **SPOHR**

"In der Berge Riesenschatten" *see Liebe-Glühen* Gubitz **WEBER**

In der Campagna see Mackay **STRAUSS**

"In der Dämmerung, um Glock zwei" *see Heimgang in der Frühe* Liliencron **WEBERN**

In der Ferne see Cornelius **CORNELIUS** Two settings: 1856 without opus number and op. 15 no. 3 (1865).

In der Ferne see Rellstab **SCHUBERT**

In der Ferne see Uhland *WANDERLIEDER.* **BRAHMS**

In der Ferne see Unknown **RIEGGER**

In der Fremde see Eichendorff **BRAHMS, SCHOECK, SCHUMANN, WOLF** Two Schumann settings: Op. 39 no. 1 and op. 39 no. 8; three Wolf settings: 1881 and two in 1883.

In der Fremde see Heine **FRANZ**

"In der Früh" *see Über Nacht und Tag* Roquette **BERG**

In der Früh, wenn die Sonne kommen will see Volkmann **PFITZNER**

In der Frühe see Mörike **REGER, WOLF**

In der Gasse see Hebbel **BRAHMS**

In der Heimat see Trakl *IM DORF.* **WEBERN**

In der Herberge see Li Po **SCHOECK**
"In der hohen Hall' sass König Sifrid" *see*
  Ballade Uhland **SCHUMANN**
"In der hohen Hall' sass König Sifried" *see*
  Die drei Lieder Uhland **LOEWE**
"In der Kindheit frühen Tagen" *see Der Engel*
  Wesendonck **WAGNER**
In der Kirche see Rückert **LOEWE**
In der Mitternacht see Jacobi **SCHUBERT**
"In der Mondesnacht, in der stillen Nacht" *see*
  Liebespost Wildenbruch **LASSEN**
In der Mondnacht see Heyse **CORNELIUS**
In der Nacht see Unknown **LASSEN**
"In der Nacht, die die Bäume mit Blüten
  deckt" *see Liederseelen* Meyer
  SCHOECK
"In der Nacht, in der Nacht da rauschen die
  Bäume so traurig" *see Nachtlied* Hahn-
  Hahn **FRANZ**
"In der Ruhe Thal geboren" *see Lied der
  Königin Elisabeth* Shenstone **LOEWE**
In der Trauer see Keller, G. **SCHOECK**
"In der Väter Hallen ruhte" *see Romanze*
  Stolberg **SCHUBERT**
"In des Meeres kühle Wogen taucht die
  Sonne" *see Abendlied* Müchler **ZELTER**
"In des Sees Wogenspiele" *see Am See*
  Bruchmann **SCHUBERT**
"In des Südens heissen Zonen Blumen giebt"
  see Spirito santo Goltz **LOEWE**
"In des Todes Feierstunde" *see Todesmusik*
  Schober **SCHUBERT**
"In die blaue Luft hinaus einen stillen Gruss
  nach Haus" *see Unterwegs* Dingelstedt
  SPOHR
"In die braunen, rauschenden Nächte" *see*
  Waldsonne Schlaf **SCHÖNBERG**
"In die dunkle Bergsschlucht" *see Geheimnis*
  Dehmel **SZYMANOWSKI**
In die Ferne see Kletke **LOEWE**
"In die tiefsten Felsengründe" *see Irrlicht*
  Müller, Wilhelm **SCHUBERT**
"In diesen Silberhainen von Oliven" *see*
  Riviera Leuthold **SCHOECK**
In diesen Wintertagen see Henckel
  SCHÖNBERG
"In diesen Wintertagen" *see Winterweihe*
  Henckell **STRAUSS**
In dreams see Stevenson, Robert Louis
  SONGS OF TRAVEL, IV.
  VAUGHAN WILLIAMS
"In dreams unhappy I behold you" *see*
  In dreams Stevenson, Robert Louis
  VAUGHAN WILLIAMS
"In düstrer Nacht" *see Blondel zu Marien*
  Unknown **SCHUBERT**

In ein Autographen-Album see Mörike
  SCHOECK
"In ein freundliches Städtchen tret ich ein" *see*
  Auf einer Wanderung Mörike **WOLF**
"In einem Bächlein helle, da schoss in froher
  Eil" *see Die Forelle* Schubart
  SCHUBERT
"In einem Dorf' am frühen Morgen" *see*
  Die Dorfkirche Zedlitz **LOEWE**
In einem Rosengärtelein see Friderici
  REGER
"In einem stillen Garten" *see Leises Lied*
  Dehmel **STRAUSS**
"In einem Tal bei armen Hirten" *see*
  Das Mädchen aus der Fremde Schiller
  SCHUBERT
  Two settings: D. 117 and D. 252.
"In einem Tal, bei einem Bach" *see Romanze*
  André **LOEWE**
In einer Sturmnacht see Meyer **SCHOECK**
"In einsamen Stunden" *see Stiller Vorwurf*
  Wolff **SCHUMANN**
"In evenings of the summer days" *see Vanity*
  Carpenter, Rue **CARPENTER**
"In Feindesland die graue Spätherbstnacht"
  see Nacht auf Posten Zwehl, Hans Fritz
  von **KILPINEN**
In flaming gold see MacDowell
  MACDOWELL
"In flaming gold thou goest" *see In flaming
  gold* MacDowell **MACDOWELL**
In Flanders fields see McCrae **IVES**
"In Flanders fields the poppies blow" *see*
  In Flanders fields McCrae **IVES**
IN FOLK TONE, no. 1
  DVOŘÁK Anon. *Dobrú noc, má milá*
IN FOLK TONE, no. 2
  DVOŘÁK Anon. *Žalo dievča, žalo trávu*
IN FOLK TONE, no. 3
  DVOŘÁK Anon. *Ach není, není tu*
IN FOLK TONE, no. 4
  DVOŘÁK Anon. *Ej, mám já koňa faku*
"In frohen Tagen such' ich dich" *see*
  Verbundenheit Huber, B. **KILPINEN**
"In from the ocean the white fog creeps" *see*
  Fog-wraiths Howells, M. **CARPENTER**
"In Frühlings Heiligtume" *see Blume und Duft*
  Hebbel **LISZT**
"In gloom of night I stand alone" *see By the
  fresh grave* Nadson **RACHMANINOFF**
"In Gold und Purpur tief verhüllt" *see*
  Sonnenuntergang Keller, G. **SCHOECK**
In goldener Fülle see Remer **STRAUSS**
"In goldnen Abendschein getaucht" *see*
  Gestillte Sehnsucht Rückert **BRAHMS**
"In Grün will ich mich kleiden" *see Die liebe
  Farbe* Müller, Wilhelm **SCHUBERT**

COMPOSER Poet *Title* "First Line"

"In grüner Landschaft Sommerflor" *see Auf ein altes Bild* Mörike WOLF

In hellen Träumen hab ich Dich oft geschaut see Gold SCHÖNBERG

"In hoher Hall' sass König Sifrid" *see Die drei Lieder* Uhland STRAUSS

"In jener Nacht" *see Fünf Sinnspüche Omars des Zeltmachers* Omar Khayyam BLACHER

"In jüng'ren Tagen war ich des Morgens froh" *see Ehmals und jetzt* Hölderlin HINDEMITH

In lectulo meo see Canticum Canticorum PIZZETTI

In Leid versunken see Mörike FRANZ

"In Liebe sich begegnen" *see Polterabendlied* Bartholdy, Dr. LOEWE

"In Liebesarmen ruht ihr trunken" *see Hohe Liebe* Uhland LISZT

In Liebeslust see Hoffmann von Fallersleben LISZT

In Linden Lea see Barnes VAUGHAN WILLIAMS *Linden Lea*

"In love she fell" *see The blue-bell* Deland MACDOWELL

In love with you see Koch ROREM

"In luftiger Trinkkemenaten" *see Der Fünfundsechziger* Scheffel JENSEN

In Lust und Schmerzen see Cornelius CORNELIUS

In meinem Garten die Nelken see Geibel FRANZ

"In meinem Garten die Nelken" *see Lied eines Mädchens* Geibel LASSEN

"In meinem Garten die Nelken" *see Mädchenlied* Geibel SCHÖNBERG

"In meinem Herzen ist's öd' und leer" *see Hoffnungslos* Obst, Willibald REGER

"In meinem Herzen regte" *see Ein Myrtenreis* Cornelius CORNELIUS

"In meinem Lebensringe bist du der Edelstein" *see An Edlitam, zur silbernen Hochzeit* Bodenstedt LISZT

In meinen Armen wieg ich dich see Natorp FRANZ

"In meiner Brust eine Glocke klingt" *see O nimm dich in Acht* Scheffler FRANZ

"In meiner Jugend als ich liebte" *see Totengräberlied* Shakespeare LOEWE

In meiner Nächte Sehnen see Daumer *FRAUENBILDER UND HULDIGUNGEN.* BRAHMS

"In meines Herzens Trauerlied" *see Gesang der Königin Maria Stuart auf den Tod Franz II* Anon. LOEWE

"In meines Vaters Garten da stehen zwei Bäumelein" *see Hoffnungstrost* Anon. REGER

In memoria d'un amico see Cavalca MALIPIERO

"In mir nur Tod" *see Die Verklärende* Buonarroti SCHOECK

In moment to delight devoted see Byron *PORTUGUESE IMITATION.* RIMSKIĬ-KORSAKOV *V poryve nezhnosti serdechnoĭ*

"In monderhellten Nächten" *see Die Sternennächte* Mayrhofer SCHUBERT

"In my distress I cried unto the Lord" *see A song of David* Bible ROREM

In my dream I seemed to see you see Gombossy, K? BARTÓK *In vivid dreams*

In my garden see Bal'mont PROKOFIEV *V moem sadu*

In my garden at night see Isaakian *IVANUSHKA.* RACHMANINOFF

In my sage moments see Hardy IRELAND

In my soul see Vilenkin RACHMANINOFF

In nature see Hálek MARTINŮ

"In one of the fights before Atlanta" *see An incident* Whitman ROREM

In one sweet rush of tender feeling see Byron *PORTUGUESE IMITATION.* RIMSKIĬ-KORSAKOV *V poryve nezhnosti serdechnoĭ*

"In Paris on a corner of an outer boulevard" *see Film: Two sisters not sisters* Stein THOMSON

"In poetischer Epistel" *see Auftrag* Mörike WOLF

In principio erat Verbum see Anon. HINDEMITH

In questa notte carica di stelle see Dazzi, Manlio PIZZETTI

In questa tomba oscura see Carpani BEETHOVEN, ZELTER

In remembrance of the sun see Akhmatova PROKOFIEV *Pamiat' o solnt͡sie*

"In Rumelia c'è un albero frondoso" *see Augurio* Anon. PIZZETTI

In Saint Blaise see Musset RUBINSTEIN *À Saint-Blaize à la Zuecca*

"In seinem schimmernden Gewand" *see Gott im Frühlinge* Uz SCHUBERT

In solitaria stanza see Vittorelli VERDI

"In Sonnenglut, in Mittagsruh" *see Alt Mütterlein* Nietzsche MEDTNER

"In spite of every thing which breathes and moves" *see Song* Cummings COPLAND

In spring see Dowson QUILTER

In spring see Shakespeare *AS YOU LIKE IT.* CARPENTER

IN SPRING, no. 1
  RIMSKIĬ-KORSAKOV Tolstoĭ *Zvonche zhavoronka pen'e*
IN SPRING, no. 2
  RIMSKIĬ-KORSAKOV Tolstoĭ *Ne veter, veia s vysoty*
IN SPRING, no. 3
  RIMSKIĬ-KORSAKOV Shenshin *Svezh i dushist tvoĭ*
IN SPRING, no. 4
  RIMSKIĬ-KORSAKOV Tolstoĭ *To bylo ranneiu vesnoĭ*
"In spring for sheer delight" *see A feast of lanterns* Yuan Mei **GRIFFES**
"In stagnant gloom I toil through day" *see Poetry* De La Mare **BERKELEY**
In stiller Nacht see Tolstoĭ **RUBINSTEIN**
"In Stunden der Entmutigung" *see Gebet* Lermontov **LISZT**
In summer fields see Allmers **IVES**
In tausend Formen see Goethe *WESTÖSTLICHER DIVAN.* **ZELTER**
"In tausend Formen magst du dich verstekken" *see In tausend Formen* Goethe **ZELTER**
In the album of a society lady see Golenishchev-Kutuzov **MUSORGSKIĬ** *Skuchaĭ*
In the alley see Ives **IVES**
In the bud of the morning-O see Stephens, James **QUILTER**
"In the cave which wild weeds cover" *see A Roman's chamber* Shelley **LUENING**
In the church-yard see Bryusov **MEDTNER**
In the corner see Musorgskiĭ **MUSORGSKIĬ** *V uglu*
In the dark grove the nightingale is silent see Nikitin **RIMSKIĬ-KORSAKOV** *V temnoĭ roshche zamolk soloveĭ*
"In the dim light of the golden lamp" *see The singer* Shanks **HESELTINE**
"In the evening as far as the eye can see" *see A green lowland of pianos* Harasymowicz **BARBER**
In the field a maiden sings see Susman, Margarete **SIBELIUS** *Im Feld ein Mädchen singt*
In the forest see Eichendorff **MEDTNER** *Im Walde*
In the garden at the castle see Anon. **MARTINŮ**
In the harem see Chu Ch'ing-yu **GRIFFES**
In the highlands see Stevenson, Robert Louis **QUILTER**
In the kingdom of roses and wine see Shenshin *GAFIZ.* **RIMSKIĬ-KORSAKOV** *V tsarstvo rozy i vina-pridi*

In the morning see Housman *LAST POEMS*: XXIII. **VAUGHAN WILLIAMS**
"In the morning let me face the east!" *see Hymn to light* Blake, James **IRELAND**
In the night see Rydberg **SIBELIUS** *I natten*
in the rain see Cummings **ROREM**
"in the rain darkness" *see in the rain* Cummings **ROREM**
"In the roomy oak among the fluttering leaves" *see Absalom* Goodman **ROREM**
"In the scented bud of the morning O" *see The daisies* Stephens, James **BARBER**
"In the scented bud of the morning-O" *see In the bud of the morning-O* Stephens, James **QUILTER**
In the seraglio garden see Jacobsen *I SERAILLETS HAVE.* **DELIUS**
In the silence of the secret night see Shenshin **RACHMANINOFF**
In the silent night see Shenshin **RACHMANINOFF** *In the silence of the secret night*
In the sky, where stars are glowing see Heine **MACDOWELL** *Oben, wo die Sterne glühen*
"In the slow world of dream" *see Memory* Roethke **ROREM**
In the soul of each of us see Korinfskiĭ **RACHMANINOFF**
"In the southern village the boy who minds the ox" *see The herd-boy* Lu Yu **BRITTEN**
In the spring see Barnes **VAUGHAN WILLIAMS**
"In the third class seat sat the journeying boy" *see Midnight on the Great Western* Hardy **BRITTEN**
In the valley see Gombossy **BARTÓK**
In the West see Burns **SCHUMANN** *Im Westen*
In the west the horizon is growing pale see Tolstoĭ **RIMSKIĬ-KORSAKOV** *Zapad gasnet v dali bledno-rozovoĭ*
In the wilderness see Graves, Robert **BARBER**
In the woods see Goethe *IM WALDE.* **MACDOWELL**
In this moonlight see Rathaus **CHAĬKOVSKIĬ** *O, du mondhelle Nacht*
In this summer see Lord, James **ROREM**
In tiefe Sklaverei lag ich gebunden see Goethe *EPIMENIDES ERWACHEN.* **ZELTER**
"In tiefer Ruh liegt und mich her" *see Kriegers Ahnung* Rellstab **SCHUBERT**
"In tiefster Erde ruht ein alt Gesetz" *see Schatzgräbers Begehr* Schober **SCHUBERT**

"In tiefster Schlucht, in Waldesschoss" *see*
Moosröslein Chezy LOEWE

"In Todesängsten hängst du da" *see*
Passionslied Unknown REGER

In trüber Stund' see Rathaus
CHAÏKOVSKIÏ

"In vain to me the clowslips blaw" *see Menie*
Burns MACDOWELL

In Vaters Garten heimlich steht see Heine
STRAUSS

In Verborgenen see Träger JENSEN

In verschwiegener Nacht see Ritter REGER

In vier Wänden see Golenishchev-Kutuzov
MUSORGSKIÏ *V chetyrekh stenakh*

In vivid dreams see Gombossy, K?
BARTÓK

"In vivid dreams I've seen you before" *see*
In vivid dreams Gombossy, K?
BARTÓK

In Weihnachtzeiten see Hesse LUENING

"In Weinberg auf der Höhe" *see Der Knabe*
und das Immlein Mörike WOLF

"In weite Ferne will ich träumen" *see Ferne*
Droysen MENDELSSOHN-
BARTHOLDY

"In winter I get up at night" *see Bed in*
summer Stevenson, Robert Louis
IRELAND

In your chamber see Pushkin PROKOFIEV
V tvoĭu svetlĭtsu

"In youth, when I did love" *see Song for the*
Gravedigger from *Hamlet* Shakespeare
THOMSON

Inauguration ball see Whitman *SPECIMEN*
DAYS. ROREM

Incantation see Byron IVES *from the*
"Incantation"

Incantation de la nuit see Jacqueton, Henry
SAUGUET

An incantation for fire and water see
Bal'mont PROKOFIEV *Zaklinanie vody i*
ornia

L'incanto degli occhi see Metastasio
SCHUBERT

Incertitud see Mompou MOMPOU

"Incertitud del meu cami" *see Incertitud*
Mompou MOMPOU

"Incertitude, O! mes delices" *see L'écrevisse*
Apollinaire POULENC

An incident see Whitman *SPECIMEN DAYS.*
ROREM

Incomprehensible see Musorgskiĭ
MUSORGSKIÏ *Neponiatnaia*

L'inconnu see Tonquédec, Marthe de
AUBERT

Incontro di Marzo see Cocconi, Ildebrando
PIZZETTI

The incredible hour see Louchheim *WITH*
OR WITHOUT ROSES. DIAMOND

L'incrédule see Verlaine *CHANSONS POUR*
ELLE, no. 20. HAHN

Indian love see Bryan BENNETT

Indian love song see Shelley *THE INDIAN*
SERENADE. DELIUS

THE INDIAN SERENADE. see Shelley
Indian love song DELIUS

The Indians see Sprague IVES

"The Indians descend from Mixco" *see Mixco*
Asturias GIDEON

LOS INDIOS BAJAN DE MIXCO. see
Asturias *Mixco* GIDEON

INDISCHE LEGENDE. see Goethe
Der Gott und die Bajadere LOEWE,
SCHOECK, SCHUBERT, ZELTER

Der Individualist see Krzyzanowski
KRENEK

Indomptablement a dû see Mallarmé
MILHAUD

INDY, VINCENT D', 1851-1931.
Baudelaire, Charles Pierre, 1821-1867.
LES FLEURS DU MAL.
L'amour et le crane, op. 20 (1884)
[Schott] "L'amour est assis sur le
crâne de l'Humanité"
Bazenery, F.
Angoisse (1871) [Marcel Colombier]
"Pitié! Mon coeur est gonflé
d'amertume"
Bonnières, Robert de, 1850-1905.
Au galop, op. 11 (1875) [unpubl.] "Ma
cavale et ma lance"
Baritone & piano.
Madrigal, op. 4 (1872-76) [Hamelle,
1887] "Qui jamais fut de plus
charmant visage"
Delaporte, R. P.
Les noces d'Or du Sacerdoce, op. 46
(1898) [Schola Cantorum, 191__]
"Heure du ciel, jour de Dieu"
Voice & harmonium; also for unison
chorus.
Gravollet, Paul
LES FRISSONS, no. 9.
Mirage, op. 56 (1903) [Hamelle, 1903]
"De loin, tu parais-sais très grande"
Hugo, Victor Marie, comte, 1802-1885.
LES ORIENTALES.
Attente, op. 3 (1872-76) [Hamelle,
1876] "Monte, écureuil, monte au
grand chêne"
Clair de lune, op. 13 (1872) [Hamelle,
ca.1898]
"La lune était sereine et jouait"
Also voice & orchestra, 1881.

Indy, Vincent d', 1851-1931.
  L'Académie Française nous a nommés
    tous trois (1888) [***Cent moins un,***
    1888] same
    Text by d'Indy?
  Ariette pour Tina (1927) [unpubl.]
    "Fidèle à ma maîtresse et toujours sur
      ses pas"
  Lied maritime, op. 43 (1896) [Rouart
    Lerolle, 1897] "Au loin, dans la mer"
  Marche du panache à la grande
    Maréchale (1871-72?) [unpubl.]
    "D'ici voyez sur ce sommet"
  Les yeux de l'Aimée, op. 58 (1904)
    [Gramophone Michaelis, 1904]
    "Nous étions assis côte á côte"
La Laurencie, Marie-Berband-Lionel
  de, 1861-1933.
  La première dent, op. 48 (1898) [Durand,
    1898] "Fille du sourirc pur"
Legrand, Marc
  La bonne terre (1896) [***L'âme enfantine,***
    ed. M. Legrand, 1897, pp.38-39]
    "La terre est blanche aux mois d'hiver"
    Voice alone.
  Mon père travaille [***L'âme enfantine,*** ed.
    M. Legrand, 1897, pp. 84-85]
    "Où va mon père, le matin"
    Voice alone.
Musset, Alfred de, 1810-1857.
  Adieu (1872) [unpubl.] "Adieu! je crois
    qu'en cette vie"
No author
  Vocalise, op. 64 (1907) [Leduc, 1907]
    In Collection Hettich, v. 2, no. 18.
    Wordless.
Orléans, Charles d', Comte
  d'Angoulème, 1391-1465.
  Madrigal à deux voix, op. 94 (1928)
    [Heugel, 1928]
    "Dieu, qu'il la faict bon regarder"
    Soprano & cello.
Schiller, Johann Christoph Friedrich
  von, 1759-1805.
  Plainte de Thécla, op. 10 (1880)
    [Hamelle, 1880] "La forêt gémit, le
    nuage roule"
    Text adapted by Bonnières.
Unknown
  Berceuse populaire [***L'illustration.***
    Suppl.-Musicale 27 Aug.1904]
    "Une poule blanche, qui est dans la
    grange"
Indy, Vincent d', 1851-1931.
  INDY
  L'Académie Française nous a nommés
    tous trois

Ariette pour Tina
Lied maritime
Marche du panache à la grande
  Maréchale
Les yeux de l'Aimée
Infant joy see Blake, William **LUENING,**
  VAUGHAN WILLIAMS
Infelice ch'io son see Unknown **ROSSINI**
L'infidèle see Chalupt **MILHAUD**
L'infidèle see Maeterlinck **SÉVERAC**
Infidélité see Gautier **HAHN**
Infini fais que je t'oublie . . . see Toulet
  KOECHLIN
"Infinite consanguinity it bears" *see Voyage*
  Crane **CARTER**
The infinite shining heavens see Stevenson,
  Robert Louis *SONGS OF TRAVEL,* VI.
  VAUGHAN WILLIAMS
INGALILL. see Fröding
  Säf, säf, susa **SIBELIUS**
Ingebjørg see Drachmann **GRIEG**
Ingemann, Bernhard Severin, 1789-
  1862.
  NIELSEN
  Guldfloden
  Jeg sa kun tilbage
  Den store Mester kommer
  Tidt er jeg glad, og vil dog gerne graede
Ingenting får störa vår stund med varandra
  see Lagerkvist **KILPINEN**
Ingénuité see Carême **SAUGUET**
Les Ingénus see Verlaine *FÊTES*
  GALANTES. **DEBUSSY**
The innate see Ives **IVES**
Der innere Friede see Rochlitz **WEBER** *Es*
  stürmt auf der Flur
Inneres Wühlen ewig zu fühlen see Goethe
  ERWIN UND ELMIRE. **MEDTNER**
Innhyllet i mørke skyer see Heine **GRIEG**
  Eingehüllt in graue Wolken
Inno a Maria Nostra Donna see Poliziano
  MALIPIERO
L'Innocence see Châteaubriand **MILHAUD**
"Innocentes jeunes filles" *see La double*
  rougeur Richter **SAUGUET**
In's Freie see Schöpff **SCHUMANN**
"Ins Grüne, ins Grüne, da lockt uns der
  Frühling" *see Das Lied im Grünen* Reil
  SCHUBERT
"In's Joch beug'ich den Nacken" *see*
  Madrigal Buonarroti **STRAUSS**
"Ins Joch beug'ich den Nakken demutvoll"
  see Madrigal Buonarroti **SCHOECK**
"In's stille Land" *see Lied* Salis-Seewis
  SCHUBERT
Ins stille Land see Salis-Seewis
  SCHUBERT *Lied*

Inscription sur le sable see Lerberghe
FAURÉ
L'insinuant see Valéry MOMPOU
"Insolemment à la beauté je me voue" *see*
  Les joues en feu Radiguet AURIC
Insomnia see Bishop ROREM
Insomnie see Tardieu SAUGUET
Interlude see Roethke ROREM
Intermezzo see Eichendorff SCHUMANN
INTERMEZZO. see HEINE
  Le bonheur SAUGUET
  Le malheur SAUGUET
Into my heart an air see Housman
  BLITZSTEIN
"Into my heart an air that kills" *see Into my
  heart an air* Housman BLITZSTEIN
"Into Thy hands, O Lord" *see Watchful's song*
  Bible VAUGHAN WILLIAMS
Introduced to flame see Josephs, Laurence
  ROREM
Invasion see D'Harcourt, Antoniette
  SAUGUET
"Invid palatsen lagunens vatten" *see
  Vattenplask* Rydberg SIBELIUS
Invitation see Koch ROREM
L'invitation au voyage see Baudelaire
  LES FLEURS DU MAL. CHABRIER,
  DUPARC
L'invto see Pepoli ROSSINI
Invito alla danza see Zangarini RESPIGHI
Invocation see Goethe *FAUST.* SEIBER
Invocation see Pradère-Niquet GOUNOD
Invocation see Pushkin RIMSKIĬ-
  KORSAKOV *Zaklinanie*
Invocation see Régnier ROUSSEL
Invocation see Rodès BLOCH
Invocation à Vesta see Barbier, J.
  GOUNOD
Invocation to sleep see Ogarev
  CHAĬKOVSKIĬ *Na son" griadushchiĭ*
Invocations aux Parques see Anon.
  POULENC
Invokation see Goethe LISZT *Der du von
  dem Himmel bist*
"Io lle diceva: – Sienteme!" *see Assunta*
  Giacomo PIZZETTI
"Io non odo imiei passi nel viale muto" *see
  Un sogno* Annunzio RESPIGHI
Io sono la Madre see Zarian RESPIGHI
"Io sono tanto stanca di lottare" *see
  Abbandono* Vivanti RESPIGHI
"Io sonoun'arida fonte" *see E il mio dolore io
  canto* Bocchialini, Jacopo PIZZETTI
Iphigenia see Mayrhofer SCHUBERT
Irdisches Glück see Seidl SCHUBERT

IRELAND, JOHN, 1879-1962.
Anon.
  Friendship in misfortune (1926)
    [Augener, 1928] "Give me the depth of
    love that springs"
  I have twelve oxen (1918) [Winthrop
    Rogers, 1919; Boosey & Hawkes]
    same
    Also a French version *J'ai douze
      boeufs,* Boosey & Hawkes.
  The three ravens (ca.1920) [Stainer &
    Bell] "There were three ravens sat on a
    tree"
  Variations sur "Cadet rousselle"
    (ca.1920) [J. & W. Chester, 1920]
    "Cadet-Rousselle a trois chapeaux"
Beddoes, Thomas Lovell, 1803-1849.
  If there were dreams to sell (1918)
    [Winthrop Rogers, 1918; Boosey &
    Hawkes] same
Blake, Ernest
  The journey (ca.1920) [Enoch, 1920;
    Ashdown]
    "Do you see the road awinding through
    the dear green fields below?"
Blake, James Vila, 1842-1925.
  Hymn to light (ca.1911) [Chappell, 1911]
    "In the morning let me face the east!"
  I will walk on the earth [Boosey &
    Hawkes, 1912] "Up to the top o' the
    trees"
  When lights go rolling round the sky
    (ca.1911) [Chappell, 1911] same
Blake, William, 1757-1827.
  Memory [Boosey & Hawkes, 1912]
    "Memory, hither come and tune your
    merry notes"
Breton, Nicholas, 1542-1626.
  A report song (1938) [Hawkes, 1938]
    "Shall we go dance the hay, the hay?"
Brontë, Emily Jane, 1818-1848.
  Love and friendship (1926) [Augener,
    1928] "Love is like the wild rosebriar"
Brooke, Rupert, 1887-1915.
  Blow out, you bugles (1918) [Winthrop
    Rogers, 1918; Boosey & Hawkes]
    same
  The soldier [Winthrop Rogers, 1917;
    Boosey & Hawkes]
    "If I should die, think only this of me"
  Spring sorrow (1918) [Winthrop Rogers,
    1918; Boosey & Hawkes]
    "All suddenly the wind comes soft"
Brown, Herbert S.
  The holy boy (1913; arr. 1938)
    [Boosey & Hawkes, 1938] "Lowly,
    laid in a manger"

Chilman, Eric, b. 1893.
The east riding (ca.1920) [Enoch, 1920; Ashdown] "Salt laden, sad with cry of ships"

Coleridge, Mary Elizabeth, 1861-1907.
Remember (1918) [Winthrop Rogers, 1918; Boosey & Hawkes]
"Time brought me many another friend"
The sacred flame (1918) [Winthrop Rogers, 1918; Boosey & Hawkes]
"Thy hand in mine, thy hand in mine"

Cooper, Eric Thirkell
Blind (1916) [Winthrop Rogers, 1917; Boosey & Hawkes]
"God, who gave the world its fairness"
The cost (1916) [Winthrop Rogers, 1917; Boosey & Hawkes]
"Take back the honour and the fame"

Daniel, Samuel, 1562-1619.
Love is a sickness full of woes (1921) [Winthrop Rogers, 1921; Boosey & Hawkes] same

Dekker, Thomas, 1570-1641.
The merry month of May (1921) [Winthrop Rogers, 1921]
"O, the month of May, the merry month of May"

Dowson, Ernest Christopher, 1867-1900.
I was not sorrowful [Boosey & Hawkes, 1912] same
If we must part [Stainer & Bell, 1976] same

Edwardes, Richard, 1523-1566.
The sweet season (1938) [Hawkes, 1938] "When May is in his prime"

Hardy, Thomas, 1840-1928.
Beckon to me to come (1926) [Oxford, 1927] same
Dear, think not that they will forget you (1926) [Oxford, 1927] same
Great things (1925) [Augener, 1935; Galliard] "Sweet cyder is a great thing"
Her song (1925) [J.B.Cramer, 1925] "I sang that song on Sunday"
In my sage moments (1926) [Oxford, 1927] same
It was what you bore with you, woman (1926) [Oxford, 1927] same
Summer schemes (1925) [J.B.Cramer, 1925] "When a friendly summer calls again"
The tragedy of that moment (1926) [Oxford, 1927] same

Weathers (1925) [J.B.Cramer, 1925]
"This is the weather the cuckoo likes"

Henry VIII, king of England, 1491-1547.
An aside (1938) [Hawkes, 1938] "These women all both great and small"

Housman, Alfred Edward, 1859-1936.
In boyhood (1926-27) [Oxford, 1928]
"When I would muse in boyhood"
Spring will not wait (1926-27) [Oxford, 1928]
Piano alone.
LAST POEMS: Prologue.
We'll to the woods no more (1926-17) [Oxford, 1928] same
THE SHROPSHIRE LAD.
The encounter [Augener, 1921] "The street sounds to the soldiers' tread"
Epilogue [Augener, 1921] "You smile upon your friend today"
Goal and wicket [Augener, 1921] "Twice a week the winter through"
Hawthorn time (1919) [Winthrop Rogers, 1919; Boosey & Hawkes]
" 'Tis time, I think, by Wenlock town"
The heart's desire (ca.1917) [Winthrop Rogers, 1917; Boosey & Hawkes]
"The boys are up the woods with day"
Ladslove [Augener, 1921] "Look not in my eyes"
The Lent lily [Augener, 1921] " 'Tis spring; come out to ramble"
The vain desire [Augener, 1921] "If truth in heart that perish"

Howell, Thomas, fl.1568.
All in a garden green (1938) [Hawkes, 1938] "Whenas the mildest month of jolly June"

Huxley, Aldous Leonard, 1894-1963.
The trellis (1920) [Augener, 1920]
"Thick-flow'r'd is the trellis"

Johanus Bassus, Frater, 16th cent.
A thanksgiving (1938) [Hawkes, 1938]
"Pleasure it is to hear"

Joyce, James, 1882-1941.
Tutto è sciolto (ca.1932) [Oxford]
"A birdless heaven, sea-dusk"

Linton, William James, 1812-1897.
O happy land (1941) [Boosey & Hawkes, 1941] same

Masefield, John, 1878-1967.
The Bells of San Marie (1919) [Augener, 1919; Galliard] "It's pleasant in Holy Mary"

IRELAND, JOHN, 1879-1962 *(continued)*
Masefield, John, 1878-1967 *(continued)*
Sea fever (1913) [Augener, 1915;
Galliard] "I must go down to the seas
again"
Vagabond (1922) [Augener, 1922;
Galliard] "Dunno a heap about the
what an' why"
Meynell, Alice Christiana (Thompson),
1847-1922.
The advent [Schott, 1934] "No sudden
thing of glory and fear"
My fair [Schott, 1934] "My Fair, no
beauty of thine will last"
Monro, Harold Edward, 1879-1932.
Earth's call (1918) [Winthrop Rogers,
1918; Doric Music Co., 1966]
"The fresh air moves like water round
a boat"
Newbolt, Sir Henry John, 1862-1938.
Hope the hornblower (ca.1911) [Boosey,
1921; Augener, 1961]
"Hark ye, hark to the winding horn"
O'Reilly, P. J.
Song from o'er the hill (1913)
[Leonard & Co., 1913; Cramer]
"A song came over the hill to me"
Rossetti, Christina Georgina, 1830-
1894.
Baby (1918) [Winthrop Rogers, 1918]
"Love me, I love you"
The blind boy (1918) [Winthrop Rogers,
1918] "Blind from my birth"
Death-parting (1918) [Winthrop Rogers,
1918]
"Goodbye in fear, goodbye in sorrow"
The garland (1918) [Winthrop Rogers,
1918] "Roses blushing red and white"
Hope (1918) [Winthrop Rogers, 1918]
"I dug and dug amongst the snow"
Newborn (1918) [Winthrop Rogers, 1918]
"Your brother has a falcon"
Published separately as *Your brother
has a falcon* (Boosey & Hawkes).
The only child (1918) [Winthrop Rogers,
1918] "Crying my little one, footsore
and weary?"
Skylark and nightingale (1918) [Winthrop
Rogers, 1918] "When a mounting
skylark sings in the sunlit summer
morn"
When I am dead, my dearest (1924)
[Oxford, 1928] same
Rossetti, Dante Gabriel, 1828-1882.
During music (1928) [Oxford, 1929]
"O cool unto the sense of pain"

English May [Boosey & Hawkes, 1912]
"Would God your health were as this
month of May"
The one hope (1926) [Augener, 1928]
"When vain desire at last and vain
regret"
Penumbra (1913) [Doric Music Co.,
1965] "I did not look upon her eyes"
Youth's spring-tribute (1913) [Doric
Music Co., 1965]
"On this sweet bank your head thrice
sweet and dear I lay"
Shakespeare, William, 1564-1616.
A WINTER'S TALE.
When daffodils begin to peer
[Boosey & Hawkes, 1912] same
Sidney, Sir Philip, 1554-1586.
My true love hath my heart (1920)
[Augener, 1921] same
Stevenson, Robert Louis, 1850-1894.
Bed in summer (ca.1912-13) [Curwen,
1915] "In winter I get up at night"
Symons, Arthur, 1865-1945.
The adoration (1918) [Chester, 1919]
"Why have you brought me myrrh"
The rat (1918) [Chester, 1919] "Pain
gnaws at my heart like a rat that
gnaws"
Rest (1919) [Chester, 1920] "The peace
of a wandering sky, silence"
Santa Chiara (Palm Sunday; Naples,
1925) [Augener, 1925; Galliard]
"Because it is the day of palms"
Tryst (1928) [Oxford, 1929] "The
fountain murmuring of sleep"
Verlaine, Paul, 1844-1896.
AQUARELLES.
Spleen (1913) [Doric Music Co., 1965]
"Around were all the roses red"
Text adapted by Dowson.
Warner, Sylvia Townsend, 1893-1978.
Hymn for a child [Schott, 1934]
"Flocking to the Temple"
The scapegoat [Schott, 1934] "See the
scapegoat, happy beast"
The soldier's return [Schott, 1934] "Jump
through the hedge, lass!"
Yeats, William Butler, 1865-1939.
The salley gardens [Schott, 1934]
"Down by the salley gardens my love
and I did meet"
Irène see Giraudoux *SUZANNE ET LA
PACIFIQUE.* **HONEGGER**
IRLANDE, no. 1
BERLIOZ Moore, T. *Le coucher du
soleil!*

IRLANDE, no. 4
    BERLIOZ Moore, T. *La belle voyageuse*
IRLANDE, no. 7
    BERLIOZ Moore, T. *L'origine de la
    harpe*
IRLANDE, no. 8
    BERLIOZ Moore, T. *Adieu, Bessy!*
IRLANDE, no. 9
    BERLIOZ Moore, T. *Élégie*
Irmelin see Jacobsen *IRMELIN ROSE.*
    DELIUS
IRMELIN ROSE. see Jacobsen
    Irmelin **DELIUS**
    Irmelin Rose **NIELSEN**
Irmelin Rose see Jacobsen *IRMELIN ROSE.*
    NIELSEN
"Irrémédiable vie" *see Jacques Villon* Éluard
    POULENC
L'irrésolue see Chalupt **MILHAUD**
Irrlicht see Müller, Wilhelm **SCHUBERT**
Irrlichter see Rückert **LOEWE**
"Irrlichter, die Knaben, die laufen und traben"
    see Irrlichter Rückert **LOEWE**
"Ein Irrsal kam in die Mondscheingärten" *see
    Peregrina II* Mörike **SCHOECK**
IRRWEGE: Lied. *see* Michell
    Verlassen **LISZT**
Irvine, John, d. 1964.
    QUILTER *Wind from the south*
IS 5. *see* Cummings
    Four uncles **DIAMOND**
IS 5 SONGS FOR SOPRANO, no. 1
    BLITZSTEIN Cummings *after all white
    horses are in bed*
IS 5 SONGS FOR SOPRANO, no. 2
    BLITZSTEIN Cummings *Jimmie's got a
    goil*
IS 5 SONGS FOR SOPRANO, no. 3
    BLITZSTEIN Cummings *when life is
    quite through with*
IS 5 SONGS FOR SOPRANO, no. 4
    BLITZSTEIN Cummings *mister, youse
    needn't be so spry*
IS 5 SONGS FOR SOPRANO, no. 5
    BLITZSTEIN Cummings *you are like
    the snow*
"Is it summer?" *see I cannot come to you*
    Ady **BARTÓK**
"Is it the shrewd October wind" *see Folksong*
    Howells, W. D. **MACDOWELL**
"Is it the tinkling of mandolins that disturbs
    you?" *see Little ivory figures pulled with
    string* Lowell, A. **GIDEON**
Is my team ploughing? see Housman
    A SHROPSHIRE LAD: XXVII.
    VAUGHAN WILLIAMS

"Is that Mister Riley" *see The side show* Ives
    IVES
Isaakian, Avetik Saakovich, 1875-1957.
    IVANUSHKA.
        RACHMANINOFF *In my garden at
        night*
Isis poignardée see Lanoux **SAUGUET**
Iskusstvo see Maĭkov **RIMSKIĬ-
    KORSAKOV**
THE ISLE. see Shelley
    The isle **RACHMANINOFF**
The isle see Shelley *THE ISLE.*
    RACHMANINOFF
"Isled in the midnight air" *see The moth*
    De La Mare **BERKELEY**
L'Isolement see Lamartine **MILHAUD**
Ispanskaya pensyna see Mikhailov
    BALAKIREV
Ispanskiĭ romans see Pushkin **MEDTNER**
    Spanish romance
    Two settings: Op. 36 no. 4 and op. 52 no.
    5.
Israël est vivant see Cohen, A. **MILHAUD**
Isstupleniye see Kol'tsov **BALAKIREV**
"Ist alles eins, was liegt doran!" *see Tot*
    Haringer **SCHÖNBERG**
"Ist auch schmuck nicht mein Rösslein" *see
    Der Soldat I* Eichendorff **WOLF**
"Ist der alte Schiffsherr endlich heimgekehrt"
    see Der alte Schiffsherr Vogl **LOEWE**
Ist der Himmel darum im Lenz so blau see
    Volkmann **PFITZNER**
"Ist der holde Lenz erschienen?" *see Klage
    der Ceres* Schiller **SCHUBERT**
"Ist dies Tauris" *see Orest auf Tauris*
    Mayrhofer **SCHUBERT**
"Ist es wahr?" *see Frage* Voss
    MENDELSSOHN-BARTHOLDY
"Ist mir's doch, als sei mein Leben" *see Am
    Strome* Mayrhofer **SCHUBERT**
"Ist nicht heilig mein Herz" *see
    Menschenbeifall* Hölderlin **BRITTEN**
Isten veled! see Horváth, P. **LISZT**
"Ist's dein Wille, süsse Maid" *see Serenade*
    Tellez **MAHLER**
"Ist's möglich?" *see Der Geprüste* Mörike
    SCHOECK
It cannot be see Maĭkov **RACHMANINOFF**
"It has broken us" *see Sea-snatch* O'Faolain,
    Sean, translator **BARBER**
"It is a whisper among the hazel bushes" *see
    The twilight people* Starkey
    VAUGHAN WILLIAMS
"It is holiday time in the woods" *see The
    somber pine* Arens, Egmont **RIEGGER**
It is not always May see Longfellow
    GOUNOD

COMPOSER Poet *Title* "First Line"

It is of other planets see Bal'mont
PROKOFIEV *Est' drugie planety*
"It is such a beautiful day I had to write you a
letter" *see Thoughts of a young girl*
Ashbery **ROREM**
"It strikes me that" *see An election* Ives **IVES**
"It was a lover and his lass" *see In spring*
Shakespeare **CARPENTER**
"It was a lover and his lass" *see Pretty ring
time* Shakespeare **HESELTINE**
It was a lover and his lass see Shakespeare
AS YOU LIKE IT. **DELIUS, QUILTER,
RIETI**
It was in the early spring see Tolstoĭ
CHAĬKOVSKIĬ *To bylo ranneiu vesnoĭ*
"It was not in the winter" *see The time of
roses* Hood **QUILTER**
"It was the time of flowers" *see In the harem*
Chu Ch'ing-yu **GRIFFES**
It was thy choice, for journey taking see
Pushkin **BORODIN**
For the shores of thy far native land
It was what you bore with you, woman see
Hardy **IRELAND**
"It was your faither and mither" *see A riddle*
Soutar **BRITTEN**
"I-tis-kit, i-tas-ket, a green and yellow basket"
see Homage to Paul Klee Deutsch
DIAMOND
Italien see Grillparzer **MENDELSSOHN-
BARTHOLDY**
ITALIENISCHES LIEDERBUCH. see Heyse
Am Sonntag Morgen **BRAHMS**
Italienisches Ständchen see Anon. **WEBER**
Canzonetta: Italienisches Ständchen
"Its clinging, mournful leaves, I said" *see
The myrtle* Deland **MACDOWELL**
It's nae thy bonnieface see Burns **LASSEN**
It's not the breezes in their flight see Tolstoĭ
RIMSKIĬ-KORSAKOV *Ne veter, veĩa s
vysoty*
"Its oh, and oh 'tis merry to go" *see Little
John's song* Chesson **CARPENTER**
"It's pleasant in Holy Mary" *see The Bells of
San Marie* Masefield **IRELAND**
Itt lent a vőlgyben see Gombossy **BARTÓK**
In the valley
Itzerott, Marie, b. 1857.
REGER
An dich
Rosen
Sehnsucht
Verklärung
Volkslied
IUzhnaia noch' see Shcherbina **RIMSKIĬ-
KORSAKOV**

IVAN. see Bodenstedt
Lied **BRAHMS**
IVANHOE. see Scott
Romanze des Richard Löwenherz
SCHUBERT
IVANUSHKA. see Isaakian
In my garden at night **RACHMANINOFF**
"I've done a very frightful thing" *see The liar*
Carpenter, Rue **CARPENTER**
I've heard an organ talk sometimes see
Dickinson **COPLAND**
Ives, A. L., Miss
IVES *Cradle song*
IVES, CHARLES EDWARD, 1874-1954.
Aldrich, Thomas Bailey, 1836-1907.
Maple leaves (1920) [114 songs, p. 56]
"October turned my maple's leaves to
gold"
Alford, Henry, 1810-1871.
Forward into light (1898) [114 songs,
p. 228] "Forward flock of Jesus"
Aria from *The celestial country*, 1898-
99 cantata by Ives.
Naught that country needeth (1899) [114
songs, p. 224] same
Aria from *The celestial country*,
cantata (1898-99) by Ives.
Allmers, Hermann, 1821-1902.
In summer fields (1900) [114 songs,
p. 186] "Quite still I lie where green
the grass and tall"
Anon.
Charlie Rutlage (ca.1921) [114 songs,
p. 19] "Another good cow-puncher has
gone"
Text from John A. Lomax, collector
Cowboy songs . . . , 1920.
A Christmas carol (1900) [114 songs,
p. 234] "Little star of Bethlehem"
My native land (1897) [114 songs,
p. 235] "My native land now meets my
eye"
A son of a gambolier (1895) [114 songs,
p. 122] "Come join my humble ditty"
Ariosto, Lodovico, 1474-1533.
La fède (1920) [114 songs, p. 77]
"La fède mai non debbe esser corrotta"
Arnold, Matthew, 1822-1888.
West London (1921) [114 songs, p. 244]
"Crouc'd on the pavement"
Bowring, Sir John, 1792-1872.
Watchman (1913) [114 songs, p. 93]
"Watchman, tell us of the night"
Brewster, Lyman Dennison, 1832-
1904, supposed author.
The all-enduring (1902) [unpubl.] "Man
passes down the way of years"

Brooke, Rupert, 1887-1915.
Grantchester (1920) [114 songs, p. 37]
"Would I were in Grantchester"

Browning, Robert, 1812-1889.
PARACELSUS.
from *"Paracelsus"* (1921) [114 songs,
p. 71] "For God is glorified in man"

Byron, George Gordon Byron, 6th
baron, 1778-1824.
from the *"Incantation"* (1921) [114
songs, p. 40] "When the moon is on
the wave"
CHILDE HAROLD'S PILGRIMAGE.
A farewell to land (1925) [18 songs,
p. 8] "Adieu, adieu! my native shore
fades"

Chezy, Wilhelmine Christiane von,
1783-1856.
Rosamunde (1898) [114 songs, p. 178]
"J'attends, helas! dans la douleur"
Text translated by Bélanger.

Collins, Anne
The greatest man (1921) [114 songs,
p. 43] "My teacher said us boys should
write"
Text in the **Evening Sun,** New York,
1921.

Cooper, James Fenimore, 1789-1851.
Afterglow (1919) [114 songs, p. 86]
"At the quiet close of day"

Cowper, William, 1731-1800.
The waiting soul (1908) [114 songs,
p. 139] "Breathe from the gentle
south"

Elliot, Lady Charlotte, d.1880.
The camp meeting (1912) [114 songs, p.
99] "Across the summer meadows fair"

Emerson, Ralph Waldo, 1803-1882.
Duty (1921) [114 songs, p. 18] "So nigh
is grandeur to our dust"

Florian, Jean Pierre Claris de, 1755-
1794.
Chanson de Florian (1901) [114 songs,
p. 174] "Ah! s'il est dans votre
village"

Gallet, Louis, 1835-1898.
Elégie (1901) [114 songs, p. 171]
"O, doux printemps d'autrefois"

Goethe, Johann Wolfgang von, 1749-
1832.
Ilmenau: over all the treetops (1902)
[114 songs, p. 153]
"Over all the treetops is rest"
Text translated by Harmony Twichell
Ives.

Gottschall, Rudolf von, 1823-1909.
Marie (1896) [114 songs, p. 212] "Marie,
I see thee fairest one"

Hadley, Arthur Twining, 1856-1930.
*SOME INFLUENCES IN MODERN
PHILOSOPHIC THOUGHT.*
Tolerance (1921?) [114 songs, p. 135]
"How can I turn from any fire"

Heine, Heinrich, 1797-1856.
Ich grolle nicht (1899) [114 songs,
p. 190] same

Heyduk, Adolf, 1835-1923, translator.
Songs my mother taught me (1895) [114
songs, p. 250] same

Hill, Susan Benedict
William Will, a Republican campaign
song (1896) [Willis Woodward & Co.]
"What we want is honest money"

Holmes, Oliver Wendell, 1809-1894.
The last reader (1921) [114 songs, p. 8]
"I sometimes sit beneath a tree"

Hunt, Leigh, 1784-1859.
Romanzo di Central Park (1900) [114
songs, p. 219] "Grove, rove, night,
delight"

Ives, A. L., Miss
Cradle song (1919) [114 songs, p. 77]
"Hush thee, dear child to slumbers"

Ives, Charles Edward, 1874-1954.
Berceuse (1900) [114 songs, p. 214]
"O'er the mountain towards the west"
The cage (1906) [114 songs, p. 144]
"A leopard went around his cage"
Circus band (1894) [114 songs, p. 128]
"All summer long we boys dreamed"
Disclosure (1921) [114 songs, p. 15]
"Thoughts, which deeply rest at
evening"
Down east (1919) [114 songs, p. 126]
"Songs! visions of my homeland"
An election (1921) [114 songs, p. 50]
"It strikes me that"
Evidence (1910) [114 songs, p. 133]
"There comes o'er the valley a
shadow"
He is there! (1917) [114 songs, p. 107]
"Fifteen years ago today"
Immortality (1921) [114 songs, p. 11]
"Who dares to say the spring is dead"
In the alley (1896) [114 songs, p. 119]
"On my way to work one summer
day"
The innate (1916) [114 songs, p. 87]
"Voices live in every finite being"
The majority (1921) [114 songs, p. 1]
"The masses! The masses!"

COMPOSER   Poet   *Title*   "First Line"

IVES, CHARLES EDWARD, 1874-1954
(*continued*)
Ives, Charles Edward, 1874-1954
(*continued*)
Memories (1897) [114 songs, p. 236]
"We're sitting in the opera house"
Nature's way (1908) [114 songs, p. 138]
"When the distant eveningbell calmly
breaths its blessing"
The new river (1921) [114 songs, p. 13]
"Down the river comes a noise!"
An old flame (1896) [114 songs, p. 202]
"When dreams enfold me"
Old home day (1920) [114 songs, p. 115]
"Go my songs!"
On the counter (1920) [114 songs, p. 68]
"Tunes we heard in 'ninety-two'"
One-two-three (1921) [114 songs, p. 88]
"Why doesn't one, two, three"
Remembrance (1921) [114 songs, p. 27]
"A sound of a distant horn"
Resolution (1921) [114 songs, p. 28]
"Walking stronger under distant skies"
The see'r (1920) [114 songs, p. 69] "An
old man, with a straw in his mouth"
The side show (1921) [114 songs, p. 76]
"Is that Mister Riley"
Slow march (1888) [114 songs, p. 259]
"One evening just at sunset we laid
him in the grave"
Soliloquy (1907) [34 songs, p. 50] "When
a man is sitting"
A song (1892) [114 songs, p. 206] "When
the waves softly sigh"
The things our fathers loved (1917) [114
songs, p. 91] "I think there must be a
place in the soul"
Thoreau (1915) [114 songs, p. 103] "He
grew in those seasons like corn in the
night"
Tom sails away (1917) [114 songs,
p. 112] "Scenes from my childhood are
with me"
Walking (1902) [114 songs, p. 149]
"A big October morning"
Waltz (1895) [114 songs, p. 252] "Round
and round the old dance ground"
Ives, Harmony Twichell, 1876-1969.
Allegro (1900) [114 songs, p. 216]
"By morning's brightest beams"
Autumn (1908) [114 songs, p. 136]
"Earth rests!"
Mists (1910) [114 songs, p. 131]
"Low lie the mists"
The south wind (1899) [114 songs,
p. 221] "When gently blows the south
wind"

Spring song (1904) [114 songs, p. 145]
"Across the hill of late"
There is a lane (1902) [114 songs,
p. 159] "There is a lane which winds
towards the bay"
To Edith (1892) [114 songs, p. 256] "So
like a flower, thy little four year face"
Two little flowers (1921) [114 songs, p.
242] "On sunny days in our backyard"
The world's highway (1893) [114 songs,
p. 207] "For long I wander'd happily"
Johnson, Robert Underwood, 1853-
1937.
At sea (1921) [114 songs, p. 10] "Some
things are undivined except by love"
The Housatonic at Stockbridge (1921)
[114 songs, p. 31]
"Contented river! in thy dreamy realm"
Luck and work (1920) [114 songs, p. 49]
"While one will search the season
over"
Premonitions (1921) [114 songs, p. 57]
"There's a shadow on the grass"
Keats, John, 1795-1821.
Like a sick eagle (1920) [114 songs,
p. 61] "The spirit is too weak"
Kipling, Rudyard, 1865-1936.
Tarrant moss (1902) [114 songs, p. 160]
"I closed and drew"
Published in *18 songs* as "Slugging a
vampire," text by Ives.
Lenau, Nicolaus, 1802-1850.
Weil' auf mir (1902) [114 songs, p. 180]
same
Lindsay, Nicholas Vachel, 1879-1931.
*General William Booth enters into
Heaven* (1914) [18 songs, p. 2]
"Booth led boldly with his big bass
drum"
Longfellow, Henry Wadsworth, 1807-
1882.
The children's hour (1901) [114 songs,
p. 163] "Between the dark and the
daylight"
Lowry, Robert, 1826-1899.
At the river (1916) [114 songs, p. 95]
"Shall we gather at the river"
Lyle, Henry Francis, 1793-1847.
Abide with me (ca.1890) [Peer
International, 1958] same
Lytton, Edward George Earle Lytton
Bulwer-Lytton, 1st baron, 1803-
1873.
When stars are in the quiet skies (1891)
[114 songs, p. 257] same

COMPOSER Poet *Title* "First Line"

McCrae, John, 1872-1918.
  In Flanders fields (1919) [114 songs,
    p. 104] "In Flanders fields the poppies
    blow"
Manilius, Marcus, d. 384 B.C.
  ASTRONOMICA, Book 4, livre 16.
    Vita (1921) [114 songs, p. 18]
      "Nascentes morimur finisque"
Markham, Edwin, 1852-1940.
  from *"Lincoln, the great commoner"*
    (1921) [114 songs, p. 23] "And so he
    came from the prairie cabin"
Meredith, George, 1828-1909.
  from *"Night of frost in May"* (1899) [114
    songs, p. 193]
      "There was the lyre of earth beheld"
Milton, John, 1608-1674.
  PARADISE LOST.
    Evening (ca.1921) [114 songs, p. 6]
      "Now came still evening on"
Moore, Thomas, 1779-1852.
  Canon (1894) [114 songs, p. 254]
      "Oh, the days are gone"
  A night song (1895) [114 songs, p. 204]
      "The young May moon"
  A night thought (1895) [114 songs,
    p. 249] "How oft a cloud, with envious
    veil"
  Those evening bells (1907) [114 songs,
    p. 142] same
Percy, Thomas, 1729-1811.
  RELIQUES.
    Harpalus (1902) [114 songs, p. 161]
      "Oh, Harpalus! (thus would he say)"
Peterson, Frederic, 1859-1938.
  At parting (1889) [34 songs, p. 71]
      "The sweetest flow'r that blows"
Pool, Morris W.
  Ann street (1921) [114 songs, p. 59]
      "Quaint name Ann street"
Robinson, Robert, 1735-1790.
  His exaltation (1913) [114 songs, p. 97]
      "For the grandeur of Thy nature"
Root, George Frederick, 1820-1895.
  Religion (1920) [114 songs, p. 36] "There
    is no unbelief"
Rossetti, Christina Georgina, 1830-
1894.
  Mirage (1902) [114 songs, p. 158] "The
    hope I dreamed of was a dream"
San Geminiano, Folgore da, 13th
cent.
  August (1920) [114 songs, p. 78] "For
    August, for August"
  December (1920) [114 songs, p. 83]
      "Last, for December"
September (1920) [114 songs, p. 81]
  "And in September"
Shelley, Percy Bysshe, 1792-1822.
  Rough wind (1902) [114 songs, p. 155]
      "Rough wind, that moanest loud"
  The world's wanderers (1895) [114
    songs, p. 253]
      "Tell me, star whose wings of light"
Sprague, Charles, 1791-1875.
  The Indians (1921) [114 songs, p. 29]
      "Alas! for them their day is o'er"
Stevenson, Robert Louis, 1850-1894.
  Requiem (1911) [18 songs, p. 9] "Under
    the wide and starry sky"
Tennyson, Alfred Tennyson, 1st
baron, 1809-1892.
  from *"Amphion"* (1896) [114 songs,
    p. 247] "The mountain stirred its bushy
    crown"
Tersteegen, Gerhardt, 1697-1769.
  Hymn (1921) [114 songs, p. 47] "Thou
    hidden love of God"
Turnbull, Monica Peveril, 1879-1901.
  Where the eagle (1900) [114 songs, p.
    215] "Where the eagle cannot see"
Unknown
  The collection (1920) [114 songs, p. 85]
      "Now help us, Lord"
  Dreams (1897) [114 songs, p. 195]
      "When twilight comes, when twilight
      comes"
  Kären (1894) [114 songs, p. 210] "Do'st
    remember child!"
  Omens and oracles (1900) [114 songs,
    p. 197] "Phantoms of the future"
  On the Antipodes (1923) [18 songs,
    p. 44] "Nature's relentless; nature is
    kind"
    Voice & 2 pianos.
  Qu'il m'irait bien (1901) [114 songs,
    p. 168] same
  The white gulls (1921) [114 songs,
    p. 240] "The white gulls dip and
    wheel"
    Russian text translated by Morris W.
    Pool (Maurice Morris, pseud.);
    poem and its author not identified.
Untermeyer, Louis, 1885-1977.
  from *"The swimmers"* (1921) [114 songs,
    p. 62] "Then the swift plunge"
    Poem appeared in the *Yale Review*,
    July 1915.
Vinje, Aasmund Olavsson, 1818-1870.
  The old mother (1900) [114 songs,
    p. 183] "My dear old mother, poor
    thou art"

IVES, CHARLES EDWARD, 1874-1954
(continued)
Whitman, Walt, 1819-1892.
  LEAVES OF GRASS.
    Walt Whitman (1921) [114 songs,
      p. 74] "Who goes there?"
Whittier, John Greenleaf, 1807-1892.
  The light that is felt (1904) [114 songs,
    p. 147] "A tender child of summers
    three"
  Serenity (1919) [114 songs, p. 89]
    "O Sabbath rest of Galilee!"
Wordsworth, William, 1770-1850.
  I travelled among unknown men (1901)
    [114 songs, p. 166] same
  So may it be (1921) [114 songs, p. 16]
    "My heart leaps up when I behold"
Ives, Charles Edward, 1874-1954.
  IVES
    Berceuse
    The cage
    Circus band
    Disclosure
    Down east
    An election
    Evidence
    He is there!
    Immortality
    In the alley
    The innate
    The majority
    Memories
    Nature's way
    The new river
    An old flame
    Old home day
    On the counter
    One-two-three
    Remembrance
    Resolution
    The see'r
    The side show
    Slow march
    Soliloquy

A song
The things our fathers loved
Thoreau
Tom sails away
Walking
Waltz
Ives, Harmony Twichell, 1876-1969.
  IVES
    Allegro
    Autumn
    Mists
    The south wind
    Spring song
    There is a lane
    To Edith
    Two little flowers
    The world's highway
Ivre d'amour see Akhtamar, Grégoire d'
  MASSENET
Iwaszkiewicz, Jaroslaw, 1894-1980.
  SZYMANOWSKI
    Allah, Allah, Akbar
    Bialy krag ksiezyca olbrzymi
    Ledwie blask slońca zloci dachy wiez
    O tej godzinie, w której miasto śpi
    O, ukochana ma
    Odeszlaś w pustynie zachodnia
    Pochyl sie cicho nad kolyska
    Śpiewam morzu, gwiazdom i tobie
    W poludnie miasto biale od goraca
Iz evangeliia ot Ioanna see Bible
  RACHMANINOFF *From the Gospel of St.*
    John, XV: 13
Iz slĕz moikh see Heine *LYRICAL*
  INTERMEZZO. **BORODIN** *Aus meinen*
    Tränen
Iz slĕz moikh mnogo, maliutka see Heine
  LYRICAL INTERMEZZO. **RIMSKIĬ-**
  KORSAKOV
Iz slez moikh vyroslo mnogo see Heine
  MUSORGSKIĬ
Iz-pod tainstvennoy kholodnoy polumaski see
  Lermontov **BALAKIREV**

J

Ja, die Schönst! see Hoffmann von
Fallersleben
*DES FAHRENDEN SCHÜLERS LIEBEN
UND LEIDEN.* **WOLF**
Ja, du bist elend see Heine **FRANZ,
SCHOECK**
"Ja, du weisst es, teure Seele" *see Zueignung*
Gilm zu Rosenegg **STRAUSS**
*Ja Heil und Dank dir die den Segen brachte!
see* George
DAS JAHR DER SEELE: Nach der Lese.
WEBERN
"Ja, ich bin krank, ich weiss" *see Die einzige
Arzenei* Hafiz **SZYMANOWSKI**
"Ja, ich weiss es" *see Vergebliche Liebe*
Bernard **SCHUBERT**
Já jstem ten rytîr zpohádky see Hálek
DVOŘÁK
"Ja, mein Glück, das langgewohnte" *see Trost*
Mörike **SCHOECK**
"Ja, spanne nur den Bogen mich zu töten" *see
Der zürnenden Diana* Mayrhofer
SCHUBERT
Já vím, že v sladké naději see Pfleger-
Moravský **DVOŘÁK**
Two settings: B. 11 no. 6 and B. 160 no. 4.
"Ja, wann gleich wär das Firmament" *see
Böses Weib* Anon. **REGER**
Jaboune, pseud. *see* Nohain, Jean
Les jacinthes see Daudet, L. **MILHAUD**
Jack L'Eventreur see Noailles, Marie Laure
de **ROREM**
The jackdaw see Unknown **STRAVINSKIĬ**
Tchitcher-Iatcher
Jackson, Kenneth, translator.
A CELTIC MISCELLANY.
BARBER *Promiscuity*
Jacob, Max, 1876-1944.
AURIC
Il se peut qu'un rêve étrange . . .
Lord Bolingbroke
Pour demain soir . . .
POULENC
Berceuse
Chanson bretonne
Cimetière
Jouer du bugle
La petite servante
Souric et Mouric
Vous n'écrivez plus?
RIETI
La crise
Monsieur le Duc

Le noyer fatal
Soir d'été
SAUGUET
A une sainte le jour de sa fête
Exhortation
Jardin mystérieux
Marine à Roscoff
Le petit paysan
Ports de l'enfer
Que penser de mon salut
Régates mystérieuses
La ville
Voisinage
Voyage
Jacob, Therese Amalie Louise von,
1797-1870.
LOEWE
Beim Tanze
Des Jünglings Segen
Ihr Spaziergang
Kapitulation
Liebesliedchen
Mädchen und Rose
Der Mutter Geist
Überraschung
Jacobi, Johann Georg, 1740-1814.
MOZART *An Chloe*
SCHUBERT
Am Tage aller Seelen
An Chloen
Hochzeitlied
In der Mitternacht
*Lied des Orpheus, als er in die Hölle
ging*
Die Perle
Trauer der Liebe
SCHUMANN *Erinnerung*
Jacobowski, Ludwig, 1868-1900.
BERG *Grabschrift*
PFITZNER
*Ich aber weiss, ich seh' dich manche
Nacht*
Leuchtende Tage
REGER
Dein Bild
Kindergeschichte
Maienblüten
Der Narr
Das Ringlein
Eine Seele
Sehnsucht
Totensprache
*VOM GESCHLECHT DER
PROMETHIDEN.*
REGER *Hymnus der Liebe*

Jacobsen, Jens Peter, 1847-1885.
  DELIUS *The page sat in the lofty tower*
  NIELSEN
    Det bødes der for
    Genrebillede
    Har Dagen sanket al sin Sorg
    I Drømmes Land
    Seraferne
    Solnedgang
    Til Asali
    Vise af "Mogens"
  SCHÖNBERG *Hochzeitslied*
DET BØDES DER FOR.
  DELIUS *Through long, long years*
I SERAILLETS HAVE.
  DELIUS *In the seraglio garden*
  NIELSEN *I Seraillets Have*
IRMELIN ROSE.
  DELIUS *Irmelin*
  NIELSEN *Irmelin Rose*
LAD VAAREN KOMME.
  DELIUS *Let springtime come then*
LØFT DE KLINGRE GLASPOKALER.
  DELIUS *Wine roses*
SILKESKO OVER GYLDEN LAEST.
  DELIUS *Silken shoes*
  NIELSEN *Silkesko over gylden Laest!*
Jacquelin Gray see Pitchford **ROREM**
Jacques Villon see Éluard **POULENC**
Jacquet, Mme. M.
  MASSENET *Heure vécue*
Jacqueton, Henry
  SAUGUET
    Cette cigarette d'ombre
    Incantation de la nuit
    Plain-ciel
"Jadis, aux jours du feu" *see Clair de lune*
  Haraucourt **KOECHLIN**
"J'adore Suzette" *see Suzette et Suzon* Hugo
  SAINT-SAËNS
"Jää hyvästi" ja "näkemiin" see
  Koskenniemi **KILPINEN**
" 'Jää hyvästi' me sanomme" *see "Jää*
  hyvästi" ja "näkemiin" Koskenniemi
  KILPINEN
Jägargossen see Runeberg **SIBELIUS**
Der Jäger see Mahlmann **ZELTER**
Der Jäger see Mörike **WOLF**
Der Jäger see Müller, Wilhelm
  SCHUBERT
Der Jäger see Münch-Bellinghausen
  BRAHMS
Der Jäger see Schultz **GRIEG**
Jaeger, Johannes
  SCHOECK *Wiegenlied*
Jäger, Maria, pseud. *see* Förster, Marie
  Laura, 1817-1856.

"Jäger, ruhe von der Jagd" *see Ellens Gesang*
  II Scott **SCHUBERT**
"Der Jäger ziehn in grünen Wald" *see*
  Studentenfahrt Eichendorff **PFITZNER**
Jaegeren see Schultz **GRIEG** *Der Jäger*
Jägerlied see Mörike **WOLF**
Jägerlied see Uhland **GRIEG**
Jägerlied see Unknown **SPOHR**
Jägers Abendlied see Goethe **MEDTNER,**
  SCHUBERT, ZELTER
  Two Schubert settings: D. 215 and D. 368.
Jägers Liebeslied see Schober **SCHUBERT**
Jaegersang see Uhland **GRIEG** *Jägerlied*
Jänckendorf *see* Nostitz und
  Jänckendorf, Gottlob Adolf Ernst von,
  1765-1836.
Jänka see Törmänen **KILPINEN**
Jag see Josephson, E. **KILPINEN**
Jag är ett träd see Josephson, E.
  SIBELIUS
"Jag ber ej om en kyss" *see Till Elektra*
  Blomberg **KILPINEN**
"Jag gråter blodiga tårar" *see Jag*
  Josephson, E. **KILPINEN**
Jag har haft en stor, tyst sorg see Blomberg
  KILPINEN
"Jag längtar dit bort till mitt hjärtas mö" *see*
  Min längtans Ö Cnattingius, Thor
  KILPINEN
"Jag läser om klockan" *see Klockan*
  Bergman **KILPINEN**
"Jag lefver min dag i drömmar" *see Dolce far*
  niente Tavaststjerna **SIBELIUS**
"Jag sade ej ett ord till dig" *see Kärlek*
  Josephson, E. **KILPINEN**
"Jag ser vad du tänker vid stranden" *see Vid*
  stranden Josephson, E. **KILPINEN**
"Jag sluter ögonen" *see Sommarens ljud*
  Österling **KILPINEN**
"Jag vandrar fram pa skogens ban" *see*
  Fågelfängaren Runeberg **SIBELIUS**
Jag väntar ingen lycka see Blomberg
  KILPINEN
Jag ville bygga ett litet bo see Cnattingius,
  Thor **KILPINEN**
Jag ville jag vore i Indialand see Fröding
  SIBELIUS
Jag ville vara tårar see Blomberg
  KILPINEN
Der Jagd see Unknown **LOEWE**
Jagdchor see Werner **SCHUBERT** *Jagdlied*
Jagdlied see Des Knaben Wunderhorn
  MENDELSSOHN-BARTHOLDY
Jagdlied see Eichendorff **FRANZ**
Jagdlied see Werner *WANDA, KÖNIGIN*
  DER SARMATEN. **SCHUBERT**

Jahody see Unknown **DVOŘÁK**
DAS JAHR DER SEELE, p. 27. *see* George
  Ich darf nicht dankend **SCHÖNBERG**
DAS JAHR DER SEELE: Nach der Lese. *see*
  George
  Ja Heil und Dank dir die den Segen
    brachte! **WEBERN**
DAS JAHR DER SEELE: Nachtwachen. *see*
  George
  Erwachen aus dem tiefsten Traumesschosse
  WEBERN
DAS JAHR DER SEELE: Traurige Tänze. *see*
  George
  Ihr tratet zu dem Herde **WEBERN**
DAS JAHR DER SEELE: Waller im Schnee.
  see George
  Noch zwingt mich Treue über dir zu wachen
  WEBERN
Jahrestag see Hesse **SCHOECK**
"J'ai bu deux flacons" *see Chanson hongroise*
  Petöfi **DELIBES**
"J'ai bu tout le printemps sur la fleur de ton
  rire" *see Fleuramye* Van Ormelingen
  MASSENET
"J'ai cherché dans mon coeur" *see Je t'aime*
  Bozzani, Suzanne **MASSENET**
"J'ai compris ta détresse" *see Je te veux*
  Pacory **SATIE**
"J'ai construit dans mon âme" *see La*
  splendeur vide Renaud **SAINT-SAËNS**
"J'ai cueilli ce brin de bruyère" *see L'adieu*
  Apollinaire **HONEGGER, RIVIER**
"J'ai des coeurs à vendre" *see La marchand*
  de coeurs Luka, Madeleine **SAUGUET**
J'ai douze boeufs see Anon. **IRELAND**
  I have twelve oxen
"J'ai fait ce rêve, Ô ma chérie" *see Le Rouge-*
  gorge Theuriet **LALO**
"J'ai fait un triste rêve" *see Jérôme et Alissa*
  Gide **MILHAUD**
"J'ai longtemps habité sous de vastes
  portiques" *see La vie antérieure*
  Baudelaire **DUPARC**
"J'ai mis à mon cheval sa bride" *see Sabre en*
  main Renaud **SAINT-SAËNS**
"J'ai mis dans un coffret d'ébène" *see*
  Le coffret d'ébène Jannet, Victor
  MASSENET
"J'ai perdu la forêt, la plaine" *see L'aveu*
  Villiers **CHAUSSON**
J'ai perdu ma force et ma vie see Musset
  TRISTESSE. **LISZT**
"J'ai perdu ma poulette" *see Chanson*
  bretonne Jacob, M. **POULENC**
"J'ai pleuré j'ai lutté" *see Sur le bord* Oeris
  AUBERT

"J'ai pour page un bel escholier" *see Mon*
  page Théus, Maurice de **MASSENET**
J'ai presque peur, en vérité see Verlaine
  FAURÉ
"J'ai quelque jour dans l'océan" *see Le vin*
  Valéry **SAUGUET**
"J'ai, quelque jour, dans l'Océan" *see Le vin*
  perdu Valéry **MOMPOU**
J'ai quelqu'un dans le coeur see Jammes
  TRISTESSES. **MILHAUD**
J'ai rêvé cette nuit see Samain **KOECHLIN**
"J'ai rêvé que mon coeur était comme jadis"
  see Rêve de la bien-aimée Courmont
  BIZET
"J'ai rêvé tellement fort de toi" *see Dernier*
  poeme Desnos **POULENC**
"J'ai revê-tu, ce soir" *see Comme autrefois*
  Dortzal **MASSENET**
"J'ai revu le cimetière" *see Cimetière de*
  campagne Vicaire **HAHN**
"J'ai traversé les pontes de Cé" *see C*
  Aragon **POULENC**
"J'ai voulu le revoir" *see Le sentier perdu*
  Choudens **MASSENET**
"J'ai vu décliner comme un songe" *see Elégie*
  Contamine **SATIE**
"J'ai vu des fleurs qui dans les plaines" *see Si*
  vous n'ouvrez vôtre fenêtre
  Dumas the younger **GOUNOD**
"J'ai vu reluire" *see Nuage* Beylié,
  Laurence de **POULENC**
J'ai vu revenir les choses see Jammes
  MILHAUD
"J'ai vu tous les yeux qu'on aime en ce
  monde" *see Souvenance* Mariéton
  MASSENET
Jail-bait blues see Goodman **ROREM**
J'aime see Musset **MILHAUD**
"J'aime dous lc rayon de la limpide aurore"
  see Sérénade Collin **CHAĭKOVSKIĭ**
J'aime l'âne see Jammes **MILHAUD**
"J'aime tes yeux" *see Chanson d'amour*
  Silvestre **FAURÉ**
Jak sie najlepiej opedzać od szerszenia see
  Iłłakowiczówna **SZYMANOWSKI**
"Jak velké požehnání" *see Při vyšívání*
  Kleinschrod **DVOŘÁK**
"Jakby sie dobrze spalo" *see Przed*
  zaśnieciem Iłłakowiczówna
  SZYMANOWSKI
Jakobowski, Ludwig *see* Jacobowski,
  Ludwig, 1868-1900.
Jalkanen, Huugo, 1880-1969.
  KILPINEN
  Aamu
  Aamulaulu

Jalkanen, Huugo, 1880-1969. *(continued)*
  KILPINEN *(continued)*
    Ah, missä lienet nyt
    Eheu fugaces!
    Eron hetki
    Erotessa
    Hiljaisuus
    Ihmisen osa
    Illanrusko
    Ilta
    Joulukirkkoon
    Kerran
    Kesäisenä päivänä
    Kevät on mennyt
    Koditon
    Kuutamo-oodi
    Lemmenlaulu
    Muistoja
    Nocturnus
    Odotus
    Oh, päivät, te päivät
    Per aspera
    Pitkä on tuskan tie
    Prologi
    Pyhäin miesten päivänä
    Syyslaulu
    Tytön laulu
    Uusi Aladdin
    Uutisraivaaja
    Y"
    Yli hohtavan hangen
"J'allais dans la campagne" *see Air romantique* Moréas **POULENC**
J'allais par des chemins perfides *see* Verlaine **FAURÉ**
"Jamais ne cesserai" *see Psalm XXXIV* Bible **HONEGGER**
Jamais plus *see* Olga de Sarmento **MASSENET**
Jamais un tel bonheur *see* Lebey **MASSENET**
James, Edward Frank Willis, 1907- **SAUGUET** *Aria*
Jammes, Francis, 1868-1938
  HONEGGER *Prière*
  MILHAUD
    Almaïde d'Étremont
    Au beau soleil
    Au bord de l'eau verte
    Avec ton parapluie
    Bernadette
    C'était affreux
    Clara d'Ellebeuse
    La gomme coule
      Two settings: Op. 50 no. 1 and op. 50 no. 2.

    J'ai vu revenir les choses
    J'aime l'âne
    Je crève de pitié
    Je le trouvai
    Ne me console pas
    Notre-Dame de Sarrance
    Pomme d'anis
    Pourquoi les boeufs
    Prière pour aller au Paradis
    Prière pour demander une étoile
    Prière pour être simple
    Prière pour qu'un enfant ne meure pas
    Printemps lointain
    Les processions des campagnes
    Quatrain
    Si tu pouvais
    Tristesse
    Viens, je te mettrai
TRISTESSES.
  BOULANGER
    Au pied de mon lit
    Demain fera un an qu' à Audaux
    Deux ancolies se balançaient
    Elle est gravement gaie
    Elle était descendue au bas de la prairie
    Je garde une médaille d'elle
    Les lilas qui avaient fleuri
    Nous nous aimerons tant que nous tairons
    Par ce que j'ai souffert
    Parfois, je suis triste
    Un poète disait que
    Si tout ceci n'est qu'un pauvre rêve
    Vous m'avez regardé avec tout votre âme
  MILHAUD
    Dans le chemin toujours trempé
    Demain fera un an qu'à Audaux
    Deux ancolies se balançaient
    Elle avait emporté des brasées de lilas
    Elle est gravement gaie
    Elle était descendue au bord de la prairie
    Faisait-il beau quand elle est morte
    J'ai quelqu'un dans le coeur
    Je garde une médaille d'elle
    Je la désire dans cette ombreuse lumière
    Je ne désire point ces ardeurs
    Je songe à ce jour là
    Les lilas qui avaient fleuri
    Nous nous aimerons tant que nous tairons
    O mon coeur, ce sera dans l'Aoûte bleu

Par ce que j'ai souffert
Parfois, je suis triste
Un poète disait que
Si tout ceci n'est qu'un pauvre rêve
Son souvenir emplit l'air si clair
Venez sous la tonnelle
Venez, ma bien aimée
Vous m'avez regardé avec tout votre
âme

JANÁČEK, LEOŠ, 1854-1928.
Rypáček, František J
Jarní píseň (1897; rev. 1905) [O.
Pazdírek, 1944] "Ó vitej vesno
kouzelná"
Printed in *Pazdírek's vocal repértoire,*
no. 1.
Jane see Leconte de Lisle *POÈMES*
ANTIQUES. **DEBUSSY**
Jane Grey see Ammann **SCHÖNBERG**
Janés, Clara, 1940-
MOMPOU *Primeros pasos*
Janés i Olivé, Josep, 1913-1959.
MOMPOU
Aquesta nit un mateix vent
Damunt de tu només les flors
Fes me la vida transparent
Jo et pressentia com la mar
Jannet, Victor
MASSENET *Le coffret d'ébène*
Janov, M. L. *see* Yanova, Mariya, 1840-
1875.
Janson, Kristofer Nagel, 1841-1917.
GRIEG
Millom Roser
Vesle Gut
Japansk akvarell see Josephson, E.
KILPINEN
Le jardin see Unknown **SÉVERAC**
Le jardin see Wilde *IMPRESSIONS I:* Le
jardin. **GRIFFES**
LE JARDIN CLOS, no. 1
FAURÉ Lerberghe *Exaucement*
LE JARDIN CLOS, no. 2
FAURÉ Lerberghe *Quand tu plonges tes*
yeux dans mes yeux
LE JARDIN CLOS, no. 3
FAURÉ Lerberghe *La messagère*
LE JARDIN CLOS, no. 4
FAURÉ Lerberghe *Je me poserai sur ton*
coeur
LE JARDIN CLOS, no. 5
FAURÉ Lerberghe *Dans la Nymphée*
LE JARDIN CLOS, no. 6
FAURÉ Lerberghe *Dans la pénombre*
LE JARDIN CLOS, no. 7
FAURÉ Lerberghe *Il m'est cher, Amour,*
le bandeau

LE JARDIN CLOS, no. 8
FAURÉ Lerberghe *Inscription sur le*
sable
Le jardin de Virigine see Luka, Madeleine
SAUGUET
JARDIN DES CARESSES. see Toussaint
L'adieu **AUBERT**
Le destin **AUBERT**
Le mirage **AUBERT**
Le sommeil des colombes **AUBERT**
Le vaincu **AUBERT**
Le visage penché **AUBERT**
Le jardin du ciel see Mendès **IBERT**
Le jardin mouillé see Régnier **ROUSSEL**
Jardin mystérieux see Jacob, M.
SAUGUET
Jardin nocturne see Brimont **FAURÉ**
Le jardinier impatient see Vildrac
MILHAUD
JARDINS D'HIVER, no. 1
JOLIVET Lefilleul, G. *Aube*
JARDINS D'HIVER, no. 2
JOLIVET Lefilleul, G. *La maison du*
bonheur
JARDINS D'HIVER, no. 3
JOLIVET Lefilleul, G. *Combien de bras*
se sont ouverts
JARDINS D'HIVER, no. 4
JOLIVET Lefilleul, G. *Quiétide*
Jarní píseň see Rypáček **JANÁČEK**
Jaro see Kleinschrod **DVOŘÁK**
Jašek's song see Tetmajer **MARTINŮ**
Jaškova zpěvanka see Tetmajer **MARTINŮ**
Jašek's song
Jasminenstrauch see Rückert **SCHUMANN**
"J'attends, helas! dans la douleur" *see*
Rosamunde Chezy **IVES**
Ein Jauchzer see Spitteler **SCHOECK**
"Jauchzet dem Herrn" *see Psalm 100* Bible
SCHOECK
"J'aurais pu dire mon Amour" *see Odelette*
Régnier **ROUSSEL**
Java de la femme see Bloch **MILHAUD**
Jazz dans la nuit see Dommange
ROUSSEL
Jazz-boys see Hughes, L. *THE WEARY*
BLUES. **CARPENTER**
Jazz-man see Farjeon **BRITTEN**
"Jde má milá na jahody na zelená borka" *see*
Jahody Unknown **DVOŘÁK**
"Je bois l'eau froide par saccades" *see Aglaé*
Cocteau **AURIC**
"Je cheminais, seul et rèveur . . . " *see*
Blessures Turpin, Henri **GOUNOD**
"Je cherche paix" *see Sonnet* Magny
ROREM

COMPOSER Poet *Title* ''First Line''

Je cours après le bonheur **see** Maupassant
MASSENET

"Je crains tes baisers" **see** *Déclaration*
Chouquet MASSENET

Je crève de pitié **see** Jammes MILHAUD

"Je crois aux choses éternelles" **see** *Credo
d'amour* Silvestre CHABRIER

Je crois en vous **see** Guérin, L. BERLIOZ

"Je dirai la rose aux plis gracieux" **see**
La rose Leconte de Lisle FAURÉ

"Je fais parfois ce rêve étrange" **see** *Mon rêve
familier* Verlaine KOECHLIN

Je garde une médaille d'elle **see** Jammes
TRISTESSES. BOULANGER, MILHAUD

"Je höher die Glocke" **see** *Liebesgedanken*
Müller, Wilhelm LOEWE

"Je jure, tant que je vivrai" **see** *Invocations
aux Parques* Anon. POULENC

Je la désire dans cette ombreuse lumière **see**
Jammes *TRISTESSES.* MILHAUD

"Je l'ai rencontrée un jour de vendange" **see**
Trois jours de vendange Daudet HAHN

Je l'ai suivie **see** Zaffira GOUNOD *L'ho
compagnata*

"Je languis nuit et jour et ma peine est
extrême" **see** *Sérénade du Bourgeois
gentilhomme* Molière FAURÉ

"Je le possède, il m'aime" **see** *Sainte Thérèse
prie* Sylvestre, Pierre MASSENET

Je le trouvai **see** Jammes MILHAUD

"Je lui rends la rose fletrie" **see** *Peine
d'amour* Silvestre DELIBES

Je marcherai pour toi **see** Carême
SAUGUET

"Je m'arrête: il y a un point à ma promenade"
see *Le point* Claudel MILHAUD

Je me metz en vostre mercy **see** Charles,
Duke of Orleans HAHN

Je me poserai sur ton coeur **see** Lerberghe
FAURÉ

Je me souviens **see** Guillot de Saix HAHN

Je me suis embarqué **see** *La Ville de
Mirmont* FAURÉ

Je me suis plaint aux tourterelles **see**
Robiquet MASSENET

Je m'en suis allé vers l'amour **see** Maurer
MASSENET

"Je m'étais endormi, et je faisais un rêve" **see**
Le mirage Toussaint AUBERT

"Je mets sur le papier luisant" **see** *La lettre*
Mendès, Jane MASSENET

"Je mettrai mes deux mains sur ma bouche"
see *Le don silencieux* Closset FAURÉ

Je n'ai envie que de t'aimer **see** Éluard
POULENC

"Je n'ai jamais connu la couleur de ses yeux"
see *Fièvre jaune* Frank, J. H.
HONEGGER

"Je n'ai pas soif, vieillard, merci!" **see** *Boire à
l'ombre* Augier GOUNOD

Je n'ai plus que les os **see** Ronsard
POULENC

"Je n'aime plus la rue St Martin" **see**
Le disparu Desnos POULENC

Je n'avais d'yeux et de courage **see** Éluard
SAUGUET

Je ne désire point ces ardeurs **see** Jammes
TRISTESSES. MILHAUD

"Je ne peux plus rien dire" **see** *Dans l'herbe*
Vilmorin POULENC

Je ne puis espérer **see** Delpit GOUNOD

Je ne sais pas t'aimer **see** Silvestre
MASSENET

"Je ne suis pas bien grand" **see** *Pas bien
grand* Kriéger, Jacqueline MILHAUD

"Je ne veux que te meurtrir de caresses" **see**
Le vaincu Toussaint AUBERT

"Je n'emporte avec moi sur la mer sans
retour" **see** *Le Départ* Régnier ROUSSEL

"Je n'entends que le bruit de la rive et de
l'eau" **see** *Sur l'eau* Sully-Prudhomme
HAHN

Je nommerai ton front **see** Éluard
POULENC

"Je pâlis et tombe en langeur" **see** *Jane*
Leconte de Lisle DEBUSSY

"Je pars! Adieu ma chere àme" **see**
Complainte Silvestre MASSENET

Je penais épouser un fier à bras **see** Aguet,
William IBERT

"Je pense à cette chambre" **see** *La chambre de
juin* Laporte SAUGUET

"Je regardais dans le jardin" **see** *Dans le
jardin* Gravollet, Paul DEBUSSY

"Je rêve d'une île ancienne" **see** *L'ile
ancienne* Samain KOECHLIN

Je sais qu'il existe **see** Carême SAUGUET

JE SAIS QU'IL EXISTE, no. 1
SAUGUET Carême *Je sais qu'il existe*

JE SAIS QU'IL EXISTE, no. 2
SAUGUET Carême *L'adolescent*

JE SAIS QU'IL EXISTE, no. 3
SAUGUET Carême *Le semeur*

JE SAIS QU'IL EXISTE, no. 4
SAUGUET Carême *Seul sur la terre*

JE SAIS QU'IL EXISTE, no. 5
SAUGUET Carême *Celui que j'aime*

JE SAIS QU'IL EXISTE, no. 6
SAUGUET Carême *Je suis un oiseau*

JE SAIS QU'IL EXISTE, no. 7
SAUGUET Carême *Simplicité*

JE SAIS QU'IL EXISTE, no. 8
SAUGUET Carême *Ingénuité*

JE SAIS QU'IL EXISTE, no. 9
SAUGUET Carême *Je serai toujours là*

JE SAIS QU'IL EXISTE, no. 10
   SAUGUET Carême *Nul ne se lasse d'être soi*
JE SAIS QU'IL EXISTE, no. 11
   SAUGUET Carême *Il vieillissait*
JE SAIS QU'IL EXISTE, no. 12
   SAUGUET Carême *Je marcherai pour toi*
"Je sais sur la colline" *see Solitude* Lamartine GOUNOD
Je serai toujours là see Carême SAUGUET
Je songe à ce jour là see Jammes *TRISTESSES.* MILHAUD
Je suis dans le fillet see Supervielle *LA PREMIÈRE FAMILLE.* MILHAUD
Je suis hereux see Hugnet SAUGUET
Je suis heureuse see Deharme, Lise SAUGUET
"Je suis ici, l'autre est ailleurs" *see Ténèbres* Claudel MILHAUD
"Je suis ivre, je suis ivre, ivre d'amour" *see Ivre d'amour* Akhtamar, Grégoire d' MASSENET
Je suis jaloux see Corneille *PSYCHÉ.* KOECHLIN
"Je suis, je suis le cri de joie" *see La chanson de l'alouette* Leprade LALO
"Je suis la blonde fleur d'amour qui resplendis" *see Hélène* Bengy-Puyvallée AUBERT
"Je suis l'inaltérable image" *see La sérénité* Barbier, M. SAINT-SAËNS
"Je suis née un mauvais mardi" *see Complainte de Florinde* Arnoux IBERT
"Je suis près de la porte" *see Flammes* Jean-Aubry ROUSSEL
"Je suis tant que dure le jour" *see Couplets bachiques* Anon. POULENC
Je suis tombé de mal en peine see Valmy-Baysse MILHAUD
Je suis un oiseau see Carême SAUGUET
"Je suis un sylphe, une ombre, un rien" *see Le sylphe* Dumas the elder FRANCK
Je t'adore see Hugnet SAUGUET
Je t'aime see Bozzani, Suzanne MASSENET
"Je t'aime tant, frêle mignonne" *see Douceur* Docquois SAINT-SAËNS
Je te l'ai dit see Eluard AURIC
Je te rends grâce, Ô Dieu see Collin GOUNOD
"Je te salue, heureuse Paix" *see Ode* Ronsard ROREM
Je te salue jeunesse see Noailles, Marie Laure de ROREM
"Je te salue, Ô Marguerite" *see Ave Margarita* (prière d'amour, 1902) Noël, Édouard MASSENET

Je te veux see Pacory SATIE
Je te vis, je t'aimais see Kahn LOEFFLER
Je te vois en rêve see Shakespeare SAUGUET
"Je t'écris de dessous la tente" *see Carte postale* Apollinaire RIVIER
"Je t'écris et la lampe écoute" *see La lettre* Barbusse AUBERT
Je tremble en voyant ton visage see Tristan L'Hermite DEBUSSY
"Je vais revoir la beauté que j'adore" *see Le maure jaloux* Florian BERLIOZ
"Je vais vous parler d'un Rien" *see Chanson du rien* Constantin-Weyer IBERT
"Je veux louer la Paix" *see L'Hymne de la paix* Baïf ROREM
"Je veux oublier" *see Départ* Augier DELIBES
"Je veux oublier, oublier" *see Départ* Augier GOUNOD
"Je veux prier: l'heure est propice" *see Prière du soir* Manuel GOUNOD
"Je veux que le matin l'ignore" *see Le secret* Silvestre FAURÉ
Je veux te voir see Émié JOLIVET
"Je voudrais être un fleuve calme" *see Le fleuve* Audigier, Georges SAINT-SAËNS
"Je voudrais pour tes yeux" *see Voeu* Régnier ROUSSEL
"Je voudrais qu'à ma fenêtre" *see Le gloxinia* Chalupt AURIC
"Je voudrais te parler à mi-voix" *see Love poem* Clift, William SAUGUET
"Je vous ai assiégé" *see Obsession* Claudel MILHAUD
"Je vous aime, Ô ma fiancée!" *see À Cécile* Dubufe GOUNOD
"Je vous salue, Marie" *see Salutation angelique* Unknown SAUGUET
The jealous lover see Rochester QUILTER
"Jean Martin prit sa besace Vive le passant qui passe" *see Le mendiant* Fombeure POULENC
"Jean Pierre sait bien qu'il fait obéir" *see Il faut obéir* Kriéger, Jacqueline MILHAUD
Jean Renaud see Anon. VAUGHAN WILLIAMS
Jean-Aubry, Georges, 1882-1950.
   AUBERT *Sérénade mélancolique*
   IBERT *Romance*
   MALIPIERO
      Light
      Song
      Stream

Jean-Aubry, Georges, 1882-1950
(continued)
ROUSSEL
Flammes
Light
SCHMITT Star
Jeanne see Giraudoux SUZANNE ET LA
PACIFIQUE. **HONEGGER**
Jeanne d'Arc au bûcher see Dumas the
elder **LISZT**
"Jeanne Houhou la très gentille" see
L'anguille Apollinaire **POULENC**
JEANNE LA ROUSSE, OU, LA FEMME DU
BRACONNIER. see Béranger
Die rothe Hanne **SCHUMANN**
"Jeanneton où irons-nous garder" see Chanson
française Anon. **RAVEL**
Jean-Paul see Richter, Johann Paul
Friedrich, 1763-1825.
"J'écoute la voix de mon rêve" see L'abri
Rodès **BLOCH**
Jedem das Seine see Colly **SCHÖNBERG**
Jedem Werke bin ich fürder tot see George
DAS BUCH DER HÄNGENDEN GÄRTEN.
SCHÖNBERG
"Ein jeder hat zu diesem Feste" see Mir fehlt
das Beste Heine **FRANZ**
"Jedes Ding in jeder Sache" see Sonett
Gerhardt **ZELTER**
Jeduch see Löns **SCHÖNBERG**
Jeg baerer med Smil min Byrde see Aakjaer
SUNDT BLOD. **NIELSEN**
Jeg elsker Dig! see Andersen **GRIEG**
"Jeg elsker dig, du blonde Pige" see
Den blonde Pige Bjørnson **GRIEG**
"Jeg elsker dig, du blonde Pige" see
Den blonde Pige II Bjørnson **GRIEG**
Jeg elsket see Bjørnson **GRIEG**
Jeg giver mit digt til våren see Bjørnson
FISKERJENTEN. **GRIEG**
"Jeg havde betalt, hvad jeg skyldte" see Jeg
lever et Liv i Laengsel Benzon **GRIEG**
Jeg havde en nyskaaren seljefløjte see Krag
DELIUS
Jeg hører i natten see Drachmann **DELIUS**
"Jeg kaldte dig mit lykkebud" see
Stambogsrim Ibsen **GRIEG**
"Jeg kunde juble for alle Vinde min Glaede
ud!" see Et Håb Paulsen **GRIEG**
Jeg laegger mig saa trygt til Ro see Winther
NIELSEN
Jeg lever et Liv i Laengsel see Benzon
GRIEG
"Jeg priser vort ringe" see Claras Sang
Feddersen **GRIEG**
Jeg reiste en deilig Sommerkvaeld see
Paulsen **GRIEG**

JEG REISTE ENDEILIG SOMMERKVAELD.
see Paulsen
Am schönsten Sommerabend war's
DELIUS
Jeg sa kun tilbage see Ingemann **NIELSEN**
Jeg stod i dunkle drømmer see Heine
LIEDERSTRAUSS. **GRIEG**
Ich stand in dunkeln Träumen
"Jeg stod på daekket og jeg så" see
Hjemkomst Paulsen **GRIEG**
Jeg synes om din lette Gang see Nielsen
NIELSEN
"Jeg takker dig for hver en Stund" see
Taksigelse Winther **GRIEG**
"Jeg vandrer gennem Skoven ved Jule-tid" see
Jule-Sne Drachmann **GRIEG**
"Jeg vandrer over mine Faedres Jord" see
Hjemstavn Poulsen, Frederik **NIELSEN**
"Jeg ved ej hvad der rører sig" see Prolog
Drachmann **GRIEG**
Jeg ved en Laerkerede see Bergstedt
NIELSEN
Jeg ved, min Tanke, ved see Geibel **GRIEG**
Dereinst, Gedanke mein
Jeitteles, Alois, 1794-1858.
BEETHOVEN
Auf dem Hügel sitz ich spähend
Diese Wolken in den Höhen
Es kehret der Maien
Leichte Segler in den Höhen
Nimm sie hin denn diese Lieder
Wo die Berge so blau
Jelínek, F. L.
DVOŘÁK Ukolébavka
Jemand see Burns **SCHUMANN**
J'en appelle à l'alchimiste see Raphaël,
Cluzel **SAUGUET**
Den jenn a den anden see Berntsen
NIELSEN
"Den jenn ska studier badde Graesk" see Den
jenn a den anden Bernsten **NIELSEN**
Jenny Gray see Anon. **HESELTINE**
Jens Madsen a An-Sofi see Berntsen
NIELSEN
"Jens Madsen wa en Feskermand" see Jens
Madsen a An-Sofi Berntsen **NIELSEN**
Jens Vejmand see Aakjaer **NIELSEN**
JENSEIT DES TWEED. see Anon.
Thomas der Reimer **LOEWE**
JENSEN, ADOLF, 1837-1879.
Alvaro Fernandez de Almeida
SPANISCHES LIEDERBUCH: Tango
vos, el mi pandero.
Klinge, klinge, mein Pandero, op. 21
no. 1 [J. Rieter-Biedermann, 1864]
same
Translated by Geibel.

Anon.
Wenn ich ein Vöglein wär', op. 1 no. 5 [Leuckart, 1859] same

SPANISCHES LIEDERBUCH: Aunque con semblante airado.
Ob auch finstre Blicke glitten, op. 21 no. 7 [J. Rieter-Biedermann, 1864] same
Translated by Heyse.

SPANISCHES LIEDERBUCH: Ay ojuelos verdes.
Ach ihr lieben Aeuglein, op. 21 no. 2 [J. Rieter-Biedermann, 1864] same
Translated by Heyse.

SPANISCHES LIEDERBUCH: Celestina.
Dulces árboles sombrosos, op. 4 no. 1 [Fritz Schuberth, 1860]
"Holde, schattenreiche Baüme"
Translated by Heyse.

SPANISCHES LIEDERBUCH: En campaña madre.
En campaña, madre, op. 4 no. 4 [Fritz Schuberth, 1860]
"Sie blasen zum Abmarsch"
Translated by Heyse.

SPANISCHES LIEDERBUCH: Niña, si la huerta vas.
Wenn du zu den Blumen gehst, op. 21 no. 5 [J. Rieter-Biedermann, 1864] same
Translated by Heyse.

SPANISCHES LIEDERBUCH: Pensamientos me quitan.
Pensamientos me quitan, op. 4 no. 6 [Fritz Schuberth, 1860]
"Es rauben Gedanken den Schlaf"
Translated by Heyse.

SPANISCHES LIEDERBUCH: Ribcricas del rio.
Am Ufer des Flusses, des Manzanares, op. 21 no. 6
[J. Rieter-Biedermann, 1864] same
Translated by Geibel.

SPANISCHES LIEDERBUCH: Ventecico murmurador.
Murmelndes Lüftchen, op. 21 no. 4 [J. Rieter-Biedermann, 1864] same
Translated by Heyse.

Antonio de Villegas
SPANISCHES LIEDERBUCH: En la peña, suso la peña.
En la peña, suso la peña, op. 4 no. 5 [Fritz Schuberth, 1860]
"Unter den Bäumen"

Beck, Karl Isidor, 1817-1879.
Über Nacht, op. 24 no. 3 [Senff, 1864]
"Ich glaubte, die Schwalbe träumte schon"

Wo Tauben sind [Ries & Erler, 1882]
"Lass mich mit meinem Weh"
EINE THRÄNE.
Eine Thräne, op. 57 no. 2 [L. Hoffarth, 1878] "Rinne, rinne leise"

Brandenburg, Otto von, 1266-1308.
Räumt den Weg! op. 55 no. 1 [Hermann Erler, 1875] same

Burns, Robert, 1759-1796.
Du süsse Dirn' von Inverness, op. 49 no. 4 [Jul. Hainauer, 1874] same
Einen schlimmen Weg ging gestern ich, op. 49 no. 3 [Jul. Hainauer, 1874] same
Für Einen, op. 49 no. 2 [Jul. Hainauer, 1874] "Mein Herz ist schwer"
John Anderson, mein Lieb, op. 49 no. 5 [Jul. Hainauer, 1874] same
Leb' wohl mein Ayr! op. 49 no. 7 [Jul. Hainauer, 1874] "Die finstere Nacht bricht schnell herein"
Mein Herz ist im Hochland, op. 49 no. 1 [Jul. Hainauer, 1874] same
O säh' ich auf der Heide dort, op. 49 no. 6 [Jul. Hainauer, 1874] same

Castillejo, Christoval De, 1490-1556.
SPANISCHES LIEDERBUCH: Alguna vez.
Alguna vez, op. 4 no. 7 [Fritz Schuberth, 1860]
"Dereinst, dereinst, Gedanke mein"
Translated by Geibel.

Chamisso, Adelbert von, 1781-1838.
Denke, denke, mein Geliebter, op. 30 no. 4 [Robert Forberg, 1868] same
Ich hab' ihn im Schlafe, op. 30 no. 5 [Robert Forberg, 1868] same
Ich habe, bevor der Morgen, op. 30 no. 2 [Robert Forberg, 1868] same
Nicht der Tau und nicht der Regen, op. 30 no. 3 [Robert Forberg, 1868] same
Was ist's, O Vater, op. 30 no. 1 [Robert Forberg, 1868] same
Wie so bleich, op. 30 no. 6 [Robert Forberg, 1868] same

Cunningham, Allan, 1784-1842.
Carlisle Tor, op. 51 no. 4 [Jul. Hainauer, 1876]
"Weiss war die Ros' auf seinem Hut"
Der Geächtete, op. 51 no. 2 [Jul. Hainauer, 1876]
"Geht, suchet in der Waldschlucht"
Gordon von Brakley, op. 51 no. 1 [Jul. Hainauer, 1876]
"Dee abwärts kam Inveraye"
Das Mädchen von Inverness, op. 51 no. 3 [Jul. Hainauer, 1876]
"Ein Mädchen lebt in Inverness"

JENSEN, ADOLF, 1837-1879 *(continued)*
Eichendorff, Joseph Karl Benedikt, Freiherr von, 1788-1857.
Der Bote, op. 57 no. 4 [L. Hoffarth, 1878] "Am Himmelsgrund da schiessen so lustig die Stern'"
Frühlingsnacht, op. 1 no. 6 [Leuckart, 1859]
"Ueber'm Garten, durch die Lüfte"
Nacht, op. 5 no. 3 [Fritz Schuberth, 1861]
"Die Vöglein, die so fröhlich sangen"
Waldesgespräch, op. 5 no. 4 [Fritz Schuberth, 1861] "Es ist schon spät"
Geibel, Emanuel, i.e., Franz Emanuel August, 1815-1884.
Du feuchter Frühlingsabend, op. 6 no. 1 [Senff, 1862] same
Durch die wolkige Maiennacht, op. 57 no. 5 [L. Hoffarth, 1878] same
Im Gebirg, op. 6 no. 5 [Senff, 1862]
"Nun rausch im Morgenwinde sacht so"
Der Knabe mit dem Wunderhorn, op. 24 no. 1 [Senff, 1864]
"Ich bin ein lust'ger Gesell"
Lied des Mädchens, op. 6 no. 4 [Senff, 1862]
"Lasst schlafen mich und träumen"
Lied des Mädchens, op. 57 no. 1 [L. Hoffarth, 1878]
"Wohl waren es Tage der Sonne"
Nun die Schatten dunkeln, op. 6 no. 2 [Senff, 1862] same
O schneller, mein Ross, op. 6 no. 6 [Senff, 1862] same
Der Page, op. 6 no. 3 [Senff, 1862]
"Da ich nun entsagen müssen"
Wanderlied [Emil Sommermeyer, 1899]
"Fort, fort, mich duldet's nicht"
Goethe, Johann Wolfgang von, 1749-1832.
Schweizerlied, op. 57 no. 6 [L. Hoffarth, 1878] "Uf'm Bergli bin i g'sässe"
FAUST.
Der König in Thule, op. 23 no. 6 [Peters, 1865]
"Es war ein König in Thule"
WILHELM MEISTER. Mignon's song: Kennst du das Land?
Mignon [Ries & Erler, 1882] "Kennst du das Land"
Gottschall, Rudolf von, 1823-1909.
Marie, op. 1 no. 2 [Leuckart, 1859]
"Marie am Fenster sitzest du"

Grimmelshausen, Hans Jacob Christoffel von, 1625-1676.
SIMPLICIUS SIMPLICISSIMUS.
Gesang des Einsiedlers, op. 61 no. 2 [Jul. Hainauer, 1880] "Komm, Trost der Nacht, O Nachtigall"
Grosse, Julius Waldemar, 1828-1902.
Bei dir, op. 13 no. 5 [Senff, 1863]
"Die Nächte stürmen"
Hafiz, Muhammad Shums al-Din, d.1388.
Als einst von deiner Schöne, op. 11 no. 1 [Fritz Schuberth, 1863] same
Ich bin ein armes Lämpchen nur, op. 11 no. 2 [Fritz Schuberth, 1863] same
Ich will bis in die Sterne, op. 11 no. 3 [Fritz Schuberth, 1863] same
Lockenstricke sollst du wissen, op. 11 no. 5 [Fritz Schuberth, 1863] same
Wehe mir mein Rosenkränzlein, op. 11 no. 7 [Fritz Schuberth, 1863] same
Wehre nicht, O Lieb, op. 11 no. 4 [Fritz Schuberth, 1863] same
Zu der Rose, zu dem Weine, op. 11 no. 6 [Fritz Schuberth, 1863] same
Hamerling, Robert, 1830-1889.
An die Vögel, op. 41 no. 5 [J. P. Gotthard, 1871]
"Zwitschert nicht vor meinem Fenster"
Die Braut, op. 41 no. 2 [J. P. Gotthard, 1871]
"Schön Liebchen komm' hernieder"
Geister der Nacht, op. 24 no. 4 [Senff, 1864]
"Ich kenne die Geister, die düstern"
Im Schlosshof, op. 41 no. 1 [J. P. Gotthard, 1871] same
Lebe wohl, op. 41 no. 3 [J. P. Gotthard, 1871]
"Nun ich dein Auge feucht gesehn"
Liebe im Schnee, op. 41 no. 6 [J. P. Gotthard, 1871]
"Sassen zwei Liebende kosend"
Rübezahl, op. 41 no. 4 [J. P. Gotthard, 1871]
"Es rauschen die Tannen und Föhren"
Heiberg, Johann Ludvig, 1791-1860.
Barcarole, op. 23 no. 4 [Peters, 1865]
"Süsse Nacht!"
Heine, Heinrich, 1797-1856.
Lehn' deine Wang' an meine Wang', op. 1 no. 1 [Leuckart, 1859] same
Nacht liegt auf den fremden Wegen (1857) [publisher unknown]

Hemans, Felicia Dorothea (Browne), 1793-1835.

Der letzte Wunsch, op. 53 no. 6 [Jul. Hainauer, 1876]
"Eil' in des Waldes Ruh' "

Mutter, O sing' mich zur Ruh, op. 53 no. 5 [Jul. Hainauer, 1876] same

Weit entfernt, op. 53 no. 4 [Jul. Hainauer, 1876] same

Herder, Johann Gottfried von, 1744-1803.

STIMMEN DER VÖLKER.

Darthula's Grabesgesang, op. 58 no. 2 [Jul. Hainauer, 1877]
"Mädchen von Kola, du schläfst"

Edward, op. 58 no. 3 [Jul. Hainauer, 1877] "Dein Schwert, wie ist's von Blut so rot"

Erlkönigs Tochter, op. 58 no. 1 [Jul. Hainauer, 1877]
"Herr Oluf reitet spät und weit"
Translated by Herder.

Lied der Desdemona, op. 58 no. 4 [Jul. Hainauer, 1877]
"An einem Baum, am Weidenbaum"
Subtitle: *aus "Les consolations des misères de ma vie."*

Hertz, Henrik, 1798-1870.

Engelgesang, op. 23 no. 3 [Peters, 1865]
"Dem Armen, dem niemals die Freude gelacht"

Mich treibt's hinaus in's lichte Frühlingsrauschen, op. 23 no. 1 [Peters, 1865] same

Hertz, Wilhelm, 1855-1902.

Fernsicht, op. 14 no. 2 [J. Rieter-Biedermann, 1864]
"Auf des Berges höchstem Scheitel"

Letzter Wunsch, op. 14 no. 1 [J. Rieter-Biedermann, 1864]
"Mein Schatz will Hochzeit halten"

Lied der verlassenen Liebe, op. 14 no. 6 [J. Rieter-Biedermann, 1864]
"Lieblos ist mein Lieb geworden, war mir treu doch manchen Tag"

Mein Engel hüte dein, op. 14 no. 4 [J. Rieter-Biedermann, 1864]
"Und willst du von mir scheiden, mein herzgeliebter Knab"

Mein Herz, op. 14 no. 3 [J. Rieter-Biedermann, 1864]
"Mein Herz ist ein stiller Tempel"

Sternbotschaft, op. 14 no. 5 [J. Rieter-Biedermann, 1864]
"Ich sass in finstrer Trauer, mir war das Herz so schwer"

Herwegh, George, 1817-1875.

Ob die Locken eine Glorie quellen, op. 5 no. 2 [Fritz Schuberth, 1861] same

Heyse, Paul Johann Ludwig von, 1830-1914.

Abschied, op. 22 no. 9 [Peters, 1864]
"Als wir Beiden mussten scheiden"

Durch die Ferne, durch die Nacht, op. 22 no. 11 [Peters, 1864]
"Hab Erbarmen, hab Erbarmen!"

Die Einsame, op. 22 no. 6 [Peters, 1864]
"Auf die Nacht in den Spinnstuben"

Geheimnis, op. 22 no. 12 [Peters, 1864]
"Lass uns leise bekennen"

Im Walde, op. 22 no. 4 [Peters, 1864]
"Waldesnacht, du wunderkühle"

Mädchenlied, op. 22 no. 8 [Peters, 1864]
"Drunten auf der Gassen stand ich"

Rosenzeit, op. 22 no. 1 [Peters, 1864]
"Nun stehn die Rosen in Blüthe"

Schlaf nur ein, op. 22 no. 10 [Peters, 1864] "Ach, was bin ich aufgewacht?"

Sonnenschein, op. 22 no. 2 [Peters, 1864]
"Mühlen still die Flügel drehn"

Über ein Stündlein [Ries & Erler, 1882]
"Dulde, gedulde dich fein!"

Ueber Nacht, op. 22 no. 7 [Peters, 1864]
"Dein Herzlein mild"

Unter den Zweigen in tiefer Nacht, op. 22 no. 3 [Peters, 1864] same

Vergangnes Glück [Ries & Erler, 1882]
"Einst warst du meiner Seele Hoffnungsstern"

MELEAGER.

Über die Welt, op. 22 no. 5 [Peters, 1864] same

SPANISCHES LIEDERBUCH (1852).

Spanisches Lied, op. 1 no. 4 [Leuckart, 1859] "In dem Schatten meiner Locken"

TOSCANISCHER RISPETTO.

Toskanischer Rispetto, op. 57 no. 3 [L. Hoffarth, 1878] "Mein Liebster singt am Haus im Mondenscheine"

Hoffmann von Fallersleben, August Heinrich, 1798-1874.

Lasst mich ruhen [Breitkopf & Härtel, **Liederkreis** no. 227, 1869?]

Kühne, Ferdinand Gustav, 1806-1888.

Was nennst du deine Liebe schwer und gross, op. 13 no. 6 [Senff, 1863] same

Kugler, Franz Theodor, 1808-1858.

Nachtgruss [Ries & Erler, 1882]
"Vor meinem Fenster dämmert das trübe Mondenlicht"

Lemcke, Karl von, 1831-1913.

Auf den Bergen, op. 61 no. 4 [Jul. Hainauer, 1880] same

JENSEN, ADOLF, 1837-1879 *(continued)*
Manuel del Rio, Don
SPANISCHES LIEDERBUCH: Cojo
jazmin y clavel.
 Cojo jazmin y clavel, op. 4 no. 3 [Fritz
  Schuberth, 1860]
  "Nelken wind' ich und Jasmin"
  Translated by Geibel.
Molbech, Christian Knud Frederik,
1821-1888.
 Frieden, op. 23 no. 2 [Peters, 1865]
  "Wass fasst dich an, O Tochter mein!"
Moore, Thomas, 1779-1852.
 Die Bowle fort! op. 50 no. 5 [Jul.
  Hainauer, 1876] same
 Es kommt eine Zeit, eine trübe Zeit! op.
  50 no. 2 [Jul. Hainauer, 1876] same
 Friede den Schlummerern! op. 50 no. 7
  [Jul. Hainauer, 1876] same
 Leis rudern hier (1864) [facsimile in
  Niggli *Adolf Jensen,* 1900, after
  p.108]
  "Leis rudern hier mein Gondolier!"
 Leis rudern hier, mein Gondolier! op. 50
  no. 4 [Jul. Hainauer, 1876] same
 Licht sie dein Traum! op. 50 no. 1 [Jul.
  Hainauer, 1876] same
 Wie manchmal, wenn des Mondes Strahl,
  op. 50 no. 6 [Jul. Hainauer, 1876]
  same
 WHEN THROUGH THE PIAZZETTA.
  Wenn durch die Piazzetta, op. 50 no. 3
  [Jul. Hainauer, 1876] same
Müller, Wilhelm, 1794-1827.
 Es hat so grün gesäuselt, op. 61 no. 3
  [Jul. Hainauer, 1880] same
Pfarrius, Gustav, 1800-1884.
 Sie war die Schönste von Allen, op. 1 no.
  3 [Leuckart, 1859]
  "Wohl war im Busch und Rasen"
Pushkin, Aleksandr Sergeevich, 1799-
1837.
 O sing, du Schöne, op. 39 no. 1 [J. P.
  Gotthard, 1871] same
 Ständchen, op. 39 no. 2 [J. P. Gotthard,
  1871] "Nächtlicher Duft"
Roquette, Otto, 1824-1896.
 Abschied, op. 35 no. 6 [L. Hoffarth,
  1870] "Nun ist mein' beste Zeit
  vorbei"
 An der Linden, op. 35 no. 4 [L. Hoffarth,
  1870]
  "So viel Laub an der Linden ist"
 Fröhliche Gesellen, op. 35 no. 1 [L.
  Hoffarth, 1870] "Hier im Kruge"
 Margreth am Thore, op. 35 no. 5 [L.
  Hoffarth, 1870]
  "Das beste Bier im ganzen Nest"

Morgens am Brunnen, op. 35 no. 2 [L.
 Hoffarth, 1870] "Er kam in der Frühe
 wie der Morgenwind"
Noch ist die blühende, goldene Zeit, op.
 55 no. 2 [Hermann Erler, 1875] same
O lass dich halten, gold'ne Stunde, op.
 35 no. 3 [L. Hoffarth, 1870] same
Perlenfischer, op. 61 no. 1 [Jul.
 Hainauer, 1880]
 "Du liebes Auge willst dich tauchen"
Unruhe, op. 13 no. 2 [Senff, 1863]
 "Bei den Bienenkörben im Garten"
Weisst du noch? op. 24 no. 5 [Senff,
 1864] same
Rückert, Friedrich, 1788-1866.
 Canzonette, op. 24 no. 2 [Senff, 1864]
  "Dort, wo ich bei ihr sass"
 LIEBESFRÜHLING.
  Da ich dich einmal gefunden, op. 13
  no. 1 [Senff, 1863] same
Scheffel, Joseph Victor von, 1826-
1886.
 Alt Heidelberg, du feine, op. 34 [J.
  Schuberth, 1867] same
 GAUDEAMUS.
  Altassyrisch, op. 40 no. 3 [L. Hoffarth,
  1870] "Im schwarzen Wallfisch zu
  Ascalon"
  Ausfahrt, op. 40 no. 1 [L. Hoffarth,
  1870] "Berggipfel erglühen"
  Die drei Dörfer, op. 40 no. 9 [L.
  Hoffarth, 1870]
  "Wer reit't mit zwanzig Knappen"
  Der Fünfundsechziger, op. 40 no. 8 [L.
  Hoffarth, 1870]
  "In luftiger Trinkkemenaten"
  Die Heimkehr, op. 40 no. 6 [L.
  Hoffarth, 1870] "Der Pfarrer von
  Assmannshausen sprach"
  Hildebrandlied, op. 40 no. 5 [L.
  Hoffarth, 1870] "Hildebrand und
  sein Sohn Hadubrand"
  Includes chorus.
  Lied fahrender Schüler, op. 40 no. 2
  [L. Hoffarth, 1870] "Pfarrherr, du
  kühler, öffne dein Thor"
  Die Malbronner Fuge, op. 40 no. 4 [L.
  Hoffarth, 1870]
  "Im Winterrefektorium zu
  Maulbronn in dem Kloster"
  Perkêo, op. 40 no. 7 [L. Hoffarth,
  1870] "Das war der Zwerg Perkêo
  im Heidelberger Schloss"
  Wer reit't mit sieben Knappen, op. 40
  no. 10 [L. Hoffarth, 1870] same
  Wer wankt zu Fusse, op. 40 no. 11 [L.
  Hoffarth, 1870] same

Der Willekumm, op. 40 no. 12 [L.
Hoffarth, 1870]
"Und als der Herr von Rodenstein"
Nos. 9-12 of opus 40 carry cycle
title "Lieder vom Rodenstein."
**Schiller, Johann Christoph Friedrich
von, 1759-1805.**
Thekla's Gesang, op. 23 no. 5 [Peters,
1865] "Der Eichwald brauset"
Scott, Sir Walter, bart., 1771-1832.
Klage der Grenzerwittwe, op. 52 no. 6
[Jul. Hainauer, 1875]
"Mein Liebster baut' ein Laube mir"
Das Mädchen von Isla, op. 52 no. 3 [Jul.
Hainauer, 1875]
"Mädchen von Isla, hoch vom Riff"
O sag' mir, wie dich frein, mein Lieb, op.
52 no. 5 [Jul. Hainauer, 1875]
"Steht meiner Dam Kühnheit an"
JOCK OF HAZELDEAN: Why weep ye
by the tide, ladie?
Jock von Hazeldean, op. 52 no. 1 [Jul.
Hainauer, 1875] "Sprich, Fraülein,
warum härmst du dich?"
LULLABY OF AN INFANT CHIEF: O
hush thee, my babie.
Wiegenlied, op. 52 no. 2 [Jul.
Hainauer, 1875] "Schlaf, Söhnchen!"
*MINSTRELSY OF THE SCOTISH
BORDER.*
Berthrams Grablied, op. 52 no. 4 [Jul.
Hainauer, 1875] "Sie schossen ihn
tot am Neunsteinberg"
Shelley, Percy Bysshe, 1792-1822.
An die Nacht, op. 61 no. 6 [Jul. Hainauer,
1880] "Göttin der Nacht"
Storm, Theodor, 1817-1888.
Loose [Ries & Erler, 1882] "Der einst er
seine junge sonnige Lieb' gebracht"
**Tennyson, Alfred Tennyson, 1st
baron, 1809-1892.**
Claribel, op. 53 no. 3 [Jul. Hainauer,
1876] "Wo Claribel gestorben"
Die Schwestern, op. 53 no. 1 [Jul.
Hainauer, 1876] "Wir waren zwei
Töchter aus einem Haus"
SWEET AND LOW.
Wiegenlied, op. 53 no. 2 [Jul.
Hainauer, 1876] "Süss und Sacht"
Träger, Albert, 1820-1912.
Als mich dein Blick beim Scheiden traf,
op. 9 no. 6 [Breitkopf & Härtel, 1863]
same
*An deinem Finger, dem weissen,
schlanken,* op. 13 no. 4 [Senff, 1863]
same

Ein Frühlingstraum, op. 9 no. 2
[Breitkopf & Härtel, 1863]
"Noch liegt der Winter"
Ihr Sternlein, op. 9 no. 5 [Breitkopf &
Härtel, 1863] same
Im Herbst, op. 9 no. 3 [Breitkopf &
Härtel, 1863]
"Vorbei der Rosen Prangen"
In Verborgenen, op. 9 no. 4 [Breitkopf &
Härtel, 1863]
"Die Welt weiss deinen Namen nicht"
Morgenständchen, op. 9 no. 8
[Breitkopf & Härtel, 1863] "Steh' auf
und öffne das Fenster schnell"
Paulinzelle, op. 9 no. 7 [Breitkopf &
Härtel, 1863]
"Der Nonne Gebete verhallten"
Wie Lenzeshauch, op. 9 no. 1
[Breitkopf & Härtel, 1863] same
Uhland, Ludwig, 1787-1862.
Der Schmied, op. 24 no. 6 [Senff, 1864]
"Ich hör' meinen Schatz"
Ulrich, Titus, 1813-1891.
Notturno, op. 13 no. 3 [Senff, 1863]
"Wir gingen einsam durch die
Gartenflur"
Unknown
*O heiss mich nicht vor deinem Antlitz
fliehn,* op. 5 no. 1
[Fritz Schuberth, 1861] same
Urban, Robert
Die Heimatglokken, op. 61 no. 5 [Jul.
Hainauer, 1880]
"Des Dorfes heimische Stille that
meinem trotzigen Sinne weh"
Valdivielso, Jose de, 1560?-1638.
SPANISCHES LIEDERBUCH.
Feridas teneis [Emil Sommermeyer,
1899]
**Vega Carpio, Lope Félix de, 1562-
1635.**
SPANISCHES LIEDERBUCH: Madre,
unos ojuelos vi.
Madre, unos ojuelos vi, op. 4 no. 2
[Fritz Schuberth, 1860]
"Mutter, ich hab' zwei Aeugelein"
Translated by Heyse.
Vicente, Gil, ca.1470-ca.1536.
SPANISCHES LIEDERBUCH: Si dormis,
doncella.
Und schläfst du, mein Mädchen, op. 21
no. 3
[J. Rieter-Biedermann, 1864] same
Translated by Geibel.
Jensen, Johannes Vilhelm, 1873-1950.
NIELSEN
Godnat
Husvild

Jenta see Vinje **GRIEG**

"J'entendais sa voix si touchante" *see Aimer* Méry **FRANCK**

"J'entends s'égrener ton rire" *see Star* Jean-Aubry **SCHMITT**

"Jenton' breier der Gutan' slaer" *see Veslemøy undrast* Garborg **GRIEG**

Jephtas see Byron *HEBREW MELODIES.* **SCHUMANN** *Die Tochter Jephtha's*

Jephta's daughter see Byron *HEBREW MELODIES.* **SCHUMANN** *Die Tochter Jephtha's*

Jephthas Tochter see Byron **LOEWE**

Jérôme see Gide *LA PORTE ETROITE.* **MILHAUD**

Jérôme et Alissa see Gide *LA PORTE ETROITE.* **MILHAUD**
    Three settings: Op. 9 no. 2, op. 9 no. 3, and op. 9 no. 5.

Jerusalem, my happy home see Anon. **THOMSON**

"Jérusalem nous est rendue" *see Hymne de Sion* Cohen, A. **MILHAUD**

Jerusalems Zerstörung durch Titus see Byron **LOEWE**

Jesenská, Ružena, 1863-1940. **MARTINŮ**
    Where have I been?
    Where was I?

Jestem i placze . . . see Kasprowicz, Jan *ŚWIETY BOZE.* **SZYMANOWSKI**

"Jestem! Jestem i placze" *see Jestem i placze . . .* Kasprowicz, Jan **SZYMANOWSKI**

"Jesu Christ's mild mother stood" *see The mild mother* Anon. **ROREM**

Jésus à la crêche see Unknown **GOUNOD**

Jesus als Kind see Unknown **LOEWE**

Jesus auf Golgatha see Sturm, C. **LOEWE**

"Jésus Christ s'habille en pauvre" *see La ballade de Jésus Christ* Anon. **VAUGHAN WILLIAMS**

Jésus de Nazareth see Porte, A. **GOUNOD**

Jesus ist mein Hirt see Hus **LOEWE**

Jesus mit seinen Jüngern auf dem Meere see Anon. **LOEWE**

Le Jet d'eau see Baudelaire *FLEURS DU MAL.* **DEBUSSY**

"J'étais encore au printemps de ma vie" *see Le pèlerin* Schiller **SAUGUET**

"J'étais seul près des flots" *see Extase* Hugo **WAGNER**

"J'étais toute petite" *see Mon histoire* Supervielle **MILHAUD**

"J'étais triste et pensif" *see Rencontre* Grandmougin **FAURÉ**

"J'étais un petit bois de France" *see Le petit bois* Supervielle **AURIC**

"Les jets d'eau dansent des sarabandes" *see Sarabande* Chalupt **ROUSSEL**

"Jetzt kommt der Frühling, der Himmel isch blau" *see Frühlingslied* Robert, F. **MENDELSSOHN-BARTHOLDY**

Jetzt rede du! see Meyer **SCHOECK**

"Jetzt steh' ich auf der höchsten Höh' " *see Vom Berge* Osterwald **FRANZ**

Jetzt und immer see Dehmel **REGER**

"Jetzt wird mein Elend voll" *see Pietà* Rilke **HINDEMITH**

Le jeu du camp fou see Unknown **JOLIVET**

"Jeune fille aux lèvres roses" *see Ta main* Guillot de Saix **HAHN**

La jeune fille de Budapest see Michaux **SAUGUET**

La jeune fille et la fauvette see Chauvinière, Edmond de **GOUNOD**

"Jeune homme de vingt ans" *see Bleuet* Apollinaire **POULENC**

Le jeune pâtre breton see Brizeux **BERLIOZ**

Le jeune paysan breton see Brizeux **BERLIOZ** *Le jeune pâtre breton*

"Une jeune pucelette, Pucelette grassouillette" *see Grasselette et maigrelette* Ronsard **SAINT-SAËNS**

"Une jeune sanguine" *see La jeune sanguine* Vilmorin **AURIC**

La jeune sanguine see Vilmorin **AURIC**

La jeune tarentine see Chénier **KOECHLIN**

Jeunesse see Anon. **MILHAUD**

Jeunesse see Vaillant-Couturier **HONEGGER**

Jewish song see Mei **RIMSKIĬ-KORSAKOV** *Evreĭskaia pesnia*

"J'habite avec toi seule un sommet de lumière" *see Première* Bengy-Puyvallée **AUBERT**

Jillian of Berry see Anon. **HESELTINE**

"Jillian of Berry she dwells on a hill" *see Jillian of Berry* Anon. **HESELTINE**

The jilted maiden see Grossmanová-Brodská **MARTINŮ**

Jimenez, Juan Ramón, 1881-1958. **MOMPOU**
    Llueve sobre el rio
    Pastoral
RODRIGO
    Pajaro del agua
    Verde, verderol

Jimmie's got a goil see Cummings **BLITZSTEIN**

"Jimmie's got a goil goil goil" *see Jimmie's got a goil* Cummings **BLITZSTEIN**

Jó Csönd herceg elött see Ady **SEIBER**
Jo et pressentia com la mar see Janès i
  Olivé **MOMPOU**
Jo joutuu ilta see Topelius **SIBELIUS**
  Det mörknar ute
Jo luovutko luotani see Lehtinen **KILPINEN**
Jo muistot taivaltani varjostaa see Lehtinen
  KILPINEN
Jo on joulu täällä see Topelius **SIBELIUS**
  Nu så kommer julen
"Jo pilvihin taivas peittyy" *see Syyslaulu*
  Lönnbohm **KILPINEN**
Jo tulenki see Kanteletar **KILPINEN**
"Jo za wodom, ty za wodom" *see Idom se*
  siuhaje, dołu, śpiewajecy Anon.
  SZYMANOWSKI
Jock von Hazeldean see Scott *JOCK OF*
  HAZELDEAN:
  Why weep ye by the tide, ladie? **JENSEN**
JOCK OF HAZELDEAN: Why weep ye by
  the tide, ladie? *see* Scott
  Jock von Hazeldean **JENSEN**
The jocund dance see Blake, William
  QUILTER
Johann Kepler see Mörike **SCHOECK**
Johann von Nepomuk see Anschütz **LOEWE**
Johanna Sebus see Goethe **SCHUBERT**
Johanna von Arc vor dem Scheiterhaufen see
  Dumas the elder **LISZT**
  Jeanne d'Arc au bûcher
Johanne see Drachmann **GRIEG**
"Johannes ging am hellen Bach" *see St.*
  Johannes und das Würmlein Chezy
  LOEWE
Johannes von der Ostee, pseud. *see* Falk,
  Johannes, 1768-1826.
Johanneswürmlein see Chezy **LOEWE** *St.*
  Johannes und das Würmlein
Johanus Bassus, Frater, 16th cent.
  IRELAND *A thanksgiving*
John Anderson see Burns **STRAUSS**
John Anderson, mein Lieb see Burns
  JENSEN
"John Anderson, mein Lieb" *see John*
  Anderson Burns **STRAUSS**
JOHN OF DAMASCUS. see Tolstoï
  Blagoslavlyayu vas, lesa **CHAĭKOVSKIĭ**
John Peel see Graves, John **THOMSON**
John, Saint, apostle
  MOMPOU *Cantar del alma*
"Johnnie cam' to our toun" *see Johnnie wi'*
  the tye Anon. **HESELTINE**
Johnnie wi' the tye see Anon. **HESELTINE**
Johnny see Auden **BRITTEN**

Johnson, Robert Underwood, 1853-
1937.
  IVES
  At sea
  The Housatonic at Stockbridge
  Luck and work
  Premonitions
Johs. Jørgensens Ungdommssang see
  Unknown **NIELSEN**
JOLIVET, ANDRÉ, 1905-1974.
  Boudry, R
    La vie est plate (1930-34) [unpubl.]
  Émié, Louis, 1900-1967.
    Amour (1944) [Heugel, 1949] "Ici et là,
      partout et même"
    Je veux te voir (1944) [Heugel, 1949]
      same
    Nous baignons dans une eau tranquille
      (1944) [Heugel, 1949] same
    Pour te parler (1944) [Heugel, 1949]
      same
    Tu dors (1944) [Heugel, 1949] same
  Germain-Colin Bucher, 1475-1545.
    Epître imprécatoire (1951) [Heugel,
      1954]
      "Après ma mort, je te feray la guerre"
  Huidobro, Vicente, 1893-1948.
    Voyage imaginaire (1930-34) [unpubl.]
  Le Père Le Moyne, 1602-1672.
    Sonnet à Madeleine Repentie (1951)
      [Heugel, 1954]
      "Ici, d'un repentir célèbre et glorieux"
  Lefilleul, G
    Aube (1951) [unpubl.]
    Combien de bras se sont ouverts (1951)
      [unpubl.]
    La maison du bonheur (1951) [unpubl.]
    Quiétide (1951) [unpubl.]
  Mellin de Saint-Gelais, 1487-1558.
    Sonnet à une lunatique (1951) [Heugel,
      1954] "Il n'est point tant de barques à
      Venise"
  Ribemont Dessaignes, Georges, 1884-
  1974.
    March funèbre (1930-34) [unpubl.]
  Unknown
    Le jeu du camp fou (1938) [Editions
      sociales internat., 1938]
The jolly shepherd see Anon. **HESELTINE**
Jone, Hildegard, 1891-1963.
  DIE FREUNDE.
    WEBERN
    Des Herzens Purpurvogel
    Sterne
    Wie bin ich Froh!

Jone, Hildegard, 1891-1963 *(continued)*
VIAE INVIAE.
 WEBERN
  Das dunkle Herz
  Es stürzt aus Höhen Frische
  Herr Jesus mein
Jones, Howard Mumford, 1892-1980.
 translator.
ROMANESQUE LYRIC.
 BARBER
  Church bell at night
  The crucifixion
Jones, William, pseud. *see* Hayes,
 Marvin, ca.1924-
Jonson, Ben, 1573?-1637.
 BLITZSTEIN *Song of the glove*
 QUILTER *By a fountainside*
 ROREM *Echo's song*
 UNDERWOODS.
  DELIUS *So white, so soft, so sweet is*
  she
"Jopa joutuikin suvi armaisin" *see Suvilaulu*
 Törmänen **KILPINEN**
Jord, i hvis favn see Richardt **NIELSEN**
Jordans Ufer see Byron **LOEWE**
Jørgensen, Johannes, 1866-1956.
 NIELSEN
  Bornehjaelpsdagens Sang
  Nu lyser Løv i Lunde
  Saenk kun dit Høved
Jos ma lauluille rupean see Kanteletar
 KILPINEN
Josef, lieber Josef mein see Geibel
 BRAHMS *Geistliches Wiegenlied*
Josephs, Laurence
 ROREM *Introduced to flame*
Josephson, Ernst Abraham, 1851-1906.
 KILPINEN
  Älvan och kardinalen
  Beständighet
  Blomman
  Fågelungarna
  Jag
  Japansk akvarell
  Kärlek
  Liten gosse
  Med strömmen
  Min grav
  Näcken
  Svanesång
  Till havet
  Vaggvisa
  Vid stranden
 SIBELIUS
  Älvan och snigeln
  En blomma stod vid vägen

Hertig Magnus
Jag är ett träd
Jubal
Kvarnhjulet
Maj
Necken
Vänskapens blomma
SVARTA ROSOR OCH GULA.
 DELIUS *Schwarze Rosen*
 SIBELIUS *Svarta rosor*
"Jospahan poloinen lienen" *see Mitäpä suren*
 sanoista Kanteletar **KILPINEN**
Jota see Anon. **FALLA**
Jouer du bugle see Jacob, M. **POULENC**
Les joues en feu see Radiguet **AURIC**
LES JOUES EN FEU, no. 1
 AURIC Radiguet *Les joues en feu*
LES JOUES EN FEU, no. 2
 AURIC Radiguet *Déjeuner de soleil*
LES JOUES EN FEU, no. 3
 AURIC Radiguet *Pelouse*
Joukahainen, Wilkku
 SIBELIUS *On hanget korkeat*
Joulukirkkoon see Jalkanen **KILPINEN**
Joulupukki kolkuttaa see Topelius
 SIBELIUS *Nu står jul vid snöig port*
Jounet, Albert, 1863-1923.
 CHAUSSON *Cantique à l'épouse*
Le jour see Banville **KOECHLIN**
Jour de chaleur aux bains de mer see Rohan
 THOMSON
"Un jour de fête au Paradis" *see La légende*
 du baiser Hardÿ de Périni **MASSENET**
Un jour de juin, que j'étais soucieux see
 Verlaine *LA BONNE CHANSON.*
 KOECHLIN
Jour de noces see Bordèse **MASSENET**
Jour de pluie see Docquois **SAINT-SAËNS**
"Un jour de printemps" *see Pastorale*
 Regnard **BIZET**
Le jour de tristesse see Richter **SAUGUET**
Le jour des prix see Scribe **GOUNOD**
"Un jour, menant ma chevrette" *see Chanson*
 de l'oiseleur Lockroy **DELIBES**
Le jour où le more see Tagore **SAUGUET**
"Le jour paraît à l'horizon" *see Aubade*
 Prévost, Gabriel **MASSENET**
"Le jour s'annonce à l'Orient" *see Pastorale*
 des cochons roses Rostand **CHABRIER**
"Le jour s'assombrit, lugubre et glacé" *see*
 Jour de pluie Docquois **SAINT-SAËNS**
Journal d'Alissa see Gide *LA PORTE*
 ETROITE. **MILHAUD**
THE JOURNAL OF KATHERINE
 MANSFIELD. see Mansfield
 My little Mother **DIAMOND**
 Souvent j'ai dit a mon mari **DIAMOND**

"La journée est plus dure que l'enfer" *see*
  Ardeur Claudel **MILHAUD**
Les journées d'Août see Chalupt **MILHAUD**
The journey see Blake, Ernest **IRELAND**
A journey see Glaze **ROREM**
Journey to the beloved see Unknown
  MARTINŮ *Cesta k milé*
The journeying boy see Hardy **BRITTEN**
  Midnight on the Great Western
"Jours passés, Ô jeunesse envolée" *see*
  Regrets! Silvestre **DELIBES**
LES JOURS SE SUIVENT, no. 1
  SAUGUET Baron *La tour prends garde*
LES JOURS SE SUIVENT, no. 2
  SAUGUET Baron *Lied*
LES JOURS SE SUIVENT, no. 3
  SAUGUET Baron *En attendant*
Joy, shipmate, joy! see Whitman *SONGS OF
  PARTING.* **VAUGHAN WILLIAMS**
Joyce, James, 1882-1941.
  CARTER *My love is in a light attire*
  GIDEON *She weeps over Rahoon*
  IRELAND *Tutto è sciolto*
  SZYMANOWSKI
    Gentle lady . . .
    Lean out of the window
    My dove, my beautiful one
    Strings in the earth
    Winds of May
  CHAMBER MUSIC.
    BARBER
      I hear an army
      Rain has fallen
      Sleep now
    ROREM *Dear heart*
    SZYMANOWSKI
      Rain has fallen
      Sleep now . . .
  FINNEGANS WAKE.
    BARBER *Nuvoletta*
  POMES PENYEACH.
    DIAMOND, ROUSSEL *A flower given
      to my daughter*
  *A PORTRAIT OF THE ARTIST AS A
    YOUNG MAN.*
    DIAMOND *Brigid's song*
  ULYSSES.
    BARBER *Solitary hotel*
"Joyeux et clair, le soleil luit" *see Les belles
  de nuit* Maquet, Thérèse **MASSENET**
Le joyeux ramoneur see Olivier, Pierre
  SAUGUET
"Joyós cassador, passa" *see Cançó del teuladí*
  Llorente **RODRIGO**
Jsem jako lípa košatá see Hálek **DVOŘÁK**
Juan Gris see Éluard **POULENC**

Juan Miró see Éluard **POULENC**
Jubal see Josephson, E. **SIBELIUS**
"Jubal sag en svana fly öfver vattnet högt mot
  sky" *see Jubal* Josephson, E.
  SIBELIUS
Juble, schöne junge Rose see Unknown
  SCHÖNBERG
Juchhe! see Reinick **BRAHMS**
"Judäa, hochgelobtes Land" *see Sehnsucht*
  Kannegiesser **WEBER**
Jünger des Weins I see Gamper **SCHOECK**
Jünger des Weins II see Gamper
  SCHOECK
Der Jüngling see Klopstock **GLUCK**
Der Jüngling am Bache see Schiller
  SCHUBERT
  Three settings: D. 30, D. 192, and D. 638.
Der Jüngling an der Quelle see Salis-
  Seewis **SCHUBERT**
Der Jüngling auf dem Hügel see
  Hüttenbrenner, Heinrich **SCHUBERT**
Der Jüngling in der Fremde see Reissig
  BEETHOVEN
Ein Jüngling liebt ein Mädchen see Heine
  SCHUMANN
Der Jüngling und der Tod see Spaun
  SCHUBERT
Der Jüngling und die Spröde see Gubitz
  WEBER
Jünglings Gebet see Rückert
  LIEBESFRÜHLING. **LOEWE**
Der Jünglings Liebe see Tieck **BRAHMS**
  Keinen hat es noch gereut
Jüngst, als ich über'n Friedhof ging see
  Ahlefeldt, Ottilie von **LASSEN**
Jüngst hört ich, welchen süssen lohn see
  Unknown **SPOHR**
"Jüngst lasest du ich merkt' es wohl heimlich
  in meinen Zügen" *see Wiedersehen*
  Wallner **WEBER**
"Jüngst sass ich am Grabe der Trauten allein"
  see Wiedersehen Wallner **WEBER**
"Jüngst träumte mir, ich sah auf lichten" *see
  Das war ich* Körner **SCHUBERT**
Die Jugend see Hölderlin **BRITTEN**
JUGEND. see Ritter
  Vom Küssen! **REGER**
"Jugend, dich hab' ich so lieb" *see Jugend
  und Alter* Hoffmann von Fallersleben
  LOEWE
Jugend und Alter see Hoffmann von
  Fallersleben **LOEWE**
Jugendflucht see Hesse **KILPINEN**
Jugendgedenken see Keller, G. **SCHOECK**
Jugendglück see Pohl **LISZT**
JUGENDLIEDER, no. 82
  BERG Mombert *Aus dem "Glühenden"*

COMPOSER Poet *Title* "First Line"

Le juif errant see Béranger *LE JUIF
ERRANT*: Chrétien, au voyageur souffrant.
GOUNOD, LISZT
LE JUIF ERRANT: Chrétien, au voyageur
souffrant. *see* Béranger
Le juif errant **GOUNOD, LISZT**
Juin see Leconte de Lisle **KOECHLIN**
Julens Vuggesang see Langsted **GRIEG**
Julesang see Falck, Mogens **NIELSEN**
Julesang see Wiberg, Ohs **NIELSEN**
Jule-Sne see Drachmann **GRIEG**
Julia's hair see Herrick **QUILTER**
Julius an Theone see Matthisson
SCHUBERT
Les jumeaux de la nuit see Obaldia
SAUGUET
"Jump through the hedge, lass!" *see
The soldier's return* Warner **IRELAND**
June see Chesson **QUILTER**
Jung Hexenlied see Bierbaum
DER JUNGEN HEXE LIED. **STRAUSS**
"Jung stritt ich einst um Accons Schloss" *see
Sankt Mariens Ritter* Giesebrecht
LOEWE
"Jung vermähle mich, O Mutter!" *see
Der Knabe an die Mutter* Anon. **REGER**
"Jung Volker ist der Räuberhauptmann" *see
Volker spielt auf!* Mörike **FRANZ**
Jung Volkers Lied see Mörike **SCHUMANN**
Jung, Walter
LASSEN *Grüssen*
Die junge Birke see Moe **GRIEG** *Ungbirken*
Junge Ehe see Ubell **REGER**
Der junge Herr und das Mädchen see
Mickiewicz **LOEWE**
Der junge Jäger see Goethe **ZELTER**
"Der junge König Heinrich schlief" *see Kaiser
Heinrich's Waffenweihe* Schwab
LOEWE
Der junge König und sein Gemahl see Kugler
LOEWE
Junge Lieder I see Schumann, F. **BRAHMS**
Junge Lieder II see Schumann, F.
BRAHMS

Die junge Nonne see Craigher **SCHUBERT**
Der junge Prinz I see Tagore *OGRODNIK.*
SZYMANOWSKI
Der junge Prinz II see Tagore *OGRODNIK.*
SZYMANOWSKI
Der junge Tag erwacht see Osterwald
FRANZ
DER JUNGEN HEXE LIED. see Bierbaum
Jung Hexenlied **STRAUSS**
"Ein junges Birklein am Ufer" *see Die junge
Birke* Moe **GRIEG**
"Ein junges Glöcklein klagte" *see Glöckleins
Klage* Spitteler **SCHOECK**
Jungfer Ssawischna see Musorgskiĭ
MUSORGSKIĭ *Svetik Savishna*
Jungfräulein Annika see Rückert **LOEWE**
"Jungfräulein Annika sass an dem
Brückenrande" *see Jungfräulein Annika*
Rückert **LOEWE**
Die Jungfrau see Meyer **SCHOECK**
Jungfrau Lorenz see Kugler **LOEWE**
Die Jungfrau und der Tod see Kugler
LOEWE
Der Junggesell see Pfizer **LOEWE**
Der Junggesell und der Mühlbach see
Goethe **ZELTER**
Junggesellenschwur see Des Knaben
Wunderhorn **STRAUSS**
Jupiter has seven moons see Bernstein
BERNSTEIN
"Jusqu'à ta bouche, j'ai levé" *see Coupe
d'ivresse* Simoni, H. Ernest **MASSENET**
"Just a span and half a span from head to
heel" *see A midget* De La Mare
CHANLER
Just like the sky your gaze is beaming see
Lermontov **RIMSKIĭ-KORSAKOV**
Kak nebesa, tvoĭ vzor blistaet
"Just think of little heathen boys!" *see Happy
heathen* Carpenter, Rue **CARPENTER**
JYLLAND. see Aakjaer
Der dukker af Disen min Faedrenejord
NIELSEN

K

K detiam *see* Khomyakov
  RACHMANINOFF *To the children*
K moeĭ pesne *see* Heine **RIMSKIĭ-KORSAKOV**
K. R., pseud. *see* Konstantin Konstantinovich, Grand Duke of Russia, 1858-1915.
"K T V = er, seht die Farben" *see* Kantonsschul-Turnverein-Kantus Schoeck **SCHOECK**
" 'k Zit voor mijn venster" *see* Meiliedje Bruyn, Bertha de **PIJPER**
Kaalund, Hans Vilhelm, 1818-1885.
  NIELSEN *Pa det jaevne, pa det jaevne*
Kaby znala ia *see* Tolstoĭ **CHAĭKOVSKIĭ**
Kaddisch *see* Anon. **RAVEL**
Der Käfer *see* Musorgskiĭ **MUSORGSKIĭ** Zhuk
"Käki kukkua käkesi" *see* Ikuinen suru Kanteletar **KILPINEN**
"Käki kukkui kuusikossa" *see* Väjä ilo emottomalle käestä Kanteletar **KILPINEN**
"Käki kukkuu, kultarinta" *see* Käköä kuullessa Larin-Kyösti **KILPINEN**
Käköä kuullessa *see* Larin-Kyösti **KILPINEN**
Kämpfte er nicht genug? *see* Kafka **KRENEK**
Kären *see* Unknown **IVES**
Kärlek *see* Josephson, E. **KILPINEN**
Das Käuzlein *see* Des Knaben Wunderhorn **SCHUMANN**
  Two settings: Op. 79 no. 10 and a 2nd without number.
Kafiristan
  COPLAND *Pastorale*
Kafka, Franz, 1883-1924.
  KRENEK
    Ach, was wird uns hier bereitet?
    Du kannst dich zurückhalten . . .
    Kämpfte er nicht genug?
    Noch spielen die Jaghunde im Hof
    Nur ein Wort
Kahl reckt der Baum *see* George DER SIEBENTE RING. **WEBERN**
Kahlert, Karl August Timothens, 1807-1864.
  LOEWE *Sankt Helena*
Kahn, Gustave, 1859-1936.
  LOEFFLER
    Boléro triste
    Je te vis, je t'aimais

LES PALAIS NOMADES: Intermède IV.
  LOEFFLER *Timbres oubliés*
LES PALAIS NOMADES: Intermède IX.
  LOEFFLER *Les paons*
LES PALAIS NOMADES: Intermède XIV.
  LOEFFLER *Adieu pour jamais*
LES PALAIS NOMADES: Lied IV.
  LOEFFLER *Les soirs d'automne*
Kahnlied *see* Unknown **LOEWE**
Kaikissa yksin *see* Kanteletar **KILPINEN**
Kaiser Heinrich's Waffenweihe *see* Schwab **LOEWE**
Kaiser Karl V. in Wittenberg *see* Hohlfeld HARFENKLÄNGEN: Kaiser Karl V. an Luthers Grabe. **LOEWE**
KAISER OTTO I. *see* Mühler Kaiser Ott's Weihnachtsfeier **LOEWE**
Kaiser Ott's Weihnachtsfeier *see* Mühler KAISER OTTO I. **LOEWE**
Die Kaiserjagd im Wienerwald *see* Vogl **LOEWE**
Kaiutar *see* Larin-Kyösti **SIBELIUS**
"Kaiutar, korea neito astui illalla ahoa" *see* Kaiutar Larin-Kyösti **SIBELIUS**
Kak griby na voĭnu sobirlis' *see* Unknown **STRAVINSKIĭ** *How the mushrooms went to war*
"Kak khorosho bylo vderevne!" *see* Gadkiĭ utenok" Andersen **PROKOFIEV**
"Kak loshel" ias" kazakami" *see* Korol'ki Kondratowicz **CHAĭKOVSKIĭ**
Kak mne bol'no *see* Einerling **RACHMANINOFF** *How painful for me*
"Kak moĭ sadik svezh i zelen!" *see* Moĭ sadik Pleshcheyev **CHAĭKOVSKIĭ**
Kak" nad" goriacheiu zoloĭ *see* Tiutchev **CHAĭKOVSKIĭ**
Kak naladidi: Durak *see* Mei PESNYA. **BALAKIREV, CHAĭKOVSKIĭ**
Kak nebesa, tvoĭ vzor blistaet *see* Lermontov **RIMSKIĭ-KORSAKOV**
Kak tolko wostok *see* Davidov, Dmitri **SZYMANOWSKI**
"Kak u duniushki, u golubushki" *see* Duniushka Anon. **PROKOFIEV**
"Kak za lesikom, za lesochkom" *see* Za lesochkom Anon. **PROKOFIEV**
Kakoe schast'e *see* Shenshin **RACHMANINOFF** *What happiness*
Kaks' oli meitä kaunokaista *see* Kanteletar **KILPINEN**
Kalbeck, Max, 1850-1921.
  RUBINSTEIN *Der einsame See* NÄCHTE.
  BRAHMS *Nachtwandler*

Kalchberg, Johann Nepomuk von, 1765-
1827.
   SCHUBERT *Die Macht der Liebe*
Kalhus
   MARTINŮ *Song of Hanička*
Kalinowe dwory see Tuwim
   SZYMANOWSKI
Kalistrat see Nekrasov **MUSORGSKIĭ**
   Kalistratushka
Kalistratushka see Nekrasov **MUSORGSKIĭ**
Kallistrat see Nekrasov **MUSORGSKIĭ**
   Kalistratushka
Kallman, Chester Simon, 1921-1975,
translator.
   BARBER *St. Ita's vision*
Kalt und schneidend see Lingg **PFITZNER**
"Kalter Regen peitscht die kahle Flur" *see*
   Wanderlied im Herbst Krenek **KRENEK**
"Kam ein Wanderer" *see Romanze*
   Mahlmann **ZELTER**
Kamhi, Victoria, 1905-1997.
   RODRIGO
      Barcarola
      Cancion del cucu
      Copillas de Belen
      La espera
Kaminský, Bohdan, 1859-1929.
   MARTINŮ *Pastel*
Kampaspe see Schlegel **ZELTER**
Der Kampf see Schiller **SCHUBERT**
Der Kampf mit dem Drachen see Schiller
   ZELTER
"Kampfmüd und sonnverbrannt" *see Biterolf*
   (Im Lager von Akkon 1190) Scheffel
   WOLF
"Kan latsipor" *see The nest* Bialik **GIDEON**
Kanareyka see Mei **CHAĭKOVSKIĭ**
"Kangastuksina katoovat minun mieleni
   unelmat" *see Ikuinen kevät* Lönnbohm
   KILPINEN
"Kann auch ein Mensch des andern auf der
   Erde ganz" *see Neue Liebe* Mörike **WOLF**
Kannegiesser, Karl Ludwig, 1781-1861.
   WEBER
      Elfenlied
      Sehnsucht
"Kanonen donnern, es blitzt das Tal" *see*
   Heimatliebe Claus, Nicolo **LASSEN**
Kanteletar
   KILPINEN
      Aina laulan
      Anna Kiesus antajalle
      Anna Maata Maariainen
      Armas arkussa ajavi
      Armottoman osa
      Ei minusta lienekänä

Ei runo rahatta laula
Ei sula syän suruinen
Erotus mielillä
Ikävä omia maita
Ikuinen suru
Jo tulenki
Jos ma lauluille rupean
Kaikissa yksin
Kaks' oli meitä kaunokaista
Kiitos emännästä
Köyhän lapset
Kukkalatva kuusi
Kummaistako kuuleminen
Kun ma kerran
Kun mun kultani tulisi
Kuti, kuti, kultaseni
Kuusen juuret kuivettuvat
Laulan ilman lainehilta
Maassa marjani makaavi
Makaaja onni
Mikäs on poikana eleä
Miksi en väsyisi
Millä maksan maammon maion
Missä armahani
Mitä tuosta, jos mä laulan
Mitäpä suren sanoista
Mont' on mulla morsianta
Muinainen käkeni
Muut kuuli kirkonkellon
Niin on meitä piikasia
Noin sanoi minun emoni
Nyt on kaikki kallistunna
Ohoh kullaista kotia
Oi Ukko ylinen herra
Oisi mulla vallan miekka
Omat on virret oppimani
On kumpiaki
Onpa tietty tietyssäni
Otettiin minusta outo
Pah' on orjana eleä
Paimenlaulu
Paista päivänen Jumala
Parempi syntymättä
Pimeä isoton pirtti
Saisinko käeltä kielen
Sanoissa kuluva
Siitä sinne tie menevi
Silloin laulan
Soitapas
Sopivaisia
Soria sotahan kuolla
Tanssi
Tule meille Tuomas kulta
Tule tänne
Tuuti, tuuti tummaistani
Tuutulaulu

COMPOSER Poet *Title* "First Line"

KANTELETAR-LAULUJA LIEDER, no. 44
  KILPINEN Kanteletar *Kuti, kuti,
  kultaseni*
KANTELETAR-LAULUJA LIEDER, no. 45
  KILPINEN Kanteletar *Mont' on mulla
  morsianta*
KANTELETAR-LAULUJA LIEDER, no. 46
  KILPINEN Kanteletar *Voi minua
  mieskulua*
KANTELETAR-LAULUJA LIEDER, no. 47
  KILPINEN Kanteletar *Makaaja onni*
KANTELETAR-LAULUJA LIEDER, no. 48
  KILPINEN Kanteletar *Laulan ilman
  lainehilta*
KANTELETAR-LAULUJA LIEDER, no. 49
  KILPINEN Kanteletar *Kaks' oli meitä
  kaunokaista*
KANTELETAR-LAULUJA LIEDER, no. 50
  KILPINEN Kanteletar *Saisinko käeltä
  kielen*
KANTELETAR-LAULUJA LIEDER, no. 51
  KILPINEN Kanteletar *Tuuti, tuuti
  tummaistani*
KANTELETAR-LAULUJA LIEDER, no. 52
  KILPINEN Kanteletar *Väjä ilo
  emottomalle käestä*
KANTELETAR-LAULUJA LIEDER, no. 53
  KILPINEN Kanteletar *Kuusen juuret
  kuivettuvat*
KANTELETAR-LAULUJA LIEDER, no. 54
  KILPINEN Kanteletar *Pah' on orjana
  eleä*
KANTELETAR-LAULUJA LIEDER, no. 55
  KILPINEN Kanteletar *Soria sotahan
  kuolla*
KANTELETAR-LAULUJA LIEDER, no. 56
  KILPINEN Kanteletar *Oi Ukko ylinen
  herra*
KANTELETAR-LAULUJA LIEDER, no. 57
  KILPINEN Kanteletar *Armas arkussa
  ajavi*
KANTELETAR-LAULUJA LIEDER, no. 58
  KILPINEN Kanteletar *Pimeä isoton pirtti*
KANTELETAR-LAULUJA LIEDER, no. 59
  KILPINEN Kanteletar *Sanoissa kuluva*
KANTELETAR-LAULUJA LIEDER, no. 60
  KILPINEN Kanteletar *Ikuinen suru*
KANTELETAR-LAULUJA LIEDER, no. 61
  KILPINEN Kanteletar *Omat on virret
  oppimani*
KANTELETAR-LAULUJA LIEDER, no. 62
  KILPINEN Kanteletar *Kiitos emännästä*
KANTELETAR-LAULUJA LIEDER, no. 63
  KILPINEN Kanteletar *Miksi en väsyisi*
KANTELETAR-LAULUJA LIEDER, no. 64
  KILPINEN Kanteletar *Siitä sinne tie
  menevi*

Kantonsschul-Turnverein-Kantus see
  Schoeck **SCHOECK**
Kanzonette see Goethe **LOEWE**
Kao, Shih, 707?-765.
  GRIFFES *Impressions of a traveler*
Die Kapelle see Uhland **SCHOECK**
Kapitulation see Jacob, T. **LOEWE**
Kapper, Siegfried, 1821-1879.
  BRAHMS
    Ade! (Nach dem Böhmischen)
    Das Mädchen
    Mädchenlied
    Vorschneller Schwur
  FRANZ *Abschied*
  DIE GESÄNGE DER SERBEN.
    BRAHMS *Mädchenfluch,* Nach dem
    Serbischen
Karadžić, Vuk Stefanović, 1787-1864.
  CHAĬKOVSKIĬ *Soloveĭ*
Kari glazki see Anon. **PROKOFIEV**
Karl der Grosse und Wittekind see Vogl
  WITEKIND. **LOEWE**
Karlfeldt, Erik Axel, 1864-1931.
  SIBELIUS *Längtan heter min arvedel*
Karlopago, pseud. *see* Ziegler, Karl, 1812-
  1877.
Die Kartenlegerin see Béranger *LES
  CARTES, OU L'HOROSCOPE.*
  SCHUMANN
Kartscher, Moritz, ca.1793-1834.
  SPOHR *Der erste Kuss*
Karwoche see Mörike **WOLF**
Kasprowicz, Jan, 1860-1926.
  MOJA PIEŚŃ WIECZORNA.
    SZYMANOWSKI *Blogoslawiona niech
    bedzie ta chwila*
  ŚWIETY BOZE.
    SZYMANOWSKI
      Jestem i placze . . .
      Świety Boze
"Kastagnetten lustig schwingen" *see*
  Die Tänzerin Unknown **LASSEN**
Kastropp, Gustav, 1844-1925.
  LASSEN *Trennung*
"Kasvoi kummulla kuusi tuores" *see Kuusi ja
  lintunen* Lönnbohm **KILPINEN**
Katchikatchi les étoiles see Messiaen
  MESSIAEN
Der Kater see Iłłakowiczówna
  SZYMANOWSKI *Kot*
Kater Murr see Musorgskiĭ **MUSORGSKIĬ**
  Kot matros
Katerina see Anon. **PROKOFIEV**
Katso yli kedon kukkain see Larin-Kyösti
  KILPINEN
Die Katzenkönigin see Chamisso
  KATZENNATUR. **LOEWE**

COMPOSER   Poet   *Title*   "First Line"

KATZENNATUR. see Chamisso
  Die Katzenkönigin **LOEWE**
Kaufmann, Alexander, 1817-1893.
  PFITZNER *Verrat*
Kaufmann, Johann Philipp, 1802-1846.
  LISZT *Die tote Nachtigall*
"Kaum an dem blaueren Himmel erblickt'
  ich" *see Epigramm* Goethe **SCHOECK**
"Kaum sind die ersten Blüten da" *see*
  Die Bienen Kiesekamo **REGER**
Kaupungilla sataa see Koskenniemi
  KILPINEN
Kaupunkimatka see Lönnbohm **KILPINEN**
Kde jsem to byla? see Jesenská **MARTINŮ**
  Where have I been?
Kde jsem to byla? see Jesenská **MARTINŮ**
  Where was I?
Kdybys, milé děvče, sedalo na truno see
  Heyduk **DVOŘÁK**
Kdysi see Grossmanová-Brodská
  MARTINŮ *Once upon a time*
Když bůh byl nejvíc rozkochán see Hálek
  DVOŘÁK
Když jsem se díval do nebe see Hálek
  DVOŘÁK
Když mne stará matka see Heyduk
  DVOŘÁK
Když tě vidim see Anon. **DVOŘÁK**
Keats, John, 1795-1821.
  DIAMOND *Chatterton*
  HINDEMITH *La belle dame sans merci*
  IVES *Like a sick eagle*
  QUILTER *Where be you going*
"The keen stars were twinkling" *see Music*
  and moonlight Shelley **QUILTER**
"The keen stars were twinkling" *see To Jane*
  Shelley **ROREM**
Keep that school girl complexion see
  Koechlin **KOECHLIN** *Gardez ce teint de*
  jeune fille
KEEPSAKE, no. 1
  MALIPIERO Jean-Aubry *Light*
KEEPSAKE, no. 2
  MALIPIERO Jean-Aubry *Song*
KEEPSAKE, no. 3
  MALIPIERO Jean-Aubry *Stream*
KEHR EIN BEI MIR. see Rückert
  Du bist die Ruh **SCHUBERT**
"Kehr' ich zum heimischen Rhein" *see*
  Gedenken Cornelius **CORNELIUS**
"Kehre nicht in diesem Kreise" *see Sorge*
  Goethe **SCHOECK**
Kehtolaulu see Koskenniemi **KILPINEN**
Keim', holde Blume see Bryan **BENNETT**
  Dawn, gentle flower
"Kein Auge hat Dein Angesicht geschaut" *see*
  An Gott Hohlfeld **SCHUBERT**

"Kein' bess're Lust in dieser Zeit" *see*
  Jägerlied Uhland **GRIEG**
Kein entrinnen see Anon. **DVOŘÁK** *Lásce*
  neujdeš
Kein Haus, keine Heimat see Münch-
  Bellinghausen **BRAHMS**
"Kein Meister fällt vom Himmel" *see*
  Gesellenlied Reinick **WOLF**
"Kein Pfad mehr" *see Der Wanderer*
  Nietzsche **DELIUS**
"Kein Rosenschimmerleuchtet" *see*
  Todtenopfer Matthisson **SCHUBERT**
"Kein Schlaf noch kühlt das Auge mir" *see*
  In der Frühe Mörike **REGER, WOLF**
"Keine Blumen blühn" *see Winterlied* Hölty
  SCHUBERT
Keine Frühlingsluft see Kol'tsov
  RUBINSTEIN
Keine gleicht von allen Schönen see Byron
  WOLF
"Keine Klage soll erschallen" *see*
  Abschiedsgesang an Wiens Bürger
  Friedelberg **BEETHOVEN**
"Keine Lust ohn' treues Lieben!" *see Triolett*
  Förster, K. **WEBER**
Keine Rast see Hesse **SCHOECK**
Keine Rettung see Mörike **SCHOECK**
"Keine Stimme hör' ich schallen" *see Um*
  Mitternacht Schulze **SCHUBERT**
Keinen hat es noch gereut see Tieck
  WUNDERSCHÖNE
  LIEBESGESCHICHTE . . . **BRAHMS**
"Keinen Reimer wird man finden" *see Unmut*
  Goethe **SCHOECK**
"Keinen Vater, der das Kinn mir hebt" *see*
  Der Narr Jacobowski **REGER**
Keller, Gottfried, 1819-1890.
  BARBER *Now have I fed and eaten up the*
    rose
  BRAHMS
    Abendregen
    Salome
    Therese
  HINDEMITH *Das Köhlerweib*
  PFITZNER
    Du milchjunger Knabe
    Ich fürcht' nit Gespenster
    Rös'chen biss den Apfel an
    Singt mein Schatz wie ein Fink
    Tretet ein, hoher Krieger
    Wandl' ich in dem Morgentau
    Wie glänzt der helle Mond
  SCHOECK
    Abendlied
    Abendlied an die Natur
    An das Herz

COMPOSER Poet *Title* "First Line"

Keller, Gottfried, 1819-1890 *(continued)*
  SCHOECK *(continued)*
    Aus den Waldliedern I
    Aus den Waldliedern II
    Aus: Ein Tagewerk I
    Aus: Ein Tagewerk II
    Den Zweifellosen I
    Den Zweifellosen II
    Die Entschwundene
    Fahrewohl
    Flack're ew'ges Licht im Tal
    Frühgesicht
    Frühlingsglaube
    In der Trauer
    Jugendgedenken
    Schifferliedchen
    Siehst du den Stern
    Sonnenuntergang
    Stille der Nacht
    Stilleben
    Das Tal
    Tod und Dichter
    Trost der Kreatur
    Trübes Wetter
    Uhruhe der Nacht
    Unter Sternen
    Wie wähnten lange recht zu leben
    Die Zeit geht nicht
  SCHÖNBERG
    Die Aufgeregten
    Geübtes Herz
    Ghasel
  WOLF
    Du milchjunger Knabe
    Das Köhlerweib ist trunken
    Singt mein Schatz wie ein Fink
    Tretet ein, hoher Krieger
    Wandl' ich in dem Morgentau
    Wie glänzt der helle Mond
  ALTE WEISEN.
    PFITZNER, SCHOECK *Mir glänzen die Augen*
Ken, Thomas, Bishop of Bath and Wells, 1637-1711.
  GOUNOD *Glory to Thee my God*
Kenner, Josef, 1794-1868.
  SCHUBERT
    Ballade
    Grablied
    Der Liedler
Kennst du das auch? see Hesse **SCHOECK**
Kennst du das Land? see Goethe *WILHELM MEISTER.* Mignon's song: Kennst du das Land?
  CHAĬKOVSKIĬ *Pesnya Min'ony*
  GOUNOD *Mignon*
  SCHUMANN, ZELTER *Kennst du das Land?*

"Kennst du das Land" *see Mignon* Goethe
  BEETHOVEN, BERG, JENSEN, SCHUBERT, SCHUMANN
"Kennst du das Land" *see Mignon IV* Goethe
  WOLF
"Kennst du das Land" *see Mignons Lied*
  Goethe **LISZT, SPOHR**
"Kennst du die Blume" *see Wasserrose* Dahn
  STRAUSS
"Kennst du nicht das Gluth verlangen" *see Geständniss* Devrient, Eduard
  MENDELSSOHN-BARTHOLDY
Kerdyk, René
  HONEGGER
    Chanson de la route
    Le naturaliste
    On est heureux
  SCHMITT *Octroi*
Le Kérioklépte see Theocritus **ROUSSEL**
KERKER UND KRONE. see Zedlitz
  Lied **SPOHR**
Kerner, Justinus, 1786-1862.
  SCHUMANN
    Alte Laute
    An Anna I
    An Anna II
    Aus das Trinkglas eines verstorbenen Freundes
    Erstes Grün
    Frage
    Gesanges Erwachen
    Im Herbste
    Kurzes Erwachen
    Lust der Sturmnacht
    Sängers Trost
    Sehnsucht nach der Waldgegend
    Stille Liebe
    Stille Thränen
    Stirb, Lieb' und Freud!
    Trost im Gesang
    Wanderlust
    Wanderung
    Wer machte dich so krank?
  SPOHR *Die Himmelsbraut*
  STRAUSS *Alphorn*
  WOLF *Zur Ruh, zur Ruh!*
KEROB-SHAL, no. 1
  SCHMITT Kerdyk, René *Octroi*
KEROB-SHAL, no. 2
  SCHMITT Jean-Aubry *Star*
KEROB-SHAL, no. 3
  SCHMITT Chalupt *Vendredi XIII*
Kerr, Alfred, 1867-1948.
  STRAUSS
    Drei Masken sah ich
    Einst kam der Bock

Es liebt einst ein Hase
Es war einmal ein Bock
Es war mal eine Wanze
Der Händler und die Maher
Hast du ein Tongedicht
Die Künstler sind die Schöpfer
O, lieber Künstler
O Schröpferschwarm
Unser Feind ist, grosser Gott
Von Händlern wird die Kunst bedroht
Kerran see Jalkanen **KILPINEN**
"Kerran lienen sun lasna ma nähnyt" *see*
    Elegia kaunneudelle Koskenniemi
    KILPINEN
Die Kerze see Matthisson **WEBER**
Kesäisenä päivänä see Jalkanen **KILPINEN**
Kesäyö see Koskenniemi **KILPINEN**
Kesäyössä see Koskenniemi **KILPINEN**
Kessel, Joseph, 1898-1979.
    HONEGGER *La chanson de l'Escadrille*
Kevät keralla see Koskenniemi **KILPINEN**
"Kevät keralla paiväin kuulakkain" *see Kevät*
    keralla Koskenniemi **KILPINEN**
Kevät on mennyt see Jalkanen **KILPINEN**
Kevätlaulu see Lehtinen **KILPINEN**
Kevättä see Lamberg **KILPINEN**
Kéž duch muj sám . . . see Kleinschrod
    DVOŘÁK
"Kéž sám a sám duch muj" *see Kéž duch muj*
    sám . . . Kleinschrod **DVOŘÁK**
Khaki Sammy see Carpenter, John
    CARPENTER
"Khbdit spes' naduvaiuchis' " *see Spes'*
    Tolstoĭ **BORODIN**
"Kherya pou dhen idhen ilyos" *see Tripatos*
    Anon. **RAVEL**
"Khodit Spes', nadyvaiuchis' " *see Spes'*
    Tolstoĭ **MUSORGSKIĭ**
Khomiakov *see* Khomyakov, Aleksyeĭ
    Stepanovich, 1804-1860.
Khomyakov, Aleksyeĭ Stepanovich,
    1804-1860.
    BALAKIREV
        Bezzvezdnaya polnoch'
        Nachstück
        Sem' noyabrya
        Spi!
        Zarya
    CHAĭKOVSKIĭ
        Podvig
        Vcherashniaia noch'
    RACHMANINOFF
        The raising of Lazarus
        To the children
"Khorosho vam, detki" *see Zimniĭ vecher*
    Pleshcheyev **CHAĭKOVSKIĭ**

Khotel by v edinoe slovo see Heine
    DIE HEIMKEHR. **CHAĭKOVSKIĭ**
"Khotel oy v edinoe slovo ia slit' " *see*
    Zhelanie Heine **MUSORGSKIĭ**
Khristos voskres see Merezhkovski
    RACHMANINOFF *Christ is risen*
Kianto, Ilmari, 1874-1970.
    SIBELIUS *Lastu lainehilla*
Kiddenes Dans see Garborg *HAUGTUSSA.*
    GRIEG *Killingdans*
Kiesekamo, Hedwig, 1846-1921.
    REGER
        An den Frühlingsregen
        Die Bienen
        Das Brüderchen
        Das Kindes Gebet
        Kindeslächeln
        Der Postillon
        Das Schwesterchen
Kiitos emännästä see Kanteletar **KILPINEN**
Killingdans see Garborg *HAUGTUSSA.*
    GRIEG
KILPINEN, YRJÖ, 1892-1959.
    Bergman, Bo Hjalmar, 1869-1967.
        Adagio, op. 31 no. 1 [W. Hansen, 1924]
            "Vattnet rörs och vinden spelar"
        Du och jag, op. 30 no. 5 [W. Hansen,
            1924] "Det var en gammal, gammal
            man"
        Hjärtat, op. 31 no. 5 [W. Hansen, 1924]
            "Hjärtat skall gro av drömmar"
        Klockan, op. 30 no. 1 [W. Hansen, 1924]
            "Jag läser om klockan"
        Lillebarn, op. 30 no. 4 [W. Hansen,
            1924] "Lillebarn lilla"
        Lyss till det djupa och stora, op. 32 no. 1
            [W. Hansen, 1924] same
        Melodi, op. 30 no. 3 [W. Hansen, 1924]
            "Bara du går över markerna"
        Den sista stjärnan, op. 31 no. 4 [W.
            Hansen, 1924] "Skyarna sakta"
        Skogen spelar. Älven rinner, op. 32 no. 2
            [W. Hansen, 1924] same
        En sommarafton, op. 31 no. 2 [W.
            Hansen, 1924]
            "Min lilla älskade så vit"
        Stjärnöga, op. 30 no. 2 [W. Hansen,
            1924] "Stjärnöga, du som jag mött"
        Stormen kör i fjällen, op. 32 no. 3 [W.
            Hansen, 1924] same
        Under vintergatan, op. 31 no. 3 [W.
            Hansen, 1924] "Högt i det höga slår"
    Blomberg, Erik Axel, 1894-1965.
        Äppelträd och päronträd, op. 49 no. 4
            [R.E.Westerlund Oy, 1947] same

KILPINEN, YRJÖ, 1892-1959 *(continued)*
Blomberg, Erik Axel, 1894-1965.
(continued)
Desdemonas sång, op. 51 no. 1
[R.E.Westerlund Oy, 1947]
"Och flickan satt sjungande invid ett fikonträd"
Den djupa källen, op. 49 no. 5
[R.E.Westerlund Oy, 1947]
"Grunda bäckar, där de fara"
Dyningen, op. 48 no. 1 [R.E.Westerlund Oy, 1947]
"Dyningen susar med langa slag"
Förledde vän, op. 51 no. 8
[R.E.Westerlund Oy, 1947] same
Förr ägde jag intet, op. 49 no. 1
[R.E.Westerlund Oy, 1947] same
Gravskrift över ett litet barn, op. 51 no. 2
[R.E.Westerlund Oy, 1947]
"Här hon göms, en vacker knopp"
Gullvivan, op. 51 no. 6 [R.E.Westerlund Oy, 1947] "Fråga mig, varför jag ger den första primulan åt er"
I dina händers mjuka fågelbo, op. 50 no. 1 [R.E.Westerlund Oy, 1947]
"I dina ögons klara morgonljus"
Jag har haft en stor, tyst sorg, op. 49 no. 2 [R.E.Westerlund Oy, 1947] same
Jag väntar ingen lycka, op. 48 no. 6
[R.E.Westerlund Oy, 1947] same
Jag ville vara tårar, op. 50 no. 4
[R.E.Westerlund Oy, 1947] same
Körsbär, op. 51 no. 5 [R.E.Westerlund Oy, 1947] same
Lärksång, op. 51 no. 9 [R.E.Westerlund Oy, 1947]
"Hör, hör, hör en kör av lärkor"
Den ljusa nattens ljusa fågeldrillar, op. 49 no. 3 [R.E.Westerlund Oy, 1947] same
Människans hem, op. 48 no. 5
[R.E.Westerlund Oy, 1947]
"Nu är det natt över jorden"
Modern, op. 50 no. 3 [R.E.Westerlund Oy, 1947]
"Framför en Mariabild vid vägkanten"
Och stod du i den kalla blåst, op. 51 no. 7 [R.E.Westerlund Oy, 1947] same
Snöblommor, op. 48 no. 2
[R.E.Westerlund Oy, 1947]
"I dag är luften blå"
Stjärnorna äro så stilla, op. 48 no. 3
[R.E.Westerlund Oy, 1947] same
Till Elektra, op. 51 no. 4
[R.E.Westerlund Oy, 1947]
"Jag ber ej om en kyss"

Till en diktare, op. 50 no. 6
[R.E.Westerlund Oy, 1947]
"Du samlar, och du samlar"
Till några påskliljor, op. 51 no. 3
[R.E.Westerlund Oy, 1947]
"Påskliljor, suckande vi se"
En ung mor, op. 50 no. 2
[R.E.Westerlund Oy, 1947]
"Dina gropia fingrar"
Var stilla hjärta, op. 49 no. 6
[R.E.Westerlund Oy, 1947] same
Vem är du? op. 48 no. 4 [R.E.Westerlund Oy, 1947] same
Visa, op. 50 no. 5 [R.E.Westerlund Oy, 1947] "Varför smeker jag ibland päronträdets gren"
Cnattingius, Thor, 1880-1929.
Det borde vara skatter, op. 44 no. 3 [W. Hansen, 1929] same
Danslek, op. 43 no. 5 [W. Hansen, 1929]
"Nu solen skiner på himlen blå"
Dödens vila, op. 46 no. 2 [W. Hansen, 1929]
"Stilla, stilla trädens kronor susa"
Jag ville bygga ett litet bo, op. 44 no. 2
[W. Hansen, 1929] same
Lilla Olles visa, op. 44 no. 5 [W. Hansen, 1929] "Mor, Mor, lilla mor, säg var lyckan bor"
Liten jungfru, op. 43 no. 2 [W. Hansen, 1929] same
En liten visa om våren, op. 43 no. 3 [W. Hansen, 1929]
"När solen skiner och lärkan slår"
Min längtans ö, op. 44 no. 1 [W. Hansen, 1929] "Jag längtar dit bort till mitt hjärtas mö"
Minnen, op. 45 no. 3 [W. Hansen, 1929]
"Minnen, minnen, hel'ga minnen"
Mitt gagoland, op. 47 no. 1 [Fazer, 1928]
"Det ligger ett land, mitt sagoland"
Önskekransen, op. 43 no. 4 [W. Hansen, 1929]
"Gullmor, Gullmor, min hjärtans kär"
Ring, ring, op. 46 no. 3 [W. Hansen, 1929] "Ring, ring till sabbatstid"
Rosa lill', op. 47 no. 5 [Fazer, 1928]
"Rosa lill' nu solen far"
Rosor, op. 45 no. 1 [W. Hansen, 1929]
"Det väser röda rosor"
Så dansa! op. 47 no. 6 [Fazer, 1928] same
Sjung mitt hjärta, op. 47 no. 3 [Fazer, 1928]
"Snön faller tät bland en och ljung"
Slumra, slumra sakta, op. 44 no. 4 [W. Hansen, 1929] same

Solstrålen, op. 47 no. 2 [Fazer, 1928]
"Det glider en liten stråle"
Stämmingsvisa, op. 47 no. 4 [Fazer,
1928] "Solen ler, och skogen susar"
Svanevit, op. 46 no. 1 [W. Hansen, 1929]
"Svanevit! svanevit! Vi sjunger du i
natten"
Det var i vårens ljusa tid, op. 45 no. 2
[W. Hansen, 1929] same
En vårmelodie, op. 43 no. 1 [W. Hansen,
1929]
"Susa min björk, och grönska min rag"

Hesse, Hermann, 1877-1962.
Allein, op. 97 no. 5 [Bote & Bock]
"Es führen über die Erde"
Aufstieg, op. 99 no. 1 [Bote & Bock]
"Und ringsum Schnee"
Aus zwei Tälern, op. 98 no. 4 [Bote &
Bock] "Ein Glocke läutet"
Berggeist, op. 99 no. 3 [Botc & Bock]
"Ein starker Geist"
Drüben, op. 98 no. 5 [Bote & Bock]
"Drüben überm Berge"
Dunkle Augen, op. 97 no. 3 [Bote &
Bock]
"Mein Heimweh und meine Liebe"
Gebet der Fischer, op. 98 no. 3 [Bote &
Bock]
"Die Stunden eilen–Mitternacht"
Glück, op. 97 no. 6 [Bote & Bock]
"So lang du nach dem Glücke jagst"
Grindelwald, op. 99 no. 2 [Bote & Bock]
"Schon manche selige Nacht"
Herbst, op. 98 no. 2 [Bote & Bock]
"Ihr Vögel im Gesträuch"
Ich fragte dich, op. 97 no. 4 [Bote &
Bock] same
Jugendflucht, op. 98 no. 1 [Bote & Bock]
"Der müde Sommer senkt das Haupt"
Die Kindheit, op. 98 no. 7 [Bote & Bock]
"Du bist mein fernes Tal"
Liebeslied, op. 97 no. 1 [Bote & Bock]
"Ich wollt' ich wär' eine Blume"
Nach dem Fest, op. 98 no. 6 [Bote &
Bock] "Von der Tafel rinnt der Wein"
Schlittenfahrt, op. 99 no. 4 [Bote &
Bock] "Der Schneewind packt mich"
Traum, op. 97 no. 7 [Bote & Bock]
"Es ist immer derselbe Traum"
Vergänglichkeit, op. 98 no. 8 [Bote &
Bock] "Vom Baum des Lebens fällt"
Wo mag meine Heimat sein? op. 97 no. 2
[Bote & Bock] same

**Huber, Berta (Bindschedler), 1893-
1958.**
Am Fenster, op. 95 no. 3 [Bote & Bock]
"Draussen im Winde"

Ausklang, op. 95 no. 14 [Bote & Bock]
"Wenn du am Abend müde bist"
Das Ende, op. 95 no. 13 [Bote & Bock]
"Es löst ein Blatt sich"
Feldblumen, op. 95 no. 7 [Bote & Bock]
"Feldblumen, zarte, kleine"
Frühling, op. 95 no. 5 [Bote & Bock]
"Du wunderbare Frühlingszeit"
Der Kirchturm, op. 95 no. 15 [Bote &
Bock] "Regungslos, ein grosser
Schweiger"
Kleinstadt im Frühling, op. 95 no. 8
[Bote & Bock] "Der Marktplatz liegt
vom Mond erhellt"
Das Licht, op. 95 no. 2 [Bote & Bock]
"Ich stand in deiner Strasse"
Mein Stübchen, op. 95 no. 4 [Bote &
Bock] "Leise geht der Tag zu Ende"
Nacht, op. 95 no. 1 [Bote & Bock]
"Alles dunkel, alles still"
Regen I, op. 95 no. 11 [Bote & Bock]
"Es tropft auf die Dächer"
Regen II, op. 95 no. 12 [Bote & Bock]
"Regen falle"
Der Ruhelose, op. 95 no. 10 [Bote &
Bock] "Mein Weg ist weit"
Strom bei Nacht, op. 95 no. 9 [Bote &
Bock] "Es wälzt der Strom"
Verbundenheit, op. 95 no. 6 [Bote &
Bock]
"In frohen Tagen such' ich dich"

Jalkanen, Huugo, 1880-1969.
Aamu, op. 18 no. 2 [Breitkopf & Härtel]
"Kuu painuu taakse taivaanrannan"
Aamulaulu, op. 15 no. 5 [Breitkopf &
Härtel] "Miten kirkas ja kuulas on
amunkoi"
Ah, missä lienet nyt, op. 16 no. 2
[Breitkopf & Härtel] same
Eheu fugaces! op. 18 no. 4 [Breitkopf &
Härtel] "Kymmenen pitkää vuotta"
Eron hetki, op. 16 no. 1 [Breitkopf &
Härtel] "On mennyt lemmenkevät
kultainen"
Erotessa, op. 15 no. 7 [Breitkopf &
Härtel] "Pois täytyy mun"
Hiljaisuus, op. 17 no. 10 [Breitkopf &
Härtel] "Hiljaisuus, mi henkii"
Ihmisen osa, op. 16 no. 8 [Breitkopf &
Härtel]
"Kuin lehdet tuulessa ihmiset on"
Illanrusko, op. 18 no. 1 [Breitkopf &
Härtel] same
Ilta, op. 17 no. 1 [Breitkopf & Härtel]
"Pois painuu päivä"
Joulukirkkoon, op. 17 no. 7 [Breitkopf &
Härtel] "Helisten soi tiu'ut, kellot"

KILPINEN, YRJÖ, 1892-1959 *(continued)*
Jalkanen, Huugo, 1880-1969.
(continued)
Kerran, op. 16 no. 4 [Breitkopf & Härtel]
"Miksi milloinkaan sinut nähdä
sainkaan"
Kesäisenä päivänä, op. 15 no. 3
[Breitkopf & Härtel] "Sa neito nuori,
sa ruususuu"
Kevät on mennyt, op. 17 no. 8
[Breitkopf & Härtel] same
Koditon, op. 17 no. 4 [Breitkopf &
Härtel] "Niin oudot on tiet, niin
vieraita maat"
Kuutamo-oodi, op. 17 no. 9 [Breitkopf &
Härtel] "Yö ja hiljaisuus"
Lemmenlaulu, op. 15 no. 2 [Breitkopf &
Härtel]
"Siunattu olkoon, armas, sun tiesi"
Muistoja, op. 16 no. 5 [Breitkopf &
Härtel] "Leyhy tuuli"
Nocturnus, op. 16 no. 6 [Breitkopf &
Härtel] "Tyhjä on puisto, autio,
lohduton"
Odotus, op. 16 no. 3 [Breitkopf & Härtel]
"Raskaat pilvet, mun murheeni varjot"
Oh, päivät, te päivät, op. 17 no. 5
[Breitkopf & Härtel] same
Per aspera, op. 17 no. 6 [Breitkopf &
Härtel] "En unta saa"
Pitkä on tuskan tie, op. 17 no. 3
[Breitkopf & Härtel] same
Prologi, op. 15 no. 1 [Breitkopf &
Härtel] "Tuomet valkeina kukkii"
Pyhäin miesten päivänä, op. 18 no. 5
[Breitkopf & Härtel] "Kolea tuuli
tohisee"
Syyslaulu, op. 16 no. 7 [Breitkopf &
Härtel] "Syyssävelet soi yli kaupungin"
Tytön laulu, op. 15 no. 4 [Breitkopf &
Härtel] "Niin monta on sortunut
murheeseen"
Uusi Aladdin, op. 18 no. 3 [Breitkopf &
Härtel] "Yön ystävä, ruhtinas unten"
Uutisraivaaja, op. 15 no. 6 [Breitkopf &
Härtel] "Soikaatte koivikossa tuulet"
Y", op. 17 no. 2 [Breitkopf & Härtel]
"Vaiti on metsä"
Yli hohtavan hangen, op. 18 no. 6
[Breitkopf & Härtel] same
Josephson, Ernst Abraham, 1851-
1906.
Älvan och kardinalen, op. 27 no. 5 [W.
Hansen, 1924] "När kardinaln en
vacker dag"
Beständighet, op. 28 no. 1 [W. Hansen,
1924]
"Låt vem som vill av sin flicka skryta"

Blomman, op. 27 no. 4 [W. Hansen,
1924] "Blomman i solen stod"
Fågelungarna, op. 27 no. 3 [W. Hansen,
1924] "Fågelungarna flögo ur bo"
Jag, op. 29 no. 4 [W. Hansen, 1924]
"Jag gråter blodiga tårar"
Japansk akvarell, op. 29 no. 3 [W.
Hansen, 1924]
"En fågel genom natten far"
Kärlek, op. 28 no. 3 [W. Hansen, 1924]
"Jag sade ej ett ord till dig"
Liten gosse, op. 27 no. 1 [W. Hansen,
1924] "Liten gosse smyckades nyss"
Med strömmen, op. 29 no. 1 [W. Hansen,
1924] "Stupande strand, al och ek"
Min grav, op. 29 no. 2 [W. Hansen,
1924] "O, gräv mig en grav,
dödgrävare snäll"
Näcken, op. 29 no. 5 [W. Hansen, 1924]
"Djup stod färgen på fura och på sten"
Svanesång, op. 28 no. 4 [W. Hansen,
1924] "Säg, varför giva vi de kval åt
världen"
Till havet, op. 28 no. 5 [W. Hansen,
1924] "Kommen, svallande vågor till
stranden"
Vaggvisa, op. 27 no. 2 [W. Hansen,
1924] "Susa, susa björk och lind"
Vid stranden, op. 28 no. 2 [W. Hansen,
1924] "Jag ser vad du tänker vid
stranden"
Kanteletar
Aina laulan, op. 100 no. 9 [Fazer, 1953]
same
Anna Kiesus antajalle, op. 100 no. 30
[Fazer, 1953] same
Anna Maata Maariainen, op. 3 no. 2
[R.E.Westerlund Oy] "Tuuvitan
tuhoista lasta"
Armas arkussa ajavi, op. 100 no. 57
[Fazer, 1954] "Muien turvaset tulevat"
Armottoman osa, op. 100 no. 27 [Fazer,
1953] "Alahan' on allin mieli"
Ei minusta lienekänä, op. 100 no. 12
[Fazer, 1953] same
Ei runo rahatta laula, op. 100 no. 29
[Fazer, 1953] "Laulaisinpa, taitaisinpa"
Ei sula syän suruinen, op. 100 no. 25
[Fazer, 1953] "Suot sulavi, maat
valuvi"
Erotus mielillä, op. 100 no. 24 [Fazer,
1953] "Miten on mieli miekkoisien"
Ikävä omia maita, op. 100 no. 26 [Fazer,
1953] "Laulan, laulan pieni piika"
Ikuinen suru, op. 100 no. 60 [Fazer,
1954] "Käki kukkua käkesi"

Jo tulenki, op. 100 no. 37 [Fazer, 1954]
same
Jos ma lauluille rupean, op. 100 no. 13
[Fazer, 1953] same
Kaikissa yksin, op. 100 no. 42 [Fazer,
1954] "Yksin vieno veet vetelen"
Kaks' oli meitä kaunokaista, op. 100 no.
49 [Fazer, 1954] same
Kiitos emännästä, op. 100 no. 62 [Fazer,
1954] "Kittos kaunoisen Jumalan"
Köyhän lapset, op. 100 no. 18 [Fazer,
1953] "Voi nuo narrit nuoret miehet"
Kukkalatva kuusi, op. 100 no. 3 [Fazer,
1953] "Marisenki, marjasenko"
Kummaistako kuuleminen, op. 100 no. 14
[Fazer, 1953] "Kukkuipa käkeä kaksi"
Kun ma kerran, op. 100 no. 23 [Fazer,
1953] same
Kun mun kultani tulisi, op. 100 no. 43
[Fazer, 1954] same
Kuti, kuti, kultaseni, op. 100 no. 44
[Fazer, 1954] same
Kuusen juuret kuivettuvat, op. 100 no. 53
[Fazer, 1954] same
Laulan ilman lainehilta, op. 100 no. 48
[Fazer, 1954] "Kuka kuuli laulavani"
Maassa marjani makaavi, op. 3 no. 3
[R.E.Westerlund OY]
"Ikävät on illat pitkät"
Makaaja onni, op. 100 no. 47 [Fazer,
1954] "Muilla onni työn tekevi"
Mikäs on poikana eleä, op. 100 no. 16
[Fazer, 1953] same
Miksi en väsyisi, op. 100 no. 63 [Fazer,
1954] "Heponenki hengähtävi matkan
pitkän mentyämsä"
Millä maksan maammon maion, op. 100
no. 39 [Fazer, 1954] same
Missä armahani, op. 100 no. 2 [Fazer,
1953] "Miss' on, kussa minun hyväni"
Mitä tuosta, jos mä laulan, op. 100 no.
36 [Fazer, 1954] same
Mitäpä suren sanoista, op. 100 no. 21
[Fazer, 1953]
"Jospahan poloinen lienen"
Mont' on mulla morsianta, op. 100 no.
45 [Fazer, 1954] same
Muinainen käkeni, op. 100 no. 35 [Fazer,
1954] "Kukkui muinainen käkeni"
Muut kuuli kirkonkellon, op. 100 no. 41
[Fazer, 1954]
"Muut ne kuuli kirkonkellon"
Niin on meitä piikasia, op. 100 no. 10
[Fazer, 1953] same
Noin sanoi minun emoni, op. 100 no. 33
[Fazer, 1954] same

Nyt on kaikki kallistunna, op. 100 no. 31
[Fazer, 1953]
"Kun olin miessä nuorempana"
Ohoh kullaista kotia, op. 100 no. 38
[Fazer, 1954]
"Lämmin paita liinainenki"
Oi Ukko ylinen herra, op. 100 no. 56
[Fazer, 1954] same
Oisi mulla vallan miekka, op. 100 no. 8
[Fazer, 1953] same
Omat on virret oppimani, op. 100 no. 61
[Fazer, 1954] same
On kumpiaki, op. 100 no. 6 [Fazer, 1953]
"Niin on noita poikasia"
Onpa tietty tietyssäni, op. 100 no. 28
[Fazer, 1953] same
Otettiin minusta outo, op. 100 no. 34
[Fazer, 1954] same
Pah' on orjana eleä, op. 100 no. 54
[Fazer, 1954] same
Paimenlaulu, op. 100 no. 1 [Fazer, 1953]
"Mipä meiän paimenien"
Paista päivänen Jumala, op. 100 no. 17
[Fazer, 1953] same
Parempi syntymättä, op. 100 no. 22
[Fazer, 1953] "Parempi minun olisi"
Pimeä isoton pirtti, op. 100 no. 58
[Fazer, 1954]
"Oli mulla muoto muinen"
Saisinko käeltä kielen, op. 100 no. 50
[Fazer, 1954] "Kukkua käkesin kälkö"
Sanoissa kuluva, op. 100 no. 59 [Fazer,
1954] "En kulu minä kutsuissa"
Siitä sinne tie menevi, op. 100 no. 64
[Fazer, 1954]
"Laulun tiean, ehk' en laula"
Silloin laulan, op. 100 no. 5 [Fazer,
1953] "Tupa on täynnä tuppisuita"
Soitapas, op. 100 no. 40 [Fazer, 1954]
"Soitapas soria likka"
Sopivaisia, op. 100 no. 7 [Fazer, 1953]
"Noin kuulin saneltavaksi"
Soria sotahan kuolla, op. 100 no. 55
[Fazer, 1954] "Suku suuresti surevi"
Tanssi, op. 100 no. 15 [Fazer, 1953]
"Likka tanssivi somasti"
Tule meille Tuomas kulta, op. 100 no. 32
[Fazer, 1953] same
Tule tänne, op. 100 no. 4 [Fazer, 1953]
same
Tuuti, tuuti tummaistani, op. 100 no. 51
[Fazer, 1954] same
Tuutulaul, op. 100 no. 20 [Fazer, 1953]
"Tuuti lasta, tuuti pientä"
Väjä ilo emottomalle käestä, op. 100 no.
52 [Fazer, 1954]
"Käki kukkui kuusikossa"

COMPOSER   Poet   *Title*   "First Line"

KILPINEN, YRJÖ, 1892-1959 *(continued)*
Kanteletar *(continued)*
Viikon vuottelin käkeä, op. 100 no. 11
[Fazer, 1953]
"Kun oisin paimenna paloinen"
Voi jos mie tok' miehen saisin, op. 100
no. 19 [Fazer, 1953] same
Voi minua mieskulua, op. 100 no. 46
[Fazer, 1954] same
Koskenniemi, Veikko Antero, 1885-
1962.
Auringon nousu, op. 26 no. 5 [Fazer]
"Nää, oi mun sieluni, auringon korkea
nousa"
Elegia kaunneudelle, op. 20 no. 1 [Fazer,
1928] "Kerran lienen sun lasna ma
nähnyt"
Elegia satakielelle, op. 21 no. 1 [Fazer,
1928] "Oi, kesän yhden sa mullekin
laulanut oot"
Elegia yksinäisyydelle, op. 25 no. 4
[Fazer] "Kysin oot sinä, ihminen"
Elegia yölle, op. 20 no. 5 [Fazer, 1928]
"Tähtien hiljaisuutta ja rauhaa"
Endymion, op. 20 no. 2 [Fazer, 1928]
"Sua koskaan saavuta ei ajan uvo"
Fiat nox, op. 25 no. 5 [Fazer]
"Niin tulkoon yö ja kuolo"
Hyökyaalto, op. 23 no. 6 [Fazer, 1928]
"Sinä hyöky hurja ja vaahtopää"
Ihme, op. 21 no. 6 [Fazer, 1928]
"Tule aamuhun hymyilevään"
Ikarus, op. 24 no. 5 [Fazer]
"Ah, Ikharus sa oot, et enempää"
"Jää hyvästi" ja "näkemiin," op. 25 no.
3 [Fazer] " 'Jää hyvästi' me sanomme"
Kaupungilla sataa, op. 24 no. 1 [Fazer]
"Vasten kivitystä kadun soipi syyttäen"
Kehtolaulu, op. 23 no. 4 [Fazer, 1928]
"Iltarusko jo sammunut on"
Kesäyö, op. 23 no. 3 [Fazer, 1928]
"Tutut aitat jo kaikki unelmoi"
Kesäyössä, op. 21 no. 4 [Fazer, 1928]
"Minä kuljen tuttua polkuain"
Kevät keralla, op. 20 no. 3 [Fazer, 1928]
"Kevät keralla paiväin kuulakkain"
Kuutamolla, op. 21 no. 2 [Fazer, 1928]
"Oi, armas, mikä ilta kuutamon"
Lakeus I, op. 22 no. 1 [Fazer, 1928]
"Mun sieluni sun ylläs väräjää"
Lakeus II, op. 22 no. 2 [Fazer, 1928]
"Sun rauhaas lemmin kuin en muuta
mitääm"
Lakeus III, op. 22 no. 3 [Fazer, 1928]
"Yön ihmeelliseen valoon"

Lakeus IV, op. 22 no. 4 [Fazer, 1928]
"Ikävässä kenttäin huojuvaisten"
Lakeus V, op. 22 no. 5 [Fazer, 1928]
"Päivän viime säteet lankee"
Lehdokki, op. 21 no. 3 [Fazer, 1928]
"En joukoin kulkevalle näy"
Leivonen, op. 26 no. 4 [Fazer]
"Sua nähnyt en ma"
Olit tuskasta väristen herännyt syön, op.
26 no. 1 [Fazer] same
On kaikki syksyn tähdet syttyneet, op. 24
no. 2 [Fazer] same
Rannalta I, op. 23 no. 1 [Fazer, 1928]
"On suuri sun rantas autius"
Rannalta II, op. 23 no. 2 [Fazer, 1928]
"Iltaruskon leimu läikehtii"
Sa mykkä matkalainen maan, op. 25 no.
2 [Fazer] same
Sonetti sadun linnusta, op. 20 no. 4
[Fazer, 1928]
"Niin moen äänen kaiku kuollet on"
Sun tuskin huomasin ma siihen aikaan,
op. 26 no. 2 [Fazer] same
Syyskuun sonetti, op. 21 no. 5 [Fazer,
1928] "Näin oomme, armas, syksyyn
saapuneet"
Syyssonetti, op. 24 no. 3 [Fazer] "Nyt
sumu harmaa nousee korven soissa"
Valkeat kaupungit, op. 26 no. 3 [Fazer]
"Nään usein unessa ma kaupungin"
Vanha laulu, op. 23 no. 5 [Fazer, 1928]
"En ma tiennyt, kun sun luota läksin"
Yksin, op. 24 no. 4 [Fazer]
"Taivas välkkyväisin jalokivin"
Ystävien piiri pienentyy, op. 25 no. 1
[Fazer] same
Lagerkvist, Pär Fabian, 1891-1974.
Det är du som skall bliva den yppersta,
op. 33 no. 5 [W. Hansen, 1924] same
Barn, som jag smekt, op. 33 no. 8 [W.
Hansen, 1924] same
Befriad är dagen, op. 34, no. 6 [W.
Hansen, 1924] same
Din mun är ljusare än min, op. 33 no. 4
[W. Hansen, 1924] same
Ett enda ord är mitt, op. 33 no. 9 [W.
Hansen, 1924] same
*En gång skall det brinna ett ljus på min
grav,* op. 33 no. 6 [W. Hansen, 1924]
same
Hela världen är mig så kär, op. 34, no. 1
[W. Hansen, 1924] same
*Ingenting får störa vår stund med
varandra,* op. 34 no. 2 [W. Hansen,
1924] same
Mitt liv går bort, jag vet ej varthäm, op.
33 no. 1 [W. Hansen, 1924] same

O vinternatt, op. 34 no. 4 [W. Hansen, 1924] same

Om tiotusen år, op. 33 no. 7 [W. Hansen, 1924] same

Regnet slår och slår, op. 34 no. 3 [W. Hansen, 1924] same

Så gamla äro alla moln, op. 34 no. 5 [W. Hansen, 1924] same

Som ett blommande mandelträd, op. 33 no. 3 [W. Hansen, 1924] same

Var är den djupa glädje, op. 33 no. 2 [W. Hansen, 1924] same

Lamberg, Eila Sylvia, 1921-

Eikö totta, no op. no., no. 5 [Fazer] same

Eräs, no op. no., no. 3 [Fazer] "Eräs on, on eräs, eräs on"

Kevättä, no op. no., no. 4 [Fazer] "Aallot solisevat"

Muisto, no op. no., no. 2 [Fazer] "Eilen kuulsi pilvet, talot, ihmissydämet"

Nocturno, no op. no., no. 1 [Fazer] "Läpäjävä veden kalvo"

Larin-Kyösti, 1873-1948.

Käköä kuullessa, op. 7 no. 2 [R.E.Westerlund Oy] "Käki kukkuu, kultarinta"

Katso yli kedon kukkain, op. 7 no. 1 [R.E.Westerlund Oy] same

Tarhassa hiipii hienohelma, op. 7 no. 3 [R.E.Westerlund Oy] same

Lehtinen, Hilja Onerva, 1882-1972.

Ilta, op. 10 no. 2 [R.E.Westerlund Oy] "Päivä laskee metsän taa"

Jo luovutko luotani, op. 10 no. 5 [R.E.Westerlund Oy] same

Jo muistot taivaltani varjostaa, op. 10 no. 6 [R.E.Westerlund Oy] same

Kevätlaulu, op. 10 no. 9 [R.E.Westerlund Oy] "Ah, miten kimmeltää keväinen hanki"

Kirkkotie, op. 10 no. 1 [R.E.Westerlund Oy] "Outo tähti silmähäni"

Nuori Apollo, op. 10 no. 8 [R.E.Westerlund Oy] "Ei maailman rikkaan riemuista"

Suruni, op. 10 no. 4 [R.E.Westerlund Oy] "Suruni on syvempi syvintä merta"

Syyshuokaus, op. 10 no. 7 [R.E.Westerlund Oy] "Soi soi syksyinen sade"

Vanitas vanitatum, op. 10 no. 3 [R.E.Westerlund Oy] "Niinkuin raskahat rattaiden raiteet"

Lönnbohm, Eino, 1878-1926.

Aamulla, op. 19 no. 12 [W. Hansen] "Yli metsän koitti jo päivän koi"

Ikuinen kevät, op. 19 no. 11 [W. Hansen] "Kangastuksina katoovat minun mieleni unelmat"

Illalla, op. 19 no. 7 [W. Hansen] "Illalla kävelin ma kangasta pitkin"

Kaupunkimatka, op. 19 no. 8 [W. Hansen] "Poika nuori kaupunkihin läksi myötätuulta"

Kuu Kalpea, op. 19 no. 6 [W. Hansen] same

Kuusi ja lintunen, op. 19 no. 1 [W. Hansen] "Kasvoi kummulla kuusi tuores"

Omenakukat, op. 19 no. 4 [W. Hansen] "Mun onneni kukkii kuin omenapuu"

Pieni ballaadi, op. 19 no. 10 [W. Hansen] "Honka se humisi ikkunan alla"

Rakastunut, op. 19 no. 3 [W. Hansen] "Raikkahasti laulaa aamun aalto"

Rannalla, op. 19 no. 9 [W. Hansen] "Näkinkengät ne rannalla karskui"

Syyslaulu, op. 19 no. 5 [W. Hansen] "Jo pilvihin taivas peittyy"

Yöperhonen, op. 19 no. 2 [W. Hansen] same

Löns, Hermann, 1866-1914.

Am Haidenhügel geht ein Singen [Fazer, 1967] same

Das bittersüsse Lied [Fazer, 1966] "In dem Grünebusch"

Goldenes Lied [Fazer, 1967] "Die goldene Mittagssonne durch zitternde Wipfel dringt"

Der Kuckuck [Fazer, 1966] "Der Kuckuck rief die ganze Nacht"

Küssekraut [Fazer, 1966] "In den Grünenwald bin ich gegangen"

Liebessuche [Fazer, 1966] "Ich hab mir einen Kranz gepflückt"

Männertreu [Fazer, 1966] "Es ging einmal ein Wind"

Rosenbüsche [Fazer, 1967] "Die Rosenbüsche sind behangen"

Schäferlied [Fazer, 1967] "Wenn ich meine Schafe weide"

Der schönste Platz [Fazer, 1967] "Wo die weissen Tauben fliegen"

Der Spuk [Fazer, 1966] "Ach Schwester, liebe Schwester"

Der Verehrung [Fazer, 1967] "Ich ging im grünen Walde"

KILPINEN, YRJÖ, 1892-1959 *(continued)*
Löns, Hermann, 1866-1914 *(continued)*
Der Vollmond scheint [Fazer, 1966]
"Der Vollmond scheint in mein
Fenster"
Zur Erinnerung [Fazer, 1967]
"Über die Haide sind wir gegangen"
**Morgenstern, Christian Otto Joseph
Wolfgang, 1871-1914.**
Anmutiger Vertrag, op. 61 no. 5 [Bote &
Bock, 1934] "Auf der Bank im Walde"
Auf einem verfallenen Kirchhof, op. 62
no. 2 [Bote & Bock, 1934]
"Was gehst du, armer, bleicher Kopf"
Deine Rosen an der Brust, op. 61 no. 3
[Bote & Bock, 1934] same
Es ist Nacht, op. 60 no. 2 [Bote & Bock,
1934] same
Die Fusswaschung, op. 59 no. 1 [Bote &
Bock, 1934]
"Ich danke dir, du stummer Stein"
Heimat, op. 61 no. 1 [Bote & Bock,
1934] "Nach all dem Menschenlärm"
Kleines Lied, op. 61 no. 2 [Bote & Bock,
1934] "Und werden wir uns nie
besitzen"
Mein Herz ist leer, op. 60 no. 1 [Bote &
Bock, 1934] same
O, Nacht, op. 59 no. 2 [Bote & Bock,
1934] "O, Nacht, du Sternenbronnen"
Der Säemann, op. 62 no. 5 [Bote &
Bock, 1934]
"Durch die Lande auf und ab"
Schicksal der Liebe, op. 60 no. 5 [Bote &
Bock, 1934] "Wir sind zwei Rosen"
Siehe, auch ich–lebe, op. 59 no. 5
[Bote & Bock, 1934]
"Also ihr lebt noch"
Thalatta, op. 59 no. 6 [Bote & Bock,
1934] "Es stürzen der Jugend Altäre
zusammen"
Der Tod und der einsame Trinker, op. 62
no. 3 [Bote & Bock, 1934]
"Guten abend, Freund"
Über die tausend Berge, op. 61 no. 4
[Bote & Bock, 1934] same
Unsere Liebe, op. 60 no. 3 [Bote &
Bock, 1934] "Diese Rose von
heimlichen Küssen schwer"
Unverlierbare Gewähr, op. 62 no. 6
[Bote & Bock, 1934] "Eines gibt's,
darauf ich mich freuen darf"
Vöglein Schwermut, op. 62 no. 1 [Bote &
Bock, 1934] "Ein schwarzes Vöglein
fliegt über die Welt"
Von zwei Rosen, op. 59 no. 3 [Bote &
Bock, 1934] same

Wie vieles ist denn Wort geworden, op.
59 no. 4 [Bote & Bock, 1934] same
Winternacht, op. 62 no. 4 [Bote & Bock,
1934] "Flockendichte Winternacht"
Wir sitzen im Dunkeln, op. 60 no. 4
[Bote & Bock, 1934] same
No author
Vocalise-étude [Alphonse Leduc, 1929]
In *Répertoire moderne de vocalises-
etudes* publiées sous la direction de
A.L.Hettich.
Wordless.
Österling, Anders, 1884-1981.
Dryaden I, op. 40 no. 5a [W. Hansen,
1929] "Du, som bland jasminer medan
natten går"
Dryaden II, op. 40 no. 5b [W. Hansen,
1929]
"Den första gråt för mig du grät"
Dryaden III, op. 40 no. 5c [W. Hansen,
1929] "Nu skall hos mig lik en dryad"
Efter lång sorg, op. 41 no. 2 [W. Hansen,
1929] "Som slätten vid havet"
Facklor, op. 41 no. 5 [W. Hansen, 1929]
"Facklor i stormen, hell er"
Förgätmigejer, op. 39 no. 3 [W. Hansen,
1929] "Kransen av förgätmigejer"
Gammal sorg, op. 41 no. 1 [W. Hansen,
1929] "Gammal sorg kan länge sjunga"
Hälsning till ett nytt år, p. 41 no. 7 [W.
Hansen, 1929] "År, som stundar, aldrig
kände jag nyår"
Morgonens hjärta, op. 41 no. 6 [W.
Hansen, 1929]
"Komma den eviga morgonen nära"
Och tröskorna tego, op. 41 no. 4 [W.
Hansen, 1929] same
Pingst, op. 39 no. 5 [W. Hansen, 1929]
"Som fulla hjärtans kvällsdröm"
Sången, op. 39 no. 1 [W. Hansen, 1929]
"Böljan och stormen förenade skrida"
Slätten, op. 41 no. 3 [W. Hansen, 1929]
"Var tid, som kommer, ymnigt sår på
gott"
Sommarens ljud, op. 39 no. 4 [W.
Hansen, 1929] "Jag sluter ögonen"
Sorglöshetens vingar, op. 39 no. 2 [W.
Hansen, 1929] "Som ett brödraskap
med glada händer"
Svanor, op. 39 no. 6 [W. Hansen, 1929]
"Nio svanor såg jag flyga"
Tala, älskade, tala, op. 40 no. 3 [W.
Hansen, 1929] same
Trasten, op. 40 no. 2 [W. Hansen, 1929]
"Trasten sjöng på skorstenskransen"
En vårrefräng, op. 40 no. 1 [W. Hansen,
1929] "Mars, april och maj"

Vid en brunn, op. 40 no. 4 [W. Hansen, 1929] "Med bergfriskt vatten lockar här en brunn"

Sergel, Albert, 1876-1946.

Eingeschneite stille Felder, op. 77 no. 2 [Bote & Bock, 1934] same

Heiligendamm, op. 75 no. 3 [Bote & Bock, 1934] "Ich weiss es nicht, was es wohl war"

Ich sang mich durch das deutsche Land, op. 77 no. 8 [Bote & Bock, 1934] same

Ihr ewigen Sterne, op. 77 no. 1 [Bote & Bock, 1934] same

Im Walde liegt ein stiller See, op. 75 no. 1 [Bote & Bock, 1934] same

Mein Herz, der wilde Rosenstrauch, op. 75 no. 4 [Bote & Bock, 1934] "Das war des Frühlings warmer Hauch"

Sommesegen, op. 75 no. 5 [Bote & Bock, 1934] "Wir gehn durch goldenes Ährenfeld"

Spiel ich wo zum Tanze auf, op. 77 no. 3 [Bote & Bock, 1934] same

Spielmannssehen, op. 77 no. 5 [Bote & Bock, 1934] "Küssen und Kosen steht euch an"

Tanzlied, op. 77 no. 4 [Bote & Bock, 1934] "Nun wind um deine Stirne"

Tausend stille, weisse, blaue Blumen, op. 75 no. 2 [Bote & Bock, 1934] same

Unter Blüten, op. 75 no. 6 [Bote & Bock, 1934] "Rings weisse Blütendolden"

Vor Tau und Tag, op. 77 no. 6 [Bote & Bock, 1934] "Der Frost in letzter Nacht"

Wenn der Wein nicht wär', op. 77 no. 7 [Bote & Bock, 1934] same

Tegengren, Jacob August, 1875-1956.

Fred, op. 4 no. 1 [R.E.Westerlund Oy] "Solen nickat sitt sista farväl"

Törmänen, Vilho Edvard, b. 1886.

Hillankukka, op. 53 no. 1 [Fazer, 1927] same

Jänka, op. 52 no. 1 [Fazer, 1927] "On jänka aava, jäinen"

Kirkkorannassa, op. 54 no. 2 [Fazer, 1927] "Tule, aaltonen, kirkkorantaan"

Laululle, op. 52 no. 3 [Fazer, 1927] "Kuin tunturilla puro hiljaa helää"

Murheen kellot, op. 53 no. 2 [Fazer, 1927] "Nyt värjyvät murheen kellot"

Muuttolintu, op. 53 no. 3 [Fazer, 1927] "Tuli lintunen laakson puuhun"

Sä menit, op. 53 no. 4 [Fazer, 1927] same

Suvilaulu, op. 54 no. 3 [Fazer, 1927] "Jopa joutuikin suvi armaisin"

Tunturilähde, op. 52 no. 2 [Fazer, 1927] same

Tunturilaulu, op. 54 no. 4 [Fazer, 1927] "Oi, ainoisin, mun armahin"

Tunturille, op. 52 no. 4 [Fazer, 1927] "Tunturille mennä tahdon"

Vanha kirkko, op. 54 no. 1 [Fazer, 1927] same

Ullman, Gustav Daniel, 1881-1945.

Alla dem som vilse fara, op. 42 no. 6 [W. Hansen, 1931] same

Kvällning, op. 42 no. 4 [W. Hansen, 1931] "Ett ensamt stilla segel lyser"

Landskap, op. 42 no. 3 [W. Hansen, 1931] "Långeliga, dunkelgrå bergsstränder"

Låt vara, op. 42 no. 2 [W. Hansen, 1931] same

En runa, op. 42 no. 1 [W. Hansen, 1931] "Måste jag döma den, mig svek"

Sol, sol! op. 42 no. 5 [W. Hansen, 1931] "Sol, sol på öde vikar"

Zwehl, Hans Fritz von, 1883-1966.

Grabstein, op. 80 no. 1 [Bote & Bock, 1959] "Hier grub man ein"

Der Heimatlose, op. 79 no. 2 [Bote & Bock, 1934] " 'Wandernd fremd und unbekannt in der Stadt"

Lied der Renate, op. 79 no. 5 [Bote & Bock, 1934] "Die goldene Wage des Lebens"

Mancher Stunden Wehen, op. 79 no. 1 [Bote & Bock, 1934] same

Marienkirche zu Danzig im Gerüst, op. 79 no. 7 [Bote & Bock, 1934] "Du Trotz des Glaubens"

Nacht auf Posten, op. 79 no. 6 [Bote & Bock, 1934] "In Feindesland die graue Spätherbstnacht"

Nirwana, op. 80 no. 2 [Bote & Bock, 1959] "Nun hat Deines Herzens Geige"

Todsüsses Gespenst, op. 80 no. 3 [Bote & Bock, 1959] "Warum kommst Du zu mir"

Venezianisches Intermezzo, op. 79 no. 4 [Bote & Bock, 1934] "Durch alte Marmorhallen"

Vorfrühling, op. 79 no. 3 [Bote & Bock, 1934] "Durch hohe Tannen"

Wenn der Bann gebrochen, op. 80 no. 4 [Bote & Bock, 1959] same

Kinanti see Anon. **GRIFFES**

Das Kind see Droste-Hülshoff **CORNELIUS**

Das Kind am Brunnen see Hebbel WOLF
Das Kind der Berge see Garborg
  HAUGTUSSA. **GRIEG** *Veslemøy*
Kind, Friedrich, 1768-1843.
  LOEWE *Der grosse Christoph*
  SCHUBERT *Hänflings Liebeswerbung*
  SPOHR *Das Mädchens Sehnsucht*
  WEBER
    Das Licht im Tale
    Lied der Hirtin
    Das Veilchen im Tale
  ZELTER
    Abendlied im Freien
    Lied bei Sonnenuntergang
  DER ABEND AM WALDBRUNNEN.
    WEBER *Bach, Echo, Kuss*
  DAS NACHTLAGER VON GRANADA.
    WEBER *Alkanzor und Zaide*
Kind ich komme see Shenshin
  BALAKIREV *Ya prishol k tebe s privetom*
"Das Kind ist krank zum Sterben" *see*
  Der Gast Fontane, T. **SCHOECK**
Kind, Johann Friedrich *see* Kind,
  Friedrich, 1768-1843.
"Das Kind ruht aus vom Spielen" *see Gottes*
  Segen Eichendorff **REGER, SCHOECK**
"Das Kind schläft unter dem Rosenstrauch"
  see Der Rosenstrauch Schulz **SPOHR**
Kind und Mädchen see Rückert **LOEWE**
Kindergeschichte see Jacobowski **REGER**
Kindergottesdienst see Gerok **SCHOECK**
Kinderliedchen see Blüthgen *ACH, WER*
  DOCH DAS KÖNNTE! **SCHOECK**
Kinderliedchen see Mei *RUTHENISCHE*
  LIEDER: No. 2. Nane. **MUSORGSKİİ**
  Detskaia pesenka
Das Kinderspiel see Overbeck **MOZART**
Kinderwacht see Unknown **SCHUMANN**
Das Kindes Gebet see Kiesekamo **REGER**
Kindeslächeln see Kiesekamo **REGER**
Die Kindheit see Hesse **KILPINEN,
  SCHOECK**
Die Kindheit see Matthisson **ZELTER**
KING HENRY VIII. see Shakespeare
  Lied aus Heinrich VIII **LASSEN**
  Orpheus with his lute **QUILTER,
    VAUGHAN WILLIAMS**
      Two Vaughan Williams settings: 1902
      and 1925.
The King in Thule see Goethe *FAUST.*
  SEIBER *Es war ein König in Thule*
The King of love my shepherd see Baker
  GOUNOD
King Saul see Byron *HEBREW MELODIES.*
  MUSORGSKİİ *TSar' Saul*
"The King's three blind daughters" *see*
  Maeterlinck *PELLÉAS ET MÉLISANDE.*
  FAURÉ *Mélisande's song*

Kingsley, Charles, 1819-1875.
  GOUNOD *Oh! that we two are maying*
Kinkel, Gottfried, 1815-1882.
  LASSEN
    Ein geistlich Abendlied
    Tröst der Nacht
  SCHUMANN *Abendlied*
Kipling, Rudyard, 1865-1936.
  GRIEG *Gentlemen-Menige*
  IVES *Tarrant moss*
  QUILTER *Non nobis, domine*
Der Kirchhof im Frühling see Uhland
  SCHOECK
Der Kirchturm see Huber, B. **KILPINEN**
Kirkkorannassa see Törmänen **KILPINEN**
Kirkkotie see Lehtinen **KILPINEN**
Kirschenweiss see Tuwim **SZYMANOWSKI**
  Słowisień
Kirschkerne see Wolf, F. **BLACHER**
The kiss see Rydberg **SIBELIUS** *Kyssen*
Kiss, my sweetheart, kiss see Manin, P.
  MARTINŮ
"Kisses! my lips now cry for kisses!" *see*
  Night of desire Gleiman, W. **BARTÓK**
"Kissing her hair" *see Rondel* Swinburne
  VAUGHAN WILLIAMS
The kiss's hope see Runeberg **SIBELIUS**
  Kyssens hopp
"Kittos kaunoisen Jumalan" *see Kiitos*
  emännästä Kanteletar **KILPINEN**
Kivikk'aho, Eila, pseud. *see* Lamberg, Eila
  Sylvia, 1921-
Kjaerlighed see Andersen **GRIEG**
Kjerulf, Theodor, 1825-1888.
  LAENGSEL.
  DELIUS *Sehnsucht*
Klärchen's Lied see Goethe **SCHUBERT**
  Die Liebe
Klärchens Lied see Goethe **ZELTER**
  Clärchen
Klage see Anon. **BRAHMS**
Klage see Asenijeff **REGER**
Klage see Goethe *WILHELM MEISTER.*
  ZELTER
Klage see Hölty **BEETHOVEN**
Klage see Kol'tsov **RUBINSTEIN**
Klage see Matthisson **SCHUBERT**
Klage see Müchler **WEBER**
Klage see Unknown **SCHUBERT**
  Two settings: D. 292 and D. 371.
Klage see Unknown **SCHUBERT**
  Der Leidende
  Two settings: D. 432 and D. 512.
Klage see Zincgref **ZELTER**
Klage I, Aus dem Böhmischen *see* Wenzig
  WESTSLAWISCHEM MÄRCHENSCHATZ.
  BRAHMS

Klage II, Slowakisch see Wenzig
  WESTSLAWISCHEM MÄRCHENSCHATZ.
  BRAHMS
Klage an den Mond see Hölty **SCHUBERT**
Klage der Ceres see Schiller **SCHUBERT**
Klage der Grenzerwittwe see Scott **JENSEN**
"Klage, meine Flöte" see Der Sänger am
  Felsen Pichler **SCHUBERT**
Klage nicht see Unknown **LASSEN**
"Klage nicht, betrübtes Kind" see Klage nicht
  Unknown **LASSEN**
Klage vor Gottes Leiden see Unknown
  REGER
Klagegesang: Jrisch see Goethe **ZELTER**
Klaglied see Rochlitz **SCHUBERT**
Klagelied von den drei Rosen see Buri
  SPOHR
Klassik see Musorgskiĭ **MUSORGSKIĭ**
Der Klassiker see Musorgskiĭ
  MUSORGSKIĭ Klassik
Klášterský, Antonín, 1866-1938.
  MARTINŮ
    Nokturno
    When we are old
"Klavier und Geige, die ich wahrlich schätze"
  see Pfeifen Hesse **SCHOECK**
Klein Evelinde see Weber **REGER**
"Klein Lieschen, ich hab' dich so lieb" see
  Einrichtung Gruppe **LOEWE**
Klein Marie see Trojan **REGER**
Die Kleine see Eichendorff **WOLF**
"Kleine Blumen" see Er klagt, dass der
  Frühling so kurtz blüht Holz **BERG**
"Kleine Blumen, kleine Blätter" see Mit einem
  gemalten Band Goethe **BEETHOVEN,**
  SCHOECK
DER KLEINE, FEINE ALMANACH. see
  Nicolai Alte Weiber **WEBER**
Die kleine Fritz an seine jungen Freunde see
  Anon. **WEBER**
"Kleine Gäste, kleine Haus" see Mausfallen-
  Sprüchlein Mörike **WOLF**
Kleine Lieder see Schulze **LASSEN**
"Kleine Lieder geht nur immer" see Kleine
  Lieder Schulze **LASSEN**
Der kleine Schiffer see Plönnies **LOEWE**
Die kleine Spinnerin see Unknown
  MOZART
"Kleine Spinnerin hinter deinem Rädchen" see
  An die fleissige Spinnerin Krauseneck
  LOEWE
Kleine Stadt in den Südlichen Alpen see
  Krenek **KRENEK**
"Kleine Tränen seh' ich zittern" see Tränen
  Braungart **REGER**
"Kleine Tropfen, seid ihr Thränen" see
  Mädchen-Schwermuth Bernhard, Lily,
  fl.1840. **SCHUMANN**

Kleine Venevil see Bjørnson ARNE. **DELIUS**
"Kleine Venevil hüpfte mit leichtem Sinn" see
  Kleine Venevil Bjørnson **DELIUS**
Kleine Vögelein, du zwitscherst fein see
  Unknown **SCHÖNBERG**
"Ein kleine Weil, da ohn' Gefähr" see
  Ein Rundum (An die grosse Fürstin)
  Weckherlin **KRENEK**
"Die kleine Welt" see Widmung Mörike
  SCHOECK
Kleine Wolke see Kol'tsov **RUBINSTEIN**
Kleiner Haushalt see Rückert **LOEWE**
"Kleiner, kühler Wiesenquell" see Die Quelle
  Unknown **LOEWE**
Kleines Lied see Morgenstern **KILPINEN**
Kleinschmid, Friedrich August, b. 1749.
  BEETHOVEN Der Mann von Wort
  REGER Friedhofsgang
Kleinschrod, Ottilie (Stieler), 1836-1914.
  DVOŘÁK
    Jaro
    Kéž duch muj sám . . .
    Při vyšívání
    U potoka
Kleinstadt im Frühling see Huber, B.
  KILPINEN
Das kleinste Lied see Hamerling **REGER**
Kleist, Ewald Christian von, 1715-1759.
  LOEWE Gross ist der Herr
  ZELTER An Lina
Klemperer, Viktor, 1881-1960.
  SCHÖNBERG Der verlorene Haufen
Klen, V.
  MARTINŮ Picture of a mood
Klenke, Karoline Louise von, 1754-1812.
  SCHUBERT Heimliches Lieben
Klepht song see Anon. **DVOŘÁK** Koljas
Kletke, Hermann, 1813-1886.
  LOEWE In die Ferne
  SCHUMANN Der Sandmann
Kling see Henckell **STRAUSS**
"Kling' die Nacht durch, klinge" see
  Das Zügenglöcklein Seidl **SCHUBERT**
Kling leise, mein Lied see Nordmann
  STÄNDCHEN (?) **LISZT**
"Kling, meine Seele gibt reinen Ton" see
  Kling Henckell **STRAUSS**
Klinge, klinge, mein Pandero see Alvaro
  Fernandez de Almeida
  SPANISCHES LIEDERBUCH: Tango vos,
  el mi pandero. **JENSEN, RUBINSTEIN,**
  WOLF
Klingemann, Carl, 1798-1862.
  MENDELSSOHN-BARTHOLDY
    Bei der Wiege
    Der Blumenstrauss

Klingemann, Carl, 1798-1862 *(continued)*
MENDELSSOHN-BARTHOLDY
(continued)
   Es lauschte das Laub so dunkelgrün
   Frühlingslied
      Two settings: Op. 34 no. 3 and op. 71
      no. 2.
   Herbstlied
   Im Herbst
   Sonntagslied
   Der Wasserfall
WALDEINSAMKEIT.
   BENNETT *As lonesome through the*
     woods I stray
"Klingend schlagen hier die Finken" *see*
   Schöner Ort Frey **SCHOECK**
"Det klinger som fra fine Instrumenter" *see*
   Forårsregn Drachmann **GRIEG**
Klingsor, Tristan L., pseud. *see* Leclère,
   Léon, 1874-1966, translator.
Ein Klippeneiland liegt im Meer see Kugler
   LOEWE
Klockan see Bergman **KILPINEN**
Kloentrup, Johann Aegidius, 1755-1830.
   ZELTER *Der Garten des Lebens*
Klopstock, Friedrich Gottlieb, 1724-1803.
   GLUCK
     Die frühen Gräber
     Der Jüngling
     Schlachtgesang
     Die Sommernacht
       Two settings: one undated, one 1785.
     Der Tod
     Vaterlandslied
     Wir und Sie
   KRENEK *Die frühen Gräber*
   LOEWE *Dem Dreieinigen*
   SCHUBERT
     Dem Unendlichen
     Edone
     Die frühen Gräber
     Die Gestirne
     Das grosse Halleluja
     Hermann und Thusnelda
     Schlachtgesang
     Selma und Selmar
     Die Sommernacht
     Vaterlandslied
   ZELTER *Selmar und Dora*
AN CIDLI.
   SCHUBERT *Furcht der Geliebten*
AN FANNY.
   LOEWE *Wenn einst ich tot bin*
ODE.
   MACDOWELL, SCHUBERT,
     STRAUSS, ZELTER *Das Rosenband*
   SCHUBERT, STRAUSS *An Sie*

Kloster in den Alpen see Krenek **KRENEK**
Klyatve tankista see Mendel'son
   PROKOFIEV
Der Knabe see Schlegel, F. *ABENDRÖTE.*
   SCHUBERT
Der Knabe an die Mutter see Anon. **REGER**
"Knabe dir gefiel" *see Verlassen* No author
   BERG
Der Knabe in der Wiege see Ottenwalt
   SCHUBERT
Der Knabe mit dem Wunderhorn see Geibel
   JENSEN, SCHUMANN
"Knabe sass ich, Fischerknabe" *see Lust und*
   Qual Goethe **STRAUSS**
"Der Knabe seufzt über's grüne Meer" *see*
   Atys Mayrhofer **SCHUBERT**
"Der Knabe träumt" *see Ballade vom*
   Haidenknaben Hebbel **SCHUMANN**
Der Knabe und das Immlein see Mörike
   WOLF
Der Knabe vom Berge see Uhland **LOEWE**
Knaben Wunderhorn *see* Des Knaben
   Wunderhorn
Knabentod see Hebbel **WOLF**
Die Knabenzeit see Hölty **SCHUBERT**
Knäblein see Janson **GRIEG** *Vesle Gut*
"Das Knäblein nach acht Tagen" *see Simeon*
   Cornelius **CORNELIUS**
Knapp, Albert, 1798-1864.
   LOEWE *Die Einladung*
Knecht Ruprecht see Boelitz **REGER**
Das Knie see Morgenstern **SEIBER**
"Ein Knie geht einsam durch die Welt" *see*
   Das Knie Morgenstern **SEIBER**
"Knieend im Staube" *see Liebeslied*
   Rosenbaum **BERG**
The knight see Wilde, Ch. **BALAKIREV**
   Rÿsar
Knight of the Grail see Anon. **ROREM**
Knobel, Betty Wehrli, b. 1904.
   STRAUSS *Malven*
Knodt, Karl Ernst, 1856-1917.
   BERG *Süss sind mir die Schollen des Tales*
"Die Knospe träumte von Sonnenschein" *see*
   Die erwachte Rose Sallet **STRAUSS**
Knoxville, Tennessee see Giovanni
   WEISGALL
Knudsen, Jakob Christian Lindberg,
   1858-1917.
   NIELSEN *Tunge, mørke natteskyer*
Koch, Ernst, 1808-1858.
   SPOHR *An*
Koch, Kenneth, 1925-2002.
   ROREM
     Down at the docks
     Hearing

COMPOSER Poet *Title* "First Line"

In love with you
Invitation
Poem
Spring
THOMSON
Collected poems
Down at the docks
Let's take a walk
Love song
A prayer to Saint Catherine
Koditon see Jalkanen **KILPINEN**
KOECHLIN, CHARLES, 1867-1950.
Banville, Théodore Faullain de, 1823-1891.
L'air, op. 8 no. 5 [Rouart Lerolle]
"Dans l'air s'en vont les ailes"
L'automne, op. 14 no. 7 [Philippo]
La chasse, op. 1 no. 6 [Rouart Lerolle]
"Les cris des chiens"
L'eau, op. 14 no. 3 [Philippo]
L'été, op. 1 no. 5 [Rouart Lerolle]
"Il brille le sauvage Eté"
Les étoiles, op. 14 no. 8 [Philippo]
La guerre, op. 14 no. 9 [Philippo]
L'hiver, op. 8 no. 2 [Rouart Lerolle]
"Aus Bois de Boulogne, l'hiver"
Le jour, op. 14 no. 1 [Philippo]
La lune, op. 8 no. 4 [Rouart Lerolle]
"Avec ses caprices la lune"
Le matin, op. 8 no. 6 [Rouart Lerolle]
"Lorsque s'éveille le matin"
Les métaux, op. 14 no. 5 [Philippo]
Le midi, op. 14 no. 2 [Philippo]
La nuit, op. 1 no. 2 [Rouart Lerolle]
"Nous bénissons la douce nuit"
La paix, op. 8 no. 7 [Rouart Lerolle]
"La paix, au milieu des moissons"
2 voices & piano.
La pêche, op. 8 no. 1[Rouart Lerolle]
"Le pêcheur vidant ses filets"
Les Pierreries, op. 8 no. 3 [Rouart Lerolle] "Les flamboyantes Pierreries"
Le printemps, op. 1 no. 4 [Rouart Lerolle] "Te voilà, rire du printemps!"
Le terre, op. 14 no. 6 [Philippo]
Le Thé, op. 1 no. 3 [Rouart Lerolle]
"Miss Ellen, ver sez moile thé"
Le vin, op. 14 no. 4 [Philippo]
RIMES DORÉES.
Promenade galante, op. 5 no. 1 [Rouart Lerolle]
"Dans le parc au noble dessin"
Mezzo & piano with optional female chorus.
Bonnard, A.
Choeur des voleurs, op. 44 no. 3 [unpubl.]

Bouilhet, Louis Hyacinthe, 1822-1869.
Chanson d'amour, op. 5 no. 3 [R. Deiss]
Moisson prochaine, op. 5 no. 2 [Rouart Lerolle] "O vierge, ta beauté semble un champ de blé mûr"
Bourget, Paul Charles Joseph, 1852-1935.
Novembre, op. 22 no. 2 [Philippo]
"Novembre approche, et c'est le mois charmant"
Chénier, André Marie, 1762-1794.
La jeune tarentine, op. 23 no. 1 [Philippo]
"Pleurez, doux alcyons, Ô vous"
Néère, op. 23 no. 2 [Philippo]
"Mais, telle qu'à sa mort"
Claudel, Paul, 1868-1955.
Dissolution, op. 68 no. 2 [unpubl.]
Corneille, Pierre, 1606-1684.
PSYCHÉ.
Je suis jaloux, op. 104 no. 2 [unpubl.]
Gregh, Fernand, 1873-1960.
Menuet, op. 5 no. 4 [R. Deiss]
"La tristesse des menuets"
Haraucourt, Edmond, 1857-1941.
Aux temps des fées, op. 7 no. 4 [Philippo; Leduc]
"Aux temps jadis, aux temps rêveurs"
Clair de lune, op. 7 no. 1 [Philippo; Leduc] "Jadis, aux jours du feu"
Dame du ciel, op. 7 no. 3 [Philippo; Leduc]
"Madame la Lune, en robe gris pâle"
Le nénuphar, op. 13 op. 3 [Philippo]
"L'air s'embrume"
Accompaniment for piano & flute obbligato ad lib.
Plein eau, op. 7 no. 2 [Philippo; Leduc]
"Rire au matin, courir dans l'ondoiement des herbes"
Le vaisseau, op. 28 no. 4 [Philippo]
"En un rêve, en un rêve étrange"
Hérédia, José María, 1842-1905.
La prière du mort, op. 17 no. 2 [Hachette]
"Arrête! écoute-moi voyageur!"
Humières, Robert, Vicomte d', 1868-1915.
Sur la grève, op. 28 no. 1 [Philippo]
"Bruit profond de la mer"
Koechlin, Charles, 1867-1950.
La Colombe, op. 151 no. 6 [Eschig]
Le cyclone, op. 151 no. 5 [Eschig]
Fatum, op. 151 no. 7 [Eschig]
Gardez ce teint de jeune fille, op. 139 no. 1 [Eschig]

KOECHLIN, CHARLES, 1867-1950
(continued)
Koechlin, Charles, 1867-1950
(continued)
M'a dit amour . . . , op. 151 no. 1
[Eschig]
Prise au piège, op. 151 no. 3 [Eschig]
Quand tu nageois emmy Sirènes et Tritons, op. 151 no. 4 [Eschig]
Tout va bien, op. 139 no. 2 [Eschig]
Tu croyais le tenir, et il t'a prise, op. 151 no. 2 [Eschig]
Leclère, Léon, 1874-1966, translator.
SHÉHÉRAZADE.
Chanson de flûte, op. 84 no. 5 [Eschig]
Chanson d'Engaddi, op. 56 no. 1 [Eschig]
La chanson des beaux amants, op. 84 no. 4 [Eschig]
Chanson d'Ishak de Mossoul, op. 84 no. 8 [Eschig]
Dédicace, op. 84 no. 1 [Eschig]
La neige, op. 56 no. 4 [Eschig]
Offrande, op. 84 no. 7 [Eschig]
L'oiseau en cage, op. 84 no. 6 [Eschig]
Paysage, op. 56 no. 2 [Eschig]
Le potier, op. 84 no. 3 [Eschig]
La rose du rameau sec, op. 56 no. 3 [Eschig]
Le ventre merveilleux, op. 56 no. 5 [Eschig]
Le voyage, op. 84 no. 2 [Eschig]
Leconte de Lisle, Charles Marie René, 1818-1894.
L'astre rouge, op. 13 no. 4 [Philippo] "Sur les continents morts, les houles léthargiques"
Le colibri, op. 17 no. 1 [Hachette] "Le vert colibri, le roi des collines"
Épiphanie, op. 17 no. 3 [Hachette] "Elle passe, tranquille, en un rêve divin"
Juin, op. 15 no. 1 [Hachette] "Les prés ont une odeur d'herbe verte et mouillée"
Midi, op. 15 no. 2 [Hachette] "Midi, Roides étés, épandu sur la plaine"
Nox, op. 15 no. 3 [Philippo] "Sur les pentes des monts les brises apaisées"
Les rêves morts, op. 13 no. 2 [Philippo] "Vois! cette mer si calme a comme un bouclier"
Villanelle, op. 21 no. 1 [Philippo] "Le temps, l'étendue et le nombre"
Villanelle, op. 21 no. 2 [Philippo] "Dans l'air léger, dans l'azur rose"

Louÿs, Pierre, 1870-1925.
CHANSONS DE BILITIS.
Chant funèbre, op. 39 no. 3 [Senart, 1923] "Chantez un chant funèbre"
Épitaphe de Bilitis, op. 39 no. 5 [Senart, 1923] "Sous les feuilles noires des lauriers"
Hymne à Astarté, op. 39 no. 1 [Senart, 1923] "Mère iné puisable"
Hymne à la nuit, op. 39 no. 4 [Senart, 1923] "Les masses noires des arbes ne bougent pas"
Pluie au matin, op. 39 no. 2 [Senart, 1923] "La nuit s'efface"
Samain, Albert Victor, 1858-1900.
Accompagnement, op. 28 no. 3 [Philippo] "Comme de longs cheveux peignés au vent du soir"
Améthyste, op. 35 no. 2 [Philippo] "L'ombre noyait les bois"
Automne, op. 28 no. 2 [Philippo] "A pas lents, et suivis du chien de la maison"
J'ai rêvé cette nuit, op. 35 no. 1 [Philippo]
Rhodante, op. 35 no. 3 [Philippo] "Dans l'après midi chaud où dorment les oiseaux"
Soir païen, op. 35 no. 4 [Philippo] "C'est un beau soir couleur de rose"
AUX FLANCS DU VASE.
Amphise et Melitta, op. 31 no. 6 [Philippo] "Assis au bord du lac où baignent leurs pieds nus"
Le cortège d'amphitrite, op. 31 no. 2 [Philippo] "Le cortège léger glisse aux plaines liquides"
L'ile ancienne, op. 31 no. 3 [Philippo] "Je rêve d'une île ancienne"
La maison du matin, op. 31 no. 4 [Philippo] same
Le repas préparé, op. 31 no. 5 [Philippo] "Ma fille, laisse là ton aiguille ta laine"
Le sommeil de canope, op. 31 no. 1 [Philippo] "Accoudés sur la table et déjà noyés d'ombre"
Silvestre, Paul Armond, 1837-1901.
En Avignon, pays d'amour, op. 5 no. 5 [R. Deiss]
Sully-Prudhomme, René François Armand, 1839-1907.
Déclin d'amour, op. 13 no. 1 [Philippo] "Dans le mortel soupir de l'automne"
Toulet, Paul Jean, 1867-1920.
Infini fais que je t'oublie . . . , op. 104 no. 1 [unpubl.]

Verlaine, Paul, 1844-1896.
> *La chanson des ingénues,* op. 22 no. 1
> [Philippo]
> "Nous sommes les Ingénucs"
> *Il pleure dans mon coeur,* op. 22 no. 4
> [Philippo] same
> *Mon rêve familier,* op. 22 no. 3
> [Philippo]
> "Je fais parfois ce rêve étrange"
> *Le paysage dans le cadre des portières,*
> op. 44 no. 1 [unpubl.]
> *LA BONNE CHANSON.*
> > *Un jour de juin, que j'étais soucieux,*
> > op. 24 no. 2 [Philippo]
> > "En robe grise et verte"
> > *N'est-ce pas?* op. 24 no. 3 [Philippo]
> > same
> > *Le soleil du matin,* op. 24 no. 1
> > [Philippo] same
> > *Va, chanson,* op. 24 no. 4 [Philippo]
> > same
> > Accompaniment for piano &
> > optional string quartet.

Villiers de l'Isle-Adam, Jean Marie
Mathias . . . , comte de, 1838-1889.
> *Hymne à Venus,* op. 68 no. 1 [unpubl.]

Vivien, Renée, 1877-1907.
> *Des roses sur la mer,* op. 44 no. 2
> [unpubl.]

Koechlin, Charles, 1867-1950.
KOECHLIN
> *La Colombe*
> *Le cyclone*
> *Fatum*
> *Gardez ce teint de jeune fille*
> *M'a dit amour . . .*
> *Prise au piège*
> *Quand tu nageois emmy Sirènes et*
> *Tritons*
> *Tout va bien*
> *Tu croyais le tenir, et il t'a prise*

Das Köhlerweib see Keller, G.
HINDEMITH

Das Köhlerweib ist trunken see Keller, G.
WOLF

"Kömmt mit dem Lenz auch die Lieb
gegangen" *see Immerdar Liebe*
Göchhausen **SPOHR**

"Der Kön'ge Herzen, Rath und Sinn" *see Bitte
zu Gott um Frieden* Telschow **LOEWE**

Der König auf dem goldnen Stuhle see
Giesebrecht **LOEWE**

Der König auf dem Thurme see Uhland
LOEWE

Der König aus dem Morgenland see
Schellenberg **REGER**

Der König bei der Krönung see Mörike
REGER, WOLF

Ein König einst gefangen sass see Castelli
DIANA VON POITIERS. **WEBER**

Der König in Thule see Goethe *FAUST.*
JENSEN, SCHUBERT

"König ist spazieren gangen" *see Einfältiges
Lied* Salus **SCHÖNBERG**

"Der König sass beim frohen Mahle" *see
Die drei Sänger* Bobrik **SCHUBERT**

"Ein König sass im Norden" *see Der König
und der Sänger* Bechstein **CORNELIUS**

König Saul see Byron *HEBREW MELODIES.*
MUSORGSKIĬ *TSar' Saul*

"Der König thront" *see Belsazar's Gesicht*
Byron **LOEWE**

Der König und der Sänger see Bechstein
CORNELIUS

Der König von Tule see Goethe *FAUST.*
ZELTER

König Wilhelm see Emsmann **LOEWE**

"König Wilhelm, unsre Sonne, Hohenzollern,
unser Stern!" *see König Wilhelm*
Emsmann **LOEWE**

Die Könige see Cornelius **CORNELIUS**
Two settings: 1856 and op. 8 no. 3 (1870).

"Die Königin steht im hohen Saal" *see
Wirkung in die Ferne* Goethe **LOEWE**

Königlich Gebet see Goethe **WOLF**

"Königliche Morgensonne" *see An die Sonne*
Tiedge **SCHUBERT**

Der Königssohn see Plönnies **LOEWE**
Der kleine Schiffer

"Die Königstochter sticket" *see Der kleine
Schiffer* Plönnies **LOEWE**

Königswinter, Wolfgang Müller von *see*
Müller von Königswinter, Wolfgang,
1816-1873.

"Könnt' ich dich in Liedern preisen" *see Stille
Liebe* Kerner **SCHUMANN**

"Könnt' ich doch stets in deine blauen Augen"
see Lied Benediktov **RUBINSTEIN**

"Könnt' ich einmal wieder singen" *see
Gesanges Erwachen* Kerner **SCHUMANN**

"Könnt' ich mit dem Vöglein fliegen" *see
Vergebener Wunsch* Unknown **LASSEN**

Könnt ich mit den Vöglein fliegen see
Ahlefeldt, Ottilie von **LASSEN**

Könnt ich mit dir dort oben gehen see Mosen
NACHTLIED. **GRIFFES**

Könnt' ich zu dir, mein Licht see Pfau
SCHÖNBERG

"Könnt'st du meine Äuglein seh'n" *see
Rote Äuglein* Anon. **FRANZ**

"Köpfchen, Köpfchen" *see Preziosas
Sprüchlein gegen Kopfweh* Cervantes
CORNELIUS

COMPOSER Poet *Title* "First Line"

Köpfchen, Köpfchen, nicht gewimmert see
Cervantes **WOLF**
Köpken, Friedrich von, 1737-1811.
SCHUBERT *Freude der Kinderjahre*
Körner, Theodor, i.e., Karl Theodor,
1791-1813.
FRANZ *Waldfahrt*
LOEWE
  Sängers Wanderlied
  Treuröschen
  Wallhaide
SCHUBERT
  Amphiaraos
  Auf der Riesenkoppe
  Das war ich
  Gebet während der Schlacht
  Das gestörte Glück
  Liebesrausch
    Two settings: D. 164 and D. 179.
  Liebeständelei
  Sängers Morgenlied
    Two settings: D. 163 and D. 165.
  Schwertlied
  Sehnsucht der Liebe
  Trinklied vor der Schlacht
  Wiegenlied
STRAUSS *Spielmann und Zither*
WEBER
  Abschied vom Leben
  Gebet während der Schlacht
  Leyer und Schwert
  Mein Vaterland
  Trost, "Herz, lass dich nicht zerspalten"
WOLF *Ständchen*
"Das Körnlein springt" *see Frühlingslied*
Braun **SCHUMANN**
Körsbär see Blomberg **KILPINEN**
Köstlin, Christian Reinhold, 1813-1856.
BRAHMS
  Auf dem Schiffe
  Auf dem See
  Nachtigall
  Ein Wanderer
FRANZ *Ach, ich denke*
Köyhän lapset see Kanteletar **KILPINEN**
Kogda bezzabotno, ditya, tĭ rezvish'sya see
Wilde, Ch. **BALAKIREV**
Kogda, chto zvali my svoim see Tiutchev
MEDTNER *We lost all that was once our
own*
Kogda glĭazhu tebe v glaza see Heine
LYRICAL INTERMEZZO. **RIMSKIĭ-
KORSAKOV**
"Kogda menĭa v usta i ochi Ty" *see Taina*
Chamisso **RIMSKIĭ-KORSAKOV**
Kogda volnuetsĭa zhelteĭushchaĭa niva see
Lermontov **RIMSKIĭ-KORSAKOV**

Kogda volnuyetsya zhelteyushchaya niva see
Lermontov **BALAKIREV**
"Koho jen bych se zeptala" *see Přemítání*
Pech **DVOŘÁK**
Kol domu se ted' potácím see Pfleger-
Moravský **DVOŘÁK**
Two settings: B. 123 no. 3 and B. 160 no.
3.
Kol domuse see Pfleger-Moravský
DVOŘÁK
Kolbe, Hanna, fl. 1892.
REGER *Wenn ich's nur wüsst*
"Kolea tuul tohisee" *see Pyhäin miesten
päivänä* Jalkanen **KILPINEN**
Koleda milostná see Anon. **MARTINŮ**
  A love carol
Kolibel'naya pesnya see Arsen'ev
BALAKIREV
Kolibel'naya pesnya see Maĭkov
NOVOGRECHESKIYE PESNI.
CHAĭKOVSKIĭ
Koljas see Anon. **DVOŘÁK**
Kolma's Klage see Macpherson
THE SONGS OF SELMA. **SCHUBERT**
Kol'tͦso see Kol'tsov **RACHMANINOFF**
  The ring
Kol'tsov, Aleseĭ Vasil'yevich, 1809-1842.
BALAKIREV
  ĬA lͦiubila ego
  Isstupleniye
  Mne li, molodtsu razudalomu
  Oboymi, potsaluy
  Pesnya razboynika
  Pesnya starika
  Pridi ko mne
  Tak i rvetsya dusha
MUSORGSKIĭ
  Duͦiut vetry, vetry buĭnye
  Mnogo est' u menͦia teremov i sadov
  Pirushka
  Po nad Donom sad tͦsvetet
  Zastol'naĭa pesn'
RACHMANINOFF
  I was with her
  The ring
  Two partings, a dialogue
RIMSKIĭ-KORSAKOV *Plenivshis' pozoĭ,
  soloveĭ*
RUBINSTEIN
  Fliehe hin, Nachtigall
  Gieb' O heil'ge Geisternacht
  Keine Frühlingsluft
  Klage
  Kleine Wolke
  Lebewohl
  Die Nachtigall und die Rose

Das Ringelein
Sturmeswinde
Wenn ich kommen dich seh'
Koltzov, Aleksey *see* Kol'tsov, Alekseĭ
Vasil'yevich, 1809-1842.
Kolybel'naia see Golenishchev-Kutuzov
MUSORGSKIĭ
Kolybel'naia Eremushki see Nekrasov
MUSORGSKIĭ
Kolybel'naia pesn' v see Pleshcheyev
CHAĭKOVSKIĭ
Kolybel'naia pesnia see Mei RIMSKIĭ-
KORSAKOV
Kolybel'naia pesnia see Ostrovski
MUSORGSKIĭ
Kolysanka gniadego konia see
Iłłakowiczówna SZYMANOWSKI
Kolysanka Krzysi see Iłłakowiczówna
SZYMANOWSKI
Kolysanka lalek see Iłłakowiczówna
SZYMANOWSKI
Kolysanka lalki see Iłłakowiczówna
SZYMANOWSKI
Kolyshetsia more see Tolstoĭ RIMSKIĭ-
KORSAKOV
"Kom, bukken til gutten" *see Lok* Bjørnson
GRIEG
"Kom du sorgsna nordan!" *see Hennes*
budskap Runeberg SIBELIUS
"Kom, i Dag maa alle synge" *see Barnets*
Sang Dam NIELSEN
"Kom Jul til Jord" *see Julesang* Wiberg,
Ohs NIELSEN
Kom nu hit, död see Shakespeare
TWELFTH NIGHT. SIBELIUS
"Kom nu hit, kom nu hit dod" *see Kom nu hit,*
död Shakespeare SIBELIUS
Komárova svatba see Anon. MARTINŮ
The gnat's wedding
Komedianti see Apollinaire MARTINŮ
Saltimbanques
Der Komet see Gerstenberg LOEWE
Komisches musikalisches Sendschreiben see
Weber, Karl WEBER
"Komm, ambrosische Nacht" *see Nacht, Muse*
und Tod Leuthold SCHOECK
Komm bald see Groth BRAHMS
Komm herbei, komm herbei, Tod! see
Shakespeare *AS YOU LIKE IT.* LOEWE
"Komm' ich längs der grünen Wiese" *see*
Die Verschmähte Falke REGER
"Komm in den Garten, ich harre dein" *see*
Erwartung Bassewitz SPOHR
"Komm' in die stille Nacht" *see Ständchen*
Reinick LASSEN, SCHUMANN, WOLF
"Komm, komm, Geselle mein" *see Lied eines*
Mädchens Anon. REGER

"Komm, komm mit nur einen Schritt!" *see*
Lockung Fischer, H. SCHÖNBERG
Komm, Liebchen, komm! see Goethe
WESTÖSTLICHER DIVAN: Buch Sulcika.
WOLF
Komm, liebe Zither, komm see Unknown
MOZART
"Komm, lieber Mai" *see Sehnsucht nach dem*
Frühlinge Overbeck MOZART
"Komm, O Bruder, in die helle Sonne" *see*
Überraschung Jacob, T. LOEWE
Komm, O Tod see Escriva Comendador
WOLF
Komm, O Verina see Heyse LASSEN
"Komm, Trost der Nacht O Nachtigall" *see*
Gesang des Einsiedlers Grimmelshausen
JENSEN
"Komm Trost der Nacht, O Nachtigall" *see*
Der Waldbruder Grimmelshausen
ZELTER
"Komm, Trost der Welt" *see Der Einsiedler*
Eichendorff SCHUMANN
"Komm, und senke die umflorten Schwingen"
see An den Schlaf Unknown SCHUBERT
Komm, wir wandeln zusammen in Mondschein
see Cornelius CORNELIUS
"Komm' zum Garten" *see Frühlingsliebe*
Hoffmann von Fallersleben FRANZ
"Komm zum Garten, denn" *see Serenade*
Eichendorff MEDTNER
"Komma den eviga morgonen nära" *see*
Morgonens hjärta Österling KILPINEN
"Kommen, svallande vågor till stranden" *see*
Till havet Josephson, E. KILPINEN
Kommen und Scheiden see Lenau
SCHUMANN
"Kommen und Scheiden, Suchen und Meiden"
see Lebenslied Matthisson SCHUBERT
Kommt feins Liebchen heut'? see Heine
FRANZ
Kommt herzu! see Unknown LOEWE
"Kommt herzu, ihr seid geladen" *see Kommt*
herzu! Unknown LOEWE
"Kommt, wir wollen uns begeben" *see Vom*
Schlaraffenland Hoffmann von
Fallersleben SCHUMANN
"Komnatka tesnaia, t'khaia" *see V chetyrekh*
stenakh Golenishchev-Kutuzov
MUSORGSKIĭ
Kon' see Pushkin MEDTNER *The war*
horse
Kondratowicz, Ludwik, 1823-1862.
CHAĭKOVSKIĭ *Korol'ki*
Konec všemu see Mužik MARTINŮ *The end*
of all
"Kong Christian stod paa Slotsholmens
Grund" *see Christianshavn* Bauditz, O.
NIELSEN

COMPOSER Poet *Title* "First Line"

KONGS-EMNERNE. *see* Ibsen
  Margretes Vuggesang **GRIEG**
  Wiegenlied **DELIUS**
"Konnte sie denn anders" *see* Vor der
  Hochzeit zu Kana Rilke **HINDEMITH**
Konstantin Konstantinovich, Grand
  Duke of Russia, 1858-1915.
  CHAĬKOVSKIĬ
    IA snachala tebia ne liubila
    IA vam ne nravlius'
    Pervoe svidanie
    Rastvoril ia okno
    Serenada
    Uzh gasli v" komnatakh ogni
Kopisch, August, 1799-1853.
  BRAHMS
    Blinde Kuh
    Die Spröde
    Während des Regens
  LOEWE
    Die Heinzelmännchen
    Landgraf Philipp der Grossmüthige
    Der Nöck
Korinfskiĭ, Apollon Apollonovich, 1868-
  1937.
    RACHMANINOFF *In the soul of each of*
      us
Kornblumen see Dahn **STRAUSS**
Kornblumen see Geibel **LASSEN**
"Kornblumen flecht' ich dir zum Kranz" *see*
  Kornblumen Geibel **LASSEN**
"Kornblumen nenn' ich die Gestalten" *see*
  Kornblumen Dahn **STRAUSS**
Der Kornblumenstrauss see Wildenbruch
  REGER
Korol'ki see Kondratowicz **CHAĬKOVSKIĬ**
Kosegarten, Ludwig Gotthard, 1758-
  1818.
  LOEWE *Wenn du wärst mein eigen*
  SCHUBERT
    Abends unter der Linde
      Two settings: D. 235 and D. 237.
    Alles um Liebe
    An die untergehende Sonne
    An Rosa I
    An Rosa II
    Das Finden
    Idens Nachtgesang
    Idens Schwanenlied
    Luisens Antwort
    Die Mondnacht
    Nachtgesang
    Schwangesang
    Das Sehnen
    Die Sterne
  ZELTER *Lied*

DER ABEND BLÜHT, TEMORA GLÜHT.
  SCHUBERT *Der Abend*
AGNES.
  SCHUBERT *Von Ida*
ICH LAG AUF GRÜNEN MATTEN.
  SCHUBERT *Die Erscheinung*
IM ERLENBUSCH, IM TANNENHAIN.
  SCHUBERT *Die Täuschung*
MINNESANG.
  SCHUBERT *Huldigung*
WER BIST DU.
  SCHUBERT *Geist der Liebe*
Koskenniemi, Veikko Antero, 1885-1962.
  KILPINEN
    Auringon nousu
    Elegia kaunneudelle
    Elegia satakielelle
    Elegia yksinäisyydelle
    Elegia yölle
    Endymion
    Fiat nox
    Hyökyaalto
    Ihme
    Ikarus
    "Jää hyvästi" ja "näkemiin"
    Kaupungilla sataa
    Kehtolaulu
    Kesäyö
    Kesäyössä
    Kevät keralla
    Kuutamolla
    Lakeus I
    Lakeus II
    Lakeus III
    Lakeus IV
    Lakeus V
    Lehdokki
    Leivonen
    Olit tuskasta väristen herännyt syön
    On kaikki syksyn tähdet syttyneet
    Rannalta I
    Rannalta II
    Sa mykkä matkalainen maan
    Sonetti sadun linnusta
    Sun tuskin huomasin ma siihen aikaan
    Syyskuun sonetti
    Syyssonetti
    Valkeat kaupungit
    Vanha laulu
    Yksin
    Ystävien piiri pienentyy
Koskimies, Aukusti Valdemar, 1856-
  1929.
  SIBELIUS
    Illalle
    Souda, souda sinisorsa

Koster, Edward Bernard, 1861-1937.
  PIJPER
    Nacht
    Over den eenzamen vijver
Kot see Iłlakowiczówna **SZYMANOWSKI**
Kot matros see Musorgskiĭ **MUSORGSKIĭ**
Kotzebue, August Friedrich Ferdinand
  von, 1761-1819.
  DER ARME MINNESINGER.
    WEBER
      Lass mich schlummern
      Rase, Sturmwind, blase
      Über die Berge mit Ungestüm
      Umringt vom muterfüllten Heere
Kozel see Musorgskiĭ **MUSORGSKIĭ**
Die Krähe see Müller, Wilhelm
  SCHUBERT
    "Eine Krähe war mit mir" *see Die Krähe*
  Müller, Wilhelm **SCHUBERT**
Die Krähen see Lingg **LASSEN**
KRÄMERSPIEGEL, no. 1
  STRAUSS Kerr *Es war einmal ein Bock*
KRÄMERSPIEGEL, no. 2
  STRAUSS Kerr *Einst kam der Bock*
KRÄMERSPIEGEL, no. 3
  STRAUSS Kerr *Es liebt einst ein Hase*
KRÄMERSPIEGEL, no. 4
  STRAUSS Kerr *Drei Masken sah ich*
KRÄMERSPIEGEL, no. 5
  STRAUSS Kerr *Hast du ein Tongedicht*
KRÄMERSPIEGEL, no. 6
  STRAUSS Kerr *O, lieber Künstler*
KRÄMERSPIEGEL, no. 7
  STRAUSS Kerr *Unser Feind ist, grosser*
    Gott
KRÄMERSPIEGEL, no. 8
  STRAUSS Kerr *Von Händlern wird die*
    Kunst bedroht
KRÄMERSPIEGEL, no. 9
  STRAUSS Kerr *Es war mal eine Wanze*
KRÄMERSPIEGEL, no. 10
  STRAUSS Kerr *Die Künstler sind die*
    Schöpfer
KRÄMERSPIEGEL, no. 11
  STRAUSS Kerr *Der Händler und die*
    Macher
KRÄMERSPIEGEL, no. 12
  STRAUSS Kerr *O Schröpferschwarm*
Die Kränze see Daumer *POLYDORA.*
  BRAHMS
    "Ein Kränzlein sollst du tragen" *see*
    Brautkranzlied Goldtammer, Frau
  LOEWE
Kraft
  LOEWE *Lasst uns mit erhfurchtvollem*
    Dank

Kraftliedchen see Unknown **WAGNER**
Krag, Vilhelm Andreas Wexels, 1871-
  1933.
  DELIUS *Jeg havde en nyskaaren seljeflØjte*
  GRIEG
    Der skreg en Fugl
    Liden Kirsten
    Mens jeg venter
    Moderen synger
    Og jeg vil ha mig en Hjertenskjaer
"Krank nun vollends und matt!" *see Muse und*
  Dichter Mörike **SCHOECK**
Der Kranke see Eichendorff **SCHOECK**
"Kransen av förgätmigejer" *see Förgätmigejer*
  Österling **KILPINEN**
Der Kranz see Schmidt, Hans **BRAHMS**
Krasavitsa see Pushkin **RIMSKIĭ-**
  KORSAKOV
Krasavitsa rybachka see Heine **BORODIN**
  Das schöne Fischermädchen
Krasiński, Zygmunt, 1812-1859.
  CHOPIN *Melodia*
Krásnohorská, Eliška, pseud. *see* Pech,
  Jindřiška, 1847-1926.
Krasov, V
  BALAKIREV *Vzglyani, moy drug*
Kraus, Karl, 1874-1936.
  WORTE IN VERSEN.
    KRENEK
      Durch die Nacht
      Die Nachtigall
Krause, Helene von (née Boddien),
  1841-1915.
  LASSEN *Das Epheublatt*
Krauseneck, Johann Christoph, 1738-
  1799.
  AN DIE FLEISIGE CHLOE.
    LOEWE *An die fleissige Spinnerin*
KRENEK, ERNST, 1900-1991.
Barth, Emil, 1900-1958.
  Heller als Glassteine, op. 189 no. 6
    (1965) [Bärenreiter, 1966] same
  Ihr Schwüre, op. 189 no. 3 (1964)
    [Bärenreiter, 1966]
    "Ihr Schwüre gegen das Vergessen"
  Der Schatten, op. 189 no. 2 (1965)
    [Bärenreiter, 1966]
    "Einziger Augenblick, unbemerkt"
  Schwarze Muse, op. 189 no. 1 (1965)
    [Bärenreiter, 1966]
    "Einflüstrerin, Stimme"
  Spruchband, op. 189 no. 4 (1964)
    [Bärenreiter, 1966] "Den Geborenen
    schreckt das Licht der Welt"
  Wechselrahmen, op. 189 no. 5 (1964)
    [Bärenreiter, 1966] "Ein Totenhafen"

KRENEK, ERNST, 1900-1991 *(continued)*
Bible
  The light is sweet, op. 132, no. 1 (1952)
    [Bärenreiter, 1959]
    "Truly the light is sweet"
  The 104th Psalm, op. 132 no. 2 (1952)
    [Bärenreiter, 1959]
    "Bless the Lord, O my soul"
Donne, John, 1573-1631.
  The flea, op. 175 (1960) [E. B. Marks,
    1964] "Mark but this flea"
Fleming, Paul, 1606-1640.
  An Sich, op. 53 no. 4 (1927) [Universal-
    Edition, 1927]
    "Sei dennoch umverzagt"
  Während der Trennung, op. 76 (1933)
    [unpubl.]
    2 voices & piano.
Gemmingen, Eberhard Friedrich,
  Freiherr von, 1726-1791.
  Das Schweigen, op. 75 (1933) [unpubl.]
Goering, Gerd Hans, 1900-ca.1932.
  Die Ballade vom König Lobesam, op. 9
    no. 7 [Universal-Edition, 1924]
    "Es war ein König Lobesam"
  Erinnerungen, op. 9 no. 4 (1922)
    [Universal-Edition, 1924]
    "Und oft war's nur ein Hauch"
  Im Spiegel, op. 9 no. 1 (1921)
    [Universal-Edition, 1924] "Wir sind
    nicht droben, doch wir sind am Ziel"
  Rätelspiel, op. 9 no. 6 (1922) [Universal-
    Edition, 1924] "Du ewig Wandelbare,
    sieh, du bist die Brükke"
  Räume, op. 9 no. 2 (1921) [Universal-
    Edition, 1924]
    "Gross wuchsen alle Räume"
Goethe, Johann Wolfgang von, 1749-
  1832.
  Fragment, op. 56 no. 3 (1927)
    [Universal-Edition, 1928]
    "Von mehr als einer Seite verwaist"
    Baritone & piano.
  Der neue Amadis, op. 56 no. 2 (1927)
    [Universal-Edition, 1928]
    "Als ich noch Knabe war"
    Baritone & piano.
  Die Zerstörung Magdeburgs, op. 56 no. 1
    (1927) [Universal-Edition, 1928]
    "O Magdeburg, die Stadt"
    Baritone & piano.
  STELLA: Act 4 scene 1.
    Stella's Monologue, op. 57 (1928)
      [Universal-Edition, 1928]
      "Du blühst schön, schöner als sonst"

Günther, Johann Christian, 1695-
  1723.
  Das unerkannte Gedicht, op. 53 no. 1
    (1927) [Universal-Edition, 1927]
    "Man lauert, sitzt und sinnt"
Hopkins, Gerard Manley, 1844-1889.
  Moonrise, op. 112 no. 4 (1946/47)
    [Bärenreiter, 1970] "I awoke in the
    midsummer not to call night"
  On a piece of music, op. 112 no. 3 (1946/
    47) [Bärenreiter, 1970]
    "How all's to one thing wrought!"
  Patience, op. 112 no. 2 (1946/47)
    [Bärenreiter, 1970]
    "Patience, hard thing!"
  Peace, op. 112 no. 1 (1946/47)
    [Bärenreiter, 1970]
    "When will you ever, Peace"
Kafka, Franz, 1883-1924.
  Ach, was wird uns hier bereitet? op. 82
    no. 5 (1937/38)
    [Schott; Universal-Edition, 1958] same
  Du kannst dich zurückhalten . . . , op. 82
    no. 4 (1937/38)
    [Schott; Universal-Edition, 1958] same
  Kämpfte er nicht genug? op. 82 no. 2
    (1937/38) [Schott; Universal-Edition,
    1958] same
  Noch spielen die Jaghunde im Hof, op.
    82 no. 3 (1937/38)
    [Schott; Universal-Edition, 1958]
    same
  Nur ein Wort, op. 82 no. 1 (1937/38)
    [Schott; Universal-Edition, 1958]
    "Nur ein Wort, nur eine Bitte"
Klopstock, Friedrich Gottlieb, 1724-
  1803.
  Die frühen Gräber, op. 19 no. 5 (1923)
    [Universal-Edition, 1924]
    "Wilkommen, O silberner Mond"
Kraus, Karl, 1874-1936.
  WORTE IN VERSEN.
    Durch die Nacht, op. 67 (1930-31)
      [Universal-Edition, 1931]
      "So spät ist es"
    Die Nachtigall, op. 68 (1931)
      [Universal-Edition, 1931]
      "Ihr Menschenkinder, seid ihr nicht
      Laub"
Krenek, Ernst, 1900-1991.
  Albumblatt, op. 228 (1977) [unpubl.]
    "Land zwischen Bergen und Wüsten"
    Holograph at the University of
      California at San Diego, La Jolla,
      CA.

COMPOSER Poet *Title* "First Line"

Alpenbewohner, op. 62 no. 11 (1929)
[Universal-Edition, 1929]
"Die Alpen werden von wilden
Nomaden bewohnt"

Auf und Ab, op. 62 no. 10 (1929)
[Universal-Edition, 1929]
"Auf und ab wie die Narren ennen die
Menschen"

Ausblick nach Süden, op. 62 no. 17
(1929) [Universal-Edition, 1929]
"Und über den Bergen liegt
Welschland"

The ballad of the railroads, op. 98 (1944)
[Bärenreiter, 1961] "Railroads,
railroads, dinning in my ear"
Originally written in English, translated
into German with Krenek's
cooperation.

Ballade vom Fest, op. 71 no. 4 (1931)
[Universal-Edition, 1972]
"Wir haben von Anbeginn her eine
Einladung zu Fest"

Ballade von den Schiffen, op. 71 no. 3
(1931) [Universal-Edition, 1972]
"Ich habe alle meine Schiffe
ausgesendet"

Dort, wo in leichter Kurve, op. 218 no. 6
(1973) [Bärenreiter, 1975] same

Entscheidung, op. 62 no. 18 (1929)
[Universal-Edition, 1929]
"Die Sehnsucht wird immer weiter
bohren"

Epilog, op. 62 no. 20 [Universal-Edition,
1929] "Am Tag nich meiner Heimkehr
geh' ich"

Friedhof im Gebirgsdorf, op. 62 no. 6
(1929) [Universal-Edition, 1929]
"Selbst die Toten in dem kleinen
Kirchhof"

Der Genuss des Unendlichen, op. 71 no.
11 (1931) [Universal-Edition, 1972]
"Einmal, einmal, in viellen
hunderttausend Tagen oder Jahren"

Gewitter, op. 62 no. 13 (1929)
[Universal-Edition, 1929]
"Plötzlich wird es schwarz zwischen
den weissen Gipfeln"

Heimatgefühl, op. 71 no. 5 (1931)
[Universal-Edition, 1972]
"Und ob mein Leben auch eingegraben
sie wie ein Höllenfuss"

Heimkehr, op. 62 no. 19 (1929)
[Universal-Edition, 1929]
"So trägt der schnelle Zug mich wieder
heimwärts"

Heimweh, op. 62 no. 14 (1929)
[Universal-Edition, 1929]
"Manchmal, in all dem Grossen"

Heisser Tag am See, op. 62 no. 15 (1929)
[Universal-Edition, 1929]
"Hier ist alles weich und südlich"

Im Gefälle der Zeit, op. 218 no. 4 (1973)
[Bärenreiter, 1975] same

Kleine Stadt in den Südlichen Alpen, op.
62 no. 16 (1929) [Universal-Edition,
1929] "Schmale Gassen, tief und
dunkel"

Kloster in den Alpen, op. 62 no. 3 (1929)
[Universal-Edition, 1929]
"Reisengross liegt das Kloster da im
Tal"

Liebeslied, op. 71 no. 7 (1931)
[Universal-Edition, 1972] "Dass Liebe
Raum noch hat in solcher Zeit"

Mauern wachsen, op. 71 no. 2 (1931)
[Universal-Edition, 1972]
"Rings um uns wachsen Mauern"

Motiv, op. 62 no. 1 (1929) [Universal-
Edition, 1929] "Ich reise aus, meine
Heimat zu entdekken"

Politik, op. 62 no. 12 (1929) [Universal-
Edition, 1929]
"Ihr Brüder, hört ein ernstes Wort"

Regentag, op. 62 no. 7 (129) [Universal-
Edition, 1929] "Es gibt Regentage die
sehr schön sind"

Rosalinde, op. 45A (1926) [private print]
"Ach, wie ich mich doch schinde"

Rückblick, op. 62 no. 9 (1929)
[Universal-Edition, 1929]
"Was hab' ich bis jetzt non gefunden?"

So spät, so spät, op. 218 no. 1 (1973)
[Bärenreiter, 1975] same

Ein später Gast tritt ein, op. 218 no. 3
(1973) [Bärenreiter, 1975] same

Spätlese, noch am Stock, op. 218 no. 2
(1973) [Bärenreiter, 1975] same

Traurige Stunde, op. 62 no. 5 (1929)
[Universal-Edition, 1929]
"Nicht jeder Reisetag ist schön und
festlich"

Trinklied, op. 71 no. 6 (1931) [Universal-
Edition, 1972] "Allein in sonniger
Herbstlaube sitz' ich beim Wein"

Und Herbstlaub und Regenschauer, op.
71 no. 8 (1931) [Universal-Edition,
1972]
"Wie traurig du am Gartentore standst"

Unser Wein, op. 62 no. 8 (1929)
[Universal-Edition, 1929]
"Von Süd und Ost belagert stürmisch
unsre Alpen"

Verkehr, op. 62 no. 2 (1929) [Universal-
Edition, 1929] "Mit der Bergbahn
geht's elektrisch immer höher"

COMPOSER   Poet   *Title*   "First Line"

KRENEK, ERNST, 1900-1991 *(continued)*
Krenek, Ernst, 1900-1991 *(continued)*
Vor dem Tod, op. 71 no. 9 (1931)
[Universal-Edition, 1972]
"Immer leiser verrinnst du"
Wanderlied im Herbst, op. 71 no. 1
(1931) [Universal-Edition, 1972]
"Kalter Regen peitscht die kahle Flur"
No. 10 for piano only.
Wetter, op. 62 no. 4 (1929) [Universal-
Edition, 1929] "Unverbindlich ist das
Wetter in den Alpen"
Zu Boden gedrückt, op. 218 no. 5 (1973)
[Bärenreiter, 1975] same
Krzyzanowski, Otfried, d. 1918.
Erinnerung, op. 19 no. 1 (1923)
[Universal-Edition, 1924] "Es will kein
Baum so wie die Linde blühen!"
Der Individualist, op. 19 no. 2 (1923)
[Universal-Edition, 1924]
"Ein Weib zu suchen! Wozu"
Wunsch, op. 19 no. 4 (1923) [Universal-
Edition, 1924] "Ein einfaches lichtes
Kleid, ein leichter Gang"
Mommsen, Theodor, 1817-1903.
Im Walde, op. 64 no. 3 [Universal-
Edition, 1930] same
Meine Laute nehm'ich wieder, op. 64 no.
1 [Universal-Edition, 1930] same
Die Saiten weiss ich zu rühren, op. 64
no. 6 [Universal-Edition, 1930] same
Und so lasst mich weider wandern, op.
64 no. 4 [Universal-Edition, 1930]
same
Wiederum lebt wohl, op. 64 no. 7
[Universal-Edition, 1930] same
Paul, Saint, apostle
The night is far spent, op. 84a (1939)
[unpubl.]
Holograph at G. Schirmer's, not
printed (1983).
Rilke, Rainer Maria, 1875-1926.
Aber die Winter! op. 48 no. 3 (1926)
[Universal-Edition, 1926] same
Nichts als ein Athemzug ist das Leere,
op. 48 no. 2 (1926) [Universal-Edition,
1926] same
Oh Thränenvolle, op. 48 no. 1 (1926)
[Universal-Edition, 1926] same
Ô Lacrimosa, no. 1
Rudulph, Mimi, 1923-
Two silent watchers, op. 222 (1975)
[unpubl.] same
Holograph at the University of
California at San Diego, La Jolla,
CA.

Sauter, Lilly von, d. ca. 1970.
Aber die Nächte, op. 216 no. 1 (1972)
[unpubl.] "Quer durch die Felder"
Beschwörung, op. 216 no. 2 (1972)
[unpubl.] "Wenn Nebel zur Au sinkt"
Der Sternenhimmel, op. 216 no. 3 (1972)
[unpubl.] "Der Tag nimmt nur noch"
Storm, Theodor, 1817-1888.
*Musikanten wollen wandern durch die
Saiten*, op. 64 no. 2 [Universal-Edition,
1930] same
Nun ein Scherflein in der Runde, op. 64
no. 5 [Universal-Edition, 1930] same
Weckherlin, Georg Rodolf, 1584-1653.
Ein Anderes, op. 53 no. 3 (1927)
[Universal-Edition, 1927]
"Ihr wisset, was für schwere Klagen"
Ein Rundum (An eine grosse Fürstin), op.
53 no. 2 (1927) [Universal-Edition,
1927]
"Ein kleine Weil, da ohn' Gefähr"
Werfel, Franz, 1890-1945.
Elevation, op. 15 no. 3 (1922)
[Universal-Edition, 1924]
"Welchen Weg bist du gegangen"
Krenek, Ernst, 1900-1991.
KRENEK
Albumblatt
Alpenbewohner
Auf und Ab
Ausblick nach Süden
The ballad of the railroads
Ballade vom Fest
Ballade von den Schiffen
Dort, wo in leichter Kurve
Entscheidung
Epilog
Friedhof im Gebirgsdorf
Der Genuss des Unendlichen
Gewitter
Heimatgefühl
Heimkehr
Heimweh
Heisser Tag am See
Im Gefälle der Zeit
Kleine Stadt in den Südlichen Alpen
Kloster in den Alpen
Liebeslied
Mauern wachsen
Motiv
Politik
Regentag
Rosalinde
Rückblick
So spät, so spät

COMPOSER Poet *Title* "First Line"

Ein später Gast tritt ein
Spätlese, noch am Stock
Traurige Stunde
Trinklied
Und Herbstlaub und Regenschauer
Unser Wein
Verkehr
Vor dem Tod
Wanderlied im Herbst
Wetter
Zu Boden gedrückt
Der Kreuzzug see Leitner **SCHUBERT**
Kreymborg, Alfred, 1883-1966.
   THOMSON *Chamber music*
Der Krieg see Claudius, M. **SCHOECK**
Kriéger, Jacqueline
   MILHAUD
   Haut comme trois pommes
   Il faut obéir
   Pas bien grand
   La tortue naine
"Krieger und Feldherrn, ereilt mich der Tod"
   see Saul vor seiner letzten Schlacht Byron
   LOEWE
Kriegers Ahnung see Rellstab **SCHUBERT**
Kriegslied der Österreicher see Friedelberg
   BEETHOVEN
Kriegst die Peitsche, Pferdchen see Anon.
   SZYMANOWSKI *Bzicem kunia*
Kriloff, I *see* Krylov, Ivan Andreevich,
   1768-1844.
Krohn, Johan Jacob, 1841-1925.
   GRIEG *Sang til juletraeet*
"Królewna od zlotni ka obraczke pozycza" *see*
   Ślub królewny Iłłakowiczówna
   SZYMANOWSKI
Kroughloff, Alexandre V *see* Kruglov,
   Aleksandr Vasil'evich, 1853-1915.
Kroung (La Cigogne, 1930?) *see* Unknown
   RESPIGHI
Kruglov, Aleksandr Vasil'evich, 1853-
   1915.
   RACHMANINOFF *No prophet I*
Krummacher, Friedrich Adolph, 1767-
   1845.
   LOEWE
   Alplied
   Die Auferstehung
   Gebet
   FESTBÜCHLEIN.
   LOEWE *Die Lerche*
   SONNTAGSLIED IM SOMMER.
   LOEWE *Sonntagslied*
Kruse, E. von
   BORODIN *Listen to my song, little friend*

Krylov, Ivan Andreevich, 1768-1844.
   RUBINSTEIN
   Der Adler und der Kukuk
   Die Ameise und die Libelle
   Der Esel und die Nachtigall
   Der Parnass
   Das Quartett
Krysolov see Bryusov **RACHMANINOFF**
   The rat-catcher
Krzyzanowski, Otfried, d. 1918.
   KRENEK
   Erinnerung
   Der Individualist
   Wunsch
Kto idyot? see Apukhtin **CHAÏKOVSKIĭ**
KTV-Kantus see Schoeck **SCHOECK**
   Kantonsschul-Turnverein-Kantus
Kubly, Herbert, 1915-1996.
   ROREM *Anniversary*
Kuckuck see Claudius, M. **SCHOECK**
Der Kuckuck see Löns **KILPINEN**
"Kuckuk, Kuckuk ruft aus dem Wald" *see*
   Frühlingsbotschaft Hoffmann von
   Fallersleben **SCHUMANN**
"Der Kuckuck rief die ganze Nacht" *see*
   Der Kuckuck Löns **KILPINEN**
Kudesnik see Agnivtsev **PROKOFIEV**
"Kühle auf dem schönen Rheine" *see Auf dem*
   Rhein Eichendorff **SCHOECK**
"Ein kühler Hauch" *see Müde* Falke **REGER**
Der Kühne see Eichendorff **PFITZNER**
Kühne, Ferdinand Gustav, 1806-1888.
   JENSEN *Was nennst du deine Liebe*
   schwer und gross
Kühne, Gustav *see* Kühne, Ferdinand
   Gustav, 1806-1888.
Die Künstler sind die Schöpfer see Kerr
   STRAUSS
Künstlers Abendlied see Goethe **ZELTER**
Der Küss see Hölty **BRAHMS**
Küssekraut see Löns **KILPINEN**
"Küssen und Kosen steht euch an" *see*
   Spielmannssehen Sergel **KILPINEN**
Küster, Elieser Gottlieb, 1732-1799.
   LOEWE *Vater unser*
Kuffner, Christoph, 1780-1846.
   SCHUBERT *Glaube, Hoffnung und Liebe*
Kugler, Franz Theodor, 1808-1858.
   JENSEN *Nachtgruss*
   LOEWE
   Herolde ritten von Ort zu Ort
   Im Schloss, da brennen der Kerzen viel
   Der junge König und sein Gemahl
   Jungfrau Lorenz
   Die Jungfrau und der Tod

Kugler, Franz Theodor, 1808-1858
(continued)
LOEWE *(continued)*
Ein Klippeneiland liegt im Meer
Wie bräutlich glänzt das heilige Rom
SKIZZENBUCH.
BRAHMS *Ständchen*
Kugler, Johann, Consul in Stettin
LOEWE
Beim Scheiden
Letztes Lied
Otto-Lied
Kuh, Emil, 1828-1876.
CORNELIUS
Du kleine Biene, verfolg mich nicht
Frühling im Sommer
Hirschlein ging im Wald spazieren
Mir ist, als zögen Arme mich schaurig
himmelwärts
LISZT *Ihr Glocken von Marling*
Kuhreigen see Garborg *HAUGTUSSA.*
GRIEG *Ku-Lok*
"Kuin lehdet tuulessa ihmiset on" *see Ihmisen*
osa Jalkanen **KILPINEN**
"Kuin tunturilla puro hiljaa helää" *see*
Laululle Törmänen **KILPINEN**
Kuining Chuonrat der Junge see Unknown
ZELTER
"Kuka kuuli laulavani" *see Laulan ilman*
lainehilta Kanteletar **KILPINEN**
Kukkalatva kuusi see Kanteletar **KILPINEN**
"Kukkua käkesin kälkö" *see Saisinko käeltä*
kielen Kanteletar **KILPINEN**
"Kukkui muinainen käkeni" *see Muinainen*
käkeni Kanteletar **KILPINEN**
"Kukkuipa käkeä kaksi" *see Kummaistako*
kuuleminen Kanteletar **KILPINEN**
Der Kukuk see Herder **LOEWE**
"Kukuk hat sich zu Tode gefallen" *see*
Ablösung im Sommer Anon. **MAHLER**
Kukushka see Gellert **CHAïKOVSKIï**
Kulchinsky, V
BALAKIREV *Dogorayet rumyaniy zakat*
Kulmann, Elisabeth, 1808-1825.
SCHUMANN
Du nennst mich armes Mädchen
Gekämpft hat meine Barke
Die letzten Blumen starben
Mond, meiner Seele Liebling
Reich' mir die Hand, O Wolke
Viel Glück zur Reise, Schwalben
Der Zeisig
Ku-Lok see Garborg *HAUGTUSSA.* **GRIEG**
Kummaistako kuuleminen see Kanteletar
KILPINEN

Kumpf, Johann Gottfried, 1781-1862.
SCHUBERT
Mein Gruss an den Mai
Der Mondabend
Kun ma kerran see Kanteletar **KILPINEN**
Kun mun kultani tulisi see Kanteletar
KILPINEN
"Kun oisin paimenna paloinen" *see Viikon*
vuottelin käkeä Kanteletar **KILPINEN**
"Kun olin miessä nuorempana" *see Nyt on*
kaikki kallistunna Kanteletar **KILPINEN**
Kunfttag I see George *DER SIEBENTE*
RING: Maximin. **WEBERN**
"Kunst! O in deine Arme" *see Keine Rettung*
Mörike **SCHOECK**
Kunze, W
RUBINSTEIN *Gebet*
Kuriose Geschichte see Reinick **PFITZNER**
Kurochkin, Vasili Stepanovich, 1831-
1875.
MUSORGSKIï *No esli by s toboiu ia*
vstretit'sia mogla
Kurowski-Eichen, Friedrich Carl Anton
Bernhard von, 1780-1853.
LOEWE
Der grosse Kurfürst und die
Spreejungfrau
Die Heldenbraut
Wach auf!
Kurz, Isolde, 1853-1944.
REGER *Um Dich*
Kurze Fahrt see Eichendorff **SCHOECK**
Kurzes Erwachen see Kerner **SCHUMANN**
Kurzes Wiedersehen see Osterwald **FRANZ**
Der Kuss see Weisse **BEETHOVEN**
Kuti, kuti, kultaseni see Kanteletar
KILPINEN
Kuu Kalpea see Lönnbohm **KILPINEN**
"Kuu painuu taakse taivaanrannan" *see Aamu*
Jalkanen **KILPINEN**
Kuusen juuret kuivettuvat see Kanteletar
KILPINEN
Kuusi ja lintunen see Lönnbohm
KILPINEN
Kuutamolla see Koskenniemi **KILPINEN**
Kuutamo-oodi see Jalkanen **KILPINEN**
Kvällning see Ullman **KILPINEN**
Kvarnhjulet see Josephson, E. **SIBELIUS**
Kveldssang for Blakken see Rolfsen **GRIEG**
Kvitko, L
PROKOFIEV *Porosiata*
"Kymmenen pitkää vuotta" *see Eheu fugaces!*
Jalkanen **KILPINEN**
Kynaston, Sir Francis, 1587-1642.
THOMSON *If thou a reason dost desire to*
know

Kyösti, Larin, pseud. *see* Larin-Kyösti, 1873-1948.

Kyrie see Anon. **LOEWE**

"Kyrie, fons bonitatis" *see Kyrie* Anon. **LOEWE**

"Kyrie, Kyrie, Kyrie eleison" *see Mass for solo voice* Anon. **THOMSON**

Kyrie, O Herr Gott Vater! see Unknown **LOEWE**

"Kysin oot sinä, ihminen" *see Elegia yksinäisyydelle* Koskenniemi **KILPINEN**

Kyssen see Rydberg **SIBELIUS**

Kyssens hopp see Runeberg **SIBELIUS**

Kytice see Unknown **DVOŘÁK**

L

La Fontaine, Jean de, 1621-1695.
   DIAMOND *Sister Jane*
   GOUNOD
      Les deux pigeons
      Tout l'univers obéit à l'amour
   SAINT-SAËNS *La cigale et la fourmi*
   THOMSON *Le singe et le léopard*
   PHILÉMON ET BAUCIS.
      GOUNOD *Ni l'or ni la grandeur*
"La la la la la" *see Chant de folie* Vallery-Radot, Pasteur **IBERT**
"La la la! La vie a mal guidé mes pas" *see La verdadera vida* Saix, Guillot de **MASSENET**
La Laurencie, Lionel de *see* La Laurencie, Marie-Berband-Lionel de, 1861-1933.
La Laurencie, Marie-Berband-Lionel de, 1861-1933.
   INDY *La première dent*
La Morvonnais, Hippolyte Michel de, 1802-1853.
   MILHAUD *Sonnet*
La Motte-Fouque, Friedrich Heinrich Karl, freiherr, 1777-1843.
   SPOHR *Lied aus Aslauga's Ritter*
La non vuol esser piu mia see Poliziano **RIETI**
La Ville de Mirmont, Jean de, 1886-1914.
   FAURÉ
      Diane, Séléné
      Je me suis embarqué
      La mer est infinie
      Vaisseaux, nous vous aurons aimés
Là-bas see Croze, J. L. **SAINT-SAËNS**
"Là-bas, dans un ciel de turquoise" *see Désir de l'Orient* Saint-Saëns **SAINT-SAËNS**
"Là-bas, là-bas" *see Elle s'en est allée* Solvay, Lucien **MASSENET**

Là-bas vers l'èglise see Anon. **RAVEL**
Le labbra ella compose see Zaffira **GOUNOD**
Labé, Louise Charly, called, 1526-1566.
   BERKELEY *Tant que mes yeux* (A memory)
   MILHAUD *Sonnet*
   SAUGUET
      A Vénus
      Amour
      Chasse
      Printemps
      Songe
      Tant que mes yeux
Labetrank der Liebe see Stoll **SCHUBERT**
Labutě see Nebesky, Jan **MARTINŮ**
   The swan
Le lac see Lamartine **SAINT-SAËNS**
Le lac see Unknown **POULENC**
"Le lac comme un gros bijou bleu" *see Paysage* Messiaen **MESSIAEN**
Lachen und Weinen see Rückert *LACHENS UND WEINENS GRUND.* **SCHUBERT**
LACHENS UND WEINENS GRUND. see **RÜCKERT**
   Lachen und Weinen **SCHUBERT**
LACRIMAS. see Schütz
   Delphine **SCHUBERT**
   Florio **SCHUBERT**
LAD VAAREN KOMME. see Jacobsen
   Let springtime come then **DELIUS**
A laddie's sang see Soutar **BRITTEN**
Lads of Zvolyn see Anon. **MARTINŮ**
   Zvolenovcí chlapci
Ladslove see Housman *THE SHROPSHIRE LAD.* **IRELAND**
THE LADY OF THE LAKE. see Scott
   Ellens Gesang I **SCHUBERT**
   Ellens Gesang II **SCHUBERT**
   Ellens Gesang III **SCHUBERT**

COMPOSER Poet *Title* ''First Line''

THE LADY OF THE LAKE *(continued)*
  Lied des gefangenen Jägers **SCHUBERT**
  Normans Gesang **SCHUBERT**
  "Lady, when I behold the roses sprouting" *see*
    Damask roses Anon. **QUILTER**
  "Lächeln ist des Mundes Sache" *see*
    Mund und Auge Hamerling **LASSEN**
  "Läg' dort ich unterm Firneschein" *see*
    Ich würd' es hören Meyer **SCHOECK**
  "Lämmin paita liinainenki" *see*
    Ohoh kullaista kotia Kanteletar
    KILPINEN
LAENGSEL. see Kjerulf
    Sehnsucht **DELIUS**
  "Längst schon flog zu Nest der Vogel" *see*
    Abendbild Ernst **LASSEN**
Längtan see Weiss **SIBELIUS** *Sehnsucht*
Längtan heter min arvedel see Karlfeldt
    SIBELIUS
  "Läpäjävä veden kalvo" *see Nocturno*
    Lamberg **KILPINEN**
Laer mig, nattens stjerne see Richardt
    NIELSEN
Lärksång see Blomberg **KILPINEN**
  "Läuten kaum die Maienglocken leise" *see*
    Der Schalk Eichendorff **FRANZ**
Läuterung see Hohenberg **BERG**
Lafait-Gontié, Antoinette
    MASSENET *Voix suprême*
Laforgue, Jules, 1860-1887.
    HONEGGER *Petite Chapelle*
    SAUGUET
      Clair de lune de Novembre
      Crépuscule de mi juillet, huit heures
Lagerkvist, Pär Fabian, 1891-1974.
    KILPINEN
      Det är du som skall bliva den yppersta
      Barn, som jag smekt
      Befriad är dagen
      Din mun är ljusare än min
      Ett enda ord är mitt
      *En gång skall det brinna ett ljus på min
        grav*
      Hela världen är mig så kär
      *Ingenting får störa vår stund med
        varandra*
      Mitt liv går bort, jag vet ej varthäm
      O vinternatt
      Om tiotusen år
      Regnet slår och slår
      Så gamla äro alla moln
      Som ett blommande mandelträd
      Var är den djupa glädje
Lagrime! see Negri **RESPIGHI**
Lahor, Jean, pseud. *see* Cazalis, Henri,
    1840-1909.

Le Lai du Chevrefeuille see France, Marie
    de **MILHAUD**
  "Laisons le litet le sommiel" *see Ode du
    premier jour de Mai* Passerat
    BERKELEY
Laisse ta hanche blonde see Hugnet
    SAUGUET
  "Laissez moi, mes amis, laissez moi solitaire"
    see Reverie Unknown **LOEFFLER**
  "Laissez-moi partir bien vite" *see Le départ*
    Unknown **POULENC**
  "Laissons le lit et le sommeil" *see Le premier
    jour de Mai* Passerat **GOUNOD**
A lake and a fairy boat see Hood *MINOR
    POEMS* (1846): For music. **HESELTINE**
Lakeus I see Koskenniemi **KILPINEN**
Lakeus II see Koskenniemi **KILPINEN**
Lakeus III see Koskenniemi **KILPINEN**
Lakeus IV see Koskenniemi **KILPINEN**
Lakeus V see Koskenniemi **KILPINEN**
Lalanne, Louise, pseud. *see* Apollinaire,
    Guillaume, 1880-1918.
  "Lalka do spizarni sie zakrada" *see* Nikczemny
    szpak Iłłakowiczówna
    SZYMANOWSKI
LALO, EDOUARD, 1823-1892.
  Anon.
    Veni Creator [Hamelle] "Veni creator
      spiritus"
      Piano or organ accompaniment.
  Beauquier, Charles, 1833-1916.
    Humoresque (1867?) [Hamelle, 1867]
      "Que me fait la politique!"
  Béranger, Pierre Jean de, 1780-1857.
    Beaucoup d'amour (1849) [Girod, 1849;
      Launer, 1849]
      "Malgré la voix de la sagesse"
    La pauvre femme (1849) [Girod, 1849;
      Launer, 1849]
      "Il neige, il neige et là devant l'église"
    Les petits coups (1849) [Girod, 1849;
      Launer, 1849]
      "Maitres de tous nos désirs"
    Si j'étais petit oiseau (1849) [Girod,
      1849; Launer, 1849]
      "Moi qui même au près des belles"
    Le suicide (1849) [Girod, 1849; Launer,
      1849] "Quoi! morts tous deux! dans
      cette chambre close"
    Le vieux vagabond (1849) [Girod, 1849;
      Launer, 1849]
      "Dans ce fossé cessons de vivre"
  Delpit, Albert, 1849-1893.
    Chant Breton, op. 31 (ca.1884) [Hamelle,
      1884; Heugel, 1988]
      "Mon ami vient de s'en aller!"
      With oboe obbligato.

Devereux, Penelope, 1562?-1607,
supposed author.
La Fénaison (1872) [G. Hartmann, 1873;
Heugel, 1988]
"Venez fillettes et garçons"

Flobert, A.
Adieux au désert (1848) [Girod, 1849;
Launer]
"La nuit disparait, l'oiseau chante"

Gautier, Théophile, 1811-1872.
L'Esclave (1872) [G. Hartmann, 1873;
Heugel, 1988]
"Captive, et peut-être oubliée"

Hugo, Victor Marie, comte, 1802-1885.
L'aube nait et ta porte est close, op. 17
no. 3 (1854) [Hamelle, 1854; Heugel,
1988] same
Chanson à boire, op. 17 no. 6 (1854)
[Hamelle, 1854; Heugel, 1988]
"Amis, vive l'orgie"
Dieu qui sourit et qui donne, op. 17 no. 4
(1854) [Hamelle, 1854; Heugel, 1988]
same
Guitare, op. 17 no. 1 (1854) [Hamelle,
1854; Heugel, 1988]
"Comment, disaient-ils?"
Oh! quand je dors, op. 17 no. 5 (1854)
[Hamelle, 1854; Heugel, 1988] same
Puisqu'ici-bas toute âme, op. 17 no. 2
(1854) [Hamelle, 1854; Heugel, 1988]
same
Souvenir (1872?) [G. Hartmann, 1873;
Heugel, 1988]
"Comme un ange qui se dévoile"

Lamartine, Alphonse Marie Louis de
Prat de, 1790-1869.
Prière de l'enfant a son réveil (1884)
[Schott, 1884; Heugel, 1988]
"O Père qu'adore mon père"
Viens! (1884) [Schott, 1884; Heugel,
1988] "Viens! cherchons une ombre
propice, viens!"

Lehugeur, A.
L'ombre de Dieu (1848) [Girod, 1849;
Launer]
"Si Dieu bénit la naissance des roses"

Leprade, Pierre Marin Victor Richard
de, 1812-1883.
La chanson de l'alouette (1884) [Schott,
1884; Heugel, 1988]
"Je suis, je suis le cri de joie"

Musset, Alfred de, 1810-1857.
À une fleur (1870) [Heugel, 1873, 1988]
"Que me veux-tu, chère fleurette"
La Zuecca (1870) [Heugel, 1873, 1988]
"A Saint Blaise, à la Zuecca, vous
étiez"

BARBERINE.
Chanson de Barberine (1870) [Heugel,
1873, 1988] "Beau chevalier qui
partez pour la guerre"
CONTES D'ESPAGNE ET D'ITALIE.
Ballade à la lune (1860) [Hamelle,
1860] "C'était dans la nuit brune"

Silvestre, Paul Armond, 1837-1901.
À celle qui part (1884) [Schott, 1884;
Heugel, 1988] "Lorsque la mer et toi
vous serez face à face"
Tristesse (1884) [Schott, 1884; Heugel,
1988]
"Nous sommes passés ce me semble"

Stupuy, Hippolyte
Le novice, op. 5 (1849) [Girod, 1849;
Launer] "Dans la brume où se perd la
lointaine colline"
Baritone & piano.

Theuriet, André, 1833-1907.
Marine, op. 33 (1884) [Hamelle, 1884;
Heugel, 1988]
"Souvent je rêve, O chère enfant"
Also voice & orchestra.
Le Rouge-gorge (1884) [G. Hartmann;
Heugel, 1988]
"J'ai fait ce rêve, Ô ma chérie"

Wilder, Victor van, 1835-1892.
Aubade (1872) [Hamelle, 1872; Heugel,
1988] "Mignonne blonde aux yeux de
flamme"

Lamartine, Alphonse Marie Louis de
Prat de, 1790-1869.
BIZET
L'âme humaine est pareille au doux ciel
Chant d'amour
Douce mer
Le grillon
GOUNOD
Au rossignol
Premier prélude de Bach
Le soir
Solitude
Le vallon
LALO
Prière de l'enfant a son réveil
Viens!
MILHAUD *L'Isolement*
RUBINSTEIN *La prière de femme*
SAINT-SAËNS
L'automne
Le golfe de Baya
Le lac
Le poète mourant
SATIE *Elégie*
SAUGUET *A des roses sous la neige*

Lamartine, Alphonse Marie Louis de Prat de, 1790-1869 *(continued)*
LA PENSÉE DES MORTS.
   GOUNOD *Seul*
The lamb see Blake, William **CHANLER, VAUGHAN WILLIAMS**
Lamberg, Eila Sylvia, 1921-
   KILPINEN
     Eikö totta
     Eräs
     Kevättä
     Muisto
     Nocturno
Lambertine see Stoll **SCHUBERT**
Lament see Anon. **SEIBER**
Lament see Unknown **PROKOFIEV**
Lament for a city see Anon. **DVOŘÁK**
     Žalozpěv Pargy
"*Lament him, Mauchline husbands a' " see*
     Epitaph for a wag in Mauchline Burns
     GIDEON
The lament of Ian the proud see Sharp, W.
   FOAM OF THE PAST. **GRIFFES**
Lamentation see Unknown **MILHAUD**
Lamento see Gautier *LA COMÉDIE DE LA MORT.* **DUPARC**
Lamento see Gautier **FAURÉ** *Chanson du pêcheur;* **GOUNOD** *La chanson du pêcheur*
Lamento see Gautier **SAINT-SAËNS**
Lamotte, Antoine Houdart de, 1672-1731.
   MOZART *Ariette*
The lamplighter see Stevenson, Robert Louis *A CHILD'S GARDEN OF VERSES.* **QUILTER**
The land of dreams see Blake, William **THOMSON**
The land of fear see Capetanakis **ROREM**
THE LAND OF LOST CONTENT, no. 1
   IRELAND Housman *The Lent lily*
THE LAND OF LOST CONTENT, no. 2
   IRELAND Housman *Ladslove*
THE LAND OF LOST CONTENT, no. 3
   IRELAND Housman *Goal and wicket*
THE LAND OF LOST CONTENT, no. 4
   IRELAND Housman *The vain desire*
THE LAND OF LOST CONTENT, no. 5
   IRELAND Housman *The encounter*
THE LAND OF LOST CONTENT, no. 6
   IRELAND Housman *Epilogue*
A land of silence see Dowson **QUILTER**
"*Land zwischen Bergen und Wüsten" see*
   Albumblatt Krenek **KRENEK**
"*Die Lande durch träumt der Schlaf" see*
   Nachtsegen Evers **REGER**
Landgraf Ludwig see Gruppe **LOEWE**

Landgraf Philipp der Grossmüthige see
   Kopisch **LOEWE**
Die Landlust see Voss **ZELTER**
Landon, Letitia, 1802-1838.
   BENNETT *Forget-me-not*
Landor, Walter Savage, 1775-1864.
   ROREM *Mother, I cannot mind my wheel*
Landscape see Sada-Ihe, 13th cent.
   GRIFFES
Landskap see Ullman **KILPINEN**
Die Landstreicherin see Rodès **BLOCH**
   La vagabonde
LANGAGE. see Ganzo
   C'est l'heure **SCHMITT**
Langbein, August Friedrich Ernst, 1757-1835.
   ZELTER *Die Fahrt ins Heu*
"*Lange begehrten wir ruhig allein zu sein" see*
   Ode Platen-Hallermünde **CORNELIUS**
"*Lange harrt' ich: aber endlich breiten ausein"*
   see An Anna I Kerner **SCHUMANN**
Langelandsk Folkemelodi see Andersen
   GRIEG
"*Långeliga, dunkelgrå bergsstränder" see*
   Landskap Ullman **KILPINEN**
"*Langes de tous les fils, Manteau de tous les pères" see Hymne pour le "Salut Drapeau" du "Prince de Byzance"...* Péladin **SATIE**
Langs ei Å see Vinje **GRIEG**
Langs en A see Vinje **GRIEG** *Langs ei Å*
"*Langsam erzählet der rauschende Wald" see*
   Im Walde Bjørnson **BERG**
"*Langsam und schimmernd fiel ein Regen" see Abendregen* Keller, G. **BRAHMS**
"*Langsam wird mein Kindchen müde" see*
   Abendlied Unknown **REGER**
Långsamt som qvällskyn see Tavaststjerna
   SIBELIUS
Langsted, Adolf, 1864-1919.
   GRIEG *Julens Vuggesang*
"*Langt bortom fjärdens vag" see Hvem styrde hit din väg?* Runeberg **SIBELIUS**
Lanier, Sidney, 1842-1881.
   CARPENTER *May, the maiden*
   RIEGGER *The violet sea*
   AN EVENING SONG.
   GRIFFES *Evening song*
Lanoux, Armand, 1913-1983.
   SAUGUET
     Chanson de l'oiseleur
     Isis poignardée
LE LANTERNE MAGIQUE. see Carême
   Le cerisier **SCHMITT**
Laporte, René, b. 1905
   SAUGUET
     L'amoire de campagne
     La chambre de juin
     Présence

Lappe, Carl *see* Lappe, Karl, 1773-1843.
Lappe, Karl, 1773-1843.
    BEETHOVEN *So oder so*
    SCHUBERT
       Der Einsame
       Im Abendrot
Lapping waters see Rydberg **SIBELIUS**
    Vattenplask
Der Lappländer see Marggraff **LOEWE**
Lappländers Lied see Marggraff **LOEWE**
    Der Lappländer
Larin-Kyösti, 1873-1948.
    KILPINEN
       Käköä kuullessa
       Katso yli kedon kukkain
       Tarhassa hiipii hienohelma
    SIBELIUS *Kaiutar*
The lark see Unknown **DVOŘÁK** *Skřivánek*
The lark see Unknown **RUBINSTEIN**
    Die Lerche
The lark sings louder see Tolstoĭ **RIMSKIĬ-**
    KORSAKOV *Zvonche zhavoronka pen'e*
LARKSPUR; ed. by Victor Neuburg
    (Steyning, Sussex: Vine Press, 1922). *see*
    Smith, Dr. James
       Milkmaids **HESELTINE**
The larky lad see Soutar **BRITTEN**
"The larky lad frae the pantry" *see The larky*
    lad Soutar **BRITTEN**
Larme see Rimbaud **RIVIER**
Les larmes see Blanchecotte
    CHAĬKOVSKIĬ
Larmes see Richepin **CASELLA**
    NB: Not seen.
Larmes see Richepin *LA MER.* **FAURÉ**
Larmes maternelles see Nekrasov
    MASSENET
Laroche, Ernest
    MASSENET *Mienne!*
Larsen, Thøger, 1875-1928.
    NIELSEN *Danmark, nu blunder den lyse*
    Nat
Larson, Jack, b. 1933.
    DIAMOND, ROREM *Do I love you?*
"Las, Colombine a fermé le volet" *see*
    Sérénade Banville **DEBUSSY**
"Las! nous n'avons pas l'avantage" *see*
    Cant per Nadal Goudouli **SÉVERAC**
Lásce neujdeš see Anon. **DVOŘÁK**
Lasker, Ignaz Julius, 1811-1876.
    LOEWE *Hinaus! Hinauf! Hinab!*
Lasker-Schüler, Else, 1869-1945.
    HINDEMITH
       Du machst mich traurig-hör'
       Traum
"Lass Akaziendüfte schaukeln" *see*
    Hochzeitlich Lied Lindner, Anton
    STRAUSS

"Lass' das Zagen" *see Nur Mut!* Schack
    STRAUSS
"Lass deine Sichel rauschen" *see Lied der*
    Schnitterin Pfau **SCHÖNBERG**
"Lass dich mit gelinden Schlägen rühren" *see*
    Sprache der Liebe Schlegel **SCHUBERT**
Lass dich nur nichts nicht dauern see
    Fleming **REGER**
"Lass dich nur nichts nicht dauern" *see*
    Pilgerspruch Fleming
    MENDELSSOHN-BARTHOLDY
Lass' die Rose schlummern see Hamerling
    LASSEN
Lass mich deine Augen see Cornelius
    RUBINSTEIN
"Lass mich ihm am Busen hangen" *see Lieder*
    der Braut Rückert **SCHUMANN**
"Lass mich in den dunklen Grund" *see*
    Trennung Kastropp **LASSEN**
"Lass mich knien, lass mich schauen!" *see*
    Thurmwächter Lynceus Goethe **LOEWE**
"Lass mich mit meinem Weh" *see Wo Tauben*
    sind Beck **JENSEN**
"Lass mich noch einmal dir ins schwarze
    Auge sehn" *see Letzte Bitte* Bierbaum
    REGER
Lass mich schlummern see Kotzebue *DER*
    ARME MINNESINGER. **WEBER**
"Lass', O Welt, O lass mich sein!" *see*
    Verborgenheit Mörike **FRANZ, WOLF**
Lass ruh'n die Toten see Chamisso
    STRAUSS
Lass scharren deiner Rosse Hug see Meyer
    PFITZNER
Lass sie nur gehn see Heyse **WOLF**
"Lass' tief in dir mich lesen" *see Ihre Stimme*
    Platen-Hallermünde **SCHUMANN**
"Lass tief in dir mich lesen" *see Mein Herz*
    und deine Stimme Platen-Hallermünde
    BRUCKNER
"Lass uns leise bekennen" *see Geheimnis*
    Heyse **JENSEN**
"Lass uns noch die Nacht erwarten" *see Alles*
    Dehmel **SCHÖNBERG**
Lasse liten see Topelius **SIBELIUS**
LASSEN, EDUARD, 1830-1904.
    Ahlefeldt, Ottilie von
       Die Erde steht in süssem Beben, op. 82
         no. 1 [Hainauer]
       Ich gehe durch die stille Nacht, op. 82
         no. 5 [Hainauer]
       Jüngst, als ich über'n Friedhof ging, op.
         82 no. 3 [Hainauer]
       Könnt ich mit den Vöglein fliegen, op. 82
         no. 4 [Hainauer]
       Still ist's auf dem Erdenkreise, op. 82 no.
         2 [Hainauer]

LASSEN, EDUARD, 1830-1904 *(continued)*
Ahlefeldt, Ottilie von *(continued)*
    See also his *Ein Frühlingsnacht,*
      author of text unknown (below).
  Wenn ich ein kleines Mücklein wär
    [Weimar: T.F.A.Kühn, 188__] same
Aldrich, Thomas Bailey, 1836-1907.
  THE BETROTHAL.
    Verlobung, op. 62 no. 2 [Hainauer]
      "Einen Ring von Golde steckt' ich
      an die Hand"
Ali, pasha, of Janima, 1741-1822.
  Die Rosen von Jericho, op. 65 no. 4
    [Hainauer]
      "Es blühen die Rosen von Jericho"
Arndt, Ernst Moritz, 1769-1860.
  Ballade, op. 85 no. 2 [Hainauer]
    "Und die Sonne macht den weiten Ritt
    um die Welt"
Bernays, Michael, 1834-1897.
  An die Nacht, op. 85 no. 5 [Hainauer]
    "Beginne deine heilige Feier"
Blüthgen, Viktor, 1844-1920.
  DAS ERSTE LIED.
    Wer hat das erste Lied erdacht, op. 92
      no. 4 [Hainauer; Oliver Ditson,
      1894] same
**Bodenstedt, Friedrich Martin von,
1819-1892.**
  Die Gletscher leuchten im Mondenlicht,
    op. 60 no. 2 [Hainauer; G. Schirmer]
    same
  Die helle Sonne leuchtet, op. 60 no. 6
    [Hainauer; G. Schirmer] same
  Hoch auf fliegt mein Herz, op. 60 no. 3
    [Hainauer; G. Schirmer] same
  Ich fühle deinen Odem, op. 45 no. 4
    [Hainauer; G. Schirmer, 1883] same
  Nun liegt die Welt im Traume, op. 60 no.
    1 [Hainauer] same
  Wenn der Frühling auf die Berge steigt,
    op. 60 no. 5 [Hainauer; G. Schirmer]
    same
  Wenn ich dich seh', op. 60 no. 4
    [Hainauer; G. Schirmer] same
Bornowski, Theodor, 1829-1892.
  Seufzer, op. 52 no. 4 [Hainauer] "O gib
    mir meinen Frieden"
Burns, Robert, 1759-1796.
  It's nae thy bonnieface, op. 66 no. 6
    [Hainauer] same
    Text adapted by J. Feis.
**Byron, George Gordon Byron, 6th
baron, 1778-1824.**
  Mein Leben, ich liebe dich, op. 68 no. 6
    [Hainauer]
      "Mädchen von Athen, geschwind"

There was a time, op. 68 no. 5
  [Hainauer]
    "Es war die Zeit, du kennst das Jahr"
Claus, Nicolo
  Das Elternhaus, op. 72 no. 1 [Hainauer]
    "So herzig, wie mein Elternhaus"
  Heimatliebe, op. 72 no. 2 [Hainauer]
    "Kanonen donnern, es blitzt das Tal"
Cornelius, Peter, 1824-1874.
  Du meiner Seele schönster Traum, op. 58
    no. 3 [Hainauer; G. Schirmer] same
  Ich ging hinaus, um dich zu sehen, op. 58
    no. 2 [Hainauer] same
  Ich weil' in tiefer Einsamkeit, op. 5 no. 4
    [J. Schuberth] same
  In deiner Nähe weil' ich noch, op. 58 no.
    6 [Hainauer; G. Schirmer] same
  Der Lenz, op. 45 no. 6 [Hainauer; G.
    Schirmer, 1883]
    "Nun wollen Knospen sich entfalten"
  Lilienblüthe, op. 58 no. 5 [Hainauer; G.
    Schirmer] "Lilienblüthe! Mädchen
    schön und zart"
  Löse, Himmel, meine Seele, op. 5 no. 3
    [J. Schuberth] same
  Mein Lied verklingt, op. 5 no. 6
    [J. Schuberth] same
  Nur eine Viertelstund! op. 5 no. 2
    [J. Schuberth]
    "Ich mochte zu Fussen liegen dir"
  Der Sänger, op. 67 no. 1 [Hainauer; G.
    Schirmer]
    "Der Dichter singt dem Frühling"
  Schönste Rast, op. 5 no. 5 [J. Schuberth]
    "Macht heim Wandern obn' Erharmen
    Staub"
  Schon grüsst auf dämmerndem Pfade, op.
    89 no. 4 [Hainauer] same
  Seit du gesagt dein strenges Wort, op. 58
    no. 4 [Hainauer] same
  Vergissmeinnicht, op. 5 no. 1 [J.
    Schuberth]
    "Ich bin eine Blume an Baches Band"
  Wieder möcht' ich dir begegnen, op. 58
    no. 1 [Hainauer; G. Schirmer, 1883]
    same
  Wiegenlied, op. 54 no. 1 [Hainauer]
    "Fragst du mit den Äugelein"
**Dahn, Felix Ludwig Sophus, 1834-
1912.**
  Germanensang [John Church Co., 1901]
    "Thor stand am Mitternachtsende der
    Welt"
  SIND GÖTTER.
    Weisse Rose, op. 85 no. 1 [Hainauer]
      "Weisse Rose nickt an Zweigen
      sehnend durch die Maienluft"

Eelbo, Bruno H., 1853-1917.
Siehe, noch blühen die Tage der Rose,
op. 88 no. 4 [Hainauer] same

Eichendorff, Joseph Karl Benedikt,
Freiherr von, 1788-1857.
Der Abend, op. 81 no. 5 [Hainauer]
"Schweigt der Menschen laute Lust"
Im Herbst, op. 45 no. 3 [Hainauer; G.
Schirmer, 1883] "Der Wald wird falb,
die Blätter fallen"
Mittagsruh, op. 81 no. 4 [Hainauer]
"Über Bergen, Fluss und Talen"
Der Morgen, op. 81 no. 3 [Hainauer]
"Fliegt der erste Morgenstrahl"
Morgengebet, op. 52 no. 1 [Hainauer]
"O wunderbares, tiefes Schweigen"
Die Nacht, op. 81 no. 6 [Hainauer]
"Wie schön hier zu verträumen"
Das Ständchen [Hainauer] "Auf die
Dächer zwischen blassen Wolken"
Verschwiegene Liebe, op. 83 no. 3
[Hainauer] "Über Wipfel und Saaten"
Vom Strande, op. 83 no. 6 [Hainauer]
"Ich rufe vom Ufer verlorenes Glück"

Eisenmayer, W.
Meine Devise, op. 52 no. 6 [Hainauer; G.
Schirmer, 1883]
"Was ich mir still gelobte"

Ernst, Heinrich Wilhelm, 1814-1865.
Abendbild, op. 68 no. 3 [Hainauer]
"Längst schon flog zu Nest der Vogel"
Ewig jung, op. 75 no. 6 [Hainauer]
"Mädchen, lass uns trinken, lachen"
Holger's Brautritt, op. 75 no. 5
[Hainauer]
"Über die Heide bergauf, bergab"
Immer bei dir, op. 68 no. 1 [Hainauer; G.
Schirmer]
"In deine Augen will ich schauen"
Mein Alles du, op. 68 no. 2 [Hainauer]
"Deiner gedenk ich im Reden und
Schweigen"
Sonntagsruhe, op. 62 no. 3 [Hainauer; G.
Schirmer] "So still und mild der Tag
und feierlich"
Trüber Morgen, op. 75 no. 4 [Hainauer;
G. Schirmer] "Die ersten Tropfen
fallen aus trübem Morgenroth"

Fitger, Arthur, 1840-1909.
Es war doch schön, op. 88 no. 3
[Hainauer] "Mir fallen alte Blätter"
Ich liege dir zu Füssen, op. 89 no. 1
[Hainauer] same
Die Memnonsäule, op. 89 no. 5
[Hainauer]
"Das ist der Liebe schönes Licht"

Fitzau, Heinrich, 1810-1859.
Der seltne Beter, op. 61 no. 2 [Hainauer,
1877] "Im Abendgolde glänzet zu
Bärenburg das Schloss"

Gautier, Théophile, 1811-1872.
LA COMÉDIE DE LA MORT.
Chinoiserie [Otto Junne]
"Ce n'est pas vous"

Geibel, Emanuel, i.e., Franz Emanuel
August, 1815-1884.
Des Woiewoden Tochter, op. 71 no. 6
[Hainauer]
"Es steht im Wald, im tiefen Wald"
Drei Bitten, op. 81 no. 2 [Hainauer]
"Drei Bitten hab ich"
Frühlingslied, op. 46 no. 1 [Hainauer]
"Tief im grünen Frühlingstag"
2 voices & piano.
Herbstnacht, op. 54 no. 4 [Hainauer]
"Ich schreit' hin an die Waldesbahn"
Der Hidalgo [Hainauer]
"Es ist so süss zu scherzen"
Ich sprach zur Taube, op. 67 no. 3
[Hainauer] same
Music says "Geibel, nach Coppée."
Im April, op. 46 no. 2 [Hainauer; G.
Schirmer, 1883]
"Du feuchter Frühlingsabend"
Kornblumen, op. 48 no. 3 [Hainauer]
"Kornblumen flecht' ich dir zum
Kranz"
Lied eines Mädchens, op. 83 no. 1
[Hainauer; G. Schirmer, 1887]
"In meinem Garten die Nelken"
Mein Herz ist wie die dunkle Nacht, op.
12 no. 3 [R. Sulzer; G. Schirmer,
1883] same
Schweigsamkeit, op. 65 no. 3 [Hainauer;
G. Schirmer] "Du fragst mich, du mein
blondes Lieb"
Vöglein wohin so schnell? op. 12 no. 4
[R. Sulzer; G. Schirmer, 1882] same
Zigeunerbub' im Norden, op. 52 no. 5
[Hainauer; G. Schirmer, 1883]
"Fern im Süd' das schöne Spanien"
Castanets *ad lib.*

Gilm zu Rosenegg, Hermann von,
1812-1864.
LETZTE BLÄTTER.
Allerseelen, op. 85 no. 3 [Hainauer]
"Stellt auf den Tisch die duftenden
Reseden"

Goethe, Johann Wolfgang von, 1749-
1832.
Maienlied, op. 85 no. 6 [Hainauer]
"Wie herrlich leuchtet mir die Natur"

COMPOSER Poet *Title* "First Line"

LASSEN, EDUARD, 1830-1904 *(continued)*
Goethe, Johann Wolfgang von, 1749-1832 *(continued)*
Nähe des Geliebten, op. 62 no. 1 [Hainauer; G. Schirmer] "Ich denke dein"
Grosse, Julius Waldemar, 1828-1902.
Sehnsucht, op. 83 no. 2 [Hainauer] "Sehnsucht, auf dem Knieen"
Groth, Klaus, 1819-1899.
Duftet die Lindenblüt', op. 93 no. 3 [Hainauer; Steingräber] same
Mir war das Leben blass und schal, op. 93 no. 2 [Hainauer; Steingräber] same
Mit Ahnungsschauern, O Natur! op. 93 no. 1 [Hainauer; Steingräber] same
Guilliaume, Jules Louis, 1825-1900.
Autrefois, à présent [Schott, 1856] "Autrefois, autrefois souviens t'en farouche"
Mon fils est couché là [Schott, 1856; Otto Junne] "Mon fils dort sous la mousse"
Pourquoi? [Schott; Otto Junne] "Vous m'avez dit en mots de flamme"
Question grave [Schott; Otto Junne] "Lorsque sa voix enchanteresse"
Hamerling, Robert, 1830-1889.
An die Vögel, op. 59 no. 2 [Hainauer, 1877] "Zwitschert nicht an meinem Fenster"
Die beiden Wolken, op. 59 no. 3 [Hainauer, 1877] "Eine Wolke seh' ich wandern"
Ich seh' dich heut zum ersten Mal, op. 71 no. 3 [Hainauer] same
Lass' die Rose schlummern, op. 59 no. 6 [Hainauer, 1877] same
Lebenslied, op. 67 no. 5 [Hainauer] "O himmlische Wonne des Lebens"
Die Lerchen, op. 59 no. 4 [Hainauer, 1877] "Es ziehen die Wolken"
Meine Lilie, op. 67 no. 4 [Hainauer; G. Schirmer] "Es flimmert der Kranz der Sterne"
Mit den Sternen, op. 71 no. 4 [Hainauer] "Mit den Sternen kehrt die Liebe"
Mund und Auge, op. 67 no. 6 [Hainauer] "Lächeln ist des Mundes Sache"
O selig, op. 72 no. 3 [Hainauer] "O selig, wem in stiller Nacht"
O trockne diese Tränen nicht, op. 59 no. 5 [Hainauer, 1877] same
Reisebild, op. 72 no. 4 [Hainauer] "O sieh, wie golden die Blümlein"
Sei nur ruhig, lieber Robin, op. 66 no. 3 [Hainauer; G. Schirmer] "Nur ein Wörtchen spricht, O Mädchen"

Trost, op. 59 no. 1 [Hainauer, 1877] "Ich will mit Leides Tönen"
Um Mitternacht, op. 66 no. 2 [Hainauer] "Mein liebes Kind, komm"
Viel Träume, op. 66 no. 1 [Hainauer] "Viel Vögel sind geflogen"
Heine, Heinrich, 1797-1856.
Das alte Lied [Hainauer; G. Schirmer, 1885] "Ei! Kennt ihr noch das alte Lied"
Childe Harold [Hainauer] "Eine starke, schwarze Barke"
Der Fichtenbaum [Hainauer; G. Schirmer, 1883] "Ein Fichtenbaum steht einsam"
Ich hab' im Traum geweinet, op. 48 no. 2 [Hainauer; G. Schirmer, 1885] same
Im Wald [Hainauer] "Wandl' ich in dem Wald des Abends"
Mein Liebchen, op. 48 no. 1 [Hainauer] "Mein Liebchen wir sassen beisammen"
Mit deinen blauen Augen, op. 12 no. 5 [R. Sulzer; G. Schirmer, 1882] same
Heyse, Paul Johann Ludwig von, 1830-1914.
Dornröschen (Das Mädchen spricht) op. 45 no. 1 [Hainauer] "Und wie sie kam zur Hexe"
Komm, O Verina, op. 89 no. 6 [Hainauer] same
Hoffmann von Fallersleben, August Heinrich, 1798-1874.
Alles scheidet liebes Herz, op. 4 no. 5 [Schlesinger]
Armes Blünchen, op. 4 no. 2 [Schlesinger]
Der Frühling und die Liebe, op. 46 no. 5 [Hainauer] "Im Rosenbusch die Liebe schlief" 2 voices & piano.
Im Liebeslust, op. 4 no. 3 [Schlesinger]
Lasst mich ruhen, op. 4 no. 1 [Schlesinger]
Mein Liebchen, op. 84 no. 1 [Hainauer] "Wie könnt' ich dein vergessen"
Mein Lied, op. 4 no. 4 [Schlesinger]
Und die Lerchen singen wieder, op. 4 no. 6 [Schlesinger] Titles of nos. 7 & 8 of this opus are unknown.
Wiegenlied, op. 54 no. 2 [Hainauer] "Schlaf' ein, mein Kind"
Holm, Mia, 1845-1912.
März, op. 81 no. 1 [Hainauer] "Im Wald der erste Vogel singt"

Hugo, Victor Marie, comte, 1802-1885.
  La Coccinelle [Schott; G. Schirmer,
    1891] "Elle me dit: quelque chose me
    tourmente"
  Hier au soir [Otto Junne; Schott]
    "Hier le vent du soir"
  Si mes vers avaient des ailes [Schott;
    Otto Junne; G. Schirmer, 1891]
    "Mes vers fuiraient doux et frêles"
  Si vous n'avez rien à me dire, op. 46
    no. 3 [Hainauer] same
    2 voices & piano.
Jung, Walter
  Grüssen, op. 52 no. 3 [Hainauer; G.
    Schirmer, 1883]
    "Des Abends Rosen sind abgeblüht"
Kastropp, Gustav, 1844-1925.
  Trennung, op. 88 no. 6 [Hainauer]
    "Lass mich in den dunklen Grund"
Kinkel, Gottfried, 1815-1882.
  Ein geistlich Abendlied, op. 84 no. 2
    [Hainauer] "Es ist so still geworden"
  Tröst der Nacht, op. 84 no. 4 [Hainauer]
    "Es heilt die Nacht des Tages
    Wunden"
Krause, Helene von (née Boddien),
  1841-1915.
  Das Epheublatt [John Church Co., 1899]
    "Ich faud im Buch ein Epheublatt"
Lenau, Nicolaus, 1802-1850.
  Frühlingsgedränge, op. 83 no. 4
    [Hainauer]
    "Frühlingskinder im bunten Gedränge"
Leo, Friedrich August, 1820-1898.
  Blaue Augen, op. 75 no. 1 [Hainauer; G.
    Schirmer]
    "Wenn kein Windchen weht"
  Das Nest, op. 75 no. 3 [Hainauer; G.
    Schirmer]
    "Was ist des Vögleins Dach"
  Schlummerlied, op. 75 no. 2 [Hainauer;
    G. Schirmer]
    "Die Wipfel säuseln Abendruh' "
Lingg, Hermann, 1820-1905.
  Die Krähen, op. 66 no. 4 [Hainauer]
    "Feldein nach einem dürren Baum"
  Lied, op. 61 no. 1 [Hainauer, 1877]
    "Wenn etwas in dir leise spricht"
  Mondmythus, op. 71 no. 5 [Hainauer]
    "Ich sah heut früh im Brunnen tief"
  Seerose, op. 66 no. 5 [Hainauer]
    "Rote Rosen, stolz und prächtig"
Lüdt, Rosa, 1842-1912.
  Ich habe den Glauben verloren, op. 62
    no. 2 [Hainauer] "Du hast mich
    belogen, du warst nicht treu"

Michell, Nicholas, 1807-1880.
  Allein, op. 74 no. 2 [Hainauer] "Es senkt
    sich der Abend über das Meer"
Mörike, Eduard Friedrich, 1804-1875.
  Frühling [Hainauer; G. Schirmer, 1883]
    "Frühling lässt ein blaues Band"
  Das verlassene Mägdlein, op. 54 no. 3
    [Hainauer]
    "Früh, wenn die Hähne kräh'n"
Musset, Alfred de, 1810-1857.
  Pepa [Schott, 1857; Otto Junne]
    "Pepa, Pepa, quand la nuit est venue"
Prölss, Robert, 1821-1906, supposed
  author.
  Barcarolle, op. 93 no. 6 [Hainauer;
    Steingräber]
    "Leis' wogt die weite Fläche"
  Brevier, op. 89 no. 3 [Hainauer]
    "Ihr müsst den Becher trinken"
  Einsamkeit, op. 89 no. 2 [Hainauer]
    "Eingeschmiegt in Klippenwände"
  Es lebt kein König! op. 93 no. 4
    [Hainauer; Steingräber] same
  Ritornell, op. 93 no. 5 [Hainauer;
    Steingräber]
    "Zum Ritornelle wird, Liebste"
Prutz, Robert Eduard, 1816-1872.
  O willkommen, op. 72 no. 6 [Hainauer]
    "Sei gegrüsst, O Frühlingsstunde"
  Vorsatz, op. 48 no. 4 [Hainauer; G.
    Schirmer, 1882]
    "Ich will dir's nimmer sagen"
Reinick, Robert, 1805-1852.
  LIEDERBUCH EINES MALERS.
    Ständchen [Hainauer]
      "Komm' in die stille Nacht"
Roquette, Otto, 1824-1896.
  Noch ist die blühende, goldene Zeit, op.
    84 no. 6 [Hainaucr] samc
Rückert, Friedrich, 1788-1866.
  SCHWANENGESANG.
    Abendglockenläuten, op. 65 no. 5
      [Hainauer] "Abendglokkenläuten"
Schack, Adolf Friedrich, Graf von,
  1815-1894.
  Abenddämmerung, op. 88 no. 1
    [Hainauer]
    "Sei willkommen, Zwielichtstunde"
Schiller, Johann Christoph Friedrich
  von, 1759-1805.
  Rekrutenlied aus Wallensteins Lager, op.
    61 no. 6 [Hainauer, 1877] "Trommeln
    und Pfeifen, kriegerischer Klang"
Scholz, Bernhard E., 1835-1916.
  Dein Auge ist mein Himmel, op. 62 no. 5
    [Hainauer] same

LASSEN, EDUARD, 1830-1904 *(continued)*
Scholz, Bernhard E., 1835-1916.
   (continued)
   Die grossen stillen Augen, op. 71 no. 1
      [Hainauer; G. Schirmer]
      "Ob ich dich auch verloren"
   Sommerabend, op. 61 no. 4 [Hainauer,
      1877; G. Schirmer]
      "Das ist die Zeit der Rosenpracht"
Schorn, Henriette (von Stein) von,
   1807-1869.
   Sei stille, op. 71 no. 2 [Hainauer; G.
      Schirmer]
      "Ach! was ist Leben doch so schwer"
Schulenburg, Ehrengarde Melusina
   von der, Countess, ca. 1667-1743.
   Herbstgefühl, op. 52 no. 2 [Hainauer]
      "Wenn der Sturm die Blätter jaget"
Schulze, Ernst Konrad Friedrich, 1789-
   1817.
   Kleine Lieder, op. 83 no. 5 [Hainauer]
      "Kleine Lieder geht nur immer"
Shakespeare, William, 1564-1616.
   HAMLET.
   Auf Morgen ist Sanct Valentinstag, op.
      74 no. 1/6 [Hainauer] same
   *Denn traut lieb Robin ist all' mein
      Lust!* op. 74 no. 1/5 [Hainauer]
      same
   Sein Bahrtuch weiss wie Bergesschnee,
      op. 74 no. 1/2 [Hainauer] same
   Sein Bart war weiss wie Bergesschnee,
      op. 74 no. 1/3 [Hainauer] same
   Sie trugen ihn barhaupt auf der Bahr,
      op. 74 no. 1/4 [Hainauer] same
   Und kommt er denn nimmer zurück?
      op. 74 no. 1/7 [Hainauer] same
   Wie erkenn' ich dein Treulieb, op. 74
      no. 1/1 [Hainauer] same
   KING HENRY VIII.
   Lied aus Heinrich VIII, op. 61 no. 3
      [Hainauer, 1877]
      "Orpheus' Laute hiess der
         Wipfel"
Stieler, Karl, 1842-1885.
   Am Strande, op. 88 no. 2 [Hainauer]
      "Mein Liebling ist ein Lindenbaum"
Storm, Theodor, 1817-1888.
   Als ich dich kaum gesehn [John Church
      Co.] same
   Die Waldbrüder, op. 46 no. 4 [Hainauer]
      "Die Drossel pfeift ihr letztes Stück"
Stotterfoth, Adelheid von
   Einsamkeit, op. 48 no. 5 [Hainauer]
      "Allein zu sein!"

Strachwitz, Moritz Karl Wilhelm
   Anton, Graf von, 1822-1847.
   Gebet auf den Wassern, op. 72 no. 5
      [Hainauer]
      "Die Nacht ist hehr und heiter"
   Der gefangene Admiral [Hainauer; G.
      Schirmer, 1889]
      "Sind heute dreiunddreissig Jahr"
   Heimkehr, op. 62 no. 4 [Hainauer]
      "Sei mir gegrüsst am Strassenrand"
   Meeresabend, op. 85 no. 4 [Hainauer]
      "Sie hat die ganze Nacht getobt"
Sturm, Julius Karl Reinholdt, 1816-
   1896.
   Nur einmal möcht ich dir noch sagen, op.
      67 no. 2 [Hainauer] same
   Über Nacht, op. 84 no. 5 [Hainauer]
      "Über Nacht, über Nacht kommt still
         das Leid"
   Wenn dein Auge freundlich, op. 68 no. 4
      [Hainauer] same
Tieck, Johann Ludwig, 1773-1853.
   Herbstlied, op. 84 no. 3 [Hainauer]
      "Feldeinwärts flog ein Vögelein"
Träger, Albert, 1820-1912.
   Im Verborgnen, op. 54 no. 5 [Hainauer]
      "Die Welt weiss deinen Namen nicht"
   Märzenblume, op. 65 no. 1 [Hainauer]
      same
   Wie durch die stille Mondesnacht, op. 65
      no. 2 [Hainauer]
      "Noch ruhest du ganz in meinem Arm"
Unknown
   Abendlandschaft [Hainauer; G. Schirmer,
      1883] "Der Hirt bläst seine Weise"
      Text may be by Eichendorff; song not
      seen.
   An den Mond [G. Schirmer, 1887]
      "Ich gehe durch die stille Nacht"
      Text may be by Ottilie von Ahlefeldt.
   Ave Maria [Hainauer]
      "Lenz ist gekommen"
   Einst, op. 92 no. 3 [Hainauer]
   Frithjofs Glück [Hainauer]
      "Nicht irdisch ist"
   Frühlingsgruss, op. 45 no. 2 [Hainauer;
      G. Schirmer, 1885]
      "Es steht ein Berg im Feuer"
   Ein Frühlingsnacht [G. Schirmer, 1887]
      "Still ist's auf dem Erdenkreise"
      See also his op. 82 no. 2: *Still ist's auf
         dem Erdenkr denkreise,* text by
         Ahlefeldt.
   Harfenklänge [Hainauer]
      "Eine Harfe ist mein Herz"
   Ich wandle unter Blumen, op. 12 no. 1
      [R. Sulzer; Augener] same

In der Nacht [R. Sulzer]
Klage nicht [Hainauer]
 "Klage nicht, betrübtes Kind"
Lebe Wohl! [R. Sulzer]
Das Lieblingslied [R. Sulzer]
Mirza Schaffy [Hainauer]
 "Ich dachte dein in tiefer Nacht"
Mondnacht [R. Sulzer]
Die Musikantin [Hainauer]
 "Schwirrend Tambourin"
Nacht in Rom, op. 92 no. 5 [Hainauer]
Nachtlied, op. 92 no. 1 [Hainauer]
O wär' ich du [Hainauer; G. Schirmer,
 1883] "O wär' ich du, mein Falke"
Romance [G. Schirmer, 1883]
 "Quand vous me montrez une rose"
Sommernacht [Hainauer]
 "Der laute Tag ist fort gezogen"
Spanische Romanze, op. 92 no. 6
 [Hainauer]
Spielmannslied, op. 45 no. 5 [Hainauer]
 "Und legt ihr zwischen mich und sie"
Die Spinnerin [Hainauer]
 "Schnurre, schnurre, meine Spindel"
Die Tänzerin [Hainauer]
 "Kastagnetten lustig schwingen"
Vergebener Wunsch [G. Schirmer, 1887]
 "Könnt' ich mit dem Vöglein fliegen"
Vorbei [R. Sulzer]
Waldasyl, op. 92 no. 2 [Hainauer]
Welle und Wind [R. Sulzer]
Die Zigeunerin [Hainauer]
 "Heute, nur heute bin ich so schön"
**Vega Carpio, Lope Félix de, 1562-
1635.**
Wiegenlied der Jungfrau Maria, op. 48
 no. 6 [Hainauer]
 "Die ihr dort wallet unter den Palmen"
Wildenbruch, Ernst von, 1845-1909.
Abendlied, op. 79 no. 3 [Hainauer]
 "Wie ist der Abend stille"
Bitteres Gedenken, op. 79 no. 2
 [Hainauer]
 "Rosen ging ich aus zu pflücken"
Ewige Liebe, op. 79 no. 4 [Hainauer]
 "Was soll ich anders sagen dir"
Liebespost, op. 79 no. 5 [Hainauer]
 "In der Mondesnacht, in der stillen
 Nacht"
Nicht weinen, op. 79 no. 1 [Hainauer]
 "Nicht weinen, Tränen tun so weh"
Seneschall's Lied, op. 74 no. 3
 [Hainauer]
 "Seht an die Erde in ihrer Pracht"
Ständchen, op. 79 no. 6 [Hainauer]
 "Rosen und duftende Veilchen"

Trost im Leid [Gebrüder Reinecke, 1893]
 "Will die Seele dir verzagen in der
 Leiden Übermass"
Wilder, Victor van, 1835-1892.
Ich hatte einst ein schönes Vaterland, op.
 12 no. 2 [R. Sulzer; Augener; G.
 Schirmer, 1883] same
**Wolzogen und Neuhaus, Alfred,
Freiherr von, 1823-1883.**
Lied aus Sakuntala, op. 61 no. 5
 [Hainauer, 1877]
 "Nach dir, O Biene, schauet die Amra"
**Zitelmann, Ernst Otto Conrad, 1854-
1897.**
Das sind so traumheft schöne Stunden,
 op. 88 no. 5 [Hainauer] same
"Lasset Gelehrte sich zanken und streiten" *see*
 Cophtisches Lied I Goethe **WOLF**
Lassitude see Collet, Louise **MILHAUD**
Lassitude see Maeterlinck **CHAUSSON**
"Lasst im Morgenstrahl des Mai'n" *see Skolie*
 Deinhardstein **SCHUBERT**
"Lasst mich nur auf meinem Sattel gelten!"
 see Freisinn Goethe
 RUBINSTEIN, SCHUMANN
"Lasst mich, ob ich auch still verglüh" *see*
 Hippolit's Lied Schopenhauer
 SCHUBERT
Lasst mich ruhen see Hoffmann von
 Fallersleben **JENSEN, LASSEN, LISZT**
Lasst mich sterben see Gleim **ZELTER**
"Lasst schlafen mich und träumen" *see Lied
 des Mädchens* Geibel **JENSEN**
"Lasst uns beten: Vater unser" *see Das Gebet
 des Herrn und die Einsetzungsworte*
 Unknown **LOEWE**
"Lasst uns das Kindlein wiegen" *see
 Christkindleins Wiegenlied* Unknown
 REGER
"Lasst uns, ihr Himmlischen, ein Fest
 begehen!" *see Uraniens Flucht* Mayrhofer
 SCHUBERT
Lasst uns mit erhrfurchtvollem Dank see Kraft
 LOEWE
"Last, for December" *see December* San
 Geminiano **IVES**
"A last little bird on a palm feather riding"
 see Silhouette Bernstein **BERNSTEIN**
Last night see Khomyakov **CHAĬKOVSKIĬ**
 Vcherashniaia noch'
A LAST POEM. see Graves, Robert
 A last song **BARBER**
LAST POEMS: Prologue. *see* Housman
 We'll go to the woods no more
 VAUGHAN WILLIAMS
 We'll to the woods no more **IRELAND**

COMPOSER Poet *Title* "First Line"

LAST POEMS: XXIII. *see* Housman
  In the morning **VAUGHAN WILLIAMS**
LAST POEMS: XXVI. *see* Housman
  The half-moon westers low **BERKELEY,**
    VAUGHAN WILLIAMS
LAST POEMS: XXVII. *see* Housman
  The sigh that heaves the grasses
    RIEGGER, VAUGHAN WILLIAMS
LAST POEMS: XLI. *see* Housman
  Fancy's knell **VAUGHAN WILLIAMS**
The last reader see Holmes, O. **IVES**
A last song see Graves, Robert *A LAST*
  POEM. **BARBER**
"A last song, and a very last" *see A last song*
  Graves, Robert **BARBER**
A last year's rose see Henley **QUILTER**
Lastochka see Lenartowicz **CHAĬKOVSKIĬ**
"Lastochke legko rezvit'sĭa" *see Zhelanie*
  serdtsa Unknown **MUSORGSKIĬ**
Lastu lainehilla see Kianto **SIBELIUS**
Låt vara see Ullman **KILPINEN**
"Låt vem som vill av sin flicka skryta" *see*
  Beständighet Josephson, E. **KILPINEN**
Late spring see Yang Knang **BERKELEY**
Late summer see Shanks *THE QUEEN OF*
  CHINA AND OTHER POEMS (1919).
  HESELTINE
"The late wind failed" *see The fleeting*
  De La Mare **BERKELEY**
Latil, Léo, 1890-1915.
  MILHAUD
    L'abandon
    Clair de lune
    Il pleut doucement
    Ma douleur et sa compagne
    Poème du journal intime de Léo Latil
    Prière à mon poète
    Le rossignol
    La tourterelle
Latini, Brunetto, 1230-1295.
  MALIPIERO *Lauda per un morto*
Die Laube see Hölty **SCHUBERT**
Laubsch, Frieda
  REGER *Süsse Ruh'*
Lauda per un morto see Latini **MALIPIERO**
LAUDI. see Annunzio
  I Pastori **PIZZETTI**
Lauds see Auden **BERKELEY**
"Laue Lüfte, Blumendüfte" *see Lob der*
  Thränen Schlegel **SCHUBERT**
"Laue Luft kommt blau geflossen" *see*
  Wanderlied Eichendorff
  MENDELSSOHN-BARTHOLDY
Die Lauer see Mickiewicz **LOEWE**
  Der Woywode
Lauf der Welt see Uhland **GRIEG**

"Laulaisinpa, taitaisinpa" *see Ei runo rahatta*
  laula Kanteletar **KILPINEN**
Laulan ilman lainehilta see Kanteletar
  KILPINEN
"Laulan, laulan pieni piika" *see Ikävä omia*
  maita Kanteletar **KILPINEN**
LAULUJA KANTELETTAREN RUNOIHIN,
  no. 2
  KILPINEN Kanteletar *Anna Maata*
    Maariainen
LAULUJA KANTELETTAREN RUNOIHIN,
  no. 3
  KILPINEN Kanteletar *Maassa marjani*
    makaavi
Laululle see Törmänen **KILPINEN**
"Laulun tieän, ehk' en laula" *see Siitä sinne*
  tie menevi Kanteletar **KILPINEN**
Laura am Klavier see Schiller **SCHUBERT**
"Laura betet!" *see Die Betende* Matthisson
  SCHUBERT, ZELTER
"Laura, Laura, über diese Welt" *see*
  Die Entzückung an Laura Schiller
  SCHUBERT
"Laura, über diese Welt" *see Die Entzückung*
  an Laura Schiller **SCHUBERT**
Laure, Marie *see* Noailles, Marie Laure
  de
Laurence de Beylié *see* Beylié, Laurence
  de
Laurencin, Marie, 1885-1956.
  POULENC
    Hier
    Le Présent
"Laut gesungen sei das Feuer" *see Jünger des*
  Weins II Gamper **SCHOECK**
Die laute Klage see Herder **BEETHOVEN**
"Der laute Tag ist fort gezogen" *see*
  Sommernacht Unknown **LASSEN**
"Lauter Freude fühl' ich" *see Lied eines*
  Kindes Unknown **SCHUBERT**
The Lawd is smilin' through the do' see
  Unknown **CARPENTER**
"Lawn as white as driven snow" *see Vendor's*
  song Shakespeare **BLITZSTEIN**
Lawrence, David Herbert, 1885-1930.
  RIETI
    Aware
    December night
    Quite forsaken
    Thomas Earp
Lay see Regnier, J. **ROREM**
"Lay a garland on my hearse" *see A sad song*
  Fletcher **HESELTINE**
"The lazy mid-day mist is rising" *see*
  Mid-day Tiutchev **MEDTNER**
Le lazzarone see Unknown **ROSSINI**
  Chansonette de cabaret ("Le lazzarone")

Le Barillier, Mme. Berthe, 1868-1927.
  MASSENET *Dans le sentier, parmi les roses*
Le Moyne, Paul, 1663-1704.
  MASSENET *Vers Béthléem*
Le Père Le Moyne, 1602-1672.
  JOLIVET *Sonnet à Madeleine Repentie*
Lead me, O night! see Maĭkov
  BALAKIREV *Vvedi menya, O noch, taykom*
Lean out of the window see Joyce
  SZYMANOWSKI
Lean thy cheek to mine see Heine *LYRICAL INTERMEZZO.* **RIMSKIĭ-KORSAKOV**
  Shchekoĭu k shcheke ty moeĭ prilozhis'
Leander, Richard, pseud. *see* Volkmann, Richard von, 1830-1889.
Lear, Edward, 1812-1888.
  STRAVINSKIĭ *The owl and the pussy-cat*
  THOMSON *The courtship of the Yongly Bongly Bo*
Leave me alone see Kleinschrod **DVOŘÁK**
  Kéž duch muj sám . . .
Leaves are falling see Pol **CHOPIN** *Leci liście z drzewa*
LEAVES OF GRASS. see Whitman
  Only themselves **LUENING**
  Walt Whitman **IVES**
"*Leb' wohl du schöne Erde" see Abschied von der Erde* Pratobevera **SCHUBERT**
Leb' wohl mein Ayr! see Burns **JENSEN**
"*Leb wohl mein Lieb" see Abschied*
  Unknown **MENDELSSOHN-BARTHOLDY**
"*Leb' wohl, und sehen wir uns wieder" see Wiedersehen* Rückert **FRANZ**
Lebe wohl see Hamerling **JENSEN**
Lebe wohl! see Horváth, P. **LISZT**
  Isten veled!
"*Lebe wohl!" see Liebewohl!* Lenau **SCHOECK**
Lebe wohl see Mörike **WOLF**
Lebe Wohl! see Unknown **LASSEN**
"*Lebe wohl! Du fühlest nicht" see Lebe wohl* Mörike **WOLF**
"*Lebe wohl, du Mann der Lust und Schmerzen" see Mollys Abschied* Bürger **BEETHOVEN**
"*Lebe wohl, lebe wohl" see Abschied* Schubert **SCHUBERT**
"*Lebe wohl, lebe wohl mein Lieb!" see Lebewohl* Uhland **SCHOECK**
"*Lebe wohl! wenn je ein brünstig Flehen" see Lebewohl* Byron **LOEWE**
Lebedź see Berent **SZYMANOWSKI**
Leben see Evers **BERG**

"*Leben, das nur Leben scheinet" see Naturfreiheit* Uhland **PFITZNER**
Lebensansicht see Anon. **WEBER**
"*Lebensfunke, vom Himmel entglüht" see Verklärung* Pope **SCHUBERT**
Lebens-Genuss see Metastasio *LA PACE FRA LA VIRTÙ E LA BELLEZZA.* **BEETHOVEN**
Lebenslied see Hamerling **LASSEN**
Lebenslied see Matthisson **SCHUBERT**
Lebenslied see Schmidt, Heinrich **SPOHR**
Lebensmelodien see Schlegel **SCHUBERT**
Lebensmut see Rellstab **SCHUBERT**
Lebensmut see Schulze **SCHUBERT**
Lebewohl see Byron **LOEWE**
Lebewohl see Kol'tsov **RUBINSTEIN**
Lebewohl! see Lenau **SCHOECK** *Liebewohl!*
Lebewohl see Uhland **SCHOECK**
"*Lebewohl, Ade" see Lebewohl* Kol'tsov **RUBINSTEIN**
Lebey, André, 1877-1938.
  MASSENET
    En même temps que ton amour
    Jamais un tel bonheur
    Quand nous nous sommes vus
Lebret, Karl August, 1809-1855.
  FRANZ *Frühlingsklage*
Leć, glosie, po rosie see Anon. **SZYMANOWSKI**
Leche, Renée de
  SAINT-SAËNS *Papillons*
Leci liście z drzewa see Pol **CHOPIN**
Lecioly zurazie see Anon. **SZYMANOWSKI**
Leclère, Léon, 1874-1966, translator.
  SHÉHÉRAZADE.
  KOECHLIN
    Chanson de flûte
    Chanson d'Engaddi
    La chanson des beaux amants
    Chanson d'Ishak de Mossoul
    Dédicace
    La neige
    Offrande
    L'oiseau en cage
    Paysage
    Le potier
    La rose du rameau sec
    Le ventre merveilleux
    Le voyage
Lecocq, Charles, 1832-1918.
  SAINT-SAËNS *Elle*
Leconte de Lisle, Charles Marie René, 1818-1894.
  CHAUSSON
    La cigale
    Le colibri

Leconte de Lisle, Charles Marie René,
   1818-1894 (continued)
DUPARC Phidylé
FAURÉ
   Lydia
   Nell
   Le parfum impérissable
   La rose
   Les roses d'Ispahan
GIDEON Les elfes
HAHN
   Lydé
   Néère
   Pholoé
   Phyllis
   Salinum
   Tyndaris
   Vile potabis
KOECHLIN
   L'astre rouge
   Le colibri
   Épiphanie
   Juin
   Midi
   Nox
   Les rêves morts
   Villanelle
      Two settings: Op. 21 no. 1 and op. 21
      no. 2.
CHANSONS ÉCOSSAISES.
   RAVEL Chanson du rouet
ÉTUDES LATINES.
   HAHN A Phidylé
POÈMES ANTIQUES.
   CHAUSSON Nanny
   DEBUSSY
      La fille aux cheveux de lin
      Jane
Ledwie blask słońca zloci dachy wiez see
   Iwaszkiewicz **SZYMANOWSKI**
Leezie Lindsay see Burns **BRITTEN**
Lefèbvre, Louis, 1871-1947.
   MASSENET La dernière chanson
Lefilleul, G.
   JOLIVET
      Aube
      Combien de bras se sont ouverts
      La maison du bonheur
      Quiétide
"Leg' in den Sarg mir mein grünes Gewand"
   see Todeslied der Bojaren Immermann
   MENDELSSOHN-BARTHOLDY
"Lege den Schmuck nun an, schöne Gulhinde"
   see Abendgesang Stieglitz **LOEWE**
Legend: Christ had a garden see
   Pleshcheyev **CHAÏKOVSKIÏ** Legenda

A LEGEND OF MONTROSE. see Scott
   Lied der Anne Lyle **SCHUBERT**
Legenda see Pleshcheyev **CHAÏKOVSKIÏ**
Legende see Goethe **LOEWE**
Légende see Marès **AUBERT**
Légende see Mauclair **BLOCH**
Légende californienne see Contamine
   SATIE
La légende du baiser see Hardÿ de Périni
   MASSENET
"La légère ondulation des feuilles berce des
   lacs" see Stream Jean-Aubry
   MALIPIERO
Legouvé, Ernest, 1807-1903.
   GOUNOD Tombez mes ailes
   SAINT-SAËNS
      Maria Lucrezia
      La mort d'Ophélie
Legrand, Marc
   INDY
      La bonne terre
      Mon père travaille
L'Egru, Christian
   SCHUMANN Aufträge
"Legt mir unter's Haupt" see Schlummerlose
   Nächte Frey, F. **BERG**
Lehdokki see Koskenniemi **KILPINEN**
Lehn' deine Wang' an meine Wang' see
   Heine **JENSEN, SCHUMANN**
"Lehnst du deine bleichgehärmte Wange" see
   Trost an Elisa Matthisson **SCHUBERT**
Lehr, Hofrath
   WEBER
      Er an Sie
      Meine Farben
      Trinklied
Lehre see Heine **FRANZ**
Lehtinen, Hilja Onerva, 1882-1972.
   KILPINEN
      Ilta
      Jo luovutko luotani
      Jo muistot taivaltani varjostaa
      Kevätlaulu
      Kirkkotie
      Nuori Apollo
      Suruni
      Syyshuokaus
      Vanitas vanitatum
Lehugeur, A.
   LALO L'ombre de Dieu
Die Leiche zu St. Just see Auersperg
   LOEWE
Eine Leichenphantasie see Schiller
   SCHUBERT
"Leicht Silberwolken schweben" see Mai
   Goethe **WOLF**

"Leicht wie gaukelnde Sylphiden" *see Lied für XXX* Schumann **SCHUMANN**

Leichte Segler in den Höhen see Jeitteles **BEETHOVEN**

Der Leichtmütige see Gubitz **WEBER**

Leichtsinniger Rat see Saul, D. **REGER**

Leiden der Trennung see Metastasio *ARTASERSE.* **SCHUBERT**

Der Leidende see Unknown **SCHUBERT**
Two settings: D. 432 and D. 512.

"Leidener, komm, denn dies ist dein Gott" *see Le crucifix* Hugo **LISZT**

Leidenschaft see Leuthold **SCHOECK**

Der leidige Frieden hat lange gewährt see Lenau **SCHUMANN**

Leierkastenmann see Busse **PFITZNER**

Der Leiermann see Müller, Wilhelm **SCHUBERT**

Leinhard, Friedrich
PFITZNER *Abendrot*

Leino, Eino, pseud. *see* Lönnbohm, Eino, 1878-1926.

"Leis dem Schmeichellied der Lauten" *see Mandolinen* Unknown **SCHOECK**

Leis rudern hier see Moore, T. **JENSEN**

"Leis rudern hier mein Gondolier!" *see Leis rudern hier* Moore, T. **JENSEN**

Leis rudern hier, mein Gondolier! see Moore, T. **JENSEN**

"Leis' rudern hier, mein Gondolier" *see Zwei Venetianische Lieder* Moore, T. **SCHUMANN**

"Leis' wogt die weite Fläche" *see Barcarolle* Prölss **LASSEN**

"Leise deinen Namen flüstern" *see Verklärung* Itzerott **REGER**

"Leise fällt ein Schnee auf das Land" *see Schlummerlied* Mombert **SZYMANOWSKI**

"Leise flehen meine Lieder" *see Ständchen* Rellstab **SCHUBERT**

"Leise geht der Tag zu Ende" *see Mein Stübchen* Huber, B. **KILPINEN**

Leise, leise weht ihr Lüfte see Brentano, F. **REGER**

Leise Lieder see Morgenstern **REGER, STRAUSS**

"Leise Lieder sing ich dir bei Nacht" *see Leise Lieder* Morgenstern **REGER, STRAUSS**

"Leise, rieseln der Quell" *see Der Jüngling an der Quelle* Salis-Seewis **SCHUBERT**

"Leise tritt auf nicht mehr in tiefem Schlaf" *see Vorfrühling* Avenarius **WEBERN**

"Leise tritt der Mond heraus" *see Schlaf ein* Boelitz **REGER**

"Leise, um dich nicht zu wecken" *see Serenade* Schack **BRAHMS**

"Leise weht es" *see Alkanzor und Zaide* Kind, F. **WEBER**

"Leise zieht durch mein Gemüt" *see Frühlingslied* Heine **BRUCKNER**

"Leise zieht durch mein Gemüt" *see Gruss* Heine **GRIEG**

Leise zieht, durch mein Gemüt see Heine **FRANZ, GIDEON**

"Leise zieht durch mein Gemüth" *see Gruss* Heine **MENDELSSOHN-BARTHOLDY**

Leise zieht durch mein Gemüth see Heine **LOEWE**

"Leise zieht durch mein Gemüthe" *see Frühlingslied* Heine **RUBINSTEIN**

"Leiser, leiser, kleine Laute" *see An die Laute* Rochlitz **SCHUBERT**

"Leiser schwanken die Aste" *see Heimkehr* Schack **STRAUSS**

Leises Lied see Dehmel **STRAUSS**

"Leisse streichen Nebelschleier über Flur und Wiesen hin" *see Maiennacht* Metternich-Winneburg **REGER**

Leitner, Karl Gottfried, Ritter von, 1800-1890.
SCHUBERT
  Des Fischers Liebesglück
  Drang in die Ferne
  Der Kreuzzug
  Die Sterne
  Vor meiner Wiege
  Der Wallensteiner Lanzknecht beim Trunk
  Der Winterabend

Leivonen see Koskenniemi **KILPINEN**

Leixner, Otto von *see* Leixner-Grünberg, Otto von, 1847-1907.

Leixner-Grünberg, Otto von, 1847-1907.
RUBINSTEIN *Liebeslied*

Lemaire, Ferdinand
SAINT-SAËNS
  Souvenances
  Tristesse

Lemcke, Karl von, 1831-1913.
BRAHMS
  Im Garten am Seegestade
  Im Waldeseinsamkeit
  Salamander
  Über die See
  Verrat
  Verzagen
  Willst du, dass ich geh'?
JENSEN *Auf den Bergen*
RUBINSTEIN
  Veilchen vom Berg, woran mahnest du mich?
  Verlust

Lemene, Francesco, conte de, 1634-
1704.
  MALIPIERO *Capriccio*
Lemmenlaulu see Jalkanen **KILPINEN**
Léna, Maurice, d. 1928.
  MASSENET *Fourvières*
Lenartovich, T *see* Lenartowicz, Teofil,
1822-1893.
Lenartowicz, Teofil, 1822-1893.
  CHAÏKOVSKIĬ *Lastochka*
Lenau, Nicolaus, 1802-1850.
  BARTÓK *Diese Rose pflück ich hier*
  FRANZ
    An die Wolke
    Bitte
    Drüben geht die Sonne scheiden
    Der Eichwald
    Frage
    Frühlingsblick
    Frühlingsgedränge
    Lenz
    Liebesfeier
    Liebesfrühling
    Nebel
    Der schwere Abend
    Sonnenuntergang; schwarze Wolken
     zieh'n
    Stille sicherheit
    Trübe wird's, die Wolken jagen
    Winternacht
  GIDEON *Einsamkeit*
  IVES *Weil' auf mir*
  LASSEN *Frühlingsgedränge*
  LISZT *Die drei Zigeuner*
  LUENING *Der Eichwald*
  MENDELSSOHN-BARTHOLDY
    An die Entfernte
    Frühlingslied
  PFITZNER *Sehnsucht nach Vergessen*
  RUBINSTEIN
    An den Frühling
    Bitte
    Die drei Zigeuner
    Frühlingsblick
  SCHOECK
    Der Abend
    An die Entfernte
     Two settings: Op. 5 no. 2 and op. 24a
      no. 3.
    Aufbruch
    Die drei Zigeuner
    Drüben geht die Sonne scheiden
    Der Eichwald
    Einsamkeit
    Erinnerung
    Der Ferne

    Frühlingsblick
    Das Gewitter
    Himmelstrauer
    Der Hirte
    Lenz
    Die Lerche
    Liebewohl!
    Scheideblick
    Der Schlaf
    Stumme Liebe
    Trübe wird's, die Wolken jagen
    Vergangenheit
  SCHUMANN
    Da liegt der Feinde gestreckte Schaar
    Den grünen Zeigern
    Einsamkeit
    Frühlingsgrüsse
    Der Husar, trara!
    Kommen und Scheiden
    Der leidige Frieden hat lange gewährt
    Lied eines Schmiedes
    Meine Rose
    Der schwere Abend
    Die Sennin
  STRAUSS
    Frühlingsgedränge
    Nebel
  WOLF
    Abendbilder
    An**
    Frage nicht
    Frühlingsgrüsse
    Herbst
    Herbstenschluss
    Herbstklage
    Liebesfrühling
    Meeresstille
    Nächtliche Wanderung
    Der Raubschütz
    Scheideblick
    Stille sicherheit
    Traurige Wege
    Wunsch
BITTE.
  LOEWE *Das dunkle Auge*
LIEBESKLÄNGE.
  FRANZ, GRIFFES *An den Wind*
  MENDELSSOHN-BARTHOLDY *Auf*
    der Wanderschaft
SCHILFLIEDER.
  BERG, MENDELSSOHN-
    BARTHOLDY, SCHÖNBERG
    Schilflied
  FRANZ, GRIFFES *Auf dem Teich, dem*
    regungslosen

COMPOSER   Poet   *Title*   "First Line"

FRANZ, GRIFFES, SCHOECK *Auf geheimem Waldespfade*
PIJPER *Auf geheimen Waldespfade*
SOPHIE.
    STRAUSS *O wärst du mein!*
Lenfaut, A.
    SAINT-SAËNS *Heures passées*
Lenormand, René, 1846-1932.
    FOLLE DU CIEL.
    MILHAUD
        Blancs sont les jours d'été
        Mes amis les cygnes
The Lent lily see Housman *THE SHROPSHIRE LAD.* **IRELAND**
Der Lenz see Cornelius **LASSEN**
Lenz see Lenau **FRANZ, SCHOECK**
"*Der Lenz ist angekommen*" *see Frühlings Ankunst* Anon. **FRANZ**
"*Der Lenz ist da*" *see Liederfrühling* Leuthold **SCHOECK**
"*Lenz ist gekommen*" *see Ave Maria* Unknown **LASSEN**
Lenz, Jakob Michael Reinhold, 1751-1792.
    GIDEON *Ach du, um die Blumen sich verliebt*
Lenz, Ludwig Friedrich, 1717-1780.
    MOZART *Lobgesang auf die feierliche Johannisloge*
"*Lenz nacht, so still und so kühl*" *see Norwegische Frühlingsnacht* Welhaven **FRANZ**
Lenzfahrt see Meyer **SCHOECK**
Lenzgesang see Fitger **SIBELIUS**
Leo, Friedrich August, 1820-1898.
    LASSEN
        Blaue Augen
        Das Nest
        Schlummerlied
LÉOCADIA. see Anouilh
    Les chemins de l'amour **POULENC**
Leon, Gottlieb von, 1757-1832.
    SCHUBERT *Die Liebe*
"*Leon und Castilien waffnen*" *see Zumalacarregui* Schleifer **LOEWE**
"*A leopard went around his cage*" *see The cage* Ives **IVES**
Leprade, Pierre Marin Victor Richard de, 1812-1883.
    CHABRIER
        Chants d'oiseaux
        Couplets de Mariette
        L'enfant
    LALO *La chanson de l'alouette*
Lerberghe, Charles van, 1861-1907.
    FAURÉ
        L'aube blanche
        Comme Dieu rayonne . . .
        Crépuscule
        Dans la Nymphée
        Dans la pénombre
        Dans un parfum de roses blanches
        Eau vivante
        Exaucement
        Il m'est cher, Amour, le bandeau
        Inscription sur le sable
        Je me poserai sur ton coeur
        La messagère
        O mort, poussière d'étoiles
        Paradis
        Prima verba
        Quand tu plonges tes yeux dans mes yeux
        Roses ardentes
        Veilles-tu, ma senteur de soleil
Die Lerche see Krummacher *FESTBÜCHLEIN.* **LOEWE**
Die Lerche see Lenau **SCHOECK**
Die Lerche see Sacken **RUBINSTEIN**
Die Lerche see Unknown **RUBINSTEIN**
"*Die Lerche singt ihr Morgenlied*" *see Wanderlied* Lua **LOEWE**
"*Lerche steiget im Gesang*" *see Die Lerche* Sacken **RUBINSTEIN**
"*Lerche wiegt sich im Gesange*" *see Frühling* Tolstoĭ **RUBINSTEIN**
"*Der Lerche wolkennahe Lieder*" *see Sehnsucht* Mayrhofer **SCHUBERT**
"*Lerche zu des Frühlings Ruhme*" *see Die Schlüsselblume* Mickiewicz **LOEWE**
Die Lerchen see Hamerling **LASSEN**
Lerchengesang see Candidus **BRAHMS**
Lermontov, Mikhail Yuryevich, 1814-1841.
    BALAKIREV
        Evreyskaya melodiya
        Iz-pod tainstvennoy kholodnoy polumaski
        Kogda volnuyetsya zhelteyushchaya niva
        Otchevo
        Pesnya Selima
        Pesnya: Zholtĭy list
        Pesnya zolotoy rĭbki
        Slĭshu li golos tvoy
        Son
        Sosna
        Utes
    CHAĬKOVSKIĬ *Liubov' mertvetsa*
    LISZT *Gebet*
    MEDTNER
        The angel
        At the cloister gate
        The prayer
    MUSORGSKIĬ *Molitva*
    PROKOFIEV *Skazhi mne*
    RIMSKIĬ-KORSAKOV
        Kak nebesa, tvoĭ vzor blistaet

Lermontov, Mikhail Yuryevich, 1814-
1841 *(continued)*
  RIMSKIĬ-KORSAKOV *(continued)*
    Kogda volnuetsia zheltëiushchaia niva
    Mne grustno
    Nochevala tuchka zolotaia
    Po nebu polunochi
  RUBINSTEIN
    Der Dolch
    Der Felsen
    Gebet
    Das Schiff
    Sehnsucht
    Wenn deine Stimme mir tönt
    Die Wolken
  NISCHCHIY.
      RACHMANINOFF *At the gate of the*
      Holy Abode
LeRoy, Grégoire, 1862-1941.
    LA CHANSON DU PAUVRE...
      DEBUSSY *Les Angélus*
"Les, da poliany" *see Trepak* Golenishchev-
  Kutuzov MUSORGSKIĬ
Lesbia Illa see Pound DIAMOND
Lesbos see Durrell, L. BERKELEY
LEŠETÍNSKÝ KOVÁR. see Čech
    Zpěv z Lešetínského kováře DVOŘÁK
Lessing, Gotthold Ephraim, 1729-1781.
    BEETHOVEN *Die Liebe*
    ZELTER *Die drei Reiche der Natur*
Let beauty awake see Stevenson, Robert
  Louis *SONGS OF TRAVEL, IX.*
  VAUGHAN WILLIAMS
"Let beauty awake in the morn" *see Let
  beauty awake* Stevenson, Robert Louis
  VAUGHAN WILLIAMS
*Let children ride the year's sweet carrousel
  see* Olson DIAMOND
Let me confess that we two must be twain see
  Shakespeare DIAMOND
Let me rest here alone see Shevchenko
  RACHMANINOFF *Again I am alone*
"Let not death boast his conquering power"
  see Epitaph Anon. ROREM
Let nothing disturb thee see Teresa of Avila
  DIAMOND
Let springtime come then see Jacobsen *LAD
  VAAREN KOMME.* DELIUS
Let the florid music praise! see Auden
  LOOK, STRANGER! BRITTEN
Let there be light, O God see Anon.
  MARTINŮ
Let us leave, my dear see Golenishchev-
  Kutuzov RACHMANINOFF
    Beloved, let us fly

Let us rest see Chekhov *UNCLE VANYA,*
  Act IV. RACHMANINOFF
"Let us walk in the white snow" *see Velvet
  shoes* Wylie THOMPSON, R.
"Lethe! Brich die Fesseln des Ufers" *see
  Sehnsucht nach Vergessen* Lenau
  PFITZNER
Die Lethe des Lebens see Baggesen
  WEBER
Let's take a walk see Hopkins ROREM
  Spring
Let's take a walk see Koch ROREM *Spring;*
  THOMSON
Let's take a walk see O'Hara ROREM
"Let's take a walk in the city" *see Spring*
  Koch ROREM
"L'etsia solntse priamo vokna sgoluboĭ" *see
  Stakhanovka* Blagov, A.
  PROKOFIEV
Letter to K. S. Stanislavsky from S. R. see
  Rachmaninoff RACHMANINOFF
Letter to New York see Bishop ROREM
La lettre see Barbusse AUBERT
La lettre see Mendès, Jane MASSENET
Lettre d'Alissa see Gide *LA PORTE
  ETROITE.* MILHAUD
Lettres d'Alissa see Gide *LA PORTE
  ETROITE.* MILHAUD
Letzte Bitte see Bierbaum REGER
LETZTE BLÄTTER. see Gilm zu Rosenegg
    Allerseelen LASSEN, PIJPER, STRAUSS
    Geduld STRAUSS
    Die Georgine STRAUSS
    Die Nacht STRAUSS
    Nichts STRAUSS
    Die Verschwiegenen STRAUSS
    Die Zeitlose STRAUSS
Letzte Hoffnung see Müller, Wilhelm
  SCHUBERT
Das letzte Lied see Tagore *OGRODNIK.*
  SZYMANOWSKI
DER LETZTE RITTER. see Auersperg
    Max' Abschied von Augsburg LOEWE
    Max in Augsburg LOEWE
    Max und Dürer LOEWE
Die letzte Rose see Gottschall FRANZ
Der letzte Wunsch see Hemans JENSEN
Die letzten Blumen starben see Kulmann
  SCHUMANN
Letzter Frühling see Benn BLACHER
Letzter Frühling see Vinje GRIEG *Våren*
Letzter Seufzer see Briesen, Otto von
  LOEWE
Letzter Wunsch see Hertz JENSEN
Letztes Lied see Kugler, Johann, Consul in
  Stettin LOEWE

Leuchtende Tage see Jacobowski
  PFITZNER
"Leucht't heller als die Sonne" *see Minnelied*
  Anon. **MENDELSSOHN-BARTHOLDY**
Leukon see Gleim **BERG** *An Leukon*
Leuthold, Heinrich, 1827-1879.
  SCHOECK
    Abkehr
    An meine Grossmutter
    Aus dem Süden
    Distichen
    Einst
    Heimweh
    Ich bin ein Spielmann von Beruf
    Im Klosterkeller
    Leidenschaft
    Liederfrühling
    Mein Herz ist wie ein Saitenspiel
    Muttersprache
    Nacht, Muse und Tod
    O Frühlingshauch, O Liederlust
    O Lebensfrühling, Blütendrang
    Rechtfertigung
    Riviera
    Rückkehr
    Sapphische Strophe
    Sonnenuntergang
    Spruch
    Die Ströme zieh'n zum fernen Meer
    Trauer
    Trinklied
    Trost
    Und wieder nehm ich die Harfe zur Hand
    Unmut
    Vorwurf
    Waldeinsamkeit
    Der Waldsee
      Two settings: Op. 15 no. 1 and op. 57
      no. 20.
    Waldvögelein
    Warnung
Leutnand
  ZELTER *Wehmut*
Leuven, Adolphe de, grefve Ribbing,
  called, 1800-1884.
  BERLIOZ *Le chasseur danois*
Le lever see Musset **GOUNOD**
Le lever de la lune see Anon. **SAINT-
SAËNS**
Levertin, Oskar Ivar, 1862-1906.
  SIBELIUS *En slända*
Lève-toi, lève-toi see Silvestre **MASSENET**
"Lève-toi! lève-toi! le printemps vient de
  maitre!" *see Chanson d'avril* Bouilhet
  BIZET

Levetzow, Karl Michael, Freiherr von,
  1871-1945.
  HÖHENLIEDER, pp. 39-40.
    SCHÖNBERG *Abschied*
  HÖHENLIEDER, pp. 41-42.
    SCHÖNBERG *Dank*
Levommi il mio pensier see Petrarca
  PIZZETTI
Les lèvres closes see Dierx **CHABRIER**
"Lèvres, Ô mères du baiser" *see La chanson
  des lèvres* Cazalis **MASSENET**
Leyer und Schwert see Körner **WEBER**
LEYER UND SCHWERT, no. 1
  WEBER Körner *Gebet während der
    Schlacht*
LEYER UND SCHWERT, no. 2
  WEBER Körner *Abschied vom Leben*
LEYER UND SCHWERT, no. 3
  WEBER Körner *Trost, "Herz, lass dich
    nicht zerspalten"*
LEYER UND SCHWERT, no. 4
  WEBER Körner *Mein Vaterland*
"Leyhy tuuli" *see Muistoja* Jalkanen
  KILPINEN
Li Po, 701-762.
  CARPENTER *On a screen*
  HESELTINE *Along the stream*
  SCHOECK *In der Herberge*
  WEBERN *Die geheimnisvolle Flöte*
Liane see Mayrhofer **SCHUBERT**
The liar see Carpenter, Rue **CARPENTER**
Líbej, milá, líbej see Manin, P. **MARTINŮ**
  Kiss, my sweetheart, kiss
La libellule see Saint-Saëns **SAINT-SAËNS**
Les Libellules see Lunel **MILHAUD**
LA LIBÉRATION DES ANTILLES, no. 1
  MILHAUD Anon. *Bonjour, messieurs les
    libérateurs*
LA LIBÉRATION DES ANTILLES, no. 2
  MILHAUD Anon. *Trois ans de souffrance*
Lichnowsky, Felix Maria Vincenz
  Andreas, Fürst von, 1814-1848.
  LISZT *Nonnenwerth*
Das Licht see Huber, B. **KILPINEN**
"Licht gewiekte vlinders zweven" *see
  Vlinderliedje* Bruyn, Bertha de **PIJPER**
Das Licht im Tale see Kind, F. **WEBER**
"Ein Licht im Traum hat mich besucht" *see
  Traumlicht* Rückert **LOEWE**
Licht sie dein Traum! see Moore, T.
  JENSEN
"Ein Licht tanzt freundlich vor mir her" *see
  Täuschung* Müller,Wilhelm **SCHUBERT**
Licht und Liebe see Collin, M. **SCHUBERT**
Lichte Nacht see Benzon **ANNA BRYDE.**
  GRIEG *Lys Nat*

Lichtenstein, Ulrich von, fl.1255.
MENDELSSOHN-BARTHOLDY
Frühlingslied
"Lichtlein schwimmen auf dem Strome" *see*
Sct. Nepomuks Vorabend Goethe
ZELTER
"Lichtlein schwimmen auf dem Strome" *see*
St. Nepomuk's Vorabend Goethe **WOLF**
Liden Kirsten see Krag **GRIEG**
"Liden Kirsten hun sad så silde" *see Liden*
Kirsten Krag **GRIEG**
Lie, Jonas Lauritz Idemil., 1833-1909.
GRIEG *I Liden højt deroppe*
"Lie thou where Life hath lain" *see Cleopatra*
to the asp Tabb **GRIFFES**
Lieb' ist die Perle see Cornelius
CORNELIUS
Lieb' Liebchen see Heine **FRANZ,**
MEDTNER, SCHUMANN
"Lieb Liebchen, leg's Händchen" *see Lieb*
Liebchen Heine **MEDTNER**
Lieb Minna see Stadler **SCHUBERT**
Lieb Seelchen, lass das Fragen sein see
Hopfen, Hans **SCHOECK**
"Lieb' sei ferne" *see Liebesnähe* Arndt
LOEWE
Lieb und Leben see Schütze **ZELTER**
"Liebchen, als wir Nachts uns küssten" *see*
Neugriechisches Lied Mikhailov
RUBINSTEIN
"Ein Liebchen hatt' ich" *see Hinkende Jamben*
Rückert **LOEWE**
Liebchen ist da! see Schröer **FRANZ**
Das Liebchen von der Ruhe see Ueltzen
BEETHOVEN
"Liebchen, was willst du?" *see Aprillaunen*
Osterwald **FRANZ**
Liebchen, wo bist du? see Reinick **WOLF**
Liebe see Andersen **GRIEG** *Kjaerlighed*
Die Liebe see Claudius, M. **SCHOECK**
Die Liebe see Dehmel **REGER**
Liebe see Garborg *HAUGTUSSA.* **GRIEG**
Elsk
Die Liebe see Goethe *EGMONT.*
SCHUBERT
Die Liebe see Leon **SCHUBERT**
Die Liebe see Lessing **BEETHOVEN**
Liebe see Rilke **BERG**
Liebe see Röser, Otto **FRANZ**
"Der Liebe bangen Sorgen erbleicht der
Freude Strahl!" *see Getrennte Liebe*
Schmidt, Heinrich **SPOHR**
Die Liebe des Nächsten see Gellert
BEETHOVEN
Die liebe Farbe see Müller, Wilhelm
SCHUBERT

Die Liebe hat gelogen see Osterwald
FRANZ
Die Liebe hat gelogen see Platen-
Hallermünde **SCHUBERT**
"Die Liebe hemmet nichts" *see Die Liebe*
Claudius, M. **SCHOECK**
Liebe im Schnee see Hamerling **JENSEN**
"Liebe ist ein süsses Licht" *see Licht und*
Liebe Collin, M. **SCHUBERT**
"Liebe ist Wahrheit!" *see Psalm* Schoeck, P.
SCHOECK
Liebe kam aus fernen Landen see Tieck
BRAHMS
"Eine Liebe kenn ich, die ist treu" *see*
Wo find' ich Trost Mörike **WOLF**
"Liebe l'amour amor amoris, Some say that
Love's a little boy" *see*
Tell me the truth about love Auden
BRITTEN
Der Liebe Lohn see Cornelius **CORNELIUS**
Liebe mir im Busen zündet see Anon.
WOLF
Liebe mit Schmerzen see Schmidt, Friedrich
ZELTER
"Liebe Mutter, heut Nacht heulte Regen und
Wind" *see Walpurgisnacht* Häring
LOEWE
Liebe ohne Heimat see Bürger **CORNELIUS**
"Die Liebe, sagt man" *see Peregrina* Mörike
SCHOECK
"Die Liebe sass als Nachtigall" *see*
Waldesgesang Geibel **STRAUSS**
Der liebe Traum see Loest **ZELTER**
Liebe und Frühling see Hoffmann von
Fallersleben **BRAHMS**
Two settings: Op. 3 no. 2 and op. 3 no. 3.
Liebe-Glühen see Gubitz **WEBER**
Lieben, Frau von
REGER *Ich stehe hoch über'm See*
Lieben und Schweigen see Tischendorf
MENDELSSOHN-BARTHOLDY
"Lieben von ganzer Seele" *see Resignation*
Buddeus **SCHUMANN**
"Lieben, warum sollt' ich's nicht?" *see*
Warum nicht? Unknown **SPOHR**
Der Liebende see Hölty *LIED EINES*
LIEBENDEN. **SCHUBERT**
Der Liebende see Reissig **BEETHOVEN**
Die Liebende schreibt see Goethe
BRAHMS, MENDELSSOHN-
BARTHOLDY, SCHUBERT
"Liebendes Wort, dich send ich fort" *see*
Botschaft Cornelius **CORNELIUS**
Lieber alles see Eichendorff **WOLF**
Lieber Schatz see Osterwald
MACDOWELL

Lieber Schatz, wie wieder gut mir see
Osterwald FRANZ
"Liebes goldnes Ringelein" *see Das Ringelein*
Kol'tsov RUBINSTEIN
"Liebes Haus auf Berges Höh!" *see Gruss an*
Züllchow Gerstenberg LOEWE
"Liebes leichtes luft'ges Ding, Schmetterling!"
see Die Sylphide Herder LOEWE
"Liebes Töchterlein" *see Die Mutter spricht*
Seyboth, Sofie REGER
Liebesbotschaft see Reinick *LIEDERBUCH*
EINES MALERS. SCHUMANN, WOLF
Liebesbotschaft see Rellstab SCHUBERT
Der Liebescheue see Unknown LOEWE
Liebesfeier see Lenau FRANZ
Liebesfrühling see Hoffmann von
Fallersleben WOLF
Liebesfrühling see Lenau FRANZ, WOLF
Liebesfrühling see Rückert FRANZ
LIEBESFRÜHLING. see Rückert
  Da ich dich einmal gefunden JENSEN
  Flügel! Flügel! SCHUMANN
  Der Himmel hat eine Thräne geweint
    SCHUMANN
  Der Himmel hat eine Träne geweint
    REGER
  Ich hab' in mich gesogen den Frühling treu
    SCHUMANN
  Jünglings Gebet LOEWE
  Liebster, deine Worte stehlen SCHUMANN
  Lieder der Braut SCHUMANN
      Two settings: Op. 25 no. 11 and op. 25
      no. 12.
  Mein schöner Stern! SCHUMANN
  Meine Töne still und heiter SCHUMANN
  O Freund, mein Schirm, mein Schutz!
    SCHUMANN
  O ihr Herren SCHUMANN
  O Sonn', O Meer, O Rose! SCHUMANN
  Die Perle FRANZ
  Rose, Meer und Sonne sind ein Bild
    SCHUMANN
LIEBESFRÜHLUNG, no. 48.
  Anbetung STRAUSS
Liebesgedanken see Müller, Wilhelm
LOEWE
Liebesgeschenk see Anon. STRAUSS
Liebesglück see Eichendorff WOLF
Liebesglück see Goethe MARTINŮ
Liebesglut see Daumer *HAFIS.* BRAHMS
Die Liebesgötter see Uz SCHUBERT
Liebesgruss aus der Ferne see Anon.
FLIEGENDES BLATT. WEBER
Liebeshändel see Löwenstein
RUBINSTEIN
Liebeshymnus see Henckell *STEH' ICH IN*
SEL'GEM TRAUME. STRAUSS

LIEBESKLÄNGE. see Lenau
  An den Wind FRANZ, GRIFFES
  Auf der Wanderschaft MENDELSSOHN-
    BARTHOLDY
Liebes-Klage see Metastasio *AMOR*
TIMIDO (Cantata XVI). BEETHOVEN
Liebesklage des Mädchens see Des Knaben
Wunderhorn BRAHMS
Liebeslauschen see Schlechta SCHUBERT
Liebeslied see Anon. *FLIEGENDES BLATT.*
WEBER
Liebeslied see Böhm WEBERN
Liebeslied see Goethe *WESTÖSTLICHER*
DIVAN. SCHUMANN
Liebeslied see Hesse KILPINEN
Liebeslied see Krenek KRENEK
Liebeslied see Leixner-Grünberg
RUBINSTEIN
Liebeslied see Rosenbaum BERG
Liebesliedchen see Calderon *EL ALCALDE*
DE ZALAMEA. STRAUSS
Liebesliedchen see Jacob, T. LOEWE
LIEBESLIEDER, no. 1
  BARTÓK Goethe *Du meine Liebe, du*
    mein Herz
  CORNELIUS Cornelius *In Lust und*
    Schmerzen
  JENSEN Rückert *Da ich dich einmal*
    gefunden
  REGER Ritter *Brautring*
  WEISGALL Trustman, Deborah *Sound*
    is simple
LIEBESLIEDER, no. 2
  BARTÓK Lenau *Diese Rose pflück ich*
    hier
  CORNELIUS Cornelius *Komm, wir*
    wandeln zusammen in Mondschein
  JENSEN Roquette *Unruhe*
  REGER Ritter *Geheimnis*
  WEISGALL Trustman, Deborah *Listen:*
    you were the victim
LIEBESLIEDER, no. 3
  BARTÓK Unknown *Du geleitest mich*
    zum Grave
  CORNELIUS Hood *Dich lieb ich*
  JENSEN Ulrich *Notturno*
  REGER Evers *Nachtgeflüster*
  WEISGALL Trustman, Deborah *You*
    were like a song
LIEBESLIEDER, no. 4
  BARTÓK Bodenstedt *Ich fühle deinen*
    Odem
  CORNELIUS Cornelius *Möcht' im Walde*
    mit dir geh'n
  JENSEN Träger *An deinem Finger, dem*
    weissen, schlanken

LIEBESLIEDER, no. 4 *(continued)*
> **REGER** Laubsch, Frieda *Süsse Ruh'*
> **WEISGALL** Trustman, Deborah *Play for me*

LIEBESLIEDER, no. 5
> **BARTÓK** Goethe *Wie herrlich leuchtet*
> **CORNELIUS** Cornelius *Ich bin so froh geworden*
> **JENSEN** Grosse *Bei dir*
> **REGER** Puttkamer *Mädchenlied*

LIEBESLIEDER, no. 6
> **BARTÓK** Rückert *Herr! der du alles wohl gemacht*
> **CORNELIUS** Cornelius *Lieb' ist die Perle*
> **JENSEN** Kühne *Was nennst du deine Liebe schwer und gross*
> **REGER** Obst, Willibald *Hoffnungslos*

LIEBESLIEDER, no. 7
> **REGER** Benz *Schlummerlied*

LIEBESLIEDER, no. 8
> **REGER** Ritter *Sonnenregen*

Liebesnacht see Frey, F. **SZYMANOWSKI**

Liebesnähe see Arndt **LOEWE**

Liebesode see Hartleben **BERG**

Liebespost see Wildenbruch **LASSEN**

"Liebesqual verschmäht mein Herz" *see Frech und Froh II* Goethe **WOLF**

Liebesrausch see Körner **SCHUBERT**
> Two settings: D. 164 and D. 179.

Liebesschwärmerei see W., Cäcilie von **SPOHR**

Liebessuche see Löns **KILPINEN**

Liebeständelei see Körner **SCHUBERT**

Liebestreu see Reinick **BRAHMS**

Liebeswunder see Hugo **RUBINSTEIN**

Liebeszauber see Bürger, J. H. **WEBER**

Liebewohl! see Lenau **SCHOECK**

Der Liebewütige see Gubitz **WEBER**

Liebhaber in allen Gestalten see Goethe **SCHUBERT**

"Lieblich blüh'n die Bäume voller Schmelz und Duft" *see Träume* Osterwald **FRANZ**

Lieblich in der Rosenzeit see Hafiz **SCHOECK**

Liebliche Maid! see Burns **FRANZ** *Lovely maid!*

Der liebliche Stern see Schulze **SCHUBERT**

"Liebliches Kind" *see Serenate* Goethe **BRAHMS**

"Liebliches Kind, kannst du mir sagen" *see Aus "Claudine von Villa-Bella"* Goethe **MEDTNER**

Das Lieblingslied see Unknown **LASSEN**

Lieblingsplätzchen see Des Knaben Wunderhorn **MENDELSSOHN-BARTHOLDY**

"Lieblos ist mein Lieb geworden, war mir treu doch manchen Tag" *see Lied der verlassenen Liebe* Hertz **JENSEN**

Liebster, deine Worte stehlen see Rückert *LIEBESFRÜHLING.* **SCHUMANN**

Liebt er mich? see Unknown **SPOHR**

Lied see Banville **CHABRIER**

Lied see Baron **SAUGUET**

Lied see Benediktov **RUBINSTEIN**

Lied see Bodenstedt *IVAN.* **BRAHMS**

Lied see Claudius, M. **SCHUBERT**
> Two settings: D. 362 and D. 501.

Lied see Eichendorff **BRAHMS**

Lied see Fouqué *UNDINE.* **SCHUBERT**

Lied see Geibel **RUBINSTEIN**

Lied see Hardenberg **ZELTER**

Lied see Heine **RUBINSTEIN**
> Two settings: Op. 32 no. 4 and op. 32 no. 5.

Lied see Hoffmann von Fallersleben **RUBINSTEIN**
> Two settings: Op. 33 no. 2 and op. 33 no. 5.

Lied see Hugo **LASSEN** *Si vous n'avez rien à me dire*

Lied see Kosegarten **ZELTER**

Lied see Lingg **LASSEN**

Lied see Lingg **PFITZNER** *Kalt und schneidend*

Lied see Löwenstein-Wertheim **WEBER**

Lied see Luhden *MORGENS AUF BETAUTER WEIDE.* **ZELTER**

Lied see Mauclair **SCHMITT**

Lied see Mayrhofer **SCHUBERT** *Ueber allen Zauber Liebe*

Lied see Mendès **CHABRIER**

Lied see Müchler **WEBER**

Lied see Paté **FRANCK**

Lied see Pichler **SCHUBERT**

Lied see Polonsky **RUBINSTEIN**

Lied see Pushkin **RUBINSTEIN**

Lied see Recke, Ewald von der **ZELTER**

Lied see Rothmaler *LIED.* **ZELTER**

Lied see Salis-Seewis **SCHUBERT**

Lied see Schiller **SCHUBERT**

Lied see Seida und Landenberg **WEBER**

Lied see Steigentesch **ZELTER**

Lied see Stolberg **SCHUBERT**

Lied see Swoboda **WEBER**

Lied see Zedlitz *KERKER UND KRONE.* **SPOHR**

Lied am Felsen see Winther **GRIEG** *Sang paa Fjeldet*

Lied am Grabe see Berlepsch *DAS GRAB.* **LOEWE**

Lied an den Tod see Schubart **SCHUBERT** *An den Tod*

COMPOSER Poet *Title* "First Line"

Lied an meinen Sohn see Dehmel **STRAUSS**

Lied aus Aslauga's Ritter see La Motte-Fouque **SPOHR**

Lied aus dem "Märlein von der Wasserfee" see Bekmann, Mathilde **SPOHR**

Lied aus der Ferne see Matthisson **SCHUBERT, ZELTER**

Lied aus der Ferne see Reissig **BEETHOVEN**

Lied aus Heinrich VIII see Shakespeare *KING HENRY VIII.* **LASSEN**

Lied aus Sakuntala see Wolzogen und Neuhaus **LASSEN**

Lied bei Sonnenuntergang see Kind, F. **ZELTER**

Lied beim Rundetanz see Salis-Seewis **SPOHR**

Lied der Anne Lyle see Scott *A LEGEND OF MONTROSE.* **SCHUBERT**

Lied der Chispa see Calderon *EL ALCALDE DE ZALAMEA.* **STRAUSS**

Lied der Desdemona see Herder *STIMMEN DER VÖLKER.* **JENSEN**

Lied der Desdemona see Shakespeare *OTELLO.* **LOEWE**

Lied der Frauen see Brentano **STRAUSS**

Lied der Freiheit see Blumauer **MOZART**

Lied der Freude see Gross, E. **SPOHR**

Lied der Freundin see Goethe **MENDELSSOHN-BARTHOLDY**

Lied der Harfnerin see Unknown **SPOHR**

Lied der Hirtin see Kind, F. **WEBER**

Lied der Königin Elisabeth see Shenstone **LOEWE**

Lied der Liebe see Matthisson **SCHUBERT**

Lied der Mignon see Goethe *WILHELM MEISTER.* **SCHUBERT**

Lied der Mignon see Goethe *WILHELM MEISTER.* Mignon's song: Heiss mich nicht reden. **SCHUBERT**

Lied der Mignon see Goethe *WILHELM MEISTER.* Mignon's song: Nur wer die Sehnsucht kennt. **SCHUBERT**
    Three settings: D. 359, D. 481, and D. 877 no. 4.

Lied der Renate see Zwehl, Hans Fritz von **KILPINEN**

Lied der Schnitterin see Pfau **SCHÖNBERG**

Lied der Soldaten see Goethe *FAUST.* **WAGNER**

Lied der Suleika see Goethe *WESTÖSTLICHER DIVAN.* **SCHUMANN**

Das Lied der Trennung see Schmidt, Klamer **MOZART**

Lied der verlassenen Liebe see Hertz **JENSEN**

Das Lied der Waise see Steinebach **WOLF**

Das Lied der Welle see Szymanowska, Zafia **SZYMANOWSKI** *Pieśń o fali*

Lied des Balearers see Musorgskiï, M. *SALAMMBÔ.* **MUSORGSKIï** *Pesn' Baleartsa*

Lied des düsteren Waldes see Borodin **BORODIN** *Song of the dark forest*

Lied des gefangenen Jägers see Scott *THE LADY OF THE LAKE.* **SCHUBERT**

Lied des Harfenspielers see Goethe *WILHELM MEISTER.* Harfenspieler. **MUSORGSKIï**

Lied des Mädchens see Geibel **JENSEN**
    Two settings: Op. 6 no. 4 and op. 57 no. 1.

Lied des Mädchens am Fenster see Paquet **SZYMANOWSKI**

Lied des Mephistopheles see Goethe *FAUST* **WAGNER**
    Two settings: Op. 5 no. 4 and op. 5 no. 5.

Lied des Mephistopheles in Auerbachs Keller see Goethe **MUSORGSKIï** *Pesnia Mefistofelia v pogrebke Auerbakha*

Lied des Orpheus, als er in die Hölle ging see Jacobi **SCHUBERT**

Lied des Schiffermädels see Bierbaum **BERG**

Das Lied des Steinklopfers see Henckell **STRAUSS**

Lied des transferierten Zettel see Shakespeare *MIDSUMMER NIGHT'S DREAM:* Bottom's song. **WOLF**

Lied des verlassenen Mädchens see Deinhardstein **SPOHR**

Lied eines Kindes see Unknown **SCHUBERT**

LIED EINES LIEBENDEN. see Hölty *Der Liebende* **SCHUBERT**

Lied eines Mädchens see Anon. **REGER**

Lied eines Mädchens see Geibel **LASSEN**

Lied eines Schiffers an die Dioskuren see Mayrhofer *SCHIFFERS NACHTLIED.* **SCHUBERT**

Lied eines Schmiedes see Lenau **SCHUMANN**

Lied eines Verliebten see Mörike **WOLF**

Lied eines Vögleins in der Oasis see Stieglitz **LOEWE**

Lied fahrender Schüler see Scheffel *GAUDEAMUS.* **JENSEN**

Lied für preussischen Patrioten see Gleim **ZELTER**

Lied für XXX see Schumann **SCHUMANN**

Ein Lied, hinterm Ofen zu singen see Claudius, M. **SCHOECK**

Das Lied im Grünen see Reil **SCHUBERT**

Lied in der Abwesenheit see Stolberg
   SCHUBERT
Lied in der Fremde see Winkler **ZELTER**
   Text may be from Winkler's *Sängers Reise*;
   cf. Weber setting.
Lied in der Fremde see Winkler *SÄNGERS
   REISE.* **WEBER**
Lied Lynceus des Thürmers see Goethe
   FAUST. **SCHUMANN**
Lied maritime see Indy **INDY**
Lied mit russischem Text see Lermontov
   RUBINSTEIN *Gebet*
Das Lied vom Reifen see Claudius, M.
   SCHUBERT
Lied vom Winde see Mörike **WOLF**
Lied von Clotilde see Nostitz **WEBER**
Das Lied von den Türen see Weisenborn
   BLACHER
Das Lied von Herrn von Falkenstein see
   Uhland **BRAHMS**
Lied zum Geburtstage meines guten Vaters see
   Mendelssohn-Bartholdy
   MENDELSSOHN-BARTHOLDY
Lied zur Gesellenreise see Ratschky
   MOZART
LIEDER ALS INTERMEZZO, no. 2. *see*
   Geibel *Wohl lag ich einst in Gram und
   Schmerz* **GRIFFES**
LIEDER ALS INTERMEZZO, no. 19. *see*
   Geibel *So halt' ich endlich dich umfangen*
   GRIFFES
Lieder aus dem Schenkenbuch . . . see
   Goethe *WESTÖSTLICHER DIVAN.*
   SCHUMANN
      Two settings: Op. 25 no. 5 and op. 25
      no. 6.
LIEDER DER AMARANTH. see Redwitz
   Brautlied **LOEWE**
Lieder der Braut see Rückert
   LIEBESFRÜHLING. **SCHUMANN**
      Two settings: Op. 25 no. 11 and op. 25
      no. 12.
LIEDER DER LIEBE, no. 1
   KILPINEN Morgenstern *Mein Herz ist
   leer*
LIEDER DER LIEBE, no. 2
   KILPINEN Morgenstern *Es ist Nacht*
LIEDER DER LIEBE, no. 3
   KILPINEN Morgenstern *Unsere Liebe*
LIEDER DER LIEBE, no. 4
   KILPINEN Morgenstern *Wir sitzen im
   Dunkeln*
LIEDER DER LIEBE, no. 5
   KILPINEN Morgenstern *Schicksal der
   Liebe*
LIEDER DER LIEBE, no. 6
   KILPINEN Morgenstern *Heimat*

LIEDER DER LIEBE, no. 7
   KILPINEN Morgenstern *Kleines Lied*
LIEDER DER LIEBE, no. 8
   KILPINEN Morgenstern *Deine Rosen an
   der Brust*
LIEDER DER LIEBE, no. 9
   KILPINEN Morgenstern *Über die
   tausend Berge*
LIEDER DER LIEBE, no. 10
   KILPINEN Morgenstern *Anmutiger
   Vertrag*
LIEDER DER OPHELIA, no. 1
   STRAUSS Shakespeare *Wie erkenn' ich
   mein Treulieb?*
LIEDER DER OPHELIA, no. 2
   STRAUSS Shakespeare *Guten Morgen,
   's ist Sankt Valentinstag*
LIEDER DER OPHELIA, no. 3
   STRAUSS Shakespeare *Sie trugen ihn
   auf der Bahre bloss*
LIEDER EINES FAHRENDEN GESELLEN,
   no. 1
   MAHLER Mahler *Wenn mein Schatz
   Hochzeit macht*
LIEDER EINES FAHRENDEN GESELLEN,
   no. 2
   MAHLER Mahler *Ging heut' Morgens
   übers Feld*
LIEDER EINES FAHRENDEN GESELLEN,
   no. 3
   MAHLER Mahler *Ich hat' ein glühend
   Messer*
LIEDER EINES FAHRENDEN GESELLEN,
   no. 4
   MAHLER Mahler *Die zwei blauen Augen
   von meinem Schatz*
LIEDER EINES SÜNDERS. 1. Teil, "Inferno."
   see Conradi *Verlassen* **SCHÖNBERG**
Lieder in Aargauer Mundart see Anon.
   HINDEMITH
LIEDER UM DEN TOD, no. 1
   KILPINEN Morgenstern *Vöglein
   Schwermut*
LIEDER UM DEN TOD, no. 2
   KILPINEN Morgenstern *Auf einem
   verfallenen Kirchhof*
LIEDER UM DEN TOD, no. 3
   KILPINEN Morgenstern *Der Tod und
   der einsame Trinker*
LIEDER UM DEN TOD, no. 4
   KILPINEN Morgenstern *Winternacht*
LIEDER UM DEN TOD, no. 5
   KILPINEN Morgenstern *Der Säemann*
LIEDER UM DEN TOD, no. 6
   KILPINEN Morgenstern *Unverlierbare
   Gewähr*

COMPOSER Poet *Title* ''First Line''

LIEDERBUCH EINES MALERS (continued)
  Nichts Schöneres **SCHUMANN, SPOHR**
  Sonntags am Rhein **SCHUMANN**
  Ständchen **LASSEN, SCHUMANN,
    WOLF**
Liederfrühling see Leuthold **SCHOECK**
LIEDERKREIS, no. 1
  SCHUMANN Eichendorff *In der Fremde*
  SCHUMANN Heine *Morgens steh' ich
    auf und frage*
LIEDERKREIS, no. 2
  SCHUMANN Eichendorff *Intermezzo*
  SCHUMANN Heine *Es treibt mich hin, es
    treibt mich her*
LIEDERKREIS, no. 3
  SCHUMANN Eichendorff
    Waldesgespräch
  SCHUMANN Heine *Ich wandelte unter
    den Bäumen*
LIEDERKREIS, no. 4
  SCHUMANN Eichendorff *Die Stille*
  SCHUMANN Heine *Lieb' Liebchen*
LIEDERKREIS, no. 5
  SCHUMANN Eichendorff *Mondnacht*
  SCHUMANN Heine *Schöne Wiege meiner
    Leiden*
LIEDERKREIS, no. 6
  SCHUMANN Eichendorff *Schöne
    Fremde*
  SCHUMANN Heine *Warte, warte, wilder
    Schiffsmann*
LIEDERKREIS, no. 7
  SCHUMANN Eichendorff *Auf einer Burg*
  SCHUMANN Heine *Berg' und Burgen
    schau'n herunter*
LIEDERKREIS, no. 8
  SCHUMANN Eichendorff *In der Fremde*
  SCHUMANN Heine *Anfangs wollt' ich
    fast verzagen*
LIEDERKREIS, no. 9
  SCHUMANN Eichendorff *Wehmuth*
  SCHUMANN Heine *Mit Myrthen und
    Rosen*
LIEDERKREIS, no. 10
  SCHUMANN Eichendorff *Zwielicht*
LIEDERKREIS, no. 11
  SCHUMANN Eichendorff *Im Walde*
LIEDERKREIS, no. 12
  SCHUMANN Eichendorff *Frühlingsnacht*
Liederseelen see Meyer **SCHOECK**
LIEDERSTRAUSS. see Heine
  Aus meinen grossen Schmerzen **FRANZ,
    WOLF**
  Es blasen die blauen Husaren **WOLF**
  Ich stand in dunkeln Träumen **GRIEG,
    WOLF**

Ihr Bild **SCHUBERT**
Mein Liebchen wir sassen beisammen
  WOLF
Mir träumte von einem Königskind **WOLF**
Sie haben heut' Abend Gesellschaft
  PFITZNER, WOLF
Spätherbstnebel, kalte Träume **WOLF**
Sterne mit den goldnen Füsschen **FRANZ,
  WOLF**
Vielgeliebte schöne Frau **BERG**
Wie des Mondes Abbild zittert **FRANZ,
  WOLF**
Liedesend see Mayrhofer **SCHUBERT**
Der Liedler see Kenner **SCHUBERT**
"Liegt ein Dorf im Abendleuchten" *see
  Dämmer* Boelitz **REGER**
"Liegt eine Stadt im Tale" *see Die stille Stadt*
  Dehmel **PFITZNER, SIBELIUS**
"Liegt nun so still die weite Welt" *see Mein
  Traum* Ritter **REGER**
"Liesse doch ein hold Geschick" *see Stumme
  Liebe* Lenau **SCHOECK**
"Lieve, reine, witte Klokjes" *see
  Sneeuwklokjes* Bruyn, Bertha de **PIJPER**
Le lièvre et le blé see Carême **MILHAUD**
Life and death see Tichborne **DIAMOND**
LIFE & DEATH (Echoes). *see* Henley
  The nightingale has a lyre of gold **DELIUS**
"Life has outdistanced all my yearnings" *see
  Lost hopes* Pushkin **MEDTNER**
"The life of a shepherd is void of all care-a"
  see The jolly shepherd Anon.
  HESELTINE
Lift not the painted veil see Shelley
  DIAMOND
"Lift on high & clink the glasses" *see Wine
  roses* Jacobsen **DELIUS**
Light see Jean-Aubry **MALIPIERO,
  ROUSSEL**
The light is sweet see Bible **KRENEK**
Light, my light see Tagore *GITANJALI.*
  CARPENTER
The light that is felt see Whittier **IVES**
"The lights from the parlour and kitchen
  shone out" *see The stars*
  Stevenson, Robert Louis **HAHN**
The lights were being dimmed see
  Konstantin **CHAĬKOVSKIĬ**
  Uzh gasli v″ komnatakh ogni
Ligny, Charles
  GOUNOD
    La fleur du foyer
    Prière du soir
Liguori, Alfonso Maria de', Saint, 1696-
  1787.
  SAINT-SAËNS *La Madonna col bambino*

Li-Ho, 9th cent.
ROUSSEL *Des fleurs font un broderie*
Li-I, d. 827?
ROUSSEL *Favorite abandonnée*
Like a sick eagle see Keats **IVES**
Like blossom dew-freshen'd to gladness see
Heine **RACHMANINOFF**
Child, thou art as beautiful as a flower
Like to a linden tree I am see Hálek
DVOŘÁK *Jsem jako lípa košatá*
Like to like see Goethe **MEDTNER** *Gleich und Gleich*
"*Likka tanssivi somasti" see Tanssi*
Kanteletar **KILPINEN**
LILA. see Goethe
So tanzet **MEDTNER**
The lilacs see Beketova *SIREN'*
RACHMANINOFF
"*The lilacs are out" see Spring talk*
Louchheim **DIAMOND**
Les lilas see Banville *LES CARIATIDES,*
livre 3, no. XVII. **DEBUSSY**
Les lilas blancs see Bourguignat, Paul
GOUNOD
"*Les lilas donneront bientôt" see Le jardin de*
Virigine Luka, Madeleine **SAUGUET**
Les lilas qui avaient fleuri see Jammes
TRISTESSES. **BOULANGER, MILHAUD**
Lilas, vos frissons sous le ciel see Bouchor,
M. *DANS LA FORÊT.* **CHAUSSON**
Die Lilien glühn in Düften see Geibel
STRAUSS
Lilienblüthe see Cornelius **LASSEN**
"*Lilienblüthe! Mädchen schön und zart" see*
Lilienblüthe Cornelius **LASSEN**
Liliencron, Detlov, Freiherr von, 1844-1909.
BERG *Tiefe Sehnsucht*
BRAHMS
Auf dem Kirchhofe
Maienkätzchen
MARTINŮ
Enough of happiness
From childhood
The spinning top's lullaby
PFITZNER
Müde
Sehnsucht
REGER *Glückes genug*
STRAUSS
Bruder Liederlich
Glückes genug
Ich liebe dich
Sehnsucht

ADJUTANTENRITTE UND ANDERE
GEDICHTE.
WEBERN *Meiner Mutter*
BUNTE BEUTE.
WEBERN *Heimgang in der Frühe*
Lilla an die Morgenröte see Unknown
SCHUBERT
Lilla Olles visa see Cnattingius, Thor
KILPINEN
Lillebarn see Bergman **KILPINEN**
"*Lillebarn lilla" see Lillebarn* Bergman
KILPINEN
LILLYGAY, no. 1
HESELTINE Anon. *The distracted maid*
LILLYGAY, no. 2
HESELTINE Anon. *Johnnie wi' the tye*
LILLYGAY, no. 3
HESELTINE Anon. *The shoemaker*
LILLYGAY, no. 4
HESELTINE Anon. *Burd Ellen and*
young Tamlane
LILLYGAY, no. 5
HESELTINE Neuburg *Rantum Tantum*
"*The lily floated white and red" see The water*
lily Nichols **HESELTINE**
"*The lily's withered chalice falls" see*
Le jardin Wilde **GRIFFES**
Lime trees see Pech **DVOŘÁK** *Lípy*
La limousine see Chalupt **MILHAUD**
Lincoln, the great commoner see Markham
IVES *from "Lincoln, the great commoner"*
Linda see Apollinaire *IL Y A*: *Les dicts*
d'amour à Linda. **RIVIER**
Linden, Auguste, pseud. *see* Harnier,
Auguste, 1826-1855.
Linden Lea see Barnes *MY ORCHA'D IN*
LINDEN LEA. **VAUGHAN WILLIAMS**
"*Die linden Lüfte sind erwacht" see*
Frühlingsglaube Uhland
MENDELSSOHN-BARTHOLDY,
SCHUBERT, SPOHR
Der Lindenbaum see Müller, Wilhelm
SCHUBERT
"*Ein linder Südhauch sprengt die Riegel" see*
Ostern Boelitz **REGER**
"*Lindes Rauschen in den Wipfeln" see*
Erinnerung Eichendorff **SCHOECK**
"*Lindes Rauschen in den Wipfeln" see Lied*
Eichendorff **BRAHMS**
Lindner, Anton 1874-1915.
STRAUSS *Hochzeitlich Lied*
Lindsay, Nicholas Vachel, 1879-1931.
IVES *General William Booth enters into*
Heaven
The line gang see Frost **CARTER**
Lines written during a sleepless night see
Pushkin **BRITTEN**

COMPOSER Poet *Title* "First Line"

Lingg, Hermann, 1820-1905.
    BRAHMS *Immer leiser wird mein*
        Schlummer
    LASSEN
      Die Krähen
      Lied
      Mondmythus
      Seerose
    PFITZNER
      Immer leiser wird mein Schlummer
      Kalt und schneidend
    REGER *Aeolsharfe*
    RUBINSTEIN *Hüte dich*
    SCHÖNBERG
      Freihold
      Gruss in die Ferne
Die Linien des Lebens see Hölderlin
    BRITTEN
The link see Tumanskiĭ **BALAKIREV**
    Zveno
Linton, William James, 1812-1897.
    IRELAND *O happy land*
Lipiner, Siegfried, 1856-1911.
    RUBINSTEIN *Was tut's*
"Die Lippe brennt, die Wange glüht" *see*
    Der erste Kuss Kartscher **SPOHR**
Lípy see Pech **DVOŘÁK**
Liricheskoe intermetstso see Heine
    MEDTNER *Lyrisches Intermezzo*
"Lisch aus, lisch aus, mein Licht!" *see*
    Resignation Haugwitz **BEETHOVEN**
Lish' rozy uvĭadaiut see Pushkin
    MEDTNER *When roses fade*
Lish' ty odin" see Pleshcheyev
    CHAĬKOVSKIĬ
Li-Shê, 9th cent.
    CARPENTER *Highwaymen*
Lisle, Charles Marie René Leconte de
    see
    Leconte de Lisle, Charles Marie René,
      1818-1894.
"A lissome maid with towseled hair" *see*
    To the golden rod MacDowell
    MACDOWELL
Listen beloved see Cummings **ROREM**
Listen, little friend see Kruse **BORODIN**
    Listen to my song, little friend
Listen to my song, little friend see Kruse
    BORODIN
"Listen when late at night" *see Song from*
    without the world Anon. **GIDEON**
Listen: you were the victim see Trustman,
    Deborah **WEISGALL**
"Listener, can you hear the silence howl" *see*
    Guilt Capetanakis **ROREM**

List'ia shumeli unylo see Pleshcheyev
    MUSORGSKIĬ
LISZT, FRANZ, 1811-1886.
    Ábrányi, Kornél, 1822-1903.
      Magyar király-dal (1883) [GA, v. 7³,
        p. 117]
        "Áldott légyen Magyarok királya!"
    Béranger, Pierre Jean de, 1780-1857.
      Le vieux vagabond (1848) [GA, v. 7¹,
        p. 1] "Dans ce fossé cessons de vivre"
      LE JUIF ERRANT: Chrétien, au voyageur
        souffrant.
      Le juif errant (1847) [unpubl.]
    Biegeleben, Rüdiger, Freiherr von
      Und sprich (1874; rev.1878) [GA, v. 7³,
        p. 55] "Sieh auf dem Meer den Glanz"
    Bocella, Marchese Cesare
      Angiolin dal biondo crin (1856) [GA,
        v. 7², p. 31] same
    Bodenstedt, Friedrich Martin von,
      1819-1892.
      An Edlitam, zur silbernen Hochzeit
        (ca.1878) [GA, v. 7³, p. 84]
        "In meinem Lebensringe bist du der
        Edelstein"
      Einst (ca.1878) [GA, v. 7³, p. 83] "Einst
        wollt ich einen Kranz dir winden"
    Cornelius, Peter, 1824-1874.
      Weimars Volkslied (1857) [GA, v. 7², p.
        58] "Von der Wartburg Zinnen nieder"
      Wieder möcht' ich dir begegnen (1860)
        [GA, v. 7³, p. 24] same
    Coronini, Carl, graf von Cronberg,
      b.1818.
      Die Fischerstochter (1871) [GA, v. 7³,
        p. 42] "Die Fischerstochter sitzt am
        Strand"
    Dingelstedt, Franz, Freiherr von, 1814-
      1881.
      Schwebe, schwebe, blaues Auge (1845)
        [GA, v. 7¹, p. 127] same
      Schwebe, schwebe, blaues Auge (ca.1860)
        [GA, v. 7², p. 99] same
    Dumas, Alexandre, the elder, 1803-
      1870.
      Jeanne d'Arc au bûcher (1874) [GA,
        v. 7³, p. 1] "Mon Dieu! j'étais une
        bergère"
      Earlier version, 1845.
    Freiligrath, Ferdinand, 1810-1876.
      O lieb (ca.1845) [GA, v. 7², p. 6]
        "O Lieb, O lieb"
      TROMPETE VON VIONVILLE.
      Und wir dachten der Toten (ca.1884)
        [GA, v. 7³, p. 111]
        "Und nun kam die Nacht"

Geibel, Emanuel, i.e., Franz Emanuel August, 1815-1884.
Die stille Wasserrose (ca.1860) [GA, v. 7^3, p. 20] same

Girardin, Delphine (Gay) de, "Mme. Émile de Girardin," 1804-1855.
Il m'aimait tant! (ca.1840) [GA, v. 7^1, p. 13] "Non, je ne l'aimais pas"

Goethe, Johann Wolfgang von, 1749-1832.
Über allen Gipfeln ist Ruh' (ca.1859) [GA, v. 7^2, p. 143] same
  Earlier version, ca.1848.
EGMONT.
  Freudvoll und leidvoll (1st setting, ca.1844) [GA, v. 7^1, p. 110] same
  Rev., ca.1860: GA, v. 7^2, p. 66; 2nd setting, ca.1848: v. 7^1, p. 114.
FAUST.
  Es war ein König in Thule (ca.1856) [GA, v. 7^2, p. 41] same
  Earlier version, 1842.
WANDRERS NACHTLIED I.
  Der du von dem Himmel bist (1842) [GA, v. 7^1, p. 30] same
  2nd version, ca.1856: GA, v. 7^2, p. 47; 3rd, ca.1860: p. 145.
WILHELM MEISTER.
  Wer nie sein Brot mit Tränen ass (ca.1845) [GA, v. 7^2, p. 139] same
  2nd version, ca.1860: GA, v. 7^3, p. 35.
WILHELM MEISTER. Mignon's song: Kennst du das Land?
  Mignons Lied (1856) [GA, v. 7^2, p. 23] "Kennst du das Land"
  Earlier version, 1842; later version, 1860: GA, v. 7^2, p. 68.

Hagn, Charlotte von, 1809-1891.
Was Liebe sei? (ca.1843) [GA, v. 7^1, p. 80] "Dichter! was Liebe sei, mir nicht verhehle!"
  2nd version, ca.1855: GA, v. 7^2, p. 96; 3rd, ca.1878: v. 7^3, p. 69.

Hebbel, Christian Friedrich, 1813-1863.
Blume und Duft (ca.1860) [GA, v. 7^3, p. 31] "In Frühlings Heiligtume"

Heine, Heinrich, 1797-1856.
Anfangs wollt' ich fast verzagen (1856; rev. ca.1880) [GA, v. 7^2, p. 109] same
Du bist wie eine Blume (ca.1842-43) [GA, v. 7^2, p. 133] same
Ein Fichtenbaum steht einsam (ca.1855) [GA, v. 7^2, p. 90] same
  2nd version, ca.1860: GA, v. 7^2, p. 93.
Im Rhein, im schönen Strome (ca.1840) [GA, v. 7^1, p. 20] same
  2nd version, ca.1856: GA, v. 7^2, p. 37.
Die Loreley (ca.1856) [GA, v. 7^2, p. 16] "Ich weiss nicht, was soll's bedeuten"
  Earlier version, 1841.
Morgens steh' ich auf und frage (ca.1843) [GA, v. 7^1, p. 82] same
  2nd version, ca.1855: GA, v. 7^2, p. 137.
Vergiftet sind meine Lieder (1842) [GA, v. 7^2, p. 135] same

Herwegh, George, 1817-1875.
Ich möchte hingehn (ca.1845) [GA, v. 7^2, p. 125] same

Hoffmann von Fallersleben, August Heinrich, 1798-1874.
Ich scheide (1860) [GA, v. 7^2, p. 175] "Die duftenden Kräuter auf der Au' "
In Liebeslust (ca.1858) [GA, v. 7^2, p. 121] same
Lasst mich ruhen (ca.1858) [GA, v. 7^2, p. 118] same
Wie singt die Lerche schön (ca.1856) [GA, v. 7^2, p. 51] same

Hohenlohe, Prinzessin Therese von
La perla (1872) [GA, v. 7^3, p. 57] "Sono del mare bianca la figlia"

Horváth, P.
Isten veled! (1846-47) [GA, v. 7^3, p. 78] same

Hugo, Victor Marie, comte, 1802-1885.
Comment, disaient-ils (1842) [GA, v. 7^1, p. 42] same
  2nd version, ca.1859: GA, v. 7^2, p. 164.
Le crucifix (1884) [GA, v. 5^6, p. 69] "Leidener, komm, denn dies ist dein Gott"
Enfant, si j'étais roi (ca.1844) [GA, v. 7^1, p. 47] same
  2nd version, ca.1859: GA, v. 7^2, p. 167.
Gastibelza (ca.1844) [GA, v. 7^1, p. 64] "Gastibelza, der greise, kühne Jäger"
Oh! quand je dors (1842) [GA, v. 7^1, p. 36] same
  2nd version, ca.1859: GA, v. 7^2, p. 159.
Quand tu chantes bercée (1849) [Budapest, 1973]
La tombe et la rose (ca.1844) [GA, v. 7^1, p. 60] "La tombe dit à la rose"

LISZT, FRANZ, 1811-1886 *(continued)*
Hugo, Victor Marie, comte, 1802-
1885 *(continued)*
CHANTS DU CRÉPUSCULE.
S'il est un charmant gazon (1844)
[GA, v. 7^1, p. 53] same
2nd version, ca.1859: GA, v. 7^2,
p. 171.
Kaufmann, Johann Philipp, 1802-
1846.
Die tote Nachtigall (ca.1843) [GA, v. 7^1,
p. 84] "Du arme, kleine Nachtigall"
2nd version, 1878: GA, v. 7^3, p. 65.
Kuh, Emil, 1828-1876.
Ihr Glocken von Marling (1874) [GA,
v. 7^3, p. 52] same
Lenau, Nicolaus, 1802-1850.
Die drei Zigeuner (1860) [GA, v. 7^3,
p. 13] "Drei Zigeuner fand ich einmal"
Lermontov, Mikhail Yuryevich, 1814-
1841.
Gebet (ca.1878) [GA, v. 7^3, p. 81]
"In Stunden der Entmutigung"
Text "after Lermontov" by Bodenstedt.
Lichnowsky, Felix Maria Vincenz
Andreas, Fürst von, 1814-1848.
Nonnenwerth (1860) [GA, v. 7^3, p. 37]
"Ach, nun taucht die Klosterzelle
einsam aus des Wassers Welle"
Earlier version, 1841.
Metschersky, Fürst Elim.
Bist du! (1843; rev. 1877-78) [GA, v. 7^3,
p. 70] "Mild wie ein Lufthauch"
Michell, Gustav, b. 1842.
IRRWEGE: Lied.
Verlassen (1880) [GA, v. 7^3, p. 90]
"Mir ist die Welt so freudenleer"
Monnier, Etienne
Élégie [Bernard-Latte] "En ces lieux tout
me parle delle"
Printed in Noske **French song** ... , pp.
305-309.
En ces lieux [Paris, before 1855]
Same song as his *Élégie?*
Müller, Joseph, 1802-1872.
Das Schlüsselblumen (1857) [GA, v. 7^2,
p. 114] "Dort am grünen Hügel
glänzen schmucke Blümchen"
Das Veilchen (1857) [GA, v. 7^2, p. 111]
"Spende, Veilchen, deine Düfte zu
Marias Preis und Ruhm!"
Musset, Alfred de, 1810-1857.
TRISTESSE.
J'ai perdu ma force et ma vie (1872)
[GA, v. 7^3, p. 49] same

Nordmann, Johannes Rumpelmaier,
1820-1887.
STÄNDCHEN (?)
Kling leise, mein Lied (1848) [GA,
v. 7^1, p. 118] same
2nd version, ca.1860: GA, v. 7^2, p.
76.
Orléans, Hélène Louise Élisabeth,
Duchesse d', 1814-1858.
Die Macht der Musik (1848-49) [GA,
v. 7^1, p. 156]
"Wer einsam steht . . . im bunten
Lebenskreise"
Pavloff, Mme.
Oh pourquoi donc (1848) [Moscow:
1844]
Publ. as "Les pleurs des femmes."
Petöfi, Sándor, 1823-1849.
A magyarok Istene (1881) [GA, v. 7^3,
p. 112]
"Félre Kislelküek, félre kislelküek"
May include chorus.
Petrarca, Francesco, 1304-1374.
Benedetto sia'l giorno (1838-39) [GA,
v. 7^1, p. 98] same
2nd version, 1861: GA, v. 7^3, p. 96.
Pace non trove (1838-39) [GA v. 7^1,
p. 89] same
2nd version, 1861: GA, v. 7^3, p. 101.
I vidi in terra angelicicostumi (1838-39)
[GA, v. 7^1, p. 104] same
2nd version, 1861: GA, v. 7^3, p. 106.
Pohl, Richard, 1826-1896.
Jugendglück (ca.1860) [GA, v. 7^3, p. 27]
"O süsser Zauber im Jugendmut"
Redwitz, Oskar, Freiherr von, 1823-
1891.
Es muss ein Wunderbares sein (1857)
[GA, v. 7^2, p. 14] same
Rellstab, Ludwig, 1799-1868.
Es rauschen die Winde (ca.1845) [GA,
v. 7^2, p. 53] same
2nd version, ca.1860: GA, v. 7^2, p. 83.
Ihr Auge (ca.1855) [GA, v. 7^2, p. 97]
"Nimm einen Strahl der Sonne"
Wo weilt er? (ca.1845) [GA, v. 7^2, p. 87]
same
Rückert, Friedrich, 1788-1866.
Ich liebe dich (1857) [GA, v. 7^3, p. 33]
same
Saar, Ferdinand von, 1833-1906.
Des Tages laute Stimmen schweigen
(1880) [GA, v. 7^3, p. 93] same
Scheffel, Joseph Victor von, 1826-
1886.
*DER BRAUTWILLKOMM AUF
WARTBURG.*

Biterolf und der Schmied von Ruhla
(1872) [GA, v. 7³, p. 142]
"Thüringens Wälder senden den
Waidmann und den Schmied"
Heinrich von Ofterdingen (1872) [GA,
v. 7³, p. 134] "Hab ich geträumt?"
Reimar der Alte (1872) [GA, v. 7³,
p. 146] "Wo liebende Herzen sich
innig vermählt"
Der tugendhafte Schreiber (1872) [GA,
v. 7³, p. 140]
"Ich schrieb allzeit nur wenig"
Walther von der Vogelweide (1872)
[GA, v. 7³, p. 137]
"Beim Scheiden der Sonne
erschimmert der Metilstein"
Schiller, Johann Christoph Friedrich
von, 1759-1805.
WILHELM TELL.
Der Alpenjäger (ca.1845) [GA, v. 7¹,
p. 149] "Es donnern die Höhn"
2nd version, ca.1859: GA, v. 7²,
p. 156.
Die Fischerknabe (ca.1845) [GA, v. 7¹,
p. 132] "Es lächelt der See"
2nd version, ca.1859: GA, v. 7²,
p. 147.
Der Hirt (ca.1845) [GA, v. 7¹, p. 142]
"Ihr Matten, lebt wohl"
2nd version, ca.1859: GA, v. 7²,
p. 152.
Schober, Franz von, 1798-1882.
Weimars Toten (1848) [GA, v.7¹, p. 172]
"Weimars Toten will ich's bringen"
Schorn, Henriette (von Stein) von,
1807-1869.
Sei still (1877) [GA, v.7³, p. 63] "Ach,
was ist Leben doch so schwer"
Tennyson, Alfred Tennyson, 1st
baron, 1809-1892.
Go not, happy day (1879) [GA, v. 7³,
p. 74] same
Also in W.G.Cusius, ed. *Songs from
the published writings of Alfred
Tennyson* ... 1880; p. 315.
Uhland, Ludwig, 1787-1862.
Gestorben war ich (ca.1849) [GA, v. 7²,
p. 4]
"Gestorben war ich vor Liebeswonne"
Hohe Liebe (ca.1849) [GA, v. 7², p. 1]
"In Liebesarmen ruht ihr trunken"
Die Vätergruft (1844) [GA, v. 7², p. 104]
"Es schritt wohl über die Heide"
Wilbrandt, Adolf, 1837-1911.
Der Glückliche (ca.1878) [GA, v. 7³,
p. 87] "Wie glänzt nun die Welt im
Abendstrahl"

Li-Tai-Pe *see* Li Po, 701-762.
Litanei auf das Fest Aller Seelen see Jacobi
SCHUBERT *Am Tage aller Seelen*
Liten gosse see Josephson, E. KILPINEN
"Liten gosse smyckades nyss" *see Liten gosse*
Josephson, E. KILPINEN
Liten jungfru see Cnattingius, Thor
KILPINEN
En liten visa om våren see Cnattingius,
Thor KILPINEN
A Lithuanian song see Anon. CHOPIN
Piosnka litewska
The little bird see Pleshcheyev
PODSNEZHNIK. CHAÏKOVSKIÏ *Ptichka*
The little black boy see Blake, William
THOMSON
Little elegy see Wylie ROREM
The little flower see Ratisbonne
CHAÏKOVSKIÏ *Tsvetok*
Little fly see Blake, William CARPENTER
"Little fly, little fly" *see The fly* Blake,
William BRITTEN
"Little fly, thy summer's play" *see Little fly*
Blake, William CARPENTER
The little graveyard see Havet
CARPENTER *Le petit cimetière*
The little gray dress see Gippius
PROKOFIEV *Seroe plat'itse*
The little green grove see Anon.
PROKOFIEV *Zelenaia roshchitsa*
The little horses see Anon. COPLAND
"Little Indian, Sioux or Crow" *see Foreign
children* Stevenson, Robert Louis
QUILTER
The little island see Shelley
RACHMANINOFF *The isle*
"A little island set in sea" *see The isle*
Shelley RACHMANINOFF
Little ivory figures pulled with string see
Lowell, A. GIDEON
Little Jack Jingle see Anon. *NURSE
LOVECHILD'S LEGACY* (London: The
Poetry Bookshop, 1916). HESELTINE
Little John's song see Chesson
CARPENTER
"Little lamb, who made thee?" *see The lamb*
Blake, William CHANLER,
VAUGHAN WILLIAMS
Little lasse see Topelius SIBELIUS *Lasse
liten*
Little old mother see Nietzsche MEDTNER
Alt Mütterlein
The little old table see Hardy BRITTEN
The little orphan girl see Musorgskiï
MUSORGSKIÏ *Sirotka*
The little pigs see Kvitko, L. PROKOFIEV
Porosiata

COMPOSER Poet *Title* "First Line"

The little prayer of I see Simpson, A.
CARPENTER
"The little pretty nightingale" *see*
The nightingale Anon. **ROREM**
Little red bootees see Des Knaben
Wunderhorn **MARTINŮ**
"Little star of Bethlehem" *see A Christmas
carol* Anon. **IVES**
Little Tommy Tucker see Anon. *NURSE
LOVECHILD'S LEGACY* (London: The
Poetry Bookshop, 1916). **HESELTINE**
"little tree little silent Christmas tree" *see
Christmas tree* Cummings **DIAMOND**
The little vagabond see Blake, William
LUENING
LITURGIE COMTADINE, cinq chants de
Rosch Haschanah, no. 1
  MILHAUD Anon. *Prenez courage, Ô
  enfants d'Israël!*
LITURGIE COMTADINE, cinq chants de
Rosch Haschanah, no. 2
  MILHAUD Anon. *Seigneur par le son du
  schophar vous ferez entendre*
LITURGIE COMTADINE, cinq chants de
Rosch Haschanah, no. 3
  MILHAUD Anon. *Le seigneur est roi*
LITURGIE COMTADINE, cinq chants de
Rosch Haschanah, no. 4
  MILHAUD Anon. *Toute l'année*
LITURGIE COMTADINE, cinq chants de
Rosch Haschanah, no. 5
  MILHAUD Anon. *Maintenant que les
  portes de bienveillance*
Liubimía see Goethe **MEDTNER** *Sie liebt
mich!*
Liubliu tebia, mesiats see Maïkov **RIMSKIĬ-
KORSAKOV**
Liubov' mertvetsa see Lermontov
CHAĬKOVSKIĬ
Livingstone, Mabel
  CARPENTER *If*
LIVRE D'AMOUR. see Vildrac
  Après minuit **IBERT**
  Comme elle a les yeux bandés **IBERT**
  Elle était venue sur les marches tièdes
    IBERT, SCHMITT
Ljubljaschtschi, C. Dorr-
  REGER *Mägdleins Frage*
Den ljusa nattens ljusa fågeldrillar see
  Blomberg **KILPINEN**
Llorente, Teodoro, 1826-1911.
  RODRIGO *Cançó del teuladí*
Llueve sobre el rio see Jimenez **MOMPOU**
Lob der Thränen see Schlegel **SCHUBERT**
Lob des Leidens see Schack **STRAUSS**
Lob des Tokayers see Batsányi **SCHUBERT**

Lobgesang see Buerde **LOEWE**
Lobgesang auf die feierliche Johannisloge see
  Lenz, L. **MOZART**
Las locas por amor see Campoamor y
  Campoosorio **TURINA**
Locations and times see Whitman
  LUENING
The lock see Unknown **MARTINŮ** *Otevření
sloveckem*
Locken, haltet mich gefangen see Goethe
  WESTÖSTLICHER DIVAN: Buch Suleika.
  WOLF
Lockenstricke sollst du wissen see Hafiz
  JENSEN
Das lockere Saatgefilde see George *DER
  SIEBENTE RING*: Gezeiten. **WEBERN**
Lockroy, Joseph Philippe Simon, 1803-
1891.
  DELIBES *Chanson de l'oiseleur*
Lockung see Eichendorff **GIDEON,
PFITZNER, SCHOECK**
Lockung see Fischer, H. **SCHÖNBERG**
Lockung see Garborg *HAUGTUSSA*. **GRIEG**
  Det synge
Lockweise see Bjørnson **GRIEG** *Lok*
Locutions see Cocteau **HONEGGER**
Loda's Gespenst see Macpherson *CARRIC-
THURA*: Spirit of Loda. **SCHUBERT**
Lodge, George Cabot, 1873-1909.
  LOEFFLER *Sonnet*
Lodge, Thomas, 1558-1625.
  RIETI *Montanus' sonnet*
  ROREM *Love*
LOEFFLER, CHARLES MARTIN, 1861-
1935.
Anon.
  By-an'-by [unpubl.] same
    Holograph at Library of Congress.
  Credo [unpubl.] "Credo in unum Deum"
    Voice & piano or organ. Holograph at
    Library of Congress.
  Old love song (1925) [unpubl.] "Alas!
    my heart is not my own"
    Holograph at Library of Congress.
Baudelaire, Charles Pierre, 1821-1867.
  La cloche fêlée, op. 5 no. 1 [G. Schirmer,
    1904] "Il est amer et doux"
    Voice, viola & piano.
  Le flambeau vivant (1902) [unpubl.]
    Holograph at Library of Congress.
Bourget, Paul Charles Joseph, 1852-
1935.
  Madrigal [unpubl.] "Si les roses
    poussaient nous rendre le baiser"
    Holograph at Library of Congress.

Dévigne, Roger, 1885-1965.
Prayer (192__) [C. C. Birchard, 1936]
"God of the tender young"
d'Hotelier, A.
Les Hirondelles [unpubl.] "Voltigez
Hirondelles voltigez près de moi"
Holograph at Library of Congress.
Hefferman, William, ca. 1720-1803.
The song of Catilin Ni Uallachain (1922)
[G. Schirmer, 1934]
"How tossed how lost with all hopes
crossed we have been!"
Also voice & orchestra.
Kahn, Gustave, 1859-1936.
Boléro triste (1908) [unpubl.] "Taut que
l'enfant me prétéra tel joucur de fleè"
Voice, violin & piano. Holograph at
Library of Congress.
Je te vis, je t'aimais (1908) [unpubl.]
same
Holograph at Library of Congress.
LES PALAIS NOMADES: Intermède IV.
Timbres oubliés, op. 10 no. 1 [G.
Schirmer, 1903] same
LES PALAIS NOMADES: Intermède IX.
Les paons, op. 10 no. 4 [G. Schirmer,
1903]
"Se penchant vers les dahlias"
LES PALAIS NOMADES: Intermède XIV.
Adieu pour jamais, op. 10 no. 2 [G.
Schirmer, 1903] "Chère apparence
viens aux couchants illuminés"
LES PALAIS NOMADES: Lied IV.
Les soirs d'automne, op. 10 no. 3 [G.
Schirmer, 1903] same
Lodge, George Cabot, 1873-1909.
Sonnet, op. 15 no. 4 [G. Schirmer, 1906]
"Tell me again, and then lift up to me
those frail white arms"
Musset, Alfred de, 1810-1857.
Marie [unpubl.] "Aiusi quand la fleur
printa-nière dans le bois"
Holograph at Library of Congress.
Poe, Edgar Allan, 1809-1849.
A dream within a dream, op. 15 no. 2
[G. Schirmer, 1906]
"Take this kiss upon the brow!"
To Helen, op. 15 no. 3 [G. Schirmer,
1906] "Helen, thy beauty is to me like
those Nicéan barks of yore"
Rossetti, Dante Gabriel, 1828-1882.
Sudden light, op. 15 no. 1 [G. Schirmer,
1906] "I have been here before"
Unknown
Busslied [unpubl.] "Gott, wie sind meine
Sünden so schwer"
Holograph at Library of Congress.

Las moyares corralera, cancion española
[unpubl.] "Tus ojos y los mios se
miran y hablau"
May be voice & guitar. Holograph at
Library of Congress.
Reverie [unpubl.] "Laissez moi, mes
amis, laissez moi solitaire"
Holograph at Library of Congress.
Tandis que l'Enfant [unpubl.]
*Ton souvenir est comme un livre bien
aimé* [unpubl.] same
Holograph at Library of Congress.
Verlaine, Paul, 1844-1896.
A une femme (1904) [unpubl.] "A vous
ces vers de par la grâce consolante"
One version for voice, violin & piano.
Holograph at Library of Congress.
Dansons la gigue! op. 5 no. 2
[G. Schirmer, 1904] same
Voice, viola & piano.
Sérénade, op. 5 no. 4 [G. Schirmer,
1904] "Comme la voix d'un mort qui
chanterait"
Voice, viola & piano.
SAGESSE.
Le son du cor s'afflige vers les bois,
op. 5 no. 3 [G. Schirmer, 1904]
same
Voice, viola & piano.
Yeats, William Butler, 1865-1939.
Ballad of the foxhunter [G. Schirmer,
1934]
"Now lay me in a cushioned chair"
Also voice & orchestra.
The fiddler of Dooney (1922) [G.
Schirmer, 1934]
"When I play on my fiddle in Dooney"
Also voice & orchestra.
THE WIND AMONG THE REEDS.
The host of the air (1907) [G.
Schirmer, 1908]
"O'Driscoll drove with a song"
Also voice & orchestra.
The hosting of the Sidhe (1907) [G.
Schirmer, 1908] "The Host is riding
from Knocknarea"
Also voice & orchestra.
"Löfvende falla sjöarna frysa" *see Norden*
Runeberg **SIBELIUS**
Lönnbohm, Eino, 1878-1926.
KILPINEN
Aamulla
Ikuinen kevät
Illalla
Kaupunkimatka
Kuu Kalpea

COMPOSER Poet *Title* "First Line"

Lönnbohm, Eino, 1878-1926 *(continued)*
  KILPINEN *(continued)*
    Kuusi ja lintunen
    Omenakukat
    Pieni ballaadi
    Rakastunut
    Rannalla
    Syyslaulu
    Yöperhonen
Löns, Hermann, 1866-1914.
  KILPINEN
    Am Haidenhügel geht ein Singen
    Das bittersüsse Lied
    Goldenes Lied
    Der Kuckuck
    Küssekraut
    Liebessuche
    Männertreu
    Rosenbüsche
    Schäferlied
    Der schönste Platz
    Der Spuk
    Der Verehrung
    Der Vollmond scheint
    Zur Erinnerung
  SCHÖNBERG *Jeduch*
Löper, Lina
  LOEWE *Wolkenbild*
Löse, Himmel, meine Seele see Cornelius
  LASSEN
Loest, Heinrich, 1778-1848.
  ZELTER *Der liebe Traum*
"Der Löw' ist los! der Löw' ist frei!" *see*
  Landgraf Ludwig Gruppe **LOEWE**
Loewe, Helene
  LOEWE
    Das Blümlein
    Ida's Wunsch
LOEWE, KARL, 1796-1869.
  Anacreon, b.ca.570 B.C.
    An die Grille, op. H. IX no. 5 [GA,
      v. 16, p. 203]
      "Du bist glücklich, O Cicade"
    An die Leier [GA, v. 1, p. 6] "Ich will
      von den Atriden"
    Auf sich selbst [GA, v. 1, p. 8] "Es sagen
      mir die Weiber"
    Auf sich selbst [GA, v. 1, p. 10] "Weil
      ich sterblich bin geboren"
  André, Johann, 1741-1799.
    Mädchen sind wie der Wind, op. 9 H. VI
      no. 4 [GA, v. 16, p. 182] same
      Text also by Friedrich Ludwig
        Aemilius Kunzen, 1761-1817.
    Romanze [GA, v. 1, p. 47] "In einem Tal,
      bei einem Bach"

Anon.
  Elvershöh, op. 3 no. 2 [GA, v. 3, p. 66]
    "Ich legte mein Haupt auf Elvershöh"
    Translated by Herder.
  Friede und Ruhe in Gott [GA, v. 2,
    p. 40] "Du Unruh' meiner Seelen"
    Voice & organ.
  *Gesang der Königin Maria Stuart auf den
    Tod Franz II* [GA, v. 2, p. 146]
    "In meines Herzens Trauerlied"
  Jesus mit seinen Jüngern auf dem Meere
    [GA, v. 16, p. 61]
    "Süsser Schlaf umfing den Müden"
    Text a Biblical folk legend.
  Kyrie [GA, v. 16, p. 70] "Kyrie, fons
    bonitatis"
  Der Treuergebene, op. 9 H. III no. 4
    [GA, v. 16, p. 167]
    "Der ich von den Frauen allen bis"
    An old German poem; translated from
      Mittelhochdeutsch.
  JENSEIT DES TWEED.
    Thomas der Reimer, op. 135 or 135a
      [GA, v. 3, p. 51]
      "Der Reimer Thomas lag am Bach"
      Translated by T. Fontane.
  THE NUT-BROWNE MAYD.
    Das braune Mädchen, op. 43 no. 3
      [GA, v. 3, p. 21]
      "Es kam zu ihr, leis an die Thür"
      Translated by Herder.
Anschütz, Ernst, 1797-1855.
  Johann von Nepomuk, op. 35 no. 2 [GA,
    v. 13, p. 58] "Ha, Priester, zitt're!"
Arndt, Ernst Moritz, 1769-1860.
  Liebesnähe [GA, v. 1, p. 30] "Lieb' sei
    ferne"
Auersperg, Anton Alexander, Graf
  von, 1806-1876.
  Die Leiche zu St. Just, op. 99 no. 4 [GA,
    v. 4, p. 124]
    "Aus Sanct Justi Klosterhallen"
  Die Reigerbaize, op. 106 [GA, v. 4,
    p. 68] "Als Lenz die Erde wieder mit
    erstem Kuss umschloss"
  Das Wiegenfest zu Gent, op. 99 no. 1
    [GA, v. 4, p. 106]
    "Es steht eine gold'ne Wiege"
  EIN FRIEDHOFKRANZ.
    Die Grabrose [GA, v. 2, p. 28]
      "Du Grabesrose wurzelst wohl"
  DER LETZTE RITTER.
    Max' Abschied von Augsburg, op. 124
      no. 3 [GA, v. 4, p. 101]
      "Max wollt' aus Augsburg reiten"
    Max in Augsburg, op. 124 no. 1 [GA,
      v. 4, p. 77]
      "Es hat das Herz des Menschen"

Max und Dürer, op. 124 no. 2 [GA,
v. 4, p. 88]
"Fürst, Trossbub, Ritter, Gauner"
**Augustinus, Aurelius, Saint, Bp. of
Hippo, 354-430.**
Wie du deine Sonne hast lassen aufgehn
[GA, v. 16, p. 56] same
Bartholdy, Dr.
Dem Herrscher (1859) [GA, v. 5, p. 81]
"Über Wolken Herr der Herren"
Bartholdy was a teacher at the Stettiner
Gymnasium.
Polterabendlied [GA, v. 2, p. 14]
"In Liebe sich begegnen"
Berlepsch, Emilie von, 1757-1830.
DAS GRAB.
Lied am Grabe [GA, v. 16, p. 69]
"Ruhig ist des Todes Schlummer"
**Binder, Franz Rudolf Immanuel, 1810-
1846.**
Das Grab zu Ephesus, op. 75 no. 1 [GA,
v. 14, p. 35]
"Es ziehet den Pilgrim rastlos fort"
Blankenfeldt, Otto
Frühlingsweihe [GA, v. 2, p. 24] "Holder
Lenz, mit reichen Gaben"
Text by Blankenfeldt and Frau
Blankenfeldt.
**Blankensee, Georg Friedrich
Alexander von, count, 1792-1867.**
Blumen-Evangelium [GA, v. 16, p. 118]
"Hoffe, liebe, glaube"
Böhmer, Wilhelm, 1791-1842.
*Ad Jesum Christum, Dominum et
Salvatorem meum* [GA, v. 1, p. 65]
"Fuit tempus, cum plorarem"
**Branco, Frau Helene [von Rödlich]
1818-1894.**
Alles in dir, op. 107 no. 2 [GA, v. 17,
p. 135] "Du giebst die Freude"
Allmacht Gottes, op. 89 no. 3 [GA, v. 17,
p. 122] "Blättlein so fein und rund"
Dein Auge, op. 89 no. 2 [GA, v. 17,
p. 121] "Ein Himmelreich dein Auge
ist"
Des Mädchens Wunsch und Geständnis,
op. 89 no. 4 [GA, v. 17, p. 124]
"O nimm mich an als deine Magd!"
Du Geist der reinsten Güte, op. 89 no. 5
[GA, v. 17, p. 126]
"Ich sinke dir ans volle Herz"
Frühling, op. 107 no. 3 [GA, v. 17,
p. 137] "Der Frühling begrüsset"
Das Glockenspiel der Phantasie, op. 89
no. 1 [GA, v. 17, p. 118] same

Mit jedem Pulsschlag leb' ich dir, op. 89
no. 6 [GA, v. 17, p. 128] same
Mondlicht, op. 107 no. 1 [GA, v. 17,
p. 132] "Wie ein Schwan still die
Bahn"
Briesen, Otto von
Letzter Seufzer [GA, v. 2, p. 73]
"Regenwetter ziehen trübe"
Brumm, Pauline
Brautlied [GA, v. 2, p. 16] "Von der
zarten Kinder Händen"
Budy, Friedrich, 1809-1856.
Deutsche Flotte (1848) [GA, v. 5, p. 74]
"Deutschlands Adler liegt gebunden"
Buerde, Samuel Gottlieb, 1753-1831.
Lobgesang [GA, v. 1, p. 61] "Alles, was
Odem hat, lobe den Herrn!"
Burns, Robert, 1759-1796.
Findlay [GA, v. 2, p. 96] "Nun, wer
klopft an meine Thür?"
**Byron, George Gordon Byron, 6th
baron, 1778-1824.**
Alles ist eitel, spricht der Prediger, op. 4
no. 4 [GA, v. 15, p. 109]
"Es waren Ruhm und Weisheit mein"
An den Wassern zu Babel, op. 4 no. 2
[GA, v. 15, p. 106]
"An Babylons Wassern gefangen"
Davids Harfe, op. 14 no. 3 [GA, v. 15,
p. 146]
"O Harfe, die des Gottgeliebten Hand"
Herodes' Klage um Mariamne, op. 4 no.
1 [GA, v. 15, p. 98]
"O Mariamne, dieses Herz"
Die höh're Welt, op. 13 no. 3 [GA, v. 15,
p. 134] "O höh're Welt"
Jephthas Tochter, op. 5 no. 2 [GA, v. 15,
p. 119] "Soll nach des Volkes und
nach Gottes Willen"
Jerusalems Zerstörung durch Titus, op.
14 no. 5 [GA, v. 15, p. 150]
"Von dem Berg"
Jordans Ufer, op. 13 no. 4 [GA, v. 15,
p. 135] "Auf Jordans Ufer streifen
wilde Horden"
Lebewohl [GA, v. 1, p. 38] "Lebe wohl!
wenn je ein brünstig Flehen"
Text adapted by Therese von Jacob.
Mein Geist ist trüb', op. 5 no. 5 [GA,
v. 15, p. 126] same
Sanherib's Niederlage, op. 13 no. 1 [GA,
v. 15, p. 132]
"Es kam des Assyers gewaltige Macht"
Saul, op. 14 no. 4 [GA, v. 15, p. 148]
"Dein Leben schliesst, dein Ruhm
begann"

COMPOSER Poet *Title* "First Line"

LOEWE, KARL, 1796-1869 (continued)
Byron, George Gordon Byron, 6th
baron, 1778-1824 (continued)
Saul vor seiner letzten Schlacht, op. 5 no.
6 [GA, v. 15, p. 130] "Krieger und
Feldherrn, ereilt mich der Tod"
Sie geht in Schönheit, op. 5 no. 1 [GA,
v. 15, p. 118] same
Die Sonne der Schlaflosen, op. 13 no. 6
[GA, v. 15, p. 144] "Schlafloser Augen
Sonne, zitternd Licht"
Thränen und Lächeln, op. 4 no. 6 [GA,
v. 15, p. 116] "Ich sah die volle
Thräne glüh'n in deines Auges Blau"
Todtenklage, op. 4 no. 5 [GA, v. 15,
p. 113] "Du in der Schönheit
strahlendem Scheim Entschwundne"
Wär' ich wirklich so falsch? op. 4 no. 3
[GA, v. 15, p. 108] same
Weint um Israel! op. 5 no. 4 [GA, v. 15,
p. 125] "Beweint die, so geweint in
Babels Land!"
Die wilde Gazelle, op. 5 no. 3 [GA,
v. 15, p. 122] "Gazelle, die so wild
und schnell"
Wohin, O Seele, wirst du eilen? op. 13
no. 5 [GA, v. 15, p. 140] same
HEBREW MELODIES.
Belsazar's Gesicht, op. 13 no. 2 [GA,
v. 8, p. 60] "Der König thront"
Text adapted by Franz Theremin.
Eliphas' Gesicht, op. 14 no. 2 [GA,
v. 8, p. 72]
"An mir vorüber ging ein Geist"
Text adapted by Franz Theremin.
Saul und Samuel, op. 14 no. 1 [GA,
v. 8, p. 66]
"Du, deren Kunst die Todten ruft"
Text adapted by Franz Theremin.
Chamisso, Adelbert von, 1781-1838.
An meinem Herzen, an meiner Brust, op.
60 no. 7 [GA, v. 17, p. 54] same
Du Ring an meinem Finger, op. 60 no. 4
[GA, v. 17, p. 39] same
Er, der Herrlichste von allen, op. 60 no.
2 [GA, v. 17, p. 34] same
Helft mir, ihr Schwestern! op. 60 no. 5
[GA, v. 17, p. 42] same
Ich kann's nicht fassen, nicht glauben,
op. 60 no. 3 [GA, v. 17, p. 37] same
*Nun hast du mir den ersten Schmerz
gethan* (1836) [GA, v. 17, p. 56] same
*Süsser Freund, du blickest mich
verwundert an,* op. 60 no. 6
[GA, v. 17, p. 50] same
Traum der eignen Tage, op. 60 no. 9
[GA, v. 17, p. 58] same

FRAUENLIEBE UND LEBEN.
Seit ich ihn gesehn, op. 60 no. 1 [GA,
v. 17, p. 32] same
KATZENNATUR.
Die Katzenkönigin, op. 64 no. 3 [GA,
v. 9, p. 102]
" 's war mal 'ne Katzenkönigin"
Chezy, Wilhelmine Christiane von,
1783-1856.
Moosröslein, op. 37 no. 2 [GA, v. 13,
p. 96]
"In tiefster Schlucht, in Waldesschoss"
St. Johannes und das Würmlein, op. 35
no. 1 [GA, v. 13, p. 51]
"Johannes ging am hellen Bach"
Claudius, Matthias, 1740-1815.
Die Mutter an der Wiege (1840) [GA,
v. 16, p. 132]
"Schlaf, holder Knabe, süss und mild"
ASMUS.
Der Zahn [GA, v. 1, p. 91] "Victoria!
der kleine weisse Zahn ist da"
DAS BAUERNLIED.
Im Anfang und jetzt [GA, v. 1, p. 70]
"Im Anfang war's auf Erden"
Cramer, Johann Andreas, 1723-1788.
Der Herr ist Gott [GA, v. 1, p. 62]
"Der Herr ist Gott und keiner mehr"
Die Himmel rufen [GA, v. 1, p. 64] same
Dionysius, 2nd c. after Christ
An die Muse [GA, v. 16, p. 197]
"O Muse, mir Vertraute"
Loewe GA equivocates on identifying
the Dionysius.
Text from **Poetae lyrici Graeci** 4
3,316. [sic]
Emsmann, August Hugo, 1810-1889.
König Wilhelm, op. 139 [GA, v. 5, p. 35]
"König Wilhelm, unsre Sonne,
Hohenzollern, unser Stern!"
Enslin, Karl, 1819-1875.
Der Abendstern [GA, v. 1, p. 58] "Bist ja
noch ganz allein"
Schlittschuhlauf [GA, v. 1, p. 85]
"Herbei, heran, auf die glänzende
Bahn!"
Der Schwimmer [GA, v. 1, p. 83] "O
Freude, O Wonne!"
Falk, Johannes, 1768-1826.
Nordisches Seelied [GA, v. 1, p. 69]
"Nach dem Sturme fahren wir"
Fick, Heinrich
THE MEETING ON THE SEASHORE.
Die Begegnung am Meeresstrand, op.
120 B [GA, v. 10, p. 166]
"Des Jünglings Blick erkennt der
Liebe Zeichen"

Fink, Gottfried Wilhelm, 1783-1847.
HÄUSLICHEN ANDACHTEN.
   Dem Ew'gen [GA, v. 1, p. 71]
      "Dem Ew'gen unsre Lieder!"
Fitzau, Heinrich, 1810-1859.
DER SELTENE BETER.
   Der alte Dessauer, op. 141 [GA, v. 5,
      p. 18]
      "Im Abendgolde glänzet zu
         Bärenburg das Schloss"
Förster, Friedrich, 1791-1868.
   Der alte Goethe, op. 9 H. IX no. 2 [GA,
      v. 11, p. 83]
      "Als ich ein junger Geselle war"
Fontane, Theodor, 1819-1898.
   Archibald Douglas, op. 128 [GA, v. 3,
      p. 37]
      "Ich hab' es getragen sieben Jahr"
Frankl, Ludwig August, 1810-1894.
   Menschenlose, op. 103 no. 2 [GA, v. 15,
      p. 42] "Vom Himmel zogen rauschend
      viel runde Tropfen sacht"
Freiligrath, Ferdinand, 1810-1876.
   Der Blumen Rache, op. 68 no. 3 [GA,
      v. 9, p. 134] "Auf des Lagers weichem
      Kissen ruht die Jungfrau"
   Der Edelfalk, op. 68 no. 2 [GA, v. 9,
      p. 128] "Die Fürstin zog zu Walde"
   Meerfahrt, op. 93 [GA, v. 10, p. 159]
      "Da schwimm ich allein auf dem
         stillen Meer"
   Der Mohrenfürst, op. 97 no. 1 [GA, v. 6,
      p. 76] "Sein Heer durchwogte das
      Palmenthal"
   Der Mohrenfürst auf der Messe, op. 97
      no. 3 [GA, v. 6, p. 91]
      "Auf der Messe, da zieht es"
   Die Mohrenfürstin, op. 97 no. 2 [GA,
      v. 6, p. 84]
      "Fern tobt der Kampf im Palmenthal"
   Nebo, op. 136 (135b) [GA, v. 14, p. 85]
      "Auf Jordan's grünen Borden"
   Prinz Eugen, der edle Ritter, op. 92 [GA,
      v. 5, p. 14]
      "Zelte, Posten, Werda-Rufer!"
   Schwalbenmärchen, op. 68 no. 1 [GA,
      v. 9, p. 122] "Auf dem stillen,
      schwülen Pfuhle tanzt"
Friedrich Wilhelm IV, King of Prussia,
   1795-1861? supposed author.
   Preussisches Hurrahlied (1848) [GA,
      v. 5, p. 48] "Wer droht unserm
      deutschen Vaterland"
Gellert, Christian Fürchtegott, 1715-
   1769.
   Busslied, op. 22 H. I no. 4 [GA, v. 16,
      p. 9] "Ich komme vor dein Angesicht"

Gott ist mein Lied [GA, v. 16, p. 45]
   same
Wie gross ist des Allmächt'gen Güte! op.
   22 H. II no. 4 [GA, v. 16, p. 14]
   same
PREIS DES SCHÖPFERS.
   Wenn ich, O Schöpfer, deine Macht
      [GA, v. 1, p. 63] same
Geppert family: father or one of the
   daughters, Therese or Luise
Engelsstimmen am Krankenbette, op. 22
   H. II no. 2 [GA, v. 16, p. 11]
   "Nimm sie willig und geduldig"
Gerstenberg
*Abendgebet, nach einer erlittenen
   Kränkung,* op. 69 no. 3 [GA, v. 17,
   p. 104] "Die mich recht erkennen"
   GA cannot identify the poet; the op. 69
      and op. 9 songs listed here are
      known as Gerstenberg-Lieder. Poet
      may be Heinrich Wilhelm von
      Gerstenberg, 1737-1823.
Abschied, op. 9 H. IV no. 2 [GA, v. 17,
   p. 97]
   "Noch einmal muss ich vor dir stehn"
Der Fernen, op. 9 H. IX no. 6 [GA,
   v. 17, p. 116]
   "So viel Blumen allwärts blühen"
Gruss an Züllchow, op. 69 no. 1 [GA,
   v. 17, p. 99]
   "Liebes Haus auf Berges Höh!"
Gute Nacht! [GA, v. 2, p. 4] "Sonst
   konnt' ich dein nicht denken"
   GA cannot identify poet; may be
      Heinrich Wilhelm von Gerstenberg,
      1737-1823.
Herzen und Augen, op. 69 no. 5 [GA,
   v. 17, p. 108] "Dich blendet
   Kerzenlicht!"
Himmelsblüthen, op. 69 no. 2 [GA, v. 17,
   p. 101] "Auch das schönste
   Blumenleben"
Der Komet, op. 69 no. 6 [GA, v. 17,
   p. 111] "Wo kommst du her?"
Die Sterne, op. 69 no. 4 [GA, v. 17,
   p. 106]
   "Welch Leuchten auf den Wogen!"
Giesebrecht, Ludwig, 1792-1873.
Abendlied [GA, v. 16, p. 112] "Schatten
   deckt, vom Tau befeuchtet"
Als Weibesarm in jungen Jahren, op. 39
   no. 5 [GA, v. 10, p. 132] same
Bienenweben (1862) [GA, v. 15, p. 28]
   "Bienen summen, wie schwer zu
   tragen"
Einsegnungslied [GA, v. 2, p. 38]
   "O Lämmlein bleibt"

LOEWE, KARL, 1796-1869 (*continued*)

Giesebrecht, Ludwig, 1792-1873
(*continued*)

Es steht ein Kelch in der Kapelle, op. 39
no. 4 [GA, v. 10, p. 130] same

Frühlings Seele [GA, v. 16, p. 104]
"Es hat der schimmernde
Sonnenstrahl"

Das heilige Haus in Loretto, op. 33 no. 2
[GA, v. 13, p. 14]
"Wolke lichtweiss in dem Blauen"

Im Schacht der Adern und der Stufen, op.
39 no. 1 [GA, v. 10, p. 120] same

Der König auf dem goldnen Stuhle, op.
52 no. 2 [GA, v. 7, p. 98] same

Nun auf dem fremden Boden, op. 52 no.
3 [GA, v. 7, p. 103] same

Sang des Moses [GA, v. 2, p. 42]
"Der Sabbath hebt, ein grössrer
Sabbath an"

Sankt Mariens Ritter, op. 36 no. 2 [GA,
v. 13, p. 80] "Jung stritt ich einst um
Accons Schloss"

Scholastica, op. 76 no. 2 [GA, v. 14,
p. 60] "Bleib, mein Bruder!"

Spielt, Mägdlein, unter eurer Weide! op.
52 no. 4 [GA, v. 7, p. 107] same

Taubenlied [GA, v. 16, p. 90] "Hat mit
frischem Birkenlaube"

*Unser Herzog hat herrliche Taten
vollbracht,* op. 39 no. 3 [GA, v. 10,
p. 125] same

Von meines Hauses engen Wänden, op.
39 no. 2 [GA, v. 10, p. 123] same

Wie früh das enge Pförtchen knarre, op.
52 no. 1 [GA, v. 7, p. 94] same

Wie wohnst du in des Reiches Städten,
op. 52 no. 5 [GA, v. 7, p. 112] same

SANFT RUHENDE FLUR.
Der Friedhof [GA, v. 8, p. 91] "Euer
Herz erschrecke nicht"

Gleim, Johann Wilhelm Ludwig,
1719-1803.

Naturgenuss [GA, v. 16, p. 95]
"Da kommt ja der liebliche Mai"

Goethe, Johann Wolfgang von, 1749-
1832.

Alpin's Klage um Morar, op. 95 (94)
[GA, v. 12, p. 62]
"Ullin trat auf mit der Harfe"

Auf dem See, op. 80 H. I no. 2 [GA,
v. 11, p. 26]
"Und frische Nahrung, neues Blut"

*Ballade vom vertriebenen und
zurückkehrenden Grafen,* op. 44 no. 1
[GA, v. 11, p. 131] "Herein, O du
Guter!"

Die Braut von Corinth, op. 29 [GA,
v. 12, p. 122]
"Nach Corinthus von Athen gezogen"

Dank des Paria, op. 58 no. 3 [GA, v. 12,
p. 121]
"Grosser Brama! nun erkenn' ich"

Erlkönig, op. 1 no. 3 [GA, v. 11, p. 85]
"Wer reitet so spät durch Nacht und
Wind?"

Die erste Walpurgisnacht, op. 25 [GA,
v. 12, p. 156] "Es lacht der Mai!"

Der Fischer, op. 43 no. 1 [GA, v. 11, p.
122] "Das Wasser rauscht', das Wasser
schwoll"

Freibeuter (1836) [GA, v. 11, p. 80]
"Mein Haus hat kein' Thür"

Frühling übers Jahr, op. 75 no. 5 [GA,
v. 11, p. 20] "Das Beet, schon lockert
sich's in die Höh'!"

Frühzeitiger Frühling, op. 79 no. 1 [GA,
v. 11, p. 18] "Tage der Wonne, kommt
ihr so bald?"

Ganymed, op. 81 no. 5 [GA, v. 12, p. 34]
"Wie im Morgenglanze du rings mich
anglühst"

Gebet des Paria, op. 58 no. 1 [GA, v. 12,
p. 96]
"Grosser Brama, Herr der Mächte!"

Gesang der Geister über den Wassern,
op. 88 [GA, v. 12, p. 16]
"Des Menschen Seele gleicht dem
Wasser"

Der getreue Eckart, op. 44 no. 2 [GA,
v. 11, p. 147] "O wären wir weiter"

Gottes ist der Orient! op. 22 H. I no. 5
[GA, v. 11, p. 70] same

Gutmann und Gutweib, op. 9 H. VIII no.
5 [GA, v. 11, p. 116]
"Und morgen fällt St. Martins Fest"

Hochzeitlied, op. 20 no. 1 [GA, v. 11,
p. 94] "Wir singen und sagen vom
Grafen so gern"

Ich denke dein, op. 9 H. III no. 1 [GA,
v. 11, p. 6] same

Im Vorübergehen, op. 81 no. 1 [GA,
v. 11, p. 24]
"Ich ging im Felde so für mich hin"

Kanzonette (1835) [GA, v. 11, p. 64]
"War schöner als der schönste Tag"

Legende, op. 58 no. 2 [GA, v. 12, p. 99]
"Wasser holen geht die reine"

Mädchenwünsche, op. 9 H. VIII no. 4
[GA, v. 11, p. 77] "O fände für mich
ein Bräutigam sich!"

Mahomet's Gesang, op. 85 [GA, v. 12,
p. 2] "Seht den Felsenquell"

Mailied, op. 79 no. 4 [GA, v. 11, p. 22]
"Wie herrlich leuchtet mir die Natur!"
Der Schatzgräber, op. 59 no. 3 [GA,
v. 11, p. 173]
"Arm am Beutel, krank am Herzen"
Der Todtentanz, op. 44 no. 3 [GA, v. 11,
p. 154] "Der Thürmer, der schaut zu
Mitten der Nacht"
Trost in Tränen, op. 80 H. II no. 2 [GA,
v. 11, p. 16] "Wie kommt's, dass du so
traurig bist?"
Der verliebte Schäferin Scapine, op. 9 H.
IX no. 3 [GA, v. 11, p. 73]
"Gern in stillen Melancholien"
Die wandelnde Glocke, op. 20 no. 3 [GA,
v. 11, p. 113]
"Es war ein Kind, das wollte nie"
Wechsel (1835) [GA, v. 11, p. 66]
"Auf Kieseln im Bache"
Wirkung in die Ferne, op. 59 no. 1 [GA,
v. 11, p. 162]
"Die Königin steht im hohen Saal"
Der Zauberlehrling, op. 20 no. 2 [GA,
v. 11, p. 104] "Hat der alte
Hexenmeister sich doch einmal
wegbegeben!"
FAUST.
Lynceus, der Helene, op. 9 H. VIII no.
2 [GA, v. 11, p. 52]
"Du siehst mich, Königin, zurück"
Lynceus, der Thürmer, op. 9 H. VIII
no. 3 [GA, v. 11, p. 61]
"Zum Sehen geboren"
Mädchen, als du kamst ans Licht [GA,
v. 11, p. 38] same
Meine Ruh' ist hin, op. 9 H. III no. 2
[GA, v. 11, p. 30] same
Nur Platz, nur Blösse! [GA, v. 11,
p. 40] same
2 voices & piano.
Sei mir heute nichts zuwider! [GA,
v. 11, p. 43] same
Szene aus "Faust," op. 9 H. IX no. 1
[GA, v. 11, p. 34]
"Ach neige, du Schmerzenreiche!"
Thurmwächter Lynceus, op. 9 H. VIII
no. 1 [GA, v. 11, p. 47] "Lass mich
knien, lass mich schauen!"
Wenn der Blüten Frühlingsregen [GA,
v. 11, p. 37] same
INDISCHE LEGENDE.
Der Gott und die Bajadere, op. 45 no.
2 [GA, v. 12, p. 80]
"Mahadöh, der Herr der Erde"
WANDRERS NACHTLIED I.
Wandrers Nachtlied, op. 9 H. I no. 3b
[GA, v. 11, p. 3]
"Der du von dem Himmel bist"

WANDRERS NACHTLIED II.
Wandrers Nachtlied, op. 9 H. I no. 3a
[GA, v. 11, p. 2]
"Über allen Gipfeln ist Ruh' "
WILHELM MEISTER.
Der Sänger, op. 59 no. 2 [GA, v. 11,
p. 168] "Was hör' ich draussen vor
dem Thor?"
WILHELM MEISTER. Mignon's song:
Nur wer die Sehnsucht kennt.
Sehnsucht, op. 9 H. III no. 5 [GA,
v. 11, p. 14]
"Nur wer die Sehnsucht kennt"
Goldtammer, Frau
Brautkranzlied [GA, v. 2, p. 12]
"Ein Kränzlein sollst du tragen"
Goltz, Emily von der, d. 1893.
Spirito santo, op. 143 [GA, v. 15, p. 63]
"In des Südens heissen Zonen Blumen
giebt"
Gotter, Friedrich Wilhelm, 1746-1797.
An die Geliebte, op. 9 H. III no. 3 [GA,
v. 16, p. 158] "Wie der Tag mir
schleichet ohne dich vollbracht"
**Gramberg, Gerhard Anton Hermann,
1772-1816.**
Frühlingserwachen, op. 9 H. IV no. 3
[GA, v. 16, p. 161] "Es schauet der
Morgen mit funkelndem Schein"
Grassmann, Newton von, 1809-1877.
Das "Dolce far niente" [GA, v. 2,
p. 108] "O dolce far niente"
Gruppe, Otto Friedrich, 1804-1876.
Der Apotheker als Nebenbuhler, op. 9 H.
X no. 6 [GA, v. 16, p. 150]
" 's ist wahr, mit blanken Scheiben"
Der Bräutigam, op. 9 H. X no. 3 [GA,
v. 16, p. 178] "Wie pocht mir vor Lust
das Herz in der Brust"
Einrichtung, op. 9, H. X, no. 5 [GA, v. 1,
p. 88]
"Klein Lieschen, ich hab' dich so lieb"
Der Feldherr, op. 67 no. 1 [GA, v. 6,
p. 2] "O lass, Geliebter, dich erflehen"
Landgraf Ludwig, op. 67 no. 3 [GA,
v. 14, p. 8]
"Der Löw' ist los! der Löw' ist frei!"
Niemand hat's gesehn, op. 9 H. X no. 4
[GA, v. 16, p. 146]
"Die Trepp' hinunter geschwungen"
Häring, Wilhelm, 1798-1871.
Fridericus Rex, op. 61 no. 1 [GA, v. 5,
p. 29] "Fridericus Rex, unser König
und Herr"
Rüberettig [GA, v. 16, p. 126] "Sie liebte
ihn, er liebte sie"

COMPOSER Poet *Title* "First Line"

LOEWE, KARL, 1796-1869 *(continued)*
Häring, Wilhelm, 1798-1871 *(continued)*
Schneiderlied [GA, v. 2, p. 98] "Es war
einmal ein Schneidergesell"
Der späte Gast, op. 7 no. 2 [GA, v. 8,
p. 50] "Was klopft ans Thor?"
Walpurgisnacht, op. 2 no. 3 [GA, v. 8,
p. 15]
"Liebe Mutter, heut Nacht heulte
Regen und Wind"
Wer ist Bär? op. 64 no. 4 [GA, v. 9,
p. 108] "Mach auf, mach auf, mach auf
deine Thür"
*SCHWERIN, MEIN GENERAL, IST
TODT, SCHWERIN IST TODT!*
General Schwerin, op. 61 no. 2 [GA,
v. 5, p. 24] "Schwerin ist todt,
Schwerin, mein General, ist todt"
**Hardenberg, Friedrich Leopold,
Freiherr von, 1772-1801.**
Wenn alle untreu werden, op. 22 H. I no.
2 [GA, v. 16, p. 4] same
Wenn ich ihn nur habe, op. 22 H. I no. 1
[GA, v. 16, p. 2] same
Heine, Heinrich, 1797-1856.
Der Asra, op. 133 [GA, v. 6, p. 98]
"Täglich ging die winderschöne
Sultanstochter"
Du schönes Fischermädchen, op. 9
H. VII no. 5 [GA, v. 17, p. 11] same
Erste Liebe, op. 9 H. VII no. 3 [GA,
v. 17, p. 9] "Sie liebten sich beide"
Ich hab' im Traume geweinet, op. 9
H. VII no. 6 [GA, v. 17, p. 14] same
Im Traum sah ich die Geliebte, op. 9
H. VII no. 2 [GA, v. 17, p. 6] same
Leise zieht durch mein Gemüth (1838)
[GA, v. 17, p. 16] same
Die Lotosblume, op. 9 H. I no. 1 [GA,
v. 17, p. 2] "Die Lotosblume ängstigt
sich"
Neuer Frühling, op. 9 H. VII no. 4 [GA,
v. 17, p. 10] "Herz, mein Herz, sei
nicht beklommen"
Die schlanke Wasserlilie (1847) [GA,
v. 2, p. 62] same
Helmbold, Ludwig, 1532-1598.
Pfingslied [GA, v. 2, p. 36] "Der heilig
Geist vom Himmel kam"
**Herder, Johann Gottfried von, 1744-
1803.**
Der Kukuk, op. 64 no. 2 [GA, v. 9, p. 96]
"Einmal in einem tiefen Thal"
Das Paradies in der Wüste, op. 37 no. 3
[GA, v. 13, p. 102]
"Mein Freund Antonius"
Tenor, men's chorus & piano.

Die Sylphide, op. 9 H. X no. 2 [GA, v.
16, p. 187] "Liebes leichtes luft'ges
Ding, Schmetterling!"
STIMMEN DER VÖLKER.
Edward, op. 1 no. 1 [GA, v. 3, p. 2]
"Dein Schwert, wie ist's von Blut so
roth"
Herr Oluf, op. 2 no. 2 [GA, v. 3, p.
58] "Herr Oluf reitet spät und weit"
Translated by Herder.
Hildebrandt
Dem Könige [GA, v. 5, p. 83] "Auf,
Preussenherz! mit deinen Jubeltönen"
Hildebrandt was a minister in Stettin.
**Hölty, Ludwig Heinrich Christoph,
1748-1776.**
O wunderschön ist Gottes Erde [GA,
v. 16, p. 100] same
**Hoffmann von Fallersleben, August
Heinrich, 1798-1874.**
Jugend und Alter, op. 9, H. X, no. 1
[GA, v. 1, p. 87]
"Jugend, dich hab' ich so lieb"
**Hohlfeld, Christoph Christian, 1776-
1849.**
HARFENKLÄNGEN: Kaiser Karl V. an
Luthers Grabe.
Kaiser Karl V. in Wittenberg, op. 99
no. 2 [GA, v. 4, p. 114]
"Ernst ritt der Kaiser"
Huber, Victor Aimé, 1800-1869.
SKIZZEN AUS SPANIEN.
Der Sturm von Alhama, op. 54 [GA,
v. 6, p. 48]
"Durch die Strassen von Granada"
Hus, Jan, 1369-1415.
Jesus ist mein Hirt [GA, v. 2, p. 35]
same
**Jacob, Therese Amalie Louise von,
1797-1870.**
Beim Tanze, op. 15 no. 2 [GA, v. 17,
p. 20] "Trallallala, mein Liebchen"
Des Jünglings Segen, op. 15 no. 4 [GA,
v. 17, p. 26]
"Singt ein Falk all' die Nacht durch"
Ihr Spaziergang, op. 9 H. IV no. 4 [GA,
v. 16, p. 163]
"Will die Holde sich ergehen"
Kapitulation, op. 15 no. 6 [GA, v. 17,
p. 30] "Hinterm Berge dort"
Liebesliedchen, op. 15 no. 5 [GA, v. 17,
p. 28] "Winter vorbei, Herzchen, mein
Liebchen!"
Mädchen und Rose, op. 15 no. 1 [GA,
v. 17, p. 18]
"Ach! mein kühler Wasserquell!"

Der Mutter Geist, op. 8 no. 2 [GA, v. 3, p. 10] "Herr Dyring ritt wohl durch das Land"

Überraschung, op. 15 no. 3 [GA, v. 17, p. 22]
"Komm, O Bruder, in die helle Sonne"

Kahlert, Karl August Timothens, 1807-1864.
Sankt Helena, op. 126 [GA, v. 6, p. 7]
"Hier steh' ich einsam auf dem Fels im Meer"

Kind, Friedrich, 1768-1843.
Der grosse Christoph, op. 34 [GA, v. 13, p. 26] "Offerus war ein Lanzenknecht"

Kleist, Ewald Christian von, 1715-1759.
Gross ist der Herr [GA, v. 16, p. 46] same

Kletke, Hermann, 1813-1886.
In die Ferne (1837) [GA, v. 15, p. 83]
"Siehst du am Abend die Wolken ziehn"

Klopstock, Friedrich Gottlieb, 1724-1803.
Dem Dreieinigen [GA, v. 1, p. 66] "Preis ihm! Er schuf und er erhäLT"
AN FANNY.
Wenn einst ich tot bin [GA, v. 16, p. 67] same

Knapp, Albert, 1798-1864.
Die Einladung, op. 76 no. 1 [GA, v. 14, p. 52] "Ein frommer Landmann in der Kirche sass"

Körner, Theodor, i.e., Karl Theodor, 1791-1813.
Sängers Wanderlied (1835) [*Der Minnesänger,* ii (1835)]
"Gar fröhlich tret ich in die Welt"
Treuröschen, op. 2 no. 1 [GA, v. 8, p. 2]
"Es war ein Jäger wohl keck und kühn"
Wallhaide, op. 6 [GA, v. 8, p. 20]
"Wo dort die alten Gemäuer stehn"

Kopisch, August, 1799-1853.
Die Heinzelmännchen, op. 83 [GA, v. 9, p. 50]
"Wie war zu Cölln es doch vordem"
Landgraf Philipp der Grossmüthige, op. 125 no. 1 [GA, v. 4, p. 130]
"O wehe, Heinz von Lüder"
Der Nöck, op. 129 no. 2 [GA, v. 9, p. 20]
"Es tönt des Nöcken Harfenschall"

Kosegarten, Ludwig Gotthard, 1758-1818.
Wenn du wärst mein eigen, op. 9 H. IV no. 1 [GA, v. 15, p. 92] same

Kraft
Lasst uns mit erhfurchtvollem Dank [GA, v. 16, p. 48] same
Text from A.H.Niemeyer *Gesangbuch für höhere Schulen und Erziehungsanstalten* 4.Aufl. (Halle: 1800), p.57.

Krauseneck, Johann Christoph, 1738-1799.
AN DIE FLEISIGE CHLOE.
An die fleissige Spinnerin, op. 9 H. V no. 5 [GA, v. 16, p. 175] "Kleine Spinnerin hinter deinem Rädchen"

Krummacher, Friedrich Adolph, 1767-1845.
Alplied [GA, v. 1, p. 72] "Auf hoher Alp wohnt auch der liebe Gott"
Die Auferstehung [GA, v. 16, p. 70]
"Mag auch die Liebe weinen!"
Gebet [GA, v. 16, p. 66] "Wenn einst mein Lebenstag sich neiget"
FESTBÜCHLEIN.
Die Lerche [GA, v. 16, p. 99]
"Hört die Lerche, sie singt"
SONNTAGSLIED IM SOMMER.
Sonntagslied [GA, v. 1, p. 59]
"Der Sonntag ist da"

Küster, Elieser Gottlieb, 1732-1799.
Vater unser [GA, v. 16, p. 64]
"Vater unser beten wir"

Kugler, Franz Theodor, 1808-1858.
Herolde ritten von Ort zu Ort, op. 38 no. 1 [GA, v. 13, p. 115] same
Im Schloss, da brennen der Kerzen viel, op. 38 no. 2 [GA, v. 13, p. 118] same
Der junge König und sein Gemahl, op. 38 no. 3 [GA, v. 13, p. 124] same
Jungfrau Lorenz, op. 33 no. 1 [GA, v. 13, p. 2] "Guten Morgen, du Sonntagsglockenschall!"
Die Jungfrau und der Tod, op. 9 H. II no. 5 [GA, v. 8, p. 113]
"Wie ist so heiss im Busen mir"
2 voices & piano.
Ein Klippeneiland liegt im Meer, op. 38 no. 4 [GA, v. 13, p. 134] same
Wie bräutlich glänzt das heilige Rom, op. 38 no. 5 [GA, v. 13, p. 139] same

Kugler, Johann, Consul in Stettin
Beim Scheiden [GA, v. 16, p. 107]
"Wehmut weckt der fernen Wolkenwandrer Gruss"
Letztes Lied [GA, v. 16, p. 106] "Durch die Freundschaft fest verbunden"
Otto-Lied [GA, v. 16, p. 119] "Als noch dem blinden Heidenwahn"

COMPOSER Poet *Title* "First Line"

LOEWE, KARL, 1796-1869 *(continued)*
Kurowski-Eichen, Friedrich Carl Anton Bernhard von, 1780-1853.
Der grosse Kurfürst und die Spreejungfrau, op. 7 no. 1 [GA, v. 5, p. 2] "Die Nacht ist so dunkel, der Sturm so laut"
Die Heldenbraut (after 1825) [GA, v. 5, p. 59] "Freiwillige vor! Auch du, lieb Mädchen"
Wach auf! op. 9 H. VI no. 1 [GA, v. 16, p. 141] "Der Hahn hat gekräht"
Lasker, Ignaz Julius, 1811-1876.
Hinaus! Hinauf! Hinab! (1840) [GA, v. 16, p. 171]
"Hinaus, hinaus! in freie Luft"
Lenau, Nicolaus, 1802-1850.
BITTE.
Das dunkle Auge (1839) [GA, v. 16, p. 152]
"Weil' auf mir, du dunkles Auge"
Löper, Lina
Wolkenbild, op. 110 no. 2 [GA, v. 15, p. 80] "Es lag auf meiner Stirn einst eine Wolke so schwer und trüb"
Loewe, Helene
Das Blümlein [GA, v. 16, p. 93] "Stille, stille, dass ich höre"
Ida's Wunsch [GA, v. 16, p. 92] "Steigt empor, ihr Wünsche mein"
Loewe, Karl, 1796-1869.
Salvum fac regem (after 1850) [GA, v. 5, p. 38] "Segne den König, ihn, unsern gütigen"
Also for orchestra or 4 men's voices.
Lua, August Ludwig, 1819-1876.
Wanderlied (1847) [GA, v. 16, p. 173] "Die Lerche singt ihr Morgenlied"
Lutze, Arthur, 1813-1870.
Der Drachenfels, op. 121 no. 1 [GA, v. 14, p. 11] "Sag an, was hinauf zur Drachenkluft die buntbewegte Menge ruft"
Gottesbote [GA, v. 2, p. 50] "Ein Engel zog durch Flur und Haus"
Mahlmann, Siegfried August, 1771-1826.
NACHT-LIED.
Die Nacht [GA, v. 1, p. 58] "Die Erde ruht, das Herz erwacht"
Marggraff, Rudolph, 1805-1880.
Der Lappländer, op. 63 no. 2 [GA, v. 15, p. 73] "Durch Schneegestöber und eisigen Wind"
Die Schneeflocke, op. 63 no. 1 [GA, v. 15, p. 67]
"Ein Sternlein fiel vom Himmel her"

Matthisson, Friedrich von, 1761-1831.
Die Elfenkönigin, op. 9 H. I no. 5 [GA, v. 16, p. 190] "Nichts unterm Monde gleicht uns Elfen"
Mayer, Dr.
Nachtständchen [GA, v. 2, p. 6] "Von deinem Bilde nur umschwebet"
Mickiewicz, Adam, 1798-1855.
Die drei Budrisse, op. 49 no. 3 [GA, v. 7, p. 20] "In den Schlosshof hernieder rief Held Budris die Brüder"
Frau Twardowska, op. 51 no. 2 [GA, v. 7, p. 77]
"Ei, das tanzt, das lärmt und trinket!"
Der junge Herr und das Mädchen, op. 50 no. 2 [GA, v. 7, p. 38]
"Mägdlein pflücket Beeren in des Waldes Mitten"
Die Schlüsselblume, op. 49 no. 2 [GA, v. 7, p. 12]
"Lerche zu des Frühlings Ruhme"
Das Switesmädchen, op. 51 no. 1 [GA, v. 7, p. 47] "Wer ist der Jüngling, lieblich zu schauen?"
Wilia und das Mädchen, op. 50 no. 1 [GA, v. 7, p. 32] "Wilia, sie, der unsre Ström' entsprangen"
Der Woywode, op. 49 no. 1 [GA, v. 7, p. 2] "Von dem Garten altan keucht zum Schlosse"
Moehrcke
Trommel-Ständchen, op. 123 no. 2 [GA, v. 15, p. 88]
"Ich bin der Trommelschläger laut"
Poet unidentified; Moehrcke (Möhricke?) on title-page.
Mühler, Heinrich von, 1813-1874.
KAISER OTTO I.
Kaiser Ott's Weihnachtsfeier, op. 121 no. 1 [GA, v. 4, p. 18]
"Zu Quedlinburg im Dome"
Müller, Wilhelm, 1794-1827.
Liebesgedanken, op. 9 H. VI no. 2 [GA, v. 16, p. 143] "Je höher die Glocke"
Münch-Bellinghausen, Eligius Franz Joseph, freiherr von, 1806-1871.
DER SOHN DU WILDNISS.
Mein Herz, ich will dich fragen, op. 86 [GA, v. 16, p. 114] same
Münter, Balthasar, b. 1734.
Unsere Auferstehung durch Christum [GA, v. 16, p. 53]
"Er ist erstanden, Jesus Christ"
Naumann, L. G.
Frühlingslust [GA, v. 16, p. 100]
"Sei willkommen, Frühlingswehen"

Neus, Jakob, b. 1767.
  Abendmahlslied [GA, v. 2, p. 39]
    "Wir beten an, hier unter Brot- und
      Weingestalten"
    Soprano, alto & organ.
Niemeyer, August Hermann, 1754-
1828.
  Der nahe Retter, op. 22 H. II no. 3 [GA,
    v. 16, p. 12] "Wenn immer trüber
    deine Morgen tagen"
  Werfet alle eure Sorgen auf ihn! op. 22
    H. II no. 1 [GA, v. 16, p. 10]
    "Warum dein Blick so trübe?"
Oër, Max von, 1806-1846.
  Die Glocken zu Speier, op. 67 no. 2 [GA,
    v. 4, p. 31]
    "Zu Lüttich, im letzten Häuselein"
Olearius, Johann, 1611-1684.
  Wunderbarer Gnadenthron [GA, v. 16,
    p. 49] same
Orléans, Hélène Louise Élisabeth,
  Duchesse d', 1814-1858.
  Musik [GA, v. 2, p. 68] "Wer einsam
    steht im bunten Lebenskreise"
Percy, Thomas, 1729-1811.
  RELIQUES.
    *Des Bettlers Tochter von Bednall
      Green* (1834) [GA, v. 2, p. 152]
      "Ein Bettelmann, schon lange blind"
Pfizer, Gustav, 1807-1890.
  Der Junggesell (1842) [GA, v. 10, p. 90]
    "Ich bin ein leichter Junggesell"
Platen-Hallermünde, August, Graf
  von, 1796-1835.
  Der Pilgrim vor St. Just, op. 9 no. 1
    [GA, v. 4, p. 120] "Nacht ist's, und
    Stürme sausen für und für"
Plönnies, Louise von, 1803-1872.
  Agnete, op. 134 [GA, v. 3, p. 104]
    "Es schaute in die Wogen"
  Der kleine Schiffer, op. 127 [GA, v. 3,
    p. 91] "Die Königstochter sticket"
Prechtler, Otto, 1813-1881.
  Deutsche Barkarole, op. 103 no. 3 [GA,
    v. 10, p. 184]
    "Wellen säuseln, Winde locken"
Puttkamer-Plauth, Eugen von, 1800-
1874, supposed author.
  Die Gruft der Liebenden, op. 21 [GA,
    v. 6, p. 28] "Da, wo des Tajo
    gründlich blauer Strom"
Randow, Carl
  Preussisches Marinelied (1856) [GA,
    v. 5, p. 76] "Ihr deutschen Länder alle"
    Text by Randow and Loewe.

Recke, Elisa von der, 1756-1833.
  Christi Huld gegen Petrus [GA, v. 2,
    p. 44] "Mitten unter deinen
    Schmerzen"
  MANCHERLEI FREUDEN.
    Rundgesang im Freien [GA, v. 1,
      p. 74] "Mit tausendfacher Schöne"
Redwitz, Oskar, Freiherr von, 1823-
1891.
  AMARANTH.
    Reiterlied, op. 145 no. 5 [GA, v. 17,
      p. 164] "Der Wald ist schwarz"
    Sängers Gebet, op. 123 no. 1 [GA,
      v. 15, p. 58]
      "Du, der Du bist der Geister Hort"
  LIEDER DER AMARANTH.
    Brautlied [GA, v. 2, p. 18] "Ich will
      die lauten Freuden nicht"
Reinick, Robert, 1805-1852.
  Der verliebte Maikäfer, op. 64 no. 1
    [GA, v. 9, p. 86] "Glühwürmchen,
    steck's Laternchen an"
Reissig, Christian Ludwig, 1783-1822.
  Sehnsucht [GA, v. 1, p. 54]
    "Die stille Nacht umdunkelt"
Rist, Johann, 1607-1667.
  Bleiches Antlitz, sei gegrüsset [GA, v. 2,
    p. 34] same
Rose, Karl, b. 1774.
  Abendstunde, op. 130 Lief. I no. 3 [GA,
    v. 17, p. 146] "Die Amsel flötet"
Rosemann
  Der Garten des Lebens [GA, v. 16,
    p. 97] "Der Garten des Lebens ist
    lieblich und schön"
    Text in R.Z.Becker *Mildheimisches
      Liederbuch* (1815): Nr. 162. Poet
      may be Johann Aegidius Kloentrup,
      1755-1830.
Rudolphi, Karoline, 1754-1811.
  Morgenlied [GA, v. 1, p. 56] "Auf,
    Brüder, auf! Der Tag bricht an"
Rückert, Friedrich, 1788-1866.
  Abendlied, op. 62 H. II no. 1 [GA, v. 17,
    p. 76] "Ich stand auf Berges Halde"
  Bescheidung, op. 62 H. I no. 2 [GA,
    v. 17, p. 62]
    "Sei bescheiden, nimm fürliebe"
  Die Blume der Ergebung, op. 62 H. II
    no. 6 [GA, v. 17, p. 92]
    "Ich bin die Blum' im Garten"
  Dem Allmächtigen [GA, v. 2, p. 46]
    "Mächtiger, der du die Wipfel"
  Des fremden Kindes heiliger Christ,
    op. 33 no. 3 [GA, v. 13, p. 20]
    "Es läuft ein fremdes Kind"

LOEWE, KARL, 1796-1869 *(continued)*
Rückert, Friedrich, 1788-1866
(continued)
Des Glockenthürmers Töchterlein,
op. 112 A [GA, v. 10, p. 16]
"Mein hochgebornes Schätzelein"
Die Göttin im Putzzimmer, op. 73 [GA,
v. 15, p. 12]
"Welche chaotische Haushälterei"
Die Gottesmauer, op. 140 [GA, v. 14,
p. 73] "O Mutter, wie stürmen die
Flocken vom Himmel"
Die Herzensrose, op. 130 Lief. I no. 2
[GA, v. 17, p. 144]
"Mein Gemüthe blühte"
Hinkende Jamben, op. 62 H. I no. 5 [GA,
v. 17, p. 72] "Ein Liebchen hatt' ich"
Ich und mein Gevatter, op. 62 H. II no. 3
[GA, v. 17, p. 80]
"Zwei wunderliche Gevattern"
In der Kirche, op. 62 H. II no. 2 [GA,
v. 17, p. 78]
"Auf der Bank, wo sie sonst"
Irrlichter, op. 62 H. I no. 6 [GA, v. 17,
p. 73] "Irrlichter, die Knaben, die
laufen und traben"
Jungfräulein Annika, op. 78 no. 1 [GA,
v. 9, p. 46] "Jungfräulein Annika sass
an dem Brückenrande"
Kind und Mädchen, op. 62 H. II no. 5
[GA, v. 17, p. 88]
"Die mich hält am Fädchen"
Kleiner Haushalt, op. 71 [GA, v. 15,
p. 2] "Einen Haushalt klein und fein
hab' ich angestellt"
O süsse Mutter, op. 62 H. I no. 3 [GA,
v. 17, p. 64] same
Der Papagei, op. 111 [GA, v. 6, p. 24]
"Das war die Schlacht von Waterloo"
Das Pfarrjüngferchen, op. 62 H. II no. 4
[GA, v. 17, p. 84]
"Herr Pfarrer hat zwei Fräulchen"
Die Riesen und die Zwerge, op. 84 no. 4
[GA, v. 17, p. 95]
"Es ging die Riesentochter"
Süsses Begräbnis, op. 62 H. I no. 4 [GA,
v. 17, p. 69]
"Schäferin, ach, wie haben sie"
Der Traum der Wittwe, op. 142 [GA,
v. 14, p. 95]
"In Basra eine Wittwe war"
Traumlicht (1842) [GA, v. 16, p. 153]
"Ein Licht im Traum hat mich
besucht"
Der Weichdorn, op. 75 no. 2 [GA, v. 14,
p. 40] "Als Maria heut' entwich"

Das Wunder auf der Flucht, op. 75 no. 4
[GA, v. 14, p. 48] "Auf jener Flucht,
von welcher nun das Morgenland"
LIEBESFRÜHLING.
Jünglings Gebet [GA, v. 2, p. 10]
"Herr, der du alles wohl gemacht"
ZEISIG.
Zeislein, op. 62 H. I no. 1 [GA, v. 17,
p. 61] "Zeislein, Zeislein, Zeislein"
Rüling, Georg Ernst von, 1748-1807.
Dich soll mein Lied erheben, op. 80 H. I
no. 3 [GA, v. 16, p. 113] same
Salis-Seewis, Johann Gaudenz,
Freiherr von, 1762-1834.
Das Fischergewerbe [GA, v. 16, p. 111]
"Das Fischergewerbe gibt rüstigen
Mut"
Sappho, 625? B.C.-570 B.C.
An Aphrodite, op. 9 H. IX no. 4 [GA,
v. 16, p. 198]
"Golden thronend, ewige Aphrodite"
Scherenberg, Christian Friedrich,
1798-1881.
Der Feind, op. 145 no. 2 [GA, v. 9,
p. 152]
"Der Adler lauscht auf seinem Horst"
Schiller, Johann Christoph Friedrich
von, 1759-1805.
Der Gang nach dem Eisenhammer, op.
17 [GA, v. 10, p. 21]
"Ein frommer Knecht war Fridolin"
Der Graf von Habsburg, op. 98 [GA,
v. 4, p. 48]
"Zu Aachen, in seiner Kaiserpracht"
Schleifer, Matthias L., 1771-1842.
Zumalacarregui (1837) [GA, v. 5, p. 85]
"Leon und Castilien waffnen"
Schmid, Konr. Arnold, 1716-1789.
Der Siegesfürst [GA, v. 16, p. 51]
"Erhöhet die prächtigen Pforten der
Siege"
Schmidt, Friederike, 1801-1837.
An die Nachtigall [GA, v. 1, p. 48]
"Deinem sanft flötenden Ton"
Schnezler, August, 1809-1853.
Der Mummelsee, op. 116 no. 3 [GA, v. 9,
p. 78]
"Im Mummelsee, im dunkeln See"
Schreiber, Aloys Wilhelm, 1763-1841.
Der ewige Jude, op. 36 no. 3 [GA, v. 13,
p. 86]
"Von des Hügels kahlem Rücken"
Maria und das Milchmädchen, op. 36 no.
1 [GA, v. 13, p. 75]
"Maria kam auf ihrer Flucht"
Odins Meeres-Ritt, op. 118 [GA, v. 3,
p. 85] "Meister Oluf, der Schmied auf
Helgoland"

Schubart, Christian Friedrich Daniel, 1739-1791.
> *Gute Nacht* (1826) [GA, v. 16, p. 151]
> same
> *Der Hirten Lied am Krippelein,* op. 22 H.
> I no. 3 [GA, v. 16, p. 6]
> "Schlaf wohl, du Himmelsknabe du"

Schulz, Johann Gottlob, 1762-1810.
> *Der Herbst* [GA, v. 16, p. 101] "Der
> Herbst beginnt, schon saust der Wind"
> Text in R.Z.Becker *Mildheimischem*
> *Liederbuch* (1815): Nr. 135.

Schwab, Gustav, 1792-1850.
> *Kaiser Heinrich's Waffenweihe,* op. 122
> [GA, v. 4, p. 35]
> "Der junge König Heinrich schlief"

Schwarzenberg, Friedrich, Fürst, 1800-1872.
> *Gruss vom Meere,* op. 103 no. 1 [GA,
> v. 10, p. 188]
> "Sei mir gegrüsst in deiner Pracht"

Segelbach, Christian Friedrich, 1763- after 1834.
> *Wir spielen und hüpfen* [GA, v. 16,
> p. 89] same
> Text in R.Z.Becker *Mildheimisches*
> *Liederbuch* (1815): Nr. 294.

Seidl, Johann Gabriel, 1804-1875.
> *Die Uhr,* op. 123 no. 3 [GA, v. 15, p. 53]
> "Ich trage, wo ich gehe"

Shakespeare, William, 1564-1616.
> *AS YOU LIKE IT.*
> > *Komm herbei, komm herbei, Tod!* [GA,
> > v. 2, p. 78] same
> *HAMLET.*
> > *Totengräberlied,* op. 9 H. II no. 1 [GA,
> > v. 8, p. 101]
> > "In meiner Jugend als ich liebte"
> *OTELLO.*
> > *Lied der Desdemona,* op. 9 H. II no. 2
> > [GA, v. 8, p. 104] "Der Arme, wie
> > seufzend am Ahorn sass sie!"

Shenstone, William, 1714-1763.
> *Lied der Königin Elisabeth,* op. 119 [GA,
> v. 3, p. 32] "In der Ruhe Thal
> geboren"
> Translated by Herder.

Siebel, Carl, 1836-1868.
> *Heimlichkeit,* op. 145 no. 4 [GA, v. 17,
> p. 162]
> "Mein Herz, O schliess' dich ein!"
> *Im Sturme,* op. 145 no. 3 [GA, v. 17,
> p. 160] "Bangt dir mein Lieb?"
> *Meeresleuchten,* op. 145 no. 1 [GA,
> v. 17, p. 158]
> "Wieviel Sonnenstrahlen fielen"

Der Teufel, op. 129 no. 1 [GA, v. 9,
p. 13]
"Und als der Mensch geschaffen war"
Die Waldkapelle, op. 130 Lief. I no. 1
[GA, v. 17, p. 140]
"Es ist mein Herz ein kleines Haus"

Simrock, Karl Joseph, 1802-1876.
> *Zwist und Sühne* [GA, v. 16, p. 128]
> "Schnür den Bündel"

Stieglitz, Heinrich Wilhelm August, 1801-1849.
> *Abendgesang,* op. 10 Heft II, no. 6 [GA,
> v. 6, p. 136] "Lege den Schmuck nun
> an, schöne Gulhinde"
> *Ali im Garten,* op. 10 Heft II, no. 2 [GA,
> v. 6, p. 120]
> "Deine Stimme lass ertönen"
> *Assad mit dem Selam,* op. 10 Heft II, no.
> 3 [GA, v. 6, p. 126]
> "Geht nun, ihr Blüthen"
> *Die Geister der Wüste,* op. 10 Heft I, no.
> 1 [GA, v. 6, p. 102] "Hui! wie die
> Wolke von Staub und Brand"
> *Gulhinde am Putztische,* op. 10 Heft II,
> no. 5 [GA, v. 6, p. 129]
> "Reich' mir den Schleier, Emina"
> *Lied eines Vögleins in der Oasis,* op. 10
> Heft I, no. 5 [GA, v. 6, p. 114]
> "Ich schaukle leicht mich im grünen
> Laub"
> *Maisuna am Brunnen,* op. 10 Heft II, no.
> 1 [GA, v. 6, [. 119]
> "Ihr habt genug getrunken"
> *Melek am Quell,* op. 10 Heft I, no. 6
> [GA, v. 6, p. 114]
> "O wie du schnaubst aus voller Brust"
> *Melek in der Wüste,* op. 10 Heft I, no. 3
> [GA, v. 6, p. 106]
> "Heiss glüht der Pfad"
> *Die Oasis,* op. 10 Heft I, no. 4 [GA, v. 6,
> p. 112]
> "Wie lockt der Palmen grünes Dach"
> *Taubenpost,* op. 10 Heft II, no. 4 [GA,
> v. 6, p. 128] "Ein Täubchen bringt mir
> täglich Grüsse"
> *Der verschmachtende Pilger,* op. 10 Heft
> I, no. 2 [GA, v. 6, p. 105]
> "Einmal Mekka noch zu sehen"

Stolberg, Friedrich Leopold, Graf zu Stolberg, 1750-1819.
> *An die Natur* [GA, v. 16, p. 94] "Süsse
> heilige Natur"

Strachwitz, Moritz Karl Wilhelm Anton, Graf von, 1822-1847.
> *Der gefangene Admiral,* op. 115 [GA,
> v. 10, p. 137]

LOEWE, KARL, 1796-1869 *(continued)*
Strachwitz, Moritz Karl Wilhelm
Anton, Graf von, 1822-1847
(continued)
" 's sind heute dreiunddreissig Jahr"
Sturm, Christoph Christian, 1740-
1786.
Busslied [GA, v. 16, p. 55] "Sei gnädig
mir nach deiner Güte!"
Jesus auf Golgatha [GA, v. 16, p. 50]
"Sieh Jesum Christum leiden!"
SCHULGESANG.
Segne, Vater, meinen Fleiss [GA, v. 1,
p. 84] same
Tegnér, Esaias, bp., 1782-1846.
Die Zugvögel, op. 74 [GA, v. 15, p. 20]
"Nun brennet am Nilstrom die Sonne
so sehr"
Telschow, Wilhelm, 1809-1872.
Bitte zu Gott um Frieden (1854) [GA,
v. 5, p. 88]
"Der Kön'ge Herzen, Rath und Sinn"
Accompaniment for organ and four-
part men's chorus.
Des Königs Zuversicht, op. 118 [GA,
v. 5, p. 78]
"Der Feinde Scharen rüsten sich"
Preussentreue (1848 or 49) [GA, v. 5,
p. 42] "Was rüttelt die Säulen und
schüttelt am Thron"
Tieck, Johann Ludwig, 1773-1853.
WALD, GARTEN UND BERG.
Vogelgesang, op. 9 H. VI no. 3 [GA,
v. 16, p. 185] "Wir lustigen Bürger
in grüner Stadt"
Trinius, Karl Bernhard, 1778-1844.
Feuersgedanken, op. 70 [GA, v. 15,
p. 32] "Dürft' ich einmal dies Dach
durchbrechen!"
Tschabuschnigg, Adolf Ritter von,
1809-1877.
Tod und Tödin, op. 105 [GA, v. 8, p. 82]
"Wer ist so spät noch fleissig wach?"
Uhland, Ludwig, 1787-1862.
Die Abgeschiedenen, op. 9 H. II no. 3
[GA, v. 8, p. 107]
"So hab' ich endlich dich gerettet"
Abschied, op. 3 no. 1 [GA, v. 10, p. 77]
"Was klinget und singet die Strassen
herauf?"
Bauernregel, op. 9 H. V no. 3 [GA,
v. 16, p. 138]
"Im Sommer such ein Liebchen dir"
Die drei Lieder, op. 3 no. 3 [GA, v. 3,
p. 72] "In der hohen Hall' sass König
Sifried"

Geisterleben, op. 9 H. I no. 4 [GA, v. 8,
p. 11]
"Von dir getrennet, liege ich begraben"
Goldschmieds Töchterlein, op. 8 no. 1
[GA, v. 10, p. 6]
"Ein Goldschmied in der Bude stand"
Graf Eberhards Weissdorn, op. 9 H. IV
no. 5 [GA, v. 14, p. 2]
"Graf Eberhard im Bart"
Graf Eberstein, op. 9 no. 5 [GA, v. 4,
p. 25] "Zu Speier im Saale, da hebt
sich ein Klingen"
Hans und Grete, op. 9 H. V no. 2 [GA,
v. 1, p. 86]
"Guckst du mir denn immer nach"
Harald, op. 45 no. 1 [GA, v. 3, p. 78]
"Vor seinem Heergefolge ritt der
kühne Held Harald!"
Der Knabe vom Berge [GA, v. 1, p. 73]
"Ich bin vom Berg der Hirtenknab' "
Der König auf dem Thurme, op. 9 H. I
no. 2 [GA, v. 16, p. 155]
"Da liegen sie alle, die grauen Höhn"
Der Räuber, op. 43 no. 2 [GA, v. 10,
p. 94]
"Einst am schönen Frühlingsmorgen"
Das Schifflein (1835) [GA, v. 10, p. 176]
"Ein Schifflein ziehet leise den Strom"
Das Ständchen, op. 9 H. II no. 4 [GA,
v. 8, p. 110]
"Was wecken aus dem Schlummer
mich"
Der Wirthin Töchterlein, op. 1 no. 2
[GA, v. 10, no. 2] "Es zogen drei
Bursche wohl über den Rhein"
Die Zufriedenen, op. 9 H. V no. 4 [GA,
v. 16, p. 139]
"Ich sass bei jener Linde"
AUF DER ÜBERFAHRT.
Die Überfahrt, op. 94 no. 1 [GA,
v. 10, p. 180] "Über diesen Strom"
Unknown
Amanda [GA, v. 1, p. 94]
"Um die blütenvollen Äste"
An die Grille [GA, v. 1, p. 81]
"Zirpe, liebe kleine Sängerin"
An die Natur [GA, v. 1, p. 41]
"Sanft mit seligem Entzücken"
Beim Maitrank [GA, v. 16, p. 124]
"Waldmeisterlein!"
Der Bergmann [GA, v. 1, p. 75]
"Der Bergmann lebt beim Grubenlicht"
Bethlehem [GA, v. 1, p. 68]
"Dir, kleines Bethlehem, erklang"
Dich bet' ich an, erstand'ner Held [GA,
v. 16, p. 54] same

Text from *Schlesinger Allgem.*
   Gesangbuch (Altona: 1780),
   Nr.302.
Die engste Nähe [GA, v. 2, p. 22]
   "Wir hatten einander so gerne"
Erdbeerliedchen [GA, v. 1, p. 78]
   "Ein Mägdlein an des Felsen Rand"
Fischerin und Jägerbursch [GA, v. 16,
   p. 109] "Fischchen schwimmt wohl hin
   und her"
Frage nicht! [GA, v. 2, p. 2]
   "Frage nicht, wie es gekommen"
Früh-Lied am Meere [GA, v. 1, p. 56]
   "Der Meeresflut mit Purpurglut"
Frühlingslied [GA, v. 1, p. 76]
   "An Birkenzweigen blättert"
Der fünfte Mai (1837) [GA, v. 6, p. 13]
   "Die Feuerschlünde am Seinstrand"
Das Gebet des Herrn und die
   Einsetzungsworte, op. 2 [GA, v. 1,
   p. 2] "Lasst uns beten: Vater unser"
Gelobt sei Gott! (1850) [GA, v. 5, p. 80]
   same
Geruhig seines Weges gehn [GA, v. 16,
   p. 96] same
Heimweh [GA, v. 1, p. 52]
   "Elysium, du Land, wo Friede wird"
Der Jagd [GA, v. 1, p. 49]
   "Hört ihr die Hörner erschallen"
Jesus als Kind [GA, v. 1, p. 67]
   "Herab kamst du auf Erden"
Kahnlied [GA, v. 1, p. 80]
   "Gleite hinan die glänzende Bahn!"
Kommt herzu! [GA, v. 16, p. 60]
   "Kommt herzu, ihr seid geladen"
Kyrie, O Herr Gott Vater! [GA, v. 2,
   p. 32] same
Der Liebescheue [GA, v. 1, p. 33]
   "Mag Toren hienieden"
Maiblümelein [GA, v. 2, p. 64]
   "Aufthaute die Erde vom Strahle"
Nachtlied [GA, v. 2, p. 72]
   "Seh' ich dort die Sternlein blinken"
O meine Blumen, ihr, meine Freude!
   [GA, v. 2, p. 66] same
Ein Preussenlied (before 1840) [GA,
   v. 5, p. 65]
   "Man geht aus Nacht in Sonne"
Die Quelle [GA, v. 1, p. 79]
   "Kleiner, kühler Wiesenquell"
Der Sorglose [GA, v. 2, p. 101]
   "Ich habe keine Schulden"
Ständchen [GA, v. 1, p. 28]
   "Gute Nacht! Im Mondenschein"
Stille Liebe [GA, v. 2, p. 20]
   "Ich trag' eine Liebe im Herzen"

Trost [GA, v. 16, p. 103]
   "Es wird wohl Winter"
Das Vöglein [GA, v. 16, p. 97]
   "Flieg doch fort, du kleines Tier!"
Weihnachts-Kantate [GA, v. 1, p. 60]
   "Ehre sei Gott in der Höhe"
Winterlied [GA, v. 16, p. 102]
   "Schöpfer, deine Herrlichkeit"
Zu dir, dem Weltenmeister (1862) [GA,
   v. 15, p. 62] same

Urner, Anna Barbara, 1760-1803.
Die Abendsonne [GA, v. 1, p. 57]
   "Goldne Abendsonne"

Vogl, Johann Nepomuk, 1802-1866.
Der alte König, op. 116 no. 2 [GA, v. 10,
   p. 72] "Es geht ein alter König"
Der alte Schiffsherr, op. 125 no. 3 [GA,
   v. 10, p. 147] "Ist der alte Schiffsherr
   endlich heimgekehrt"
Am Klosterbrunne, op. 110 no. 1 [GA,
   v. 15, p. 48] "Im düstern Klostergarten
   ein einsam Brünnlein steht"
Das Erkennen, op. 65 no. 2 [GA, v. 10,
   p. 116] "Ein Wanderbursch' mit dem
   Stab in der Hand"
Der Gesang, op. 56 no. 2 [GA, v. 9,
   p. 114] "Erschaffen schon die Erde
   lag"
Heinrich der Vogler, op. 56 no. 1 [GA,
   v. 4, p. 14]
   "Herr Heinrich sitzt am Vogelherd"
Heuska, op. 108 no. 2 [GA, v. 6, p. 61]
   "Vor dem Schlosse Don Loranca's"
Die Kaiserjagd im Wienerwald, op. 108
   no. 1 [GA, v. 4, p. 136]
   "Horch, Hörnerklang"
Der Mönch zu Pisa, op. 114 [GA, v. 4,
   p. 63]
   "Zu Pisa in dem Klostergarten"
Die Schwanenjungfrau, op. 129 no. 3
   [GA, v. 9, p. 32]
   "Ging Herr Walther hin im Freien"
Die schwarzen Augen, op. 94 no. 2 [GA,
   v. 10, p. 63]
   "Das war der Junker Emerich"
Urgrossvaters Gesellschaft, op. 56 no. 3
   [GA, v. 10, p. 103]
   "Sie waren alle zum Tanzplatz hinaus"
Das Vaterland, op. 125 no. 2 [GA, v. 10,
   p. 82]
   "Fahr hin! fahr hin für alle Zeiten"
Die verfallene Mühle, op. 109 [GA, v. 9,
   p. 68] "Es reitet schweigend und allein
   der alte Graf"
Das vergessene Lied, op. 65 no. 1 [GA,
   v. 10, p. 111] "Maria sitzt und stimmet
   die Harfe zum Gesang"

LOEWE, KARL, 1796-1869 *(continued)*
Vogl, Johann Nepomuk, 1802-1866
(continued)
SCHNEEGLÖCKCHEN.
Blumenballade (1846) [GA, v. 9,
p. 146]
"Noch ziehn die Wolken düster"
WITEKIND.
Karl der Grosse und Wittekind, op. 65
no. 3 [GA, v. 4, p. 2] "Es steht der
Sachsenführer, Herr Wittekind"
Voss, Johann Heinrich, 1751-1826.
Frühlingslied [GA, v. 1, p. 77]
"Willkommen im Grünen!"
Minnelied, op. 9 H. V no. 1 [GA, v. 16,
p. 134]
"Der Holdseligen sonder Wank"
Wessenberg, Ignaz Heinrich Karl,
Freiherr von, 1774-1860.
Der heilige Franziskus, op. 75 no. 3 [GA,
v. 14, p. 46]
"Franziskus einst, der Heil'ge"
Wetzel, Friedrich Gottlob, 1779-1819.
Das Muttergottesbild im Teiche, op. 37
no. 1 [GA, v. 13, p. 94]
"Im schönen Land Tirol"
Zedlitz, Joseph Christian von, 1790-
1862.
Die Dorfkirche, op. 116 no. 1 [GA, v. 10,
p. 98]
"In einem Dorf' am frühen Morgen"
Die nächtliche Heerschau, op. 23 [GA,
v. 6, p. 16]
"Nachts um die zwölfte Stunde"
Ziegler, Karl, 1812-1877.
Der Hirt auf der Brücke, op. 130 Lief. I
no. 4 [GA, v. 17, p. 148]
"Der Waldbach tost"
HIMMEL UND ERDE.
Frühlingsankunft, op. 130 Lief. II no. 5
[GA, v. 17, p. 152]
"Es ist mein Herz verengt, verdorrt"
Zinserling, W.
Die treuen Schwalben [GA, v. 1, p. 42]
"Wenn am kleinen Kammerfenster"
Zitzmann, Heinrich Gottfried, 1775-
1839.
Das Blumenopfer [GA, v. 1, p. 43]
"Noch schmückten zarte Blüten"
Zuccalmaglio, Anton Wilhelm
Florentin von, 1803-1869.
DES KNABEN WUNDERHORN.
Die verlorene Tochter, op. 78 no. 2
[GA, v. 9, p. 3] "Es flogen drei
Schwälbelein über den Rhein"

Loewe, Karl, 1796-1869.
LOEWE *Salvum fac regem*
Die Löwenbraut see Chamisso
SCHUMANN
Löwenstein, Rudolf, 1819-1891.
RUBINSTEIN
Abschied
Beim Fenstergehn
Beruhigung
Das gebrochene Herz
Liebeshändel
Unerklärlich
Löwenstein-Wertheim-Freudenberg,
Wilhelm, Prinz du, 1817-1877.
WEBER *Lied*
LØFT DE KLINGRE GLASPOKALER. see
Jacobsen *Wine roses* **DELIUS**
"Løft mig kun bort, du staerke Død" *see*
En Digters sidste Sang Andersen **GRIEG**
"Loin de la ville sitôt crépite" *see Nuit*
blanche Fargue **AURIC**
"Loin de mai, loin de mai" *see Chanson*
d'amour Shakespeare **CHAUSSON**
Loin de moi ta lèvre qui ment see Aicard
MASSENET
"Loin de toi, loin de toi" *see Adieu, Bessy!*
Moore, T. **BERLIOZ**
"Loin des oiseaux, des troupeaux" *see Larme*
Rimbaud **RIVIER**
"Loin des yeux du monde" *see Flots, palmes,*
sables Renaud **DEBUSSY**
"Loin du bruit des humaines fêtes" *see*
Prélude Docquois **SAINT-SAËNS**
Loin du pays see Gounod **GOUNOD**
Lok see Bjørnson **GRIEG**
Lollipop song see Sakonskaya, N.
PROKOFIEV *Sladkaïa pesenka*
Lombard, F.
SAINT-SAËNS *Bergeronnette*
Lomir zikh bafrayen see Anon. **WEISGALL**
London see Blake, William **BRITTEN,**
VAUGHAN WILLIAMS
London Atheneum, pseud.
CARPENTER *Memory*
LONDON NIGHTS. see Symons
A prayer to Saint Anthony of Padua
HESELTINE
LONDON NIGHTS: "12 Sep 1891" (1895-97).
see Symons
Autumn twilight **HESELTINE**
The lone-ganger see Nietzsche *DIE*
FRÖHLICHE WISSENSCHAFT. **DELIUS**
Der Einsame
Loneliness see Musset *LA NUIT DE MAI:*
stanza 4,"Pourquoi mon coeur bat-il si
vite?" **RACHMANINOFF**

COMPOSER Poet   *Title*   "First Line"

Lonesome tree *see* Tree, Iris **ROREM**
Long ago sweetheart mine see MacDowell **MACDOWELL**
"Le long des blés que la brise" *see Fleur des blés* Girod **DEBUSSY**
Long distance see Anon. **MILHAUD**
"Le long du bois couvert de givre je marchais" *see Le tombeau des Naïdes* Louÿs **DEBUSSY**
"Le long du ciel grenat" *see A l'aube dans la Montagne* Séverac **SÉVERAC**
"Le long du Qaui" *see Les berceaux* Sully-Prudhomme **FAURÉ**
"Long, long is the night" *see To Chloe in sickness* Burns **BENNETT**
A long pilgrimage see Hafiz **MARTINŮ**
"The long September evening dies" *see Autumn twilight* Symons **HESELTINE**
Long time ago see Anon. **COPLAND**
Longfellow, Henry Wadsworth, 1807-1882.
  BRITTEN *Beware*
  GOUNOD
    The arrow and the song
    Beware
    If thou art sleeping maiden, awake
    It is not always May
    The sea hath its pearls
  IVES *The children's hour*
Longing see Golenishchev-Kutuzov **MUSORGSKIĬ** *Skuchaĭ*
Longing see Kjerulf *LAENGSEL.* **DELIUS** *Sehnsucht*
Longing see Weiss **SIBELIUS** *Sehnsucht*
Longing for home see Nietzsche **MEDTNER** *Heimweh*
Longing is my heritage see Karlfeldt **SIBELIUS** *Längtan heter min arvedel*
"Longtemps au pied du perron de la maison" *see Rosemonde* Apollinaire **POULENC**
"Longtemps captifs chez le Russe loin tain" *see Les deux grenadiers* Heine **WAGNER**
"La longue nuit, le jeux ouverts" *see Insomnie* Tardieu **SAUGUET**
La lontananza see Torre, G. **ROSSINI**
Look down, fair moon see Whitman **ROREM**
Look, how the floor of heav'n see Shakespeare *MERCHANT OF VENICE.* **THOMSON**
Look in thy garden see Maĭkov **RIMSKIĬ-KORSAKOV** *Posmotri v svoĭ vertograd*
Look into your garden fair see Maĭkov **RIMSKIĬ-KORSAKOV** *Posmotri v svoĭ vertograd*

Look, my friend see Krasov, V. **BALAKIREV** *Vzglyani, moy drug*
Look not in my eyes see Housman **BERKELEY**
"Look not in my eyes" *see Ladslove* Housman **IRELAND**
"Look off, dear Love, across the sallow sands" *see Evening song* Lanier **GRIFFES**
LOOK, STRANGER! see Auden
  Let the florid music praise! **BRITTEN**
  Now the leaves are falling fast **BRITTEN**
"Look, stranger, at this island now" *see Seascape* Auden **BRITTEN**
Look stranger, on this island see Auden *ON THIS ISLAND.* **ROREM**
Look, yonder cloud see Grekov *STANSĬ.* **CHAĬKOVSKIĬ** *Smotri, von oblako*
"Looking as I've looked before" *see The stranger* Rich **ROREM**
The looking-glass see Eristavi, D. **RUBINSTEIN**
Looking-glass river see Stevenson, Robert Louis **CARPENTER**
THE LOOM OF DREAMS. see Symons *The sick heart* **HESELTINE**
Loose see Storm **JENSEN**
Lope de Vega see Vega Carpio, Lope Félix de, 1562-1635.
López de Ubeda, Juan, fl.1579-1582.
  WOLF *Ach, des Knaben Augen sind*
Lorca, Federico Garcia *see* Garcia Lorca, Federico, 1899-1936.
Lord Bolingbroke see Jacob, M. **AURIC**
"Lord Bolingbroke est en voyage" *see Lord Bolingbroke* Jacob, M. **AURIC**
Lord, have not by custom see Goodman **ROREM**
"The Lord is my shepherd" *see The bird's song* Bible **VAUGHAN WILLIAMS**
Lord, James
  ROREM *In this summer*
Lord my shield, my refuge see Bible **DVOŘÁK** *Skrýše má paveza má Ty jsi*
"Lord of the Mountain, reared within the Mountain" *see Young man, chieftan!* Austin, Mary **CARPENTER**
"Le Lord prévôt d'Edinbourg" *see Irène* Giraudoux **HONEGGER**
The lordly Hudson see Goodman **ROREM**
The Lord's prayer see Bible *MATTHEW 6: 9-13.* **ROREM**
Die Loreley see Heine **LISZT**
Loreley see Lorenz **SCHUMANN**
Lorenz, Auguste Wilhelmine, 1784-1861.
  SCHUMANN *Loreley*
Lorenz, F.
  BERG *Wo der Goldregen steht*

Lorenzen, H.
 NIELSEN *Gry*
Lorma see Macpherson *BATTLE OF LORA.*
 SCHUBERT
 Two settings: D. 327 and D. 376.
"Lorma sass in der Halle von Aldo" *see*
 Lorma Macpherson **SCHUBERT**
Lorrain, Jehan, pseud. *see* Duval, Paul
 Alexander Martin, 1856-1906.
"Lorsque au soleil couchant les riviéres sont
 roses" *see Beau soir* Bourget **DEBUSSY**
"Lorsque je regarde mes mains" *see Les mains*
 Bazan, Noël **MASSENET**
"Lorsque je voy en ordre la brunette" *see*
 D'Anne jouant de l'espinette Marot
 RAVEL
"Lorsque la mer et toi vous serez face à face"
 see À celle qui part Silvestre **LALO**
"Lorsque le ciel de saphir" *see Les roses*
 Banville **DEBUSSY**
"Lorsque le nuit" *see Les Ecrevisses* Hugnet
 THOMSON
"Lorsque le vent du soir l'agite" *see Plus vite*
 Văcărescu **MASSENET**
"Lorsque mes yeux se ferment" *see Je te vois*
 en rêve Shakespeare **SAUGUET**
"Lorsque mon ombre fugitive voltige autour
 de toi" *see L'apparition* Schiller
 SAUGUET
"Lorsque Ninon courait dans la forêt
 prochaine" *see Elle sait!* Boyer, Georges
 GOUNOD
"Lorsque nous sermons seuls" *see Poésie de*
 Mytis Anon. **MASSENET**
"Lorsque sa voix enchanteresse" *see Question*
 grave Guilliaume **LASSEN**
"Lorsque s'éveille le matin" *see Le matin*
 Banville **KOECHLIN**
"Lorsque t'environne la triste journée" *see*
 Le jour de tristesse Richter **SAUGUET**
"Lorsque vous dormez, petite Mireille" *see*
 Petite mireille Beissier **MASSENET**
"Lorsqu'elle met la main" *see L'amoire de*
 campagne Laporte **SAUGUET**
"Lorsqu'on sera très pressé" *see Civet à toute*
 vitesse Dumont **BERNSTEIN**
Lose Ware see Mörike **SCHOECK**
Lost content see Ady **BARTÓK**
Lost hopes see Pushkin **MEDTNER**
"The lost one" *see Afterthought* Bernstein
 BERNSTEIN
Lotarev, Igor' Vasil'evich, 1887-1941.
 RACHMANINOFF *Daisies*
LOTOSBLÄTTER. see Schack
 Breit' über mein Haupt **STRAUSS**

 Hoffen und wieder verzagen **STRAUSS**
 Mein Herz ist stumm **STRAUSS**
 Schön sind, doch kalt **STRAUSS**
 Wie sollten wir geheim sie halten
 STRAUSS
 Wozu noch, Mädchen **STRAUSS**
LOTOSBLÄTTER, no. 1
 STRAUSS Schack *Wozu noch, Mädchen*
LOTOSBLÄTTER, no. 2
 STRAUSS Schack *Breit' über mein Haupt*
LOTOSBLÄTTER, no. 3
 STRAUSS Schack *Schön sind, doch kalt*
LOTOSBLÄTTER, no. 4
 STRAUSS Schack *Wie sollten wir geheim*
 sie halten
LOTOSBLÄTTER, no. 5
 STRAUSS Schack *Hoffen und wieder*
 verzagen
LOTOSBLÄTTER, no. 6
 STRAUSS Schack *Mein Herz ist stumm*
Die Lotosblume see Geibel **FRANZ**
Die Lotosblume see Heine **FRANZ,**
 LOEWE, SCHUMANN
Die Lotosblume see Ives, Harmony **IVES**
 The south wind
"Die Lotosblume ängstigt sich" *see*
 Die Lotosblume Heine
 FRANZ, LOEWE, SCHUMANN
Louchheim, Katie, 1903-1991.
 WITH OR WITHOUT ROSES.
 DIAMOND
 The incredible hour
 Love's worth
 Spring talk
 Whither thou goest
"Loud blaw the frosty breezes" *see Castle*
 Gordon, or The young Highland rover
 Burns **BENNETT**
Louvencourt, Comtesse Maurice Roch
 de
 MASSENET *Les nuages*
Louÿs, Pierre, 1870-1925.
 CHANSONS DE BILITIS.
 DEBUSSY
 Le chevelure
 La flûte de Pan
 Le tombeau des Naïdes
 GIDEON
 Chanson
 La pluie au matin
 IBERT *Le petit âne blanc*
 KOECHLIN
 Chant funèbre
 Épitaphe de Bilitis
 Hymne à Astarté

Hymne à la nuit
Pluie au matin
Love see Lodge, T. **ROREM**
Love and friendship see Brontë **IRELAND**
LOVE AND TIME, no. 1
   DIAMOND Louchheim *The incredible hour*
LOVE AND TIME, no. 2
   DIAMOND Louchheim *Whither thou goest*
LOVE AND TIME, no. 3
   DIAMOND Louchheim *Love's worth*
LOVE AND TIME, no. 4
   DIAMOND Louchheim *Spring talk*
A love carol see Anon. **MARTINŮ**
Love concealed see Bjørnson **DELIUS**
   Verborg'ne Liebe
Love for love see Anon. **HESELTINE**
"Love I come today to tender" *see Greeting*
   Shenshin **MEDTNER**
Love in a life see Browning, R. **ROREM**
Love is a bable see Anon. **QUILTER**
Love is a sickness full of woes see Daniel,
   Samuel **IRELAND**
"Love is like a wind upon the water" *see*
   Siciliano Rhinelander **THOMPSON, R.**
"Love is like the wild rosebriar" *see Love and friendship* Brontë **IRELAND**
Love is more see Cummings **DIAMOND**
"Love is more thicker than forget" *see Love is more* Cummings **DIAMOND**
"LOVE is of nothing made" *see Love's worth* Louchheim **DIAMOND**
"Love me, I love you" *see Baby* Rossetti, Christina **IRELAND**
Love me little, love me long see Anon. **RIETI**
Love, my heart longs day and night see Tagore **MILHAUD**
The love of a dead man see Lermontov **CHAĬKOVSKIĬ** *Liubov' mertvetsa*
The love of one dead see Lermontov **CHAĬKOVSKIĬ** *Liubov' mertvetsa*
A love paean see Mickiewicz **CHAĬKOVSKIĬ** *Moia balovnitsa*
Love poem see Clift, William **SAUGUET**
Love song see Koch **THOMSON**
LOVE SONGS, no. 1
   DVOŘÁK Pfleger-Moravský *Ó, naší lásce nekvete*
LOVE SONGS, no. 2
   DVOŘÁK Pfleger-Moravský *Vtak mnohém srdci mrtvojest*
LOVE SONGS, no. 3
   DVOŘÁK Pfleger-Moravský *Kol domu se ted potácím*

LOVE SONGS, no. 4
   DVOŘÁK Pfleger-Moravský *Já vím, že v sladké naději*
LOVE SONGS, no. 5
   DVOŘÁK Pfleger-Moravský *Nad krajem vévodí lehký spánek*
LOVE SONGS, no. 6
   DVOŘÁK Pfleger-Moravský *Zde v lese u potoka*
LOVE SONGS, no. 7
   DVOŘÁK Pfleger-Moravský *Vté sladké moci očí tvých*
LOVE SONGS, no. 8
   DVOŘÁK Pfleger-Moravský *Ó, duše drahá, jediná*
"Love to his singer held a glistening leaf" *see Love's last gift* Rossetti, Dante **VAUGHAN WILLIAMS**
Love whom I have never seen see Unknown **CARPENTER**
Lovelace, Richard, 1618-1658.
   DIAMOND *To Lucasta, on going to the wars*
   QUILTER *To Althea from prison*
Loveliest lass see Goethe *CLAUDINE VON VILLA-BELLA.* **MEDTNER**
   Aus "Claudine von Villa-Bella"
"Lovely kind, and kindly loving" *see Fair and true* Breton **HESELTINE**
Lovely maid! see Burns **FRANZ**
Lovely Savishna see Musorgskiĭ **MUSORGSKIĬ** *Svetik Savishna*
The lover as mirror see Stringham **DIAMOND**
"Lover divine and perfect comrade" *see Gods* Whitman **ROREM**
Lover, Samuel, 1797-1868.
   HINDEMITH *The whistlin' thief*
The lover's maze see Campion *GILES EARLE, HIS BOOKE* (1616-1625). **HESELTINE**
Love's bower see Anon. **VAUGHAN WILLIAMS** *L'amour de moy*
Love's flame see Vilenkin **RACHMANINOFF** *In my soul*
LOVE'S LABOUR'S LOST. see Shakespeare
   Mockery **HESELTINE**
   When icicles hang by the wall **QUILTER, VAUGHAN WILLIAMS**
Love's last gift see Rossetti, Dante *THE HOUSE OF LIFE,* no. LIX. **VAUGHAN WILLIAMS**
Love's minstrels see Rossetti, Dante *THE HOUSE OF LIFE,* no. IX. **VAUGHAN WILLIAMS**

Love's philosophy see Shelley **DELIUS, QUILTER**
Love's secret see Blake, William *NEVER PAIN TO TELL THY LOVE.* **LUENING**
Love's stricken "Why" see Dickinson **ROREM**
Love's worth see Louchheim *WITH OR WITHOUT ROSES.* **DIAMOND**
Lovesight see Rossetti, Dante *THE HOUSE OF LIFE*, no. IV.
   VAUGHAN WILLIAMS
"Low lie the mists" see Mists Ives, Harmony **IVES**
Lowell, Amy, 1814-1925.
   GIDEON *Little ivory figures pulled with string*
   THOMSON *Vernal equinox*
The Lowlands of Holland see Unknown **BERKELEY**
"Lowly, laid in a manger" see The holy boy Brown, Herbert S. **IRELAND**
Lowry, Robert, 1826-1899.
   COPLAND, IVES *At the river*
Lu Yu, 1125-1210.
   BRITTEN *The herd-boy*
Lua, August Ludwig, 1819-1876.
   LOEWE *Wanderlied*
   SPOHR *Der Herbst*
Lubi, Michael, 1757-1808.
   SCHUBERT *Ammenlied*
Luce see Negri **RESPIGHI**
Lucie see Musset **MARTINŮ**
Luck and work see Johnson **IVES**
Ludana
   AUBERT *Péché véniel*
   MASSENET
    Menteuse chérie
    Orphelines
    Si vous vouliez bien me le dire
LUDIONS. see Fargue
  Air du Poète **SATIE**
  Air du Rat **SATIE**
  Chanson du chat **SATIE**
  La Grenouille américaine **SATIE**
  Spleen **SATIE**
LUDIONS, no. 1
  SATIE Fargue *Air du Rat*
LUDIONS, no. 2
  SATIE Fargue *Spleen*
LUDIONS, no. 3
  SATIE Fargue *La Grenouille américaine*
LUDIONS, no. 4
  SATIE Fargue *Air du Poète*
LUDIONS, no. 5
  SATIE Fargue *Chanson du chat*

Lübeck, Schmidt von *see* Schmidt, Georg Philipp, 1766-1849.
Lüdt, Rosa, 1842-1912.
   LASSEN *Ich habe den Glauben verloren*
"Die Lüfte werden heller" see Aufbruch Osterwald **FRANZ**
Lühe, Caroline von der (geb. von Brandenstein), b. 1755.
   ZELTER *Die unsichtbare Welt*
LUENING, OTTO, 1900-1996.
  Anon.
   The dawn (1932) [Highgate Press]
    "Oh, the dawn is coming high!"
   For like a chariot's wheel (1929) [Highgate Press] same
  Bible
   Answer not a fool according to his folly (1973) [Highgate Press] same
   The mouth of the righteous man (1973) [Highgate Press] same
   A righteous man falling down before the wicked (1973) [Highgate Press] same
   The slothful man saith (1973) [Highgate Press] same
   There is a generation that curseth their father (1973) [Highgate Press] same
   These six things doth the Lord hate (1973) [Highgate Press] same
  Blake, William, 1757-1827.
   Auguries of innocence (1928) [G. Schirmer, 1944]
    "To see a world in a grain of sand" Publication rights reverted to composer.
   The Divine image (1949) [E. B. Marks]
    "To mercy, pity, peace, and love"
   Earth's answer (1928) [ACA, 1957]
    "Earth rais'd up her head"
   Hear the voice of the Bard (1928) [unpubl.] same
   Infant joy (1928) [Highgate Press]
    "I have no name"
   The little vagabond (1981) [ACA]
    "Dear mother, dear mother, the church is cold"
   Silent, silent night (1981) [ACA] same
   To morning (1928) [Highgate Press]
    "O holy Virgin! clad in purest white"
   Young love (1928) [G. Schirmer, 1944]
    "Are not the joys of morning sweeter" Publication rights reverted to composer.
   NEVER PAIN TO TELL THY LOVE.
    Love's secret (1949) [E. B. Marks, 1951] "Never seek to tell thy love"

Bodenstedt, Friedrich Martin von, 1819-1892.
Wir wandeln alle den Weg (1915) [ACA]
Byron, George Gordon Byron, 6th baron, 1778-1824.
The harp the monarch minstrel swept (1951) [Highgate Press] same
She walks in beauty (1951) [Highgate Press] same
Cornelius, Peter, 1824-1874.
An dem Traume (1915) [ACA]
Dickinson, Emily, 1830-1866.
Experiment to me Is every one I meet (1942-51) [Highgate Press] same
Few get enough (1942-51) [Highgate Press] same
Hope is the thing with feathers (1942-51) [Highgate Press] same
I felt a cleavage in my mind (1942-51) [Highgate Press] same
If I can stop one heart from breaking (1942-51) [Highgate Press] same
Our share of night to bear (1942-51) [Highgate Press] samc
The show is not the show (1942-51) [Highgate Press] same
Soul, wilt thou toss again? (1942-51) [Highgate Press] same
When I hoped I feared (1942-51) [Highgate Press] samc
Frey, Adolf, 1855-1920.
Mysterium (1917) [ACA]
Hesse, Hermann, 1877-1962.
At Christmas time (1937) [Highgate Press] "At Christmas time I travel far"
Also voice & orchestra.
Frühling (1918) [ACA]
In Weihnachtzeiten (1917) [ACA]
Wie sind die Tage (1918) [ACA]
Lenau, Nicolaus, 1802-1850.
Der Eichwald (1915) [ACA]
Mörike, Eduard Friedrich, 1804-1875.
Semptembermorgen (1915) [ACA]
NB: Title spelled correctly.
Naidu, Sarojini (Chattopadhyay), 1879-1949.
Transience (1922) [Highgate Press] "Nay do not grieve tho' life be full of sadness"
Also voice & orchestra.
No author
Evening song (1936-37) [Highgate Press, 1966]
Morning song (1936-37) [Highgate Press, 1966]
Night song (1936-37) [Highgate Press, 1966]

Sharp, William, 1885-1905.
Noon silence (1922) [Highgate Press] "A lyre bird sings a low monotonous song"
Also voice & orchestra.
Venilia (1922) [Highgate Press] "Along the faint shores of the foamless gulf"
Also voice & orchestra.
Shelley, Percy Bysshe, 1792-1822.
Goodnight (1929) [Highgate Press] "Goodnight! ah no; the hour is ill"
I faint, I perish (1929) [Highgate Press] "I faint, I perish with my love!"
A Roman's chamber (1928) [Highgate Press] "In the cave which wild weeds cover"
Wake the serpent not (1928) [Highgate Press] same
Taggard, Genevieve, 1894-1948.
Swing, swing and swoon (1936) [Highgate Press]
Unknown
The birth of pleasure (1928) [Highgate Press]
Forever lost (1936) [Highgate Press]
Two songs for soprano and piano (1916) [ACA]
Luening reported "not available" in Feb. 1984.
Whitman, Walt, 1819-1892.
At the last (1936) [Highgate Press]
A farm picture (1929) [Associated] "Through the ample open door"
Gliding o'er all (1928) [G. Schirmer, 1944] same
Publication rights reverted to composer.
Hast never come to thee (1936) [Highgate Press] same
Soprano & flute.
Here the frailest leaves of me (1929) [Associated] same
Locations and times (1928) [Highgate Press] same
Visored (1928) [Highgate Press] "A mask, a perpetual natural disguiser of herself"
LEAVES OF GRASS.
Only themselves (1928 or 1934) [New Music Edition, 1935] "Only themselves understand themselves"
Wilde, Oscar, 1854-1900.
Requiescat (1917) [ACA]
"Die Luft ist blau" **see** *Frühlingslied*
Unknown **SCHUBERT**

COMPOSER Poet *Title* "First Line"

"Die Luft ist kühl" *see Vorüber* Wisbacher
BERG
"Luften är solig och skyarna tindra" *see Maj*
Josephson, E. **SIBELIUS**
"Luften tung och dagen varm" *see*
Harpolekaren och hans son Rydberg
SIBELIUS
Lugnier, Antonin
MASSENET *Soir de rêve*
Lugovskoĭ, Vladimir Aleksandrovich,
1901-1957.
PROKOFIEV *Soldatskaia poxodnaia*
Luhden
ES HEBT DER WALLENDE BUSEN.
ZELTER *Sehnsucht*
MORGENS AUF BETAUTER WEIDE.
ZELTER *Lied*
Luis el Chico, Don
WOLF *Deine Mutter, süsses Kind*
Luisens Antwort see Kosegarten
SCHUBERT
Luka, Madeleine, 1894–1989.
SAUGUET
Chanson des amoureux
Le jardin de Virigine
La marchand de coeurs
Voici le chemin de la vie
LUKE 2: 9-15. see Bible
An angel speaks to the shepherds **ROREM**
"Lulla, lulla, lullaby" *see Lullaby*
Shakespeare **BLITZSTEIN**
LULLABIES, no. 1
MARTINŮ Falke *To my child*
LULLABIES, no. 2
MARTINŮ Liliencron *The spinning top's
lullaby*
LULLABIES, no. 3
MARTINŮ Raabe *Sleep, my little one*
LULLABIES, no. 4
MARTINŮ Des Knaben Wunderhorn
Thanks to God the Creator
LULLABIES, no. 5
MARTINŮ Des Knaben Wunderhorn
My little angel
LULLABIES, no. 6
MARTINŮ Des Knaben Wunderhorn
Sleep, infant, sleep
LULLABIES, no. 7
MARTINŮ Des Knaben Wunderhorn
Little red bootees
LULLABIES, no. 8
MARTINŮ Des Knaben Wunderhorn
Fourteen little angels
Lullaby see Dekker *THE PLEASANT
COMOEDY OF PATIENT GRISSILL*
(1603). **HESELTINE**

Lullaby see Jelínek, F. L. **DVOŘÁK**
Ukolébavka
Lullaby see Maĭkov *NOVOGRECHESKIYE
PESNI.* **CHAĬKOVSKIĬ**
Kolibel'naya pesnya
Lullaby see Mei **RIMSKIĬ-KORSAKOV**
Kolybel'naia pesnia
Lullaby see Schulz, G. **RIEGGER**
Lullaby see Shakespeare **BLITZSTEIN**
Lullaby see Yeats **ROREM**
"Lullaby baby, lullabylaby bady" *see*
The nurse's song Phillip, John **BRITTEN**
Lullaby during the storm see Pleshcheyev
CHAĬKOVSKIĬ *Kolybel'naia pesn' v*
Lullaby in a storm see Pleshcheyev
CHAĬKOVSKIĬ *Kolybel'naia pesn' v*
LULLABY OF AN INFANT CHIEF: O hush
thee, my babie. *see* Scott
Wiegenlied **JENSEN**
Lullaby of the woman of the mountain see
Pearse **ROREM**
La luna con le Pleiadi see Sappho **RIETI**
La lune see Banville **KOECHLIN**
"Lune, belle lune" *see Lune d'Avril* Carême
POULENC
La lune blanche see Verlaine *LA BONNE
CHANSON.* **DELIUS**
"La lune blanche luit dans les bois" *see*
Apaisement Verlaine **CHAUSSON**
"La lune blanche luit dans les bois" *see*
La bonne chanson Verlaine
STRAVINSKIĬ
"La lune blanche luit dans les bois" *see*
L'heure exquise Verlaine **HAHN**
"La lune blanche luit dans les bois" *see*
La lune blanche Verlaine **DELIUS**
La lune blanche luit dans les bois see
Verlaine *LA BONNE CHANSON.* **FAURÉ**
Lune d'Avril see Carême **POULENC**
"La lune était sereine et jouait" *see Clair de
lune* Hugo **INDY**
"La lune s'attristait" *see Apparition*
Mallarmé **DEBUSSY**
"La lune se levait, pure, mais plus glacée" *see*
Musique Bourget **DEBUSSY**
"La lune s'est bâti dans les flots cette nuit"
see Sérénade Văcărescu **AUBERT**
Lunel, Armand, b. 1892
MILHAUD
L'adieu
L'agriculteur
Le cavalier
Les châtelaines
Les enfants
Les Libellules
L'Octobre
Le sifflet

LUNZ. see Mayrhofer
  Abschied **SCHUBERT**
Lust am Liebchen see Bürger **ZELTER**
Lust der Sturmnacht see Kerner
  SCHUMANN
"Lust entfloh und hin ist hin!" *see*
  Der Leichtmütige Gubitz **WEBER**
Lust und Qual see Goethe **STRAUSS**
"Lust'ge Vögel in dem Wald" *see Nachklang*
  Eichendorff **SCHOECK**
Lusty juventus see Wever *AN ENTERLUDE*
  CALLED LUSTY JUVENTUS (1565).
  HESELTINE
Luther, Martin, 1483-1546.
  HESELTINE *Balulalow*
Lutheri Vespera see Vergilius *AENEID.*
  ZELTER
Lutschemäulchen see Boelitz **REGER**
"Lutschemund, Lutschemund, treib's nur nicht
  gar zu bunt" *see Lutschemäulchen*
  Boelitz **REGER**
Lutze, Arthur, 1813-1870.
  LOEWE
    Der Drachenfels
    Gottesbote
Lybeck, Mikael, 1864-1925.
  SIBELIUS *I systrar, I bröder*
Lydé see Leconte de Lisle **HAHN**
Lydia see Leconte de Lisle **FAURÉ**
"Lydia sur tes roses joues" *see Lydia*
  Leconte de Lisle **FAURÉ**
"Lying and longing, thirsting for breezes" *see*
  Summer Gombossy **BARTÓK**
Lyle, Henry Francis, 1793-1847.
  IVES *Abide with me*
Lynceus, der Helene see Goethe *FAUST.*
  LOEWE
Lynceus, der Thürmer see Goethe *FAUST.*
  LOEWE

"A lyre bird sings a low monotonous song"
  see Noon silence Sharp, W. **LUENING**
LYRICAL INTERMEZZO. see Heine
  Aus meinen Tränen **BORODIN**
  El' i pal'ma **RIMSKIĭ-KORSAKOV**
  Iz slēz moikh mnogo, maliutka **RIMSKIĭ-KORSAKOV**
  Kogda gliazhu tebe v glaza **RIMSKIĭ-KORSAKOV**
  Shchekoiu k shcheke ty moeĭ prilozhis' **RIMSKIĭ-KORSAKOV**
Lyrical intermezzo see Heine **MEDTNER**
  Lyrisches Intermezzo
Lyrisches Intermezzo see Heine **MEDTNER**
LYRISCHES INTERMEZZO, no. 63. *see*
  Heine *Das ist ein Brausen und Heulen*
  FRANZ, GRIFFES, WOLF
LYRISCHES INTERMEZZO, no. 67. *see*
  Heine *Am Kreuzweg wird begraben*
  GRIFFES
LYRISCHES INTERMEZZO, no. 68. *see*
  Heine *Wo ich bin, mich rings umdunkelt*
  GRIFFES, WOLF
Lys Nat see Benzon *ANNA BRYDE.* **GRIEG**
Lyse naetter see Drachmann **DELIUS**
  Dreamy nights
LYSE NAETTER. see Drachmann
  Summer nights **DELIUS**
Lyss till det djupa och stora see Bergman
  KILPINEN
"Lyt nu, du ludende Sanger" *see Serenade til*
  Welhaven Bjørnson **GRIEG**
Lytton, Edward George Earle Lytton
  Bulwer-Lytton, 1st baron, 1803-1873.
  IVES *When stars are in the quiet skies*
Lyubov voyna see Mendel'son
  PROKOFIEV

"Ma belle amie est morte" *see Chanson du pêcheur* Gautier **FAURÉ, GOUNOD**

Ma belle amie est morte see Gautier **GOUNOD**

"Ma belle amie est morte" *see Sur les lagunes* Gautier **BERLIOZ**

"Ma belle, le jour va paraitre" *see Aubade* Ferrier **BIZET**

"Ma campagne est semée de tours" *see Tours* Richaud **SAUGUET**

"Ma cavale et ma lance" *see Au galop* Bonnières **INDY**

"Ma chambre a la forme d'une cage" *see Hôtel* Apollinaire **POULENC**

Ma chérie, aimons-nous see Catullus **MILHAUD**

Ma chérie, en présence de son mari see Catullus **MILHAUD**

"Ma colombe, Ô ma tourterelle" *see La tourterelle* Latil **MILHAUD**

Ma come potrei . . . see Boccaccio *IL NINFALE FIESOLANO*, 287. **RESPIGHI**

M'a dit amour . . . see Koechlin **KOECHLIN**

Ma douleur et sa compagne see Latil **MILHAUD**

"Ma fille, laisse là ton aiguille ta laine" *see Le repas préparé* Samain **KOECHLIN**

Ma fille, souviens-toi see Unknown **GOUNOD**

"Ma gentille fauvette" *see La jeune fille et la fauvette* Chauvinière, Edmond de **GOUNOD**

"Ma guitare, je te chante" *see À sa guitare* Ronsard **POULENC**

Ma jeunesse see Văcărescu **HAHN**

"Ma jeunesse, toujours brisée" *see Ma jeunesse* Văcărescu **HAHN**

"Ma maîtresse est volage" *see La maîtresse volage* Anon. **POULENC**

Má matička see Sládek **MARTINŮ** *Mother dear*

"Ma mie à son toit fidèle" *see Les fées* Banville **SAINT-SAËNS**

"Ma Osot Haayalot Balalot?" *see Morning star* Goldberg **GIDEON**

"Ma patrie est comme une barque" *see Richard II* Quarante Aragon **AURIC**

"Ma pensée est un cygne harmonieux et sage" *see Cygne sur l'éau* Brimont **FAURÉ**

Ma petite mère a pleuré see Gravollet, Paul **MASSENET**

Má píseň zas mi láskouzní see Heyduk **DVOŘÁK**

Ma poupée chérie see Séverac **SÉVERAC**

"Ma tourte relle, mon amie" *see La révoltée* Chalupt **MILHAUD**

Ma vie a son secret see Arvers **BIZET**

Ma vie est la feuille see Gabory **AURIC**

"Ma ville, ma belle ville" *see Zäide* (Boléro) Beauvoir **BERLIOZ**

Maassa marjani makaavi see Kanteletar **KILPINEN**

Mabbe, James, 1572-1642? translator.
  THE SPANISH BAWD (1631): Now sleepe, and take thy rest.
    HESELTINE *The contented lover*

Macdonald, Jacques Etienne Joseph Alexandre, duc de Tarente, 1765-1840.
    MASSENET *Les amoureuses sont des folles*

MACDOWELL, EDWARD ALEXANDER, 1861-1908.
Burns, Robert, 1759-1796.
  Deserted, op. 9 no. 1 (1894)
    [Breitkopf & Härtel, 1894; Arthur P. Schmidt,1899]
    "Ye banks and braes o' bonnie Doon"
  Menie, op. 34 no. 1 [Arthur P. Schmidt, 1889]
    "In vain to me the clowslips blaw"
  My Jean, op. 34 no. 2 [Arthur P. Schmidt, 1889]
    "Of a' the airts the wind can blow"
Deland, Margaret Wade (Campbell), 1857-1945.
  The blue-bell, op. 26 no. 5 [G. Schirmer, 1887] "In love she fell"
  The clover, op. 26 no. 3 [G. Schirmer, 1887] "O ruddy lover!"
  The mignonette, op. 26 no. 6 [G. Schirmer, 1887]
    "A dame of high degree, is she"
  The myrtle, op. 26 no. 2 [G. Schirmer, 1887]
    "Its clinging, mournful leaves, I said"
  The pansy, op. 26 no. 1 [G. Schirmer, 1887] "O dainty pansy!"
  The yellow daisy, op. 26 no. 4 [G. Schirmer, 1887] "What's his heart?"
Gardner, William Henry, 1865-1932.
  For sweet love's sake, op. 40 no. 4 [Arthur P. Schmidt, 1890] same
  I ask but this, op. 40 no. 6 [Arthur P. Schmidt, 1890] same

O lovely rose, op. 40 no. 5 [Arthur P.
Schmidt, 1890] same
Sweet blue-eyed maid, op. 40 no. 1
[Arthur P. Schmidt, 1890] same
Sweetheart tell me, op. 40 no. 2 [Arthur
P. Schmidt, 1890] same
Thy beaming eyes, op. 40 no. 3 [Arthur
P. Schmidt, 1890] same

**Geibel, Emanuel, i.e., Franz Emanuel
August, 1815-1884.**
Nachtlied, op. 12 no. 1 [Kahnt, 1883]
"Der Mond kommt still gegangen"

**Glücklich, Johann Christian, 1839-
1920.**
Bitte, op. 33 no. 1 [Jul. Hainauer, 1889]
"O, nenn mich nicht dein Leben"

**Goethe, Johann Wolfgang von, 1749-
1832.**
Idylle, op. 33 no. 3 [Jul. Hainauer, 1889]
"Ein Blumen Glöckchen"
Midsummer lullaby, op. 47 no. 2
[Breitkopf & Härtel, 1893]
"Silver clouds are lightly sailing"
Music says "after Goethe."
IM WALDE.
In the woods, op. 47 no. 6
[Breitkopf & Härtel, 1893] same

Heine, Heinrich, 1797-1856.
Du liebst mich nicht, op. 11 no. 2 (1881)
[Kahnt, 1883] same
Der Fichtenbaum [unpubl.]
"Der Fichtenbaum steht einsam"
Holograph at Butler Library, Columbia
University.
Mein Liebchen, op. 11 no. 1 (1881)
[Kahnt, 1883] same
Oben, wo die Sterne glühen, op. 11 no. 3
(1881) [Kahnt, 1883] same

Howells, William Dean, 1837-1920.
Folksong, op. 47 no. 3 [Breitkopf &
Härtel, 1893]
"Is it the shrewd October wind"
The sea, op. 47 no. 7 [Breitkopf &
Härtel, 1893] "One sails away to sea"
Through the meadow, op. 47 no. 8
[Breitkopf & Härtel, 1893]
"The summer sun was soft and
bland"

**Klopstock, Friedrich Gottlieb, 1724-
1803.**
ODE.
Das Rosenband, op. 12 no. 2
[Kahnt, 1883]
"Im Frühlings Schatten fand ich sie"

**MacDowell, Edward Alexander, 1861-
1908.**

Around a twisted snake of flame
[unpubl.] same
Holograph at Library of Congress.
As the gloaming shadows creep, op. 56
no. 4 [P.L. Jung, 1898; Arthur P.
Schmidt, 1899] same
Confidence, op. 47 no. 4 [Breitkopf &
Härtel, 1893] "Noonday sun or night"
Constancy, op. 58 no. 1 [Arthur P.
Schmidt, 1899]
"Old lilac bushes thin and grey"
Fair springtide, op. 60 no. 2 [Arthur P.
Schmidt, 1902]
"Fair springtide cometh once again"
In flaming gold [unpubl.]
"In flaming gold thou goest"
Location of holograph unknown.
Long ago sweetheart mine, op. 56 no. 1
[P.L. Jung, 1898; Arthur P. Schmidt,
1899] same
A maid sings light, op. 56 no. 3 [P.L.
Jung, 1898; Arthur P. Schmidt, 1899]
same
Merry maiden spring, op. 58 no. 3
[Arthur P. Schmidt, 1899]
"A winsome morning measure"
O thistle-leafed flame [unpubl.] same
Holograph owned by Margery Lowens.
The robin sings in the apple-tree, op. 47
no. 1 [Breitkopf & Härtel, 1893] same
Slumber song, op. 9 no. 2 (1894)
[Breitkopf & Härtel, 1894; Arthur P.
Schmidt, 1899]
"Dearest, sleep sound"
Sunrise, op. 58 no. 2 [Arthur P. Schmidt,
1899] "Sunrise gilds the crested sea"
The swan bent low to the lily, op. 56 no.
2 [P.L. Jung, 1898; Arthur P. Schmidt,
1899] same
To the golden rod, op. 60 no. 3 [Arthur
P. Schmidt, 1902]
"A lissome maid with towseled hair"
Tyrant love, op. 60 no. 1 [Arthur P.
Schmidt, 1902] "Where e'er love be"
The westwind croons in the cedar trees,
op. 47 no. 5 [Breitkopf & Härtel,
1893] same

Osterwald, Karl Wilhelm, 1820-1887.
Lieber Schatz [unpubl.] "In dem
Dornbusch blüht ein Röslein"
Holograph at Butler Library, Columbia
University.

Unknown
Geistliches Wiegenlied, op. 33 no. 2 [Jul.
Hainauer, 1889] "Dormi Jesu!"

COMPOSER Poet *Title* "First Line"

MacDowell, Edward Alexander, 1861-
  1908.
  MACDOWELL
    Around a twisted snake of flame
    As the gloaming shadows creep
    Confidence
    Constancy
    Fair springtide
    In flaming gold
    Long ago sweetheart mine
    A maid sings light
    Merry maiden spring
    O thistle-leafed flame
    The robin sings in the apple-tree
    Slumber song
    Sunrise
    The swan bent low to the lily
    To the golden rod
    Tyrant love
    The westwind croons in the cedar trees
"Mach auf, mach auf" *see Ständchen* Schack
  STRAUSS
"Mach auf, mach auf, mach auf deine Thür"
  see Wer ist Bär? Häring **LOEWE**
Machado, Antonio *see* Machado y Ruiz,
  Antonio, 1875-1939.
Machado y Ruiz, Antonio, 1875-1939.
  RODRIGO
    Abril galan
    Canción del duero
    Cantaban los niños
    Fiesta en el Prado
    Mañana de Abril
    Mi corazon te aguarda
    Preludio
    Recuerdas?
    Los sueños
    Tu voz y tu mano
Die Macht ader Augen see Metastasio
  SCHUBERT *L'incanto degli occhi*
Macht der Liebe see Herder **ZELTER**
Die Macht der Liebe see Kalchberg
  SCHUBERT
Die Macht der Musik see Orléans, Hélène
  LISZT
"Macht heim Wandern obn' Erharmen Staub"
  see Schönste Rast Cornelius **LASSEN**
Mackay, John Henry, 1864-1933.
  REGER *Morgen*
  SCHÖNBERG *Am Wegrand*
  STRAUSS
    Heimliche Aufforderung
    In der Campagna
    Morgen
MacLeish, Archibald, 1892-1982.
  CHANLER *These, my Ophelia*

  Two versions: 1925 and revised, 1937.
  GIDEON *The too-late born*
  HARRIS *Freedom's land*
Macleod, Fiona, pseud. *see*
  Sharp, William, 1885-1905.
MacLow, Jackson, 1922-
  ROREM *The nipples of the rain*
Macpherson, James, 1736-1796.
  SCHUBERT
    Die Nacht
    Der Tod Oskar's
  ZELTER *Colma von Ossian*
  BATTLE OF LORA.
    SCHUBERT *Lorma*
      Two settings: D. 327 and D. 376.
  CARRIC-THURA.
    SCHUBERT
      Cronnan
      Shilrik und Vinvela
  CARRIC-THURA: Spirit of Loda.
    SCHUBERT *Loda's Gespenst*
  DARTHULA.
    SCHUBERT *Ossians Lied nach dem*
      Falle Nathos'
  FINGAL.
    SCHUBERT *Das Mädchen von Inistore*
  THE SONGS OF SELMA.
    SCHUBERT *Kolma's Klage*
Mad as the mist and snow see Yeats
  ROREM
Mad nights see Apukhtin **CHAЇKOVSKIЇ**
  Nochi bezumnye
Madame see Cocteau **HONEGGER**
"Madame Eustache a dix-sept filles" *see Nous*
  voulons une petit soeur Nohain, Jean
  POULENC
"Madame Henri Rousseau monte en ballon
  captif" *see Hommage à Erik Satie* Cocteau
  AURIC
"Madame la Lune, en robe gris pâle" *see*
  Dame du ciel Haraucourt **KOECHLIN**
"Madame, vous voyez des hommes" *see*
  Amour viril Boyer, Georges
  SAINT-SAËNS
Madeleine see Tranchant, Alfred
  SAINT-SAËNS
Madeleine, Marie, i.e., Marie Madeleine
  Freifrau von Puttkamer *see*
  Puttkamer, Marie Madeleine
  (Günther), Freifrau, 1881-
Madmaselle Pimpernelle see No author
  BLACHER
La Madonna col bambino see Liguori
  SAINT-SAËNS
"Madonna, d'un braccio soa ve ch'io cinga"
  see Invito alla danza Zangarini
  RESPIGHI

La Madre al figlio lontano see Pàntini,
Romualdo *CANTILENE ALL'ARIA
APERTA.* **PIZZETTI**
"Madre, todas las noches junto a mis rejas"
see Preludios Trueba **FALLA**
Madre, unos ojuelos vi see Vega Carpio
SPANISCHES LIEDERBUCH:
Madre, unos ojuelos vi. **JENSEN**
MADRIALE. see Buonarroti
Madrigal **SCHOECK, STRAUSS**
Madrid, Princesse des Espagnes see Musset
CONTES D'ESPAGNE ET D'ITALIE.
DEBUSSY
Madrigal see Anon. **POULENC, RIETI**
Two Rieti settings: 1949 and 1967.
Madrigal see Bonnières **INDY**
Madrigal see Bourget **LOEFFLER**
Madrigal see Buonarroti *MADRIALE.*
SCHOECK, STRAUSS
Madrigal see Molière **SAINT-SAËNS**
Madrigal see Rivas **TURINA**
Madrigal see Silvestre **MASSENET**
Madrigal à deux voix see Orléans, Charles
d' **INDY**
Madrigal lyrique see Régnier **ROUSSEL**
"Mächtiger, der du die Wipfel" *see
Dem Allmächtigen* Rückert **LOEWE**
Das Mädchen see Kapper **BRAHMS**
Das Mädchen see Schlegel, F.
ABENDRÖTE. **SCHUBERT**
Das Mädchen see Schlegel, F. **SCHUBERT**
Blanka
Das Mädchen see Vinje **GRIEG** *Jenta*
Mädchen, als du kamst ans Licht see Goethe
FAUST. **LOEWE**
*Das Mädchen an das erste Schneeglöckchen
see* Gerstenberg, Friedrich von
WEBER
Das Mädchen an den Mai see Mörike
SCHOECK
Das Mädchen aus der Fremde see Schiller
SCHUBERT
Two settings: D. 117 and D. 252.
"Mädchen entsiegelten, Brüder, die Flaschen"
see Skolie Matthisson **SCHUBERT**
"Ein Mädchen ging die Wies' entlang" *see
Bach, Echo, Kuss* Kind, F. **WEBER**
Das Mädchen im Kampf mit sich selbst see
Hebbel **GIDEON**
"Mädchen Inistores" *see Das Mädchen von
Inistore* Macpherson **SCHUBERT**
"Ein Mädchen ist's, das früh und spät mir"
see Das Bild Unknown **SCHUBERT**
"Mädchen, lass uns trinken, lachen" *see
Ewig jung* Ernst **LASSEN**
"Ein Mädchen lebt in Inverness" *see
Das Mädchen von Inverness* Cunningham
JENSEN

Mädchen mit dem roten Mündchen see Heine
FRANZ, WOLF
Mädchen sind wie der Wind see André
LOEWE
"Ein Mädchen so schön aus himmlischen
Höh'n" *see Was ich sah* Vinje **GRIEG**
Das Mädchen spricht see Gruppe **BRAHMS**
Das Mädchen spricht see Heyse **LASSEN**
Dornröschen (Das Mädchen spricht)
Das Mädchen spricht see Prutz **REGER**
Das Mädchen und das Gras see Anon.
DVOŘÁK *Panenka a tráva*
Mädchen und Rose see Jacob, T. **LOEWE**
"Mädchen von Athen, geschwind" *see Mein
Leben, ich liebe dich* Byron **LASSEN**
Das Mädchen von Inistore see Macpherson
FINGAL. **SCHUBERT**
Das Mädchen von Inverness see
Cunningham **JENSEN**
Das Mädchen von Isla see Scott **JENSEN**
"Mädchen von Isla, hoch vom Riff" *see
Das Mädchen von Isla* Scott **JENSEN**
"Mädchen von Kola, du schläfst" *see
Darthula's Grabesgesang* Herder **JENSEN**
MÄDCHENBLUMEN, no. 1
STRAUSS Dahn *Kornblumen*
MÄDCHENBLUMEN, no. 2
STRAUSS Dahn *Mohnblumen*
MÄDCHENBLUMEN, no. 3
STRAUSS Dahn *Efeu*
MÄDCHENBLUMEN, no. 4
STRAUSS Dahn *Wasserrose*
Mädchenfluch, Nach dem Serbischen *see*
Kapper *DIE GESÄNGE DER SERBEN.*
BRAHMS
Mädchenfrühling see Dehmel
ERLÖSUNGEN. **SCHÖNBERG**
Mädchenlied see Boelitz **REGER**
Mädchenlied see Geibel **SCHÖNBERG**
Mädchenlied see Haringer *ABSCHIED.*
SCHÖNBERG
Mädchenlied see Heyse **BRAHMS,
JENSEN, SCHÖNBERG**
Two Brahms settings: Op. 95 no. 6 and op.
107 no. 5.
Mädchenlied see Kapper **BRAHMS**
Mädchenlied see Morgenstern **REGER**
Mädchenlied see Puttkamer **REGER**
Mädchenlied see Remer **SCHÖNBERG**
Mädchens Abendgedanken see Vischer
RUBINSTEIN
Mädchens Held see Goethe **ZELTER**
Das Mädchens Sehnsucht see Kind, F.
SPOHR
Mädchen-Schwermuth see Bernhard, Lily
SCHUMANN

Mädchenwünsche see Goethe LOEWE

"Mädel, halt die Rökke fest" *see*
   Der Sausewind Busse REGER

"Mädel, lass das Stricken geh" *see*
   Nicht doch! Dehmel SCHÖNBERG

"Mädel, schau' mir ins Gesicht" *see*
   Liebeszauber Bürger, J. H. WEBER

"Mädel, sei kein eitles Ding" *see Mahnung*
   Hochstetter SCHÖNBERG

"Mäderl mit dem goldnen Latz" *see*
   Liebeshändel Löwenstein RUBINSTEIN

"Ein Mägdlein an des Felsen Rand" *see*
   Erdbeerliedchen Unknown LOEWE

"Mägdlein pflücket Beeren in des Waldes
   Mitten" *see Der junge Herr und das
   Mädchen* Mickiewicz LOEWE

"Ein Mägdlein sass am Meeresstrand" *see*
   Treue Liebe Schulz BRAHMS

"Das Mägdlein sprach" *see Mein und Dein*
   Fischer, J. REGER

"Das Mägdlein trat aus dem Fischerhaus" *see*
   Phantasie Tellez MAHLER

Das Mägdlein und der Spatz see Anon.
   REGER

"Das Mägdlein will ein'n Freier hab'n" *see*
   Für fünfzehn Pfennige Des Knaben
   Wunderhorn STRAUSS

Mägdleins Frage see Ljubljaschtschi
   REGER

Die Männer sind méchant see Seidl
   SCHUBERT

"Männer suchen stets zu naschen" *see*
   Warnung Unknown REGER

Männertreu see Löns KILPINEN

Människans hem see Blomberg KILPINEN

Märchenland see Evers REGER

Märchenwunder see Cornelius
   CORNELIUS

März see Holm LASSEN

Märzenblume see Träger LASSEN

Märzveilchen see Andersen SCHUMANN

Mäuschen see Iłłakowiczówna
   SZYMANOWSKI *Myszy*

Maeterlinck, Maurice, 1862-1949.
   BOULANGER
      Attente
      Reflets
   CHAUSSON
      Fauves las
      Lassitude
      Oraison
      Serre chaude
      Serre d'ennui
   IBERT *Chanson*
   SCHMITT *Ils ont tué trois petites filles*
   SÉVERAC *L'infidèle*

PELLÉAS ET MÉLISANDE.
   FAURÉ *Mélisande's song*

Maffei, Andrea, 1798-1885.
   RUBINSTEIN *La prima viola*
   VERDI
      Ad una stella
      Brindisi
         Two versions: 1835? And 1845.
      Il tramonto

"Mag auch die Liebe weinen!" *see*
   Die Auferstehung Krummacher LOEWE

"Mag Toren hienieden" *see Der Liebescheue*
   Unknown LOEWE

Maggioni, S. Manfredo
   VERDI
      Il poveretto
      Lo spazzacamino
      La zingara

The magic of thy presence see Bodenstedt
   QUILTER *Und was die Sonne glüht*

Magie der Farben see Hesse SCHOECK

Magny, Olivier de, d. ca. 1560.
   ROREM *Sonnet*
      Two settings, both 1953.

The magpie see Unknown STRAVINSKĬ
   La petite pie

Magre, Maurice, 1877-1941.
   HAHN
      Chanson au bord de la fontaine, extraite
         de *Méduse*
      Le plus beau présent
   L' OUVRIER QUI PLEURE.
      SÉVERAC *La chanson de blaisine*

Magyar király-dal see Ábrányi LISZT

Magyarisch see Daumer POLYDORA.
   BRAHMS

Mahadöh see Goethe LOEWE *Der Gott und
   die Bajadere*

"Mahadöh, der Herr der Erde" *see Der Gott
   und die Bajadere* Goethe LOEWE,
   SCHOECK, SCHUBERT, ZELTER

Mahaut
   RIVIER
      Le Cheichi
      En rêve
      Le quatrain de la rose

"Ein Mahl für uns und ein Licht für dich" *see*
   Sankt Michael Weinheber STRAUSS

MAHLER, GUSTAV, 1860-1911.
   Anon.
      Es fiel ein Reif in der Frühlingsnacht
         (1876-?79) [unpubl.] same
      Text may be from Erk & Böhme
         Deutscher Liederhort, pp. 587-89.
   DES KNABEN WUNDERHORN:
      Ablösung.

Ablösung im Sommer [Schott, 1892;
Universal]
"Kukuk hat sich zu Tode gefallen"
DES KNABEN WUNDERHORN:
Abschied für immer.
Aus! Aus! [Schott, 1892; Universal]
"Heute marschieren wir!"
DES KNABEN WUNDERHORN: Drei
Reiter am Tor.
Scheiden und Meiden [Schott, 1892;
Universal] "Es ritten drei Reiter zum
Thore hinaus!"
DES KNABEN WUNDERHORN: Nicht
Wiedersehen.
Nicht Wiedersehen! [Schott, 1892;
Universal] "Und nun ade"
DES KNABEN WUNDERHORN: Der
Schweizer.
Zu Strassburg auf der Schanz [Schott,
1892; Universal] same
DES KNABEN WUNDERHORN:
Selbstgefühl.
Selbstgefühl [Schott, 1892; Universal]
"Ich weiss nicht, wie mir ist!"
DES KNABEN WUNDERHORN: Starke
Einbildungskraft.
Starke Einbildungskraft [Schott, 1892;
Universal] "Hast gesagt, du willst
mich nehmen"
DES KNABEN WUNDERHORN: Um die
Kinder still und artig zu machen.
Um schlimme Kinder artig zu machen
[Schott, 1892; Universal]
"Es kam ein Herr zum Schlösseli"
DES KNABEN WUNDERHORN:
Waldvöglein.
*Ich ging mit Lust durch einen grünen
Wald* [Schott, 1892; Universal] same
Heine, Heinrich, 1797-1856.
Im wunderschönen Monat Mai (1876-
?79) [unpubl.] same
Microfilm at the New York Public
Library.
Mahler, Gustav, 1860-1911.
Ging heut' Morgens übers Feld (1883-
85) [Weinberger, 1897] same
Orchestrated in the 1890s.
Hans und Grethe [Schott, 1885;
Universal] "Ringel, ringel Reihn'n!"
Ich hat' ein glühend Messer (1883-85)
[Weinberger, 1897] same
Orchestrated in the 1890s.
Im Lenz (1880) [unpubl.] "Sag' an, du
Träumer am lichten Tag"
Maitanz im Grünen (1880) [unpubl.]
"Ringel, ringel Reih'n"

In his *Lieder und Gesange,* v.1,
Schott, as *Hans und Grethe*; see
above.
Wenn mein Schatz Hochzeit macht (1883-
85) [Weinberger, 1897] same
Orchestrated in the 1890s.
Winterlied (1880) [unpubl.]
"Über Berg und Tal"
*Die zwei blauen Augen von meinem
Schatz* (1883-85) [Weinberger, 1897]
same
Orchestrated in the 1890s.
Tellez, Gabriel, 1570?-1648.
EL BURLADOR DE SEVILLA.
Phantasie [Schott, 1885; Universal]
"Das Mägdlein trat aus dem
Fischerhaus"
Serenade [Schott, 1885; Universal]
"Ist's dein Wille, süsse Maid"
Volkmann, Richard von, 1830-1889.
Erinnerung [Schott, 1885; Universal] "Es
wecket meine Liebe die Lieder immer
wieder!"
Frühlingsmorgen [Schott, 1885;
Universal] "Es klopft an das Fenster
der Lindenbaum"
Mahler, Gustav, 1860-1911.
MAHLER
Ging heut' Morgens übers Feld
Hans und Grethe
Ich hat' ein glühend Messer
Im Lenz
Maitanz im Grünen
Wenn mein Schatz Hochzeit macht
Winterlied
*Die zwei blauen Augen von meinem
Schatz*
**Mahlmann, Siegfried August, 1771-
1826.**
SPOHR *Schwermut*
ZELTER
Der Jäger
Romanze
NACHT-LIED.
LOEWE *Die Nacht*
Mahnung see Anon. **DVOŘÁK**
Připamatování
Mahnung see Hochstetter **SCHÖNBERG**
Mahomet's Gesang see Goethe **LOEWE,
SCHUBERT**
Two Schubert settings: D. 549 and D. 721.
Mahot, A.
SAINT-SAËNS *Fière beauté*
Mai see Coppée **HAHN**
Mai see Docquois **SAINT-SAËNS**
Mai see Goethe **WOLF**

Mai see Hugo FAURÉ
"Mai! Les arbres du verger" *see Mai*
   Docquois SAINT-SAËNS
Der Mai tritt ein mit Freuden see Anon.
   SCHÖNBERG
Maiakovskii, Vladimir Vladimirovich,
   1894-1930.
   PROKOFIEV *Pesnya*
Maiblümelein see Unknown LOEWE
Maid of Athens see Byron GOUNOD
Maid quiet see Yeats RIETI, ROREM
A maid sings light see MacDowell
   MACDOWELL
The maiden and the grass see Anon.
   DVOŘÁK *Panenka a tráva*
The maiden and the sun see Maĭkov
   RIMSKIĭ-KORSAKOV *Deva i solntse*
The maiden blush see Herrick QUILTER
The maiden came from her lover's tryst see
   Runeberg SIBELIUS
    Flickan kom ifrån sin älsklings möte
Maiden mine see Case BENNETT
"Maiden mine with lips so rosy" *see Maiden*
   mine Case BENNETT
"The maidens came when I was in my
   mother's bow'r" *see The bayly berith the*
   bell away Anon. HESELTINE
Maiden's dreams see Huch MARTINŮ
A maiden's song see Sládek MARTINŮ
MAIDMENT'S NORTH COUNTRIE
   GARLAND (1824). *see* Anon.
    Burd Ellen and young Tamlane
    HESELTINE
THE MAID'S TRAGEDY (1619): Aspatia's
   song. *see* Fletcher
    A sad song HESELTINE
Der Maien ist gestorben see Gerheusser,
   Rosa REGER
Maienblümlein see Eckschlager WEBER
Maienblüten see Jacobowski REGER
Maienkätzchen see Liliencron BRAHMS
"Maienkätzchen, erster Gruss" *see*
   Maienkätzchen Liliencron BRAHMS
"Maienkätzchen, erster Gruss" *see*
   Tiefe Sehnsucht Liliencron BERG
Maienlied see Goethe LASSEN
Maienlied see Wart MENDELSSOHN-
   BARTHOLDY
Maiennacht see Metternich-Winneburg
   REGER
Maigesang see Goethe BEETHOVEN
Maigret, Henri
   MASSENET *Chanson pour elle*
Maĭkov, Apollon Nikolayevich, 1821-
   1897.
    BALAKIREV *Vvedi menya, O noch,*
    taykom

   PROKOFIEV *Mastitĭye, vetvistĭye, dubĭ*
   RACHMANINOFF *It cannot be*
   RIMSKIĭ-KORSAKOV
    Deva i solntse
    Eshche ĭa poln, o drug moĭ milyĭ
    IA v grote zhdal tebĭa v urochnyĭ chas
    Iskusstvo
    Liubliu tebĭa, mesĭats
    Nimfa
    O chem v tishi nocheĭ
    Oktava
    Pevets
    Posmotri v svoĭ vertograd
    Somnenie
    Son v letniuĭu noch'
    Tikho more goluboe!
   RUBINSTEIN *Elegie*
   NOVOGRECHESKIYE PESNI.
    CHAĭKOVSKIĭ
     Kolibel'naya pesnya
     Novogrecheskiye pesni
Mailied see Goethe FRANZ, LOEWE,
   MEDTNER, PFITZNER, SCHOECK,
   SCHÖNBERG, ZELTER
MAILIED. see Goethe
   Wo geht's Liebchen? ZELTER
Mailied see Goethe ZELTER *Wo geht's*
   Liebchen?
Mailied see Hölty SCHUBERT, WOLF
Mailied see Unknown MENDELSSOHN-
   BARTHOLDY
Main dominée par le coeur see Éluard
   POULENC
Die Mainacht see Hölty BRAHMS,
   SCHUBERT
Les mains see Bazan, Noël MASSENET
"Mains agitées, aux grimaces nouées" *see* . . .
   Mais mourir Éluard POULENC
"Les mains lentes sous la lampe" *see*
   Brodeuses Mauclair AUBERT
Maintenant que les portes de bienveillance see
   Anon. MILHAUD
. . . *Mais mourir see* Éluard POULENC
"Mais, telle qu'à sa mort" *see Néère* Chénier
   KOECHLIN
"Mais vers qui marchez-vous" *see Je sais*
   qu'il existe Carême SAUGUET
Maĭ skaĭa pesn' see Goethe MEDTNER
   Mailied
La maison see Messiaen MESSIAEN
La maison du bonheur see Lefilleul, G.
   JOLIVET
La maison du matin see Samain
   AUX FLANCS DU VASE. KOECHLIN
La maison inachevée see Paliard MILHAUD
Maisuna am Brunnen see Stieglitz LOEWE

COMPOSER Poet *Title* "First Line"

Maitanz im Grünen see Mahler **MAHLER**
Maitiak bilhoa holli see Unknown
SZYMANOWSKI
Maitland, Edward, 1824-1897.
   GOUNOD *Oh, happy home*
"Maitre du vivre et du morir" *see Prière dans*
   le soir Pépin, Edwige **SAUGUET**
"Maitres de tous nos désirs" *see*
   Les petits coups Béranger **LALO**
La maîtresse volage see Anon. **POULENC**
Maj see Josephson, E. **SIBELIUS**
The majority see Ives **IVES**
Makaaja onni see Kanteletar **KILPINEN**
"Make a fuss and be tedious" *see English*
   usage Moore, M. **THOMSON**
"Make a joyful noise unto the Lord" *see*
   A psalm of praise Bible **ROREM**
Making calls see Carpenter, Rue
   CARPENTER
Die Malbronner Fuge see Scheffel
   GAUDEAMUS. **JENSEN**
MALER NOLTEN. see Mörike
   Peregrina **SCHOECK**
"Malgré la voix de la sagesse" *see Beaucoup*
   d'amour Béranger **LALO**
Malherbe, François de, 1555-1628.
   POULENC *Épitaphe*
Le malheur see Heine *INTERMEZZO.*
   SAUGUET
"Le malheur, mon grand laboureur" *see Repos*
   dan le malheur Michaux **SAUGUET**
MALIPIERO, GIAN FRANCESCO, 1882-
1973.
   Annunzio, Gabriele d', 1863-1938.
      ALCYONE.
         Ditirambo terzo (dalle laudi di
            Gabriele d'Annunzio, 1923)
            [Ricordi, 1924]
            "O grande Estate, delizio grande"
      LA CHIMERA.
         Eliana (1909) [Carisch, 1914] "Dorme
            a notte il palagio d'Eliana"
         Grasinda (1909) [Carisch, 1914]
            "Dorme Grasinda in mezzo a'suoi
            tesori"
         Melusina (1909) [Carisch, 1914]
            "Guarda, assisa, la vaga Melusina"
         Mirinda (1909) [Carisch, 1914]
            "Mirinda e il fido"
         Morgana (1909) [Carisch, 1914]
            "Or tremule, su i marie su learene"
         Oriana–Oriana infedele (1909)
            [Carisch, 1914]
            "Oriana tenea l'incantamento"
   Anon.
      Canto della neve (1923) [Ricordi, 1924]
         "Chi colla neve solazzarsi verole"

Berni, Francesco, 1497 or 8-1535.
   Cancheri e beccafichi magri arosto
      (1922) [Ricordi, 1922] same
      Also voice & orchestra.
   Chiome d'argento fine, irte e attorte
      (1922) [Ricordi, 1922] same
      Also voice & orchestra.
Burchiello, Domenico di Giovanni,
   known as, 1404-1448.
   Andando a uccellare (1921) [Pizzi, 1922;
      Bongiovanni] same
   Cacio stillato (1921) [Pizzi, 1922;
      Bongiovanni] same
   Rose spinose (1921) [Pizzi, 1922;
      Bongiovanni] same
   Va in mercato, Giorgin (1921) [Pizzi,
      1922; Bongiovanni] same
Cavalca, Domenico, d.1342.
   In memoria d'un amico (1949) [Suvini
      Zerboni, 1949]
      "Oh vita del mondo, non se' vita"
Cros, Charles, 1842-1888.
   LE COFFRET DE SANTAL, CHANSONS
      PERPÉTUELLES (1873).
      L'archet (1916) [Senart, 1918;
         Salabert]
         "Elle avait de beaux cheveux"
Jean-Aubry, Georges, 1882-1950.
   Light (1918) [J. & W. Chester, 1919]
      "Des larmes ont coulé d'un coeur
      secret"
   Song (1918) [J. & W. Chester, 1919]
      "Un chant s'élance, fleur du silence"
   Stream (1918) [J. & W. Chester, 1919]
      "La légère ondulation des feuilles
      berce des lacs"
Latini, Brunetto, 1230-1295.
   Lauda per un morto (1923) [Ricordi,
      1924] "O fratel nostro, che se' morto"
Lemene, Francesco, conte de, 1634-
   1704.
   Capriccio (1923) [Ricordi, 1924]
      "Son troppo sazia, non ne vo'più"
Margueritte, Victor, 1866-1942.
   Chanson morave (1914) [Senart, 1918;
      Salabert] "Ecoute, écoute . . . On dirait
      un glas qui dans l'air frissonne"
   Pégase (1914) [Senart, 1918; Salabert]
      "Cabré devant la noire escallade du
      mur"
   Les yeux coleur du temps (1914) [Senart,
      1918; Salabert]
      "Silencieuse, sur les arbes"
Moréas, Jean, 1856-1910.
   Ariette (1916) [Senart, 1918; Salabert]
      "Tu me lias de tes mains blanches"

MALIPIERO, GIAN FRANCESCO, 1882-1973 *(continued)*
No author
> *Tre vocalizzi nello stile moderno* (1929) [Ricordi, 1929]
> > Wordless.

Pàntini, Romualdo
> *La cavalcata della morte* (c.1908) [Rahter] "Morte, non io ti temo"

Poliziano, Angelo, 1454-1494.
> *Ballata* (1920) [J. & W. Chester, 1922] "Donne mie voi non sapete"
> *L'Eco* [J. & W. Chester, 1922] "Che fai tu, Eco, mentre io ti chiamo?"
> *Inno a Maria Nostra Donna* (1920) [J. & W. Chester, 1922] "Vergine santa, immacolata"

Unknown
> *Dialogo no. 3 'con Jacopone da Todi'* (1956) [Ricordi, 1957] "O iubilo del core, che fai cantar d'amore!"
> > Voice & 2 pianos.

Mallarmé see Radiguet **AURIC**
Mallarmé, Stéphane, 1842-1898.
DEBUSSY
> *Apparition*
> *Éventail*
> *Placet futile*
> *Soupir*

MILHAUD
> *Le cantonnier*
> *Le crieur d'imprimés*
> *La femme de l'ouvrier*
> *Indomptablement a dû*
> *Le Marchand d'ail et d'oignons*
> *La Marchande d'habits*
> *La Marchande d'herbes aromatiques*
> *Quatrain*
> *Quelconque une solitude*
> *Le savetier*
> *Le vitrier*

RAVEL
> *Placet futile*
> *Sainte*
> *Soupir*
> *Surgi de la croupe et du bond*

SAUGUET
> *Renouveau*
> *Senteurs*
> *Tristesse d'été*

MALOROSSYSKAYA PESNYA. see Surikov
ÍA li v poke da ne travushka byla
CHAĬKOVSKIĬ
Le malpropre see Vildrac **MILHAUD**
Maltworms see Stevenson, W. *GAMMER GURTON'S NEEDLE* (1575).
HESELTINE

Malven see Knobel **STRAUSS**
Malybrok-Stieler, O., pseud. *see* Kleinschrod, Ottilie (Stieler), 1836-1914.
Malyutka see Pleshcheyev **MUSORGSKIĬ**
> *Akh, zachem tvoi glazki poroĭu*
Mám staré parky rád see Borecký, Jaromír **MARTINŮ** *I love old parks*
La maman see Tastu **SAINT-SAËNS**
"Maman, le gros Bébé t'appelle, il a bobo" *see La chanson du Bébé* Pacini **ROSSINI**
La mamma è come il pane caldo see Zarian **RESPIGHI**
"Man geht aus Nacht in Sonne" *see Ein Preussenlied* Unknown **LOEWE**
"Man lauert, sitzt und sinnt" *see Das unerkannte Gedicht* Günther **KRENEK**
"Man passes down the way of years" *see The all-enduring* Brewster, Lyman **IVES**
Man sagt mir see Heyse **WOLF**
"Man soll hören süsses Singen" *see Maienlied* Wart **MENDELSSOHN-BARTHOLDY**
"Man soll seinem Herzen gehorchen" *see Herzensverstand* Wolf, F. **BLACHER**
Man strebt die Flamme zu verhehlen see Unknown **BEETHOVEN**
Mañana de Abril see Machado y Ruiz **RODRIGO**
Manch Bild vergessener Zeiten see Heine **WOLF**
Manche Nacht see Dehmel **SCHOECK, SZYMANOWSKI**
"Manche Thrän' aus meinen Augen" *see Wasserflut* Müller, Wilhelm **SCHUBERT**
Mancher Stunden Wehen see Zwehl, Hans Fritz von **KILPINEN**
MANCHERLEI FREUDEN. see Recke *Rundgesang im Freien* **LOEWE**
"Manchmal, in all dem Grossen" *see Heimweh* Krenek **KRENEK**
Mandoline see Verlaine *FÊTES GALANTES.* **DEBUSSY, FAURÉ**
Mandoline see Verlaine **HAHN** *Fêtes galantes*
Mandolinen see Unknown **SCHOECK**
"Le manège a vapeur regarde s'en aller" *see Fête de Bordeaux* Cocteau **MILHAUD**
Mangeot, L
SAINT-SAËNS *Sérénade*
Manilius, Marcus, d.384 B.C.
ASTRONOMICA, Book 4, livre 16.
IVES *Vita*
Manin, J.
MARTINŮ
> *Povĕra*
> *We erred in the morning*
> *Kiss, my sweetheart, kiss*

Man-like, my God *see* Goodman **ROREM**
Manlius *see* Manilius, Marcus, d. 384
   B. C.
Der Mann von Wort see Kleinschmid
   BEETHOVEN
Mannesbangen see Dehmel *WEIB UND*
   WELT. **SCHÖNBERG**
Le manoir de Rosemonde see Bonnières
   CONTES DE FÉES. **DUPARC**
Mansfield, Katherine, 1890-1923.
   THE JOURNAL OF KATHERINE
      MANSFIELD.
      DIAMOND
         My little Mother
         Souvent j'ai dit a mon mari
Mansilla, Daniel Garcia, 1838-1892.
   MASSENET *Si tu l'oses*
Manteau de fleurs see Gravollet, Paul *LES*
   FRISSONS. **RAVEL**
Manuel del Rio, Don
   WOLF *Mühvoll komm' ich und beladen*
   SPANISCHES LIEDERBUCH: Cojo jazmin
      y clavel.
      JENSEN *Cojo jazmin y clavel*
Manuel, Eugène, 1823-1901.
   GOUNOD *Prière du soir*
   MASSENET
      Quand on aime
      Sérénade
Many chambers and gardens have I see
   Kol'tsov **MUSORGSKIÏ**
   Mnogo est' u menia teremov i sadov
"Manzanita colorada" *see De ronda* Anon.
   RODRIGO
Maple leaves see Aldrich **IVES**
Maquarie, Arthur
   QUILTER *Autumn evening*
Maquet, Thérèse
   MASSENET
      Beaux yeux que j'aime
      Les belles de nuit
Marc Chagall see Éluard **POULENC**
Marc, Gabriel
   DUPARC *Sérénade*
March funèbre see Ribemont Dessaignes
   JOLIVET
March snow see Wecksell **SIBELIUS**
   Marssnön
Le Marchand d'ail et d'oignons see
   Mallarmé **MILHAUD**
La marchand de coeurs see Luka,
   Madeleine **SAUGUET**
La marchande d'anémondes see Sidery
   SAUGUET
La marchande des rêves see Silvestre
   MASSENET

La Marchande d'habits see Mallarmé
   MILHAUD
La Marchande d'herbes aromatiques see
   Mallarmé **MILHAUD**
Marche Américaine see Unknown
   SÉVERAC
Marche du panache à la grande Maréchale
   see Indy **INDY**
"Marcher dans un sentier de pierres et de
   roses" *see Tristesse* Carrier, P.
   MASSENET
Marcy, Claude
   SAUGUET *Les amoureux sont seuls au*
      monde
Marées, Adolf von, 1801-1874.
   SPOHR *Das wirtshaus zu*
Marès, Roland de, 1874-1955.
   AUBERT *Légende*
   ARIETTES DOULOUREUSES.
      RAVEL *Ballade de la reine morte*
         d'aimer
"Margaret, are you grieving" *see Spring and*
   fall (to a young child) Hopkins **ROREM**
Margarethe see Goethe *FAUST.* **ZELTER**
Margarethlein see Krag **GRIEG** *Liden*
   Kirsten
Margaritki see Lotarev **RACHMANINOFF**
   Daisies
Marggraff, Rudolph, 1805-1880.
   LOEWE
      Der Lappländer
      Die Schneeflocke
Margolin, Anna, 1887-1952.
   WEISGALL *A city by the sea*
Margot la pie a fait son nid see Anon.
   MOMPOU
Margreta see Roquette **JENSEN** *Margreth*
   am Thore
Margretens Wiegenlied see Ibsen *KONGS-*
   EMNERNE. **GRIEG** *Margretes Vuggesang*
Margretes Vuggesang see Ibsen *KONGS-*
   EMNERNE. **GRIEG**
Margreth am Thore see Roquette **JENSEN**
Marguerite see Pradère-Niquet **GOUNOD**
"Une marguerite à la bouche" *see*
   Le beau navire Carême **MILHAUD**
Marguerite d'Angoulême, Queen of
   Navarre, 1492-1549.
   SÉVERAC *Albado*
"Marguerite de Navarre" *see La promenade*
   Bédat de Monlaur, Pierre **HONEGGER**
Margueritte, Victor, 1866-1942.
   MALIPIERO
      Chanson morave
      Pégase
      Les yeux coleur du temps

Maria see Unknown **SPOHR**
   Two settings: Op. 139 no. 2 and WoO 107.
Maria am Rosenstrauch see Schellenberg
   REGER
Maria, glutton see Carpenter, Rue
   CARPENTER
"Maria kam auf ihrer Flucht" *see Maria und*
   das Milchmädchen Schreiber **LOEWE**
Maria Lucrezia see Legouvé
   SAINT-SAËNS
"Maria sits in her high chair" *see Maria,*
   glutton Carpenter, Rue **CARPENTER**
"Maria sitzt am Rosenbusch" *see Maria am*
   Rosenstrauch Schellenberg **REGER**
"Maria sitzt am Rosenhag und wiegt ihr
   Jesuskind" *see Mariä Wiegenlied* Boelitz
   REGER
"Maria sitzt und stimmet die Harfe zum
   Gesang" *see Das vergessene Lied* Vogl
   LOEWE
Maria und das Milchmädchen see Schreiber
   LOEWE
Mariä Heimsuchung see Rilke **HINDEMITH**
Mariä Verkündigung see Rilke **HINDEMITH**
Mariä Wiegenlied see Boelitz **REGER**
Le mariage des roses see David **FRANCK**
Mariazang see Unknown **PIJPER**
Marie see Gottschall **FRANZ, IVES,**
   JENSEN
Marie see Hardenberg **SCHUBERT**
Marie see Musset **LOEFFLER**
"Marie, am Fenster sitzest du" *see Marie*
   Gottschall **FRANZ, JENSEN**
"Marie auf der Wiese, auf der Wiese Marie"
   see Klein Marie Trojan **REGER**
"Marie, I see thee fairest one" *see Marie*
   Gottschall **IVES**
Marie Laurencin see Cocteau **AURIC**
Marienbad see No author **SATIE**
Das Marienbild see Schreiber **SCHUBERT**
Marienkirche zu Danzig im Gerüst see
   Zwehl, Hans Fritz von **KILPINEN**
DAS MARIENLEBEN, no. 1
   HINDEMITH Rilke *Geburt Mariä*
DAS MARIENLEBEN, no. 2
   HINDEMITH Rilke *Die Darstellung*
    Mariä im Tempel
DAS MARIENLEBEN, no. 3
   HINDEMITH Rilke *Mariä Verkündigung*
DAS MARIENLEBEN, no. 4
   HINDEMITH Rilke *Mariä Heimsuchung*
DAS MARIENLEBEN, no. 5
   HINDEMITH Rilke *Argwohn Josephs*
DAS MARIENLEBEN, no. 6
   HINDEMITH Rilke *Verkündigung über*
    den Hirten

DAS MARIENLEBEN, no. 7
   HINDEMITH Rilke *Geburt Christi*
DAS MARIENLEBEN, no. 8
   HINDEMITH Rilke *Rast auf der Flucht in*
    Ägypten
DAS MARIENLEBEN, no. 9
   HINDEMITH Rilke *Vor der Hochzeit zu*
    Kana
DAS MARIENLEBEN, no. 10
   HINDEMITH Rilke *Vor der Passion*
DAS MARIENLEBEN, no. 11
   HINDEMITH Rilke *Pietà*
DAS MARIENLEBEN, no. 12
   HINDEMITH Rilke *Stillung Mariä mit*
    dem Auferstandenen
DAS MARIENLEBEN, no. 13
   HINDEMITH Rilke *Vom Tode Mariä*
DAS MARIENLEBEN, no. 14
   HINDEMITH Rilke *Vom Tode Mariä*
DAS MARIENLEBEN, no. 15
   HINDEMITH Rilke *Vom Tode Mariä*
Marienlied see Hardenberg **SCHOECK**
Marienwürmchen see Des Knaben
   Wunderhorn **SCHUMANN**
Das Marienwürmchen see Hugo **LASSEN**
   La Coccinelle
"Marienwürmchen, setze dich" *see*
   Marienwürmchen Des Knaben
   Wunderhorn **SCHUMANN**
Mariéton, Paul, 1862-1911.
   MASSENET
    Ne donne pas ton coeur
    Séparation
    Souvenance
MARIGOLD, no. 1
   IRELAND Rossetti, Dante *Youth's*
    spring-tribute
MARIGOLD, no. 2
   IRELAND Rossetti, Dante *Penumbra*
MARIGOLD, no. 3
   IRELAND Verlaine *Spleen*
Marin, Francisco Rodríguez *see*
   Rodríguez Marin, Francisco, 1855-
   1943.
Marine see Rimbaud **MILHAUD**
Marine see Theuriet **LALO**
Marine à Roscoff see Jacob, M. **SAUGUET**
"Marisenki, marjasenko" *see Kukkalatva kuusi*
   Kanteletar **KILPINEN**
"Mark but this flea" *see The flea* Donne
   KRENEK
Markham, Charles Edwin *see* Markham,
   Edwin, 1852-1940.
Markham, Edwin, 1852-1940.
   IVES *from "Lincoln, the great commoner"*
"Der Marktplatz liegt vom Mond erhellt" *see*
   Kleinstadt im Frühling Huber, B.
   KILPINEN

Marlowe, Christopher, 1564-1593.
  *THE PASSIONATE SHEEPHERD TO HIS
    LOVE.*
  HESELTINE *The passionate shepherd*
Marmotte see Goethe **BEETHOVEN**
Marot, Clément, 1495?-1544.
  RAVEL
    D'Anne jouant de l'espinette
    D'Anne qui me jecta de la neige
  RIVIER *Dedans Paris, ville jolie . . .*
  ROREM *Rondeau de sa grande amie*
  *TRENTE ET HUYT CHANSONS
    MUSICALES . . . :* Chanson
    vingtcinquiesme . . .
  HESELTINE *Chanson du Jour de Noël*
Marqués de Santillana *see*
  Santillana, Iñigo López de Mendoza,
    marqués de, 1398-1458.
Marquise see Silvestre **MASSENET**
"La marquise a dit: 'Mon beau Puyjoli'" *see*
  La gavotte de Puyjoli Noël, Édouard
  MASSENET
Marquise vous souvenez-vous? see Coppée
  SAINT-SAËNS
Marrant see Gélin **ROREM**
Marronniers see Anon. **MILHAUD**
Les marronniers see Collin **MASSENET**
Marry me, mother, as long as I'm young see
  Tetmajer **MARTINŮ**
"Mars, april och maj" *see En vårrefräng*
  Österling **KILPINEN**
Marsan, Maurice de, 1852-1929.
  MILHAUD *Les temps faciles*
MARSH, ROMNEY, pseud. *see* **QUILTER,
  ROGER, 1877-1953.**
Marssnön see Wecksell **SIBELIUS**
La martiale see Chalupt **MILHAUD**
Martin, Gabriel, 1862-
  MASSENET *Soir de printemps*
Martin, Paul
  SAINT-SAËNS *Les sapins*
Martínek, Vojtěch, 1887-1960.
  MARTINŮ *Dead eyes*
Martinelli?
  BRUCKNER *Wild wie Bäche*
Martinez Sierra, Gregorio, 1881-1947.
  FALLA
    Canzon Andaluza: El pan de ronda
    Oración de las madres que tienen . . .
Le Martin-Pêcheur see Renard *HISTOIRES
  NATURELLES.* **RAVEL**
MARTINŮ, BOHUSLAV, 1890-1959.
  Aicard, Jean François Victor, 1848-
    1921.
    La poule a couvé (1929) [unpubl.]
    NB: Information about the unpublished
      songs is from Kenneth Thompson,

*Dictionary of Twentieth-century
  Composers (1911-1971).* (New
  York: St. Martin's Press, 1973).
Anon.
  Bohatá milá (1942) [Melantrich, 1948]
    "Dybych věděl já"
  Boží muka (1944) [Melantrich, 1948]
    "U Brněnské Boží moke"
  Děvče z Moravy (1944) [Melantrich,
    1948] "Přiletěl ptáček zcizí krajiny"
  The gnat's wedding (1912) [unpubl.]
  Hlásný (1944) [Melantrich, 1948]
    "Chodí hlásný po dědině"
  In the garden at the castle (1912)
    [unpubl.]
  Let there be light, O God (1912)
    [unpubl.]
  A love carol (1937) [Melantich; musical
    appendix to *Eva,* 1937, no. 3]
  Mother mine, I have a laddie (1913)
    [unpubl.]
  Naděje (1944) [Melantrich, 1948]
    "Hlavěnka mě bolí"
  Opuštěný milý (1942) [Melantrich, 1948]
    "Ach, vychodí, vychodí"
  Le petit oiseau (1913) [unpubl.]
  Prosba (1942) [Melantrich, 1948]
    "Dej mně, Bože, ten dar"
  Le sapin de Noel (1913) [unpubl.]
  Smutný milý (1942) [Melantrich, 1948]
    "Ej, smutno je mně, smutno"
  Le soir (1913) [unpubl.]
    Reciter & harp.
  Súsedova stajńa (1944) [Melantrich,
    1948] "U súseda nová stajńa"
  Tajná láska (1944) [Melantrich, 1948]
    "Chceme my se, chccmc"
  Touha (1932) [Supraphon, 1976]
  Touha (1942) [Mclantrich, 1948]
    "A já mám doma bratra rybáře"
  Ukolébavka (1932) [Supraphon, 1976]
  Veselá dievča (1942) [Melantrich, 1948]
    "Dybych já měla sukńu červenú"
  Vysoká veža (1942) [Melantrich,
    1948]"Aj, veža, veža"
  Zvědavá dievča (1942) [Melantrich,
    1948] "Dievča umíralo, ešte zavolalo"
  Zvolenovcí chlapci (1944) [Melantrich,
    1948] "Zvolenovcí hezcí chlapci"
Apollinaire, Guillaume, 1880-1918.
  La blanche neige (1930) [unpubl.]
  Saltimbanques (1930) [unpubl.]
    Text may be from Apollinaire's
      Alcools; cf. Honegger and Rivier
      settings.
  ALCOOLS.

MARTINŮ, BOHUSLAV, 1890-1959
(continued)
Apollinaire, Guillaume, 1880-1918
(continued)
ALCOOLS (continued)
L'adieu (1930) [unpubl.]
Borecký, Jaromír, 1869-1951.
I love old parks (1912) [unpubl.]
Červenka, Jan, 1861-1908.
Before you know (1910) [unpubl.]
DES KNABEN WUNDERHORN
Fourteen little angels (1916-18) [unpubl.]
Little red bootees (1916-18) [unpubl.]
My little angel (1916-18) [unpubl.]
Sleep, infant, sleep (1916-18) [unpubl.]
Thanks to God the Creator (1916-1918)
[unpubl.]
Dreman, J.
Bar (1918?) [Panton, 1966]
Text also by J. Herold.
Eben, Bedřich
Píseň na starošpanělský text (1914)
[Supraphon, 1973]
"Srdéčko mé, všechno spí"
Erben, Karel Jaromír, 1811-1870.
Easter (1933) [Musical appendix to
Lidove Noviny, April 16, 1933]
"God's blessing on this house, to God
we sing"
Falke, Gustav, 1853-1916.
To my child (1916-18) [unpubl.]
Gellner, František, 1881-1914.
Miners' song (1918?) [Panton, 1966]
Goethe, Johann Wolfgang von, 1749-
1832.
Glückliche Fahrt (1914-15) [unpubl.]
"Die Nebel zerreisen"
Liebesglück (1914-15) [unpubl.]
"Bleibe, bleibe bei mir"
ELFENLIED.
Elfenliedchen (1914-15) [unpubl.]
"Um Mitternacht"
Gramont, T. de
Le poulet (1929) [unpubl.]
Grossmanová-Brodská, Ludmila,
1859-
The jilted maiden (1912) [unpubl.]
Once upon a time (1912) [unpubl.]
Hafiz, Muhammad Shums al-Din,
d.1388.
A long pilgrimage (1917-18) [unpubl.]
Restored to health (1917-18) [unpubl.]
Sweet death (1917-18) [unpubl.]
Hálek, Vitezslav, 1835-1874.
In nature (1910) [unpubl.]
Heine, Heinrich, 1797-1856.

Hoar-frost fallen in the field (1912)
[unpubl.]
I see you every night, my dear (1912)
[unpubl.]
Herold, Jíří, 1875-1934.
Summer ballad (1918?) [Panton, 1966]
Heyduk, Adolf, 1835-1923.
A winter's night (1910) [unpubl.]
You write to me (1912) [unpubl.]
Hlavsa, Vrat.
The fiery man (1912) [unpubl.]
Song of the First of November (1912)
[unpubl.]
Three maidens on a bright night (1912)
[unpubl.]
Houdek, V.
Why have you laughed at me? (1910)
[unpubl.]
Huch, Ricarda Octavia, 1864-1947.
Maiden's dreams (1910) [unpubl.]
Jesenská, Ružena, 1863-1940.
Where have I been? (1910) [unpubl.]
Where was I? (1912) [unpubl.]
Kalhus
Song of Hanička (1912) [unpubl.]
Kaminský, Bohdan, 1859-1929.
Pastel (1910) [unpubl.]
Klášterský, Antonín, 1866-1938.
Nokturno (1910) [unpubl.]
When we are old (1910) [unpubl.]
Klen, V.
Picture of a mood (1910) [unpubl.]
Liliencron, Detlov, Freiherr von, 1844-
1909.
Enough of happiness (1912) [unpubl.]
From childhood (1912) [unpubl.]
The spinning top's lullaby (1916-18)
[unpubl.]
Manin, J.
Pověra (1910) [unpubl.]
We erred in the morning (1911) [unpubl.]
Manin, P.
Kiss, my sweetheart, kiss (1910) [unpubl.]
Martínek, Vojtěch, 1887-1960.
Dead eyes (1912) [unpubl.]
Mayer, Rudolf, 1837-1865, supposed
author.
At night (1910) [unpubl.]
Moore, G.
Evening (1917) [unpubl.]
Musset, Alfred de, 1810-1857.
Lucie (1912) [unpubl.]
Mužik, August Eugen, 1859-1925.
Dead love (1912) [unpubl.]
The end of all (1912) [unpubl.]
First love (1911) [unpubl.]

The right number (1911) [unpubl.] "As I
  walked with my love, one evening"
The rose (1912) [unpubl.]
Song (1911) [unpubl.]
Nebesky, Jan, b. 1880
  The swan (1912) [unpubl.]
No author
  Vocalise-étude (1930) [Leduc, 1930]
    Wordless. Also for violin & piano or
    cello & piano as "Ariette."
Poe, Edgar Allan, 1809-1849.
  The sleeper (1910) [unpubl.]
Raabe, Wilhelm Karl, 1831-1910.
  Sleep, my little one (1916-18) [unpubl.]
Sládek, Josef Václav, 1845-1912.
  All this is what only remains (1912)
    [unpubl.]
  Dívčí píseň (1910) [unpubl.]
  The drowned maiden (1910) [unpubl.]
  A maiden's song (1911) [unpubl.]
  Mother dear (1911) [unpubl.]
  Tears (1911) [unpubl.]
  When the day comes (1911) [unpubl.]
Tetmajer, Kazimierz, 1865-1940.
  Jašek's song (1911) [unpubl.]
  Marry me, mother, as long as I'm young
    (1912) [unpubl.]
  Speak on! (1912) [unpubl.]
Toman, Karel, 1877-1946.
  DIE MONATE: Januar.
    On snow-swept paths (1922) [unpubl.]
  DIE MONATE: September.
    My brother has finished ploughing
      (1922) [unpubl.]
Uhland, Ludwig, 1787-1862.
  A shepherd's Sunday song (1917)
    [unpubl.]
Unknown
  Cesta k milé (1943) [Melantrich, 1948]
    "Aj! Stupaj, stupaj, stupaj"
  Chodníček (1943) [Melantrich, 1948]
    "Pujdeme, pujdeme"
  Early in the morning I weed the grain
    (1912) [unpubl.]
  Otevření slovečkem (1943) [Melantrich,
    1948] "Zamykaj, maměnko, zamykaj"
  Rosička (1943) [Melantrich, 1948]
    "Slunéčko zachodí za les javorový"
  Rozmarýn (1943) [Melantrich, 1948]
    "Pod našima oknama"
  Sen Panny Marie (1943) [Melantrich,
    1948] "Usnula, usnula, ja"
  Thou, who dwellest in Heaven (1922)
    [unpubl.]
  U maměnky (1943) [Melantrich, 1948]
    "Dyž sem u maměnky byla"

Villiers de l'Isle-Adam, Jean Marie
  Mathias . . . , comte de, 1838-1889.
  Old song (1912) [unpubl.]
Xaurof, L
  Le petit chat (1929) [unpubl.]
Mary Lee, Lady Chudleigh *see*
  Chudleigh, Mary (Lee), lady, 1656-
  1710.
Mary, Queen of Scots, 1542-1568.
  SCHUMANN
    Abschied von der Welt
    Abschied von Frankreich
    An die Königin Elisabeth
    Gebet
    Nach der Geburt ihres Sohnes
"Mary that was the Child's mother" *see*
  The frostbound wood Blunt **HESELTINE**
"Más quiero yoa Peribá Nez con su capa la
  pardilla queal" *see Romance del
  comendador de ocaña* Vega Carpio
  RODRIGO
Masefield, John, 1878-1967.
  GRIFFES *An old song re-sung*
  IRELAND
    The Bells of San Marie
    Sea fever
    Vagabond
    BALLADS AND POEMS (1903).
      HESELTINE *Captain Stratton's fancy*
    SALT WATER BALLADS.
      GRIFFES *Sorrow of Mydath*
"A mask, a perpetual natural disguiser of
  herself" *see Visored* Whitman **LUENING**
Mass for solo voice see Anon. **THOMSON**
MASSENET, JULES, 1842-1912.
  Aicard, Jean François Victor, 1848-
  1921.
    Chant de nourrice (1905) [Heugel, 1905]
      "Dors, mon petit enfant, dors"
    Loin de moi ta lèvre qui ment (ca.1888)
      [Heugel] same
    Le Noël des humbles (1908) [Heugel,
      1908] "L'enfant est nu, Tout en peuple
      est venu"
  Akhtamar, Grégoire d'
    Ivre d'amour (1906) [Heugel, 1906]
      "Je suis ivre, je suis ivre, ivre
      d'amour"
  Alexandre, André
    Amours bénis (1899) [Heugel]
      "Une aube fraîche . . . et printanière"
    Extase printanière (1902) [Heugel, 1902]
      "O je t'implore à genoux!"
    La mélodie des baisers [G. Astruc
      (Editions de la Societé musicale)]
      "Toujours les lilas fleuriront"

MASSENET, JULES, 1842-1912 *(continued)*
  Alexandre, André *(continued)*
    Mousmé (1901) [Heugel, 1901]
      "Au jardin de ma fantaisie"
  Allievo, Biago
    L'hymne des fleurs (1907) [Heugel]
  Allorge, Henri
    Effusion [Heugel, 1912]
  Anon.
    Mélancolie (1913) [Heugel, 1913]
      "Sur les flots de la vie"
    Poésie de Mytis [*Musica* no. 120, Sept.
      1912 (Paris: P.Lafitte); Heugel]
      "Lorsque nous sermons seuls"
    Le poète et le fantôme (1891) [Heugel,
      1891] "Qui donc es-tu, forme légère"
    Sévillana (1895) [Heugel]
      "A Séville, belles Señoras"
      Text adapted by Jules Ruelle.
  Autran, Joseph Antoine, 1813-1877.
    Les Alcyons (1887) [G. Hartmann;
      Heugel]
      "Vos destins sont pour l'homme"
  Barbier, Marie Anne, d. 1742.
    L'ange et l'enfant (1899) [Heugel]
      "L'ange Amabed a cueilli des roses"
  Bazan, Noël
    Les mains (1899) [Heugel]
      "Lorsque je regarde mes mains"
  Beissier, Fernand, 1858-1936.
    Petite mireille (1899) [Heugel, 1899]
      "Lorsque vous dormez, petite Mireille"
  Biron, Armand de Gontaut, baron de
    La dernière lettre de Werther à Charlotte
      (1913) [Heugel, 1913]
      "Il faut nous séparer . . . "
  Blanchecotte, Augustine-Malvina,
    1830-before 1895.
    Non, tu n'as pas fini d'aimer (1871) [G.
      Hartmann] same
  Bordèse, Stéphan, b. 1847.
    Jour de noces (1886) [G. Hartmann;
      Heugel]
      "Il fait beau, le ciel nous protège"
    La neige (1891) [A. Durand]
    Le sais-tu? (1880) [G. Hartmann]
      "N'as-tu pas vu l'hirondelle"
  Bourguignat, Paul
    Où que s'envole (1884) [unpubl.?]
    Pour Antoinette (1899) [Heugel]
      "Quand je m'en vais par les sentiers"
    Vous qui passez (1899) [Heugel]
      "O vous qui passez solitaire"
  Boyer, Georges, 1850-1931.
    En chantant (1906) [Heugel, 1906]
      "Dans la familiale demeure"
    Les enfants (1881) [G. Hartmann;
      Heugel]
      "On ne devrait faire aux enfants"
      Also voice & orchestra.
    Les mères (1891) [A. Quinzard, 1892]
      "Celle qui devient mère"
    Les mères (2nd version, 1901) [unpubl.?]
      "Celle qui devient mère"
      Manuscript in the Bibliothèque
      nationale, Paris.
    Le pauv' petit (1903) [Heugel, 1903;
      Supplément au *Ménestrel,* 2/7/04]
      "Il était un petit enfant"
    Le petit Jésus (1899) [Heugel]
      "Le petit Jésus, en habits de neige"
      Also voice & orchestra.
    Royauté (1889) [G. Hartmann]
      "Le poète est roi"
    Si tu veux, Mignonne (1876) [G.
      Hartmann; Heugel] same
    Souvenez-vous, Vierge Marie! [G.
      Schirmer, 1888] same
  Bozzani, Suzanne
    Je t'aime (1893) [Heugel, 1893]
      "J'ai cherché dans mon coeur"
      Also voice & orchestra.
  Bricourt, Louis
    Fleurs cueillies (1888) [A. Klein, 1888]
  Bruno, Camille
    La rivière (1900) [Heugel, 1900]
      "La rivière chantait ainsi"
      Also voice & orchestra.
    Tes cheveux (1905) [Heugel, 1905]
      "Tels que des brins de paille fine"
    Tout passé (1909) [Heugel, 1909]
      "Les plus ardentes amours"
  Buchillot, G.
    Oh! si les fleurs avaient des yeux (1903)
      [Heugel, 1903] same
    Les yeux clos (1905) [Heugel, 1905]
      "Quand tes yeux clos ne verront plus"
  Carré, Michel, 1819-1872.
    Chant provençal (1871) [G. Hartmann;
      Heugel] "Mireille ne sait pas encore"
    Néère [G. Schirmer, 1888]
      "Au détour du chemin"
      Extrait des *Erynnies*.
  Carrier, P.
    Tristesse (1894) [Heugel, 1894] "Marcher
      dans un sentier de pierres et de roses"
  Cazalis, Henri, 1840-1909.
    La chanson des lèvres (1897) [Heugel,
      1897] "Lèvres, Ô mères du baiser"
  Chabroux, Ernest
    L'heure douce (1907) [Heugel, 1907]
      "Ainsi qu'un fier guerrier"

Chaffotte, Jeanne
Le printemps visite la terre (1901)
[Heugel, 1901] same

Champsaur, Félicien, 1859-1934.
Chanson juanesque (1905) [Heugel,
1905] "Toujours! Et, demain, plus
jamais!"

Chantepie, J
Dors, ami [G. Hartmann] "Dors, ami,
dors et que les songes"
Not in Noske or *New Grove* lists.

Chassang, Maurice
Et puis (1905) [Heugel, 1905]
"Vous aurez la fleur d'oranger"

Choudens, Paul de, 1850-1925.
Le sentier perdu (1877) [G. Hartmann;
Heugel] "J'ai voulu le revoir"

Chouquet, Gustave, 1819-1886.
À Mignonne (1869) [G. Hartmann, 1869;
Heugel] "Pour qui sera, Mignonne"
Ballade de David Rizzio (1863) [Heugel,
1899]
Berceuse (1869) [G. Hartmann, 1869;
Heugel] "Enfant rose, Fleur éclose"
Déclaration (1866) [G. Hartmann;
Heugel] "Je crains tes baisers"

Collin, Paul Adrien François, b. 1845-
1915.
Automne (1876) [G. Hartmann, 1882;
Heugel]
"Profitons bien des jours d'Octobre"
Les marronniers (1876) [G. Hartmann,
1882; Heugel] "Hélas! les marronniers
qui bordent les allées"
Narcisse à la fontaine [G. Schirmer,
1888] "Enfin, elles s'en vont"
Pareils à des oiseaux (1876) [G.
Hartmann, 1882; Heugel] same
Prelude (1876) [G. Hartmann, 1882;
Heugel] "Qu'il est doux d'éveiller
lentement les pensées"
Qu'importe que l'hiver (1876) [G.
Hartmann, 1882; Heugel] same
Roses d'Octobre (1876) [G. Hartmann,
1882; Heugel]
"Belles frileuses qui sont nées"

Coppée, François Édouard Joachim,
1842-1908.
Sérénade de Zanetto (1869) [G.
Hartmann] "Mignonne, voici l'Avril!"
Also voice & orchestra.

Croze, J. L.
À deux pleurer! (1897) [Heugel, 1899]
"Comme vous dormiez, je n'ai pas
osé"

Delair, Paul, 1842-1894.
L'âme des fleurs (1891) [A. Quinzard]
"Gardez les fleurs que je vous ai
données"
Also in *L'Illustration. Supplément-
musical,* 1905 no. 5, pp. 37-39.

Demouth, Paul
Les âmes (1898) [Heugel]
"Dites-moi ce que sont les âmes"
Le nid (1898) [Heugel]
"Si j'étais le bon Dieu qui donne"

Desachy, Paul, 1872-1906.
Hymne d'amour (1895) [Heugel]
"Comme un lierre grimpant"

Dessirier, Annie
Les extases (1912) [Heugel, 1912]
"Des chants, des fleurs et du soleil"
Authorship of text on music: Annie
Dessirier (Jean du Clos), as though a
pseudonym.

Distel, Camille
Les bois de pins (1868) [Durand, 1906]
"L'ombre descend de leurs rameaux"
Op. 2 no. 2.
Bonne nuit (1868) [Durand, 1913]
"La terre dort au ciel pur"
Op. 2 no. 1.
Le verger (1868) [Durand, 1906]
"Oh! combien j'aime le verger"
Op. 2 no. 3.

Dortzal, Jeanne, 1878-
Battements d'ailes (1913) [Heugel, 1913]
"Les soirs d'été si doux"
Comme autrefois (1913) [Heugel, 1913]
"J'ai revê-tu, ce soir"
Nocturne (1913) [Heugel, 1913]
"Il est minuit"
Parfums [Heugel, 1914] "Mon coeur
d'enfant était un paradis"

Dubor, Georges de, b. 1848
Amoureux appel (1900) [Heugel, 1900]
"Viena, Ô le désiré"

Duer, Caroline King, b. 1865
Au très aimé (1900) [Heugel]

Duverne, Anne Girard
Si tu m'aimes [Heugel]

Faure, Maurice Louis Émile, 1850-
1919.
La mort de la cigale (1911) [Heugel,
1911] "Quand les blonds èpis mûrs
ondoyant dans la plaine"

Feillet, Émilie
Ton souvenir (1909) [Heugel, 1909]
"Mon coeur n'est pas déposé de"

Ferrand, François
Avril est là! (1899) [Heugel] same

Fleury-Daunizeau, Georges
Dites-lui que je l'aime (1910) [Heugel,
1910] "Dites-lui que les fleurs ont
ouvert leur calice"

MASSENET, JULES, 1842-1912 (*continued*)

Florian, Jean Pierre Claris de, 1755-1794.
  Musette (1872) [G. Hartmann, ca.1873; Heugel] "L' autre jour, sous l'ombrage"
    Also voice & orchestra.

France, Anatole, 1844-1924.
  Âmes obscures [Heugel, 1912] "Tout, dans l'immuable nature"

Fuster, Charles, 1866-1929.
  Passionnément (1899) [Heugel, 1899] "Tout recevoir de toi me charme"

Gallet, Louis, 1835-1898.
  À Colombine (1872) [G. Hartmann; Heugel] "Colombine charmante"
  Chanson de Capri (1872) [G. Hartmann; Heugel]
    "Connaissez-vous qui m'a charmé?"
  Elégie (between 1866 and 1872) [E. & A. Girod; G. Hartmann; Heugel] "Ô doux printemps d'autrefois"
  Les femmes de Magdala [G. Hartmann; Heugel] "Le soleil effleure la plaine"
  Nuit d'Espagne (1872) [G. Hartmann; Heugel] "L'air est embaumé"

Gassier, Alfred, 1849-1907.
  Éveil (1906) [Heugel, 1906] "La vierge étoile est effacée"

Gautier, Théophile, 1811-1872.
  L'esclave (1868) [E. & A. Girod, 1868] "Captive et peut-être oubliée"
    Op. 12 no. 1.

Gibout, Henri
  Berceuse (1896) [Heugel, 1896] "Ton rêve est plain de chases folles"

Gilbert, Laurent, 1751-1780.
  Stances (between 1866-1872) [G. Hartmann; Heugel] "Au banquet de la vie"

Gille, Philippe Emile François, 1831-1901.
  Printemps dernier (1884) [G. Hartmann; Heugel] "Vous en souvient-il, Madeleine"

Gillouin, Adrien, 1861-
  C'est le printemps (1906) [Heugel, 1906] "L'azur sourit; le vent tiédit"

Girard, Marguerite
  Eternité (1899) [Béziers, 1899] "L'éternité! je l'ai comprise"

Grain, Madeleine
  Dieu créa le désert (1910) [Heugel, 1910] same
  Feux follets d'amour (1913) [Heugel, 1913]
    "Mes soeurs! dans cette nuit d'étoiles"

Gravollet, Paul
  Ma petite mère a pleuré [Hamelle, 1902; Heugel, 1903]

Grieumard, Édouard
  Ce sont les petits que je veux chanter (1899) [Heugel] same

Gruaz, Julien
  Avec toi (1902) [Heugel, 1902] "Avec toi courir dans les plaines"
  Rondel de la belle au bois (1900) [Heugel, 1900] "Ouvrez vos tendres yeux la belle au bois dormant"

Guérin-Catelin, Émile-Jean, 1856-after 1905.
  Départ (1893) [Heugel, 1893] "Puisque pour moi le temps a sonné"
    Also voice & orchestra.

Halmont, Jacques d'
  Avril est amoureux (1900) [Heugel, 1900] "Avril dort sous la lune blanche"
    Also voice & orchestra.

Hardÿ de Périni, Édouard, 1843-1908.
  La légende du baiser (1903) [Heugel, 1903; Supplément au **Ménestrel** 12/11/04] "Un jour de fête au Paradis"

Hasselt, André Henri Constant van, 1806-1874.
  Sur une poésie de Van Hasselt (1902) [Heugel, 1902] "L'azur si pur des cieux joyeux ruisselle"

Henri IV, king of France, 1553-1610.
  L'heureuse souffrance (1902) [Heugel, 1902] "Coeur, va vite, pauvre coeur"

Hirsch, Gaston, b. 1830.
  Au delà du rêve (1903) [Heugel, 1903] "Où n'atteindrai-je pas?"

Hugo, Victor Marie, comte, 1802-1885.
  C'est l'amour (1908) [Heugel, 1908] "Oh oui! la terre est belle"
  Être aimé (1893) [Heugel, 1893] same
  Guitare (1886) [G. Hartmann; Heugel] "Comment, disaient-ils"
  Nouvelle chanson sur un vieil air (1869) [unpubl.?]
  La nuit [Heugel, 1914] "Parfois, lorsque tout dort"
  Soleil couchant [Heugel]

Jacquet, Mme. M.
  Heure vécue [Heugel]

Jannet, Victor
  Le coffret d'ébène [Heugel, 1914] "J'ai mis dans un coffret d'ébène"

Lafait-Gontié, Antoinette
  Voix suprême [Heugel]

Laroche, Ernest
Mienne! (1894) [Heugel, 1894]
"De ce soir, je serai joyeux"
Le Barillier, Mme. Berthe, 1868-1927.
Dans le sentier, parmi les roses (1891)
[Heugel] same
Le Moyne, Paul, 1663-1704.
Vers Béthléem (1903) [Heugel, 1903;
Supplément au *Ménestrel* 3/20/04]
"Ils cheminent depuis longtemps"
Lebey, André, 1877-1938.
En même temps que ton amour (1902)
[Heugel, 1902] same
Jamais un tel bonheur (1902) [Heugel,
1902] same
Quand nous nous sommes vus (1902)
[Heugel, 1902] same
Lefèbvre, Louis, 1871-1947.
La dernière chanson (1898) [Heugel,
1908] "Si désormais vivre ensemble"
Léna, Maurice, d. 1928.
Fourvières (1893) [Heugel, 1896]
"Dans la brume rêveuse où dort"
Louvencourt, Comtesse Maurice Roch
de
Les nuages (1913) [Heugel, 1913]
"Les voyez-vous passer"
Ludana
Menteuse chérie [Heugel, 1912]
"Menteuse chérie, lorsque tu màs dit"
Orphelines (1906) [Heugel, 1906]
"Elles marchent deux par deux"
Si vous vouliez bien me le dire (1907)
[Heugel, 1907] same
Lugnier, Antonin
Soir de rêve [Heugel, 1914]
"Au bosquet de ta lèvre"
Macdonald, Jacques Etienne Joseph
Alexandre, duc de Tarente, 1765-
1840.
Les amoureuses sont des folles (1902)
[Heugel, 1902] same
Maigret, Henri
Chanson pour elle (1897) [Heugel]
"Pour toi, j'écris cette chanson"
Mansilla, Daniel Garcia, 1838-1892
Si tu l'oses (1897) [Heugel, 1897]
"Viens plus près, tout près t'asseoir"
Manuel, Eugène, 1823-1901.
Quand on aime (1887) [G. Hartmann;
Heugel] same
Sérénade (1886) [unpubl.]
"Quand on aime, on ete tout léger!"
Facsimile of 1st page of the holograph
in L. Schneider *Massenet* (Paris:
1908), p. 357.

Maquet, Thérèse
Beaux yeux que j'aime (1891) [Heugel,
1891] "Il est des étoiles aux cieux"
Les belles de nuit (1887) [Heugel]
"Joyeux et clair, le soleil luit"
Mariéton, Paul, 1862-1911.
Ne donne pas ton coeur (1892) [Heugel,
1892] same
Séparation (1886) [Heugel]
"Puisque tu ne veux pas m'attendre"
Souvenance (1897) [Heugel] "J'ai vu tous
les yeux qu'on aime en ce monde"
Martin, Gabriel, b. 1862
Soir de printemps (1894) [Heugel, 1894]
"Douce! Faut-il t'aimer, te chanter tour
à tour?"
Maupassant, Guy de, 1850-1893.
Je cours après le bonheur (ca.1888)
[Heugel] same
Maurer, Théodore, b. 1844, supposed
author.
En voyage (1913) [Heugel, 1913]
"Où donc allez-vous, Madame"
Je m'en suis allé vers l'amour (1902)
[Heugel, 1902]
"Pleins d'un concert de fraîches voix"
Max, Paul
Toujours (1910) [Heugel, 1910]
"Les fleurs passent au gré du temps"
Mendès, Catulle Abraham, 1841-1909.
L'heure volée (1902) [Heugel, 1902]
"Sonneur qui sonnes l'heure et
l'heure"
Mendès, Jane (Primitive-Mette)
Catulle, d. 1955.
La lettre (1907) [Heugel, 1907]
"Je mets sur le papier luisant"
Molière, Jean Baptiste Poquelin,
1622-1673.
Sérénade de Molière [G. Schirmer, 1888]
"C'est un amant"
Monrousseau, Lucien
Rien ne passe (1911) [Heugel, 1911]
same
Morel-Retz, Louis Pierre Gabriel
Bernard, 1825-1899.
Amoureuse (1898) [Heugel, 1898]
"Tu voudrais lire dans mon âme"
L'éventail [Heugel, 1892]
"Aimable bijou de famille"
Musset, Alfred de, 1810-1857.
Souvenir de Venise (1865) [G. Hartmann;
Heugel] "A Saint Blaise à la Zuecca
vous étiez"
Also for 2 sopranos under title *À la
Zuecca.*

MASSENET, JULES, 1842-1912 (*continued*)
Nekrasov, Nikolaiï Aleksyeyevich, 1821-1877.
  Larmes maternelles (1893) [Heugel]
    "La guerre a fait une victime!"
    Also voice & orchestra.
Noël, Édouard
  Ave Margarita (prière d'amour, 1902) [Heugel, 1902]
    "Je te salue, Ô Marguerite"
  La gavotte de Puyjoli (1909) [Heugel, 1909] "La marquise a dit: 'Mon beau Puyjoli' "
Normand, Jacques Clary Jean, 1848-1931.
  Les oiselets (1877) [G. Hartmann; Heugel] "Sous le brouillard léger"
  Pitchounette (1897) [Heugel, 1897]
    "Pitchounette, entends-tu pas"
    Also voice & orchestra.
  Première danse (1899) [Heugel, 1899]
    "Des bons vieux airs très connus"
    Also voice & orchestra.
  Souhait (1880) [G. Hartmann; Heugel]
    "Si vous étiez fleur"
  Vieilles lettres (1898) [Heugel]
    "Quand chauffant nos pieds aux tisons"
Olga de Sarmento
  Jamais plus [Heugel]
Pélissier, Léon G.
  Regard d'enfant (1898) [Heugel]
    "Petit enfant, fragile et beau"
Peyre, Mathylde
  Rêverie sentimentale (1910) [Heugel, 1910] "Ce soir, mon bien aimé"
Picard, Hélène
  Dormons parmi les lis (1908) [Heugel, 1908] "C'est toi qui me diras les saisons infinies"
Pierre d'Amor
  Voix de femmes (1901) [Heugel, 1901]
    "Voix des mamans, voix câlineuses"
Poirson, S. Cuthbert
  Rose de Mai (1913) [Heugel, 1913] "Ce n'est pas ta beauté qui m'attire . . . "
Postel, Madeleine
  L'amour pleure [Heugel, 1912]
    "Le pauvre amour est tout en larmes"
Pradel, Georges
  Sonnet (1869) [G. Hartmann; Heugel]
    "Les grands bois s'éveillaient"
Prévost, Gabriel
  Aubade (1877) [G. Hartmann; Heugel]
    "Le jour paraît à l'horizon"

Princet, Jules
  L'oiseau de paradis [Heugel, 1913]
    "Sur les routes de l'infini"
Robiquet, Paul Pierre, 1848-1928.
  Je me suis plaint aux tourterelles (1878-79) [G. Hartmann; Heugel] same
  La nuit sans doute était trop belle (1878-79) [G. Hartmann; Heugel] same
  Oh! ne finis jamais (1878-79) [G. Hartmann; Heugel] same
    2 voices & piano.
  Ouvre tes yeux bleus (1878-79) [G. Hartmann; Heugel] same
    2 voices & piano; also with orchestra.
  Pourquoi pleures-tu? (1878-79) [G. Hartmann; Heugel] same
  Puisqu'elle a pris ma vie (1878-79) [G. Hartmann; Heugel] same
Rocha, Lucien
  Aube païenne [Heugel, 1914]
    "Quand de mon tertre en fleur"
Ronsard, Pierre de, 1524-1585.
  Portret d'un enfant (1868) [Girod, 1868]
    "Quand je voy tant de couleurs"
    Op. 12 no. 4.
Roux, Jean
  On dit! (1901) [Heugel, 1901] "On dit . . . , on dit beaucoup de choses . . ."
Ruelle, Jules, d. 1892.
  Enchantement! (1890) [G. Hartmann; Heugel] "Comme un rayon qui luit"
  Sérénade aux mariés (1868) [Girod, 1868] "Voici l'heure du mystère"
    Op. 12 no. 2.
  La vie d'une rose (1868) [Girod, 1868]
    "Par un beau matin Pimpante et ravie"
    Op. 12 no. 3.
Saix, Guillot de
  La verdadera vida [Heugel, 1933; Supplément au **Ménestrel** 10/19/34]
    "La la la! La vie a mal guidé mes pas"
Schneider, Louis, 1861-1934.
  Noël des fleurs [Heugel, 1912] "Il pleut des iris, des jasmins, des roses"
Silvestre, Paul Armond, 1837-1901.
  Un adieu (between 1866-1872) [G. Hartmann; Heugel]
    "Sur ta bouche avec le désir"
  Adieux à la prairie (1872) [G. Hartmann, ca.1873; Heugel]
    "Adieu! Adieu! bergère chérie"
    With 3-part chorus; also orchestrated.
  L'air du soir emportait (1868) [G. Hartmann; Heugel] same
  Anniversaire (1880) [Heugel; G. Schirmer, 1888] "Le poète dort"

Aurore (1872) [G. Hartmann, ca.1873; Heugel] "Cocorico, le coq chante"
Also voice & orchestra.
C'est au temps de la Chrysantheme (1882) [G. Hartmann; Heugel] same
Crépuscule (1872) [G. Hartmann, ca.1873; Heugel]
"Comme un rideau sous la blancheur"
Also voice & orchestra.
Dans l'air plein de fils de soie (1868) [G. Hartmann; Heugel] same
Dors, Magda (1905) [Heugel, 1905]
"Dors, Magda, si blanche et si rose"
Epitaphe (1868) [G. Hartmann; Heugel]
"Souvenir éternel, regret inconsolé"
Il pleuvait (1871) [G. Hartmann; Heugel] same
Je ne sais pas t'aimer (1882) [G. Hartmann; Heugel] "Tu l'as bien dit: Je ne sais pas t'aimer!"
Lève-toi, lève-toi (1868) [G. Hartmann; Heugel] same
Madrigal (between 1866 and 1872) [G. Hartmann; Heugel]
"Le soir frissonne au coeur des roses"
La marchande des rêves (1905) [Heugel, 1905]
"Pour faire mes heures plus brèves"
Marquise (1888) [G. Hartmann; Heugel]
"Vous en souvenez-vous, Marquise?"
Mon amour l'a bien mérité (1882) [G. Hartmann; Heugel]
"Ah! du moins, pour toi je veux être"
Mon coeur est plein de toi (1882) [G. Hartmann; Heugel] same
Noël (1882) [G. Hartmann; Heugel]
"Noël! En voyant dans ses langes"
Noël païen (between 1866 and 1872) [G. Hartmann; Heugel] "Noël! Noël!"
Pastorale (1872) [G. Hartmann, ca.1873; Heugel]
"Voici venir le doux printemps"
With 3-part chorus; also orchestrated.
Paysage (1872) [G. Hartmann, ca.1873; Heugel]
"Arbre charmant qui me rappelle"
Also voice & orchestra.
Pensée d'automne (1888) [G. Hartmann; Heugel] "L'An fuit vers son déclin"
Also voice & orchestra.
Pensée de printemps (1893) [Heugel]
"C'est l'espoir des beaux jours qui luit dans le ciel bleu"
Also voice & orchestra.
Pour qu'à l'Espérance il ne céde (1868) [G. Hartmann; Heugel] same

Rien n'est que de France [C. Delagrave, 1891]
"Où sont, sous les matins en pleurs"
Facsimile of holograph printed after p. 176 of Silvestre's *Floréal*.
Sonnet païen (between 1866-1872) [G. Hartmann; Heugel]
"Rosa, Rosa, l'air est plus deux"
Un souffle de parfums s'élève (1868) [G. Hartmann; Heugel] same
Sous les branches (1868) [G. Hartmann; Heugel] "En Avril sous les branches"
MIGNONNE.
Complainte (1866) [G. Hartmann, ca.1891]
"Je pars! Adieu ma chere âme"
Prélude (1866) [G. Hartmann, ca.1891]
Text printed, no singing.
Que l'heure est donc brève (1866) [G. Hartmann, ca.1891] same
Riez-vous? (1866) [G. Hartmann, ca.1891]
Text printed, no singing.
Sonnet matinal (1866) [G. Hartmann, ca.1891] "Les étoiles effarouchées"
Sur la source (1866) [G. Hartmann, ca.1891] same
Voici que les grand lys (1866) [G. Hartmann, ca.1891] same
Vous aimerez demain (1866) [G. Hartmann, ca.1891] "Le doux printemps a bu dans le creux"
Simoni, H. Ernest
Coupe d'ivresse (1899) [Heugel]
"Jusqu'à ta bouche, j'ai levé"
Solvay, Lucien
Elle s'en est allée (1895) [Heugel, 1895]
"Là-bas, là-bas"
Stuart, Paul
Retour d'oiseau [Heugel, 1911]
"La forêt semble tout en fête"
Sylvestre, Pierre
Sainte Thérèse prie (1902) [Heugel, 1902] "Je le possède, il m'aime"
Also voice & orchestra.
Tennyson, Alfred Tennyson, 1st baron, 1809-1892.
Come into the garden, Maud [London: C. Kegan Paul, 1880] same
In *Songs from the published writings of Alfred Tennyson . . . set to music by various composers,* ed. by W. G. Cusius, p. 323.
Teulet, Edmond
Chanson désespérée (1905) [Heugel, 1910] "Si je pouvais chanter encore"

MASSENET, JULES, 1842-1912 *(continued)*
Theuriet, André, 1833-1907.
  La veillée du petit Jésus (1876) [G.
    Hartmann; Heugel]
    "Il est minuit l'étable est sombre"
    Also in Supplément au *Ménestrel*,
    Dec. 24, 1926.
Théus, Maurice de
  Mon page (1900) [Heugel, 1900]
    "J'ai pour page un bel escholier"
Troillet, Émile
  Devant l'infini (ca.1892) [Heugel]
    "Les feuilles dans les airs"
  Soeur d'élection (1900) [Heugel, 1900]
    "O ma soeur d'idéal"
    Also voice & orchestra under the title
    Cantique.
Unknown
  Chanson andalouse (1891) [Heugel,
    1891] "Pourquoi chanter l'amoureuse
    ivresse?"
    Words adapted by Jules Ruelle.
Văcărescu, Elena, 1868-1947.
  L'âme oiseaux (1895) [Heugel]
    "Le printemps a jeté sa lyre"
  Chant de guerre cosaque (1893) [Heugel]
    "Vierge, tes cheveux noirs dépassent ta
    ceinture"
  Plus vite (1892) [Heugel, 1892]
    "Lorsque le vent du soir l'agite"
  Septembre (1891) [Heugel, 1891]
    "Que les premiers jours de Septembre"
Valendre, Marie de
  Premiers fils d'argent (1897) [Heugel]
    "Le soir, quand pour dormir"
Van Ormelingen, Georges, 1865-1906.
  GLOSES ORPHIQUES.
  Antienne (1895) [Heugel, 1895]
    "Tes yeux aux leurs fières"
  Defuncta nascuntur (1895) [Heugel,
    1895] "Les roses se sont refermées"
  Fleuramye (1895) [Heugel, 1895]
    "J'ai bu tout le printemps sur la
    fleur de ton rire"
Varenne, Marc
  Dialogue [Heugel, 1913]
    "Pourquoi donc ne distu plus rien?"
Vingtrie, Jean de
  Ce que disent les cloches (1900) [Heugel,
    1900]
    "Les cloches tintent dans l'air triste"
Zaffira, Giuseppe
  L'improvisatore (1864) [G. Hartmann;
    Heugel] "Vois-tu là-bas sur le chemin"
The masses see Ives **IVES** *The majority*

"Les masses noires des arbes ne bougent pas"
  see Hymne à la nuit Louÿs **KOECHLIN**
"The masses! The masses!" *see The majority*
  Ives **IVES**
"Måste jag döma den, mig svek" *see En runa*
  Ullman **KILPINEN**
Mastitĭye, vetvistĭye, dubĭ see Maĭkov
  PROKOFIEV
"M'as-tu connu marchand d'journaux à
  Barbès" *see Vous n'écrivez plus?* Jacob,
  M. **POULENC**
"Un mât invisible couronné de ciel" *see*
  Jeunesse Anon. **MILHAUD**
Les matelots see Gautier **FAURÉ**
Matičko má, hocha mám see Anon.
  MARTINŮ *Mother mine, I have a laddie*
Le matin see Banville **KOECHLIN**
Le matin see Bouclon **BERLIOZ**
Le matin see Hugo **SAINT-SAËNS**
Le matin les branches attisent see Éluard
  POULENC
MATTHEW 6: 9-13. see Bible
  The Lord's prayer **ROREM**
MATTHEW 27: 62-66; 28. see Bible
  The resurrection **ROREM**
"Matthew, Mark, Luke and John" *see*
  Before sleeping Anon. **THOMSON**
Matthisson, Friedrich von, 1761-1831.
  BEETHOVEN
    Adelaide
    An Laura
    Andenken
    Opferlied
  GLUCK *Siegsgesang für Freie*
  LOEWE *Die Elfenkönigin*
  SCHUBERT
    Der Abend
    Adelaide
    An Laura
    Andenken
    Die Betende
    Entzückung
    Geist der Liebe
    Geisternähe
    Der Geistertanz
      Two settings: D. 15 and D. 116.
    Julius an Theone
    Klage
    Lebenslied
    Lied aus der Ferne
    Lied der Liebe
    Naturgenuss
    Die Schatten
    Skolie
    Die Sterbende
    Totenkranz für ein Kind
    Trost an Elisa

WEBER
  Ich denke dein
  Die Kerze
WOLF *Andenken*
ZELTER
  Adelaide
  Beruhigung
  Die Betende
  Die Elfenkönigin
  Feenreigen
  Die Kindheit
  Lied aus der Ferne
  Opferlied
ABENDGEWÖLKE SCHWEBEN HELL.
  SCHUBERT *Stimme der Liebe*
    Two settings: D. 187 and D. 418.
AM SEEGESTAD'.
  SCHUBERT *Erinnerungen*
DAS FRAULEIN IM THURME.
  SCHUBERT *Romanze*
TODTENOPFER.
  SCHUBERT *Todtenopfer*
Mattinata see Annunzio *LA CHIMERA.*
  RESPIGHI
Mattino di luce see Nerses **RESPIGHI**
Mauclair, Camille, 1872-1945.
  AUBERT *Brodeuses*
  BLOCH
    Complainte
    Les fleurs
    Légende
    Rondo
  CHAUSSON
    Ballade
    Les couronnes
    Les heures
  SCHMITT *Lied*
Mauern wachsen see Krenek **KRENEK**
La Maumariée see Unknown **PIJPER**
La Maumariée II see Unknown **PIJPER**
Maupassant, Guy de, 1850-1893.
  MASSENET *Je cours après le bonheur*
Le maure jaloux see Florian **BERLIOZ**
Maurer, Théodore, b. 1844
  MASSENET
    En voyage
    Je m'en suis allé vers l'amour
Mausefangen see Schellenberg **REGER**
Mausfallen-Sprüchlein see Mörike **WOLF**
La mauvaise prière see Chalupt **AUBERT**
Max' Abschied von Augsburg see Auersperg
  DER LETZTE RITTER. **LOEWE**
Max in Augsburg see Auersperg
  DER LETZTE RITTER. **LOEWE**
Max, Paul
  MASSENET *Toujours*

Max und Dürer see Auersperg
  DER LETZTE RITTER. **LOEWE**
"Max wollt' aus Augsburg reiten" *see*
  Max' Abschied von Augsburg Auersperg
  LOEWE
May see Anon. **BRITTEN**
May see Josephson, E. **SIBELIUS** *Maj*
May, the maiden see Lanier **CARPENTER**
"May, the maiden, violet laden" *see May, the*
  maiden Lanier **CARPENTER**
Mayakovsky, V *see* Maíakovskii, Vladimir
  Vladimirovich, 1894-1930.
May-dew see Uhland **BENNETT** *O'er the*
  woodlands
Mayer, Dr.
  LOEWE *Nachtständchen*
Mayer, K
  FRANZ *O Herz in meiner Brust!*
Mayer, Rudolf, 1837-1865, supposed
  author.
  MARTINŮ *At night*
"Mayerke, mon fils, Mayerke, mon fils" *see*
  Chanson hébraïque Anon. **RAVEL**
Maykov *see* Maĭkov, Apollon
  Nikolayevich, 1821-1897.
Mayláth, Johann, Count, 1786-1855.
  SCHUBERT *Der Blumen Schmerz*
"Mayn harts, mayn harts veynt in mir" *see*
  Mayn harts veynt in mir Anon.
  WEISGALL
Mayn harts veynt in mir see Anon.
  WEISGALL
Mayr, Anton, 1855-1935.
  REGER *Abgeguckt*
Mayrhofer, Johann, 1787-1836.
  SCHUBERT
    Abendlied der Fürstin
    Abendstern
    Der Alpenjäger
    Alte Liebe rostet nie
    Am Strome
    An die Freunde
    Antigone und Oedip
    Atys
    Auf der Donau
    Auflösung
    Augenlied
    Aus "Heliopolis"
      Two settings: D. 753 and D. 754.
    Beim Winde
    Einsamkeit
    Der entsühnte Orest
    Erlafsee
    Fahrt zum Hades
    Freiwilliges Versinken
    Geheimnis. An Franz Schubert

COMPOSER   Poet   *Title*   ''First Line''

Mayrhofer, Johann, 1787-1836
(continued)
SCHUBERT *(continued)*
  Gondelfahrer
  Der Hirt
  Iphigenia
  Liane
  Liedesend
  Memnon
  Nachtstück
  Nachtviolen
  Orest auf Tauris
  Piloktet
  Rückweg
  Schlaflied
  Sehnsucht
  Der Sieg
  Die Sternennächte
  Trost
  Ueber allen Zauber Liebe
  Uraniens Flucht
  Wie Ulfru fischt
  Der zürnenden Diana
  Zum Punsche
IM WINDE.
  SCHUBERT *Der Schiffer*
LUNZ.
  SCHUBERT *Abschied*
NACH DEM GEWITTER.
  SCHUBERT *Nach einem Gewitter*
SCHIFFERS NACHTLIED.
  SCHUBERT *Lied eines Schiffers an die*
    Dioskuren
SITZ' ICH IM GRAS.
  SCHUBERT *Am See*
Mazatsumi see Mazatsumi **STRAVINSKĬ**
Mazatsumi
  STRAVINSKĬ *Mazatsumi*
Mazurka see Vilmorin **POULENC**
McCrae, John, 1872-1918.
  IVES *In Flanders fields*
McCullers, Carson, 1917-1967.
  DIAMOND *The twisted Trinity*
McDonald, George
  CARPENTER *Alas, how easily things go*
    wrong
"Me siats zadumchivyĭ" *see Nad ozerom*
  Golenishchev-Kutuzov **BALAKIREV**
Mé srdce často vbolesti see Pfleger-
  Moravský **DVOŘÁK**
  Three settings: B. 11 no. 11, B. 123 no. 6,
    and B. 124 no. 3.
MEASURE FOR MEASURE. see
  Shakespeare
  Take, O take those lips away
    HESELTINE, QUILTER, THOMSON,
    VAUGHAN WILLIAMS

    Two Heseltine settings: 1916-17 and
      1918-19.
MEASURE FOR MEASURE: Take, O take
  those lips away. *see* Shakespeare
  Chanson d'amour **CHAUSSON**
Mechtateliu see Pushkin **MEDTNER**
  To a dreamer
"Mechty, mechty! Gde vashasladost'?" *see*
  Probuzhden'e Pushkin **RIMSKĬ-**
  KORSAKOV
"Meczennica, biedna świeta Krystynka" *see*
  Świetz Krystyna Iłłakowiczówna
  SZYMANOWSKI
"Med bergfriskt vatten lockar här en brunn"
  see Vid en brunn Österling **KILPINEN**
"Med daempede Hvirvler Trommerne gaa" *see*
  Soldaten Andersen **GRIEG**
Med en Primula veris see Paulsen **GRIEG**
Med en vandlilje see Ibsen **GRIEG**
Med strömmen see Josephson, E.
  KILPINEN
Medina, Salvador Jacinto Polo de *see*
  Polo de Medina, Salvador Jacinto,
  1603-1676.
Meditation see Pech **DVOŘÁK** *Přemítání*
Meditation see Shevchenko
  RACHMANINOFF
"Mediterranean suns!" *see Invitation* Koch
  ROREM
Medjé see Barbier, J. **GOUNOD**
Medlitel'no vlekutsia dni moi see Pushkin
  ZHELANIE. **RIMSKĬ-KORSAKOV**
MEDTNER, NIKOLAĬ KARLOVICH,
1880-1951.
Bryusov, Valery Yakovlevich, 1873-1924.
  In the church-yard, op. 28 no. 4
    {*Tiazhela bestsvetna i pusta*}
    [GA, v. 5, p. 196] "Blank and dull the
      dingy, heavy stone"
Bugayev, Boris Nikolaevich, 1880-
  1934.
  DRUZBIAM.
    Epitaph, op. 13 no. 2 {*Epitazhiia*}
    [GA, v. 5, p. 74]
    "I aspired to soar in sun-light"
Chamisso, Adelbert von, 1781-1838.
  Frisch gesungen, op. 46 no. 7 {*Pesnia*}
    [GA, v. 6, p. 187]
    "Hab' oft im Kreise der Lieben"
  Die Quelle, op. 46 no. 6 {*Ruchei*} [GA,
    v. 6, p. 183]
    "Unsre Quelle kommt im Schatten"
Eichendorff, Joseph Karl Benedikt,
  Freiherr von, 1788-1857.
  Im Walde, op. 46 no. 4 {*V lesu*} [GA,
    v. 6, p. 176] "Es zog eine Hochzeit
    den Berg entlang"

Nachtgruss, op. 61 no. 2 {*Nochnoĭ privet*}
[GA, v. 6, p. 237]
"Weill jetzo alles stille ist"
Reiselied, op. 61 no. 1 {*Pesn' strannika*}
[GA, v. 6, p. 234]
"So ruhig geh ich meinen Pfad so still"
Winternacht, op. 46 no. 5 {*Zimniaia
noch'*} [GA, v. 6, p. 178]
"Verschneit liegt rings die ganze Welt"
AUSSICHT.
   Serenade, op. 46 no. 3 {*Serenada*}
   [GA, v. 6, p. 174]
   "Komm zum Garten, denn"

Goethe, Johann Wolfgang von, 1749-1832.

Auf dem See, op. 3 no. 3 {*Na ozere*} [GA,
v. 5, p. 15]
"Und frische Nahrung, neues Blut"
Die Bekehrte, op. 18 no. 2
{*Obrashchennaia*} [GA, v. 5, p. 135]
"Bei dem Glanze der Abendröte"
Einsamkeit, op. 18 no. 3 {*Odinochestvo*}
[GA, v. 5, p. 140]
"Die ihr Felsen und Bäume bewohnt"
Erster Verlust, op. 6 no. 8 {*Pervaia
utrata*} [GA, v. 5, p. 46]
"Ach! Wer bringt die schöner Tage"
Gefunden, op. 6 no. 9 {*Nakhodka*} [GA,
v. 5, p. 49]
"Ich ging im Walde so für mich hin"
Geistergruss, op. 15 no. 12 {*Privetstvie
dukha*} [GA, v. 5, p. 122]
"Hoch auf dem alten Turme"
Gleich und Gleich, op. 15 no. 11 {*Drug
dlia druga*} [GA, v. 5, p. 120]
"Ein Blumenglöckchen vom Boden
hervor"
Glückliche Fahrt, op. 15 no. 8
{*Schastlivoe plavan'e*} [GA, v. 5,
p. 103] "Die Nebel zerreissen"
Im Vorübergehen, op. 6 no. 4
{*Mimokhodom*} [GA, v. 5, p. 30]
"Ich ging im Felde so für mich hin"
Jägers Abendlied, op. 18 no. 6
{*Vecherniaia pesn' okhotnika*}
[GA, v. 5, p. 152] "Im Felde schleich'
ich still und wild"
Mailied, op. 6 no. 2 {*Maĭskaia pesn'*}
[GA, v. 5, p. 22]
"Zwischen Weizen und Korn"
Nähe des Geliebten, op. 15 no. 9
{*Blizost' milogo*} [GA, v. 5, p. 108]
"Ich denke dein"
Selbstbetrug, op. 15 no. 3
{*Samoobol'shchenie*} [GA, v. 5, p. 84]
"Der Vorhang schwebet hin und her"

Die Spröde, op. 18 no. 1 {*Nedostupnaia*}
[GA, v. 5, p. 132]
"An dem reinsten Frühlingsmorgen"
Das Veilchen, op. 18 no. 5 {*Fialka*} [GA,
v. 5, p. 145]
"Ein Veilchen auf der Wiese stand"
Vor Gericht, op. 15 no. 6 {*Pered sudom*}
[GA, v. 5, p. 94]
"Von wem ich's habe"
CLAUDINE VON VILLA-BELLA.
   Aus "Claudine von Villa-Bella," op. 6
   no. 5 {*Pesenka iz "Klaudiny"*}
   [GA, v. 5, p. 37] "Liebliches Kind,
   kannst du mir sagen"
   Der untreue Knabe, op. 15 no. 10
   {*Nevernyĭ iunosha*}
   [GA, v. 5, p. 113] "Es war ein
   Knabe frech gerug"
ELFENLIED.
   Elfenliedchen, op. 6 no. 3 {*Pesenka
   el'fov*} [GA, v. 5, p. 26]
   "Um Mitternacht, wenn die
   Menschen erst schlafen"
ERWIN UND ELMIRE.
   Inneres Wühlen ewig zu fühlen, op. 6
   no. 6 {*Vechno smiuten'e*}
   [GA, v. 5, p. 40] same
   Sie liebt mich! op. 15 no. 4 {*Liubimia*}
   [GA, v. 5, p. 87] same
   Sieh mich, Heil'ger, wie ich bin, op. 6
   no. 7 {*Veor skloni otets sviatoĭ*}
   [GA, v. 5, p. 42] same
GEWEIHTER PLATZ.
   Geweihter Platz, op. 41 no. 1
   {*Sviashchennoe mesto*} [GA, v. 6,
   p. 98] "Wenn zu den Reihen der
   Nymphen versammelt"
LILA.
   So tanzet, op. 15 no. 5 {*Akh igry i
   tantsy*} [GA, v. 5, p. 91]
   "So tanzet und springet"
MEERESSTILLE.
   Meeresstille, op. 15 no. 7 {*Tish' na
   more*} [GA, v. 5, p. 100]
   "Tiefe Stille herrscht im Wasser"
WANDRERS NACHTLIED I.
   Wandrers Nachtlied, op. 15 no. 1
   {*Nochnaia pesn' strannika I*}
   [GA, v. 5, p. 78]
   "Der du von dem Himmel bist"
WANDRERS NACHTLIED II.
   Wandrers Nachtlied, op. 6 no. 1
   {*Nochnaia pesni strannika II*}
   [GA, v. 5, p. 19]
   "Über allen Gipfeln ist Ruh"

**MEDTNER, NIKOLAĬ KARLOVICH,
1880-1951** *(continued)*
Goethe, Johann Wolfgang von, 1749-
1832 *(continued)*
WILHELM MEISTER. Harfenspieler.
An die Türen will ich schleichen, op.
15 no. 2 {*Tikho postoĭu u vkhoda*}
[GA, v. 5, p. 81] same
WILHELM MEISTER. Mignon's song:
Nur wer die Sehnsucht kennt.
Mignon, op. 18 no. 4 {*Pesnia Min'ony*}
[GA, v. 5, p. 142]
"Nur wer die Sehnsucht kennt"
ZAHME XENIEN.
Geweihter Platz, op. 46 no. 2
{*Sviashchennoe mesto*}
[GA, v. 6, p. 169] "Wenn zu den
Reihen der Nymphen versammelt"
Praeludium, op. 46 no. 1 {*Preliudiia*}
[GA, v. 6, p. 163]
"Wenn im Unendlichen dasselbe"
Heine, Heinrich, 1797-1856.
Bergstimme, op. 12 no. 3 {*Gornyĭ golos*}
[GA, v. 5, p. 59]
"Ein Reiter durch das Bergthal zieht"
Lieb Liebchen, op. 12 no. 1 [GA, v. 5,
p. 52] "Lieb Liebchen, leg's
Händchen"
Lyrisches Intermezzo, op. 12 no. 2
{*Liricheskoe intermetstso*} [GA, v. 5,
p. 55]
"Ein Fichtenbaum steht einsam"
Lermontov, Mikhail Yuryevich, 1814-
1841.
The angel, op. 1a [GA, v. 5, p. 125] "At
midnight an angel flew over the sky"
At the cloister gate, op. 3 no. 1 {*U vrat
obiteli sviatoĭ*} [GA, v. 5, p. 7]
"Before the holy cloister gate"
The prayer, op. 61 no. 5 {*Molitva*} [GA,
v. 6, p. 246]
"When life becomes unbearable"
Nietzsche, Friedrich Wilhelm, 1844-
1900.
Alt Mütterlein, op. 19 no. 2 [Edition
russe de musique, 1911]
"In Sonnenglut, in Mittagsruh"
Not in Collected works.
Gruss, op. 19 no. 1 [Edition russe de
musique, 1911]
"Ihr Vöglein in den Lüften"
Not in Collected works.
Heimkehr, op. 19a no. 1 (1910?) [Edition
russe de musique, 192_]
"Das war ein Tag der Schmerzen"
Not in Collected works.

Heimweh, op. 19 no. 3 [Edition russe de
musique, 1911]
"Das milde Abendläuten"
Not in Collected works.
Verzweiflung, op. 19a no. 2 (1910?)
[Edition russe de musique, 192_]
"Von Ferne tönt der Glokkenschlag"
Not in Collected works.
No author
Sonata vocalise [GA, v. 6, p. 101]
Wordless.
Suite vocalise, op. 41 no. 2 [GA, v. 6,
p. 117]
Wordless; movements entitled
Introduzione, Gesang der Nymphen,
Geheimnisse, Zug der Grazien and
Was der Dichter spricht.
Pushkin, Aleksandr Sergeevich, 1799-
1837.
Alas, for I outlive my yearnings, op. 3
no. 2 {*IA perezhil svoi zhelan'ia*}
[GA, v. 5, p. 11] same
The angel, op. 36 no. 1 [GA, v. 6, p. 42]
"At Heaven's gate there stood an
angel"
Arion, op. 36 no. 6 [GA, v. 6, p. 62]
"Ah, there were many of us there"
The coach of life, op. 45 no. 2 {*Telega
zhizni*} [GA, v. 6, p. 146]
"Although at times the load is heavy"
Echo, op. 32 no. 1 {*Ekho*} [GA, v. 6,
p. 7] "Tho be it cry of baying hounds"
Elegy, op. 45 no. 1 {*Elegiia*} [GA, v. 6,
p. 137]
"I love your secret hidden flowers"
Elegy, op. 52 no. 3 {*Elegiia*} [GA, v. 6,
p. 206] "The fire of youth is gone, its
madness jaded"
The faded flower, op. 36 no. 2 {*TSvetok*}
[GA, v. 6, p. 47]
"A faded flower, dried and scentless"
I loved you well, op. 32 no. 4 {*IA vac
liubil*} [GA, v. 6, p. 22] same
If one day you're disillusioned, op. 61
no. 4 {*Esli zhizn' tebia obmanet*}
[GA, v. 6, p. 244] same
Lost hopes, op. 29 no. 5 {*Elegiia: IA
perezhil svoi zhelan'ia*}
[GA, v. 5, p. 237] "Life has
outdistanced all my yearnings"
Message, op. 32 no. 3 {*Pokhoronnaia
pesnia*} [GA, v. 6, p. 17]
"Far from home are you, my brother"
The muse, op. 29 no. 1 {*Muza*} [GA, v. 5,
p. 217] "She loved me as a child"
Night, op. 36 no. 5 {*Nach'*} [GA, v. 6,
p. 58] "For you my voice is filled
tonight with love and longing"

The prisoner, op. 52 no. 7 {*Uznik*} [GA, v. 6, p. 230] "Alone by the bars at the window I lay"

The ravens, op. 52 no. 2 {*Voron*} [GA, v. 6, p. 201]
"Ravens high aloft are soaring"

Retrospect, op. 32 no. 2 {*Vospominanie*} [GA, v. 6, p. 12]
"When thru the world at last there comes the close of day"

The rose, op. 29 no. 6 {*Roza*} [GA, v. 5, p. 241] "Where, where is the rose-bud, the child of dawn"

Serenade, op. 52 no. 6 {*Serenada*} [GA, v. 6, p. 222] "I come, Inesilla, my sweetest and best"

The singer, op. 29 no. 2 {*Pevets*} [GA, v. 5, p. 224] "And have you heard the singer in the night"

Sleepless, op. 29 no. 3 {*Stikhi, sochinennye noch'iu vo vremia bessonnitsy*} [GA, v. 5, p. 227] "All is darkness, naught I see"

Spanish romance, op. 36 no. 4 {*Ispanskiĭ romans*} [GA, v. 6, p. 53]
"The night is still, a soft breeze blows"

Spanish romance, op. 52 no. 5 {*Ispanskiĭ romans*} [GA, v. 6, p. 216]
"To the noble senorita"

The summons, op. 29 no. 7 {*Zaklinanie*} [GA, v. 5, p. 243]
"O if it be that, in the night"

To a dreamer, op. 32 no. 6 {*Mechtateliu*} [GA, v. 6, p. 34] "To surge in passion's mighty throes is your enjoyment"

Visions, op. 52 no. 40 {*Primety*} [GA, v. 6, p. 212]
"I ride to you, and happy dreams"

The waltz, op. 32 no. 5 {*Mogu l' zabyt' to sladkoe magnoven'e*} [GA, v. 6, p. 27]
"O moment of rapt'rous bliss!"
Collected works cites words by A. Delwig.

The war horse, op. 29 no. 4 {*Kon'*} [GA, v. 5, p. 232]
"Say, my noble steed, why neigh you"

What means to thee my humble name? op. 61 no. 3 {*Chto v imeni tebe moem?*} [GA, v. 6, p. 240] same

When roses fade, op. 36 no. 3 {*Lish' rozy uviadaiut*} [GA, v. 6, p. 51]
"When roses are about to fade"

The window, op. 52 no. 1 {*Okno*} [GA, v. 6, p. 191] "Where is the world that harks to fancy?"

Winter evening, op. 13 no. 1 {*Zimniĭ vecher*} [GA, v. 5, p. 63]
"Whirling winter snow and vapor"

Shenshin, Afanasiĭ Afanas'evich, 1820-1892.

Beauty, op. 24 no. 6 {*Tol'ko vstrechu ulybku tvoiu*} [GA, v. 5, p. 174]
"When your glances, enchanting, you fling"

Butterfly, op. 28 no. 3 {*Babochka*} [GA, v. 5, p. 191] "You're right, whatever of me charms and pleases"

Dawn in the garden, op. 24 no. 7 {*Shepot robkoe dykhan'e*} [GA, v. 5, p. 177]
"Whisp'ring, timid, softly breathing"

Greeting, op. 24 no. 8 {*IA prishel k tebe s privetom*} [GA, v. 5, p. 179]
"Love I come today to tender"

Humble yet valiant, op. 24 no. 5 {*IA potriasen, kogda krugom*} [GA, v. 5, p. 169] "Humble am I when thunder roars"

Impromptu, op. 37 no. 3 {*Moego tot bezumstva zhelal*} [GA, v. 6, p. 81]
"He would have me go mad who invented this rose"

Prayer for rain, op. 28 no. 1 {*Nezhdannyĭ dozhd'*} [GA, v. 5, p. 183]
"Ye vapors, rain-clouds, hear ye me"

Serenade, op. 28 no. 2 {*Ne moqu ia slyshat' etoĭ*} [GA, v. 5, p. 188]
"All the little birds I see that flutter"

Waltz, op. 37 no. 4 {*Val's*} [GA, v. 6, p. 86]
"So lithe and so dainty and slender"

Tiutchev, Fëdor Ivanovich, 1803-1873.

Behold my visionary soul, op. 61 no. 7 {*O, veshchaia dusha moia*} [GA, v. 6, p. 252] same

Day and night, op. 24 no. 1 {*Deu'i noch'*} [GA, v. 5, p. 155]
"Above the gulf that has no name"

Dejection, op. 28 no. 6 {*Sizhu zadumchiv i odin*} [GA, v. 5, p. 204]
"I sit dejected and apart"

Elegy, op. 28 no. 5 {*Vesennee uspokoenie*} [GA, v. 5, p. 201]
"O, not with cold earth, alas, cover me over"

Mid-day, op. 61 no. 6 {*Polden'*} [GA, v. 6, p. 248]
"The lazy mid-day mist is rising"

Night winds, op. 37 no. 5 {*O chem ty voesh' vetr nochnoĭ*} [GA, v. 6, p. 92]
"And why your moaning, winds of night?"

COMPOSER   Poet   *Title*   ''First Line''

**MEDTNER, NIKOLAÏ KARLOVICH,
1880-1951** (*continued*)

Tiutchev, Fëdor Ivanovich, 1803-1873
(*continued*)

Our time, op. 45 no. 4 {*Nash vek*} [GA,
v. 6, p. 158]

" 'Tis not our flesh that now-a-days is
weak"

The pauper, op. 28 no. 7 {*Poshli gospod'
svoĭu otradu*} [GA, v. 5, p. 212]

"Vouch-safe, O Lord, to bless the
pauper"

Sleepless, op. 37 no. 1 {*Bessonnitsa*}
[GA, v. 6, p. 70]

"Monotonous the hours toll"

Song of night, op. 45 no. 3 {*Pesn' nochi*}
[GA, v. 6, p. 152] "Around the globe
the mighty seas extend"

Tears, op. 37 no. 2 {*Slëzy*} [GA, v. 6,
p. 77] "Tears never ending, forever
descending"

Twilight, op. 24 no. 4 {*Dumerki*} [GA,
v. 5, p. 164] "Dark, grey twilight
comes descending"

Waves and thoughts, op. 24 no. 3 {*Duma
za dumoĭ, volna za volnoĭ*}
[GA, v. 5, p. 162] "Wave follows
wave as does thought follow
thought"

We lost all that was once our own, op.
61 no. 8 {*Kogda, chto zvali my svoim*}
[GA, v. 6, p. 255] same

Willow, op. 24 no. 2 {*Chto ty klonish'
nad vodami*} [GA, v. 5, p. 160]

"Why, O willow, are you bending"

Das Meer see
Rolfsen **GRIEG** *Havet*

"Das Meer erglänzte weit hinaus" *see
Am Meer* Heine **SCHUBERT**

Das Meer erstrahlt im Sonnenschein see
Heine **FRANZ**

"Das Meer hat seine Perlen" *see Auf dem
Meere* Heine **FRANZ**

Meeres Stille see Goethe **SCHUBERT**
Two settings: D. 215A and D. 216.

Meeresabend see Strachwitz **LASSEN**

"Der Meeresflut mit Purpurglut" *see Früh-
Lied am Meere* Unknown **LOEWE**

Meeresleuchten see Siebel **LOEWE**

Meeresstille see Eichendorff **FRANZ**

MEERESSTILLE. see Goethe
Meeresstille **GRIFFES, MEDTNER**

Meeresstille see Goethe *MEERESSTILLE.*
GRIFFES, MEDTNER

Meeresstille see Lenau **WOLF**

Meerfahrt see Freiligrath **LOEWE**

Meerfahrt see Heine *TRAGÖDIEN NEBST
EINEM LYRISCHEN INTERMEZZO.*
BRAHMS, FRANZ

Die Meerfee see Buddeus **SCHUMANN**

THE MEETING ON THE SEASHORE. see
Fick, Heinrich
Die Begegnung am Meeresstrand **LOEWE**

"Még azt vetik a szememre" *see Még azt vetik
szememre* Pósa **BARTÓK**

Még azt vetik szememre see Pósa **BARTÓK**

Mei Bua see Sommerstorff **REGER**

Mei, Lev Aleksandrovich, 1822-1862.
BALAKIREV *Zapevka*
CHAÏKOVSKIĬ
Kanareyka
Zachem?
MUSORGSKIĬ
Po griby
RIMSKIĬ-KORSAKOV
Evreĭ skaĭa pesnia
Kolybel'naia pesnia
Vstan', soĭ di! davno dennitsa
OKTAVI.
CHAÏKOVSKIĬ *Ya s neyu nikogda ne
govoril*
PESNYA.
BALAKIREV, CHAÏKOVSKIĬ *Kak
naladili: Durak*
RUTHENISCHE LIEDER: No. 2. Nane.
MUSORGSKIĬ *Detskaia pesenka*

"Mei Mueter mag mi net" *see Die Trauernde*
Anon. **BRAHMS, FRANZ**

"Mei Schätzel das hat mi verlassen" *see Wird
er wohl noch meiner gedenken?* Anon.
FRANZ

Meier, Daniel Eduard, 1812-1873.
SPOHR *Sehnsucht*

Meiliedje see Bruyn, Bertha de **PIJPER**

Le meilleur moment des amours see
Sully-Prudhomme **DELIBES**

Mein! see Müller, Wilhelm **SCHUBERT**

Mein Alles du see Ernst **LASSEN**

Mein altes Ross see Strachwitz
SCHUMANN

"Mein Aug' ist trüb" *see Was soll ich sagen?*
Chamisso **GRIEG, SCHUMANN,
WOLF**

Mein Auge see Dehmel **STRAUSS**

"Mein Auge schliess mit deinem Kuse zu" *see
Mutter, tote Mutter* Hartwig **REGER**

Mein Bett ruft see Ady **BARTÓK** *Lost
content*

"Mein Blümchenklein" *see Das Veilchen*
Holstein **DELIUS**

Mein Engel hüte dein see Hertz **JENSEN**

"Mein feines Lieb ist fern von mir" *see Klage*
Zincgref **ZELTER**

"Mein Fleiss und Müh hab ich nie gespart"
*see Wie Georg von Frundsberg von sich
selber sang* Des Knaben Wunderhorn
   SCHÖNBERG
Mein Fluss see Mörike **SCHOECK**
"Mein Freund Antonius" *see Das Paradies in
der Wüste* Herder **LOEWE**
"Mein Freund ist mein, und ich bin sein!" *see
Aus dem hohen Liede* Cornelius
   CORNELIUS
Mein Garten see Hoffmann von
   Fallersleben **SCHUMANN**
Mein Geist ist trüb' see Byron **LOEWE**
"Mein Geist ist trüb und schwer" *see
Hebräische Melodie* Byron **RUBINSTEIN**
"Mein Geliebter ist ein Sohn des Hügels" *see
Shilrik und Vinvela* Macpherson
   SCHUBERT
"Mein Gemüthe blühte" *see Die Herzensrose*
Rückert **LOEWE**
Mein Gruss an den Mai see Kumpf
   SCHUBERT
"Mein Handwerk geht durch alle Welt" *see
Tischlerlied* Unknown **SCHUBERT**
"Mein Haus hat kein' Thür" *see Freibeuter*
Goethe **LOEWE**
"Mein Heimweh und meine Liebe" *see Dunkle
Augen* Hesse **KILPINEN**
Mein Herz see Hertz **JENSEN**
Mein Herz see Tagore *OGRODNIK.*
   SZYMANOWSKI
Mein Herz see Wiener, Oskar **REGER**
Mein Herz, das ist ein tiefer Schacht see
Unknown **SCHÖNBERG**
"Mein Herz, der Vogel der Wildnis" *see Mein
Herz* Tagore **SZYMANOWSKI**
Mein Herz, der wilde Rosenstrauch see
Sergel **KILPINEN**
Mein Herz, ich will dich fragen see Münch-
Bellinghausen *DER SOHN DU
WILDNISS.* **LOEWE**
Mein Herz in steten Treuen see Anon.
   SCHÖNBERG
"Mein Herz ist betrübt" *see Jemand* Burns
   SCHUMANN
"Mein Herz ist ein stiller Tempel" *see Mein
Herz* Hertz **JENSEN**
Mein Herz ist im Hochland see Burns
   FRANZ *My heart is in the Highland;*
   JENSEN
"Mein Herz ist im Hochland" *see Hochländers
Abschied* Burns **SCHUMANN**
Mein Herz ist leer see Morgenstern
   KILPINEN
Mein Herz ist mir gemenget see Anon.
   SCHÖNBERG

"Mein Herz ist schwer!" *see Aus den
"Hebräischen Gesängen"* Byron
   SCHUMANN
"Mein Herz ist schwer" *see Für Einen* Burns
   FRANZ, JENSEN
Mein Herz ist schwer see Geibel
   SPÄTHERBSTBLÄTTER. **BRAHMS**
Mein Herz ist stumm see Schack
   LOTOSBLÄTTER. **STRAUSS**
Mein Herz ist wie die dunkle Nacht see
   Geibel **GRIFFES, LASSEN, PFITZNER**
"Mein Herz ist wie die dunkle Nacht" *see
Der Mond* Geibel
   MENDELSSOHN-BARTHOLDY
Mein Herz ist wie ein Saitenspiel see
   Leuthold **SCHOECK**
"Mein Herz ist wie ein See so weit" *see
Heiter* Nietzsche **WEBERN**
"Mein Herz ist zerrissen" *see Du liebst mich
nicht* Platen-Hallermünde **SCHUBERT**
"Mein Herz, O schliess' dich ein!" *see
Heimlichkeit* Siebel **LOEWE**
Mein Herz schmückt sich mit dir see
   Bodenstedt **RUBINSTEIN**
Mein Herz und deine Stimme see Platen-
Hallermünde **BRUCKNER**
Mein Herzensschatz see Oelschläger,
   Hermann **RUBINSTEIN**
"Mein hochgebor'ne Schätzelein" *see
Glockentürmers Töchterlein* Rückert
   SCHUMANN
"Mein hochgebornes Schätzelein" *see
Des Glockenthürmers Töchterlein* Rückert
   LOEWE
Mein Hochland-Kind see Burns **FRANZ**
"Mein Hoffen du und Seligkeit" *see Furcht*
Busse-Palma **BERG**
"Mein Hund, du, hat dich bloss beknurrt" *see
Warnung* Dehmel **SCHÖNBERG**
"Mein Kind, in welchem Krieg hast du" *see
Auf ein Kind* Mörike **SCHOECK**
Mein Kind schläft unterm Moose see
   Guilliaume **LASSEN**
   Mon fils est couché là
Mein Kind, wär' ich König see Hugo **LISZT**
   Enfant, si j'étais roi
"Mein Kindchen ist fein" *see Elternstolz*
   Anon. **REGER**
Mein kleiner Vogel see Andersen **GRIEG**
   Min lille Fugl
Mein Leben, ich liebe dich see Byron
   LASSEN
"Mein Leben wälzt sich murrend fort" *see
Der Strom* Unknown **SCHUBERT**
"Mein Lieb ist ein Jäger, und grün ist sein
Kleid" *see Der Jäger*
   Münch-Bellinghausen **BRAHMS**

Mein Lieb ist eine rote Ros' see Burns
FRANZ *My love is like a red rose*
Mein Liebchen see Heine LASSEN,
MACDOWELL
Mein Liebchen see Hoffmann von
Fallersleben LASSEN
Mein Liebchen wir sassen beisammen see
Heine *LIEDERSTRAUSS*. WOLF
"Mein Liebchen, wir sassen beisammen" *see*
Im Kahn Heine
MENDELSSOHN-BARTHOLDY
"Mein Liebchen, wir sassen beisammen" *see*
Meerfahrt Heine BRAHMS, FRANZ
"Mein Liebchen wir sassen beisammen" *see*
Mein Liebchen Heine LASSEN
"Mein liebes Kind, komm" *see*
Um Mitternacht Hamerling LASSEN
"Mein liebes Kind, schlaf ein!" *see*
Wiegenlied Jaeger, Johannes
SCHOECK
"Mein Liebling ist ein Lindenbaum" *see*
Am Strande Stieler LASSEN
"Mein Liebster baut' ein Laube mir" *see*
Klage der Grenzerwittwe Scott JENSEN
Mein Liebster hat es Tische mich geladen see
Heyse WOLF
Mein Liebster ist so klein see Heyse WOLF
Mein Liebster singt am see Heyse WOLF
"Mein Liebster singt am Haus im
Mondenscheine" *see Toskanischer Rispetto*
Heyse JENSEN
Mein Lied see Hoffmann von Fallersleben
LASSEN
"Mein Lied ist klein" *see Untreu* Cornelius
CORNELIUS
Mein Lied verklingt see Cornelius LASSEN
"Mein Liedlein ward ein Büblein" *see Wunsch*
Michaeli REGER
"Mein Ross so müd' in dem Stalle sich steht"
see Lied des gefangenen Jägers Scott
SCHUBERT
"Mein rotes Herz, mein totes Herz" *see*
Mein Herz Wiener, Oskar REGER
"Mein Schäfer, ach!" *see Der bescheidene*
Schäfer Weisse REGER
Mein Schätzelein see Huggenberger
REGER
"Mein Schätzelein ist ein gar köstliches Ding"
see Mein Schätzelein Huggenberger
REGER
"Mein Schatz, der ist auf die Wanderschaft
hin" *see Heimlicher Liebe Pein* Anon.
WEBER
Mein Schatz ist auf der Wanderschaft see
Osterwald FRANZ
"Mein Schatz ist auf die Wanderschaft wohl
in die weite Welt" *see Schwäbische Treue*

Seyboth, Sofie REGER
"Mein Schatz ist nicht da" *see Sehnsucht*
Anon. BRAHMS
Mein Schatz ist wie ein Schneck see Pfau
SCHÖNBERG
"Mein Schatz will Hochzeit halten" *see*
Letzter Wunsch Hertz JENSEN
"Mein Schatzerl is hübsch" *see Volkslied*
Anon. WEBER
Mein schöner Stern! see Rückert
LIEBESFRÜHLING. SCHUMANN
Mein Sinn ist wie der mächt'ge Fels see
Andersen GRIEG *Min Tanke er et*
maegtigt Fjeld
"Mein Sohn, wo willst du hin so spät?" *see*
Winterlied Anon.
MENDELSSOHN-BARTHOLDY
Mein Stübchen see Huber, B. KILPINEN
Mein Traum see Ritter REGER
Mein und Dein see Fischer, J. REGER
"Mein Vater hat gesagt" *see*
Hat gesagt—bleibt's nicht dabei
Des Knaben Wunderhorn
REGER, STRAUSS
Mein Vaterland see Hoffmann von
Fallersleben SPOHR
Mein Vaterland see Körner WEBER
Mein Verlangen see Förster, F. WEBER
Mein Verlangen see Müller von der Werra
SPOHR
"Mein Verstand und armes Herz" *see*
Verschliedene Wege Bodenstedt
RUBINSTEIN
Mein Wagen rollet langsam see Heine
SCHUMANN
"Mein Wagen rollet langsam durch lustiges
Waldesgrün" *see Waldesfahrt* Heine
STRAUSS
"Mein Wappen ist nicht adelig" *see In ein*
Autographen-Album Mörike SCHOECK
"Mein Weg ist weit" *see Der Ruhelose*
Huber, B. KILPINEN
Mein wundes Herz verlangt see Groth
HUNDERT BLÄTTER . . . BRAHMS
Mein Wunsch see Anon. ZELTER
Mein Ziel see Vinje GRIEG *Fyremål*
"Meine armen, kleinen Lieder halten Wacht"
see Abschied Wiener, Oskar REGER
"Meine Blüten sind zernagt" *see Lied*
Kosegarten ZELTER
Meine Devise see Eisenmayer, W. LASSEN
"Meine eingelegten Ruder triefen" *see*
Eingelegte Ruder Meyer PFITZNER
Meine Farben see Lehr, Hofrath WEBER
"Meine Freundin hat ein schwarze Katze" *see*
Der genügsame Liebhaber Salus
SCHÖNBERG

Meine höchste Wonne see Reissig **ZELTER**
"Meine Laute hab' ich gehängt an die Wand"
    see Pause Müller, Wilhelm **SCHUBERT**
Meine Laute nehm'ich wieder see
    Mommsen **KRENEK**
Meine Lebenszeit verstreicht see Hafiz
    SCHOECK
"Meine Lebenszeit verstreicht" *see Vom Tode*
    Gellert **BEETHOVEN**
"Meine Liebe ist grün wie der Fliederbusch"
    see Junge Lieder I Schumann, F.
    BRAHMS
"Meine Liebe, lange wie die Taube" *see Liebe*
    ohne Heimat Bürger **CORNELIUS**
Meine Lieder see Frey **BRAHMS**
"Meine Lieder, meine Sänge" *see Lied*
    Löwenstein-Wertheim **WEBER**
Meine Lilie see Hamerling **LASSEN**
"Meine Mutter hat gewollt" *see Ach, wär' es*
    nie geschehen Anon. **FRANZ**
Meine Rose see Lenau **SCHUMANN**
"Meine Ruh' ist dahin" *see Klaglied* Rochlitz
    SCHUBERT
Meine Ruh' ist hin see Goethe *FAUST.*
    LOEWE, SEIBER
"Meine Ruh ist hin" *see Gretchen* Goethe
    MENDELSSOHN-BARTHOLDY,
    SPOHR
"Meine Ruh' ist hin" *see Gretchen am*
    Spinnrade Goethe **SCHUBERT,**
    WAGNER
"Meine Ruh ist hin" *see Margarethe* Goethe
    ZELTER
Meine Seele see Evers **REGER**
Meine Seele ist still zu Gott see Bible *PSALM*
    62. **REGER**
"Meine Sehnsucht ist zum Licht" *see*
    Sternenfall Wilhelm, Carl **BERG**
"Meine Selinde" *see Stimme der Liebe*
    Stolberg **SCHUBERT**
Meine Töne still und heiter see Rückert
    LIEBESFRÜHLING. **SCHUMANN**
Meinem Kinde see Falke **REGER,**
    STRAUSS
Meiner Mutter see Liliencron
    ADJUTANTENRITTE UND ANDERE
    GEDICHTE. **WEBERN**
Meines Herzens Sehnsucht see Unknown
    MUSORGSKIĬ *Zhelanie serdt̄sa*
Meissner, Alfred, 1822-1885.
    BRAHMS *Nachwirkung*
"Ein Meister bin ich worden" *see In der*
    Trauer Keller, G. **SCHOECK**
"Meister Oluf, der Schmied auf Helgoland"
    see Odins Meeres-Ritt Schreiber **LOEWE**
Lo mejor del amor see Arteaga, Cristina de
    TURINA

Melancholia see Hettich **AUBERT**
MELANCHOLIC HUMOURS (1600). *see*
    Breton *Fair and true* **HESELTINE**
Melancholie see Miranda **SCHUMANN**
Melancholy: a song "à la Debussy" see
    Farnol *BETHANE THE SMITH:* Chapter
    XVI. **COPLAND**
Mélancolie see Anon. **MASSENET**
Mélancolie see Chabaneix **IBERT**
Mélancolie see Coppée **GOUNOD**
Mélancolie see Renaud **SAINT-SAËNS**
    La solitaire
"Melde mir die Nachtgeräusche, Muse" *see*
    Nachtgeräusche Meyer **SCHOECK**
MELEAGER. see Heyse
    Über die Welt **JENSEN**
Melek am Quell see Stieglitz **LOEWE**
Melek in der Wüste see Stieglitz **LOEWE**
Mélisande's song see Maeterlinck *PELLÉAS*
    ET MÉLISANDE. **FAURÉ**
Mell, Max, 1882-1971.
    BERG *Der milde Herbst von Anno 45*
Mellin de Saint-Gelais, 1487-1558.
    JOLIVET *Sonnet à une lunatique*
Melodi see Bergman **KILPINEN**
Melodia see Krasiński **CHOPIN**
Mélodie see Nadson **RACHMANINOFF**
    Melody
La mélodie des baisers see Alexandre,
    André **MASSENET**
Mélodie espagnole see Mikhailov
    BALAKIREV *Ispanskaya pensyna*
Eine Melodie singt mein Herz see Huch
    PFITZNER
MÉLODIES PASSAGÈRES, no. 1
    BARBER Rilke *Puisque tout passe*
MÉLODIES PASSAGÈRES, no. 2
    BARBER Rilke *Un cygne*
MÉLODIES PASSAGÈRES, no. 3
    BARBER Rilke *Tombeau dans un parc*
MÉLODIES PASSAGÈRES, no. 4
    BARBER Rilke *Le clocher chante*
MÉLODIES PASSAGÈRES, no. 5
    BARBER Rilke *Départ*
MÉLODIES PERSANES, no. 1
    SAINT-SAËNS Renaud *La brise*
MÉLODIES PERSANES, no. 2
    SAINT-SAËNS Renaud *La splendeur*
    vide
MÉLODIES PERSANES, no. 3
    SAINT-SAËNS Renaud *La solitaire*
MÉLODIES PERSANES, no. 4
    SAINT-SAËNS Renaud *Sabre en main*
MÉLODIES PERSANES, no. 5
    SAINT-SAËNS Renaud *Au cimetière*

MÉLODIES PERSANES, no. 5 *(continued)*
SAINT-SAËNS *(continued)*
MÉLODIES PERSANES, no. 6
SAINT-SAËNS Renaud *Tournoiement*
MÉLODIES POPULAIRES GRECQUES
RAVEL Anon.
  A vous, oiseau des plaines
  Chanson de pâtre épirote
  Mon mouchoir, hélas, est perdu
  NB: Unnumbered; lost.
MÉLODIES POPULAIRES GRECQUES, no. 1
RAVEL Anon. *Le réveil de la mariée*
MÉLODIES POPULAIRES GRECQUES, no. 2
RAVEL Anon. *Là-bas vers l'èglise*
MÉLODIES POPULAIRES GRECQUES, no. 3
RAVEL Anon. *Quel galant*
MÉLODIES POPULAIRES GRECQUES, no. 4
RAVEL Anon. *Chanson des cueilleuses de lentisques*
MÉLODIES POPULAIRES GRECQUES, no. 5
RAVEL Anon. *Tout gai!*
MÉLODIES SUR LES POÈMES SYMBOLISTES, no. 1
SAUGUET Mallarmé *Renouveau*
MÉLODIES SUR LES POÈMES SYMBOLISTES, no. 2
SAUGUET Mallarmé *Tristesse d'été*
MÉLODIES SUR LES POÈMES SYMBOLISTES, no. 3
SAUGUET Laforgue *Crépuscule de mi juillet, huit heures*
MÉLODIES SUR LES POÈMES SYMBOLISTES, no. 4
SAUGUET Laforgue *Clair de lune de Novembre*
MÉLODIES SUR LES POÈMES SYMBOLISTES, no. 5
SAUGUET Baudelaire *Le chat*
MÉLODIES SUR LES POÈMES SYMBOLISTES, no. 6
SAUGUET Baudelaire *Le chat*
MELODII. see Shenshin
  Ne otkhodi ot menia **CHAĬKOVSKIĬ**
Melodiia see Nadson **RACHMANINOFF**
  Melody
Melodram Gretchens see Goethe *FAUST.*
  WAGNER
Melody see Nadson **RACHMANINOFF**
Melpómene see Attard, Josefina de
  TURINA
Melusina see Annunzio *LA CHIMERA.*
  MALIPIERO

Melville, Herman, 1819-1891.
DIAMOND
  Monody
  A portrait; the Marchioness of Brinvilliers
ROREM *Shelly's vision*
BILLY BUD, FORETOPMAN.
  DIAMOND *Billy in the Darbies*
ON THE GRAVE OF A YOUNG CAVALRY OFFICER.
  DIAMOND *Epitaph*
Memnon see Mayrhofer **SCHUBERT**
"Memnon, Memnon, That Lady who used to walk about" *see Lesbia Illa* Pound
  DIAMOND
Die Memnonsäule see Fitger **LASSEN**
Memories see Ives **IVES**
Memory see Blake, William **CHANLER, IRELAND**
Memory see London Atheneum **CARPENTER**
Memory see Roethke **ROREM**
"Memory, hither come, and tune your merry notes" *see Dream valley* Blake, William **QUILTER**
"Memory, hither come, & tune your merry notes" *see Memory* Blake, William **CHANLER, IRELAND**
Mému ditěti see Falke **MARTINŮ** *To my child*
Men min fågel märks dock icke see Fröding **SIBELIUS**
La menace see Régnier **ROUSSEL**
Mendel'son, Mira Aleksandrovna, 1915-1968.
PROKOFIEV
  Frits
  Klyatve tankista
  Lyubov voyna
  Podruga boytsa
  Sin Kabordi
  Smelo vpered!
MENDELSSOHN, FELIX *see* **MENDELSSOHN-BARTHOLDY, FELIX, 1809-1847.**
MENDELSSOHN-BARTHOLDY, FELIX, 1809-1847.
Anon.
  Erntelied, op. 8 no. 4 [GA, v. 19, p. 8] "Es ist ein Schnitter"
  Minnelied, op. 34 no. 1 [GA, v. 19, p. 58] "Leucht't heller als die Sonne"
  O Jugend, O schöne Rosenzeit! op. 57 no. 4 [GA, v. 19, p. 96] "Von allen schönen Kindern auf der Welt"
  Winterlied, op. 19a no. 3 [GA, v. 19, p. 46] "Mein Sohn, wo willst du hin so spät?"

Baur, Albert, 1803-1886.
Weihnachtslied (1832) [H.Gerber *Albert Baur* (Freiburg, 1971): pp. 162-63] "Auf schicke dich recht feierlich"

Bible
Der du die Menschen lässest sterben, op. 112 no. 2 [GA, v. 14, no. 100] same
Doch der Herr, er leitet die Irrenden recht, op. 112 no. 1 [GA, v. 14, no. 100] same

Böttger, Adolf, 1816-1870.
Ich hör' ein Vöglein (1841) [GA, v. 19, p. 164] same

Byron, George Gordon Byron, 6th baron, 1778-1824.
Sun of the sleepless (1834) [GA, v. 19, p. 157] same
There be none of beauty's daughters (1833) [GA, v. 19, p. 154] same

DES KNABEN WUNDERHORN
Jagdlied, op. 84 no. 3 [GA, v. 19, p. 151] "Mit Lust thät ich ausreiten durch einen grünen Wald"
Lieblingsplätzchen, op. 99 no. 3 [GA, v. 19, p. 135] "Wisst ihr wo ich gerne weil' in der Abendkühle?"

Devrient, Eduard, 1801-1877.
Geständniss, op. 9 no. 2 [GA, v. 19, p. 27] "Kennst du nicht das Gluth verlangen"

Droysen, Johann Gustav, 1808-1884.
Entsagung, op. 9 no. 11 [GA, v. 19, p. 39] "Herr, zu dir will ich mich retten"
Ferne, op. 9 no. 9 [GA, v. 19, p. 36] "In weite Ferne will ich träumen"
Sehnsucht, op. 9 no. 7 [GA, v. 19, p. 34] "Fern und ferner schallt der Reigen"

Ebert, Karl Leopold Felix Egon (Ritter von), 1801-1882.
Das erste Veilchen, op. 19a no. 2 [GA, v. 19, p. 44] "Als ich das erste Veilchen erblickt"
Reiselied, op. 19a no. 6 [GA, v. 19, p. 53] "Bringet des treusten Herzens Grüsse"

Eichendorff, Joseph Karl Benedikt, Freiherr von, 1788-1857.
Es weiss und räth es doch Keiner, op. 99 no. 6 [GA, v. 19, p. 140] same
Nachtlied, op. 71 no. 6 [GA, v. 19, p. 116] "Vergangen ist der lichte Tag"
Pagenlied [GA, v. 19, p. 161] "Wenn die Sonne lieblich schiene wie im Wälschland lau und blau"
Das Waldschloss (1835) [GA, v. 19, p. 159] "Wo noch kein Wandrer gegangen"

Wanderlied, op. 57 no. 6 [GA, v. 19, p. 101] "Laue Luft kommt blau geflossen"

Feuchtersleben, Ernst, Freiherr von, 1806-1849.
Volkslied, op. 47 no. 4 [GA, v. 19, p. 82] "Es ist bestimmt in Gottes Rath"

Fleming, Paul, 1606-1640.
Pilgerspruch, op. 8 no. 5 [GA, v. 19, p. 10] "Lass dich nur nichts nicht dauern"

Geibel, Emanuel, i.e., Franz Emanuel August, 1815-1884.
Der Mond, op. 86 no. 5 [GA, v. 19, p. 126] "Mein Herz ist wie die dunkle Nacht"
Wenn sich zwei Herzen scheiden, op. 99 no. 5 [GA, v. 19, p. 139] same

Goethe, Johann Wolfgang von, 1749-1832.
Erster Verlust, op. 99 no. 1 [GA, v. 19, p. 130] "Ach wer bringt die schönen Tage"
Die Liebende schreibt, op. 86 no. 3 [GA, v. 19, p. 121] "Ein Blick von deinen Augen in die meinen"
Lied der Freundin (1837) [Düsseldorf, 1960 (facsimile of holograph)] "Zarter Blumen leicht Gewinde" Introduction to facsimile by Max F. Schneider.
Suleika, op. 34 no. 4 [GA, v. 19, p. 64] "Ach, um deine feuchten Schwingen"
FAUST.
  Gretchen [unpubl.] "Meine Ruh ist hin"
WESTÖSTLICHER DIVAN.
  Suleika, op. 57 no. 3 [GA, v. 19, p. 92] "Was bedeutet die Bewegung?"

Grillparzer, Franz, 1791-1872.
Italien, op. 8 no. 3 [GA, v. 19, p. 6] "Schöner und schöner schmückt sich der Plan"

Heine, Heinrich, 1797-1856.
Allnächtlich im Traume, op. 86 no. 4 [GA, v. 19, p. 124] same
Auf Flügeln des Gesanges, op. 34 no. 2 [GA, v. 19, p. 59] same
Gruss, op. 19a no. 5 [GA, v. 19, p. 52] "Leise zieht durch mein Gemüth"
Im Kahn (1837) [unpubl.] "Mein Liebchen, wir sassen beisammen" In F. Mendelssohn *Briefe an Ignaz und Charlotte Moscheles* (Leipzig, 1888): p. 148; American edition (Boston, 1888): p. 161.

MENDELSSOHN-BARTHOLDY, FELIX, 1809-1847 *(continued)*

Heine, Heinrich, 1797-1856 *(continued)*

Morgengruss, op. 47 no. 2 [GA, v. 19, p. 76] "Über die Berge steigt schon die Sonne"

Neue Liebe, op. 19a no. 4 [GA, v. 19, p. 49] "In dem Mondenschein im Walde sah ich"

Reiselied, op. 34 no. 6 [GA, v. 19, p. 69] "Der Herbstwind rüttelt die Bäume"

Verlust, op. 9 no. 10 [GA, v. 19, p. 38] "Und wüssten's die Blumen"

Hölty, Ludwig Heinrich Christoph, 1748-1776.

Andres Maienlied, op. 8 no. 8 [GA, v. 19, p. 15] "Die Schwalbe fliegt"

Minnelied, op. 8 no. 1 [GA, v. 19, p. 3] "Holder klingt der Vogelsang"

Hoffmann von Fallersleben, August Heinrich, 1798-1874.

Seemanns Scheidelied [GA, v. 19, p. 174] "Es freut sich Alles weit und breit"

Tröstung, op. 71 no. 1 [GA, v. 19, p. 104] "Werde heiter mein Gemüthe und vergiss der Angst und Pein!"

Immermann, Karl Leberecht, 1796-1840.

Todeslied der Bojaren (1834) [GA, v. 19, p. 166] "Leg' in den Sarg mir mein grünes Gewand"

Klingemann, Carl, 1798-1862.

Bei der Wiege, op. 47 no. 6 [GA, v. 19, p. 86] "Schlummre! Schlummre und träume von kommender Zeit"

Der Blumenstrauss, op. 47 no. 5 [GA, v. 19, p. 83] "Sie wandelt im Blumengarten"

Es lauschte das Laub so dunkelgrün, op. 86 no. 1 [GA, v. 19, p. 118] same

Frühlingslied, op. 34 no. 3 [GA, v. 19, p. 62] "Es brechen im schallenden Reigen"

Frühlingslied, op. 71 no. 2 [GA, v. 19, p. 106] "Der Frühling naht mit Brausen"

Herbstlied, op. 84 no. 2 [GA, v. 19, p. 147] "Im Walde rauschen dürre Blätter"

Im Herbst, op. 9 no. 5 [GA, v. 19, p. 31] "Ach wie schnell die Tage fliehen"

Sonntagslied, op. 34 no. 5 [GA, v. 19, p. 67] "Ringsum erschallt in Wald und Flur"

Der Wasserfall (1820-23?) [unpubl.] "Rieselt hernieder"

In Luise Leven *Mendelssohn als Lyriker . . .* (Krefeld, 1926): p. 164.

Lenau, Nicolaus, 1802-1850.

An die Entfernte, op. 71 no. 3 [GA, v. 19, p. 110] "Diese Rose pflück' ich hier"

Frühlingslied, op. 47 no. 3 [GA, v. 19, p. 78] "Durch den Wald, den dunkeln"

LIEBESKLÄNGE.

Auf der Wanderschaft, op. 71 no. 5 [GA, v. 19, p. 114] "Ich wandre fort in's ferne Land"

SCHILFLIEDER.

Schilflied, op. 71 no. 4 [GA, v. 19, p. 111] "Auf dem Teich, dem regungslosen"

Lichtenstein, Ulrich von, fl.1255.

Frühlingslied, op. 19a no. 1 [GA, v. 19, p. 42] "In dem Walde, süsse Töne singen kleine Vöglein"

Mendelssohn-Bartholdy, Felix, 1809-1847.

Lied zum Geburtstage meines guten Vaters [unpubl.] "Ihr Töne schwingt euch"

In Ernst Wolff *Felix Mendelssohn Bartholdy* (Berlin, 1906), p. 13.

Moore, Thomas, 1779-1852.

Der Blumenkranz (1829) [GA, v. 19, p. 168] "An Celia's Baum in stiller Nacht hängt"

Venetianisches Gondellied, op. 57 no. 5 [GA, v. 19, p. 98] "Wenn durch die Piazzetta die Abendluft weht"

Robert, Friederike (Braun), 1795-1832.

Frühlingslied, op. 8 no. 6 [GA, v. 19, p. 11] "Jetzt kommt der Frühling, der Himmel isch blau"

Das Heimweh, op. 8 no. 2 [GA, v. 19, p. 4] "Was ist's, das mir den Athem hemmet"

Schiller, Johann Christoph Friedrich von, 1759-1805.

DIE PICCOLOMINI.

Des Mädchens Klage [GA, v. 19, p. 171] "Der Eichwald brauset"

Schlippenbach, Albert, Graf von, 1800-1886.

Die Sterne schau'n in stiller Nacht, op. 99 no. 2 [GA, v. 19, p. 132] same

Schreiber, Heinrich, 1793-1872.

Altdeutsches Lied, op. 57 no. 1 [GA, v. 19, p. 88] "Es ist in den Wald gesungen"

Scott, Sir Walter, bart., 1771-1832.

Ave Maria (1820) [unpubl.]
"Ave Maria, Jungfrau mild"
In Luise Leven **Mendelssohn als**
   Lyriker . . . (Krefeld, 1926): p. 155.
Raste Krieger, Krieg ist aus (1820)
[unpubl.] same
In Luise Leven **Mendelssohn als**
   Lyriker . . . (Krefeld, 1926): p. 157.
Simrock, Karl Joseph, 1802-1876.
Warnung vor dem Rhein [GA, v. 19,
   p. 176] "An den Rhein, an den Rhein"
Spee, Friedrich, 1591-1635.
Altdeutsches Frühlingslied, op. 86 no. 6
   [GA, v. 19, p. 128]
   "Der trübe Winter ist vorbei"
Tieck, Johann Ludwig, 1773-1853.
Minnelied, op. 47 no. 1 [GA, v. 19,
   p. 74] "Wie der Quell so lieblich
   klinget"
Tischendorf, Lobegott Friedrich
  Konstantin von, 1815-1874.
Lieben und Schweigen (1840 or 41)
   [Henry Litolff, n.d.] "Ich flocht ein
   Kränzlein schöner Lieder"
Uhland, Ludwig, 1787-1862.
Frühlingsglaube, op. 9 no. 8 [GA, v. 19,
   p. 35] "Die linden Lüfte sind erwacht"
Hirtenlied, op. 57 no. 2 [GA, v. 19, p.
   90] "O Winter, schlimmer Winter"
Die Nonne, op. 9 no. 12 [GA, v. 19,
   p. 41] "Im stillen Klostergarten eine
   bleiche Jungfrau ging"
Das Schifflein, op. 99 no. 4 [GA, v. 19,
   p. 136] "Ein Schlifflein ziehet leise
   den Strom hin seine Gleise"
Unknown
Der Abendsegen (18__?) [Schuberth,
   1854?]
Abschied (1830) [unpubl.]
   "Leb wohl mein Lieb"
An Marie (18__?) [Aibl, 1882]
   "Weiter, rastlos, athemlos, vorüber
   festlich helles Schloss"
Der Bettler (1830) [unpubl.]
   "Ich danke Gott dir"
Da lieg' ich unter den Bäumen, op. 84
   no. 1 [GA, v. 19, p. 144] same
Erwartung (18__?) [Aibl, 1882]
   "Bist auf ewig du gegangen"
Es rauscht der Wald (18__?) [unpubl.]
Im Frühling, op. 9 no. 4 [GA, v. 19,
   p. 29] "Ihr frühlings trunknen Blumen"
Mailied (1834) [unpubl.]
   "Ich weiss mir'n Mädchen"
Die Nachtigall (1821) [unpubl.]
   "Da ging ich hin"

O könnt ich zu dir fliegen (1838)
   [unpubl.]
Reiterlied (1830) [unpubl.] "Immer fort"
Romanze, op. 8 no. 10 [GA, v. 19, p. 20]
   "Einmal aus seinen Blicken"
Sanft weh'n im Hauch der Abendluft
   (1822) [unpubl.]
   Author of text may be Matthisson.
Der Tag (1830) [unpubl.]
   "Sanft entschwanden mir"
Der Verlassene (1821) [unpubl.]
   "Nacht ist um mich her"
In Luise Leven **Mendelssohn als**
   Lyriker . . . (Krefeld, 1926): p. 158.
Vier trübe Monden sind entfloh'n
   (18__?) [Aibl, 1882]
   "Auf ihrem Grabe"
Von allen deinen zarten Gaben (1822)
   [unpubl.] same
In Luise Leven **Mendelssohn als**
   Lyriker . . . (Krefeld, 1926): p. 160.
Wartend, op. 9 no. 3 [GA, v. 19, p. 28]
   "Sie trug einen Falken auf ihrer Hand"
Warum ich weine (18__?) [Aibl, 1882]
   "Weinend seh' ich in die Nacht"
Wiegenlied (1822) [unpubl.]
   "Schlummre sanft"
In Luise Leven **Mendelssohn als**
   Lyriker . . . (Krefeld, 1926): p. 162.
Voss, Johann Heinrich, 1751-1826.
Abendlied, op. 8 no. 9 [GA, v. 19, p. 19]
   "Das Tagewerk ist abgethan"
Frage, op. 9 no. 1 [GA, v. 19, p. 26]
   "Ist es wahr?"
Im Grünen, op. 8 no. 11 [GA, v. 19,
   p. 22] "Willkommen im Grünen!"
Morgenlied, op. 86 no. 2 [GA, v. 19,
   p. 120] "Erwacht in neuer Stärke
   begrüss' ich, Gott"
Scheidend, op. 9 no. 6 [GA, v. 19, p. 32]
   "Wie so gelinde die Fluth bewegt"
Wart, Jakob von, fl. 1272-1331.
Maienlied, op. 8 no. 7 [GA, v. 19, p. 14]
   "Man soll hören süsses Singen"
Mendelssohn-Bartholdy, Felix, 1809-
1847.
  MENDELSSOHN-BARTHOLDY *Lied*
   zum Geburtstage meines guten Vaters
Mendès, Catulle Abraham, 1841-1909.
  BIZET
   L'abandonnée
   Le gascon
   La sirène
  CHABRIER
   Chanson pour Jeanne
   Lied

Mendès, Catulle Abraham, 1841-1909
(continued)
FAURÉ
  Dans la forêt de Septembre
  La fleur qui va sur l'eau
HAHN
  Chanson
  Naguère, au temps des églantines
  Le souvenir d'avoir chanté
IBERT *Le jardin du ciel*
MASSENET *L'heure volée*
ROUSSEL *Pendant l'attente*
SAINT-SAËNS *Clair de lune*
SATIE *Chanson médiévale*
Mendès, Jane (Primitive-Mette) Catulle,
d. 1955.
MASSENET *La lettre*
Mendès, Mme. Catulle *see* Mendès,
Jane (Primitive-Mette) Catulle, d.
1955.
Le mendiant see Fombeure *CHANSONS DE
LA GRANDE HUNE.* **POULENC**
Menelaus see Vaughan Williams, U.
VAUGHAN WILLIAMS
Menia ty v tolpe ne uznala see
  Golenishchev-Kutuzov **MUSORGSKIĬ**
Menie see Burns **MACDOWELL**
Mens jeg venter see Krag **GRIEG**
Der Mensch see Claudius, M. **SCHOECK**
Der Mensch see Scherenberg **LOEWE**
  Der Feind
"Der Mensch lebt und bestehet" *see Spruch*
  Claudius, M. **SCHOECK**
Mensch und Natur see Braungart **REGER**
Menschenbeifall see Hölderlin **BRITTEN**
Menschenherz see Grazie **BERG** *Was zucken
die braunen Geigen*
Menschenlose see Frankl **LOEWE**
*MENSCHLICHES, ALLZUMENSCHLICHES.
see* Nietzsche
  Der Wanderer und sein Schatten **DELIUS**
Menteuse chérie see Ludana **MASSENET**
"Menteuse chérie, lorsque tu màs dit" *see
  Menteuse chérie* Ludana **MASSENET**
Menuet see Coppée **SAINT-SAËNS**
  Marquise vous souvenez-vous?
Menuet see Gregh **KOECHLIN**
*Mephistopheles' Song in Auerbach's Cellar
  see* Goethe **MUSORGSKIĬ**
  Pesnia Mefistofelia v pogrebke Auerbakha
LA MER. see Richepin
  Larmes **FAURÉ**
La mer see Wilde *IMPRESSIONS II:* La mer.
  GRIFFES *The sea*
La mer see Wilde *IMPRESSIONS II:* La mer.
  GRIFFES

La mer est infinie see La Ville de Mirmont
  FAURÉ
La mer est plus belle see Verlaine
  DEBUSSY
"La mer n'a pas d'oranges" *see Adelina à la
  promenade* Garcia Lorca **POULENC**
MERCHANT OF VENICE. see Shakespeare
  Fancie **BRITTEN**
  Fancy **POULENC**
  Look, how the floor of heav'n **THOMSON**
  Tell me where is fancy bred? **CARTER,
  QUILTER, THOMSON**
Merciful God see Anon. **BORODIN**
"Mére des souvenirs" *see Le Balcon*
  Baudelaire **DEBUSSY**
"Mère iné puisable" *see Hymne à Astarté*
  Louÿs **KOECHLIN**
Mère, me diras-tu? see Anon.
  SZYMANOWSKI *Uwoz, mamo*
Mereau, Sophie (Schubert), 1773?-1806.
  BEETHOVEN
    Feuerfarb'
      Two settings: Hess 144 and op. 52 no.
      2.
  ZELTER *Erinnerung an einen Freund*
Meredith, George, 1828-1909.
  COPLAND *Dirge in woods*
  IVES *from "Night of frost in May"*
Les mères see Boyer, Georges
  MASSENET
    Two settings: 1891 and 1901.
Merezhkovski, Dmitriĭ Sergyeyevich,
1865-1941.
  CHAĬKOVSKIĬ
    Smert'
    Usni!
  RACHMANINOFF
    Christ is risen
    I beg for mercy
    Oh no, I beg you, forsake me not
  RUBINSTEIN *O child, dear heart*
Merezhkovsky, Dmitry *see* Merezhkovski,
Dmitriĭ Sergyeyevich, 1865-1941.
Meri
  RUBINSTEIN *The return*
"Merk dir's in vollster Kraft" *see Merkspruch*
  Weigand **REGER**
Merkenstein see Rupprecht **BEETHOVEN**
"Merkenstein, Merkenstein! Wo ich wandle
  denk' ich dein" *see Merkenstein*
  Rupprecht **BEETHOVEN**
Merkspruch see Weigand **REGER**
Merry maiden spring see MacDowell
  MACDOWELL
The merry month of May see Dekker
  IRELAND

Méry, Joseph, 1798-1865.
FRANCK
Aimer
L'émir de Bengador
Mes amis les cygnes see Lenormand *FOLLE DU CIEL.* **MILHAUD**
"Mes frères, ne l'oubliez pas" *see Ne l'oubliez pas* Regnault, Mme. Félix
SAINT-SAËNS
MES PRISONS: Sagesse III, no. 6. *see* Verlaine *D'une prison* **HAHN**
"Mes soeurs! dans cette nuit d'étoiles" *see Feux follets d'amour* Grain, Madeleine
MASSENET
Mes vers fuiraient, doux et freles see Hugo
GRIFFES *Si mes vers avaient des ailes*
"Mes vers fuiraient, doux et frêles" *see Si mes vers avaient des ailes!* Hugo **HAHN, LASSEN**
Mesa, Juan Bautista de, 1583-1627.
RODRIGO *Soneto*
"Mescetemi il vino!" *see Brindisi* Maffei
VERDI
Two settings: 1835? And 1845.
"Mesiats plyvet I tikh i spokocn" *see Pesnya Selima* Lermontov **BALAKIREV**
"Mesiats zadumchivyï" *see Nad rekoï* Golenishchev-Kutuzov **MUSORGSKIï**
Message see Pushkin **MEDTNER**
Message d'amour see Giebel **LASSEN**
Vöglein wohin so schnell?
La messagère see Lerberghe **FAURÉ**
Messe solennelle: O salutaris see Anon.
FRANCK
The messenger see Heine **RIMSKIï-KORSAKOV** *Goneẗs*
The messenger see Witwicki **CHOPIN** *Posel*
MESSIAEN, OLIVIER, 1908-1992.
Messiaen, Olivier, 1908-1992.
Action de grâces (1936) [Durand, 1937]
"Le ciel, et l'eau qui suit les variations des nuages"
Adieu (1945) [Leduc, 1948-49]
"Adieu toi, colombe verte"
L'amour de Piroutcha (1945) [Leduc, 1948-49] "Toungou, ahi, toungou"
Amour oiseau d'étoile (1945) [Leduc, 1948-49] "Oiseau d'étoile"
Antienne du silence (1938) [Durand, 1939] "Ange silencieux"
Soprano & piano.
Arc-en-ciel d'innocence (1938) [Durand, 1939] "Philule, tu t'étires comme une majuscule de vieux missel"
Soprano & piano.
Bail avec Mi (1938) [Durand, 1939] "Ton oeil de terre"

Soprano & piano.
Bonjour toi, colombe vert (1945) [Leduc, 1948-49] same
Le collier (1936) [Durand, 1937] "Printemps enchaîné"
Dans le noir (1945) [Leduc, 1948-49] same
Danse du bébé-Phile (1938) [Durand, 1939] "Pilule, viens, dansons"
Soprano & piano.
Les deux guerriers (1936) [Durand, 1937] "De deux nous voici un"
Doundou tchil (1945) [Leduc, 1948-49] same
L'épouse (1936) [Durand, 1937] "Va où l'Esprit te mène"
Épouvante (1936) [Durand, 1937] "ha, ha, ha, ha, ha, ha, ha, ho!"
L'escalier redit, gestes du soleil (1945) [Leduc, 1948-49] "Il ne parle plus"
La fiancée perdue (1930) [Durand, 1930] "C'est la douce fiancée"
Katchikatchi les étoiles (1945) [Leduc, 1948-49] same
La maison (1936) [Durand, 1937] "Cette maison nous allons la quitter"
Minuit pile et face (1938) [Durand, 1939] "Ville, oeil puant, minuits obliques"
Soprano & piano.
Montagnes (1945) [Leduc, 1948-49] "Rouge-violet, noir sur noir"
Paysage (1936) [Durand, 1937] "Le lac comme un gros bijou bleu"
Pourquoi? (1930) [Durand, 1930] "Pourquoi les oiseaux de l'air"
Prière exaucée (1936) [Durand, 1937] "Ebranlez la solitaire"
Répétition planétaire (1945) [Leduc, 1948-49] "Ahi! Ahi! Ahi! Ahi!"
Résurrection (1938) [Durand, 1939] "Alleluia, alleluia"
Soprano & piano.
Syllabes (1945) [Leduc, 1948-49] "Colombe, colombe verte"
Ta voix (1936) [Durand, 1937] "Fenêtre pleine d'après-midi"
La ville qui dormait, toi (1945) [Leduc, 1948-49] same
No author
Vocalise (1935) [Leduc, 1935; Durand, 1937]
Soprano & piano.
Sauvage, Cécile, 1883-1927.
Le sourire (1930) [Durand, 1930] "Certain mot murmuré Par vous est un baiser"

MESSIAEN, OLIVIER, 1908-1992
(continued)
Villon, François, b.1431.
  Ballade des pendus (1921) [unpubl.]
  Epître à ses amis (1921) [unpubl.]
Messiaen, Olivier, 1908-1992.
  MESSIAEN
  Action de grâces
  Adieu
  L'amour de Piroutcha
  Amour oiseau d'étoile
  Antienne du silence
  Arc-en-ciel d'innocence
  Bail avec Mi
  Bonjour toi, colombe vert
  Le collier
  Dans le noir
  Danse du bébé-Phile
  Les deux guerriers
  Doundou tchil
  L'épouse
  Épouvante
  L'escalier redit, gestes du soleil
  La fiancée perdue
  Katchikatchi les étoiles
  La maison
  Minuit pile et face
  Montagnes
  Paysage
  Pourquoi?
  Prière exaucée
  Répétition planétaire
  Résurrection
  Syllabes
  Ta voix
  La ville qui dormait, toi
MESSIAH. see Händel
  Doch du liessest ihn im Grabe nicht
  REGER
MESSINES . . . see Cammaerts
  Berceuse de la guerre **CARPENTER**
Mestres, Apeles, 1854-1936.
  SÉVERAC *La cançо dels invadits*
MÉTAMORPHOSES, no. 1
  POULENC Vilmorin *Reine des mouettes*
MÉTAMORPHOSES, no. 2
  POULENC Vilmorin *C'est ainsi que tu es*
MÉTAMORPHOSES, no. 3
  POULENC Vilmorin *Paganini*
Metastasio, Pietro Antonio Domenico
  Buonaventura, 1698-1782.
  BEETHOVEN
  O care selve
  La partenza
  GOUNOD *Quanti Mai*
  ROSSINI

Aragonese
Arietta all'antica, dedotta dal "O
  salutaris Hostia"
La dichiarazione
Mi lagnerò tacendo
La partenza
Pour album: Sogna il guerrier
La promessa
Il rimprovero
Tirana alla spagnola (Rossinizzata)
  SCHUBERT
  Da quel sembiante appresi
  L'incanto degli occhi
  Mio ben, ricordati
  Il traditor deluso
  WEBER *Ch'io mai vi possa*
ADRIANO: Act II, scene 6.
  BEETHOVEN *L'amante impatiente*
  Two settings: Op. 82 no. 3 and op. 82
  no. 4.
ALCIDE AL BIVIO.
  SCHUBERT *Pensa, che questo istante*
AMOR TIMIDO (Cantata XVI).
  BEETHOVEN *Liebes-Klage*
ARTASERSE.
  SCHUBERT *Leiden der Trennung*
DEMOFOONTE.
  SCHUBERT *Misero pargoletto*
DIDONE ABBANDONATA.
  SCHUBERT *Arie*
GLI ORTI ESPERIDI.
  SCHUBERT *Son fra l'onde*
LA PACE FRA LA VIRTÙ E LA
  BELLEZZA.
  BEETHOVEN *Lebens-Genuss*
Les métaux **see** Banville **KOECHLIN**
Metschersky, Fürst Elim.
  LISZT *Bist du!*
Metternich *see*
  Metternich-Winneburg, Clemens
  Wenzel Lothar, Fürst von, 1773-
  1859.
Metternich-Winneburg, Clemens Wenzel
  Lothar, Fürst von, 1773-1859.
  REGER *Maiennacht*
Mew, Charlotte, 1870-1928.
  ROREM *Smile, death*
Mey *see* Mei, Lev Aleksandrovich, 1822-
  1862.
Mey, Lev *see* Mei, Lev Aleksandrovich,
  1822-1862.
Meyer, Conrad Ferdinand, 1825-1898.
  PFITZNER
  Eingelegte Ruder
  Hussens Kerker
  Lass scharren deiner Rosse Hug
  Säerspruch

COMPOSER   Poet   *Title*   "First Line"

SCHOECK
  Abendwolke
  Alle
  Am Himmelstor
  Das Ende des Festes
  Firnelicht
  Frühling Triumphator
  Der Gesang des Meeres
  Göttermahl
  Das Heilige Feuer
  Hochzeitslied
  Ich würd' es hören
  Im Harmesnächten
  In einer Sturmnacht
  Jetzt rede du!
  Die Jungfrau
  Lenzfahrt
  Liederseelen
  Mit einem Jugendbildnis
  Nachtgeräusche
  Neujahrsglocken
  Der Reisebecher
  Reisephantasie
  Requiem
  Der römische Brunnen
  Schwarzschattende Kastanie
  Unruhige Nacht
  Vor der Ernte
  Was treibst du, Wind?
  Das weisse Spitzchen
  STRAUSS *Im Spätboot*
Meyer, Karl, b. 1845.
  REGER *Spatz und Spätzin*
Meynell, Alice Christiana (Thompson),
  1847-1922.
  IRELAND
  The advent
  My fair
  MILHAUD *The roaring frost*
"Mezhtremia moriami bashnia" *see Deva i*
  solntse Maïkov **RIMSKIĭ-KORSAKOV**
"Mezi květy dlela zlatá včela" *see Proto* Pech
  DVOŘÁK
Mezza notte see Shenshin **CHAĬKOVSKIĭ**
"Mgla mi do oczu zawiewa zlona" *see Dumka*
  Zaleski **CHOPIN**
"Mgla mi do oczu zawiewa zlona" *see Nie ma*
  czego trzeba Zaleski **CHOPIN**
"Mi amor es desmayo de luz y reflejos" *see*
  Melpómene Attard, Josefina de
  TURINA
"Mi amor! Recuerdas dime" *see Recuerdas?*
  Machado y Ruiz **RODRIGO**
Mi corazon te aguarda see Machado y Ruiz
  RODRIGO
"Mi Hasbond wa en Piinwon Rad" *see*
  AE Lastrae Berntsen **NIELSEN**

Mi lagnerò tacendo see Deschamps
  ROSSINI *Nizza*
Mi lagnerò tacendo see Metastasio
  ROSSINI
"Mi lagnerò tacendo" *see Il rimprovero*
  Metastasio **ROSSINI**
Mi lagnerò tacendo see Ucceili, F. **ROSSINI**
  La separazione
"Mi lagnerò tacendo della mia sorte amara"
  see Aragonese Metastasio **ROSSINI**
"Mi lagnerò tacendo della mia sorte amara"
  see Arietta all'antica, dedotta dal "O
  salutaris Hostia" Metastasio **ROSSINI**
"Mi lagneró tacendo della mia sorte amara"
  see Tirana alla spagnola (Rossinizzata)
  Metastasio **ROSSINI**
"Mi nuit! le flat murmure el le ciel étincè le"
  see La nuit Ferrier **BIZET**
"Mi parve, un giorno" *see Perchè piangi?*
  Pavesi, Corrado Marchese **GOUNOD**
MICH ERGREIFT, ICH WEISS NICHT WIE.
  see Goethe
  Tischlied **SCHUBERT, ZELTER**
"Mich ergreift, ich weiss nicht wie" *see*
  Tischlied Goethe **SCHUBERT, ZELTER**
"Mich führt mein Weg wohl meilenlang" *see*
  Gesang der Norna Scott **SCHUBERT**
"Mich hat der Herbst betrogen" *see*
  Winterahnung Rückert **REGER**
Mich treibt's hinaus in's lichte
  Frühlingsrauschen see Hertz, H. **JENSEN**
"Mich umduftet deine Seele" *see Nachtseele*
  Evers **REGER**
Michaeli, Otto, 1870-1941.
  REGER
  Gruss
  Wunsch
Michaelskirchplatz see Busse **PFITZNER**
Michaux, Henri, 1899-1984.
  SAUGUET
  Dans la nuit
  La jeune fille de Budapest
  Repos dan le malheur
Michelangelo *see* Buonarroti, Michel
  Angelo, 1475-1564.
Michell, Gustav, b.1842.
  IRRWEGE: Lied.
  LISZT *Verlassen*
Michell, Nicholas, 1807-1880.
  LASSEN *Allein*
Miciński, Tadeusz, 1873-1921.
  SZYMANOWSKI
  Nade mna leci w szafir morza
  Rycz, burzo!
  Tak jestem smetny
  W zaczarowanym lesie

COMPOSER Poet *Title* "First Line"

Miciński, Tadeusz, 1873-1921 *(continued)*
W MROKU GWIAZD.
SZYMANOWSKI
Na ksiezycu czarnym
Na pustej trzcinie
Pachna mi dziwnie twoje zlote wlosy
Święty Franciszek mówi
W mym sercu
Z maurytańskich śpiewnych sal
Mickiewicz, Adam, 1798-1855.
CHAïKOVSKIï
Ali mat' menia rozhala
Moia balovnĩtsa
Na zemlĩu sumrak pal
CHOPIN *Moja pieszczotka*
LOEWE
Die drei Budrisse
Frau Twardowska
Der junge Herr und das Mädchen
Die Schlüsselblume
Das Switesmädchen
Wilia und das Mädchen
Der Woywode
RIMSKIï-KORSAKOV
Moia balovnĩtsa
Sviteziãnka
Mid autumn flowers see Aksakov
BALAKIREV *Sredi tsvetov pori osenney*
Mid sombre days see Rathaus
CHAïKOVSKIï *In trüber Stund'*
Mid-day see Tiutchev **MEDTNER**
A midget see De La Mare *DING DONG*
BELL: Benighted. **CHANLER**
Le midi see Banville **KOECHLIN**
Midi see Leconte de Lisle **KOECHLIN**
"*Midi, Roides étés, épandu sur la plaine" see*
Midi Leconte de Lisle **KOECHLIN**
Midnight see Prokosch **ROREM**
Midnight: I pluck the curtains back see Olson
DIAMOND
THE MIDNIGHT MEDITATION, no. 1
DIAMOND Olson *Midnight: I pluck the*
curtains back
THE MIDNIGHT MEDITATION, no. 2
DIAMOND Olson *Immensity, like the*
darkness cast from the cloud above
THE MIDNIGHT MEDITATION, no. 3
DIAMOND Olson *Let children ride the*
year's sweet carrousel
THE MIDNIGHT MEDITATION, no. 4
DIAMOND Olson *I thought once I should*
have at a man's age
Midnight on the Great Western see Hardy
BRITTEN
The midnight sun see Goodman **ROREM**

Midsummer lullaby see Goethe
MACDOWELL
Midsummer nights see Rathaus
RACHMANINOFF *These summer nights*
MIDSUMMER NIGHT'S DREAM: Bottom's
song. *see* Shakespeare
Lied des transferierten Zettel **WOLF**
Miel de Narbonne see Cocteau **POULENC**
"Mien tras danzá is en corro" *see Abril galan*
Machado y Ruiz **RODRIGO**
Mienne! see Laroche, Ernest **MASSENET**
"Mientras la sombra pasa de un santo amor"
see Preludio Machado y Ruiz
RODRIGO
Mieszkanie see Iłlakowiczówna
SZYMANOWSKI
"Mieux qu'une tour profane" *see Le clocher*
chante Rilke **BARBER**
"Mig ej lockar din skatt" *see Till Frigga*
Runeberg **SIBELIUS**
The mighty thoughts of an old world see
Beddoes **BERKELEY**
Mignon see Goethe **SCHUMANN** *Kennst du*
das Land
Mignon see Goethe *WILHELM MEISTER.*
SCHUBERT
Two settings: D. 469 nd D. 727.
Mignon see Goethe *WILHELM MEISTER.*
Mignon's song: Heiss mich nicht reden.
SCHUBERT
Mignon see Goethe *WILHELM MEISTER.*
Mignon's song: Kennst du das Land?
BEETHOVEN, BERG, GOUNOD,
JENSEN, SCHUBERT, SCHUMANN
Mignon see Goethe *WILHELM MEISTER.*
Mignon's song: Nur wer die Sehnsucht
kennt. **MEDTNER**
Mignon I see Goethe *WILHELM MEISTER.*
Mignon's song: Heiss mich nicht reden.
WOLF
Mignon II see Goethe *WILHELM MEISTER.*
Mignon's song: Nur wer die Sehnsucht
kennt. **WOLF**
Mignon III see Goethe *WILHELM MEISTER.*
WOLF
Mignon IV see Goethe *WILHELM MEISTER.*
Mignon's song: Kennst du das Land?
WOLF
Mignon, 1 see Goethe **ZELTER** *Kennst du*
das Land?
Mignon, 3 see Goethe **ZELTER** *Geheimnis*
Mignon als Engel verkleidet see Goethe
ZELTER
Mignon und der Harfner see Goethe
WILHELM MEISTER. Mignon's song:
Nur wer die Sehnsucht kennt. **SCHUBERT**

The mignonette see Deland **MACDOWELL**
Mignonne see Ronsard **WAGNER**
MIGNONNE. see Silvestre
  Complainte **MASSENET**
  Prélude **MASSENET**
  Que l'heure est donc brève! **DELIBES,
    MASSENET**
  Riez-vous? **MASSENET**
  Sonnet matinal **MASSENET**
  Sur la source **MASSENET**
  Voici que les grand lys **MASSENET**
  Vous aimerez demain **MASSENET**
"Mignonne, allons voir, si la rose" *see*
  Mignonne Ronsard **WAGNER**
"Mignonne blonde aux yeux de flamme" *see*
  Aubade Wilder **LALO**
"Mignonne, sais-tu comment" *see Le mariage*
  des roses David **FRANCK**
"Mignonne, viens voir, ce soir" *see À ma*
  mignonne Renaut, J. **DELIBES**
"Mignonne, voici l'Avril!" *see Chanson*
  d'Avril Coppée **GOUNOD**
"Mignonne, voici l'Avril!" *see Sérénade de*
  Zanetto Coppée **MASSENET**
Mignons Lied see Goethe **WILHELM
  MEISTER.** Mignon's song: Kennst du das
  Land? **LISZT, SPOHR**
Mignon's Lied see Goethe **ZELTER** *Kennst
  du das Land?*
Mignon's song see Goethe **BEETHOVEN,
  LOEWE** *Sehnsucht*
Mignon's song see Goethe **MEDTNER**
  Mignon
Mignon's song see Goethe **SCHUBERT**
  Lied der Mignon
  Five settings: D. 359, D. 481, and D. 877
    nos. 2-4.
Mignon's song see Goethe **SCHUBERT**
  Mignon und der Harfner
Mignon's song see Goethe **SCHUBERT**
  Sehnsucht
Mignon's song see Goethe **SCHUMANN**
  Nur wer die Sehnsucht kennt
Mignon's song see Goethe **WILHELM
  MEISTER.** Mignon's song: Kennst du das
  Land? **CHAÏKOVSKIï** *Pesnya Min'ony*
Mignon's song see Goethe **WOLF** *Mignon II*
Mignon's song see Goethe **ZELTER**
  Nur wer die Sehnsucht kennt
Mignon's song see Goethe **ZELTER**
  Sehnsucht
The migrant wind see Bal'mont
  RACHMANINOFF
Mikäs on poikana eleä see Kanteletar
  KILPINEN

Mikan, Johann Christian, 1769-1844.
  SCHUBERT *Die Befreier Europas in Paris*
Mikhaël, Ephraïm, 1866-1890.
  CHABRIER *L' île heureuse*
Mikhailov, Mikhail Larionovich, 1826-
  1865.
  BALAKIREV
    Ispanskaya pensyna
    Son
  RUBINSTEIN *Neugriechisches Lied*
"Mikouchka, Mikouchka, voilà qu'on a fait tes
  boucles" *see Berceuse* Stravinskiï
  STRAVINSKIï
Miksi en väsyisi see Kanteletar **KILPINEN**
"Miksi milloinkaan sinut nähdä sainkaan" *see*
  Kerran Jalkanen **KILPINEN**
The mild mother see Anon. **ROREM**
The mild stars shone for us see Pleshcheyev
  SLOVA DLYA MUZÏKI. **CHAÏKOVSKIï**
  Nam zvezdy krotkie siïali
"Mild wie ein Lufthauch" *see Bist du!*
  Metschersky **LISZT**
"Das milde Abendläuten" *see Heimweh*
  Nietzsche **MEDTNER**
Der milde Herbst von Anno 45 see Mell
  BERG
MILHAUD, DARIUS, 1892-1974.
  Anon.
    Beata viscera Mariae, op. 231c no. 4
      (1942) [Heugel, 1946] same
      Voice & organ or piano.
    Berceuse, op. 86 no. 4 (1925) [Heugel,
      1925] "Dors, dors, dors, ton papa ira
      au village"
      Also voice & orchestra.
    Bonjour, messieurs les libérateurs, op.
      246 no. 1 (1944) [Leeds, 1949]
      "Le navire qui est sur la rade"
      Text adapted by Alice Joyau-Dormoy.
    Le chant du veilleur, op. 86 no. 2 (1925)
      [Heugel, 1925] "Holà! Qui va là?"
      Also voice & orchestra.
    Chant Hassidique, op. 86 no. 6 (1925)
      [Heugel, 1925]
      "Que te dirai je et que te raconterai je"
      Also voice & orchestra.
    Chante de délivrance, op. 86 no. 3
      (1925) [Heugel, 1925]
      "Pour le grâce de mon ami mon coeur"
      Also voice & orchestra.
    Confidence, op. 233 no. 3 (1942)
      [Heugel, 1946]
      "Le silence est plume d'ange et flotte"
    Le Funeste Retour: chanson de marin,
      op. 123 (1933) [unpubl.]
    Gam hayom, op. 179 no. 2 (1937)
      [Masada Nigun]

MILHAUD, DARIUS, 1892-1974 *(continued)*
Anon *(continued)*

Gloire à Dieu, op. 86 no. 5 (1925)
[Heugel, 1925]
"Mon Dieu est ma force"
Also voice & orchestra.

Hodie nobis de coelo, op. 231c no. 2
(1942) [Heugel, 1946] same
Voice & organ or piano.

Holem tsaudi, op. 179 no. 1 (1937)
[Masada Nigun]

Jeunesse, op. 233 no. 6 (1942) [Heugel,
1946]
"Un mât invisible couronné de ciel"

Long distance, op. 233 no. 5 (1942)
[Heugel, 1946] "Ta voix, vibration si
douce à mon oreille"

*Maintenant que les portes de
bienveillance,* op. 125 no. 5 (1933)
[Heugel, 1934] same
Also voice & small orchestra.

Marronniers, op. 233 no. 1 (1942)
[Heugel, 1946]
"Chandelier du mystère"

Le mistral, op. 233 no. 4 (1942) [Heugel,
1946] "Il s'éveille en chantant"

O magnum mysterium, op. 231c no. 3
(1942) [Heugel, 1946] same
Voice & organ or piano.

Prenez courage, Ô enfants d'Israël! op.
125 no. 1 (1933) [Heugel, 1934] same
Also voice & small orchestra.

Prière de l'après-dîner, op. 96 no. 2
(1927) [Heugel, 1927]
"Que vos tabernacles sont aimables, O
Seigneur des armées"

Prière du matin, op. 96 no. 1 (1927)
[Heugel, 1927] "Mon Dieu, l'âme que
vous m'avez donnée est pure"

Prière du soir, op. 96 no. 3 (1927)
[Heugel, 1927]
"Béni soit le Seigneur, notre Dieu"

Salve Regina mater, op. 231c no. 1
(1942) [Heugel, 1946] same
Voice & organ or piano.

Le seigneur est roi, op. 125 no. 3 (1933)
[Heugel, 1934] same
Also voice & small orchestra.

*Seigneur par le son du schophar vous
ferez entendre,* op. 125 no. 2 [Heugel,
1934] same
Also voice & small orchestra.

La séparation, op. 86 no. 1 (1925)
[Heugel, 1925] "Celui qui distingue le
sacré du profane"
Also voice & orchestra.

Toi, op. 233 no. 2 (1942) [Heugel, 1946]
"Pauvre de joie"

Toute l'année, op. 125 no. 4 (1933)
[Heugel, 1934] same
Also voice & small orchestra.

Trois ans de souffrance, op. 246 no. 2
(1944) [Leeds, 1949] "En mil neuf
cent quarante on nous a dit"
Text adapted by Alice Joyau-Dormoy.

Verbum caro factum, op. 231c no. 5
(1942) [Heugel, 1946] same
Voice & organ or piano.

**Aubigné, Théodore Agrippa d', 1552-
1630.**

*Préparatif a la mort en allégorie
maritime,* op. 403 (1963) [unpubl.]

Bard, Chevalier

La chanson du printemps, op. 128d no. 2
(1933) [Enoch, 1934]
"Ah! reste, reste dans mon coeur"
Song from the film ***Mme. Bovary.***

Bloch, Jean Richard, 1884-1947.

Chanson du capitaine, op. 173 (1937)
[Deiss, 1937; Salabert]
"Ce paqu'bot ci s'appell' 'La Julie' "

Java de la femme, op. 173b no. 2 (1937)
[Deiss, 1937; Salabert]
"Quatre ans, j'avais quatre ans"

Carême, Maurice, 1899-1978.

L'amoureux, op. 319 no. 3 (1952)
[Heugel, 1954] "Il l'aimait tellement"

Le beau navire, op. 319 no. 11 (1952)
[Heugel, 1954]
"Une marguerite à la bouche"

La bise, op. 319 no. 9 (1952) [Heugel,
1954] "Ce sont des feuilles mortes"

La chance, op. 319 no. 7 (1952) [Heugel,
1954] "Qui ne la connut riche"

Le charme, op. 319 no. 12 (1952)
[Heugel, 1954]
"Il ne tient plus qu'a un fil"

Destinée, op. 319 no. 10 (1952) [Heugel,
1954] "Sans même détourner la tête"

La dormeuse, op. 319 no. 5 (1952)
[Heugel, 1954]
"Elle dormait depuis cent ans"

Les feuilles, op. 319 no. 2 (1952)
[Heugel, 1954] "Au ciel, en
d'immenses vergers"

Le lièvre et le blé, op. 319 no. 8 (1952)
[Heugel, 1954]
"Le blé jaunissant craint les rêves"

La peine, op. 319 no. 6 (1952) [Heugel,
1954] "On vendit le chien et la chaîne"

La prière, op. 319 no. 4 (1952) [Heugel,
1954] "Prière abandonnée au tournant
du chemin"

Sortilège, op. 319 no. 1 (1952) [Heugel, 1954] "Il prit un reste de brouillard"
Catullus, Caius Valerius, 87-57 B. C.
La femme que j'aime, op. 80 no. 1 (1923) [Heugel, 1926] same
Voice & violin.
Ma chérie, aimons-nous, op. 80 no. 3 (1923) [Heugel, 1926] same
Voice & violin.
Ma chérie, en présence de son mari, op. 80 no. 4 (1923) [Heugel, 1926] same
Voice & violin.
Voilà où mon âme en est venue, op. 80 no. 2 (1923) [Heugel, 1926] same
Voice & violin.
Chalupt, René, 1885-1957.
Le Colonel Romanoff, op. 55 no. 12 (1919) [Durand, 1920]
"Le soir vient"
Le convive, op. 55 no. 10 (1919) [Durand, 1920]
"Elles t'aiment plus que la vie"
La Grand'Mère de la Révolution, op. 55 no. 7 (1919) [Durand, 1920]
"Qu'un jour à la gare Alexandre"
L'infidèle, op. 55 no. 4 (1919) [Durand, 1920] "O Catherine Ivanowna"
L'irrésolue, op. 55 no. 6 (1919) [Durand, 1920] "N'ecoute pas, Anastasie"
Les journées d'Août, op. 55 no. 8 (1919) [Durand, 1920]
"C'est vous qu'au Palais de Tauride"
La limousine, op. 55 no. 11 (1919) [Durand, 1920]
"Sous la neige, la Rolls Royce"
La martiale, op. 55 no. 3 (1919) [Durand, 1920]
"Le grand Turc apprend ce qu'il cuit"
Monsieur Protopopoff, op. 55 no. 9 (1919) [Durand, 1920] "Regardez ce Monsieur qui va Monter en limousine"
L'orgueilleuse, op. 55 no. 1 (1919) [Durand, 1920]
"Pourquoi, Princesse de Ballet"
La perverse, op. 55 no. 5 (1919) [Durand, 1920]
"Qu'elle était donc tentatrice"
La révoltée, op. 55 no. 2 (1919) [Durand, 1920] "Ma tourte relle, mon amie"
Châteaubriand, François Auguste René, vicomte de,1768-1848.
À la lune, op. 10 no. 2 (1913) [Mathot; Salabert, 1914]
"Chaste déese! déesse si pure"
L'aurore, op. 10 no. 1 (1913) [Mathot; Salabert, 1914] "Quelle douce clarté vient éclairer l'Orient"

L'Innocence, op. 10 no. 3 (1913) [Mathot; Salabert, 1914]
"Fille du ciel, aimable innocence"
Claudel, Paul, 1868-1955.
Ardeur, op. 7 no. 4 [Mathot, 1913; Salabert, 1947]
"La journée est plus dure que l'enfer"
Chanson d'automne, op. 26 no. 1 (1915-17) [Durand, 1920]
"Dans la lumière éclatante d'automne"
Baritone & piano.
Le cygne, op. 142 (1935) [unpubl.]
Décembre, op. 7 no. 2 [Mathot, 1913; Salabert, 1947] "Balayant la contrée et ce vallon feuillu"
La descente, op. 7 no. 6 [Mathot, 19913; Salabert, 1947] "Ah! que ces gens continuent à dormir!"
Dissolution, op. 7 no. 3 [Mathot, 1913; Salabert, 1947] "Et je suis de nouveau reporté sur la mer"
La nuit à la vérandah, op. 7 no. 1 [Mathot, 1913; Salabert, 1947]
"Certains Sauvages croient que l'âme des enfantes mortnés"
Obsession, op. 26 no. 4 (1915-17) [Durand, 1920] "Je vous ai assiégé"
Baritone & piano.
Le point, op. 7 no. 7 [Mathot, 1913; Salabert, 1947] "Je m'arrête: il y a un point à ma promenade"
Also voice & orchestra.
Le sombre Mai, op. 26 no. 3 (1915-17) [Durand, 1920]
"Les Princesses aux yeux de chevreuil"
Baritone & piano.
Suivies d'un verso Canioca (1917?) [unpubl.]
Ténèbres, op. 26 no. 2 (1915-17) [Durand, 1920]
"Je suis ici, l'autre est ailleurs"
Baritone & piano.
Tristesse de l'eau, op. 7 no. 5 [Mathot, 1913; Salabert, 1947]
"Il est une conception dans la joie"
Cocteau, Jean, 1889-1963.
Chat, op. 356 (1956) [unpubl.]
Fête de Bordeaux, op. 59 no. 2 (1920) [La Sirène Musicale, 1920; Eschig]
"Le manège a vapeur regarde s'en aller"
Fête de Montmartre, op. 59 no. 3 (1920) [La Sirène Musicale, 1920; Eschig]
"Ne vous balancez pas si fort"
Fumée, op. 59 no. 1 (1920) [La Sirène Musicale, 1920; Eschig]

COMPOSER Poet *Title* "First Line"

MILHAUD, DARIUS, 1892-1974 *(continued)*
  Cocteau, Jean, 1889-1963 *(continued)*
    "C'est permis de fumer gare"
    Pièce de circonstance, op. 90 (1926)
      [unpubl.?]
      Milhaud autobiography says "not for
        sale."
  Cohen, Albert, 1895-1981.
    Hymne de Sion, op. 88a no. 1 (1925)
      [Universal-Edition, 1926]
      "Jérusalem nous est rendue"
    Israël est vivant, op. 88a no. 2 (1925)
      [Universal-Edition, 1926] "Le blanc
      Messie chevauche devant nous"
  Collet, Louise, 1810-1876.
    Lassitude, op. 19 no. 3 (1914) [unpubl.]
  Corneille, Pierre, 1606-1684.
    Poème de Corneille, op. 178 (1937)
      [unpubl.]
  Daudet, Lucien Alphonse, 1883-1946.
    Le bégonia, op. 60 no. 2 (1920) [Durand,
      1923] "Bégonia Aurora"
      Also for voice & 7 instruments.
    Le brachycome, op. 60 no. 6 (1920)
      [Durand, 1923] "Brachycome
      Ibéridifolia étoile bleue nouveauté"
      Also for voice & 7 instruments.
    Les crocus, op. 60 no. 5 (1920) [Durand,
      1923] "Les crocus se forcent en potées
      ou dans des soucoupes"
      Also for voice & 7 instruments.
    L'eremurus, op. 60 no. 7 (1920) [Durand,
      1923] "Eremurus Isabellinus"
      Also for voice & 7 instruments.
    Les fritillaires, op. 60 no. 3 (1920)
      [Durand, 1923] "Les fritillaires aiment
      les endroits exposés"
      Also for voice & 7 instruments.
    Les jacinthes, op. 60 no. 4 (1920)
      [Durand, 1923] "Albertine blanc pur"
      Also for voice & 7 instruments.
    La violette, op. 60 no. 1 (1920) [Durand,
      1923] "La violette cyclope se force"
      Also for voice & 7 instruments.
  Du Bellay, Joachim, ca.1525-1560.
    De sa peine, et des beautés de sa Dame,
      op. 409 no. 4 (1964) [T.Presser, 1966]
      "C'est mon feu, c'est ma cordelle"
    Le vrai amour, op. 409 no. 1 (1964)
      [T.Presser, 1966] same
  Dufrénoy, Mme. Adélaide Gillette
    (Billet), 1765-1825.
    Élégie, op. 19 no. 2 (1914) [unpubl.]
  Flament, Albert, 1877-1956.
    Quatrain, op. 143 (1935) [unpubl.]
  Flaubert, Gustave, 1821-1880.

    Chanson de l'aveugle, op. 128d no. 1
      (1933) [Enoch, 1934]
    "Souvent la chaleur d'un beau jour"
    Song from the film *Mme Bovary.*
  Fluchère, Henri, 1914-
    Cours de solfège: Papillon, Papillonnette,
      op. 217 (1940) [unpubl.]
  France, Marie de
    Le Lai du Chevrefeuille, op. 409 no. 9
      (1964) [T.Presser, 1966]
    "D'eux deux il était ainsi comme du
      chèvre feuille était"
  Gide, André Paul Guillaume, 1869-
    1951.
    LA PORTE ETROITE.
      Jérôme, op. 9 no. 1 [Heugel, 1947]
        "Efforcez vous d'entrer par la porte
        étroite"
        Composed 1913; revised, 1931.
      Jérôme et Alissa, op. 9 no. 2 [Heugel,
        1947]
        "Elle devint tout-à-coup très grave"
        Composed 1913; revised, 1931.
      Jérôme et Alissa, op. 9 no. 3 [Heugel,
        1947] "J'ai fait un triste rêve"
        Composed 1913; revised, 1931.
      Jérôme et Alissa, op. 9 no. 5 [Heugel,
        1947]
        "C'est ta lettre qui m'a fait revenir"
        Composed 1913; revised, 1931.
      Journal d'Alissa, op. 9 no. 8 [Heugel,
        1947]
        "Mon Dieu, vous savez bien que j'ai
        besoin de lui pour vous aimer"
        Composed 1913; revised, 1931.
        Alissa, no. 7, is prelude for
        piano only.
      Lettre d'Alissa, op. 9 no. 4 [Heugel,
        1947] "Mon cher, Jérôme, j'ai
        beaucoup réfléchi"
        Composed 1913; revised, 1931.
      Lettres d'Alissa, op. 9 no. 6 [Heugel,
        1947]
        "Ici rien n'est changé dans le jardin"
        Composed 1913; revised, 1931.
  Gosse, Chevalier
    L'arbre exotique, op. 28 (1915) [unpubl.]
  Guérin, Eugénie de, 1805-1848.
    A mesure qu'on avance, op. 27 no. 3
      (1915) [Roudanez, 1922; Philippo;
      Combre] same
    Cette promenade avec toi, op. 27 no. 1
      (1915) [Roudanez, 1922; Philippo;
      Combre] same
    Nous voilà donc exilés, op. 27 no. 2
      (1915) [Roudanez, 1922; Philippo;
      Combre] same

Guérin, Maurice de, 1810-1839.
 Les siècles ont creusé, op. 11 no. 1
  (1913-14) [unpubl.]
Jammes, Francis, 1868-1938.
 Almaïde d'Étremont, op. 6 no. 2
  [unpubl.]
 Au beau soleil, op. 1 no. 5 [unpubl.]
 Au bord de l'eau verte, op. 1 no. 3
  [unpubl.]
 Avec ton parapluie, op. 1 no. 1 [unpubl.]
 Bernadette, op. 6 no. 4 [unpubl.]
 C'était affreux, op. 1 no. 6 [unpubl.]
 Clara d'Ellebeuse, op. 6 no. 1 [unpubl.]
 La gomme coule, op. 50 nos. 1 and 2
  (1918) [unpubl.]
 J'ai vu revenir les choses, op. 1 no. 2
  [unpubl.]
 J'aime l'âne, op. 1 no. 7 [unpubl.]
 Je crève de pitié, op. 1 no. 8 [unpubl.]
 Je le trouvai, op. 50 no. 4 (1918)
  [unpubl.]
 Ne me console pas, op. 1 no. 16
  [unpubl.]
 Notre-Dame de Sarrance, op. 29 (1915)
  [unpubl.]
 Pomme d'anis, op. 6 no. 3 [unpubl.]
 Pourquoi les boeufs, op. 1 no. 9 [unpubl.]
 Prière pour aller au Paradis, op. 1 no.
  11 [unpubl.]
 Prière pour demander une étoile, op. 1
  no. 13 [unpubl.]
 Prière pour être simple, op. 1 no. 10
  [unpubl.]
 Prière pour qu'un enfant ne meure pas,
  op. 1 no. 12 [unpubl.]
 Printemps lointain, op. 253 (1945)
  [unpubl.]
 Les processions des campagnes, op. 1 no.
  4 [unpubl.]
 Quatrain, op. 106 (1929) [*La Revue
  Musicale,* Suppl., April 1929, p. 31]
  "Des noms sont exaltés un à un"
  Also in *La Revue Musicale,* no. 400-
  401 (1987): "Albert Roussel, 1869-
  1937."
 Si tu pouvais, op. 1 no. 15 [unpubl.]
 Tristesse, op. 1 no. 14 [unpubl.]
 Viens, je te mettrai, op. 50 no. 3 (1918)
  [unpubl.]
 TRISTESSES.
  Dans le chemin toujours trempé, op.
   355 no. 4 (1956) [Heugel, 1957]
   same
  Demain fera un an qu'à Audaux, op.
   355 no. 24 (1956) [Heugel, 1957]
   same

Deux ancolies se balançaient, op. 355
 no. 20 (1956) [Heugel, 1957] same
Elle avait emporté des brasées de lilas,
 op. 355 no. 9 (1956) [Heugel, 1957]
 same
Elle est gravement gaie, op. 355 no. 5
 (1956) [Heugel, 1957] same
*Elle était descendue au bord de la
 prairie,* op. 355 no. 3 (1956)
 [Heugel, 1957] same
Faisait-il beau quand elle est morte,
 op. 355 no. 14 (1956) [Heugel,
 1957]
 same
J'ai quelqu'un dans le coeur, op. 355
 no. 16 (1956) [Heugel, 1957] same
Je garde une médaille d'elle, op. 355
 no. 15 (1956) [Heugel, 1957] same
*Je la désire dans cette ombreuse
 lumière,* op. 355 no. 2 (1956)
 [Heugel, 1957] same
Je ne désire point ces ardeurs, op. 355
 no. 11 (1956) [Heugel, 1957] same
Je songe à ce jour là, op. 355 no. 18
 (1956) [Heugel, 1957] same
Les lilas qui avaient fleuri, op. 355 no.
 19 (1956) [Heugel, 1957] same
*Nous nous aimerons tant que nous
 tairons,* op. 355 no. 13 (1956)
 [Heugel, 1957] same
*O mon coeur, ce sera dans l'Aoûte
 bleu,* op. 355 no. 12 (1956) [Heugel,
 1957] same
Par ce que j'ai souffert, op. 355 no. 21
 (1956) [Heugel, 1957] same
Parfois, je suis triste, op. 355 no. 6
 (1956) [Heugel, 1957] same
Un poète disait que, op. 355 no. 7
 (1956) [Heugel, 1957] same
Si tout ceci n'est qu'un pauvre rêve,
 op. 355 no. 10 (1956) [Heugel,
 1957] same
Son souvenir emplit l'air si clair, op.
 355 no. 8 (1956) [Heugel, 1957]
 same
Venez sous la tonnelle, op. 355 no. 22
 (1956) [Heugel, 1957] same
Venez, ma bien aimée, op. 355 no. 23
 (1956) [Heugel, 1957] same
*Vous m'avez regardé avec tout votre
 âme,* op. 355 no. 17 (1956)
 [Heugel, 1957] same
Kriéger, Jacqueline
 Haut comme trois pommes, op. 195 no. 2
  (1938) [Heugel, 1955]
  "Tu n'est qu'un tout petit bonhomme"

COMPOSER Poet *Title* "First Line"

MILHAUD, DARIUS, 1892-1974 *(continued)*
Kriéger, Jacqueline *(continued)*
Il faut obéir, op. 195 no. 4 (1938)
[Heugel, 1955]
"Jean Pierre sait bien qu'il fait obéir"
Pas bien grand, op. 195 no. 1 (1938)
[Heugel, 1955]
"Je ne suis pas bien grand"
La tortue naine, op. 195 no. 3 (1938)
[Heugel, 1955]
"On ne peut que trouver vilaine"
La Morvonnais, Hippolyte Michel de,
1802-1853.
Sonnet, op. 11 no. 3 (1913-14) [unpubl.]
Labé, Louise Charly, called, 1526-
1566.
Sonnet, op. 409 no. 3 (1964) [T.Presser,
1966] same
Lamartine, Alphonse Marie Louis de
Prat de, 1790-1869.
L'Isolement, op. 11 no. 2 (1913-14)
[unpubl.]
Latil, Léo, 1890-1915.
L'abandon, op. 20 no. 1 (1914) [Durand,
1920] "Pourquoi, pourquoi m'avez-
vous abandonné?"
Clair de lune, op. 2 no. 2 [unpubl.]
Il pleut doucement, op. 2 no. 3 [unpubl.]
Ma douleur et sa compagne, op. 20 no. 2
(1914) [Durand, 1920]
"Quand vous avez laissé"
Poème du journal intime de Léo Latil,
op. 73 (1921) [Eschig, 1927]
"Qu'ils sont beaux ces enfants des
hommes"
Prière à mon poète, op. 2 no. 1 [unpubl.]
Le rossignol, op. 20 no. 3 (1914)
[Durand, 1920] "Nous sommes aux
portes du printemps"
La tourterelle, op. 20 no. 4 (1914)
[Durand, 1920]
"Ma colombe, Ô ma tourterelle"
Lenormand, René, 1846-1932.
FOLLE DU CIEL.
Blancs sont les jours d'été, op. 149 no.
2 (1936) [Heugel, 1954] same
Mes amis les cygnes, op. 149 no. 1
(1936) [Heugel, 1954] same
Lunel, Armand, b. 1892
L'adieu, op. 21 no. 8 (1914) [unpubl.]
L'agriculteur, op. 21 no. 6 (1914)
[unpubl.]
Le cavalier, op. 21 no. 4 (1914) [unpubl.]
Les châtelaines, op. 21 no. 3 (1914)
[unpubl.]
Les enfants, op. 21 no. 1 (1914) [unpubl.]

Les Libellules, op. 21 no. 5 (1914)
[unpubl.]
L'Octobre, op. 21 no. 7 (1914) [unpubl.]
Le sifflet, op. 21 no. 2 (1914) [unpubl.]
Mallarmé, Stéphane, 1842-1898.
Le cantonnier, op. 44 no. 3 (1917) [La
Sirène Musicale, 1920; Eschig]
"Tes cailloux tu les nivelles"
Le crieur d'imprimés, op. 44 no. 7 (1917)
[La Sirène Musicale, 1920; Eschig]
"Toujours n'importe le titre"
La femme de l'ouvrier, op. 44 no. 5
(1917) [La Sirène Musicale, 1920;
Eschig]
"La femme l'enfant la soupe"
Indomptablement a dû, op. 51 no. 1
(1918) [*La Revue Musicale*, Suppl. 1
Jan. 1921; Eschig, 1927] same
Le Marchand d'ail et d'oignons, op. 44
no. 4 (1917) [La Sirène Musicale,
1920; Eschig]
"L'ennui d'aller en visite"
La Marchande d'habits, op. 44 no. 8
(1917) [La Sirène Musicale, 1920;
Eschig]
"Le vif oeil dont tu regardes"
La Marchande d'herbes aromatiques, op.
44 no. 2 (1917) [La Sirène Musicale,
1920; Eschig]
"Ta paille azur de lavande"
Quatrain, op. 180 (1937) [unpubl.]
Quelconque une solitude, op. 51 no. 2
(1918) [*La Revue Musicale*, Suppl. 1
Jan. 1921; Eschig, 1927] same
Le savetier, op. 44 no. 1 (1917) [La
Sirène Musicale, 1920; Eschig]
"Hors de la poix rien à faire"
Le vitrier, op. 44 no. 6 (1917) [La Sirène
Musicale, 1920; Eschig]
"Le pur soleil qui remise"
Marsan, Maurice de, 1852-1929.
Les temps faciles, op. 305 (1950)
[unpubl.]
Meynell, Alice Christiana (Thompson),
1847-1922.
The roaring frost, op. 37 no. 3 (1916)
[unpubl.]
Morand, Paul, 1889-1976.
Don Juan, op. 65 no. 1 (1920) [unpubl.]
Étrennes, op. 65 no. 3 (1920) [unpubl.]
Révérence, op. 65 no. 2 (1920) [unpubl.]
Moreno
SE PLAIRE SUR LA MÊME FLEUR.
Ritournelle et six chansons, op. 131
[unpubl.]
Musset, Alfred de, 1810-1857.

J'aime, op. 409 no. 2 (1964) [T.Presser, 1966] same

No author

Vocalise, op. 105 (1928) [Leduc, 1929]

Paliard, Camille Marie José, b. 1892

Le boulanger, op. 216 no. 3 (1940) [Heugel, 1947] "Dans le village il y a un petit homme tout sec"

Cet hiver, op. 265 no. 1 (1946) [Heugel] same

Cette douleur, op. 265 no. 2 (1946) [Heugel] same

Les champignons, op. 216 no. 14 (1940) [Heugel, 1947] "Quand les premières pluies de Septembre"

Le château, op. 216 no. 9 (1940) [Heugel, 1947] "Les automobilistes qui pasent sur la route"

Les conscrits, op. 216 no. 8 (1940) [Heugel, 1947] "Le tambour roule"

Les deux hôtels, op. 216 no. 2 (1940) [Heugel, 1947] "Dans le village, il v a deux hôtels"

L'horizon, op. 216 no. 10 (1940) [Heugel, 1947] "Derrière les vallons a peine creusés"

La maison inachevée, op. 216 no. 4 (1940) [Heugel, 1947] "Dans un pré en pente"

Modestes vacances, op. 216 no. 1 (1940) [Heugel, 1947] "Nous prenons la route qui monte"

Monsieur le Curé, op. 216 no. 5 (1940) [Heugel, 1947] "Si vous cherchez Monsieur le Curé"

Paresse, op. 216 no. 7 (1940) [Heugel, 1947] "Etendue dans le vallon étroit"

Le pêcheur, op. 216 no. 11 (1940) [Heugel, 1947] "Pêcheur, horrible pêcheur blond et doux"

La petite bergère, op. 216 no. 13 (1940) [Heugel, 1947] "Elle est menue comme une puce"

Le retour, op. 216 no. 15 (1940) [Heugel, 1947] "Voici de nouveau la petite voiture devant la porte"

Le ruisseau, op. 216 no. 12 (1940) [Heugel, 1947] "Si je me penche sur le pont"

Silence au fond de l'allée, op. 265 no. 3 (1946) [Heugel] same

Tant de vagabonds, op. 265 no. 4 (1946) [Heugel] same

Les trois peupliers, op. 216 no. 6 (1940) [Heugel, 1947] "Trois peupliers au milieu d'un champ"

Patmore, Coventry Kersey Dighton, 1823-1896.

THE UNKNOWN EROS: The azalea.

L'azalée, op. 31 no. 2 (1915) [Heugel, 1955] "A cette place, chez nous"

THE UNKNOWN EROS: Departure.

Le départ, op. 31 no. 1 (1915) [Heugel, 1955] "Ce n'étaient pas là vos grandes et gracieuses manières"

Pitoëff, Georges, 1886-1939.

TU NE M'ÉCHAPPERAS JAMAIS.

La bohémienne la main n'a pris, op. 151 no. 1 (1936) [Heugel, 1954] same

Un petit pas, deux petits pas, op. 151 no. 2 (1936) [Heugel, 1954] same

Rimbaud, Jean Nicolas Arthur, 1854-1891.

Aube, op. 45 no. 2 (1917) [unpubl.]

Marine, op. 45 no. 1 (1917) [unpubl.]

Veillées, op. 409 no. 7 (1964) [T.Presser, 1966] "C'est le repos éclairé"

Ronsard, Pierre de, 1524-1585.

Plusieurs de leurs corps dénués, op. 409 no. 8 (1964) [T.Presser, 1966] "Plusieurs de leurs corps dénués"

Rossetti, Christina Georgina, 1830-1894.

A birthday, op. 37 no. 2 (1916) [unpubl.]

Song, op. 37 no. 1 (1916) [unpubl.]

Scève, Maurice, 16th century.

Moins je la vois, op. 409 no. 5 (1964) [T.Presser, 1966] same

Supervielle, Jules, 1884-1960.

Abandonnée, op. 148b no. 2 (1935-36) [Deiss, 1937; Salabert] "En attendant je serai" Also voice & orchestra.

Ce bruit de la mer, op. 276 no. 3 (1947) [Heugel, 1947] same

Ce peu, op. 276 no. 1 (1947) [Heugel, 1947] "Ce peu d'océan"

Compagnons du silence, op. 276 no. 2 (1947) [Heugel, 1947] same

Mon histoire, op. 148b no. 1 (1935-36) [Deiss, 1937; Salabert] "J'étais toute petite" Also voice & orchestra.

Sans feu ni lieu, op. 148b no. 3 (1935-36) [Deiss, 1937; Salabert] "Pour les enfants san feu ni lieu" Also voice & orchestra.

LA PREMIÈRE FAMILLE.

Chacun son tour, les animaux, op. 193 no. 2 (1938) [Heugel, 1954] same

Je suis dans le fillet, op. 193 no. 1 (1938) [Heugel, 1954] same

MILHAUD, DARIUS, 1892-1974 *(continued)*
Tagore, Rabindranath, 1861-1941.
Defamation, op. 36 no. 2 (1916)
[Composers' Music Corp., 1923]
"Why are those tears in your eyes, my child?"
The gift, op. 36 no. 5 (1916) [Composers' Music Corp., 1923] "I want to give you something, my child"
Love, my heart longs day and night, op. 30 no. 1 (1915) [G. Schirmer] "Amour, mon coeur languit tout le jour"
Paper boats, op. 36 no. 3 (1916) [Composers' Music Corp., 1923] "Day by day I float my paper boats"
Peace, my heart, op. 30 no. 2 (1915) [G. Schirmer] "Paix, mon coeur"
Sympathy, op. 36 no. 4 (1916) [Composers' Music Corp., 1923] "If I were only a little puppy"
GARDENER.
Ayez pitié de votre serviteur, op. 35 no. 2 (1916-17) [unpubl.]
Ne gardez pas, op. 35 no. 1 (1916-17) [unpubl.]
GITANJALI.
Poème du "Gitanjali" op. 22 (1914) [**Revue Française de Musique** 12 pt.2 (1913-14): 505] "Les nuages s'entassent sur les nuages" Text translated and adapted by Gide.
When and why, op. 36 no. 1 (1916) [Composers' Music Corp., 1923] "When I bring you coloured toys"
Tastu, Mme. Amable, 1798-1885.
Plainte, op. 19 no. 1 (1914) [unpubl.]
Thompson, Francis, 1859-1907.
Poèmes de Francis Thompson, op. 54 (1919) [unpubl.] Text translated by Claudel.
Unknown
Chant d'amour, op. 34 no. 6 (1916) [Eschig, 1920] "En même temps que tous les bourgeons la rose"
Chant de forgeron, op. 34 no. 7 (1916) [Eschig, 1920] "Près du Jourdain il y a une maison de forgeron"
Chant de la pitié, op. 34 no. 4 (1916) [Eschig, 1920] "Dans les champs de Bethléem"
Chant de nourrice, op. 34 no. 1 (1916) [Eschig, 1920] "Dors, ma fleur, mon fils chéri"
Chant de résignation, op. 34 no. 5 (1916) [Eschig, 1920] "Prends mon âme fais en une lyre brillante"

Chant de Sion, op. 34 no. 2 (1916) [Eschig, 1920] "Ce n'est la rosée ni la pluie"
Chant du laboureur, op. 34 no. 3 (1916) [Eschig, 1920] "Mon espérance n'est pas encore perdue"
Ecoutez mes enfants, op. 359 (1957) [unpubl.] Voice & organ.
Lamentation, op. 34 no. 8 (1916) [Eschig, 1920] "Au ciel sept chérubins silencieux comme les rêves"
Valmy-Baysse, Jean, b. 1874
Belle dame de mon émoi, op. 152b no. 2 (1936) [Deiss, 1937; Salabert] same Also voice & orchestra.
Je suis tombé de mal en peine, op. 152b no. 3 (1936) [Deiss, 1937; Salabert] same Also voice & orchestra.
Rassa, ma dame est fraîche et fine, op. 152b no. 1 (1936) [Deiss, 1937; Salabert] same Also voice & orchestra.
Verlaine, Paul, 1844-1896.
Nevermore, op. 409 no. 6 (1964) [T.Presser, 1966] "Souvenir, souvenir, que me veux-tu?"
Vildrac, Charles, 1882-1971.
Le jardinier impatient, op. 167 no. 5 (1937) [Deiss; Salabert] "Dans son potager ma grand mère"
Le malpropre, op. 167 no. 4 (1937) [Deiss; Salabert] "Un fermier du voisinage"
La pomme et l'escargot, op. 167 no. 3 (1937) [Deiss; Salabert] "Il y avait une pomme"
Poupette et Patata, op. 167 no. 2 (1937) [Deiss; Salabert] "Au beau milieu de l'ile verte"
Les quatre petits lions, op. 167 no. 1 (1937) [Deiss; Salabert] "Partis d'une ménagerie"
Vilmorin, Louise de, 1902-1969.
Ballade-nocturne, op. 296 (1949) [Heugel, 1949] "Dame du soir les anémones"
Milkmaids see Smith, Dr. James
LARKSPUR. **HESELTINE**
Millä maksan maammon maion see
Kanteletar **KILPINEN**
Millay, Edna St. Vincent, 1892-1950.
FATAL INTERVIEW.

GIDEON
Gone in good sooth you are
Moon, that against the lintel of the
West
Night is my sister
The millennium see Blixen *OUT OF AFRICA.*
DIAMOND
Miller, Johann Martin, 1750-1814.
MOZART *Die Zufriedenheit*
Millevoye, Charles Hubert, 1782-1816.
BIZET
Rose d'amour
Vieille chanson
GOUNOD *La fauvette*
"Millionen öder Jahre" *see Reminiszenz*
Hebbel **CORNELIUS**
Millom Roser see Janson **GRIEG**
The millwheel see Josephson, E.
SIBELIUS *Kvarnhjulet*
Milton, John, 1608-1674.
PARADISE LOST
IVES *Evening*
Mimaamaquim see Bible **HONEGGER**
"Mimaamaquim queratikha Adornaï" *see*
Mimaamaquim Bible **HONEGGER**
Mimokhodom see Goethe **MEDTNER**
Im Vorübergehen
"Min bleka sjukling skall luta" *see Sof in!*
Tavaststjerna **SIBELIUS**
Min grav see Josephson, E. **KILPINEN**
"Min hvide svane" *see En svane* Ibsen
GRIEG
"Min kaere lille Gentleman" *see Til min*
Dreng Benzon **GRIEG**
Min längtans ö see Cnattingius, Thor
KILPINEN
"Min lilla älskade så vit" *see En sommarafton*
Bergman **KILPINEN**
Min lille Fugl see Andersen **GRIEG**
Min lille Fugl, hvor flyver du see Andersen
NIELSEN
Min Sjael er mørk see Byron **NIELSEN**
"Min søde Brud, min unge Viv" *see Vandring*
i Skoven Andersen **GRIEG**
Min Tanke er et maegtigt Fjeld see
Andersen **GRIEG**
"Min Tankes Tanke ene du er vorden" *see Jeg*
elsker Dig! Andersen **GRIEG**
"Minä kuljen tuttua polkuain" *see Kesäyössä*
Koskenniemi **KILPINEN**
Mine is a hot and fiery steed see Anon.
DVOŘÁK *Ej, mám já koňa faku*
Miners' song see Gellner **MARTINŮ**
Minnelied see Anon. **MENDELSSOHN-**
BARTHOLDY, REGER
Minnelied see Hölty **BRAHMS,**
MENDELSSOHN-BARTHOLDY,
SCHUBERT

Minnelied see Hölty **SCHUBERT** *Seligkeit*
Minnelied see Tieck **MENDELSSOHN-**
BARTHOLDY
Minnelied see Voss **LOEWE, WEBER**
Minnen see Cnattingius, Thor **KILPINEN**
"Minnen, minnen, hel'ga minnen" *see Minnen*
Cnattingius, Thor **KILPINEN**
MINNESANG. see Kosegarten
Huldigung **SCHUBERT**
MINNESPIEL, no. 1
SCHUMANN Rückert *Meine Töne still*
und heiter
MINNESPIEL, no. 2
SCHUMANN Rückert *Liebster, deine*
Worte stehlen
MINNESPIEL, no. 4
SCHUMANN Rückert *Mein schöner*
Stern!
MINNESPIEL, no. 6
SCHUMANN Rückert *O Freund, mein*
Schirm, mein Schutz!
MINNEWEISEN, no. 1
JENSEN Geibel *Du feuchter*
Frühlingsabend
MINNEWEISEN, no. 2
JENSEN Geibel *Nun die Schatten dunkeln*
MINNEWEISEN, no. 3
JENSEN Geibel *Der Page*
MINNEWEISEN, no. 4
JENSEN Geibel *Lied des Mädchens*
MINNEWEISEN, no. 5
JENSEN Geibel *Im Gebirg*
MINNEWEISEN, no. 6
JENSEN Geibel *O schneller, mein Ross*
"Minns du de skimrande böljornas suck" *see*
På verandan vid havet Rydberg
SIBELIUS
Minona see Bertrand **SCHUBERT**
MINOR POEMS (1846): For music. *see* Hood
A lake and a fairy boat **HESELTINE**
Minsky, Nikolai, pseud. *see* Vilenkin,
Nikolay Maksimovich, 1855-1937.
Minstrels see Ibsen **SPILLEMAEND. BERG,**
DELIUS *Spielleute*
MINSTRELSY OF THE SCOTISH BORDER.
see Scott *Berthrams Grablied* **JENSEN**
Minuit see Guichard, Abeille **SAUGUET**
Minuit pile et face see Messiaen
MESSIAEN
Mio ben, ricordati see Metastasio
SCHUBERT
"Mipä meiän paimenien" *see Paimenlaulu*
Kanteletar **KILPINEN**
Mir bist du tot see Graf-Bartholomew, M.
PFITZNER
"Mir fallen alte Blätter" *see Es war doch*
schön Fitger **LASSEN**

Mir fehlt das Beste see Heine **FRANZ**
Mir glänzen die Augen see Keller, G. *ALTE WEISEN.* **PFITZNER, SCHOECK**
"Mir ist, als müsst ich dir was sagen" *see Schottisch Lied* Unknown **SPOHR**
Mir ist, als zögen Arme mich schaurig himmelwärts see Kuh **CORNELIUS**
"Mir ist, da ich dich habe" *see Widmung* Rückert **REGER**
"Mir ist die Welt so freudenleer" *see Verlassen* Michell **LISZT**
"Mir ist nach einer Heimat weh" *see Abendrot* Leinhard, Friedrich **PFITZNER**
"Mir ist so weh ums Herz" *see Schwermut* Candidus **BRAHMS**
"Mir ist so wohl, so weh' " *see Erlafsee* Mayrhofer **SCHUBERT**
"Mir ist's so eng allüberall!" *see In's Freie* Schöpff **SCHUMANN**
"Mir klingt ein Ton so wunderbar" *see Ein Ton* Cornelius **CORNELIUS**
"Mir träumt', ich komm' ans Himmelstor" *see Am Himmelstor* Meyer **SCHOECK**
"Mir träumt', ich war ein Vögelein" *see Der Traum* Hölty **SCHUBERT**
"Mir träumte" *see Sehnsucht II* Heine **BERG**
"Mir träumte einst ein schöner Traum" *see Ein Traum* Bodenstedt **GRIEG**
"Mir träumte einst von wildem Liebesglüh'n" *see Traumbild* Heine **FRANZ**
Mir träumte von einem Königskind see Heine *LIEDERSTRAUSS.* **WOLF**
Mir war als müsste ich graven see Unknown **GRIFFES**
Mir war das Leben blass und schal see Groth **LASSEN**
Mir ward gesagt see Heyse **WOLF**
Mirage see Gravollet, Paul *LES FRISSONS,* no. 9. **INDY**
Mirage see Rossetti, Christina **IVES**
Le mirage see Toussaint *JARDIN DES CARESSES.* **AUBERT**
MIRAGES, no. 1
    FAURÉ Brimont *Cygne sur l'éau*
MIRAGES, no. 2
    FAURÉ Brimont *Reflets dans l'éau*
MIRAGES, no. 3
    FAURÉ Brimont *Jardin nocturne*
MIRAGES, no. 4
    FAURÉ Brimont *Danseuse*
Miranda see Fogazzaro, Antonio **RESPIGHI**
Miranda, Francisco Saa de, fl.1550. **SCHUMANN** *Melancholie*
Mireille see Carré **MASSENET** *Chant provençal*

"Mireille ne sait pas encore" *see Chant provençal* Carré **MASSENET**
Mirinda see Annunzio *LA CHIMERA.* **MALIPIERO**
"Mirinda e il fido" *see Mirinda* Annunzio **MALIPIERO**
Mirmont, Jean de la Ville de *see* La Ville de Mirmont, Jean de, 1886-1914.
Miroir see Gabory **AURIC**
"Miroir puisque le temps emporte" *see Miroir* Gabory **AURIC**
MIROIRS BRÛLANTS, no. 1
    POULENC Éluard *Tu vois le feu du soir*
MIROIRS BRÛLANTS, no. 2
    POULENC Éluard *Je nommerai ton front*
Mirologio per un bambino see Anon. **PIZZETTI**
Mirza Schaffy see Unknown **LASSEN**
Mirza-Schaffy, pseud. *see* Bodenstedt, Friedrich Martin von, 1819-1892.
Der Misanthrop see Goethe **ZELTER**
Misero pargoletto see Metastasio *DEMOFOONTE.* **SCHUBERT**
"Miss Ellen, ver sez moile thé" *see Le Thé* Banville **KOECHLIN**
"Miss' on, kussa minun hyväni" *see Missä armahani* Kanteletar **KILPINEN**
Missä armahani see Kanteletar **KILPINEN**
"Mistä lastu lainehilla?" *see Lastu lainehilla* Kianto **SIBELIUS**
mister, youse needn't be so spry see Cummings **BLITZSTEIN**
Il mistero see Romani **VERDI**
Mistletoe see De La Mare **BERKELEY**
Le mistral see Anon. **MILHAUD**
Mistress mine see Shakespeare *TWELFTH NIGHT.* **CARPENTER**
"Mistress mine, where are you roaming" *see Mistress mine* Shakespeare **CARPENTER**
Mists see Ives, Harmony **IVES**
Mit Ahnungsschauern, O Natur! see Groth **LASSEN**
"Mit Alt var du blevet" *see Drømme* Benzon **GRIEG**
Mit deinen blauen Augen see Heine **DELIUS, LASSEN, STRAUSS**
"Mit dem grauen Felsensaal" *see Das Tal* Keller, G. **SCHOECK**
Mit dem grünen Lautenband see Müller, Wilhelm **SCHUBERT**
MIT DEM LEBEN. see Falke Fromm **BERG, REGER, WEBERN**
Mit dem Meere allein see Ady **BARTÓK** *Alone with the sea*
"Mit dem Pfeil, dem Bogen" *see Des Buben Schützenlied* Schiller **SCHUMANN**

Mit den Sternen see Hamerling **LASSEN**

"Mit den Sternen kehrt die Liebe" *see Mit den Sternen* Hamerling **LASSEN**

"Mit der Bergbahn gcht's elektrisch immer höher" *see Verkehr* Krenek **KRENEK**

Mit der Kinderfrau see Musorgskiĭ **MUSORGSKIĬ** *S nianeĭ*

"Mit der Myrthe geschmückt" *see Die Löwenbraut* Chamisso **SCHUMANN**

Mit der Puppe see Musorgskiĭ **MUSORGSKIĬ** *S kukloĭ*

"Mit des Bräutigams Gehagen" *see Ritter Kurt's Brautfahrt* Goethe **WOLF**

Mit einem gemalten Band see Goethe **BEETHOVEN, SCHOECK**

Mit einem Jugendbildnis see Meyer **SCHOECK**

Mit einer Primula veris see Paulsen **GRIEG** *Med en Primula veris*

Mit einer Wasserlilie see Ibsen **GRIEG** *Med en vandlilje*

"Mit erstorbnem Scheinen" *see Eine Leichenphantasie* Schiller **SCHUBERT**

"Mit geheimnisvollen Düften" *see Frühlingslied* Geibel **BRAHMS**

"Mit gelben Birnen hänget" *see Hälfte des Lebens* Hölderlin **BRITTEN**

"Mit Gesang und Tanz" *see Friedensreigen* Voss **ZELTER**

"Mit hellem Sang und Harfenspiel" *see In der Ferne* Cornelius **CORNELIUS**

"Mit Hjerte er en Himmel graa" *see Taaren* Andersen **GRIEG**

Mit jedem Pulsschlag leb' ich dir see Branco **LOEWE**

"Mit leisen Harfentönen" *see Wehmut* Salis-Seewis **SCHUBERT**

"Mit Liebesblick und Spiel und Sang" *see Gretels Warnung* Halem **BEETHOVEN**

"Mit Lust thät ich ausreiten durch einen grünen Wald" *see Jagdlied* Des Knaben Wunderhorn **MENDELSSOHN-BARTHOLDY**

"Mit Mädchen sich vertragen" *see Frech und Froh I* Goethe **WOLF**

"Mit meinem Gott geh ich zur Ruh" *see Am Abend* Unknown **REGER**

Mit meinem Mädchen kann sich keine messen see Dante **RUBINSTEIN** *Tanto gentile e tanto onesta*

"Mit meinem Saitenspiele" *see Rückkehr* Eichendorff **WOLF**

Mit Myrthen und Rosen see Heine **SCHUMANN**

"Mit Regen und Sturmgebrause" *see Winternacht* Schack **STRAUSS**

Mit Rosen bestreut see Bern **REGER**

Mit schwarzen Segeln see Heine *VERSCHIEDENE-SERAPHINE, no. 12.* **FRANZ, GRIFFES, WOLF**

"Mit tausendfacher Schöne" *see Rundgesang im Freien* Recke **LOEWE**

"Mit unserm Arm ist nichts gethan" *see Schlachtgesang* Klopstock **SCHUBERT**

Mit vierzig Jahren see Rückert **BRAHMS**

Mitä tuosta, jos mä laulan see Kanteletar **KILPINEN**

Mitäpä suren sanoista see Kanteletar **KILPINEN**

"Miten kirkas ja kuulas on aamunkoi" *see Aamulaulu* Jalkanen **KILPINEN**

"Miten on mieli miekkoisien" *see Erotus mielillä* Kanteletar **KILPINEN**

Mitt gagoland see Cnattingius, Thor **KILPINEN**

"Mitt Hjarta har vori i Livets Strid" *see Den Saerde* Vinje **GRIEG**

Mitt liv går bort, jag vet ej varthäm see Lagerkvist **KILPINEN**

Mittag see Schellenberg **REGER**

Mittag im September see Hesse **SCHOECK**

Mittagsruh see Eichendorff **LASSEN**

"Mittagsruhe haltend auf den Matten" *see Reisephantasie* Meyer **SCHOECK**

"Mitten im Schimmcr der spiegelnden Wellen" *see Auf dem Wasser zu singen* Stolberg **SCHUBERT**

Mitten ins Herz see Chamisso **FRANZ**

"Mitten unter deinen Schmerzen" *see Christi Huld gegen Petrus* Recke **LOEWE**

Mitternacht see Dingelstedt **SPOHR**

Mitternacht see Rückert **RUBINSTEIN**

"Die Mitternacht zog näher schon" *see Belsatzar* Heine **SCHUMANN**

Mixco see Asturias *LOS INDIOS BAJAN DE MIXCO.* **GIDEON**

Mluv ke mně dál see Tetmajer **MARTINŮ** *Speak on!*

Mne často týrá pochyba see Pfleger-Moravský **DVOŘÁK**

Mne grustno see Lermontov **RIMSKIĬ-KORSAKOV**

"Mne grustno, lotomu" *see Otchevo* Lermontov **BALAKIREV**

Mne li, molodtsu razudalomu see Kol'tsov **BALAKIREV**

"Mne snilis' " *see K moeĭ pesne* Heine **RIMSKIĬ-KORSAKOV**

Mně zdálo se žes umřela see Hálek **DVOŘÁK**

Mnogo est' u menia teremov i sadov see Kol'tsov **MUSORGSKIĬ**

"Moça tan fermosa non vien la frontera" *see*
  Serranilla Santillana **RODRIGO**
Mockery see Shakespeare *LOVE'S*
  LABOUR'S LOST. **HESELTINE**
Møde see Garborg *HAUGTUSSA.* **GRIEG**
  Møte
Moderen synger see Krag **GRIEG**
Modéré-Plus lent see Shakespeare
  THE TEMPEST. **HONEGGER**
Modern see Blomberg **KILPINEN**
Modersorg see Richardt **GRIEG**
Modestes vacances see Paliard **MILHAUD**
Il modo di prender mogli see Unknown
  SCHUBERT
Moe, Jørgen Engebretsen, 1813-1882.
  GRIEG *Ungbirken*
Möcht' im Walde mit dir geh'n see Cornelius
  CORNELIUS
Möcht' wissen, was sie schlagen see
  Eichendorff **FRANZ**
"Möcht' wissen, was sie schlagen" *see*
  Die Nachtigallen Eichendorff **PFITZNER**
"Möchten viele Seelen dies verstehen" *see*
  Verwelkende Rosen Hesse **SCHOECK**
Mögen alle bösen Zungen see Anon. **WOLF**
Moego tot bezumstva zhelal see Shenshin
  MEDTNER *Impromptu*
Moehrcke
  LOEWE *Trommel-Ständchen*
Der Mönch zu Pisa see Vogl **LOEWE**
"Mönchin! schliess mich in dein Dunkel" *see*
  Nachtergebund Trakl **WEBERN**
Mörike, Eduard Friedrich, 1804-1875.
  BERG *Die Soldatenbraut*
  BRAHMS
    Agnes
    An eine Äolsharfe
  FRANZ
    Er ist's!
    Herz, ich habe schwer an dir zu tragen
    In Leid versunken
    Rosenzeit
    Ein Stündlein wohl vor Tag
    Ein Tännlein grünet wo
    Um Mitternacht
    Verborgenheit,
    Volker spielt auf!
  LASSEN
    Frühling
    Das verlassene Mägdlein
  LUENING *Semptembermorgen*
  PFITZNER
    Denk es, O Seele
    Das verlassene Mägdelein
      Two settings: No. 5 of *Sechs*
        Jugendlieder (1884/87) and op. 30
        no. 2.

REGER
  Begegnung
  In der Frühe
  Der König bei der Krönung
SCHOECK
  Am Walde
  An einem Wintermorgan, vor
    Sonnenaufgang
  An meine Mutter
  An Philomele
  Antike Poesie
  Auf dem Krankenbette
  Auf der Teck
  Auf ein Ei geschrieben
  Auf ein Kind
  Auf eine Lampe
  Auf einen Klavierspieler
  Aus der Ferne
  Besuch in Urach
  Die Enthusiasten
  Er ist's
  Erinna an Sappho
  Gebet
  Der Geprüste
  Gesang zu zweien in der Nacht
  Der Hirtenknabe
  Im Park
  Impromptu
  In ein Autographen-Album
  Johann Kepler
  Keine Rettung
  Lose Ware
  Das Mädchen an den Mai
  Mein Fluss
  Muse und Dichter
  Nach dem Kriege
  Nachts
  Nachts am Schreibepult
  Nur zu!
  Peregrina
  Peregrina II
  Restauration
  Ritterliche Werbung
  Schön-Rohtraut
  Die Schwestern
  Septembermorgen
    Two settings: Op. 7 no. 2 and op. 51
      no. 5.
  Spruch
  Trost
  Widmung
  Zu einer Konfirmation
  Zu viel
SCHUMANN
  Er ist's
  Der Gärtner

Jung Volkers Lied
Die Soldatenbraut
Das verlassne Mägdelein
WOLF
Abschied
Agnes
An den Schlaf
An die Geliebte
An eine Äolsharfe
Auf ein altes Bild
Auf eine Christblume
    Two settings: M. 20 and M. 21.
Auf einer Wanderung
Auftrag
Begegnung
Bei einer Trauung
Denk es, O Seele!
Elfenlied
Er ist's
Erstes Liebeslied eines Mädchens
Der Feuerreiter
Frage und Antwort
Fussreise
Der Gärtner
Gebet
Die Geister am Mummelsee
Der Genesene an die Hoffung
Gesang Weylas
Heimweh
Im Frühling
In der Frühe
Der Jäger
Jägerlied
Karwoche
Der Knabe und das Immlein
Der König bei der Krönung
Lebe wohl
Lied eines Verliebten
Lied vom Winde
Mausfallen-Sprüchlein
Neue Liebe
Nimmersatte Liebe
Nixe Binsefuss
Perigrina I
Perigrina II
Rat einer Alter
Schlafendes Jesuskind
Selbstgeständnis
Seufzer
Storchenbotschaft
Ein Stündlein wohl vor Tag
Suschens Vogel
Der Tambour
Die Tochter der Haide
Um Mitternacht
Verborgenheit

Das verlassene Mägdlein
Wo find' ich Trost
Zitronenfalter im April
Zum neuen Jahr
Zur Warnung
MALER NOLTEN.
    SCHOECK *Peregrina*
"Mörker radde i mitt sinne" *see Hjärtats*
    morgon Runeberg **SIBELIUS**
Det mörknar ute see Topelius **SIBELIUS**
Mogu l' zabyt' to sladkoe magnoven'e see
    Pushkin **MEDTNER** *The waltz*
Mohnblumen see Dahn **STRAUSS**
"Mohnblumen sind die runden" *see*
    Mohnblumen Dahn **STRAUSS**
Der Mohrenfürst see Freiligrath **LOEWE**
Der Mohrenfürst auf der Messe see
    Freiligrath **LOEWE**
Die Mohrenfürstin see Freiligrath **LOEWE**
Moĭ golos dlia tebia see Pushkin *NOCH'*
    RIMSKIĭ-KORSAKOV
"Moĭ golos, dlia tebia" *see Noch'* Pushkin
    MUSORGSKIĭ
Moi j'irai dans la lune see Obaldia
    SAUGUET
"Moĭ koster v tumane svetit" *see Pesu'*
    Polonsky **CHAĭKOVSKIĭ**
"Moĭ lizochek tak uzh mal" *see Detskaya*
    pesnya Aksakov **CHAĭKOVSKIĭ**
"Moi qui même au près des belles" *see Si*
    j'étais petit oiseau Béranger **LALO**
Moĭ sadik see Pleshcheyev **CHAĭKOVSKIĭ**
Moia balovnitsa see Mickiewicz
    CHAĭKOVSKIĭ, RIMSKIĭ-KORSAKOV
Le moineau est assis see Anon.
    STRAVINSKIĭ
"Le moineau est assis sur la haie d'autrui" *see*
    Le moineau est assis Anon.
    STRAVINSKIĭ
Moins je la vois see Scève **MILHAUD**
Le mois de Marie see Anon. **GOUNOD**
    Prière à la Vierge
Moisson prochaine see Bouilhet
    KOECHLIN
MOJA PIEŚŃ WIECZORNA. see
    Kasprowicz, Jan
    Blogoslawiona niech bedzie ta chwila
    SZYMANOWSKI
Moja pieszczotka see Mickiewicz **CHOPIN**
Molbech, Christian Knud Frederik, 1821-
    1888.
    JENSEN *Frieden*
Molière, Jean Baptiste Poquelin, 1622-
    1673.
    MASSENET *Sérénade de Molière*
    SAINT-SAËNS *Madrigal*

COMPOSER   Poet   *Title*   "First Line"

Molière, Jean Baptiste Poquelin, 1622-1673 *(continued)*
LE BOURGEOIS GENTILHOMME.
> **FAURÉ** *Sérénade du Bourgeois gentilhomme*

"Molineroes mi amante" *see Canción del duero* Machado y Ruiz **RODRIGO**

Molitva see Goethe **RACHMANINOFF**
> *A prayer*

Molitva see Lermontov **MEDTNER**
> *The prayer*

Molitva see Lermontov **MUSORGSKIĭ**

Molitva see Romanov **RACHMANINOFF**
> *Prayer*

"Mollement accoudée" *see La reine de coeur* Carême **POULENC**

Møller, Poul Martin, 1794-1838.
> **NIELSEN**
>> *Farvel, min velsignede Fødeby!*
>> *Grøn er Vaarens Haek*
>> *Rosen blusser alt i Danas Have*
>> *Sov ind mit lille Nusseben!*
>> *Vor Verden priser jeg tusindfold*

Møllerdatteren see Chamisso **GRIEG**
> *Die Müllerin*

Mollys Abschied see Bürger **BEETHOVEN**

Mombert, Alfred, 1872-1942.
> **BERG**
>> *Aus dem "Glühenden"*
>> *Spaziergang*
> **SZYMANOWSKI**
>> *Fragment: Der Glühende*
>> *Schlummerlied*
> *DER GLÜHENDE.*
>> **BERG**
>>> *Nun ich der Riesen Stärksten*
>>> *Schlafend trägt man mich*
>>> *Warm die Lüfte*

Mommsen, Theodor, 1817-1903.
> **KRENEK**
>> *Im Walde*
>> *Meine Laute nehm'ich wieder*
>> *Die Saiten weiss ich zu rühren*
>> *Und so lasst mich weider wandern*
>> *Wiederum lebt wohl*

MOMPOU, FEDERICO, 1893-1987.
> Anon.
>> *Aserrin, aserran* (1943) [Salabert, 1955] same
>> *D'alt d'un cotxe n'hi ha una nina qu'en* (1931) [Salabert, 1931] same
>> *Hevist dins la lluna tres petits conills* (1931) [Salabert, 1931] same
>> *Margot la pie a fait son nid* (1931) [Salabert, 1931] same
>> *Petite fille de Paris* (1943) [Salabert, 1955] same
>> *Pito, pito, colorito* (1943) [Salabert, 1955] same

Blancafort, Manuel, 1897-
> *L'hora grisa* (1915) [Union Musical Española, 1954]
>> "Tot dorm a l'hora grisa"

Cabanillas, Ramón, 1876-1959.
> *Aureana do sil* (1951) [Salabert, 1962]
>> "As areas de ouro aureana do Sil"

Carner, José, 1884-1971.
> *Cançoneta incerta* (1926) [Union Musical Española, 1953] "Aquest cami tan fi tan fi qui sap ou mena"

Garcés, Tomás, b. 1901
> *Cançó de la Fira* (1949) [Salabert, 1949]
>> "Els seus tresors mostra la fira"

Janés, Clara, 1940-
> *Primeros pasos* (1964) [Salabert, 1967]
>> "Tu cuerpo como un arbol"

Janés i Olivé, Josep, 1913-1959.
> *Aquesta nit un mateix vent* (1946) [Salabert, 1949] same
> *Damunt de tu només les flors* (1942) [Salabert, 1949] same
> *Fes me la vida transparent* [Salabert, 1989] same
> *Jo et pressentia com la mar* (1948) [Salabert, 1949] same

Jimenez, Juan Ramón, 1881-1958.
> *Llueve sobre el rio* (1945) [Salabert, 1956] same
> *Pastoral* (1945) [Salabert, 1956]
>> "Los caminos de la tarde"

John, Saint, apostle
> *Cantar del alma* (1961) [Salabert, 1961]
>> "Aquella eterna fuerte esta escondida"

Mompou, Federico, 1893-1987.
> *Fortina de fullatge* (1926-28) [Salabert, 1931] "Encare veig al lluny"
> *Incertitud* (1926-28) [Salabert, 1931]
>> "Incertitud del meu cami"
> *Neu* (1926-28) [Salabert, 1931]
>> "No es neu són flors de cel"
> *Rosa del cami* (1926-28) [Salabert, 1931]
>> "En dolç desmai durant la nit"

Pomès, Mathilde
> *Le nuage* (1928) [Rouart Lerolle, 1931; Salabert] "S'embarquer, Ô lente nef"

Ribot, Theodule, 1839-1916.
> *Sant Marti* (1962) [unpubl.?]

Valéry, Paul Ambroise, 1871-1945.
> *La fausse morte* [Eschig, 1985]
>> "Humblement, tendrement, sur le tombeau charmant"
> *L'insinuant* [Eschig, 1985] "O Courbes, méandres, secrets du menteur"

COMPOSER Poet *Title* "First Line"

Les pas [Eschig, 1985]
"Tes pas, enfants de mon silence"
Le sylphe [Eschig, 1985]
"Ni vu ni connu"
Le vin perdu [Eschig, 1985]
"J'ai, quelque jour, dans l'Océan"
Mompou, Federico, 1893-1987.
MOMPOU
Fortina de fullatge
Incertitud
Neu
Rosa del cami
"Mon amant m'a baisée au cou" *see Les fleurs*
Mauclair BLOCH
Mon amante a les vertus de l'eau see
Ségalen IBERT
"Mon âme a joint ses mains étranges" *see*
Attente Maeterlinck BOULANGER
"Mon âme vers ton front où rêve" *see Soupir*
Mallarmé DEBUSSY, RAVEL
"Mon ami vient de s'en aller!" *see Chant*
Breton Delpit LALO
"Mon amie, il faut que je parte" *see Départ*
Rilke BARBER
Mon amour . . . see Eluard AURIC
Mon amour a mon coeur see Barbier, J.
GOUNOD
"Mon amour d'antan" *see Amour d'antan*
Bouchor, M. CHAUSSON
Mon amour est bon à dire see Hugnet
THOMSON
Mon amour l'a bien mérité see Silvestre
MASSENET
"Mon amour pour avoir figuré mes désirs" *see*
Mon amour . . . Eluard AURIC
"Mon beau tzigane mon amant" *see*
Les cloches Apollinaire HONEGGER
MON BIEN, no. 1
SAUGUET Clancier *Comme autrefois*
MON BIEN, no. 2
SAUGUET Clancier *Le temps et les pays*
MON BIEN, no. 3
SAUGUET Clancier *Bergère*
"Mon bien aimé" *see L'âme délaissée*
Delavigne ROSSINI
"Mon bien aimé" *see Cantique pour la*
première communion Dulong de Rosnay,
R. P. GOUNOD
"Mon bien aimé, dans mes douleurs" *see Vous*
ne priez pas Delavigne BIZET
Mon bien aimé siffle bien see Aguet,
William IBERT
Mon cadavre est doux comme un gant see
Vilmorin POULENC
"Mon cher, Jérôme, j'ai beaucoup réfléchi"
see Lettre d'Alissa Gide MILHAUD

"Mon coeur blessé gémit tout bas" *see*
L'amour à Pekin Pacini ROSSINI
"Mon coeur d'enfant était un paradis" *see*
Parfums Dortzal MASSENET
Mon coeur est plein de toi see Silvestre
MASSENET
"Mon coeur lassé de tout" *see Le vallon*
Lamartine GOUNOD
"Mon coeur n'est pas déposé de" *see Ton*
souvenir Feillet, Émilie MASSENET
"Mon Dieu est ma force" *see Gloire à Dieu*
Anon. MILHAUD
"Mon Dieu faites que je m'abandonne
constamment" *see Prière* Peyrissac, Jean
RIVIER
"Mon Dieu! j'étais une bergère" *see Jeanne*
d'Arc au bûcher Dumas the elder LISZT
"Mon Dieu, l'âme que vous m'avez donnée
est pure" *see Prière du matin* Anon.
MILHAUD
"Mon Dieu, Seigneur et Père" *see Que ta*
volonté soit faite Gounod GOUNOD
"Mon Dieu vous m'avez appelé parmi les
hommes" *see Prière* Jammes
HONEGGER
"Mon Dieu, vous savez bien que j'ai besoin
de lui pour vous aimer" *see Journal*
d'Alissa Gide MILHAUD
Mon elué see Unknown RESPIGHI
"Mon enfant, ma soeur" *see L'invitation au*
voyage Baudelaire CHABRIER,
DUPARC
"Mon espérance n'est pas encore perdue" *see*
Chant du laboureur Unknown
MILHAUD
"Mon fils dort sous la mousse" *see Mon fils*
est couché là Guilliaume LASSEN
Mon fils est couché là see Guilliaume
LASSEN
"Mon fils, roseéphémère, endors ta plainte a
mère" *see Le dodo des enfants* Unknown
ROSSINI
Mon habit see Béranger GOUNOD
Mon histoire see Supervielle MILHAUD
Mon mouchoir, hélas, est perdu see Anon.
RAVEL
Mon page see Théus, Maurice de
MASSENET
"Mon père me marie à l'âge de quinze ans"
see La Maumariée II Unknown PIJPER
Mon père travaille see Legrand, Marc
INDY
Mon petit bateau see Stevenson, Robert
Louis *A CHILD'S GARDEN OF VERSES.*
HAHN *My ship and I*
Mon rêve familier see Verlaine KOECHLIN

DIE MONATE: Januar. *see* Toman
   On snow-swept paths **MARTINŮ**
DIE MONATE: September. *see* Toman
   My brother has finished ploughing
     MARTINŮ
Der Mond see Geibel **MENDELSSOHN-**
   BARTHOLDY
"*Der Mond, der scheint*" *see Die Ammenuhr*
   Des Knaben Wunderhorn
   SCHUMANN
Der Mond glüht see Diederich **REGER**
"*Mond, hast du auch gesehen*" *see*
   Das Mädchen spricht Prutz **REGER**
Der Mond hat eine schwere Klag' see Heyse
   WOLF
"*Der Mond ist aufgegangen*" *see Abendlied*
   Claudius, M. **SCHOECK, SCHUBERT**
"*Der Mond ist schlafen 'gangen*" *see*
   Ständchen Osterwald **FRANZ**
"*Der Mond kommt still gegangen*" *see*
   Nachtlied Geibel **FRANZ, GRIFFES,**
   MACDOWELL
Mond, meiner Seele Liebling see Kulmann
   SCHUMANN
"*Der Mond scheint auf mein Lager*" *see*
   Fromm Falke **BERG, REGER, WEBERN**
"*Der Mond steht über dem Berge*" *see*
   Ständchen Kugler **BRAHMS**
"*Der Mond streut durch die Zweige sein*
   silberblaues Licht" *see Sommernacht* Evers
   REGER
Der Mondabend see Kumpf **SCHUBERT**
"*Monde tu nous interroges*" *see L'Enigme*
   éternelle Anon. **RAVEL**
Mondenschein see Heine *HEIMKEHR.*
   BRAHMS
Mondlicht see Branco **LOEWE**
Mondmythus see Lingg **LASSEN**
Mondnacht see Eichendorff **BRAHMS,**
   SCHUMANN
Mondnacht see Evers **REGER**
Die Mondnacht see Kosegarten
   SCHUBERT
Mondnacht see Unknown **LASSEN**
"*Der Mondschein, der ist schon verblichen*"
   see Himmelsboten zu Liebchens Himmelbett
   Des Knaben Wunderhorn **STRAUSS**
"*Der Mondschein lag auf dem Wasser*" *see*
   Traum Semler **BERG**
Mongolian idiot see Shapiro **ROREM**
The monk see Anon. **PROKOFIEV** *Chernets*
The monk and his cat see Auden, W. H.,
   translator **BARBER**
Monks and raisins see Villa, J. G. *HAVE*
   COME, AM HERE. **BARBER**
Monnier, Etienne

LISZT
   Élégie
   En ces lieux
Monnier, Marc, 1829-1885.
   FAURÉ *Barcarolle*
Monody see Melville **DIAMOND**
Monody on a lady famed for her caprice see
   Burns **GIDEON**
"*Monotonous the hours toll*" *see Sleepless*
   Tiutchev **MEDTNER**
Monrad, Olaf Peder, 1849-1920.
   GRIEG *Ved en ung Hustrus Båre*
Monro, Harold Edward, 1879-1932.
   IRELAND *Earth's call*
Monroe, Marilyn, 1926-1962.
   DIAMOND *Don't cry*
Monrousseau, Lucien
   MASSENET *Rien ne passe*
Monsieur le Curé see Paliard **MILHAUD**
Monsieur le Duc see Jacob, M. **RIETI**
"*Monsieur le Duc vint à point nommeé*" *see*
   Monsieur le Duc Jacob, M. **RIETI**
Monsieur Protopopoff see Chalupt
   MILHAUD
Monsieur sans-souci see Nohain, Jean
   POULENC
Monsterberg-Münckeman, Elimar von,
   b.1877.
   BERG *Abschied*
Mont' on mulla morsianta see Kanteletar
   KILPINEN
Montagnes see Messiaen **MESSIAEN**
Montanus' sonnet see Lodge, T. **RIETI**
"*Monte, écureuil, monte au grand chêne*" *see*
   Attente Hugo **INDY; SAINT-SAËNS,**
   WAGNER *L'attente*
Montesquiou-Fezensac, Robert, comte
   de, 1855-1921.
   SCHMITT
     Les barques
     Un cantique
"*Montez à Dieu, chants d'allé gresse!*" *see*
   Chantez noël Barbier, J. **GOUNOD**
Montgomery, James, 1771-1854.
   BENNETT *Resignation*
   GOUNOD *For ever with the Lord*
Montgomery-Gretchen see Burns **FRANZ**
Montparnasse see Apollinaire *IL Y A.*
   POULENC
Moo is a cow see Feeney **CHANLER**
The moon see Shelley **HINDEMITH**
Moon, that against the lintel of the West see
   Millay *FATAL INTERVIEW.* **GIDEON**
Moonlight see Quilter **QUILTER**
Moonrise see Hopkins **KRENEK**

Moore, G.
  MARTINŮ *Evening*
Moore, Marianne Craig, 1887-1972.
  THOMSON
    English usage
    My crow Pluto
Moore, Thomas, 1779-1852.
  BERLIOZ
    Adieu, Bessy!
    La belle voyageuse
    Le coucher du soleil!
    Élégie
    L'origine de la harpe
  DUPARC *Élégie*
  HINDEMITH *Echo*
  IVES
    Canon
    A night song
    A night thought
    Those evening bells
  JENSEN
    Die Bowle fort!
    Es kommt eine Zeit, eine trübe Zeit!
    Friede den Schlummerern!
    Leis rudern hier
    Leis rudern hier, mein Gondolier!
    Licht sie dein Traum!
    Wie manchmal, wenn des Mondes Strahl
  MENDELSSOHN-BARTHOLDY
    Der Blumenkranz
    Venetianisches Gondellied
  RUBINSTEIN
    A dream
    Good Night!
    The tear
  SCHUMANN *Zwei Venetianische Lieder*
  WEBER *From Chindara's warbling fount*
  WHEN THROUGH THE PIAZZETTA.
    JENSEN *Wenn durch die Piazzetta*
    SCHUMANN *Zwei Venetianische Lieder*
Moosröslein see Chezy **LOEWE**
"Mor, Mor, lilla mor, säg var lyckan bor" *see*
  Lilla Olles visa Cnattingius, Thor
  KILPINEN
Morand, Paul, 1889-1976.
  MILHAUD
    Don Juan
    Étrennes
    Révérence
  RAVEL
    Chanson à boire
    Chanson épique
    Chanson romantique
Moravian girl see Anon. **MARTINŮ** *Děvče z Moravy*
"Morceau pour piston seul" *see Enfant de troupe* Cocteau **POULENC**

More see Borodin **BORODIN** *The sea*
"More dim than waning moon Thy face" *see*
  Old love Crapsey **WEISGALL**
More, Elisa, lo stanco poeta see Bianchi,
  Tommaso **VERDI**
MORE TRIVIA. see Smith, Logan
  The epitaph **DIAMOND**
  Somewhere **DIAMOND**
Moréas, Jean, 1856-1910.
  CHAUSSON *Dans la forêt du Charme et
    de l'Enchantement*
  HAHN
    Aux rayons du couchant
    Belle lune d'argent
    Compagne de l'éther
    Dans la nuit
    Dans le ciel est dressé le chéne séculaire
    Donc, vous allez fleurir encor
    Eau printanière
    *Encor sur le pavé sonne mon pas
      nocturne*
    Fumée
    Pendant que je médite
    Quand je viendrai m'asseoir
    Quand reviendra l'automne
    Roses en bracelet
    Théone
  MALIPIERO *Ariette*
  POULENC
    Air champêtre
    Air grave
    Air romantique
    Air vif
  RESPIGHI *Au milieu du jardin*
  SAINT-SAËNS *L'arbre*
Morel-Retz, Louis Pierre Gabriel
  Bernard, 1825-1899.
  MASSENET
    Amoureuse
    L'éventail
"*Morena*" *me llaman see* Anon. **RODRIGO**
Moreno
  SE PLAIRE SUR LA MÊME FLEUR.
    MILHAUD *Ritournelle et six chansons*
Morgana see Annunzio *LA CHIMERA.*
  MALIPIERO
Der Morgen see Eichendorff **LASSEN**
Morgen see Mackay **REGER, STRAUSS**
Der Morgen see Sallet **STRAUSS**
"Der Morgen blüht; der Osten glüht" *see Von
  Ida* Kosegarten **SCHUBERT**
"Der Morgen steigt und glüht und steigt" *see
  Zwischen zwei Nächten* Falke **REGER**
Morgenbøn paa Skolen see Gjertsen **GRIEG**
Morgendug see Chamisso **GRIEG**
  Morgentau

Morgendug, der sagte baever see Hauch
  NIELSEN
Morgengebet see Eichendorff **LASSEN**
Morgengebet in der Schule see Gjertsen
  GRIEG *Morgenbøn paa Skolen*
Morgengesang see Alberus *MORGENLIED.*
  REGER
Morgengruss see Heine **MENDELSSOHN-
  BARTHOLDY**
Morgengruss see Müller, Wilhelm
  SCHUBERT
Morgengruss an Serena see Nostitz und
  Jänckendorf **ZELTER**
Der Morgenkuss see Batsányi *DER
  MORGENKUSS NACH EINEM BALL.*
  SCHUBERT
DER MORGENKUSS NACH EINEM BALL.
  see Batsányi
  Der Morgenkuss **SCHUBERT**
MORGENLIED. see Alberus
  Morgengesang **REGER**
  O Jesu Christ, wir warten dein **REGER**
Morgenlied see Rudolphi **LOEWE**
Morgenlied see Stolberg **SCHUBERT**
Morgenlied see Uhland **RUBINSTEIN**
Morgenlied see Unknown **SCHUBERT**
Morgenlied see Voss **MENDELSSOHN-
  BARTHOLDY, ZELTER**
Morgenlied see Werner *DIE SÖHNE DES
  TALES.* **SCHUBERT**
Morgenrot see Rückert **STRAUSS**
Morgens see Storm **RUBINSTEIN**
Morgens am Brunnen see Roquette
  JENSEN
"Morgens auf betauter Weide" *see Lied*
  Luhden **ZELTER**
MORGENS AUF BETAUTER WEIDE. see
  Luhden *Lied* **ZELTER**
Morgens steh' ich auf und frage see Heine
  LISZT, SCHUMANN
"Morgens steh' ich auf und frage" *see Kommt
  feins Liebchen heut'?* Heine **FRANZ**
Morgenständchen see Scheffel **LISZT**
  Reimar der Alte
Morgenständchen see Träger **JENSEN**
Morgenstern, Christian Otto Joseph
  Wolfgang, 1871-1914.
  HINDEMITH
    Auf der Treppe sitzen meine Öhrchen
    Vor dir schein' ich aufgewacht
    Wie Sankt Franciscus schweb' in der Luft
  KILPINEN
    Anmutiger Vertrag
    Auf einem verfallenen Kirchhof
    Deine Rosen an der Brust
    Es ist Nacht

Die Fusswaschung
Heimat
Kleines Lied
Mein Herz ist leer
O, Nacht
Der Säemann
Schicksal der Liebe
Siehe, auch ich—lebe
Thalatta
Der Tod und der einsame Trinker
Über die tausend Berge
Unsere Liebe
Unverlierbare Gewähr
Vöglein Schwermut
Von zwei Rosen
Wie vieles ist denn Wort geworden
Winternacht
Wir sitzen im Dunkeln
  REGER
    Anmutiger Vertrag
    Frühlingsregen
    Gleich einer versunkenen Melodie
    Hymnus des Hasses
    Leise Lieder
    Mädchenlied
    Pflügerin Sorge
    Weisse Tauben
  SEIBER
    Das Knie
    Das Nasobem
    Die Trichter
  STRAUSS *Leise Lieder*
Morgenstimmung see Reinick **WOLF**
Morgentau see Anon. **WOLF**
Morgentau see Chamisso **GRIEG**
Morgenwind see Heyse **CORNELIUS**
"Morgenwölkchen, leichte weben" *see Frieden*
  Grun, James **PFITZNER**
Morgonen see Runeberg **SIBELIUS**
Morgonens hjärta see Österling **KILPINEN**
"Mørket viger, Dagen stiger" *see Gry*
  Lorenzen, H. **NIELSEN**
"Mormora nel giardino" *see Nel giardino*
  Rocchi, Francesco **RESPIGHI**
The morn of live see Tiutchev
  RACHMANINOFF *I remember that day*
MORNING. see Blake, William
  Daybreak **QUILTER**
The morning see Runeberg **SIBELIUS**
  Morgonen
Morning see Yanova **RACHMANINOFF**
Morning fair see Agee *SONNET XX.*
  CARPENTER
Morning song see Heywood **QUILTER**
Morning song see No author **LUENING**
Morning star see Goldberg **GIDEON**

Morning star see Verlaine *LA BONNE
CHANSON.* **DELIUS** *Avant que tu ne t'en
ailles*
MORNING STAR, no. 1
   GIDEON Bialik *The nest*
MORNING STAR, no. 2
   GIDEON Yalan-Stekelis *The cat is angry*
MORNING STAR, no. 3
   GIDEON Goldberg *Morning star*
MORNING STAR, no. 4
   GIDEON Bialik *The swing*
Morris, Maurice, pseud. *see* Pool, Morris
W.
MORS ROK. see Aakjaer
   Spurven sidder stum bag Kvist **NIELSEN**
Morskaya tsarevna see Borodin **BORODIN**
La mort de la cigale see Faure, M.
   MASSENET
La Mort des amants see Baudelaire *FLEURS
DU MAL.* **DEBUSSY**
La mort d'Ophélie see Legouvé
   SAINT-SAËNS
La mort d'Ophélie see Shakespeare
   BERLIOZ
Le mort maudit see Richepin **CHAUSSON**
La mort passe see Chobanian **HONEGGER**
Mort, ta servante est à ma porte see Tagore
GITANJALI. **CASELLA**
Morta tu giacerai see Sappho **RIETI**
"Morte, non io ti temo" *see La cavalcata della
morte* Pàntini, Romualdo **MALIPIERO**
Mortenson, Norma Jean *see* Monroe,
Marilyn, 1926-1962.
Les morts see Richepin **CHAUSSON**
Mosen, Julius, 1803-1867.
   GRIFFES *Der träumende See*
   SCHUMANN *Der Nussbaum*
   NACHTLIED.
      GRIFFES *Könnt ich mit dir dort oben
gehen*
Mosenthal, Salomon Hermann, Ritter
von, 1821-1877.
   RUBINSTEIN *Nachhall*
Moses, Elizabeth Ann
   THOMPSON, R.
      A ballad
      Southwind
Moskhos
   ROUSSEL *Pan ainmait Ekho*
Moss, Howard, 1922-1987.
   ROREM
      The air is the only
      A body without love
      I know so many stories
      Only lover's rest
      See how they love me

      They rise up shining
      Tourist's song
"Most high, omnipotent Lord" *see From the
canticle of the sun* Francis of Assisi
   THOMSON
"Most holy night, that still dost keep" *see
The night* Belloc, Hilaire **HESELTINE**
"The most unpleasant thing to do" *see Making
calls* Carpenter, Rue **CARPENTER**
MOSTLY ABOUT LOVE, no. 1
   THOMSON Koch *Love song*
MOSTLY ABOUT LOVE, no. 2
   THOMSON Koch *Down at the docks*
MOSTLY ABOUT LOVE, no. 3
   THOMSON Koch *Let's take a walk*
MOSTLY ABOUT LOVE, no. 4
   THOMSON Koch *A prayer to Saint
Catherine*
Møte see Garborg *HAUGTUSSA.* **GRIEG**
The moth see De La Mare **BERKELEY**
MOTHER AND CHILD, no. 1
   IRELAND Rossetti, Christina *Newborn*
MOTHER AND CHILD, no. 2
   IRELAND Rossetti, Christina
   The only child
MOTHER AND CHILD, no. 3
   IRELAND Rossetti, Christina *Hope*
MOTHER AND CHILD, no. 4
   IRELAND Rossetti, Christina
   Skylark and nightingale
MOTHER AND CHILD, no. 5
   IRELAND Rossetti, Christina
   The blind boy
MOTHER AND CHILD, no. 6
   IRELAND Rossetti, Christina *Baby*
MOTHER AND CHILD, no. 7
   IRELAND Rossetti, Christina
   Death-parting
MOTHER AND CHILD, no. 8
   IRELAND Rossetti, Christina
   The garland
Mother dear see Sládek **MARTINŮ**
Mother dear, oh was I born see Mickiewicz
   CHAÏKOVSKIĬ *Ali mat' menia rozhala*
Mother, I cannot mind my wheel see Landor
   ROREM
Mother mine, I have a laddie see Anon.
   MARTINŮ
Motion & stillness see Shove
   VAUGHAN WILLIAMS
Motiv see Krenek **KRENEK**
Motto see Eichendorff **SCHOECK**
Mou celou duší zádumně bolestné see
   Pfleger-Moravský **DVOŘÁK**
"The mountain stirred its bushy crown" *see
from "Amphion"* Tennyson **IVES**

COMPOSER   Poet   *Title*   "First Line"

Mourn no moe see Fletcher **HESELTINE**
Mousmé see Alexandre, André
MASSENET
MOUSSORGSKY, MODEST PETROVICH
see
MUSORGSKIĭ, MODEST PETROVICH,
1839-1881.
The mouth of the righteous man see Bible
LUENING
Mouton Blanc see Bibesco **SAUGUET**
MOUVEMENTS DU COEUR, no. 1
SAUGUET Vilmorin *Prelude*
MOUVEMENTS DU COEUR, no. 7
SAUGUET Vilmorin *Postlude: Polonaise*
Moy geniy, moy angel, moy drug see
Shenshin **CHAĬKOVSKIĭ**
Las moyares corralera, cancion española *see*
Unknown **LOEFFLER**
Moyne, Paul le *see* Le Moyne, Paul,
1663-1704.
MOZART, WOLFGANG AMADEUS,
1756-1791.
Batsányi, Gabriele (von Baumberg),
1775-1839.
Als Luise die Briefe ihres ungetreuen
Liebhabers verbrannte, K. 520
[GA, v. 7, p. 58; NMA, v. 8, p. 40]
"Erzeugt von heisser Phantasie"
Blumauer, Aloys, 1755-1798.
Lied der Freiheit, K. 506 [GA, v. 7,
p. 48; NMA, v. 8, p. 28]
"Wer unter eines Mädchens Hand"
Campe, Joachim Heinrich, 1746-1818.
Abendempfindung an Laura, K. 523 [GA,
v. 7, p. 60; NMA, v. 8, p. 42]
"Abend ist's"
Denis, Johann Nepomuk Cosmas
Michael, 1729-1800.
Gibraltar, K. Anh. 25 (386d) [NMA,
v. 8, p. 72]
"O Calpe! dir donnert's am Fusse"
Ferrand, Antoine, 1678-1719.
Ariette, K. 284d (307) [GA, v. 7, p. 12;
NMA, v. 8, p. 6]
"Oiseaux, si tous les ans"
Goethe, Johann Wolfgang von, 1749-
1832.
Das Veilchen, K. 476 [GA, v. 7, p. 42;
NMA, v. 8, p. 26]
"Ein Veilchen auf der Wiese stand"
Hagedorn, Friedrich von, 1708-1754.
Die Alte, K. 517 [GA, v. 7, p. 50; NMA,
v. 8, p. 32] "Zu meiner Zeit"
Hermes, Johann Timotheus, 1738-
1821.
SOPHIENS REISE.

Ich würd' auf meinem Pfad, K. 340c
(390) [GA, v. 7, p. 22; NMA, v. 8,
p. 17] same
Sei du mein Trost, K. 340b (391) [GA,
v. 7, p. 23; NMA, v. 8, p. 16] same
Verdankt sei es dem Glanz der
Grossen, K. 340a (392)
[GA, v. 7, p. 24; NMA, v. 8, p. 15]
same
Hölty, Ludwig Heinrich Christoph,
1748-1776.
Das Traumbild, K. 530 [GA, v. 7, p. 70;
NMA, v. 8, p. 52] "Wo bist du, Bild"
Jacobi, Johann Georg, 1740-1814.
An Chloe, K. 524 [GA, v. 7, p. 64;
NMA, v. 8, p. 46] "Wenn die Lieb'
aus deinen blauen Augen"
Lamotte, Antoine Houdart de, 1672-
1731.
Ariette, K. 295b (308) [GA, v. 7, p. 14;
NMA, v. 8, p. 8]
"Dans un bois solitaire"
Lenz, Ludwig Friedrich, 1717-1780.
Lobgesang auf die feierliche
Johannisloge, K. 125h (148)
[GA, v. 7, p. 5; NMA, v. 8, p. 4]
"O heiliges Band"
Miller, Johann Martin, 1750-1814.
Die Zufriedenheit, K. 367a (349) [GA,
v. 7, p. 18; NMA, v. 8, p. 12]
"Was graf' ich viel nach Geld und
Gut"
Also with mandolin accompaniment.
Overbeck, Christian Adolf, 1755-1821.
Das Kinderspiel, K. 598 [GA, v. 7, p. 80;
NMA, v. 8, p. 60]
"Wir Kinder, wir schmecken"
Sehnsucht nach dem Frühlinge, K. 596
[GA, v. 7, p. 77; NMA, v. 8, p. 58]
"Komm, lieber Mai"
Ratschky, Franz Joseph von, 1757-
1810.
Lied zur Gesellenreise, K. 468 [GA, v. 7,
p. 34; NMA, v. 8, p. 18]
"Die ihr einem neuen Grade"
Voice & piano or organ.
Schall, Johann Eberhard Friedrich,
1742-1790.
Des kleinen Friedrichs Geburtstag,
K. 529 [GA, v. 7, p. 68; NMA, v. 8,
p. 50] "Es war einmal, ihr Leute"
Schmidt, Klamer Eberhard Karl, 1746-
1824.
Das Lied der Trennung, K. 519 [GA,
v. 7, p. 54; NMA, v. 8, p. 36]
"Die Engel Gottes weinen"

Sturm, Christoph Christian, 1740-
1786.
  Der Frühling, K. 597 [GA, v. 7, p. 78;
    NMA, v. 8, p. 59]
    "Erwacht zum neuen Leben"
Unknown
  Beim Auszug in das Feld, K. 552 [NMA,
    v. 8, p. 56]
    "Dem hohen Kaiser-Worte treu"
  Die kleine Spinnerin, K. 531 [GA, v. 7,
    p. 72; NMA, v. 8, p. 54]
    "Was spinnst du?"
  Komm, liebe Zither, komm, K. 367b (351)
    [GA, v. 7, p. 21; NMA, v. 8, p. 14]
    same
    Voice & mandolin.
  Wie unglücklich bin ich nit, K. 125g
    (147) [GA, v. 7, p. 4; NMA, v. 8, p. 4]
    same
Uz, Johann Peter, 1720-1796.
  An die Freude, K. 43b (53) [GA, v. 7,
    p. 2; NMA, v. 8, p. 2]
    "Freude, Königin der Weisen"
Weisse, Christian Felix, 1726-1804.
  Die betrogene Welt, K. 474 [GA, v. 7,
    p. 40; NMA, v. 8, p. 24]
    "Der reiche Tor, mit Gold
      geschmücket"
  Die Verschweigung, K. 518 [GA, v. 7,
    p. 52; NMA, v. 8, p. 34]
    "Sobald Damoetas Chloen sieht"
  Der Zauberer, K. 472 [GA, v. 7, p. 36;
    NMA, v. 8, p. 20]
    "Ihr Mädchen, flieht Damöten ja"
  Die Zufriedenheit, K. 473 [GA, v. 7,
    p. 38; NMA, v. 8, p. 22]
    "Wie sanft, wie ruhig fühl' ich hier"
Ziegenhagen, Franz Heinrich, 1753-
1806.
  *Die ihr des unermesslichen Weltalls
    Schöpfer ehrt*, K. 619
    [GA, v. 7, p. 82; NMA, v. 4⁴, p. 59]
    same
    Cantata for voice & piano.
Mr. Belloc's fancy see Squire, Sir John
TRICKS OF THE TRADE (1917).
  HESELTINE
Mrtvá láska see Mužik **MARTINŮ**
  Dead love
MUCH ADO ABOUT NOTHING. see
  Shakespeare
  Pardon, Goddess of the night **THOMSON**
  Sigh no more, ladies **HESELTINE,
    QUILTER, THOMSON**
"Una muchacha guapa, llamada" *see Adela*
  Anon. **RODRIGO**

Müchler, Karl Friedrich, 1763-1857.
  WEBER
    Klage
    Lied
    Das Röschen
  ZELTER
    Abendlied
    An junge spröde Schöne
Müde see Falke **REGER**
Müde see Liliencron **PFITZNER**
"Der müde Sommer senkt das Haupt" *see*
  Jugendflucht Hesse **KILPINEN**
Die müde Wanderer see Hoffmann von
  Fallersleben **STRAUSS**
"Die Mühle, die dreht ihre Flügel" see
  Die Müllerin Chamisso **GRIEG**
"Eine Mühle seh' ich blinken" *see Halt!*
  Müller, Wilhelm **SCHUBERT**
"Mühlen still die Flügel drehn" *see*
  Sonnenschein Heyse **JENSEN**
Mühler, Heinrich von, 1813-1874.
  KAISER OTTO I.
    LOEWE *Kaiser Ott's Weihnachtsfeier*
Mühvoll komm' ich und beladen see Manuel
  del Rio, Don **WOLF**
"Die Mükke sitzt am Fenster" *see Abend- und
  Morgenrot* Hoffmann von Fallersleben
  STRAUSS
Müller, Joseph, 1802-1872.
  LISZT
    Das Schlüsselblumen
    Das Veilchen
"Ein Müller mahlte" *see Zwiesprach* Boelitz
  REGER
Der Müller und der Bach see Müller,
  Wilhelm **SCHUBERT**
Müller von der Werra, Friedrich Konrad
  Mueller, known as, 1823-1881.
  SPOHR *Mein Verlangen*
Müller von Königswinter, Wolfgang,
1816-1873.
  FRANZ
    Im Herbst
    Im Walde
    Widmung
  PFITZNER *Hast du von den
    Fischerkindern*
  SCHUMANN *Im Wald*
Müller, Wilhelm, 1794-1827.
  JENSEN *Es hat so grün gesäuselt*
  LOEWE *Liebesgedanken*
  SCHUBERT
    Am Feierabend
    Auf dem Flusse
    Die böse Farbe
    Danksagung an den Bach

Müller, Wilhelm, 1794-1827 *(continued)*
  SCHUBERT *(continued)*
    Des Baches Wiegenlied
    Des Müllers Blumen
    Eifersucht und Stolz
    Einsamkeit
    Erstarrung
    Frühlingstraum
    Gefror'ne Thränen
    Der greise Kopf
    Gute Nacht
    Halt!
    Der Hirt auf dem Felsen
    Im Dorfe
    Irrlicht
    Der Jäger
    Die Krähe
    Der Leiermann
    Letzte Hoffnung
    Die liebe Farbe
    Der Lindenbaum
    Mein!
    Mit dem grünen Lautenband
    Morgengruss
    Der Müller und der Bach
    Mut
    Die Nebensonne
    Der Neugierige
    Pause
    Die Post
    Rast
    Rückblick
    Der stürmische Morgen
    Täuschung
    Thränenregen
    Trockne Blumen
    Ungeduld
    Das Wandern
    Wasserflut
    Der Wegweiser
    Die Wetterfahne
    Das Wirtshaus
    Wohin?
  SPOHR *Ungeduld*
Die Müllerin see Chamisso **GRIEG**
Münch-Bellinghausen, Eligius Franz Joseph, freiherr von, 1806-1871.
  BRAHMS
    Bei dir sind meine Gedanken
    Beim Abschied
    Der Jäger
    Kein Haus, keine Heimat
    Steig' auf, geliebter Schatten
  SCHUMANN *Geisternähe*
  DER SOHN DU WILDNISS.
    LOEWE *Mein Herz, ich will dich fragen*

Mündel, Curt
  ELSÄSSISCHE VOLKSLIEDER.
    STRAUSS
      Ach was Kummer, Qual und Schmerzen
      Wer lieben will, muss leiden
"Ein Münich steht in seiner Zell" *see*
    Der Kreuzzug Leitner **SCHUBERT**
Münter, Balthasar, b. 1734.
  LOEWE *Unsere Auferstehung durch Christum*
"Mütterchen, das führ zu Grab" *see*
    Wanderlied Beta **SCHÖNBERG**
Le muguet see Richter **SAUGUET**
MUI GRACIOSA ES LA DONCELLA. see
    Vicente, Gil
    O wie lieblich ist das Mädchen
      SCHUMANN
"Muien turvaset tulevat" *see Armas arkussa ajavi* Kanteletar **KILPINEN**
"Muilla onni työn tekevi" *see Makaaja onni* Kanteletar **KILPINEN**
Muinainen käkeni see Kanteletar
    KILPINEN
Muisto see Lamberg **KILPINEN**
Muistoja see Jalkanen **KILPINEN**
Muj bratr dooral see Toman *DIE MONATE:* September. **MARTINŮ**
    My brother has finished ploughing
The mulberry tree see Unknown
    PROKOFIEV
Der Mummelsee see Schnezler **LOEWE**
"Mun onneni kukkii kuin omenapuu" *see*
    Omenakukat Lönnbohm **KILPINEN**
"Mun sieluni sun ylläs väräjää" *see Lakeus I* Koskenniemi **KILPINEN**
Munch, Andreas, 1811-1884.
  GRIEG
    Harpen
    Udfarten
    Vuggesang
  SOLNEDGANG.
    DELIUS *Beim Sonnenuntergang*
    GRIEG *Solnedgang*
Mund und Auge see Hamerling **LASSEN**
"Der muntern Hüpferin Libell" *see*
    Die Ameise und die Libelle Krylov
      RUBINSTEIN
"Muore il giorno invernale tra un pio lamentar di campane" *see Sera d'Inverno* Silvani, Mario **PIZZETTI**
Murheen kellot see Törmänen **KILPINEN**
Murmelndes Lüftchen see Anon.
  SPANISCHES LIEDERBUCH: Ventecico murmurador. **JENSEN**
"Murmure autour de ma nacelle" *see Douce mer* Lamartine **BIZET**

Murray, Gilbert, 1866-1957.
VAUGHAN WILLIAMS *Where is the home for me?*
Murrays Ermordung see Anon. **BRAHMS**
"Musa of the seablue eyes" *see On a singing girl* Wylie **ROREM**
LAS MUSAS DE ANDALUCIA, no. 5
TURINA Attard, Josefina de
Melpómene
The muse see Pushkin **MEDTNER, RACHMANINOFF**
Muse und Dichter see Mörike **SCHOECK**
Musen und Grazien in der Mark see Goethe **ZELTER**
Der Musensohn see Goethe **SCHUBERT, ZELTER**
Musette see Florian **MASSENET**
Music see Polonsky **RACHMANINOFF**
Music see Shelley **QUILTER**
Music and moonlight see Shelley **QUILTER**
Music for voice and flute see No author **RIEGGER**
Music I heard see Aiken *DISCORDANTS.* **COPLAND**
"Music I heard with you was more than music" *see Discordants* Aiken **ROREM**
"Music I heard with you was more than music" *see Music I heard* Aiken **COPLAND**
Music, when soft voices die see Shelley *POSTHUMOUS POEMS* (1824).
DIAMOND, HESELTINE, QUILTER
Musica in horto see Rubino **RESPIGHI**
Musik see Orléans, Hélène **LOEWE**
Die Musik see Uhland **STRAUSS** *Einkehr*
Der Musikant see Eichendorff **WOLF**
Musikanten wollen wandern durch die Saiten see Storm **KRENEK**
Die Musikantin see Unknown **LASSEN**
Musing on the roaring ocean see Burns **BENNETT**
Musique see Bourget *LES AVEUX:* Amour. **DEBUSSY**
Musique sur l'eau see Samain **SCHMITT**
Musje Morgenrots Lied see Heyse **CORNELIUS**
MUSORGSKIĬ, MODEST PETROVICH, 1839-1881.
Ammosov, A.
Chto vam slova liubvi (1860) [GA, v. 5^{1-2}, p. 36] same
Byron, George Gordon Byron, 6th baron, 1778-1824.
HEBREW MELODIES.
Tsar' Saul (1863) [GA, v. 5^{1-2}, pp. 58, 66] "O, vozhdi! Esli vyĭdet na doliu moiu"

Goethe, Johann Wolfgang von, 1749-1832.
Pesnia Mefistofelia v pogrebke Auerbakha (1879) [GA, v. 5^8, p. 24] "Zhil byl korol' kogdato, pri nem blokha zhila"
WILHELM MEISTER. Harfenspieler.
Lied des Harfenspielers (1863) {*Pesn' Startsa*} [GA, v. 5^{1-2}, p. 55] "An die Türen will ich schleichen"
Golenishchev-Kutuzov, Arseniĭ Arkad'yevich, graf, 1848-1913.
Elegiia (1874) [GA, v. 5^7, p. 10] "V tumane dremlet noch' "
Kolybel'naia (1875, 1877) [GA, v. 9, p. 6] "Stonet rebenok"
Menia ty v tolpe ne uznala (1874) [GA, v. 5^7, p. 4] same
Nad rekoĭ (1874) [GA, v. 5^7, p. 19] "Mesiats zadumchivyĭ"
Okon'en prazdnyĭ, shumnyĭ den' (1874) [GA, v. 5^7, p. 6] same
Polkovodets (1875, 1877) [GA, v. 5^9, p. 30] "Grokhochet bitva"
Serenada (1875, 1877) [GA, v. 5^9, p. 12] "Nega valshebnaia"
Skuchaĭ (1874) [GA, v. 5^7, p. 10] "Skuchaĭ. Ty sozdana dlia skuki"
Trepak (1875, 1877) [GA, v. 5^9, p. 20] "Les, da poliany"
V chetyrekh stenakh (1874) [GA, v.5^7, p. 2] "Komnatka tesnaia, t'khaia"
Zebytyĭ (1874) [GA, v. 5^4, p. 66] "On smert' nashel v kraiu chuzhom"
SOMMERNACHT.
Videnie (1877) [GA, v. 5^8, p. 18] "IA videl noch' "
Gol'ts-Miller, Ivan Ivanovich, 1842-1871.
Otverzhennaia (1865) [GA, v. 5^{1-2}, p. 104] "Ne smotri na nee ty sprezren'em"
Grekov, Nikolay, 1810-1866.
Gde ty, zvezdochka? (1858) [GA, v. 5^{1-2}, pp. 1, 4] same
Heine, Heinrich, 1797-1856.
Iz slez moikh vyroslo mnogo (1866) [GA, v. 5^3, p. 29] same
Zhelanie (1866) [GA, v. 5^3, pp. 5, 9] "Khotel oy v edinoe slovo ia slit' "
Kol'tsov, Alekseĭ Vasil'yevich, 1809-1842.
Duiut vetry, vetry buĭnye (1864) [GA, v. 5^{1-2}, p. 40] same
Mnogo est' u menia teremov i sadov (1863) [GA, v. 5^{1-2}, p. 22] same

MUSORGSKIĬ, MODEST PETROVICH,
1839-1881 *(continued)*
Kol'tsov, Alekseĭ Vasil'yevich, 1809-
1842 *(continued)*
  Pirushka (1867) [GA, v. 5^4, p. 20]
    "Vorota tesovy rastvorilisia"
  Po nad Donom sad tsvetet (1867) [GA,
    v. 5^4, p. 42] same
  Zastol'naia pesn' (1859) [GA, v. 5$^{1-2}$,
    pp. 7, 12] "Daĭte bokaly!"
Kurochkin, Vasili Stepanovich, 1831-
1875.
  No esli by s toboiu ia vstretit'sia mogla
    (1863) [GA, v. 5$^{1-2}$, p. 47]
    "Rasstalis' gordo my"
Lermontov, Mikhail Yuryevich, 1814-
1841.
  Molitva (1865) [GA, v. 5$^{1-2}$, p. 27]
    "IA, matey' bozhiia"
Mei, Lev Aleksandrovich, 1822-1862.
  Po griby (1867?) [GA, v. 5^4, pp. 12, 16]
    "Pyzhichkov, volvianochek"
  RUTHENISCHE LIEDER: No. 2. Nane.
    Detskaia pesenka (1868) [GA, v. 5^4,
    pp. 60, 62]
    "Vo sadu, akh, vo sadochke"
Musorgskiĭ, Modest Petrovich, 1839-
1881.
  Akh, ty, p'ianaia teteria! (1866) [GA,
    v. 5^3, p. 37] same
  Klassik (1867) [GA, v. 5^4, pp. 34, 38]
    "IA prost, ia iasen, ia skromen"
  Kot matros (1868-72) [GA, v. 5^6, p. 33]
    "Aĭ, aĭ, aĭ, aĭ, mama!"
  Kozel (1867) [GA, v. 5^4, p. 30]
    "Shla devitsa proguliat'sia"
  Na son griadushiĭ' [GA, v. 5^6, p. 29]
    "Gospodi pomiluĭ papu i mamu"
  Neponiatnaia (1875) [GA, v. 5^8, p. 1]
    "Tikha i molchaliva"
  Ozoruik (1867) [GA, v. 5^4, p. 24]
    "Okh, baushka, okh, rodnaia"
  Poekhal na polochke (1868-72) [GA,
    v. 5^6, pp. 37, 46] "Geĭ! Gop, gop,
    gop!"
  Raëk (1870) [GA, v.5^5, pp. 9, 35]
    "Eĭ, pochtenny gospoda"
  S kukloĭ (1868-72) [GA, v. 5^6, p. 26]
    "Tiapa, baĭ, baĭ"
  S nianeĭ (1868-72) [GA, v.5^6, p. 9]
    "Rasskazhi mne, nia niushka"
  Seminarist (1866) [GA, v. 5^3, pp. 46, 59]
    "Panis, piscis, crinis, finis"
  Sirotka (1868) [GA, v. 5^4, pp. 46, 49]
    "Barin moĭ milen'kiia"
  Svetik Savishna (1866) [GA, v. 5^3, p. 33]
    "Svet moĭ, Savishna"

V uglu (1868-72) [GA, v. 5^6, p. 13]
    "Akh, ty, prokaznik!"
  Zhuk (1868-72) [GA, v. 5^6, p. 17]
    "Niania, nianiaka!"
Musorgskiĭ, Modest Petrovich, 1839-
1881, supposed author.
  SALAMMBÔ.
    Pesn' Baleartsa (1864) [GA, v. 5$^{1-2}$, p.
    122] "Vobia t'iakh devy molodoĭ"
Nekrasov, Nikolaiĭ Aleksyeyevich,
1821-1877.
  Kalistratushka (1864) [GA, v. 5$^{1-2}$,
    pp. 84, 94] "Nado mnoĭ pe vala
    matuska"
  Kolybel'naia Eremushki (1868) [GA,
    v. 5^4, pp. 52, 56] "Baiu bai, baĭ"
Ostrovski, Aleksandr Nikolayevich,
1823-1886.
  Kolybel'naia pesnia (1865) [GA, v. 5$^{1-2}$,
    pp. 109, 116]
    "Baiu, baiu, milvnu chenochek"
Pleshcheyev, Alekseĭ Nikolayevich,
1825-1893.
  Akh, zachem tvoi glazki poroiu (1866)
    [GA, v. 5$^{1-2}$, p. 50] same
  List'ia shumeli unylo (1859) [GA, v. 5$^{1-2}$,
    p. 16] same
  Vecherniaia pesenka (1871) [GA, v. 5^4,
    p. 64]
    "Vecher otradnyĭ Leg na kholmakh"
Pushkin, Aleksandr Sergeevich, 1799-
1837.
  Noch' (1864) [GA, v.5$^{1-2}$, pp. 72, 79]
    "Moĭ golos, dlia tebia"
    Orchestrated, 1868.
  Strekotun'ia beloboka (1867) [GA, v. 5^4,
    p. 6] same
Rückert, Friedrich, 1788-1866.
  Strannik (1878) [GA, v. 5^8, p. 22]
    "Teni gor vyso kikh na vodu legli"
Shevchenko, Taras, 1814-1861.
  Na Dnepre (1879) [GA, v. 5^8, p. 29]
    "Stoĭ, Dnepr! Slushaĭ, Dnepr!"
  GAĬDAMAKI.
    Gopak (1866) [GA, v. 5^3, pp. 13, 23]
    "Goĭ! gol, gol, go laka!"
Solomon
  Evreĭskaia pesnia (1867) [GA, v. 5^4,
    pp. 2, 4] "IA, tsvetok polevoĭ"
Tolstoĭ, Alekseĭ Konstantinovich, Graf,
1817-1875.
  Gornimi tikho letela dusha nebesami
    (1877) [GA, v. 5^8, p. 6] same
  Ne bozhiim gromom gore udarilo (1877)
    [GA, v. 5^8, p. 3] same
  Oĭ, chest' li to molodtsu len priasti?
    (1877) [GA, v. 5^8, p. 13] same

Rassevaetsia, rasstupaetsia (1877) [GA,
  v. 5[8], p. 16] same
Spes' (1877) [GA, v.5[8], p. 10]
  "Khodit Spes', nadyvaiuchis' "
Unknown
  IA v subbotu zatepliu svechu (1864) [GA,
    v. 5[1-2], p. 130] "O prechistaia deva"
    Music by Goradigiani; arranged for
      soprano, baritone & piano by
      Musorgskiĭ.
  Otchego, skazhi, dusha devitsa (1858)
    [GA, v. 5[1-2], p. 31] same
  Zhelanie serdtsa (1858) [GA, v. 5[3], p. 1]
    "Lastochke legko rezvit'sia"
Musorgskiĭ, Modest Petrovich, 1839-
  1881.
  MUSORGSKIĬ
    Akh, ty, p'ianaia teteria!
    Klassik
    Kot matros
    Kozel
    Na son griadushiĭ'
    Neponiatnaia
    Ozoruik
    Poekhal na polochke
    Raëk
    S kukloĭ
    S nianeĭ
    Seminarist
    Sirotka
    Svetik Savishna
    V uglu
    Zhuk
Musorgskiĭ, Modest Petrovich, 1839-
  1881, supposed author.
  SALAMMBÔ.
    MUSORGSKIĬ *Pesn' Balearisa*
Muss es eine Trennung geben see Tieck
  BRAHMS
Musset, Alfred de, 1810-1857.
  BIZET
    À une fleur
    Adieux à Suzon
  CHABRIER
    Adieux à Suzon
    Ah! Petit démons!
  CHAUSSON *Le rideau de ma voisine*
  DELIBES
    Bonjour, Suzon!
    Les filles de Cadix
  FRANCK *Ninon*
  GOUNOD
    Le lever
    Venise
  INDY *Adieu*
  LALO
    À une fleur
    La Zuecca

  LASSEN *Pepa*
  LOEFFLER *Marie*
  MARTINŮ *Lucie*
  MASSENET *Souvenir de Venise*
  MILHAUD *J'aime*
  RUBINSTEIN
    À Saint-Blaize à la Zuecca
    Rappelle-toi quand l'aurore craintive
    Romance
  SAINT-SAËNS *Chanson de Fortunio*
A QUOI RÊVENT LES JEUNES FILLES.
  DELIBES *Sérénade à Ninon*
BARBERINE.
  DELIBES *Beau chevalier qui partez
    pour la guerre*
  LALO, RUBINSTEIN *Chanson de
    Barberine*
LE CHANDELIER.
  DELIUS *Chanson de Fortunio*
CHANSON DE FORTUNIO.
  CHAĬKOVSKIĬ *Net, nikogda ne nazovu*
CONTES D'ESPAGNE ET D'ITALIE.
  DEBUSSY
    Ballade à la lune
    Madrid, Princesse des Espagnes
  LALO *Ballade à la lune*
LA NUIT DE MAI: stanza 4,"Pourquoi mon
  coeur bat-il si vite?"
  RACHMANINOFF *Loneliness*
POÉSIES NOUVELLES (1842).
  DEBUSSY *Rondeau*
TRISTESSE.
  LISZT *J'ai perdu ma force et ma vie*
"*Musst nicht allein im Freien*" *see Im Mai*
  Osterwald **FRANZ**
"*Musst's auch grad' so dunkel sein an der
  Weissdornhekke!*" *see Schlimme Geschichte*
  Ritter **REGER**
Mut see Abschatz **ZELTER**
Mut see Müller, Wilhelm **SCHUBERT**
Mutation see Apollinaire *CALLIGRAMMES.*
  POULENC
Muth, Franz Alfred, 1839-1890.
  REGER *Engelwacht*
Mutig trägst du die Last see Unknown
  WEBERN
"*Muto rima se il labbro*" *see La separazione*
  Ucceili, F. **ROSSINI**
Die Mutter an der Wiege see Claudius, M.
  LOEWE
"*Die Mutter betet herzig*" *see Muttertraum*
  Andersen **SCHUMANN**
"*Mutter, draussen ist es Frühling worden*" *see
  Mägdleins Frage* Ljubljaschtschi **REGER**
Die Mutter Erde see Stolberg **SCHUBERT**
  Lied

COMPOSER Poet *Title* "First Line"

"Mutter geht durch ihre Kammern" *see Lied*
Fouqué **SCHUBERT**
Der Mutter Geist see Jacob, T. **LOEWE**
"Die Mutter hat mich jüngst Gescholten" *see*
Die Unterscheidung Seidl **SCHUBERT**
"Mutter, hilf mir armen Tochter" *see*
Der Kranz Schmidt, Hans **BRAHMS**
"Mutter, ich hab' zwei Aeugelein" *see Madre,*
unos ojuelos vi Vega Carpio **JENSEN**
"Mutter, liebe Mutter, komm rasch einmal
hier" *see Furchthäschen* Schellenberg
REGER
"Mutter, Mutter!" *see Lieder der Braut*
Rückert **SCHUMANN**
Mutter, O sing mich zur Ruh! see Hemans
FRANZ, JENSEN
Mutter, schau gut an see Anon.
SZYMANOWSKI *Uwoz, mamo*
"Die Mutter sie sass mit dem Kind" *see Unter*
Rosen Janson **GRIEG**
Die Mutter singt see Krag **GRIEG** *Moderen*
synger
Die Mutter spricht see Seyboth, Sofie
REGER
Mutter, tote Mutter see Hartwig **REGER**
"Mutter zum Bienelein" *see Lehre* Heine
FRANZ
Das Muttergottesbild im Teiche see Wetzel
LOEWE
MUTTERGOTTES-STRÄUSSLEIN ZUM
MAIMONATE, no. 1
LISZT Müller, J. *Das Veilchen*
MUTTERGOTTES-STRÄUSSLEIN ZUM
MAIMONATE, no. 2
LISZT Müller, J. *Das Schlüsselblumen*
Mutterschmerz see Richardt **GRIEG**
Modersorg
Muttersprache see Leuthold **SCHOECK**
Muttertändelei see Bürger **STRAUSS**
Muttertraum see Andersen **SCHUMANN**
Muut kuuli kirkonkellon see Kanteletar
KILPINEN
"Muut ne kuuli kirkonkellon" *see Muut kuuli*
kirkonkellon Kanteletar **KILPINEN**
Muuttolintu see Törmänen **KILPINEN**
"Muy graciosa es la doncella" *see Cantiga*
Vicente, Gil **RODRIGO**
Muza see Pushkin **MEDTNER,**
RACHMANINOFF *The muse*
Mužik, August Eugen, 1859-1925.
MARTINŮ
Dead love
The end of all
First love
The right number
The rose

Song
Muzyka see Polonsky **RACHMANINOFF**
Music
My bed calls me see Ady **BARTÓK** *Lost*
content
My beloved is mine and I am his see Quarles
BRITTEN *Canticle I*
My beloved spake see Bible **GOUNOD**
My blood burns see Pushkin **RIMSKIĭ-**
KORSAKOV *V krovi gorit*
My blood so red see Anon. **ROREM**
The call
"My blood so red for thee was shed" *see*
The call Anon. **ROREM**
"My brother Cain, the wounded, liked to sit"
see Abel Capetanakis **ROREM**
My brother has finished ploughing see
Toman *DIE MONATE:* September.
MARTINŮ
"My brother he's a funny one" *see Brother*
Carpenter, Rue **CARPENTER**
My country is growing see Afinogenov
PROKOFIEV *Chetyre pesni*
My crow Pluto see Moore, M. **THOMSON**
My cry see Dalliba **PIZZETTI**
My daddy is a cankered carl see Anon.
GOUNOD
My days are spent in yearning see Pushkin
ZHELANIE. **RIMSKIĭ-KORSAKOV**
Medlitel'no vlekutsia dni moi
"My dear mistress has a heart" *see*
The jealous lover Rochester **QUILTER**
"My dear, my dear I know" *see To a young*
girl Yeats **ROREM**
"My dear old mother, poor thou art" *see*
The old mother Vinje **IVES**
My dearest friend, my heart is singing see
Maĭkov **RIMSKIĭ-KORSAKOV**
Eshche ia poln, O drug moĭ milyĭ
My dove, my beautiful one see Joyce
SZYMANOWSKI
My early walk see Burns **BRITTEN**
My eyes will I to the hills lift up see Bible
DVOŘÁK *Pozdvihuji oči svých k horám*
"My faint spirit was sitting in the light" *see*
Arab love song Shelley **QUILTER**
My fair see Meynell **IRELAND**
"My Fair, no beauty of thine will last" *see*
My fair Meynell **IRELAND**
My favorite see Mickiewicz **CHAĭKOVSKIĭ**
Moia balovnitsa
"My fever is not new" *see Phaedra's farewell*
Racine **THOMSON**
"My first day in Paris I walked" *see*
For Poulenc O'Hara **ROREM**
"My fishing done, I have returned" *see*
The riverside village Ssu-k'ung Shu
BERKELEY

COMPOSER Poet *Title* "First Line"

My shadow see Stevenson, Robert Louis
RIEGGER
My Shepherd will supply my need see Watts
THOMSON
My ship and I see Stevenson, Robert
Louis *A CHILD'S GARDEN OF VERSES.*
HAHN
My sideli s toboĭ see Rathaus
CHAĬKOVSKIĬ *An dem schlummernden
Strom*
My song is fierce and bitter see Heine
BORODIN *Vergiftet sind meine Lieder*
My song of love rings through the dusk see
Heyduk **DVOŘÁK** *Má píseň zas mi
láskouzní*
My song resounds see Heyduk **DVOŘÁK**
Má píseň zas mi láskouzní
My songs are filled with poison see Heine
BORODIN *Vergiftet sind meine Lieder*
My songs are poisoned see Heine **BORODIN**
Vergiftet sind meine Lieder
My soul is dark see Byron **DIAMOND**
MY SOUL IS DARK. see Byron
Hebräische Melodie **RUBINSTEIN**
My soul is dark! see Byron **SCHUMANN**
Aus den "Hebräischen Gesängen"
"My, sovetskie soldaty" see Soldatskaia
poxodnaĭa Lugovskoĭ **PROKOFIEV**
My spirit will not haunt the mound see Hardy
DIAMOND
My spoiled darling see Mickiewicz
CHAĬKOVSKIĬ, RIMSKIĬ-KORSAKOV
Moĭa balovnitsa
My spoiled little darling see Mickiewicz
RIMSKIĬ-KORSAKOV *Moĭa balovnitsa*
My sweetheart see Alexander, G.
CARPENTER
My sweetheart see Mickiewicz **CHOPIN**
Moja pieszczotka
"My tea is nearly ready" see The lamplighter
Stevenson, Robert Louis **QUILTER**
*"My teacher said us boys should write" see
The greatest man* Collins, Anne **IVES**
My true love hath my heart see Sidney, Sir
Philip **IRELAND**
My true love is a bird see Rorem **ROREM**
*"My Uncle Daniel fought in the Civil War
band" see Four uncles* Cummings
DIAMOND
My voice calls out to you see Pushkin
NOCH' **RIMSKIĬ-KORSAKOV**
Moĭ golos dlĭa tebĭa
My voice for thee is sweet and languid see
Pushkin *NOCH'* **RIMSKIĬ-KORSAKOV**
Moĭ golos dlĭa tebĭa
Ein Myrtenreis see Cornelius **CORNELIUS**

MYRTHEN, no. 1
SCHUMANN Rückert *Widmung*
MYRTHEN, no. 2
SCHUMANN Goethe *Freisinn*
MYRTHEN, no. 3
SCHUMANN Mosen *Der Nussbaum*
MYRTHEN, no. 4
SCHUMANN Burns *Jemand*
MYRTHEN, no. 5
SCHUMANN Goethe *Lieder aus dem
Schenkenbuch . . .*
MYRTHEN, no. 6
SCHUMANN Goethe *Lieder aus dem
Schenkenbuch . . .*
MYRTHEN, no. 7
SCHUMANN Heine *Die Lotosblume*
MYRTHEN, no. 8
SCHUMANN Goethe *Talismane*
MYRTHEN, no. 9
SCHUMANN Goethe *Lied der Suleika*
MYRTHEN, no. 10
SCHUMANN Burns *Die Hochländer-
Wittwe*
MYRTHEN, no. 11
SCHUMANN Rückert *Lieder der Braut*
MYRTHEN, no. 12
SCHUMANN Rückert *Lieder der Braut*
MYRTHEN, no. 13
SCHUMANN Burns *Hochländers
Abschied*
MYRTHEN, no. 14
SCHUMANN Burns *Hochländisches
Wiegenlied*
MYRTHEN, no. 15
SCHUMANN Byron *Aus den
"Hebräischen Gesängen"*
MYRTHEN, no. 16
SCHUMANN Fanshawe *Räthsel*
MYRTHEN, no. 17
SCHUMANN Moore, T. *Zwei
Venetianische Lieder*
MYRTHEN, no. 18
SCHUMANN Moore, T. *Zwei
Venetianische Lieder*
MYRTHEN, no. 19
SCHUMANN Burns *Hauptmann's Weib*
MYRTHEN, no. 20
SCHUMANN Burns *Weit, weit*
MYRTHEN, no. 21
SCHUMANN Heine *Was will die einsame
Thräne*
MYRTHEN, no. 22
SCHUMANN Burns *Niemand*
MYRTHEN, no. 23
SCHUMANN Burns *Im Westen*
MYRTHEN, no. 24

SCHUMANN Heine *Du bist wie eine*
Blume
MYRTHEN, no. 25
  SCHUMANN Rückert *Aus den "Östlichen*
  Rosen"
MYRTHEN, no. 26
  SCHUMANN Rückert *Zum Schluss*
"Les myrtilles sont pour la dame" *see*
  Chanson Apollinaire POULENC
The myrtle see Deland MACDOWELL
Myrto see Silvestre DELIBES
"Myrto ne sait pas de chansons" *see Myrto*
  Silvestre DELIBES

Myself see De La Mare ROREM
Mysterium see Frey LUENING
Mystic song of the ancient Russian flagellants
  see Gorodetski STRAVINSKIĬ
  A song of the dew
"Mystiques barcarolles" *see A Clymène*
  Verlaine FAURÉ
"Myszki pod podloga mieszkaly" *see Myszy*
  Iłłakowiczówna SZYMANOWSKI
Myszy see Iłłakowiczówna
  SZYMANOWSKI

N

Na beregu see Pleshcheyev CHAĬKOVSKIĬ
Na Dnepre see Shevchenko MUSORGSKIĬ
Na gore-to kalina see Anon. PROKOFIEV
Na horách ticho a vúdolí ticho see Pfleger-
  Moravský DVOŘÁK
Na horách ticho a vúdolích ticho see Pfleger-
  Moravský DVOŘÁK
Na horách ticho, vúdolí ticho see Pfleger-
  Moravský DVOŘÁK
Na kholmakh Gruzii see Pushkin RIMSKIĬ-
  KORSAKOV
Na ksiezycu czarnym see Miciński *W*
  MROKU GWIAZD. SZYMANOWSKI
"Na ma cześć" *see Uczta* Szymanowska,
  Zafia SZYMANOWSKI
"Na malej wysepce" *see Kot*
  Iłłakowiczówna SZYMANOWSKI
Na nivy zhelty see Tolstoĭ CHAĬKOVSKIĬ
Na nivy zheltye niskhodit tishina see Tolstoĭ
  RIMSKIĬ-KORSAKOV
Na ozere see Goethe MEDTNER
  Auf dem See
Na pustej trzcinie see Miciński *W MROKU*
  GWIAZD. SZYMANOWSKI
"Na razdol'i nebes" *see IUzhnaia noch'*
  Shcherbina RIMSKIĬ-KORSAKOV
"Na severe dikom stoit" *see Sosna*
  Lermontov BALAKIREV
"Na severnom golom utese" *see El' i pal'ma*
  Heine RIMSKIĬ-KORSAKOV
Na smert' chizhika see Zhukovski
  RACHMANINOFF *On the death of a*
  linnet
Na son" griadushiĭ see Ogarev
  CHAĬKOVSKIĬ

Na son griadushiĭ' see Musorgskiĭ
  MUSORGSKIĬ
"Na vysoké skále sama sedí matka Koljova"
  see Koljas Anon. DVOŘÁK
Na zemliu sumrak pal see Mickiewicz
  CHAĬKOVSKIĬ
Naar Odin vinker see Oehlenschläger
  NIELSEN
Naar Smaabørn klynker ved Aftentide see
  Dabelsteen, Chr. NIELSEN
"Naar trofast, varm og redelig jeg bejle vil til
  dig" *see Simpel Sang* Drachmann GRIEG
Nach' see Pushkin MEDTNER *Night*
"Nach all dem Menschenlärm" *see Heimat*
  Morgenstern KILPINEN
"Nach Corinthus von Athen gezogen" *see*
  Die Braut von Corinth Goethe
  LOEWE, ZELTER
Nach dem Abschiede see Hoffmann von
  Fallersleben WOLF
Nach dem Fest see Hesse KILPINEN
NACH DEM GEWITTER. see Mayrhofer
  Nach einem Gewitter SCHUBERT
Nach dem Kriege see Mörike SCHOECK
"Nach dem Sturme fahren wir" *see Nordisches*
  Seelied Falk LOEWE
Nach der Geburt ihres Sohnes see Mary
  SCHUMANN
"Nach diesen trüben Tagen" *see Frühlings*
  Ankunft Hoffmann von Fallersleben
  SCHUMANN
"Nach dir, O Biene, schauet die Amra" *see*
  Lied aus Sakuntala Wolzogen und
  Neuhaus LASSEN
Nach einem Gewitter see Mayrhofer *NACH*
  DEM GEWITTER. SCHUBERT

Nach einem Regen see Dehmel
SZYMANOWSKI

"Nach Frankreich zogen zwei Grenadier'" *see*
Die beiden Grenadiere Heine
SCHUMANN

"Nach langem Frost, wie weht die Luft so
lind!" *see Frühlingsgrüsse* Lenau
SCHUMANN, WOLF

"Nach Mittage sassen mir junges Volk im
Kühlen" *see Stirbt der Fuchs, so gilt der
Balg* Goethe ZELTER

Nach neuen Meeren see Nietzsche *DIE
FRÖHLICHE WISSENSCHAFT.* DELIUS

Nach oben grüne Bergweid' see Lie GRIEG
I Liden højt deroppe

Nach Pilzen see Mei MUSORGSKIĬ
Po griby

"Nach so vielen trüben Tagen send'" *see
Cora an die Sonne* Batsányi SCHUBERT

"Nach Süden nun sich lenken" *see Wanderlied
der Prager Studenten* Eichendorff
SCHOECK

"Der Nachen dröhnt, Cypressen flüstern" *see
Fahrt zum Hades* Mayrhofer SCHUBERT

Nachgefühl see Goethe SPOHR, ZELTER

Nachhall see Mosenthal RUBINSTEIN

"Die Nachigallen schlafen" *see Aus "Pfingsten
ein Gedichtsreigen"* Evers BERG

Nachklang see Eichendorff SCHOECK

Nachklang see Goethe *WESTÖSTLICHER
DIVAN.* SCHOECK

Nachklang see Groth BRAHMS

Nachruf see Eichendorff SCHOECK,
WOLF

Nachstück see Khomyakov BALAKIREV

Nacht see Eichendorff JENSEN, LASSEN,
RUBINSTEIN, SCHOECK, WOLF

Die Nacht see Gilm zu Rosenegg *LETZTE
BLÄTTER.* STRAUSS

Nacht see Hauptmann BERG

Nacht see Huber, B. KILPINEN

Nacht see Koster PIJPER

Die Nacht see Macpherson SCHUBERT

Die Nacht see Mahlmann *NACHT-LIED.*
LOEWE

Nacht see Pushkin MUSORGSKIĬ *Noch'*

Nacht see Rathaus CHAĬKOVSKIĬ

Die Nacht see Uz SCHUBERT

Nacht am Rheine see Siebel BARTÓK

Nacht auf Posten see Zwehl, Hans Fritz
von KILPINEN

"Die Nacht bergeht nach süsser Ruh" *see
Am Morgen* Cornelius CORNELIUS

"Die Nacht bricht an' " *see Der Unglückliche*
Pichler SCHUBERT

"Die Nacht bricht bald herein" *see Normans
Gesang* Scott SCHUBERT

"Nacht, dem Zauber" *see Wolkennacht*
Avenarius WEBERN

"Die Nacht fällt ein" *see Vorwurf* Hesse
SCHOECK

Nacht in Rom see Unknown LASSEN

"Die Nacht ist dumpfig und finster" *see
Die Nacht* Macpherson SCHUBERT

"Die Nacht ist finster, schwül und bang" *see
Nächtliche Wanderung* Lenau WOLF

"Die Nacht ist hehr und heiter" *see Gebet auf
den Wassern* Strachwitz LASSEN

"Die Nacht ist keines Menschen Freund" *see
Das hat die Sommernacht getan* Ritter
SZYMANOWSKI

"Die Nacht ist so dunkel, der Sturm so laut"
*see Der grosse Kurfürst und die
Spreejungfrau* Kurowski-Eichen
LOEWE

"Nacht ist um mich her" *see Der Verlassene*
Unknown MENDELSSOHN-
BARTHOLDY

"Nacht ist wie ein stilles Meer" *see Die Nacht*
Eichendorff WOLF

"Nacht ist's, und Stürme sausen für und für"
see Der Pilgrim vor St. Just Platen-
Hallermünde LOEWE

Nacht liegt auf den fremden Wegen see Heine
DIE HEIMKEHR, no. 98. GRIFFES,
JENSEN

"Nacht liegt auf den fremden Wegen" *see
Mondenschein* Heine BRAHMS

Nacht, Muse und Tod see Leuthold
SCHOECK

"Nacht umhüllt mit wehendem Flügel" *see
Bertha's Lied in der Nacht* Grillparzer
SCHUBERT

Nacht und Grab see Zschokke WOLF

Nacht und Träume see Collin, M.
SCHUBERT

"Die Nacht war kaum verblühet" *see Sonntag*
Eichendorff FRANZ

"Die Nacht war tief und die Mutter schlief"
see Die Betrogene spricht Ritter REGER

Nachtergebund see Trakl *OFFENBARUNG
UND UNTERGAND.* WEBERN

Nachtgang see Bierbaum BERG
Nachtgesang; REGER, STRAUSS

Nachtgebet der Braut see Dehmel WEBERN

Nachtgeflüster see Evers REGER

Nachtgefühl see Hesse SCHOECK

Nachtgeräusche see Meyer SCHOECK

Nachtgesang see Bierbaum BERG

Nachtgesang see Collin, M. SCHUBERT
Licht und Liebe

Nachtgesang see Goethe SCHOECK,
SCHUBERT, ZELTER

Nachtgesang see Kosegarten SCHUBERT
Nachtgruss see Eichendorff MEDTNER,
SCHOECK, WOLF
Nachtgruss see Kugler JENSEN
Nachtgruss see Reinick WOLF
Nachthymne see Hardenberg SCHUBERT
DIE NACHTIGALL. see Hölty
Seufzer SCHUBERT
Nachtigall see Köstlin BRAHMS
Die Nachtigall see Kraus *WORTE IN*
VERSEN. KRENEK
Die Nachtigall see Storm BERG
Die Nachtigall see Szymanowska, Zafia
SZYMANOWSKI *Slowik*
Die Nachtigall see Unknown
MENDELSSOHN-BARTHOLDY,
RUBINSTEIN
"Nachtigall, hüte dich" *see Hüte dich* Lingg
RUBINSTEIN
"Die Nachtigall singt überall" *see Seufzer*
Hölty SCHUBERT
Die Nachtigall spielt auf goldener Leier see
Henley *LIFE & DEATH (ECHOES).*
DELIUS *The nightingale has a lyre of gold*
Die Nachtigall und die Rose see Kol'tsov
RUBINSTEIN
Die Nachtigallen see Eichendorff
PFITZNER
Nachtigallen schwingen see Hoffmann von
Fallersleben BRAHMS
DAS NACHTLAGER VON GRANADA. see
Kind, F.
Alkanzor und Zaide WEBER
Nachtlied see Eichendorff
MENDELSSOHN-BARTHOLDY,
SCHOECK
Nachtlied see Geibel FRANZ, GRIFFES,
MACDOWELL
Nachtlied see Goethe SCHUMANN
Nachtlied see Hahn-Hahn FRANZ
NACHT-LIED. see Mahlmann
Die Nacht LOEWE
NACHTLIED. see Mosen
Könnt ich mit dir dort oben gehen
GRIFFES
Nachtlied see Unknown LASSEN, LOEWE
Nachtliedje see Bruyn, Bertha de PIJPER
Nachts see Cornelius CORNELIUS
Nachts see Eichendorff PFITZNER
Nachts see Mörike SCHOECK
Nachts am Schreibepult see Mörike
SCHOECK
"Nachts bin vom Traum schlaftrunken ich
erwacht" *see Nachts* Cornelius
CORNELIUS
"Nachts in der zwölften Stunde" *see*
Die nächtliche Heerschau Zedlitz
SCHUMANN

"Nachts um der zwölfte Stunde" *see*
Die nächtliche Heerschau Zedlitz
LOEWE
"Nachts, wenn die Bäume rauschen im
verschwiegnen Sommerwind" *see*
Märchenland Evers REGER
"Nachts zu unbekannter Stunde" *see*
Heimliches Verschwinden Schöpff
SCHUMANN
Nachtseele see Evers REGER
Nachtsegen see Evers REGER
Nachtständchen see Mayer, Dr. LOEWE
Nachtstück see Khomyakov BALAKIREV
Nachstück
Nachtstück see Mayrhofer SCHUBERT
Nachtviolen see Mayrhofer SCHUBERT
"Nachtviolen, Nachtviolen!" *see Nachtviolen*
Mayrhofer SCHUBERT
Nachtwanderer see Eichendorff PFITZNER
Nachtwandler see Kalbeck *NÄCHTE.*
BRAHMS
Nachtzauber see Eichendorff WOLF
Nachwirkung see Meissner BRAHMS
Nad krajem vévodí lehký spánek see Pfleger-
Moravský DVOŘÁK
Two settings: B. 11 no. 17 and B. 160 no.
5.
"Nad, nad" *see The swing* Bialik GIDEON
Nad ozerom see Golenishchev-Kutuzov
BALAKIREV
Nad poliarnym morem see Svetlova
PROKOFIEV
Nad rekoǐ see Golenishchev-Kutuzov
MUSORGSKIǏ
Nad svezheǐ mogiloǐ see Nadson
RACHMANINOFF *By the fresh grave*
Nadaud, Gustave, 1820-1893.
GOUNOD *Pauvre Braga*
Nade mna leci w szafir morza see Miciński
SZYMANOWSKI
Naděje see Anon. MARTINŮ
Nadie lo oye como ellos see Rivas, Reyna
THOMSON
"Nado mnoǐ pe vala matuska" *see*
Kalistratushka Nekrasov MUSORGSKIǏ
Nadson, Semen IAkovlevich, 1862-1887.
RACHMANINOFF
By the fresh grave
Melody
'Tis time
Nadson, Semyon *see* Nadson, Semen
IAkovlevich, 1862-1887.
"Nää, oi mun sieluni, auringon korkea nousa"
see Auringon nousu Koskenniemi
KILPINEN
"Nään usein unessa ma kaupungin" *see*
Valkeat kaupungit Koskenniemi
KILPINEN

NÄCHTE. see Kalbeck
  Nachtwandler **BRAHMS**
"Die Nächte stürmen" *see Bei dir* Grosse
  JENSEN
Nächtens klang die süsse Laute see Fouqué
  DER ZAUBERRING. **SCHUBERT**
"Nächtlich macht der Herr die Rund" *see*
  Der Weckruf Eichendorff **PFITZNER**
Die nächtliche Heerschau see Zedlitz
  LOEWE, SCHUMANN
Nächtliche Pfade see Stieler **REGER**
Nächtliche Scheu see Dehmel *ABER DIE*
  LIEBE. **WEBERN**
Nächtliche Wanderung see Lenau **WOLF**
"Nächtlicher Duft" *see Ständchen* Pushkin
  JENSEN
Näcken see Josephson, E. **KILPINEN;**
  SIBELIUS *Necken*
Näcken see Wennerberg **SIBELIUS**
Nähe des Geliebten see Goethe **LASSEN,**
  MEDTNER, SCHUBERT, ZELTER
Die Näherin see Rilke **BERG**
"Näin oomme, armas, syksyyn saapuneet" *see*
  Syyskuun sonetti Koskenniemi
  KILPINEN
"Näkinkengät ne rannalla karskui" *see*
  Rannalla Lönnbohm **KILPINEN**
Naeman see Burns **SCHUMANN** *Niemand*
När jag drömmer see Tavaststjerna
  SIBELIUS
"När kardinaln en vacker dag" *see Älvan och*
  kardinalen Josephson, E. **KILPINEN**
"När solen skiner och lärkan slår" *see En liten*
  visa om våren Cnattingius, Thor
  KILPINEN
Naguère, au temps des églantines see
  Mendès **HAHN**
Nahandove see Parny, Evariste **RAVEL**
"Nahandove, Ô belle Nahandove" *see*
  Nahandove Parny, Evariste **RAVEL**
Der nahe Retter see Niemeyer **LOEWE**
"Naht die jubelvolle Zeit" *see*
  Weihnachtsgefühl Frey, F. **STRAUSS**
Naidu, Sarojini (Chattopadhyay), 1879-
1949.
  LUENING *Transience*
Naïs see Unknown **HAHN**
"Naïs vierge blonde à l'oeil noir" *see Naïs*
  Unknown **HAHN**
La najade see Annunzio *POEMA*
  PARADISIACO. **RESPIGHI**
"Naked & brave thou goest" *see Farewell*
  tablet to Agathocles Evans **GIDEON**
Nakhodka see Goethe **MEDTNER** *Gefunden*
Náladová kresba see Klen, V. **MARTINŮ**
  Picture of a mood

Nam zvezdy krotkie siiali see Pleshcheyev
  SLOVA DLYA MUZÏKI. **CHAÏKOVSKIÏ**
Namenstagslied see Stadler **SCHUBERT**
Nana see Anon. **FALLA**
Nani, nani see Anon. **RODRIGO**
Nanny see Leconte de Lisle *POÈMES*
  ANTIQUES. **CHAUSSON**
Nantucket see Williams, W. **ROREM**
NANTUCKET SONGS, no. 1
  ROREM Roethke *From whence cometh*
  song?
NANTUCKET SONGS, no. 2
  ROREM Williams, W. *The dance*
NANTUCKET SONGS, no. 3
  ROREM Williams, W. *Nantucket*
NANTUCKET SONGS, no. 4
  ROREM Waller *Go, lovely rose*
NANTUCKET SONGS, no. 5
  ROREM Rossetti, Christina *Up-hill*
NANTUCKET SONGS, no. 6
  ROREM Landor *Mother, I cannot mind*
  my wheel
NANTUCKET SONGS, no. 7
  ROREM Ashbery *Fear of death*
NANTUCKET SONGS, no. 8
  ROREM Ashbery *Thoughts of a young*
  girl
NANTUCKET SONGS, no. 9
  ROREM Rossetti, Christina *Ferry me*
  across the water
NANTUCKET SONGS, no. 10
  ROREM Waller *The dancer*
Når jeg vil dø see Paulsen **GRIEG**
"Når løvet falder traet fra skogens kroner" *see*
  Når jeg vil dø Paulsen **GRIEG**
"Nar nat udvaelder" *see Syndfloden*
  Grundtvig **NIELSEN**
Nar somrens sang er sungen see Hostrup
  NIELSEN
Narciss see Gripenberg **SIBELIUS** *Narsissi*
Narcisse à la fontaine see Collin
  MASSENET
Der Narr see Jacobowski **REGER**
Narsissi see Gripenberg **SIBELIUS**
Narzeczony see Witwicki **CHOPIN**
"Nascentes morimur finisque" *see Vita*
  Manilius **IVES**
Nash vek see Tiutchev **MEDTNER** *Our time*
Nashe, Thomas, 1567-1601.
  SUMMER'S LAST WILL AND
  TESTAMENT (1600).
  DELIUS *Spring, the sweet Spring*
  HESELTINE *Spring*
Das Nasobem see Morgenstern **SEIBER**
Nastoïashchuiu see Akhmatova
  PROKOFIEV

"N'as-tu pas vu l'hirondelle" *see Le sais-tu?*
 Bordèse **MASSENET**
NATIONAL ODES OF CHINA. see
 Confucius
 To a young gentleman **CARPENTER**
Natorp, Bernard Christoph Ludwig,
 1774-1846.
 FRANZ *In meinen Armen wieg ich dich*
Nattergalen see Walther von der
 Vogelweide **GRIEG** *Die verschwiegene
 Nachtigall*
Die Natur see Claudius, M. **SCHOECK**
Le naturaliste see Kerdyk, René
 HONEGGER
*Nature lies peaceful in slumber and dreaming
 see* Pfleger-Moravský **DVOŘÁK**
 Nad krajem vévodí lehký spánek
 Two settings: B. 11 no. 17 and B. 160
 no. 5.
Nature morte see Ganivet **SCHMITT**
Nature morte see Richaud **SAUGUET**
Nature, the gentlest mother see Dickinson
 COPLAND
"Nature's relentless; nature is kind" *see
 On the Antipodes* Unknown **IVES**
Nature's way see Ives **IVES**
Naturens aedle dyrker see Hauch **NIELSEN**
Naturfreiheit see Uhland **PFITZNER**
Naturgenuss see Gleim **LOEWE**
Naturgenuss see Matthisson **SCHUBERT**
Naught that country needeth see Alford,
 Henry **IVES**
The naughty boy see Musorgskiĭ
 MUSORGSKIĬ *Ozoruik*
Naumann, L. G.
 LOEWE *Frühlingslust*
"N'avez-vous pas un porte plume?" *see
 "A traduire en esthonien . . . "* Chalupt
 RIVIER
"Le navire qui est sur la rade" *see Bonjour,
 messieurs les libérateurs* Anon.
 MILHAUD
"Nay do not grieve tho' life be full of
 sadness" *see Transience* Naidu **LUENING**
Ne bozhiim gromom gore udarilo see Tolstoĭ
 MUSORGSKIĬ
"Ne crois pas que les morts soient morts!" *see
 Les morts* Richepin **CHAUSSON**
"Né dans une crèche" *see Jésus de Nazareth*
 Porte, A. **GOUNOD**
Ne dolgo nam gulyat see Grekov
 CHAĬKOVSKIĬ
Ne donne pas ton coeur see Mariéton
 MASSENET
Ne gardez pas see Tagore *GARDENER.*
 MILHAUD

"Ne jamais la voir ni l'entendre" *see Soupir*
 Sully-Prudhomme **DUPARC,
 RESPIGHI**
Ne l'oubliez pas see Regnault, Mme. Félix
 SAINT-SAËNS
Ne me console pas see Jammes
 MILHAUD
"Ne me fuis pas, Ô jeune fille" *see Sur une
 jeune fille* Anacreon **ROUSSEL**
Ne moqu ia slyshat' etoĭ see Shenshin
 MEDTNER *Serenade*
Ne mozhet byt' see Maĭkov
 RACHMANINOFF *It cannot be*
Ne otkhodi ot menia see Shenshin
 MELODII. **CHAĬKOVSKIĬ**
"Ne parlons plus" *see L'heure captive*
 Dommange **AUBERT**
Ne penitsia more see Tolstoĭ **RIMSKIĬ-
 KORSAKOV**
Ne penitsya more see Tolstoĭ **BALAKIREV**
"Ne poĭ, krasavitsa" *see Gruzinskaya pesnya*
 Pushkin **BALAKIREV**
Ne poĭ, krasavitsa, pri mne see Pushkin
 RACHMANINOFF *Sing not to me,
 beautiful maiden;* **RIMSKIĬ-KORSAKOV**
"Ne smotri na nee ty sprezren'em" *see
 Otverzhennaia* Gol'ts-Miller
 MUSORGSKIĬ
Ne sprashivaĭ see Goethe *WILHELM
 MEISTER.* Mignon's song: Heiss mich nicht
 reden. **CHAĬKOVSKIĬ**
"Ne strashna mne" *see Pesnya razboynika*
 Kol'tsov **BALAKIREV**
Ne suis que grain de sable see Satie **SATIE**
Ne ver', mne drug! see Tolstoĭ
 RACHMANINOFF *Believe me not, friend;*
 RIMSKIĬ-KORSAKOV
Ne ver', moĭ drug see Tolstoĭ
 CHAĬKOVSKIĬ
Ne veter, veia s vysoty see Tolstoĭ **RIMSKIĬ-
 KORSAKOV**
"Ne vous arrêtez pas nuage sur la ville
 horrible" *see La ville* Jacob, M.
 SAUGUET
"Ne vous balancez pas si fort" *see Fête de
 Montmartre* Cocteau **MILHAUD**
"Ne zdes' li ty legkoiu ten'iu" *see Moy geniy,
 moy angel, moy drug* Shenshin
 CHAĬKOVSKIĬ
Near closing time see Goodman **ROREM**
Near the beloved see Goethe **MEDTNER**
 Nähe des Geliebten
'Neath the fir trees *see* Runeberg
 SIBELIUS *Under strandens granar*
Nebbie see Negri **RESPIGHI**
Nebel see Lenau **FRANZ, STRAUSS**

COMPOSER Poet *Title* "First Line"

Nebel see Sandburg **BLACHER**
Nebel und Gram see Tolstoĭ **RUBINSTEIN**
"Die Nebel zerreisen" *see Glückliche Fahrt*
   Goethe **MARTINŮ, MEDTNER**
"Nebelgrau die weite Welt" *see Unterwegs*
   Boelitz **REGER**
Die Nebensonne see Müller, Wilhelm
   SCHUBERT
Nebesky, Jan, 1880-
   MARTINŮ *The swan*
Nebo see Freiligrath **LOEWE**
NECESSITIES OF LIFE. see Rich
   Song **WEISGALL**
Necken see Josephson, E. **SIBELIUS**
"N'ecoute pas, Anastasie" *see L'irrésolue*
   Chalupt **MILHAUD**
"Nedavno, obol'shen" *see Snovidenie*
   Pushkin **RIMSKIĬ-KORSAKOV**
Nedostupnaia see Goethe **MEDTNER**
   Die Spröde
Nèère see Carré **MASSENET**
Nèère see Chénier **KOECHLIN**
Nèère see Leconte de Lisle **HAHN**
La nef see Guichard, Abeille **SAUGUET**
"Nega valshebnaia" *see Serenada*
   Golenishchev-Kutuzov **MUSORGSKIĬ**
Le Nègre see Cocteau *TEMPÉRATURES.*
   HONEGGER
"Le nègre mineur de l'azure" *see Le Nègre*
   Cocteau **HONEGGER**
Negri, Ada, 1870-1945.
   RESPIGHI
    Lagrime!
    Luce
    Nebbie
    Notte
    Notturno
    Storia breve
    L'ultima ebbrezza!
   FATALITÀ.
   RESPIGHI *Nevicata*
NÉGY DAL PÓSA LAJOR, no. 1
   BARTÓK Pósa *Őszi szellő*
NÉGY DAL PÓSA LAJOR, no. 2
   BARTÓK Pósa *Még azt vetik szememre*
NÉGY DAL PÓSA LAJOR, no. 3
   BARTÓK Pósa *Nincs olyan bú*
NÉGY DAL PÓSA LAJOR, no. 4
   BARTÓK Pósa *Ejnye! Ejnye!*
Négy Petöfi dal see Petöfi **SEIBER**
"Nehmt hin die Welt!" *see Die Theilung der*
   Erde Schiller **ZELTER**
"Nei sjå, kor det blåner her!" *see Blåbaer-Li*
   Garborg **GRIEG**
Neig' schöne Knospe Dich zu mir see
   Bodenstedt **QUILTER**

La neige see Bordèse **MASSENET**
La neige see Leclère, translator
   SHÉHÉRAZADE. **KOECHLIN**
Neige, coeur et lys see Ganivet **SCHMITT**
NEIGES, no. 1
   SAUGUET D'Harcourt, Antoniette
    Au bord de la cheminée
NEIGES, no. 2
   SAUGUET D'Harcourt, Antoniette
    Sommeil
NEIGES, no. 3
   SAUGUET D'Harcourt, Antoniette
    Fenêtre ouverte le soir
NEIGES, no. 4
   SAUGUET D'Harcourt, Antoniette
    Dormeur suspendu
NEIGES, no. 5
   SAUGUET D'Harcourt, Antoniette
    Invasion
NEIGES, no. 6
   SAUGUET D'Harcourt, Antoniette
    Les gens distraits
The neighbour's stable see Anon.
   MARTINŮ *Súsedova stajňa*
Neigl, schöne Knospe, dich zu mir see
   Bodenstedt **RUBINSTEIN**
Die Neigung see Unknown **GLUCK**
"Nein, ich wiederstrebe nicht mehr" *see*
   Die Neigung Unknown **GLUCK**
Nein, junger Herr, so triebt see Heyse
   WOLF
"Nein, länger werd'ich diesen Kampf nicht
   kämpfen" *see Der Kampf* Schiller
   SCHUBERT
Nejkrásnější smrt see Hafiz **MARTINŮ**
   Sweet death
"Nekrasiv ia, znaiu sam" *see Pevets* Maĭkov
   RIMSKIĬ-KORSAKOV
Nekrasov, Nikolaĭ Aleksyeyevich, 1821-
   1877.
   BORODIN *U lyudey-to v domu*
   CHAĬKOVSKIĬ *Prosti*
   MASSENET *Larmes maternelles*
   MUSORGSKIĬ
    Kalistratushka
    Kolybel'naia Eremushki
   RIMSKIĬ-KORSAKOV *Prosti! Ne pomni*
    dneĭ paden'ia
Nel giardino see Rocchi, Francesco
   RESPIGHI
Nelken see Storm **REGER**
"Nelken wind' ich und Jasmin" *see Cojo*
   jazmin y clavel Manuel del Rio, Don
   JENSEN
Nell see Leconte de Lisle **FAURÉ**
Nell' orror di notte oscura see Angiolini,
   Carlo **VERDI**

"Nella sala gialla una tazza d'ambra" *see*
   La danza Olkienizkaia-Naldi **CASELLA**
"Nell'orto abbandonato ora l'edace muschio"
   see Crepuscolo Rubino **RESPIGHI**
Nem mehetek hozzád see Ady **BARTÓK**
   I cannot come to you
Nenastnyĭ den' potukh see Pushkin
   RIMSKIĭ-KORSAKOV
"Nenne soll ich, sagt ihr" *see Nichts* Gilm zu
   Rosenegg **STRAUSS**
"N'entrez pas, Monsieur" *see Ode à un jeune*
   gentilhomme Roché **ROUSSEL**
Le nénuphar see Haraucourt **KOECHLIN**
Neponiatnaia see Musorgskiĭ
   MUSORGSKIĭ
"Ner mejo che un signore" *see Er coccodrillo*
   Salustri **CASELLA**
Nérac en fête see Bédat de Monlaur,
   Pierre **HONEGGER**
Nereids see Anon. **DVOŘÁK** *Nereidy*
Nereidy see Anon. **DVOŘÁK**
Nerses (Lampronetsi), 1143-1198.
   RESPIGHI *Mattino di luce*
Nesliashchikh solntse see Tolstoĭ **RIMSKIĭ-**
   KORSAKOV
Nessun maggior, page d'album see Dante
   BERLIOZ
The nest see Bialik **GIDEON**
Das Nest see Leo **LASSEN**
N'est-ce pas? see Verlaine LA BONNE
   CHANSON. **FAURÉ, KOECHLIN**
"N'est-il pour le coeur rien d'autre" *see*
   Le vide de l'instant Richter **SAUGUET**
"Net na svete kraĭa" *see Pesnia o rodine*
   Prokof'yev, A. **PROKOFIEV**
"Net, ne liubila ĭa" *see On tak menia liubil*
   Apukhtin **CHAĬKOVSKIĭ**
Net, nikogda ne nazovu see Musset
   CHANSON DE FORTUNIO.
   CHAĬKOVSKIĭ
Neu see Mompou **MOMPOU**
Neuburg, Victor B., 1873-1940.
   HESELTINE *Rantum Tantum*
   QUILTER *Trollie, lollie, laughter*
Der neue Amadis see Goethe **KRENEK,**
   WOLF, ZELTER
Der neue Amor see Goethe **ZELTER**
Neue Fülle see Zweig **REGER**
Neue Liebe see Eichendorff **PFITZNER**
Neue Liebe see Geibel **RUBINSTEIN**
Neue Liebe see Heine **MENDELSSOHN-**
   BARTHOLDY
Neue Liebe see Mörike **WOLF**
Neue Liebe, neues Leben see Goethe
   BEETHOVEN, SPOHR, ZELTER
   Two Beethoven settings: Op. 75 no. 2 and
   WoO 127.

Das neue Lied see Herder **WEBER**
Neuer Frühling see Heine **LOEWE**
"Ein neues Lied" *see Das neue Lied* Herder
   WEBER
NEUF MÉLODIES RETROUVÉES, no. 1
   HAHN Guillot de Saix *Je me souviens*
NEUF MÉLODIES RETROUVÉES, no. 2
   HAHN Guillot de Saix *La vie est belle*
NEUF MÉLODIES RETROUVÉES, no. 3
   HAHN Paté *L'amitié*
NEUF MÉLODIES RETROUVÉES, no. 4
   HAHN Mendès *Chanson*
NEUF MÉLODIES RETROUVÉES, no. 5
   HAHN Unknown *Naïs*
NEUF MÉLODIES RETROUVÉES, no. 6
   HAHN Unknown *La nymphe de la source*
NEUF MÉLODIES RETROUVÉES, no. 7
   HAHN Guillot de Saix *Au rossignol*
NEUF MÉLODIES RETROUVÉES, no. 8
   HAHN Guillot de Saix *Ta main*
NEUF MÉLODIES RETROUVÉES, no. 9
   HAHN Guillot de Saix *Sous l'oranger*
Der Neugierige see Müller, Wilhelm
   SCHUBERT
Neugriechisches Lied see Mikhailov
   RUBINSTEIN
Neujahrsglocken see Meyer **SCHOECK**
Neun, Wilfried von der, pseud. *see*
   Schöpff, Wilhelm, 1826-1916.
Neus, Jakob, b.1767.
   LOEWE *Abendmahlslied*
NEVER PAIN TO TELL THY LOVE. see
   Blake, William
   Love's secret **LUENING**
"Never seek to tell thy love" *see Love's secret*
   Blake, William **LUENING**
"Never the nightingale, Oh my dear" *see*
   Dirge Crapsey **WEISGALL**
Never will love lead us to that glad goal for
   which we languish see Pfleger-Moravský
   DVOŘÁK *Ó, naší lásce*
Never will love lead us to that glad goal for
   which we languish see Pfleger-Moravský
   DVOŘÁK *Ó, naší lásce nekvete*
   Two settings: B. 123 no. 4 and B. 160
      no. 1.
Nevermore see Verlaine **MILHAUD**
Nevernyĭ iunosha see Goethe **MEDTNER**
   Der untreue Knabe
Nevicata see Negri *FATALITÀ.* **RESPIGHI**
The new ghost see Shove **VAUGHAN**
   WILLIAMS
The new river see Ives **IVES**
A new year carol see Anon. **BRITTEN**
Newbolt, Sir Henry John, 1862-1938.
   IRELAND *Hope the hornblower*

COMPOSER   Poet   *Title*   "First Line"

Newborn see Rossetti, Christina **IRELAND**
"Nez au vent, coeur plein d'ai se" *see Lied*
Mendès **CHABRIER**
Než se nadějěš *see* Červenka, Jan
MARTINŮ *Before you know*
"Nezabudoochka-tsvetochek" *see* Bal'mont
STRAVINSKIĭ *Forget-me-nots*
"Nezapomeň, družičko má, nikdy" *see*
Připamatování Anon. **DVOŘÁK**
Nezhdannyĭ dozhd' see Shenshin
MEDTNER *Prayer for rain*
Ni l'or ni la grandeur see La Fontaine
PHILÉMON ET BAUCIS. **GOUNOD**
Ni otzyva, ni slova see Tolstoĭ
CHAĭKOVSKIĭ
Ni slova, O drug" moĭ see Pleshcheyev
CHAĭKOVSKIĭ
"Ni vu ni connu" *see Le sylphe* Valéry
MOMPOU
"Niania, nianiaka!" *see Zhuk* Musorgskĭ
MUSORGSKIĭ
Nichols, Robert Malise Bowyer, 1893-
1944.
ARBOURS AND ENDURANCES (1917).
HESELTINE *The water lily*
"Nicht allein in Rathaussälen" *see Aus dem*
Süden Leuthold **SCHOECK**
"Nicht dass ein Engel eintrat" *see Mariä*
Verkündigung Rilke **HINDEMITH**
"Nicht, dass ich dies Bestreben nicht erfasse"
see Rechtfertigung Leuthold **SCHOECK**
Nicht der Tau und nicht der Regen see
Chamisso **JENSEN**
"Nicht der Thau und nicht der Regen" *see*
Tränen Chamisso **FRANZ**
Nicht doch! see Dehmel *ERLÖSUNGEN.*
SCHÖNBERG
Nicht düstre, Theosoph, so tief! see Hafiz
SCHOECK
"Nicht ein Lüftchen regt sich leise" *see Ruhe,*
meine Seele Henckell **STRAUSS**
Nicht Gelegenheit macht Diebe see Goethe
WESTÖSTLICHER DIVAN: Buch Suleika.
WOLF
"Nicht im Schlafe hab' ich das geträumt" *see*
Freundliche Vision Bierbaum **STRAUSS**
"Nicht im Thale der süssen Heimath" *see*
An Anna II Kerner **SCHUMANN**
"Nicht irdisch ist" *see Frithjofs Glück*
Unknown **LASSEN**
"Nicht jeder Reisetag ist schön und festlich"
see Traurige Stunde Krenek **KRENEK**
Nicht länger kann ich singen see Heyse
WOLF
Nicht mehr zu dir zu gehen Beschloss ich see
Daumer *HAFIS.* **BRAHMS**

"Nicht mehr zurück?" *see Der Wanderer und*
sein Schatten Nietzsche **DELIUS**
Nicht mit Engeln im blauen Himmelszelt see
Bodenstedt **RUBINSTEIN**
"Nicht mit Engeln im blauen Himmelszeit"
see Zuleikha Bodenstedt **SPOHR,**
SZYMANOWSKI
"Nicht so düster und so bleich" *see*
Totengräber-Weise Schlechta
SCHUBERT
"Nicht so schnelle, war' ein wenig" *see*
Aufträge L'Egru **SCHUMANN**
Nicht weinen see Wildenbruch **LASSEN**
"Nicht weinen, Tränen tun so weh" *see Nicht*
weinen Wildenbruch **LASSEN**
Nicht Wiedersehen! see Anon. *DES KNABEN*
WUNDERHORN: Nicht Wiedersehen.
MAHLER
Nichts see Gilm zu Rosenegg *LETZTE*
BLÄTTER. **STRAUSS**
Nichts als ein Athemzug ist das Leere see
Rilke **KRENEK**
Nichts Schöneres see Reinick *LIEDERBUCH*
EINES MALERS. **SCHUMANN, SPOHR**
"Nichts unterm Monde gleicht uns Elfen" *see*
Die Elfenkönigin Matthisson **LOEWE**
"Nichts vom Vergänglichen" *see Xenion*
Goethe **STRAUSS**
Nicolai, Christoph Friedrich, 1733-1811.
DER KLEINE, FEINE ALMANACH.
WEBER *Alte Weiber*
Nicolai, Friedrich *see* Nicolai, Christoph
Friedrich, 1733-1811.
Le nid see Demouth, Paul **MASSENET**
Le nid see Quételart, A. **GOUNOD**
Nie ma czego trzeba see Zaleski **CHOPIN**
NIE MA CZEGO TRZEBA. see Zalenski
Dumka **CHOPIN**
"Niebo bez gwiazd" *see Niebo biez zwiozd*
Davidov, Dmitri **SZYMANOWSKI**
Niebo biez zwiozd see Davidov, Dmitri
SZYMANOWSKI
NIELSEN, CARL, 1865-1931.
Aakjaer, Jeppe, 1866-1930.
Det danske Brød paa Sletten gror (1917-
1921) [W. Hansen, 1921] same
Den føreste laerke, op. 21 no. 5 [W.
Hansen, 1907] same
Høgen, op. 21 no. 2 [W. Hansen, 1907]
"Vaer hilset Høg over Granetop"
Jens Vejmand, op. 21 no. 3 [W. Hansen,
1907] "Hvem sidder der bag
Skjaermen med Klude om sin Haand"
HISTORIENS SANG.
Som dybest Brønd (1917-1921) [W.
Hansen, 1921] same

JYLLAND.
  Der dukker af Disen min Faedrenejord
  (1916-1917) [W. Hansen, 1917]
  same
MORS ROK.
  Spurven sidder stum bag Kvist
  [Borups, 1926] same
PIGER PAA ENGEN.
  Nu er Dagen fuld af Sang (1913-1915)
  [W. Hansen, 1915] same
SE DIGUD.
  Se dig ud en Sommerdag (1916-1917)
  [W. Hansen, 1917] same
SUNDT BLOD.
  Jeg baerer med Smil min Byrde (1913-
  1915) [W. Hansen, 1915] same
SVALEN.
  Hør, hvor let dens Vinger smaekker
  (1916-1917) [W. Hansen, 1917]
  same
Aarestrup, Emil, 1800-1856.
  Angst (1887) [unpubl.]
  "Hold fastere omkring mig"
Almquist, C. J. L., 1793-1866.
  Balladen om Bjørnen, op. 47 (1923) [W.
  Hansen, 1924]
  "De draebte Bjørnens Unger"
  Text adapted by Aage Bernsten.
Andersen, Hans Christian, 1805-1875.
  Højt ligger paa Marken den hvide Sne
  (1916-17) [W. Hansen, 1917] same
  Hun har mig glemt! (1916-17) [W.
  Hansen, 1917] same
  Min lille Fugl, hvor flyver du (1916-17)
  [W. Hansen, 1917] same
  Studie efter Naturen (1916) [W. Hansen,
  1916]
  "Solen skinner i Naboens Gaard"
Anon.
  Der boede en Mand i Ribe By (1916-17)
  [W. Hansen, 1917] same
Balslev, Harald
  Der gaar et stille Tog (1929) [***Ubberup
  Hojskoles Aarsskrift***, 1953, p. 58]
  "Vi ser ud over hver en egn"
  Text also by Uffe Hansen.
Bartrumsen
  FRA ROLD TIL REBILD.
  Vi Jyder (1929) [A. Kaaber, 1929]
  "Vi er Jyder, Børn af Landet"
Bauditz, O.
  Christianshavn (ca. 1918) [Copenhagen:
  Nodetrykkeriet Presto, 1918]
  "Kong Christian stod paa Slotsholmens
  Grund"
Bergstedt, Harald Alfred, 1877-1965.

  Jeg ved en Laerkerede [Borups, 1926]
  same
  Solen er saa rød, Mor [Borups, 1926]
  same
Berntsen, Anton
  AE Lastrae [Borups, 1941]
  "Mi Hasbond wa en Piinwon Rad"
  Den jenn a den anden [Borups, 1941]
  "Den jenn ska studier badde Graesk"
  Jens Madsen a An-Sofi [Borups, 1941]
  "Jens Madsen wa en Feskermand"
  Wo Daetter [Borups, 1941]
  "Hun ae sa møjen hwalle Piig"
Bjørnson, Bjornstjerne, 1832-1910.
  Fremtidens Land (1929) [***Ubberup
  Højskoles Aarsskrift***, 1929, pp. 4-5]
  "Fremtidens Land! Derhen de styrer,
  de tusinde Savn"
  Sangen har lysning (1922) [W. Hansen,
  1925] same
Blicher, Steen Steensen, 1782-1848.
  De Refsnaesdrenge, de Samsøpiger
  (1913-15) [W. Hansen, 1915] same
  Ud gaar du nu paa Livets Vej (1913-15)
  [W. Hansen, 1915] same
Bønnelycke, Emil, 1893-1953.
  Hjemlige Jul (1923) [***Magasinet***, Dec. 23,
  1923; Peder Friis, 1926]
Burns, Robert, 1759-1796.
  Tag Jer i Agt for Anna (1887) [unpubl.]
  "I Knøse, tag, det raader jeg"
**Byron, George Gordon Byron, 6th
  baron, 1778-1824.**
  Min Sjael er mørk (1887) [unpubl.]
Callanau, I.
  Serenade (1887) [unpubl.]
  "See Luften er stille"
Dabelsteen, Chr.
  Naar Smaabørn klynker ved Aftentide
  [Borups, 1926] same
Dam, Johannes, 1866-1926.
  Barnets Sang (1915) [W. Hansen, 1915]
  "Kom, i Dag maa alle synge"
Damm, M.
  Den Spillemand spiller paa Strenge
  [Borups, 1926] same
**Drachmann, Holger Henrik Herholdt,
  1846-1908.**
  Faedrelandssang (1906) [W. Hansen,
  1906] "Du danske Mand"
Falck, Mogens
  Julesang (1923) [W. Hansen, 1923]
  "Himlen mørkner stor og stum"
**Grundtvig, Nicolai Frederik Severin,
  1783-1872.**
  Der sad en fisker sa tankefuld (1917-21)
  [W. Hansen, 1921] same

COMPOSER Poet *Title* "First Line"

NIELSEN, CARL, 1865-1931 (continued)
Grundtvig, Nicolai Frederik Severin,
1783-1872 (continued)
Der snaekker mødtes (1917-21) [W.
Hansen, 1921] same
Nu skal det abenbares (1922) [W.
Hansen, 1925] same
Syndfloden (1917-21) [W. Hansen, 1921]
"Nar nat udvaelder"
Udrundne er de gamle Dage (1917-19)
[*Nordens Musik*, July 1919, pp. 97-98]
same
Choral arrangement published 1921,
W. Hansen.
Hauch, Johannes Carsten, 1790-1872.
Morgendug, der sagte baever (1917-21)
[W. Hansen, 1921] same
Naturens aedle dyrker (1917-21) [W.
Hansen, 1921] same
Vender sig Lykken fra dig (1913-15) [W.
Hansen, 1915] same
Hoffmann, Kai, 1874-1949.
Den danske Sang er en ung, blond Pige
[Borups, 1926] same
Holstein, Ludvig Ditlef, greve, 1864-
1943.
AEbleblomst, op. 10 no. 1 [W. Hansen,
1897] "Du fine, hvide"
Blomstervise (1917) [unpubl.]
"Danmarks Sommer gik sin Gang"
Erindringens Sø, op. 10 no. 2 [W.
Hansen, 1897]
"Traed stille, min Veninde"
Hilsen, op. 10 no. 6 [W. Hansen, 1897]
"Den dovne Fjord som gynger og
straekker"
I Aften, op. 10 no. 5 [W. Hansen, 1897]
"Det gyldenhvide Himmellys"
Sang bag Ploven, op. 10 no. 4 [W.
Hansen, 1897]
"I Solen gaar jeg bag min Plov"
Sommersang, op. 10 no. 3 [W. Hansen,
1897] "Fyldt med Blomster blusser
AEbletraeets Gren"
Hostrup, Jens Christian, 1818-1892.
Dér, hvor vi stred og sang (1917-21) [W.
Hansen, 1921] same
Hvad synger du om (1922) [W. Hansen,
1925] same
Nar somrens sang er sungen (1917-21)
[W. Hansen, 1921] same
Den traenger ud til hvert et sted (1927)
[*Tidsskrift for dansk Folkeoplysning*,
April 1928, p. 309] same
De unges Sang (1908) [W. Hansen, 1910]
"Vi fik ej under Tidernes"

Also arranged for men's chorus.
Det vi ved at siden Slangens Gift (1923-
24) [unpubl.]
Ingemann, Bernhard Severin, 1789-
1862.
Guldfloden (1927) [*Ubberup Hojskoles
Aarsskrift*, 1928, p. 4]
"Der strømmer en Flod"
Jeg sa kun tilbage (1917-21) [W. Hansen,
1921] same
Den store Mester kommer (1917-19)
[*Nordens Musik*, July 1919, pp. 97-98]
same
Tidt er jeg glad, og vil dog gerne graede
(1916-17) [W. Hansen, 1917] same
Jacobsen, Jens Peter, 1847-1885.
Det bødes der for, op. 6 no. 4 [W.
Hansen, 1893] same
Genrebillede, op. 6 no. 1 [W. Hansen,
1893] "Pagen højt paa Taarnet sad"
Har Dagen sanket al sin Sorg, op. 4 no.
5 [W. Hansen, 1892] same
I Drømmes Land (1891) [unpubl.] "Det
er herligt at leve i Drømmenes Land"
Seraferne, op. 6 no. 2 [W. Hansen, 1893]
"Seraferne har rullet bort de klare
Stjerner"
Solnedgang, op. 4 no. 1 [W. Hansen,
1892]
"Svømmende Skyer, dejlige Cyclader"
Til Asali, op. 4 no. 3 [W. Hansen, 1892]
"Før drømte jeg fast hver eneste Nat"
Vise af "Mogens," op. 6 no. 5 [W.
Hansen, 1893]
"Havde Jeg, O havde jeg en Dattersøn"
I SERAILLETS HAVE.
I Seraillets Have, op. 4 no. 2 [W.
Hansen, 1892] "Rosen saenker sit
Hoved tungt af Dug og Duft"
IRMELIN ROSE.
Irmelin Rose, op. 4 no. 4 [W. Hansen,
1892]
"Se, der var en Gang en Konge"
SILKESKO OVER GYLDEN LAEST.
Silkesko over gylden Laest! op. 6 no. 3
[W. Hansen, 1893] same
Jensen, Johannes Vilhelm, 1873-1950.
Godnat, op. 21 no. 7 [W. Hansen, 1907]
"No wil a sej Jer Godnaet"
Husvild, op. 21 no. 6 [W. Hansen, 1907]
"Gi Husly til to Persowner"
Jørgensen, Johannes, 1866-1956.
Bornehjaelpsdagens Sang (1911) [W.
Hansen, 1911] "Vi Børn, vi vaagner"
Nu lyser Løv i Lunde (1917-21) [W.
Hansen, 1921] same

Saenk kun dit Høved, op. 21 no. 4 [W. Hansen, 1907] same

Kaalund, Hans Vilhelm, 1818-1885.
Pa det jaevne, pa det jaevne (1917-21) [W. Hansen, 1921] same

Knudsen, Jakob Christian Lindberg, 1858-1917.
Tunge, mørke natteskyer (1917-21) [W. Hansen, 1921] same

Larsen, Thøger, 1875-1928.
Danmark, nu blunder den lyse Nat (1929) [unpubl.; facsimile in *Politiken*, I.I.1930]

Lorenzen, H.
Gry (1919-20) [W. Hansen, 1920] "Mørket viger, Dagen stiger"

Møller, Poul Martin, 1794-1838.
Farvel, min velsignede Fødeby! (1913-15) [W. Hansen, 1915] same
Grøn er Vaarens Haek [Borups, 1926] same
Rosen blusser alt i Danas Have (1913-15) [W. Hansen, 1915] same
Sov ind mit lille Nusseben! (1913-15) [W. Hansen, 1915] same
Vor Verden priser jeg tusindfold (1913-15) [W. Hansen, 1915] same

Nielsen, Carl, 1865-1931.
Jeg synes om din lette Gang (1906) [unpubl.]
  Facsimile of holograph in Meyer and Petersen *Carl Nielsen, kunstneren og mennesket; en biografi* (Nyt nordisk forlag, 1947-48).
Vuggevise (ca.1883) [unpubl.]

No author
Vocalise-étude (1927) [Alphonse Leduc, 1928]
  Soprano & piano. In Hettich *Répertoire Moderne de Vocalises-Etudes* . . . , v. 6, p. 57.

Oehlenschläger, Adam Gottlob, 1779-1850.
Betragt mit svage spind (1917-21) [W. Hansen, 1921] same
Hvor sødt i Sommer-Aftenstunden (1916-17) [W. Hansen, 1917] same
I Skyggen vi vanke (1913-15) [W. Hansen, 1915] same
Naar Odin vinker (1913-15) [W. Hansen, 1915] same
Nu er da Vaaren kommen (1916-17) [W. Hansen, 1917] same
Underlige Aftenlufte! (1913-15) [W. Hansen, 1915] same

Paludan-Müller, Frederik, 1809-1876.

Gensyn (1930) [*Højskolebladet*, 1930, 4.IV., nr.14, pp.435-36] "Hvor blev den Blomst"

Ploug, Carl, 1813-1894.
St. St. Blicher (1917-21) [W. Hansen, 1921] "Hederlaerken, den liden fugl"

Poulsen, Frederik, 1876-1950.
Det, som lysner over Vangen (1931) [unpubl.] same
Hjemstavn (1929) [W. Hansen, 1940] "Jeg vandrer over mine Faedres Jord"

Richardt, Christian Ernst, 1831-1892.
Derfor kan vort øje Glaedes (1917-21) [W. Hansen, 1921] same
Jord, i hvis favn (1917-21) [W. Hansen, 1921] same
Laer mig, nattens stjerne (1922) [W. Hansen, 1925] same
Velkommen Laerkelil (1928) [unpubl.]

Rode, Helge, 1870-1927.
Skal Blomsterne da visne? op. 21 no. 1 [W. Hansen, 1907] same
Tyst som Aa i Engen rinder [Borups, 1926] same

Rode, Ove, 1867-1933.
Dansk Vejr (1927) [Borups, 1927]

Rogberg, Alma
Det är höst (1926) [unpubl.]

Rørdam, Valdemar
Dansk Arbejde (1923) [W. Hansen, 1923] "Føden og Klaeden, Baaden og Teltet"

Rosing, Michael, 1756-1818.
O, hvor jeg er glad i Dag [Borups, 1926] same

Shelley, Percy Bysshe, 1792-1822.
Til mit Hjertes Dronning (1887) [unpubl.] "Skal vi vandre en Stund"

Stuckenberg, Viggo Henrik Fog, 1863-1905.
Nu springer Vaaren fra sin Seng (1916-17) [W. Hansen, 1917] same

Thomas af Strengnaes
Frihed er det bedste guld (1917-21) [W. Hansen, 1921] same

Unknown
Aldrig hans Ord kan jeg glemme (1891) [unpubl.]
Johs. Jørgensens Ungdommsang (1913) [*Nordisk Ugeblad for Katholske Kristne*, 61.Aarg.Nr.24,15.VI.1913] "Velsignet vaere du, vor Herre, Gud"
Sof sött (1922) [unpubl.] "Sof sött, du lilla Sonja"

NIELSEN, CARL, 1865-1931 *(continued)*
Welhaven, Johann Sebastian
Cammermeyer, 1807-1873.
Vejviseren synger (1887) [unpubl.]
"Til Fjelds over Bygden"
Wiberg, Ohs
Julesang (1923) [W. Hansen, 1923]
"Kom Jul til Jord"
Wied, Gustav Johannes, 1858-1914.
ATALANTA.
Gudhjaelp (1901) [unpubl.]
"Den Sol, som dukker op i Øst"
Jens Petersen, 1856-1902, joint
author of text.
Winther, Christian, 1796-1876.
Jeg laegger mig saa trygt til Ro [Borups,
1926] same
Nielsen, Carl, 1865-1931.
NIELSEN
Jeg synes om din lette Gang
Vuggevise
Niemand see Burns **SCHUMANN**
Niemand hat's gesehn see Gruppe **LOEWE**
Niemeyer, August Hermann, 1754-1828.
LOEWE
Der nahe Retter
Werfet alle eure Sorgen auf ihn!
Niet", tol'ko tot", kto znal" see Goethe
WILHELM MEISTER. Mignon's song: Nur
wer die Sehnsucht kennt.
CHAÏKOVSKIÏ
Nietzsche, Friedrich Wilhelm, 1844-
1900.
HINDEMITH *Three songs*
MEDTNER
Alt Mütterlein
Gruss
Heimkehr
Heimweh
Verzweiflung
SCHÖNBERG *Der Wanderer*
WEBERN *Heiter*
DIE FRÖHLICHE WISSENSCHAFT.
DELIUS
Der Einsame
Nach neuen Meeren
Der Wanderer
MENSCHLICHES,
ALLZUMENSCHLICHES.
DELIUS *Der Wanderer und sein*
Schatten
The night see Belloc, Hilaire **HESELTINE**
Night see Pleshcheyev **RIMSKIÏ-**
KORSAKOV *Noch'*
Night see Polonsky **CHAÏKOVSKIÏ** *Noch'*

Night see Pushkin **MEDTNER;**
MUSORGSKIÏ *Noch'*
Night see Rathaus **CHAÏKOVSKIÏ** *Nacht;*
RACHMANINOFF
Night see Schaffer **COPLAND**
A night battle see Whitman *SPECIMEN*
DAYS. **ROREM**
Night crow see Roethke **ROREM**
Night flew over the world see Pleshcheyev
RIMSKIÏ-KORSAKOV *Noch'*
Night flowers see Cronyn **RIEGGER**
The night is far spent see Paul, Saint,
apostle **KRENEK**
Night is mournful see Bunin
RACHMANINOFF
Night is my sister see Millay *FATAL*
INTERVIEW. **GIDEON**
"The night is still, a soft breeze blows" *see*
Spanish romance Pushkin **MEDTNER**
Night of desire see Gleiman, W. **BARTÓK**
Night of frost in May see Meredith **IVES**
from "Night of frost in May"
Night on ways unknown has fallen see Heine
DIE HEIMKEHR. **GRIFFES**
Nacht liegt auf den fremden Wegen
Night song see Geibel **GRIFFES,**
MACDOWELL *Nachtlied*
A night song see Moore, T. **IVES**
Night song see No author **LUENING**
Night song to preciosa see Ginner, Isaac
SAINT-SAËNS
A night thought see Moore, T. **IVES**
The night watchman see Anon. **MARTINŮ**
Hlásný
Night winds see Tiutchev **MEDTNER**
The nightingale see Anon. **ROREM**
The nightingale see Karadžić
CHAÏKOVSKIÏ *Soloveǐ*
The nightingale see Rorem **ROREM** *Poem:*
The nightingale
The nightingale see Unknown
RUBINSTEIN *Die Nachtigall*
The nightingale see Welhaven **DELIUS**
Sing, sing
The nightingale and the rose see Pushkin
BRITTEN
The nightingale has a lyre of gold see Henley
LIFE & DEATH (ECHOES). **DELIUS**
"The nightingale has a lyre of gold" *see* Song
of the blackbird Henley **QUILTER**
A nightingale sings to the rose see Kol'tsov
RIMSKIÏ-KORSAKOV
Plenivshis' pozoǐ, soloveǐ
The nightingale unheard see Peabody
GIDEON
Nightmare see Soutar **BRITTEN**

The night-piece see Herrick **QUILTER**
Night's revelation see Eichendorff
   MEDTNER *Nachtgruss*
"Niin moen äänen kaiku kuollet on" *see*
   Sonetti sadun linnusta Koskenniemi
   KILPINEN
"Niin monta on sortunut murheeseen" *see*
   Tytön laulu Jalkanen **KILPINEN**
Niin on meitä piikasia see Kanteletar
   KILPINEN
"Niin on noita poikasia" *see On kumpiaki*
   Kanteletar **KILPINEN**
"Niin oudot on tiet, niin vieraita maat" *see*
   Koditon Jalkanen **KILPINEN**
"Niin tulkoon yö ja kuolo" *see Fiat nox*
   Koskenniemi **KILPINEN**
"Niinkuin raskahat rattaiden raiteet" *see*
   Vanitas vanitatum Lehtinen **KILPINEN**
Nikczemny szpak see Iłłakowiczówna
   SZYMANOWSKI
Nikitin, Ivan Savvich, 1824-1861.
   RIMSKIĭ-KORSAKOV *V temnoĭ roshche*
      zamolk soloveĭ
Nikolajesen, V
   GRIEG *Til L.M. Lindemans Sølvbryllup*
Nimfa see Maĭkov **RIMSKIĭ-KORSAKOV**
"Nimm die Forsythien tief in dich hinein" *see*
   Letzter Frühling Benn **BLACHER**
"Nimm die letzten Abschiedsküsse" *see*
   Auf dem Strome Rellstab **SCHUBERT**
"Nimm einen Strahl der Sonne" *see Ihr Auge*
   Rellstab **LISZT**
Nimm sie hin denn diese Lieder see Jeitteles
   BEETHOVEN
"Nimm sie willig und gedulgig" *see*
   Engelsstimmen am Krankenbette Geppert
   family **LOEWE**
"Nimmer, das glaubt mir, erscheinen die
   Götter" *see Dithyrambe* Schiller
   SCHUBERT
"Nimmer länger trag' ich dieser Leiden Last"
   see Der Leidende Unknown **SCHUBERT**
"Nimmer lange weil'ich hier" *see Trost*
   Unknown **SCHUBERT**
"Nimmer, nimmer darf ich dir gestehen" *see*
   Julius an Theone Matthisson
   SCHUBERT
"Nimmer trag' ich länger dieser Leiden Last"
   see Der Leidende Unknown **SCHUBERT**
"Nimmer werd' ich, nimmer dein vergessen"
   see Die Laube Hölty **SCHUBERT**
Nimmer will ich dich verlieren! see Goethe
   WESTÖSTLICHER DIVAN: Buch Suleika.
   WOLF
Nimmersatte Liebe see Mörike **WOLF**
Nincs olyan bú see Pósa **BARTÓK**

1904 see Apollinaire *IL Y A.* **POULENC**
Ninety-six see Hunt **IVES** *Romanzo di*
   Central Park
IL NINFALE FIESOLANO, 287. *see*
   Boccaccio
   Ma come potrei . . . **RESPIGHI**
Ninfe se liete see Unknown **WEBER**
Ninna nanna corbellina see Anon.
   CASELLA
Nino, pseud. *see* Frank, Jacques Henri,
   1904-
Ninon see Musset **FRANCK**
"Ninon! Ninon! que fais-tu de la vie?" *see*
   Ninon Musset **FRANCK**
"Ninon, Ninon, que fais-tu de la vie?" *see*
   Sérénade à Ninon Musset **DELIBES**
"Nio svanor såg jag flyga" *see Svanor*
   Österling **KILPINEN**
The nipples of the rain see MacLow
   ROREM
Nirwana see Zwehl, Hans Fritz von
   KILPINEN
NISCHCHIY. see Lermontov
   At the gate of the Holy Abode
   RACHMANINOFF
Die Nixe see Falke **REGER**
Nixe Binsefuss see Mörike **WOLF**
Nizza see Deschamps **ROSSINI**
"Nizza, je puis sans peine" *see Nizza*
   Deschamps **ROSSINI**
No author *see*
   AURIC *Vocalise*
   BERG *Verlassen*
   BIZET *Vocalise pour ténor*
   BLACHER
      A b c d e f und g
      Anzkiis kwanzkiis kurschpiis kluus
      Guete Tag, mon cher Papa!
      Ich und du und dem Müller sein Kuh
      Madmaselle Pimpernelle
      Quunk, quai quenni monni denni monni
      Unser Schaulmester es en gelärden Mann
   CASELLA
      Ecce Deus salvator meus
      Ecce odor filii mei
      Respice, Domine, familiam tuam
      Tre vocalizzi
   CHANLER *Agnus Dei*
   COPLAND *Vocalise*
   DIAMOND *Vocalises*
   DVOŘÁK
      Ave Maria
      Ave maris stella
      Hymnus k Nejsvětější Trojici
   FAURÉ *Vocalise*
   GRIEG *Ave Maris Stella*

COMPOSER   Poet   *Title*   "First Line"

No author *(continued)*
  HONEGGER *Vocalise-etude*
  IBERT *Vocalise-étude*
  INDY *Vocalise*
  KILPINEN *Vocalise-étude*
  LUENING
    Evening song
    Morning song
    Night song
  MALIPIERO *Tre vocalizzi nello stile moderno*
  MARTINŮ *Vocalise-étude*
  MEDTNER
    Sonata vocalise
    Suite vocalise
  MESSIAEN *Vocalise*
  MILHAUD *Vocalise*
  NIELSEN *Vocalise-Étude*
  PIZZETTI
    Tre vocalizzi
    Vocalise-étude
    Vocalizzo
  POULENC *Vocalise*
  PROKOFIEV *Piat' pesen bez slov*
  RACHMANINOFF *Vocalise*
  RAVEL *Vocalise-Étude en forme de Habanera*
  RESPIGHI *Tre vocalizzi*
  RIEGGER *Music for voice and flute*
  ROREM *Alleluia*
  ROSSINI *Gorgheggi e solfeggi*
  ROUSSEL
    Vocalise no. 1
    Vocalise no. 2
  SATIE
    Marienbad
    Les oiseaux
    Rambouillet
  SAUGUET *Valse des Si*
  SCHMITT *Vocalise en si bémol*
  SÉVERAC *Canzone dans le mode hypolidien*
  STRAUSS *Der Graf von Rom*
  STRAVINSKĬ *Pastorale*
  SZYMANOWSKI *Vocalise-etude*
  TURINA *Vocalizaciones*
  VAUGHAN WILLIAMS *Three vocalises*
"No corè, puti" *see L'avertimento* Anon.
  HAHN
"No es neu són flors de cel" *see Neu* Mompou **MOMPOU**
No escape see Anon. **DVOŘÁK**
    Lásce neujdeš
No esli by s toboĭu ĭa vstretit'sĭa mogla see Kurochkin **MUSORGSKĬ**
No, I have never loved see Apukhtin **CHAĬKOVSKĬ** *On tak menĭa lĭubil*

No, I shall never tell see Musset *CHANSON DE FORTUNIO.* **CHAĬKOVSKĬ**
    Net, nikogda ne nazovu
"No leaflet stirs upon the silent shore" *see Summer nights* Drachmann **DELIUS**
"No Ljåen han syng på den saftige Voll" *see I Slåtten* Garborg **GRIEG**
No longer mourn for me when I am dead see Shakespeare **DIAMOND**
No more dams I'll make for fish see Shakespeare *THE TEMPEST.* **DIAMOND**
No more I will thy love importune see Anon. **WEISGALL**
No, non è morto il figlio tuo see Zarian **RESPIGHI**
No one can hear him the way they can see Rivas, Reyna **THOMSON**
    Nadie lo oye como ellos
No, only he who has known see Goethe **CHAĬKOVSKĬ**
    Nieť, tol'ko toť, kto znaľ
No prophet I see Kruglov **RACHMANINOFF**
No response, or word, or greeting see Tolstoĭ **CHAĬKOVSKĬ** *Ni otzyva, ni slova*
"No ser eg atter slike Fjell og Dalar" *see Ved Rondane* Vinje **GRIEG**
"No song, no song from far or near" *see Rest* Simpson, M. **CARPENTER**
"No stend ho steller i Kjøkenkrå" *see Veslemøy lengtar* Garborg **GRIEG**
"No sudden thing of glory and fear" *see The advent* Meynell **IRELAND**
No tidings came from Thee see Tolstoĭ **CHAĬKOVSKĬ** *Ni otzyva, ni slova*
No voice to scold see De La Mare *DING DONG BELL:* Benighted. **CHANLER**
No, whom I love I will not name see Musset *CHANSON DE FORTUNIO.* **CHAĬKOVSKĬ** *Net, nikogda ne nazovu*
"No wil a sej Jer Godnaet" *see Godnat* Jensen, J. **NIELSEN**
Noailles, Anna Elisabeth (de Brancovan), comtesse de, 1876-1933. **SAINT-SAËNS**
    Soir romantique
    Violons dans le soir
Noailles, Marie Laure de, 1902-1970. **ROREM**
    Jack L'Eventreur
    Je te salue jeunesse
Noblesse obligé, my Lord see Goodman **ROREM**
Noc každou tebe drahá zřím see Heine **MARTINŮ** *I see you every night, my dear*

Les noces d'Or du Sacerdoce see Delaporte, R. P. INDY

Noch' see Pleshcheyev RIMSKIï-KORSAKOV

Noch' see Polonsky CHAïKOVSKIï

NOCH' see Pushkin
  Moï golos dlia tebia RIMSKIï-KORSAKOV

Noch' see Pushkin MUSORGSKIï

Noch' see Rathaus CHAïKOVSKIï Nacht

Noch' see Rathaus RACHMANINOFF
  Night

"Noch ahnt man kaum" see Morgenlied Uhland RUBINSTEIN

"Noch eine Stunde lasst mich hier" see
  Im Sonnenschein Rückert STRAUSS

"Noch einmal muss ich vor dir stehn" see
  Abschied Gerstenberg LOEWE

"Noch einmal ton', O Harfe" see Abschied
  von der Harfe Salis-Seewis SCHUBERT

"Noch erging sie's leicht im Anbeginne" see
  Mariä Heimsuchung Rilke HINDEMITH

"Noch immer Frühling" see An den Frühling
  Lenau RUBINSTEIN

"Noch immer halt ich dich umfasst" see
  Scheiden Saul, D. REGER

"Noch immcr lag ein tiefes Schweigen" see
  Das Gewitter Lenau SCHOECK

"Noch in meines Lebens Lenze" see
  Der Pilgrim Schiller SCHUBERT

Noch ist die blühende, goldene Zeit see
  Roquette JENSEN, LASSEN

"Noch liegt der Winter" see
  Ein Frühlingstraum Träger JENSEN

Noch' pechal'na see Bunin
  RACHMANINOFF Night is mournful

"Noch' proletala nad mirom" see Noch'
  Pleshcheyev RIMSKIï-KORSAKOV

"Noch ruhest du ganz in meinem Arm" see
  Wie durch die stille Mondesnacht Träger
  LASSEN

"Noch schmückten zarte Blüten" see
  Das Blumenopfer Zitzmann LOEWE

Noch spielen die Jaghunde im Hof see Kafka
  KRENEK

"Noch unverrückt, O schöne Lampe" see
  Auf eine Lampe Mörike SCHOECK

"Noch weisst du nicht wess Kind du bist" see
  An einen Säugling Döhring
  BEETHOVEN

"Noch ziehn die Wolken düster" see
  Blumenballade Vogl LOEWE

Noch zwingt mich Treue über dir zu wachen
  see George DAS JAHR DER SEELE:
  Waller im Schnee. WEBERN

Nochevala tuchka zolotaia see Lermontov
  RIMSKIï-KORSAKOV

"Nochevala tuchka zolotaia" see Utes
  Lermontov BALAKIREV

Nochi bezumnye see Apukhtin
  CHAïKOVSKIï

Noch'iu v sadu u menia see Isaakian
  RACHMANINOFF
  In my garden at night

Nochnaia pesn' strannika I see Goethe
  MEDTNER Wandrers Nachtlied

Nochnaia pesni strannika II see Goethe
  MEDTNER Wandrers Nachtlied

"Nochniia t'ma bezmolvie" see Na son"
  griadushchii Ogarev CHAïKOVSKIï

Nochnoï privet see Eichendorff MEDTNER
  Nachtgruss

Nocturne see Auden THE DOG BENEATH
  THE SKIN. BRITTEN

Nocturne see Bouchor, M. CHAUSSON

Nocturne see Cazalis HAHN

Nocturne see Dortzal MASSENET

Nocturne see Fourcaud FRANCK

Nocturne see Prokosch THE CARNIVAL.
  BARBER

Nocturne see Quinault SAINT-SAËNS

Nocturne see Villiers FAURÉ

Nocturne see Whitman WHISPERS OF
  HEAVENLY DEATH.
  VAUGHAN WILLIAMS

"Nocturne jardin" see Jardin nocturne
  Brimont FAURÉ

NOCTURNES, POÈMES IMITÉS DE H.
  HEINE. see Valade
  Tragédie DEBUSSY

Nocturno see Lamberg KILPINEN

Nocturnus see Jalkanen KILPINEN

Der Nöck see Kopisch LOEWE

Noël see Barbier, J. GOUNOD Chantez noël

Noël see Silvestre MASSENET

Noël see Wilder FAURÉ

Noël ancien see Panzacchi RESPIGHI

Noël des enfants qui n'ont plus de maisons
  see Debussy DEBUSSY

Noël des fleurs see Schneider MASSENET

Le Noël des humbles see Aicard
  MASSENET

Le Noël des jouets see Ravel RAVEL

Noël, Édouard
  MASSENET
    Ave Margarita
    La gavotte de Puyjoli

"Noël! En voyant dans ses langes" see Noël
  Silvestre MASSENET

"Noël! Noël!" see Noël païen Silvestre
  MASSENET

"Noël nouvelet Noël chantons ici" see
  Noël ancien Panzacchi RESPIGHI

"Noël nouvelet Noël chantons ici" *(continued)*
  NB: No author of text on music; Ricordi
    catalogue names F. Panzacchi.
    Two settings: This 1912, following entry
    1909.
"Noël nouvelet, Noël chantons ici" *see*
  Noël ancien Unknown **RESPIGHI**
Noël païen see Silvestre **MASSENET**
Noël pastoral see Hettich **AUBERT**
Noel see Unknown **RIEGGER**
Noel ancien see Unknown **RESPIGHI**
Nohain, Jean
  POULENC
    Monsieur sans-souci
    Nous voulons une petit soeur
    Le petit garçon trop bien portant
    La tragique histoire du petit René
"Noin kuulin saneltavaksi" *see Sopivaisia*
  Kanteletar **KILPINEN**
Noin sanoi minun emoni see Kanteletar
  KILPINEN
"La noire terre boit la pluie" *see Qu'il faut*
  boire Anacreon **ROUSSEL**
Nokturno see Klášterský **MARTINŮ**
"Un nom: Cromac, nous fait parler" *see*
  Au pays Fargue **AUBERT**
Le nom de Marie see Ségur **GOUNOD**
Non contrastar cogl'nomini see Chaĭkovskiĭ
  CHAĬKOVSKIĬ *Pimpinella*
"Non, je ne l'aimais pas" *see Il m'aimait tant!*
  Girardin **LISZT**
"Non nella bella estate" *see Mirologio per un*
  bambino Anon. **PIZZETTI**
Non nobis, domine see Kipling **QUILTER**
"Non so qual io mi voglia" *see Ballata*
  Boccaccio **RESPIGHI**
"Non sorgono 'ascolta ascolta" *see Sopra*
  un'aria antica Annunzio **RESPIGHI**
Non t'accostar all'urna see Vittorelli
  SCHUBERT
Non t'accostare all'urna see Vittorelli
  ROREM, VERDI
Non, tu n'as pas fini d'aimer see
  Blanchecotte **MASSENET**
None but the lonely heart see Goethe
  WILHELM MEISTER. Mignon's song: Nur
  wer die sehnsucht kennt.
  CHAĬKOVSKIĬ *Niet'', tol'ko tot'', kto znal''*
Die Nonne see Fröhlich **SCHUMANN**
Die Nonne see Hölty **SCHUBERT**
Die Nonne see Uhland **MENDELSSOHN-**
  BARTHOLDY
"Der Nonne Gebete verhallten" *see*
  Paulinzelle Träger **JENSEN**
Nonnenwerth see Lichnowsky **LISZT**
Noon silence see Sharp, W. **LUENING**

"Noonday sun or night" *see Confidence*
  MacDowell **MACDOWELL**
"Nord oder Süd!" *see So oder so* Lappe
  BEETHOVEN
Norden see Runeberg **SIBELIUS**
Nordheim, H., pseud. *see* Schorn,
  Henriette (von Stein) von, 1807-1869.
Nordisches Seelied see Falk **LOEWE**
Nordmann, Johannes Rumpelmaier,
  1820-1887.
  STÄNDCHEN (?)
    LISZT *Kling leise, mein Lied*
NORGE, no. 1
  GRIEG Paulsen *Hjemkomst*
NORGE, no. 2
  GRIEG Paulsen *Til Norge*
NORGE, no. 3
  GRIEG Paulsen *Henrik Wergeland*
NORGE, no. 4
  GRIEG Paulsen *Turisten*
NORGE, no. 5
  GRIEG Paulsen *Udvandreren*
Normand, Jacques Clary Jean, 1848-
  1931.
  MASSENET
    Les oiselets
    Pitchounette
    Première danse
    Souhait
    Vieilles lettres
Normans Gesang see Scott *THE LADY OF*
  THE LAKE. **SCHUBERT**
Norse, Harold, 1916-
  ROREM
    The flea's lament
    Freak show
    Goodbye to penny fate
    The gypsy
    The Hebrides
    Song of the third duck from the right
    Test your skill
Norse lullaby see Field, Eugene
  CARPENTER
De norske fjelde see Rolfsen **GRIEG**
The North see Runeberg **SIBELIUS** *Norden*
Norwegische Frühlingsnacht see Welhaven
  FRANZ
"Nos sentiers aimés s'en vont refleurir" *see*
  Printemps triste Bouchor, M.
  CHAUSSON
Nos souvenirs see Bouchor, M.
  CHAUSSON
Nos souvenirs qui chantent see Tatry,
  Robert **POULENC**
"Nos souvenirs, toutes ces choses" *see*
  Nos souvenirs Bouchor, M. **CHAUSSON**

Nostitz und Jänkendorf, Gottlob Adolf
  Ernst von, 1765-1836.
  ZELTER *Morgengruss an Serena*
Nostitz und Jänkendorf, Klothilde
  Septimia von, 1801-1852.
  WEBER *Lied von Clotilde*
Nostiz, Clotilde *see* Nostitz und
  Jänkendorf, Klothilde Septimia von,
  1801-1852.
Not a sound from the sea see Tolstoĭ
  RIMSKĬĬ-KORSAKOV *Ne penitsia more*
Not one nightingale sings in the dark see
  Nikitin **RIMSKĬĬ-KORSAKOV**
  V temnoĭ roshche zamolk soloveĭ
Not the wind, blowing from the heights see
  Tolstoĭ **RIMSKĬĬ-KORSAKOV**
  Ne veter, veĭa s vysoty
"La note è bela" *see La barcheta* Anon.
  HAHN
"Nothing is so beautiful as spring" *see Spring*
  Hopkins **ROREM**
"Nothing would sleep in that cellar" *see*
  Root cellar Roethke **ROREM**
Notre amour see Silvestre **FAURÉ**
"Notre amour est chose légere" *see*
  Notre amour Silvestre **FAURÉ**
"Notre amour cst règlé" *see Sanglots*
  Apollinaire **POULENC**
Notre Dame de France see Boyer, Georges
  GOUNOD
Notre Dame des petits enfants see Ségur
  GOUNOD
Notre-Dame de Sarrance see Jammes
  MILHAUD
Notschrei aus den Gefilden Lapplands see
  Strauss, R. **STRAUSS**
Notte see Negri **RESPIGHI**
Notturno see Boelitz **REGER**
Notturno see Negri **RESPIGHI**
Notturno see Ulrich **JENSEN**
N'oublions pas! see Barbier, J. **BIZET**
Nought to my heart can bring relief see
  Pfleger-Moravský **DVOŘÁK**
  Mé srdce často vbolesti
    Three settings: B. 11 no. 11, B. 123
    no. 6, and B. 124 no. 3.
"Nous aimer, à quoi bon, hélas!" *see Fleurs*
  décloses Blée, Catulle **SCHMITT**
"Nous aurons des lits pleins d'odeurs légères"
  see La Mort des amants Baudelaire
  DEBUSSY
Nous avions si chaud see Hugnet
  SAUGUET
Nous avons fait la nuit see Éluard
  POULENC
"Nous avons pensé à des choses pures" *see*
  Le vois amical Valéry **SAUGUET**

Nous baignons dans une eau tranquille see
  Émié **JOLIVET**
"Nous bénissons la douce nuit" *see La nuit*
  Banville **HAHN, KOECHLIN**
"Nous étions assis côte á côte" *see Les yeux*
  de l'Aimée Indy **INDY**
"Nous n'avons plus de maisons!" *see Noël des*
  enfants qui n'ont plus de maisons
  Debussy **DEBUSSY**
Nous ne vous chantons pas see Eluard
  AURIC
Nous nous aimerons see Anon. **CHAUSSON**
Nous nous aimerons tant que nous tairons see
  Jammes *TRISTESSES.*
  BOULANGER, MILHAUD
"Nous prenons la route qui monte" *see*
  Modestes vacances Paliard **MILHAUD**
Nous qu'en ces lieux see Anon.
  SAINT-SAËNS
"Nous sommes aux portes du printemps" *see*
  Le rossignol Latil **MILHAUD**
"Nous sommes filles du village" *see Villanelle*
  Vauquelin **SAINT-SAËNS**
"Nous sommes la jeunesse ardente" *see*
  Jeunesse Vaillant-Couturier
  HONEGGER
"Nous sommes les Ingénues" *see La chanson*
  des ingénues Verlaine **KOECHLIN**
"Nous sommes passés ce me semble" *see*
  Tristesse Silvestre **LALO**
"Nous sommes tous accourus petits et grands"
  see Petit Ramusianum harmonique
  Stravinskiĭ **STRAVINSKIĬ**
"Nous venions de voir le taureau" *see*
  Les filles de Cadix Musset **DELIBES**
Nous voilà donc exilés see Guérin, E.
  MILHAUD
Nous voulons une petit soeur see Nohain,
  Jean **POULENC**
Nouvelle chanson sur un vieil air see Hugo
  MASSENET
Novalis, pseud. *see* Hardenberg, Friedrich
  Leopold, Freiherr von, 1772-1801.
November 2, 1920 see Ives **IVES** *An election*
Novembre see Bourget **KOECHLIN**
"Novembre approche, et c'est le mois
  charmant" *see Novembre* Bourget
  KOECHLIN
Le novice see Stupuy, Hippolyte **LALO**
NOVOGRECHESKIYE PESNI. see Maĭkov
  Kolibel'naya pesnya **CHAĬKOVSKIĬ**
Novogrecheskiye pesni see Maĭkov
  NOVOGRECHESKIYE PESNI.
  CHAĬKOVSKIĬ
"Now came still evening on" *see Evening*
  Milton **IVES**

COMPOSER Poet *Title* "First Line"

Now Christmas comes see Topelius
SIBELIUS *Nu så kommer julen*
Now Christmas stands at the snowy gate see
Topelius SIBELIUS
Nu står jul vid snöig port
"Now green comes springing o'er the heath"
see Consider Ford HESELTINE
Now have I fed and eaten up the rose see
Keller, G. BARBER
"Now help us, Lord" *see The collection*
Unknown IVES
"Now I come, lonely bed, lonely bed" *see*
Lost content Ady BARTÓK
Now I make a circle see Boultenhouse,
Charles ROREM
"Now is the month of maying" *see May*
Anon. BRITTEN
"Now lay me in a cushioned chair" *see Ballad*
of the foxhunter Yeats LOEFFLER
Now let no charitable hope see Wylie
ROREM
"Now on another land I turn two quiet eyes"
see The beacon barn O'Malley, Patrick
BERKELEY
"Now sleep and take thy rest" *see*
The contented lover Mabbe HESELTINE
Now sleeps the crimson petal see Tennyson
QUILTER, ROREM
Now stands our love see Agee SONNET 20.
DIAMOND
"Now stands our love on that still verge of
day" *see Morning fair* Agee
CARPENTER
"Now swallows build" *see Spring song*
Antipater BERKELEY
"Now that there's no more fighting on" *see*
Chez Eitingon Unknown BLITZSTEIN
Now the leaves are falling fast see Auden
LOOK, STRANGER! BRITTEN
Now the lusty spring is seen see Fletcher
ROREM
"Now the next day" *see The resurrection*
Bible ROREM
"Now thro' night's caressing grip" *see*
Nocturne Auden BRITTEN
"Now what do you think of little Jack Jingle?"
see Little Jack Jingle Anon.
HESELTINE
Nox see Leconte de Lisle KOECHLIN
Le noyer fatal see Jacob, M. RIETI
"Nu är det natt över jorden" *see Människans*
hem Blomberg KILPINEN
"Nu daler Solen sagte ned" *see Solnedgang*
Munch GRIEG
Nu er da Vaaren kommen see
Oehlenschläger NIELSEN

Nu er Dagen fuld af Sang see Aakjaer
PIGER PAA ENGEN. NIELSEN
Nu hviler du i jorden see Paulsen GRIEG
"Nu løftes Laft og Lofte" *see Margretes*
Vuggesang Ibsen GRIEG
Nu lyser Løv i Lunde see Jørgensen
NIELSEN
Nu så kommer julen see Topelius SIBELIUS
Nu skal det abenbares see Grundtvig
NIELSEN
"Nu skall hos mig lik en dryad" *see Dryaden*
III Österling KILPINEN
"Nu solen skiner på himlen blå" *see Danslek*
Cnattingius, Thor KILPINEN
Nu springer Vaaren fra sin Seng see
Stuckenberg NIELSEN
Nu står jul vid snöig port see Topelius
SIBELIUS
"Nu susar var genom solbla luft" *see Vårtagen*
Gripenberg SIBELIUS
"Nu synker Solen i Asiens Dale" *see*
Odalisken synger Brun GRIEG
"Nu vist det våres i Norges dale" *see*
Udvandreren Paulsen GRIEG
Nuage see Beylié, Laurence de POULENC
Le nuage see Pomès, Mathilde MOMPOU
Nuage, premier pas de mon élévation see
Éluard SAUGUET
Nuageries see Richepin CASELLA
Les nuages see Louvencourt MASSENET
Nuages see Richepin DELIUS
"Les nuages là-haut vont rêvant" *see*
Nuageries Richepin CASELLA
"Nuages, nuages que . . . " *see Nuages*
Richepin DELIUS
"Les nuages s'entassent sur les nuages" *see*
Poème du "Gitanjali" Tagore MILHAUD
La nuit see Banville HAHN, KOECHLIN
La nuit see Ferrier BIZET
La nuit see Hugo MASSENET
"La nuit a des douceurs de femme" *see*
De rêve Debussy DEBUSSY
La nuit à la vérandah see Claudel
MILHAUD
Nuit blanche see Fargue AURIC
Nuit d'automne see Régnier ROUSSEL
LA NUIT DE MAI: stanza 4, "Pourquoi mon
coeur bat-il si vite?" *see* Musset
Loneliness RACHMANINOFF
"La nuit descend du haut des cieux" *see Noël*
Wilder FAURÉ
Nuit d'Espagne see Gallet MASSENET
Nuit d'été, nuit sombre see Anon.
SZYMANOWSKI *Ciamna nocka, ciamna*
Nuit d'étoiles see Banville *LES*
STALACTITES. La Dernière Pensée de
Weber. DEBUSSY

"La nuit disparait, l'oiseau chante" *see Adieux au désert* Flobert, A. **LALO**

"La nuit est blue . . . et chaude" *see Le repos en Égypte* Samain **RESPIGHI**

"La nuit est descendue, voici l'heure attendue" *see Sérénade* Mangeot, L. **SAINT-SAËNS**

"La nuit est façonée avec un art subtil" *see Nuit mauresque* Vivien **AUBERT**

"La nuit était pensive et ténébreuse" *see Nocturne* Bouchor, M. **CHAUSSON**

"La nuit était venue" *see Comme à la lumière de la lune* Proust **SAUGUET**

"La nuit, la pluie, Paris" *see La marchande d'anémondes* Sidery **SAUGUET**

Nuit mauresque see Vivien **AUBERT**

"La nuit règne à Grenade" *see À Grenade* Pacini **ROSSINI**

La nuit sans doute était trop belle see Robiquet **MASSENET**

"La nuit s'efface" *see Pluie au matin* Louÿs **KOECHLIN**

"Nuit, sommeil des souffles" *see Incantation de la nuit* Jacqueton, Henry **SAUGUET**

"La nuit, sur le grand mystère" *see Nocturne* Villiers **FAURÉ**

Nuits blanches see Debussy **DEBUSSY**

Nuits de grand vent see Stevenson, Robert Louis *A CHILD'S GARDEN OF VERSES.* **HAHN** *Windy nights*

LES NUITS D'ÉTÉ, no. 1 **BERLIOZ** Gautier *Villanelle*

LES NUITS D'ÉTÉ, no. 2 **BERLIOZ** Gautier *La spectre de la rose*

LES NUITS D'ÉTÉ, no. 3 **BERLIOZ** Gautier *Sur les lagunes*

LES NUITS D'ÉTÉ, no. 4 **BERLIOZ** Gautier *Absence*

LES NUITS D'ÉTÉ, no. 5 **BERLIOZ** Gautier *Au cimetière*

LES NUITS D'ÉTÉ, no. 6 **BERLIOZ** Gautier *L'Île inconnue*

NUITS PERSANES. see Renaud *Flots, palmes, sables* **DEBUSSY**

Nul ne se lasse dêtre soi see Carême **SAUGUET**

"Nulla cosa quaggiù e più triste" *see Remember* Cocconi, Ildebrando **PIZZETTI**

Nun auf dem fremden Boden see Giesebrecht **LOEWE**

Nun bin ich dein see Ruiz **WOLF**

"Nun bin ich untreu worden" *see Unruhe der Nacht* Keller, G. **SCHOECK**

"Nun brennet am Nilstrom die Sonne so sehr" *see Die Zugvögel* Tegnér **LOEWE**

"Nun da die Bäum' in Blüten steh'n" *see In Blüten* Osterwald **FRANZ**

"Nun da Schatten niedergleiten" *see Florio* Schütz **SCHUBERT**

"Nun, da sie Alle eingeschlafen" *see Verlorne Liebe* Galli **REGER**

Nun, da so warm der Sonnenschein see Redwitz **PFITZNER**

Nun der Abend licht und lang see Drachmann **GRIEG** *Nur er Aftnen lys og lang*

"Nun die Schatten dunkeln" *see Für Musik* Geibel **FRANZ, STRAUSS**

Nun die Schatten dunkeln see Geibel **JENSEN**

"Nun die Schatten dunkeln" *see Lied* Geibel **RUBINSTEIN**

"Nun du wie Licht durch meine Träume gehst" *see Traum* Evers **REGER**

Nun ein Scherflein in der Runde see Storm **KRENEK**

"Nun gieb ein Morgenküsschen" *see Morgens* Storm **RUBINSTEIN**

"Nun grünt der Berg" *see Im Mai* Osterwald **FRANZ**

"Nun hängt nur noch am Kirchturmknopf der letzte Sonnenschein" *see Gegen Abend* Bierbaum **REGER**

Nun hast du mir den ersten Schmerz gethan see Chamisso **LOEWE, SCHUMANN**

Nun hat das Lied ein Ende see Osterwald **FRANZ**

"Nun hat Deines Herzens Geige" *see Nirwana* Zwehl, Hans Fritz von **KILPINEN**

Nun hat mein Stecken gute Rast see Osterwald **FRANZ**

"Nun hebt sich Dach und Dekke zum Sternenhimmel auf" *see Wiegenlied* Ibsen **DELIUS**

Nun holt mir eine Kanne Wein see Burns **FRANZ**

"Nun, ich bin befreit!" *see Der Geleichmütige* Gubitz **WEBER**

"Nun ich dein Auge feucht gesehn" *see Lebe wohl* Hamerling **JENSEN**

Nun ich der Riesen Stärksten see Mombert *DER GLÜHENDE.* **BERG**

"Nun ist es Herbst, die Blätter fallen" *see Herbst* Lenau **WOLF**

"Nun ist mein' beste Zeit vorbei" *see Abschied* Roquette **JENSEN**

"Nun kommt die Nacht gegangen" *see Wiegenlied* Braungart **REGER**

"Nun lass' das Lamentieren" *see Trost* Leuthold **SCHOECK**

COMPOSER Poet *Title* "First Line"

"Nun lass' das Lamentieren" *(continued)*

"Nun lass mich träumen" *see Märchenwunder*
Cornelius **CORNELIUS**

Nun lass uns Frieden schliessen see Heyse
WOLF

"Nun legen sich die Wogen" *see*
Sterbeglocken Eichendorff **SCHOECK**

"Nun, Liebster, geh', nun scheide!" *see*
Vorabend Cornelius **CORNELIUS**

Nun liegt die Welt im Traume see
Bodenstedt **LASSEN**

"Nun merk' ich erst, wie Müd'ich bin" *see*
Rast Müller, Wilhelm **SCHUBERT**

Nun quill aus meiner Seele see Schoeck, P.
SCHOECK

"Nun rausch im Morgenwinde sacht so" *see*
Im Gebirg Geibel **JENSEN**

Nun ruhest du im Grabe see Paulsen
GRIEG *Nu hviler du i jorden*

"Nun ruhst du sanft in meinem Arm" *see*
Abendfrieden Braungart **REGER**

"Nun ruht der Sommerabend lind" *see*
Hochgebirgsleben Ibsen **DELIUS**

"Nun scheidet vom sterbenden Walde" *see*
Abschied vom Walde Schöpff
SCHUMANN

"Nun seh' ich meine Berg' und Täler wieder"
see Auf der Reise zur Heimat Vinje
DELIUS

"Nun sinkt hinab die Sonne" *see Beim*
Sonnenuntergang Munch **DELIUS**

"Nun steh' ich über Grat und Kluft" *see*
Der Alte Falke **REGER**

"Nun stehen die Rosen in Blüthe" *see*
Frühlingslust Heyse **SCHUMANN**

"Nun stehn die Rosen in Blüthe" *see*
Rosenzeit Heyse **JENSEN**

Nun steht der Wald in Blüten see Unknown
SCHOECK

A nun takes the veil see Hopkins **BARBER**

Nun, wandre, Maria, nun wandre nur fort see
Ocaña **WOLF**

Nun weiss man erst, was Rosenknospe sei see
Goethe
CHINESISCH- DEUTSCHE JAHRES- UND
TAGESZEITEN. **WEBERN**

"Nun, wer klopft an meine Thür?" *see Findlay*
Burns **LOEWE**

"Nun wind um deine Stirne" *see Tanzlied*
Sergel **KILPINEN**

"Nun wir uns lieben" *see Gefunden*
Avenarius **WEBERN**

"Nun wird es wieder grün auf allen Wiesen"
see Frühlingsklage Lebret **FRANZ**

"Nun wollen Berg' und Tale wieder blüh'n"
see Wasserfahrt Geibel **FRANZ**

"Nun wollen Knospen sich entfalten" *see*
Der Lenz Cornelius **LASSEN**

"Nun ziehen Tage über die Welt" *see*
Sommertag Hohenberg **BERG**

Nunca olvida see Campoamor y
Campoosorio **TURINA**

Nuñez, Nicolas, fl.1550.
WOLF *Die du Gott gebarst, du Reine*

"Nunmehr, da Himmel, Erde" *see Sonett III*
Petrarca **SCHUBERT**

Nuori Apollo see Lehtinen **KILPINEN**

Nuptiae factae sunt see Bible **HINDEMITH**

Nuptial song see Anon. **WEISGALL**

"Nur bei dir, an deinem Herzen" *see*
An Minna Unknown **BEETHOVEN**

Nur das thut mir so bitterweh' see Redwitz
AMARANTH. **SCHÖNBERG**

"Nur ein Gedanke" *see An die Königin*
Elisabeth Mary **SCHUMANN**

Nur ein lächelnder Blick see Zimmermann
SCHUMANN

"Nur ein Wörtchen spricht, O Mädchen" *see*
Sei nur ruhig, lieber Robin Hamerling
LASSEN

Nur ein Wort see Kafka **KRENEK**

"Nur ein Wort, nur eine Bitte" *see Nur ein*
Wort Kafka **KRENEK**

Nur eine Viertelstund! see Cornelius
LASSEN

"Nur einen Sommer gönnt, ihr Gewaltigen!"
see An die Parzen Hölderlin
HINDEMITH

Nur Eines wünscht see Rambach **ZELTER**

Nur einmal möcht ich dir noch sagen see
Sturm, J. **LASSEN**

Nur er Aftnen lys og lang see Drachmann
GRIEG

"Nur fast so wie im Traum ist mir's
geschehen" *see Besuch in Urach* Mörike
SCHOECK

Nur Mut! see Schack **STRAUSS**

Nur Platz, nur Blösse! see Goethe *FAUST.*
LOEWE

Nur wer die Sehnsucht kennt see Goethe
WILHELM MEISTER. Mignon's song: Nur
wer die sehnsucht kennt.
CHAÏKOVSKIĬ *Niet", tol'ko tot", kto znal"*

Nur wer die Sehnsucht kennt see Goethe
WILHELM MEISTER. Mignon's song: Nur
wer die sehnsucht kennt.
SCHUMANN, ZELTER

"Nur wer die Sehnsucht kennt" *see Lied der*
Mignon Goethe **SCHUBERT**
Three settings: D. 359, D. 481, and D. 877
no. 4.

"Nur wer die Sehnsucht kennt" *see Mignon*
Goethe **MEDTNER**

COMPOSER   Poet   *Title*   ''First Line''

"Nur wer die Sehnsucht kennt" *see Mignon II*
Goethe **WOLF**

"Nur wer die Sehnsucht kennt" *see Mignon
und der Harfner* Goethe **SCHUBERT**

"Nur wer die Sehnsucht kennt" *see Sehnsucht*
Goethe **BEETHOVEN, LOEWE,
SCHUBERT, ZELTER**

Nur zu! see Mörike **SCHOECK**

"La nurse était bleu et la brique rose" *see
Passage d'une nurse* Gilson **RIVIER**

NURSE LOVECHILD'S LEGACY (London:
The Poetry Bookshop, 1916). *see* Anon.
  Arthur o' Bower **HESELTINE**
  How many miles to Babylon? **HESELTINE**
  I had a little pony **HESELTINE**
  I won't be my father's Jack **HESELTINE**
  Little Jack Jingle **HESELTINE**
  Little Tommy Tucker **HESELTINE**
  O my kitten **HESELTINE**
  Robin and Richard **HESELTINE**
  Suky, you shall be my wife **HESELTINE**
  There was a man of Thessaly **HESELTINE**

There was an old man **HESELTINE**
There was an old woman **HESELTINE**
The nurse's song see Phillip, John
BRITTEN

Der Nussbaum see Mosen **SCHUMANN**
THE NUT-BROWNE MAYD. see Anon.
  Das braune Mädchen **LOEWE**
Nuvole see Unknown **PIZZETTI**
Nuvoletta see Joyce *FINNEGANS WAKE.*
BARBER

"Nuvoletta in her light dress" *see Nuvoletta*
Joyce **BARBER**

Nyár see Gombossy **BARTÓK** *Summer*
The nymph see Maïkov **RIMSKIǏ-
KORSAKOV** *Nimfa*

La nymphe de la source see Unknown
HAHN

Nyt on kaikki kallistunna see Kanteletar
KILPINEN

"Nyt sumu harmaa nousee korven soissa" *see
Syyssonetti* Koskenniemi **KILPINEN**

"Nyt värjyvät murheen kellot" *see Murheen
kellot* Törmänen **KILPINEN**

O

"O, Anblick der Glanznacht, Sternheere" *see
Der Tod* Klopstock **GLUCK**

"O banger Traum" *see Erinnerung*
Osterwald **FRANZ**

"O be still, be still, unquiet thoughts" *see
The lover's maze* Campion **HESELTINE**

"O beau lac, Ô limpide azur" *see Le lac*
Unknown **POULENC**

Ô belle blonde see Zaffira **GOUNOD**
  Biondina bella

"O blaa nätter i var ungdomspark" *see
Narsissi* Gripenberg **SIBELIUS**

"O blanche Tyndaris" *see Tyndaris* Leconte
de Lisle **HAHN**

"O blanches colombes du soir" *see Chanson
au bord de la fontaine, extraite de Méduse*
Magre **HAHN**

"O blaue Luft" *see An einem heitern Morgen*
Uhland **SCHOECK**

"O Blümlein, das den Wiesenrand einst zierte"
see Die Blume Zhukovski **RUBINSTEIN**

"O bon vin, bon vin, bon vin" *see O bon vin,
où as-tu crû?* Anon. **ROUSSEL**

O bon vin, où as-tu crû? see Anon.
ROUSSEL

O boundless, boundless evening see Heym
BARBER

"O brich nicht Steg, du zitterst sehr" *see
Heimkehr* Uhland **BRAHMS**

o by the by see Cummings **BLITZSTEIN**
Ó byl to krásný, zlatý sen see Pfleger-
Moravský **DVOŘÁK**
  Three settings: B. 11 no. 5, B. 123 no. 2,
  and B. 124 no. 2.

"O Calpe! dir donnert's am Fusse" *see
Gibraltar* Denis **MOZART**

O care selve see Metastasio **BEETHOVEN**
"O Catherine Ivanowna" *see L'infidèle*
Chalupt **MILHAUD**

"O cet ennui bleu dans le coeur!" *see Serre
d'ennui* Maeterlinck **CHAUSSON**

"O Chatterton! How very sad thy fate!" *see
Chatterton* Keats **DIAMOND**

O chem ty voesh' vetr nochnoǐ see Tiutchev
MEDTNER *Night winds*

O chem v tishi nocheǐ see Maïkov **RIMSKIǏ-
KORSAKOV**

O child, dear heart see Merezhkovski
RUBINSTEIN

"O Cigale, née avec les beaux jours" *see
La cigale* Leconte de Lisle **CHAUSSON**

"O, come with me into my wall'd-in garden"
see The walled-in garden Heald, Arthur
QUILTER

"O cool unto the sense of pain" *see During music* Rossetti, Dante **IRELAND**

"O Courbes, méandres, secrets du menteur"
see L'insinuant Valéry **MOMPOU**

"O dainty pansy!" *see The pansy* Deland
MACDOWELL

"O danke nicht, für diese Lieder" *see Widmung* Müller von Königswinter
FRANZ

"O dass ich dir vom stillen Auge" *see An die Geliebte* Stoll **BEETHOVEN, SCHUBERT**

"O Dieu, de tes soldats la cauronne et la gloire!" *see L'anniversaire des martyrs* Dallet **GOUNOD**

"O Dieu donne-moi délivrance" *see Psalm CXI* Bible **HONEGGER**

"O Dieu, pourquoi viens-tu en fraude" *see Petite musique* Richaud **SAUGUET**

"O ditya, pod okoshkom tvoim" *see Serenada* Konstantin **CHAÏKOVSKIÏ**

O do not love too long see Yeats **ROREM**

"O dolce far niente" *see Das "Dolce far niente"* Grassmann **LOEWE**

"Ô, doux printemps d'autrefois" *see Elégie* Gallet **IVES, MASSENET**

"O Du, der ich erblühte, die mich er quick te Tag um Tag" *see Mädchenlied* Boelitz **REGER**

"O du Entriss'ne mir und meinem Kusse!" *see Sei mir gregrüsst!* Rückert **SCHUBERT**

"O du leichter, loser Wind" *see Frühlingsgefühl* Zhukovski **RUBINSTEIN**

O du liebes Jesukind see Unknown
BRUCKNER

O, du mondhelle Nacht see Rathaus
CHAÏKOVSKIÏ

O, du, Säfer! see Musorgskiï
MUSORGSKIÏ *Akh, ty, p'ianaïa teteriaï!*

"O du, wenn deine Lippen mich berühen"
seeHeimliches Lieben Klenke **SCHUBERT**

Ó, duše drahá, jedinká see Pfleger-Moravský **DVOŘÁK**

Ó duše drahá jedinkájež see Pfleger-Moravský **DVOŘÁK**

O, esli b ty mogla see Tolstoï
CHAÏKOVSKIÏ, RIMSKIÏ-KORSAKOV

"O, esli pravda" *see Zaklinanie* Pushkin
RIMSKIÏ-KORSAKOV

O, eslib" znali vy see Pleshcheyev
CHAÏKOVSKIÏ

"O fände für mich ein Bräutigam sich!" *see Mädchenwünsche* Goethe **LOEWE**

O falce di luna see Annunzio *CANTO NOVO*: Canto dell'Ospite, no. VII.
RESPIGHI

"O Felsen, lieber Felsen" *see Klage II, Slowakisch* Wenzig **BRAHMS**

"Ô fier jeune homme, Ô tueur de gazelles" *see La solitaire* Renaud **SAINT-SAËNS**

"O figlio, figlio, in che mondo ti trovi?" *see La Madre al figlio lontano* Pàntini, Romualdo **PIZZETTI**

"O fior del prato!" *see Stornello* Donini
RESPIGHI

"O flaumenleichte Zeit der dunkeln Frühe!" *see An einem Wintermorgan, vor Sonnenaufgang* Mörike **SCHOECK**

"O floraison divine des lilas" *see Les lilas* Banville **DEBUSSY**

"O Fluss, mein Fluss im Morgenstrahl!" *see Mein Fluss* Mörike **SCHOECK**

O frage nicht see Woskresensky
RUBINSTEIN

"O fraîche nuit, nuit transparente" *see Nocturne* Fourcaud **FRANCK**

"O fratel nostro, che se' morto" *see Lauda per un morto* Latini **MALIPIERO**

"O Freude, O Wonne!" *see Der Schwimmer* Enslin **LOEWE**

O Freund, mein Schirm, mein Schutz! see Rückert *LIEBESFRÜHLING.* **SCHUMANN**

O from what power hast thou this powerful might see Shakespeare **DIAMOND**

"O Frühlingsabenddämmerung!" *see Geheimnis* Candidus **BRAHMS**

O Frühlingshauch, O Liederlust see Leuthold **SCHOECK**

"O Geist der heil'gen Liebe" *see Gebet* Kunze, W. **RUBINSTEIN**

"O gib mir meinen Frieden" *see Seufzer* Bornowski **LASSEN**

"O gib vom weichen Pfühle" *see Nachtgesang* Goethe **SCHOECK, SCHUBERT**

"O gieb, vom weichen Pfühle" *see Nachtgesang* Goethe **ZELTER**

"O Gott, mein gebieter" *see Gebet* Mary
SCHUMANN

"O, gräv mig en grav, dödgrävare snäll" *see Min grav* Josephson, E. **KILPINEN**

"O grande Estate, delizio grande" *see Ditirambo terzo* (dalle laudi di Gabriele d'Annunzio, 1923) Annunzio
MALIPIERO

O happy land see Linton **IRELAND**

"O Harfe, die des Gottgeliebten Hand" *see Davids Harfe* Byron **LOEWE**

"O hast du dies gewollt" *see Vor der Passion* Rilke **HINDEMITH**

"O, heart of mine" *see Loneliness* Musset
RACHMANINOFF

"O heiliges Band" *see Lobgesang auf die
feierliche Johannisloge* Lenz, L.
MOZART

*O heiss mich nicht vor deinem Antlitz fliehn
see* Unknown **JENSEN**

O Herre Gott, nimm du von mir see
Unknown **REGER**

O Herz in meiner Brust! see Mayer, K.
FRANZ

"O Herz, sei endlich stille!" *see An mein Herz*
Schulze **SCHUBERT**

"O himmlische Wonne des Lebens" *see
Lebenslied* Hamerling **LASSEN**

"O Hochland und O Südland!" *see Murrays
Ermordung* Anon. **BRAHMS**

"O höh're Welt" *see Die höh're Welt* Byron
LOEWE

"O Hoffnung!" *see An die Hoffnung*
Hölderlin **REGER**

"O holy Virgin! clad in purest white" *see
To morning* Blake, William **LUENING**

O, hvor jeg er glad i Dag see Rosing
NIELSEN

O Hymen! O Hymenee! see Whitman
BLITZSTEIN

"O Hymen! O Hymenee! why do you tantalize
me thus?" *see O Hymen! O Hymenee!*
Whitman **BLITZSTEIN**

"O if it be that, in the night" *see
The summons* Pushkin **MEDTNER**

O, if only you knew see Pleshcheyev
CHAĬKOVSKIĬ *O, eslib" znali vy*

O ihr Herren see Rückert
LIEBESFRÜHLING. **SCHUMANN**

"O it's I that am the captain of a tidy little
ship" *see My ship and I*
Stevenson, Robert Louis **HAHN**

"O! it's owre the braes abüne our toun" *see
A laddie's sang* Soutar **BRITTEN**

"O iubilo del core, che fai cantar d'amore!"
see Dialogo no. 3 "con Jacopone da Todi"
Unknown **MALIPIERO**

"O je t'implore à genoux!" *see Extase
printanière* Alexandre, André
MASSENET

O Jesu Christ, wir warten dein see Alberus
MORGENLIED. **REGER**

"O Jesulein zart, O Jesulein zart" *see
Christkindleins Wiegenlied* Des Knaben
Wunderhorn **SZYMANOWSKI**

O jeunes filles see Gabory **SAUGUET**

"Ô joi de mon âme" *see Chanson des
cueilleuses de lentisques* Anon. **RAVEL**

O Jugend, O schöne Rosenzeit! see Anon.
MENDELSSOHN-BARTHOLDY

O könnt ich zu dir fliegen see Unknown
MENDELSSOHN-BARTHOLDY

"O köstlicher Tokayer" *see Lob des Tokayers*
Batsányi **SCHUBERT**

O komm im Traum see Hugo **LISZT**
Oh! quand je dors

O Komme, holde Sommernacht see Grohe
BRAHMS

O kühler Wald see Brentano **BRAHMS**

Ô LACRIMOSA, no. 2
KRENEK Rilke *Nichts als ein Athemzug
ist das Leere*

Ô LACRIMOSA, no. 3
KRENEK Rilke *Aber die Winter!*

"O Lady Judith, spröder Schatz" *see
Entführung* Häring **BRAHMS**

"O lächle, Freund der Liebe" *see Abends*
Unknown **FRANZ**

"Ô Lämmlein bleibt" *see Einsegnungslied*
Giesebrecht **LOEWE**

O lass dich halten, gold'ne Stunde see
Roquette **JENSEN**

"O lass, Geliebter, dich erflehen" *see
Der Feldherr* Gruppc **LOEWE**

"O lass mich die trunkenen Blicke erheben"
see Was tut's Lipiner **RUBINSTEIN**

O Lebensfrühling, Blütendrang see Leuthold
SCHOECK

"O, legt mich nicht ins dunkle Grab" *see
Frühlingsruhe* Uhland **SCHOECK**

"O les passions en allées" *see Fauves las*
Maeterlinck **CHAUSSON**

"O l'heure douce!" *see Temps de neige*
Gauthier-Villars **SÉVERAC**

O lieb see Freiligrath **LISZT**

"O Lieb, O lieb" *see O lieb* Freiligrath
LISZT

"O Liebe, die mein Herz erfüllet" *see
Lambertine* Stoll **SCHUBERT**

O, lieber Künstler see Kerr **STRAUSS**

O liebliche Wangen see Fleming **BRAHMS**

"O Life, thy name to me's a galling sound"
see On death Clare **DIAMOND**

"O little head of gold!" *see Lullaby of the
woman of the mountain* Pearse **ROREM**

"O Lord of grace! I stand before Thee self-
confessed" *see A prayer* Goethe
RACHMANINOFF

"O Lord of Heaven!" *see The raising of
Lazarus* Khomyakov **RACHMANINOFF**

O lovely rose see Gardner, W.
MACDOWELL

O lüge nicht! see Heine **FRANZ**

O lurcher-loving collier, black as night see
Auden **BERKELEY**

"O, Lust am Rheine, am heimischen Strande"
see Am Rhein Cornelius **CORNELIUS**

COMPOSER Poet *Title* ''First Line''

O ma belle rebelle **see** Baïf **GOUNOD**

"O ma soeur d'idéal" **see** *Soeur d'élection*
Trolliet, Emile **MASSENET**

"O Madame voilà ce qu'il faudrait
comprendre vous me" **see** *Madame*
Cocteau **HONEGGER**

"O Magdeburg, die Stadt" **see** *Die Zerstörung
Magdeburgs* Goethe **KRENEK**

O magnum mysterium **see** Anon.
MILHAUD

"O Mariamne, dieses Herz" **see** *Herodes'
Klage um Mariamne* Byron **LOEWE**

"O Medjé, qui d'un sourire" **see** *Medjé*
Barbier, J. **GOUNOD**

"O mein Geliebter in die Kissen bet ich nach
dir" **see** *Nachtgebet der Braut* Dehmel
WEBERN

O, mein Sternelein **see** Grekov
MUSORGSKIĭ *Gde ty, zvezdochka?*

O meine Blumen, ihr, meine Freude! **see**
Unknown **LOEWE**

"O Menschheit, O Leben, wass soll's?" **see**
Totengräbers Heimwehe Craigher
SCHUBERT

"Ô mer, ouvre-toi" **see** *Arioso* Silvestre
DELIBES

O might those sighes and teares **see** Donne
BRITTEN

"O mio povero cor" **see** *Povero core* Graf
RESPIGHI

"O misère de trop aimer" **see** *Regrets* Fargue
AURIC

O mistress mine! **see** Shakespeare
TWELFTH NIGHT. **CHANLER,
QUILTER**

"O mistress mine, where are you roaming?"
see *O mistress mine!* Shakespeare
CHANLER, QUILTER

"O mistress mine, where are you roaming?"
see *Sweet-and-twenty* Shakespeare
HESELTINE

"O moment of rapt'rous bliss!" **see** *The waltz*
Pushkin **MEDTNER**

"O mon bonheur, ma vie" **see** *Chant de
bonheur* Berlioz **BERLIOZ**

"O mon cher rouet" **see** *Chanson du rouet*
Leconte de Lisle **RAVEL**

O mon coeur, ce sera dans l'Aoûte bleu **see**
Jammes *TRISTESSES.* **MILHAUD**

"O mon tzigane mon amant" **see** *Les cloches*
Apollinaire **RIVIER**

O Mond, O lösch' dein gold'nes Licht **see**
Förster, M. **FRANZ**

"Ô monde! Ô vie! Ô temps!" **see** *Plainte*
Tastu **SAINT-SAËNS**

O moon, how I love you **see** Maïkov
RIMSKIĭ-KORSAKOV
Liubliu tebia, mesiats

O mort, poussière d'étoiles **see** Lerberghe
FAURÉ

"O mother earth, O dear one" **see** *A song of
the dew* Gorodetski **STRAVINSKIĭ**

O mrtvých očích **see** Martínek **MARTINŮ**
Dead eyes

"O Muse, mir Vertraute" **see** *An die Muse*
Dionysius **LOEWE**

"O Mutter, der junge Prinz ist un unsrer Tür"
see *Der junge Prinz II* Tagore
SZYMANOWSKI

"O Mutter, der junge Prinz muss an unsrer
Tür" **see** *Der junge Prinz I* Tagore
SZYMANOWSKI

"O Mutter, wie stürmen die Flocken vom
Himmel" **see** *Die Gottesmauer* Rückert
LOEWE

"O my deir hert, young Jesus sweit" **see**
Balulalow Luther **HESELTINE**

O, my dove **see** Bible **THOMSON**

O my kitten **see** Anon. *NURSE
LOVECHILD'S LEGACY* (London: The
Poetry Bookshop, 1916). **HESELTINE**

"O my kitten, a kitten" **see** *O my kitten*
Anon. **HESELTINE**

O, Nacht **see** Morgenstern **KILPINEN**

"O, Nacht, du Sternenbronnen" **see** *O, Nacht*
Morgenstern **KILPINEN**

"O Nachtigall, dein süsser Schall" **see**
Nachtigall Köstlin **BRAHMS**

Ó, naší lásce **see** Pfleger-Moravský
DVOŘÁK

Ó, naší lásce nekvete **see** Pfleger-Moravský
DVOŘÁK
Two settings: B. 123 no. 4 and B. 160 no.
1.

O, ne grusti! **see** Apukhtin
RACHMANINOFF *Oh, do not grieve!*

"O, nenn mich nicht dein Leben" **see** *Bitte
Glücklich* **MACDOWELL**

O net, moliu, ne ukhodi! **see** Merezhkovski
RACHMANINOFF
Oh no, I beg you, forsake me not

O net, ne Figner **see** Unknown
PROKOFIEV

"O, niezglebione, nieobjete moce!" **see** *Święty
Boże* Kasprowicz, Jan **SZYMANOWSK**

O nimm dich in Acht **see** Scheffler **FRANZ**

"O nimm mich an als deine Magd!" **see**
Des Mädchens Wunsch und Geständnis
Branco **LOEWE**

O not for long are we to stroll **see** Grekov
CHAĭKOVSKIĭ *Ne dolgo nam gulyat*

"O, not with cold earth, alas, cover me over"
see *Elegy* Tiutchev **MEDTNER**

COMPOSER   Poet   *Title*   ''First Line''

"O nuit! que j'aime ton mystère" *see Nocturne* Quinault **SAINT-SAËNS**

O, nun heb du an, dort in deinem Moor see Whitman **HINDEMITH**

"O Père qu'adore mon père" *see Prière de l'enfant a son réveil* Lamartine **LALO**

O platano felice see Vittorelli **ROREM**

"O porte de l'hôtel" *see Montparnasse* Apollinaire **POULENC**

"O prechistaïa deva" *see ÍA v subbotu zatepliu svechu* Unknown **MUSORGSKĬĬ**

"Ô premier rossignol qui viens dans les lilas" *see Le rossignol des lilas* Dauphin **HAHN**

"O presse deine Hand in meine Hand" *see Junge Ehe* Ubell **REGER**

O quand je dors see Hugo **LISZT**
Oh! quand je dors

O Quell, was strömst du rasch und wild see Schulze **SCHUBERT**

"O Ragna, hvor dog Tiden går" *see Ragna* Drachmann **GRIEG**

"O rêveuse, pour que je plonte" *see Éventail* Mallarmé **DEBUSSY**

"O ruddy lover!" *see The clover* Deland **MACDOWELL**

"O Sabbath rest of Galilee!" *see Serenity* Whittier **IVES**

O säh ich auf der Heide dort see Burns **FRANZ** *O wert thou in the cauld blast*

O säh' ich auf der Heide dort see Burns **JENSEN**

O sag' mir, wie dich frein, mein Lieb see Scott **JENSEN**

"O sagt, ihr Lie ben mir einmal" *see Der blinde Knabe* Cibber **SCHUBERT**

O Salutaris see Anon. **FAURÉ, FRANCK** *Messe solennelle*: O salutaris; **HAHN, HONEGGER**

O salutaris see Unknown **SCHMITT**

O salutaris, de campagne see Unknown **ROSSINI**

"O Salutaris hostia" *see O Salutaris* Anon. **FAURÉ, HAHN, HONEGGER**

"O, schmäht des Lebens Leiden nicht" *see Lob des Leidens* Schack **STRAUSS**

"O Schmetterling, sprich" *see Schmetterling* Hoffmann von Fallersleben **SCHUMANN**

O schneller mein Ross see Geibel **DELIUS, JENSEN, STRAUSS**

O Schröpferschwarm see Kerr **STRAUSS**

O selig see Hamerling **LASSEN**

"O selig, wem in stiller Nacht" *see O selig* Hamerling **LASSEN**

"O serre au milieu des forêts!" *see Serre chaude* Maeterlinck **CHAUSSON**

"O sick heart, be at rest!" *see The sick heart* Symons **HESELTINE**

"O sieh, wie golden dic Blümlcin" *see Reisebild* Hamerling **LASSEN**

"O silence des nuits dont la voix seule est douce" *see L'absent* Gounod **GOUNOD**

O sing, du Schöne see Pushkin **JENSEN**

O sing that song see Pleshcheyev **CHAÏKOVSKĬĬ** *O, spoĭ zhe tu pesniu*

O Sonn', O Meer, O Rose! see Rückert *LIEBESFRÜHLING.* **SCHUMANN**

"O Sonnenschein, O Sonnenschein!" *see An den Sonnenschein* Reinick **SCHUMANN**

O, spoĭ zhe tu pesniu see Pleshcheyev **CHAÏKOVSKĬĬ**

O sposo, noi fanciulle see Sappho **RIETI**

O süsser Mai! see Henckell **STRAUSS**

O süsse Mutter see Rückert **LOEWE**

"O süsse Mutter, ich kann nicht spinnen" *see Die Spinnerin* Rückert **WOLF**

"O süsser Zauber im Jugendmut" *see Jugendglück* Pohl **LISZT**

"O sweet everlasting voices, be still" *see The everlasting voices* Yeats **HESELTINE**

"O taliga vagor vandra" *see Fåfäng önskan* Runeberg **SIBELIUS**

O tej godzinie, w której miasto śpi see Iwaszkiewicz **SZYMANOWSKI**

O that I'd ne'er been married see Burns **BRITTEN**

"O the high valley, the little low hill" *see The valley and the hill* Coleridge **QUILTER**

O, the month of May see Dekker **QUILTER**

"O, the month of May, the merry month of May" *see The merry month of May* Dekker **IRELAND**

"O the valley in the summer when I and my John" *see Johnny* Auden **BRITTEN**

O thistle-leafed flame see MacDowell **MACDOWELL**

O thou, my field see Tolstoĭ **RACHMANINOFF**

"Ô toi que berce un rêve enchanteur" *see Sérénade toscane* Anon. **FAURÉ**

O toi, suprême accomplissement de ma vie see Tagore *GITANJALI.* **CASELLA**

O triste était mon âme see Verlaine **SCHMITT**

O trockne diese Tränen nicht see Hamerling **LASSEN**

O, ukochana ma see Iwaszkiewicz **SZYMANOWSKI**

"O unbewölktes Leben!" *see Der Sieg* Mayrhofer **SCHUBERT**

"O Ursprung aller Brunen" *see Klage vor Gottes Leiden* Unknown **REGER**

COMPOSER Poet *Title* ''First Line''

"O versenk', O versenk' dein Leid" *see*
  Liebestreu Reinick **BRAHMS**
O, veshchaia dusha moia *see* Tiutchev
  MEDTNER *Behold my visionary soul*
"Ô Vierge Sante Virge mère" *see Notre Dame*
  des petits enfants Ségur **GOUNOD**
"O vierge, ta beauté semble un champ de blé
  mûr" *see Moisson prochaine* Bouilhet
  KOECHLIN
O vinternatt see Lagerkvist **KILPINEN**
"Ó vitej vesno kouzelná" *see Jarní píseň*
  Rypáček **JANÁČEK**
"Ô vous que Dieu bénit entre toutes les
  femmes" *see Notre Dame de France*
  Boyer, Georges **GOUNOD**
"O vous qui passez solitaire" *see Vous qui*
  passez Bourguignat, Paul **MASSENET**
"O, vozhdi! Esli vyĭdet na doliu moiu" *see*
  TSar' Saul Byron **MUSORGSKIĬ**
O wär' dein Haus durchsichtig see Heyse
  WOLF
O wär' ich du see Unknown **LASSEN**
"O wär' ich du, mein Falke" *see O wär' ich*
  du Unknown **LASSEN**
O wär' mein Lieb' jen' Röslein rot see Burns
  BERG
"O wären wir weiter" *see Der getreue Eckart*
  Goethe **LOEWE, ZELTER**
O wärst du mein! see Lenau **SOPHIE.**
  STRAUSS
"O wag' es nicht" *see An*** Lenau **WOLF**
"O was muss es die Engel gekostet haben" *see*
  Geburt Mariä Rilke **HINDEMITH**
"O wehe, Heinz von Lüder" *see Landgraf*
  Philipp der Grossmüthige Kopisch
  LOEWE
"O weile, süsser Geliebter!" *see Liebesnacht*
  Frey, F. **SZYMANOWSKI**
"O welche Glühn in fremde Hülle" *see*
  Neue Fülle Zweig **REGER**
O wert thou in the cauld blast see Burns
  FRANZ
"O what a physical effect it has on me" *see*
  In love with you Koch **ROREM**
"O what can ail thee, knight-at-arms" *see*
  La belle dame sans merci Keats
  HINDEMITH
"O what if the fowler my blackbird has
  taken?" *see The fuchsia tree* Anon.
  QUILTER
"O what would I give" *see Aspiration*
  Carpenter, Rue **CARPENTER**
"O when I shut my eyes in spring" *see Four*
  nights Shove **VAUGHAN WILLIAMS**
"O wie dringt das junge Leben" *see*
  Lebensmut Schulze **SCHUBERT**

"O wie du schnaubst aus voller Brust" *see*
  Melek am Quell Stieglitz **LOEWE**
"O wie greulich, wie abscheulich ist der
  Winter" *see Schlecht' Wetter* Braungart
  REGER
O wie lieblich ist das Mädchen see Vicente,
  Gil *MUI GRACIOSA ES LA DONCELLA.*
  SCHUMANN
"O, wie öde, sonder Freudenschall" *see*
  Trauerstille Bürger **PFITZNER**
"O, wie schön ist deine Welt" *see*
  Im Abendrot Lappe **SCHUBERT**
"O wie schwer die Pein" *see Klage* Kol'tsov
  RUBINSTEIN
"O wie träumte es sich süss" *see*
  Sonnenuntergang Leuthold **SCHOECK**
O willkommen see Prutz **LASSEN**
"O Winter, schlimmer Winter" *see Hirtenlied*
  Uhland **MENDELSSOHN-**
  BARTHOLDY
"O Woche, Zeugin heiliger Beschwerde!" *see*
  Karwoche Mörike **WOLF**
"O wunderbares, tiefes Schweigen" *see*
  Morgengebet Eichendorff **LASSEN**
O wunderschön ist Gottes Erde see Hölty
  LOEWE
"O wüsst ich doch den Weg zurück" *see*
  Heimweh II Groth **BRAHMS**
O wüsstest du, wie viel ich deinetwegen see
  Heyse **WOLF**
"O ye snowflakes covering the earth" *see*
  Lament Unknown **PROKOFIEV**
O you whom I often and silently come see
  Whitman **ROREM**
"O zasni moe serdtse gluboko!" *see*
  Primiren'e Shcherbina **CHAĬKOVSKIĬ**
O zawiedzionym zolnierzu see Unknown
  SZYMANOWSKI
"Ó zda vmysli mám jen tebe?" *see*
  Vzpomínání Pech **DVOŘÁK**
Ó zlatá ruže, spatnilá see Pfleger-
  Moravský **DVOŘÁK**
Die Oasis see Stieglitz **LOEWE**
Ob auch finstre Blicke glitten see Anon.
  SPANISCHES LIEDERBUCH:
  Aunque con semblante airado. **JENSEN,**
  WOLF
Ob der Koran von Ewigkeit sei? see Goethe
  SCHENKENBUCH. **WOLF**
Ob die Locken eine Glorie quellen see
  Herwegh **JENSEN**
"Ob ein Gott sei" *see An die Hoffnung*
  Tiedge **BEETHOVEN**
"Ob ich dich auch verloren" *see Die grossen*
  stillen Augen Scholz, B. **LASSEN**
"Ob ich lach" *see Liebeslied* Böhm
  WEBERN

"Ob mein Mund auch dürfte" *see Lass mich deine Augen* Cornelius **RUBINSTEIN**
Obaldia, René de, 1918-
  SAUGUET
    Les jumeaux de la nuit
    Moi j'irai dans la lune
    Le secret
Ein Obdach gegen Sturm und Regen see Rückert **STRAUSS**
"Oben auf des Berges Spitze" *see Die feindlichen Brüder* Heine **SCHUMANN**
"Oben drehen sich die grossen" *see Die Sternenwelten* Fellinger **SCHUBERT**
"Oben in dem Birnenbaum sitzt ein Vöglein" *see Zum Schlafen* Schellenberg **REGER**
Oben, wo die Sterne glühen see Heine **MACDOWELL**
Oblak a mrákota see Bible **DVOŘÁK**
"Obloczna góra ciagnie ptak" *see Lebedź* Berent **SZYMANOWSKI**
Oboymi, potsaluy see Kol'tsov **BALAKIREV**
Obrashchennaïa see Goethe **MEDTNER**
    Die Bekehrte
Obrochnik see Shenshin **RACHMANINOFF** *The peasant*
Obsession see Claudel **MILHAUD**
Obst, Willibald
  REGER *Hoffnungslos*
Obstacles see Pech **DVOŘÁK** *Překážky*
OBUS COULEUR DE LUNE. see Apollinaire *Carte postale* **RIVIER**
Ocaña, Francisco de, fl.1603.
  WOLF *Nun, wandre, Maria, nun wandre nur fort*
The ocean is heaving, as wave after wave see Tolstoï **RIMSKIĬ-KORSAKOV** *Kolyshetsia more*
"Ocean thunders and raves" *see The sea* Borodin **BORODIN**
Och finns det en tanke? see Tavaststjerna **SIBELIUS**
"Och flickan satt sjungande invid ett fikonträd" *see Desdemonas sång* Blomberg **KILPINEN**
Och stod du i den kalla blåst see Blomberg **KILPINEN**
Och tröskorna tego see Österling **KILPINEN**
Ock nör som jag ver en liten smadrang see Shakespeare *TWELFTH NIGHT.* **SIBELIUS**
The octave see Maĭkov **RIMSKIĬ-KORSAKOV** *Oktava*
"October turned my maple's leaves to gold" *see Maple leaves* Aldrich **IVES**

L'Octobre see Lunel **MILHAUD**
Octroi see Kerdyk, René **SCHMITT**
Die Odaliske see Brun **GRIEG** *Odalisken synger*
Odalisken synger see Brun **GRIEG**
The Odalisque see Yü-hsi **CARPENTER**
ODE. see Klopstock
  An Sie **SCHUBERT, STRAUSS**
  Das Rosenband **MACDOWELL, SCHUBERT, STRAUSS, ZELTER**
Ode see O'Shaughnessy **DIAMOND**
Ode see Platen-Hallermünde **CORNELIUS**
Ode see Ronsard **ROREM**
Ode à un jeune gentilhomme see Roché **ROUSSEL**
Ode an den Tod see Klopstock **GLUCK** *Der Tod*
Ode chinoise see Roché **ROUSSEL** *Ode à un jeune gentilhomme*
Ode du premier jour de Mai see Passerat **BERKELEY**
ODE TO AN EXPIRING FROG. see Dickens *Recitativo e aria romantica* **HINDEMITH**
Odelette see Régnier **AUBERT, ROUSSEL**
ODELETTES. see Banville
  Aimons-nous **SAINT-SAËNS**
  Aimons-nous et dormons **DEBUSSY**
"Der Odem Gottes weht" *see Himmelsfunken* Silbert **SCHUBERT**
ODEN UND LIEDER VON KLOPSTOCK, no. 1
  GLUCK Klopstock *Vaterlandslied*
ODEN UND LIEDER VON KLOPSTOCK, no. 2
  GLUCK Klopstock *Wir und Sie*
ODEN UND LIEDER VON KLOPSTOCK, no. 3
  GLUCK Klopstock *Schlachtgesang*
ODEN UND LIEDER VON KLOPSTOCK, no. 4
  GLUCK Klopstock *Der Jüngling*
ODEN UND LIEDER VON KLOPSTOCK, no. 5
  GLUCK Klopstock *Die Sommernacht*
ODEN UND LIEDER VON KLOPSTOCK, no. 6
  GLUCK Klopstock *Die frühen Gräber*
ODEN UND LIEDER VON KLOPSTOCK, no. 7
  GLUCK Unknown *Die Neigung*
    Text not by Klopstock according to A. Einstein.
ODES ANACRÉONTIQUES
  ROUSSEL
    Anacreon

ODES ANACRÉONTIQUES *(continued)*
  ROUSSEL *(continued)*
    Anacreon *(continued)*
      Qu'il faut boire
      Sur lui-même
        Two settings: op. 31 no. 1 and op. 32 no. 1.
      Sur une jeune fille
        Two settings: op. 31 no. 3 and op. 32 no. 2.
      Sur une songe
Odeszlaś w pustynie zachodnia see
  Iwaszkiewicz **SZYMANOWSKI**
"Une odeur délicate de thé" *see De Ceylan*
  Chalupt **AUBERT**
"Odi di un uom che muore" *see L'ultimo ricordo* Redaelli, G. **ROSSINI**
"Odi l'aura che dolce sospira" *see Lebens-Genuss* Metastasio **BEETHOVEN**
"Odia la pastorella" *see La pastorella* Santo-Magno, N di **ROSSINI**
Odinochestvo see Goethe **MEDTNER**
  Einsamkeit
Odins Meeres-Ritt see Schreiber **LOEWE**
O'Donnell, G. M.
  ROREM *Epigram*
"Odorosa foriera d'aprile" *see La prima viola*
  Maffei **RUBINSTEIN**
Odotus see Jalkanen **KILPINEN**
"O'Driscoll drove with a song" *see The host of the air* Yeats **LOEFFLER**
"Odsédé par ces mots le veuvage et l'automne" *see Mélancolie* Coppée
  GOUNOD
Oër, Max von, 1806-1846.
  LOEWE *Die Glocken zu Speier*
"Öfver drifvans iskristall" *see Vår förnimmelser* Tavaststjerna **SIBELIUS**
Oehlenschläger, Adam Gottlob, 1779-1850.
  NIELSEN
    Betragt mit svage spind
    Hvor sødt i Sommer-Aftenstunden
    I Skyggen vi vanke
    Naar Odin vinker
    Nu er da Vaaren kommen
    Underlige Aftenlufte!
  ZELTER *Pilgers Tod*
  AXEL UND WALBURG: Romanze.
    ZELTER *Romanze*
Öhqvist
  SIBELIUS *Segelfahrt*
Oelschläger, Hermann
  RUBINSTEIN *Mein Herzensschatz*
Önskekransen see Cnattingius, Thor
  KILPINEN

"O'er the mountain towards the west" *see Berceuse* Ives **IVES**
O'er the tarn's unruffled mirror see Lenau **SCHILFLIEDER. GRIFFES**
  Auf dem Teich, dem regungslosen
O'er the woodlands see Uhland **BENNETT**
O'er thee I bend see Shenshin **MEDTNER**
  Humble yet valiant
Oeris, Arsène
  AUBERT
    Fatum
    Sur le bord
Österling, Anders, 1884-1981.
  KILPINEN
    Dryaden I
    Dryaden II
    Dryaden III
    Efter lång sorg
    Facklor
    Förgätmigejer
    Gammal sorg
    Hälsning till ett nytt år
    Morgonens hjärta
    Och tröskorna tego
    Pingst
    Sången
    Slätten
    Sommarens ljud
    Sorglöshetens vingar
    Svanor
    Tala, älskade, tala
    Trasten
    En vårrefräng
    Vid en brunn
"Of a' the airts the wind can blow" *see My Jean* Burns **MACDOWELL**
"Of cord and cassiawood is the lute compounded" *see The old lute* Po Chü-i **BRITTEN**
Of God, angels . . . see Goodman **ROREM**
Of him I love day and night see Whitman **ROREM**
Of what I dream in the quiet night see Maïkov **RIMSKIï-KORSAKOV**
  O chem v tishi nocheĭ
Of what, through silent night see Maïkov **RIMSKIï-KORSAKOV**
  O chem v tishi nocheĭ
O'Faolain, Sean, 1900-1991, translator.
  BARBER *Sea-snatch*
  THE SILVER BRANCH.
    BARBER
      At St. Patrick's Purgatory
      The desire for hermitage
      The heavenly banquet
OFFENBARUNG UND UNTERGAND. see Trakl *Nachtergebund* **WEBERN**

"Offerus war ein Lanzenknecht" *see*
  Der grosse Christoph Kind, F. **LOEWE**
"Officiers de la Garde Blanche" *see*
  Aux officiers de la Garde Blanche
  Vilmorin **POULENC**
"Offne mir die goldne Pforte" *see An den*
  Traum Cornelius **CORNELIUS**
L'Offrande see Anon. **POULENC**
Offrande see Leclère, translator
  SHÉHÉRAZADE. **KOECHLIN**
Offrande see Verlaine *GREEN.* **HAHN**
"Offre un encens modeste aux Lares
  familiers" *see A Phidylé* Leconte de Lisle
  HAHN
"Oft am langen Tage seufz' ich, ach!" *see*
  Sehnsucht Weiss **SIBELIUS**
"Oft in einsam stillen Stunden" *see*
  Das Heimweh Winkler **SCHUBERT**
"Oft in my garden at night" *see In my garden*
  at night Isaakian **RACHMANINOFF**
Og jeg vil ha mig en Hjertenskjaer see Krag
  GRIEG
"Og jeg vil ha mig en Silkevest" *see Og jeg*
  vil ha mig en Hjertenskjaer Krag **GRIEG**
Ogarev, Nikolai Platonovich, 1813-1877.
  CHAïKOVSKIï *Na son″ grïadushchiï*
Ogaryov *see* Ogarev, Nikolai
  Platonovich, 1813-1877.
"Oggi, Demo, gli è pasqua, oggi fiera" *see*
  Il Clefta prigione Anon. **PIZZETTI**
"Oggi tremi ne l'aria profumata" *see Vigilia*
  Nuziale Cocconi, Ildebrando **PIZZETTI**
Ogni sabato avrete il lune accesso see
  Unknown **MUSORGSKIï**
  IA v subbotu zatepliu svechu
OGRODNIK. see Tagore
  Der junge Prinz I **SZYMANOWSKI**
  Der junge Prinz II **SZYMANOWSKI**
  Das letzte Lied **SZYMANOWSKI**
  Mein Herz **SZYMANOWSKI**
"Oh! children only think of it" *see*
  For careless children Carpenter, Rue
  CARPENTER
"Oh! combien j'aime le verger" *see Le verger*
  Distel, Camille **MASSENET**
Oh, could you but for one short hour see
  Tolstoï **CHAïKOVSKIï**
  O, esli b ty mogla
Oh, could you but forget see Tolstoï
  RIMSKIï-KORSAKOV *O, esli b ty mogla*
Oh! dille tu! see Zaffira **GOUNOD**
Oh, do not grieve! see Apukhtin
  RACHMANINOFF
"Oh! écoute la symphonie" *see Musique sur*
  l'eau Samain **SCHMITT**
"Oh excelso muro, oh torres coronadas" *see*
  Soneto a Córdoba Góngora y Argote
  FALLA

Oh, happy home see Ligny, Charles
  GOUNOD *La fleur du foyer*
 Oh, happy home see Maitland **GOUNOD**
"Oh, Harpalus! (thus would he say)" *see*
  Harpalus Percy **IVES**
"Oh, heavenly Poesey, Heavenward mount on
  high!" *see Epilogue* Goethe **SEIBER**
"Oh, heavenly Poesey, Heavenward mount on
  high!" *see Invocation* Goethe **SEIBER**
Oh, if only you could for one moment see
  Tolstoï **CHAïKOVSKIï** *O, esli b ty mogla*
Oh, if thou couldst for one moment see
  Tolstoï **RIMSKIï-KORSAKOV**
  O, esli b ty mogla
Oh, lady, let the sad tears fall see Crapsey
  WEISGALL
"Oh, little Ellen never did" *see Good Ellen*
  Carpenter, Rue **CARPENTER**
Oh, Lord, have mercy and turn Thy face to me
  see Bible **DVOŘÁK**
  Popatřiž na mne a smiluj se nade mnou
"Oh, Lord, I'm lonesome" *see Waitin'* Harris
  HARRIS
"Oh, love, whom I have never seen" *see*
  Love whom I have never seen Unknown
  CARPENTER
"Oh! ma petite princesse de clarté" *see*
  Chanson de la nuit durable Espinasse-
  Mongenet **SÉVERAC**
"Oh mark how high the fountains play" *see*
  The fountains Tiutchev
  RACHMANINOFF
Oh my blacke Soule! see Donne **BRITTEN**
Oh, my shepherd is the Lord see Bible
  DVOŘÁK *Hospodin jest muj pastýř*
Oh! ne finis jamais see Robiquet
  MASSENET
"Oh! ne murmurez pas son nom!" *see Élégie*
  Moore, T. **DUPARC**
Oh, never leave me, sweet friend see
  Shenshin *MELODII.* **CHAïKOVSKIï**
  Ne otkhodi ot menia
Oh never sing to me again see Pushkin
  RACHMANINOFF
  Sing not to me, beautiful maiden
Oh no, I beg you, forsake me not see
  Merezhkovski **RACHMANINOFF**
"Oh, nuit, nuit de Delos" *see Carte postale à*
  Délos Richaud **SAUGUET**
"Oh oui! la terre est belle" *see C'est l'amour*
  Hugo **MASSENET**
Oh, päivät, te päivät see Jalkanen
  KILPINEN
Oh pourquoi donc see Pavloff, Mme **LISZT**
Oh, quand je dors see Hugo **BIZET**
  Sérénade: Oh, quand je dors; **LALO,**
  LISZT

COMPOSER Poet *Title* "First Line"

"Oh! quand la mort, que rien ne saurait apaiser" *see Dernier voeu* Banville **HAHN**

"Oh! quand la mort que rien ne saurait apaiser" *see Souhait* Banville **DEBUSSY**

"Oh see how thick the gold cup flowers" *see Goodbye* Housman **VAUGHAN WILLIAMS**

Oh! si les fleurs avaient des yeux see Buchillot, G. **MASSENET**

Oh! si tu pouvais see Tolstoï **CHAÏKOVSKIÏ** *O, esli b ty mogla*

Oh, sing unto the Lord a joyful song see Bible **DVOŘÁK** *Zpívejte Hospodinu píseň novou*

"Oh, some are fond of red wine and some are fond of white" *see Captain Stratton's fancy* Masefield **HESELTINE**

Oh! that we two are maying see Kingsley **GOUNOD**

"Oh, the dawn is coming high!" *see The dawn* Anon. **LUENING**

"Oh, the days are gone" *see Canon* Moore, T. **IVES**

"Oh, the gallant fisher's life" *see Fishing song* Walton, I. **BRITTEN**

"Oh, the sweet contentment" *see The countryman* Chalkhill **HESELTINE**

"Oh these midsummer nights" *see These summer nights* Rathaus **RACHMANINOFF**

"Oh thou whose mercy" *see Resignation* Montgomery **BENNETT**

Oh Thränenvolle see Rilke **KRENEK**

Oh, to vex me see Donne **BRITTEN**

"Oh! viens, la fleur déjà fanée" *see Chant d'automne* Anon. **GOUNOD**

"Oh vita del mondo, non se' vita" *see In memoria d'un amico* Cavalca **MALIPIERO**

Oh, wert thou here see Dehmel **SIBELIUS** *Aus banger Brust*

Oh! what a perfect golden dream see Pfleger-Moravský **DVOŘÁK** *Ó, byl to krásný, zlatý sen*

"Oh, would not it be funny, and would not people stare" *see If* Livingstone, Mabel **CARPENTER**

O'Hara, Frank, 1926-1966. **ROREM**
   For Poulenc
   Let's take a walk
   Poem: I will always love you
   SNEDEN'S LANDING VARIATIONS.
      THOMSON *From "Sneden's Landing Variations"*

"Ohn' Lieb' bist du durchs Leben kommen" *see Widmung* Cossmann **PFITZNER**

"Ohne das Schöne" *see Spruch* Mörike **SCHOECK**

"Ohne Liebe lebe wer da kann" *see Die Liebe* Lessing **BEETHOVEN**

Ohnivý muž see Hlavsa, Vrat. **MARTINŮ** *The fiery man*

Ohoh kullaista kotia see Kanteletar **KILPINEN**

"Oi, ainoisin, mun armahin" *see Tunturilaulu* Törmänen **KILPINEN**

"Oi, armas, mikä ilta kuutamon" *see Kuutamolla* Koskenniemi **KILPINEN**

Oï, chest' li to molodtsu len priasti? see Tolstoï **MUSORGSKIÏ**

"Oi, kesän yhden sa mullekin laulanut oot" *see Elegia satakielelle* Koskenniemi **KILPINEN**

"Oi, terve! tumma, vieno tähtiilta" *see Illalle* Koskimies **SIBELIUS**

Oi Ukko ylinen herra see Kanteletar **KILPINEN**

"Oï, vchera my pesni peli da guliali" *see Provody* Anon. **PROKOFIEV**

Oiseau see Éluard **SAUGUET**

"L'oiseau dans le buisson" *see Aubade* Pommey, Louis **FAURÉ**

L'oiseau de paradis see Princet, Jules **MASSENET**

"Oiseau d'étoile" *see Amour oiseau d'étoile* Messiaen **MESSIAEN**

L'oiseau en cage see Leclère, translator. *SHÉHÉRAZADE.* **KOECHLIN**

"L'oiseau m'a dit" *see Faut-il chanter?* Borrelli **DELIBES**

"Un oiseau s'envole" *see Georges Braque* Éluard **POULENC**

Les oiseaux see No author **SATIE**

"Oiseaux, si tous les ans" *see Ariette* Ferrand, A. **MOZART**

Les oiselets see Normand **MASSENET**

Oisi mulla vallan miekka see Kanteletar **KILPINEN**

"Okh, baushka, okh, rodnaïa" *see Ozoruik* Musorgskiï **MUSORGSKIÏ**

"Okh, pora tebe na voliu" *see Zapevka* Mei **BALAKIREV**

Okno see Pushkin **MEDTNER** *The window*

Okon'en prazdnyï, shumnyï den' see Golenishchev-Kutuzov **MUSORGSKIÏ**

Oktava see Maïkov **RIMSKIÏ-KORSAKOV**

OKTAVI. see Mei
   Ya s neyu nikogda ne govoril **CHAÏKOVSKIÏ**

Olas gigantes see Bécquer **FALLA, TURINA**

"Olas gigantes que os rompeis bramando" *see Olas gigantes* Bécquer **FALLA, TURINA**

COMPOSER   Poet   *Title*   "First Line"

Old Abram Brown see Anon. **BRITTEN**
OLD AMERICAN SONGS (First set), no. 1
  COPLAND Emmett *The boatmen's dance*
OLD AMERICAN SONGS (First set), no. 2
  COPLAND Anon. *The dodger*
OLD AMERICAN SONGS (First set), no. 3
  COPLAND Anon. *Long time ago*
OLD AMERICAN SONGS (First set), no. 4
  COPLAND Anon. *Simple gifts*
OLD AMERICAN SONGS (First set), no. 5
  COPLAND Anon. *I bought me a cat*
OLD AMERICAN SONGS (Second set), no. 1
  COPLAND Anon. *The little horses*
OLD AMERICAN SONGS (Second set), no. 2
  COPLAND Anon. *Zion's walls*
OLD AMERICAN SONGS (Second set), no. 3
  COPLAND Anon. *The golden willow tree*
OLD AMERICAN SONGS (Second set), no. 4
  COPLAND Lowry *At the river*
OLD AMERICAN SONGS (Second set), no. 5
  COPLAND Anon. *Ching-a-ring chaw*
An old carol see Anon. **QUILTER**
OLD ENGLISH SONGS, no. 1
  THOMSON Donne *Consider, Lord*
OLD ENGLISH SONGS, no. 1
  THOMSON Shakespeare *Look, how the floor of heav'n*
OLD ENGLISH SONGS, no. 2
  THOMSON Anon. *The holly and the ivy, a carol of Nativity and Lent*
OLD ENGLISH SONGS, no. 2
  THOMSON Heywood *The bell doth toll*
OLD ENGLISH SONGS, no. 3
  THOMSON Anon. *Remember Adam's fall*
OLD ENGLISH SONGS, no. 3
  THOMSON Fisher, J. *At the spring*
OLD ENGLISH SONGS, no. 4
  THOMSON Graves, John *John Peel*
An old flame see Ives **IVES**
Old home day see Ives **IVES**
"Old King Caraway supped on cake" *see Cake and Sack* De La Mare **CHANLER**
The old letter in my book see Pfleger-Moravský **DVOŘÁK** *Zde hledím na tendrahý list*
"Old lilac bushes thin and grey" *see Constancy* MacDowell **MACDOWELL**
Old love see Crapsey **WEISGALL**
Old love song see Anon. **LOEFFLER**
The old lute see Po Chü-i **BRITTEN**

"An old man, with a straw in his mouth" *see The see'r* Ives **IVES**
Old man's song see Goethe *WILHELM MEISTER*. Harfenspieler. **MUSORGSKIĬ** *Lied des Harfenspielers*
Old man's song see Kol'tsov **BALAKIREV** *Pesnya starika*
The old mother see Vinje **IVES**
Old poem see Waley, Arthur **COPLAND**
Old Shellover see De La Mare *PEACOCK PIE*. **CHANLER**
An old song see Borodin **BORODIN** *Song of the dark forest*
Old song see Villiers **MARTINŮ**
An old song re-sung see Masefield **GRIFFES**
The old temple among the mountains see Chang Wen-chang **GRIFFES**
"Old Tillie Turveycombe sat to sew" *see Tillie* De La Mare **CHANLER**
THE OLD WIVES' TALE (1595). *see* Peele *Chopcherry* **HESELTINE** *Whenas the rye reach to the chin* **HESELTINE**
Oldys, William, 1696-1761.
  HINDEMITH *On a fly drinking out of his cup*
Olearius, Johann, 1611-1684.
  LOEWE *Wunderbarer Gnadenthron*
O'Leary, Joseph
  ROREM *Whiskey drink divine*
Olga de Sarmento
  MASSENET *Jamais plus*
"Oli mulla muoto muinen" *see Pimeä isoton pirtti* Kanteletar **KILPINEN**
Oliphant, Ernest Henry Clark, 1862-1936.
  ROUSSEL *A farewell*
Olit tuskasta väristen herännyt syön see Koskenniemi **KILPINEN**
OLIVIER. see Pichler *Der Unglückliche* **SCHUBERT**
Olivier de Magny *see* Magny, Olivier de, d. ca. 1560.
Olivier, Pierre
  SAUGUET *L'enfant qui dort* *Le joyeux ramoneur*
Olkienizkaia-Naldi, Raissa
  LO SPECCHIO. **CASELLA** *La danza* *Volutta*
Olson, Elder, 1909-1992.
  DIAMOND *I thought once I should have at a man's age*

Olson, Elder, 1909-1992. *(continued)*
DIAMOND *(continued)*
*Immensity, like the darkness cast from
the cloud above*
*Let children ride the year's sweet
carrousel*
Midnight: I pluck the curtains back
"Om du en natt helt plötsligt hörde strängar"
see Romeo Tavaststjerna **SIBELIUS**
Om tiotusen år see Lagerkvist **KILPINEN**
O'Malley, Patrick
BERKELEY *The beacon barn*
"Omar, der Zeltmacher hat von früh bis spät"
*see Fünf Sinnsprüche Omars des
Zeltmachers* Omar Khayyam **BLACHER**
Omar Khayyam, 11th c.
BLACHER
Fünf Sinnsprüche Omars des Zeltmachers
NB: Five settings with this title, op. 3
nos. 1-5.
Omar the tentmaker *see* Omar
Khayyam, 11th c.
Omat on virret oppimani see Kanteletar
KILPINEN
L'ombre de Dieu see Lehugeur, A. **LALO**
"L'ombre de la très douce est évoquée" *see
Carte postale* Apollinaire **POULENC**
"L'ombre de la très douce est évoquée" *see
Linda* Apollinaire **RIVIER**
L'ombre des arbres see Verlaine
ROMANCES SANS PAROLES. **DEBUSSY**
"L'ombre des arbres dans la rivière
embrumée" *see Paysage triste* Verlaine
HAHN
L'ombre des rues see Hornez, André
SAUGUET
"L'ombre descent de leurs rameaux" *see
Les bois de pins* Distel, Camille
MASSENET
"L'ombre noyait les bois" *see Améthyste*
Samain **KOECHLIN**
Omenakukat see Lönnbohm **KILPINEN**
Omens and oracles see Unknown **IVES**
"An omnibus across the bridge" *see Symphony
in yellow* Wilde **GRIFFES**
L'omnibus automobile see Hyspa **SATIE**
On a balcony by the sea see Rydberg
SIBELIUS *På verandan vid havet*
On a fly drinking out of his cup see Oldys
HINDEMITH
On a little bird see Armstrong **ROREM**
On a piece of music see Hopkins **KRENEK**
"On a remplacé les coquillages" *see Une carte
postale* Radiguet **SAUGUET**
On a screen see Li Po **CARPENTER**
On a singing girl see Wylie **ROREM**

"On aime bien ce grand vin" *see Pensées
d'octobre* Follain **SAUGUET**
"On beds of snow the moonbeam slept" *see
The tear* Moore, T. **RUBINSTEIN**
On death see Clare **DIAMOND**
On dit! see Roux, Jean **MASSENET**
"On dit . . . , on dit beaucoup de choses . . . "
see On dit! Roux, Jean **MASSENET**
"On entend un chant sur l'eau dans la brume"
see Chanson triste Bouchor, M.
DEBUSSY
On est heureux see Kerdyk, René
HONEGGER
*On golden fields of wheat the quiet now
descends see* Tolstoï **RIMSKĬ-
KORSAKOV**
Na nivy zheltye niskhodit tishina
On hanget korkeat see Joukahainen,
Wilkku **SIBELIUS**
On hearing "The last rose of summer" see
Wolfe, C. **HINDEMITH**
"On jänka aava, jäinen" *see Jänka*
Törmänen **KILPINEN**
On kaikki syksyn tähdet syttyneet see
Koskenniemi **KILPINEN**
On kumpiaki see Kanteletar **KILPINEN**
On l'a placée see Zaffira **GOUNOD**
Ier fù mandata
On me dit: . . . see Ségalen **IBERT**
"On mennyt lemmenkevät kultainen" *see
Eron hetki* Jalkanen **KILPINEN**
"On my flute, when ev'ning darkens" *see The
rat-catcher* Bryusov **RACHMANINOFF**
"On my way to work one summer day" *see
In the alley* Ives **IVES**
"On ne devrait faire aux enfants" *see
Les enfants* Boyer, Georges **MASSENET**
"On ne mène pas la vache" *see Vache* Éluard
SAUGUET
On ne peut me connaitre . . . see Eluard
AURIC
"On ne peut que trouver vilaine" *see La tortue
naine* Kriéger, Jacqueline **MILHAUD**
"On shore how still, all nature seems asleep"
see Dreamy nights Drachmann **DELIUS**
"On slumber-laden wings" *see Melody*
Nadson **RACHMANINOFF**
"On smert' nashel v kraiu chuzhom" *see
Zebytyĭ* Golenishchev-Kutuzov
MUSORGSKĬ
On snow-swept paths see Toman
DIE MONATE: Januar. **MARTINŮ**
"On sonne, on sonne!" *see Le réveil . . .*
Desbordes-Valmore **AURIC**
"On sunny days in our backyard" *see
Two little flowers* Ives, Harmony **IVES**

"On suuri sun rantas autius" *see Rannalta I*
Koskenniemi **KILPINEN**
On tak menia liubil see Apukhtin
CHAĬKOVSKIĬ
On the Antipodes see Unknown **IVES**
On the bank see Pleshcheyev
CHAĬKOVSKIĬ *Na beregu*
"On the coast of Coromandel" *see*
The courtship of the Yongly Bongly Bo
Lear **THOMSON**
On the counter see Ives **IVES**
On the day when death will knock at thy door
see Tagore *GITANJALI.* **CARPENTER**
On the death of a linnet see Zhukovski
RACHMANINOFF
On the Dnieper see Shevchenko
MUSORGSKIĬ *Na Dnepre*
On the Don the gardens bloom see Kol'tsov
MUSORGSKIĬ *Po nad Donom sad t͡svetet*
On the golden cornfields see Tolstoĭ
CHAĬKOVSKIĬ *Na nivy zhelty*
ON THE GRAVE OF A YOUNG CAVALRY
OFFICER. *see* Melville
Epitaph **DIAMOND**
On the hills of Georgia see Pushkin
RIMSKIĬ-KORSAKOV
Na kholmakh Gruzii
On the lake see Goethe **MEDTNER**
Auf dem See
"On the lake where droop'd the willow" *see*
Long time ago Anon. **COPLAND**
On the seashore see Drachmann **DELIUS**
Summer nights
On the seashore of endless worlds see
Tagore *GITANJALI.* **CARPENTER**
On the yellow field see Tolstoĭ
CHAĬKOVSKIĬ *Na nivy zhelty*
ON THIS ISLAND. *see* Auden
Look stranger, on this island **ROREM**
Seascape **BRITTEN**
ON THIS ISLAND, no. 1
BRITTEN Auden *Let the florid music*
praise!
ON THIS ISLAND, no. 2
BRITTEN Auden *Now the leaves are*
falling fast
ON THIS ISLAND, no. 3
BRITTEN Auden *Seascape*
ON THIS ISLAND, no. 4
BRITTEN Auden *Nocturne*
ON THIS ISLAND, no. 5
BRITTEN Auden *As it is, plenty*
"On this sweet bank your head thrice sweet
and dear I lay" *see Youth's spring-tribute*
Rossetti, Dante **IRELAND**
"On vendit le chien et la chaîne" *see La peine*
Carême **MILHAUD**

"On voit des marquis sur des bicyclettes" *see*
Fêtes galantes Aragon **POULENC**
Ona, kak polden', khorosha see Vilenkin
RACHMANINOFF *She is as lovely as the*
moon
"Ona vse vliubviuveriala" *see Fal'shivaya*
nota Borodin **BORODIN**
Once upon a dream see Rorem **ROREM**
Once upon a time see Feeney **CHANLER**
Once upon a time see Grossmanová-
Brodská **MARTINŮ**
"Once, when weary, on my bed I laid me" *see*
Drömmen Runeberg **SIBELIUS**
Ond Dag see Garborg *HAUGTUSSA.*
GRIEG *Vond Dag*
"L'onde frémit, lónde s'agite" *see Le pêcheur*
Du Boys **BERLIOZ**
"L'onde porte le poids des feuilles en
détresse" *see Feuilles sur l'eau* Vivien
AUBERT
"Ondeggiano i letti di rose" *see Erotica*
Annunzio **PIZZETTI**
Les ondines see Heine **SAUGUET**
"One evening just at sunset we laid him in the
grave" *see Slow march* Ives **IVES**
"One flame-winged brought a white-winged
harp-player" *see Love's minstrels*
Rossetti, Dante
VAUGHAN WILLIAMS
The one hope see Rossetti, Dante
IRELAND
The 104th Psalm see Bible **KRENEK**
"One morning very early, one morning in the
spring" *see The distracted maid* Anon.
HESELTINE
"One night, as Dick lay fast asleep" *see*
Full moon De La Mare **BERKELEY**
One of us see Feeney **CHANLER**
"One sails away to sea" *see The sea*
Howells, W. D. **MACDOWELL**
One word is too often profaned see Shelley
QUILTER
A one-eyed tailer see De La Mare
CHANLER
Onerva, L., pseud. *see* Lehtinen, Hilja
Onerva, 1882-1972.
One-two-three see Ives **IVES**
Ongaro, Francesco dall, 1808-1873.
VERDI *Il Brigidino*
Oni otvechali see Hugo **RACHMANINOFF**
They answered
The only child see Rossetti, Christina
IRELAND
Only lover's rest see Moss **ROREM**
Only themselves see Whitman *LEAVES OF*
GRASS. **LUENING**

COMPOSER Poet *Title* "First Line"

"Only themselves understand themselves" *see*
 Only themselves Whitman **LUENING**
Only thou alone see Pleshcheyev
 CHAĬKOVSKIĬ *Lish' ty odin"*
Onpa tietty tietyssäni see Kanteletar
 KILPINEN
open your heart see Cummings
 BLITZSTEIN
Opferlied see Matthisson **BEETHOVEN,**
 ZELTER
OPHELIA-LIEDER, no. 1
 LASSEN Shakespeare *Wie erkenn' ich*
 dein Treulieb
OPHELIA-LIEDER, no. 2
 LASSEN Shakespeare *Sein Bahrtuch*
 weiss wie Bergesschnee
OPHELIA-LIEDER, no. 3
 LASSEN Shakespeare *Sein Bart war*
 weiss wie Bergesschnee
OPHELIA-LIEDER, no. 4
 LASSEN Shakespeare *Sie trugen ihn*
 barhaupt auf der Bahr
OPHELIA-LIEDER, no. 5
 LASSEN Shakespeare *Denn traut lieb*
 Robin ist all' mein Lust!
OPHELIA-LIEDER, no. 6
 LASSEN Shakespeare *Auf Morgen ist*
 Sanct Valentinstag
OPHELIA-LIEDER, no. 7
 LASSEN Shakespeare *Und kommt er*
 denn nimmer zurück?
Ophelia's lament see Shakespeare
 HAMLET. **ROREM**
Opiat' vstrepenulos' ty, serdtse see Grekov
 RACHMANINOFF
 Again you leapt, my heart
Opitz, Martin, 1597-1639.
 WEBER *Gelahrtheit*
Opuščená see Unknown **DVOŘÁK**
Opuštěná milá see Grossmanová-Brodská
 MARTINŮ *The jilted maiden*
Opuštěný milý see Anon. **MARTINŮ**
"Or che di fiori adorno" *see La passeggiata*
 Unknown **ROSSINI**
"Or sù! non ci pensiamo" *see Il modo di*
 prender mogli Unknown **SCHUBERT**
"Or tremule, su i marie su learene" *see*
 Morgana Annunzio **MALIPIERO**
Oración de las madres que tienen . . . see
 Martinez Sierra **FALLA**
"L'orage mugis sait dans une nuit profonde"
 see The worker Weatherly **GOUNOD**
Oraison see Maeterlinck **CHAUSSON**
Oraison funèbre see Bossuet **THOMSON**
Orchids see Roethke **ROREM**
O'Reilly, P J

IRELAND *Song from o'er the hill*
Orest auf Tauris see Mayrhofer
 SCHUBERT
L'orgia see Pepoli **ROSSINI**
L'orgueilleuse see Chalupt **MILHAUD**
"Oriana tenea l'incantamento" *see*
 Oriana–Oriana infedele Annunzio
 MALIPIERO
Oriana–Oriana infedele see Annunzio
 LA CHIMERA. **MALIPIERO**
LES ORIENTALES. see Hugo
 Attente **INDY**
 L'attente **SAINT-SAËNS, WAGNER**
 Clair de lune **INDY**
 Extase **WAGNER**
L' origine de la harpe see Moore, T.
 BERLIOZ
Orion see Unknown **GIDEON**
Orions bälte see Topelius **SIBELIUS**
Orion's girdle see Topelius **SIBELIUS**
 Orions bälte
Orléans, Charles d', Comte
 d'Angoulème, 1391-1465.
 INDY *Madrigal à deux voix*
Orléans, Hélène Louise Élisabeth,
 Duchesse d', 1814-1858.
 LISZT *Die Macht der Musik*
 LOEWE *Musik*
The orphan see Erben **DVOŘÁK** *Sirotek*
The orphan girl in the pleasure garden see
 Broughten **ROREM**
L'orpheline du Tyrol, ballade élégie *see*
 Unknown **ROSSINI**
Orphelines see Ludana **MASSENET**
Orpheus see Jacobi **SCHUBERT** *Lied des*
 Orpheus, als er in die Hölle ging
"Orpheus' Laute hiess der Wipfel" *see Lied*
 aus Heinrich VIII Shakespeare **LASSEN**
Orpheus with his lute see Shakespeare
 KING HENRY VIII.
 QUILTER, VAUGHAN WILLIAMS
 NB: Two Vaughan Williams settings:
 1902 and 1925.
"Orpheus with his lute made trees" *see*
 Orpheus with his lute Shakespeare
 VAUGHAN WILLIAMS
 Two settings: 1902 and 1925.
GLI ORTI ESPERIDI. see Metastasio
 Son fra l'onde **SCHUBERT**
Oscuro è il ciel see Sappho **PIZZETTI**
"Osedlaĭu konia, Konia bystrova" *see Pesnya*
 starika Kol'tsov **BALAKIREV**
Osen' see Pleshcheyev **CHAĬKOVSKIĬ**
O'Shaughnessy, Arthur William Edgar,
 1844-1881.
 DIAMOND *Ode*

Osiennieje solnce see Davidov, Dmitri
   SZYMANOWSKI
Ossian, pseud. *see* Macpherson, James,
   1736-1796.
Ossians Lied nach dem Falle Nathos' see
   Macpherson *DARTHULA*. **SCHUBERT**
Osterlied see Böttger **GRIEG**
Ostern see Boelitz **REGER**
"Ostern ist zwar schon vorbei" *see*
   Auf ein Ei geschrieben Mörike
   SCHOECK
Osterwald, Karl Wilhelm, 1820-1887.
   FRANZ
   Abends
   Ach, dass du kamst
   Ach, wenn ich doch ein Immchen wär
   Ade denn, du stolze
   Aprillaunen
   Aufbruch
   Bei der Linde
   Da die Stunde kam
   Dornröschen
   Dort unterm Lindenbaum
   Du grüne Rast im Haine
   Durch säuselnde Bäume
   Entschluss
   Erinnerung
      Two settings: Op. 5 no. 10 and op. 51
      no. 10.
   Erster Verlust
   Frühe Klage
   Gewitternacht
   Gleich wie der Mond
   Die Harrende
   Herbstsorge
   Ich lobe mir die Vögelein
   Im Frühling
   Im Mai
      Two settings: Op. 11 no. 3 and op. 22
      no. 5.
   Im Sommer
   In Blüten
   Der junge Tag erwacht
   Kurzes Wiedersehen
   Die Liebe hat gelogen
   Lieber Schatz, wie wieder gut mir
   Mein Schatz ist auf der Wanderschaft
   Nun hat das Lied ein Ende
   Nun hat mein Stecken gute Rast
   Der Schnee ist zergangen
   Schöner Mai, bist über Nacht
   Sonnenwende
   Ständchen
   Träume
   Treibt der Sommer seinen Rosen
   Um Mitternacht

   Umsonst
   Und die Rosen, sie prangen
   Und welche Rose blüten treibt
   Vergiss mein nicht
   Verlass' mich nicht!
   Vom Berge
   Wanderlied
   Wenn ich's nur wüsste
   Will über Nacht wohl übers Tal
   Zu spät
   MACDOWELL *Lieber Schatz*
Ostrovok see Shelley **RACHMANINOFF**
   The isle
Ostrovski, Aleksandr Nikolayevich,
   1823-1886.
   MUSORGSKIĬ *Kolybel'naĭa pesnĭa*
O'Sullivan, Seumas *see* Starkey, James,
   1879-1958.
Őszi szellő see Pósa **BARTÓK**
"Ot lastochki do solov'ia" *see Golos" ptĭts"*
   Bal'mont **PROKOFIEV**
Otchalila lodka see Apukhtin **PROKOFIEV**
"Otchego ĭa lĭublĭu tebĭa" *see Noch'*
   Polonsky **CHAĬKOVSKIĬ**
Otchego, skazhi, dusha devĭtsa see Unknown
   MUSORGSKIĬ
Otchevo? see Heine *WARUM SIND DANN*
   DIE ROSEN SO BLASS? **CHAĬKOVSKIĬ**
Otchevo see Lermontov **BALAKIREV**
"Otchevo poblednela vesnoy" *see Otchevo?*
   Heine **CHAĬKOVSKIĬ**
OTELLO. see Shakespeare
   Lied der Desdemona **LOEWE**
Otettiin minusta outo see Kanteletar
   KILPINEN
Otevření slovečkem see Unknown
   MARTINŮ
"The other night I saw a light!" *see*
   A Christmas carol Anon. **ROREM**
Otravoĭ polny moi pĭesni} see Heine
   BORODIN *Vergiftet sind meine Lieder*
Otryvok iz A Mĭusse see Musset
   RACHMANINOFF *Loneliness*
Ottenwalt, Anton, 1789-1845.
   SCHUBERT *Der Knabe in der Wiege*
Otto-Lied see Kugler, Johann, Consul in
   Stettin **LOEWE**
Otverzhennaĭa see Gol'ts-Miller
   MUSORGSKIĬ
"Où allez-vous?" *see Pour demain soir . . .*
   Jacob, M. **AURIC**
"Où butine l'abeille je butine aussi" *see*
   Un peu animé Shakespeare
   HONEGGER
"Où donc allez-vous, Madame" *see En voyage*
   Maurer **MASSENET**

COMPOSER   Poet   *Title*   ''First Line''

"Où le bedeau a passé" *see Chanson du clair tamis* Fombeure **POULENC**

"Où n'atteindrai-je pas?" *see Au delà du rêve* Hirsch **MASSENET**

Où nous avons aimé see Aguétant, Pierre **SAINT-SAËNS**

Où que s'envole see Bourguignat, Paul **MASSENET**

"Où sont nos amoureuses?" *see Les cydalises* Gérard de Nerval **AURIC**

"Où sont, sous les matins en pleurs" *see Rien n'est que de France* Silvestre **MASSENET**

"Où t'envoles-tu, si, frêle, petit papillon léger" *see Papillons* Leche, Renée de **SAINT-SAËNS**

"Où va mon père, le matin" *see Mon père travaille* Legrand, Marc **INDY**

"Où vas-tu, toi qui passes si tard" *see Le bachelier de Salamanque* Chalupt **ROUSSEL**

Où vivre? see Richepin **SCHMITT**

Où voulez-vous aller? see Gautier **GOUNOD**

"Oublie, Ô Pholoé" *see Pholoé* Leconte de Lisle **HAHN**

"Oui, Messieurs, c'est alors" *see Vieille chanson* Hugo **DELIBES**

"Oui, nous sommes encor les hommes d'Armorique" *see Le chant des Bretons* Brizeux **BERLIOZ**

Our doom is in our being see Agee **SONNET 2. DIAMOND**

"Our Father . . . " *see The Lord's prayer* Bible **ROREM**

Our share of night to bear see Dickinson **LUENING**

Our time see Tiutchev **MEDTNER**

"Out across the wave all is bare" *see Landscape* Sada-Ihe, 13th cent. **GRIFFES**

"Out in the sun my garden stands" *see About my garden* Carpenter, Rue **CARPENTER**

OUT OF AFRICA. see Blixen *The millennium* **DIAMOND**

Out of my sight see Witwicki **CHOPIN** *Precz z moich oczu . . .*

"Out of the tulip tree, the boy who had green eyes" *see The tulip tree* Goodman **ROREM**

"Out upon it, I have loved" *see The constant lover* Suckling **QUILTER**

The outcast see Gol'ts-Miller **MUSORGSKIĭ** *Otverzhennaĭa*

"Outo tähti silmähäni" *see Kirkkotie* Lehtinen **KILPINEN**

Outside it grows dark see Topelius **SIBELIUS** *Det mörknar ute*

Ouvre tes yeux bleus see Robiquet **MASSENET**

"Ouvrez vos tendres yeux la belle au bois dormant" *see Rondel de la belle au bois* Gruaz, Julien **MASSENET**

L'ouvrier see Weatherly **GOUNOD** *The worker*

L'OUVRIER QUI PLEURE. see Magre *La chanson de blaisine* **SÉVERAC**

Ovčákova píseň nedělní see Uhland **MARTINŮ** *A shepherd's Sunday song*

"Over all the treetops is rest" *see Ilmenau: Over all the treetops* Goethe **IVES**

Over de høje fjaelle see Bjørnson **ARNE. DELIUS** *Over the mountains high*

Over den eenzamen vijver see Koster **PIJPER**

Over her embroidery see Kleinschrod **DVOŘÁK** *Při vyšívání*

Over the Artic Ocean see Svetlova **PROKOFIEV** *Nad poliarnym morem*

Over the lake see Golenishchev-Kutuzov **BALAKIREV** *Nad ozerom*

Over the land is April see Stevenson, Robert Louis **QUILTER**

Over the mountains high see Bjørnson **ARNE. DELIUS**

"Over the sea, over the sea" *see The half-ring moon* Tabb **GRIFFES**

Overbeck, Christian Adolf, 1755-1821. **MOZART** *Das Kinderspiel Sehnsucht nach dem Frühlinge*

The owl and the pussy-cat see Lear **STRAVINSKIĭ**

"The owl & the pussy-cat went to sea" *see The owl and the pussy-cat* Lear **STRAVINSKIĭ**

"Ox and ass at Bethlehem" *see The first mercy* Blunt **HESELTINE**

The oxen, a Christmas carol see Hardy **ROREM**

"Oy vey Rebenyu" *see Undzer Rebenyu* Anon. **WEISGALL**

Oyème see Sully-Prudhomme **GOUNOD** *Prière*

Ozoruik see Musorgskiĭ **MUSORGSKIĭ**

P

"Pa den lugna skogs sjöns vatten satt jag hela"
see *Sommarnatten* Runeberg **SIBELIUS**
Pa det jaevne, pa det jaevne see Kaalund
NIELSEN
"Pa drifvans snö där glimmar" *see Demanten*
på marssnön Wecksell **SIBELIUS**
"Pa fjärdens silfverbricka en fläck det syns"
see När jag drömmer Tavaststjerna
SIBELIUS
På Norges nøgne fjelde see Paulsen
GRIEG
På Skogstien see Paulsen **GRIEG**
"På Tunet gik Smågutten med Hugen tung af
Nag" *see Blåbaeret* Grønvold **GRIEG**
På verandan vid havet see Rydberg
SIBELIUS
"Paa Fjeldet Huldren siddcr" *see Til L.M.*
Lindemans Sølvbryllup Nikolajesen, V.
GRIEG
Paa Hamars Ruiner see Vinje **GRIEG**
Ein Paar see Braungart **REGER**
Pablo Picasso see Eluard **POULENC**
LA PACE FRA LA VIRTÙ E LA BELLEZZA.
see Metastasio
Lebens-Genuss **BEETHOVEN**
Pace non trove see Petrarca **LISZT**
Pachna mi dziwnie twoje zlote wlosy see
Miciński *W MROKU GWIAZD.*
SZYMANOWSKI
Pacini, Emilio, 1810-1898.
ROSSINI
À Grenade
L'amour à Pekin
Amour sans espoir ("Tirana
all'espagnole rossinize")
Au chevet d'un mourant (élégie)
La chanson du Bébé
Pompadour, la grande coquette
Roméo
Le sylvain
La veuve andalouse
"Pack, clouds, away!" *see Morning song*
Heywood **QUILTER**
Pacory, Henry, b. 1873.
SATIE *Je te veux*
Padlo jíní na pole see Heine **MARTINŮ**
Hoar-frost fallen in the field
Padrilla, Pedro de, fl.1580.
LA SIERRA ES ALTA.
SCHUMANN *Hoch, hoch sind die Berge*
"Päivä laskee metsän taa" *see Ilta* Lehtinen
KILPINEN
"Päivän viime säteet lankee" *see Lakeus V*
Koskenniemi **KILPINEN**

Pagan see Phemister, Bruce **ROREM**
Paganini see Vilmorin **POULENC**
Der Page see Geibel **JENSEN,**
SCHUMANN
The page sat in the lofty tower see Jacobsen
DELIUS
"Pagen højt paa Taarnet sad" *see Genrebillede*
Jacobsen **NIELSEN**
Pagen højt paa taarnet sad see Jacobsen
DELIUS *The page sat in the lofty tower*
Pagenlied see Eichendorff
MENDELSSOHN-BARTHOLDY
Pah' on orjana eleä see Kanteletar
KILPINEN
Pailleron, Édouard Jules Henri, 1834-
1899.
BIZET *Tarantelle*
AVRIL: Chanson.
RACHMANINOFF *Aprel'! veshniĭ*
prazdnichnyĭ den'
Paimenlaulu see Kanteletar **KILPINEN**
"Pain gnaws at my heart like a rat that gnaws"
see The rat Symons **IRELAND**
Painfully & sweetly see Rostopchina
CHAĬKOVSKIĬ *I bol'no, i sladko*
Paista päivänen Jumala see Kanteletar
KILPINEN
La paix see Banville **HAHN, KOECHLIN**
"La paix, au milieu des moissons" *see*
La paix Banville **HAHN, KOECHLIN**
La paix de Dieu see Henry, Maurice
GOUNOD
"Paix, mon coeur" *see Peace, my heart*
Tagore **MILHAUD**
Pajaro del agua see Jimenez **RODRIGO**
LES PALAIS NOMADES: Intermède IV. *see*
Kahn *Timbres oubliés* **LOEFFLER**
LES PALAIS NOMADES: Intermède IX. *see*
Kahn *Les paons* **LOEFFLER**
LES PALAIS NOMADES: Intermède XIV. *see*
Kahn *Adieu pour jamais* **LOEFFLER**
LES PALAIS NOMADES: Lied IV. *see* Kahn
Les soirs d'automne **LOEFFLER**
"Pâle espionne de l'amour" *see L'espionne*
Apollinaire **POULENC**
"Pâle rose, le soleil t'a donné" *see A une rose*
pâlissant au soleil Richter **SAUGUET**
"Les pâles heures, sous la lune" *see*
Les heures Mauclair **CHAUSSON**
Palgrave, Francis Turner, 1824-1897.
GOUNOD *Queen of love*
Paliard, Camille Marie José, b. 1892
MILHAUD
Le boulanger

Paliard, Camille Marie José, b. 1892
  (*continued*)
    MILHAUD (*continued*)
      Cet hiver
      Cette douleur
      Les champignons
      Le château
      Les conscrits
      Les deux hôtels
      L'horizon
      La maison inachevée
      Modestes vacances
      Monsieur le Curé
      Paresse
      Le pêcheur
      La petite bergère
      Le retour
      Le ruisseau
      Silence au fond de l'allée
      Tant de vagabonds
      Les trois peupliers
Palma, Georg Busse *see* Busse-Palma,
  Georg, 1876-1915.
"Palomicas de oro" *see Sobre el cupey*
  Hernández Aquino **RODRIGO**
Una Palomita blanca see Anon. **RODRIGO**
Paludan-Müller, Frederik, 1809-1876.
  NIELSEN *Gensyn*
Pamiat' o solntse see Akhmatova
  PROKOFIEV
Pan ainmait Ekho see Moskhos **ROUSSEL**
El pan de ronda see Martinez Sierra
  FALLA *Canzon Andaluza: El pan de ronda*
Panch, Petro, b. 1891.
  PROKOFIEV *Shel stanitseiu kazak*
Panchenko, Petro Iosifovich *see* Panch,
  Petro, 1891-
Panenka a tráva see Anon. **DVOŘÁK**
"Pangur, white Pangur, how happy we are"
  see The monk and his cat
  Auden, W. H., translator. **BARBER**
Pani Twardowski see Mickiewicz **LOEWE**
  Frau Twardowska
Panicz i dziewczyna see Mickiewicz
  LOEWE *Der junge Herr und das Mädchen*
"Panis, piscis, crinis, finis" *see Seminarist*
  Musorgskiĭ **MUSORGSKIĬ**
Panizza, Oskar, 1853-1921.
  STRAUSS *Sie wissen's nicht*
El pano moruno see Anon. **FALLA**
The pansy see Deland **MACDOWELL**
Pàntini, Romualdo
  MALIPIERO *La cavalcata della morte*
  CANTILENE ALL'ARIA APERTA.
    PIZZETTI *La Madre al figlio lontano*
Pantomime see Verlaine *FÊTES GALANTES.*
  DEBUSSY

Panzacchi, Enrico, 1841-1904.
  RESPIGHI
    In alto mare
    Noël ancien
Paoli, Betty, pseud. *see* Glück, Barbara
  Elisabeth, 1814-1894.
Le Paon see Renard *HISTOIRES*
  NATURELLES. **RAVEL**
Les paons see Kahn *LES PALAIS*
  NOMADES: Intermède IX. **LOEFFLER**
Papadiamantopoulos, Ioannes *see*
  Moréas, Jean, 1856-1910.
Der Papagei see Rückert **LOEWE**
Paper boats see Tagore **MILHAUD**
Le papillon et la fleur see Hugo **FAURÉ**
"Papillon, tu es inhumain!" *see Filet à*
  papillons Radiguet **AURIC**
Les papillons see Gautier **CHAUSSON**
Papillons see Leche, Renée de
  SAINT-SAËNS
"Les papillons couleur de neige" *see*
  Les papillons Gautier **CHAUSSON**
Papini, Giovanni, 1881-1956.
  PIZZETTI *Passeggiata*
La Pâquerette see Dumas the younger
  GOUNOD
"Pâquerette gentille, sur qui brille" *see*
  La Pâquerette Dumas the younger
  GOUNOD
Les pâquerettes see Hirtz **AURIC**
"Les pâquerettes trop simplettes" *see*
  Les pâquerettes Hirtz **AURIC**
Pâques see Docquois **SAINT-SAËNS**
"Pâques! Pâques!" *see Pâques* Docquois
  SAINT-SAËNS
Paquet, Alfons Hermann, 1881-1944.
  SZYMANOWSKI *Lied des Mädchens am*
    Fenster
Par ce que j'ai souffert see Jammes
  TRISTESSES. **BOULANGER, MILHAUD**
"Par delà la mer d'azur" *see Là-bas* Croze, J.
  L. **SAINT-SAËNS**
"Par les chemins de l'aurore chevauche" *see*
  Berceuse de Galiane Arnoux **IBERT**
"Par les corps endormis" *see Jack L'Eventreur*
  Noailles, Marie Laure de **ROREM**
"Par les portes d'Orkenise" *see Chanson*
  d'Orkenise Apollinaire **POULENC**
Par les soirs . . . see Fersen, I. de
  RESPIGHI
"Par les soirs bleus d'été" *see Sensation*
  Rimbaud **RIVIER**
Par l'étreinte . . . see Fersen, I. de
  RESPIGHI
"Par Saint Gilles, Viens nous-en" *see La pas*
  d'armes du roi Jean Hugo **SAINT-SAËNS**

"Par un beau matin Pimpante et ravie" *see*
   La vie d'une rose Ruelle **MASSENET**
"Par un souris, l'amour" *see Philis* Anon.
   SÉVERAC
Parabase see Goethe **SCHOECK**
PARACELSUS. see Browning, R.
   from "Paracelsus" **IVES**
Parade see Banville *LES CARIATIDES*, livre
   3, no. X. **AURIC**
Das Paradies in der Wüste see Herder
   LOEWE
Le paradis see Anon.
   VAUGHAN WILLIAMS
Paradis see Lerberghe **FAURÉ**
PARADISE LOST. see Milton
   Evening **IVES**
Pardon see Hölderlin **SAUGUET**
Pardon, Goddess of the night see
   Shakespeare *MUCH ADO ABOUT
   NOTHING.* **THOMSON**
Pareils à des oiseaux see Collin **MASSENET**
"Parempi minun olisi" *see Parempi syntymättä*
   Kanteletar **KILPINEN**
Parempi syntymättä see Kanteletar
   KILPINEN
"Paren' prigozhiĭ moĭ" *see Svitez͠ianka*
   Mickiewicz **RIMSKIĬ-KORSAKOV**
Paresse see Paliard **MILHAUD**
Parfois, je suis triste see Jammes
   TRISTESSES. **BOULANGER, MILHAUD**
"Parfois, lorsque tout dort" *see La nuit* Hugo
   MASSENET
"Parfois, pendant les longues heures" *see*
   Les cloches de la mer Saint-Saëns
   SAINT-SAËNS
Le parfum impérissable see Leconte de
   Lisle **FAURÉ**
Parfums see Dortzal **MASSENET**
Parga's lament see Anon. **DVOŘÁK**
   Žalozpěv Pargy
PARIA, no. 1
   LOEWE Goethe *Gebet des Paria*
PARIA, no. 2
   LOEWE Goethe *Legende*
PARIA, no. 3
   LOEWE Goethe *Dank des Paria*
PARISIANA, no. 1
   POULENC Jacob, M. *Jouer du bugle*
PARISIANA, no. 2
   POULENC Jacob, M. *Vous n'écrivez
   plus?*
Parlez pour moi see Barbier, J. **GOUNOD**
"Parmi les neiges du grand nord" *see*
   Chanson de la fille de bar Aguet, William
   SAUGUET
"Parmi l'ombre où bat la lampe" *see Solitude*
   Gaillard, Roger **SAUGUET**

Der Parnass see Krylov **RUBINSTEIN**
Parny, Evariste, 1753-1814.
   RAVEL
   Aoua!
   Il est doux . . .
   Nahandove
Parole see Eichendorff *DICHTER UND
   IHRE GESELLEN* (1834). **BRAHMS**
La partenza see Metastasio **BEETHOVEN,
   ROSSINI**
"Partis d'une ménagerie" *see Les quatre petits
   lions* Vildrac **MILHAUD**
Partis les vaisseaux see Hugnet **THOMSON**
Partizan Zhelezni͠ak see Golodny, Mikhail
   PROKOFIEV
"Partons en barque sur la mer" *see Sérénade
   italienne* Bourget **CHAUSSON**
Les pas see Valéry **MOMPOU**
Pas bien grand see Kriéger, Jacqueline
   MILHAUD
La pas d'armes du roi Jean see Hugo
   SAINT-SAËNS
Påskesang see Böttger **GRIEG** *Osterlied*
"Påskliljor, suckande vi se" *see Till några
   påskliljor* Blomberg **KILPINEN**
Passage d'une nurse see Gilson **RIVIER**
Passed away see Saunders, E. **GOUNOD**
"Passegger, che al dolce aspetto" *see
   Il poveretto* Maggioni, S. Manfredo
   VERDI
Passeggiata see Papini, Giovanni
   PIZZETTI
La passeggiata see Unknown **ROSSINI**
The passenger see Howe **THOMPSON, R.**
Passerat, Jean, 1534-1602.
   BERKELEY *Ode du premier jour de Mai*
   GOUNOD *Le premier jour de Mai*
Passez, passez toujours see Hugo **FRANCK**
Passiflora see Chambrun **GOUNOD**
Passing see Pound **DIAMOND**
Passing by see Anon. **HESELTINE**
Passing dreams see Dowson **QUILTER**
*THE PASSIONATE SHEEPHERD TO HIS
   LOVE. see* Marlowe
   The passionate shepherd **HESELTINE**
The passionate shepherd see Marlowe *THE
   PASSIONATE SHEEPHERD TO HIS
   LOVE.* **HESELTINE**
Passionnément see Fuster **MASSENET**
Passionslied see Unknown **REGER**
The past see Shelley **BENNETT**
Pastel see Gille **BIZET**
Pastel see Kaminský **MARTINŮ**
Una pastora yo ami see Anon. **RODRIGO**
Pastoral see Jimenez **MOMPOU**
Pastorale see Kafiristan **COPLAND**

Pastorale see Lockroy **DELIBES** *Chanson de l'oiseleur*
Pastorale see No author **STRAVINSKII**
Pastorale see Regnard **BIZET**
Pastorale see Silvestre **MASSENET**
Pastorale des cochons roses see Rostand
   CHABRIER
Pastorcito Santo see Vega Carpio
   RODRIGO
La pastorella see Goldoni *IL FILOSOFO DI CAMPAGNA.* **SCHUBERT**
La pastorella see Santo-Magno, N di
   ROSSINI
"La pastorella al prato" *see La pastorella*
   Goldoni **SCHUBERT**
La pastorella dell'Alpi see Pepoli **ROSSINI**
Pastores loquebantur see Bible
   HINDEMITH
I Pastori see Annunzio *LAUDI.* **PIZZETTI**
"Une pastourelle gentille" *see Chanson du Jour de Noël* Marot **HESELTINE**
Patchen, Kenneth, 1911-1972.
   DIAMOND *Be music, night*
Paté, Lucien, 1845-1939.
   FRANCK *Lied*
   HAHN *L'amitié*
"Pathétique au commandement" *see Gymnaste aérien* Copperie, Adrien **SAUGUET**
Patience see Hopkins **KRENEK**
"Patience, distu, patience" *see Le noyer fatal* Jacob, M. **RIETI**
"Patience, hard thing!" *see Patience* Hopkins
   KRENEK
The patient sleeps see Henley **CHANLER**
Patmore, Coventry Kersey Dighton, 1823-1896.
   THE UNKNOWN EROS: The azalea.
     MILHAUD *L'azalée*
   THE UNKNOWN EROS: Departure.
     MILHAUD *Le départ*
Patria, consorti, figli see Cerutti, L. F.
   ROSSINI *L'ultimo pensiero*
   ("Patria, consorti, figli")
Patte de velours see Spenner, M.
   GOUNOD
Paul et Virginie see Radiguet **POULENC**
Paul Klee see Eluard **POULENC**
Paul, Saint, apostle
   KRENEK *The night is far spent*
Paulinzelle see Träger **JENSEN**
PAUL'S BLUES, no. 1
   ROREM Goodman *Near closing time*
PAUL'S BLUES, no. 2
   ROREM Goodman *Bawling blues*
PAUL'S BLUES, no. 3
   ROREM Goodman *Jail-bait blues*

Paulsen, John Olaf, 1851-1924.
   GRIEG
   Den aergjerrige
   Et Håb
   Faedrelandssang
   Farvel
   Henrik Wergeland
   Hjemkomst
   Jeg reiste en deilig Sommerkvaeld
   Med en Primula veris
   Når jeg vil dø
   Nu hviler du i jorden
   På Norges nøgne fjelde
   På Skogstien
   Til Én. I
   Til Én. II
   Til Norge
   Turisten
   Udvandreren
   JEG REISTE ENDEILIG SOMMERKVAELD.
     DELIUS *Am schönsten Sommerabend war's*
The pauper see Tiutchev **MEDTNER**
Pause see Müller, Wilhelm **SCHUBERT**
Le pauv' petit see Boyer, Georges
   MASSENET
"Le pauvre amour est tout en larmes" *see L'amour pleure* Postel, Madeleine
   MASSENET
Pauvre Braga see Nadaud **GOUNOD**
"Pauvre de joie" *see Toi* Anon. **MILHAUD**
"Pauvre enfant qui voulez combattre la nature" *see À une jeune fille* Augier
   GOUNOD
La pauvre femme see Béranger **LALO**
"La pauvre fleur disait au papillon céleste" *see Le papillon et la fleur* Hugo **FAURÉ**
Pavesi, Corrado Marchese
   GOUNOD *Perchè piangi?*
Pavloff, Mme
   LISZT *Oh pourquoi donc*
Pax vobiscum see Schober **SCHUBERT**
Le pays bienheureux see Gounod **GOUNOD**
Le pays des rêves see Silvestre **FAURÉ**
Pays sans nom see Schneider **AUBERT**
"Les pays, tu sais bien" *see Pays sans nom* Schneider **AUBERT**
Paysage see Leclère, translator.
   SHÉHÉRAZADE. **KOECHLIN**
Paysage see Messiaen **MESSIAEN**
Paysage see Silvestre **MASSENET**
Paysage see Theuriet **HAHN**
Le paysage dans le cadre des portières see Verlaine **KOECHLIN**
Paysage sentimental see Bourget
   LES AVEUX: Amour. **DEBUSSY**

COMPOSER Poet *Title* "First Line"

Paysage triste *see* Verlaine **HAHN**
PAYSAGES BELGES. see Verlaine
  Chevaux de bois **DEBUSSY**
PAYSAGES TRISTES. see Verlaine
  Soleils couchants **CASELLA, SÉVERAC**
Peabody, Josephine Preston, 1874-1922.
  GIDEON *The nightingale unheard*
Peace *see* Hopkins **KRENEK**
Peace, my heart *see* Tagore **MILHAUD**
"The peace of a wandering sky, silence" *see*
  Rest Symons **IRELAND**
Peacefully slumber *see* Barbier, J.
  GOUNOD *Clos ta paupière*
PEACOCK PIE. see De La Mare
  Cake and Sack **CHANLER**
  Old Shellover **CHANLER**
  The ship of Rio **BRITTEN, CHANLER**
  Tillie **CHANLER**
"A peal is that mountain" *see Portrait of F. B.*
  [Frances Blood] Stein **THOMSON**
Pearse, Padriac, 1879-1916.
  ROREM *Lullaby of the woman of the mountain*
The peasant see Shenshin
  RACHMANINOFF
Pech, Jindřiška, 1847-1926.
  DVOŘÁK
    Lípy
    Překážky
    Přemítání
    Proto
    Vzpomínání
La pêche see Banville **HAHN, KOECHLIN**
Péché véniel see Ludana **AUBERT**
Le pêcheur see Du Boys **BERLIOZ**
Le pêcheur see Paliard **MILHAUD**
"Pêcheur, horrible pêcheur blond et doux" *see*
  Le pêcheur Paliard **MILHAUD**
"Le pêcheur vidant ses filets" *see La pêche*
  Banville **HAHN, KOECHLIN**
Peele, George, 1558?-1597?
  THE OLD WIVES' TALE (1595).
    HESELTINE
      Chopcherry
      Whenas the rye reach to the chin
Pégase see Margueritte **MALIPIERO**
La peine see Carême **MILHAUD**
Peine d'amour see Silvestre **DELIBES**
Peitl, Paul, 1853-
  WOLF *Ein Grab*
Péladin, Joséphin, 1858-1918.
  LE PRINCE DE BYZANCE.
    SATIE *Hymne pour le "Salut Drapeau" du "Prince de Byzance..."*
Le pèlerin see Schiller **SAUGUET**
Pélissier, Léon G.

MASSENET *Regard d'enfant*
PELLÉAS ET MÉLISANDE. see
  Maeterlinck
    Mélisande's song **FAURÉ**
Pelouse see Radiguet **AURIC**
Pemberton, May
  QUILTER *Come, lady-day*
"Penchée à ma fenêtre" *see Chanson italienne*
  Anon. **RAVEL**
"Pendant la nuit une rose avance sous feux
  éteints" *see Souvenirs d'enfance* Cocteau
  HONEGGER
Pendant l'attente see Mendès **ROUSSEL**
Pendant le bal see Tolstoï **CHAĬKOVSKIĬ**
  Sred' shumnago bala
Pendant que je médite see Moréas **HAHN**
"Pendant qu'ils étaient partis pour la guerre"
  see C'est la paix Debladis, Georgette
  FAURÉ
LES PÉNITENTS EN MAILLOT ROSE, no. 1
  SAUGUET Jacob, M. *A une sainte le jour de sa fête*
LES PÉNITENTS EN MAILLOT ROSE, no. 2
  SAUGUET Jacob, M. *Jardin mystérieux*
LES PÉNITENTS EN MAILLOT ROSE, no. 3
  SAUGUET Jacob, M. *Marine à Roscoff*
LES PÉNITENTS EN MAILLOT ROSE, no. 4
  SAUGUET Jacob, M. *La ville*
LES PÉNITENTS EN MAILLOT ROSE, no. 5
  SAUGUET Jacob, M. *Ports de l'enfer*
Penmarch, G. de
  SAINT-SAËNS *Le sommeil des fleurs*
PENNY ARCADE: A cyclical melodrama for voice & piano, no. 1
  ROREM Norse *Freak show*
PENNY ARCADE: A cyclical melodrama for voice & piano, no. 2
  ROREM Norse *The gypsy*
PENNY ARCADE: A cyclical melodrama for voice & piano, no. 3
  ROREM Norse *The flea's lament*
PENNY ARCADE: A cyclical melodrama for voice & piano, no. 4
  ROREM Norse *Test your skill*
PENNY ARCADE: A cyclical melodrama for voice & piano, no. 5
  ROREM Norse *Song of the third duck from the right*
PENNY ARCADE: A cyclical melodrama for voice & piano, no. 6
  ROREM Norse *Goodbye to penny fate*

COMPOSER Poet *Title* "First Line"

Penny paradise see Musorgskiĭ
  MUSORGSKIĭ *Raëk*
Pensa, che questo istante see Metastasio
  ALCIDE AL BIVIO. **SCHUBERT**
Pensamientos me quitan see Anon.
  SPANISCHES LIEDERBUCH:
  Pensamientos me quitan.
  JENSEN
Pensée d'automne see Silvestre
  MASSENET
Pensée de printemps see Silvestre
  MASSENET
LA PENSÉE DES MORTS. see Lamartine
  Seul **GOUNOD**
Pensées d'octobre see Follain **SAUGUET**
Penumbra see Rossetti, Dante **IRELAND**
People hide their love see Wu-Ti, Liang
  dynasty **BERKELEY**
Pepa see Musset **LASSEN**
"Pepa, Pepa, quand la nuit est venue" *see*
  Pepa Musset **LASSEN**
Pépin, Edwige
  SAUGUET *Prière dans le soir*
"Pépita reine de Venise" *see Toréador*
  Cocteau **POULENC**
Pepoli, Carlo, Conte, 1796-1881.
  ROSSINI
    La danza
    La gita in gondola
    L'invito
    L'orgia
    La pastorella dell'Alpi
Per aspera see Jalkanen **KILPINEN**
"Per una vela en el mar blau" *see Canticel*
  Carner **RODRIGO**
Perchè piangi? see Pavesi, Corrado
  Marchese **GOUNOD**
Percy, Thomas, 1729-1811.
  RELIQUES.
    IVES *Harpalus*
    LOEWE *Des Bettlers Tochter von*
      Bednall Green
Perduta ho la pace see Goethe *FAUST.*
  VERDI
Pered sudom see Goethe **MEDTNER** *Vor*
  Gericht
"Pered voevodoĭ molcha on stoit" *see Ballada*
  Turgenev **RUBINSTEIN**
Peregrina see Mörike **SCHOECK**
Peregrina see Mörike *MALER NOLTEN.*
  SCHOECK
Perigrina I see Mörike **WOLF**
Peregrina II see Mörike **SCHOECK, WOLF**
Perkêo see Scheffel *GAUDEAMUS.*
  JENSEN
La perla see Hohenlohe **LISZT**

Die Perle see Hohenlohe **LISZT** *La perla*
Die Perle see Jacobi **SCHUBERT**
Die Perle see Rückert *LIEBESFRÜHLING.*
  FRANZ
"La perle est aux ondes" *see À toi mon coeur*
  Barbier, J. **GOUNOD**
"Die Perlen meiner Seele" *see Huldigung*
  Hafiz **STRAUSS**
Perlenfischer see Roquette **JENSEN,**
  WOLF
PERMIT ME VOYAGE. Description of
  Elysium. *see* Agee
  Sure on this shining night **BARBER**
Peros, Sándor
  BARTÓK *Evening song*
Perpina, D. Francisco
  DESEO DE AMOR.
    SAINT-SAËNS *Désir d'amour*
Perpińan, Don Francesco *see* Perpina, D.
  Francisco
Der Perserkönig Cai-Caius see Schink
  ZELTER
Personne ne saura jamais see Derème
  IBERT
Pervaĭa utrata see Goethe **MEDTNER**
  Erster Verlust
La perverse see Chalupt **MILHAUD**
Pervigilium Veneris see Anon. **THOMSON**
  The feast of love
Pervoe svidanie see Konstantin
  CHAĭKOVSKIĭ
El pescador see Espronceda **TURINA**
"Pescadorcita mía" *see El pescador*
  Espronceda **TURINA**
Pesenka el'fov see Goethe **MEDTNER**
  Elfenliedchen
Pesenka iz "Klaudiny" see Goethe
  MEDTNER *Aus "Claudine von Villa-*
  Bella"
Pesn' Baleartsa see Musorgskiĭ, M.,
  supposed author. *SALAMMBÔ.*
  MUSORGSKIĭ
Pesn' nochi see Tiutchev **MEDTNER**
  Song of night
Pesn' Startsa see Goethe **MUSORGSKIĭ**
  Lied des Harfenspielers
Pesn' strannika see Eichendorff **MEDTNER**
  Reiselied
Pesnia see Chamisso **MEDTNER**
  Frisch gesungen
Pesnia Mefistofelia v pogrebke Auerbakha see
  Goethe **MUSORGSKIĭ**
Pesnia Min'ony see Goethe **MEDTNER**
  Mignon
Pesnia o rodine see Prokof'yev, A.
  PROKOFIEV

Pesnia o Voroshilove see Sikorskaya, Tatyana **PROKOFIEV**
Pesnia razocharovannogo see Rathaus **RACHMANINOFF** *Song of the disillusioned*
Pesnia smelykh see Surkov **PROKOFIEV**
Pesnia Ziuleĭki see Byron **RIMSKIĭ-KORSAKOV**
Pesnya see Maĭakovskii **PROKOFIEV**
PESNYA. see Mei
  Kak naladidi: Durak **BALAKIREV, CHAĭKOVSKIĭ**
Pesnya Min'ony see Goethe *WILHELM MEISTER.* Mignon's song: Kennst du das Land? **CHAĭKOVSKIĭ**
Pesnya razboynika see Kol'tsov **BALAKIREV**
Pesnya Selima see Lermontov **BALAKIREV**
Pesnya starika see Kol'tsov **BALAKIREV**
Pesnya tyomnovo lesa see Borodin **BORODIN** *Song of the dark forest*
Pesnya Zemfiri see Pushkin **CHAĭKOVSKIĭ**
Pesnya: Zholtĭy list see Lermontov **BALAKIREV**
Pesnya zolotoy rĭbki see Lermontov **BALAKIREV**
Pesu' see Polonsky **CHAĭKOVSKIĭ**
Peter, René
  DEBUSSY *Berceuse*
Peter Warlock's fancy see Anon. **HESELTINE**
PETERISMS, set one, no. 1
  HESELTINE Peele *Chopcherry*
PETERISMS, set one, no. 2
  HESELTINE Fletcher *A sad song*
PETERISMS, set one, no. 3
  HESELTINE Skelton, J. *Rutterkin*
PETERISMS, set two, no. 1
  HESELTINE Udall *Roister doister*
PETERISMS, set two, no. 2
  HESELTINE Nashe *Spring*
PETERISMS, set two, no. 3
  HESELTINE Wever *Lusty juventus*
Peterson, Frederic, 1859-1938.
  IVES *At parting*
Le petit âne blanc see Lorys, Pierre **IBERT**
Le petit bois see Supervielle **AURIC**
Le petit chat see Xaurof, L. **MARTINŮ**
"Petit cheval, qui m'es si cher" *see Cansón pel cabalet* Estieu **SÉVERAC**
Le petit cimetière see Havet **CARPENTER**
PETIT COURS DE MORALE, no. 1
  HONEGGER Giraudoux *Jeanne*
PETIT COURS DE MORALE, no. 2
  HONEGGER Giraudoux *Adèle*

PETIT COURS DE MORALE, no. 3
  HONEGGER Giraudoux *Cécile*
PETIT COURS DE MORALE, no. 4
  HONEGGER Giraudoux *Irène*
PETIT COURS DE MORALE, no. 5
  HONEGGER Giraudoux *Rosemonde*
"Le petit enfant Amour" *see L'amour blessé* Ronsard **SAINT-SAËNS**
"Petit enfant, fragile et beau" *see Regard d'enfant* Pélissier, Léon G. **MASSENET**
Le petit garçon trop bien portant see Nohain, Jean **POULENC**
Le petit Jésus see Boyer, Georges **MASSENET**
Le petit oiseau see Anon. **MARTINŮ**
Petit oiseau see Bouclon **BERLIOZ**
Un petit pas, deux petits pas see Pitoëff *TU NE M'ÉCHAPPERAS JAMAIS.* **MILHAUD**
Le petit paysan see Jacob, M. **SAUGUET**
"Le petit pèr'combes s'en va chez le docteur" *see Chez le docteur* Hyspa **SATIE**
Petit Ramusianum harmonique see Stravinskiĭ **STRAVINSKIĭ**
"Petit ruisseau qui cours à travers la prairie" *see Soir d'automne* Gounod **GOUNOD**
Le petit sentier see Bouchor, M. **CHAUSSON**
La petite bergère see Paliard **MILHAUD**
La petite Bohémienne see Deschamps **ROSSINI** *Chanson de Zora* (La petite Bohémienne)
Petite Chapelle see Laforgue **HONEGGER**
Petite écuyère see Copperie, Adrien **SAUGUET**
Petite fille de Paris see Anon. **MOMPOU**
"Petite fourmi sérieuse" *see Tombez mes ailes* Legouvé **GOUNOD**
Petite main see Docquois **SAINT-SAËNS**
Petite Marguerite see Rolland **BIZET**
Petite mireille see Beissier **MASSENET**
Petite musique see Richaud **SAUGUET**
La petite pie see Unknown **STRAVINSKIĭ**
Une petite pomme see Hirtz **AURIC**
La petite princesse see Fargue *TANCRÈDE.* **SCHMITT**
"La petite princesse guette" *see La petite princesse* Fargue **SCHMITT**
La petite servante see Jacob, M. **POULENC**
"Les petites fleurs n'ont pu vivre" *see Tragédie* Valade **DEBUSSY**
PETITES LÉGENDES, no. 1
  MILHAUD Carême *Sortilège*
PETITES LÉGENDES, no. 2
  MILHAUD Carême *Les feuilles*
PETITES LÉGENDES, no. 3
  MILHAUD Carême *L'amoureux*

PETITES LÉGENDES, no. 4
  MILHAUD Carême *La prière*
PETITES LÉGENDES, no. 5
  MILHAUD Carême *La dormeuse*
PETITES LÉGENDES, no. 6
  MILHAUD Carême *La peine*
PETITES LÉGENDES, no. 7
  MILHAUD Carême *La chance*
PETITES LÉGENDES, no. 8
  MILHAUD Carême *Le lièvre et le blé*
PETITES LÉGENDES, no. 9
  MILHAUD Carême *La bise*
PETITES LÉGENDES, no. 10
  MILHAUD Carême *Destinée*
PETITES LÉGENDES, no. 11
  MILHAUD Carême *Le beau navire*
PETITES LÉGENDES, no. 12
  MILHAUD Carême *Le charme*
Les petits ânes see Hirtz **AURIC**
Les petits coups see Béranger **LALO**
Petöfi, Alexander *see* Petöfi, Sándor,
  1823-1849.
Petöfi, Sándor, 1823-1849.
  DELIBES *Chanson hongroise*
  FRANZ
    Blätter lässt die Blume fallen
    Selige Nacht!
  LISZT *A magyarok Istene*
  SEIBER *Négy Petöfi dal*
Petrarca, Francesco, 1304-1374.
  LISZT
    Benedetto sia'l giorno
    Pace non trove
    I vidi in terra angelicicostumi
  PFITZNER *Zweiundneunzigstes Sonnet*
    von Petrarca
  PIZZETTI
    Levommi il mio pensier
    Quel Rosignuol
    La vita fugge
  SCHUBERT
    Sonett I
    Sonett II
    Sonett III
Petrarch *see* Petrarca, Francesco, 1304-
  1374.
Un peu animé see Shakespeare
  THE TEMPEST. **HONEGGER**
"Peuple du Christ j'expose" *see Petite*
  Chapelle Laforgue **HONEGGER**
Peut-être see Croze, J. L. **SAINT-SAËNS**
"Peut-il se reposer" *see Celui qui dort, à la*
  mémoire de Francis Poulenc Eluard
  SAUGUET
Peut-il se reposer? see Eluard **POULENC**
Pevets see Maïkov **RIMSKIĬ-KORSAKOV**

Pevets see Pushkin **MEDTNER** *The singer*
PEVITSE: Unosi moe serdtse *see* Shenshin
  Unosi moe serdtse **CHAĬKOVSKIĬ**
Peyre, L. de
  GOUNOD *Ce que je suis sans toi*
Peyre, Mathylde
  MASSENET *Rêverie sentimentale*
Peyrissac, Jean, 1895-1974.
  RIVIER *Prière*
"Der Pfarrer von Assmannshausen sprach" *see*
  Die Heimkehr Scheffel **JENSEN**
"Pfarrherr, du kühler, öffne dein Thor" *see*
  Lied fahrender Schüler Scheffel **JENSEN**
Pfarrius, Gustav, 1800-1884.
  JENSEN *Sie war die Schönste von Allen*
  WALDLIEDERN.
  SCHUMANN
    Der Bräutigam und die Birke
    Die Hütte
    Warnung
Das Pfarrjüngferchen see Rückert **LOEWE**
Pfau, Ludwig, 1821-1894.
  SCHÖNBERG
    Du kehrst mir den Rücken
    Einsam bin ich und allein
    Einst hat vor deines Vaters haus
    Gott grüss dich, Marie!
    Könnt' ich zu dir, mein Licht
    Lied der Schnitterin
    Mein Schatz ist wie ein Schneck
    Der Pflanze, die dort über dem Abgrund
      schwebt
    Vergissmeinnicht
    Warum bist du aufgewacht
    Zweifler
Pfeffel, Gottlieb Conrad, 1736-1809.
  BEETHOVEN *Der freie Mann*
  SCHUBERT *Der Vatermörder*
Pfeifen see Hesse **SCHOECK**
Pfingslied see Helmbold **LOEWE**
PFITZNER, HANS, 1869-1949.
  Anon.
    Untreu und Trost (1903) [Brockhaus]
    "Da dob'n auf jener Linden"
  Bartels, Adolf, 1862-1945.
    Wenn sich Liebes von dir lösen will, op.
      40 no. 2 [Peters, 1932] same
  Böttger, Adolf, 1816-1870.
    Ich hör ein Vöglein locken, op. 2 no. 5
      [Brockhaus, 1889] same
  Bürger, Gottfried August, 1747-1794.
    An die Bienen, op. 22 no. 5 [Brockhaus,
      1907]
    "Wollt ihr wissen, holde Bienen"
    An die Morgenröte, op. 41 no. 1 [Peters,
      1932]

"Wenn die goldne Frühe neu geboren"
Gegenliebe, op. 22 no. 4 [Brockhaus,
1907]
"Wenn, O Mädchen, wenn dein Blut"
Schön Suschen, op. 22 no. 3 [Brockhaus,
1907]
"Schön Suschen kannt' ich lange Zeit"
Trauerstille, op. 26 no. 4 [Brockhaus,
1916] "O, wie öde, sonder
Freudenschall"

Busse, Carl, 1872-1918.
Gretel, op. 11 no. 5 [Brockhaus, 1901]
"Vor der Tür im Sonnenscheine"
Leierkastenmann, op. 15 no. 1
[Brockhaus, 1904]
"Wo der Weiser steht an der Strass"
Michaelskirchplatz, op. 19 no. 2
[Brockhaus, 1905]
"Abendschwärmer zogen um die
Linden"
Stimme der Sehnsucht, op. 19 no. 1
[Brockhaus, 1905]
"Ich raun' dir am Bette"

Chamisso, Adelbert von, 1781-1838.
Tragische Geschichte, op. 22 no. 2
[Brockhaus, 1907]
" 's war einer, dem's zu Herzen ging"

Cossmann, Paul Nikolaus, 1869-1942.
Die Bäume wurden gelb, op. 6 no. 5
[Fürstner, 1894; Boosey & Hawkes]
same
Widmung, op. 6 no. 4 [Fürstner, 1894;
Boosey & Hawkes] "Ohn' Lieb' bist
du durchs Leben kommen"

Dehmel, Richard, 1863-1920.
Der Arbeitsmann, op. 30 no. 4 [Fürstner,
1922; Boosey & Hawkes]
"Wir haben ein Bett"
Die stille Stadt, op. 29 no. 4 [Fürstner,
1922] "Liegt eine Stadt im Tale"
Venus mater, op. 11 no. 4 [Brockhaus,
1901] "Träume, träume du mein süsses
Leben"

**Eichendorff, Joseph Karl Benedikt,
Freiherr von, 1788-1857.**
Abschied, op. 9 no. 5 [Brockhaus, 1898]
"Abendlich schon rauscht der Wald"
Das Alter, op. 41 no. 3 [Peters, 1932]
"Hoch mit den Wolken geht der Vögel
Reise"
Der Bote, op. 5 no. 3 [Fürstner;
Boosey & Hawkes]
"Am Himmelsgrund schiessen lustig
die Stern"
Die Einsame, op. 9 no. 2 [Brockhaus,
1898]
"Wär's dunkel, ich läg' im Walde"

Der Gärtner, op. 9 no. 1 [Brockhaus,
1898] "Wohin ich geh' und schaue"
Im Herbst, op. 9 no. 3 [Brockhaus, 1898]
"Der Wald wird falb, die Blätter
fallen"
In Danzig, op. 22 no. 1 [Brockhaus,
1907] "Dunkle Giebel, hohe Fenster"
Der Kühne, op. 9 no. 4 [Brockhaus,
1898] "Und wo noch kein Wandrer
gegangen"
Lockung, op. 7 no. 4 [Ries & Erler,
1894] "Hörst du nicht die Bäume
rauschen"
Die Nachtigallen, op. 21 no. 2 [Kahnt,
1907]
"Möcht' wissen, was sie schlagen"
Nachts, op. 26 no. 2 [Brockhaus, 1916]
"Ich stehe im Waldesschatten"
Nachtwanderer, op. 7 no. 2 [Ries &
Erler, 1894] "Er reitet nachts auf
einem braunen Ross"
Neue Liebe, op. 26 no. 3 [Brockhaus,
1916]
"Herz, mein Herz, warum so fröhlich"
Sonst, op. 15 no. 4 [Brockhaus, 1904]
"Es glänzt der Tulpenflor"
Studentenfahrt, op. 11 no. 3 [Brockhaus,
1901]
"Der Jäger ziehn in grünen Wald"
Der verspätete Wanderer, op. 41 no. 2
[Peters, 1932] "Wo aber werd' ich sein
im künft'gen Lenze"
Der Weckruf, op. 40 no. 6 [Peters, 1932]
"Nächtlich macht der Herr die Rund"
Zorn, op. 15 no. 2 [Brockhaus, 1904]
"Seh ich im verfallenen, dunkeln
Haus"
Zum Abschied meiner Tochter, op. 10 no.
3 [Brockhaus, 1898]
"Der Herbstwind schüttelt die Linde"

Frey, Friedrich Hermann, 1830-1911.
Herbstgefühl, op. 40 no. 4 [Peters, 1932]
"Wie ferne Tritte hörst du's schallen"

**Geibel, Emanuel, i.e., Franz Emanuel
August, 1815-1884.**
Mein Herz ist wie die dunkle Nacht, op. 3
no. 3 [Tischer & Jagenberg, 1889]
same

**Goethe, Johann Wolfgang von, 1749-
1832.**
An den Mond, op. 18 [Brockhaus, 1906]
"Füllest wieder Busch und Tal"
Mailied, op. 26 no. 5 [Brockhaus, 1916]
"Wie herrlich leuchtet mir die Natur"
Willkommen und Abschied, op. 29 no. 3
[Fürstner, 1922] "Es schlug mein Herz,
geschwind zu Pferde"

PFITZNER, HANS, 1869-1949 *(continued)*
Goethe, Johann Wolfgang von, 1749-
1832 *(continued)*
WANDRERS NACHTLIED I.
Wanderers Nachtlied, op. 40 no. 5
[Peters, 1932]
"Der du von dem Himmel bist"
Graf-Bartholomew, M
Mir bist du tot [Ries & Erler, 1933] same
Grun, James
Frieden, op. 5 no. 1 [Fürstner; Boosey &
Hawkes]
"Morgenwölkchen, leichte weben"
*Wie Frühlingsahnung weht es durch die
Lande,* op. 7 no. 5 [Ries & Erler,
1894] same
Wiegenlied, op. 5 no. 2 [Fürstner;
Boosey & Hawkes] "Schlaf' ein,
gewieget an meiner Brust"
Zugvogel, op. 6 no. 3 [Fürstner, 1894;
Boosey & Hawkes]
"Schon will der Abend sinken"
Hebbel, Christian Friedrich, 1813-
1863.
Gebet, op. 26 no. 1 [Brockhaus, 1916]
"Die du über die Sterne weg"
Herbstbild, op. 21 no. 1 [Kahnt, 1907]
"Dies ist ein Herbsttag, wie ich keinen
sah"
Ich und Du, op. 11 no. 1 [Brockhaus,
1901] "Wir träumten von einander"
Heine, Heinrich, 1797-1856.
Es fällt ein Stern herunter, op. 4 no. 3
[Tischer & Jagenberg, 1889] same
Es fasst mich wieder der alte Mut, op. 4
no. 4 [Tischer & Jagenberg, 1889]
same
Es glänzt so schön die sinkende Sonne,
op. 4 no. 1 [Tischer & Jagenberg,
1889] same
Ich will mich im grünen Wald ergehn, op.
6 no. 2 [Fürstner, 1894; Boosey &
Hawkes] same
Die schlanke Wasserlilie
[Notenbeilage der **Neuen Musik-
Zeitschrift** III, 1949, Nr. 5/6] same
Wasserfahrt, op. 6 no. 6 [Fürstner, 1894;
Boosey & Hawkes]
"Ich stand gelehnet an den Mast"
LIEDERSTRAUSS.
Sie haben heut' Abend Gesellschaft,
op. 4 no. 2
[Tischer & Jagenberg, 1889] same
Heyse, Paul Johann Ludwig von,
1830-1914.
Über ein Stündlein, op. 7 no. 3 [Ries &
Erler, 1894]
"Dulde, gedulde dich fein"

Hölderlin, Friedrich, 1770-1843.
Abbitte, op. 29 no. 1 [Fürstner, 1922]
"Heilig Wesen"
Huch, Ricarda Octavia, 1864-1947.
Bestimmung, op. 35 no. 1 [Fürstner,
1924; Boosey & Hawkes]
"Was ist in deiner Seele"
Denn unsere Liebe hat zu heiss geflammt,
op. 35 no. 6 [Fürstner, 1924;
Boosey & Hawkes] same
Ich werde nicht an deinem Herzen satt,
op. 35 no. 2 [Fürstner, 1924;
Boosey & Hawkes] same
Eine Melodie singt mein Herz, op. 35 no.
5 [Fürstner, 1924; Boosey & Hawkes]
same
Schwill an, mein Strom, op. 35 no. 4
[Fürstner, 1924; Boosey & Hawkes]
same
Sehnsucht, op. 40 no. 3 [Peters, 1932]
"Um bei dir zu sein"
*Wo hast du all die Schönheit
hergenommen,* op. 35 no. 3
[Fürstner, 1924; Boosey & Hawkes]
same
Jacobowski, Ludwig, 1868-1900.
*Ich aber weiss, ich seh' dich manche
Nacht,* op. 11 no. 2 [Brockhaus, 1901]
same
Leuchtende Tage, op. 40 no. 1 [Peters,
1932] "Ach unsre leuchtenden Tage"
Kaufmann, Alexander, 1817-1893.
Verrat, op. 2 no. 7 [Brockhaus, 1889]
"Die Wasserlilie kichert leis"
Keller, Gottfried, 1819-1890.
Du milchjunger Knabe, op. 33 no. 3
[Fürstner, 1923; Boosey & Hawkes]
same
Ich fürcht' nit Gespenster, op. 33 no. 2
[Fürstner, 1923; Boosey & Hawkes]
same
Rös'chen biss den Apfel an, op. 33 no. 6
[Fürstner, 1923; Boosey & Hawkes]
same
Singt mein Schatz wie ein Fink, op. 33
no. 5 [Fürstner, 1923; Boosey &
Hawkes] same
Tretet ein, hoher Krieger, op. 33 no. 7
[Fürstner, 1923; Boosey & Hawkes]
same
Wandl' ich in dem Morgentau, op. 33 no.
4 [Fürstner, 1923; Boosey & Hawkes]
same
Wie glänzt der helle Mond, op. 33 no. 8
[Fürstner, 1923; Boosey & Hawkes]
same

ALTE WEISEN.
   Mir glänzen die Augen, op. 33 no. 1
    [Fürstner, 1923; Boosey & Hawkes]
    same
Leinhard, Friedrich
   Abendrot, op. 24 no. 4 [Brockhaus, 1909]
    "Mir ist nach einer Heimat weh"
Lenau, Nicolaus, 1802-1850.
   Sehnsucht nach Vergessen, op. 30 no. 1
    [Fürstner, 1922; Boosey & Hawkes]
    "Lethe! Brich die Fesseln des Ufers"
Liliencron, Detlov, Freiherr von, 1844-1909.
   Müde, op. 10 no. 2 [Brockhaus, 1898]
    "Auf dem Wege vom Tanzsaal nach
    Haus"
   Sehnsucht, op. 10 no. 1 [Brockhaus,
    1898] "Ich ging den Weg entlang"
Lingg, Hermann, 1820-1905.
   Immer leiser wird mein Schlummer, op. 2
    no. 6 [Brockhaus, 1889] same
   Kalt und schneidend, op. 2 no. 3
    [Brockhaus, 1889] same
Meyer, Conrad Ferdinand, 1825-1898.
   Eingelegte Ruder, op. 32 no. 3 [Fürstner,
    1923; Boosey & Hawkes]
    "Meine eingelegten Ruder triefen"
   Hussens Kerker, op. 32 no. 1 [Fürstner,
    1923; Boosey & Hawkes]
    "Es geht mit mir zu Ende"
   Lass scharren deiner Rosse Hug, op. 32
    no. 4 [Fürstner, 1923; Boosey &
    Hawkes]
      "Geh nicht, die Gott für mich
      erschuf"
   Säerspruch, op. 32 no. 2 [Fürstner, 1923;
    Boosey & Hawkes]
    "Bemesst den Schritt"
Mörike, Eduard Friedrich, 1804-1875.
   Denk es, O Seele, op. 30 no. 3 [Fürstner,
    1922; Boosey & Hawkes]
    "Ein Tännlein grünet wo"
   Das verlassene Mägdelein [Ries & Erler,
    1933] "Früh, wann die Hähne krähen"
    NB: No. 5 of *Sechs Jugendlieder*
    (1884/87).
   Das verlassene Mägdlein, op. 30 no. 2
    [Fürstner, 1922; Boosey & Hawkes]
    "Früh, wann die Hähne krähen"
Müller von Königswinter, Wolfgang, 1816-1873.
   Hast du von den Fischerkindern, op. 7
    no. 1 [Ries & Erler, 1894] same
Petrarca, Francesco, 1304-1374.
   Zweiundneunzigstes Sonnet von Petrarca,
    op. 24 no. 3 [Brockhaus, 1909]

    "Voll jener Süsse"
Redwitz, Oskar, Freiherr von, 1823-1891.
   Nun, da so warm der Sonnenschein
    [Ries & Erler, 1933] same
Reinick, Robert, 1805-1852.
   Kuriose Geschichte [Ries & Erler, 1933]
    "Ich bin einmal etwas hinausspaziert"
Rückert, Friedrich, 1788-1866.
   Herbsthauch, op. 29 no. 2 [Fürstner,
    1922] "Herz, nun so alt"
   Warum sind deine Augen denn so nass,
    op. 3 no. 1 [Tischer & Jagenberg,
    1889] same
Sallet, Friedrich von, 1812-1843.
   Herbstlied, op. 3 no. 2 [Tischer &
    Jagenberg, 1889]
    "Durch die Wälder streif ich munter"
Sturm, Julius Karl Reinholdt, 1816-1896.
   Abendlied [Ries & Erler, 1933]
    "Der Tag neigt sich zu Ende"
Uhland, Ludwig, 1787-1862.
   Naturfreiheit [Ries & Erler, 1933]
    "Leben, das nur Leben scheinet"
Unknown
   Im tiefen Wald verborgen, op. 2 no. 4
    [Brockhaus, 1889] same
   Zweifelnde Liebe, op. 6 no. 1 [Fürstner,
    1894; Boosey & Hawkes]
    "Blau der See, vom hohen Schilfe"
Volkmann, Richard von, 1830-1889.
   *In der Früh, wenn die Sonne kommen
    will,* op. 2 no. 1 [Brockhaus, 1889]
    same
   Ist der Himmel darum im Lenz so blau,
    op. 2 no. 2 [Brockhaus, 1889] same
Wackernagel, Ilse (Stach von Goltzheim), 1879-1941.
   An die Mark, op. 15 no. 3 [Brockhaus,
    1904] "Bereifte Kiefern, atemlose
    Seen"
Walther von der Vogelweide, 12th cent.
   Gewalt der Minne, op. 24 no. 2
    [Brockhaus, 1909]
    "Wer gab dir, Minne, die Gewalt"
   Unter der Linden bei der Haide, op. 24
    no. 1 [Brockhaus, 1909] same
Pfizer, Gustav, 1807-1890.
   LOEWE *Der Junggesell*
*Der Pflanze, die dort über dem Abgrund
  schwebt see* Pfau **SCHÖNBERG**
Pfleger-Moravský, Gustav, 1833-1875.
   DVOŘÁK
   Já vím, že v sladké naději

COMPOSER Poet *Title* "First Line"

Pfleger-Moravský, Gustav, 1833-1875
   (continued)
   DVOŘÁK *(continued)*
      Two settings: B. 11 no. 6 and B. 160
      no. 4.
   Kol domu se ted' potácím
      Two settings: B. 123 no. 3 and B. 160
      no. 3.
   Kol domuse
   Mé srdce často vbolesti
      Three settings: B. 11 no. 11, B. 123
      no. 6, and B. 124 no. 3.
   Mne často tỳrá pochyba
   Mou celou duší zádumně bolestné
   Na horách ticho a vúdolí ticho
   Na horách ticho a vúdolích ticho
   Na horách ticho, vúdolí ticho
   Nad krajem vévodí lehký spánek
      Two settings: B. 11 no. 17 and B. 160
      no. 5.
   Ó byl to krásný zlatý sen
      Three settings: B.11 no. 5, B. 123 no.
      2, and B. 124 no. 2.
   Ó, duše drahá, jedinká
   Ó duše drahá jedinkájež
   Ó, naší lásce
   Ó, naší lásce nekvete
      Two settings: B. 123 no. 4 and B. 160
      no. 1.
   Ó zlatá ruže, spatnilá
   Tam stojí stará skála
   Ty se ptáš pročmoje zpěvy bouří
   Vtak mnohém srdci mrtvojest
      Two settings: B. 11 no. 3 and B. 160
      no. 2.
   Vté sladké moci
   Vté sladké moci očí tvých
   Vy vroucí písně pějte
      Two settings: B. 11 no. 1 and B. 123
      no. 1.
   Vy vroucí písně spějte
   Zde hledím na tendrahý list
   Zde v lese u potoka
      Two settings: B. 11 no. 14 and B. 160
      no. 6.
Pflicht und Liebe see Gotter **SCHUBERT**
Pflügerin Sorge see Morgenstern **REGER**
Pflügerlied see Salis-Seewis **SCHUBERT**
Phaedra's farewell see Racine **THOMSON**
Phanomen see Goethe *WESTÖSTLICHER*
   DIVAN: Buch des Sängers. **WOLF**
Phantasie see Tellez *EL BURLADOR DE*
   SEVILLA. **MAHLER**
Phantoms see Giovannitti **GRIFFES**
Phantoms see Tabb **GRIFFES**
"Phantoms of the future" *see* Omens and
   oracles Unknown **IVES**

Phemister, Bruce
   ROREM *Pagan*
Phidile see Claudius, M. **SCHOECK,**
   SCHUBERT
Phidylé see Leconte de Lisle **DUPARC**
PHILÉMON ET BAUCIS. see La Fontaine
   Ni l'or ni la grandeur **GOUNOD**
Philine see Goethe *WILHELM MEISTER.*
   WOLF
Philip, John *see* Phillip, John
Philis see Anon. **SÉVERAC**
Phillip, John
   BRITTEN *The nurse's song*
   THE COMMODYE OF PACIENT AND
      MEEKE GRISSILL (1566).
   HESELTINE *Cradle song*
Philomel see Barnefield **ROREM**
"Philosophes rêveurs, qui pensez tout savoir"
   see Chanson à boire du vieux temp
   Boileau-Despréaux **SAINT-SAËNS**
"Philule, tu t'étires comme une majuscule de
   vieux missel" *see Arc-en-ciel d'innocence*
   Messiaen **MESSIAEN**
"Phoebe sat, sweet she sat" *see Montanus'*
   sonnet Lodge, T. **RIETI**
"Phöbus, mit lokkerem Zügel" *see Abendlied*
   im Freien Kind, F. **ZELTER**
"Phoebus tucks all his arrows away" *see*
   Chamber music Kreymborg **THOMSON**
Pholoé see Leconte de Lisle **HAHN**
Phyllis see Leconte de Lisle **HAHN**
"Piange lenta la luna" *see Contrasto*
   Zangarini **RESPIGHI**
"Piangea un di pensando" *see Canzonetta*
   spagnuola "En medio a mis colores"
   Unknown **ROSSINI**
Pianto antico see Carducci **CASELLA**
Piat' pesen bez slov see No author
   PROKOFIEV
Piave, Francesco Maria, 1810-1876.
   VERDI *Barcarola*
Picard, Hélène
   MASSENET *Dormons parmi les lis*
Piccola mano bianca see Rocchi, Francesco
   RESPIGHI
Piccola serenata see Bernstein
   BERNSTEIN
DIE PICCOLOMINI. see Schiller
   Des Mädchens Klage **MENDELSSOHN-**
      BARTHOLDY, SCHUBERT, ZELTER
      Three Schubert settings: D. 6, D. 191,
      and D. 389.
Pichler, Karoline (Greiner), 1769-1843.
   SCHUBERT
   Lied
   Der Sänger am Felsen

OLIVIER.
SCHUBERT *Der Unglückliche*
Picture of a mood see Klen, V. **MARTINŮ**
"Pie au nid, tchi, tchi, tchi" *see La petite pie*
Unknown **STRAVINSKĬĬ**
Pièce de circonstance see Cocteau
MILHAUD
Pièce en forme de Habanera see No author
RAVEL *Vocalise-étude en forme de*
Habanera
The pied piper see Bryusov
RACHMANINOFF *The rat-catcher*
"Les pieds les chevaux emportés par la mer"
see Invasion D'Harcourt, Antoniette
SAUGUET
Pielgrzym see Tetmajer **SZYMANOWSKI**
Pieni ballaadi see Lönnbohm **KILPINEN**
Pierre d'Amor
MASSENET *Voix de femmes*
Pierre d'Amour *see* Pierre d'Amor
Pierre de Ronsard *see* Ronsard, Pierre
de, 1524-1585.
Les Pierreries see Banville **KOECHLIN**
Pierrot see Banville *LES CARIATIDES,* livre
3, no. VI. **DEBUSSY**
Pierrot see Teasdale **GRIFFES**
"Pierrot qui n'a rien d'un Clitandre" *see*
Pantomime Verlaine **DEBUSSY**
"Pierrot stands in the garden" *see Pierrot*
Teasdale **GRIFFES**
Pierścien see Witwicki **CHOPIN**
Piérwiosnek see Mickiewicz **LOEWE**
Die Schlüsselblume
Piesenka medviedia see Anon.
STRAVINSKĬĬ *Chanson de l'ours*
Pieśń o fali see Szymanowska, Zafia
SZYMANOWSKI
PIEŚNI KURPIOWSKIE, no. 1
SZYMANOWSKI Anon. *Lecioly zurazie*
PIEŚNI KURPIOWSKIE, no. 2
SZYMANOWSKI Anon. *Wysla burzycka*
PIEŚNI KURPIOWSKIE, no. 3
SZYMANOWSKI Anon. *Uwoz, mamo*
PIEŚNI KURPIOWSKIE, no. 4
SZYMANOWSKI Anon. *U jeziorecka*
PIEŚNI KURPIOWSKIE, no. 5
SZYMANOWSKI Anon.
A pod borem siwe kunie
PIEŚNI KURPIOWSKIE, no. 6
SZYMANOWSKI Anon. *Bzicem kunia*
PIEŚNI KURPIOWSKIE, no. 7
SZYMANOWSKI Anon. *Ściani dumbek*
PIEŚNI KURPIOWSKIE, no. 8
SZYMANOWSKI Anon.
Leć, glosie, po rosie
PIEŚNI KURPIOWSKIE, no. 9

SZYMANOWSKI Anon. *Zarzyjze, kuniu*
PIEŚNI KURPIOWSKIE, no. 10
SZYMANOWSKI Anon.
Ciamna nocka, ciamna
PIEŚNI KURPIOWSKIE, no. 11
SZYMANOWSKI Anon.
Wysly rybki, sysly
PIEŚNI KURPIOWSKIE, no. 12
SZYMANOWSKI Anon.
Wsyscy przyjechali
Pietà see Rilke **HINDEMITH**
Pietà, Signor see Boito *AGNUS DEI.* **VERDI**
"Pietà, Signor, Pietà Signor" *see Pietà, Signor*
Boito **VERDI**
Pigeons on the grass see Stein *FOUR*
SAINTS IN 3 ACTS. **THOMSON**
PIGER PAA ENGEN. see Aakjaer
Nu er Dagen fuld af Sang **NIELSEN**
Piggesnie see Anon. **HESELTINE**
PIJPER, WILLEM, 1894-1947.
Anon.
Het wasser te nacht (1923) [Amsterdam:
Broekmans & Van Poppel, 1923] same
Het windetje die uyt den oosten waeyt
(1923) [Amsterdam: Broekmans &
Van Poppel, 1923] same
Bruyn, Bertha de
Meiliedje (1916) [Donemus, 1950]
" 'k Zit voor mijn venster"
Nachtliedje (1914) [Donemus, 1950]
"Slaap, lief kind-je, zacht"
Sneeuwklokjes (1916) [Donemus, 1950]
"Lieve, reine, witte Klokjes"
Vlinderliedje (1915) [Donemus, 1950]
"Licht gewiekte vlinders zweven"
Clercq, René de
Douwdeuntje (1916) [Donemus, 1950]
"Ik hoor hem nog"
Van den Oever [unpubl.?]
"Ronk, bonk klitse klets"
A fragment, no date.
Fitger, Arthur, 1840-1909.
Ich liege Dir zu Füssen (1913)
[Donemus, 1954] same
Die Spinnerin [unpubl.?]
"Rolle liebe Spindel"
A fragment.
Die Spinnerin (1913) [Donemus, 1954]
"Gestern sasz ich wie ich sasz"
LIEDER VOM MAURERGESELLEN.
Wanderschaft (1912) [unpubl.?]
"Ich bin ein jung jung Malergesell"
Gilm zu Rosenegg, Hermann von,
1812-1864.
LETZTE BLÄTTER.
Allerseelen, op. 9b (1914) [Donemus,
1950] "Stell' auf den Tisch die
duftenden Reseden"

PIJPER, WILLEM, 1894-1947 *(continued)*
Koster, Edward Bernard, 1861-1937.
Nacht (1912) [Donemus, 1953]
"De rosse mann trekt langzaam"
Over den eenzamen vijver, op. 1 no. 3
(1912) [Donemus, 1953] same
Lenau, Nicolaus, 1802-1850.
SCHILFLIEDER.
Auf geheimen Waldespfade, op. 1 no. 5
(1913) [unpubl.?] same
Unknown
Mariazang (1929) [Amsterdam:
Broekmans & Van Poppel]
"God groet u coninghinne"
16th century text.
La Maumariée I (1919) [Senart, 1923]
"Un soir me promenant dans mon
jardin"
La Maumariée II (1920) [Senart, 1923]
"Mon père me marie à l'âge de quinze
ans"
Der Schäfer (1911) [lost]
Schiftlieder [lost]
Pilgers Tod see Oehlenschläger ZELTER
Pilgerspruch see Fleming
MENDELSSOHN-BARTHOLDY
Pilgerweise see Schober SCHUBERT
Der Pilgrim see Schiller SCHUBERT
Der Pilgrim vor St. Just see Platen-
Hallermünde LOEWE
The pilgrim's psalm see Bible
VAUGHAN WILLIAMS
The pillars see Bal'mont PROKOFIEV
Stolby
Piloktet see Mayrhofer SCHUBERT
"Pilule, viens, dansons" *see Danse du bébé-
Phile* Messiaen MESSIAEN
Pimeä isoton pirtti see Kanteletar
KILPINEN
Pimpinella see Chaïkovskiĭ CHAĬKOVSKIĬ
The pine and the palm see Heine *LYRICAL
INTERMEZZO.* RIMSKIĬ-KORSAKOV
El' i pal'ma
The pine-tree see Lermontov BALAKIREV
Sosna
Pingst see Österling KILPINEN
Pink flush of dawn see Pushkin
PROKOFIEV *Rumianoĭ zareĭu pokrylsis
vostok*
La Pintade see Renard *HISTOIRES
NATURELLES.* RAVEL
Pintos, Carlos Rodriguez *see* Rodriguez-
Pintos, Carlos, b. 1895
Pioggia see Aganoor-Pompilj RESPIGHI
Piosnka litewska see Anon. CHOPIN

"Piovea; per le finestre spalancate" *see
Pioggia* Aganoor-Pompilj RESPIGHI
The piper see Blake, William *SONGS OF
INNOCENCE:* Introduction.
VAUGHAN WILLIAMS
A piper see Starkey
VAUGHAN WILLIAMS
"The piper came to our town" *see The piper
of Dundee* Unknown RESPIGHI
"A piper in the streets today" *see A piper*
Starkey VAUGHAN WILLIAMS
The piper of Dundee see Unknown
RESPIGHI
"Piping down the valleys wild" *see The piper*
Blake, William VAUGHAN WILLIAMS
THE PIRATE. see Scott
Gesang der Norna SCHUBERT
Pirushka see Kol'tsov MUSORGSKIĬ
Píseň see Mužik MARTINŮ *Song*
Píseň na starošpanělský text see
Eben, Bedřich MARTINŮ
Píseň prvního listopadu see Hlavsa, Vrat.
MARTINŮ *Song of the First of November*
*Pis'mo K. S. Stanislavskomer ot S.
Rakhmaninova see* Rachmaninoff
RACHMANINOFF
Letter to K. S. Stanislavsky from S. R.
Písnička O Haničce see Kalhus MARTINŮ
Song of Hanička
Písnička skřítku see Goethe *ELFENLIED.*
MARTINŮ *Elfenliedchen*
PÍSNIČKY NA DVĚ STRÁNKY, no. 1
MARTINŮ Anon. *Děvče z Moravy*
PÍSNIČKY NA DVĚ STRÁNKY, no. 2
MARTINŮ Anon. *Súsedova stajňa*
PÍSNIČKY NA DVĚ STRÁNKY, no. 3
MARTINŮ Anon. *Naděje*
PÍSNIČKY NA DVĚ STRÁNKY, no. 4
MARTINŮ Anon. *Hlásný*
PÍSNIČKY NA DVĚ STRÁNKY, no. 5
MARTINŮ Anon. *Tajná láska*
PÍSNIČKY NA DVĚ STRÁNKY, no. 6
MARTINŮ Anon. *Boží muka*
PÍSNIČKY NA DVĚ STRÁNKY, no. 7
MARTINŮ Anon. *Zvolenovcí chlapci*
PÍSNIČKY NA JEDNU STRÁNKU, no. 1
MARTINŮ Unknown *Rosička*
PÍSNIČKY NA JEDNU STRÁNKU, no. 2
MARTINŮ Unknown *Otevření slovečkem*
PÍSNIČKY NA JEDNU STRÁNKU, no. 3
MARTINŮ Unknown *Cesta k milé*
PÍSNIČKY NA JEDNU STRÁNKU, no. 4
MARTINŮ Unknown *Chodníček*
PÍSNIČKY NA JEDNU STRÁNKU, no. 5
MARTINŮ Unknown *U maměnky*

PÍSNIČKY NA JEDNU STRÁNKU, no. 6
   MARTINŮ Unknown *Sen Panny Marie*
PÍSNIČKY NA JEDNU STRÁNKU, no. 7
   MARTINŮ Unknown *Rozmarýn*
Pitchford, Kenneth Lee, 1930-
   ROREM
     Jacquelin Gray
     Song for lying in bed during a night rain
Pitchounette *see* Normand **MASSENET**
"Pitchounette, entends-tu pas" *see*
   Pitchounette Normand **MASSENET**
"Pitié! Mon coeur est gonflé d'amertume" *see*
   Angoisse Bazenery, F. **INDY**
Pitkä on tuskan tie see Jalkanen **KILPINEN**
Pito, pito, colorito see Anon. **MOMPOU**
Pitoëff, Georges, 1886-1939.
   TU NE M'ÉCHAPPERAS JAMAIS.
   MILHAUD
     La bohémienne la main n'a prls
     Un petit pas, deux petits pas
"Pity me on my pilgrimage to Loch Derg!"
   see At St. Patrick's Purgatory
   O'Faolain, Sean, translator. **BARBER**
"I più bei fior comprate" *see La fioraja*
   fiorentina Unknown **ROSSINI**
"Piubovnik rozysoloveĭ" *see Pesnia Ziuleĭki*
   Byron **RIMSKIĬ-KORSAKOV**
PIZZETTI, ILDEBRANDO, 1880-1968.
Annunzio, Gabriele d', 1863-1938.
   Erotica (1911) [Pizzi, 1922;
     Bongiovanni, 1924]
     "Ondeggiano i letti di rose"
   LAUDI.
     I Pastori (1908) [Forlivesi, 1916]
       "Settembre, andiamo"
       Also for voice & orchestra.
Anon.
   Augurio (1932-33) [Ricordi, 1933]
     "In Rumelia c'è un albero frondoso"
     Also published as no. 1, *Tre canti*
     grechi.
   Bebro e il suo cavallo (1944) [Forlivesi,
     1945] "A Vardari, a Vardari, nel
     campo di Vardari"
     Also for voice and orchestra.
   Bella lucente luna [Forlivesi, 1960] same
   Canzone per ballo (1932-33) [Ricordi,
     1933] "Godete, giovani, godete"
     Also published as no. 3, *Tre canti*
     grechi.
   Il Clefta prigione (1912) [Forlivesi, 1916]
     "Oggi, Demo, gli è pasqua, oggi fiera"
   Mirologio per un bambino (1932-33)
     "Non nella bella estate"
     Also published as no. 2, *Tre canti*
     grechi.

San Basilio (1912) [Forlivesi, 1916]
   "San Basilio viene di Cesarea"
Bocchialini, Jacopo
   E il mio dolore io canto (1940)
     [Forlivesi, 1945]
     "Io sonoun'arida fonte"
   Sei tornato da me (1951) [unpubl.]
Buonarroti, Michel Angelo, 1475-1564.
   Vorrei voler, Signor, quel ch'io non
     voglio (1944) [Forlivesi, 1945] same
Canticum Canticorum
   Adjuro vos, filiae Jerusalem (1908)
     [unpubl.]
     Antiphon (Song of Songs).
   Adjuro vos, filiae Jerusalem (1932-33)
     [Ricordi, 1933]
   In lectulo meo (1908) [unpubl.]
     Antiphon (Song of Songs).
   Surge, propera, amica mia [Forlivesi,
     1960] "Surge, surge, surge, propera
     amica mea"
Cocconi, Ildebrando
   Incontro di Marzo (1904)
     [Trieste: Schmidl; Milano: Casa
       Editricc Musicale Italiana, 1908]
       "Guardami dunque! Io sono sempre
       quella"
   Remember (1904)
     [Trieste: Schmidl; Milano: Casa
       Editrice Musicale Italiana, 1908]
       "Nulla cosa quaggiù e più triste"
   Vigilia Nuziale (1904)
     [Trieste: Schmidl; Milano: Casa
       Editricc Musicale Italiana, 1908]
       "Oggi tremi ne l'aria profumata"
Dalliba, Gerda, 1885-1913.
   My cry (1919) [unpubl.]
Dazzi, Manlio
   In questa notte carica di stelle (1944)
     [Forlivesi, 1945] same
     Also for voice and orchestra.
Giacomo, Salvatore di, 1862-1934.
   Angeleca (1916-18) [Forlivesi, 1918]
     "È 'a notte 'e Pasca. A ll'unnece"
     Also with orchestra, unpublished.
   Assunta (1916-18) [Forlivesi, 1918]
     "Io lle diceva: – Sienteme!"
     Also with orchestra, unpublished.
Hugo, Victor Marie, comte, 1802-1885.
   Epitaphe (1903) [Firenze, **La nuova**
     musica, p. 14 (Album 1911)]
     Information from **New Grove.**
No author
   Tre vocalizzi (1929) [Ricordi, 1929:
     Vocalizzi nell stile moderno . . .]

COMPOSER Poet *Title* "First Line"

PIZZETTI, ILDEBRANDO, 1880-1968
(continued)
No author *(continued)*
Vocalise-étude (1929) [Leduc, 1929]
In *Répertoire moderne de Vocalises-Etudes,* v. 7, no. 68.
Vocalizzo (1957) [Curci, 1958]
Revised, 1960, for mezzo-soprano & orchestra.
Pàntini, Romualdo
CANTILENE ALL'ARIA APERTA.
La Madre al figlio lontano (1910) [Forlivesi, 1916] "O figlio, figlio, in che mondo ti trovi?"
Papini, Giovanni, 1881-1956.
Passeggiata (1915) [Forlivesi, 1916] "Due in confidenzo, dritti come re"
Petrarca, Francesco, 1304-1374.
Levommi il mio pensier (1922) [Ricordi, 1923] same
Quel Rosignuol (1922) [Ricordi, 1923] same
La vita fugge (1922) [Ricordi, 1923] same
Sappho, 625? B.C.-570 B.C.
Oscuro è il ciel (1931) [Ricordi, 1933] same
Also for voice and orchestra.
Scuote amore il mio cuori [Forlivesi, 1960] same
Silvani, Mario, 1884-1913.
Sera d'Inverno (1907) [Trieste: Schmidl; Milano: Casa Editrice Musicale Italiana, 1908] "Muore il giorno invernale tra un pio lamentar di campane" NYPL copy's imprint covered by label of Casa musicale Giuliana, Trieste.
Teresa of Avila, Saint, 1515-1582.
L'annuncio (1908) [Firenze: Grandi Magazzini di Musica Estera e Italiana, 1912?]
Unknown
Nuvole (1899) [unpubl.]
Zerbini, Alfredo
Al Marchesén, povrén, ch'l'era un bulot (1947-49) [unpubl.]
Che cälma in gir! Che päza sepolcräla! (1947-49) [unpubl.]
La va pian pian cla portanten'na scura (1947-49) [unpubl.]
Place des Invalides see Cocteau AURIC
Placet futile see Mallarmé DEBUSSY, RAVEL
"Placez à mon côté ma plume" *see Dernières volontés* Veuillot GOUNOD

Plain-ciel see Jacqueton, Henry SAUGUET
Plainte see Tastu MILHAUD, SAINT-SAËNS
Plainte de Thécla see Schiller INDY
Plaisir d'aimer see Unknown BEETHOVEN
A plan see Carpenter, Rue CARPENTER
Platen, August von *see* Platen-Hallermünde, August, Graf von, 1796-1835.
Platen-Hallermünde, August, Graf von, 1796-1835.
BRAHMS
Du sprichst, dass ich mich täuschte
Ich schleich umher betrübt
Der Strom, der neben mir verrauschte
Wehe, so willst du mich wieder
Wie rafft' ich mich auf in der Nacht
BRUCKNER *Mein Herz und deine Stimme*
CORNELIUS
Ode
Vision
LOEWE *Der Pilgrim vor St. Just*
SCHUBERT
Du liebst mich nicht
Die Liebe hat gelogen
SCHUMANN *Ihre Stimme*
WOLF *Ghazél*
Platner, Anton, 1787-1855.
SCHUBERT *Die Blumensprache*
Plato, ca.429-347 B.C.
BERKELEY *To Aster*
ROREM *Two songs on words of Plato*
Play acting see Anon. HESELTINE
"Play de blues for me" *see That soothin' song* Hughes, L. CARPENTER
Play for me see Trustman, Deborah WEISGALL
The player queen see Yeats CARPENTER
THE PLEASANT COMOEDY OF PATIENT GRISSILL (1603). *see* Dekker
Lullaby HESELTINE
Sweet content HESELTINE
The pleasant summer's come see Burns FRANZ
"Pleasure it is to hear" *see A thanksgiving* Johanus Bassus IRELAND
"The Pleiades are sinking cool as paint" *see Lesbos* Durrell, L. BERKELEY
Plein eau see Haraucourt KOECHLIN
"Pleins d'un concert de fraîches voix" *see Je m'en suis allé vers l'amour* Maurer MASSENET
"Pleje děva konopí u panskéhe sada" *see Skřivánek* Unknown DVOŘÁK

Plenivshis' pozoĭ, soloveĭ see Kol'tsov
RIMSKIĭ-KORSAKOV
Pleshcheyev, Alekseĭ Nikolayevich,
1825-1893.
   CHAĭKOVSKIĭ
     Babushka i vnuchek
     Kolybel'naĭa pesn' v
     Legenda
     Lish' ty odin"
     Moĭ sadik
     Na beregu
     Ni slova, O drug" moĭ
     O, eslib" znali vy
     O, spoĭ zhe tu pesniu
     Osen'
     Vesennyaya pesnya
     Vesna
       Two settings: Op. 54 no. 3 and op. 54
       no. 9.
     Zima
     Zimniĭ vecher
   MUSORGSKIĭ
     Akh, zachem tvoi glazki poroiu
     List'ia shumeli unylo
     Vecherniaia pesenka
   RIMSKIĭ-KORSAKOV *Noch'*
   PODSNEZHNIK.
     CHAĭKOVSKIĭ *Ptichka*
   SLOVA DLYA MUZĬKI.
     CHAĭKOVSKIĭ *Nam zvezdy krotkie*
     siiali
Pletzsch, Oskar
   STRAUSS *Der böhmische Musikant*
"Pleurez, doux alcyons, Ô vous" *see La jeune*
   tarentine Chénier **KOECHLIN**
"Pleurons nos chagrins, chacun le nôtre" *see*
   Larmes Richepin **FAURÉ**
Les pleurs des femmes see Pavloff, Mme.
   LISZT *Oh pourquoi donc*
Plönnies, Louise von, 1803-1872.
   LOEWE
     Agnete
     Der kleine Schiffer
"Plötzlich wird es schwarz zwischen den
   weissen Gipfeln" *see Gewitter* Krenek
   KRENEK
Ploug, Carl, 1813-1894.
   NIELSEN *St. St. Blicher*
La pluie see Richepin **CHAUSSON**
La pluie au matin see Louÿs *CHANSONS DE*
   BILITIS. **GIDEON, KOECHLIN**
"La pluie, hésitante et sans bruit" *see Grisaille*
   Catteau **AUBERT**
"La pluie, la pluie aux doigts verts" *see*
   La pluie Richepin **CHAUSSON**
Plum pudding see Dumont *LA BONNE*
   CUISINE FRANÇAISE. **BERNSTEIN**

Plume d'eau clair see Éluard **POULENC**
PLUMES, no. 1
   SAUGUET Gabory *O jeunes filles*
PLUMES, no. 2
   SAUGUET Gabory *Puisque Vénus*
PLUMES, no. 3
   SAUGUET Gabory *Tombé du ciel dans la*
     mansarde
"Les plus ardentes amours" *see Tout passé*
   Bruno, Camille **MASSENET**
Le plus beau présent see Magre **HAHN**
Le plus doux chemin see Silvestre **FAURÉ**
Plus rien ne me tient aux pieds see Éluard
   SAUGUET
Plus vite see Văcărescu **MASSENET**
Plus vite, mon cheval see Geibel **DELIUS**
   O schneller mein ross
Plusieurs de leurs corps dénués see Ronsard
   MILHAUD
Po cestách zavátých see Toman
   DIE MONATE: Januar. **MARTINŮ**
   On snow-swept paths
Po Chü-i, 772-846.
   BRITTEN
     Depression
     The old lute
Po griby see Mei **MUSORGSKIĭ**
Po nad Donom sad tsvetet see Kol'tsov
   MUSORGSKIĭ
Po nebu polunochi see Lermontov
   RIMSKIĭ-KORSAKOV
Pochyl sie cicho nad kolyska see
   Iwaszkiewicz **SZYMANOWSKI**
"Poco è l'ora omai lontana" *see Mezza notte*
   Shenshin **CHAĭKOVSKIĭ**
Pod krysheĭ see Gorianskogo, V.
   PROKOFIEV
"Pod murami Szirazu lezy piekna Mozella"
   see Grób Hafiza Hafiz **SZYMANOWSKI**
"Pod našima oknama" *see Rozmarýn*
   Unknown **MARTINŮ**
"Pod oknom, chulok starushka" *see*
   Babushka i vnuchek Pleshcheyev
   CHAĭKOVSKIĭ
Podbliudnaia see Anon. **STRAVINSKIĭ**
   Le moineau est assis
Podruga boytsa see Mendel'son
   PROKOFIEV
PODSNEZHNIK. see Pleshcheyev
   Ptichka **CHAĭKOVSKIĭ**
Podvig see Khomyakov **CHAĭKOVSKIĭ**
"Podvig est' iv srazhen' i" *see Podvig*
   Khomyakov **CHAĭKOVSKIĭ**
Poe, Edgar Allan, 1809-1849.
   LOEFFLER
     A dream within a dream
     To Helen

Poe, Edgar Allan, 1809-1849 *(continued)*
MARTINŮ *The sleeper*
A DREAM.
    SÉVERAC *Un rêve*
Poekhal na polochke see **Musorgskiĭ**
    MUSORGSKIĬ
Poem see Dropkin **WEISGALL**
    Two settings: 197_ and 1972.
Poem see Goodman **ROREM**
    The lordly Hudson
Poem see Koch **ROREM**
Poem for F see Roditi **ROREM**
Poem: I will always love you see O'Hara
    ROREM
Poem: The nightingale see Rorem **ROREM**
POEMA EN FORMA DE CANCIONES, no.
    2
    TURINA Campoamor y Campoosorio
    Nunca olvida
POEMA EN FORMA DE CANCIONES, no.
    3
    TURINA Campoamor y Campoosorio
    Cantares
POEMA EN FORMA DE CANCIONES, no.
    4
    TURINA Campoamor y Campoosorio
    Los dos miedos
POEMA EN FORMA DE CANCIONES, no.
    5
    TURINA Campoamor y Campoosorio
    Las locas por amor
POEMA PARADISIACO. see Annunzio
    La najade **RESPIGHI**
    La sera **RESPIGHI**
    Un sogno **RESPIGHI**
    Sopra un'aria antica **RESPIGHI**
Un poème see Apollinaire *IL Y A.*
    POULENC
POÈME D'AMOUR, no. 1
    MASSENET Robiquet *Je me suis plaint
    aux tourterelles*
POÈME D'AMOUR, no. 2
    MASSENET Robiquet *La nuit sans doute
    était trop belle*
POÈME D'AMOUR, no. 3
    MASSENET Robiquet *Ouvre tes yeux
    bleus*
POÈME D'AMOUR, no. 4
    MASSENET Robiquet *Puisqu'elle a pris
    ma vie*
POÈME D'AMOUR, no. 5
    MASSENET Robiquet *Pourquoi pleures-
    tu?*
POÈME D'AMOUR, no. 6
    MASSENET Robiquet *Oh! ne finis
    jamais*

POÈME D'AVRIL, no. 1
    MASSENET Silvestre *Prélude*
POÈME D'AVRIL, no. 2
    MASSENET Silvestre *Sonnet matinal*
POÈME D'AVRIL, no. 3
    MASSENET Silvestre *Voici que les
    grand lys*
POÈME D'AVRIL, no. 4
    MASSENET Silvestre *Riez-vous?*
POÈME D'AVRIL, no. 5
    MASSENET Silvestre *Vous aimerez
    demain*
POÈME D'AVRIL, no. 6
    MASSENET Silvestre *Que l'heure est
    donc brève*
POÈME D'AVRIL, no. 7
    MASSENET Silvestre *Sur la source*
POÈME D'AVRIL, no. 8
    MASSENET Silvestre *Complainte*
Poème de Corneille see Corneille
    MILHAUD
POÈME D'HIVER, no. 1
    MASSENET Silvestre *C'est au temps de
    la Chrysantheme*
POÈME D'HIVER, no. 2
    MASSENET Silvestre *Mon coeur est
    plein de toi*
POÈME D'HIVER, no. 3
    MASSENET Silvestre *Noël*
POÈME D'HIVER, no. 4
    MASSENET Silvestre *Je ne sais pas
    t'aimer*
POÈME D'HIVER, no. 5
    MASSENET Silvestre *Mon amour l'a
    bien mérité*
Poème d'Octobre (IV) see Collin
    CHAÏKOVSKIĬ *Qu'importe que l'hiver*
POÈME D'OCTOBRE
    MASSENET Collin *Prelude*
POÈME D'OCTOBRE, no. 1
    MASSENET Collin *Automne*
POÈME D'OCTOBRE, no. 2
    MASSENET Collin *Les marronniers*
POÈME D'OCTOBRE, no. 3
    MASSENET Collin *Qu'importe que
    l'hiver*
POÈME D'OCTOBRE, no. 4
    MASSENET Collin *Roses d'Octobre*
POÈME D'OCTOBRE, no. 5
    MASSENET Collin *Pareils à des oiseaux*
Poème du "Gitanjali" see Tagore
    GITANJALI. **MILHAUD**
Poème du journal intime de Léo Latil see
    Latil **MILHAUD**
POÈME DU SOUVENIR, no. 1
    MASSENET Silvestre *Lève-toi, lève-toi*

COMPOSER   Poet   *Title*   ''First Line''

"Le poète dort" *see Anniversaire* Silvestre
  MASSENET
"Le poète est roi" *see Royauté* Boyer,
  Georges **MASSENET**
Le poète et le fantôme see Anon.
  MASSENET
Le poète mourant see Lamartine
  SAINT-SAËNS
POETISCHES TAGEBUCH. see Schulze
  Im Walde **SCHUBERT**
Poetry see De La Mare **BERKELEY**
THE POET'S ECHO, no. 1
  BRITTEN Pushkin *Echo*
THE POET'S ECHO, no. 2
  BRITTEN Pushkin *My heart . . .*
THE POET'S ECHO, no. 3
  BRITTEN Pushkin *Angel*
THE POET'S ECHO, no. 4
  BRITTEN Pushkin *The nightingale and
    the rose*
THE POET'S ECHO, no. 5
  BRITTEN Pushkin *Epigram*
THE POET'S ECHO, no. 6
  BRITTEN Pushkin *Lines written during a
    sleepless night*
Poet's song see Cummings **COPLAND**
  Song
Pogodi! see Grekov **CHAÏKOVSKIÏ**
Pohl, Richard, 1826-1896.
  LISZT *Jugendglück*
"Poika nuori kaupunkihin läksi myötätuulta"
  see Kaupunkimatka Lönnbohm
  KILPINEN
"Les poils de cette chèvre et mêmc" *see La
  chèvre du Thibet* Apollinaire **POULENC**
"Poïmi khot'raz″ tosklivoe priznan'e" *see
  Poymi khotraz* Shenshin **CHAÏKOVSKIÏ**
Le point see Claudel **MILHAUD**
Poirson, S. Cuthbert
  MASSENET *Rose de Mai*
"Pois painuu päivä" *see Ilta* Jalkanen
  KILPINEN
"Pois täytyy mun" *see Erotessa* Jalkanen
  KILPINEN
A poison tree see Blake, William
  BRITTEN, VAUGHAN WILLIAMS
Les poissons se jouent see Anon.
  SZYMANOWSKI *Wysly rybki, sysly*
"Poka ne trebuet pozta" *see Poet* Pushkin
  RIMSKIÏ-KORSAKOV
Der Pokal see Arnim **STRAUSS**
Pokhoronnaïa pesnia see Pushkin
  MEDTNER *Message*
Pokinem, milaïa see Golenishchev-Kutuzov
  RACHMANINOFF
  Beloved, let us fly

Pol, Wincenty, 1807-1872.
  CHOPIN *Leci liście z drzewa*
Pola, Wincentego *see* Pol, Wincenty,
  1807-1872.
Polden' see Tiutchev **MEDTNER** *Mid-day*
The policeman in the park see Feeney
  CHANLER
Politik see Krenek **KRENEK**
Poliubila ia na pechal' svoiu see
  Shevchenko **RACHMANINOFF**
  I have grown fond of sorrow
Poliziano, Angelo, 1454-1494.
  MALIPIERO
  Ballata
  L'Eco
  Inno a Maria Nostra Donna
  RIETI
  Canti oghun
  La non vuol esser piu mia
  ZELTER *Die Schäferinn*
Polkovodets see Golenishchev-Kutuzov
  MUSORGSKIÏ
Pollak, Aaron
  SCHUBERT *Frühlingslied*
Polo see Anon. **FALLA**
Polo de Medina, Salvador Jacinto,
  1603-1676.
  RODRIGO *Estribillo*
Polonsky, Yakov Petrovich, 1819-1898.
  CHAÏKOVSKIÏ
  Noch'
  Pesu'
  RACHMANINOFF
  Discord
  Music
  When yesterday we met
  RUBINSTEIN
  Lied
  The prisoner
  Sinngedicht
  VIZOV.
  CHAÏKOVSKIÏ *Za oknom v teni
    mel'kaet*
Polovtsev, A.
  RUBINSTEIN *Romance*
Polterabendlied see Bartholdy, Dr. **LOEWE**
POLYDORA. see Daumer
  Es träumte mir **BRAHMS**
  Eine gute, gute Nacht **BRAHMS**
  Die Kränze **BRAHMS**
  Magyarisch **BRAHMS**
  Schön war, das ich dir weihte **BRAHMS**
  Die Schnur, die Perl an Perle **BRAHMS**
  Wir wandelten **BRAHMS**
POLYMÈTRES, no. 1
  SAUGUET Richter *La double rougeur*

COMPOSER Poet *Title* "First Line"

POLYMÈTRES, no. 2
  SAUGUET Richter *Le muguet*
POLYMÈTRES, no. 3
  SAUGUET Richter *Le vide de l'instant*
POLYMÈTRES, no. 4
  SAUGUET Richter *A une rose pâlissant au soleil*
POLYMÈTRES, no. 5
  SAUGUET Richter *Le jour de tristesse*
POLYMÈTRES, no. 6
  SAUGUET Richter *Le bal d'enfants*
Pomès, Mathilde
  MOMPOU *Le nuage*
POMES PENYEACH. see Joyce
  A flower given to my daughter **DIAMOND, ROUSSEL**
Pomey, Louis *see* Pommey, Louis
Pomme d'anis see Jammes **MILHAUD**
La pomme et l'escargot see Vildrac
  MILHAUD
Pommey, Louis
  FAURÉ *Aubade*
Pomni menia! see Bal'mont **PROKOFIEV**
Pompadour, la grande coquette see Pacini
  ROSSINI
Pompili, Aganoor *see* Aganoor-Pompilj, Vittoria Antonia Maria, 1855-1910.
Le pont see Apollinaire *IL Y A.* **POULENC**
Le pont Mirabeau see Apollinaire
  ALCOOLS. **RIVIER**
Pool, Morris W.
  IVES *Ann street*
The pools of peace see Campbell, Joan
  CARPENTER
Poor Henry see De La Mare **BERKELEY**
"Poor youth, so handsome" *see Specimen case*
  Whitman **ROREM**
Popatřiž na mne a smiluj se nade mnou see
  Bible **DVOŘÁK**
Pope, Alexander, 1688-1744.
  THE DYING CHRISTIAN TO HIS SOUL.
  SCHUBERT *Verklärung*
"Por mayo, era por mayo" *see Romancillo*
  Anon. **RODRIGO**
"Por traidores, tus ojos" *see Cancion* Anon.
  FALLA
"Por un allegre prado de flores esmaltado" *see*
  Cantilena Rivas **TURINA**
"Por ver si me consolaba" *see Asturiana*
  Anon. **FALLA**
Pora! see Nadson **RACHMANINOFF**
  'Tis time
Porc see Eluard **SAUGUET**
Porosiata see Kvitko, L. **PROKOFIEV**
Porque toco el pandero see Anon.
  RODRIGO

La porta dell'inferno see Dante
  SAINT-SAËNS
Porte, A.
  GOUNOD *Jésus de Nazareth*
LA PORTE ETROITE. see Gide
  Jérôme **MILHAUD**
  Jérôme et Alissa **MILHAUD**
    Three settings: Op. 9 no. 2, op. 9 no. 3, and op. 9 no. 5.
  Journal d'Alissa **MILHAUD**
  Lettre d'Alissa **MILHAUD**
  Lettres d'Alissa **MILHAUD**
"La porte s'ouvre!" *see Voisinage* Jacob, M.
  SAUGUET
Porter, Katherine Anne, 1894-1980.
  DIAMOND *Anniversary in a country cemetery*
Le portrait see Colette **POULENC**
Portrait d'Henri Rousseau see Cocteau
  AURIC
Portrait of F. B. [Frances Blood] see Stein
  THOMSON
A PORTRAIT OF THE ARTIST AS A YOUNG MAN. see Joyce
  Brigid's song **DIAMOND**
A portrait; the Marchioness of Brinvilliers see
  Melville **DIAMOND**
Portret d'un enfant see Ronsard
  MASSENET
Ports de l'enfer see Jacob, M. **SAUGUET**
PORTUGUESE IMITATION. see Byron
  V poryve nezhnosti serdechnoĭ
  RIMSKIĬ-KORSAKOV
Pósa, Lajos, 1850-1914.
  BARTÓK
    Ejnye! Ejnye!
    Még azt vetik szememre
    Nincs olyan bú
    Őszi szellő
Posel see Witwicki **CHOPIN**
Poshli gospod' svoĭu otradu see Tiutchev
  MEDTNER *The pauper*
Posmotri v svoĭ vertograd see Maĭkov
  RIMSKIĬ-KORSAKOV
Die Post see Müller, Wilhelm **SCHUBERT**
Postel, Madeleine
  MASSENET *L'amour pleure*
"Posthorn, wie so keck und fröhlich" *see*
  Kurze Fahrt Eichendorff **SCHOECK**
POSTHUMOUS POEMS (1824). *see* Shelley
  Music, when soft voices die **DIAMOND, HESELTINE, QUILTER**
Der Postillon see Kiesekamo **REGER**
Postlude: Polonaise see Vilmorin
  SAUGUET
Posts see Bal'mont **PROKOFIEV** *Stolby*

Le potier see Leclère, translator.
SHÉHÉRAZADE. **KOECHLIN**
Le pouf see Chalupt **AURIC**
Poule see Eluard **SAUGUET**
La poule a couvé see Aicard **MARTINŮ**
"Une poule blanche, qui est dans la grange"
  see Berceuse populaire Unknown **INDY**
La poule noire see Hirtz **AURIC**
Poulenc: A gymnopédie see O'Hara **ROREM**
  For Poulenc

POULENC, FRANCIS, 1899-1963.

Anon.
La belle jeunesse (1926) [Heugel, 1926]
  "Il faut s'aimer toujours"
Chanson à boire (1926) [Heugel, 1926]
  "Les rois d'Egypte et de Syrie"
Couplets bachiques (1926) [Heugel,
  1926] "Je suis tant que dure le jour"
Invocations aux Parques (1926) [Heugel,
  1926] "Je jure, tant que je vivrai"
Madrigal (1926) [Heugel, 1926]
  "Vous êtes belle comme un ange"
La maîtresse volage (1926) [Heugel,
  1926] "Ma maîtresse est volage"
L'Offrande (1926) [Heugel, 1926]
  "Au Dieu d'Amour"
Sérénade (1926) [Heugel, 1926]
  "Avec une si belle main"

Anouilh, Jean, 1910-1987.
LÉOCADIA.
Les chemins de l'amour (1940)
  [Eschig, 1945]
  "Les chemins qui vont à la mer"

Apollinaire, Guillaume, 1880-1918.
L'anguille (1931) [Rouart Lerolle, 1931]
  "Jeanne Houhou la très gentille"
Avant le cinéma (1931) [Rouart Lerolle,
  1931] "Et puis ce soir"
Bleuet (1939) [Durand, 1940]
  "Jeune homme de vingt ans"
Carte postale (1931) [Rouart Lerolle,
  1931] "L'ombre de la très douce est
  évoquée"
Chanson d'Orkenise (1940) [Eschig,
  1941] "Par les portes d'Orkenise"
Voyage à Paris (1940) [Eschig, 1941]
  "Ah! la charmante chose"
ALCOOLS.
Rosemonde (1954) [Eschig, 1955]
  "Longtemps au pied du perron de la
  maison"
LE BESTIAIRE.
Le carpe (1919) [Editions de la Sirène,
  1920; Eschig, 1944]
  "Dans vos viviers dans vos étangs"
  Originally for voice & chamber
  ensemble.

La chèvre du Thibet (1919) [Editions
  de la Sirène, 1920; Eschig, 1944]
  "Les poils de cette chèvre et même"
  Originally for voice & chamber
  ensemble.
Le dauphin (1919) [Editions de la
  Sirène, 1920; Eschig, 1944]
  "Dauphins, vous jouez dans la mer"
  Originally for voice & chamber
  ensemble.
Le dromadaire (1919) [Editions de la
  Sirène, 1920; Eschig, 1944]
  "Avec ses quatre dromadaires"
  Originally for voice & chamber
  ensemble.
L'écrevisse (1919) [Editions de la
  Sirène, 1920; Eschig, 1944]
  "Incertitude, O! mes delices"
  Originally for voice & chamber
  ensemble.
La sauterelle (1919) [Editions de la
  Sirène, 1920; Eschig, 1944]
  "Voici la fine sauterelle"
  Originally for voice & chamber
  ensemble.
La souris (1956) [Eschig, 1957]
  "Belles journées"
CALLIGRAMMES.
Aussi bien que les cigales (1948)
  [Heugel, 1948]
  "Gens du midi, gens du midi"
L'espionne (1948) [Heugel, 1948]
  "Pâle espionne de l'amour"
La grâce exilée (1948) [Heugel, 1948]
  "Va-t'en, va-t'en mon arc-en-ciel"
Il pleut (1948) [Heugel, 1948]
  "Il pleut des voix de femmes"
Mutation (1948) [Heugel, 1948]
  "Une femme qui pleurait"
Vers le sud (1948) [Heugel, 1948]
  "Zénith Tous ces regrets"
Voyage (1948) [Heugel, 1948]
  "Adieu, amour nuage qui fuis"
LE GUETTEUR MÉLANCOLIQUE.
Hôtel (1940) [Eschig, 1941] "Ma
  chambre a la forme d'une cage"
IL Y A.
Allons plus vite (1938) [Rouart Lerolle,
  1939]
  "Et le soir vient et les lys meurent"
Chanson (1931) [Rouart Lerolle, 1931]
  "Les myrtilles sont pour la dame"
Dans le jardin d'Anna (1938) [Rouart
  Lerolle, 1939]
  "Certes si nous avions vécu"
Fagnes de Wallonie (1940) [Eschig,
  1941] "Tant de tristesses plénières"

POULENC, FRANCIS, 1899-1963
(continued)
Apollinaire, Guillaume, 1880-1918
(continued)
IL Y A (continued)
La grenouillère (1938) [Salabert, 1939]
"Au bord de l'île on voit"
Hyde Park (1945) [Eschig, 1945]
"Les Faiseurs de religions"
Montparnasse (1941-45) [Eschig,
1945] "O porte de l'hôtel"
1904 (1931) [Rouart Lerolle, 1931] "A
Strasbourg en dix-neuf-cent-quatre"
Un poème (1946) [Eschig, 1947]
"Il est entré"
Le pont (1946) [Eschig, 1947] "Deux
dames, le long le long du fleuve"
Sanglots (1940) [Eschig, 1941]
"Notre amour est réglé"
Aragon, Louis, 1897-1982.
C (1943) [Rouart Lerolle, 1944]
"J'ai traversé les pontes de Cé"
Fêtes galantes (1943) [Rouart Lerolle,
1944] "On voit des marquis sur des
bicyclettes"
Beylié, Laurence de
Nuage (1956) [Eschig, 1957]
"J'ai vu reluire"
Carême, Maurice, 1899-1978.
Les anges musiciens (1960) [Eschig,
1960] "Sur les fils de la pluie"
Ba, be, bi, bo, bu (1960) [Eschig, 1960]
same
Le carafon (1960) [Eschig, 1960]
"Pourquoi, se plaignait la carafe?"
Lune d'Avril (1960) [Eschig, 1960]
"Lune, belle lune"
Quelle aventure! (1960) [Eschig, 1960]
"Une puce, dans sa voiture"
La reine de coeur (1960) [Eschig, 1960]
"Mollement accoudée"
Le sommeil (1960) [Eschig, 1960]
"Le sommeil en voyage"
Charles, Duke of Orleans, 1391-1465.
Priez pour paix (1938) [Rouart Lerolle,
1939] same
Cocteau, Jean, 1889-1963.
Donne d'enfant (1919) [Editions de la
Sirène, 1920; Eschig]
"Técla notre âge d'or"
Enfant de troupe (1919) [Editions de la
Sirène, 1920; Eschig]
"Morceau pour piston seul"
Miel de Narbonne (1919) [Editions de la
Sirène, 1920; Eschig] "Use ton coeur"
Toréador (1918; rev. 1932) [Salabert,
1918; R. Deiss, 1933]

"Pépita reine de Venise"
Colette, Sidonie Gabrielle, 1873-1954.
Le portrait (1938) [Salabert, 1939]
"Belle, méchante, menteuse, injuste"
Desnos, Robert, 1900-1945.
Dernier poeme (1956) [Eschig, 1957]
"J'ai rêvé tellement fort de toi"
Le disparu (1947) [Rouart Lerolle, 1947]
"Je n'aime plus la rue St Martin"
Eluard, Paul, 1895-1952.
A toutes brides (1937) [Durand, 1937]
same
Amoureuses (1935) [Durand, 1935]
"Elles ont les épaules hautes"
Bonne journée (1937) [Durand, 1937]
same
Ce doux petit visage (1939) [Rouart
Lerolle, 1941]
"Rien que ce doux petit visage"
Une chanson de porcelaine (1958)
[Eschig, 1959] same
Dans les ténèbres du jardin (1950)
[Eschig, 1951] same
Figure de force brûlante et farouche
(1937) [Durand, 1937] same
Le front comme un drapeau perdu (1937)
[Durand, 1937] same
Georges Braque (1956) [Eschig, 1957]
"Un oiseau s'envole"
La grande rivière qui va (1950) [Eschig,
1951] same
Une herbe pauvre (1937) [Durand, 1937]
same
Homme au sourire tendre (1950) [Eschig,
1951] same
Il la prend dans ses bras (1935) [Durand,
1935] same
Jacques Villon (1956) [Eschig, 1957]
"Irrémédiable vie"
Je n'ai envie que de t'aimer (1937)
[Durand, 1937] same
Je nommerai ton front (1938) [Salabert,
1939] same
Juan Gris (1956) [Eschig, 1957]
"De jour merci"
Juan Miró (1956) [Eschig, 1957]
"Soleil de proie prisonnier de ma tête"
Main dominée par le coeur (1947)
[Rouart Lerolle, 1947] same
. . . Mais mourir (1947) [Heugel, 1948]
"Mains agitées, aux grimaces nouées"
Marc Chagall (1956) [Eschig, 1957]
"Ane ou vache coq ou cheval"
Le matin les branches attisent (1950)
[Eschig, 1951] same
Nous avons fait la nuit (1937) [Durand,
1937] same

Pablo Picasso (1956) [Eschig, 1957]
"Entoure ce citron de blanc d'oeuf
informe"

Paul Klee (1956) [Eschig, 1957]
"Sur la pente fatale"

Peut-il se reposer? (1935) [Durand,
1935] same

Plume d'eau clair (1935) [Durand, 1935]
same

Rayon des yeux (1950) [Eschig, 1951]
same

Rôdeuse au front de verre (1935)
[Durand, 1935] same

Une roulotte couverte en tuiles (1937)
[Durand, 1937] same

Une ruine coquille vide (1937) [Durand,
1937] same

Tout disparut (1950) [Eschig, 1951] same

Tu vois le feu du soir (1938) [Salabert,
1939] same

Unis la fraîcheur et le feu (1950)
[Eschig, 1951] same

Fombeure, Maurice, 1906-1981.
CHANSONS DE LA GRANDE HUNE.
C'est le joli printemps (1942) [Eschig,
1943] same
Originally voice & orchestra; piano
arrangement made by Poulenc.

Chanson de la fille frivole (1942)
[Eschig, 1943] "Ah dit la fille
frivole que le vent y vire"
Originally voice & orchestra; piano
arrangement made by Poulenc.

Chanson du clair tamis (1942) [Eschig,
1943] "Où le bedeau a passé"
Originally voice & orchestra; piano
arrangement made by Poulenc.

Les gars qui vont à la fête (1942)
[Eschig, 1943] same
Originally voice & orchestra; piano
arrangement made by Poulenc.

Le mendiant (1942) [Eschig, 1943]
"Jean Martin prit sa besace Vive le
passant qui passe"
Originally voice & orchestra; piano
arrangement made by Poulenc.

Le retour du sergent (1942) [Eschig,
1943]
"Le sergent s'en revient de guerre"
Originally voice & orchestra; piano
arrangement made by Poulenc.

Garcia Lorca, Federico, 1899-1936.
Adelina à la promenade (1947) [Heugel,
1947] "La mer n'a pas d'oranges"

Chanson de l'oranger sec (1947)
[Heugel, 1947]
"Bûcheron Abats mon ombre"

L'enfant muet (1947) [Heugel, 1947]
"L'enfant cherche sa voix"

Jacob, Max, 1876-1944.
Berceuse (1931) [Rouart Lerolle, 1932]
"Ton père est à la messe"

Chanson bretonne (1931) [Rouart
Lerolle, 1932] "J'ai perdu ma poulette"

Cimetière (1931) [Rouart Lerolle, 1932]
"Si mon marin vous le chassez"

Jouer du bugle (1954) [Salabert, 1954]
"Les trois dames qui jouaient"

La petite servante (1931) [Rouart Lerolle,
1932]
"Préservez-nous du feu et du tonnerre"

Souric et Mouric (1931) [Rouart Lerolle,
1932] "Souric et Mouric, rat blanc,
souris noire"

Vous n'écrivez plus? (1954) [Salabert,
1954] "M'as-tu connu marchand
d'journaux à Barbès"

Laurencin, Marie, 1885-1956.
Hier (1931) [Rouart Lerolle, 1931]
"Hier, c'est ce chapeau fané"

Le Présent (1931) [Rouart Lerolle, 1931]
"Si tu veux je te donnerai"

Malherbe, François de, 1555-1628.
Épitaphe (1930) [Rouart Lerolle, 1930]
"Belle âme qui fus mon flambeau"
Baritone or mezzo-soprano & piano.

Moréas, Jean, 1856-1910.
Air champêtre (1927-28) [Rouart Lerolle,
1928] "Belle source, belle source"

Air grave (1927-28) [Rouart Lerolle,
1928] "Ah! fuyez à présent"

Air romantique (1927-28) [Rouart
Lerolle, 1928]
"J'allais dans la campagne"

Air vif (1927-28) [Rouart Lerolle, 1928]
"Le trésor du verger et le jardin en
fête"

No author
Vocalise (1927) [Leduc, 1929]

Nohain, Jean
Monsieur sans-souci (1934) [Enoch,
1937] "Quand les gens"

Nous voulons une petit soeur (1934)
[Enoch, 1935]
"Madame Eustache a dix-sept filles"

Le petit garçon trop bien portant (1934)
[Enoch, 1937] "Ah! mon cher docteur"

La tragique histoire du petit René (1934)
[Enoch, 1935]
"Avec mon face à main"

Racine, Jean Baptiste, 1639-1699.
Hymne (1947) [Salabert, 1949]
"Sombre nuit, aveugles ténébres"

POULENC, FRANCIS, 1899-1963
(continued)
Radiguet, Raymond, 1903-1923.
Paul et Virginie (1946) [Eschig, 1947]
"Ciel! les colonies"
Ronsard, Pierre de, 1524-1585.
À sa guitare (1935) [Durand, 1935]
"Ma guitare, je te chante"
A son page (1924-25) [Heugel, 1925]
"Fais rafraîchir mon vin"
Attributs (1924-25) [Heugel, 1925]
"Les épis sont à Cérès"
Ballet (1924-25) [Heugel, 1925]
"Le soir qu'Amour"
Je n'ai plus que les os (1924-25)
[Heugel, 1925] same
Le tombeau (1924-25) [Heugel, 1925]
"Quand le ciel et mon heure"
Shakespeare, William, 1564-1616.
MERCHANT OF VENICE.
Fancy [London: Anthony Blond, 1962,
p. 255]
"Tell me where is fancy bred"
In *Classical songs for children,*
edited by the Countess of
Harewood and Donald Duncan.
Tatry, Robert
Nos souvenirs qui chantent (19__)
[Heugel, 1962]
"Sous les reflets de lune vaporeuse"
Composed by Poulenc and Paul
Bonneau.
Unknown
L'adieu (1934) [Rouart Lerolle, 1934]
"Vois ma belle sur ma lance"
Text translated by Jacques Lerolle.
La couronne (1934) [Rouart Lerolle,
1934]
"Toute en pleurs la belle jette sa
couronne"
Text translated by Jacques Lerolle.
Le départ (1934) [Rouart Lerolle, 1934]
"Laissez-moi partir bien vite"
Text translated by Jacques Lerolle.
Le dernier mazour (1934) [Rouart
Lerolle, 1934]
"Encore un mazour avant"
Text translated by Jacques Lerolle.
Le drapeau blanc (1934) [Rouart Lerolle,
1934]
"Pour son amant un drapeau blanc"
Text translated by Jacques Lerolle.
Les gars polonais (1934) [Rouart Lerolle,
1934] "Vivent les gars polonais que
personne n'égale"
Text translated by Jacques Lerolle.

Le lac (1934) [Rouart Lerolle, 1934]
"O beau lac, Ô limpide azur"
Text translated by Jacques Lerolle.
La Vistule (1934) [Rouart Lerolle, 1934]
"La Vistule arrose toute la Pologne"
Text translated by Jacques Lerolle.
Vilmorin, Louise de, 1902-1969.
Aus-delà (1937) [Durand, 1938]
"Eau-de-vie!"
Aux officiers de la Garde Blanche (1937)
[Durand, 1938]
"Officiers de la Garde Blanche"
C'est ainsi que tu es (1943) [Rouart
Lerolle, 1944] "Ta chair, d'âme mêlée"
La dame d'André (1939) [Rouart Lerolle,
1940] "André ne connaît pas la dame"
Dans l'herbe (1939) [Rouart Lerolle,
1940] "Je ne peux plus rien dire"
Fleurs (1939) [Rouart Lerolle, 1940]
"Fleurs promises"
Le garçon de Liège (1937) [Durand,
1938] "Un garçon de conte de fée"
Il vole (1939) [Rouart Lerolle, 1940]
"En allant se coucher le soleil"
Mazurka (1949) [Heugel, 1949]
"Les bijoux aux poitrines"
One of seven songs by French
composers to Vilmorin poems,
united under title "Mouvements du
coeur" in memory of Chopin.
Mon cadavre est doux comme un gant
(1939) [Rouart Lerolle, 1940] same
Paganini (1943) [Rouart Lerolle, 1944]
"Violon, hippocampe et sirène"
Reine des mouettes (1943) [Rouart
Lerolle, 1944] same
Violon (1939) [Rouart Lerolle, 1940]
"Couple amoureux aux accents
méconnus"
Le poulet see Gramont, T de **MARTINŮ**
Poulsen, Frederik, 1876-1950.
NIELSEN
Det, som lysner over Vangen
Hjemstavn
Pound, Ezra, 1885-1972.
DIAMOND
Agathas
Lesbia Illa
Passing
Young lady
Poupette et Patata see Vildrac **MILHAUD**
Pour album: Sogna il guerrier see
Metastasio **ROSSINI**
Pour Antoinette see Bourguignat, Paul
MASSENET
Pour ce que plaisance est morte see
Charles, Duke of Orleans **DEBUSSY**

"Pour chanter le retour du jour" *see Le matin*
  Bouclon **BERLIOZ**
"Pour chanter le retour du jour" *see*
  Petit oiseau Bouclon **BERLIOZ**
Pour chercher sur la carte des mers see
  Hugnet **THOMSON**
Pour demain soir . . . see Jacob, M.
  AURIC
"Pour faire mes heures plus breves" *see*
  La marchande des rêves Silvestre
  MASSENET
Pour la chanter see Zaffira **GOUNOD**
  Ho messo nuove
"Pour le grâce de mon ami mon coeur" *see*
  Chante de délivrance Anon. **MILHAUD**
"Pour le jour des Hyacinthies" *see*
  La flûte de Pan Louÿs **DEBUSSY**
"Pour le retour du Soleil honorer" *see*
  Printemps Labé **SAUGUET**
"Pour les enfants san feu ni lieu" *see*
  Sans feu ni lieu Supervielle **MILHAUD**
Pour les victims see Unknown **FRANCK**
"Pour moi sa main cueillait des roses" *see*
  Lied Paté **FRANCK**
"Pour ne poser qu'un doigt dessus" *see Chat*
  Eluard **SAUGUET**
Pour Nicolas see Alix, Marie **SAUGUET**
Pour qu'à l'Espérance il ne céde see
  Silvestre **MASSENET**
"Pour que la nuit soit douce" *see Invocation*
  Régnier **ROUSSEL**
"Pour que le vent te les apporte" *see*
  Testament Silvestre **DUPARC**
"Pour que ton rire clair, jeune" *see*
  Les fontaines Régnier **HAHN**
"Pour qui sera, Mignonne" *see À Mignonne*
  Chouquet **MASSENET**
"Pour son amant un drapeau blanc" *see*
  Le drapeau blanc Unknown **POULENC**
Pour te parler see Émié **JOLIVET**
"Pour toi j'ai toute donné" *see Tendresse*
  Champlay, R. **AUBERT**
"Pour toi, j'écris cette chanson" *see Chanson*
  pour elle Maigret, Henri **MASSENET**
Pour un arbre de Noël see Anon.
  CHAUSSON
Pour un cyprés see Desnoux, Lucienne
  SAUGUET
Pourquoi? see Guilliaume **LASSEN**
Pourquoi? see Messiaen **MESSIAEN**
"Pourquoi chanter l'amoureuse ivresse?" *see*
  Chanson andalouse Unknown
  MASSENET
"Pourquoi donc ne distu plus rien?" *see*
  Dialogue Varenne, Marc **MASSENET**
Pourquoi les boeufs see Jammes
  MILHAUD

"Pourquoi les oiseaux de l'air" *see Pourquoi?*
  Messiaen **MESSIAEN**
Pourquoi pleures tu? see Robiquet
  MASSENET
"Pourquoi, pourquoi m'avez-vous
  abandonné?" *see L'abandon* Latil
  MILHAUD
"Pourquoi, Princesse de Ballet" *see*
  L'orgueilleuse Chalupt **MILHAUD**
Pourquoi rester seulette? see Croze, J. L.
  SAINT-SAËNS
"Pourquoi, se plaignait la carafe?" *see*
  Le carafon Carême **POULENC**
Pourquoi t'exiler see Anon. **SAINT-SAËNS**
Pourtant il y a encore autre chose see Birot,
  P. A. **SAUGUET**
Povĕra see Manin, J. **MARTINŮ**
Il poveretto see Maggioni, S. Manfredo
  VERDI
Povero core see Graf **RESPIGHI**
Poymi khotraz see Shenshin
  CHAïKOVSKIï
Pozdvihuji očí svých k horám see Bible
  DVOŘÁK
Practising see Carpenter, Rue
  CARPENTER
Pradel, Georges
  MASSENET *Sonnet*
Pradère, Onésime *see* Pradère-Niquet,
  Onésime
Pradère-Niquet, Onésime
  GOUNOD
    À une soeur
    Invocation
    Marguerite
Präludium see Boelitz **REGER**
Praeludium see Goethe *ZAHME XENIEN.*
  MEDTNER
"Praise ye the Lord" *see Psalm 148* Bible
  ROREM
"Praise ye the Lord" *see Psalm 150* Bible
  ROREM
PRAISES AND PRAYERS, no. 1
  THOMSON Francis of Assisi *From the*
    canticle of the sun
PRAISES AND PRAYERS, no. 2
  THOMSON Anon. *My Master hath a*
    garden
PRAISES AND PRAYERS, no. 3
  THOMSON Crashaw *Sung by the*
    shepherds
PRAISES AND PRAYERS, no. 4
  THOMSON Anon. *Before sleeping*
PRAISES AND PRAYERS, no. 5
  THOMSON Anon. *Jerusalem, my happy*
    home

COMPOSER Poet *Title* ''First Line''

The praises of God see Auden, W. H.
   translator. **BARBER**
Prandstetter, Martin Josef, b.1750.
   SCHUBERT *Die Fröhlichkeit*
"Přání svá, duše, zasázej" *see Výklad znamení*
   Anon. **DVOŘÁK**
Pratobevera, Adolf von, 1806-1875.
   SCHUBERT *Abschied von der Erde*
Pravý počet see Mužik **MARTINŮ**
   The right number
Prayer see Dévigne **LOEFFLER**
Prayer see Glücklich **MACDOWELL** *Bitte*
A prayer see Goethe **RACHMANINOFF**
The prayer see Lermontov **MEDTNER,**
   MUSORGSKIĭ *Molitva;* **RUBINSTEIN**
   Gebet
Prayer see Mary **SCHUMANN** *Gebet*
Prayer see Roethke **DIAMOND**
Prayer see Romanov **RACHMANINOFF**
Prayer for rain see Shenshin **MEDTNER**
Prayer from "The dry salvages" see Eliot
   THE DRY SALVAGES. **ROREM**
Prayer on Great Island see Davis, Rev. O.
   S. **RIEGGER**
A prayer to Saint Anthony of Padua see
   Symons *LONDON NIGHTS.*
   HESELTINE
A prayer to Saint Catherine see Koch
   THOMSON
"Le pré est vénéneux mais joli en automne"
   see Les colchiques Apollinaire **RIVIER**
Prechtler, Otto, 1813-1881.
   LOEWE *Deutsche Barkarole*
PRECIOSILLA. see Stein
   Preciosilla **THOMSON**
Preciosilla see Stein *PRECIOSILLA.*
   THOMSON
Precz z moich oczu . . . see Witwicki
   CHOPIN
Pred ikoniĭ see Golenishchev-Kutuzov
   RACHMANINOFF *Before the icon*
"Prédit me fut, que devais fermement" *see*
   Amour Labé **SAUGUET**
Preetzman, Caspara, 1792-1876.
   GRIEG *Dig elsker jeg!*
Il preghiera del poeta see Sole **VERDI**
PREIS DES SCHÖPFERS. see Gellert
   Wenn ich, O Schöpfer, deine Macht
   LOEWE
"Preis ihm! Er schuf und er erhält" *see*
   Dem Dreieinigen Klopstock **LOEWE**
Překážky see Pech **DVOŘÁK**
"Prelestna ia rybachka" *see Barkarola*
   Arsen'ev **BALAKIREV**
Preliudiia see Goethe **MEDTNER**
   Praeludium

Prelude see Collin **MASSENET**
Prélude see Docquois **SAINT-SAËNS**
Prélude see Hérold **AUBERT**
Prélude see Silvestre *MIGNONNE.*
   MASSENET
Prelude see Vilmorin **SAUGUET**
Preludio see Machado y Ruiz **RODRIGO**
Preludios see Trueba **FALLA**
Le premier amour see
   Desbordes-Valmore **AURIC**
Le premier jour de Mai see Passerat
   GOUNOD
Premier prélude de Bach see Lamartine
   GOUNOD
Première see Bengy-Puyvallée **AUBERT**
Première danse see Normand **MASSENET**
La première de toutes see Hugnet
   THOMSON
La première dent see La Laurencie **INDY**
LA PREMIÈRE FAMILLE. see Supervielle
   Chacun son tour, les animaux **MILHAUD**
   Je suis dans le fillet **MILHAUD**
PREMIÈRES MÉLODIES, no. 1
   AUBERT Hettich *Noël pastoral*
PREMIÈRES MÉLODIES, no. 2
   AUBERT Tonquédec, Marthe de
   L'inconnu
PREMIÈRES MÉLODIES, no. 3
   AUBERT Oeris *Sur le bord*
PREMIÈRES MÉLODIES, no. 4
   AUBERT Marès *Légende*
PREMIÈRES MÉLODIES, no. 5
   AUBERT Ludana *Péché véniel*
Premiers fils d'argent see Valendre, Marie
   de **MASSENET**
Premiers transports see Deschamps
   BERLIOZ
"Premiers transports que nul n'oublie" *see*
   Premiers transports Deschamps
   BERLIOZ
Přemítání see Pech **DVOŘÁK**
Premonitions see Johnson **IVES**
Prends bien soin de mourir see Gélin
   ROREM
Prends garde see Barbier, J. **GOUNOD**
Prends mon âme see Audigier, Georges
   SÉVERAC
"Prends mon âme fais en une lyre brillante"
   see Chant de résignation Unknown
   MILHAUD
Prenez courage, Ô enfants d'Israël! see
   Anon. **MILHAUD**
Préparatif a la mort en allégorie maritime see
   Aubigné **MILHAUD**
"Près de l'enfant Dieu fait descendre" *see*
   L'ange gardien Quételart, A. **GOUNOD**

COMPOSER   Poet   *Title*   "First Line"

"Près de l'étang, sur la prêle vole" *see La libellule* Saint-Saëns **SAINT-SAËNS**

"Près de son nid jeune fauvette" *see Patte de velours* Spenner, M. **GOUNOD**

"Près de toi garde-moi toute" *see Peut-être* Croze, J. L. **SAINT-SAËNS**

"Près du Jourdain il y a une maison de forgeron" *see Chant de forgeron* Unknown **MILHAUD**

"Près du pêcheur qui ruisselle" *see Soirée en mer* Hugo **SAINT-SAËNS**

"Les prés ont une odeur d'herbe verte et mouillée" *see Juin* Leconte de Lisle **KOECHLIN**

Présage de la croix see Bordèse **SAINT-SAËNS**

Présence see Laporte **SAUGUET**

Le Présent see Laurencin **POULENC**

Les présents see Villiers **FAURÉ**

"Préservez-nous du feu et du tonnerre" *see La petite servante* Jacob, M. **POULENC**

Pressat, André **SAINT-SAËNS** *Soeur Anne*

The pretty girl no longer loves me see Vinogradov **BORODIN** *Razlyubila krasna devitsa*

Pretty ring time see Shakespeare *AS YOU LIKE IT.* **HESELTINE**

Ein Preussenlied see Unknown **LOEWE**

Preussentreue see Telschow **LOEWE**

Die preussiche Kriegerin see Kurowski-Eichen **LOEWE** *Die Heldenbraut*

Preussisches Hurrahlied see Friedrich Wilhelm IV **LOEWE**

Preussisches Marinelied see Randow, Carl **LOEWE**

Prévost, Gabriel **MASSENET** *Aubade*

Preziosas Sprüchlein gegen Kopfweh see Cervantes **CORNELIUS**

"Pri more chernom stoĭat stolby" *see Stolby* Bal'mont **PROKOFIEV**

Při řekách babylonských see Bible **DVOŘÁK**

Při vyšívání see Kleinschrod **DVOŘÁK**

Pride see Tolstoĭ **BORODIN** *Spes'*

"The pride of the peacock is the glory of God" *see Proverb I* Blake, William **BRITTEN**

Pride passes by, puffed up see Tolstoĭ **MUSORGSKIĭ** *Spes'*

Pridi ko mne see Kol'tsov **BALAKIREV**

"Pridi ko mne nochnoĭ poroĭ" *see Morskaya tsarevna* Borodin **BORODIN**

La prière see Carême **MILHAUD**

Prière see Dévigne **LOEFFLER** *Prayer*

Prière see Jammes **HONEGGER**

Prière see Peyrissac, Jean **RIVIER**

Prière see Sully-Prudhomme **GOUNOD**

Prière à la Vierge see Anon. **GOUNOD**

Prière à mon poète see Latil **MILHAUD**

"Prière abandonnée au tournant du chemin" *see La prière* Carême **MILHAUD**

Prière d'Abraham see Barbier, J. **GOUNOD**

Prière d'amour see Noël, Édouard **MASSENET** *Ave Margarita* (prière d'amour, 1902)

Prière dans le soir see Pépin, Edwige **SAUGUET**

La prière de femme see Lamartine **RUBINSTEIN**

Prière de l'après-dîner see Anon. **MILHAUD**

Prière de l'enfant a son réveil see Lamartine **LALO**

Prière du matin see Anon. **MILHAUD**

La prière du mort see Hérédia **KOECHLIN**

Prière du soir see Anon. **MILHAUD**

Prière du soir see Ligny, Charles **GOUNOD**

Prière du soir see Manuel **GOUNOD**

Prière exaucée see Messiaen **MESSIAEN**

Prière pour aller au Paradis see Jammes **MILHAUD**

Prière pour demander une étoile see Jammes **MILHAUD**

Prière pour être simple see Jammes **MILHAUD**

Prière pour l'Empereur et la famille impériale see Baëlen, Mme. **GOUNOD**

Prière pour qu'un enfant ne meure pas see Jammes **MILHAUD**

PRIÈRES JOURNALIÈRES À L'USAGE DES JUIFS . . . , no. 1 **MILHAUD** Anon. *Prière du matin*

PRIÈRES JOURNALIÈRES À L'USAGE DES JUIFS . . . , no. 2 **MILHAUD** Anon. *Prière de l'après-dîner*

PRIÈRES JOURNALIÈRES À L'USAGE DES JUIFS . . . , no. 3 **MILHAUD** Anon. *Prière du soir*

Priez pour paix see Charles, Duke of Orleans **POULENC**

"Přiletěl ptáček zcizí krajiny" *see Děvče z Moravy* Anon. **MARTINŮ**

Přílítlo jaro zdaleka see Hálek **DVOŘÁK**

Prima verba see Lerberghe **FAURÉ**

La prima viola see Maffei **RUBINSTEIN**

La primavera see Anon. **HAHN, HARRIS**

Primavera see Charles, Duke of Orleans **SAINT-SAËNS**

Primavera see Gautier **GOUNOD**

Primavera see Stuart, Paul SAINT-SAËNS
"Primel und Stern und Syringe von einsamer
Kerze beleuchtet" *see*
Nachts am Schreibepult Mörike
SCHOECK
Die Primeln see Hamerling REGER
Primeros pasos see Janés MOMPOU
Primety see Pushkin MEDTNER *Visions*
Primiren'e see Shcherbina CHAïKOVSKIï
The primrose see Runeberg SIBELIUS
Sippan
"The primrose in the sheäde do blow" *see*
Blackmwore by the Stour Barnes
VAUGHAN WILLIAMS
LE PRINCE DE BYZANCE. see Péladin
Hymne pour le "Salut Drapeau" du
"Prince de Byzance.". SATIE
THE PRINCESS. see Tennyson
The bugle song THOMSON
The splendour falls
VAUGHAN WILLIAMS
THE PRINCESS: IV, 1. 21. *see* Tennyson
Tears, idle tears VAUGHAN WILLIAMS
"Princesse! à jalouser le destin d'une Hébé"
see Placet futile Mallarmé DEBUSSY,
RAVEL
"Les Princesses aux yeux de chevreuil" *see*
Le sombre Mai Claudel MILHAUD
Princet, Jules
MASSENET *L'oiseau de paradis*
"Prinsessan är du och prinsen är jag" *see*
Romance Tavaststjerna SIBELIUS
PRINSESSEN. see Bjørnson
Prinsessen GRIEG
Prinsessen see Bjørnson *PRINSESSEN.*
GRIEG
"Prinsessen sad højt i sit Jomfrubur" *see*
Prinsessen Bjørnson GRIEG
Le printemps see Banville HAHN,
KOECHLIN
Le printemps see Hölderlin SAUGUET
Printemps see Labé SAUGUET
Printemps see Ronsard AURIC
"Le printemps a jeté sa lyre" *see*
L'âme oiseaux Văcărescu MASSENET
"Le printemps chasse les hivers" *see*
Au printemps Barbier, J. GOUNOD
Printemps dernier see Gille MASSENET
"Printemps enchaîné" *see Le collier*
Messiaen MESSIAEN
Printemps lointain see Jammes MILHAUD
"Le printemps maladif a chassé tristement
l'hiver" *see Renouveau* Mallarmé
SAUGUET
Printemps triste see Bouchor, M.
CHAUSSON

Le printemps visite la terre see
Chaffotte, Jeanne MASSENET
Printemps-jeunesse see Tolstoï
CHAïKOVSKIï *To bylo ranneiu vesnoï*
Prinz Eugen, der edle Ritter see Freiligrath
LOEWE
Die Prinzessin see Bjørnson *PRINSESSEN.*
GRIEG *Prinsessen*
Prinzessin macht Hochzeit see
Iłłakowiczówna SZYMANOWSKI
Ślub królewny
"Prinzesslein tanzt durch die Wiese" *see*
Klein Evelinde Weber REGER
"Prions trestous, jeunes et vieulx" *see Lay*
Regnier, J. ROREM
Připamatování see Anon. DVOŘÁK
Prise au piège see Koechlin KOECHLIN
Prise aux réseaux d'or see Bengoechea
CRÉPUSCULES DU MATIN. SCHMITT
Prison see Verlaine *SAGESSE.* FAURÉ
The prisoner see Polonsky RUBINSTEIN
The prisoner see Pushkin MEDTNER
"Prisons are built with stones of Law" *see*
Proverb II Blake, William BRITTEN
Privetstvie dukha see Goethe MEDTNER
Geistergruss
Privilèges see Ronsard SCHMITT
Probuzhden'e see Pushkin
RIMSKIï-KORSAKOV
Proč zoubky Tvé tak smály se? see
Houdek, V. MARTINŮ
Why have you laughed at me?
La procession see Brizeux, Ch. FRANCK
Les processions des campagnes see Jammes
MILHAUD
Procopé, Hjalmar, 1868-1927.
SIBELIUS *Små flickorna*
Procris see Vaughan Williams, U.
VAUGHAN WILLIAMS
"Procris is lying at the waterside" *see Procris*
Vaughan Williams, U.
VAUGHAN WILLIAMS
"Prodaet menia v palatke nash sovetskiï
prodavets" *see Sladkaia pesenka*
Sakonskaya, N. PROKOFIEV
Prölss, Robert, 1821-1906, supposed
author.
LASSEN
Barcarolle
Brevier
Einsamkeit
Es lebt kein König!
Ritornell
Proelsz *see* Prölss, Robert, 1821-1906,
supposed author.
"Profitons bien des jours d'Octobre" *see*
Automne Collin MASSENET

Prokhodit vse see Rathaus
RACHMANINOFF *All things pass by*
Prokofiev, A. *see* Prokof'yev, Aleksandr
Andreyevich, b. 1900.
**PROKOFIEV, SERGEĬ SERGEEVICH,
1891-1953.**
Afinogenov, Aleksandr Nikolaevich,
1904-1941.
   Chetyre pesni, op. 66 no. 3 (1935) [GA,
   v. 17, p. 166]
   "Rastet strana, rastet strana"
   Skvoz' shega i tumany, op. 66 no. 4
   (1935) [GA, v. 17, p. 171] same
Agnivt͡sev, Nikolaĭ I͡Akovlevich, d.
1932.
   Kudesnik, op. 23 no. 5 (1915) [GA,
   v. 17, p. 89]
   "V starom zamke, za goroi͡u"
Akhmatova, Anna Andreevna, 1888-
1966.
   Nastoi͡ashchui͡u, op. 27 no. 2 (1916) [GA,
   v. 17, p. 101] same
   Pamiat' o solnt͡se, op. 27 no. 3 (1916)
   [GA, v. 17, p. 103] same
   Seroglazyĭ korol', op. 27 no. 5 (1916)
   [GA, v. 17, p. 109]
   "Slava tebe, bezyskhodnai͡a bol'! "
   Solnt͡se komnatu napolnilo, op. 27 no. 1
   (1916) [GA, v. 17, p. 98] same
   Zdravstvuĭ! op. 27 no. 4 (1916) [GA,
   v. 17, p. 106] same
Andersen, Hans Christian, 1805-1875.
   Gadkiĭ utenok'', op. 18 (1914) [GA, v. 17,
   pp. 11 and 32]
   "Kak khorosho bylo vderevne!"
   Based on Andersen's fairy tale.
Anon.
   Aniutka, op. 66 no. 2 (1935) [GA, v. 17,
   p. 162] same
   Chernet͡s, op. 104 no. 12 (1944) [GA,
   v. 17, p. 270]
   "Zaxotelos' chernet͡su poguliati"
   Duni͡ushka, op. 104 no. 11 (1944) [GA,
   v. 17, p. 264]
   "Kak u duni͡ushki, u golubushki"
   Geĭ, po doroge, op. 79 no. 7 (1939) [GA,
   v. 17, p. 230] same
   Text published in **Pravda,** Nov. 9,
   1937.
   I͡A nigde druzhka ne vizhu, op. 104 no. 7
   (1944) [GA, v. 17, p. 251]
   "Akh, a to nigde"
   Kari glazki, op. 104 no. 10 (1944) [GA,
   v. 17, p. 257] "Akh, kari glazki"
   Katerina, op. 104 no. 4 (1944) [GA,
   v. 17, p. 243] "I͡A sidela do sumerek"

Na gore-to kalina, op. 104 no. 3 (1944)
   [GA, v. 17, p. 241] same
Provody, op. 79 no. 4 (1939) [GA, v. 17,
   p. 225]
   "Oĭ, vchera my pesni peli da guliali"
Sashen'ka, op. 104 no. 6 (1944) [GA,
   v. 17, p. 248]
   "Chto zhe ty, Sashen'kara dost' "
Snezhki belye, op. 104 no. 5 (1944) [GA,
   v. 17, p. 246] same
Son, op. 104 no. 9 (1944) [GA, v. 17,
   p. 255] "Son moĭ milyĭ, son
   schastlivyĭ"
V lete kalina, op. 104 no. 1 (1944) [GA,
   v. 17, p. 233] same
Za goroiu, op. 66 no. 5 (1935) [GA,
   v. 17, p. 175]
   "Za goroi͡u u krinit͡sy"
Za lesochkom, op. 104 no. 8 (1944) [GA,
   v. 17, p. 254]
   "Kak za lesikom, za lesochkom"
Zelenai͡a roshchit͡sa, op. 104 no. 2 (1944)
   [GA, v. 17, p. 237] same
Apukhtin, Aleksyeĭ Nikolayevich,
1841-1893.
   Otchalila lodka, op. 9 no. 2 [GA, v. 17,
   p. 6] same
Bal'mont, Konstantin Dmitriyevich,
1867-1943.
   Babochka, op. 36 no. 3 (1921) [GA,
   v. 17, p. 144] "Zheltokrylai͡a
   babochka"
   Est' drugie planety, op. 9 no. 1 [GA,
   v. 17, p. 1] same
   Golos'' ptit͡s'', op. 36 no. 2 (1921) [GA,
   v. 17, p. 138]
   "Ot lastochki do solov'i͡a"
   Pomni meni͡a! op. 36 no. 4 (1921) [GA,
   v. 17, p. 147]
   "I͡A prines tebe vkradchibyĭ list"
   Stolby, op. 36 no. 5 (1921) [GA, v. 17,
   p. 154]
   "Pri more chernom stoi͡at stolby"
   V moem sadu, op. 23 no. 4 (1915) [GA,
   v. 17, p. 82] same
   Zaklinanie vody i ornia, op. 36 no. 1
   (1921) [GA, v. 17, p. 133]
   "I͡A svet zazhgu, ia svet zazhgu na
   etom beregu"
Barto, A.
   Boltun'i͡a, op. 68 no. 1 [GA, v. 17,
   p. 183] "Eto vovka vydumal"
Blagov, A.
   Stakhanovka, op. 79 no. 2 (1939) [GA,
   v. 17, p. 218] "L'etsi͡a solnt͡se priamo
   vokna sgoluboĭ"

PROKOFIEV, SERGEĬ SERGEEVICH,
1891-1953 *(continued)*
Gippius, Zinaida Nikolaevna, 1869-
1945.
  Seroe plat'itse, op. 23 no. 2 (1915) [GA,
    v. 17, p. 73]
  "Devochka vseren' kom plat'itse"
Golodny, Mikhail
  Partizan Zhelezniak, op. 66 no. 1 (1935)
    [GA, v. 17, p. 160] "V stepi pod
    khersonom vysokie travy"
Gorianskogo, V.
  Pod kryshei, op. 23 no. 1 (1915) [GA,
    v. 17, p. 58]
  "IA ne znaiu chto takoe"
Kvitko, L.
  Porosiata, op. 68 no. 3 [GA, v. 17,
    p. 197] "Anna Banna, nash otriad"
Lermontov, Mikhail Yuryevich, 1814-
1841.
  Skazhi mne (1903) [unpubl.]
Lugovskoĭ, Vladimir Aleksandrovich,
1901-1957.
  Soldatskaia poxodnaia, op. 121 (1950)
    [GA, v. 17, p. 285]
  "My, sovetskie soldaty"
Maiakovskii, Vladimir Vladimirovich,
1894-1930.
  Pesnya, op. 89 no. 1 (1941) [unpubl.]
Maĭkov, Apollon Nikolayevich, 1821-
1897.
  Mastitiye, vetvistiye, dubĭ (1906-07)
    [unpubl.]
Mendel'son, Mira Aleksandrovna,
1915-1968.
  Frits, op. 89 no. 6 [Muzfond, 1942]
  Klyatve tankista, op. 89 no. 3 (1941-42)
    [Muzfond, 1942]
  Lyubov voyna, op. 89 no. 7 [unpubl.]
  Podruga boytsa, op. 89 no. 5 [Muzfond,
    1942]
  Sin Kabordi, op. 89 no. 4 (1941-42)
    [Muzfond, 1942]
  Smelo vpered! op. 79 no. 5 (1939) [GA,
    v. 17, p. 226]
  "Ty, Rodina, pomnish' surovye byli"
No author
  Piat' pesen bez slov, op. 35 (1920) [GA,
    v. 17, p. 113]
Panch, Petro, b. 1891.
  Shel stanitseiu kazak, op. 79 no. 6 (1939)
    [GA, v. 17, p. 228] same
Prokofiev, Sergeĭ Sergeevich, 1891-
1953.
  Smotri, pushinki (1903) [unpubl.]
Prokof'yev, Aleksandr Andreyevich, b.
1900.

Pesnia o rodine, op. 79 no. 1 (1939)
    [GA, v. 17, p. 214]
  "Net na svete kraia"
Pushkin, Aleksandr Sergeevich, 1799-
1837.
  Rumianoĭ zareiu pokrylsia vostok, op. 73
    no. 2 (1936)
    [GA, v. 17, p. 204] same
  Sosny, op. 73 no. 1 (1936) [GA, v. 17,
    p. 199]
  "Vnov' ia posetil tot ugolok zemlia"
  Uzh ya ne tot (1903) [unpubl.]
  V tvoiu svetlitsu, op. 73 no. 3 (1936)
    [GA, v. 17, p. 212] same
Sakonskaya, N
  Sladkaia pesenka, op. 68 no. 2 [GA,
    v. 17, p. 194] "Prodaet menia v palatke
    nash sovetskiĭ prodavets"
Sikorskaya, Tatyana
  Pesnia o Voroshilove, op. 66 no. 6
    (1935) [GA, v. 17, p. 179]
  "My pomnim stepnye pokhody"
Surkov, Alekseĭ Aleksandrovich, 1899-
1983.
  Pesnia smelykh, op. 89 no. 2 (1941)
    [GA, v. 17, p. 231]
  "Steliutsia chernye tuchi"
Svetlova, Marina, 1922-
  Nad poliarnym morem, op. 79 no. 3
    (1939) [GA, v. 17, p. 222] same
Unknown
  Lament [Enoch, 1923] "O ye snowflakes
    covering the earth"
    Arranged by Prokofiev; published in
      Swan, ed. *Songs from many lands,*
      p. 39.
  The mulberry tree [Enoch, 1923]
    "Will you come to the mulberry tree in
      the dawning"
    Arranged by Prokofiev; published in
      Swan, ed. *Songs from many lands,*
      p. 42.
  O net, ne Figner (1903) [unpubl.]
Vérine, Boris
  Dover'sia mne, op. 23 no. 3 (1915) [GA,
    v. 17, p. 79] same
Prokofiev, Sergeĭ Sergeevich, 1891-
1953.
PROKOFIEV
  Smotri, pushinki
Prokof'yev, Aleksandr Andreyevich, b.
1900.
PROKOFIEV
  Pesnia o rodine
Prokosch, Frederic, 1908-1989.
ROREM
  Evening
  Midnight

THE CARNIVAL.
   BARBER *Nocturne*
Prolog see Drachmann **GRIEG**
Prologi see Jalkanen **KILPINEN**
Prologue see Mei **BALAKIREV** *Zapevka*
Prologue and Epilogue: from "The Rain" see
   Windham *EMBLEMS OF CONDUCT.*
   Chapter "The Rain." **ROREM**
La promenade see Bédat de Monlaur,
   Pierre **HONEGGER**
Promenade galante see Banville
   RIMES DORÉES. **KOECHLIN**
Promeneur see Follain **SAUGUET**
LE PROMENOIR DES DEUX AMANTS,
   no. 2
   DEBUSSY Tristan L'Hermite *Crois mon*
     conseil
LE PROMENOIR DES DEUX AMANTS,
   no. 3
   DEBUSSY Tristan L'Hermite *Je tremble*
     en voyant ton visage
La promessa see Metastasio **ROSSINI**
Prometheus see Goethe **SCHUBERT,**
   WOLF
Promiscuity see Jackson, Kenneth,
   translator. *A CELTIC MISCELLANY.*
   BARBER
The prophet see Pushkin
   RIMSKIĬ-KORSAKOV *Prorok*
Prorok see Pushkin **RIMSKIĬ-KORSAKOV**
Prosba see Anon. **MARTINŮ**
PROSE LYRIQUES
   DEBUSSY Debussy *De fleurs*
   DEBUSSY Debussy *De grève*
   DEBUSSY Debussy *De rêve*
   DEBUSSY Debussy *De soir*
Prosie see Iłłakowiczówna
   SZYMANOWSKI
"Prosie przebrało sie i poszło spacerować" *see*
   Prosie Iłłakowiczówna
   SZYMANOWSKI
Prosti see Nekrasov **CHAĬKOVSKIĬ**
Prosti! Ne pomni dneĭ paden'ia see
   Nekrasov **RIMSKIĬ-KORSAKOV**
Prostye solva see Chaĭkovskiĭ
   CHAĬKOVSKIĬ
Proto see Pech **DVOŘÁK**
Proud songsters see Hardy **BRITTEN**
Proust, Marcel, 1871-1922.
   SAUGUET *Comme à la lumière de la lune*
Provençalisches Lied see Uhland
   SCHUMANN
Proverb I see Blake, William
   PROVERBS OF HELL. **BRITTEN**
Proverb II see Blake, William
   PROVERBS OF HELL. **BRITTEN**

Proverb III see Blake, William
   PROVERBS OF HELL. **BRITTEN**
Proverb IV see Blake, William
   PROVERBS OF HELL. **BRITTEN**
Proverb V see Blake, William **BRITTEN**
Proverb VI see Blake, William
   PROVERBS OF HELL. **BRITTEN**
Proverb VII see Blake, William
   AUGURIES OF INNOCENCE. **BRITTEN**
PROVERBS OF HELL. see Blake, William
   Proverb I **BRITTEN**
   Proverb II **BRITTEN**
   Proverb III **BRITTEN**
   Proverb IV **BRITTEN**
   Proverb VI **BRITTEN**
PROVERBS 31. see Bible
   Eishet chayil **GIDEON**
Provody see Anon. **PROKOFIEV**
Prutz, Robert Eduard, 1816-1872.
   FRANZ *Wohl viele tausend Vögelein*
   LASSEN
     O willkommen
     Vorsatz
   REGER
     Das Mädchen spricht
První láska see Mužik **MARTINŮ** *First love*
Przed zaśnięciem see Iłłakowiczówna
   SZYMANOWSKI
"Przyszła do łózka bosa kaczuszka" *see*
   Kołysanka lalki Iłłakowiczówna
   SZYMANOWSKI
Psalm see Schoeck, P. **SCHOECK**
Psalm 23 see Bible **SCHOECK**
Psalm XXXIV see Bible **HONEGGER**
PSALM 62. see Bible
   Meine Seele ist still zu Gott **REGER**
PSALM 86. see Bible
   Psalm 86: A prayer of David **ROREM**
Psalm 86: A prayer of David see Bible
   PSALM 86. **ROREM**
PSALM 100. see Bible
   A psalm of praise **ROREM**
Psalm 100 see Bible **SCHOECK**
Psalm CXI see Bible **HONEGGER**
PSALM 119. see Bible
   Geistliches Lied "Wohl denen" **REGER**
PSALM 120. see Bible
   A song of David **ROREM**
Psalm 121 see Bible **BLACHER**
PSALM 127. see Bible
   Hinei nachalat adonai baním **GIDEON**
PSALM 128. see Bible
   Y' gia kapecha ki Tocheil **GIDEON**
Psalm 134 see Bible **ROREM**
Psalm CXXXVIII see Bible **HONEGGER**
Psalm 141 see Bible **BLACHER**

Psalm 142 see Bible **BLACHER, ROREM**

Psalm 148 see Bible **ROREM**

Psalm 150 see Bible **ROREM**

Psalm für das Vaterland see Rolfsen **GRIEG**
  Faedrelandssalme

A psalm of praise see Bible *PSALM 100.*
  ROREM

PSYCHÉ. see Corneille
  Je suis jaloux **KOECHLIN**

"Ptakowie, kwiatowie, lanie weseli" *see*
  Święty Franciszek Tuwim
  SZYMANOWSKI

"Ptaszki leca pytać sie" *see Święty Franciszek
  mówi* Miciński **SZYMANOWSKI**

Ptichka see Pleshcheyev *PODSNEZHNIK.*
  CHAĬKOVSKIĬ

"Une puce, dans sa voiture" *see
  Quelle aventure!* Carême **POULENC**

"Puis qu'ici-bàs toute âme" *see Rêverie* Hugo
  SAINT-SAËNS

Puisque j'ai mis ma lèvre see Hugo **HAHN**

"Puisque j'ai mis ma lèvre à ta coupe" *see
  Extase* Hugo **SAINT-SAËNS**

"Puisque j'ai mis ma lèvre à ta coupe" *see
  Passez, passez toujours* Hugo **FRANCK**

"Puisque j'ai mis ma lèvre à ta coupe" *see
  Puisque j'ai mis ma lèvre* Hugo **HAHN**

Puisque l'aube grandit see Verlaine **FAURÉ**

"Puisque les roses sont jolies" *see Chanson
  pour Jeanne* Mendès **CHABRIER**

"Puisque Mai tout en fleurs" *see Mai* Hugo
  FAURÉ

"Puisque pour moi le temps a sonné" *see
  Départ* Guérin-Catelin **MASSENET**

"Puisque rien ne t'arrête en cet heureux pays"
  see Adieux de l'hôtesse arabe Hugo
  BIZET

Puisque tout passe see Rilke
  POÈMES FRANCAIS. **BARBER**

"Puisque tu ne veux pas m'attendre" *see
  Séparation* Mariéton **MASSENET**

Puisque Vénus see Gabory **SAUGUET**

Puisqu'elle a pris ma vie see Robiquet
  MASSENET

Puisqu'ici-bas toute âme see Hugo **LALO**

"Puisqu'ici-bas toute âme" *see Rêverie* Hugo
  HAHN

"Pujdeme, pujdeme" *see Chodníček*
  Unknown **MARTINŮ**

"Pullula ne l'opaco bosco" *see La najade*
  Annunzio **RESPIGHI**

"Pulse höret auf zu schlagen durch den
  sturmgehobnen Busen" *see
  Sonatine, B flat minor, op. 138 "An sie am
    Klavier"* Braun von Braunthal
  SPOHR

Punschlied see Unknown **BEETHOVEN**

Punschlied. Im Norden zu singen see
  Schiller **SCHUBERT**

"Le pur soleil qui remise" *see Le vitrier*
  Mallarmé **MILHAUD**

"Purpur malt die Tannenhügel" *see
  Der Abend* Matthisson **SCHUBERT**

Pushař zima see Collin **CHAĬKOVSKIĬ**
  Qu'importe que l'hiver

Pushkin, Aleksandr Sergeevich, 1799-
1837.
  BALAKIREV *Gruzinskaya pesnya*
  BORODIN *For the shores of thy far native
    land*
  BRITTEN
    Angel
    Echo
    Epigram
    Lines written during a sleepless night
    My heart . . .
    The nightingale and the rose
  CHAĬKOVSKIĬ *Pesnya Zemfiri*
  JENSEN
    O sing, du Schöne
    Ständchen
  MEDTNER
    Alas, for I outlive my yearnings
    The angel
    Arion
    The coach of life
    Echo
    Elegy
      Two settings: Op. 45 no. 1 and op. 52
      no. 3.
    The faded flower
    I loved you well
    If one day you're disillusioned
    Lost hopes
    Message
    The muse
    Night
    The prisoner
    The ravens
    Retrospect
    The rose
    Serenade
    The singer
    Sleepless
    Spanish romance
      Two settings: Op. 36 no. 4 and op. 52
      no. 5.
    The summons
    To a dreamer
    Visions
    The waltz
    The war horse

COMPOSER   Poet   *Title*   "First Line"

What means to thee my humble name?
When roses fade
The window
Winter evening
MUSORGSKIĭ
Noch'
Strekotun'ia beloboka
PROKOFIEV
Rumianoĭ zareiu pokrylsia vostok
Sosny
Uzh ya ne tot
V tvoiu svetlitsu
RACHMANINOFF
Arion
The muse
Sing not to me, beautiful maiden
The storm
RIMSKIĭ-KORSAKOV
Anchar-drevo smerti
Chto v imeni tebe moem?
Dlia beregov otchizuy dal'noi
Ekho
Grechanke
IA veriu iu liubim
Krasavitsa
Na kholmakh Gruzii
Ne poĭ, krasavitsa, pri mne
Nenastnyĭ den' potukh
Poet
Probuzhden'e
Prorok
Redeet oblakov letuchaia griada
Snovidenie
Tsvetok zasokhshiĭ
Ty i my
V krovi gorit
Zaklinanie
RUBINSTEIN
Auf dein Wohl trink'ich
Bacchisches Lied
Der Engel
Der Gefangene
Lied

Der Sturm
Vernehmet ihr?
STRAVINSKIĭ *Storm cloud*
NOCH'
 RIMSKIĭ-KORSAKOV *Moĭ golos dlia*
 tebia
ZHELANIE.
 RIMSKIĭ-KORSAKOV *Medlitel'no*
 vlekutsia dni moi
DIE ZIGEUNER.
 RUBINSTEIN *Scene...*
"Puskaĭ kholodnoiu zemleiu" **see**
 Liubov' mertvetsa Lermontov
 CHAĭKOVSKIĭ
"Pust' govoriat poeziia mechta" **see** *Somnenie*
 Maĭkov **RIMSKIĭ-KORSAKOV**
Pustĭnya **see** Zhemchuzhnikov
 BALAKIREV
"Pustoe serdechnym Ona" **see** *Ty i my*
 Pushkin **RIMSKIĭ-KORSAKOV**
Put your cheek so tenderly next to my own **see**
 Heine *LYRICAL INTERMEZZO.*
 RIMSKIĭ-KORSAKOV *Shchekoiu k*
 shcheke ty moeĭ prilozhis'
The putting right **see** Mei *PESNYA.*
 BALAKIREV *Kak naladidi: Durak*
Puttkamer, Marie Madeleine (Günther),
 Freifrau, 1881-
 BERG *Vom Ende*
 REGER *Mädchenlied*
Puttkamer-Plauth, Eugen von, 1800-
 1874, supposed author.
 LOEWE *Die Gruft der Liebenden*
Pyhäin miesten päivänä **see** Jalkanen
 KILPINEN
Pyrker, Johann Ladislaus, 1772-1847.
 SCHUBERT
 Die Allmacht
 Das Heimweh
Pyrker von Felsö-Eör *see* Pyrker,
 Johann Ladislaus, 1772-1847.
Pythia **see** Ritter **REGER**
"Pyzhichkov, volvianochek" *see* *Po griby* Mei
 MUSORGSKIĭ

COMPOSER Poet *Title* "First Line"

Q

"Qu' as-tu vu dans ton exil?" *see Rosemonde* Giraudoux **HONEGGER**

"Quälend ungestillltes Sehnen" *see Die verfehlte Stunde* Schlegel **SCHUBERT**

"Quaint name Ann street" *see Ann street* Pool, Morris W. **IVES**

Qual voce, quai note see Unknown **ROSSINI**

Quand, à tes genoux! see Silvestre **AUBERT**

"Quand ce beau printemps je voy" *see Printemps* Ronsard **AURIC**

"Quand celui qui t'adore" *see Élégie* Moore, T. **BERLIOZ**

"Quand chauffant nos pieds aux tisons" *see Vieilles lettres* Normand **MASSENET**

"Quand de mon tertre en fleur" *see Aube païenne* Rocha, Lucien **MASSENET**

"Quand Dieu laisse sortir" *see Oraison funèbre* Bossuet **THOMSON**

"Quand je baise, pâle de fièvre" *see Caprice* Banville **DEBUSSY**

"Quand je chemine, le soir" *see Séraphine* Heine **HAHN**

Quand je fus pris au pavillon see Charles, Duke of Orleans **HAHN**

"Quand je m'en vais par les sentiers" *see Pour Antoinette* Bourguignat, Paul **MASSENET**

"Quand je mourrai, que l'on me mette" *see Coquetterie posthume* Gautier **DEBUSSY**

"Quand je suis loin quand je suis triste" *see J'en appelle à l'alchimiste* Raphaël, Cluzel **SAUGUET**

Quand je viendrai m'asseoir see Moréas **HAHN**

"Quand je viendrai m'asseoir dans le vent" *see Dans la nuit* Moréas **HAHN**

"Quand je viens sur la prairie" *see La vie gaie* Hölderlin **SAUGUET**

"Quand je voy tant de couleurs" *see Portret d'un enfant* Ronsard **MASSENET**

"Quand la fleur du soleil" *see Le parfum impérissable* Leconte de Lisle **FAURÉ**

Quand la nuit n'est pas étoilé see Hugo **HAHN**

"Quand l'aube va paritre" *see Etoile du matin* Distel, Camille **SAINT-SAËNS**

"Quand le ciel couleur d'une joue" *see La ceinture* Valéry **SAUGUET**

"Quand le ciel et mon heure" *see Le tombeau* Ronsard **POULENC**

"Quand le feu brûle encore" *see Eaux douces* Beaumont **SAUGUET**

"Quand le matin l'homme est bien reposé" *see Hommage au travail* Senart **HONEGGER**

Quand le rossignol see Anon. **VAUGHAN WILLIAMS**

"Quand le son du cor sendort" *see Le chasseur perdu en forêt* Fort **HONEGGER**

Quand l'enfant prie see Boyer, Charles **GOUNOD**

"Quand les anges se sont perdus" *see Ballade* Mauclair **CHAUSSON**

"Quand les blonds èpis mûrs ondoyant dans la plaine" *see La mort de la cigale* Faure, M. **MASSENET**

"Quand les bruns matelots des mers orientales" *see Épithalame* Grenier **DELIBES**

"Quand les cloches du soir" *see Les cloches du soir* Desbordes-Valmore **FRANCK**

"Quand les gens" *see Monsieur sans-souci* Nohain, Jean **POULENC**

"Quand les moutons sont dans la bergerie" *see Robin Gray* Florian **FRANCK**

"Quand les premières pluies de Septembre" *see Les champignons* Paliard **MILHAUD**

"Quand l'étranger envahissant la France" *see Les trois exiles* Delfosse **FRANCK**

"Quand mon âme ravie" *see Je crois en vous* Guérin, L. **BERLIOZ**

Quand nous nous sommes vus see Lebey **MASSENET**

Quand on aime see Manuel **MASSENET**

"Quand on aime, on ete tout léger!" *see Sérénade* Manuel **MASSENET**

"Quand on se rencontre" *see La prière de femme* Lamartine **RUBINSTEIN**

"Quand, pour me faire ce geste" *see L'adieu* Toussaint **AUBERT**

Quand reviendra l'automne see Moréas **HAHN**

"Quand sur la colline" *see Crépuscule* Anon. **GOUNOD**

"Quand ta voix céleste prélude" *see Au rossignol* Lamartine **GOUNOD**

"Quand tes yeux clos ne verront plus" *see Les yeux clos* Buchillot, G. **MASSENET**

"Quand ton sourire me surprit" *see Le charme* Silvestre **CHAUSSON**

"Quand tu arrives, garçon" *see La tour prends garde* Baron **SAUGUET**

Quand tu chantes bercée see Hugo **LISZT**

"Quand tu chantes bercée" *see Sérénade* Hugo **GOUNOD**

Quand tu nageois emmy Sirènes et Tritons see Koechlin **KOECHLIN**

Quand tu plonges tes yeux dans mes yeux see Lerberghe **FAURÉ**

Quand tu verras les hirondelles see Zimmer, Bernard **HONEGGER**

"Quand un regard que rien ne voile" *see Compliment* Dumas the younger **GOUNOD**

"Quand viendra la saison nouvelle" *see Villanelle* Gautier **BERLIOZ**

"Quand vous avez laissé" *see Ma douleur et sa compagne* Latil **MILHAUD**

"Quand vous me montrez une rose" *see Romance* Unknown **LASSEN**

"Quando dal tuo verone, fra l'ombre della sera" *see La lontananza* Torre, G. **ROSSINI**

Quando nasceste voi see Birga, Arturo *RISPETTI TOSCANI.* **RESPIGHI**

Quanti Mai see Metastasio **GOUNOD**

"Qu'apercoiton si blanc au loin?" *see Tsaraiuki* Tsaraiuki **STRAVINSKIĬ**

Quarles, Francis, 1592-1644.
    BRITTEN *Canticle I*

Quarrel see Anon. **SEIBER**

Das Quartett see Krylov **RUBINSTEIN**

"Les quartiers retirés" *see La wagon immobile* Hugnet **THOMSON**

Quatrain see Flament **MILHAUD**

Quatrain see Jammes **MILHAUD**

Quatrain see Mallarmé **MILHAUD**

Le quatrain de la rose see Mahaut **RIVIER**

"Quatre ans, j'avais quatre ans" *see Java de la femme* Bloch **MILHAUD**

QUATRE CHANSONS DE CÉRULEUM, no. 1
    SAUGUET Luka, Madeleine *La marchand de coeurs*

QUATRE CHANSONS DE CÉRULEUM, no. 2
    SAUGUET Luka, Madeleine *Voici le chemin de la vie*

QUATRE CHANSONS DE CÉRULEUM, no. 3
    SAUGUET Luka, Madeleine *Chanson des amoureux*

QUATRE CHANSONS DE CÉRULEUM, no. 4
    SAUGUET Luka, Madeleine *Le jardin de Virigine*

QUATRE CHANSONS POUR ENFANTS, no. 1
    POULENC Nohain, Jean *Nous voulons une petit soeur*

QUATRE CHANSONS POUR ENFANTS, no. 2
    POULENC Nohain, Jean *La tragique histoire du petit René*

QUATRE CHANSONS POUR ENFANTS, no. 3
    POULENC Nohain, Jean *Le petit garçon trop bien portant*

QUATRE CHANSONS POUR ENFANTS, no. 4
    POULENC Nohain, Jean *Monsieur sans-souci*

QUATRE CHANTS DE LA FRANCE MALHEUREUSE, no. 1
    AURIC Aragon *Richard II Quarante*

QUATRE CHANTS DE LA FRANCE MALHEUREUSE, no. 2
    AURIC Supervielle *Le petit bois*

QUATRE CHANTS DE LA FRANCE MALHEUREUSE, no. 3
    AURIC Eluard *Nous ne vous chantons pas*

QUATRE CHANTS DE LA FRANCE MALHEUREUSE, no. 4
    AURIC Aragon *La rose et la Réséda*

QUATRE MÉLODIES, no. 1
    CHAUSSON Bouchor, M. *Nocturne*

QUATRE MÉLODIES, no. 2
    CHAUSSON Bouchor, M. *Amour d'antan*

QUATRE MÉLODIES, no. 3
    CHAUSSON Bouchor, M. *Printemps triste*

QUATRE MÉLODIES, no. 4
    CHAUSSON Bouchor, M. *Nos souvenirs*
    NB: The above series is op. 8.

QUATRE MÉLODIES, no. 1
    CHAUSSON Verlaine *Apaisement*

QUATRE MÉLODIES, no. 2
    CHAUSSON Cazalis *Sérénade*

QUATRE MÉLODIES, no. 3
    CHAUSSON Villiers *L'aveu*

QUATRE MÉLODIES, no. 4
    CHAUSSON Leconte de Lisle *La cigale*
    NB: The above series is op. 13.

QUATRE MONOCANTES, no. 1
    SCHMITT Bengoechea *Prise aux réseaux d'or*

QUATRE MONOCANTES, no. 2
    SCHMITT Fargue *La petite princesse*

QUATRE MONOCANTES, no. 3
    SCHMITT Vincendon, Mireille *Antennes*

QUATRE MONOCANTES, no. 4
    SCHMITT Carême *Le cerisier*

QUATRE PETITES MÉLODIES, no. 1
    SATIE Lamartine *Elégie*

QUATRE PETITES MÉLODIES, no. 2
    SATIE Cocteau *Danseuse*

QUATRE PETITES MÉLODIES, no. 3
    SATIE Anon. *Chanson*

QUATRE PETITES MÉLODIES, no. 4
    SATIE Radiguet *Adieu*

COMPOSER   Poet   *Title*   "First Line"

Les quatre petits lions see Vildrac
  MILHAUD
QUATRE POÈMES, no. 1
  AURIC Gabory *La voix*
QUATRE POÈMES, no. 2
  AURIC Gabory *L'ange a perdu son
  auréole*
QUATRE POÈMES, no. 3
  AURIC Gabory *Miroir*
QUATRE POÈMES, no. 4
  AURIC Gabory *Ma vie est la feuille*
QUATTRO ARIE SCOZZESI
  ARMONIZZATE, no. 1
  RESPIGHI Unknown *When the kye come
  hame*
QUATTRO ARIE SCOZZESI
  ARMONIZZATE, no. 2
  RESPIGHI Unknown *Within a mile of
  Edinburgh town*
QUATTRO ARIE SCOZZESI
  ARMONIZZATE, no. 3
  RESPIGHI Unknown *My heart's in the
  Highlands*
QUATTRO ARIE SCOZZESI
  ARMONIZZATE, no. 4
  RESPIGHI Unknown *The piper of
  Dundee*
    Texts by Robert Burns?
QUATTRO FAVOLE ROMANESCHE, no. 1
  CASELLA Salustri *Er coccodrillo*
QUATTRO FAVOLE ROMANESCHE, no. 2
  CASELLA Salustri *La carità*
QUATTRO FAVOLE ROMANESCHE, no. 3
  CASELLA Salustri *Er gatto e er cane*
QUATTRO FAVOLE ROMANESCHE, no. 4
  CASELLA Salustri *L'elezzione der
  presidente*
QUATTRO LIRICHE ITALIANE, no. 1
  RIETI Anon. *E per un bel cantar*
QUATTRO LIRICHE ITALIANE, no. 2
  RIETI Poliziano *La non vuol esser piu
  mia*
QUATTRO LIRICHE ITALIANE, no. 3
  RIETI Anon. *E lo mio cor s'inchina*
QUATTRO LIRICHE ITALIANE, no. 4
  RIETI Poliziano *Canti oghun*
QUATTRO RISPETTI TOSCANI, no. 1
  RESPIGHI Birga, Arturo *Quando
  nasceste voi*
QUATTRO RISPETTI TOSCANI, no. 2
  RESPIGHI Birga, Arturo *Venitelo a
  vedere 'l mi'piccino . . .*
QUATTRO RISPETTI TOSCANI, no. 3
  RESPIGHI Birga, Arturo *Viene di là,
  lontan lontano . . .*
QUATTRO RISPETTI TOSCANI, no. 4

RESPIGHI Birga, Arturo *Razzolan, sopra
  a l'aja, le galline . . .*
Que Dieu se montre seulement see Anon.
  VAUGHAN WILLIAMS
"Que j'aime à vous voir, belles fleurs" *see
  Les fleurs* Contamine **SATIE**
"Que j'aime cette heure rêveuse" *see
  Le coucher du soleil!* Moore, T.
  BERLIOZ
"Que la vie est ennuyeuse" *see École de
  guerre* Cocteau **AURIC**
"Que le jour me dure! Passé loin de toi" *see
  Ariette à l'ancienne* Rousseau **ROSSINI**
"Que le jour me dure! Passé loin de toi" *see
  Ariette villageoise* Rousseau **ROSSINI**
Que le temps me dure see Rousseau
  BEETHOVEN
"Que lentement passent les heures" *see
  A la Santé* Apollinaire **HONEGGER**
"Que les premiers jours de Septembre" *see
  Septembre* Văcărescu **MASSENET**
Que l'heure est donc brève! see Silvestre
  MIGNONNE. **DELIBES, MASSENET**
"Que me fait la politique!" *see Humoresque*
  Beauquier **LALO**
"Que me fait toute la terre" *see Chanson*
  Régnier **FAURÉ**
"Que me font ces vallons, ces palais" *see
  Elégie* Lamartine **SATIE**
"Que me veux-tu, chère fleurette" *see
  À une fleur* Musset **BIZET, LALO**
"Que m'importe que l'Infante de Portugal" *see
  Coeur en péril* Chalupt **ROUSSEL**
Que penser de mon salut see Jacob, M.
  SAUGUET
"Que ta gloire, Ô Roi des rois" *see Kaddisch*
  Anon. **RAVEL**
Que ta volonté soit faite see Gounod
  GOUNOD
"Que te dirai je et que te raconterai je" *see
  Chant Hassidique* Anon. **MILHAUD**
"Que ton coeur prenne sa défense" *see
  La dernière fleur* Desbordes-Valmore
  SAUGUET
"Que tu es simple et claire" *see Eau vivante*
  Lerberghe **FAURÉ**
"Que vos tabernacles sont aimables, O
  Seigneur des armées" *see Prière de l'après-
  dîner* Anon. **MILHAUD**
Quedito see Anon. **RODRIGO**
"Quedito, pasito" *see Quedito* Anon.
  RODRIGO
*THE QUEEN OF CHINA AND OTHER
  POEMS* (1919). *see* Shanks
  Late summer **HESELTINE**
  The singer **HESELTINE**

COMPOSER Poet *Title* ''First Line''

Queen of love see Palgrave **GOUNOD**
The queen of the sea see Borodin
   BORODIN Morskaya tsarevna
The queen's face on the summery coin see
   Horan **BARBER**
"Quel feu s'allu me dans mon coeur!" see
   L'esprit saint Unknown **BIZET**
Quel galant see Anon. **RAVEL**
Quel Rosignuol see Petrarca **PIZZETTI**
Quelconque une solitude see Mallarmé
   MILHAUD
Die Quelle see Chamisso **MEDTNER**
Die Quelle see Unknown **LOEWE**
Quelle aventure! see Carême **POULENC**
"Quelle douce clarté vient éclairer l'Orient"
   see L'aurore Châteaubriand **MILHAUD**
"Qu'elle était donc tentatrice" see La perverse
   Chalupt **MILHAUD**
"Quellen rauschen, Lüfte schweigen" see
   Sehnsucht Itzerott **REGER**
QUELQUE CHANSONS MAUVES, no. 1
   MASSENET Lebey En même temps que
   ton amour
QUELQUE CHANSONS MAUVES, no. 2
   MASSENET Lebey Quand nous nous
   sommes vus
QUELQUE CHANSONS MAUVES, no. 3
   MASSENET Lebey Jamais un tel bonheur
"Quer durch die Felder" see Aber die Nächte
   Sauter, Lilly von, d. ca. 1970.
   KRENEK
The quest see Bal'mont **RACHMANINOFF**
"Qu'est ce donc sur la garenne?" see
   Nérac en fête Bédat de Monlaur, Pierre
   HONEGGER
"Qu'est-il besoin de tant la Paix crier" see
   Sonnet Daurat, Jean **ROREM**
Question grave see Guilliaume **LASSEN**
Questo palpito soave see Unknown
   ROSSINI
"Qu'es-tu donc" see Le souvenir Collin, H.
   GOUNOD
Quételart, A
   GOUNOD
      L'ange gardien
      Le nid
"La queue de boeuf n'est pas" see
   Queues de boeuf Dumont **BERNSTEIN**
Queues de boeuf see Dumont LA BONNE
   CUISINE FRANÇAISE. **BERNSTEIN**
"Qui donc es-tu, forme légère" see Le poète et
   le fantôme Anon. **MASSENET**
"Qui donc porte manteau" see Promeneur
   Follain **SAUGUET**
"Qui jamais fut de plus charmant visage" see
   Madrigal Bonnières **INDY**

"Qui ne la connut riche" see La chance
   Carême **MILHAUD**
"Qui saura t'émouvoir, âme triste" see
   Âme triste Docquois **SAINT-SAËNS**
"Qui sempre ride il cielo" see L'esule Torre,
   G. **ROSSINI**
Quiet girl see Blitzstein **BLITZSTEIN**
Quiet is the blue sea see Maïkov **RIMSKIï-
   KORSAKOV** Tikho more goluboe!
Quiet is the leaves' evening song see Hálek
   DVOŘÁK Umlklo stromu šumění
Quiet lie the deep blue waters see Maïkov
   RIMSKIï-KORSAKOV Tikho more
   goluboe!
"The quiet pools of peace lie far" see
   The pools of peace Campbell, Joan
   CARPENTER
"Quiet sleep! or I will make Erinnys whip
   thee" see A charm Randolph, T.
   BRITTEN
Quiétide see Lefilleul, G. **JOLIVET**
Quietly evening falls see Shenshin
   RIMSKIï-KORSAKOV Tikho vecher
   dogoraet
"Qu'il est doux d'éveiller lentement les
   pensées" see Prelude Collin **MASSENET**
Qu'il faut boire see Anacreon **ROUSSEL**
Qu'il m'irait bien see Unknown **IVES**
"Qu'il vienne cclui que j'aime" see Celui que
   j'aime Carême **SAUGUET**
"Qu'ils sont beaux ces enfants des hommes"
   see Poème du journal intime de Léo Latil
   Latil **MILHAUD**
QUILTER, ROGER, 1877-1953.
Anon.
   Amaryllis at the fountain, op. 15 no. 2
      (1914) [Boosey, 1914] "Crowned with
      flowers I saw fair amaryllis"
   Brown is my love, op. 12 no. 5 (1908)
      [Boosey, 1908] same
   Damask roses, op. 12 no. 3 (1908)
      [Boosey, 1908] "Lady, when I behold
      the roses sprouting"
   Fair house of joy, op. 12 no. 7 (1908)
      [Boosey, 1908]
      "Fain would I change that note"
   The faithless shepherdess, op. 12 no. 4
      (1908) [Boosey, 1908] "While that the
      sun with his beams hot"
   The fuchsia tree, op. 25 no. 2 (1923)
      [Boosey & Hawkes, 1923] "O what if
      the fowler my blackbird has taken?"
   Love is a bable [unpubl.]
   An old carol, op. 25 no. 3 (1924)
      [Boosey & Hawkes, 1924]
      "I sing of a maiden that is matchless"

QUILTER, ROGER, 1877-1953 *(continued)*
 Anon *(continued)*
  Weep you no more, op. 12 no. 1 (1908)
   [Boosey, 1908] same
 Beddoes, Thomas Lovell, 1803-1849.
  If thou would'st ease thine heart
   [unpubl.]
 Bennett, Rodney, 1890-1948.
  The cradle in Bethlehem (1945) [Curwen,
   1949; G. Schirmer] "There was no
   cradle for Jesus when he was small"
   Also with strings.
  Freedom (1941) [Boosey, 1941]
   Also with piano and strings.
 Bickle, Judith Brundrett
  Daisies after rain (1951) [Ascherberg,
   Hopwood & Crew, 1951]
   "The daisy stars are swaying lakes"
 Binyon, Laurence, 1869-1943.
  The answer [Boosey, 1904] "Ask me not,
   dear, what thing it is"
  At close of day (1904) [Boosey, 1904]
   "Warm, the deserted evening"
 Blake, William, 1757-1827.
  Dream valley, op. 20 no. 1 (1917)
   [Boosey & Hawkes, 1917]
   "Memory, hither come, and tune your
    merry notes"
  The jocund dance, op. 18 no. 3 [Elkin,
   1914] "I love the jocund dance"
  The wild flower's song, op. 20 no. 2
   (1917) [Boosey & Hawkes, 1917]
   "As I wandered in the forest"
  MORNING.
   Daybreak, op. 20 no. 3 (1917)
    [Boosey & Hawkes, 1917]
    "To find the western path, right
     through the gates"
 Bodenstedt, Friedrich Martin von,
  1819-1892.
  Die helle Sonne leuchtet, op. 2 no. 4
   [Elkin, 1903] same
  Ich fühle deinen Odem, op. 2 no. 3
   [Elkin, 1903] same
  My heart adorned with thee (1952)
   [Elkin, 1953] same
  Neig' schöne Knospe Dich zu mir, op. 2
   no. 1 [Elkin, 1903] same
  Und was die Sonne glüht, op. 2 no. 2
   [Elkin, 1903] same
 Byron, George Gordon Byron, 6th
  baron, 1778-1824.
  There be none of beauty's daughters, op.
   24 no. 1 (1922) [Chappell, 1922] same
 Campion, Thomas, 1567-1619.
  My life's delight, op. 12 no. 2 (1908)
   [Boosey, 1908]

   "Come, O come, my life's delight!"
 Chesson, Mrs. Nora (Hopper), 1871-
  1906.
  Blossom time, op. 15 no. 3 (1914)
   [Boosey, 1914] "Blossom on the plum"
  June (1905) [Boosey & Hawkes, 1905]
   "Dark red roses in a honeyed wind
    swinging"
  Spring is at the door, op. 18 no. 4 [Elkin,
   1914] same
 Coleridge, Mary Elizabeth, 1861-1907.
  Through the sunny garden, op. 18 no. 5
   [Elkin, 1916] same
  The valley and the hill, op. 18 no. 6
   [Elkin, 1916]
   "O the high valley, the little low hill"
 Dekker, Thomas, 1570-1641.
  O, the month of May, op. 24 no. 4 (1927)
   [Chappell, 1927] same
 Denson, Olive M.
  Wild cherry (1938) [Ascherberg,
   Hopwood & Crew, 1938]
 Dowson, Ernest Christopher, 1867-
  1900.
  A coronal, op. 10 no. 1 (1908) [Boosey,
   1908] "Violets and leaves of vine"
  In spring, op. 10 no. 4 (1908) [Boosey,
   1908] "See how the trees and the
   osiers lithe"
  A land of silence, op. 10 no. 3 (1908)
   [Boosey, 1908] "What land of silence"
  Passing dreams, op. 10 no. 2 (1908)
   [Boosey, 1908] "They are not long, the
   weeping and the laughter"
 Heald, Arthur
  The walled-in garden (1952) [Chappell,
   1952] "O, come with me into my
   wall'd-in garden"
 Henley, William Ernest, 1849-1903.
  Fill a glass with golden wine, op. 3 no. 3
   (1905) [Boosey, 1905] same
  A last year's rose, op. 14 no. 3 (1910)
   [Boosey, 1910]
   "From the brake the nightingale"
  Song of the blackbird, op. 14 no. 4
   (1910) [Boosey, 1910]
   "The nightingale has a lyre of gold"
 Herrick, Robert, 1591-1674.
  The bracelet, op. 8 no. 1 (1906) [Boosey,
   1906]
   "Why I tie about thy wrist, Julia"
  Cherry-ripe, op. 8 no. 6 (1906) [Boosey,
   1906] " 'Cherry-ripe, ripe, ripe,' I cry"
  I dare not ask a kiss, op. 28 no. 3
   [Boosey, 1926] same
  Julia's hair, op. 8 no. 5 (1906) [Boosey,
   1906] "Dew sat on Julia's hair"

The maiden blush, op. 8 no. 2 (1906)
[Boosey, 1906]
"So look the mornings when the sun"
The night-piece, op. 8 no. 4 (1906)
[Boosey, 1906]
"Her eyes the glow-worm lend thee"
To daisies, op. 8 no. 3 (1906) [Boosey,
1906] "Shut not so soon, the dull-eyed
night"
Tulips (1947) [Ascherberg, Hopwood &
Crew, 1947]
From a partsong, 1946.

Heywood, Thomas, d. 1641.
Morning song, op. 24 no. 2 (1922)
[Chappell, 1922] "Pack, clouds, away!"

Hood, Thomas, 1799-1845.
The time of roses, op. 24 no. 5 (1928)
[Chappell, 1928]
"It was not in the winter"

Irvine, John, d. 1964.
Wind from the south (1936) [Ascherberg,
Hopwood & Crew, 1936] "The wind
comes softly out of the south"

Jonson, Ben, 1573?-1637.
By a fountainside, op. 12 no. 6 (1908)
[Boosey, 1908]
"Slow, slow, fresh fount, keep time
with my salt tears"

Keats, John, 1795-1821.
Where be you going, op. 18 no. 2 [Elkin,
1914] same

Kipling, Rudyard, 1865-1936.
Non nobis, domine (1934) [Boosey,
1938] same
Also for chorus, strings and piano.

Lovelace, Richard, 1618-1658.
To Althea from prison, op. 28 no. 4
[Boosey, 1926]
"When love with unconfined wings"

Maquarie, Arthur
Autumn evening, op. 14 no. 1 (1910)
[Boosey, 1910] "The yellow poplar
leaves have strown"

Neuburg, Victor B., 1873-1940.
Trollie, lollie, laughter (1939)
[Ascherberg, Hopwood & Crew, 1939]

Pemberton, May
Come, lady-day (1938) [Ascherberg,
Hopwood & Crew, 1938]
"When the snow is off the mountains"

Quilter, Roger, 1877-1953.
April love (1952) [Ascherberg,
Hopwood & Crew, 1952]
"The buds are bursting in the brake"
By the sea, op. 1 no. 4 [Forsyth, 1901] "I
stood today by the shimm'ring sea"

Come spring! sweet spring! [Weeks &
Co., 1897]
Fair lullaby (1921) [Chappell, 1921]
"Close thine eyes in slumber sweet"
I have a friend, op. 1 no. 1 [Forsyth,
1901] same
Moonlight, op. 1 no. 3 [Forsyth, 1901]
"Under the silver moonlight"
The reign of the stars [Weeks & Co.,
1897]
The sea-bird, op. 1 no. 2 [Forsyth, 1901]
"I watched a sea-bird flying"
A secret
No information available.
Spring voices (1936) [Ascherberg,
Hopwood & Crew, 1936] "I heard a
throstle singing at the dawn of day"

**Rochester, John Wilmot, 2d earl of,
1647-1680.**
The jealous lover, op. 28 no. 1 [Boosey,
1923] "My dear mistress has a heart"
To wine and beauty, op. 18 no. 1 [Elkin,
1914]
"Vulcan! provide me such a cup"

**Rossetti, Christina Georgina, 1830-
1894.**
A song at parting (1952) [Elkin; Galaxy,
1952] "When I am dead, my dearest,
sing no sad songs for me"

Shakespeare, William, 1564-1616.
Blow, blow, thou winter wind, op. 6 no. 3
[Boosey, 1905] same
Hark, hark the lark (1946) [Boosey &
Hawkes, 1946] same
AS YOU LIKE IT.
It was a lover and his lass, op. 23 no.
3 (1921) [Boosey, 1921] same
Under the greenwood tree, op. 23 no.
2 (1921) [Boosey, 1921] same
CYMBELINE.
Fear no more the heat o' the sun, op.
23 no. 1 (1921) [Boosey, 1921]
same
HAMLET.
How should I your true love know? op.
30 no. 3 [Boosey, 1927, 1933] same
KING HENRY VIII.
Orpheus with his lute, op. 32 no. 1
(1939) [Boosey, 1939] same
LOVE'S LABOUR'S LOST.
When icicles hang by the wall, op. 32
no. 2 (1939) [Boosey, 1939] same
MEASURE FOR MEASURE.
Take, O take those lips away, op. 23
no. 4 (1921) [Boosey, 1921] same

COMPOSER Poet *Title* "First Line"

Quilter, Roger, 1877-1953 *(continued)*.
  Shakespeare, William, 1564-1616
  (continued).
    MERCHANT OF VENICE.
      Tell me, where is fancy bred? (1951)
        [Boosey, 1951] same
    MUCH ADO ABOUT NOTHING.
      Sigh no more, ladies, op. 30 no. 4
        [Boosey, 1927, 1933] same
    THE TEMPEST.
      Come unto these yellow sands (1951)
        [Booscy, 1951] same
      Full fathom five [unpubl.]
      Where the bee sucks [unpubl.]
    TWELFTH NIGHT.
      Come away, Death, op. 6 no. 1
        [Boosey, 1905]
        "Come away, come away, death"
      Hey, ho, the wind and the rain, op. 23
        no. 5 (1921) [Boosey, 1921]
        "When that I was & a little tiny
          boy"
      O mistress mine, op. 6 no. 2 [Boosey,
        1905] "O mistress mine, where are
        you roaming?"
    TWO GENTLEMEN OF VERONA.
      Who is Silvia? op. 30 no. 1 [Boosey,
        1927, 1933] same
    A WINTER'S TALE.
      When daffodils begin to peer, op. 30
        no. 2 [Boosey, 1927, 1933] same
  Shelley, Percy Bysshe, 1792-1822.
    Arab love song, op. 25 no. 4 (1927)
      [Hawkes & Son, 1927] "My faint spirit
      was sitting in the light"
    Love's philosophy, op. 3 no. 1 ((1905)
      [Boosey, 1905]
      "The fountains mingle with the river"
    Music (1947) [Curwen, 1948] "I pant for
      the music which is divine"
    Music and moonlight (1935) [Curwen,
      1948] "The keen stars were twinkling"
    One word is too often profaned (1946)
      [Curwen, 1947; G. Schirmer] same
    POSTHUMOUS POEMS (1824).
      Music, when soft voices die, op. 25 no.
        5 (1927) [Winthrop Rogers, 1927]
        same
  Stephens, James, 1882-1950.
    In the bud of the morning-O, op. 25 no. 6
      (1927) [Winthrop Rogers, 1927]
      "In the scented bud of the morning-O"
  Sterling-Levis, Edith
    Drooping wings (1945) [Chappell, 1945]
      "Dreamily the night comes"
  Stevenson, Robert Louis, 1850-1894.

    In the highlands, op. 26 no. 1 (1922)
      [Elkin, 1922] same
    Over the land is April, op. 26 no. 2
      (1922) [Elkin, 1922] same
    A CHILD'S GARDEN OF VERSES.
      Foreign children, op. 5 no. 4
        [Chappell, 1914] "Little Indian,
        Sioux or Crow"
      A good child, op. 5 no. 1 [Chappell,
        1914] "I woke before the morning"
      The lamplighter, op. 5 no. 2 [Chappell,
        1914] "My tea is nearly ready"
      Where go the boats? op. 5 no. 3
        [Chappell, 1914]
        "Dark brown is the river"
  Suckling, Sir John, 1609-1642.
    The constant lover, op. 28 no. 5 [Boosey,
      1928] "Out upon it, I have loved"
    Why so pale and wan? op. 28 no. 2
      [Boosey, 1926] same
  Tennyson, Alfred Tennyson, 1st
  baron, 1809-1892.
    Now sleeps the crimson petal, op. 3 no. 2
      (1904) [Boosey, 1904] same
  Unknown
    Come back (1903) [Elkin, 1903]
      "I dreamed I heard your voice in the
        night"
      Text may be by Quilter.
    The secret (1903) [Elkin, 1903] "My
      heart, my heart. No one may see"
      Text may be by Quilter.
  Waller, Edmund, 1606-1687.
    Go, lovely rose, op. 24 no. 3 (1923)
      [Chappell, 1923] same
  Watson, Sir William, 1858-1935.
    April, op. 14 no. 2 (1910) [Boosey, 1910]
      "April, April, Laugh thy girlish
        laughter"
  Williams, Alfred, 1877-1930.
    Cuckoo song, op. 15 no. 1 (1913)
      [Boosey, 1913]
      "Blow, blow, winds of May"
    Song of the stream, op. 25 no. 1 (1922)
      [Winthrop Rogers, 1922]
      "Flow on! happy stream"
Quilter, Roger, 1877-1953.
  QUILTER
    April love
    By the sea
    Come spring! sweet spring!
    Fair lullaby
    I have a friend
    Moonlight
    The reign of the stars

The sea-bird

A secret

Spring voices

Qu'importe que l'hiver **see** Collin
CHAĬKOVSKIĬ, MASSENET

Quinault, Jeanne-Francoise, 1700?-1783.
SAINT-SAËNS *Nocturne*

Quinton, Ronald, pseud. *see* Quilter,
Roger, 1877-1953.

Quite forsaken see Lawrence **RIETI**

"Quite still I lie where green the grass and
tall" *see In summer fields* Allmers **IVES**

"Quoi! morts tous deux! dans cette chambre
close" *see Le suicide* Béranger **LALO**

"Quoique tes yeux ne la voient pas" *see*
Dans la Nymphée Lerberghe **FAURÉ**

"Quoy qu'on tient belles langagières" *see*
Ballade des femmes de Paris Villon
DEBUSSY

"Qu'un jour à la gare Alexandre" *see*
La Grand'Mère de la Révolution Chalupt
MILHAUD

Quunk, quai quenni monni denni monni see
No author **BLACHER**

R

Raabe, Wilhelm Karl, 1831-1910.
MARTINŮ *Sleep, my little one*

"Rab' zum Raben fliegt daher" *see Lied*
Pushkin **RUBINSTEIN**

Rachel see De La Mare **BERKELEY**

"Rachel, c'est vous la dame blonde" *see*
Cartomancie Chalupt **RIVIER**

"Rachel sings sweet, Oh, yes, at night" *see*
Rachel De La Mare **BERKELEY**

RACHMANINOFF, SERGEI, 1873-1943.

Apukhtin, Aleksyeĭ Nikolayevich,
1841-1893.

Fate, op. 21 no. 1 (1900) {*Sud'ba*} [State
Music Publ., 1947, 1963, p.126]
"With pilgrim's staff, with weary gait"

Oh, do not grieve! op. 14 no. 8 (1896)
{*O, ne grusti!*}
[State Music Publ., 1947, 1963, p.107]
same

Bal'mont, Konstantin Dmitriyevich,
1867-1943.

The migrant wind, op. 34 no. 4 (1912)
{*Veter pereletnyĭ*}
[State Music Publ., 1947, 1963, p.251]
same

The quest, op. 38 no. 6 (1916) {*Au!*}
[State Music Publ., 1947, 1963, p.325]
"Was it a dream?"

Beketova, Ekaterina Andreevna, 1855-
1892.
SIREN'

The lilacs, op. 21 no. 5 (1902) [State
Music Publ., 1947, 1963, p.144]
"At the red of the dawn"

Bible

From the Gospel of St. John, XV: 13
(1915) {*Iz evangeliĭa ot Ioanna*}
[State Music Publ., 1947, 1963, p.304]
"Bol'shi seĭa liubve nikto zhe imat' "

Bryusov, Valery Yakovlevich, 1873-
1924.

The rat-catcher, op. 38 no. 4 (1916)
{*Krysolov*}
[State Music Publ., 1947, 1963, p.315]
"On my flute, when ev'ning
darkens"

Bugayev, Boris Nikolaevich, 1880-
1934.

To her, op. 38 no. 2 (1916) [State Music
Publ., 1947, 1963, p.308]
"Grasses dewpearl'd so tearfully"

Bunin, Ivan Alekseevich, 1870-1953.

Night is mournful, op. 26 no. 12 (1906)
{*Noch' pechal'na*}
[State Music Publ., 1947, 1963, p.215]
same

Chekhov, Anton Pavlovich, 1860-1909.
UNCLE VANYA, Act IV.

Let us rest, op. 26 no. 3 (1906)
{*My otdoxnem*}
[State Music Publ., 1947, 1963,
p.183] same

RACHMANINOFF, SERGEI, 1873-1943
(continued)
Davidova, Mariya A.
I wait for thee! op. 14 no. 1 (1894)
{*IA zhdu tebia*}
[State Music Publ., 1947, 1963, p.86]
same
Einerling, Countess Adolfovna, 1873-1942.
Before my window, op. 26 no. 10 (1906)
{*U moego okna*}
[State Music Publ., 1947, 1963, p.209]
same
How fair this spot, op. 21 no. 7 (1902)
{*Zodes' khorosho*}
[State Music Publ., 1947, 1963, p.150]
same
How painful for me, op. 21 no. 12 (1902)
{*Kak mne bol'no*}
[State Music Publ., 1947, 1963, p.170]
"How? my heart aches!"
Goethe, Johann Wolfgang von, 1749-1832.
A prayer, op. 8 no. 6 (1893) {*Molitva*}
[State Music Publ., 1947, 1963, p.82]
"O Lord of grace! I stand before Thee
self-confessed"
Golenishchev-Kutuzov, Arseniĭ
Arkad'yevich, graf, 1848-1913.
Before the icon, op. 21 no. 10 (1902)
{*Pred ikoniĭ*}
[State Music Publ., 1947, 1963, p.162]
"She stood by the image"
Beloved, let us fly, op. 26 no. 5 (1906)
{*Pokinem, milaia*}
[State Music Publ., 1947, 1963, p.192]
same
How long, my friend, op. 4 no. 6 (1893)
{*Davno l', moĭ drut*}
[State Music Publ., 1947, 1963, p.65]
same
Grekov, Nikolay, 1810-1866.
Again you leapt, my heart (1890)
{*Opiat' vstrepenulos' ty, serdtse*}
[State Music Publ., 1947, 1963, p.15]
same
Guyot, Jean-Marie, 1854-1888.
Twilight, op. 21 no. 3 (1902) {*Sumerki*}
[State Music Publ., 1947, 1963, p.138]
"Alone and lost in dreams"
Heine, Heinrich, 1797-1856.
DU BIST WIE EINE BLUME.
*Child, thou art as beautiful as a
flower,* op. 8 no. 2 (1893)
{*Ditia! kak tsbetok . . .* } [State
Music Publ., 1947, 1963, p.71]
same

*ICH HATTE EINST EIN SCHÖNES
VATERLAND.*
A dream, op. 8 no. 5 (1893) {*Son*}
[State Music Publ., 1947, 1963,
p.80]
"My native land I once enjoyed"
DIE SCHLANKE WASSERLILIE.
The water lily, op. 8 no. 1 (1893)
{*Rechnaia lileia*}
[State Music Publ., 1947, 1963,
p.69] "From reeds on the river"
Hugo, Victor Marie, comte, 1802-1885.
They answered, op. 21 no. 4 (1902)
{*Oni otvechali*}
[State Music Publ., 1947, 1963, p.141]
"They wonder'd a while"
Isaakian, Avetik Saakovich, 1875-1957.
IVANUSHKA.
In my garden at night, op. 38 no. 1
(1916) {*Noch'iu v sadu u menia*}
[State Music Publ., 1947, 1963,
p.306]
"Oft in my garden at night"
Khomyakov, Aleksyeĭ Stepanovich,
1804-1860.
The raising of Lazarus, op. 34 no. 6
(1912) {*Voskreshenie lazaria*}
[State Music Publ., 1947, 1963, p.265]
"O Lord of Heaven!"
To the children, op. 26 no. 7 (1906)
{*K detiam*}
[State Music Publ., 1947, 1963, p.198]
"How often at midnight"
Kol'tsov, Alekseĭ Vasil'yevich, 1809-1842.
I was with her, op. 14 no. 4 (1896) {*IA
byl u neĭ*}
[State Music Publ., 1947, 1963, p.93]
same
The ring, op. 26 no. 14 (1906) {*Kol'tso*}
[State Music Publ., 1947, 1963, p.221]
"Here the tapers I hold"
Two partings, a dialogue, op. 26 no. 4
(1906) {*Dva proshchaniia*}
[State Music Publ., 1947, 1963, p.185]
"Two lovers hadst Thou in thy lead"
Baritone, soprano & piano.
Korinfskiĭ, Apollon Apollonovich,
1868-1937.
In the soul of each of us, op. 34 no. 2
(1912) {*V Dushe u kazhdogo iaz*}
[State Music Publ., 1947, 1963, p.243]
"The soul at all times would
conceal"
Kruglov, Aleksandr Vasil'evich, 1853-1915.

No prophet I, op. 21 no. 11 (1902)
{*IA ne prorok*}
[State Music Publ., 1947, 1963, p.167]
same

Lermontov, Mikhail Yuryevich, 1814-1841.
NISCHCHIY.
At the gate of the Holy Abode (1890)
{*U vrat obiteli sviatoĭ*}
[State Music Publ., 1947, 1963, p.7]
same

Lotarev, Igor' Vasil'evich, 1887-1941.
Daisies, op. 38 no. 3 (1916) {*Margaritki*}
[State Music Publ., 1947, 1963, p.312]
"Behold, my friend, the daisies sweet and tender"

Maĭkov, Apollon Nikolayevich, 1821-1897.
It cannot be, op. 34 no. 7 (1910; rev. 1912) {*Ne mozhet byt'* }
[State Music Publ., 1947, 1963, p.268]
same

Merezhkovski, Dmitriĭ Sergyeyevich, 1865-1941.
Christ is risen, op. 26 no. 6 (1906)
{*Khristos voskres*}
[State Music Publ., 1947, 1963, p.195]
same
I beg for mercy, op. 26 no. 8 (1906)
{*Roshchady ia moliu!*}
[State Music Publ., 1947, 1963, p.202]
same
Oh no, I beg you, forsake me not, op. 4 no. 1 (1892)
{*O net, moliu, ne ukhodi!*} [State Music Publ., 1947, 1963, p.46] same

Musset, Alfred de, 1810-1857.
LA NUIT DE MAI: stanza 4,"Pourquoi mon coeur bat-il si vite?"
Loneliness, op. 21 no. 6 (1902)
{*Otryvok iz A Miusse*}
[State Music Publ., 1947, 1963, p.147] "O, heart of mine"

Nadson, Semen IAkovlevich, 1862-1887.
By the fresh grave, op. 21 no. 2 (1902)
{*Nad svezheĭ mogiloĭ*}
[State Music Publ., 1947, 1963, p.136]
"In gloom of night I stand alone"
Melody, op. 21 no. 9 (1902) {*Melodiia*}
[State Music Publ., 1947, 1963, p.156]
"On slumber-laden wings"
'Tis time, op. 14 no. 12 (1896) {*Pora!*}
[State Music Publ., 1947, 1963, p.122]
same

No author

Vocalise, op. 34 no. 14 (1912; rev. 1915)
[State Music Publ., 1947, 1963, p.300]
Wordless.

Pailleron, Édouard Jules Henri, 1834-1899.
AVRIL: Chanson.
Aprel'! veshniĭ prazdnichnyĭ den' (1891) [State Music Publ., 1947, 1963, p.20] same

Polonsky, Yakov Petrovich, 1819-1898.
Discord, op. 34 no. 13 (1912)
{*Dissonans*}
[State Music Publ., 1947, 1963, p.291]
"What if fate should decree that apart we remain"
Music, op. 34 no. 8 (1912) {*Muzyka*}
[State Music Publ., 1947, 1963, p.271]
"How it flows, how it grows!"
When yesterday we met, op. 26 no. 13 (1906) {*Vchera my vstretilis'*}
[State Music Publ., 1947, 1963, p.218]
same

Pushkin, Aleksandr Sergeevich, 1799-1837.
Arion, op. 34 no. 5 (1912) [State Music Publ., 1947, 1963, p.257]
"Full many souls the vessels held"
The muse, op. 34 no. 1 (1912) {*Muza*}
[State Music Publ., 1947, 1963, p.231]
"From childhood's early days"
Sing not to me, beautiful maiden, op. 4 no. 4 (1893)
{*Ne poĭ, krasavitsa, pri mne*} [State Music Publ., 1947, 1963, p.57]
same
The storm, op. 34 no. 3 (1912) {*Buria*}
[State Music Publ., 1947, 1963, p.246]
"I saw the maid on rocky strand"

Rachmaninoff, Sergei, 1873-1943.
Letter to K. S. Stanislavsky from S. R. (1908)
{*Pis'mo K. S. Stanislavskomer ot S. Rakhmaninova*} [State Music Publ., 1947, 1963, p.232]
"Dorogoĭ Konstantin Sergeevich"
Rachmaninoff's letter of greeting to Stanislavsky on the 10 years' jubilee of the Moscow Arts Theatre, 1909.

Rathaus, Daniil, 1869-1937.
All things pass by, op. 26 no. 15 (1906)
{*Prokhodit vse*}
[State Music Publ., 1947, 1963, p.230]
same
The flower has faded (1893)
{*Uvial tsvetok*}
[State Music Publ., 1947, 1963, p.34]
same

RACHMANINOFF, SERGEI, 1873-1943
(continued)
Rathaus, Daniil, 1869-1937 *(continued)*
Night (1903-04) {*Noch'*} [State Music
Publ., 1963, p.174]
"Snova son na ustalye ochi neĭdet"
Song of the disillusioned (1893)
{*Pesnia razocharovannogo*}
[State Music Publ., 1947, 1963, p.28]
"Umri! tverdit mne den'"
These summer nights, op. 14 no. 5 (1896)
{*Eti letnie nochi*}
[State Music Publ., 1947, 1963, p.96]
"Oh these midsummer nights"
Romanov, Konstantin, 1858-1916
(Grand Duke Konstantin
Konstantinovich)
Prayer (1916) {*Molitva*} [Belwin-Mills,
1973] "Teach me, teach me, oh God"
Op. 38, although not included in
original publication of that opus.
Shelley, Percy Bysshe, 1792-1822.
THE ISLE.
The isle, op. 14 no. 2 (1896)
{*Ostrovok*}
[State Music Publ., 1947, 1963,
p.88] "A little island set in sea"
Shenshin, Afanasiĭ Afanas'evich,
1820-1892.
*For long there has been little
consolation*, op. 14 no. 3 (1896)
{*Davno v liubni*} [State Music Publ.,
1947, 1963, p.90] same
I shall tell you nothing (1890)
{*IA tebe nichego ne skazhu*}
[State Music Publ., 1947, 1963, p.10]
same
In the silence of the secret night, op. 4
no. 3 (1890)
{*V molchan'i nochi taĭnoĭ*}
[State Music Publ., 1947, 1963, p.53]
"When silent night doth hold me"
The peasant, op. 34 no. 11 (1912)
{*Obrochnik*}
[State Music Publ., 1947, 1963, p.279]
"With holy banner firmly held"
What happiness, op. 34 no. 12 (1912)
{*Kakoe schast'e*}
[State Music Publ., 1947, 1963, p.285]
"What wealth of rapture"
Shevchenko, Taras, 1814-1861.
Again I am alone, op. 26 no. 9 (1906)
{*IA opiat' odinok*}
[State Music Publ., 1947, 1963, p.206]
"Spring is come"
I have grown fond of sorrow, op. 8 no. 4
(1893) {*Poliubila ia na pechal' svoiu*}

[State Music Publ., 1947, 1963,
p.78]
"For a life of pain I have giv'n my
love"
Meditation, op. 8 no. 3 (1893) {*Duma*}
[State Music Publ., 1947, 1963, p.73]
"The days in turn pass all too soon"
Teternikov, Fyodor, 1863-1927.
A dream, op. 38 no. 5 (1916) {*Son*} [State
Music Publ., 1947, 1963, p.320]
"Say, oh wither art bound?"
Glory to God, op. 38 (1916) {*Vsë khochet
pet'*} [Belwin-Mills, 1973]
"All nature sings to God Almighty"
Tiutchev, Fëdor Ivanovich, 1803-1873.
The fountains, op. 26 no. 11 (1906)
{*Fontan*}
[State Music Publ., 1947, 1963, p.211]
"Oh mark how high the fountains
play"
He took all from me, op. 26 no. 2 (1906)
{*Vse otnial u menia*}
[State Music Publ., 1947, 1963, p.181]
same
I remember that day, op. 34 no. 10
(1912) {*Seĭ den'ia pomniu*}
[State Music Publ., 1947, 1963, p.277]
"The hour I mind me"
Spring waters, op. 14 no. 11 (1896)
{*Vesennie vody*}
[State Music Publ., 1947, 1963, p.117]
"Tho' still the fields are white with
snow"
You knew him, op. 34 no. 9 (1912)
{*Ty znal ego*}
[State Music Publ., 1947, 1963, p.274]
"You knew him well"
Tolstoĭ, Alekseĭ Konstantinovich, Graf,
1817-1875.
Believe me not, friend, op. 14 no. 7
(1896) {*Ne ver' mne, drug!*}
[State Music Publ., 1947, 1963, p.104]
same
Do you remember the evening? (1893)
{*Ty pomnish' li vecher*}
[State Music Publ., 1947, 1963, p.37]
same
How everyone loves thee, op. 14 no. 6
(1896) {*Tebia tak liubiat vse*}
[State Music Publ., 1947, 1963, p.101]
same
O thou, my field, op. 4 no. 5 (1893)
{*Uzh ty, niva moia*}
[State Music Publ., 1947, 1963, p.61]
"Thou, my field, my beloved harvest
field"

There are many sounds, op. 26 no. 1
(1906) {*Est' mnogo zvukov*}
[State Music Publ., 1947, 1963, p.179]
"Within the heart what treasures lie
concealed"
Twilight has fallen (1891) {*Smerkalos'*}
[State Music Publ., 1947, 1963, p.24]
"Zharkiĭ den'blednel neulovimo, nad
ozerom tuman"
Unknown
Apple tree, O apple tree (1920)
[Swan, Alfred J., ed. *Songs from many
lands* (Enoch: 1923)] same
Facsimile in *Musical Quarterly* Jan.
1944; no words there.
Vilenkin, Nikolay Maksimovich, 1855-
1937.
In my soul, op. 14 no. 10 (1896)
{*V moeĭ dushe*}
[State Music Publ., 1947, 1963, p.114]
"Within my soul"
She is as lovely as the moon, op. 14 no. 9
(1896) {*Ona, kak polden', khorosha*}
[State Music Publ., 1947, 1963, p.111]
same
Vyazemsky, Pyotr, 1792-1878.
Were you hiccuping? (1899)
{*Ikalos' li tebe, Natasha?*}
[State Music Publ., 1947, 1963, p.42]
same
Yanova, Mariya, 1840-1875.
Morning, op. 4 no. 2 (1891) {*Utro*} [State
Music Publ., 1947, 1963, p.50]
"I love thee well"
Zhukovski, Vasiliĭ Andreyevich, 1783-
1852.
On the death of a linnet, op. 21 no. 8
(1902) {*Na smert' chizhika*}
[State Music Publ., 1947, 1963, p.152]
"My linnet lies within his grave"
Rachmaninoff, Sergei, 1873-1943.
RACHMANINOFF *Letter to K. S.
Stanislavsky from S. R.*
Racine, Jean Baptiste, 1639-1699.
HAHN *Cantique sur le bonheur des
justes . . .*
POULENC *Hymne*
THOMSON *Phaedra's farewell*
Radiguet, Raymond, 1903-1923.
AURIC
Album
Bateau
Déjeuner de soleil
Domino
Escarpin
Filet à papillons

Hirondelle
Les joues en feu
Mallarmé
Pelouse
POULENC *Paul et Virginie*
SATIE *Adieu*
SAUGUET
Une carte postale
Chansons de marins
Halte
"Räck mig de väna läpparnes Kalk" *see*
Kyssen Rydberg **SIBELIUS**
Raëk see Musorgskiĭ **MUSORGSKIĭ**
Rätelspiel see Goering **KRENEK**
Räthsel see Anon. **RUBINSTEIN**
Räthsel see Fanshawe **SCHUMANN**
Rätselhaft see Unknown **SPOHR**
DIE RÄUBER. see Schiller
Amalia **SCHUBERT**
Der Räuber see Uhland **LOEWE**
Die Räuberbrüder see Eichendorff
CORNELIUS
Räume see Goering **KRENEK**
Räumt den Weg! see Brandenburg **JENSEN**
Rafael, L., pseud. *see* Kiesekamo, Hedwig,
1846-1921.
Ragna see Drachmann **GRIEG**
Ragnhild see Drachmann **GRIEG**
"Raikkahasti laulaa aamun aalto" *see*
Rakastunut Lönnbohm **KILPINEN**
"Railroads, railroads, dinning in my ear" *see*
The ballad of the railroads Krenek
KRENEK
Rain has fallen see Joyce **CHAMBER**
MUSIC. BARBER, SZYMANOWSKI
"Rain has fallen all the day" *see Rain has
fallen* Joyce **BARBER,
SZYMANOWSKI**
Rain in spring see Goodman **ROREM**
The rainbow see Wordsworth **IVES**
So may it be
The rainy day has waned see Pushkin
RIMSKIĭ-KORSAKOV
Nenastnyĭ den' potukh
The rainy day is done see Pushkin
RIMSKIĭ-KORSAKOV
Nenastnyĭ den' potukh
"The rainy mist sweeps gently o'er the village
by the stream" *see Highwaymen* Li-Shê
CARPENTER
The raising of Lazarus see Khomyakov
RACHMANINOFF
Rakastunut see Lönnbohm **KILPINEN**
RALPH ROISTER DOISTER (1550). *see*
Udall *Roister doister* **HESELTINE**
Rambach, Friedrich Eberhard, 1767-
1826.
ZELTER *Nur Eines wünscht*

Rambouillet see No author **SATIE**
Rameau, Jean Philippe, 1683-1764.
   GOUNOD *L'aveu*
Le ramier see Silvestre **FAURÉ**
"Ramure aux rumeurs amollies" *see Dans la*
   forêt de Septembre Mendès **FAURÉ**
La rançon see Baudelaire **FAURÉ**
Randolph, Thomas, 1605-1635.
   BRITTEN *A charm*
Randow, Carl
   LOEWE *Preussisches Marinelied*
Rannalla see Lönnbohm **KILPINEN**
Rannalta I see Koskenniemi **KILPINEN**
Rannalta II see Koskenniemi **KILPINEN**
Ráno raníčko, pleju obilíčko see Unknown
   MARTINŮ
   Early in the morning I weed the grain
Rantum Tantum see Neuburg **HESELTINE**
Raphaël, Cluzel
   SAUGUET
      L'alchimiste a la voix d'ambre
      L'alchimiste au cher visage
      L'alchimiste au regard d'ambre
      L'alchimiste est dans le grenier
      Dans le jardin de l'alchimiste
      J'en appelle à l'alchimiste
      Les yeux d'ambre de l'alchimiste
"Le rapide Bordeaux Trieste" *see Hommage à*
   Valery-Larbaud Chalupt **RIVIER**
Rappelle-toi quand l'aurore craintive see
   Musset **RUBINSTEIN**
Rapture see Kol'tsov **BALAKIREV**
   Isstupleniye
Rase, Sturmwind, blase see Kotzebue
   DER ARME MINNESINGER. **WEBER**
"Raskaat pilvet, mun murheeni varjot" *see*
   Odotus Jalkanen **KILPINEN**
Raskas huokaus see Dehmel **SIBELIUS**
   Aus banger Brust
Rassa, ma dame est fraîche et fine see
   Valmy-Baysse **MILHAUD**
Rassevaetsia, rasstupaetsia see Tolstoĭ
   MUSORGSKIĬ
"Rasskazhi mne, niâ niǔshka" *see S niâneĭ*
   Musorgskiĭ **MUSORGSKIĬ**
"Rasstalis' gordo my" *see No esli by s toboiu*
   ia vstretit'sia mogla Kurochkin
   MUSORGSKIĬ
Rast see Müller, Wilhelm **SCHUBERT**
Rast auf der Flucht in Ägypten see Rilke
   HINDEMITH
"Raste, Krieger, Krieg ist aus" *see Ellens*
   Gesang I Scott **SCHUBERT**
Raste Krieger, Krieg ist aus see Scott
   MENDELSSOHN-BARTHOLDY
"Rastet strana, rastet strana" *see Chetyre pesni*
   Afinogenov **PROKOFIEV**

Rastlose Liebe see Goethe **FRANZ,**
   SCHOECK, SCHUBERT, ZELTER
Rastvoril ia okno see Konstantin
   CHAĬKOVSKIĬ
The rat see Symons **IRELAND**
Rat einer Alter see Mörike **WOLF**
The rat-catcher see Bryusov
   RACHMANINOFF
Rathaus, Daniil, 1869-1937.
   CHAĬKOVSKIĬ
      An dem schlummernden Strom
      In trüber Stund'
      Nacht
      O, du mondhelle Nacht
      Sonne ging zur Ruhe
      Weil' ich wie einstmals allein
   RACHMANINOFF
      All things pass by
      The flower has faded
      Night
      Song of the disillusioned
      These summer nights
Rathaus, Daniil Maksimovich *see*
   Rathaus, Daniil, 1869-1937.
Ratisbonne, Louis Gustave Fortuné,
   1827-1900.
   CHAĬKOVSKIĬ *Tsvetok*
Ratschky, Franz Joseph von, 1757-1810.
   MOZART *Lied zur Gesellenreise*
Der Rattenfänger see Goethe **SCHUBERT,**
   WOLF
Der Raubschütz see Lenau **WOLF**
Rauhe Winde wehn see Kol'tsov
   MUSORGSKIĬ *Duiut vetry, vetry buǐ nye*
"Rauschen der Strom" *see Aufenthalt*
   Rellstab **SCHUBERT**
"Rauschen des Bächlein" *see Liebesbotschaft*
   Rellstab **SCHUBERT**
"Rauschet ihr Meere und wehet ihr Winde!"
   see Lied der Freude Gross, E. **SPOHR**
"Rauscht die See im Sturme springend" *see*
   Der Schiffer Davidov **RUBINSTEIN**
RAVEL, MAURICE, 1875-1937.
   Anon.
      A vous, oiseau des plaines (1904) [lost]
      Chanson de pâtre épirote (1904) [lost]
      Chanson des cueilleuses de lentisques
         (1904) [Durand, 1906]
         "Ô joi de mon âme"
         Also voice & orchestra; orchestration
            by M. Rosenthal.
      Chanson espagnole (1910) [Jurgenson,
         1910; Durand, 1925]
         "Adieu, va, mon homme, adieu"
      Chanson française (1910) [Jurgenson,
         1910; Durand, 1925]

"Jeanneton où irons-nous garder"

Chanson hébraïque (1910) [Jurgenson, 1910; Durand, 1925] "Mayerke, mon fils, Mayerke, mon fils"

Chanson italienne (1910) [Jurgenson, 1910; Durand, 1925] "Penchée à ma fenêtre"

L'Enigme éternelle (1914) [Durand, 1915] "Monde tu nous interroges"

Kaddisch (1914) [Durand, 1915] "Que ta gloire, Ô Roi des rois"

Là-bas vers l'èglise (1906) [Durand, 1906] same
　Also voice & orchestra; orchestration by M. Rosenthal.

Mon mouchoir, hélas, est perdu (1904) [lost]

Quel galant (1904) [Durand, 1906] same
　Also voice & orchestra; orchestration by M. Rosenthal.

Le réveil de la mariée (1906) [Durand, 1906] "Réveille-toi, réveille-toi"
　Also voice & orchestra; orchestration by Ravel.

Tout gai! (1906) [Durand, 1906] "Tout gai! gai"
　Also voice & orchestra; orchestration by Ravel.

Tripatos (1909) [**Revue musicale**, Dec. 1938; Salabert, 1975] "Kherya pou dhen idhen ilyos"

Burns, Robert, 1759-1796.

Chanson écossaise (1910) [Salabert, 1975] "Ye banks and braes o' bonnie Doon"

Fargue, Léon-Paul, 1878-1947.

Rêves (1927) [Durand, 1927] "Un enfant court Autour des marhres"

Gravollet, Paul

LES FRISSONS.

Manteau de fleurs (1903) [Hamelle, 1906, 1920] "Toutes les fleurs de mon jardin sont roses"
　Also voice & orchestra.

Leconte de Lisle, Charles Marie René, 1818-1894.

CHANSONS ÉCOSSAISES.

Chanson du rouet (1898) [Salabert, 1975] "O mon cher rouet"

Mallarmé, Stéphane, 1842-1898.

Placet futile (1913) [Durand, 1914] "Princesse! à jalouser le destin d'une Hébé"
　Also for voice with chamber ensemble.

Sainte (1896) [Durand, 1907] "A la fenêtre recélant"

Soupir (1913) [Durand, 1914] "Mon âme vers ton front où rêve"
　Also for voice with chamber ensemble.

Surgi de la croupe et du bond (1913) [Durand, 1914] same
　Also for voice with chamber ensemble.

Marès, Roland de, 1874-1955.

ARIETTES DOULOUREUSES.

Ballade de la reine morte d'aimer (ca.1893) [Salabert, 1975] "En Bohème était une Reine"

Marot, Clément, 1495?-1544.

D'Anne jouant de l'espinette (1898) [Demets, 1900; Eschig, 1923] "Lorsque je voy en ordre la brunette"

D'Anne qui me jecta de la neige (1898) [Demets, 1900; Eschig, 1923] "Anne por jeu me jecta de la neige"

Morand, Paul, 1889-1976.

Chanson à boire (1932-33) [Durand, 1934] "Foin du bâtard, illustre Dame"

Chanson épique (1932-33) [Durand, 1934] "Bon Saint Michel qui me donnez loisir"

Chanson romantique (1932-33) [Durand, 1934] "Si vous me disiez que la terre"

No author

Vocalise-étude en forme de Habanera (1907) [Leduc, 1909]

Parny, Evariste, 1753-1814.

Aoua! (1926) [Durand, 1926] "Aoua! Aoua!"
　For voice, piano, flute, and 'cello.

Il est doux . . . (1926) [Durand, 1926] same
　For voice, piano, flute, and 'cello.

Nahandove (1926) [Durand, 1926] "Nahandove, Ô belle Nahandove"
　For voice, piano, flute, and 'cello.

Ravel, Maurice, 1875-1937.

Le Noël des jouets (1905) [Mathot, 1914; Salabert] "Le troupeau verni des moutons"
　Also voice & orchestra.

Régnier, Henri François Joseph de, 1864-1936.

Les Grands Vents venus d'outre-mer (1906 or 07) [Durand, 1907] same

Renard, Jules, 1864-1910.

HISTOIRES NATURELLES.

Le Cygne (1906) [Durand, 1907] "Il glisse sur le bassin"
　Also voice & orchestra; orchestration by Manuel Rosenthal.

Le Grillon (1906) [Durand, 1907] "C'est l'heure où"

RAVEL, MAURICE, 1875-1937 *(continued)*
  Renard, Jules, 1864-1910 *(continued)*
    HISTOIRES NATURELLES (continued)
      Also voice & orchestra;
        orchestration by Manuel
        Rosenthal.
      Le Martin-Pêcheur (1906) [Durand,
        1907] "Ĉa n'a pas mordu, ce soir"
      Also voice & orchestra;
        orchestration by Manuel
        Rosenthal.
      Le Paon (1906) [Durand, 1907] "Il va
        sûrement se marier aujourd'hui"
      Also voice & orchestra;
        orchestration by Manuel
        Rosenthal.
      La Pintade (1906) [Durand, 1907]
        "C'est la bossue de ma cour"
      Also voice & orchestra;
        orchestration by Manuel
        Rosenthal.
  Ronsard, Pierre de, 1524-1585.
    Ronsard à son âme (1923-24) [Durand,
      1924 "Amelette Ronsardelette,
      Mignonnelette"
    Also published in Supplément à la
      Revue Musicale, May 1924.
  Unknown
    Chanson flamande (1910) [lost]
    Chanson russe (1910) [lost]
  Verhaeren, Emile, 1855-1916.
    LES DÉBÂCLES.
      Si morne! (1898) [Salabert, 1975]
        "Se replier toujours, sur soimême"
  Verlaine, Paul, 1844-1896.
    Un grand sommeil noir (1895) [Durand,
      1953] same
    Sur l'Herbe (1907) [Durand, 1907]
      "L'abbé divague"
Ravel, Maurice, 1875-1937.
  RAVEL *Le Noël des jouets*
Ravenna see Hesse **SCHOECK**
The ravens see Pushkin **MEDTNER**
"Ravens high aloft are soaring" *see*
  The ravens Pushkin **MEDTNER**
Rayon des yeux see Éluard **POULENC**
Razlyubila krasna devitsa see Vinogradov
  BORODIN
Razocharovanie see Collin **CHAĬKOVSKIĬ**
  Déception
Razzolan, sopra a l'aja, le galline . . . see
  Birga, Arturo *RISPETTI TOSCANI.*
  RESPIGHI
The real war will never get in the books see
  Whitman *SPECIMEN DAYS.* **ROREM**
The reason see Pech **DVOŘÁK** *Proto*

Der Rebe Elimeylekh see Anon. **WEISGALL**
The rebel see Evans, M. *I AM A BLACK*
  WOMAN. **WEISGALL**
REBENKRANZ ZU WALDMEISTERS
  SILBERNER HOCHZEIT: In der Früh. *see*
  Roquette *Über Nacht und Tag* **BERG**
"Rebhahnruf und Glockenlaut" *see Ich und du*
  Busse **BERG**
Reboul, Jean, 1795-1864.
  FRANCK *L'ange et l'enfant*
  WAGNER *Tout n'est qu'images fugitives*
Rechnaĭa lileĭa see Heine
  RACHMANINOFF *The water lily*
"Die Rechte streckt' ich schmerzlich oft" *see*
  Im Harmesnächten Meyer **SCHOECK**
Rechtfertigung see Leuthold **SCHOECK**
Recitativo e aria romantica see Dickens *ODE*
  TO AN EXPIRING FROG. **HINDEMITH**
Recitativo ritmato see Dante **ROSSINI**
Recke, Elisa von der, 1756-1833.
  LOEWE *Christi Huld gegen Petrus*
  MANCHERLEI FREUDEN.
  LOEWE *Rundgesang im Freien*
Recke, Ewald von der
  ZELTER
    Bilder schon entflohner Stunden
    Lied
    Sehnsucht nach dem Geliebten
Reçois mes hommages see Anon.
  SAINT-SAËNS
Reconciliation see Shcherbina
  CHAĬKOVSKIĬ *Primiren'e*
Reconciliation see Whitman **ROREM**
RÉCRÉATION, no. 1
  MILHAUD Kriéger, Jacqueline
    Pas bien grand
RÉCRÉATION, no. 2
  MILHAUD Kriéger, Jacqueline
    Haut comme trois pommes
RÉCRÉATION, no. 3
  MILHAUD Kriéger, Jacqueline
    La tortue naine
RÉCRÉATION, no. 4
  MILHAUD Kriéger, Jacqueline
    Il faut obéir
Recueillement see Baudelaire *FLEURS DU*
  MAL. **DEBUSSY**
Recuerdas? see Machado y Ruiz
  RODRIGO
Red chimneys see Havet **CARPENTER**
  Les cheminées rouge
RED FLAG. see Ridge
  Electrocution **ROREM**
Red hair see Carpenter, Rue **CARPENTER**
Red roses see Jacobsen **DELIUS** *Through*
  long, long years

Redaelli, G
ROSSINI *L'ultimo ricordo*
Redeet oblakov letuchaĭa griada see Pushkin
RIMSKIĬ-KORSAKOV
Redwitz, Oskar, Freiherr von, 1823-1891.
  BRUCKNER *Amaranths' Waldeslieder*
  LISZT *Es muss ein Wunderbares sein*
  PFITZNER *Nun, da so warm der*
    Sonnenschein
  AMARANTH.
    LOEWE
      Reiterlied
      Sängers Gebet
    SCHÖNBERG
      Nur das thut mir so bitterweh'
  LIEDER DER AMARANTH.
    LOEWE *Brautlied*
"Reed, reed, rustle!" *see Säf, säf, susa*
  Fröding **SIBELIUS**
Reflets see Maeterlinck **BOULANGER**
Reflets dans l'éau see Brimont **FAURÉ**
REFLEXER, no. 1
  KILPINEN Lagerkvist *Mitt liv går bort,*
    jag vet ej varthäm
REFLEXER, no. 2
  KILPINEN Lagerkvist *Var är den djupa*
    glädje
REFLEXER, no. 3
  KILPINEN Lagerkvist *Som ett*
    blommande mandelträd
REFLEXER, no. 4
  KILPINEN Lagerkvist *Din mun är*
    ljusare än min
REFLEXER, no. 5
  KILPINEN Lagerkvist *Det är du som*
    skall bliva den yppersta
REFLEXER, no. 6
  KILPINEN Lagerkvist *En gång skall det*
    brinna ett ljus på min grav
REFLEXER, no. 7
  KILPINEN Lagerkvist *Om tiotusen år*
REFLEXER, no. 8
  KILPINEN Lagerkvist *Barn, som jag*
    smekt
REFLEXER, no. 9
  KILPINEN Lagerkvist *Ett enda ord är*
    mitt
REFLEXER, no. 10
  KILPINEN Lagerkvist *Hela världen är*
    mig så kär
REFLEXER, no. 11
  KILPINEN Lagerkvist *Ingenting får störa*
    vår stund med varandra
REFLEXER, no. 12
  KILPINEN Lagerkvist *Regnet slår och*
    slår

REFLEXER, no. 13
  KILPINEN Lagerkvist *O vinternatt*
REFLEXER, no. 14
  KILPINEN Lagerkvist *Så gamla äro alla*
    moln
REFLEXER, no. 15
  KILPINEN Lagerkvist *Befriad är dagen*
De Refsnaesdrenge, de Samsøpiger see
  Blicher **NIELSEN**
"Un regard caressant, une bouche rieuse" *see*
  Elle Lecocq **SAINT-SAËNS**
Regard d'enfant see Pélissier, Léon G.
  MASSENET
"Regardez ce Monsieur qui va Monter en
  limousine" *see Monsieur Protopopoff*
  Chalupt **MILHAUD**
LA REGATA VENEZIANA, no. 1
  ROSSINI Unknown *Anzoleta avanti la*
    regata
LA REGATA VENEZIANA, no. 2
  ROSSINI Unknown *Anzoleta co passa la*
    regata
LA REGATA VENEZIANA, no. 3
  ROSSINI Unknown *Anzoleta dopo la*
    regata
Régates mystérieuses see Jacob, M.
  SAUGUET
Regen see Schlaf *HELLDUNKEL* (1899).
  BERG
Regen I see Huber, B. **KILPINEN**
Regen II see Huber, B. **KILPINEN**
"Regen falle" *see Regen II* Huber, B.
  KILPINEN
"Regen, linder Frühlingsregen" *see An den*
  Frühlingsregen Kiesekamo **REGER**
"Der Regen rasselt, es saust der Sturm" *see*
  Trostlos Hochwald, A. von **SPOHR**
Regenlied see Groth **BRAHMS**
Regenlied see Groth *HUNDERT*
  BLÄTTER . . . **BRAHMS**
  NB: The two Brahms songs have variant
  texts.
Regentag see Krenek **KRENEK**
"Regentropfen aus den Bäumen fallen" *see*
  Nachklang Groth **BRAHMS**
"Regentropfen aus den Bäumen fallen" *see*
  Regenlied Groth **BRAHMS**
"Regenwetter ziehen trübe" *see Letzter Seufzer*
  Briesen, Otto von **LOEWE**
REGER, MAX, 1873-1916.
  Alberus, Erasmus, d. 1553.
    MORGENLIED.
      Morgengesang, op. 137 no. 8 (1914)
      [GA, v. 34, p. 188]
      "Steht auf ihr lieben Kinderlein!"
      Text from Will Vesper, comp. ***Der***
        deutsche Psalter, ein Jahrtausend

REGER, MAX, 1873-1916 (*continued*)
  Alberus, Erasmus, d. 1553 (*continued*)
    MORGENLIED (*continued*)
      geistlicher Dichtung (Verlag W.
        Langewiesche-Brandt)
      O Jesu Christ, wir warten dein, op.
        137 no. 12 (1914) [GA, v. 34,
        p. 192] same
        Text from Will Vesper, comp. **Der
        deutsche Psalter, ein Jahrtausend
        geistlicher Dichtung** (Verlag W.
        Langewiesche-Brandt)
  Annunzio, Gabriele d', 1863-1938.
    Wenn lichter Mondenschein, op. 35 no. 6
      (1899) [GA, v. 31, p. 111] same
  Anon.
    Böses Weib, op. 75 no. 5 (1903) [GA,
      v. 32, p. 158]
      "Ja, wann gleich wär das Firmament"
    Elternstolz, op. 70 no. 6 (1902-03) [GA,
      v. 32, p. 116]
      "Mein Kindchen ist fein"
    Hoffnungstrost, op. 70 no. 10 (1902-03)
      [GA, v. 32, p. 131]
      "In meines Vaters Garten da stehen
        zwei Bäumelein"
    Der Knabe an die Mutter, op. 75 no. 3
      (1903) [GA, v. 32, p. 154]
      "Jung vermähle mich, O Mutter!"
    Lied eines Mädchens, op. 104 no. 4
      (1907) [GA, v. 34, p. 80]
      "Komm, komm, Geselle mein"
    Das Mägdlein und der Spatz, op. 76 no.
      38 [GA, v. 33, p. 108]
      "Früh am Morgen ging die Maid aus
        der Tür hinaus"
    Minnelied, op. 76 no. 21[GA, v. 33,
      p. 53] "Herzchen, mein Schätzchen"
    Schlimm für die Männer, op. 75 no. 7
      (1903) [GA, v. 32, p. 164]
      "Sprachen Königin und König
        einstens"
    Wären wir zwei kleine Vögel, op. 55 no.
      10 (1900/01) [GA, v. 31, p. 233] same
    Waldeinsamkeit, op. 76 no. 3 [GA, v. 33,
      p. 8]
      "Gestern Abend in der stillen Ruh' "
    Wenn alle Welt so einig wär', op. 76 no.
      17 [GA, v. 33, p. 43] same
    Wiegenlied (1909) [GA, v. 34, p. 159]
      "Schlaf, Kindlein, balde"
  Arndt, Ernst Moritz, 1769-1860.
    Grablied, op. 137 no. 7 (1914) [GA,
      v. 34, p. 187]
      "Geht nun hin und grabt mein Grab"
      Text from Will Vesper, comp. **Der
      deutsche Psalter, ein Jahrtausend**

      geistlicher Dichtung (Verlag W.
      Langewiesche-Brandt)
  Asenijeff, Elsa von
    Amselliedchen (1912) [GA, v. 34, p. 165]
      "Amselchen mein"
    An eine Mutter (1912) [GA, v. 34,
      p. 163]
      "Der Himmel ist so weit und hehr"
    Klage (1912) [GA, v. 34, p. 161]
      "Wo ich bin"
  Auersperg, Anton Alexander, Graf
    von, 1806-1876.
    Das Blatt im Buche, op. 15 no. 2 (1894)
      [GA, v. 31, p. 52]
      "Ich hab eine alte Muhme"
  Baumbach, Rudolf, 1840-1905.
    Der Schwur, op. 76 no. 26 [GA, v. 33,
      p. 70]
      "Zum Hänschen sprach das Gretchen"
  Benz, Friedrich, 1878-1904.
    Schlummerlied (1902) [GA, v. 34, p. 132]
      "Schlaf wohl, schlaf wohl!"
  Bern, Maximilian, 1849-1923.
    Mit Rosen bestreut, op. 76 no. 12 [GA, v.
      33, p. 29] "Ich habe mein Kindlein in
      Schlaf gewiegt"
  Bible
    PSALM 62.
      Meine Seele ist still zu Gott, op. 105
        no. 2 (1907) [GA, v. 34, p. 179]
        same
    PSALM 119.
      Geistliches Lied "Wohl denen" (1903)
        [GA, v. 34, p. 200]
        "Wohn denen, die ohne Tadel leben"
        Voice and organ.
  Bierbaum, Otto Julius, 1865-1910.
    Aus der Ferne in der Nacht, op. 66 no. 3
      (1902) [GA, v. 32, p. 56]
      "Wenn im braunen Hafen alle Schiffe
        schlafen"
    Flieder, op. 35 no. 4 (1899) [GA,
      v. 31, p. 106]
      "Stille, träumende Frühlingsnacht"
    Frauenhaar, op. 37 no. 4 (1899) [GA,
      v. 31, p. 120]
      "Frauenhaar trag' ich am Hute"
    Freundliche Vision, op. 66 no. 2 (1902)
      [GA, v. 32, p. 54]
      "Eine Wiese voller Margeriten"
    Gegen Abend, op. 70 no. 11 (1902-03)
      [GA, v. 32, p. 133]
      "Nun hängt nur noch am
        Kirchturmknopf der letzte
        Sonnenschein"
    Letzte Bitte (1899) [GA, v. 34, p. 117]

"Lass mich noch einmal dir ins schwarze Auge sehn"

Nachtgang, op. 51 no. 7 (1900) [GA, v. 31, p. 187]
"Wir gingen durch die stille Nacht"

Ritter rät dem Knappen dies, op. 70 no. 3 (1902-03) [GA, v. 32, p. 105]
"Sitz im Sattel, reite, reite auf die Freite"

Schmied Schmerz, op. 51 no. 6 (1900) [GA, v. 31, p. 184]
"Der Schmerz ist ein Schmied"

Traum durch die Dämmerung, op. 35 no. 3 (1899) [GA, v. 31, p. 104]
"Weite Wiesen im Dämmergrau"

Blüthgen, Viktor, 1844-1920.

Die fünf Hühnerchen, op. 76 no. 51 [GA, v. 33, p. 139]
"Ich war mal in dem Dorfe"

Stampelchen, op. 62 no. 9 (1901) [GA, v. 32, p. 27] "Still, wie so still!"

Boelitz, Martin, 1874-1921.

Dämmer, op. 75 no. 4 (1903) [GA, v. 32, p. 156]
"Liegt ein Dorf im Abendleuchten"

Das Dorf, op. 97 no. 1 (1906) [GA, v. 34, p. 35] "Wie ist die Nacht voll holder Heimlichkeiten!"

Du bist mir gut! op. 66 no. 4 (1902) [GA, v. 32, p. 59] same

Erlöst, op. 66 no. 9 (1902) [GA, v. 32, p. 73] "Das dank' ich deiner Güte"

Es blüht ein Blümlein rosenrot, op. 76 no. 20 [GA, v. 33, p. 51] same

Knecht Ruprecht, op. 76 no. 50 [GA, v. 33, p. 137]
"Draussen weht es bitterkalt"

Lutschemäulchen, op. 76 no. 45 [GA, v. 33, p. 126]
"Lutschemund, Lutschemund, treib's nur nicht gar zu bunt"

Mädchenlied, op. 104 no. 6 (1907) [GA, v. 34, p. 89] "O Du, der ich erblühte, die mich er quick te Tag um Tag"

Mariä Wiegenlied, op. 76 no. 52 [GA, v. 33, p. 141] "Maria sitzt am Rosenhag und wiegt ihr Jesuskind"

Notturno, op. 88 no. 1 (1905) [GA, v. 34, p. 19] "Vor meinem Fenster schläft die Nacht"

Ostern (1902) [GA, v. 34, p. 141] "Ein linder Südhauch sprengt die Riegel"

Präludium, op. 70 no. 1 (1902-03) [GA, v. 32, p. 97] "Sturm, wie lieb ich dich wilden Gesellen"

Reinheit, op. 62 no. 6 (1901) [GA, v. 32, p. 19] "Deiner Liebe goldane Güte trägst du Lächelnd"

Reiterlied, op. 76 no. 34 [GA, v. 33, p. 97] "Ein Reiter muss haben ein Rösslein zu traben"

Schlaf ein, op. 76 no. 47 [GA, v. 33, p. 130] "Leise tritt der Mond heraus"

Soldatenlied, op. 76 no. 46 [GA, v. 33, p. 128] "So ein rechter Soldat fürcht' nicht Kugel und Streit"

Ein Tänzchen, op. 76 no. 49 [GA, v. 33, p. 134]
"Auf der schönen, schönen Wiese"

Tragt, blaue Träume (1901) [GA, v. 34, p. 138] same

Unterwegs, op. 68 no. 2 (1902) [GA, v. 32, p. 84] "Nebelgrau die weite Welt"

Der verliebte Jäger, op. 76 no. 13 [GA, v. 33, p. 31]
"Es zog ein Jäger in den Wald"

Vor dem Sterben, op. 62 no. 7 (1901) [GA, v. 32, p. 21]
"Wenn dich die tiefe Sehnsucht rührt"

Vorbeimarsch, op. 76 no. 30 [GA, v. 33, p. 84] "Es haben die liebjungen Mädchen"

Wehe, op. 62 no. 1 (1901) [GA, v. 32, p. 2] "Dröhnende Hämmer in russiger Hand"

Das Wölklein, op. 76 no. 33 [GA, v. 33, p. 95] "Ich geh' auf stillen Auen"

Zwei Mäuschen, op. 76 no. 48 [GA, v. 33, p. 132]
"Es waren mal zwei Mäuschen"

Zwiesprach, op. 76 no. 23 [GA, v. 33, p. 58] "Ein Müller mahlte"

Braungart, Richard, 1872-1963.

Abendfrieden (1906) [GA, v. 34, p. 150]
"Nun ruhst du sanft in meinem Arm"

Du brachtest mir deiner Seele Trank, op. 75 no. 17 (1903) [GA, v. 32, p. 192] same

Gebet, op. 62 no. 8 (1901) [GA, v. 32, p. 24] "Du ewigkalter Himmel"

Mensch und Natur, op. 62 no. 4 (1901) [GA, v. 32, p. 12] "Was tragen wir unsere Leiden in diesen Glanz hinein?"

Ein Paar, op. 55 no. 9 (1900/01) [GA, v. 31, p. 231]
"Schweigend geht die junge Frau an dem Arm des greisen Gatten"

Schlecht' Wetter, op. 76 no. 7 [GA, v. 33, p. 16] "O wie greulich, wie abscheulich ist der Winter"

Tränen, op. 70 no. 15 (1902-03) [GA, v. 32, p. 141]
"Kleine Tränen seh' ich zittern"

Warte nur! op. 76 no. 10 [GA, v. 33, p. 24] "Wenn die Buben recht böse sind"

REGER, MAX, 1873-1916 *(continued)*
Braungart, Richard, 1872-1963.
(continued)
Wiegenlied (1903) [GA, v. 34, p. 144]
"Nun kommt die Nacht gegangen"
Brentano, Fritz, 1840-1914.
Leise, leise weht ihr Lüfte, op. 97 no. 2
(1906) [GA, v. 34, p. 37] same
Busse, Carl, 1872-1918.
Der Sausewind, op. 104 no. 5 (1907)
[GA, v. 34, p. 83]
"Mädel, halt die Rökke fest"
Schlafliedchen, op. 75 no. 14 (1903)
[GA, v. 32, p. 184]
"Sum, sum der Sandmann geht"
Wenn die Linde blüht, op. 76 no. 4 [GA,
v. 33, p. 10] same
Chamisso, Adelbert von, 1781-1838.
Scherz, op. 8 no. 4 (1892) [GA, v. 31,
p. 25] "Es stehn in unserm Garten"
Dahn, Felix Ludwig Sophus, 1834-
1912.
*All' mein Gedanken, mein Herz und mein
Sinn,* op. 75 no. 9 (1903)
[GA, v. 32, p. 171] same
Dein Auge, op. 35 no. 1 (1899) [GA,
v. 31, p. 99] "Seit ganz mein Aug' ich
durft' in deines tauchen"
SCHLICHTE WEISEN, no. 7.
Du meines Herzens Krönelein, op. 76
no. 1 [GA, v. 33, p. 2] same
Dehmel, Richard, 1863-1920.
Jetzt und immer, op. 66 no. 11 (1902)
[GA, v. 32, p. 77] "Seit wann du mein,
ich weiss es nicht"
Die Liebe, op. 66 no. 7 (1902) [GA,
v. 32, p. 68] "Du sahst durch meine
Seele in die Welt"
Waldseligkeit, op. 62 no. 2 (1901) [GA,
v. 32, p. 8]
"Der Wald beginnt zu rauschen"
Wiegenlied, op. 43 no. 5 (1900) [GA,
v. 31, p. 136]
"Bienchen, Bienchen, Bienchen wiegt
sich im Sonnenschein"
DIE VERWANDLUNGEN DER VENUS:
Venus Mater.
Wiegenlied, op. 51 no. 3 (1900) [GA,
v. 31, p. 172] "Träume, träume, du
mein süsses Leben!"
WEIB UND WELT.
Helle Nacht, op. 37 no. 1 (1899) [GA,
v. 31, p. 114] "Weich küsst die
Zweige der weisse Mond"
Text erroneously attributed to
Verlaine in the Reger GA.
DES KNABEN WUNDERHORN

Hat gesagt- bleibt's nicht dabei, op. 75
no. 12 (1903) [GA, v. 32, p. 177]
"Mein Vater hat gesagt"
Diederich, Franz, 1865-1921.
Der Mond glüht, op. 51 no. 1 (1900)
[GA, v. 31, p. 167] same
Eichendorff, Joseph Karl Benedikt,
Freiherr von, 1788-1857.
Dein Wille, Herr, geschehe! op. 137 no.
2 (1914) [GA, v. 34, p. 182] same
Text from Will Vesper, comp. **Der
deutsche Psalter, ein Jahrtausend
geistlicher Dichtung** (Verlag W.
Langewiesche-Brandt)
Gottes Segen, op. 76 no. 31 [GA, v. 33,
p. 89]
"Das Kind ruht aus vom Spielen"
Traum, op. 15 no. 4 (1894) [GA, v. 31,
p. 56] "Was ist mir denn so wehe?"
Engel, Franz, 1834-1920.
Verlassen hab ich mein Lieb, op. 15 no. 9
(1894) [GA, v. 31, p. 66] same
Enslin, Karl, 1819-1875.
Herzenstausch, op. 76 no. 5 [GA, v. 33,
p. 12]
"Du sagst, mein liebes Mütterlein"
Evers, Franz, 1871-1947.
Das Fenster klang im Winde, op. 75 no.
16 (1903) [GA, v. 32, p. 190] same
Flötenspielerin, op. 88 no. 3 (1905) [GA,
v. 34, p. 27] "Weiche Flötentöne
tiefverträumtes Girren"
Geheimnis, op. 51 no. 4 (1900) [GA,
v. 31, p. 178]
"Die andern Mädchen wissen's nicht"
Märchenland, op. 68 no. 3 (1902) [GA,
v. 32, p. 86]
"Nachts, wenn die Bäume rauschen im
verschwiegnen Sommerwind"
Meine Seele, op. 70 no. 7 (1902-03) [GA,
v. 32, p. 119] same
Mondnacht, op. 75 no. 2 (1903) [GA, v.
32, p. 151] "Es ist ein seliges Prangen"
Nachtgeflüster (1900) [GA, v. 34, p. 124]
"Wie geheimes Lispeln rieselt's durch
die Nacht"
Nachtseele, op. 68 no. 5 (1902) [GA, v.
32, p. 92] "Mich umduftet deine Seele"
Nachtsegen, op. 55 no. 12 (1900/01)
[GA, v. 31, p. 239]
"Die Lande durch träumt der Schlaf"
Ruhe, op. 62 no. 3 (1901) [GA, v. 32, p.
10] "Hältst mich nun ganz in den
Armen"
Sommernacht, op. 70 no. 17 (1902-03)
[GA, v. 32, p. 147]

"Der Mond streut durch die Zweige
sein silberblaues Licht"
Traum, op. 55 no. 2 (1900/01) [GA,
v. 31, p. 209 "Nun du wie Licht durch
meine Träume gehst"

Falke, Gustav, 1853-1916.
Der Alte, op. 55 no. 15 (1900/01) [GA,
v. 31, p. 248]
"Nun steh' ich über Grat und Kluft"
An die Geliebte, op. 68 no. 6 (1902)
[GA, v. 32, p. 95]
"Immer bleibst du lieblich mir"
Die bunten Kühe, op. 70, no. 4 (1902-03)
[GA, v. 32, p. 110]
"Drei bunte Kühe in guter Ruh"
Gute Nacht, op. 55 no. 13 (1900/01)
[GA, v. 31, p. 242]
"Das war der Junker"
Heimat, op. 76 no. 37 [GA, v. 33, p. 105]
"Ich habe lieb die helle Sonne"
Meinem Kinde, op. 43 no. 3 (1900) [GA,
v. 31, p. 131]
"Du schläfst und sachte neig' ich"
Müde, op. 43 no. 2 (1900) [GA, v. 31,
p. 128] "Ein kühler Hauch"
Die Nixe, op. 62 no. 10 (1901) [GA,
v. 32, p. 30]
"Aus der Tiefe tauchte sie nach oben"
Der tapfere Schneider, op. 55 no. 3
(1900/01) [GA, v. 31, p. 211]
"Ich wollt', ich wär' ein Held"
Trost, op. 15 no. 10 (1894) [GA, v. 31,
p. 70] "Still, still! 's ist nur ein Traum"
Die Verschmähte, op. 70 no. 8 (1902-03)
[GA, v. 32, p. 122]
"Komm' ich längs der grünen Wiese"
Viola d'amour, op. 55 no. 11 (1900/01)
[GA, v. 31, p. 236]
"Holde Königin der Geigen"
Wäsche im Wind, op. 75 no. 8 (1903)
[GA, v. 32, p. 168]
"Tollt der Wind über Feld und Wiese"
Wir zwei, op. 62 no. 5 (1901) [GA, v. 32,
p. 14]
"Wir haben oft beim Wein gesessen"
Zwischen zwei Nächten, op. 43 no. 1
(1900) [GA, v. 31, p. 124]
"Der Morgen steigt und glüht und
steigt"
MIT DEM LEBEN.
Fromm, op. 62 no. 11 (1901) [GA,
v. 32, p. 34]
"Der Mond scheint auf mein Lager"

Fick, K.
Der Bote, op. 70 no. 14 (1902-03) [GA,
v. 32, p. 139] "Die Erde schläft, des
Mondes Schein verklärend sie bedeckt"

Author of text may be Karl Fick,
1887-
Des Durstes Erklärung, op. 70 no. 16
(1902-03) [GA, v. 32, p. 143]
"Immer schwitzend, immer sitzend"
Author of text may be Karl Fick,
1887-

Fischer, Johann Georg, 1816-1897.
Mein und Dein, op. 70 no. 13 (1902-03)
[GA, v. 32, p. 137]
"Das Mägdlein sprach"

Flemes, Bernhard, 1875-1940.
Brunnensang, op. 76 no. 43 [GA, v. 33,
p. 122] "Aus dunkler Nacht ein
Brunnenlied klang hell"

Fleming, Paul, 1606-1640.
Lass dich nur nichts nicht dauern, op.
137 no. 9 (1914) [GA, v. 34, p. 189]
same
Text from Will Vesper, comp. ***Der
deutsche Psalter, ein Jahrtausend
geistlicher Dichtung*** (Verlag W.
Langewiesche-Brandt)

Förstner, Clara (Müller), 1850-1907.
Frühlingsmorgen, op. 51 no. 11 (1900)
[GA, v. 31, p. 198] "Vom Himmel ist
der Frühlingsregen herabgerauscht"

Frey, Adolf, 1855-1920.
Unvergessen, op. 48 no. 7 (1900) [GA,
v. 31 p. 165] "Im Gefild zum Strausse
wand wilde Blüt' ich sonder Acht"

Friderici, Daniel, 1584-1638.
In einem Rosengärtelein, op. 76 no. 18
[GA, v. 33, p. 46] same

**Galli, Eugenie Tugendreich (nee von
Loos), 1849-1917.**
Verlorne Liebe, op. 51 no. 10 (1900)
[GA, v. 31, p. 196]
"Nun, da sie Alle eingeschlafen"

**Geibel, Emanuel, i.e., Franz Emanuel
August, 1815-1884.**
Hütet euch, op. 48 no. 1 (1900) [GA,
v. 31, p. 147]
"Wo am Herd ein Brautpaar siedelt"
Im April, op. 4 no. 4 (1891) [GA, v. 31,
p. 9] "Du feuchter Frühlingsabend"
Das sterbende Kind, op. 23 no. 3 (1898)
[GA, v. 31, p. 77]
"Wie doch so still dir am Herzen"

Gensichen, Otto Franz, 1847-1933.
Gruss, op. 70 no. 5 (1902-03) [GA,
v. 32, p. 113]
"Unter blühenden Bäumen hab' bei"

Gerheusser, Rosa
Der Maien ist gestorben (1906) [GA,
v. 34, p. 147] same

REGER, MAX, 1873-1916 *(continued)*
Gersdorff, Julius, 1849-1907.
 Am Brünnele, op. 76 no. 9 [GA, v. 33,
   p. 21] "An dem Brünnle"
Gilm zu Rosenegg, Hermann von,
 1812-1864.
 Das arme Vögelein, op. 12 no. 2 (1893)
   [GA, v. 31, p. 32] "Es lokket und
   zwitschert von Haus zu Haus"
Ginzkey, Franz Karl, 1871-1963.
 Von der Liebe, op. 76 no. 32 [GA, v. 33,
   p. 91] "Schrieb dic schöne Adelheid"
Glücklich, Johann Christian, 1839-
 1920.
 Am Meer! (1894) [GA, v. 34, p. 106]
   "Unendlich dehnt sich das brausende
   Meere"
 An Zeppelin (1909) [GA, v. 34, p. 157]
   "Du, der die Menschheit stolz"
Goethe, Johann Wolfgang von, 1749-
 1832.
 Einsamkeit, op. 75 no. 18 (1903) [GA,
   v. 32, p. 194]
   "Die ihr Felsen und Bäume bewohnt"
Händel, Georg Friedrich, 1685-1759.
 MESSIAH.
   Doch du liessest ihn im Grabe nicht,
   op. 19 no. 2 [GA, v. 34, p. 173]
   "Die Schmach bricht ihm das Herz"
   Voice and organ.
Hamann, Ludwig, 1867-died between
 1930 and 1936.
 Ehre sei Gott in der Höhe! (1905) [GA,
   v. 34, p. 303] "Hoch am dunklen
   Himmelsbogen glänzt ein Stern"
   Voice and organ.
Hamerling, Robert, 1830-1889.
 Das kleinste Lied, op. 23 no. 1 (1898)
   [GA, v. 31, p. 71] "Wie's aussieht im
   ew'gen Freudenhain"
 Die Primeln, op. 66 no. 6 (1902) [GA,
   v. 32, p. 64]
   "Sieh, Liebchen, hier im Waldestal"
Hardenberg, Friedrich Leopold,
 Freiherr von, 1772-1801.
 Ich sehe dich in tausend Bildern, op. 105
   no. 1 (1907) [GA, v. 34, p. 177] same
 Wenn in bangen, trüben Stunden (1900)
   [GA, v. 34, p. 193] same
   Voice and organ.
Hartleben, Otto Erich, 1864-1905.
 Im Arm der Liebe, op. 48 no. 3 (1900)
   [GA, v. 31, p. 154] same
Hartwig, Dora, b. 1913.
 Mutter, tote Mutter, op. 104 no. 3 (1907)
   [GA, v. 34, p. 77] "Mein Auge schliess
   mit deinem Kuse zu"

Hauptmann, Carl Ferdinand
 Maximilian, 1858-1921.
 Es schläft ein stiller Garten, op. 98 no. 4
   (1906) [GA, v. 34, p. 62] same
Hebbel, Christian Friedrich, 1813-
 1863.
 Gebet, op. 4 no. 1 (1890) [GA, v. 31,
   p. 2] "Die du, über den Sterne weg"
Heine, Heinrich, 1797-1856.
 Aus den Himmelsaugen, op. 98 no. 1
   (1906) [GA, v. 34, p. 49] same
 DIE HEIMKEHR.
   Der Tod, das ist die kühle Nacht
   (1899) [GA, v. 34, p. 115] same
Henckell, Karl Friedrich, 1864-1929.
 Ich schwebe, op. 62 no. 14 (1901) [GA,
   v. 32, p. 43] "Ich schwebe wie auf
   Engelsschwingen"
Herman, Nikolaus, d. 1561.
 Bitte um einen seligen Tod, op. 137 no. 1
   (1914) [GA, v. 34, p. 181]
   "Wenn mein Stündlein für handen ist"
   Text from Will Vesper, comp. *Der
   deutsche Psalter, ein Jahrtausend
   geistlicher Dichtung* (Verlag W.
   Langewiesche-Brandt)
Hertz, Wilhelm, 1855-1902.
 Daz iuwer min engel walte! op. 76 no. 2
   [GA, v. 33, p. 5]
   "Und willst du von mir scheiden, mein
   herzgeliebter Knab' "
Hölderlin, Friedrich, 1770-1843.
 An die Hoffnung, op. 124 (1912) [GA,
   v. 35, p. 1] "O Hoffnung!"
   For alto and orchestra or piano; GA
   includes orchestral version only.
 DIE EICHBÄUME.
   Ihr, ihr Herrlichen! op. 75 no. 6
   (1903) [GA, v. 32, p. 160] same
Hörmann, Ludwig von, 1837-1924.
 Stelldichein, op. 88 no. 2 (1905) [GA,
   v. 34, p. 23]
   "Husch, husch, husch, husch"
Holst, Adolf, 1867-1945.
 Bitte, op. 142 no. 5 (1915) [GA, v. 34,
   p. 103] "Alle Sternelein, die am
   Himmel steh'n"
Huggenberger, Josef, 1865-c. 1938.
 Auf mondbeschienenen Wegen, op. 79c
   no. 5 (1903) [GA, v. 34, p. 12] same
 Friede, op. 76 no. 25 [GA, v. 33, p. 67]
   "Tief im Talgrund überm Bach"
 Friede, op. 79c no. 4 (1903) [GA, v. 34,
   p. 10] "Tief im Talgrund überm Bach"
 Mein Schätzelein, op. 76 no. 14 [GA,
   v. 33, p. 35] "Mein Schätzelein ist ein
   gar köstliches Ding"

Schmeichelkätzchen, op. 76 no. 29 [GA,
v. 33, p. 80]
"Ein Schmeichelkätzchen nenn'ich
mein"
Züge, op. 79c no. 8 [GA, v. 34, p. 18]
"Jüngst lasest du ich merkt' es wohl
heimlich in meinen Zügen"

Itzerott, Marie, b. 1857.
An dich, op. 66 no. 8 (1902) [GA, v. 32,
p. 71] "Deine Seele hat die meine einst
so wunderbar berührt"
Rosen, op. 55 no. 4 (1900/01) [GA,
v. 31, p. 215]
"Eine Schale blühender Rosen"
Sehnsucht, op. 66 no. 1 (1902) [GA,
v. 32, p. 52]
"Quellen rauschen, Lüfte schweigen"
Verklärung, op. 55 no. 6 (1900/01) [GA,
v. 31, p. 224]
"Leise deinen Namen flüstern"
Volkslied, op. 79c no. 3 (1901) [GA, v.
34, p. 8] "Wenn Gott es hätt' gewollt"

Jacobowski, Ludwig, 1868-1900.
Dein Bild, op. 70 no. 12 (1902-03) [GA,
v. 32, p. 135] "Auf deinem Bild in
schwarzem Rahmen"
Kindergeschichte, op. 66 no. 12 (1902)
[GA, v. 32, p. 79]
"Und der Nachbarssohn, der Ruprecht"
Maienblüten, op. 66 no. 5 (1902) [GA,
v. 32, p. 61] "Duld' es still"
Der Narr, op. 55 no. 5 (1900/01) [GA,
v. 31, p. 221]
"Keinen Vater, der das Kinn mir hebt"
Das Ringlein, op. 75 no. 13 (1903) [GA,
v. 32, p. 181]
"Es ist ein Ring gebogen"
Eine Seele, op. 68 no. 1 (1902) [GA,
v. 32, p. 81]
"In deinen Liedern lebt mein Leben"
Sehnsucht, op. 70 no. 9 (1902-03) [GA,
v. 32, p. 128]
"Alte Gruben schaufle um"
Totensprache, op. 62 no. 12 (1901) [GA,
v. 32, p. 36] "Ich weiss, ich träume im
Grabe schon vielle tausend Jahre"
*VOM GESCHLECHT DER
PROMETHIDEN.*
Hymnus der Liebe, op. 136 (1914)
[GA, v. 35, p. 29]
"Höre mich, Ewiger" For baritone
and orchestra or piano; GA includes
orchestral version only.

Kiesekamo, Hedwig, 1846-1921.
An den Frühlingsregen, op. 76 no. 41
[GA, v. 33, p. 115]

"Regen, linder Frühlingsregen"
Die Bienen, op. 76 no. 57 [GA, v. 33, p.
151] "Kaum sind die ersten Blüten da"
Das Brüderchen, op. 76 no. 53 [GA,
v. 33, p. 143] "Ich werde Soldat"
Das Kindes Gebet, op. 76 no. 22 [GA,
v. 33, p. 56]
"Wenn die kleinen Kinder beten"
Kindeslächeln, op. 76 no. 27 [GA, v. 33,
p. 74] "Wenn mein Kindlein in der
Wiegen lächelt still"
Der Postillon, op. 76 no. 42 [GA, v. 33,
p. 118]
"Trara, trara, mein Hörnlein hell"
Das Schwesterchen, op. 76 no. 54 [GA,
v. 33, p. 145] "Ich werde Mama"

Kleinschmidt, Albert, 1847-1924.
Friedhofsgang, op. 12 no. 1 (1893) [GA,
v. 31, p. 30] "Tiefes, tiefes Schweigen"

Kolbe, Hanna, fl. 1892.
Wenn ich's nur wüsst, op. 12 no. 3
(1893) [GA, v. 31, p. 35]
"Er hat mich im Traum geküsst"

Kurz, Isolde, 1853-1944.
Um Dich, op. 12 no. 5 (1893) [GA,
v. 31, p. 41] "Was hat des Schlummers
Band zerrissen"

Laubsch, Frieda
Süsse Ruh' (1900) [GA, v. 34, p. 126]
"Der goldne Morgen kommt herauf mit
Glut"

Lieben, Frau von
Ich stehe hoch über'm See, op. 14b [GA,
v. 31, p. 43] same

**Liliencron, Detlov, Freiherr von, 1844-
1909.**
Glückes genug, op. 37 no. 3 (1899) [GA,
v. 31, p. 118]
"Wenn sanft du mir im Arme schliefst"

Lingg, Hermann, 1820-1905.
Aeolsharfe, op. 75 no. 11 (1903) [GA,
v. 32, p. 175] "Geheimnisvoller Klang"

Ljubljaschtschi, C. Dorr-
Mägdleins Frage, op. 51 no. 2 (1900)
[GA, v. 31, p. 169] "Mutter, draussen
ist es Frühling worden"

Mackay, John Henry, 1864-1933.
Morgen, op. 66 no. 10 (1902) [GA, v. 32,
p. 75] "Und morgen wird die Sonne
wieder scheinen"

Mayr, Anton, 1855-1935.
Abgeguckt, op. 76 no. 24 [GA, v. 33,
p. 64] "Es liegt ein alter Mühlenstein"

**Metternich-Winneburg, Clemens
Wenzel Lothar, Fürst von, 1773-
1859.**

REGER, MAX, 1873-1916 *(continued)*
Metternich-Winneburg, Clemens
Wenzel Lothar, Fürst von, 1773-
1859 *(continued)*
Maiennacht, op. 76 no. 15 [GA, v. 33,
p. 38] "Leisse streichen Nebelschleier
über Flur und Wiesen hin"
Meyer, Karl, b. 1845.
Spatz und Spätzin, op. 88 no. 4 (1905)
[GA, v. 34, p. 31]
"Auf dem Dache sitzt der Spatz"
Michaeli, Otto, 1870-1941.
Gruss, op. 12 no. 4 (1893) [GA, v. 31,
p. 38]
"Am Kirchhof ging ich jüngst vorbei"
Wunsch, op. 76 no. 40 [GA, v. 33, p.
113] "Mein Liedlein ward ein Büblein"
Mörike, Eduard Friedrich, 1804-1875.
Begegnung, op. 62 no. 13 (1901) [GA,
v. 32, p. 38] "Was doch heut Nacht ein
Sturm gewesen"
In der Frühe (1908?) [GA, v. 34, p. 154]
"Kein Schlaf noch kühlt das Auge mir"
Der König bei der Krönung, op. 70 no. 2
(1902-03) [GA, v. 32, p. 101]
"Dir angetrauet am Altare, O
Vaterland"
Morgenstern, Christian Otto Joseph
Wolfgang, 1871-1914.
Anmutiger Vertrag, op. 62 no. 16 (1901)
[GA, v. 32, p. 49]
"Auf der Bank im Walde"
Frühlingsregen, op. 51 no. 9 (1900) [GA,
v. 31, p. 193]
"Regne, regne, Frühlingsregen"
Gleich einer versunkenen Melodie, op. 51
no. 8 (1900) [GA, v. 31, p. 191] same
Hymnus des Hasses, op. 55 no. 1 (1900/
01) [GA, v. 31, p. 205]
"Heil dir, der du hassen kannst"
Leise Lieder, op. 48 no. 2 (1900) [GA,
v. 31, p. 150]
"Leise Lieder sing ich dir bei Nacht"
Mädchenlied, op. 51 no. 5 (1900) [GA,
v. 31, p. 182]
"Draussen im weiten Krieg"
Pflügerin Sorge, op. 62 no. 15 (1901)
[GA, v. 32, p. 46]
"Über der Erde Stirne"
Weisse Tauben, op. 51 no. 12 (1900)
[GA, v. 31, p. 201]
"Weisse Tauben fliegen"
Muth, Franz Alfred, 1839-1890.
Engelwacht, op. 68 no. 4 (1902) [GA,
v. 32, p. 89]
"Wenn alle Blumen träumen"

Obst, Willibald
Hoffnungslos (1901) [GA, v. 34, p. 130]
"In meinem Herzen ist's öd' und leer"
Prutz, Robert Eduard, 1816-1872.
Das Mädchen spricht, op. 15 no. 5
(1894) [GA, v. 31, p. 58]
"Mond, hast du auch gesehen"
Puttkamer, Marie Madeleine
(Günther), Freifrau, 1881-
Mädchenlied (1901) [GA, v. 34, p. 128]
"Die fernen, fernen Berge mit ihren
Nebelschleiern"
Reinick, Robert, 1805-1852.
Schwalbenmütterlein, op. 142 no. 2
(1915) [GA, v. 34, p. 95]
"Schwalbenmütterlein,
Schwalbenmütterlein!"
Ritter, Anna (Nuhn), 1865-1921.
Allein, op. 31 no. 1 (1898) [GA, v. 31,
p. 81] "Wie zerrissner Saiten Klingen"
Die Betrogene spricht, op. 43 no. 6
(1900) [GA, v. 31, p. 139]
"Die Nacht war tief und die Mutter
schlief"
Brautring (1900) [GA, v. 34, p. 120]
"Als über den Flieder das Mondlicht
rann"
Geheimnis (1900) [GA, v. 34, p. 122]
"Ich trag' ein glückselig Geheimnis"
Die Glocke des Glücks, op. 79c no. 6
(1903-04) [GA, v. 34, p. 14]
"Viele Glokken hör ich läuten"
Ich glaub', lieber Schatz, op. 31 no. 2
(1898) [GA, v. 31, p. 83]
"Unter den blühenden Linden"
In verschwiegener Nacht (1898) [GA,
v. 34, p. 111] same
Mein Traum, op. 31 no. 5 (1898) [GA,
v. 31, p. 91]
"Liegt nun so still die weite Welt"
Pythia, op. 23 no. 2 (1898) [GA, v. 31,
p. 74] "Hat einmal ein Mädel die
Muhme gefragt"
Schlimme Geschichte, op. 31 no. 6 (1898)
[GA, v. 31, p. 96]
"Musst's auch grad' so dunkel sein an
der Weissdornhekke!"
Sonnenregen (1902) [GA, v. 34, p. 136]
"Ich gehe fremd durch die Menge"
Sterne, op. 55 no. 7 (1900/01) [GA,
v. 31, p. 226]
"Die ihr den Aether mit seligen
Schwingen durch schneidet"
Unbegehrt, op. 31 no. 3 (1898) [GA,
v. 31, p. 86] "Es stand eine Rose im
tieftiefen Grund"

Und hab' so grosse Sehnsucht doch, op.
　31 no. 4 (1898) [GA, v. 31, p. 89]
　"Ich hab' kein' Mutter"
Volkslied, op. 37 no. 2 (1899) [GA,
　v. 31, p. 116]
　"Ein Vöglein singt im Wald"
JUGEND.
　Vom Küssen! op. 23 no. 4 (1898) [GA,
　　v. 31, p. 79]
　　"War ich gar so jung und dumm"
Rohrscheidt, Kurt von, 1857-1935.
　Glück, op. 15 no. 1 (1894) [GA, v. 31,
　　p. 51] "Es ruht mit ernstem Sinnen auf
　　mir dein Blick"
Roquette, Otto, 1824-1896.
　Du liebes Auge, op. 35 no. 5 (1899) [GA,
　　v. 31, p. 109] same
Rückert, Friedrich, 1788-1866.
　Widmung, op. 4 no. 2 (1891) [GA, v. 31,
　　p. 5] "Mir ist, da ich dich habe"
　Winterahnung, op. 4 no. 3 (1891) [GA,
　　v. 31, p. 7]
　　"Mich hat der Herbst betrogen"
　LIEBESFRÜHLING.
　　Der Himmel hat eine Träne geweint,
　　　op. 35 no. 2 (1899)
　　　[GA, v. 31, p. 101] same
Saul, Daniel, 1854-1903.
　Leichtsinniger Rat, op. 15 no. 8 (1894)
　　[GA, v. 31, p. 64]
　　"Wo du triffst ein Mündlein hold"
　Scheiden, op. 15 no. 6 (1894) [GA, v. 31,
　　p. 60]
　　"Noch immer halt ich dich umfasst"
Schäfer, Theo, b. 1872.
　Abend, op. 79c no. 1 (1903) [GA, v. 34,
　　p. 2]
　　"Es blüht um mich des Abends Stille"
　Erinnerung, op. 79c no. 7 (1906-07)
　　[GA, v. 34, p. 17]
　　"Eine stille Melodie"
**Schatz, Josef, 1871-1950, supposed
author.**
　Der gute Rat, op. 98 no. 2 (1906) [GA,
　　v. 34, p. 53] "Hier ein Weilchen! dort
　　ein Weilchen!"
**Schellenberg, Ernst Ludwig, 1883-
1964.**
　Der Dieb (1906?) [GA, v. 34, p. 152]
　　"Ich bin ein Dieb geworden"
　Furchthäschen, op. 76 no. 55 [GA, v. 33,
　　p. 147] "Mutter, liebe Mutter, komm
　　rasch einmal hier"
　Glück, op. 76 no. 16 [GA, v. 33, p. 40]
　　"Das machte dein stiller, keuscher
　　Blick"

Der Igel, op. 76 no. 56 [GA, v. 33,
　p. 149] "Der Igel, der Igel"
Der König aus dem Morgenland, op. 76
　no. 60 [GA, v. 33, p. 157]
　"Ich bin der König vom Morgenland"
Maria am Rosenstrauch, op. 142 no. 3
　(1915) [GA, v. 34, p. 97]
　"Maria sitzt am Rosenbusch"
Mausefangen, op. 76 no. 58 [GA, v. 33,
　p. 153] "Eins, zwei, drei"
Mittag, op. 76 no. 35 [GA, v. 33, p. 101]
　"Zwischen Mohn und Rittersporn hab'
　ich träumend heut' "
Schelmenliedchen, op. 76 no. 36 [GA,
　v. 33, p. 103]
　"Wenn hell die liebe Sonne lacht"
Zum Schlafen, op. 76 no. 59 [GA, v. 33,
　p. 155] "Oben in dem Birnenbaum
　sitzt ein Vöglein"
Scholz, Maria, 1861-1944.
　Ach, Liebster, in Gedanken, op. 48 no. 4
　　(1900) [GA, v. 31, p. 157] same
　Allen Welten abgewandt, op. 55 no. 14
　　(1900/01) [GA, v. 31, p. 246]
　　"An den Mondes strahlen gleiten
　　meine Küsse"
　Um Mitternacht blühen die Blumen, op.
　　79c no. 2 (1901) [GA, v. 34, p. 4]
　　same
Seyboth, Sofie
　Darum, op. 75 no. 15 (1903) [GA, v. 32,
　　p. 187]
　　"Hab' Singen für mein Leben gern"
　Die Mutter spricht, op. 76 no. 28 [GA,
　　v. 33, p. 76] "Liebes Töchterlein"
　Schwäbische Treue, op. 75 no. 10 (1903)
　　[GA, v. 32, p. 173]
　　"Mein Schatz ist auf die Wanderschaft
　　wohl in die weite Welt"
Sommerstorff, Otto, 1859-1934.
　Mei Bua, op. 76 no. 11 [GA, v. 33,
　　p. 27] "A' Versle, a' g'spassig's"
Stein, Gretel
　Wiegenlied, op. 142 no. 1 (1915) [GA,
　　v. 34, p. 92]
　　"Schlaf' ein, mein liebes Kindlein du"
　　Author of text may be Gertrude Stein.
Stieler, Karl, 1842-1885.
　Nächtliche Pfade, op. 37 no. 5 (1899)
　　[GA, v. 31, p. 122]
　　"In dem Bäumen regt sich's leise"
Storm, Theodor, 1817-1888.
　Einen Brief soll ich schreiben, op. 76 no.
　　8 [GA, v. 33, p. 19] same
　　Text not by R. Burns as Reger
　　attributed.

REGER, MAX, 1873-1916 *(continued)*
Storm, Theodor, 1817-1888 *(continued)*
Nelken, op. 15 no. 3 (1894) [GA, v. 31,
p. 54] "Ich wand ein Sträusschen
morgens früh"
Sturm, Julius Karl Reinholdt, 1816-
1896.
Heimweh (1900) [GA, v. 34, p. 196]
"Unser Schifflein treibt umher auf des
Lebens"
Voice and organ.
Zwei Gänse, op. 55 no. 8 (1900/01) [GA,
v. 31, p. 229]
"Zur weissen Gans sprach einst
vertraulich eine graue"
Träger, Albert, 1820-1912.
Wiegenlied (1898) [GA, v. 34, p. 113]
"Schliesse, mein Kind"
Triepel, Gertrud. b. 1863.
Sommernacht, op. 98 no. 5 (1906) [GA,
v. 34, p. 66]
"Im Garten rauscht die Sommernacht"
Trojan, Johannes, 1837-1915.
Klein Marie, op. 76 no. 44 [GA, v. 33,
p. 124] "Marie auf der Wiese, auf der
Wiese Marie"
Ubell, Hermann, 1876-1947.
Junge Ehe, op. 48 no. 5 (1900) [GA,
v. 31, p. 159]
"O presse deine Hand in meine Hand"
Uhland, Ludwig, 1787-1862.
Bauernregel, op. 8 no. 5 (1892) [GA,
v. 31, p. 28]
"Im Sommer such' ein Liebchen dir"
Hans und Grete, op. 76 no. 19 [GA,
v. 33, p. 48]
"Guckst du mir denn immer nach"
Sonntag, op. 98 no. 3 (1906) [GA, v. 34,
p. 58]
"So hab' ich doch die ganze Woche"
Waldlied, op. 8 no. 1 (1892) [GA, v. 31,
p. 18] "Im Walde geh' ich wohlgemut"
Unknown
Abendlied, op. 76 no. 39 [GA, v. 33,
p. 111]
"Langsam wird mein Kindchen müde"
Am Abend, op. 137 no. 4 (1914) [GA,
v. 34, p. 184]
"Mit meinem Gott geh ich zur Ruh"
Text from Will Vesper, comp. *Der
deutsche Psalter, ein Jahrtausend
geistlicher Dichtung* (Verlag W.
Langewiesche-Brandt)
Beim Schneewetter, op. 76 no. 6 [GA,
v. 33, p. 14]
"Die Englein haben's Bett gemacht"

Bitte, op. 4 no. 6 (1891) [GA, v. 31,
p. 15] "Du siehst mich nun schon drei
Tage heut"
Christ, deines Geistes Süssigkeit, op. 137
no. 6 (1914) [GA, v. 34, p. 186] same
Text from Will Vesper, comp. *Der
deutsche Psalter, ein Jahrtausend
geistlicher Dichtung* (Verlag W.
Langewiesche-Brandt)
Christkindleins Wiegenlied, op. 137 no.
10 (1914) [GA, v. 34, p. 190]
"Lasst uns das Kindlein wiegen"
Text from Will Vesper, comp. *Der
deutsche Psalter, ein Jahrtausend
geistlicher Dichtung* (Verlag W.
Langewiesche-Brandt)
Klage vor Gottes Leiden, op. 137 no. 11
(1914) [GA, v. 34, p. 191]
"O Ursprung aller Brunen"
Text from Will Vesper, comp. *Der
deutsche Psalter, ein Jahrtausend
geistlicher Dichtung* (Verlag W.
Langewiesche-Brandt)
O Herre Gott, nimm du von mir, op. 137
no. 5 (1914) [GA, v. 34, p. 185] same
Text from Will Vesper, comp. *Der
deutsche Psalter, ein Jahrtausend
geistlicher Dichtung* (Verlag W.
Langewiesche-Brandt)
Passionslied, op. 19 no. 1 [GA, v. 34, p.
167] "In Todesängsten hängst du da"
Voice and organ.
Der Schelm, op. 15 no. 7 (1894) [GA,
v. 31, p. 62]
"Veilchen wollt ich pflükken"
Uns ist geboren ein Kindelein, op. 137
no. 3 (1914) [GA, v. 34, p. 183] same
Text from Will Vesper, comp. *Der
deutsche Psalter, ein Jahrtausend
geistlicher Dichtung* (Verlag W.
Langewiesche-Brandt)
Warnung, op. 104 no. 2 (1907) [GA,
v. 34, p. 73]
"Männer suchen stets zu naschen"
Der zerrissne Grabkranz, op. 4 no. 5
(1891) [GA, v. 31, p. 13]
"Auf einem Grab in Stükken liegt ein
zerrissner Kranz"
Weber, Cläre Henrika, 1881-1954.
Klein Evelinde, op. 142 no. 4 (1915)
[GA, v. 34, p. 99]
"Prinzesslein tanzt durch die Wiese"
Wegerer, Asta von
Es soll mein Gebet dich tragen (1893-94)
[GA, v. 34, p. 105] same
Weigand, Wilhelm, 1862-1949.

Merkspruch, op. 75 no. 1 (1903) [GA,
v. 32, p. 149]
"Merk dir's in vollster Kraft"
Weisse, Christian Felix, 1726-1804.
Der bescheidene Schäfer, op. 97 no. 4
(1906) [GA, v. 34, p. 46]
"Mein Schäfer, ach!"
Wiener, Oskar
Abschied, op. 43 no. 4 (1900) [GA, v. 31,
p. 134] "Meine armen, kleinen Lieder
halten Wacht"
Am Dorfsee, op. 48 no. 6 (1900) [GA,
v. 31, p. 163] "Am Dorfsee neigt die
Weide ihr kahles Haupt"
Mein Herz, op. 43 no. 7 (1900) [GA,
v. 31, p. 142]
"Mein rotes Herz, mein totes Herz"
Sag es nicht, op. 43 no. 8 (1900) [GA,
v. 31, p. 144] same
Wildenbruch, Ernst von, 1845-1909.
Der Kornblumenstrauss, op. 8 no. 3
(1892) [GA, v. 31, p. 22]
"Auf meinem Tische stehn"
Tränen im Auge, op. 8 no. 2 (1892) [GA,
v. 31, p. 20]
"Warum so bleich und blass"
Zweig, Stefan, 1881-1942.
Ein Drängen, op. 97 no. 3 (1906) [GA,
v. 34, p. 41] same
Neue Fülle, op. 104 no. 1 (1907) [GA,
v. 34, p. 70]
"O welche Glühn in fremde Hülle"
Regnard, Jean François, 1655-1709.
BIZET *Pastorale*
Regnault, Mme. Félix
SAINT-SAËNS *Ne l'oubliez pas*
"Regne, regne, Frühlingsregen" *see*
Frühlingsregen Morgenstern **REGER**
Regnet slår och slår see Lagerkvist
KILPINEN
**Régnier, Henri François Joseph de,
1864-1936.**
AUBERT *Odelette*
FAURÉ *Chanson*
HAHN *Les fontaines*
RAVEL *Les Grands Vents venus d'outre-*
mer
ROUSSEL
Adieux
Le Départ
Invocation
Le jardin mouillé
Madrigal lyrique
La menace
Nuit d'automne
Odelette

Voeu
Regnier, Jehan, fl.1392-1468.
ROREM *Lay*
Regret: Devant le ciel see Bourget
LES AVEUX: Amour. **DEBUSSY**
Regrets see Fargue **AURIC**
Regrets! see Silvestre **DELIBES**
"Regungslos, ein grosser Schweiger" *see*
Der Kirchturm Huber, B. **KILPINEN**
"Reich' den Pokal mir" *see Skolie* Reinick
WOLF
"Reich' mir den Schleier, Emina" *see*
Gulhinde am Putztische Stieglitz **LOEWE**
Reich' mir die Hand, O Wolke see Kulmann
SCHUMANN
Reichardt, Heinrich
ZELTER *Gefilde des Todes*
Reiche mir aus blauer Ferne see Schink
ZELTER
"Der reiche Tor, mit Gold geschmücket" *see*
Die betrogene Welt Weisse **MOZART**
"Der Reif hat einen weissen Schein" *see*
Der greise Kopf Müller, Wilhelm
SCHUBERT
Reigen see Voss **WEBER**
Die Reigerbaize see Auersperg **LOEWE**
The reign of the stars see Quilter **QUILTER**
Reiher flogen see Anon. **SZYMANOWSKI**
Lecioly zurazie
**Reil, Johann Anton Friedrich, 1773-
1843.**
SCHUBERT *Das Lied im Grünen*
Reimar der Alte see Scheffel *DER*
BRAUTWILLKOMM AUF WARTBURG.
LISZT
"Der Reimer Thomas lag am Bach" *see*
Thomas der Reimer Anon. **LOEWE**
"Rein und freundlich lacht der Himmel" *see*
Der Mondabend Kumpf **SCHUBERT**
Reinbeck, Georg, 1766-1849.
WEBER
Romanze: Die Ruinen
Sanftes Licht
GORDON UND MONTROSE ODER DER
KAMPFDER GEFÜHLE.
WEBER *Ballade*
La reine de coeur see Carême **POULENC**
Reine des cieux see Anon. **SAINT-SAËNS**
Reine des mouettes see Vilmorin **POULENC**
La reine m'a livré see Hugnet **SAUGUET**
Reinheit see Boelitz **REGER**
Reinhold, C., pseud. see Köstlin, Christian
Reinhold, 1813-1856.
Reinick, Robert, 1805-1852.
BRAHMS
Juchhe!

Reinick, Robert, 1805-1852 *(continued)*
 BRAHMS *(continued)*
  Liebestreu
 LOEWE *Der verliebte Maikäfer*
 PFITZNER *Kuriose Geschichte*
 REGER *Schwalbenmütterlein*
 SCHÖNBERG *Im Fliederbusch ein*
  Vöglein sass
 SPOHR
  Der Bleicherin Nachtlied
  Frühlingsglocken
  Schweigen ist ein schönes Ding
 WOLF
  Dem Vaterland
  Frohe Botschaft
  Frühlingsglocken
  Gesellenlied
  Liebchen, wo bist du?
  Morgenstimmung
  Nachtgruss
  Skolie
  Wiegenlied im Sommer
  Wiegenlied im Winter
  Wohin mit der Freud?
 LIEDERBUCH EINES MALERS.
  LASSEN *Ständchen*
  SCHUMANN
   An den Sonnenschein
   Dichters Genesung
   Liebesbotschaft
   Nichts Schöneres
   Sonntags am Rhein
   Ständchen
  SPOHR *Nichts Schöneres*
  WOLF
   Liebesbotschaft
   Ständchen
Der Reisebecher see Meyer **SCHOECK**
Reisebild see Hamerling **LASSEN**
REISEBUCH AUS DEN OESTERREICHEN ALPEN, no. 1
 KRENEK Krenek *Motiv*
REISEBUCH AUS DEN OESTERREICHEN ALPEN, no. 2
 KRENEK Krenek *Verkehr*
REISEBUCH AUS DEN OESTERREICHEN ALPEN, no. 3
 KRENEK Krenek *Kloster in den Alpen*
REISEBUCH AUS DEN OESTERREICHEN ALPEN, no. 4
 KRENEK Krenek *Wetter*
REISEBUCH AUS DEN OESTERREICHEN ALPEN, no. 5
 KRENEK Krenek *Traurige Stunde*
REISEBUCH AUS DEN OESTERREICHEN ALPEN, no. 6

 KRENEK Krenek *Friedhof im Gebirgsdorf*
REISEBUCH AUS DEN OESTERREICHEN ALPEN, no. 7
 KRENEK Krenek *Regentag*
REISEBUCH AUS DEN OESTERREICHEN ALPEN, no. 8
 KRENEK Krenek *Unser Wein*
REISEBUCH AUS DEN OESTERREICHEN ALPEN, no. 9
 KRENEK Krenek *Rückblick*
REISEBUCH AUS DEN OESTERREICHEN ALPEN, no. 10
 KRENEK Krenek *Auf und Ab*
REISEBUCH AUS DEN OESTERREICHEN ALPEN, no. 11
 KRENEK Krenek *Alpenbewohner*
REISEBUCH AUS DEN OESTERREICHEN ALPEN, no. 12
 KRENEK Krenek *Politik*
REISEBUCH AUS DEN OESTERREICHEN ALPEN, no. 13
 KRENEK Krenek *Gewitter*
REISEBUCH AUS DEN OESTERREICHEN ALPEN, no. 14
 KRENEK Krenek *Heimweh*
REISEBUCH AUS DEN OESTERREICHEN ALPEN, no. 15
 KRENEK Krenek *Heisser Tag am See*
REISEBUCH AUS DEN OESTERREICHEN ALPEN, no. 16
 KRENEK Krenek *Kleine Stadt in den Südlichen Alpen*
REISEBUCH AUS DEN OESTERREICHEN ALPEN, no. 17
 KRENEK Krenek *Ausblick nach Süden*
REISEBUCH AUS DEN OESTERREICHEN ALPEN, no. 18
 KRENEK Krenek *Entscheidung*
REISEBUCH AUS DEN OESTERREICHEN ALPEN, no. 19
 KRENEK Krenek *Heimkehr*
REISEBUCH AUS DEN OESTERREICHEN ALPEN, no. 20
 KRENEK Krenek *Epilog*
Reiselied see Ebert **MENDELSSOHN-BARTHOLDY**
Reiselied see Eichendorff **MEDTNER, SCHOECK**
Reiselied see Heine **MENDELSSOHN-BARTHOLDY**
Reiselied see Hofmannsthal **BERG**
REISEMINDER FRA FJELD OG FJORD, no. 1
 GRIEG Drachmann *Prolog*
REISEMINDER FRA FJELD OG FJORD, no. 2

GRIEG Drachmann *Johanne*
REISEMINDER FRA FJELD OG FJORD, no. 3

GRIEG Drachmann *Ragnhild*
REISEMINDER FRA FJELD OG FJORD, no. 4

GRIEG Drachmann *Ingebjørg*
REISEMINDER FRA FJELD OG FJORD, no. 5

GRIEG Drachmann *Ragna*
REISEMINDER FRA FJELD OG FJORD, no. 6

GRIEG Drachmann *Epilog*
"Reisengross liegt das Kloster da im Tal" *see*
  Kloster in den Alpen Krenek **KRENEK**
Reisephantasie see Meyer **SCHOECK**
Reissig, Christian Ludwig, 1783-1822.
  BEETHOVEN
    An den fernen Geliebten
    Des Kriegers Abschied
    Der Jüngling in der Fremde
    Der Liebende
    Lied aus der Ferne
    Sehnsucht
    Der Zufriedene
  LOEWE *Sehnsucht*
  SCHUBERT *Der Zufriedene*
  ZELTER *Meine höchste Wonne*
"Ein Reiter durch das Bergthal zieht" *see*
  Bergstimme Heine **MEDTNER**
"Ein Reiter muss haben ein Rösslein zu
  traben" *see Reiterlied* Boelitz **REGER**
"Der Reiter reitet durch's helle Thal" *see*
  Der Reiter und der Bodensee Schwab
  SCHUMANN
Der Reiter und der Bodensee see Schwab
  SCHUMANN
Reiterlied see Boelitz **REGER**
Reiterlied see Redwitz *AMARANTH.*
  LOEWE
Reiterlied see Unknown **MENDELSSOHN-
  BARTHOLDY**
"Řekla bych vám, ruže, něco" *see Překážky*
  Pech **DVOŘÁK**
Rekrutenlied aus Wallensteins Lager see
  Schiller **LASSEN**
Religion see Root **IVES**
LE RELIQUAIRE. see Coppée
  La vague et la cloche **DUPARC**
RELIQUES. see Percy
  Des Bettlers Tochter von Bednall Green
    LOEWE
  Harpalus **IVES**
Rellstab, Ludwig, 1799-1868.
  LISZT
    Es rauschen die Winde

  Ihr Auge
  Wo weilt er?
SCHUBERT
  Abschied
  Auf dem Strome
  Aufenthalt
  Frühlingssehnsucht
  Herbst
  In der Ferne
  Kriegers Ahnung
  Lebensmut
  Liebesbotschaft
  Ständchen
Remember see Cocconi, Ildebrando
  PIZZETTI
Remember see Coleridge **IRELAND**
Remember Adam's fall see Anon.
  THOMSON
"Remember Adam's fall, O thou man" *see*
  Remember Adam's fall Anon. **THOMSON**
Remember me see Bal'mont **PROKOFIEV**
  Pomni menia!
Remembrance see Ives **IVES**
Remembrance see Pech **DVOŘÁK**
  Vzpomínání
Remembrance see Pushkin **MEDTNER**
  Retrospect
Remer, Paul, 1867-1943.
  SCHÖNBERG *Mädchenlied*
  STRAUSS *In goldener Fülle*
Reminiszenz see Hebbel **CORNELIUS**
Renard, Jules, 1864-1910.
  HISTOIRES NATURELLES.
    RAVEL
      Le Cygne
      Le Grillon
      Le Martin-Pêcheur
      Le Paon
      La Pintade
Renaud, Armand, 1836-1895.
  HAHN *Les cygnes*
  SAINT-SAËNS
    Au cimetière
    La brise
    Sabre en main
    La solitaire
    La splendeur vid
    Tournoiement
  NUITS PERSANES (1870).
    DEBUSSY *Flots, palmes, sables*
Renaudière, M de La
  CHABRIER *Le sentier sombre*
Renaut, J.
  DELIBES *À ma mignonne*
Rencontre see Grandmougin **FAURÉ**
"Rendete a gli occhi miei, O fonte O fiume"
  see Sonetto XXXVIII Buonarroti
  BRITTEN

COMPOSER Poet *Title* "First Line"

La rendez-vous see Claudel **HONEGGER**
Le rendez-vous see Fiéffé **SAINT-SAËNS**
"Une renoncule Âcre" *see Vie des campagnes*
   Follain **SAUGUET**
Renouveau see Mallarmé **SAUGUET**
Le repas préparé see Samain *AUX FLANCS DU VASE.* **KOECHLIN**
Repentir see Anon. **GOUNOD**
Répétition planétaire see Messiaen
   MESSIAEN
Réponse de Medjé see Barbier, M.
   GOUNOD
Réponse d'une épouse sage see Chang-Chi
   ROUSSEL
A report song see Breton **IRELAND**
Repos dan le malheur see Michaux
   SAUGUET
Le repos en Égypte see Samain **RESPIGHI**
A request see Glücklich **MACDOWELL**
   Bitte
Requiem see Anon. **SCHUMANN**
Requiem see Meyer **SCHOECK**
Requiem see Stevenson, Robert Louis
   IVES, ROREM
"Requiem Eterna dona ei Domine" *see A ma belle mère* Unknown **ROSSINI**
Requiescat see Wilde **LUENING**
"Resedenduft durchs kranke Fenster irrt" *see In der Heimat* Trakl **WEBERN**
Resignation see Buddeus **SCHUMANN**
Resignation see Haugwitz **BEETHOVEN**
Resignation see Montgomery **BENNETT**
Resolution see Ives **IVES**
Respice, Domine, familiam tuam see
   No author **CASELLA**
RESPIGHI, OTTORINO, 1879-1936.
   Aganoor-Pompilj, Vittoria Antonia
      Maria, 1855-1910.
      E se un Giorno Tornasse (1911) [Ricordi, 1919] same
      Pioggia (1909) [Bongiovanni, 1906]
         "Piovea; per le finestre spalancate"
   Annunzio, Gabriele d', 1863-1938.
      La donna sul sarcofago (1919) [Ricordi, 1986] "La donna in attitudine regale"
      La statua (1919) [Ricordi, 1986]
         "Chi scenderà dal'alta scala"
      CANTO NOVO: Canto dell'Ospite, no. VI.
         Van li effluvi de le rose (1909) [Bongiovanni, 1912] same
      CANTO NOVO: Canto dell'Ospite, no. VII.
         O falce di luna (1909) [Bongiovanni, 1912] same
      LA CHIMERA.

      Mattinata (1909) [Bongiovanni, 1910]
         "Spandono le campane a la prim'alba l'ave"
      POEMA PARADISIACO.
      La najade (1920) [Bongiovanni, 1927]
         "Pullula ne l'opaco bosco"
      La sera (1920) [Bongiovanni, 1927]
         "Rimanete, vi prego, rimanete qui"
      Un sogno (1920) [Bongiovanni, 1927]
         "Io non odo imiei passi nel viale muto"
      Sopra un'aria antica (1920) [Bongiovanni, 1927]
         "Non sorgono 'ascolta ascolta"
   Birga, Arturo
      RISPETTI TOSCANI.
      Quando nasceste voi (1914) [Bongiovanni, 1915] same
      Razzolan, sopra a l'aja, le galline . . . (1914) [Bongiovanni, 1915] same
      Venitelo a vedere 'l mi'piccino . . . (1914) [Bongiovanni, 1915] same
      Viene di là, lontan lontano . . . (1914) [Bongiovanni, 1915] same
   Boccaccio, Giovanni, 1313-1375.
      Ballata (1906) [Bongiovanni, 1907]
         "Non so qual io mi voglia"
      L'udir talvolta . . . (1906) [Bongiovanni, 1907] same
      IL NINFALE FIESOLANO, 287.
         Ma come potrei . . . (1906) [Bongiovanni, 1907] same
   Donini, Alberto, 1887-
      Canzone (1906) [Bongiovanni, 1907]
         "Amor mi fa sovente"
         From the comic opera *Re Enzo.*
      Stornello (1906?) [Bongiovanni, 1949]
         "O fior del prato!"
         From the comic opera *Re Enzo.* For 1 or 2 voices & piano.
   Fersen, I. de
      Par les soirs . . . (1917) [Ricordi, 1918]
         "Vaguement et longtemps aux mauves crepuscules"
      Par l'étreinte . . . (1917) [Ricordi, 1918]
         "Tu es venu, la chambre est parfumée"
      L'HYMNAIRE D'ADONIS.
         Il pleut, bergère (1920) [unpubl.?]
   Fogazzaro, Antonio
      Miranda (1902) [unpubl.]
   Graf, Arturo, 1848-1913.
      Povero core (1909) [Bongiovanni, 1910]
         "O mio povero cor"
   Hugo, Victor Marie, comte, 1802-1885.
      Si tu beux (1909) [Bongiovanni, 1910] same

Moréas, Jean, 1856-1910.
Au milieu du jardin (1909) [Bongiovanni, 1912] same
Negri, Ada, 1870-1945.
Lagrime! (1896) [Bongiovanni, 1982] "Tornai: la bocca tiepida"
Luce (1906) [Bongiovanni, 1982] "A fasci s'effonde per l'aria tranquilla"
Nebbie (1906?) [Bongiovanni, 1906] "Soffro, Lontan lontano"
Notte (1912) [Bongiovanni, 1912] "Sul giardino fantastico"
Notturno (1896) [Bongiovanni, 1982] "Su'cespugli, vezzose, in un sopor beato"
Storia breve (1904) [Bongiovanni, 1982] "Ella pareva un so gno di poeta"
L'ultima ebbrezza! (1896) [Bongiovanni, 1982] "Un ultimo profumo innebriante versa"
FATALITÀ.
Nevicata (1906?) [Bongiovanni, 1906] "Sui campi e sulle strade"
Nerses (Lampronetsi), 1143-1198.
Mattino di luce (1921) [Ricordi, 1922] same
No author
Tre vocalizzi (1930) [unpubl.?]
Panzacchi, Enrico, 1841-1904.
In alto mare (1909) [Bongiovanni, 1910] "È sdruscito il navil"
Noël ancien (1912) [Bongiovanni, 1912] "Noël nouvelet Noël chantons ici"
No author of text on the music; attribution from Ricordi catalogue.
Rocchi, Francesco
Nel giardino (1912) [Bongiovanni, 1919] "Mormora nel giardino"
Piccola mano bianca (1912) [Bongiovanni, 1919]
Rubino, Antonio, 1880-1964.
Acqua (1917) [Ricordi, 1917] "Acqua, e tu ancora sul tuo flauto lene"
Arranged for voice & 11 instruments, 1925.
Crepuscolo (1917) [Ricordi, 1917] "Nell'orto abbandonato ora l'edace muschio"
Arranged for voice & 11 instruments, 1925.
Egle (1917) [Ricordi, 1917] "Frondeggia il bosco d'uberi verzure"
Arranged for voice & 11 instruments, 1925.
I fauni (1917) [Ricordi, 1917] "S'odono al monte i saltellanti rivi"

Arranged for voice & 11 instruments, 1925.
Musica in horto (1917) [Ricordi, 1917] "Uno squillo di cròtali clangenti rompe"
Arranged for voice & 11 instruments, 1925.
Samain, Albert Victor, 1858-1900.
Le repos en Égypte (1912) [Bongiovanni] "La nuit est blue . . . et chaude"
Shelley, Percy Bysshe, 1792-1822.
Canto funebre (1917) [Ricordi, 1918] "Rude vento, che diffondi in suon di pianto"
Serenata indiana (1909) [Bongiovanni, 1912] "Del sonno tra i fantasimi di te sognavo"
Su una violetta morta (1912) [Bongiovanni, 1919] "È vanito l'odor di questo fiorc, chc"
I tempi assai lontani (1917) [Ricordi, 1918] "Come l'ombra di cara estinta vita"
Sully-Prudhomme, René François Armand, 1839-1907.
LES SOLITUDES.
Soupir (1909) [Bongiovanni, 1910] "Ne jamais la voir ni l'entendre"
Tagore, Rabindranath, 1861-1941.
La fine (1917) [Ricordi, 1918] "È tempo per me d'andare, mamma, me ne vado"
Unknown
Bella porta di rubini (1906) [Bongiovanni, 1907] same
Canzone sacra (1928) [unpubl.?]
Le funtanelle, canzone dell'Abruzzo (1930) [unpubl.?]
Kroung (La Cigogne, 1930?) [unpubl.?]
Mon elué (1930?) [unpubl.?]
My heart's in the Highlands (1924) [Universal, 1925] same
Text by Robert Burns?
Noel ancien (1909) [Bongiovanni, 1912] "Noël nouvelet, Noël chantons ici"
The piper of Dundee (1924) [Universal, 1925] "The piper came to our town"
Tanto bella (1897) [Bongiovanni, 1982] "A la tua culla vennero le fate"
Voici noël (1920) [unpubl.?]
When the kye come hame (1924) [Universal, 1925] "Come all ye jolly shepherds that whistle thro' the glen"
Within a mile of Edinburgh town (1924) [Universal, 1925] " 'Twas within a mile of Edinburgh town"

COMPOSER   Poet   *Title*   "First Line"

RESPIGHI, OTTORINO, 1879-1936
(continued)
Vivanti, Annie, 1868-1942.
  Abbandono (1909) [Bongiovanni, 1910]
    "Io sono tanto stanca di lottare"
Zangarini, Carlo, 1874-1943.
  Contrasto (1906?) [Bongiovanni, 1906]
    "Piange lenta la luna"
  Invito alla danza (1906?) [Bongiovanni,
    1906] "Madonna, d'un braccio soa ve
    ch'io cinga"
  Scherzo (1906?) [Bongiovanni, 1906]
    "Una notte, al davanzale"
  Stornellatrice (1906?) [Bongiovanni,
    1936]
    "Che mi giova cantar: 'Fior di betulla' "
    Text also by Alberto Donini.
Zarian, Kostan, 1885-1969.
  Io sono la Madre (1921) [Ricordi, 1922]
    same
  La mamma è come il pane caldo (1921)
    [Ricordi, 1922] same
  No, non è morto il figlio tuo (1921)
    [Ricordi, 1922] same
Respóndemos see Anon. **RODRIGO**
Rest see Simpson, M. *THE DIAL.*
  CARPENTER
Rest see Symons **IRELAND**
Rest in the valley see Pfleger-Moravský
  DVOŘÁK *Na horách ticho a vúdolí
  ticho*
Rest in the valley see Pfleger-Moravsky
  DVOŘÁK *Na horách
  ticho a vúdolích ticho*
Rest in the valley see Pfleger-Moravsky
  DVOŘÁK *Na horách ticho, vúdolí ticho*
Rest, sweet nymphs see Anon. **HESELTINE**
"Rest, sweet nymphs, let golden sleep" *see*
  Rest, sweet nymphs Anon. **HESELTINE**
Rest well . . . see Goodman **ROREM**
Restauration see Mörike **SCHOECK**
"Reste ainsi, penchée sur ton coeur" *see*
  Le visage penché Toussaint **AUBERT**
Restored to health see Hafiz **MARTINŮ**
The resurrection see Bible *MATTHEW 27:
  62-66; 28.* **ROREM**
Résurrection see Messiaen **MESSIAEN**
Le retour see Delaquys **BOULANGER**
Le retour see Paliard **MILHAUD**
Retour d'oiseau see Stuart, Paul
  MASSENET
Le retour du sergent see Fombeure
  CHANSONS DE LA GRANDE HUNE.
  POULENC
Retrospect see Pushkin **MEDTNER**
The return see Meri **RUBINSTEIN**

Return, O Shulamite see Bible **THOMSON**
  Two settings: 1924 and 1926.
"Return, return, O Shulamite" *see Return, O
  Shulamite!* Bible **THOMSON**
Returning home see Nietzsche **MEDTNER**
  Heimkehr
Un rêve see Poe *A DREAM.* **SÉVERAC**
Un rêve see Spenner, M. **GOUNOD**
Rêve d'amour see Hugo **FAURÉ**
Rêve de la bien-aimée see Courmont **BIZET**
Réveil see Cocteau **AURIC**
Le réveil . . . see Desbordes-Valmore
  AURIC
Le réveil de la mariée see Anon. **RAVEL**
"Réveille-toi, réveille-toi" *see Le réveil de la
  mariée* Anon. **RAVEL**
Réveillez-vous, Piccarz see Anon.
  VAUGHAN WILLIAMS
Le Réveillon see Wilde *THE FOURTH
  MOVEMENT.* Impression: Le Réveillon.
  GRIFFES *Dawn*
Le revenant see Baudelaire **HINDEMITH**
Révérence see Morand **MILHAUD**
Rêverie see Banville *LES CARIATIDES*, livre
  2, Amours d'Élise . . . no. V. **DEBUSSY**
Rêverie see Barbier, J. **GOUNOD**
Rêverie see Croisset **CASELLA**
Rêverie see Hugo **HAHN, SAINT-SAËNS**
Reverie see Unknown **LOEFFLER**
Rêverie sentimentale see Peyre, Mathylde
  MASSENET
Rêves see Fargue **RAVEL**
Les rêves see Silvestre **ROUSSEL**
RÊVES, no. 1
  MILHAUD Anon. *Marronniers*
RÊVES, no. 2
  MILHAUD Anon. *Toi*
RÊVES, no. 3
  MILHAUD Anon. *Confidence*
RÊVES, no. 4
  MILHAUD Anon. *Le mistral*
RÊVES, no. 5
  MILHAUD Anon. *Long distance*
RÊVES, no. 6
  MILHAUD Anon. *Jeunesse*
Rêves d'or pour ton sommeil see Anon.
  CASELLA
Les rêves morts see Leconte de Lisle
  KOECHLIN
"Revet li zvor' vlesu glukhom" *see Ekho*
  Pushkin **RIMSKII-KORSAKOV**
Reviens (Epilogue) *see* Docquois
  SAINT-SAËNS
"Reviens, reviens, ma bien aimée" *see
  Absence* Gautier **BERLIOZ, BIZET**
La révoltée see Chalupt **MILHAUD**

Rey, Paul
SÉVERAC
  Albada a l'Estela
  Les cors
ANOMALIE.
  SÉVERAC *Le chevrier*
Rhapsodie see Haug **WEBER** *Die Blume*
RHEINISCHE LIEDER I
  CORNELIUS Cornelius *In der Ferne*
RHEINISCHE LIEDER II
  CORNELIUS Cornelius *Botschaft*
RHEINISCHE LIEDER III
  CORNELIUS Cornelius *Am Rhein*
RHEINISCHE LIEDER IV
  CORNELIUS Cornelius *Gedenken*
Rhinelander, Philip Hamilton, 1908-
  THOMPSON, R. *Siciliano*
Rhodante see Samain **KOECHLIN**
Ribemont Dessaignes, Georges, 1884-
1974.
  JOLIVET *March funèbre*
Ribot, Theodule, 1839-1916.
  MOMPOU *Sant Marti*
Rich, Adrienne Cecile, 1929-
  DIVING INTO THE WRECK.
  ROREM *The stranger*
  NECESSITIES OF LIFE.
  WEISGALL *Song*
Rich and poor see Nekrasov **BORODIN**
  U lyudey-to v domu
Rich days see Davies, W. H. **BERKELEY**
Richard II Quarante see Aragon **AURIC**
Richardt, Christian Ernst, 1831-1892.
  GRIEG
    Efteraarsstormen
    Modersorg
  NIELSEN
    Derfor kan vort øje Glaedes
    Jord, i hvis favn
    Laer mig, nattens stjerne
    Velkommen Laerkelil
Richaud, André de, b. 1907.
  SAUGUET
    Carte postale à Délos
    Coeur noir du vent qui passe
    Nature morte
    Petite musique
    Ritournelle
    Tours
Richepin, Jean, 1849-1926.
  CASELLA
    En ramant
    Larmes
    Nuageries
  CHAUSSON
    Le mort maudit

  Les morts
  La pluie
  DELIUS *Nuages*
  FAURÉ *Au cimetière*
  GOUNOD *La chanson de la glu*
  HONEGGER
    Chanson de la route
    Chanson de l'eau
  SCHMITT
    Evocation
    Où vivre?
  LA MER.
    FAURÉ *Larmes*
Richter, Johann Paul Friedrich, 1763-
1825.
  SAUGUET
    A une rose pâlissant au soleil
    Le bal d'enfants
    La double rougeur
    Le jour de tristesse
    Le muguet
    Le vide de l'instant
A riddle see Soutar **BRITTEN**
  Two settings: Op. 84 no. 1 and op. 84 no.
  7.
Le rideau de ma voisine see Musset
  CHAUSSON
Ridge, Lola, 1883-1941.
  RED FLAG.
    ROREM *Electrocution*
Riding on a stick see Musorgskiĭ
  MUSORGSKIĬ *Poekhal na polochke*
RIEGGER, WALLINGFORD, 1885-1961.
  Anon.
    Charmant bocage (1920) [Peer, 1950]
      same
    Toi, dont les yeux (1920) [Peer, 1950]
      same
  Arens, Egmont
    The somber pine (1902) [Associated,
      1961] "It is holiday time in the woods"
  Burns, Robert, 1759-1796.
    Ye banks and braes o' Bonnie Doon
      (1910) [Peer, 1951] same
  Cronyn, George William, 1888-1969.
    Fairy song (1910) [unpubl.]
    Hi Hi Hi (1910) [unpubl.]
    Night flowers (1910) [unpubl.]
    Song of the woman of the wood (1910)
      [unpubl.]
  Davis, Rev. O. S.
    Prayer on Great Island (1910) [unpubl.]
  Housman, Alfred Edward, 1859-1936.
    We'll to the woods so move (1925)
      [unpubl.]
    LAST POEMS: XXVII.

RIEGGER, WALLINGFORD, 1885-1961
(continued)
Housman, Alfred Edward, 1859-1936
(continued)
LAST POEMS (continued)
The sigh that heaves the grasses
(1925) [unpubl.]
Text assumed to be that of Vaughan
Williams' song by the same title.
A SHROPSHIRE LAD: LIV.
With rue my heart is laden (1925)
[unpubl.]
Lanier, Sidney, 1842-1881.
The violet sea (1909) [unpubl.]
No author
Music for voice and flute, op. 23 (1936)
[Broude Bros.; Bomart, 1950]
Vocalise on syllable "Ah."
Rossetti, Christina Georgina, 1830-
1894.
Who has seen the wind (1910) [unpubl.]
Schulz, G.
Lullaby (1911) [unpubl.]
Stevenson, Robert Louis, 1850-1894.
My shadow (1910) [unpubl.]
Symons, Arthur, 1865-1945.
After sunset (1925) [unpubl.]
Thomas, Dylan, 1914-1953.
DO NOT GO GENTLE.
The dying of the light, op. 59 (1954)
[Associated, 1956]
"Do not go gentle into that good
night"
Also voice & orchestra.
Unknown
Am Strand (1913) [unpubl.]
In der Ferne (1913) [unpubl.]
Noel (1910) [unpubl.]
Under the greenwood tree (1908)
[unpubl.]
Text may be from Shakespeare's *As
you like it.* Cf. Quilter setting, op.
23 no. 2.
Un rien see Unknown **ROSSINI**
Rien ne passe see Monrousseau, Lucien
MASSENET
Rien n'est que de France see Silvestre
MASSENET
"Rien que ce doux petit visage" *see Ce doux
petit visage* Eluard **POULENC**
"Rieselt hernieder" *see Der Wasserfall*
Klingemann **MENDELSSOHN-
BARTHOLDY**
Die Riesen und die Zwerge see Rückert
LOEWE
RIETI, VITTORIO, 1898-1994.

Anon.
Balow (1949) [unpubl.] "Balow, my
babe, lie still and sleep!"
Photocopy of holograph at Vassar
College.
E lo mio cor s'inchina (1945) [General
Music, 1966] same
E per un bel cantar (1945) [General
Music, 1966] same
Fain would I have a pretty thing (1967)
[General Music, 1968] same
Love me little, love me long (1967)
[General Music, 1968] same
Madrigal (1949) [unpubl.] "My love in
her attire doth show her wit"
Photocopy of holograph at Vassar
College. Published in revised form,
1967, as no. 1 of *5 Elizabethan
songs.*
Madrigal (1967) [General Music, 1968]
"My love in her attire doth show her
wit"
Revision of 1949 *Madrigal.*
Herrick, Robert, 1591-1674.
To the virgins, to make much of time
(1949) [unpubl.]
"Gather ye rosebuds while ye may"
Photocopy of holograph at Vassar
College.
Howell, Thomas, fl. 1568.
To his lady, of her doubtful answer
(1967) [General Music, 1968]
" 'Twixt death and doubtfulness"
Jacob, Max, 1876-1944.
La crise (1933) [General Music, 1975]
"Caravelle de mes rêves"
Monsieur le Duc (1933) [General Music,
1975] "Monsieur le Duc vint à point
nommeé"
Le noyer fatal (1933) [General Music,
1975] "Patience, distu, patience"
Soir d'été (1933) [General Music, 1975]
"Vos yeux clos, votre main lasse"
Lawrence, David Herbert, 1885-1930.
Aware (1960) [General Music, 1964]
"Slowly the moon is rising"
December night (1960) [General Music,
1964]
"Take off your cloak and your hat"
Quite forsaken (1960) [General Music,
1964]
"What pain to wake and miss you!"
Thomas Earp (1960) [General Music,
1964] "I heard a little chicken chirp"
Lodge, Thomas, 1558-1625.
Montanus' sonnet (1967) [General Music,
1968] "Phoebe sat, sweet she sat"

Poliziano, Angelo, 1454-1494.
  Canti oghun (1945) [General Music, 1966] same
  La non vuol esser piu mia (1945) [General Music, 1966] same
Sappho, 625? B.C.-570 B.C.
  A goccia a goccia (1974) [unpubl.; photocopy of holograph available from General Music] same
  Aspergi il corpo tuo (1974) [unpubl.; photocopy of holograph available from General Music] same
  La luna con le Pleiadi (1974) [unpubl.; photocopy of holograph available from General Music] same
  Morta tu giacerai (1974) [unpubl.; photocopy of holograph available from General Music] same
  O sposo, noi fanciulle (1974) [unpubl.; photocopy of holograph available from General Music] same
  Se il mio seno (1974) [unpubl.; photocopy of holograph available from General Music] same
  Sei giunta alfine (1974) [unpubl.; photocopy of holograph available from General Music] same
Shakespeare, William, 1564-1616.
  AS YOU LIKE IT.
    It was a lover and his lass (1949) [unpubl.] same
      Photocopy of holograph at Vassar College.
Sidney, Sir Philip, 1554-1586.
  Voices at the window (1949) [unpubl.] "Who is it that, this dark night" Photocopy of holograph at Vassar College.
Yeats, William Butler, 1865-1939.
  Brown penny (1957) [General Music, 1964] "I whispered, 'I am too young' "
  The fiddler of Dooney (1957) [General Music, 1964] "When I play on my fiddle in Dooney"
  Maid quiet (1957) [General Music, 1964] "Where has Maid Quiet gone to"
  When you are old (1957) [General Music, 1964] same
Riez-vous? see Silvestre *MIGNONNE.*
  MASSENET
The right number see Mužik **MARTINŮ**
A righteous man falling down before the wicked see Bible **LUENING**
Rilke, Rainer Maria, 1875-1926.
  BERG
    Liebe
    Die Näherin
    Traumgekrönt
  BERNSTEIN
    Extinguish my eyes
    When my soul touches yours
  HINDEMITH
    Argwohn Josephs
    Die Darstellung Mariä im Tempel
    Geburt Christi
    Geburt Mariä
    Mariä Heimsuchung
    Mariä Verkündigung
    Pietà
    Rast auf der Flucht in Ägypten
    Stillung Mariä mit dem Auferstandenen
    Verkündigung über den Hirten
    Vom Tode Mariä
      Three settings: Op. 27 nos. IVa, IVb, and IVc.
    Vor der Hochzeit zu Kana
    Vor der Passion
  KRENEK
    Aber die Winter!
    Nichts als ein Athemzug ist das Leere
    Oh Thränenvolle
  SAUGUET *Herbst*
  SCHÖNBERG *Am Strande*
  POÈMES FRANCAIS.
    BARBER
      Le clocher chante
      Un cygne
      Départ
      Puisque tout passe
      Tombeau dans un parc
  SONETTE AN ORPHEUS.
    DIAMOND *Even though the world keeps changing*
Rima see Bécquer **TURINA**
  Two settings: Op. 6 and op. 26 no. 3.
"Rimanete, vi prego, rimanete qui" *see La sera* Annunzio **RESPIGHI**
RIMAS, no. 1
  FALLA Bécquer *Olas gigantes*
RIMAS, no. 2
  FALLA Bécquer *Dios mio, que solos se quedan los muertos!*
Rimbaud, Arthur *see* Rimbaud, Jean Nicolas Arthur, 1854-1891.
Rimbaud, Jean Nicolas Arthur, 1854-1891.
  HINDEMITH *Bal des pendus*
  MILHAUD
    Aube
    Marine
    Veillées
  RIVIER

Rimbaud, Jean Nicolas Arthur, 1854-
1891 *(continued)*
  RIVIER *(continued)*
    Larme
    Sensation
    Tête de faune
Rimembranza del Trastevere see Zaffira
  MASSENET *L'improvisatore*
RIMES DORÉES. see Banville
  Promenade galante **KOECHLIN**
RIMES TENDRES, no. 1
  AUBERT Silvestre *Quand, à tes genoux!*
RIMES TENDRES, no. 2
  AUBERT Silvestre *Si de mon premier*
    rêve
RIMES TENDRES, no. 3
  AUBERT Silvestre *Souvent de nos biens*
    le meilleur
Il rimprovero see Metastasio **ROSSINI**
Il rimprovero ('Se fra le trecce d'Ebano') *see*
  Unknown **ROSSINI**
RIMSKIĬ-KORSAKOV, NIKOLAĬ
ANDREEVICH, 1844-1908.
  Anon.
    Gde ty, tam mysl' moia letaet, op. 8 no. 1
      [GA, v. 45, p. 85] same
    Vikhodi ko mne, signora (1861)
      [unpubl.?]
  Byron, George Gordon Byron, 6th
  baron, 1778-1824.
    Pesnia Ziuleĭki, op. 26 no. 4 [GA, v. 45,
      p. 152] "Piubovnik rozysoloveĭ"
    PORTUGUESE IMITATION.
      V poryve nezhnosti serdechnoĭ, op. 26
        no. 1 [GA, v. 45, p. 131] same
  Chamisso, Adelbert von, 1781-1838.
    Taina, op. 8 no. 3 [GA, v. 45, p. 92]
      "Kogda menia v usta i ochi Ty"
  Coppée, François Édouard Joachim,
  1842-1908.
    Ekho, op. 27 no. 2 [GA, v. 45, p. 162]
      "IA gor'ko setoval v pustyne"
  Heine, Heinrich, 1797-1856.
    Gonets, op. 4 no. 2 [GA, v. 45, p. 44]
      "Vstavaĭ, sluga! Konia sedlaĭ!"
    K moeĭ pesne, op. 25 no. 1 [GA, v. 45,
      p. 119] "Mne snilis' "
    LYRICAL INTERMEZZO.
      El' i pal'ma, op. 3 no. 1 [GA, v. 45,
        pp. 19 and 23]
        "Na severnom golom utese"
      Iz sléz moikh mnogo, maliutka, op. 2
        no. 4 [GA, v. 45, p. 14] same
      Kogda gliazhu tebe v glaza, op. 25 no.
        2 [GA, v. 45, p. 125] same
      Shchekoiu k shcheke ty moeĭ prilozhis',
        op. 2 no. 1 [GA, v. 45, p. 3]
        same

Kol'tsov, Alekseĭ Vasil'yevich, 1809-
1842.
  Plenivshis' pozoĭ, soloveĭ, op. 2 no. 2
    [GA, v. 45, p. 5] same
Lermontov, Mikhail Yuryevich, 1814-
1841.
  Kak nebesa, tvoĭ vzor blistaet, op. 7 no. 4
    [GA, v. 45, p. 78] same
  Kogda volnuetsia zhelteiushchaia niva,
    op. 40 no. 1 [GA, v. 45, p. 199]
    same
  Mne grustno, op. 41 no. 2 [GA, v. 45,
    p. 235] same
  Nochevala tuchka zolotaia, op. 3 no. 3
    [GA, v. 45, p. 32] same
  Po nebu polunochi, op. 40 no. 2 [GA,
    v. 45, p. 208] same
Maĭkov, Apollon Nikolayevich, 1821-
1897.
  Deva i solntse, op. 50 no. 1 [GA, v. 45,
    p. 395]
    "Mezhtremia moriami bashnia"
  Eshche ia poln, O drug moĭ milyĭ, op. 50
    no. 4 [GA, v. 45, p. 409] same
  IA v grote zhdal tebia v urochnyĭ chas,
    op. 40 no. 4 [GA, v. 45, p. 223]
    same
  Iskusstvo, op. 45 no. 2 [GA, v. 45,
    p. 308] "Srezal sebe ia trostnik"
  Liubliu tebia, mesiats, op. 41 no. 3 [GA,
    v. 45, p. 239] same
  Nimfa, op. 56 no. 1 [GA, v. 45, p. 467]
    "IA znaiu, otchego"
    Also voice (soprano) and orchestra,
      1905.
  O chem v tishi nocheĭ, op. 40 no. 3 [GA,
    v. 45, p. 218] same
  Oktava, op. 45 no. 3 [GA, v. 45, p. 313]
    "Garmonii stikha bozhestvennye"
  Pevets, op. 50 no. 2 [GA, v. 45, p. 399]
    "Nekrasiv ia, znaiu sam"
  Posmotri v svoĭ vertograd, op. 41 no. 4
    [GA, v. 45, p. 245] same
  Somnenie, op. 45 no. 4 [GA, v. 45,
    p. 317]
    "Pust' govoriat poeziia mechta"
  Son v letniuiu noch', op. 56 no. 2 [GA,
    v. 45, p. 474] "Dolgo noch'iu vchera"
    Also voice (soprano) and orchestra,
      1906.
  Tikho more goluboe! op. 50 no. 3 [GA,
    v. 45, p. 404] same
Mei, Lev Aleksandrovich, 1822-1862.
  Evreĭskaia pesnia, op. 7 no. 2 [GA,
    v. 45, p. 63] "Spliu, no serdtse moe"
  Kolybel'naia pesnia, op. 2 no. 3 [GA,
    v. 45, p. 9] "Baiu, baiushki, baiu"

Inserted into the second version of *The Maid of Pskov* and into *Boyarina Vera Sheloga*.

Vstan', soĭ di! davno dennitsa, op. 8 no. 4 [GA, v. 45, p. 98] same

Mickiewicz, Adam, 1798-1855.

Moia balovnitsa, op. 42 no. 4 [GA, v. 45, p. 274] same

Svitezianka, op. 7 no. 3 [GA, v. 45, p. 68] "Paren' prigozhiĭ moĭ"

Nekrasov, Nikolaĭ Aleksyeyevich, 1821-1877.

Prosti! Ne pomni dneĭ paden'ia, op. 27 no. 4 [GA, v. 45, p. 169] same

Nikitin, Ivan Savvich, 1824-1861.

V temnoĭ roshche zamolk soloveĭ, op. 4 no. 3 [GA, v. 45, p. 48] same

Pleshcheyev, Alekseĭ Nikolayevich, 1825-1893.

Noch', op. 8 no. 2 [GA, v. 45, p. 87] "Noch' proletala nad mirom"

Pushkin, Aleksandr Sergeevich, 1799-1837.

Anchar-drevo smerti, op. 49 no. 1 [GA, v. 45, p. 369]
"Vpustyne chakholoĭ i skupoĭ"
Also voice (bass) and orchestra, 1906.

Chto v imeni tebe moem? op. 4 no. 1 [GA, v. 45, p. 41] same

Dlia beregov otchizuy dal'noi, op. 26 no. 3 [GA, v. 45, p. 142] same

Ekho, op. 45 no. 1 [GA, v. 45, p. 305] "Revet li zvor' vlesu glukhom"

Grechanke, op. 55 no. 2 [GA, v. 45, p. 451] "Ty rozhdena vosplameniat' "

IA veriu ia liubim, op. 8 no. 6 [GA, v. 45, p. 113] same

Krasavitsa, op. 51 no. 4 [GA, v. 45, p. 431] "Vsĕ vneĭ garmoniia"

Na kholmakh Gruzii, op. 3 no. 4 [GA, v. 45, p. 35] same

Ne poĭ, krasavitsa, pri mne, op. 51 no. 2 [GA, v. 45, p. 420] same

Nenastnyĭ den' potukh, op. 51 no. 5 [GA, v. 45, p. 437] same

Poet, op. 45 no. 5 [GA, v. 45, p. 325] "Poka ne trebuet pozta"

Probuzhden'e, op. 55 no. 1 [GA, v. 45, p. 447]
"Mechty, mechty! Gde vashasladost'? "

Prorok, op. 49 no. 2 [GA, v. 45, p. 382] "Dukhovnoĭ zhazhdoĭu tomim"
Also voice (bass) and orchestra, 1899.

Redeet oblakov letuchaia griada, op. 42 no. 3 [GA, v. 45, p. 262] same

Snovidenie, op. 55 no. 3 [GA, v. 45, p. 455] "Nedavno, obol'shen"

Tsvetok zasokhshi, op. 51 no. 3 [GA, v. 45, p. 426] same

Ty i my, op. 27 no. 3 [GA, v. 45, p. 166] "Pustoe serdechnym Ona"

V krovi gorit (1865) [unpubl.?].

Zaklinanie, op. 26 no. 2 [GA, v. 45, p. 134] "O, esli pravda"

NOCH'
Moĭ golos dlia tebia, op. 7 no. 1 [GA, v. 45, p. 59] same

ZHELANIE.
Medlitel'no vlekutsia dni moi, op. 51 no. 1 [GA, v. 45, p. 415] same

Shcherbina, Nikelaĭ Fedorovich, 1821-1869.

IUzhnaia noch', op. 3 no. 2 [GA, v. 45, p. 27] "Na razdol'i nebes"

Shenshin, Afanasiĭ Afanas'evich, 1820-1892.

IA prishel k tebe s privetom, op. 42 no. 2 [GA, v. 45, p. 257] same

Shopot, robkoe dykhan'e, op. 42 no. 1 [GA, v. 45, p. 253] same

Svezh i dushist tvoĭ, op. 43 no. 3 [GA, v. 45, p. 291] same

Tikho vecher dogoraet, op. 4 no. 4 [GA, v. 45, p. 52] same

GAFIZ.
V tsarstvo rozy i vina-pridi, op. 8 no. 5 [GA, v. 45, p. 107] same

Tolstoĭ, Alekseĭ Konstantinovich, Graf, 1817-1875.

Drobitsia, i pleshchet, op. 46 no. 1 [GA, v. 45, p. 335] same

Gornimi tikho letela dusha nebesami, op. 27 no. 1 [GA, v. 45, p. 157] same

Kolyshetsia more, op. 46 no. 3 [GA, v. 45, p. 345] same

Na nivy zheltye niskhodit tishina, op. 39 no. 3 [GA, v. 45, p. 185] same

Ne penitsia more, op. 46 no. 2 [GA, v. 45, p. 340] same

Ne ver' mne, drug, op. 46 no. 4 [GA, v. 45, p. 352] same

Ne veter, veia s vysoty, op. 43 no. 2 [GA, v. 45, p. 287] same

Nesliashchikh solntse, op. 41 no. 1 [GA, v. 45, p. 231] same
Text after Byron.

O, esli b ty mogla, op. 39 no. 1 [GA, v. 45, p. 175] same

To bylo ranneiu vesnoĭ, op. 43 no. 4 [GA, v. 45, p. 296] same

Usni, pechal'nyĭ drug, op. 39 no. 4 [GA, v. 45, p. 189] same

RIMSKIĭ-KORSAKOV, NIKOLAĭ ANDREEVICH, 1844-1908 *(continued)*
   Tolstoĭ, Alekseĭ Konstantinovich, Graf, 1817-1875 *(continued)*
     Vzdymaĭutsia volny, op. 46 no. 5 [GA, v. 45, p. 358] same
     Zapad gasnet v dali bledno-rozovoĭ, op. 39 no. 2 [GA, v. 45, p. 179] same
     Zvonche zhavoronka pen'e, op. 43 no. 1 [GA, v. 45, p. 283] same
   Uhland, Ludwig, 1787-1862.
     IA umer ot schast'ia, op. 55 no. 4 [GA, v. 45, p. 460] same
The ring see Kol'tsov **RACHMANINOFF**
The ring see Witwicki **CHOPIN** Pierścien
Ring out, wild bells see Tennyson **GOUNOD**
Ring, ring see Cnattingius, Thor **KILPINEN**
"Ring, ring till sabbatstid" *see Ring, ring* Cnattingius, Thor **KILPINEN**
"Einen Ring von Golde steckt' ich an die Hand" *see Verlobung* Aldrich **LASSEN**
"Ringel, ringel Reih'n" *see Maitanz im Grünen* Mahler **MAHLER**
"Ringel, ringel Reihn'n!" *see Hans und Grethe* Mahler **MAHLER**
Das Ringelein see Kol'tsov **RUBINSTEIN**
Das Ringlein see Jacobowski **REGER**
"Rings um uns wachsen Mauern" *see Mauern wachsen* Krenek **KRENEK**
"Rings weisse Blütendolden" *see Unter Blüten* Sergel **KILPINEN**
"Ringsum erschallt in Wald und Flur" *see Sonntagslied* Klingemann **MENDELSSOHN-BARTHOLDY**
Ringwaldt, Bartholomäus, ca.1530-1599.
   WEBER *Die fromme Magd*
Ringwall, Bartholomäus *see* Ringwaldt, Bartholomäus, ca.1530-1599.
"Rinne, rinne leise" *see Eine Thräne* Beck **JENSEN**
"Rire au matin, courir dans l'ondoiement des herbes" *see Plein eau* Haraucourt **KOECHLIN**
"Rire étant si jolie, c'est mal" *see Sommation irrespectueuse* Hugo **CHABRIER**
RISPETTI TOSCANI. see Birga, Arturo
   Quando nasceste voi **RESPIGHI**
   Razzolan, sopra a l'aja, le galline . . . **RESPIGHI**
   Venitelo a vedere 'l mi'piccino . . . **RESPIGHI**
   Viene di là, lontan lontano . . . **RESPIGHI**
Rist, Johann, 1607-1667.
   LOEWE *Bleiches Antlitz, sei gegrüsset*

Ritornell see Prölss **LASSEN**
Ritournelle see Coppée **SÉVERAC**
Ritournelle see Richaud **SAUGUET**
Ritournelle et six chansons see Moreno *SE PLAIRE SUR LA MÊME FLEUR.* **MILHAUD**
Ritter, Anna (Nuhn), 1865-1921.
   REGER
     Allein
     Die Betrogene spricht
     Brautring
     Geheimnis
     Die Glocke des Glücks
     Ich glaub', lieber Schatz
     In verschwiegener Nacht
     Mein Traum
     Pythia
     Schlimme Geschichte
     Sonnenregen
     Sterne
     Unbegehrt
     Und hab' so grosse Sehnsucht doch
     Volkslied
   SIBELIUS *Rosenlied*
   SZYMANOWSKI *Das hat die Sommernacht getan JUGEND.*
   REGER *Vom Küssen!*
Ritter Kurt's Brautfahrt see Goethe **WOLF**
Ritter rät dem Knappen dies see Bierbaum **REGER**
Ritter Toggenburg see Schiller **SCHUBERT**
"Ritter, treue Schwesterliebe" *see Ritter Toggenburg* Schiller **SCHUBERT**
Ritterliche Werbung see Mörike **SCHOECK**
Rivas, Duque de, 1791-1865.
   TURINA
     Cantilena
     Madrigal
     Romance
Rivas, Reyna
   THOMSON
     Nadie lo oye como ellos
     Son amigos de todos
     Todas las horas
Rive d'amour see Silvestre **BIZET**
The riverside village see Ssu-k'ung Shu **BERKELEY**
RIVIER, JEAN, 1896-1987.
   Apollinaire, Guillaume, 1880-1918.
     Crépuscule (1944) [unpubl.]
     ALCOOLS.
       L'adieu (1925-26) [Salabert, 1929]
         "J'ai cueilli ce brin de bruyère"
       Aubade (1925-26) [Salabert, 1929]
         "C'est le printemps viens t'en Pâquette"

Automne (1925-26) [Salabert, 1929]
"Dans le brouillard s'en vont un
paysan cagneux"
Les cloches (1925-26) [Salabert, 1929]
"O mon tzigane mon amant"
Clothilde (1925-26) [Salabert, 1929]
"L'anémone et l'ancolie"
Les colchiques (1934-35)
[Société d'éditions musicales
internationales, 1959] "Le pré est
vénéneux mais joli en automne"
Le pont Mirabeau (1934-35)
[Société d'éditions musicales
internationales, 1959] "Sous le
pont Mirabeau coule la Seine"
Saltimbanques (1925-26) [Salabert,
1929] "Dans la plaine les baladins"
IL Y A. Les dicts d'amour à Linda.
Linda (1925-26) [Salabert, 1929]
"L'ombre de la trés douce est
évoquée"
OBUS COULEUR DE LUNE.
Carte postale (1929) [Senart, 1930;
Salabert]
"Je t'écris de dessous la tente"
LA TÊTE ÉTOILÉE.
Le départ (1925-26) [Salabert, 1929]
"Et leurs visages étaient pâles"
Chalupt, René, 1885-1957.
"A traduire en esthonien . . . " (1949)
[Salabert, 1952]
"N'avez-vous pas un porte plume?"
Cartomancie (1949) [Salabert, 1952]
"Rachel, c'est vous la dame blonde"
Hommage à Valery-Larbaud (1949)
[Salabert, 1952]
"Le rapide Bordeaux Trieste"
Le vivier (1949) [Salabert, 1952]
"En le frais silence nageant"
Gilson, Paul, 1865-1942.
La fable du village (1956) [Salabert,
1958] "Le che val blanc de Barneville"
Passage d'une nurse (1956) [Salabert,
1958] "La nurse était bleu et la brique
rose"
La sirène de Scheveningue (1956)
[Salabert, 1958] "A Scheveningue sur
la plage òu l'ensable le vent du nord"
Mahaut
Le Cheichi (1944) [unpubl.]
En rêve (1944) [unpubl.]
Le quatrain de la rose (1929) [Senart,
1930; Salabert]
"Rose tu es la fleur de chair"
Marot, Clément, 1495?-1544.
Dedans Paris, ville jolie . . . (1945)
[Salabert, 1947] same

Peyrissac, Jean, 1895-1974.
Prière (1969) [Editions musicales
transatlantiques, 1977]
"Mon Dieu faites que je m'abandonne
constamment"
**Rimbaud, Jean Nicolas Arthur, 1854-
1891.**
Larme (1935) [Société d'éditions
musicales internationales, 1959]
"Loin des oiseaux, des troupeaux"
Sensation (1929) [Senart, 1930; Salabert]
"Par les soirs bleus d'été"
Tête de faune (1935) [Société d'éditions
musicales internationales, 1959]
"Dans la feuillée écrin vert tàché d'or"
Ronsard, Pierre de, 1524-1585.
Bel aubépin (1945) [Salabert, 1947]
"Bel aubépin verdissant fleurissant"
Heureux qui comme Ulysse [Gérard
Billaudot, 1968] same
Rossignol, mon mignon . . . (1945)
[Salabert, 1947] "Rossignol mon
mignon qui par cette saulaie"
Terre, ouvre-moi ton sein [Gérard
Billaudot, 1968] same
Le tombeau de Ronsard (1945) [Salabert,
1947] "Ronsard repose ici qui hardi
dès l'enfance"
Unknown
Doloroso e giocoso (1969) [Salabert]
Riviera see Leuthold **SCHOECK**
La rivière see Bruno, Camille **MASSENET**
"La rivière chantait ainsi" see La rivière
Bruno, Camille **MASSENET**
Rýsar see Wilde, Ch. **BALAKIREV**
The roadside fire see Stevenson, Robert
Louis *SONGS OF TRAVEL*, XI.
VAUGHAN WILLIAMS
The roaring frost see Meynell **MILHAUD**
Robert, Friederike (Braun), 1795-1832.
MENDELSSOHN-BARTHOLDY
Frühlingslied
Das Heimweh
ZELTER *Was soll ich mich mit Worten
quälen?*
Robin and Richard see Anon. *NURSE
LOVECHILD'S LEGACY* (London: The
Poetry Bookshop, 1916). **HESELTINE**
"Robin and Richard were two pretty men" see
Robin and Richard Anon. **HESELTINE**
Robin Good-fellow see Anon. **HESELTINE**
Robin Gray see Florian **FRANCK**
The robin sings in the apple-tree see
MacDowell **MACDOWELL**
Robinson, Robert, 1735-1790.
IVES *His exaltation*

COMPOSER Poet *Title* ''First Line''

Robiquet, Paul Pierre, 1848-1928.
  MASSENET
    Je me suis plaint aux tourterelles
    La nuit sans doute était trop belle
    Oh! ne finis jamais
    Ouvre tes yeux bleus
    Pourquoi pleures-tu?
    Puisqu'elle a pris ma vie
Rocchi, Francesco
  RESPIGHI
    Nel giardino
    Piccola mano bianca
Rocha, Lucien
  MASSENET *Aube païenne*
Roché, Henri Pierre, 1879-1959.
  ROUSSEL
    Amoureux séparés
    Ode à un jeune gentilhomme
Rochester, John Wilmot, 2d earl of,
  1647-1680.
  QUILTER
    The jealous lover
    To wine and beauty
Rochlitz, Friedrich *see* Rochlitz, Johann
  Friedrich, 1770-1842.
Rochlitz, Johann Friedrich, 1770-1842.
  SCHUBERT
    Alinde
    An die Laute
    Klaglied
  WEBER *Es stürmt auf der Flur*
The rock see Lermontov **BALAKIREV**
    Utes
Rode, Helge, 1870-1927.
  NIELSEN
    Skal Blomsterne da visne?
    Tyst som Aa i Engen rinder
Rode, Ove, 1867-1933.
  NIELSEN *Dansk Vejr*
Rodenbach, G
  SCHMITT *Dans l'air fraîchi*
Rodenstein see Scheffel **JENSEN**
    Die drei Dörfer
    Wer reit't mit sieben Knappen
    Wer wankt zu Fusse
    Der Willekumm
Rodès, Béatrix
  BLOCH
    L'abri
    Le déclin
    Invocation
    La vagabonde
Rôdeuse au front de verre see Eluard
  POULENC
Roditi, Edouard, 1910-1992.
  ROREM *Poem for F*

RODRIGO, JOAQUÍN, 1901-1999.
Anon.
  Adela (1951) [Schott, 1959]
    "Una muchacha guapa, llamada"
  Aire y Donaire (1952) [Schott, 1959]
    "Airey donaire!"
  Canción de baile con pandero (1951)
    [Schott, 1959]
    "En el mar, hay un pescado"
  Canción de cuna (1951) [Schott, 1959]
    "En tu puerta, Teresa"
  Cancion del grumete [Madrid: Ed.
    Joaquín Rodrigo, 1980]
    "En la mar hay una torre"
  Con qué la lavaré? (1947) [Madrid: Ed.
    Joaquín Rodrigo, 1957] same
  Corderito blanco (1973) [Unión Musical
    Española, 1973] same
  De dónde venis, amore? (1947) [Madrid:
    Ed. Joaquín Rodrigo, 1957] same
  De los álamos vengo, madre! (1947)
    [Madrid: Ed. Joaquín Rodrigo, 1957]
    same
  De ronda (1951) [Schott, 1959]
    "Manzanita colorada"
  En Jerez de la Frontera (1951) [Schott,
    1959] same
  En las montañas de Asturias (1951)
    [Schott, 1959] same
  Estando yo en mi majada (1951) [Schott,
    1959] same
  Folias Canarias (1948) [Schott, 1959]
    "Gran Canaria, Gran Canaria se ha
      dormido"
    Voice & guitar.
  "Morena" me llaman (1968) [Eschig,
    1968] same
  Nani, nani (Cancion de cuna, 1968)
    [Eschig, 1968] same
  Una Palomita blanca (1951) [Schott,
    1959] same
  Una pastora yo ami (1968) [Eschig,
    1968] same
  Porque toco el pandero (1951) [Schott,
    1959] same
  Quedito (1973) [Unión Musical Española,
    1973] "Quedito, pasito"
  Respóndemos (1968) [Eschig, 1968] same
  Romance de la infantina de francia
    (1928) [Salabert]
  Romancillo [Madrid: Ed. Joaquín
    Rodrigo, 1980]
    "Por mayo, era por mayo"
  San José y Maria (1951) [Schott, 1959]
    same
  Tararán (1951) [Schott, 1959]
    "Tararán, si viés a la una"

Viva la novia y el novio! (1951) [Schott, 1959] same

Vos me matásteis (1947) [Madrid: Ed. Joaquín Rodrigo, 1957] same

Carner, José, 1884-1971.
Canticel [Madrid: Ed. Joaquín Rodrigo, 1980] "Per una vela en el mar blau"

Castro, Rosalía de, 1837-1885.
Un home, San Antonio! [Madrid: Ed. Joaquín Rodrigo, 1980] "San Antonio bendito"

Émié, Louis, 1900-1967.
Homenaje a Debussy: "La grotte" (1962) [Éditions de France, 1962?] "Dans cette grotte où le silence ignore encor"

Figueroa, Francisco de, 1536?-1620.
Esta niña se lleva la flor [Madrid: Ed. Joaquín Rodrigo, 1980] same

Hernández Aquino, Luis, b. 1907
Sobre el cupey [Madrid: Ed. Joaquín Rodrigo, 1980] "Palomicas de oro"

Jimenez, Juan Ramón, 1881-1958.
Pajaro del agua (1961) [Union Musical Española, 1963] same
Voice & flute or voice & piano.

Verde, verderol (1961) [Union Musical Española, 1963] same
Voice & flute or voice & piano.

Kamhi, Victoria, 1905-1997.
Barcarola [Madrid: Ed. Joaquín Rodrigo, 1980] "Corre, corre, mi barquito"

Cancion del cucu [Madrid: Ed. Joaquín Rodrigo, 1980] "Cuclillo, cuclillo canta"

Copillas de Belen (1952) [Schott, 1959] "Si la palmera supiera que el Niño"
Voice & guitar.

La espera (1952) [Madrid: Ed. Joaquín Rodrigo, 1972] "Cuando llegue, ay, yo no sé"

Llorente, Teodoro, 1826-1911.
Cançó del teuladí [Madrid: Ed. Joaquín Rodrigo, 1980] "Joyós cassador, passa"

Machado y Ruiz, Antonio, 1875-1939.
Abril galan (1972) [Unión Musical Española, 1972] "Mien tras danzá is en corro"

Canción del duero (1972) [Unión Musical Española, 1972] "Molineroes mi amante"

Cantaban los niños (1972) [Unión Musical Española, 1972] "Yo escucho los cantos de viejas cadencias"

Fiesta en el Prado (1972) [Unión Musical Española, 1972] "Hay fiesta en el prado verde"

Mañana de Abril (1972) [Unión Musical Española, 1972] "Era una mañana y abril sonrcía"

Mi corazon te aguarda (1972) [Unión Musical Española, 1972] "Amada, el aura dice"

Preludio (1972) [Unión Musical Española, 1972] "Mientras la sombra pasa de un santo amor"

Recuerdas? (1972) [Unión Musical Española, 1972] "Mi amor! Recuerdas dime"

Los sueños (1972) [Unión Musical Española, 1972] "El hada más hermosa ha soureido"

Tu voz y tu mano (1972) [Unión Musical Española, 1972] "Soñé que tú me llevabas"

Mesa, Juan Bautista de, 1583-1627.
Soneto [Madrid: Ed. Joaquín Rodrigo, 1980] "Dormía en un prado mi pastora hermosa"

Polo de Medina, Salvador Jacinto, 1603-1676.
Estribillo [Madrid: Ed. Joaquín Rodrigo, 1980] "Y muera yo de amor por Perinarda"

Rodriguez-Pintos, Carlos, b. 1895.
Fino cristal [Madrid: Ed. Joaquín Rodrigo, 1980] "Fino cristal, mi niño"

San Juan de la Cruz
Cantico de la esposa [Madrid: Ed. Joaquín Rodrigo, 1980] "A dónde te escondiste, Amado"

Santillana, Iñigo López de Mendoza, marqués de, 1398-1458.
Serranilla (1928) [Salabert, 1929] "Moça tan fermosa non vien la frontera"

Vega Carpio, Lope Félix de, 1562-1635.
Coplas del pastor enamorado (1935) [Madrid: Ed. Joaquín Rodrigo, 1966] "Verdes ribe ras amenas"
Voice & guitar.

Pastorcito Santo (1952) [Schott, 1959] "Zagalejo de perlas hijo del alba"
Voice & guitar.

Romance del comendador de ocaña (1948) [Unión Musical Española, 1962] "Más quiero yoa Peribá Nez con su capa la pardilla queal"

Vicente, Gil, ca.1470-ca.1536.
Cantiga (1925) [Salabert] "Muy graciosa es la doncella"

Rodríguez Marin, Francisco, 1855-1943.
TURINA
A unos ojos

Rodríguez Marin, Francisco, 1855-1943
  (continued)
  TURINA *(continued)*
    Anhelos
    Vade retro!
Rodriguez-Pintos, Carlos, b. 1895.
  RODRIGO *Fino cristal*
Die Römer see Claudius, M. **SCHOECK**
Der römische Brunnen see Meyer
  SCHOECK
Das Röschen see Müchler **WEBER**
Rös'chen biss den Apfel an see Keller, G.
  PFITZNER
Röselein, Röselein see Schöpff
  SCHUMANN
  "Röselein, Röselein! müssen denn Dornen
  sein?" *see Röselein, Röselein* Schöpff
  SCHUMANN
Röser, Otto
  FRANZ
    Als trüg' man die Liebe zu Grab
    Liebe
Das Röslein see Hoffmann von
  Fallersleben **STRAUSS**
    Ein Röslein zog ich mir im Garten
Ein Röslein zog ich mir im Garten see
  Hoffmann von Fallersleben **STRAUSS**
Roethke, Theodore, 1908-1963.
  DIAMOND
    My papa's waltz
    Prayer
  ROREM
    The apparition
    The beast
    Interlude
    Memory
    My Papa's waltz
    Night crow
    Orchids
    Root cellar
    The serpent
    Snake
    The surly one
    The waking
  THE FAR FIELD.
    ROREM *From whence cometh song?*
  THE WAKING.
    ROREM *I strolled across an open field*
  WISH FOR A YOUNG WIFE.
    BARBER *My lizard*
Rogberg, Alma
  NIELSEN *Det är höst*
Rogers, Robert Cameron, 1862-1912.
  THOMPSON, R. *Serenade in Seville*
"Rogez, Rogez" *see The cat is angry*
  Yalan-Stekelis **GIDEON**

Rohan, Catherine de Parthenay-
  Larchevêque, duchesse de, 1554-
  1631.
  THOMSON
    A son Altesse la Princesse Antoinette
      Murat
    Jour de chaleur aux bains de mer
    La Seine
Rohrscheidt, Kurt von, 1857-1935.
  REGER *Glück*
Le Roi d'amour est mon pasteur see Baker
  GOUNOD *The King of love my shepherd*
Le roi de Thulé see Gérard de Nerval
  BERLIOZ
LE ROI S'AMUSE. see Hugo
  Vieille chanson **DELIBES**
  "Le roi vieilli s'accoude au balcon du palais"
    see Conte Ferrier **BIZET**
  "Les rois d'Egypte et de Syrie" *see Chanson à*
    boire Anon. **POULENC**
Roister doister see Udall *RALPH ROISTER*
  DOISTER (1550). **HESELTINE**
  "Rok sie kochali, a wiek sie nie widzieli" *see*
    Dwojaki koniec Zaleski **CHOPIN**
Rolfsen, Nordahl, 1848-1928.
  GRIEG
    Faedrelandssalme
    Havet
    Kveldssang for Blakken
    De norske fjelde
    Under Juletraeet
Rolland, Olivier
  BIZET
    Petite Marguerite
    La rose et l'abeille
  "Rolle liebe Spindel" *see Die Spinnerin*
    Fitger **PIJPER**
Rollinat, Maurice, 1853-1903.
  CHABRIER *Tes yeux bleus*
Romance see Jean-Aubry **IBERT**
Romance see Musset **RUBINSTEIN**
Romance see Polovtsev, A. **RUBINSTEIN**
Romance see Rivas **TURINA**
Romance see Stevenson, Robert Louis
  SONGS OF TRAVEL (1895). **HESELTINE**
Romance see Tavaststjerna **SIBELIUS**
Romance see Unknown **LASSEN**
Romance, "Comment disait-il" see Hugo
  RUBINSTEIN
La Romance d'Ariel see Bourget
  LES AVEUX: Souvenirs du Nord, no. 5.
  DEBUSSY
Romance de la infantina de francia see
  Anon. **RODRIGO**
Romance de Mignon see Goethe *WILHELM*
  MEISTER. Mignon's song: Kennst du das
  Land? **DUPARC**

COMPOSER Poet *Title* "First Line"

RONDELS SUR DES POÉSIES DE
    CHARLES D'ORLÉANS . . . , no. 3
    HAHN Banville *Le printemps*
RONDELS SUR DES POÉSIES DE
    CHARLES D'ORLÉANS . . . , no. 4
    HAHN Banville *L'air*
RONDELS SUR DES POÉSIES DE
    CHARLES D'ORLÉANS . . . , no. 5
    HAHN Banville *La paix*
        NB: No. 6 for SATB and piano.
RONDELS SUR DES POÉSIES DE
    CHARLES D'ORLÉANS . . . , no. 7
    HAHN Banville *La pêche*
RONDELS SUR DES POÉSIES DE
    CHARLES D'ORLÉANS . . . , no. 8
    HAHN Charles, Duke of Orleans
        Quand je fus pris au pavillon
RONDELS SUR DES POÉSIES DE
    CHARLES D'ORLÉANS . . . , no. 9
    HAHN Banville *Les étoiles*
RONDELS SUR DES POÉSIES DE
    CHARLES D'ORLÉANS . . . , no. 10
    HAHN Banville *L'automne*
        NB: No. 11 for SAT and piano.
RONDELS SUR DES POÉSIES DE
    CHARLES D'ORLÉANS . . . , no. 12
    HAHN Mendès
        Le souvenir d'avoir chanté
RONDELS, troisième série, no. 1
    KOECHLIN Banville *Le jour*
RONDELS, troisième série, no. 2
    KOECHLIN Banville *Le midi*
RONDELS, troisième série, no. 3
    KOECHLIN Banville *L'eau*
RONDELS, troisième série, no. 4
    KOECHLIN Banville *Le vin*
RONDELS, troisième série, no. 5
    KOECHLIN Banville *Les métaux*
RONDELS, troisième série, no. 6
    KOECHLIN Banville *Le terre*
RONDELS, troisième série, no. 7
    KOECHLIN Banville *L'automne*
RONDELS, troisième série, no. 8
    KOECHLIN Banville *Les étoiles*
RONDELS, troisième série, no. 9
    KOECHLIN Banville *La guerre*
La rondinella see Banville **GOUNOD** *L'âme
    d'un ange*
Rondo see Mauclair **BLOCH**
"Ronk, bonk klitse klets" *see* Van den Oever
    Clercq, René de **PIJPER**
Ronsard à son âme see Ronsard **RAVEL**
Ronsard, Pierre de, 1524-1585.
    AUBERT *La fontaine d'Hélène*
    AURIC *Printemps*
    BIZET, CASELLA *Sonnet*

GOUNOD *Heureux sera le jour*
HONEGGER *La terre, l'eau, l'air et le
    vent*
MASSENET *Portret d'un enfant*
MILHAUD *Plusieurs de leurs corps
    dénués*
POULENC
    À sa guitare
    A son page
    Attributs
    Ballet
    Je n'ai plus que les os
    Le tombeau
RAVEL *Ronsard à son âme*
RIVIER
    Bel aubépin
    Heureux qui comme Ulysse
    Rossignol, mon mignon . . .
    Terre, ouvre-moi ton sein
    Le tombeau de Ronsard
ROREM *Ode*
ROUSSEL
    Ciel, aer et vens
    Rossignol, mon mignon
SAINT-SAËNS
    À Saint-Blaise
    L'amant malheureux
    L'amour blessé
    L'amour oyseau
    Grasselette et maigrelette
SCHMITT
    Privilèges
    Ses deux yeux . . .
    Si . . .
    Le soir qu'amour
SÉVERAC *Les amours*
WAGNER *Mignonne*
"Ronsard repose ici qui hardi dès l'enfance"
    see Le tombeau de Ronsard Ronsard
    RIVIER
The rook see Unknown **STRAVINSKIĬ**
    Le corbeau
"Room after room, I hunt the house through"
    see Love in a life Browning, R. **ROREM**
Roos, Richard, pseud. *see* Engelhardt,
    Karl August, 1768-1834.
Root cellar see Roethke **ROREM**
Root, George Frederick, 1820-1895.
    IVES *Religion*
Rooted firm see Goethe **MEDTNER**
    Gefunden
Roquette, Otto, 1824-1896.
    FRANZ
        Das macht das dunkelgrüne Laub
        Du liebes Auge
        Die Sonn' ist hin

COMPOSER   Poet   *Title*   ''First Line''

Weisst du noch?
Willkommen, mein Wald
JENSEN
Abschied
An der Linden
Fröhliche Gesellen
Margreth am Thore
Morgens am Brunnen
Noch ist die blühende, goldene Zeit
O lass dich halten, gold'ne Stunde
Perlenfischer
Unruhe
Weisst du noch?
LASSEN *Noch ist die blühende, goldene*
Zeit
REGER *Du liebes Auge*
WOLF *Perlenfischer*
REBENKRANZ ZU WALDMEISTERS
SILBERNER HOCHZEIT: In der Früh.
BERG *Über Nacht und Tag*
Rørdam, Valdemar
NIELSEN *Dansk Arbejde*
ROREM, NED, 1923-
Aiken, Conrad Potter, 1889-1973.
DISCORDANTS.
Discordants (1946) [unpubl.]
"Music I heard with you was more
than music"
Anne Boleyn, queen consort of Henry
VIII, 1507-1536.
Defiled is my name (1975-76) [Boosey &
Hawkes, 1979] same
Anon.
Ave Maria, op. 1 no. 2 (1940-41)
[unpubl.]
The call (1950) [Elkan-Vogel, 1953;
Southern, 1963]
"My blood so red for thee was shed"
Now included as no. 3, *My blood so
red*, in the cycle **From an unknown
past.**
A Christmas carol (1952) [Elkan-Vogel,
1953; T.Presser]
"The other night I saw a light!"
Epitaph (1953) [Elkan-Vogel, 1953;
T.Presser, 1965] "Let not death boast
his conquering power"
Knight of the Grail (1944) [Private
edition with cover by Morris Golde]
The mild mother (1952) [E. C. Schirmer,
1968]
"Jesu Christ's mild mother stood"
The nightingale (1951) [Boosey, 1956]
"The little pretty nightingale"
Roundel (1948) [unpubl.]
Apollinaire, Guillaume, 1880-1918.

ALCOOLS.
Automne (1949) [unpubl.]
Armstrong, Martin Donisthorpe, 1882-
1974.
On a little bird (1951) [unpubl.]
Ashbery, John, 1927-
*SELF PORTRAITS IN A CONVEX
MIRROR.*
Fear of death [Boosey & Hawkes,
1981] "What is it now with me"
TENNIS COURT OATH.
Thoughts of a young girl [Boosey &
Hawkes, 1981]
"It is such a beautiful day I had to
write you a letter"
Voice unaccompanied.
Auden, Wystan Hugh, 1907-1973.
Stop all the clocks [Boosey, 1965] same
ON THIS ISLAND.
Look stranger, on this island (1947)
[unpubl.]
Ayer, Ethan
After Atlantis (1963) [unpubl.]
Blood is not blood (1963) [unpubl.]
Baïf, Jean Antoine de, 1532-1589.
L'Hymne de la paix (1953) [C. F. Peters,
1953; Boosey & Hawkes, 1970]
"Je veux louer la Paix"
Also arranged with string
accompaniment, 1956.
Barnefield, Richard, 1574-1627.
Philomel (1950) [Hargail Music Press,
1952; Boosey & Hawkes]
"As it fell upon a day"
Bible
LUKE 2: 9-15.
An angel speaks to the shepherds
(1952) [Southern, 1956]
"And, lo, the Angel of the Lord"
MATTHEW 6: 9-13.
The Lord's prayer (1957) [C. F. Peters,
1957] "Our Father . . . "
MATTHEW 27: 62-66; 28.
The resurrection (1952) [Southern,
1956] "Now the next day"
PSALM 86.
Psalm 86: A prayer of David (1945)
[unpubl.]
PSALM 100.
A psalm of praise (1945) [Associated,
1946]
"Make a joyful noise unto the Lord"
PSALM 120.
A song of David (1945) [Associated,
1946] "In my distress I cried unto
the Lord"

ROREM, NED, 1923- *(continued)*
 Bible *(continued)*
  PSALM 134.
   Psalm 134 (1951) [Southern, 1955]
    "Behold, bless ye the Lord"
  PSALM 142.
   Psalm 142 (1951) [Southern, 1955] "I
    cried unto the Lord with my voice"
  PSALM 148.
   Psalm 148 (1951) [Southern, 1955]
    "Praise ye the Lord"
  PSALM 150.
   Psalm 150 (1951) [Southern, 1955]
    "Praise ye the Lord"
 Bishop, Elizabeth, 1911-1979.
  Casabianca (1957) [unpubl.]
  Conversation (1957) [Boosey & Hawkes,
   1969] "The tumult in the heart keeps
   asking questions"
  Detective story (1954) [unpubl.]
  Insomnia (1957) [unpubl.]
  Letter to New York (1957) [unpubl.]
  Visits to St. Elizabeths (1957) [Boosey,
   1964] "This is the house of Bedlam"
   Poem from **The Partisan Review,**
   1957.
  SONGS FOR A COLORED SINGER, VI.
   What's that shining in the leaves
   (1957) [unpubl.]
 Blake, William, 1757-1827.
  The sick rose (1944) [unpubl.]
 Bogan, Louise, 1897-1970.
  Solitary observation brought back from a
   soujourn in hell (1963) [unpubl.]
 Boultenhouse, Charles
  Boy into animal (1948) [Boosey &
   Hawkes, 1969] same
   Composed for **Fire Boy,** incidental
    music for a puppet show..
  Cloudless blue claw (1948) [Boosey &
   Hawkes, 1969] same
   Composed for **Fire Boy.**
  Now I make a circle (1948) [Boosey &
   Hawkes, 1969] same
   Composed for **Fire Boy.**
  Squirrel song (1948) [unpubl.]
  Sun song (1948) [unpubl.]
   Composed for **Fire boy.**
 Bradstreet, Anne, 1612-1672.
  To my dear and loving husband (1976)
   [Boosey & Hawkes, 1979]
   "If ever two were one, then surely we"
 Broughten, James Richard, 1913-
 1999.
  The orphan girl in the pleasure garden
   (1955) [unpubl.]
 Browning, Robert, 1812-1889.

  Love in a life (1951) [Boosey & Hawkes,
   1972] "Room after room, I hunt the
   house through"
 Capetanakis, Demetrios, 1912-1944.
  Abel (1954) [Boosey & Hawkes, 1968]
   "My brother Cain, the wounded, liked
   to sit"
  Angel (1954) [unpubl.]
  Experienced by two stones (1954)
   [unpubl.]
  Guilt (1954) [Boosey & Hawkes, 1968]
   "Listener, can you hear the silence
   howl"
  The land of fear (1954) [Boosey &
   Hawkes, 1968] "Before we leave this
   deadly Land of Fear"
 Castleman, Marion
  From "The return" (1947) [unpubl.]
 Catullus, Caius Valerius, 87-57 B. C.
  Catullus: On the burial of his brother
   (1947) [Boosey & Hawkes, 1969]
   "By ways remote and distant waters
   sped"
 Chaucer, Geoffrey, d. 1400.
  Song (1944) [Private edition]
   Printed with *Knight of the grail* and
    The appeal in a private edition with
    cover by Morris Golde.
 Chudleigh, Mary (Lee), lady, 1656-
 1710.
  To the ladies (1976) [Boosey & Hawkes,
   1979] "Wife and servant are the same"
 Cocteau, Jean, 1889-1963.
  De Don Juan (1944) [unpubl.]
 Coleridge, Mary Elizabeth, 1861-1907.
  We never said farewell (1975) [Boosey &
   Hawkes, 1979] same
 Cummings, Edward Estlin, 1894-1962.
  All in green my love went riding, op. 1
   no. 5 (1940-41) [unpubl.]
  Doll's boy (1944) [private edition]
   Published in a private edition with
    cover sketch by Alvin Ross.
    Extremely rare.
  in the rain [Boosey, 1965]
   "in the rain darkness"
  Listen beloved (1944) [unpubl.]
  Spring song, op. 1 no. 3 (1940-41)
   [unpubl.]
 Daurat, Jean, 1507-1588.
  Sonnet (1953) [C. F. Peters, 1953;
   Boosey & Hawkes, 1970]
   "Qu'est-il besoin de tant la Paix crier"
   Also arranged with string
    accompaniment, 1956.
 De La Mare, Walter, 1873-1956.

Myself (1950) [unpubl.]
Denby, Edward, 1903-1983.
First warm days (1953-54) [unpubl.]
Dickinson, Emily, 1830-1866.
Love's stricken "Why" [Boosey, 1965]
same
What inn is this (1975-76) [Boosey &
Hawkes, 1979] same
Donne, John, 1573-1631.
A burnt ship (1945) [unpubl.]
Dryden, John, 1631-1700.
From "Cleomenes" (1953) [unpubl.]
Hidden flames (1953) [unpubl.]
Eagel, Paul
The freedom song (1948) [unpubl.]
Eddy, Mary Baker, 1821-1910.
Feed my sheep (1966) [unpubl.]
Eliot, Thomas Stearns, 1888-1965.
THE DRY SALVAGES.
Prayer from "The dry salvages"
(1946) [unpubl.]
Fletcher, John, 1579-1625.
Come hither, you that love (1951-52)
[unpubl.] same
Come, shepherds, come (1951-52)
[unpubl.] same
Hold back thy hours, dark night (1951-
52) [unpubl.] same
Now the lusty spring is seen (1951-52)
[unpubl.] same
Sing his praises (1951-52) [unpubl.] same
Follain, Jean, 1903-1971.
L'ile (1953) [unpubl.]
Frost, Robert, 1874-1963.
Stopping by woods on a snowy evening
(1946) [unpubl.]
Garrigue, Jean, 1914-1972.
Where we came (1974) [Boosey &
Hawkes, 1976] "Where we came the
grasses were high"
Gélin, Daniel, 1921-
Marrant (1953) [unpubl.]
Prends bien soin de mourir (1953)
[unpubl.]
Toute une ville (1953) [unpubl.]
Gibbons, Orlando, 1583-1625.
The silver swan (1949) [Peer; Southern,
1950] same
1950 edition incorrectly cites Ben
Jonson as author of text.
Glaze, Andrew, 1920-
A journey (1976) [Boosey & Hawkes,
1977] "I was five years old and I
stepped up into the street car"
Goodman, Paul, 1911-1972.
Absalom (1946) [Boosey & Hawkes,
1972] "In the roomy oak among the
fluttering leaves"

All men are mad some way (1946)
[unpubl.]
Bawling blues (1947) [Red Ozier Press,
1984] "Why am I bawling?"
Boy with a baseball glove (1953)
[unpubl.]
The boy with the ax (1953) [unpubl.]
Clouds (1953) [Boosey & Hawkes, 1968]
"So effortlessly we are not given"
Epitaph for Janet (1947) [unpubl.]
For Janet (1947) [unpubl.]
For Susan (1953) [Boosey & Hawkes,
1968] "How like a wildflower
untended"
Hallowed be the ordainer (1946)
[unpubl.]
Jail-bait blues (1947) [Red Ozier Press,
1984] "I used to be jail-bait"
Lord, have not by custom (1946)
[unpubl.]
The lordly Hudson (1947) [Mercury
Music Corp., 1947; T. Presser]
"Driver, what stream is it?"
Man-like, my God (1946) [unpubl.]
The midnight sun (1953) [E. C. Schirmer,
1968] "I thought I woke: the midnight
sun flooded"
Near closing time (1947) [Red Ozier
Press, 1984] "With unerring finger"
Noblesse obligé, my Lord (1946)
[unpubl.]
Of God, angels . . . (1946) [unpubl.]
Rain in spring (1949) [Boosey, 1956]
"There fell a beautiful clear rain"
Rest well . . . (1946) [unpubl.]
Sally's smile (1953) [C. F. Peters, 1957]
"Sara has smiled upon me such a
smile"
Such beauty as hurts to behold (1957)
[C. F. Peters, 1961] same
The tulip tree (1953) [E. C. Schirmer,
1968] "Out of the tulip tree, the boy
who had green eyes"
What sparks and wiry cries (1956)
[Boosey & Hawkes, 1968] same
Green, Julien, 1900-1998.
He thinks upon his death (1951)
[unpubl.]
He walks beneath the stars (1951)
[unpubl.]
Hearing music at his mother's funeral
(1951) [unpubl.]
Hanson, Pauline
So beautiful is the tree of night (1964)
[unpubl.]
Hardy, Thomas, 1840-1928.

ROREM, NED, 1923- *(continued)*
Hardy, Thomas, 1840-1928 *(continued)*
The oxen, a Christmas carol (1947)
[unpubl.]
Herbert, Mary Sidney, Countess of
Pembroke, 1561-1621.
If ever hapless woman had a cause
(1976) [Boosey & Hawkes, 1979]
same
Herrick, Robert, 1591-1674.
Another epitaph (1950) [Mercury Music
Corp., 1952; T. Presser]
"Here a pretty baby lies"
Cherry-ripe (1950) [Mercury Music
Corp., 1952; T. Presser]
"Cherry-ripe, ripe, ripe, I cry"
Comfort to a youth that had lost his love
(1950) [Mercury Music Corp., 1952; T.
Presser] "What needs complaints"
Epitaph upon a child that died (1950)
[Mercury Music Corp., 1952; T.
Presser] "Here she lies, a pretty bud"
*To Anthea, who may command him
anything* (1950) [Mercury Music
Corp., 1952; T. Presser] "Bid me to
live"
To daisies, not to shut so soon (1950)
[Mercury Music Corp., 1952; T.
Presser] "Shut not so soon"
To music, to becalm his fever (1950)
[Mercury Music Corp., 1952; T.
Presser]
"Charm me asleep, and melt me so"
To the willow-tree (1950) [Mercury
Music Corp., 1952; T. Presser]
"Thou art to all lost love the best"
Upon Julia's clothes (1950) [Mercury
Music Corp., 1952; T. Presser]
"Whenas in silks my Julia goes"
Hillyer, Robert Silliman, 1895-1961.
Early in the morning (1955) [C. F.
Peters, 1958] same
Hopkins, Gerard Manley, 1844-1889.
Felix Randal (1946) [unpubl.]
Spring (1947) [Boosey & Hawkes, 1953]
"Nothing is so beautiful as spring"
Spring and fall (to a young child, 1946)
[Mercury Music Corp., 1947;
T.Presser] "Margaret, are you
grieving"
Hugnet, Georges, 1906-1974.
Abandonée, je suis abandonée (1953)
[unpubl.]
Tout beau mon coeur (1953) [unpubl.]
Jonson, Ben, 1573?-1637.
Echo's song (1948) [Boosey & Hawkes,
1953] "Slow, slow, fresh fount, keep
time with my salt tears"

Josephs, Laurence
Introduced to flame (1948) [unpubl.]
Joyce, James, 1882-1941.
CHAMBER MUSIC.
Dear heart (1948) [unpubl.]
Koch, Kenneth, 1925-2002.
Down at the docks (1965-66) [Boosey &
Hawkes, 1969] same
Hearing (1966) [Boosey & Hawkes,
1969] "Hear the beautiful tinny voices
of the trumpets"
In love with you (1965-66) [Boosey &
Hawkes, 1969] "O what a physical
effect it has on me"
Invitation (1966) [Boosey & Hawkes,
1969] "Mediterranean suns!"
Poem (1966) [Boosey & Hawkes, 1969]
"And so unless I'm going to see your
face"
Spring (1966) [Boosey & Hawkes, 1969]
"Let's take a walk in the city"
Kubly, Herbert, 1915-1996.
Anniversary (1946) [unpubl.]
Landor, Walter Savage, 1775-1864.
Mother, I cannot mind my wheel
[Boosey & Hawkes, 1981] same
Larson, Jack, b. 1933.
Do I love you [Boosey, 1965] "Do I love
you more than a day?"
Lodge, Thomas, 1558-1625.
Love (1953) [Boosey & Hawkes, 1969]
"Turn I my looks unto the skies"
Lord, James
In this summer (1954) [unpubl.]
MacLow, Jackson, 1922-
The nipples of the rain (1947) [unpubl.]
Magny, Olivier de, d. ca. 1560.
Sonnet (1953) [C. F. Peters, 1953;
Boosey & Hawkes, 1970]
"Gordes, que ferons-nous?"
Also arranged with string
accompaniment, 1956.
Sonnet (1953) [C. F. Peters, 1953;
Boosey & Hawkes, 1970]
"Je cherche paix"
Also arranged with string
accompaniment, 1956.
Marot, Clément, 1495?-1544.
Rondeau de sa grande amie (1953)
[unpubl.]
Melville, Herman, 1819-1891.
Shelly's vision (1947) [unpubl.]
Mew, Charlotte, 1870-1928.
Smile, death (1975) [Boosey & Hawkes,
1979] "Smile, death, see I smile as I
come to you"

Moss, Howard, 1922-1987.
The air is the only [Boosey, 1965] same
A body without love (1960) [unpubl.]
I know so many stories (1960) [unpubl.]
Only lover's rest (1960) [unpubl.]
See how they love me (1956) [C. F.
Peters, 1958] same
Later used as "The Princess's Lover"
in **King Midas.**
They rise up shining (1960) [unpubl.]
Tourist's song (1948) [unpubl.]
No author
Alleluia (1946) [Hargail Music Press,
1949; Boosey & Hawkes, 1977]
"Alleluia . . . "
Noailles, Marie Laure de, 1902-1970.
Jack L'Eventreur (1953) [**Folder
Magazine,** 1956; Boosey & Hawkes,
1972] "Par les corps endormis"
Je te salue jeunesse (1953) [unpubl.]
Norse, Harold, 1916-
The flea's lament (1948) [unpubl.]
Freak show (1948) [unpubl.]
Goodbye to penny fate (1948) [unpubl.]
The gypsy (1948) [unpubl.]
The Hebrides (1948) [unpubl.]
Song of the third duck from the right
(1948) [unpubl.]
Test your skill (1948) [unpubl.]
O'Donnell, G. M.
Epigram (1947) [unpubl.]
O'Hara, Frank, 1926-1966.
For Poulenc (1963) [E. C. Schirmer,
1968] "My first day in Paris I walked"
Originally published with title:
Poulenc: A gymnopédie.
Let's take a walk (1952-53) [unpubl.]
Poem: I will always love you (1957)
[unpubl.]
O'Leary, Joseph
Whiskey drink divine (1950) [unpubl.]
Pearse, Padriac, 1879-1916.
Lullaby of the woman of the mountain
(1950) [Boosey & Hawkes, 1956]
"O little head of gold!"
Phemister, Bruce
Pagan, op. 1 no. 4 (1940-41) [unpubl.]
Pitchford, Kenneth Lee, 1930-
Jacquelin Gray ((1958) [unpubl.]
Song for lying in bed during a night rain
[Boosey, 1965]
"How can I wash the lightning away"
Plato, ca. 429-347 B.C.
Two songs on words of Plato (1964)
[unpubl.]
Prokosch, Frederic, 1908-1989.

Evening (1947?) [unpubl.]
Midnight (1957) [unpubl.]
Regnier, Jehan, fl. 1392-1468.
Lay (1953) [C. F. Peters, 1953;
Boosey & Hawkes, 1970]
"Prions trestous, jeunes et vieulx"
Also arranged with string
accompaniment, 1956.
Rich, Adrienne Cecile, 1929-
DIVING INTO THE WRECK.
The stranger (1975) [Boosey &
Hawkes, 1979]
"Looking as I've looked before"
Ridge, Lola, 1883-1941.
RED FLAG.
Electrocution (1976) [Boosey &
Hawkes, 1979]
"He shudders . . . feeling on the
shaven spot"
Roditi, Edouard, 1910-1992.
Poem for F (1955) [unpubl.]
Roethke, Theodore, 1908-1963.
The apparition [Boosey, 1965] "My
pillow won't tell me where he is gone"
The beast (1959) [unpubl.]
Interlude [Boosey, 1965]
"The element of air was out of hand"
Memory (1959) [C. F. Peters, 1961]
"In the slow world of dream"
My Papa's waltz (1959) [C. F. Peters,
1963] "The whiskey on your breath
could make a small boy dizzy"
Night crow (1959) [C. F. Peters, 1963]
"When I saw that clumsy crow"
Orchids (1959) [Boosey & Hawkes,
1969] "They lean over the path"
Root cellar (1959) [C. F. Peters, 1963]
"Nothing would sleep in that cellar"
The serpent (1972) [Boosey & Hawkes,
1974]
"There was a serpent who had to sing"
Snake (1959) [C. F. Peters, 1963]
"I saw a young snake glide"
The surly one (1959) [unpubl.]
The waking (1959) [C. F. Peters, 1961]
"I wake to sleep"
THE FAR FIELD.
From whence cometh song?
[Boosey & Hawkes, 1981] same
THE WAKING.
I strolled across an open field (1959)
[Boosey & Hawkes, 1969] same
Ronsard, Pierre de, 1524-1585.
Ode (1953) [C. F. Peters, 1953;
Boosey & Hawkes, 1970]
"Je te salue, heureuse Paix"

COMPOSER Poet *Title* "First Line"

ROREM, NED, 1923- *(continued)*
Ronsard, Pierre de, 1524-1585
(continued)
Also arranged with string
accompaniment, 1956.
Rorem, Ned, 1923-
My true love is a bird (1944) [unpubl.]
Once upon a dream (1950) [unpubl.]
Poem: The nightingale, op. 1 no. 1
(1940-41) [unpubl.]
The soul sings (1947) [unpubl.]
Rossetti, Christina Georgina, 1830-
1894.
A birthday (1976) [Boosey & Hawkes,
1979] "My heart is like a singing bird"
Ferry me across the water [Boosey &
Hawkes, 1981] same
Up-hill [Boosey & Hawkes, 1981] "Does
the road wind uphill all the way?"
Sappho, 625? B.C.-570 B.C.
Evening (1947) [unpubl.]
Sappho: Fragment (1949) [unpubl.]
Shakespeare, William, 1564-1616.
HAMLET.
Ophelia's lament (1948) [unpubl.]
Shapiro, Karl Jay, 1913-2000.
Mongolian idiot (1947) [unpubl.]
Shelley, Percy Bysshe, 1792-1822.
To Jane (1974) [Boosey & Hawkes,
1976] "The keen stars were twinkling"
Sitwell, Edith, Dame, 1887-1964.
You, the young rainbow of my tears
(1948) [Boosey & Hawkes, 1982]
same
The youth with the red-gold hair (1948)
[Galaxy, 1982; Boosey & Hawkes,
1982] "The gold-armoured ghost from
the Roman road"
Spenser, Edmund, 1552?-1599.
What if some little pain (1949) [Hargail
Music Press, 1952; Boosey & Hawkes]
same
Stein, Gertrude, 1874-1946.
I am rose (1955) [C. F. Peters, 1963]
same
Stevenson, Robert Louis, 1850-1894.
Requiem (1948) [Peer, 1950]
"Under the wide & starry sky"
Tennyson, Alfred Tennyson, 1st
baron, 1809-1892.
Ask me no more (1963) [Boosey &
Hawkes, 1969] same
Far, far away (1963) [Boosey & Hawkes,
1969] "What sight so lured him thro'
the fields"
Now sleeps the crimson petal (1963)
[Boosey & Hawkes, 1969] same

THE DAY DREAM.
The sleeping palace (1949) [Boosey &
Hawkes, 1969] "The varying-year
with blade and sheaf"
Tree, Iris
Lonesome tree (1955) [unpubl.]
Tyler, Parker, 1907-1974.
Dawn angel (1945) [unpubl.]
Vittorelli, Jacopo, 1749-1835.
Guarda che bianca luna! (1954 or 55)
[unpubl.] same
Non t'accostare all'urna (1954 or 55)
[unpubl.] same
O platano felice (1954 or 55) [unpubl.]
same
Zitto, La Bella Irene (1954 or 55)
[unpubl.] same
Waller, Edmund, 1606-1687.
The dancer [Boosey & Hawkes, 1981]
"Behold the brand of beauty tossed!"
Go, lovely rose [Boosey & Hawkes,
1981] same
Whitman, Walt, 1819-1892.
As Adam early in the morning (1957) [C.
F. Peters, 1961] same
Gliding o'er all (1957) [Boosey &
Hawkes, 1970] same
Gods (1957) [Boosey & Hawkes, 1970]
"Lover divine and perfect comrade"
I saw in Louisiana a live-oak growing
(1982) [Boosey & Hawkes, 1982]
same
Look down, fair moon (1957) [Boosey &
Hawkes, 1970] same
O you whom I often and silently come
(1957) [C. F. Peters, 1961] same
Of him I love day and night (1982)
[Boosey & Hawkes, 1982] same
Reconciliation (1946) [Boosey &
Hawkes, 1970]
"Word over all, beautiful as the sky!"
Sometimes with one I love (1957)
[Boosey & Hawkes, 1970] same
To a common prostitute (1982)
[Boosey & Hawkes, 1982]
"Be composed–be at ease with me"
To you (1957) [Elkan-Vogel, 1965;
T.Presser] "Stranger, if you passing
meet me"
Youth, day, old age, and night (1954) [C.
F. Peters, 1958]
"Youth, large, lusty, loving youth"
SPECIMEN DAYS.
Inauguration ball (1969) [Boosey &
Hawkes, 1971]
"At the dance and supper room I
could not help thinking"

Freely excised from *Specimen Days* (1882) by Rorem.
An incident (1969) [Boosey & Hawkes, 1971]
"In one of the fights before Atlanta"
Freely excised from *Specimen Days* (1882) by Rorem.
A night battle (1969) [Boosey & Hawkes, 1971]
"What scene is this?"
Freely excised from *Specimen Days* (1882) by Rorem.
The real war will never get in the books (1969) [Boosey & Hawkes, 1971] "And so goodbye to the war"
Freely excised from *Specimen Days* (1882) by Rorem.
Specimen case (1969) [Boosey & Hawkes, 1971]
"Poor youth, so handsome"
Freely excised from *Specimen Days* (1882) by Rorem.

Williams, William Carlos, 1883-1963.
The dance [Boosey & Hawkes, 1981] "In Breughel's great picture, The Kermess"
Nantucket [Boosey & Hawkes, 1981]
"Flowers through the window lavender and yellow"

Windham, Donald, 1920-
EMBLEMS OF CONDUCT. Chapter "The Rain."
Prologue and Epilogue: from "The Rain" [Boosey, 1965]
"Everywhere, the impossible is happening"

Wyatt, Sir Thomas, 1503?-1542.
The appeal (1944) [private edition]
Printed with *Song* and *Knight of the Grail* in a private edition with cover by Morris Golde; extremely rare.
Forget not yet (1952) [unpubl.]

Wylie, Elinor, 1885-1928.
Little elegy (1949) [Hargail Music Press, 1952; Boosey & Hawkes]
"Without you no rose can grow"
Now let no charitable hope (1975) [Boosey & Hawkes, 1979] same
On a singing girl (1946) [Hargail Music Press, 1952; Boosey & Hawkes]
"Musa of the seablue eyes"

Yeats, William Butler, 1865-1939.
Cradle song (1951) [unpubl.]
I know that I shall meet my fate (1948) [unpubl.]
Lullaby (1951) [unpubl.]
Mad as the mist and snow (1951) [unpubl.]

Maid quiet (1951) [unpubl.]
O do not love too long (1951) [unpubl.]
Sweet dancer (1951) [unpubl.]
To a young girl (1951) [Boosey & Hawkes, 1972]
"My dear, my dear I know"

Rorem, Ned, 1923-
ROREM
My true love is a bird
Once upon a dream
Poem: The nightingale
The soul sings

Rosa del cami see Mompou **MOMPOU**
"Rosa, denkst du an mich" *see An Rosa II* Kosegarten **SCHUBERT**
Rosa lill' see Cnattingius, Thor **KILPINEN**
"Rosa lill' nu solen far" *see Rosa lill'* Cnattingius, Thor **KILPINEN**
"Rosa, Rosa, l'air est plus deux" *see Sonnet païen* Silvestre **MASSENET**
Rosalinde see Krenek **KRENEK**
Rosamunde see Chezy **IVES**
Die Rose see Bodenstedt **RUBINSTEIN**
The rose see Feeney **CHANLER**
La rose see Leconte de Lisle **FAURÉ**
The rose see Mužik **MARTINŮ**
The rose see Pushkin **MEDTNER**
Die Rose see Schlegel, F. *ABENDRÖTE.* **SCHUBERT**
The rose see Unknown **DVOŘÁK** *Růže*
"A rose bud by my early walk" *see My early walk* Burns **BRITTEN**
Rose cheek'd Laura, come see Campion **THOMSON**
Rose d'amour see Millevoye **BIZET**
Rose de Mai see Poirson, S. Cuthbert **MASSENET**
Die Rose, die Lilie see Heine **FRANZ, SCHUMANN**
La rose du rameau sec see Leclère, translator *SHÉHÉRAZADE.* **KOECHLIN**
La rose et la Réséda see Aragon **AURIC**
La rose et l'abeille see Rolland **BIZET**
The rose family see Frost **CARTER**
"Rose is a rose" *see Le Berceau de Gertrude Stein* Hugnet **THOMSON**
"The rose is a rose, and was always a rose" *see The rose family* Frost **CARTER**
Rose, Karl, b.1774.
LOEWE *Abendstunde*
Rose, Meer und Sonne sind ein Bild see Rückert *LIEBESFRÜHLING.* **SCHUMANN**
The rose of the night see Sharp, W. *THE HOUR OF BEAUTY.* **GRIFFES**
"Rose, partons! voici l'aurore" *see Les champs* Béranger **BERLIOZ, GOUNOD**

COMPOSER Poet *Title* "First Line"

Rose spinose see Burchiello **MALIPIERO**

"Rose tu es la fleur de chair" *see Le quatrain
de la rose* Mahaut **RIVIER**

"Rose, un voile rose" *see Petite écuyère*
Copperie, Adrien **SAUGUET**

Roseate dawn see Pushkin **PROKOFIEV**
Rumianoĭ zareiu pokrylsīa vostok

La Rosée see Hugnet **THOMSON**

Rosemann
LOEWE *Der Garten des Lebens*
Poet may be J A Kloentrup.

Rosemann, pseud. *see* Kloentrup, Johann
Aegidius, 1755-1830.

Rosemary see Unknown **MARTINŮ**
Rozmarýn

Rosemonde see Apollinaire *ALCOOLS.*
POULENC

Rosemonde see Giraudoux *SUZANNE ET LA
PACIFIQUE.* **HONEGGER**

"Rosen!" *see Ferne Lieder* Rückert **BERG**

Rosen see Itzerott **REGER**

Rosen blusser alt i Danas Have see Møller
NIELSEN

"Rosen brach ich Nachts mir am dunklen
Hage" *see Sappische Ode* Schmidt, Hans
BRAHMS

"Rosen fliehen nicht allein" *see
An die Entfernte* Lenau **SCHOECK**

"Rosen ging ich aus zu pflücken" *see Bitteres
Gedenken* Wildenbruch **LASSEN**

Rosen in Haare see Hafiz **WEBER**

"Rosen, ja, Rosen likväl är skönast" *see
De bägge rosorna* Franzén **SIBELIUS**

"Die Rosen leuchten immer noch" *see
Aus banger Brust* Dehmel **SIBELIUS**

"Rosen pflücken, Rosen blüh'n" *see
An Leukon* Gleim **BERG**

"Rosen saenker sit Hoved tungt af Dug og
Duft" *see I Seraillets Have* Jacobsen
NIELSEN

"Rosen und duftende Veilchen" *see Ständchen*
Wildenbruch **LASSEN**

Die Rosen von Jericho see Ali **LASSEN**

Das Rosenband see Klopstock *ODE.*
**MACDOWELL, SCHUBERT,
STRAUSS, ZELTER**

Rosenbaum, Kory Elizabeth, 1868-1930.
BERG *Liebeslied*

Rosenbüsche see Löns **KILPINEN**

"Die Rosenbüsche sind behangen" *see
Rosenbüsche* Löns **KILPINEN**

Rosendufte füllen rings die Lüfte see
Unknown **RUBINSTEIN**

"Rosenknop saa fast og rund" *see
Rosenknoppen* Andersen **GRIEG**

Rosenknoppen see Andersen **GRIEG**

Die Rosenknospe see Andersen **GRIEG**
Rosenknoppen

Rosenlied see Ritter **SIBELIUS**

Der Rosenstrauch see Schulz **SPOHR**

Rosenzeit see Heyse **JENSEN**

Rosenzeit see Mörike **FRANZ**

"Rosenzeit, wie schnell vorbei" *see Agnes*
Mörike **BRAHMS, WOLF**

"Rosenzeit, wie schnell vorbei" *see Rosenzeit*
Mörike **FRANZ**

Les roses see Banville *LES CARIATIDES,*
livre 3, no. XV. **DEBUSSY**

Roses ardentes see Lerberghe **FAURÉ**

"Roses blushing red and white" *see The
garland* Rossetti, Christina **IRELAND**

"Les roses de l'autre année" *see Lied*
Mauclair **SCHMITT**

Les roses d'Ispahan see Leconte de Lisle
FAURÉ

"Les roses d'Ispahan dans leur gaîne de
mousse" *see Les roses d'Ispahan* Leconte
de Lisle **FAURÉ**

Roses d'Octobre see Collin **MASSENET**

Roses du soir see Vivien **AUBERT**

Roses en bracelet see Moréas **HAHN**

Roses et papillons see Hugo **FRANCK**

"Les roses étaient toules rouges" *see Spleen*
Verlaine **DEBUSSY**

"Les roses se sont refermées" *see Defuncta
nascuntur* Van Ormelingen **MASSENET**

Roshchady ia moliu! see Merezhkovski
RACHMANINOFF *I beg for mercy*

Rosička see Unknown **MARTINŮ**

Le rosier blanc see Spenner, M. **GOUNOD**

"Rosig ist das Lebensfädgeu" *see Lied*
Rothmaler **ZELTER**

Rosing, Michael, 1756-1818.
NIELSEN *O, hvor jeg er glad i Dag*

Rosmarin see Erben **DVOŘÁK** *Rozmarýna*

Rosmarin see Hauenschild **FRANZ**

Rosmarine see Erben **DVOŘÁK** *Rozmarýna*

"Rośnie trawka, ziólko, zimne dni sie mienia"
see Posel Witwicki **CHOPIN**

Rosor see Cnattingius, Thor **KILPINEN**

Rosornas sang see Ritter **SIBELIUS**
Rosenlied

"De rosse mann trekt langzaam" *see Nacht*
Koster **PIJPER**

Rossetti, Christina Georgina, 1830-1894.
IRELAND
Baby
The blind boy
Death-parting
The garland
Hope
Newborn

The only child
Skylark and nightingale
When I am dead, my dearest
IVES *Mirage*
MILHAUD
   A birthday
   Song
QUILTER *A song at parting*
RIEGGER *Who has seen the wind*
ROREM
   A birthday
   Ferry me across the water
   Up-hill
VAUGHAN WILLIAMS
   Boy Johnny
   Dreamland
   If I were a queen
   When I am dead, my Dearest
Rossetti, Dante Gabriel, 1828-1882.
   IRELAND
      During music
      English May
      The one hope
      Penumbra
      Youth's spring-tribute
   LOEFFLER *Sudden light*
   VAUGHAN WILLIAMS *Willow-wood*
   THE HOUSE OF LIFE, no. IV.
      VAUGHAN WILLIAMS *Lovesight*
   THE HOUSE OF LIFE, no. IX.
      VAUGHAN WILLIAMS
         Love's minstrels
   THE HOUSE OF LIFE, no. XIX.
      VAUGHAN WILLIAMS *Silent noon*
   THE HOUSE OF LIFE, no. XXII.
      VAUGHAN WILLIAMS *Heart's haven*
   THE HOUSE OF LIFE, no. XLVIII.
      VAUGHAN WILLIAMS *Death in love*
   THE HOUSE OF LIFE, no. LIX.
      VAUGHAN WILLIAMS
         Love's last gift
Le rossignol see Anon. **DELIBES**
Le rossignol see Banville *AMÉTHYSTES.*
   SAINT-SAËNS
Le rossignol see Latil **MILHAUD**
Le rossignol des lilas see Dauphin **HAHN**
Rossignol, mon mignon . . . see Ronsard
   RIVIER, ROUSSEL
"Rossignol mon mignon qui dansces te
   saulair" *see Rossignol, mon mignon*
   Ronsard **ROUSSEL**
"Rossignol mon mignon qui par cette saulaie"
   see Rossignol, mon mignon . . . Ronsard
   RIVIER
ROSSINI, GIOACCHINO, 1792-1868.
   Castellani, A.

Il fanciullo smarrito [Rome: 1881]
   In *Strenna del giornale la lega della
      democrazia.*
Cerutti, L. F.
   L'ultimo pensiero ("Patria, consorti,
      figli") [unpubl.?]
Dante Aligheri, 1265-1321.
   Recitativo ritmato (1848) [Florence, n.d.]
      "Farò come colui che piange e dice"
      Holograph: Fondazione Rossini.
Delavigne, Jean François Casimir,
   1793-1843.
   Les adieux à Rome (1827) [Paris: C.
      Delavigne *7 messéniennes nouvelles,*
      1827] "Rome pour la dernière fois"
      Tenor & piano or harp.
   L'âme délaissée (ca.1844) [Paris: 1844]
      "Mon bien aimé"
Deschamps, Émile, 1791-1871.
   Chanson de Zora (La petite Bohémienne)
      [Quaderni Rossiniani, v. 5, p. 49]
      "Gens de la plaine ou de l'âpre
         montagne"
   Nizza (ca.1836) [Paris: ca.1837]
      "Nizza, je puis sans peine"
      Text by Deschamps and Metastasio.
Metastasio, Pietro Antonio Domenico
   Buonaventura, 1698-1782.
   Aragonese [Quaderni Rossiniani, v. 4,
      p. 44] "Mi lagnerò tacendo della mia
      sorte amara"
   *Arietta all'antica, dedotta dal "O
      salutaris Hostia"* [Quaderni
      Rossiniani, v. 4, p. 60]
         "Mi lagnerò tacendo della mia sorte
            amara"
   La dichiarazione (ca.1834) [Milan: 1834-
      35] "Ch'io mai vi possa lasciar
      d'amare"
   Mi lagnerò tacendo [cf. *New Grove*,
      v. 16, p. 247 for various settings]
      Numerous versions composed as
         albumleaves.
   La partenza [G. Ricordi, reprint 1980]
      "Ecco quel fiero istante"
   Pour album: Sogna il guerrier [unpubl.?]
   La promessa [G. Ricordi, reprint 1980]
      "Ch'io mai vi possa lasciar d'amare"
   Il rimprovero [G. Ricordi, reprint 1980]
      "Mi lagnerò tacendo"
   Tirana alla spagnola (Rossinizzata)
      [Quaderni Rossiniani, v. 4, p. 30]
      "Mi lagneró tacendo della mia sorte
         amara"
No author
   Gorgheggi e solfeggi (ca.1827) [Paris:
      1827]

ROSSINI, GIOACCHINO, 1792-1868
(continued)
Pacini, Emilio, 1810-1898.
À Grenade (ca.1860) [Quaderni
   Rossiniani, v. 5, p. 90]
   "La nuit règne à Grenade"
L'amour à Pekin [Quaderni Rossiniani,
   v. 5, p. 85]
   "Mon coeur blessé gémit tout bas"
Amour sans espoir ("Tirana all'espagnole
   rossinize") [unpubl.?]
   Music identical with *Tirana alla
      spagnola,* Quaderni Rossiniani, v. 4,
      p. 30.
Au chevet d'un mourant (élégie)
   [Quaderni Rossiniani, v. 5, p. 17]
   "De la douleur n'aît l'espérance"
La chanson du Bébé [Quaderni
   Rossiniani, v. 5, p. 25] "Maman, le
   gros Bébé t'appelle, il a bobo"
Pompadour, la grande coquette
   [unpubl.?]
Roméo [unpubl.?]
Le sylvain [Quaderni Rossiniani, v. 5,
   p. 1] "Belle nymphes blondes des
   forêts profondes"
La veuve andalouse (ca.1860) [unpubl.?]
   "Toi pour jamais"
Pepoli, Carlo, Conte, 1796-1881.
La danza [G. Ricordi, reprint 1980]
   "Già la luna è in mezzo al mare"
La gita in gondola [G. Ricordi, reprint
   1980] "Voli l'agile barchetta"
L'invito [G. Ricordi, reprint 1980]
   "Vieni O Ruggiero"
L'orgia [G. Ricordi, reprint 1980]
   "Amiamo, cantiamo"
La pastorella dell'Alpi [G. Ricordi,
   reprint 1980] "Son bella pastorella"
Redaelli, G.
L'ultimo ricordo [Quaderni Rossiniani,
   v. 4, p. 19] "Odi di un uom che
   muore"
Rousseau, Jean Jacques, 1712-1778.
Ariette à l'ancienne [Quaderni
   Rossiniani, v. 5, p. 69] "Que le jour
   me dure! Passé loin de toi"
Ariette villageoise [Quaderni Rossiniani,
   v. 5, p. 72] "Que le jour me dure!
   Passé loin de toi"
Santo-Magno, N. di
Beltà crudele (1821) [Naples: 1847]
   "Amori scendete"
   Facsimile in J. Subirá *La música en la
      Casa de Alba* (Madrid: 1927).
La pastorella (ca.1821) [Milan: ca.1850,
   2nd ed.] "Odia la pastorella"

Torre, G.
L'esule [Quaderni Rossiniani, v. 4, p. 25]
   "Qui sempre ride il cielo"
La lontananza [Quaderni Rossiniani, v. 4,
   p. 12] "Quando dal tuo verone, fra
   l'ombre della sera"
Ucceili, F.
La separazione (ca.1858) [Paris: ca.1858]
   "Muto rima se il labbro"
   Originally composed as *Mi lagnerò
      tacendo.*
Unknown
A ma belle mère [Quaderni Rossiniani,
   v. 11, p. 58]
   "Requiem Eterna dona ei Domine"
Addio ai viennesi (1822) [Vienna: 1822]
   "Da voi parto, amate sponde"
Adieux à la vie! (Élégie sur une seule
   note) [Quaderni Rossiniani, v. 5, p. 75]
   "Salut! dernière aurore qui viens pour
   moi d'eclore!"
Anzoleta avanti la regata [Milan: 1878]
Anzoleta co passa la regata [Milan:
   1878]
Anzoleta dopo la regata [Milan: 1878]
Ave Maria (su due note) [Quaderni
   Rossiniani, v. 4, p. 51] "A te, che
   benedetta fra tutte sei, Maria"
*Canzonetta spagnuola "En medio a mis
   colores"* (1821) [Milan: ca.1850]
   "Piangea un di pensando"
Chansonette de cabaret ("Le lazzarone")
   [unpubl.?]
Le dodo des enfants [Quaderni
   Rossiniani, v. 5, p. 9]
   "Mon fils, roseéphémère, endors ta
   plainte a mère"
La fioraja fiorentina [Quaderni
   Rossiniani, v. 4, p. 5]
   "I più bei fior comprate"
Infelice ch'io son (1821) [unpubl.?]
   Facsimile in L. Schmidt *Emil
      Naumanns illustrierte Musik-
      geschichte* (Dresden: 9/1928).
O salutaris, de campagne [unpubl.?]
L'orpheline du Tyrol, ballade élégie
   [Quaderni Rossiniani, v. 5, p. 31]
   "Seule, une pauvre enfant sans
   parents"
La passeggiata (1831) [Madrid: *Cartas
   espanolas,* 11 April 1831]
   "Or che di fiori adorno"
   Also known as *Anacreontica.*
Qual voce, quai note (1813) [unpubl.]
Questo palpito soave [unpubl.?]
Un rien [Quaderni Rossiniani, v. 11,
   p. 60] "Ave Maria gratia plena gratia"

Il rimprovero ("Se fra le trecce
d'Ebano") [Florence: 1944]
Se il vuol la molinara (1801?) [Milan:
1821]
Holograph: New York: Pierpont
Morgan Library.
Il trovatore (1818) [Naples: 1818]
"Chi m'ascolta il canto usato"
Holograph: Library of Congress.
Rossinizzata see Metastasio **ROSSINI**
Tirana alla spagnola (Rossinizzata)
Rostand, Edmond, 1868-1918.
CHABRIER
Ballade des gros dindons
Pastorale des cochons roses
Toutes les fleurs
Rostand, Rosemonde Gérard, b. 1871.
CHABRIER
Les cigales
Villanelle des petits canards
Rostopchina, Evdokiia, grafinia, 1811-
1858.
CHAĬKOVSKIĬ *I bol'no, i sladko*
RUBINSTEIN
Der fallende Stern
Sie singt ein Lied
Weht es, heult es trüb'
The rosy sunset fades see Kulchinsky, V.
BALAKIREV *Dogorayet rumyaniÿ zakat*
Rosyanka see Gorodetski **STRAVINSKIĬ**
A song of the dew
Rote Äuglein see Anon. **FRANZ**
Rote Rosen see Stieler **STRAUSS**
"Rote Rosen, stolz und prächtig" *see Seerose*
Lingg **LASSEN**
Rotes Lied see Tuwim **SZYMANOWSKI**
Kalinowe dwory
Die rothe Hanne see Béranger *JEANNE LA
ROUSSE, OU, LA FEMME DU
BRACONNIER.* **SCHUMANN**
Rothmaler
LIED.
ZELTER *Lied*
Le Rouet see Leconte de Lisle **RAVEL**
Chanson du rouet
Le Rouge-gorge see Theuriet **LALO**
"Rouge-violet, noir sur noir" *see Montagnes*
Messiaen **MESSIAEN**
Rough wind see Shelley **IVES**
"Rough wind, that moanest loud" *see Rough
wind* Shelley **IVES**
Une roulotte couverte en tuiles see Éluard
POULENC
"Round and round the old dance ground" *see
Waltz* Ives **IVES**
Roundel see Anon. **ROREM**

Rounds, Emma
THOMPSON, R. *The wild home pussy*
Rousseau, Jean Jacques, 1712-1778.
BEETHOVEN *Que le temps me dure*
ROSSINI
Ariette à l'ancienne
Ariette villageoise
*LES CONSOLATIONS DES MISÈRES DE
MA VIE.*
ZELTER *Félicité passée*
Rousseau, Johann Baptist, 1802-1867.
BRAHMS *Der Frühling*
Rousseil, R.
GOUNOD *Voix d'Alsace-Lorraine*
ROUSSEL, ALBERT, 1869-1937.
Anacreon, b.ca.570 B.C.
Qu'il faut boire, op. 31 no. 2 (1926)
[Durand, 1927]
"La noire terre boit la pluie"
Translated by Leconte de Lisle.
Sur lui-même, op. 31 no. 1 (1926)
[Durand, 1927]
"Tu chantes les guerres Thébaines"
Translated by Leconte de Lisle.
Sur lui-même, op. 32 no. 1 (1926)
[Durand, 1927]
"Dès que Bakkhos me tient"
Translated by Leconte de Lisle.
Sur une jeune fille, op. 31 no. 3 (1926)
[Durand, 1927]
"La fille de Tantalos fut"
Translated by Leconte de Lisle.
Sur une jeune fille, op. 32 no. 2 (1926)
[Durand, 1927]
"Ne me fuis pas, Ô jeune fille"
Translated by Leconte de Lisle.
Sur une songe, op. 32 no. 3 (1926)
[Durand, 1927] "Il me semblait"
Translated by Leconte de Lisle.
Anon.
O bon vin, où as-tu crû? (1928) [Durand,
1935] "O bon vin, bon vin, bon vin"
Traditional chanson harmonized by
Roussel.
Chalupt, René, 1885-1957.
Le bachelier de Salamanque, op. 20 no. 1
(1919) [Durand, 1919]
"Où vas-tu, toi qui passes si tard"
Also voice & orchestra.
Coeur en péril, op. 50 no. 2 (1933-34)
[Durand, 1934] "Que m'importe que
l'Infante de Portugal"
L'heure du retour, op. 50 no. 1 (1933-34)
[Durand, 1934]
"Une bise aigre et monotone fait
grincer les girouettes des maisons"

ROUSSEL, ALBERT, 1869-1937 *(continued)*
  Chalupt, René, 1885-1957 *(continued)*
    Sarabande, op. 20 no. 2 (1919) [Durand,
      1919] "Les jets d'eau dansent des
      sarabandes"
    Also voice & orchestra.
  Chang-Chi, 8-9th cent.
    Réponse d'une épouse sage, op. 35 no. 2
      (1927) [Durand, 1927] "Connaissant,
      seigneur, mon état d'épouse"
    Also voice & orchestra.
  Dommange, René Auguste Louis
    Henri, b. 1888.
    Jazz dans la nuit, op. 38 (1928) [Durand,
      1929] "Le bal, sur le parc incendié"
    Also voice & orchestra; orchestration
      by P. Vellones.
  Huang-Fu-Ian
    Vois, de belles filles, op. 47 no. 2 (1932)
      [Durand, 1934] same
  Jean-Aubry, Georges, 1882-1950.
    Flammes, op. 10 (1908) [Rouart Lerolle]
      "Je suis près de la porte"
    Light, op. 19 no. 1 (1918) [Durand, 1919]
      "Des larmes ont coulé"
  Joyce, James, 1882-1941.
    POMES PENYEACH.
    A flower given to my daughter (1931)
      [Durand, 1948] "Frail the white rose
      and frail are her hands"
      First published in **The Joyce Book**
        (London: Sylvan Press, 1932).
  Li-Ho, 9th cent.
    Des fleurs font un broderie, op. 35 no. 1
      (1927) [Durand, 1927] same
  Li-I, d. 827?
    Favorite abandonnée, op. 47 no. 1 (1932)
      [Durand, 1934]
      "Sous la lune le palais résonne"
  Mendès, Catulle Abraham, 1841-1909.
    Pendant l'attente (ca.1900) [destroyed,
      by Roussel?]
  Moskhos
    Pan ainmait Ekho, op. 44 no. 2 (1931)
      [Durand, 1931] same
  No author
    Vocalise no. 1 (1927) [Lemoine, 1928]
      First published in **L'Art du Chant:**
        Recueil de Vocalises modernes
        (Paris: 1928).
    Vocalise no. 2 (1928) [Leduc, 1930]
      First published in Hettich, ed.,
        Répertoire moderne de
        Vocalises–Etudes, v. 10 (Paris:
        1930). Orchestrated by A. Hoérée.
  Oliphant, Ernest Henry Clark, 1862-
    1936.

    A farewell, op. 19 no. 2 (1918) [Durand,
      1919] "If thou insist then we will say
      farewell"
  Régnier, Henri François Joseph de,
    1864-1936.
    Adieux, op. 8 no. 1 (1907) [Rouart
      Lerolle, 1921] "Il est de doux adieux
      au seuil des portes"
    Also voice & orchestra.
    Le Départ, op. 3 no. 1 (1903) [Rouart
      Lerolle, 1921] "Je n'emporte avec moi
      sur la mer sans retour"
    Invocation, op. 8 no. 3 (1907) [Rouart
      Lerolle, 1921]
      "Pour que la nuit soit douce"
    Le jardin mouillé, op. 3 no. 3 (1903)
      [Rouart Lerolle, 1921]
      "La croisée est ouverte"
    Madrigal lyrique, op. 3 no. 4 (1903)
      [Rouart Lerolle, 1921]
      "Vous êtes grande de tout"
    La menace, op. 9 (1907) [Rouart Lerolle,
      1910, 1921] "Vous aimerez un jour
      peutêtre ce vivagre"
    Also voice & orchestra, 1908.
    Nuit d'automne, op. 8 no. 2 (1907)
      [Rouart Lerolle, 1921]
      "Le couchant est si beau"
    Odelette, op. 8 no. 4 (1907) [Rouart
      Lerolle, 1921] "J'aurais pu dire mon
      Amour"
    Voeu, op. 3 no. 2 (1903) [Rouart Lerolle,
      1921] "Je voudrais pour tes yeux"
  Roché, Henri Pierre, 1879-1959.
    Amoureux séparés, op. 12 no. 2 [Rouart
      Lerolle, 1921] "Dans le royaume de
      Yen"
    Ode à un jeune gentilhomme, op. 12 no.
      1 [Rouart Lerolle, 1921]
      "N'entrez pas, Monsieur"
  Ronsard, Pierre de, 1524-1585.
    Ciel, aer et vens, op. 26 no. 2 (1924)
      [Durand, 1924] same
      Voice & flute.
    Rossignol, mon mignon, op. 26 no. 1
      (1924) [**Revue Musicale,** Supplement,
      May 1924; Durand, 1924] "Rossignol
      mon mignon qui dansces te saulair"
      Voice & flute.
  Silvestre, Paul Armond, 1837-1901.
    Les rêves (ca.1900) [destroyed, by
      Roussel?]
  Tailhade, Laurent, 1854-1919.
    Tristesse au jardin (ca.1900) [destroyed,
      by Roussel?]
  Theocritus, 310? B.C.-250? B.C.

Le Kérioklépte, op. 44 no. 1 (1931)
  [Durand, 1931]
  "Une cruelle abeille piqua une fois"
Ville, Georges, 1824-1897.
  Si quelquefois tu pleures . . . , op. 55 no.
    2 (1935) [Durand, 1936] same
  Vieilles cartes, vieilles mains, op. 55 no.
    1 (1935) [Durand, 1936] same
Roux, Jean
  MASSENET *On dit!*
Row gently here, my gondolier see **Moore, T.**
  SCHUMANN *Zwei Venetianische Lieder*
Row, row duck see **Koskimies SIBELIUS**
  Souda, souda sinisorsa
Roy, Camille
  GOUNOD *Le temps des roses*
Royauté see **Boyer, Georges MASSENET**
Roy's wife of Aldivalloch see **Anon.**
  GOUNOD
Roza see **Pushkin MEDTNER** *The rose*
Róže see **Unknown DVOŘÁK**
Rozmarýn see **Unknown MARTINŮ**
Rozmarýna see **Erben DVOŘÁK**
Rubino, Antonio, 1880-1964.
  RESPIGHI
  Acqua
  Crepuscolo
  Egle
  I fauni
  Musica in horto
RUBINSTEIN, ANTON, 1829-1894.
  Alvaro Fernandez de Almeida
  SPANISCHES LIEDERBUCH: Tango
    vos, el mi pandero.
    Klinge, klinge, mein Pandero, op. 76
      no. 6 (1867) [Senff, 1867] same
      Translated by Geibel.
  Anon.
    Räthsel, op. 33 no. 4 (1856) [Kistner,
      1870] "Es schmachtet eine Blume"
    SPANISCHES LIEDERBUCH.
    Bedeckt mich mit Blumen, op. 76 no. 5
      (1867) [Senff, 1867] same
      Text by M. Doceo? translated by
      Geibel.
  Backody
    Wir drei (1891) [Senff] "Es steht ein
      Blümchen dort im Thal"
  Baumbach, Rudolf, 1840-1905.
    Das begraben Lied (1890) [Senff;
      Jurgenson] "Hell schimmert das alte
      Königsschloss"
    Seefahrt, op. 115 no. 4 (1890) [Senff]
      "Hör auf deinen Fahrgesellen"
  Benediktov, Vladimir Grigor'evich,
    1807-1873.

Lied, op. 78 no. 2 (1868) [Senff, 1869]
    "Könnt' ich doch stets in deine blauen
      Augen"
Boddien, G. von
  Es blinkt der Thau, op. 72 no. 1 (1864)
    [Senff] same
  Die Heimath meiner Lieder (1891)
    [Senff] "Wenn ich des Donners
    Stimme höre"
    Op. 76 no. 10.
  Die Waldhexe, op. 72 no. 3 (1864)
    [Senff] "Vorbei, vorbei durch Feld und
    Wald"
  Wie eine Lerch' in blauer Luft, op. 72 no.
    2 (1864) [Senff] same
Bodenstedt, Friedrich Martin von,
  1819-1892.
  Gelb rollt mir zu Füssen, op. 34 no. 9
    (1854) [Kistner, 1870] same
  Gott hiess die Sonne glühen, op. 34 no.
    12 (1854) [Kistner, 1870] same
  Die helle Sonne leuchtet, op. 34 no. 10
    (1854) [Kistner, 1870] same
  Ich fühle deinen Odem, op. 34 no. 6
    (1854) [Kistner, 1870] same
  Mein Herz schmückt sich mit dir, op. 34
    no. 2 (1854) [Kistner, 1870] same
  Neigl, schöne Knospe, dich zu mir, op. 34
    no. 8 (1854) [Kistner, 1870] same
  Nicht mit Engeln im blauen Himmelszelt,
    op. 34 no. 1 (1854) [Kistner, 1870]
    same
  Die Rose, op. 34 no. 4 (1854) [Kistner,
    1870] "Es hat die Rose sich beklagt"
  Schlag' die Tschadra zurück, op. 34 no.
    7 (1854) [Kistner, 1870] same
  Seh' ich deine zarte Füsschen an, op. 34
    no. 3 (1854) [Kistner, 1870] same
  Thu nicht so spröde, schönes Kind, op.
    34 no. 11 (1854) [Kistner, 1870] same
  Verschliedene Wege (1891) [Senff]
    "Mein Verstand und armes Herz"
  Die Weise guter Zecher ist, op. 34 no. 5
    (1854) [Kistner, 1870] same
Byron, George Gordon Byron, 6th
  baron, 1778-1824.
  MY SOUL IS DARK.
    Hebräische Melodie, op. 78 no. 1
      (1868) [Senff, 1869]
      "Mein Geist ist trüb und schwer"
      Translated by Lermontov (Russian),
      Osterwald (German).
Ciampoli, Domenico, 1855-1929.
  Fanciula mia [Ricordi]
Cornelius, Peter, 1824-1874.
  Lass mich deine Augen, op. 115 no. 8
    (1890) [Senff] "Ob mein Mund auch
    dürfte"

RUBINSTEIN, ANTON, 1829-1894
(continued)
Dahn, Felix Ludwig Sophus, 1834-
1912.
Fatme (1881) [Senff] "Schlanke Fatme,
hohe Palme"
Dante Aligheri, 1265-1321.
Tanto gentile e tanto onesta, op. 83 no. 5
[Bote & Bock, ca.1871] same
Davidov
Der Schiffer, op. 8 no. 6 (1850) [Senff,
1874] "Rauscht die See im Sturme
springend"
Unable to verify Davidov same as
Dmitri Davidov set by
Szymanowski.
Eichendorff, Joseph Karl Benedikt,
Freiherr von, 1788-1857.
Nacht, op. 76 no. 2 (1867) [Senff, 1867]
"Hörst du die Gründe rufen"
Waldeinsamkeit, op. 76 no. 1 (1867)
[Senff, 1867]
"Waldeinsamkeit, du grünes Revier"
Eristavi, D.
Autumn (1891)
Listed in *New Grove;* not located
elsewhere.
The looking-glass (1891)
Listed in *New Grove;* not located
elsewhere.
Frey, Friedrich Hermann, 1830-1911.
Das erste Sommergras; Vor der Ernte,
op. 115 no. 1 (1890) [Senff]
"Ich weiss es nicht"
Geibel, Emanuel, i.e., Franz Emanuel
August, 1815-1884.
Frühmorgens, op. 57 no. 1 (1864) [Senff]
"Ich weiss nicht"
Lied, op. 57 no. 2 (1864) [Senff]
"Nun die Schatten dunkeln"
Neue Liebe, op. 57 no. 3 (1864) [Senff]
"Hinaus in's Weite"
Goethe, Johann Wolfgang von, 1749-
1832.
EGMONT.
Clärchens Lied, op. 57 no. 4 (1864)
[Senff] "Freudvoll und leidvoll"
WESTÖSTLICHER DIVAN.
Freisinn, op. 57 no. 5 (1864) [Senff]
"Lasst mich nur auf meinem Sattel
gelten!"
Grossi, Tommaso, 1791-1853.
Die Wanderschwalbe, op. 83 no. 6
[Bote & Bock, ca.1871] same
Grot, Yakov Karlovich, 1812-1893.
The Siskin (1843-44)

Listed in *New Grove;* not located
elsewhere.
Hamerling, Robert, 1830-1889.
An die Vögel, op. 115 no. 5 (1890)
[Senff] "Zwitschert nicht vor meinem
Fenster"
Heine, Heinrich, 1797-1856.
Der Asra, op. 32 no. 6 (1856) [Kistner]
"Täglich ging die wunderschöne
Sultanstochter"
Frühlingslied, op. 32 no. 1 (1856)
[Kistner] "Leise zieht durch mein
Gemüthe"
Frühlingslied, op. 32 no. 2 (1856)
[Kistner] "Die blauen Frühlingsaugen"
Frühlingslied, op. 32 no. 3 (1856)
[Kistner]
"In dem Walde spriesst's und grünt es"
Lied, op. 32 no. 4 (1856) [Kistner]
"Es war ein alter König"
Lied, op. 32 no. 5 (1856) [Kistner]
"Du bist wie eine Blume"
Tragödie, op. 57 no. 6 (1864) [Senff]
"Entflieh mit mir und sei mein Weib"
Wo? (1893) [Senff]
"Wo wird einst des Wandermüden"
Hoffmann von Fallersleben, August
Heinrich, 1798-1874.
Lied, op. 33 no. 2 (1856) [Kistner, 1870]
"An der Rose Busen schmiegt"
Lied, op. 33 no. 5 (1856) [Kistner, 1870]
"Siehe, der Frühling währet"
Hugo, Victor Marie, comte, 1802-1885.
Chanson d'amour (1879)
Listed in *New Grove;* not located
elsewhere.
Liebeswunder [Senff, ca.1885] "A quoi
bon entendre les oiseaux des bois?"
Romance, "Comment disait-il," op. 3
(youthful no.; 1843-44) [Moscow:
Gresser]
Information from Otto Albrecht's list
in Bowen *Free Artist, the Story of
Anton and Nicholas Rubinstein.*
Kalbeck, Max, 1850-1921.
Der einsame See, op. 115 no. 7 (1890)
[Senff] "Wo Gletscherhöhen starren"
Kol'tsov, Alekseĭ Vasil'yevich, 1809-
1842.
Fliehe hin, Nachtigall, op. 27 no. 1
(1849) [Spina, ca.1866; A. Cranz]
"Singe, Nachtigall"
Gieb' O heil'ge Geisternacht, op. 27 no.
3 (1849) [Spina, ca.1866]
Keine Frühlingsluft, op. 27 no. 7 (1849)
[Spina, ca.1866] same

Klage, op. 78 no. 5 (1868) [Senff, 1869]
"O wie schwer die Pein"
Kleine Wolke, op. 27 no. 6 (1849) [Spina,
ca.1866]
Lebewohl, op. 27 no. 2 (1849) [Spina,
ca.1866] "Lebewohl, Ade"
Die Nachtigall und die Rose, op. 27 no. 4
(1849) [Spina, ca.1866]
"Es singt der Ros' in Liebesdrang"
Das Ringelein, op. 27 no. 5 (1849)
[Spina, ca.1866]
"Liebes goldnes Ringelein"
Sturmeswinde, op. 27 no. 9 (1849)
[Spina, ca.1866] same
Wenn ich kommen dich seh', op. 27 no. 8
(1849) [Spina, ca.1866] same

Krylov, Ivan Andreevich, 1768-1844.
Der Adler und der Kukuk, op. 64 no. 4
[Senff] "Der Aar den Kukuk"
Die Ameise und die Libelle, op. 64 no. 5
[Senff] "Der muntern Hüpferin Libell"
Der Esel und die Nachtigall, op. 64 no. 1
[Senff] "Ein Esel sah die Nachtigall"
Der Parnass, op. 64 no. 3 [Senff] "Zur
Zeit als Griechenland der Götter satt"
Das Quartett, op. 64 no. 2 [Senff]
"Der Affe, Herr von Putzig"

Kunze, W.
Gebet, op. 115 no. 9 (1890) [Senff]
"O Geist der heil'gen Liebe"

**Lamartine, Alphonse Marie Louis de
Prat de, 1790-1869.**
La prière de femme, op. 83 no. 4 [Bote &
Bock, ca.1871] "Quand on se
rencontre"

**Leixner-Grünberg, Otto von, 1847-
1907.**
Liebeslied, op. 115 no. 6 (1890) [Senff]
"Und bist du auch ferne"

Lemcke, Karl von, 1831-1913.
*Veilchen vom Berg, woran mahnest du
mich?* op. 72 no. 5 (1864) [Senff]
same
Verlust, op. 72 no. 6 (1864) [Senff]
"Ich hatte eine Nachtigall"

Lenau, Nicolaus, 1802-1850.
An den Frühling, op. 76 no. 3 (1867)
[Senff, 1867] "Noch immer Frühling"
Bitte (1891) [Senff]
"Weil auf mir, du dunkles Auge"
Die drei Zigeuner (1891) [Senff]
"Drei Zigeuner fand ich einmal"
Frühlingsblick, op. 76 no. 4 (1867)
[Senff, 1867]
"Durch den Wald, den dunkeln"

**Lermontov, Mikhail Yuryevich, 1814-
1841.**

Der Dolch, op. 36 no. 5 [Spina, 1856-57]
Der Felsen, op. 36 no. 1 [Spina, 1856-
57] "Eine Wolke liess beim Glanz der
Sterne"
Gebet, op. 4 (youthful no.; 1843-44)
[Moscow: Gresser]
Das Schiff, op. 36 no. 3 [Spina, 1856-57]
"Einsam auf blauer Wasserwüste"
Sehnsucht, op. 8 no. 5 (1850) [Senff,
1874] "Gönnt mir goldne Tageshelle"
Wenn deine Stimme mir tönt, op. 36 no. 2
[Spina, 1856-57] same
Die Wolken, op. 36 no. 4 [Spina, 1856-
57] "Wolken am Himmelszelt"

Lingg, Hermann, 1820-1905.
Hüte dich (1881) [Bote & Bock]
"Nachtigall, hüte dich"

Lipiner, Siegfried, 1856-1911.
Was tut's, op. 115 no. 2 (1890) [Senff]
"O lass mich die trunkenen Blicke
erheben"

Löwenstein, Rudolf, 1819-1891.
Abschied, op. 1 no. 5 (1848) [Spina]
"I hab gedacht, dass i allei"
Beim Fenstergehn, op. 1 no. 2 (1848)
[Spina] "Schlafst scho mei Greterl"
Beruhigung, op. 1 no. 6 (1848) [Spina]
"I hat e schön's Schatzerl"
Das gebrochene Herz, op. 1 no. 4 (1848)
[Spina] "I sah mal a Blimle"
Liebeshändel, op. 1 no. 3 (1848) [Spina]
"Mäderl mit dem goldnen Latz"
Unerklärlich, op. 1 no. 1 (1848) [Spina;
A. Cranz]
"Weiss nit, was mir g'scheh"

Maffei, Andrea, 1798-1885.
La prima viola, op. 83 no. 7 [Bote &
Bock, ca.1871]
"Odorosa foriera d'aprile"

**Maïkov, Apollon Nikolayevich, 1821-
1897.**
Elegie, op. 78 no. 8 (1868) [Senff, 1869]
"Wenn stets in stiller Nacht"

**Merezhkovski, Dmitriï Sergyeyevich,
1865-1941.**
O child, dear heart (1891)
Listed in *New Grove;* not located
elsewhere.

Meri
The return (1854)
Listed in *New Grove;* not located
elsewhere.
Poet may be Joseph Méry, 1798-1865.

**Mikhailov, Mikhail Larionovich, 1826-
1865.**
Neugriechisches Lied, op. 78 no. 7
(1868) [Senff, 1869]

RUBINSTEIN, ANTON, 1829-1894
(continued)
Mikhailov, Mikhail Larionovich, 1826-
1865 *(continued)*
"Liebchen, als wir Nachts uns küssten"
Moore, Thomas, 1779-1852.
A dream, op. 83 no. 10 [Bote & Bock,
ca.1871]
"I thought this heart enkindled lay"
Good Night! op. 83 no. 9 [Bote & Bock,
ca.1871]
"Good night! good night! and is it so?"
The tear, op. 83 no. 8 [Bote & Bock,
ca.1871] "On beds of snow the
moonbeam slept"
Mosenthal, Salomon Hermann, Ritter
von, 1821-1877.
Nachhall, op. 33 no. 6 (1856) [Kistner,
1870] "Ich sah' dich einmal"
Musset, Alfred de, 1810-1857.
À Saint-Blaize à la Zuecca, op. 83 no. 2
[Bote & Bock, ca.1871] same
Rappelle-toi quand l'aurore craintive, op.
83 no. 1 [Bote & Bock, ca.1871] same
Romance [St. Petersburg: Bernard]
"Dors pendant que je veille"
BARBERINE.
Chanson de Barberine, op. 83 no. 3
[Bote & Bock, ca.1871]
"Beau chevalier qui partez pour la
guerre"
Oelschläger, Hermann
Mein Herzensschatz (1891) [Senff]
"Wie bist du nur"
Polonsky, Yakov Petrovich, 1819-1898.
Lied, op. 78 no. 9 (1868) [Senff, 1869]
"Wie der Quell ist mein Lied"
The prisoner (ca.1878)
Listed in *New Grove;* not located
elsewhere.
Sinngedicht, op. 78 no. 10 (1868) [Senff,
1869] "Zur Kirche rufet ernst"
Polovtsev, A.
Romance (1849)
Listed in *New Grove;* not located
elsewhere.
Pushkin, Aleksandr Sergeevich, 1799-
1837.
Auf dein Wohl trink'ich, op. 36 no. 8
[Spina] same
Bacchisches Lied [Bote & Bock; Senff]
"Was schweigt unser fröhlicher Chor?"
Der Engel, op. 78 no. 3 (1868) [Senff,
1869] "An Edens Thor ein Engel"
Der Gefangene, op. 78 no. 6 (1868)
[Senff, 1869] "Im Kerker gefangen"

Lied, op. 78 no. 11 (1868) [Senff, 1869]
"Rab' zum Raben fliegt daher"
Der Sturm, op. 78 no. 4 (1868) [Senff,
1869] "Auf steilem Felsen steht"
Vernehmet ihr? op. 36 no. 7 [Spina]
same
DIE ZIGEUNER.
Scene . . . op. 78 no. 12 (1868) [Senff,
1869] "Alter Mann, grimmer Mann"
Rostopchina, Evdokiia, grafinia, 1811-
1858.
Der fallende Stern, op. 36 no. 11 [Spina]
"Er schoss herab"
Sie singt ein Lied, op. 36 no. 10 [Spina]
same
Weht es, heult es trüb', op. 36 no. 12
[Spina] same
Rückert, Friedrich, 1788-1866.
Die Blume der Ergebenheit (1881)
[Bote & Bock]
"Ich bin die Blume im Garten"
Mitternacht (1881) [Bote & Bock]
"Um Mitternacht hab' ich gewacht"
Sacken, Th. von
Die Lerche, op. 33 no. 3 (1856) [Kistner,
1870] "Lerche steiget im Gesang"
Scherer, Georg, 1828-1909.
Am Strande, op. 115 no. 3 (1890) [Senff]
"Ich sass am Strand"
Storm, Theodor, 1817-1888.
Morgens, op. 72 no. 4 (1864) [Senff]
"Nun gieb ein Morgenküsschen"
Strauss, David Friedrich, 1808-1874.
Wem ich dieses klage (1881) [Bote &
Bock] same?
Sturm, Julius Karl Reinholdt, 1816-
1896.
Der Dichter, op. 115 no. 10 (1890)
[Senff]
"Du merkst nicht, wie so flüchtig"
Sukhanov, Mikhail Dmitrievich, 1801-
1843.
The swallow (1849)
Listed in *New Grove;* not located
elsewhere.
Tolstoĭ, Alekseĭ Konstantinovich, Graf,
1817-1875.
Am Meeresstrand, op. 101 no. 3 (1877)
[Senff, 1879] "Es brandet die Welle"
Des Baches Geplauder, op. 101 no. 12
(1877) [Senff, 1879]
"Weithin dehnt sich ein Forst"
Frühling, op. 101 no. 5 (1877) [Senff,
1879] "Lerche wiegt sich im Gesange"
Fürst Rostislav, op. 101 no. 11 (1877)
[Senff, 1879] "Im fremden Land, im
Bett des Stroms"

Hätt' ich das gewusst, hätt' ich das gehant, op. 101 no. 10 [Senff, 1879] same

In stiller Nacht, op. 101 no. 4 (1877) [Senff, 1879] "Es glitten nach rauschendem Regen"

Nebel und Gram, op. 101 no. 2 (1877) [Senff, 1879] "Es wallt und woget schwer"

Sanftes Walten, op. 101 no. 7 (1877) [Senff, 1879] "Wie bei des Zephyrs leisem Hauch"

Schlaf' ein, op. 101 no. 9 (1877) [Senff, 1879] "Schlaf' ein, mein trauernd Lieb"

Vergängliches, op. 101 no. 8 (1877) [Senff, 1879] "Hoch bäumen sich auf in die Lüfte"

Wie es sein muss, op. 101 no. 1 (1877) [Senff, 1879] "Wer da liebt, lieb' überm Maasse"

Die Wölfe, op. 101 no. 6 (1877) [Senff, 1879] "Wenn kein Lied mehr erschallet"

Turgenev, Ivan Sergyeyevich, 1818-1883.

Ballada (1891) [Jurgenson; State Music Publ., 1965] "Pered voevodoĭ molcha on stoit"

Die Erde ruht, op. 36 no. 9 [Spina] same

Spring evening (1885) Listed in **New Grove;** not located elsewhere.

Uhland, Ludwig, 1787-1862.

Morgenlied, op. 33 no. 1 (1856) [Kistner, 1870] "Noch ahnt man kaum"

Unknown

Einen Bruder hatt' ich, einen Geliebten, op. 105 no. 6 (1877) [Bote & Bock] same Translated from Serbish by Th. Hauptner.

Eben brach der Mond durch Wolkenschatten, op. 105 no. 4 (1877) [Bote & Bock] same Translated from Serbish by Th. Hauptner.

Geh' bei Tagesanbruch auf die Strasse, op. 105 no. 10 (1877) [Bote & Bock] same Translated from Serbish by Th. Hauptner.

Gott, O Gott, wo ist, wo ist mein Auserwählter? op. 105 no. 7 [Bote & Bock] same Translated from Serbish by Th. Hauptner.

Herbstgedanken [Schuberth, 1871] "Wenn die Stürme schaurig tosen"

Die Lerche, op. 6 (youthful no.; 1843-44) [Moscow: Gresser]

Die Nachtigall, op. 5 (youthful no.; 1843-44) [Moscow: Gresser]

Rosendufte füllen rings die Lüfte, op. 105 no. 3 (1877) [Bote & Bock] same Translated from Serbish by Th. Hauptner.

Ständchen [Schuberth, 1871] "Durch die laue Nacht"

Warum musst du welken, schöne, Rose, op. 105 no. 2 (1877) [Bote & Bock] same Translated from Serbish by Th. Hauptner.

Weithin rief die Mutter nach der Tochter, op. 105 no. 5 (1877) [Bote & Bock] same Translated from Serbish by Th. Hauptner.

Wie so launisch bist du, O Sonnenschein, op. 105 no. 8 (1877) [Bote & Bock] same Translated from Serbish by Th. Hauptner.

Wie wart ihr fröhlich, gold'ne Mädchentage, op. 105 no. 1 [Bote & Bock] same Translated from Serbish by Th. Hauptner.

Willst du einen Ehemann erkennen, op. 105 no. 9 (1877) [Bote & Bock] same Translated from Serbish by Th. Hauptner.

Vilenkin, Nikolay Maksimovich, 1855-1937.

Serenada (1891) [Jurgenson; State Music Publ., 1965] "Tianutsia po neby tuchi tiazhelye"

Vischer, Friedrich Theodor von, 1807-1887.

Mädchens Abendgedanken (1882) [Bote & Bock] "Wer der Meine wohl wird werden"

Weiden, E.

Zuruf aus der Ferne, op. 2 (youthful no.; 1841-42) [Cöln: Schloss]

Woskresensky

O frage nicht, op. 36 no. 6 [Spina, 1856-57) same

Zhukovski, Vasiliĭ Andreyevich, 1783-1852.

Das Blättchen, op. 8 no. 3 (1850) [Senff, 1874] "Vom Freundeszweig getrennt"

COMPOSER Poet *Title* "First Line"

RUBINSTEIN, ANTON, 1829-1894
  (*continued*)
  Zhukovski, Vasiliĭ Andreyevich, 1783-
  1852 (*continued*)
    Die Blume, op. 8 no. 4 (1850) [Senff,
      1874] "O Blümlein, das den
      Wiesenrand einst zierte"
    Frühlingsgefühl, op. 8 no. 2 (1850)
      [Senff, 1874]
      "O du leichter, loser Wind"
    Der Traum, op. 8 no. 1 (1850) [Senff,
      1874] "Am Wiesenhügel schlummert'
      ich"
Rucheĭ see Chamisso **MEDTNER**
  Die Quelle
"Rude vento, che diffondi in suon di pianto"
  see Canto funebre Shelley **RESPIGHI**
Rudolf, Carl, pseud. *see* Gottschall, Rudolf
  von, 1823-1909.
Rudolphi, Karoline, 1754-1811.
  LOEWE *Morgenlied*
  ZELTER *An die welke Rose*
Rudulph, Mimi, 1923-
  KRENEK *Two silent watchers*
Rüberettig see Häring **LOEWE**
Rübezahl see Hamerling **JENSEN**
Rückblick see Krenek **KRENEK**
Rückblick see Müller, Wilhelm
  SCHUBERT
Rückert, Friedrich, 1788-1866.
  BARTÓK *Herr! der du alles wohl gemacht*
  BERG
    Ferne Lieder
    Ich will die Fluren meiden
  BRAHMS
    Gestillte Sehnsucht
    Mit vierzig Jahren
  FRANZ
    Er ist gekommen
    Ich hab' in deinem Auge
    Liebesfrühling
    Ständchen
    Vom Auge zum Herzen
    Wiedersehen
  HINDEMITH
    Das Ganze, nicht das Einzelne
    Vier Lieder
  JENSEN *Canzonette*
  LISZT *Ich liebe dich*
  LOEWE
    Abendlied
    Bescheidung
    Die Blume der Ergebung
    Dem Allmächtigen
    Des fremden Kindes heiliger Christ
    Des Glockenthürmers Töchterlein

  Die Göttin im Putzzimmer
  Die Gottesmauer
  Die Herzensrose
  Hinkende Jamben
  Ich und mein Gevatter
  In der Kirche
  Irrlichter
  Jungfräulein Annika
  Kind und Mädchen
  Kleiner Haushalt
  O süsse Mutter
  Der Papagei
  Das Pfarrjüngferchen
  Die Riesen und die Zwerge
  Süsses Begräbnis
  Der Traum der Wittwe
  Traumlicht
  Der Weichdorn
  Das Wunder auf der Flucht
  MUSORGSKIĬ *Strannik*
  PFITZNER
    Herbsthauch
    Warum sind deine Augen denn so nass
  REGER
    Widmung
    Winterahnung
  RUBINSTEIN
    Die Blume der Ergebenheit
    Mitternacht
  SCHUBERT
    Dass sie hier gewesen
    Sei mir gregrüsst!
  SCHUMANN
    Aus den "Östlichen Rosen"
    Die Blume der Ergebung
    Glockentürmers Töchterlein
    Jasminenstrauch
    Schneeglöckchen
    Volksliedchen
    Widmung
    Zum Schluss
  STRAUSS
    Gestern war ich Atlas
    Ich sehe wie in einem Spiegel
    Im Sonnenschein
    Morgenrot
    Ein Obdach gegen Sturm und Regen
    Die sieben Siegel
    Und dann nicht mehr
    Vom künftigen Alter
  WOLF
    Frühling, Liebster
    So wahr die Sonne scheinet
    Die Spinnerin
  KEHR EIN BEI MIR.
    SCHUBERT *Du bist die Ruh*

LACHENS UND WEINENS GRUND.
 SCHUBERT *Lachen und Weinen*
LIEBESFRÜHLING.
 FRANZ *Die Perle*
 JENSEN *Da ich dich einmal gefunden*
 LOEWE *Jünglings Gebet*
 REGER *Der Himmel hat eine Träne*
  geweint
 SCHUMANN
  Flügel! Flügel!
  Der Himmel hat eine Thräne geweint
  Ich hab' in mich gesogen den Frühling
   treu
  Liebster, deine Worte stehlen
  Lieder der Braut
   Two settings: Op. 25 no. 11 and op.
   25 no. 12.
  Mein schöner Stern!
  Meine Töne still und heiter
  O Freund, mein Schirm, mein Schutz!
  O ihr Herren
  O Sonn', O Meer, O Rose!
  Rose, Meer und Sonne sind ein Bild
 STRAUSS *Anbetung*
SCHWANENGESANG.
 LASSEN *Abendglockenläuten*
VOM KÜNFTIGEN ALTER.
 SCHUBERT *Greisengesang*
ZEISIG.
 LOEWE *Zeislein*
Rückkehr see Eichendorff **WOLF**
Rückkehr see Leuthold **SCHOECK**
Rückleben see Uhland **STRAUSS**
Rückweg see Mayrhofer **SCHUBERT**
Rüeger, Armin
 SCHOECK *Bei der Kirche*
Rüling, Georg Ernst von, 1748-1807.
 LOEWE *Dich soll mein Lied erheben*
Ruelle, Jules, d. 1892.
 MASSENET
  Enchantement!
  Sérénade aux mariés
  La vie d'une rose
Ruf vom Berge see Treitschke
 BEETHOVEN
"Ruft die Mutter, ruft der Tochter" *see*
  Mädchenfluch, Nach dem Serbischen
  Kapper **BRAHMS**
"Ruh' von schmerzensreichen Mühen aus" *see*
  Requiem Anon. **SCHUMANN**
Ruhe see Evers **REGER**
Ruhe see Goethe **ZELTER**
Ruhe, meine Seele see Henckell **STRAUSS**
"Ruhe, süss Liebchen, im Schatten der grauen
  dämmernden Nacht" *see Schlaflied* Tieck
 SPOHR

"Ruhe Süssliebchen" *see Schlummerlied*
 Tieck **FRANZ**
Ruhe, Süssliebchen see Tieck **BRAHMS**
Der Ruhelose see Huber, B. **KILPINEN**
Ruheplatz see Anacreon **SCHOECK**
Ruhetal see Uhland **SCHOECK**
Ruhethal see Uhland **SAINT-SAËNS**
"Ruhig ist des Todes Schlummer" *see Lied am*
  Grabe Berlepsch **LOEWE**
"Ruh'n in Frieden" *see Am Tage aller Seelen*
  Jacobi **SCHUBERT**
Une ruine coquille vide see Eluard
 POULENC
Die Ruinen see Reinbeck **WEBER** *Romanze:*
  Die Ruinen
Le ruisseau see Paliard **MILHAUD**
Ruiz de Alarcón y Mendoza, Juan, 1581-
 1639.
 WOLF *Nun bin ich dein*
Rumianoĭ zareĭu pokrylsia vostok see
 Pushkin **PROKOFIEV**
En runa see Ullman **KILPINEN**
"Rund um mich Nacht, ich irr' allein" *see*
  Kolma's Klage Macpherson **SCHUBERT**
Rundgesang auf dem Wasser see Voss
 ZELTER
Rundgesang beim Rheinwein see Voss
 ZELTER
Rundgesang im Freien see Recke
  MANCHERLEI FREUDEN. **LOEWE**
Ein Rundum (An eine grosse Fürstin) see
 Weckherlin **KRENEK**
Runeberg, Johann Ludvig, 1804-1877.
 SIBELIUS
  Arioso
  Blommans öde
  Drömmen
  Fåfäng önskan
  Fågelfängaren
  Flickan kom ifrån sin älsklings möte
  Den första kyssen
  Hennes budskap
  Hjärtats morgon
  Hundra vägar
  Hvem styrde hit din väg?
  Jägargossen
  Kyssens hopp
  Morgonen
  Norden
  Se'n har jag ej frågat mera
  Serenade
  Sippan
  Sommarnatten
  Till Frigga
  Törnet
  Under strandens granar
  Våren flyktar hastigt

Rupprecht, Johann Baptist, 1776-1846.
  BEETHOVEN *Merkenstein*
"The rustling nightfall strews my gown with
  roses" *see Along the stream* Li Po
  HESELTINE
RUTHENISCHE LIEDER: No. 2. Nane. *see*
  Mei *Detskaia pesenka* **MUSORGSKIĭ**
Rutterkin see Skelton, J. **HESELTINE**
"Rutterkin is come unto our town" *see*
  Rutterkin Skelton, J. **HESELTINE**
Ruy Blas see Hugo **CHABRIER**
RUY BLAS. see Hugo
  An die Geliebte **SPOHR**
Ruže see Mužik **MARTINŮ** *The rose*
Rycz, burzo! see Miciński **SZYMANOWSKI**
Rydberg, Abraham Viktor *see* Rydberg,
  Viktor, 1828-1895.

Rydberg, Viktor, 1828-1895.
  SIBELIUS
    Harpolekaren och hans son
    Höstkväll
    I natten
    Kyssen
    På verandan vid havet
    Vattenplask
    Vi ses igen
Rypáček, František J.
  JANÁČEK *Jarní píseň*
Rytsar' see Wilde, Ch. **BALAKIREV** *Rȳsar*
"Rzeko z cudzoziemców strony" *see Smutna
  rzeka* Witwicki **CHOPIN**
"Róży mój gniady, ziemie grzebie" *see Wojak*
  Witwicki **CHOPIN**

S

" 's is nichts mit den alten Weibern" *see Alte
  Weiber* Nicolai **WEBER**
's ist nicht dein holdes Angesicht see Burns
  LASSEN *It's nae thy bonnieface*
" 's ist wahr, mit blanken Scheiben" *see
  Der Apotheker als Nebenbuhler* Gruppe
  LOEWE
S kukloĭ see Musorgskiĭ **MUSORGSKIĭ**
S nianeĭ see Musorgskiĭ **MUSORGSKIĭ**
" 's sind heute dreiunddreissig Jahr" *see Der
  gefangene Admiral* Strachwitz **LOEWE**
" 's war einer, dem's zu Herzen ging" *see
  Tragische Geschichte* Chamisso
  PFITZNER
" 's war mal 'ne Katzenkönigin" *see
  Die Katzenkönigin* Chamisso **LOEWE**
Så dansa! see Cnattingius, Thor
  KILPINEN
Så gamla äro alla moln see Lagerkvist
  KILPINEN
Sa mykkä matkalainen maan see
  Koskenniemi **KILPINEN**
"Sa neito nuori, sa ruususuu" *see Kesäisenä
  päivänä* Jalkanen **KILPINEN**
"Saa du ham min lille Dreng" *see Modersorg*
  Richardt **GRIEG**

Saa du Knøsen, som strøg forbi see
  Drachmann **GRIEG**
Saar, Ferdinand von, 1833-1906.
  LISZT *Des Tages laute Stimmen schweigen*
"Der Sabbath hebt, ein grössrer Sabbath an"
  see Sang des Moses Giesebrecht
  LOEWE
Sabre en main see Renaud **SAINT-SAËNS**
Sacken, Th. von
  RUBINSTEIN *Die Lerche*
The sacred flame see Coleridge **IRELAND**
"Sad am I on autumn mornings" *see Autumn
  tears* Ady **BARTÓK**
Sad river see Witwicki **CHOPIN** *Smutna rzeka*
A sad song see Fletcher *THE MAID'S
  TRAGEDY* (1619): Aspatia's song.
  HESELTINE
Sada-lhe, 13th cent.
  GRIFFES *Landscape*
Sade, Comte Donatien Alphonse
  François de, 1740-1814.
  THOMSON *Commentaire sur Saint
    Jérome*
Sade, Marquis de *see* Sade, Comte
  Donatien Alphonse François de, 1740-
  1814.

Sadly rustle the leaves see Pleshcheyev
MUSORGSKÏÏ *List'ia shumeli unylo*
Sä menit see Törmänen **KILPINEN**
Der Säemann see Morgenstern **KILPINEN**
Säerspruch see Meyer **PFITZNER**
Säf, säf, susa see Fröding *INGALILL.*
SIBELIUS
"Säg hvarför är du sa ledsen i dag" *see Svarta*
rosor Josephson, E. **SIBELIUS**
"Säg, varför giva vi de kval åt världen" *see*
Svanesång Josephson, E. **KILPINEN**
Der Sänger see Cornelius **LASSEN**
Der Sänger see Goethe *WILHELM*
MEISTER. **LOEWE, SCHUBERT,**
WOLF, ZELTER
DER SÄNGER, no. 1
SCHOECK Leuthold *Leidenschaft*
DER SÄNGER, no. 2
SCHOECK Leuthold *Muttersprache*
DER SÄNGER, no. 3
SCHOECK Leuthold *Liederfrühling*
DER SÄNGER, no. 4
SCHOECK Leuthold *Waldeinsamkeit*
DER SÄNGER, no. 5
SCHOECK Leuthold *Vorwurf*
DER SÄNGER, no. 6
SCHOECK Leuthold *Rechtfertigung*
DER SÄNGER, no. 7
SCHOECK Leuthold *Abkehr*
DER SÄNGER, no. 8
SCHOECK Leuthold *Waldvögelein*
DER SÄNGER, no. 9
SCHOECK Leuthold *Aus dem Süden*
DER SÄNGER, no. 10
SCHOECK Leuthold *Riviera*
DER SÄNGER, no. 11
SCHOECK Leuthold *Nacht, Muse und*
Tod
DER SÄNGER, no. 12
SCHOECK Leuthold *Sapphische Strophe*
DER SÄNGER, no. 13
SCHOECK Leuthold *Sonnenuntergang*
DER SÄNGER, no. 14
SCHOECK Leuthold *Warnung*
DER SÄNGER, no. 15
SCHOECK Leuthold *Heimweh*
DER SÄNGER, no. 16
SCHOECK Leuthold *Rückkehr*
DER SÄNGER, no. 17
SCHOECK Leuthold *Einst*
DER SÄNGER, no. 18
SCHOECK Leuthold *An meine*
Grossmutter
DER SÄNGER, no. 19
SCHOECK Leuthold *Trauer*
DER SÄNGER, no. 20
SCHOECK Leuthold *Der Waldsee*

DER SÄNGER, no. 21
SCHOECK Leuthold *Im Klosterkeller*
DER SÄNGER, no. 22
SCHOECK Leuthold *Trinklied*
DER SÄNGER, no. 23
SCHOECK Leuthold *Distichen*
DER SÄNGER, no. 24
SCHOECK Leuthold *Spruch*
DER SÄNGER, no. 25
SCHOECK Leuthold *Unmut*
DER SÄNGER, no. 26
SCHOECK Leuthold *Trost*
Der Sänger am Felsen see Pichler
SCHUBERT
Der Sänger der Vorwelt see Schiller
ZELTER
Der Sänger und der Maler see Anon.
WEBER
"Der Sänger zog durch Wald und Flur" *see*
Maria Unknown **SPOHR**
Two settings: Op. 139 no. 2 and WoO 107.
Sängers Gebet see Redwitz *AMARANTH.*
LOEWE
Sängers Morgenlied see Körner **SCHUBERT**
Two settings: D. 163 and D. 165.
SÄNGERS REISE. see Winkler
Lied in der Fremde **WEBER**
Sängers Trost see Kerner **SCHUMANN**
Sängers Wanderlied see Körner **LOEWE**
Saenk kun dit Høved see Jørgensen
NIELSEN
Den Saerde see Vinje **GRIEG**
Saeta en forma de Salve a la Virgen de la
Esperanza see Alvarez Quintero, S.
TURINA
"Säuselnde Lüfte wehend so mild" *see*
Frühlingssehnsucht Rellstab **SCHUBERT**
Säusle, liebe Myrthe see Brentano
STRAUSS
Säv, säv, susa see Fröding *INGALILL.*
SIBELIUS *Säf, säf, susa*
Saffo *see* Sappho, 625? B.C.-570 B.C.
"Sag' an, du Träumer am lichten Tag" *see*
Im Lenz Mahler **MAHLER**
Sag' an, O lieber Vogel mein see Hebbel
SCHUMANN
"Sag an, was hinauf zur Drachenkluft die
buntbewegte Menge ruft" *see*
Der Drachenfels Lutze **LOEWE**
"Sag an, wer lehrt dich Lieder" *see*
Geheimnis. An Franz Schubert Mayrhofer
SCHUBERT
Sag es nicht see Wiener, Oskar **REGER**
Sag mir! Sag mir, wer einst die Uhren erfand
see Heine **FRANZ**
Sag', O sag', warum, liebes Mägdelein see
Unknown **MUSORGSKÏÏ**
Otchego, skazhi, dusha devĩtsa

COMPOSER Poet *Title* "First Line"

"Sag, warum bist du so traurig heut?" *see*
  Schwarze Rosen Josephson, E. **DELIUS**
"Sag', welch wunderbare Träume" *see Träume*
  Wesendonck **WAGNER**
SAGESSE. see Verlaine
  Le ciel **CARPENTER**
  Le ciel est, par-dessus la toit **DELIUS,**
    SÉVERAC
  Prison **FAURÉ**
  Le son du cor s'afflige **DEBUSSY**
  Le son du cor s'afflige vers les bois
    LOEFFLER
Sagesse see Verlaine **STRAVINSKIĬ**
Saget mir auf welchem Pfade see George
  DAS BUCH DER HÄNGENDEN GÄRTEN.
  SCHÖNBERG
"Sagt es niemand, nur den Weisen" *see Selige*
  Sehnsucht Goethe **SCHOECK, ZELTER**
Sagt ihm, dass er zu mir komme see Anon.
  WOLF
"Sagt mir an, was schmunzelt ihr?" *see*
  Reigen Voss **WEBER**
Sagt, seid Ihr es, feiner Herr see Anon.
  WOLF
"Sagt, wo sind die Vortrefflichen hin" *see*
  Der Sänger der Vorwelt Schiller **ZELTER**
"Sah' dem edlen Bildnis in des Auges" *see*
  Magyarisch Daumer **BRAHMS**
"Sah ein Knab' ein Röslein stehn" *see*
  Heidenröslein Goethe **SCHUBERT**
Sahst vorbei mit dem Glutblick du see
  Drachmann **GRIEG** *Saa du Knøsen, som*
  strøg forbi
Sailing see Öhqvist **SIBELIUS** *Segelfahrt*
Sailor' the cat see Musorgskiĭ
  MUSORGSKIĬ *Kot matros*
"Saint Anthony of Padua whom I bear in
  effigy" *see A prayer to Saint Anthony of*
  Padua Symons **HESELTINE**
"Saint Blaise qui vis aux cieux" *see À Saint-*
  Blaise Ronsard **SAINT-SAËNS**
"Saint Jérome racconte" *see Commentaire sur*
  Saint Jérome Sade **THOMSON**
Saint-Beuve *see* Sainte-Beuve, Charles
  Augustin, 1804-1869.
Sainte see Mallarmé **RAVEL**
Une sainte en son auréole see Verlaine
  FAURÉ
"Sainte, Sainte, quand m'opprime la tentation
  du péché" *see A une sainte le jour de sa*
  fête Jacob, M. **SAUGUET**
Sainte Thérèse prie see Sylvestre, Pierre
  MASSENET
Sainte-Beuve, Charles Augustin, 1804-
  1869.
  GRIFFES *Sur ma lyre l'autre foix*
  SAINT-SAËNS *Dans les coins bleus*

SAINT-SAËNS, CAMILLE, 1835-1921.
Aguétant, Pierre
  Angélus (1918) [Durand, 1918]
    "Les clochers, souverains du soir"
    Also voice & orchestra.
  Où nous avons aimé (1918) [Durand,
    1918] same
    Also voice & orchestra.
Aicard, Jean François Victor, 1848-
1921.
  Vogue, vogue la galère (ca.1877)
    [Richault; Durand] same
    Accompaniment for piano with
    harmonium ad lib.
Anon.
  À la lune (1856) [unpubl.?]
  Alla riva del tebro (ca.1860) [G.
    Hartmann; Durand, 1899] same
    Arrangement, by Saint-Saëns, of
    Palestrina madrigal.
  Ariel (1841) [unpubl.?]
  Canzonetta toscana (ca.1863) [G.
    Hartmann; Durand]
  La chasse du Burgrave [Richault]
    Scène for mezzo-soprano & piano.
  Dans ce beau mois [unpubl.?]
  L'echo de la harpe [unpubl.?]
  Heureux qui du coeur de Marie (ca.1860)
    [Richault? 1865]
  Le lever de la lune (1855) [Richault;
    Durand] "Ainsi qu'une jeune beauté"
  Nous qu'en ces lieux (ca.1844) [unpubl.?]
  Pourquoi t'exiler (1858) [unpubl.?]
  Reçois mes hommages (ca.1844)
    [unpubl.?]
  Reine des cieux (ca.1860) [Richault,
    1865; Durand, 188_] same
  Tandis que sur vos ans (1844) [unpubl.?]
Audigier, Georges
  Le fleuve (1906) [Durand, 1906]
    "Je voudrais être un fleuve calme"
Banville, Théodore Faullain de, 1823-
1891.
  Les fées (1892) [Durand, 1906]
    "Ma mie à son toit fidèle"
    Accompaniment for piano, 4 hands;
    also voice & orchestra.
  AMÉTHYSTES.
    Le rossignol (1892) [Durand, 1901]
      "Vois, sur les violettes"
  ODELETTES.
    Aimons-nous (1892) [Durand, 1892]
      same
      Also voice & orchestra.

Barbier, Marie Anne, d.1742.
CONTES BLANCS.
La sérénité (1893) [Durand, 1895]
"Je suis l'inaltérable image"
Belleau, Rémy, 1527?-1577.
Avril (ca.1921) [Durand, 1921]
"Avril, l'honneur et des bois"
Bergerat, Émile, 1845-1923.
Romance pour *** (1892) [unpubl.?]
Voice & harp.
Boileau-Despréaux, Nicolas, 1636-
1711.
Chanson à boire du vieux temps (1885)
[Durand] "Philosophes rêveurs, qui
pensez tout savoir"
Bordèse, Stéphan, b. 1847.
Présage de la croix (1890) [Durand]
"Alors vers sa douzième année"
Boyer, Georges, 1850-1931.
Amour viril (1891) [Durand, 1891?]
"Madame, vous voyez des hommes"
Cazalis, Henri, 1840-1909.
Danse macabre (1873) [Enoch; Durand]
"Zit et zig et zig, la mort en cadence"
2nd version: voice & orchestra; 3rd
version: orchestra.
CHANSON TRISTE.
Dans ton coeur (1872) [Durand, 1884]
same
Charles, Duke of Orleans, 1391-1465.
Primavera [unpubl.?]
Written to the same words as *Temps
nouveau.*
Temps nouveau (1921) [Durand, 1921]
"Le temps a laissé son manteau"
Text the same as the song *Primavera.*
Collerville, Vicomte de
Les fleurs (1892) [unpubl.?]
Coppée, François Édouard Joachim,
1842-1908.
Marquise vous souvenez-vous? (ca.1869)
[G. Hartmann, 1870] same
Ronde (1885) [unpubl.?]
Croze, J. L.
Là-bas (1892) [Durand]
"Par delà la mer d'azur"
Peut-être (1893) [Durand, 1894]
"Près de toi garde-moi toute"
Pourquoi rester seulette? (1894)
[Durand] same
Dante Aligheri, 1265-1321.
La porta dell'inferno (ca.1854) [unpubl.?]
Davis, F.
My land (1871) [Boosey, 1871]
New Grove says Davis, T., author of
text.

Desbordes-Valmore, Marceline
Félicité Josèphe, 1786-1859.
Le soir (1841) [Durand, 1896]
Deschoulières, Mme.
Idylle (1852) [unpubl.?]
Distel, Camille
Etoile du matin (ca.1860) [Durand, 1869]
"Quand l'aube va paritre"
Docquois, Georges, 1863-1927.
Âme triste [Durand, 1915]
"Qui saura t'émouvoir, âme triste"
Amoroso [Durand, 1915] "Elle me
demandait: 'Que de viennent les roses' "
Douceur [Durand, 1915]
"Je t'aime tant, frêle mignonne"
Jour de pluie (1914) [Durand, 1915]
"Le jour s'assombrit, lugubre et glacé"
Mai [Durand, 1915]
"Mai! Les arbres du verger"
Pâques [Durand, 1915]
"Pâques! Pâques!"
Petite main [Durand, 1915] "Dans mon
indigne main lorsque je t'emprisonne"
Prélude [Durand, 1915]
"Loin du bruit des humaines fêtes"
Reviens (Epilogue) [Durand, 1915]
"Amour, amour cruel et tendre"
Silence [Durand, 1915]
"A quoi bon vouloir m'exprimer"
Fiéffé, Eugène, 1821-1862.
Le rendez-vous (1851) [unpubl.?]
Fournier, Paul, 1853-1935.
Honneur à l'Amérique (1917) [Durand]
Victoire (1918) [Durand, 1918]
Vive la France (1914) [Durand, 1915]
Gautier, Théophile, 1811-1872.
Lamento (1850) [unpubl.?]
Ginner, Isaac
Night song to preciosa (1879) [Boosey,
1879]
Haïdar-Pacha, Prince
L'etoile (1907) [Durand, 1907] "Etoile, Ô
feu du soir qui te lèves la première"
Hugo, Victor Marie, comte, 1802-1885.
À quoi bon entendre les oiseaux des bois
(ca.1869) [[G. Hartmann, 1870] same
Le chant de ceux qui s'en vont sur mer
(1868) [G. Hartmann; Choudens, 1870]
"Adieu, patrie, l'onde est en furie!"
La cloche (ca.1855) [Richault; Durand]
"Seule en ta sombre tour aux faîtes
dentelés"
Also voice & orchestra.
La coccinelle (1868) [Durand] "Elle me
dit: quelque chose me tourmente"
L'enlèvement (1865) [Richault, 1866;
Durand] "Si tu veux, faisons un rêve"

SAINT-SAËNS, CAMILLE, 1835-1921
(continued)
Hugo, Victor Marie, comte, 1802-1885
(continued)
Also voice & orchestra.
Extase (ca.1860) [G. Flaxland; Durand]
"Puisque j'ai mis ma lèvre à ta coupe"
Also voice & orchestra.
Une flûte invisible (1885) [Durand]
With flute obbligato.
Guitare (1851)[Choudens] "Comment,
disaient-ils, avec nos nacelles"
Le matin (ca.1864) [Richault; Durand]
"L'aurore s'allume"
La pas d'armes du roi Jean (1852)
[Richault, 1855; Durand]
"Par Saint Gilles, Viens nous-en"
Also voice & orchestra.
Rêverie (1851) [Richault; Durand]
"Puis qu'ici-bàs toute âme"
Also voice & orchestra.
Si vous n'avez rien à me dire (1870)
[Durand] same
Soirée en mer (1862) [G. Flaxland;
Durand]
"Près du pêcheur qui ruisselle"
Suzette et Suzon (1888) [Durand, 1906]
"J'adore Suzette"
CHANTS DU CRÉPUSCULE.
S'il est un charmant gazon (1915, 2nd
version) [Durand, 1915] same
First version entitled *Chanson.*
LES ORIENTALES.
L'attente (ca.1855) [Richault; Durand]
"Monte, écureuil, monte au grand
chêne"
Also voice & orchestra.
La Fontaine, Jean de, 1621-1695.
La cigale et la fourmi [Arno Volk
Verlag, 1958]
"La cigale ayant chanté 'Tout l'été' "
In **Anthology of Music,** v. 16
(Cologne: Arno Volk Verlag, 1958).
Lamartine, Alphonse Marie Louis de Prat de, 1790-1869.
L'automne (ca.1852) [unpubl.?]
Le golfe de Baya (ca.1847) [unpubl.?]
Le lac (1850) [Richault]
Le poète mourant (1851) [unpubl.?]
Leche, Renée de
Papillons (1918) [Durand, 1918]
"Où t'envoles-tu, si, frêle, petit
papillon léger"
Also voice & orchestra.
Lecocq, Charles, 1832-1918.
Elle (1901) [Durand, 1901] "Un regard
caressant, une bouche rieuse"

Legouvé, Ernest, 1807-1903.
Maria Lucrezia (1868) [G. Hartmann]
"Le doux printemps vient d'éclater!"
La mort d'Ophélie (ca.1857) [Richault,
1858; Durand]
"Au bord d'un torrent, Ophélie"
Lemaire, Ferdinand
Souvenances (ca.1858) [Richault;
Durand]
Tristesse (ca.1868) [Richault; Durand]
"De tristesse amère et profonde"
Lenfaut, A.
Heures passées (1865) [unpubl.?]
Liguori, Alfonso Maria de', Saint, 1696-1787.
La Madonna col bambino (ca.1855)
[Mme. Mayens-Couvreur, 1868;
Durand]
Lombard, F.
Bergeronnette (1850) [unpubl.?]
Mahot, A.
Fière beauté (1893) [Durand]
"Vous avez la splendeur sereine des
grandes dames d'autrefois"
Also voice & orchestra.
Mangeot, L.
Sérénade, op. 15 [Choudens] "La nuit est
descendue, voici l'heure attendue"
Also voice & chamber ensemble or
voice & orchestra.
Martin, Paul
Les sapins (1914) [Durand, 1914]
"Sombres et fiers sapins, j'admire en
vous la race"
Mendès, Catulle Abraham, 1841-1909.
Clair de lune (ca.1865) [Richault;
Durand]
"Dans la forêt que orée un rêve"
Molière, Jean Baptiste Poquelin, 1622-1673.
Madrigal (1897) [unpubl.?]
Cited as song in **New Grove;** Durand
catalogue says from **Psyché** de
Moliere, for tenor & men's chorus.
Not seen.
Moréas, Jean, 1856-1910.
L'arbre (1903) [Durand, 1903]
"Sur la plaine sans fin"
Musset, Alfred de, 1810-1857.
Chanson de Fortunio [unpubl.?]
Noailles, Anna Elisabeth (de Brancovan), comtesse de, 1876-1933.
Soir romantique (1907) [Durand, 1907]
"Eté, j'ai cherché trop longtemps"
Violons dans le soir (1907) [Durand]
Accompaniment for violin & piano.

Penmarch, G. de
  Le sommeil des fleurs (1855) [Richault;
  Durand] "Le soir, quand le soleil
  l'horizon s'incline"
Perpina, D. Francisco
  DESEO DE AMOR.
    Désir d'amour (1901) [Durand, 1901]
      "Un vide étrange et martel est dans
      mon âme"
        Also bass & orchestra as
        "Romanza."
Pressat, André
  Soeur Anne (1903) [Durand, 1903] "Sur
  l'aîle des fuyantes grives las! hélas!"
Quinault, Jeanne-Francoise, 1700?-
  1783.
  Nocturne (1900) [Durand, 1915]
    "O nuit! que j'aime ton mystère"
Regnault, Mme. Félix
  Ne l'oubliez pas (ca.1915) [Durand,
  1915] "Mes frères, ne l'oubliez pas"
Renaud, Armand, 1836-1895.
  Au cimetière (ca.1870) [Durand, 1872]
    "Assis sur cette blanche tombe"
  La brise (ca.1870) [Durand, 1872]
    "Comme des chevreaux piqués parun
    taon"
  Sabre en main (ca.1870) [Durand, 1872]
    "J'ai mis à mon cheval sa bride"
  La solitaire (1870) [Durand, 1872] "Ô
    fier jeune homme, Ô tueur de gazelles"
  La splendeur vide (1870) [Durand, 1872]
    "J'ai construit dans mon âme"
  Tournoiement (ca.1870) [Durand, 1872]
    "Sans que nulle part je séjourne"
Ronsard, Pierre de, 1524-1585.
  À Saint-Blaise (1921) [Durand, 1921]
    "Saint Blaise qui vis aux cieux"
  L'amant malheureux (1921) [Durand,
  1921] "A ce malheur qui jour et jour
  me point"
  L'amour blessé (1921) [Durand, 1921]
    "Le petit enfant Amour"
  L'amour oyseau (1907) [Durand, 1907]
    "Un enfant de dans un bocage"
  Grasselette et maigrelette (1920)
  [Durand, 1921]
    "Une jeune pucelette, Pucelette
    grassouillette"
Sainte-Beuve, Charles Augustin, 1804-
  1869.
  Dans les coins bleus (1880) [Durand]
    same
Saint-Saëns, Camille, 1835-1921.
  Les cloches de la mer (1900) [Durand,
  1906]
    "Parfois, pendant les longues heures"
    Also voice & orchestra.

Désir de l'Orient (1871) [Durand, 1895]
  "Là-bas, dans un ciel de turquoise"
Guitares et mandolines (1890) [Durand]
  same
La libellule (1894) [Durand, 1894]
  "Près de l'étang, sur la prêle vole"
  Also voice & orchestra.
Sonnet (1898) [Durand] "Ce tendre
  sentiment, dans mon âme il habite"
Thème varié (1900) [Durand]
St. Chaffray, Édouard
  Toi (ca.1856) [Richault]
Stuart, Paul
  Primavera (1893) [Durand]
    "Salut, Ô gai printemps!"
Tastu, Mme. Amable, 1798-1885.
  La feuille du peuplier (1853) [Richault;
  Durand] "Feuille mobile et tremblante"
  Also voice & orchestra.
  La maman (ca.1841) [unpubl.?]
  Plainte (ca.1855) [Richault; Durand]
    "Ô monde! Ô vie! Ô temps!"
    Also voice & orchestra.
  Télesille (1849) [unpubl.?]
Tennyson, Alfred Tennyson, 1st
  baron, 1809-1892.
  A voice by the cedar tree (1871)
    [Augener, 1871] same
    Also published in **Songs from the
    published writings of Alfred
    Tennyson** (London: C. Kegan Paul,
    1880), 305.
Tranchant, Alfred
  Madeleine (1892) [Durand]
    "Elle est gentille, Madeleine"
  Si je l'osais (1898) [Durand]
  Vive Paris, vive la France (1893)
    [Margueritat, 1894]
    Unison song.
Uhland, Ludwig, 1787-1862.
  Antwort [unpubl.?]
  Ruhethal (1854) [unpubl.?]
Unknown
  Fomicacicadéide (1908) [unpubl.?]
    Holograph in Kreis- und
    Studienbibliothek, Dillingen an der
    Donau, Germany.
Vauquelin de La Fresnaye, Jean,
  1536-1607.
  Villanelle (1921) [Durand, 1921]
    "Nous sommes filles du village"
Verlaine, Paul, 1844-1896.
  ROMANCES SANS PAROLES.
    Le vent dans la plaine (1912) [Durand,
    1913] "C'est l'extase langoureuse"
Zamacoïs, Miguel, 1866-1939.
  La française [**Le petit Parisien,** 1915]

Saint-Saëns, Camille, 1835-1921.
  SAINT-SAËNS
    Les cloches de la mer
    Désir de l'Orient
    Guitares et mandolines
    La libellule
    Sonnet
    Thème varié
Saisinko käeltä kielen see Kanteletar
  KILPINEN
Le sais-tu? see Bordèse **MASSENET**
"Sais-tu bien le destin" *see Légende* Marès
  AUBERT
Die Saiten weiss ich zu rühren see
  Mommsen **KRENEK**
Saix, Guillot de
  MASSENET *La verdadera vida*
Sakonskaya, N.
  PROKOFIEV *Sladkaĩa pesenka*
Salamander see Lemcke **BRAHMS**
SALAMMBÔ. see Musorgskiĭ, M.
  Pesn' Baleartsa **MUSORGSKIĭ**
Salinum see Leconte de Lisle **HAHN**
Salis-Seewis, Johann Gaudenz, Freiherr
  von, 1762-1834.
  LOEWE *Das Fischergewerbe*
  SCHOECK *Das Grab*
  SCHUBERT
    Abschied von der Harfe
    Die Einsiedelei
      Two settings: D. 393 and D. 563.
    Der Entfernten
    Fischerlied
      Two settings: D. 351 and D. 562.
    Gesang an die Harmonie
    Das Grab
      Three settings: D. 330, D. 377, and D.
      569.
    Der Herbstabend
    Herbstlied
    Der Jüngling an der Quelle
    Lied
    Pflügerlied
    Wehmut
  SPOHR *Lied beim Rundetanz*
Sallet, Friedrich von, 1812-1843.
  PFITZNER *Herbstlied*
  STRAUSS
    Die erwachte Rose
    Der Morgen
The salley gardens see Yeats **IRELAND**
"Sally is gone that was so kindly" *see*
  Ha'nacker mill Belloc, Hilaire
  HESELTINE
Sally's smile see Goodman **ROREM**

Salmon, André, 1881-
  SAUGUET *Cinq mars, à la mémoire de*
    Max Jacob
Salome see Keller, G. **BRAHMS**
"Salt laden, sad with cry of ships" *see*
  The east riding Chilman **IRELAND**
SALT WATER BALLADS. see Masefield
  Sorrow of Mydath **GRIFFES**
"La Saltimbanque aux yeux pleins de
  douceur" *see Parade* Banville **AURIC**
Saltimbanques see Apollinaire **MARTINŮ**
  NB: Unpublished; text not compared with
    the following settings.
Saltimbanques see Apollinaire *ALCOOLS.*
  HONEGGER, RIVIER
Salus, Hugo, 1866-1929.
  SCHÖNBERG
    Einfältiges Lied
    Der genügsame Liebhaber
Salustri, Carlo Alberto, 1871-1950.
  LE FAVOLE ROMANESCHE.
    CASELLA
      La carità
      L'elezzione der presidente
      Er coccodrillo
      Er gatto e er cane
"Salut! dernière aurore qui viens pour moi
  d'eclore!" *see*
  Adieux à la vie! (élégie sur une seule note)
    Unknown **ROSSINI**
Salut drapeau! see Péladin **SATIE**
  Hymne pour le "Salut Drapeau" du
    "Prince de Byzance . . ."
"Salut, Ô gai printemps!" *see Primavera*
  Stuart, Paul **SAINT-SAËNS**
Salutation angelique see Unknown
  SAUGUET
Salve Regina see Anon. **FAURÉ**
Salve Regina mater see Anon. **MILHAUD**
"Salve Regina Mater" *see Salve Regina*
  Anon. **FAURÉ**
Salvum fac regem see Loewe **LOEWE**
Samain, Albert Victor, 1858-1900.
  AUBERT
    L'âme errante
    Silence
  CASELLA *Soir païen*
  FAURÉ
    Accompagnement
    Arpège
    Soir
  KOECHLIN
    Accompagnement
    Améthyste
    Automne
    J'ai rêvé cette nuit

Rhodante
Soir païen
RESPIGHI *Le repos en Égypte*
SCHMITT *Musique sur l'eau*
AUX FLANCS DU VASE.
   KOECHLIN
     Amphise et Melitta
     Le cortège d'amphitrite
     L'ile ancienne
     La maison du matin
     Le repas préparé
     Le sommeil de canope
Samoobol'shchenie see Goethe **MEDTNER**
   Selbstbetrug
Samotny ksiezyc see Szymanowska, Zafia
   SZYMANOWSKI
"San Antonio bendito" *see Un home, San*
   Antonio! Castro, R. **RODRIGO**
San Basilio see Anon. **PIZZETTI**
"San Basilio viene di Cesarea" *see San Basilio*
   Anon. **PIZZETTI**
San Geminiano, Folgore da, 13th cent.
   IVES
     August
     December
     September
San José y Maria see Anon. **RODRIGO**
San Juan de la Cruz
   RODRIGO *Cantico de la esposa*
Sandburg, Carl, 1878-1967.
   BLACHER *Nebel*
   CHICAGO POEMS.
   HARRIS *Fog*
Der Sandmann see Kletke **SCHUMANN**
"Sanft entschwanden mir" *see Der Tag*
   Unknown **MENDELSSOHN-**
   BARTHOLDY
"Sanft ertönen Morgenglokken" *see*
   Glockenklänge Unknown **SPOHR**
"Sanft glänzt die Abendsonne" *see Abendlied*
   Unknown **SCHUBERT**
"Sanft mit seligem Entzücken" *see*
   An die Natur Unknown **LOEWE**
SANFT RUHENDE FLUR. see Giesebrecht
   Der Friedhof **LOEWE**
"Sanft wehn, im Hauch der Abendluft" *see*
   Totenkranz für ein Kind Matthisson
   SCHUBERT
Sanft weh'n im Hauch der Abendluft see
   Unknown **MENDELSSOHN-**
   BARTHOLDY
"Sanftes Clavier, sanftes Clavier!" *see*
   Seraphine an ihr Klavier Schubart
   SCHUBERT
Sanftes Licht see Reinbeck **WEBER**
"Sanftes Licht, weiche nicht" *see Sanftes Licht*
   Reinbeck **WEBER**

Sanftes Walten see Tolstoï **RUBINSTEIN**
Sang bag Ploven see Holstein **NIELSEN**
Sang des Moses see Giesebrecht **LOEWE**
"Sang ein Bettlerpärlein am Schenkentor" *see*
   Mädchenlied Heyse **SCHÖNBERG**
Sang paa Fjeldet see Winther **GRIEG**
Sang til juletraeet see Krohn **GRIEG**
Sångarlön see Snoilsky **SIBELIUS**
"Les sangelots longs des violons de
   l'automne" *see Chanson d'automne*
   Verlaine **DELIUS**
Sången see Österling **KILPINEN**
Sangen har lysning see Bjørnson **NIELSEN**
Sangeslust see Eberwein **SPOHR**
   Two settings: Op. 101 no. 2 and WoO 95.
Sanglier, Charles
   SCHMITT *La tortue et le lièvre*
Sanglots see Apollinaire *IL Y A.* **POULENC**
"Les sanglots longs des violons de l'automne"
   see Chanson d'automne Verlaine
   CARPENTER, HAHN
Sanherib's Niederlage see Byron **LOEWE**
Sankt Helena see Kahlert **LOEWE**
Sankt Mariens Ritter see Giesebrecht
   LOEWE
Sankt Michael see Weinheber **STRAUSS**
Sankt Nepomucks Vorabend see Goethe
   ZELTER *Sct. Nepomuks Vorabend*
SANNOSA ESTA LA NINNA. see Vicente,
   Gil *Weh, wie zornig ist das Mädchen*
   SCHUMANN
Sanoissa kuluva see Kanteletar **KILPINEN**
Sans feu ni lieu see Supervielle **MILHAUD**
"Sans même détourner la tête" *see Destinée*
   Carême **MILHAUD**
"Sans que nulle part je séjourne" *see*
   Tournoiement Renaud **SAINT-SAËNS**
Sant Marti see Ribot **MOMPOU**
Santa Chiara (Palm Sunday; Naples, 1925)
   see Symons **IRELAND**
Santillana, Iñigo López de Mendoza,
   marqués de, 1398-1458.
   RODRIGO *Serranilla*
Santo-Magno, N. di
   ROSSINI
     Beltà crudele
     La pastorella
Le sapin de Noel see Anon. **MARTINŮ**
Les sapins see Martin, Paul **SAINT-SAËNS**
Sapphische Strophe see Leuthold
   SCHOECK
Sappho, 625? B.C.-570 B.C.
   BERKELEY *Epitaph of Timas*
   GOUNOD *À une jeune grecque*
   LOEWE *An Aphrodite*
   PIZZETTI
     Oscuro è il ciel
     Scuote amore il mio cuori

Sappho, 625? B.C.-570 B.C. *(continued)*
RIETI
  A goccia a goccia
  Aspergi il corpo tuo
  La luna con le Pleiadi
  Morta tu giacerai
  O sposo, noi fanciulle
  Se il mio seno
  Sei giunta alfine
ROREM
  Evening
  Sappho: Fragment
Sappho: Fragment see Sappho **ROREM**
Sappische Ode see Schmidt, Hans
BRAHMS
"Sara has smiled upon me such a smile" *see*
  Sally's smile Goodman **ROREM**
Sarabande see Chalupt **ROUSSEL**
Sashen'ka see Anon. **PROKOFIEV**
"Sassen zwei Liebende kosend" *see*
  Liebe im Schnee Hamerling **JENSEN**
"S'asseoir tous deux au bord du flot qui
  passe" *see Au bord de l'eau*
  Sully-Prudhomme **FAURÉ**
Sassoon, Siegfried Lorraine, 1886-1967.
CARPENTER
  Serenade
  Slumber-song
GIDEON *Slumber song*
SATIE, ERIK, 1866-1925.
Anon.
  Chanson (1920) [Eschig, 1920; Ed. de la
    Sirène, 1922] "C'est mon trésor, c'est
    mon bijou le joli trou par où"
Bonnaud, Dominique, b.1864.
  La diva de l'Empire (1904) [Bellon
    Ponscarme, 1904; Salabert, 1976]
    "Sous le grand chapeau Greenaway"
    Text by Bonnaud and Numa Blès.
Chalupt, René, 1885-1957.
  Le Chapelier (1916) [Rouart Lerolle,
    1917; Salabert] "Le chapelier s'étonne
    de constater que sa montre"
    Text after Lewis Carroll's *Alice in
    Wonderland.*
Cocteau, Jean, 1889-1963.
  Danseuse (1920) [Eschig, 1920; Ed. de la
    Sirène, 1922]
    "Le crabe sort sur ses points"
Contamine, José-Maria Patricio
  Manuel, 1867-1926.
  Les anges (1886) [Alfred Satie, 1887;
    Salabert, 1968]
    "Vétus de blanc, Dans l'azur clair"
    Published as op. 20 no. 1 (1887).
  Chanson (1887) [Alfred Satie, 1887;
    Salabert, 1968]

"Bien courte, hélas! est l'espérance"
    Published as op. 52 (1887).
Elégie (1886) [Alfred Satie, 1887;
    Salabert, 1968]
    "J'ai vu décliner comme un songe"
    Published as op. 19 (1887).
Les fleurs (1886) [Alfred Satie, 1887;
    Salabert, 1968]
    "Que j'aime à vous voir, belles fleurs"
    Published as op. 20 no. 2 (1887).
Imperial-Oxford (ca.1900-1905) [unpubl.]
    Excerpt in Nigel Wilkins *Writings of
    Erik Satie* (London: Eulenburg,
    1980), 153.
Légende californienne (ca.1905)
    [unpubl.]
    Excerpt in Nigel Wilkins *Writings of
    Erik Satie* (London: Eulenburg,
    1980), 155.
Sylvie (1886) [Alfred Satie, 1887;
    Salabert, 1968]
    "Elle est si belle, Ma Sylvie"
    Published as op. 20 no. 3 (1887).
Durante, D.
  Allons-y Chochotte (1905) [Salabert,
    1978]
Fargue, Léon-Paul, 1878-1947.
  La statue de bronze (1916) [Rouart
    Lerolle, 1917; Salabert]
    "La grenouille du jeu de tonneau"
  LUDIONS.
    Air du Poète (1923) [Rouart Lerolle,
      1926; Salabert]
      "Au pays de Papouasie, J'ai caressé
      la Pouasie . . . "
    Air du Rat (1923) [Rouart Lerolle,
      1926; Salabert] "Abi Abirounère, qui
      que tu n'etais don?"
    Chanson du chat (1923) [Rouart
      Lerolle, 1926; Salabert]
      "Il est une bébête Tili petit n'enfant"
    La Grenouille américaine (1923)
      [Rouart Lerolle, 1926; Salabert]
      "La gouénouille améouicaine Me
      regarde par dessus"
    Spleen (1923) [Rouart Lerolle, 1926;
      Salabert]
      "Dans un vieux square où l'océan"
Godebska, Mimie
  Daphénéo (1916) [Rouart Lerolle, 1917;
    Salabert] "Dis-moi, Daphénéo, quel est
    donc cet arbre"
Hyspa, Vincent, 1865-1938.
  Chez le docteur (ca.1905-1906) [Salabert,
    1976] "Le petit pèr'combes s'en va
    chez le docteur"

Un dîner à l'Élysée (ca.1900) [V. Hyspa **Chansons d'amour** (Enoch: 1903)]

L'omnibus automobile (ca.1900-1906) [Salabert, 1976] "C'était pendant l'horreur du Quatorze Juillet"

Tendrement (ca.1902) [Baudoux, 1902; Salabert] "D'un amour tendre et pur"

Le veuf (ca.1900-1902) [Patrick Gowers "Erik Satie . . . " Ph.D. diss., Univ. of Cambridge, 1966]

Lamartine, Alphonse Marie Louis de Prat de, 1790-1869.

Elégie (1920) [Eschig, 1920; Ed. de la Sirène, 1922]
"Que me font ces vallons, ces palais"
Also published in *Tombeau de Claude Debussy,* **La Revue musicale. Suppl. musicale** Dec. 1920.

Mendès, Catulle Abraham, 1841-1909.

Chanson médiévale (1906) [Salabert, 1968] "Comme je m'en retournais de la fontaine"

No author

Marienbad (1905) [Salabert, 1978]
Les oiseaux (1905) [Salabert, 1978]
Rambouillet (1905) [Salabert, 1978]
NB: These are **Trois mélodies sans paroles,** nos. 1-3.

Pacory, Henry, b. 1873.

Je te veux (1897) [Baudoux, 1902; Salabert, 1971]
"J'ai compris ta détresse"

Péladin, Joséphin, 1858-1918.

LE PRINCE DE BYZANCE.

Hymne pour le "Salut Drapeau" du "Prince de Byzance . . ." (1891) [Salabert, 1968]
"Langes de tous les fils, Manteau de tous les pères"

Radiguet, Raymond, 1903-1923.

Adieu (1920) [Eschig, 1920]
"Amiral, ne crois pas déchoir"

Satie, Erik, 1866-1925.

Ne suis que grain de sable (1914) [Rouart Lerolle, 1916; Salabert] same
Suis chauve de naissance (1914) [Rouart Lerolle, 1916; Salabert] same
Ta parure est secrète (1914) [Rouart Lerolle, 1916; Salabert] same

Satie, Erik, 1866-1925.

SATIE

Ne suis que grain de sable
Suis chauve de naissance
Ta parure est secrète

SAUDADES, no. 1

HESELTINE Li Po *Along the stream*

SAUDADES, no. 2

HESELTINE Shakespeare *Take, O take those lips away*

SAUDADES, no. 3

HESELTINE Callimachus *Heracleitus*

SAUGUET, HENRI, 1901-1989.

Aguet, William

Chanson de la fille de bar (1953) [unpubl.]
"Parmi les neiges du grand nord"

Alix, Marie

Pour Nicolas (1979) [unpubl.] "D'un même moule, les jours s'écoulent"

Anon.

Cette attirance de la brume (1947) [ms. lost]

Auriol, J.-G.

Chanson de Calypso (1933) [unpubl.] Song from the film **L'Epervier.**

Balzac, Honoré de, 1799-1850.

Sur une page d'Album (1954) [unpubl.]

Baron, Jacques, b. 1905.

En attendant (1970) [unpubl.]
"Ils vont arriver, la nuit est tombée"
Lied (1970) [unpubl.]
"Il n'y avait qu'un lit"
La tour prends garde (1970) [unpubl.]
"Quand tu arrives, garçon"

Baudelaire, Charles Pierre, 1821-1867.

Le chat (1938) [Amphion, 1944]
"Dans ma cervelle se promène"
Le chat (1938) [Amphion, 1944]
"De sa fourrure blonde et brune"

Beaumont, Germaine, 1891-1983.

Eaux douces (1945) [unpubl.]
"Quand le feu brûle encore"

Bibesco, Marthe Lucie (Lahovary), Princesse, 1887-1945.

Mouton Blanc (1953) [Salabert]
"Achille aux pieds légers"

Birot, Pierre-Albert

Bête me veut, bête me prend (1968) [unpubl.] same
Démon des mains, parfait visage (1968) [unpubl.] same
Pourtant il y a encore autre chose (1968) [unpubl.] same

Boulanger, Daniel, 1922-

Imploration (1981) [unpubl.]
"Bonté, sagesse et le savoir"

Brimont, Renée de, Baronne, 1880-1943.

La belle morte (1937) [unpubl.]

Capri, Agnès

Un bouquet à la main (1941) [unpubl.]

Carême, Maurice, 1899-1978.

L'adolescent (1973) [unpubl.]
"Il voulait que ce soit mon pied"

SAUGUET, HENRI, 1901-1989 *(continued)*
　Carême, Maurice, 1899-1978.
　　(continued)
　　Celui que j'aime (1973) [unpubl.]
　　　"Qu'il vienne celui que j'aime"
　　Il vieillissait (1973) [unpubl.]
　　　"Il se disait si je pouvais"
　　Image (1956) [unpubl.]
　　Ingénuité (1973) [unpubl.]
　　　"Il aimait se déshabiller"
　　Je marcherai pour toi (1973) [unpubl.]
　　　same
　　Je sais qu'il existe (1973) [unpubl.]
　　　"Mais vers qui marchez-vous"
　　Je serai toujours là (1973) [unpubl.]
　　　same
　　Je suis un oiseau (1973) [unpubl.] same
　　Nul ne se lasse d'être soi (1973)
　　　[unpubl.] "Il voulait sortir de lui"
　　Le semeur (1973) [unpubl.]
　　　"Il plongea ses deux mains"
　　Seul sur la terre (1973) [unpubl.]
　　　"Donc il se tourna vers le mur"
　　Simplicité (1973) [unpubl.]
　　　"Ils n'avait qu'une table"
　Chabrillac, Léon
　　Bergerie (1946) [ms. lost]
　Chalupt, René, 1885-1957.
　　Le chalet tyrolien (1948) [unpubl.]
　　　"Dans le parc de cette demoiselle"
　Clancier, Georges Emmanuel, 1914-
　　Bergère (1958) [unpubl.]
　　　"Bergère, bergère dans l'herbe . . . "
　　Comme autrefois (1958) [unpubl.]
　　　"Comme autrefois la douceur . . . "
　　Le temps et les pays (1958) [unpubl.]
　　　same
　Clift, William
　　Love poem (1976) [unpubl.]
　　　"Je voudrais te parler à mi-voix"
　Cocteau, Jean, 1889-1963.
　　Chansons de marins (1933) [Smyth,
　　　1933] "Ils sont tous jeunes et beaux
　　　sur la 'belle cubaine' "
　　　　Text also by Radiguet.
　Copperie, Adrien
　　Cloune étoilé (1925) [Rouart Lerolle,
　　　1926] "Cloune, étoile de mer"
　　Ecuyère voltige (1925) [Rouart Lerolle,
　　　1926] "Tombée du ciel de papier"
　　Fausse alerte (1922) [**Revue Horizon**
　　　(Bordeaux) 1922]
　　Gymnaste aérien (1925) [Rouart Lerolle,
　　　1926] "Pathétique au commandement"
　　Haute ecole (1925) [Rouart Lerolle,
　　　1926] "Sous les flots crus d'une
　　　trompette"

　　Petite écuyère (1925) [Rouart Lerolle,
　　　1926] "Rose, un voile rose"
　D'Harcourt, Antoniette
　　Au bord de la cheminée (1942) [Éditions
　　　de France]
　　Dormeur suspendu (1942) [Éditions de
　　　France]
　　Fenêtre ouverte le soir (1942) [Éditions
　　　de France]
　　Les gens distraits (1942) [Éditions de
　　　France]
　　Invasion (1942) [Éditions de France]
　　　"Les pieds les chevaux emportés par la
　　　mer"
　　Sommeil (1942) [Éditions de France]
　　　"Cette main abattue sur mon visage"
　Deharme, Lise, d. 1990.
　　Je suis heureuse (1950) [unpubl.]
　　　No information provided by the
　　　composer.
　Desbordes-Valmore, Marceline
　Félicité Josèphe, 1786-1859.
　　Adieu (1959) [unpubl.]
　　　"Tout, quittez mon coeur"
　　La dernière fleur (1959) [unpubl.]
　　　"Que ton coeur prenne sa défense"
　　Souvenir (1959) [unpubl.]
　　　"Son image comme un songe"
　Desnoux, Lucienne
　　Pour un cyprés [unpubl.]
　　　"Au cyprès que j'ai fait planter là-bas"
　　　Medium voice, viola, & piano.
　Dréjac, Jean
　　Le chemin des forains (1955) [Salabert]
　　　"Ils ont troué la nuit de paillettes
　　　d'argent"
　Eluard, Paul, 1895-1952.
　　Bêtes et méchants (1944) [unpubl.]
　　　"Venant du dehors, venant du dedans"
　　*Celui qui dort, à la mémoire de Francis
　　　Poulenc* (1963) [unpubl.]
　　　"Peut-il se reposer"
　　Chat (1921) [Jobert, 1926]
　　　"Pour ne poser qu'un doigt dessus"
　　Cheval (1921) [Jobert, 1926]
　　　"Cheval seul, cheval perdu"
　　Chien (1921) [Jobert, 1926]
　　　"Chien chaud, tout entier dans la voix"
　　Une écluse sans brouillard (1943)
　　　[unpubl.]
　　Fenêtre illusoire à ma taille (1943)
　　　[unpubl.]
　　Il est midi, il est minuit (1943) [unpubl.]
　　Je n'avais d'yeux et de courage (1943)
　　　[unpubl.]
　　Nuage, premier pas de mon élévation
　　　(1943) [unpubl.]

Oiseau (1921) [Jobert, 1926]
"Charmé . . . Oh! pauvre fille!"
Plus rien ne me tient aux pieds (1943)
[unpubl.]
Porc (1921) [Jobert, 1926]
"Du soleil sur le dos"
Poule (1921) [Jobert, 1926]
"Hélas! ma soeur, bête bête"
Tout est un grand secret (1943) [unpubl.]
Vache (1921) [Jobert, 1926]
"On ne mène pas la vache"

Fernandez, Jeanne
A une élégante sans fortune (1947) [ms.
lost]

Follain, Jean, 1903-1971.
Au pays (1961) [unpubl.]
"Ils avaient décidé de s'en aller"
Domaine d'homme (1961) [unpubl.]
"L'homme éternel cultive"
Effacement (1961) [unpubl.]
"L'herbe a grandi au fossé"
Eglogue (1961) [unpubl.]
"Dans la maison refermée"
Les images (1961) [unpubl.]
"Une enfant qui soulève un peu"
Pensées d'octobre (1961) [unpubl.]
"On aime bien ce grand vin"
Promeneur (1961) [unpubl.]
"Qui donc porte manteau"
Vie des campagnes (1961) [unpubl.]
"Une renoncule Âcre"

Gabory, Georges, 1899-
O jeunes filles (1922) [Eschig, 1924]
same
Puisque Vénus (1922) [Eschig, 1924]
same
Tombé du ciel dans la mansarde (1922)
[Eschig, 1924] same

Gaillard, Roger
Amitié (1958) [unpubl.]
"Il ne faut pas prier pour les morts"
Solitude (1958) [unpubl.]
"Parmi l'ombre où bat la lampe"

Gautier, Théophile, 1811-1872.
Le spectre de la rose (1930) [unpubl.,
ms. lost]

Gengenbach, Eric de
La sirène au coquillage (1956) [unpubl.]
"Carillon funèbre"

Guichard, Abeille
La nef (1943) [unpubl.]
Minuit (1943) [unpubl.]
Toi (1943) [unpubl.]

Heine, Heinrich, 1797-1856.
Les ondines (1932) [unpubl.]
"Les flots battent la plage solitaire"

INTERMEZZO.
Le bonheur (1932) [unpubl.]
Le malheur (1932) [unpubl.]

Hölderlin, Friedrich, 1770-1843.
Chant du Destin (1933) [unpubl.]
"Vous passez la-haut dans la lumière"
L'hiver (1933) [unpubl.]
"L'aire est chauve"
Pardon (1933) [unpubl.]
"Divine créature"
Le printemps (1933) [unpubl.]
"L'homme oublie les soucis de
l'esprit"
La vie gaie (1933) [unpubl.]
"Quand je viens sur la prairie"

Hornez, André
L'ombre des rues (1949) [Ed.
Transatlantiques]
From the film, ***Entre onze heures et
minuit.***

Hugnet, Georges, 1906-1974.
Cache la fée (1944) [unpubl.] same
Facsimile of ms. in ***La Table Ronde***
(Paris, 1945), Cahier 3, following
p. 230.
Ces mots qui n'ont plus de sens (1944)
[unpubl.] same
Et voici des ans (1944) [unpubl.] same
Ici seront nées mes saisons (1944)
[unpubl.] same
Je suis hereux (1944) [unpubl.] same
Je t'adore (1944) [unpubl.] same
Laisse ta hanche blonde (1944) [unpubl.]
same
Nous avions si chaud (1944) [unpubl.]
same
La reine m'a livré (1944) [unpubl.] same
Sois mon amie (1944) [unpubl.] same

Jacob, Max, 1876-1944.
A une sainte le jour de sa fête (1944)
[Heugel, 1949]
"Sainte, Sainte, quand m'opprime la
tentation du péché"
Exhortation (1948) [Heugel, 1950]
"Vous, si beaux qui passez!"
Jardin mystérieux (1944) [Heugel, 1949]
"Coquilles d'ailes!"
Marine à Roscoff (1944) [Heugel, 1949]
"Le ciel et la mer couleur de tableau"
Le petit paysan (1948) [Heugel, 1950]
"Sous les ormeaux"
Ports de l'enfer (1944) [Heugel, 1949]
"Le cor appelle comme une cloche"
Que penser de mon salut (1948) [Heugel,
1950] "Il est comme la tige au milieu
des herbes"

COMPOSER Poet *Title* "First Line"

SAUGUET, HENRI, 1901-1989 *(continued)*
  Jacob, Max, 1876-1944 *(continued)*
    Régates mystérieuses (1948) [Heugel, 1950] "Galères! les proues et les poupes s'avancent"
    La ville (1944) [Heugel, 1949] "Ne vous arrêtez pas nuage sur la ville horrible"
    Voisinage (1948) [Heugel, 1950] "La porte s'ouvre!"
    Voyage (1948) [Heugel, 1950] "Chemin de nuit"
  Jacqueton, Henry
    Cette cigarette d'ombre (1969) [Editions françaises de musique, 1973]
    Incantation de la nuit (1969) [Editions françaises de musique, 1973] "Nuit, sommeil des souffles"
    Plain-ciel (1969) [Editions françaises de musique, 1973] "Ciel et mer, homme et femme"
  James, Edward Frank Willis, 1907-
    Aria (1934) [In James *The bones of my hand . . .* (London: Oxford Univ. Press, 1938), 83-86] "Dans la plus haute Eughillydie"
  Labé, Louise Charly, called, 1526-1566.
    A Vénus (1927) [Rouart Lerolle, 1928] "Claire Vénus, qui erres par les Cieux"
    Amour (1927) [Rouart Lerolle, 1928] "Prédit me fut, que devais fermement"
    Chasse (1927) [Rouart Lerolle, 1928] "Diane étant en l'épaisseur d'un bois"
    Printemps (1927) [Rouart Lerolle, 1928] "Pour le retour du Soleil honorer"
    Songe (1927) [Rouart Lerolle, 1928] "Toute aussitôt que je commence à prendre"
    Tant que mes yeux (1927) [Rouart Lerolle, 1928] same
  Laforgue, Jules, 1860-1887.
    Clair de lune de Novembre (1938) [Amphion, 1944] "Voyez un clair de lune de Novembre"
    Crépuscule de mi juillet, huit heures (1938) [Amphion, 1944] "Après un temps d'averse pas trop épaisse"
  Lamartine, Alphonse Marie Louis de Prat de, 1790-1869.
    A des roses sous la neige (1930) [unpubl., ms. lost]
  Lanoux, Armand, 1913-1983.
    Chanson de l'oiseleur (1950) [unpubl.] No information provided by the composer.
    Isis poignardée (1953) [unpubl.] "La veuve au corps de jeune fille"

Laporte, René, b. 1905.
    L'amoire de campagne (1954) [unpubl.] "Lorsqu'elle met la main"
    La chambre de juin (1954) [unpubl.] "Je pense à cette chambre"
    Présence (1929) [Rouart Lerolle, 1930] "Tu peux m'abandonner me dire adieu"
  Luka, Madeleine, 1894-1989.
    Chanson des amoureux (1946) [unpubl.] "Il étaient deux amoureux"
    Le jardin de Virigine (1946) [unpubl.] "Les lilas donneront bientôt"
    La marchand de coeurs (1946) [unpubl.] "J'ai des coeurs à vendre"
    Voici le chemin de la vie (1946) [unpubl.]
        No additional information available from the composer.
  Mallarmé, Stéphane, 1842-1898.
    Renouveau (1938) [Amphion, 1944] "Le printemps maladif a chassé tristement l'hiver"
    Senteurs (1947) [ms. lost]
    Tristesse d'été (1938) [Amphion, 1944] "Ce soleil sur la sable"
  Marcy, Claude
    Les amoureux sont seuls au monde (1947) [Ed. Transatlantiques, 1948] "Ils se sont recontrés dans le flot du métro"
        Song from the film, *Les amoureux sont seuls au monde.*
  Michaux, Henri, 1899-1984.
    Dans la nuit (1965) [Eschig, 1966] same
        For bass voice alone.
    La jeune fille de Budapest (1965) [Eschig, 1966] "Dans la brûme tiède d'une haleine"
        For bass voice alone.
    Repos dan le malheur (1965) [Eschig, 1966] "Le malheur, mon grand laboureur"
        For bass voice alone.
  No author
    Valse des Si (1956) [unpubl.] "Si, si, si. . . . ."
  Obaldia, René de, 1918-
    Les jumeaux de la nuit (1969) [unpubl.] "Dans le ventre de Maman"
    Moi j'irai dans la lune (1969) [unpubl.]
    Le secret (1969) [unpubl.] "Le chemin près du bois"
  Olivier, Pierre
    L'enfant qui dort (1951) [unpubl.] "Sur la pointe des pieds"

Le joyeux ramoneur (1951) [unpubl.]
   "Sautant d'un toit à l'autre toit"
Pépin, Edwige
   Prière dans le soir (1966) [unpubl.]
      "Maitre du vivre et du morir"
Proust, Marcel, 1871-1922.
   Comme à la lumière de la lune (1967)
      [unpubl.] "La nuit était venue"
Radiguet, Raymond, 1903-1923.
   Une carte postale (1922) [unpubl.]
      "On a remplacé les coquillages"
   Halte (1923) [unpubl.]
      "Cycliste en jupe culotte"
Raphaël, Cluzel
   L'alchimiste a la voix d'ambre (1978)
      [unpubl.]
   L'alchimiste au cher visage (1978)
      [unpubl.]
   L'alchimiste au regard d'ambre (1978)
      [unpubl.]
   L'alchimiste est dans le grenier (1978)
      [unpubl.]
   Dans le jardin de l'alchimiste (1978)
      [unpubl.]
   J'en appelle à l'alchimiste (1978)
      [unpubl.] "Quand je suis loin quand je
      suis triste"
   Les yeux d'ambre de l'alchimiste (1978)
      [unpubl.]
Richaud, André de, b. 1907.
   Carte postale à Délos (1946) [unpubl.]
      "Oh, nuit, nuit de Delos"
   Coeur noir du vent qui passe (1946)
      [unpubl.] same
   Nature morte (1946) [unpubl.]
      "La tête de cire, sur la table"
   Petite musique (1946) [unpubl.]
      "O Dieu, pourquoi viens-tu en fraude"
   Ritournelle (1946) [unpubl.]
      "Arbre de marbre où je sais"
   Tours (1946) [unpubl.]
      "Ma campagne est semée de tours"
Richter, Johann Paul Friedrich, 1763-
1825.
   A une rose pâlissant au soleil (1931)
      [unpubl.]
      "Pâle rose, le soleil t'a donné"
   Le bal d'enfants (1931) [unpubl.]
      "Ah, comme vous souriez"
   La double rougeur (1931) [unpubl.]
      "Innocentes jeunes filles"
   Le jour de tristesse (1931) [unpubl.]
      "Lorsque t'environne la triste journée"
   Le muguet (1931) [unpubl.]
      "Blanche clochette au bal"
   Le vide de l'instant (1931) [unpubl.]
      "N'est-il pour le coeur rien d'autre"

Rilke, Rainer Maria, 1875-1926.
   Herbst (1932) [unpubl., ms. lost]
Salmon, André, 1881-
   Cinq mars, à la mémoire de Max Jacob
      (1953) [unpubl.]
      "A la chapelle Notre Dâme"
Schiller, Johann Christoph Friedrich
von, 1759-1805.
   L'apparition (1928) [Rouart Lerolle,
      1929] "Lorsque mon ombre fugitive
      voltige autour de toi"
   Les guides de la vie (1928) [Rouart
      Lerolle, 1929]
      "Il est deux génies qui te guident"
   Le pèlerin (1928) [Rouart Lerolle, 1929]
      "J'étais encore au printemps de ma
      vie"
   Le souvenir (1928) [Rouart Lerolle,
      1929]
      "Il éclipsait tous les jeunes gens"
Seghers, Pierre, 1906-1987.
   Chant funèbre pour de nouveaux héros
      (1944) [unpubl.]
Senghor, Léopold Sedar, Pres.
Senegal, 1906-
   Chant de feu (1976) [unpubl.] "Feu que
      les hommes regardent dans la nuit"
Shakespeare, William, 1564-1616.
   Chanson (1929) [Jobert, 1930]
      "Eloigne, oh! éloigne ces lèvres"
   Je te vois en rêve (1929) [Jobert, 1930]
      "Lorsque mes yeux se ferment"
   To my fair friend you never can be old
      (1964) [unpubl.]
   Weary with toil (1964) [unpubl.]
Sidery
   La marchande d'anémondes (1957)
      [unpubl.] "La nuit, la pluie, Paris"
      Text also by Grendel.
Swinburne, Algernon Charles, 1837-
1909.
   Amour et sommeil (1929) [Rouart
      Lerolle, 1930] "Gisant endormi entre
      les battements de la nuit"
Tagore, Rabindranath, 1861-1941.
   Es-tu sorti par cette nuit d'orage? (1937)
      [Éditions de France] same
   Le jour où le more (1937) [Éditions de
      France] same
Tardieu, Jean, 1903-1995.
   L'Aventure (1982) [unpubl.] "Était-ce
      hier ou dans un temps lontain"
   Le chevalier à l'armure étincelante
      (1982) [unpubl.]
      "Vieil homme, vieil homme"
   Insomnie (1982) [unpubl.]
      "La longue nuit, le jeux ouverts"

COMPOSER   Poet   *Title*   "First Line"

SAUGUET, HENRI, 1901-1989 *(continued)*
Thoreau, Henry David, 1817-1862.
  Fumée légère (1943) [unpubl.]
    "Fumée légère, ailée"
Unknown
  Salutation angelique (1943) [Rouart
    Lerolle; Salabert, 1951]
    "Je vous salue, Marie"
      Voice & organ.
Valéry, Paul Ambroise, 1871-1945.
  La ceinture (1945) [unpubl.]
    "Quand le ciel couleur d'une joue"
  Le vin (1953) [unpubl.]
    "J'ai quelque jour dans l'océan"
  Le vois amical (1945) [unpubl.]
    "Nous avons pensé à des choses pures"
Vaucaire, Michel, b. 1904.
  Les enfants du Ruisseau (1936)
    [L'Echiquier, 1936]
    "Tu étais jeune et moi gamine"
Vilmorin, Louise de, 1902-1969.
  Postlude: Polonaise (1949) [Heugel,
    1949] "Dans les campagnes de
    Pologne"
      Composite suite to honor Chopin's
      centenary.
  Prelude (1949) [Heugel, 1949]
    "Une forêt surgit des flots"
      Composite suite to honor Chopin's
      centenary.
Saul see Byron **DIAMOND, LOEWE**
Saul, Daniel, 1854-1903.
  REGER
    Leichtsinniger Rat
    Scheiden
Saul und Samuel see Byron *HEBREW*
  MELODIES. **LOEWE**
Saul vor seiner letzten Schlacht see Byron
  LOEWE
Saunders, E
  GOUNOD *Passed away*
"Sausendes, brausendes Rad der Zeit" *see*
  Stehe still Wesendonck **WAGNER**
Der Sausewind see Busse **REGER**
"Sausewind, Brausewind! dort und hier!" *see*
  Lied vom Winde Mörike **WOLF**
"Sautant d'un toit à l'autre toit" *see Le joyeux
  ramoneur* Olivier, Pierre **SAUGUET**
Sauter, Lilly von, d. ca. 1970.
  KRENEK
    Aber die Nächte
    Beschwörung
    Der Sternenhimmel
Sauter, Samuel Friedrich, 1766-1846.
  IL CANTO DELLA QUAGLIA.
    BEETHOVEN, SCHUBERT
    Der Wachtelschlag

La sauterelle see Apollinaire
  LE BESTIAIRE. **POULENC**
Sauvage, Cécile, 1883-1927.
  MESSIAEN *Le sourire*
"Sauvons-nous du souci d'un jour!" *see*
  Théone Moréas **HAHN**
Le savetier see Mallarmé **MILHAUD**
"Say, my noble steed, why neigh you" *see*
  The war horse Pushkin **MEDTNER**
"Say, oh wither art bound?" *see A dream*
  Teternikov **RACHMANINOFF**
Sbohem see Apollinaire *ALCOOLS.*
  MARTINŮ *L'adieu*
The scapegoat see Warner **IRELAND**
"Scaramouche et Pulcinella" *see Fantoches*
  Verlaine **DEBUSSY**
  Two settings: 1882 and 1892?
Scene . . . see Pushkin *DIE ZIGEUNER.*
  RUBINSTEIN
SCENES FROM "ANOTHER SLEEP" no. 1
  ROREM Green *Hearing music at his
    mother's funeral*
SCENES FROM "ANOTHER SLEEP" no. 2
  ROREM Green *He walks beneath the
    stars*
SCENES FROM "ANOTHER SLEEP" no. 3
  ROREM Green *He thinks upon his death*
"Scenes from my childhood are with me" *see
  Tom sails away* Ives **IVES**
"The scent of hyacinths like a pale mist" *see
  Vernal equinox* Lowell, A. **THOMSON**
Scève, Maurice, 16th century.
  MILHAUD *Moins je la vois*
Schack, Adolf Friedrich, Graf von, 1815-
  1894.
  BRAHMS
    Abenddämmerung
    Herbstgefühl
    Serenade
  LASSEN *Abenddämmerung*
  STRAUSS
    Barkarole
    Dem Herzen ähnlich
    Das Geheimnis
    Heimkehr
    Lob des Leidens
    Nur Mut!
    Seitdem dein Aug' in meines schaute
    Ständchen
    Von dunklem Schleier umsponnen
    Winternacht
  LOTOSBLÄTTER.
    STRAUSS
    Breit' über mein Haupt
    Hoffen und wieder verzagen
    Mein Herz ist stumm

Schön sind, doch kalt
Wie sollten wir geheim sie halten
Wozu noch, Mädchen
"Schad' um das schöne, grüne Band" *see Mit*
dem grünen Lautenband Müller, Wilhelm
SCHUBERT
Der Schäfer see Goethe **WOLF**
Der Schäfer see Unknown **PIJPER**
"Der Schäfer putzte sich zum Tanz" *see*
Bauern unter der Linde Goethe
WAGNER
"Ein Schäfer sass im Grünen" *see Der Schäfer*
und der Reiter Fouqué **SCHUBERT**
Schäfer, Theo, b. 1872.
   REGER
      Abend
      Erinnerung
Der Schäfer und der Reiter see Fouqué
SCHÄFER UND REITER. **SCHUBERT**
SCHÄFER UND REITER. see Fouqué
   Der Schäfer und der Reiter **SCHUBERT**
"Schäferin, ach, wie haben sie" *see*
   Süsses Begräbnis Rückert **LOEWE**
Die Schäferinn see Poliziano **ZELTER**
Schäferlied see Löns **KILPINEN**
Schäfers Klagelied see Goethe **SCHUBERT,**
   ZELTER
Schäfers Nachtlied see Heyse **CORNELIUS**
Die Schäferstunde see Hiemer **WEBER**
   Damon und Chloe
"Schaff', das Tagwerk meiner Hände" *see*
   Hoffnung Goethe **SCHUBERT**
Schaffer, Aaron, 1894-1957.
   COPLAND
      My heart is in the east
      Night
      A summer vacation
"Eine Schale blühender Rosen" *see Rosen*
   Itzerott **REGER**
Die Schale der Vergessenheit see Hölty
   BRAHMS
"Eine Schale des Stroms" *see Die Schale der*
   Vergessenheit Hölty **BRAHMS**
Der Schalk see Eichendorff **FRANZ**
Schall, Johann Eberhard Friedrich,
   1742-1790.
   MOZART *Des kleinen Friedrichs*
      Geburtstag
Schastlivoe plavan'e see Goethe **MEDTNER**
   Glückliche Fahrt
Der Schatten see Barth **KRENEK**
Die Schatten see Matthisson **SCHUBERT**
"Schatten deckt, vom Tau befeuchtet" *see*
   Abendlied Giesebrecht **LOEWE**
Schattenleben see Frey, F. **BERG**
Schatz, Josef, 1871-1950, supposed author.
   REGER *Der gute Rat*

Der Schatzgräber see Eichendorff
   SCHUMANN
Der Schatzgräber see Goethe **LOEWE,**
   SCHUBERT
Schatzgräbers Begehr see Schober
   SCHUBERT
Der Schaukasten see Musorgskiĭ
   MUSORGSKIĬ *Raëk*
"Ein scheckiges Pferd" *see Soldatenlied*
   Hoffmann von Fallersleben
   SCHUMANN
Scheffel, Joseph Victor von, 1826-1886.
   JENSEN *Alt Heidelberg, du feine*
   WOLF
      Biterolf (Im Lager von Akkon 1190)
      Wächterlied auf der Wartburg
      DER BRAUTWILLKOMM AUF
      WARTBURG.
   LISZT
      Biterolf und der Schmied von Ruhla
      Heinrich von Ofterdingen
      Reimar der Alte
      Der tugendhafte Schreiber
      Walther von der Vogelweide
   GAUDEAMUS.
   JENSEN
      Altassyrisch
      Ausfahrt
      Die drei Dörfer
      Der Fünfundsechziger
      Die Heimkehr
      Hildebrandlied
      Lied fahrender Schüler
      Die Malbronner Fuge
      Perkêo
      Wer reit't mit sieben Knappen
      Wer wankt zu Fusse
      Der Willekumm
Scheffler, Johann, 1624-1677.
   FRANZ *O nimm dich in Acht*
   HINDEMITH *Vier Lieder*
"Die Scheibe friert, der Wind ist rauh" *see*
   Sehnsucht Seidl **SCHUBERT**
Scheideblick see Lenau **SCHOECK, WOLF**
Scheidelied see Baumbach **BERG**
Scheiden see Saul, D. **REGER**
Scheiden und Meiden see Anon.
   DES KNABEN WUNDERHORN: Drei
   Reiter am Tor. **MAHLER**
Scheiden und Meiden see Uhland
   WANDERLIEDER. **BRAHMS, SCHOECK**
Scheidend see Voss **MENDELSSOHN-**
   BARTHOLDY
Schellenberg, Ernst Ludwig, 1883-1964.
   REGER
      Der Dieb

COMPOSER   Poet   *Title*   "First Line"

Schellenberg, Ernst Ludwig, 1883-1964
  (*continued*)
  REGER (*continued*)
    Furchthäschen
    Glück
    Der Igel
    Der König aus dem Morgenland
    Maria am Rosenstrauch
    Mausefangen
    Mittag
    Schelmenliedchen
    Zum Schlafen
Der Schelm see Unknown **REGER**
Schelmenliedchen see Schellenberg
  REGER
"Schemen erloschener Flammen" *see*
  Ein Friedhof Hauenschild **FRANZ**
Schenk mir deinen goldenen Kamm see
  Dehmel **SCHÖNBERG**
SCHENKENBUCH. see Goethe
  Ob der Koran von Ewigkeit sei? **WOLF**
Schenkendorf, Max von, 1783-1817.
  BRAHMS
    An die Trauben
    An ein Bild
    Erinnerung
    Frühlingstrost
    Todessehnen
  WEBER *Die gefangenen Sänger*
Scherenberg, Christian Friedrich, 1798-
  1881.
  LOEWE *Der Feind*
Scherer, Georg, 1828-1909.
  BERG, RUBINSTEIN *Am Strande*
Scherz see Chamisso **REGER**
Scherzo see Zangarini **RESPIGHI**
Scheurlein, Georg, 1802-1872.
  WAGNER *Der Tannenbaum*
"Scheust dich noch immer" *see Entschluss*
  Osterwald **FRANZ**
Schicksal der Liebe see Morgenstern
  KILPINEN
Schien mir's, als ich sah die Sonne see
  Strindberg *GESPENSTER SONATE.*
  WEBERN
Das Schiff see Lermontov **RUBINSTEIN**
Der Schiffer see Davidov **RUBINSTEIN**
Der Schiffer see Mayrhofer *IM WINDE.*
  SCHUBERT
Der Schiffer see Schlegel, F.
  FRÜHLINGSGEDICHTE. **SCHUBERT**
Schifferlied der Wasserfee see Tieck **SPOHR**
Schifferliedchen see Keller, G. **SCHOECK**
Das Schiffermädchen see Geyer **SPOHR**
SCHIFFERS NACHTLIED. see Mayrhofer
  Lied eines Schiffers an die Dioskuren
  SCHUBERT

Schiffers Scheidelied see Schober
  SCHUBERT
Das Schifflein see Uhland **LOEWE,**
  MENDELSSOHN-BARTHOLDY
"Ein Schifflein ziehet leise den Strom" *see*
  Das Schifflein Uhland
  LOEWE, MENDELSSOHN-
  BARTHOLDY
Schiftlieder see Unknown **PIJPER**
Schikaneder, Emanuel Johann, 1751-
  1812.
  SPIEGEL VON ARCADUA.
    SCHÖNBERG *Arie aus dem Spiegel von*
    Arcadien
"Schildern, willst du Freund, soll ich dir
  Elisen?" *see Schilderung eines Mädchens*
  Unknown **BEETHOVEN**
Schilderung eines Mädchens see Unknown
  BEETHOVEN
Schilflied see Lenau *SCHILFLIEDER.*
  BERG, MENDELSSOHN-
  BARTHOLDY, SCHÖNBERG
SCHILFLIEDER. see Lenau
  Auf dem Teich, dem regungslosen **FRANZ,**
  GRIFFES
  Auf geheimem Waldespfade **FRANZ,**
  GRIFFES
  Auf geheimen Waldespfade **PIJPER,**
  SCHOECK
  Schilflied **BERG, MENDELSSOHN-**
  BARTHOLDY, SCHÖNBERG
SCHILFLIEDER, no. 1
  FRANZ Lenau *Auf geheimem*
  Waldespfade
  SCHOECK Lenau *Drüben geht die Sonne*
  scheiden
SCHILFLIEDER, no. 2
  FRANZ Lenau *Drüben geht die Sonne*
  scheiden
  SCHOECK Lenau *Trübe wird's, die*
  Wolken jagen
SCHILFLIEDER, no. 3
  FRANZ Lenau *Trübe wird's, die Wolken*
  jagen
  SCHOECK Lenau *Auf geheimen*
  Waldespfade
SCHILFLIEDER, no. 4
  FRANZ Lenau *Sonnenuntergang;*
  schwarze Wolken zieh'n
SCHILFLIEDER, no. 5
  FRANZ Lenau *Auf dem Teich, dem*
  Regungslosen
Schiller, Johann Christoph Friedrich
  von, 1759-1805.
  INDY *Plainte de Thécla*
  JENSEN *Thekla's Gesang*

COMPOSER   Poet   *Title*   "First Line"

LASSEN *Rekrutenlied aus Wallensteins Lager*

LOEWE
Der Gang nach dem Eisenhammer
Der Graf von Habsburg

SAUGUET
L'apparition
Les guides de la vie
Le pèlerin
Le souvenir

SCHUBERT
Der Alpenjäger
An den Frühling
Three settings: D. 245, D. 283, and D. 587.
An die Freude
An Emma
Die Bürgschaft
Elysium
Die Entzückung an Laura
Two settings: D. 390 and D. 577.
Die Erwartung
Der Flüchtling
Gruppe aus dem Tartarus
Hektors Abschied
Der Jüngling am Bache
Three settings: D. 30, D. 192, and D. 638.
Der Kampf
Klage der Ceres
Laura am Klavier
Eine Leichenphantasie
Lied
Das Mädchen aus der Fremde
Two settings: D. 117 and D. 252.
Der Pilgrim
Punschlied. Im Norden zu singen
Ritter Toggenburg
Der Taucher
Thekla (Eine Geisterstimme)
Two settings: D. 73 and D. 595.
Die vier Weltalter

SCHUMANN
Des Sennen Abschied
Der Handschuh

STRAUSS *Des Alpenhirten Abschied*

ZELTER
An die Freude
Berglied
Elegie an Emma
Der Graf von Habsburg
Der Handschuh; eine Erzälung
Die Ideale
Der Kampf mit dem Drachen
Der Sänger der Vorwelt
Der Taucher

Die Theilung der Erde
Die vier Weltalter

ACH! AUS DIESES TALES GRÜNDEN.
SCHUBERT *Sehnsucht*
Two settings: D. 52 and D. 636.

DER BESUCH.
SCHUBERT *Dithyrambe*

DIE ERWARTUNG.
ZELTER *Im Garten*

ES REDEN UND TRÄUMEN DIE MENSCHEN.
SCHUBERT *Hoffnung*
Two settings: D. 251 and D. 637.

DIE GÖTTER GRIECHENLANDS: 12th stanza.
SCHUBERT *Die Götter Griechenlands*

DIE PICCOLOMINI.
MENDELSSOHN-BARTHOLDY, SCHUBERT, ZELTER
Des Mädchens Klage
Three Schubert settings: D. 6, D. 191, and D. 389

DIE RÄUBER.
SCHUBERT *Amalia*

SIE KONNTE MIR KEIN WÖRTCHEN SAGEN.
SCHUBERT *Das Geheimniss*
Two settings: D. 250 and D. 793.

WILHELM TELL.
LISZT
Der Alpenjäger
Die Fischerknabe
Der Hirt
SCHUMANN *Des Buben Schützenlied*

Schilling, Heinar, 1894-1955.
HINDEMITH *Durch die abendlichen Gärten*

Schink, Johann Friedrich, 1755-1835.
ZELTER
An den Mond
Erkennung
Der Perserkönig Cai-Caius
Reiche mir aus blauer Ferne

"Schlacht, du brichst an!" *see Trinklied vor der Schlacht* Körner **SCHUBERT**
Schlachtgesang see Klopstock **GLUCK, SCHUBERT**
Der Schlaf see Bjørnson **DELIUS**
Schlaf! see Khomyakov **BALAKIREV** *Spi!*
Der Schlaf see Lenau **SCHOECK**
Schlaf ein see Boelitz **REGER**
Schlaf' ein see Tolstoĭ **RUBINSTEIN**
"Schlaf' ein, gewieget an meiner Brust" *see Wiegenlied* Grun, James **PFITZNER**
"Schlaf' ein, mein Kind" *see Wiegenlied* Hoffmann von Fallersleben **LASSEN**

"Schlaf' ein, mein liebes Kindlein du" *see*
  Wiegenlied Stein, Gretel REGER
"Schlaf ein, mein süsses Kind" *see*
  Wiegenlied im Winter Reinick WOLF
"Schlaf' ein, mein trauernd Lieb" *see*
  Schlaf' ein Tolstoï RUBINSTEIN
"Der Schlaf entführte mich in deine Gärten"
  see Traum Lasker-Schüler HINDEMITH
"Schlaf, Herzenssöhnchen, mein Liebling bist
  du!" *see Wiegenlied* Hiemer WEBER
"Schlaf, holder Knabe, süss und mild" *see*
  Die Mutter an der Wiege Claudius, M.
  LOEWE
Schlaf, Johannes, 1862-1941.
  SCHÖNBERG *Waldsonne*
  HELLDUNKEL (1899).
    BERG
      Im Zimmer
      Regen
      Winter
"Schlaf, Kindlein, balde" *see Wiegenlied*
  Anon. REGER
Schlaf, mein Kind, in Ruh' *see* Anon.
  DVOŘÁK *Spi, mé ditě, spi*
Schlaf nur ein *see* Heyse JENSEN
"Schlaf, Söhnchen!" *see Wiegenlied* Scott
  JENSEN
"Schlaf! süsser Schlaf!" *see An den Schlaf*
  Mörike WOLF
"Schlaf wohl, du Himmelsknabe du" *see*
  Der Hirten Lied am Krippelein Schubart
  LOEWE
"Schlaf' wohl du Himmelsknabe du" *see*
  Weihnachtslied Schubart STRAUSS
"Schlaf wohl, schlaf wohl!" *see*
  Schlummerlied Benz REGER
"Schlafe, schlafe, holder, süsser Knabe" *see*
  Wiegenlied Unknown SCHUBERT
"Schlafe, süsser kleiner Donald" *see*
  Hochländisches Wiegenlied Burns
  SCHUMANN
Schlafen, schlafen *see* Hebbel
  DEM SCHMERZ SEIN RECHT. BERG
Schlafen, schlafen, nichts als schlafen *see*
  Hebbel *DEM SCHMERZ SEIN RECHT.*
  SCHOECK
"Schlafen, schlafen, nichts als schlafen!" *see*
  Schlafen, schlafen Hebbel BERG
Schlafend trägt man mich *see* Mombert
  DER GLÜHENDE. BERG
"Schlafend trägt man mich in mein
  Heimatland" *see Fragment: Der Glühende*
  Mombert SZYMANOWSKI
Die schlafende Prinzessin *see* Borodin
  BORODIN
Schlafendes Jesuskind *see* Mörike WOLF

Schlaflied *see* Mayrhofer SCHUBERT
Schlaflied *see* Tieck SPOHR
Schlafliedchen *see* Busse REGER
"Schlafloser Augen Sonne, zitternd Licht" *see*
  Die Sonne der Schlaflosen Byron LOEWE
"Schlafloser Sonne, melanchol'scher Stern!"
  see An den Mond Byron SCHUMANN
"Schlafst scho mei Greterl" *see Beim*
  Fenstergehn Löwenstein RUBINSTEIN
Schlag' die Tschadra zurück *see* Bodenstedt
  RUBINSTEIN
Schlagende Herzen *see* Bierbaum STRAUSS
"Schlagt mein ganzes Glück in Splitter" *see*
  Des Sängers Habe Schlechta
  SCHUBERT
Schlagt! Schlagt! Trommeln! *see* Whitman
  HINDEMITH
"Schlanke Fatme, hohe Palme" *see Fatme*
  Dahn RUBINSTEIN
Die schlanke Wasserlilie *see* Heine FRANZ,
  LOEWE, PFITZNER
DIE SCHLANKE WASSERLILIE. *see* Heine
  The water lily RACHMANINOFF
Schlecht' Wetter *see* Braungart REGER
Schlechta, Franz Xaver von Wssehrd,
  1796-1875.
  SCHUBERT
    Aus Diego Manazares
    Des Sängers Habe
    Fischerweise
    Liebeslauschen
    Totengräber-Weise
    Widerschein
      Two settings: D. 639 and D. 949.
    IM KIRCHHOF.
      SCHUBERT *Auf einen Kirchhof*
Der schlechte Moses *see* Iłłakowiczówna
  SZYMANOWSKI *Zly Lejba*
Schlechtes Wetter *see* Heine STRAUSS
Schlegel, August Wilhelm von, 1767-
  1845.
  SCHUBERT
    Abendlied für die Entfernte
    Die gefangenen Sänger
    Lebensmelodien
    Lob der Thränen
    Sprache der Liebe
    Die verfehlte Stunde
    Wiedersehn
  ZELTER
    Gesang und Kuss
    Der Heilige Lukas
    Kampaspe
Schlegel, Friedrich von, 1772-1829.
  SCHUBERT
    Blanka

COMPOSER   Poet   *Title*   "First Line"

Fülle der Liebe
Im Walde
Vom Mitleiden Mariae
ABENDRÖTE.
SCHUBERT
Abendröte
Die Berge
Der Fluss
Die Gebüsche
Der Knabe
Das Mädchen
Die Rose
Der Schmetterling
Die Sterne
Die Vögel
Der Wanderer
FRÜHLINGSGEDICHTE.
SCHUBERT Der Schiffer
Schlegel, Karl Wilhelm Friedrich von,
1772-1829. see
Schlegel, Friedrich von, 1772-1829.
Schleifer, Matthias L., 1771-1842.
LOEWE Zumalacarregui
SCHLICHTE WEISEN, no. 1
REGER Dahn Du meines Herzens
Krönelein
STRAUSS Dahn All mein Gedanken
SCHLICHTE WEISEN, no. 2
REGER Hertz Daz iuwer min engel walte!
STRAUSS Dahn Du meines Herzens
Krönelein
SCHLICHTE WEISEN, no. 3
REGER Anon. Waldeinsamkeit
STRAUSS Dahn Ach Lieb', nun muss ich
scheiden
SCHLICHTE WEISEN, no. 4
REGER Busse Wenn die Linde blüht
STRAUSS Dahn Ach, weh mir
verglückhaftem Mann
SCHLICHTE WEISEN, no. 5
REGER Enslin Herzenstausch
STRAUSS Dahn Die Frauen sind oft
fromm und still
SCHLICHTE WEISEN, no. 6
REGER Unknown Beim Schneewetter
SCHLICHTE WEISEN, no. 7 see Dahn
Du meines Herzens Krönelein **REGER,**
STRAUSS
SCHLICHTE WEISEN, no. 7
REGER Braungart Schlecht' Wetter
SCHLICHTE WEISEN, no. 8
REGER Storm Einen Brief soll ich
schreiben
SCHLICHTE WEISEN, no. 9
REGER Gersdorff Am Brünnele
SCHLICHTE WEISEN, no. 10 see Dahn
Ach, weh mir verglückhaftem Mann
STRAUSS

SCHLICHTE WEISEN, no. 10
REGER Braungart Warte nur!
SCHLICHTE WEISEN, no. 11 see Dahn
All mein Gedanken **STRAUSS**
SCHLICHTE WEISEN, no. 11
REGER Sommerstorff Mei Bua
SCHLICHTE WEISEN, no. 12 (?) see Dahn
Ach Lieb', nun muss ich scheiden
STRAUSS
SCHLICHTE WEISEN, no. 12
REGER Bern Mit Rosen bestreut
SCHLICHTE WEISEN, no. 13 see Dahn
Die Frauen sind oft fromm und still
STRAUSS
SCHLICHTE WEISEN, no. 13
REGER Boelitz Der verliebte Jäger
SCHLICHTE WEISEN, no. 14
REGER Huggenberger Mein Schätzelein
SCHLICHTE WEISEN, no. 15
REGER Metternich-Winneburg
Maiennacht
SCHLICHTE WEISEN, no. 16
REGER Schellenberg Glück
SCHLICHTE WEISEN, no. 17
REGER Anon. Wenn alle Welt so einig
wär'
SCHLICHTE WEISEN, no. 18
REGER Friderici In einem Rosengärtelein
SCHLICHTE WEISEN, no. 19
REGER Uhland Hans und Grete
SCHLICHTE WEISEN, no. 20
REGER Boelitz Es blüht ein Blümlein
rosenrot
SCHLICHTE WEISEN, no. 21
REGER Anon. Minnelied
SCHLICHTE WEISEN, no. 22
REGER Kiesekamo Das Kindes Gebet
SCHLICHTE WEISEN, no. 23
REGER Boelitz Zwiesprach
SCHLICHTE WEISEN, no. 24
REGER Mayr Abgeguckt
SCHLICHTE WEISEN, no. 25
REGER Huggenberger Friede
SCHLICHTE WEISEN, no. 26
REGER Baumbach Der Schwur
SCHLICHTE WEISEN, no. 27
REGER Kiesekamo Kindeslächeln
SCHLICHTE WEISEN, no. 28
REGER Seyboth, Sofie Die Mutter
spricht
SCHLICHTE WEISEN, no. 29
REGER Huggenberger
Schmeichelkätzchen
SCHLICHTE WEISEN, no. 30
REGER Boelitz Vorbeimarsch
SCHLICHTE WEISEN, no. 31
REGER Eichendorff Gottes Segen

COMPOSER Poet Title "First Line"

SCHLICHTE WEISEN, no. 32
 REGER Ginzkey *Von der Liebe*
SCHLICHTE WEISEN, no. 33
 REGER Boelitz *Das Wölklein*
SCHLICHTE WEISEN, no. 34
 REGER Boelitz *Reiterlied*
SCHLICHTE WEISEN, no. 35
 REGER Schellenberg *Mittag*
SCHLICHTE WEISEN, no. 36
 REGER Schellenberg *Schelmenliedchen*
SCHLICHTE WEISEN, no. 37
 REGER Falke *Heimat*
SCHLICHTE WEISEN, no. 38
 REGER Anon. *Das Mägdlein und der Spatz*
SCHLICHTE WEISEN, no. 39
 REGER Unknown *Abendlied*
SCHLICHTE WEISEN, no. 40
 REGER Michaeli *Wunsch*
SCHLICHTE WEISEN, no. 41
 REGER Kiesekamo *An den Frühlingsregen*
SCHLICHTE WEISEN, no. 42
 REGER Kiesekamo *Der Postillon*
SCHLICHTE WEISEN, no. 43
 REGER Flemes *Brunnensang*
SCHLICHTE WEISEN, no. 44
 REGER Trojan *Klein Marie*
SCHLICHTE WEISEN, no. 45
 REGER Boelitz *Lutschemäulchen*
SCHLICHTE WEISEN, no. 46
 REGER Boelitz *Soldatenlied*
SCHLICHTE WEISEN, no. 47
 REGER Boelitz *Schlaf ein*
SCHLICHTE WEISEN, no. 48
 REGER Boelitz *Zwei Mäuschen*
SCHLICHTE WEISEN, no. 49
 REGER Boelitz *Ein Tänzchen*
SCHLICHTE WEISEN, no. 50
 REGER Boelitz *Knecht Ruprecht*
SCHLICHTE WEISEN, no. 51
 REGER Blüthgen *Die fünf Hühnerchen*
SCHLICHTE WEISEN, no. 52
 REGER Boelitz *Mariä Wiegenlied*
SCHLICHTE WEISEN, no. 53
 REGER Kiesekamo *Das Brüderchen*
SCHLICHTE WEISEN, no. 54
 REGER Kiesekamo *Das Schwesterchen*
SCHLICHTE WEISEN, no. 55
 REGER Schellenberg *Furchthäschen*
SCHLICHTE WEISEN, no. 56
 REGER Schellenberg *Der Igel*
SCHLICHTE WEISEN, no. 57
 REGER Kiesekamo *Die Bienen*
SCHLICHTE WEISEN, no. 58
 REGER Schellenberg *Mausefangen*

SCHLICHTE WEISEN, no. 59
 REGER Schellenberg *Zum Schlafen*
SCHLICHTE WEISEN, no. 60
 REGER Schellenberg *Der König aus dem Morgenland*
Ein schlichter Sang see Drachmann **GRIEG** *Simpel Sang*
"Schlief die Mutter endlich ein" *see Die Kartenlegerin* Béranger **SCHUMANN**
"Schliesse, mein Kind" *see Wiegenlied* Träger **REGER**
Schliesse mir die Augen beide see Storm **BERG**
"Ein Schlifflein ziehet leise den Strom hin seine Gleise" *see Das Schifflein* Uhland **MENDELSSOHN-BARTHOLDY**
Schlimm für die Männer see Anon. **REGER**
Schlimme Geschichte see Ritter **REGER**
Schlippenbach, Albert, Graf von, 1800-1886. **MENDELSSOHN-BARTHOLDY** *Die Sterne schau'n in stiller Nacht*
Schlittenfahrt see Hesse **KILPINEN**
Schlittschuhlauf see Enslin **LOEWE**
Schlof mayn kind, schlof keseyder zingen see Anon. **WEISGALL**
Schloss Gordon see Burns **BENNETT** *Castle Gordon, or The young Highland rover*
Die Schlüsselblume see Mickiewicz **LOEWE**
Das Schlüsselblumen see Müller, J. **LISZT**
Schlummerlied see Benz **REGER**
Das Schlummerlied see Frey **SCHOECK**
Schlummerlied see Leo **LASSEN**
Schlummerlied see Mayrhofer **SCHUBERT** *Schlaflied*
Schlummerlied see Mombert **SZYMANOWSKI**
Schlummerlied see Tieck **FRANZ**
Schlummerlose Nächte see Frey, F. **BERG**
"Schlummre sanft" *see Wiegenlied* Unknown **MENDELSSOHN-BARTHOLDY**
"Schlumm're sanft! Noch an dem Mutterherzen" *see Wiegenlied* Körner **SCHUBERT**
"Schlummre! Schlummre und träume von kommender Zeit" *see Bei der Wiege* Klingemann **MENDELSSOHN-BARTHOLDY**
Schlusslied des Narren see Shakespeare *TWELFTH NIGHT*: When that I was and a little tiny boy **SCHUMANN**
"Die Schmach bricht ihm das Herz" *see Doch du liessest ihn im Grabe nicht* Händel **REGER**

COMPOSER Poet *Title* ''First Line''

"Schmale Gassen, tief und dunkel" *see Kleine Stadt in den Südlichen Alpen* Krenek
KRENEK
Schmeichelkätzchen see Huggenberger
REGER
"Ein Schmeichelkätzchen nenn'ich mein" *see Schmeichelkätzchen* Huggenberger
REGER
Schmerz see Blankensee **WEBER**
"Der Schmerz ist ein Schmied" *see Schmied Schmerz* Bierbaum **REGER**
Schmerzen see Wesendonck **WAGNER**
"Schmerzen und Freuden reift jede Stunde" *see Freunde* Avenarius **WEBERN**
Schmerzliche Wonnen see Anon. **WOLF**
Schmetterling see Cornelius **CORNELIUS**
Schmetterling see Hoffmann von Fallersleben **SCHUMANN**
Der Schmetterling see Schlegel, F. *ABENDRÖTE.* **SCHUBERT**
Der Schmetterling ist in die Rose verliebt see Heine **FRANZ**
Schmid, Konr. Arnold, 1716-1789.
　　LOEWE *Der Siegesfürst*
Schmidt, Friederike, 1801-1837.
　　LOEWE *An die Nachtigall*
Schmidt, Friedrich Wilhelm August, 1764-1838.
　　ZELTER *Liebe mit Schmerzen*
Schmidt, Georg Philipp, 1766-1849.
　　SCHUBERT
　　　　Der Unglückliche
　　　　Der Wanderer
　　ZELTER
　　　　Dauerhafte Farben
　　　　Das Fremdlings Abendlied
　　　　Todes Wiegenlied
Schmidt, Hans, 1854-1923.
　　BRAHMS
　　　　In den Beeren
　　　　Der Kranz
　　　　Sappische Ode
　　　　Sommerabend
Schmidt, Heinrich, 1779-1857.
　　SPOHR
　　　　Getrennte Liebe
　　　　Lebenslied
Schmidt, Klamer Eberhard Karl, 1746-1824.
　　MOZART *Das Lied der Trennung*
Der Schmied see Uhland **BRAHMS, JENSEN**
Der Schmied auf Helgoland see Schreiber
　　LOEWE *Odins Meeres-Ritt*
Schmied Schmerz see Bierbaum **REGER**
SCHMITT, FLORENT, 1870-1958.

Arosa, Paul, b. 1874.
　　Belle Meunière (1904) [unpubl.]
　　Chanson bretonne, op. 18 no. 2 [Hamelle, 1903]
　　　　"Il etait un pauv' petit gas"
Aubanel, T.
　　Si mon coeur avait des ailes . . . , op. 21 no. 3 [Hamelle]
Bengoechea, Hernando de, 1889-1915.
　　CRÉPUSCULES DU MATIN.
　　　　Prise aux réseaux d'or, op. 115 no. 1 [Durand, 1957] same
Blée, Catulle
　　Chanson, op. 2 no. 2 [Rouart Lerolle; Salabert]
　　Fleurs décloses, op. 45 no. 3 [S. Chapelier, 1912]
　　　　"Nous aimer, à quoi bon, hélas!"
Carême, Maurice, 1899-
　　LE LANTERNE MAGIQUE.
　　　　Le cerisier, op. 115 no. 4 [Durand, 1957] " 'Le cerisier,' fable"
Chalupt, René, 1885-1957.
　　Vendredi XIII, op. 67 no. 3 [Durand, 1925] "Dans le jardin du Luxembourg"
Colombeau, Eugène Adenis de, 1854-
　　Sémiramis, op. 14 [Rouart Lerolle; Salabert]
Dampierre, Leila de, comtesse, 1891-1955.
　　La citerne des mille colonnes, op. 98 no. 2 [Durand, 1943] "Colonnes sans soleil, pâles prisonnières"
Fargue, Léon-Paul, 1878-1947.
　　TANCRÈDE.
　　　　La petite princesse, op. 115 no. 2 [Durand, 1957]
　　　　"La petite princesse guette"
Forestier, J.
　　Demande, op. 20 [Hamelle]
Ganivet, Maurice, 1849-1884.
　　Fils de la Vierge, op. 4 no. 3 [Durand]
　　　　"Comme les fils étincelants"
　　Nature morte, op. 2 no. 1 [Rouart Lerolle; Salabert]
　　Neige, coeur et lys, op. 18 no. 1 [Hamelle]
Ganzo, Robert, 1898-1995.
　　. . . de pleurs d'égrène, op. 118 no. 1 [Durand, 1951]
　　　　"L'humide été de pleurs dégrène"
　　Les dîners se font en courant, op. 118 no. 2 [Durand, 1951] same
　　LANGAGE.
　　　　C'est l'heure, op. 118 no. 3 [Durand, 1951] same

SCHMITT, FLORENT, 1870-1958
(continued)
Gauthier-Villars, Henry, 1859-1931.
 Soir sur le lac, op. 9 [Grus; Lemoine]
Jean-Aubry, Georges, 1882-1950.
 Star, op. 67 no. 2 [Durand, 1925]
  "J'entends s'égrener ton rire"
Kerdyk, René
 Octroi, op. 67 no. 1 [Durand, 1925]
  "Tout un paysage en lignes blanches"
Maeterlinck, Maurice, 1862-1949.
 Ils ont tué trois petites filles, op. 45 no. 4
  [S. Chapelier, 1912] same
Mauclair, Camille, 1872-1945.
 Lied, op. 4 no. 1 [Durand]
  "Les roses de l'autre année"
Montesquiou-Fezensac, Robert, comte
 de, 1855-1921.
 Les barques, op. 8 [Salabert]
  "Les barques sont les cygnes blancs"
 Un cantique, op. 21 no. 1 [Hamelle]
No author
 Vocalise en si bémol, op. 30 [Leduc]
  Soprano & piano. In Hettich, ed.,
  Répertoire moderne de
  Vocalises–Etudes, v. 1.
Richepin, Jean, 1849-1926.
 Evocation, op. 45 no. 2 [S. Chapelier,
  1912] "Te souviens-tu du baiser"
 Où vivre? op. 45 no. 1 [S. Chapelier,
  1912] same
Rodenbach, G.
 Dans l'air fraîchi, op. 55 no. 1 [unpubl.]
Ronsard, Pierre de, 1524-1585.
 Privilèges, op. 100 no. 2 [Durand, 1942]
  "Les épis sont à Cérès"
 Ses deux yeux . . . , op. 100 no. 3
  [Durand, 1942] "Ses deux yeux bruns"
 Si . . . , op. 100 no. 1 [Durand, 1942] "Si
  mille oeillets, si mille lys j'embrasse"
 Le soir qu'amour, op. 100 no. 4 [Durand,
  1942] same
Samain, Albert Victor, 1858-1900.
 Musique sur l'eau, op. 33 [Mathot, 1913]
  "Oh! écoute la symphonie"
Sanglier, Charles
 La tortue et le lièvre, op. 98 no. 3
  [Durand, 1943]
  "Entre le lièvre et la tortue"
Tailhade, Laurent, 1854-1919.
 Tristesse au jardin, op. 52 [Mathot, 1910;
  Salabert] "Le doux rêve que tu nias"
Unknown
 La grenade entr'ouverte [Hamelle]
 O salutaris, op. 1 [Heugel]
Verlaine, Paul, 1844-1896.
 Femme et chatte, op. 21 no. 2 [Hamelle]

Il pleure dans mon coeur, op. 4 no. 2
 [Durand] same
O triste était mon âme, op. 55 no. 2 [S.
 Chapelier, 1912] same
Vildrac, Charles, 1882-1971.
 LIVRE D'AMOUR.
 Elle était venue sur les marches tièdes,
  op. 98 no. 1 [Durand, 1943] same
Vincendon, Mireille
 ALEXANDRIE.
 Antennes, op. 115 no. 3 [Durand,
  1957] "Antennes du silence"
Schneck', Schneck'! see Benzon **GRIEG**
 Snegl, Snegl!
"Der Schnee, der gestern noch in Flöckchen"
 see Schneeglöckchen Rückert
 SCHUMANN
Der Schnee ist zergangen see Osterwald
 FRANZ
Die Schneeflocke see Marggraff **LOEWE**
Schneeglöckchen see Anon. **SCHUMANN**
Schneeglöckchen see Rückert **SCHUMANN**
SCHNEEGLÖCKCHEN. see Vogl
 Blumenballade **LOEWE**
"Schneeglöckchen tut läuten" *see*
 Frühlingsglocken Reinick **SPOHR, WOLF**
"Schneeglöcklein, O Schneeglöcklein" *see*
 Viola Schober **SCHUBERT**
"Der Schneewind packt mich" *see*
 Schlittenfahrt Hesse **KILPINEN**
Schneider, Édouard
 AUBERT *Pays sans nom*
Schneider, Louis, 1861-1934.
 MASSENET *Noël des fleurs*
Schneiderlied see Häring **LOEWE**
"Schnell fliegt der Aar am Himmel hell" *see*
 Sehnsucht Kjerulf **DELIUS**
"Schnell geniesst die schnellen Stunden" *see*
 Lebenslied Schmidt, Heinrich **SPOHR**
Schnezler, August, 1809-1853.
 LOEWE *Der Mummelsee*
Schnezler, Ferdinand Alexander August
 see Schnezler, August, 1809-1853.
"Schnür den Bündel" *see Zwist und Sühne*
 Simrock **LOEWE**
Die Schnur, die Perl an Perle see Daumer
 POLYDORA. **BRAHMS**
"Schnurre, schnurre, meine Spindel" *see*
 Die Spinnerin Unknown **LASSEN**
Schober, Franz von, 1798-1882.
 LISZT *Weimars Toten*
 SCHUBERT
 Am Bach im Frühling
 An die Musik
 Genügsamkeit
 Jägers Liebeslied

Pax vobiscum
Pilgerweise
Schatzgräbers Begehr
Schiffers Scheidelied
Todesmusik
Trost im Liede
Vergissmeinnicht
Viola
Die Wolkenbraut

SCHOECK, OTHMAR, 1886-1957.

Anacreon, b. ca. 570 B.C.
Ruheplatz, op. 31 no. 4 (1915)
[Breitkopf & Härtel, 1921]
"Hier im Schatten, O Batyllos"
Translated by Mörike.

Anon.
Die Verlassene, op. 6 no. 1 (1905) [Hug,
1907] "Wenn i zum Brünnle geh"
High voice & piano.

Bible
Psalm 23, op. 11 no. 2 (1907) [Hug,
1907] "Der Herr ist mein Hirte"
Baritone & organ.
Psalm 100, op. 11 no. 3 (1907) [Hug,
1907] "Jauchzet dem Herrn"
Baritone & organ.

Blüthgen, Viktor, 1844-1920.
ACH, WER DOCH DAS KÖNNTE!
Kinderliedchen, o. op. Nr. 6 (1902)
[unpubl.] "Gemäht sind die Felder"

Buonarroti, Michel Angelo, 1475-1564.
Die Verklärende, op. 9 no. 1 (1907)
[Hug, 1907] "In mir nur Tod"
Baritone & piano.
MADRIALE.
Madrigal, op. 31 no. 1 (1917)
[Breitkopf & Härtel, 1921]
"Ins Joch beug' ich den Nakken
demutvoll"

Busch, Wilhelm, 1832-1908.
Dilemma, op. 13 no. 3 (1907) [Hug,
1908] "Das glaube mir, so sagte er"

Busse, Carl, 1872-1918.
Über den Bergen, o. op. Nr. 11 (1903)
[unpubl.] same

Claudius, Matthias, 1740-1815.
Abendlied, op. 52 no. 10 (1937)
[Universal-Edition, 1937]
"Der Mond ist aufgegangen"
*Als er sein Weib und 's Kind schlafend
fand,* op. 52 no. 4 (1937)
[Universal-Edition, 1937]
"Das heiss' ich rechte Augenweide"
Auf den Tod einer Kaiserin, op. 52 no. 15
(1937) [Universal-Edition, 1937]
"Sie machte Frieden!"

Der Frühling, op. 52 no. 6 (1937)
[Universal-Edition, 1937]
"Heute will ich fröhlich, fröhlich sein"
Der Krieg, op. 52 no. 14 (1937)
[Universal-Edition, 1937]
" 'sist Krieg!"
Kuckuck, op. 52 no. 8 (1937) [Universal-
Edition, 1937]
"Wir Vögel singen nicht egal"
Die Liebe, op. 52 no. 1 (1937)
[Universal-Edition, 1937]
"Die Liebe hemmet nichts"
Ein Lied, hinterm Ofen zu singen, op.
52 no. 9 (1937) [Universal-Edition,
1937]
"Der Winter ist ein rechter Mann"
Der Mensch, op. 52 no. 11 (1937)
[Universal-Edition, 1937]
"Empfangen und genähret"
Die Natur, op. 52 no. 5 (1937)
[Universal-Edition, 1937]
"Tausend Blumen um mich her"
Phidile, op. 52 no. 2 (1937) [Universal-
Edition, 1937]
"Ich war erst sechzehn Sommer alt"
Die Römer, op. 52 no. 12 (1937)
[Universal-Edition, 1937]
"Die Römer, die"
Der Schwarze in der Zuckerplantage, op.
52 no. 13 (1937) [Universal-Edition,
1937]
"Weit von meinem Vaterlande"
Spruch, op. 52 no. 17 (1937) [Universal-
Edition, 1937]
"Der Mensch lebt und bestehet"
Die Sternseherin, op. 52 no. 7 (1937)
[Universal-Edition, 1937]
"Ich sehe oft um Mitternacht"
Der Tod, op. 52 no. 16 (1937)
[Universal-Edition, 1937]
"Ach, es ist so dunkel in des Todes
Kammer"
*Ein Wiegenlied, bei Mondschein zu
singen,* op. 52 no. 3 (1937)
[Universal-Edition, 1937]
"So schlafe nun, du Kleine!"

Dante Aligheri, 1265-1321.
VITA NUOVA.
*Du, des Erbarmens Feind, grausamer
Tod,* op. 9 no. 2 (1906) [Hug, 1907]
same
Baritone & piano.

Dehmel, Richard, 1863-1920.
Manche Nacht, op. 24a no. 6 (1911)
[Breitkopf & Härtel, 1917]
"Wenn die Felder sich verdunkeln"

SCHOECK, OTHMAR, 1886-1957
(continued)
Eichendorff, Joseph Karl Benedikt, Freiherr von, 1788-1857
Abendlandschaft, op. 20 no. 10 (1914)
[Breitkopf & Härtel, 1917]
"Der Hirt bläst seine Weise"
Abschied, op. 20 no. 7 (1909)
[Breitkopf & Härtel, 1917]
"Abendlich schon rauscht der Wald"
An die Lützowschen Jäger, op. 30 no. 11
(1917) [Breitkopf & Härtel, 1921]
"Wunderliche Spiessgesellen"
Auf dem Rhein, op. 30 no. 12 (1917)
[Breitkopf & Härtel, 1921]
"Kühle auf dem schönen Rheine"
Auf einer Burg, op. 17 no. 6 (1909)
[Hug, 1909]
"Eingeschlafen auf der Lauer"
Auf meines Kindes Tod, op. 20 no. 8
(1914) [Breitkopf & Härtel, 1917]
"Von fern die Uhren schlagen"
Die Einsame, op. 10 no. 2 (1907) [Hug,
1907]
"Wär's dunkel, ich läg' im Walde"
Ergebung, op. 30 no. 6 (1918)
[Breitkopf & Härtel, 1921]
"Es wandelt, was wir schauen"
Erinnerung, op. 10 no. 1 (1907) [Hug,
1907]
"Lindes Rauschen in den Wipfeln"
Erinnerung, op. 17 no. 7 (1909) [Hug,
1909] "Ich hör' die Bächlein rauschen"
Der frohe Wandersmann, op. 17 no. 8
(1909) [Hug, 1909]
"Wem Gott will rechte Gunst
erweisen"
Der Gärtner, op. 20 no. 11 (1914)
[Breitkopf & Härtel, 1917]
"Wohin ich geh' und schaue"
Gottes Segen, op. 35 no. 3 (1928)
[Breitkopf & Härtel, 1931]
"Das Kind ruht aus vom Spielen"
Guter Rat, op. 10 no. 3 (1907) [Hug,
1907] "Springer, der in luft'gem
Schreiten"
Im Wandern, op. 30 no. 4 (1918)
[Breitkopf & Härtel, 1921]
"So ruhig geh ich meinen Pfad"
In der Fremde, op. 15 no. 4 (1908) [Hug,
1908] "Da fahr' ich still im Wagen"
Der Kranke, op. 20 no. 9 (1913)
[Breitkopf & Härtel, 1917]
"Soll ich dich denn nun verlassen"
Kurze Fahrt, op. 30 no. 2 (1918)
[Breitkopf & Härtel, 1921]
"Posthorn, wie so keck und fröhlich"
Lockung, op. 30 no. 10 (1917)
[Breitkopf & Härtel, 1921]
"Über gelb' und rote Streifen"
Motto, op. 51 no. 2 (1934) [Hug, 1946]
"Aus schweren Träumen"
Nachklang, op. 30 no. 7 (1917)
[Breitkopf & Härtel, 1921]
"Lust'ge Vögel in dem Wald"
Nachruf, op. 20 no. 14 (1910)
[Breitkopf & Härtel, 1917]
"Du liebe, treue Laute"
Nacht, op. 30 no. 9 (1917) [Breitkopf &
Härtel, 1921]
"Hörst du die Gründe rufen"
Nachtgruss, op. 51 no. 1 (1931) [Hug,
1946] "Weil jetzo alles stille ist"
Nachtlied, op. 20 no. 13 (1914)
[Breitkopf & Härtel, 1917]
"Vergangen ist der lichte Tag"
Reiselied, op. 12 no. 1 (1908) [Hug,
1908] "Durch Feld u. Buchenhallen"
Sterbeglocken, op. 30 no. 5 (1918)
[Breitkopf & Härtel, 1921]
"Nun legen sich die Wogen"
Trost, op. 51 no. 3 (1935) [Hug, 1946]
"Es haben viel Dichter gesungen"
Umkehr, op. 20 no. 12 (1914)
[Breitkopf & Härtel, 1917]
"Hier bin ich"
Der verspätete Wanderer, op. 30 no. 8
(1917) [Breitkopf & Härtel, 1921]
"Wo aber werd' ich sein im künft'gen
Lenze?"
Waldeinsamkeit, op. 30 no. 1 (1918)
[Breitkopf & Härtel, 1921]
"Waldeinsamkeit! Du grünes Revier"
Wanderlied der Prager Studenten, op. 12
no. 2 (1907) [Hug, 1908]
"Nach Süden nun sich lenken"
Winternacht, op. 30 no. 3 (1918)
[Breitkopf & Härtel, 1921]
"Verschneit liegt rings die ganze Welt"
Fontane, Theodor, 1819-1898.
Der Gast, o. op. Nr. 9 (1903) [unpubl.]
"Das Kind ist krank zum Sterben"
Frey, Adolf, 1855-1920.
Das Schlummerlied, op. 14 no. 2 (1907)
[Hug, 1908]
"In begrünter Sommerlaube"
Low voice & piano.
Schöner Ort, op. 14 no. 3 (1907) [Hug,
1908] "Klingend schlagen hier die
Finken"
Low voice & piano.

Gamper, Gustav, 1873-1948.

Jünger des Weins I, op. 24b no. 2 (1915)
[Breitkopf & Härtel, 1917]
"Führe mich zum Rosenhaine"

Jünger des Weins II, op. 24b no. 3 (1915)
[Breitkopf & Härtel, 1917]
"Laut gesungen sei das Feuer"

Gerok, Karl, 1815-1890.

Kindergottesdienst, o. op. Nr. 13 (1903?)
[unpubl.]
"Es läuten zur Kirche die Glokken"

Goethe, Johann Wolfgang von, 1749-1832.

Epigramm, op. 31 no. 5 (1906)
[Breitkopf & Härtel, 1921]
"Kaum an dem blaueren Himmel
erblickt' ich"

Erster Verlust, op. 15 no. 5 (1908) [Hug,
1908]
"Ach, wer bringt die schönen Tage"

Geistesgruss, o. op. Nr. 5 (1902?)
[unpubl.] "Hoch auf dem alten Turme"

Gleich und gleich, o. op. Nr. 10 (1903)
[unpubl.] "Ein Blumenglöckchen vom
Boden hervor"

Herbstgefühl, op. 19a no. 1 (1909)
[Breitkopf & Härtel, 1917]
"Fetter grüne, du Laub"

Im Sommer, op. 17 no. 1 (1909) [Hug,
1909] "Wie Feld und Au so blinkend
im Tau"

Mailied, op. 19a no. 3 (1911)
[Breitkopf & Härtel, 1917]
"Wie herrlich leuchtet mir die Natur"

Mit einem gemalten Band, op. 19a no. 4
(1912) [Breitkopf & Härtel, 1917]
"Kleine Blumen, kleine Blätter"

Nachtgesang, o. op. Nr. 2 (1901?)
[unpubl.] "O gib vom weichen Pfühle"

Parabase, op. 19a no. 8 (1914)
[Breitkopf & Härtel, 1917]
"Freudig war vor viellen Jahren"

Rastlose Liebe, op. 19a no. 5 (1912)
[Breitkopf & Härtel, 1917]
"Dem Schnee, dem Regen"

Selbstbetrug, o. op. Nr. 8 (1903)
[unpubl.]
"Der Vorhang schwebet hin und her"

Sorge, op. 19a no. 6 (1910) [Breitkopf &
Härtel, 1917]
"Kehre nicht in diesem Kreise"

Ungeduld, op. 19a no. 7 (1914?)
[Breitkopf & Härtel, 1917]
"Immer wieder in die Weite"

*CHINESISCH- DEUTSCHE JAHRES-
UND TAGESZEITEN.*

Dämmrung senkte sich von oben, op.
19a no. 2 (1911)
[Breitkopf & Härtel, 1917] same

INDISCHE LEGENDE.

Der Gott und die Bajadere, op. 34
(1921) [Breitkopf & Härtel, 1921]
"Mahadöh, der Herr der Erde"
Baritone or alto & piano; also
voice & orchestra.

WESTÖSTLICHER DIVAN.

Diese Gondel vergleich ich, op. 19b
no. 7 V (1906)
[Breitkopf & Härtel, 1917] same

Eine einzige Nacht an deinem Herzen!
op. 19b no. 7 II (1907)
[Breitkopf & Härtel, 1917] same

Haben sie von deinen Fehlen, op. 19b
no. 4 I (1915)
[Breitkopf & Härtel, 1917] same

Höre den Rat, op. 19b no. 4 II (1915)
[Breitkopf & Härtel, 1917] same

Nachklang, op. 19b no. 1 (1915)
[Breitkopf & Härtel, 1917]
"Es klingt so prächtig"

Seh' ich den Pilgrim, op. 19b no. 7 IV
(1906) [Breitkopf & Härtel, 1917]
same

Selige Sehnsucht, op. 19b no. 6 (1911)
[Breitkopf & Härtel, 1917]
"Sagt es nicmand, nur den Weisen"

Suleika, op. 19b no. 3 (1915)
[Breitkopf & Härtel, 1917]
"Deinem Blick mich zu bequemen"

Suleika und Hatem, op. 19b no. 2
(1915) [Breitkopf & Härtel, 1917]
"An des lust'gen Brunnens Rand"

Unmut, op. 19b no. 5 (1915)
[Breitkopf & Härtel, 1917]
"Keinen Reimer wird man finden"

Warum leckst du dein Mäulchen, op.
19b no. 7 I (1906)
[Breitkopf & Härtel, 1917] same

Wie ich so ehrlich war, op. 19b no. 4
III (1915)
[Breitkopf & Härtel, 1917] same

Wie sie klingeln, die Pfaffen! op. 19b
no. 7 III (1906)
[Breitkopf & Härtel, 1917] same

**Hafiz, Muhammad Shums al-Din, d.
1388.**

Ach, wie richtete, so klagt ich, op. 33 no.
4 [Breitkopf & Härtel, 1921] same

*Ach, wie schön ist Nacht und
Dämmerschein,* op. 33 no. 1
[Breitkopf & Härtel, 1921] same

Das Gescheh'ne, nicht bereut's Hafis, op.
33 no. 3 [Breitkopf & Härtel, 1921]
same

SCHOECK, OTHMAR, 1886-1957
(continued)
Hafiz, Muhammad Shums al-Din, d.
   1388 *(continued)*
   Höre mir den Prediger, op. 33 no. 2
      [Breitkopf & Härtel, 1921] same
   Horch, hörst du nicht vom Himmel her,
      op. 33 no. 10 [Breitkopf & Härtel,
      1921] same
   Ich habe mich dem Heil entschworen, op.
      33 no. 8 [Breitkopf & Härtel, 1921]
      same
   Ich roch der Liebe himmlischers Arom,
      op. 33 no. 7 [Breitkopf & Härtel,
      1921] same
   Lieblich in der Rosenzeit, op. 33 no. 9
      [Breitkopf & Härtel, 1921] same
   Meine Lebenszeit verstreicht, op. 33 no. 6
      [Breitkopf & Härtel, 1921] same
   Nicht düstre, Theosoph, so tief! op. 33
      no. 11 [Breitkopf & Härtel, 1921]
      same
   Sing, O lieblicher Sängermund, op. 33
      no. 12 [Breitkopf & Härtel, 1921]
      same
   Wie stimmst du mich zur Andacht, op. 33
      no. 5 [Breitkopf & Härtel, 1921] same
Hardenberg, Friedrich Leopold,
   Freiherr von, 1772-1801.
   Marienlied, op. 6 no. 5 (1907) [Hug,
      1907]
      "Ich sehe dich in tausend Bildern"
      High voice & piano.
Hebbel, Christian Friedrich, 1813-
   1863.
   Das Heiligste, op. 24a no. 5 (1914)
      [Breitkopf & Härtel, 1917]
      "Wenn zwei sich ineinander still
      versenken"
   DEM SCHMERZ SEIN RECHT.
      Schlafen, schlafen, nichts als schlafen,
         op. 14 no. 4 (1907) [Hug, 1908]
         same
         Low voice & piano.
Heine, Heinrich, 1797-1856.
   Das Fräulein am Meere, o. op. Nr. 16
      (1905) [unpubl.]
      "Ein Fräulein stand am Meere"
   Gekommen ist der Maie, op. 17 no. 5
      (1904) [Hug, 1909] same
   Ja, du bist elend, op. 13 no. 2 (1907)
      [Hug, 1908] same
   Vergiftet sind meine Lieder, op. 13 no. 1
      (1907) [Hug, 1908] same
   Warum sind denn die Rosen so blass? op.
      4 no. 2 (1906) [Hug, 1907] same

Wo? op. 4 no. 3 (1906) [Hug, 1907]
      "Wo wird einst des Wandermüden"
HEIMKEHR.
   Sommerabend, op. 4 no. 1 (1904)
      [Hug, 1907]
      "Dämmernd liegt der Sommerabend"
Hesse, Hermann, 1877-1962.
   Abends, op. 44 no. 4 (1929) [Breitkopf &
      Härtel, 1931]
      "Abends gehn die Liebespaare"
   Aus zwei Tälern, op. 8 no. 2 (1906)
      [Hug, 1907] "Eine Glokke läutet"
   Auskunst, op. 8 no. 3 (1906) [Hug, 1907]
      "Im Welschland, wo die braunen"
   Blauer Schmetterling, op. 44 no. 6 (1929)
      [Breitkopf & Härtel, 1931]
      "Flügelt ein kleiner blauer"
   Elisabeth, op. 8 no. 1 (1906) [Hug, 1907]
      "Wie eine weisse Wolke"
   Frühling, op. 24b no. 6 (1911)
      [Breitkopf & Härtel, 1917]
      "Wieder schreitet er den braunen Pfad"
   Für Ninon, op. 44 no. 9 (1929)
      [Breitkopf & Härtel, 1931]
      "Dass du bei mir magst weilen"
   Im Krauzgang von St. Stefano, op. 31 no.
      3 (1917) [Breitkopf & Härtel, 1921]
      "Ein Wändeviereck, blass, vergilbt und
      alt"
   Im Nebel, o. op. Nr. 45 (1952)
      [*Schweizerische Musikzeitung,* April
      1, 1954, pp. 136-37]
      "Seltsam, im Nebel zu wandern!"
   Jahrestag, op. 8 no. 4 (1906) [Hug,
      1907] "Im alten loderlohen Glanze"
   Keine Rast, op. 24b no. 7 (1914-15)
      [Breitkopf & Härtel, 1917]
      "Seele, banger Vogel du"
   Kennst du das auch? op. 24b no. 4
      (1906) [Breitkopf & Härtel, 1917]
      same
   Die Kindheit, op. 31 no. 2 (1914-15)
      [Breitkopf & Härtel, 1921]
      "Du bist mein fernes Tal"
   Magie der Farben, op. 44 no. 2 (1929)
      [Breitkopf & Härtel, 1931]
      "Gottes Atem hin und wieder"
   Mittag im September, op. 44 no. 5 (1929)
      [Breitkopf & Härtel, 1931]
      "Es hält der blaue Tag"
   Nachtgefühl, op. 44 no. 1 (1929)
      [Breitkopf & Härtel, 1931]
      "Tief mit blauer Nachtgewalt"
   Pfeifen, op. 44 no. 7 (1929) [Breitkopf &
      Härtel, 1931] "Klavier und Geige, die
      ich wahrlich schätze"

Ravenna, op. 24b no. 9 (1913)
[Breitkopf & Härtel, 1917]
"Ich bin auch in Ravenna gewesen"
Sommernacht, op. 44 no. 8 (1929)
[Breitkopf & Härtel, 1931]
"Die Bäume tropfen vom
Gewittergruss"
Vergänglichkeit, op. 44 no. 10 (1929)
[Breitkopf & Härtel, 1931]
"Vom Baum des Lebens fällt"
Verwelkende Rosen, op. 44 no. 3 (1929)
[Breitkopf & Härtel, 1931]
"Möchten viele Seelen dies verstehen"
Vorwurf, o. op. Nr. 27 (1907) [unpubl.]
"Die Nacht fällt ein"
Was lachst du so? op. 24b no. 5 (1906)
[Breitkopf & Härtel, 1917] same
Das Ziel, op. 24b no. 8 (1914)
[Breitkopf & Härtel, 1917]
"Immer bin ich ohne Ziel gegangen"

**Hoffmann von Fallersleben, August
Heinrich, 1798-1874.**
Wiegenlied, o. op. Nr. 15 (1904-5?)
[unpubl.]
"Wer hat die schönsten Schäfchen?"

Hopfen, Hans
Lieb Seelchen, lass das Fragen sein, o.
op. Nr. 7 (1903) [unpubl.] same

Jaeger, Johannes
Wiegenlied, o. op. Nr. 44 (1947) [Basel:
Heinrich Majer, 1952]
"Mein liebes Kind, schlaf ein!"
Text and music by Jaeger,
movement for voice and piano by
Schoeck.

Keller, Gottfried, 1819-1890.
Abendlied, op. 55 no. 12 (1941-43)
[Universal-Edition, 1945]
"Augen, meine lieben Fensterlein"
Abendlied an die Natur, op. 55 no. 6
(1941-43) [Universal-Edition, 1945]
"Hüll' ein mich in die grünen Dekken"
An das Herz, op. 55 no. 23 (1941-43)
[Universal-Edition, 1945]
"Willst du nicht dich schliessen"
Aus den Waldliedern I, op. 55 no. 8
(1941-43) [Universal-Edition, 1945]
"Arm in Arm und Kron' an Krone"
Aus den Waldliedern II, op. 55 no. 9
(1941-43) [Universal-Edition, 1945]
"Aber auch den Föhrenwald"
Aus: Ein Tagewerk I, op. 55 no. 24
(1941-43) [Universal-Edition, 1945]
"Vom Lager stand ich mit dem
Frühlicht auf"
Aus: Ein Tagewerk II, op. 55 no. 25
(1941-43) [Universal-Edition, 1945]
"Aber ein kleiner goldener Stern"

Den Zweifellosen I, op. 55 no. 20 (1941-
43) [Universal-Edition, 1945]
"Wer ohne Leid"
Den Zweifellosen II, op. 55 no. 21 (1941-
43) [Universal-Edition, 1945]
"Es ist nicht Selbstsucht und nicht
Eitelkeit"
Die Entschwundene, o. op. Nr. 37
(1923?) [unpubl.]
"Es war ein heit'res, gold'nes Jahr"
Low voice & piano.
Fahrewohl, op. 35 no. 1 (1928)
[Breitkopf & Härtel, 1931]
"Den Linden ist zu Füssen tief"
Flack're ew'ges Licht im Tal, op. 55 no.
14 (1941-43) [Universal-Edition, 1945]
same
Frühgesicht, op. 55 no. 17 (1941-43)
[Universal-Edition, 1945]
"Es donnert über der Pfaffengass"
Frühlingsglaube, op. 55 no. 18 (1941-43)
[Universal-Edition, 1945]
"Es wandert eine schöne Sage"
In der Trauer, op. 55 no. 19 (1941-43)
[Universal-Edition, 1945]
"Ein Meister bin ich worden"
Jugendgedenken, op. 24b no. 10 (1914)
[Breitkopf & Härtel, 1917] "Ich will
spiegeln mich in jenen Tagen"
Schifferliedchen, op. 6 no. 2 (1906) [Hug,
1907] "Schon hat die Nacht den
Silberschrein"
High voice & piano.
Siehst du den Stern, op. 55 no. 3 (1941-
43) [Universal-Edition, 1945] same
Sonnenuntergang, op. 55 no. 2 (1941-43)
[Universal-Edition, 1945]
"In Gold und Purpur tief verhüllt"
Stille der Nacht, op. 55 no. 4 (1941-43)
[Universal-Edition, 1945]
"Willkommen, klare Sommernacht"
Stilleben, op. 55 no. 10 (1941-43)
[Universal-Edition, 1945]
"Durch Bäume dringt ein leiser Ton"
Das Tal, op. 55 no. 11 (1941-43)
[Universal-Edition, 1945]
"Mit dem grauen Felsensaal"
Tod und Dichter, op. 55 no. 22 (1941-43)
[Universal-Edition, 1945]
"Deiner bunten Blasen Kinderfreude"
Trost der Kreatur, op. 55 no. 1 (1941-43)
[Universal-Edition, 1945]
"Wie schlafend unterm Flügel"
Trübes Wetter, op. 55 no. 16 (1941-43)
[Universal-Edition, 1945]
"Es ist ein stiller Regentag"

COMPOSER Poet *Title* "First Line"

SCHOECK, OTHMAR, 1886-1957
(continued)
Keller, Gottfried, 1819-1890 *(continued)*
Uhruhe der Nacht, op. 55 no. 7 (1941-
43) [Universal-Edition, 1945]
"Nun bin ich untreu worden"
Unter Sternen, op. 55 no. 5 (1941-43)
[Universal-Edition, 1945]
"Wende dich, du kleiner Stern"
Wie wähnten lange recht zu leben, op. 55
no. 13 (1941-43)
[Universal-Edition, 1945] same
Die Zeit geht nicht, op. 55 no. 15 (1941-
43) [Universal-Edition, 1945] same
ALTE WEISEN.
Mir glänzen die Augen, o. op. Nr. 31
(1910?) [unpubl.] same
Lenau, Nicolaus, 1802-1850.
Der Abend, op. 45 no. 10 (1930) [Hug,
1934]
"Die Wolken waren fortgezogen"
An die Entfernte, op. 5 no. 2 (1907)
[Hug, 1907]
"Rosen fliehen nicht allein"
An die Entfernte, op. 24a no. 3 (1914)
[Breitkopf & Härtel, 1917]
"Diese Rose pflück' ich hier"
Aufbruch, op. 45 no. 2 (1930) [Hug,
1934]
"Des Himmels frohes Antlitz brannte"
Die drei Zigeuner, op. 24a no. 4 (1914)
[Breitkopf & Härtel, 1917]
"Drei Zigeuner fand ich einmal"
Drüben geht die Sonne scheiden, op. 2
no. 1 (1905) [Hug, 1907, 1946] same
Der Eichwald, op. 45 no. 4 (1930) [Hug,
1934] "Ich trat in einen heilig düstern
Eichwald"
Einsamkeit, op. 45 no. 6 (1930) [Hug,
1934] "Schon seh'ich Hirt' und Herde
nimmer"
Erinnerung, op. 45 no. 1 (1930) [Hug,
1934] "Du warst mir ein gar trauter"
Der Ferne, op. 45 no. 7 (1930) [Hug,
1934]
"Des Berges Gipfel war erschwungen"
Frühlingsblick, op. 5 no. 3 (1907) [Hug,
1907] "Durch den Wald, den dunkeln"
Das Gewitter, op. 45 no. 8 (1930) [Hug,
1934] "Noch immer lag ein tiefes
Schweigen"
Himmelstrauer, op. 5 no. 1 (1905) [Hug,
1907] "Am Himmelsantlitz wandelt ein
Gedanke"
Der Hirte, op. 45 no. 5 (1930) [Hug,
1934] "Schon zog vom Wald ich ferne
wieder"

Lenz, op. 24a no. 1 (1910) [Breitkopf &
Härtel, 1917] "Die Bäume blühn, die
Vöglein singen"
Die Lerche, op. 45 no. 3 (1930) [Hug,
1934]
"Froh summte nach der Süssen Beute"
Liebewohl! o. op. Nr. 19 (1905) [Corrodi
Othmar Schoeck . . . , 2. Aufl.
(Frauenfeld/Leipzig: Verlag Huber,
1936), 47-49] "Lebe wohl!"
Scheideblick, o. op. Nr. 17 (1905)
[unpubl.] "Als ein unergründlich
Wonnemeer"
Der Schlaf, op. 45 no. 9 (1930) [Hug,
1934]
"Ein Greis trat lächelnd mir entgegen"
Stumme Liebe, op. 24a no. 2 (1913)
[Breitkopf & Härtel, 1917]
"Liesse doch ein hold Geschick"
Trübe wird's, die Wolken jagen, op. 2 no.
2 (1905) [Hug, 1907] same
Vergangenheit, o. op. Nr. 14 (1904)
[Corrodi **Othmar Schoeck . . . ,** 2 Aufl.
(Frauenfeld/Leipzig: Verlag Huber,
1936), 44-45]
"Hesperus, der bleiche Funken"
SCHILFLIEDER.
Auf geheimem Waldespfade, op. 2 no.
3 (1905) [Hug, 1907] same
Leuthold, Heinrich, 1827-1879.
Abkehr, op. 57 no. 7 (1944-45)
[Universal-Edition, 1951]
"Wie einst den Knaben lacht ihr noch
heut mich an"
High voice & piano.
An meine Grossmutter, op. 57 no. 18
(1944-45) [Universal-Edition, 1951]
"Wie floss von deiner Lippe milde
Güte!"
High voice & piano.
Aus dem Süden, op. 57 no. 9 (1944-45)
[Universal-Edition, 1951]
"Nicht allein in Rathaussälen"
High voice & piano.
Distichen, op. 57 no. 23 (1944-45)
[Universal-Edition, 1951]
"Selbstzweck sei sich die Kunst"
High voice & piano.
Einst, op. 57 no. 17 (1944-45)
[Universal-Edition, 1951]
"Ihr Bilder, die die Zeit begrub"
High voice & piano.
Heimweh, op. 57 no. 15 (1944-45)
[Universal-Edition, 1951]
"Hier pflegt Natur mit ihren goldnen
Auen"
High voice & piano.

Ich bin ein Spielmann von Beruf, op. 56
  no. 3 (1944) [Universal-Edition, 1946]
  same
    High voice & harp or piano.
Im Klosterkeller, op. 57 no. 21 (1944-45)
  [Universal-Edition, 1951]
  "Hier scheidet die Klosterpforte"
    High voice & piano.
Leidenschaft, op. 57 no. 1 (1944-45)
  [Universal-Edition, 1951]
  "Was immer mir die Feindschaft
    unterschoben"
    High voice & piano.
Liederfrühling, op. 57 no. 3 (1944-45)
  [Universal-Edition, 1951]
  "Der Lenz ist da"
    High voice & piano.
Mein Herz ist wie ein Saitenspiel, op. 56
  no. 5 (1944) [Universal-Edition, 1946]
  same
Muttersprache, op. 57 no. 2 (1944-45)
  [Universal-Edition, 1951]
  "Dich vor allem, heilige
    Muttersprache"
    High voice & piano.
Nacht, Muse und Tod, op. 57 no. 11
  (1944-45) [Universal-Edition, 1951]
  "Komm, ambrosische Nacht"
    High voice & piano.
O Frühlingshauch, O Liederlust, op. 56
  no. 1 (1944) [Universal-Edition, 1946]
  same
    High voice & harp or piano.
O Lebensfrühling, Blütendrang, op. 56
  no. 6 (1944) [Universal-Edition, 1946]
  same
    High voice & harp or piano.
Rechtfertigung, op. 57 no. 6 (1944-45)
  [Universal-Edition, 1951] "Nicht, dass
  ich dies Bestreben nicht erfasse"
    High voice & piano.
Riviera, op. 57 no. 10 (1944-45)
  [Universal-Edition, 1951]
  "In diesen Silberhainen von Oliven"
    High voice & piano.
Rückkehr, op. 57 no. 16 (1944-45)
  [Universal-Edition, 1951]
  "Schon verstummt das Lied der Grille"
    High voice & piano.
Sapphische Strophe, op. 57 no. 12 (1944-
  45) [Universal-Edition, 1951]
  "Schweigen rings"
    High voice & piano.
Sonnenuntergang, op. 57 no. 13 (1944-
  45) [Universal-Edition, 1951]
  "O wie träumte es sich süss"
    High voice & piano.

Spruch, op. 57 no. 24 (1944-45)
  [Universal-Edition, 1951] "Ein guter
  Ruf ist wie ein wohnlich Haus"
    High voice & piano.
Die Ströme zieh'n zum fernen Meer, op.
  56 no. 2 (1944) [Universal-Edition,
  1946] same
    High voice & harp or piano.
Trauer, op. 57 no. 19 (1944-45)
  [Universal-Edition, 1951]
  "Ein unbezwingbar dunkler Hang"
    High voice & piano.
Trinklied, op. 57 no. 22 (1944-45)
  [Universal-Edition, 1951]
  "Greift zum Becher und lasst das
    Schelten!"
    High voice & piano.
Trost, op. 57 no. 26 (1944-45)
  [Universal-Edition, 1951]
  "Nun lass' das Lamentieren"
    High voice & piano.
*Und wieder nehm ich die Harfe zur
  Hand,* op. 56 no. 4 (1944)
  [Universal-Edition, 1946] same
    High voice & harp or piano.
Unmut, op. 57 no. 25 (1944-45)
  [Universal-Edition, 1951]
  "Du sahst mich schwelgen oft im
    Tonregister"
    High voice & piano.
Vorwurf, op. 57 no. 5 (1944-45)
  [Universal-Edition, 1951]
  "Wohl ist es schön, auf fauler Haut"
    High voice & piano.
Waldeinsamkeit, op. 57 no. 4 (1944-45)
  [Universal-Edition, 1951]
  "Wo über mir die Wald nacht finster"
    High voice & piano.
Der Waldsee, op. 15 no. 1 (1907) [Hug,
  1908] "Wie bist du schön"
Der Waldsee, op. 57 no. 20 (1944-45)
  [Universal-Edition, 1951]
  "Wie bist du schön"
    High voice & piano.
Waldvögelein, op. 57 no. 8 (1944-45)
  [Universal-Edition, 1951]
  "Waldvögelein, wohin ziehst du?"
    High voice & piano.
Warnung, op. 57 no. 14 (1944-45)
  [Universal-Edition, 1951]
  "Wenn ein Gott dir gab für's Schöne"
    High voice & piano.
Li Po, 701-762.
In der Herberge, op. 7 no. 3 (1907)
  [Hug, 1907]
  "Vor mein Bett wirft der Mond"
    Low voice & piano.

SCHOECK, OTHMAR, 1886-1957
(continued)
Meyer, Conrad Ferdinand, 1825-1898.

Abendwolke, op. 60 no. 26 (1946)
[Universal-Edition, 1949]
"So stille ruht im Hafen"
Middle voice & piano.

Alle, op. 60 no. 18 (1946) [Universal-
Edition, 1949]
"Es sprach der Geist: Sieh auf!"
Middle voice & piano.

Am Himmelstor, op. 60 no. 5 (1946)
[Universal-Edition, 1949]
"Mir träumt', ich komm' ans
Himmelstor"
Middle voice & piano.

Das Ende des Festes, op. 60 no. 15
(1946) [Universal-Edition, 1949]
"Da mit Sokrates die Freunde tranken"
Middle voice & piano.

Firnelicht, op. 60 no. 23 (1946)
[Universal-Edition, 1949]
"Wie pocht' das Herz mir in der
Brust"
Middle voice & piano.

Frühling Triumphator, op. 60 no. 9
(1946) [Universal-Edition, 1949]
"Frühling, der die Welt umblaut"
Middle voice & piano.

Der Gesang des Meeres, op. 60 no. 13
(1946) [Universal-Edition, 1949]
"Wolken, meine Kinder"
Middle voice & piano.

Göttermahl, op. 60 no. 21 (1946)
[Universal-Edition, 1949] "Wo die
Tannen finstre Schatten werfen"
Middle voice & piano.

Das Heilige Feuer, op. 60 no. 1 (1946)
[Universal-Edition, 1949] "Auf das
Feuer mit dem goldnen Strahle"
Middle voice & piano.

Hochzeitslied, op. 60 no. 12 (1946)
[Universal-Edition, 1949]
"Aus der Eltern Macht und Haus"
Middle voice & piano.

Ich würd' es hören, op. 60 no. 22 (1946)
[Universal-Edition, 1949]
"Läg' dort ich unterm Firneschein"
Middle voice & piano.

Im Harmesnächten, op. 60 no. 7 (1946)
[Universal-Edition, 1949] "Die Rechte
streckt' ich schmerzlich oft"
Middle voice & piano.

In einer Sturmnacht, op. 60 no. 6 (1946)
[Universal-Edition, 1949] "Es fährt der
Wind gewaltig durch die Nacht"
Middle voice & piano.

Jetzt rede du! op. 60 no. 28 (1946)
[Universal-Edition, 1949] "Du warest
mir ein täglich Wanderziel"
Middle voice & piano.

Die Jungfrau, op. 60 no. 16 (1946)
[Universal-Edition, 1949]
"Wo sah ich, Mädchen, deine Züge"
Middle voice & piano.

Lenzfahrt, op. 60 no. 8 (1946)
[Universal-Edition, 1949]
"Am Himmel wächst der Sonne Glut"
Middle voice & piano.

Liederseelen, op. 60 no. 2 (1946)
[Universal-Edition, 1949]
"In der Nacht, die die Bäume mit
Blüten deckt"
Middle voice & piano.

Mit einem Jugendbildnis, op. 60 no. 4
(1946) [Universal-Edition, 1949]
"Hier doch keinem darfst du's zeigen"
Middle voice & piano.

Nachtgeräusche, op. 60 no. 27 (1946)
[Universal-Edition, 1949]
"Melde mir die Nachtgeräusche, Muse"
Middle voice & piano.

Neujahrsglocken, op. 60 no. 17 (1946)
[Universal-Edition, 1949]
"In den Lüften schwellen des
Gedröhne"
Middle voice & piano.

Der Reisebecher, op. 60 no. 19 (1946)
[Universal-Edition, 1949]
"Gestern fand ich"
Middle voice & piano.

Reisephantasie, op. 60 no. 3 (1946)
[Universal-Edition, 1949]
"Mittagsruhe haltend auf den Matten"
Middle voice & piano.

Requiem, op. 60 no. 25 (1946)
[Universal-Edition, 1949]
"Bei der Abendsonne Wandern"
Middle voice & piano.

Der römische Brunnen, op. 60 no. 14
(1946) [Universal-Edition, 1949]
"Aufsteigt der Strahl und fallend
giesst"
Middle voice & piano.

Schwarzschattende Kastanie, op. 60 no.
24 (1946) [Universal-Edition, 1949]
same
Middle voice & piano.

Unruhige Nacht, op. 60 no. 10 (1946)
[Universal-Edition, 1949]
"Heut ward mir bis zum jungen Tag"
Middle voice & piano.

Vor der Ernte, op. 6 no. 3 (1905) [Hug, 1907]
"An wolken reinem Himmel geht"
High voice & piano.

Was treibst du, Wind? op. 60 no. 11 (1946) [Universal-Edition, 1949] same
Middle voice & piano.

Das weisse Spitzchen, op. 60 no. 20 (1946) [Universal-Edition, 1949]
"Ein blenden des Spitzchen blickt über den Wald"
Middle voice & piano.

Mörike, Eduard Friedrich, 1804-1875.

Am Walde, op. 62 no. 4 [Universal-Edition, 1956] "Am Waldsaum kann ich lange Nachmittage"

An einem Wintermorgan, vor Sonnenaufgang, op. 62 no. 2 [Universal-Edition, 1956]
"O flaumenleichte Zeit der dunkeln Frühe!"

An meine Mutter, op. 14 no. 1 (1907) [Hug, 1908]
"Stiehe, von allen den Liedern"
Low voice & piano.

An Philomele, op. 62 no. 5 [Universal-Edition, 1956] "Tonleiterähnlich steiget dein Klaggesang"

Antike Poesie, op. 62 no. 21 [Universal-Edition, 1956]
"Ich sah den Helikon in Wolkendunst"

Auf dem Krankenbette, op. 62 no. 38 [Universal-Edition, 1956]
"Gleich wie ein Vogel am Fenster vorbei"

Auf der Teck, op. 62 no. 6 [Universal-Edition, 1956]
"Hier ist Freude, hier ist Lust"

Auf ein Ei geschrieben, op. 62 no. 30 [Universal-Edition, 1956]
"Ostern ist zwar schon vorbei"

Auf ein Kind, op. 62 no. 35 [Universal-Edition, 1956] "Mein Kind, in welchem Krieg hast du"

Auf eine Lampe, op. 62 no. 19 [Universal-Edition, 1956]
"Noch unverrückt, O schöne Lampe"

Auf einen Klavierspieler, op. 62 no. 31 [Universal-Edition, 1956]
"Hört ihn und seht sein dürftig Instrument!"

Aus der Ferne, op. 62 no. 17 [Universal-Edition, 1956]
"Weht, O wehet, liebe Morgenwinde!"

Besuch in Urach, op. 62 no. 40 [Universal-Edition, 1956]

"Nur fast so wie im Traum ist mir's geschehen"

Die Enthusiasten, op. 62 no. 28 [Universal-Edition, 1956]
"Die Welt wär' ein Sumpf"

Er ist's, op. 51 no. 4 (1937) [Hug, 1946]
"Frühling lässt sein blaues Band"

Erinna an Sappho, op. 62 no. 22 [Universal-Edition, 1956]
"Vielfach sind zum Hades die Pfade"

Gebet, op. 62 no. 33 [Universal-Edition, 1956] "Herr! schikke, was du willt"

Der Geprüste, op. 62 no. 39 [Universal-Edition, 1956] "Ist's möglich?"

Gesang zu zweien in der Nacht, op. 62 no. 3 [Universal-Edition, 1956]
"Wie süss der Nachtwind nun die Wiese streift"

Der Hirtenknabe, op. 62 no. 34 [Universal-Edition, 1956]
"Vesperzeit, Betgeläut'"

Im Park, op. 62 no. 8 [Universal-Edition, 1956]
"Sieh, der Kastanie kindliches Laub"

Impromptu, op. 62 no. 27 [Universal-Edition, 1956]
"Die ganz' Welt ist in dich verliebt"

In ein Autographen-Album, op. 62 no. 26 [Universal-Edition, 1956]
"Mein Wappen ist nicht adelig"

Johann Kepler, op. 62 no. 23 [Universal-Edition, 1956] "Gestern, als ich vom nächtlichen Lager"

Keine Rettung, op. 62 no. 24 [Universal-Edition, 1956]
"Kunst! O in deine Arme"

Lose Ware, op. 62 no. 10 [Universal-Edition, 1956]
"Tinte! Tinte, wer braucht!"

Das Mädchen an den Mai, op. 62 no. 7 [Universal-Edition, 1956]
"Es ist doch im April fürwahr"

Mein Fluss, op. 62 no. 9 [Universal-Edition, 1956] "O Fluss, mein Fluss im Morgenstrahl!"

Muse und Dichter, op. 62 no. 37 [Universal-Edition, 1956]
"Krank nun vollends und matt!"

Nach dem Kriege, op. 62 no. 25 [Universal-Edition, 1956]
"Bei euren Taten, euren Siegen"

Nachts, op. 62 no. 20 [Universal-Edition, 1956] "Horch! auf der Erde feuchtem Grund gelegen"

Nachts am Schreibepult, op. 62 no. 16 [Universal-Edition, 1956]

SCHOECK, OTHMAR, 1886-1957
(continued)
Mörike, Eduard Friedrich, 1804-1875
(continued)
"Primel und Stern und Syringe von
einsamer Kerze beleuchtet"
Nur zu! op. 62 no. 18 [Universal-Edition,
1956] "Schön prangt im Silbertau die
junge Rose"
Peregrina, op. 62 no. 14 [Universal-
Edition, 1956]
"Aufgeschmückt ist der Freudensaal"
Peregrina II, op. 17 no. 4 (1909?) [Hug,
1909] "Ein Irrsal kam in die
Mondscheingärten"
Restauration, op. 62 no. 32 [Universal-
Edition, 1956]
"Das süsse Zeug ohne Saft und Kraft!"
Ritterliche Werbung, op. 62 no. 11
[Universal-Edition, 1956]
"Wo gehst du hin, du schönes Kind?"
Schön-Rohtraut, op. 62 no. 13
[Universal-Edition, 1956]
"Wie heisst König Ringangs
Töchterlein?"
Die Schwestern, op. 62 no. 12
[Universal-Edition, 1956]
"Wir Schwestern zwei, wir schönen"
Septembermorgen, op. 7 no. 2 (1905)
[Hug, 1907]
"Im Nebel ruhet noch die Welt"
Low voice & piano.
Septembermorgen, op. 51 no. 5 (1937)
[Hug, 1946]
"Im Nebel ruhet noch die Welt"
Spruch, op. 51 no. 6 (1943) [Hug, 1946]
"Ohne das Schöne"
Trost, op. 62 no. 29 [Universal-Edition,
1956]
"Ja, mein Glück, das langgewohnte"
Widmung, op. 62 no. 1 [Universal-
Edition, 1956] "Die kleine Welt"
Zu einer Konfirmation, op. 62 no. 36
[Universal-Edition, 1956]
"Bei jeder Wendung deiner
Lebensbahn"
Zu viel, op. 62 no. 15 [Universal-Edition,
1956] "Der Himmel glänzt vom
reinsten Frühlingslichte"
MALER NOLTEN.
Peregrina, op. 15 no. 6 (1908) [Hug,
1908] "Die Liebe, sagt man"
Rüeger, Armin
Bei der Kirche, op. 7 no. 1 (1905) [Hug,
1907] "Es gehen zur Kirche die Leute"
Low voice & piano.

Salis-Seewis, Johann Gaudenz,
Freiherr von, 1762-1834.
Das Grab, o. op. Nr. 1 (1901?) [unpubl.]
"Das Grab ist tief und stille"
Schoeck, Othmar, 1886-1957.
Kantonsschul-Turnverein-Kantus, o. op.
Nr. 3 (1901?) [*Liederbuch,* hrsg. vom
Altherrenverband des KTV Zürich,
1909]
"K T V = er, seht die Farben"
Printed by V. Kobold, Zürich.
Schoeck, Paul, 1882-1952.
Alle meine Wünsche schweigen, op. 6 no.
4 (1906) [Hug, 1907] same
High voice & piano.
Nun quill aus meiner Seele, op. 15 no. 2
(1907) [Hug, 1908] same
Psalm, op. 11 no. 1 (1906) [Hug, 1907]
"Liebe ist Wahrheit!"
Baritone & organ.
Spitteler, Carl, 1845-1924.
Das bescheidene Wünschlein, op. 24a no.
7 (1910) [Breitkopf & Härtel, 1917]
"Damals, ganz zuerst am Anfang"
Glöckleins Klage, op. 24a no. 8 (1910)
[Breitkopf & Härtel, 1917]
"Ein junges Glöcklein klagte"
Der Hufschmied, op. 24a no. 9 (1909)
[Breitkopf & Härtel, 1917]
"Schwarzbrauner Hufschmied"
Ein Jauchzer, op. 24b no. 1 (1910)
[Breitkopf & Härtel, 1917]
"Was ist's, das der Gedanken mutigen
Tritt"
Eine Unbekanntschaft, op. 24a no. 10
(1910) [Breitkopf & Härtel, 1917]
"Der Denker rechnet wohl einmal"
Storm, Theodor, 1817-1888.
April, op. 35 no. 2 (1928) [Breitkopf &
Härtel, 1931]
"Das ist die Drossel, die da schlägt"
Uhland, Ludwig, 1787-1862.
Abendwolken, op. 20 no. 6 (1910)
[Breitkopf & Härtel, 1917]
"Wolken seh' ich abendwärts"
Abschied, op. 3 no. 3 (1905) [Hug, 1907]
"Was klinget und singet die Strass'
herauf?"
An einem heitern Morgen, op. 20 no. 2
(1910) [Breitkopf & Härtel, 1917]
"O blaue Luft"
Auf den Tod eines Kindes, op. 3 no. 6
(1907) [Hug, 1907]
"Du kamst, du gingst mit leiser Spur"
Auf ein Kind, op. 20 no. 1 (1908)
[Breitkopf & Härtel, 1917]
"Aus der Bedrängnis"

COMPOSER Poet *Title* "First Line"

Dichtersegen, op. 20 no. 3 (1910)
[Breitkopf & Härtel, 1917]
"Als ich ging die Flur entlang"
Frühlingsfeier, op. 15 no. 3 (1908) [Hug,
1908] "Süsser goldner Frühlingstag!"
Frühlingsruhe, op. 20 no. 4 (1905)
[Breitkopf & Härtel, 1917]
"O, legt mich nicht ins dunkle Grab"
Im Herbste, op. 17 no. 2 (1908) [Hug,
1909]
"Seid gegrüsst mit Frühlingswonne"
Die Kapelle, op. 3 no. 2 (1905) [Hug,
1907] "Droben stehet die Kapelle"
Der Kirchhof im Frühling, op. 17 no. 3
(1908) [Hug, 1909]
"Stiller Garten, eile nur"
Lebewohl, op. 3 no. 4 (1905) [Hug, 1907]
"Lebe wohl, lebe wohl mein Lieb!"
Ruhetal, op. 3 no. 1 (1903) [Hug, 1907]
"Wann im letzten Abendstrahl"
Wein und Brot, op. 20 no. 5 (1910)
[Breitkopf & Härtel, 1917]
"Solche Düfte sind mein Leben"
WANDERLIEDER.
Scheiden und Meiden, op. 3 no. 5
(1908) [Hug, 1907]
"So soll ich nun dich meiden"
Unknown
Farbenkantus (ca.1901) [unpubl.?]
Listed in *New Grove*; cannot identify
in thematic catalog.
Mandolinen, op. 6 no. 6 (1907) [Hug,
1907]
"Leis dem Schmeichellied der Lauten"
High voice & piano. Verlaine,
translator?
Nun steht der Wald in Blüten, o. op. Nr.
12 (1903?) [unpubl.] same
Stummer Abschied, o. op. Nr. 18 (1905)
[Corrodi *Othmar Schoeck . . .* , 2.
Aufl. (Frauenfeld/Leipzig: Verlag
Huber, 1936), 46] "Es tat den
Beiden so weh das Scheiden"
Schoeck, Othmar, 1886-1957.
SCHOECK *Kantonsschul-Turnverein-*
Kantus
Schoeck, Paul, 1882-1952.
SCHOECK
Alle meine Wünsche schweigen
Nun quill aus meiner Seele
Psalm
Schön Hedwig see Hebbel **SCHUMANN**
"Schön Liebchen komm' hernieder" *see*
Die Braut Hamerling **JENSEN**
"Schön prangt im Silbertau die junge Rose"
see Nur zu! Mörike **SCHOECK**

Schön sind, doch kalt see Schack
LOTOSBLÄTTER. **STRAUSS**
Schön Suschen see Bürger **PFITZNER**
"Schön Suschen kannt' ich lange Zeit" *see*
Schön Suschen Bürger **PFITZNER**
Schön war, das ich dir weihte see Daumer
POLYDORA. **BRAHMS**
"Schön wie Engel voll Walhalla's Wonne" *see*
Amalia Schiller **SCHUBERT**
SCHOENBERG, ARNOLD, 1874-1951. *see*
SCHÖNBERG, ARNOLD, 1874-1951.
SCHÖNBERG, ARNOLD, 1874-1951.
Ammann, Heinrich
Jane Grey, op. 12 no. 1 (1907) [GA, v.
1^1 p. 93]
"Sie führten ihn durch den grauen
Hof"
Text in *Neuer deutscher*
Balladenschatz, p. 1.
Anon.
Es gingen zwei Gespielen gut (1929)
[GA, v.1^1 p. 172] same
Der Mai tritt ein mit Freuden (1929)
[GA, v.1^1 p. 171] same
Mein Herz in steten Treuen (1929) [GA,
v.1^1 p. 174] same
Mein Herz ist mir gemenget (1929) [GA,
v.1^1 p. 173] same
Beta, Ottomar, 1845-1913.
Wanderlied (before 1897?) [GA, v.1^2 p.
145] "Mütterchen, das führ zu Grab"
Poet identified as Oskar Beta in
Journal of the Schönberg Institute 2
(Oct. 1977): 72-80.
Bierbaum, Otto Julius, 1865-1910.
Gigerlette (1901) [GA, v.1^2 p. 134]
"Fräulein Gigerlette lud mich ein zum
Thee"
Text in Bierbaum *Deutsche*
Chansons (Brettl-Lieder) (1900),
pp. 3-4.
Breden, Christiane (Friderik), 1844-
1901.
Dass schon die Maienzeit vorüber (before
9/11/1895) [GA, v.1^2 p. 34] same
Colly
Jedem das Seine (1901) [GA, v.1^2 p.
117] "Ebenes Paradefeld"
Conradi, Hermann, 1862-1890.
LIEDER EINES SÜNDERS. 1. Teil,
"Inferno."
Verlassen, op. 6 no. 4 (1903) [GA,
v.1^1 p. 71]
"Im Morgen grauen schritt ich fort"
Dehmel, Richard, 1863-1920.
Erhebung, op. 2 no. 3 (1899) [GA, v.1^1
p. 29] "Gib mir deine Hand"

SCHÖNBERG, ARNOLD, 1874-1951
(continued)
Dehmel, Richard, 1863-1920 *(continued)*
Erwartung, op. 2 no. 1 (1899) [GA, v.1^1
p. 23] "Aus dem meergrünen Teiche"
Schenk mir deinen goldenen Kamm, op. 2
no. 2 [GA, v.1^1 p. 26] same
Warnung, op. 3 no. 3 (1899) [GA, v.1^1 p.
44]
"Mein Hund, du, hat dich bloss
beknurrt"
ERLÖSUNGEN.
Mädchenfrühling (1897) [GA, v.1^2 p.
86] "Aprilwind; alle Knospen"
Nicht doch! (ca.1897?) [GA, v.1^2 p.
89] "Mädel, lass das Stricken geh"
IM ZWIELICHT.
Alles, op. 6 no. 2 (1905) [GA, v.1^1 p. 64]
"Lass uns noch die Nacht erwarten"
WEIB UND WELT.
Mannesbangen (ca.1897?) [GA, v.1^2 p.
99] "Du musst nicht meinen"
DES KNABEN WUNDERHORN
*Wie Georg von Frundsberg von sich
selber sang,* op. 3 no. 1 (1903)
[GA, v.1^1 p. 37] "Mein Fleiss und
Müh hab ich nie gespart"
P. 541 in 1962 reprint edition.
Fischer, Hans, 1869-1934.
Lockung, op. 6 no. 7 (1905) [GA, v.1^1 p.
82]
"Komm, komm mit nur einen Schritt!"
Frey, Friedrich Hermann, 1830-1911.
Das zerbrochene Krüglein (before 1895?)
[GA, v.1^2 p. 11]
"Ich hab' zum Brunnen ein Krüglein
gebracht"
Geibel, Emanuel, i.e., Franz Emanuel
August, 1815-1884.
Mädchenlied (before 3/9/1896) [GA, v.1^2
p. 63] "In meinem Garten die Nelken"
George, Stefan, 1868-1933.
*DAS BUCH DER HÄNGENDEN
GÄRTEN.*
*Als Neuling trat ich ein in dein
Gehege,* op. 15 no. 3 [GA, v.1^1 p.
119] same
Als wir hinter dem beblümten Tore, op.
15 no. 11 [GA, v.1^1 p. 137] same
*Angst und Hoffen wechselnd mich
beklemmen,* op. 15 no. 7
[GA, v.1^1 p. 128] same
*Da meine Lippen reglos sind und
brennen,* op. 15 no. 4 [GA, v.1^1
p. 122] same
Du lehnest wider eine Silberweide, op.
15 no. 13 [GA, v.1^1 p. 142] same

Hain in diesen Paradiesen, op. 15 no.
2 [GA, v.1^1 p. 117] same
Jedem Werke bin ich fürder tot, op. 15
no. 6 [GA, v.1^1 p. 126] same
Saget mir auf welchem Pfade, op. 15
no. 5 [GA, v. 1^1 p. 124] same
*Das schöne Beet betracht ich mir im
Harren,* op. 15 no. 10 [GA, v.1^1 p.
134] same
Sprich nicht immer, op. 15 no. 14 [GA,
v.1^1 p. 144] same
Streng ist uns das Glück und spröde,
op. 15 no. 9 [GA, v.1^1 p. 132] same
*Unterm schutz von dichten
Blättergründen,* op. 15 no. 1 [GA,
v.1^1 p. 115] same
*Wenn ich heut nicht deinen Leib
berühre,* op. 15 no. 8 [GA, v.1^1
p. 130] same
*Wenn sich bei heiliger Ruh in tiefen
Matten,* op. 15 no. 12 [GA, v.1^1 p.
140] same
Wir bevölkerten die abend-düstern,
op. 15 no. 15 [GA, v.1^1 p. 145]
same
DAS JAHR DER SEELE, p. 27.
Ich darf nicht dankend, op. 14 no. 1
(1907) [GA, v.1^1 p. 107] same
Goethe, Johann Wolfgang von, 1749-
1832.
Mailied [GA, v.1^2 p. 102]
"Zwischen Weizen und Korn"
WESTÖSTLICHER DIVAN.
Deinem Blick mich zu bequemen
(1903) [GA, v.1^2 p. 148] same
Gold, Alfred, b. 1874.
*In hellen Träumen hab ich Dich oft
geschaut* (1893) [GA, v.1^2 p. 1] same
Facsimile in *60. Geburtstag Festschrift*
(Universal Edition, 1934), 32.
Haringer, Jakob, 1883-1948.
ABSCHIED.
Mädchenlied, op. 48 no. 3 (1933) [GA,
v.1^1 p. 159]
"Es leuchtet so schön die Sonne"
Tot, op. 48 no. 2 (1933) [GA, v.1^1
p. 157]
"Ist alles eins, was liegt doran!"
DIE DENKMÄLER: Der Reisende oder
Die Träne.
Summermüd, op. 48 no. 1 (1933) [GA,
v.1^1 p. 153] "Wenn du schon
glaubst"
Hart, Julius, 1859-1930.
Traumleben, op. 6 no. 1 (1903) [GA, v.1^1
p. 61] "Um meinen Nacken schlingt
sich ein blütenweisser Arm"

Henckel, Georg
   In diesen Wintertagen, op. 14 no. 2 [GA,
      v.1¹ p. 109] same
Heyse, Paul Johann Ludwig von,
   1830-1914.
   Mädchenlied (ca.1897?) [GA, v.1² p. 79]
      "Sang ein Bettlerpärlein am
      Schenkentor"
   Waldesnacht (ca.1897?) [GA, v.1² p. 81]
      "Waldesnacht, du wunderkühle"
Hochstetter, Gustav, 1873-1944.
   Mahnung (1901) [GA, v.1² p. 124]
      "Mädel, sei kein eitles Ding"
Hofmannsthal, Hugo Hofmann, Edler
   von, 1874-1929.
   Die Beiden (1899) [GA, v.1² p. 96, 146
      (2 versions)]
      "Sie trug den Becher in der Hand"
Jacobsen, Jens Peter, 1847-1885.
   Hochzeitslied, op. 3 no. 4 [GA, v.1¹
      p. 48 "So voll und reich wand noch
      das Leben nimmer euch seinen Kranz"
Keller, Gottfried, 1819-1890.
   Die Aufgeregten, op. 3 no. 2 (1903) [GA,
      v.1¹ p. 41] "Welche tief bewegten
      Lebensläufchen"
   Geübtes Herz, op. 3 no. 5 (1903) [GA,
      v.1¹ p. 51] "Weise nicht von dir mein
      schlichtes Herz"
   Ghasel, op. 6 no. 5 (1904) [GA, v.1¹
      p. 75] "Ich halte dich in meinem Arm"
Klemperer, Viktor, 1881-1960.
   Der verlorene Haufen, op. 12 no. 2
      (1907) [GA, v.1¹ p. 99] "Trinkt aus,
      ihr zechtet zum letzten mal"
      Text in *Neuer deutscher*
      Balladenschatz, p. 59.
Lenau, Nicolaus, 1802-1850.
   SCHILFLIEDER.
   Schilflied (1893) [GA, v.1² p. 4]
      "Drüben geht die Sonne scheiden"
Levetzow, Karl Michael, Freiherr von,
   1871-1945.
   HÖHENLIEDER, pp. 39-40.
   Abschied, op. 1 no. 2 [GA, v.1¹ p. 10]
      "Aus den Trümmern einer hohen
      Schönheit"
   HÖHENLIEDER, pp. 41-42.
   Dank, op. 1 no. 1 (1898) [GA, v.1¹
      p. 3] "Grosses hast du mir gegeben
      in jenen Hochstunden"
Lingg, Hermann, 1820-1905.
   Freihold, op. 3 no. 6 (1900) [GA, v.1¹
      p. 55] "Soviel Raben nachts
      auffliegen"
   Gruss in die Ferne (1900) [GA, v.1²
      p. 106] "Dunkelnd über den See"

Löns, Hermann, 1866-1914.
   Jeduch [GA, v.1² p. 151]
      "Ich stehe hier am Jammerstein"
Mackay, John Henry, 1864-1933.
   Am Wegrand, op. 6 no. 6 (1905) [GA,
      v.1¹ p. 78] "Tausend Menschen ziehen
      vorüber, den ich ersehne"
Nietzsche, Friedrich Wilhelm, 1844-
   1900.
   Der Wanderer, op. 6 no. 8 (1905) [GA,
      v.1¹ p. 85] "Wandrer durch die Nacht
      mit gutem Schritt"
Pfau, Ludwig, 1821-1894.
   Du kehrst mir den Rücken (before
      9/11/1895) [GA, v.1² p. 55] same
   Einsam bin ich und allein (before
      9/11/1895) [GA, v.1² p. 47] same
   Einst hat vor deines Vaters haus
      (ca.1893) [GA, v.1² p. 8] same
   Gott grüss dich, Marie! (before
      9/11/1895) [GA, v.1² p. 43] same
   Könnt' ich zu dir, mein Licht (before
      9/11/1895) [GA, v.1² p. 37] same
   Lied der Schnitterin (before 1897?) [GA,
      v.1² p. 26]
      "Lass deine Sichel rauschen"
   Mein Schatz ist wie ein Schneck (before
      9/11/1895) [GA, v.1² p. 41] same
   Der Pflanze, die dort über dem Abgrund
      schwebt (before 9/11/1895)
      [GA, v.1² p. 45] same
   Vergissmeinnicht (1895?) [GA, v.1²
      p. 20] "War ein Blümlein wunderfein"
   Warum bist du aufgewacht (before
      1895?) [GA, v.1² p. 18] same
   Zweifler (1895?) [GA, v.1² p. 53]
      "Du kleine bist so lieb und hold"
      Facsimile in Stuckenschmidt
      Schönberg (1974), p. 35.
Redwitz, Oskar, Freiherr von, 1823-
   1891.
   AMARANTH.
   Nur das thut mir so bitterweh' (before
      9/11/1895) [GA, v.1² p. 50] same
Reinick, Robert, 1805-1852.
   Im Fliederbusch ein Vöglein sass (before
      9/11/1895) [GA, v.1² p. 30] same
Remer, Paul, 1867-1943.
   Mädchenlied, op. 6 no. 3 (1905) [GA,
      v.1¹ p. 68]
      "Ach, wenn es nun die Mutter wüsst'"
Rilke, Rainer Maria, 1875-1926.
   Am Strande (1908) [GA, v.1¹ p. 167]
      "Vorüber die Flut"
Salus, Hugo, 1866-1929.
   Einfältiges Lied (1901) [GA, v.1² p. 109]
      "König ist spazieren gangen"

COMPOSER   Poet   *Title*   "First Line"

SCHÖNBERG, ARNOLD, 1874-1951
(*continued*)
Salus, Hugo, 1866-1929 (*continued*)
Der genügsame Liebhaber (1901) [GA, v.1^2 p. 113] "Meine Freundin hat ein schwarze Katze"
Schikaneder, Emanuel Johann, 1751-1812.
SPIEGEL VON ARCADUA.
Arie aus dem Spiegel von Arcadien (1901) [GA, v.1^2 p. 138] "Seit ich so viele Weiber sah"
Schlaf, Johannes, 1862-1941.
Waldsonne, op. 2 no. 4 [GA, v.1^1 p. 31] "In die braunen, rauschenden Nächte"
Unknown
Dass gestern eine Wespe Dich (before 1895?) [GA, v.1^2 p. 13] same
Gedenken [GA, v.1^1 p. 165] "Es steht sein Bild noch immer da"
Juble, schöne junge Rose (before 1895?) [GA, v.1^2 p. 16] same
Kleine Vögelein, du zwitscherst fein (ca.1893) [unpubl.] same
Partial facsimile in *Musical Quarterly* 60 (1974): 415.
Mein Herz, das ist ein tiefer Schacht (before 9/11/1895) [GA, v.1^2 p. 60] same
Vrchlický, Jaroslav
Ekloge (1893-97) [GA, v.1^2 p. 67, 73 (2 versions)] "Duftreich ist die Erde"
Wackernagel, Wilhelm, 1806-1869.
Ich grüne wie die Weide grünt (before 9/11/1895) [GA, v.1^2 p. 57] same
Wedekind, Frank, 1864-1918.
Galathea (1901) [GA, v.1^2 p. 129] "Ach, wie brenn' ich vor Verlangen"
Text in Bierbaum *Deutsche Chansons (Brettl-Lieder)* (1900), pp. 201-02.
Zedlitz, Joseph Christian von, 1790-1862.
Sehnsucht (before 3/9/1896) [GA, v.1^2 p. 65] "Als mein Auge sie fand"
Das schöne Beet betracht ich mir im Harren
see George *DAS BUCH DER HÄNGENDEN GÄRTEN.* **SCHÖNBERG**
Das schöne Fischermädchen see Heine **BORODIN**
Schöne Fremde see Eichendorff *DICHTER UND IHRE GESELLEN.* **SCHUMANN**
DIE SCHÖNE MÜLLERIN, no. 1
SCHUBERT Müller, Wilhelm
Das Wandern
DIE SCHÖNE MÜLLERIN, no. 2
SCHUBERT Müller, Wilhelm *Wohin?*
DIE SCHÖNE MÜLLERIN, no. 3
SCHUBERT Müller, Wilhelm *Halt!*

DIE SCHÖNE MÜLLERIN, no. 4
SCHUBERT Müller, Wilhelm
Danksagung an den Bach
DIE SCHÖNE MÜLLERIN, no. 5
SCHUBERT Müller, Wilhelm
Am Feierabend
DIE SCHÖNE MÜLLERIN, no. 6
SCHUBERT Müller, Wilhelm
Der Neugierige
DIE SCHÖNE MÜLLERIN, no. 7
SCHUBERT Müller, Wilhelm
Ungeduld
DIE SCHÖNE MÜLLERIN, no. 8
SCHUBERT Müller, Wilhelm
Morgengruss
DIE SCHÖNE MÜLLERIN, no. 9
SCHUBERT Müller, Wilhelm
Des Müllers Blumen
DIE SCHÖNE MÜLLERIN, no. 10
SCHUBERT Müller, Wilhelm
Thränenregen
DIE SCHÖNE MÜLLERIN, no. 11
SCHUBERT Müller, Wilhelm *Mein!*
DIE SCHÖNE MÜLLERIN, no. 12
SCHUBERT Müller, Wilhelm *Pause*
DIE SCHÖNE MÜLLERIN, no. 13
SCHUBERT Müller, Wilhelm *Mit dem grünen Lautenband*
DIE SCHÖNE MÜLLERIN, no. 14
SCHUBERT Müller, Wilhelm *Der Jäger*
DIE SCHÖNE MÜLLERIN, no. 15
SCHUBERT Müller, Wilhelm *Eifersucht und Stolz*
DIE SCHÖNE MÜLLERIN, no. 16
SCHUBERT Müller, Wilhelm *Die liebe Farbe*
DIE SCHÖNE MÜLLERIN, no. 17
SCHUBERT Müller, Wilhelm *Die böse Farbe*
DIE SCHÖNE MÜLLERIN, no. 18
SCHUBERT Müller, Wilhelm *Trockne Blumen*
DIE SCHÖNE MÜLLERIN, no. 19
SCHUBERT Müller, Wilhelm
Der Müller und der Bach
DIE SCHÖNE MÜLLERIN, no. 20
SCHUBERT Müller, Wilhelm
Des Baches Wiegenlied
"Schöne Sennin, noch einmal singe" *see Die Sennin* Lenau **SCHUMANN**
"Schöne Welt, wo bist du?" *see Die Götter Griechenlands* Schiller **SCHUBERT**
Schöne Wiege meiner Leiden see Heine **SCHUMANN**
Die schönen Augen der Frühlingsnacht see Heine **FRANZ**

Schöner Mai, bist über Nacht see Osterwald
   FRANZ
Schöner Ort see Frey **SCHOECK**
Ein schöner Stern geht auf in meiner Nacht
   see Heine **DELIUS**
"*Ein schöner Stern geht auf in meiner Nacht*"
   see O lüge nicht! Heine **FRANZ**
"*Schöner und schöner schmückt sich der Plan*"
   see Italien Grillparzer
   MENDELSSOHN-BARTHOLDY
"*Schönheit ist dem Muth beschieden Lieb'*
   erobert sich der Held" *see Kampaspe*
   Schlegel **ZELTER**
Schön-Rohtraut see Mörike **SCHOECK**
"*Der schönste Cherub kommt*" *see Winter*
   Schlaf **BERG**
Der schönste Platz see Löns **KILPINEN**
Schönste Rast see Cornelius **LASSEN**
"*Schöpfer, deine Herrlichkeit*" *see Winterlied*
   Unknown **LOEWE**
"*Schöpferin beseelter Töne!*" *see Gesang an*
   die Harmonie Salis-Seewis **SCHUBERT**
Schöpff, Wilhelm, 1826-1916.
   SCHUMANN
     Abschied vom Walde
     Es stürmet am Abendhimmel
     Gesungen
     Heimliches Verschwinden
     Herbstlied
     Himmel und Erde
     In's Freie
     Röselein, Röselein
Der Scholar see Eichendorff **WOLF**
Scholastica see Giesebrecht **LOEWE**
Scholz, Bernhard E., 1835-1916.
   LASSEN
     Dein Auge ist mein Himmel
     Die grossen stillen Augen
     Sommerabend
Scholz, Maria, 1861-1944.
   REGER
     Ach, Liebster, in Gedanken
     Allen Welten abgewandt
     Um Mitternacht blühen die Blumen
"*Schon erlischt der Kerze Schein*" *see Nacht*
   Rathaus **CHAĬKOVSKIĬ**
Schon grüsst auf dämmerndem Pfade see
   Cornelius **LASSEN**
"*Schon hat die Nacht den Silberschrein*" *see*
   Schifferliedchen Keller, G. **SCHOECK**
"*Schon im bunten Knabenkleide*" *see*
   Die frühe Liebe Hölty **SCHUBERT**
"*Schon manche selige Nacht*" *see Grindelwald*
   Hesse **KILPINEN**
"*Schon sank die Sonne*" *see Die müde*
   Wanderer Hoffmann von Fallersleben
   STRAUSS

"*Schon seh'ich Hirt' und Herde nimmer*" *see*
   Einsamkeit Lenau **SCHOECK**
Schon streckt' ich aus see Heyse **WOLF**
"*Schon verstummt das Lied der Grille*" *see*
   Rückkehr Leuthold **SCHOECK**
"*Schon will der Abend sinken*" *see Zugvogel*
   Grun, James **PFITZNER**
"*Schon zog vom Wald ich ferne wieder*" *see*
   Der Hirte Lenau **SCHOECK**
Schopenhauer, Johanna, 1766-1838.
   GABRIELE.
     SCHUBERT *Hippolit's Lied*
Schorn, Henriette (von Stein) von, 1807-
   1869.
   LASSEN *Sei stille*
   LISZT *Sei still*
Schottisch Lied see Unknown **SPOHR**
"*Das Schratlein hockt*" *see Holophan*
   Wallpach zu Schwanenfeld **BERG**
Der Schreckenberger see Eichendorff
   WOLF
Schreiber, Aloys Wilhelm, 1763-1841.
   LOEWE
     Der ewige Jude
     Maria und das Milchmädchen
     Odins Meeres-Ritt
   SCHUBERT
     Das Abendrot
     An den Mond in einer Herbstnacht
     Der Blumenbrief
     Das Marienbild
   ZELTER *Der Schüchterne*
Schreiber, Heinrich, 1793-1872.
   MENDELSSOHN-BARTHOLDY
     Altdeutsches Lied
"*Schrieb die schöne Adelheid*" *see*
   Von der Liebe Ginzkey **REGER**
Schröer, Karl Julius, 1825-1900.
   FRANZ
     Genesung
     Liebchen ist da!
     Stiller Abend
Schterbinah *see* Shcherbina, Nikelaĭ
   Fedorovich, 1821-1869.
Schubart, Christian Friedrich Daniel,
   1739-1791.
   LOEWE
     Gute Nacht
     Der Hirten Lied am Krippelein
   SCHUBERT
     An den Tod
     Die Forelle
     Grablied auf einen Soldaten
     Seraphine an ihr Klavier
   STRAUSS *Weihnachtslied*
Schubert an sein Klavier see Schubart
   SCHUBERT *Seraphine an ihr Klavier*

COMPOSER Poet *Title* "First Line"

SCHUBERT, FRANZ, 1797-1828.
Aeschylus ca. 525-456 B.C.
Fragment aus dem Aeschylus, D. 450
[GA, v. 20⁴, pp. 128, 131]
"So wird der Mann, der sonder Zwang
gerecht ist"
Anacreon, b. ca. 570 B.C.
An die Leyer, D. 737 [GA, v. 20⁷, p. 42]
"Ich will von Atreus Söhnen"
Text translated by Bruchmann.
Batsányi, Gabriele (von Baumberg),
1775-1839.
Abendständchen: An Lina, D. 265 [GA,
v. 20³, p. 52]
"Sei sanft wie ihre Seele"
An die Sonne, D. 270 [GA, v. 20³, p. 56]
"Sinke, liebe Sonne, sinke"
Cora an die Sonne, D. 263 [GA, v. 20³,
p. 50]
"Nach so vielen trüben Tagen send"
Lob des Tokayers, D. 248 [GA, v. 20³,
p. 66] "O köstlicher Tokayer"
*DER MORGENKUSS NACH EINEM
BALL.*
Der Morgenkuss, D. 264 [GA, v. 20³,
p. 51] "Durch eine ganze Nacht sich
nah zu sein"
Bauernfeld, Eduard von, 1802-1890.
Der Vater mit dem Kind, D. 906 [GA,
v. 20⁸, p. 261]
"Dem Vater liegt das Kind im Arm"
Bernard, Josef Karl, 1780-1850.
Vergebliche Liebe, D. 177 [GA, v. 20²,
p. 88] "Ja, ich weiss es"
Bertrand, Friedrich Anton Franz, 1787-
1830.
Adelwold und Emma, D. 211 [GA, v. 20²,
p. 132]
"Hoch, und ehern schier von Dauer"
Minona, D. 152 [GA, v. 20², p. 6]
"Wie treiben die Wolken so finster und
schwer"
Bible
Der 13. Psalm, D. 663 [**Festblätter . . .
10.Deutsche Sängerbundesfest**]
"Ach, Herr, wie lange willst du mein
so ganz vergessen?"
Festblätter no. 1, pp. 8-9 (Wien:
1928); edited by Deutsch.
Bobrik, Johann Friedrich Ludwig,
1781-1844.
Die drei Sänger, D. 329 [GA, v. 20¹⁰,
p. 97] "Der König sass beim frohen
Mahle"
Bruchmann, Franz, Ritter von, 1798-
1867.
Am See, D. 746 [GA, v. 20⁷, p. 74]
"In des Sees Wogenspiele"

Im Haine, D. 738 [GA, v. 20⁷, p. 46]
"Sonnenstrahlen durch die Tannen"
Schwestergruss, D. 762 [GA, v. 20⁷,
p. 38] "Im Mondenschein wall' ich auf
und ab"
Der zürnende Barde, D. 785 [GA, v. 20⁷,
p. 71]
"Wer wagt's, wer wagt's, wer wagt's"
Castelli, Ignaz Franz, 1781-1862.
Das Echo, D. 868 [GA, v. 20⁸, p. 258]
"Herzliebe, gute Mütter"
Frohsinn, D. 520 [GA, v. 20⁵, p. 2]
"Ich bin von lockerem Schlage"
Cibber, Colley, 1671-1757.
Der blinde Knabe, D. 833 [GA, v. 20⁸,
pp. 54, 58]
"O sagt, ihr Lie ben mir einmal"
Claudius, Matthias, 1740-1815.
Abendlied, D. 499 [GA, v. 20⁴, p. 240]
"Der Mond ist aufgegangen"
Am ersten Maimorgen, D. 344 [Published
privately by Reinhold van Hoorickx]
"Heute will ich fröhlich, fröhlich sein"
Am Grabe Anselmo's, D. 504 [GA,
v. 20⁴, p. 236]
"Dass ich dich verloren habe"
An die Nachtigall, D. 497 [GA, v. 20⁴,
p. 238] "Er liegt und schläft"
An eine Quelle, D. 530 [GA, v. 20⁴,
p. 232] "Du kleine grünumwachs'ne
Quelle"
Bei dem Grabe meines Vaters, D. 496
[GA, v. 20⁴, p. 234]
"Friede sei um diesen Grabstein her"
Lied, D. 362 [GA, v. 20⁴, p. 244]
"Ich bin vergnügt, im Siegeston"
Lied, D. 501 [GA, v. 20⁴, p. 246]
"Ich bin vergnügt, im Siegeston"
2nd setting; see also D. 362.
Das Lied vom Reifen, D. 532 [GA,
v. 20⁵, p. 36]
"Seht meine lieben Bäume an"
Phidile, D. 500 [GA, v. 20⁴, p. 242]
"Ich war erst sechzehn Sommer alt"
Täglich zu singen, D. 533 [GA, v. 20⁵,
p. 38] "Ich danke Gott und freue
mich"
Der Tod und das Mädchen, D. 531 [GA,
v. 20⁵, p. 35] "Vorüber, ach vorüber"
Collin, Matthäus, 1779-1824.
Herrn Josef Spaun, D. 749 [GA, v. 20¹⁰,
p. 84] "Und nimmer schreibst du?"
Licht und Liebe, D. 352 [GA, v. 20⁴,
p. 253] "Liebe ist ein süsses Licht"
Nacht und Träume, D. 827 [GA, v. 20⁸,
p. 68]
"Heilige Nacht, du sinkest nieder"

Wehmut, D. 772 [GA, v. 20^7, p. 102]
"Wenn ich durch Wald und Fluren
geh' "

Der Zwerg, D. 771 [GA, v. 20^7, p. 95]
"Im trüben Licht verschwinden schon
die Berge"

Cowley, Abraham, 1618-1667.
Der Weiberfreund, D. 271 [GA, v. 20^3,
p. 57] "Hoch fand von Evens Töchter
scharen ich keine"

Craigher, Jacob Nicolaus de
Jachelutta, 1797-1855.
Die junge Nonne, D. 828 [GA, v. 20^8,
p. 62] "Wie braust durch die Wipfel
der heulende Sturm"

Totengräbers Heimwehe, D. 842 [GA,
v. 20^8, p. 50]
"O Menschheit, O Leben, wass soll's?"

Deinhardstein, Johann Ludwig
Ferdinand von, 1794-1859.
Skolie, D. 306 [GA, v. 20^3, p. 120]
"Lasst im Morgenstrahl des Mai'n"

Ehrlich, Bernhard Ambros, ca.1765-
1827.
Als ich sie erröten sah, D. 153 [GA,
v. 20^2, p. 15] "All' mein Wirken"

Engelhardt, Karl August, 1768-1834.
Ihr Grab, D. 736 [GA, v. 20^7, p. 4]
"Dort ist ihr Grab, did einst im
Schmelz"

Fellinger, Johann Georg, 1781-1886.
Die erste Liebe, D. 182 [GA, v. 20^2,
p. 94] same

Die Sternenwelten, D. 307 [GA, v. 20^3,
p. 121] "Oben drehen sich die grossen"
WAS FUNKELT IHR SO MILD.
Die Sterne, D. 176 [GA, v. 20^2, p. 86]
"Was funkelt ihr so mild mich an?"

Fouqué, Friedrich Heinrich, Baron de
la Motte, 1777-1843.
SCHÄFER UND REITER.
Der Schäfer und der Reiter, D. 517
[GA, v. 20^5, p. 6]
"Ein Schäfer sass im Grünen"
UNDINE.
Lied, D. 373 [GA, v. 20^4, p. 3]
"Mutter geht durch ihre Kammern"
DER ZAUBERRING.
An dem jungen Morgenhimmel, D. 93
no. 3 [GA, v. 20^1, p. 141] same
Don Gayseros, Don Gayseros, D. 93
no. 1 [GA, v. 20^1, p. 132] same
Nächtens klang die süsse Laute, D. 93
no. 2 [GA, v. 20^1, p. 137] same

Goethe, Johann Wolfgang von, 1749-
1832.
Am Flusse, D. 160 [GA, v. 20^2, p. 58]
"Verfliesset, vielgeliebte Lieder"

Am Flusse, D. 766 [GA, v. 20^7, p. 56]
"Verfliesset, vielgeliebte Lieder"
2nd setting; see also D. 160.

An den Mond, D. 259 [GA, v. 20^3, p. 40]
"Füllest wieder Busch und Tal"

An den Mond, D. 296 [GA, v. 20^3, p.
195] "Füllest wieder Busch und Tal"
2nd setting; see also D. 259.

An die Entfernte, D. 765 [GA, v. 20^7,
p. 54] "So hab' ich wirklich dich
verloren?"

An Schwager Kronos, D. 369 [GA,
v. 20^4, p. 204] "Spute dich, Kronos!"

Auf dem See, D. 543 [GA, v. 20^5, pp. 66,
70] "Und frische Nahrung, neues Blut"

Bundeslied, D. 258 [GA, v. 20^3, p. 38]
"In allen guten Stunden"

Erlkönig, D. 328 [GA, v. 20^3, pp. 202,
208, 214, 219] "Wer reitet so spät
durch Nacht und Wind?"

Erster Verlust, D. 226 [GA, v. 20^2,
p. 172] "Ach, wer bringt die schönen
Tage"

Der Fischer, D. 225 [GA, v. 20^2, p. 171]
"Das Wasser rauscht, das Wasser
schwoll"

Ganymed, D. 544 [GA, v. 20^5, p. 75]
"Wie im Morgenglanze du rings mich
anglühst"

Geistesgruss, D. 142 [GA, v. 20^3,
pp. 189, 190, 191, 192]
"Hoch auf dem alten Thurme"

Gesang der Geister über den Wassern,
D. 484 [GA, v. 20^{10}, p. 106]
"Des Menschen Seele gleicht dem
Wasser"
Fragment; see D. 538, 704, 705, 714
for other settings.

Der Goldschmiedsgesell, D. 560 [GA,
v. 20^3, p. 49]
"Es ist doch meine Nachbarin"

Grenzen der Menschheit, D. 716 [GA,
v. 20^6, p. 185]
"Wenn der uralte heilige Vater"

Heidenröslein, D. 257 [GA, v. 20^3, p. 37]
"Sah ein Knab' ein Röslein stehn"

Hoffnung, D. 295 [GA, v. 20^3, pp. 193,
194]
"Schaff', das Tagwerk meiner Hände"

Jägers Abendlied, D. 215 [*Die Musik,*
v. 6 no. 7 (Jan. 15, 1907): Suppl., pp.
2-3]
"Im Felde schleich' ich still und wild"
First version; see also D. 368.

Jägers Abendlied, D. 368 [GA, v. 20^4,
p. 203] "Im Felde schleich' ich still
und wild"
2nd setting; see also D. 215.

COMPOSER Poet *Title* "First Line"

SCHUBERT, FRANZ, 1797-1828
(continued)
Goethe, Johann Wolfgang von, 1749-1832 *(continued)*

Johanna Sebus, D. 728 [GA, v. 20^{10}, p. 128] "Der Damm zerreisst, das Feld erbraust"

Die Liebende schreibt, D. 673 [GA, v. 20^6, p. 68] "Ein Blick von deinen Augen in die meinen"

Liebhaber in allen Gestalten, D. 558 [GA, v. 20^3, p. 46] "Ich wollt', ich wär' ein Fisch"

Mahomets Gesang, D. 549 [GA, v. 20^{10}, p. 110] "Seht den Felsenquell"

Mahomets Gesang, D. 721 [GA, v. 20^{10}, p. 125] "Seht den Felsenquell" 2nd setting; see also D. 549.

Meeres Stille, D. 215A [NGA, IV, 1, p. 197] "Tiefe Stille herrscht im Wasser"

Meeres Stille, D. 216 [GA, v. 20^2, p. 160] "Tiefe Stille herrscht im Wasser" 2nd setting; see also D. 215A.

Der Musensohn, D. 764 [GA, v. 20^7, pp. 48, 51] "Durch Feld und Wald zu schweifen"

Nachtgesang, D. 119 [GA, v. 20^1, p. 197] "O gib vom weichen Pfühle"

Nähe des Geliebten, D. 162 [GA, v. 20^2, pp. 62, 63] "Ich denke dein"

Prometheus, D. 674 [GA, v. 20^6, p. 71] "Bedecke deinen Himmel, Zeus"

Rastlose Liebe, D. 138 [GA, v. 20^3, p. 198] "Dem Schnee, dem Regen"

Der Rattenfänger, D. 255 [GA, v. 20^3, p. 34] "Ich bin der wohlbekannte Sänger"

Schäfers Klagelied, D. 121 [GA, v. 20^1, pp. 200, 203] "Da droben auf jenem Berge"

Der Schatzgräber, D. 256 [GA, v. 20^3, p. 35] "Arm am Beutel, krank am Herzen"

Schweizerlied, D. 559 [GA, v. 20^3, p. 48] "Uf'm Bergli bin i g'sässe"

Die Spinnerin, D. 247 [GA, v. 20^3, p. 44] "Als ich still und ruhig spann"

Trost in Thränen, D. 120 [GA, v. 20^1, p. 198] "Wie kommt's, dass du so traurig bist"

Wer kauft Liebesgötter? D. 261 [GA, v. 20^3, p. 43] "Von allen schönen Waren"

Willkommen und Abschied, D. 767 [GA, v. 20^7, pp. 58, 64] "Es schlug mein Herz, geschwind zu Pferde!"

Wonne der Wehmut, D. 260 [GA, v. 20^3, p. 42] "Trocknet nicht, trocknet nicht"

EGMONT.
Die Liebe, D. 210 [GA, v. 20^2, p. 130] "Freudvoll und leidvoll"

FAUST.
Gretchen am Spinnrade, D. 118 [GA, v. 20^1, p. 191] "Meine Ruh' ist hin"

Gretchen vor der Mater dolorosa, D. 564 [GA, v. 20^{10}, p. 116] "Ach neige, du Schmerzenreiche"

Der König in Thule, D. 367 [GA, v. 20^4, p. 202] "Es war ein König in Thule"

Szene aus Goethe's "Faust" D. 126 [GA, v. 20^1, pp. 215, 219] "Wie anders, Gretchen, war dir's"

INDISCHE LEGENDE.
Der Gott und die Bajadere, D. 254 [GA, v. 20^3, p. 32] "Mahadöh, der Herr, der Erde"

MICH ERGREIFT, ICH WEISS NICHT WIE.
Tischlied, D. 234 [GA, v. 20^2, p. 182] "Mich ergreift, ich weiss nicht wie"

SEHNSUCHT.
Sehnsucht, D. 123 [GA, v. 20^1, p. 206] "Was zieht mir das Herz so?"

WANDRERS NACHTLIED I.
Wandrers Nachtlied, D. 224 [GA, v. 20^2, p. 170] "Der du von dem Himmel bist"

WANDRERS NACHTLIED II.
Wandrers Nachtlied, D. 768 [GA, v. 20^7, p. 70] "Über allen Gipfeln ist Ruh' "

WESTÖSTLICHER DIVAN.
Geheimes, D. 719 [GA, v. 20^6, p. 183] "Über meines Liebchens Äugeln"

Suleika, D. 720 [GA, v. 20^6, p. 194] "Was bedeutet die Bewegung"

Versunken, D. 715 [GA, v. 20^6, p. 178] "Voll Locken kraus ein Haupt so rund"

WILHELM MEISTER.
An Mignon, D. 161 [GA, v. 20^2, pp. 59, 60] "Über Tal und Fluss getragen"

Harfenspieler, D. 325 [GA, v. 20^3, p. 187] "Wer sich der Einsamkeit ergiebt"

Harfenspieler I, D. 478 [GA, v. 20^4, pp. 181, 189] "Wer sich der Einsamkeit ergiebt"

Harfenspieler III, D. 480 [GA, v. 20^4, pp. 186, 187, 192] "Wer nie sein Brot mit Thränen ass"

Lied der Mignon, D. 877 no. 3 [GA, v. 20^8, p. 172] "So lasst mich scheinen, bis ich werde"
Mignon, D. 469 [GA, v. 20^6, p. 191] "So lasst mich scheinen, bis ich werde"
Mignon, D. 727 [GA, v. 20^6, p. 191] "So lasst mich scheinen, bis ich werde"
2nd setting; see also D. 469.
Der Sänger, D. 149 [GA, v. 20^2, pp. 33, 41] "Was hör' ich draussen vor dem Thor"
WILHELM MEISTER. Harfenspieler.
Harfenspieler II, D. 479 [GA, v. 20^4, pp. 184, 196] "An die Thüren will ich schleichen"
WILHELM MEISTER. Mignon's song: Heiss mich nicht reden.
Lied der Mignon, D. 877 no. 2 [GA, v. 20^8, p. 169] "Heiss mich nicht reden"
Mignon, D. 726 [GA, v. 20^6, p. 189] "Heiss mich nicht reden"
WILHELM MEISTER. Mignon's song: Kennst du das Land?
Mignon, D. 321 [GA, v. 20^3, p. 155] "Kennst du das Land?"
WILHELM MEISTER. Mignon's song: Nur wer die Sehnsucht kennt.
Lied der Mignon, D. 359 [GA, v. 20^4, p. 200] "Nur wer die Schnsucht kennt"
Lied der Mignon, D. 481 [GA, v. 20^4, p. 198] "Nur wer die Sehnsucht kennt"
Lied der Mignon, D. 877 no. 4 [GA, v. 20^8, p. 174] "Nur wer die Sehnsucht kennt"
Mignon und der Harfner, D. 877 no. 1 [GA, v. 20^8, p. 166] "Nur wer die Sehnsucht kennt"
Sehnsucht, D. 310 [GA, v. 20^3, pp. 126, 128] "Nur wer die Sehnsucht kennt"
Goldoni, Carlo, 1707-1793.
IL FILOSOFO DI CAMPAGNA.
La pastorella, D. 528 [GA, v. 20^{10}, p. 46] "La pastorella al prato"
Gotter, Friedrich Wilhelm, 1746-1797.
Pflicht und Liebe, D. 467 [GA, v. 20^{10}, p. 104] "Du, der ewig um mich trauert"
Grillparzer, Franz, 1791-1872.
Bertha's Lied in der Nacht, D. 653 [GA, v. 20^6, p. 18] "Nacht umhüllt mit wehendem Flügel"

Hardenberg, Friedrich Leopold, Freiherr von, 1772-1801.
Hymne I, D. 659 [GA, v. 20^6, p. 42] "Wenige wissen das Geheimnis der Liebe"
Hymne II, D. 660 [GA, v. 20^6, p. 49] "Wenn ich ihn nur habe"
Hymne III, D. 661 [GA, v. 20^6, p. 50] "Wenn alle untreu werden"
Hymne IV, D. 662 [GA, v. 20^6, p. 52] "Ich sag' es jedem"
Marie, D. 658 [GA, v. 20^6, p. 53] "Ich sehe dich in tausend Bildern"
Nachthymne, D. 687 [GA, v. 20^6, p. 80] "Hirüber wall' ich"
Heine, Heinrich, 1797-1856.
Am Meer, D. 957 no. 12 [GA, v. 20^9, p. 178] "Das Meer erglänzte weit hinaus"
Der Atlas, D. 957 no. 8 [GA, v. 20^9, p. 167] "Ich unglücksel'ger Atlas"
Der Doppelgänger, D. 957 no. 13 [GA, v. 20^9, p. 180] "Still ist die Nacht"
Das Fischermädchen, D. 957 no. 10 [GA, v. 20^9, p. 172] "Du schönes Fischermädchen"
Die Stadt, D. 957 no. 11 [GA, v. 20^9, p. 175] "Am fernen Horizonte"
LIEDERSTRAUSS.
Ihr Bild, D. 957 no. 9 [GA, v. 20^9, p. 170] "Ich stand in dunkeln Träumen"
Herder, Johann Gottfried von, 1744-1803.
Ein altschottische Ballade, D. 923 [GA, v. 20^9, pp. 102, 104] "Dein Schwert, wie ist's von Blut so rot"
Text published in Thomas Percy *Reliques of ancient English poetry;* German translation by Herder.
Hölty, Ludwig Heinrich Christoph, 1748-1776.
An den Mond, D. 193 [GA, v. 20^2, p. 110] "Geuss, lieber Mond"
An den Mond, D. 468 [GA, v. 20^4, p. 148] "Was schauest du so hell und klar"
An die Apfelbäume, wo ich Julien erblickte, D. 197 [GA, v. 20^2, p. 117] "Ein heilig Säuseln, und ein Gesangeston"
Auf den Tod einer Nachtigall, D. 399 [GA, v. 20^4, p. 98] "Sie ist dahin"
Blumenlied, D. 431 [GA, v. 20^4, p. 105] "Es ist ein halbes Himmelreich"
Erntelied, D. 434 [GA, v. 20^4, p. 109] "Sicheln schallen, Ähren fallen"

SCHUBERT, FRANZ, 1797-1828
(continued)
Hölty, Ludwig Heinrich Christoph,
1748-1776 *(continued)*
Die frühe Liebe, D. 430 [GA, v. 20⁴, p.
104] "Schon im bunten Knabenkleide"
Klage an den Mond, D. 436 [GA, v. 20⁴,
p. 95]
"Dein Silber schien durch Eichengrün"
A second version, D. 437, unpublished.
Die Knabenzeit, D. 400 [GA, v. 20⁴,
p. 100] "Wie glücklich, wem das
Knabenkleid"
Die Laube, D. 214 [GA, v. 20², p. 159]
"Nimmer werd' ich, nimmer dein
vergessen"
Mailied, D. 503 [Privately published by
R. van Hoorickx] "Grüner wird die Au
und der Himmel blau"
Die Mainacht, D. 194 [GA, v. 20²,
p. 112] "Wann der silberne Mond"
Minnelied, D. 429 [GA, 20⁴, p. 103]
"Holder klingt der Vogelsang"
Die Nonne, D. 208 [GA, v. 20², p. 124;
2nd version to be in NGA, IV, 8]
"Es liebt' in Welschland irgendwo"
Seligkeit, D. 433 [GA, v. 20⁴, p. 108]
"Freuden sonder Zahl"
Todtengräberlied, D. 44 [GA, v. 20¹,
p. 54] "Grabe, Spaten, grabe!"
Winterlied, D. 401 [GA, v. 20⁴, p. 102]
"Keine Blumen blühn"
BALLADE.
Der Traum, D. 213 [GA, v. 20², p.
158] "Mir träumt', ich war ein
Vögelein"
GEUSS NICHT SO LAUT.
An die Nachtigall, D. 196 [GA, v. 20²,
p. 116] "Geuss nicht so laut"
LIED EINES LIEBENDEN.
Der Liebende, D. 207 [GA, v. 20²,
p. 123] "Beglückt, beglückt, wer
dich erblickt"
DIE NACHTIGALL.
Seufzer, D. 198 [GA, v. 20², p. 120]
"Die Nachtigall singt überall"
Hohlfeld, Christoph Christian, 1776-
1849.
An Gott, D. 863 [**Lieder für Blinde und
von Blinden,** 1827, p. 9] "Kein Auge
hat Dein Angesicht geschaut"
Poem published in **Lieder . . . ,**
edited by Johann Wilhelm Klein;
song lost.
Hüttenbrenner, Heinrich
Der Jüngling auf dem Hügel, D. 702
[GA, v. 20⁶, p. 126]
"Ein Jüngling auf dem Hügel"

Jacobi, Johann Georg, 1740-1814.
Am Tage aller Seelen, D. 343 [GA,
v. 20⁵, p. 216] "Ruh'n in Frieden"
An Chloen, D. 462 [GA, v. 20⁴, p. 149]
"Bei der Liebe reinsten Flammen"
Hochzeitlied, D. 463 [GA, v. 20⁴, p. 150]
"Will singen euch im alten Ton"
In der Mitternacht, D. 464 [GA, v. 20⁴,
p. 151] "Todesstille deckt das Tal"
*Lied des Orpheus, als er in die Hölle
ging,* D. 474 [GA, v. 20⁴, pp. 164,
170] "Wälze dich hinweg, du wildes
Feuer!"
Die Perle, D. 466 [GA, v. 20⁴, p. 153]
"Es ging ein Mann zur Frühlingszeit"
Trauer der Liebe, D. 465 [GA, v. 20⁴, p.
152] "Wo die Taub' in stillen Buchen"
Kalchberg, Johann Nepomuk von,
1765-1827.
Die Macht der Liebe, D. 308 [GA,
v. 20³, p. 123]
"Überall, wohin mein Auge blicket"
Kenner, Josef, 1794-1868.
Ballade, D. 134 [GA, v. 20², p. 198]
"Ein Fräulein schaut vom hohen
Thurm"
Grablied, D. 218 [GA, v. 20², p. 166]
"Er fiel den Tod fürs Vaterland"
Der Liedler, D. 209 [GA, v. 20², p. 184]
"Gieb, Schwester, mir die Harf' herab"
Kind, Friedrich, 1768-1843.
Hänflings Liebeswerbung, D. 552 [GA,
v. 20⁵, p. 90]
"Ahidi, ich liebe, Ahidi, ich liebe!"
Klenke, Karoline Louise von, 1754-
1812.
Heimliches Lieben, D. 922 [GA, v. 20⁹,
pp. 92, 97] "O du, wenn deine Lippen
mich berühen"
Klopstock, Friedrich Gottlieb, 1724-
1803.
Dem Unendlichen, D. 291 [GA, v. 20³,
pp. 85, 90, 95] "Wie erhebt sich das
Herz, wenn es dich"
Edone, D. 445 [GA, v. 20⁴, p. 116]
"Dein süsses Bild, Edone"
Die frühen Gräber, D. 290 [GA, v. 20³,
p. 84]
"Willkommen, O silberner Mond"
Die Gestirne, D. 444 [GA, v. 20⁴, p. 114]
"Es tönet sein Lob Feld und Wald"
Das grosse Halleluja, D. 442 [GA,
v. 20⁴, p. 110]
"Ehre sei dem Hocherhab'nen"
Hermann und Thusnelda, D. 322 [GA,
v. 20³, p. 159] "Ha, dort kömmt er, mit
Schweiss, mit Römerblut"

Schlachtgesang, D. 443 [GA, v. 20⁴, p. 112]
"Mit unserm Arm ist nichts gethan"

Selma und Selmar, D. 286 [GA, v. 20³, pp. 74, 75]
"Weine du nicht O, die ich innig liebe"

Die Sommernacht, D. 289 [GA, v. 20³, pp. 80, 82] "Wenn der Schimmer von dem Monde nun herab"

Vaterlandslied, D. 287 [GA, v. 20³, pp. 76, 77]
"Ich bin ein deutsches Mädchen!"

AN CIDLI.

    Furcht der Geliebten, D. 285 [GA, v. 20³, pp. 70, 71] "Cidli, du weinest, und ich schlumm're sicher"

ODE.

    An Sie, D. 288 [GA, v. 20³, p. 78]
    "Zeit, Verkündigerin der besten Freuden"

    Das Rosenband, D. 280 [GA, v. 20³, p. 72]
    "Im Frühlingsgarten fand ich sie"

Köpken, Friedrich von, 1737-1811.

Freude der Kinderjahre, D. 455 [GA, v. 20⁴, p. 142]
"Freude, die im frühen Lenze"

Körner, Theodor, i.e., Karl Theodor, 1791-1813.

Amphiaraos, D. 166 [GA, v. 20², p. 68]
"Vor Thebens siebenfach gähnenden Toren"

Auf der Riesenkoppe, D. 611 [GA, v. 20⁵, p. 184]
"Hoch auf dem Gipfel deiner Gebirge"

Das war ich, D. 174 [GA, v. 20², p. 84]
"Jüngst träumte mir, ich sah auf lichten"

Gebet während der Schlacht, D. 171 [GA, v. 20², p. 80]
"Vater, ich rufe dich!"

Das gestörte Glück, D. 309 [GA, v. 20³, p. 124]
"Ich hab' ein heisses junges Blut"

Liebesrausch, D. 164 [*Musik aus aller Welt* v. 1 no. 1 (Jan. 1928): 7]
"Glanz des Guten und des Schönen strahlt mir dein hohes Bild"

Liebesrausch, D. 179 [GA, v. 20², p. 90]
"Dir, Mädchen, schlägt mit leisem Behen"

Liebeständelei, D. 206 [GA, v. 20², p. 122]
"Süsses Liebchen! komm zu mir!"

Sängers Morgenlied, D. 163 [GA, v. 20², p. 64]
"Süsses Licht! Aus goldnen Pforten"

Sängers Morgenlied, D. 165 [GA, v. 20², p. 66]
"Süsses Licht! Aus goldnen Pforten"

Schwertlied, D. 170 [GA, v. 20², p. 78]
"Du Schwert an meiner Linken"

Sehnsucht der Liebe, D. 180 [GA, v. 20², p. 92]
"Wie die Nacht mit heil'gem Beben"

Trinklied vor der Schlacht, D. 169 [GA, v. 20², p. 76]
"Schlacht, du brichst an!"
Unison song.

Wiegenlied, D. 304 [GA, v. 20³, p. 117]
"Schlumm're sanft! Noch an dem Mutterherzen"

Kosegarten, Ludwig Gotthard, 1758-1818.

Abends unter der Linde, D. 235 [GA, v. 20², p. 204]
"Woher, O namenloses Sehnen"

Abends unter der Linde, D. 237 [GA, v. 20², p. 206]
"Woher, O namenloses Sehnen"

Alles um Liebe, D. 241 [GA, v. 20², p. 212] "Was ist es, das die Seele füllt?"

An die untergehende Sonne, D. 457 [GA, v. 20⁴, p. 134]
"Sonne, du sinkst, Sonne, du sinkst"

An Rosa I, D. 315 [GA, v. 20³, p. 145]
"Warum bist du nicht hier?"

An Rosa II, D. 316 [GA, v. 20³, pp. 146, 147] "Rosa, denkst du an mich"

Das Finden, D. 219 [GA, v. 20², p. 167]
"Ich hab' ein Mädchen funden"

Idens Nachtgesang, D. 227 [GA, v. 20², p. 173] "Vernimm es, Nacht, was Ida dir vertrauet"

Idens Schwanenlied, D. 317 [GA, v. 20³, p. 148]
"Wie schaust du aus dem Nebelflor"

Luisens Antwort, D. 319 [GA, v. 20³, p. 152] "Wohl weinen Gottes Engel"

Die Mondnacht, D. 238 [GA, v. 20², p. 208] "Siehe, wie die Mondesstrahlen"

Nachtgesang, D. 314 [GA, v. 20³, p. 144]
"Tiefe Feier schauert um die Welt"

Schwangesang, D. 318 [GA, v. 20³, p. 150] "Endlich steh'n die Pforten offen"

Das Sehnen, D. 231 [GA, v. 20², p. 177]
"Wehmut die mich hüllt"

Die Sterne, D. 313 [GA, v. 20³, p. 142]
"Wie wohl ist mir im Dunkeln"

DER ABEND BLÜHT, TEMORA GLÜHT.

SCHUBERT, FRANZ, 1797-1828
(continued)
Kosegarten, Ludwig Gotthard, 1758-1818 *(continued)*
DER ABEND BLÜHT, TEMORA GLÜHT *(continued)*
    Der Abend, D. 221 [GA, v. 20^2, p. 178]
      "Der Abend blüht, Temora glüht"
AGNES.
    Von Ida, D. 228 [GA, v. 20^2, p. 174]
      "Der Morgen blüht; der Osten glüht"
ICH LAG AUF GRÜNEN MATTEN.
    Die Erscheinung, D. 229 [GA, v. 20^2, p. 175] "Ich lag auf grünen Matten"
IM ERLENBUSCH, IM TANNENHAIN.
    Die Täuschung, D. 230 [GA, v. 20^2, p. 176]
      "Im Erlenbusch, im Tannenhain"
MINNESANG.
    Huldigung, D. 240 [GA, v. 20^2, p. 210]
      "Ganz verloren, ganz versunken"
WER BIST DU.
    Geist der Liebe, D. 233 [GA, v. 20^2, p. 180] "Wer bist du, Geist der Liebe"
Kuffner, Christoph, 1780-1846.
    Glaube, Hoffnung und Liebe, D. 955 [GA, v. 20^8, p. 28]
      "Glaube, hoffe, liebe!"
Kumpf, Johann Gottfried, 1781-1862.
    Mein Gruss an den Mai, D. 305 [GA, v. 20^3, p. 118]
      "Sei mir gegrüsst, O Mai"
    Der Mondabend, D. 141 [GA, v. 20^2, p. 20] "Rein und freundlich lacht der Himmel"
Lappe, Karl, 1773-1843.
    Der Einsame, D. 800 [GA, v. 20^8, pp. 36, 41] "Wenn meine Grillen schwirren, bei Nacht"
    Im Abendrot, D. 799 [GA, v. 20^8, p. 30] "O, wie schön ist deine Welt"
Leitner, Karl Gottfried, Ritter von, 1800-1890.
    Des Fischers Liebesglück, D. 933 [GA, v. 20^9, p. 116]
      "Dort blinket durch Weiden"
    Drang in die Ferne, D. 770 [GA, v. 20^7, p. 91] "Vater, du glaubst es nicht"
    Der Kreuzzug, D. 932 [GA, v. 20^9, p. 114]
      "Ein Münich steht in seiner Zell"
    Die Sterne, D. 939 [GA, v. 20^9, p. 125]
      "Wie blitzen die Sterne so hell durch die Nacht!"

    Vor meiner Wiege, D. 927 [GA, v. 20^9, p. 108]
      "Das also, das ist der enge Schrein"
Der Wallensteiner Lanzknecht beim Trunk, D. 931 [GA, v. 20^9, p. 112]
      "He! schenket mir im Helme ein!"
Der Winterabend, D. 938 [GA, v. 20^9, p. 118]
      "Es ist so still, so heimlich um mich"
Leon, Gottlieb von, 1757-1832.
    Die Liebe, D. 522 [GA, v. 20^5, p. 4]
      "Wo weht der Liebe hoher Geist?"
Lubi, Michael, 1757-1808.
    Ammenlied, D. 122 [GA, v. 20^1, p. 224]
      "Am hohen, hohen Thurm"
Macpherson, James, 1736-1796.
    Die Nacht, D. 534 [GA, v. 20^5, p. 39]
      "Die Nacht ist dumpfig und finster"
    Der Tod Oskar's, D. 375 [GA, v. 20^4, p. 7] "Warum öffnest du wieder, Erzeugter von Alpin"
BATTLE OF LORA.
    Lorma, D. 327 [Privately printed: Stuttgart, Walter Schulz, 1928]
      "Lorma sass in der Halle von Aldo"
    Lorma, D. 376 [GA, v. 20^{10}, p. 102]
      "Lorma sass in der Halle von Aldo"
CARRIC-THURA.
    Cronnan, D. 282 [GA, v. 20^4, p. 21]
      "Ich sitz' bei der moosigten Quelle"
    Shilrik und Vinvela, D. 293 [GA, v. 20^3, p. 100] "Mein Geliebter ist ein Sohn des Hügels"
CARRIC-THURA: Spirit of Loda.
    Loda's Gespenst, D. 150 [GA, v. 20^2, p. 21] "Der bleiche, kalte Mond erhob sich in Osten"
DARTHULA.
    Ossians Lied nach dem Falle Nathos', D. 278 [GA, v. 20^3, p. 108; Revisionsbericht to Series 20, pp. 34-36] "Beugt euch aus euren Wolken nieder"
FINGAL.
    Das Mädchen von Inistore, D. 281 [GA, v. 20^3, p. 110]
      "Mädchen Inistores"
THE SONGS OF SELMA.
    Kolma's Klage, D. 217 [GA, v. 20^2, p. 161] "Rund um mich Nacht, ich irr' allein"
Matthisson, Friedrich von, 1761-1831.
    Der Abend, D. 108 [GA, v. 20^1, p. 161]
      "Purpur malt die Tannenhügel"
    Adelaide, D. 95 [GA, v. 20^1, p. 169]
      "Einsam wandelt dein Freund im Frühlingsgarten"

An Laura, D. 115 [GA, v. 20¹, p. 183]
"Herzen, die gen Himmel sich
erheben"

Andenken, D. 99 [GA, v. 20¹, p. 144]
"Ich denke dein, wenn durch den
Hain"

Die Betende, D. 102 [GA, v. 20¹, p. 156]
"Laura betet!"

Entzückung, D. 413 [GA, v. 20⁴, p. 84]
"Tag voll Himmel!"

Geist der Liebe, D. 414 [GA, v. 20⁴,
p. 87]
"Der Abend schleiert Flur und Hain"

Geisternähe, D. 100 [GA, v. 20¹, p. 147]
"Der Dämm'rung Schein durchblinkt
den Hain"

Der Geistertanz, D. 15 [GA, v. 20¹⁰,
pp. 92, 94] "Die bretterne Kammer der
Toten erbedt"

Der Geistertanz, D. 116 [GA, v. 20¹,
p. 186] "Die bretterne Kammer der
Toten erbedt"

Julius an Theone, D. 419 [GA, v. 20⁴,
p. 91] "Nimmer, nimmer darf ich dir
gestehen"

Klage, D. 415 [GA, v. 20⁴, p. 88]
"Die Sonne steigt"

Lebenslied, D. 508 [GA, v. 20⁴, p. 250]
"Kommen und Scheiden, Suchen und
Meiden"

Lied aus der Ferne, D. 107 [GA, v. 20¹,
p. 158]
"Wenn in des Abends letztem Scheine"

Lied der Liebe, D. 109 [GA, v. 20¹,
p. 163] "Durch Fichten am Hügel,
durch Erlen am Bach"

Naturgenuss, D. 188 [GA, v. 20², p. 99]
"Im Abendschimmer wallt der Quell"

Die Schatten, D. 50 [GA, v. 20¹, p. 58]
"Freunde, deren Grüfte sich schon
bemoosten"

Skolie, D. 507 [GA, v. 20⁴, p. 249]
"Mädchen entsiegelten, Brüder, die
Flaschen"

Die Sterbende, D. 186 [GA, v. 20²,
p. 100] "Heil! dies ist die letzte Zähre"

Totenkranz für ein Kind, D. 275 [GA,
v. 20³, p. 61]
"Sanft wehn, im Hauch der Abendluft"

Trost an Elisa, D. 97 [GA, v. 20¹,
p. 154] "Lehnst du deine
bleichgehärmte Wange"

ABENDGEWÖLKE SCHWEBEN HELL.
Stimme der Liebe, D. 187 [GA, v. 20²,
p. 98]
"Abendgewölke schweben hell"

Stimme der Liebe, D. 418 [GA, v. 20⁴,
p. 90]
"Abendgewölke schweben hell"

AM SEEGESTAD'.
Erinnerungen, D. 98 [GA, v. 20¹,
p. 166] "Am Seegestad', in lauden
Vollmondsnächten"

DAS FRÄULEIN IM THURME.
Romanze, D. 114 [GA, v. 20¹, p. 178]
"Ein Fräulein klagt'"

TODTENOPFER.
Todtenopfer, D. 101 [GA, v. 20¹, p.
151] "Kein Rosenschimmerleuchtet"

Mayláth, Johann, Count, 1786-1855.
Der Blumen Schmerz, D. 731 [GA, v.
20⁶, p. 210]
"Wie tönt es mir so schaurig"

Mayrhofer, Johann, 1787-1836.
Abendlied der Fürstin, D. 495 [GA,
v. 20⁴, p. 227]
"Der Abend röthet nun das Thal"

Abendstern, D. 806 [GA, v. 20⁸, p. 18]
"Was weilst du einsam an dem
Himmel"

Der Alpenjäger, D. 524 [GA, v. 20⁵,
pp. 12, 16] "Auf hohem Bergesrücken"

Alte Liebe rostet nie, D. 477 [GA, v. 20⁴,
p. 180] same

Am Strome, D. 539 [GA, v. 20⁵, p. 54]
"Ist mir's doch, als sei mein Leben"

An die Freunde, D. 654 [GA, v. 20⁶,
p. 20]
"Im Wald, im Wald, da grabt mich
ein"

Antigone und Oedip, D. 542 [GA, v. 20⁵,
p. 62] "Ihr hohen Himmlischen,
erhöret der Tochter"

Atys, D. 585 [GA, v. 20⁵, p. 159]
"Der Knabe seufzt über's grüne Meer"

Auf der Donau, D. 553 [GA, v. 20⁵,
p. 92] "Auf der Wellen Spiegel
schwimmt der Kahn"

Auflösung, D. 807 [GA, v. 20⁸, p. 20]
"Verbirg dich, Sonne"

Augenlied, D. 297 [GA, v. 20³, p. 168]
"Süsse Augen, klare Bronnen!"

Aus "Heliopolis" D. 753 [GA, v. 20⁷,
p. 8] "Im kalten rauhen Norden"

Aus "Heliopolis" D. 754 [GA, v. 20⁷,
p. 10] "Fels auf Felsen hingewälzet"

Beim Winde, D. 669 [GA, v. 20⁶, p. 54]
"Es träumen die Wolken"

Einsamkeit, D. 620 [GA, v. 20⁵, p. 196]
"Gib mir die Fülle der Einsamkeit!"

Der entsühnte Orest, D. 699 [GA, v. 20⁶,
p. 121]
"Zu meinen Füssen brichst du dich"

SCHUBERT, FRANZ, 1797-1828
(continued)
Mayrhofer, Johann, 1787-1836
(continued)

Erlafsee, D. 586 [GA, v. 20^5, p. 164]
"Mir ist so wohl, so weh'"

Fahrt zum Hades, D. 526 [GA, v. 20^5,
p. 20] "Der Nachen dröhnt,
Cypressen flüstern"

Freiwilliges Versinken, D. 700 [GA,
v. 20^6, p. 124] "Wohin? O Helios!"

Geheimnis. An Franz Schubert, D. 491
[GA, v. 20^4, p. 223]
"Sag an, wer lehrt dich Lieder"

Gondelfahrer, D. 808 [GA, v. 20^8, p. 26]
"Es tanzen Mond und Sterne"

Der Hirt, D. 490 [GA, v. 20^4, p. 220]
"Du Thurm! zu meinem Leide"

Iphigenia, D. 573 [GA, v. 20^5, p. 127]
"Blüht denn hier an Tauris Strande"

Liane, D. 298 [GA, v. 20^3, p. 165]
"Hast du Lianen nicht gesehen?"

Liedesend, D. 473 [GA, v. 20^4, pp. 154,
159] "Auf seinem gold'nen Throne"

Memnon, D. 541 [GA, v. 20^5, p. 59]
"Den Tag hindurch nur einmal mag ich
sprechen"

Nachtstück, D. 672 [GA, v. 20^6, p. 62]
"Wenn über Berge sich der Nebel
breitet"

Nachtviolen, D. 752 [GA, v. 20^7, p. 6]
"Nachtviolen, Nachtviolen!"

Orest auf Tauris, D. 548 [GA, v. 20^6,
p. 118] "Ist dies Tauris"

Piloktet, D. 540 [GA, v. 20^5, p. 56]
"Da sitz' ich ohne Bogen"

Rückweg, D. 476 [GA, v. 20^4, p. 178]
"Zum Donaustrom, zur Kaiserstadt"

Schlaflied, D. 527 [GA, v. 20^5, p. 24]
"Es mahnt der Wald"

Sehnsucht, D. 516 [GA, v. 20^6, p. 130]
"Der Lerche wolkennahe Lieder"

Der Sieg, D. 805 [GA, v. 20^8, p. 16]
"O unbewölktes Leben!"

Die Sternennächte, D. 670 [GA, v. 20^6,
p. 58] "In monderhellten Nächten"

Trost, D. 671 [GA, v. 20^6, p. 60]
"Hörnerklänge rufen klagend"
Deutsch notes poem not in Mayhofer's
published works.

Ueber allen Zauber Liebe, D. 682 [GA,
v. 20^{10}, p. 125]
"Sie hüpfte mit mir auf grünem Plan"

Uraniens Flucht, D. 554 [GA, v. 20^5,
p. 99] "Lasst uns, ihr Himmlischen, ein
Fest begehen!"

Wie Ulfru fischt, D. 525 [GA, v. 20^5, p.
18] "Die Angel zuckt, die Rute bebt"

Der zürnenden Diana, D. 707 [GA,
v. 20^6, pp. 133, 141] "Ja, spanne nur
den Bogen mich zu töten"

Zum Punsche, D. 492 [GA, v. 20^4, p.
226] "Woget brausend, Harmonieen"

IM WINDE.
Der Schiffer, D. 536 [GA, v. 20^5,
p. 95] "Im Winde, im Sturme
befahr' ich den Fluss"

LUNZ.
Abschied, D. 475 [GA, v. 20^4, p. 176]
"Über die Berge zieht ihr fort"

NACH DEM GEWITTER.
Nach einem Gewitter, D. 561 [GA,
v. 20^5, p. 116] "Auf den Blumen"

SCHIFFERS NACHTLIED.
Lied eines Schiffers an die Dioskuren,
D. 360 [GA, v. 20^4, p. 221]
"Dioskuren, Zwillingssterne"

SITZ' ICH IM GRAS.
Am See, D. 124 [GA, v. 20^1, p. 210]
"Sitz' ich im Gras"

Metastasio, Pietro Antonio Domenico Buonaventura, 1698-1782.

Da quel sembiante appresi, D. 688 no. 3
[GA, v. 20^{10}, p. 52] same

L'incanto degli occhi, D. 902 no. 1 [GA,
v. 20^{10}, p. 54] "Da voi cari lumi"

Mio ben, ricordati, D. 688 no. 4 [GA,
v. 20^{10}, p. 53] same

Il traditor deluso, D. 902, no. 2 [GA,
v. 20^{10}, p. 58] "Aimè, io tremo!"

ALCIDE AL BIVIO.
Pensa, che questo istante, D. 76 [GA,
v. 20^{10}, p. 34] same

ARTASERSE.
Leiden der Trennung, D. 509 [GA,
v. 20^4, p. 251]
"Vom Meere trennt sich die Welle"
Text translated by Heinrich von
Collin.

DEMOFOONTE.
Misero pargoletto, D. 42 [GA, v. 20^{10},
p. 31] same

DIDONE ABBANDONATA.
Arie, D. 510 [GA, v. 20^{10}, p. 40]
"Vedi, quanto adoro"

GLI ORTI ESPERIDI.
Son fra l'onde, D. 78 [GA, v. 20^{10},
p. 36] same

Mikan, Johann Christian, 1769-1844.
Die Befreier Europas in Paris, D. 104
[GA, v. 20^{10}, p. 76]
"Sie sind in Paris!"

Müller, Wilhelm, 1794-1827.

Am Feierabend, D. 795 no. 5 [GA, v. 20[7], p. 145]
"Hätt' ich tausend Arme zu rühen"

Auf dem Flusse, D. 911 no. 7 [GA, v. 20[9], p. 22]
"Der du so lustig rauschtest"

Die böse Farbe, D. 795 no. 17 [GA, v. 20[7], p. 174]
"Ich möchte zieh'n in die Welt hinaus"

Danksagung an den Bach, D. 795 no. 4 [GA, v. 20[7], p. 143]
"War es also gemeint"

Des Baches Wiegenlied, D. 795 no. 20 [GA, v. 20[7], p. 184]
"Gute Ruh', gute Ruh', tu' die Augen zu"

Des Müllers Blumen, D. 795 no. 9 [GA, v. 20[7], p. 155]
"Am Bach viel kleine Blumen steh'n"

Eifersucht und Stolz, D. 795 no. 15 [GA, v. 20[7], p. 168]
"Wohin so schnell, so kraus und wild"

Einsamkeit, D. 911 no. 12 [GA, v. 20[9], pp. 40, 42] "Wie eine trübe Wolke"

Erstarrung, D. 911 no. 4 [GA, v. 20[9], p. 10] "Ich such' im Schnee vergebens"

Frühlingstraum, D. 911 no. 11 [GA, v. 20[9], p. 36]
"Ich träumte von bunten Blumen"

Gefror'ne Thränen, D. 911 no. 3 [GA, v. 20[9], p. 8] "Gefror'ne Tropfen fallen"

Der greise Kopf, D. 911 no. 14 [GA, v. 20[9], p. 48]
"Der Reif hat einen weissen Schein"

Gute Nacht, D. 911 no. 1 [GA, v. 20[9], p. 2] "Fremd bin ich eingezogen"

Halt! D. 795 no. 3 [GA, v. 20[7], p. 140]
"Eine Mühle seh' ich blinken"

Der Hirt auf dem Felsen, D. 965 [GA, v. 20[10], p. 16] "Wenn auf dem höchsten Fels ich steh"
Voice & piano with clarinet obbligato.

Im Dorfe, D. 911 no. 17 [GA, v. 20[9], p. 56] "Es bellen die Hunde, es rasseln die Ketten"

Irrlicht, D. 911 no. 9 [GA, v. 20[9], p. 30] "In die tiefsten Felsengründe"

Der Jäger, D. 795 no. 14 [GA, v. 20[7], p. 166] "Was sucht denn der Jager am Mühlbach hier?"

Die Krähe, D. 911 no. 15 [GA, v. 20[9], p. 50] "Eine Krähe war mit mir"

Der Leiermann, D. 911 no. 24 [GA, v. 20[9], p. 74] "Drüben hinterm Dorfe steht ein Leiermann"

Letzte Hoffnung, D. 911 no. 16 [GA, v. 20[9], p. 53]
"Hie und da ist an den Bäumen"

Die liebe Farbe, D. 795 no. 16 [GA, v. 20[7], p. 172]
"In Grün will ich mich kleiden"

Der Lindenbaum, D. 911 no. 5 [GA, v. 20[9], p. 16]
"Am Brunnen vor dem Thore"

Mein! D. 795 no. 11 [GA, v. 20[7], p. 158]
"Bächlein, lass dein Rauschen sein"

Mit dem grünen Lautenband, D. 795 no. 13 [GA, v. 20[7], p. 165]
"Schad' um das schöne, grüne Band"

Morgengruss, D. 795 no. 8 [GA, v. 20[7], p. 154]
"Guten Morgen, schöne Müllerin!"

Der Müller und der Bach, D. 795 no. 19 [GA, v. 20[7], p. 181] "Wo ein treues Herze in Liebe vergeht"

Mut, D. 911 no. 22 [GA, v. 20[9], p. 70]
"Fliegt der Schnee mir in's Gesicht"

Die Nebensonne, D. 911 no. 23 [GA, v. 20[9], p. 72] "Drei Sonne sah ich am Himmel steh'n"

Der Neugierige, D. 795 no. 6 [GA, v. 20[7], p. 149] "Ich frage keine Blume"

Pause, D. 795 no. 12 [GA, v. 20[7], p. 162] "Meine Laute hab' ich gehängt an die Wand"

Die Post, D. 911 no. 13 [GA, v. 20[9], p. 44] "Von der Strasse her ein Posthorn klingt"

Rast, D. 911 no. 10 [GA, v. 20[9], pp. 32, 34]
"Nun merk' ich erst, wie Müd'ich bin"

Rückblick, D. 911 no. 8 [GA, v. 20[9], p. 26] "Es brennt mir unter beiden Sohlen"

Der stürmische Morgen, D. 911 no. 18 [GA, v. 20[9], p. 60]
"Wie hat der Sturm zerrissen"

Täuschung, D. 911 no. 19 [GA, v. 20[9], p. 62]
"Ein Licht tanzt freundlich vor mir her"

Thränenregen, D. 795 no. 10 [GA, v. 20[7], p. 156]
"Wir sassen so traulich beisammen"

Trockne Blumen, D. 795 no. 18 [GA, v. 20[7], p. 178]
"Ihr Blümlein alle, die sie mir gab"

Ungeduld, D. 795 no. 7 [GA, v. 20[7], p. 152] "Ich schnitt' es gern in alle Rinden ein"

Das Wandern, D. 795 no. 1 [GA, v. 20[7], p. 134]
"Das Wandern ist des Müllers Lust"

SCHUBERT, FRANZ, 1797-1828
(continued)
Müller, Wilhelm, 1794-1827 *(continued)*
Wasserflut, D. 911 no. 6 [GA, v. 20^9,
   p. 20] "Manche Thrän' aus meinen
   Augen"
Der Wegweiser, D. 911 no. 20 [GA,
   v. 20^9, p. 64]
   "Was vermeid' ich denn die Wege"
Die Wetterfahne, D. 911 no. 2 [GA,
   v. 20^9, p. 6]
   "Der Wind spielt mit der Wetterfahne"
Das Wirtshaus, D. 911 no. 21 [GA,
   v. 20^9, p. 68] "Auf einen Totenacker"
Wohin? D. 795 no. 2 [GA, v. 20^7, p. 136]
   "Ich hört' ein Bächlein rauschen"
Ottenwalt, Anton, 1789-1845.
Der Knabe in der Wiege, D. 579 [GA,
   v. 20^5, p. 180] "Er schläft so süss"
Petrarca, Francesco, 1304-1374.
Sonett I, D. 628 [GA, v. 20^5, p. 225]
   "Apollo, lebet noch dein hold
      Verlangen"
Sonett II, D. 629 [GA, v. 20^5, p. 228]
   "Allein, nachdenklich, wie gelähmt
      vom Krampfe"
Sonett III, D. 630 [GA, v. 20^5, p. 231]
   "Nunmehr, da Himmel, Erde"
Pfeffel, Gottlieb Conrad, 1736-1809.
Der Vatermörder, D. 10 [GA, v. 20^1,
   p. 40] "Ein Vater starb von des Sohnes
   Hand"
Pichler, Karoline (Greiner), 1769-1843.
Lied, D. 483 [GA, v. 20^4, p. 212]
   "Ferne von der grossen Stadt"
Der Sänger am Felsen, D. 482 [GA,
   v. 20^4, p. 210] "Klage, meine Flöte"
OLIVIER.
   Der Unglückliche, D. 713 [GA, v. 20^6,
      pp. 168, 173] "Die Nacht bricht an'"
Platen-Hallermünde, August, Graf
von, 1796-1835.
Du liebst mich nicht, D. 756 [GA, v. 20^7,
   pp. 24, 26] "Mein Herz ist zerrissen"
Die Liebe hat gelogen, D. 751 [GA,
   v. 20^7, p. 28] same
Platner, Anton, 1787-1855.
Die Blumensprache, D. 519 [GA, v. 20^5,
   p. 25] "Es deuten die Blumen des
   Herzens Gefühle"
Pollak, Aaron
Frühlingslied, D. 919 [GA, v. 21, p. 325]
   "Geöffnet sind des Winters Riegel"
   Also for 4-part men's chorus,
   unaccompanied.

Pope, Alexander, 1688-1744.
THE DYING CHRISTIAN TO HIS SOUL.
   Verklärung, D. 59 [GA, v. 20^1, p. 68]
   "Lebensfunke, vom Himmel
      entglüht"
Prandstetter, Martin Josef, b. 1750.
Die Fröhlichkeit, D. 262 [GA, v. 20^3,
   p. 64] "Wess' Adern leichtes Blut
   durchspringt"
Pratobevera, Adolf von, 1806-1875.
Abschied von der Erde, D. 829 [GA, v.
   20^{10}, p. 136]
   "Leb' wohl du schöne Erde"
Pyrker, Johann Ladislaus, 1772-1847.
Die Allmacht, D. 852 [GA, v. 20^8,
   p. 128] "Gross ist Jehovah, der Herr"
Das Heimweh, D. 851 [GA, v. 20^8,
   pp. 112, 120] "Ach, der Gebirgssohn
   hängt mit kindlicher Lieb' "
Reil, Johann Anton Friedrich, 1773-
1843.
Das Lied im Grünen, D. 917 [GA, v. 20^9,
   p. 85] "Ins Grüne, ins Grüne, da lockt
   uns der Frühling"
Reissig, Christian Ludwig, 1783-
1822.
Der Zufriedene, D. 320 [GA, v. 20^3,
   p. 154] "Zwar schuf das Glück
   hienieden"
Rellstab, Ludwig, 1799-1868.
Abschied, D. 957 no. 7 [GA, v. 20^9,
   p. 160]
   "Ade! du muntre, do fröhliche Stadt"
Auf dem Strome, D. 943 [GA, v. 20^{10}, p.
   2] "Nimm die letzten Abschiedsküsse"
   Accompaniment for piano & horn or
   cello.
Aufenthalt, D. 957 no. 5 [GA, v. 20^9,
   p. 151] "Rauschen der Strom"
Frühlingssehnsucht, D. 957 no. 3 [GA,
   v. 20^9, p. 144]
   "Säuselnde Lüfte wehend so mild"
Herbst, D. 945 [GA, v. 20^{10}, p. 90]
   "Es rauschen die Winde so herbstlich
   und kalt"
In der Ferne, D. 957 no. 6 [GA, v. 20^9,
   p. 156] "Wehe dem Fliehenden, Welt
   hinaus Ziehenden!"
Kriegers Ahnung, D. 957 no. 2 [GA,
   v. 20^9, p. 139]
   "In tiefer Ruh liegt und mich her"
Lebensmut, D. 937 [GA, v. 20^{10}, p. 134]
   "Frölicher Lebensmut"
Liebesbotschaft, D. 957 no. 1 [GA, v.
   20^9, p. 134] "Rauschen des Bächlein"
Ständchen, D. 957 no. 4 [GA, v. 20^9,
   p. 148] "Leise flehen meine Lieder"

Rochlitz, Johann Friedrich, 1770-1842.

Alinde, D. 904 [GA, v. 204, p. 257]
"Die Sonne sinkt in's tiefe Mecr"

An die Laute, D. 905 [GA, v. 20^4, p. 262]
"Leiser, leiser, kleine Laute"

Klaglied, D. 23 [GA, v. 20^1, p. 52]
"Meine Ruh' ist dahin"

Rückert, Friedrich, 1788-1866.

Dass sie hier gewesen, D. 775 [GA,
v. 20^8, p. 2] "Dass der Ostwind Düfte"

Sei mir gregrüsst! D. 741 [GA, v. 20^6,
p. 214] "O du Entriss'ne mir und
meinem Kusse!"

KEHR EIN BEI MIR.

Du bist die Ruh, D. 776 [GA, v. 20^8,
p. 4] same

LACHENS UND WEINENS GRUND.

Lachen und Weinen, D. 777 [GA,
v. 20^8, p. 7] same

VOM KÜNFTIGEN ALTER.

Greisengesang, D. 778 [GA, v. 20^8,
p. 10] "Der Frost hat mir bereifet
des Hauses Dach"

Salis-Seewis, Johann Gaudenz,
Freiherr von, 1762-1834.

Abschied von der Harfe, D. 406 [GA,
v. 20^4, p. 80]
"Noch einmal tön', O Harfe"

Die Einsiedelei, D. 393 [GA, v. 20^4,
p. 60] "Es rieselt, klar und wehend"

Die Einsiedelei, D. 563 [GA, v. 20^5,
p. 120] "Es rieselt, klar und wehend"
2nd setting; see also D. 393.

Der Entfernten, D. 350 [GA, v. 20^4,
p. 69] "Wohl denk' ich allenthalben"

Fischerlied, D. 351 [GA, v. 20^4, p. 70]
"Das Fischergewerbe gibt rüstigen
Muth!"

Fischerlied, D. 562 [GA, v. 20^5, p. 118]
"Das Fischergewerbe gibt rüstigen
Muth!"
2nd setting; see also D. 351.

Gesang an die Harmonie, D. 394 [GA,
v. 20^4, p. 62]
"Schöpferin beseelter Töne!"

Das Grab, D. 330 [GA, v. 20^3, p. 231]
"Das Grab ist tief und stille"
First version; see also D. 377, D. 569.

Das Grab, D. 377 [GA, v. 20^4, p. 6]
"Das Grab ist tief und stille"
2nd setting; see also D. 330, D. 569.

Das Grab, D. 569 [GA, v. 20^5, p. 122]
"Das Grab ist tief und stille"
3rd setting; see also D. 330, D. 377.

Der Herbstabend, D. 405 [GA, v. 20^4,
p. 68] "Abendglockenhalle zittern"

Herbstlied, D. 502 [GA, v. 20^4, p. 248]
"Bunt sind schon die Wälder"

Der Jüngling an der Quelle, D. 300 [GA,
v. 20^3, p. 208]
"Leise, rieseln der Quell"

Lied, D. 403 [GA, v. 20^4, pp. 66, 67]
"In's stille Land"

Pflügerlied, D. 392 [GA, v. 20^4, p. 58]
"Arbeitsam und wacker"

Wehmut, D. 404 [GA, v. 20^4, p. 64]
"Mit leisen Harfentönen"

Sauter, Samuel Friedrich, 1766-1846.

IL CANTO DELLA QUAGLIA.

Der Wachtelschlag, D. 742 [GA,
v. 20^7, p. 2] "Ach! mir schallt's
dorten so lieblich hervor"

Schiller, Johann Christoph Friedrich
von, 1759-1805.

Der Alpenjäger, D. 588 [GA, v. 20^5,
p. 168]
"Willst du nicht das Lämmlein hüten"

An den Frühling, D. 245 [GA, v. 20^3, p.
6] "Willkommen, schöner Jüngling!"
1st setting; see also D. 283, D. 587.

An den Frühling, D. 283 [GA, v. 20^3, p.
68] "Willkommen, schöner Jüngling!"
2nd setting; see also D. 245, D. 587.

An den Frühling, D. 587 [GA, v. 20^3, p.
8] "Willkommen, schöner Jüngling!"
3rd setting; see also D. 245, D. 283.

An die Freude, D. 189 [GA, v. 20^2, p.
102] "Freude, schöner Götterfunken"

An Emma, D. 113 [GA, v. 20^1, pp. 172,
174, 176] "Weit in nebelgrauer Ferne"

Die Bürgschaft, D. 246 [GA, v. 20^3,
p. 11] "Zu Dionys, dem Tyrannen"

Elysium, D. 584 [GA, v. 20^5, p. 149]
"Vorüber die stöhnende Klage!"

Die Entzückung an Laura, D. 390 [GA,
v. 20^4, p. 54] "Laura, über diese Welt"

Die Entzückung an Laura, D. 577 [GA,
v. 20^{10}, pp. 119, 120]
"Laura, Laura, über diese Welt"
2nd setting; see also D. 390.

Die Erwartung, D. 159 [GA, v. 20^2,
p. 47] "Hör' ich das Pförtchen nicht
gehen?"

Der Flüchtling, D. 402 [GA, v. 20^4,
p. 35] "Frisch atmet des Morgens
lebendiger Hauch"

Gruppe aus dem Tartarus, D. 583 [GA,
v. 20^5, p. 144] "Horch, wie Murmeln
des empörten Meeres"

Hektors Abschied, D. 312 [GA, v. 20^3,
pp. 130, 136] "Will sich Hektor ewig
von mir wenden"

SCHUBERT, FRANZ, 1797-1828
(continued)
Schiller, Johann Christoph Friedrich
von, 1759-1805 *(continued)*
Der Jüngling am Bache, D. 30 [GA, v.
20^1, p. 48]
"An der Quelle sass der Knabe"
1st setting; see also D. 192, D. 638.
Der Jüngling am Bache, D. 192 [GA,
v. 20^2, p. 108]
"An der Quelle sass der Knabe"
2nd setting; see also D. 30, D. 638.
Der Jüngling am Bache, D. 638 [GA,
v. 20^6, pp. 38, 40]
"An der Quelle sass der Knabe"
3rd setting; see also D. 30, D. 192.
Der Kampf, D. 594 [GA, v. 20^5, p. 171]
"Nein, länger werd'ich diesen Kampf
nicht kämpfen"
Klage der Ceres, D. 323 [GA, v. 20^3, p.
171] "Ist der holde Lenz erschienen?"
Laura am Klavier, D. 388 [GA, v. 20^4,
pp. 41, 46] "Wenn dein Finger durch
die Saiten meistert"
Eine Leichenphantasie, D. 7 [GA, v. 20^1,
p. 22] "Mit erstorbnem Scheinen"
Lied, D. 284 [GA, v. 20^3, p. 69]
"Es ist so angenehm"
Das Mädchen aus der Fremde, D. 117
[GA, v. 20^1, p. 189]
"In einem Tal bei armen Hirten"
Das Mädchen aus der Fremde, D. 252
[GA, v. 20^3, p. 10]
"In einem Tal bei armen Hirten"
2nd setting; see also D. 117.
Der Pilgrim, D. 794 [GA, v. 20^7, p. 130]
"Noch in meines Lebens Lenze"
Punschlied. Im Norden zu singen, D. 253
[GA, v. 20^3, p. 30]
"Auf der Berge freien Höhen"
Ritter Toggenburg, D. 397 [GA, v. 20^4,
p. 31] "Ritter, treue Schwesterliebe"
Der Taucher, D. 77 & D. 111 [GA,
v. 20^1, pp. 73, 102] "Wer wegt es,
Rittersmann oder Knapp?"
Thekla (Eine Geisterstimme), D. 73 [GA,
v. 20^1, p. 70] "Wo ich sei, und wo
mich hingewendet"
Thekla (Eine Geisterstimme), D. 595
[GA, v. 20^5, pp. 177, 178]
"Wo ich sei und wo mich
hingewendet"
2nd setting; see also D. 73.
Die vier Weltalter, D. 391 [GA, v. 20^4,
p. 56] "Wohl perlet im Glase der
purpurne Wein"

ACH! AUS DIESES TALES GRÜNDEN.
Sehnsucht, D. 52 [GA, v. 20^1, p. 62]
"Ach, aus dieses Tales Gründen"
Sehnsucht, D. 636 [GA, v. 20^6, pp. 23,
29] "Ach, aus dieses Tales Gründen"
2nd setting; see also D. 52.
DER BESUCH.
Dithyrambe, D. 801 [GA, v. 20^8,
p. 14] "Nimmer, das glaubt mir,
erscheinen die Götter"
ES REDEN UND TRÄUMEN DIE
MENSCHEN.
Hoffnung, D. 251 [GA, v. 20^3, p. 4]
"Es reden und träumen die
Menschen viel"
Hoffnung, D. 637 [GA, v. 20^6, p. 36]
"Es reden und träumen die
Menschen viel"
2nd setting; see also D. 251.
DIE GÖTTER GRIECHENLANDS: 12th
stanza.
Die Götter Griechenlands, D. 677
[GA, v. 20^6, pp. 76, 78]
"Schöne Welt, wo bist du?"
DIE PICCOLOMINI.
Des Mädchens Klage, D. 6 [GA, v.
20^1, p. 16] "Der Eichwald brauset"
1st setting; see also D. 191, D. 389.
Des Mädchens Klage, D. 191 [GA,
v. 20^2, pp. 104, 106]
"Der Eichwald braust"
2nd setting; see also D. 6, D. 389.
Des Mädchens Klage, D. 389 [GA, v.
20^4, p. 52] "Der Eichwald braust"
3rd setting; see also D. 6, D. 191.
DIE RÄUBER.
Amalia, D. 195 [GA, v. 20^2, p. 113]
"Schön wie Engel voll Walhalla's
Wonne"
SIE KONNTE MIR KEIN WÖRTCHEN
SAGEN.
Das Geheimniss, D. 250 [GA, v. 20^3,
p. 2] "Sie konnte mir kein Wörtchen
sagen"
Das Geheimniss, D. 793 [GA, v. 20^7,
p. 125] "Sie konnte mir kein
Wörtchen sagen"
2nd setting; see also D. 250.
Schlechta, Franz Xaver von Wssehrd,
1796-1875.
Aus Diego Manazares, D. 458 [GA,
v. 20^4, p. 146] "Wo irrst du durch
einsame Schatten der Nacht"
Des Sängers Habe, D. 832 [GA, v. 20^8,
p. 46] "Schlagt mein ganzes Glück in
Splitter"

Fischerweise, D. 881 [GA, v. 20^8,
  pp. 190, 194]
  "Den Fischer fechten Sorgen"
Liebeslauschen, D. 698 [GA, v. 20^6,
  p. 113] "Hier unten steht ein Ritter im
  hellen Mondenstrahl"
Totengräber-Weise, D. 869 [GA, v. 20^8,
  p. 198] "Nicht so düster und so bleich"
Widerschein, D. 639 [NGA, v. 4^{5a}, p.
  138] "Fischer harrt am Brückenbogen"
  Also published in **Taschenbuch zum
    geselligen Vernügen,** Leipzig:
    G.J.Göschen, 1820. Ed. by Friedrich
    Kind.
Widerschein, D. 949 [GA, v. 20^9, p. 130;
  NGA, v. 4^{5a}, p. 143]
  "Tom lehnt harrend auf der Brücke"
  Alternatiave text begins: "Fischer
    harrt am Brückenbagen"
IM KIRCHHOF.
  Auf einen Kirchhof, D. 151 [GA,
    v. 20^2, p. 1]
    "Sei gegrüsst, geweihte Stille"
Schlegel, August Wilhelm von, 1767-
1845.
  Abendlied für die Entfernte, D. 856 [GA,
    v. 20^8, p. 138]
    "Hinaus, mein Blick! hinaus in's Tal!"
  Die gefangenen Sänger, D. 712 [GA,
    v. 20^6, p. 164]
    "Hörst du von den Nachtigallen"
  Lebensmelodien, D. 395 [GA, v. 20^4,
    p. 72] "Auf den Wassern wohnt mein
    stilles Leben"
  Lob der Thränen, D. 711 [GA, v. 20^5,
    p. 10] "Laue Lüfte, Blumendüfte"
  Sprache der Liebe, D. 410 [GA, v. 20^4,
    p. 78] "Lass dich mit gelinden
    Schlägen rühren"
  Die verfehlte Stunde, D. 409 [GA, v. 20^4,
    p. 76] "Quälend ungestilltes Sehnen"
  Wiedersehn, D. 855 [GA, v. 20^8, p. 136]
    "Der Frühlingssonne holdes Lächeln"
Schlegel, Friedrich von, 1772-1829.
  Blanka, D. 631 [GA, v. 20^5, p. 236]
    "Wenn mich einsam Lüfte fächeln"
  Fülle der Liebe, D. 854 [GA, v. 20^8,
    p. 132]
    "Ein sehnend Streben teilt mir das
    Herz"
  Im Walde, D. 708 [GA, v. 20^6, p. 149]
    "Windes Rauschen"
  Vom Mitleiden Mariae, D. 632 [GA,
    v. 20^5, p. 238]
    "Als bei dem Kreuz Maria stand"

ABENDRÖTE.
  Abendröte, D. 690 [GA, v. 20^6, p. 94]
    "Tiefer sinket schon die Sonne"
  Die Berge, D. 634 [GA, v. 20^4, p. 227]
    "Sieht uns der Blick gehoben"
  Der Fluss, D. 693 [GA, v. 20^6, p. 91]
    "Wie rein Gesang sich windet"
  Die Gebüsche, D. 646 [GA, v. 20^6,
    p. 1] "Es wehet kühl und leise"
  Der Knabe, D. 692 [GA, v. 20^6, p. 88]
    "Wenn ich nur ein Vöglein wäre"
  Das Mädchen, D. 652 [GA, v. 20^6, p.
    16] "Wie so innig, möcht'ich sagen"
  Die Rose, D. 745 [GA, v. 20^7, pp. 18,
    21] "Es lockte schöne Wärme"
  Der Schmetterling, D. 633 [GA, v. 20^3,
    p. 225] "Wie soll ich nicht tanzen"
  Die Sterne, D. 684 [GA, v. 20^6,
    p. 102] "Du staunest, O Mensch"
  Die Vögel, D. 691 [GA, v. 20^6, p. 86]
    "Wie lieblich und fröhlich"
  Der Wanderer, D. 649 [GA, v. 20^6, p.
    5] "Wie deutlich des Mondes Licht"
FRÜHLINGSGEDICHTE.
  Der Schiffer, D. 694 [GA, v. 20^6, p.
    98] "Friedlich lieg' ich hingegossen"
Schmidt, Georg Philipp, 1766-1849.
  Der Unglückliche, D. 489 [GA, v. 20^4,
    p. 214] "Ich komme vom Gebirge her"
    See also D. 493.
  Der Wanderer, D. 493 [GA, v. 20^4,
    p. 217] "Ich komme vom Gebirge her"
    See also D. 489.
Schober, Franz von, 1798-1882.
  Am Bach im Frühling, D. 361 [GA,
    v. 20^4, p. 230]
    "Du brachst sie nun, die kalte Rinde"
  An die Musik, D. 547 [GA, v. 20^5,
    pp. 86, 87] "Du holde Kunst, in wie
    viel grauen Stunden"
  Genügsamkeit, D. 143 [GA, v. 20^3,
    p. 230] "Dort raget ein Berg aus den
    Wolken hehr"
  Jägers Liebeslied, D. 909 [GA, v. 20^8,
    p. 264] "Ich schiess' den Hirsch im
    grünen Forst"
  Pax vobiscum, D. 551 [GA, v. 20^5, p. 88]
    "Der Friede sei mit euch!"
  Pilgerweise, D. 789 [GA, v. 20^7, p. 108]
    "Ich bin ein Waller auf der Erde"
  Schatzgräbers Begehr, D. 761 [GA,
    v. 20^7, p. 35]
    "In tiefster Erde ruht ein alt Gesetz"
  Schiffers Scheidelied, D. 910 [GA, v. 20^8,
    p. 267]
    "Die Wogen am Gestade schwellen"

SCHUBERT, FRANZ, 1797-1828
(continued)
Schober, Franz von, 1798-1882
(continued)
Todesmusik, D. 758 [GA, v. 20⁷, p. 30]
"In des Todes Feierstunde"
Trost im Liede, D. 546 [GA, v. 20⁵,
p. 84]
"Braust des Unglücks Sturm empor"
Vergissmeinnicht, D. 792 [GA, v. 20⁷,
p. 114] "Als der Frühling sich vom"
Viola, D. 786 [GA, v. 20⁷, p. 76]
"Schneeglöcklein, O Schneeglöcklein"
Die Wolkenbraut, D. 683 [lost]
Schopenhauer, Johanna, 1766-1838.
GABRIELE.
Hippolit's Lied, D. 890 [GA, v. 20⁸,
p. 230] "Lasst mich, ob ich auch
still verglüh"
Schreiber, Aloys Wilhelm, 1763-1841.
Das Abendrot, D. 627 [GA, v. 20⁵,
p. 220] "Du heilig, glühend Abendrot!"
An den Mond in einer Herbstnacht,
D. 614 [GA, v. 20⁵, p. 188]
"Freundlich ist dein Antlitz"
Der Blumenbrief, D. 622 [GA, v. 20⁵,
p. 213] "Euch Blümlein will ich
senden zur schönen Jungfrau dort"
Das Marienbild, D. 623 [GA, v. 20⁵, p.
214] "Sei gegrüsst, du Frau der Huld"
Schubart, Christian Friedrich Daniel,
1739-1791.
An den Tod, D. 518 [GA, v. 20⁵, p. 130]
"Tod, du Schrecken der Natur"
Die Forelle, D. 550 [GA, v. 20⁵, pp. 132,
135, 138, 141] "In einem Bächlein
helle, da schoss in froher Eil"
Grablied auf einen Soldaten, D. 454
[GA, v. 20⁴, p. 140]
"Zieh hin, du braver Krieger du!"
Seraphine an ihr Klavier, D. 342 [GA,
v. 20⁴, p. 138]
"Sanftes Clavier, sanftes Clavier!"
Schubert, Franz, 1797-1828.
Abschied, D. 578 [GA, v. 20¹⁰, p. 80]
"Lebe wohl, lebe wohl"
Schücking, Clemens August, 1759-
1790.
Hagar's Klage, D. 5 [GA, v. 20¹, p. 1]
"Hier am Hügel heissen Sandes sitz'
ich"
Schütz, Christian Wilhelm von, 1776-
1847.
LACRIMAS.
Delphine, D. 857 no. 2 [GA, v. 20⁸,
p. 146] "Ach was soll ich beginnen"

Florio, D. 857 no. 1 [GA, v. 20⁸,
p. 143]
"Nun da Schatten niedergleiten"
Schulze, Ernst Konrad Friedrich, 1789-
1817.
An mein Herz, D. 860 [GA, v. 20⁸,
p. 154] "O Herz, sei endlich stille!"
Auf der Bruck, D. 853 [GA, v. 20⁸,
p. 106]
"Frisch trabe sonder Ruh' und Rast"
Im Frühling, D. 882 [GA, v. 20⁸, p. 202]
"Still sitz' ich an des Hügels Hang"
Lebensmut, D. 883 [GA, v. 20⁸, p. 206]
"O wie dringt das junge Leben"
Der liebliche Stern, D. 861 [GA, v. 20⁸,
p. 160]
"Ihr Sternlein, still in der Hohe"
O Quell, was strömst du rasch und wild,
D. 874 [unpubl.] same
Tiefes Leid, D. 876 [GA, v. 20⁸, p. 164]
"Ich bin von aller Ruh' geschieden"
Über Wildemann, D. 884 [GA, v. 20⁸,
p. 216] "Die Winde sausen am
Tannenhang"
Um Mitternacht, D. 862 [GA, v. 20⁸, p.
212] "Keine Stimme hör' ich schallen"
POETISCHES TAGEBUCH.
Im Walde, D. 834 [GA, v. 20⁸, p. 96]
"Ich wandre über Berg und Tal"
Scott, Sir Walter, bart., 1771-1832.
IVANHOE.
Romanze des Richard Löwenherz,
D. 907 [GA, v. 20⁸, p. 220]
"Grosser Taten tat der Ritter"
THE LADY OF THE LAKE.
Ellens Gesang I, D. 837 [GA, v. 20⁸,
p. 70]
"Raste, Krieger, Krieg ist aus"
Ellens Gesang II, D. 838 [GA, v. 20⁸,
p. 78] "Jäger, ruhe von der Jagd"
Ellens Gesang III, D. 839 [GA, v. 20⁸,
p. 90] "Ave Maria! Jungfrau mild!"
Lied des gefangenen Jägers, D. 843
[GA, v. 20⁸, p. 92] "Mein Ross so
müd' in dem Stalle sich steht"
Normans Gesang, D. 846 [GA, v. 20⁸,
p. 82]
"Die Nacht bricht bald herein"
A LEGEND OF MONTROSE.
Lied der Anne Lyle, D. 830 [GA,
v. 20⁹, p. 78]
"Wärst du bei mir um Lebenstal"
THE PIRATE.
Gesang der Norna, D. 831 [GA,
v. 20⁹, p. 82] "Mich führt mein Weg
wohl meilenlang"

Seidl, Johann Gabriel, 1804-1875.
 Am Fenster, D. 878 [GA, v. 20^8, p. 176]
  "Ihr lieben Mauern hold und traut"
 Bei dir allein, D. 866 no. 2 [GA, v. 20^8,
  p. 243] "Bei dir allein empfind' ich"
 Im Freien, D. 880 [GA, v. 20^8, p. 184]
  "Draussen in der weiten Nacht"
 Irdisches Glück, D. 866, no. 4 [GA,
  v. 20^8, p. 250]
  "So Mancher sieht mit finstrer Miene"
 Die Männer sind méchant, D. 866 no. 3
  [GA, v. 20^8, p. 248]
  "Du sagtest mir es, Mutter"
 Sehnsucht, D. 879 [GA, v. 20^8, p. 179]
  "Die Scheibe friert, der Wind ist rauh"
 Die Taubenpost, D. 957 no. 14 [GA,
  v. 20^9, p. 182] "Ich hab' eine
  Brieftaub' in meinem Sold"
 Die Unterscheidung, D. 866 no. 1 [GA,
  v. 20^8, p. 240] "Die Mutter hat mich
  jüngst gescholten"
 Der Wanderer an den Mond, D. 870
  [GA, v. 20^8, p. 234]
  "Ich auf der Erd', am Himmel du"
 Wiegenlied, D. 867 [GA, v. 20^8, p. 252]
  "Wie sich der Äuglein kindlicher
  Himmel"
 Das Zügenglöcklein, D. 871 [GA, v. 20^8,
  p. 237]
  "Kling' die Nacht durch, klinge"
Senn, Johann Chrysostomus, 1792-
1857.
 Schwanengesang, D. 744 [GA, v. 20^7,
  p. 16] "Wie klag' ich's aus"
 Selige Welt, D. 743 [GA, v. 20^7, p. 14]
  "Ich treibe auf des Lebens Meer"
Shakespeare, William, 1564-1616.
 ANTONY AND CLEOPATRA.
  Trinklied, D. 888 [GA, v. 20^8, p. 227]
   "Bacchus, feister Furst des Wiens"
 CYMBELINE.
  Ständchen, D. 889 [GA, v. 20^8, p. 228]
   "Horch, horch! die Lerch' im
   Ätherblau"
 TWO GENTLEMEN OF VERONA.
  An Sylvia, D. 891 [GA, v. 20^8, p. 232]
   "Was ist Sylvia, saget an"
Silbert, Johann Petrus, 1772-1844.
 Abendbilder, D. 650 [GA, v. 20^6, p. 7]
  "Still beginnt's im Hain zu thauen"
 Himmelsfunken, D. 651 [GA, v. 20^6,
  p. 14] "Der Odem Gottes weht"
Spaun, Josef, Freiherr von, 1788-
1865.

 Der Jüngling und der Tod, D. 545 [GA,
  v. 20^5, pp. 80, 82] "Die Sonne sinkt"
Stadler, Albert, 1794-1888.
 Lieb Minna, D. 222 [GA, v. 20^2, p. 168]
  "Schwüler Hauch weht mir herüber"
 Namenstagslied, D. 695 [GA, v. 20^{10}, p.
  81] "Vater, schenk' mir diese Stunde"
Stolberg, Friedrich Leopold, Graf zu
Stolberg, 1750-1819.
 Abendlied, D. 276 [GA, v. 20^3, p. 62]
  "Gross und rotentflammet schwebet"
 An die Natur, D. 372 [GA, v. 20^4, p. 2]
  "Süsse, heilige Natur"
 Auf dem Wasser zu singen, D. 774 [GA,
  v. 20^7, p. 106] "Mitten im Schimmer
  der spiegelnden Wellen"
 Daphne am Bach, D. 411 [GA, v. 20^4,
  p. 81] "Ich hab' ein Bächlein funden"
 Lied, D. 788 [GA, v. 20^7, p. 104]
  "Des Lebens Tag ist schwer und
  schwül"
 Lied in der Abwesenheit, D. 416
  [*Moderne Welt*, Dec. 1925, Suppl., pp.
  1-2]
  "Ach, mir ist das Herz so schwer"
 Morgenlied, D. 266 [GA, v. 20^3, p. 54]
  "Willkommen, rotes Morgenlicht!"
 Romanze, D. 144 [GA, XX
  Revisionsbericht no. 209, p. 46; NGA
  IV, 7, p. 201]
  "In der Väter Hallen ruhte"
 Stimme der Liebe, D. 412 [GA, v. 20^4,
  p. 82] "Meine Selinde"
Stoll, Johann Ludwig, 1778-1815.
 An die Geliebte, D. 303 [GA, v. 20^3,
  p. 116]
  "O, dass ich dir vom stillen Auge"
 Labetrank der Liebe, D. 302 [GA, v. 20^3,
  p. 114] "Wenn im Spiele leiser Töne"
 Lambertine, D. 301 [GA, v. 20^3, p. 112]
  "O Liebe, die mein Herz erfüllet"
Széchényi, Ludwig, Count von, 1781-
1855.
 Die abgeblühte Linde, D. 514 [GA,
  v. 20^5, p. 29]
  "Wirst du halten, was du schwurst"
 Der Flug der Zeit, D. 515 [GA, v. 20^5,
  p. 33] "Es floh die Zeit im
  Wirbelfluge"
Tiedge, Christoph August, 1752-1841.
 An die Sonne, D. 272 [GA, v. 20^3, p. 58]
  "Königliche Morgensonne"
Uhland, Ludwig, 1787-1862.
 Frühlingsglaube, D. 686 [GA, v. 20^6, pp.
  108, 110]
  "Die linden Lüfte sind erwacht"

SCHUBERT, FRANZ, 1797-1828
(continued)
Unknown
Abendlied, D. 384 [GA, v 20^4, p. 30]
"Sanft glänzt die Abendsonne"
An den Schlaf, D. 447 [GA, v. 20^4, p. 120] "Komm, und senke die umflorten Schwingen"
Text may be by Uz.
Auf der Sieg der Deutschen, D. 81 [GA, v. 20^{10}, p. 74]
"Verschwunden sind die Schmerzen"
Accompaniment for 2 violins & cello.
Das Bild, D. 155 [GA, v. 20^2, p. 19]
"Ein Mädchen ist's, das früh und spät mir"
Blondel zu Marien, D. 626 [GA, v. 20^5, p. 218] "In düstrer Nacht"
Frühlingslied, D. 398 [GA, v. 20^4, p. 97]
"Die Luft ist blau"
Text variantly attributed to Hölty.
Grablied für die Mutter, D. 616 [GA, v. 20^5, p. 194]
"Hauche milder, Abendluft"
Klage, D. 292 [GA, v. 20^3, p. 4]
"Trauer umfliesst mein Leben"
Text incorrectly attributed to Hölty.
Klage, D. 371 [GA, v. 20^4, p. 5]
"Trauer umfliesst mein Leben"
2nd setting; see also D. 292.
Der Leidende, D. 432 [GA, v. 20^4, pp. 106, 107] "Nimmer trag' ich länger dieser Leiden Last"
Der Leidende, D. 512 [*Nachlass . . .* v. 50 (Vienna: Diabelli, 1850)]
"Nimmer länger trag' ich dieser Leiden Last"
2nd setting; see also D. 432.
Lied eines Kindes, D. 596 [GA, v. 20^{10}, p. 122] "Lauter Freude fühl' ich"
Lilla an die Morgenröte, D. 273 [GA, v. 20^3, p. 59]
"Wie schön bist du, du güldne Morgenröte"
Il modo di prender mogli, D. 902 no. 3 [GA, v. 20^{10}, p. 65]
"Or sù! non ci pensiamo"
Morgenlied, D. 381 [GA, v. 20^4, p. 29]
"Die frohe neubelebte Flur"
Der Strom, D. 565 [GA, v. 20^5, p. 123]
"Mein Leben wälzt sich murrend fort"
Text attributed variously to Schubert or Stadler.
Tischlerlied, D. 274 [GA, v. 20^3, p. 60]
"Mein Handwerk geht durch alle Welt"

Trost, D. 523 [GA, v. 20^5, p. 5]
"Nimmer lange weil'ich hier"
Wiegenlied, D. 498 [GA, v. 20^4, p. 239]
"Schlafe, schlafe, holder, süsser Knabe"
Zur Namensfeier des Herrn Andreas Siller, D. 83 [GA, v. 20^{10}, p. 72]
"Des Phöbus Strahlen sind dem Aug'entschwunden"
Accompaniment for violin & harp.
Uz, Johann Peter, 1720-1796.
Gott im Frühlinge, D. 448 [GA, v. 20^4, p. 121] "In seinem schimmernden Gewand"
Der gute Hirte, D. 449 [GA, v. 20^4, p. 124] "Was sorgest du?"
Die Liebesgötter, D. 446 [GA, v. 20^4, p. 118] "Cypris, meiner Phyllis gleich"
Die Nacht, D. 358 [GA, v. 20^4, p. 127]
"Du verstörst uns nicht, O Nacht!"
Vittorelli, Jacopo, 1749-1835.
Guarda, che bianca luna, D. 688 no. 2 [GA, v. 20^{10}, p. 50] same
Non t'accostare all'urna, D. 688 no. 1 [GA, v. 20^{10}, p. 48] same
Werner, Friedrich Ludwig Zacharias, 1768-1823.
DIE SÖHNE DES TALES.
Morgenlied, D. 685 [GA, v. 20^6, p. 104] "Eh' die Sonne früh aufersteht"
WANDA, KÖNIGIN DER SARMATEN.
Jagdlied, D. 521 [GA, v. 20^5, p. 3]
"Trarah! Trarah! wie kehren daheim"
Willemer, Marianne Jung von, 1784-1860.
Suleika II, D. 717 [GA, v. 20^6, p. 201]
"Ach, um deine feuchten Schwingen"
Text erroneously attributed to Goethe.
Winkler, Karl Gottfried Theodor, 1775-1856.
Das Heimweh, D. 456 [GA, v. 20^4, p. 144] "Oft in einsam stillen Stunden"
Zettler, Alois, 1778-1828.
IHR FREUNDE UND DU, GOLD'NER WEIN.
Trinklied, D. 183 [GA, v. 20^2, p. 97]
"Ihr Freunde und du gold'ner Wein"
Schubert, Franz, 1797-1828.
SCHUBERT *Abschied*
Der Schüchterne see Schreiber ZELTER
Schücking, Clemens August, 1759-1790.
SCHUBERT *Hagar's Klage*
Schütz, Christian Wilhelm von, 1776-1847.

LACRIMAS.
   SCHUBERT
     Delphine
     Florio
Schütze, Stephan, 1771-1839.
   ZELTER
     Lieb und Leben
     Seufzer des Gefangnen
     Das Wandernde Lied
Der Schützling see Vogl **LOEWE**
   Die Kaiserjagd im Wienerwald
Schulenburg, Ehrengarde Melusina von
   der, Countess, ca. 1667-1743.
   LASSEN *Herbstgefühl*
SCHULGESANG. see Sturm, C.
   Segne, Vater, meinen Fleiss **LOEWE**
Schultz, Wilhelm, 1854-1921.
   GRIEG *Der Jäger*
Schulz, Eduard, 1813-1842.
   BRAHMS *Treue Liebe*
   SCHUMANN *Ein Gedanke*
   SPOHR *Der Rosenstrauch*
Schulz, G
   RIEGGER *Lullaby*
Schulz, Johann Gottlob, 1762-1810.
   LOEWE *Der Herbst*
Schulze, Ernst Konrad Friedrich, 1789-
   1817.
   LASSEN *Kleine Lieder*
   SCHUBERT
     An mein Herz
     Auf der Bruck
     Im Frühling
     Lebensmut
     Der liebliche Stern
     O Quell, was strömst du rasch und wild
     Tiefes Leid
     Über Wildemann
     Um Mitternacht
   SCHUMANN *Verwandlung*
POETISCHES TAGEBUCH.
   SCHUBERT *Im Walde*
Schumann, Felix, 1854-1879.
   BRAHMS
     Junge Lieder I
     Junge Lieder II
     Versunken
SCHUMANN, ROBERT, 1810-1856.
   Andersen, Hans Christian, 1805-1875.
     Märzveilchen, op. 40 no. 1 (1840) [GA,
       v. 13^2, p. 50] "Der Himmel wölbt sich
       rein und blau"
     Muttertraum, op. 40 no. 2 (1840) [GA,
       v. 13^2, p. 52] "Die Mutter betet herzig"
     Der Soldat, op. 40 no. 3 (1840) [GA,
       v. 13^2, p. 54] "Es geht bei gedämpfter
       Trommeln Klang"

Der Spielmann, op. 40 no. 4 (1840) [GA,
   v. 13^2, p. 57]
   "Im Städtchen giebt es des Jubels vicl"
Weihnachtlied, op. 79 no. 16 (1849) [GA,
   v. 13^3, p. 52] "Als das Christkind ward
   zur Welt gebracht"
Anon.
   Requiem, op. 90 no. 7 (1850) [GA,
     v. 133, p. 120] "Ruh' von
     schmerzensreichen Mühen aus"
   Schneeglöckchen, op. 96 no. 2 (1850)
     [GA, v. 13^3, p. 137]
     "Die Sonne sah die Erde an"
   Verrathene Liebe, op. 40 no. 5 (1840)
     [GA, v. 13^2, p. 60] "Da Nachts wir uns
     küssten O Mädchen"
   Vom Reitersmann [unpubl.; ms. in
     Robert-Schumann-Haus, Zwickau]
   Zigeunerliedchen, op. 79 no. 7 (1849)
     [GA, v. 13^3, p. 36]
     "Unter die Soldaten"
   EBRO CAUDOLOSE.
     Flutenreicher Ebro, op. 138 no. 5
       (1849) [GA, v. 10, p. 138] same
       Accompaniment for piano, 4 hands.
   Béranger, Pierre Jean de, 1780-1857.
     LES CARTES, OU L'HOROSCOPE.
       Die Kartenlegerin, op. 31 no. 2 (1840)
         [GA, v. 13^1, p. 98]
         "Schlief die Mutter endlich ein"
         Text translated by Chamisso.
     *JEANNE LA ROUSSE, OU, LA FEMME
     DU BRACONNIER.*
       Die rothe Hanne, op. 31 no. 3 (1840)
         [GA, v. 13^1, p. 103]
         "Den Sängling an der Brust"
         Text translated by Chamisso.
   Bernhard, Lily, fl. 1840.
     Mädchen-Schwermuth, op. 142 no. 3
       (1840) [GA, v. 13^4, p. 101]
       "Kleine Tropfen, seid ihr Thränen"
   Braun, Ferdinand, fl. 1841.
     Frühlingslied, op. 125 no. 4 (1850) [GA,
       v. 13^4, p. 68] "Das Körnlein springt"
     Op. 125 no. 1 in GA.
   Buddeus, Julius, fl. 1850.
     Die Meerfee, op. 125 no. 1 (1850) [GA,
       v. 13^4, p. 72]
       "Helle Silberglöcklein klingen"
       Op. 125 no. 3 in GA.
     Resignation, op. 83 no. 1 (1850) [GA, v.
       13^3, p. 78] "Lieben von ganzer Seele"
   Burns, Robert, 1759-1796.
     Dem rothen Röslein gleicht mein Lieb,
       op. 27 no. 2 (ca.1840) [GA, v. 13^1,
       p. 73] same

SCHUMANN, ROBERT, 1810-1856
(continued)

Burns, Robert, 1759-1796 *(continued)*
Hauptmann's Weib, op. 25 no. 19 (1840)
[GA, v. 13¹, p. 61] "Hoch zu Pferd!"
Hochländers Abschied, op. 25 no. 13
(1840) [GA, v. 13¹, p. 49]
"Mein Herz ist im Hochland"
Die Hochländer-Wittwe, op. 25 no. 10
(1840) [GA, v. 13¹, p. 43]
"Ich bin gekommen ins Niederland"
Text translated by Wilhelm Gerhard.
Hochländisches Wiegenlied, op. 25 no.
14 (1840) [GA, v. 13¹, p. 51]
"Schlafe, süsser kleiner Donald"
Im Westen, op. 25 no. 23 (1840) [GA,
v. 13¹, p. 67] "Ich schau' über Forth"
Jemand, op. 25 no. 4 (1840) [GA, v. 13¹,
p. 32] "Mein Herz ist betrübt"
Text translated by Wilhelm Gerhard.
Niemand, op. 25 no. 22 (1840) [GA,
v. 13¹, p. 66]
"Ich hab' mein Weib allein"
Part of same poem as op. 25 no. 4,
Jemand.
Weit, weit, op. 25 no. 20 (1840) [GA,
v. 13¹, p. 63]
"Wie kann ich froh und munter sein"

Byron, George Gordon Byron, 6th
baron, 1778-1824.
Aus den "Hebräischen Gesängen" op. 25
no. 15 (1840) [GA, v. 13¹, p. 52]
"Mein Herz ist schwer!"
Die Weinende, WoO 21,2 (1827)
[Universal, 1933]
"Ich sah dich weinen! ach!"
HEBREW MELODIES.
An den Mond, op. 95 no. 2 (1849)
[GA, v. 13³, p. 130] "Schlafloser
Sonne, melanchol'scher Stern!"
Dem Helden, op. 95 no. 3 (1849) [GA,
v. 13³, p. 132] "Dein Tag ist aus,
dein Ruhm fing an"
Die Tochter Jephtha's, op. 95 no. 1
(1849) [GA, v. 13³, p. 126]
"Da die Heimath, O Vater"

Camoens, Luis de, ca.1524-1580.
DE DENTRO TENGO MI MAL.
Tief im Herzen, op. 138 no. 2 (1849)
[GA, v. 10, p. 126]
"Tief im Herzen trag' ich Pein"
Accompaniment for piano, 4
hands.

Candidus, Karl August, 1817-1872.
Husarenabzug, op. 125 no. 2 (1850) [GA,
v. 13⁴, p. 76]

"Aus dem dunkeln Thor wallt"
Op. 125 no. 5 in GA.

Chamisso, Adelbert von, 1781-1838.
An meinem Herzen, an meiner Brust, op.
42 no. 7 (1840) [GA, v. 13², p. 74]
same
Du Ring an meinem Finger, op. 42 no. 4
(1840) [GA, v. 13², p. 68] same
Er, der Herrlichste von allen, op. 42 no.
2 (1840) [GA, v. 13², p. 63] same
Helft mir, ihr Schwestern, op. 42 no. 5
(1840) [GA, v. 13², p. 70] same
Ich kann's nicht fassen, op. 42 no. 3
(1840) [GA, v. 13², p. 66] same
Die Löwenbraut, op. 31 no. 1 (1840)
[GA, v. 13¹, p. 92]
"Mit der Myrthe geschmückt"
*Nun hast du mir den ersten Schmerz
gethan,* op. 42 no. 8 (1840) [GA,
v. 13², p. 76] same
*Süsser Freund, du blickest mich
verwundert an,* op. 42 no. 6 (1840)
[GA, v. 13², p. 72] same
Was soll ich sagen! op. 27 no. 3 (1840)
[GA, v. 13¹, p. 75]
"Mein Aug' ist trüb' "
FRAUENLIEBE UND LEBEN.
Seit ich ihn gesehen, op. 42 no. 1
(1840) [GA, v. 13², p. 62] same

Christern, Carl, fl. 1840.
Ich wand're nicht, op. 51 no. 3 (1840)
[GA, v. 13², p. 137]
"Warum soll ich denn wandern"
DES KNABEN WUNDERHORN
Die Ammenuhr (1848) [unpubl.]
"Der Mond, der scheint"
Das Käuzlein, op. 79 no. 10 (1849) [GA,
v. 13³, p. 42]
"Ich armes Käuzlein kleine"
Das Käuzlein [unpubl.; ms.: Zwickau,
Robert-Schumann-Haus]
"Ich armes Käuzlein kleine"
2nd setting.
Marienwürmchen, op. 79 no. 13 (1849)
[GA, v. 13³, p. 46]
"Marienwürmchen, setze dich"

Eichendorff, Joseph Karl Benedikt,
Freiherr von, 1788-1857.
Auf einer Burg, op. 39 no. 7 (1840) [GA,
v. 13², p. 40]
"Eingeschlafen auf der Lauer"
Der Einsiedler, op. 83 no. 3 (1850) [GA,
v. 13³, p. 86] "Komm, Trost der Welt"
Der frohe Wandersmann, op. 77 no. 1
(1840) [GA, v. 13³, p. 18] "Wem Gott
will rechte Gunst erweisen"

Frühlingsfahrt, op. 45 no. 2 (1840) [GA,
v. 13², p. 81]
"Es zogen zwei rüst'ge Gesellen"
Frühlingsnacht, op. 39 no. 12 (1840)
[GA, v. 13², p. 48]
"Ueber'm Garten durch die Lüfte"
Im Walde, op. 39 no. 11 (1840) [GA,
v. 13², p. 46] "Es zog eine Hochzeit
den Berg entlang"
In der Fremde, op. 39 no. 1 (1840) [GA,
v. 13², p. 28]
"Aus der Heimath hinter den Blitzen"
In der Fremde, op. 39 no. 8 (1840) [GA,
v. 13², p. 41]
"Ich hör' die Bächlein rauschen"
Intermezzo, op. 39 no. 2 (1840) [GA,
v. 13², p. 30] "Dein Bildniss
wunderselig hab' ich im Herzens
grund"
Mondnacht, op. 39 no. 5 (1840) [GA,
v. 13², p. 36]
"Es war, als hätt' der Himmel"
Der Schatzgräber, op. 45 no. 1 (1840)
[GA, v. 13², p. 78]
"Wenn alle Wälder schliefen"
Die Stille, op. 39 no. 4 (1840) [GA,
v. 13², p. 34]
"Es weiss und räth es doch Keiner"
Waldesgespräch, op. 39 no. 3 (1840)
[GA, v. 13², p. 31] "Es ist schon spät"
AHNUNG UND GEGENWART.
Wehmuth, op. 39 no. 9 (1840) [GA,
v. 13², p. 43]
"Ich kann wohl manchmal singen"
Zwielicht, op. 39 no. 10 (1840) [GA, v.
13², p. 44] "Dämm'rung will die
Flügel spreiten"
DICHTER UND IHRE GESELLEN.
Schöne Fremde, op. 39 no. 6 (1840)
[GA, v. 13², p. 38] "Es rauschen die
Wipfel und schauern"

Fanshawe, Catharine, 1765-1834.
Räthsel, op. 25 no. 16 (1840) [GA,
v. 13¹, p. 55] "Es flüstert's der
Himmel"

Fröhlich, Abraham, 1796-1865.
Die Nonne, op. 49 no. 3 (1840) [GA,
v. 13², p. 130]
"Im Garten steht die Nonne"

Geibel, Emanuel, i.e., Franz Emanuel
August, 1815-1884.
Der Hidalgo, op. 30 no. 3 (1840) [GA,
v. 13¹, p. 88]
"Es ist so süss, zu scherzen"
Der Knabe mit dem Wunderhorn, op. 30
no. 1 (1840) [GA, v. 13¹, p. 80]
"Ich bin ein lust'ger Geselle"

Der Page, op. 30 no. 2 (1840) [GA,
v. 13¹, p. 84]
"Da ich nun entsagen müssen"
Sehnsucht, op. 51 no. 1 (1840) [GA,
v. 13², p. 132] "Ich blick' in mein
Herz"

Goethe, Johann Wolfgang von, 1749-
1832.
Der Fischer, WoO 19 (1829) [*Zeitschrift
für Musik,* Jan.1933, Notenbeilage
N.1] "Das Wasser rauscht, das Wasser
schwoll"
Nachtlied, op. 96 no. 1 (1850) [GA, v.
13³, p. 136]
"Ueber allen Gipfeln ist Ruh' "
Die wandelnde Glocke, op. 79 no. 17
(1849) [GA, v. 13³, p. 54]
"Es war ein Kind, das wollte nie"
FAUST.
Lied Lynceus des Thürmers, op. 79 no.
27 (1849) [GA, v. 13³, p. 72]
"Zum Sehen geboren"
WESTÖSTLICHER DIVAN.
Freisinn, op. 25 no. 2 (1840) [GA,
v. 13¹, p. 26] "Lasst mich nur auf
meinem Sattel gelten!"
Liebeslied, op. 51 no. 5 (1840?) [GA,
v. 13², p. 139] "Dir zu eröffnen
mein Herz verlangt mich"
Lied der Suleika, op. 25 no. 9 (1840)
[GA, v. 13¹, p. 40]
"Wie, mit innigstem Behagen"
Text attributed to Marianne von
Willemer.
Lieder aus dem Schenkenbuch . . . , op.
25 no. 5 (1840) [GA, v. 13¹, p. 34]
"Sitz' ich allein"
Lieder aus dem Schenkenbuch . . . , op.
25 no. 6 (1840) [GA, v. 13¹, p. 35]
"Setze mir nicht"
Talismane, op. 25 no. 8 (1840) [GA,
v. 13¹, p. 38]
"Gottes ist der Orient!"
WILHELM MEISTER.
Ballade des Harfners, op. 98a no. 2
(1849) [GA, v. 13⁴, p. 6] "Was hör
ich draussen vor dem Thor"
Singet nicht in Trauertönen, op. 98a
no. 7 (1849) [GA, v. 13⁴, p. 20]
same
So lasst mich scheinen, bis ich werde,
op. 98a no. 9 (1849) [GA, v. 13⁴, p.
24] same
Wer nie sein Brod mit Thränen ass, op.
98a no. 4 (1849) [GA, v. 13⁴, p. 13]
same

SCHUMANN, ROBERT, 1810-1856
(continued)
Goethe, Johann Wolfgang von, 1749-
1832 *(continued)*
WILHELM MEISTER (continued)
Wer sich der Einsamkeit ergiebt, op.
98a no. 6 (1849) [GA, v. 13⁴, p. 18]
same
WILHELM MEISTER. Harfenspieler.
An die Thüren will ich schleichen, op.
98a no. 8 (1849) [GA, v. 13⁴, p. 22]
same
WILHELM MEISTER. Mignon's song:
Heiss mich nicht reden.
Heiss' mich nicht reden, op. 98a no. 5
(1849) [GA, v. 13⁴, p. 15] same
WILHELM MEISTER. Mignon's song:
Kennst du das Land?
Kennst du das Land, op. 98a no. 1
(1849) [GA, v. 134, p. 2] same
Mignon, op. 79 no. 28 (1849) [GA,
v. 13³, p. 74] "Kennst du das Land"
WILHELM MEISTER. Mignon's song:
Nur wer die Sehnsucht kennt.
Nur wer die Sehnsucht kennt, op. 98a
no. 3 (1849) [GA, v. 13⁴, p. 11]
same
Hebbel, Christian Friedrich, 1813-
1863.
Ballade vom Haideknaben, op. 122 no. 1
[GA, v. 13⁴, p. 113]
"Der Knabe träumt"
Speaker & piano.
Sag'an, O lieber Vogel mein, op. 27 no.
1 (ca.1840) [GA, v. 13¹, p. 72] same
Schön Hedwig, op. 106 (1849) [GA,
v. 13⁴, p. 107] "Im Kreise der Vasallen
sitzt der Ritter"
Speaker & piano.
Heine, Heinrich, 1797-1856.
Abends am Strand, op. 45 no. 3 (1840)
[GA, v. 13², p. 84]
"Wir sassen am Fischerhause"
Allnächtlich im Traume, op. 48 no. 14
(1840) [GA, v. 13², p. 112] same
Die alten, bösen Lieder, op. 48 no. 16
(1840) [GA, v. 13², p. 118] same
Am leuchtenden Sommermorgen, op. 48
no. 12 (1840) [GA, v. 13², p. 108]
same
Anfangs wollt' ich fast verzagen, op. 24
no. 8 (1840) [GA, v. 13¹, p. 19] same
Der arme Peter, op. 53 no. 3 (1840)
[GA, v. 13², p. 148] "Der Hans und
die Grete tanzen herum"
Aus alten Märchen winkt es, op. 48 no.
15 (1840) [GA, v. 13², p. 114] same

Aus meinen Thränen spriessen, op. 48 no.
2 (1840) [GA, v. 13², p. 89] same
Die beiden Grenadiere, op. 49 no. 1
(1840) [GA, v. 13², p. 122]
"Nach Frankreich zogen zwei
Grenadier'"
Berg' und Burgen schau'n herunter, op.
24 no. 7 (1840) [GA, v. 13¹, p. 17]
same
Das ist ein Flöten und Geigen, op. 48 no.
9 (1840) [GA, v. 13², p. 101] same
Dein Angesicht, op. 127 no. 2 (1840)
[GA, v. 13⁴, p. 82] same
Du bist wie eine Blume, op. 25 no. 24
(1840) [GA, v. 13¹, p. 68] same
Es leuchtet meine Liebe, op. 127 no. 3
(1840) [GA, v. 13⁴, p. 83] same
Es treibt mich hin, es treibt mich her, op.
24 no. 2 (1840) [GA, v. 13¹, p. 4]
same
Die feindlichen Brüder, op. 49 no. 2
(1840) [GA, v. 132, p. 126]
"Oben auf des Berges Spitze"
Hör' ich das Liedchen klingen, op. 48 no.
10 (1840) [GA, v. 13², p. 104] same
Ich grolle nicht, op. 48 no. 7 (1840) [GA,
v. 13², p. 96] same
Ich hab' im Traum geweinet, op. 48 no.
13 (1840) [GA, v. 13², p. 110] same
Ich wandelte unter den Bäumen, op. 24
no. 3 (1840) [GA, v. 13¹, p. 6] same
Ich will meine Seele tauchen, op. 48 no.
5 (1840) [GA, v. 13², p. 92] same
Im Rhein, im heiligen Strome, op. 48 no.
6 (1840) [GA, v. 13², p. 94] same
Im wunderschönen Monat Mai, op. 48
no. 1 (1840) [GA, v. 13², p. 88] same
Ein Jüngling liebt ein Mädchen, op. 48
no. 11 (1840) [GA, v. 13², p. 106]
same
Lehn' deine Wang' an meine Wang', op.
142 no. 2 (1840) [GA, v. 13⁴, p. 100]
same
Lieb' Liebchen, op. 24 no. 4 (1840) [GA,
v. 13¹, p. 8] same
Die Lotosblume, op. 25 no. 7 (1840)
[GA, v. 13¹, p. 36]
"Die Lotosblume ängstigt sich"
Mein Wagen rollet langsam, op. 142 no.
4 (1840) [GA, v. 13⁴, p. 103] same
Mit Myrthen und Rosen, op. 24 no. 9
(1840) [GA, v. 13¹, p. 20] same
Morgens steh' ich auf und frage, op. 24
no. 1 (1840) [GA, v. 13¹, p. 3] same
Die Rose, die Lilie, op. 48 no. 3 (1840)
[GA, v. 13², p. 90] same

Schöne Wiege meiner Leiden, op. 24 no.
5 (1840) [GA, v. 131, p. 9] same
Tragödie, op. 64 no. 3 (1841?) [GA,
v. 13³, p. 14]
"Entflieh' mit mir und sei mein Weib"
Und wüssten's die Blumen, op. 48 no. 8
(1840) [GA, v. 13², p. 98] same
Warte, warte, wilder Schiffsmann, op. 24
no. 6 (1840) [GA, v. 13¹, p. 13] same
Was will die einsame Thräne, op. 25 no.
21 (1840) [GA, v. 13¹, p. 64] same
Wenn ich in deine Augen seh', op. 48 no.
4 (1840) [GA, v. 13², p. 91] same
BELSATZAR.
Belsatzar, op. 57 (1840) [GA, v. 13³,
p. 2]
"Die Mitternacht zog näher schon"

Heyse, Paul Johann Ludwig von, 1830-1914.

Frühlingslust, op. 125 no. 5 (1850) [GA,
v. 13⁴, p. 70]
"Nun stehen die Rosen in Blüthe"
Op. 125 no. 2 in GA.
Die Spinnerin, op. 107 no. 4 (1851) [GA,
v. 13⁴, p. 46]
"Auf dem Dorf' in den Spinnstuben"

Hoffmann von Fallersleben, August Heinrich, 1798-1874.

Der Abendstern, op. 79 no. 1 (1849)
[GA, v. 13³, p. 30]
"Du lieblicher Stern"
Frühlings Ankunft, op. 79 no. 19 (1849)
[GA, v. 13³, p. 58]
"Nach diesen trüben Tagen"
Frühlingsbotschaft, op. 79 no. 3 (1849)
[GA, v. 13³, p. 31]
"Kuckuk, Kuckuk ruft aus dem Wald"
Frühlingsgruss, op. 79 no. 4 (1849) [GA,
v. 13³, p. 32]
"So sei gegrüsst vieltausendmal"
Hinaus ins Freie, op. 79 no. 11 (1849)
[GA, v. 13³, p. 43]
"Wie blüht es im Thale"
Mein Garten, op. 77 no. 2 (1850) [GA,
v. 13³, p. 20]
"Veilchen, Rosmarin, Mimosen"
Schmetterling, op. 79 no. 2 (1849) [GA,
v. 13³, p. 30]
"O Schmetterling, sprich"
Soldatenlied, WoO 7 (1844) [GA, v. 13⁴,
p. 122] "Ein scheckiges Pferd"
Sonntag, op. 79 no. 6 (1849) [GA, v. 13³,
p. 34] "Der Sonntag ist gekommen"
Vom Schlaraffenland, op. 79 no. 5 (1849)
[GA, v. 13³, p. 33]
"Kommt, wir wollen uns begeben"

Die Waise, op. 79 no. 14 (1849) [GA,
v. 13³, p. 48]
"Der Frühling kehrct wieder"

Immermann, Karl Leberecht, 1796-1840.

Auf dem Rhein, op. 51 no. 4 (1846?)
[GA, v. 13², p. 138]
"Auf deinem Grunde"

Jacobi, Johann Georg, 1740-1814.

Erinnerung, WoO 21,3 (1828) [Universal,
1933]
"Glück der Engel! wo geblieben?"

Kerner, Justinus, 1786-1862.

Alte Laute, op. 35 no. 12 (1840) [GA,
v. 13¹, p. 131]
"Hörst du den Vogel singen?"
An Anna I, WoO 21,6 (1828) [Universal,
1933] "Lange harrt' ich: aber endlich
breiten ausein"
An Anna II, WoO 10,2 (1828) [GA,
v. 14, p. 34]
"Nicht im Thale der süssen Heimath"
*Aus das Trinkglas eines verstorbenen
Freundes,* op. 35 no. 6 (1840)
[GA, v. 13¹, p. 120]
"Du herrlich Glas"
Erstes Grün, op. 35 no. 4 (1840) [GA,
v. 13¹, p. 116] "Du junges Grün"
Frage, op. 35 no. 9 (1840) [GA, v. 13¹,
p. 126] "Wärst du nicht"
Gesanges Erwachen, WoO 21,5 (1828)
[Universal, 1933]
"Könnt' ich einmal wieder singen"
Im Herbste, WoO 10,3 (1828) [GA,
v. 14, p. 36] "Zieh' nur, du Sonne,
zieh' eilend von hier"
Kurzes Erwachen, WoO 21,4 (1828)
[Universal, 1933] "Ich bin im Mai
gegangen und hab' es nicht gewusst"
Lust der Sturmnacht, op. 35 no. 1 (1840)
[GA, v. 13¹, p. 108]
"Wenn durch Berg' und Thale
draussen Regen schauert"
Sängers Trost, op. 127 no. 1 (1840) [GA,
v. 13⁴, p. 80]
"Weint auch einst kein Liebchen"
Sehnsucht nach der Waldgegend, op. 35
no. 5 (1840) [GA, v. 13¹, p. 118]
"Wär' ich nie aus euch gegangen"
Stille Liebe, op. 35 no. 8 (1840) [GA,
v. 13¹, p. 124]
"Könnt' ich dich in Liedern preisen"
Stille Thränen, op. 35 no. 10 (1840) [GA,
v. 13¹, p. 127]
"Du bist vom Schlaf erstanden"
Stirb, Lieb' und Freud! op. 35 no. 2
(1840) [GA, v. 13¹, p. 110]
"Zu Augsburg steht ein hohes Haus"

SCHUMANN, ROBERT, 1810-1856
(continued)
Kerner, Justinus, 1786-1862 *(continued)*
Trost im Gesang, op. 142 no. 1 (1840)
[GA, v. 13^4, p. 98]
"Der Wandrer, dem verschwunden so
Sonn'als Mondenlicht"
Wanderlust, op. 35 no. 3 (1840) [GA,
v. 13^1, p. 113] "Wohlauf! noch
getrunken den funkelnden Wein!"
Wanderung, op. 35 no. 7 (1840) [GA,
v. 13^1, p. 122]
"Wohlauf und frisch gewandert"
Wer machte dich so krank? op. 35 no. 11
(1840) [GA, v. 13^1, p. 130]
"Dass du so krank geworden"
Kinkel, Gottfried, 1815-1882.
Abendlied, op. 107 no. 6 (1851) [GA,
v. 13^4, p. 50] "Es ist so still geworden"
Kletke, Hermann, 1813-1886.
Der Sandmann, op. 79 no. 12 (1849)
[GA, v. 13^3, p. 44]
"Zwei feine Stieflein hab' ich an"
Kulmann, Elisabeth, 1808-1825.
Du nennst mich armes Mädchen, op. 104
no. 3 (1851) [GA,
v. 13^4, p. 32] same
Gekämpft hat meine Barke, op. 104 no. 7
(1851) [GA, v. 13^4, p. 38] same
Die letzten Blumen starben, op. 104 no. 6
(1851) [GA, v. 13^4, p. 37] same
Mond, meiner Seele Liebling, op. 104 no.
1 (1851) [GA, v. 13^4, p. 28] same
Reich' mir die Hand, O Wolke, op. 104
no. 5 (1851) [GA, v. 13^4, p. 35] same
Viel Glück zur Reise, Schwalben, op. 104
no. 2 (1851) [GA, v. 13^4, p. 30] same
Der Zeisig, op. 104 no. 4 (1851) [GA,
v. 13^4, p. 34] "Wir sind ja, Kind"
L'Egru, Christian
Aufträge, op. 77 no. 5 (1850) [GA,
v. 13^3, p. 26]
"Nicht so schnelle, war' ein wenig"
Lenau, Nicolaus, 1802-1850.
Da liegt der Feinde gestreckte Schaar,
op. 117 no. 4 (1851) [GA, v. 13^4,
p. 58] same
Den grünen Zeigern, op. 117 no. 3
(1851) [GA, v. 13^4, p. 56] same
Einsamkeit, op. 90 no. 5 (1850) [GA,
v. 13^3, p. 114]
"Wild verwachs'ne dunkle Fichten"
Frühlingsgrüsse, WoO 26,2 (1851)
[**Musical Quarterly** 28 (1942): 58-60]
"Nach langem Frost"
Der Husar, trara! op. 117 no. 1 (1851)
[GA, v. 13^4, p. 52] same

Kommen und Scheiden, op. 90 no. 3
(1850) [GA, v. 133, p. 111]
"So oft sie kam, erschien mir die
Gestalt"
Der leidige Frieden hat lange gewährt,
op. 117 no. 2 (1851) [GA, v. 13^4,
p. 54] same
Lied eines Schmiedes, op. 90 no. 1
(1850) [GA, v. 13^3, p. 108]
"Fein Rösslein, ich beschlage dich"
Meine Rose, op. 90 no. 2 (1850) [GA,
v. 13^3, p. 109]
"Der holden Lenzgeschmeide"
Der schwere Abend, op. 90 no. 6 (1850)
[GA, v. 13^3, p. 118]
"Die dunklen Wolken hingen"
Die Sennin, op. 90 no. 4 (1850) [GA,
v. 13^3, p. 112]
"Schöne Sennin, noch einmal singe"
Lorenz, Auguste Wilhelmine, 1784-
1861.
Loreley, op. 53 no. 2 (1840) [GA, v. 13^2,
p. 147]
"Es flüstern und rauschen die Wogen"
Mary, Queen of Scots, 1542-1568.
Abschied von der Welt, op. 135 no. 4
(1852) [GA, v. 13^4, p. 95]
"Was nützt die mir noch zugemess'ne
Zeit?"
Abschied von Frankreich, op. 135 no. 1
(1852) [GA, v. 13^4, p. 90]
"Ich zieh' dahin"
An die Königin Elisabeth, op. 135 no. 3
(1852) [GA, v. 13^4, p. 93]
"Nur ein Gedanke"
Gebet, op. 135 no. 5 (1852) [GA, v. 13^4,
p. 97] "O Gott, mein gebieter"
Nach der Geburt ihres Sohnes, op. 135
no. 2 (1852) [GA, v. 13^4, p. 92]
"Herr Jesu Christ"
Miranda, Francisco Saa de, fl.1550.
Melancholie, op. 74 no. 6 (1849) [GA,
v. 10, p. 64]
"Wann, wann erscheint der Morgen"
Mörike, Eduard Friedrich, 1804-1875.
Er ist's, op. 79 no. 23 (1849) [GA,
v. 13^3, p. 64]
"Frühling lässt sein blaues Band"
Der Gärtner, op. 107 no. 3 (1851) [GA,
v. 13^4, p. 44] "Auf ihrem Leibrösslein"
Jung Volkers Lied, op. 125 no. 3 (1851)
[GA, v. 13^4, p. 74]
"Und die mich trug im Mutterarm"
Op. 125 no. 4 in GA.
Die Soldatenbraut, op. 64 no. 1 (1847)
[GA, v. 13^3, p. 10] "Ach, wenn's nur
der König auch wüsst'"

Das verlassne Mägdelein, op. 64 no. 2
(1847) [GA, v. 13³, p. 13]
"Früh wann die Hähne kräh'n"

Moore, Thomas, 1779-1852.

Zwei Venetianische Lieder, op. 25 no. 17
(1840) [GA, v. 13¹, p. 58]
"Leis' rudern hier, mein Gondolier"

WHEN THROUGH THE PIAZZETTA.

Zwei Venetianische Lieder, op. 25 no.
18 (1840) [GA, v. 13¹, p. 60]
"Wenn durch die Piazetta die
Abendluft weht"

Mosen, Julius, 1803-1867.

Der Nussbaum, op. 25 no. 3 (1840) [GA,
v. 13¹, p. 28] "Es grünet ein Nussbaum
vor dem Haus"

**Müller von Königswinter, Wolfgang,
1816-1873.**

Im Wald, op. 107 no. 5 (1851) [GA,
v. 13⁴, p. 48] "Ich zieh' so allein in
den Wald hinein!"

**Münch-Bellinghausen, Eligius Franz
Joseph, freiherr von, 1806-1871.**

Geisternähe, op. 77 no. 3 (1850) [GA,
v. 13³, p. 22]
"Was weht um meine Schläfe"

Padrilla, Pedro de, fl.1580.

LA SIERRA ES ALTA.

Hoch, hoch sind die Berge, op. 138 no.
8 (1849) [GA, v. 10, p. 150] same
Accompaniment for piano, 4 hands.

Pfarrius, Gustav, 1800-1884.

WALDLIEDERN.

Der Bräutigam und die Birke, op. 119
no. 3 (1851) [GA, v. 13⁴, p. 65]
"Birke, Birke, des Waldes Zier"

Die Hütte, op. 119 no. 1 (1851) [GA,
v. 13⁴, p. 60]
"Im Wald, in grüner Runde"

Warnung, op. 119 no. 2 (1851) [GA,
v. 13⁴, p. 64]
"Es geht der Tag zur Neige"

**Platen-Hallermünde, August, Graf
von, 1796-1835.**

Ihre Stimme, op. 96 no. 3 (1850) [GA,
v. 13³, p. 141]
"Lass' tief in dir mich lesen"

Reinick, Robert, 1805-1852.

LIEDERBUCH EINES MALERS.

An den Sonnenschein, op. 36 no. 4
(1840) [GA, v. 13¹, p. 138]
"O Sonnenschein, O Sonnenschein!"

Dichters Genesung, op. 36 no. 5
(1840) [GA, v. 13¹, p. 140]
"Und wieder hatt' ich der Schönsten
gedacht"

Liebesbotschaft, op. 36 no. 6 (1840)
[GA, v. 13¹, p. 144]
"Wolken die ihr nach Osten Eilt"

Nichts Schöneres, op. 36 no. 3 (1840)
[GA, v. 13¹, p. 136]
"Als ich zuerst dich hab' geseh'n"

Sonntags am Rhein, op. 36 no. 1
(1840) [GA, v. 13¹, p. 132]
"Des Sonntags in der Morgenstund' "

Ständchen, op. 36 no. 2 (1840) [GA,
v. 13¹, p. 134]
"Komm' in die stille Nacht"

Rückert, Friedrich, 1788-1866.

Aus den "Östlichen Rosen", op. 25 no.
25 (1840) [GA, v. 13¹, p. 69]
"Ich sende einen Gruss"

Die Blume der Ergebung, op. 83 no. 2
(1850) [GA, v. 13³, p. 82]
"Ich bin die Blum' im Garten"

Glockentürmers Töchterlein [unpubl.]
"Mein hochgebor'ne Schätzelein"

Jasminenstrauch, op. 27 no. 4 (1840)
[GA, v. 13¹, p. 76]
"Grün ist der Jasminenstrauch"

Schneeglöckchen, op. 79 no. 26 (1849)
[GA, v. 13³, p. 70] "Der Schnee, der
gestern noch in Flöckchen"

Volksliedchen, op. 51 no. 2 (1840) [GA,
v. 13², p. 135]
"Wenn ich früh in den Garten geh' "

Widmung, op. 25 no. 1 (1840) [GA,
v. 13¹, p. 24] "Du meine Seele, du
mein Herz"

Zum Schluss, op. 25 no. 26 (1840) [GA,
v. 13¹, p. 71]
"Hier in diesen erdbeklommen Lüften"

LIEBESFRÜHLING.

Flügel! Flügel! op. 37 no. 8 (1841)
[GA, v. 13², p. 14] same

Der Himmel hat eine Thräne geweint,
op. 37 no. 1 (1841) [GA, v. 13²,
p. 2] same

*Ich hab' in mich gesogen den Frühling
treu,* op. 37 no. 5 (1841) [GA, v.
13², p. 10] same

Liebster, deine Worte stehlen, op. 101
no. 2 (1849) [GA, v. 10, p. 92] same

Lieder der Braut, op. 25 no. 11 (1840)
[GA, v. 13¹, p. 46]
"Mutter, Mutter!"

Lieder der Braut, op. 25 no. 12 (1840)
[GA, v. 13¹, p. 48]
"Lass mich ihm am Busen hangen"

Mein schöner Stern! op. 101 no. 4
(1849) [GA, v. 10, p. 98] same

O Freund, mein Schirm, mein Schutz!
op. 101 no. 6 (1849) [GA, v. 10,
p. 108] same

SCHUMANN, ROBERT, 1810-1856
(continued)
Rückert, Friedrich, 1788-1866
(continued)
LIEBESFRÜHLING (continued)
O ihr Herren, op. 37 no. 3 (1841)
[GA, v. 13², p. 7] same
O Sonn', O Meer, O Rose! op. 37 no.
10 (1841) [GA, v. 13², p. 22] same
Rose, Meer und Sonne sind ein Bild,
op. 37 no. 9 (1841) [GA, v. 13²,
p. 18] same
Schiller, Johann Christoph Friedrich
von, 1759-1805.
Des Sennen Abschied, op. 79 no. 22
(1849) [GA, v. 13³, p. 62]
"Ihr Matten, lebt wohl"
Der Handschuh, op. 87 (1850) [GA,
v. 13³, p. 88] "Vor seinem
Löwengarten"
WILHELM TELL.
Des Buben Schützenlied, op. 79 no. 25
(1849) [GA, v. 13³, p. 68]
"Mit dem Pfeil, dem Bogen"
Schöpff, Wilhelm, 1826-1916.
Abschied vom Walde, op. 89 no. 4 (1850)
[GA, v. 13³, p. 102]
"Nun scheidet vom sterbenden Walde"
Es stürmet am Abendhimmel, op. 89 no.
1 (1850) [GA, v. 13³, p. 94] same
Gesungen, op. 96 no. 4 (1850) [GA,
v. 13³, p. 144]
"Hört ihr im Laube des Regens"
Heimliches Verschwinden, op. 89 no. 2
(1850) [GA, v. 13³, p. 96]
"Nachts zu unbekannter Stunde"
Herbstlied, op. 89 no. 3 (1850) [GA,
v. 13³, p. 99]
"Durch die Tannen und die Linden"
Himmel und Erde, op. 96 no. 5 (1850)
[GA, v. 13³, p. 146]
"Wie der Bäume kühne Wipfel"
In's Freie, op. 89 no. 5 (1850) [GA,
v. 13³, p. 103]
"Mir ist's so eng allüberall!"
Röselein, Röselein, op. 89 no. 6 (1850)
[GA, v. 13³, p. 106]
"Röselein, Röselein! müssen denn
Dornen sein?"
Schulz, Eduard, 1813-1842.
Ein Gedanke, WoO 26,1 (1840) [*Musical
Quarterly* 28 (1942): 57-58]
"Sie schlingt um meinen Nacken"

Schulze, Ernst Konrad Friedrich, 1789-
1817.
Verwandlung (1827) [unpubl.] "Wenn der
Winter sonst entschwand"
Schumann, Robert, 1810-1856.
Hirtenknabe, WoO 10,4 (1828) [GA,
v. 14, p. 37]
"Bin nur ein armer Hirtenknab"
Lied für XXX (1827) [unpubl.]
"Leicht wie gaukelnde Sylphiden"
Die Sehnsucht, WoO 21,1 (1827)
[Universal, 1933]
"Sterne der blauen himmlischen Auen"
Schwab, Gustav, 1792-1850.
Der Reiter und der Bodensee, WoO 11,1
(1840) [*Jahrbuch der Musikbibliothek
Peters,* 1897] "Der Reiter reitet durch's
helle Thal"
Seidl, Johann Gabriel, 1804-1875.
Blondel's Lied, op. 53 no. 1 (1840) [GA,
v. 13², p. 142]
"Spähend nach dem Eisengitter"
Shakespeare, William, 1564-1616.
TWELFTH NIGHT: When that I was and
a little tiny boy.
Schlusslied des Narren, op. 127 no. 5
(1840) [GA, v. 13⁴, p. 88] "Und als
ich ein winzig Bübchen war"
Shelley, Percy Bysshe, 1792-1822.
Die Flüchtlinge, op. 122 no. 2 [GA,
v. 13⁴, p. 119] "Der Hagel klirrt
nieder"
Speaker & piano.
Strachwitz, Moritz Karl Wilhelm
Anton, Graf von, 1822-1847.
Mein altes Ross, op. 127 no. 4 (1850)
[GA, v. 13⁴, p. 86] same
Uhland, Ludwig, 1787-1862.
Ballade, op. 139 no. 7 [GA, v. 9¹², p. 17]
"In der hohen Hall' sass König Sifrid"
Voice & harp.
Des Knaben Berglied, op. 79 no. 8
(1849) [GA, v. 13³, p. 39]
"Ich bin vom Berg der Hirtenknab' "
Provençalisches Lied, op. 139 no. 4
(1852) [GA, v. 9¹², p. 11]
"In den Thalen der Provence"
Voice & harp.
Das Schwert (1848) [unpubl.]
"Zur Schmiede ging ein junger Held"
Der weisse Hirsch (1848) [unpubl.]
"Es gingen drei Jäger"
Ulrich, Titus, 1813-1891.
Die Fensterscheibe, op. 107 no. 2 (1851)
[GA, v. 13⁴, p. 42]
"Die Fenster klär'ich zum Feiertag"

Herzeleid, op. 107 no. 1 (1851) [GA, v. 13^4, p. 40] "Die Weiden lassen matt die Zweige hangen"

Unknown

Der Contrabandiste, op. 74 Anhang (1849) [GA, v. 10, p. 84] "Ich bin der Contrabandiste"

Kinderwacht, op. 79 no. 21 (1849) [GA, v. 13^3, p. 61] "Wenn fromme Kindlein schlafen geh'n"

Vicente, Gil, ca.1470-ca.1536.

MUI GRACIOSA ES LA DONCELLA.

O wie lieblich ist das Mädchen, op. 138 no. 3 (1849) [GA, v. 10, p. 128] same

Accompaniment for piano, 4 hands.

SANNOSA ESTA LA NINNA.

Weh, wie zornig ist das Mädchen, op. 138 no. 7 (1849) [GA, v. 10, p. 148] same

Accompaniment for piano, 4 hands.

Vimioso, Francisco de Portugal, conde de, d.1549.

Geständnis, op. 74 no. 7 (1849) [GA, v. 10, p. 66] "Also lieb' ich euch, Geliebte"

Wolff, Oskar Ludwig, 1799-1851.

Stiller Vorwurf, op. 77 no. 4 (1850) [GA, v. 13^3, p. 24] "In einsamen Stunden"

Zedlitz, Joseph Christian von, 1790-1862.

Die nächtliche Heerschau, WoO 11, 2 (1840) [*Jahrbuch der Musikbibliothek Peters,* 1897] "Nachts in der zwölften Stunde"

Zimmermann, Georg Wilhelm, 1794-1835.

Nur ein lächelnder Blick, op. 27 no. 5 (1840) [GA, v. 13^1, p. 77] same

Schumann, Robert, 1810-1856.

SCHUMANN

Hirtenknabe

Lied für XXX

Die Sehnsucht

Schwab, Gustav, 1792-1850.

LOEWE *Kaiser Heinrich's Waffenweihe*

SCHUMANN *Der Reiter und der Bodensee*

Schwäbische Treue see Seyboth, Sofie **REGER**

"Die Schwälble ziehet fort, ziehet fort" *see Volkslied* Anon. **BRAHMS**

"Die Schwalbe, die den Sommer bringt" *see Lied des transferierten Zettel* Shakespeare **WOLF**

"Die Schwalbe fliegt" *see Andres Maienlied* Hölty **MENDELSSOHN-BARTHOLDY**

"Schwalbc, sag' mir an" *see Das Mädchen spricht* Gruppe **BRAHMS**

"Die Schwalbe zieht, der Sommer flieht" *see Verlass' mich nicht!* Osterwald **FRANZ**

Der Schwalben Heimkehr see Herlossohn **WOLF**

"Die Schwalben zieh'n" *see Scheidelied* Baumbach **BERG**

Schwalbenmärchen see Freiligrath **LOEWE**

Schwalbenmütterlein see Reinick **REGER**

"Schwalbenmütterlein, Schwalbenmütterlein!" *see Schwalbenmütterlein* Reinick **REGER**

Ein Schwan see Ibsen **GRIEG** *En svane*

SCHWANENGESANG. see Rückert *Abendglockenläuten* **LASSEN**

Schwanengesang see Senn **SCHUBERT**

SCHWANENGESANG, no. 1

SCHUBERT Rellstab *Liebesbotschaft*

SCHWANENGESANG, no. 2

SCHUBERT Rellstab *Kriegers Ahnung*

SCHWANENGESANG, no. 3

SCHUBERT Rellstab *Frühlingssehnsucht*

SCHWANENGESANG, no. 4

SCHUBERT Rellstab *Ständchen*

SCHWANENGESANG, no. 5

SCHUBERT Rellstab *Aufenthalt*

SCHWANENGESANG, no. 6

SCHUBERT Rellstab *In der Ferne*

SCHWANENGESANG, no. 7

SCHUBERT Rellstab *Abschied*

SCHWANENGESANG, no. 8

SCHUBERT Heine *Der Atlas*

SCHWANENGESANG, no. 9

SCHUBERT Heine *Ihr Bild*

SCHWANENGESANG, no. 10

SCHUBERT Heine *Das Fischermädchen*

SCHWANENGESANG, no. 11

SCHUBERT Heine *Die Stadt*

SCHWANENGESANG, no. 12

SCHUBERT Heine *Am Meer*

SCHWANENGESANG, no. 13

SCHUBERT Heine *Der Doppelgänger*

SCHWANENGESANG, no. 14

SCHUBERT Seidl *Die Taubenpost*

Die Schwanenjungfrau see Vogl **LOEWE**

Schwangesang see Kosegarten **SCHUBERT**

"Schwarz wie Nacht brausest du auf" *see Die Braut am Gestade* Voss **ZELTER**

"Schwarzbrauner Hufschmied" *see Der Hufschmied* Spitteler **SCHOECK**

Der Schwarze in der Zuckerplantage see Claudius, M. **SCHOECK**

Die schwarze Laute see Bierbaum **SZYMANOWSKI**

Schwarze Muse see Barth **KRENEK**
Schwarze Rosen see Josephson, E. *SVARTA
  ROSOR OCH GULA.* **DELIUS**
Die schwarzen Augen see Vogl **LOEWE**
Schwarzenberg, Friedrich, Fürst, 1800-
  1872.
  LOEWE *Gruss vom Meere*
"Ein schwarzes Vöglein fliegt über die Welt"
  see Vöglein Schwermut Morgenstern
  KILPINEN
Schwarzschattende Kastanie see Meyer
  SCHOECK
"Schwebe, mein tanzender Kahn" *see
  Das Schiffermädchen* Geyer **SPOHR**
Schwebe, schwebe, blaues Auge see
  Dingelstedt **LISZT**
  Two settings: 1845 and ca. 1860.
"Schwebst du nieder aus den Weiten" *see
  Himmelfahrt* Dehmel **WEBERN**
Schweig' einmal still see Heyse **WOLF**
"Schweig, O Herz! warum dies bange
  Schnen" *see Lied der Harfnerin* Unknown
  SPOHR
Das Schweigen see Gemmingen **KRENEK**
Schweigen ist ein schönes Ding see Reinick
  SPOHR
"Schweigen rings" *see Sapphische Strophe*
  Leuthold **SCHOECK**
Schweigend durchflog eine Seele see Tolstoï
  MUSORGSKIĭ
  Gornimi tikho letela dusha nebesami
"Schweigend geht die junge Frau an dem Arm
  des greisen Gatten" *see Ein Paar*
  Braungart **REGER**
"Schweigend sahe der May die bekränzte" *see
  Der Jüngling* Klopstock **GLUCK**
Schweigsamkeit see Geibel **LASSEN**
"Schweigt der Menschen laute Lust" *see
  Der Abend* Eichendorff **LASSEN**
Schweizer, Karl Friedrich, Freiherr von,
  1797-1847.
  SPOHR
    Des Mädchens Klage
    Ermutigung
Schweizer Lied see Goethe *UF'M BERGLI.*
  ZELTER
Schweizerlied see Goethe **FRANZ,
  JENSEN, SCHUBERT**
Der schwere Abend see Lenau **FRANZ,
  SCHUMANN**
"Schwerin ist todt, Schwerin, mein General,
  ist todt" *see General Schwerin* Häring
  LOEWE
*SCHWERIN, MEIN GENERAL, IST TODT,
  SCHWERIN IST TODT! see* Häring
  General Schwerin **LOEWE**

Der Schwermütige see Gubitz **WEBER**
Schwermut see Candidus **BRAHMS**
Schwermut see Mahlmann **SPOHR**
Das Schwert see Uhland **SCHUMANN**
Schwertlied see Körner **SCHUBERT**
Das Schwesterchen see Kiesekamo **REGER**
Schwestergruss see Bruchmann
  SCHUBERT
Die Schwestern see Mörike **SCHOECK**
Die Schwestern see Tennyson **JENSEN**
Schwill an, mein Strom see Huch
  PFITZNER
Der Schwimmer see Enslin **LOEWE**
"Schwingt euch auf, Posannenchöre" *see
  Wächterlied auf der Wartburg* Scheffel
  WOLF
"Schwirrend Tambourin" *see Die Musikantin*
  Unknown **LASSEN**
"Schwor ein junges Mädchen" *see
  Vorschneller Schwur* Kapper **BRAHMS**
"Schwüler Hauch weht mir herüber" *see
  Lieb Minna* Stadler **SCHUBERT**
Schwung see Hafiz **STRAUSS**
Der Schwur see Baumbach **REGER**
Ściani dumbek see Anon. **SZYMANOWSKI**
Scollard, Clinton, 1860-1932.
  GRIFFES *Come love, across the sunlit
    land*
Scott, Sir Walter, bart., 1771-1832.
  JENSEN
    Klage der Grenzerwittwe
    Das Mädchen von Isla
    O sag' mir, wie dich frein, mein Lieb
  MENDELSSOHN-BARTHOLDY
    Ave Maria
    Raste Krieger, Krieg ist aus
  SIBELIUS *The sun upon the lake is low*
IVANHOE.
  SCHUBERT *Romanze des Richard
    Löwenherz*
JOCK OF HAZELDEAN: Why weep ye by
  the tide, ladie?
  JENSEN *Jock von Hazeldean*
THE LADY OF THE LAKE.
  SCHUBERT
    Ellens Gesang I
    Ellens Gesang II
    Ellens Gesang III
    Lied des gefangenen Jägers
    Normans Gesang
A LEGEND OF MONTROSE.
  SCHUBERT *Lied der Anne Lyle*
LULLABY OF AN INFANT CHIEF: O hush
  thee, my babie.
  JENSEN *Wiegenlied*
*MINSTRELSY OF THE SCOTISH
  BORDER.*
  JENSEN *Berthrams Grablied*

COMPOSER Poet *Title* "First Line"

THE PIRATE.
  SCHUBERT *Gesang der Norna*
Scribe, Augustin Eugène, 1791-1861.
  GOUNOD *Le jour des prix*
Sct. Nepomuks Vorabend see Goethe
  ZELTER
Scuote amore il mio cuori see Sappho
  PIZZETTI
"Se a ciascun l'interno affanno" *see Quanti*
  Mai Metastasio **GOUNOD**
Se come io son poeta see Zaffira **GOUNOD**
"Se, der var en Gang en Konge" *see Irmelin*
  Rose Jacobsen **NIELSEN**
Se dig for, når du vaelger din Vej see
  Benzon *ANNA BRYDE.* **GRIEG**
Se dig ud en Sommerdag see Aakjaer
  SE DIGUD. **NIELSEN**
SE DIGUD. see Aakjaer
  Se dig ud en Sommerdag **NIELSEN**
Se fra le trecce d'Ebano see Unknown
  ROSSINI *Il rimprovero* ("Se fra le trecce
  d'Ebano")
"Se hvitsippan hur täck hon är" *see*
  Hvitsippan Franzén **SIBELIUS**
Se il mio seno see Sappho **RIETI**
Se il vuol la molinara see Unknown
  ROSSINI
"Se, Marie, hvad jeg bringer" *see Med en*
  vandlilje Ibsen **GRIEG**
"Se penchant vers les dahlias" *see Les paons*
  Kahn **LOEFFLER**
"Se peut-il qu'autrefois" *see Romance*
  Jean-Aubry **IBERT**
SE PLAIRE SUR LA MÊME FLEUR. see
  Moreno
  Ritournelle et six chansons **MILHAUD**
"Se replier toujours, sur soimême" *see*
  Si morne! Verhaeren **RAVEL**
"Se, Solen blusser saa elskovsrød" *see*
  Kjaerlighed Andersen **GRIEG**
"Se tranquillo a te deecanto" *see Il mistero*
  Romani **VERDI**
The sea see Borodin **BORODIN**
The sea see Howells, W. D.
  MACDOWELL
The sea see Wilde *IMPRESSIONS II:* La mer.
  GRIFFES
Sea calm see Goethe *MEERESSTILLE.*
  MEDTNER *Meeresstille*
The sea does not foam see Tolstoĭ
  BALAKIREV *Ne penitsya more*
Sea fever see Masefield **IRELAND**
The sea hath its pearls see Longfellow
  GOUNOD
"The sea is flecked with bars of gray" *see*
  Les silhouettes Wilde **CARPENTER**

The sea is not foaming, the waves are all still
  see Tolstoĭ **RIMSKIĬ-KORSAKOV**
  Ne penitsia more
The sea is tossing see Tolstoĭ **RIMSKIĬ-**
  KORSAKOV *Kolyshetsia more*
The sea princess see Borodin **BORODIN**
  Morskaya tsarevna
The sea-bird see Quilter **QUILTER**
Seascape see Auden *ON THIS ISLAND.*
  BRITTEN
"The seashells lie as cold as death" *see*
  Motion & stillness Shove
  VAUGHAN WILLIAMS
Sea-snatch see O'Faolain, Sean, translator
  BARBER
Sea-swell see Tiutchev **MEDTNER**
  Waves and thoughts
SECHS HÖLDERLIN-FRAGMENTE, no. 1
  BRITTEN Hölderlin *Menschenbeifall*
SECHS HÖLDERLIN-FRAGMENTE, no. 2
  BRITTEN Hölderlin *Die Heimat*
SECHS HÖLDERLIN-FRAGMENTE, no. 3
  BRITTEN Hölderlin *Sokrates und*
    Alcibiades
SECHS HÖLDERLIN-FRAGMENTE, no. 4
  BRITTEN Hölderlin *Die Jugend*
SECHS HÖLDERLIN-FRAGMENTE, no. 5
  BRITTEN Hölderlin *Hälfte des Lebens*
SECHS HÖLDERLIN-FRAGMENTE, no. 6
  BRITTEN Hölderlin *Die Linien des*
    Lebens
SECHS JUGENDLIEDER, no. 1
  PFITZNER Sturm, J. *Abendlied*
SECHS JUGENDLIEDER, no. 2
  PFITZNER Graf-Bartholomew, M.
    Mir bist du tot
SECHS JUGENDLIEDER, no. 3
  PFITZNER Uhland *Naturfreiheit*
SECHS JUGENDLIEDER, no. 4
  PFITZNER Redwitz *Nun, da so warm der*
    Sonnenschein
SECHS JUGENDLIEDER, no. 5
  PFITZNER Mörike *Das verlassene*
    Mägdelein
SECHS JUGENDLIEDER, no. 6
  PFITZNER Reinick *Kuriose Geschichte*
SECHS LIEDER AUS DEM NACHLASS,
  no. 1
  JENSEN Heyse *Vergangnes Glück*
SECHS LIEDER AUS DEM NACHLASS,
  no. 2
  JENSEN Beck *Wo Tauben sind*
SECHS LIEDER AUS DEM NACHLASS,
  no. 3
  JENSEN Storm *Loose*
SECHS LIEDER AUS DEM NACHLASS,
  no. 4
  JENSEN Kugler *Nachtgruss*

COMPOSER Poet *Title* ''First Line''

"Sei sanft wie ihre Seele" *see*
  Abendständchen: An Lina Batsányi
  SCHUBERT
Sei still see Schorn **LISZT, LASSEN**
Sei tornato da me see Bocchialini, Jacopo
  PIZZETTI
"Sei willkommen, Frühlingswehen" *see*
  Frühlingslust Naumann, L. G. **LOEWE**
"Sei willkommen, Zwielichtstunde" *see*
  Abenddämmerung Schack **BRAHMS,**
  LASSEN
SEIBER, MÁTYÁS, 1905-1960.
  Ady, Endre, 1877-1918.
    Jó Csönd herceg elött (1925) [unpubl.?]
      Neither located nor examined.
    Tüzes seb vagyok (1925) [unpubl.?]
      Neither located nor examined.
  Anon.
    Farewell (1936) [Augener, 1956]
      Baritone & violin.
    Lament (1936) [Augener, 1956]
      Baritone & violin.
    Quarrel (1936) [Augener, 1956]
      Baritone & violin.
    Soldier's song (1936) [Augener, 1956]
      Baritone & violin.
    Tears (1952) [Schott, 1954]
      "Weep, weep you no more"
      Text by Dowland?
  Dunbar, William, 1460?-1520?
    Timor mortis (1952) [Schott, 1954]
      "I that in heill was and gladness am"
  Goethe, Johann Wolfgang von, 1749-
  1832.
    FAUST.
      Epilogue (1952) [Schott, 1954]
        "Oh, heavenly Poesey, Heavenward
        mount on high!"
      Es war ein König in Thule (1949)
        [Augener, 1951]
      Invocation (1952) [Schott, 1954]
        "Oh, heavenly Poesey, Heavenward
        mount on high!"
      Meine Ruh' ist hin (1949) [Augener,
        1951]
  Morgenstern, Christian Otto Joseph
  Wolfgang, 1871-1914.
    Das Knie (1927) [Universal, 1956] "Ein
      Knie geht einsam durch die Welt"
      Soprano & clarinet.
    Das Nasobem (1927) [Universal, 1956]
      "Auf seinen Nasen schreitet"
      Soprano & clarinet.
    Die Trichter (1927) [Universal, 1956]
      "Zwei Trichter wandeln durch die
      Nacht"
      Soprano & clarinet.

Petöfi, Sándor, 1823-1849.
  Négy Petöfi dal (1922-23) [unpubl.?]
    Cycle includes 4 songs; neither located
    nor examined.
Shakespeare, William, 1564-1616.
  Sonnet (1952) [Schott, 1954] "Shall I
    compare thee to a summer's day?"
Unknown
  By the fountains of Rome (1956)
    [unpubl.?]
    Neither located nor examined.
"Seid gegrüsst, ihr grünen Hallen" *see*
  Lenzgesang Fitger **SIBELIUS**
"Seid gegrüsst mit Frühlingswonne" *see*
  Im Herbste Uhland **SCHOECK**
Seida und Landenberg, Franz Eugen
Joseph, Freiherr von, b. 1772.
  WEBER *Lied*
Seidl, Johann Gabriel, 1804-1875.
  LOEWE *Die Uhr*
  SCHUBERT
    Am Fenster
    Bei dir allein
    Im Freien
    Irdisches Glück
    Die Männer sind méchant
    Sehnsucht
    Die Taubenpost
    Die Unterscheidung
    Der Wanderer an den Mond
    Wiegenlied
    Das Zügenglöcklein
  SCHUMANN *Blondel's Lied*
Le seigneur est roi see Anon. **MILHAUD**
Seigneur par le son du schophar vous ferez
  entendre see Anon. **MILHAUD**
Sein Bahrtuch weiss wie Bergesschnee see
  Shakespeare *HAMLET.* **LASSEN**
  Two settings: Op. 74 no.1/2 and op. 74 no.
  1/3.
"Sein Heer durchwogte das Palmenthal" *see*
  Der Mohrenfürst Freiligrath **LOEWE**
La Seine see Rohan **THOMSON**
SEIS MÉLODIES, no. 1
  GOUNOD Passerat *Le premier jour de*
  Mai
SEIS MÉLODIES, no. 2
  GOUNOD Baïf *O ma belle rebelle*
SEIS MÉLODIES, no. 3
  GOUNOD Hugo *Aubade*
SEIS MÉLODIES, no. 4
  GOUNOD Anon. *Chant d'automne*
SEIS MÉLODIES, no. 5
  GOUNOD Musset *Le lever*
SEIS MÉLODIES, no. 6
  GOUNOD Musset *Venise*

COMPOSER   Poet   *Title*   "First Line"

SEIS MÉLODIES ENFANTINES, no. 1
    GOUNOD Spenner, M. *Bon jour, bon soir*
SEIS MÉLODIES ENFANTINES, no. 2
    GOUNOD Spenner, M. *Le rosier blanc*
SEIS MÉLODIES ENFANTINES, no. 4
    GOUNOD Scribe *Le jour des prix*
SEIS MÉLODIES ENFANTINES, no. 5
    GOUNOD Quételart, A. *L'ange gardien*
SEIS MÉLODIES ENFANTINES, no. ?
    GOUNOD Spenner, M. *Un rêve*
        NB: The 6th song in this cycle could not be identified.
Seit du gesagt dein strenges Wort see
    Cornelius **LASSEN**
"Seit ganz mein Aug' ich durft' in deines tauchen" *see Dein Auge* Dahn **REGER**
Seit ich ihn gesehen see Chamisso
    FRAUENLIEBE UND LEBEN.
    SCHUMANN
Seit ich ihn gesehn see Chamisso
    FRAUENLIEBE UND LEBEN. **LOEWE**
"Seit ich so viele Weiber sah" *see Arie aus dem Spiegel von Arcadien* Schikaneder
    SCHÖNBERG
"Seit wann du mein, ich weiss es nicht" *see Jetzt und immer* Dehmel **REGER**
Seitdem dein Aug' in meines schaute see
    Schack **STRAUSS**
Sektantskaĩa see Anon. **STRAVINSKIĬ**
    Chant dissident
"Der selbe grosse Engel" *see Vom Tode Mariä*
    Rilke **HINDEMITH**
"Selbst die Toten in dem kleinen Kirchhof"
    see Friedhof im Gebirgsdorf Krenek
    KRENEK
Selbstbetrug see Goethe **MEDTNER,**
    SCHOECK
Selbstgefühl see Anon. *DES KNABEN WUNDERHORN*: Selbstgefühl. **MAHLER**
Selbstgespräch see Gleim **BEETHOVEN**
Selbstgeständnis see Mörike **WOLF**
"Selbstzweck sei sich die Kunst" *see Distichen* Leuthold **SCHOECK**
Selezen see Anon. **STRAVINSKIĬ** *Canard*
SELF PORTRAITS IN A CONVEX MIRROR.
    see Ashbery
    Fear of death **ROREM**
Self-deceit see Goethe **MEDTNER**
    Selbstbetrug
"Sel'ge Abende nieder steigen in mein Herz"
    see Stiller Abend Schröer **FRANZ**
"Selge Zeiten" *see Der Schwermütige* Gubitz
    WEBER
Selig ihr Blinden see Heyse **WOLF**
"Selig, O Mutter, wer stirbt!" *see Auf den Tod eines Kindes* Anon. **ZELTER**

Selige Nacht! see Petöfi **FRANZ**
"Selige Nacht! Ich bin nun bei der Liebsten hier" *see Selige Nacht!* Petöfi **FRANZ**
Selige Sehnsucht see Goethe
    WESTÖSTLICHER DIVAN. **SCHOECK,**
    ZELTER
Selige Welt see Senn **SCHUBERT**
Seligkeit see Hölty **SCHUBERT**
Selim's song see Lermontov **BALAKIREV**
    Pesnya Selima
Selma und Selmar see Klopstock
    SCHUBERT
Selmar und Dora see Klopstock **ZELTER**
DER SELTENE BETER. see Fitzau
    Der alte Dessauer **LOEWE**
Der seltne Beter see Fitzau **LASSEN**
Die selt'ne Beter see Fitzau **LOEWE**
    Der alte Dessauer
"Seltsam, im Nebel zu wandern!" *see Im Nebel* Hesse **SCHOECK**
Seltsam ist Juanas Weise see Anon. **WOLF**
Sem' noyabrya see Khomyakov
    BALAKIREV
"S'embarquer, Ô lente nef" *see Le nuage* Pomès, Mathilde **MOMPOU**
Le semeur see Carême **SAUGUET**
Seminarist see Musorgskiĭ **MUSORGSKIĬ**
Sémiramis see Colombeau **SCHMITT**
Semler, Frida (Mrs. Mortimer Seabury)
    BERG *Traum*
Semmler *see* Semler, Frida (Mrs. Mortimer Seabury)
Semptembermorgen see Mörike **LUENING**
Se'n har jag ej frågat mera see Runeberg
    SIBELIUS
Sen Panny Marie see Unknown **MARTINŮ**
Senart, Maurice, 1878-1962.
    HONEGGER *Hommage au travail*
Send thy comfort! see Tiutchev **MEDTNER**
    The pauper
Send-off see Anon. **PROKOFIEV** *Provody*
Sendschreiben see Collin, M. **SCHUBERT**
    Herrn Josef Spaun
Seneschall's Lied see Wildenbruch
    LASSEN
Senghor, Léopold Sedar, Pres. Senegal, 1906-
    SAUGUET *Chant de feu*
Senn, Johann Chrysostomus, 1792-1857.
    SCHUBERT
        Schwanengesang
        Selige Welt
Die Sennerin see Paulsen **GRIEG** *Turisten*
Die Sennin see Lenau **SCHUMANN**
Sensation see Rimbaud **RIVIER**

Senteurs see Mallarmé **SAUGUET**
Le sentier perdu see Choudens
  MASSENET
Le sentier sombre see Renaudière
  CHABRIER
"Sentiers où l'herbe se balance" *see L'absent*
  Hugo **FAURÉ**
La séparation see Anon. **MILHAUD**
Séparation see Mariéton **MASSENET**
Séparation see Tolstoï **CHAïKOVSKIï**
  Ni otzyva, ni slova
La separazione see Ucceili, F. **ROSSINI**
Sephestia's lullaby see Greene, R.
  BRITTEN
SEPT CHANSONS DE L'ALCHIMISTE, no.
  1
  SAUGUET Raphaël, Cluzel *L'alchimiste*
    au regard d'ambre
SEPT CHANSONS DE L'ALCHIMISTE, no.
  2
  SAUGUET Raphaël, Cluzel *L'alchimiste*
    est dans le grenier
SEPT CHANSONS DE L'ALCHIMISTE, no.
  3
  SAUGUET Raphaël, Cluzel *L'alchimiste*
    au cher visage
SEPT CHANSONS DE L'ALCHIMISTE, no.
  4
  SAUGUET Raphaël, Cluzel *L'alchimiste*
    a la voix d'ambre
SEPT CHANSONS DE L'ALCHIMISTE, no.
  5
  SAUGUET Raphaël, Cluzel *Dans le*
    jardin de l'alchimiste
SEPT CHANSONS DE L'ALCHIMISTE, no.
  6
  SAUGUET Raphaël, Cluzel *Les yeux*
    d'ambre de l'alchimiste
SEPT CHANSONS DE L'ALCHIMISTE, no.
  7
  SAUGUET Raphaël, Cluzel *J'en appelle*
    à l'alchimiste
SEPT MÉLODIES, no. 1
  CHAUSSON Leconte de Lisle *Nanny*
SEPT MÉLODIES, no. 2
  CHAUSSON Silvestre *Le charme*
SEPT MÉLODIES, no. 3
  CHAUSSON Gautier *Les papillons*
SEPT MÉLODIES, no. 4
  CHAUSSON Gautier *La dernière feuille*
SEPT MÉLODIES, no. 5
  CHAUSSON Bourget *Sérénade italienne*
SEPT MÉLODIES, no. 6
  CHAUSSON Ackermann *Hébé*
SEPT MÉLODIES, no. 7
  CHAUSSON Leconte de Lisle *Le colibri*

SEPT POÈMES DE LA CONNAISSANCE
  DE L'EST, no. 1
  MILHAUD Claudel *La nuit à la vérandah*
SEPT POÈMES DE LA CONNAISSANCE
  DE L'EST, no. 2
  MILHAUD Claudel *Décembre*
SEPT POÈMES DE LA CONNAISSANCE
  DE L'EST, no. 3
  MILHAUD Claudel *Dissolution*
SEPT POÈMES DE LA CONNAISSANCE
  DE L'EST, no. 4
  MILHAUD Claudel *Ardeur*
SEPT POÈMES DE LA CONNAISSANCE
  DE L'EST, no. 5
  MILHAUD Claudel *Tristesse de l'eau*
SEPT POÈMES DE LA CONNAISSANCE
  DE L'EST, no. 6
  MILHAUD Claudel *La descente*
SEPT POÈMES DE LA CONNAISSANCE
  DE L'EST, no. 7
  MILHAUD Claudel *Le point*
SEPTAIN. see Collen, G.
  Chudnyĭ sad" **BORODIN**
September see San Geminiano **IVES**
SEPTEMBER SONGS, no. 5
  QUILTER Coleridge *Through the sunny*
    garden
SEPTEMBER SONGS, no. 6
  QUILTER Coleridge *The valley and the*
    hill
Septembermorgen see Mörike **SCHOECK**
  Two settings: Op. 7 no. 2 and op. 51 no. 5.
Septembre see Văcărescu **MASSENET**
Ser du havet? see Geibel **GRIEG**
  Siehst du das Meer?
La sera see Annunzio *POEMA*
  PARADISIACO. **RESPIGHI**
Sera d'Inverno see Silvani, Mario
  PIZZETTI
La sera fiesolana see Annunzio *ALCYONE.*
  CASELLA
Seraferne see Jacobsen **NIELSEN**
"Seraferne har rullet bort de klare Stjerner"
  see Seraferne Jacobsen **NIELSEN**
"Le Séraphin des soirs passe le long des
  fleurs" *see L'âme errante* Samain
  AUBERT
Séraphine see Heine **HAHN**
Seraphine an ihr Klavier see Schubart
  SCHUBERT
Serenada see Collin **CHAïKOVSKIï**
  Sérénade
Serenada see Eichendorff **MEDTNER**
  Serenade
Serenada see Golenishchev-Kutuzov
  MUSORGSKIï

Serenada *see* Konstantin **CHAÏKOVSKIÏ**
Serenada *see* Pushkin **MEDTNER** *Serenade*
Serenada see Turquety *AURORE.*
  CHAÏKOVSKIÏ
Serenada *see* Vilenkin **RUBINSTEIN**
Serenada Don-Zhuana see Tolstoï
  CHAÏKOVSKIÏ
Sérénade see Anon. **POULENC**
Serenade *see* Baggesen **WEBER**
Sérénade see Banville *LES CARIATIDES,*
  livre 3, no. VII. **DEBUSSY**
Serenade *see* Callanau, I. **NIELSEN**
Sérénade see Cazalis **CHAUSSON**
Sérénade see Châtillon **CHABRIER**
Sérénade see Chauvinière, Edmond de
  GOUNOD
Sérénade see Collin **CHAÏKOVSKIÏ**
Serenade *see* Eichendorff *AUSSICHT.*
  MEDTNER
Serenade *see* Golenishchev-Kutuzov
  MUSORGSKIÏ *Serenada*
Sérénade see Hugo **GOUNOD**
Sérénade see Konstantin **CHAÏKOVSKIÏ**
  Serenada
Sérénade see Mangeot, L. **SAINT-SAËNS**
Sérénade see Manuel **MASSENET**
Sérénade see Marc, Gabriel **DUPARC**
Serenade *see* Pushkin **MEDTNER**
Serenade *see* Runeberg **SIBELIUS**
Serenade *see* Sassoon **CARPENTER**
Serenade *see* Schack **BRAHMS**
Serenade *see* Shenshin **MEDTNER**
Serenade *see* Tellez *EL BURLADOR DE*
  SEVILLA. **MAHLER**
Sérénade see Turquety *AURORE.*
  CHAÏKOVSKIÏ *Serenada*
Sérénade see Văcărescu **AUBERT**
Sérénade see Verlaine **LOEFFLER**
Sérénade à Ninon see Musset *A QUOI*
  RÊVENT LES JEUNES FILLES. **DELIBES**
Sérénade aux mariés see Ruelle
  MASSENET
Sérénade d'Arlequin see Gallet **MASSENET**
  À Colombine
Sérénade d'automne see Blanchecotte
  MASSENET *Non, tu n'as pas fini d'aimer*
Sérénade de Molière see Molière
  MASSENET
Sérénade de Ruy Blas see Hugo **CHABRIER**
  Ruy Blas
Sérénade de Zanetto see Coppée
  MASSENET
Sérénade du Bourgeois gentilhomme see
  Molière *LE BOURGEOIS*
  GENTILHOMME. **FAURÉ**
Sérénade du passant see Coppée
  MASSENET *Sérénade de Zanetto*

Sérénade Florentine see Cazalis **DUPARC**
Serenade in Seville *see* Rogers
  THOMPSON, R.
Sérénade italienne see Bourget **CHAUSSON**
Sérénade mélancolique see Jean-Aubry
  AUBERT
Sérénade: Oh, quand je dors see Hugo
  BIZET
Serenade til Welhaven *see* Bjørnson **GRIEG**
Sérénade toscane see Anon. **FAURÉ**
Serenata indiana see Shelley **RESPIGHI**
Serenate see Goethe *CLAUDINE VON*
  VILLA BELLA. **BRAHMS**
La sérénité see Barbier, M. *CONTES*
  BLANCS. **SAINT-SAËNS**
Serenity *see* Whittier **IVES**
Sergel, Albert, 1876-1946.
  KILPINEN
    Eingeschneite stille Felder
    Heiligendamm
    Ich sang mich durch das deutsche Land
    Ihr ewigen Sterne
    Im Walde liegt ein stiller See
    Mein Herz, der wilde Rosenstrauch
    Sommersegen
    Spiel ich wo zum Tanze auf
    Spielmannssehen
    Tanzlied
    Tausend stille, weisse, blaue Blumen
    Unter Blüten
    Vor Tau und Tag
    Wenn der Wein nicht wär'
"Le sergent s'en revient de guerre" *see*
    Le retour du sergent Fombeure
    POULENC
Seroe plat'itse see Gippius **PROKOFIEV**
Seroglazyĭ korol' see Akhmatova
  PROKOFIEV
The serpent see Roethke **ROREM**
Serranilla see Santillana **RODRIGO**
Serre chaude see Maeterlinck **CHAUSSON**
Serre d'ennui see Maeterlinck **CHAUSSON**
SERRES CHAUDES, no. 1
  CHAUSSON Maeterlinck *Serre chaude*
SERRES CHAUDES, no. 2
  CHAUSSON Maeterlinck *Serre d'ennui*
SERRES CHAUDES, no. 3
  CHAUSSON Maeterlinck *Lassitude*
SERRES CHAUDES, no. 4
  CHAUSSON Maeterlinck *Fauves las*
SERRES CHAUDES, no. 5
  CHAUSSON Maeterlinck *Oraison*
Ses deux yeux... see Ronsard **SCHMITT**
"Ses deux yeux bruns" *see Ses deux yeux...*
  Ronsard **SCHMITT**
"Settembre, andiamo" *see I Pastori*
  Annunzio **PIZZETTI**

COMPOSER Poet *Title* "First Line"

"Setze mir nicht" *see Lieder aus dem
Schenkenbuch . . .* Goethe **SCHUMANN**
Seufzer see Bjørnson **GRIEG** Suk
Seufzer see Bornowski **LASSEN**
Seufzer see Hölty *DIE NACHTIGALL.*
SCHUBERT
Seufzer see Mörike **WOLF**
Seufzer des Gefangnen see Schütze
ZELTER
Seufzer eines Ungeliebten see Bürger
BEETHOVEN
Seul see Lamartine *LA PENSÉE DES
MORTS.* **GOUNOD**
Seul sur la terre see Carême **SAUGUET**
Seule see Gautier **FAURÉ, HAHN**
"Seule en ta sombre tour aux faîtes dentelés"
see La cloche Hugo **SAINT-SAËNS**
"Seule, une pauvre enfant sans parents" *see
L'orpheline du Tyrol,* ballade élégie
Unknown **ROSSINI**
"Seuls, tous deux, ravis, chantants" *see
Dans les ruines d'une abbaye* Hugo
FAURÉ
SEVEN DANISH SONGS, no. 1
DELIUS Jacobsen *Silken shoes*
SEVEN DANISH SONGS, no. 2
DELIUS Jacobsen *Irmelin*
SEVEN DANISH SONGS, no. 3
DELIUS Drachmann *Summer nights*
SEVEN DANISH SONGS, no. 4
DELIUS Jacobsen *In the seraglio garden*
SEVEN DANISH SONGS, no. 5
DELIUS Jacobsen *Wine roses*
SEVEN DANISH SONGS, no. 6
DELIUS Jacobsen *Through long, long
years*
SEVEN DANISH SONGS, no. 7
DELIUS Jacobsen *Let springtime come
then*
SEVEN ELIZABETHAN LYRICS, no. 1
QUILTER Anon. *Weep you no more*
SEVEN ELIZABETHAN LYRICS, no. 2
QUILTER Campion *My life's delight*
SEVEN ELIZABETHAN LYRICS, no. 3
QUILTER Anon. *Damask roses*
SEVEN ELIZABETHAN LYRICS, no. 4
QUILTER Anon. *The faithless
shepherdess*
SEVEN ELIZABETHAN LYRICS, no. 5
QUILTER Anon. *Brown is my love*
SEVEN ELIZABETHAN LYRICS, no. 6
QUILTER Jonson *By a fountainside*
SEVEN ELIZABETHAN LYRICS, no. 7
QUILTER Anon. *Fair house of joy*
SEVEN LITTLE PRAYERS, no. 1
ROREM Goodman *All men are mad
some way*

SEVEN LITTLE PRAYERS, no. 2
ROREM Goodman *Noblesse obligé, my
Lord*
SEVEN LITTLE PRAYERS, no. 3
ROREM Goodman *Rest well . . .*
SEVEN LITTLE PRAYERS, no. 4
ROREM Goodman *Lord, have not by
custom*
SEVEN LITTLE PRAYERS, no. 5
ROREM Goodman *Hallowed be the
ordainer*
SEVEN LITTLE PRAYERS, no. 6
ROREM Goodman *Man-like, my God*
SEVEN LITTLE PRAYERS, no. 7
ROREM Goodman *Of God, angels . . .*
Seven merry songs in the Aargau dialect see
Anon. **HINDEMITH** *Lieder in Aargauer
Mundart*
Seven November see Khomyakov
BALAKIREV *Sem' noyabrya*
SEVEN SONGS FROM "THE PILGRIM'S
PROGRESS," no. 1
VAUGHAN WILLIAMS Bible
Watchful's song
SEVEN SONGS FROM "THE PILGRIM'S
PROGRESS," no. 2
VAUGHAN WILLIAMS Bunyan
The song of the pilgrims
SEVEN SONGS FROM "THE PILGRIM'S
PROGRESS," no. 3
VAUGHAN WILLIAMS Bible
The pilgrim's psalm
SEVEN SONGS FROM "THE PILGRIM'S
PROGRESS," no. 4
VAUGHAN WILLIAMS Bible *The song
of the leaves of life and the water of life*
SEVEN SONGS FROM "THE PILGRIM'S
PROGRESS," no. 5
VAUGHAN WILLIAMS Vaughan
Williams, U. *The song of Vanity Fair*
SEVEN SONGS FROM "THE PILGRIM'S
PROGRESS," no. 6
VAUGHAN WILLIAMS Bunyan
The woodcutter's song
SEVEN SONGS FROM "THE PILGRIM'S
PROGRESS," no. 7
VAUGHAN WILLIAMS Bible
The bird's song
SEVEN SONNETS OF MICHELANGELO,
no. 1
BRITTEN Buonarroti *Sonetto XVI*
SEVEN SONNETS OF MICHELANGELO,
no. 2
BRITTEN Buonarroti *Sonetto XXXI*
SEVEN SONNETS OF MICHELANGELO,
no. 3
BRITTEN Buonarroti *Sonetto XXX*

SEVEN SONNETS OF MICHELANGELO,
no. 4
BRITTEN Buonarroti *Sonetto LV*
SEVEN SONNETS OF MICHELANGELO,
no. 5
BRITTEN Buonarroti *Sonetto XXXVIII*
SEVEN SONNETS OF MICHELANGELO,
no. 6
BRITTEN Buonarroti *Sonetto XXXII*
SEVEN SONNETS OF MICHELANGELO,
no. 7
BRITTEN Buonarroti *Sonetto XXIV*
SÉVERAC, DÉODAT DE, 1872-1921.
Anon.
Philis (1907) [Rouart Lerolle]
"Par un souris, l'amour"
Audigier, Georges
Prends mon âme (1898) [unpubl.]
Baudelaire, Charles Pierre, 1821-1867.
Les hiboux (1898) [S. Chapelier, 1913;
Rouart Lerolle, 1924]
"Sous les ifs noirs qui les abritent"
Coppée, François Édouard Joachim,
1842-1908.
Ritournelle (before 1898) [unpubl.]
Espinasse-Mongenet, Mme. Louise
Chanson de la nuit durable (1910)
[Rouart Lerolle, 1911]
"Oh! ma petite princesse de clarté"
Estieu, Prosper, 1860-1939.
Cansón pel cabalet [Philippo, 1913;
Rouart Lerolle]
"Petit cheval, qui m'es si cher"
Gauthier-Villars, Henry, 1859-1931.
Temps de neige (1904) [Rouart Lerolle]
"O l'heure douce!"
Goudouli, Pierre, 1580-1649.
Cant per Nadal [Philippo, 1913; Rouart
Lerolle]
"Las! nous n'avons pas l'avantage"
Maeterlinck, Maurice, 1862-1949.
L'infidèle (1900) [Eschig]
Magre, Maurice, 1877-1941.
L'OUVRIER QUI PLEURE.
La chanson de blaisine (1900) [Eschig]
Marguerite d'Angoulême, Queen of
Navarre, 1492-1549.
Albado [Philippo, 1913; Rouart Lerolle]
"Voici ton Jean, ton Jean"
Mestres, Apeles, 1854-1936.
La cançó dels invadits (1917 or 18)
[unpubl.]
No author
Canzone dans le mode hypolidien (1911)
[Leduc]
Vocalise-étude; Collection Hettich.

Poe, Edgar Allan, 1809-1849.
A DREAM.
Un rêve (1902) [Rouart Lerolle, 1903?]
"En des visions de la sombre nuit"
Rey, Paul
Albada a l'Estela (1898) [unpubl.]
Les cors (1898) [Eschig]
ANOMALIE.
Le chevrier (1898) [Eschig]
Ronsard, Pierre de, 1524-1585.
Les amours (1909) [unpubl.?]
May include 3 songs.
Séverac, Déodat de, 1873-1921.
A l'aube dans la Montagne (1903)
[Edition Mutuelle; Rouart Lerolle,
1906] "Le long du ciel grenat"
Ma poupée chérie (1914) [Rouart Lerolle,
1921] same
Unknown
Les Gosses dans les ruines (1918)
[Edition française illustrée]
Le jardin (before 1898) [Édition
Mutuelle; Rouart Lerolle]
Marche Américaine (1918) [unpubl.]
Vabre
Deux mélodies en Langue d'Oc (1910)
[J. Robert]
Verhaeren, Emile, 1855-1916.
LES VIGNES DANS MURAILLE.
L'éveil de Pâques (1899) [Eschig]
Verlaine, Paul, 1844-1896.
PAYSAGES TRISTES.
Soleils couchants (1901) [unpubl.]
SAGESSE.
Le ciel est, par-dessus le toit (1897)
[Édition Mutuelle; Rouart Lerolle,
ca.1904] same
Séverac, Déodat de, 1872-1921.
SÉVERAC
A l'aube dans la Montagne
Ma poupée chérie
Severyanin, Igor, pseud. *see* Lotarev,
Igor' Vasil'evich, 1887-1941.
Sévillana see Anon. **MASSENET**
"Sex, as they harshly call it" *see Song* Rich
WEISGALL
Seyboth, Sofie
REGER
Darum
Die Mutter spricht
Schwäbische Treue
Shadow see Golenishchev-Kutuzov
MUSORGSKIĭ
Okon'en prazdnyĭ, shumnyĭ den'
Shake your brown feet, Honey see Hughes,
L. *THE WEARY BLUES.* **CARPENTER**

COMPOSER Poet *Title* "First Line"

SHAKESPEARE SONGS, no. 1
  THOMSON Shakespeare *Was this fair face*
SHAKESPEARE SONGS, no. 2
  THOMSON Shakespeare *Take, O take those lips away*
SHAKESPEARE SONGS, no. 3
  THOMSON Shakespeare *Tell me where is fancy bred*
SHAKESPEARE SONGS, no. 4
  THOMSON Shakespeare *Pardon, Goddess of the night*
SHAKESPEARE SONGS, no. 5
  THOMSON Shakespeare *Sigh no more, ladies*
Shakespeare, William, 1564-1616.
  BERLIOZ *La mort d'Ophélie*
  BLITZSTEIN
    Lullaby
    Vendor's song
  DIAMOND
    For shame deny that thou bear'st love to any
    Let me confess that we two must be twain
    My love is as a fever longing still
    No longer mourn for me when I am dead
    O from what power hast thou this powerful might
    Shall I compare thee to a summer's day?
    Those pretty wrongs that liberty commits
    When in disgrace with fortune and men's eyes
    When to the sessions of set silent thought
  QUILTER
    Blow, blow, thou winter wind
    Hark, hark the lark
  SAUGUET
    Chanson
    Je te vois en rêve
    To my fair friend you never can be old
    Weary with toil
  SEIBER *Sonnet*
ALL'S WELL THAT ENDS WELL.
  THOMSON *Was this fair face*
ANTONY AND CLEOPATRA.
  SCHUBERT *Trinklied*
AS YOU LIKE IT.
  CARPENTER *In spring*
  DELIUS *It was a lover and his lass*
  HESELTINE *Pretty ring time*
  LOEWE *Komm herbei, komm herbei, Tod!*
  QUILTER
    It was a lover and his lass
    Under the greenwood tree
  RIETI *It was a lover and his lass*

CYMBELINE.
  QUILTER *Fear no more the heat o' the sun*
  SCHUBERT *Ständchen*
HAMLET.
  LASSEN
    Auf Morgen ist Sanct Valentinstag
    Denn traut lieb Robin ist all' mein Lust!
    Sein Bahrtuch weiss wie Bergesschnee
    Sein Bart war weiss wie Bergesschnee
    Sie trugen ihn barhaupt auf der Bahr
    Und kommt er denn nimmer zurück?
    Wie erkenn' ich dein Treulieb
  LOEWE *Totengräberlied*
  QUILTER *How should I your true love know?*
  ROREM *Ophelia's lament*
  STRAUSS
    Guten Morgen, 's ist Sankt Valentinstag
    Sie trugen ihn auf der Bahre bloss
    Wie erkenn' ich mein Treulieb?
  THOMSON
    How should I your true love know
    Song for the Gravedigger
    They bore him barefac'd on the bier
    Tomorrow is Saint Valentine's day
HAMLET: He is dead & gone, lady.
  CHAUSSON *Chanson d'Ophélie*
KING HENRY VIII.
  LASSEN *Lied aus Heinrich VIII*
  QUILTER, VAUGHAN WILLIAMS
    Orpheus with his lute
      Two Vaughan Williams settings: 1902 and 1925.
LOVE'S LABOUR'S LOST.
  HESELTINE *Mockery*
  QUILTER, VAUGHAN WILLIAMS
    When icicles hang by the wall
MEASURE FOR MEASURE.
  HESELTINE, QUILTER, THOMSON, VAUGHAN WILLIAMS
    Take, O take those lips away
      Two Heseltine settings: 1916-17 and 1918-19.
MEASURE FOR MEASURE: Take, O take those lips away.
  CHAUSSON *Chanson d'amour*
MERCHANT OF VENICE.
  BRITTEN *Fancie*
  CARTER *Tell me where is fancy bred?*
  POULENC *Fancy*
  QUILTER *Tell me, where is fancy bred?*
  THOMSON
    Look, how the floor of heav'n
    Tell me where is fancy bred

COMPOSER Poet *Title* ''First Line''

MIDSUMMER NIGHT'S DREAM: Bottom's song.
> **WOLF** *Lied des transferierten Zettel*

MUCH ADO ABOUT NOTHING.
> **HESELTINE, QUILTER** *Sigh no more, ladies*
> **THOMSON**
>> *Pardon, Goddess of the night*
>> *Sigh no more, ladies*

OTELLO.
> **LOEWE** *Lied der Desdemona*

ROMEO AND JULIET.
> **BLACHER**
>> *Die einst'ge Sehnsucht*
>> *So wilde Freude nimmt ein wildes Ende*
>> *Zwei hohe Häuser, gleich an Würdigkeit*

THE TEMPEST.
> **DIAMOND**
>> *Come unto these yellow sands*
>> *Full fathom five*
>> *No more dams I'll make for fish*
>> *Where the bee sucks*
>> *While you here do snoring lie*
> **HONEGGER**
>> *Modéré-Plus lent*
>> *Un peu animé*
> **QUILTER**
>> *Come unto these yellow sands*
>> *Full fathom five*
>> *Where the bee sucks*

TWELFTH NIGHT.
> **CARPENTER** *Mistress mine*
> **CHANLER** *O mistress mine!*
> **HESELTINE** *Sweet-and-twenty*
> **QUILTER**
>> *Come away, Death*
>> *Hey, ho, the wind and the rain*
>> *O mistress mine*
> **SIBELIUS**
>> *Kom nu hit, död*
>> *Ock nör som jag ver en liten smadrang*

TWELFTH NIGHT: Come away, come away, death.
> **CHAUSSON** *Chanson de clown*

TWELFTH NIGHT: When that I was and a little tiny boy.
> **SCHUMANN** *Schlusslied des Narren*

TWO GENTLEMEN OF VERONA.
> **QUILTER** *Who is Silvia?*
> **SCHUBERT** *An Sylvia*

A WINTER'S TALE.
> **BLITZSTEIN** *Shepherd's song*
> **HESELTINE** *The sweet o' the year*
> **IRELAND, QUILTER** *When daffodils begin to peer*

Shall I compare thee to a summer's day? see Shakespeare **DIAMOND**
"Shall I compare thee to a summer's day?" *see Sonnet* Shakespeare **SEIBER**
Shall I forget thee? see Tavaststjerna **SIBELIUS** *Långsamt som qvällskyn*
"Shall we gather at the river" *see At the river* Lowry **IVES**
"Shall we gather by the river" *see At the river* Lowry **COPLAND**
"Shall we go dance the hay, the hay?" *see A report song* Breton **IRELAND**
"Shall we roam, my love, to the twilight grove" *see To the queen of my heart* Shelley **DELIUS**
Shanks, Edward Buxton, 1892-1953.
> *THE QUEEN OF CHINA AND OTHER POEMS* (1919).
>> **HESELTINE**
>>> *Late summer*
>>> *The singer*

Shapiro, Karl Jay, 1913-2000.
> **ROREM** *Mongolian idiot*

Sharp, William, 1885-1905.
> **LUENING**
>> *Noon silence*
>> *Venilia*
> **SIBELIUS** *A cavalry catch*
> *FOAM OF THE PAST.*
>> **GRIFFES** *The lament of Ian the proud*
> *FROM THE HILLS OF DREAMS.*
>> **GRIFFES** *Thy dark eyes to mine*
> *THE HOUR OF BEAUTY.*
>> **DELIUS** *I-Brasil*
>> **GRIFFES** *The rose of the night*

Sharpe, William *see* Sharp, William, 1885-1905.
Shchekoiu k shcheke ty moeĭ prilozhis' see Heine *LYRICAL INTERMEZZO.*
> **RIMSKIĬ-KORSAKOV**

Shcherbina, Nikelaĭ Fedorovich, 1821-1869.
> **CHAĬKOVSKIĬ** *Primiren'e*
> **RIMSKIĬ-KORSAKOV** *IUzhnaia noch'*

"She is all so slight" *see After two years* Aldington **HESELTINE**
She is as lovely as the moon see Vilenkin **RACHMANINOFF**
"She is gentle and also wise" *see As ever I saw* Anon. **HESELTINE**
"She is so proper and so pure" *see Piggesnie* Anon. **HESELTINE**
"She loved me as a child" *see The muse* Pushkin **MEDTNER**
She loves me! see Goethe *ERWIN UND ELMIRE.* **MEDTNER** *Sie liebt mich!*

"She stood by the image" *see Before the icon*
    Golenishchev-Kutuzov
    RACHMANINOFF
She walks in beauty see Byron **LUENING**
She weeps over Rahoon see Joyce **GIDEON**
SHÉHÉRAZADE. see Leclère, translator
    Chanson de flûte **KOECHLIN**
    Chanson d'Engaddi **KOECHLIN**
    La chanson des beaux amants **KOECHLIN**
    Chanson d'Ishak de Mossoul **KOECHLIN**
    Dédicace **KOECHLIN**
    Offrande **KOECHLIN**
    L'oiseau en cage **KOECHLIN**
    La neige **KOECHLIN**
    Paysage **KOECHLIN**
    Le potier **KOECHLIN**
    La rose du rameau sec **KOECHLIN**
    Le ventre merveilleux **KOECHLIN**
    Le voyage **KOECHLIN**
Shel stanitseiu kazak see Panch
    PROKOFIEV
Shelley, Percy Bysshe, 1792-1822.
    BENNETT *The past*
    DELIUS
        Love's philosophy
        To the queen of my heart
    DIAMOND *Lift not the painted veil*
    GOUNOD
        The fountain mingles with the river
        Good night
    HINDEMITH *The moon*
    IVES
        Rough wind
        The world's wanderers
    JENSEN *An die Nacht*
    LUENING
        Goodnight
        I faint, I perish
        A Roman's chamber
        Wake the serpent not
    NIELSEN *Til mit Hjertes Dronning*
    QUILTER
        Arab love song
        Love's philosophy
        Music
        Music and moonlight
        One word is too often profaned
    RESPIGHI
        Canto funebre
        Serenata indiana
        Su una violetta morta
        I tempi assai lontani
    ROREM *To Jane*
    SCHUMANN *Die Flüchtlinge*
    THE INDIAN SERENADE.
        DELIUS *Indian love song*

THE ISLE.
    RACHMANINOFF *The isle*
POSTHUMOUS POEMS (1824).
    DIAMOND, HESELTINE, QUILTER
        Music, when soft voices die
Shelly's vision see Melville **ROREM**
Shenshin, Afanasiĭ Afanas'evich, 1820-
    1892.
    BALAKIREV
        Shopot, robkoye dĭkhan'ye
        Ya prishol k tebe s privetom
    CHAĬKOVSKIĬ
        IA tebe nichego ne skazhu'
        Mezza notte
        Moy geniy, moy angel, moy drug
        Poymi khotraz
    MEDTNER
        Beauty
        Butterfly
        Dawn in the garden
        Greeting
        Humble yet valiant
        Impromptu
        Prayer for rain
        Serenade
        Waltz
    RACHMANINOFF
        For long there has been little consolation
        I shall tell you nothing
        In the silence of the secret night
        The peasant
        What happiness
    RIMSKIĬ-KORSAKOV
        IA prishel k tebe s privetom
        Shopot, robkoe dykhan'e
        Svezh i dushist tvoĭ
        Tikho vecher dogoraet
GAFIZ.
    RIMSKIĬ-KORSAKOV *V tsarstvo rozy*
        i vina-pridi
MELODII.
    CHAĬKOVSKIĬ *Ne otkhodi ot menia*
PEVITSE: Unosi moe Serdtse.
    CHAĬKOVSKIĬ *Unosi moe serdtse*
Shenstone, William, 1714-1763.
    LOEWE *Lied der Königin Elisabeth*
Shên-Yo, 441-513.
    BERKELEY *Dreaming of a dead lady*
The shepherd see Blake, William
    VAUGHAN WILLIAMS
A shepherd see De La Mare **CHANLER**
The shepherd boy sings in the valley of
    humiliation see Bunyan **DIAMOND**
"A shepherd, Ned Vaughan" *see A shepherd*
    De La Mare **CHANLER**
Shepherd's song see Shakespeare
    A WINTER'S TALE. **BLITZSTEIN**

A shepherd's Sunday song *see* Uhland
  MARTINŮ
Shepot robkoe dykhan'e see Shenshin
  MEDTNER *Dawn in the garden*
"She's neither scholarly nor wise" *see My*
  sweetheart Alexander, G. **CARPENTER**
Shevchenko, Taras, 1814-1861.
  CHAĬKOVSKIĬ *Vecher*
  MUSORGSKIĬ *Na Dnepre*
  RACHMANINOFF
    Again I am alone
    I have grown fond of sorrow
    Meditation
    GAĬDAMAKI.
      MUSORGSKIĬ *Gopak*
Shilrik und Vinvela see Macpherson
  CARRIC-THURA. **SCHUBERT**
The ship of Rio see De La Mare *PEACOCK*
  PIE. **BRITTEN, CHANLER**
The ship starting see Whitman
  THOMPSON, R.
"Shla devītsa proguliat'sia" *see Kozel*
  Musorgski **MUSORGSKIĬ**
The shoemaker see Anon. **HESELTINE**
"Shoemaker, shoemaker, are ye within?" *see*
  The shoemaker Anon. **HESELTINE**
Shopot, robkoe dykhan'e see Shenshin
  RIMSKIĬ-KORSAKOV
Shopot, robkoye dīkhan'ye see Shenshin
  BALAKIREV
Shoukovsky *see* Zhukovski, Vasiliĭ
  Andreyevich, 1783-1852.
Shove, Fredegond, 1889-1949.
  VAUGHAN WILLIAMS
    Four nights
    Motion & stillness
    The new ghost
    The water mill
The show is not the show see Dickinson
  LUENING
THE SHROPSHIRE LAD. see Housman
  The encounter **IRELAND**
  Epilogue **IRELAND**
  Goal and wicket **IRELAND**
  Hawthorn time **IRELAND**
  The heart's desire **IRELAND**
  Ladslove **IRELAND**
  The Lent lily **IRELAND**
  The vain desire **IRELAND**
A SHROPSHIRE LAD: V. *see* Housman
  Goodbye **VAUGHAN WILLIAMS**
A SHROPSHIRE LAD: XXVI. *see* Housman
  Along the field **VAUGHAN WILLIAMS**
A SHROPSHIRE LAD: XXVII. *see*
  Housman *Is my team ploughing?*
  VAUGHAN WILLIAMS

A SHROPSHIRE LAD: LIV. *see* Housman
  With rue my heart is laden **BARBER,**
    RIEGGER, VAUGHAN WILLIAMS
"Shut not so soon" *see*
  To daisies, not to shut so soon Herrick
  ROREM
"Shut not so soon, the dull-eyed night" *see*
  To daisies Herrick **QUILTER**
Si . . . see Ronsard **SCHMITT**
"Sì come nella penna e nell'inchiostro" *see*
  Sonetto XVI Buonarroti **BRITTEN**
Si con mis deseos see Vega Carpio
  LA ESTRELLA DE SEVILLA. **TURINA**
Si de mon premier rêve see Silvestre
  AUBERT
"Si désormais vivre ensemble" *see*
  La dernière chanson Lefèbvre
  MASSENET
"Si Dieu bénit la naissance des roses" *see*
  L'ombre de Dieu Lehugeur, A. **LALO**
"Si j'ai parlé de mon amour" *see Odelette*
  Régnier **AUBERT**
"Si j'avais le talent de Constantin Guys" *see*
  Le tilbury Chalupt **AURIC**
Si j'avais l'univers see Zaffira **GOUNOD**
  Se come io son poeta
Si je l'osais see Tranchant, Alfred
  SAINT-SAËNS
"Si je me penche sur le pont" *see Le ruisseau*
  Paliard **MILHAUD**
"Si je n'étais captive" *see La captive* Hugo
  BERLIOZ
"Si je pouvais chanter encore" *see Chanson*
  désespérée Teulet, Edmond **MASSENET**
"Si j'étais le bon Dieu qui donne" *see Le nid*
  Demouth, Paul **MASSENET**
"Si j'étais le Zéphyr ailé" *see Zéphyr*
  Banville **DEBUSSY**
"Si j'étais, O mon amoureuse" *see Sérénade*
  Marc, Gabriel **DUPARC**
Si j'étais petit oiseau see Béranger **LALO**
Si la mort est le but see Bertin **GOUNOD**
"Si la palmera supiera que el Niño" *see*
  Copillas de Belen Kamhi, Victoria
  RODRIGO
"Si la voix d'un enfant peut monter jusqu'à
  vous" *see En prière* Bordèse **FAURÉ**
"Si le bonheur à sourire t'invite" *see À une*
  soeur Pradère-Niquet **GOUNOD**
"Si le bonheur à sourire t'invite" *see*
  Marguerite Pradère-Niquet **GOUNOD**
Si le mal d'amour see Zimmer, Bernard
  HONEGGER
"Si l'enfant som meille" *see Berceuse*
  Desbordes-Valmore **BIZET**
"Si les roses poussaient nous rendre le baiser"
  see Madrigal Bourget **LOEFFLER**

"Si l'on veut savoir qui m'envoie" *see Envoi de fleurs* Augier **GOUNOD**

Si mes vers avaient des ailes see Hugo **GRIFFES, HAHN, LASSEN**

"Si mille oeillets, si mille lys j'embrasse" *see Si...* Ronsard **SCHMITT**

Si mon coeur avait des ailes... see Aubanel, T. **SCHMITT**

"Si mon marin vous le chassez" *see Cimetière* Jacob, M. **POULENC**

Si morne! see Verhaeren *LES DÉBÂCLES.* **RAVEL**

Si quelquefois tu pleures... see Ville **ROUSSEL**

"Si, si, si. . . . ." *see Valse des Si* No author **SAUGUET**

"Si tes pas t'ont conduit vers l'heureuse vallée" *see La nymphe de la source* Unknown **HAHN**

"Si ton front est comme un roseau" *see Chanson* Mendès **HAHN**

Si tout ceci n'est qu'un pauvre rêve see Jammes *TRISTESSES.* **BOULANGER, MILHAUD**

Si tu beux see Hugo **RESPIGHI**

"Si tu demandes quelque soir" *see Les présents* Villiers **FAURÉ**

"Si tu dors, jeune fille" *see Viens, les gazons sont verts* Barbier, J. **GOUNOD**

Si tu l'oses see Mansilla, Daniel Garcia **MASSENET**

Si tu m'aimes see Duverne, Anne Girard **MASSENET**

Si tu pouvais see Jammes **MILHAUD**

"Si tu savais que je t'adore" *see L'émir de Bengador* Méry **FRANCK**

"Si tu veux, faisons un rêve" *see L'enlèvement* Hugo **SAINT-SAËNS**

"Si tu veux je te donnerai" *see Le Présent* Laurencin **POULENC**

Si tu veux, Mignonne see Boyer, Georges **MASSENET**

"Si tu veux savoir ma belle" *see Sylvie* Choudens **FAURÉ**

Si vous aimez! see Gille **BIZET**

"Si vous cherchez Monsieur le Curé" *see Monsieur le Curé* Paliard **MILHAUD**

"Si vous donnez le calme aprés tant de secousses" *see Les larmes* Blanchecotte **CHAïKOVSKIï**

"Si vous étiez fleur" *see Souhait* Normand **MASSENET**

"Si vous me disiez que la terre" *see Chanson romantique* Morand **RAVEL**

Si vous n'avez rien à me dire see Hugo **LASSEN, SAINT-SAËNS**

Si vous n'ouvrez vôtre fenêtre see Dumas the younger **GOUNOD**

Si vous vouliez bien me le dire see Ludana **MASSENET**

Siam' iti l'altro giorno see Zaffira **GOUNOD**

SIBELIUS, JEAN, 1865-1957.

Borgström
Hymn to Thais (1900) [unpubl.]

Busse-Palma, Georg, 1876-1915.
Erloschen (1906) [Suomen Musiikkilehti]

Dehmel, Richard, 1863-1920.
Aus banger Brust, op. 50 no. 4 (1906) [Robert Lienau, 1907] "Die Rosen leuchten immer noch"
Die stille Stadt, op. 50 no. 5 (1906) [Robert Lienau, 1907] "Liegt eine Stadt im Tale"

Dixon, Richard Watson, 1833-1900.
Autumn song (1913) [Silver Burdett *Progressive music series,* 1915] "The feathers of the willow"

Fitger, Arthur, 1840-1909.
Lenzgesang, op. 50 no. 1 (1906) [Robert Lienau, 1907] "Seid grüsst, ihr grünen Hallen"

Franzén, Franz Mikael, bishop, 1772-1847.
De bägge rosorna, op. 88 no. 2 (1917) [W. Hansen, 1923] "Rosen, ja, Rosen likväl är skönast"
Blåsippan, op. 88 no. 1 (1917) [W. Hansen, 1923] "Hvad lärkan bådat har från skyn"
Hvitsippan, op. 88 no. 3 (1917) [W. Hansen, 1923] "Se hvitsippan hur täck hon är"

Frey, Friedrich Hermann, 1830-1911.
Der Wanderer und der Bach, op. 72 no. 5 (1915) [Breitkopf & Härtel, 1916] "Wohin, O Bächlein, schnelle?"

Fröding, Gustaf, 1860-1911.
Bollspelet vid Trianon, op. 36 no. 3 (1899) [Breitkopf & Härtel, 1904] "Gossip and tennis and clash and clatter"
Also voice & orchestra, unpublished.
Jag ville jag vore i Indialand, op. 38 no. 5 (1904) [Breitkopf & Härtel, 1904] same
Men min fågel märks dock icke, op. 36 no. 2 (1899) [Breitkopf & Härtel, 1904] "Svanen speglas re'n i sundet"
Music attributes text to Rundberg.
INGALILL.
Säf, säf, susa, op. 36 no. 4 (1899) [Breitkopf & Härtel, 1904] "Reed, reed, rustle!"

Gripenberg, Bertil, 1878-1947.
Narsissi (1918?) [R. E. Westerlund Oy;
Ed. Fazer, 1967]
"O blaa nätter i var ungdomspark"
Teodora, op. 35 no. 2 (1907-08)
[Breitkopf & Härtel, 1910]
"Det frasar af silke"
Vårtagen, op. 61 no. 8 (1910)
[Breitkopf & Härtel, 1911]
"Nu susar var genom solbla luft"

Hedberg, Tor Harald, 1862-1931.
Soluppgång, op. 37 no. 3 (1902)
[Breitkopf & Härtel, 1904]
"Under himlens purpurbrand"

Josephson, Ernst Abraham, 1851-1906.
Älvan och snigeln, op. 57 no. 1 (1909)
[Robert Lienau, 1910]
"Den breda elf genom skogens barm"
En blomma stod vid vägen, op. 57 no. 2
(1909) [Robert Lienau, 1910] same
Hertig Magnus, op. 57 no. 6 (1909)
[Robert Lienau, 1910]
"Hertig Magnus fran sitt fönster"
Jag är ett träd, op. 57 no. 5 (1909)
[Robert Lienau, 1910] same
Jubal, op. 35 no. 1 (1907-08)
[Breitkopf & Härtel, 1910]
"Jubal sag en svana fly öfver vattnet
högt mot sky"
Also voice & orchestra.
Kvarnhjulet, op. 57 no. 3 (1909) [Robert
Lienau, 1910]
"Dränkt i tjära qvarn hjulet gar"
Maj, op. 57 no. 4 (1909) [Robert Lienau,
1910]
"Luften är solig och skyarna tindra"
Necken, op. 57 no. 8 (1909) [Robert
Lienau, 1910]
"Djup stod färgen pa fura och pa sten"
Vänskapens blomma, op. 57 no. 7 (1909)
[Robert Lienau, 1910]
"Ack, vänskap, ljufva blomma"
SVARTA ROSOR OCH GULA.
Svarta rosor, op. 36 no. 1 (1899)
[Breitkopf & Härtel, 1904]
"Säg hvarför är du sa ledsen i dag"

Joukahainen, Wilkku
On hanget korkeat, op. 1 no. 5 [R. E.
Westerlund Oy, 1919; Ed. Fazer, 1967]
same

Karlfeldt, Erik Axel, 1864-1931.
Längtan heter min arvedel, op. 86 no. 2
(1916) [W. Hansen, 1923] same

Kianto, Ilmari, 1874-1970.
Lastu lainehilla, op. 17 no. 7 (1898)
[Breitkopf & Härtel, 1906]
"Mistä lastu lainehilla?"

Koskimies, Aukusti Valdemar, 1856-1929.
Illalle, op. 17 no. 6 (1898) [Brcitkopf &
Härtel, 1906]
"Oi, terve! tumma, vieno tähtiilta"
Souda, souda sinisorsa (1899) [Frazerin
Musiikkikaupa Oy, 1899] same

Larin-Kyösti, 1873-1948.
Kaiutar, op. 72 no. 4 (1915)
[Breitkopf & Härtel, 1916]
"Kaiutar, korea neito astui illalla ahoa"

Levertin, Oskar Ivar, 1862-1906.
En slända, op. 17 no. 5 (1894?)
[Breitkopf & Härtel, 1907]
"Du vackra slända, som till mig flög
in"

Lybeck, Mikael, 1864-1925.
I systrar, I bröder, op. 86 no. 6 (1916)
[W. Hansen, 1923]
"Tre systrar de häkla sin moders lin"

Öhqvist
Segelfahrt (1899) [*Brohige blad*, 1899]

Procopé, Hjalmar, 1868-1927.
Små flickorna (1920) [*Lucifer*, 1920]

Ritter, Anna (Nuhn), 1865-1921.
Rosenlied, op. 50 no. 6 (1906) [Robert
Lienau, 1907] "Wir senkten die
Wurzeln in Moos und Gestein"

Runeberg, Johann Ludvig, 1804-1877.
Arioso, op. 3 (1893; rev. 1913) [R. E.
Westerlund Oy]
"Talviaamull'astui tyttö huurteisessa"
Also voice & string orchestra.
Blommans öde, op. 88 no. 6 (1917)
[W. Hansen, 1923] "Barn af våren"
Drömmen, op. 13 no. 5 (1891)
[Breitkopf & Härtel, 1904]
"Once, when weary, on my bed I laid
me"
Fåfäng önskan, op. 61 no. 7 (1910)
[Breitkopf & Härtel, 1911]
"O taliga vagor vandra"
Fågelfängaren, op. 90 no. 4 (1917)
[R. E. Westerlund Oy; W. Hansen]
"Jag vandrar fram pa skogens ban"
Flickan kom ifrån sin älsklings möte, op.
37 no. 5 (1901) [Breitkopf & Härtel]
same
Den första kyssen, op. 37 no. 1 (1898)
[Breitkopf & Härtel]
"Thro' silver clouds the ev'ning star
was stealing"
Hennes budskap, op. 90 no. 2 (1917)
[R. E. Westerlund Oy; W. Hansen]
"Kom du sorgsna nordan!"
Hjärtats morgon, op. 13 no. 3 (1891)
[Breitkopf & Härtel, 1906]
"Mörker radde i mitt sinne"

SIBELIUS, JEAN, 1865-1957 *(continued)*
  Runeberg, Johann Ludvig, 1804-1877
  (continued)
    Hundra vägar, op. 72 no. 6 (1907)
      [Breitkopf & Härtel, 1916]
      "Store skapare, förlåt det"
    Hvem styrde hit din väg? op. 90 no. 6
      (1917) [R. E. Westerlund Oy; W.
      Hansen]
      "Langt bortom fjärdens vag"
    Jägargossen, op. 13 no. 7 (1891)
      [Breitkopf & Härtel, 1904]
      "The birds take cover on the ground"
    Kyssens hopp, op. 13 no. 2 (1892)
      [Breitkopf & Härtel, 1906]
      "Der jag satt i drömmar vid en källa"
    Morgonen, op. 90 no. 3 (1917) [R. E.
      Westerlund Oy; W. Hansen]
      "Solennagra purpurdroppar re'n pa
      österns skyar stänkt"
    Norden, op. 90 no. 1 (1917) [R. E.
      Westerlund Oy; W. Hansen]
      "Löfvende falla sjöarna frysa"
    Se'n har jag ej fr\aagat mera, op. 17 no.
      1 (1894) [Breitkopf & Härtel, 1904-
      1908] "Hvarför är sa flyktig varen"
      Also voice & orchestra, unpublished.
    Serenade (1888) [*Det sjungande
      Finland,* no. 45, 1888]
    Sippan, op. 88 no. 4 (1917) [W. Hansen,
      1923] "Sippa, vårens första blomma"
    Sommarnatten, op. 90 no. 5 (1917) [R. E.
      Westerlund Oy; W. Hansen]
      "Pa den lugna skogs sjöns vatten satt
      jag hela"
    Till Frigga, op. 13 no. 6 (1892)
      [Breitkopf & Härtel, 1906]
      "Mig ej lockar din skatt"
    Törnet, op. 88 no. 5 (1917) [W. Hansen,
      1923] "Törne du min syskonplanta"
    Under strandens granar, op. 13 no. 1
      (1892) [Breitkopf & Härtel, 1906]
      same
    Våren flyktar hastigt, op. 13 no. 4 (1891)
      [Breitkopf & Härtel, 1904] same
      Also voice & orchestra, unpublished.
  Rydberg, Viktor, 1828-1895.
    Harpolekaren och hans son, op. 38 no. 4
      (1904) [Breitkopf & Härtel, 1904]
      "Luften tung och dagen varm"
    Höstkväll, op. 38 no. 1 (1903)
      [Breitkopf & Härtel, 1906]
      "Solen gar ned"
      Also voice & orchestra, 1907.
    I natten, op. 38 no. 3 (1903)
      [Breitkopf & Härtel, 1906]
      "Tyst är lunden och sjön"

      Also voice & orchestra, unpublished.
    Kyssen, op. 72 no. 3 (1915) [Breitkopf &
      Härtel, 1916]
      "Räck mig de väna läpparnes Kalk"
    På verandan vid havet, op. 38 no. 2
      (1902) [Breitkopf & Härtel, 1904-
      1908] "Minns du de skimrande
      böljornas suck"
      Also voice & orchestra, unpublished.
    Vattenplask, op. 61 no. 2 (1910)
      [Breitkopf & Härtel, 1911]
      "Invid palatsen lagunens vatten"
    Vi ses igen, op. 72 no. 1 (1914)
      [Breitkopf & Härtel, 1916]
  Scott, Sir Walter, bart., 1771-1832.
    The sun upon the lake is low (1913)
      [Silver Burdett *Progressive music
      series,* 1915] same
  Shakespeare, William, 1564-1616.
    TWELFTH NIGHT.
      Kom nu hit, död, op. 60 no. 1 (1909)
        [Breitkopf & Härtel, 1911]
        "Kom nu hit, kom nu hit dod"
        Voice & piano or guitar.
      *Ock nör som jag ver en liten
        smadrang,* op. 60 no. 2 (1909)
        [Breitkopf & Härtel, 1911] same
        Voice & piano or guitar.
  Sharp, William, 1885-1905.
    A cavalry catch (1913) [Silver Burdett
      Progressive music series, 1915]
      "Up! for the bugles are calling"
  Snoilsky, Karl Johan Gustaf, grefve,
  1841-1903.
    Dold förening, op. 86 no. 3 (1916) [W.
      Hansen, 1923]
      "Två vattenliljor ur svallet stå"
    Sångarlön, op. 86 no. 5 (1916) [W.
      Hansen, 1923]
      "Gick du en morgon i vårsols sken"
  Susman, Margarete, 1872-1966.
    Im Feld ein Mädchen singt, op. 50 no. 3
      (1906) [Robert Lienau, 1907] same
  Tavaststjerna, Karl August, 1860-1898.
    Dolce far niente, op. 61 no. 6 (1910)
      [Breitkopf & Härtel, 1911]
      "Jag lefver min dag i drömmar"
    Fågellek, op. 17 no. 3 (1891)
      [Breitkopf & Härtel, 1904-1908]
      "Daggen har duggat"
      Also voice & orchestra, unpublished.
    Långsamt som qvällskyn, op. 61 no. 1
      (1910) [Breitkopf & Härtel, 1911]
      same
    När jag drömmer, op. 61 no. 3 (1910)
      [Breitkopf & Härtel, 1911]

"Pa fjärdens silfverbricka en fläck det syns"
Och finns det en tanke? op. 86 no. 4 (1916) [W. Hansen, 1923] same
Romance, op. 61 no. 5 (1910) [Breitkopf & Härtel, 1911] "Prinsessan är du och prinsen är jag"
Romeo, op. 61 no. 4 (1910) [Breitkopf & Härtel, 1911] "Om du en natt helt plötsligt hörde strängar"
Sof in! op. 17 no. 2 (1894) [Breitkopf & Härtel, 1904-1908] "Min bleka sjukling skall luta" Also voice & orchestra, unpublished.
Vår förnimmelser, op. 86 no. 1 (1916) [W. Hansen, 1923] "Öfver drifvans iskristall"
Vilse, op. 17 no. 4 (1894) [Breitkopf & Härtel, 1904] "Vi gingo väl vilse ifran hvarann hvar togo de andra vägen?"
Topelius, Zacharius, 1818-1898.
Giv mig ej glans, op. 1 no. 4 [R. E. Westerlund Oy, 1919; Ed. Fazer, 1967] same
Lasse liten, op. 37 no. 2 (1902) [Breitkopf & Härtcl, 1906] "Werlden är sa stor, sa stor"
Det mörknar ute, op. 1 no. 3 [R. E. Westerlund Oy, 1919; Ed. Fazer, 1967] same
Nu så kommer julen, op. 1 no. 2 [R. E. Westerlund Oy, 1919; Ed. Fazer, 1967] same
Nu står jul vid snöig port, op. 1 no. 1 [R. E. Westerlund Oy, 1919; Ed. Fazer, 1967] same
Orions bälte, op. 72 no. 2 (1914) [Breitkopf & Härtel, 1916]
Wecksell, Josef Julius, 1838-1907.
Demanten på marssnön, op. 36 no. 6 (1899) [Breitkopf & Härtel, 1912] "Pa drifvans snö där glimmar"
Marssnön, op. 36 no. 5 (1899) [Breitkopf & Härtel, 1912] "Den svala snön därute faller och täcker marken mer"
Var det en dröm? op. 37 no. 4 (1902) [Breitkopf & Härtel, 1906] same
Weiss, Emil Rudolf, 1875-1942.
Sehnsucht, op. 50 no. 2 (1906) [Robert Lienau, 1907] "Oft am langen Tage seufz' ich, ach!"
Wennerberg, Gunnar, 1817-1901.
Näcken (1888) [unpubl.]
Sicche t'inganni, O Clori see **Anon. WEBER**
Canzonetta: Italienisches Ständchen

"Sicheln schallen, Ähren fallen" *see Erntelied* Hölty **SCHUBERT**
Sicilian lullaby see Field, Eugene **CARPENTER**
Siciliano see Rhinelander **THOMPSON, R.**
The sick heart see Symons *THE LOOM OF DREAMS.* **HESELTINE**
The sick rose see Blake, William **ROREM**
The side show see Ives **IVES**
Sidery **SAUGUET** *La marchande d'anémondes*
Sidney, Sir Philip, 1554-1586. **IRELAND** *My true love hath my heart* **RIETI** *Voices at the window ASTROPHEL AND STELLA* (1591): First song. **HESELTINE** *Dedication*
"Sie blasen zum Abmarsch" *see En campaña, madre* Anon. **JENSEN**
Sie blasen zum Abmarsch, lieb Mütterlein see Anon. **WOLF**
Sie floh vor mir see Heine **FRANZ**
"Sie führten ihn durch den grauen Hof" *see Jane Grey* Ammann **SCHÖNBERG**
Sie geht in Schönheit see Byron **LOEWE**
Sie haben heut' Abend Gesellschaft see Heine *LIEDERSTRAUSS.* **PFITZNER, WOLF**
"Sie haben mich geheissen" *see Die Waise* Chamisso **GRIEG**
Sie haben wegen der Trunkenheit see Goethe *WESTÖSTLICHER DIVAN:* Schenkenbuch. **WOLF**
"Sie hat die ganze Nacht getobt" *see Meeresabend* Strachwitz **LASSEN**
"Sie hüpfte mit mir auf grünem Plan" *see Ueber allen Zauber Liebe* Mayrhofer **SCHUBERT**
"Sie ist dahin" *see Auf den Tod einer Nachtigall* Hölty **SCHUBERT**
"Sie ist gegangen" *see Nachwirkung* Meissner **BRAHMS**
"Sie konnte mir kein Wörtchen sagen" *see Das Geheimniss* Schiller **SCHUBERT** Two settings: D. 250 and D. 793.
SIE KONNTE MIR KEIN WÖRTCHEN SAGEN. see Schiller *Das Geheimniss* **SCHUBERT** Two settings: D. 250 and D. 793.
Sie liebt mich! see Goethe *ERWIN UND ELMIRE.* **MEDTNER**
"Sie liebte ihn, er liebte sie" *see Rüberettig* Häring **LOEWE**
"Sie liebten sich beide" *see Erste Liebe* Heine **LOEWE**
Sie liebten sich beide see Heine **FRANZ**
"Sie machte Frieden!" *see Auf den Tod einer Kaiserin* Claudius, M. **SCHOECK**

COMPOSER   Poet   *Title*   ''First Line''

"Sie schlingt um meinen Nacken" *see*
  Ein Gedanke Schulz **SCHUMANN**
"Sie schossen ihn tot am Neunsteinberg" *see*
  Berthrams Grablied Scott **JENSEN**
"Sie sind in Paris!" *see Die Befreier Europas*
  in Paris Mikan **SCHUBERT**
Sie singt ein Lied see Rostopchina
  RUBINSTEIN
"Sie stand wohl am Fensterbogen" *see Parole*
  Eichendorff **BRAHMS**
"Sie trug den Becher in der Hand" *see Die*
  Beiden Hofmannsthal **SCHÖNBERG**
"Sie trug einen Falken auf ihrer Hand" *see*
  Wartend Unknown
  MENDELSSOHN-BARTHOLDY
Sie trugen ihn auf der Bahre bloss see
  Shakespeare *HAMLET.* **STRAUSS**
Sie trugen ihn barhaupt auf der Bahr see
  Shakespeare *HAMLET.* **LASSEN**
"Sie wandeln durch des Waldes Grün" *see*
  Spaziergang Mombert **BERG**
"Sie wandelt im Blumengarten" *see*
  Der Blumenstrauss Klingemann
  MENDELSSOHN-BARTHOLDY
Sie war die Schönste von Allen see Pfarrius
  JENSEN
"Sie waren alle zum Tanzplatz hinaus" *see*
  Urgrossvaters Gesellschaft Vogl **LOEWE**
Sie wissen's nicht see Panizza **STRAUSS**
Siebel, Carl, 1836-1868.
  BARTÓK *Nacht am Rheine*
  LOEWE
    Heimlichkeit
    Im Sturme
    Meeresleuchten
    Der Teufel
    Die Waldkapelle
SIEBEN BRETTL-LIEDER, no. 1
  SCHÖNBERG Wedekind *Galathea*
SIEBEN BRETTL-LIEDER, no. 2
  SCHÖNBERG Bierbaum *Gigerlette*
SIEBEN BRETTL-LIEDER, no. 3
  SCHÖNBERG Salus *Der genügsame*
    Liebhaber
SIEBEN BRETTL-LIEDER, no. 4
  SCHÖNBERG Salus *Einfältiges Lied*
SIEBEN BRETTL-LIEDER, no. 5
  SCHÖNBERG Hochstetter *Mahnung*
SIEBEN BRETTL-LIEDER, no. 6
  SCHÖNBERG Colly *Jedem das Seine*
SIEBEN BRETTL-LIEDER, no. 7
  SCHÖNBERG Schikaneder *Arie aus*
    dem Spiegel von Arcadien
SIEBEN FRÜHE LIEDER, no. 1
  BERG Hauptmann *Nacht*
SIEBEN FRÜHE LIEDER, no. 2
  BERG Lenau *Schilflied*

SIEBEN FRÜHE LIEDER, no. 3
  BERG Storm *Die Nachtigall*
SIEBEN FRÜHE LIEDER, no. 4
  BERG Rilke *Traumgekrönt*
SIEBEN FRÜHE LIEDER, no. 5
  BERG Schlaf *Im Zimmer*
SIEBEN FRÜHE LIEDER, no. 6
  BERG Hartleben *Liebesode*
SIEBEN FRÜHE LIEDER, no. 7
  BERG Hohenberg *Sommertag*
SIEBEN LIEDER AUS DEM
  NORWEGISCHEN, no. 1
  DELIUS Ibsen *Wiegenlied*
SIEBEN LIEDER AUS DEM
  NORWEGISCHEN, no. 2
  DELIUS Vinje *Auf der Reise zur Heimat*
SIEBEN LIEDER AUS DEM
  NORWEGISCHEN, no. 3
  DELIUS Bjørnson *Abendstimmung*
SIEBEN LIEDER AUS DEM
  NORWEGISCHEN, no. 4
  DELIUS Bjørnson *Kleine Venevil*
SIEBEN LIEDER AUS DEM
  NORWEGISCHEN, no. 5
  DELIUS Ibsen *Spielleute*
SIEBEN LIEDER AUS DEM
  NORWEGISCHEN, no. 6
  DELIUS Bjørnson *Verborg'ne Liebe*
SIEBEN LIEDER AUS DEM
  NORWEGISCHEN, no. 7
  DELIUS Ibsen *Eine Vogelweise*
Die sieben Schwestern see Wihl **SPOHR**
Die sieben Siegel see Rückert **STRAUSS**
SIEBENGESANG DES TODES. see Trakl
  Verklärung **WEBERN**
DER SIEBENTE RING. see George
  An Bachesranft die einzigen Frühen
    WEBERN
  Dies ist ein Lied für dich allein **WEBERN**
  Im Morgentaun trittst du hervor **WEBERN**
  Im Windesweben war meine Frage
    WEBERN
  Kahl reckt der Baum **WEBERN**
DER SIEBENTE RING: Gezeiten. *see*
  George
  Das lockere Saatgefilde **WEBERN**
DER SIEBENTE RING: Maximin. *see*
  George
  Kunfttag I **WEBERN**
  Trauer I **WEBERN**
DER SIEBENTE RING: Traumdunkel. *see*
  George
  Eingang **WEBERN**
Der siebte November see Khomyakov
  BALAKIREV *Sem' noyabrya*
Les siècles ont creusé see Guérin, M.
  MILHAUD

COMPOSER   Poet   *Title*   "First Line"

Der Sieg see Mayrhofer **SCHUBERT**
Der Siegesfürst see Schmid **LOEWE**
Siegsgesang für Freie see Matthisson
   GLUCK
"Sieh, an letzten Himmels Saum schwebt die
   Blume" *see Die trunkene Tänzerin* Bock,
   K. **HINDEMITH**
"Sieh auf dem Meer den Glanz" *see
   Und sprich* Biegeleben **LISZT**
"Sieh, der Himmel wird blau" *see Nach einem
   Regen* Dehmel **SZYMANOWSKI**
"Sieh, der Kastanie kindliches Laub" *see
   Im Park* Mörike **SCHOECK**
Sieh' dich vor see Benzon *ANNA BRYDE.*
   GRIEG *Se dig for, når du vaelger din Vej*
"Sieh, Du musst es mir vergeben" *see Wenn
   Gespenster auferstehen* Dörmann **BERG**
"Sieh Jesum Christum leiden!" *see Jesus auf
   Golgatha* Sturm, C. **LOEWE**
"Sieh, Liebchen, hier im Waldestal" *see
   Die Primeln* Hamerling **REGER**
Sieh mich, Heil'ger, wie ich bin see Goethe
   ERWIN UND ELMIRE. **MEDTNER**
"Sich, wie wir zu den Sternen aufsteigen!" *see
   Hoch in der Frühe* Dehmel
   SZYMANOWSKI
Siehe, auch ich–lebe see Morgenstern
   KILPINEN
"Siehe, der Frühling währet" *see Lied*
   Hoffmann von Fallersleben
   RUBINSTEIN
Siehe, noch blühen die Tage der Rose see
   Eelbo **LASSEN**
"Siehe, wie die Mondesstrahlen" *see
   Die Mondnacht* Kosegarten **SCHUBERT**
"Siehst du am Abend die Wolken ziehn" *see
   In die Ferne* Kletke **LOEWE**
Siehst du das Meer? see Geibel **GRIEG**
Siehst du den Stern see Keller, G.
   SCHOECK
"Sieht uns der Blick gehoben" *see Die Berge*
   Schlegel, F. **SCHUBERT**
LA SIERRA ES ALTA. see Padrilla
   Hoch, hoch sind die Berge **SCHUMANN**
Sierra, Gregorio Martinez *see* Martinez
   Sierra, Gregorio, 1881-1947.
La sieste see Claudel **HONEGGER**
SIETE CANCIONES POPULARES
   ESPAÑOLAS, no. 1
   FALLA Anon. *El pano moruno*
SIETE CANCIONES POPULARES
   ESPAÑOLAS, no. 2
   FALLA Anon. *Seguidilla Murciana*
SIETE CANCIONES POPULARES
   ESPAÑOLAS, no. 3
   FALLA Anon. *Asturiana*

SIETE CANCIONES POPULARES
   ESPAÑOLAS, no. 4
   FALLA Anon. *Jota*
SIETE CANCIONES POPULARES
   ESPAÑOLAS, no. 5
   FALLA Anon. *Nana*
SIETE CANCIONES POPULARES
   ESPAÑOLAS, no. 6
   FALLA Anon. *Cancion*
SIETE CANCIONES POPULARES
   ESPAÑOLAS, no. 7
   FALLA Anon. *Polo*
Le sifflet see Lunel **MILHAUD**
"Sig, husker du i Sommer" *see På Skogstien*
   Paulsen **GRIEG**
The sigh see Maïkov **RIMSKIĭ-
   KORSAKOV** *Pevets*
Sigh no more, ladies see Shakespeare
   MUCH ADO ABOUT NOTHING.
   HESELTINE, QUILTER, THOMSON
Sigh, sedges, sigh see Fröding *INGALILL.*
   SIBELIUS *Säf, säf, susa*
The sigh that heaves the grasses see
   Housman *LAST POEMS*: XXVII.
   RIEGGER, VAUGHAN WILLIAMS
      Riegger setting unpublished; assumed to
      be the same text set by Vaughan
      Williams.
Siitä sinne tie menevi see Kanteletar
   KILPINEN
Sikorskaya, Tatyana
   PROKOFIEV *Pesnia o Voroshilove*
S'il est un charmant gazon see Hugo
   CHANTS DU CRÉPUSCULE.
   FRANCK, LISZT, SAINT-SAËNS
"S'il est un charmant gazon" *see
   Rêve d'amour* Hugo **FAURÉ**
"S'il est vrai, Chloris, que tu m'aimes" *see
   A Chloris* Théophile **HAHN**
"Silbermond, mit bleichen Strahlen" *see
   An den Mond* Simrock **BRAHMS**
Silbert, Johann Petrus, 1772-1844.
   SCHUBERT
      Abendbilder
      Himmelsfunken
Silence see Docquois **SAINT-SAËNS**
Silence see Samain **AUBERT**
Silence au fond de l'allée see Paliard
   MILHAUD
"Le silence descend en nous" *see Silence*
   Samain **AUBERT**
Silence descends on the golden cornfields see
   Tolstoï **RIMSKIĭ-KORSAKOV**
      Na nivy zheltye niskhodit tishina
"Le silence est plume d'ange et flotte" *see
   Confidence* Anon. **MILHAUD**

Silence ineffable see Bourget **DEBUSSY**
  Romance, musique pour éventail
"Silence ineffable de l'heure" *see Romance,*
  musique pour éventail Bourget **DEBUSSY**
"Silencieuse, sur les arbes" *see Les yeux*
  coleur du temps Margueritte
  MALIPIERO
The silent city see Dehmel **SIBELIUS**
  Die stille Stadt
Silent noon see Rossetti, Dante
  THE HOUSE OF LIFE, no. XIX.
  VAUGHAN WILLIAMS
Silent, silent night see Blake, William
  LUENING
silent unday by silently not night see
  Cummings **BLITZSTEIN**
Silent woods see Heyduk
  DVOŘÁK *A les je tichý kolem kol*
Silesius, Angelus, pseud. *see* Scheffler,
  Johann, 1624-1677.
Silhouette see Bernstein **BERNSTEIN**
Les silhouettes see Wilde **CARPENTER**
Silken shoes see Jacobsen *SILKESKO OVER*
  GYLDEN LAEST. **DELIUS**
"Silken shoes upon golden lasts!" *see Silken*
  shoes Jacobsen **DELIUS**
SILKESKO OVER GYLDEN LAEST. see
  Jacobsen
  Silken shoes **DELIUS**
  Silkesko over gylden Laest! **NIELSEN**
Silkesko over gylden Laest! see Jacobsen
  SILKESKO OVER GYLDEN LAEST.
  NIELSEN
Silloin laulan see Kanteletar **KILPINEN**
Silvani, Mario 1884-1913.
  PIZZETTI *Sera d'Inverno*
Silver see De La Mare **BERKELEY,**
  BRITTEN
THE SILVER BRANCH. see O'Faolain,
  Sean, translator
  At St. Patrick's Purgatory **BARBER**
  The desire for hermitage **BARBER**
  The heavenly banquet **BARBER**
"Silver clouds are lightly sailing" *see*
  Midsummer lullaby Goethe
  MACDOWELL
The silver swan see Gibbons **ROREM**
Silvestre, Paul Armond, 1837-1901.
  AUBERT
    Quand, à tes genoux!
    Si de mon premier rêve
    Souvent de nos biens le meilleur
  BIZET
    En Avril
    Rive d'amour
  CHABRIER *Credo d'amour*

DELIBES
  Arioso
  Blanche et Rose
  Heure du soir
  Myrto
  Peine d'amour
  Regrets!
DUPARC *Textament*
FAURÉ
  Aurore
  Automne
  Chanson d'amour
  Le Fée aux chansons
  Fleur jetée
  Notre amour
  Le pays des rêves
  Le plus doux chemin
  Le ramier
  Le secret
  Le voyageur
KOECHLIN *En Avignon, pays d'amour*
LALO
  À celle qui part
  Tristesse
MASSENET
  Un adieu
  Adieux à la prairie
  L'air du soir emportait
  Anniversaire
  Aurore
  C'est au temps de la Chrysantheme
  Crépuscule
  Dans l'air plein de fils de soie
  Dors, Magda
  Epitaphe
  Il pleuvait
  Je ne sais pas t'aimer
  Lève-toi, lève-toi
  Madrigal
  La marchande des rêves
  Marquise
  Mon amour l'a bien mérité
  Mon coeur est plein de toi
  Noël
  Noël païen
  Pastorale
  Paysage
  Pensée d'automne
  Pensée de printemps
  Pour qu'à l'Espérance il ne céde
  Rien n'est que de France
  Sonnet païen
  Un souffle de parfums s'élève
  Sous les branches
ROUSSEL *Les rêves*
CHANSON DES HEURES.
  CHAUSSON *Le charme*

COMPOSER Poet *Title* "First Line"

MIGNONNE.
> **DELIBES** *Que l'heure est donc brève!*
> **MASSENET**
>> *Complainte*
>> *Prélude*
>> *Que l'heure est donc brève*
>> *Riez-vous?*
>> *Sonnet matinal*
>> *Sur la source*
>> *Voici que les grand lys*
>> *Vous aimerez demain*

Simeon see Cornelius **CORNELIUS**
Simone see Gourmont **COPLAND**
"Simone, white as thy throat the snow I see"
> *see Simone* Gourmont **COPLAND**
Simoni, H. Ernest
> **MASSENET** *Coupe d'ivresse*
Simpel Sang see Drachmann **GRIEG**
Simple gifts see Anon. **COPLAND**
Simple words see Chaïkovskiĭ
> **CHAÏKOVSKIĬ** *Prostye solva*
Simplicité see Carême **SAUGUET**
SIMPLICIUS SIMPLICISSIMUS. see
> Grimmelshausen
> *Gesang des Einsiedlers* **JENSEN**
Simpson, Archibald
> **CARPENTER** *The little prayer of I*
Simpson, Mabel
> *THE DIAL.*
> **CARPENTER** *Rest*
Simrock, Karl Joseph, 1802-1876.
> **BRAHMS**
>> *An den Mond*
>> *Auf dem See*
> **LOEWE** *Zwist und Sühne*
> **MENDELSSOHN-BARTHOLDY**
>> *Warnung vor dem Rhein*
> **SPOHR** *Ständchen*
>> Two settings: Op. 139 no. 1 and WoO
>> 94.
Sin Kabordi see Mendel'son **PROKOFIEV**
"Sinä hyöky hurja ja vaahtopää" *see*
> *Hyökyaalto* Koskenniemi **KILPINEN**
"Since I am coming to that holy room" *see*
> *Consider, Lord* Donne **THOMSON**
Since she whom I loved see Donne
> **BRITTEN**
"Since you love me and I love you the rest
> matters not" *see Pastorale* Kafiristan
> **COPLAND**
Sind es Schmerzen see Tieck **BRAHMS**
Sind es Schmerzen, sind es Freuden see Tieck
> **WEBER**
SIND GÖTTER. see Dahn
> *Weisse Rose* **LASSEN**
"Sind heute dreiunddreissig Jahr" *see*
> *Der gefangene Admiral* Strachwitz
> **LASSEN**

"Sind wir geschieden" *see Liebesgruss aus der*
> *Ferne* Anon. **WEBER**
"Sing a Hymn of Freedom, fling the banner
> high!" *see The home-road* Carpenter,
> John **CARPENTER**
"Sing, Belgian's [sic] sing" *see After Antwerp*
> Cammaerts **COPLAND**
Sing fervent songs at nightfall see Pfleger-
> Moravský **DVOŘÁK** *Vy vroucí písně*
> *spějte*
Sing his praises see Fletcher **ROREM**
Sing, Madchen, sing see Bryan **BENNETT**
> *Sing, maiden, sing*
Sing, maiden, sing see Bryan **BENNETT**
Sing not those songs see Pushkin **RIMSKIĬ-**
> **KORSAKOV** *Ne poĭ, krasavīt͡sa, pri mne*
Sing not to me, beautiful maiden see Pushkin
> **RACHMANINOFF**
Sing, O lieblicher Sängermund see Hafiz
> **SCHOECK**
Sing on there in the swamp see Whitman
> **HINDEMITH**
Sing, sing see Welhaven **DELIUS**
"Sing, sing Nachtigall Du" *see Sing, sing*
> Welhaven **DELIUS**
"Le singe avec le léopard" *see Le singe et le*
> *léopard* La Fontaine **THOMSON**
Le singe et le léopard see La Fontaine
> **THOMSON**
"Singe, Mädchen, hell und klar" *see In den*
> *Beeren* Schmidt, Hans **BRAHMS**
"Singe, Nachtigall" *see Fliehe hin, Nachtigall*
> Kol'tsov **RUBINSTEIN**
Die singende Gemeinde see Grundtvig
> **GRIEG** *Den syngende Menighed*
The singer see Maĭkov **RIMSKIĬ-**
> **KORSAKOV** *Pevets*
The singer see Pushkin **MEDTNER**
The singer see Shanks *THE QUEEN OF*
> *CHINA AND OTHER POEMS* (1919).
> **HESELTINE**
The singer's reward see Snoilsky **SIBELIUS**
> *Sångarlön*
"Singet die Nachtigall im dunkeln Wald" *see*
> *Lied* Zedlitz **SPOHR**
Singet nicht in Trauertönen see Goethe
> *WILHELM MEISTER.* **SCHUMANN**
"Singet nicht in Trauertönen" *see Philine*
> Goethe **WOLF**
Singing see Chamisso **MEDTNER**
> *Frisch gesungen*
"Singt ein Falk all' die Nacht durch" *see*
> *Des Jünglings Segen* Jacob, T. **LOEWE**
Singt mein Schatz wie ein Fink see Keller, G.
> **PFITZNER, WOLF**
"Singt mein Schatz wie ein Fink" *see Salome*
> Keller, G. **BRAHMS**

COMPOSER Poet *Title* "First Line"

Sinite parvulos see Unknown **FRANCK**
"Sinke, liebe Sonne, sinke" *see An die Sonne*
   Batsányi **SCHUBERT**
Sinngedicht see Polonsky **RUBINSTEIN**
Sinnspruch see Goethe **STRAUSS**
"Sippa, vårens första blomma" *see Sippan*
   Runeberg **SIBELIUS**
Sippan see Runeberg **SIBELIUS**
SIREN' see Beketova
   The lilacs **RACHMANINOFF**
La sirène see Mendès **BIZET**
La sirène au coquillage see Gengenbach,
   Eric de **SAUGUET**
La sirène de Scheveningue see Gilson
   RIVIER
Široké rukávy see Heyduk **DVOŘÁK**
Sirotek see Erben **DVOŘÁK**
Sirotka see Musorgskiĭ **MUSORGSKIĭ**
"Siršĭ jiskry, sršĭ, skovadliny prší" *see Zpěv z*
   Lešetínského kováře Čech **DVOŘÁK**
The Siskin see Grot **RUBINSTEIN**
" 'sist Krieg!" *see Der Krieg* Claudius, M.
   SCHOECK
Den sista stjärnan see Bergman **KILPINEN**
Sister Jane see La Fontaine **DIAMOND**
"Sitting under the mistletoe" *see Mistletoe*
   De La Mare **BERKELEY**
Sitwell, Edith, Dame, 1887-1964.
   ROREM
      You, the young rainbow of my tears
      The youth with the red-gold hair
   THE CANTICLE OF THE ROSE.
      BRITTEN *Canticle III*
"Sitz' ich allein" *see Lieder aus dem*
   Schenkenbuch . . . Goethe **SCHUMANN**
"Sitz' ich im Gras" *see Am See* Mayrhofer
   SCHUBERT
SITZ' ICH IM GRAS. see Mayrhofer
   Am See **SCHUBERT**
"Sitz im Sattel, reite, reite auf die Freite" *see*
   Ritter rät dem Knappen dies Bierbaum
   REGER
"Siunattu olkoon, armas, sun tiesi" *see*
   Lemmenlaulu Jalkanen **KILPINEN**
SIX CHANSONS DE THÉÂTRE, no. 1
   MILHAUD Pitoëff *La bohémienne la*
   main n'a pris
SIX CHANSONS DE THÉÂTRE, no. 2
   MILHAUD Pitoëff *Un petit pas, deux*
   petits pas
SIX CHANSONS DE THÉÂTRE, no. 3
   MILHAUD Supervielle *Je suis dans le*
   fillet
SIX CHANSONS DE THÉÂTRE, no. 4
   MILHAUD Supervielle *Chacun son tour,*
   les animaux

SIX CHANSONS DE THÉÂTRE, no. 5
   MILHAUD Lenormand *Mes amis les*
   cygnes
SIX CHANSONS DE THÉÂTRE, no. 6
   MILHAUD Lenormand *Blancs sont les*
   jours d'été
SIX CHANTS POPULAIRES
   HÉBRAÏQUES, no. 1
   MILHAUD Anon. *La séparation*
SIX CHANTS POPULAIRES
   HÉBRAÏQUES, no. 2
   MILHAUD Anon. *Le chant du veilleur*
SIX CHANTS POPULAIRES
   HÉBRAÏQUES, no. 3
   MILHAUD Anon. *Chante de délivrance*
SIX CHANTS POPULAIRES
   HÉBRAÏQUES, no. 4
   MILHAUD Anon. *Berceuse*
SIX CHANTS POPULAIRES
   HÉBRAÏQUES, no. 5
   MILHAUD Anon. *Gloire à Dieu*
SIX CHANTS POPULAIRES
   HÉBRAÏQUES, no. 6
   MILHAUD Anon. *Chant Hassidique*
SIX ELIZABETHAN SONGS, no. 1
   BLITZSTEIN Spenser *Sweet is the rose*
SIX ELIZABETHAN SONGS, no. 2
   BLITZSTEIN Shakespeare *Shepherd's*
   song
SIX ELIZABETHAN SONGS, no. 3
   BLITZSTEIN Jonson *Song of the glove*
SIX ELIZABETHAN SONGS, no. 4
   BLITZSTEIN Anon. *Court song*
SIX ELIZABETHAN SONGS, no. 5
   BLITZSTEIN Shakespeare *Lullaby*
SIX ELIZABETHAN SONGS, no. 6
   BLITZSTEIN Shakespeare *Vendor's*
   song
SIX LOVE SONGS, no. 1
   MACDOWELL Gardner, W. *Sweet blue-*
   eyed maid
SIX LOVE SONGS, no. 2
   MACDOWELL Gardner, W. *Sweetheart*
   tell me
SIX LOVE SONGS, no. 3
   MACDOWELL Gardner, W.
   Thy beaming eyes
SIX LOVE SONGS, no. 4
   MACDOWELL Gardner, W. *For sweet*
   love's sake
SIX LOVE SONGS, no. 5
   MACDOWELL Gardner, W. *O lovely*
   rose
SIX LOVE SONGS, no. 6
   MACDOWELL Gardner, W. *I ask but*
   this

COMPOSER Poet *Title* "First Line"

SIX MÉLODIES-MINUTE, no. 1
  HONEGGER Bédat de Monlaur, Pierre
    Le château du Bartas
SIX MÉLODIES-MINUTE, no. 2
  HONEGGER Bédat de Monlaur, Pierre
    Tout le long de la Baïse
SIX MÉLODIES-MINUTE, no. 3
  HONEGGER Bédat de Monlaur, Pierre
    Le départ
SIX MÉLODIES-MINUTE, no. 4
  HONEGGER Bédat de Monlaur, Pierre
    La promenade
SIX MÉLODIES-MINUTE, no. 5
  HONEGGER Bédat de Monlaur, Pierre
    Nérac en fête
SIX MÉLODIES-MINUTE, no. 6
  HONEGGER Bédat de Monlaur, Pierre
    Duo
SIX POÈMES, no. 1
  AURIC Eluard *Je te l'ai dit*
SIX POÈMES, no. 2
  AURIC Eluard *Mon amour . . .*
SIX POÈMES, no. 3
  AURIC Eluard *Elle se penche sur moi . . .*
SIX POÈMES, no. 4
  AURIC Eluard *Le front aux vitres . . .*
SIX POÈMES, no. 5
  AURIC Eluard *On ne peut me
    connaitre . . .*
SIX POÈMES, no. 6
  AURIC Eluard *Tout disparut . . .*
SIX POÈMES ARABES, no. 1
  AUBERT Toussaint *Le mirage*
SIX POÈMES ARABES, no. 2
  AUBERT Toussaint *Le vaincu*
SIX POÈMES ARABES, no. 3
  AUBERT Toussaint *Le visage penché*
SIX POÈMES ARABES, no. 4
  AUBERT Toussaint *Le sommeil des
    colombes*
SIX POÈMES ARABES, no. 5
  AUBERT Toussaint *L'adieu*
SIX POÈMES ARABES, no. 6
  AUBERT Toussaint *Le destin*
SIX PROVERBS, no. 1
  LUENING Bible *There is a generation
    that curseth their father*
SIX PROVERBS, no. 2
  LUENING Bible *Answer not a fool
    according to his folly*
SIX PROVERBS, no. 3
  LUENING Bible *A righteous man falling
    down before the wicked*
SIX PROVERBS, no. 4
  LUENING Bible *The slothful man saith*

SIX PROVERBS, no. 5
  LUENING Bible *These six things doth the
    Lord hate*
SIX PROVERBS, no. 6
  LUENING Bible *The mouth of the
    righteous man*
SIX ROMANCES POPULAIRES, no. 1
  LALO Béranger *La pauvre femme*
SIX ROMANCES POPULAIRES, no. 2
  LALO Béranger *Beaucoup d'amour*
SIX ROMANCES POPULAIRES, no. 3
  LALO Béranger *Le suicide*
SIX ROMANCES POPULAIRES, no. 4
  LALO Béranger *Si j'étais petit oiseau*
SIX ROMANCES POPULAIRES, no. 5
  LALO Béranger *Les petits coups*
SIX ROMANCES POPULAIRES, no. 6
  LALO Béranger *Le vieux vagabond*
*Sizhu zadumchiv i odin **see** *Tiutchev
  MEDTNER *Dejection*
*Sjung mitt hjärta **see** Cnattingius, Thor
  KILPINEN
*Skal Blomsterne da visne? **see** Rode, Helge
  NIELSEN
"Skal vi vandre en Stund" **see** *Til mit Hjertes
  Dronning* Shelley **NIELSEN**
*Skazhi mne **see** Lermontov **PROKOFIEV**
*Skazhi, O chem v teni vetveĭ **see** Sollogub
  CHAĬKOVSKIĬ
"A skelp frae his teacher" **see** *Black day*
  Soutar **BRITTEN**
Skelton, John, 1460?-1529.
  HESELTINE *Rutterkin*
Skelton, Philipp, 1707-1787.
  GOUNOD *To God, ye choir above*
*SKIZZEN AUS SPANIEN. **see** Huber, V.
  Der Sturm von Alhama **LOEWE**
*SKIZZENBUCH. **see** Kugler
  Ständchen **BRAHMS**
"Skjaer og ø!" **see** *Havet* Rolfsen **GRIEG**
*Skogen gir susende, langsom besked **see**
  Bjørnson **DELIUS**
*Skogen spelar. älven rinner **see** Bergman
  KILPINEN
*Skolie **see** Deinhardstein **SCHUBERT**
*Skolie **see** Matthisson **SCHUBERT**
*Skolie **see** Reinick **WOLF**
*Skovsang **see** Winther **GRIEG**
*Skřivánek **see** Unknown **DVOŘÁK**
*Skrýše má paveza má Ty jsi **see** Bible
  DVOŘÁK
*Skuchaĭ **see** Golenishchev-Kutuzov
  MUSORGSKIĬ
"Skuchaĭ. Ty sozdana dlia skuki" **see** *Skuchaĭ*
  Golenishchev-Kutuzov **MUSORGSKIĬ**
"Skuchnaia kartina!" **see** *Osen'* Pleshcheyev
  CHAĬKOVSKIĬ

COMPOSER Poet *Title* "First Line"

Skvoz' shega i tumany see Afinogenov
   PROKOFIEV
The sky above the roof see Verlaine *LE CIEL
   EST PARDESSUS LE TOIT.*
   VAUGHAN WILLIAMS
"The sky is dark and the hills are white" *see
   Norse lullaby* Field, Eugene
   CARPENTER
"The sky is laced with fitful red" *see Dawn*
   Wilde **GRIFFES**
"Skyarna sakta" *see Den sista stjärnan*
   Bergman **KILPINEN**
Skylark and nightingale see Rossetti,
   Christina **IRELAND**
"Slaap, lief kind-je, zacht" *see Nachtliedje*
   Bruyn, Bertha de **PIJPER**
Sládek, Josef Václav, 1845-1912.
   MARTINŮ
   All this is what only remains
   Dívčí píseň
   The drowned maiden
   A maiden's song
   Mother dear
   Tears
   When the day comes
Sladkaia pesenka see Sakonskaya, N.
   PROKOFIEV
Slätten see Österling **KILPINEN**
Slaughter see Soutar **BRITTEN**
"Slava tebe, bezyskhodnaia bol'!" *see
   Sieroglazyĭ korol'* Akhmatova
   PROKOFIEV
"Sleek black boys in a cabaret" *see Jazz-boys*
   Hughes, L. **CARPENTER**
Sleep see Feeney **CHANLER**
Sleep see Fletcher *THE WOMAN HATER*
   (1607). **HESELTINE**
Sleep! see Khomyakov **BALAKIREV** *Spi!*
Sleep! see Merezhkovski **CHAĬKOVSKIĬ**
   Usni!
"Sleep, and I'll be still as another sleeper" *see
   Tired* Vaughan Williams, U.
   VAUGHAN WILLIAMS
"Sleep; and my song shall build about your
   bed" *see Slumber-song* Sassoon
   CARPENTER
"Sleep forsakes me with the light" *see Lines
   written during a sleepless night* Pushkin
   BRITTEN
Sleep, infant, sleep see Des Knaben
   Wunderhorn **MARTINŮ**
"Sleep is not something you worry about" *see
   Sleep* Feeney **CHANLER**
Sleep is supposed to be see Dickinson
   COPLAND
"Sleep, my honey, sleep" *see The Lawd is
   smilin' through the do'* Unknown
   CARPENTER

Sleep, my little one see Raabe **MARTINŮ**
Sleep, my poor friend see Tolstoĭ **RIMSKIĬ-
   KORSAKOV** *Usni, pechal'nyĭ drug*
Sleep now see Joyce *CHAMBER MUSIC.*
   BARBER, SZYMANOWSKI
"Sleep now, O sleep now" *see Sleep now*
   Joyce **BARBER**
Sleep on, my mournful friend see Tolstoĭ
   RIMSKIĬ-KORSAKOV *Usni, pechal'nyĭ
   drug*
Sleep, poor friend see Tolstoĭ
   CHAĬKOVSKIĬ *Usni pechal'nyĭ drug"*
"Sleep, sleep, beauty bright" *see A cradle-
   song* Blake, William **CARPENTER**
Sleep, sleep, peasant's son see Ostrovski
   MUSORGSKIĬ *Kolybel'naia pesnia*
The sleep that flits on baby's eyes see Tagore
   GITANJALI. **CARPENTER**
"Sleep! sleep! beauty bright" *see A cradle
   song* Blake, William **BRITTEN**
The sleeper see Poe **MARTINŮ**
The sleeping palace see Tennyson *THE DAY
   DREAM.* **ROREM**
The sleeping princess see Borodin
   BORODIN *Die schlafende Prinzessin*
Sleepless see Pushkin **MEDTNER**
Sleepless see Tiutchev **MEDTNER**
Sleza drozhit" see Tolstoĭ **CHAĬKOVSKIĬ**
Slezy see Blanchecotte **CHAĬKOVSKIĬ**
   Les larmes
Slězy see Tiutchev **MEDTNER** *Tears*
Śliczny chlopiec see Zaleski **CHOPIN**
"Slipping through the rushes in a green &
   gray canoe" *see The echo child* Baker,
   Mary Ely **THOMPSON, R**.
Slíshu li golos tvoy see Lermontov
   BALAKIREV
"Slonca jesieni blade promienie" *see
   Osiennieje solnce* Davidov, Dmitri
   SZYMANOWSKI
SLOPIEWNIE, no. 1
   SZYMANOWSKI Tuwim *Slowisień*
SLOPIEWNIE, no. 2
   SZYMANOWSKI Tuwim *Zielone slowa*
SLOPIEWNIE, no. 3
   SZYMANOWSKI Tuwim *Świety
   Franciszek*
SLOPIEWNIE, no. 4
   SZYMANOWSKI Tuwim *Kalinowe
   dwory*
SLOPIEWNIE, no. 5
   SZYMANOWSKI Tuwim *Wanda*
The slothful man saith see Bible **LUENING**
SLOVA DLYA MUZĬKI. see Pleshcheyev
   Nam zvezdy krotkie siiali **CHAĬKOVSKIĬ**
Slow march see Ives **IVES**

"Slow, slow, fresh fount, keep time with my salt tears" *see By a fountainside* Jonson **QUILTER**

"Slow, slow, fresh fount, keep time with my salt tears" *see Echo's song* Jonson **ROREM**

Slowik see Szymanowska, Zafia **SZYMANOWSKI**

Słowisień see Tuwim **SZYMANOWSKI**

Slowly as the evening sun see Tavaststjerna **SIBELIUS** *Långsamt som qvällskyn*

Slowly drag my days see Pushkin *ZHELANIE.* **RIMSKĬĬ-KORSAKOV** *Medlitel'no vlekutsia dni moi*

"Slowly, silently, now the moon" *see Silver* De La Mare **BERKELEY, BRITTEN**

"Slowly the moon is rising" *see Aware* Lawrence **RIETI**

Ślub królewny see Iłłakowiczówna **SZYMANOWSKI**

Slugging a vampire see Kipling **IVES** *Tarrant moss*

Slumber see Tavaststjerna **SIBELIUS** *Sof in!*

Slumber song see Bjørnson **DELIUS** *Der Schlaf*

Slumber song see MacDowell **MACDOWELL**

Slumber song see Sassoon **CARPENTER, GIDEON**

Slumra, slumra sakta see Cnattingius, Thor **KILPINEN**

"Slunéčko zachodí za les javorový" *see Rosička* Unknown **MARTINŮ**

"Slunka svit jak líbá zemi" *see Jaro* Kleinschrod **DVOŘÁK**

Slushayte, podruzhen'ki, pesenku moyu see Kruse **BORODIN** *Listen to my song, little friend*

Slyš, Ó Bože! slyš modlitbu mou see Bible **DVOŘÁK**

Slyš, Ó Bože, volání mé see Bible **DVOŘÁK**

Slyszalem ciebie see Tetmajer **SZYMANOWSKI**

Slzy see Sládek **MARTINŮ** *Tears*

Små flickorna see Procopé **SIBELIUS**

Small girls see Procopé **SIBELIUS** *Små flickorna*

"Småsporven gjeng i" *see Sporven* Garborg **GRIEG**

Smelo vpered! see Mendel'son **PROKOFIEV**

Smerkalos' see Tolstoĭ **RACHMANINOFF** *Twilight has fallen*

Smert' see Merezhkovski **CHAĬKOVSKĬĬ**

Smile, death see Mew **ROREM**

"Smile, death, see I smile as I come to you" *see Smile, death* Mew **ROREM**

Smith, Dr. James, 1605-1667. *LARKSPUR;* ed. by Victor Neuburg (Steyning, Sussex: Vine Press, 1922). **HESELTINE** *Milkmaids*

Smith, Logan Pearsall, 1865-1946. *MORE TRIVIA.* **DIAMOND** *The epitaph* *Somewhere*

"Smooth it slides upon its travel" *see Looking-glass river* Stevenson, Robert Louis **CARPENTER**

Smotri, pushinki see Prokofiev **PROKOFIEV**

Smotri, von oblako see Grekov *STANSĬ.* **CHAĬKOVSKĬĬ**

Smutek see Iłłakowiczówna **SZYMANOWSKI**

Smutna rzeka see Witwicki **CHOPIN**

"Smutno niańki ci śpiewaly" *see Pierścien* Witwicki **CHOPIN**

Smutný milý see Anon. **MARTINŮ**

Snake see Roethke **ROREM**

SNEDEN'S LANDING VARIATIONS. see O'Hara *From "Sneden's Landing Variations"* **THOMSON**

Sneeuwklokjes see Bruyn, Bertha de **PIJPER**

Snegl, Snegl! see Benzon **GRIEG**

Snezhki belye see Anon. **PROKOFIEV**

"Snilas' mne devushka" *see Son* Mikhailov **BALAKIREV**

Snöblommor see Blomberg **KILPINEN**

"Snön faller tät bland en och ljung" *see Sjung mitt hjärta* Cnattingius, Thor **KILPINEN**

Snoilsky, Karl Johan Gustaf, grefve, 1841-1903. **SIBELIUS** *Dold förening* *Sångarlön*

Snova, kak prezhde see Rathaus **CHAĬKOVSKĬĬ** *Weil' ich wie einstmals allein*

"Snova son na ustalye ochi neĭdet" *see Night* Rathaus **RACHMANINOFF**

Snovidenie see Pushkin **RIMSKĬĬ-KORSAKOV**

"Snow in winter's wind" *see Image* Cox, Oscar **HINDEMITH**

So beautiful is the tree of night see Hanson **ROREM**

So dance ye see Goethe *LILA.* **MEDTNER** *So tanzet*

So dread a fate I'll never believe **see** Maïkov
  RACHMANINOFF *It cannot be*
So early in the spring-time air **see** Tolstoĭ
  RIMSKIĭ-KORSAKOV *To bylo ranneiu
  vesnoĭ*
"So effortlessly we are not given" **see** *Clouds*
  Goodman **ROREM**
"So ein rechter Soldat fürcht' nicht Kugel und
  Streit" **see** *Soldatenlied* Boelitz **REGER**
So far away **see** Burns **FRANZ**
"So hab' ich doch die ganze Woche" **see**
  Sonntag Uhland **BRAHMS, REGER**
"So hab' ich endlich dich gerettet" **see**
  Die Abgeschiedenen Uhland **LOEWE**
"So hab' ich wirklich dich verloren?" **see**
  An die Entfernte Goethe **SCHUBERT,
  ZELTER**
So halt' ich endlich dich umfangen **see**
  Geibel *LIEDER ALS INTERMEZZO*, no.
  19. **GRIFFES**
"So harre ich schweigend" **see**
  Im Morgengrauen Stieler **BERG**
"So herzig, wie mein Elternhaus" **see**
  Das Elternhaus Claus, Nicolo **LASSEN**
So ich traurig bin weiss ich nur ein Ding **see**
  George
  DAS BUCH DER SAGEN UND SÄNGE:
  Sänge eines fahrenden Spielmanns.
  WEBERN
"So ist die Lieb! So ist die Lieb!" **see**
  Nimmersatte Liebe Mörike **WOLF**
So it begins **see** Agee *SONNET 1.*
  DIAMOND
"So jemand spricht: ich liebe Gott" **see**
  Die Liebe des Nächsten Gellert
  BEETHOVEN
So land man nüchtern ist **see** Goethe
  WESTÖSTLICHER DIVAN: Schenkenbuch.
  WOLF
"So lang du nach dem Glücke jagst" **see**
  Glück Hesse **KILPINEN**
So lasst mich scheinen, bis ich werde **see**
  Goethe *WILHELM MEISTER.*
  SCHUMANN
"So lasst mich scheinen, bis ich werde" **see**
  Lied der Mignon Goethe **SCHUBERT**
"So lasst mich scheinen, bis ich werde" **see**
  Mignon Goethe **SCHUBERT**
  Two settings: D. 469 and D. 727.
"So lasst mich scheinen, bis ich werde" **see**
  Mignon III Goethe **WOLF**
"So like a flower, thy little four year face" **see**
  To Edith Ives, Harmony **IVES**
"So lithe and so dainty and slender" **see** *Waltz*
  Shenshin **MEDTNER**
"So look the mornings when the sun" **see**
  The maiden blush Herrick **QUILTER**

"So Mancher sieht mit finstrer Miene" **see**
  Irdisches Glück Seidl **SCHUBERT**
So many hours, so many fancies **see**
  Golenishchev-Kutuzov
  RACHMANINOFF *How long, my friend*
So many sweet delicate flowers **see** Heine
  LYRICAL INTERMEZZO. **RIMSKIĭ-
  KORSAKOV**
  Iz sléz moikh mnogo, maliutka
So may it be **see** Wordsworth **IVES**
"So nigh is grandeur to our dust" **see** *Duty*
  Emerson **IVES**
So oder so **see** Lappe **BEETHOVEN**
"So oft sie kam, erschien mir die Gestalt" **see**
  Kommen und Scheiden Lenau
  SCHUMANN
So pretty **see** Comden **BERNSTEIN**
So regnet es sich langsam ein **see** Flaischlen
  BERG
"So ruhig geh ich meinen Pfad" **see**
  Im Wandern Eichendorff **SCHOECK**
"So ruhig geh ich meinen Pfad so still" **see**
  Reiselied Eichendorff **MEDTNER**
"So schlafe nun, du Kleine!" **see**
  Ein Wiegenlied, bei Mondschein zu singen
  Claudius, M. **SCHOECK**
"So sei gegrüsst vieltausendmal" **see**
  Frühlingsgruss Hoffmann von
  Fallersleben **SCHUMANN**
"So singet laut den Phillalu" **see** *Klagegesang:
  Jrisch* Goethe **ZELTER**
"So soll ich dich nun meiden" **see** *Scheiden
  und Meiden* Uhland **BRAHMS,
  SCHOECK**
So soon forgotten **see** Apukhtin
  CHAĭKOVSKIĭ *Zabyt' tak skoro!*
"So spät ist es" **see** *Durch die Nacht* Kraus
  KRENEK
So spät, so spät **see** Krenek **KRENEK**
So stehn wir, ich und meine Weide **see**
  Daumer *HAFIS.* **BRAHMS**
"So still und mild der Tag und feierlich" **see**
  Sonntagsruhe Ernst **LASSEN**
"So stille ruht im Hafen" **see** *Abendwolke*
  Meyer **SCHOECK**
So sweet love seemed **see** Bridges, R. S.
  BERKELEY
So tanzet **see** Goethe *LILA.* **MEDTNER**
"So tanzet und springet" **see** *So tanzet*
  Goethe **MEDTNER**
"So tönet denn, schäumende Wellen" **see**
  Verzweiflung Tieck **BRAHMS**
"So trägt der schnelle Zug mich wieder
  heimwärts" **see** *Heimkehr* Krenek
  KRENEK
"So trieb sie mich" **see** *So far away* Burns
  FRANZ

"So viel Blumen allwärts blühen" *see*
  Der Fernen Gerstenberg **LOEWE**
"So viel Laub an der Linden ist" *see An der*
  Linden Roquette **JENSEN**
"So voll und reich wand noch das Leben
  nimmer euch seinen Kranz" *see*
  Hochzeitslied Jacobsen **SCHÖNBERG**
"So wälz' ich ohne Unterlass" *see Genialisch*
  Treiben Goethe **WOLF**
So wahr die Sonne scheinet see Rückert
  WOLF
"So wart, bis ich dies" *see Trauer I* George
  WEBERN
So weit von Hier see Burns **FRANZ** *So far*
  away
So white, so soft, so sweet is she see Jonson
  UNDERWOODS. **DELIUS**
So wilde Freude nimmt ein wildes Ende see
  Shakespeare *ROMEO AND JULIET.*
  BLACHER
So willst du des Armen see Tieck **BRAHMS**
"So willst du treulos von mir scheiden" *see*
  Die Ideale Schiller **ZELTER**
"So wird der Mann, der sonder Zwang gerecht
  ist" *see Fragment aus dem Aeschylus*
  Aeschylus **SCHUBERT**
"Sobald Damoetas Chloen sieht" *see*
  Die Verschweigung Weisse **MOZART**
Sobre el cupey see Hernández Aquino
  RODRIGO
"S'odono al monte i saltellanti rivi" *see*
  I fauni Rubino **RESPIGHI**
DIE SÖHNE DES TALES. see Werner
  Morgenlied **SCHUBERT**
Soeur Anne see Pressat, André
  SAINT-SAËNS
Soeur d'élection see Trolliet, Emile
  MASSENET
"Soeur des Soeurs tisseuses de violettes" *see*
  Danseuse Brimont **FAURÉ**
Sof in! see Tavaststjerna **SIBELIUS**
Sof sött see Unknown **NIELSEN**
"Sof sött, du lilla Sonja" *see Sof sött*
  Unknown **NIELSEN**
So-fei gathering flowers see Wang **GRIFFES**
"Soffro, Lontan lontano" *see Nebbie* Negri
  RESPIGHI
Softly the forest see Bjørnson **DELIUS**
  Skogen gir susende, langsom besked
Softly the spirit flew up to Heaven see Tolstoï
  CHAÏKOVSKIÏ *Gornimi tikho letela;*
  RIMSKIÏ-KORSAKOV *Gornimi tikho*
  letela dusha nebesami
Sogna il guerrier see Metastasio **ROSSINI**
  Pour album: Sogna il guerrier
Un sogno see Annunzio *POEMA*
  PARADISIACO. **RESPIGHI**

"Sohn der Jungfrau, Himmelskind" *see*
  Schlafendes Jesuskind Mörike **WOLF**
DER SOHN DU WILDNISS. see
  Münch-Bellinghausen
  Mein Herz, ich will dich fragen **LOEWE**
"Soi soi syksyinen sade" *see Syyshuokaus*
  Lehtinen **KILPINEN**
"Soikaatte koivikossa tuulet" *see*
  Uutisraivaaja Jalkanen **KILPINEN**
Le soir see Anon. **MARTINŮ**
Le soir see Desbordes-Valmore
  SAINT-SAËNS
Le soir see Lamartine **GOUNOD**
Soir see Samain **FAURÉ**
Soir d'automne see Gounod **GOUNOD**
Soir de printemps see Martin, Gabriel
  MASSENET
Soir de rêve see Lugnier, Antonin
  MASSENET
Soir d'été see Jacob, M. **RIETI**
"Le soir frissonne au coeur des roses" *see*
  Madrigal Silvestre **MASSENET**
"Un soir me promenant dans mon jardin" *see*
  La Maumariée I Unknown **PIJPER**
Soir païen see Samain **CASELLA,**
  KOECHLIN
"Le soir qu'Amour" *see Ballet* Ronsard
  POULENC
Le soir qu'amour see Ronsard **SCHMITT**
"Le soir, quand le soleil l'horizon s'incline"
  see Le sommeil des fleurs Penmarch, G.
  de **SAINT-SAËNS**
"Le soir, quand pour dormir" *see Premiers fils*
  d'argent Valendre, Marie de
  MASSENET
"Un soir que j'etais endormie" *see Un rêve*
  Spenner, M. **GOUNOD**
"Le soir ramène le silence" *see Le soir*
  Lamartine **GOUNOD**
Soir romantique see Noailles **SAINT-**
  SAËNS
"Le soir s'afaisse sur lui même" *see Sérénade*
  mélancolique Jean-Aubry **AUBERT**
"Le soir sous l'abri de ses voiles" *see*
  Voguons sur les flots Unknown
  GOUNOD
Soir sur le lac see Gauthier-Villars
  SCHMITT
"Le soir vient" *see Le Colonel Romanoff*
  Chalupt **MILHAUD**
"Soirée du dimanche" *see Les soirées*
  bagnolaises Hugnet **THOMSON**
Soirée en mer see Hugo **SAINT-SAËNS**
Les soirées bagnolaises see Hugnet
  THOMSON
SOIRÉES DE PÉTROGRAD, no. 1
  MILHAUD Chalupt *L'orgueilleuse*

COMPOSER Poet *Title* "First Line"

SOIRÉES DE PÉTROGRAD, no. 2
  MILHAUD Chalupt *La révoltée*
SOIRÉES DE PÉTROGRAD, no. 3
  MILHAUD Chalupt *La martiale*
SOIRÉES DE PÉTROGRAD, no. 4
  MILHAUD Chalupt *L'infidèle*
SOIRÉES DE PÉTROGRAD, no. 5
  MILHAUD Chalupt *La perverse*
SOIRÉES DE PÉTROGRAD, no. 6
  MILHAUD Chalupt *L'irrésolue*
SOIRÉES DE PÉTROGRAD, no. 7
  MILHAUD Chalupt *La Grand'Mère de la Révolution*
SOIRÉES DE PÉTROGRAD, no. 8
  MILHAUD Chalupt *Les journées d'Aoüt*
SOIRÉES DE PÉTROGRAD, no. 9
  MILHAUD Chalupt *Monsieur Protopopoff*
SOIRÉES DE PÉTROGRAD, no. 10
  MILHAUD Chalupt *Le convive*
SOIRÉES DE PÉTROGRAD, no. 11
  MILHAUD Chalupt *La limousine*
SOIRÉES DE PÉTROGRAD, no. 12
  MILHAUD Chalupt *Le Colonel Romanoff*
LES SOIRÉES MUSICALES, no. 1
  ROSSINI Metastasio *La promessa*
LES SOIRÉES MUSICALES, no. 2
  ROSSINI Metastasio *Il rimprovero*
LES SOIRÉES MUSICALES, no. 3
  ROSSINI Metastasio *La partenza*
LES SOIRÉES MUSICALES, no. 4
  ROSSINI Pepoli *L'orgia*
LES SOIRÉES MUSICALES, no. 5
  ROSSINI Pepoli *L'invito*
LES SOIRÉES MUSICALES, no. 6
  ROSSINI Pepoli *La pastorella dell'Alpi*
LES SOIRÉES MUSICALES, no. 7
  ROSSINI Pepoli *La gita in gondola*
LES SOIRÉES MUSICALES, no. 8
  ROSSINI Pepoli *La danza*
Les soirs d'automne see Kahn *LES PALAIS NOMADES*: Lied IV. **LOEFFLER**
"Les soirs d'été si doux" *see Battements d'ailes* Dortzal **MASSENET**
"Sois le bienvenu, rouge automne" *see L'automne* Banville **HAHN**
Sois mon amie see Hugnet **SAUGUET**
"Sois sage, Ô ma Douleur" *see Recueillement* Baudelaire **DEBUSSY**
"Sois-moi fidèle, Ô pauvre habit que j'aime!" *see Mon habit* Béranger **GOUNOD**
Soitapas see Kanteletar **KILPINEN**
"Soitapas soria likka" *see Soitapas* Kanteletar **KILPINEN**
Sokrates und Alcibiades see Hölderlin **BRITTEN**

Sol, sol! see Ullman **KILPINEN**
"Sol, sol på öde vikar" *see Sol, sol!* Ullman **KILPINEN**
"Solche Düfte sind mein Leben" *see Wein und Brot* Uhland **SCHOECK**
Der Soldat see Andersen **GRIEG** *Soldaten;* **SCHUMANN**
Der Soldat I see Eichendorff **WOLF**
Der Soldat II see Eichendorff **WOLF**
"Soldat sein ist gefährlich" *see Lieber alles* Eichendorff **WOLF**
Soldaten see Andersen **GRIEG**
Die Soldatenbraut see Mörike **BERG, SCHUMANN**
Soldatenlied see Boelitz **REGER**
Soldatenlied see Hoffmann von Fallersleben **SCHUMANN, STRAUSS**
Soldatskaia poxodnaia see Lugovskoï **PROKOFIEV**
The soldier see Andersen **GRIEG** *Soldaten*
The soldier see Brooke **IRELAND**
A soldier's love see Mendel'son **PROKOFIEV** *Lyubov voyna*
Soldiers' marching song see Lugovskoï **PROKOFIEV** *Soldatskaia poxodnaia*
The soldier's return see Warner **IRELAND**
Soldier's song see Anon. **SEIBER**
The soldier's sweetheart see Mendel'son **PROKOFIEV** *Podruga boytsa*
The soldier's wife see Shevchenko **RACHMANINOFF** *I have grown fond of sorrow*
Sole, Nicola, 1821-1859.
  VERDI *Il preghiera del poeta*
Soleil couchant see Hugo **MASSENET**
"Soleil de proie prisonnier de ma tête" *see Juan Miró* Éluard **POULENC**
Le soleil du matin see Verlaine *LA BONNE CHANSON.* **KOECHLIN**
"Le soleil effleure la plaine" *see Les femmes de Magdala* Gallet **MASSENET**
"Le soleil est droit sur la sente" *see Les cigales* Rostand, R. **CHABRIER**
"Le soleil rayonnait encore" *see Déception* Collin **CHAÏKOVSKIÏ**
"Le soleil vient de paraître" *see Vincenette* Barbier, Pierre **GOUNOD**
Soleils couchants see Verlaine *PAYSAGES TRISTES.* **CASELLA, SÉVERAC**
Solen er saa rød, Mor see Bergstedt **NIELSEN**
"Solen gar ned" *see Höstkväll* Rydberg **SIBELIUS**
"Solen ler, och skogen susar" *see Stämmingsvisa* Cnattingius, Thor **KILPINEN**

COMPOSER Poet *Title* "First Line"

"Solen nickat sitt sista farväl" *see Fred
  Tegengren* KILPINEN
"Solen skinner i Naboens Gaard" *see Studie
  efter Naturen* Andersen NIELSEN
"Solennagra purpurdroppar re'n pa österns
  skyar stänkt" *see Morgonen* Runeberg
  SIBELIUS
Solèra, Temistocle, 1815-1878.
  VERDI *L'esule*
Soliloquy see Ives IVES
La solitaire see Renaud SAINT-SAËNS
Solitary hotel see Joyce *ULYSSES.* BARBER
"Solitary hotel in mountain pass" *see Solitary
  hotel* Joyce BARBER
*Solitary observation brought back from a
  soujourn in hell see* Bogan ROREM
Solitude see Gaillard, Roger SAUGUET
Solitude see Goethe MEDTNER *Einsamkeit*
Solitude see Lamartine GOUNOD
LES SOLITUDES. see Sully-Prudhomme
  Soupir DUPARC, RESPIGHI
"Soll ich dich denn nun verlassen" *see
  Der Kranke* Eichendorff SCHOECK
"Soll nach des Volkes und nach Gottes
  Willen" *see Jephthas Tochter* Byron
  LOEWE
"Soll sich der Mond nicht heller scheinen" *see
  Vor dem Fenster* Anon. BRAHMS
Sollogub, Vladimir Aleksandrovich,
  graf, 1814-1882.
  CHAĭKOVSKIĭ *Skazhi, O chem v teni
    vetveĭ*
Solnedgang see Jacobsen NIELSEN
SOLNEDGANG. see Munch
  Beim Sonnenuntergang DELIUS
  Solnedgang GRIEG
Solnedgang see Munch *SOLNEDGANG.*
  GRIEG
Solntse komnatu napolnilo see Akhmatova
  PROKOFIEV
Sologoub, Fyodor, pseud. *see* Teternikov,
  Fyodor, 1863-1927.
Solomon
  MUSORGSKIĭ *Evreĭskaia pesnia*
Soloveĭ see Karadžić CHAĭKOVSKIĭ
Soloveĭ i roza see Pushkin BRITTEN
  The nightingale and the rose
"Solovei msĭ, soloveiko!" *see Soloveĭ*
  Karadžić CHAĭKOVSKIĭ
Solov'yov, S.
  BORODIN *Why art thou so early, Dawn?*
Solstice see Wolff, R. L. THOMPSON, R.
Solstrålen see Cnattingius, Thor
  KILPINEN
Soluppgång see Hedberg SIBELIUS
Solvay, Lucien
  MASSENET *Elle s'en est allée*

Som dybest Brønd see Aakjaer *HISTORIENS
  SANG.* NIELSEN
Som ett blommande mandelträd see
  Lagerkvist KILPINEN
"Som ett brödraskap med glada händer" *see
  Sorglöshetens vingar* Österling
  KILPINEN
"Som fulla hjärtans kvällsdröm" *see Pingst*
  Österling KILPINEN
"Som slätten vid havet" *see Efter lång sorg*
  Österling KILPINEN
The somber pine see Arens, Egmont
  RIEGGER
Le sombre Mai see Claudel MILHAUD
"Sombre nuit, aveugles ténébres" *see Hymne*
  Racine POULENC
"Sombres et fiers sapins, j'admire en vous la
  race" *see Les sapins* Martin, Paul
  SAINT-SAËNS
*SOME INFLUENCES IN MODERN
  PHILOSOPHIC THOUGHT. see* Hadley
  Tolerance IVES
Some one see De La Mare THOMPSON, R.
"Some one came knocking" *see Some one*
  De La Mare THOMPSON, R.
Some say that Love's a little boy see Auden
  BRITTEN *Tell me the truth about love*
"Some things are undivined except by love"
  see At sea Johnson IVES
Someone see Burns SCHUMANN *Jemand*
"Sometimes she is a child within mine arms"
  see Heart's haven Rossetti, Dante
  VAUGHAN WILLIAMS
Sometimes with one I love see Whitman
  ROREM
Somewhere see Smith, Logan *MORE
  TRIVIA.* DIAMOND
"Somewhere, far below the horizon" *see
  Somewhere* Smith, Logan DIAMOND
En sommarafton see Bergman KILPINEN
Sommarens ljud see Österling KILPINEN
Sommarnatten see Runeberg SIBELIUS
Sommation irrespectueuse see Hugo
  CHANSONS DES RUES ET DES BOIS.
  CHABRIER
Le sommeil see Carême POULENC
Sommeil see D'Harcourt, Antoniette
  SAUGUET
Le sommeil de canope see Samain *AUX
  FLANCS DU VASE.* KOECHLIN
Le sommeil des colombes see Toussaint
  JARDIN DES CARESSES. AUBERT
Le sommeil des fleurs see Penmarch, G. de
  SAINT-SAËNS
"Le sommeil en voyage" *see Le sommeil*
  Carême POULENC

"Sommer entschwand, Herbstluft durchwehet das Land" *see Der Herbst* Lua **SPOHR**

Sommer i Guerre see Drachmann **DELIUS**
  Summer landscape

Der Sommer ist so schön see Burns **FRANZ**
  The pleasant summer's come

"Der Sommer ist zu Ende" *see Sonnenwende* Osterwald **FRANZ**

Der Sommerabend see Becker, K. **ZELTER**

Sommerabend see Heine *HEIMKEHR.* **BRAHMS, SCHOECK**

Sommerabend see Schmidt, Hans **BRAHMS**

Sommerabend see Scholz, B. **LASSEN**

Sommerabend see Weigand **WEBERN**

Sommerfäden see Candidus **BRAHMS**

"Sommerfäden hin und wieder" *see Sommerfäden* Candidus **BRAHMS**

Sommernacht see Evers **REGER**

SOMMERNACHT. see Golenishchev-Kutuzov *Videnie* **MUSORGSKIĬ**

Sommernacht see Hesse **SCHOECK**

Die Sommernacht see Klopstock **GLUCK, SCHUBERT**
  Two Gluck settings, second 1785.

Sommernacht see Triepel, Gertrud **REGER**

Sommernacht see Unknown **LASSEN**

Sommersang see Holstein **NIELSEN**

Sommersegen see Sergel **KILPINEN**

SOMMERSEGEN, no. 1
  KILPINEN Sergel *Im Walde liegt ein stiller See*

SOMMERSEGEN, no. 2
  KILPINEN Sergel *Tausend stille, weisse, blaue Blumen*

SOMMERSEGEN, no. 3
  KILPINEN Sergel *Heiligendamm*

SOMMERSEGEN, no. 4
  KILPINEN Sergel *Mein Herz, der wilde Rosenstrauch*

SOMMERSEGEN, no. 5
  KILPINEN Sergel *Sommersegen*

SOMMERSEGEN, no. 6
  KILPINEN Sergel *Unter Blüten*

Sommerstorff, Otto, 1859-1934.
  REGER *Mei Bua*

Sommertag see Hohenberg **BERG**

"Sommerträume ihr purpurne Abende" *see Heilige Himmel* Evers **BERG**

Somnenie see Maĭkov **RIMSKIĬ-KORSAKOV**

Son see Anon. **PROKOFIEV**

Son see Heine **RACHMANINOFF** *A dream*

Son see Lermontov **BALAKIREV**

Son see Mikhailov **BALAKIREV**

Son see Teternikov **RACHMANINOFF**
  A dream

Son amigos de todos see Rivas, Reyna **THOMSON**

"Son bella pastorella" *see La pastorella dell'Alpi* Pepoli **ROSSINI**

Le son du cor s'afflige see Verlaine *SAGESSE.* **DEBUSSY**

"Le son du cor s'afflige vers les bois" *see Le son du cor s'afflige* Verlaine **DEBUSSY**

Le son du cor s'afflige vers les bois see Verlaine *SAGESSE.* **LOEFFLER**

Son fra l'onde see Metastasio *GLI ORTI ESPERIDI.* **SCHUBERT**

"Son image comme un songe" *see Souvenir* Desbordes-Valmore **SAUGUET**

"Son moĭ milyĭ, son schastlivyĭ" *see Son* Anon. **PROKOFIEV**

A son of a gambolier see Anon. **IVES**

Son of Kabarda see Mendel'son **PROKOFIEV** *Sin Kabordi*

Son souvenir emplit l'air si clair see Jammes *TRISTESSES.* **MILHAUD**

"Son troppo sazia, non ne vo'più" *see Capriccio* Lemene **MALIPIERO**

Son v letniuiu noch' see Maĭkov **RIMSKIĬ-KORSAKOV**

Sonata vocalise see No author **MEDTNER**

Sonatine, B flat minor, op. 138 "An sie am Klavier" see Braun von Braunthal **SPOHR**

"Soñé que tù me llevabas" *see Tu voz y tu mano* Machado y Ruiz **RODRIGO**

Soneto see Mesa, Juan Bautista de **RODRIGO**

SONETO, no. 1
  TURINA Rodríguez Marin, Francisco *Anhelos*

SONETO, no. 2
  TURINA Rodríguez Marin, Francisco *Vade retro!*

SONETO, no. 3
  TURINA Rodríguez Marin, Francisco *A unos ojos*

SONETO A CÓRDOBA. see Góngora y Argote *Soneto a Córdoba* **FALLA**

Soneto a Córdoba see Góngora y Argote *SONETO A CÓRDOBA.* **FALLA**

Sonett see Gerhardt **ZELTER**

Sonett see Streckfuss **WEBER**

Sonett I see Petrarca **SCHUBERT**

Sonett II see Petrarca **SCHUBERT**

Sonett III see Petrarca **SCHUBERT**

Sonett aus dem 13. Jahrhundert see Thibaut IV **ZELTER**

SONETTE AN ORPHEUS. see Rilke *Even though the world keeps changing* **DIAMOND**

I SONETTI DELLA FATE, no. 1
   MALIPIERO Annunzio *Eliana*
I SONETTI DELLA FATE, no. 2
   MALIPIERO Annunzio *Mirinda*
I SONETTI DELLA FATE, no. 3
   MALIPIERO Annunzio *Melusina*
I SONETTI DELLA FATE, no. 4
   MALIPIERO Annunzio *Grasinda*
I SONETTI DELLA FATE, no. 5
   MALIPIERO Annunzio *Morgana*
I SONETTI DELLA FATE, no. 6-7
   MALIPIERO Annunzio *Oriana–Oriana
   infedele*
Sonetti sadun linnusta see Koskenniemi
   KILPINEN
Sonetto XVI see Buonarroti **BRITTEN**
Sonetto XXIV see Buonarroti **BRITTEN**
Sonetto XXX see Buonarroti **BRITTEN**
Sonetto XXXI see Buonarroti **BRITTEN**
Sonetto XXXII see Buonarroti **BRITTEN**
Sonetto XXXVIII see Buonarroti **BRITTEN**
Sonetto LV see Buonarroti **BRITTEN**
Song see Chaucer **ROREM**
Song see Crapsey **WEISGALL**
Song see Cummings **COPLAND**
A song see Ives **IVES**
Song see Jean-Aubry **MALIPIERO**
Song see Lermontov **BALAKIREV** *Pesnya:
   Zholtíy list*
Song see Mužik **MARTINŮ**
Song see Rich *NECESSITIES OF LIFE.*
   WEISGALL
Song see Rossetti, Christina **MILHAUD**
Song see Zaleski *NIE MA CZEGO TRZEBA.*
   CHOPIN *Dumka*
A song at parting see Rossetti, Christina
   QUILTER
Song based on an old Spanish text see Eben,
   Bedřich **MARTINŮ** *Píseň na
   starošpanělský text*
"A song came over the hill to me" *see Song
   from o'er the hill* O'Reilly, P. J.
   IRELAND
Song for lying in bed during a night rain see
   Pitchford **ROREM**
Song for the Gravedigger from *Hamlet see*
   Shakespeare *HAMLET.* **THOMSON**
Song from o'er the hill see O'Reilly, P. J.
   IRELAND
Song from "The Smith of Lešetín" see Čech
   LEŠETINSKÝ KOVÁR. **DVOŘÁK**
   Zpěv z Lešetínského kováře
Song from without the world see Anon.
   GIDEON
The song of Catilin Ni Uallachain see
   Hefferman **LOEFFLER**

A song of David see Bible *PSALM 120.*
   ROREM
A song of enchantment see De La Mare
   BRITTEN
"A song of enchantment I sang me there" *see
   A song of enchantment* De La Mare
   BRITTEN
Song of gladness will I sing Thee see Bible
   DVOŘÁK *Bože! Bože! Píseň novou*
Song of Hanička see Kalhus **MARTINŮ**
Song of night see Tiutchev **MEDTNER**
Song of Selim see Lermontov **BALAKIREV**
   Pesnya Selima
Song of the Balearic Islander see
   Musorgskiĭ, M. *SALAMMBÔ.*
   MUSORGSKIĬ *Pesn' Balearĭsa*
Song of the blackbird see Henley **QUILTER**
The song of the brave see Surkov
   PROKOFIEV *Pesnia smelykh*
Song of the dagger see Anon. **GRIFFES**
Song of the dark forest see Borodin
   BORODIN
A song of the dew see Gorodetski
   STRAVINSKIĬ
Song of the disillusioned see Rathaus
   RACHMANINOFF
Song of the elves see Goethe *ELFENLIED.*
   MEDTNER *Elfenliedchen*
Song of the First of November see Hlavsa,
   Vrat. **MARTINŮ**
Song of the glove see Jonson **BLITZSTEIN**
Song of the golden fish see Lermontov
   BALAKIREV *Pesnya zolotoy rïbki*
Song of the gypsy girl see Polonsky
   CHAĬKOVSKIĬ *Pesu'*
Song of the homeland see Prokof'yev, A.
   PROKOFIEV *Pesnia O rodine*
*The song of the leaves of life and the water of
   life see* Bible **VAUGHAN WILLIAMS**
The song of the pilgrims see Bunyan
   VAUGHAN WILLIAMS
Song of the roses see Ritter **SIBELIUS**
   Rosenlied
The song of the soldiers see De La Mare
   BERKELEY
Song of the stream see Williams **QUILTER**
Song of the third duck from the right see
   Norse **ROREM**
Song of the woman of the wood see Cronyn
   RIEGGER
The song of Vanity Fair see Vaughan
   Williams, U. **VAUGHAN WILLIAMS**
Song of Voroshilov see Sikorskaya,
   Tatyana **PROKOFIEV** *Pesnia O
   Voroshilove*
The song that you sang long ago see
   Pleshcheyev **CHAĬKOVSKIĬ** *O, spoĭ zhe
   tu pesniu*

COMPOSER Poet *Title* "First Line"

Songe see Labé **SAUGUET**
SONGS & PROVERBS OF WILLIAM
  BLAKE
  BRITTEN Blake, William
    Ah! Sun-flower
    The chimney-sweeper
    Every night and every morn
    The fly
    London
    A poison tree
    Proverb I
    Proverb II
    Proverb III
    Proverb IV
    Proverb V
    Proverb VI
    Proverb VII
    The tyger
      NB: The music of *Songs & Proverbs* is
      continuous; these are the titles of the
      individual songs.
SONGS FOR A COLORED SINGER, VI. *see*
  Bishop
  What's that shining in the leaves **ROREM**
SONGS FOR A MEDIUM VOICE, no. 1
  IRELAND Symons *The adoration*
SONGS FOR A MEDIUM VOICE, no. 2
  IRELAND Symons *The rat*
SONGS FOR A MEDIUM VOICE, no. 3
  IRELAND Symons *Rest*
SONGS FOR ALICE ESTY, no. 1
  THOMSON Koch *Love song*
SONGS FOR ALICE ESTY, no. 2
  THOMSON Koch *Down at the docks*
SONGS FOR ALICE ESTY, no. 3
  THOMSON Koch *Let's take a walk*
SONGS FOR ALICE ESTY, no. 4
  THOMSON Koch *A prayer to Saint
    Catherine*
SONGS FOR "CERVENÁ SEDMA," no. 1
  MARTINŮ Herold, Jiří *Summer ballad*
SONGS FOR "CERVENÁ SEDMA," no. 2
  MARTINŮ Dreman, J. *Bar*
SONGS FOR "CERVENÁ SEDMA," no. 3
  MARTINŮ Gellner *Miners' song*
SONGS FOR OPHELIA, no. 1
  THOMSON Shakespeare *How should I
    your true love know*
SONGS FOR OPHELIA, no. 2
  THOMSON Shakespeare *Tomorrow is
    Saint Valentine's day*
SONGS FOR OPHELIA, no. 3
  THOMSON Shakespeare *They bore him
    barefac'd on the bier*
SONGS FROM THE CHINESE, no. 1
  BRITTEN Unknown *The big chariot*

SONGS FROM THE CHINESE, no. 2
  BRITTEN Po Chü-i *The old lute*
SONGS FROM THE CHINESE, no. 3
  BRITTEN Wu-Ti, Liang dynasty
    The autumn wind
SONGS FROM THE CHINESE, no. 4
  BRITTEN Lu Yu *The herd-boy*
SONGS FROM THE CHINESE, no. 5
  BRITTEN Po Chü-i *Depression*
SONGS FROM THE CHINESE, no. 6
  BRITTEN Unknown *Dance song*
Songs my mother taught me see Heyduk
  DVOŘÁK *Když mne stará matka*; **IVES**
SONGS OF A WAYFARER, no. 1
  IRELAND Blake, William *Memory*
SONGS OF A WAYFARER, no. 2
  IRELAND Shakespeare *When daffodils
    begin to peer*
SONGS OF A WAYFARER, no. 3
  IRELAND Rossetti, Dante *English May*
SONGS OF A WAYFARER, no. 4
  IRELAND Dowson *I was not sorrowful*
SONGS OF A WAYFARER, no. 5
  IRELAND Blake, James *I will walk on
    the earth*
SONGS OF EXPERIENCE, no. 1
  LUENING Blake, William *Earth's
    answer*
SONGS OF EXPERIENCE, no. 2
  LUENING Blake, William *Hear the voice
    of the Bard*
SONGS OF INNOCENCE: Introduction. *see*
  Blake, William
  The piper **VAUGHAN WILLIAMS**
SONGS OF PARTING. see Whitman
  Joy, shipmate, joy!
  VAUGHAN WILLIAMS
THE SONGS OF SELMA. see Macpherson
  Kolma's Klage **SCHUBERT**
SONGS OF THE HALF-LIGHT, no. 1
  BERKELEY De La Mare *Rachel*
SONGS OF THE HALF-LIGHT, no. 2
  BERKELEY De La Mare *Full moon*
SONGS OF THE HALF-LIGHT, no. 3
  BERKELEY De La Mare *All that's past*
SONGS OF THE HALF-LIGHT, no. 4
  BERKELEY De La Mare *The moth*
SONGS OF THE HALF-LIGHT, no. 5
  BERKELEY De La Mare *The fleeting*
SONGS OF TRAVEL (1895). *see* Stevenson,
  Robert Louis
  Romance **HESELTINE**
  To the memory of a great singer
  HESELTINE
SONGS OF TRAVEL, I. *see* Stevenson,
  Robert Louis
  The vagabond **VAUGHAN WILLIAMS**

SONGS OF TRAVEL, II. *see* Stevenson, Robert Louis
Youth and love **VAUGHAN WILLIAMS**
SONGS OF TRAVEL, IV. *see* Stevenson, Robert Louis
In dreams **VAUGHAN WILLIAMS**
SONGS OF TRAVEL, VI. *see* Stevenson, Robert Louis
The infinite shining heavens **VAUGHAN WILLIAMS**
SONGS OF TRAVEL, IX. *see* Stevenson, Robert Louis *Let beauty awake* **VAUGHAN WILLIAMS**
SONGS OF TRAVEL, XI. *see* Stevenson, Robert Louis
The roadside fire **VAUGHAN WILLIAMS**
SONGS OF TRAVEL, XIV. *see* Stevenson, Robert Louis *Bright is the ring of words* **VAUGHAN WILLIAMS**
SONGS OF TRAVEL, XVI. *see* Stevenson, Robert Louis *Whither must I wander?* **VAUGHAN WILLIAMS**
SONGS OF TRAVEL, XXII. *see* Stevenson, Robert Louis
I have trod the upward and the downward slope **VAUGHAN WILLIAMS**
SONGS OF TRAVEL, no. 1
VAUGHAN WILLIAMS Stevenson, Robert Louis *The vagabond*
SONGS OF TRAVEL, no. 2
VAUGHAN WILLIAMS Stevenson, Robert Louis *Let beauty awake*
SONGS OF TRAVEL, no. 3
VAUGHAN WILLIAMS Stevenson, Robert Louis *The roadside fire*
SONGS OF TRAVEL, no. 4
VAUGHAN WILLIAMS Stevenson, Robert Louis *Youth and love*
SONGS OF TRAVEL, no. 5
VAUGHAN WILLIAMS Stevenson, Robert Louis *In dreams*
SONGS OF TRAVEL, no. 6
VAUGHAN WILLIAMS Stevenson, Robert Louis *The infinite shining heavens*
SONGS OF TRAVEL, no. 7
VAUGHAN WILLIAMS Stevenson, Robert Louis *Whither must I wander?*
SONGS OF TRAVEL, no. 8
VAUGHAN WILLIAMS Stevenson, Robert Louis *Bright is the ring of words*
SONGS OF TRAVEL, no. 9
VAUGHAN WILLIAMS Stevenson, Robert Louis *I have trod the upward and the downward slope*

SONGS OF VOYAGE, no. 1
GIDEON Evans *Farewell tablet to Agathocles*
SONGS OF VOYAGE, no. 2
GIDEON Peabody *The nightingale unheard*
SONGS ON CZECH FOLK POETRY, no. 1
MARTINŮ Anon. *Bohatá milá*
SONGS ON CZECH FOLK POETRY, no. 2
MARTINŮ Anon. *Opuštěný milý*
SONGS ON CZECH FOLK POETRY, no. 3
MARTINŮ Anon. *Touha*
SONGS ON CZECH FOLK POETRY, no. 4
MARTINŮ Anon. *Zvědavá dievča*
SONGS ON CZECH FOLK POETRY, no. 5
MARTINŮ Anon. *Veselá dievča*
SONGS ON CZECH FOLK POETRY, no. 6
MARTINŮ Anon. *Smutný milý*
SONGS ON CZECH FOLK POETRY, no. 7
MARTINŮ Anon. *Prosba*
SONGS ON CZECH FOLK POETRY, no. 8
MARTINŮ Anon. *Vysoká veža*
SONGS SACRED AND PROFANE, no. 1
IRELAND Meynell *The advent*
SONGS SACRED AND PROFANE, no. 2
IRELAND Warner *Hymn for a child*
SONGS SACRED AND PROFANE, no. 3
IRELAND Meynell *My fair*
SONGS SACRED AND PROFANE, no. 4
IRELAND Yeats *The salley gardens*
SONGS SACRED AND PROFANE, no. 5
IRELAND Warner *The soldier's return*
SONGS SACRED AND PROFANE, no. 6
IRELAND Warner *The scapegoat*
"Songs! visions of my homeland" *see Down east* Ives **IVES**
Die Sonn' ist hin see Roquette **FRANZ**
Die Sonne der Schlaflosen see Byron **LOEWE**
Sonne der Schlummerlosen see Byron *SUN OF THE SLEEPLESS!* **WOLF**
"Sonne der Schlummerlosen, bleicher bleicher Stern!" *see Sonne der Schlummerlosen* Byron **WOLF**
"Sonne, du sinkst, Sonne, du sinkst" *see An die untergehende Sonne* Kosegarten **SCHUBERT**
"Der Sonne entgegen" *see Winterliebe* Henckell **STRAUSS**
Sonne ging zur Ruhe see Rathaus **CHAĬKOVSKIĬ**
"Die Sonne glüht wie ein Liebestraum" *see Liebe* Andersen **GRIEG**
"Die Sonne hebt an" *see Frühlingsanfang* Geibel **STRAUSS**
"Sonne, herbstlich dünn und zag" *see In den Nachtmittag geflüstert* Trakl **WEBERN**

COMPOSER Poet *Title* "First Line"

"Die Sonne sah die Erde an" *see*
Schneeglöckchen Anon. **SCHUMANN**
"Die Sonne sinkt" *see Der Jüngling und der*
Tod Spaun **SCHUBERT**
"Die Sonne sinkt in's tiefe Meer" *see Alinde*
Rochlitz **SCHUBERT**
"Die Sonne steigt" *see Klage* Matthisson
SCHUBERT
"Sonne, weinest jeden Abend dir die schönen
Augen rot" *see Schmerzen* Wesendonck
WAGNER
Sonnenregen see Ritter **REGER**
Sonnenschein see Heyse **JENSEN**
"Sonnenstrahlen durch die Tannen" *see*
Im Haine Bruchmann **SCHUBERT**
Sonnenuntergang see Hölderlin
CORNELIUS, HINDEMITH
Sonnenuntergang see Keller, G. **SCHOECK**
Sonnenuntergang see Leuthold **SCHOECK**
Sonnenuntergang; schwarze Wolken zieh'n see
Lenau **FRANZ**
Sonnenwende see Osterwald **FRANZ**
Sonnet see Cummings **GIDEON**
Sonnet see Daurat, Jean **ROREM**
Sonnet see La Morvonnais **MILHAUD**
Sonnet see Labé **MILHAUD**
Sonnet see Lodge, G. **LOEFFLER**
Sonnet see Magny **ROREM**
Two settings, variant texts; both 1953.
Sonnet see Pradel, Georges **MASSENET**
Sonnet see Ronsard **BIZET, CASELLA**
Sonnet see Saint-Saëns **SAINT-SAËNS**
Sonnet see Shakespeare **SEIBER**
SONNET 1. see Agee
So it begins **DIAMOND**
SONNET 2. see Agee
Our doom is in our being **DIAMOND**
SONNET 4. see Agee
I have been fashioned **DIAMOND**
SONNET 8. see Agee
What curious thing is love **DIAMOND**
SONNET 9. see Agee
Why am I here **DIAMOND**
SONNET 10. see Agee
Wring me no more **DIAMOND**
SONNET 17. see Agee
I nothing saw in you **DIAMOND**
SONNET XX. see Agee
Morning fair **CARPENTER**
SONNET 20. see Agee
Now stands our love **DIAMOND**
SONNET 23. see Agee
This little time **DIAMOND**
SONNET, no. 1
SAUGUET Shakespeare *Weary with toil*

SONNET, no. 2
SAUGUET Shakespeare *To my fair friend you never can be old*
Sonnet à Madeleine Repentie see Le Père **JOLIVET**
Sonnet à une lunatique see Mellin **JOLIVET**
Sonnet matinal see Silvestre *MIGNONNE.* **MASSENET**
Sonnet païen see Silvestre **MASSENET**
Sonnet to Cordova see Góngora y Argote *SONETO A CÓRDOBA.* **FALLA** *Soneto a Córdoba*
SONNETS DE LOUISE LABÉ, no. 1
SAUGUET Labé *Chasse*
SONNETS DE LOUISE LABÉ, no. 2
SAUGUET Labé *A Vénus*
SONNETS DE LOUISE LABÉ, no. 3
SAUGUET Labé *Songe*
SONNETS DE LOUISE LABÉ, no. 4
SAUGUET Labé *Amour*
SONNETS DE LOUISE LABÉ, no. 5
SAUGUET Labé *Printemps*
SONNETS DE LOUISE LABÉ, no. 6
SAUGUET Labé *Tant que mes yeux*
SONNETS FROM "FATAL INTERVIEW," no. 1
GIDEON Millay *Gone in good sooth you are*
SONNETS FROM "FATAL INTERVIEW," no. 2
GIDEON Millay *Night is my sister*
SONNETS FROM "FATAL INTERVIEW," no. 3
GIDEON Millay *Moon, that against the lintel of the West*
Ein Sonnett see Thibaut IV **BRAHMS**
"Sonneur qui sonnes l'heure et l'heure" *see L'heure volée* Mendès **MASSENET**
Sonnleithner, Joseph Ferdinand, 1766-1835.
ZELTER *An eine Mutter, deren Tochter als Kind starb*
Sonntag see Eichendorff **FRANZ**
Sonntag see Hoffmann von Fallersleben **SCHUMANN**
Sonntag see Uhland **BRAHMS, REGER**
"Der Sonntag ist da" *see Sonntagslied* Krummacher **LOEWE**
"Der Sonntag ist gekommen" *see Sonntag* Hoffmann von Fallersleben **SCHUMANN**
Sonntag und Montag see Unknown **SPOHR**
Sonntags am Rhein see Reinick *LIEDERBUCH EINES MALERS.* **SCHUMANN**
Sonntagslied see Klingemann **MENDELSSOHN-BARTHOLDY**

Sonntagslied see Krummacher
  SONNTAGSLIED IM SOMMER. **LOEWE**
SONNTAGSLIED IM SOMMER. see
  Krummacher *Sonntagslied* **LOEWE**
Sonntagsruhe see Ernst **LASSEN**
"Sono del mare bianca la figlia" *see La perla*
  Hohenlohe **LISZT**
Sons of Uncle Sam see Harris **HARRIS**
Sonst see Eichendorff **PFITZNER**
"Sonst konnt' ich dein nicht denken" *see*
  Gute Nacht! Gerstenberg **LOEWE**
SOPHIE. see Lenau
  O wärst du mein! **STRAUSS**
SOPHIENS REISE. see Hermes
  Ich würd' auf meinem Pfad **MOZART**
  Sei du mein Trost **MOZART**
  Verdankt sei es dem Glanz der Grossen
    MOZART
Sopivaisia see Kanteletar **KILPINEN**
Sopra l'acqua indormenzada . . . see Anon.
  HAHN
Sopra un'aria antica see Annunzio *POEMA*
  PARADISIACO. **RESPIGHI**
"Les sorciers et les fées dansent sur le côteau"
  see Chanson de fol Fort **HONEGGER**
Sorge see Goethe **SCHOECK**
Die Sorglichen see Falke **BERG**
Sorgloshetens vingar see Österling
  KILPINEN
Der Sorglose see Unknown **LOEWE**
Soria sotahan kuolla see Kanteletar
  KILPINEN
Sorochen'ka see Unknown **STRAVINSKIĬ**
  La petite pie
Sorrow in springtime see Einerling
  RACHMANINOFF *How painful for me*
Sorrow of Mydath see Masefield *SALT*
  WATER BALLADS. **GRIFFES**
The sorrowful maiden see Burns **FRANZ**
Sortilège see Carême **MILHAUD**
Sosna see Lermontov **BALAKIREV**
Sosny see Pushkin **PROKOFIEV**
"Le souci plus léger que les vents de l'Epire"
  see Salinum Leconte de Lisle **HAHN**
Souda, souda sinisorsa see Koskimies
  SIBELIUS
Un souffle de parfums s'élève see Silvestre
  MASSENET
"Un souffle d'ombre éteint" *see Le jardin du*
  ciel Mendès **IBERT**
Souhait see Banville *LES STALACTITES.*
  DEBUSSY
Souhait see Normand **MASSENET**
"The soul at all times would conceal" *see*
  In the soul of each of us Korinfskiĭ
  RACHMANINOFF

The soul calmly floated through the heavenly
  Empyrean see Tolstoĭ **MUSORGSKIĬ**
  Gornimi tikho letela dusha nebesami
The soul flew Heavenward see Tolstoĭ
  CHAĬKOVSKIĬ *Gornimi tikho letela*
The soul sings see Rorem **ROREM**
Soul, wilt thou toss again? see Dickinson
  LUENING
"Souléve ta paupière close" *see La spectre de*
  la rose Gautier **BERLIOZ**
The soul's concealment see Korinfskiĭ
  RACHMANINOFF
In the soul of each of us
Sound is simple see Trustman, Deborah
  WEISGALL
"A sound of a distant horn" *see Remembrance*
  Ives **IVES**
"Sound the flute" *see Spring* Blake, William
  THOMPSON, R.
Sounds of autumn see Ady **BARTÓK**
  Autumn echoes
The sounds of day are still see Tolstoĭ
  CHAĬKOVSKIĬ *Usni pechal'nyĭ drug"*
Soupir see Mallarmé **DEBUSSY, RAVEL**
Soupir see Sully-Prudhomme
  LES SOLITUDES. **DUPARC, RESPIGHI**
Souric et Mouric see Jacob, M. **POULENC**
"Souric et Mouric, rat blanc, souris noire" *see*
  Souric et Mouric Jacob, M. **POULENC**
Sourikoff *see* Surikov, Ivan Zakharovich,
  1841-1880.
Le sourire see Sauvage **MESSIAEN**
Un sourire éclaira see Zaffira **GOUNOD**
  Le labbra ella compose
La souris see Apollinaire *LE BESTIAIRE.*
  POULENC
"Sous la lune le palais résonne" *see Favorite*
  abandonnée Li-I **ROUSSEL**
"Sous la neige, la Rolls Royce" *see*
  La limousine Chalupt **MILHAUD**
"Sous le brouillard léger" *see Les oiselets*
  Normand **MASSENET**
"Sous le flot qui déferle" *see La sirène*
  Mendès **BIZET**
"Sous le grand chapeau Greenaway" *see*
  La diva de l'Empire Bonnaud **SATIE**
"Sous le pont Mirabeau coule la Seine" *see*
  Le pont Mirabeau Apollinaire **RIVIER**
"Sous le saule de la prairie" *see Toi qui*
  l'amais, verse des pleurs Du Boys
  BERLIOZ
"Sous l'eau du songe qui s'éllève" *see Reflets*
  Maeterlinck **BOULANGER**
Sous les branches see Silvestre **MASSENET**
"Sous les décombres entassés" *see Pour les*
  victims Unknown **FRANCK**

COMPOSER Poet *Title* "First Line"

"Sous les feuilles noires des lauriers" *see*
   Épitaphe de Bilitis Louÿs **KOECHLIN**
"Sous les flots crus d'une trompette" *see*
   Haute ecole Copperie, Adrien
   SAUGUET
"Sous les grands peupliers" *see Le banc de*
   pierre Choudens **GOUNOD**
"Sous les ifs noirs qui les abritent" *see*
   Les hiboux Baudelaire **SÉVERAC**
"Sous les ormeaux" *see Le petit paysan*
   Jacob, M. **SAUGUET**
"Sous les reflets de lune vaporeuse" *see*
   Nos souvenirs qui chantent Tatry, Robert
   POULENC
Sous l'oranger see Guillot de Saix **HAHN**
"Sous vos sombres chevelures petites fées"
   see Dans la forêt du Charme et de
   l'Enchantement Moréas **CHAUSSON**
Sous-bois see Unknown **AUBERT**
Soutar, William, 1898-1943.
   BRITTEN
      The auld aik
      Bed-time
      Black day
      The children
      A laddie's sang
      The larky lad
      Nightmare
      A riddle
         Two settings: Op. 84 no. 1 and op. 84
         no. 7.
      Slaughter
      Supper
      Who are these children?
The south wind see Ives, Harmony **IVES**
Southern night see Shcherbina **RIMSKIĬ-**
   KORSAKOV *IŪzhnaiá noch'*
Southern road see Brown, S. **GIDEON**
Southwind see Moses, Elizabeth Ann
   THOMPSON, R.
Souvenance see Châteaubriand **FRANCK**
Souvenance see Mariéton **MASSENET**
Souvenances see Lemaire, Ferdinand
   SAINT-SAËNS
Souvenez-vous, Vierge Marie! see Boyer,
   Georges **MASSENET**
Le souvenir see Collin, H. **GOUNOD**
Souvenir see Desbordes-Valmore
   SAUGUET
Souvenir see Hugo **LALO**
Le souvenir see Schiller **SAUGUET**
Le souvenir d'avoir chanté see Mendès
   HAHN
Souvenir de Venise see Musset **MASSENET**
Souvenir du transtevère see Zaffira
   MASSENET *L'improvisatore*

"Souvenir éternel, regret inconsolé" *see*
   Epitaphe Silvestre **MASSENET**
"Souvenir, souvenir, que me veux-tu?" *see*
   Nevermore Verlaine **MILHAUD**
Souvenirs d'enfance see Cocteau
   HONEGGER
Souvent de nos biens le meilleur see
   Silvestre **AUBERT**
Souvent j'ai dit a mon mari see Mansfield
   THE JOURNAL OF KATHERINE
   MANSFIELD. **DIAMOND**
"Souvent je rêve, O chère enfant" *see Marine*
   Theuriet **LALO**
"Souvent la chaleur d'un beau jour" *see*
   Chanson de l'aveugle Flaubert
   MILHAUD
Sov ind mit lille Nusseben! see Møller
   NIELSEN
"Sov, min Søn, O slumre sødt" *see Vuggesang*
   Munch **GRIEG**
"Sov nu sødt, du lille Mor" *see Ved Moders*
   Grav Benzon **GRIEG**
"Soviel Raben nachts auffliegen" *see Freihold*
   Lingg **SCHÖNBERG**
"Spähend nach dem Eisengitter" *see Blondel's*
   Lied Seidl **SCHUMANN**
Der späte Gast see Häring **LOEWE**
"Später der Linden bei der Haide" *see Unter*
   der Linden Walther von der
   Vogelweide **BERG**
Ein später Gast tritt ein see Krenek
   KRENEK
SPÄTHERBSTBLÄTTER. see Geibel
   Mein Herz ist schwer **BRAHMS**
Spätherbstnebel, kalte Träume see Heine
   LIEDERSTRAUSS. **WOLF**
"Spätherbstnebel, kalte Träume" *see*
   Vielgeliebte schöne Frau Heine **BERG**
SPÄTLESE, no. 1
   KRENEK Krenek *So spät, so spät*
SPÄTLESE, no. 2
   KRENEK Krenek *Spätlese, noch am Stock*
SPÄTLESE, no. 3
   KRENEK Krenek *Ein später Gast tritt ein*
SPÄTLESE, no. 4
   KRENEK Krenek *Im Gefälle der Zeit*
SPÄTLESE, no. 5
   KRENEK Krenek *Zu Boden gedrückt*
SPÄTLESE, no. 6
   KRENEK Krenek *Dort, wo in leichter*
      Kurve
Spätlese, noch am Stock see Krenek
   KRENEK
"Spandono le campane a la prim'alba l'ave"
   see Mattinata Annunzio **RESPIGHI**
Spanische Romanze see Unknown **LASSEN**

COMPOSER Poet *Title* "First Line"

Spanisches Lied see Heyse *SPANISCHES LIEDERBUCH* (1852). **BRAHMS, JENSEN**

SPANISCHES LIEDERBUCH. see Anon.
  Bedeckt mich mit Blumen **RUBINSTEIN, WOLF**

SPANISCHES LIEDERBUCH. see Geibel
  Geistliches Wiegenlied **BRAHMS**

SPANISCHES LIEDERBUCH. see Heyse
  Spanisches Lied **BRAHMS, JENSEN**

SPANISCHES LIEDERBUCH. see
  Valdivielso *Feridas teneis* **JENSEN**

SPANISCHES LIEDERBUCH: Alguna vez.
  see Castillejo
  Alguna vez **JENSEN**
  Dereinst, Gedanke mein **GRIEG**
  Dereinst, dereinst, Gedanke mein **WOLF**

SPANISCHES LIEDERBUCH: Aunque con
  semblante airado. *see* Anon.
  Ob auch finstre Blicke glitten **JENSEN, WOLF**

SPANISCHES LIEDERBUCH: Ay ojuelos
  verdes. *see* Anon.
  Ach ihr lieben Aeuglein **JENSEN**

SPANISCHES LIEDERBUCH: Celestina. *see*
  Unknown
  Dulces árboles sombrosos **JENSEN**

SPANISCHES LIEDERBUCH: Cojo jazmin y
  clavel. *see* Manuel del Rio, Don
  Cojo jazmin y clavel **JENSEN**

SPANISCHES LIEDERBUCH: En campaña
  madre. *see* Anon.
  En campaña, madre **JENSEN**

SPANISCHES LIEDERBUCH: En la peña,
  suso la peña. *see* Antonio de Villegas
  En la peña, suso la peña **JENSEN**

SPANISCHES LIEDERBUCH: Madre, unos
  ojuelos vi. *see* Vega Carpio
  Madre, unos ojuelos vi **JENSEN**

SPANISCHES LIEDERBUCH: Niña, si la
  huerta vas. *see* Anon.
  Wenn du zu den Blumen gehst **JENSEN, WOLF**

SPANISCHES LIEDERBUCH: Pensamientos
  me quitan. *see* Anon.
  Pensamientos me quitan **JENSEN**

SPANISCHES LIEDERBUCH: Ribericas del
  rio. *see* Anon.
  Am Ufer des Flusses, des Manzanares **JENSEN**

SPANISCHES LIEDERBUCH: Si dormis,
  doncella. *see* Vicente, Gil
  Und schläfst du, mein Mädchen **JENSEN, WOLF**

SPANISCHES LIEDERBUCH: Tango vos, el
  mi pandero. *see* Alvaro Fernandez de
  Almeida

Klinge, klinge, mein Pandero **JENSEN, RUBINSTEIN, WOLF**

SPANISCHES LIEDERBUCH: Ventecico
  murmurador. *see* Anon.
  Murmelndes Lüftchen **JENSEN**

THE SPANISH BAWD (1631): Now sleepe,
  and take thy rest. *see* Mabbe
  The contented lover **HESELTINE**

The Spanish ladies see Anon.
  VAUGHAN WILLIAMS

Spanish romance see Pushkin **MEDTNER**
  Two settings: Op. 36 no. 4 and op. 52 no.
  5.

Spanish song see Mikhailov **BALAKIREV**
  Ispanskaya pensyna

Spannung see Anon. **BRAHMS**

Sparklet,pseud. *see* Flament, Albert, 1877-
  1956.

Der Spassvogel see Musorgskiĭ
  MUSORGSKIĬ *Ozoruik*

Der Spatz see Garborg *HAUGTUSSA.*
  GRIEG *Sporven*

Spatz und Spätzin see Meyer, K. **REGER**

Spaun, Josef, Freiherr von, 1788-1865.
  SCHUBERT *Der Jüngling und der Tod*

Spaziergang see Mombert **BERG**

"Lo spazzacamin! Son d'aspetto brutto" *see*
  Lo spazzacamino Maggioni, S.
  Manfredo **VERDI**

Lo spazzacamino see Maggioni, S.
  Manfredo **VERDI**

Speak on! see Tetmajer **MARTINŮ**

LO SPECCHIO. see Olkienizkaia-Naldi
  La danza **CASELLA**
  Volutta **CASELLA**

Specimen case see Whitman *SPECIMEN
  DAYS.* **ROREM**

SPECIMEN DAYS. see Whitman
  Inauguration ball **ROREM**
  An incident **ROREM**
  A night battle **ROREM**
  The real war will never get in the books
  ROREM
  Specimen case **ROREM**

La spectre de la rose see Gautier
  BERLIOZ, SAUGUET

Spee, Friedrich, 1591-1635.
  MENDELSSOHN-BARTHOLDY
  Altdeutsches Frühlingslied

Spell of Springtide see Gripenberg
  SIBELIUS *Vårtagen*

"Spende, Veilchen, deine Düfte zu Marias
  Preis und Ruhm!" *see Das Veilchen*
  Müller, J. **LISZT**

Spenner, M.
  GOUNOD
  Bon jour, bon soir

Spenner, M. *(continued)*
  GOUNOD *(continued)*
    Patte de velours
    Un rêve
    Le rosier blanc
Spenser, Edmund, 1552?-1599.
  ROREM *What if some little pain*
  AMORETTI.
    BLITZSTEIN *Sweet is the rose*
Spes' see Tolstoĭ **BORODIN,**
  MUSORGSKIĭ
Spi! see Khomyakov **BALAKIREV**
Spi, dítě, spi see Des Knaben Wunderhorn
  MARTINŮ *Sleep, infant, sleep*
"Spi, ditia moe" *see Kolibel'naya pesnya*
  Maĭkov **CHAĭKOVSKIĭ**
"Spi, maliutka moĭ prekrasnyĭ" *see*
  Kolibel'naya pesnya Arsen'ev
  BALAKIREV
Spi, mé ditě, spi see Anon. **DVOŘÁK**
"Spi, mé zaté boubelaté malé dětátko" *see*
  Ukolébavka Jelínek, F. L. **DVOŘÁK**
Spící see Poe **MARTINŮ** *The sleeper*
Spick and span see Feeney **CHANLER**
"Der Spiegel dieser treuen, braunen Augen"
  see Peregrina I Mörike **WOLF**
SPIEGEL VON ARCADUA. see Schikaneder
  Arie aus dem Spiegel von Arcadien
  SCHÖNBERG
Spiel ich wo zum Tanze auf see Sergel
  KILPINEN
Spielleute see Ibsen *SPILLEMAEND.* **BERG,**
  DELIUS
Der Spielmann see Andersen **SCHUMANN**
Spielmann see Ibsen **BERG, DELIUS**
  Spielleute
"Ein Spielmann, der muss reisen" *see*
  Abschied Monsterberg-Münckeman
  BERG
"Der Spielmann sass am Felsen" *see*
  Spielmann und Zither Körner **STRAUSS**
Der Spielmann und sein Kind see Hoffmann
  von Fallersleben **STRAUSS**
Spielmann und Zither see Körner **STRAUSS**
Spielmannslied see Ibsen **GRIEG**
  Spillemaend
Spielmannslied see Unknown **LASSEN**
SPIELMANNSLIEDER, no. 1
  KILPINEN Sergel *Ihr ewigen Sterne*
SPIELMANNSLIEDER, no. 2
  KILPINEN Sergel *Eingeschneite stille*
  Felder
SPIELMANNSLIEDER, no. 3
  KILPINEN Sergel *Spiel ich wo zum*
  Tanze auf
SPIELMANNSLIEDER, no. 4
  KILPINEN Sergel *Tanzlied*

SPIELMANNSLIEDER, no. 5
  KILPINEN Sergel *Spielmannssehen*
SPIELMANNSLIEDER, no. 6
  KILPINEN Sergel *Vor Tau und Tag*
SPIELMANNSLIEDER, no. 7
  KILPINEN Sergel *Wenn der Wein nicht*
  wär'
SPIELMANNSLIEDER, no. 8
  KILPINEN Sergel *Ich sang mich durch*
  das deutsche Land
Spielmannssehen see Sergel **KILPINEN**
SPIELMANNSWEISEN, no. 1
  SCHOECK Leuthold *O Frühlingshauch,*
  O Liederlust
SPIELMANNSWEISEN, no. 2
  SCHOECK Leuthold *Die Ströme zieh'n*
  zum fernen Meer
SPIELMANNSWEISEN, no. 3
  SCHOECK Leuthold *Ich bin ein*
  Spielmann von Beruf
SPIELMANNSWEISEN, no. 4
  SCHOECK Leuthold *Und wieder nehm*
  ich die Harfe zur Hand
SPIELMANNSWEISEN, no. 5
  SCHOECK Leuthold *Mein Herz ist wie*
  ein Saitenspiel
SPIELMANNSWEISEN, no. 6
  SCHOECK Leuthold *O Lebensfrühling,*
  Blütendrang
Spielt, Mägdlein, unter eurer Weide! see
  Giesebrecht **LOEWE**
Śpiewam morzu, gwiazdom i tobie see
  Iwaszkiewicz **SZYMANOWSKI**
"Śpij, śpij, gniady koniu roboczy!" *see*
  Kolysanka gniadego konia
  Iłłakowiczówna **SZYMANOWSKI**
"Śpij, syneczku, na drewnianym lozeczku" *see*
  Kolysanka Krzysi Iłłakowiczówna
  SZYMANOWSKI
Spillemaend see Ibsen **GRIEG**
SPILLEMAEND. see Ibsen *Spielleute*
  BERG, DELIUS
Den Spillemand spiller paa Strenge see
  Damm, M. **NIELSEN**
Die Spinnerin see Fitger **PIJPER**
  Two settings, one 1913.
Die Spinnerin see Goethe **SCHUBERT,**
  ZELTER
Die Spinnerin see Heyse **SCHUMANN**
Die Spinnerin see Rückert **WOLF**
Die Spinnerin see Unknown **LASSEN**
The spinning top's lullaby see Liliencron
  MARTINŮ
"The spirit is too weak" *see Like a sick eagle*
  Keats **IVES**
Spirito santo see Goltz **LOEWE**

COMPOSER Poet *Title* "First Line"

The spirit's greeting see Goethe **MEDTNER**
   Geistergruss
Spiritual: I wan' my friends see Wright,
   Merle St. Croix **THOMPSON, R.**
"Spirto ben nato, in cui si specchia e vede"
   see Sonetto XXIV Buonarroti **BRITTEN**
"Spish'li ty, moĭadeviťsa?" *see Ispanskaya*
   pensyna Mikhailov **BALAKIREV**
Spitteler, Carl, 1845-1924.
   SCHOECK
      Das bescheidene Wünschlein
      Glöckleins Klage
      Der Hufschmied
      Ein Jauchzer
      Eine Unbekanntschaft
Spleen see Fargue *LUDIONS.* **SATIE**
Spleen see Verlaine **FAURÉ**
   Text variant from the following songs.
Spleen see Verlaine *AQUARELLES.*
   DEBUSSY, IRELAND
La splendeur vide see Renaud
   SAINT-SAËNS
The splendour falls see Tennyson
   THE PRINCESS. **VAUGHAN WILLIAMS**
"The splendor falls on castle walls" *see*
   The bugle song Tennyson **THOMSON**
"The splendour falls on castle walls" *see*
   The splendour falls Tennyson
   VAUGHAN WILLIAMS
"Spliu, no serdťse moe" *see Evreĭskaia pesnia*
   Mei **RIMSKIĭ-KORSAKOV**
SPOHR, LOUIS, 1784-1859.
   Adil
      *Ghasel,*op. 72 no. 3 [C. F. Peters, 1827]
         "Wer hätte sie gesehn und nicht auch
         sie geliebt?"
   Anna Amalia von Sachsen-Weimar,
   1739-1807.
      An Rosa Maria, op. 72 no. 5 [C. F.
         Peters, 1827] "Du gabst mir längst
         dein schönes Herz"
   Bassewitz, Karl, 1809-1907.
      Erwartung, WoO 121 [Wigand, 1854]
         "Komm in den Garten, ich harre dein"
   Becker, Julius, 1811-1859.
      *Abendlied,*WoO 104 [H. Hotop, 1841]
         "Sternennacht, heil'ge Nacht!"
   Bekmann, Mathilde
      *Lied aus dem "Märlein von der
         Wasserfee,"* op. 139 no. 4 [Luckhardt,
         1848] "Über die Wellen zieht zagend
         und trauernd mein Lied"
   Bodenstedt, Friedrich Martin von,
   1819-1892.
      Fatima beim Saitenspiel, WoO 119, no. 3
         [Peters, 1855]

"Deine Finger rühren die Saiten, und
   die Saiten mein Herz"
*Trinklied,*WoO 119, no. 2 [Peters, 1855]
   "Füllt mir das Trinkhorn! reicht es
   herum!"
Zuleikha, WoO 119, no. 1 [Peters, 1855]
   "Nicht mit Engeln im blauen
   Himmelszelt"
Braun von Braunthal, Johann Karl,
1802-1866.
   Gruss, WoO 110 [Haslinger, 1844]
      "Immortelle! bring' mein 'gute Nacht'
      ihr hin"
   *Sonatine, B flat minor, op. 138 "An sie
      am Klavier"* [Luckhardt, 1848]
      "Pulse höret auf zu schlagen durch den
      sturmgehobnen Busen"
Buri
   *Klagelied von den drei Rosen,*op. 41 no.
      4 [C. F. Peters, 1817]
      "Drei Rosen hielt ich in Händen, um
      eine der Liebsten zu spenden"
      Author of text may be Ludwig
         Ysenburg von Buri (1747-1806).
Chamisso, Adelbert von, 1781-1838.
   Tränen, WoO 108 [Bösenberg, 1842]
      "Was ist's, O Vater, was ich
      verbrach?"
Deinhardstein, Johann Ludwig
Ferdinand von, 1794-1859.
   Lied des verlassenen Mädchens, WoO 90
      [Wien: Schaumburgsche,
      Schellbachersche u. Mayersche
      Buchhandlung, 1815]
      "Wie weil' ich so gern, wo die
      Trauer webt"
Dingelstedt, Franz, Freiherr von, 1814-
1881.
   Mitternacht, WoO 97 [Paul, 1839]
      "Die Wolken ziehen schwarz und
      hoch"
   Unterwegs, WoO 101 [Spehr, 1842]
      "In die blaue Luft hinaus einen stillen
      Gruss nach Haus"
Eberwein, Julius, 1801-1870.
   Sangeslust, op. 101 no. 2 [Breitkopf &
      Härtel, 1837]
      "Das Vöglein singt den ganzen Tag"
      Voice & piano, 4 hands.
   Sangeslust, WoO 95 [Breitkopf & Härtel,
      1836]
      "Das Vöglein singt den ganzen Tag"
Geibel, Emanuel, i.e., Franz Emanuel
August, 1815-1884.
   *Gondelfahrt,*op. 101 no. 6 [Breitkopf &
      Härtel, 1837]
      "In den Wassern der Laguna"

SPOHR, LOUIS, 1784-1859 *(continued)*
  Geibel, Emanuel, i.e., Franz Emanuel
  August, 1815-1884 *(continued)*
    Voice & piano, 4 hands.
    Wolle keiner mich fragen, WoO 106
      [Göpel, 1842] same
  Geyer, Agnes Emerita, b. 1787.
    Das Schiffermädchen, op. 25 no. 6 [J. A.
      Böhme, 1810]
      "Schwebe, mein tanzender Kahn"
  Göchhausen, Karl Emil Konstantin
  von, 1778-1855.
    Immerdar Liebe, WoO 113 [Rudolstadt:
      Müller, 1845] "Kömmt mit dem Lenz
      auch die Lieb gegangen"
    Wiegenlied, op. 25 no. 1 [J. A. Böhme,
      1810] "Elia popeia, so leise, so lind"
  Goethe, Johann Wolfgang von, 1749-
  1832.
    Nachgefühl, WoO 91 [**Amphion,** edited
      by J.J.F.Dotzauer (Meissen bei Friedr.
      Wihl. Goedsche, 1824): 61-63]
      "Wenn die Reben wieder blühen,
        rühret sich der Wein im Fasse"
    Neue Liebe, neues Leben, WoO 127
      [Beilage zu **Deutscher
        Musenalmanach . . . ,** 9. Jhrg., 1859]
      "Herz, mein Herz, was soll das
        geben"
    Vanitas! Vanitatum vanitas, op. 41 no. 6
      [C. F. Peters, 1817]
      "Ich hab' meine Sach' auf nichts
        gestellt, juchhe!"
    Zigeunerlied, op. 25 no. 5 [J. A. Böhme,
      1810] "Im Nebelgeriesel, im tiefen
      Schnee"
    FAUST.
      Gretchen, op. 25 no. 3 [J. A. Böhme,
        1810] "Meine Ruh ist hin"
    WILHELM MEISTER.
      An Mignon, op. 41 no. 3 [C. F. Peters,
        1817] "Über Tal und Fluss getragen
        ziehet"
    WILHELM MEISTER. Mignon's song:
      Kennst du das Land?
      Mignon's Lied, op. 37 no. 1 [C. F.
        Peters, 1816] "Kennst du das Land?"
  Gross, E.
    Lied der Freude, op. 25 no. 4 [J. A.
      Böhme, 1810] "Rauschet ihr Meere
      und wehet ihr Winde!"
  Harnier, Auguste, 1826-1855.
    Grüsse, WoO 123 [Kahnt, 1862]
      "Fliege auf Windes Schwingen,
        Blättlein, zu ihr!"
    BÜHNE UND HAUS.

Immer dasselbe, WoO 124 [Payne,
  1858] "Es wogt wie steigende
  Wellen im Herzen hin"
Hochwald, A. von
  Trostlos, op. 101 no. 4 [Breitkopf &
    Härtel, 1837] "Der Regen rasselt, es
    saust der Sturm"
    Voice & piano, 4 hands.
Hoffmann von Fallersleben, August
Heinrich, 1798-1874.
  Mein Vaterland, WoO 111 [Bassermann,
    1845] "Treue Liebe bis zum Grabe
    schwör ich"
  Was mir wohl übrig bliebe, op. 139 no. 5
    [Luckhardt, 1848] same
  Was mir wohl übrig bliebe, WoO 96
    [Friese, 1838] same
Hugo, Victor Marie, comte, 1802-1885.
  RUY BLAS.
    An die Geliebte, WoO 100 [Fritz
      Schuberth, 1850] "Immer mag
      verklingen muntrer Bögel Sang"
Kartscher, Moritz, ca. 1793-1834.
  Der erste Kuss, op. 41 no. 5 [C. F.
    Peters, 1817]
    "Die Lippe brennt, die Wange glüht"
Kerner, Justinus, 1786-1862.
  Die Himmelsbraut, op. 105 no. 1
    [Helmuth, 1839]
    "Zu Augsburg steht ein hohes Haus"
Kind, Friedrich, 1768-1843.
  Das Mädchens Sehnsucht, op. 41 no. 1
    [C. F. Peters, 1817] "Das Herz ist
    gewachsen, Es pocht in der Brust"
Koch, Ernst, 1808-1858.
  An, op. 105 no. 4 [Helmuth, 1839] "Was
    treibt mich hin zu dir mit Macht?"
La Motte-Fouque, Friedrich Heinrich
Karl, freiherr, 1777-1843.
  Lied aus Aslauga's Ritter, op. 41 no. 2
    [C. F. Peters, 1817]
    "Ach, wär' ich nur ein Vögelein!"
Lua, August Ludwig, 1819-1876.
  Der Herbst, WoO 115 [Bote & Bock,
    1848] "Sommer entschwand, Herbstluft
    durchwehet das Land"
Mahlmann, Siegfried August, 1771-
1826.
  Schwermut, op. 94 no. 5 [Simrock, 1837]
    "Als mein Leben vol Blumen hing"
Marées, Adolf von, 1801-1874.
  Das wirtshaus zu, WoO 93 [Schott, 1836]
    "Im Wirthshaus geht es aus und ein"
Meier, Daniel Eduard 1812-1873.
  Sehnsucht, WoO 114 [Wessel, 1848]
    "Ev'ry where, far and near, whether
    resting, whether walking"

Müller, Wilhelm, 1794-1827.
   Ungeduld, op. 94 no. 4 [Simrock, 1837]
      "Ich schnitt es gern in alle Rinden ein"
Müller von der Werra, Friedrich
   Konrad Mueller, known as,1823-
   1881.
   *Mein Verlangen,*WoO 122 [St. Gallen:
      Scheitlin u. Zollikofer, 1855]
      "Es ist ein süsses Wähnen im Trauern
      und in Tränen"
Reinick, Robert, 1805-1852.
   Der Bleicherin Nachtlied, op. 94 no. 3
      [Simrock, 1837]
      "Wellen blinkten durch die Nacht"
   Frühlingsglocken, op. 101 no. 1
      [Breitkopf & Härtel, 1837]
      "Schneeglöckchen tut läuten"
   Schweigen ist ein schönes Ding, op. 101
      no. 5 [Breitkopf & Härtel, 1837] same
   LIEDERBUCH EINES MALERS.
      Nichts Schöneres, op. 101 no. 3
      [Breitkopf & Härtel, 1837]
      "Als ich zuerst dich hab gesehn"
Salis-Seewis, Johann Gaudenz,
   Freiherr von, 1762-1834.
   Lied beim Rundetanz, op. 37 no. 6 [C. F.
      Peters, 1816]
      "Auf! es dunkelt; silbern funkelt"
Schmidt, Heinrich, 1779-1857.
   *Getrennte Liebe,*op. 37 no. 4 [C. F.
      Peters, 1816] "Der Liebe bangen
      Sorgen erbleicht der Freude Strahl!"
   Lebenslied, op. 37 no. 2 [C. F. Peters,
      1816] "Schnell geniesst die schnellen
      Stunden"
Schulz, Eduard, 1813-1842.
   Der Rosenstrauch, op. 105 no. 2
      [Helmuth, 1839] "Das Kind schläft
      unter dem Rosenstrauch"
Schweizer, Karl Friedrich, Freiherr
   von, 1797-1847.
   Des Mädchens Klage, op. 105 no. 5
      [Helmuth, 1839]
      "Ich bin so bleich, du bist so rot"
   Ermutigung, WoO 112 [Kassel:
      Selbstverlag, 1845] "Freundig zum
      Himmel auf blikke mein Herz!"
Simrock, Karl Joseph, 1802-1876.
   *Ständchen,*op. 139 no. 1 [Luckhardt,
      1848] "Atme nur leise zieh ich die
      Kreise hier"
   Ständchen, WoO 94 [Kandern: Verlag
      des oberrheinischen Comptoirs, 1837]
      "Atme nur leise, zieh ich die Kreise
      hier"

Sturm, Julius Karl Reinholdt, 1816-
   1896.
   Wohin, WoO 125 [unpubl.] "Wohin, du
      rauschender Strom, wohin, wohin?"
      Holograph in Berlin,
      Staatsbibliothek.
Tieck, Johann Ludwig, 1773-1853.
   *Schifferlied der Wasserfee,*op. 72 no. 2
      [C. F. Peters, 1827] "Auf Wogen
      gezogen, von Klängen, Gesängen"
   *Schlaflied,*op. 72 no. 6 [C. F. Peters,
      1827] "Ruhe, süss Liebchen, im
      Schatten der grauen dämmernden
      Nacht"
Uhland, Ludwig, 1787-1862.
   Frühlingsglaube, op. 72 no. 1 [C. F.
      Peters, 1827]
      "Die linden Lüfte sind erwacht"
   Das Ständchen, op. 105 no. 3 [Helmuth,
      1839] "Was wekken aus dem
      Schlummer mich für süsse Klänge
      doch?"
Unknown
   Beruhigung, op. 72 no. 4 [C. F. Peters,
      1827]
      "Du armes Herz, was wünschest du?"
   Bitte, bitte! op. 94 no. 2 [Simrock, 1837]
      same
      Text may be by Heinrich Schmidt.
   Glockenklänge, WoO 118 [Oehme und
      Müller, 1852]
      "Sanft ertönen Morgenglokken"
   Jägerlied, op. 139 no. 3 [Luckhardt,
      1848] "Wenn Eos am Morgen mit
      rosigem Finger das Dunkel erhellt"
   Jüngst hört ich, welchen süssen lohn,
      WoO 139 [unpubl.] same
   Liebt er mich? WoO 109 [Göpel, 1843]
      same
   Lied der Harfnerin, op. 94 no. 1
      [Simrock, 1837] "Schweig, O Herz!
      warum dies bange Schnen"
   Maria, op. 139 no. 2 [Luckhardt, 1848]
      "Der Sänger zog durch Wald und Flur"
   Maria, WoO 107 [Chr. Fr. Müller, 1842]
      "Der Sänger zog durch Wald und Flur"
   Rätselhaft, WoO 103 [Spehr, 1841]
      "Der Frühling ist herangekommen"
      Voice & piano, 4 hands.
   Schottisch Lied, op. 25 no. 2 [J. A.
      Böhme, 1810]
      "Mir ist, als müsst ich dir was sagen"
   *Sonntag und Montag,*op. 94 no. 6
      [Simrock, 1837] "Heute ist Sonntag"
   Warum nicht? op. 105 no. 6 [Helmuth,
      1839]
      "Lieben, warum sollt' ich's nicht?"

SPOHR, LOUIS, 1784-1859 *(continued)*
W., Cäcilie von
  Liebesschwärmerei, op. 37 no. 5 [C. F.
    Peters, 1816] "Wär ich ein Vogelein,
    flög ich zu ihm!"
  Die Stimme der Nacht, op. 37 no. 3 [C.
    F. Peters, 1816]
    "Dort im Tal hör ich verhallen"
Walther von der Vogelweide, 12th
  cent.
  Die verschwiegene Nachtigall, WoO 126
    [Beilage zu *Deutscher*
      Musenalmanach . . . , 8 Jhrg., 1858]
    "Unter der Linden an der Heide"
Wihl, Ludwig, 1806-1882.
  Die sieben Schwestern, WoO 102 [Dunst,
    1840] "Die Wogen ergriffen vom
    Loreley-Sang"
Zedlitz, Joseph Christian von, 1790-
  1862.
  KERKER UND KRONE.
    Lied, WoO 105 [Bösenberg, 1841]
      "Singet die Nachtigall im dunkeln
      Wald"
Zimmermann, Balthasar Friedrich
  Wilhelm, 1807-1878.
  Verlust, WoO 99 [Riedl, 1839] "Am
    Bach, am Bach, im flüsternden Gras"
Sporven see Garborg *HAUGTUSSA.* **GRIEG**
Spottlied see Goethe *WILHELM MEISTER.*
  WOLF
Sprache der Liebe see Schlegel
  SCHUBERT
"Sprachen Königin und König einstens" *see*
  Schlimm für die Männer Anon. **REGER**
Sprague, Charles, 1791-1875.
  IVES *The Indians*
Die Spree-Nonne see Kurowski-Eichen
  LOEWE *Der grosse Kurfürst und die*
    Spreejungfrau
"Sprich, Fraülein, warum härmst du dich?" *see*
  Jock von Hazeldean Scott **JENSEN**
Sprich nicht immer see George *DAS BUCH*
  DER HÄNGENDEN GÄRTEN.
  SCHÖNBERG
Spring see Blake, William **THOMPSON, R.**
Spring see Carpenter, Rue **CARPENTER**
The spring see Chamisso **MEDTNER**
  Die Quelle
Spring see Gorodetski **STRAVINSKIĭ**
Spring see Hopkins **ROREM**
Spring see Koch **ROREM**
Spring see Nashe *SUMMER'S LAST WILL*
  AND TESTAMENT (1600). **HESELTINE**
Spring see Tennyson
  VAUGHAN WILLIAMS

Spring and fall (to a young child, 1946) *see*
  Hopkins **ROREM**
The spring came flying from afar see Hálek
  DVOŘÁK *Přílítlo jaro zdaleka*
Spring evening see Turgenev **RUBINSTEIN**
Spring flew hither from afar see Hálek
  DVOŘÁK *Přílítlo jaro zdaleka*
Spring is at the door see Chesson
  QUILTER
"Spring is come" *see Again I am alone*
  Shevchenko **RACHMANINOFF**
Spring is flying see Runeberg **SIBELIUS**
  Våren flyktar hastigt
Spring solace see Tiutchev **MEDTNER**
  Elegy
Spring song see Antipater **BERKELEY**
Spring song see Cummings **ROREM**
Spring song see Fitger **SIBELIUS**
  Lenzgesang
Spring song see Goethe **MEDTNER** *Mailied*
Spring song see Ives, Harmony **IVES**
Spring song see Pleshcheyev
  CHAĬKOVSKIĭ *Vesennyaya pesnya*
Spring song see Rypáček **JANÁČEK** *Jarní*
  píseň
Spring song see Witwicki **CHOPIN** *Wiosna*
Spring sorrow see Brooke **IRELAND**
Spring talk see Louchheim *WITH OR*
  WITHOUT ROSES. **DIAMOND**
Spring: the grass grows green see
  Pleshcheyev **CHAĬKOVSKIĭ** *Vesna*
Spring: the snow is melting see Pleshcheyev
  CHAĬKOVSKIĭ *Vesna*
Spring, the sweet Spring see Nashe
  SUMMER'S LAST WILL AND
  TESTAMENT (1600). **DELIUS**
"Spring, the sweet spring is the year's
  pleasant king" *see Spring* Nashe
  HESELTINE
Spring voices see Quilter **QUILTER**
Spring waters see Tiutchev
  RACHMANINOFF
Spring will not wait see Housman
  IRELAND
"Springer, der in luft'gem Schreiten" *see*
  Guter Rat Eichendorff **SCHOECK**
Spring-tide see Kleinschrod **DVOŘÁK** *Jaro*
Die Spröde see Goethe **MEDTNER,**
  WOLF, ZELTER
Die Spröde see Kopisch **BRAHMS**
Spruch see Claudius, M. **SCHOECK**
Spruch see Goethe *WESTÖSTLICHER*
  DIVAN. **STRAUSS**
Spruch see Leuthold **SCHOECK**
Spruch see Mörike **SCHOECK**
Spruchband see Barth **KRENEK**

Spuk see Hebbel **BERG**
Der Spuk see Löns **KILPINEN**
Spurned love see Aldrich *TWO SONGS
    FROM THE PERSIAN*, II. **COPLAND**
Spurven sidder stum bag Kvist see Aakjaer
    MORS ROK. **NIELSEN**
"*Spute dich, Kronos!" see An Schwager
    Kronos* Goethe **SCHUBERT**
Spyashchaya knyazhna see Borodin
    BORODIN *Die schlafende Prinzessin*
Squire, Sir John Collings, 1884-1958.
    TRICKS OF THE TRADE (1917).
        HESELTINE *Mr. Belloc's fancy*
Squirrel song see Boultenhouse, Charles
    ROREM
"*Srdéčko mé, všechno spí" see Píseň na
    starošpanělský text* Eben, Bedřich
    MARTINŮ
Sred' mrachnykh dneǐ see Rathaus
    CHAǏKOVSKIǏ *In trüber Stund'*
Sred' shumnago bala see Tolstoǐ
    CHAǏKOVSKIǏ
Sredi tsvetov pori osenney see Aksakov
    BALAKIREV
"*Srezal sebe ia trostnik" see Iskusstvo*
    Maǐkov **RIMSKIǏ-KORSAKOV**
Ssu-k'ung Shu, 8th century A. D.
    BERKELEY *The riverside village*
St. Chaffray, Édouard
    SAINT-SAËNS *Toi*
St. Francis of Assisi *see* Francis of
    Assisi, Saint, 1182-1226.
St. Ita's vision see Kallman **BARBER**
St. Johannes und das Würmlein see Chezy
    LOEWE
St. Nepomucks Vorabend see Goethe
    ZELTER *Sct. Nepomuks Vorabend*
St. Nepomuk's Vorabend see Goethe **WOLF**
St. St. Blicher see Ploug **NIELSEN**
Stach-Lerner, Ilse von *see* Wackernagel,
    Ilse (Stach von Goltzheim), 1879-1941.
Stadler, Albert, 1794-1888.
    SCHUBERT
        Lieb Minna
        Namenstagslied
Die Stadt see Heine **SCHUBERT**
Stämmingsvisa see Cnattingius, Thor
    KILPINEN
Ständchen see Anon. **BRAHMS, ZELTER**
Das Ständchen see Eichendorff **LASSEN,
    WOLF**
Ständchen see Körner **WOLF**
Ständchen see Kugler *SKIZZENBUCH.*
    BRAHMS
STÄNDCHEN (?) *see* Nordmann
    Kling leise, mein Lied **LISZT**

Ständchen see Osterwald **FRANZ**
Ständchen see Pushkin **JENSEN**
Ständchen see Reinick *LIEDERBUCH EINES
    MALERS.* **LASSEN, SCHUMANN,
    WOLF**
Ständchen see Rellstab **SCHUBERT**
Ständchen see Rückert **FRANZ**
Ständchen see Schack **STRAUSS**
Ständchen see Shakespeare *CYMBELINE.*
    SCHUBERT
Ständchen see Simrock **SPOHR**
    Two settings: Op. 139 no. 1 and WoO 94.
Das Ständchen see Uhland **LOEWE,
    SPOHR**
Ständchen see Unknown **LOEWE,
    RUBINSTEIN**
Ständchen see Wildenbruch **LASSEN**
Ein Ständchen Euch zu bringen see Heyse
    WOLF
LE STAGIONI ITALICHE, no. 1
    MALIPIERO Latini *Lauda per un morto*
LE STAGIONI ITALICHE, no. 2
    MALIPIERO Anon. *Canto della neve*
LE STAGIONI ITALICHE, no. 3
    MALIPIERO Lemene *Capriccio*
LE STAGIONI ITALICHE, no. 4
    MALIPIERO Annunzio *Ditirambo terzo*
        (dalle laudi di Gabriele d'Annunzio)
Stakhanovite girl see Blagov, A.
    PROKOFIEV *Stakhanovka*
Stakhanovka see Blagov, A. **PROKOFIEV**
LES STALACTITES. see Banville
    Souhait **DEBUSSY**
LES STALACTITES: La Dernière Pensée de
    Weber. *see* Banville
    Nuit d'étoiles **DEBUSSY**
Stambogsrim see Ibsen **GRIEG**
Stammbuchsreim see Ibsen **GRIEG**
    Stambogsrim
Stampelchen see Blüthgen **REGER**
Stances see Bertin **GOUNOD** *Si la mort est
    le but*
Stances see Gilbert **MASSENET**
Stances à la mémoire de Livingstone see
    Houghton **GOUNOD** *Ilala*
"Stand das Mädchen, stand am Bergesabhang"
    see Das Mädchen Kapper **BRAHMS**
"Stand, stand against the rising night" *see
    Freedom's land* MacLeish **HARRIS**
STANSǏ. see Grekov
    Smotri, von oblako **CHAǏKOVSKIǏ**
Star see Jean-Aubry **SCHMITT**
"Star of day" *see Sunset* Case **BENNETT**
Stará píseň see Villiers **MARTINŮ** *Old song*
Starke Einbildungskraft see Anon. *DES
    KNABEN WUNDERHORN*: Starke
    Einbildungskraft. **MAHLER**

"Eine starke schwarze Barke" *see Childe Harold* Heine **FRANZ, LASSEN**

"Ein starker Geist" *see Berggeist* Hesse **KILPINEN**

Starkey, James, 1879-1958.
VAUGHAN WILLIAMS
A piper
The twilight people

The star-flower see Franzén **SIBELIUS**
Hvitsippan

Starless midnight coldly breathed see Khomyakov **BALAKIREV** *Bezzvezdnaya polnoch'*

Starry night see Pleshcheyev *SLOVA DLYA MUZÏKI.* **CHAĬKOVSKIĬ**
Nam zvezdy krotkie siiali

The stars see Stevenson, Robert Louis *A CHILD'S GARDEN OF VERSES.* **HAHN**

The stars that twinkle in the sky see Hálek **DVOŘÁK** *Ty hvězdičky tam na nebi to veliké*

The stars upon the firmament see Hálek **DVOŘÁK** *Ty hvězdičky tam na nebi to veliké*

"Staryĭ muzh, groznyĭ muzh" *see Pesnya Zemfiri* Pushkin **CHAĬKOVSKIĬ**

Šťastná jízda see Goethe **MARTINŮ**
Glückliche Fahrt

La statua see Annunzio **RESPIGHI**

La statue de bronze see Fargue **SATIE**

Stay, my charmer see Burns **BENNETT**

"Steepies for the bairnie" *see Supper* Soutar **BRITTEN**

"Steh' auf und öffne das Fenster schnell" *see Morgenständchen* Träger **JENSEN**

STEH' ICH IN SEL'GEM TRAUME. see Henckell *Liebeshymnus* **STRAUSS**

Stehe still see Wesendonck **WAGNER**

"Steht auf ihr lieben Kinderlein!" *see Morgengesang* Alberus **REGER**

"Steht meiner Dam Kühnheit an" *see O sag' mir, wie dich frein, mein Lieb* Scott **JENSEN**

Steig' auf, geliebter Schatten see Münch-Bellinghausen **BRAHMS**

Steigentesch, August Ernst, Freiherr von, 1774-1826.
ZELTER *Lied*

"Steigt empor, ihr Wünsche mein" *see Ida's Wunsch* Loewe, Helene **LOEWE**

Stein, Gertrude, 1874-1946.
DIAMOND, ROREM *I am rose*
THOMSON
Deux soeurs qui sont pas soeurs
Film: Two sisters not sisters
Portrait of F. B. [Frances Blood]
Susie Asado

FOUR SAINTS IN 3 ACTS.
THOMSON *Pigeons on the grass*
PRECIOSILLA.
THOMSON *Preciosilla*

Stein, Gretel
REGER *Wiegenlied*
NB: Poet may be Gertrude Stein.

Steinebach, Friedrich, 1821-1899.
WOLF *Das Lied der Waise*

"Steliutsia chernye tuchi" *see Pesnia smelykh* Surkov **PROKOFIEV**

"Stell' auf den Tisch die duftenden Reseden" *see Allerseelen* Gilm zu Rosenegg **PIJPER, STRAUSS**

Stella *see* Devereux, Penelope, 1562?-1607, supposed author.

STELLA: Act 4 scene 1. *see* Goethe *Stella's Monologue* **KRENEK**

Stella's Monologue see Goethe *STELLA:* Act 4 scene 1. **KRENEK**

Stelldichein see Garborg *HAUGTUSSA.* **GRIEG** *Møte*

Stelldichein see Hörmann **REGER**

"Stellt auf den Tisch die duftenden Reseden" *see Allerseelen* Gilm zu Rosenegg **LASSEN**

Stephens, James, 1882-1950.
BARBER
Bessie Bobtail
The daisies
QUILTER *In the bud of the morning-O*

Sterb' ich, so hüllt in Blumen see Heyse **WOLF**

Sterbeglocken see Eichendorff **SCHOECK**

Die Sterbende see Matthisson **SCHUBERT**

Das sterbende Kind see Geibel **GRIFFES, REGER**

Sterling-Levis, Edith
QUILTER *Drooping wings*

Der Stern see Arnim **STRAUSS**

Der Stern ist die Liebe see Unknown **FRANZ**

Sternbotschaft see Hertz **JENSEN**

"Sternchen mit dem trüben Schein" *see Gold überwiegt die Liebe* Anon. **BRAHMS**

STERNDALE BENNETT, WILLIAM *see* **BENNETT, WILLIAM STERNDALE, 1816-1875.**

Die Sterne see Fellinger *WAS FUNKELT IHR SO MILD.* **SCHUBERT**

Die Sterne see Gerstenberg **LOEWE**

Sterne see Jone *DIE FREUNDE.* **WEBERN**

Die Sterne see Kosegarten **SCHUBERT**

Die Sterne see Leitner **SCHUBERT**

Sterne see Ritter **REGER**

Die Sterne see Schlegel, F. *ABENDRÖTE.* **SCHUBERT**

"Sterne der blauen himmlischen Auen" *see*
  Die Sehnsucht Schumann **SCHUMANN**
"Die Sterne flimmern und prangen" *see*
  Erinnerung Osterwald **FRANZ**
Sterne mit den goldnen Füsschen see Heine
  LIEDERSTRAUSS. **FRANZ, WOLF**
Die Sterne schau'n in stiller Nacht see
  Schlippenbach **MENDELSSOHN-
  BARTHOLDY**
Sternenfall see Wilhelm, Carl **BERG**
Der Sternenhimmel see Sauter, Lilly von, d.
  ca. 1970. **KRENEK**
"Sternennacht, heil'ge Nacht!" *see Abendlied*
  Becker, J. **SPOHR**
Die Sternennächte see Mayrhofer
  SCHUBERT
Die Sternenwelten see Fellinger
  SCHUBERT
"Ein Sternlein fiel vom Himmel her" *see*
  Die Schneeflocke Marggraff **LOEWE**
Die Sternseherin see Claudius, M.
  SCHOECK
Štěstí lásky see Goethe **MARTINŮ**
  Liebesglück
Štěstí to dost see Liliencron **MARTINŮ**
  Enough of happiness
"Ein steter Kampf ist unser Leben" *see Klage*
  Müchler **WEBER**
Stevenson, Robert Louis, 1850-1894.
  CARPENTER
    The cock shall crow
    Looking-glass river
  IRELAND *Bed in summer*
  IVES *Requiem*
  QUILTER
    In the highlands
    Over the land is April
  RIEGGER *My shadow*
  ROREM *Requiem*
  A CHILD'S GARDEN OF VERSES.
    HAHN
      A good boy
      My ship and I
      The stars
      The swing
      Windy nights
    QUILTER
      Foreign children
      A good child
      The lamplighter
      Where go the boats?
  SONGS OF TRAVEL (1895).
    HESELTINE
      Romance
      To the memory of a great singer

SONGS OF TRAVEL, I.
  VAUGHAN WILLIAMS *The vagabond*
SONGS OF TRAVEL, II.
  VAUGHAN WILLIAMS *Youth and
    love*
SONGS OF TRAVEL, IV.
  VAUGHAN WILLIAMS *In dreams*
SONGS OF TRAVEL, VI.
  VAUGHAN WILLIAMS *The infinite
    shining heavens*
SONGS OF TRAVEL, IX.
  VAUGHAN WILLIAMS *Let beauty
    awake*
SONGS OF TRAVEL, XI.
  VAUGHAN WILLIAMS *The roadside
    fire*
SONGS OF TRAVEL, XIV.
  VAUGHAN WILLIAMS *Bright is the
    ring of words*
SONGS OF TRAVEL, XVI.
  VAUGHAN WILLIAMS *Whither must
    I wander?*
SONGS OF TRAVEL, XXII.
  VAUGHAN WILLIAMS *I have trod
    the upward and the downward slope*
Stevenson, William, 1521-1575.
  GAMMER GURTON'S NEEDLE (1575).
    HESELTINE *Maltworms*
Die Stickerin see Kleinschrod **DVOŘÁK**
  Při vyšívání
Stickney
  GIDEON *Be still, the hanging gardens
    were a dream*
Stieglitz, Heinrich Wilhelm August,
  1801-1849.
  LOEWE
    Abendgesang
    Ali im Garten
    Assad mit dem Selam
    Die Geister der Wüste
    Gulhinde am Putztische
    Lied eines Vögleins in der Oasis
    Maisuna am Brunnen
    Melek am Quell
    Melek in der Wüste
    Die Oasis
    Taubenpost
    Der verschmachtende Pilger
"Stiehe, von allen den Liedern" *see An meine
  Mutter* Mörike **SCHOECK**
Stieler, Karl, 1842-1885.
  BERG *Im Morgengrauen*
  LASSEN *Am Strande*
  REGER *Nächtliche Pfade*
  STRAUSS *Rote Rosen*

COMPOSER   Poet   *Title*   "First Line"

*Stikhi, sochinennye noch'iu vo vremia
   bessonnitsy see* Pushkin **BRITTEN**
   Lines written during a sleepless night;
   MEDTNER *Sleepless*
"Still beginnt's im Hain zu thauen" *see
   Abendbilder* Silbert **SCHUBERT**
"Still falls the rain" *see Canticle III* Sitwell
   BRITTEN
"Still ist die Nacht" *see Der Doppelgänger*
   Heine **SCHUBERT**
Still ist's auf dem Erdenkreise see Ahlefeldt,
   Ottilie von **LASSEN**
"Still ist's auf dem Erdenkreise" *see
   Ein Frühlingsnacht* Unknown **LASSEN**
"Still ist's wo die Gräber sind" *see
   Schattenleben* Frey, F. **BERG**
"Still sitz' ich an des Hügels Hang" *see
   Im Frühling* Schulze **SCHUBERT**
"Still, still! 's ist nur ein Traum" *see Trost*
   Falke **REGER**
"Still, wie so still!" *see Stampelchen*
   Blüthgen **REGER**
Den stilla staden see Dehmel **SIBELIUS**
   Die stille Stadt
"Stilla, stilla trädens kronor susa" *see Dödens
   vila* Cnattingius, Thor **KILPINEN**
Die Stille see Eichendorff **SCHUMANN**
Stille der Nacht see Keller, G. **SCHOECK**
Das stille Königreich see Busse **BERG**
DAS STILLE LEUCHTEN, no. 1
   SCHOECK Meyer *Das Heilige Feuer*
DAS STILLE LEUCHTEN, no. 2
   SCHOECK Meyer *Liederseelen*
DAS STILLE LEUCHTEN, no. 3
   SCHOECK Meyer *Reisephantasie*
DAS STILLE LEUCHTEN, no. 4
   SCHOECK Meyer *Mit einem
   Jugendbildnis*
DAS STILLE LEUCHTEN, no. 5
   SCHOECK Meyer *Am Himmelstor*
DAS STILLE LEUCHTEN, no. 6
   SCHOECK Meyer *In einer Sturmnacht*
DAS STILLE LEUCHTEN, no. 7
   SCHOECK Meyer *Im Harmesnächten*
DAS STILLE LEUCHTEN, no. 8
   SCHOECK Meyer *Lenzfahrt*
DAS STILLE LEUCHTEN, no. 9
   SCHOECK Meyer *Frühling Triumphator*
DAS STILLE LEUCHTEN, no. 10
   SCHOECK Meyer *Unruhige Nacht*
DAS STILLE LEUCHTEN, no. 11
   SCHOECK Meyer *Was treibst du, Wind?*
DAS STILLE LEUCHTEN, no. 12
   SCHOECK Meyer *Hochzeitslied*
DAS STILLE LEUCHTEN, no. 13
   SCHOECK Meyer *Der Gesang des
   Meeres*

DAS STILLE LEUCHTEN, no. 14
   SCHOECK Meyer *Der römische Brunnen*
DAS STILLE LEUCHTEN, no. 15
   SCHOECK Meyer *Das Ende des Festes*
DAS STILLE LEUCHTEN, no. 16
   SCHOECK Meyer *Die Jungfrau*
DAS STILLE LEUCHTEN, no. 17
   SCHOECK Meyer *Neujahrsglocken*
DAS STILLE LEUCHTEN, no. 18
   SCHOECK Meyer *Alle*
DAS STILLE LEUCHTEN, no. 19
   SCHOECK Meyer *Der Reisebecher*
DAS STILLE LEUCHTEN, no. 20
   SCHOECK Meyer *Das weisse Spitzchen*
DAS STILLE LEUCHTEN, no. 21
   SCHOECK Meyer *Göttermahl*
DAS STILLE LEUCHTEN, no. 22
   SCHOECK Meyer *Ich würd' es hören*
DAS STILLE LEUCHTEN, no. 23
   SCHOECK Meyer *Firnelicht*
DAS STILLE LEUCHTEN, no. 24
   SCHOECK Meyer *Schwarzschattende
   Kastanie*
DAS STILLE LEUCHTEN, no. 25
   SCHOECK Meyer *Requiem*
DAS STILLE LEUCHTEN, no. 26
   SCHOECK Meyer *Abendwolke*
DAS STILLE LEUCHTEN, no. 27
   SCHOECK Meyer *Nachtgeräusche*
DAS STILLE LEUCHTEN, no. 28
   SCHOECK Meyer *Jetzt rede du!*
Stille Liebe see Kerner **SCHUMANN**
Stille Liebe see Röser, Otto **FRANZ** *Liebe*
Stille Liebe see Unknown **LOEWE**
"Die stille Lotosblume steigt aus dem blauen
   See" *see Die Lotosblume* Geibel **FRANZ**
"Eine stille Melodie" *see Errinerung*
   Schäfer, T. **REGER**
"Die stille Nacht umdunkelt" *see Sehnsucht*
   Reissig **BEETHOVEN, LOEWE**
Stille sicherheit see Lenau **FRANZ, WOLF**
Die stille Stadt see Dehmel **PFITZNER,
   SIBELIUS**
"Stille, stille, dass ich höre" *see Das Blümlein*
   Loewe, Helene **LOEWE**
Stille Thränen see Kerner **SCHUMANN**
"Stille, träumende Frühlingsnacht" *see Flieder*
   Bierbaum **REGER**
Die stille Wasserrose see Geibel **LISZT**
Stilleben see Keller, G. **SCHOECK**
Stiller Abend see Schröer **FRANZ**
Stiller Gang see Dehmel **STRAUSS**
"Stiller Garten, eile nur" *see Der Kirchhof im
   Frühling* Uhland **SCHOECK**
Stiller Vorwurf see Wolff **SCHUMANN**
Stillung Mariä mit dem Auferstandenen see
   Rilke **HINDEMITH**

Stimme der Liebe see Matthisson
ABENDGEWÖLKE SCHWEBEN HELL.
SCHUBERT
    Two settings: D. 187 and D. 418.
Stimme der Liebe see Stolberg **SCHUBERT**
Die Stimme der Nacht see W., Cäcilie von
    SPOHR
Stimme der Sehnsucht see Busse **PFITZNER**
Stimme im Dunkeln see Dehmel
    SZYMANOWSKI
STIMMEN DER VÖLKER. see Herder
    Darthula's Grabesgesang **JENSEN**
    Edward **JENSEN, LOEWE**
    Erlkönigs Tochter **JENSEN**
    Herr Oluf **LOEWE**
    Lied der Desdemona **JENSEN**
STIMMEN UND BILDER. see Avenarius
    Wolkennacht **WEBERN**
STIMMEN UND BILDER. Ehe. *see*
  Avenarius
    Freunde **WEBERN**
    Gefunden **WEBERN**
STIMMEN UND BILDER. Jahrbuch. *see*
  Avenarius
    Vorfrühling **WEBERN**
    Vorfrühling II **WEBERN**
    Wehmut **WEBERN**
STIMMEN UND BILDER. Stimmungen. *see*
  Avenarius
    Gebet **WEBERN**
"Stirb immerhin, es welken ja so viele der
  Freuden" *see Elegie auf den Tod eines*
  Pudels Unknown **BEETHOVEN**
Stirb, Lieb' und Freud! see Kerner
  SCHUMANN
Stirbt der Fuchs, so gilt der Balg see Goethe
  ZELTER
Stjärnöga see Bergman **KILPINEN**
"Stjärnöga, du som jag mött" *see Stjärnöga*
  Bergman **KILPINEN**
Stjärnorna äro så stilla see Blomberg
  KILPINEN
"Störe nicht den leisen Schlummer" *see*
  Nachtwandler Kalbeck **BRAHMS**
"Stoĭ, Dnepr! Slushaĭ, Dnepr!" *see Na Dnepre*
  Shevchenko **MUSORGSKIĭ**
Stolberg, Friedrich Leopold, Graf zu
  Stolberg, 1750-1819.
  LOEWE *An die Natur*
  SCHUBERT
    Abendlied
    An die Natur
    Auf dem Wasser zu singen
    Daphne am Bach
    Lied
    Lied in der Abwesenheit

    Morgenlied
    Romanze
    Stimme der Liebe
  ZELTER *Ach! Mir ist das Herz so schwer*
Stolby see Bal'mont **PROKOFIEV**
Stoll, Johann Ludwig, 1778-1815.
  BEETHOVEN *An die Geliebte*
  SCHUBERT
    An die Geliebte
    Labetrank der Liebe
    Lambertine
  WEBER *Die Zeit*
Stoll, Joseph Ludwig *see* Stoll, Johann
  Ludwig, 1778-1815.
Stona, Maria, pseud. *see* Scholz, Maria,
  1861-1944.
"Stonet rebenok" *see Kolybel'naia*
  Golenishchev-Kutuzov **MUSORGSKIĭ**
Stop all the clocks see Auden **ROREM**
"Stop all the clocks" *see Funeral blues*
  Auden **BRITTEN**
STOP, pseud. *see* Morel-Retz, Louis Pierre
  Gabriel Bernard, 1825-1899.
Stopping by woods on a snowy evening see
  Frost **ROREM**
Storchenbotschaft see Mörike **WOLF**
Den store Mester kommer see Ingemann
  NIELSEN
"Store skapare, förlåt det" *see Hundra vägar*
  Runeberg **SIBELIUS**
Storia breve see Negri **RESPIGHI**
The storm see Pushkin **RACHMANINOFF**
Storm cloud see Pushkin **STRAVINSKIĭ**
Storm, Theodor, 1817-1888.
  BERG
    Die Nachtigall
    Schliesse mir die Augen beide
  BRAHMS *Über die Heide*
  JENSEN *Loose*
  KRENEK
    Musikanten wollen wandern durch die
      Saiten
    Nun ein Scherflein in der Runde
  LASSEN
    Als ich dich kaum gesehn
    Die Waldbrüder
  REGER
    Einen Brief soll ich schreiben
    Nelken
  RUBINSTEIN *Morgens*
  SCHOECK *April*
  WEBERN *Dämmerstunde*
Stormen kör i fjällen see Bergman
  KILPINEN
Stornellatrice see Zangarini **RESPIGHI**
Stornello see Anon. **VERDI**

COMPOSER Poet *Title* "First Line"

Stornello see Donini **RESPIGHI**
Stotterfoth, Adelheid von
   LASSEN *Einsamkeit*
Stout see Carpenter, Rue **CARPENTER**
Strachwitz, Moritz Karl Wilhelm Anton,
   Graf von, 1822-1847.
   LASSEN
      Gebet auf den Wassern
      Der gefangene Admiral
      Heimkehr
      Meeresabend
   LOEWE *Der gefangene Admiral*
   SCHUMANN *Mein altes Ross*
Das Sträusschen see Goethe **ZELTER**
Strafpredigt über die französische Musik see
   Unknown **WEBER**
Strahlt zuweilen auch ein mildes Licht see
   Daumer *FRAUENBILDER UND*
   HULDIGUNGEN. **BRAHMS**
The Strand lullaby see Unknown **RIEGGER**
   Am Strand
The stranger see Rich *DIVING INTO THE*
   WRECK. **ROREM**
"Stranger, here lies Ann Poverty" *see*
   Ann Poverty De La Mare **CHANLER**
"Stranger, if you passing meet me" *see To you*
   Whitman **ROREM**
Strannik see Rückert **MUSORGSKIĬ**
Strashnaia minuta see Chaĭkovskiĭ
   CHAĬKOVSKIĬ
Strauss, David Friedrich, 1808-1874.
   RUBINSTEIN *Wem ich dieses klage*
"Der Strauss, den ich gepflücket" *see*
   Blumengruss Goethe **WOLF**
"Der Strauss, den ich gepflücket" *see*
   Willkommen dem 28. August 1749 Goethe
   ZELTER
"Der Strauss, den ich gepflükket" *see*
   Blumengruss Goethe **WEBERN**
STRAUSS, RICHARD, 1864-1949.
   Anon.
      Liebesgeschenk, op. 77 no. 3 [Lieder GA,
         v. 3, p. 90]
         "Ich pflückte eine kleine Pfirsichblüte"
   Arnim, Ludwig Achim, Freiherr von,
      1781-1831.
      Einerlei, op. 69 no. 3 [Lieder GA, v. 3,
         p. 17] "Ihr Mund ist stets derselbe"
      Der Pokal, op. 69 no. 2 [Lieder GA, v. 3,
         p. 14] "Freunde, weihet den Pokal"
      Der Stern, op. 69 no. 1 [Lieder GA, v. 3,
         p. 11] "Ich stehe ihn wieder, den
         lieblichen Stern"
   Bierbaum, Otto Julius, 1865-1910.
      Freundliche Vision, op. 48 no. 1 [Lieder
         GA, v. 2, p. 141] "Nicht im Schlafe
         hab' ich das geträumt"
         Also voice & orchestra, 1918.

Nachtgang, op. 29 no. 3 [Lieder GA,
   v. 1, p. 154] "Wir gingen durch die
   dunkle, milde Nacht"
Schlagende Herzen, op. 29 no. 2 [Lieder
   GA, v. 1, p. 150] "Über Wiesen und
   Felder ein Knabe ging"
Traum durch die Dämmerung, op. 29 no.
   1 [Lieder GA, v. 1, p. 147]
   "Weite Wiesen im Dämmergrau"
Wir beide wollen springen, AV 90 (1896)
   [Lieder GA, v. 3, p. 174] "Es ging ein
   Wind durch's weite Land"
DER JUNGEN HEXE LIED.
   Jung Hexenlied, op. 39 no. 2 [Lieder
      GA, v. 1, p. 287]
      "Als nachts ich überm Gebirge ritt"
Bodmann, Emanuel von, 1874-1946.
   Herr Lenz, op. 37 no. 5 [Lieder GA, v. 1,
      p. 271] "Herr Lenz springt heute durch
      die Stadt"
Brentano, Clemens Maria, 1778-1842.
   Als mir dein Lied erklang, op. 68 no. 4
      [Lieder GA, v. 2, p. 328]
      "Dein Lied erklang! Ich hab' es
      gehört!"
      Also voice & orchestra, 1940.
   Amor, op. 68 no. 5 [Lieder GA, v. 2,
      p. 336] "An dem Feuer sass das Kind
      Amor"
      Also voice & orchestra, 1940.
   An die Nacht, op. 68 no. 1 [Lieder GA,
      v. 2, p. 309]
      "Heilige Nacht! Heil'ge Nacht!
      Sternengeschlossner
      Himmelsfriede!"
      Also voice & orchestra, 1940.
   Ich wollt' ein Sträusslein binden, op. 68
      no. 2 [Lieder GA, v. 2, p. 314] same
      Also voice & orchestra, 1940.
   Lied der Frauen, op. 68 no. 6 [Lieder
      GA, v. 2, p. 342]
      "Wenn es stürmt auf den Wogen"
      Also voice & orchestra, 1933.
   Säusle, liebe Myrthe, op. 68 no. 3 [Lieder
      GA, v. 2, p. 320] same
      Also voice & orchestra, 1940.
Bürger, Gottfried August, 1747-1794.
   Muttertändelei, op. 43 no. 2 [Lieder GA,
      v. 2, p. 10]
      "Seht mir doch mein schönes Kind"
      Also voice & orchestra, 1900.
Buonarroti, Michel Angelo, 1475-1564.
   MADRIALE.
   Madrigal, op. 15 no. 1 [Lieder GA,
      v. 1, p. 25]
      "In's Joch beug'ich den Nacken"

Burns, Robert, 1759-1796.
> *John Anderson*, AV 73 (1880) [Boosey &
> Hawkes, 1968]
>> "John Anderson, mein Lieb"

Busse, Carl, 1872-1918.
> *Blauer Sommer*, op. 31 no. 1 [Lieder GA,
> v. 1, p. 159]
>> "Ein blauer Sommerglanz"
> *Weisser Jasmin*, op. 31 no. 3 [Lieder GA,
> v. 1, p. 167]
>> "Bleiche Blüte, Blüte der Liebe"
> *HEDWIG.*
>> *Wenn*, op. 31 no. 2 [Lieder GA, v. 1,
>> p. 162] "Und wärst du mein Weib"

Calderon de la Barca, Pedro, 1600-1681.
> *EL ALCALDE DE ZALAMEA.*
>> *Liebesliedchen*, AV 96 no. 1 (1904)
>> [Lieder GA, v. 3, p. 176]
>>> "Hör mein Liebesliedchen ziehn
>>> Isabel"
>>> Tenor, guitar & harp.
>> *Lied der Chispa*, AV 96 no. 2 (1904)
>> [Lieder GA, v. 3, p. 178]
>>> "Es war ein Bruder Liederlich"
>>> Mezzo-soprano, unison male
>>> voices, guitar & 2 harps; voices
>>> sing sequentially with soloist.

Chamisso, Adelbert von, 1781-1838.
> *Lass ruh'n die Toten*, AV 35 (1877)
> [Lieder GA, v. 3, p. 242]
>> "Es steht ein altes Gemäuer"

Dahn, Felix Ludwig Sophus, 1834-1912.
> *Efeu*, op. 22 no. 3 [Lieder GA, v. 1,
> p. 107] "Aber Efeu nenn' ich jene
> Mädchen"
> *Kornblumen*, op. 22 no. 1 [Lieder GA,
> v. 1, p. 101]
>> "Kornblumen nenn' ich die Gestalten"
> *Mohnblumen*, op. 22 no. 2 [Lieder GA,
> v. 1, p. 104]
>> "Mohnblumen sind die runden"
> *Wasserrose*, op. 22 no. 4 [Lieder GA,
> v. 1, p. 111] "Kennst du die Blume"
> *SCHLICHTE WEISEN*, no. 7.
>> *Du meines Herzens Krönelein*, op. 21
>> no. 2 [Lieder GA, v. 1, p. 89] same
> *SCHLICHTE WEISEN*, no. 10.
>> *Ach, weh mir verglückhaftem Mann*,
>> op. 21 no. 4 [Lieder GA, v. 1, p. 93]
>> same
> *SCHLICHTE WEISEN*, no. 11.
>> *All mein Gedanken*, op. 21 no. 1
>> [Lieder GA, v. 1, p. 87] same

SCHLICHTE WEISEN, no. 12 (?).
> *Ach Lieb', nun muss ich scheiden*, op.
> 21 no. 3 [Lieder GA, v. 1, p. 91]
> same
SCHLICHTE WEISEN, no. 13.
> *Die Frauen sind oft fromm und still*,
> op. 21 no. 5 [Lieder GA, v. 1, p. 97]
> same

Dehmel, Richard, 1863-1920.
> *Der Arbeitsmann*, op. 39 no. 3 [Lieder
> GA, v. 1, p. 291] "Wir haben ein Bett"
> *Befreit*, op. 39 no. 4 [Lieder GA, v. 1,
> p. 296] "Du wirst nicht weinen"
> Also voice & orchestra, 1933.
> *Leises Lied*, op. 39 no. 1 [Lieder GA,
> v. 1, p. 283] "In einem stillen Garten"
> *Lied an meinen Sohn*, op. 39 no. 5
> [Lieder GA, v. 1, p. 301]
>> "Der Sturm behorcht mein Vaterhaus"
> *Mein Auge*, op. 37 no. 4 [Lieder GA,
> v. 1, p. 268] "Du bist mein Auge"
> Also voice & orchestra, 1933.
> *Stiller Gang*, op. 31 no. 4 [Lieder GA,
> v. 1, p. 172] "Der Abend graut"
> *Waldseligkeit*, op. 49 no. 1 [Lieder GA,
> v. 2, p. 161]
>> "Der Wald beginnt zu rauschen"
>> Also voice & orchestra, 1918.
> *Wiegenliedchen*, op. 49 no. 3 [Lieder GA,
> v. 2, p. 171] "Bienchen, Bienchen
> wiegt sich im Sonnenschein"
> *DIE VERWANDLUNGEN DER VENUS*:
> Venus Mater.
>> *Wiegenlied*, op. 41 no. 1 [Lieder GA,
>> v. 1, p. 313]
>>> "Träume du mein süsses Leben"
>>> Also voice & orchestra, 1916?
> *WEIB UND WELT.*
>> *Am Ufer*, op. 41 no. 3 [Lieder GA,
>> v. 1, p. 330] "Die Welt verstummt"

DES KNABEN WUNDERHORN
> *Für fünfzehn Pfennige*, op. 36 no. 2
> [Lieder GA, v. 1, p. 238]
>> "Das Mägdlein will ein'n Freier hab'n"
> *Hat gesagt—bleibt's nicht dabei*, op. 36
> no. 3 [Lieder GA, v. 1, p. 243]
>> "Mein Vater hat gesagt"
> *Himmelsboten zu Liebchens Himmelbett*,
> op. 32 no. 5 [Lieder GA, v. 1, p. 190]
>> "Der Mondschein, der ist schon
>> verblichen"
> *Junggesellenschwur*, op. 49 no. 6 [Lieder
> GA, v. 2, p. 185]
>> "Weine, weine, weine nur nicht"

Falke, Gustav, 1853-1916.
> *Meinem Kinde*, op. 37 no. 3 [Lieder GA,
> v. 1, p. 264]

COMPOSER Poet *Title* "First Line"

STRAUSS, RICHARD, 1864-1949
(continued)
Falke, Gustav, 1853-1916 *(continued)*
  "Du schläfst und sachte neig' ich"
    Also voice & orchestra, 1897.
Frey, Friedrich Hermann, 1830-1911.
  Weihnachtsgefühl, AV 94 (1899) [Lieder
    GA, v. 3, p. 273]
    "Naht die jubelvolle Zeit"
Geibel, Emanuel, i.e., Franz Emanuel
August, 1815-1884.
  Es rauscht des Laub zu meinem Füssen,
    AV 161 (1879) [lost] same
  Frühlingsanfang, AV 162 (1879) [lost]
    "Die Sonne hebt an"
  Für Musik, AV 158 (1879) [lost]
    "Nun die Schatten dunkeln"
  Herz, mein Herz, AV 8 (1871) [unpubl.]
    "Herz, mein Herz, sei nicht
      beklommen"
  Im Walde, AV 43 (1878) [Lieder GA,
    v. 3, p. 260] same
  Die Lilien glühn in Düften, AV 160
    (1879) [lost]
  O schneller, mein Ross, AV 159 (1879)
    [lost]
  Waldesgesang, AV 55 (1879) [Lieder
    GA, v. 3, p. 269]
    "Die Liebe sass als Nachtigall"
Gilm zu Rosenegg, Hermann von,
1812-1864.
  Wer hat's gethan? AV 84a (1885)
    [unpubl.] "Es steht mein Lied in Nacht
    und Frost"
  IM FRÜHLING.
    Zueignung, op. 10 no. 1 [Lieder GA,
      v. 1, p. 3]
      "Ja, du weisst es, teure Seele"
      Also voice & orchestra, 1940.
  LETZTE BLÄTTER.
    Allerseelen, op. 10 no. 8 [Lieder GA,
      v. 1, p. 20] "Stell' auf den Tisch die
      duftenden Reseden"
    Geduld, op. 10 no. 5 [Lieder GA, v. 1,
      p. 12] "Geruld, sagst du"
    Die Georgine, op. 10 no. 4 [Lieder
      GA, v. 1, p. 9]
      "Warum so spät erst, Georgine?"
    Die Nacht, op. 10 no. 3 [Lieder GA,
      v. 1, p. 7]
      "Aus dem Walde tritt die Nacht"
    Nichts, op. 10 no. 2 [Lieder GA, v. 1,
      p. 5] "Nenne soll ich, sagt ihr"
    Die Verschwiegenen, op. 10 no. 6
      [Lieder GA, v. 1, p. 17]
      "Ich habe wohl"

Die Zeitlose, op. 10 no. 7 [Lieder GA,
  v. 1, p. 19]
  "Auf frisch gemähtem Weideplatz"
Goethe, Johann Wolfgang von, 1749-
1832.
  Das Bächlein, op. 88 no. 1 (1933)
    [Lieder GA, v. 3, p. 143]
    "Du Bächlein silberhell und klar"
    Also voice & orchestra, 1935.
  Der Fischer, AV 33 (1877) [Lieder GA,
    v. 3, p. 232] "Das Wasser rauscht' das
    Wasser schwoll"
  Gefunden, op. 56 no. 1 [Lieder GA, v. 2,
    p. 211] "Ich ging im Walde so für
    mich hin"
  Lust und Qual, AV 36 (1877) [Lieder
    GA, v. 3, p. 244]
    "Knabe sass ich, Fischerknabe"
  Sinnspruch, AV 105 (1919) [Lieder GA,
    v. 3, p. 181]
    "Alle Menschen gross und klein"
  Xenion, AV 131 (1942) [Lieder GA, v. 3,
    p. 187] "Nichts vom Vergänglichen"
  WESTÖSTLICHER DIVAN.
    Durch allen Schall und Klang, AV 111
      (1925) [Lieder GA, v. 3, p. 183]
      same
    Hab' ich euch denn je geraten, op. 67
      no. 5 [Lieder GA, v. 2, p. 301] same
    Spruch, AV 116 (1930) [Boosey &
      Hawkes, 1969] "Wie etwas sei leicht"
    Wanderers Gemütsruhe, op. 67 no. 6
      [Lieder GA, v. 2, p. 304]
      "Übers Niederträchtige niemand sich
      beklage"
    Wer wird von der Welt verlangen, op.
      67 no. 4 [Lieder GA, v. 2, p. 298]
      same
    Zugemessne Rhythmen, AV 122 (1935)
      [Lieder GA, v. 3, p. 185]
      "Zugemessne Rhythmen reizen
      freilich"
  WESTÖSTLICHER DIVAN:
  Schenkenbuch.
    Erschaffen und Beleben, op. 87 no. 2
      (1922) [Lieder GA, v. 3, p. 119]
      "Hans Adam war ein Erdenkloss"
      AV 106.
Gruppe, Otto Friedrich, 1804-1876.
  Begegnung, AV 72 (1880) [Lieder GA,
    v. 3, p. 169]
    "Die Treppe hinunter gesprungen"
Hafiz, Muhammad Shums al-Din, d.
1388.
  Die Allmächtige, op. 77 no. 4 [Lieder
    GA, v. 3, p. 97]
    "Die höchste Macht der Erde"

Huldigung, op. 77 no. 5 [Lieder GA,
 v. 3, p. 102] "Die Perlen meiner Seele"
Ihre Augen, op. 77 no. 1 [Lieder GA,
 v. 3, p. 83] "Deine gewälbten Brauen"
Schwung, op. 77 no. 2 [Lieder GA, v. 3,
 p. 86] "Gebt mir meinen Becher"

Hart, Julius, 1859-1930.
Cäcilie, op. 27 no. 2 [Lieder GA, v. 1,
 p. 133] "Wenn du es wüsstest"
 Also voice & orchestra, 1897.

Heine, Heinrich, 1797-1856.
Frühlingsfeier, op. 56 no. 5 [Lieder GA,
 v. 2, p. 226]
 "Das ist des Frühlings traurige Lust"
 Also voice & orchestra, 1933.
Die heiligen drei Könige, op. 56 no. 6
 [Lieder GA, v. 2, p. 234]
 "Die heiligen drei Könige aus
 Morgenland"
 Also voice & orchestra, 1906.
In Vaters Garten heimlich steht, AV 64
 (1879) [Boosey & Hawkes, 1968]
 same
Mit deinen blauen Augen, op. 56 no. 4
 [Lieder GA, v. 2, p. 223] same
Schlechtes Wetter, op. 69 no. 5 [Lieder
 GA, v. 3, p. 27]
 "Das ist ein schlechtes Wetter"
Waldesfahrt, op. 69 no. 4 [Lieder GA,
 v. 3, p. 22] "Mein Wagen rollet
 langsam durch lustiges Waldesgrün"

Henckell, Karl Friedrich, 1864-1929.
Blindenklage, op. 56 no. 2 [Lieder GA,
 v. 2, p. 214] "Wenn ich dich frage,
 dem das Leben blüht"
Ich schwebe, op. 48 no. 2 [Lieder GA,
 v. 2, p. 144] "Ich schwebe wie auf
 Engelsschwingen"
Ich trage meine Minne, op. 32 no. 1
 [Lieder GA, v. 1, p. 177] same
Kling, op. 48 no. 3 [Lieder GA, v. 2,
 p. 148]
 "Kling, meine Seele gibt reinen Ton"
Das Lied des Steinklopfers, op. 49 no. 4
 [Lieder GA, v. 2, p. 175]
 "Ich bin kein Minister"
O süsser Mai! op. 32 no. 4 [Lieder GA,
 v. 1, p. 186] same
Ruhe, meine Seele, op. 27 no. 1 [Lieder
 GA, v. 1, p. 131]
 "Nicht ein Lüftchen regt sich leise"
 Also voice & orchestra, 1948.
Winterliebe, op. 48 no. 5 [Lieder GA,
 v. 2, p. 155] "Der Sonne entgegen"
 Also voice & orchestra, 1918.

Winterweihe, op. 48 no. 4 [Lieder GA,
 v. 2, p. 152] "In diesen Wintertagen"
 Voice & orchestra, 1918.
STEH' ICH IN SEL'GEM TRAUME.
Liebeshymnus, op. 32 no. 3 [Lieder
 GA, v. 1, p. 184] "Heil jenem Tag"
 Also voice & orchestra, 1897.

Hoffmann von Fallersleben, August
Heinrich, 1798-1874.
Abend- und Morgenrot, AV 42 (1878)
 [Lieder GA, v. 3, p. 257]
 "Die Mükke sitzt am Fenster"
Husarenlied, AV 14 (1873?) [Lieder GA,
 v. 3, p. 230] "Husaren müssen reiten"
Die müde Wanderer, AV 13 (1873?)
 [Lieder GA, v. 3, p. 226]
 "Schon sank die Sonne"
Ein Röslein zog ich mir im Garten, AV
 49 (1878?) [Lieder GA, v. 3, p. 267]
 same
Soldatenlied, AV 48 (1878?) [Lieder GA,
 v. 3, p. 264]
 "Die Trommeln und Pfeifen"
Der Spielmann und sein Kind, AV 46
 (1878) [Boosey & Hawkes, 1968]
 "Es blitzt und kracht"
 Also voice & orchestra, 1878.
Wiegenlied, AV 41 (1878) [Lieder GA,
 v. 3, p. 254]
 "Die Ähren nur noch niken"

Kerner, Justinus, 1786-1862.
Alphorn, AV 29 (1876) [Lieder GA, v. 3,
 p. 274]
 "Ein Alphorn hör' ich schallen"
 Voice, horn & piano.

Kerr, Alfred, 1867-1948.
Drei Masken sah ich, op. 66 no. 4
 [Lieder GA, v. 2, p. 253] same
Einst kam der Bock, op. 66 no. 2 [Lieder
 GA, v. 2, p. 245] same
Es liebt einst ein Hase, op. 66 no. 3
 [Lieder GA, v. 2, p. 251] same
Es war einmal ein Bock, op. 66 no. 1
 [Lieder GA, v. 2, p. 241] same
Es war mal eine Wanze, op. 66 no. 9
 [Lieder GA, v. 2, p. 273] same
Der Händler und die Macher, op. 66 no.
 11 [Lieder GA, v. 2, p. 279] same
Hast du ein Tongedicht, op. 66 no. 5
 [Lieder GA, v. 2, p. 256] same
Die Künstler sind die Schöpfer, op. 66
 no. 10 [Lieder GA, v. 2, p. 276] same
O, lieber Künstler, op. 66 no. 6 [Lieder
 GA, v. 2, p. 259] same
O Schröpferschwarm, op. 66 no. 12
 [Lieder GA, v. 2, p. 281] same
Unser Feind ist, grosser Gott, op. 66 no.
 7 [Lieder GA, v. 2, p. 264] same

COMPOSER Poet *Title* "First Line"

STRAUSS, RICHARD, 1864-1949
(continued)
Kerr, Alfred, 1867-1948 *(continued)*
Von Händlern wird die Kunst bedroht,
op. 66 no. 8 [Lieder GA, v. 2, p. 267]
same
Klopstock, Friedrich Gottlieb, 1724-1803.
ODE.
An Sie, op. 43 no. 1 [Lieder GA, v. 2, p. 3] "Zeit, Verkündigerin der besten Freuden"
Das Rosenband, op. 36 no. 1 [Lieder GA, v. 1, p. 235]
"Im Frühlingsschatten fand ich sie"
Also voice & orchestra, 1897.
Knobel, Betty Wehrli, b. 1904.
Malven (1948) [Boosey & Hawkes, 1985]
"Aus Rosen, Phlox, Zinienflor"
Körner, Theodor, i.e., Karl Theodor, 1791-1813.
Spielmann und Zither, AV 40 (1878) [Lieder GA, v. 3, p. 246]
"Der Spielmann sass am Felsen"
Lenau, Nicolaus, 1802-1850.
Frühlingsgedränge, op. 26 no. 1 [Lieder GA, v. 1, p. 121]
"Frühlingskinder im bunten Gedränge"
Nebel, AV 47 (1878?) [Lieder GA, v. 3, p. 263] "Du trüber Nebel hüllst mir das Tal"
SOPHIE.
O wärst du mein! op. 26 no. 2 [Lieder GA, v. 1, p. 125] same
Liliencron, Detlov, Freiherr von, 1844-1909.
Bruder Liederlich, op. 41 no. 4 [Lieder GA, v. 1, p. 333]
"Die Feder am Sturmhut"
Glückes genug, op. 37 no. 1 [Lieder GA, v. 1, p. 257]
"Wenn sanft du mir im Arme schliefst"
Ich liebe dich, op. 37 no. 2 [Lieder GA, v. 1, p. 260] "Vier adlige Rosse voran unserm Wagen"
Also voice & orchestra, 1943.
Sehnsucht, op. 32 no. 2 [Lieder GA, v. 1, p. 180] "Ich ging den Weg entlang"
Lindner, Anton, 1874-1915.
Hochzeitlich Lied, op. 37 no. 6 [Lieder GA, v. 1, p. 274]
"Lass Akaziendüfte schaukeln"
Mackay, John Henry, 1864-1933.
Heimliche Aufforderung, op. 27 no. 3 [Lieder GA, v. 1, p. 137]
"Auf hebe die funkelnde Schale"

In der Campagna, op. 41 no. 2 [Lieder GA, v. 1, p. 325]
"Ich grüsse die Sonne"
Morgen, op. 27 no. 4 [Lieder GA, v. 1, p. 143] "Und morgen wird die Sonne wieder scheinen"
Also voice & orchestra, 1897.
Meyer, Conrad Ferdinand, 1825-1898.
Im Spätboot, op. 56 no. 3 [Lieder GA, v. 2, p. 219] "Aus der Schiffsbank mach' ich neinen Pfühl"
Morgenstern, Christian Otto Joseph Wolfgang, 1871-1914.
Leise Lieder, op. 41 no. 5 [Lieder GA, v. 1, p. 341]
"Leise Lieder sing ich dir bei Nacht"
Mündel, Curt
ELSÄSSISCHE VOLKSLIEDER.
Ach was Kummer, Qual und Schmerzen, op. 49 no. 8 [Lieder GA, v. 2, p. 193] same
Wer lieben will, muss leiden, op. 49 no. 7 [Lieder GA, v. 2, p. 190] same
No author
Der Graf von Rom, AV 102 (1906) [unpubl.]
Facsimile ed.: Program of Berlin State Opera, new production of *Der Rosenkavalier,* 1961.
Panizza, Oskar, 1853-1921.
Sie wissen's nicht, op. 49 no. 5 [Lieder GA, v. 2, p. 181]
"Es wohnt ein kleines Vögelein"
Pletzsch, Oskar
Der böhmische Musikant, AV 7 (1871?) [Boosey & Hawkes, 1968]
"Es kommt aus fernem Böhmerland"
Remer, Paul, 1867-1943.
In goldener Fülle, op. 49 no. 2 [Lieder GA, v. 2, p. 165]
"Wir schreiten in goldener Fülle"
Rückert, Friedrich, 1788-1866.
Gestern war ich Atlas, op. 46 no. 2 [Lieder GA, v. 2, p. 71] same
Ich sehe wie in einem Spiegel, op. 46 no. 5 [Lieder GA, v. 2, p. 88] same
Im Sonnenschein, op. 87 no. 4 (1935) [Lieder GA, v. 3, p. 134]
"Noch eine Stunde lasst mich hier"
AV 121.
Morgenrot, op. 46 no. 4 [Lieder GA, v. 2, p. 80]
"Dort, wo der Morgenstern"
Ein Obdach gegen Sturm und Regen, op. 46 no. 1 [Lieder GA, v. 2, p. 67] same

Die sieben Siegel, op. 46 no. 3 [Lieder
GA, v. 2, p. 75]
"Weil ich dich nicht legen kann"
Und dann nicht mehr, op. 87 no. 3
(1929) [Lieder GA, v. 3, p. 125]
"Ich sah sie nur ein einzigmal"
AV 114.
Vom künftigen Alter, op. 87 no. 1 (1929)
[Lieder GA, v. 3, p. 113] "Der Frost
hat mir bereifet des Hauses Dach"
AV 115.
LIEBESFRÜHLING, no. 48.
  Anbetung, op. 36 no. 4 [Lieder GA,
  v. 1, p. 247] "Die Liebste steht mir
  von den Gedanken"
Sallet, Friedrich von, 1812-1843.
Die erwachte Rose, AV 66 (1880)
[Lieder GA, v. 3, p. 163]
"Die Knospe träumte von
Sonnenschein"
Der Morgen, AV 165 (1880) [lost]
"Der erste Strahl vom Osten her"
Schack, Adolf Friedrich, Graf von, 1815-1894.
Barkarole, op. 17 no. 6 [Lieder GA, v. 1,
p. 62]
"Um der fallenden Ruders Spitzen"
Dem Herzen ähnlich, op. 15 no. 4
[Lieder GA, v. 1, p. 36] same
Das Geheimnis, op. 17 no. 3 [Lieder GA,
v. 1, p. 53] "Du fragst mich, Mädchen"
Heimkehr, op. 15 no. 5 [Lieder GA, v. 1,
p. 40] "Leiser schwanken die Äste"
Lob des Leidens, op. 15 no. 3 [Lieder
GA, v. 1, p. 32]
"O, schmäht des Lebens Leiden nicht"
Nur Mut! op. 17 no. 5 [Lieder GA, v. 1,
p. 58] "Lass' das Zagen"
Seitdem dein Aug' in meines schaute, op.
17 no. 1 [Lieder GA, v. 1, p. 45] same
Ständchen, op. 17 no. 2 [Lieder GA, v. 1,
p. 47] "Mach auf, mach auf"
Von dunklem Schleier umsponnen, op. 17
no. 4 [Lieder GA, v. 1, p. 56] same
Winternacht, op. 15 no. 2 [Lieder GA,
v. 1, p. 28]
"Mit Regen und Sturmgebrause"
LOTOSBLÄTTER.
  Breit' über mein Haupt, op. 19 no. 2
  [Lieder GA, v. 1, p. 71] same
  Hoffen und wieder verzagen, op. 19
  no. 5 [Lieder GA, v. 1, p. 79] same
  Mein Herz ist stumm, op. 19 no. 6
  [Lieder GA, v. 1, p. 82] same
  Schön sind, doch kalt, op. 19 no. 3
  [Lieder GA, v. 1, p. 73] same
  Wie sollten wir geheim sie halten, op.
  19 no. 4 [Lieder GA, v. 1, p. 75]
  same
  Wozu noch, Mädchen, op. 19 no. 1
  [Lieder GA, v. 1, p. 69] same
Schiller, Johann Christoph Friedrich von, 1759-1805.
Des Alpenhirten Abschied, AV 151
(1872) [lost]
Schubart, Christian Friedrich Daniel, 1739-1791.
Weihnachtslied, AV 2 (1871) [Lieder
GA, v. 3, p. 221]
"Schlaf' wohl du Himmelsknabe du"
Shakespeare, William, 1564-1616.
HAMLET.
  *Guten Morgen, 's ist Sankt
  Valentinstag,* op. 67 no. 2
  [Lieder GA, v. 2, p. 290] same
  Sie trugen ihn auf der Bahre bloss, op.
  67 no. 3 [Lieder GA, v. 2, p. 293]
  same
  Wie erkenn' ich mein Treulieb? op. 67
  no. 1 [Lieder GA, v. 2, p. 287] same
Stieler, Karl, 1842-1885.
Rote Rosen, AV 76 (1883) [Lieder GA,
v. 3, p. 159] "Weisst Du die Rose"
Strauss, Richard, 1864-1949.
Hab Dank, du güt'ger Weisheitspender,
AV 126 (1939)
[fac. ed.: **Richard Strauss Jahrbuch,**
1959/60, p. 132] same
Bass alone.
Notschrei aus den Gefilden Lapplands,
AV 127 (1940) [unpubl.]
"Im ganzen Ort gibts keine Kohlen"
Soprano/tenor alone.
Wer tritt herein, AV 136 (1943) [fac. ed.:
Los Angeles Times, July 1, 1945]
"Wer tritt herein so fesch und
schlank?"
Soprano/tenor alone.
Uhland, Ludwig, 1787-1862.
Auf ein Kind, op. 47 no. 1 [Lieder GA,
v. 2, p. 97] "Aus der Bedrängnis"
Des Dichters Abendgang, op. 47 no. 2
[Lieder GA, v. 2, p. 99]
"Ergehst du dich im Abendlicht"
Also voice & orchestra, 1918.
Die drei Lieder, AV 164 (1879) [lost]
"In hoher Hall' sass König Sifrid"
Die Drossel, AV 34 (1877) [Lieder GA,
v. 3, p. 240]
"Ich will ja nicht in Gerten geh'n"
Einkehr, AV 3 (1871) [Lieder GA, v. 3,
p. 222] "Bei einem Wirte wundermild"
Einkehr, op. 47 no. 4 [Lieder GA, v. 2,
p. 113] "Bei einem Wirte wundermild"

STRAUSS, RICHARD, 1864-1949
(continued)
Uhland, Ludwig, 1787-1862 *(continued)*
Rückleben, op. 47 no. 3 [Lieder GA, v. 2, p. 107]
"An ihrem Grabe kniet ich fest"
Die Ulme zu Hirsau, op. 43 no. 3 [Lieder GA, v. 2, p. 17]
"Zu Hirsau in den Trümmern"
Von den sieben Zechbrüdern, op. 47 no. 5 [Lieder GA, v. 2, p. 119]
"Ich kenne sieben lustige Brüder"
Der weisse Hirsch, AV 6 (1871?) [Boosey & Hawkes, 1968]
"Es gingen drei Jäger"
ATB & piano; voices sing sequentially, not ensemble.
Winterreise, AV 4 (1871) [Lieder GA, v. 3, p. 224]
"Bei diesen kalten Wehen"
Vogl, Johann Nepomuk, 1802-1866.
Waldkonzert, AV 5 (1871?) [Boosey & Hawkes, 1968]
"Herr Frühling gibt jetzt ein Konzert"
Weinheber, Josef, 1892-1945.
Blick vom oberen Belvedere, op. 88 no. 2 (1942) [Lieder GA, v. 3, p. 147]
"Fülle du!"
Sankt Michael, op. 88 no. 3 (1942) [Lieder GA, v. 3, p. 152]
"Ein Mahl für uns und ein Licht für dich"
Strauss, Richard, 1864-1949.
STRAUSS
Hab Dank, du güt'ger Weisheitspender
Notschrei aus den Gefilden Lapplands
Wer tritt herein
STRAVINSKIĭ, IGOR' FEDOROVICH, 1882-1971.
Akahito, 8th cent.
Akahito (1912) [Edition russe de musique, 1913; Boosey & Hawkes]
"Descendons au jardin"
Also voice & chamber ensemble.
Anon.
Canard (1918) {*Selezen*} [J. & W. Chester, 1920]
"Vieux canard, vieux canard, sors"
Les canards, les cygnes, les oies . . . (1917) {*Gusi, lebedi . . .*} [J. & W. Chester, 1920] same
Chanson de l'ours (1915) {*Piesenka medviedia*} [J. & W. Chester, 1920]
"Grince, grince, grince patte en bouleau"
Chanson pour compter (1919) {*Zapevnaya*} [J. & W. Chester, 1920)

"Un, moi qui l'ai, deux, toi qui l'as"
Chant dissident (1919) {*Sektantskaia*} [J. & W. Chester, 1920]
"Vent, neige, obscurité"
Le moineau est assis (1919) {*Podbliudnaia*} [J. & W. Chester, 1920) "Le moineau est assis sur la haie d'autrui"
Tilim-bom (1915-17) {*Tilim'-bom'*} [J. & W. Chester, 1920] same
Bal'mont, Konstantin Dmitriyevich, 1867-1943.
The dove (1911; rev. 1947) {*Golub'*} [Boosey & Hawkes, 1947]
"Flew once where he saw a tow'r"
Also voice & chamber ensemble, 1954.
Forget-me-nots (1911; rev. 1947) {*Nezabudoochka-tsvetochek'*} [Boosey & Hawkes, 1947] "Blue forget-me-not, sweet blossom"
Also voice & chamber ensemble, 1954.
Gorodetski, Sergey Mitrofanovich, 1884-1967.
A song of the dew, op. 6 no. 2 (1908) {*Rosyanka*} [Jurgenson, 1912; Boosey, 1968] "O mother earth, O dear one"
Spring, op. 6 no. 1 (1908) {*Vesna*} [Jurgenson, 1912; Boosey, 1968] "Chimes of gladness, chimes of sadness"
Lear, Edward, 1812-1888.
The owl and the pussy-cat (1966) [Boosey, 1967]
"The owl & the pussy-cat went to sea"
Mazatsumi
Mazatsumi (1912) [Edition russe de musique, 1913; Boosey & Hawkes]
"Avril parait"
Also voice & chamber ensemble.
No author
Pastorale (1907) [Jurgenson, 1910; J. & W. Chester]
Also voice & chamber ensemble.
Pushkin, Aleksandr Sergeevich, 1799-1837.
Storm cloud (1902) [unpubl.]
Stravinskiĭ, Igor' Fedorovich, 1882-1971.
Berceuse (1917) [in his ***Expositions & Developments,*** Faber, 1962]
"Mikouchka, Mikouchka, voilà qu'on a fait tes boucles"
Petit Ramusianum harmonique (1937) [***Hommage à C.-F.Ramuz*** Lausanne: V. Porchet, 1938] "Nous sommes tous accourus petits et grands"

Tsaraiuki
  Tsaraiuki (1913) [Edition russe de
    musique, 1913; Boosey & Hawkes]
    "Qu'apercoiton si blanc au loin?"
      Also voice & chamber ensemble.
Unknown
  Le corbeau (ca.1906; rev.1913] {*Vorona*}
    [Edition russe de musique, 1914;
      Boosey & Hawkes, 1947]
      "Sur le pont un jour passant"
        Also voice & orchestra, 1929-30.
        Also in Harewood, ed. ***Classical***
          songs for children, p.235.
  How the mushrooms went to war (1904)
    {*Kak griby na voĭnu sobirlis'*}
    [Boosey & Hawkes, 1980]
      Bass & piano.
  La petite pie (ca.1906; rev.1913)
    {*Sorochen'ka*}
    [Edition russe de musique, 1914;
      Boosey & Hawkes, 1947]
      "Pie au nid, tchi, tchi, tchi"
        Also voice & orchestra, 1929-30.
  Tchitcher-Iatcher (ca.1906; rev.1913)
    {*Chicher" IAcher" Sobiralsia na
      vecher"*}
    [Edition russe de musique, 1914;
      Boosey & Hawkes, 1947] same
      Also voicc & orchcstra, 1929-30.
  Tom the cat [Harewood, ed. ***Classical***
    songs for children, p.234] same
Verlaine, Paul, 1844-1896.
  Sagesse, op. 9 no. 2 (1910) [Jurgenson,
    1911; Boosey & Hawkes, 1954]
    "Un grand sommeil noir"
      Also baritone & orchestra, 1951.
  LA BONNE CHANSON.
    La bonne chanson, op. 9 no. 1 (1910)
      [Jurgenson, 1911; Boosey &
        Hawkes, 1954] "La lune blanche
        luit dans les bois"
          Also baritone & orchestra, 1951.
Stravinskiĭ, Igor' Fedorovich, 1882-1971.
  STRAVINSKIĬ
    Berceuse
    Petit Ramusianum harmonique
The strawberries see Unknown **DVOŘÁK**
  Jahody
Stream see Jean-Aubry **MALIPIERO**
Streckfuss, Adolf Friedrich Karl, 1778-
  1844.
  WEBER *Sonett*
"The street sounds to the soldiers' tread" *see*
  The encounter Housman **IRELAND**
The street sounds to the soldiers' tread see
  Housman **BERKELEY**

Strekotun'ia beloboka see Pushkin
  MUSORGSKIĬ
Streng ist uns das Glück und spröde see
  George *DAS BUCH DER HÄNGENDEN
  GÄRTEN.* **SCHÖNBERG**
Strindberg, August, 1849-1912.
  GESPENSTER SONATE.
    WEBERN *Schien mir's, als ich sah die
      Sonne*
Stringham, Edward, 1918-
  DIAMOND *The lover as mirror*
Strings in the earth see Joyce
  SZYMANOWSKI
Die Ströme zieh'n zum fernen Meer see
  Leuthold **SCHOECK**
STROFISKE SANGE, no. 1
  NIELSEN Rode, Helge *Skal Blomsterne
    da visne?*
STROFISKE SANGE, no. 2
  NIELSEN Aakjaer *Høgen*
STROFISKE SANGE, no. 3
  NIELSEN Aakjaer *Jens Vejmand*
STROFISKE SANGE, no. 4
  NIELSEN Jørgensen *Saenk kun dit
    Høved*
STROFISKE SANGE, no. 5
  NIELSEN Aakjaer *Den føreste laerke*
STROFISKE SANGE, no. 6
  NIELSEN Jensen, J. *Husvild*
STROFISKE SANGE, no. 7
  NIELSEN Jensen, J. *Godnat*
Der Strom see Unknown **SCHUBERT**
Strom bei Nacht see Huber, B. **KILPINEN**
Der Strom, der neben mir verrauschte see
  Platen-Hallermünde **BRAHMS**
"Der Strom glitt einsam hin" *see Am Strom*
  Eichendorff **FRANZ**
Strophe von Schiller see Schiller
  SCHUBERT *Die Götter Griechenlands*
"Strumyk lubi wdolinie" *see Gdzie lubi . . .*
  Witwicki **CHOPIN**
Struna naladěna see Heyduk **DVOŘÁK**
Stuart, Paul
  MASSENET *Retour d'oiseau*
  SAINT-SAËNS *Primavera*
Stuckenberg, Viggo Henrik Fog, 1863-
  1905.
  NIELSEN *Nu springer Vaaren fra sin Seng*
Studentenfahrt see Eichendorff **PFITZNER**
Studie efter Naturen see Andersen
  NIELSEN
"Studieren will nichts bringen" *see*
  Der verzweifelte Liebhaber Eichendorff
  WOLF
Ein Stündlein wohl vor Tag see Mörike
  FRANZ, WOLF

Der stürmische Morgen see Müller,
    Wilhelm **SCHUBERT**
Stumme Liebe see Lenau **SCHOECK**
Stummer Abschied see Unknown
    SCHOECK
"Die Stunden eilen–Mitternacht" *see Gebet
    der Fischer* Hesse **KILPINEN**
"Stupande strand, al och ek" *see Med
    strömmen* Josephson, E. **KILPINEN**
Stupuy, Hippolyte
    LALO *Le novice*
Der Sturm see Pushkin **RUBINSTEIN**
"Der Sturm behorcht mein Vaterhaus" *see
    Lied an meinen Sohn* Dehmel **STRAUSS**
Sturm, Christoph Christian, 1740-1786.
    LOEWE
        Busslied
        Jesus auf Golgatha
    MOZART *Der Frühling*
    SCHULGESANG.
        LOEWE *Segne, Vater, meinen Fleiss*
Sturm, Julius Karl Reinholdt, 1816-1896.
    LASSEN
        Nur einmal möcht ich dir noch sagen
        Über Nacht
        Wenn dein Auge freundlich
    PFITZNER *Abendlied*
    REGER
        Heimweh
        Zwei Gänse
    RUBINSTEIN *Der Dichter*
    SPOHR *Wohin*
    WOLF *Über Nacht*
"Sturm mit seinen Donnerschlägen kann mir
    nicht wie du" *see Meeresstille* Lenau
    WOLF
Der Sturm von Alhama see Huber, V.
    SKIZZEN AUS SPANIEN. **LOEWE**
"Sturm, wie lieb ich dich wilden Gesellen"
    see Präludium Boelitz **REGER**
Sturmeswinde see Kol'tsov **RUBINSTEIN**
Su una violetta morta see Shelley
    RESPIGHI
"Sua koskaan saavuta ei ajan uvo" *see
    Endymion* Koskenniemi **KILPINEN**
"Sua nähnyt en ma" *see Leivonen*
    Koskenniemi **KILPINEN**
"Su'cespugli, vezzose, in un sopor beato" *see
    Notturno* Negri **RESPIGHI**
Such beauty as hurts to behold see
    Goodman **ROREM**
Suckling, Sir John, 1609-1642.
    QUILTER
        The constant lover
        Why so pale and wan?
Sud'ba see Apukhtin **RACHMANINOFF**
    Fate

Sudden light see Rossetti, Dante
    LOEFFLER
Los sueños see Machado y Ruiz **RODRIGO**
Süss sind mir die Schollen des Tales see
    Knodt **BERG**
"Süss tönt Gesanges Hauch" *see Der Liebe
    Lohn* Cornelius **CORNELIUS**
"Süss und Sacht" *see Wiegenlied* Tennyson
    JENSEN
"Süsse Ahnung dehnt den Busen" *see
    Romanze: Die Ruinen* Reinbeck **WEBER**
"Süsse Augen, klare Bronnen!" *see Augenlied*
    Mayrhofer **SCHUBERT**
Die süsse Dirn' von Inverness see Burns
    FRANZ
"Süsse heilige Natur" *see An die Natur*
    Stolberg **LOEWE, SCHUBERT**
"Süsse Nacht!" *see Barcarole* Heiberg
    JENSEN
Süsse Ruh' see Laubsch, Frieda **REGER**
"Das süsse Zeug ohne Saft und Kraft!" *see
    Restauration* Mörike **SCHOECK**
*Süsser Freund, du blickest mich verwundert
    an see* Chamisso **LOEWE, SCHUMANN**
"Süsser goldner Frühlingstag!" *see
    Frühlingsfeier* Uhland **SCHOECK**
Süsser Mond see Heine **WEISGALL**
"Süsser Schlaf umfing den Müden" *see Jesus
    mit seinen Jüngern auf dem Meere* Anon.
    LOEWE
Süsses Begräbnis see Rückert **LOEWE**
"Süsses Bild, schwebst mir vor mit leisem
    Sehnen" *see Abendphantasie* Brun, S.
    ZELTER
"Süsses Licht! Aus goldnen Pforten" *see
    Sängers Morgenlied* Körner **SCHUBERT**
    Two settings: D. 163 and D. 165.
"Süsses Liebchen! komm zu mir!" *see
    Liebeständelei* Körner **SCHUBERT**
"Sui campi e sulle strade" *see Nevicata* Negri
    RESPIGHI
Le suicide see Béranger **LALO**
Suis chauve de naissance see Satie **SATIE**
SUITE FOR SOPRANO AND FLUTE, no. 1
    LUENING No author *Night song*
        NB: No. 2 for flute alone.
SUITE FOR SOPRANO AND FLUTE, no. 3
    LUENING No author *Morning song*
SUITE FOR SOPRANO AND FLUTE, no. 4
    LUENING No author *Evening song*
Suite vocalise see No author **MEDTNER**
Suivies d'un verso Canioca see Claudel
    MILHAUD
Suk see Bjørnson **GRIEG**
Sukhanov, Mikhail Dmitrievich, 1801-
    1843.

RUBINSTEIN *The swallow*
"Suku suuresti surevi" *see Soria sotahan
kuolla* Kanteletar **KILPINEN**
Suky, you shall be my wife see Anon.
NURSE LOVECHILD'S LEGACY (London:
The Poetry Bookshop, 1916).
HESELTINE
"Sul giardino fantastico" *see Notte* Negri
RESPIGHI
Suleika see Goethe **MENDELSSOHN-
BARTHOLDY, ZELTER**
Suleika see Goethe *WESTÖSTLICHER
DIVAN.*
**MENDELSSOHN-BARTHOLDY,
SCHOECK, SCHUBERT**
Suleika II see Willemer **SCHUBERT**
Suleika und Hatem see Goethe
WESTÖSTLICHER DIVAN. **SCHOECK**
Sulima see Tieck **BRAHMS**
Sully-Prudhomme, René François
Armand, 1839-1907.
AUBERT
Chanson de mer
Les yeux
DELIBES *Le meilleur moment des amours*
DUPARC *Le galop*
FAURÉ
Au bord de l'eau
Les berceaux
Ici-bas
FRANCK *Le vase brisé*
GOUNOD *Prière*
HAHN *Sur l'eau*
KOECHLIN *Déclin d'amour*
LES SOLITUDES.
DUPARC, RESPIGHI *Soupir*
"Sum, sum der Sandmann geht" *see
Schlafliedchen* Busse **REGER**
Sumerki see Guyot **RACHMANINOFF**
Twilight
"Šumí potok v tichém lkání" *see U potoka*
Kleinschrod **DVOŘÁK**
Summer see Gombossy **BARTÓK**
Summer ballad see Herold, Jíří **MARTINŮ**
"Summer ends now" *see Hurrahing in harvest*
Hopkins **BERKELEY**
Summer eve see Paulsen *JEG REISTE
ENDEILIG SOMMERKVAELD.* **DELIUS**
Am schönsten Sommerabend war's
Summer landscape see Drachmann **DELIUS**
A summer love tale see Pleshcheyev
CHAĬKOVSKIĬ *Ni slova, O drug″ moĭ*
Summer night see Runeberg **SIBELIUS**
Sommarnatten
Summer nights see Drachmann *LYSE
NAETTER.* **DELIUS**

Summer night's dream see Maĭkov
RIMSKIĬ-KORSAKOV *Son v letniuiu
noch'*
Summer schemes see Hardy **IRELAND**
"The summer sun was soft and bland" *see
Through the meadow* Howells, W. D.
MACDOWELL
A summer vacation see Schaffer **COPLAND**
Summermüd see Haringer *DIE
DENKMÄLER*: Der Reisende oder Die
Träne. **SCHÖNBERG**
SUMMER'S LAST WILL AND TESTAMENT
(1600). *see* Nashe
Spring **HESELTINE**
Spring, the sweet Spring **DELIUS**
The summons see Pushkin **MEDTNER**
"S'un casto amor, s'una pietà superna" *see
Sonetto XXXII* Buonarroti **BRITTEN**
The sun fills my room see Akhmatova
PROKOFIEV *Solntse komnatu napolnilo*
The sun has set see Rathaus **CHAĬKOVSKIĬ**
Sonne ging zur Ruhe
"The sun is at rest: its rays are gone" *see
Summer landscape* Drachmann **DELIUS**
Sun of the sleepless see Byron
MENDELSSOHN-BARTHOLDY
SUN OF THE SLEEPLESS! see Byron
Sonne der Schlummerlosen **WOLF**
Sun of the sleepless see Tolstoĭ **RIMSKIĬ-
KORSAKOV** *Nesliashchikh solntse*
"Sun rauhaas lemmin kuin en muuta mitääm"
see Lakeus II Koskenniemi **KILPINEN**
Sun song see Boultenhouse, Charles
ROREM
Sun tuskin huomasin ma siihen aikaan see
Koskenniemi **KILPINEN**
The sun upon the lake is low see Scott
SIBELIUS
SUNDT BLOD. see Aakjaer
Jeg baerer med Smil min Byrde **NIELSEN**
The sunflower see Blake, William
THOMSON
Sung by the shepherds see Crashaw
A HYMN TO THE NATIVITY. **THOMSON**
Sunrise see Hedberg **SIBELIUS** *Soluppgång*
Sunrise see MacDowell **MACDOWELL**
"Sunrise gilds the crested sea" *see Sunrise*
MacDowell **MACDOWELL**
Sunset see Case **BENNETT**
Sunset see Munch *SOLNEDGANG.* **DELIUS**
Beim Sonnenuntergang
"Suot sulavi, maat valuvi" *see Ei sula syän
suruinen* Kanteletar **KILPINEN**
"Superimpose on the petals of a rose" *see
The rose* Feeney **CHANLER**
Supervielle, Jules, 1884-1960.

COMPOSER   Poet   *Title*   "First Line"

Supervielle, Jules, 1884-1960 *(continued)*
AURIC *Le petit bois*
MILHAUD
  Abandonnée
  Ce bruit de la mer
  Ce peu
  Compagnons du silence
  Mon histoire
  Sans feu ni lieu
LA PREMIÈRE FAMILLE.
  MILHAUD
    Chacun son tour, les animaux
    Je suis dans le fillet
Supper see Soutar BRITTEN
"Sur cette croix jadis immonde" *see Sur la montagne* Barbier, J. GOUNOD
Sur la grève see Humières KOECHLIN
Sur la Grève see Unknown BIZET
"Sur la luzerne en fleur" *see La fille aux cheveux de lin* Leconte de Lisle DEBUSSY
"Sur la mer les crépuscules tombent" *see De grève* Debussy DEBUSSY
"Sur la mer qui brame" *see En ramant* Richepin CASELLA
"Sur la mer voilée" *see La fleur qui va sur l'eau* Mendès FAURÉ
Sur la montagne see Barbier, J. GOUNOD
"Sur la pente fatale" *see Paul Klee* Éluard POULENC
"Sur la plaine sans fin" *see L'arbre* Moréas SAINT-SAËNS
"Sur la pointe des pieds" *see L'enfant qui dort* Olivier, Pierre SAUGUET
Sur la source see Silvestre *MIGNONNE.* MASSENET
"Sur l'aîle des fuyantes grives las! hélas!" *see Soeur Anne* Pressat, André SAINT-SAËNS
Sur le basalte see Fontaines, A. HONEGGER
Sur le bord see Oeris AUBERT
"Sur le coteau" *see Les Colombes* Gautier FALLA
"Sur le flot des rêves" *see Rêverie* Barbier, J. GOUNOD
"Sur le lac bordé d'azalée" *see Rondel chinois* Anon. DEBUSSY
"Sur le pont un jour passant" *see Le corbeau* Unknown STRAVINSKIĬ
Sur l'eau see Sully-Prudhomme HAHN
"Sur l'eau bleue et profonde" *see Les matelots* Gautier FAURÉ
"Sur les continents morts, les houles léthargiques" *see L'astre rouge* Leconte de Lisle KOECHLIN

"Sur les fils de la pluie" *see Les anges musiciens* Carême POULENC
"Sur les flots de la vie" *see Mélancolie* Anon. MASSENET
"Sur les grands bois noyés de brume" *see Heure du soir* Silvestre DELIBES
Sur les lagunes see Gautier BERLIOZ
"Sur les pentes des monts les brises apaisées" *see Nox* Leconte de Lisle KOECHLIN
"Sur les routes de l'infini" *see L'oiseau de paradis* Princet, Jules MASSENET
Sur l'Herbe see Verlaine RAVEL
Sur lui-même see Anacreon ROUSSEL
  Two settings: Op. 31 no. 1 and op. 32 no. 1.
Sur ma lyre l'autre foix see Sainte-Beuve GRIFFES
"Sur ta bouche avec le désir" *see Un adieu* Silvestre MASSENET
"Sur ton sein pâle, mon coeur" *see Nocturne* Cazalis HAHN
"Sur un lys pàle mon coeur dort" *see Extase* Cazalis DUPARC
"Sur un trois-mâts de la Marine" *see La mauvaise prière* Chalupt AUBERT
Sur une jeune fille see Anacreon ROUSSEL
  Two settings: Op. 31 no. 3 and op. 32 no. 2.
Sur une page d'Album see Balzac SAUGUET
Sur une poésie de Van Hasselt see Hasselt MASSENET
Sur une songe see Anacreon ROUSSEL
Sure on this shining night see Agee *PERMIT ME VOYAGE*: Description of Elysium. BARBER
Surge, propera, amica mia see Canticum Canticorum PIZZETTI
"Surge, surge, surge, propera amica mea" *see Surge, propera, amica mia* Canticum Canticorum PIZZETTI
Surgi de la croupe et du bond see Mallarmé RAVEL
Surikov, Ivan Zakharovich, 1841-1880.
MALOROSSYSKAYA PESNYA.
  CHAĬKOVSKIĬ *IA li v poke da ne travushka byla*
Surkov, Alekseĭ Aleksandrovich, 1899-1983.
  PROKOFIEV *Pesniā smelykh*
The surly one see Roethke ROREM
Suruni see Lehtinen KILPINEN
"Suruni on syvempi syvintä merta" *see Suruni* Lehtinen KILPINEN
"Susa min björk, och grönska min rag" *see En vårmelodie* Cnattingius, Thor KILPINEN

"Susa, susa björk och lind" *see Vaggvisa*
Josephson, E. **KILPINEN**
Susannah Fry see De La Mare *DING DONG
BELL*: Benighted. **CHANLER**
Suschens Vogel see Mörike **WOLF**
Súsedova stajňa see Anon. **MARTINŮ**
Susie Asado see Stein **THOMSON**
Susman, Margarete, 1872-1966.
SIBELIUS *Im Feld ein Mädchen singt*
Suvilaulu see Törmänen **KILPINEN**
SUZANNE ET LA PACIFIQUE. see
Giraudoux
Adèle **HONEGGER**
Cécile **HONEGGER**
Irène **HONEGGER**
Jeanne **HONEGGER**
Rosemonde **HONEGGER**
Suzette et Suzon see Hugo **SAINT-SAËNS**
"Den svala snön därute faller och täcker
marken mer" *see Marssnön* Wecksell
SIBELIUS
SVALEN. see Aakjaer
Hør, hvor let dens Vinger smaekker
NIELSEN
En svane see Ibsen **GRIEG**
"En svane strøg mod syd" *see Farvel*
Paulsen **GRIEG**
"Svanen speglas re'n i sundet" *see Men min
fågel märks dock icke* Fröding **SIBELIUS**
Svanesång see Josephson, E. **KILPINEN**
Svanevit see Cnattingius, Thor **KILPINEN**
"Svanevit! svanevit! Vi sjunger du i natten"
see Svanevit Cnattingius, Thor
KILPINEN
Svanor see Österling **KILPINEN**
Svarta rosor see Josephson, E. *SVARTA
ROSOR OCH GULA.* **SIBELIUS**
SVARTA ROSOR OCH GULA. see
Josephson, E.
Schwarze Rosen **DELIUS**
Svarta rosor **SIBELIUS**
"Svet moĭ, Savishna" *see Svetik Savishna*
Musorgskiĭ **MUSORGSKIĬ**
Svetik Savishna see Musorgskiĭ
MUSORGSKIĬ
Svetlova, Marina, 1922-
PROKOFIEV *Nad poliarnym morem*
Svezh i dushist tvoĭ see Shenshin **RIMSKIĬ-
KORSAKOV**
Sviashchennoe mesto see Goethe
MEDTNER *Geweihter Platz*
Two settings: Op. 41 no. 1 and op. 46 no.
2.
Svítaj, bože see Anon. **MARTINŮ** *Let there
be light, O God*
Svitezianka see Mickiewicz **RIMSKIĬ-
KORSAKOV**

Svitezyanka see Mickiewicz **RIMSKIĬ-
KORSAKOV** *Sviteziãnka*
"Svømmende Skyer, dejlige Cyclader" *see
Solnedgang* Jacobsen **NIELSEN**
The swallow see Lenartowicz
CHAĬKOVSKIĬ *Lastochka*
The swallow see Sukhanov **RUBINSTEIN**
The swan see Nebesky, Jan **MARTINŮ**
The swan bent low to the lily see MacDowell
MACDOWELL
SWEET AND LOW. see Tennyson
Wiegenlied **JENSEN**
"Sweet and low, sweet and low" *see Evening
song* Tennyson **HARRIS**
Sweet baby, sleep! see Wither **GOUNOD**
Sweet blue-eyed maid see Gardner, W.
MACDOWELL
Sweet content see Dekker *THE PLEASANT
COMOEDY OF PATIENT GRISSILL*
(1603). **HESELTINE**
"Sweet cyder is a great thing" *see Great
things* Hardy **IRELAND**
Sweet dancer see Yeats **ROREM**
Sweet death see Hafiz **MARTINŮ**
Sweet is the rose see Spenser *AMORETTI.*
BLITZSTEIN
"Sweet little bell" *see Church bell at night*
Jones, Howard Mumford, translator.
BARBER
Sweet maid, give answer see Chaĭkovskiĭ
CHAĬKOVSKIĬ *Strashnaia minuta*
Sweet melody see Sakonskaya, N.
PROKOFIEV *Sladkaia pesenka*
The sweet o' the year see Shakespeare
A WINTER'S TALE. **HESELTINE**
The sweet season see Edwardes **IRELAND**
"Sweet, sweet, sweet, sweet, sweet tea" *see
Susie Asado* Stein **THOMSON**
Sweet Venevil see Bjørnson *ARNE.* **DELIUS**
Kleine Venevil
Sweet-and-twenty see Shakespeare
TWELFTH NIGHT. **HESELTINE**
"The sweetest flow'r that blows" *see
At parting* Peterson **IVES**
Sweetheart tell me see Gardner, W.
MACDOWELL
ŚWIETY BOZE. see Kasprowicz, Jan
Jestem i placze . . . **SZYMANOWSKI**
Świety Boze **SZYMANOWSKI**
Świety Boze see Kasprowicz, Jan *ŚWIETY
BOZE.* **SZYMANOWSKI**
Świety Franciszek see Tuwim
SZYMANOWSKI
Świety Franciszek mówi see Miciński
W MROKU GWIAZD. **SZYMANOWSKI**
Świetz Krystyna see Iłlakowiczówna
SZYMANOWSKI

The swimmers see Untermeyer **IVES** *from*
"*The swimmers*"
Swinburne, Algernon Charles, 1837-
1909.
   SAUGUET *Amour et sommeil*
   VAUGHAN WILLIAMS *Rondel*
The swing see Bialik **GIDEON**
The swing see Stevenson, Robert Louis
  A CHILD'S GARDEN OF VERSES. **HAHN**
Swing, swing and swoon see Taggard
   LUENING
Das Switesmädchen see Mickiewicz
   LOEWE
Switezianka see Mickiewicz **LOEWE**
  Das Switesmädchen
Swoboda, Wenzel, 1764-1822, supposed
author.
   WEBER *Lied*
Swollen head see Tolstoĭ **BORODIN** *Spes'*
Sydney, Sir Philip *see* Sidney, Sir Philip,
1554-1586.
Syllabes see Messiaen **MESSIAEN**
Le sylphe see Dumas the elder **FRANCK**
Le sylphe see Valéry **MOMPOU**
Die Sylphide see Herder **LOEWE**
Le sylvain see Pacini **ROSSINI**
Sylvestre, Pierre
   MASSENET *Sainte Thérèse prie*
Sylvie see Choudens **FAURÉ**
Sylvie see Contamine **SATIE**
Symons, Arthur, 1865-1945.
   IRELAND
    The adoration
    The rat
    Rest
    Santa Chiara
    Tryst
   RIEGGER *After sunset*
   LONDON NIGHTS.
    HESELTINE *A prayer to Saint Anthony
     of Padua*
   LONDON NIGHTS: "12 Sep 1891" (1895-
   97).
    HESELTINE *Autumn twilight*
   THE LOOM OF DREAMS.
    HESELTINE *The sick heart*
Sympathy see Tagore **MILHAUD**
Symphony in yellow see Wilde **GRIFFES**
Syndfloden see Grundtvig **NIELSEN**
Det synge see Garborg *HAUGTUSSA.*
   GRIEG
Den syngende Menighed see Grundtvig
   GRIEG
Syrokomla, Wladyslaw, pseud. *see*
  Kondratowicz, Ludwik, 1823-1862.
Syyshuokaus see Lehtinen **KILPINEN**

Syyskuun sonetti see Koskenniemi
   KILPINEN
Syyslaulu see Jalkanen **KILPINEN**
Syyslaulu see Lönnbohm **KILPINEN**
"Syyssävelet soi yli kaupungin" *see Syyslaulu*
  Jalkanen **KILPINEN**
Syyssonetti see Koskenniemi **KILPINEN**
Széchényi, Lajas, gróf *see* Széchényi,
  Ludwig, Count von, 1781-1855.
Széchényi, Ludwig, Count von, 1781-
1855.
   SCHUBERT
    Die abgeblühte Linde
    Der Flug der Zeit
Szene aus "Faust" see Goethe *FAUST.*
   LOEWE
Szene aus Goethe's "Faust" see Goethe
  FAUST. **SCHUBERT**
"Szerszeniu, szerszeniu, nie siadaj mi" *see*
  Jak sie n ajlepiej opedzać od szerszenia
  Iłlakowiczówna **SZYMANOWSKI**
Színes álomban see Gombossy, K ?
   BARTÓK *In vivid dreams*
Sztankó, Béla
   BARTÓK *Bell sound*
Szymanowska, Zafia
   SZYMANOWSKI
    Pieśń o fali
    Samotny ksiezyc
    Slowik
    Taniec
    Uczta
    Zlote trzewiczki
Szymanowska-Grzybowska, Sophie *see*
  Szymanowska, Zafia
SZYMANOWSKI, KAROL, 1882-1937.
Anon.
   A pod borem siwe kunie, op. 58 no. 5
    [GA, v. C/11, p. 177] same
   Bzicem kunia, op. 58 no. 6 [GA, v. C/11,
    p. 179] same
   Ciamna nocka, ciamna, op. 58 no. 10
    [GA, v. C/11, p. 189] same
   Dans les pré fleuris (1925?) [GA,
    v. C/11, p. 228]
    "Ah! Ah! Dans les prés fleuris"
   Four folk songs, op. 47 (1928-30)
    [unpubl.; no. 1 in **Muzyka,** No. 1-2
    (1938)]
   Idom se siuhaje, dołu, śpiewajecy (1924)
    [GA, v. C/11, p. 204]
    "Jo za wodom, ty za wodom"
     Facsimile: Warsaw: **Pani,** 1924, nos.
     8/9, pp. 11-13.
   Leć, glosie, po rosie, op. 58 no. 8 [GA,
    v. C/11, p. 184] same

Lecioly zurazie, op. 58 no. 1 [GA,
v. C/11, p. 167] same
Ściani dumbek, op. 58 no. 7 [GA,
v. C/11, p. 182] same
U jeziorecka, op. 58 no. 4 [GA, v. C/11,
p. 174] same
Uwoz, mamo, op. 58 no. 3 [GA, v. C/11,
p. 172] same
Wsyscy przyjechali, op. 58 no. 12 [GA,
v. C/11, p. 195] same
Wysla burzycka, op. 58 no. 2 [GA,
v. C/11, p. 169] same
Wysly rybki, sysly, op. 58 no. 11 [GA,
v. C/11, p. 192] same
Zarzyjze, kuniu, op. 58 no. 9 [GA,
v. C/11, p. 186] same
Berent, Waclav, 1873-1941.
Lebedź, op. 7 (1904) [Universal-Edition,
1913] "Obloczna góra ciagnie ptak"
Bierbaum, Otto Julius, 1865-1910.
Die schwarze Laute, op. 13 no. 5 [A.
Piwarski, 1911]
"Aus dem Rosenstokke vom Grabe des
Christ"
**Bodenstedt, Friedrich Martin von,
1819-1892.**
Zuleikha, op. 13 no. 4 [A. Piwarski,
1911] "Nicht mit Engeln im blauem
Himmelszeit"
Bulcke, Carl, 1875-1936.
Einsiedel, op. 22 no. 1 (1910) [Universal-
Edition, 1912] "Da droben am Berge"
Czyzowskiego, Kazimierza Andrzeja
Wyszywala raz Hanka (1920?) [**Muzyka,**
No. 1-2 (1938): p. 21] same
Davidov, Dmitri
Kak tolko wostok, op. 32 no. 1 (1915)
[GA, v. C/11, p. 45]
"Gdy zorza zablysnie na niebie"
Niebo biez zwiozd, op. 32 no. 2 (1915)
[GA, v. C/11, p. 47]
"Niebo bez gwiazd"
Osiennieje solnce, op. 32 no. 3 (1915)
[GA, v. C/11, p. 50]
"Slonca jesieni blade promienie"
Unable to verify Dmitri Davidov as
the same Davidov set by
Rubinstein.
Dehmel, Richard, 1863-1920.
Auf See, op. 13 no. 3 [A. Piwarski, 1911]
"Doch hatte niemals tiefere Macht dein
Blick"
Aufblick, op. 17 no. 5 (1907) [Universal-
Edition, 1913] "Über uns'rer Liebe
hängt eine tiefe Trauerweide"
Enführung, op. 17 no. 8 (1907)
[Universal-Edition, 1913]

"Ach! aus Träumen fahr ich in die
graue Luft"
Geheimnis, op. 17 no. 2 (1907)
[Universal-Edition, 1913]
"In die dunkle Bergsschlucht"
Hoch in der Frühe, op. 17 no. 1 (1907)
[Universal-Edition, 1913] "Sieh, wie
wir zu den Sternen aufsteigen!"
Manche Nacht, op. 17 no. 4 (1907)
[Universal-Edition, 1913]
"Wenn die Felder sich verdunkeln"
Nach einem Regen, op. 17 no. 7 (1907)
[Universal-Edition, 1913]
"Sieh, der Himmel wird blau"
Stimme im Dunkeln, op. 13 no. 1 [A.
Piwarski, 1911]
"Es klagt im Dunkeln irgendwo"
Verkündigung, op. 17 no. 6 (1907)
[Universal-Edition, 1913]
"Du tatest mir die Tür auf, ernstes
Kind"
Werbung, op. 17 no. 3 (1907) [Universal-
Edition, 1913]
"Und du kamest in mein Haus"
DES KNABEN WUNDERHORN
Christkindleins Wiegenlied, op. 13 no. 2
[A. Piwarski, 1911]
"O Jesulein zart, O Jesulein zart"
Faktor, Emil, 1876-1942.
An kleine Mädchen, op. 22 no. 3 (1910)
[Universal-Edition, 1912]
"Ich weiss ihr liebt das Dunkel nicht"
Falke, Gustav, 1853-1916.
Seele, op. 17 no. 10 (1907) [Universal-
Edition, 1913] "Dämmesung löscht die
letzten Lichter"
Frey, Friedrich Hermann, 1830-1911.
Liebesnacht, op. 17 no. 12 (1907)
[Universal-Edition, 1913]
"O weile, süsser Geliebter!"
**Hafiz, Muhammad Shums al-Din, d.
1388.**
Die brennenden Tulpen, op. 24 no. 3
(1911) [GA, v. C/11, p. 6]
"Einst aus meinem Grabe werden
ungezählte rote Tulpen"
Die einzige Arzenei, op. 24 no. 2 (1911)
[GA, v. C/11, p. 4]
"Ja, ich bin krank, ich weiss"
Grób Hafiza, op. posth. [GA, v. C/11,
p. 18] "Pod murami Szirazu lezy
piekna Mozella"
Tanz, op. 24 no. 4 (1911) [GA, v. C/11,
p. 8] "Heute tanzt alles"
Also voice & orchestra, op. 26 no. 3.
Trauriger Frühling, op. 24 no. 6 (1911)
[GA, v. C/11, p. 15]
"Der Frühling ist erschienen"

COMPOSER   Poet   *Title*   "First Line"

SZYMANOWSKI, KAROL, 1882-1937
(continued)

Hafiz, Muhammad Shums al-Din, d.
1388 (continued)
Der verliebte Ostwind, op. 24 no. 5
(1911) [GA, v. C/11, p. 11]
"Ich, Unglückseliger!"
Also voice & orchestra, op. 26 no.
2.
Wünsche, op. 24 no. 1 (1911) [GA,
v. C/11, p. 2] "Ich wollt, ich wär ein
morgenklarer See und du"
Also voice & orchestra, op. 26 no.
1.

Huch, Ricarda Octavia, 1864-1947.
Bestimmung, op. 22 no. 5 (1910)
[Universal-Edition, 1912]
"Was ist in deiner Seele"

Iłłakowiczówna, Kazimiera, 1892-1983.
Gil i sroka, op. 49 no. 11 (1922-23) [GA,
v. C/11, p. 127] "Urodzil sie gil z
czerwonym brzuszkiem"
Gwiazdka, op. 49 no. 5 (1922-23) [GA,
v. C/11, p. 118]
"U córeczki, u córeczki"
Jak sie najlepiej opedzać od szerszenia,
op. 49 no. 2 (1922-23) [GA, v. C/11,
p. 114]
"Szerszeniu, szerszeniu, nie siadaj mi"
Kolysanka gniadego konia, op. 49 no. 19
(1922-23) [GA, v. C/11, p. 142]
"Śpij, śpij, gniady koniu roboczy!"
Kolysanka Krzysi, op. 49 no. 14 (1922-
23) [GA, v. C/11, p. 132]
"Śpij, syneczku, na drewnianym
lozeczku"
Kolysanka lalek, op. 49 no. 10 (1922-23)
[GA, v. C/11, p. 126]
"U naszego synka nieba okruszynka"
Kolysanka lalki, op. 49 no. 16 (1922-23)
[GA, v. C/11, p. 136]
"Przyszla do lózka bosa kaczuszka"
Kot, op. 49 no. 15 (1922-23) [GA,
v. C/11, p. 134] "Na malej wysepce"
Mieszkanie, op. 49 no. 3 (1922-23) [GA,
v. C/11, p. 116]
"Gdyby sie tak zmieścić w kwiatku"
Myszy, op. 49 no. 17 (1922-23) [GA,
v. C/11, p. 137]
"Myszki pod podloga mieszkaly"
Nikczemny szpak, op. 49 no. 20 (1922-
23) [GA, v. C/11, p. 144]
"Lalka do spizarni sie zakrada"
Prosie, op. 49 no. 4 (1922-23) [GA,
v. C/11, p. 117] "Prosie przebralo sie i
poszlo spacerować"

Przed zaśnieciem, op. 49 no. 1 (1922-23)
[GA, v. C/11, p. 112]
"Jakby sie dobrze spalo"
Ślub królewny, op. 49 no. 6 (1922-23)
[GA, v. C/11, p. 120]
"Królewna od zlotni ka obraczke
pozycza"
Smutek, op. 49 no. 12 (1922-23) [GA,
v. C/11, p. 128]
"Wino dzikie u okna chwieje"
Świetz Krystyna, op. 49 no. 8 (1922-23)
[GA, v. C/11, p. 123]
"Meczennica, biedna świeta
Krystynka"
Trzmiel i zuk, op. 49 no. 7 (1922-23)
[GA, v. C/11, p. 122]
"Czupirzy sie, czupurzy kosmaty
trzmiel na rózy"
Wiosna, op. 49 no. 9 (1922-23) [GA,
v. C/11, p. 124]
"W pasiece az dzwoni"
Wizyta u krowy, op. 49 no. 13 (1922-23)
[GA, v. C/11, p. 130]
"Czy zdrowa pani krowa"
Zly Lejba, op. 49 no. 18 (1922-23) [GA,
v. C/11, p. 139] "Ach, Lejbo, Lejbo,
jakze ci nie wstyd?"

Iwaszkiewicz, Jaroslaw, 1894-1980.
Allah, Allah, Akbar, op. 42 no. 1 (1918)
[GA, v. C/11, p. 71] same
Also voice & orchestra, 1934.
Bialy krag ksiezyca olbrzymi, op. 48 no.
3 [GA, v. C/11, p. 108] same
Ledwie blask slońca zloci dachy wiez, op.
42 no. 3 (1918) [GA, v. C/11, p. 76]
same
Also voice & orchestra, 1934.
O tej godzinie, w której miasto śpi, op.
42 no. 5 (1918) [GA, v. C/11, p. 82]
same
Also voice & orchestra, 1934.
O, ukochana ma, op. 42 no. 2 (1918)
[GA, v. C/11, p. 74] same
Also voice & orchestra, 1934.
Odeszlaś w pustynie zachodnia, op. 42
no. 6 (1918) [GA, v. C/11, p. 86] same
Also voice & orchestra, 1934.
Pochyl sie cicho nad kolyska, op. 48 no.
1 [GA, v. C/11, p. 106] same
Śpiewam morzu, gwiazdom i tobie, op. 48
no. 2 [GA, v. C/11, p. 107] same
W poludnie miasto biale od goraca, op.
42 no. 4 (1918) [GA, v. C/11, p. 77]
same
Also voice & orchestra, 1934.

Joyce, James, 1882-1941.
Gentle lady . . . , op. 54 no. 1 (1926)
[GA, v. C/11, p. 150] same
Lean out of the window, op. 54 no. 3
(1926) [GA, v. C/11, p. 154] same
My dove, my beautiful one, op. 54 no. 4
(1926) [GA, v. C/11, p. 156] same
Strings in the earth, op. 54 no. 5 (1926)
[GA, v. C/11, p. 159] same
Winds of May, op. 54 no. 6 (1926) [GA,
v. C/11, p. 160] same
CHAMBER MUSIC.
Rain has fallen, op. 54 no. 7 (1926)
[GA, v. C/11, p. 163] same
Sleep now . . . , op. 54 no. 2 (1926)
[GA, v. C/11, p. 152] same
Kasprowicz, Jan, 1860-1926.
MOJA PIEŚŃ WIECZORNA.
Blogoslawiona niech bedzie ta chwila,
op. 5 no. 3 (1902)
[Gebethner & Wolff, 19__] same
ŚWIETY BOZE.
Jestem i placze . . . , op. 5 no. 2 (1902)
[Gebethner & Wolff, 19__]
"Jestem! Jestem i placze"
Świety Boze, op. 5 no. 1 (1902)
[Gebethner & Wolff, 19__]
"O, niezglebione, nieobjete moce!"
Miciński, Tadeusz, 1873-1921.
Nade mna leci w szafir morza, op. 11 no.
3 (1904-05) [Universal-Edition, 1913]
same
Rycz, burzo! op. 11 no. 4 (1904-05)
[Universal-Edition, 1913] same
Tak jestem smetny, op. 11 no. 1 (1904-
05) [Universal-Edition, 1913] same
W zaczarowanym lesie, op. 11 no. 2
(1904-05) [Universal-Edition, 1913]
same
W MROKU GWIAZD.
Na ksiezycu czarnym, op. 20 no. 1
(1909) [Gebethner & Wolff, 1925]
same
Na pustej trzcinie, op. 20 no. 6 (1909)
[Gebethner & Wolff, 1925] same
Pachna mi dziwnie twoje zlote wlosy,
op. 20 no. 3 (1909)
[Gebethner & Wolff, 1925] same
Świety Franciszek mówi, op. 20 no. 2
(1909) [Gebethner & Wolff, 1925]
"Ptaszki leca pytać sie"
W mym sercu, op. 20 no. 4 (1909)
[Gebethner & Wolff, 1925] same
Z maurytańskich śpiewnych sal, op. 20
no. 5 (1909)
[Gebethner & Wolff, 1925] same

Mombert, Alfred, 1872-1942.
Fragment: Der Glühende, op. 17 no. 11
(1907) [Universal-Edition, 1913]
"Schlafend trägt man mich in mein
Heimatland"
Schlummerlied, op. 17 no. 9 (1907)
[Universal-Edition, 1913]
"Leise fällt ein Schnee auf das Land"
No author
Vocalise-etude (1928) [GA, v. C/11,
p. 200]
Paquet, Alfons Hermann, 1881-1944.
Lied des Mädchens am Fenster, op. 22
no. 2 (1910) [Universal-Edition, 1912]
"Ein Wand'rer in der Gassen"
Ritter, Anna (Nuhn), 1865-1921.
Das hat die Sommernacht getan, op. 22
no. 4 (1910) [Universal-Edition, 1912]
"Die Nacht ist keines Menschen
Freund"
Szymanowska, Zafia
Pieśń o fali, op. 31 no. 5 (1915) [GA,
v. C/11, p. 36] "Ach! ach!"
Samotny ksiezyc, op. 31 no. 1 (1915)
[GA, v. C/11, pp. 25, 225] "Ach! ach!"
Slowik, op. 31 no. 2 (1915) [GA, v. C/11,
p. 28] "Ach! ach! ach!"
Taniec, op. 31 no. 4 (1915) [GA, v. C/11,
p. 33] "Ach!"
Uczta, op. 31 no. 6 (1915) [GA, v. C/11,
p. 38] "Na ma cześć"
Zlote trzewiczki, op. 31 no. 3 (1915)
[GA, v. C/11, p. 31]
"Ach! Od wrót mojego palacu"
Tagore, Rabindranath, 1861-1941.
OGRODNIK.
Der junge Prinz I, op. 41 no. 2 [GA,
v. C/11, p. 57] "O Mutter, der junge
Prinz muss an unsrer Tür"
Der junge Prinz II, op. 41 no. 3 [GA,
v. C/11, p. 61] "O Mutter, der junge
Prinz ist un unsrer Tür"
Das letzte Lied, op. 41 no. 4 [GA,
v. C/11, p. 66]
"Vollende denn das letzte Lied"
Mein Herz, op. 41 no. 1 [GA, v. C/11,
p. 55]
"Mein Herz, der Vogel der Wildnis"
Tetmajer, Kazimierz, 1865-1940.
Czasem gdy dlugo na pól sennie marze,
op. 2 no. 4 [Gebethner & Wolff, 1907,
1911] same
Daleko zostal caly świat, op. 2 no. 1
[Gebethner & Wolff, 1907, 1911] same
Pielgrzym, op. 2 no. 6 [Gebethner &
Wolff, 1907, 1911]
"Gdziekolwiek zwróce krok"

SZYMANOWSKI, KAROL, 1882-1937
(continued)
Tetmajer, Kazimierz, 1865-1940
(continued)
Slyszalem ciebie, op. 2 no. 5
[Gebethner & Wolff, 1907, 1911] same
Tyś nie umarla, op. 2 no. 2 [Gebethner &
Wolff, 1907, 1911] same
We mglach strumienie szumia wód, op. 2
no. 3 [Gebethner & Wolff, 1907, 1911]
same
Tuwim, Juljan, 1894-1953.
Kalinowe dwory, op. 46 bis, no. 4 (1921)
[GA, v. C/11, p. 99] same
Slowisień, op. 46 bis, no. 1 (1921) [GA,
v. C/11, p. 93] "W bialodrzewiu jasnie
dzni sloneczno"
Świety Franciszek, op. 46 bis, no. 3
(1921) [GA, v. C/11, p. 98]
"Ptakowie, kwiatowie, lanie weseli"

Wanda, op. 46 bis no. 5 (1921) [GA,
v. C/11, p. 102]
"Woda Wanda wislana"
Zielone slowa, op. 46 bis, no. 2 (1921)
[GA, v. C/11, p. 95]
"A gdzie pod lasem podlasina"
Unknown
Argizagi ederra, op. 44 no. 1 (ca.1920)
[unpubl.]
Do dziewczyny (1920) [unpubl.] "Czemu
tak lzy ronisz, dziewczyno droga"
Maitiak bilhoa holli, op. 44 no. 2
(ca.1920) [unpubl.]
O zawiedzionym zolnierzu (1920)
[unpubl.] "Byl raz sobie zolnierz, co
mial dwie kochanki"
"Szynkareczko, szafareczko, bój sie Boga,
stój!" *see Hulanka* Witwicki CHOPIN

T

T
VAUGHAN WILLIAMS *Wishes*
"Ta chair, d'âme mêlée" *see C'est ainsi que tu
es* Vilmorin POULENC
Ta main see Guillot de Saix HAHN
"Ta paille azur de lavande" *see La Marchande
d'herbes aromatiques* Mallarmé
MILHAUD
Ta parure est secrète see Satie SATIE
"Ta rose de pourpre à ton clair soleil" *see Nell*
Leconte de Lisle FAURÉ
Ta voix see Messiaen MESSIAEN
"Ta voix, vibration si douce à mon oreille"
see Long distance Anon. MILHAUD
Taaren see Andersen GRIEG
Tabb, John Banister, 1845-1909.
GRIFFES
Cleopatra to the asp
The first snowfall
The half-ring moon
Phantoms
The water lily
Table-mat song see Anon. STRAVINSKIĭ
Le moineau est assis
"Täglich ging die winderschöne
Sultanstochter" *see Der Asra* Heine
LOEWE, RUBINSTEIN

Täglich zu singen see Claudius, M.
SCHUBERT
"Tähtien hiljaisuutta ja rauhaa" *see Elegia
yölle* Koskenniemi KILPINEN
"Ein Tännlein grünet wo" *see Denk es, O
Seele* Mörike PFITZNER, WOLF
Ein Tännlein grünet wo see Mörike FRANZ
Ein Tänzchen see Boelitz REGER
Die Tänzerin see Unknown LASSEN
"Ein Täubchen bringt mir täglich Grüsse" *see
Taubenpost* Stieglitz LOEWE
Die Täuschung see Kosegarten *IM
ERLENBUSCH, IM TANNENHAIN.*
SCHUBERT
Täuschung see Müller, Wilhelm
SCHUBERT
Der Tag see Unknown MENDELSSOHN-
BARTHOLDY
"Der Tag beginnt zu dunkeln" *see Abends*
Osterwald FRANZ
"Der Tag ging regenschwer und sturmbewegt"
see Auf dem Kirchhofe Liliencron
BRAHMS
"Der Tag hat seinen Schmuck" *see
Abendsegen* Anon. WEBER
Der Tag ist vergangen see Anon. WEBERN
Tag Jer i Agt for Anna see Burns NIELSEN

"Der Tag neigt sich zu Ende" *see Abendlied*
  Sturm, J. **PFITZNER**
"Der Tag nimmt nur noch" *see*
  Der Sternenhimmel Sauter, Lilly von, d.
  ca. 1970. **KRENEK**
"Tag voll Himmel!" *see Entzückung*
  Matthisson **SCHUBERT**
"Tage der Wonne, kommt ihr so bald?" *see*
  Frühzeitiger Frühling Goethe
  LOEWE, ZELTER
"Das Tagewerk ist abgetan" *see Abendlied*
  Voss **ZELTER**
Das Tagewerk ist abgetan see Voss
  ZELTER
"Das Tagewerk ist abgethan" *see Abendlied*
  Voss **MENDELSSOHN-BARTHOLDY**
Taggard, Genevieve, 1894-1948.
  LUENING *Swing, swing and swoon*
Tagore, Rabindranath, 1861-1941.
  MILHAUD
    Defamation
    The gift
    Love, my heart longs day and night
    Paper boats
    Peace, my heart
    Sympathy
  RESPIGHI *La fine*
  SAUGUET
    Es-tu sorti par cette nuit d'orage?
    Le jour où le more
  GARDENER.
    MILHAUD
      Ayez pitié de votre serviteur
      Ne gardez pas
  GITANJALI.
    CARPENTER
      The day is no more
      I am like a remnant of a cloud of
        autumn
      Light, my light
      On the day when death will knock at
        thy door
      On the seashore of endless worlds
      The sleep that flits on baby's eyes
      When I bring to you colour'd toys
    CASELLA
      A cette heure du départ
      Dans une salutation suprême
      Mort, ta servante est à ma porte
      O toi, suprême accomplissement de ma
        vie
    MILHAUD
      Poème du "Gitanjali"
      When and why
  OGRODNIK.
    SZYMANOWSKI
      Der junge Prinz I

      Der junge Prinz II
      Das letzte Lied
      Mein Herz
Tailhade, Laurent, 1854-1919.
  ROUSSEL, SCHMITT *Tristesse au jardin*
Taina see Chamisso **RIMSKIĬ-**
KORSAKOV
"Taivas välkkyväisin jalokivin" *see Yksin*
  Koskenniemi **KILPINEN**
Tajná láska see Anon. **MARTINŮ**
Tak chto zhe? see Chaĭkovskiĭ
  CHAĬKOVSKIĬ
Tak i rvetsya dusha see Kol'tsov
  BALAKIREV
Tak jak ten měsíc vnebes báň see Hálek
  DVOŘÁK
Tak jestem smetny see Miciński
  SZYMANOWSKI
Take away my heart see Shenshin *PEVITSE:*
  Unosi moe serdtse. **CHAĬKOVSKIĬ** *Unosi*
  moe serdtse
"Take back the honour and the fame" *see*
  The cost Cooper, Eric Thirkell
  IRELAND
"Take heed of this small child of earth" *see*
  The children of the poor Hugo **DIAMOND**
Take my heart away see Shenshin *PEVITSE:*
  Unosi moe serdtse. **CHAĬKOVSKIĬ** *Unosi*
  moe serdtse
"Take off your cloak and your hat" *see*
  December night Lawrence **RIETI**
Take the sun and keep the stars see Harris
  HARRIS
"Take this kiss upon the brow!" *see A dream*
  within a dream Poe **LOEFFLER**
Take, O take those lips away see
  Shakespeare **CHAUSSON**
  Chanson d'amour
Take, O take those lips away see
  Shakespeare *MEASURE FOR*
  MEASURE. **HESELTINE, QUILTER,**
  THOMSON, VAUGHAN WILLIAMS
    Two Heseltine settings: 1916-17 and
    1918-19.
Takk for dit råd see Bjørnson
  FISKERJENTEN. **GRIEG**
Taksigelse see Winther **GRIEG**
Das Tal see Keller, G. **SCHOECK**
Tala, älskade, tala see Österling **KILPINEN**
Talismane see Goethe *WESTÖSTLICHER*
  DIVAN. **SCHUMANN**
"Talviaamull'astui tyttö huurteisessa" *see*
  Arioso Runeberg **SIBELIUS**
Talvj *see* Jacob, Therese Amalie Louise
  von, 1797-1870.
Tam stojí stará skála see Pfleger-Moravský
  DVOŘÁK

COMPOSER Poet *Title* "First Line"

Der Tambour see Mörike **WOLF**
"Le tambour roule" *see Les conscrits* Paliard
   MILHAUD
Tambourliedchen see Candidus **BRAHMS**
"T'amo, o pio bove" *see Il bove* Carducci
   CASELLA
TANCRÈDE. see Fargue
   La petite princesse **SCHMITT**
"Tandis qu'à leurs oeuvres perverses" *see*
   Primavera Gautier **GOUNOD**
Tandis que l'Enfant see Unknown
   LOEFFLER
Tandis que sur vos ans see Anon.
   SAINT-SAËNS
Taniec see Szymanowska, Zafia
   SZYMANOWSKI
The tankman's vow see Mendel'son
   PROKOFIEV *Klyatve tankista*
Der Tannenbaum see Scheurlein **WAGNER**
"Der Tannenbaum steht schweigend" *see*
   Der Tannenbaum Scheurlein **WAGNER**
Tanssi see Kanteletar **KILPINEN**
"Tant de tristesses plénières" *see Fagnes de*
   Wallonie Apollinaire **POULENC**
Tant de vagabonds see Paliard **MILHAUD**
Tant que mes yeux see Labé **BERKELEY,**
   SAUGUET
   Berkeley setting subtitled: A Memory.
Tanto bella see Unknown **RESPIGHI**
Tanto gentile e tanto onesta see Dante
   RUBINSTEIN
Tantum Ergo see Anon. **FRANCK**
Tanz see Hafiz **SZYMANOWSKI**
Der Tanz see Szymanowska, Zafia
   SZYMANOWSKI *Taniec*
Tanzlied see Golenishchev-Kutuzov
   MUSORGSKIǐ *Trepak*
Tanzlied see Sergel **KILPINEN**
Tanzlied im Mai see Hoffmann von
   Fallersleben **FRANZ**
Tapestry see Douglas, William
   THOMPSON, R.
Der tapfere Schneider see Falke **REGER**
Tarantelle see Pailleron **BIZET**
Tararán see Anon. **RODRIGO**
"Tararán, si viés a la una" *see Tararán* Anon.
   RODRIGO
Tardieu, Jean, 1903-1995.
   SAUGUET
    L'Aventure
    Le chevalier à l'armure étincelante
    Insomnie
Tarente, Jacques Etienne Joseph
   Alexandre, Macdonald, duc de *see*
   Macdonald, Jacques Etienne Joseph
    Alexandre, duc de Tarente, 1765-
    1840

Tarhassa hiipii hienohelma see Larin-Kyösti
   KILPINEN
Tarrant moss see Kipling **IVES**
Tastu, Mme. Amable, 1798-1885.
   MILHAUD *Plainte*
   SAINT-SAËNS
    La feuille du peuplier
    La maman
    Plainte
    Télesille
Tatry, Robert
   POULENC *Nos souvenirs qui chantent*
Taubenlied see Giesebrecht **LOEWE**
Die Taubenpost see Seidl **SCHUBERT**
Taubenpost see Stieglitz **LOEWE**
Der Taucher see Schiller **SCHUBERT,**
   ZELTER
"Tausend Blumen um mich her" *see*
   Die Natur Claudius, M. **SCHOECK**
"Tausend Menschen ziehen vorüber, den ich
   ersehne" *see Am Wegrand* Mackay
   SCHÖNBERG
Tausend stille, weisse, blaue Blumen see
   Sergel **KILPINEN**
"Taut que l'enfant me prétéra tel joucur de
   fleè" *see Boléro triste* Kahn **LOEFFLER**
Tavaststjerna, Karl August, 1860-1898.
   SIBELIUS
    Dolce far niente
    Fågellek
    Långsamt som qvällskyn
    När jag drömmer
    Och finns det en tanke?
    Romance
    Romeo
    Sof in!
    Vår förnimmelser
    Vilse
Tavouk gueunksis see Dumont *LA BONNE*
   CUISINE FRANÇAISE. **BERNSTEIN**
Taylor, Jane, 1783-1824.
   BRITTEN *Cuckoo!*
TCHAIKOVSKY, PETER ILICH *see*
   CHAǏKOVSKIǏ, PETR IL'ICH, 1840-
   1893.
Tchitcher-Iatcher see Unknown
   STRAVINSKIǏ
Tchobanian, Archag *see* Chobanian,
   Arshag, 1872-1954.
"Te amaré diosa Venus" *see Las locas por*
   amor Campoamor y Campoosorio
   TURINA
"Te recordistu, Nina" *see Che pecà!* Anon.
   HAHN
"Te souviens-tu du baiser" *see Evocation*
   Richepin **SCHMITT**

"Te vi un punto y flotando ante mis ojos" *see*
Rima Bécquer **TURINA**
"Te voilà, rire du printemps" *see Le printemps*
Banville **HAHN, KOECHLIN**
"Teach me, teach me, oh God" *see Prayer*
Romanov **RACHMANINOFF**
The tear see Moore, T. **RUBINSTEIN**
A tear trembles see Tolstoĭ **CHAĬKOVSKIĬ**
  Sleza drozhit"
Tears see Anon. **SEIBER**
Tears see Sládek **MARTINŮ**
Tears see Tiutchev **MEDTNER**
Tears see Wang Seng-ju **GRIFFES**
Tears, idle tears see Tennyson
  THE PRINCESS: IV, 1. 21.
  VAUGHAN WILLIAMS
"Tears never ending, forever descending" *see*
  Tears Tiutchev **MEDTNER**
Teasdale, Sara, 1884-1933.
  GRIFFES *Pierrot*
Tebia tak liubiat vse see Tolstoĭ
  RACHMANINOFF
  How everyone loves thee
"Técla notre âge d'or" *see Donne d'enfant*
  Cocteau **POULENC**
Tegengren, Jacob August, 1875-1956.
  KILPINEN *Fred*
Tegnér, Esaias, 1761-1846. *see* Tegnér,
  Esaias, bp., 1782-1846.
Tegnér, Esaias, bp., 1782-1846.
  LOEWE *Die Zugvögel*
TEL JOUR TELLE NUIT, no. 1
  POULENC Éluard *Bonne journée*
TEL JOUR TELLE NUIT, no. 2
  POULENC Éluard *Une ruine coquille*
  vide
TEL JOUR TELLE NUIT, no. 3
  POULENC Éluard *Le front comme un*
  drapeau perdu
TEL JOUR TELLE NUIT, no. 4
  POULENC Éluard *Une roulotte couverte*
  en tuiles
TEL JOUR TELLE NUIT, no. 5
  POULENC Éluard *A toutes brides*
TEL JOUR TELLE NUIT, no. 6
  POULENC Éluard *Une herbe pauvre*
TEL JOUR TELLE NUIT, no. 7
  POULENC Éluard *Je n'ai envie que de*
  t'aimer
TEL JOUR TELLE NUIT, no. 8
  POULENC Éluard *Figure de force*
  brûlante et farouche
TEL JOUR TELLE NUIT, no. 9
  POULENC Éluard *Nous avons fait la nuit*
Telega zhizni see Pushkin **MEDTNER**
  The coach of life

Télesille see Tastu **SAINT-SAËNS**
"Tell me again, and then lift up to me those
  frail white arms" *see Sonnet* Lodge, G.
  LOEFFLER
"Tell me not, Sweet" *see To Lucasta, on*
  going to the wars Lovelace **DIAMOND**
"Tell me not that thou dost love me" *see*
  Indian love Bryan **BENNETT**
"Tell me, star whose wings of light" *see*
  The world's wanderers Shelley **IVES**
"Tell me, tell me, where is fancie bred" *see*
  Fancie Shakespeare **BRITTEN**
Tell me the truth about love see Auden
  BRITTEN
Tell me, what are you thinking? see
  Sollogub **CHAĬKOVSKIĬ**
  Skazhi, O chem v teni vetveĭ
Tell me, what in the shade of the branches see
  Sollogub **CHAĬKOVSKIĬ**
  Skazhi, O chem v teni vetveĭ
"Tell me where is fancy bred" *see Fancy*
  Shakespeare **POULENC**
Tell me where is fancy bred? see
  Shakespeare *MERCHANT OF VENICE.*
  CARTER, QUILTER, THOMSON
Tell me where, ye summer breezes see Case
  BENNETT
Tell me why, dearest maiden see Unknown
  MUSORGSKIĬ
  Otchego, skazhi, dusha devitsa
"Tell me why do wagons frown" *see To cross*
  the street Carpenter, Rue **CARPENTER**
Tellez, Gabriel, 1570?-1648.
  EL BURLADOR DE SEVILLA.
  MAHLER
  Phantasie
  Serenade
Tellow, pseud. *see* Kosegarten, Ludwig
  Gotthard, 1758-1818.
"Tels que des brins de paille fine" *see Tes*
  cheveux Bruno, Camille **MASSENET**
Telschow, Wilhelm, 1809-1872.
  LOEWE
  Bitte zu Gott um Frieden
  Des Königs Zuversicht
  Preussentreue
DIE TEMPERAMENTE BEIM VERLUSTE
  DER GELIEBTEN, no. 1
  WEBER Gubitz *Der Leichtmütige*
DIE TEMPERAMENTE BEIM VERLUSTE
  DER GELIEBTEN, no. 2
  WEBER Gubitz *Der Schwermütige*
DIE TEMPERAMENTE BEIM VERLUSTE
  DER GELIEBTEN, no. 3
  WEBER Gubitz *Der Liebewütige*
DIE TEMPERAMENTE BEIM VERLUSTE
  DER GELIEBTEN, no. 4
  WEBER Gubitz *Der Geleichmütige*

TEMPÉRATURES. see Cocteau
  Le Nègre **HONEGGER**
THE TEMPEST. see Shakespeare
  Come unto these yellow sands **DIAMOND, QUILTER**
  Full fathom five **DIAMOND, QUILTER**
  Modéré-Plus lent **HONEGGER**
  No more dams I'll make for fish
    DIAMOND
  Un peu animé **HONEGGER**
  Where the bee sucks **DIAMOND, QUILTER**
  While you here do snoring lie **DIAMOND**
I tempi assai lontani see Shelley **RESPIGHI**
"The temple courts with grasses rank abound"
  see The old temple among the mountains
  Chang Wen-chang **GRIFFES**
Le temps a laissié son manteau see Charles,
  Duke of Orleans **DEBUSSY**
"Le temps a laissé son manteau" *see Temps
  nouveau* Charles, Duke of Orleans
  SAINT-SAËNS
Temps de neige see Gauthier-Villars
  SÉVERAC
Temps de neige see Hettich **CASELLA**
Le temps des roses see Roy, Camille
  GOUNOD
Le temps et les pays see Clancier **SAUGUET**
Les temps faciles see Marsan **MILHAUD**
"Le temps, l'étendue et le nombre" *see
  Villanelle* Leconte de Lisle **KOECHLIN**
Temps nouveau see Charles, Duke of
  Orleans **SAINT-SAËNS**
Le temps qui fuit see Anon. **GOUNOD**
"The ten hours' light is abating" *see At day-
  close in November* Hardy **BRITTEN**
Ten ptáček, ten se nazpívá see Hálek
  DVOŘÁK
"A tender child of summers three" *see
  The light that is felt* Whittier **IVES**
Tendrement see Hyspa **SATIE**
Tendresse see Champlay, R. **AUBERT**
Ténèbres see Claudel **MILHAUD**
"Teni gor vyso kikh na vodu legli" *see
  Strannik* Rückert **MUSORGSKIï**
Tennis at Trianon see Fröding **SIBELIUS**
  Bollspelet vid Trianon
TENNIS COURT OATH. see Ashbery
  Thoughts of a young girl **ROREM**
Tennyson, Alfred Tennyson, 1st baron,
  1809-1892.
  BERKELEY *Tonight the winds begin to
    rise*
  GOUNOD *Ring out, wild bells*
  HARRIS *Evening song*
  IVES *from "Amphion"*

JENSEN
  Claribel
  Die Schwestern
LISZT *Go not, happy day*
MASSENET *Come into the garden, Maud*
QUILTER *Now sleeps the crimson petal*
ROREM
  Ask me no more
  Far, far away
  Now sleeps the crimson petal
SAINT-SAËNS *A voice by the cedar tree*
VAUGHAN WILLIAMS
  Claribel
  Spring
THE DAY DREAM.
  ROREM *The sleeping palace*
THE PRINCESS.
  THOMSON *The bugle song*
  VAUGHAN WILLIAMS *The splendour
    falls*
THE PRINCESS: IV, 1. 21.
  VAUGHAN WILLIAMS *Tears, idle
    tears*
SWEET AND LOW.
  JENSEN *Wiegenlied*
THE WINDOW.
  VAUGHAN WILLIAMS *Winter*
The tenor man's story see Hardy **BRITTEN**
  The choirmaster's burial
Teodora see Gripenberg **SIBELIUS**
Teresa of Avila, Saint, 1515-1582.
  DIAMOND *Let nothing disturb thee*
  PIZZETTI *L'annuncio*
Le terre see Banville **KOECHLIN**
"La terre dort au ciel pur" *see Bonne nuit*
  Distel, Camille **MASSENET**
"La terre est blanche aux mois d'hiver" *see
  La bonne terre* Legrand, Marc **INDY**
La terre, l'eau, l'air et le vent see Ronsard
  HONEGGER
"La terre les eaux va bruvant" *see La terre,
  l'eau, l'air et le vent* Ronsard
  HONEGGER
Terre, ouvre-moi ton sein see Ronsard
  RIVIER
Terrible moment see Chaïkovskiï
  CHAïKOVSKIï *Strashnaia minuta*
Tersteegen, Gerhardt, 1697-1769.
  IVES *Hymn*
"Tes beaux yeux sont las" *see Le Jet d'eau*
  Baudelaire **DEBUSSY**
"Tes cailloux tu les nivelles" *see
  Le cantonnier* Mallarmé **MILHAUD**
Tes cheveux see Bruno, Camille
  MASSENET
"Tes grands yeux doux semblent des îles" *see
  Sérénade* Cazalis **CHAUSSON**

COMPOSER Poet *Title* "First Line"

"Tes pas, enfants de mon silence" *see Les pas* Valéry **MOMPOU**

"Tes yeux aux leurs fières" *see Antienne* Van Ormelingen **MASSENET**

Tes yeux bleus see Rollinat **CHABRIER**

"Tes yeux sont de claires fontaines" *see Déclaration* Giraud, Henri **AUBERT**

Test your skill see Norse **ROREM**

LE TESTAMENT. see Villon
  Ballade de Villon à s'amye **DEBUSSY**
  Ballade des femmes de Paris **DEBUSSY**
  Ballade que Villon feit à requeste de sa mère . . . **DEBUSSY**

Tête de faune see Rimbaud **RIVIER**

LA TÊTE ÉTOILÉE. see Apollinaire
  Le départ **RIVIER**

Teternikov, Fyodor, 1863-1927.
  RACHMANINOFF
  A dream
  Glory to God

Tetmajer, Kazimierz, 1865-1940.
  MARTINŮ
  Jašek's song
  Marry me, mother, as long as I'm young
  Speak on!
  SZYMANOWSKI
  Czasem gdy dlugo na pól sennie marze
  Daleko zostal caly świat
  Pielgrzym
  Slyszalem ciebie
  Tyś nie umarla
  We mglach strumienie szumia wód

Der Teufel see Siebel **LOEWE**

Teulet, Edmond
  MASSENET *Chanson désespérée*

Textament see Silvestre **DUPARC**

Thackeray, William Makepeace, 1811-1863.
  BRITTEN *A tragic story*

Thalatta see Morgenstern **KILPINEN**

"The Thames nocturne of blue and gold" *see Early morning in London* Wilde **GRIFFES**

Thanks to God the Creator see DES KNABEN WUNDERHORN **MARTINŮ**

A thanksgiving see Johanus Bassus **IRELAND**

That soothin' song see Hughes, L. *FINE CLOTHES TO THE JEW.* **CARPENTER**

"That strain again?" *see On hearing "The last rose of summer"* Wolfe, C. **HINDEMITH**

Le Thé see Banville **KOECHLIN**

Die Theilung der Erde see Schiller **ZELTER**

Thekla (Eine Geisterstimme) *see* Schiller **SCHUBERT**
  Two settings: D. 73 and D. 595.

Thekla's Gesang see Schiller **JENSEN**

Thème varié see Saint-Saëns **SAINT-SAËNS**

"Then the swift plunge" *see from "The swimmers"* Untermeyer **IVES**

"Then they bid you close your eyelids" *see The patient sleeps* Henley **CHANLER**

Theocritus, 310? B.C.-250? B.C.
  ROUSSEL *Le Kérioklépte*

Théone see Moréas **HAHN**

Théophile de Viau, 1590-1626.
  HAHN *A Chloris*

There are many sounds see Tolstoï **RACHMANINOFF**

There be none of beauty's daughters see Byron **MENDELSSOHN-BARTHOLDY, QUILTER**

There be none of beauty's daughters see Byron **WOLF**
  Keine gleicht von allen Schönen

There came a wind like a bugle see Dickinson **COPLAND**

"There came an image in Life's retinue" *see Death in love* Rossetti, Dante **VAUGHAN WILLIAMS**

"There comes o'er the valley a shadow" *see Evidence* Ives **IVES**

"There fell a beautiful clear rain" *see Rain in spring* Goodman **ROREM**

There is a garden in her face see Campion **THOMSON**

There is a generation that curseth their father see Bible **LUENING**

There is a green hill far away see Alexander, C. **GOUNOD**

There is a lady sweet and kind see Anon. **HESELTINE**

"There is a lady sweet and kind" *see Passing by* Anon. **HESELTINE**

There is a lane see Ives, Harmony **IVES**

"There is a lane which winds towards the bay" *see There is a lane* Ives, Harmony **IVES**

"There is a mill, an ancient one" *see The water mill* Shove **VAUGHAN WILLIAMS**

There is a tumult and howling see Heine *LYRISCHES INTERMEZZO,* no. 63. **GRIFFES** *Das ist ein Brausen und Heulen*

"There is a wind where the rose was" *see Autumn* De La Mare **BRITTEN**

There is dew my tone love see Hood **GOUNOD**

There is much that grows from my tears see Heine **MUSORGSKIĬ**
  Iz slez moikh vyroslo mnogo

There is no such sorrow see Pósa **BARTÓK**
  Nincs olyan bú
"There is no unbelief" *see Religion* Root
  IVES
"There is not much that I can do" *see At the*
  railway station, Upway Hardy **BRITTEN**
"There Liddy zot bezide her cow" *see*
  The winter's willow, a country song
  Barnes **VAUGHAN WILLIAMS**
"There liv'd a sage" *see A tragic story*
  Thackeray **BRITTEN**
There stands an ancient crag see Pfleger-
  Moravský **DVOŘÁK**
  Tam stojí stará skála
"There was a King in days of old" *see Irmelin*
  Jacobsen **DELIUS**
"There was a little ship in South Amerikee"
  see The golden willow tree Anon.
  COPLAND
There was a man of Newington see Anon.
  BRITTEN
There was a man of Thessaly see Anon.
  NURSE LOVECHILD'S LEGACY.
  (London: The Poetry Bookshop, 1916).
    HESELTINE
There was a monkey see Anon. **BRITTEN**
"There was a serpent who had to sing" *see*
  The serpent Roethke **ROREM**
"There was a ship of Rio sail'd out into the
  blue" *see The ship of Rio* De La Mare
  BRITTEN
"There was a ship of Rio sailed" *see The ship
  of Rio* De La Mare **CHANLER**
There was a time see Byron **LASSEN**
"There was a time when stone was stone" *see*
  The twisted Trinity McCullers **DIAMOND**
There was an old man see Anon. *NURSE
  LOVECHILD'S LEGACY.*
  (London: The Poetry Bookshop, 1916).
    HESELTINE
There was an old woman see Anon. *NURSE
  LOVECHILD'S LEGACY.*
  (London: The Poetry Bookshop, 1916).
    HESELTINE
"There was no cradle for Jesus when he was
  small" *see The cradle in Bethlehem*
  Bennett **QUILTER**
"There was the lyre of earth beheld" *see from
  "Night of frost in May"* Meredith **IVES**
"There were three ravens sat on a tree" *see
  The three ravens* Anon. **IRELAND**
"There's a jolly lot o' laughter" *see
  Play acting* Anon. **HESELTINE**
"There's a shadow on the grass" *see
  Premonitions* Johnson **IVES**

"There's pairt o' it young" *see A riddle*
  Soutar **BRITTEN**
"There's sorrow on the wind, my grief" *see
  I-Brasil* Sharp, W. **DELIUS**
Therese see Keller, G. **BRAHMS**
Theresens letztes Lied see Woltmann
  ZELTER
These, my Ophelia see MacLeish
  CHANLER
  Two settings: 1925; rev. 1937
These six things doth the Lord hate see Bible
  LUENING
These summer nights see Rathaus
  RACHMANINOFF
"These women all both great and small" *see
  An aside* Henry VIII **IRELAND**
"Theuerster Herr Kapellmeister" *see
  Komisches musikalisches Sendschreiben*
  Weber, Karl **WEBER**
Theuriet, André, 1833-1907.
  HAHN *Paysage*
  LALO
    Marine
    Le Rouge-gorge
  MASSENET *La veillée du petit Jésus*
Théus, Maurice de
  MASSENET *Mon page*
They answered see Hugo
  RACHMANINOFF
They are ev'ryone's friends see Rivas,
  Reyna **THOMSON** *Son amigos de todos*
"They are not long, the weeping and the
  laughter" *see Passing dreams* Dowson
  QUILTER
They bore him barefac'd on the bier see
  Shakespeare *HAMLET.* **THOMSON**
"They lean over the path" *see Orchids*
  Roethke **ROREM**
They rise up shining see Moss **ROREM**
"They told me, Heracleitus, you were dead"
  see Heracleitus Callimachus
  HESELTINE
"They wonder'd a while" *see They answered*
  Hugo **RACHMANINOFF**
Thibault *see* Thibaut IV, King of Navarre,
  1201-1253.
Thibaut IV, King of Navarre, 1201-1253.
  BRAHMS *Ein Sonnett*
  ZELTER *Sonett aus dem 13. Jahrhundert*
"Thick-flow'r'd is the trellis" *see The trellis*
  Huxley **IRELAND**
The things our fathers loved see Ives **IVES**
"Think in it's glass" *see Poor Henry*
  De La Mare **BERKELEY**
"Think in the morning" *see Proverb IV*
  Blake, William **BRITTEN**

Think of me! see Bal'mont **PROKOFIEV**
  Pomni meniá!
Thirstily I wait see Gombossy **BARTÓK**
  Summer
THIS BOOK OF HOURS. *see* Crane, W.
  This book of hours **GRIFFES**
This book of hours see Crane, W.
  THIS BOOK OF HOURS. **GRIFFES**
This is my love see Gombossy **BARTÓK**
  My love
"This is the house of Bedlam" *see Visits to St.*
  Elizabeths Bishop **ROREM**
"This is the summer's incredible hour" *see*
  The incredible hour Louchheim
  DIAMOND
"This is the time when the days have
  shortened" *see Solstice* Wolff, R. L.
  THOMPSON, R.
"This is the weather the cuckoo likes" *see*
  Weathers Hardy **IRELAND**
"This is thy hour, O Saul" *see*
  A clear midnight Whitman
  VAUGHAN WILLIAMS
This little time see Agee *SONNET 23.*
  DIAMOND
"This time of year" *see Anniversary in a*
  country cemetery Porter **DIAMOND**
This world is not my home see Anon.
  DIAMOND
This would I ask of each, tiny bird see Hálek
  DVOŘÁK *Vy malí, drobní ptáčkové*
"Tho be it cry of baying hounds" *see Echo*
  Pushkin **MEDTNER**
"Tho' still the fields are white with snow" *see*
  Spring waters Tiutchev
  RACHMANINOFF
Thomas af Strengnaes
  NIELSEN *Frihed er det bedste guld*
Thomas der Reimer see Anon. *JENSEIT*
  DES TWEED. **LOEWE**
Thomas, Dylan, 1914-1953.
  DIAMOND *I have longed to move away*
  DO NOT GO GENTLE.
  RIEGGER *The dying of the light*
Thomas Earp see Lawrence **RIETI**
Thomas Logge see De La Mare *DING*
  DONG BELL: Benighted. **CHANLER**
Thompson, Francis, 1859-1907.
  HINDEMITH *Envoy*
  MILHAUD *Poèmes de Francis Thompson*
THOMPSON, RANDALL, 1899-1984.
  Anon.
    My master hath a garden (1927) [*New*
      songs for new voices, edited by Louis
      Untermeyer, Clara & David Mannes.
      Harcourt, Brace, 1928] same

Baker, Mary Ely
  The echo child (1927) [*New songs for*
    new voices, edited by Louis
    Untermeyer, Clara & David Mannes.
    Harcourt, Brace, 1928]
    "Slipping through the rushes in a
    green & gray canoe"
Blake, William, 1757-1827.
  Spring (1920) [unpubl.] "Sound the flute"
De La Mare, Walter, 1873-1956.
  Some one (1927) [*New songs for new*
    voices, edited by Louis Untermeyer,
    Clara & David Mannes. Harcourt,
    Brace, 1928]
    "Some one came knocking"
Dougherty, Eleanor
  Doubts (1926) [unpubl.]
Douglas, William
  Tapestry (1925) [unpubl.]
    Scheduled for publication by E. C.
    Schirmer, 1984; not yet published,
    1990.
Howe, Mark Antony De Wolfe, 1864-
  1960.
  The passenger (1957) [E. C. Schirmer,
    1961] "I sit alone in a way station"
  Veritas (1954) [unpubl.]
Moses, Elizabeth Ann
  A ballad (1926) [unpubl.]
  Southwind (1926) [unpubl.]
Rhinelander, Philip Hamilton, 1908-
  Siciliano (1952) [E. C. Schirmer, 1980]
    "Love is like a wind upon the water"
Rogers, Robert Cameron, 1862-1912.
  Serenade in Seville (1920) [unpubl.]
Rounds, Emma
  The wild home pussy (1927) [*New songs*
    for new voices, edited by Louis
    Untermeyer, Clara & David Mannes.
    Harcourt, Brace, 1928] "I love little
    pussy, her coat is so warm"
Whitman, Walt, 1819-1892.
  The ship starting (1922) [unpubl.]
    High voice & piano.
Wolff, R. L.
  Solstice (1966) [E. C. Schirmer, 1984]
    "This is the time when the days have
    shortened"
Wright, Merle St. Croix
  Discipleship (1925) [unpubl.]
  Drought (1925) [unpubl.]
  The Heavens declare (1925) [unpubl.]
  Spiritual: I wan' my friends (1925)
    [unpubl.]
  White moth at twilight (1925) [unpubl.]
Wylie, Elinor, 1885-1928.
  Velvet shoes (1927) [*New songs for new*
    voices, edited by Louis Untermeyer,

THOMPSON, RANDALL, 1899-1984
(continued)
Wylie, Elinor, 1885-1928 *(continued)*
Clara & David Mannes. Harcourt,
Brace, 1928]
"Let us walk in the white snow"
Song also published by E. C.
Schirmer, 1938.
"Thoms sass am hallenden See" *see*
Der arme Thoms Falk ZELTER
THOMSON, VIRGIL, 1896-1989.
Anon.
Before sleeping (1963) [G. Schirmer,
1963] "Matthew, Mark, Luke and
John"
The feast of love (1964) [G. Schirmer,
1965] "Tomorrow all know love"
Baritone & piano; also with orchestra.
The holly and the ivy, a carol of Nativity
and Lent (1955) [unpubl.]
"The holly and the ivy, now both are
full well grown"
Soprano & piano; choral version
published 1964.
Jerusalem, my happy home (1963) [G.
Schirmer, 1963]
"Hierusalem, my happie home"
Anon. verses based on St.
Augustine.
Mass for solo voice (1961) [G. Schirmer,
1962] "Kyrie, Kyrie, Kyrie eleison"
Also voice & orchestra, 1962.
My Master hath a garden (1963) [G.
Schirmer, 1963] same
Remember Adam's fall (1955) [H. W.
Gray, 1963]
"Remember Adam's fall, O thou man"
Baritone & piano.
Bible
By night (1926) [American Music
Edition, 1953]
"By night on my bed I sought him"
Soprano & percussion.
I am my beloved's (1924) [unpubl.]
Tenor & piano.
I am my beloved's (1926) [American
Music Edition, 1953] same
Soprano & percussion.
O, my dove (1926) [American Music
Edition, 1953] same
Soprano & percussion.
Return, O Shulamite (1924) [unpubl.]
Tenor & piano.
Return, O Shulamite! (1926) [American
Music Edition, 1953]
"Return, return, O Shulamite"
Soprano & percussion.

Thou that dwellest in the gardens (1924)
[unpubl.]
Tenor & piano.
Thou that dwellest in the gardens (1926)
[American Music Edition, 1953]
same
Soprano & percussion.
Blake, William, 1757-1827.
And did those feet (1951) [Ricordi, 1953]
same
Baritone & piano; also with orchestra.
The divine image (1951) [Ricordi, 1953]
"To mercy, pity, peace, and love"
Baritone & piano; also with orchestra.
The land of dreams (1951) [Ricordi,
1953] "Awake, awake, my little boy!"
Baritone & piano; also with orchestra.
The little black boy (1951) [Ricordi,
1953] "My mother bore me in the
southern wild"
Baritone & piano; also with
orchestra.
The sunflower (1920) [unpubl.]
"Ah, sunflower weary of love"
Soprano & piano.
THE TYGER.
The tiger (1926) [G. Schirmer, 1967]
"Tiger, tiger burning bright"
Soprano & piano.
Tiger! Tiger! (1951) [Ricordi, 1953]
same
Baritone & piano; also with
orchestra.
Bossuet, Jacques Bénigne, bishop of
Meaux, 1627-1704.
Oraison funèbre (1930) [unpubl.]
"Quand Dieu laisse sortir"
Tenor & piano.
Campion, Thomas, 1567-1619.
Follow thy fair sun (1951) [Ricordi,
1953] same
Mezzo-soprano & piano; also with
clarinet, viola & harp.
Follow your saint (1951) [Ricordi, 1953]
same
Mezzo-soprano & piano; also with
clarinet, viola & harp.
Rose cheek'd Laura, come (1951)
[Ricordi, 1953] same
Mezzo-soprano & piano; also with
clarinet, viola & harp.
There is a garden in her face (1951)
[Ricordi, 1953] same
Mezzo-soprano & piano; also with
clarinet, viola & harp.
What is it? (1980) [T.Presser, 1981]
"What is it all that men possess"

Crashaw, Richard, 1613?-1649.
A HYMN TO THE NATIVITY.
 Sung by the shepherds (1963) [G.
  Schirmer, 1963]
  "Welcome to our wond'ring sight"
Donne, John, 1573-1631.
 Consider, Lord (1955) [Southern, 1962]
  "Since I am coming to that holy room"
  Baritone & piano.
Fisher, Jasper, fl. 1639.
 At the spring (1955) [H. W. Gray, 1965]
  "At the spring birds do sing"
  Soprano & piano.
Francis of Assisi, Saint, 1182-1226.
 From the canticle of the sun (1963) [G.
  Schirmer, 1963]
  "Most high, omnipotent Lord"
Graves, John Woodcock, 1795-1886.
 John Peel (1955) [Southern, 1962] "D'ye
  ken John Peel with his coat so gay"
  Baritone & piano.
Heywood, Thomas, d. 1641.
 The bell doth toll (1955) [Southern,
  1962] "Come list and hark"
  Baritone & piano.
Hugnet, Georges, 1906-1974.
 Le Berceau de Gertrude Stein (1928)
  [Southern, 1979] "Rose is a rose"
  Soprano & piano.
 Les Ecrevisses (1927) [privately printed,
  1940; Southern, 1980] "Lorsque le
  nuit"
  Soprano & piano.
 Grenadine (1927) [privately printed,
  1940; Southern, 1980]
  "Grenade grenadine"
   Soprano & piano.
 Mon amour est bon à dire (1931) [G.
  Schirmer, 1950] same
  Soprano or mezzo-soprano & piano.
 Partis les vaisseaux (1931) [G. Schirmer,
  1950] same
  Soprano or mezzo-soprano & piano.
 Pour chercher sur la carte des mers
  (1931) [G. Schirmer, 1950] same
  Soprano or mezzo-soprano & piano.
 La première de toutes (1931) [G.
  Schirmer, 1950] same
  Soprano or mezzo-soprano & piano.
 La Rosée (1927) [privately printed, 1940;
  Southern, 1980]
  "Tout l'oiseaux ce matin"
   Soprano & piano.
 Les soirées bagnolaises (1928) [unpubl.]
  "Soirée du dimanche"
  Soprano & piano.

La wagon immobile (1927) [privately
 printed, 1940; Southern, 1980]
 "Les quartiers retirés"
 Soprano & piano.
Koch, Kenneth, 1925-2002.
 Collected poems (1959) [Southern, 1978]
  "I was asleep when they worked up the
  buffalo"
  Soprano, baritone & piano; also with
  orchestra.
 Down at the docks (1959) [G. Schirmer,
  1964] same
 Let's take a walk (1959) [G. Schirmer,
  1964] same
 Love song (1959) [G. Schirmer, 1964]
  "I love you as a sheriff searches for a
  walnut"
 A prayer to Saint Catherine (1959) [G.
  Schirmer, 1964] "If I am to be
  preserved from heartache and shyness"
Kreymborg, Alfred, 1883-1966.
 Chamber music (1931) [unpubl.]
  "Phoebus tucks all his arrows away"
Kynaston, Sir Francis, 1587-1642.
 If thou a reason dost desire to know
  (1955) [Southern, 1962] same
La Fontaine, Jean de, 1621-1695.
 Le singe et le léopard (1930) [Southern,
  1973] "Le singe avec le léopard"
  Soprano & piano.
Lear, Edward, 1812-1888.
 The courtship of the Yongly Bongly Bo
  (1973-74) [G. Schirmer, 1977]
  "On the coast of Coromandel"
Lowell, Amy, 1814-1925.
 Vernal equinox (1920) [unpubl.] "The
  scent of hyacinths like a pale mist"
  Soprano & piano.
Moore, Marianne Craig, 1887-1972.
 English usage (1963) [G. Schirmer,
  1966] "Make a fuss and be tedious"
 My crow Pluto (1963) [G. Schirmer,
  1966] same
O'Hara, Frank, 1926-1966.
 SNEDEN'S LANDING VARIATIONS.
  From "Sneden's Landing Variations"
   (1972) [Lingua Press, ca.1977]
   "What and each in and they their the
   and poor not to with all in in"
Racine, Jean Baptiste, 1639-1699.
 Phaedra's farewell (1932) [Southern,
  1974] "My fever is not new"
  Soprano or mezzo-soprano & piano.
Rivas, Reyna
 Nadie lo oye como ellos (1957)
  [Southern, 1962] same
  Soprano & piano.

COMPOSER Poet *Title* "First Line"

THOMSON, VIRGIL, 1896-1989
(continued)
Rivas, Reyna *(continued)*
Son amigos de todos (1957) [Southern, 1962] same
Soprano & piano.
Todas las horas (1957) [Southern, 1962] same
Soprano & piano.
Rohan, Catherine de Parthenay-Larchevêque, duchesse de, 1554-1631.
A son Altesse la Princesse Antoinette Murat (1928) [unpubl.]
"Elle partit, le grande errante"
Soprano & piano.
Jour de chaleur aux bains de mer (1928) [unpubl.] "Tout le monde se baigne"
Soprano & piano.
La Seine (1928) [unpubl.; facsimile in *Parnassus: Poetry in Review*, 1977]
"Est-il rien de plus beau"
Sade, Comte Donatien Alphonse François de, 1740-1814.
Commentaire sur Saint Jérome (1928) [unpubl.] "Saint Jérome raconte"
Soprano & piano.
Shakespeare, William, 1564-1616.
ALL'S WELL THAT ENDS WELL.
Was this fair face (1957) [Southern, 1961] same
Tenor & piano.
HAMLET.
How should I your true love know (1936) [unpubl.] same
Song for the Gravedigger from *Hamlet* (1936) [unpubl.]
"In youth, when I did love"
They bore him barefac'd on the bier (1936) [unpubl.] same
Tomorrow is Saint Valentine's day (1936) [unpubl.] same
MEASURE FOR MEASURE.
Take, O take those lips away (1956) [Southern, 1961] same
MERCHANT OF VENICE.
Look, how the floor of heav'n (1955) [H. W. Gray, 1963] same
Soprano & piano.
Tell me where is fancy bred (1957) [Southern, 1961] same
Tenor & piano.
MUCH ADO ABOUT NOTHING.
Pardon, Goddess of the night (1957) [Southern, 1961] same
Tenor & piano.

Sigh no more, ladies (1957) [Southern, 1961] same
Tenor & piano.
Stein, Gertrude, 1874-1946.
Deux soeurs qui sont pas soeurs (1929) [unpubl.] "Au coin d'une rue"
Soprano & piano.
Film: Two sisters not sisters (1930) [Southern, 1981] "In Paris on a corner of an outer boulevard"
Portrait of F. B. [Frances Blood] (1929) [G. Schirmer, 1971]
"A peal is that mountain"
Mezzo-soprano & piano.
Susie Asado (1926) [Boosey & Hawkes]
"Sweet, sweet, sweet, sweet, sweet tea"
Soprano & piano.
FOUR SAINTS IN 3 ACTS.
Pigeons on the grass (1928) [Mercury Music Corp., 1934] same
Included at the composer's request because "it is a pastiche, not an excerpt."
PRECIOSILLA.
Preciosilla (1926) [G. Schirmer, 1948]
"Cousin to Clare washing"
Soprano & piano.
Tennyson, Alfred Tennyson, 1st baron, 1809-1892.
THE PRINCESS.
The bugle song (1941) [Holt, Rinehart, Winston, 1966]
"The splendor falls on castle walls"
Unison children's song; in *Exploring music 5*, 1966 ed. only.
Thomson, Virgil, 1896-1989.
Go to sleep, Alexander Smallers, Jr. (1935) [unpubl.]
Voice alone.
Go to sleep, Pare McTaggett Lorentz (1937) [unpubl.]
Voice alone.
Watts, Isaac, 1674-1748.
My Shepherd will supply my need (1959) [H. W. Gray, 1959] same
Webster, John, 1580?-1625?
THE WHITE DEVIL.
Dirge (1939) [G. Schirmer, 1947]
"Call for the robin red-breast and the wren"
Mezzo-soprano & piano.
Thomson, Virgil, 1896-1989.
THOMSON
Go to sleep, Alexander Smallers, Jr.
Go to sleep, Pare McTaggett Lorentz
"Thor stand am Mitternachtsende der Welt"
see Germanensang Dahn **LASSEN**

Thoreau see Ives **IVES**
Thoreau, Henry David, 1817-1862.
  SAUGUET *Fumée légère*
The thorn see Runeberg **SIBELIUS** *Törnet*
Those evening bells see Moore, T. **IVES**
Those folk see Nekrasov **BORODIN**
  U lyudey-to v domu
Those pretty wrongs that liberty commits see
  Shakespeare **DIAMOND**
Thou and you see Pushkin **RIMSKIĬ-
  KORSAKOV** *Ty i my*
Thou art so captivating see Golovinsky
  BALAKIREV *Ti plenitel'noy negi polna*
"Thou art to all lost love the best" *see*
  To the willow-tree Herrick **ROREM**
Thou gav'st me leave to kiss see Herrick
  HESPERIDES (1648): Chop-cherry.
  HESELTINE
"Thou gazest on the stars" *see To Aster* Plato
  BERKELEY
Thou hast left me ever, Jame see Burns
  FRANZ
Thou hast made me see Donne **BRITTEN**
"Thou hidden love of God" *see Hymn*
  Tersteegen **IVES**
"Thou more than most sweet glove" *see*
  Song of the glove Jonson **BLITZSTEIN**
"Thou, my field, my beloved harvest field"
  see O thou, my field Tolstoĭ
  RACHMANINOFF
Thou only dear one, but for thee see
  Pfleger-Moravský **DVOŘÁK**
  Ó, duše drahá, jedinká
  Ó, duše drahá, jedinkájež
Thou that dwellest in the gardens see Bible
  THOMSON
  Two settings: 1924 and 1926
Thou, who dwellest in Heaven see Unknown
  MARTINŮ
"Thou whose spell can raise the dead" *see*
  Saul Byron **DIAMOND**
Thoughts of a young girl see Ashbery
  TENNIS COURT OATH. **ROREM**
"Thoughts, which deeply rest at evening" *see*
  Disclosure Ives **IVES**
EINE THRÄNE. see Beck
  Eine Thräne **JENSEN**
Eine Thräne see Beck *EINE THRÄNE.*
  JENSEN
Die Thräne see Moore, T. **RUBINSTEIN**
  The tear
Thränen und Lächeln see Byron **LOEWE**
Thränenregen see Müller, Wilhelm
  SCHUBERT
Three autumn tears see Ady **BARTÓK**
  Autumn tears

THREE CALAMUS POEMS, no. 1
  ROREM Whitman *Of him I love day and
  night*
THREE CALAMUS POEMS, no. 2
  ROREM Whitman *I saw in Louisiana a
  live-oak growing*
THREE CALAMUS POEMS, no. 3
  ROREM Whitman *To a common
  prostitute*
THREE CHRISTMAS SONGS, no. 1
  MARTINŮ Aicard *La poule a couvé*
THREE CHRISTMAS SONGS, no. 2
  MARTINŮ Gramont, T de *Le poulet*
THREE CHRISTMAS SONGS, no. 3
  MARTINŮ Xaurof, L. *Le petit chat*
THREE EPITAPHS, no. 1
  CHANLER De La Mare *A shepherd*
THREE EPITAPHS, no. 2
  CHANLER De La Mare *A one-eyed
  tailor*
THREE EPITAPHS, no. 3
  CHANLER De La Mare *Three husbands*
THREE FIRE SONGS, no. 1
  MACDOWELL MacDowell *O thistle-
  leafed flame*
THREE FIRE SONGS, no. 2
  MACDOWELL MacDowell *In flaming
  gold*
THREE FIRE SONGS, no. 3
  MACDOWELL MacDowell *Around a
  twisted snake of flame*
THREE FORGOTTEN SONGS, no. 1
  BALAKIREV Golovinsky *Ti plenitel'noy
  negi polna*
THREE FORGOTTEN SONGS, no. 2
  BALAKIREV Tumanskiĭ *Zveno*
THREE FORGOTTEN SONGS, no. 3
  BALAKIREV Mikhailov *Ispanskaya
  pensyna*
THREE GREEK SONGS, no. 1
  BERKELEY Sappho *Epitaph of Timas*
THREE GREEK SONGS, no. 2
  BERKELEY Antipater *Spring song*
THREE GREEK SONGS, no. 3
  BERKELEY Plato *To Aster*
Three husbands see De La Mare *HERE LIES
  MY THREE HUSBANDS.* **CHANLER**
THREE INCANTATIONS FROM A
  MARIONETTE TALE, no. 1
  ROREM Boultenhouse, Charles
  Cloudless blue claw
THREE INCANTATIONS FROM A
  MARIONETTE TALE, no. 2
  ROREM Boultenhouse, Charles
  Now I make a circle

COMPOSER Poet *Title* "First Line"

THREE INCANTATIONS FROM A
MARIONETTE TALE, no. 3
  ROREM Boultenhouse, Charles
  Boy into animal
Three maidens on a bright night see
  Hlavsa, Vrat. **MARTINŮ**
THREE MODERN GREEK SONGS, no. 1
  DVOŘÁK Anon. *Koljas*
THREE MODERN GREEK SONGS, no. 2
  DVOŘÁK Anon. *Nereidy*
THREE MODERN GREEK SONGS, no. 3
  DVOŘÁK Anon. *Žalozpěv Pargy*
Three Offenbach songs see Blitzstein
  BLITZSTEIN
THREE POEMS, no. 1
  GRIFFES Blake, William *In a myrtle
  shade*
THREE POEMS, no. 2
  GRIFFES Brooke *WaiKiKi*
THREE POEMS, no. 3
  GRIFFES Giovannitti *Phantoms*
The three ravens see Anon. **IRELAND**
THREE SENTENCES FROM THE SONG
OF SOLOMON, no. 1
  THOMSON Bible *Thou that dwellest in
  the gardens*
THREE SENTENCES FROM THE SONG
OF SOLOMON, no. 2
  THOMSON Bible *Return, O Shulamite*
THREE SENTENCES FROM THE SONG
OF SOLOMON, no. 3
  THOMSON Bible *I am my beloved's*
THREE SHAKESPEARE SONGS, no. 1
  QUILTER Shakespeare *Come away,
  Death*
THREE SHAKESPEARE SONGS, no. 2
  QUILTER Shakespeare *O mistress mine*
THREE SHAKESPEARE SONGS, no. 3
  QUILTER Shakespeare *Blow, blow,
  thou winter wind*
THREE SHELLEY LYRICS, no. 1
  DELIUS Shelley *Indian love song*
THREE SHELLEY LYRICS, no. 2
  DELIUS Shelley *Love's philosophy*
THREE SHELLEY LYRICS, no. 3
  DELIUS Shelley *To the queen of my heart*
Three sisters see De La Mare *DING DONG
BELL*: Benighted. **CHANLER**
"Three sisters rest beneath this cypress shade"
  see Three sisters De La Mare **CHANLER**
Three songs see Nietzsche **HINDEMITH**
THREE SONGS FOR AMERICAN
SCHOOLS, no. 1
  SIBELIUS Dixon *Autumn song*
THREE SONGS FOR AMERICAN
SCHOOLS, no. 2

SIBELIUS Scott *The sun upon the lake is
low*
THREE SONGS FOR AMERICAN
SCHOOLS, no. 3
  SIBELIUS Sharp, W. *A cavalry catch*
THREE SONGS SET TO POEMS FROM
"CHAMBER MUSIC" BY JAMES JOYCE,
no. 1
  BARBER Joyce *Rain has fallen*
THREE SONGS SET TO POEMS FROM
"CHAMBER MUSIC" BY JAMES JOYCE,
no. 2
  BARBER Joyce *Sleep now*
THREE SONGS SET TO POEMS FROM
"CHAMBER MUSIC" BY JAMES JOYCE,
no. 3
  BARBER Joyce *I hear an army*
Three vocalises see No author
  VAUGHAN WILLIAMS
The thresher see Du Bellay
  D'UN VANNEUR DE BLÉ AUX VENTS: A
  vous troppe légère. **BERKELEY**
"Thro' silver clouds the ev'ning star was
  stealing" *see Den första kyssen* Runeberg
  SIBELIUS
"Thro' the forest dark" *see Song of the dark
  forest* Borodin **BORODIN**
Through long, long years see Jacobsen
  DET BØDES DER FOR. **DELIUS**
Through snow and fog see Afinogenov
  PROKOFIEV *Skvoz' shega i tumany*
"Through the ample open door" *see
  A farm picture* Whitman **LUENING**
Through the meadow see Howells, W. D.
  MACDOWELL
Through the sunny garden see Coleridge
  QUILTER
"The thrushes sing as the sun is going" *see
  Proud songsters* Hardy **BRITTEN**
Thu nicht so spröde, schönes Kind see
  Bodenstedt **RUBINSTEIN**
"Thüringens Wälder senden den Waidmann
  und den Schmied" *see Biterolf und der
  Schmied von Ruhla* Scheffel **LISZT**
"Der Thürmer, der schaut zu Mitten der
  Nacht" *see Der Todtentanz* Goethe
  LOEWE
"Der Thürmer der schaut zu Mitten der
  Nacht" *see Der Totentanz* Goethe
  ZELTER
Thu-Fu see **WEBERN** *Der Frühlingsregen*
The thunderstorm see Carpenter, Rue
  CARPENTER
Thurmwächter Lynceus see Goethe *FAUST.*
  LOEWE
Thy beaming eyes see Gardner, W.
  MACDOWELL

Thy dark eyes to mine see Sharp, W. *FROM THE HILLS OF DREAMS.* **GRIFFES**
Thy glance is radiant as the heavens see
  Just like the sky your gaze is beaming
  Lermontov **RIMSKĬ-KORSAKOV**
  Kak nebesa, tvoĭ vzor blistaet
"Thy hand in mine, thy hand in mine" see
  The sacred flame Coleridge **IRELAND**
Thy pity I implore! see Merezhkovski
  RACHMANINOFF *I beg for mercy*
Thy radiant image see Chaĭkovskiĭ
  CHAĬKOVSKIĬ *Tak chto zhe?*
Ti plenitel'noy negi polna see Golovinsky
  BALAKIREV
"Tianutsia po neby tuchi tiazhelye" see
  Serenada Vilenkin **RUBINSTEIN**
"Tiapa, baĭ, baĭ" see *S kukloĭ* Musorgskiĭ
  MUSORGSKIĬ
Tiazhela bestsvetna i pusta see Bryusov
  MEDTNER *In the church-yard*
Tichborne, Chidiock, 1558?-1586.
  DIAMOND *Life and death*
Tichý, Jaroslav, pseud. see Rypáček,
  František J.
Tidt er jeg glad, og vil dog gerne graede see
  Ingemann **NIELSEN**
Tieck, Johann Ludwig, 1773-1853.
  BRAHMS
    Liebe kam aus fernen Landen
    Muss es eine Trennung geben
    Ruhe, Süssliebchen
    Sind es Schmerzen
    So willst du des Armen
    Sulima
    Traun, Bogen und Pfeil sind gut für den Feind
    Treue Liebe dauert lange
    Verzweiflung
    War es dir, dem dies Lippen bebten?
    Wie froh und frisch
    Wie schnell verschwindet so Licht als Glanz
    Wie soll ich die Freude
    Wir müssen uns trennen
  CORNELIUS *Herbstlied*
  FRANZ *Schlummerlied*
  LASSEN *Herbstlied*
  MENDELSSOHN-BARTHOLDY
    Minnelied
  SPOHR
    Schifferlied der Wasserfee
    Schlaflied
  WEBER *Sind es Schmerzen, sind es Freuden*
  ZELTER *Herbstlied*
  WALD, GARTEN UND BERG.
    LOEWE *Vogelgesang*

WUNDERSCHÖNE LIEBESGESCHICHTE...
  BRAHMS *Keinen hat es noch gereut*
Tiède azur see Derème **IBERT**
Tiedge, Christoph August, 1752-1841.
  SCHUBERT *An die Sonne*
  ZELTER *Wiedersehen*
  URANIA.
    BEETHOVEN *An die Hoffnung*
  URANIA: Klagen des Zweiflers.
    BEETHOVEN *An die Hoffnung*
"Tief im Gemüt mir Liebe glüht" see
  Sei mein! Cornelius **CORNELIUS**
"Tief im grünen Frühlingstag" see
  Frühlingslied Geibel **LASSEN**
Tief im Herzen see Camoens *DE DENTRO TENGO MI MAL.* **SCHUMANN**
Tief im Herzen trag' ich Pein see Camoens *DE DENTRO TENGO MI MAL.* **WOLF**
"Tief im Herzen trag' ich Pein" see
  Tief im Herzen Camoens **SCHUMANN**
"Tief im Talgrund überm Bach" see *Friede* Huggenberger **REGER**
  Two settings: Op. 76 no. 25 and op. 79c no. 4.
"Tief in des Waldes Nacht liegt" see *Die schlafende Prinzessin* Borodin **BORODIN**
"Tief mit blauer Nachtgewalt" see
  Nachtgefühl Hesse **SCHOECK**
Tief von fern see Dehmel *ERLÖSUNGEN.* **WEBERN**
"Tiefe Feier schauert um die Welt" see
  Nachtgesang Kosegarten **SCHUBERT**
Tiefe grauenvolle Stille see Anon. **ZELTER**
Tiefe Sehnsucht see Liliencron **BERG**
"Tiefe Stille herrscht im Wasser" see
  Meeres Stille Goethe **SCHUBERT**
  Two settings: D. 215A and D. 216.
"Tiefe Stille herrscht im Wasser" see
  Meeresstille Goethe **GRIFFES, MEDTNER**
"Tiefer sinket schon die Sonne" see *Abendröte* Schlegel, F. **SCHUBERT**
Tiefes Leid see Schulze **SCHUBERT**
"Tiefes, tiefes Schweigen" see *Friedhofsgang* Kleinschmidt **REGER**
The tiger see Blake, William *THE TYGER.* **THOMSON**
"The tiger in the tiger pit" see *For an old man* Eliot **DIAMOND**
Tiger! Tiger! see Blake, William *THE TYGER.* **THOMSON**
"Tiger, tiger burning bright" see *The tiger* Blake, William **THOMSON**
"Tikha i molchaliva" see *Neponiatnaia* Musorgskiĭ **MUSORGSKIĬ**

Tikho more goluboe! see Maĭkov **RIMSKIĭ-KORSAKOV**

Tikho postoĭu u vkhoda see Goethe **MEDTNER** *An die Türen will ich schleichen*

Tikho vecher dogoraet see Shenshin **RIMSKIĭ-KORSAKOV**

Til Asali see Jacobsen **NIELSEN**

"Til de tabtes Legioner" *see Gentlemen-Menige* Kipling **GRIEG**

Til Deg du hei see Garborg *HAUGTUSSA.* **GRIEG**

Til en hunndjevel see Benzon **GRIEG** *To a devil*

Til Én. I see Paulsen **GRIEG**

Til Én. II see Paulsen **GRIEG**

"Til Fjelds over Bygden" *see Vejviseren synger* Welhaven **NIELSEN**

Til Generalkonsul Chr. Tønsberg see Bøgh, Johan **GRIEG**

"Til hende stod mine tanker" *see Spillemaend* Ibsen **GRIEG**

Til Kirken hun vandrer see Groth **GRIEG** *Beim Kirchgang von allen*

Til L.M. Lindemans Sølvbryllup see Nikolajesen, V. **GRIEG**

Til min Dreng see Benzon **GRIEG**

Til mit Hjertes Dronning see Shelley **NIELSEN**

Til Norge see Paulsen **GRIEG**

Le tilbury see Chalupt **AURIC**

Tilim-bom see Anon. **STRAVINSKIĭ**

Till Elektra see Blomberg **KILPINEN**

Till en diktare see Blomberg **KILPINEN**

Till Frigga see Runeberg **SIBELIUS**

Till havet see Josephson, E. **KILPINEN**

Till några påskliljor see Blomberg **KILPINEN**

Tillie see De La Mare *PEACOCK PIE.* **CHANLER**

Timbres oubliés see Kahn *LES PALAIS NOMADES*: Intermède IV. **LOEFFLER**

"Time brought me many another friend" *see Remember* Coleridge **IRELAND**

The time of roses see Hood **QUILTER**

"A time there was as one may guess" *see Before life and after* Hardy **BRITTEN**

Time was, when I in anguish lay see Geibel *LIEDER ALS INTERMEZZO*, no. 2. **GRIFFES** *Wohl lag ich einst in Gram und Schmerz*

Timor mortis see Dunbar, William **SEIBER**

"Tinte! Tinte, wer braucht!" *see Lose Ware* Mörike **SCHOECK**

"T'intendo, si, mio cor" *see Liebes-Klage* Metastasio **BEETHOVEN**

"Tintez, tintez, cloches de deuil" *see Les cloches* Gounod **GOUNOD**

Tirana alla spagnola (Rossinizzata) see Metastasio **ROSSINI**

Tirana all'espagnole rossinize see Pacini **ROSSINI** *Amour sans espoir*

La tiranna see Unknown **BEETHOVEN**

Tired see Vaughan Williams, U. **VAUGHAN WILLIAMS**

Tirso de Molina, pseud. *see* Tellez, Gabriel, 1570?-1648.

" 'Tis not our flesh that now-a-days is weak" *see Our time* Tiŭtchev **MEDTNER**

" 'Tis spring; come out to ramble" *see The Lent lily* Housman **IRELAND**

"'Tis the gift to be simple" *see Simple gifts* Anon. **COPLAND**

'Tis time see Nadson **RACHMANINOFF**

" 'Tis time, I think, by Wenlock town" *see Hawthorn time* Housman **IRELAND**

Tischendorf, Lobegott Friedrich Konstantin von, 1815-1874. **MENDELSSOHN-BARTHOLDY** *Lieben und Schweigen*

Tischlerlied see Unknown **SCHUBERT**

Tischlied see Goethe *MICH ERGREIFT, ICH WEISS NICHT WIE.* **SCHUBERT, ZELTER**

Tish' na more see Goethe **MEDTNER** *Meeresstille*

Tit for tat see De La Mare **BRITTEN**

TIT FOR TAT, no. 1 **BRITTEN** De La Mare *A song of enchantment*

TIT FOR TAT, no. 2 **BRITTEN** De La Mare *Autumn*

TIT FOR TAT, no. 3 **BRITTEN** De La Mare *Silver*

TIT FOR TAT, no. 4 **BRITTEN** De La Mare *Vigil*

TIT FOR TAT, no. 5 **BRITTEN** De La Mare *Tit for tat*

Tiŭtchev, Fëdor Ivanovich, 1803-1873. **CHAĭKOVSKIĭ** *Kak" nad" goriacheĭu zoloĭ* **MEDTNER**
Behold my visionary soul
Day and night
Dejection
Elegy
Mid-day
Night winds
Our time
The pauper
Sleepless
Song of night
Tears

COMPOSER   Poet   *Title*   "First Line"

Twilight
Waves and thoughts
We lost all that was once our own
Willow
   RACHMANINOFF
    The fountains
    He took all from me
    I remember that day
    Spring waters
    You knew him
To a common prostitute see Whitman
   ROREM
To a devil see Benzon **GRIEG**
To a dreamer see Pushkin **MEDTNER**
To a Grecian girl see Pushkin **RIMSKIĬ-**
   KORSAKOV *Grechanke*
To a Greek woman see Pushkin **RIMSKIĬ-**
   KORSAKOV *Grechanke*
"*To a lovely myrtle bound*" *see In a myrtle*
   shade Blake, William **GRIFFES**
To a young gentleman see Confucius
   NATIONAL ODES OF CHINA.
   CARPENTER
To a young girl see Yeats **ROREM**
TO A YOUNG GIRL, no. 1
   ROREM Yeats *Mad as the mist and snow*
TO A YOUNG GIRL, no. 2
   ROREM Yeats *Cradle song*
TO A YOUNG GIRL, no. 3
   ROREM Yeats *O do not love too long*
TO A YOUNG GIRL, no. 4
   ROREM Yeats *Maid quiet*
TO A YOUNG GIRL, no. 5
   ROREM Yeats *Lullaby*
TO A YOUNG GIRL, no. 6
   ROREM Yeats *To a young girl*
To Althea from prison see Lovelace
   QUILTER
To Anthea, who may command him anything
   see Herrick **ROREM**
To Aster see Plato **BERKELEY**
To brune Øjne see Andersen **GRIEG**
"*To brune Øjne jeg nylig saa*" *see*
   To brune Øjne Andersen **GRIEG**
To bylo ranneiu vesnoĭ see Tolstoĭ
   CHAĬKOVSKIĬ, RIMSKIĬ-KORSAKOV
To Chloe in sickness see Burns **BENNETT**
To cross the street see Carpenter, Rue
   CARPENTER
To daffodils see Herrick *HESPERIDES.*
   DELIUS
To daisies see Herrick **QUILTER**
To daisies, not to shut so soon see Herrick
   ROREM
To Edith see Ives, Harmony **IVES**
To evening see Koskimies **SIBELIUS** *Illalle*

"To find the western path, right through the
   gates" *see Daybreak* Blake, William
   QUILTER
To forget so soon see Apukhtin
   CHAĬKOVSKIĬ *Zabyt' tak skoro!*
To Frigga see Runeberg **SIBELIUS**
   Till Frigga
To God, ye choir above see Skelton
   GOUNOD
"To have known him" *see Monody* Melville
   DIAMOND
To Helen see Poe **LOEFFLER**
To her see Bugayev **RACHMANINOFF**
To his lady, of her doubtful answer see
   Howell, Thomas **RIETI**
To Jane see Shelley **ROREM**
TO JULIA, no. 1
   QUILTER Herrick *The bracelet*
TO JULIA, no. 2
   QUILTER Herrick *The maiden blush*
TO JULIA, no. 3
   QUILTER Herrick *To daisies*
TO JULIA, no. 4
   QUILTER Herrick *The night-piece*
TO JULIA, no. 5
   QUILTER Herrick *Julia's hair*
TO JULIA, no. 6
   QUILTER Herrick *Cherry-ripe*
To kiss see Gleiman, W. **BARTÓK**
   Night of desire
To Lucasta, on going to the wars see
   Lovelace **DIAMOND**
"To mercy, pity, peace, and love" *see*
   The Divine image Blake, William
   LUENING, THOMSON,
    VAUGHAN WILLIAMS
To morning see Blake, William **LUENING**
To music see Herrick **GIDEON**
To music, to becalm his fever see Herrick
   HINDEMITH, ROREM
To my child see Falke **MARTINŮ**
To my dear and loving husband see
   Bradstreet **ROREM**
To my fair friend you never can be old see
   Shakespeare **SAUGUET**
To my song see Heine **RIMSKIĬ-**
   KORSAKOV *K moeĭ pesne*
To one unknown see Dudley, Helen
   CARPENTER
"To outer senses there is peace" *see*
   La fuite de la lune Wilde **GRIFFES**
TO POETRY, no. 1
   SEIBER Goethe *Invocation*
TO POETRY, no. 2
   SEIBER Shakespeare *Sonnet*
TO POETRY, no. 3
   SEIBER Anon. *Tears*

COMPOSER Poet *Title* "First Line"

TO POETRY, no. 4
SEIBER Dunbar, William *Timor mortis*
TO POETRY, no. 5
SEIBER Goethe *Epilogue*
To Queen Elizabeth see Mary **SCHUMANN**
An die Königin Elisabeth
"To sa czary, pewno czary!" *see Czary*
Witwicki **CHOPIN**
"To see a world in a grain of sand" *see*
Auguries of innocence Blake, William
LUENING
"To see a world in a grain of sand" *see*
Proverb VII Blake, William **BRITTEN**
To some far shore you have departed see
Pushkin **RIMSKIĬ-KORSAKOV**
Dlia beregov otchizuy dal'noi
"To surge in passion's mighty throes is your
enjoyment" *see To a dreamer* Pushkin
MEDTNER
To the children see Khomyakov
RACHMANINOFF
To the forests see Tolstoĭ *JOHN OF
DAMASCUS.* **CHAĬKOVSKIĬ**
Blagoslavlyayu vas, lesa
To the golden rod see MacDowell
MACDOWELL
"To the heart of youth the world is a highway
side" *see Youth and love* Stevenson,
Robert Louis
VAUGHAN WILLIAMS
To the ladies see Chudleigh **ROREM**
To the land of roses and wine see Shenshin
GAFIZ. **RIMSKIĬ-KORSAKOV**
V tsarstvo rozy i vina-pridi
To the memory of a great singer see
Stevenson, Robert Louis *SONGS OF
TRAVEL.* **HESELTINE**
To the moon see Byron *HEBREW
MELODIES.* **SCHUMANN** *An den Mond*
"To the noble senorita" *see Spanish romance*
Pushkin **MEDTNER**
TO THE POET, no. 1
RIMSKIĬ-KORSAKOV Pushkin *Ekho*
TO THE POET, no. 2
RIMSKIĬ-KORSAKOV Maĭkov *Iskusstvo*
TO THE POET, no. 3
RIMSKIĬ-KORSAKOV Maĭkov *Oktava*
TO THE POET, no. 4
RIMSKIĬ-KORSAKOV Maĭkov *Somnenie*
TO THE POET, no. 5
RIMSKIĬ-KORSAKOV Pushkin *Poet*
To the queen of my heart see Shelley
DELIUS
To the virgins, to make much of time see
Herrick **RIETI**
To the willow-tree see Herrick **ROREM**

To všechno už jen zbylo see Sládek
MARTINŮ *All this is what only remains*
To wine and beauty see Rochester
QUILTER
To you see Whitman **ROREM**
Die Tochter der Haide see Mörike **WOLF**
"Tochter des Walds, du Lilienverwandte" *see*
Auf eine Christblume Mörike **WOLF**
Die Tochter Jephtha's see Byron *HEBREW
MELODIES.* **SCHUMANN**
Der Tod see Claudius, M. **SCHOECK,
WEBERN**
Der Tod see Klopstock **GLUCK**
Der Tod see Spaun **SCHUBERT**
Der Jüngling und der Tod
Der Tod, das ist die kühle Nacht see Heine
DIE HEIMKEHR. **BRAHMS, REGER**
"Tod, du Schrecken der Natur" *see*
An den Tod Schubart **SCHUBERT**
Der Tod Oskar's see Macpherson
SCHUBERT
Der Tod und das Mädchen see Claudius, M.
SCHUBERT
Der Tod und der einsame Trinker see
Morgenstern **KILPINEN**
Tod und Dichter see Keller, G. **SCHOECK**
Tod und Tödin see Tschabuschnigg
LOEWE
Todas las horas see Rivas, Reyna
THOMSON
Todes Wiegenlied see Schmidt, Georg
ZELTER
Todeslied der Bojaren see Immermann
MENDELSSOHN-BARTHOLDY
Todesmusik see Schober **SCHUBERT**
Todessehnen see Schenkendorf **BRAHMS**
"Todesstille deckt das Tal" *see*
In der Mitternacht Jacobi **SCHUBERT**
Todsüsses Gespenst see Zwehl, Hans Fritz
von **KILPINEN**
Todtengräberlied see Hölty **SCHUBERT**
Todtenklage see Byron **LOEWE**
TODTENOPFER. see Matthisson
Todtenopfer **SCHUBERT**
Todtenopfer see Matthisson
TODTENOPFER. **SCHUBERT**
Der Todtentanz see Goethe **LOEWE**
"Tödlich graute mir der Morgen" *see Der
Genesene an die Hoffung* Mörike **WOLF**
Törmänen, Vilho Edvard, b. 1886.
KILPINEN
Hillankukka
Jänka
Kirkkorannassa
Laululle
Murheen kellot

Muuttolintu
Sä menit
Suvilaulu
Tunturilähde
Tunturilaulu
Tunturille
Vanha kirkko
"Törne du min syskonplanta" *see* Törnet
Runeberg **SIBELIUS**
Törnet see Runeberg **SIBELIUS**
Toi see Anon. **MILHAUD**
Toi see Guichard, Abeille **SAUGUET**
Toi see St. Chaffray, Édouard
SAINT-SAËNS
Toi, dont les yeux see Anon. **RIEGGER**
"Toi pour jamais" *see La veuve andalouse*
Pacini **ROSSINI**
Toi qui l'amais, verse des pleurs see
Du Boys **BERLIOZ**
Tolerance see Hadley *SOME INFLUENCES*
IN MODERN PHILOSOPHIC THOUGHT.
IVES
Tol'ko vstrechu ulybku tvoiu see Shenshin
MEDTNER *Beauty*
"Tollt der Wind über Feld und Wiese" *see*
Wäsche im Wind Falke **REGER**
Tolstoĭ, Alekseĭ Konstantinovich, Graf,
1817-1875.
BALAKIREV *Ne penitsya more*
BORODIN *Spes'*
CHAĬKOVSKĬ
Gornimi tikho letela dusha nebesami
Kaby znala ia
Na nivy zhelty
Ne ver', moĭ drug
Ni otzyva, ni slova
O, esli b ty mogla
Serenada Don-Zhuana
Sleza drozhiť
Sred' shumnago bala
To bylo ranneiu vesnoĭ
Usni pechal'nyĭ drug'
MUSORGSKĬ
Gornimi tikho letela dusha nebesami
Ne bozhiim gromom gore udarilo
Oĭ, chest' li to molodtsu len priasti?
Rassevaetsia, rasstupaetsia
Spes'
RACHMANINOFF
Believe me not, friend
Do you remember the evening?
How everyone loves thee
O thou, my field
There are many sounds
Twilight has fallen

RIMSKĬ-KORSAKOV
Drobitsia, i pleshchet
Gornimi tikho letela dusha nebesami
Kolyshetsia more
Na nivy zheltye niskhodit tishina
Ne penitsia more
Ne ver' mne, drug
Ne veter, veia s vysoty
Nesliashchikh solntse
O, esli b ty mogla
To bylo ranneiu vesnoĭ
Usni, pechal'nyĭ drug
Vzdymaiutsia volny
Zapad gasnet v dali bledno-rozovoĭ
Zvonche zhavoronka pen'e
RUBINSTEIN
Am Meeresstrand
Des Baches Geplauder
Frühling
Fürst Rostislav
Hätt' ich das gewusst, hätt' ich das
gehant
In stiller Nacht
Nebel und Gram
Sanftes Walten
Schlaf' ein
Vergängliches
Wie es sein muss
Die Wölfe
JOHN OF DAMASCUS.
CHAĬKOVSKĬ *Blagoslavlyayu vas, lesa*
Tom lehnt harrend auf der Brücke see
Schlechta **SCHUBERT** *Widerschein*
"Tom lehnt harrend auf der Brücke" *see*
Widerschein Schlechta **SCHUBERT**
Tom sails away see Ives **IVES**
Tom the cat see Unknown **STRAVINSKĬ**
Tom Tyler see Anon. **HESELTINE**
Toman, Karel, 1877-1946.
DIE MONATE: Januar.
MARTINŮ
On snow-swept paths
My brother has finished ploughing
La tombe dit à la rose see Hugo *LES VOIX*
INTÉRIEURES. **WAGNER**
"La tombe dit à la rose" *see*
La tombe et la rose Hugo **LISZT**
Tombé du ciel dans la mansarde see Gabory
SAUGUET
La tombe et la rose see Hugo **LISZT**
Le tombeau see Ronsard **POULENC**
Tombeau dans un parc see Rilke *POÈMES*
FRANCAIS. **BARBER**
Le tombeau de Ronsard see Ronsard
RIVIER
Le tombeau des Naïdes see Louÿs
CHANSONS DE BILITIS. **DEBUSSY**

"Tombée du ciel de papier" *see Ecuyère voltige* Copperie, Adrien **SAUGUET**

Tombez mes ailes see Legouvé **GOUNOD**

"Tomorrow all know love" *see The feast of love* Anon. **THOMSON**

Tomorrow is Saint Valentine's day see Shakespeare *HAMLET.* **THOMSON**

Ein Ton see Cornelius **CORNELIUS**

"Ton âme est un lac d'amour" *see Les cygnes* Renaud **HAHN**

"Ton image que mon coeur garde" *see Sous l'oranger* Guillot de Saix **HAHN**

"Ton oeil de terre" *see Bail avec Mi* Messiaen **MESSIAEN**

"Ton père est à la messe" *see Berceuse* Jacob, M. **POULENC**

"Ton rêve est plain de chases folles" *see Berceuse* Gibout, Henri **MASSENET**

"Ton sourire infini m'est cher" *see Chanson de mer* Sully-Prudhomme **AUBERT**

Ton souvenir see Feillet, Émilie **MASSENET**

Ton souvenir est comme un livre bien aimé see Unknown **LOEFFLER**

TONE-IMAGES FOR A MEZZO-SOPRANO, no. 1
GRIFFES Wilde *La fuite de la lune*

TONE-IMAGES FOR A MEZZO-SOPRANO, no. 2
GRIFFES Wilde *Symphony in yellow*

TONE-IMAGES FOR A MEZZO-SOPRANO, no. 3
GRIFFES Henley *We'll to the woods and gather May*

Tonight the winds begin to rise see Tennyson **BERKELEY**

"Tonleiterähnlich steiget dein Klaggesang" *see An Philomele* Mörike **SCHOECK**

Tonquédec, Marthe de
AUBERT *L'inconnu*

The too-late born see MacLeish **GIDEON**

Topelius, Zacharius, 1818-1898.
SIBELIUS
   Giv mig ej glans
   Lasse liten
   Det mörknar ute
   Nu så kommer julen
   Nu står jul vid snöig port
   Orions bälte

Toréador see Cocteau **POULENC**

"Tornai: la bocca tiepida" *see Lagrime!* Negri **RESPIGHI**

Torre, G.
ROSSINI
   L'esule
   La lontananza

"A tortoise I see on a lotus-flower resting" *see On a screen* Li Po **CARPENTER**

La tortue et le lièvre see Sanglier, Charles **SCHMITT**

La tortue naine see Kriéger, Jacqueline **MILHAUD**

TOSCANISCHER RISPETTO. see Heyse *Toskanischer Rispetto* **JENSEN**

Toskanischer Rispetto see Heyse *TOSCANISCHER RISPETTO.* **JENSEN**

Tot see Haringer *ABSCHIED.* **SCHÖNBERG**

"Tot dorm a l'hora grisa" *see L'hora grisa* Blancafort **MOMPOU**

Die tote Nachtigall see Kaufmann, J. **LISZT**

Totengräberlied see Shakespeare *HAMLET.* **LOEWE**

Totengräbers Heimwehe see Craigher **SCHUBERT**

Totengräber-Weise see Schlechta **SCHUBERT**

"Ein Totenhafen" *see Wechselrahmen* Barth **KRENEK**

Totenkranz für ein Kind see Matthisson **SCHUBERT**

Totensprache see Jacobowski **REGER**

Der Totentanz see Goethe **ZELTER**

Touha see Anon. **MARTINŮ**
   Two settings: 1932 and 1942

Toujours see Grandmougin **FAURÉ**

Toujours see Nax, Paul **MASSENET**

"Toujours! Et, demain, plus jamais!" *see Chanson juanesque* Champsaur **MASSENET**

"Toujours les lilas fleuriront" *see La mélodie des baisers* Alexandre, André **MASSENET**

"Toujours n'importe le titre" *see Le crieur d'imprimés* Mallarmé **MILHAUD**

Toulet, Paul Jean, 1867-1920.
KOECHLIN *Infini fais que je t'oublie . . .*

"Toungou, ahi, toungou" *see L'amour de Piroutcha* Messiaen **MESSIAEN**

La tour prends garde see Baron **SAUGUET**

Tourist's song see Moss **ROREM**

Tourneux, Eugène
GOUNOD *Chanson de printemps*

"Tournez, tournez, bons chevaux de bois" *see Chevaux de bois* Verlaine **DEBUSSY**

Tournoiement see Renaud **SAINT-SAËNS**

Tours see Richaud **SAUGUET**

La tourterelle see Latil **MILHAUD**

Tous deux see Verlaine **HAHN**

"Tous deux vers la rive lointaine" *see Voyage* Gille **BIZET**

Toussaint, Franz, 1879-1955.
JARDIN DES CARESSES.
AUBERT
   L'adieu
   Le destin
   Le mirage
   Le sommeil des colombes
   Le vaincu
   Le visage penché
"Tout à l'heure ses mains plus délicates" *see*
   Nuits blanches Debussy **DEBUSSY**
Tout beau mon coeur see Hugnet **ROREM**
"Tout, dans l'immuable nature" *see*
   Âmes obscures France **MASSENET**
Tout disparut . . . see Éluard **AURIC,**
   POULENC
"Tout disparut même les toits" *see*
   Tout disparut . . . Éluard **AURIC**
Tout est un grand secret see Éluard
   SAUGUET
Tout gai! see Anon. **RAVEL**
"Tout gai! gai" *see Tout gai!* Anon. **RAVEL**
Tout le long de la Baïse see Bédat de
   Monlaur, Pierre **HONEGGER**
"Tout le monde se baigne" *see Jour de
   chaleur aux bains de mer* Rohan
   THOMSON
"Tout l'oiseaux ce matin" *see La Rosée*
   Hugnet **THOMSON**
Tout l'univers obéit à l'amour see
   La Fontaine **GOUNOD**
Tout n'est qu'images fugitives see Reboul
   WAGNER
Tout passé see Bruno, Camille **MASSENET**
"Tout, quittez mon coeur" *see Adieu*
   Desbordes-Valmore **SAUGUET**
"Tout recevoir de toi me charme" *see*
   Passionnément Fuster **MASSENET**
"Tout revit, ma bien aimée!" *see Après l'hiver*
   Hugo **BIZET**
"Tout un paysage en lignes blanches" *see*
   Octroi Kerdyk, René **SCHMITT**
Tout va bien see Koechlin **KOECHLIN**
"Toute aussitôt que je commence à prendre"
   see Songe Labé **SAUGUET**
"Toute, avec sa robe et ses fleurs" *see*
   Inscription sur le sable Lerberghe
   FAURÉ
"Toute en pleurs la belle jette sa couronne"
   see La couronne Unknown **POULENC**
Toute l'année see Anon. **MILHAUD**
"Toute pure comme le ciel" *see La delphinium*
   Claudel **HONEGGER**
"Toute senle silencieuse les yeux" *see*
   La mort passe Chobanian **HONEGGER**
Toute une ville see Gélin **ROREM**

Toutes les fleurs see Rostand **CHABRIER**
"Toutes les fleurs, certes" *see Toutes les fleurs*
   Rostand **CHABRIER**
"Toutes les fleurs de mon jardin sont roses"
   see Manteau de fleurs Gravollet, Paul
   RAVEL
Towska, Kory, pseud. *see* Rosenbaum,
   Kory Elizabeth, 1868-1930.
"Tra la la . . . " *see Tarantelle* Pailleron
   BIZET
"Tra, la, la, la, la, la, comment, disaient-ils"
   see Guitare Hugo **BIZET**
Il traditor deluso see Metastasio
   SCHUBERT
"Traed stille, min Veninde" *see Erindringens
   Sø* Holstein **NIELSEN**
Träger, Albert, 1820-1912.
   JENSEN
      Als mich dein Blick beim Scheiden traf
      *An deinem Finger, dem weissen,
         schlanken*
      Ein Frühlingstraum
      Ihr Sternlein
      Im Herbst
      In Verborgenen
      Morgenständchen
      Paulinzelle
      Wie Lenzeshauch
   LASSEN
      Im Verborgnen
      Märzenblume
      Wie durch die stille Mondesnacht
   REGER *Wiegenlied*
Tränen see Andersen **GRIEG** *Taaren*
Tränen see Braungart **REGER**
Tränen see Chamisso **FRANZ, SPOHR**
   Four Franz settings: Op. 6 no. 6, op. 50 no.
      5, op. 51 no. 2, and op. 52 no. 4
Tränen im Auge see Wildenbruch **REGER**
Den traenger ud til hvert et sted see Hostrup
   NIELSEN
Träume see Benzon **GRIEG** *Drømme*
Träume see Osterwald **FRANZ**
Träume see Wesendonck **WAGNER**
"Träume du mein süsses Leben" *see*
   Wiegenlied Dehmel **STRAUSS**
"Träume, träume du mein süsses Leben" *see*
   Venus mater Dehmel **PFITZNER**
"Träume, träume, du mein süsses Leben!" *see*
   Wiegenlied Dehmel **REGER**
Der träumende See see Mosen **GRIFFES**
Tragédie see Valade **NOCTURNES,**
   POÈMES IMITÉS DE H. HEINE.
   DEBUSSY
The tragedy of that moment see Hardy
   IRELAND

A tragic story see Thackeray **BRITTEN**
La tragique histoire du petit René see
  Nohain, Jean **POULENC**
Tragische Geschichte see Chamisso
  PFITZNER
Tragödie see Heine **RUBINSTEIN,**
  SCHUMANN
TRAGÖDIE. see Heine
  Auf ihrem Grab **GRIFFES**
  Tragödie I **GRIFFES**
  Tragödie II **GRIFFES**
Tragödie I see Heine *TRAGÖDIE.* **GRIFFES**
Tragödie II see Heine *TRAGÖDIE.*
  GRIFFES
TRAGÖDIEN NEBST EINEM LYRISCHEN
  INTERMEZZO. *see* Heine
  Meerfahrt **BRAHMS, FRANZ**
Tragt, blaue Träume see Boelitz **REGER**
Trakl, Georg, 1887-1914.
  HINDEMITH *Trompeten*
  IM DORF.
    WEBERN *In der Heimat*
  OFFENBARUNG UND UNTERGAND.
    WEBERN *Nachtergebund*
  SIEBENGESANG DES TODES.
    WEBERN *Verklärung*
  TRAUM DES BÖSEN.
    WEBERN *In den Nachtmittag geflüstert*
"Trallallala, mein Liebchen" *see Beim Tanze*
  Jacob, T. **LOEWE**
Il tramonto see Maffei **VERDI**
Tranchant, Alfred
  SAINT-SAËNS
    Madeleine
    Si je l'osais
    Vive Paris, vive la France
Tranchant, Jean
  HONEGGER *Le grand étang*
Transience see Naidu **LUENING**
TRANSLATIONS, no. 1
  WEISGALL Giovanni
    Knoxville, Tennessee
TRANSLATIONS, no. 2
  WEISGALL Rich *Song*
TRANSLATIONS, no. 3
  WEISGALL Trustman, Deborah
    Child song
TRANSLATIONS, no. 4
  WEISGALL Dropkin *Poem*
TRANSLATIONS, no. 5
  WEISGALL Dropkin *Poem*
TRANSLATIONS, no. 6
  WEISGALL Evans, M. *The rebel*
TRANSLATIONS, no. 7
  WEISGALL Margolin *A city by the sea*
"Trara, trara, mein Hörnlein hell" *see*
  Der Postillon Kiesekamo **REGER**

"Trarah! Trarah! wie kehren daheim" *see*
  Jagdlied Werner **SCHUBERT**
Trasten see Österling **KILPINEN**
"Trasten sjöng på skorstenskransen" *see*
  Trasten Österling **KILPINEN**
Trau' nicht der Liebe see Anon. **WOLF**
Trauer see Cornelius **CORNELIUS**
Trauer see Leuthold **SCHOECK**
Trauer der Liebe see Jacobi **SCHUBERT**
Trauer I see George *DER SIEBENTE RING*:
  Maximin. **WEBERN**
"Trauer umfliesst mein Leben" *see Klage*
  Unknown **SCHUBERT**
  Two settings: D. 292 and D. 371
TRAUER UND TROST, no. 1
  CORNELIUS Cornelius *Trauer*
TRAUER UND TROST, no. 2
  CORNELIUS Cornelius *Angedenken*
TRAUER UND TROST, no. 3
  CORNELIUS Cornelius *Ein Ton*
TRAUER UND TROST, no. 4
  CORNELIUS Cornelius *An den Traum*
TRAUER UND TROST, no. 5
  CORNELIUS Cornelius *Treue*
TRAUER UND TROST, no. 6
  CORNELIUS Cornelius *Trost*
Die Trauernde see Anon. **BRAHMS,**
  FRANZ
Trauerstille see Bürger **PFITZNER**
Ein Traum see Bodenstedt **GRIEG**
Traum see Eichendorff **REGER**
Traum see Evers **REGER**
Traum see Hesse **KILPINEN**
Der Traum see Hölty *BALLADE.*
  SCHUBERT
Traum see Lasker-Schüler **HINDEMITH**
Ein Traum see Lermontov **BALAKIREV**
  Son
Ein Traum see Moore, T. **RUBINSTEIN**
  A dream
Traum see Semler **BERG**
Der Traum see Zhukovski **RUBINSTEIN**
Traum der eignen Tage see Chamisso
  LOEWE
Der Traum der Wittwe see Rückert **LOEWE**
TRAUM DES BÖSEN. see Trakl
  In den Nachtmittag geflüstert **WEBERN**
Traum durch die Dämmerung see Bierbaum
  REGER, STRAUSS
Traum rosen see Heinitz, Marie **DELIUS**
Traumbild see Heine **FRANZ**
Das Traumbild see Hölty **MOZART**
Traumgekrönt see Rilke **BERG**
Traumleben see Hart, J. **SCHÖNBERG**
Traumlicht see Rückert **LOEWE**
Traun, Bogen und Pfeil sind gut für den Feind
  see Tieck **BRAHMS**

"Traurig, einsam welkst du hin" *see*
Die Blume Haug **WEBER**
Der traurige Jäger see Eichendorff **FRANZ**
Romanze
Das traurige Mädchen see Burns **FRANZ**
The sorrowful maiden
Traurige Stunde see Krenek **KRENEK**
Traurige Wege see Lenau **WOLF**
Trauriger Frühling see Hafiz
SZYMANOWSKI
Traurigkeit see Altenberg *WAS DER TAG*
MIR ZUTRÄGT': Traurigkeit. **BERG**
Traute Henriette see Unknown
BEETHOVEN
LE TRAVAIL DU PEINTRE, no. 1
POULENC Éluard *Pablo Picasso*
LE TRAVAIL DU PEINTRE, no. 2
POULENC Éluard *Marc Chagall*
LE TRAVAIL DU PEINTRE, no. 3
POULENC Éluard *Georges Braque*
LE TRAVAIL DU PEINTRE, no. 4
POULENC Éluard *Juan Gris*
LE TRAVAIL DU PEINTRE, no. 5
POULENC Éluard *Paul Klee*
LE TRAVAIL DU PEINTRE, no. 6
POULENC Éluard *Juan Miró*
LE TRAVAIL DU PEINTRE, no. 7
POULENC Éluard *Jacques Villon*
Traveller's song see Eichendorff
MEDTNER *Reiselied*
"Travka zeleneet" *see Vesna* Pleshcheyev
CHAĬKOVSKIĬ
TRE CANTI SACRI, no. 1
CASELLA No author *Ecce odor filii mei*
TRE CANTI SACRI, no. 2
CASELLA No author *Respice, Domine,*
familiam tuam
TRE CANTI SACRI, no. 3
CASELLA No author *Ecce Deus salvator*
meus
TRE CANZONI TRECENTESCHE, no. 1
CASELLA Cino da Pistoia *Giovane*
bella luce del mio core
TRE CANZONI TRECENTESCHE, no. 2
CASELLA Anon. *Fuor de la bella gaiba*
TRE CANZONI TRECENTESCHE, no. 3
CASELLA Anon. *Amante sono, vaghiccia,*
di voi
"Tré ptáku letí Prevezy" *see Žalozpěv Pargy*
Anon. **DVOŘÁK**
TRE SONETTI DI PETRARCA
LISZT Petrarca
Benedetto sia'l giorno
Pace non trove
I vidi in terra angelicicostumi
"Tre systrar de häkla sin moders lin" *see*
I systrar, I bröder Lybeck **SIBELIUS**

Tre vocalizzi see No author **CASELLA,**
PIZZETTI, RESPIGHI
Tre vocalizzi nello stile moderno see
No author **MALIPIERO**
Treat me nice see Dunbar **CARPENTER**
"Treat me nice, Miss Mandy Jane" *see*
Treat me nice Dunbar **CARPENTER**
Tree, Iris
ROREM *Lonesome tree*
"The tree stood flowering in a dream" *see*
Nightmare Soutar **BRITTEN**
Treibe nur mit Lieben Spott see Anon.
WOLF
Treibt der Sommer seinen Rosen see
Osterwald **FRANZ**
Treitschke, Georg Friedrich, 1776-1842.
BEETHOVEN *Ruf vom Berge*
The trellis see Huxley **IRELAND**
"Tremble argenté, til-leul, bouleau . . ." *see*
Accompagnement Samain **FAURÉ**
Trennung see Anon. **BRAHMS**
Two settings: Op. 14 no. 5 and op. 97 no.
6.
Trennung see Kastropp **LASSEN**
TRENTE ET HUYT CHANSONS
MUSICALES . . . : Chanson
vingtcinquiesme . . . *see* Marot
Chanson du Jour de Noël **HESELTINE**
Trepak see Golenishchev-Kutuzov
MUSORGSKIĬ
"Die Trepp' hinunter geschwungen" *see*
Niemand hat's gesehn Gruppe **LOEWE**
"Die Treppe hinunter gesprungen" *see*
Begegnung Gruppe **STRAUSS**
TRES ESTAMPAS DE NIÑEZ, no. 1
THOMSON Rivas, Reyna *Todas las*
horas
TRES ESTAMPAS DE NIÑEZ, no. 2
THOMSON Rivas, Reyna *Son amigos de*
todos
TRES ESTAMPAS DE NIÑEZ, no. 3
THOMSON Rivas, Reyna *Nadie lo oye*
como ellos
TRES POEMAS, no. 1
TURINA Bécquer *Olas gigantes*
TRES POEMAS, no. 2
TURINA Bécquer *Tu pupila es azul y*
cuando ríes
TRES POEMAS, no. 3
TURINA Bécquer *Besa el aura que gimé*
blandamente
"Le trésor du verger et le jardin en fête" *see*
Air vif Moréas **POULENC**
Tretet ein, hoher Krieger see Keller, G.
PFITZNER, WOLF

Treue see Cornelius **CORNELIUS**
Treue Liebe see Schulz **BRAHMS**
"Treue Liebe bis zum Grabe schwör ich" *see*
  Mein Vaterland Hoffmann von
  Fallersleben **SPOHR**
Treue Liebe dauert lange see Tieck
  BRAHMS
Die treuen Schwalben see Zinserling, W.
  LOEWE
Der Treuergebene see Anon. **LOEWE**
Treuröschen see Körner **LOEWE**
Tři panny za světlé noci see Hlavsa, Vrat.
  MARTINŮ *Three maidens on a bright*
  night
Die Trichter see Morgenstern **SEIBER**
TRICKS OF THE TRADE (1917). *see*
  Squire, Sir John
  Mr. Belloc's fancy **HESELTINE**
Triepel, Gertrud, b. 1863.
  REGER *Sommernacht*
Trilussa, pseud. *see* Salustri, Carlo
  Alberto, 1871-1950.
Trinius, Karl Bernhard, 1778-1844.
  LOEWE *Feuersgedanken*
Trinklied see Baggesen **WEBER**
  Die Lethe des Lebens
Trinklied see Bodenstedt **SPOHR**
Trinklied see Henckell **BERG**
Trinklied see Kol'tsov **MUSORGSKĬ**
  Zastol'naĭa pesn'
Trinklied see Krenek **KRENEK**
Trinklied see Lehr, Hofrath **WEBER**
Trinklied see Leuthold **SCHOECK**
Trinklied see Shakespeare *ANTONY AND*
  CLEOPATRA. **SCHUBERT**
Trinklied see Unknown **BEETHOVEN**
Trinklied see Zettler *IHR FREUNDE UND*
  DU, GOLD'NER WEIN. **SCHUBERT**
Trinklied vor der Schlacht see Körner
  SCHUBERT
"Trinkt aus, ihr zechtet zum letzten mal" *see*
  Der verlorene Haufen Klemperer
  SCHÖNBERG
Triolet à Philis see Banville **DEBUSSY**
  Zéphyr
Triolett see Förster, K. **WEBER**
Triolett see Gleim *TRIOLETT*: Gebt mir
  Blumen. **ZELTER**
TRIOLETT: Gebt mir Blumen. *see* Gleim
  Triolett **ZELTER**
Tripatos see Anon. **RAVEL**
TRIPTICO, no. 1
  TURINA Campoamor y Campoosorio
  Farruca
TRIPTICO, no. 2
  TURINA Rivas *Cantilena*

TRIPTICO, no. 3
  TURINA Rivas *Madrigal*
Tristan L'Hermite François, 1601-1655.
  DEBUSSY
  Crois mon conseil
  La grotte
  Je tremble en voyant ton visage
Tristesse see Carrier, P. **MASSENET**
Tristesse see Gautier **FAURÉ**
Tristesse see Jammes **MILHAUD**
Tristesse see Lemaire, Ferdinand
  SAINT-SAËNS
TRISTESSE. see Musset
  J'ai perdu ma force et ma vie **LISZT**
Tristesse see Musset **LISZT**
  J'ai perdu ma force et ma vie
Tristesse see Silvestre **LALO**
Tristesse au jardin see Tailhade **ROUSSEL,**
  SCHMITT
Tristesse de l'eau see Claudel **MILHAUD**
"La tristesse des menuets" *see Menuet* Gregh
  KOECHLIN
Tristesse d'été see Mallarmé **SAUGUET**
TRISTESSES. see Jammes
  Au pied de mon lit **BOULANGER**
  Dans le chemin toujours trempé
  MILHAUD
  Demain fera un an qu'à Audaux
  BOULANGER, MILHAUD
  Deux ancolies se balançaient
  BOULANGER, MILHAUD
  Elle avait emporté des brasées de lilas
  MILHAUD
  Elle est gravement gaie **BOULANGER,**
  MILHAUD
  Elle était descendue au bas de la prairie
  BOULANGER, MILHAUD
  Faisait-il beau quand elle est morte
  MILHAUD
  J'ai quelqu'un dans le coeur **MILHAUD**
  Je garde une médaille d'elle
  BOULANGER, MILHAUD
  Je la désire dans cette ombreuse lumière
  MILHAUD
  Je ne désire point ces ardeurs **MILHAUD**
  Je songe à ce jour là **MILHAUD**
  Les lilas qui avaient fleuri **BOULANGER,**
  MILHAUD
  Nous nous aimerons tant que nous tairons
  BOULANGER, MILHAUD
  O mon coeur, ce sera dans l'Aoûte bleu
  MILHAUD
  Par ce que j'ai souffert **BOULANGER,**
  MILHAUD
  Parfois, je suis triste **BOULANGER,**
  MILHAUD

Un poète disait que **BOULANGER, MILHAUD**
Si tout ceci n'est qu'un pauvre rêve
BOULANGER, MILHAUD
Son souvenir emplit l'air si clair
MILHAUD
Venez, ma bien aimée **MILHAUD**
Venez sous la tonnelle **MILHAUD**
Vous m'avez regardé avec tout votre âme
BOULANGER, MILHAUD
TRISTESSES, no. 2
MILHAUD Jammes *Je la désire dans cette ombreuse lumière*
    NB: No. 1 for piano alone.
TRISTESSES, no. 3
MILHAUD Jammes *Elle était descendue au bord de la prairie*
TRISTESSES, no. 4
MILHAUD Jammes *Dans le chemin toujours trempé*
TRISTESSES, no. 5
MILHAUD Jammes *Elle est gravement gaie*
TRISTESSES, no. 6
MILHAUD Jammes *Parfois, je suis triste*
TRISTESSES, no. 7
MILHAUD Jammes *Un poète disait que*
TRISTESSES, no. 8
MILHAUD Jammes *Son souvenir emplit l'air si clair*
TRISTESSES, no. 9
MILHAUD Jammes *Elle avait emporté des brasées de lilas*
TRISTESSES, no. 10
MILHAUD Jammes *Si tout ceci n'est qu'un pauvre rêve*
TRISTESSES, no. 11
MILHAUD Jammes *Je ne désire point ces ardeurs*
TRISTESSES, no. 12
MILHAUD Jammes *O mon coeur, ce sera dans l'Aoûte bleu*
TRISTESSES, no. 13
MILHAUD Jammes *Nous nous aimerons tant que nous tairons*
TRISTESSES, no. 14
MILHAUD Jammes *Faisait-il beau quand elle est morte*
TRISTESSES, no. 15
MILHAUD Jammes *Je garde une médaille d'elle*
TRISTESSES, no. 16
MILHAUD Jammes *J'ai quelqu'un dans le coeur*
TRISTESSES, no. 17
MILHAUD Jammes *Vous m'avez regardé avec tout votre âme*

TRISTESSES, no. 18
MILHAUD Jammes *Je songe à ce jour là*
TRISTESSES, no. 19
MILHAUD Jammes *Les lilas qui avaient fleuri*
TRISTESSES, no. 20
MILHAUD Jammes *Deux ancolies se balançaient*
TRISTESSES, no. 21
MILHAUD Jammes *Par ce que j'ai souffert*
TRISTESSES, no. 22
MILHAUD Jammes *Venez sous la tonnelle*
TRISTESSES, no. 23
MILHAUD Jammes *Venez, ma bien aimée*
TRISTESSES, no. 24
MILHAUD Jammes *Demain fera un an qu'à Audaux*
"Tro ei Venner" see Et Vennestykke Vinje
GRIEG
Trockne Blumen see Müller, Wilhelm
SCHUBERT
*"Trocknet nicht, trocknet nicht" see
Wonne der Wehmut* Goethe
BEETHOVEN, SCHUBERT, ZELTER
*"Trocknet nicht, trocknet nicht" see
Wonne der Wehmuth* Goethe **FRANZ**
Tröst der Nacht see Kinkel **LASSEN**
Tröstung see Hoffmann von Fallersleben
MENDELSSOHN-BARTHOLDY
Troillet, Émile
MASSENET *Devant l'infini*
Trois ans de souffrance see Anon.
MILHAUD
TROIS CAPRICES, no. 1
AURIC Banville *Fête galante*
TROIS CAPRICES, no. 2
AURIC Banville *Les bergers*
TROIS CAPRICES, no. 3
AURIC Banville *Parade*
TROIS CHANSONS DE FRANCE
DEBUSSY
    Tristan L'Hermite *La grotte*
    Charles, Duke of Orleans
        Pour ce que plaisance est morte
        Le temps a laissié son manteau
TROIS CHANSONS DE NEGRESSE, no. 1
MILHAUD Supervielle *Mon histoire*
TROIS CHANSONS DE NEGRESSE, no. 2
MILHAUD Supervielle *Abandonnée*
TROIS CHANSONS DE NEGRESSE, no. 3
MILHAUD Supervielle *Sans feu ni lieu*

TROIS CHANSONS DE TROUBADOUR, no. 1
  MILHAUD Valmy-Baysse *Rassa, ma dame est fraîche et fine*
TROIS CHANSONS DE TROUBADOUR, no. 2
  MILHAUD Valmy-Baysse *Belle dame de mon émoi*
TROIS CHANSONS DE TROUBADOUR, no. 3
  MILHAUD Valmy-Baysse *Je suis tombé de mal en peine*
TROIS CHANTS D'OMBRE, no. 1
  SAUGUET Jacqueton, Henry *Cette cigarette d'ombre*
TROIS CHANTS D'OMBRE, no. 2
  SAUGUET Jacqueton, Henry *Plain-ciel*
TROIS CHANTS D'OMBRE, no. 3
  SAUGUET Jacqueton, Henry *Incantation de la nuit*
"Les trois dames qui jouaient" *see Jouer du bugle* Jacob, M. **POULENC**
Les trois exiles see Delfosse **FRANCK**
"Les trois filles allèrent danser au clair de lune" *see Rondo* Mauclair **BLOCH**
TROIS INNOCENTINES, no. 1
  SAUGUET Obaldia *Le secret*
TROIS INNOCENTINES, no. 2
  SAUGUET Obaldia *Moi j'irai dans la lune*
TROIS INNOCENTINES, no. 3
  SAUGUET Obaldia *Les jumeaux de la nuit*
TROIS INTERLUDES, no. 1
  AURIC Chalupt *Le pouf*
TROIS INTERLUDES, no. 2
  AURIC Chalupt *Le gloxinia*
TROIS INTERLUDES, no. 3
  AURIC Chalupt *Le tilbury*
Trois jours de vendange see Daudet **HAHN**
TROIS MÉLODIES DE 1886, no. 1
  SATIE Contamine *Les anges*
TROIS MÉLODIES DE 1886, no. 2
  SATIE Contamine *Les fleurs*
TROIS MÉLODIES DE 1886, no. 3
  SATIE Contamine *Sylvie*
TROIS MÉLODIES SANS PAROLES, no. 1
  SATIE No author *Rambouillet*
TROIS MÉLODIES SANS PAROLES, no. 2
  SATIE No author *Les oiseaux*
TROIS MÉLODIES SANS PAROLES, no. 3
  SATIE No author *Marienbad*
Les trois peupliers see Paliard **MILHAUD**
"Trois peupliers au milieu d'un champ" *see Les trois peupliers* Paliard **MILHAUD**

TROIS POÈMES, no. 1
  AURIC
  Fargue *Nuit blanche*
  Jacob, M. *Lord Bolingbroke*
  Vilmorin *Le châle*
TROIS POÈMES, no. 2
  AURIC
  Fargue *Enfance*
  Jacob, M. *Pour demain soir...*
  Vilmorin *La jeune sanguine*
TROIS POÈMES, no. 3
  AURIC
  Fargue *Regrets*
  Jacob, M. *Il se peut qu'un rêve étrange...*
  Vilmorin *Attendez le prochain bateau*
  NB: There are 3 sets of *Trois poèmes.*
TROIS POEMES CHASTES, no. 1
  MASSENET Boyer, Georges *Le pauv' petit*
TROIS POEMES CHASTES, no. 2
  MASSENET Le Moyne *Vers Béthléem*
TROIS POEMES CHASTES, no. 3
  MASSENET Hardý de Périni *La légende du baiser*
TROIS POÈMES DE MALLARMÉ, no. 1
  DEBUSSY Mallarmé *Soupir*
TROIS POÈMES DE MALLARMÉ, no. 2
  DEBUSSY Mallarmé *Placet futile*
TROIS POÈMES DE MALLARMÉ, no. 3
  DEBUSSY Mallarmé *Éventail*
TROIS POÈMES GALANTS, no. 1
  JOLIVET Mellin *Sonnet à une lunatique*
TROIS POÈMES GALANTS, no. 2
  JOLIVET Germain-Colin *Epître imprécatoire*
TROIS POÈMES GALANTS, no. 3
  JOLIVET Le Père *Sonnet à Madeleine Repentie*
TROIS PSAUMES, no. 1
  HONEGGER Bible *Psalm XXXIV*
TROIS PSAUMES, no. 2
  HONEGGER Bible *Psalm CXI*
TROIS PSAUMES, no. 3
  HONEGGER Bible *Psalm CXXXVIII*
Trojan, Johannes, 1837-1915.
  REGER *Klein Marie*
Trollie, lollie, laughter see Neuburg **QUILTER**
Trolliet, Emile
  MASSENET *Soeur d'élection*
"Die Trommeln und Pfeifen" *see Soldatenlied* Hoffmann von Fallersleben **STRAUSS**
"Trommeln und Pfeifen, kriegerischer Klang" *see Rekrutenlied aus Wallensteins Lager* Schiller **LASSEN**

Trommel-Ständchen see Moehrcke **LOEWE**
TROMPETE VON VIONVILLE. see
  Freiligrath
  Und wir dachten der Toten **LISZT**
Trompeten see Trakl **HINDEMITH**
Trost see Cornelius **CORNELIUS**
Trost see Eichendorff **SCHOECK**
Trost see Falke **REGER**
Trost see Hamerling **LASSEN**
Trost see Leuthold **SCHOECK**
Trost see Mayrhofer **SCHUBERT**
Trost see Mörike **SCHOECK**
Trost see Unknown **LOEWE, SCHUBERT**
Trost an Elisa see Matthisson **SCHUBERT**
Trost der Kreatur see Keller, G. **SCHOECK**
Trost, "Herz, lass dich nicht zerspalten" see
  Körner **WEBER**
Trost im Gesang see Kerner **SCHUMANN**
Trost im Leid see Wildenbruch **LASSEN**
Trost im Liede see Schober **SCHUBERT**
Trost in Thränen see Goethe **SCHUBERT**
Trost in Tränen see Goethe **BRAHMS,**
  LOEWE, ZELTER
Trostlos see Hochwald, A. von **SPOHR**
"Le troupeau verni des moutons" *see Le Noël*
  des jouets Ravel **RAVEL**
Il trovatore see Unknown **ROSSINI**
Trudom see Vinje **GRIEG**
True tenderness see Akhmatova
  PROKOFIEV *Nastoiashchuiu*
TRUE TOPER'S TUNES . . . no. 1
  HESELTINE Masefield *Captain*
  Stratton's fancy
TRUE TOPER'S TUNES . . . no. 2
  HESELTINE Squire, Sir John *Mr.*
  Belloc's fancy
Trueba, Antonio de, 1821-1899.
  FALLA *Preludios*
"Der trübe Winter ist vorbei" *see Altdeutsches*
  Frühlingslied Spee
  MENDELSSOHN-BARTHOLDY
Trübe wird's, die Wolken jagen see Lenau
  FRANZ, SCHOECK
"Trübe Wolken, Herbstesluft" *see*
  Herbstenschluss Lenau **WOLF**
Trüber Morgen see Ernst **LASSEN**
Trübes Wetter see Keller, G. **SCHOECK**
"Truly the light is sweet" *see The light is*
  sweet Bible **KRENEK**
Trunken müssen wir alle sein! see Goethe
  WESTÖSTLICHER DIVAN: Schenkenbuch.
  WOLF
Die trunkene Tänzerin see Bock, K.
  HINDEMITH
Trust me see Vérine, Boris **PROKOFIEV**
  Dover'sia mne

Trustman, Deborah
  WEISGALL
  Child song
  Listen: you were the victim
  Play for me
  Sound is simple
  You were like a song
Tryst see Symons **IRELAND**
Trzech Budrysów see Mickiewicz **LOEWE**
  Die drei Budrisse
Trzmiel i zuk see Iłłakowiczówna
  SZYMANOWSKI
TSar' Saul see Byron *HEBREW MELODIES.*
  MUSORGSKIĬ
Tsaraiuki
  STRAVINSKIĬ *Tsaraiuki*
Tsaraiuki see Tsaraiuki **STRAVINSKIĬ**
The Tsar's drinking house see Mei *PESNYA.*
  CHAĬKOVSKIĬ *Kak naladili: Durak*
Tschabuschnigg, Adolf Ritter von, 1809-
  1877.
  LOEWE *Tod und Tödin*
TSvetok see Pushkin **MEDTNER**
  The faded flower
Tsvetok see Ratisbonne **CHAĬKOVSKIĬ**
Tsvetok zasokhshiĭ see Pushkin **RIMSKIĬ-**
  KORSAKOV
"Tu aimais les raisins" *see Familière*
  Chabaneix **IBERT**
"Tu chantes les guerres Thébaines" *see*
  Sur lui-même Anacreon **ROUSSEL**
"Tu crois au mare de café" *see L'incrédule*
  Verlaine **HAHN**
Tu croyais le tenir, et il t'a prise see
  Koechlin **KOECHLIN**
"Tu cuerpo como un arbol" *see Primeros*
  pasos Janés **MOMPOU**
"Tu dici che non m'ami" *see Stornello* Anon.
  VERDI
Tu dors see Émié **JOLIVET**
"Tu es venu, la chambre est parfumée" *see*
  Par l'étreinte . . . Fersen, I. de
  RESPIGHI
"Tu étais jeune et moi gamine" *see Les*
  enfants du Ruisseau Vaucaire **SAUGUET**
"Tu l'as bien dit: Je ne sais pas t'aimer!" *see*
  Je ne sais pas t'aimer Silvestre
  MASSENET
"Tu m'aimes!" *see Réponse de Medjé*
  Barbier, M. **GOUNOD**
"Tu m'as donné un coussin de soie" *see*
  Le plus beau présent Magre **HAHN**
"Tu me lias de tes mains blanches" *see Ariette*
  Moréas **MALIPIERO**
"Tu me parles toujours d'un pays radieux" *see*
  Le pays bienheureux Gounod **GOUNOD**

TU NE M'ÉCHAPPERAS JAMAIS. see
    Pitoëff
    La bohémienne la main n'a pris
        MILHAUD
    Un petit pas, deux petits pas **MILHAUD**
    "Tu n'est qu'un tout petit bonhomme" *see*
        Haut comme trois pommes
        Kriéger, Jacqueline **MILHAUD**
    "Tu peux m'abandonner me dire adieu" *see*
        Présence Laporte **SAUGUET**
    "Tu peux m'oublier dans la joie" *see L'amitié*
        Paté **HAHN**
    Tu pupila es azul y cuando ríes see Bécquer
        TURINA
    "Tu sa' ch'io so, signior mie, che tu sai" *see*
        Sonetto LV Buonarroti **BRITTEN**
    "Tu seras loin, loin de moi" *see Berceuse du*
        marin Champlay, R. **AUBERT**
    "Tu te penches et tu souris" *see Mélancolie*
        Chabaneix **IBERT**
    "Tu Trinitatis unitas" *see Hymnus k*
        Nejsvětější Trojici No author **DVOŘÁK**
    "Tu vas, cruel navire, m'emporter là-bas!" *see*
        Le départ du mousse Barbier, Pierre
        GOUNOD
    Tu vois le feu du soir see Éluard **POULENC**
    "Tu voudrais lire dans mon âme" *see*
        Amoureuse Morel-Retz **MASSENET**
    Tu voz y tu mano see Machado y Ruiz
        RODRIGO
    Tüzes seb vagyok see Ady **SEIBER**
    Der tugendhafte Schreiber see Scheffel *DER*
        BRAUTWILLKOMM AUF WARTBURG.
        LISZT
    "Tule, aaltonen, kirkkorantaan" *see*
        Kirkkorannassa Törmänen **KILPINEN**
    "Tule aamuhun hymyilevään" *see Ihme*
        Koskenniemi **KILPINEN**
    Tule meille Tuomas kulta see Kanteletar
        KILPINEN
    Tule tänne see Kanteletar **KILPINEN**
    "Tuli lintunen laakson puuhun" *see*
        Muuttolintu Törmänen **KILPINEN**
    The tulip tree see Goodman **ROREM**
    Tulips see Herrick **QUILTER**
    Tumanskiĭ, Vasiliĭ Ivanovich, 1800-1860.
        BALAKIREV *Zveno*
    "The tumult in the heart keeps asking
        questions" *see Conversation* Bishop
        ROREM
    Tune thy fiddle, gipsy! see Heyduk
        DVOŘÁK *Struna naladěna*
    "Tunes we heard in 'ninety-two' " *see*
        On the counter Ives **IVES**
    Tunge, mørke natteskyer see Knudsen
        NIELSEN

Tunturilähde see Törmänen **KILPINEN**
Tunturilaulu see Törmänen **KILPINEN**
TUNTURILAULUJA, no. 1
    KILPINEN Törmänen *Jänka*
TUNTURILAULUJA, no. 2
    KILPINEN Törmänen *Tunturilähde*
TUNTURILAULUJA, no. 3
    KILPINEN Törmänen *Laululle*
TUNTURILAULUJA, no. 4
    KILPINEN Törmänen *Tunturille*
TUNTURILAULUJA, no. 5
    KILPINEN Törmänen *Hillankukka*
TUNTURILAULUJA, no. 6
    KILPINEN Törmänen *Murheen kellot*
TUNTURILAULUJA, no. 7
    KILPINEN Törmänen *Muuttolintu*
TUNTURILAULUJA, no. 8
    KILPINEN Törmänen *Sä menit*
TUNTURILAULUJA, no. 9
    KILPINEN Törmänen *Vanha kirkko*
TUNTURILAULUJA, no. 10
    KILPINEN Törmänen *Kirkkorannassa*
TUNTURILAULUJA, no. 11
    KILPINEN Törmänen *Suvilaulu*
TUNTURILAULUJA, no. 12
    KILPINEN Törmänen *Tunturilaulu*
Tunturille see Törmänen **KILPINEN**
"Tunturille mennä tahdon" *see Tunturille*
    Törmänen **KILPINEN**
"Tuomet valkeina kukkii" *see Prologi*
    Jalkanen **KILPINEN**
"Tupa on täynnä tuppisuita" *see Silloin laulan*
    Kanteletar **KILPINEN**
Turgenev, Ivan Sergyeyevich, 1818-
    1883.
    RUBINSTEIN
    Ballada
    Die Erde ruht
    Spring evening
TURINA, JOAQUÍN, 1882-1949.
    Alvarez Quintero, Serafín, 1871-1938.
        *Saeta en forma de Salve a la Virgen de
        la Esperanza, op. 60*
        [Union Musical Española, 1931]
            "Dios te salve, Macarena"
            Text also by Joaquín Alvarez
            Quintero, 1873-1944.
    Arteaga, Cristina de
        Corazón de mujer, op. 39 [Union Musical
        Española, 1927] same
        Also voice & orchestra.
        Cunas, op. 38 no. 2 [Union Musical
        Española, 1927]
            "Cunas de los niños misteriosas arcas"
        Lo mejor del amor, op. 38 no. 1 [Union
        Musical Española, 1927] same

Attard, Josefina de
  Melpómene, op. 93 no. 5 [Union Musical
    Española, 1943] "Mi amor es desmayo
    de luz y reflejos"
Bécquer, Gustavo Adolfo, 1836-1870.
  Besa el aura que gimé blandamente, op.
    81 no. 3 [Union Musical Española,
    1935] same
  Olas gigantes, op. 81 no. 1 [Union
    Musical Española, 1935]
    "Olas gigantes que os rompeis
    bramando"
  Rima, op. 6 [Eschig, 1914]
    "Yo soy ardiente yo soy mo rena"
  Rima, op. 26 no. 3 [Union Musical
    Española, 1923] "Te vi un punto y
    flotando ante mis ojos"
  Tu pupila es azul y cuando ríes, op. 81
    no. 2 [Union Musical Española, 1935]
    same
Campoamor y Campoosorio, Ramón
  María . . . , 1817-1901.
  Cantares, op. 19 no. 3 [Union Musical
    Española, 1923]
    "Ay! Ay! Más cerca de mí te siento"
  Los dos miedos, op. 19 no. 4 [Union
    Musical Española, 1923]
    "Al comenzar la noche de aquel dia"
  Farruca, op. 45 no. 1 [Union Musical
    Española, 1929]
    "Está tuimagen, que admiro"
  Las locas por amor, op. 19 no. 5 [Union
    Musical Española, 1923]
    "Te amaré diosa Venus"
  Nunca olvida, op. 19 no. 2 [Union
    Musical Española, 1923]
    "Ya que este mundo abandono"
Espronceda, José de, 1808-1842.
  El pescador, op. 26 no. 2 [Union Musical
    Española, 1923] "Pescadorcita mía"
No author
  Vocalizaciones, op. 74 [Union Musical
    Española, 1932]
Rivas, Duque de, 1791-1865.
  Cantilena, op. 45 no. 2 [Union Musical
    Española, 1929] "Por un allegre prado
    de flores esmaltado"
  Madrigal, op. 45 no. 3 [Union Musical
    Española, 1929]
    "Tus ojos, ojos no son, niña"
  Romance, op. 26 no. 1 [Union Musical
    Española, 1923]
    "En una yegua tordilla"
Rodríguez Marin, Francisco, 1855-
  1943.
  A unos ojos, op. 54 no. 3 [Union Musical
    Española, 1930]
    "Ah! Luceros radiantes"

  Anhelos, op. 54 no. 1 [Union Musical
    Española, 1930] "Agua quisiera ser"
  Vade retro! op. 54 no. 2 [Union Musical
    Española, 1930] "Amaste á Pedro"
Unknown
  Ave Maria, op. 95 [Union Musical
    Española]
Vega Carpio, Lope Félix de, 1562-
  1635.
  LA DISCRETA ENAMORADA.
    Cuando tan hermosa os miro, op. 90
      no. 1 [Union Musical Española,
      1936] same
  LA ESTRELLA DE SEVILLA.
    Si con mis deseos, op. 90 no. 2 [Union
      Musical Española, 1936] same
  FUENTE OVEJUNA.
    Al val de Fuente Ovejuna, op. 90 no. 3
      [Union Musical Española, 1936]
      same
Turisten see Paulsen **GRIEG**
"Turn I my looks unto the skies" *see Love*
  Lodge, T. **ROREM**
Turnbull, Monica Peveril, 1879-1901.
  IVES *Where the eagle*
"Turned to jade are the boy's rosy cheeks" *see*
  Depression Po Chü-i **BRITTEN**
Turpin, Charles
  GOUNOD *L'arithmétique*
Turpin, Henri
  GOUNOD *Blessures*
Turquety, Edouard, 1807-1867.
  AURORE.
    CHAÏKOVSKI *Serenada*
"Turteltaube, du klagest so laut" *see Die laute*
  Klage Herder **BEETHOVEN**
Tus ojillos negros see Castro **FALLA**
"Tus ojos, ojos no son, niña" *see Madrigal*
  Rivas **TURINA**
"Tus ojos y los mios se miran y hablau" *see*
  Las moyares corralera, cancion española
  Unknown **LOEFFLER**
Tutto è sciolto see Joyce **IRELAND**
"Tutut aitat jo kaikki unelmoi" *see Kesäyö*
  Koskenniemi **KILPINEN**
"Tuuti lasta, tuuti pientä" *see Tuutulaulu*
  Kanteletar **KILPINEN**
Tuuti, tuuti tummaistani see Kanteletar
  KILPINEN
Tuutulaulu see Kanteletar **KILPINEN**
"Tuuvitan tuhoista lasta" *see Anna Maata*
  Maariainen Kanteletar **KILPINEN**
Tuwim, Juljan, 1894-1953.
  SZYMANOWSKI
    Kalinowe dwory
    Slowisień

COMPOSER Poet *Title* "First Line"

Tuwim, Juljan, 1894-1953 *(continued)*
  Świety Franciszek
  Wanda
  Zielone slowa
"Två vattenliljor ur svallet stå" *see*
  Dold förening Snoilsky **SIBELIUS**
"Tvoĭ obraz svetlyĭ" *see Tak chto zhe?*
  Chaĭkovskiĭ **CHAĬKOVSKIĬ**
" 'Twas within a mile of Edinburgh town" *see*
  Within a mile of Edinburgh town
  Unknown **RESPIGHI**
'Twas wondrous sweet that dream of ours see
  Pfleger-Moravský **DVOŘÁK** *Ó byl to
  krásný zlatý sen*
    Three settings: B. 11 no. 5, B. 123 no. 2,
    and B. 124 no. 2.
TWELFTH NIGHT. see Shakespeare
  Come away, Death **QUILTER**
  Hey, ho, the wind and the rain **QUILTER**
  Kom nu hit, död **SIBELIUS**
  Mistress mine **CARPENTER**
  O mistress mine! **CHANLER, QUILTER**
  Ock nör som jag ver en liten smadrang
    SIBELIUS
  Sweet-and-twenty **HESELTINE**
TWELFTH NIGHT: Come away, come away,
  death. *see* Shakespeare
  Chanson de clown **CHAUSSON**
TWELFTH NIGHT: When that I was and a
  little tiny boy. *see* Shakespeare
  Schlusslied des Narren **SCHUMANN**
Twelve oxen see Anon. **HESELTINE**
TWELVE POEMS OF EMILY DICKINSON,
  no. 1
  COPLAND Dickinson *Nature, the
  gentlest mother*
TWELVE POEMS OF EMILY DICKINSON,
  no. 2
  COPLAND Dickinson *There came a wind
  like a bugle*
TWELVE POEMS OF EMILY DICKINSON,
  no. 3
  COPLAND Dickinson *Why do they shut
  me out of Heaven?*
TWELVE POEMS OF EMILY DICKINSON,
  no. 4
  COPLAND Dickinson *The world feels
  dusty*
TWELVE POEMS OF EMILY DICKINSON,
  no. 5
  COPLAND Dickinson *Heart, we will
  forget him*
TWELVE POEMS OF EMILY DICKINSON,
  no. 6
  COPLAND Dickinson *Dear March, come
  in!*

TWELVE POEMS OF EMILY DICKINSON,
  no. 7
  COPLAND Dickinson *Sleep is supposed
  to be*
TWELVE POEMS OF EMILY DICKINSON,
  no. 8
  COPLAND Dickinson *When they come
  back*
TWELVE POEMS OF EMILY DICKINSON,
  no. 9
  COPLAND Dickinson *I felt a funeral in
  my brain*
TWELVE POEMS OF EMILY DICKINSON,
  no. 10
  COPLAND Dickinson *I've heard an
  organ talk sometimes*
TWELVE POEMS OF EMILY DICKINSON,
  no. 11
  COPLAND Dickinson *Going to Heaven!*
TWELVE POEMS OF EMILY DICKINSON,
  no. 12
  COPLAND Dickinson *The chariot*
"Twice a week the winter through" *see*
  Goal and wicket Housman **IRELAND**
Twilight see Guyot **RACHMANINOFF**
Twilight see Tiutchev **MEDTNER**
Twilight fancies see Bjørnson **DELIUS**
  Abendstimmung
Twilight has fallen see Tolstoĭ
  RACHMANINOFF
The twilight people see Starkey
  VAUGHAN WILLIAMS
The twisted Trinity see McCullers
  DIAMOND
" 'Twixt death and doubtfulness" *see*
  To his lady, of her doubtful answer
  Howell, Thomas **RIETI**
TWO BERGERETTES, no. 1
  RIEGGER Anon. *Charmant bocage*
TWO BERGERETTES, no. 2
  RIEGGER Anon. *Toi, dont les yeux*
Two birds flew into the sunset glow see
  Anon. **GRIFFES**
Two brown eyes see Andersen **DELIUS**
  Zwei braune Augen
TWO BY MARIANNE MOORE, no. 1
  THOMSON Moore, M. *English usage*
TWO BY MARIANNE MOORE, no. 2
  THOMSON Moore, M. *My crow Pluto*
TWO GENTLEMEN OF VERONA. see
  Shakespeare
  An Sylvia **SCHUBERT**
  Who is Silvia? **QUILTER**
Two kings sat together in Orkadal see Geibel
  GRIFFES *Zwei Könige sassen auf Orkadal*
Two little flowers see Ives, Harmony **IVES**

TWO LOVE SONGS, no. 1
BERNSTEIN Rilke *Extinguish my eyes*
TWO LOVE SONGS, no. 2
BERNSTEIN Rilke *When my soul touches yours*
"Two lovers hadst Thou in thy lead" *see Two partings,* a dialogue Kol'tsov **RACHMANINOFF**
Two partings, a dialogue *see* Kol'tsov **RACHMANINOFF**
TWO POEMS BY JOHN MASEFIELD, no. 1
GRIFFES Masefield *An old song re-sung*
TWO POEMS BY JOHN MASEFIELD, no. 2
GRIFFES Masefield *Sorrow of Mydath*
TWO RONDELS FOR A SOPRANO, no. 1
GRIFFES Crane, W. *This book of hours*
TWO RONDELS FOR A SOPRANO, no. 2
GRIFFES Scollard *Come love, across the sunlit land*
The two roses see Franzén **SIBELIUS** *De bägge rosorna*
TWO SHORT SONGS, no. 1
HESELTINE Herrick *I held Love's head*
TWO SHORT SONGS, no. 2
HESELTINE Herrick *Thou gav'st me leave to kiss*
Two silent watchers see Rudulph, Mimi, 1923- **KRENEK**
Two sisters not sisters see Stein **THOMSON** *Film: Two sisters not sisters*
Two slants see Manilius **IVES** *Vita*
TWO SONGS BETWEEN TWO WALTZES, no. 1
RIETI Yeats *The fiddler of Dooney*
TWO SONGS BETWEEN TWO WALTZES, no. 2
RIETI Yeats *When you are old*
TWO SONGS BETWEEN TWO WALTZES, no. 3
RIETI Yeats *Maid quiet*
TWO SONGS BETWEEN TWO WALTZES, no. 4
RIETI Yeats *Brown penny*
Two songs for soprano and piano see Unknown **LUENING**
TWO SONGS FROM THE PERSIAN, II. *see* Aldrich *Spurned love* **COPLAND**
Two songs on words of Plato see Plato **ROREM**
Ty hvězdičky tam na nebi to veliké see Hálek **DVOŘÁK**
Ty i my see Pushkin **RIMSKIĬ-KORSAKOV**
Ty jenž sídlíš v nebesích see Unknown **MARTINŮ** *Thou, who dwellest in Heaven*

"Ty kuda letish', kak" ptitsa" *see Serenada* Turquety **CHAĬKOVSKIĬ**
Ty píšeš mi see Heyduk **MARTINŮ** *You write to me*
Ty pomnish' li vecher see Tolstoĭ **RACHMANINOFF** *Do you remember the evening?*
"Ty priletel iz goroda" *see Kukushka* Gellert **CHAĬKOVSKIĬ**
"Ty, Rodina, pomnish' surovye byli" *see Smelo vpered!* Mendel'son **PROKOFIEV**
"Ty rozhdena vosplameniat' " *see Grechanke* Pushkin **RIMSKIĬ-KORSAKOV**
Ty se ptáš pročmoje zpěvy bouří see Pfleger-Moravský **DVOŘÁK**
"Ty znaesh' kraĭ" *see Pesnya Min'ony* Goethe **CHAĬKOVSKIĬ**
Ty znal ego see Tiutchev **RACHMANINOFF** *You knew him*
"Ty zvezda na polnochnom nebe" *see Prostye solva* Chaĭkovskiĭ **CHAĬKOVSKIĬ**
THE TYGER. see Blake, William *The tiger* **THOMSON** *Tiger! Tiger!* **THOMSON** *The tyger* **BRITTEN**
The tyger see Blake, William *THE TYGER.* **BRITTEN**
"Tyger! Tyger! burning bright" *see The tyger* Blake, William **BRITTEN**
"The tygers of wrath are wiser than the horses of instruction" *see Proverb V* Blake, William **BRITTEN**
"Tyhjä on puisto, autio, lohduton" *see Nocturnus* Jalkanen **KILPINEN**
Tyler, Parker, 1907-1974.
ROREM *Dawn angel*
Tyndaris see Leconte de Lisle **HAHN**
Tyrant love see MacDowell **MACDOWELL**
Tyrley Tyrlow see Anon. **HESELTINE**
Tyś nie umarla see Tetmajer **SZYMANOWSKI**
"Tyst är lunden och sjön" *see I natten* Rydberg **SIBELIUS**
Tyst som Aa i Engen rinder see Rode, Helge **NIELSEN**
"Tytebaeret opp på Tuva" *see Tyteberet* Vinje **GRIEG**
Tyteberet see Vinje **GRIEG**
Tytön laulu see Jalkanen **KILPINEN**
Tyutchev, Fyodor *see* Tiutchev, Fĕdor Ivanovich, 1803-1873.
"Tyvnimaesh', vniz skloniv golovku" *see Strashnaia minuta* Chaĭkovskiĭ **CHAĬKOVSKIĬ**

U

"U Brněnské Boží moke" *see Boží muka*
Anon. **MARTINŮ**
"U córeczki, u córeczki" *see Gwiazdka*
Iłłakowiczówna **SZYMANOWSKI**
U jeziorecka see Anon. **SZYMANOWSKI**
U lyudey-to v domu see Nekrasov
BORODIN
U maměnky see Unknown **MARTINŮ**
U moego okna see Einerling
RACHMANINOFF *Before my
window*
"U naszego synka nieba okruszynka" *see
Kolysanka lalek* Iłłakowiczówna
SZYMANOWSKI
U potoka see Kleinschrod **DVOŘÁK**
"U súseda nová stajňa" *see Súsedova stajňa*
Anon. **MARTINŮ**
U vrat obiteli sviatoĭ see Lermontov
MEDTNER *At the cloister gate;*
RACHMANINOFF *At the gate of the Holy
Abode*
"U zhe davno idu ĭa utomlennyĭ" *see Pustĭnya*
Zhemchuzhnikov **BALAKIREV**
Ubell, Hermann, 1876-1947.
REGER *Junge Ehe*
Ucceili, F
ROSSINI *La separazione*
Uczta see Szymanowska, Zafia
SZYMANOWSKI
Ud gaar du nu paa Livets Vej see Blicher
NIELSEN
Udall, Nicholas, 1505-1556.
BRITTEN *I must be married on Sunday
RALPH ROISTER DOISTER (1550).*
HESELTINE *Roister doister*
Udfarten see Munch **GRIEG**
L'udir talvolta . . . see Boccaccio
RESPIGHI
Udrundne er de gamle Dage see Grundtvig
NIELSEN
Udvandreren see Paulsen **GRIEG**
Ueber allen Gipfeln ist Ruh! see Goethe
IVES *Ilmenau: over all the treetops*
Über allen Gipfeln ist Ruh' see Goethe
LISZT
"Ueber allen Gipfeln ist Ruh' " *see Nachtlied*
Goethe **SCHUMANN**
"Über allen Gipfeln ist Ruh" *see Ruhe*
Goethe **ZELTER**
"Über allen Gipfeln ist Ruh' " *see Wandrers
Nachtlied* Goethe **LOEWE, MEDTNER,
SCHUBERT**
Ueber allen Zauber Liebe see Mayrhofer
SCHUBERT

"Über Berg und Tal" *see Winterlied* Mahler
MAHLER
"Über Bergen, Fluss und Talen" *see
Mittagsruh* Eichendorff **LASSEN**
Über den Bergen see Busse **BERG,
SCHOECK**
Über den Wiesentau see Anon.
SZYMANOWSKI *Leć, glosie, po rosie*
"Über der Erde Stirne" *see Pflügerin Sorge*
Morgenstern **REGER**
Über die Berge mit Ungestüm see Kotzebue
DER ARME MINNESINGER. **WEBER**
"Über die Berge steigt schon die Sonne" *see
Morgengruss* Heine
MENDELSSOHN-BARTHOLDY
"Über die Berge zieht ihr fort" *see Abschied*
Mayrhofer **SCHUBERT**
"Über die Haide sind wir gegangen" *see
Zur Erinnerung* Löns **KILPINEN**
Über die Heide see Storm **BRAHMS**
"Über die Heide bergauf, bergab" *see
Holger's Brautritt* Ernst **LASSEN**
"Über die hellen funkelnden Wellen" *see
Wasserfahrt* Hoffmann von Fallersleben
FRANZ
"Über die Hügel und über die Berge hin" *see
Auf der Wanderung*
Hoffmann von Fallersleben **WOLF**
Über die See see Lemcke **BRAHMS**
Über die tausend Berge see Morgenstern
KILPINEN
"Über die Wellen zieht zagend und trauernd
mein Lied" *see Lied aus dem "Märlein von
der Wasserfee"* Bekmann, Mathilde
SPOHR
Über die Welt see Heyse *MELEAGER.*
JENSEN
"Über diesen Strom" *see Die Überfahrt*
Uhland **LOEWE**
Über ein Stündlein see Heyse **JENSEN,
PFITZNER**
"Über gelb' und rote Streifen" *see Lockung*
Eichendorff **SCHOECK**
Über meinen Nächten see Eichhorn **BERG**
"Über meines Liebchens Äugeln" *see
Geheimes* Goethe **SCHUBERT**
Über Nacht see Beck **JENSEN**
Ueber Nacht see Heyse **JENSEN**
Über Nacht see Sturm, J. **LASSEN, WOLF**
"Über Nacht, über Nacht kommt still das
Leid" *see Über Nacht* Sturm, J.
LASSEN, WOLF

Über Nacht und Tag see Roquette
*REBENKRANZ ZU WALDMEISTERS
SILBERNER HOCHZEIT:* In der Früh.
BERG
"Über Tal und Fluss getragen" *see An Mignon*
Goethe **SCHUBERT, SPOHR, ZELTER**
"Über unsre Liebe hängt eine tief
Trauerweide" *see Aufblick* Dehmel
WEBERN
"Über uns'rer Liebe hängt eine tiefe
Trauerweide" *see Aufblick* Dehmel
SZYMANOWSKI
"Über Wiesen und Felder ein Knabe ging" *see*
Schlagende Herzen Bierbaum **STRAUSS**
Über Wildemann see Schulze **SCHUBERT**
"Über Wipfel und Saaten" *see Verschwiegene*
Liebe Eichendorff **LASSEN, WOLF**
"Über Wolken Herr der Herren" *see*
Dem Herrscher Bartholdy, Dr. **LOEWE**
"Überall, wohin mein Auge blicket" *see Die*
Macht der Liebe Kalchberg **SCHUBERT**
Die Überfahrt see Uhland *AUF DER*
ÜBERFAHRT. **LOEWE**
Der Überläufer see Des Knaben
Wunderhorn **BRAHMS**
"Ueber'm Garten, durch die Lüfte" *see*
Frühlingsnacht Eichendorff **JENSEN,**
SCHUMANN
Überraschung see Jacob, T. **LOEWE**
"Übers Niederträchtige niemand sich beklage"
see Wanderers Gemütsruhe Goethe
STRAUSS
Ueltzen, Hermann Wilhelm Franz, 1759-
1808.
BEETHOVEN *Das Liebchen von der Ruhe*
UF'M BERGLI. see Goethe
Schweizer Lied **ZELTER**
"Uf'm Bergli bin i gsässe" *see Schweizerlied*
Goethe **FRANZ, JENSEN, SCHUBERT**
The ugly duckling see Andersen
PROKOFIEV *Gadkiĭ utenok"*
Uhland, Ludwig, 1787-1862.
BENNETT *O'er the woodlands*
BRAHMS
Heimkehr
Das Lied von Herrn von Falkenstein
Der Schmied
Sonntag
GRIEG
Jägerlied
Lauf der Welt
JENSEN *Der Schmied*
LISZT
Gestorben war ich
Hohe Liebe
Die Vätergruft

LOEWE
Die Abgeschiedenen
Abschied
Bauernregel
Die drei Lieder
Geisterleben
Goldschmieds Töchterlein
Graf Eberhards Weissdorn
Graf Eberstein
Hans und Grete
Harald
Der Knabe vom Berge
Der König auf dem Thurme
Der Räuber
Das Schifflein
Das Ständchen
Der Wirthin Töchterlein
Die Zufriedenen
MARTINŮ *A shepherd's Sunday song*
MENDELSSOHN-BARTHOLDY
Frühlingsglaube
Hirtenlied
Die Nonne
Das Schifflein
PFITZNER *Naturfreiheit*
REGER
Bauernregel
Hans und Grete
Sonntag
Waldlied
RIMSKIĬ-KORSAKOV
IA umer ot schast'ia
RUBINSTEIN *Morgenlied*
SAINT-SAËNS
Antwort
Ruhethal
SCHOECK
Abendwolken
Abschied
An einem heitern Morgen
Auf den Tod eines Kindes
Auf ein Kind
Dichtersegen
Frühlingsfeier
Frühlingsruhe
Im Herbste
Die Kapelle
Der Kirchhof im Frühling
Lebewohl
Ruhetal
Wein und Brot
SCHUBERT *Frühlingsglaube*
SCHUMANN
Ballade
Des Knaben Berglied
Provençalisches Lied

Uhland, Ludwig, 1787-1862 (continued)
  SCHUMANN (continued)
    Das Schwert
    Der weisse Hirsch
  SPOHR
    Frühlingsglaube
    Das Ständchen
  STRAUSS
    Auf ein Kind
    Des Dichters Abendgang
    Die drei Lieder
    Die Drossel
    Einkehr
      Two settings: AV 3 and op. 47 no. 4.
    Rückleben
    Die Ulme zu Hirsau
    Von den sieben Zechbrüdern
    Der weisse Hirsch
    Winterreise
  AUF DER ÜBERFAHRT.
    LOEWE Die Überfahrt
  WANDERLIEDER.
    BRAHMS In der Ferne
    BRAHMS, SCHOECK Scheiden und
      Meiden
Die Uhr see Seidl LOEWE
Uhruhe der Nacht see Keller, G.
  SCHOECK
Ukolébavka see Anon. MARTINŮ
Ukolébavka see Jelínek, F. L. DVOŘÁK
"Ullin trat auf mit der Harfe" see Alpin's
  Klage um Morar Goethe LOEWE
Ullman, Gustav Daniel, 1881-1945.
  KILPINEN
    Alla dem som vilse fara
    Kvällning
    Landskap
    Låt vara
    En runa
    Sol, sol!
Ullrich, Titus see Ulrich, Titus, 1813-
  1891.
Die Ulme zu Hirsau see Uhland STRAUSS
Ulrich, Titus, 1813-1891.
  JENSEN Notturno
  SCHUMANN
    Die Fensterscheibe
    Herzeleid
L'ultima ebbrezza! see Negri RESPIGHI
L'ultimo pensiero ("Patria, consorti, figli") see
  Cerutti, L. F. ROSSINI
"Un ultimo profumo innebriante versa" see
  L'ultima ebbrezza! Negri RESPIGHI
L'ultimo ricordo see Redaelli, G. ROSSINI
ULYSSES. see Joyce
  Solitary hotel BARBER

"Ulysses part la voile au vent" see Le retour
  Delaquys BOULANGER
"Um bei dir zu sein" see Sehnsucht Huch
  PFITZNER
"Um der fallenden Ruders Spitzen" see
  Barkarole Schack STRAUSS
Um Dich see Kurz REGER
"Um die blütenvollen Äste" see Amanda
  Unknown LOEWE
"Um meinen Nacken schlingt sich ein
  blütenweisser Arm" see Traumleben
  Hart, J. SCHÖNBERG
"Um mich ist Nacht" see Colma von Ossian
  Macpherson ZELTER
"Um Mitternacht" see Elfenliedchen Goethe
  MARTINŮ
Um Mitternacht see Goethe ZELTER
Um Mitternacht see Hamerling LASSEN
Um Mitternacht see Mörike FRANZ, WOLF
Um Mitternacht see Osterwald FRANZ
Um Mitternacht see Schulze SCHUBERT
Um Mitternacht blühen die Blumen see
  Scholz REGER
"Um Mitternacht ging ich" see
  Um Mitternacht Goethe ZELTER
"Um Mitternacht hab' ich gewacht" see
  Mitternacht Rückert RUBINSTEIN
"Um Mitternacht ruht die ganze Erde nun" see
  Um Mitternacht Osterwald FRANZ
"Um Mitternacht, wenn die Menschen erst
  schlafen" see Elfenliedchen Goethe
  MEDTNER
Um Rettung biete ein güld'nes Geschmeide
  see August WEBER
Um schlimme Kinder artig zu machen see
  Anon. DES KNABEN WUNDERHORN:
  Um die Kinder still und artig zu machen.
  MAHLER
"Um zu begreifen, wie sie damals war" see
  Die Darstellung Mariä im Tempel Rilke
  HINDEMITH
Umkehr see Eichendorff SCHOECK
Umlklo stromu šumění see Hálek DVOŘÁK
"Umri! tverdit mne den' " see Song of the
  disillusioned Rathaus RACHMANINOFF
Umringt vom muterfüllten Heere see
  Kotzebue DER ARME MINNESINGER.
  WEBER
Umsonst see Anon. WEBER
Umsonst see Osterwald FRANZ
"Umsonst, umsonst entsagt'ich der lockenden
  Liebe" see Umsonst Anon. WEBER
"Umwallt vom hellem Wimpel schwebt das
  Boot im Wellentanz" see Rundgesang auf
  dem Wasser Voss ZELTER
"Un, deux, trois et quat' " see Chanson des
  quatre Bloch HONEGGER

COMPOSER   Poet   Title   "First Line"

Un home, San Antonio! see Castro, R.
RODRIGO
"Un, moi qui l'ai, deux, toi qui l'as" *see*
Chanson pour compter Anon.
STRAVINSKIĬ
"Una notte, al davanzale" *see Scherzo*
Zangarini **RESPIGHI**
"Unangeklopft ein Herr tritt abends bei mir
ein" *see Abschied* Mörike **WOLF**
Unbefangenheit see Anon. **WEBER**
Unbegehrt see Ritter **REGER**
Die Unbegreifliche see Musorgskiĭ
MUSORGSKIĬ *Neponiatnaia*
Eine Unbekanntschaft see Spitteler
SCHOECK
Unbewegte laue Luft see Daumer
FRAUENBILDER UND HULDIGUNGEN.
BRAHMS
"Ein unbezwingbar dunkler Hang" *see Trauer*
Leuthold **SCHOECK**
UNCLE VANYA, Act IV. see Chekhov
Let us rest **RACHMANINOFF**
"Und als der Herr von Rodenstein" *see*
Der Willekumm Scheffel **JENSEN**
"Und als der Mensch geschaffen war" *see*
Der Teufel Siebel **LOEWE**
"Und als ich ein winzig Bübchen war" *see*
Schlusslied des Narren Shakespeare
SCHUMANN
"Und bist du auch ferne" *see Liebeslied*
Leixner-Grünberg **RUBINSTEIN**
"Und bist du jung an Jahren" *see Schäfers*
Nachtlied Heyse **CORNELIUS**
Und dann nicht mehr see Rückert **STRAUSS**
"Und der Engel sprach" *see Argwohn Josephs*
Rilke **HINDEMITH**
"Und der Nachbarssohn, der Ruprecht" *see*
Kindergeschichte Jacobowski **REGER**
Und die Lerchen singen wieder see
Hoffmann von Fallersleben **LASSEN**
"Und die mich trug im Mutterarm" *see*
Jung Volkers Lied Mörike **SCHUMANN**
Und die Rosen, sie prangen see Osterwald
FRANZ
"Und die Sonne macht den weiten Ritt um die
Welt" *see Ballade* Arndt **LASSEN**
"Und du kamest in mein Haus" *see Werbung*
Dehmel **SZYMANOWSKI**
"Und frische Nahrung, neues Blut" *see*
Auf dem See Goethe **LOEWE,
MEDTNER, SCHUBERT, WOLF**
"Und gleichwohl kann ich anders nicht" *see*
An die Stolze Fleming **BRAHMS**
Und hab' so grosse Sehnsucht doch see Ritter
REGER
Und Herbstlaub und Regenschauer see
Krenek **KRENEK**

"Und Kinder wachsen auf" *see Ballade des
äusseren Lebens* Hofmannsthal **BERG**
"Und kommt der Frühling wieder her" *see
Wanderlied* Osterwald **FRANZ**
Und kommt er denn nimmer zurück? see
Shakespeare *HAMLET.* **LASSEN**
"Und legt ihr zwischen mich und sie" *see
Spielmannslied* Unknown **LASSEN**
"Und morgen fällt Sanct Martins Fest" *see
Gutmann und Gutweib* Goethe **WOLF**
"Und morgen fällt St. Martins Fest" *see
Gutmann und Gutweib* Goethe **LOEWE**
"Und morgen wird die Sonne wieder
scheinen" *see Morgen* Mackay **REGER,
STRAUSS**
"Und nimmer schreibst du?" *see Herrn Josef
Spaun* Collin, M. **SCHUBERT**
"Und nun ade" *see Nicht Wiedersehen!* Anon.
MAHLER
"Und nun ein End' dem Trauern" *see
Genesung* Schröer **FRANZ**
"Und nun kam die Nacht" *see Und wir
dachten der Toten* Freiligrath **LISZT**
"Und ob mein Leben auch eingegraben sie
wie ein Höllenfuss" *see Heimatgefühl*
Krenek **KRENEK**
"Und oft war's nur ein Hauch" *see
Erinnerungen* Goering **KRENEK**
"Und rausch' auch alles umgedreht dem
Untergange zu" *see Die Bewegung* Voss
ZELTER
"Und ringsum Schnee" *see Aufstieg* Hesse
KILPINEN
"Und sängen die Vögel dir laut meine Lieb"
see Wie lieb ich dich hab' Cornelius
CORNELIUS
Und schläfst du, mein Mädchen see Vicente,
Gil *SPANISCHES LIEDERBUCH:*
Si dormis, doncella. **JENSEN, WOLF**
Und so lasst mich weider wandern see
Mommsen **KRENEK**
Und sprich see Biegeleben **LISZT**
Und steht Ihr früh am Morgen auf see Heyse
WOLF
"Und über den Bergen liegt Welschland" *see
Ausblick nach Süden* Krenek **KRENEK**
"Und wärst du mein Weib" *see Wenn* Busse
STRAUSS
"Und was bedeuten diese Zwänge" *see
Gedichte* Benn **BLACHER**
Und was die Sonne glüht see Bodenstedt
QUILTER
Und welche Rose blüten treibt see Osterwald
FRANZ
"Und werden wir uns nie besitzen" *see
Kleines Lied* Morgenstern **KILPINEN**

"Und wie mag die Liebe" *see Liebe* Rilke
  BERG
"Und wie sie kam zur Hexe" *see Dornröschen*
  (Das Mädchen spricht) Heyse **LASSEN**
"Und wieder hatt' ich der Schönsten gedacht"
  see Dichters Genesung Reinick
  SCHUMANN
Und wieder nehm ich die Harfe zur Hand see
  Leuthold **SCHOECK**
Und willst du deinen Liebsten see Heyse
  WOLF
"Und willst du von mir scheiden, mein
  herzgeliebter Knab' " *see Daz iuwer min
  engel walte!* Hertz **REGER**
"Und willst du von mir scheiden, mein
  herzgeliebter Knab" *see Mein Engel hüte
  dein* Hertz **JENSEN**
Und wir dachten der Toten see Freiligrath
  TROMPETE VON VIONVILLE. **LISZT**
"Und wo noch kein Wand'rer 'gangen" *see
  Romanze* Eichendorff **FRANZ**
"Und wo noch kein Wandrer gegangen" *see
  Der Kühne* Eichendorff **PFITZNER**
Und wüssten's die Blumen see Heine
  FRANZ, SCHUMANN
"Und wüssten's die Blumen" *see Verlust*
  Heine **MENDELSSOHN-BARTHOLDY**
"Under himlens purpurbrand" *see Soluppgång*
  Hedberg **SIBELIUS**
Under Juletraeet see Rolfsen **GRIEG**
Under strandens granar see Runeberg
  SIBELIUS
Under the greenwood tree see Shakespeare
  AS YOU LIKE IT. **QUILTER**
Under the greenwood tree see Unknown
  RIEGGER
    Unpublished; text may be from
      Shakespeare's *As you like it.* Cf. Quilter
      setting above.
Under the mysterious mask see Lermontov
  BALAKIREV
    Iz-pod tainstvennoy kholodnoy polumaski
Under the roof see Gorianskogo, V.
  PROKOFIEV *Pod krysheĭ*
"Under the silver moonlight" *see Moonlight*
  Quilter **QUILTER**
"Under the wide and starry sky" *see Requiem*
  Stevenson, Robert Louis **IVES,
  ROREM**
Under vintergatan see Bergman **KILPINEN**
Underlige Aftenlufte! see Oehlenschläger
  NIELSEN
Understand but once see Shenshin
  CHAĬKOVSKIĬ *Poymi khotraz*
UNDERWOODS. see Jonson
    So white, so soft, so sweet is she **DELIUS**

UNDINE. see Fouqué
  Lied **SCHUBERT**
Undzer Rebenyu see Anon. **WEISGALL**
"Unendlich dehnt sich das brausende Meere"
  see Am Meer! Glücklich **REGER**
Unerhört see Droste-Hülshoff
  CORNELIUS
Das unerkannte Gedicht see Günther
  KRENEK
Unerklärlich see Löwenstein **RUBINSTEIN**
Unexpected rain see Shenshin **MEDTNER**
  Prayer for rain
Unfall see Eichendorff **WOLF**
En ung mor see Blomberg **KILPINEN**
Ungarisches Königslied see Ábrányi **LISZT**
  Magyar király-dal
Ungarns Gott see Petöfi **LISZT**
  A magyarok Istene
Ungbirken see Moe **GRIEG**
Ungeduld see Goethe **SCHOECK**
Ungeduld see Müller, Wilhelm
  SCHUBERT, SPOHR
UNGEREIMTES NACH KINDERREIMEN,
  no. 1
  BLACHER No author *A b c d e f und g*
UNGEREIMTES NACH KINDERREIMEN,
  no. 2
  BLACHER No author *Unser
    Schaulmester es en gelärden Mann*
UNGEREIMTES NACH KINDERREIMEN,
  no. 3
  BLACHER No author *Madmaselle
    Pimpernelle*
UNGEREIMTES NACH KINDERREIMEN,
  no. 4
  BLACHER No author *Guete Tag, mon
    cher Papa!*
UNGEREIMTES NACH KINDERREIMEN,
  no. 5
  BLACHER No author *Quunk, quai
    quenni monni denni monni*
UNGEREIMTES NACH KINDERREIMEN,
  no. 6
  BLACHER No author *Anzkiis kwanzkiis
    kurschpiis kluus*
UNGEREIMTES NACH KINDERREIMEN,
  no. 7
  BLACHER No author *Ich und du und
    dem Müller sein Kuh*
"Ungern flieht das süsse Leben" *see
  Die Kerze* Matthisson **WEBER**
De unges Sang see Hostrup **NIELSEN**
Der Unglückliche see Pichler *OLIVIER.*
  SCHUBERT
Der Unglückliche see Schmidt, Georg
  SCHUBERT

Ungmöen *see* Garborg *HAUGTUSSA.*
  GRIEG *Veslemøy*
"The unicorn's hoofs! The unicorn's hoofs!"
  see Dance song Unknown **BRITTEN**
Unis la fraîcheur et le feu see Éluard
  POULENC
Unknown
  AUBERT *Sous-bois*
  BARTÓK *Du geleitest mich zum Grave*
  BEETHOVEN
    An Minna
    Elegie auf den Tod eines Pudels
    Gedenke mein
    Das Glück der Freundschaft
    Hoffnung
    Man strebt die Flamme zu verhehlen
    Plaisir d'aimer
    Punschlied
    Schilderung eines Mädchens
    La tiranna
    Traute Henriette
    Trinklied
  BENNETT *Gentle Zephyr*
  BERKELEY *The Lowlands of Holland*
  BERLIOZ *Le dépit de la bergère*
  BIZET
    L'esprit saint
    Sur la Grève
  BLITZSTEIN
    Chez Eitingon
    A child writes a letter
  BRUCKNER *O du liebes Jesukind*
  CARPENTER
    The Lawd is smilin' through the do'
    Love whom I have never seen
  CHABRIER *Ronde gauloise*
  DIAMOND *L'âme de Claude Debussy*
  DVOŘÁK
    Jahody
    Kytice
    Opuščená
    Róže
    Skřivánek
    Zezhulice
  FRANCK
    Pour les victims
    Sinite parvulos
  FRANZ
    Abends
    Das Grab der Liebe
    Der Stern ist die Liebe
  GIDEON *Orion*
  GLUCK *Die Neigung*
  GOUNOD
    À la brise
    Jésus à la crêche

Ma fille, souviens-toi
Venez, douces compagnes
Voguons sur les flots
When in the early morning
GRIFFES *Mir war als müsste ich graven*
HAHN
  Chansons espagnoles
  Naïs
  La nymphe de la source
HINDEMITH
  Achtzehn Lieder
  Drei Lieder
INDY *Berceuse populaire*
IVES
  The collection
  Dreams
  Kären
  Omens and oracles
  On the Antipodes
  Qu'il m'irait bien
  The white gulls
JENSEN *O heiss mich nicht vor deinem*
  Antlitz fliehn
JOLIVET *Le jeu du camp fou*
LASSEN
  Abendlandschaft
  An den Mond
  Ave Maria
  Einst
  Frithjofs Glück
  Frühlingsgruss
  Ein Frühlingsnacht
  Harfenklänge
  Ich wandle unter Blumen
  In der Nacht
  Klage nicht
  Lebe Wohl!
  Das Lieblingslied
  Mirza Schaffy
  Mondnacht
  Die Musikantin
  Nacht in Rom
  Nachtlied
  O wär' ich du
  Romance
  Sommernacht
  Spanische Romanze
  Spielmannslied
  Die Spinnerin
  Die Tänzerin
  Vergebener Wunsch
  Vorbei
  Waldasyl
  Welle und Wind
  Die Zigeunerin
LOEFFLER
  Busslied

Unknown *(continued)*
 LOEFFLER *(continued)*
  Las moyares corralera, cancion española
  Reverie
  Tandis que l'Enfant
  Ton souvenir est comme un livre bien
    aimé
 LOEWE
  Amanda
  An die Grille
  An die Natur
  Beim Maitrank
  Der Bergmann
  Bethlehem
  Dich bet' ich an, erstand'ner Held
  Die engste Nähe
  Erdbeerliedchen
  Fischerin und Jägerbursch
  Frage nicht!
  Früh-Lied am Meere
  Frühlingslied
  Der fünfte Mai
  Das Gebet des Herrn und die
    Einsetzungsworte
  Gelobt sei Gott!
  Geruhig seines Weges gehn
  Heimweh
  Der Jagd
  Jesus als Kind
  Kahnlied
  Kommt herzu!
  Kyrie, O Herr Gott Vater!
  Der Liebescheue
  Maiblümelein
  Nachtlied
  O meine Blumen, ihr, meine Freude!
  Ein Preussenlied
  Die Quelle
  Der Sorglose
  Ständchen
  Stille Liebe
  Trost
  Das Vöglein
  Weihnachts-Kantate
  Winterlied
  Zu dir, dem Weltenmeister
 LUENING
  The birth of pleasure
  Forever lost
  Two songs for soprano and piano
 MACDOWELL *Geistliches Wiegenlied*
 MALIPIERO
  Dialogo no. 3 'con Jacopone da Todi'
 MARTINŮ
  Cesta k milé
  Chodníček

  Early in the morning I weed the grain
  Otevření slovečkem
  Rosička
  Rozmarýn
  Sen Panny Marie
  Thou, who dwellest in Heaven
  U maměnky
 MASSENET *Chanson andalouse*
 MENDELSSOHN-BARTHOLDY
  Der Abendsegen
  Abschied
  An Marie
  Der Bettler
  Da lieg' ich unter den Bäumen
  Erwartung
  Es rauscht der Wald
  Im Frühling
  Mailied
  Die Nachtigall
  O könnt ich zu dir fliegen
  Reiterlied
  Romanze
  Sanft weh'n im Hauch der Abendluft
  Der Tag
  Der Verlassene
  Vier trübe Monden sind entfloh'n
  Von allen deinen zarten Gaben
  Wartend
  Warum ich weine
  Wiegenlied
 MILHAUD
  Chant d'amour
  Chant de forgeron
  Chant de la pitié
  Chant de nourrice
  Chant de résignation
  Chant de Sion
  Chant du laboureur
  Ecoutez mes enfants
  Lamentation
 MOZART
  Beim Auszug in das Feld
  Die kleine Spinnerin
  Komm, liebe Zither, komm
  Wie unglücklich bin ich nit
 MUSORGSKIĬ
  IA v subbotu zatepliu svechu
  Otchego, skazhi, dusha devitsa
  Zhelanie serdtsa
 NIELSEN
  Aldrig hans Ord kan jeg glemme
  Johs. Jørgensens Ungdommsang
  Sof sött
 PFITZNER
  Im tiefen Wald verborgen
  Zweifelnde Liebe

COMPOSER Poet *Title* ''First Line''

PIJPER
Mariazang
La Maumariée I
La Maumariée II
Der Schäfer
Schiftlieder

PIZZETTI *Nuvole*

POULENC
L'adieu
La couronne
Le départ
Le dernier mazour
Le drapeau blanc
Les gars polonais
Le lac
La Vistule

PROKOFIEV
Lament
The mulberry tree
O net, ne Figner

QUILTER
Come back
The secret

RACHMANINOFF
Apple tree, O apple tree

RAVEL
Chanson flamande
Chanson russe

REGER
Abendlied
Am Abend
Beim Schneewetter
Bitte
Christ, deines Geistes Süssigkeit
Christkindleins Wiegenlied
Klage vor Gottes Leiden
O Herre Gott, nimm du von mir
Passionslied
Der Schelm
Uns ist geboren ein Kindelein
Warnung
Der zerrissne Grabkranz

RESPIGHI
Bella porta di rubini
Canzone sacra
Le funtanelle, canzone dell'Abruzzo
Kroung (La Cigogne)
Mon elué
My heart's in the Highlands
    Text by Robert Burns?
Noel ancien
The piper of Dundee
Tanto bella
Voici noël
When the kye come hame
Within a mile of Edinburgh town

RIEGGER
Am Strand
In der Ferne
Noel
Under the greenwood tree

RIVIER
Doloroso e giocoso

ROSSINI
A ma belle mère
Addio ai viennesi
Adieux à la vie! (élégie sur une seule
    note)
Anzoleta avanti la regata
Anzoleta co passa la regata
Anzoleta dopo la regata
Ave Maria (su due note)
*Canzonetta spagnuola "En medio a mis
    colores"*
Chansonette de cabaret ("Le lazzarone")
Le dodo des enfants
La fioraja fiorentina
Infelice ch'io son
O salutaris, de campagne
L'orpheline du Tyrol, ballade élégie
La passeggiata
Qual voce, quai note
Questo palpito soave
Un rien
*Il rimprovero ("Se fra le trecce
    d'Ebano")*
Se il vuol la molinara
Il trovatore

RUBINSTEIN
Einen Bruder hatt' ich, einen Geliebten
*Eben brach der Mond durch
    Wolkenschatten*
Geh' bei Tagesanbruch auf die Strasse
*Gott, O Gott, wo ist, wo ist mein
    Auserwählter?*
Herbstgedanken
Die Lerche
Die Nachtigall
Rosendufte füllen rings die Lüfte
Ständchen
Warum musst du welken, schöne, Rose
Weithin rief die Mutter nach der Tochter
Wie so launisch bist du, O Sonnenschein
*Wie wart ihr fröhlich, gold'ne
    Mädchentage*
Willst du einen Ehemann erkennen

SAINT-SAËNS *Fomicacicadéide*

SAUGUET *Salutation angelique*

SCHMITT
La grenade entr'ouverte
O salutaris

SCHOECK
Farbenkantus

COMPOSER Poet *Title* ''First Line''

Unknown (*continued*)
  SCHOECK (*continued*)
    Mandolinen
    Nun steht der Wald in Blüten
    Stummer Abschied
  SCHÖNBERG
    Dass gestern eine Wespe Dich
    Gedenken
    Juble, schöne junge Rose
    Kleine Vögelein, du zwitscherst fein
    Mein Herz, das ist ein tiefer Schacht
  SCHUBERT
    Abendlied
    An den Schlaf
    Auf der Sieg der Deutschen
    Das Bild
    Blondel zu Marien
    Frühlingslied
    Grablied für die Mutter
    Klage
      Two settings: D. 292 and D. 371.
    Der Leidende
      Two settings: D. 432 and D. 512.
    Lied eines Kindes
    Lilla an die Morgenröte
    Il modo di prender mogli
    Morgenlied
    Der Strom
    Tischlerlied
    Trost
    Wiegenlied
    Zur Namensfeier des Herrn Andreas
      Siller
  SCHUMANN
    Der Contrabandiste
    Kinderwacht
  SEIBER *By the fountains of Rome*
  SÉVERAC
    Les Gosses dans les ruines
    Le jardin
    Marche Américaine
  SPOHR
    Beruhigung
    Bitte, bitte!
    Glockenklänge
    Jägerlied
    Jüngst hört ich, welchen süssen lohn
    Liebt er mich?
    Lied der Harfnerin
    Maria
      Two settings: Op. 139 no. 2 and WoO
      107.
    Rätselhaft
    Schottisch Lied
    Sonntag und Montag
    Warum nicht?

  STRAVINSKIĬ
    Le corbeau
    How the mushrooms went to war
    La petite pie
    Tchitcher-Iatcher
    Tom the cat
  SZYMANOWSKI
    Argizagi ederra
    Do dziewczyny
    Maitiak bilhoa holli
    O zawiedzionym zolnierzu
  TURINA *Ave Maria*
  VERDI
    Cupo e il sepolcro mutolo
    È la vita
  WAGNER
    Dors, mon enfant
    Kraftliedchen
  WEBER
    Ah dove siete?
    Ninfe se liete
    Strafpredigt über die französische Musik
    Vatergruss
  WEBERN
    Christkindlein trägt die Sünden der Welt
    Du träumst so heiss im Sommerwind
    Mutig trägst du die Last
    Verderben, sterben–ich leb' ohne Trost
  WOLF
    Bescheidene Liebe
    Der goldene Morgen
    Die Verlassene
  ZELTER
    Abschied
    Ach könnt' ich nimmer vergessen'
    Come potrei ma vivere
    Dove sei mia bella
    Der Friede
    Kuining Chuonrat der Junge
  THE BOOK OF SONGS.
    BRITTEN
      The big chariot
      Dance song
  SPANISCHES LIEDERBUCH: Celestina.
    JENSEN *Dulces árboles sombrosos*
  THE UNKNOWN EROS: The azalea. *see*
    Patmore *L'azalée* **MILHAUD**
  THE UNKNOWN EROS: Departure. *see*
    Patmore *Le départ* **MILHAUD**
  Unmut see Goethe *WESTÖSTLICHER*
    DIVAN. **SCHOECK**
  Unmut see Leuthold **SCHOECK**
  "Uno squillo di cròtali clangenti rompe" *see*
    Musica in horto Rubino **RESPIGHI**
  Unosi moe serdtse see Shenshin *PEVITSE*:
    Unosi moe serdtse. **CHAĬKOVSKIĬ**

Unruhe see Roquette **JENSEN**
Unruhige Nacht see Meyer **SCHOECK**
Uns ist geboren ein Kindelein see Unknown
  REGER
Unser Feind ist, grosser Gott see Kerr
  STRAUSS
Unser Herzog hat herrliche Taten vollbracht
  see Giesebrecht **LOEWE**
Unser Schaulmester es en gelärden Mann see
  No author **BLACHER**
"Unser Schifflein treibt umher auf des
  Lebens" *see Heimweh* Sturm, J. **REGER**
Unser süsster Beruf see Gotter **ZELTER**
"Unser täglich Brot gib uns heute" *see*
  Vater unser V Cornelius **CORNELIUS**
Unser Wein see Krenek **KRENEK**
Unsere Auferstehung durch Christum see
  Münter **LOEWE**
Unsere Liebe see Morgenstern **KILPINEN**
Die unsichtbare Welt see Lühe **ZELTER**
"Unsre Quelle kommt im Schatten" *see*
  Die Quelle Chamisso **MEDTNER**
"Unter blühenden Bäumen hab' bei" *see*
  Gruss Gensichen **REGER**
Unter Blüten see Sergel **KILPINEN**
"Unter Blüten des Mai's" *see Der Küss* Hölty
  BRAHMS
Unter dem Weihnachtsbaum see Rolfsen
  GRIEG *Under Juletraeet*
Unter den Bäumen see Antonio de Villegas
  JENSEN *En la peña, suso la peña*
"Unter den Bäumen" *see En la peña, suso la*
  peña Antonio de Villegas **JENSEN**
"Unter den blühenden Linden" *see Ich glaub',*
  lieber Schatz Ritter **REGER**
"Unter den Linden, an der Haide" *see*
  Die verschwiegene Nachtigall
  Walther von der Vogelweide **GRIEG**
Unter den Zweigen in tiefer Nacht see Heyse
  JENSEN
Unter der Linden see Walther von der
  Vogelweide **BERG**
"Unter der Linden an der Heide" *see*
  Die verschwiegene Nachtigall
  Walther von der Vogelweide **SPOHR**
Unter der Linden bei der Haide see Walther
  von der Vogelweide **PFITZNER**
"Unter die Soldaten" *see Zigeunerliedchen*
  Anon. **SCHUMANN**
Unter Rosen see Janson **GRIEG**
  Millom Roser
Unter Sternen see Keller, G. **SCHOECK**
UNTER STERNEN, no. 1
  SCHOECK Keller, G. *Trost der Kreatur*
UNTER STERNEN, no. 2
  SCHOECK Keller, G. *Sonnenuntergang*

UNTER STERNEN, no. 3
  SCHOECK Keller, G. *Siehst du den Stern*
UNTER STERNEN, no. 4
  SCHOECK Keller, G. *Stille der Nacht*
UNTER STERNEN, no. 5
  SCHOECK Keller, G. *Unter Sternen*
UNTER STERNEN, no. 6
  SCHOECK Keller, G. *Abendlied an die*
  Natur
UNTER STERNEN, no. 7
  SCHOECK Keller, G. *Uhruhe der Nacht*
UNTER STERNEN, no. 8
  SCHOECK Keller, G. *Aus den*
  Waldliedern I
UNTER STERNEN, no. 9
  SCHOECK Keller, G. *Aus den*
  Waldliedern II
UNTER STERNEN, no. 10
  SCHOECK Keller, G. *Stilleben*
UNTER STERNEN, no. 11
  SCHOECK Keller, G. *Das Tal*
UNTER STERNEN, no. 12
  SCHOECK Keller, G. *Abendlied*
UNTER STERNEN, no. 13
  SCHOECK Keller, G. *Wie wähnten lange*
  recht zu leben
UNTER STERNEN, no. 14
  SCHOECK Keller, G. *Flack're ew'ges*
  Licht im Tal
UNTER STERNEN, no. 15
  SCHOECK Keller, G. *Die Zeit geht nicht*
UNTER STERNEN, no. 16
  SCHOECK Keller, G. *Trübes Wetter*
UNTER STERNEN, no. 17
  SCHOECK Keller, G. *Frühgesicht*
UNTER STERNEN, no. 18
  SCHOECK Keller, G. *Frühlingsglaube*
UNTER STERNEN, no. 19
  SCHOECK Keller, G. *In der Trauer*
UNTER STERNEN, no. 20
  SCHOECK Keller, G. *Den Zweifellosen I*
UNTER STERNEN, no. 21
  SCHOECK Keller, G. *Den Zweifellosen II*
UNTER STERNEN, no. 22
  SCHOECK Keller, G. *Tod und Dichter*
UNTER STERNEN, no. 23
  SCHOECK Keller, G. *An das Herz*
UNTER STERNEN, no. 24
  SCHOECK Keller, G. *Aus: Ein Tagewerk*
  I
UNTER STERNEN, no. 25
  SCHOECK Keller, G. *Aus: Ein Tagewerk*
  II
"Unter verschnittenen Weiden" *see Trompeten*
  Trakl **HINDEMITH**
Unterm schutz von dichten Blättergründen see
  George *DAS BUCH DER HÄNGENDEN*
  GÄRTEN. **SCHÖNBERG**

COMPOSER Poet *Title* "First Line"

Unter'm weissen Baume sitzend see Heine
  FRANZ
Untermeyer, Louis, 1885-1977.
  IVES *from "The swimmers"*
Die Unterscheidung see Seidl **SCHUBERT**
Unterwegs see Boelitz **REGER**
Unterwegs see Dingelstedt **SPOHR**
until and i heard see Cummings
  BLITZSTEIN
"Unto him that overcometh shall be given"
  *see The song of the leaves of life and the
  water of life* Bible
  VAUGHAN WILLIAMS
Untreu see Cornelius **CORNELIUS**
Untreu und Trost see Anon. **PFITZNER**
Der untreue Knabe see Goethe *CLAUDINE
  VON VILLA BELLA.* **MEDTNER**
Unüberwindlich see Goethe **BRAHMS**
"Unverbindlich ist das Wetter in den Alpen"
  see Wetter Krenek **KRENEK**
Unvergessen see Frey **REGER**
Unverlierbare Gewähr see Morgenstern
  KILPINEN
"Up! for the bugles are calling" *see A cavalry
  catch* Sharp, W. **SIBELIUS**
"Up to the top o' the trees" *see I will walk on
  the earth* Blake, James **IRELAND**
The Upas-Tree see Pushkin **RIMSKĬĬ-
  KORSAKOV** *Anchar-drevo smerti*
Up-hill see Rossetti, Christina **ROREM**
Upon Julia's clothes see Herrick **ROREM**
"Upon the street they lie" *see The children*
  Soutar **BRITTEN**
Upon their grave see Heine *TRAGÖDIE.*
  GRIFFES *Auf ihrem Grab*
Urania see Mayrhofer **SCHUBERT**
  Uraniens Flucht
URANIA. see Tiedge
  An die Hoffnung **BEETHOVEN**
URANIA: Klagen des Zweiflers. *see* Tiedge
  An die Hoffnung **BEETHOVEN**
Uraniens Flucht see Mayrhofer
  SCHUBERT
Urban, Robert
  JENSEN *Die Heimatglokken*
Urgrossvaters Gesellschaft see Vogl **LOEWE**

Urians Reise um die Welt see Claudius, M.
  BEETHOVEN
Urner, Anna Barbara, 1760-1803.
  LOEWE *Die Abendsonne*
"Urodzil sie gil z czerwonym brzuszkiem" *see
  Gil i sroka* Iłłakowiczówna
  SZYMANOWSKI
"Use ton coeur" *see Miel de Narbonne*
  Cocteau **POULENC**
The useful plough see Anon. **BRITTEN**
Usni! see Merezhkovski **CHAĬKOVSKĬĬ**
Usni pechal'nyĭ drug" see Tolstoĭ
  CHAĬKOVSKĬĬ, RIMSKĬĬ-KORSAKOV
"Usnula panenka usnula vtravičce" *see
  Panenka a tráva* Anon. **DVOŘÁK**
"Usnula, usnula, ja" *see Sen Panny Marie*
  Unknown **MARTINŮ**
"Usnut' by mne navek v trave" *see Usni!*
  Merezhkovski **CHAĬKOVSKĬĬ**
Utes see Lermontov **BALAKIREV**
Utonulá see Sládek **MARTINŮ**
  The drowned maiden
Utro see Yanova **RACHMANINOFF**
  Morning
Utyos see Lermontov **BALAKIREV** *Utes*
Uusi Aladdin see Jalkanen **KILPINEN**
Uutisraivaaja see Jalkanen **KILPINEN**
Uvial tsvetok see Rathaus
  RACHMANINOFF *The flower has faded*
Uwoz, mamo see Anon. **SZYMANOWSKI**
Uz, Johann Peter, 1720-1796.
  MOZART *An die Freude*
  SCHUBERT
    Gott im Frühlinge
    Der gute Hirte
    Die Liebesgötter
    Die Nacht
Uzdraven see Hafiz **MARTINŮ** *Restored to
  health*
Uzh gasli v" komnatakh ogni see Konstantin
  CHAĬKOVSKĬĬ
"Uzh taet sneg" *see Vesna* Pleshcheyev
  CHAĬKOVSKĬĬ
Uzh ty, niva moĩa see Tolstoĭ
  RACHMANINOFF *O thou, my field*
Uzh ya ne tot see Pushkin **PROKOFIEV**
Uznik see Pushkin **MEDTNER** *The prisoner*

V

V chetyrekh stenakh see Golenishchev-
Kutuzov **MUSORGSKIĭ**
V Dushe u kazhdogo iaz see Korinfskiĭ
RACHMANINOFF
In the soul of each of us
V etu lunnuiu noch' see Rathaus
CHAĭKOVSKIĭ *O, du mondhelle Nacht*
V krovi gorit see Pushkin **RIMSKIĭ-
KORSAKOV**
V lesu see Eichendorff **MEDTNER**
Im Walde
V lete kalina see Anon. **PROKOFIEV**
V moeĭ dushe see Vilenkin
RACHMANINOFF *In my soul*
V moem sadu see Bal'mont **PROKOFIEV**
V molchan'i nochi taĭnoĭ see Shenshin
RACHMANINOFF
In the silence of the secret night
"*V poldnevnyĭ zhar" see Son* Lermontov
BALAKIREV
V poryve nezhnosti serdechnoĭ see Byron
PORTUGUESE IMITATION.
RIMSKIĭ-KORSAKOV
V přírodě see Hálek **MARTINŮ** *In nature*
"*V starom zamke, za goroiu" see Kudesnik*
Agnivtsev **PROKOFIEV**
"*V staryĭ sad vykhozhu ia" see Vesennyaya*
pesnya Pleshcheyev **CHAĭKOVSKIĭ**
"*V stepi pod khersonom vysokie travy" see*
Partizan Zhelezniak Golodny, Mikhail
PROKOFIEV
V temnoĭ roshche zamolk soloveĭ see Nikitin
RIMSKIĭ-KORSAKOV
"*V temnom ade, pod zemleĭ" see*
Novogrecheskiye pesni Maĭkov
CHAĭKOVSKIĭ
V tsarstvo rozy i vina-pridi see Shenshin
GAFIZ. **RIMSKIĭ-KORSAKOV**
"*V tumane dremlet noch' " see Elegiia*
Golenishchev-Kutuzov **MUSORGSKIĭ**
V tvoiu svetlitsu see Pushkin **PROKOFIEV**
V uglu see Musorgskiĭ **MUSORGSKIĭ**
V zahradě na hradě see Anon. **MARTINŮ**
In the garden at the castle
Va, chanson see Anon. **SZYMANOWSKI**
Leć, głosie, po rosie
Va, chanson see Verlaine *LA BONNE*
CHANSON. **KOECHLIN**
Va in mercato, Giorgin see Burchiello
MALIPIERO
Va, mon cheval see Anon.
SZYMANOWSKI *Zarzyjze, kuniu*
"*Va où l'Esprit te mène" see L'épouse*
Messiaen **MESSIAEN**

La va pian pian cla portanten'na scura see
Zerbini, Alfredo **PIZZETTI**
"*Va! trotte sans fin, trotte sans trêve" see*
Le petit âne blanc Lorys, Pierre **IBERT**
Vabre
SÉVERAC *Deux mélodies en Langue d'Oc*
Les vacances see Bigorie, L. **GOUNOD**
Vacaresco, Hélène *see* Văcărescu, Elena,
1868-1947.
Văcărescu, Elena, 1868-1947.
AUBERT *Sérénade*
HAHN *Ma jeunesse*
MASSENET
L'âme oiseaux
Chant de guerre cosaque
Plus vite
Septembre
Vache see Éluard **SAUGUET**
Vade retro! see Rodríguez Marin,
Francisco **TURINA**
Väjä ilo emottomalle käestä see Kanteletar
KILPINEN
Vänskapens blomma see Josephson, E.
SIBELIUS
"*Vaer hilset Høg over Granetop" see Høgen*
Aakjaer **NIELSEN**
Vaer hilset, I Damer see Drachmann
GRIEG
Die Vätergruft see Uhland **LISZT**
Vagabond see Masefield **IRELAND**
The vagabond see Stevenson, Robert
Louis *SONGS OF TRAVEL,* I.
VAUGHAN WILLIAMS
La vagabonde see Rodès **BLOCH**
Vaggvisa see Josephson, E. **KILPINEN**
La vague et la cloche see Coppée *LE*
RELIQUAIRE. **DUPARC**
"*Vaguement et longtemps aux mauves*
crepuscules" see Par les soirs . . . Fersen,
I. de **RESPIGHI**
Vaillant-Couturier, Paul, 1892-1937.
HONEGGER *Jeunesse*
The vain desire see Housman *THE*
SHROPSHIRE LAD. **IRELAND**
Le vaincu see Toussaint *JARDIN DES*
CARESSES. **AUBERT**
Le vaisseau see Haraucourt **KOECHLIN**
Vaisseaux, nous vous aurons aimés see
La Ville de Mirmont **FAURÉ**
"*Vaiti on metsä" see Y"* Jalkanen
KILPINEN
Valade, Léon, 1841-1884.
NOCTURNES, poèmes imités de H. Heine.
DEBUSSY *Tragédie*

Valdivielso, Jose de, 1560?-1638.
  WOLF *Wunden trägst du, mein Geliebter*
  SPANISCHES LIEDERBUCH.
    JENSEN *Feridas teneis*
Valendre, Marie de
  MASSENET *Premiers fils d'argent*
Valéry, Paul Ambroise, 1871-1945.
  MOMPOU
    La fausse morte
    L'insinuant
    Les pas
    Le sylph
    Le vin perdu
  SAUGUET
    La ceinture
    Le vin
    Le vois amical
Valgsang see Bjørnson **GRIEG**
Valkeat kaupungit see Koskenniemi
  KILPINEN
Vallery-Radot, Pasteur
  IBERT *Chant de folie*
The valley and the hill see Coleridge
  QUILTER
Le vallon see Lamartine **GOUNOD**
"*Vallons de ma montagne*" *see Loin du pays*
  Gounod **GOUNOD**
Valmy-Baysse, Jean, b. 1874.
  MILHAUD
    Belle dame de mon émoi
    Je suis tombé de mal en peine
    Rassa, ma dame est fraîche et fine
Val's see Shenshin **MEDTNER** *Waltz*
Valse des Si see No author **SAUGUET**
LA VALSE GRÉGORIENNE, no. 1
  THOMSON Hugnet *Les Ecrevisses*
LA VALSE GRÉGORIENNE, no. 2
  THOMSON Hugnet *Grenadine*
LA VALSE GRÉGORIENNE, no. 3
  THOMSON Hugnet *La Rosée*
LA VALSE GRÉGORIENNE, no. 4
  THOMSON Hugnet *La wagon immobile*
Van den Oever see Clercq, René de
  PIJPER
Van Doren, Mark, 1894-1972.
  CARTER *The difference*
Van Hasselt, André Henri Constant *see*
  Hasselt, André Henri Constant van,
  1806-1874.
Van Lerberghe, Charles *see* Lerberghe,
  Charles van, 1861-1907.
Van li effluvi de le rose see Annunzio
  CANTO NOVO: Canto dell'Ospite, no. VI.
  RESPIGHI
Van Ormelingen, Georges, 1865-1906.
  GLOSES ORPHIQUES.

MASSENET
  Antienne
  Defuncta nascuntur
  Fleuramye
"Vandrer jeg i granskogen stille" *see* Henrik
  Wergeland Paulsen **GRIEG**
Vandring i Skoven see Andersen **GRIEG**
Vanha kirkko see Törmänen **KILPINEN**
Vanha laulu see Koskenniemi **KILPINEN**
Vanitas vanitatum see Lehtinen **KILPINEN**
Vanitas! Vanitatum vanitas see Goethe
  SPOHR, ZELTER
Vanity see Carpenter, Rue **CARPENTER**
Vanor, Georges, pseud. *see* Van
  Ormelingen, Georges, 1865-1906.
Var är den djupa glädje see Lagerkvist
  KILPINEN
"Var det ej nylig, Solen sank" *see Lys Nat*
  Benzon **GRIEG**
Var det en dröm? see Wecksell **SIBELIUS**
Vår förnimmelser see Tavaststjerna
  SIBELIUS
Det var i vårens ljusa tid see Cnattingius,
  Thor **KILPINEN**
Var stilla hjärta see Blomberg **KILPINEN**
"Var tid, som kommer, ymnigt sår på gott"
  see Slätten Österling **KILPINEN**
Våren see Vinje **GRIEG**
Våren flyktar hastigt see Runeberg
  SIBELIUS
Varenne, Marc
  MASSENET *Dialogue*
VARÈSE, EDGAR, 1883-1965.
  Verlaine, Paul, 1844-1896.
    Un grand sommeil noir (1906) [Salabert]
    same
"Varför smeker jag ibland päronträdets gren"
  see Visa Blomberg **KILPINEN**
Variations sur "Cadet rousselle" see Anon.
  IRELAND
En vårmelodie see Cnattingius, Thor
  KILPINEN
En vårrefräng see Österling **KILPINEN**
Varsang see Fitger **SIBELIUS** *Lenzgesang*
Vårtagen see Gripenberg **SIBELIUS**
"The varying-year with blade and sheaf" *see*
  The sleeping palace Tennyson **ROREM**
Le vase brisé see Sully-Prudhomme
  FRANCK
"Le vase, où meurt cette verveine" *see Le*
  vase brisé Sully-Prudhomme **FRANCK**
"Vasten kivitystä kadun soipi syyttäen" *see*
  Kaupungilla sataa Koskenniemi
  KILPINEN
"Va-t'en, va-t'en mon arc-en-ciel" *see*
  La grâce exilée Apollinaire **POULENC**

"Vater, du glaubst es nicht" *see Drang in die Ferne* Leitner **SCHUBERT**

"Vater, ich rufe dich!" *see Gebet während der Schlacht* Körner **SCHUBERT, WEBER**

Der Vater mit dem Kind see Bauernfeld **SCHUBERT**

"Vater, schenk' mir diese Stunde" *see Namenstagslied* Stadler **SCHUBERT**

"Ein Vater starb von des Sohnes Hand" *see Der Vatermörder* Pfeffel **SCHUBERT**

Vater unser see Küster **LOEWE**

Vater unser I see Cornelius **CORNELIUS**

Vater unser II see Cornelius **CORNELIUS**

Vater unser III see Cornelius **CORNELIUS**

Vater unser IV see Cornelius **CORNELIUS**

Vater unser V see Cornelius **CORNELIUS**

Vater unser VI see Cornelius **CORNELIUS**

Vater unser VII see Cornelius **CORNELIUS**

Vater unser VIII see Cornelius **CORNELIUS**

Vater unser IX see Cornelius **CORNELIUS**

"Vater unser beten wir" *see Vater unser* Küster **LOEWE**

"Vater unser, der du bist im Himmel" *see Vater unser I* Cornelius **CORNELIUS**

"Vater, wo fliegen die Schwänehin?" *see Herbst* Holstein **DELIUS**

Vatergruss see Unknown **WEBER**

Vaterländisches Lied see Paulsen **GRIEG** *Faedrelandssang*

Das Vaterland see Vogl **LOEWE**

Vaterlandslied see Klopstock **GLUCK, SCHUBERT**

Der Vatermörder see Pfeffel **SCHUBERT**

Vattenplask see Rydberg **SIBELIUS**

"Vattnet rörs och vinden spelar" *see Adagio* Bergman **KILPINEN**

Vaucaire, Michel, b. 1904.
   SAUGUET *Les enfants du Ruisseau*

VAUGHAN WILLIAMS, RALPH, 1872-1958.

Anon.

L'amour de moy (1904) [Boosey, 1907] same
   Text old French, adapted by Paul England.

La ballade de Jésus Christ (1904?) [Oxford Univ. Press, 1935] "Jésus Christ s'habille en pauvre"

Chanson de quête (1904) [Oxford Univ. Press, 1935] "Voici venir le joli mai"

Entlaubet ist der Walde (1902) [Oxford Univ. Press, 1937] same

Jean Renaud (1904) [unpubl.]
   Text old French, adapted by Paul England.

Le paradis (1952) [unpubl.]
   Voice & harp or piano.

Quand le rossignol (1904) [unpubl.]

Que Dieu se montre seulement (1904) [unpubl.]

Réveillez-vous, Piccarz (1903) [Boosey, 1907] same
   Text from French battle-song, adapted by Paul England.

The Spanish ladies (1912) [Boosey, 1912] "Fare you well and adieu to you, Spanish ladies"

Wanderlied [Oxford Univ. Press, 1937] "Wol auf, gut G'sell, von hinnen"

The willow song (1897) [unpubl.]

Barnes, William, 1801-1886.

In the spring (1952) [Oxford Univ. Press, 1952] "My love is the maïd ov all maïdens"

The winter's willow, a country song (1903) [*The Vocalist,* Nov. 1903; Boosey & Hawkes, 1914] "There Liddy zot bezide her cow"

BLACKMWORE MAIDENS.

Blackmwore by the Stour (1900) [*The Vocalist,* May 1902; Boosey & Hawkes, 1912] "The primrose in the sheäde do blow"

MY ORCHA'D IN LINDEN LEA.

Linden Lea (1901) [*The Vocalist,* April 1902; Boosey & Hawkes, 1912] "Within the woodlands, flow'ry gladed"

Bible

The bird's song (1951) [Oxford Univ. Press, 1952] "The Lord is my shepherd"
   Concert version differs from the opera.

The pilgrim's psalm (1951) [Oxford Univ. Press, 1952] "I will put on the whole armour of light"
   Concert version differs from that in the opera.

The song of the leaves of life and the water of life (1951) [Oxford Univ. Press, 1952] "Unto him that overcometh shall be given"
   Concert version differs from that in the opera. 2 voices & piano.

Watchful's song (1951) [Oxford Univ. Press, 1952] "Into Thy hands, O Lord"
   Concert version differs from that in the opera.

Blake, William, 1757-1827.

The divine image (1957) [Oxford Univ. Press, 1958]

VAUGHAN WILLIAMS, RALPH, 1872-1958 *(continued)*

Blake, William, 1757-1827 *(continued)*

"To mercy, pity, peace, and love"
Voice & oboe.

Eternity (1957) [Oxford Univ. Press, 1958] "He who binds to himself a joy"
Voice & oboe.

Infant joy (1957) [Oxford Univ. Press, 1958] "I have no name"
Voice & oboe.

The lamb (1957) [Oxford Univ. Press, 1958] "Little lamb, who made thee?"
Voice & oboe.

London (1957) [Oxford Univ. Press, 1958] "I wander thro' each charter'd street"
Voice & oboe.

A poison tree (1957) [Oxford Univ. Press, 1958]
"I was angry with my friend"
Voice & oboe.

The shepherd (1957) [Oxford Univ. Press, 1958]
"How sweet is the shepherd's sweet lot!"
Voice & oboe.

AH! SUN-FLOWER.
Ah! sun-flower (1957) [Oxford Univ. Press, 1958] same
Voice & oboe.

A DIVINE IMAGE.
Cruelty has a human heart (1957) [Oxford Univ. Press, 1958] same
Voice & oboe.

SONGS OF INNOCENCE: Introduction.
The piper (1957) [Oxford Univ. Press, 1958] "Piping down the valleys wild"
Voice & oboe.

Bunyan, John, 1628-1688.

The song of the pilgrims (1951) [Oxford Univ. Press, 1952]
"Who would true valour see"
Concert version differs from that in the opera.

The woodcutter's song (1951) [Oxford Univ. Press, 1952]
"He that is down need fear no fall"
Concert version differs from that in the opera.

Coleridge, Mary Elizabeth, 1861-1907.

Cradle song (1905) [**The Vocalist,** April 1905]
Translation of "The Virgin's cradle song" 1894?

Hardy, Thomas, 1840-1928.

THE DYNASTS.
Buonaparty (1908) [Boosey & Hawkes, 1909]
"We be the King's men"

Heywood, Thomas, d. 1641.

Ye little birds (1905) [unpubl., lost?]

Housman, Alfred Edward, 1859-1936.

LAST POEMS: Prologue.
We'll go to the woods no more (1926? rev. 1954] [Oxford Univ. Press, 1954] same
Voice & violin.

LAST POEMS: XXIII.
In the morning (1926? rev. 1954] [Oxford Univ. Press, 1954] same
Voice & violin.

LAST POEMS: XXVI.
The half-moon westers low (1926? rev. 1954] [Oxford Univ. Press, 1954] same
Voice & violin.

LAST POEMS: XXVII.
The sigh that heaves the grasses (1926? rev. 1954] [Oxford Univ. Press, 1954] same
Voice & violin.

LAST POEMS: XLI.
Fancy's knell (1926? rev. 1954] [Oxford Univ. Press, 1954]
"When lads were home from labour"
Voice & violin.

A SHROPSHIRE LAD: V.
Goodbye (1926? rev. 1954] [Oxford Univ. Press, 1954]
"Oh see how thick the gold cup flowers"
Voice & violin.

A SHROPSHIRE LAD: XXVI.
Along the field (1926? rev. 1954] [Oxford Univ. Press, 1954]
"Along the field as we came by"
Voice & violin.

A SHROPSHIRE LAD: XXVII.
Is my team ploughing? (1908) [unpubl.]
Eventually incorporated into **On Wenlock edge.**

A SHROPSHIRE LAD: LIV.
With rue my heart is laden (1926? rev. 1954] [Oxford Univ. Press, 1954] same
Voice & violin.

Murray, Gilbert, 1866-1967.

Where is the home for me? (ca.1911-14) [Ashdown, 1922]
Text after **The Bacchae** of Euripides.

No author
> *Three vocalises* (1958) [Oxford Univ.
> Press, 1960]
>> Movements entitled Prelude, Scherzo
>> and Quasi menuetto.
>> Soprano & B-flat clarinet.

Rossetti, Christina Georgina, 1830-1894.
> *Boy Johnny* (1902?) [*The Vocalist,* Sept.
> 1902; Boosey & Hawkes, 1914]
> "If you'll busk you as a bride"
> *Dreamland* (1905) [Boosey & Hawkes,
> 1906] "Where sunless rivers weep"
> *If I were a queen* (1902?) [*The Vocalist,*
> Nov. 1902; Boosey & Hawkes, 1914]
> same
> *When I am dead, my Dearest* (before
> 1903) [K. Prowse, 1903] same

Rossetti, Dante Gabriel, 1828-1882.
> *Willow-wood* (1903) [unpubl.?]
>> Revised version, 1908-9: voice &
>> orchestra with chorus, Breitkopf &
>> Härtel, 1909.
> THE HOUSE OF LIFE, no. IV.
>> *Lovesight* (1903) [J. Willcocks, 1904;
>> Ashdown, 1933] "When do I see
>> thee most, beloved one?"
> THE HOUSE OF LIFE, no. IX.
>> *Love's minstrels* (1903) [J. Willcocks,
>> 1904; Ashdown, 1933]
>> "One flame-winged brought a white-
>> winged harp-player"
> THE HOUSE OF LIFE, no. XIX.
>> *Silent noon* (1903) [J. Willcocks, 1904;
>> Ashdown, 1933]
>> "Your hands lie open in the long
>> fresh grass"
> THE HOUSE OF LIFE, no. XXII.
>> *Heart's haven* (1903) [J. Willcocks,
>> 1904; Ashdown, 1933]
>> "Sometimes she is a child within
>> mine arms"
> THE HOUSE OF LIFE, no. XLVIII.
>> *Death in love* (1903) [J. Willcocks,
>> 1904; Ashdown, 1933]
>> "There came an image in Life's
>> retinue"
> THE HOUSE OF LIFE, no. LIX.
>> *Love's last gift* (1903) [J. Willcocks,
>> 1904; Ashdown, 1933] "Love to his
>> singer held a glistening leaf"

Shakespeare, William, 1564-1616.
> KING HENRY VIII.
>> *Orpheus with his lute* (1902) [K.
>> Prowse, 1903]
>> "Orpheus with his lute made trees"

> *Orpheus with his lute* (2nd setting,
> 1925) [Oxford Univ. Press, 1926]
> "Orpheus with his lute made
> trees"
> LOVE'S LABOUR'S LOST.
>> *When icicles hang by the wall* (1925)
>> [Oxford Univ. Press, 1926]
>> same
> MEASURE FOR MEASURE.
>> *Take, O take those lips away* (1925)
>> [Oxford Univ. Press, 1926]
>> same

Shove, Fredegond, 1889-1949.
> *Four nights* (1925) [Oxford Univ. Press,
> 1925]
> "O when I shut my eyes in spring"
> *Motion & stillness* (1925) [Oxford Univ.
> Press, 1925]
> "The seashells lie as cold as death"
> *The new ghost* (1925) [Oxford Univ.
> Press, 1925] "And he cast it down,
> down, on the green grass"
> *The water mill* (1925) [Oxford Univ.
> Press, 1925]
> "There is a mill, an ancient one"

Starkey, James, 1879-1958.
> *A piper* (1925) [Oxford Univ. Press,
> 1925] "A piper in the streets
> today"
> *The twilight people* (1925) [Oxford Univ.
> Press, 1925] "It is a whisper among
> the hazel bushes"

Stevenson, Robert Louis, 1850-1894.
> SONGS OF TRAVEL, I.
>> *The vagabond* (1904) [Boosey &
>> Hawkes, 1905, 1907, 1960]
>> "Give to me the life I love"
> SONGS OF TRAVEL, II.
>> *Youth and love* (1904) [Boosey &
>> Hawkes, 1907, 1960]
>> "To the heart of youth the world is a
>> highway side"
> SONGS OF TRAVEL, IV.
>> *In dreams* (1904) [Boosey & Hawkes,
>> 1907, 1960]
>> "In dreams unhappy I behold you"
> SONGS OF TRAVEL, VI.
>> *The infinite shining heavens* (1904)
>> [Boosey & Hawkes, 1907, 1960]
>> same
> SONGS OF TRAVEL, IX.
>> *Let beauty awake* (1904) [Boosey &
>> Hawkes, 1907, 1960]
>> "Let beauty awake in the morn"
> SONGS OF TRAVEL, XI.
>> *The roadside fire* (1904) [Boosey &
>> Hawkes, 1905, 1907, 1960]
>> "I will make you brooches"

COMPOSER   Poet   *Title*   "First Line"

VAUGHAN WILLIAMS, RALPH, 1872-1958 *(continued)*
Stevenson, Robert Louis, 1850-1894 *(continued)*
SONGS OF TRAVEL, XIV.
Bright is the ring of words (1904) [Boosey & Hawkes, 1905, 1907, 1960] same
SONGS OF TRAVEL, XVI.
Whither must I wander? (1901?) [Boosey & Hawkes, 1912, 1960] "Home no more home to me"
SONGS OF TRAVEL, XXII.
I have trod the upward and the downward slope (1904) [Boosey & Hawkes, 1960] same
Swinburne, Algernon Charles, 1837-1909.
Rondel (1895/96?) [unpubl.] "Kissing her hair"
T
Wishes (1893) [*Cambridge Observer,* Aug. 1893]
Tennyson, Alfred Tennyson, 1st baron, 1809-1892.
Claribel (1896) [Boosey & Hawkes, 1906] "Where Claribel low lieth"
Spring (1896) [unpubl.]
Text from "The window" or "The song of the wrens."
THE PRINCESS.
The splendour falls (1905) [*The Vocalist,* May 1905;
Boosey & Hawkes, 1914] "The splendour falls on castle walls"
THE PRINCESS: IV, 1. 21.
Tears, idle tears (1903) [*The Vocalist,* June 1903; Boosey & Hawkes, 1903] same
THE WINDOW.
Winter (1896) [unpubl.]
Vaughan Williams, Ursula (Wood), 1911-
Hands, eyes and heart (1956?) [Oxford Univ. Press, 1960] "Hands, give him all the measure of my love"
Menelaus (1954) [Oxford Univ. Press, 1960] "You will come home"
Procris (1958) [Oxford Univ. Press, 1960] "Procris is lying at the waterside"
The song of Vanity Fair (1951) [Oxford Univ. Press, 1952]
"Come and buy from our booths"
Concert version differs from that in the opera.
Tired (1956) [Oxford Univ. Press, 1960] "Sleep, and I'll be still as another sleeper"

Vaux, Thomas, 2d baron, 1510-1556.
How can the tree but wither? (1896) [Oxford Univ. Press, 1934] "How can the tree but waste and wither away"
Verlaine, Paul, 1844-1896.
LE CIEL EST PARDESSUS LE TOIT.
The sky above the roof (1908) [Boosey & Hawkes, 1909] same
Text adapted by Mabel Dearmer, 1872-1915.
Whitman, Walt, 1819-1892.
FROM NOON TO STARRY NIGHT.
A clear midnight (1925) [Oxford Univ. Press, 1925] "This is thy hour, O Saul"
SONGS OF PARTING.
Joy, shipmate, joy! (1925) [Oxford Univ. Press, 1925] same
WHISPERS OF HEAVENLY DEATH.
Darest thou now, O soul (1925) [Curwen, 1925] same
Also voice & strings.
Nocturne (1925) [Oxford Univ. Press, 1925] "Whispers of heavenly death murmur'd I hear"
Vaughan Williams, Ursula (Wood), 1911-
VAUGHAN WILLIAMS
Hands, eyes and heart
Menelaus
Procris
The song of Vanity Fair
Tired
Vauquelin de La Fresnaye, Jean, 1536-1607.
SAINT-SAËNS *Villanelle*
Vauvert, Mme. Espinasse-Mongenet *see* Espinasse-Mongenet, Mme. Louise
Vaux, Thomas, 2d baron, 1510-1556.
VAUGHAN WILLIAMS *How can the tree but wither?*
Vchera my vstretilis' *see* Polonsky
RACHMANINOFF
When yesterday we met
Vcherashniaia noch' *see* Khomyakov
CHAĬKOVSKIĬ
"*Vcherashniaia noch' byla tak svetna*" *see* *Nachstück* Khomyakov **BALAKIREV**
Vdejte mne, matičko see Tetmajer
MARTINŮ
Marry me, mother, as long as I'm young
Večer see Moore, G. **MARTINŮ** *Evening*
Vecher see Shevchenko **CHAĬKOVSKIĬ**
"*Vecher otradnyĭ Leg na kholmakh*" *see* *Vecherniaia pesenka* Pleshcheyev
MUSORGSKIĬ

Vecherniaĩa pesenka *see* Pleshcheyev
MUSORGSKIĬ
Vecherniaĩa pesn' okhotnika *see* Goethe
MEDTNER *Jägers Abendlied*
Vechno smiaten'e *see* Goethe MEDTNER
Inneres Wühlen ewig zu fühlen
Ved en ung Hustrus Båre *see* Monrad
GRIEG
Ved Gjaetle-Baekken *see* Garborg
HAUGTUSSA. GRIEG *Ved Gjaetle-Bekken*
Ved Gjaetle-Bekken *see* Garborg
HAUGTUSSA. GRIEG
Ved Moders Grav *see* Benzon GRIEG
Ved Rondane *see* Vinje *FERDAMINNI.*
GRIEG
"Vedi! la bianca luna splende sui colli" *see*
L'esule Solèra VERDI
"Vedi, quanto adoro" *see* *Arie* Metastasio
SCHUBERT
Vega Carpio, Lope Félix de, 1562-1635.
LASSEN *Wiegenlied der Jungfrau Maria*
RODRIGO
Coplas del pastor enamorado
Pastorcito Santo
Romance del comendador de ocaña
WOLF
Die ihr schwebet um diese Palmen
Weint nicht, ihr Äuglein
LA DISCRETA ENAMORADA.
TURINA *Cuando tan hermosa os miro*
LA ESTRELLA DE SEVILLA.
TURINA *Si con mis deseos*
FUENTE OVEJUNA.
TURINA *Al val de Fuente Ovejuna*
SPANISCHES LIEDERBUCH: Madre, unos
ojuelos vi.
JENSEN *Madre, unos ojuelos vi*
"Vegen vita, på Villstig venda" *see* *Fyremål*
Vinje GRIEG
"Veggio co' bei vostri occhi un dolce lume"
see *Sonetto XXX* Buonarroti BRITTEN
The veil of night has fall'n *see* Mickiewicz
CHAĬKOVSKIĬ *Na zemliu sumrak pal*
Das Veilchen *see* Anon. ZELTER
Veilchen *see* Cornelius CORNELIUS
Das Veilchen *see* Goethe MEDTNER,
MOZART
Das Veilchen *see* Holstein DELIUS
Das Veilchen *see* Müller, J. LISZT
"Ein Veilchen auf der Wiese stand" *see*
Das Veilchen Goethe MEDTNER,
MOZART
"Ein Veilchen blüht im Thale" *see*
Das Veilchen im Tale Kind, F. WEBER
Das Veilchen im Tale *see* Kind, F. WEBER
"Veilchen, Rosmarin, Mimosen" *see* *Mein*
Garten Hoffmann von Fallersleben
SCHUMANN

Veilchen vom Berg, woran mahnest du mich?
see Lemcke RUBINSTEIN
"Veilchen wollt ich pflükken" *see*
Der Schelm Unknown REGER
La veillée du petit Jésus *see* Theuriet
MASSENET
Veillées *see* Rimbaud MILHAUD
Veilles-tu, ma senteur de soleil *see*
Lerberghe FAURÉ
"Věje větříček zkniežeckých lesév" *see* *Kytice*
Unknown DVOŘÁK
Vejviseren synger *see* Welhaven NIELSEN
Velikonoční *see* Erben MARTINŮ *Easter*
Velkommen Laerkelil *see* Richardt NIELSEN
"Velsignet vaere du, vor Herre, Gud" *see*
Johs. Jørgensens Ungdommsang Unknown
NIELSEN
Velvet shoes *see* Wylie THOMPSON, R.
Vem är du? *see* Blomberg KILPINEN
"Vcnant du dchors, vcnant du dcdans" *see*
Bêtes et méchants Éluard SAUGUET
Vender sig Lykken fra dig *see* Hauch
NIELSEN
Vendor's song *see* Shakespeare
BLITZSTEIN
Vendredi XIII *see* Chalupt SCHMITT
Venetianisches Gondellied *see* Moore, T.
MENDELSSOHN-BARTHOLDY
Venevil *see* Bjørnson DELIUS *Kleine*
Venevil
Venez, douces compagnes *see* Unknown
GOUNOD
"Venez fillettes et garçons" *see* *La Fénaison*
Devereux LALO
"Venez jusqu'à ces sables d'or" *see* *Modéré-*
Plus lent Shakespeare HONEGGER
Venez, ma bien aimée *see* Jammes
TRISTESSES. MILHAUD
Venez sous la tonnelle *see* Jammes
TRISTESSES. MILHAUD
VENEZIA, no. 1
HAHN Anon. *Sopra l'acqua*
indormenzada . . .
VENEZIA, no. 2
HAHN Anon. *La barcheta*
VENEZIA, no. 3
HAHN Anon. *L'avertimento*
VENEZIA, no. 4
HAHN Anon. *La Biondina in gondoleta*
VENEZIA, no. 5
HAHN Anon. *Che pecà!*
VENEZIA, no. 6
HAHN Anon. *La primavera*
Venezianisches Intermezzo *see* Zwehl, Hans
Fritz von KILPINEN
Veni Creator *see* Anon. LALO

COMPOSER Poet *Title* "First Line"

"Veni creator spiritus" *see Veni Creator*
Anon. **LALO**
Venilia see Sharp, W. **LUENING**
Venise see Musset **GOUNOD**
Venise see Verlaine **FAURÉ**
    A Clymène
    C'est l'extase . . .
    En sourdine
    Green
    Mandoline
Venitelo a vedere 'l mi'piccino . . . see Birga,
    Arturo *RISPETTI TOSCANI.* **RESPIGHI**
Le vent dans la plaine see Verlaine
    ROMANCES SANS PAROLES.
    SAINT-SAËNS
"Vent, neige, obscurité" *see Chant dissident*
    Anon. **STRAVINSKIĭ**
Le ventre merveilleux see Leclère, translator
    SHÉHÉRAZADE. **KOECHLIN**
Venus mater see Dehmel **PFITZNER**
Veor skloni otets sviatoĭ see Goethe
    MEDTNER *Sieh mich, Heil'ger, wie ich*
    bin
"Ver ikkje so modlaus" *see Jenta* Vinje
    GRIEG
Der Verbannte see Kahlert **LOEWE**
    Sankt Helena
"Verbirg dich, Sonne" *see Auflösung*
    Mayrhofer **SCHUBERT**
Verborgenheit see Mörike **FRANZ, WOLF**
Verborg'ne Liebe see Bjørnson **DELIUS;**
    GRIEG *Dulgt Kjaerlighed*
Verbum caro factum see Anon. **MILHAUD**
Verbundenheit see Huber, B. **KILPINEN**
La verdadera vida see Saix, Guillot de
    MASSENET
Verdankt sei es dem Glanz der Grossen see
    Hermes *SOPHIENS REISE.* **MOZART**
Verde, verderol see Jimenez **RODRIGO**
Verdens Gang see Uhland **GRIEG**
    Lauf der Welt
Verderben, sterben—ich leb' ohne Trost see
    Unknown **WEBERN**
"Verdes ribe ras amenas" *see Coplas del*
    pastor enamorado Vega Carpio
    RODRIGO
VERDI, GIUSEPPE, 1813-1901.
    Angiolini, Carlo
        Nell' orror di notte oscura (1838) [Gio.
            Canti, 1838?] same
    Anon.
        Stornello (1869) [Ricordi, 1869]
            "Tu dici che non m'ami"
    Balestra, Luigi
        La seduzione (1839) [Gio. Canti, 1839?]
            "Era bella com'angiol del cielo"
            Bass & piano.

Bianchi, Tommaso
    More, Elisa, lo stanco poeta (1838) [Gio.
        Canti, 1838?] same
Boito, Arrigo, 1842-1918.
    AGNUS DEI.
        Pietà, Signor (1894) [**Harmonia**
            (Rome) Oct. 15, 1913]
            "Pietà, Signor, Pietà Signor"
                1st published in facsimile in **Fata**
                Morgana, late 1894; later in
                Rassegna dorico (Rome) March
                1941.
Escudier, Marie Pierre Yves, 1819-
1880.
    L'abandonée (1849) [Schott, ca.1849;
        Heugel, 1882]
        "Beaux jours que le coeur envie"
        Text may be by Marie or Léon
        Escudier (1821-1881).
Goethe, Johann Wolfgang von, 1749-
1832.
    Chi i bei di m'adduce ancora (1842)
        [**Music Review** 9 (Feb. 1948): 13]
        same
    FAUST.
        Deh, pietoso, oh addolorata (1838)
            [Gio. Canti, 1838?] same
        Perduta ho la pace (1838) [Gio. Canti,
            1838?] same
Maffei, Andrea, 1798-1885.
    Ad una stella (1845) [F. Lucca, 1845]
        "Bell'astro della terra"
    Brindisi (1st version, 1835?) [Ricordi,
        1935] "Mescetemi il vino!"
        Two versions; same words, different
        music.
    Brindisi (2nd version, 1845) [F. Lucca,
        1845] "Mescetemi il vino!"
        Two versions; same words, different
        music.
    Il tramonto (2nd version, 1845) [F.
        Lucca, 1845]
        "Amo l'ora del giorno che muore"
            1st version in manuscript in the New
            York Public Library.
Maggioni, S. Manfredo
    Il poveretto (1847) [F. Lucca, 1847]
        "Passegger, che al dolce aspetto"
        Bass & piano.
    Lo spazzacamino (1845) [F. Lucca, 1845]
        "Lo spazzacamin! Son d'aspetto
        brutto"
    La zingara (1845) [F. Lucca, 1845]
        "Chi padre mi fosse"
Ongaro, Francesco dall, 1808-1873.
    Il Brigidino (1863) [**Scenario** (Rome)
        Feb. 1941; Casa Musicale Sonzogno,
        1948]
        "E lo mio damo se n'è ito a Siena"

Piave, Francesco Maria, 1810-1876.
  Barcarola (1850) [facsimile in G. Stefani
    Verdi e Trieste (1951)]
      "Fiorellin che sorgi appena cosi fresco"
Romani, Felice, 1788-1865.
  Il mistero (1845) [F. Lucca, 1845]
    "Se tranquillo a te deecanto"
Sole, Nicola, 1821-1859.
  Il preghiera del poeta (1858) [*Rivista*
    Musicale Italiana 45 (1941): 230]
      "Del tuo celeste foco eterno Iddio un
        core accendi"
Solèra, Temistocle, 1815-1878.
  L'esule (1839) [Gio. Canti, 1839?]
    "Vedi! la bianca luna splende sui colli"
    Bass & piano.
Unknown
  Cupo e il sepolcro mutolo (1873)
    [unpubl.'?]
      Listed in *New Grove;* not located in
        Hopkinson.
  È la vita (1844) [Boccaccini & Spada,
    1985] same
Vittorelli, Jacopo, 1749-1835.
  In solitaria stanza (1838) [Gio. Canti,
    1838?] same
  Non t'accostare all'urna (1838) [Gio.
    Canti, 1838?] same
Verdruss see Iłłakowiczówna
  SZYMANOWSKI *Smutek*
LA VERDURE DORÉE, no. 1
  IBERT Derème *Comme j'allais*
LA VERDURE DORÉE, no. 2
  IBERT Derème *Tiède azur*
LA VERDURE DORÉE, no. 3
  IBERT Derème *Cette grande chambre*
LA VERDURE DORÉE, no. 4
  IBERT Derème *Personne ne saura jamais*
Der Verehrung see Löns **KILPINEN**
Die verfallene Mühle see Vogl **LOEWE**
Verfehlte Liebe see Heine **FRANZ**
Die verfehlte Stunde see Schlegel
  SCHUBERT
"Verfliesset, vielgeliebte Lieder" *see*
  Am Flusse Goethe **SCHUBERT**
    Two settings: D. 160 and D. 766.
Vergängliches see Tolstoï **RUBINSTEIN**
Vergänglichkeit see Hesse **KILPINEN,**
  SCHOECK
"Vergangen ist der lichte Tag" *see Nachtlied*
  Eichendorff **MENDELSSOHN-**
  BARTHOLDY, SCHOECK
Vergangen ist mir Glück und Heil see Anon.
  BRAHMS
Vergangenheit see Lenau **SCHOECK**
Vergangnes Glück see Heyse **JENSEN**

Vergebener Wunsch see Unknown **LASSEN**
Vergebliche Liebe see Bernard **SCHUBERT**
Vergebliches Standchen see Anon.
  BRAHMS
Vergeb'ner Wunsch see Unknown **LASSEN**
  Vergebener Wunsch
Le verger see Distel, Camille **MASSENET**
Vergessen see Osterwald **FRANZ**
  Erinnerung
Der Vergessene see Golenishchev-Kutuzov
  MUSORGSKIĬ *Zebytyĭ*
Das vergessene Lied see Vogl **LOEWE**
"Vergib uns unsre Schuld" *see Vater unser VI*
  Cornelius **CORNELIUS**
Vergiftet sind meine Lieder see Heine
  BORODIN, GIDEON, LISZT,
  SCHOECK
Vergilius Maro, Publius, 70 B.C.-19 B.C.
  AENEID.
    ZELTER *Lutheri Vespera*
Vergine d'Atene see Byron **GOUNOD**
  Maid of Athens
"Vergine santa, immacolata" *see Inno a Maria*
  Nostra Donna Poliziano **MALIPIERO**
Vergiss mein nicht see Osterwald **FRANZ**
Vergissmeinnicht see Cornelius **LASSEN**
Vergissmeinnicht see Pfau **SCHÖNBERG**
Vergissmeinnicht see Schober **SCHUBERT**
"Verglommen ist das Abendrot" *see*
  Des müden Abendlied Geibel **FRANZ,**
  GRIFFES
Verhaeren, Emile, 1855-1916.
  LES DÉBÂCLES.
    RAVEL *Si morne!*
  LES VIGNES DANS MURAILLE.
    SÉVERAC *L'éveil de Pâques*
"Verhasst ist mir das Folgen und das Führen"
  see Der Einsame Nietzsche **DELIUS**
Verin, Boris *see* Vérine, Boris
Vérine, Boris
  PROKOFIEV *Dover'sĩa mne*
Veritas see Howe **THOMPSON, R.**
Verkehr see Krenek **KRENEK**
Die Verklärende see Buonarroti **SCHOECK**
Verklärung see Itzerott **REGER**
Verklärung see Pope *THE DYING*
  CHRISTIAN TO HIS SOUL. **SCHUBERT**
Verklärung see Trakl *SIEBENGESANG DES*
  TODES. **WEBERN**
Verkündigung see Dehmel
  SZYMANOWSKI
Verkündigung über den Hirten see Rilke
  HINDEMITH

Verlaine, Paul, 1844-1896.

CARPENTER
Dansons la gigue
Il pleure dans mon coeur
CHAUSSON
La chanson bien douce
Le chevalier Malheur
DEBUSSY
L'échelonnement des haies
Il pleure dans mon coeur
La mer est plus belle
DELIUS *Il pleure dans mon coeur*
FAURÉ
A Clymène
Donc, ce sera par un clair jour d'été
L'hiver a cessé
J'ai presque peur, en vérité
J'allais par des chemins perfides
Puisque l'aube grandit
Une sainte en son auréole
Spleen
HAHN
L'allée est sans fin
La bonne chanson
Paysage triste
Tous deux
HONEGGER *Un grand sommeil noir*
KOECHLIN
La chanson des ingénues
Il pleure dans mon coeur
Mon rêve familier
Le paysage dans le cadre des portières
LOEFFLER
A une femme
Dansons la gigue!
Sérénade
MILHAUD *Nevermore*
RAVEL
Un grand sommeil noir
Sur l'Herbe
SCHMITT
Femme et chatte
Il pleure dans mon coeur
O triste était mon âme
STRAVINSKÏ *Sagesse*
VARÈSE *Un grand sommeil noir*
AQUARELLES.
DEBUSSY
Green
Spleen
FAURÉ *Green*
IRELAND *Spleen*
LA BONNE CHANSON.
CHAUSSON *Apaisement*
DELIUS
Avant que tu ne t'en ailles
La lune blanche

FAURÉ
Avant que tu ne t'en ailles
La lune blanche luit dans les bois
N'est-ce pas?
HAHN *L'heure exquise*
KOECHLIN
Un jour de juin, que j'étais soucieux
N'est-ce pas?
Le soleil du matin
Va, chanson
STRAVINSKÏ *La bonne chanson*
CHANSONS POUR ELLE, no. 20.
HAHN *L'incrédule*
LE CIEL EST PARDESSUS LE TOIT.
VAUGHAN WILLIAMS *The sky above the roof*
EN SOURDINE.
CARPENTER *When the misty shadows glide*
FÊTES GALANTES.
DEBUSSY
Clair de lune
Two settings: 1882 and 1892.
Colloque sentimental
En sourdine
Two settings: 1882 and 1892.
Fantoches
Two settings: 1882 and 1892?
Le faune
Les Ingénus
Mandoline
Pantomime
FAURÉ
Clair de lune
En sourdine
Mandoline
HAHN
En sourdine
Fêtes galantes
GREEN.
HAHN *Offrande*
MES PRISONS: Sagesse III, no. 6.
HAHN *D'une prison*
PAYSAGES BELGES.
DEBUSSY *Chevaux de bois*
PAYSAGES TRISTES.
CASELLA, SÉVERAC *Soleils couchants*
POÈMES SATURNIENS.
CARPENTER, DELIUS, HAHN
Chanson d'automne
ROMANCES SANS PAROLES.
DEBUSSY
C'est l'extase langoureuse
L'ombre des arbres
FAURÉ *C'est l'extase . . .*
SAINT-SAËNS *Le vent dans la plaine*

COMPOSER Poet *Title* ''First Line''

SAGESSE.
> **CARPENTER** *Le ciel*
> **DEBUSSY** *Le son du cor s'afflige*
> **DELIUS** *Le ciel est, par-dessus la toit*
> **FAURÉ** *Prison*
> **LOEFFLER** *Le son du cor s'afflige vers les bois*
> **SÉVERAC** *Le ciel est, par-dessus le toit*

Verlass' mich nicht! see Osterwald **FRANZ**

Verlassen see Conradi *LIEDER EINES SÜNDERS.* 1. Teil, "Inferno."
> **SCHÖNBERG**

Verlassen see Michell *IRRWEGE*: Lied.
> **LISZT**

Verlassen see No author **BERG**

Verlassen hab ich mein Lieb see Engel, F.
> **REGER**

Der Verlassene see Anon. **FRANZ, SCHOECK**

Der Verlassene see Unknown
> **MENDELSSOHN-BARTHOLDY, WOLF**

Das verlassene Mägdlein see Mörike
> **PFITZNER**

Das verlassene Mägdlein see Mörike
> **LASSEN, PFITZNER, WOLF**

Das verlassne Mägdelein see Mörike
> **SCHUMANN**

Der Verliebte see Goethe **ZELTER** *Christel*
Der verliebte Jäger see Boelitz **REGER**
Der verliebte Maikäfer see Reinick **LOEWE**
Der verliebte Ostwind see Hafiz
> **SZYMANOWSKI**

Der verliebte Schäferin Scapine see Goethe
> **LOEWE**

Verlobung see Aldrich *THE BETROTHAL.*
> **LASSEN**

Der verlorene Haufen see Klemperer
> **SCHÖNBERG**

Die verlorene Tochter see Zuccalmaglio
> *DES KNABEN WUNDERHORN.* **LOEWE**

Verlorne Liebe see Galli **REGER**

Verlust see Heine **MENDELSSOHN-BARTHOLDY**

Verlust see Lemcke **RUBINSTEIN**
Verlust see Zimmermann, B. **SPOHR**
Verlust (Auf Mollys Tod, 1859) see Bürger
> **CORNELIUS**

Vernal equinox see Lowell, A. **THOMSON**
Vernehmet ihr? see Pushkin **RUBINSTEIN**
"Vernimm es, Nacht, was Ida dir vertrauet"
> *see Idens Nachtgesang* Kosegarten
> **SCHUBERT**

Verrat see Kaufmann **PFITZNER**
Verrat see Lemcke **BRAHMS**
Verrat see Vinje **GRIEG** *Et Vennestykke*
"Verrathen!" *see Der Liebewütige* Gubitz
> **WEBER**

Verrathene Liebe see Anon. **SCHUMANN**
Vers Béthléem see Le Moyne **MASSENET**
Vers le sud see Apollinaire
> *CALLIGRAMMES.* **POULENC**

VERSCHIEDENE-SERAPHINE, no. 12. *see*
> Heine *Mit schwarzen Segeln* **FRANZ, GRIFFES, WOLF**

Verschliedene Wege see Bodenstedt
> **RUBINSTEIN**

*Verschling' der Abgrund meines Liebste Hütte
see* Heyse **WOLF**

Der verschmachtende Pilger see Stieglitz
> **LOEWE**

Die Verschmähte see Falke **REGER**

"Verschneit liegt rings die ganze Welt" *see*
> *Winternacht* Eichendorff
> **MEDTNER, SCHOECK**

Die Verschweigung see Weisse **MOZART**
Verschwiegene Liebe see Eichendorff
> **LASSEN, WOLF**

Die verschwiegene Nachtigall see Walther
> von der Vogelweide **GRIEG, SPOHR**

Die Verschwiegenen see Gilm zu Rosenegg
> *LETZTE BLÄTTER.* **STRAUSS**

"Verschwunden sind die Schmerzen" *see*
> *Auf der Sieg der Deutschen* Unknown
> **SCHUBERT**

Der verspätete Wanderer see Eichendorff
> **PFITZNER, SCHOECK**

Die Verstossene see Gol'ts-Miller
> **MUSORGSKĬ** *Otverzhennaĭa*

Versuch in achtzeiligen Strophen see Goethe
> **ZELTER**

Versunken see Goethe *WESTÖSTLICHER DIVAN.* **SCHUBERT**

Versunken see Schumann, F. **BRAHMS**
"Le vert colibri, le roi des collines" *see*
> *Le colibri* Leconte de Lisle
> **CHAUSSON, KOECHLIN**

Verurteilt see Garborg *HAUGTUSSA.*
> **GRIEG** *Dømd*

Verwandlung see Schulze **SCHUMANN**
DIE VERWANDLUNGEN DER VENUS:
> Venus Mater. *see* Dehmel
> *Wiegenlied* **REGER, STRAUSS**

Verwelkende Rosen see Hesse **SCHOECK**
"Verwelkte Blätter, entseelte Götter" *see*
> *Herbstgefühl* Fleischer **BERG**

Der Verwundete see Vinje **GRIEG**
> *Den Saerde*

"Very old are the woods" *see All that's past*
> De La Mare **BERKELEY**

Verzagen see Lemcke **BRAHMS**
Der verzweifelte Liebhaber see Eichendorff
> **WOLF**

Verzweiflung see Nietzsche **MEDTNER**

COMPOSER Poet *Title* "First Line"

Verzweiflung see Tieck **BRAHMS**

Veselá dievča see Anon. **MARTINŮ**

"Veselo tsvetiki v pole pestreiut" *see Tsvetok*
Ratisbonne **CHAïKOVSKIï**

Veselyĭ chas see Kol'tsov **MUSORGSKIï**
Zastol'naĭa pesn'

Vesennee uspokoenie see Tiutchev
MEDTNER *Elegy*

Vesennie vody see Tiutchev
RACHMANINOFF *Spring waters*

Vesennyaya pesnya see Pleshcheyev
CHAïKOVSKIï

Vesle Gut see Janson **GRIEG**

Veslemøy see Garborg *HAUGTUSSA.*
GRIEG

Veslemøy Am Spinnrad see Garborg
HAUGTUSSA. **GRIEG** *Veslemøy ved
rokken*

Veslemøy lengtar see Garborg *HAUGTUSSA.*
GRIEG

Veslemøy sehnt sich see Garborg
HAUGTUSSA. **GRIEG** *Veslemøy lengtar*

Veslemøy undrast see Garborg
HAUGTUSSA. **GRIEG**

Veslemøy ved rokken see Garborg
HAUGTUSSA. **GRIEG**

Veslemøy's wandering see Garborg
HAUGTUSSA. **GRIEG** *Veslemøy undrast*

Vesna see Gorodetski **STRAVINSKIï**
Spring

Vesna see Pleshcheyev **CHAïKOVSKIï**
Two settings: Op. 54 no. 3 and op. 54 no.
9.

"Vesperzeit, Betgeläut' " *see Der Hirtenknabe*
Mörike **SCHOECK**

Veter pereletnyĭ see Bal'mont
RACHMANINOFF *The migrant wind*

"Vétus de blanc, Dans l'azur clair" *see
Les anges* Contamine **SATIE**

Le veuf see Hyspa **SATIE**

Veuillot, Louis François, 1813-1883.
GOUNOD *Dernières volontés*

La veuve andalouse see Pacini **ROSSINI**

"La veuve au corps de jeune fille" *see
Isis poignardée* Lanoux **SAUGUET**

"Veux-tu qu'au beau pays des rêves" *see
Le pays des rêves* Silvestre **FAURÉ**

"Vi Børn, vi vaagner" *see Bornehjaelpsdagens
Sang* Jørgensen **NIELSEN**

"Vi er Jyder, Børn af Landet" *see Vi Jyder*
Bartrumsen **NIELSEN**

"Vi fik ej under Tidernes" *see De unges Sang*
Hostrup **NIELSEN**

"Vi gik en dejlig vårdag" *see En fuglevise*
Ibsen **GRIEG**

"Vi gingo väl vilse ifran hvarann hvar togo de
andra vägen?" *see Vilse* Tavaststjerna
SIBELIUS

Vi Jyder see Bartrumsen *FRA ROLD TIL
REBILD.* **NIELSEN**

"Vi løfted din Rod!" *see Under Juletraeet*
Rolfsen **GRIEG**

"Vi ser på Taersklen os tilbage" *see Epilog*
Drachmann **GRIEG**

"Vi ser ud over hver en egn" *see Der gaar et
stille Tog* Balslev, Harald **NIELSEN**

Vi ses igen see Rydberg **SIBELIUS**

"Vi står og synge på Hamars Grav" *see
Paa Hamars Ruiner* Vinje **GRIEG**

Det vi ved at siden Slangens Gift see
Hostrup **NIELSEN**

VIAE INVIAE. see Jone
Das dunkle Herz **WEBERN**
Es stürzt aus Höhen Frische **WEBERN**
Herr Jesus mein **WEBERN**

Vicaire, Gabriel, 1848-1900.
HAHN *Cimetière de campagne*

Vicente, Gil, ca.1470-ca.1536.
RODRIGO *Cantiga*
WOLF *Wehe der, die mir verstrickte
meinen Geliebten!*
MUI GRACIOSA ES LA DONCELLA.
SCHUMANN *O wie lieblich ist das
Mädchen*
SANNOSA ESTA LA NINNA.
SCHUMANN *Weh, wie zornig ist das
Mädchen*
SPANISCHES LIEDERBUCH: Si dormis,
doncella.
JENSEN, WOLF *Und schläfst du, mein
Mädchen*

Victoire see Fournier **SAINT-SAËNS**

"Victoria! der kleine weisse Zahn ist da" *see
Der Zahn* Claudius, M. **LOEWE**

Vid en brunn see Österling **KILPINEN**

Vid stranden see Josephson, E. **KILPINEN**

Le vide de l'instant see Richter **SAUGUET**

"Un vide étrange et martel est dans mon âme"
see Désir d'amour Perpina, D. Francisco
SAINT-SAËNS

Videnie see Golenishchev-Kutuzov
SOMMERNACHT. **MUSORGSKIï**

I vidi in terra angelicicostumi see Petrarca
LISZT

Vidit Joannes Jesum venientem see Bible
HINDEMITH

La vie antérieure see Baudelaire **DUPARC**

Vie des campagnes see Follain **SAUGUET**

VIE DES CAMPAGNES, no. 1
SAUGUET Follain *Les images*

VIE DES CAMPAGNES, no. 2
SAUGUET Follain *Vie des campagnes*

VIE DES CAMPAGNES, no. 3
  SAUGUET Follain *Au pays*
VIE DES CAMPAGNES, no. 4
  SAUGUET Follain *Domaine d'homme*
VIE DES CAMPAGNES, no. 5
  SAUGUET Follain *Pensées d'octobre*
VIE DES CAMPAGNES, no. 6
  SAUGUET Follain *Eglogue*
VIE DES CAMPAGNES, no. 7
  SAUGUET Follain *Promeneur*
VIE DES CAMPAGNES, no. 8
  SAUGUET Follain *Effacement*
La vie d'une rose see Ruelle **MASSENET**
La vie est belle see Guillot de Saix **HAHN**
La vie est plate see Boudry, R. **JOLIVET**
La vie gaie see Hölderlin **SAUGUET**
"Vieil homme, vieil homme" *see Le chevalier*
  à l'armure étincelante Tardieu **SAUGUET**
Vieille chanson see Hugo *LE ROI S'AMUSE.*
  DELIBES
Vieille chanson see Millevoye **BIZET**
Vieille chanson d'amour (XV. siècle) see
  Anon. **LOEFFLER** *Old love song*
Vieille chanson espagnole see Houssaye
  AUBERT
Vieilles cartes, vieilles mains see Ville
  ROUSSEL
VIEILLES CHANSONS, no. 1
  SAINT-SAËNS Charles, Duke of
  Orleans *Temps nouveau*
VIEILLES CHANSONS, no. 2
  SAINT-SAËNS Belleau *Avril*
VIEILLES CHANSONS, no. 3
  SAINT-SAËNS Vauquelin *Villanelle*
Vieilles lettres see Normand **MASSENET**
Viel Glück zur Reise, Schwalben see
  Kulmann **SCHUMANN**
Viel Träume see Hamerling **BERG,**
  LASSEN
"Viel Vögel sind geflogen" *see Viel Träume*
  Hamerling **LASSEN**
"Viele Gaeste wüns ich heut" *see*
  Das Gastmahl Goethe **ZELTER**
"Viele Glokken hör ich läuten" *see*
  Die Glocke des Glücks Ritter **REGER**
"Viele Vögel sind geflogen" *see Viel Träume*
  Hamerling **BERG**
"Vielfach sind zum Hades die Pfade" *see*
  Erinna an Sappho Mörike **SCHOECK**
Vielgeliebte schöne Frau see Heine
  LIEDERSTRAUSS. **BERG**
Der vielschönen Fraue see Eichendorff
  FRANZ
"Viena, Ô le désiré" *see Amoureux appel*
  Dubor **MASSENET**
Viene di là, lontan lontano . . . see Birga,
  Arturo *RISPETTI TOSCANI.* **RESPIGHI**

"Vieni O Ruggiero" *see L'invito* Pepoli
  ROSSINI
Viens! see Lamartine **LALO**
"Viens à moi! viens à moi!" *see La chanson*
  de la rose Barbier, J. **BIZET**
"Viens! c'est le jour d'un Dieu" *see Lydé*
  Leconte de Lisle **HAHN**
"Viens, cherchons une ombre propice" *see*
  Chant d'amour Lamartine **BIZET**
"Viens! cherchons une ombre propice, viens!"
  see Viens! Lamartine **LALO**
"Viens enfant, la terre s'éveille" *see Chanson*
  de printemps Tourneux, Eugène
  GOUNOD
Viens, je te mettrai see Jammes **MILHAUD**
Viens, les gazons sont verts see Barbier, J.
  GOUNOD
"Viens! l'heure est procice" *see Barcarolle*
  Guinand **DEBUSSY**
"Viens, lorsque dans l'azur" *see Hymne à la*
  nuit Barbier, J. **GOUNOD**
Viens, mon coeur see Bible **GOUNOD**
  My beloved spake
"Viens plus près, tout près t'asseoir" *see*
  Si tu l'oses Mansilla, Daniel Garcia
  MASSENET
"Viens tout près et chante" *see Au rossignol*
  Guillot de Saix **HAHN**
"Viens! une flûte invisible" *see L'Églogue*
  Hugo **DELIBES**
"Vier adlige Rosse voran unserm Wagen" *see*
  Ich liebe dich Liliencron **STRAUSS**
VIER DEUTSCHE VOLKSLIEDER, no. 1
  SCHÖNBERG Anon. *Der Mai tritt ein*
  mit Freuden
VIER DEUTSCHE VOLKSLIEDER, no. 2
  SCHÖNBERG Anon. *Es gingen zwei*
  Gespielen gut
VIER DEUTSCHE VOLKSLIEDER, no. 3
  SCHÖNBERG Anon. *Mein Herz ist mir*
  gemenget
VIER DEUTSCHE VOLKSLIEDER, no. 4
  SCHÖNBERG Anon. *Mein Herz in steten*
  Treuen
Vier Lieder see Claudius, M., Hardenberg,
  Rückert, Scheffler **HINDEMITH**
  NB: 4 sets of unpublished songs; apparently
  the texts of each set are by a single poet.
VIER LIEDER NACH GEDICHTEN VON
  FRIEDRICH NIETZSCHE, no. 1
  DELIUS Nietzsche *Nach neuen Meeren*
VIER LIEDER NACH GEDICHTEN VON
  FRIEDRICH NIETZSCHE, no. 2
  DELIUS Nietzsche *Der Wanderer*
VIER LIEDER NACH GEDICHTEN VON
  FRIEDRICH NIETZSCHE, no. 3
  DELIUS Nietzsche *Der Einsame*

COMPOSER Poet *Title* "First Line"

VIER LIEDER NACH GEDICHTEN VON FRIEDRICH NIETZSCHE, no. 4
DELIUS Nietzsche *Der Wanderer und sein Schatten*
Vier trübe Monden sind entfloh'n see
Unknown **MENDELSSOHN-BARTHOLDY**
Die vier Weltalter see Schiller **SCHUBERT, ZELTER**
Vierge d'Athènes see Byron **GOUNOD**
Maid of Athens
"La vierge étoile est effacée" *see Éveil*
Gassier **MASSENET**
"Vierge, tes cheveux noirs dépassent ta ceinture" *see Chant de guerre cosaque*
Văcărescu **MASSENET**
"Les vierges fleurs ouvrant leur minces corsets verts" *see Secret aveu* Haraucourt
AUBERT
"Vieux canard, vieux canard, sors" *see Canard* Anon. **STRAVINSKIĭ**
"Un vieux faune de terre cuite" *see Le faune*
Verlaine **DEBUSSY**
Le vieux vagabond see Béranger **LALO, LISZT**
"Le vif oeil dont tu regardes" *see La Marchande d'habits* Mallarmé
MILHAUD
Vigil see De La Mare **BRITTEN**
Vigilia Nuziale see Cocconi, Ildebrando
PIZZETTI
LES VIGNES DANS MURAILLE. see
Verhaeren *L'éveil de Pâques* **SÉVERAC**
Viikon vuottelin käkeä see Kanteletar
KILPINEN
Vikhodi ko mne, signora see Anon.
RIMSKIĭ-KORSAKOV
Le vilain petit canard see Andersen
PROKOFIEV *Gadkiĭ utenok"*
Vilde, K. *see* Wilde, Ch.
"Vildgjaes, Vildgjaes i hvide Flokker" *see Mens jeg venter* Krag **GRIEG**
Vildrac, Charles, 1882-1971.
MILHAUD
Le jardinier impatient
Le malpropre
La pomme et l'escargot
Poupette et Patata
Les quatre petits lions
LIVRE D'AMOUR.
IBERT
Après minuit
Comme elle a les yeux bandés
Elle était venue sur les marches tièdes
SCHMITT *Elle était venue sur les marches tièdes*

Vile potabis see Le conte de Lisle **HAHN**
Vilenkin, Nikolay Maksimovich, 1855-1937.
RACHMANINOFF
In my soul
She is as lovely as the moon
RUBINSTEIN *Serenada*
Villa, José Garcia, 1914-1997.
HAVE COME, AM HERE.
BARBER *Monks and raisins*
Villanelle see Gautier **BERLIOZ**
Villanelle see Leconte de Lisle
KOECHLIN
Two settings: Op. 21 no. 1 and op. 21 no. 2.
Villanelle see Vauquelin **SAINT-SAËNS**
Villanelle des petits canards see Rostand, R.
CHABRIER
La ville see Jacob, M. **SAUGUET**
Ville, Georges, 1824-1897.
ROUSSEL
Si quelquefois tu pleures . . .
Vieilles cartes, vieilles mains
"Ville, oeil puant, minuits obliques" *see Minuit pile et face* Messiaen **MESSIAEN**
La ville qui dormait, toi see Messiaen
MESSIAEN
Villeurs, Jean de *see* Hardÿ de Périni, Édouard, 1843-1908.
Villiers de l'Isle-Adam, Jean Marie Mathias . . . , comte de, 1838-1889.
CHAUSSON *L'aveu*
FAURÉ
Nocturne
Les présents
KOECHLIN *Hymne à Venus*
MARTINŮ *Old song*
Villon, François, b.1431.
MESSIAEN
Ballade des pendus
Epître à ses amis
LE TESTAMENT.
DEBUSSY
Ballade de Villon à s'amye
Ballade des femmes de Paris
Ballade que Villon feit à requeste de sa mère . . .
Vilmorin, Louise de, 1902-1969.
AURIC
Attendez le prochain bateau
Le châle
La jeune sanguine
MILHAUD *Ballade-nocturne*
POULENC
Aus-delà
Aux officiers de la Garde Blanche

COMPOSER Poet *Title* "First Line"

C'est ainsi que tu es
La dame d'André
Dans l'herbe
Fleurs
Le garçon de Liège
Il vole
Mazurka
Mon cadavre est doux comme un gant
Paganini
Reine des mouettes
Violon
  SAUGUET
  Postlude: Polonaise
  Prelude
Vilse see Tavaststjerna **SIBELIUS**
Vimioso, Francisco de Portugal, conde
  de, d.1549.
  SCHUMANN *Geständnis*
Le vin see Banville **KOECHLIN**
Le vin see Valéry **SAUGUET**
Le vin perdu see Valéry **MOMPOU**
Vincendon, Mireille
  ALEXANDRIE.
  SCHMITT *Antennes*
Vincenette see Barbier, Pierre **GOUNOD**
"Vingt-huit cheminées rouges dansent sur le
  toit" *see Les cheminées rouge* Havet
  CARPENTER
Vingtrie, Jean de
  MASSENET *Ce que disent les cloches*
Vinje, Aasmund Olavsson, 1818-1870.
  GRIEG
  Attegløyma
  Eit Syn
  Et Vennestykke
  Det Første
  Fyremål
  Gamle Mor
  Guten
  Jenta
  Langs ei Å
  Paa Hamars Ruiner
  Den Saerde
  Trudom
  Tyteberet
  Våren
  IVES *The old mother*
  FERDAMINNI.
  DELIUS *Auf der Reise zur Heimat*
  GRIEG *Ved Rondane*
Vinogradov
  BORODIN *Razlyubila krasna devitsa*
Viol, Wilhelm, i.e., Friedrich Wilhelm,
  1817-1874.
  FRANZ *Ein Gruss von Ihr!*
Viola see Schober **SCHUBERT**

Viola d'amour see Falke **REGER**
The violet see Goethe **MEDTNER**
  Das Veilchen
The violet see Holstein **DELIUS**
  Das Veilchen
The violet sea see Lanier **RIEGGER**
"Violets and leaves of vine" *see A coronal*
  Dowson **QUILTER**
La violette see Daudet, L. **MILHAUD**
"La violette cyclope se force" *see La violette*
  Daudet, L. **MILHAUD**
Violon see Vilmorin **POULENC**
"Violon, hippocampe et sirène" *see Paganini*
  Vilmorin **POULENC**
Violons dans le soir see Noailles
  SAINT-SAËNS
Virgil see Vergilius Maro, Publius, 70
  B.C.-19 B.C.
The Virgin's cradle song see Coleridge
  VAUGHAN WILLIAMS *Cradle song*
Visa see Blomberg **KILPINEN**
Le visage penché see Toussaint *JARDIN*
  DES CARESSES. **AUBERT**
Vischer, Friedrich Theodor von, 1807-
  1887.
  RUBINSTEIN *Mädchens Abendgedanken*
Vise af "Mogens" see Jacobsen **NIELSEN**
"Vishnevyĭ sadik vozle khaty" *see Vecher*
  Shevchenko **CHAĬKOVSKIĬ**
Vision see Golenishchev-Kutuzov
  SOMMERNACHT. **MUSORGSKIĬ** *Videnie*
Vision see Khomyakov **BALAKIREV**
  Bezzvezdnaya polnoch'
Vision see Platen-Hallermünde
  CORNELIUS
Visions see Pushkin **MEDTNER**
VISIONS INFERNALES, no. 1
  SAUGUET Jacob, M. *Voyage*
VISIONS INFERNALES, no. 2
  SAUGUET Jacob, M. *Voisinage*
VISIONS INFERNALES, no. 3
  SAUGUET Jacob, M. *Que penser de mon*
  salut
VISIONS INFERNALES, no. 4
  SAUGUET Jacob, M. *Régates*
  mystérieuses
VISIONS INFERNALES, no. 5
  SAUGUET Jacob, M. *Le petit paysan*
VISIONS INFERNALES, no. 6
  SAUGUET Jacob, M. *Exhortation*
Visions of heaven I fondly paint see Hálek
  DVOŘÁK *Když jsem se díval do*
  nebe
Visits to St. Elizabeths see Bishop **ROREM**
Visored see Whitman **LUENING**
La Vistule see Unknown **POULENC**

COMPOSER Poet *Title* "First Line"

"La Vistule arrose toute la Pologue" *see*
  La Vistule Unknown **POULENC**
Vita see Manilius *ASTRONOMICA,* Book 4,
  livre 16. **IVES**
La vita fugge see Petrarca **PIZZETTI**
VITA NUOVA. see Dante
  Du, des Erbarmens Feind, grausamer Tod
    SCHOECK
Le vitrier see Mallarmé **MILHAUD**
Vitsippan see Franzén **SIBELIUS** *Hvitsippan*
Vittorelli, Jacopo, 1749-1835.
  ROREM
    Guarda che bianca luna!
    Non t'accostare all'urna
    O platano felice
    Zitto, La Bella Irene
  SCHUBERT
    Guarda, che bianca luna
    Non t'accostare all'urna
  VERDI
    In solitaria stanza
    Non t'accostare all'urna
Viva la novia y el novio! see Anon.
  RODRIGO
Vivanti, Annie, 1868-1942.
  RESPIGHI *Abbandono*
Vive la France see Dérouléde **GOUNOD**
Vive la France see Fournier **SAINT-SAËNS**
"Vive la France! O mon pays" *see Vive la*
  France Dérouléde **GOUNOD**
Vive Paris, vive la France see Tranchant,
  Alfred **SAINT-SAËNS**
"Vivent les gars polonais que personne
  n'égale" *see Les gars polonais* Unknown
  POULENC
"Vivent les vacances!" *see Les vacances*
  Bigorie, L. **GOUNOD**
Vivien, Renée, 1877-1907.
  AUBERT
    Aigues-Marines
    Feuilles sur l'eau
    Nuit mauresque
    Roses du soir
  KOECHLIN *Des roses sur la mer*
Le vivier see Chalupt **RIVIER**
VIZOV. see Polonsky
  Za oknom v teni mel'kaet **CHAЇKOVSKIЇ**
"Vlaty zakovan, Vshleme zlatom" *see Rȳsar*
  Wilde, Ch. **BALAKIREV**
Vlčkova ukolébavka see Liliencron
  MARTINŮ *The spinning top's lullaby*
Vlinderliedje see Bruyn, Bertha de **PIJPER**
Vnoci see Mayer, R. **MARTINŮ** *At night*
"Vnov' ia posetil tot ugolok zemlia" *see Sosny*
  Pushkin **PROKOFIEV**
"Vo sadu, akh, vo sadochke" *see Detskaia*
  pesenka Mei **MUSORGSKIЇ**

"Vobia t'iakh devy molodoĭ" *see Pesn'*
  Baleartsa Musorgskiĭ, M.
  MUSORGSKIЇ
Vocalise see No author **AURIC,**
  COPLAND, FAURÉ, INDY, MESSIAEN,
  MILHAUD, POULENC,
  RACHMANINOFF
Vocalise en si bémol see No author
  SCHMITT
Vocalise no. 1 see No author **ROUSSEL**
Vocalise no. 2 see No author **ROUSSEL**
Vocalise pour ténor see No author **BIZET**
Vocalise-etude see No author **HONEGGER,**
  SZYMANOWSKI
Vocalise-étude see No author **IBERT,**
  KILPINEN, MARTINŮ, NIELSEN,
  PIZZETTI
Vocalise-Étude en forme de Habanera see
  No author **RAVEL**
Vocalises see
  No author **DIAMOND**
Vocalizaciones see No author **TURINA**
Vocalizzo see No author **PIZZETTI**
Die Vögel see Schlegel, F. *ABENDRÖTE.*
  SCHUBERT
"Ein Vögelein fliegt über den Rhein" *see*
  Auf dem Schiffe Köstlin **BRAHMS**
Das Vöglein see Hebbel **WOLF**
Das Vöglein see Unknown **LOEWE**
"Das Vöglein auf dem Baum" *see O Herz in*
  meiner Brust! Mayer, K. **FRANZ**
"Die Vöglein, die so fröhlich sangen" *see*
  Nacht Eichendorff **JENSEN**
"Vöglein, einsam in dem Bauer" *see*
  Die gefangenen Sänger Schenkendorf
  WEBER
"Vöglein fliegt dem Nestchen zu" *see*
  Wiegenlied Cornelius **CORNELIUS**
"Vöglein hüpfet in dem Haine" *see Die freien*
  Sänger Förster, F. **WEBER**
Vöglein Schwermut see Morgenstern
  KILPINEN
"Das Vöglein singt den ganzen Tag" *see*
  Sangeslust Eberwein **SPOHR**
  Two settings: Op. 101 no. 2 and WoO 95.
"Ein Vöglein singt im Wald" *see Volkslied*
  Ritter **REGER**
"Vöglein vom Zweig gaukelt hernieder" *see*
  Das Vöglein Hebbel **WOLF**
Vöglein, wohin so schnell? see Geibel
  FRANZ, LASSEN
Voeu see Hugo **BIZET**
Voeu see Régnier **ROUSSEL**
"Ein Vogel auf dem Buchenzweig" *see*
  Waldlied Winther **GRIEG**
Ein Vogel schrie see Krag **GRIEG**
  Der skreg en Fugl

Vogelgesang see Tieck *WALD, GARTEN UND BERG.* **LOEWE**
Ein Vogellied see Ibsen **GRIEG** *En fuglevise*
Eine Vogelweise see Ibsen *EN FUGLEVISE.*
    DELIUS
Vogl, Johann Nepomuk, 1802-1866.
    LOEWE
       Der alte König
       Der alte Schiffsherr
       Am Klosterbrunne
       Das Erkennen
       Der Gesang
       Heinrich der Vogler
       Heuska
       Die Kaiserjagd im Wienerwald
       Der Mönch zu Pisa
       Die Schwanenjungfrau
       Die schwarzen Augen
       Urgrossvaters Gesellschaft
       Das Vaterland
       Die verfallene Mühle
       Das vergessene Lied
    STRAUSS *Waldkonzert*
    SCHNEEGLÖCKCHEN.
    LOEWE *Blumenballade*
    WITEKIND.
    LOEWE *Karl der Grosse und Wittekind*
Vogue, vogue la galère see Aicard
    SAINT-SAËNS
Voguons sur les flots see Unknown
    GOUNOD
Voi jos mie tok' miehen saisin see Kanteletar
    KILPINEN
Voi minua mieskulua see Kanteletar
    KILPINEN
"*Voi nuo narrit nuoret miehet*" *see Köyhän lapset* Kanteletar **KILPINEN**
A voice by the cedar tree see Tennyson
    SAINT-SAËNS
The voice of the birds see Bal'mont
    PROKOFIEV *Golos'' ptits''*
The voice of the mountain see Heine
    MEDTNER *Bergstimme*
VOICE, VIOLA & PIANO.
    LASSEN *Storm Die Waldbrüder*
Voices at the window see Sidney, Sir Philip
    RIETI
"*Voices live in every finite being*" *see The innate* Ives **IVES**
"*Voici de nouveau la petite voiture devant la porte*" *see Le retour* Paliard **MILHAUD**
"*Voici des fruits, des fleurs, des feuilles et des branches*" *see Green* Verlaine **DEBUSSY, FAURÉ, HAHN**
"*Voici la fine sauterelle*" *see La sauterelle* Apollinaire **POULENC**

Voici le chemin de la vie see Luka, Madeleine **SAUGUET**
"*Voici le soleil qui se lève*" *see Bon jour, bon soir* Spenner, M. **GOUNOD**
"*Voici l'heure du mystère*" *see Sérénade aux mariés* Ruelle **MASSENET**
"*Voici l'orme qui balance*" *see Infidélité* Gautier **HAHN**
"*Voici mes plus beaux*" *see Enfance* Fargue **AURIC**
Voici noël see Unknown **RESPIGHI**
"*Voici que le printemps, ce fils léger d'Avril*" *see Romance: Voici que le printemps* Bourget **DEBUSSY**
Voici que les grand lys see Silvestre *MIGNONNE.* **MASSENET**
"*Voici que les jardins de la nuit vont fleurir*" *see Soir* Samain **FAURÉ**
"*Voici, sur mon déclin*" *see Passiflora* Chambrun **GOUNOD**
"*Voici ton Jean, ton Jean*" *see Albado* Marguerite d'Angoulême **SÉVERAC**
"*Voici venir le doux printemps*" *see Pastorale* Silvestre **MASSENET**
"*Voici venir le joli mai*" *see Chanson de quête* Anon. **VAUGHAN WILLIAMS**
"*Voici venir les temps où vibrant sur sa tige*" *see Harmonie du soir* Baudelaire **DEBUSSY**
Voigt, Christian Friedrich Traugott, 1770-1814.
    WEBER *An eine Freudin*
"*Voilà les feuilles sans sève qui tombent sur le gazon*" *see Seul* Lamartine **GOUNOD**
Voilà où mon âme en est venue see Catullus **MILHAUD**
"*Voilà Silvandre et Lycas et Myrtil*" *see Fête galante* Banville **AURIC**
"*Voilà Sylvandre et Lucas et Myrtil*" *see Fête galante* Banville **DEBUSSY**
Le vois amical see Valéry **SAUGUET**
"*Vois! cette mer si calme a comme un bouclier*" *see Les rêves morts* Leconte de Lisle **KOECHLIN**
Vois, de belles filles see Huang-Fu-Ian **ROUSSEL**
"*Vois ma belle sur ma lance*" *see L'adieu* Unknown **POULENC**
"*Vois, sur les violettes*" *see Le rossignol* Banville **SAINT-SAËNS**
Voisinage see Jacob, M. **SAUGUET**
"*Vois-tu là-bas sur le chemin*" *see L'improvisatore* Zaffira **MASSENET**
La voix see Gabory **AURIC**
Voix d'Alsace-Lorraine see Rousseil, R. **GOUNOD**

Voix de femmes see Pierre d'Amor
   MASSENET
"Voix des mamans, voix câlineuses" *see Voix*
   de femmes Pierre d'Amor **MASSENET**
"La voix d'un démon familier" *see La voix*
   Gabory **AURIC**
LES VOIX INTÉRIEURES. see Hugo
   La tombe dit à la rose **WAGNER**
Voix suprême see Lafait-Gontié, Antoinette
   MASSENET
"Voli l'agile barchetta" *see La gita in gondola*
   Pepoli **ROSSINI**
Volker spielt auf! see Mörike **FRANZ**
Volkmann, Richard von, 1830-1889.
   MAHLER
      Erinnerung
      Frühlingsmorgen
   PFITZNER
      In der Früh, wenn die Sonne kommen
         will
      Ist der Himmel darum im Lenz so blau
Volkslied see Anon. **BRAHMS, FRANZ,**
   WEBER
      Two Weber settings: Op. 54 no. 6 and op.
      54 no. 7.
Volkslied see Anon. *FLIEGENDES BLATT.*
   WEBER
Volkslied see Feuchtersleben
   MENDELSSOHN-BARTHOLDY
Volkslied see Itzerott **REGER**
Volkslied see Ritter **REGER**
Volksliedchen see Rückert **SCHUMANN**
Volksmelodie aus Langeland see Andersen
   GRIEG *Langelandsk Folkemelodi*
"Voll jener Süsse" *see Zweiundneunzigstes*
   Sonnet von Petrarca Petrarca **PFITZNER**
"Voll Locken kraus ein Haupt so rund" *see*
   Versunken Goethe **SCHUBERT**
"Vollende denn das letzte Lied" *see Das letzte*
   Lied Tagore **SZYMANOWSKI**
"Voller, dichter tropft ums Dach da" *see*
   Während des Regens Kopisch **BRAHMS**
Der Vollmond scheint see Löns **KILPINEN**
"Der Vollmond scheint in mein Fenster" *see*
   Der Vollmond scheint Löns **KILPINEN**
"Voltigez Hirondelles voltigez près de moi"
   see Les Hirondelles d'Hotelier, A.
   LOEFFLER
THE VOLUNTEER. see Asquith
   Epitaph: The clerk **BRITTEN**
Volutta see Olkienizkaia-Naldi
   LO SPECCHIO. **CASELLA**
Vom Auge zum Herzen see Rückert **FRANZ**
"Vom Baum des Lebens fällt" *see*
   Vergänglichkeit Hesse **KILPINEN,**
   SCHOECK

"Vom Berg der Knab, der zieht hinab" *see*
   Knabentod Hebbel **WOLF**
"Vom Berg hinab gestiegen" *see Wiegenlied*
   im Sommer Reinick **WOLF**
Vom Berge see Osterwald **FRANZ**
"Vom Berge was kommt dort um Mitternacht
   spät" *see Die Geister am Mummelsee*
   Mörike **WOLF**
Vom Ende see Puttkamer **BERG**
"Vom Freundeszweig getrennt" *see*
   Das Blättchen Zhukovski **RUBINSTEIN**
VOM GESCHLECHT DER PROMETHIDEN.
   see Jacobowski
   Hymnus der Liebe **REGER**
"Vom Himmel ist der Frühlingsregen
   herabgerauscht" *see Frühlingsmorgen*
   Förstner **REGER**
"Vom Himmel zogen rauschend viel runde
   Tropfen sacht" *see Menschenlose* Frankl
   LOEWE
Vom künftigen Alter see Rückert **STRAUSS**
VOM KÜNFTIGEN ALTER. see Rückert
   Greisengesang **SCHUBERT**
Vom Küssen! see Ritter *JUGEND.* **REGER**
"Vom Lager stand ich mit dem Frühlicht auf"
   see Aus: Ein Tagewerk I Keller, G.
   SCHOECK
"Vom Meere trennt sich die Welle" *see*
   Leiden der Trennung Metastasio
   SCHUBERT
Vom Mitleiden Mariae see Schlegel, F.
   SCHUBERT
Vom Monte Pincio see Bjørnson **GRIEG**
   Fra Monte Pincio
Vom Reitersmann see Anon. **SCHUMANN**
Vom Schlaraffenland see Hoffmann von
   Fallersleben **SCHUMANN**
Vom Strande see Eichendorff **LASSEN**
Vom Strande, Nach dem Spanischen *see*
   Eichendorff **BRAHMS**
"Vom Taue glänzt der Rasen" *see*
   Des Morgens Hölderlin **HINDEMITH**
Vom Tode see Gellert **BEETHOVEN**
Vom Tode Mariä see Rilke **HINDEMITH**
   Three settings: Op. 27 IVa, IVb, and IVc.
Vom verwundeten Knaben see Anon.
   BRAHMS
Von allen deinen zarten Gaben see Unknown
   MENDELSSOHN-BARTHOLDY
"Von allen schönen Kindern auf der Welt" *see*
   O Jugend, O schöne Rosenzeit! Anon.
   MENDELSSOHN-BARTHOLDY
"Von allen schönen Waaren zum Markte" *see*
   Wer kauft Liebesgötter? Goethe **ZELTER**
"Von allen schönen Waren" *see Wer kauft*
   Liebesgötter? Goethe **SCHUBERT**

COMPOSER   Poet   *Title*   "First Line"

"Von deinem Bilde nur umschwebet" *see*
Nachtständchen Mayer, Dr. LOEWE

"Von dem Berg" *see Jerusalems Zerstörung
durch Titus* Byron LOEWE

"Von dem Berge zu den Hügeln" *see
Wanderlied* Goethe WOLF

"Von dem Garten altan keucht zum Schlosse"
see Der Woywode Mickiewicz LOEWE

Von den sieben Zechbrüdern see Uhland
STRAUSS

"Von der Last" *see Flötenspielerin*
Altenberg BERG

Von der Liebe see Ginzkey REGER

"Von der Strasse her ein Posthorn klingt" *see
Die Post* Müller, Wilhelm SCHUBERT

"Von der Tafel rinnt der Wein" *see Nach dem
Fest* Hesse KILPINEN

"Von der Wartburg Zinnen nieder" *see
Weimars Volkslied* Cornelius LISZT

"Von der zarten Kinder Händen" *see Brautlied*
Brumm, Pauline LOEWE

"Von des Hügels kahlem Rücken" *see
Der ewige Jude* Schreiber LOEWE

"Von diesem Kreis" *see Fünf Sinnsprüche
Omars des Zeltmachers* Omar Khayyam
BLACHER

"Von dir getrennet, liege ich begraben" *see
Geisterleben* Uhland LOEWE

Von dunklem Schleier umsponnen see Schack
STRAUSS

Von ewiger Liebe see Wenzig BRAHMS

"Von fern die Uhren schlagen" *see Auf meines
Kindes Tod* Eichendorff SCHOECK

"Von Ferne tönt der Glokkenschlag" *see
Verzweiflung* Nietzsche MEDTNER

Von Händlern wird die Kunst bedroht see
Kerr STRAUSS

Von Ida see Kosegarten *AGNES.*
SCHUBERT

"Von mehr als einer Seite verwaist" *see
Fragment* Goethe KRENEK

Von meines Hauses engen Wänden see
Giesebrecht LOEWE

von Salis, Johann Gaudenz *see*
Salis-Seewis, Johann Gaudenz,
Freiherr von, 1762-1834.

"Von stillem Ort" *see Angedenken* Cornelius
CORNELIUS

"Von Süd und Ost belagert stürmisch unsre
Alpen" *see Unser Wein* Krenek KRENEK

"Von Wald umgeben ein Blütenbaum" *see
Bild der Liebe* Frey, F. WEBERN

Von waldbekränzter Hohe see Daumer
FRAUENBILDER UND HULDIGUNGEN.
BRAHMS

"Von wem ich es habe" *see Geheimnis*
Goethe ZELTER

"Von wem ich's habe" *see Vor Gericht*
Goethe MEDTNER

Von zwei Rosen see Morgenstern
KILPINEN

Vond Dag see Garborg *HAUGTUSSA.*
GRIEG

Vor dem Fenster see Anon. BRAHMS

Vor dem Schlafengehen see Musorgskiĭ
MUSORGSKIĬ *Na son griadushiĭ'*

"Vor dem Schlosse Don Loranca's" *see
Heuska* Vogl LOEWE

Vor dem Sterben see Boelitz REGER

Vor dem Tod see Krenek KRENEK

Vor der Ernte see Meyer SCHOECK

Vor der Hochzeit zu Kana see Rilke
HINDEMITH

Vor der Passion see Rilke HINDEMITH

"Vor der Tür im Sonnenscheine" *see Gretel*
Busse PFITZNER

"Vor dir, O Gott" *see Gebet* Voss ZELTER

Vor dir schein' ich aufgewacht see
Morgenstern HINDEMITH

Vor Gericht see Goethe MEDTNER

"Vor Kälte ist die Luft erstarrt" *see
Winternacht* Lenau FRANZ

"Vor lauter hochadligen Zeugen" *see
Bei einer Trauung* Mörike WOLF

"Vor mein Bett wirft der Mond" *see
In der Herberge* Li Po SCHOECK

"Vor meinem Fenster dämmert das trübe
Mondenlicht" *see Nachtgruss* Kugler
JENSEN

"Vor meinem Fenster regt" *see Wenn ich's
nur wüsste* Osterwald FRANZ

"Vor meinem Fenster schläft die Nacht" *see
Notturno* Boelitz REGER

Vor meiner Wiege see Leitner SCHUBERT

"Vor seinem Heergefolge ritt der kühne Held
Harald!" *see Harald* Uhland LOEWE

"Vor seinem Löwengarten" *see
Der Handschuh* Schiller SCHUMANN

"Vor seinem Löwengarten" *see
Der Handschuh; eine Erzälung* Schiller
ZELTER

"Vor seiner Hütte ruhig im Schatten sitzt" *see
Abendphantasie* Hölderlin HINDEMITH

Vor Tau und Tag see Sergel KILPINEN

"Vor Thebens siebenfach gähnenden Toren"
see Amphiaraos Körner SCHUBERT

Vor Verden priser jeg tusindfold see Møller
NIELSEN

Vorabend see Cornelius CORNELIUS

Vorbei see Unknown LASSEN

"Vorbei der Rosen Prangen" *see Im Herbst*
Träger JENSEN

"Vorbei, vorbei durch Feld und Wald" *see
Die Waldhexe* Boddien, G. von
RUBINSTEIN

Vorbeimarsch see Boelitz **REGER**

Vorfrühling see Avenarius *STIMMEN UND BILDER.* Jahrbuch. **WEBERN**

Vorfrühling see Zwehl, Hans Fritz von **KILPINEN**

Vorfrühling II see Avenarius *STIMMEN UND BILDER.* Jahrbuch. **WEBERN**

Vorgesang see Mei **BALAKIREV** *Zapevka*

"Der Vorhang schwebet hin und her" *see Selbstbetrug* Goethe **MEDTNER, SCHOECK**

Voron see Pushkin **MEDTNER** *The ravens*

Vorona see Unknown **STRAVINSKĬ** *Le corbeau*

"Vorota tesovy rastvorilisia" *see Pirushka* Kol'tsov **MUSORGSKĬ**

Vorrei voler, Signor, quel ch'io non voglio see Buonarroti **PIZZETTI**

Vorsatz see Prutz **LASSEN**

Vorschneller Schwur see Kapper **BRAHMS**

Vorüber see Hebbel **BRAHMS**

Vorüber see Wisbacher **BERG**

"Vorüber, ach vorüber" *see Der Tod und das Mädchen* Claudius, M. **SCHUBERT**

Vorüber der Mai see Förster, M. **FRANZ**

"Vorüber die Flut" *see Am Strande* Rilke **SCHÖNBERG**

"Vorüber die stöhnende Klage!" *see Elysium* Schiller **SCHUBERT**

"Vorüber ist der blut'ge Strauss" *see Die Räuberbrüder* Eichendorff **CORNELIUS**

Vorwurf see Hesse **SCHOECK**

Vorwurf see Leuthold **SCHOECK**

"Vos destins sont pour l'homme" *see Les Alcyons* Autran **MASSENET**

Vos me matásteis see Anon. **RODRIGO**

"Vos yeux clos, votre main lasse" *see Soir d'été* Jacob, **M. RIETI**

Voskreshenie lazaria see Khomyakov **RACHMANINOFF** *The raising of Lazarus*

Vospominanie see Pushkin **MEDTNER** *Retrospect*

Voss, Johann Heinrich, 1751-1826.
  LOEWE
    Frühlingslied
    Minnelied
  MENDELSSOHN-BARTHOLDY
    Abendlied
    Frage
    Im Grünen
    Morgenlied
    Scheidend
  WEBER
    Minnelied
    Reigen

ZELTER
  Abendlied
  Die Bewegung
  Die Braut am Gestade
  Friedensreigen
  Gebet
  Die Gegend am Meer
  Die Landlust
  Morgenlied
  Rundgesang auf dem Wasser
  Rundgesang beim Rheinwein
  Das Tagewerk ist abgetan

"Vot" minovala razluka unylaia" *see Pervoe svidanie* Konstantin **CHAĬKOVSKĬ**

"Votre âme est un paysage choisi" *see Clair de lune* Verlaine **DEBUSSY, FAURÉ** Two Debussy settings: 1882 and 1892.

"Vouch-safe, O Lord, to bless the pauper" *see The pauper* Tiutchev **MEDTNER**

Vous aimerez demain see Silvestre *MIGNONNE.* **MASSENET**

"Vous aimerez un jour peutêtre ce vivagre" *see La menace* Régnier **ROUSSEL**

"Vous aurez la fleur d'oranger" *see Et puis* Chassang, Maurice **MASSENET**

"Vous avez la splendeur sereine des grandes dames d'autrefois" *see Fière beauté* Mahot, A. **SAINT-SAËNS**

"Vous en souvenez-vous, Marquise?" *see Marquise* Silvestre **MASSENET**

"Vous en souvient-il, Madeleine" *see Printemps dernier* Gille **MASSENET**

"Vous êtes belle comme un ange" *see Madrigal* Anon. **POULENC**

"Vous êtes grande de tout" *see Madrigal lyrique* Régnier **ROUSSEL**

"Vous m'avez dit en mots de flamme" *see Pourquoi?* Guilliaume **LASSEN**

Vous m'avez regardé avec tout votre âme see Jammes *TRISTESSES.* **BOULANGER, MILHAUD**

"Vous me demandez de me taire" *see Toujours* Grandmougin **FAURÉ**

"Vous méprisez nature!" *see Sonnet* Ronsard **BIZET**

Vous ne priez pas see Delavigne **BIZET**

Vous n'écrivez plus? see Jacob, M. **POULENC**

"Vous passez la-haut dans la lumière" *see Chant du Destin* Hölderlin **SAUGUET**

Vous qui passez see Bourguignat, Paul **MASSENET**

"Vous savez, seigneur, ma misère!" *see Oraison* Maeterlinck **CHAUSSON**

"Vous, si beaux qui passez!" *see Exhortation* Jacob, M. **SAUGUET**

COMPOSER Poet *Title* ''First Line''

"Vous souvient-il de cette jeune amie" *see*
    Le premier amour Desbordes-Valmore
    AURIC
Voyage see Apollinaire *CALLIGRAMMES.*
    POULENC
Voyage see Crane *VOYAGES III.* **CARTER**
Voyage see Gille **BIZET**
Voyage see Jacob, M. **SAUGUET**
Le voyage see Leclère, translator
    SHÉHÉRAZADE. **KOECHLIN**
Voyage à Paris see Apollinaire **POULENC**
LE VOYAGE D'ÉTÉ, no. 1
    MILHAUD Paliard *Modestes vacances*
LE VOYAGE D'ÉTÉ, no. 2
    MILHAUD Paliard *Les deux hôtels*
LE VOYAGE D'ÉTÉ, no. 3
    MILHAUD Paliard *Le boulanger*
LE VOYAGE D'ÉTÉ, no. 4
    MILHAUD Paliard *La maison inachevée*
LE VOYAGE D'ÉTÉ, no. 5
    MILHAUD Paliard *Monsieur le Curé*
LE VOYAGE D'ÉTÉ, no. 6
    MILHAUD Paliard *Les trois peupliers*
LE VOYAGE D'ÉTÉ, no. 7
    MILHAUD Paliard *Paresse*
LE VOYAGE D'ÉTÉ, no. 8
    MILHAUD Paliard *Les conscrits*
LE VOYAGE D'ÉTÉ, no. 9
    MILHAUD Paliard *Le château*
LE VOYAGE D'ÉTÉ, no. 10
    MILHAUD Paliard *L'horizon*
LE VOYAGE D'ÉTÉ, no. 11
    MILHAUD Paliard *Le pêcheur*
LE VOYAGE D'ÉTÉ, no. 12
    MILHAUD Paliard *Le ruisseau*
LE VOYAGE D'ÉTÉ, no. 13
    MILHAUD Paliard *La petite bergère*
LE VOYAGE D'ÉTÉ, no. 14
    MILHAUD Paliard *Les champignons*
LE VOYAGE D'ÉTÉ, no. 15
    MILHAUD Paliard *Le retour*
Voyage imaginaire see Huidobro **JOLIVET**
VOYAGES III. see Crane
    Voyage **CARTER**
Le voyageur see Silvestre **FAURÉ**
"Voyageur, où vas-tu?" *see Le voyageur*
    Silvestre **FAURÉ**
"Voyez un clair de lune de Novembre" *see*
    Clair de lune de Novembre Laforgue
    SAUGUET
"Les voyez-vous passer" *see Les nuages*
    Louvencourt **MASSENET**

"Vpustyne chakholoĭ i skupoĭ" *see Anchar-*
    drevo smerti Pushkin
    RIMSKIĬ-KORSAKOV
Le vrai amour see Du Bellay **MILHAUD**
Vrchlický, Jaroslav
    SCHÖNBERG *Ekloge*
Vsĕ khochet pet' see Teternikov
    RACHMANINOFF *Glory to God*
Vse otnĭal u menĭa see Tiutchev
    RACHMANINOFF *He took all from me*
"Vsĕ vneĭ garmoniia" *see Krasavĭtsa* Pushkin
    RIMSKIĬ-KORSAKOV
"Všírém poli dubec stojí" *see Zezhulice*
    Unknown **DVOŘÁK**
Vstan', soĭdi! davno dennĭtsa see Mei
    RIMSKIĬ-KORSAKOV
"Vstavaĭ, sluga! Konia sedlaĭ!" *see Goneĭs*
    Heine **RIMSKIĬ-KORSAKOV**
Vtak mnohém srdci mrtvojest see Pfleger-
    Moravský **DVOŘÁK**
    Two settings: B. 11 no. 3 and B. 160 no. 2.
Vté sladké moci see Pfleger-Moravský
    DVOŘÁK
Vté sladké moci očí tvých see Pfleger-
    Moravský **DVOŘÁK**
Vug, O Vove see Drachmann **GRIEG**
Vuggesang see Munch **GRIEG**
Vuggevise see Nielsen **NIELSEN**
"Vulcan! provide me such a cup" *see To wine*
    and beauty Rochester **QUILTER**
Vvedi menya, O noch, taykom see Maĭkov
    BALAKIREV
"Vvozdushnykh vysotakh" *see Zarya*
    Khomyakov **BALAKIREV**
Vy malí, drobní ptáčkové see Hálek
    DVOŘÁK
Vy vroucí písně pějte! see Pfleger-Moravský
    DVOŘÁK
    Two settings: B. 11 no. 1 and B. 123 no. 1.
Vy vroucí písně spějte see Pfleger-
    Moravský **DVOŘÁK**
Vy všichni kdo jste stísněni see Hálek
    DVOŘÁK
Vyazemsky, Pyotr, 1792-1878.
    RACHMANINOFF *Were you hiccuping?*
Výklad znamení see Anon. **DVOŘÁK**
Vysoká veža see Anon. **MARTINŮ**
Vzdymaiutsĭa volny see Tolstoĭ **RIMSKIĬ-**
    KORSAKOV
Vzglyani, moy drug see Krasov, V.
    BALAKIREV
Vzoshol na nebo mesyats yasnĭy see
    ĬAtsevicha **BALAKIREV**
Vzpomínání see Pech **DVOŘÁK**

W

"W bialodrzewiu jasnie dzni sloneczno" *see*
Slowisień Tuwim **SZYMANOWSKI**
W., Cäcilie von
SPOHR
Liebesschwärmerei
Die Stimme der Nacht
W MROKU GWIAZD. *see* Miciński
Na ksiezycu czarnym **SZYMANOWSKI**
Na pustej trzcinie **SZYMANOWSKI**
Pachna mi dziwnie twoje zlote wlosy
SZYMANOWSKI
Świety Franciszek mówi **SZYMANOWSKI**
W mym sercu **SZYMANOWSKI**
Z maurytańskich śpiewnych sal
SZYMANOWSKI
W mym sercu see Miciński *W MROKU
GWIAZD.* **SZYMANOWSKI**
"W pasiece az dzwoni" *see Wiosna*
Iłłakowiczówna **SZYMANOWSKI**
W poludnie miasto biale od goraca see
Iwaszkiewicz **SZYMANOWSKI**
W zaczarowanym lesie see Miciński
SZYMANOWSKI
Wach auf! see Kurowski-Eichen **LOEWE**
"Wach auf, wach auf, du junger Gesell" *see
Trennung* Anon. **BRAHMS**
Der Wachtelschlag see Sauter *IL CANTO
DELLA QUAGLIA.* **BEETHOVEN,
SCHUBERT**
Die wackelnde Glocke see Goethe
WANDERERS NACHTLIED. **ZELTER**
Wackernagel, Ilse (Stach von
Goltzheim), 1879-1941.
PFITZNER *An die Mark*
Wackernagel, Wilhelm, 1806-1869.
SCHÖNBERG *Ich grüne wie die Weide
grünt*
Wächterlied auf der Wartburg see Scheffel
WOLF
Während der Trennung see Fleming
KRENEK
Während des Regens see Kopisch **BRAHMS**
"Wälze dich hinweg, du wildes Feuer!" *see
Lied des Orpheus, als er in die Hölle ging*
Jacobi **SCHUBERT**
"Ein Wändeviereck, blass, vergilbt und alt"
see Im Krauzgang von St. Stefano Hesse
SCHOECK
"Wär' ich ein Kind" *see Das Kind* Droste-
Hülshoff **CORNELIUS**
"Wär ich ein Vogelein, flög ich zu ihm!" *see
Liebesschwärmerei* W., Cäcilie von
SPOHR

"Wär' ich nie aus euch gegangen" *see
Sehnsucht nach der Waldgegend* Kerner
SCHUMANN
Wär' ich wirklich so falsch? see Byron
LOEWE
Wären wir zwei kleine Vögel see Anon.
REGER
"Wär's dunkel, ich läg' im Walde" *see
Die Einsame* Eichendorff **PFITZNER,
SCHOECK**
"Wärst du bei mir um Lebenstal" *see Lied der
Anne Lyle* Scott **SCHUBERT**
"Wärst du nicht" *see Frage* Kerner
SCHUMANN
Wäsche im Wind see Falke **REGER**
"Wagen musst du und fluchtig erbeuten" *see
Der Soldat II* Eichendorff **WOLF**
WAGNER, RICHARD, 1813-1883.
Apel, Theodor
DER ENTFERNTEN.
Glockentöne (1832) [unpubl.]
Béranger, Pierre Jean de, 1780-1857.
Les adieux de Marie Stuart (1840) [GA,
XV, p. 32; SW, XVII, p. 52]
"Adieu, charmant pays de France"
Goethe, Johann Wolfgang von, 1749-
1832.
FAUST.
Bauern unter der Linde, op. 5 no. 2
(1832) [GA, XV, p. 4; SW, XVII,
p. 4]
"Der Schäfer putzte sich zum Tanz"
Branders Lied, op. 5 no. 3 (1832) [GA,
XV, p. 11; SW XVII, p. 11]
"Es war eine Ratt' im Kellernest"
Gretchen am Spinnrade, op. 5 no. 6
(1832)
[GA, XV, p. 19; SW, XVII, p. 19]
"Meine Ruh ist hin"
Lied der Soldaten, op. 5 no. 1 (1832)
[GA, XV, p. 1; SW, XVII, p. 1]
"Burgen mit hohen Mauern und
Zinnen"
Lied des Mephistopheles, op. 5 no. 4
(1832)
[GA, XV, p. 14; SW, XVII, p. 14]
"Es war einmal ein König"
Lied des Mephistopheles, op. 5 no. 5
(1832) [GA, XV, p. 17; SW, XVII,
p. 17]
"Was machst du mir von Liebchens
Tür"

Melodram Gretchens, op. 5 no. 7
(1832) [GA, XV, p. 22; SW, SVII,
p. 22]
"Ach neige, du Schmerzenreiche"
Heine, Heinrich, 1797-1856.
Les deux grenadiers (1839-40) [GA, XV,
p. 54; SW, XVII, p. 45]
"Longtemps captifs chez le Russe loin
tain"
Hugo, Victor Marie, comte, 1802-1885.
LES ORIENTALES.
L'attente (1840) [GA, XV, p. 50; SW,
XVII, p. 34] "Monte, écureuil,
monte au grand chêne"
Extase [SW, XVII, p. 32]
"J'étais seul près des flots"
LES VOIX INTÉRIEURES.
La tombe dit à la rose [SW, XVII,
p. 37] same
Reboul, Jean, 1795-1864.
Tout n'est qu'images fugitives (1840)
[GA, XV, p. 28; SW, XVII, p. 42]
same
Ronsard, Pierre de, 1524-1585.
Mignonne (1840) [GA, XV, p. 46; SW,
XVII, p. 38]
"Mignonne, allons voir, si la rose"
Scheurlein, Georg, 1802-1872.
Der Tannenbaum (1838) [GA, XV, p. 25;
SW, XVII, p. 25]
"Der Tannenbaum steht schweigend"
Unknown
Dors, mon enfant (1840) [GA, XV, p. 42;
SW, XVIII, p. 28] "Dors entre mes
bras, enfant plein de charmés"
Kraftliedchen (1871) [***Wiener Illustrierte
Zeitung,*** Oct. 14, 1877]
"Der Worte viele sind gemacht"
Also in ***Monthly Musical Record*** 13
(Apr. 1, 1883): 90. Voice alone.
Wagner, Richard, 1813-1883.
*Gruss seiner Treuen an Friedrich August
den Geliebten* (1844)
[GA, XV, p. 62; SW, XVII, p. 62]
"Im treuen Sachsenland ertönt die
frohe Kunde"
Also for men's chorus,
unaccompanied.
**Wesendonck, Mathilde (Luckmeyer),
1828-1902.**
Der Engel (1857) [GA, XV, p. 64; SW,
XVII, pp. 64 and 86]
"In der Kindheit frühen Tagen"
Im Treibhaus (1858) [GA, XV, p. 72;
SW, XVII, pp. 78, 82 and 94]
"Hoch gewölbte Blätterkronen"

Schmerzen (1857) [GA, XV, p. 76; SW,
XVII, pp. 70 and 98]
"Sonne, weinest jeden Abend dir die
schönen Augen rot"
Stehe still (1858) [GA, XV, p. 67; SW,
XVII, pp. 73 and 89]
"Sausendes, brausendes Rad der Zeit"
Träume (1857) [GA, XV, p. 78; SW,
XVII, pp. 67 and 100]
"Sag', welch wunderbare Träume"
Wagner, Richard, 1813-1883.
WAGNER *Gruss seiner Treuen an
Friedrich August den Geliebten*
La wagon immobile see Hugnet **THOMSON**
Wagtail and baby see Hardy **BRITTEN**
Wahllied see Bjørnson **GRIEG** *Valgsang*
WaiKiKi see Brooke **GRIFFES**
Wailly, Léon de, 1804-1863.
BERLIOZ *Chansonette*
Die Waise see Chamisso **GRIEG**
Die Waise see Hoffmann von Fallersleben
SCHUMANN
Das Waisenkind see Musorgskiĭ
MUSORGSKIĬ *Sirotka*
Wait! see Grekov **CHAĬKOVSKIĬ** *Pogodi!*
Waitin' see Harris **HARRIS**
The waiting soul see Cowper **IVES**
Wake the serpent not see Shelley **LUENING**
The waking see Roethke **ROREM**
THE WAKING. see Roethke
I strolled across an open field **ROREM**
"Der Wald beginnt zu rauschen" *see*
Waldseligkeit Dehmel **REGER,
STRAUSS**
WALD, GARTEN UND BERG. see Tieck
Vogelgesang **LOEWE**
"Der Wald ist schwarz" *see Reiterlied*
Redwitz LOEWE
"Der Wald wird falb, die Blätter fallen" *see*
Im Herbst Eichendorff **LASSEN,
PFITZNER**
Waldasyl see Unknown **LASSEN**
Waldau, Max, pseud. *see* Hauenschild,
Georg von, 1825-1855.
"Der Waldbach tost" *see Der Hirt auf der
Brücke* Ziegler, K. **LOEWE**
WALDBLUMEN, no. 1
LOEWE Branco *Das Glockenspiel der
Phantasie*
WALDBLUMEN, no. 2
LOEWE Branco *Dein Auge*
WALDBLUMEN, no. 3
LOEWE Branco *Allmacht Gottes*
WALDBLUMEN, no. 4
LOEWE Branco *Des Mädchens Wunsch
und Geständnis*

COMPOSER Poet *Title* "First Line"

WALDBLUMEN, no. 5
  LOEWE Branco *Du Geist der reinsten Güte*
WALDBLUMEN, no. 6
  LOEWE Branco *Mit jedem Pulsschlag leb' ich dir*
Der Waldbruder see Grimmelshausen **ZELTER**
Die Waldbrüder see Storm **LASSEN**
Waldeinsamkeit see Anon. **REGER**
Waldeinsamkeit see Eichendorff **RUBINSTEIN, SCHOECK**
WALDEINSAMKEIT. see Klingemann
  As lonesome through the woods I stray
  BENNETT
Waldeinsamkeit see Leuthold **SCHOECK**
"*Waldeinsamkeit, du grünes Revier*" *see*
  Waldeinsamkeit Eichendorff
  RUBINSTEIN, SCHOECK
Waldesfahrt see Heine **STRAUSS**
Waldesgesang see Geibel **STRAUSS**
Waldesgespräch see Eichendorff **JENSEN,**
  SCHUMANN
Waldesnacht see Heyse **SCHÖNBERG**
Waldesnacht see Schlegel, F. **SCHUBERT**
  Im Walde
"*Waldesnacht, du wunderkühle*" *see Im Walde*
  Heyse **JENSEN**
"*Waldesnacht, du wunderkühle*" *see*
  Waldesnacht Heyse **SCHÖNBERG**
Waldfahrt see Körner **FRANZ**
Die Waldhexe see Boddien, G. von
  RUBINSTEIN
Die Waldkapelle see Siebel **LOEWE**
Waldkonzert see Vogl **STRAUSS**
Waldlied see Uhland **REGER**
Waldlied see Winther **GRIEG** *Skovsang*
WALDLIEDERN. see Pfarrius
  Der Bräutigam und die Birke
  SCHUMANN
  Die Hütte **SCHUMANN**
  Warnung **SCHUMANN**
Waldmädchen see Eichendorff **WOLF**
"*Waldmeisterlein!*" *see Beim Maitrank*
  Unknown **LOEWE**
Das Waldschloss see Eichendorff
  MENDELSSOHN-BARTHOLDY
Der Waldsee see Leuthold **SCHOECK**
  Two settings: Op. 15 no. 1 and op. 57 no. 20.
Waldseligkeit see Dehmel **REGER,**
  STRAUSS
Waldsonne see Schlaf **SCHÖNBERG**
Waldvögelein see Leuthold **SCHOECK**
"*Waldvögelein, wohin ziehst du?*" *see*
  Waldvögelein Leuthold **SCHOECK**

Waldwanderung see Andersen **GRIEG**
  Vandring i Skoven
Waley, Arthur, 1889-1966, translator.
  COPLAND *Old poem*
"Walkeing betimes close by a green wood
  side" *see Milkmaids* Smith, Dr. James
  HESELTINE
Walking see Ives **IVES**
"Walking stronger under distant skies" *see*
  Resolution Ives **IVES**
Walking the woods see Anon. **HESELTINE**
"Walle, Regen, walle nieder" *see Regenlied*
  Groth **BRAHMS**
The walled-in garden see Heald, Arthur
  QUILTER
Der Wallensteiner Lanzknecht beim Trunk see
  Leitner **SCHUBERT**
Waller, Edmund, 1606-1687.
  CARPENTER, QUILTER *Go, lovely
    rose*
  ROREM
    The dancer
    Go, lovely rose
Wallhaide see Körner **LOEWE**
Wallner
  WEBER *Wiedersehen*
Wallpach zu Schwanenfeld, Arthur,
  ritter von, 1866-1946.
  BERG *Holophan*
Walpurgisnacht see Häring **LOEWE**
Walt Whitman see Whitman *LEAVES OF
  GRASS.* **IVES**
Walther von der Vogelweide see Scheffel
  *DER BRAUTWILLKOMM AUF
  WARTBURG.* **LISZT**
Walther von der Vogelweide, 12th cent.
  BERG *Unter der Linden*
  GRIEG *Die verschwiegene Nachtigall*
  PFITZNER
    Gewalt der Minne
    Unter der Linden bei der Haide
  SPOHR *Die verschwiegene Nachtigall*
Walton, Izaak, 1593-1683.
  BRITTEN *Fishing song*
Waltz see Ives **IVES**
The waltz see Pushkin **MEDTNER**
Waltz see Shenshin **MEDTNER**
Wanda see Tuwim **SZYMANOWSKI**
WANDA, KÖNIGIN DER SARMATEN. see
  Werner *Jagdlied* **SCHUBERT**
Die wandelnde Glocke see Goethe **LOEWE,**
  SCHUMANN
Wandelt sich rasch auch die Welt see Rilke
  SONETTE AN ORPHEUS. **DIAMOND**
  Even though the world keeps changing
"Ein Wanderbursch' mit dem Stab in der
  Hand" *see Das Erkennen* Vogl **LOEWE**

Ein Wanderer see Köstlin **BRAHMS**
Der Wanderer see Nietzsche **SCHÖNBERG**
  NB: Text variant from the Delius setting
  below.
Der Wanderer see Nietzsche *DIE
  FRÖHLICHE WISSENSCHAFT.* **DELIUS**
Wanderer see Rückert **MUSORGSKIï**
  Strannik
Der Wanderer see Schlegel, F.
  ABENDRÖTE. **SCHUBERT**
Der Wanderer see Schmidt, Georg
  SCHUBERT
Der Wanderer see Schmidt, Georg
  SCHUBERT *Der Unglückliche*
Der Wanderer an den Mond see Seidl
  SCHUBERT
The wanderer and his shadow see Nietzsche
  *MENSCHLICHES,
  ALLZUMENSCHLICHES.*
  DELIUS *Der Wanderer und sein Schatten*
Der Wanderer und der Bach see Frey, F.
  SIBELIUS
Der Wanderer und sein Schatten see
  Nietzsche *MENSCHLICHES,
  ALLZUMENSCHLICHES.* **DELIUS**
Wanderers Gemütsruhe see Goethe
  WESTÖSTLICHER DIVAN. **STRAUSS**
WANDERERS NACHTLIED. see Goethe
  Die wuckelnde Glocke **ZELTER**
Wanderers Nachtlied see Goethe
  WANDRERS NACHTLIED I. **PFITZNER,
  WOLF**
Wanderer's night-song see Goethe
  WANDRERS NACHTLIED I. **MEDTNER**
  Wanderers Nachtlied
Wanderer's night-song see Goethe
  WANDRERS NACHTLIED II. **MEDTNER**
  Wanderers Nachtlied
Wanderlied see Anon.
  VAUGHAN WILLIAMS, WOLF
Wanderlied see Beta **SCHÖNBERG**
Wanderlied see Eichendorff
  MENDELSSOHN-BARTHOLDY
Wanderlied see Geibel **JENSEN**
Wanderlied see Goethe **WOLF**
Wanderlied see Kerner **SCHUMANN**
  Wanderlust
Wanderlied see Lua **LOEWE**
Wanderlied see Osterwald **FRANZ**
Wanderlied der Prager Studenten see
  Eichendorff **SCHOECK**
Wanderlied im Herbst see Krenek **KRENEK**
WANDERLIEDER. see Uhland
  In der Ferne **BRAHMS**
  Scheiden und Meiden **BRAHMS,
  SCHOECK**

Wanderlust see Kerner **SCHUMANN**
Das Wandern see Müller, Wilhelm
  SCHUBERT
"*Das Wandern ist des Müllers Lust*" *see Das
  Wandern* Müller, Wilhelm **SCHUBERT**
"*Wandern lieb ich für mein Leben*" *see
  Der Musikant* Eichendorff **WOLF**
" *'Wandernd fremd und unbekannt in der
  Stadt*" *see Der Heimatlose* Zwehl, Hans
  Fritz von **KILPINEN**
Das Wandernde Lied see Schütze **ZELTER**
Wanderschaft see Fitger *LIEDER VOM
  MAURERGESELLEN.* **PIJPER**
Die Wanderschwalbe see Grossi
  RUBINSTEIN
Wandert ihr Wolken see Avenarius **BERG**
Wanderung see Kerner **SCHUMANN**
WANDERUNG IM GEBIRGE, no. 1
  SCHOECK Lenau *Erinnerung*
WANDERUNG IM GEBIRGE, no. 2
  SCHOECK Lenau *Aufbruch*
WANDERUNG IM GEBIRGE, no. 3
  SCHOECK Lenau *Die Lerche*
WANDERUNG IM GEBIRGE, no. 4
  SCHOECK Lenau *Der Eichwald*
WANDERUNG IM GEBIRGE, no. 5
  SCHOECK Lenau *Der Hirte*
WANDERUNG IM GEBIRGE, no. 6
  SCHOECK Lenau *Einsamkeit*
WANDERUNG IM GEBIRGE, no. 7
  SCHOECK Lenau *Der Ferne*
WANDERUNG IM GEBIRGE, no. 8
  SCHOECK Lenau *Das Gewitter*
WANDERUNG IM GEBIRGE, no. 9
  SCHOECK Lenau *Der Schlaf*
WANDERUNG IM GEBIRGE, no. 10
  SCHOECK Lenau *Der Abend*
Wandl' ich in dem Morgentau see Keller, G.
  PFITZNER, WOLF
Wandl' ich in dem Wald des Abends see
  Heine **FRANZ**
"*Wandl' ich in dem Wald des Abends*" *see
  Im Wald* Heine **LASSEN**
"*Der Wandrer, dem verschwunden so Sonn'als
  Mondenlicht*" *see Trost im Gesang*
  Kerner **SCHUMANN**
"*Wandrer durch die Nacht mit gutem Schritt*"
  see Der Wanderer Nietzsche
  SCHÖNBERG
"*Ein Wand'rer in der Gassen*" *see Lied des
  Mädchens am Fenster* Paquet
  SZYMANOWSKI
Wandrers Nachtlied see Goethe *WANDRERS
  NACHTLIED I.* **LOEWE, MEDTNER,
  SCHUBERT, ZELTER**

COMPOSER Poet *Title* "First Line"

Wandrers Nachtlied see Goethe *WANDRERS
NACHTLIED II.* **LOEWE, MEDTNER,
SCHUBERT**
Wandrers Nachtlied see Goethe **ZELTER**
Ruhe
WANDRERS NACHTLIED I. see Goethe
Der du von dem Himmel bist **LISZT**
Wanderers Nachtlied **PFITZNER, WOLF**
Wandrers Nachtlied **LOEWE, MEDTNER,
SCHUBERT, ZELTER**
WANDRERS NACHTLIED II. see Goethe
Wandrers Nachtlied **LOEWE, MEDTNER,
SCHUBERT**
WANDSBECKER LIEDERBUCH, no. 1
SCHOECK Claudius, M. *Die Liebe*
WANDSBECKER LIEDERBUCH, no. 2
SCHOECK Claudius, M. *Phidile*
WANDSBECKER LIEDERBUCH, no. 3
SCHOECK Claudius, M. *Ein Wiegenlied,
bei Mondschein zu singen*
WANDSBECKER LIEDERBUCH, no. 4
SCHOECK Claudius, M. *Als er sein
Weib und 's Kind schlafend fand*
WANDSBECKER LIEDERBUCH, no. 5
SCHOECK Claudius, M. *Die Natur*
WANDSBECKER LIEDERBUCH, no. 6
SCHOECK Claudius, M. *Der Frühling*
WANDSBECKER LIEDERBUCH, no. 7
SCHOECK Claudius, M.
Die Sternseherin
WANDSBECKER LIEDERBUCH, no. 8
SCHOECK Claudius, M. *Kuckuck*
WANDSBECKER LIEDERBUCH, no. 9
SCHOECK Claudius, M. *Ein Lied,
hinterm Ofen zu singen*
WANDSBECKER LIEDERBUCH, no. 10
SCHOECK Claudius, M. *Abendlied*
WANDSBECKER LIEDERBUCH, no. 11
SCHOECK Claudius, M. *Der Mensch*
WANDSBECKER LIEDERBUCH, no. 12
SCHOECK Claudius, M. *Die Römer*
WANDSBECKER LIEDERBUCH, no. 13
SCHOECK Claudius, M. *Der Schwarze
in der Zuckerplantage*
WANDSBECKER LIEDERBUCH, no. 14
SCHOECK Claudius, M. *Der Krieg*
WANDSBECKER LIEDERBUCH, no. 15
SCHOECK Claudius, M. *Auf den Tod
einer Kaiserin*
WANDSBECKER LIEDERBUCH, no. 16
SCHOECK Claudius, M. *Der Tod*
WANDSBECKER LIEDERBUCH, no. 17
SCHOECK Claudius, M. *Spruch*
Wang, Chang-ling, fl.ca.750.
GRIFFES *So-fei gathering flowers*
Wang Seng-ju, fl. 6th cent.
GRIFFES *Tears*

"Wann der silberne Mond" *see Die Mainacht*
Hölty **BRAHMS, SCHUBERT**
"Wann im letzten Abendstrahl" *see Ruhetal*
Uhland **SCHOECK**
"Wann, wann erscheint der Morgen" *see
Melancholie* Miranda **SCHUMANN**
War see Carpenter, Rue **CARPENTER**
"War ein Blümlein wunderfein" *see
Vergissmeinnicht* Pfau **SCHÖNBERG**
"War es also gemeint" *see Danksagung an
den Bach* Müller, Wilhelm **SCHUBERT**
War es dir, dem dies Lippen bebten? see
Tieck **BRAHMS**
The war horse see Pushkin **MEDTNER**
"War ich gar so jung und dumm" *see Vom
Küssen!* Ritter **REGER**
WAR SCENES, no. 1
ROREM Whitman *A night battle*
WAR SCENES, no. 2
ROREM Whitman *Specimen case*
WAR SCENES, no. 3
ROREM Whitman *An incident*
WAR SCENES, no. 4
ROREM Whitman *Inauguration ball*
WAR SCENES, no. 5
ROREM Whitman *The real war will
never get in the books*
"War schöner als der schönste Tag" *see
Kanzonette* Goethe **LOEWE**
Warble for lilac time see Whitman
CARTER
"Warble me now for joy of lilac-time" *see
Warble for lilac time* Whitman **CARTER**
Wargentin
WEBER *An Sie*
WARLOCK, PETER, pseud. *see*
HESELTINE, PHILIP, 1894-1930.
"Warm die Lüfte" *see Aus dem "Glühenden"*
Mombert **BERG**
Warm die Lüfte see Mombert
DER GLÜHENDE. **BERG**
"Warm perfumes like a breath from vine and
tree" *see WaiKiKi* Brooke **GRIFFES**
"Warm, the deserted evening" *see At close of
day* Binyon **QUILTER**
Warner, Sylvia Townsend, 1893-1978.
IRELAND
Hymn for a child
The scapegoat
The soldier's return
Warning see Anon. **DVOŘÁK**
Připamatování
Warnung see Dehmel **SCHÖNBERG**
Warnung see Leuthold **SCHOECK**
Warnung see Pfarrius *WALDLIEDERN.*
SCHUMANN

COMPOSER Poet *Title* "First Line"

Warnung see Unknown **REGER**
Warnung vor dem Rhein see Simrock
MENDELSSOHN-BARTHOLDY
The warrior see Witwicki **CHOPIN** *Wojak*
Wart, Jakob von, fl. 1272-1331.
  MENDELSSOHN-BARTHOLDY
    Maienlied
DIE WARTBURG-LIEDER
  LISZT Scheffel
    Biterolf und der Schmied von Ruhla
    Heinrich von Ofterdingen
    Reimar der Alte
    Der tugendhafte Schreiber
    Walther von der Vogelweide
Warte, Jacob von *see* Wart, Jakob von,
  fl. 1272-1331.
Warte nur! see Braungart **REGER**
Warte, warte, wilder Schiffsmann see Heine
  SCHUMANN
Wartend see Unknown **MENDELSSOHN-**
  BARTHOLDY
Warum? see Guilliaume **LASSEN**
  Pourquoi?
Warum? see Heine *WARUM SIND DANN*
  DIE ROSEN SO BLASS? **CHAÏKOVSKÏÏ**
  Otchevo?
Warum bist du aufgewacht see Pfau
  SCHÖNBERG
"Warum bist du nicht hier?" *see An Rosa I*
  Kosegarten **SCHUBERT**
"Warum dein Blick so trübe?" *see Werfet alle*
  eure Sorgen auf ihn! Niemeyer **LOEWE**
"Warum denn warten von Tag zu Tag?" *see*
  Komm bald Groth **BRAHMS**
"Warum, Geliebte, denk ich dein" *see*
  Perigrina II Mörike **WOLF**
"Warum huldigest du, heiliger Sokrates" *see*
  Sokrates und Alcibiades Hölderlin
  BRITTEN
"Warum ich bleibe" *see Seufzer des*
  Gefangnen Schütze **ZELTER**
Warum ich weine see Unknown
  MENDELSSOHN-BARTHOLDY
"Warum kommst Du zu mir" *see Todsüsses*
  Gespenst Zwehl, Hans Fritz von
  KILPINEN
Warum leckst du dein Mäulchen see Goethe
  WESTÖSTLICHER DIVAN. **SCHOECK**
Warum musst du welken, schöne, Rose see
  Unknown **RUBINSTEIN**
Warum nicht? see Unknown **SPOHR**
"Warum öffnest du wieder, Erzeuger von
  Alpin" *see Der Tod Oskar's* Macpherson
  SCHUBERT
Warum schimmert dein Auge see Paulsen
  GRIEG *Til én. II*

Warum sind dann die Rosen so blass? see
  Heine *OTCHEVO?* **CHAÏKOVSKÏÏ**
Warum sind deine Augen denn so nass see
  Rückert **PFITZNER**
Warum sind denn die Rosen so blass? see
  Heine **CORNELIUS, SCHOECK**
"Warum so bleich und blass" *see Tränen im*
  Auge Wildenbruch **REGER**
"Warum so spät erst, Georgine?" *see Die*
  Georgine Gilm zu Rosenegg **STRAUSS**
"Warum soll ich denn wandern" *see*
  Ich wand're nicht Christern **SCHUMANN**
"Was bedeutet die Bewegung?" *see Suleika*
  Goethe **MENDELSSOHN-**
  BARTHOLDY, SCHUBERT
"Was bricht hervor wie Blüthen weiss" *see*
  Das Mädchen an das erste Schneeglöckchen
  Gerstenberg, Friedrich von **WEBER**
WAS DER TAG MIR ZUTRÄGT':
  Flötenspielerin. see Altenberg
  Flötenspielerin **BERG**
WAS DER TAG MIR ZUTRÄGT': Hoffnung.
  see Altenberg *Hoffnung* **BERG**
WAS DER TAG MIR ZUTRÄGT': Traurigkcit.
  see Altenberg *Traurigkeit* **BERG**
"Was doch heut Nacht ein Sturm gewesen"
  see Begegnung Mörike **REGER, WOLF**
"Was erhofftest Du Dir" *see Hoffnung*
  Altenberg **BERG**
Was für ein Lied soll dir gesungen werden see
  Heyse **WOLF**
WAS FUNKELT IHR SO MILD. see
  Fellinger *Die Sterne* **SCHUBERT**
"Was funkelt ihr so mild mich an?" *see*
  Die Sterne Fellinger **SCHUBERT**
"Was gehst du, armer, bleicher Kopf" *see*
  Auf einem verfallenen Kirchhof
  Morgenstern **KILPINEN**
"Was graf' ich viel nach Geld und Gut" *see*
  Die Zufriedenheit Miller, J. **MOZART**
"Was hab' ich bis jetzt non gefunden?" *see*
  Rückblick Krenek **KRENEK**
"Was hat des Schlummers Band zerrissen" *see*
  Um Dich Kurz **REGER**
"Was hör ich draussen vor dem Thor" *see*
  Ballade des Harfners Goethe
  SCHUMANN
"Was hör' ich draussen vor dem Thor?" *see*
  Der Sänger Goethe **LOEWE,**
  SCHUBERT, WOLF, ZELTER
Was I not a blade of grass? see Surikov
  MALOROSSYSKAYA PESNYA.
  CHAÏKOVSKÏÏ
  ÎA li v poke da ne travushka byla
"Was ich mir still gelobte" *see Meine Devise*
  Eisenmayer, W. **LASSEN**

COMPOSER Poet *Title* "First Line"

Was ich sah see Vinje **GRIEG** *Eit Syn*

"Was im Netze? Schau einmal!" *see Erstes Liebeslied eines Mädchens* Mörike **WOLF**

"Was immer mir die Feindschaft unterschoben" *see Leidenschaft* Leuthold **SCHOECK**

Was in der Schenke waren heute see Goethe *WESTÖSTLICHER DIVAN*: Schenkenbuch. **WOLF**

"Was ist des Sängers Vaterland?" *see Mein Vaterland* Körner **WEBER**

"Was ist des Vögleins Dach" *see Das Nest* Leo **LASSEN**

"Was ist es, das die Seele füllt?" *see Alles um Liebe* Kosegarten **SCHUBERT**

"Was ist in deiner Seele" *see Bestimmung* Huch **PFITZNER, SZYMANOWSKI**

"Was ist mir denn so wehe?" *see Traum* Eichendorff **REGER**

"Was ist Sylvia, saget an" *see An Sylvia* Shakespeare **SCHUBERT**

"Was ist's, das der Gedanken mutigen Tritt" *see Ein Jauchzer* Spitteler **SCHOECK**

"Was ist's, das mir den Athem hemmet" *see Das Heimweh* Robert, F. **MENDELSSOHN-BARTHOLDY**

Was ist's, O Vater see Chamisso **JENSEN**

"Was ist's, O Vater" *see Tränen* Chamisso **FRANZ**

"Was ist's, O Vater, was ich verbrach?" *see Tränen* Chamisso **SPOHR**

"Was it a dream?" *see The quest* Bal'mont **RACHMANINOFF**

Was it a dream? see Wecksell **SIBELIUS** *Var det en dröm?*

Was it the mother who bore me? see Mickiewicz **CHAĬKOVSKIĬ** *Ali mat' menia rozhala*

"Was klinget und singet die Strass' herauf?" *see Abschied* Uhland **SCHOECK**

"Was klinget und singet die Strassen herauf?" *see Abschied* Uhland **LOEWE**

"Was klopft ans Thor?" *see Der späte Gast* Häring **LOEWE**

Was lachst du so? see Hesse **SCHOECK**

Was Liebe sei? see Hagn **LISZT**

"Was machst du mir von Liebchens Tür" *see Lied des Mephistopheles* Goethe **WAGNER**

Was mir wohl übrig bliebe see Hoffmann von Fallersleben **SPOHR**
Two settings: Op. 139 no. 5 and WoO 96.

Was nennst du deine Liebe schwer und gross see Kühne **JENSEN**

"Was nützt die mir noch zugemess'ne Zeit?" *see Abschied von der Welt* Mary **SCHUMANN**

Was pocht mein Herz so sehr see Burns **FRANZ**

"Was rennt das Volk, was wälzt sich dart die langen Gaffen" *see Der Kampf mit dem Drachen* Schiller **ZELTER**

"Was rüttelt die Säulen und schüttelt am Thron" *see Preussentreue* Telschow **LOEWE**

"Was schauest du so hell und klar" *see An den Mond* Hölty **SCHUBERT**

"Was schaust du mich so freundlich an" *see An ein Bild* Schenkendorf **BRAHMS**

"Was schweigt unser fröhlicher Chor?" *see Bacchisches Lied* Pushkin **RUBINSTEIN**

"Was sie damals empfanden" *see Stillung Mariä mit dem Auferstandenen* Rilke **HINDEMITH**

Was soll der Zorn see Heyse **WOLF**

"Was soll ich anders sagen dir" *see Ewige Liebe* Wildenbruch **LASSEN**

Was soll ich mich mit Worten quälen? see Robert, F. **ZELTER**

Was soll ich sagen? see Chamisso **GRIEG, SCHUMANN, WOLF**

"Was sorgest du?" *see Der gute Hirte* Uz **SCHUBERT**

"Was spinnst du?" *see Die kleine Spinnerin* Unknown **MOZART**

"Was stürmet die Heide herauf?" *see Ballade* Reinbeck **WEBER**

"Was sucht denn der Jager am Mühlbach hier?" *see Der Jäger* Müller, Wilhelm **SCHUBERT**

"Was that dir, Thor" *see Wir und Sie* Klopstock **GLUCK**

Was this fair face see Shakespeare *ALL'S WELL THAT ENDS WELL.* **THOMSON**

"Was tragen wir unsere Leiden in diesen Glanz hinein?" *see Mensch und Natur* Braungart **REGER**

Was treibst du, Wind? see Meyer **SCHOECK**

"Was treibt mich hier von hinnen?" *see Dämmerempfindung* Hebbel **CORNELIUS**

"Was treibt mich hin zu dir mit Macht?" *see An* Koch, E. **SPOHR**

Was tun? see Hugo **LISZT** *Comment, disaient-ils*

Was tut's see Lipiner **RUBINSTEIN**

"Was unterm Monde Gleicht" *see Die Elfenkönigin* Matthisson **ZELTER**

"Was vermeid' ich denn die Wege" *see Der Wegweiser* Müller, Wilhelm **SCHUBERT**

"Was wecken aus dem Schlummer mich" *see Das Ständchen* Uhland **LOEWE**

COMPOSER Poet *Title* "First Line"

"Was weht um meine Schläfe" *see*
Geisternähe Münch-Bellinghausen
SCHUMANN

"Was weilst du einsam an dem Himmel" *see*
Abendstern Mayrhofer **SCHUBERT**

"Was wekken aus dem Schlummer mich für
süsse Klänge doch?" *see Das Ständchen*
Uhland **SPOHR**

Was will die einsame Thräne see Heine
SCHUMANN

"Was will die einsame Träne" *see*
Die Heimkehr Heine **CORNELIUS**

Was will die einsame Träne see Heine
FRANZ

"Was will die Nacht" *see Leben* Evers
BERG

"Was zieht mir das Herz so?" *see Sehnsucht*
Goethe **BEETHOVEN, SCHUBERT,
WOLF, ZELTER**

"Was zieht zu deinem Zauberkreise" *see Lied*
Müchler **WEBER**

Was zucken die braunen Geigen see Grazie
BERG

"Wasch dich, mein Schwesterchen, wasch
dich!" *see Die Tochter der Haide* Mörike
WOLF

"Wass fasst dich an, O Tochter mein!" *see*
Frieden Molbech **JENSEN**

"Wasser holen geht die reine" *see Legende*
Goethe **LOEWE**

"Das Wasser rauscht', das Wasser schwoll"
see Der Fischer Goethe **LOEWE,
SCHUBERT, SCHUMANN, STRAUSS,
WOLF, ZELTER**

"Wasser stürzt uns" *see Reiselied*
Hofmannsthal **BERG**

Wasserfahrt see Geibel **FRANZ**

Wasserfahrt see Heine **FRANZ, PFITZNER**

Wasserfahrt see Hoffmann von
Fallersleben **FRANZ**

Der Wasserfall see Klingemann
MENDELSSOHN-BARTHOLDY

Wasserflut see Müller, Wilhelm
SCHUBERT

"Die Wasserlilie kichert leis" *see Verrat*
Kaufmann **PFITZNER**

Wasserrose see Dahn **STRAUSS**

Watchful's song see Bible **VAUGHAN
WILLIAMS**

Watchman see Bowring **IVES**

"Watchman, tell us of the night" *see*
Watchman Bowring **IVES**

The water lily see Heine *DIE SCHLANKE
WASSERLILIE.* **RACHMANINOFF**

The water lily see Nichols *ARBOURS AND
ENDURANCES* (1917). **HESELTINE**

The water lily see Tabb **GRIFFES**

The water mill see Shove
VAUGHAN WILLIAMS

WATERCOLORS, no. 1
CARPENTER Li Po *On a screen*

WATERCOLORS, no. 2
CARPENTER Yü-hsi *The Odalisque*

WATERCOLORS, no. 3
CARPENTER Li-Shê *Highwaymen*

WATERCOLORS, no. 4
CARPENTER Confucius *To a young
gentleman*

The water's full of swimmers see Rohan
THOMSON *Jour de chaleur aux bains de
mer*

The watersprite see Josephson, E.
SIBELIUS *Necken*

The watersprite see Wennerberg **SIBELIUS**
Näcken

Watson, Sir William, 1858-1935.
QUILTER *April*

Watts, Isaac, 1674-1748.
THOMSON *My Shepherd will supply my
need*

The wave breaks into spray see Tolstoĭ
RIMSKIĬ-KORSAKOV *Drobitsia, i
pleshchet*

"Wave follows wave as does thought follow
thought" *see Waves and thoughts* Tiutchev
MEDTNER

"Wave that wand'rest" *see Forget-me-not*
Landon **BENNETT**

Waves and thoughts see Tiutchev
MEDTNER

The waves rise up like mountains see Tolstoĭ
RIMSKIĬ-KORSAKOV *Vzdymaiutsia
volny*

"The way a crow shook down on me" *see*
The dust of snow Frost **CARTER**

The way you are see Blitzstein
BLITZSTEIN

The wayside cross see Anon. **MARTINŮ**
Boží muka

"We are the children who play in the park"
see The children Feeney **CHANLER**

"We are the music-makers" *see Ode*
O'Shaughnessy **DIAMOND**

"We be the King's men" *see Buonaparty*
Hardy **VAUGHAN WILLIAMS**

We erred in the morning see Manin, J.
MARTINŮ

"We guide the ships, we scan the skies" *see*
Take the sun and keep the stars Harris
HARRIS

We have not far to walk see Grekov
CHAĬKOVSKIĬ *Ne dolgo nam gulyat*

COMPOSER Poet *Title* "First Line"

We lost all that was once our own **see**
Tiutchev **MEDTNER**
"We man the ships, we fire the guns" **see**
Sons of Uncle Sam Harris **HARRIS**
We mglach strumienie szumia wód **see**
Tetmajer **SZYMANOWSKI**
We never said farewell **see** Coleridge
ROREM
We sat together **see** Rathaus
CHAĬKOVSKIĬ *An dem schlummernden
Strom*
WE TWO, no. 1
DIAMOND Shakespeare *Shall I
compare thee to a summer's day?*
WE TWO, no. 2
DIAMOND Shakespeare *Let me confess
that we two must be twain*
WE TWO, no. 3
DIAMOND Shakespeare *Those pretty
wrongs that liberty commits*
WE TWO, no. 4
DIAMOND Shakespeare *For shame
deny that thou bear'st love to any*
WE TWO, no. 5
DIAMOND Shakespeare *O from what
power hast thou this powerful might*
WE TWO, no. 6
DIAMOND Shakespeare *My love is as a
fever longing still*
WE TWO, no. 7
DIAMOND Shakespeare *No longer
mourn for me when I am dead*
WE TWO, no. 8
DIAMOND Shakespeare *When in
disgrace with fortune and men's eyes*
WE TWO, no. 9
DIAMOND Shakespeare *When to the
sessions of sweet silent thought*
"We were learning in our school today" **see**
So pretty Comden **BERNSTEIN**
We'll go to the woods no more **see** Housman
LAST POEMS: Prologue.
VAUGHAN WILLIAMS
We'll to the woods and gather May **see**
Henley **GRIFFES**
We'll to the woods no more **see** Housman
LAST POEMS: Prologue. **IRELAND**
WE'LL TO THE WOODS NO MORE, no. 1
Ireland **HOUSMAN** *We'll to the woods no
more*
WE'LL TO THE WOODS NO MORE, no. 2
IRELAND Housman *In boyhood*
WE'LL TO THE WOODS NO MORE, no. 3
IRELAND Housman *Spring will not wait*
We'll to the woods so move **see** Housman
RIEGGER

THE WEARY BLUES. see Hughes, L.
The cryin' blues **CARPENTER**
Jazz-boys **CARPENTER**
Shake your brown feet, Honey
CARPENTER
The weary one's evensong **see** Geibel
GRIFFES *Des müden Abendlied*
"Weary the cry of the wind is" **see** *Sorrow of
Mydath* Masefield **GRIFFES**
Weary with toil **see** Shakespeare
SAUGUET
Weatherly, Frederick Edward, 1848-
1929.
GOUNOD
The holy vision
The worker
Weathers **see** Hardy **IRELAND**
Weber, Cläre Henrika, 1881-1954.
REGER *Klein Evelinde*
WEBER, KARL MARIA VON, 1786-1826.
Anon.
Bettlerlied, op. 25 no. 4 (1812)
[Gröbenschütz u. Seiler; Schuberth;
Hofmeister]
"I und mein junges Weib"
Voice & guitar.
Canzonetta: Italienisches Ständchen
(1810) [Peters]
"Wie sehr du mich verkanntest"
Bass & piano or harp.
Heimlicher Liebe Pein, op. 64 no. 3
(1818) [Schlesinger]
"Mein Schatz, der ist auf die
Wanderschaft hin"
Herzchen, mein Schätzchen, op. 64 no. 8
(1819) [Schlesinger] same
Die kleine Fritz an seine jungen Freunde,
op. 15 no. 3 (1809) [Simrock]
"Ach wenn ich nur ein Liebchen hätt"
Lebensansicht, op. 66 no. 4 (1812)
[Schlesinger]
"Frei und froh mit muntern Sinnen"
Bass & piano.
Der Sänger und der Maler, op. 80 no. 6
(1820) [Schlesinger]
"Ei, wenn ich doch ein Maler wär'"
Umsonst, op. 71 no. 4 (1802)
[Schlesinger] "Umsonst, umsonst
entsagt' ich der lockenden Liebe"
Unbefangenheit, op. 30 no. 3 (1813)
[Schlesinger]
"Frage mich immer, fragest umsonst!"
Volkslied, op. 54 no. 6 (1818) [Peters]
"Wenn ich ein Vöglein wär' "
Volkslied, op. 54 no. 7 (1818) [Peters]
"Weine, weine, weine nur nicht!"

COMPOSER Poet *Title* "First Line"

May be from *Des Knaben
Wundehorn;* cf. Strauss
Junggesellenschur, op. 49 no. 6.
FLIEGENDES BLATT.
 Abendsegen, op. 64 no. 5 (1819)
  [Schlesinger]
  "Der Tag hat seinen Schmuck"
 Liebesgruss aus der Ferne, op. 64 no.
  6 (1819) [Schlesinger]
  "Sind wir geschieden"
 Liebeslied, op. 54 no. 3 (1817) [Peters]
  "Ich hab' mir eins erwählet"
 Volkslied, op. 64 no. 1 (1818)
  [Schlesinger]
  "Mein Schatzerl is hübsch"
**August, Emil Leopold, Herzog von
Sachsen-Gotha und Altenburg,
1772-1822.**
 *Um Rettung biete ein güld'nes
 Geschmeide* (1812) [**Reliquienschrein,**
 p. 78] same
Baggesen, Jens, 1764-1826.
 Die Lethe des Lebens, op. 66 no. 5
  (1809) [Schlesinger]
  "Wenn, Brüder, wie wir täglich sehen"
  Bass, choir & piano.
 Serenade (1809) [Concha; Simrock;
  Cranz] "Horch, leise horch!"
  Voice & piano or guitar.
**Blankensee, Georg Friedrich
Alexander von, count, 1792-1867.**
 Schmerz, op. 80 no. 4 (1820)
  [Schlesinger]
  "Herz, mein Herz, ermanne dich!"
Bürger, J. H.
 Liebeszauber, op. 13 no. 3 (1807)
  [Gombart]
  "Mädel, schau' mir ins Gesicht"
  Voice & guitar.
Castelli, Ignaz Franz, 1781-1862.
 Wunsch und Entsagung, op. 66 no. 6
  (1817) [Schlesinger]
  "Wenn ich die Blümlein schau' "
 DIANA VON POITIERS.
  Ein König einst gefangen sass (1816)
   [Schlesinger] same
   Voice & guitar.
**Cussy, Ferdinand de Cornot, baron
de, 1795-1866.**
 Elle était simple et gentillette (1824)
  [Schlesinger] same
Dusch, Alexander von, 1789-1876.
 Des Künstlers Abschied, op. 71 no. 6
  (1810) [Schlesinger]
  "Auf die stürm'sche See hinaus"
  Voice & guitar.

Eckschlager, Joseph August, b. 1784.
 Maienblümlein, op. 23 no. 3 (1811)
  [Schlesinger] same
Förster, Friedrich, 1791-1868.
 Die freien Sänger, op. 47 no. 2 (1816)
  [Schlesinger]
  "Vöglein hüpfet in dem Haine"
 Mein Verlangen, op. 47 no. 5 (1816)
  [Schlesinger]
  "Ach, wär' ich doch zu dieser Stund"
Förster, Karl Albert Eleon, 1794-1833.
 Triolett, op. 71 no. 1 (1819) [Schlesinger]
  "Keine Lust ohn' treues Lieben!"
Gerstenberg, Friedrich von
 *Das Mädchen an das erste
 Schneeglöckchen,* op. 71 no. 3 (1819)
  [Schlesinger]
  "Was bricht hervor wie Blüthen weiss"
Gubitz, Friedrich Wilhelm, 1786-1870.
 Gebet um die Geliebte, op. 47 no. 6
  (1814) [Schlesinger]
  "Alles in mir glühet, zu lieben!"
 Der Geleichmütige, op. 46 no. 4 (1816)
  [Schlesinger] "Nun, ich bin befrcit!"
 Der Jüngling und die Spröde, op. 47 no.
  4 (1816) [Schlesinger] "Weile, Kind"
 Der Leichtmütige, op. 46 no. 1 (1816)
  [Schlesinger]
  "Lust entfloh und hin ist hin!"
 Liebe-Glühen, op. 25 no. 1 (1812)
  [Gröbenschütz u. Seiler; Schuberth;
  Hofmeister]
  "In der Berge Riesenschatten"
  Voice & guitar.
 Der Liebewütige, op. 46 no. 3 (1816)
  [Schlesinger] "Verrathen!"
 Der Schwermütige, op. 46 no. 2 (1816)
  [Schlesinger] "Selge Zeiten"
**Hafiz, Muhammad Shums al-Din,
d.1388.**
 Rosen in Haare, op. 66 no. 2 (1818)
  [Schlesinger] same
Haug, Friedrich, 1761-1829.
 Die Blume, op. 23 no. 2 (1809)
  [Schlesinger]
  "Traurig, einsam welkst du hin"
**Herder, Johann Gottfried von, 1744-
1803.**
 Das neue Lied (1810) [**Reliquienschrein,**
 p. 63] "Ein neues Lied"
  Voice alone.
Hiemer, Franz Karl, 1768-1822.
 Damon und Chloe, op. 13 no. 1 (1810)
  [Gombart]
  "Endlich hatte Damon sie gefunden"
  Voice & guitar.

WEBER, KARL MARIA VON, 1786-1826
(continued)
Hiemer, Franz Karl, 1768-1822
  (continued)
  Wiegenlied, op. 13 no. 2 (1810)
    [Gombart]
    "Schlaf, Herzenssöhnchen, mein
      Liebling bist du!"
    Voice & guitar.
Kannegiesser, Karl Ludwig, 1781-
1861.
  Elfenlied, op. 80 no. 3 (1819)
    [Schlesinger]
    "Ich tummle mich auf der Haide"
  Sehnsucht, op. 80 no. 2 (1819)
    [Schlesinger]
    "Judäa, hochgelobtes Land"
Kind, Friedrich, 1768-1843.
  Das Licht im Tale (1822) [Schlesinger]
    "Der Gaishirt steht am Felsenrand"
  Lied der Hirtin, op. 71 no. 5 (1818)
    [Schlesinger]
    "Wenn die Maien grün sich kleiden"
  Das Veilchen im Tale, op. 66 no. 1
    (1817) [Schlesinger]
    "Ein Veilchen blüht im Thale"
  DER ABEND AM WALDBRUNNEN.
    Bach, Echo, Kuss, op. 71 no. 2 (1818)
      [Schlesinger] "Ein Mädchen ging die
      Wies' entlang"
      Voice & guitar.
  DAS NACHTLAGER VON GRANADA.
    Alkanzor und Zaide (1818) [Friese]
      "Leise weht es"
      Voice & guitar.
Körner, Theodor, i.e., Karl Theodor,
1791-1813.
  Abschied vom Leben, op. 41 no. 2 (1814)
    [Schlesinger] "Die Wunde brennt"
  Gebet während der Schlacht, op. 41 no. 1
    (1814) [Schlesinger]
    "Vater, ich rufe dich!"
  Leyer und Schwert, op. 43 (1816)
    [Schlesinger]
    "Düst're Harmonieen hör' ich klingen"
  Mein Vaterland, op. 41 no. 4 (1814)
    [Schlesinger]
    "Was ist des Sängers Vaterland?"
  Trost, "Herz, lass dich nicht zerspalten"
    op. 41 no. 3 (1814) [Schlesinger] same
Kotzebue, August Friedrich Ferdinand
von, 1761-1819.
  DER ARME MINNESINGER.
    Lass mich schlummern, op. 25 no. 3
      (1811)
      [Gröbenschütz u. Seiler; Schuberth;
      Hofmeister] same
      Voice & guitar or piano.

Rase, Sturmwind, blase (1811)
  [*Reliquienschrein*, p. 63] same
  Voice & guitar.
Über die Berge mit Ungestüm, op. 25
  no. 2 (1811)
  [Gröbenschütz u. Seiler; Schuberth;
  Hofmeister] same
  Voice & guitar or piano.
Umringt vom muterfüllten Heere, op.
  25 no. 5 (1811)
  [Gröbenschütz u. Seiler; Schuberth;
  Hofmeister] same
  Voice, 4 part men's chorus &
  guitar.
Lehr, Hofrath
  Er an Sie, op. 15 no. 6 (1808) [Simrock]
    "Ein Echo kenn' ich"
  Meine Farben, op. 23 no. 1 (1808)
    [Schlesinger] "Wollt ihr sie kennen?"
  Trinklied (1809) [*Reliquienschrein*,
    p. 55] "Weil es also Gott gefügt"
    Voice, piano & chorus.
Löwenstein-Wertheim-Freudenberg,
Wilhelm, Prinz du, 1817-1877.
  Lied, op. 15 no. 1 (1809) [Simrock]
    "Meine Lieder, meine Sänge"
Matthisson, Friedrich von, 1761-1831.
  Ich denke dein, op. 66 no. 3 (1806)
    [Schlesinger] same
  Die Kerze (1802) [*Reliquienschrein*,
    p. 15] "Ungern flieht das süsse Leben"
    Also in *Jahrbuch der Musikbibliothek
    Peters für 1902*, p. 90.
Metastasio, Pietro Antonio Domenico
Buonaventura, 1698-1782.
  Ch'io mai vi possa, op. 29 no. 3 (1811)
    [Haas] same
    Voice & guitar or piano.
Moore, Thomas, 1779-1852.
  From Chindara's warbling fount (1826)
    [*Reliquienschrein*, p. 160] same
    Also in Beilage zür *Zeitschrift für
    Musik*, 1926, Heft 12.
Müchler, Karl Friedrich, 1763-1857.
  Klage, op. 15 no. 2 (1808) [Simrock]
    "Ein steter Kampf ist unser Leben"
  Lied, op. 15 no. 4 (1809) [Simrock]
    "Was zieht zu deinem Zauberkreise"
  Das Röschen, op. 15 no. 5 (1809)
    [Simrock] "Ich sah ein Röschen"
Nicolai, Christoph Friedrich, 1733-
1811.
  DER KLEINE, FEINE ALMANACH.
    Alte Weiber, op. 54 no. 5 (1817)
      [Peters]
      " 's is nichts mit den alten Weibern"

Nostitz und Jänkendorf, Klothilde
Septimia von, 1801-1852.
Lied von Clotilde, op. 80 no. 1 (1821)
[Schlesinger] "Wcnn Kindlein süssen
Schlummers Ruh"
Opitz, Martin, 1597-1639.
Gelahrtheit, op. 64 no. 4 (1818)
[Schlesinger]
"Ich empfinde fast ein Grauen"
Reinbeck, Georg, 1766-1849.
Romanze: Die Ruinen (1809)
[Hofmeister; Cranz; Schlesinger]
"Süsse Ahnung dehnt den Busen"
Sanftes Licht, op. 13 no. 4 (1809)
[Gombart]
"Sanftes Licht, weiche nicht"
Voice & guitar.
*GORDON UND MONTROSE ODER
DER KAMPFDER GEFÜIILE.*
Ballade, op. 47 no. 3 (1815)
[Schlesinger]
"Was stürmet die Heide herauf?"
Ringwaldt, Bartholomäus, ca.1530-
1599.
Die fromme Magd, op. 54 no. 1 (1818)
[Peters]
"Ein' fromme Magd von gutem Stand"
Rochlitz, Johann Friedrich, 1770-1842.
Es stürmt auf der Flur, op. 30 no. 2
(1813) [Schlesinger] same
Schenkendorf, Max von, 1783-1817.
Die gefangenen Sänger, op. 47 no. 1
(1816) [Schlesinger]
"Vöglein, einsam in dem Bauer"
Seida und Landenberg, Franz Eugen
Joseph, Freiherr von, b. 1772.
Lied (1803) [*Reliquienschrein,* p. 17]
"Entfliehet schnell von mir"
Stoll, Johann Ludwig, 1778-1815.
Die Zeit, op. 13 no. 5 (1810) [Gombart]
"Es sitzt die Zeit im weissen Kleid"
Voice & guitar.
Streckfuss, Adolf Friedrich Karl, 1778-
1844.
Sonett, op. 23 no. 4 (1812) [Schlesinger]
"Du liebes, holdes, himmelsüsses
Wesen"
Swoboda, Wenzel, 1764-1822,
supposed author.
Lied (1804) [*Reliquienschrein,* p. 18]
"Ich sah sie hingesunken"
Tieck, Johann Ludwig, 1773-1853.
Sind es Schmerzen, sind es Freuden, op.
30 no. 6 (1813) [Schlesinger] same
Unknown
Ah dove siete? op. 29 no. 1 (1811)
[Haas] "Ah dove siete?"
Voice & guitar or piano.

Ninfe se liete, op. 29 no. 2 (1811) [Haas]
same
Voice & guitar or piano.
Strafpredigt über die französische Musik
(1801) [*Reliquienschrein,* p. 14]
"Französ'sche Musika"
Vatergruss (1823) [*Reliquienschrein,*
p. 150] "Du gute, gute Mäzze"
Voigt, Christian Friedrich Traugott,
1770-1814.
An eine Freudin, op. 23 no. 6 (1812)
[Schlesinger]
"Zur Freude ward geboren"
Voss, Johann Heinrich, 1751-1826.
Minnelied, op. 30 no. 4 (1813)
[Schlesinger]
"Der Holdseligen sonder Wank"
Reigen, op. 30 no. 5 (1813) [Schlesinger]
"Sagt mir an, was schmunzelt ihr?"
Wallner
Wiedersehen, op. 30 no. 1 (1804)
[Schlesinger] "Jüngst sass ich am
Grabe der Trauten allein"
Wargentin
An Sie, op. 80 no. 5 (1820) [Schlesinger]
"Das war ein recht abscheuliches
Gesicht"
Weber, Karl Maria von, 1786-1826.
Komisches musikalisches Sendschreiben
(1808) [*Reliquienschrein,* p. 32]
"Theuerster Herr Kapellmeister"
Winkler, Karl Gottfried Theodor, 1775-
1856.
SÄNGERS REISE.
Lied in der Fremde (1817?)
[*Reliquienschrein,* p. 102]
"Einsam? einsam? nein"
Weber, Karl Maria von, 1786-1826.
WEBER *Komisches musikalisches
Sendschreiben*
WEBERN, ANTON VON, 1883-1945.
Anon.
Du bist mein, ich bin dein (1901)
[unpubl.] same
Der Tag ist vergangen, op. 12 no. 1
(1915) [Universal-Edition, 1925]
same
Avenarius, Ferdinand, 1856-1923.
STIMMEN UND BILDER.
Wolkennacht (1900) [unpubl.]
"Nacht, dem Zauber"
STIMMEN UND BILDER: Ehe.
Freunde (1904) [Carl Fischer, 1965]
"Schmerzen und Freuden reift jede
Stunde"

WEBERN, ANTON VON, 1883-1945
(continued)
Avenarius, Ferdinand, 1856-1923
(continued)
STIMMEN UND BILDER (continued)
Gefunden (1904) [Carl Fischer, 1965]
"Nun wir uns lieben"
STIMMEN UND BILDER: Jahrbuch.
Vorfrühling (1899) [Carl Fischer,
1965] "Leise tritt auf nicht mehr in
tiefem Schlaf"
Vorfrühling II (1900) [unpubl.]
"Doch schwer hinschnaubend"
Wehmut (1901) [unpubl.]
"Darf ich einer Blume still"
STIMMEN UND BILDER: Stimmungen.
Gebet (1903) [Carl Fischer, 1965]
"Ertrage du's, lass schneiden dir den
Schmerz"
Böhm, Hans, 1876-1946.
Liebeslied (1904) [unpubl.] "Ob ich lach"
Claudius, Matthias, 1740-1815.
Der Tod (1904) [Carl Fischer, 1965]
"Ach, es ist so dunkel in des Todes
Kammer"
Dehmel, Richard, 1863-1920.
Aufblick (1903) [Carl Fischer, 1965]
"Über unsre Liebe hängt eine tief
Trauerweide"
Nachtgebet der Braut (1903) [Carl
Fischer, 1965] "O mein Geliebter in
die Kissen bet ich nach dir"
ABER DIE LIEBE.
Nächtliche Scheu (1907) [Carl Fischer,
1966]
"Zaghaft vom Gewölk ins Land"
ERLÖSUNGEN.
Tief von fern (1901) [Carl Fischer,
1965] "Aus des Abends weissen
Wogen taucht ein Stern"
WEIB UND WELT.
Am Ufer (1908) [Carl Fischer, 1966]
"Die Welt verstummt"
Helle Nacht (1908) [Carl Fischer,
1966] "Weich küsst die Zweige der
weisse Mond"
Himmelfahrt (1908) [Carl Fischer,
1966] "Schwebst du nieder aus den
Weiten"
Ideale Landschaft (1906) [Carl Fischer,
1966] "Du hattest einen Glanz auf
deiner Stirn"
Falke, Gustav, 1853-1916.
MIT DEM LEBEN.
Fromm (1902) [Carl Fischer, 1965]
"Der Mond scheint auf mein Lager"

Frey, Friedrich Hermann, 1830-1911.
Bild der Liebe (1904) [Carl Fischer,
1965] "Von Wald umgeben ein
Blütenbaum"
George, Stefan, 1868-1933.
DAS BUCH DER SAGEN UND SÄNGE:
Sänge eines fahrenden Spielmanns.
*So ich traurig bin weiss ich nur ein
Ding*, op. 4 no. 4 (1909)
[Universal-Edition, 1923] same
DAS JAHR DER SEELE: Nach der Lese.
*Ja Heil und Dank dir die den Segen
brachte!* op. 4 no. 3 (1909)
[Universal-Edition, 1923] same
DAS JAHR DER SEELE: Nachtwachen.
*Erwachen aus dem tiefsten
Traumesschosse* (1908-09) [Carl
Fischer, 1970] same
DAS JAHR DER SEELE: Traurige Tänze.
Ihr tratet zu dem Herde, op. 4 no. 5
(1909) [Universal-Edition, 1923]
same
DAS JAHR DER SEELE: Waller im
Schnee.
*Noch zwingt mich Treue über dir zu
wachen*, op. 4 no. 2 (1909)
[Universal-Edition, 1923] same
DER SIEBENTE RING.
An Bachesranft die einzigen Frühen,
op. 3 no. 3 (1909)
[Universal-Edition, 1921] same
Dies ist ein Lied für dich allein, op. 3
no. 1 (1909)
[Universal-Edition, 1921] same
Im Morgentaun trittst du hervor, op. 3
no. 4 (1909)
[Universal-Edition, 1921] same
Im Windesweben war meine Frage, op.
3 no. 2 (1909)
[Universal-Edition, 1921] same
Kahl reckt der Baum, op. 3 no. 5
(1909) [Universal-Edition, 1921]
same
DER SIEBENTE RING: Gezeiten.
Das lockere Saatgefilde (1908-09)
[Carl Fischer, 1970] same
DER SIEBENTE RING: Maximin.
Kunfttag I (1908-09) [Carl Fischer,
1970] "Dem bist du Kind"
Trauer I (1908-09) [Carl Fischer,
1970] "So wart, bis ich dies"
DER SIEBENTE RING: Traumdunkel.
Eingang, op. 4 no. 1 (1909)
[Universal-Edition, 1923]
"Welt der Gestalten lang"
Goethe, Johann Wolfgang von, 1749-
1832.

Gegenwart (1917) [unpubl.]
"Alles kündigt dich an!"
Gleich und Gleich, op. 12 no. 4 (1917)
[Universal-Edition, 1925]
"Ein Blumenglöckchen vom Boden
hervor"
BLUMENGRUSS.
Blumengruss (1903) [Carl Fischer,
1965] "Der Strauss, den ich
gepflükket"
*CHINESISCH- DEUTSCHE JAHRES-
UND TAGESZEITEN.*
*Nun weiss man erst, was Rosenknospe
sei* (1929) [unpubl.] same
GOTT UND WELT: Howards
Ehrengedächtnis.
Cirrus (1930) [unpubl.] "Doch immer
höher steigt der edle Drang"
Jone, Hildegard, 1891-1963.
DIE FREUNDE.
Des Herzens Purpurvogel, op. 25 no. 2
(1934-35)
[Universal-Edition, 1956] same
Sterne, op. 25 no. 3 (1934-35)
[Universal-Edition, 1956] same
Wie bin ich Froh! op. 25 no. 1 (1934-
35) [Universal-Edition, 1956] same
VIAE INVIAE.
Das dunkle Herz, op. 23 no. 1 (1934)
[Universal-Edition, 1936] same
Es stürzt aus Höhen Frische, op. 23,
no. 2 (1934)
[Universal-Edition, 1936] same
Herr Jesus mein, op. 23 no. 3 (1934)
[Universal-Edition, 1936] same
Li Po, 701-762.
Die geheimnisvolle Flöte, op. 12 no. 2
(1917) [Universal-Edition, 1925]
"An einem Abend"
Liliencron, Detlov, Freiherr von, 1844-
1909.
*ADJUTANTENRITTE UND ANDERE
GEDICHTE.*
Meiner Mutter (1914) [unpubl.] "Wie
oft sah ich die blassen Hände nähen"
BUNTE BEUTE.
Heimgang in der Frühe (1901) [Carl
Fischer, 1965] "In der Dämmerung,
um Glock zwei"
Nietzsche, Friedrich Wilhelm, 1844-
1900.
Heiter (1904) [Carl Fischer, 1965]
"Mein Herz ist wie ein See so weit"
Storm, Theodor, 1817-1888.
Dämmerstunde (1901) [unpubl.] "Im
Sessel du, und ich zu deinen Füssen"

Strindberg, August, 1849-1912.
GESPENSTER SONATE.
Schien mir's, als ich sah die Sonne,
op. 12 no. 3 (1915)
[Universal-Edition, 1925] same
Thu-Fu
Der Frühlingsregen (1920) [unpubl.]
"Der holde liebe Frühlingsregen"
Also voice & orchestra.
Trakl, Georg, 1887-1914.
IM DORF.
In der Heimat (1915) [unpubl.]
"Resedenduft durchs kranke Fenster
irrt"
OFFENBARUNG UND UNTERGAND.
Nachtergebund (1920) [unpubl.]
"Mönchin! schliess mich in dein
Dunkel"
Also voice & orchestra.
SIEBENGESANG DES TODES.
Verklärung (1917) [unpubl.]
"Wenn es Abend wird"
TRAUM DES BÖSEN.
In den Nachtmittag geflüstert (1915)
[unpubl.]
"Sonne, herbstlich dünn und zag"
Unknown
Christkindlein trägt die Sünden der Welt
(1920) [unpubl.] same
Du träumst so heiss im Sommerwind
(1901) [unpubl.] same
Mutig trägst du die Last (1914) [unpubl.]
same
Also voice with violin, oboe &
harmonium.
Verderben, sterben–ich leb' ohne Trost
(1925) [unpubl.] same
Weigand, Wilhelm, 1862-1949.
Sommerabend (1903) [Carl Fischer,
1965] "Du Sommerabend! Heilig,
goldnes Licht!"
Webster, John, 1580?-1625?
THE WHITE DEVIL.
THOMSON *Dirge*
Wechsel see Goethe **LOEWE**
Wechselrahmen see Barth **KRENEK**
WECHSELRAHMEN, no. 1
KRENEK Barth *Schwarze Muse*
WECHSELRAHMEN, no. 2
KRENEK Barth *Der Schatten*
WECHSELRAHMEN, no. 3
KRENEK Barth *Ihr Schwüre*
WECHSELRAHMEN, no. 4
KRENEK Barth *Spruchband*
WECHSELRAHMEN, no. 5
KRENEK Barth *Wechselrahmen*

WECHSELRAHMEN, no. 6
  KRENEK Barth *Heller als Glassteine*
Weckherlin, Georg Rodolf, 1584-1653.
  KRENEK
    Ein Anderes
    Ein Rundum (An eine grosse Fürstin)
Der Weckruf see Eichendorff **PFITZNER**
Wecksell, Josef Julius, 1838-1907.
  SIBELIUS
    Demanten på marssnön
    Marssnön
    Var det en dröm?
Wedekind, Frank, 1864-1918.
  SCHÖNBERG *Galathea*
Wee Willie see Burns **BRITTEN**
"Wee Willie Gray, and his leather wallet" *see*
  Wee Willie Burns **BRITTEN**
"Weep no more, nor sigh, nor groan" *see*
  Mourn no moe Fletcher **HESELTINE**
"Weep not, my wanton, smile upon my knee"
  see Sephestia's lullaby Greene, R.
  BRITTEN
"Weep, weep you no more" *see Tears* Anon.
  SEIBER
Weep you no more see Anon. **QUILTER**
Weg mit allen euren Klagen see Gleim
  ZELTER
Wegerer, Asta von
  REGER *Es soll mein Gebet dich tragen*
Der Wegweiser see Müller, Wilhelm
  SCHUBERT
Weh, wie zornig ist das Mädchen see
  Vicente, Gil *SANNOSA ESTA LA NINNA.*
  SCHUMANN
Wehe see Boelitz **REGER**
"Wehe dem Fliehenden, Welt hinaus
  Ziehenden!" *see In der Ferne* Rellstab
  SCHUBERT
*Wehe der, die mir verstrickte meinen
  Geliebten! see* Vicente, Gil **WOLF**
"Wehe Luftchen, lind und lieblich" *see
  Botschaft* Daumer **BRAHMS**
Wehe mir mein Rosenkränzlein see Hafiz
  JENSEN
Wehe, so willst du mich wieder see Platen-
  Hallermünde **BRAHMS**
Wehmut see Avenarius *STIMMEN UND
  BILDER*: Jahrbuch. **WEBERN**
Wehmut see Collin, M. **SCHUBERT**
Wehmuth see Eichendorff *AHNUNG UND
  GEGENWART.* **SCHUMANN**
Wehmut see Leutnand **ZELTER**
Wehmut see Salis-Seewis **SCHUBERT**
"Wehmut die mich hüllt" *see Das Sehnen*
  Kosegarten **SCHUBERT**
"Wehmut weckt der fernen Wolkenwandrer
  Gruss" *see Beim Scheiden*

Kugler, Johann, Consul in Stettin
  LOEWE
Wehre nicht, O Lieb see Hafiz **JENSEN**
Wehrli-Knobel, Betty *see* Knobel, Betty
  Wehrli, 1904-
Weht es, heult es trüb' see Rostopchina
  RUBINSTEIN
"Weht, O wehet, liebe Morgenwinde!" *see
  Aus der Ferne* Mörike **SCHOECK**
WEIB UND WELT. see Dehmel
    Am Ufer **STRAUSS, WEBERN**
    Helle Nacht **REGER, WEBERN**
    Himmelfahrt **WEBERN**
    Ideale Landschaft **WEBERN**
    Mannesbangen **SCHÖNBERG**
"Ein Weib zu suchen! Wozu" *see
  Der Individualist* Krzyzanowski
  KRENEK
Der Weiberfreund see Cowley **SCHUBERT**
"Weich küsst die Zweige der weisse Mond"
  see Helle Nacht Dehmel
  REGER, WEBERN
Der Weichdorn see Rückert **LOEWE**
"Weiche Flötentöne tiefverträumtes Girren"
  see Flötenspielerin Evers **REGER**
Weiden, E
  RUBINSTEIN *Zuruf aus der Ferne*
"Die Weiden lassen matt die Zweige hangen"
  see Herzeleid Ulrich **SCHUMANN**
Weigand, Wilhelm, 1862-1949.
  REGER *Merkspruch*
  WEBERN *Sommerabend*
Weihnachtlied see Andersen **SCHUMANN**
Der Weihnachtsbaum see Krohn **GRIEG**
    Sang til juletraeet
Weihnachtsgefühl see Frey, F. **STRAUSS**
Weihnachts-Kantate see Unknown **LOEWE**
Weihnachtslied see Baur, Albert
  MENDELSSOHN-BARTHOLDY
Weihnachtslied see Schubart **STRAUSS**
WEIHNACHTSLIEDER I
  CORNELIUS Cornelius *Christbaum*
WEIHNACHTSLIEDER IIa
  CORNELIUS Cornelius *Die Hirten*
    NB: 1856 setting.
WEIHNACHTSLIEDER IIb
  CORNELIUS Cornelius *Die Hirten*
    NB: 1870 setting, op. 8 no. 2.
WEIHNACHTSLIEDER IIIa
  CORNELIUS Cornelius *Die Könige*
    NB: 1856 setting.
WEIHNACHTSLIEDER IIIb
  CORNELIUS Cornelius *Die Könige*
    NB: 1870 setting, op. 8 no. 3.
WEIHNACHTSLIEDER IV
  CORNELIUS Cornelius *Simeon*

WEIHNACHTSLIEDER V
CORNELIUS Cornelius *Christus der
Kinderfreund*
WEIHNACHTSLIEDER VI
CORNELIUS Cornelius *Christkind*
Weihnachtsschnee see Drachmann **GRIEG**
Jule-Sne
Weihnachts-Wiegenlied see Langsted
GRIEG *Julens Vuggesang*
Weil' auf mir see Lenau **IVES**
"Weil' auf mir, du dunkles Auge" *see Bitte*
Lenau **FRANZ, RUBINSTEIN**
"Weil' auf mir, du dunkles Auge" *see
Das dunkle Auge* Lenau **LOEWE**
"Weil es also Gott gefügt" *see Trinklied* Lehr,
Hofrath **WEBER**
"Weil ich dich nicht legen kann" *see
Die sieben Siegel* Rückert **STRAUSS**
"Weil ich sterblich bin geboren" *see Auf sich
selbst* Anacreon **LOEWE**
Weil' ich wie einstmals allein see Rathaus
CHAÏKOVSKIï
"Weil jetzo alles stille ist" *see Nachtgruss*
Eichendorff **SCHOECK**
Weil noch, Sonnenstrahl see Tennyson
LISZT *Go not, happy day*
"Weile, Kind" *see Der Jüngling und die
Spröde* Gubitz **WEBER**
"Weill jetzo alles stille ist" *see Nachtgruss*
Eichendorff **MEDTNER**
Weimars Toten see Schober **LISZT**
"Weimars Toten will ich's bringen" *see
Weimars Toten* Schober **LISZT**
Weimars Volkslied see Cornelius **LISZT**
Wein und Brot see Uhland **SCHOECK**
"Weine du nicht O, die ich innig liebe" *see
Selma und Selmar* Klopstock **SCHUBERT**
"Weine, weine der nicht, O die ich innig
liebe" *see Selmar und Dora* Klopstock
ZELTER
"Weine, weine, weine nur nicht" *see
Junggesellenschwur* Des Knaben
Wunderhorn **STRAUSS**
"Weine, weine, weine nur nicht!" *see
Volkslied* Anon. **WEBER**
"Weinend seh' ich in die Nacht" *see Warum
ich weine* Unknown
MENDELSSOHN-BARTHOLDY
Die Weinende see Byron **SCHUMANN**
"Weinet, sanfte Mädchen" *see Traurigkeit*
Altenberg **BERG**
Weinheber, Josef, 1892-1945.
STRAUSS
*Blick vom oberen Belvedere
Sankt Michael*
"Weint auch einst kein Liebchen" *see Sängers
Trost* Kerner **SCHUMANN**

Weint nicht, ihr Äuglein see Vega Carpio
WOLF
Weint um Israel! see Byron **LOEWE**
Die Weise guter Zecher ist see Bodenstedt
RUBINSTEIN
"Weise nicht von dir mein schlichtes Herz"
see Geübtes Herz Keller, G.
SCHÖNBERG
Weisenborn, Günther, 1902-
BLACHER *Das Lied von den Türen*
WEISGALL, HUGO, 1912-1997.
Anon.
   Baleboste Zisinke (1976) [T.Presser,
     1980] "Balesboste zisinke, zisinke zise
     Baleboste"
   Di goldene pave (1976) [T.Presser, 1980]
     "Es kumt tsu flien di goldene pave"
   Lomir zikh bafrayen (1976) [T.Presser,
     1980] same
   Mayn harts veynt in mir (1976)
     [T.Presser, 1980] "Mayn harts, mayn
     harts veynt in mir"
   No more I will thy love importune (1945)
     [T.Presser, 1958] same
   Nuptial song (1955) [T.Presser, 1958]
     "Be nimble, quick, away"
   Der Rebe Elimeylekh (1976) [T.Presser,
     1980] "Az der Rebe Elimeylekh iz
     gevorn zeyer freylekh"
   Schlof mayn kind, schlof keseyder zingen
     (1976) [T.Presser, 1980] same
   Undzer Rebenyu (1976) [T.Presser, 1980]
     "Oy vey Rebenyu"
Crapsey, Adelaide, 1878-1914.
   Dirge, op. 1 no. 4 [T.Presser, 1940]
     "Never the nightingale, Oh my dear"
   Oh, lady, let the sad tears fall, op. 1 no.
     3 [T.Presser, 1940] same
   Old love, op. 1 no. 1 [T.Presser, 1940]
     "More dim than waning moon Thy
     face"
   Song, op. 1 no. 2 [T.Presser, 1940]
     "I make my shroud but no one know"
Dropkin, Celia (Levin), 1888-1956.
   Poem (1972) [T.Presser, 1977]
     "I haven't yet seen you asleep"
   Poem (197_) [T.Presser, 1977] "You
     sowed in me, not a child but yourself"
Evans, Mari E., 1923-
   I AM A BLACK WOMAN.
     The rebel (197_) [T.Presser, 1977]
       "When I die I'm sure I will have a
       Big Funeral"
Giovanni, Nikki, 1943-
   Knoxville, Tennessee (1972) [T.Presser,
     1977] "I always like summer best"

WEISGALL, HUGO, 1912-1997 *(continued)*
Giraud, Albert, 1860-1929.
Eine blasse Wäscherin (1929) [unpubl.;
ms. at Library of Congress] same
Heine, Heinrich, 1797-1856.
Süsser Mond (1929) [unpubl.; ms. at
Library of Congress]
"Ah, ah, ah, nacht liegt auf den
fremden Wegen"
Margolin, Anna, 1887-1952.
A city by the sea (1971) [T.Presser, 1977]
"When did it all happen?"
Rich, Adrienne Cecile, 1929-
NECESSITIES OF LIFE.
Song (1972) [T.Presser, 1977]
"Sex, as they harshly call it"
Trustman, Deborah
Child song (1972) [T.Presser, 1977]
"How will I know"
Listen: you were the victim (1979)
[T.Presser, 1979] same
Play for me (1979) [T.Presser, 1979]
same
Sound is simple (1979) [T.Presser, 1979]
same
You were like a song (1979) [T.Presser,
1979] same
Wolfe, Humbert, 1885-1940.
I looked back suddenly (1943) [unpubl.]
Weiss, Emil Rudolf, 1875-1942.
SIBELIUS *Sehnsucht*
"Weiss nit, was mir g'scheh" *see Unerklärlich*
Löwenstein **RUBINSTEIN**
"Weiss war die Ros' auf seinem Hut" *see*
Carlisle Tor Cunningham **JENSEN**
Weisse, Christian Felix, 1726-1804.
BEETHOVEN *Der Kuss*
MOZART
Die betrogene Welt
Die Verschweigung
Der Zauberer
Die Zufriedenheit
REGER *Der bescheidene Schäfer*
Der weisse Hirsch see Uhland
SCHUMANN, STRAUSS
Weisse Rose see Dahn *SIND GÖTTER.*
LASSEN
"Weisse Rose nickt an Zweigen sehnend
durch die Maienluft" *see Weisse Rose*
Dahn **LASSEN**
Die weisse, rote Rose see Bjørnson **GRIEG**
Den hvide, røde Rose
Das weisse Spitzchen see Meyer **SCHOECK**
Weisse Tauben see Morgenstern **REGER**
"Weisse Tauben fliegen" *see Weisse Tauben*
Morgenstern **REGER**

Weisser Jasmin see Busse **STRAUSS**
"Weisst Du die Rose" *see Rote Rosen* Stieler
STRAUSS
Weisst du noch? see Hafiz **FRANZ**
Weisst du noch? see Roquette **FRANZ,
JENSEN**
Weit entfernt see Hemans **JENSEN**
"Weit in nebelgrauer Ferne" *see An Emma*
Schiller **SCHUBERT**
"Weit über das Feld" *see Lied* Bodenstedt
BRAHMS
"Weit von meinem Vaterlande" *see*
Der Schwarze in der Zuckerplantage
Claudius, M. **SCHOECK**
Weit, weit see Burns **SCHUMANN**
"Weite Wiesen im Dämmergrau" *see Traum
durch die Dämmerung* Bierbaum
REGER, STRAUSS
"Weiter, rastlos, athemlos, vorüber festlich
helles Schloss" *see An Marie* Unknown
MENDELSSOHN-BARTHOLDY
"Weithin dehnt sich ein Forst" *see Des Baches
Geplauder* Tolstoï **RUBINSTEIN**
Weithin rief die Mutter nach der Tochter see
Unknown **RUBINSTEIN**
"Welch ein wunderbares Leben" *see*
Der Liebende Reissig **BEETHOVEN**
"Welch Leuchten auf den Wogen!" *see
Die Sterne* Gerstenberg **LOEWE**
"Welche chaotische Haushälterei" *see
Die Göttin im Putzzimmer* Rückert
LOEWE
"Welche tief bewegten Lebensläufchen" *see
Die Aufgeregten* Keller, G. **SCHÖNBERG**
"Welchen Weg bist du gegangen" *see
Elevation* Werfel **KRENEK**
"Welcome to our wond'ring sight" *see Sung
by the shepherds* Crashaw **THOMSON**
Welcome to Skye see Anon. **GOUNOD**
"Welcome to you rich autumn days" *see Rich
days* Davies, W. H. **BERKELEY**
Welhaven, Johann Sebastian
Cammermeyer, 1807-1873.
DELIUS *Sing, sing*
FRANZ *Norwegische Frühlingsnacht*
NIELSEN *Vejviseren synger*
Welken see Rodès **BLOCH** *Le déclin*
Welkes Blatt bebt see Lermontov
BALAKIREV *Pesnya: Zholtïy list*
Well, well! see Pósa **BARTÓK** *Ejnye! Ejnye!*
Welle und Wind see Unknown **LASSEN**
"Die Wellen blinken und fliessen" *see Es liebt
sich so lieblich im Lenze* Heine **BRAHMS**
"Die Wellen blinken und fliessen" *see
Frühling* Heine **FRANZ**
"Wellen blinkten durch die Nacht" *see
Der Bleicherin Nachtlied* Reinick **SPOHR**

"Wellen säuseln, Winde locken" *see Deutsche Barkarole* Prechtler LOEWE

"Welt der Gestalten lang" *see Eingang* George WEBERN

"Die Welt verstummt" *see Am Ufer* Dehmel STRAUSS, WEBERN

"Die Welt wär' ein Sumpf" *see Die Enthusiasten* Mörike SCHOECK

"Die Welt weiss deinen Namen nicht" *see In Verborgenen* Träger JENSEN, LASSEN

"Wem Gott will rechte Gunst erweisen" *see Der frohe Wandersmann* Eichendorff SCHOECK, SCHUMANN

Wem ich dieses klage see Strauss, D. RUBINSTEIN

"Wende dich, du kleiner Stern" *see Unter Sternen* Keller, G. SCHOECK

"Wenige wissen das Geheimnis der Liebe" *see Hymne I* Hardenberg SCHUBERT

Wenn see Busse *HEDWIG.* STRAUSS

"Wenn alle Blumen träumen" *see Engelwacht* Muth REGER

Wenn alle untreu werden see Hardenberg LOEWE

"Wenn alle untreu werden" *see Hymne III* Hardenberg SCHUBERT

"Wenn alle Wälder schliefen" *see Der Schatzgräber* Eichendorff SCHUMANN

Wenn alle Welt so einig wär' see Anon. REGER

"Wenn am kleinen Kammerfenster" *see Die treuen Schwalben* Zinserling, W. LOEWE

"Wenn auf dem höchsten Fels ich steh" *see Der Hirt auf dem Felsen* Müller, Wilhelm SCHUBERT

"Wenn, Brüder, wie wir täglich sehen" *see Die Lethe des Lebens* Baggesen WEBER

Wenn dein Auge freundlich see Sturm, J. LASSEN

"Wenn dein Finger durch die Saiten meistert" *see Laura am Klavier* Schiller SCHUBERT

Wenn deine Stimme mir tönt see Lermontov RUBINSTEIN

Wenn der Bann gebrochen see Zwehl, Hans Fritz von KILPINEN

Wenn der Blüten Frühlingsregen see Goethe *FAUST.* LOEWE

Wenn der Frühling auf die Berge steigt see Bodenstedt FRANZ, LASSEN

"Wenn der Schimmer von dem Monde nun herab" *see Die Sommernacht* Klopstock GLUCK, SCHUBERT
    Two Gluck settings: One undated, the other 1785.

"Wenn der Sturm die Blätter jaget" *see Herbstgefühl* Schulenburg LASSEN

"Wenn der uralte, heilige Vater" *see Grenzen der Menschheit* Goethe BERG, SCHUBERT, WOLF

Wenn der Wein nicht wär' see Sergel KILPINEN

"Wenn der Winter sonst entschwand" *see Verwandlung* Schulze SCHUMANN

"Wenn des Mondes bleiches Licht" *see Ein Grab* Peitl WOLF

"Wenn dich die tiefe Sehnsucht rührt" *see Vor dem Sterben* Boelitz REGER

"Wenn die Abendröte" *see Die Kindheit* Matthisson ZELTER

"Wenn die Buben recht böse sind" *see Warte nur!* Braungart REGER

"Wenn die Erde leise aufgewacht" *see Im Frühling* Arndt, J. FRANZ

"Wenn die Felder sich verdunkeln" *see Manche Nacht* Dehmel SCHOECK, SZYMANOWSKI

"Wenn die goldne Frühe neu geboren" *see An die Morgenröte* Bürger PFITZNER

"Wenn die Hahnen frühe krähen" *see Morgenwind* Heyse CORNELIUS

"Wenn die kleinen Kinder beten" *see Das Kindes Gebet* Kiesekamp REGER

"Wenn die Lieb' aus deinen blauen Augen" *see An Chloe* Jacobi MOZART

Wenn die Linde blüht see Busse REGER

"Wenn die Maien grün sich kleiden" *see Lied der Hirtin* Kind, F. WEBER

"Wenn die Nacht sich über die Welt senkt" *see Sehnsucht III* Hohenberg BERG

"Wenn die Reben wieder blühen, rühret sich der Wein im Fasse" *see Nachgefühl* Goethe SPOHR, ZELTER

"Wenn die Schwalben heimwärts ziehn" *see Der Schwalben Heimkehr* Herlossohn WOLF

"Wenn die Sonne lieblich schiene wie im Wälschland lau und blau" *see Pagenlied* Eichendorff MENDELSSOHN-BARTHOLDY

"Wenn die Sonne nieder sinket" *see Abendlied unterm gestirnten Himmel* Goeble BEETHOVEN

"Wenn die Stürme schaurig tosen" *see Herbstgedanken* Unknown RUBINSTEIN

Wenn doch mein Lied ein Vöglein wäre see Hugo LASSEN *Si mes vers avaient des ailes*

Wenn drüben die Glocken klingen see Hauenschild FRANZ

"Wenn du am Abend müde bist" *see Ausklang* Huber, B. KILPINEN

"Wenn du es wüsstest" *see Cäcilie* Hart, J.
    STRAUSS
Wenn du, mein Liebster see Heyse WOLF
Wenn du mich mit den Augen streifst und
    lachst see Heyse WOLF
Wenn du nur zuweilen lächelst see Daumer
    HAFIS. BRAHMS
"Wenn du schon glaubst" *see Summermüd*
    Haringer SCHÖNBERG
Wenn du wärst mein eigen see Kosegarten
    LOEWE
Wenn du zu den Blumen gehst see Anon.
    SPANISCHES LIEDERBUCH: Niña, si la
    huerta vas. JENSEN, WOLF
"Wenn durch Berg' und Thale draussen Regen
    schauert" *see Lust der Sturmnacht*
    Kerner SCHUMANN
"Wenn durch die Piazetta die Abendluft weht"
    see Zwei Venetianische Lieder Moore, T.
    SCHUMANN
Wenn durch die Piazzetta see Moore, T.
    WHEN THROUGH THE PIAZZETTA.
    JENSEN
"Wenn durch die Piazzetta die Abendluft
    weht" *see Venetianisches Gondellied*
    Moore, T.
    MENDELSSOHN-BARTHOLDY
"Wenn ein Gott dir gab für's Schöne" *see*
    Warnung Leuthold SCHOECK
Wenn einst ich tot bin see Klopstock *AN*
    FANNY. LOEWE
"Wenn einst mein Lebenstag sich neiget" *see*
    Gebet Krummacher LOEWE
Wenn einst sie lag an meiner Brust see
    Andersen GRIEG *Hun er saa hvid*
"Wenn Eos am Morgen mit rosigem Finger
    das Dunkel erhellt" *see Jägerlied*
    Unknown SPOHR
"Wenn es Abend wird" *see Verklärung* Trakl
    WEBERN
"Wenn es stürmt auf den Wogen" *see Lied*
    der Frauen Brentano STRAUSS
"Wenn etwas in dir leise spricht" *see Lied*
    Lingg LASSEN
"Wenn Fortuna spröde tut" *see*
    Der Glücksritter Eichendorff WOLF
"Wenn fremde Blikke wachsam uns umgeben"
    see Gesang und Kuss Schlegel ZELTER
"Wenn fromme Kindlein schlafen geh'n" *see*
    Kinderwacht Unknown SCHUMANN
Wenn Gespenster auferstehen see Dörmann
    BERG
"Wenn Gott es hätt' gewollt" *see Volkslied*
    Itzerott REGER
"Wenn hell die liebe Sonne lacht" *see*
    Schelmenliedchen Schellenberg REGER

"Wenn i zum Brünnle geh" *see*
    Die Verlassene Anon. SCHOECK
Wenn ich auf dem Lager liege see Heine
    FRANZ
Wenn ich dein gedenke see Goethe
    WESTÖSTLICHER DIVAN: Buch Suleika.
    WOLF
"Wenn ich des Donners Stimme höre" *see Die*
    Heimath meiner Lieder Boddien, G. von
    RUBINSTEIN
"Wenn ich dich frage, dem das Leben blüht"
    see Blindenklage Henckell STRAUSS
Wenn ich dich seh' see Bodenstedt
    LASSEN
"Wenn ich die Blümlein schau' " *see Wunsch*
    und Entsagung Castelli WEBER
"Wenn ich durch Wald und Fluren geh' " *see*
    Wehmut Collin, M. SCHUBERT
Wenn ich ein kleines Mücklein wär see
    Ahlefeldt, Ottilie von LASSEN
Wenn ich ein Vöglein wär' see Anon.
    JENSEN
"Wenn ich ein Vöglein wär" *see Ruf vom*
    Berge Treitschke BEETHOVEN
"Wenn ich ein Vöglein wär' " *see Volkslied*
    Anon. WEBER
"Wenn ich früh in den Garten geh' " *see*
    Volksliedchen Rückert SCHUMANN
Wenn ich heut nicht deinen Leib berühre see
    George *DAS BUCH DER HÄNGENDEN*
    GÄRTEN. SCHÖNBERG
Wenn ich ihn nur habe see Hardenberg
    LOEWE
"Wenn ich ihn nur habe" *see Hymne II*
    Hardenberg SCHUBERT
Wenn ich in deine Augen seh see Heine
    FRANZ, SCHUMANN, WOLF
Wenn ich kommen dich seh' see Kol'tsov
    RUBINSTEIN
"Wenn ich meine Schafe weide" *see*
    Schäferlied Löns KILPINEN
"Wenn ich nur ein Vöglein wäre" *see*
    Der Knabe Schlegel, F. SCHUBERT
"Wenn ich, O Kindlein" *see Auf ein*
    schlummerndes Kind Hebbel
    CORNELIUS
Wenn ich, O Schöpfer, deine Macht see
    Gellert *PREIS DES SCHÖPFERS.*
    LOEWE
"Wenn ich, von deinem Anschaun tief gestillt"
    see An die Geliebte Mörike WOLF
Wenn ich's nur wüsst see Kolbe REGER
Wenn ich's nur wüsste see Osterwald
    FRANZ
"Wenn im braunen Hafen alle Schiffe
    schlafen" *see Aus der Ferne in der Nacht*
    Bierbaum REGER

"Wenn im Hauch der Abend kühle" *see*
  Die unsichtbare Welt Lühe ZELTER
"Wenn im Spiele leiser Töne" *see Labetrank
  der Liebe* Stoll SCHUBERT
"Wenn im Unendlichen dasselbe" *see
  Praeludium* Goethe MEDTNER
"Wenn immer trüber deine Morgen tagen" *see
  Der nahe Retter* Niemeyer LOEWE
Wenn in bangen, trüben Stunden see
  Hardenberg REGER
"Wenn in des Abends letztem Scheine" *see
  Lied aus der Ferne* Matthisson
  SCHUBERT, ZELTER
"Wenn jemand eine Reise tut" *see Urians
  Reise um die Welt* Claudius, M.
  BEETHOVEN
"Wenn kein Lied mehr erschallet" *see
  Die Wölfe* Tolstoï RUBINSTEIN
"Wenn kein Windchen weht" *see Blaue Augen*
  Leo LASSEN
"Wenn Kindlein süssen Schlummers Ruh" *see
  Lied von Clotilde* Nostitz WEBER
Wenn lichter Mondenschein see Annunzio
  REGER
"Wenn mein Herz beginnt zu klingen" *see
  Meine Lieder* Frey BRAHMS
"Wenn mein Kindlein in der Wiegen lächelt
  still" *see Kindeslächeln* Kiesekamo
  REGER
Wenn mein Schatz Hochzeit macht see
  Mahler MAHLER
"Wenn mein Stündlein für handen ist" *see
  Bitte um einen seligen Tod* Herman
  REGER
"Wenn meine Grillen schwirren, bei Nacht"
  see Der Einsame Lappe SCHUBERT
"Wenn meine Mutter hexen könnt" *see
  Der Tambour* Mörike WOLF
"Wenn mich einsam Lüfte fächeln" *see
  Blanka* Schlegel, F. SCHUBERT
"Wenn Nebel zur Au sinkt" *see Beschwörung*
  Sauter, Lilly von, d. ca. 1970.
  KRENEK
"Wenn, O Mädchen, wenn dein Blut" *see
  Gegenliebe* Bürger PFITZNER
"Wenn sanft du mir im Arme schliefst" *see
  Glückes genug* Liliencron REGER,
  STRAUSS
*Wenn sich bei heiliger Ruh in tiefen Matten
  see* George *DAS BUCH DER
  HÄNGENDEN GÄRTEN.* SCHÖNBERG
Wenn sich Liebes von dir lösen will see
  Bartels PFITZNER
Wenn sich zwei Herzen scheiden see Geibel
  FRANZ, MENDELSSOHN-
  BARTHOLDY

"Wenn stets in stiller Nacht" *see Elegie*
  Maïkov RUBINSTEIN
"Wenn über Berge sich der Nebel breitet" *see
  Nachtstück* Mayrhofer SCHUBERT
"Wenn um den Hollunder der Abendwind
  kost" *see Junge Lieder II* Schumann, F.
  BRAHMS
"Wenn zu den Reihen der Nymphen
  versammelt" *see Geweihter Platz* Goethe
  MEDTNER
  Two settings: Op. 41 no. 1 and op. 46
  no. 2.
"Wenn zu der Regenwand" *see Phanomen*
  Goethe WOLF
"Wenn zwei sich ineinander still versenken"
  see Das Heiligste Hebbel SCHOECK
Wenn Zwei von einander scheiden see Heine
  FRANZ
Wennerberg, Gunnar, 1817-1901.
  SIBELIUS *Näcken*
Wenzig, Josef, 1807-1876.
  BRAHMS *Von ewiger Liebe*
  WESTSLAWISCHEM MÄRCHENSCHATZ.
  BRAHMS
    Abschied, Böhmisch
    Des Liebsten Schwur, Aus dem
      Böhmischen
    Klage I, Aus dem Böhmischen
    Klage II, Slowakisch
"Wer auf den Wogen schliefe" *see
  Der Freund* Eichendorff WOLF
WER BIST DU. see Kosegarten
  Geist der Liebe SCHUBERT
"Wer bist du doch, O Mädchen?" *see
  Gesegnet* Droste-Hülshoff CORNELIUS
"Wer bist du, Geist der Liebe" *see Geist der
  Liebe* Kosegarten SCHUBERT
"Wer da liebt, lieb' überm Maasse" *see Wie es
  sein muss* Tolstoï RUBINSTEIN
"Wer der Meine wohl wird werden" *see
  Mädchens Abendgedanken* Vischer
  RUBINSTEIN
"Wer droht unserm deutschen Vaterland" *see
  Preussisches Hurrahlied*
  Friedrich Wilhelm IV LOEWE
"Wer einsam steht . . . im bunten
  Lebenskreise" *see Die Macht der Musik*
  Orléans, Hélène LISZT
"Wer einsam steht im bunten Lebenskreise"
  see Musik Orléans, Hélène LOEWE
"Wer gab dir, Minne, die Gewalt" *see Gewalt
  der Minne* Walther von der Vogelweide
  PFITZNER
"Wer hätte sie gesehn und nicht auch sie
  geliebt?" *see Ghasel* Adil SPOHR
"Wer hat bedacht, dass bis zu ihrem
  Kommen" *see Vom Tode Mariä* Rilke
  HINDEMITH

Wer hat das erste Lied erdacht see Blüthgen
   DAS ERSTE LIED. **LASSEN**
"Wer hat die schönsten Schäfchen?" *see*
   Wiegenlied Hoffmann von Fallersleben
   SCHOECK
"Wer hats doch durchschauet?" *see*
   Schmetterling Cornelius **CORNELIUS**
Wer hat's gethan? see Gilm zu Rosenegg
   STRAUSS
"Wer in die Fremde will wandern" *see*
   Heimweh Eichendorff **WOLF**
Wer ist Bär? see Häring **LOEWE**
"Wer ist der Jüngling, lieblich zu schauen?"
   see Das Switesmädchen Mickiewicz
   LOEWE
"Wer ist so spät noch fleissig wach?"*see Tod
   und Tödin* Tschabuschnigg **LOEWE**
Wer kauft Liebesgötter? see Goethe
   SCHUBERT, ZELTER
Wer lieben will, muss leiden see Mündel
   ELSÄSSISCHE VOLKSLIEDER. **STRAUSS**
Wer machte dich so krank? see Kerner
   SCHUMANN
"Wer nicht, wenn warm von Hand zu Hand"
   see Punschlied Unknown **BEETHOVEN**
Wer nie sein Brod mit Thränen ass see
   Goethe *WILHELM MEISTER.*
   SCHUMANN
"Wer nie sein Brod mit Thränen ass" *see*
   Harfenspieler III Goethe **WOLF**
"Wer nie sein Brot mit Thränen ass" *see*
   Harfenspieler III Goethe **SCHUBERT**
Wer nie sein Brot mit Tränen ass see Goethe
   WILHELM MEISTER. **LISZT, ZELTER**
"Wer nie sein Brot mit Tränen ass" *see Klage*
   Goethe **ZELTER**
"Wer ohne Leid" *see Den Zweifellosen I*
   Keller, G. **SCHOECK**
"Wer reitet so spät durch Nacht und Wind?"
   see Erlkönig Goethe **BEETHOVEN,
   LOEWE, SCHUBERT**
"Wer reitet so spät durch Nacht und Wind?"
   see Der Erlkönig Goethe **ZELTER**
Wer reit't mit sieben Knappen see Scheffel
   GAUDEAMUS. **JENSEN**
"Wer reit't mit zwanzig Knappen" *see*
   Die drei Dörfer Scheffel **JENSEN**
Wer rief dich denn? see Heyse **WOLF**
Wer sah einen Burschen am Spinnrad sitzen?
   see Tolstoï **MUSORGSKÏ**
   Oï, chest' li to molodtsu len priasti?
"Wer sehen will zweien lebendige Brunnen"
   see Liebesklage des Mädchens
   Des Knaben Wunderhorn **BRAHMS**
Wer sein holdes Lieb verloren see Anon.
   WOLF

"Wer sich der Einsamkeit ergiebt" *see*
   Einsamkeit Goethe **ZELTER**
Wer sich der Einsamkeit ergiebt see Goethe
   WILHELM MEISTER. **SCHUMANN**
"Wer sich der Einsamkeit ergiebt" *see*
   Harfenspieler Goethe **SCHUBERT**
"Wer sich der Einsamkeit ergiebt" *see*
   Harfenspieler I Goethe **SCHUBERT,
   WOLF**
Wer tat deinem Füsslein weh? see Anon.
   WOLF
Wer tritt herein see Strauss, R. **STRAUSS**
"Wer tritt herein so fesch und schlank?" *see*
   Wer tritt herein Strauss, R. **STRAUSS**
"Wer unter eines Mädchens Hand" *see Lied
   der Freiheit* Blumauer **MOZART**
"Wer wagt's, wer wagt's, wer wagt's" *see*
   Der zürnende Barde Bruchmann
   SCHUBERT
Wer wankt zu Fusse see Scheffel
   GAUDEAMUS. **JENSEN**
"Wer wegt es, Rittersmann oder Knapp?" *see*
   Der Taucher Schiller **SCHUBERT**
"Wer, wer ist ein freier Mann?" *see Der freie
   Mann* Pfeffel **BEETHOVEN**
Wer wird von der Welt verlangen see Goethe
   WESTÖSTLICHER DIVAN. **STRAUSS**
Werbung see Dehmel **SZYMANOWSKI**
"Werde heiter mein Gemüthe und vergiss der
   Angst und Pein!" *see Tröstung*
   Hoffmann von Fallersleben
   MENDELSSOHN-BARTHOLDY
"We're sitting in the opera house" *see*
   Memories Ives **IVES**
Were you hiccuping? see Vyazemsky
   RACHMANINOFF
Werfel, Franz, 1890-1945.
   KRENEK *Elevation*
Werfet alle eure Sorgen auf ihn! see
   Niemeyer **LOEWE**
Das Werk des Tages ist vollbracht see
   Golenishchev-Kutuzov **MUSORGSKÏ**
   Okon'en prazdny, shumnyĭ den'
"Werlden är sa stor, sa stor" *see Lasse liten*
   Topelius **SIBELIUS**
Werner, Friedrich Ludwig Zacharias,
   1768-1823.
   DIE SÖHNE DES TALES.
   SCHUBERT *Morgenlied*
   WANDA, KÖNIGIN DER SARMATEN.
   SCHUBERT *Jagdlied*
Wesendonck, Mathilde (Luckmeyer),
   1828-1902.
   WAGNER
   Der Engel
   Im Treibhaus
   Schmerzen

Stehe still
Träume
"Wess' Adern leichtes Blut durchspringt" *see*
Die Fröhlichkeit Prandstetter
SCHUBERT
Wessenberg, Ignaz Heinrich Karl,
Freiherr von, 1774-1860.
BEETHOVEN *Das Geheimnis*
LOEWE *Der heilige Franziskus*
The west dies out in pallid rose see Tolstoǐ
RIMSKIǐ-KORSAKOV
Zapad gasnet v dali bledno-rozovoǐ
West London see Arnold IVES
WESTÖSTLICHER DIVAN. see Goethe
Deinem Blick mich zu bequemen
SCHÖNBERG
Diese Gondel vergleich ich SCHOECK
Durch allen Schall und Klang STRAUSS
Eine einzige Nacht an deinem Herzen!
SCHOECK
Freisinn RUBINSTEIN, SCHUMANN
Geheimes SCHUBERT
Hab' ich euch denn je geraten STRAUSS
Haben sie von deinen Fehlen SCHOECK
Höre den Rat SCHOECK
In tausend Formen ZELTER
Liebeslied SCHUMANN
Lied der Suleika SCHUMANN
Lieder aus dem Schenkenbuch . . .
SCHUMANN
Two settings: Op. 25 no. 5 and op. 25
no. 6.
Nachklang SCHOECK
Seh' ich den Pilgrim SCHOECK
Selige Sehnsucht SCHOECK, ZELTER
Spruch STRAUSS
Suleika MENDELSSOHN-BARTHOLDY,
SCHOECK, SCHUBERT
Suleika und Hatem SCHOECK
Talismane SCHUMANN
Unmut SCHOECK
Versunken SCHUBERT
Wanderers Gemütsruhe STRAUSS
Warum leckst du dein Mäulchen
SCHOECK
Wer wird von der Welt verlangen
STRAUSS
Wie ich so ehrlich war SCHOECK
Wie sie klingeln, die Pfaffen! SCHOECK
Zugemessne Rhythmen STRAUSS
WESTÖSTLICHER DIVAN: Buch des Sängers.
see Goethe
Phanomen WOLF
WESTÖSTLICHER DIVAN: Buch Suleika. *see*
Goethe
Als ich auf dem Euphrat schiffte WOLF

Dies zu deuten bin erbötig! WOLF
Hätt' ich irgend wohl Bedenken WOLF
Hoch beglückt in deiner Liebe WOLF
Komm, Liebchen, komm! WOLF
Locken, haltet mich gefangen WOLF
Nicht Gelegenheit macht Diebe WOLF
Nimmer will ich dich verlieren! WOLF
Wenn ich dein gedenke WOLF
Wie sollt' ich heiter bleiben WOLF
WESTÖSTLICHER DIVAN: Schenkenbuch.
see Goethe
Erschaffen und Beleben STRAUSS, WOLF
Sie haben wegen der Trunkenheit WOLF
So land man nüchtern ist WOLF
Trunken müssen wir alle sein! WOLF
Was in der Schenke waren heute WOLF
WESTSLAWISCHEM MÄRCHENSCHATZ. see
Wenzig
Abschied, Böhmisch BRAHMS
Des Liebsten Schwur, Aus dem Böhmischen
BRAHMS
Klage I, Aus dem Böhmischen BRAHMS
Klage II, Slowakisch BRAHMS
Westwind see Willemer SCHUBERT
Suleika II
The westwind croons in the cedar trees see
MacDowell MACDOWELL
Wetter see Krenek KRENEK
Wetter und Wind see Anon.
SZYMANOWSKI *Wysla burzycka*
Die Wetterfahne see Müller, Wilhelm
SCHUBERT
Wetzel, Friedrich Gottlob, 1779-1819.
LOEWE *Das Muttergottesbild im Teiche*
Wever, Robert, fl. ca. 1550.
AN ENTERLUDE CALLED LUSTY
JUVENTUS (1565).
HESELTINE
In an arbour green
Lusty juventus
"What and each in and they their the and poor
not to with all in in" *see*
From "Sneden's Landing Variations"
O'Hara THOMSON
What are the words of love to you? see
Ammosov, A. MUSORGSKIǐ
Chto vam slova liubvi
What curious thing is love see Agee
SONNET 8. DIAMOND
What does it matter? see Chaǐkovskiǐ
CHAǐKOVSKIǐ *Tak chto zhe?*
What does my name now mean to you? see
Pushkin RIMSKIǐ-KORSAKOV
Chto v imeni tebe moem?
What happiness see Shenshin
RACHMANINOFF

what if a much of a which of a wind see
Cummings **BLITZSTEIN**

"What if fate should decree that apart we
remain" *see Discord* Polonsky
RACHMANINOFF

What if this present see Donne **BRITTEN**

What inn is this see Dickinson **ROREM**

What is it? see Campion **THOMSON**

"What is it all that men possess" *see What is
it?* Campion **THOMSON**

"What is it now with me" *see Fear of death*
Ashbery **ROREM**

What is my name to thee? see Pushkin
RIMSKIĬ-KORSAKOV *Chto v imeni tebe
moem?*

What if some little pain see Spenser
ROREM

"What is this crying that I hear in the wind?"
see The lament of Ian the proud Sharp, W.
GRIFFES

"What land of silence" *see A land of silence*
Dowson **QUILTER**

What means to thee my humble name? see
Pushkin **MEDTNER**

"What needs complaints" *see Comfort to a
youth that had lost his love* Herrick
ROREM

"What pain to wake and miss you!" *see Quite
forsaken* Lawrence **RIETI**

"What scene is this?" *see A night battle*
Whitman **ROREM**

"What sight so lured him thro' the fields" *see
Far, far away* Tennyson **ROREM**

What sparks and wiry cries see Goodman
ROREM

"What though the first pure snowdrop wilt and
die" *see Another spring* De La Mare
BERKELEY

What torment, what rapture see Rostopchina
CHAĬKOVSKIĬ *I bol'no, i sladko*

"What we want is honest money" *see William
Will, a Republican campaign song*
Hill, Susan Benedict **IVES**

"What wealth of rapture" *see What happiness*
Shenshin **RACHMANINOFF**

"What will I do gin my Hoggie die" *see My
Hoggie* Burns **BRITTEN**

"What's his heart?" *see The yellow daisy*
Deland **MACDOWELL**

What's in your mind, my dove see Auden
BERKELEY

What's that shining in the leaves see Bishop
SONGS FOR A COLORED SINGER, VI.
ROREM

"What's the use of practising" *see Practising*
Carpenter, Rue **CARPENTER**

"When a friendly summer calls again" *see
Summer schemes* Hardy **IRELAND**

"When a gal is breathin' sorrow cause her
man is far away" *see Blue gal* Carpenter,
John **CARPENTER**

"When a man is sitting" *see Soliloquy* Ives
IVES

"When a mounting skylark sings in the sunlit
summer morn" *see Skylark and nightingale*
Rossetti, Christina **IRELAND**

"When Abraham Lincoln was born" *see Bells*
Hayes **GIDEON**

When and why see Tagore *GITANJALI.*
MILHAUD

When daffodils begin to peer see
Shakespeare *A WINTER'S TALE.*
IRELAND, QUILTER

"When daffodils begin to peer" *see
Shepherd's song* Shakespeare
BLITZSTEIN

"When daffodils begin to peer" *see The sweet
o' the year* Shakespeare **HESELTINE**

"When daises pied, and violets blue" *see
Mockery* Shakespeare **HESELTINE**

"When did it all happen?" *see A city by the
sea* Margolin **WEISGALL**

"When do I see thee most, beloved one?" *see
Lovesight* Rossetti, Dante
VAUGHAN WILLIAMS

"When dreams enfold me" *see An old flame*
Ives **IVES**

"When gently blows the south wind" *see
The south wind* Ives, Harmony **IVES**

When God was in a happy mood see Hálek
DVOŘÁK *Když bůh byl nejvíc rozkochán*

"When He is King we will give Him the
Kings' gifts" *see Bethlehem down* Blunt
HESELTINE

When I am dead, my dearest see Rossetti,
Christina **IRELAND,
VAUGHAN WILLIAMS**

"When I am dead, my dearest, sing no sad
songs for me" *see A song at parting*
Rossetti, Christina **QUILTER**

When I behold your eyes so dear see Heine
LYRICAL INTERMEZZO.
RIMSKIĬ-KORSAKOV *Kogda gliazhu
tebe v glaza*

When I bring to you colour'd toys see
Tagore *GITANJALI.* **CARPENTER**

"When I bring you coloured toys" *see When
and why* Tagore **MILHAUD**

"When I die I'm sure I will have a Big
Funeral" *see The rebel* Evans, M.
WEISGALL

When I dream see Tavaststjerna **SIBELIUS**
När jag drömmer

When I gaze into thy eyes see Heine
LYRICAL INTERMEZZO. **RIMSKIĬ-**
KORSAKOV *Kogda gliazhu tebe v glaza*
"When I hear the blare of trumpet" *see War*
Carpenter, Rue **CARPENTER**
When I hear thy voice see Lermontov
BALAKIREV *Slĭshu li golos tvoy*
When I hoped I feared see Dickinson
LUENING
"When I peruse the conquer'd fame of heroes"
see How it was with them Whitman
DIAMOND
"When I play on my fiddle in Dooney" *see*
The fiddler of Dooney Yeats
LOEFFLER, RIETI
"When I saw that clumsy crow" *see Night*
crow Roethke **ROREM**
"When I would muse in boyhood" *see*
In boyhood Housman **IRELAND**
When icicles hang by the wall see
Shakespeare *LOVE'S LABOUR'S LOST.*
QUILTER, VAUGHAN WILLIAMS
"When I'm a big man" *see A plan*
Carpenter, Rue **CARPENTER**
When in disgrace with fortune and men's eyes
see Shakespeare **DIAMOND**
"When in my night" *see Phantoms*
Giovannitti **GRIFFES**
When in the early morning see Unknown
GOUNOD
"When Jesus Christ was four years old" *see*
The birds Belloc, Hilaire
BRITTEN, HESELTINE
"When lads were home from labour" *see*
Fancy's knell Housman
VAUGHAN WILLIAMS
"When life becomes unbearable" *see*
The prayer Lermontov **MEDTNER**
when life is quite through with see
Cummings **BLITZSTEIN**
Two settings: 1929 and 1960.
When lights go rolling round the sky see
Blake, James **IRELAND**
WHEN LITTLE BOYS SING, no. 1
CARPENTER Carpenter, Rue *About my*
garden
WHEN LITTLE BOYS SING, no. 2
CARPENTER Carpenter, Rue *Red hair*
WHEN LITTLE BOYS SING, no. 3
CARPENTER Carpenter, Rue *Aspiration*
WHEN LITTLE BOYS SING, no. 4
CARPENTER Carpenter, Rue
The thunderstorm
WHEN LITTLE BOYS SING, no. 5
CARPENTER Carpenter, Rue *A plan*
WHEN LITTLE BOYS SING, no. 6
CARPENTER Carpenter, Rue *Practising*

WHEN LITTLE BOYS SING, no. 7
CARPENTER Carpenter, Rue *Brother*
WHEN LITTLE BOYS SING, no. 8
CARPENTER Carpenter, Rue
Contemplation
WHEN LITTLE BOYS SING, no. 9
CARPENTER Carpenter, Rue *Happy*
heathen
WHEN LITTLE BOYS SING, no. 10
CARPENTER Carpenter, Rue *To cross*
the street
WHEN LITTLE BOYS SING, no. 11
CARPENTER Carpenter, Rue *Making*
calls
WHEN LITTLE BOYS SING, no. 12
CARPENTER Carpenter, Rue *When the*
night comes
"When love with unconfined wings" *see*
To Althea from prison Lovelace
QUILTER
When lovely golden fields of wheat are gently
swaying see Lermontov
RIMSKIĬ-KORSAKOV *Kogda volnuetsia*
zhelteiushchaia niva
"When May is in his prime" *see The sweet*
season Edwardes **IRELAND**
When my glances see Shenshin **MEDTNER**
Beauty
When my mother taught me see Heyduk
DVOŘÁK *Když mne stará matka*
When my soul touches yours see Rilke
BERNSTEIN
When other lips shall speak see Bunn
THE BOHEMIAN GIRL. **DELIUS**
"When Pat came over the hill" *see*
The whistlin' thief Lover **HINDEMITH**
"When roses are about to fade" *see When*
roses fade Pushkin **MEDTNER**
When roses fade see Pushkin **MEDTNER**
"When silent night doth hold me" *see In the*
silence of the secret night Shenshin
RACHMANINOFF
"When Sister Jane, who had produced a child"
see Sister Jane La Fontaine **DIAMOND**
When stars are in the quiet skies see Lytton
IVES
"When that I was & a little tiny boy" *see Hey,*
ho, the wind and the rain Shakespeare
QUILTER
When that I was and a little tiny boy see
Shakespeare *TWELFTH NIGHT.*
SCHUMANN *Schlusslied des Narren*
SIBELIUS *Ock nör som jag ver en liten*
smadrang
When the day comes see Sládek **MARTINŮ**
"When the distant eveningbell calmly breaths
its blessing" *see Nature's way* Ives **IVES**

COMPOSER Poet *Title* "First Line"

When the golden cornfield waves see
Lermontov RIMSKIĬ-KORSAKOV
Kogda volnuetsia zhelteĭushchaia niva
When the kye come hame see Unknown
RESPIGHI
When the misty shadows glide see Verlaine
EN SOURDINE. CARPENTER
"When the moon is on the wave" *see from the*
"Incantation" Byron IVES
When the night comes see Carpenter, Rue
CARPENTER
"When the snow is off the mountains" *see*
Come, lady-day Pemberton, May
QUILTER
"When the stars in crowds" *see The*
policeman in the park Feeney CHANLER
"When the waves softly sigh" *see A song* Ives
IVES
When the yellow cornfield waves see
Lermontov BALAKIREV
Kogda volnuyetsya zhelteyushchaya niva
When they come back see Dickinson
COPLAND
When thou playest, carefree child see Wilde,
Ch. BALAKIREV
Kogda bezzabotno, ditya, tĭ rezvish'sya
When through the Piazzetta night breathes her
cool air see Moore, T.
WHEN THROUGH THE PIAZZETTA.
SCHUMANN *Zwei Venetianische Lieder*
WHEN THROUGH THE PIAZZETTA. see
Moore, T.
Wenn durch die Piazzetta JENSEN
Zwei Venetianische Lieder SCHUMANN
"When thru the world at last there comes the
close of day" *see Retrospect* Pushkin
MEDTNER
When thy sweet glances on me fall see
Pfleger-Moravský DVOŘÁK *Vté sladké*
moci
Two settings: B. 11 no. 2 and B. 160 no.
7.
When to the sessions of sweet silent thought
see Shakespeare DIAMOND
"When twilight comes, when twilight comes"
see Dreams Unknown IVES
"When vain desire at last and vain regret" *see*
The one hope Rossetti, Dante IRELAND
When we are old see Klášterský MARTINŮ
When we were idlers with the loitering rills
see Coleridge, H. BERKELEY
"When will you ever, Peace" *see Peace*
Hopkins KRENEK
When yesterday we met see Polonsky
RACHMANINOFF
When you are old see Yeats RIETI

"When your glances, enchanting, you fling"
see Beauty Shenshin MEDTNER
"Whenas in silks my Julia goes" *see Upon*
Julia's clothes Herrick ROREM
"Whenas the mildest month of jolly June" *see*
All in a garden green Howell, Thomas
IRELAND
"Whenas the rye reach to the chin" *see*
Chopcherry Peele HESELTINE
Whenas the rye reach to the chin see Peele
THE OLD WIVES' TALE (1595).
HESELTINE
"Whence, O fragrant form of life" *see*
The water lily Tabb GRIFFES
"Whenever the moon and the stars are set" *see*
Windy nights Stevenson, Robert Louis
HAHN
Where art thou, little star? see Grekov
MUSORGSKIĬ *Gde ty, zvezdochka?*
Where be you going see Keats QUILTER
"Where Claribel low lieth" *see Claribel*
Tennyson VAUGHAN WILLIAMS
"Where e'er love be" *see Tyrant love*
MacDowell MACDOWELL
Where go the boats? see Stevenson,
Robert Louis *A CHILD'S GARDEN OF*
VERSES. QUILTER
"Where has Maid Quiet gone to" *see Maid*
quiet Yeats RIETI
Where have I been? see Jesenská
MARTINŮ
Where I am, the gloom surrounds see Heine
LYRISCHES INTERMEZZO, no. 68.
GRIFFES *Wo ich bin, mich rings*
umdunkelt
Where is the home for me? see Murray
VAUGHAN WILLIAMS
"Where is the world that harks to fancy?" *see*
The window Pushkin MEDTNER
"Where sunless rivers weep" *see Dreamland*
Rossetti, Christina
VAUGHAN WILLIAMS
Where the bee sucks see Shakespeare
THE TEMPEST. DIAMOND, QUILTER
Where the eagle see Turnbull IVES
"Where the eagle cannot see" *see Where the*
eagle Turnbull IVES
Where thou art, my thought flies to thee see
Anon. RIMSKIĬ-KORSAKOV
Gde ty, tam mysl' moĭa letaet
Where was I? see Jesenská MARTINŮ
Where we came see Garrigue ROREM
"Where we came the grasses were high" *see*
Where we came Garrigue ROREM
"Where, where is the rose-bud, the child of
dawn" *see The rose* Pushkin MEDTNER

"While I in western lands do pine" *see My heart is in the east* Schaffer **COPLAND**

"While larks with little wind fann'd the pure air" *see Lovely maid!* Burns **FRANZ**

"While one will search the season over" *see Luck and work* Johnson **IVES**

"While that the sun with his beams hot" *see The faithless shepherdess* Anon.
    QUILTER

While you here do snoring lie see Shakespeare *THE TEMPEST.*
    DIAMOND

"Whirling winter snow and vapor" *see Winter evening* Pushkin **MEDTNER**

Whiskey drink divine see O'Leary, Joseph
    ROREM

"The whiskey on your breath could make a small boy dizzy" *see My papa's waltz* Roethke **DIAMOND, ROREM**

A whisper, a gentle breath see Shenshin
    RIMSKIĬ-KORSAKOV *Shopot, robkoe dykhan'e*

A whisper, a timid breath see Shenshin
    BALAKIREV *Shopot, robkoye díkhan'ye*

WHISPERS OF HEAVENLY DEATH. see Whitman
    Darest thou now, O soul
        VAUGHAN WILLIAMS
    Nocturne **VAUGHAN WILLIAMS**

"Whispers of heavenly death murmur'd I hear" *see Nocturne* Whitman
    VAUGHAN WILLIAMS

Whisp'ring nature see Shenshin
    MEDTNER *Dawn in the garden*

Whisp'ring, timid breathless sighing see Shenshin **RIMSKIĬ-KORSAKOV**
    Shopot, robkoe dykhan'e

"Whisp'ring, timid, softly breathing" *see Dawn in the garden* Shenshin
    MEDTNER

The whistlin' thief see Lover **HINDEMITH**

THE WHITE DEVIL. see Webster
    Dirge **THOMSON**

The white gulls see Unknown **IVES**

"The white gulls dip and wheel" *see The white gulls* Unknown **IVES**

"A white mist drifts across the shrouds" *see La mer* Wilde **GRIFFES**

"A white mist drifts across the shrouds" *see The sea* Wilde **GRIFFES**

White moth at twilight see Wright, Merle St. Croix **THOMPSON, R.**

White snowflakes see Anon. **PROKOFIEV**
    Snezhki belye

The white-flanked magpie see Pushkin
    MUSORGSKIĬ *Strekotun'ia beloboka*

Whither must I wander? see Stevenson, Robert Louis *SONGS OF TRAVEL,* XVI.
    VAUGHAN WILLIAMS

Whither thou goest see Louchheim *WITH OR WITHOUT ROSES.* **DIAMOND**

Whitman, Walt, 1819-1892.
    BLITZSTEIN
        After the dazzle of day
        Ages and ages
        As Adam
        As if a phantom caress'd me
        I am He
        O Hymen! O Hymenee!
    CARTER *Warble for lilac time*
    DIAMOND *How it was with them*
    HINDEMITH
        Der ich, in Zwischenräumen
        O, nun heb du an, dort in deinem Moor
        Schlagt! Schlagt! Trommeln!
        Sing on there in the swamp
    LUENING
        At the last
        A farm picture
        Gliding o'er all
        Hast never come to thee
        Here the frailest leaves of me
        Locations and times
        Visored
    ROREM
        As Adam early in the morning
        Gliding o'er all
        Gods
        I saw in Louisiana a live-oak growing
        Look down, fair moon
        O you whom I often and silently come
        Of him I love day and night
        Reconciliation
        Sometimes with one I love
        To a common prostitute
        To you
        Youth, day, old age, and night
    THOMPSON, R. *The ship starting*
    FROM NOON TO STARRY NIGHT.
        VAUGHAN WILLIAMS *A clear midnight*
    LEAVES OF GRASS.
        IVES *Walt Whitman*
        LUENING *Only themselves*
    SONGS OF PARTING.
        VAUGHAN WILLIAMS *Joy, shipmate, joy!*
    SPECIMEN DAYS.
        ROREM
            Inauguration ball
            An incident
            A night battle

Whitman, Walt, 1819-1892 *(continued)*
SPECIMEN DAYS (continued)
ROREM *(continued)*
*The real war will never get in the
books*
Specimen case
WHISPERS OF HEAVENLY DEATH.
VAUGHAN WILLIAMS
Darest thou now, O soul
Nocturne
Whittier, John Greenleaf, 1807-1892.
IVES
The light that is felt
Serenity
Who are these children? see Soutar
BRITTEN
WHO ARE THESE CHILDREN? no. 1
BRITTEN Soutar *A riddle*
WHO ARE THESE CHILDREN? no. 2
BRITTEN Soutar *A laddie's sang*
WHO ARE THESE CHILDREN? no. 3
BRITTEN Soutar *Nightmare*
WHO ARE THESE CHILDREN? no. 4
BRITTEN Soutar *Black day*
WHO ARE THESE CHILDREN? no. 5
BRITTEN Soutar *Bed-time*
WHO ARE THESE CHILDREN? no. 6
BRITTEN Soutar *Slaughter*
WHO ARE THESE CHILDREN? no. 7
BRITTEN Soutar *A riddle*
WHO ARE THESE CHILDREN? no. 8
BRITTEN Soutar *The larky lad*
WHO ARE THESE CHILDREN? no. 9
BRITTEN Soutar *Who are theseF
children?*
WHO ARE THESE CHILDREN? no. 10
BRITTEN Soutar *Supper*
WHO ARE THESE CHILDREN? no. 11
BRITTEN Soutar *The children*
WHO ARE THESE CHILDREN? no. 12
BRITTEN Soutar *The auld aik*
"Who dares to say the spring is dead" *see
Immortality* Ives **IVES**
Who goes? see Apukhtin **CHAĭKOVSKIĭ**
Kto idyot?
"Who goes there?" *see Walt Whitman*
Whitman **IVES**
Who has brought you here? see Runeberg
SIBELIUS *Hvem styrde hit din väg?*
Who has seen the wind see Rossetti,
Christina **RIEGGER**
"Who is it that, this dark night" *see Voices at
the window* Sidney, Sir Philip **RIETI**
Who is Silvia? see Shakespeare *TWO
GENTLEMEN OF VERONA.* **QUILTER**
"Who says that it's by my desire" *see People
hide their love* Wu-Ti, Liang dynasty
BERKELEY

"Who would true valour see" *see The song of
the pilgrims* Bunyan
VAUGHAN WILLIAMS
"Whoe'er thou art, O reader" *see Epitaph on
wee Johnie* Burns **GIDEON**
"Who'll play at Rantum Tantum over the
fields in May?" *see Rantum Tantum*
Neuburg **HESELTINE**
Why? see Heine *WARUM SIND DANN DIE
ROSEN SO BLASS?* **CHAĭKOVSKIĭ**
Otchevo?
Why? see Lermontov **BALAKIREV**
Otchevo
Why? see Mei **CHAĭKOVSKIĭ** *Zachem?*
"Why am I bawling?" *see Bawling blues*
Goodman **ROREM**
Why am I here see Agee *SONNET 9.*
DIAMOND
"Why are those tears in your eyes, my child?"
see Defamation Tagore **MILHAUD**
Why art thou so early, Dawn? see
Solov'yov, S. **BORODIN**
Why did I dream of you? see Mei
CHAĭKOVSKIĭ *Zachem?*
Why do they shut me out of Heaven? see
Dickinson **COPLAND**
"Why doesn't one, two, three" *see One-two-
three* Ives **IVES**
"Why have you brought me myrrh" *see
The adoration* Symons **IRELAND**
Why have you laughed at me? see Houdek,
V. **MARTINŮ**
"Why I tie about thy wrist, Julia" *see
The bracelet* Herrick **QUILTER**
"Why, O willow, are you bending" *see Willow*
Tiutchev **MEDTNER**
Why so pale and wan? see Suckling
QUILTER
"Wiatr zaszumial miedzy krzewy" *see
Narzeczony* Witwicki **CHOPIN**
Wiberg, Ohs
NIELSEN *Julesang*
A wicked child see Carpenter, Rue
CARPENTER
Wide the sleeves and trousers see Heyduk
DVOŘÁK *Široké rukávy*
Widerschein see Schlechta **SCHUBERT**
Two settings: D. 639 and D. 949.
Widmung see Cossmann **PFITZNER**
Widmung see Mörike **SCHOECK**
Widmung see Müller von Königswinter
FRANZ
Widmung see Rückert **REGER,
SCHUMANN**
"Wie anders, Gretchen, war dir's" *see Szene
aus Goethe's "Faust"* Goethe
SCHUBERT

"Wie bei des Zephyrs leisem Hauch" *see
Sanftes Walten* Tolstoï RUBINSTEIN

Wie bin ich Froh! see Jone *DIE FREUNDE.*
WEBERN

"Wie bist du Frühling gut und treu" *see
Amaranths' Waldeslieder* Redwitz
BRUCKNER

Wie bist du, meine Königin see Daumer
HAFIS. BRAHMS

"Wie bist du nur" *see Mein Herzensschatz*
Oelschläger, H. RUBINSTEIN

"Wie bist du schön" *see Der Waldsee*
Leuthold SCHOECK

   Two settings: Op. 15 no. 1 and op. 57
   no. 20.

"Wie blitzen die Sterne so hell durch die
Nacht!" *see Die Sterne* Leitner
SCHUBERT

"Wie blüht es im Thale" *see Hinaus ins Freie*
Hoffmann von Fallersleben
SCHUMANN

Wie bräutlich glänzt das heilige Rom see
Kugler LOEWE

"Wie braust durch die Wipfel der heulende
Sturm" *see Die junge Nonne* Craigher
SCHUBERT

"Wie der Bäume kühne Wipfel" *see Himmel
und Erde* Schöpff SCHUMANN

"Wie der Quell ist mein Lied" *see Lied*
Polonsky RUBINSTEIN

"Wie der Quell so lieblich klinget" *see
Minnelied* Tieck MENDELSSOHN-
BARTHOLDY

"Wie der Tag mir schleichtet ohne dich
vollbracht" *see An die Geliebte* Gotter
LOEWE

Wie des Mondes Abbild zittert see Heine
LIEDERSTRAUSS. FRANZ, WOLF

"Wie deutlich des Mondes Licht" *see
Der Wanderer* Schlegel, F. SCHUBERT

"Wie die Nacht mit heil'gem Beben" *see
Sehnsucht der Liebe* Körner SCHUBERT

Wie die Wolke nach der Sonne see
Hoffmann von Fallersleben BRAHMS

"Wie doch so still dir am Kerzen" *see
Das sterbende Kind* Geibel GRIFFES,
REGER

Wie du deine Sonne hast lassen aufgehn see
Augustinus LOEWE

Wie durch die stille Mondesnacht see Träger
LASSEN

"Wie ein Goldadler reisst der Blitz" *see Ich
liebe dich!* Grabbe BERG

"Wie ein Schwan still die Bahn" *see
Mondlicht* Branco LOEWE

Wie eine Lerch' in blauer Luft see Boddien,
G. von RUBINSTEIN

"Wie eine trübe Wolke" *see Einsamkeit*
Müller, Wilhelm SCHUBERT

"Wie eine weisse Wolke" *see Elisabeth*
Hesse SCHOECK

"Wie einst den Knaben lacht ihr noch heut
mich an" *see Abkehr* Leuthold
SCHOECK

"Wie erhebt sich das Herz, wenn es dich" *see
Dem Unendlichen* Klopstock SCHUBERT

Wie erkenn' ich dein Treulieb see
Shakespeare *HAMLET.* LASSEN

Wie erkenn' ich mein Treulieb? see
Shakespeare *HAMLET.* STRAUSS

"Wie erscholl der Gang" *see Schlachtgesang*
Klopstock GLUCK

Wie es sein muss see Tolstoï RUBINSTEIN

"Wie etwas sei leicht" *see Spruch* Goethe
STRAUSS

"Wie Feld und Au' so blinkend im Tau" *see
Im Sommer* Goethe FRANZ, SCHOECK

"Wie ferne Tritte hörst du's schallen" *see
Herbstgefühl* Frey, F. PFITZNER

"Wie floss von deiner Lippe milde Güte!" *see
An meine Grossmutter* Leuthold
SCHOECK

Wie froh und frisch see Tieck BRAHMS

Wie früh das enge Pförtchen knarre see
Giesebrecht LOEWE

*Wie Frühlingsahnung weht es durch die Lande
see* Grun, James PFITZNER

"Wie geheimes Lispeln rieselt's durch die
Nacht" *see Nachtgeflüster* Evers REGER

*Wie Georg von Frundsberg von sich selber
sang see* Des Knaben Wunderhorn
SCHÖNBERG

Wie glänzt der helle Mond see Keller, G.
PFITZNER, WOLF

"Wie glänzt nun die Welt im Abendstrahl"
see Der Glückliche Wilbrandt LISZT

"Wie glücklich, wem das Knabenkleid" *see
Die Knabenzeit* Hölty SCHUBERT

Wie gross ist des Allmächt'gen Güte! see
Gellert LOEWE

"Wie hat der Sturm zerrissen" *see
Der stürmische Morgen* Müller, Wilhelm
SCHUBERT

"Wie heimlicher Weise" *see Zum neuen Jahr*
Mörike WOLF

"Wie heisst König Ringangs Töchterlein?"
see Schön-Rohtraut Mörike SCHOECK

Wie herrlich leuchtet see Goethe BARTÓK

"Wie herrlich leuchtet mir die Natur" *see
Maienlied* Goethe LASSEN

"Wie herrlich leuchtet mir die Natur" *see
Maigesang* Goethe BEETHOVEN

"Wie herrlich leuchtet mir die Natur!" *see
Mailied* Goethe LOEWE, PFITZNER,
SCHOECK

Wie ich so ehrlich war see Goethe
WESTÖSTLICHER DIVAN. SCHOECK
"Wie im Morgenglanze du rings mich
anglühst" *see Ganymed* Goethe
LOEWE, SCHUBERT, WOLF
"Wie ist der Abend stille" *see Abendlied*
Wildenbruch LASSEN
"Wie ist die Nacht voll holder
Heimlichkeiten!" *see Das Dorf* Boelitz
REGER
"Wie ist doch die Erde so schön, so schön!"
see Juchhe! Reinick BRAHMS
"Wie ist so heiss im Busen mir" *see Die
Jungfrau und der Tod* Kugler LOEWE
"Wie kann ich froh und munter sein" *see
Weit, weit* Burns SCHUMANN
"Wie klag' ich's aus" *see Schwanengesang*
Senn SCHUBERT
"Wie könnt' ich dein vergessen" *see Mein
Liebchen* Hoffmann von Fallersleben
LASSEN
"Wie kommt's, dass du so traurig bist" *see
Trost in Thränen* Goethe SCHUBERT
"Wie kommt's, dass du so traurig bist" *see
Trost in Tränen* Goethe BRAHMS,
LOEWE, ZELTER
"Wie kühl schweift sich's" *see Nachtgruss*
Eichendorff WOLF
Wie lange schon see Heyse WOLF
Wie Lenzeshauch see Träger JENSEN
Wie lieb ich dich hab' see Cornelius
CORNELIUS
"Wie lieblich und fröhlich" *see Die Vögel*
Schlegel, F. SCHUBERT
"Wie lockt der Palmen grünes Dach" *see
Die Oasis* Stieglitz LOEWE
Wie man eine Hummel verjagt see
Iłłakowiczówna SZYMANOWSKI
Jak sie najlepiej opędzać od szerszenia
Wie manchmal, wenn des Mondes Strahl see
Moore, T. JENSEN
Wie Melodien zieht es mir see Groth
HUNDERT BLÄTTER... BRAHMS
"Wie, mit innigstem Behagen" *see Lied der
Suleika* Goethe SCHUMANN
Wie öd! see Golenishchev-Kutuzov
MUSORGSKIĭ *Skuchaĭ*
"Wie oft sah ich die blassen Hände nähen"
see Meiner Mutter Liliencron WEBERN
"Wie oft schon ward es Frühling wieder" *see
Liebesfrühling* Hoffmann von
Fallersleben WOLF
"Wie pocht' das Herz mir in der Brust" *see
Firnelicht* Meyer SCHOECK
"Wie pocht mir vor Lust das Herz in der
Brust" *see Der Bräutigam* Gruppe
LOEWE

Wie rafft' ich mich auf in der Nacht see
Platen-Hallermünde BRAHMS
"Wie rein Gesang sich windet" *see Der Fluss*
Schlegel, F. SCHUBERT
"Wie sanft, wie ruhig fühl' ich hier" *see
Die Zufriedenheit* Weisse MOZART
Wie Sankt Franciscus schweb' in der Luft see
Morgenstern HINDEMITH
"Wie schaust du aus dem Nebelflor" *see Idens
Schwanenlied* Kosegarten SCHUBERT
"Wie schienen die Sternlein so hell, so hell"
see Abschied Kapper FRANZ
"Wie schienen die Sternlein so hell, so hell"
see Ade! (Nach dem Böhmischen) Kapper
BRAHMS
"Wie schlafend unterm Flügel" *see Trost der
Kreatur* Keller, G. SCHOECK
Wie schnell verschwindet so Licht als Glanz
see Tieck BRAHMS
"Wie schön bist du, du güldne Morgenröte"
see Lilla an die Morgenröte Unknown
SCHUBERT
"Wie schön geschmückt der festliche Raum"
see Christbaum Cornelius CORNELIUS
"Wie schön hier zu verträumen" *see
Die Nacht* Eichendorff LASSEN
"Wie sehr du mich verkanntest" *see
Canzonetta: Italienisches Ständchen* Anon.
WEBER
"Wie sehr ich dein, soll ich dir sagen" *see
Frage* Lenau FRANZ
"Wie sehr ich Dein, soll ich dir sagen?" *see
Frage nicht* Lenau WOLF
"Wie sich der Äuglein kindlicher Himmel" *see
Wiegenlied* Seidl SCHUBERT
"Wie sich Rebenranken schwingen" *see Liebe
und Frühling* Hoffmann von
Fallersleben BRAHMS
Wie sie klingeln, die Pfaffen! see Goethe
WESTÖSTLICHER DIVAN. SCHOECK
Wie sind die Tage see Hesse LUENING
Wie singt die Lerche schön see Hoffmann
von Fallersleben LISZT
"Wie sisst mir das Liebchen?" *see Im Fernen*
Goethe ZELTER
Wie so bleich see Chamisso JENSEN
"Wie so gelinde die Fluth bewegt" *see
Scheidend* Voss MENDELSSOHN-
BARTHOLDY
"Wie so innig, möcht'ich sagen" *see
Das Mädchen* Schlegel, F. SCHUBERT
Wie so launisch bist du, O Sonnenschein see
Unknown RUBINSTEIN
Wie soll ich die Freude see Tieck BRAHMS
Wie soll ich fröhlich sein und lachen gar see
Heyse WOLF

"Wie soll ich nicht tanzen" *see Der Schmetterling* Schlegel, F. **SCHUBERT**

Wie sollt' ich heiter bleiben see Goethe *WESTÖSTLICHER DIVAN*: Buch Suleika. **WOLF**

Wie sollten wir geheim sie halten see Schack *LOTOSBLÄTTER.* **STRAUSS**

Wie stimmst du mich zur Andacht see Hafiz **SCHOECK**

"Wie süss der Nachtwind nun die Wiese streift" *see Gesang zu zweien in der Nacht* Mörike **SCHOECK**

"Wie tönt es mir so schaurig" *see Der Blumen Schmerz* Mayláth **SCHUBERT**

"Wie trag ich doch im Sinne" *see Musje Morgenrots Lied* Heyse **CORNELIUS**

"Wie traulich war das Fleckchen" *see Heimweh I* Groth **BRAHMS**

"Wie traurig du am Gartentore standst" *see Und Herbstlaub und Regenschaue* Krenek **KRENEK**

"Wie traurig sind wir Mädchen dran" *see Dies und Das* Anon. **FRANZ**

"Wie treiben die Wolken so finster und schwer" *see Minona* Bertrand **SCHUBERT**

Wie Ulfru fischt see Mayrhofer **SCHUBERT**

Wie unglücklich bin ich nit see Unknown **MOZART**

Wie viele Zeit verlor ich see Heyse **WOLF**

Wie vieles ist denn Wort geworden see Morgenstern **KILPINEN**

Wie wähnten lange recht zu leben see Keller, G. **SCHOECK**

"Wie war zu Cölln es doch vordem" *see Die Heinzelmännchen* Kopisch **LOEWE**

Wie wart ihr fröhlich, gold'ne Mädchentage see Unknown **RUBINSTEIN**

"Wie weil' ich so gern, wo die Trauer webt" *see Lied des verlassenen Mädchens* Deinhardstein **SPOHR**

"Wie wenn im frost'gen Windhauch tödtlich" *see Herbstgefühl* Schack **BRAHMS**

"Wie wohl ist mir im Dunkeln" *see Die Sterne* Kosegarten **SCHUBERT**

Wie wohnst du in des Reiches Städten see Giesebrecht **LOEWE**

"Wie zerrissner Saiten Klingen" *see Allein* Ritter **REGER**

Wied, Gustav Johannes, 1858-1914. *ATALANTA.* **NIELSEN** *Gudhjaelp*

Wieder möcht' ich dir begegnen see Cornelius **LASSEN, LISZT**

"Wieder schreitet er den braunen Pfad" *see Frühling* Hesse **SCHOECK**

Wiederfinden see Goethe **ZELTER**

Wiedersehen see Rückert **FRANZ**

Wiedersehen see Tiedge **ZELTER**

Wiedersehen see Wallner **WEBER**

Wiedersehn see Schlegel **SCHUBERT**

"Wiedersehn! Wiedersehn!" *see Wiedersehen* Tiedge **ZELTER**

Wiederum lebt wohl see Mommsen **KRENEK**

Wieg' O Welle see Drachmann **GRIEG** *Vug, O Vove*

Das Wiegenfest zu Gent see Auersperg **LOEWE**

Wiegenlied see Anon. **REGER**

Wiegenlied see Braungart **REGER**

Wiegenlied see Cornelius **CORNELIUS, LASSEN**

Wiegenlied see Dehmel **REGER**

Wiegenlied see Dehmel *DIE VERWANDLUNGEN DER VENUS*: Venus Mater. **REGER, STRAUSS**

Wiegenlied see Des Knaben Wunderhorn **BRAHMS**

Wiegenlied see Göchhausen **SPOHR**

Wiegenlied see Golenishchev-Kutuzov **MUSORGSKIĬ** *Kolybel'naia*

Wiegenlied see Grun, James **PFITZNER**

Wiegenlied see Hiemer **WEBER**

Wiegenlied see Hoffmann von Fallersleben **LASSEN, SCHOECK, STRAUSS**

Wiegenlied see Ibsen *KONGS-EMNERNE.* **DELIUS**

Wiegenlied see Jaeger, Johannes **SCHOECK**

Wiegenlied see Jelínek, F. L. **DVOŘÁK** *Ukolébavka*

Wiegenlied see Körner **SCHUBERT**

Wiegenlied see Munch **GRIEG** *Vuggesang*

Wiegenlied see Ostrovski **MUSORGSKIĬ** *Kolybel'naia pesnia*

Wiegenlied see Ottenwalt **SCHUBERT** *Der Knabe in der Wiege*

Wiegenlied see Scott *LULLABY OF AN INFANT CHIEF*: O hush thee, my babie. **JENSEN**

Wiegenlied see Seidl **SCHUBERT**

Wiegenlied see Stein, Gretel **REGER**

Wiegenlied see Tennyson *SWEET AND LOW.* **JENSEN**

Wiegenlied see Träger **REGER**

Wiegenlied see Unknown **MENDELSSOHN-BARTHOLDY, SCHUBERT**

Ein Wiegenlied, bei Mondschein zu singen see Claudius, M. **SCHOECK**

COMPOSER Poet *Title* ''First Line''

Wiegenlied der Jungfrau Maria see Vega
   Carpio LASSEN
Wiegenlied der Puppe see Iłłakowiczówna
   SZYMANOWSKI *Kolysanka lalki*
Wiegenlied der Puppen see Iłłakowiczówna
   SZYMANOWSKI *Kolysanka lalek*
Wiegenlied für das braune Pferd see
   Iłłakowiczówna SZYMANOWSKI
   Kolysanka gniadego konia
Wiegenlied im Sommer see Reinick WOLF
Wiegenlied im Winter see Reinick WOLF
Wiegenlied Jeremuschkas see Nekrasov
   MUSORGSKIĬ *Kolybel'naĭa Eremushki*
Wiegenliedchen see Dehmel STRAUSS
Wiehert, ihr Pferdchen see Anon.
   SZYMANOWSKI *Zarzyjze, kuniu*
Wiener, Francis *see* Croisset, Francis de,
   1877-1937.
Wiener, Oskar
   REGER
      Abschied
      Am Dorfsee
      Mein Herz
      Sag es nicht
"Wie's aussieht im ew'gen Freudenhain" *see*
   Das kleinste Lied Hamerling REGER
"Eine Wiese voller Margeriten" *see*
   Freundliche Vision Bierbaum REGER
"Wieviel Sonnenstrahlen fielen" *see*
   Meeresleuchten Siebel LOEWE
"Wife and servant are the same" *see To the*
   ladies Chudleigh ROREM
Wihl, Ludwig, 1806-1882.
   SPOHR *Die sieben Schwestern*
Wilbrandt, Adolf, 1837-1911.
   LISZT *Der Glückliche*
"The wild bee reels from bough to bough"
   see Her voice Wilde CARPENTER
Wild cherry see Denson, Olive M.
   QUILTER
The wild flower's song see Blake, William
   HINDEMITH, QUILTER
The wild home pussy see Rounds, Emma
   THOMPSON, R.
"Wild verwachs'ne dunkle Fichten" *see*
   Einsamkeit Lenau SCHUMANN
Wild wie Bäche see Martinelli?
   BRUCKNER
Wilde, Ch
   BALAKIREV
      Kogda bezzabotno, ditya, tĭ rezvish'sya
      Rĭysar
Die wilde Gazelle see Byron LOEWE
Wilde, Oscar, 1854-1900.
   CARPENTER
      Her voice
      Les silhouettes

GRIFFES *Symphony in yellow*
LUENING *Requiescat*
FANTAISIES DÉCORATIVES, no. 2.
   GRIFFES *Les ballons*
FLOWERS OF GOLD. Impressions, no. 2.
   GRIFFES *La fuite de la lune*
THE FOURTH MOVEMENT. Impression:
   Le Réveillon.
   GRIFFES *Dawn*
IMPRESSIONS I: Le jardin.
   GRIFFES *Le jardin*
IMPRESSIONS II: La mer.
   GRIFFES
      La mer
      The sea
WIND FLOWERS: Impression du matin.
   GRIFFES *Early morning in London*
Wildenbruch, Ernst von, 1845-1909.
   LASSEN
      Abendlied
      Bitteres Gedenken
      Ewige Liebe
      Liebespost
      Nicht weinen
      Seneschall's Lied
      Ständchen
      Trost im Leid
   REGER
      Der Kornblumenstrauss
      Tränen im Auge
Wilder, Victor van, 1835-1892.
   FAURÉ *Noël*
   LALO *Aubade*
   LASSEN *Ich hatte einst ein schönes*
      Vaterland
The wilderness see Zhemchuzhnikov
   BALAKIREV *Pustĭnya*
Wilhelm, Carl
   BERG *Sternenfall*
Wilhelm, Karl *see* Wilhelm, Carl
WILHELM MEISTER. see Goethe
   An Mignon SCHUBERT, SPOHR,
      ZELTER
   Ballade des Harfners SCHUMANN
   Einsamkeit ZELTER
   Harfenspieler SCHUBERT
   Harfenspieler I SCHUBERT, WOLF
   Harfenspieler III SCHUBERT, WOLF
   Klage ZELTER
   Lied der Mignon SCHUBERT
   Mignon SCHUBERT
      Two settings: D. 469 and D. 727.
   Mignon III WOLF
   Philine WOLF
   Der Sänger LOEWE, SCHUBERT,
      WOLF, ZELTER

Singet nicht in Trauertönen **SCHUMANN**
So lasst mich scheinen, bis ich werde
SCHUMANN
Spottlied **WOLF**
Wer nie sein Brod mit Thränen ass
SCHUMANN
Wer nie sein Brot mit Tränen ass **LISZT,
ZELTER**
Wer sich der Einsamkeit ergiebt
SCHUMANN
WILHELM MEISTER. Harfenspieler. *see*
Goethe
An die Thüren will ich schleichen
SCHUMANN
An die Türen will ich schleichen
MEDTNER, ZELTER
Harfenspieler II **SCHUBERT, WOLF**
Lied des Harfenspielers **MUSORGSKĪĬ**
WILHELM MEISTER. Mignon's song: Heiss
mich nicht reden. *see* Goethe
Geheimnis **ZELTER**
Heiss' mich nicht reden **SCHUMANN**
Lied der Mignon **SCHUBERT**
Mignon **SCHUBERT**
Mignon I **WOLF**
Ne sprashivaĭ **CHAĬKOVSKĪĬ**
WILHELM MEISTER. Mignon's song: Kennst
du das Land? *see* Goethe
Kennst du das Land **SCHUMANN,
ZELTER**
Mignon **BEETHOVEN, BERG,
GOUNOD, JENSEN, SCHUBERT,
SCHUMANN**
Mignon IV **WOLF**
Mignons Lied **LISZT**
Mignon's Lied **SPOHR**
Pesnya Min'ony **CHAĬKOVSKĪĬ**
Romance de Mignon **DUPARC**
WILHELM MEISTER. Mignon's song: Nur
wer die Sehnsucht kennt. *see* Goethe
Lied der Mignon **SCHUBERT**
    Three settings: D. 359, D. 481, and D.
    877 no. 4.
Mignon **MEDTNER**
Mignon II **WOLF**
Mignon und der Harfner **SCHUBERT**
Niet'', tol'ko tot'', kto znal'' **CHAĬKOVSKĪĬ**
Nur wer die Sehnsucht kennt
SCHUMANN, ZELTER
Sehnsucht **BEETHOVEN, LOEWE,
SCHUBERT, ZELTER**
WILHELM TELL. *see* Schiller
Der Alpenjäger **LISZT**
Des Buben Schützenlied **SCHUMANN**
Die Fischerknabe **LISZT**
Der Hirt **LISZT**

"Wilia, sie, der unsre Ström' entsprangen" *see*
Wilia und das Mädchen Mickiewicz
LOEWE
Wilia und das Mädchen *see* Mickiewicz
LOEWE
Wilija i dziewica *see* Mickiewicz **LOEWE**
Wilia und das Mädchen
Wilkinson, Florence *see* Evans, Mrs.
Florence (Wilkinson)
"Wilkommen, O silberner Mond" *see*
Die frühen Gräber Klopstock **KRENEK**
"Will dic Holde sich ergehen" *see* Ihr
Spaziergang Jacob, T. **LOEWE**
"Will die Seele dir verzagen in der Leiden
Übermass" *see* Trost im Leid
Wildenbruch **LASSEN**
"Will ruhen unter den Bäumen hier" *see*
In der Ferne Uhland **BRAHMS**
"Will sich Hektor ewig von mir wenden" *see*
Hektors Abschied Schiller **SCHUBERT**
"Will singen euch im alten Ton" *see*
Hochzeitlied Jacobi **SCHUBERT**
Will über Nacht wohl übers Tal *see*
Osterwald **FRANZ**
"Will ye go to the Hielands, Leezie Lindsay?"
see Leezie Lindsay Burns **BRITTEN**
"Will you come to the mulberry tree in the
dawning" *see* The mulberry tree
Unknown **PROKOFIEV**
Der Willekumm *see* Scheffel *GAUDEAMUS.*
JENSEN
Willemer, Marianne Jung von, 1784-
1860.
SCHUBERT Suleika II
William Will, a Republican campaign song *see*
Hill, Susan Benedict **IVES**
Williams, Alfred, 1877-1930.
QUILTER
Cuckoo song
Song of the stream
Williams, William Carlos, 1883-1963.
ROREM
The dance
Nantucket
Willkommen dem 28. August 1749 *see*
Goethe *BLUMENGRUSS.* **ZELTER**
"Willkommen im Grünen!" *see* Frühlingslied
Voss **LOEWE**
"Willkommen im Grünen!" *see* Im Grünen
Voss **MENDELSSOHN-BARTHOLDY**
"Willkommen, klare Sommernacht" *see* Stille
der Nacht Keller, G. **SCHOECK**
"Willkommen, lieber schöner Mai" *see*
Mailied Hölty **WOLF**
Willkommen, mein Wald *see* Roquette
FRANZ
"Willkommen, O silbener Mond" *see*
Die frühen Gräber Klopstock **GLUCK,
SCHUBERT**

COMPOSER   Poet   *Title*   "First Line"

"Willkommen, rotes Morgenlicht!" *see*
  Morgenlied Stolberg **SCHUBERT**
"Willkommen, schöner Jüngling!" *see An den*
  Frühling Schiller **SCHUBERT**
    Three settings: D. 245, D. 283, and D.
    587.
Willkommen und Abschied see Goethe
  PFITZNER, SCHUBERT
Willow see Tiutchev **MEDTNER**
The willow song see Anon.
  VAUGHAN WILLIAMS
Willow-wood see Rossetti, Dante
  VAUGHAN WILLIAMS
Willst du, dass ich geh'? see Lemcke
  BRAHMS
Willst du einen Ehemann erkennen see
  Unknown **RUBINSTEIN**
"Willst du nicht das Lämmlein hüten" *see*
  Der Alpenjäger Schiller **SCHUBERT**
"Willst du nicht dich schliessen" *see An das*
  Herz Keller, G. **SCHOECK**
"Wilt thou forget?" *see The past* Shelley
  BENNETT
Wind see Feeney **CHANLER**
THE WIND AMONG THE REEDS. see Yeats
  The host of the air **LOEFFLER**
  The hosting of the Sidhe **LOEFFLER**
THE WIND AMONG THE REEDS (1899):
  Aedh wishes for the cloths . . . *see* Yeats
  The cloths of heaven **HESELTINE**
THE WIND AMONG THE REEDS (1899):
  Aodh to Dectora. *see* Yeats
  The everlasting voices **HESELTINE**
"The wind comes softly out of the south" *see*
  Wind from the south Irvine **QUILTER**
WIND FLOWERS: Impression du matin. *see*
  Wilde
  Early morning in London **GRIFFES**
Wind from the south see Irvine **QUILTER**
The wind from the West see Young, Ella
  POEMS (1906). **HESELTINE**
"Wind is to show how a thing can blow" *see*
  Wind Feeney **CHANLER**
"Der Wind spielt mit der Wetterfahne" *see*
  Die Wetterfahne Müller, Wilhelm
  SCHUBERT
"A wind sways the pines" *see Dirge in woods*
  Meredith **COPLAND**
"Die Winde sausen am Tannenhang" *see*
  Über Wildemann Schulze **SCHUBERT**
"Windes Rauschen" *see Im Walde* Schlegel,
  F. **SCHUBERT**
Windham, Donald, 1920-
  EMBLEMS OF CONDUCT. Chapter "The
  Rain."
    ROREM *Prologue and Epilogue: from*
    "The Rain"

The window see Pushkin **MEDTNER**
THE WINDOW. see Tennyson
  Winter **VAUGHAN WILLIAMS**
Winds of May see Joyce **SZYMANOWSKI**
Windy nights see Stevenson, Robert Louis
  A CHILD'S GARDEN OF VERSES. **HAHN**
Wine roses see Jacobsen *LØFT DE*
  KLINGRE GLASPOKALER. **DELIUS**
Winkler, Karl Gottfried Theodor, 1775-
  1856.
  SCHUBERT *Das Heimweh*
  ZELTER *Lied in der Fremde*
  SÄNGERS REISE.
    WEBER *Lied in der Fremde*
"Wino dzikie u okna chwieje" *see Smutek*
  Iłłakowiczówna **SZYMANOWSKI**
"A winsome morning measure" *see Merry*
  maiden spring MacDowell
  MACDOWELL
The winter see Burns **BRITTEN**
Winter see Pleshcheyev **CHAĬKOVSKĬĬ**
  Zima
Winter see Schlaf *HELLDUNKEL* (1899).
  BERG
Winter see Tennyson *THE WINDOW.*
  VAUGHAN WILLIAMS
Winter evening see Pleshcheyev
  CHAĬKOVSKĬĬ *Zimniĭ vecher*
Winter evening see Pushkin **MEDTNER**
"The winter is past, and the summer comes at
  last" *see The winter* Burns **BRITTEN**
"Der Winter ist ein rechter Mann" *see Ein*
  Lied, hinterm Ofen zu singen Claudius, M.
  SCHOECK
Winter night see Eichendorff **MEDTNER**
  Winternacht
"Winter vorbei, Herzchen, mein Liebchen!"
  see Liebesliedchen Jacob, T. **LOEWE**
WINTER WORDS, no. 1
  BRITTEN Hardy *At day-close in*
  November
WINTER WORDS, no. 2
  BRITTEN Hardy *Midnight on the Great*
  Western
WINTER WORDS, no. 3
  BRITTEN Hardy*Wagtail and baby*
WINTER WORDS, no. 4
  BRITTEN Hardy *The little old table*
WINTER WORDS, no. 5
  BRITTEN Hardy *The choirmaster's burial*
WINTER WORDS, no. 6
  BRITTEN Hardy *Proud songsters*
WINTER WORDS, no. 7
  BRITTEN Hardy *At the railway station,*
  Upway
WINTER WORDS, no. 8

COMPOSER Poet *Title* "First Line"

BRITTEN Hardy *Before life and after*
Winter's gone see Clare **BENNETT**
A winter's night see Heyduk **MARTINŮ**
A WINTER'S TALE. see Shakespeare
 Shepherd's song **BLITZSTEIN**
 The sweet o' the year **HESELTINE**
 When daffodils begin to peer **IRELAND, QUILTER**
The winter's willow, a country song *see*
 Barnes **VAUGHAN WILLIAMS**
Der Winterabend see Leitner **SCHUBERT**
Winterahnung see Rückert **REGER**
Winterliebe see Henckell **STRAUSS**
Winterlied see Anon. **MENDELSSOHN-BARTHOLDY**
Winterlied see Hölty **SCHUBERT**
Winterlied see Mahler **MAHLER**
Winterlied see Unknown **LOEWE**
Winternacht see Eichendorff **MEDTNER, SCHOECK**
Winternacht see Lenau **FRANZ**
Winternacht see Morgenstern **KILPINEN**
Winternacht see Schack **STRAUSS**
Winterreise see Uhland **STRAUSS**
WINTERREISE, no. 1
 SCHUBERT Müller, Wilhelm
 Gute Nacht
WINTERREISE, no. 2
 SCHUBERT Müller, Wilhelm
 Die Wetterfahne
WINTERREISE, no. 3
 SCHUBERT Müller, Wilhelm
 Gefror'ne Thränen
WINTERREISE, no. 4
 SCHUBERT Müller, Wilhelm *Erstarrung*
WINTERREISE, no. 5
 SCHUBERT Müller, Wilhelm
 Der Lindenbaum
WINTERREISE, no. 6
 SCHUBERT Müller, Wilhelm *Wasserflut*
WINTERREISE, no. 7
 SCHUBERT Müller, Wilhelm
 Auf dem Flusse
WINTERREISE, no. 8
 SCHUBERT Müller, Wilhelm *Rückblick*
WINTERREISE, no. 9
 SCHUBERT Müller, Wilhelm *Irrlicht*
WINTERREISE, no. 10
 SCHUBERT Müller, Wilhelm *Rast*
WINTERREISE, no. 11
 SCHUBERT Müller, Wilhelm
 Frühlingstraum
WINTERREISE, no. 12
 SCHUBERT Müller, Wilhelm *Einsamkeit*
WINTERREISE, no. 13
 SCHUBERT Müller, Wilhelm *Die Post*

WINTERREISE, no. 14
 SCHUBERT Müller, Wilhelm
 Der greise Kopf
WINTERREISE, no. 15
 SCHUBERT Müller, Wilhelm *Die Krähe*
WINTERREISE, no. 16
 SCHUBERT Müller, Wilhelm
 Letzte Hoffnung
WINTERREISE, no. 17
 SCHUBERT Müller, Wilhelm *Im Dorfe*
WINTERREISE, no. 18
 SCHUBERT Müller, Wilhelm
 Der stürmische Morgen
WINTERREISE, no. 19
 SCHUBERT Müller, Wilhelm *Täuschung*
WINTERREISE, no. 20
 SCHUBERT Müller, Wilhelm
 Der Wegweiser
WINTERREISE, no. 21
 SCHUBERT Müller, Wilhelm
 Das Wirtshaus
WINTERREISE, no. 22
 SCHUBERT Müller, Wilhelm *Mut*
WINTERREISE, no. 23
 SCHUBERT Müller, Wilhelm
 Die Nebensonne
WINTERREISE, no. 24
 SCHUBERT Müller, Wilhelm
 Der Leiermann
Winterweihe see Henckell **STRAUSS**
Winther, Christian, 1796-1876.
 GRIEG
 Blomsterne tale
 Sang paa Fjeldet
 Skovsang
 Taksigelse
 NIELSEN *Jeg laegger mig saa trygt til Ro*
Wiosna see Iłłakowiczówna
 SZYMANOWSKI
Wiosna see Witwicki **CHOPIN**
"Die Wipfel säuseln Abendruh' " *see*
 Schlummerlied Leo **LASSEN**
Wir beide wollen springen see Bierbaum
 STRAUSS
"Wir beten an, hier unter Brot- und
 Weingestalten" *see Abendmahlslied* Neus
 LOEWE
Wir bevölkerten die abend-düstern see
 George *DAS BUCH DER HÄNGENDEN GÄRTEN.* **SCHÖNBERG**
Wir drei see Backody **RUBINSTEIN**
"Wir gehn durch goldenes Ährenfeld" *see*
 Sommersegen Sergel **KILPINEN**
"Wir gingen an einem Maientag in schattiger
 Allee" *see Eine Vogelweise* Ibsen
 DELIUS

"Wir gingen beide" *see Lied* Steigentesch
ZELTER
"Wir gingen durch die dunkle, milde Nacht"
see Nachtgang Bierbaum **STRAUSS**
"Wir gingen durch die dunkle milde Nacht"
see Nachtgesang Bierbaum **BERG**
"Wir gingen durch die stille Nacht" *see*
Nachtgang Bierbaum **REGER**
"Wir gingen einsam durch die Gartenflur" *see*
Notturno Ulrich **JENSEN**
Wir haben beide lange Zeit see Heyse
WOLF
"Wir haben ein Bett" *see Der Arbeitsmann*
Dehmel **PFITZNER, STRAUSS**
"Wir haben oft beim Wein gesessen" *see Wir*
zwei Falke **REGER**
"Wir haben von Anbeginn her eine Einladung
zu Fest" *see Ballade vom Fest* Krenek
KRENEK
"Wir hatten einander so gerne" *see Die engste*
Nähe Unknown **LOEWE**
"Wir Kinder, wir schmecken" *see*
Das Kinderspiel Overbeck **MOZART**
"Wir lustigen Bürger in grüner Stadt" *see*
Vogelgesang Tieck **LOEWE**
Wir müssen uns trennen see Tieck **BRAHMS**
"Wir sassen am Fischerhause" *see Abends am*
Strand Heine **SCHUMANN**
"Wir sassen so traulich beisammen" *see*
Thränenregen Müller, Wilhelm
SCHUBERT
"Wir schreiten in goldener Fülle" *see*
In goldener Fülle Remer **STRAUSS**
"Wir Schwestern zwei, wir schönen" *see*
Die Schwestern Mörike **SCHOECK**
"Wir senkten die Wurzeln in Moos und
Gestein" *see Rosenlied* Ritter **SIBELIUS**
"Wir sind ja, Kind" *see Der Zeisig* Kulmann
SCHUMANN
"Wir sind nicht droben, doch wir sind am
Ziel" *see Im Spiegel* Goering **KRENEK**
"Wir sind zwei Rosen" *see Schicksal der*
Liebe Morgenstern **KILPINEN**
"Wir singen und sagen vom Grafen so gern"
see Hochzeitlied Goethe **LOEWE,**
ZELTER
Wir sitzen im Dunkeln see Morgenstern
KILPINEN
Wir spielen und hüpfen see Segelbach
LOEWE
"Wir träumten von einander" *see Ich und Du*
Hebbel **PFITZNER**
Wir und Sie see Klopstock **GLUCK**
"Wir Vögel singen nicht egal" *see Kuckuck*
Claudius, M. **SCHOECK**
Wir wandeln alle den Weg see Bodenstedt
LUENING

Wir wandelten see Daumer *POLYDORA.*
BRAHMS
"Wir waren zwei Töchter aus einem Haus"
see Die Schwestern Tennyson **JENSEN**
"Wir wollten mit Kosen und Lieben" *see*
Morgentau Chamisso **GRIEG**
Wir zwei see Falke **REGER**
Wird er wohl noch meiner gedenken? see
Anon. **FRANZ**
Wirkung in die Ferne see Goethe **LOEWE,**
ZELTER
"Wirst du halten, was du schwurst" *see Die*
abgeblühte Linde Széchényi **SCHUBERT**
Der Wirthin Töchterlein see Uhland
LOEWE
Das Wirtshaus see Müller, Wilhelm
SCHUBERT
Wisbacher, Franz, 1849-1912.
BERG *Vorüber*
Wish for a young love see Roethke
BARBER *My lizard*
WISH FOR A YOUNG WIFE. see Roethke
My lizard **BARBER**
Wishes see T **VAUGHAN WILLIAMS**
"Wisst ihr wo ich gerne weil' in der
Abendkühle?" *see Lieblingsplätzchen*
Des Knaben Wunderhorn
MENDELSSOHN-BARTHOLDY
Witchcraft see Witwicki **CHOPIN** *Czary*
WITEKIND. see Vogl
Karl der Grosse und Wittekind **LOEWE**
"With easy hands upon the rein" *see Who are*
these children? Soutar **BRITTEN**
"With holy banner firmly held" *see The*
peasant Shenshin **RACHMANINOFF**
With jet black sails see Heine
VERSCHIEDENE-SERAPHINE, no. 12.
GRIFFES *Mit schwarzen Segeln*
With nursie see Musorgskiǐ **MUSORGSKIǐ**
Snianeǐ
WITH OR WITHOUT ROSES. see
Louchheim
The incredible hour **DIAMOND**
Love's worth **DIAMOND**
Spring talk **DIAMOND**
Whither thou goest **DIAMOND**
"With perfume heavily laden the roses droop
their heads" *see In the seraglio garden*
Jacobsen **DELIUS**
"With pilgrim's staff, with weary gait" *see*
Fate Apukhtin **RACHMANINOFF**
With rue my heart is laden see Housman
A SHROPSHIRE LAD: LIV. **BARBER,**
RIEGGER, VAUGHAN WILLIAMS
With the doll see Musorgskiǐ
MUSORGSKIǐ *Skukloǐ*

"With unerring finger" *see Near closing time* Goodman **ROREM**

With you, my thoughts are ever flying! see Anon. **RIMSKIĬ-KORSAKOV** *Gde ty, tam mysl' moĩa letaet*

Wither, George, 1588-1667. **GOUNOD** *Sweet baby, sleep!*

Withered flower see Pushkin **RIMSKIĬ-KORSAKOV** *Tsvetok zasokhshiĭ*

Within a mile of Edinburgh town see Unknown **RESPIGHI**

Within four walls see Golenishchev-Kutuzov **MUSORGSKIĬ** *V chetyrekh stenakh*

"Within my soul" *see In my soul* Vilenkin **RACHMANINOFF**

"Within the heart what treasures lie concealed" *see There are many sounds* Tolstoĭ **RACHMANINOFF**

"Within the violence of the storm" *see Slaughter* Soutar **BRITTEN**

"Within the woodlands, flow'ry gladed" *see Linden Lea* Barnes **VAUGHAN WILLIAMS**

"Without you no rose can grow" *see Little elegy* Wylie **ROREM**

Witwicki, Stefan, 1802-1847. **CHOPIN** *Czary* *Gdzie lubi . . .* *Hulanka* *Narzeczony* *Pierścien* *Posel* *Precz z moich oczu . . .* *Smutna rzeka* *Wiosna* *Wojak* *Zyczenie*

The wizard see Agnivt̃sev **PROKOFIEV** *Kudesnik*

Wizyta u krowy see Iłłakowiczówna **SZYMANOWSKI**

Wo? see Heine **RUBINSTEIN, SCHOECK**

"Wo aber werd' ich sein im künft'gen Lenze" *see Der verspätete Wanderer* Eichendorff **PFITZNER, SCHOECK**

"Wo am Herd ein Brautpaar siedelt" *see Hütet euch* Geibel **REGER**

"Wo bist du, Bild" *see Das Traumbild* Hölty **MOZART**

"Wo bist du? Trunken dämmert die Seele mir" *see Sonnenuntergang* Hölderlin **CORNELIUS, HINDEMITH**

"Wo blüht das Blümchen" *see Das Geheimnis* Wessenberg **BEETHOVEN**

"Wo Claribel gestorben" *see Claribel* Tennyson **JENSEN**

Wo Daetter see Berntsen **NIELSEN**

Wo der Goldregen steht see Lorenz, F. **BERG**

"Wo der Mond mit bleichem Schimmer" *see Beruhigung* Matthisson **ZELTER**

"Wo der Weiser steht an der Strass" *see Leierkastenmann* Busse **PFITZNER**

Wo die Berge so blau see Jeitteles **BEETHOVEN**

"Wo die Rose hier blünt" *see Anakreon's Grab* Goethe **WOLF**

"Wo die Tannen finstre Schatten werfen" *see Göttermahl* Meyer **SCHOECK**

"Wo die Taub' in stillen Buchen" *see Trauer der Liebe* Jacobi **SCHUBERT**

"Wo die weissen Tauben fliegen" *see Der schönste Platz* Löns **KILPINEN**

"Wo dort die alten Gemäuer stehn" *see Wallhaide* Körner **LOEWE**

"Wo du triffst ein Mündlein hold" *see Leichtsinniger Rat* Saul, D. **REGER**

"Wo ein treues Herze in Liebe vergeht" *see Der Müller und der Bach* Müller, Wilhelm **SCHUBERT**

Wo find' ich Trost see Mörike **WOLF**

"Wo gehst du hin, du schönes Kind?" *see Ritterliche Werbung* Mörike **SCHOECK**

Wo geht's Liebchen? see Goethe *MAILIED.* **ZELTER**

"Wo Gletscherhöhen starren" *see Der einsame* See Kalbeck **RUBINSTEIN**

Wo hast du all die Schönheit hergenommen see Huch **PFITZNER**

"Wo ich bin" *see Klage* Asenijeff **REGER**

Wo ich bin, mich rings umdunkelt see Heine *LYRISCHES INTERMEZZO, no. 68.* **GRIFFES, WOLF**

"Wo ich ferne des Mikaue Ho her Gipfel ragen seh" *see Endlose Liebe* Florenz **CARPENTER**

"Wo ich sei, und wo mich hingewendet" *see Thekla (Eine Geisterstimme)* Schiller **SCHUBERT** Two settings: D. 73 and D. 595.

"Wo irrst du durch einsame Schatten der Nacht" *see Aus Diego Manazares* Schlechta **SCHUBERT**

"Wo kommst du her?" *see Der Komet* Gerstenberg **LOEWE**

"Wo liebende Herzen sich innig vermählt" *see Reimar der Alte* Scheffel **LISZT**

Wo mag meine Heimat sein? see Hesse **KILPINEN**

"Wo noch kein Wandrer gegangen" *see Das Waldschloss* Eichendorff **MENDELSSOHN-BARTHOLDY**

COMPOSER Poet *Title* "First Line"

"Wo sah ich, Mädchen, deine Züge" *see*
   Die Jungfrau Meyer **SCHOECK**
Wo sind Sie hin? see Heine **GRIEG**
"Wo stammst du her?" *see Erkennung* Schink
   ZELTER
"Wo süss in Frieden ein Herze ruht" *see*
   Das Grab der Liebe Unknown **FRANZ**
Wo Tauben sind see Beck **JENSEN**
"Wo über mir die Wald nacht finster" *see*
   Waldeinsamkeit Leuthold **SCHOECK**
"Wo weht der Liebe hoher Geist?" *see*
   Die Liebe Leon **SCHUBERT**
Wo weilt er? see Rellstab **LISZT**
"Wo willst du klares Bächlein hin so
   munter?" *see Der Junggesell und der
   Mühlbach*
   Goethe **ZELTER**
Wo wird einst? see Heine **WOLF**
"Wo wird einst des Wandermüden" *see
   Wo?* Heine **RUBINSTEIN, SCHOECK**
"Wo wird einst des Wandermüden" *see
   Wo wird einst?* Heine **WOLF**
"Woda Wanda wislana" *see Wanda* Tuwim
   SZYMANOWSKI
Die Wölfe see Tolstoï **RUBINSTEIN**
Das Wölklein see Boelitz **REGER**
Woe's me! woe's me! see Campbell
   GOUNOD
"Die Wogen am Gestade schwellen" *see*
   Schiffers Scheidelied Schober
   SCHUBERT
"Die Wogen ergriffen vom Loreley-Sang" *see*
   Die sieben Schwestern Wihl **SPOHR**
"Woget brausend, Harmonieen" *see Zum
   Punsche* Mayrhofer **SCHUBERT**
"Woher, O namenloses Sehnen" *see Abends
   unter der Linde* Kosegarten **SCHUBERT**
      Two settings: D. 235 and D. 237.
Wohin? see Müller, Wilhelm **SCHUBERT**
Wohin see Sturm, J. **SPOHR**
"Wohin, du rauschender Strom, wohin,
   wohin?" *see Wohin* Sturm, J. **SPOHR**
"Wohin ich geh' und schaue" *see Der
   Gärtner* Eichendorff **PFITZNER,
   SCHOECK**
"Wohin ich geh' und schaue" *see Der
   vielschönen Fraue* Eichendorff **FRANZ**
Wohin mit der Freud? see Reinick **WOLF**
"Wohin, O Bächlein, schnelle?" *see*
   Der Wanderer und der Bach Frey, F.
   SIBELIUS
"Wohin? O Helios!" *see Freiwilliges
   Versinken* Mayrhofer **SCHUBERT**
Wohin, O Seele, wirst du eilen? see Byron
   LOEWE

"Wohin so schnell, so kraus und wild" *see
   Eifersucht und Stolz* Müller, Wilhelm
   SCHUBERT
"Wohl denk' ich allenthalben" *see Der
   Entfernten* Salis-Seewis **SCHUBERT**
Wohl denk' ich oft see Buonarroti **WOLF**
"Wohl denk' ich oft an mein vergangnes
   Leben" *see Wohl denk' ich oft* Buonarroti
   WOLF
"Wohl ist es schön, auf fauler Haut" *see
   Vorwurf* Leuthold **SCHOECK**
Wohl kenn' ich Euren Stand see Heyse
   WOLF
Wohl lag ich einst in Gram und Schmerz see
   Geibel *LIEDER ALS INTERMEZZO*, no. 2.
   GRIFFES
"Wohl perlet im Glase der purpurne Wein"
   see Die vier Weltalter Schiller
   SCHUBERT, ZELTER
Wohl tauscht ihr Vögelein see Ferrand, A.
   MOZART *Ariette*
Wohl viele tausend Vögelein see Prutz
   FRANZ
"Wohl wandert' ich aus in trauriger Stund' "
   see Auf der Wanderschaft (2 versions,
   1878) Chamisso **WOLF**
"Wohl war im Busch und Rasen" *see Sie war
   die Schönste von Allen* Pfarrius **JENSEN**
Wohl waren es, Tage der Sonne see Geibel
   FRANZ
"Wohl waren es Tage der Sonne" *see Lied des
   Mädchens* Geibel **JENSEN**
"Wohl weinen Gottes Engel" *see Luisens
   Antwort* Kosegarten **SCHUBERT**
"Wohlauf! noch getrunken den funkelnden
   Wein!" *see Wanderlust* Kerner
   SCHUMANN
"Wohlauf und frisch gewandert" *see
   Wanderung* Kerner **SCHUMANN**
"Wohn denen, die ohne Tadel leben" *see
   Geistliches Lied "Wohl denen"* Bible
   REGER
Die Wohnung see Iłłakowiczówna
   SZYMANOWSKI *Mieszkanie*
Wojak see Witwicki **CHOPIN**
Wojkowicz, Jan z, pseud. *see* Nebesky,
   Jan, 1880-
"Wol auf, gut G'sell, von hinnen" *see
   Wanderlied* Anon.
   VAUGHAN WILLIAMS
Wolf, Friedrich, 1888-1953.
   BLACHER
      Herzensverstand
      Die Hexe
      Kirschkerne
      Das Zirkuspferdchen

WOLF, HUGO, 1860-1903.

Alvaro Fernandez de Almeida
SPANISCHES LIEDERBUCH: Tango
vos, el mi pandero.
Klinge, klinge, mein Pandero (1889)
[GA, v. 4, p. 44] same

Anon.
Ach, im Maien wär's, im Maieh (1890)
[GA, v. 4, p. 117] same
Ach, wie lang die Seele schlummert!
(1889) [GA,
v. 4, p. 32] same
Alle gingen, Herz, zu Ruh (1889) [GA,
v. 4, p. 122] same
Auf den grünen Balkon mein Mädchen
(1889) [GA, v. 4, p. 60] same
Bitt' ihn, O Mutter, bitte den Knaben
(1889) [GA, v. 4, p. 100] same
Da nur Leid und Leidenschaft (1890)
[GA,
v. 4, p. 150] same
Eide, so die Liebe schwur (1890) [GA,
v. 4, p. 77] same
Führ' mich, Kind, nach Bethlehem!
(1889) [GA, v. 4, p. 22] same
Geh, Geliebter (1890) [GA, v. 4, p. 159]
same
Herr, was trägt der Boden hier (1889)
[GA, v. 4, p. 35] same
Herz, verzage nicht geschwind (1889)
[GA, v. 4, p. 81] same
Ich fuhr über Meer (1889) [GA, v. 4,
p. 72] same
Liebe mir im Busen zündet (1890) [GA,
v. 4, p. 104] same
Mögen alle bösen Zungen (1890) [GA,
v. 4, p. 90] same
Morgentau (1877) [GA, v. 6, p. 3]
"Der Früh hauch hat gefächelt"
Sagt ihm, dass er zu mir komme (1890)
[GA, v. 4, p. 96] same
Sagt, seid Ihr es, feiner Herr (1889) [GA,
v. 4, p. 85] same
Schmerzliche Wonnen (1890) [GA, v. 4,
p. 108] same
Seltsam ist Juanas Weise (1889) [GA,
v. 4, p. 53] same
Sie blasen zum Abmarsch, lieb Mütterlein
(1889) [GA, v. 4, p. 138] same
Trau' nicht der Liebe (1890) [GA, v. 4,
p. 112] same
Treibe nur mit Lieben Spott (1889) [GA,
v. 4, p. 57] same
Wanderlied (1877) [GA, v. 7¹, p. 29]
"Es segeln die Wolken"
Wer sein holdes Lieb verloren (1889)
[GA, v. 4, p. 69] same

Wer tat deinem Füsslein weh? (1889)
[GA, v. 4, p. 143] same
SPANISCHES LIEDERBUCH.
Bedeckt mich mit Blumen (1889) [GA,
v. 4, p. 133] same
Text by M. Doceo? Translated by
Geibel.
SPANISCHES LIEDERBUCH: Aunque
con semblante airado.
Ob auch finstre Blicke glitten (1890)
[GA, v. 4, p. 131] same
Translated by Heyse.
SPANISCHES LIEDERBUCH: Niña, si la
huerta vas.
Wenn du zu den Blumen gehst (1889)
[GA, v. 4, p. 65] same

Buonarroti, Michel Angelo, 1475-1564.
Alles endet, was entstehet (1897) [GA,
v. 6, p. 96] same
Fühlt meine Seele (1897) [GA, v. 6,
p. 99] same
Wohl denk' ich oft (1897) [GA, v. 6,
p. 94] "Wohl denk' ich oft an mein
vergangnes Leben"

Byron, George Gordon Byron, 6th
baron, 1778-1824.
Keine gleicht von allen Schönen (1896)
[GA, v. 6, p. 46] same
SUN OF THE SLEEPLESS!
Sonne der Schlummerlosen (1896)
[GA, v. 6, p. 44]
"Sonne der Schlummerlosen,
bleicher bleicher Stern!"

Camoens, Luis de, ca.1524-1580.
DE DENTRO TENGO MI MAL.
Tief im Herzen trag' ich Pein (1890)
[GA, v. 4, p. 126] same

Castillejo, Christoval De, 1490-1556.
SPANISCHES LIEDERBUCH: Alguna
vez.
Dereinst, dereinst, Gedanke mein
(1890) [GA, v. 4, p. 124] same
Geibel, translator.

Cervantes Saavedra, Miguel de, 1547-
1616.
Köpfchen, Köpfchen, nicht gewimmert
(1889) [GA, v. 4, p. 94] same

Chamisso, Adelbert von, 1781-1838.
Auf der Wanderschaft (2 versions, 1878)
[GA, v. 7³, pp. 55, 57]
"Wohl wandert' ich aus in trauriger
Stund' "
Was soll ich sagen? (1878) [unpubl.;
ms. in Vienna Stadtbibliothek
Musiksammlung]
"Mein Aug ist trüb"

WOLF, HUGO, 1860-1903 *(continued)*
Chamisso, Adelbert von, 1781-1838
(continued)

Facsimiles in Werner *Der Hugo Wolf-Verein in Wien* (Regensburg: 1921) and Grasberger *Hugo Wolf...* (Vienna: 1960).

Cota, Rodrigo de, fl.15th cent.
Blindes Schauen (1889) [GA, v. 4, p. 75]
"Blindes Schauen, dunkle Leuchte"

Eichendorff, Joseph Karl Benedikt, Freiherr von, 1788-1857.
Erwartung, E 18 [GA, v. 2, p. 67]
"Grüss euch aus Herzensgrund"
Der Freund, E 1 [GA, v. 2, p. 1
"Wer auf den Wogen schliefe"
Der Glücksritter, E 10 [GA, v. 2, p. 38]
"Wenn Fortuna spröde tut"
Heimweh, E 12 [GA, v. 2, p. 45]
"Wer in die Fremde will wandern"
In der Fremde (1881) [GA, v. 7^2, p. 82]
"Da fahr ich still im Wagen"
In der Fremde (1883) [GA, v. 7^2, p. 84]
"Ich geh durch die dunklen Gassen"
In der Fremde (1883) [GA, v. 7^2, p. 86]
"Wolken, wälderwärts gegangen"
Die Kleine (1887) [GA, v. 7^2, p. 96]
"Zwischen Bergen, liebe Mutter"
Lieber alles, E 11 [GA, v. 2, p. 42]
"Soldat sein ist gefährlich"
Liebesglück, E 16 [GA, v. 2, p. 58]
"Ich hab ein Liebchen lieb recht von Herzen"
Der Musikant, E 2 [GA, v. 2, p. 5]
"Wandern lieb ich für mein Leben"
Nachruf (1880) [GA, v. 7^2, p. 78]
"Du liebe treue Laute"
Die Nacht, E 19 [GA, v. 2, p. 70]
"Nacht ist wie ein stilles Meer"
Nachtgruss (1880) [unpubl.; ms. in Vienna Stadtbibliothek Musiksammlung]
"Wie kühl schweift sich's"
Nachtzauber, E 8 [GA, v. 2, p. 28]
"Hörst du nicht die Quellen gehen"
Rückkehr (1883) [GA, v. 7^2, p. 92]
"Mit meinem Saitenspiele"
Der Scholar, E 13 [GA, v. 2, p. 49]
"Bei dem angenehmsten Wetter"
Der Schreckenberger, E 9 [GA, v. 2, p. 34] "Aufs Wohlsein meiner Dame"
Seemanns Abschied, E 17 [GA, v. 2, p. 61] "Ade, mein Schatz, du mochtst mich nicht"
Der Soldat I, E 5 [GA, v. 2, p. 16]
"Ist auch schmuck nicht mein Rösslein"

Der Soldat II, E 6 [GA, v. 2, p. 20]
"Wagen musst du und fluchtig erbeuten"
*Das Ständchen,*E 4 [GA, v. 2, p. 11]
"Auf die Dächer zwischen blassen Wolken"
Unfall, E 15 [GA, v. 2, p. 55]
"Ich ging bei Nacht einst über Land"
Verschwiegene Liebe, E 3 [GA, v. 2, p. 8] "Über Wipfel und Saaten"
Der verzweifelte Liebhaber, E 14 [GA, v. 2, p. 53]
"Studieren will nichts bringen"
Waldmädchen, E 20 [GA, v. 2, p. 72]
"Bin ein Feuer hell, das lodert"
Die Zigeunerin, E 7 [GA, v. 2, p. 22]
"Am Kreuzweg, da lausche ich"

Escriva Comendador, Joan, d. ca. 1520.
Komm, O Tod (1890) [GA, v. 4, p. 128]
same

Goethe, Johann Wolfgang von, 1749-1832.
Anakreon's Grab, G 29 (1888) [GA, v. 3^1, p. 135] "Wo die Rose hier blünt"
Auf dem See, op. 3 no. 5 (1875) [GA, v. 7^3, p. 18]
"Und frische Nahrung, neues Blut"
Beherzigung (1887) [GA, v. 6, p. 34]
"Feiger Gedanken, bängliches Schwanken"
Die Bekehrte, G 27 (1889) [GA, v. 3^1, p. 127]
"Bei dem Glanz der Abendröthe"
Benerzigung, G 18 (1888) [GA, v. 3^1, p. 95] "Ach! was soll der Mensch verlangen?"
Cophtisches Lied I, G 14 (1888) [GA, v. 3^1, p. 83] "Lasset Gelehrte sich zanken und streiten"
Cophtisches Lied II, G 15 (1888) [GA, v. 3^1, p. 87]
"Geh! gehorche meinen Winken"
Dank des Paria, G 30 (1888) [GA, v. 3^1, p. 137]
"Grosser Brama! nun erkenn' ich"
Epiphanias, G 19 (1888) [GA, v. 3^1, p. 99] "Die heiligen drei König' mit ihren Stern"
Erster Verlust, op. 9 no. 3 (1876) [GA, v. 7^3, p. 38]
"Ach, wer bringt die schönen Tage"
Der Fischer, op. 3 no. 3 (1875) [GA, v. 7^3, p. 10] "Das Wasser rauscht', das Wasser schwoll"
Frech und Froh I, G 16 (1888) [GA, v. 3^1, p. 89]
"Mit Mädchen sich vertragen"

Frech und Froh II, G 17 (1889) [GA,
v. 3¹, p. 93]
"Liebesqual verschmäht mein Herz"
Frühling übers Jahr, G 28 (1888) [GA,
v. 3¹, p. 131] "Das Beet, schon lockert
sich's in die Höh'! "
Ganymed, G 50 (1889) [GA, v. 3²,
p. 213] "Wie im Morgenglanze du
rings mich anglühst"
Genialisch Treiben, G 21 (1889) [GA,
v. 3¹, p. 109]
"So wälz' ich ohne Unterlass"
*Gleich und Gleich,*G 25 (1888) [GA,
v. 3¹, p . 121] "Ein Blumenglöckchen
vom Boden hervor"
Grenzen der Menschheit, G 51 (1889)
[GA, v. 3², p. 219]
"Wenn der uralte heilige Vater"
Gutmann und Gutweib, G 13 (1888) [GA,
v. 3¹, p. 69]
"Und morgen fällt Sanct Martins Fest"
Königlich Gebet, G 31 (1889) [GA, v. 3¹,
p. 140]
"Ha, ich bin der Herr der Welt'! "
Mai, op. 9 no. 5 (1876) [unpubl.; ms. in
Vienna Stadtbibliothek
Musiksammlung]
"Leicht Silberwolken schweben"
Der neue Amadis, G 23 (1889) [GA,
v. 3¹, p. 115]
"Als ich noch ein Knabe war"
Prometheus, G 49 (1889) [GA, v. 3²,
p. 201] "Bedecke deinen Himmel,
Zeus"
Der Rattenfänger, G 11 (1888) [GA,
v. 3¹, p. 46]
"Ich bin der wohlbekannte Sänger"
Ritter Kurt's Brautfahrt, G 12 (1888)
[GA, v. 3¹, p. 57]
"Mit des Bräutigams Gehagen"
Der Schäfer, G 22 (1888) [GA, v. 3¹,
p. 113] "Er war ein fauler Schäfer"
Die Spröde, G 26 (1889) [GA, v. 3¹,
p. 122]
"An dem reinsten Frühlingsmorgen"
St. Nepomuk's Vorabend, G 20 (1888)
[GA, v. 3¹, p. 106]
"Lichtlein schwimmen auf dem
Strome"
Wanderlied, op. 3 no. 4 (1875) [unpubl.?]
"Von dem Berge zu den Hügeln"
Not in GA.
BLUMENGRUSS.
Blumengruss, G 24 (1888) [GA, v. 3¹,
p. 120]
"Der Strauss, den ich gepflücket"

FAUST.
*Gretchen vor dem Andachtsbild der
Mater dolorosa* (1878) [GA, v. 7²,
p. 30]
"Ach neige, du Schmerzenreiche"
SCHENKENBUCH.
Ob der Koran von Ewigkeit sei? G 34
(1889) [GA, v. 3², p. 148] same
SEHNSUCHT.
Sehnsucht, op. 3 no. 2 (1875) [GA,
v. 7³, p. 6]
"Was zieht mir das Herz so?"
WANDRERS NACHTLIED I.
Wanderers Nachtlied (1887) [GA, v. 6,
p. 36]
"Der du von dem Himmel bist"
WESTÖSTLICHER DIVAN: Buch des
Sängers.
Phanomen, G 32 (1889) [GA, v. 3²,
p. 142]
"Wenn zu der Regenwand"
WESTÖSTLICHER DIVAN: Buch
Suleika.
Als ich auf dem Euphrat schiffte, G 41
(1889) [GA, v. 3², p. 174] same
Dies zu deuten bin erbötig! G 42
(1889) [GA, v. 3², p. 176] same
Hätt' ich irgend wohl Bedenken, G 43
(1889) [GA, v. 3², p. 180] same
Hoch beglückt in deiner Liebe, G 40
(1889) [GA, v. 3², p. 168] same
Komm, Liebchen, komm! G 44 (1889)
[GA, v. 3², p. 182] same
Locken, haltet mich gefangen, G 47
(1889) [GA, v. 3², p. 192] same
Nicht Gelegenheit macht Diebe, G 39
(1889) [GA, v. 3², p. 166] same
Nimmer will ich dich verlieren! G 48
(1889) [GA, v. 3², p. 198] same
Wenn ich dein gedenke, G 46 (1889)
[GA, v. 3², p. 190] same
Wie sollt' ich heiter bleiben, G 45
(1889) [GA, v. 3², p. 188] same
WESTÖSTLICHER DIVAN:
Schenkenbuch.
Erschaffen und Beleben, G 33 (1889)
[GA, v. 3², p. 144]
"Hans Adam war ein Erdenkloss"
Sie haben wegen der Trunkenheit, G
37 (1889) [GA, v. 3², p. 158] same
So land man nüchtern ist, G 36 (1889)
[GA, v. 3², p. 155] same
Trunken müssen wir alle sein! G 35
(1889) [GA, v. 3², p. 150] same
Was in der Schenke waren heute, G 38
(1889) [GA, v. 3², p. 161] same

WOLF, HUGO, 1860-1903 *(continued)*
Goethe, Johann Wolfgang von, 1749-1832 *(continued)*
WILHELM MEISTER.
  Harfenspieler I, G 1 (1888) [GA, v. 3^1, p. 1]
    "Wer sich der Einsamkeit ergiebt"
  Harfenspieler III, G 3 (1888) [GA, v. 3^1, p. 6] "Wer nie sein Brod mit Thränen ass"
  Mignon III, G 7 (1888) [GA, v. 3^1, p. 18] "So lasst mich scheinen, bis ich werde"
  Philine, G 8 (1888) [GA, v. 3^1, p. 21] "Singet nicht in Trauertönen"
  Der Sänger, G 10 (1888) [GA, v. 3^1, p. 35] "Was hör' ich draussen vor dem Thor"
  Spottlied, G 4 (1888) [GA, v. 3^1, p. 8] "Ich armer Teufel, Herr Baron"
WILHELM MEISTER. Harfenspieler.
  Harfenspieler II, G 2 (1888) [GA, v. 3^1, p. 4]
    "An die Türen will ich schleichen"
WILHELM MEISTER. Mignon's song: Heiss mich nicht reden.
  Mignon I, G 5 (1888) [GA, v. 3^1, p. 12] "Heiss mich nicht reden, heiss mich schweigen"
WILHELM MEISTER. Mignon's song: Kennst du das Land?
  Mignon IV, G 9 (1888) [GA, v. 3^1, p. 26] "Kennst du das Land"
WILHELM MEISTER. Mignon's song: Nur wer die Sehnsucht kennt.
  Mignon II, G 6 (1888) [GA, v. 3^1, p. 15]
    "Nur wer die Sehnsucht kennt"
Hebbel, Christian Friedrich, 1813-1863.
  Das Kind am Brunnen (1878) [GA, v. 7^1, p. 46] "Frau Amme, Frau Amme, das Kind ist erwacht!"
  Knabentod (1878) [GA, v. 7^2, p. 16] "Vom Berg der Knab, der zieht hinab"
  Das Vöglein (1878) [GA, v. 6, p. 5] "Vöglein vom Zweig gaukelt hernieder"
Heine, Heinrich, 1797-1856.
  Du bist wie eine Blume (1876) [GA, v. 7^2, p. 37] same
  Ernst ist der Frühling (1878) [GA, v. 7^1, p. 62] same
  Es war ein alter König (1878) [GA, v. 7^1, p. 58] same
  Mädchen mit dem roten Mündchen (1876) [GA, v. 7^2, p. 35] same

  Manch Bild vergessener Zeiten (1878) [unpubl.; ms. in Vienna Stadtbibliothek Musiksammlung] same
  Wenn ich in deinen Augen seh (1876) [GA, v. 7^2, p. 38] same
  Wo wird einst? (1888) [GA, v. 6, p. 40] "Wo wird einst des Wandermüden"
LIEDERSTRAUSS.
  Aus meinen grossen Schmerzen (1878) [GA, v. 7^1, p. 13] same
  Es blasen die blauen Husaren (1878) [GA, v. 7^1, p. 22] same
  Ich stand in dunkeln Träumen (1878) [GA, v. 7^1, p. 7] same
  Mein Liebchen wir sassen beisammen (1878) [GA, v. 7^1, p. 18] same
  Mir träumte von einem Königskind (1878, 1881) [GA, v. 7^1, p. 16] same
  Sie haben heut Abend Gesellschaft (1878) [GA, v. 7^1, p. 3] same
  Spätherbstnebel, kalte Träume (1878) [GA, v. 7^2, p. 40] same
  Sterne mit den goldnen Füsschen (1880) [GA, v. 7^2, p. 46] same
  Wie des Mondes Abbild zittert (1880) [GA, v. 7^2, p. 49] same
*LYRISCHES INTERMEZZO,*no. 63.
  Das ist ein Brausen und Heulen (1878) [GA, v. 7^1, p. 11] same
*LYRISCHES INTERMEZZO,*no. 68.
  Wo ich bin, mich rings umdunkelt (1878) [GA, v. 7^1, p. 56] same
*VERSCHIEDENE-SERAPHINE,*no. 12.
  Mit schwarzen Segeln (1878) [GA, v. 7^2, p. 44] same
Herlossohn, Karl, 1804-1849.
  Der Schwalben Heimkehr (1877) [GA, v. 7^2, p. 14] "Wenn die Schwalben heimwärts ziehn"
Heyse, Paul Johann Ludwig von, 1830-1914.
  Auch kleine Dinge, I 1 (1891) [GA, v. 5, p. 2] same
  Benedeit die sel'ge Mutter, I 35 (1896) [GA, v. 5, p. 78] same
  Dass doch gemalt all'deine Reize wären, I 9 (1891) [GA, v. 5, p. 18] same
  Du denkst mit einem Fädchen, I 10 (1891) [GA, v. 5, p. 20] same
  Du sagst mir, dass ich keine Fürstin sei, I 28 (1896) [GA, v. 5, p. 62] same
  Gesegnet sei das Grün, I 39 (1896) [GA, v. 5, p. 88] same
  Gesegnet sei, durch den die Welt entstund, I 4 (1890) [GA, v. 5, p. 8] same

Geselle, woll'n wir uns in Kutten hüllen,
I 14 (1891) [GA, v. 5, p. 28] same

Heb' auf dein blondes Haupt, I 18 (1891)
[GA, v. 5, p. 38] same

*Heut' Nacht erhob ich mich im
Mitternacht,* I 41 (1896) [GA, v. 5,
p. 92] same

Hoffärtig seid Ihr, I 13 (1891) [GA, v. 5,
p. 26] same

*Ich esse nun mein Brot nicht trocken
mehr,* I 24 (1896) [GA, v. 5, p. 54]
same

Ich hab' in Penna, I 46 (1896) [GA, v. 5,
p. 102] same

Ich liess mir sagen und mir ward erzählt,
I 26 (1896) [GA, v. 5, p. 58] same

Ihr jungen Leute, I 16 (1891) [GA, v. 5,
p. 34] same

Ihr seid die Allerschönste weit und breit,
I 3 (1890) [GA, v. 5, p. 6] same

In dem Schatten meiner Locken (1889)
[GA, v. 4, p. 49] same

Lass sie nur gehn, I 30 (1896) [GA, v. 5,
p. 66] same

Man sagt mir, I 21 (1891) [GA, v. 5,
p. 44] same

*Mein Liebster hat es Tische mich
geladen,* I 25 (1896) [GA, v. 5, p. 56]
same

Mein Liebster ist so klein, I 15 (1891)
[GA, v. 5, p. 31] same

Mein Liebster singt am Haus, I 20 (1891)
[GA, v. 5, p. 42] same

Mir ward gesagt, I 2 (1890) [GA, v. 5,
p. 4] same

Der Mond hat eine schwere Klag', I 7
(1890) [GA, v. 5, p. 14] same

Nein, junger Herr, so triebt, I 12 (1891)
[GA, v. 5, p. 24] same

Nicht länger kann ich singen, I 42 (1896)
[GA, v. 5, p. 93] same

Nun lass uns Frieden schliessen, I 8
(1890) [GA, v. 5, p. 16] same

O wär' dein Haus durchsichtig, I 40
(1896) [GA, v. 5, p. 90] same

O wüsstest du, wie viel ich deinetwegen,
I 44 (1896) [GA, v. 5, p. 96] same

Schon streckt' ich aus, I 27 (1896) [GA,
v. 5, p. 60] same

Schweig' einmal still, I 43 (1896) [GA,
v. 5, p. 94] same

Selig ihr Blinden, I 5 (1890) [GA,
v. 5, p. 10] same

Ein Ständchen Euch zu bringen, I 22
(1891) [GA, v. 5, p. 46] same

Sterb' ich, so hüllt in Blumen, I 33
(1896) [GA, v. 5, p. 72] same

Und steht Ihr früh am Morgen auf, I 34
(1896) [GA, v. 5, p. 74] same

Und willst du deinen Liebsten, I 17
(1891) [GA, v. 5, p. 36] same

*Verschling' der Abgrund meines Liebste
Hütte,* I 45 (1896) [GA, v. 5, p. 99]
same

*Was für ein Lied soll dir gesungen
werden,* I 23 (1896) [GA, v. 5, p. 52]
same

Was soll der Zorn, I 32 (1896) [GA, v. 5,
p. 70] same

Wenn du, mein Liebster, I 36 (1896)
[GA, v. 5, p. 82] same

*Wenn du mich mit den Augen streifst und
lachst,* I 38 (1896) [GA, v. 5, p. 86]
same

Wer rief dich denn? I 6 (1890) [GA, v. 5,
p. 12] same

Wie lange schon, I 11 (1891) [GA, v. 5,
p. 22] same

Wie soll ich fröhlich sein und lachen gar,
I 31 (1896) [GA, v. 5, p. 68] same

Wie viele Zeit verlor ich, I 37 (1896)
[GA, v. 5, p. 84] same

Wir haben beide lange Zeit, I 19 (1891)
[GA, v. 5, p. 40] same

Wohl kenn' ich Euren Stand, I 29 (1896)
[GA, v. 5, p. 64] same

**Hölty, Ludwig Heinrich Christoph,
1748-1776.**

Mailied (1876) [unpubl.; ms. in Vienna
Stadtbibliothek Musiksammlung]
"Willkommen, lieber schöner Mai"

**Hoffmann von Fallersleben, August
Heinrich, 1798-1874.**

Liebesfrühling (1878) [GA, v. 7², p. 18]
"Wie oft schon ward es Frühling
wieder"

Nach dem Abschiede (1878) [GA, v. 7²,
p. 28] "Dunkel sind nun alle Gassen"

*DES FAHRENDEN SCHÜLERS LIEBEN
UND LEIDEN.*

Auf der Wanderung (1878) [GA, v. 7²,
p. 20] "Über die Hügel und über die
Berge hin"

Ja, die Schönst! (1878) [GA, v. 7²,
p. 24] same

Ibsen, Henrik, 1828-1906.

DAS FEST AUF SOLHAUG.

Gesang Margit's (1891) [GA, v. 6,
p. 68]
"Bergkönig ritt durch die Lande"

Gudmund's erster Gesang (1891,
1896) [GA, v. 6, p. 74]
"Ich wandelte sinnend allein auf der
Halde"

WOLF, HUGO, 1860-1903 *(continued)*
 Ibsen, Henrik, 1828-1906 *(continued)*
  DAS FEST AUF SOLHAUG (continued)
   Gudmund's zweiter Gesang (1891)
    [GA, v. 6, p. 77]
    "Ich fuhr wohl über Wasser und in
    die Ferne weit"
 Keller, Gottfried, 1819-1890.
  Du milchjunger Knabe (1890) [GA, v. 6,
   p. 56] same
  Das Köhlerweib ist trunken (1890) [GA,
   v. 6, p. 61] same
  Singt mein Schatz wie ein Fink (1890)
   [GA, v. 6, p. 53] same
  Tretet ein, hoher Krieger (1890) [GA,
   v. 6, p. 50] same
  Wandl' ich in dem Morgentau (1890)
   [GA, v. 6, p. 58] same
  Wie glänzt der helle Mond (1890) [GA,
   v. 6, p. 65] same
 Kerner, Justinus, 1786-1862.
  Zur Ruh, zur Ruh! [GA, v. 6, p. 38] "Zur
   Ruh, zur Ruh ihr müden Glieder!"
 **Körner, Theodor, i.e., Karl Theodor,
  1791-1813.**
  Ständchen (1877) [GA, v. 7^2, p. 8]
   "Alles wiegt die stille Nacht"
 Lenau, Nicolaus, 1802-1850.
  Abendbilder (1877) [GA, v. 7^2, p. 51]
   "Friedlicher Abend"
  An** (1877) [GA, v. 7^1, p. 25]
   "O wag' es nicht"
  Frage nicht (1879) [GA, v. 7^2, p. 66]
   "Wie sehr ich Dein, soll ich dir
   sagen?"
  Frühlingsgrüsse (1876) [GA, v. 7^3, p. 24]
   "Nach langem Frost, wie weht die Luft
   so lind!"
  Herbst (1879) [GA, v. 7^2, p. 68]
   "Nun ist es Herbst, die Blätter fallen"
  Herbstenschluss (1879) [GA, v. 7^2, p. 59]
   "Trübe Wolken, Herbstesluft"
  Herbstklage (1879) [unpubl.; ms. in
   Vienna Stadtbibliothek
   Musiksammlung]
   "Holder Lenz, du bist dahin"
  Liebesfrühling, op. 9 no. 2 (1876) [GA,
   v. 7^3, p. 35] "Ich sah den Lenz einmal"
  Meeresstille, op. 9 no. 1 (1876) [GA,
   v. 7^3, p. 29]
   "Sturm mit seinen Donnerschlägen
   kann mir nicht wie du"
  Nächtliche Wanderung (1878) [GA, v. 7^1,
   p. 38] "Die Nacht ist finster, schwül
   und bang"
  *Der Raubschütz,*op. 5 (1875-76) [unpubl.;
   ms. in Vienna Stadtbibliothek

   Musiksammlung]
   "Der alte Müller Jakob"
  Scheideblick (1876) [GA, v. 7^3, p. 52]
   "Als ein unergründlich Wonnemeer
   strahlte"
  Stille sicherheit (1876) [GA, v. 7^3, p. 49]
   "Horch, wie still es wird im dunklen
   Hain"
  Traurige Wege (1878) [GA, v. 7^1, p. 32]
   "Bin mit dir im Wald gegangen"
  Wunsch (1877) [unpubl.; ms. in Vienna
   Stadtbibliothek Musiksammlung]
   "Fort möcht ich reisen weit"
 López de Ubeda, Juan, fl.1579-1582.
  Ach, des Knaben Augen sind (1889) [GA,
   v. 4, p. 26] same
 Luis el Chico, Don
  Deine Mutter, süsses Kind (1890) [GA,
   v. 4, p. 148] same
 Manuel del Rio, Don
  Mühvoll komm' ich und beladen (1890)
   [GA, v. 4, p. 28] same
 Matthisson, Friedrich von, 1761-1831.
  Andenken (1877) [GA, v. 7^2, p. 4] "Ich
   denke dein, wenn durch den Hain"
 Mörike, Eduard Friedrich, 1804-1875.
  Abschied, M 53 (1888) [GA, v. 1, p. 207]
   "Unangeklopft ein Herr tritt abends bei
   mir ein"
  Agnes, M 14 (1888) [GA, v. 1, p. 52]
   "Rosenzeit! wie schnell vorbei"
  An den Schlaf, M 29 (1888) [GA, v. 1,
   p. 103] "Schlaf! süsser Schlaf!"
  An die Geliebte, M 32 (1888) [GA, v. 1,
   p. 113] "Wenn ich, von deinem
   Anschaun tief gestillt"
  An eine Äolsharfe, M 11 (1888) [GA,
   v. 1, p. 37]
   "Angelehnt an die Efeuwand"
  Auf ein altes Bild, M 23 (1888) [GA,
   v. 1, p. 86]
   "In grüner Landschaft Sommerflor"
  Auf eine Christblume, M 20 (1888) [GA,
   v. 1, p. 76] "Tochter des Walds, du
   Lilienverwandte"
  Auf eine Christblume, M 21 (1888) [GA,
   v. 1, p. 82] "Im Winterboden schläft
   ein Blumenkeim"
  Auf einer Wanderung, M 15 (1888) [GA,
   v. 1, p. 56] "In ein freundliches
   Städtchen tret ich ein"
  Auftrag, M 50 (1888) [GA, v. 1, p. 199]
   "In poetischer Epistel"
  Begegnung, M 8 (1888) [GA, v. 1, p. 25]
   "Was doch heut Nacht ein Sturm
   gewesen"

Bei einer Trauung, M 51 (1888) [GA,
v. 1, p. 203]
"Vor lauter hochadligen Zeugen"
Denk es, O Seele! M 39 (1888) [GA,
v. 1, p. 137] "Ein Tännlein grünet wo"
Elfenlied, M 16 (1888) [GA, v. 1, p. 62]
"Bei Nacht im Dorf der Wächter rief"
Er ist's, M 6 (1888) [GA, v. 1, p. 19]
"Frühling lässt sein blaues Band"
Erstes Liebeslied eines Mädchens, M 42
(1888) [GA, v. 1, p. 151]
"Was im Netze? Schau einmal!"
Der Feuerreiter, M 44 (1888) [GA, v. 1,
p. 162] "Sehet ihr am Fensterlein"
Frage und Antwort, M 35 (1888) [GA,
v. 1, p. 123]
"Fragst du mich woher die bange"
Fussreise, M 10 (1888) [GA, v. 1, p. 32]
"Am frisch geschnittnen Wanderstab"
Der Gärtner, M 17 (1888) [GA, v. 1,
p. 66] "Auf ihrem Leibrösslein"
Gebet, M 28 (1888) [GA, v. 1, p. 101]
"Herr! schicke was du Willt"
Die Geister am Mummelsee, M 47 (1888)
[GA, v. 1, p. 181] "Vom Berge was
kommt dort um Mitternacht spät"
Der Genesene an die Hoffung, M 1
(1888) [GA, v. 1, p. 1]
"Tödlich graute mir der Morgen"
Gesang Weylas, M 46 (1888) [GA, v. 1,
p. 179] "Du bist Orplid, mein Land!"
Heimweh, M 37 (1888) [GA, v. 1,
p. 127] "Anders wird die Welt mit
jedem Schritt"
Im Frühling, M 13 (1888) [GA, v. 1,
p. 46]
"Hier lieg ich auf dem Frühlingshügel"
In der Frühe, M 24 (1888) [GA, v. 1,
p. 88]
"Kein Schlaf noch kühlt das Auge mir"
Der Jäger, M 40 (1888) [GA, v. 1,
p. 140] "Drei Tage Regen fort und
fort"
Jägerlied, M 4 (1888) [GA, v. 1, p. 13]
"Zierlich ist des Vogels Tritt"
Karwoche, M 26 (1888) [GA, v. 1, p. 93]
"O Woche, Zeugin heiliger
Beschwerde!"
Der Knabe und das Immlein, M 2 (1888)
[GA, v. 1, p. 5]
"In Weinberg auf der Höhe"
Der König bei der Krönung (1886) [GA,
v. 6, p. 31] "Die angetrauet am Altare"
Lebe wohl, M 36 (1888) [GA, v. 1,
p. 125] "Lebe wohl! Du fühlest nicht"

Lied eines Verliebten, M 43 (1888) [GA,
v. 1, p. 157]
"In aller Früh, ach lang vor Tag"
Lied vom Winde, M 38 (1888) [GA, v. 1,
p. 130] "Sausewind, Brausewind! dort
und hier!"
Mausfallen-Sprüchlein (1882) [GA, v. 6,
p. 24] "Kleine Gäste, kleine Haus"
Neue Liebe, M 30 (1888) [GA, v. 1, p.
105] "Kann auch ein Mensch des
andern auf der Erde ganz"
Nimmersatte Liebe, M 9 (1888) [GA,
v. 1, p. 29]
"So ist die Lieb! So ist die Lieb!"
Nixe Binsefuss, M 45 (1888) [GA, v. 1,
p. 173]
"Des Wassermanns sein Töchterlein"
Perigrina I, M 33 (1888) [GA, v. 1,
p. 117] "Der Spiegel dieser treuen,
braunen Augen"
Perigrina II, M 34 (1888) [GA, v. 1,
p. 119]
"Warum, Geliebte, denk ich dein"
Rat einer Alter, M 41 (1888) [GA, v. 1,
p. 147] "Bin jung gewesen, kann auch
mit reden"
Schlafendes Jesuskind, M 25 (1888) [GA,
v. 1, p. 90]
"Sohn der Jungfrau, Himmelskind"
Selbstgeständnis, M 52 (1888) [GA, v. 1,
p. 205]
"Ich bin meiner Mutter einzig Kind"
Seufzer, M 22 (1888) [GA, v. 1, p. 84]
"Dein Liebesfeuer, ach Herr!"
Storchenbotschaft, M 48 (1888) [GA,
v. 1, p. 188] "Des Schäfers sein Haus
und das steht auf zwei Rad"
Ein Stündlein wohl vor Tag, M 3 (1888)
[GA, v. 1, p. 11]
"Derweil ich schlafend lag"
Suschens Vogel (1880) [GA, v. 7^2, p. 70]
"Ich hatt ein Vöglein, ach wie fein!"
Der Tambour, M 5 (1888) [GA, v. 1,
p. 15]
"Wenn meine Mutter hexen könnt"
Die Tochter der Haide (1884) [GA, v. 7^2,
p. 73] "Wasch dich, mein
Schwesterchen, wasch dich!"
Um Mitternacht, M 19 (1888) [GA, v. 1,
p. 72]
"Gelassen stieg die Nacht aus Land"
Verborgenheit, M 12 (1888) [GA, v. 1,
p. 43]
"Lass, O Welt, O lass mich sein!"
Das verlassene Mägdlein, M 7 (1888)
[GA, v. 1, p. 23]

WOLF, HUGO, 1860-1903 *(continued)*
Mörike, Eduard Friedrich, 1804-1875
(continued)
"Früh, wann die Hähne krähn"
Wo find' ich Trost, M 31 (1888) [GA,
v. 1, p. 108]
"Eine Liebe kenn ich, die ist treu"
Zitronenfalter im April, M 18 (1888)
[GA, v. 1, p. 70]
"Grausame Frühlingssonne"
Zum neuen Jahr, M 27 (1888) [GA, v. 1,
p. 97] "Wie heimlicher Weise"
Zur Warnung, M 49 (1888) [GA, v. 1,
p. 195]
"Einmal, nach einer lustigen Nacht"
Nuñez, Nicolas, fl.1550.
Die du Gott gebarst, du Reine (1889)
[GA, v. 4, p. 6] same
Ocaña, Francisco de, fl.1603.
Nun, wandre, Maria, nun wandre nur fort
(1889) [GA, v. 4, p. 10] same
Peitl, Paul, 1853-
Ein Grab (1876) [GA, v. 7^2, p. 2]
"Wenn des Mondes bleiches Licht"
Platen-Hallermünde, August, Graf
von, 1796-1835.
Ghazél (1876) [Wolf *Nachgelassene
Werke,* v. 1, p. 39] "Im Wasser wogt
die Lilie, die blanke, hin und her"
Reinick, Robert, 1805-1852.
Dem Vaterland (1890) [unpubl.? copy in
Vienna Stadtbibliothek
Musiksammlung]
"Das ist ein hohes helles Wort"
Frohe Botschaft (1890) [GA, v. 7^2,
p. 122]
"Hielt die allerschönste Herrin"
Frühlingsglocken (1883) [GA, v. 7^2,
p. 110] "Schneeglöckchen tut läuten!"
Gesellenlied (1888) [GA, v. 6, p. 81]
"Kein Meister fällt vom Himmel"
Liebchen, wo bist du? (1883) [GA, v. 7^2,
p. 103] "Zaubrer bin ich, doch was
frommt es?"
Morgenstimmung (1896) [GA, v. 6,
p. 86] "Bald ist der Nacht ein End
gemacht"
Nachtgruss (1883) [GA, v. 7^2, p. 108]
"In dem Himmel ruht die Erde"
Skolie (1889) [GA, v. 6, p. 89]
"Reich' den Pokal mir"
Wiegenlied im Sommer (1882) [GA, v. 6,
p. 15] "Vom Berg hinab gestiegen"
Wiegenlied im Winter (1882) [GA, v. 6,
p. 18] "Schlaf ein, mein süsses Kind"
Wohin mit der Freud? (1882) [GA, v. 7^2,
p. 100] "Ach du klar blauer Himmel"

LIEDERBUCH EINES MALERS.
Liebesbotschaft (1883) [GA, v. 7^2,
p. 118]
"Wolken, die ihr nach Osten eilt"
Ständchen (1883) [GA, v. 7^2, p. 115]
"Komm in die stille Nacht!"
Roquette, Otto, 1824-1896.
Perlenfischer (1876) [GA, v. 7^3, p. 46]
"Du liebes Auge, willst dich tauchen"
Rückert, Friedrich, 1788-1866.
Frühling, Liebster (1878) [unpubl.;
ms. in Vienna Stadtbibliothek
Musiksammlung]
"Ich sass an einem Rädchen"
So wahr die Sonne scheinet (1878) [GA,
v. 7^3, p. 53] same
Die Spinnerin (1878) [GA, v. 6, p. 9] "O
süsse Mutter, ich kann nicht spinnen"
Ruiz de Alarcón y Mendoza, Juan,
1581-1639.
Nun bin ich dein (1890) [GA, v. 4, p. 2]
same
Scheffel, Joseph Victor von, 1826-
1886.
Biterolf (Im Lager von Akkon 1190)
(1886) [GA, v. 6, p. 32]
"Kampfmüd und sonnverbrannt"
Wächterlied auf der Wartburg (1887)
[GA, v. 6, p. 26]
"Schwingt euch auf, Posannenchöre"
Shakespeare, William, 1564-1616.
MIDSUMMER NIGHT'S DREAM:
Bottom's song.
Lied des transferierten Zettel (1889)
[GA, v. 6, p. 42] "Die Schwalbe, die
den Sommer bringt"
Steinebach, Friedrich, 1821-1899.
Das Lied der Waise (1877) [unpubl.;
ms. in Vienna Stadtbibliothek
Musiksammlung]
"Einsam steh ich und alleine"
Sturm, Julius Karl Reinholdt, 1816-
1896.
Über Nacht (1878) [GA, v. 7^1, p. 54]
"Über Nacht, über Nacht kommt still
das Leid"
Unknown
Bescheidene Liebe (1876 or 1877) [GA,
v. 7^1, p. 64]
"Ich bin wie and're Mädchen nicht"
Der goldene Morgen, op. 9 no. 6 (1876)
[GA, v. 7^3, p. 44]
"Golden lacht und glüht der Morgen"
Die Verlassene (1877) [unpubl.]
"Hört Ihr dort drüben"
Facsimile in R. Batka and W. Nagel
Allgemeine Geschichte der Musik,
III (Stuttgart: 1915), 252.

COMPOSER   Poet   *Title*   "First Line"

Valdivielso, Jose de, 1560?-1638.
  Wunden trägst du, mein Geliebter (1889)
    [GA, v. 4, p. 37] same
Vega Carpio, Lope Félix de, 1562-
  1635.
  Die ihr schwebet um diese Palmen (1889)
    [GA, v. 4, p. 14] same
  Weint nicht, ihr Äuglein (1890) [GA,
    v. 4, p. 141] same
Vicente, Gil, ca.1470-ca.1536.
  *Wehe der, die mir verstrickte meinen
    Geliebten!* (1890) [GA, v. 4, p. 156]
    same
  SPANISCHES LIEDERBUCH: Si dormis,
    doncella.
  Und schläfst du, mein Mädchen (1889)
    [GA, v. 4, p. 136] same
Zschokke, Heinrich, 1771-1848.
  Nacht und Grab, op. 3 no. 1 (1875) [GA,
    v. 7^3, p. 1]
  "Sei mir gegrüsst, O schöne Nacht"
Zusner, Vinzenz, 1803-1874.
  Abendglöcklein, op. 9 no. 4 (1876) [GA,
    v. 7^3, p. 40] "Des Glöckleins Schall
    durchtönt das Tal"
Wolfe, Charles, 1791-1823.
  HINDEMITH *On hearing "The last rose
    of summer"*
Wolfe, Humbert, 1885-1940.
  WEISGALL *I looked back suddenly*
Wolff, Oskar Ludwig, 1799-1851.
  SCHUMANN *Stiller Vorwurf*
Wolff, R. L.
  THOMPSON, R. *Solstice*
"Wolke lichtweiss in dem Blauen" *see
  Das heilige Haus in Loretto* Giesebrecht
  LOEWE
"Eine Wolke liess beim Glanz der Sterne" *see
  Der Felsen* Lermontov **RUBINSTEIN**
"Eine Wolke seh' ich wandern" *see
  Die beiden Wolken* Hamerling **LASSEN**
Die Wolken see Lermontov **RUBINSTEIN**
"Wolken am Himmelszelt" *see Die Wolken*
  Lermontov **RUBINSTEIN**
"Wolken die ihr nach Osten eilt" *see
  Liebesbotschaft* Reinick **SCHUMANN,
  WOLF**
"Wolken, meine Kinder" *see Der Gesang des
  Meeres* Meyer **SCHOECK**
"Wolken seh' ich abendwärts" *see
  Abendwolken* Uhland **SCHOECK**
"Wolken, wälderwärts gegangen" *see In der
  Fremde* Eichendorff **WOLF**
"Die Wolken waren fortgezogen" *see
  Der Abend* Lenau **SCHOECK**
"Die Wolken ziehen schwarz und hoch" *see
  Mitternacht* Dingelstedt **SPOHR**

Wolkenbild see Löper, Lina **LOEWE**
Die Wolkenbraut see Schober **SCHUBERT**
Wolkennacht see Avenarius *STIMMEN UND
  BILDER.* **WEBERN**
Wolle keiner mich fragen see Geibel
  FRANZ, SPOHR
"Wollt ihr sie kennen?" *see Meine Farben*
  Lehr, Hofrath **WEBER**
"Wollt ihr wissen, holde Bienen" *see An die
  Bienen* Bürger **PFITZNER**
Woltmann, Karl Ludwig von, 1770-1817,
  supposed author.
  ZELTER *Theresens letztes Lied*
Wolzogen, Alfred, freiherr von *see*
  Wolzogen und Neuhaus, Alfred,
  Freiherr von, 1823-1883.
Wolzogen und Neuhaus, Alfred,
  Freiherr von, 1823-1883.
  LASSEN *Lied aus Sakuntala*
THE WOMAN HATER (1607). *see* Fletcher
  Sleep **HESELTINE**
A WOMAN OF VALOR, no. 1
  GIDEON Bible *Hinei nachalat adonai
    baním*
A WOMAN OF VALOR, no. 2
  GIDEON Bible *Eishet chayil*
A WOMAN OF VALOR, no. 3
  GIDEON Bible *Y' gia kapecha ki Tocheil*
WOMEN'S VOICES, no. 1
  ROREM Wylie *Now let no charitable
    hope*
WOMEN'S VOICES, no. 2
  ROREM Rossetti, Christina *A birthday*
WOMEN'S VOICES, no. 3
  ROREM Bradstreet *To my dear and
    loving husband*
WOMEN'S VOICES, no. 4
  ROREM Chudleigh *To the ladies*
WOMEN'S VOICES, no. 5
  ROREM Herbert *If ever hapless woman
    had a cause*
WOMEN'S VOICES, no. 6
  ROREM Coleridge *We never said
    farewell*
WOMEN'S VOICES, no. 7
  ROREM Rich *The stranger*
WOMEN'S VOICES, no. 8
  ROREM Dickinson *What inn is this*
WOMEN'S VOICES, no. 9
  ROREM Anne Boleyn *Defiled is my
    name*
WOMEN'S VOICES, no. 10
  ROREM Ridge *Electrocution*
WOMEN'S VOICES, no. 11
  ROREM Mew *Smile, death*
The wonderful garden see Collen, G.
  SEPTAIN. **BORODIN** *Chudnyĭ sad"*

COMPOSER Poet *Title* "First Line"

The wondrous garden see Collen, G.
  SEPTAIN. **BORODIN** *Chudnyĭ sad″*
Wonne der Wehmut see Goethe
  BEETHOVEN, SCHUBERT, ZELTER
Wonne der Wehmuth see Goethe **FRANZ**
"Wonnelohn getreuer Huldigungen" *see*
  Verlust (Auf Mollys Tod, 1859) Bürger
  CORNELIUS
The woodcutter's song see Bunyan
  VAUGHAN WILLIAMS
"Word over all, beautiful as the sky!" *see*
  Reconciliation Whitman **ROREM**
Wordsworth, William, 1770-1850.
  IVES
    I travelled among unknown men
    So may it be
The worker see Weatherly **GOUNOD**
The world feels dusty see Dickinson
  COPLAND
"The world is high as a bird can fly" *see*
  Worlds Fisher, A. **CARPENTER**
The world would see thee smile see Tolstoĭ
  RACHMANINOFF *How everyone loves*
  thee
Worlds see Fisher, A. *THE COFFEE-POT*
  FACE. **CARPENTER**
The world's highway see Ives, Harmony
  IVES
The world's wanderers see Shelley **IVES**
Worte see Benn **BLACHER**
WORTE IN VERSEN. see Kraus
  Durch die Nacht **KRENEK**
  Die Nachtigall **KRENEK**
"Der Worte viele sind gemacht" *see*
  Kraftliedchen Unknown **WAGNER**
Woskresensky
  RUBINSTEIN*O frage nicht*
"Would God your health were as this month
  of May" *see English May*
  Rossetti, Dante **IRELAND**
"Would I were in Grantchester" *see*
  Grantchester Brooke **IVES**
Der Woywode see Mickiewicz **LOEWE**
Wozu? see Anon. **FRANZ**
Wozu noch, Mädchen see Schack
  LOTOSBLÄTTER. **STRAUSS**
"Wozu wozu mir sein sollte das Aug' " *see*
  Wozu? Anon. **FRANZ**
Wright, Merle St. Croix
  THOMPSON, R.
    Discipleship
    Drought
    The Heavens declare

  Spiritual: I wan' my friends
  White moth at twilight
Wring me no more see Agee *SONNET 10.*
  DIAMOND
Wsyscy przyjechali see Anon.
  SZYMANOWSKI
Wünsche see Hafiz **SZYMANOWSKI**
"Wüsst ich, dass du mich lieb" *see Gegenliebe*
  Bürger **BEETHOVEN**
Wull ye come in the eärly spring see Barnes
  COME. **CARPENTER**
"Die Wunde brennt" *see Abschied vom Leben*
  Körner **WEBER**
Wunden trägst du, mein Geliebter see
  Valdivielso **WOLF**
Das Wunder auf der Flucht see Rückert
  LOEWE
Wunderbarer Gnadenthron see Olearius
  LOEWE
"Wunderliche Spiessgesellen" *see An die*
  Lützowschen Jäger Eichendorff
  SCHOECK
WUNDERSCHÖNE
  LIEBESGESCHICHTE . . . see Tieck
  Keinen hat es noch gereut **BRAHMS**
"Wundervolle Waldeskühle, die ich
  tausendmale grüss" *see Im Walde* Heyse
  CORNELIUS
Wunsch see Krzyzanowski **KRENEK**
Wunsch see Lenau **WOLF**
Wunsch see Michaeli **REGER**
Wunsch und Entsagung see Castelli **WEBER**
Wu-Ti, Han dynasty, 157-87 B. C.
  BERKELEY, BRITTEN *The autumn*
  wind
Wu-Ti, Liang dynasty, 464-549.
  BERKELEY *People hide their love*
Wyatt, Sir Thomas, 1503?-1542.
  HESELTINE *And wilt thou leave me thus?*
  ROREM
    The appeal
    Forget not yet
    Little elegy
    Now let no charitable hope
Wylie, Elinor, 1885-1928.
  ROREM *On a singing girl*
  THOMPSON, R. *Velvet shoes*
Wysla burzycka see Anon.
  SZYMANOWSKI
Wysly rybki, sysly see Anon.
  SZYMANOWSKI
Wyszywala raz Hanka see Czyzowskiego,
  Kazimierza Andrzeja **SZYMANOWSKI**
"Wzniosly, smukly i mlody" *see Śliczny*
  chlopiec Zaleski **CHOPIN**

X

Xaurof, L.
  MARTINŮ *Le petit chat*

Xenion see Goethe **STRAUSS**

Y

Y" see Jalkanen **KILPINEN**
"Y avait un' foix un pauv' gas" *see La
  chanson de la glu* Richepin **GOUNOD**
Y' gia kapecha ki Tocheil see Bible: Psalm
  128. **GIDEON**
"Y muera yo de amor por Perinarda" *see
  Estribillo* Polo de Medina **RODRIGO**
Ya lyubila evo see Kol'tsov **BALAKIREV**
  IA liubila ego
Ya prishol k tebe s privetom see Shenshin
  BALAKIREV
"Ya que este mundo abandono" *see Nunca
  olvida* Campoamor y Campoosorio
  TURINA
Ya s neyu nikogda ne govoril see Mei
  OKTAVI. **CHAĭKOVSKIĭ**
"Ya viene la primavera" *see La primavera*
  Anon. **HARRIS**
Yalan-Stekelis, Miriam (Wilensky), 1900-
  GIDEON *The cat is angry*
Yang Knang
  BERKELEY *Late spring*
Yanova, Mariya, 1840-1875.
  RACHMANINOFF *Morning*
Yarmolinsky, Babette Deutsch *see*
  Deutsch, Babette, 1895-
Yarmouth Fair see Collins, Hal
  HESELTINE
Ye banks and braes o' Bonnie Doon see
  Burns **RIEGGER**
"Ye banks and braes o' bonnie Doon" *see
  Chanson écossaise* Burns **RAVEL**
"Ye banks and braes o' bonnie Doon" *see
  Deserted* Burns **MACDOWELL**
Ye little birds see Heywood
  VAUGHAN WILLIAMS
Ye sisters, ye brothers see Lybeck **SIBELIUS**
  I systrar, I bröder
"Ye vapors, rain-clouds, hear ye me" *see
  Prayer for rain* Shenshin **MEDTNER**

Yeats, William Butler, 1865-1939.
  BARBER *The secrets of the old*
  CARPENTER *The player queen*
  IRELAND *The salley gardens*
  LOEFFLER
    Ballad of the foxhunter
    The fiddler of Dooney
  RIETI
    Brown penny
    The fiddler of Dooney
    Maid quiet
    When you are old
  ROREM
    Cradle song
    I know that I shall meet my fate
    Lullaby
    Mad as the mist and snow
    Maid quiet
    O do not love too long
    Sweet dancer
    To a young girl
  THE WIND AMONG THE REEDS.
    LOEFFLER
      The host of the air
      The hosting of the Sidhe
  THE WIND AMONG THE REEDS (1899):
    Aedh wishes for the cloths . . .
    HESELTINE *The cloths of heaven*
  THE WIND AMONG THE REEDS (1899):
    Aodh to Dectora.
    HESELTINE *The everlasting voices*
The yellow daisy see Deland
  MACDOWELL
The yellow leaf trembles see Lermontov
  BALAKIREV *Pesnya: Zholtĭy list*
"The yellow poplar leaves have strown" *see
  Autumn evening* Maquarie, Arthur
  QUILTER
Yeremushka's cradle-song see Nekrasov
  MUSORGSKIĭ *Kolybel'naia Eremushki*
yes is a pleasant country see Cummings
  BLITZSTEIN

"Yes, nightingale thru all the summertime"
see The nightingale unheard Peabody
GIDEON
"Yes, the candidate's a dodger" *see*
The dodger Anon. **COPLAND**
Yesternight see Khomyakov **CHAĬKOVSKIĬ**
Vcherashniaia noch'
Yetsevich, M *see* ĪAtsevicha, M
Les yeux see Sully-Prudhomme **AUBERT**
"Les yeux boissés" *see Hébé* Ackermann
CHAUSSON
Les yeux clos see Buchillot, G. **MASSENET**
Les yeux coleur du temps see Margueritte
MALIPIERO
Les yeux d'ambre de l'alchimiste see
Raphaël, Cluzel **SAUGUET**
Les yeux de l'Aimée see Indy **INDY**
Yksin see Koskenniemi **KILPINEN**
"Yksin vieno veet vetelen" *see Kaikissa yksin*
Kanteletar **KILPINEN**
Yli hohtavan hangen see Jalkanen
KILPINEN
"Yli metsän koitti jo päivän koi" *see Aamulla*
Lönnbohm **KILPINEN**
"Yo escucho los cantos de viejas cadencias"
see Cantaban los niños Machado y Ruiz
RODRIGO
"Yo no se que tienen tus ojillos negros" *see*
Tus ojillos negros (Canzon Andaluza)
Castro **FALLA**
"Yo soy ardiente yo soy mo rena" *see Rima*
Bécquer **TURINA**
"Yö ja hiljaisuus" *see Kuutamo-oodi*
Jalkanen **KILPINEN**
"Yön ihmeelliseen valon" *see Lakeus III*
Koskenniemi **KILPINEN**
"Yön ystävä, ruhtinas unten" *see Uusi Aladdin*
Jalkanen **KILPINEN**
Yöperhonen see Lönnbohm **KILPINEN**
You alone see Pleshcheyev **CHAĬKOVSKIĬ**
Lish' ty odin"
you are like the snow see Cummings
BLITZSTEIN
You are my glorious rose see Pfleger-
Moravský **DVOŘÁK** *Ó zlatá ruže,*
spatnilá
"You are so wonderful, what shall I do?" *see*
I rise when you enter Feeney **CHANLER**
You ask why my songs see Pfleger-
Moravský **DVOŘÁK** *Ty se ptáš pročmoje*
zpěvy bouřýí
You didn't recognize me in the crowd see
Golenishchev-Kutuzov **MUSORGSKIĬ**
Menia ty v tolpe ne uznala
You do not love me see Konstantin
CHAĬKOVSKIĬ *ĪA vam ne nravlius'*

"You kindly winds who gaily go blowing" *see*
The thresher Du Bellay **BERKELEY**
You knew him see Tiutchev
RACHMANINOFF
"You knew him well" *see You knew him*
Tiutchev **RACHMANINOFF**
You love me not! see Heine **MACDOWELL**
Du liebst mich nicht
You recall that evening? see Tolstoĭ
RACHMANINOFF *Do you remember the*
evening?
"You smile upon your friend today" *see*
Epilogue Housman **IRELAND**
"You sowed in me, not a child but yourself"
see Poem Dropkin **WEISGALL**
You, the young rainbow of my tears see
Sitwell **ROREM**
"You were glad tonight" *see Serenade*
Sassoon **CARPENTER**
You were like a song see Trustman,
Deborah **WEISGALL**
"You will come home" *see Menelaus*
Vaughan Williams, U.
VAUGHAN WILLIAMS
You write to me see Heyduk **MARTINŮ**
Young, Ella, 1867-1956.
POEMS (1906).
HESELTINE *The wind from the West*
A young girl's wish see Witwicki **CHOPIN**
Zyczenie
The young Highland rover see Burns
BENNETT *Castle Gordon, or The young*
Highland rover
The young hunter see Runeberg **SIBELIUS**
Jägargossen
Young lady see Pound **DIAMOND**
Young love see Blake, William **LUENING**
Young man, chieftan! see Austin, Mary
CARPENTER
"The young May moon" *see A night song*
Moore, T. **IVES**
The young sportsman see Runeberg
SIBELIUS *Jägargossen*
Young Venevil see Bjørnson **ARNE. DELIUS**
Kleine Veneil
"Your brother has a falcon" *see Newborn*
Rossetti, Christina **IRELAND**
"Your hands lie open in the long fresh grass"
see Silent noon Rossetti, Dante
VAUGHAN WILLIAMS
"You're right, whatever of me charms and
pleases" *see Butterfly* Shenshin
MEDTNER
Youth and love see Stevenson, Robert
Louis *SONGS OF TRAVEL*, II.
VAUGHAN WILLIAMS

Youth, day, old age, and night see Whitman
ROREM
"*Youth, large, lusty, loving youth*" *see Youth,*
day, old age, and night Whitman
ROREM
The youth with the red-gold hair see Sitwell
ROREM
Youth's spring-tribute see Rossetti, Dante
IRELAND

Ystävien piiri pienentyy see Koskenniemi
KILPINEN
Yuan Mei, 1715-1797.
GRIFFES *A feast of lanterns*
Yü-hsi, 772-842.
CARPENTER *The Odalisque*

Z

"Z gór, gdzie dźwigali strasznych krzyzów
brzemie" *see Melodia* Krasiński **CHOPIN**
Z maurytańskich śpiewnych sal see Miciński
W MROKU GWIAZD. **SZYMANOWSKI**
Za goroĩu see Anon. **PROKOFIEV**
"*Za goroiu u krinitsy*" *see Za goroiu* Anon.
PROKOFIEV
Za lesochkom see Anon. **PROKOFIEV**
Za oknom v teni mel'kaet see Polonsky
VIZOV. **CHAĬKOVSKIĬ**
Zabyt' tak skoro! see Apukhtin
CHAĬKOVSKIĬ
Zachem? see Mei **CHAĬKOVSKIĬ**
"*Zachem zhe ty prisnilasia*" *see Zachem?* Mei
CHAĬKOVSKIĬ
Zäide (Boléro) see Beauvoir **BERLIOZ**
Zärtliche Liebe see Herrosee **BEETHOVEN**
Zaffira, Giuseppe
GOUNOD
Biondina bella
Da qualche tempo
E le campane hanno suonato
E stati al quanto
Ell' è malata!
L'ho compagnata
Ho messo nuove
Ier fù mandata
Ier l'ho scontrata
Le labbra ella compone
Oh! dille tu!
Se come io son poeta
Siam' iti l'altro giorno
MASSENET *L'improvisatore*
"*Zagalejo de perlas hijo del alba*" *see*
Pastorcito Santo Vega Carpio **RODRIGO**
"*Zaghaft vom Gewölk ins Land*" *see*
Nächtliche Scheu Dehmel **WEBERN**

ZAHME XENIEN. see Goethe
Geweihter Platz **MEDTNER**
Praeludium **MEDTNER**
Der Zahn see Claudius, M. *ASMUS.*
LOEWE
Zakatilos' solntse see Rathaus
CHAĬKOVSKIĬ *Sonne ging zur*
Ruhe
Zaklinanie see Pushkin **MEDTNER**
The summons; **RIMSKIĬ-KORSAKOV**
Zaklinanie vody i ornia see Bal'mont
PROKOFIEV
Zaleski, Josef Bohdan, 1802-1886.
CHOPIN
Dwojaki koniec
Nie ma czego trzeba
Śliczny chlopiec
NIE MA CZEGO TRZEBA.
CHOPIN *Dumka*
Žalo dievča, žalo trávu see Anon. **DVOŘÁK**
Žalozpěv Pargy see Anon. **DVOŘÁK**
Zamacoïs, Miguel, 1866-1939.
SAINT-SAËNS *La française*
"*Zamykaj, maměnko, zamykaj*" *see Otevření*
slovečkem Unknown **MARTINŮ**
Zangarini, Carlo, 1874-1943.
RESPIGHI
Contrasto
Invito alla danza
Scherzo
Stornellatrice
Zapad gasnet v dali bledno-rozovoĭ see
Tolstoĭ **RIMSKIĬ-KORSAKOV**
Zapevka see Mei **BALAKIREV**
Zapevnaya see Anon. **STRAVINSKIĬ**
Chanson pour compter
Zarian, Constant *see* Zarian, Kostan,
1885-1969.

COMPOSER Poet *Title* "First Line"

Zarian, Kostan, 1885-1969.
RESPIGHI
Io sono la Madre
La mamma è come il pane caldo
No, non è morto il figlio tuo
"Das zarte Knäblein ward ein Mann" *see*
Christus der Kinderfreund Cornelius
CORNELIUS
"Zarter Blumen leicht Gewinde" *see Lied der*
Freundin Goethe
MENDELSSOHN-BARTHOLDY
Zarya see Khomyakov **BALAKIREV**
Zarzyjze, kuniu see Anon. **SZYMANOWSKI**
Zastol'naia pesn' see Kol'tsov
MUSORGSKIĭ
Der Zauberer see Weisse **MOZART**
Der Zauberlehrling see Goethe **LOEWE,**
ZELTER
DER ZAUBERRING. see Fouqué
An dem jungen Morgenhimmel
SCHUBERT
Don Gayseros, Don Gayseros **SCHUBERT**
Nächtens klang die süsse Laute
SCHUBERT
"Zaubrer bin ich, doch was frommt es?" *see*
Liebchen, wo bist du? Reinick **WOLF**
"Zaxotelos' chernetsu poguliati" *see Chernets*
Anon. **PROKOFIEV**
Zde hledím na tendrahý list see Pfleger-
Moravský **DVOŘÁK**
Zde v lese u potoka see Pfleger-Moravský
DVOŘÁK
Two settings: B. 11 no. 14 and B. 160 no.
6.
Zdravstvuĭ! see Akhmatova **PROKOFIEV**
Zebytyĭ see Golenishchev-Kutuzov
MUSORGSKIĭ
Zedlitz, Joseph Christian von, 1790-
1862.
LOEWE
Die Dorfkirche
Die nächtlihe Heerschau
SCHÖNBERG *Sehnsucht*
SCHUMANN *Die nächtliche Heerschau*
KERKER UND KRONE.
SPOHR *Lied*
Der Zeisig see Kulmann **SCHUMANN**
ZEISIG. see Rückert
Zeislein **LOEWE**
Zeislein see Rückert *ZEISIG.* **LOEWE**
"Zeislein, Zeislein, Zeislein" *see Zeislein*
Rückert **LOEWE**
Die Zeit see Stoll **WEBER**
Die Zeit geht nicht see Keller, G.
SCHOECK
"Zeit, Verkündigerin der besten Freuden" *see*
An Sie Klopstock **SCHUBERT,**
STRAUSS

Die Zeitlose see Gilm zu Rosenegg
LETZTE BLÄTTER. **STRAUSS**
Zelenaia roshchĭtsa see Anon. **PROKOFIEV**
Die Zelle in Nonnenwerth see Lichnowsky
LISZT *Nonnenwerth*
"Zelte, Posten, Werda-Rufer!" *see Prinz*
Eugen, der edle Ritter Freiligrath
LOEWE
ZELTER, KARL FRIEDRICH, 1758-1832.
Abschatz, Johann Erasmus Assmann,
freiherr von, 1646-1699.
Mut (1803) [unpubl.]
Anon.
Am Tage der sieben Brüder (1812) [ms.
lost]
An den See (1803) [unpubl.]
An die Preisverteilerin bei einem
Ritterspiele (1812) [unpubl., lost]
Auf den Tod eines Kindes [Trautwein,
1827; Schott (Landshoff), 1932]
"Selig, O Mutter, wer stirbt!"
Beglückt, wer in des Herbstes (1792)
[unpubl., lost]
Beim lieben hellen Mondenschein (1870)
[unpubl., lost]
Chloe, kennst du noch die Stunde? (1779)
[unpubl., lost]
Mein Wunsch [unpubl., lost]
Ständchen [Kunst und Industrie
Comptoir, v. 4, 1813; Schott
(Landshoff), 1932]
"Zu meiner Laute Liebesklang"
Tiefe grauenvolle Stille (1783) [unpubl.,
lost]
Das Veilchen [Kunst und Industrie
Comptoir, v. 2, 181_; Schott
(Landshoff), 1932]
"Blümchen der Demuth, unter
dichten Blättern birgst"
Bechtolsheim, Julie, Freifrau von
(geb. Freiin von Keller), 1747-1847.
Die beiden Schalen (1805) [publ., 1806]
Becker, Karl Friedrich, 1777-1806,
supposed author.
Ahnung (1803) [publ., 1804]
Romanze [unpubl.] "Es war ein
wunderschönes Tal"
Der Sommerabend (1812) [unpubl.?]
Brun, Sophie Christiane Frederikke
(Münter), 1765-1835.
Abendphantasie [Kunst und Industrie
Comptoir, v. 4, 1813]
"Süsses Bild, schwebst mir vor mit
leisem Sehnen"
Ich denke dein (1794)
[Kunst und Industrie Comptoir, v. 1,
1810; Schott (Landshoff), 1932]
same

Bürger, Gottfried August, 1747-1794.
Lust am Liebchen (1787?)
[*Claviermagazin für Kenner und
Liebhaber*, 1787]
Carpani, Giuseppe, 1752-1825.
In questa tomba oscura (1810) [unpubl.,
lost]
Claudius, Matthias, 1740-1815.
Freimauerlied (1784) [*Claviermagazin
für Kenner und Liebhaber*, 1787]
"Füllt noch einmal die Gläser"
Diez, Heinrich Friedrich von, 1751-
1817.
Die Gegenwart (1795-96?) [Trautwein,
1796]
Falk, Johannes, 1768-1826.
Der arme Thoms (1796) [Kunst und
Industrie Comptoir, v. 4, 1813]
"Thoms sass am hallenden See"
Florian, Jean Pierre Claris de, 1755-
1794.
Helas! (1796) [unpubl., lost]
Gerhardt, Paul, 1607-1676.
Sonett (1803) [Kunst und Industrie
Comptoir, v. 2, 181_; Schott
(Landshoff), 1932]
"Jedes Ding in jeder Sache"
Gleim, Johann Wilhelm Ludwig,
1719-1803.
Das Hüttchen (1791-92?) [J.A.Böhme,
Heft 1, 1802]
"Ich hab' ein kleines Hüttchen nur"
Ich alter Pilger (1786) [unpubl., lost]
Lasst mich sterben (1791) [unpubl., lost]
Lied für preussischen Patrioten (1792)
[J.F.Reichardt ed., *Studien*, 1792]
"Erhalt uns den König"
Weg mit allen euren Klagen (1791)
[unpubl., lost]
TRIOLETT: Gebt mir Blumen.
Triolett (1791) [unpubl., lost]
Goethe, Johann Wolfgang von, 1749-
1832.
An den Mond [Kunst und Industrie
Comptoir, v. 3, 1813; Schott
(Landshoff), 1932]
"Füllest wieder Busch und Tal"
An die Entfernte (1807) [Schlesinger,
1821; Schott (Landshoff), 1932]
"So hab ich wirklich dich verloren?"
Auch mein Sinn (1814) [Schlesinger,
1821] "Ich gieng im Walde so vor
mich hin"
Aus der Ferne (1816) [Trautwein;
Heinrichshofen] "Dir zu eröffnen mein
Herz verlangt mich"

Ballade (1818) [unpubl.]
"Herein, O der Guter"
Die Bekehrte (1807)
[Kunst und Industrie Comptoir, v. 2,
181_; Martin Breslauer, 1924]
"Bey dem Glanze der Abendröthe"
Die Braut von Corinth (1798)
[J.A.Böhme, Heft 1]
"Nach Corinthus von Athen gezogen"
Christel (1810) [Kunst und Industrie
Comptoir, v. 1, 1810; Schott
(Landshoff), 1932]
"Hab oft einen dummen düstern Sinn"
Der Erlkönig (1797) [*Schriften der
Goethe-Gesellschaft*, v. 11, 1896]
"Wer reitet so spät durch Nacht und
Wind?"
Erster Verlust (1807)
[Kunst und Industrie Comptoir, v. 4,
1813; Schott (Landshoff), 1932]
"Ach! wer bringt die schönen Tage"
Der Fischer (1809) [Kunst und Industrie
Comptoir, v. 2, 181_] "Das Wasser
rauscht, das Wasser schwoll"
Frühzeitiger Frühling (1802)
[Kunst und Industrie Comptoir, v. 3,
1812; Schott (Landshoff), 1932]
"Tage der Wonne, kommt ihr so
bald?"
Das Gastmahl (1814) [Trautwein, 1832]
"Viele Gaeste wüns ich heut"
Geheimnis (1810) [unpubl.]
"Von wem ich es habe"
Die Geheimnisse (1811) [unpubl.]
Geistesgruss (1810) [Kunst und Industrie
Comptoir, v. 3, 1812]
"Hoch auf dem alten Thurme"
Der getreue Eckart [Schlesinger, 1821]
"O wären wir weiter"
Gewohnt, getan (1813) [Schott
(Landshoff), 1932] "Ich habe geliebet"
Gleich und gleich (1819) [Schott
(Landshoff), 1932]
"Ein Blumenglöckchen vom Boden
hervor"
Der Goldschmied (1810) [unpubl.]
Hochzeitlied (1802)
[Kunst und Industrie Comptoir, v. 2,
181_; Martin Breslauer, 1924]
"Wir singen und sagen vom Grafen
so gern"
Ich wollt' ich wär ein Fisch (1810)
[Kunst und Industrie Comptoir, v. 3,
1812] same
2 voices, zither & piano.
Im Fernen (1816) [Schlesinger, 1821]
"Wie sisst mir das Liebchen?"

ZELTER, KARL FRIEDRICH, 1758-1832
(continued)
Goethe, Johann Wolfgang von, 1749-1832 *(continued)*
Jägers Abendlied (1807) [Schlesinger, 1821]
 "Im Felde schleich ich still und wild"
Der junge Jäger [Kunst und Industrie Comptoir, v. 1, 1810]
 "Es ist in Schuss gefallen"
Der Junggesell und der Mühlbach [Berlin: Zelter's **Zwölf Lieder am Klavier . . .** , 1801] "Wo willst du klares Bächlein hin so munter?"
Klagegesang: Jrisch (1819) [Trautwein; Heinrichshofen]
 "So singet laut den Phillalu"
Künstlers Abendlied (1807) [unpubl.]
 "Ach, dass die innre Schöpfungskraft"
Mädchens Held (1816) [Trautwein, 1827; Heinrichshofen]
 "Flieh, flieh, flieh Täubchen, flieh"
Mailied [Martin Breslauer, 1924]
 "Zwischen Weizen und Korn"
Mignon als Engel verkleidet (1796?) [Schiller's **Musenalmanach,** 1797]
Der Misanthrop [Kunst und Industrie Comptoir, v. 4, 1813]
 "Erst sitzt er eine Weile"
Musen und Grazien in der Mark (1796) [Schiller's **Musenalmanach,** 1797]
Der Musensohn (1807) [Kunst und Industrie Comptoir, v. 4, 1813]
 "Durch Feld und Wald zu schweifen"
Nachgefühl (1798) [Schlesinger, 1821]
 "Wenn die Reben wieder blüben rübret sich der Wein im Fasse"
Nachtgesang (1804) [Schott (Landshoff), 1932] "O gieb, vom weichen Pfühle"
Nähe des Geliebten (1808) [Schott (Landshoff), 1932] "Ich denke dein"
Der neue Amadis (1802) [unpubl.]
Der neue Amor [Schlesinger, 1821]
 "Amor, nicht das Kind"
Neue Liebe, neues Leben (1812) [Kunst und Industrie Comptoir, v. 4, 1813; Schott (Landshoff), 1932]
 "Herz, mein Herz, was soll das geben?"
Rastlose Liebe (1812) [Kunst und Industrie Comptoir, v. 4, 1813; Schott (Landshoff), 1932]
 "Dem Schnee, dem Regen"
Ruhe (1814) [Schlesinger, 1821; Schott (Landshoff), 1932]
 "Über allen Gipfeln ist Ruh"

Schäfers Klagelied (1802) [Kunst und Industrie Comptoir, v. 1, 1810; Schott (Landshoff), 1932]
 "Da droben auf jenem Berge"
Sct. Nepomuks Vorabend [Trautwein, 1827] "Lichtlein schwimmen auf dem Strome"
 2 voices & piano.
Die Spinnerin (1800) [lost]
Die Spröde (1807) [Kunst und Industrie Comptoir, v. 2, 181_; Martin Breslauer, 1924]
 "An dem reinsten Frühlingsmorgen"
Stirbt der Fuchs, so gilt der Balg (1807) [Kunst und Industrie Comptoir, v. 3, 1812] "Nach Mittage sassen mir junges Volk im Kühlen"
Das Sträusschen (1822) [unpubl.]
Suleika (1820) [Schott (Landshoff), 1932]
 "Ach, um deine feuchten Schwingen"
Der Totentanz (1814) [Trautwein, 1826; Heinrichshofen] "Der Thürmer der schaut zu Mitten der Nacht"
Trost in Tränen (1803) [Schott (Landshoff), 1932]
 "Wie kommts, dass du so traurig bist"
Um Mitternacht (1818) [Schlesinger, 1821; Schott (Landshoff), 1932]
 "Um Mitternacht ging ich"
Vanitas! Vanitatum vanitas! (1806) [Kunst und Industrie Comptoir, v. 2, 181_; Schott (Landshoff), 1932]
 "Ich hab' mein Sach auf Nichts gestellt"
Versuch in achtzeiligen Strophen [Berlin: Zelter's **Sechs deutsche Lieder . . .** , 1827]
Wer kauft Liebesgötter? (1802) [Kunst und Industrie Comptoir, v. 1, 1810; Martin Breslauer, 1924]
 "Von allen schönen Waaren zum Markte"
Wiederfinden (1820?) [unpubl.]
Wirkung in die Ferne [unpubl.]
Wonne der Wehmut (1807) [Schott (Landshoff), 1932]
 "Trocknet nicht, trocknet nicht"
Der Zauberlehrling (1799) [J.A.Böhme, Heft 1] "Hat der alte Hexenmeister sich doch einmal wegbegeben"
BLUMENGRUSS.
Willkommen dem 28. August 1749 (1810) [Kunst und Industrie Comptoir, v. 2, 181_; Schott (Landshoff), 1932]
 "Der Strauss, den ich gepflücket"

2 voices with chorus & piano.
Also published by Martin
Breslauer, 1924, as
Blumengruss.
EGMONT.
  Clärchen (1804) [Kunst und Industrie
  Comptoir, v. 1, 1810;
  Schlesinger, H. 1, 1810]
    "Freudvoll, freudvoll und leidvoll,
    Gedanken voll seyn"
EPIMENIDES ERWACHEN.
  In tiefe Sklaverei lag ich gebunden
  [Trautwein, 1827; Heinrichshofen]
  same
FAUST.
  Gretchens Lied aus Faust [Schlesinger]
  Der König von Tule
  [Kunst und Industrie Comptoir, v. 3,
  1812; Schott (Landshoff), 1932]
    "Es war ein König in Tule"
  Margarethe [Kunst und Industrie
  Comptoir, v. 1, 1810]
    "Meine Ruh ist hin"
INDISCHE LEGENDE.
  Der Gott und die Bajadere (1797)
  [Kunst und Industrie Comptoir, v. 3,
  1812]
    "Mahadöh, der Herr der Erde"
    Voice & harp.
MAILIED.
  Wo geht's Liebchen? (1810)
  [Kunst und Industrie Comptoir, v. 2,
  181_; Schott (Landshoff), 1932]
    "Zwischen Weizen und Korn"
*MICH ERGREIFT, ICH WEISS NICHT
WIE.*
  Tischlied (1807) [Schott (Landshoff),
  1932]
    "Mich ergreift, ich weiss nicht wie"
SEHNSUCHT.
  Sehnsucht (1802) [unpubl.]
    "Was zieht mir das Herz so?"
UF'M BERGLI.
  Schweizer Lied (1811) [Gröbenschütz
  und Seiler, 1811]
WANDERERS NACHTLIED.
  Die wackelnde Glocke (1814)
  [Nägeli *Neue Liedersammlung,*
  1821; Schott (Landshoff)]
    2 settings; 1st unpubl., 2nd as
    above.
WANDRERS NACHTLIED I.
  Wandrers Nachtlied (1807)
  [Kunst und Industrie Comptoir, v. 4,
  1813; Schott (Landshoff), 1932]
    "Der du on dem Himmel bist"

WESTÖSTLICHER DIVAN.
  In tausend Formen (1823) [Schott
  (Landshoff), 1932] "In tausend
  Formen magst du dich verstekken"
  Selige Sehnsucht (1820) [Trautwein;
  Heinrichshofen]
    "Sagt es niemand, nur den Weisen"
WILHELM MEISTER.
  An Mignon (1797)
  [Schiller's *Musenalmanach,* 1798;
  Schott (Landshoff), 1932]
    "Über Tal und Fluss getragen"
  Einsamkeit [Schott (Landshoff), 1932]
    "Wer sich der Einsamkeit ergiebt"
  Klage (1795) [Schott (Landshoff),
  1932]
    "Wer nie sein Brot mit Tränen ass"
  Der Sänger (1803) [Kunst und
  Industrie Comptoir, v. 3, 1812]
    "Was hör' ich draussen vor dem
    Thor"
  Wer nie sein Brot mit Tränen ass
  (1795)
  [Schlesinger, 1821; Schott
  (Landshoff), 1932] same
WILHELM MEISTER. Harfenspieler.
  An die Türen will ich schleichen
  (1818) [Schott (Landshoff), 1932]
  same
*WILHELM MEISTER. Mignon's song:
Heiss mich nicht reden.*
  Geheimnis (1795) [Trautwein, 1796;
  Schott (Landshoff), 1932]
    "Heiss mich nicht reden"
*WILHELM MEISTER. Mignon's song:
Kennst du das Land?*
  Kennst du das Land? (1795)
  [J.A.Böhme; Schott (Landshoff),
  1932] same
*WILHELM MEISTER. Mignon's song:
Nur wer die Sehnsucht kennt.*
  Nur wer die Sehnsucht kennt (1812)
  [Martin Breslauer, 1924] same
  Sehnsucht (1795) [Schlesinger, 1821;
  Schott (Landshoff), 1932]
    "Nur wer die Sehnsucht kennt"
Gotter, Friedrich Wilhelm, 1746-1797.
  Unser süsster Beruf (1796) [unpubl., lost]
**Grimmelshausen, Hans Jacob
Christoffel von, 1625-1676.**
  Der Waldbruder (1800?) [Berlin: Zelter's
  Zwölf Lieder am Klavier . . . , 1801]
    "Komm Trost der Nacht, O Nachtigall"
**Hardenberg, Friedrich Leopold,
Freiherr von, 1772-1801.**
  Lied [unpubl., lost]
    "Bricht das matte Herz"

COMPOSER Poet *Title* "First Line"

ZELTER, KARL FRIEDRICH, 1758-1832
(continued)
Helvig, Amalie (von Imhof) von, 1766-1831.
Die Geister des Sees [J.A.Böhme, Heft 1]
"Dumpf rauschts vom hohen
Wogenstrand ans steile
Felsengestade"
Herder, Johann Gottfried von, 1744-1803.
Macht der Liebe (1796?) [Schiller's
Musenalmanach, 1797]
Hölty, Ludwig Heinrich Christoph, 1748-1776.
Der Frühling (1791) [unpubl., lost]
Ianke
*Gesang zum Jahresfeste der
Luisenstiftung*
[Kunst und Industrie Comptoir, v. 4,
1813] "Begrüsset mit Tönen und
Liedern den Tag"
3 voices without accompaniment.
Kind, Friedrich, 1768-1843.
Abendlied im Freien [Kunst und Industrie
Comptoir, v. 4, 1813]
"Phöbus, mit lokkerem Zügel"
Lied bei Sonnenuntergang [unpubl., lost]
Kleist, Ewald Christian von, 1715-1759.
An Lina (1791) [Reichardt, ed.
Musikalische Blumenstrauss, 1794]
Kloentrup, Johann Aegidius, 1755-1830.
Der Garten des Lebens (1791)
[Reichardt, ed. ***Liedergeselliger
Freude,*** 1794]
Klopstock, Friedrich Gottlieb, 1724-1803.
Selmar und Dora [J.A.Böhme, Heft 1]
"Weine, weine der nicht, O die ich
innig liebe"
ODE.
Das Rosenband [Kunst und Industrie
Comptoir, v. 1, 1810]
"Im Frühlingsschatten fand ich sie"
Kosegarten, Ludwig Gotthard, 1758-1818.
Lied [J.A.Böhme, Heft 1; Schott
(Landshoff), 1932]
"Meine Blüten sind zernagt"
Langbein, August Friedrich Ernst, 1757-1835.
Die Fahrt ins Heu (1807) [Moritz
Westphal, 1808]
Lessing, Gotthold Ephraim, 1729-1781.
Die drei Reiche der Natur (1809)
[unpubl., lost?]

Leutnand
Wehmut (1816) [unpubl., lost]
Loest, Heinrich, 1778-1848.
Der liebe Traum [unpubl., lost]
Lühe, Caroline von der (geb. von
Brandenstein), b. 1755.
Die unsichtbare Welt (1805) [Kunst und
Industrie Comptoir, v. 1, 1810]
"Wenn im Hauch der Abend kühle"
Luhden
ES HEBT DER WALLENDE BUSEN.
Sehnsucht (1804) [unpubl.]
MORGENS AUF BETAUTER WEIDE.
Lied (1804) [unpubl.]
"Morgens auf betauter Weide"
Macpherson, James, 1736-1796.
Colma von Ossian [Kunst und Industrie
Comptoir, v. 4, 1813]
"Um mich ist Nacht"
Mahlmann, Siegfried August, 1771-1826.
Der Jäger (1802?) [unpubl.?]
Romanze (1804) [***Taschenbuch zum
geselligen Vergnügen,*** 1805]
"Kam ein Wanderer"
Matthisson, Friedrich von, 1761-1831.
Adelaide (1793) [Berlin: Franke, 1793]
Beruhigung (1796) [J.A.Böhme, 1802;
Schott (Landhoff), 1932]
"Wo der Mond mit bleichem
Schimmer"
Die Betende (1794) [Kunst und Industrie
Comptoir, v. 1, 1810; Trautwein, 1796]
"Laura betet!"
Die Elfenkönigin (1794) [Trautwein,
1796] "Was unterm Monde Gleicht"
Feenreigen (1797?) [Schiller's
Musenalmanach, 1798]
Die Kindheit (1794) [Trautwein, 1796]
"Wenn die Abendröte"
Lied aus der Ferne (1794) [Kunst und
Industrie Comptoir, v. 1, 1810]
"Wenn in des Abends letztem Scheine"
Opferlied (1807) [Kunst und Industrie
Comptoir v. 2, 181_]
"Die Flamme lodert"
Mereau, Sophie (Schubert), 1773?-1806.
Erinnerung an einen Freund [Berlin:
1801] "Es rauscht der Strom, es weht
der Wind"
Müchler, Karl Friedrich, 1763-1857.
Abendlied [Schott (Landshoff), 1932]
"In des Meeres kühle Wogen taucht
die Sonne"
An junge spröde Schöne [Johann
Reichardt ***Lieder geselliger Freude,***
1796]

Nostitz und Jänckendorf, Gottlob
Adolf Ernst von, 1765-1836.
Morgengruss an Serena (1812) [unpubl.]

Oehlenschläger, Adam Gottlob, 1779-
1850.
Pilgers Tod (1816) [unpubl.]
AXEL UND WALBURG: Romanze.
Romanze (1816) [unpubl.]

Poliziano, Angelo, 1454-1494.
Die Schäferinn [J.A.Böhme, Heft 1]
"Frühe geht die Schäferinn, führt die
Lämmchen"
Text also ascribed to Johann
Diedrich von Gries, 1750-1818.

Rambach, Friedrich Eberhard, 1767-
1826.
Nur Eines wünscht (1796) [unpubl.]

Recke, Ewald von der
Bilder schon entflohner Stunden (1797)
[unpubl, lost]
Lied (1793?) [Berlin: Franke, 1793]
"Allgütiger, ich bringe dir"
Sehnsucht nach dem Geliebten (1796)
[unpubl.]

Reichardt, Heinrich
Gefilde des Todes (1794) [Trautwein,
1796]

Reissig, Christian Ludwig, 1783-1822.
Meine höchste Wonne [unpub.]

Robert, Friederike (Braun), 1795-1832.
Was soll ich mich mit Worten quälen?
[unpubl., lost]
Robert supposed authoress.

Rothmaler
LIED.
Lied (1796) [unpubl.]
"Rosig ist das Lebensfädgeu"

Rousseau, Jean Jacques, 1712-1778.
*LES CONSOLATIONS DES MISÈRE DE
MA VIE.*
Félicité passée (1803)
[Kunst und Industrie Comptoir, v. 3,
1812; Schott (Landshoff), 1932]
"Au bord d'une fontaine"

Rudolphi, Karoline, 1754-1811.
An die welke Rose (1796) [unpubl., lost]

Schiller, Johann Christoph Friedrich
von, 1759-1805.
An die Freude (1792) [Berlin: Franke,
1793]
Berglied (1804) [Kunst und Industrie
Comptoir, v. 3, 1812; Schott
(Landshoff), 1932] "Am Abgrund leitet
der schwindliche Steg"
Elegie an Emma (1797) [Schiller's
Musenalmanach, 1798]

Der Graf von Habsburg (1804) [unpubl.]
Der Handschuh; eine Erzälung [Kunst
und Industrie Comptoir, v. 3, 1812]
"Vor seinem Löwengarten"
Die Ideale (1797) [Schott (Landshoff),
1932] "So willst du treulos von mir
scheiden"
Der Kampf mit dem Drachen (1802)
[J.A.Böhme, Heft 1]
"Was rennt das Volk, was wälzt sich
dart die langen Gaffen"
Der Sänger der Vorwelt (1803)
[Trautwein; Heinrichshofen]
"Sagt, wo sind die Vortrefflichen hin"
Der Taucher (1802) [unpubl.]
Die Theilung der Erde (1806) [Kunst und
Industrie Comptoir, v. 2, 181_]
"Nehmt hin die Welt!"
Die vier Weltalter (1802) [J.A.Böhme,
Heft 1, 1802] "Wohl perlet im Glase
der purpurne Wein"
DIE ERWARTUNG.
Im Garten (1800?) [Berlin: Zelter's
Zwölf Lieder am Klavier . . . , 1801]
"Hör ich das Pförtchen nicht
gehen?"
DIE PICCOLOMINI.
Des Mädchens Klage (1799)
[Berlin: Zelter's **Zwölf Lieder am
Klavier . . . ,** 1801]
"Der Eichwald brauset"

Schink, Johann Friedrich, 1755-1835.
An den Mond (1817) [Berlin: Rücker]
"Endlich scheinest der wieder"
Erkennung (1817) [Berlin: Schink,
1818] "Wo stammst du her?"
Der Perserkönig Cai-Caius (1817)
[Berlin, Schink, 1818]
Reiche mir aus blauer Ferne (1817)
[Berlin: Schink, 1817]

Schlegel, August Wilhelm von, 1767-
1845.
Gesang und Kuss (1798) [Schott
(Landshoff), 1932] "Wenn fremde
Blikke wachsam uns umgeben"
Der Heilige Lukas (1815) [unpubl.]
Kampaspe [J.A.Böhme, Heft 1]
"Schönheit ist dem Muth beschieden
Lieb' erobert sich der Held"

Schmidt, Friedrich Wilhelm August,
1764-1838.
Liebe mit Schmerzen (1797) [unpubl.,
lost]

Schmidt, Georg Philipp, 1766-1849.
Dauerhafte Farben (1804) [**Taschenbuch
zum geselligen Vergnügen,** 1805]

ZELTER, KARL FRIEDRICH, 1758-1832
(continued)
Schmidt, Georg Philipp, 1766-1849
(continued)
Das Fremdlings Abendlied (1807)
[unknown]
Todes Wiegenlied (1806) [Schott
(Landshoff), 1932] "Ich hab eine
Wiege so schmuck und nett"
Schreiber, Aloys Wilhelm, 1763-1841.
Der Schüchterne (1805) [publication
information lacking]
Schütze, Stephan, 1771-1839.
Lieb und Leben (1806) [Becker's
***Taschenbuch zum geselligen
Vergnügen,*** 1807]
Seufzer des Gefangnen [Kunst und
Industrie Comptoir, v. 2, 181_]
"Warum ich bleibe"
Das Wandernde Lied (1806?) [unpubl.,
lost]
Sonnleithner, Joseph Ferdinand,
1766-1835.
*An eine Mutter, deren Tochter als Kind
starb* [J.A.Böhme] "Ia Mutter, weine
nur! das Schicksal griff und brach"
Steigentesch, August Ernst, Freiherr
von, 1774-1826.
Lied (1796?) [Schiller's
Musenalmanach, 1797]
"Wir gingen beide"
Stolberg, Friedrich Leopold, Graf zu
Stolberg, 1750-1819.
Ach! Mir ist das Herz so schwer (1797)
[unpubl., lost]
Thibaut IV, King of Navarre, 1201-
1253.
Sonett aus dem 13. Jahrhundert (1802)
[Schlesinger, 1821; Schott (Landshoff),
1932]
"Ach, könnt ich, könnt vergessen sie!"
Tieck, Johann Ludwig, 1773-1853.
Herbstlied (1800) [Schott (Landshoff),
1932]
"Feld einwärts flog ein Vögelein"
Wiedersehen (1807) [Kunst und Industrie
Comptoir, v. 1, 1810]
"Wiedersehn! Wiedersehn!"
Unknown
Abschied [Schott (Landshoff), 1932]
"Zieht die Lerch im Herbste fort"
Ach könnt' ich nimmer vergessen'
[Schlesinger]
Come potrei ma vivere [unpubl.]
Dove sei mia bella [unpubl.?]
Der Friede [unpubl., lost]

Kuining Chuonrat der Junge (1813)
[unpubl.]
Vergilius Maro, Publius, 70 B.C.-19
B.C.
AENEID.
Lutheri Vespera (1816) [unpubl.]
"Dulces exuviae, dum fata deusque
sinebat"
Voss, Johann Heinrich, 1751-1826.
Abendlied [Schott (Landshoff), 1932]
"Das Tagewerk ist abgetan"
Die Bewegung (1796) [Trautwein, 1826;
Heinrichshofen]
"Und rausch' auch alles umgedreht
dem Untergange zu"
Die Braut am Gestade (1811?) [Kunst
und Industrie Comptoir, v. 3, 1812]
"Schwarz wie Nacht brausest du auf"
Friedensreigen (1796) [Trautwein, 1796]
"Mit Gesang und Tanz"
Gebet (1796) [Trautwein, 1796]
"Vor dir, O Gott"
Die Gegend am Meer (1796) [unpubl.,
lost]
Die Landlust (before 1800?) [unpubl.,
lost]
Morgenlied (before 1800) [Johann Voss
Musenalmanach, 1800] "Erwacht in
neuer Stärke, begruss ich Gott"
Rundgesang auf dem Wasser [Berlin:
1801] "Umwallt vom hellem Wimpel
schwebt das Boot im Wellentanz"
Rundgesang beim Rheinwein [Berlin:
1801] "Ihr habt doch Wein genug im
Hause?"
Voice with violin & piano.
Das Tagewerk ist abgetan (1798?)
[Reichardt ***Neue Lieder gesselliger
Freude,*** 1799] same
Winkler, Karl Gottfried Theodor, 1775-
1856.
Lied in der Fremde [unpubl.]
Text may be from Winkler's ***Sängers
Reise***; cf. Weber setting.
Woltmann, Karl Ludwig von, 1770-
1817, supposed author.
Theresens letztes Lied (1798) [unpubl.]
Zincgref, Julius Wilhelm, 1591-1635.
Klage (1803) [Schott (Landshoff), 1932]
"Mein feines Lieb ist fern von mir"
Zemphira's song **see Pushkin**
CHAĬKOVSKIĬ *Pesnya Zemfiri*
"Zénith Tous ces regrets" **see** *Vers le sud*
Apollinaire POULENC
"Le Zéphir à la douce haleine" **see** *Rêverie*
Banville DEBUSSY

Zéphyr see Banville *LES CARIATIDES,* livre 3, no. II. **DEBUSSY**

Zerbini, Alfredo
PIZZETTI
Al Marchesén, povrén, ch'l'era un bulot
Che cälma in gir! Che päza sepolcräla!
La va pian pian cla portanten'na scura

Das zerbrochene Krüglein see Frey, F.
SCHÖNBERG

Der zerrissne Grabkranz see Unknown
REGER

Die Zerstörung Magdeburgs see Goethe
KRENEK

Zettler, Alois, 1778-1828.
IHR FREUNDE UND DU, GOLD'NER WEIN.
SCHUBERT *Trinklied*

Zezhulice see Unknown **DVOŘÁK**

"Zharkiĭ den'blednel neulovimo, nad ozerom tuman" *see Twilight has fallen* Tolstoĭ
RACHMANINOFF

Zhelanie see Heine **MUSORGSKIĭ**

ZHELANIE. see Pushkin
Medlitel'no vlekutsia dni moi **RIMSKIĭ-KORSAKOV**

Zhelanie serdtsa see Unknown
MUSORGSKIĭ

"Zheltokrylaia babochka" *see Babochka*
Bal'mont **PROKOFIEV**

"Zheltyĭ list o stebel' b'etsia" *see Pesnya: Zholtĭy list* Lermontov **BALAKIREV**

Zhemchuzhnikov, Alekseĭ Mikhaĭlovich, 1821-1908.
BALAKIREV *Pustĭnya*

"Zhil byl korol' kogdato, pri nem blokha zhila" *see Pesnia Mefistofelia v pogrebke Auerbakha* Goethe **MUSORGSKIĭ**

Zhuk see Musorgskĭ **MUSORGSKIĭ**

Zhukovski, Vasiliĭ Andreyevich, 1783-1852.
RACHMANINOFF *On the death of a linnet*
RUBINSTEIN
Das Blättchen
Die Blume
Frühlingsgefühl
Der Traum

Zickeltanz see Garborg *HAUGTUSSA.*
GRIEG *Killingdans*

Der Ziegenbock see Musorgskiĭ
MUSORGSKIĭ *Kozel*

Ziegenhaen, Franz Heinrich, 1753-1806.
MOZART *Die ihr des unermesslichen Weltalls Schöpfer ehrt*

Ziegenhagen, Karl Heinrich *see* Ziegenhagen, Franz Heinrich, 1753-1806.

Ziegler, Karl, 1812-1877.
LOEWE *Der Hirt auf der Brücke HIMMEL UND ERDE.*
LOEWE *Frühlingsankunft*

"Zieh hin, du braver Krieger du!" *see Grablied auf einen Soldaten* Schubart
SCHUBERT

"Zieh' nicht so schnell vorüber" *see An die Wolke* Lenau **FRANZ**

"Zieh' nur, du Sonne, zieh' eilend von hier" *see Im Herbste* Kerner **SCHUMANN**

"Zieht die Lerch im Herbste fort" *see Abschied* Unknown **ZELTER**

Das Ziel see Hesse **SCHOECK**

Zielone slowa see Tuwim **SZYMANOWSKI**

"Zierlich ist des Vogels Tritt" *see Jägerlied* Mörike **WOLF**

DIE ZIGEUNER. see Pushkin
Scene . . . **RUBINSTEIN**

Zigeunerbub' im Norden see Geibel
LASSEN

Die Zigeunerin see Eichendorff **WOLF**

Die Zigeunerin see Unknown **LASSEN**

Zigeunerlied see Goethe **SPOHR**

Zigeunerliedchen see Anon. **SCHUMANN**

Zima see Pleshcheyev **CHAĬKOVSKIĭ**

Zimmer, Bernard
HONEGGER
Quand tu verras les hirondelles
Si le mal d'amour

Zimmermann, Balthasar Friedrich Wilhelm, 1807-1878.
SPOHR *Verlust*

Zimmermann, Georg Wilhelm, 1794-1835.
SCHUMANN *Nur ein lächelnder Blick*

Zimní noc see Heyduk **MARTINŮ**
A winter's night

Zimniaia noch' see Eichendorff **MEDTNER**
Winternacht

Zimniĭ vecher see Pleshcheyev
CHAĬKOVSKIĭ

Zimniĭ vecher see Pushkin **MEDTNER**
Winter evening

Zincgref, Julius Wilhelm, 1591-1635.
ZELTER *Klage*

La zingara see Maggioni, S. Manfredo
VERDI

Zinkgräf, Julius Wilhelm *see* Zincgref, Julius Wilhelm, 1591-1635.

Zinserling, W
LOEWE *Die treuen Schwalben*

Zion's walls see Anon. **COPLAND**

Das Zirkuspferdchen see Wolf, F.
BLACHER

"Zirpe, liebe kleine Sängerin" *see An die Grille* Unknown **LOEWE**

"Zit et zig et zig, la mort en cadence" *see*
  Danse macabre Cazalis **SAINT-SAËNS**
Zitelmann, Ernst Otto Conrad, 1854-
  1897.
  LASSEN *Das sind so traumheft schöne*
    Stunden
Zitronenfalter im April see Mörike **WOLF**
Zitto, La Bella Irene see Vittorelli **ROREM**
Zitzmann, Heinrich Gottfried, 1775-1839.
  LOEWE *Das Blumenopfer*
Zkho see Pushkin **BRITTEN** *Echo*
Zlote trzewiczki see Szymanowska, Zafia
  SZYMANOWSKI
Zly Lejba see Iłłakowiczwna
  SZYMANOWSKI
Zodes' khorosho see Einerling
  RACHMANINOFF *How fair this spot*
Zorn see Eichendorff **PFITZNER**
Zpěv z Lešetínského kováře see Čech
  LEŠETINSKÝ KOVÁŘ. **DVOŘÁK**
Zpívejte Hospodinu píseň novou see Bible
  DVOŘÁK
Zschokke, Heinrich, 1771-1848.
  WOLF *Nacht und Grab*
"Zu Aachen, in seiner Kaiserpracht" *see*
  Der Graf von Habsburg Schiller **LOEWE**
"Zu Augsburg steht ein hohes Haus" *see*
  Die Himmelsbraut Kerner **SPOHR**
"Zu Augsburg steht ein hohes Haus" *see Stirb,*
  Lieb' und Freud! Kerner **SCHUMANN**
Zu Boden gedrückt see Krenek **KRENEK**
"Zu dem Duft, der da würzt die Lenzesluft"
  see Veilchen Cornelius **CORNELIUS**
Zu der Rose, zu dem Weine see Hafiz
  JENSEN
"Zu Dionys, dem Tyrannen" *see*
  Die Bürgschaft Schiller **SCHUBERT**
Zu dir, dem Weltenmeister see Unknown
  LOEWE
Zu einer Konfirmation see Mörike
  SCHOECK
"Zu Hirsau in den Trümmern" *see Die Ulme*
  zu Hirsau Uhland **STRAUSS**
"Zu ihr stand all' mein Sehnen" *see Spielleute*
  Ibsen **BERG, DELIUS**
Zu L.M. Lindemans Silberhochzeit see
  Nikolajesen, V. **GRIEG**
  Til L.M. Lindemans Sølvbryllup
"Zu Lüttich, im letzten Häuselein" *see*
  Die Glocken zu Speier Oër **LOEWE**
"Zu meinen Füssen brichst du dich" *see Der*
  entsühnte Orest Mayrhofer **SCHUBERT**
"Zu meiner Laute Liebesklang" *see Ständchen*
  Anon. **ZELTER**
"Zu meiner Zeit" *see Die Alte* Hagedorn
  MOZART

"Zu Pisa in dem Klostergarten" *see*
  Der Mönch zu Pisa Vogl **LOEWE**
"Zu Quedlinburg im Dome" *see Kaiser Ott's*
  Weihnachtsfeier Mühler **LOEWE**
Zu spät see Osterwald **FRANZ**
"Zu Speier im Saale, da hebt sich ein
  Klingen" *see Graf Eberstein* Uhland
  LOEWE
Zu Strassburg auf der Schanz see Anon. *DES*
  KNABEN WUNDERHORN: Der Schweizer.
  FRANZ, MAHLER
"Zu uns komme Dein Reich" *see Vater unser*
  III Cornelius **CORNELIUS**
Zu viel see Mörike **SCHOECK**
Zuccalmaglio, Anton Wilhelm Florentin
  von, 1803-1869.
  DES KNABEN WUNDERHORN.
  LOEWE *Die verlorene Tochter*
La Zuecca see Musset **LALO**
Züge see Huggenberger **REGER**
Das Zügenglöcklein see Seidl **SCHUBERT**
Zueignung see Gilm zu Rosenegg *IM*
  FRÜHLING. **STRAUSS**
Der zürnende Barde see Bruchmann
  SCHUBERT
Der zürnenden Diana see Mayrhofer
  SCHUBERT
Zuflucht see Rodès **BLOCH** *L'abri*
Der Zufriedene see Reissig **BEETHOVEN,**
  SCHUBERT
Die Zufriedenen see Uhland **LOEWE**
Zufriedenheit see Claudius, M. **SCHUBERT**
  Lied
    Two settings: D. 362 and D. 501.
Die Zufriedenheit see Miller, J. **MOZART**
Die Zufriedenheit see Weisse **MOZART**
Zugemessne Rhythmen see Goethe
  WESTÖSTLICHER DIVAN. **STRAUSS**
"Zugemessne Rhythmen reizen freilich" *see*
  Zugemessne Rhythmen Goethe **STRAUSS**
Die Zugvöge see Tegnér **LOEWE**
Zugvogel see Grun, James **PFITZNER**
Zuleika's song see Byron **RIMSKĬĬ-**
  KORSAKOV *Pesnia Ziuleĭki*
Zuleikha see Bodenstedt **SPOHR,**
  SZYMANOWSKI
Zum Abschied meiner Tochter see
  Eichendorff **PFITZNER**
"Zum Donaustrom, zur Kaiserstadt" *see*
  Rückweg Mayrhofer **SCHUBERT**
"Zum Frühling sprach ich: Weile!" *see*
  Doppelwandlung Hoffmann von
  Fallersleben **FRANZ**
"Zum Hänschen sprach das Gretchen" *see*
  Der Schwur Baumbach **REGER**
Zum Heimatstrand zurückzukehren see
  Pushkin **BORODIN** *For the shores of thy*
  far native land

Zum neuen Jahr see Mörike **WOLF**
"Zum Ossa sprach der Pelion" *see Unerhört*
   Droste-Hülshoff **CORNELIUS**
Zum Punsche see Mayrhofer **SCHUBERT**
"Zum Reigen herbei im fröhlichen Mai!" *see*
   Tanzlied im Mai Hoffmann von
   Fallersleben **FRANZ**
"Zum Ritornelle wird, Liebste" *see Ritornell*
   Prölss **LASSEN**
Zum Schlafen see Schellenberg **REGER**
Zum Schluss see Rückert **SCHUMANN**
"Zum Sehen geboren" *see Lied Lynceus des*
   Thürmers Goethe **SCHUMANN**
"Zum Sehen geboren" *see Lynceus, der*
   Thürmer Goethe **LOEWE**
Zumalacarregui see Schleifer **LOEWE**
Zur Erinnerung see Löns **KILPINEN**
"Zur ew'gen Ruh' sie sangen die schöne
   Müllerin" *see Romanze* Eichendorff
   FRANZ
"Zur Freude ward geboren" *see An eine*
   Freudin Voigt **WEBER**
Zur Johannisnacht see Krag **GRIEG** *Og jeg*
   vil ha mig en Hjertenskjaer
"Zur Kirche rufet ernst" *see Sinngedicht*
   Polonsky **RUBINSTEIN**
Zur Namensfeier des Herrn Andreas Siller see
   Unknown **SCHUBERT**
Zur Rosenzeit see Goethe **GRIEG**
Zur Ruh, zur Ruh! see Kerner **WOLF**
"Zur Ruh, zur Ruh ihr müden Glieder!" *see*
   Zur Ruh, zur Ruh! Kerner **WOLF**
"Zur Schmiede ging ein junger Held" *see*
   Das Schwert Uhland **SCHUMANN**
Zur Warnung see Mörike **WOLF**
"Zur weissen Gans sprach einst vertraulich
   eine graue" *see Zwei Gänse* Sturm, J.
   REGER
"Zur Zeit als Griechenland der Götter satt" *see*
   Der Parnass Krylov **RUBINSTEIN**
Zuruf aus der Ferne see Weiden, E.
   RUBINSTEIN
Zusner, Vinzenz, 1803-1874.
   WOLF *Abendglöcklein*
"Zuweilen dünkt es mich als trübe" *see*
   Verfehlte Liebe Heine **FRANZ**
Zvědavá dievča see Anon. **MARTINŮ**
Zveno see Tumanskiĭ **BALAKIREV**
Zvolenovcí chlapci see Anon. **MARTINŮ**
"Zvolenovcí hezcí chlapci" *see Zvolenovcí*
   chlapci Anon. **MARTINŮ**
Zvonche zhavoronka pen'e see Tolstoĭ
   RIMSKIĬ-KORSAKOV
"Zwar schuf das Glück hienieden" *see*
   Der Zufriedene Reissig **BEETHOVEN,**
   SCHUBERT

Zwehl, Hans Fritz von, 1883-1966.
   KILPINEN
      Grabstein
      Der Heimatlose
      Lied der Renate
      Mancher Stunden Wehen
      Marienkirche zu Danzig im Gerüst
      Nacht auf Posten
      Nirwana
      Todsüsses Gespenst
      Venezianisches Intermezzo
      Vorfrühling
      Wenn der Bann gebrochen
Zwehlin see Zwehl, Hans Fritz von
ZWEI BALLADEN, no. 1
   HINDEMITH Keats *La belle dame sans*
      merci
ZWEI BALLADEN, no. 2
   HINDEMITH Rimbaud *Bal des pendus*
Die zwei blauen Augen von meinem Schatz see
   Mahler **MAHLER**
Zwei braune Augen see Andersen **DELIUS;**
   GRIEG *To brune Øjne*
Zwei chansons see Brecht **BLACHER**
"Zwei feine Stieflein hab' ich an" *see*
   Der Sandmann Kletke **SCHUMANN**
Zwei Gänse see Sturm, J. **REGER**
ZWEI GEISTLICHE LIEDER, no. 1
   MENDELSSOHN-BARTHOLDY Bible
      Doch der Herr, er leitet die Irrenden
      recht
ZWEI GEISTLICHE LIEDER, no. 2
   MENDELSSOHN-BARTHOLDY Bible
      Der du die Menschen lässest sterben
Zwei hohe Häuser, gleich an Würdigkeit see
   Shakespeare **ROMEO AND JULIET.**
   BLACHER
Zwei Könige sassen auf Orkadal see Geibel
   GRIFFES
Zwei Lieder see Brentano **HINDEMITH**
Zwei Mäuschen see Boelitz **REGER**
"Zwei Trichter wandeln durch die Nacht" *see*
   Die Trichter Morgenstern **SEIBER**
Zwei Venetianische Lieder see Moore, T.
   SCHUMANN
      Two settings: Op. 25 no. 17 and op. 25
      no. 18; text for no. 18 taken from
      Moore's *WHEN THROUGH THE*
      PIAZZETTA.
Zwei welke Rosen see Hauenschild **FRANZ**
"Zwei welke Rosen träumen" *see Zwei welke*
   Rosen Hauenschild **FRANZ**
"Zwei wunderliche Gevattern" *see Ich und*
   mein Gevatter Rückert **LOEWE**
Zweifelnde Liebe see Unknown **PFITZNER**
Zweifler see Pfau **SCHÖNBERG**

COMPOSER Poet *Title* "First Line"

Zweig, Stefan, 1881-1942.
  REGER
    Ein Drängen
    Neue Fülle
Zweiundneunzigstes Sonnet von Petrarca see
  Petrarca **PFITZNER**
Der Zwerg see Collin, M. **SCHUBERT**
Zwielicht see Eichendorff *AHNUNG UND*
  GEGENWART. **SCHUMANN**
Zwiesprach see Boelitz **REGER**
"Zwischen Bergen, liebe Mutter" *see*
  Die Kleine Eichendorff **WOLF**
"Zwischen Mohn und Rittersporn hab' ich
  träumend heut' " *see Mittag* Schellenberg
  REGER
"Zwischen Weizen und Korn" see *Mailied*
  Goethe **FRANZ, MEDTNER,**
  SCHÖNBRG, ZELTER
"Zwischen Weizen und Korn" *see Wo geht's*
  Liebchen? Goethe **ZELTER**
Zwischen zwei Nächten see Falke **REGER**
Zwist und Sühne see Simrock **LOEWE**
"Zwitschert nicht an meinem Fenster" *see*
  An die Vögel Hamerling **LASSEN,**
  JENSEN, RUBINSTEIN
ZWÖLF GEISTLICHE LIEDER, no. 1
  REGER Herman *Bitte um einen seligen*
  Tod
ZWÖLF GEISTLICHE LIEDER, no. 2
  REGER Eichendorff *Dein Wille, Herr,*
  geschehe!

ZWÖLF GEISTLICHE LIEDER, no. 3
  REGER Unknown *Uns ist geboren ein*
  Kindelein
ZWÖLF GEISTLICHE LIEDER, no. 4
  REGER Unknown *Am Abend*
ZWÖLF GEISTLICHE LIEDER, no. 5
  REGER Unknown *O Herre Gott, nimm*
  du von mir
ZWÖLF GEISTLICHE LIEDER, no. 6
  REGER Unknown *Christ, deines Geistes*
  Süssigkeit
ZWÖLF GEISTLICHE LIEDER, no. 7
  REGER Arndt *Grablied*
ZWÖLF GEISTLICHE LIEDER, no. 8
  REGER Alberus *Morgengesang*
ZWÖLF GEISTLICHE LIEDER, no. 9
  REGER Fleming *Lass dich nur nichts*
  nicht dauern
ZWÖLF GEISTLICHE LIEDER, no. 10
  REGER Unknown *Christkindleins*
  Wiegenlied
ZWÖLF GEISTLICHE LIEDER, no. 11
  REGER Unknown *Klage vor Gottes*
  Leiden
ZWÖLF GEISTLICHE LIEDER, no. 12
  REGER Alberus *O Jesu Christ, wir*
  warten dein
Zyczenie see Witwicki **CHOPIN**